THE GREAT AMERICAN BASEBALL STAT BOOK 1994

Gary Gillette
The Baseball Workshop

Pete Palmer, Stuart Shea, David W. Smith
Contributing Editors

A MOUNTAIN LION/21st CENTURY SPORTS BOOK

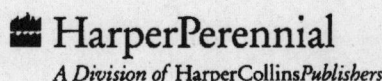
HarperPerennial
A Division of HarperCollinsPublishers

Acknowledgments

This book is dedicated to Stuart Shea for his dedication and hard work and to Cecilia Garibay for her patience.

A tip of the baseball cap to Bill Disney, Eddie Epstein, David Nichols, Gary Skoog, Tom Peters, Tom Tippett, and Jay Virshbo, all of whom helped in various important ways.

Finally, thanks to Steve Stovall and John Monteleone of Mountain Lion, to Margaret Trejo at Trejo Production, and to Robert Wilson at HarperCollins—they made this book possible

A MOUNTAIN LION/21st CENTURY BOOK

ISSN 1056-5116
ISBN 0-06-273232-3

94 95 CK 5 4 3 2 1

CONTENTS

INTRODUCTION

The Great American Stat Book 1994 is crammed with as much information as we could possibly fit into it's 544 pages. It is designed to give you more information on current players and teams than you can obtain from any other source.

Baseball reference books typically deal with only one type of statistics: either official statistics (e.g., AB, R, H, RBI; IP, W, L, ERA) or situational statistics (e.g., vs. left-handers, vs. right-handers; at home, on road). This book contains *both* types of statistics for all players active in 1993.

The *Stat Book* contains three primary types of information: situational statistics, official career statistics, and special statistics.

o Situational stats are defined by how a player performs in a specific situation: how he hits against left-handed pitchers, how he pitched on the road, how well he hit with runners on base, or how well he pitched month-by-month during the season. Comprehensive situational stats for 420 players (15 regulars per team) are found in Part 1; the most important situational stats categories are found in Part 2 for all other 1993 players. Part 3 gives team and league situational stats and park effects.

o Official statistics are the traditional baseball statistics listed in newspapers' sports sections, baseball magazines, and reference books. The career records in Part 5 of the book contain complete major-league career statistics for *all* 1993 players. This part includes extensive minor-league career information for all major-leaguers. Unlike other sources which leave out much information, the *Stat Book* includes every official batting and pitching statistics category.

o The special reports included in Part 4 are a mix of statistics on starting pitching, relief pitching, basestealing, and defense. These reports break down the official stats into categories useful for analyzing player and team performance.

One note. In order to get the *Stat Book* published as early as possible, all 1993 statistics used in the book are based on the final unofficial totals for the 1993 season. These unofficial totals are released the day after the regular season ends and aren't significantly different from the final official stats that are released two months later. Final official statistics aren't released until after this book goes to press.

You shouldn't notice many differences in the batting and pitching statistics, though. Baseball usually makes very few—and very minor—changes between the final unofficial statistics and the final official statistics. Fielding statistics are another case. Therefore, there may be small differences between some of the fielding stats in this book and the final official totals. These changes are minor and don't substantially alter any analysis based on these numbers.

Several changes have been made in the 1994 edition of the *Stat Book*. As always, these changes are made with the goal of making the book more useful and informative. The most important changes are the addition of an Index and the inclusion of new statistics in Part 6.

Part 1. This section has been expanded to include 420 regular players (15 per team) due to the addition of the Marlins and Rockies. The lists of regular players and debut players has been deleted; this information can now be found in the Index.

Part 3. The Park Effects Chart has been moved to Part 3 to accompany the team and league statistics. Final 1993 standings for both leagues have been added.

Part 4. The Basestealing Reports have been expanded to include all pitchers, catchers, and batters, instead of setting a minimum of 10 attempts. The Catcher Fielding Reports now include team totals.

Part 5. The Career Registers no longer include players who did not play in the major leagues last season. Of course, many top prospects were called up in September 1993, and their complete career records are still included in the book.

In place of these minor-leaguers, a new section of the book (Part 6) has been added. The Order Form on the last page of the book gives buyers of the Stat Book a chance to get comprehensive rankings and ratings of top 1994 prospects free of charge at the end of spring training. It also gives Stat Book readers a chance to purchase at half price a supplement to the book which includes the career records of 500 top minor-league prospects.

Part 6. This new section consists of two long reports. The first shows Pete Palmer's 1994 projections for batters and pitchers; the second gives 1993 park factors and league averages for all 18 minor leagues.

Index. Near the end of the book, you will now find alphabetical index for all players, showing the page numbers on which you can find their situational statistics and their career records.

The material at the end of the book also includes information about The Baseball Workshop and about the non-profit research organization, Retrosheet.

Send me your comments or suggestions—feedback is both welcome and appreciated. You may reach me care of the publisher or by writing to The Baseball Workshop.

—GARY GILLETTE

A USER'S GUIDE

Every baseball reference book you can buy (and there are literally hundreds of them) is chock-full of statistics set in agate type.

What's a baseball fan to do when presented with so many choices? What makes this book more useful than the others? How do you sort out the statistical wheat from the chaff?

Many of the answers to these questions are matters of personal preference. Lots of fans don't want to get bogged down in statistics, feeling that too many stats diminish their appreciation of the game. That's fine: one of the beauties of baseball is that it can be enjoyed in many, very different ways.

However, if you want to use this book to better understand and predict the performance of current players, read this essay first. It will help you to properly interpret the remarkable wealth of statistics in this book.

AFLOAT IN A SEA OF STATISTICS

Baseball has always had statistics, and its statistics have always given a more complete picture of the game than those of other sports. The familiar traditional stats—batting average, runs, home runs, runs batted in, wins, losses, earned-run average, and strikeouts—obviously have lots of merit, or they wouldn't be universally known and discussed by fans.

In recent years, as the media have been paying more and more attention to baseball statistics, more and more "new" statistics have been published and a statistical backlash has arisen. This takes different forms, but can easily be recognized by such questions as, "What's wrong with the old statistics?" and "Why do we need new stats?" or by complaints about a player's stats "in road games on Tuesdays against a southpaw with a runner on second under a full moon."

Here are some answers to those questions. What's wrong with the old familiar stats is that they haven't changed as the game has changed. They still have value, but newer stats are needed to describe and analyze the way the game is played today. Everything else in life changes over time, so why should baseball—or baseball statistics, for that matter—remain frozen?

Baseball was a radically different game in 1910 when Ty Cobb was terrorizing pitchers. It changed when Babe Ruth became king and instituted the era of the slugger in the 1920s; it changed again with the advent of night baseball and the rise of relief pitching. Maury Wills and the reintroduction of speed changed the game again in the 1960s. Artificial turf, domed stadiums, the adoption of the designated hitter rule, and the increasing specialization in player roles have altered the face of the game yet again in the past 25 years.

Scholars, doctors, lawyers, politicians, teachers, stockbrokers, mechanics, and many others play largely the same roles in society today as they did 75 years ago. Yet their training isn't the same, their tools are different, the way they approach their jobs has changed, and the amount they get paid has increased manyfold. There is no reason to assume that similar changes haven't affected our national pastime.

Just as our language has altered and our sciences have progressed, so, too, must our understanding of how baseball is played. Baseball statistics are the measure of the game, and the "new" statistics are simply an attempt to assess the modern game more accurately.

APPLY COMMON SENSE TO BASEBALL STATISTICS

Just because the average fan is not a mathematician or a so-called baseball expert doesn't mean that he or she can't use common sense when evaluating baseball stats. The key here is to apply the same rules of good judgment to baseball stats that you apply to real life.

Think critically, be skeptical, ask questions, examine the evidence carefully. If you follow these guidelines when looking at baseball stats, you should be happy with the results.

The first rule for any statistic—baseball or otherwise—is not to read any more significance into it than it was designed for. Two good examples of this are pitchers' won-lost records and ERAs. These stats serve well when evaluating starting pitchers who pitch lots of innings. For relief pitchers, however, their relevance is marginal and when relief pitching became prominent, the Save statistic was invented to better reflect the change in the way the game was played.

A corollary to this rule is never to put more weight on a statistic than it can justifiably support. If a stat doesn't show the complete picture, don't use it to make sweeping judgments. Example: a player can lead the league in homers and runs batted in but not deserve the Most Valuable Player award because of big holes in his game that are not measured by HRs and RBIs. He could be a bad fielder and a terrible baserunner, making him less valuable than a player who does everything well but doesn't quite measure up in the glamour stats categories.

The second rule is to be skeptical of small samples. Even good statistics can be very misleading when measuring small numbers of events. Sometimes a small sample will support a theory or reveal a trend, but the level of chance in small numbers is too great for any reliance to be placed on them. Scott Lusader hit .319 in his rookie year with Detroit in 1987, playing in the heat of a pennant race. Of course, he only had 47 at-bats, so it's not surprising that he has never proven himself as a big-league hitter.

Too obvious an example? Consider Dan Gladden. As a rookie with the Giants, Dan clipped NL pitchers for a .270 average in 342 at-bats in the second half of 984 after hitting .397 in Triple-A the first half of the year. Lots of people thought he was going to be a bona fide .300 hitter in the big leagues, yet he has never hit more than .295 since then and has a career average of .272. Why should this not have been a surprise to the skeptical? Because one half of a season is too small a sample to base such judgments on, and because Gladden's minor-league history before 1984 showed no such gaudy batting averages to lend additional weight to the evidence.

The third rule is to look for strong trends over time or to look for evidence from multiple sources. The stronger the trend and the longer the period of time over which it occurs, the more reliability you can place on it. The primary value of career statistics when predicting future performance is that they are a much more reliable indicator than single-season stats. The reason for this is that the good luck and bad luck, the fluke performances, and the injuries tend to even out over long periods of time. If a player has averaged 18 home runs a year for six years and then breaks loose for 30 one year, he's much more likely to revert to his average the next season than to hit 30 again.

Be especially wary of expecting too much from players coming off "career" years. For veteran players with established track records, "career" years are just that— the peaks of their careers. Because of skill, good health, favorable circumstances, and a dose of good fortune, a player may exceed his career norms by a wide margin one season. However, because all of these factors will not be present every year, the odds of players returning to normal production after a career year is very high.

PREDICTING PERFORMANCE

Baseball is an exceedingly complex game deceptively cloaked in a mantle of simplicity. If predicting the performance of players and teams were easy, there wouldn't be such delightful surprises as the 1993 Phillies. No matter how much you know about baseball, there is so much more that remains unknown.

In order to have a prayer of a chance of accurately predicting future performance, you must study the evidence carefully, consider past circumstances, try to anticipate future changes in circumstances, and then draw the proper conclusions. This is obviously a lot easier said than done for everyone involved, including managers, coaches, players, writers, and analysts. If it really were easy to predict performance, scouts wouldn't recommend many more players than succeed, managers wouldn't pencil .180 hitters into the lineup, and pitchers with ERAs over five wouldn't get out of the bullpen except in blowouts.

While predictions are admittedly imperfect, you can certainly increase the accuracy of your hunches by relying on the proper statistics. Some stats are more meaningful than others, some stats are useful only in certain situations, and most stats can mislead if not interpreted properly.

A QUICK TOUR OF THE BOOK

The first two sections of the *Stat Book* present extensive situational statistics for all 1993 major-league players. One of the most important features of this book is that it presents totals for the past ten years in all situations. No other book gives you this information— information that can make it easier to predict next year's performance.

(The reason ten-year totals are used is that Project Scoresheet's database starts with the 1984 season. Since over 90% of major-league players active today made their big-league debuts after 1984, these ten-year totals are also their career totals, which is how they will be referred to here.)

Career situational totals are very important analytical tools for many reasons. If a player was injured or didn't play much in 1993, his totals will be much more meaningful than his 1993 numbers. If you know that a player has changed in some important way (e.g., his batting stance, his pitching motion, or just in the way he is used), you can compare his 1993 stats to his career averages to see how these changes might have made a difference.

Explanations of the situational statistics categories used are listed below, using batters' statistics as examples. Abbreviations for statistics used throughout the book can be found with the introductions to each part of the book.

The situational statistics categories shown for pitchers are analogous to those for batters, but are divided into two parts. The first part uses traditional pitching statistics for the home/road, grass/turf, day/night, and monthly breakdowns. The second part shows how opposing batters hit against that pitcher in various situations.

All of the categories listed below are shown for the 420 regular players included in Part 1. The most important categories (vs. left/vs. right, home/road, and bases empty, and second half) are shown in Part 2 for all other 1993 players.

○ "Vs. Left" and "vs. Right" break down batters' statistics into how they batted against left-handed pitchers and how they batted against right-handed pitchers. For pitchers, the breakdowns represent how opposing left-handed and right-handed batters did against them.

○ "At Home" and "On Road" break players' statistics into how they performed in games in their home ballpark and how they performed in games in other ballparks.

o "On Grass" and "On Turf" break player's statistics into how they performed in venues with grass fields as opposed to those with artificial turf.

o "Day Games" and "Night Games" separate players' statistics into games starting before 5:00 p.m. local time and those starting after 5:00 p.m.

o The monthly categories are self-explanatory with the exception of the last line. September and October games are totaled and include regular-season games only. Second half statistics for non-regular players are totals of their July, August, September and October stats.

o The "Bases Empty" category breaks down players' statistics into how they batted when there was no runner on base. For regular players, the "Leadoff" line gives statistics when they were the first batter of an inning.

o The "Runners On Base" category breaks down players' statistics into how they batted when there was a runner or runners on base. For regular players, the "Scoring Position" line gives statistics separately with a runner or runners in scoring position (i.e., on second base and/or third base).

o The "Late and Close" line gives players' statistics when the score is close in the late innings of a game. Late and Close situations are defined as at-bats in the 7th inning or later when a player's team is ahead by only one run, the score is tied, or his team is behind but the tying run is at-bat, on-base, or on-deck.

This means that the game is always close if the batter's team is behind by only one run in the 7th inning or later, and that the game can never be close if his team is behind by more than five runs. While the definition of a Late and Close situation does not change, such situations can change from one at-bat to the next if the score or the runners on base change.

Essentially, the game is considered close for an at-bat if it is currently tied, if there is only a one-run difference in the score, or if the team that is currently behind would take the lead, tie the game, or come within one run of tying the game if the batter hit a home run and all runners on base scored. By the way, the Close part of the Late and Close definition is the same as used in the official Save rule for pitchers.

The team and league statistics presented in Part 3 are useful for two reasons. The league statistics give the norms so that you can see how much above or below average a particular player is. The team statistics give you a chance to see where a team was strongest and weakest—information that can help you predict what moves they're likely to make. Better yet, these numbers will help predict what the effects of those moves will be.

The Special Reports found in Part 4 have several functions. The Starting Pitching and Relief Pitching reports give much more detailed information about pitchers than the official stats. There are several key pieces of information in these reports.

For starting pitchers, look closely at their run support. If a pitcher's run support is way above his team's average runs scored per game, it's likely that his record is better than it should be, based solely on his pitching ability. This is frequently a tipoff that he will "slump" next year. The converse is also true. A pitcher who endures a season of miserable support from his mates will generally rebound smartly the following year.

The second set of numbers of value for starters represents their endurance. Looking at how often a pitcher was replaced in certain innings can give you a clue as to how he will be used next year. A starter who can't make it to the 7th inning in many of his starts is a good candidate for bullpen duty in the future. The Quality Start stats given are also excellent indicators of a starting pitcher's endurance. Starters aren't going to win every Quality Start they make, but the more they make, the longer their manager can wait to go to the bullpen.

For ace relief pitchers, look closely at the Blown Save, Save Percentage, and Inherited Runners columns. If an ace reliever blows too many Save opportunities or lets too many inherited runners score, he could be demoted to middle relief fast. For middle relievers, look at their Save opportunities, their Save Conversion Percentages and the innings in which they enter the game. Most middle relievers will have few Save opportunities compared to the number of games they pitch in relief. However, the higher the number of opportunities and the higher the conversion percentage, the greater are their chances of being auditioned for the closer's job if there is a vacancy in the future. But beware of middle relievers who rarely get into games in late innings, since this is a clear sign that they are not trusted to pitch in key situations.

The value of the last two parts of the book should be self-evident. The first point to note about the Career Register is that similar batting and pitching statistics are grouped together, allowing for easier analysis than the traditional statistics lines. The second point is that all minor-league stats lines include classifications as well as leagues. Comparing stats across the minor leagues is not easy, but the statistics included in Part 6—which show park and league differences—should make it possible to this kind of analysis.

USING SITUATIONAL STATS

Because baseball is so complex and unpredictable, experience is in many ways the best teacher. No book of statistics can substitute for years spent following baseball and studying its history and its players. Such experience gives an astute fan a valuable sense of the relative importance of particular statistics and how to apply them.

Many fans feel lost, however, when trying to ascertain the meaning of such new statistics as situationals, so some brief comments on the strengths and weaknesses of the prominent categories may be helpful.

By far the most important situational statistics categories are the left/right and home/road breakdowns. For decades now, managers have regularly been platooning hitters, which serves as an indication of how seriously the people who fill out the lineup cards take the differences between left-handed and right-handed batters. In recent years, the prevalence of what one might call "platoon pitching"—the frequent changing of relief pitchers in late innings to get the platoon advantage over the batter—has increased greatly as well.

There are many theories about why it is true, but no one disagrees with the facts that, overall, right-handed hitters hit left-handed pitchers better than right-handed pitchers, and that left-handed batters are at a distinct disadvantage when facing left-handed pitchers. because this knowledge is applied in every major-league game, the "vs. left" and "vs. right" situational stats lines are most important and enlightening.

The home/road stats breakdowns are also very meaningful, but in a rather different way. Baseball people are well aware of the effects different ballparks have on players, but it is somewhat harder to apply that information every day. For example, it might be clear that a particular starting pitcher performs substantially better in his home park than elsewhere. Even so, most teams cannot afford the luxury of benching key players in road games, so what might be termed "home/road platooning" is much less frequent than left/right platooning.

Frequently, the most valuable information to be gained from studying home/road splits for players is when they have changed teams or when their home ballpark has been radically altered in the off-season. When players are traded—especially from teams with extreme ballparks like Wrigley Field or the Oakland Coliseum—their career road statistics are usually good predictors of how they will fare in their new environment. If a team performs radical surgery on its park—like moving the fences in much closer in the power alleys—one can use home/road numbers to make an estimate of how much a player's numbers might change (by holding road stats constant and adjusting home stats for the change).

Grass/turf and day/night breakdowns are much less useful than left/right and home/road. Grass/turf numbers are always heavily influenced by a player's home park: because home games will necessarily be all grass or all turf, one of the grass/turf lines will largely reflect a player's home performance. Furthermore, because players on different teams and in different divisions play very different percentages of games on grass and turf, the numbers are even less comparable. The best use of grass/turf numbers, then, is in assessing the performances of players who move from a team with grass to a team with turf, or vice versa.

Monthly stats for one season are a useful means of seeing what happened when—but the real scope of monthly stats is evident in the career totals. Many players show pronounced patterns of playing better or worse in the cold spring and fall months (April, May, September) than in the hot summer months (June, July, August). Some are prone to hot starts and cold finishes; others start slowly and finish strongly. Check for these patterns when evaluating players who are off to especially fast or slow starts in 1994.

The bases empty/runners on base and "late and close" breakdowns are more problematical than the others. Baseball analysts are constantly arguing over the predictive value of so-called clutch statistics; no one has yet been able to do a definitive study of "clutch" performance and show that it remains constant over multiple seasons. While these stats are a lot of fun to look at for past years, their predictive value has not been established. Second-half breakdowns have become very popular in recent years, especially with fantasy players. These stats can sometimes give you a good idea of how a player will do next year, *provided* there was some significant change in his game last season. For example, if a player was injured early in the year, his second half numbers can tell you whether he's recovered or not. Ditto if he changed positions or made a substantial change in his pitching mechanics or his swing. However, don't assume that a hot or cold second half necessarily means that a player will play that way next year. Unless there is some other factor to consider, career averages are better predictors than half-year stats.

A last word of advice about the situationals: be sure to make use of the career totals, especially for players who did not play much in 1993. Because of the much larger sampling, these career totals will generally be more accurate than single-season stats in predicting future performance—although you should always consider whether a player's age, injury status, and/or changes in his batting or pitching technique may render the career numbers less useful.

Aside from all of the stats, the other very important factor to consider when evaluating a player is his age. While we'd like to believe that 30-year-old rookies can triumph against the odds, the realities are much more sobering. Great players almost always are playing regularly in the majors by their early 20s; solid, regular players almost always establish themselves by the age of 25 or 26. Although some prospects don't get a fair chance to prove themselves until they're 26 to 27, most players who surface in the big leagues that late aren't going to have much of a career. Pitchers frequently take longer to develop than position players and are more erratic in their performances, but the next Roger Clemens is much more likely to win his first 20 games before the age of 25 than after.

I hope this short guide helps you get more out of the book. Baseball seems like such a simple game, but it's fantastically complex when you try to analyze it. Baseball statistics are like a foreign language which is difficult to learn, but rewards you with many new insights when you have mastered it.

Part 1

Regular Players' Situational Statistics

This part contains situational breakdowns for major-league regulars in 1993. Players are listed alphabetically, separated into batters and pitchers.

Each player's statistics follow the same format. The first line gives the player's name, how he bats and throws, and his age, effective for the 1994 season. It also lists the team he played for and the positions he played in 1993.

A player's effective age for the season is his age on his birthday that year. So whether a player turns 30 on February 15, June 1, September 30, or December 31, 1994, his Season Effective Age is considered to be 30.

Effective age is used rather than a player's calendar age because it really is the age he is closest to for the majority of the season. (For instance, a player who turns 30 on November 1 is actually more than 29½ for the majority of the season, which means that an effective age of 30 is more accurate than his calendar age of 29.) It also standardizes all player ages, allowing for accurate comparisons.

On the left-hand side of the page are the player's situational statistics for 1993, broken down into the various categories. On the right-hand side of the page are the player's situational statistics totals from 1984–1993. If a player played in the majors every year from 1984 to 1993, it will show "10-Year Totals." If he played in the majors for only part of that period, the header will list the actual number of years he played and the first year he played. For example, a player who played in 1989, 1990, and 1993 would have "3-Year Totals" listed.

REGULAR PLAYERS

A total of 420 players, 15 per team—nine position players and six pitchers—were selected based on their playing time. Traded players had their statistics on all teams added together.

Regulars at the fielding positions were almost always determined by the most games started for a team at that position. For teams with unstable lineups (i.e., several players starting many games at multiple positions), a judgment call was made.

Regular pitchers were usually their team's top four starters (by games started) and top two relievers (by games finished). Some teams with very stable starting rotations are represented by five starters and one reliever. For a few teams with unstable starting rotations, three starters and three relievers were selected.

Two new pieces of information were added to the situational statistics for pitchers this year. **POW** or **FIN** indicates whether a pitcher was a power pitcher or a finesse pitcher in 1992. Power pitchers are above the league average in strikeouts and walks (combined); finesse pitchers are below league average. Ground-ball pitchers (**GB**) were above league average in ground outs; fly-ball pitchers (**FB**) were below league average.

SP (Starting Pitcher), **RP** (Relief Pitcher), **C** (Catcher), **1B** (First Base), **2B** (Second Base), **SS** (Shortstop), **LF** (Left Field), **CF** (Center Field), **RF** (Right Field), **OF** (Outfield), and **DH** (Designated Hitter) are the standard baseball positional abbreviations used throughout the book.

KEY TO ABBREVIATIONS

BATTING AND PITCHING STATISTICS
G	Games
H	Hits
R	Runs
HR	Home Runs
BB	Bases on Balls
IBB	Intentional Bases on Balls
SO	Strikeouts

BATTING STATISTICS
TPA	Total Plate Appearances
AB	At-Bats
2B	Doubles

3B	Triples
TB	Total Bases
RBI	Runs Batted In
HP or HBP	Hit by Pitch
SH	Sacrifice Hits
SF	Sacrifice Flies
SB	Stolen Bases
CS	Caught Stealing
SB%	Stolen Base Percentage [SB/(SB+CS)]
GDP	Grounded into Double Play
BA	Batting Average (H/AB)

OBA	On Base Average [(H+TBB+HBP)/ (AB+TBB+HBP+SF)]
SA	Slugging Average (TB/AB)

PITCHING STATISTICS
GS	Games Started
CG	Complete Games
GF	Games Finished
IP	Innings Pitched
TBF	Total Batters Faced
ER	Earned Runs
HB	Hit Batsmen

WP	Wild Pitches
BK	Balks
W	Wins
L	Losses
PCT	Winning Percentage [W/(W+L)]
SHO	Shutouts
S or SV	Saves
ERA	Earned Run Average [(ER/IP) × 9]

BATTERS

LUIS ALICEA — BB/TR — age 29 — SL 2B96, OF4, 3B1   4-YEAR TOTALS (1988–1993)

1993	BA	OBA	SA	AB	H	2B	3B	HR	RBI	BB	SO	BA	OBA	SA	AB	H	2B	3B	HR	RBI	BB	SO
Total	.279	.362	.373	362	101	19	3	3	46	47	54	.244	.320	.340	992	242	41	18	6	102	107	145
vs. Left	.367	.432	.468	79	29	5	0	1	9	9	4	.257	.317	.335	272	70	12	3	1	26	21	28
vs. Right	.254	.343	.346	283	72	14	3	2	37	38	50	.239	.321	.342	720	172	29	15	5	76	86	117
at Home	.287	.361	.371	202	58	7	2	2	25	24	26	.262	.341	.385	519	136	19	15	5	55	59	67
on Road	.269	.364	.375	160	43	12	1	1	21	23	28	.224	.297	.290	473	106	22	3	1	47	48	78
on Grass	.262	.364	.333	84	22	3	0	1	6	13	15	.213	.301	.261	253	54	9	0	1	20	31	44
on Turf	.284	.361	.385	278	79	16	3	2	40	34	39	.254	.327	.367	739	188	32	18	5	82	76	101
Day Games	.242	.333	.323	124	30	6	2	0	12	17	22	.242	.329	.360	314	76	12	8	3	36	38	55
Night Games	.298	.377	.399	238	71	13	1	3	34	30	32	.245	.316	.330	678	166	29	10	3	66	69	90
April	.318	.400	.318	22	7	0	0	0	4	3	2	.180	.257	.213	89	16	1	1	0	9	10	15
May	.333	.419	.392	51	17	1	1	0	9	8	4	.288	.370	.419	222	64	9	7	2	33	27	20
June	.304	.373	.457	46	14	4	0	1	6	5	10	.253	.305	.364	154	39	10	2	1	12	11	21
July	.291	.387	.380	79	23	5	1	0	6	12	17	.248	.324	.321	165	41	6	3	0	9	18	29
August	.265	.348	.357	98	26	3	0	2	17	14	10	.243	.339	.339	189	46	6	3	2	21	28	28
Sept-Oct	.212	.284	.333	66	14	6	1	0	4	5	11	.208	.272	.301	173	36	9	2	1	18	13	32
Bases Empty	.257	.336	.307	218	56	11	0	0	0	24	34	.246	.323	.333	568	140	26	7	3	3	60	84
Leadoff	.221	.319	.250	104	23	3	0	0	0	15	18	.213	.303	.267	240	51	8	1	1	1	29	40
Runners On Base	.313	.398	.472	144	45	8	3	3	46	23	20	.241	.316	.349	424	102	15	11	3	99	47	61
Scoring Position	.338	.431	.571	77	26	6	3	2	43	18	12	.254	.348	.377	236	60	11	6	2	90	38	39
Late and Close	.319	.425	.406	69	22	4	1	0	15	14	9	.225	.338	.293	222	50	8	2	1	26	37	35

ROBERTO ALOMAR — BB/TR — age 26 — TOR 2B150   6-YEAR TOTALS (1988–1993)

1993	BA	OBA	SA	AB	H	2B	3B	HR	RBI	BB	SO	BA	OBA	SA	AB	H	2B	3B	HR	RBI	BB	SO
Total	.326	.408	.492	589	192	35	6	17	93	80	67	.297	.364	.416	3550	1053	181	37	56	395	372	436
vs. Left	.241	.297	.373	166	40	8	1	4	24	12	29	.261	.329	.392	1090	284	54	7	25	128	103	176
vs. Right	.359	.449	.539	423	152	27	5	13	69	68	38	.313	.380	.426	2460	769	127	30	31	267	269	260
at Home	.325	.409	.498	289	94	18	4	8	38	40	30	.307	.376	.435	1732	531	82	24	31	218	192	200
on Road	.327	.407	.487	300	98	17	2	9	55	40	37	.287	.352	.397	1818	522	99	13	25	177	180	236
on Grass	.339	.411	.510	239	81	13	2	8	41	28	25	.284	.343	.379	2009	570	88	14	25	205	179	254
on Turf	.317	.406	.480	350	111	22	4	9	52	52	42	.313	.391	.464	1541	483	93	23	31	190	193	182
Day Games	.282	.373	.436	188	53	12	1	5	32	26	24	.290	.361	.411	1121	325	70	9	16	139	124	132
Night Games	.347	.425	.519	401	139	23	5	12	61	54	43	.300	.366	.418	2429	728	111	28	40	256	248	304
April	.302	.400	.407	86	26	4	1	1	8	13	11	.292	.353	.383	465	136	20	2	6	47	43	57
May	.259	.344	.389	108	28	3	1	3	18	15	13	.287	.350	.410	654	188	24	7	14	77	62	74
June	.369	.431	.563	103	38	5	0	5	15	10	10	.287	.359	.418	596	171	34	7	10	64	64	70
July	.309	.374	.495	97	30	8	2	2	12	10	14	.289	.354	.387	574	166	33	7	3	53	59	74
August	.360	.423	.514	111	40	8	0	3	20	12	13	.302	.371	.429	662	200	38	8	10	67	70	101
Sept-Oct	.357	.481	.595	84	30	7	2	3	20	20	6	.321	.396	.459	599	192	32	6	13	87	74	60
Bases Empty	.334	.411	.494	338	113	20	2	10	10	42	39	.289	.355	.409	2093	604	108	20	35	35	207	269
Leadoff	.304	.370	.416	125	38	3	1	3	3	13	11	.300	.363	.438	774	232	40	8	17	17	76	80
Runners On Base	.315	.404	.490	251	79	15	4	7	83	38	28	.308	.377	.425	1457	449	73	17	21	360	165	167
Scoring Position	.322	.416	.507	146	47	6	3	5	74	26	15	.311	.377	.434	823	256	42	10	13	325	97	103
Late and Close	.274	.344	.440	84	23	3	1	3	16	9	14	.296	.376	.399	561	166	26	4	8	71	71	84

MOISES ALOU — BR/TR — age 28 — MON OF136   3-YEAR TOTALS (1990–1993)

1993	BA	OBA	SA	AB	H	2B	3B	HR	RBI	BB	SO	BA	OBA	SA	AB	H	2B	3B	HR	RBI	BB	SO
Total	.286	.340	.483	482	138	29	6	18	85	38	53	.282	.332	.467	843	238	57	9	27	141	63	102
vs. Left	.268	.320	.445	164	44	10	2	5	24	11	10	.274	.317	.426	317	87	21	3	7	38	18	25
vs. Right	.296	.350	.503	318	94	19	4	13	61	27	43	.287	.341	.492	526	151	36	6	20	103	45	77
at Home	.252	.310	.432	222	56	8	1	10	47	20	27	.282	.331	.486	383	108	22	4	16	82	31	49
on Road	.315	.366	.527	260	82	21	5	8	38	18	26	.283	.333	.452	460	130	35	5	11	59	32	53
on Grass	.292	.343	.466	161	47	12	2	4	18	12	20	.277	.333	.435	253	70	21	2	5	28	22	32
on Turf	.283	.339	.492	321	91	17	4	14	67	26	33	.285	.332	.481	590	168	36	7	22	113	41	70
Day Games	.295	.341	.442	156	46	12	1	3	21	11	19	.309	.354	.471	278	86	25	1	6	38	20	34
Night Games	.282	.340	.503	326	92	17	5	15	64	27	34	.269	.322	.465	565	152	32	8	21	103	43	68
April	.298	.337	.464	84	25	4	2	2	10	6	9	.323	.356	.495	93	30	6	2	2	11	6	11
May	.322	.374	.422	90	29	6	0	1	13	6	7	.305	.365	.433	141	43	10	1	2	17	12	14
June	.180	.260	.360	89	16	4	0	4	15	9	8	.244	.303	.440	168	41	10	1	7	37	15	16
July	.323	.374	.646	99	32	9	1	7	24	8	12	.297	.342	.547	148	44	14	1	9	29	10	19
August	.279	.322	.442	104	29	4	2	3	20	8	17	.255	.308	.406	192	49	10	2	5	28	16	31
Sept-Oct	.438	.526	.875	16	7	2	1	1	3	1	0	.307	.346	.535	101	31	7	2	4	19	4	11
Bases Empty	.270	.314	.492	248	67	13	3	12	12	13	27	.272	.318	.460	441	120	28	5	15	15	27	59
Leadoff	.293	.333	.586	99	29	8	3	5	5	4	16	.318	.356	.582	170	54	16	4	7	7	8	26
Runners On Base	.303	.366	.474	234	71	16	3	6	73	25	26	.294	.347	.475	402	118	29	4	12	126	36	43
Scoring Position	.293	.383	.476	147	43	13	1	4	67	24	19	.291	.367	.490	261	76	21	2	9	114	35	33
Late and Close	.250	.384	.353	68	17	2	1	1	10	16	13	.255	.340	.416	137	35	6	2	4	24	19	24

RICH AMARAL — BR/TR — age 32 — SEA 2B77, 3B19, SS14, DH9, 1B3

1993

1993	BA	OBA	SA	AB	H	2B	3B	HR	RBI	BB	SO
Total	.290	.348	.367	373	108	24	1	1	44	33	54
vs. Left	.372	.411	.480	148	55	14	1	0	21	10	12
vs. Right	.236	.307	.293	225	53	10	0	1	23	23	42
at Home	.264	.353	.326	178	47	9	1	0	19	24	26
on Road	.313	.343	.405	195	61	15	0	1	25	9	28
on Grass	.306	.331	.389	157	48	10	0	1	18	6	25
on Turf	.278	.359	.352	216	60	14	1	0	26	27	29
Day Games	.245	.311	.300	110	27	6	0	0	11	10	19
Night Games	.308	.363	.395	263	81	18	1	1	33	23	35
April	.324	.377	.423	71	23	7	0	0	6	5	11
May	.330	.393	.423	97	32	6	0	1	13	10	17
June	.219	.296	.281	64	14	4	0	0	5	6	10
July	.260	.337	.286	77	20	2	0	0	8	9	8
August	.250	.235	.313	16	4	1	0	0	2	0	1
Sept-Oct	.313	.340	.438	48	15	4	1	0	10	3	7
Bases Empty	.278	.341	.352	227	63	14	0	1	1	20	29
Leadoff	.282	.336	.347	124	35	8	0	0	0	10	15
Runners On Base	.308	.358	.390	146	45	10	1	0	43	13	25
Scoring Position	.337	.375	.434	83	28	6	1	0	39	8	11
Late and Close	.281	.347	.313	64	18	2	0	0	12	7	10

3-YEAR TOTALS (1991–1993)

	BA	OBA	SA	AB	H	2B	3B	HR	RBI	BB	SO
Total	.272	.328	.344	489	133	27	1	2	51	39	75
vs. Left	.333	.373	.438	192	64	15	1	1	25	12	18
vs. Right	.232	.299	.283	297	69	12	0	1	26	27	57
at Home	.246	.331	.297	232	57	10	1	0	20	28	35
on Road	.296	.325	.385	257	76	17	0	2	31	11	40
on Grass	.301	.324	.388	206	62	12	0	2	24	7	36
on Turf	.251	.330	.311	283	71	15	1	0	27	32	39
Day Games	.250	.307	.321	140	35	7	0	1	16	11	27
Night Games	.281	.336	.352	349	98	20	1	1	35	28	48
April	.330	.374	.450	100	33	9	0	1	12	6	15
May	.275	.346	.350	120	33	6	0	1	13	12	22
June	.219	.296	.281	64	14	4	0	0	5	6	10
July	.260	.337	.286	77	20	2	0	0	8	9	8
August	.250	.235	.313	16	4	1	0	0	2	0	1
Sept-Oct	.259	.292	.321	112	29	5	1	0	11	6	19
Bases Empty	.268	.331	.332	295	79	16	0	1	1	25	43
Leadoff	.269	.325	.324	145	39	8	0	0	0	12	21
Runners On Base	.278	.322	.361	194	54	11	1	1	50	14	32
Scoring Position	.312	.350	.422	109	34	7	1	1	46	9	14
Late and Close	.253	.309	.289	83	21	3	0	0	13	7	15

BRADY ANDERSON — BL/TL — age 30 — BAL OF140, DH2

1993

1993	BA	OBA	SA	AB	H	2B	3B	HR	RBI	BB	SO
Total	.262	.363	.425	560	147	36	8	13	66	82	99
vs. Left	.259	.390	.353	170	44	10	0	2	17	32	38
vs. Right	.264	.350	.456	390	103	26	8	11	49	50	61
at Home	.242	.344	.343	265	64	17	2	2	31	40	50
on Road	.281	.381	.498	295	83	19	6	11	35	42	49
on Grass	.264	.369	.410	466	123	30	7	8	54	71	82
on Turf	.255	.333	.500	94	24	6	1	5	12	11	17
Day Games	.285	.370	.509	165	47	15	2	6	21	22	31
Night Games	.253	.360	.390	395	100	21	6	7	45	60	68
April	.287	.376	.460	87	25	7	1	2	11	12	17
May	.180	.283	.297	111	20	5	1	2	7	15	19
June	.256	.356	.500	78	20	8	1	3	10	10	12
July	.239	.341	.423	71	17	4	0	3	8	10	17
August	.319	.436	.440	91	29	6	1	1	17	20	16
Sept-Oct	.295	.383	.459	122	36	6	4	2	13	15	18
Bases Empty	.261	.354	.436	353	92	17	6	11	11	45	63
Leadoff	.262	.344	.477	214	56	10	3	10	10	25	35
Runners On Base	.266	.378	.406	207	55	19	2	2	55	37	36
Scoring Position	.260	.375	.346	127	33	9	1	0	48	24	26
Late and Close	.306	.396	.518	85	26	6	3	2	13	14	15

6-YEAR TOTALS (1988–1993)

	BA	OBA	SA	AB	H	2B	3B	HR	RBI	BB	SO
Total	.244	.343	.375	2264	553	106	29	44	234	315	407
vs. Left	.209	.334	.307	597	125	22	6	8	56	99	132
vs. Right	.257	.346	.400	1667	428	84	23	36	178	216	275
at Home	.229	.326	.348	1124	257	50	9	22	125	149	215
on Road	.260	.358	.402	1140	296	56	20	22	109	166	192
on Grass	.241	.337	.364	1873	452	84	20	35	193	250	339
on Turf	.258	.367	.430	391	101	22	9	9	41	65	68
Day Games	.270	.357	.429	652	176	34	14	14	66	81	118
Night Games	.234	.337	.353	1612	377	72	15	30	168	234	289
April	.279	.391	.451	337	94	25	9	5	44	55	69
May	.210	.297	.338	491	103	21	3	12	52	55	85
June	.237	.345	.394	287	68	17	2	8	27	44	47
July	.281	.384	.414	295	83	12	3	7	32	46	48
August	.229	.341	.327	398	91	10	4	7	44	68	70
Sept-Oct	.250	.325	.364	456	114	21	8	5	35	47	88
Bases Empty	.236	.330	.371	1434	338	64	20	30	30	180	266
Leadoff	.225	.313	.369	822	185	35	10	21	21	95	137
Runners On Base	.259	.363	.382	830	215	42	9	14	204	135	141
Scoring Position	.265	.381	.382	490	130	22	7	7	182	98	95
Late and Close	.254	.343	.368	342	87	15	6	4	35	45	70

ERIC ANTHONY — BL/TL — age 27 — HOU OF131

1993

1993	BA	OBA	SA	AB	H	2B	3B	HR	RBI	BB	SO
Total	.249	.319	.397	486	121	19	4	15	66	49	88
vs. Left	.247	.314	.380	158	39	4	1	5	25	16	38
vs. Right	.250	.321	.405	328	82	15	3	10	41	33	50
at Home	.255	.326	.382	251	64	11	3	5	31	25	46
on Road	.243	.312	.413	235	57	8	1	10	35	24	42
on Grass	.209	.273	.392	148	31	3	0	8	24	13	26
on Turf	.266	.339	.399	338	90	16	4	7	42	36	62
Day Games	.222	.300	.347	144	32	5	2	3	19	16	21
Night Games	.260	.327	.418	342	89	14	2	12	47	33	67
April	.338	.398	.512	80	27	6	1	2	13	8	11
May	.260	.327	.365	96	25	4	0	2	13	10	17
June	.217	.270	.289	83	18	1	1	1	6	6	17
July	.239	.313	.398	88	21	2	0	4	12	10	15
August	.244	.333	.511	90	22	2	2	6	16	10	18
Sept-Oct	.163	.241	.245	49	8	4	0	0	6	5	10
Bases Empty	.235	.318	.365	255	60	10	1	7	7	30	51
Leadoff	.219	.294	.395	114	25	3	1	5	5	11	19
Runners On Base	.264	.320	.433	231	61	9	3	8	59	19	37
Scoring Position	.228	.296	.362	127	29	3	1	4	44	12	24
Late and Close	.218	.279	.346	78	17	1	0	3	14	7	15

5-YEAR TOTALS (1989–1993)

	BA	OBA	SA	AB	H	2B	3B	HR	RBI	BB	SO
Total	.224	.295	.378	1344	301	50	5	49	189	137	321
vs. Left	.218	.285	.343	432	94	13	1	13	64	41	116
vs. Right	.227	.300	.395	912	207	37	4	36	125	96	205
at Home	.238	.305	.389	642	153	26	4	21	87	60	148
on Road	.211	.286	.368	702	148	24	1	28	102	77	173
on Grass	.199	.265	.379	417	83	9	0	22	69	39	99
on Turf	.235	.309	.378	927	218	41	5	27	120	98	222
Day Games	.201	.263	.353	399	80	16	3	13	53	35	86
Night Games	.234	.309	.388	945	221	34	2	36	136	102	235
April	.309	.374	.454	97	30	6	1	2	13	10	15
May	.256	.330	.404	250	64	13	0	8	40	28	55
June	.212	.276	.345	293	62	11	2	8	31	27	82
July	.201	.260	.367	264	53	8	0	12	40	23	66
August	.209	.298	.393	211	44	5	2	10	36	25	47
Sept-Oct	.210	.286	.358	229	48	7	0	9	29	24	56
Bases Empty	.198	.274	.337	733	145	20	2	26	26	74	192
Leadoff	.193	.270	.307	322	62	5	1	10	10	32	69
Runners On Base	.255	.320	.427	611	156	30	3	23	163	63	129
Scoring Position	.224	.303	.360	353	79	16	1	10	127	44	87
Late and Close	.236	.305	.393	242	57	5	0	11	42	25	62

BRAD AUSMUS — BR/TR — age 25 — SD C49

1993	BA	OBA	SA	AB	H	2B	3B	HR	RBI	BB	SO
Total	.256	.283	.412	160	41	8	1	5	12	6	28
vs. Left	.295	.340	.477	44	13	3	1	1	4	3	7
vs. Right	.241	.261	.388	116	28	5	0	4	8	3	21
at Home	.325	.341	.575	80	26	6	1	4	9	2	15
on Road	.188	.226	.250	80	15	2	0	1	3	4	13
on Grass	.286	.308	.468	126	36	6	1	5	12	4	19
on Turf	.147	.194	.206	34	5	2	0	0	0	2	9
Day Games	.286	.300	.327	49	14	2	0	0	1	1	6
Night Games	.243	.276	.450	111	27	6	1	5	11	5	22
April	.000	.000	.000	0	0	0	0	0	0	0	0
May	.000	.000	.000	0	0	0	0	0	0	0	0
June	.000	.000	.000	0	0	0	0	0	0	0	0
July	.143	.333	.143	7	1	0	0	0	0	2	3
August	.241	.259	.410	83	20	5	0	3	6	2	14
Sept-Oct	.286	.306	.443	70	20	3	1	2	6	2	11
Bases Empty	.272	.292	.417	103	28	4	1	3	3	3	14
Leadoff	.311	.326	.444	45	14	3	0	1	1	1	7
Runners On Base	.228	.267	.404	57	13	4	0	2	9	3	14
Scoring Position	.219	.242	.406	32	7	3	0	1	7	1	7
Late and Close	.190	.227	.238	21	4	1	0	0	1	1	7

1-YEAR TOTALS (1993)

	BA	OBA	SA	AB	H	2B	3B	HR	RBI	BB	SO
	.256	.283	.412	160	41	8	1	5	12	6	28
	.295	.340	.477	44	13	3	1	1	4	3	7
	.241	.261	.388	116	28	5	0	4	8	3	21
	.325	.341	.575	80	26	6	1	4	9	2	15
	.188	.226	.250	80	15	2	0	1	3	4	13
	.286	.308	.468	126	36	6	1	5	12	4	19
	.147	.194	.206	34	5	2	0	0	0	2	9
	.286	.300	.327	49	14	2	0	0	1	1	6
	.243	.276	.450	111	27	6	1	5	11	5	22
	.000	.000	.000	0	0	0	0	0	0	0	0
	.000	.000	.000	0	0	0	0	0	0	0	0
	.000	.000	.000	0	0	0	0	0	0	0	0
	.143	.333	.143	7	1	0	0	0	0	2	3
	.241	.259	.410	83	20	5	0	3	6	2	14
	.286	.306	.443	70	20	3	1	2	6	2	11
	.272	.292	.417	103	28	4	1	3	3	3	14
	.311	.326	.444	45	14	3	0	1	1	1	7
	.228	.267	.404	57	13	4	0	2	9	3	14
	.219	.242	.406	32	7	3	0	1	7	1	7
	.190	.227	.238	21	4	1	0	0	1	1	7

CARLOS BAERGA — BB/TR — age 26 — CLE 2B150, DH4

1993	BA	OBA	SA	AB	H	2B	3B	HR	RBI	BB	SO
Total	.321	.355	.486	624	200	28	6	21	114	34	68
vs. Left	.315	.345	.447	219	69	5	3	6	33	7	25
vs. Right	.323	.360	.506	405	131	23	3	15	81	27	43
at Home	.331	.356	.468	299	99	11	3	8	60	15	35
on Road	.311	.353	.502	325	101	17	3	13	54	19	33
on Grass	.318	.354	.480	531	169	22	5	18	97	30	59
on Turf	.333	.360	.516	93	31	6	1	3	17	4	9
Day Games	.342	.373	.523	199	68	6	3	8	42	10	24
Night Games	.311	.346	.468	425	132	22	3	13	72	24	44
April	.286	.313	.473	91	26	5	0	4	14	3	13
May	.274	.304	.443	106	29	4	4	2	22	5	12
June	.333	.353	.602	108	36	6	1	7	24	4	14
July	.337	.384	.462	104	35	4	0	3	15	6	10
August	.341	.390	.496	123	42	5	1	4	23	11	11
Sept-Oct	.348	.373	.424	92	32	4	0	1	16	5	8
Bases Empty	.303	.333	.465	333	101	17	2	11	11	13	34
Leadoff	.333	.365	.533	120	40	5	2	5	5	5	8
Runners On Base	.340	.377	.509	291	99	11	4	10	103	21	34
Scoring Position	.341	.385	.527	167	57	4	3	7	92	18	26
Late and Close	.292	.358	.406	96	28	2	0	3	13	9	9

4-YEAR TOTALS (1990–1993)

	BA	OBA	SA	AB	H	2B	3B	HR	RBI	BB	SO
	.301	.344	.440	2186	657	105	11	59	335	133	275
	.323	.350	.436	651	210	26	3	14	104	20	80
	.291	.342	.441	1535	447	79	8	45	231	113	195
	.322	.361	.442	1077	347	51	6	22	170	62	124
	.280	.329	.437	1109	310	54	5	37	165	71	151
	.307	.349	.450	1854	569	86	9	54	293	113	222
	.265	.319	.380	332	88	19	2	5	42	20	53
	.296	.347	.434	700	207	24	5	21	114	50	91
	.303	.343	.442	1486	450	81	6	38	221	83	184
	.274	.309	.412	274	75	9	1	9	32	13	30
	.285	.329	.400	375	107	12	5	7	63	22	38
	.288	.339	.499	351	101	21	1	17	58	27	51
	.318	.363	.454	337	107	17	1	9	43	21	43
	.312	.352	.447	414	129	21	1	11	69	21	55
	.317	.362	.425	435	138	25	2	6	70	29	58
	.284	.325	.414	1220	346	60	3	31	31	61	155
	.296	.341	.440	423	125	21	2	12	12	24	41
	.322	.367	.472	966	311	45	8	28	304	72	120
	.304	.362	.451	586	178	18	4	20	269	60	83
	.275	.338	.391	389	107	21	0	8	48	32	55

JEFF BAGWELL — BR/TR — age 26 — HOU 1B140

1993	BA	OBA	SA	AB	H	2B	3B	HR	RBI	BB	SO
Total	.320	.388	.516	535	171	37	4	20	88	62	73
vs. Left	.318	.408	.592	179	57	17	1	10	36	30	20
vs. Right	.320	.376	.478	356	114	20	3	10	52	32	53
at Home	.330	.409	.509	267	88	17	2	9	43	37	32
on Road	.310	.365	.522	268	83	20	2	11	45	25	41
on Grass	.337	.382	.596	166	56	12	2	9	34	15	26
on Turf	.312	.390	.480	369	115	25	2	11	54	47	47
Day Games	.272	.344	.463	162	44	7	0	8	26	17	26
Night Games	.340	.406	.539	373	127	30	4	12	62	45	47
April	.314	.404	.523	86	27	7	1	3	15	13	11
May	.412	.467	.676	102	42	6	0	7	25	14	13
June	.240	.292	.365	96	23	4	1	2	8	8	11
July	.289	.349	.474	114	33	7	1	4	21	10	14
August	.352	.419	.574	108	38	10	1	4	15	13	21
Sept-Oct	.276	.382	.379	29	8	3	0	0	4	4	3
Bases Empty	.306	.368	.520	294	90	20	2	13	13	27	38
Leadoff	.324	.348	.574	108	35	8	2	5	5	4	14
Runners On Base	.336	.409	.510	241	81	17	2	7	75	35	35
Scoring Position	.291	.373	.449	127	37	6	1	4	63	21	19
Late and Close	.226	.290	.357	84	19	5	0	2	9	8	14

3-YEAR TOTALS (1991–1993)

	BA	OBA	SA	AB	H	2B	3B	HR	RBI	BB	SO
	.295	.380	.464	1675	494	97	14	53	266	221	286
	.309	.406	.526	595	184	40	4	27	107	101	88
	.287	.366	.431	1080	310	57	10	26	159	120	198
	.293	.384	.456	835	245	53	7	23	126	115	134
	.296	.377	.473	840	249	44	7	30	140	106	152
	.315	.393	.498	496	156	18	5	21	97	67	89
	.287	.375	.450	1179	338	79	9	32	169	154	197
	.283	.359	.458	456	129	22	2	18	71	53	77
	.299	.388	.467	1219	365	75	12	35	195	168	209
	.278	.377	.453	223	62	14	2	7	35	35	47
	.297	.378	.490	296	88	13	1	14	55	36	62
	.283	.360	.421	297	84	16	2	7	32	38	44
	.281	.367	.477	285	80	16	5	10	49	38	47
	.289	.382	.447	318	92	21	4	7	51	46	50
	.344	.423	.504	256	88	17	0	8	44	28	36
	.291	.370	.468	914	266	59	8	29	29	104	147
	.300	.373	.474	363	109	27	3	10	10	36	64
	.300	.392	.460	761	228	38	6	24	237	117	139
	.284	.385	.435	457	130	17	5	14	206	82	90
	.316	.431	.535	269	85	19	2	12	50	49	46

HAROLD BAINES — BL/TL — age 35 — BAL DH116

1993	BA	OBA	SA	AB	H	2B	3B	HR	RBI	BB	SO		10-YEAR TOTALS (1984–1993) BA	OBA	SA	AB	H	2B	3B	HR	RBI	BB	SO
Total	.313	.390	.510	416	130	22	0	20	78	57	52		.294	.361	.464	5185	1523	260	23	193	850	575	783
vs. Left	.260	.330	.427	96	25	4	0	4	18	10	16		.275	.327	.416	1471	404	63	8	43	217	117	280
vs. Right	.328	.408	.534	320	105	18	0	16	60	47	36		.301	.374	.484	3714	1119	197	15	150	633	458	503
at Home	.345	.431	.584	197	68	11	0	12	46	32	24		.299	.368	.485	2501	749	138	11	101	471	287	363
on Road	.283	.352	.443	219	62	11	0	8	32	25	28		.288	.355	.446	2684	774	122	12	92	379	288	420
on Grass	.310	.393	.504	355	110	18	0	17	66	51	39		.296	.366	.467	4366	1294	222	16	164	739	500	653
on Turf	.328	.377	.541	61	20	4	0	3	12	6	13		.280	.336	.449	819	229	38	7	29	111	75	130
Day Games	.321	.407	.491	106	34	6	0	4	14	16	14		.306	.375	.474	1478	453	76	8	52	241	174	236
Night Games	.310	.385	.516	310	96	16	0	16	64	41	38		.289	.356	.460	3707	1070	184	15	141	609	401	547
April	.298	.349	.351	57	17	3	0	0	6	5	12		.255	.324	.387	643	164	29	1	18	87	66	110
May	.348	.516	.478	23	8	3	0	0	2	8	4		.289	.362	.424	819	237	39	1	23	118	100	113
June	.292	.347	.483	89	26	5	0	4	19	8	10		.303	.376	.507	942	285	43	6	46	173	118	142
July	.392	.448	.689	74	29	4	0	6	22	10	11		.331	.399	.517	876	290	55	3	34	162	102	142
August	.250	.371	.387	80	20	2	0	3	10	16	7		.277	.342	.448	929	257	38	8	35	147	96	132
Sept-Oct	.323	.388	.602	93	30	5	0	7	19	10	8		.297	.354	.476	976	290	56	4	37	163	93	144
Bases Empty	.289	.357	.482	228	66	11	0	11	11	24	35		.277	.340	.435	2859	791	139	10	98	98	271	448
Leadoff	.316	.386	.500	114	36	6	0	5	5	13	17		.271	.334	.408	1028	279	45	4	29	29	96	153
Runners On Base	.340	.427	.543	188	64	11	0	9	67	33	17		.315	.386	.500	2326	732	121	13	95	752	304	335
Scoring Position	.333	.412	.550	111	37	9	0	5	57	19	13		.302	.388	.482	1344	406	69	7	53	635	226	217
Late and Close	.278	.349	.463	54	15	4	0	2	9	7	9		.283	.375	.473	755	214	40	2	33	115	111	123

BRET BARBERIE — BB/TR — age 27 — FLO 2B97

1993	BA	OBA	SA	AB	H	2B	3B	HR	RBI	BB	SO		3-YEAR TOTALS (1991–1993) BA	OBA	SA	AB	H	2B	3B	HR	RBI	BB	SO
Total	.277	.344	.371	375	104	16	2	5	33	33	58		.274	.364	.363	796	218	39	4	8	75	100	142
vs. Left	.312	.370	.422	109	34	6	0	2	3	9	15		.258	.342	.357	213	55	12	0	3	15	24	38
vs. Right	.263	.334	.350	266	70	10	2	3	30	24	43		.280	.372	.365	583	163	27	4	5	60	76	104
at Home	.226	.305	.307	199	45	8	1	2	15	18	31		.253	.351	.323	372	94	12	1	4	34	50	61
on Road	.335	.391	.443	176	59	8	1	3	18	15	27		.292	.375	.399	424	124	27	3	4	41	50	81
on Grass	.246	.327	.338	293	72	11	2	4	30	31	46		.246	.330	.341	414	102	18	3	5	41	45	79
on Turf	.390	.412	.488	82	32	5	0	1	3	2	12		.304	.399	.387	382	116	21	1	3	34	55	63
Day Games	.322	.410	.425	87	28	6	0	1	10	11	11		.251	.351	.344	247	62	15	1	2	25	36	52
Night Games	.264	.324	.354	288	76	10	2	4	23	22	47		.284	.370	.372	549	156	24	3	6	50	64	90
April	.286	.390	.286	35	10	0	0	0	1	6	6		.248	.373	.286	105	26	4	0	0	2	20	24
May	.250	.357	.250	12	3	0	0	0	0	1	2		.262	.392	.262	42	11	0	0	0	5	7	12
June	.312	.407	.419	93	29	5	1	1	8	14	16		.276	.377	.374	123	34	7	1	1	14	18	23
July	.154	.185	.269	26	4	0	0	1	2	1	5		.233	.337	.360	86	20	5	0	2	12	12	17
August	.333	.381	.500	108	36	7	1	3	12	6	13		.300	.358	.438	210	63	10	2	5	20	14	38
Sept-Oct	.218	.264	.257	101	22	4	0	0	10	5	16		.278	.362	.343	230	64	13	1	0	22	29	28
Bases Empty	.275	.340	.374	222	61	11	1	3	3	19	36		.274	.358	.369	485	133	22	3	6	6	52	81
Leadoff	.310	.355	.465	71	22	5	0	2	2	4	11		.283	.330	.401	187	53	11	1	3	3	9	28
Runners On Base	.281	.351	.366	153	43	5	1	2	30	14	22		.273	.373	.354	311	85	17	1	2	69	48	61
Scoring Position	.258	.349	.326	89	23	3	0	1	26	11	16		.250	.369	.323	192	48	11	0	1	62	36	42
Late and Close	.320	.378	.373	75	24	4	0	0	6	6	13		.285	.359	.366	172	49	11	0	1	17	17	37

DEREK BELL — BR/TR — age 26 — SD OF125, 3B19

1993	BA	OBA	SA	AB	H	2B	3B	HR	RBI	BB	SO		3-YEAR TOTALS (1991–1993) BA	OBA	SA	AB	H	2B	3B	HR	RBI	BB	SO
Total	.262	.303	.417	542	142	19	1	21	72	23	122		.253	.308	.393	731	185	25	4	23	88	44	161
vs. Left	.299	.342	.520	177	53	6	0	11	30	10	31		.279	.336	.484	244	68	9	1	13	36	16	44
vs. Right	.244	.284	.367	365	89	13	1	10	42	13	91		.240	.294	.347	487	117	16	3	10	52	28	117
at Home	.252	.309	.416	274	69	9	0	12	34	17	60		.225	.298	.375	373	84	10	2	14	39	27	81
on Road	.272	.296	.418	268	73	10	1	9	38	6	62		.282	.319	.411	358	101	15	2	9	49	17	80
on Grass	.262	.306	.442	416	109	16	1	19	62	20	86		.268	.311	.435	485	130	20	2	19	70	24	100
on Turf	.262	.290	.333	126	33	3	0	2	10	3	36		.224	.302	.309	246	55	5	2	4	18	20	61
Day Games	.207	.254	.331	169	35	9	0	4	16	6	40		.211	.273	.318	242	51	12	1	4	20	12	59
Night Games	.287	.324	.456	373	107	10	1	17	56	17	82		.274	.325	.429	489	134	13	3	19	68	32	102
April	.274	.346	.521	73	20	3	0	5	11	7	25		.282	.349	.513	78	22	3	0	5	12	7	26
May	.330	.358	.495	103	34	2	0	5	17	2	19		.258	.305	.394	155	40	3	0	6	20	7	31
June	.208	.259	.317	101	21	2	0	3	11	5	28		.226	.291	.331	124	28	4	0	3	14	10	32
July	.204	.232	.301	93	19	4	1	1	8	2	20		.203	.257	.297	128	26	4	1	2	10	6	29
August	.283	.320	.467	92	26	5	0	4	17	4	20		.275	.315	.442	138	38	7	2	4	22	7	29
Sept-Oct	.275	.310	.425	80	22	3	0	3	8	3	10		.287	.352	.426	108	31	4	1	3	10	7	14
Bases Empty	.242	.270	.376	306	74	11	0	10	10	10	69		.232	.278	.355	422	98	14	1	12	12	22	94
Leadoff	.305	.345	.481	131	40	8	0	5	5	6	26		.295	.345	.459	183	54	10	1	6	6	10	33
Runners On Base	.288	.341	.470	236	68	8	1	11	62	13	53		.282	.346	.443	309	87	11	3	11	76	22	67
Scoring Position	.259	.335	.381	139	36	2	0	5	47	11	31		.257	.341	.372	183	47	4	1	5	60	18	40
Late and Close	.218	.288	.297	101	22	2	0	2	9	6	25		.233	.315	.318	129	30	2	0	3	12	11	30

JAY BELL — BR/TR — age 29 — PIT SS154

1993	BA	OBA	SA	AB	H	2B	3B	HR	RBI	BB	SO	8-YEAR TOTALS (1986–1993) BA	OBA	SA	AB	H	2B	3B	HR	RBI	BB	SO
Total	.310	.392	.437	604	187	32	9	9	51	77	122	.267	.335	.389	3048	814	157	35	48	290	299	567
vs. Left	.342	.449	.484	190	65	14	2	3	21	33	30	.305	.385	.442	1067	325	69	18	14	111	137	167
vs. Right	.295	.364	.415	414	122	18	7	6	30	44	92	.247	.307	.360	1981	489	88	17	34	179	162	400
at Home	.322	.424	.441	286	92	19	3	3	22	49	57	.273	.347	.395	1503	410	89	17	20	129	165	282
on Road	.299	.362	.434	318	95	13	6	6	29	28	65	.261	.323	.383	1545	404	68	18	28	161	134	285
on Grass	.333	.390	.493	207	69	10	4	5	20	18	42	.257	.317	.379	1005	258	47	14	16	100	85	200
on Turf	.297	.393	.408	397	118	22	5	4	31	59	80	.272	.344	.394	2043	556	110	21	32	190	214	367
Day Games	.333	.417	.477	174	58	14	1	3	15	23	29	.278	.345	.414	867	241	58	9	14	93	84	165
Night Games	.300	.382	.421	430	129	18	8	6	36	54	93	.263	.331	.379	2181	573	99	26	34	197	215	402
April	.326	.376	.465	86	28	5	2	1	6	7	16	.224	.303	.302	388	87	13	4	3	31	42	69
May	.300	.358	.445	110	33	11	1	1	10	10	27	.277	.342	.415	465	129	34	3	8	50	47	94
June	.326	.435	.442	95	31	3	1	2	11	18	20	.284	.362	.415	422	120	18	8	7	42	50	84
July	.273	.322	.382	110	30	5	2	1	7	6	18	.265	.309	.384	536	142	29	4	9	47	33	80
August	.386	.453	.526	114	44	8	1	2	13	13	22	.282	.334	.397	582	164	31	6	8	50	43	113
Sept-Oct	.236	.404	.348	89	21	0	2	2	4	23	19	.263	.352	.402	655	172	32	10	13	70	84	127
Bases Empty	.316	.386	.472	377	119	18	7	9	9	39	76	.245	.316	.364	1842	451	86	16	34	34	177	363
Leadoff	.288	.368	.500	104	30	4	3	4	4	13	22	.262	.333	.413	545	143	24	8	14	14	57	105
Runners On Base	.300	.403	.379	227	68	14	2	0	42	38	46	.301	.364	.426	1206	363	71	19	14	256	122	204
Scoring Position	.274	.411	.342	117	32	6	1	0	38	27	26	.289	.357	.422	650	188	35	12	9	226	74	121
Late and Close	.268	.383	.320	97	26	3	1	0	11	18	29	.261	.338	.360	472	123	16	8	5	50	56	98

GEORGE BELL — BR/TR — age 35 — CHA DH102

1993	BA	OBA	SA	AB	H	2B	3B	HR	RBI	BB	SO	10-YEAR TOTALS (1984–1993) BA	OBA	SA	AB	H	2B	3B	HR	RBI	BB	SO
Total	.217	.243	.363	410	89	17	2	13	64	13	49	.279	.318	.473	5848	1634	301	29	258	973	322	727
vs. Left	.193	.217	.312	109	21	4	0	3	12	4	17	.286	.330	.511	1760	504	87	9	97	308	116	208
vs. Right	.226	.252	.382	301	68	13	2	10	52	9	32	.276	.313	.457	4088	1130	214	20	161	665	206	519
at Home	.224	.249	.388	201	45	8	2	7	38	6	25	.282	.324	.470	2856	806	149	19	116	491	171	355
on Road	.211	.238	.340	209	44	9	0	6	26	7	24	.277	.312	.477	2992	828	152	10	142	482	151	372
on Grass	.231	.253	.390	364	84	15	2	13	62	10	40	.273	.307	.458	3031	826	143	7	135	519	149	374
on Turf	.109	.163	.152	46	5	2	0	0	2	3	9	.287	.330	.490	2817	808	158	22	123	454	173	353
Day Games	.254	.257	.425	134	34	6	1	5	27	2	12	.273	.315	.469	1930	526	105	13	83	321	111	254
Night Games	.199	.236	.333	276	55	11	1	8	37	11	37	.283	.320	.475	3918	1108	196	16	175	652	211	473
April	.186	.247	.233	86	16	4	0	0	8	6	8	.297	.334	.496	816	242	46	3	37	125	42	97
May	.262	.275	.427	103	27	3	1	4	18	2	8	.271	.309	.455	1014	275	41	11	41	171	55	129
June	.229	.241	.371	105	24	7	1	2	16	3	15	.281	.315	.480	1089	306	53	4	52	197	59	153
July	.217	.217	.348	23	5	0	0	1	4	0	2	.273	.320	.466	877	239	44	3	40	148	58	109
August	.000	.000	.000	0	0	0	0	0	0	0	0	.306	.348	.536	968	296	64	3	51	180	59	106
Sept-Oct	.183	.212	.409	93	17	3	0	6	18	2	16	.255	.289	.415	1084	276	53	5	37	152	49	133
Bases Empty	.192	.229	.324	213	41	10	0	6	6	8	27	.273	.316	.483	3044	831	158	15	150	150	166	400
Leadoff	.204	.228	.327	98	20	6	0	2	2	2	12	.268	.305	.472	1408	377	75	7	66	66	63	182
Runners On Base	.244	.258	.406	197	48	7	2	7	58	5	22	.286	.320	.463	2804	803	143	14	108	823	156	327
Scoring Position	.221	.230	.426	122	27	2	1	7	56	3	19	.288	.327	.480	1657	477	84	8	73	718	126	218
Late and Close	.226	.250	.321	53	12	0	1	1	6	1	4	.277	.321	.472	931	258	42	5	43	156	59	123

ALBERT BELLE — BR/TR — age 28 — CLE OF150, DH9

1993	BA	OBA	SA	AB	H	2B	3B	HR	RBI	BB	SO	5-YEAR TOTALS (1989–1993) BA	OBA	SA	AB	H	2B	3B	HR	RBI	BB	SO
Total	.290	.370	.552	594	172	36	3	38	129	76	96	.270	.330	.505	1881	507	98	10	108	376	166	384
vs. Left	.327	.412	.617	162	53	11	0	12	39	26	25	.287	.344	.551	499	143	34	1	32	113	48	99
vs. Right	.275	.353	.528	432	119	25	3	26	90	50	71	.263	.325	.488	1382	364	64	9	76	263	118	285
at Home	.306	.399	.583	271	83	11	2	20	66	42	36	.272	.336	.484	920	250	46	4	47	191	87	180
on Road	.276	.344	.526	323	89	25	1	18	63	34	60	.267	.325	.524	961	257	52	6	61	185	79	204
on Grass	.287	.371	.554	495	142	29	2	33	107	67	80	.266	.327	.499	1600	425	83	7	92	317	145	325
on Turf	.303	.363	.545	99	30	7	1	5	22	9	16	.292	.347	.537	281	82	15	3	16	59	21	59
Day Games	.340	.403	.636	206	70	16	0	15	43	22	26	.290	.349	.548	604	175	42	3	36	125	51	115
Night Games	.263	.353	.508	388	102	20	3	23	86	54	70	.260	.321	.484	1277	332	56	7	72	251	115	269
April	.302	.365	.640	86	26	5	0	8	21	6	16	.260	.324	.516	246	64	12	0	17	46	18	58
May	.276	.372	.533	105	29	6	0	7	23	14	14	.286	.361	.549	297	85	17	2	19	62	33	57
June	.298	.386	.619	84	25	8	2	5	19	12	16	.257	.321	.495	218	56	12	2	12	38	19	41
July	.341	.432	.681	91	31	4	0	9	25	17	12	.289	.345	.543	322	93	12	2	22	74	30	59
August	.282	.360	.470	117	33	7	0	5	22	15	17	.259	.315	.471	401	104	20	1	21	73	33	86
Sept-Oct	.252	.315	.432	111	28	6	1	4	19	12	21	.264	.319	.471	397	105	25	3	17	83	33	83
Bases Empty	.280	.348	.557	307	86	20	1	21	21	28	51	.255	.312	.479	967	247	47	5	53	53	71	201
Leadoff	.271	.320	.464	140	38	13	1	4	4	9	18	.269	.322	.470	453	122	26	4	19	19	31	84
Runners On Base	.300	.391	.547	287	86	16	2	17	108	48	45	.284	.348	.532	914	260	51	5	55	323	95	183
Scoring Position	.302	.408	.585	159	48	10	1	11	90	37	29	.290	.362	.560	504	146	34	3	32	265	69	112
Late and Close	.333	.444	.679	81	27	5	1	7	26	17	12	.255	.325	.456	294	75	10	2	15	70	32	71

SEAN BERRY — BR/TR — age 28 — MON 3B96

1993

	BA	OBA	SA	AB	H	2B	3B	HR	RBI	BB	SO
Total	.261	.348	.465	299	78	15	2	14	49	41	70
vs. Left	.232	.348	.379	95	22	3	1	3	9	17	15
vs. Right	.275	.347	.505	204	56	12	1	11	40	24	55
at Home	.261	.362	.410	134	35	5	0	5	22	23	34
on Road	.261	.335	.509	165	43	10	2	9	27	18	36
on Grass	.267	.368	.515	101	27	5	1	6	13	15	22
on Turf	.258	.338	.439	198	51	10	1	8	36	26	48
Day Games	.256	.346	.522	90	23	4	1	6	22	13	21
Night Games	.263	.349	.440	209	55	11	1	8	27	28	49
April	.160	.371	.160	25	4	0	0	0	4	8	6
May	.235	.278	.412	17	4	0	0	1	4	0	4
June	.302	.392	.628	43	13	2	0	4	9	7	8
July	.292	.346	.361	72	21	2	0	1	8	7	19
August	.211	.291	.500	76	16	5	1	5	15	9	20
Sept-Oct	.303	.390	.561	66	20	6	1	3	9	10	13
Bases Empty	.298	.379	.542	168	50	7	2	10	10	21	35
Leadoff	.284	.333	.507	67	19	4	1	3	3	5	11
Runners On Base	.214	.310	.366	131	28	8	0	4	39	20	35
Scoring Position	.216	.324	.375	88	19	5	0	3	34	16	24
Late and Close	.197	.254	.197	61	12	0	0	0	8	4	21

4-YEAR TOTALS (1990–1993)

	BA	OBA	SA	AB	H	2B	3B	HR	RBI	BB	SO
	.251	.326	.412	439	110	20	3	15	58	49	109
vs. Left	.227	.323	.348	141	32	4	2	3	12	20	27
vs. Right	.262	.327	.443	298	78	16	1	12	46	29	82
at Home	.264	.355	.393	178	47	8	0	5	25	26	49
on Road	.241	.304	.425	261	63	12	3	10	33	23	60
on Grass	.247	.331	.443	158	39	6	2	7	17	19	37
on Turf	.253	.323	.395	281	71	14	1	8	41	30	72
Day Games	.259	.344	.467	135	35	5	1	7	24	18	34
Night Games	.247	.318	.388	304	75	15	2	8	34	31	75
April	.160	.371	.160	25	4	0	0	0	4	8	6
May	.161	.212	.290	31	5	1	0	1	4	1	7
June	.302	.392	.628	43	13	2	0	4	9	7	8
July	.292	.346	.361	72	21	2	0	1	8	7	19
August	.212	.275	.434	99	21	5	1	5	15	9	29
Sept-Oct	.272	.340	.426	169	46	10	2	4	18	17	40
Bases Empty	.267	.337	.457	247	66	10	2	11	11	24	56
Leadoff	.293	.327	.495	99	29	6	1	4	4	5	16
Runners On Base	.229	.313	.354	192	44	10	1	4	47	25	53
Scoring Position	.213	.315	.352	122	26	6	1	3	41	20	36
Late and Close	.221	.261	.221	86	19	0	0	0	8	4	28

DAMON BERRYHILL — BB/TR — age 31 — ATL C105

1993

	BA	OBA	SA	AB	H	2B	3B	HR	RBI	BB	SO
Total	.245	.291	.382	335	82	18	2	8	43	21	64
vs. Left	.272	.315	.432	81	22	5	1	2	14	6	13
vs. Right	.236	.283	.366	254	60	13	1	6	29	15	51
at Home	.275	.306	.450	171	47	10	1	6	26	9	35
on Road	.213	.275	.311	164	35	8	1	2	17	12	29
on Grass	.249	.290	.407	253	63	14	1	8	35	16	47
on Turf	.232	.292	.305	82	19	4	1	0	8	5	17
Day Games	.214	.272	.310	84	18	5	0	1	6	6	15
Night Games	.255	.297	.406	251	64	13	2	7	37	15	49
April	.325	.364	.575	40	13	4	0	2	6	3	7
May	.132	.175	.184	38	5	2	0	0	3	2	6
June	.295	.340	.568	44	13	4	1	2	7	3	8
July	.233	.246	.317	60	14	2	0	1	7	1	11
August	.219	.321	.315	73	16	2	1	1	6	10	12
Sept-Oct	.262	.282	.387	80	21	6	0	2	14	2	20
Bases Empty	.218	.271	.341	179	39	11	1	3	3	11	40
Leadoff	.211	.273	.296	71	15	4	1	0	0	5	10
Runners On Base	.276	.314	.429	156	43	7	1	5	40	10	24
Scoring Position	.242	.299	.358	95	23	5	0	2	33	9	18
Late and Close	.203	.254	.356	59	12	3	0	2	6	4	15

7-YEAR TOTALS (1987–1993)

	BA	OBA	SA	AB	H	2B	3B	HR	RBI	BB	SO
Total	.238	.280	.366	1525	363	79	4	36	189	90	301
vs. Left	.252	.283	.363	397	100	18	1	8	53	20	53
vs. Right	.233	.279	.367	1128	263	61	3	28	136	70	248
at Home	.269	.306	.427	765	206	46	3	23	112	43	159
on Road	.207	.254	.304	760	157	33	1	13	77	47	142
on Grass	.246	.288	.386	1072	264	57	3	29	144	64	214
on Turf	.219	.263	.318	453	99	22	1	7	45	26	87
Day Games	.240	.282	.345	641	154	38	1	9	71	40	132
Night Games	.236	.279	.381	884	209	41	3	27	118	50	169
April	.240	.284	.440	125	30	7	0	6	16	8	24
May	.223	.244	.348	305	68	17	0	7	35	9	57
June	.286	.323	.394	231	66	14	1	3	35	14	46
July	.198	.239	.292	257	51	9	0	5	26	12	49
August	.258	.325	.425	252	65	14	2	8	30	24	43
Sept-Oct	.234	.279	.349	355	83	18	1	7	47	23	82
Bases Empty	.228	.271	.359	817	186	46	2	19	19	44	171
Leadoff	.234	.273	.359	320	75	17	1	7	7	15	61
Runners On Base	.250	.291	.374	708	177	33	2	17	170	46	130
Scoring Position	.251	.304	.370	419	105	23	0	9	148	38	87
Late and Close	.219	.272	.333	288	63	13	1	6	27	20	68

DANTE BICHETTE — BR/TR — age 31 — COL OF137

1993

	BA	OBA	SA	AB	H	2B	3B	HR	RBI	BB	SO
Total	.310	.348	.526	538	167	43	5	21	89	28	99
vs. Left	.286	.346	.496	119	34	11	1	4	18	10	22
vs. Right	.317	.348	.535	419	133	32	4	17	71	18	77
at Home	.373	.408	.650	260	97	29	5	11	51	13	37
on Road	.252	.291	.410	278	70	14	0	10	38	15	62
on Grass	.319	.359	.539	401	128	33	5	15	63	22	69
on Turf	.285	.313	.489	137	39	10	0	6	26	6	30
Day Games	.271	.304	.459	170	46	14	0	6	23	7	34
Night Games	.329	.368	.557	368	121	29	5	15	66	21	65
April	.314	.359	.514	70	22	5	0	3	14	5	11
May	.303	.369	.485	99	30	5	2	3	15	11	18
June	.313	.327	.500	96	30	12	0	2	13	3	20
July	.324	.352	.657	102	33	11	1	7	21	4	20
August	.309	.339	.527	110	34	8	2	4	15	4	23
Sept-Oct	.295	.338	.426	61	18	2	0	2	11	1	7
Bases Empty	.301	.337	.518	299	90	26	3	11	11	15	55
Leadoff	.297	.319	.429	91	27	7	1	1	1	3	15
Runners On Base	.322	.361	.536	239	77	17	2	10	78	13	44
Scoring Position	.308	.359	.462	143	44	6	2	4	64	11	31
Late and Close	.313	.352	.675	83	26	6	0	8	21	3	13

6-YEAR TOTALS (1988–1993)

	BA	OBA	SA	AB	H	2B	3B	HR	RBI	BB	SO
Total	.270	.303	.434	1903	514	112	11	59	265	88	390
vs. Left	.267	.311	.439	651	174	40	6	20	93	41	137
vs. Right	.272	.300	.431	1252	340	72	5	39	172	47	253
at Home	.282	.318	.469	891	251	59	9	30	141	44	167
on Road	.260	.291	.402	1012	263	53	2	29	124	44	223
on Grass	.271	.306	.437	1548	420	88	11	49	215	72	309
on Turf	.265	.293	.417	355	94	24	0	10	50	16	81
Day Games	.275	.314	.446	625	172	37	2	22	89	34	132
Night Games	.268	.298	.427	1278	342	75	9	37	176	54	258
April	.280	.311	.440	300	84	18	0	10	47	14	53
May	.264	.308	.420	421	111	21	3	13	54	27	89
June	.258	.291	.449	314	81	26	2	10	48	16	70
July	.296	.321	.509	291	86	18	1	14	49	12	64
August	.261	.307	.412	272	71	17	3	6	28	13	63
Sept-Oct	.266	.282	.377	305	81	12	2	6	39	6	51
Bases Empty	.274	.311	.441	1036	284	64	5	33	33	50	213
Leadoff	.278	.308	.412	396	110	23	3	8	8	15	84
Runners On Base	.265	.294	.424	867	230	48	6	26	232	38	177
Scoring Position	.255	.293	.411	487	124	21	5	15	200	32	115
Late and Close	.282	.314	.458	330	93	12	2	14	59	13	71

CRAIG BIGGIO — BR/TR — age 29 — HOU 2B155

6-YEAR TOTALS (1988–1993)

1993	BA	OBA	SA	AB	H	2B	3B	HR	RBI	BB	SO	BA	OBA	SA	AB	H	2B	3B	HR	RBI	BB	SO
Total	.287	.373	.474	610	175	41	5	21	64	77	93	.276	.355	.392	2890	799	147	17	51	256	333	431
vs. Left	.295	.408	.508	183	54	11	2	8	19	32	22	.266	.365	.375	966	257	42	6	17	74	146	109
vs. Right	.283	.357	.459	427	121	30	3	13	45	45	71	.282	.350	.401	1924	542	105	11	34	182	187	322
at Home	.285	.389	.444	295	84	19	2	8	30	46	50	.281	.364	.395	1426	400	81	11	20	124	177	222
on Road	.289	.358	.502	315	91	22	3	13	34	31	43	.273	.347	.389	1464	399	66	6	31	132	156	209
on Grass	.289	.371	.520	204	59	14	3	9	23	25	31	.265	.333	.381	909	241	34	4	21	79	88	126
on Turf	.286	.374	.451	406	116	27	2	12	41	52	62	.282	.365	.397	1981	558	113	13	30	177	245	305
Day Games	.276	.348	.470	185	51	9	3	7	15	17	27	.295	.371	.440	757	223	39	7	19	77	84	100
Night Games	.292	.384	.475	425	124	32	2	14	49	60	66	.270	.349	.375	2133	576	108	10	32	179	249	331
April	.250	.362	.375	80	20	5	1	1	4	14	10	.290	.371	.390	328	95	14	2	5	19	42	53
May	.324	.398	.581	105	34	9	0	6	10	11	16	.302	.368	.437	483	146	30	1	11	50	49	82
June	.212	.297	.442	104	22	7	1	5	11	11	15	.254	.343	.379	496	126	24	1	12	41	64	67
July	.291	.388	.408	103	30	7	1	1	11	13	18	.281	.355	.370	527	148	25	5	4	43	51	72
August	.318	.394	.545	110	35	10	0	5	20	15	12	.282	.371	.405	511	144	28	4	9	54	71	64
Sept-Oct	.315	.395	.463	108	34	3	2	3	8	13	22	.257	.331	.374	545	140	26	4	10	49	56	93
Bases Empty	.274	.357	.479	420	115	29	3	17	17	47	67	.271	.345	.401	1826	495	97	12	39	39	188	266
Leadoff	.271	.346	.454	251	68	13	3	9	9	26	36	.262	.336	.412	885	232	47	10	22	22	93	117
Runners On Base	.316	.408	.463	190	60	12	2	4	47	30	26	.286	.372	.376	1064	304	50	5	12	217	145	165
Scoring Position	.284	.389	.440	116	33	7	1	3	41	20	19	.273	.378	.360	619	169	26	2	8	194	107	115
Late and Close	.244	.387	.372	86	21	5	0	2	8	16	13	.254	.350	.351	496	126	23	2	7	51	65	76

LANCE BLANKENSHIP — BR/TR — age 31 — OAK OF66, 2B19, 1B6, DH5, SS2

6-YEAR TOTALS (1988–1993)

1993	BA	OBA	SA	AB	H	2B	3B	HR	RBI	BB	SO	BA	OBA	SA	AB	H	2B	3B	HR	RBI	BB	SO
Total	.190	.363	.254	252	48	8	1	2	23	67	64	.222	.350	.299	1050	233	48	3	9	92	200	218
vs. Left	.145	.336	.181	83	12	3	0	0	5	24	28	.205	.345	.264	352	72	15	0	2	30	73	70
vs. Right	.213	.377	.290	169	36	5	1	2	18	43	36	.231	.353	.317	698	161	33	3	7	62	127	148
at Home	.210	.385	.306	124	26	6	0	2	16	36	39	.220	.357	.301	509	112	25	2	4	50	105	113
on Road	.172	.342	.203	128	22	2	1	0	7	31	25	.224	.344	.298	541	121	23	1	5	42	95	105
on Grass	.176	.350	.236	199	35	6	0	2	19	53	54	.222	.351	.299	871	193	42	2	7	80	168	186
on Turf	.245	.412	.321	53	13	2	1	0	4	14	10	.223	.346	.302	179	40	6	1	2	12	32	32
Day Games	.180	.366	.252	111	20	5	0	1	13	32	31	.208	.339	.272	448	93	18	1	3	34	84	101
Night Games	.199	.362	.255	141	28	3	1	1	10	35	33	.233	.359	.319	602	140	30	2	6	58	116	117
April	.256	.396	.395	43	11	3	0	1	5	10	12	.228	.330	.323	189	43	6	0	4	24	30	38
May	.211	.360	.268	71	15	4	0	0	6	16	19	.237	.379	.300	207	49	13	0	0	16	46	44
June	.241	.450	.345	58	14	1	1	1	8	21	12	.217	.344	.320	253	55	13	2	3	21	46	56
July	.098	.281	.098	51	5	0	0	0	3	13	13	.174	.309	.203	138	24	4	0	0	11	26	30
August	.103	.278	.103	29	3	0	0	0	1	7	8	.202	.336	.284	109	22	6	0	1	9	20	22
Sept-Oct	.000	.000	.000	0	0	0	0	0	0	0	0	.260	.391	.331	154	40	6	1	1	11	32	28
Bases Empty	.147	.333	.213	136	20	4	1	1	1	36	37	.214	.351	.306	579	124	28	2	7	7	117	126
Leadoff	.179	.353	.299	67	12	3	1	1	1	18	16	.196	.334	.300	250	49	10	2	4	4	51	53
Runners On Base	.241	.399	.302	116	28	4	0	1	22	31	27	.231	.350	.291	471	109	20	1	2	85	83	92
Scoring Position	.277	.467	.354	65	18	2	0	1	22	24	14	.213	.359	.247	267	57	6	0	1	73	60	51
Late and Close	.186	.417	.233	43	8	2	0	0	5	17	12	.214	.377	.280	168	36	8	0	1	12	43	37

JEFF BLAUSER — BR/TR — age 29 — ATL SS161

7-YEAR TOTALS (1987–1993)

1993	BA	OBA	SA	AB	H	2B	3B	HR	RBI	BB	SO	BA	OBA	SA	AB	H	2B	3B	HR	RBI	BB	SO
Total	.305	.401	.436	597	182	29	2	15	73	85	109	.273	.355	.419	2366	646	119	17	64	280	278	466
vs. Left	.283	.374	.469	145	41	8	2	5	16	22	25	.291	.375	.480	821	239	51	10	28	112	114	142
vs. Right	.312	.410	.425	452	141	21	0	10	57	63	84	.263	.344	.386	1545	407	68	7	36	168	164	324
at Home	.277	.396	.369	282	78	12	1	4	27	48	55	.276	.368	.414	1125	310	57	9	27	131	149	212
on Road	.330	.407	.495	315	104	17	1	11	46	37	54	.271	.343	.423	1241	336	62	8	37	149	129	254
on Grass	.314	.417	.450	456	143	21	1	13	52	71	81	.274	.362	.428	1760	482	87	13	53	211	222	334
on Turf	.277	.350	.390	141	39	8	1	2	21	14	28	.271	.334	.391	606	164	32	4	11	69	56	132
Day Games	.329	.408	.468	158	52	8	1	4	17	18	27	.287	.364	.432	659	189	29	5	19	72	74	131
Night Games	.296	.399	.424	439	130	21	1	11	56	67	82	.268	.351	.414	1707	457	90	12	45	208	204	335
April	.330	.414	.372	94	31	4	0	0	6	13	15	.257	.314	.329	280	72	10	2	2	22	22	52
May	.344	.451	.505	93	32	6	0	3	16	15	15	.292	.390	.494	267	78	19	4	9	43	39	59
June	.276	.402	.437	87	24	6	1	2	9	17	16	.274	.357	.431	376	103	26	3	9	49	45	71
July	.258	.376	.412	97	25	0	0	5	14	17	18	.248	.347	.399	363	90	11	1	14	49	54	73
August	.350	.432	.553	103	36	7	1	4	10	11	17	.294	.371	.442	473	139	23	1	15	45	53	81
Sept-Oct	.276	.345	.350	123	34	6	0	1	18	12	28	.270	.348	.414	607	164	30	6	15	72	65	130
Bases Empty	.271	.378	.391	340	92	14	0	9	9	49	65	.254	.330	.400	1418	360	64	7	43	43	144	273
Leadoff	.267	.342	.362	105	28	4	0	2	2	11	19	.272	.321	.425	508	138	29	2	15	15	35	88
Runners On Base	.350	.431	.494	257	90	15	2	6	64	36	44	.302	.391	.447	948	286	55	10	21	237	134	193
Scoring Position	.302	.406	.381	139	42	8	0	1	50	27	28	.292	.391	.420	524	153	32	4	9	197	90	110
Late and Close	.272	.361	.359	92	25	2	0	2	17	10	20	.231	.303	.383	420	97	16	3	14	55	37	102

MIKE BLOWERS — BR/TR — age 29 — SEA 3B117, DH3, OF2, C1, 1B1

1993	BA	OBA	SA	AB	H	2B	3B	HR	RBI	BB	SO	BA	OBA	SA	AB	H	2B	3B	HR	RBI	BB	SO
Total	.280	.357	.475	379	106	23	3	15	57	44	98	.245	.318	.398	669	164	30	3	22	84	69	184
vs. Left	.357	.424	.669	154	55	14	2	10	34	17	24	.316	.391	.560	250	79	18	2	13	46	30	44
vs. Right	.227	.311	.342	225	51	9	1	5	23	27	74	.203	.273	.301	419	85	12	1	9	38	39	140
at Home	.265	.379	.454	185	49	9	1	8	23	32	53	.238	.336	.364	324	77	12	1	9	30	46	95
on Road	.294	.333	.495	194	57	14	2	7	34	12	45	.252	.300	.429	345	87	18	2	13	54	23	89
on Grass	.305	.345	.526	154	47	12	2	6	25	10	35	.246	.301	.409	357	88	15	2	13	48	27	95
on Turf	.262	.364	.440	225	59	11	1	9	32	34	63	.244	.337	.385	312	76	15	1	9	36	42	89
Day Games	.259	.317	.402	112	29	8	1	2	12	9	34	.250	.316	.387	212	53	12	1	5	21	19	65
Night Games	.288	.373	.506	267	77	15	2	13	45	35	64	.243	.319	.403	457	111	18	2	17	63	50	119
April	.258	.324	.323	31	8	0	1	0	2	3	6	.230	.306	.340	100	23	0	1	3	9	11	24
May	.313	.370	.597	67	21	10	0	3	17	6	15	.258	.313	.460	124	32	13	0	4	25	9	34
June	.220	.319	.373	59	13	4	1	1	5	9	19	.209	.303	.314	86	18	4	1	1	7	12	24
July	.324	.439	.529	34	11	1	0	2	5	5	7	.288	.373	.481	52	15	1	0	3	7	6	10
August	.319	.364	.583	72	23	4	0	5	15	5	14	.293	.337	.511	92	27	5	0	5	16	6	23
Sept-Oct	.259	.348	.414	116	30	4	1	4	13	15	37	.228	.311	.353	215	49	7	1	6	20	25	69
Bases Empty	.288	.339	.495	208	60	17	1	8	8	15	53	.249	.306	.409	374	93	19	1	13	13	30	94
Leadoff	.314	.344	.488	86	27	6	0	3	3	4	20	.288	.331	.458	153	44	8	0	6	6	10	32
Runners On Base	.269	.376	.450	171	46	6	2	7	49	29	45	.241	.332	.383	295	71	11	2	9	71	39	90
Scoring Position	.311	.438	.534	103	32	3	1	6	46	23	23	.281	.392	.455	167	47	6	1	7	65	30	47
Late and Close	.392	.475	.647	51	20	7	0	2	10	8	12	.267	.357	.436	101	27	8	0	3	13	14	24

TIM BOGAR — BR/TR — age 28 — NYN SS66, 3B7, 2B6

1993	BA	OBA	SA	AB	H	2B	3B	HR	RBI	BB	SO	BA	OBA	SA	AB	H	2B	3B	HR	RBI	BB	SO
Total	.244	.300	.351	205	50	13	0	3	25	14	29	.244	.300	.351	205	50	13	0	3	25	14	29
vs. Left	.243	.293	.357	70	17	5	0	1	7	5	9	.243	.293	.357	70	17	5	0	1	7	5	9
vs. Right	.244	.304	.348	135	33	8	0	2	18	9	20	.244	.304	.348	135	33	8	0	2	18	9	20
at Home	.204	.257	.276	98	20	4	0	1	9	5	17	.204	.257	.276	98	20	4	0	1	9	5	17
on Road	.280	.339	.421	107	30	9	0	2	16	9	12	.280	.339	.421	107	30	9	0	2	16	9	12
on Grass	.222	.273	.281	153	34	6	0	1	12	8	26	.222	.273	.281	153	34	6	0	1	12	8	26
on Turf	.308	.379	.558	52	16	7	0	2	13	6	3	.308	.379	.558	52	16	7	0	2	13	6	3
Day Games	.159	.232	.254	63	10	3	0	1	3	4	8	.159	.232	.254	63	10	3	0	1	3	4	8
Night Games	.282	.331	.394	142	40	10	0	2	22	10	21	.282	.331	.394	142	40	10	0	2	22	10	21
April	.000	.000	.000	6	0	0	0	0	0	0	1	.000	.000	.000	6	0	0	0	0	0	0	1
May	.235	.297	.382	34	8	2	0	1	4	3	2	.235	.297	.382	34	8	2	0	1	4	3	2
June	.311	.338	.393	61	19	5	0	0	9	2	10	.311	.338	.393	61	19	5	0	0	9	2	10
July	.189	.268	.216	74	14	2	0	0	3	6	11	.189	.268	.216	74	14	2	0	0	3	6	11
August	.300	.364	.633	30	9	4	0	2	9	3	5	.300	.364	.633	30	9	4	0	2	9	3	5
Sept-Oct	.000	.000	.000	0	0	0	0	0	0	0	0	.000	.000	.000	0	0	0	0	0	0	0	0
Bases Empty	.225	.285	.342	120	27	8	0	2	2	9	18	.225	.285	.342	120	27	8	0	2	2	9	18
Leadoff	.214	.254	.321	56	12	3	0	1	1	3	5	.214	.254	.321	56	12	3	0	1	1	3	5
Runners On Base	.271	.323	.365	85	23	5	0	1	23	5	11	.271	.323	.365	85	23	5	0	1	23	5	11
Scoring Position	.315	.367	.463	54	17	5	0	1	23	3	7	.315	.367	.463	54	17	5	0	1	23	3	7
Late and Close	.171	.211	.200	35	6	1	0	0	3	2	5	.171	.211	.200	35	6	1	0	0	3	2	5

WADE BOGGS — BL/TR — age 36 — NYA 3B134, DH8

1993	BA	OBA	SA	AB	H	2B	3B	HR	RBI	BB	SO	BA	OBA	SA	AB	H	2B	3B	HR	RBI	BB	SO
Total	.302	.378	.363	560	169	26	3	2	59	74	49	.331	.423	.451	5853	1939	390	40	77	629	951	462
vs. Left	.262	.323	.339	168	44	8	1	1	25	18	18	.298	.374	.401	1834	547	97	14	21	228	222	188
vs. Right	.319	.401	.372	392	125	18	0	1	34	56	31	.346	.444	.474	4019	1392	293	26	56	401	729	274
at Home	.314	.383	.373	271	85	13	0	1	24	33	23	.362	.458	.510	2856	1034	248	21	44	329	516	236
on Road	.291	.373	.353	289	84	13	1	1	35	41	26	.302	.388	.395	2997	905	142	19	33	300	435	226
on Grass	.304	.379	.367	471	143	22	1	2	53	63	44	.334	.427	.457	4921	1643	338	33	67	533	815	401
on Turf	.292	.370	.337	89	26	4	0	0	6	11	5	.318	.403	.421	932	296	52	7	10	96	136	61
Day Games	.266	.329	.317	199	53	7	0	1	23	20	22	.321	.417	.425	1995	640	121	9	23	195	333	157
Night Games	.321	.404	.388	361	116	19	1	1	36	54	27	.337	.426	.464	3858	1299	269	31	54	434	618	305
April	.300	.405	.371	70	21	5	0	0	7	13	11	.296	.413	.397	754	223	47	1	9	70	156	76
May	.296	.363	.324	108	32	3	0	0	15	13	7	.336	.433	.476	963	324	62	9	18	128	172	77
June	.323	.382	.434	99	32	6	1	1	11	9	4	.335	.423	.469	994	333	71	10	14	109	151	67
July	.304	.382	.418	79	24	6	0	1	8	10	8	.334	.417	.475	981	328	77	11	13	112	145	80
August	.326	.422	.348	92	30	2	0	0	4	16	9	.335	.415	.439	1121	375	63	6	14	104	157	85
Sept-Oct	.268	.341	.304	112	30	4	0	0	14	13	10	.342	.434	.441	1040	356	70	3	9	106	170	77
Bases Empty	.277	.367	.342	339	94	17	1	1	1	48	26	.326	.406	.450	3544	1154	241	26	49	49	470	273
Leadoff	.255	.367	.314	153	39	6	0	1	1	27	11	.331	.409	.445	1760	582	118	6	24	24	231	121
Runners On Base	.339	.395	.394	221	75	9	1	1	58	26	23	.340	.446	.453	2309	785	149	14	28	580	481	189
Scoring Position	.294	.372	.349	126	37	4	0	1	57	21	14	.336	.473	.447	1243	418	80	8	14	526	370	110
Late and Close	.297	.372	.338	74	22	0	0	1	7	10	8	.311	.413	.384	839	261	41	4	4	82	148	90

FRANK BOLICK — BB/TR — age 28 — MON 1B51, 3B24

1993	BA	OBA	SA	AB	H	2B	3B	HR	RBI	BB	SO		BA	OBA	SA	AB	H	2B	3B	HR	RBI	BB	SO
Total	.211	.298	.329	213	45	13	0	4	24	23	37		.211	.298	.329	213	45	13	0	4	24	23	37
vs. Left	.237	.333	.390	59	14	3	0	2	8	8	8		.237	.333	.390	59	14	3	0	2	8	8	8
vs. Right	.201	.283	.305	154	31	10	0	2	16	15	29		.201	.283	.305	154	31	10	0	2	16	15	29
at Home	.193	.299	.321	109	21	8	0	2	11	14	22		.193	.299	.321	109	21	8	0	2	11	14	22
on Road	.231	.296	.337	104	24	5	0	2	13	9	15		.231	.296	.337	104	24	5	0	2	13	9	15
on Grass	.219	.315	.313	64	14	3	0	1	4	8	10		.219	.315	.313	64	14	3	0	1	4	8	10
on Turf	.208	.290	.336	149	31	10	0	3	20	15	27		.208	.290	.336	149	31	10	0	3	20	15	27
Day Games	.230	.284	.311	74	17	6	0	0	6	5	11		.230	.284	.311	74	17	6	0	0	6	5	11
Night Games	.201	.304	.338	139	28	7	0	4	18	18	26		.201	.304	.338	139	28	7	0	4	18	18	26
April	.278	.333	.444	36	10	3	0	1	5	3	5		.278	.333	.444	36	10	3	0	1	5	3	5
May	.208	.317	.377	53	11	3	0	2	8	7	11		.208	.317	.377	53	11	3	0	2	8	7	11
June	.286	.419	.449	49	14	5	0	1	6	10	7		.286	.419	.449	49	14	5	0	1	6	10	7
July	.118	.151	.157	51	6	2	0	0	5	2	9		.118	.151	.157	51	6	2	0	0	5	2	9
August	.167	.200	.167	24	4	0	0	0	0	1	5		.167	.200	.167	24	4	0	0	0	0	1	5
Sept-Oct	.000	.000	.000	0	0	0	0	0	0	0	0		.000	.000	.000	0	0	0	0	0	0	0	0
Bases Empty	.211	.274	.333	114	24	11	0	1	1	8	17		.211	.274	.333	114	24	11	0	1	1	8	17
Leadoff	.259	.306	.345	58	15	5	0	0	0	2	9		.259	.306	.345	58	15	5	0	0	0	2	9
Runners On Base	.212	.322	.323	99	21	2	0	3	23	15	20		.212	.322	.323	99	21	2	0	3	23	15	20
Scoring Position	.159	.294	.203	69	11	0	0	1	18	12	15		.159	.294	.203	69	11	0	0	1	18	12	15
Late and Close	.204	.278	.286	49	10	1	0	1	4	4	9		.204	.278	.286	49	10	1	0	1	4	4	9

BARRY BONDS — BL/TL — age 30 — SFOF157

1993	BA	OBA	SA	AB	H	2B	3B	HR	RBI	BB	SO		BA	OBA	SA	AB	H	2B	3B	HR	RBI	BB	SO
Total	.336	.458	.677	539	181	38	4	46	123	126	79		.283	.391	.526	4123	1165	258	40	222	679	737	669
vs. Left	.326	.423	.619	218	71	15	2	15	45	39	29		.283	.384	.520	1578	446	108	19	76	268	258	277
vs. Right	.343	.481	.717	321	110	23	2	31	78	87	50		.283	.395	.530	2545	719	150	21	146	411	479	392
at Home	.312	.403	.613	266	83	17	0	21	58	42	36		.273	.380	.505	1991	543	114	18	104	317	346	343
on Road	.359	.507	.740	273	98	21	4	25	65	84	43		.292	.400	.546	2132	622	144	22	118	362	391	326
on Grass	.333	.453	.667	408	136	24	2	36	91	93	61		.291	.390	.536	1379	401	84	10	78	227	233	224
on Turf	.344	.476	.710	131	45	14	2	10	32	33	18		.278	.391	.521	2744	764	174	30	144	452	504	445
Day Games	.317	.437	.675	265	84	19	2	24	61	57	34		.271	.384	.517	1293	350	79	13	71	200	244	211
Night Games	.354	.479	.679	274	97	19	2	22	62	69	45		.288	.393	.530	2830	815	179	27	151	479	493	458
April	.431	.553	.889	72	31	8	2	7	25	21	12		.285	.366	.565	513	146	38	8	30	89	66	91
May	.367	.475	.684	98	36	6	2	7	16	20	19		.296	.405	.546	670	198	37	10	37	114	110	107
June	.280	.393	.559	93	26	5	0	7	19	18	14		.276	.389	.502	721	199	49	6	34	98	134	118
July	.308	.432	.692	91	28	5	0	10	22	19	9		.298	.403	.561	684	204	42	9	40	131	124	112
August	.353	.486	.682	85	30	4	0	8	19	24	15		.272	.391	.510	751	204	43	2	44	129	152	120
Sept-Oct	.300	.429	.610	100	30	10	0	7	22	24	10		.273	.384	.490	784	214	49	5	37	118	145	121
Bases Empty	.308	.402	.628	312	96	22	3	24	24	48	48		.270	.361	.506	2527	683	161	27	127	127	344	411
Leadoff	.277	.353	.569	137	38	10	3	8	8	16	23		.284	.371	.522	1312	372	93	17	62	62	174	203
Runners On Base	.374	.524	.744	227	85	16	1	22	99	78	31		.302	.433	.558	1596	482	97	13	95	552	393	258
Scoring Position	.358	.557	.675	123	44	10	1	9	70	63	18		.290	.448	.530	926	269	52	10	50	438	296	156
Late and Close	.370	.436	.827	81	30	4	0	11	24	11	12		.270	.385	.471	703	190	40	7	29	94	135	135

BOBBY BONILLA — BB/TR — age 31 — NYN OF85, 3B52, 1B6

1993	BA	OBA	SA	AB	H	2B	3B	HR	RBI	BB	SO		BA	OBA	SA	AB	H	2B	3B	HR	RBI	BB	SO
Total	.265	.352	.522	502	133	21	3	34	87	72	96		.277	.356	.474	4234	1173	245	40	169	684	535	666
vs. Left	.277	.325	.516	155	43	5	1	10	32	12	15		.268	.332	.442	1691	454	87	9	63	268	168	179
vs. Right	.259	.363	.524	347	90	16	2	24	55	60	81		.283	.371	.494	2543	719	158	31	106	416	367	487
at Home	.275	.341	.550	240	66	8	2	18	54	27	37		.267	.348	.453	2036	544	114	18	76	328	257	285
on Road	.256	.362	.496	262	67	13	1	16	33	45	59		.286	.363	.493	2198	629	131	22	93	356	278	381
on Grass	.268	.350	.529	380	102	17	2	26	75	52	66		.280	.355	.483	1665	466	81	15	76	275	202	287
on Turf	.254	.359	.500	122	31	4	1	8	12	20	30		.275	.356	.467	2569	707	164	25	93	409	333	379
Day Games	.260	.330	.495	200	52	9	1	12	30	22	37		.282	.346	.494	1390	392	87	9	63	224	138	218
Night Games	.268	.366	.540	302	81	12	2	22	57	50	59		.275	.360	.464	2844	781	158	31	106	460	397	448
April	.234	.330	.442	77	18	4	0	4	16	12	8		.284	.345	.469	606	172	34	3	24	106	59	82
May	.243	.313	.515	103	25	1	0	9	17	11	26		.278	.363	.489	713	198	33	5	36	118	96	114
June	.283	.345	.528	106	30	7	2	5	15	10	18		.271	.353	.464	722	196	56	10	21	104	93	120
July	.255	.365	.457	94	24	7	0	4	13	18	22		.257	.337	.428	717	184	34	4	27	96	91	115
August	.302	.410	.615	96	29	1	1	9	21	19	16		.299	.379	.538	768	230	50	8	39	144	103	113
Sept-Oct	.269	.321	.654	26	7	1	0	3	5	2	6		.273	.354	.448	708	193	38	10	22	116	93	122
Bases Empty	.257	.346	.521	292	75	10	2	21	21	40	56		.270	.341	.468	2288	617	114	23	98	98	239	352
Leadoff	.310	.372	.599	142	44	4	2	11	11	14	26		.292	.350	.498	1060	309	55	13	46	46	91	152
Runners On Base	.276	.360	.524	210	58	11	1	13	66	32	40		.286	.372	.480	1946	556	131	17	71	586	296	314
Scoring Position	.257	.360	.440	109	28	3	1	5	48	22	24		.279	.385	.471	1124	314	72	10	41	494	224	189
Late and Close	.241	.369	.494	83	20	3	0	6	14	18	20		.256	.365	.429	704	180	31	2	29	111	125	130

BRET BOONE — BR/TR — age 25 — SEA 2B74, DH1

1993	BA	OBA	SA	AB	H	2B	3B	HR	RBI	BB	SO	2-YEAR TOTALS (1992–1993) BA	OBA	SA	AB	H	2B	3B	HR	RBI	BB	SO
Total	.251	.301	.443	271	68	12	2	12	38	17	52	.233	.277	.403	400	93	16	2	16	53	21	86
vs. Left	.266	.337	.494	79	21	4	1	4	11	9	19	.227	.290	.387	119	27	5	1	4	12	11	31
vs. Right	.245	.285	.422	192	47	8	1	8	27	8	33	.235	.271	.409	281	66	11	1	12	41	10	55
at Home	.259	.301	.489	135	35	8	1	7	19	7	29	.257	.294	.471	191	49	12	1	9	27	9	47
on Road	.243	.300	.397	136	33	4	1	5	19	10	23	.211	.261	.340	209	44	4	1	7	26	12	39
on Grass	.245	.308	.468	94	23	4	1	5	14	8	18	.220	.279	.411	141	31	4	1	7	19	10	27
on Turf	.254	.297	.429	177	45	8	1	7	24	9	34	.239	.275	.398	259	62	12	1	9	34	11	59
Day Games	.264	.283	.494	87	23	3	1	5	18	3	16	.238	.264	.434	122	29	4	1	6	22	4	24
Night Games	.245	.309	.418	184	45	9	1	7	20	14	36	.230	.282	.388	278	64	12	1	10	31	17	62
April	.286	.333	.429	28	8	1	0	1	2	1	9	.286	.333	.429	28	8	1	0	1	2	1	9
May	.000	.000	.000	0	0	0	0	0	0	0	0	.000	.000	.000	0	0	0	0	0	0	0	0
June	.174	.286	.348	23	4	1	0	1	3	3	4	.174	.286	.348	23	4	1	0	1	3	3	4
July	.000	.000	.000	0	0	0	0	0	0	0	0	.000	.000	.000	0	0	0	0	0	0	0	0
August	.253	.295	.475	99	25	5	1	5	15	5	17	.241	.288	.431	137	33	6	1	6	20	7	25
Sept-Oct	.256	.301	.438	121	31	5	1	5	18	8	22	.226	.261	.387	212	48	8	1	8	28	10	48
Bases Empty	.235	.283	.407	162	38	6	2	6	6	10	35	.210	.261	.365	233	49	8	2	8	8	14	53
Leadoff	.259	.283	.328	58	15	1	0	1	1	2	13	.217	.261	.277	83	18	2	0	1	1	5	17
Runners On Base	.275	.325	.495	109	30	6	0	6	32	7	17	.263	.298	.455	167	44	8	0	8	45	7	33
Scoring Position	.245	.302	.321	53	13	1	0	1	21	5	8	.230	.268	.322	87	20	2	0	2	32	5	17
Late and Close	.326	.367	.435	46	15	5	0	0	4	2	9	.236	.267	.319	72	17	6	0	0	4	2	19

PAT BORDERS — BR/TR — age 31 — TOR C138

1993	BA	OBA	SA	AB	H	2B	3B	HR	RBI	BB	SO	6-YEAR TOTALS (1988–1993) BA	OBA	SA	AB	H	2B	3B	HR	RBI	BB	SO
Total	.254	.285	.371	488	124	30	0	9	55	20	66	.257	.291	.397	2000	514	114	8	50	243	96	312
vs. Left	.244	.278	.361	119	29	8	0	2	16	6	15	.263	.307	.403	875	230	54	6	19	108	57	127
vs. Right	.257	.287	.374	369	95	22	0	7	39	14	51	.252	.278	.392	1125	284	60	2	31	135	39	185
at Home	.239	.273	.352	247	59	10	0	6	33	10	32	.252	.290	.406	965	243	57	4	28	124	50	131
on Road	.270	.296	.390	241	65	20	0	3	22	10	34	.262	.291	.388	1035	271	57	4	22	119	46	181
on Grass	.271	.307	.370	181	49	9	0	3	16	10	22	.266	.299	.386	806	214	37	3	18	95	42	137
on Turf	.244	.271	.371	307	75	21	0	6	39	10	44	.251	.285	.405	1194	300	77	5	32	148	54	175
Day Games	.217	.245	.349	152	33	8	0	4	13	5	32	.225	.253	.376	652	147	37	2	19	67	25	127
Night Games	.271	.302	.381	336	91	22	0	5	42	15	34	.272	.308	.407	1348	367	77	6	31	176	71	185
April	.195	.222	.260	77	15	5	0	0	3	3	13	.253	.287	.406	308	78	17	3	8	28	15	54
May	.274	.299	.488	84	23	3	0	5	15	3	8	.249	.278	.406	389	97	17	1	14	44	16	70
June	.245	.280	.340	94	23	6	0	1	8	3	7	.262	.292	.394	325	85	20	1	7	39	12	34
July	.234	.234	.328	64	15	3	0	1	10	0	12	.282	.322	.437	284	80	20	0	8	51	17	41
August	.319	.344	.396	91	29	7	0	0	5	4	10	.283	.308	.392	332	94	21	0	5	35	13	51
Sept-Oct	.244	.306	.397	78	19	6	0	2	14	7	16	.221	.266	.356	362	80	19	3	8	46	23	62
Bases Empty	.270	.291	.381	281	76	16	0	5	5	8	37	.259	.284	.401	1139	295	64	4	30	30	39	178
Leadoff	.286	.303	.403	119	34	8	0	2	2	3	13	.279	.299	.437	469	131	28	2	14	14	13	64
Runners On Base	.232	.277	.357	207	48	14	0	4	50	12	29	.254	.299	.391	861	219	50	4	20	213	57	134
Scoring Position	.221	.276	.305	131	29	8	0	1	43	10	18	.236	.295	.358	491	116	27	3	9	179	45	75
Late and Close	.296	.338	.423	71	21	6	0	1	11	5	15	.265	.305	.396	359	95	21	1	8	45	20	74

MIKE BORDICK — BR/TR — age 29 — OAK SS159, 2B1

1993	BA	OBA	SA	AB	H	2B	3B	HR	RBI	BB	SO	4-YEAR TOTALS (1990–1993) BA	OBA	SA	AB	H	2B	3B	HR	RBI	BB	SO
Total	.249	.332	.311	546	136	21	2	3	48	60	58	.265	.333	.324	1299	344	45	7	6	117	115	158
vs. Left	.265	.351	.346	162	43	10	0	1	11	19	20	.280	.349	.353	357	100	16	2	2	32	35	40
vs. Right	.242	.324	.297	384	93	11	2	2	37	41	38	.259	.326	.313	942	244	29	5	4	85	80	118
at Home	.250	.324	.314	280	70	12	0	2	20	25	25	.261	.329	.334	631	165	21	5	5	52	51	70
on Road	.248	.341	.308	266	66	9	2	1	28	35	33	.268	.336	.314	668	179	24	2	1	65	64	88
on Grass	.252	.328	.318	453	114	17	2	3	32	43	45	.257	.320	.319	1073	276	34	7	6	82	84	130
on Turf	.237	.351	.280	93	22	4	0	0	16	17	13	.301	.390	.350	226	68	11	0	0	35	31	28
Day Games	.234	.308	.299	231	54	7	1	2	20	23	24	.278	.336	.350	514	143	14	4	5	50	40	58
Night Games	.260	.350	.321	315	82	14	1	1	28	37	34	.256	.330	.307	785	201	31	3	1	67	75	100
April	.236	.333	.327	55	13	2	0	1	4	6	6	.292	.351	.343	137	40	4	0	1	14	11	17
May	.261	.349	.326	92	24	4	1	0	7	11	10	.304	.366	.376	181	55	6	2	1	15	17	18
June	.264	.358	.341	91	24	4	0	0	9	13	8	.247	.332	.337	178	44	8	1	2	17	21	21
July	.295	.330	.337	95	28	4	0	0	10	5	9	.274	.312	.329	252	69	12	1	0	23	12	32
August	.288	.403	.365	104	30	3	1	1	7	17	10	.271	.368	.316	269	73	5	2	1	17	34	29
Sept-Oct	.156	.223	.193	109	17	4	0	0	11	8	15	.223	.284	.277	282	63	10	1	1	31	20	41
Bases Empty	.242	.318	.298	322	78	15	0	1	1	29	30	.252	.324	.310	746	188	30	2	3	3	68	83
Leadoff	.186	.274	.214	140	26	4	0	0	0	12	10	.248	.314	.307	326	81	11	1	2	2	25	32
Runners On Base	.259	.351	.330	224	58	6	2	2	47	31	28	.282	.343	.344	553	156	15	5	3	114	47	75
Scoring Position	.274	.397	.325	117	32	3	0	1	43	25	15	.283	.359	.345	325	92	10	2	2	108	39	41
Late and Close	.195	.339	.195	87	17	0	0	0	5	16	13	.222	.324	.261	176	39	3	2	0	15	23	26

DARYL BOSTON — BL/TL — age 31 — COL OF79

1993	BA	OBA	SA	AB	H	2B	3B	HR	RBI	BB	SO
Total	.261	.325	.464	291	76	15	1	14	40	26	57
vs. Left	.231	.286	.462	13	3	0	0	1	4	0	4
vs. Right	.263	.327	.464	278	73	15	1	13	36	26	53
at Home	.279	.359	.412	136	38	7	1	3	18	16	27
on Road	.245	.293	.510	155	38	8	0	11	22	10	30
on Grass	.278	.341	.493	223	62	13	1	11	31	20	44
on Turf	.206	.270	.368	68	14	2	0	3	9	6	13
Day Games	.299	.364	.570	107	32	6	1	7	18	10	25
Night Games	.239	.302	.402	184	44	9	0	7	22	16	32
April	.292	.370	.313	48	14	1	0	0	5	5	9
May	.183	.290	.400	60	11	1	0	4	6	8	9
June	.250	.333	.469	32	8	4	0	1	4	4	5
July	.167	.189	.250	36	6	0	0	1	2	1	8
August	.313	.348	.563	64	20	4	0	4	10	4	14
Sept-Oct	.333	.382	.706	51	17	5	1	4	13	4	12
Bases Empty	.305	.386	.570	151	46	8	1	10	10	18	32
Leadoff	.382	.425	.809	68	26	6	1	7	7	5	11
Runners On Base	.214	.255	.350	140	30	7	0	4	30	8	25
Scoring Position	.186	.228	.337	86	16	4	0	3	26	5	14
Late and Close	.174	.255	.217	46	8	2	0	0	2	4	11

10-YEAR TOTALS (1984–1993)

	BA	OBA	SA	AB	H	2B	3B	HR	RBI	BB	SO
	.251	.314	.412	2552	641	129	22	79	264	231	449
vs. Left	.236	.285	.337	347	82	17	3	4	31	22	85
vs. Right	.254	.318	.424	2205	559	112	19	75	233	209	364
at Home	.254	.319	.400	1254	319	60	16	30	119	119	227
on Road	.248	.308	.424	1298	322	69	6	49	145	112	222
on Grass	.252	.314	.414	2032	513	104	19	62	209	182	348
on Turf	.246	.312	.404	520	128	25	3	17	55	49	101
Day Games	.257	.327	.418	775	199	41	6	24	84	78	142
Night Games	.249	.308	.409	1777	442	88	16	55	180	153	307
April	.242	.309	.327	260	63	10	3	2	23	23	42
May	.235	.302	.419	442	104	19	4	18	40	41	72
June	.229	.289	.423	407	93	28	3	15	52	34	79
July	.247	.296	.394	340	84	19	2	9	28	24	64
August	.289	.343	.447	519	150	20	4	18	53	44	82
Sept-Oct	.252	.325	.416	584	147	33	6	17	68	65	110
Bases Empty	.261	.320	.435	1550	404	87	14	52	52	132	285
Leadoff	.293	.345	.500	714	209	47	7	29	29	56	128
Runners On Base	.237	.303	.375	1002	237	42	8	27	212	99	164
Scoring Position	.241	.323	.414	565	136	23	6	21	188	73	99
Late and Close	.212	.300	.340	438	93	25	5	7	32	52	102

JEFF BRANSON — BL/TR — age 27 — CIN SS59, 2B45, 3B14, 1B1

1993	BA	OBA	SA	AB	H	2B	3B	HR	RBI	BB	SO
Total	.241	.275	.310	381	92	15	1	3	22	19	73
vs. Left	.253	.281	.341	91	23	5	0	1	3	4	22
vs. Right	.238	.273	.300	290	69	10	1	2	19	15	51
at Home	.232	.265	.324	185	43	11	0	2	8	9	33
on Road	.250	.284	.296	196	49	4	1	1	14	10	40
on Grass	.246	.287	.295	122	30	1	1	1	8	7	28
on Turf	.239	.269	.317	259	62	14	0	2	14	12	45
Day Games	.217	.250	.302	106	23	4	1	1	7	5	28
Night Games	.251	.284	.313	275	69	11	0	2	15	14	45
April	.333	.375	.400	15	5	1	0	0	0	1	2
May	.414	.433	.552	29	12	4	0	0	3	1	8
June	.293	.323	.362	58	17	1	0	1	3	3	12
July	.211	.273	.289	90	19	5	1	0	3	8	15
August	.232	.253	.326	95	22	3	0	2	9	3	19
Sept-Oct	.181	.204	.191	94	17	1	0	0	4	3	17
Bases Empty	.258	.282	.343	233	60	12	1	2	2	8	43
Leadoff	.243	.270	.342	111	27	3	1	2	2	4	18
Runners On Base	.216	.264	.257	148	32	3	0	1	20	11	30
Scoring Position	.181	.242	.205	83	15	2	0	0	17	8	19
Late and Close	.231	.273	.231	52	12	0	0	0	2	3	14

2-YEAR TOTALS (1992–1993)

	BA	OBA	SA	AB	H	2B	3B	HR	RBI	BB	SO
	.254	.286	.325	496	126	22	2	3	37	24	89
vs. Left	.242	.269	.323	99	24	5	0	1	3	4	25
vs. Right	.257	.290	.325	397	102	17	2	2	34	20	64
at Home	.249	.279	.342	237	59	14	1	2	17	11	38
on Road	.259	.292	.309	259	67	8	1	1	20	13	51
on Grass	.263	.304	.316	152	40	3	1	1	13	9	34
on Turf	.250	.277	.328	344	86	19	1	2	24	15	55
Day Games	.242	.271	.331	157	38	9	1	1	14	7	37
Night Games	.260	.292	.322	339	88	13	1	2	23	17	52
April	.278	.316	.333	18	5	1	0	0	0	1	4
May	.357	.378	.524	42	15	7	0	0	7	2	12
June	.293	.323	.362	58	17	1	0	1	3	3	12
July	.252	.310	.330	115	29	7	1	0	10	10	17
August	.234	.261	.320	128	30	5	0	2	11	5	22
Sept-Oct	.222	.237	.244	135	30	1	1	0	6	3	22
Bases Empty	.273	.300	.357	286	78	14	2	2	2	11	48
Leadoff	.256	.288	.346	133	34	4	1	2	2	6	19
Runners On Base	.229	.268	.281	210	48	8	0	1	35	13	41
Scoring Position	.221	.270	.279	122	27	7	0	0	32	10	25
Late and Close	.280	.314	.305	82	23	2	0	0	8	4	20

GEORGE BRETT — BL/TR — age 41 — KC DH140

1993	BA	OBA	SA	AB	H	2B	3B	HR	RBI	BB	SO
Total	.266	.312	.434	560	149	31	3	19	75	39	67
vs. Left	.209	.246	.299	187	39	7	2	2	19	7	18
vs. Right	.295	.344	.501	373	110	24	1	17	56	32	49
at Home	.269	.313	.429	275	74	17	3	7	32	17	28
on Road	.263	.311	.439	285	75	14	0	12	43	22	39
on Grass	.265	.311	.449	234	62	10	0	11	35	18	33
on Turf	.267	.313	.423	326	87	21	3	8	40	21	34
Day Games	.294	.340	.506	170	50	13	1	7	26	13	21
Night Games	.254	.300	.403	390	99	18	2	12	49	26	46
April	.220	.250	.317	82	18	5	0	1	8	4	9
May	.245	.294	.394	94	23	5	0	3	14	7	10
June	.299	.346	.464	97	29	7	0	3	15	8	10
July	.310	.342	.620	71	22	5	1	5	13	3	8
August	.248	.306	.367	109	27	5	1	2	8	10	18
Sept-Oct	.280	.331	.477	107	30	4	1	5	17	7	12
Bases Empty	.281	.325	.483	292	82	17	3	12	12	16	39
Leadoff	.320	.347	.485	97	31	10	0	2	2	3	7
Runners On Base	.250	.299	.381	268	67	14	0	7	63	23	28
Scoring Position	.214	.291	.331	145	31	8	0	3	50	20	20
Late and Close	.260	.321	.390	100	26	4	0	3	8	10	10

10-YEAR TOTALS (1984–1993)

	BA	OBA	SA	AB	H	2B	3B	HR	RBI	BB	SO
	.293	.369	.471	5042	1478	324	37	167	799	622	550
vs. Left	.270	.330	.422	1715	463	87	10	51	262	155	205
vs. Right	.305	.388	.497	3327	1015	237	27	116	537	467	345
at Home	.297	.372	.468	2530	751	157	29	73	415	315	233
on Road	.289	.365	.475	2512	727	167	8	94	384	307	317
on Grass	.288	.365	.477	2006	578	129	6	79	311	246	259
on Turf	.296	.371	.468	3036	900	195	31	88	488	376	291
Day Games	.310	.377	.522	1344	417	110	9	52	234	150	142
Night Games	.287	.366	.453	3698	1061	214	28	115	565	472	408
April	.244	.353	.386	570	139	26	2	17	73	98	62
May	.300	.376	.465	693	208	49	7	17	105	86	78
June	.288	.362	.445	865	249	64	3	22	125	99	78
July	.318	.389	.524	962	306	70	7	38	166	115	104
August	.304	.375	.508	1014	308	64	13	39	177	126	123
Sept-Oct	.286	.352	.459	938	268	51	5	34	153	98	105
Bases Empty	.282	.345	.469	2707	763	177	21	96	96	247	303
Leadoff	.285	.341	.493	966	275	68	5	41	41	78	94
Runners On Base	.306	.394	.474	2335	715	147	16	71	703	375	247
Scoring Position	.295	.417	.446	1281	378	76	6	35	584	313	159
Late and Close	.273	.376	.434	781	213	45	3	25	119	131	88

STEVE BUECHELE — BR/TR — age 33 — CHN 3B129, 1B6

1993	BA	OBA	SA	AB	H	2B	3B	HR	RBI	BB	SO	BA	OBA	SA	AB	H	2B	3B	HR	RBI	BB	SO
Total	.272	.345	.437	460	125	27	2	15	65	48	87	.248	.317	.400	3797	941	170	20	122	487	354	740
vs. Left	.281	.378	.469	128	36	9	0	5	14	19	18	.277	.354	.467	1238	343	75	5	50	163	143	216
vs. Right	.268	.332	.425	332	89	18	2	10	51	29	69	.234	.299	.367	2559	598	95	15	72	324	211	524
at Home	.281	.359	.451	224	63	12	1	8	29	25	38	.251	.321	.394	1882	472	77	9	58	225	178	350
on Road	.263	.332	.424	236	62	15	1	7	36	23	49	.245	.313	.405	1915	469	93	11	64	262	176	390
on Grass	.280	.357	.449	354	99	20	2	12	50	39	64	.250	.319	.401	2863	716	125	16	92	367	262	543
on Turf	.245	.302	.396	106	26	7	0	3	15	9	23	.241	.311	.394	934	225	45	4	30	120	92	197
Day Games	.279	.349	.429	233	65	12	1	7	22	24	36	.243	.313	.388	961	234	42	5	29	104	89	175
Night Games	.264	.341	.445	227	60	15	1	8	43	24	51	.249	.318	.403	2836	707	128	15	93	383	265	565
April	.250	.310	.400	80	20	4	1	2	9	7	17	.251	.326	.435	494	124	22	3	21	62	50	104
May	.241	.272	.483	87	21	7	1	4	14	3	16	.268	.325	.462	597	160	34	2	26	79	49	118
June	.186	.234	.256	43	8	3	0	0	3	2	6	.215	.294	.336	622	134	31	1	14	69	65	124
July	.308	.361	.477	65	20	5	0	2	8	5	15	.272	.335	.412	628	171	26	4	18	84	55	105
August	.273	.385	.409	88	24	3	0	3	16	15	17	.244	.320	.389	697	170	29	6	20	105	68	136
Sept-Oct	.330	.430	.505	97	32	5	0	4	15	16	16	.240	.306	.378	759	182	28	4	23	88	67	153
Bases Empty	.268	.346	.441	261	70	15	0	10	10	28	63	.240	.305	.404	2149	516	92	9	81	81	181	425
Leadoff	.301	.352	.487	113	34	9	0	4	4	8	19	.264	.310	.455	927	245	48	3	41	41	56	160
Runners On Base	.276	.344	.432	199	55	12	2	5	55	20	24	.258	.332	.393	1648	425	78	11	41	406	173	315
Scoring Position	.283	.369	.417	120	34	7	0	3	45	16	19	.259	.343	.381	967	250	46	6	20	344	122	194
Late and Close	.242	.329	.306	62	15	2	1	0	9	8	23	.246	.314	.356	630	155	24	3	13	68	55	152

JAY BUHNER — BR/TR — age 30 — SEA OF148, DH10

1993	BA	OBA	SA	AB	H	2B	3B	HR	RBI	BB	SO	BA	OBA	SA	AB	H	2B	3B	HR	RBI	BB	SO
Total	.272	.379	.476	563	153	28	3	27	98	100	144	.253	.344	.460	2162	546	100	12	108	359	289	611
vs. Left	.320	.435	.535	172	55	10	0	9	32	35	44	.256	.354	.476	691	177	34	2	38	115	100	178
vs. Right	.251	.353	.450	391	98	18	3	18	66	65	100	.251	.339	.452	1471	369	66	10	70	244	189	433
at Home	.273	.402	.491	275	75	17	2	13	53	59	74	.248	.351	.464	1063	264	56	7	53	179	162	314
on Road	.271	.355	.462	288	78	11	1	14	45	41	70	.257	.337	.456	1099	282	44	5	55	180	127	297
on Grass	.285	.365	.487	228	65	8	1	12	32	31	48	.268	.350	.484	889	238	31	4	51	156	108	232
on Turf	.263	.388	.469	335	88	20	2	15	66	69	96	.242	.340	.443	1273	308	69	8	57	203	181	379
Day Games	.288	.393	.503	177	51	9	1	9	31	30	41	.282	.367	.538	634	179	35	2	41	115	81	182
Night Games	.264	.372	.464	386	102	19	2	18	67	70	103	.240	.334	.427	1528	367	65	10	67	244	208	429
April	.321	.412	.432	81	26	3	0	2	16	14	18	.266	.369	.422	199	53	8	1	7	28	34	54
May	.270	.327	.590	100	27	3	1	9	19	9	26	.251	.340	.481	231	58	4	2	15	47	32	58
June	.300	.422	.511	90	27	5	1	4	15	19	23	.239	.322	.452	440	105	16	3	24	86	48	127
July	.283	.404	.457	92	26	4	0	4	18	19	18	.271	.362	.521	303	82	11	1	21	53	41	79
August	.179	.343	.381	84	15	3	1	4	11	21	27	.258	.358	.491	454	117	30	5	22	75	68	143
Sept-Oct	.276	.370	.466	116	32	10	0	4	19	18	32	.245	.333	.409	535	131	31	0	19	70	66	150
Bases Empty	.274	.361	.476	307	84	16	2	14	14	42	80	.253	.341	.451	1172	297	55	4	56	56	145	345
Leadoff	.304	.394	.534	148	45	9	2	7	7	22	39	.296	.377	.521	497	147	28	3	26	26	63	127
Runners On Base	.270	.398	.477	256	69	12	1	13	84	58	64	.252	.348	.471	990	249	45	8	52	303	144	266
Scoring Position	.278	.424	.444	151	42	7	0	6	65	44	37	.273	.383	.475	554	151	25	6	25	239	107	144
Late and Close	.304	.426	.468	79	24	5	1	2	10	19	13	.232	.329	.391	358	83	12	3	13	48	54	95

ELLIS BURKS — BR/TR — age 30 — CHA OF146

1993	BA	OBA	SA	AB	H	2B	3B	HR	RBI	BB	SO	BA	OBA	SA	AB	H	2B	3B	HR	RBI	BB	SO
Total	.275	.352	.441	499	137	24	4	17	74	60	97	.280	.344	.455	3293	922	184	31	110	461	311	547
vs. Left	.281	.380	.477	153	43	4	1	8	28	25	24	.289	.364	.463	939	271	54	7	32	137	114	137
vs. Right	.272	.339	.425	346	94	20	3	9	46	35	73	.277	.335	.452	2354	651	130	24	78	324	197	410
at Home	.298	.383	.475	238	71	15	3	7	40	31	46	.296	.364	.485	1581	468	104	16	54	237	166	248
on Road	.253	.323	.410	261	66	9	1	10	34	29	51	.265	.324	.428	1712	454	80	15	56	224	145	299
on Grass	.275	.355	.451	415	114	20	4	15	67	52	77	.281	.345	.456	2767	777	152	25	94	398	269	452
on Turf	.274	.337	.393	84	23	4	0	2	7	8	20	.276	.334	.451	526	145	32	6	16	63	42	95
Day Games	.272	.376	.424	125	34	5	1	4	21	20	24	.279	.353	.442	1086	303	56	8	35	162	117	180
Night Games	.275	.344	.447	374	103	19	3	13	53	40	73	.280	.339	.461	2207	619	128	23	75	299	194	367
April	.338	.400	.507	71	24	3	3	1	9	7	13	.274	.363	.422	424	116	25	7	8	49	54	78
May	.253	.326	.493	75	19	1	1	5	14	8	18	.275	.331	.468	633	174	35	9	23	83	54	109
June	.256	.333	.407	86	22	4	0	3	15	10	15	.276	.329	.504	601	166	35	3	32	102	48	91
July	.303	.370	.528	89	27	5	0	5	14	10	15	.310	.373	.522	477	148	32	6	19	71	45	85
August	.298	.352	.479	94	28	8	0	3	16	7	18	.282	.347	.433	653	184	35	5	18	97	64	104
Sept-Oct	.202	.337	.238	84	17	3	0	0	6	18	18	.265	.327	.372	505	134	22	1	10	59	46	80
Bases Empty	.276	.354	.452	290	80	12	3	11	11	34	62	.278	.341	.448	1807	502	85	15	64	64	161	299
Leadoff	.279	.360	.396	111	31	5	0	2	2	14	19	.286	.345	.456	842	241	40	8	29	29	71	122
Runners On Base	.273	.350	.426	209	57	12	1	6	63	26	35	.283	.347	.464	1486	420	99	16	46	397	150	248
Scoring Position	.252	.331	.437	119	30	10	0	4	57	16	27	.273	.346	.468	880	240	47	10	35	364	108	165
Late and Close	.268	.357	.380	71	19	5	0	1	11	11	20	.248	.335	.391	499	124	26	6	11	62	62	112

BRETT BUTLER — BL/TL — age 37 — LA OF155

1993

	BA	OBA	SA	AB	H	2B	3B	HR	RBI	BB	SO
Total	.298	.387	.371	607	181	21	10	1	42	86	69
vs. Left	.330	.407	.374	206	68	5	2	0	17	28	18
vs. Right	.282	.378	.369	401	113	16	8	1	25	58	51
at Home	.347	.441	.409	291	101	10	4	0	22	49	32
on Road	.253	.336	.335	316	80	11	6	1	20	37	37
on Grass	.311	.404	.374	463	144	14	6	1	34	72	54
on Turf	.257	.331	.361	144	37	7	4	0	8	14	15
Day Games	.266	.359	.356	177	47	6	5	0	9	25	18
Night Games	.312	.399	.377	430	134	15	5	1	33	61	51
April	.329	.450	.390	82	27	3	1	0	5	17	9
May	.308	.356	.364	107	33	4	1	0	11	9	11
June	.315	.359	.370	108	34	4	1	0	12	8	14
July	.269	.369	.375	104	28	3	4	0	4	17	8
August	.253	.373	.354	99	25	4	3	0	2	15	13
Sept-Oct	.318	.425	.374	107	34	3	0	1	8	20	14
Bases Empty	.296	.383	.365	416	123	12	7	1	1	56	48
Leadoff	.300	.368	.381	257	77	8	5	1	1	27	35
Runners On Base	.304	.396	.382	191	58	9	3	0	41	30	21
Scoring Position	.322	.411	.405	121	39	4	3	0	40	20	13
Late and Close	.337	.444	.500	104	35	6	4	1	9	19	12

10-YEAR TOTALS (1984–1993)

	BA	OBA	SA	AB	H	2B	3B	HR	RBI	BB	SO
Total	.293	.383	.382	5861	1720	212	93	40	432	844	634
vs. Left	.295	.389	.359	2009	592	54	26	8	162	308	271
vs. Right	.293	.380	.394	3852	1128	158	67	32	270	536	363
at Home	.311	.402	.393	2845	885	97	46	15	200	434	277
on Road	.277	.365	.371	3016	835	115	47	25	232	410	357
on Grass	.301	.389	.391	4577	1376	171	73	32	352	666	472
on Turf	.268	.362	.350	1284	344	41	20	8	80	178	162
Day Games	.277	.371	.365	2042	566	69	31	16	150	303	236
Night Games	.302	.390	.391	3819	1154	143	62	24	282	541	398
April	.304	.392	.404	740	225	32	12	6	51	107	72
May	.252	.348	.314	1007	254	36	10	2	67	145	131
June	.296	.384	.379	1003	297	40	14	5	83	147	100
July	.303	.387	.386	998	302	28	20	5	78	138	95
August	.294	.385	.394	1027	302	33	17	12	79	145	126
Sept-Oct	.313	.404	.417	1086	340	43	20	10	74	162	110
Bases Empty	.290	.377	.382	4038	1173	147	67	30	30	540	437
Leadoff	.288	.372	.381	2366	682	84	41	18	18	307	254
Runners On Base	.300	.397	.381	1823	547	65	26	10	402	304	197
Scoring Position	.296	.402	.386	1113	330	42	20	6	381	213	122
Late and Close	.286	.379	.366	919	263	30	8	9	83	138	124

KEN CAMINITI — BB/TR — age 31 — HOU 3B143

1993

	BA	OBA	SA	AB	H	2B	3B	HR	RBI	BB	SO
Total	.262	.321	.390	543	142	31	0	13	75	49	88
vs. Left	.246	.319	.401	187	46	14	0	5	36	21	22
vs. Right	.270	.322	.385	356	96	17	0	8	39	28	66
at Home	.257	.308	.375	288	74	19	0	5	45	22	46
on Road	.267	.336	.408	255	68	12	0	8	30	27	42
on Grass	.264	.338	.425	174	46	7	0	7	23	20	26
on Turf	.260	.313	.374	369	96	24	0	6	52	29	62
Day Games	.276	.352	.404	156	43	11	0	3	22	19	25
Night Games	.256	.308	.385	387	99	20	0	10	53	30	63
April	.226	.286	.405	84	19	6	0	3	15	7	14
May	.260	.280	.471	104	27	7	0	5	21	3	16
June	.265	.301	.367	98	26	7	0	1	8	5	15
July	.253	.299	.304	79	20	4	0	0	12	6	14
August	.238	.330	.345	84	20	3	0	2	8	12	14
Sept-Oct	.319	.418	.426	94	30	4	0	2	11	16	15
Bases Empty	.277	.322	.416	274	76	14	0	8	8	18	46
Leadoff	.260	.292	.351	131	34	6	0	2	2	6	18
Runners On Base	.245	.320	.364	269	66	17	0	5	67	31	42
Scoring Position	.262	.351	.396	164	43	13	0	3	61	24	28
Late and Close	.287	.345	.438	80	23	6	0	2	9	7	12

7-YEAR TOTALS (1987–1993)

	BA	OBA	SA	AB	H	2B	3B	HR	RBI	BB	SO
Total	.257	.315	.371	3035	781	152	11	57	370	255	493
vs. Left	.282	.330	.427	1156	326	68	5	30	176	86	159
vs. Right	.242	.305	.336	1879	455	84	6	27	194	169	334
at Home	.272	.328	.395	1531	417	92	6	28	204	128	253
on Road	.242	.302	.346	1504	364	60	5	29	166	127	240
on Grass	.246	.305	.358	950	234	35	6	21	101	81	151
on Turf	.262	.319	.377	2085	547	117	7	36	269	174	342
Day Games	.261	.322	.368	844	220	42	5	13	94	79	153
Night Games	.256	.312	.372	2191	561	110	6	44	276	176	340
April	.264	.319	.393	349	92	21	0	8	43	27	58
May	.256	.310	.379	441	113	17	2	11	57	34	56
June	.256	.305	.365	496	127	28	1	8	56	38	80
July	.278	.329	.404	515	143	25	5	10	73	39	65
August	.241	.314	.350	614	148	36	2	9	79	65	126
Sept-Oct	.255	.313	.352	620	158	25	1	11	62	52	108
Bases Empty	.254	.304	.368	1619	411	82	6	30	30	110	277
Leadoff	.278	.316	.395	697	194	40	4	11	11	34	102
Runners On Base	.261	.327	.375	1416	370	70	5	27	340	145	216
Scoring Position	.271	.353	.392	841	228	50	2	16	303	117	146
Late and Close	.266	.323	.376	545	145	21	3	11	56	47	108

JOSE CANSECO — BR/TR — age 30 — TEX OF49, P1

1993

	BA	OBA	SA	AB	H	2B	3B	HR	RBI	BB	SO
Total	.255	.308	.455	231	59	14	1	10	46	16	62
vs. Left	.237	.302	.474	38	9	0	0	3	9	4	9
vs. Right	.259	.310	.451	193	50	14	1	7	37	12	53
at Home	.291	.331	.536	110	32	7	1	6	20	6	27
on Road	.223	.289	.380	121	27	7	0	4	26	10	35
on Grass	.273	.329	.488	205	56	12	1	10	43	15	54
on Turf	.115	.143	.192	26	3	2	0	0	3	1	8
Day Games	.343	.387	.600	70	24	7	1	3	21	4	19
Night Games	.217	.275	.391	161	35	7	0	7	25	12	43
April	.256	.311	.488	82	21	7	0	4	21	6	18
May	.274	.328	.462	106	29	6	1	4	18	8	35
June	.209	.255	.372	43	9	1	0	2	7	2	9
July	.000	.000	.000	0	0	0	0	0	0	0	0
August	.000	.000	.000	0	0	0	0	0	0	0	0
Sept-Oct	.000	.000	.000	0	0	0	0	0	0	0	0
Bases Empty	.220	.280	.379	132	29	7	1	4	4	8	40
Leadoff	.250	.273	.406	32	8	3	1	0	0	1	8
Runners On Base	.303	.345	.556	99	30	7	0	6	42	8	22
Scoring Position	.338	.370	.600	65	22	5	0	4	38	5	14
Late and Close	.182	.263	.242	33	6	2	0	0	6	3	12

9-YEAR TOTALS (1985–1993)

	BA	OBA	SA	AB	H	2B	3B	HR	RBI	BB	SO
Total	.266	.345	.507	3886	1033	185	9	245	780	449	1060
vs. Left	.285	.360	.556	1008	287	52	4	71	206	113	265
vs. Right	.259	.340	.490	2878	746	133	5	174	574	336	795
at Home	.268	.354	.501	1834	491	80	4	113	351	236	496
on Road	.264	.337	.513	2052	542	105	5	132	429	213	564
on Grass	.267	.347	.504	3247	866	145	8	203	649	382	874
on Turf	.261	.333	.524	639	167	40	1	42	131	67	186
Day Games	.277	.360	.532	1422	394	82	5	90	321	170	394
Night Games	.259	.336	.493	2464	639	103	4	155	459	279	666
April	.270	.366	.492	551	149	23	0	33	116	83	153
May	.267	.342	.496	700	187	26	1	44	135	81	193
June	.264	.345	.542	565	149	29	1	42	112	64	132
July	.288	.357	.581	618	178	29	1	50	144	63	154
August	.244	.315	.448	685	167	38	3	32	123	66	211
Sept-Oct	.265	.348	.497	767	203	40	3	44	150	92	217
Bases Empty	.246	.328	.474	2064	508	98	6	120	120	229	615
Leadoff	.264	.344	.509	727	192	36	2	46	46	80	189
Runners On Base	.288	.363	.545	1822	525	87	3	125	660	220	445
Scoring Position	.294	.371	.533	1084	319	49	3	68	528	150	281
Late and Close	.257	.331	.475	611	157	34	0	33	144	65	169

CHUCK CARR — BB/TR — age 27 — FLO OF139

1993	BA	OBA	SA	AB	H	2B	3B	HR	RBI	BB	SO
Total	.267	.327	.330	551	147	19	2	4	41	49	74
vs. Left	.254	.309	.353	173	44	9	1	2	15	13	33
vs. Right	.272	.335	.320	378	103	10	1	2	26	36	41
at Home	.284	.349	.347	271	77	8	0	3	20	28	36
on Road	.250	.305	.314	280	70	11	2	1	21	21	38
on Grass	.280	.341	.337	410	115	12	1	3	28	40	55
on Turf	.227	.283	.312	141	32	7	1	1	13	9	19
Day Games	.258	.331	.283	120	31	1	1	0	3	12	14
Night Games	.269	.326	.343	431	116	18	1	4	38	37	60
April	.226	.273	.290	62	14	4	0	0	0	4	9
May	.288	.388	.365	104	30	5	0	1	18	15	20
June	.237	.278	.330	97	23	4	1	1	12	7	14
July	.259	.286	.296	54	14	2	0	0	2	2	5
August	.303	.341	.378	119	36	3	0	2	6	7	12
Sept-Oct	.261	.341	.287	115	30	1	1	0	3	14	14
Bases Empty	.275	.328	.335	385	106	15	1	2	2	30	50
Leadoff	.293	.343	.346	246	72	8	1	1	1	19	29
Runners On Base	.247	.325	.319	166	41	4	1	2	39	19	24
Scoring Position	.239	.328	.310	113	27	2	0	2	37	16	21
Late and Close	.356	.400	.400	90	32	4	0	0	9	7	20

4-YEAR TOTALS (1990–1993)

	BA	OBA	SA	AB	H	2B	3B	HR	RBI	BB	SO
	.260	.322	.320	628	163	22	2	4	45	58	84
	.256	.306	.345	203	52	10	1	2	16	14	38
	.261	.330	.308	425	111	12	1	2	29	44	46
	.278	.345	.338	299	83	9	0	3	20	32	41
	.243	.301	.304	329	80	13	2	1	25	26	43
	.274	.333	.329	434	119	13	1	3	31	40	60
	.227	.299	.299	194	44	9	1	1	14	18	24
	.230	.301	.252	139	32	1	1	0	4	13	15
	.268	.328	.339	489	131	21	1	4	41	45	69
	.222	.269	.286	63	14	4	0	0	0	4	10
	.288	.388	.365	104	30	5	0	1	18	15	20
	.237	.278	.330	97	23	4	1	1	12	7	14
	.259	.286	.296	54	14	2	0	0	2	2	5
	.292	.328	.362	130	38	3	0	2	7	7	14
	.244	.330	.278	180	44	4	1	0	6	23	21
	.265	.323	.323	437	116	17	1	2	2	37	55
	.285	.342	.336	277	79	9	1	1	1	24	31
	.246	.321	.314	191	47	5	1	2	43	21	29
	.238	.322	.308	130	31	3	0	2	41	17	23
	.324	.388	.373	102	33	5	0	0	11	11	26

JOE CARTER — BR/TR — age 34 — TOR OF151, DH3

1993	BA	OBA	SA	AB	H	2B	3B	HR	RBI	BB	SO
Total	.254	.312	.489	603	153	33	5	33	121	47	113
vs. Left	.296	.341	.531	162	48	6	1	10	34	12	28
vs. Right	.238	.302	.474	441	105	27	4	23	87	35	85
at Home	.250	.304	.529	312	78	18	3	21	66	21	58
on Road	.258	.321	.447	291	75	15	2	12	55	26	55
on Grass	.257	.318	.487	226	58	14	1	12	44	20	44
on Turf	.252	.309	.491	377	95	19	4	21	77	27	69
Day Games	.238	.297	.519	206	49	11	1	15	42	15	46
Night Games	.262	.320	.474	397	104	22	4	18	79	32	67
April	.277	.304	.590	83	23	6	1	6	25	4	18
May	.313	.336	.617	115	36	10	2	7	16	2	20
June	.230	.349	.483	87	20	5	1	5	22	13	20
July	.219	.274	.305	105	23	6	0	1	18	8	19
August	.243	.306	.505	111	27	2	0	9	21	10	23
Sept-Oct	.235	.304	.441	102	24	4	1	5	19	10	13
Bases Empty	.256	.302	.542	277	71	16	3	19	19	14	48
Leadoff	.295	.324	.640	139	41	8	2	12	12	4	17
Runners On Base	.252	.321	.445	326	82	17	2	14	102	33	65
Scoring Position	.273	.345	.513	187	51	10	1	11	92	22	43
Late and Close	.227	.284	.375	88	20	2	1	3	9	6	15

10-YEAR TOTALS (1984–1993)

	BA	OBA	SA	AB	H	2B	3B	HR	RBI	BB	SO
	.263	.310	.471	5754	1514	296	38	275	994	349	943
	.276	.320	.479	1608	444	81	9	76	260	107	266
	.258	.306	.468	4146	1070	215	29	199	734	242	677
	.266	.314	.483	2859	760	145	19	146	502	180	479
	.260	.305	.459	2895	754	151	19	129	492	169	464
	.262	.308	.459	3932	1032	191	23	179	650	240	630
	.265	.312	.497	1822	482	105	15	96	344	109	313
	.258	.304	.465	1902	490	94	14	91	313	115	340
	.266	.312	.474	3852	1024	202	24	184	681	234	603
	.266	.307	.467	718	191	40	1	34	130	40	134
	.270	.310	.464	946	255	49	9	39	157	49	152
	.267	.327	.522	889	237	53	6	54	168	61	155
	.250	.302	.431	980	245	48	6	39	159	70	143
	.256	.300	.482	1055	270	48	5	60	183	61	166
	.271	.312	.466	1166	316	58	11	49	197	68	193
	.259	.298	.479	2961	768	156	17	153	153	136	460
	.272	.305	.518	1164	317	57	5	73	73	43	156
	.267	.321	.463	2793	746	140	21	122	841	213	483
	.272	.338	.463	1660	452	82	15	68	703	170	317
	.243	.298	.402	903	219	26	8	34	147	62	162

VINNY CASTILLA — BR/TR — age 27 — COL SS104

1993	BA	OBA	SA	AB	H	2B	3B	HR	RBI	BB	SO
Total	.255	.283	.404	337	86	9	7	9	30	13	45
vs. Left	.333	.370	.529	87	29	4	2	3	8	5	11
vs. Right	.228	.253	.360	250	57	5	5	6	22	8	34
at Home	.305	.346	.497	167	51	5	6	5	19	11	19
on Road	.206	.217	.312	170	35	4	1	4	11	2	26
on Grass	.278	.309	.456	259	72	8	7	8	28	13	34
on Turf	.179	.190	.231	78	14	1	0	1	2	0	11
Day Games	.259	.274	.472	108	28	2	3	5	15	2	16
Night Games	.253	.287	.371	229	58	7	4	4	15	11	29
April	.273	.320	.591	22	6	0	2	1	2	2	4
May	.400	.429	.500	60	24	2	2	0	4	2	3
June	.262	.279	.476	84	22	2	2	4	11	2	13
July	.167	.179	.204	54	9	2	0	0	1	1	8
August	.250	.263	.472	72	18	2	1	4	10	2	11
Sept-Oct	.156	.235	.178	45	7	1	0	0	2	4	6
Bases Empty	.291	.298	.447	206	60	6	4	6	6	2	23
Leadoff	.378	.386	.573	82	31	2	1	4	4	1	9
Runners On Base	.198	.262	.336	131	26	3	3	3	24	11	22
Scoring Position	.179	.266	.346	78	14	1	3	2	22	10	15
Late and Close	.206	.256	.353	34	7	2	0	1	3	3	4

3-YEAR TOTALS (1991–1993)

	BA	OBA	SA	AB	H	2B	3B	HR	RBI	BB	SO
	.254	.284	.397	358	91	10	7	9	31	14	51
	.323	.357	.505	93	30	4	2	3	8	5	12
	.230	.259	.358	265	61	6	5	6	23	9	39
	.299	.343	.476	187	56	6	6	5	20	12	25
	.205	.216	.310	171	35	4	1	4	11	2	26
	.276	.310	.444	279	77	9	7	8	29	14	40
	.177	.188	.228	79	14	1	0	1	2	0	11
	.259	.279	.457	116	30	2	3	5	15	2	19
	.252	.287	.368	242	61	8	4	4	16	12	32
	.273	.320	.591	22	6	0	2	1	2	2	4
	.400	.429	.500	60	24	2	2	0	4	2	3
	.262	.279	.476	84	22	2	2	4	11	2	13
	.167	.179	.204	54	9	2	0	0	1	1	8
	.250	.263	.472	72	18	2	1	4	10	2	11
	.182	.257	.212	66	12	2	0	0	3	5	12
	.286	.293	.432	220	63	6	4	6	6	2	28
	.367	.374	.544	90	33	2	1	4	4	1	13
	.203	.272	.341	138	28	4	3	3	25	12	23
	.195	.283	.366	82	16	2	3	2	23	11	16
	.211	.256	.342	38	8	2	0	1	3	3	4

ANDUJAR CEDENO — BR/TR — age 25 — HOU SS149, 3B1

1993	BA	OBA	SA	AB	H	2B	3B	HR	RBI	BB	SO	4-YEAR TOTALS (1990–1993) BA	OBA	SA	AB	H	2B	3B	HR	RBI	BB	SO
Total	.283	.346	.412	505	143	24	4	11	56	48	97	.246	.299	.380	984	242	50	8	22	105	71	247
vs. Left	.341	.400	.482	164	56	7	2	4	18	14	21	.276	.326	.391	312	86	16	4	4	32	22	65
vs. Right	.255	.320	.378	341	87	17	2	7	38	34	76	.232	.287	.375	672	156	34	4	18	73	49	182
at Home	.308	.377	.453	247	76	14	2	6	27	26	55	.254	.317	.405	511	130	31	5	12	56	44	138
on Road	.260	.316	.372	258	67	10	2	5	29	22	42	.237	.280	.353	473	112	19	3	10	49	27	109
on Grass	.272	.333	.426	169	46	7	2	5	20	16	31	.259	.307	.420	305	79	13	3	10	37	20	70
on Turf	.289	.352	.405	336	97	17	2	6	36	32	66	.240	.296	.362	679	163	37	5	12	68	51	177
Day Games	.287	.337	.438	160	46	8	2	4	24	11	29	.255	.290	.397	290	74	14	3	7	38	12	69
Night Games	.281	.350	.400	345	97	16	2	7	32	37	68	.242	.303	.373	694	168	36	5	15	67	59	178
April	.292	.347	.400	65	19	5	1	0	7	6	13	.236	.293	.340	106	25	7	2	0	7	8	29
May	.309	.363	.468	94	29	7	1	2	9	7	19	.271	.331	.413	155	42	11	1	3	14	12	40
June	.346	.402	.500	78	27	2	2	2	13	7	12	.346	.402	.500	78	27	2	2	2	13	7	12
July	.232	.295	.305	95	22	4	0	1	8	8	12	.235	.294	.322	115	27	5	1	1	10	9	18
August	.262	.351	.310	84	22	1	0	1	6	12	18	.252	.308	.385	226	57	10	1	6	27	19	58
Sept-Oct	.270	.327	.494	89	24	5	0	5	13	8	23	.211	.253	.365	304	64	15	1	10	34	16	90
Bases Empty	.313	.363	.470	281	88	16	2	8	8	22	62	.265	.306	.414	548	145	31	3	15	15	31	147
Leadoff	.322	.375	.492	118	38	5	0	5	5	10	24	.258	.300	.393	229	59	10	0	7	7	13	62
Runners On Base	.246	.326	.339	224	55	8	2	3	48	26	35	.222	.291	.337	436	97	19	5	7	90	40	100
Scoring Position	.252	.325	.329	143	36	6	1	1	43	16	24	.223	.297	.328	265	59	10	3	4	80	28	63
Late and Close	.265	.337	.337	83	22	3	0	1	10	9	15	.241	.306	.367	158	38	8	0	4	15	15	39

ARCHI CIANFROCCO — BR/TR — age 28 — MON/SD 3B64, 1B42

1993	BA	OBA	SA	AB	H	2B	3B	HR	RBI	BB	SO	2-YEAR TOTALS (1992–1993) BA	OBA	SA	AB	H	2B	3B	HR	RBI	BB	SO
Total	.243	.287	.416	296	72	11	2	12	48	17	69	.242	.282	.390	528	128	16	4	18	78	28	135
vs. Left	.282	.310	.423	78	22	5	0	2	15	5	16	.263	.297	.429	175	46	7	2	6	32	11	41
vs. Right	.229	.278	.413	218	50	6	2	10	33	12	53	.232	.275	.371	353	82	9	2	12	46	17	94
at Home	.266	.305	.455	154	41	7	2	6	21	8	32	.240	.288	.400	250	60	7	3	9	37	15	60
on Road	.218	.266	.373	142	31	4	0	6	27	9	37	.245	.277	.381	278	68	9	1	9	41	13	75
on Grass	.265	.309	.465	226	60	8	2	11	40	13	50	.266	.304	.439	289	77	10	2	12	47	15	72
on Turf	.171	.213	.257	70	12	3	0	1	8	4	19	.213	.255	.331	239	51	6	2	6	31	13	63
Day Games	.212	.255	.364	99	21	4	1	3	11	4	24	.246	.282	.400	175	43	5	2	6	28	8	50
Night Games	.259	.302	.442	197	51	7	1	9	37	13	45	.241	.282	.385	353	85	11	2	12	50	20	85
April	.235	.235	.471	17	4	1	0	1	1	0	5	.220	.233	.317	41	9	1	0	1	5	0	15
May	.000	.000	.000	0	0	0	0	0	0	0	0	.254	.294	.540	63	16	1	1	5	17	3	14
June	.095	.136	.143	21	2	1	0	0	0	1	3	.219	.235	.271	96	21	2	0	1	5	2	25
July	.247	.312	.519	81	20	5	1	5	18	7	17	.238	.303	.437	126	30	6	2	5	21	11	30
August	.312	.337	.462	93	29	2	0	4	13	4	19	.297	.328	.432	118	35	4	0	4	14	6	26
Sept-Oct	.202	.253	.321	84	17	2	1	2	16	5	25	.202	.253	.321	84	17	2	1	2	16	5	25
Bases Empty	.221	.266	.387	163	36	4	1	7	7	9	40	.237	.281	.376	295	70	9	1	10	10	16	74
Leadoff	.216	.259	.314	51	11	0	1	1	1	3	8	.243	.271	.340	103	25	2	1	2	2	4	19
Runners On Base	.271	.311	.451	133	36	7	1	5	41	8	29	.249	.283	.408	233	58	7	3	8	68	12	61
Scoring Position	.325	.360	.558	77	25	4	1	4	39	5	19	.283	.321	.449	138	39	4	2	5	61	9	41
Late and Close	.269	.333	.442	52	14	3	0	2	6	4	13	.309	.362	.433	97	30	4	1	2	11	4	27

DAVE CLARK — BL/TR — age 32 — PIT OF91

1993	BA	OBA	SA	AB	H	2B	3B	HR	RBI	BB	SO	8-YEAR TOTALS (1986–1993) BA	OBA	SA	AB	H	2B	3B	HR	RBI	BB	SO
Total	.271	.358	.444	277	75	11	2	11	46	38	58	.255	.323	.400	1045	266	37	5	35	142	109	233
vs. Left	.250	.400	.625	16	4	0	0	2	4	4	8	.216	.293	.353	51	11	1	0	2	6	6	25
vs. Right	.272	.356	.433	261	71	11	2	9	42	34	50	.257	.325	.402	994	255	36	5	33	136	103	208
at Home	.273	.356	.503	143	39	5	2	8	29	19	29	.259	.327	.429	536	139	18	5	21	81	55	120
on Road	.269	.361	.381	134	36	6	0	3	17	19	29	.250	.320	.369	509	127	19	0	14	61	54	113
on Grass	.284	.383	.370	81	23	1	0	2	10	12	17	.249	.311	.372	683	170	24	3	18	82	62	156
on Turf	.265	.348	.474	196	52	10	2	9	36	26	41	.265	.346	.453	362	96	13	2	17	60	47	77
Day Games	.224	.344	.342	76	17	3	0	2	10	14	17	.267	.342	.443	386	103	16	2	16	63	46	81
Night Games	.289	.364	.483	201	58	8	2	9	36	24	41	.247	.312	.375	659	163	21	3	19	79	63	152
April	.269	.367	.308	26	7	1	0	0	1	3	7	.266	.343	.372	94	25	4	0	2	7	10	23
May	.250	.400	.375	24	6	0	0	1	5	6	3	.180	.272	.309	139	25	0	0	6	16	18	29
June	.167	.250	.286	42	7	2	0	1	4	5	11	.211	.293	.319	185	39	7	2	3	22	22	42
July	.313	.414	.479	48	15	5	0	1	13	9	11	.333	.403	.516	126	42	11	0	4	25	16	29
August	.254	.333	.418	67	17	2	0	3	9	8	12	.243	.297	.379	177	43	4	1	6	22	14	44
Sept-Oct	.329	.390	.614	70	23	1	2	5	14	7	14	.284	.340	.460	324	92	11	2	14	50	29	66
Bases Empty	.273	.344	.460	139	38	7	2	5	5	15	33	.263	.320	.423	579	152	24	3	21	21	49	125
Leadoff	.267	.353	.467	60	16	3	0	3	3	8	8	.249	.315	.422	237	59	11	0	10	10	23	45
Runners On Base	.268	.372	.428	138	37	4	0	6	41	23	25	.245	.327	.371	466	114	13	2	14	121	60	108
Scoring Position	.293	.423	.378	82	24	4	0	1	31	20	20	.251	.358	.355	279	70	9	1	6	102	51	74
Late and Close	.263	.354	.386	57	15	1	0	2	7	8	15	.238	.308	.357	244	58	6	1	7	30	26	64

JERALD CLARK — BR/TR — age 31 — COL OF96, 1B37

1993	BA	OBA	SA	AB	H	2B	3B	HR	RBI	BB	SO		6-YEAR TOTALS (1988–1993) BA	OBA	SA	AB	H	2B	3B	HR	RBI	BB	SO
Total	.282	.324	.444	478	135	26	6	13	67	20	60		.251	.297	.398	1500	377	71	13	41	193	81	284
vs. Left	.276	.323	.422	116	32	9	1	2	15	5	15		.236	.279	.389	471	111	22	4	14	51	24	91
vs. Right	.285	.325	.450	362	103	17	5	11	52	15	45		.259	.305	.402	1029	266	49	9	27	142	57	193
at Home	.322	.387	.524	227	73	16	3	8	40	17	26		.257	.310	.438	739	190	38	6	28	114	46	126
on Road	.247	.262	.371	251	62	10	3	5	27	3	34		.246	.283	.359	761	187	33	7	13	79	35	158
on Grass	.287	.338	.462	359	103	22	4	11	54	19	44		.260	.306	.429	1105	287	56	10	37	163	62	206
on Turf	.269	.281	.387	119	32	4	2	2	13	1	16		.228	.272	.311	395	90	15	3	4	30	19	78
Day Games	.293	.350	.520	150	44	10	3	6	23	9	17		.243	.294	.382	456	111	22	4	11	50	28	82
Night Games	.277	.312	.409	328	91	16	3	7	44	11	43		.255	.298	.405	1044	266	49	9	30	143	53	202
April	.211	.262	.421	57	12	4	1	2	4	3	8		.221	.294	.392	222	49	9	1	9	25	20	45
May	.267	.337	.430	86	23	5	0	3	12	3	14		.235	.283	.325	234	55	12	0	3	20	9	49
June	.373	.427	.467	75	28	5	1	0	7	6	11		.300	.369	.456	217	65	15	2	5	27	21	30
July	.173	.214	.269	52	9	2	0	1	6	2	5		.258	.299	.402	229	59	11	2	6	31	13	44
August	.306	.333	.480	98	30	4	2	3	17	3	13		.264	.297	.400	250	66	10	3	6	29	8	40
Sept-Oct	.300	.319	.500	110	33	6	2	4	21	3	9		.239	.259	.411	348	83	14	5	12	61	10	76
Bases Empty	.257	.296	.405	269	69	12	5	6	6	6	41		.234	.279	.359	849	199	38	7	18	18	40	174
Leadoff	.252	.304	.374	107	27	7	0	2	2	4	16		.251	.296	.351	359	90	19	1	5	5	18	69
Runners On Base	.316	.360	.493	209	66	14	1	7	61	14	19		.273	.319	.449	651	178	33	6	23	175	41	110
Scoring Position	.312	.360	.536	125	39	11	1	5	57	10	14		.264	.313	.443	375	99	18	5	13	152	25	60
Late and Close	.284	.289	.473	74	21	2	0	4	16	1	7		.230	.255	.368	269	62	8	1	9	45	9	55

PHIL CLARK — BR/TR — age 26 — SD OF36, 1B24, C11, 3B5

1993	BA	OBA	SA	AB	H	2B	3B	HR	RBI	BB	SO		2-YEAR TOTALS (1992–1993) BA	OBA	SA	AB	H	2B	3B	HR	RBI	BB	SO
Total	.313	.345	.496	240	75	17	0	9	33	8	31		.330	.368	.503	294	97	21	0	10	38	14	40
vs. Left	.323	.368	.496	133	43	11	0	4	17	8	14		.360	.406	.535	172	62	15	0	5	22	12	20
vs. Right	.299	.315	.495	107	32	6	0	5	16	0	17		.287	.313	.459	122	35	6	0	5	16	2	20
at Home	.328	.365	.517	116	38	4	0	6	21	5	15		.349	.396	.510	149	52	6	0	6	24	10	21
on Road	.298	.326	.476	124	37	13	0	3	12	3	16		.310	.338	.497	145	45	15	0	4	14	4	19
on Grass	.316	.349	.497	177	56	8	0	8	29	6	25		.335	.377	.493	221	74	11	0	8	32	12	32
on Turf	.302	.333	.492	63	19	9	0	1	4	2	6		.315	.342	.534	73	23	10	0	2	6	2	8
Day Games	.271	.308	.388	85	23	4	0	2	6	3	9		.305	.339	.457	105	32	7	0	3	10	4	13
Night Games	.335	.366	.555	155	52	13	0	7	27	5	22		.344	.384	.529	189	65	14	0	7	28	10	27
April	.227	.320	.273	22	5	1	0	0	1	1	5		.227	.320	.273	22	5	1	0	0	1	1	5
May	.419	.438	.710	31	13	3	0	2	5	0	2		.417	.432	.778	36	15	4	0	3	7	0	2
June	.292	.292	.333	48	14	2	0	0	1	0	4		.338	.372	.378	74	25	3	0	0	2	4	8
July	.313	.389	.583	48	15	4	0	3	7	5	7		.306	.386	.516	62	19	4	0	4	8	7	10
August	.304	.328	.554	56	17	2	0	4	11	1	7		.304	.328	.554	56	17	2	0	4	11	1	7
Sept-Oct	.314	.316	.457	35	11	5	0	0	8	1	6		.364	.362	.523	44	16	7	0	0	9	1	8
Bases Empty	.302	.345	.540	139	42	12	0	7	7	5	19		.322	.366	.534	174	56	16	0	7	7	8	24
Leadoff	.283	.309	.453	53	15	3	0	2	2	1	10		.309	.338	.471	68	21	5	0	2	2	2	12
Runners On Base	.327	.346	.436	101	33	5	0	2	26	3	12		.342	.372	.458	120	41	5	0	3	31	6	16
Scoring Position	.265	.278	.412	68	18	4	0	2	26	2	8		.291	.318	.418	79	23	4	0	2	29	4	10
Late and Close	.289	.313	.467	45	13	2	0	2	6	1	8		.298	.339	.439	57	17	2	0	2	7	3	10

WILL CLARK — BL/TL — age 30 — SF 1B129

1993	BA	OBA	SA	AB	H	2B	3B	HR	RBI	BB	SO		8-YEAR TOTALS (1986–1993) BA	OBA	SA	AB	H	2B	3B	HR	RBI	BB	SO
Total	.283	.367	.432	491	139	27	2	14	73	63	68		.299	.373	.499	4269	1278	249	37	176	709	506	744
vs. Left	.269	.335	.330	182	49	6	1	1	28	17	22		.293	.346	.450	1572	460	82	15	45	283	125	271
vs. Right	.291	.386	.492	309	90	21	1	13	45	46	46		.303	.389	.527	2697	818	167	22	131	426	381	473
at Home	.249	.349	.362	257	64	12	1	5	31	38	39		.306	.380	.514	2160	662	136	17	93	367	267	364
on Road	.321	.389	.509	234	75	15	1	9	42	25	29		.292	.367	.483	2109	616	113	20	83	342	239	380
on Grass	.277	.365	.419	394	109	22	2	10	58	52	54		.305	.380	.503	3189	974	188	27	129	531	389	562
on Turf	.309	.380	.485	97	30	5	0	4	15	11	14		.281	.354	.487	1080	304	61	10	47	178	117	182
Day Games	.266	.357	.421	252	67	16	1	7	36	33	42		.304	.387	.518	1806	549	118	22	75	303	241	317
Night Games	.301	.379	.444	239	72	11	1	7	37	30	26		.296	.363	.484	2463	729	131	15	101	406	265	427
April	.198	.277	.275	91	18	4	0	1	10	10	13		.298	.377	.489	667	199	37	9	24	105	86	121
May	.277	.373	.362	94	26	5	0	1	12	14	12		.265	.342	.473	774	205	39	7	36	121	87	140
June	.295	.402	.500	88	26	9	0	3	18	16	15		.325	.401	.546	636	207	35	6	31	137	86	100
July	.299	.384	.464	97	29	4	0	4	13	11	14		.295	.367	.463	672	198	35	3	24	104	73	127
August	.286	.324	.524	63	18	2	2	3	14	3	9		.306	.371	.529	777	238	54	7	35	134	80	123
Sept-Oct	.379	.456	.534	58	22	3	0	2	6	9	8		.311	.386	.495	743	231	49	5	26	108	94	133
Bases Empty	.282	.392	.424	262	74	13	0	8	8	42	35		.289	.355	.470	2408	696	137	17	88	88	226	422
Leadoff	.337	.406	.512	86	29	6	0	3	3	7	11		.292	.354	.482	814	238	42	8	32	32	68	129
Runners On Base	.284	.339	.441	229	65	14	2	6	65	21	33		.313	.395	.536	1861	582	112	20	88	621	280	322
Scoring Position	.227	.294	.326	141	32	7	2	1	51	16	23		.304	.406	.517	1105	336	63	14	48	513	223	213
Late and Close	.290	.364	.493	69	20	3	1	3	11	7	9		.293	.381	.490	704	206	41	7	28	124	101	139

ROYCE CLAYTON — BR/TR — age 24 — SFSS153

1993	BA	OBA	SA	AB	H	2B	3B	HR	RBI	BB	SO	3-YEAR TOTALS (1991–1993) BA	OBA	SA	AB	H	2B	3B	HR	RBI	BB	SO
Total	.282	.331	.372	549	155	21	5	6	70	38	91	.257	.308	.343	896	230	29	9	10	96	65	160
vs. Left	.247	.286	.341	170	42	10	0	2	16	10	29	.247	.300	.336	271	67	14	2	2	20	21	51
vs. Right	.298	.350	.385	379	113	11	5	4	54	28	62	.261	.311	.346	625	163	15	7	8	76	44	109
at Home	.305	.346	.421	266	81	12	2	5	34	16	44	.279	.326	.384	451	126	15	4	8	51	31	71
on Road	.261	.316	.325	283	74	9	3	1	36	22	47	.234	.289	.301	445	104	14	5	2	45	34	89
on Grass	.285	.335	.387	421	120	17	4	6	48	30	70	.263	.316	.356	680	179	22	7	9	68	51	115
on Turf	.273	.317	.320	128	35	4	1	0	22	8	21	.236	.282	.301	216	51	7	2	1	28	14	45
Day Games	.266	.311	.339	271	72	7	2	3	32	17	48	.250	.303	.327	416	104	9	4	5	44	31	68
Night Games	.299	.350	.403	278	83	14	3	3	38	21	43	.262	.312	.356	480	126	20	5	5	52	34	92
April	.264	.261	.297	91	24	1	1	0	9	0	18	.242	.270	.291	165	40	2	3	0	15	7	33
May	.311	.385	.422	90	28	3	2	1	13	10	12	.270	.343	.405	148	40	7	2	3	21	16	24
June	.271	.293	.333	96	26	3	0	1	11	3	14	.245	.280	.329	143	35	4	1	2	13	7	23
July	.333	.394	.494	87	29	6	1	2	21	10	12	.333	.394	.494	87	29	6	1	2	21	10	12
August	.209	.258	.279	86	18	4	1	0	8	4	20	.240	.295	.289	121	29	4	1	0	11	8	23
Sept-Oct	.303	.375	.404	99	30	4	0	2	8	11	15	.246	.299	.319	232	57	6	1	3	15	17	45
Bases Empty	.297	.350	.417	290	86	18	1	5	5	22	44	.265	.323	.369	483	128	24	1	8	8	39	87
Leadoff	.320	.383	.492	128	41	11	1	3	3	12	12	.303	.364	.442	208	63	12	1	5	5	19	29
Runners On Base	.266	.309	.320	259	69	3	4	1	65	16	47	.247	.290	.312	413	102	5	8	2	88	26	73
Scoring Position	.254	.310	.312	173	44	3	2	1	63	15	34	.231	.292	.308	260	60	4	5	2	85	24	48
Late and Close	.177	.217	.203	79	14	2	0	0	2	4	22	.184	.243	.199	141	26	2	0	0	4	11	36

ALEX COLE — BL/TL — age 29 — COL OF93

1993	BA	OBA	SA	AB	H	2B	3B	HR	RBI	BB	SO	4-YEAR TOTALS (1990–1993) BA	OBA	SA	AB	H	2B	3B	HR	RBI	BB	SO
Total	.256	.339	.305	348	89	9	4	0	24	43	58	.275	.356	.331	1264	348	35	18	0	73	157	210
vs. Left	.143	.182	.286	21	3	1	1	0	3	1	9	.293	.400	.380	184	54	6	5	0	18	31	41
vs. Right	.263	.349	.306	327	86	8	3	0	21	42	49	.272	.348	.323	1080	294	29	13	0	55	126	169
at Home	.235	.315	.302	179	42	4	4	0	18	20	31	.279	.371	.346	619	173	17	12	0	54	88	111
on Road	.278	.365	.308	169	47	5	0	0	6	23	27	.271	.341	.318	645	175	18	6	0	19	69	99
on Grass	.258	.333	.316	275	71	8	4	0	22	30	46	.273	.356	.323	927	253	26	10	0	57	118	148
on Turf	.247	.360	.260	73	18	1	0	0	2	13	12	.282	.356	.356	337	95	9	8	0	16	39	62
Day Games	.252	.331	.298	131	33	4	1	0	8	16	25	.261	.346	.297	387	101	8	3	0	20	52	74
Night Games	.258	.344	.309	217	56	5	3	0	16	27	33	.282	.361	.347	877	247	27	15	0	53	105	136
April	.309	.382	.382	68	21	1	2	0	3	8	10	.281	.345	.353	153	43	5	3	0	5	15	25
May	.213	.284	.250	80	17	3	0	0	6	7	14	.231	.309	.259	147	34	4	0	0	11	15	24
June	.269	.375	.346	52	14	2	1	0	10	10	9	.270	.373	.305	141	38	3	1	0	14	24	21
July	.268	.348	.317	41	11	2	0	0	2	5	7	.273	.367	.337	187	51	4	4	0	13	28	34
August	.284	.354	.324	74	21	1	1	0	1	8	9	.309	.383	.383	298	92	10	6	0	13	35	55
Sept-Oct	.152	.282	.152	33	5	0	0	0	2	5	9	.266	.344	.317	338	90	9	4	0	17	40	51
Bases Empty	.221	.307	.261	226	50	5	2	0	0	27	40	.277	.363	.331	838	232	25	10	0	0	110	147
Leadoff	.242	.299	.303	99	24	2	2	0	0	8	15	.267	.365	.323	446	119	13	6	0	0	69	72
Runners On Base	.320	.397	.385	122	39	4	2	0	24	16	18	.272	.343	.333	426	116	10	8	0	73	47	63
Scoring Position	.315	.409	.397	73	23	4	1	0	23	12	15	.280	.374	.329	243	68	6	3	0	68	38	46
Late and Close	.239	.321	.283	46	11	0	1	0	5	6	8	.254	.339	.288	205	52	3	2	0	17	25	38

VINCE COLEMAN — BB/TR — age 33 — NYN OF90

1993	BA	OBA	SA	AB	H	2B	3B	HR	RBI	BB	SO	9-YEAR TOTALS (1985–1993) BA	OBA	SA	AB	H	2B	3B	HR	RBI	BB	SO
Total	.279	.316	.375	373	104	14	8	2	25	21	58	.266	.328	.343	4415	1175	138	70	20	280	401	774
vs. Left	.290	.333	.430	100	29	5	3	1	6	7	17	.254	.316	.366	1588	404	75	29	15	116	141	290
vs. Right	.275	.309	.355	273	75	9	5	1	19	14	41	.273	.335	.329	2827	771	63	41	5	164	260	484
at Home	.284	.328	.389	190	54	6	4	2	16	13	39	.278	.343	.369	2200	612	71	40	16	164	212	372
on Road	.273	.302	.361	183	50	8	4	0	9	8	19	.254	.312	.317	2215	563	67	30	4	116	189	402
on Grass	.290	.325	.384	307	89	9	7	2	23	17	51	.259	.320	.313	1574	408	35	16	6	96	145	295
on Turf	.227	.271	.333	66	15	5	1	0	2	4	7	.270	.332	.359	2841	767	103	54	14	184	256	479
Day Games	.268	.325	.366	142	38	9	1	1	9	12	17	.267	.327	.353	1496	399	47	26	10	103	137	272
Night Games	.286	.310	.381	231	66	5	7	1	16	9	41	.266	.328	.337	2919	776	91	44	10	177	264	502
April	.258	.289	.333	93	24	3	2	0	6	4	12	.273	.341	.366	644	176	26	14	2	47	65	102
May	.236	.298	.345	110	26	5	2	1	8	10	14	.291	.353	.372	828	241	21	17	4	59	80	144
June	.303	.333	.416	89	27	3	2	1	8	4	18	.264	.326	.350	880	232	29	16	5	54	79	156
July	.333	.353	.420	81	27	3	2	0	3	3	14	.253	.319	.311	665	168	19	7	2	32	65	122
August	.000	.000	.000	0	0	0	0	0	0	0	0	.279	.332	.355	768	214	25	11	4	51	60	124
Sept-Oct	.000	.000	.000	0	0	0	0	0	0	0	0	.229	.286	.287	630	144	18	5	3	37	52	126
Bases Empty	.297	.333	.425	259	77	13	7	2	2	14	38	.270	.335	.349	3028	819	98	47	15	15	285	551
Leadoff	.312	.350	.487	154	48	9	6	2	2	9	23	.275	.341	.359	1902	523	72	32	8	8	183	364
Runners On Base	.237	.276	.263	114	27	1	1	0	23	7	20	.257	.312	.329	1387	356	40	23	5	265	116	223
Scoring Position	.224	.289	.239	67	15	1	0	0	22	7	15	.252	.318	.337	898	226	28	17	5	256	93	167
Late and Close	.197	.219	.279	61	12	3	1	0	2	2	14	.259	.322	.321	723	187	27	6	2	63	67	126

JEFF CONINE — BR/TR — age 28 — FLO OF147, 1B43

1993	BA	OBA	SA	AB	H	2B	3B	HR	RBI	BB	SO
Total	.292	.351	.403	595	174	24	3	12	79	52	135
vs. Left	.299	.366	.455	167	50	7	2	5	28	20	36
vs. Right	.290	.345	.383	428	124	17	1	7	51	32	99
at Home	.296	.340	.381	307	91	11	0	5	41	21	71
on Road	.288	.362	.427	288	83	13	3	7	38	31	64
on Grass	.288	.341	.398	462	133	21	0	10	59	38	105
on Turf	.308	.384	.421	133	41	3	3	2	20	14	30
Day Games	.288	.371	.394	132	38	5	0	3	14	17	37
Night Games	.294	.345	.406	463	136	19	3	9	65	35	98
April	.321	.386	.346	78	25	2	0	0	7	9	20
May	.258	.383	.382	89	23	3	1	2	11	18	22
June	.292	.369	.469	96	28	6	1	3	15	10	25
July	.358	.382	.462	106	38	5	0	2	15	4	20
August	.286	.305	.420	112	32	4	1	3	20	3	23
Sept-Oct	.246	.298	.333	114	28	4	0	2	11	8	25
Bases Empty	.269	.338	.343	324	87	13	1	3	3	32	79
Leadoff	.225	.290	.325	120	27	7	1	1	1	11	32
Runners On Base	.321	.367	.476	271	87	11	2	9	76	20	56
Scoring Position	.311	.376	.459	148	46	4	0	6	66	17	31
Late and Close	.225	.283	.353	102	23	2	1	3	18	9	27

3-YEAR TOTALS (1990–1993)

	BA	OBA	SA	AB	H	2B	3B	HR	RBI	BB	SO
Total	.286	.345	.395	706	202	31	5	12	90	62	163
vs. Left	.303	.379	.443	201	61	9	2	5	33	27	44
vs. Right	.279	.331	.376	505	141	22	3	7	57	35	119
at Home	.292	.341	.378	339	99	14	0	5	47	26	76
on Road	.281	.349	.411	367	103	17	5	7	43	36	87
on Grass	.285	.336	.392	523	149	24	1	10	62	41	122
on Turf	.290	.370	.404	183	53	7	4	2	28	21	41
Day Games	.280	.364	.379	161	45	7	0	3	16	21	44
Night Games	.288	.339	.400	545	157	24	5	9	74	41	119
April	.321	.386	.346	78	25	2	0	0	7	9	20
May	.258	.383	.382	89	23	3	1	2	11	18	22
June	.292	.369	.469	96	28	6	1	3	15	10	25
July	.358	.382	.462	106	38	5	0	2	15	4	20
August	.275	.308	.397	189	52	8	3	3	29	9	41
Sept-Oct	.243	.302	.331	148	36	7	0	2	13	12	35
Bases Empty	.255	.325	.332	380	97	16	2	3	3	37	96
Leadoff	.201	.263	.285	144	29	7	1	1	1	12	41
Runners On Base	.322	.369	.469	326	105	15	3	9	87	25	67
Scoring Position	.320	.386	.466	178	57	6	1	6	77	21	36
Late and Close	.217	.278	.325	120	26	2	1	3	18	11	31

SCOTT COOPER — BL/TR — age 27 — BOS 3B154, 1B2, SS1

1993	BA	OBA	SA	AB	H	2B	3B	HR	RBI	BB	SO
Total	.279	.355	.397	526	147	29	3	9	63	58	81
vs. Left	.257	.321	.361	144	37	5	2	2	17	10	25
vs. Right	.288	.367	.411	382	110	24	1	7	46	48	56
at Home	.325	.396	.443	255	83	19	1	3	31	30	37
on Road	.236	.316	.354	271	64	10	2	6	32	28	44
on Grass	.291	.365	.400	437	127	23	2	7	50	49	67
on Turf	.225	.303	.382	89	20	6	1	2	13	9	14
Day Games	.267	.369	.364	176	47	9	1	2	19	27	27
Night Games	.286	.347	.414	350	100	20	2	7	44	31	54
April	.350	.402	.475	80	28	4	0	2	16	7	17
May	.280	.359	.341	82	23	3	1	0	6	7	12
June	.267	.371	.400	90	24	6	0	2	12	15	12
July	.253	.330	.389	95	24	4	0	3	7	11	13
August	.215	.303	.367	79	17	5	2	1	10	9	15
Sept-Oct	.310	.363	.410	100	31	7	0	1	12	9	12
Bases Empty	.257	.326	.366	292	75	13	2	5	5	25	43
Leadoff	.235	.254	.328	119	28	8	0	1	1	3	16
Runners On Base	.308	.389	.436	234	72	16	1	4	58	33	38
Scoring Position	.311	.412	.432	132	41	7	0	3	53	25	23
Late and Close	.192	.319	.282	78	15	5	1	0	6	15	14

4-YEAR TOTALS (1990–1993)

	BA	OBA	SA	AB	H	2B	3B	HR	RBI	BB	SO
Total	.285	.356	.403	899	256	54	5	14	103	97	117
vs. Left	.272	.346	.393	191	52	8	3	3	24	18	32
vs. Right	.288	.359	.405	708	204	46	2	11	79	79	85
at Home	.326	.390	.440	436	142	29	3	5	48	46	55
on Road	.246	.324	.367	463	114	25	2	9	55	51	62
on Grass	.293	.361	.407	765	224	43	4	12	86	81	98
on Turf	.239	.325	.381	134	32	11	1	2	17	16	19
Day Games	.290	.372	.404	297	86	20	1	4	34	38	36
Night Games	.282	.348	.402	602	170	34	4	10	69	59	81
April	.322	.380	.433	90	29	4	0	2	18	9	19
May	.269	.351	.328	119	32	5	1	0	9	12	13
June	.269	.346	.383	167	45	13	0	2	20	20	19
July	.254	.342	.358	134	34	5	0	3	12	18	22
August	.242	.315	.371	132	32	10	2	1	13	13	22
Sept-Oct	.327	.385	.479	257	84	17	2	6	31	25	22
Bases Empty	.273	.340	.405	524	143	33	3	10	10	48	63
Leadoff	.265	.291	.388	196	52	16	1	2	2	7	23
Runners On Base	.301	.378	.400	375	113	21	2	4	93	49	54
Scoring Position	.310	.400	.400	210	65	10	0	3	87	35	35
Late and Close	.262	.350	.375	160	42	14	2	0	17	22	23

JOEY CORA — BB/TR — age 29 — CHA 2B151, 3B3

1993	BA	OBA	SA	AB	H	2B	3B	HR	RBI	BB	SO
Total	.268	.351	.349	579	155	15	13	2	51	67	63
vs. Left	.255	.337	.292	161	41	4	1	0	8	19	19
vs. Right	.273	.356	.371	418	114	11	12	2	43	48	44
at Home	.262	.350	.333	279	73	6	7	0	24	34	29
on Road	.273	.351	.363	300	82	9	6	2	27	33	34
on Grass	.263	.355	.340	476	125	11	10	2	41	61	49
on Turf	.291	.330	.388	103	30	4	3	0	10	6	14
Day Games	.244	.315	.306	180	44	3	4	0	14	17	18
Night Games	.278	.366	.368	399	111	12	9	2	37	50	45
April	.325	.404	.422	83	27	4	2	0	7	11	11
May	.236	.340	.303	89	21	2	2	0	9	14	9
June	.278	.383	.351	97	27	2	1	1	7	14	10
July	.272	.362	.370	92	25	5	2	0	10	11	8
August	.254	.293	.333	114	29	2	2	1	11	6	17
Sept-Oct	.250	.336	.327	104	26	0	4	0	7	11	8
Bases Empty	.248	.336	.323	347	86	5	9	1	1	41	50
Leadoff	.182	.298	.256	121	22	1	2	0	0	17	15
Runners On Base	.297	.372	.388	232	69	10	4	1	50	26	13
Scoring Position	.294	.372	.365	126	37	3	3	0	43	15	10
Late and Close	.216	.293	.284	74	16	3	1	0	4	8	10

6-YEAR TOTALS (1987–1993)

	BA	OBA	SA	AB	H	2B	3B	HR	RBI	BB	SO
Total	.256	.337	.317	1289	330	35	19	2	94	144	132
vs. Left	.260	.336	.292	373	97	8	2	0	17	40	42
vs. Right	.254	.337	.328	916	233	27	17	2	77	104	90
at Home	.258	.347	.313	608	157	15	9	0	44	72	58
on Road	.254	.328	.322	681	173	20	10	2	50	72	74
on Grass	.256	.347	.315	1025	262	27	14	2	72	129	105
on Turf	.258	.296	.326	264	68	8	5	0	22	15	27
Day Games	.251	.322	.300	427	107	11	5	0	25	40	41
Night Games	.259	.344	.326	862	223	24	14	2	69	104	91
April	.275	.377	.346	182	50	9	2	0	12	28	21
May	.232	.321	.284	250	58	7	3	0	20	32	28
June	.277	.358	.356	191	53	4	4	1	13	19	20
July	.256	.332	.337	172	44	8	3	0	15	16	13
August	.232	.289	.279	190	44	2	2	1	20	16	28
Sept-Oct	.266	.345	.316	304	81	5	5	0	14	33	22
Bases Empty	.249	.333	.309	807	201	19	13	1	1	91	97
Leadoff	.212	.311	.276	340	72	8	7	0	0	42	34
Runners On Base	.268	.343	.332	482	129	16	6	1	93	53	35
Scoring Position	.234	.317	.276	290	68	6	3	0	82	36	27
Late and Close	.206	.277	.236	199	41	4	1	0	6	18	25

WIL CORDERO — BR/TR — age 23 — MON SS134, 3B2

1993	BA	OBA	SA	AB	H	2B	3B	HR	RBI	BB	SO
Total	.248	.308	.387	475	118	32	2	10	58	34	60
vs. Left	.243	.315	.365	148	36	11	2	1	14	14	18
vs. Right	.251	.304	.398	327	82	21	0	9	44	20	42
at Home	.225	.288	.423	213	48	16	1	8	26	17	35
on Road	.267	.324	.359	262	70	16	1	2	32	17	25
on Grass	.268	.333	.346	153	41	6	0	2	24	12	15
on Turf	.239	.295	.407	322	77	26	2	8	34	22	45
Day Games	.192	.231	.245	151	29	8	0	0	17	7	27
Night Games	.275	.342	.454	324	89	24	2	10	41	27	33
April	.235	.295	.420	81	19	7	1	2	10	7	12
May	.255	.282	.408	98	25	9	0	2	10	3	11
June	.220	.312	.280	82	18	5	0	0	4	8	12
July	.262	.357	.393	61	16	0	1	2	10	8	10
August	.261	.301	.391	69	18	6	0	1	7	3	6
Sept-Oct	.262	.311	.429	84	22	5	0	3	17	5	9
Bases Empty	.230	.268	.334	287	66	16	1	4	4	13	38
Leadoff	.231	.268	.347	121	28	8	0	2	2	6	12
Runners On Base	.277	.363	.468	188	52	16	1	6	54	21	22
Scoring Position	.263	.367	.432	118	31	9	1	3	44	18	15
Late and Close	.235	.279	.444	81	19	5	0	4	13	4	9

2-YEAR TOTALS (1992–1993)

	BA	OBA	SA	AB	H	2B	3B	HR	RBI	BB	SO
Total	.260	.317	.389	601	156	36	3	12	66	43	91
vs. Left	.286	.351	.390	182	52	12	1	1	16	17	22
vs. Right	.248	.302	.389	419	104	24	1	11	50	26	69
at Home	.244	.301	.415	275	67	16	2	9	29	21	44
on Road	.273	.331	.368	326	89	20	1	3	37	22	47
on Grass	.272	.330	.358	173	47	6	0	3	28	12	22
on Turf	.255	.312	.402	428	109	30	3	9	38	31	69
Day Games	.213	.253	.257	183	39	8	0	0	18	8	37
Night Games	.280	.344	.447	418	117	28	3	12	48	35	54
April	.235	.295	.420	81	19	7	1	2	10	7	12
May	.255	.282	.408	98	25	9	0	2	10	3	11
June	.220	.312	.280	82	18	5	0	0	4	8	12
July	.284	.370	.375	88	25	0	1	2	11	11	18
August	.260	.313	.356	104	27	7	0	1	8	6	17
Sept-Oct	.284	.325	.453	148	42	8	1	5	23	8	21
Bases Empty	.242	.283	.349	364	88	20	2	5	5	19	56
Leadoff	.263	.304	.388	152	40	10	0	3	3	9	15
Runners On Base	.287	.366	.451	237	68	16	1	7	61	24	35
Scoring Position	.266	.364	.432	139	37	9	1	4	51	19	20
Late and Close	.236	.283	.396	106	25	5	0	4	14	6	15

CHAD CURTIS — BR/TR — age 26 — CAL OF151, 2B3

1993	BA	OBA	SA	AB	H	2B	3B	HR	RBI	BB	SO
Total	.285	.361	.369	583	166	25	3	6	59	70	89
vs. Left	.324	.405	.446	148	48	8	2	2	11	20	19
vs. Right	.271	.347	.343	435	118	17	1	4	48	50	70
at Home	.310	.374	.403	303	94	17	1	3	35	30	44
on Road	.257	.349	.332	280	72	8	2	3	24	40	45
on Grass	.289	.363	.360	484	140	20	1	4	50	57	76
on Turf	.263	.354	.414	99	26	5	2	2	9	13	13
Day Games	.285	.376	.366	172	49	8	0	2	21	25	28
Night Games	.285	.355	.370	411	117	17	3	4	38	45	61
April	.294	.367	.324	68	20	2	0	0	6	8	7
May	.350	.463	.500	100	35	7	1	2	16	20	13
June	.241	.362	.287	87	21	4	0	0	7	16	14
July	.272	.318	.398	103	28	4	0	3	9	7	17
August	.316	.367	.342	117	37	3	0	0	12	10	20
Sept-Oct	.231	.286	.343	108	25	5	2	1	9	9	18
Bases Empty	.304	.395	.417	345	105	15	3	6	6	50	48
Leadoff	.362	.451	.552	105	38	6	1	4	4	16	9
Runners On Base	.256	.311	.298	238	61	10	0	0	53	20	41
Scoring Position	.273	.327	.322	143	39	7	0	0	50	14	27
Late and Close	.305	.383	.337	95	29	3	0	0	6	12	12

2-YEAR TOTALS (1992–1993)

	BA	OBA	SA	AB	H	2B	3B	HR	RBI	BB	SO
Total	.273	.352	.370	1024	280	41	5	16	105	121	160
vs. Left	.300	.399	.463	270	81	14	3	8	33	46	37
vs. Right	.264	.335	.337	754	199	27	2	8	72	75	123
at Home	.292	.364	.393	504	147	23	2	8	55	54	76
on Road	.256	.342	.348	520	133	18	3	8	50	67	84
on Grass	.274	.349	.356	851	233	33	2	11	81	96	136
on Turf	.272	.371	.439	173	47	8	3	5	24	25	24
Day Games	.273	.363	.372	293	80	11	0	6	34	39	45
Night Games	.274	.348	.369	731	200	30	5	10	71	82	115
April	.305	.378	.368	95	29	4	1	0	10	12	10
May	.300	.408	.456	160	48	9	2	4	19	28	23
June	.260	.357	.331	169	44	6	0	2	21	24	25
July	.251	.319	.403	191	48	8	0	7	18	17	32
August	.277	.348	.317	202	56	5	0	1	19	23	38
Sept-Oct	.266	.325	.357	207	55	9	2	2	18	17	32
Bases Empty	.287	.374	.397	614	176	24	4	12	12	82	88
Leadoff	.316	.417	.469	196	62	8	2	6	6	31	21
Runners On Base	.254	.320	.329	410	104	17	1	4	93	39	72
Scoring Position	.253	.314	.349	249	63	10	1	4	88	24	44
Late and Close	.275	.367	.339	171	47	5	0	2	11	24	25

DARREN DAULTON — BL/TR — age 32 — PHI C146

1993	BA	OBA	SA	AB	H	2B	3B	HR	RBI	BB	SO
Total	.257	.392	.482	510	131	35	4	24	105	117	111
vs. Left	.213	.346	.404	188	40	10	1	8	29	38	45
vs. Right	.283	.418	.528	322	91	25	3	16	76	79	66
at Home	.260	.375	.458	262	68	16	3	10	55	48	56
on Road	.254	.409	.508	248	63	19	1	14	50	69	55
on Grass	.259	.424	.570	158	41	14	1	11	37	48	31
on Turf	.256	.377	.443	352	90	21	3	13	68	69	80
Day Games	.274	.411	.538	117	32	11	1	6	27	28	30
Night Games	.252	.387	.466	393	99	24	3	18	78	89	81
April	.234	.438	.516	64	15	3	0	5	15	23	16
May	.260	.395	.625	96	25	6	1	9	30	22	20
June	.256	.349	.389	90	23	7	1	1	16	13	24
July	.259	.415	.481	81	21	7	1	3	17	23	15
August	.253	.388	.494	79	20	5	1	4	14	18	16
Sept-Oct	.270	.378	.400	100	27	7	0	2	13	18	20
Bases Empty	.262	.365	.484	248	65	18	2	11	11	39	53
Leadoff	.252	.357	.495	111	28	9	0	6	6	17	24
Runners On Base	.252	.415	.481	262	66	17	2	13	94	78	58
Scoring Position	.239	.424	.453	159	38	9	2	7	79	56	33
Late and Close	.284	.473	.506	81	23	6	0	4	14	29	22

9-YEAR TOTALS (1985–1993)

	BA	OBA	SA	AB	H	2B	3B	HR	RBI	BB	SO
Total	.237	.351	.414	2621	622	140	13	99	414	457	551
vs. Left	.221	.335	.379	712	157	40	2	23	97	117	172
vs. Right	.244	.356	.427	1909	465	100	11	76	317	340	379
at Home	.243	.359	.428	1274	310	76	9	47	210	230	259
on Road	.232	.342	.401	1347	312	64	4	52	204	227	292
on Grass	.237	.346	.421	768	182	38	2	33	124	129	177
on Turf	.237	.352	.411	1853	440	102	11	66	290	328	374
Day Games	.236	.343	.423	690	163	34	1	31	104	114	167
Night Games	.238	.353	.411	1931	459	106	12	68	310	343	384
April	.236	.369	.427	347	82	17	2	15	65	72	85
May	.228	.357	.415	400	91	23	2	16	67	81	93
June	.234	.345	.406	436	102	25	1	16	74	77	91
July	.224	.338	.403	486	109	24	3	19	74	84	86
August	.240	.341	.435	504	121	25	2	23	69	75	103
Sept-Oct	.261	.360	.400	448	117	26	3	10	65	68	93
Bases Empty	.217	.319	.382	1407	306	71	5	50	50	200	298
Leadoff	.221	.309	.388	588	130	35	0	21	21	70	107
Runners On Base	.260	.385	.451	1214	316	69	8	49	364	257	253
Scoring Position	.250	.392	.421	711	178	37	3	26	299	179	151
Late and Close	.225	.329	.344	494	111	20	0	13	67	75	134

CHILI DAVIS — BB/TR — age 34 — CAL DH150, P1

1993	BA	OBA	SA	AB	H	2B	3B	HR	RBI	BB	SO	10-YEAR TOTALS (1984–1993) BA	OBA	SA	AB	H	2B	3B	HR	RBI	BB	SO
Total	.243	.327	.440	573	139	32	0	27	112	71	135	.272	.355	.444	5129	1395	259	20	194	795	677	997
vs. Left	.260	.326	.496	131	34	7	0	8	31	13	32	.253	.316	.429	1539	390	65	5	65	246	148	316
vs. Right	.238	.327	.423	442	105	25	0	19	81	58	103	.280	.371	.450	3590	1005	194	15	129	549	529	681
at Home	.269	.353	.466	283	76	17	0	13	59	36	62	.275	.359	.439	2520	692	125	10	90	385	343	484
on Road	.217	.302	.414	290	63	15	0	14	53	35	73	.269	.351	.448	2609	703	134	10	104	410	334	513
on Grass	.250	.334	.443	476	119	26	0	22	94	59	115	.268	.349	.427	3622	971	168	11	129	548	464	720
on Turf	.206	.294	.423	97	20	6	0	5	18	12	20	.281	.368	.483	1507	424	91	9	65	247	213	277
Day Games	.274	.353	.553	179	49	11	0	13	44	22	47	.273	.355	.446	1789	488	84	8	70	284	239	359
Night Games	.228	.315	.388	394	90	21	0	14	68	49	88	.272	.355	.443	3340	907	175	12	124	511	438	638
April	.232	.283	.357	56	13	4	0	1	12	3	14	.271	.337	.419	731	198	40	1	22	110	76	150
May	.216	.350	.361	97	21	5	0	3	17	20	27	.274	.350	.442	921	252	51	7	30	137	112	167
June	.241	.274	.481	108	26	8	0	6	27	5	18	.256	.330	.456	957	245	43	5	46	164	110	163
July	.255	.372	.422	102	26	5	0	4	19	19	19	.278	.361	.451	832	231	38	2	34	134	112	156
August	.229	.311	.413	109	25	5	0	5	16	13	33	.265	.361	.420	916	243	49	3	29	132	139	201
Sept-Oct	.277	.348	.564	101	28	5	0	8	21	11	24	.293	.393	.475	772	226	38	2	33	118	128	160
Bases Empty	.192	.263	.334	287	55	11	0	10	10	28	80	.258	.326	.416	2819	727	134	11	97	97	282	541
Leadoff	.138	.222	.169	130	18	4	0	0	0	14	36	.258	.324	.430	1191	307	60	5	45	45	116	215
Runners On Base	.294	.388	.545	286	84	21	0	17	102	43	55	.289	.387	.477	2310	668	125	9	97	698	395	456
Scoring Position	.325	.427	.589	163	53	16	0	9	81	28	31	.285	.402	.480	1347	384	79	5	58	592	294	282
Late and Close	.278	.409	.422	90	25	4	0	3	11	19	20	.254	.370	.410	851	216	40	3	29	125	159	183

ERIC DAVIS — BR/TR — age 32 — LA/DET OF121, DH5

1993	BA	OBA	SA	AB	H	2B	3B	HR	RBI	BB	SO	10-YEAR TOTALS (1984–1993) BA	OBA	SA	AB	H	2B	3B	HR	RBI	BB	SO
Total	.237	.319	.415	451	107	18	1	20	68	55	106	.262	.355	.483	3575	935	145	20	202	632	515	930
vs. Left	.219	.323	.350	137	30	6	0	4	19	22	26	.268	.374	.506	1182	317	49	5	74	210	202	270
vs. Right	.245	.317	.443	314	77	12	1	16	49	33	80	.258	.345	.471	2393	618	96	15	128	422	313	660
at Home	.250	.342	.405	232	58	6	0	10	39	34	46	.259	.364	.470	1669	432	64	8	91	304	281	422
on Road	.224	.293	.425	219	49	12	1	10	29	21	60	.264	.346	.494	1906	503	81	12	111	328	234	508
on Grass	.235	.326	.408	370	87	14	1	16	58	52	87	.262	.351	.467	1513	397	56	8	79	246	203	368
on Turf	.247	.282	.444	81	20	4	0	4	10	3	19	.261	.357	.495	2062	538	89	12	123	386	312	562
Day Games	.222	.289	.417	144	32	8	1	6	22	14	37	.261	.346	.488	1162	303	50	11	64	205	149	304
Night Games	.244	.332	.414	307	75	10	0	14	46	41	69	.262	.359	.480	2413	632	95	9	138	427	366	626
April	.253	.320	.299	87	22	1	0	1	10	8	19	.241	.330	.425	598	144	21	4	27	81	81	162
May	.172	.280	.359	64	11	3	0	3	11	10	17	.242	.329	.487	499	121	25	2	31	108	65	138
June	.228	.338	.439	57	13	3	0	3	12	10	14	.288	.387	.542	524	151	17	4	36	107	82	130
July	.276	.327	.429	98	27	6	0	3	10	8	22	.267	.355	.463	737	197	37	4	33	106	98	189
August	.214	.267	.443	70	15	4	0	4	10	5	16	.265	.364	.487	614	163	24	2	36	110	96	156
Sept-Oct	.253	.371	.533	75	19	1	1	6	15	14	18	.264	.362	.506	603	159	21	4	39	120	93	155
Bases Empty	.231	.301	.433	247	57	11	0	13	13	25	67	.251	.334	.459	1961	493	67	8	108	108	235	518
Leadoff	.229	.267	.490	96	22	7	0	6	6	5	22	.266	.335	.519	838	223	36	4	56	56	84	187
Runners On Base	.245	.339	.392	204	50	7	1	7	55	30	39	.274	.378	.512	1614	442	78	12	94	524	280	412
Scoring Position	.230	.355	.398	113	26	5	1	4	47	23	28	.275	.401	.511	951	262	48	7	54	429	210	256
Late and Close	.209	.294	.363	91	19	2	0	4	11	11	24	.255	.357	.469	620	158	22	0	37	131	98	161

ANDRE DAWSON — BR/TR — age 40 — BOS DH97, OF20

1993	BA	OBA	SA	AB	H	2B	3B	HR	RBI	BB	SO	10-YEAR TOTALS (1984–1993) BA	OBA	SA	AB	H	2B	3B	HR	RBI	BB	SO
Total	.273	.313	.425	461	126	29	1	13	67	17	49	.277	.321	.481	5281	1463	260	38	247	909	322	754
vs. Left	.320	.356	.576	125	40	9	1	7	22	5	14	.297	.341	.526	1611	479	85	11	87	283	108	209
vs. Right	.256	.298	.369	336	86	20	0	6	45	12	35	.268	.312	.461	3670	984	175	27	160	626	214	545
at Home	.304	.340	.486	247	75	19	1	8	45	10	23	.288	.336	.500	2596	747	123	19	130	461	178	353
on Road	.238	.283	.355	214	51	10	0	5	22	7	26	.267	.306	.463	2685	716	137	19	117	448	144	401
on Grass	.276	.318	.432	391	108	26	1	11	61	15	39	.288	.330	.511	3138	903	156	24	165	583	189	434
on Turf	.257	.289	.386	70	18	3	0	2	6	2	10	.261	.307	.438	2143	560	104	14	82	326	133	320
Day Games	.251	.285	.419	179	45	9	0	7	28	6	20	.297	.343	.533	2553	759	124	21	145	491	173	356
Night Games	.287	.331	.429	282	81	20	0	6	39	11	29	.258	.300	.433	2728	704	136	17	102	418	149	398
April	.237	.286	.316	76	18	3	0	1	10	2	10	.297	.344	.533	735	218	37	10	39	137	50	90
May	.242	.235	.273	33	8	1	0	0	9	0	2	.278	.320	.489	837	233	45	7	39	146	51	118
June	.227	.257	.361	97	22	5	1	2	11	3	15	.256	.296	.419	792	203	36	3	29	116	40	112
July	.330	.383	.546	97	32	6	0	5	20	7	8	.279	.329	.458	875	244	39	2	38	154	64	130
August	.305	.348	.495	105	32	11	0	3	10	5	9	.275	.316	.487	1014	279	50	4	49	167	56	148
Sept-Oct	.264	.298	.434	53	14	3	0	2	7	1	5	.278	.322	.498	1028	286	53	7	53	189	61	156
Bases Empty	.262	.306	.426	237	62	16	1	7	7	8	24	.267	.302	.474	2725	727	125	23	131	131	110	410
Leadoff	.267	.313	.457	105	28	8	0	4	4	3	9	.250	.284	.454	1158	290	57	7	55	55	43	162
Runners On Base	.286	.321	.424	224	64	13	0	6	60	9	25	.288	.340	.489	2556	736	135	15	116	778	212	344
Scoring Position	.313	.354	.516	128	40	8	0	6	60	7	13	.293	.365	.499	1470	430	82	7	69	658	186	204
Late and Close	.303	.303	.434	76	23	4	0	2	10	0	6	.273	.327	.449	942	257	34	3	42	151	74	149

ROB DEER — BR/TR — age 34 — DET/BOS OF122, DH6

10-YEAR TOTALS (1984–1993)

1993	BA	OBA	SA	AB	H	2B	3B	HR	RBI	BB	SO		BA	OBA	SA	AB	H	2B	3B	HR	RBI	BB	SO
Total	.210	.303	.386	466	98	17	1	21	55	58	169		.220	.323	.442	3831	844	145	13	226	591	561	1379
vs. Left	.281	.397	.579	121	34	7	1	9	21	22	40		.259	.372	.551	1120	290	47	5	90	205	201	337
vs. Right	.186	.267	.319	345	64	10	0	12	34	36	129		.204	.302	.397	2711	554	98	8	136	386	360	1042
at Home	.214	.330	.438	192	41	7	0	12	34	33	66		.216	.328	.442	1843	399	67	6	112	298	288	661
on Road	.208	.281	.350	274	57	10	1	9	21	25	103		.224	.319	.442	1988	445	78	7	114	293	273	718
on Grass	.211	.316	.393	361	76	13	1	17	46	53	129		.221	.327	.444	3206	710	123	11	189	495	480	1147
on Turf	.210	.252	.362	105	22	4	0	4	9	5	40		.214	.305	.434	625	134	22	2	37	96	81	232
Day Games	.272	.366	.522	184	50	11	1	11	29	28	60		.217	.325	.447	1287	279	55	5	77	199	201	462
Night Games	.170	.260	.298	282	48	6	0	10	26	30	109		.222	.322	.439	2544	565	90	8	149	392	360	917
April	.205	.286	.466	88	18	5	0	6	16	10	33		.228	.332	.526	534	122	22	4	43	107	78	185
May	.239	.345	.380	71	17	4	0	2	8	12	24		.228	.339	.450	654	149	27	2	38	101	108	228
June	.205	.300	.409	44	9	0	0	3	6	6	16		.204	.291	.423	700	143	19	1	44	113	82	246
July	.232	.286	.329	82	19	2	0	2	6	5	32		.235	.331	.450	540	127	21	1	31	71	72	193
August	.160	.259	.253	75	12	1	0	2	6	8	27		.216	.323	.452	624	135	23	2	40	108	94	231
Sept-Oct	.217	.331	.453	106	23	5	1	6	13	17	37		.216	.327	.381	779	168	33	3	30	91	127	296
Bases Empty	.203	.288	.419	236	48	7	1	14	14	26	88		.214	.313	.439	2039	436	74	8	123	123	280	732
Leadoff	.231	.307	.495	91	21	3	0	7	7	9	37		.234	.327	.471	893	209	39	1	57	57	116	299
Runners On Base	.217	.317	.352	230	50	10	0	7	41	32	81		.228	.334	.445	1792	408	71	5	103	468	281	647
Scoring Position	.173	.302	.293	133	23	4	0	4	34	24	47		.223	.350	.435	1008	225	37	1	58	368	201	365
Late and Close	.278	.380	.595	79	22	4	0	7	18	12	26		.217	.322	.433	608	132	25	2	34	91	86	240

DELINO DESHIELDS — BL/TR — age 25 — MON 2B123

4-YEAR TOTALS (1990–1993)

1993	BA	OBA	SA	AB	H	2B	3B	HR	RBI	BB	SO		BA	OBA	SA	AB	H	2B	3B	HR	RBI	BB	SO
Total	.295	.389	.372	481	142	17	7	2	29	72	64		.277	.367	.373	2073	575	79	25	23	181	287	419
vs. Left	.311	.407	.435	161	50	8	3	2	13	24	22		.275	.371	.368	728	200	25	8	9	65	105	161
vs. Right	.287	.379	.341	320	92	9	4	0	16	48	42		.279	.364	.375	1345	375	54	17	14	116	182	258
at Home	.333	.435	.432	234	78	9	4	2	14	41	29		.296	.387	.390	969	287	42	11	9	75	140	190
on Road	.259	.343	.316	247	64	8	3	0	15	31	35		.261	.348	.358	1104	288	37	14	14	106	147	229
on Grass	.256	.322	.281	160	41	4	0	0	11	16	21		.254	.337	.338	619	157	19	6	7	60	80	131
on Turf	.315	.420	.417	321	101	13	7	2	18	56	43		.287	.379	.388	1454	418	60	19	16	121	207	288
Day Games	.406	.497	.496	133	54	6	3	0	10	24	20		.307	.397	.389	609	187	26	6	4	57	93	136
Night Games	.253	.346	.325	348	88	11	4	2	19	48	44		.265	.354	.366	1464	388	53	19	19	124	194	283
April	.273	.412	.400	55	15	4	0	1	5	13	8		.291	.383	.412	289	84	14	3	5	21	43	59
May	.276	.394	.343	105	29	4	0	1	5	20	16		.247	.361	.341	381	94	14	2	6	25	67	82
June	.243	.325	.280	107	26	2	1	0	3	12	16		.286	.383	.373	367	105	12	7	2	31	57	79
July	.393	.432	.479	117	46	4	3	0	10	8	10		.338	.401	.426	385	130	17	4	3	34	41	56
August	.306	.405	.444	36	11	1	2	0	2	6	4		.281	.360	.391	338	95	13	6	4	41	38	57
Sept-Oct	.246	.382	.311	61	15	2	1	0	4	13	10		.214	.306	.291	313	67	9	3	3	29	41	86
Bases Empty	.307	.392	.394	322	99	14	4	2	2	42	45		.281	.365	.378	1396	392	52	15	18	18	174	285
Leadoff	.330	.419	.431	188	62	10	3	1	1	26	25		.290	.365	.387	790	229	24	10	11	11	85	140
Runners On Base	.270	.382	.327	159	43	3	3	0	27	30	19		.270	.371	.362	677	183	27	10	5	163	113	134
Scoring Position	.252	.375	.288	111	28	2	1	0	25	23	17		.273	.385	.369	439	120	23	5	3	152	87	93
Late and Close	.318	.381	.353	85	27	1	1	0	10	10	16		.267	.353	.345	374	100	12	4	3	46	53	90

ORESTES DESTRADE — BB/TR — age 32 — FLO 1B152

3-YEAR TOTALS (1987–1993)

1993	BA	OBA	SA	AB	H	2B	3B	HR	RBI	BB	SO		BA	OBA	SA	AB	H	2B	3B	HR	RBI	BB	SO
Total	.255	.324	.406	569	145	20	3	20	87	58	130		.247	.320	.389	635	157	21	3	21	91	68	152
vs. Left	.294	.344	.458	177	52	5	3	6	28	13	39		.273	.323	.416	209	57	6	3	6	29	15	51
vs. Right	.237	.315	.383	392	93	15	0	14	59	45	91		.235	.318	.376	426	100	15	0	15	62	53	101
at Home	.266	.343	.422	282	75	13	2	9	46	33	60		.257	.334	.408	319	82	14	2	10	49	37	70
on Road	.244	.305	.390	287	70	7	1	11	41	25	70		.237	.305	.370	316	75	7	1	11	42	31	82
on Grass	.235	.320	.388	425	100	16	2	15	69	52	101		.233	.321	.376	455	106	16	2	15	70	58	112
on Turf	.313	.338	.458	144	45	4	1	5	18	6	29		.283	.318	.422	180	51	5	1	6	21	10	40
Day Games	.280	.348	.472	125	35	4	1	6	27	13	31		.265	.331	.450	151	40	5	1	7	30	15	36
Night Games	.248	.317	.387	444	110	16	2	14	60	45	99		.242	.316	.370	484	117	16	2	14	61	53	116
April	.273	.350	.364	88	24	3	1	1	11	11	12		.273	.350	.364	88	24	3	1	1	11	11	12
May	.202	.248	.293	99	20	3	0	2	13	5	20		.202	.248	.293	99	20	3	0	2	13	5	20
June	.316	.358	.531	98	31	5	2	4	16	8	24		.320	.360	.530	100	32	5	2	4	16	8	24
July	.215	.277	.344	93	20	6	0	2	14	7	24		.193	.254	.312	109	21	7	0	2	14	8	30
August	.301	.393	.570	93	28	1	0	8	16	14	24		.292	.377	.528	106	31	1	0	8	17	15	30
Sept-Oct	.224	.316	.337	98	22	2	0	3	17	13	26		.218	.325	.323	133	29	2	0	4	20	21	36
Bases Empty	.251	.312	.399	291	73	9	2	10	10	25	61		.249	.317	.386	321	80	10	2	10	10	31	68
Leadoff	.170	.225	.305	141	24	2	1	5	5	9	34		.182	.248	.318	148	27	3	1	5	5	12	35
Runners On Base	.259	.335	.414	278	72	11	1	10	77	33	69		.245	.322	.392	314	77	11	1	11	81	37	84
Scoring Position	.303	.395	.454	152	46	3	0	4	64	26	42		.284	.376	.420	169	48	9	1	4	66	28	50
Late and Close	.239	.340	.295	88	21	3	0	1	10	14	23		.214	.314	.256	117	25	3	1	0	11	18	33

MIKE DEVEREAUX — BR/TR — age 31 — BAL OF130

7-YEAR TOTALS (1987–1993)

1993	BA	OBA	SA	AB	H	2B	3B	HR	RBI	BB	SO		BA	OBA	SA	AB	H	2B	3B	HR	RBI	BB	SO
Total	.250	.306	.400	527	132	31	3	14	75	43	99		.257	.309	.412	2643	679	123	28	77	342	203	436
vs. Left	.276	.352	.442	156	43	9	1	5	23	19	29		.279	.335	.452	903	252	44	11	30	111	77	134
vs. Right	.240	.286	.383	371	89	22	2	9	52	24	70		.245	.296	.391	1740	427	79	17	47	231	126	302
at Home	.263	.331	.457	247	65	20	2	8	48	27	41		.252	.310	.420	1276	321	59	15	42	181	110	202
on Road	.239	.283	.350	280	67	11	1	6	27	16	58		.262	.309	.405	1367	358	64	13	35	161	93	234
on Grass	.244	.303	.404	446	109	28	2	13	68	38	80		.254	.308	.418	2214	562	100	25	71	294	175	370
on Turf	.284	.326	.383	81	23	3	1	1	7	5	19		.273	.317	.382	429	117	23	3	6	48	28	66
Day Games	.250	.278	.410	144	36	4	2	5	20	5	22		.245	.292	.381	714	175	31	6	18	74	46	115
Night Games	.251	.316	.397	383	96	27	1	9	55	38	77		.261	.316	.424	1929	504	92	22	59	268	157	321
April	.229	.245	.365	96	22	6	2	1	11	2	13		.228	.282	.378	312	71	15	4	8	32	23	43
May	.346	.393	.423	26	9	2	0	0	3	1	5		.278	.328	.451	306	85	22	2	9	39	23	46
June	.248	.331	.429	105	26	10	0	3	12	13	20		.265	.322	.427	468	124	23	7	13	57	41	70
July	.302	.348	.453	106	32	5	1	3	17	8	21		.286	.337	.445	479	137	17	7	15	66	38	84
August	.216	.294	.369	111	24	5	0	4	17	13	19		.239	.304	.394	503	120	20	5	16	74	47	80
Sept-Oct	.229	.278	.373	83	19	3	0	3	15	6	21		.247	.286	.386	575	142	26	3	16	74	31	113
Bases Empty	.236	.304	.366	276	65	16	1	6	6	26	56		.257	.312	.408	1546	398	69	16	44	44	118	266
Leadoff	.245	.327	.398	98	24	9	0	2	2	11	18		.251	.313	.406	653	164	35	6	18	18	56	108
Runners On Base	.267	.309	.438	251	67	15	2	8	69	17	43		.256	.306	.418	1097	281	54	12	33	298	85	170
Scoring Position	.291	.322	.468	158	46	12	2	4	61	9	25		.265	.309	.452	663	176	39	11	21	267	50	101
Late and Close	.197	.262	.276	76	15	3	0	1	9	7	12		.236	.287	.364	428	101	9	2	14	55	32	77

GARY DISARCINA — BR/TR — age 27 — CAL SS126

5-YEAR TOTALS (1989–1993)

1993	BA	OBA	SA	AB	H	2B	3B	HR	RBI	BB	SO		BA	OBA	SA	AB	H	2B	3B	HR	RBI	BB	SO
Total	.238	.273	.313	416	99	20	1	3	45	15	38		.236	.273	.297	1048	247	42	2	6	90	41	102
vs. Left	.210	.234	.244	119	25	4	0	0	7	3	10		.209	.239	.243	263	55	9	0	0	12	9	24
vs. Right	.249	.288	.340	297	74	16	1	3	38	12	28		.245	.284	.315	785	192	33	2	6	78	32	78
at Home	.250	.279	.324	216	54	8	1	2	28	7	19		.227	.264	.288	520	118	18	1	4	53	20	46
on Road	.225	.265	.300	200	45	12	0	1	17	8	19		.244	.281	.305	528	129	24	1	2	37	21	56
on Grass	.231	.268	.307	355	82	16	1	3	36	13	35		.227	.267	.283	874	198	32	1	5	72	36	86
on Turf	.279	.302	.344	61	17	4	0	0	9	2	3		.282	.306	.368	174	49	10	1	1	18	5	16
Day Games	.235	.273	.330	115	27	6	1	1	9	4	13		.245	.288	.347	294	72	16	1	4	23	15	31
Night Games	.239	.273	.306	301	72	14	0	2	36	11	25		.232	.267	.277	754	175	26	1	2	67	26	71
April	.227	.239	.333	66	15	4	0	1	6	1	8		.266	.307	.344	128	34	7	0	1	9	7	17
May	.231	.265	.297	91	21	3	0	1	12	4	5		.210	.255	.250	200	42	5	0	1	17	11	18
June	.281	.316	.404	89	25	6	1	1	15	5	11		.256	.288	.379	195	50	11	2	3	22	7	18
July	.229	.282	.271	96	22	4	0	0	9	4	8		.222	.267	.256	180	40	6	0	0	16	8	16
August	.216	.247	.257	74	16	3	0	0	3	1	6		.232	.255	.288	177	41	7	0	1	18	2	15
Sept-Oct	.000	.000	.000	0	0	0	0	0	0	0	0		.238	.277	.274	168	40	6	0	0	8	6	18
Bases Empty	.233	.270	.306	219	51	11	1	1	1	9	27		.243	.277	.306	602	146	28	2	2	2	23	68
Leadoff	.232	.277	.316	95	22	6	1	0	0	5	11		.250	.291	.311	244	61	13	1	0	0	12	22
Runners On Base	.244	.276	.320	197	48	9	0	2	44	6	11		.226	.267	.285	446	101	14	0	4	88	18	34
Scoring Position	.265	.305	.342	117	31	6	0	1	40	5	5		.238	.295	.290	252	60	10	0	1	79	15	22
Late and Close	.176	.218	.189	74	13	1	0	0	7	2	8		.143	.204	.170	182	26	2	0	1	14	11	23

MARIANO DUNCAN — BR/TR — age 31 — PHI 2B65, SS59

8-YEAR TOTALS (1985–1993)

1993	BA	OBA	SA	AB	H	2B	3B	HR	RBI	BB	SO		BA	OBA	SA	AB	H	2B	3B	HR	RBI	BB	SO
Total	.282	.304	.417	496	140	26	4	11	73	12	88		.259	.297	.380	3326	862	149	31	64	326	158	624
vs. Left	.273	.291	.429	198	54	11	1	6	24	5	29		.300	.331	.451	1302	391	73	12	33	143	55	214
vs. Right	.289	.312	.409	298	86	15	3	5	49	7	59		.233	.275	.335	2024	471	76	19	31	183	103	410
at Home	.289	.315	.427	211	61	8	3	5	28	5	44		.260	.298	.378	1604	417	69	14	31	145	77	308
on Road	.277	.295	.411	285	79	18	1	6	45	7	44		.258	.295	.382	1722	445	80	17	33	181	81	316
on Grass	.256	.270	.372	180	46	7	1	4	27	3	30		.244	.286	.350	1604	392	66	14	25	146	81	317
on Turf	.297	.322	.443	316	94	19	3	7	46	9	58		.273	.307	.409	1722	470	83	17	39	180	77	307
Day Games	.298	.328	.444	124	37	6	0	4	23	4	23		.274	.312	.410	978	268	43	12	22	103	48	183
Night Games	.277	.295	.409	372	103	20	4	7	50	8	65		.253	.290	.368	2348	594	106	19	42	223	110	441
April	.255	.293	.309	55	14	3	0	0	4	2	8		.270	.325	.395	488	132	29	1	10	40	32	88
May	.200	.223	.367	90	18	3	0	4	13	3	22		.221	.255	.314	621	137	21	5	9	55	27	133
June	.302	.333	.458	96	29	3	3	2	14	3	14		.267	.300	.384	555	148	23	6	10	53	21	86
July	.349	.359	.429	63	22	2	0	1	12	1	10		.258	.294	.378	500	129	23	5	9	44	24	97
August	.276	.297	.398	98	27	7	1	1	17	2	20		.292	.322	.435	572	167	25	9	13	68	24	102
Sept-Oct	.319	.326	.500	94	30	6	0	3	13	1	14		.253	.290	.383	590	149	28	5	13	66	30	118
Bases Empty	.276	.313	.431	246	68	14	0	8	8	11	44		.255	.300	.379	1999	510	93	14	42	42	112	385
Leadoff	.333	.371	.560	84	28	4	0	5	5	4	12		.241	.292	.352	874	211	32	7	17	17	55	167
Runners On Base	.288	.294	.404	250	72	12	4	3	65	1	44		.265	.292	.383	1327	352	56	17	22	284	46	239
Scoring Position	.316	.316	.441	152	48	9	2	2	60	0	31		.263	.291	.389	773	203	31	11	15	259	32	152
Late and Close	.276	.273	.474	76	21	6	0	3	14	0	14		.263	.305	.363	521	137	19	3	9	57	27	110

LENNY DYKSTRA — BL/TL — age 31 — PHI OF160

	1993 BA	OBA	SA	AB	H	2B	3B	HR	RBI	BB	SO	9-YR BA	OBA	SA	AB	H	2B	3B	HR	RBI	BB	SO
Total	.305	.420	.482	637	194	44	6	19	66	129	64	.288	.373	.421	3856	1110	233	34	71	349	513	406
vs. Left	.281	.414	.392	217	61	14	2	2	18	48	29	.271	.366	.367	1117	303	54	10	11	97	160	150
vs. Right	.317	.424	.529	420	133	30	4	17	48	81	35	.295	.376	.443	2739	807	179	24	60	252	353	256
at Home	.300	.425	.518	307	92	25	3	12	36	69	29	.295	.386	.444	1868	551	114	15	45	178	274	185
on Road	.309	.416	.448	330	102	19	3	7	30	60	35	.281	.361	.399	1988	559	119	19	26	171	239	221
on Grass	.317	.424	.459	205	65	9	1	6	18	36	20	.279	.356	.405	1769	493	105	17	28	157	204	200
on Turf	.299	.419	.493	432	129	35	5	13	48	93	44	.296	.387	.435	2087	617	128	17	43	192	309	206
Day Games	.297	.423	.429	175	52	13	2	2	13	38	17	.283	.367	.423	1243	352	82	10	24	102	159	135
Night Games	.307	.420	.502	462	142	31	4	17	53	91	47	.290	.376	.420	2613	758	151	24	47	247	354	271
April	.216	.361	.398	88	19	5	1	3	3	20	6	.290	.386	.467	469	136	33	7	12	42	71	43
May	.296	.382	.374	115	34	9	0	0	7	15	8	.300	.377	.417	630	189	38	3	10	56	74	58
June	.337	.466	.538	104	35	9	0	4	9	26	12	.318	.398	.446	639	203	42	5	10	53	85	72
July	.374	.485	.589	107	40	8	0	5	16	23	11	.305	.392	.425	760	232	44	4	13	76	107	77
August	.269	.409	.500	104	28	6	3	4	11	26	12	.254	.337	.394	807	205	46	11	15	61	97	91
Sept-Oct	.319	.410	.487	119	38	7	2	3	20	19	15	.263	.354	.392	551	145	30	4	11	61	79	65
Bases Empty	.316	.426	.515	421	133	32	5	14	14	80	41	.284	.365	.419	2668	758	164	24	49	49	324	281
Leadoff	.319	.433	.523	260	83	23	3	8	8	51	31	.274	.361	.419	1631	447	98	17	35	35	211	184
Runners On Base	.282	.410	.417	216	61	12	1	5	52	49	23	.296	.390	.427	1188	352	69	10	22	300	189	125
Scoring Position	.230	.377	.356	135	31	6	1	3	46	34	17	.283	.396	.392	720	204	40	7	8	260	144	85
Late and Close	.310	.463	.548	84	26	5	0	5	16	24	10	.307	.408	.421	589	181	35	1	10	79	101	66

Right side: 9-YEAR TOTALS (1985–1993)

JIM EISENREICH — BL/TL — age 35 — PHI OF137, 1B1

	1993 BA	OBA	SA	AB	H	2B	3B	HR	RBI	BB	SO	8-YR BA	OBA	SA	AB	H	2B	3B	HR	RBI	BB	SO
Total	.318	.363	.445	362	115	17	4	7	54	26	36	.282	.325	.397	2400	677	131	27	30	282	164	250
vs. Left	.293	.354	.414	58	17	2	1	1	11	6	11	.282	.319	.374	524	148	23	5	5	70	30	73
vs. Right	.322	.365	.451	304	98	15	3	6	43	20	25	.282	.327	.403	1876	529	108	22	25	212	134	177
at Home	.327	.371	.455	156	51	7	2	3	24	10	15	.282	.329	.407	1152	325	59	20	15	149	87	106
on Road	.311	.357	.437	206	64	10	2	4	30	16	21	.282	.322	.387	1248	352	72	7	15	133	77	144
on Grass	.323	.358	.457	127	41	6	1	3	19	8	13	.290	.329	.387	928	269	55	4	9	91	57	114
on Turf	.315	.366	.438	235	74	11	3	4	35	18	23	.277	.323	.403	1472	408	76	23	21	191	107	136
Day Games	.244	.259	.280	82	20	3	0	0	12	2	8	.305	.340	.423	683	208	43	10	6	93	41	62
Night Games	.339	.392	.493	280	95	14	4	7	42	24	28	.273	.319	.386	1717	469	88	17	24	189	123	188
April	.320	.393	.440	25	8	1	1	0	5	3	2	.274	.304	.393	318	87	18	4	4	39	17	45
May	.371	.421	.514	35	13	5	0	0	5	3	1	.292	.346	.396	391	114	29	3	2	45	33	43
June	.351	.390	.545	77	27	5	2	2	18	5	9	.277	.325	.366	451	125	22	3	4	47	35	38
July	.310	.326	.345	84	26	0	0	1	9	2	6	.275	.316	.391	448	123	22	9	4	51	28	39
August	.282	.320	.521	71	20	3	1	4	9	3	9	.314	.355	.491	328	103	17	4	11	48	21	32
Sept-Oct	.300	.378	.343	70	21	3	0	0	8	10	9	.269	.310	.369	464	125	23	4	5	52	30	53
Bases Empty	.312	.343	.445	173	54	10	2	3	3	7	18	.282	.320	.402	1326	374	81	18	14	14	72	138
Leadoff	.225	.267	.310	71	16	3	0	1	1	4	10	.294	.333	.426	585	172	45	4	8	8	34	65
Runners On Base	.323	.381	.444	189	61	7	2	4	51	19	18	.282	.331	.390	1074	303	50	9	16	268	92	112
Scoring Position	.303	.370	.426	122	37	4	1	3	47	14	12	.266	.322	.378	670	178	30	6	11	249	68	77
Late and Close	.268	.321	.296	71	19	2	0	0	10	6	8	.261	.317	.370	440	115	19	7	5	42	38	59

Right side: 8-YEAR TOTALS (1984–1993)

MIKE FELDER — BB/TR — age 33 — SEA OF95, DH6, 3B2

	1993 BA	OBA	SA	AB	H	2B	3B	HR	RBI	BB	SO	9-YR BA	OBA	SA	AB	H	2B	3B	HR	RBI	BB	SO
Total	.211	.262	.269	342	72	7	5	1	20	22	34	.250	.303	.324	2144	536	57	30	14	160	164	205
vs. Left	.190	.271	.238	63	12	1	1	0	2	5	6	.270	.320	.342	622	168	17	8	4	46	47	51
vs. Right	.215	.259	.276	279	60	6	4	1	18	17	28	.242	.296	.317	1522	368	40	22	10	114	117	154
at Home	.234	.287	.293	167	39	4	3	0	10	12	17	.249	.308	.321	1029	256	25	17	5	73	87	95
on Road	.189	.237	.246	175	33	3	2	1	10	10	17	.251	.299	.327	1115	280	32	13	9	87	77	110
on Grass	.188	.250	.256	133	25	2	2	1	7	10	14	.247	.300	.319	1602	396	36	23	11	118	122	161
on Turf	.225	.269	.278	209	47	5	3	0	13	12	20	.258	.312	.339	542	140	21	7	3	42	42	44
Day Games	.231	.311	.319	91	21	3	1	0	4	9	12	.231	.294	.314	780	180	19	8	10	61	68	86
Night Games	.203	.242	.251	251	51	4	4	0	16	13	22	.261	.308	.330	1364	356	38	22	4	99	96	119
April	.253	.325	.333	75	19	3	0	1	6	7	8	.278	.340	.332	223	62	5	2	1	16	22	25
May	.235	.284	.314	102	24	0	4	0	5	6	9	.248	.287	.339	363	90	6	12	1	32	19	37
June	.161	.200	.196	56	9	2	0	0	4	3	6	.248	.305	.312	468	116	15	6	1	29	40	39
July	.237	.293	.263	38	9	1	0	0	2	3	5	.238	.282	.310	361	86	10	2	4	28	22	33
August	.200	.200	.200	20	4	0	0	0	0	0	0	.246	.309	.333	285	70	7	3	4	23	26	21
Sept-Oct	.137	.185	.196	51	7	1	1	0	3	3	6	.252	.307	.327	444	112	14	5	3	32	35	50
Bases Empty	.207	.251	.266	188	39	5	3	0	0	11	22	.246	.294	.316	1355	333	41	15	8	8	90	134
Leadoff	.157	.205	.241	83	13	3	2	0	0	5	11	.249	.299	.322	698	174	23	5	6	6	47	65
Runners On Base	.214	.274	.273	154	33	2	2	1	20	11	12	.257	.317	.338	789	203	16	15	6	152	74	71
Scoring Position	.179	.261	.218	78	14	1	1	0	17	7	6	.239	.307	.326	457	109	13	9	3	139	50	41
Late and Close	.160	.220	.187	75	12	2	0	0	5	6	11	.234	.305	.302	440	103	11	5	3	44	45	50

Right side: 9-YEAR TOTALS (1985–1993)

FELIX FERMIN — BR/TR — age 31 — CLE SS140

1993	BA	OBA	SA	AB	H	2B	3B	HR	RBI	BB	SO		BA	OBA	SA	AB	H	2B	3B	HR	RBI	BB	SO
Total	.262	.303	.317	480	126	16	2	2	45	24	14		.256	.307	.297	2172	557	58	11	3	156	147	119
vs. Left	.293	.323	.395	157	46	9	2	1	15	6	2		.271	.328	.317	649	176	19	4	1	51	55	28
vs. Right	.248	.293	.279	323	80	7	0	1	30	18	12		.250	.297	.289	1523	381	39	7	2	105	92	91
at Home	.230	.277	.274	226	52	6	2	0	21	14	5		.261	.314	.312	1063	277	34	9	1	84	79	52
on Road	.291	.326	.354	254	74	10	0	2	24	10	9		.252	.299	.283	1109	280	24	2	2	72	68	67
on Grass	.256	.292	.298	406	104	10	2	1	36	18	12		.251	.299	.290	1740	436	46	8	2	126	114	90
on Turf	.297	.358	.419	74	22	6	0	1	9	6	2		.280	.335	.329	432	121	12	3	1	30	33	29
Day Games	.236	.280	.284	148	35	4	0	1	14	8	6		.260	.312	.292	674	175	14	1	2	44	47	46
Night Games	.274	.313	.331	332	91	12	2	1	31	16	8		.255	.304	.300	1498	382	44	10	1	112	100	73
April	.264	.329	.292	72	19	2	0	0	7	6	1		.230	.291	.265	226	52	3	1	1	20	19	9
May	.281	.304	.315	89	25	3	0	0	8	3	4		.261	.301	.303	353	92	11	2	0	25	19	20
June	.221	.286	.234	77	17	1	0	0	3	6	3		.243	.291	.267	382	93	9	0	0	15	24	19
July	.293	.341	.402	82	24	4	1	1	7	4	1		.255	.301	.305	400	102	11	3	1	29	23	22
August	.222	.243	.253	99	22	3	0	0	7	3	2		.267	.308	.309	359	96	13	1	0	35	21	15
Sept-Oct	.311	.333	.443	61	19	3	1	1	13	2	3		.270	.335	.319	452	122	11	4	1	32	41	34
Bases Empty	.221	.260	.280	271	60	11	1	1	1	12	7		.250	.297	.294	1260	315	34	8	2	2	78	70
Leadoff	.216	.269	.320	97	21	5	1	1	1	7	2		.254	.305	.300	500	127	11	3	2	2	36	26
Runners On Base	.316	.357	.364	209	66	5	1	1	44	12	7		.265	.320	.302	912	242	24	3	1	154	69	49
Scoring Position	.312	.356	.384	125	39	4	1	1	44	8	3		.253	.313	.296	533	135	14	3	1	150	45	31
Late and Close	.369	.446	.477	65	24	4	0	1	7	7	0		.261	.335	.301	306	80	9	0	1	17	29	18

7-YEAR TOTALS (1987–1993)

TONY FERNANDEZ — BB/TR — age 32 — NYN/TOR SS142

1993	BA	OBA	SA	AB	H	2B	3B	HR	RBI	BB	SO		BA	OBA	SA	AB	H	2B	3B	HR	RBI	BB	SO
Total	.279	.348	.394	526	147	23	11	5	64	56	45		.285	.339	.390	5625	1603	273	80	53	541	450	523
vs. Left	.248	.339	.321	165	41	8	2	0	14	23	7		.276	.339	.367	1829	504	83	18	16	167	176	149
vs. Right	.294	.353	.427	361	106	15	9	5	50	33	38		.290	.339	.401	3796	1099	190	62	37	374	274	374
at Home	.271	.351	.376	255	69	10	7	1	31	31	20		.288	.347	.396	2738	789	143	47	19	267	239	243
on Road	.288	.346	.410	271	78	13	4	4	33	25	25		.282	.332	.385	2887	814	130	33	34	274	211	280
on Grass	.275	.344	.407	280	77	15	5	4	39	30	20		.280	.335	.383	2701	756	122	29	33	247	220	278
on Turf	.285	.353	.378	246	70	8	6	1	25	26	25		.290	.343	.397	2924	847	151	51	20	294	230	245
Day Games	.235	.328	.301	166	39	6	1	1	21	22	14		.275	.332	.371	1783	491	82	16	19	167	147	167
Night Games	.300	.358	.436	360	108	17	10	4	43	34	31		.289	.342	.399	3842	1112	191	64	34	374	303	356
April	.203	.349	.246	69	14	1	1	0	8	15	6		.261	.319	.331	655	171	15	8	5	64	51	76
May	.191	.273	.309	68	13	3	1	1	6	8	7		.270	.334	.375	930	251	50	9	10	85	91	98
June	.330	.383	.528	106	35	7	4	2	16	9	12		.315	.377	.451	1001	315	63	20	11	108	98	88
July	.278	.343	.333	90	25	2	0	1	8	9	5		.249	.295	.340	965	240	44	10	8	79	65	91
August	.266	.308	.358	109	29	4	3	0	15	7	12		.301	.349	.417	1031	310	49	22	9	111	70	85
Sept-Oct	.369	.424	.524	84	31	6	2	1	11	8	3		.303	.350	.403	1043	316	52	11	10	94	75	85
Bases Empty	.248	.299	.350	274	68	13	3	3	3	19	21		.278	.331	.378	3487	968	163	45	32	32	261	337
Leadoff	.237	.283	.290	93	22	2	0	1	1	6	5		.273	.327	.369	1659	453	80	19	14	14	122	149
Runners On Base	.313	.397	.440	252	79	10	8	2	61	37	24		.297	.352	.411	2138	635	110	35	21	509	189	186
Scoring Position	.311	.407	.466	148	46	5	6	2	57	26	20		.308	.371	.427	1218	375	71	22	10	463	132	129
Late and Close	.293	.375	.370	92	27	4	0	1	13	12	12		.313	.367	.414	879	275	38	15	7	99	77	76

10-YEAR TOTALS (1984–1993)

CECIL FIELDER — BR/TR — age 31 — DET 1B119, DH36

1993	BA	OBA	SA	AB	H	2B	3B	HR	RBI	BB	SO		BA	OBA	SA	AB	H	2B	3B	HR	RBI	BB	SO
Total	.267	.368	.464	573	153	23	0	30	117	90	125		.259	.346	.500	2870	743	114	3	191	590	377	753
vs. Left	.324	.462	.570	142	46	11	0	8	35	38	25		.286	.386	.580	1020	292	53	2	81	221	163	264
vs. Right	.248	.333	.429	431	107	12	0	22	82	52	100		.244	.324	.456	1850	451	61	1	110	369	214	489
at Home	.283	.381	.537	283	80	12	0	20	67	44	63		.267	.358	.545	1388	370	61	1	108	311	191	351
on Road	.252	.354	.393	290	73	11	0	10	50	46	62		.252	.336	.458	1482	373	53	2	83	279	186	402
on Grass	.269	.368	.471	484	130	17	0	27	101	76	101		.258	.351	.498	2201	568	82	1	148	463	310	554
on Turf	.258	.365	.427	89	23	6	0	3	16	14	24		.262	.331	.508	669	175	32	2	43	127	67	199
Day Games	.278	.386	.488	205	57	10	0	11	47	34	48		.234	.327	.472	936	219	32	1	63	201	125	250
Night Games	.261	.357	.451	368	96	13	0	19	70	56	77		.271	.356	.514	1934	524	82	2	128	389	252	503
April	.271	.367	.376	85	23	3	0	2	17	13	21		.237	.311	.451	384	91	13	0	23	87	39	89
May	.250	.381	.511	92	23	3	0	7	16	18	22		.273	.382	.548	429	117	28	0	30	81	73	123
June	.286	.403	.622	98	28	3	0	10	32	20	18		.283	.374	.579	494	140	18	1	42	133	72	128
July	.278	.363	.537	108	30	7	0	7	24	15	23		.263	.343	.526	506	133	20	1	37	99	61	134
August	.273	.368	.404	99	27	4	0	3	17	15	20		.250	.343	.459	516	129	22	1	28	99	72	140
Sept-Oct	.242	.317	.308	91	22	3	0	1	11	9	20		.246	.322	.442	541	133	13	0	31	91	60	139
Bases Empty	.278	.372	.520	252	70	10	0	17	17	36	53		.251	.325	.489	1439	361	49	1	97	97	153	390
Leadoff	.285	.376	.472	123	35	2	0	7	7	17	23		.266	.334	.521	698	186	23	1	51	51	67	173
Runners On Base	.259	.364	.421	321	83	13	0	13	100	54	72		.267	.366	.512	1431	382	65	2	94	493	224	363
Scoring Position	.292	.407	.487	195	57	8	0	10	90	40	41		.270	.382	.492	837	226	38	2	48	384	159	217
Late and Close	.214	.333	.343	70	15	3	0	2	10	12	15		.239	.342	.370	422	101	10	0	15	66	64	121

8-YEAR TOTALS (1985–1993)

STEVE FINLEY — BL/TL — age 29 — HOU OF140

1993	BA	OBA	SA	AB	H	2B	3B	HR	RBI	BB	SO
Total	.266	.304	.385	545	145	15	13	8	44	28	65
vs. Left	.268	.297	.378	164	44	6	3	2	16	5	16
vs. Right	.265	.307	.388	381	101	9	10	6	28	23	49
at Home	.246	.280	.333	252	62	5	7	1	20	11	29
on Road	.283	.325	.430	293	83	10	6	7	24	17	36
on Grass	.270	.316	.434	196	53	7	5	5	15	13	22
on Turf	.264	.297	.358	349	92	8	8	3	29	15	43
Day Games	.258	.314	.348	178	46	3	2	3	9	13	17
Night Games	.270	.299	.403	367	99	12	11	5	35	15	48
April	.222	.315	.286	63	14	1	0	1	3	7	7
May	.262	.310	.354	65	17	2	2	0	3	4	2
June	.226	.270	.298	84	19	2	2	0	1	5	9
July	.313	.333	.455	99	31	5	3	1	11	3	10
August	.274	.299	.381	113	31	2	2	2	12	4	15
Sept-Oct	.273	.299	.463	121	33	3	4	4	14	5	22
Bases Empty	.245	.293	.372	323	79	9	7	6	6	19	40
Leadoff	.267	.315	.376	101	27	3	4	0	0	6	12
Runners On Base	.297	.321	.405	222	66	6	6	2	38	9	25
Scoring Position	.295	.317	.429	112	33	2	5	2	35	5	13
Late and Close	.306	.348	.482	85	26	2	2	3	10	4	6

5-YEAR TOTALS (1989–1993)

	BA	OBA	SA	AB	H	2B	3B	HR	RBI	BB	SO
	.274	.323	.379	2429	665	93	42	26	215	175	276
	.249	.289	.331	726	181	23	9	6	66	37	94
	.284	.338	.399	1703	484	70	33	20	149	138	182
	.261	.312	.356	1207	315	44	25	7	95	87	150
	.286	.335	.401	1222	350	49	17	19	120	88	126
	.273	.318	.372	1153	315	49	13	13	99	77	137
	.274	.328	.385	1276	350	44	29	13	116	98	139
	.254	.310	.340	677	172	26	7	6	45	54	65
	.281	.328	.394	1752	493	67	35	20	170	121	211
	.248	.310	.344	294	73	9	5	3	23	25	38
	.272	.319	.403	404	110	23	9	4	32	28	40
	.254	.317	.351	413	105	17	7	3	29	36	36
	.297	.339	.387	390	116	12	7	3	33	23	44
	.280	.334	.369	393	110	16	5	3	45	32	46
	.282	.319	.402	535	151	16	9	10	53	31	72
	.270	.322	.378	1475	398	61	21	19	19	107	169
	.273	.319	.372	597	163	26	12	3	3	38	72
	.280	.325	.379	954	267	32	21	7	196	68	107
	.282	.339	.398	515	145	14	14	6	179	52	71
	.286	.337	.377	374	107	12	2	6	43	29	42

DARRIN FLETCHER — BL/TR — age 28 — MON C127

1993	BA	OBA	SA	AB	H	2B	3B	HR	RBI	BB	SO
Total	.255	.320	.379	396	101	20	1	9	60	34	40
vs. Left	.260	.356	.377	77	20	3	0	2	11	11	11
vs. Right	.254	.311	.379	319	81	17	1	7	49	23	29
at Home	.257	.322	.404	183	47	12	0	5	30	17	16
on Road	.254	.319	.357	213	54	8	1	4	30	17	24
on Grass	.271	.347	.368	133	36	2	1	3	19	13	13
on Turf	.247	.307	.384	263	65	18	0	6	41	21	27
Day Games	.235	.273	.296	115	27	4	0	1	10	4	18
Night Games	.263	.339	.413	281	74	16	1	8	50	30	22
April	.327	.377	.469	49	16	4	0	1	9	4	4
May	.196	.226	.196	51	10	0	0	0	3	2	5
June	.196	.327	.304	46	9	2	0	1	11	8	5
July	.349	.439	.506	83	29	4	0	3	13	13	5
August	.275	.320	.418	91	25	4	0	3	16	4	12
Sept-Oct	.158	.202	.303	76	12	6	1	1	8	3	9
Bases Empty	.234	.286	.371	205	48	8	1	6	6	13	19
Leadoff	.200	.229	.412	80	16	3	1	4	4	3	8
Runners On Base	.277	.355	.387	191	53	12	0	3	54	21	21
Scoring Position	.242	.340	.383	128	31	9	0	3	51	19	15
Late and Close	.309	.390	.426	68	21	6	1	0	10	6	9

5-YEAR TOTALS (1989–1993)

	BA	OBA	SA	AB	H	2B	3B	HR	RBI	BB	SO
	.246	.299	.353	785	193	39	3	13	101	55	89
	.265	.346	.368	117	31	6	0	2	16	14	20
	.243	.290	.350	668	162	33	3	11	85	41	69
	.240	.291	.363	342	82	19	1	7	46	25	37
	.251	.306	.345	443	111	20	2	6	55	30	52
	.275	.345	.385	247	68	8	2	5	34	22	24
	.232	.277	.338	538	125	31	1	8	67	33	65
	.255	.308	.359	220	56	12	1	3	25	15	28
	.242	.295	.350	565	137	27	2	10	76	40	61
	.266	.314	.383	94	25	5	0	2	15	6	11
	.215	.236	.280	107	23	4	0	1	12	3	12
	.192	.279	.263	99	19	4	0	1	14	11	12
	.331	.404	.463	136	45	7	1	3	18	16	12
	.252	.303	.359	131	33	5	0	3	21	8	17
	.220	.260	.344	218	48	14	2	3	21	11	25
	.230	.271	.341	434	100	18	3	8	8	21	43
	.257	.274	.406	175	45	9	1	5	5	4	13
	.265	.332	.368	351	93	21	0	5	93	34	46
	.228	.316	.342	228	52	14	0	4	84	30	34
	.246	.308	.338	142	35	11	1	0	13	6	23

SCOTT FLETCHER — BR/TR — age 36 — BOS 2B116, SS2, 3B1, DH1

1993	BA	OBA	SA	AB	H	2B	3B	HR	RBI	BB	SO
Total	.285	.341	.402	480	137	31	5	5	45	37	35
vs. Left	.268	.292	.423	123	33	8	1	3	17	4	8
vs. Right	.291	.357	.395	357	104	23	4	2	28	33	27
at Home	.284	.348	.380	250	71	18	0	2	22	21	21
on Road	.287	.333	.426	230	66	13	5	3	23	16	14
on Grass	.287	.340	.390	408	117	26	2	4	35	30	31
on Turf	.278	.346	.472	72	20	5	3	1	10	7	4
Day Games	.272	.325	.372	180	49	13	1	1	16	14	12
Night Games	.293	.351	.420	300	88	18	4	4	29	23	23
April	.250	.328	.423	52	13	2	2	1	3	4	4
May	.304	.389	.481	79	24	8	0	2	11	12	6
June	.250	.298	.341	44	11	1	0	1	3	3	5
July	.299	.348	.364	107	32	5	1	0	13	7	6
August	.302	.327	.434	106	32	12	1	0	7	3	6
Sept-Oct	.272	.330	.359	92	25	3	1	1	8	8	8
Bases Empty	.298	.352	.425	322	96	23	3	4	4	25	26
Leadoff	.300	.373	.453	190	57	17	3	2	2	20	16
Runners On Base	.259	.318	.354	158	41	8	2	1	41	12	9
Scoring Position	.289	.345	.392	97	28	6	2	0	39	7	7
Late and Close	.239	.299	.282	71	17	3	0	0	6	5	8

10-YEAR TOTALS (1984–1993)

	BA	OBA	SA	AB	H	2B	3B	HR	RBI	BB	SO
	.267	.336	.343	4559	1216	204	31	27	449	444	469
	.285	.355	.364	1556	443	70	9	12	138	162	141
	.257	.327	.332	3003	773	134	22	15	311	282	328
	.280	.350	.357	2236	626	106	14	13	237	222	214
	.254	.323	.329	2323	590	98	17	14	212	222	255
	.270	.339	.345	3814	1029	172	22	24	374	368	392
	.251	.325	.332	745	187	32	9	3	75	76	77
	.270	.339	.350	1183	320	59	10	5	108	120	114
	.265	.335	.340	3376	896	145	21	22	341	324	355
	.263	.353	.343	575	151	18	8	4	62	74	69
	.262	.329	.339	829	217	33	8	5	79	84	90
	.273	.353	.358	735	201	38	6	4	66	81	77
	.284	.335	.362	778	221	42	2	5	78	58	62
	.271	.332	.333	841	228	39	2	3	84	70	83
	.247	.321	.325	801	198	34	5	6	80	77	88
	.250	.321	.324	2788	696	122	17	17	17	268	300
	.238	.316	.323	1089	259	50	5	11	11	114	110
	.294	.360	.373	1771	520	82	14	10	432	176	169
	.298	.369	.376	1070	319	54	7	5	405	122	120
	.241	.318	.288	704	170	23	2	2	84	72	93

JULIO FRANCO — BR/TR — age 36 — TEX DH140

1993	BA	OBA	SA	AB	H	2B	3B	HR	RBI	BB	SO	10-YEAR TOTALS (1984–1993) BA	OBA	SA	AB	H	2B	3B	HR	RBI	BB	SO
Total	.289	.360	.438	532	154	31	3	14	84	62	95	.303	.365	.415	5359	1623	254	35	92	678	532	677
vs. Left	.265	.330	.422	102	27	5	1	3	18	10	21	.319	.384	.485	1447	461	91	12	42	196	160	180
vs. Right	.295	.368	.442	430	127	26	2	11	66	52	74	.297	.358	.389	3912	1162	163	23	50	482	372	497
at Home	.330	.400	.500	264	87	21	3	6	45	32	42	.323	.385	.441	2647	856	143	18	44	348	270	305
on Road	.250	.321	.377	268	67	10	0	8	39	30	53	.283	.346	.389	2712	767	111	17	48	330	262	372
on Grass	.301	.374	.456	445	134	30	3	11	70	53	75	.309	.372	.423	4517	1395	227	29	77	576	459	558
on Turf	.230	.293	.345	87	20	1	0	3	14	9	20	.271	.327	.371	842	228	27	6	15	102	73	119
Day Games	.324	.377	.468	139	45	11	0	3	26	13	22	.293	.360	.388	1469	430	67	8	19	183	149	202
Night Games	.277	.355	.427	393	109	20	3	11	58	49	73	.307	.367	.425	3890	1193	187	27	73	495	383	475
April	.286	.337	.416	77	22	5	1	1	9	6	15	.280	.348	.396	714	200	40	2	13	105	73	93
May	.265	.291	.480	98	26	9	0	4	16	4	22	.294	.353	.428	951	280	48	8	21	118	89	151
June	.190	.300	.310	42	8	2	0	1	4	7	6	.296	.359	.408	936	277	40	7	17	106	92	124
July	.278	.386	.444	108	30	3	0	5	21	19	19	.311	.376	.405	880	274	39	2	13	116	93	87
August	.333	.445	.455	99	33	6	0	2	14	19	13	.320	.382	.422	947	303	43	3	16	116	92	112
Sept-Oct	.324	.350	.444	108	35	6	2	1	20	7	20	.310	.369	.424	931	289	44	13	12	117	93	110
Bases Empty	.259	.326	.408	309	80	20	1	8	8	30	60	.297	.355	.404	3058	909	145	18	48	48	261	395
Leadoff	.293	.351	.415	123	36	9	0	2	2	11	27	.301	.350	.400	1201	362	60	5	16	16	86	156
Runners On Base	.332	.405	.480	223	74	11	2	6	76	32	35	.310	.378	.430	2301	714	109	17	44	630	271	282
Scoring Position	.338	.393	.486	148	50	8	1	4	68	18	27	.311	.385	.430	1362	424	64	13	24	564	187	189
Late and Close	.243	.301	.419	74	18	3	2	2	11	7	18	.298	.363	.416	798	238	32	7	16	108	83	101

TRAVIS FRYMAN — BR/TR — age 25 — DET SS81, 3B69, DH1

1993	BA	OBA	SA	AB	H	2B	3B	HR	RBI	BB	SO	4-YEAR TOTALS (1990–1993) BA	OBA	SA	AB	H	2B	3B	HR	RBI	BB	SO
Total	.300	.379	.486	607	182	37	5	22	97	77	128	.277	.337	.451	2055	570	115	13	72	311	179	472
vs. Left	.265	.349	.482	166	44	7	1	9	29	23	32	.287	.349	.493	564	162	30	4	26	95	53	121
vs. Right	.313	.390	.488	441	138	30	4	13	68	54	96	.274	.332	.435	1491	408	85	9	46	216	126	351
at Home	.316	.402	.537	285	90	20	2	13	45	42	53	.264	.334	.435	973	257	47	7	35	135	98	225
on Road	.286	.358	.441	322	92	17	3	9	52	35	75	.289	.339	.466	1082	313	68	6	37	176	81	247
on Grass	.292	.374	.474	517	151	30	5	18	74	67	109	.279	.338	.449	1752	488	92	12	61	247	153	397
on Turf	.344	.408	.556	90	31	7	0	4	23	10	19	.271	.330	.462	303	82	23	1	11	64	26	75
Day Games	.316	.363	.500	228	72	14	2	8	31	16	50	.281	.331	.447	684	192	36	6	22	91	51	157
Night Games	.290	.388	.478	379	110	23	3	14	66	61	78	.276	.339	.453	1371	378	79	7	50	220	128	315
April	.341	.406	.560	91	31	6	1	4	21	10	23	.290	.353	.459	231	67	8	2	9	38	22	45
May	.253	.313	.374	99	25	2	2	2	13	9	26	.253	.306	.409	296	75	12	2	10	50	24	77
June	.228	.301	.386	101	23	4	0	4	13	11	19	.263	.309	.437	327	86	20	2	11	49	21	72
July	.345	.416	.564	110	38	11	2	3	17	13	22	.290	.347	.507	365	106	28	3	15	55	31	89
August	.313	.408	.518	112	35	8	0	5	20	17	18	.292	.354	.455	424	124	23	2	14	55	38	94
Sept-Oct	.319	.425	.511	94	30	6	0	4	13	17	20	.272	.345	.434	412	112	24	2	13	64	43	95
Bases Empty	.278	.354	.462	288	80	20	3	9	9	32	57	.269	.327	.446	1044	281	54	7	39	39	84	237
Leadoff	.288	.368	.423	111	32	7	1	2	2	12	18	.294	.349	.476	357	105	24	4	11	11	28	70
Runners On Base	.320	.401	.508	319	102	17	2	13	88	45	71	.286	.346	.456	1011	289	61	6	33	272	95	235
Scoring Position	.333	.410	.536	183	61	12	2	7	74	27	44	.290	.345	.454	586	170	41	5	15	227	55	149
Late and Close	.324	.417	.437	71	23	5	0	1	11	12	20	.257	.324	.410	268	69	15	1	8	40	27	75

GARY GAETTI — BR/TR — age 36 — CAL/KC 3B79, 1B24, DH6

1993	BA	OBA	SA	AB	H	2B	3B	HR	RBI	BB	SO	10-YEAR TOTALS (1984–1993) BA	OBA	SA	AB	H	2B	3B	HR	RBI	BB	SO
Total	.245	.300	.438	331	81	20	1	14	50	21	87	.255	.305	.424	5244	1339	252	22	197	758	342	912
vs. Left	.278	.365	.567	97	27	7	0	7	20	13	27	.255	.315	.430	1499	382	67	5	62	218	131	235
vs. Right	.231	.270	.385	234	54	13	1	7	30	8	60	.256	.300	.422	3745	957	185	17	135	540	211	677
at Home	.286	.342	.494	168	48	17	0	6	28	12	42	.270	.318	.445	2604	702	136	13	98	392	169	463
on Road	.202	.256	.380	163	33	3	1	8	22	9	45	.241	.291	.405	2640	637	116	9	99	366	173	449
on Grass	.213	.271	.367	150	32	5	0	6	19	9	38	.254	.305	.419	2515	640	108	5	99	351	169	434
on Turf	.271	.323	.497	181	49	15	1	8	31	12	49	.256	.304	.429	2729	699	144	17	98	407	173	478
Day Games	.216	.269	.402	97	21	4	1	4	19	7	28	.258	.306	.417	1550	400	66	3	58	247	97	279
Night Games	.256	.313	.453	234	60	16	0	10	31	14	59	.254	.304	.428	3694	939	186	19	139	511	245	633
April	.222	.286	.278	18	4	1	0	0	2	2	5	.262	.316	.437	707	185	38	4	26	100	57	135
May	.167	.242	.200	30	5	1	0	0	2	3	7	.266	.316	.452	933	248	47	4	39	150	67	157
June	.231	.286	.423	26	6	2	0	1	2	1	5	.251	.306	.415	856	215	40	2	32	114	62	141
July	.346	.414	.551	78	27	8	1	2	14	7	16	.267	.311	.437	930	248	51	4	33	147	55	158
August	.205	.211	.420	88	18	4	0	5	11	1	28	.236	.283	.408	918	217	40	5	36	126	53	172
Sept-Oct	.231	.306	.473	91	21	4	0	6	19	7	26	.251	.297	.399	900	226	36	2	31	121	48	149
Bases Empty	.238	.284	.443	185	44	12	1	8	8	9	45	.246	.290	.416	2890	710	144	13	107	107	153	493
Leadoff	.240	.296	.373	75	18	5	1	1	1	5	16	.246	.287	.428	1226	301	62	6	50	50	57	180
Runners On Base	.253	.318	.432	146	37	8	0	6	42	12	42	.267	.322	.435	2354	629	108	9	90	651	189	419
Scoring Position	.235	.294	.353	85	20	4	0	2	31	7	22	.267	.328	.449	1349	360	67	4	57	565	132	258
Late and Close	.229	.282	.357	70	16	3	0	2	8	3	23	.234	.290	.398	812	190	36	2	31	108	62	138

GREG GAGNE — BR/TR — age 33 — KC SS159

1993	BA	OBA	SA	AB	H	2B	3B	HR	RBI	BB	SO
Total	.280	.319	.406	540	151	32	3	10	57	33	93
vs. Left	.314	.364	.445	137	43	12	0	2	20	12	26
vs. Right	.268	.303	.392	403	108	20	3	8	37	21	67
at Home	.305	.340	.420	269	82	20	1	3	31	16	38
on Road	.255	.298	.391	271	69	12	2	7	26	17	55
on Grass	.262	.298	.432	206	54	10	2	7	25	11	41
on Turf	.290	.331	.389	334	97	22	1	3	32	22	52
Day Games	.219	.253	.384	146	32	7	1	5	23	7	29
Night Games	.302	.343	.414	394	119	25	2	5	34	26	64
April	.194	.270	.284	67	13	1	1	1	5	7	10
May	.321	.345	.429	84	27	4	1	1	9	3	13
June	.266	.320	.330	94	25	3	0	1	8	8	18
July	.344	.350	.500	96	33	9	0	2	15	2	15
August	.284	.318	.490	102	29	10	1	3	10	5	18
Sept-Oct	.247	.302	.361	97	24	5	0	2	10	8	19
Bases Empty	.280	.316	.402	328	92	21	2	5	5	17	58
Leadoff	.306	.350	.448	134	41	8	1	3	3	9	24
Runners On Base	.278	.323	.410	212	59	11	1	5	52	16	35
Scoring Position	.295	.348	.459	122	36	9	1	3	47	12	22
Late and Close	.237	.256	.342	114	27	4	1	2	11	3	20

10-YEAR TOTALS (1984–1993)

	BA	OBA	SA	AB	H	2B	3B	HR	RBI	BB	SO
Total	.254	.297	.390	3899	992	214	38	79	389	221	763
vs. Left	.269	.313	.425	1147	309	75	19	22	120	74	229
vs. Right	.248	.291	.375	2752	683	139	19	57	269	147	534
at Home	.255	.304	.395	1899	484	112	22	37	206	124	355
on Road	.254	.291	.384	2000	508	102	16	42	183	97	408
on Grass	.258	.295	.400	1539	397	82	13	37	139	75	307
on Turf	.252	.299	.383	2360	595	132	25	42	250	146	456
Day Games	.237	.281	.372	1176	279	60	10	26	117	65	246
Night Games	.262	.304	.397	2723	713	154	28	53	272	156	517
April	.259	.318	.395	552	143	29	5	12	49	43	106
May	.265	.310	.399	649	172	33	9	12	65	42	122
June	.237	.282	.374	721	171	38	8	15	81	42	145
July	.254	.286	.362	677	172	40	3	9	62	27	126
August	.277	.312	.443	654	181	47	10	14	74	32	128
Sept-Oct	.237	.281	.367	646	153	27	3	17	58	35	136
Bases Empty	.262	.304	.409	2236	586	135	23	49	49	117	421
Leadoff	.268	.306	.419	880	236	53	10	20	20	46	156
Runners On Base	.244	.289	.364	1663	406	79	15	30	340	104	342
Scoring Position	.248	.302	.380	920	228	50	12	16	298	77	196
Late and Close	.246	.294	.352	548	135	25	6	7	44	33	117

ANDRES GALARRAGA — BR/TR — age 33 — COL 1B119

1993	BA	OBA	SA	AB	H	2B	3B	HR	RBI	BB	SO
Total	.370	.403	.602	470	174	35	4	22	98	24	73
vs. Left	.350	.383	.573	117	41	6	1	6	25	6	16
vs. Right	.377	.410	.612	353	133	29	3	16	73	18	57
at Home	.402	.430	.647	266	107	20	3	13	64	15	33
on Road	.328	.368	.544	204	67	15	1	9	34	9	40
on Grass	.356	.389	.565	379	135	25	3	16	80	21	58
on Turf	.429	.464	.758	91	39	10	1	6	18	3	15
Day Games	.362	.400	.558	163	59	12	1	6	38	9	22
Night Games	.375	.405	.625	307	115	23	3	16	60	15	51
April	.412	.435	.647	85	35	8	0	4	25	5	9
May	.360	.385	.500	50	18	4	0	1	13	2	7
June	.420	.458	.720	100	42	8	2	6	21	6	19
July	.351	.407	.608	74	26	5	1	4	11	5	13
August	.231	.273	.436	39	9	2	0	2	5	1	9
Sept-Oct	.361	.385	.566	122	44	8	1	5	23	5	16
Bases Empty	.325	.349	.546	249	81	11	4	12	12	6	42
Leadoff	.310	.315	.527	129	40	6	2	6	6	1	23
Runners On Base	.421	.460	.665	221	93	24	0	10	86	18	31
Scoring Position	.425	.480	.701	127	54	14	0	7	76	17	21
Late and Close	.358	.414	.453	53	19	5	0	0	7	5	14

9-YEAR TOTALS (1985–1993)

	BA	OBA	SA	AB	H	2B	3B	HR	RBI	BB	SO
Total	.279	.332	.452	3877	1083	217	20	138	570	259	932
vs. Left	.294	.343	.501	1260	370	76	4	59	205	93	287
vs. Right	.272	.326	.429	2617	713	141	16	79	365	166	645
at Home	.292	.346	.474	1906	556	126	15	64	307	135	447
on Road	.267	.318	.431	1971	527	91	5	74	263	124	485
on Grass	.284	.329	.457	1281	364	61	4	51	197	80	302
on Turf	.277	.333	.450	2596	719	156	16	87	373	179	630
Day Games	.273	.340	.448	1181	323	69	4	43	158	105	287
Night Games	.282	.328	.454	2696	760	148	16	95	412	154	645
April	.305	.369	.481	501	153	34	0	18	87	42	110
May	.287	.334	.455	620	178	34	2	22	98	39	143
June	.295	.351	.493	678	200	49	5	25	101	47	160
July	.274	.330	.460	624	171	35	6	23	84	43	154
August	.235	.285	.364	637	150	21	2	19	70	36	161
Sept-Oct	.283	.327	.463	817	231	44	5	31	130	52	204
Bases Empty	.272	.314	.447	2104	572	120	13	74	74	105	493
Leadoff	.282	.324	.462	844	238	52	5	30	30	45	202
Runners On Base	.288	.352	.459	1773	511	97	7	64	496	154	439
Scoring Position	.275	.361	.428	1048	288	54	7	31	408	132	286
Late and Close	.255	.320	.416	718	183	40	2	24	94	62	193

MIKE GALLEGO — BR/TR — age 34 — NYA SS55, 2B52, 3B27

1993	BA	OBA	SA	AB	H	2B	3B	HR	RBI	BB	SO
Total	.283	.364	.412	403	114	20	1	10	54	50	65
vs. Left	.305	.376	.464	151	46	9	0	5	17	17	13
vs. Right	.270	.356	.381	252	68	11	1	5	37	33	52
at Home	.302	.394	.438	192	58	11	0	5	20	27	31
on Road	.265	.336	.389	211	56	9	1	5	34	23	34
on Grass	.290	.368	.411	348	101	16	1	8	45	42	56
on Turf	.236	.338	.418	55	13	4	0	2	9	8	9
Day Games	.317	.428	.408	142	45	5	1	2	21	26	24
Night Games	.264	.325	.414	261	69	15	0	8	33	24	41
April	.438	.438	.813	16	7	0	0	2	4	0	4
May	.302	.456	.434	53	16	4	0	1	8	13	5
June	.327	.346	.490	49	16	5	0	1	7	2	10
July	.250	.314	.283	92	23	0	0	1	9	8	13
August	.313	.367	.475	99	31	8	1	2	13	9	15
Sept-Oct	.223	.348	.351	94	21	3	0	3	13	18	18
Bases Empty	.283	.367	.447	219	62	13	1	7	7	26	36
Leadoff	.269	.358	.473	93	25	7	0	4	4	12	13
Runners On Base	.283	.360	.370	184	52	7	0	3	47	24	29
Scoring Position	.237	.303	.351	114	27	7	0	2	45	13	21
Late and Close	.217	.266	.333	60	13	1	0	2	7	3	10

9-YEAR TOTALS (1985–1993)

	BA	OBA	SA	AB	H	2B	3B	HR	RBI	BB	SO
Total	.242	.325	.337	2319	562	90	11	36	228	266	358
vs. Left	.265	.344	.378	769	204	41	2	14	76	92	105
vs. Right	.231	.316	.317	1550	358	49	9	22	152	174	253
at Home	.252	.342	.348	1141	288	44	7	17	102	146	162
on Road	.233	.309	.327	1178	274	46	4	19	126	120	196
on Grass	.243	.326	.333	1951	474	72	10	28	183	225	295
on Turf	.239	.320	.359	368	88	18	1	8	45	41	63
Day Games	.251	.343	.345	870	218	34	6	12	95	113	138
Night Games	.237	.314	.333	1449	344	56	5	24	133	153	220
April	.276	.363	.376	210	58	10	1	3	21	28	32
May	.232	.333	.346	396	92	18	3	7	51	54	57
June	.244	.309	.314	405	99	11	1	5	32	38	62
July	.231	.306	.322	432	100	14	2	7	43	41	62
August	.257	.335	.375	339	87	15	2	7	35	38	44
Sept-Oct	.235	.325	.322	537	126	22	2	7	46	67	101
Bases Empty	.230	.321	.332	1345	310	53	3	26	26	172	223
Leadoff	.219	.311	.345	589	129	21	1	17	17	77	94
Runners On Base	.259	.330	.344	974	252	37	8	10	202	94	135
Scoring Position	.235	.320	.316	532	125	25	3	4	181	63	78
Late and Close	.245	.316	.339	339	83	10	2	6	31	31	61

RON GANT — BR/TR — age 29 — ATL OF155

1993	BA	OBA	SA	AB	H	2B	3B	HR	RBI	BB	SO		BA	OBA	SA	AB	H	2B	3B	HR	RBI	BB	SO
Total	.274	.345	.510	606	166	27	4	36	117	67	117		.262	.326	.466	3192	836	158	27	147	480	300	599
												7-YEAR TOTALS (1987–1993)											
vs. Left	.295	.385	.510	149	44	6	1	8	34	23	13		.268	.346	.473	990	265	58	8	43	164	119	149
vs. Right	.267	.331	.510	457	122	21	3	28	83	44	104		.259	.317	.464	2202	571	100	19	104	316	181	450
at Home	.279	.352	.505	301	84	13	2	17	55	35	53		.271	.338	.486	1544	418	72	16	76	242	149	273
on Road	.269	.337	.515	305	82	14	2	19	62	32	64		.254	.316	.448	1648	418	86	11	71	238	151	326
on Grass	.276	.348	.502	464	128	19	4	26	92	54	85		.262	.328	.463	2352	616	101	21	110	360	224	437
on Turf	.268	.333	.535	142	38	8	0	10	25	13	32		.262	.323	.476	840	220	57	6	37	120	76	162
Day Games	.204	.280	.358	162	33	3	2	6	22	18	44		.242	.320	.421	886	214	30	9	37	126	97	212
Night Games	.300	.368	.565	444	133	24	2	30	95	49	73		.270	.329	.484	2306	622	128	18	110	354	203	387
April	.207	.286	.379	87	18	3	0	4	8	10	19		.195	.281	.359	359	70	16	2	13	41	42	83
May	.309	.389	.617	94	29	6	1	7	23	13	15		.268	.321	.491	582	156	32	4	30	100	47	109
June	.283	.343	.586	99	28	10	1	6	17	9	22		.274	.329	.514	529	145	33	8	26	74	40	94
July	.273	.350	.555	110	30	5	1	8	21	12	20		.272	.326	.480	537	146	27	5	25	79	42	99
August	.262	.314	.430	107	28	0	0	6	21	9	21		.257	.337	.450	505	130	20	4	23	74	59	98
Sept-Oct	.303	.378	.486	109	33	3	1	5	27	14	20		.278	.344	.466	680	189	30	4	30	112	70	116
Bases Empty	.260	.333	.511	319	83	10	2	22	22	34	60		.272	.333	.496	1821	495	82	15	99	99	154	343
Leadoff	.235	.311	.496	119	28	1	0	10	10	13	23		.289	.338	.544	783	226	36	4	52	52	54	129
Runners On Base	.289	.357	.509	287	83	17	2	14	95	33	57		.249	.318	.427	1371	341	76	12	48	381	146	256
Scoring Position	.301	.369	.601	173	52	14	1	12	89	23	38		.260	.336	.437	822	214	52	6	27	327	106	155
Late and Close	.253	.291	.547	95	24	5	1	7	20	6	17		.224	.292	.387	501	112	22	3	18	72	48	100

CARLOS GARCIA — BR/TR — age 27 — PIT 2B140, SS3

1993	BA	OBA	SA	AB	H	2B	3B	HR	RBI	BB	SO		BA	OBA	SA	AB	H	2B	3B	HR	RBI	BB	SO
Total	.269	.316	.399	546	147	25	5	12	47	31	67		.266	.309	.390	613	163	26	7	12	52	32	86
												4-YEAR TOTALS (1990–1993)											
vs. Left	.304	.337	.466	191	58	15	2	4	15	10	17		.296	.329	.466	206	61	15	4	4	17	11	21
vs. Right	.251	.306	.363	355	89	10	3	8	32	21	50		.251	.299	.351	407	102	11	3	8	35	21	65
at Home	.256	.294	.389	285	73	9	4	7	25	14	44		.257	.289	.384	323	83	10	5	7	29	14	53
on Road	.284	.340	.410	261	74	16	1	5	22	17	23		.276	.329	.397	290	80	16	2	5	23	18	33
on Grass	.303	.369	.461	165	50	9	1	5	18	13	14		.306	.367	.459	183	56	9	2	5	19	14	16
on Turf	.255	.292	.373	381	97	16	4	7	29	18	53		.249	.282	.360	430	107	17	5	7	33	18	70
Day Games	.311	.351	.416	161	50	6	1	3	11	8	11		.290	.330	.387	186	54	7	1	3	11	9	20
Night Games	.252	.302	.392	385	97	19	4	9	36	23	56		.255	.299	.391	427	109	19	6	9	41	23	66
April	.254	.301	.358	67	17	4	0	1	7	3	10		.254	.301	.358	67	17	4	0	1	7	3	10
May	.250	.316	.417	72	18	5	2	1	6	7	10		.260	.325	.425	73	19	5	2	1	7	7	10
June	.230	.275	.351	74	17	4	1	1	4	5	9		.213	.256	.325	80	17	4	1	1	4	5	10
July	.257	.299	.385	109	28	5	0	3	8	6	15		.250	.292	.375	112	28	5	0	3	8	6	18
August	.331	.385	.483	118	39	4	1	4	14	6	13		.331	.385	.483	118	39	4	1	4	14	6	13
Sept-Oct	.264	.295	.368	106	28	3	1	2	8	4	10		.264	.285	.362	163	43	4	3	2	12	5	25
Bases Empty	.299	.345	.471	344	103	19	5	10	10	17	41		.300	.342	.463	380	114	20	6	10	10	17	51
Leadoff	.280	.318	.410	200	56	11	0	5	5	8	23		.291	.326	.418	213	62	12	0	5	5	8	27
Runners On Base	.218	.269	.277	202	44	6	0	2	37	14	26		.210	.257	.270	233	49	6	1	2	42	15	35
Scoring Position	.232	.295	.295	112	26	4	0	1	34	11	15		.214	.274	.270	126	27	4	0	1	38	12	18
Late and Close	.242	.298	.295	95	23	3	1	0	7	7	16		.234	.284	.318	107	25	3	3	0	9	7	20

JEFF GARDNER — BL/TR — age 30 — SD 2B133, 3B1, SS1

1993	BA	OBA	SA	AB	H	2B	3B	HR	RBI	BB	SO		BA	OBA	SA	AB	H	2B	3B	HR	RBI	BB	SO
Total	.262	.337	.356	404	106	21	7	1	24	45	69		.248	.322	.330	460	114	21	7	1	25	50	83
												3-YEAR TOTALS (1991–1993)											
vs. Left	.174	.345	.217	23	4	1	0	0	0	6	7		.121	.256	.152	33	4	1	0	0	0	6	11
vs. Right	.268	.336	.365	381	102	20	7	1	24	39	62		.258	.327	.344	427	110	20	7	1	25	44	72
at Home	.236	.314	.317	199	47	7	3	1	11	22	41		.227	.304	.298	225	51	7	3	1	12	25	47
on Road	.288	.360	.395	205	59	14	4	0	13	23	28		.268	.338	.362	235	63	14	4	0	13	25	36
on Grass	.256	.329	.341	317	81	16	4	1	18	34	55		.244	.319	.320	353	86	16	4	1	19	39	64
on Turf	.287	.367	.414	87	25	5	3	0	6	11	14		.262	.331	.364	107	28	5	3	0	6	11	19
Day Games	.254	.349	.346	130	33	10	1	0	6	18	28		.245	.341	.325	151	37	10	1	0	6	21	32
Night Games	.266	.331	.361	274	73	11	6	1	18	27	41		.249	.312	.333	309	77	11	6	1	19	29	51
April	.255	.286	.383	47	12	4	1	0	3	2	9		.255	.286	.383	47	12	4	1	0	3	2	9
May	.296	.370	.395	81	24	6	1	0	4	10	11		.296	.370	.395	81	24	6	1	0	4	10	11
June	.221	.326	.286	77	17	3	1	0	1	11	13		.221	.326	.286	77	17	3	1	0	1	11	13
July	.368	.419	.500	68	25	4	1	1	8	6	13		.368	.419	.500	68	25	4	1	1	8	6	13
August	.269	.329	.343	67	18	3	1	0	2	6	12		.257	.316	.329	70	18	3	1	0	2	6	13
Sept-Oct	.156	.270	.234	64	10	1	2	0	6	10	11		.154	.248	.197	117	18	1	2	0	7	15	24
Bases Empty	.266	.347	.359	259	69	13	4	1	1	32	41		.247	.326	.328	299	74	13	4	1	1	35	52
Leadoff	.283	.377	.425	113	32	9	2	1	1	17	15		.260	.353	.382	131	34	9	2	1	1	19	20
Runners On Base	.255	.319	.352	145	37	8	3	0	23	13	28		.248	.313	.335	161	40	8	3	0	24	15	31
Scoring Position	.275	.352	.363	80	22	5	1	0	21	10	20		.264	.347	.345	87	23	5	1	0	22	12	21
Late and Close	.203	.298	.243	74	15	3	0	0	6	9	14		.188	.274	.224	85	16	3	0	0	6	9	16

BRENT GATES — BB/TR — age 24 — OAK 2B139

1993	BA	OBA	SA	AB	H	2B	3B	HR	RBI	BB	SO
Total	.290	.357	.391	535	155	29	2	7	69	56	75
vs. Left	.256	.337	.343	172	44	9	0	2	18	20	24
vs. Right	.306	.366	.413	363	111	20	2	5	51	36	51
at Home	.264	.328	.345	258	68	9	0	4	36	25	39
on Road	.314	.383	.433	277	87	20	2	3	33	31	36
on Grass	.271	.336	.363	435	118	20	1	6	54	42	62
on Turf	.370	.443	.510	100	37	9	1	1	15	14	13
Day Games	.278	.347	.361	216	60	7	1	3	23	23	33
Night Games	.298	.363	.411	319	95	22	1	4	46	33	42
April	.000	.000	.000	0	0	0	0	0	0	0	0
May	.276	.375	.391	87	24	4	0	2	10	14	11
June	.294	.350	.382	102	30	6	0	1	18	9	19
July	.276	.354	.310	116	32	1	0	1	10	13	16
August	.277	.314	.420	112	31	8	1	2	13	7	11
Sept-Oct	.322	.389	.449	118	38	10	1	1	18	13	18
Bases Empty	.289	.362	.379	280	81	17	1	2	2	30	40
Leadoff	.330	.406	.415	94	31	5	0	1	1	11	12
Runners On Base	.290	.351	.404	255	74	12	1	5	67	26	35
Scoring Position	.266	.343	.350	143	38	7	1	1	56	20	21
Late and Close	.278	.365	.378	90	25	6	0	1	18	13	19

1-YEAR TOTALS (1993)

BA	OBA	SA	AB	H	2B	3B	HR	RBI	BB	SO
.290	.357	.391	535	155	29	2	7	69	56	75
.256	.337	.343	172	44	9	0	2	18	20	24
.306	.366	.413	363	111	20	2	5	51	36	51
.264	.328	.345	258	68	9	0	4	36	25	39
.314	.383	.433	277	87	20	2	3	33	31	36
.271	.336	.363	435	118	20	1	6	54	42	62
.370	.443	.510	100	37	9	1	1	15	14	13
.278	.347	.361	216	60	7	1	3	23	23	33
.298	.363	.411	319	95	22	1	4	46	33	42
.000	.000	.000	0	0	0	0	0	0	0	0
.276	.375	.391	87	24	4	0	2	10	14	11
.294	.350	.382	102	30	6	0	1	18	9	19
.276	.354	.310	116	32	1	0	1	10	13	16
.277	.314	.420	112	31	8	1	2	13	7	11
.322	.389	.449	118	38	10	1	1	18	13	18
.289	.362	.379	280	81	17	1	2	2	30	40
.330	.406	.415	94	31	5	0	1	1	11	12
.290	.351	.404	255	74	12	1	5	67	26	35
.266	.343	.350	143	38	7	1	1	56	20	21
.278	.365	.378	90	25	6	0	1	18	13	19

KIRK GIBSON — BL/TL — age 37 — DET DH76, OF32

1993	BA	OBA	SA	AB	H	2B	3B	HR	RBI	BB	SO
Total	.261	.337	.432	403	105	18	6	13	62	44	87
vs. Left	.275	.326	.325	40	11	2	0	0	8	1	12
vs. Right	.259	.338	.444	363	94	16	6	13	54	43	75
at Home	.254	.326	.421	197	50	8	5	5	30	22	42
on Road	.267	.348	.442	206	55	10	1	8	32	22	45
on Grass	.226	.302	.354	328	74	11	5	7	47	36	72
on Turf	.413	.488	.773	75	31	7	1	6	15	8	15
Day Games	.266	.342	.364	143	38	10	2	0	16	15	38
Night Games	.258	.334	.469	260	67	8	4	13	46	29	49
April	.407	.520	.661	59	24	6	0	3	15	14	13
May	.270	.372	.459	74	20	1	2	3	10	12	18
June	.115	.146	.218	78	9	3	1	1	9	3	23
July	.328	.366	.567	67	22	5	1	3	5	3	9
August	.261	.316	.420	88	23	3	1	3	17	5	19
Sept-Oct	.189	.311	.243	37	7	0	1	0	6	7	5
Bases Empty	.250	.332	.448	212	53	8	2	10	10	26	49
Leadoff	.253	.352	.418	79	20	2	1	3	3	12	21
Runners On Base	.272	.343	.414	191	52	10	4	3	52	18	38
Scoring Position	.243	.331	.342	111	27	6	1	1	44	13	17
Late and Close	.226	.328	.321	53	12	2	0	1	4	7	14

10-YEAR TOTALS (1984–1993)

BA	OBA	SA	AB	H	2B	3B	HR	RBI	BB	SO
.267	.356	.464	4071	1088	187	35	181	617	536	906
.243	.328	.408	1261	307	52	7	47	183	138	342
.278	.368	.489	2810	781	135	28	134	434	398	564
.267	.354	.463	2004	535	82	25	87	317	262	434
.268	.358	.464	2067	553	105	10	94	300	274	472
.274	.364	.478	3042	835	137	25	144	477	409	676
.246	.331	.422	1029	253	50	10	37	140	127	230
.259	.338	.444	1272	329	63	10	51	189	141	277
.271	.364	.473	2799	759	124	25	130	428	395	629
.279	.372	.482	477	133	20	4	23	80	68	110
.282	.363	.499	553	156	29	8	25	75	66	115
.248	.334	.465	854	212	37	8	44	148	108	193
.278	.355	.456	759	211	39	3	30	106	88	149
.279	.376	.467	803	224	34	9	33	116	116	187
.243	.342	.422	625	152	28	3	26	92	90	152
.261	.345	.457	2267	591	100	18	103	103	272	526
.272	.348	.467	783	213	32	11	33	33	81	170
.275	.369	.472	1804	497	87	17	78	514	264	380
.265	.374	.466	988	262	50	11	42	418	180	214
.249	.357	.426	615	153	25	6	24	92	95	158

BERNARD GILKEY — BR/TR — age 28 — SL OF134, 1B3

1993	BA	OBA	SA	AB	H	2B	3B	HR	RBI	BB	SO
Total	.305	.370	.481	557	170	40	5	16	70	56	66
vs. Left	.343	.396	.518	137	47	8	2	4	22	11	15
vs. Right	.293	.362	.469	420	123	32	3	12	48	45	51
at Home	.325	.380	.506	265	86	21	3	7	35	23	26
on Road	.288	.361	.459	292	84	19	2	9	35	33	40
on Grass	.295	.368	.477	176	52	12	1	6	23	21	26
on Turf	.310	.371	.483	381	118	28	4	10	47	35	40
Day Games	.326	.389	.503	175	57	15	2	4	18	15	17
Night Games	.296	.361	.471	382	113	25	3	12	52	41	49
April	.339	.424	.464	56	19	5	1	0	3	9	10
May	.279	.347	.397	68	19	3	1	1	6	7	8
June	.336	.379	.589	107	36	13	1	4	16	7	15
July	.333	.387	.520	102	34	4	0	5	17	9	12
August	.257	.347	.436	101	26	7	1	3	17	13	9
Sept-Oct	.293	.353	.447	123	36	8	1	3	11	11	12
Bases Empty	.290	.356	.466	341	99	22	4	10	10	32	43
Leadoff	.344	.402	.569	195	67	14	3	8	8	17	19
Runners On Base	.329	.391	.505	216	71	18	1	6	60	24	23
Scoring Position	.313	.386	.500	134	42	8	1	5	56	18	16
Late and Close	.293	.377	.444	99	29	7	1	2	14	12	14

4-YEAR TOTALS (1990–1993)

BA	OBA	SA	AB	H	2B	3B	HR	RBI	BB	SO
.285	.357	.430	1273	363	71	13	29	136	142	156
.299	.367	.420	479	143	22	6	8	51	51	50
.277	.351	.436	794	220	49	7	21	85	91	106
.281	.345	.417	643	181	37	7	12	66	62	67
.289	.369	.443	630	182	34	6	17	70	80	89
.292	.374	.459	318	93	17	3	10	41	42	51
.283	.351	.420	955	270	54	10	19	95	100	105
.291	.351	.444	378	110	25	3	9	36	32	43
.283	.359	.423	895	253	46	10	20	100	110	113
.294	.376	.383	180	53	9	2	1	10	24	30
.249	.343	.364	173	43	7	2	3	15	25	20
.330	.375	.508	191	63	16	3	4	24	14	27
.275	.341	.397	229	63	8	1	9	30	23	33
.228	.315	.373	228	52	13	1	6	31	28	25
.327	.389	.522	272	89	18	4	9	26	28	21
.275	.341	.419	785	216	43	8	18	18	74	99
.305	.361	.489	423	129	26	5	14	14	34	42
.301	.380	.447	488	147	28	5	11	118	68	57
.305	.403	.468	282	86	15	5	7	108	53	40
.294	.380	.441	238	70	15	1	6	30	33	33

JOE GIRARDI — BR/TR — age 30 — COL C84

1993	BA	OBA	SA	AB	H	2B	3B	HR	RBI	BB	SO		BA	OBA	SA	AB	H	2B	3B	HR	RBI	BB	SO
Total	.290	.346	.397	310	90	14	5	3	31	24	41		.269	.316	.342	1203	324	53	8	6	101	77	161
vs. Left	.295	.349	.449	78	23	5	2	1	5	7	7		.293	.329	.388	441	129	28	4	2	38	26	45
vs. Right	.289	.345	.379	232	67	9	3	2	26	17	34		.256	.309	.315	762	195	25	4	4	63	51	116
at Home	.327	.385	.463	147	48	8	3	2	19	13	21		.287	.336	.364	588	169	23	5	4	65	42	81
on Road	.258	.311	.337	163	42	6	2	1	12	11	20		.252	.297	.320	615	155	30	3	2	36	35	80
on Grass	.299	.361	.425	221	66	11	4	3	26	20	29		.275	.327	.349	837	230	32	6	6	82	61	108
on Turf	.270	.309	.326	89	24	3	1	0	5	4	12		.257	.292	.325	366	94	21	2	0	19	16	53
Day Games	.318	.357	.467	107	34	7	3	1	10	6	10		.271	.314	.350	572	155	28	4	3	53	34	72
Night Games	.276	.341	.360	203	56	7	2	2	21	18	31		.268	.319	.334	631	169	25	4	3	48	43	89
April	.280	.299	.373	75	21	5	1	0	6	2	14		.269	.292	.315	216	58	8	1	0	13	5	31
May	.272	.306	.359	92	25	3	1	1	11	5	7		.265	.330	.345	238	63	9	2	2	26	23	28
June	.000	.000	.000	4	0	0	0	0	0	0	1		.272	.296	.367	147	40	6	1	2	11	4	23
July	.000	.000	.000	0	0	0	0	0	0	0	0		.298	.323	.347	124	37	6	0	0	11	6	7
August	.291	.350	.455	55	16	2	2	1	7	5	7		.247	.299	.329	255	63	12	3	1	21	19	33
Sept-Oct	.333	.434	.440	84	28	4	1	1	7	12	12		.283	.352	.359	223	63	12	1	1	19	20	39
Bases Empty	.279	.332	.385	179	50	8	1	3	3	13	19		.261	.301	.337	689	180	31	3	5	5	34	88
Leadoff	.258	.270	.403	62	16	4	1	1	1	1	5		.255	.286	.330	282	72	13	1	2	2	9	33
Runners On Base	.305	.366	.412	131	40	6	4	0	28	11	22		.280	.336	.348	514	144	22	5	1	96	43	73
Scoring Position	.286	.346	.400	70	20	4	2	0	25	7	14		.272	.347	.349	272	74	14	2	1	88	34	48
Late and Close	.234	.294	.298	47	11	1	1	0	3	3	9		.274	.309	.321	212	58	6	2	0	12	10	35

5-YEAR TOTALS (1989–1993)

DAN GLADDEN — BR/TR — age 37 — DET OF86, DH5

1993	BA	OBA	SA	AB	H	2B	3B	HR	RBI	BB	SO		BA	OBA	SA	AB	H	2B	3B	HR	RBI	BB	SO
Total	.267	.312	.433	356	95	16	2	13	56	21	50		.271	.325	.383	4438	1201	201	40	73	436	332	614
vs. Left	.261	.304	.478	138	36	6	0	8	20	8	13		.283	.343	.410	1372	388	68	10	29	137	123	165
vs. Right	.271	.316	.404	218	59	10	2	5	36	13	37		.265	.317	.371	3066	813	133	30	44	299	209	449
at Home	.251	.302	.497	167	42	8	0	11	35	12	21		.280	.341	.404	2162	605	98	21	43	219	188	274
on Road	.280	.320	.376	189	53	8	2	2	21	9	29		.262	.310	.363	2276	596	103	19	30	217	144	340
on Grass	.269	.316	.435	308	83	14	2	11	50	21	41		.259	.317	.363	2470	639	104	11	44	246	194	366
on Turf	.250	.280	.417	48	12	2	0	2	6	0	9		.286	.336	.409	1968	562	97	29	29	190	138	248
Day Games	.279	.336	.450	129	36	3	2	5	21	10	12		.265	.334	.373	1530	405	60	9	29	135	143	230
Night Games	.260	.297	.423	227	59	13	0	8	35	11	38		.274	.320	.389	2908	796	141	31	44	301	189	384
April	.313	.278	.563	16	5	2	1	0	3	0	0		.270	.320	.372	596	161	33	2	8	61	36	68
May	.000	.000	.000	0	0	0	0	0	0	0	0		.272	.321	.402	712	194	39	10	11	65	48	109
June	.256	.310	.410	78	20	3	0	3	8	6	11		.272	.333	.389	717	195	29	5	15	64	61	83
July	.271	.301	.429	70	19	5	0	2	9	2	6		.278	.330	.366	681	189	37	4	5	72	49	86
August	.278	.339	.500	108	30	4	1	6	25	10	18		.265	.322	.375	886	235	29	10	16	101	69	125
Sept-Oct	.250	.292	.345	84	21	2	0	2	11	3	15		.268	.325	.394	846	227	34	9	18	73	69	143
Bases Empty	.228	.291	.395	167	38	9	2	5	5	13	30		.267	.327	.378	2805	749	128	23	46	46	226	412
Leadoff	.229	.299	.400	70	16	4	1	2	2	7	10		.271	.333	.385	1563	424	67	12	29	29	126	214
Runners On Base	.302	.330	.466	189	57	7	0	8	51	8	20		.277	.321	.392	1633	452	73	17	27	390	106	202
Scoring Position	.282	.303	.466	103	29	1	0	6	43	3	13		.265	.315	.382	985	261	42	8	19	351	74	134
Late and Close	.258	.294	.452	31	8	0	0	2	8	2	4		.256	.324	.380	676	173	32	8	12	85	63	111

10-YEAR TOTALS (1984–1993)

JUAN GONZALEZ — BR/TR — age 25 — TEX OF129, DH10

1993	BA	OBA	SA	AB	H	2B	3B	HR	RBI	BB	SO		BA	OBA	SA	AB	H	2B	3B	HR	RBI	BB	SO
Total	.310	.368	.632	536	166	33	1	46	118	37	99		.274	.326	.535	1815	497	101	5	121	348	122	395
vs. Left	.333	.374	.657	108	36	8	0	9	20	7	20		.282	.334	.510	461	130	24	0	27	80	38	104
vs. Right	.304	.367	.626	428	130	25	1	37	98	30	79		.271	.323	.544	1354	367	77	5	94	268	84	291
at Home	.330	.386	.656	273	90	17	0	24	58	19	54		.284	.334	.528	913	259	55	3	54	161	57	218
on Road	.289	.349	.608	263	76	16	1	22	60	18	45		.264	.318	.542	902	238	46	2	67	187	65	177
on Grass	.307	.366	.607	460	141	25	1	37	102	34	85		.275	.327	.531	1515	417	79	4	100	288	104	333
on Turf	.329	.378	.789	76	25	8	0	9	16	3	14		.267	.319	.557	300	80	22	1	21	60	18	62
Day Games	.271	.349	.574	129	35	7	0	10	29	10	26		.275	.336	.565	356	98	21	2	26	78	24	76
Night Games	.322	.374	.651	407	131	26	0	36	89	27	73		.273	.324	.528	1459	399	80	3	95	270	98	319
April	.321	.391	.641	78	25	4	0	7	12	6	17		.302	.352	.549	182	55	9	0	12	32	12	38
May	.348	.434	.773	66	23	7	0	7	17	7	8		.304	.368	.560	273	83	23	1	15	55	25	49
June	.313	.353	.563	96	30	6	0	6	22	6	15		.286	.347	.544	294	84	11	1	21	63	29	66
July	.349	.402	.708	106	37	6	1	10	29	9	17		.282	.326	.598	291	82	15	1	25	70	17	68
August	.252	.314	.550	111	28	3	0	10	22	5	24		.270	.319	.593	344	93	16	1	31	71	19	78
Sept-Oct	.291	.333	.608	79	23	7	0	6	16	4	18		.232	.278	.418	431	100	27	1	17	57	20	96
Bases Empty	.290	.339	.549	286	83	18	1	18	18	13	52		.263	.312	.512	945	249	61	3	56	56	52	195
Leadoff	.380	.441	.674	129	49	12	1	8	8	7	19		.272	.323	.507	383	104	28	1	20	20	19	75
Runners On Base	.332	.400	.728	250	83	15	0	28	100	24	47		.285	.341	.560	870	248	40	2	65	292	70	200
Scoring Position	.308	.383	.667	159	49	9	0	16	76	17	33		.272	.336	.502	544	148	24	1	33	223	53	129
Late and Close	.324	.359	.649	74	24	6	0	6	18	3	17		.259	.320	.528	286	74	17	0	20	52	21	72

5-YEAR TOTALS (1989–1993)

LUIS GONZALEZ — BL/TR — age 27 — HOU OF149

4-YEAR TOTALS (1990–1993)

1993	BA	OBA	SA	AB	H	2B	3B	HR	RBI	BB	SO	BA	OBA	SA	AB	H	2B	3B	HR	RBI	BB	SO
Total	.300	.361	.457	540	162	34	3	15	72	47	83	.267	.327	.427	1421	380	83	15	38	196	113	241
vs. Left	.302	.369	.413	172	52	10	0	3	21	13	28	.269	.340	.387	375	101	23	3	5	47	32	70
vs. Right	.299	.357	.478	368	110	24	3	12	51	34	55	.267	.322	.442	1046	279	60	12	33	149	81	171
at Home	.291	.341	.445	265	77	15	1	8	40	19	43	.260	.317	.410	703	183	41	8	16	97	55	121
on Road	.309	.379	.469	275	85	19	2	7	32	28	40	.274	.336	.444	718	197	42	7	22	99	58	120
on Grass	.315	.378	.517	178	56	14	2	6	24	17	27	.280	.335	.453	461	129	25	5	15	68	34	77
on Turf	.293	.352	.428	362	106	20	1	9	48	30	56	.261	.323	.415	960	251	58	10	23	128	79	164
Day Games	.298	.360	.536	168	50	16	3	6	23	16	26	.266	.329	.455	402	107	27	5	13	49	35	63
Night Games	.301	.361	.422	372	112	18	0	9	49	31	57	.268	.326	.416	1019	273	56	10	25	147	78	178
April	.315	.381	.534	73	23	4	0	4	13	4	6	.207	.277	.348	184	38	9	1	5	20	12	36
May	.200	.282	.356	90	18	3	1	3	9	9	12	.236	.284	.445	229	54	13	4	9	34	15	37
June	.286	.359	.371	70	20	3	0	1	7	8	11	.272	.348	.438	224	61	14	1	7	31	24	33
July	.368	.431	.600	95	35	8	1	4	16	11	11	.309	.383	.502	217	67	13	4	7	34	25	34
August	.310	.346	.410	100	31	8	1	0	9	6	24	.301	.342	.429	259	78	13	4	4	33	14	51
Sept-Oct	.313	.365	.464	112	35	8	0	3	18	17	19	.266	.320	.399	308	82	21	1	6	44	23	50
Bases Empty	.317	.371	.485	293	93	18	2	9	9	20	41	.271	.325	.442	737	200	43	7	23	23	47	118
Leadoff	.368	.417	.547	106	39	6	2	3	3	7	15	.295	.347	.498	281	83	16	4	11	11	19	42
Runners On Base	.279	.349	.425	247	69	16	1	6	63	27	42	.263	.328	.411	684	180	40	8	15	173	66	123
Scoring Position	.265	.348	.415	147	39	8	1	4	55	22	25	.263	.343	.416	392	103	21	3	11	150	51	81
Late and Close	.310	.356	.417	84	26	6	0	1	9	5	15	.300	.360	.426	237	71	14	2	4	33	19	43

MARK GRACE — BL/TL — age 30 — CHN 1B154

6-YEAR TOTALS (1988–1993)

1993	BA	OBA	SA	AB	H	2B	3B	HR	RBI	BB	SO	BA	OBA	SA	AB	H	2B	3B	HR	RBI	BB	SO
Total	.325	.393	.475	594	193	39	4	14	98	71	32	.304	.377	.425	3401	1033	187	22	60	453	412	260
vs. Left	.352	.412	.528	193	68	14	1	6	41	21	12	.293	.360	.415	1161	340	59	10	21	170	122	125
vs. Right	.312	.383	.449	401	125	25	3	8	57	50	20	.309	.386	.429	2240	693	128	12	39	283	290	135
at Home	.353	.421	.480	300	106	19	2	5	52	37	18	.315	.394	.424	1723	542	94	7	27	238	231	125
on Road	.296	.364	.469	294	87	20	2	9	46	34	14	.293	.360	.425	1678	491	93	15	33	215	181	135
on Grass	.346	.412	.510	451	156	33	4	11	79	54	27	.309	.382	.425	2465	761	136	14	41	333	301	196
on Turf	.259	.331	.364	143	37	6	0	3	19	17	5	.291	.366	.423	936	272	51	8	19	120	111	64
Day Games	.338	.402	.457	317	107	16	2	8	49	37	20	.308	.387	.426	1832	565	96	10	33	245	241	140
Night Games	.310	.382	.495	277	86	23	2	6	49	34	12	.298	.365	.423	1569	468	91	12	27	208	171	120
April	.325	.379	.506	83	27	6	0	3	16	9	2	.283	.381	.420	367	104	22	2	8	51	59	19
May	.364	.416	.515	99	36	8	2	1	22	11	6	.310	.372	.429	617	191	35	6	9	86	63	54
June	.302	.370	.500	106	32	9	0	4	18	12	8	.314	.385	.421	532	167	28	4	7	66	64	38
July	.301	.376	.386	83	25	4	0	1	6	10	3	.291	.371	.416	546	159	31	2	11	62	70	35
August	.336	.410	.437	119	40	6	0	2	15	14	5	.322	.387	.456	686	221	33	4	17	95	72	59
Sept-Oct	.317	.397	.500	104	33	6	2	3	21	15	8	.292	.369	.400	653	191	38	4	8	93	84	55
Bases Empty	.322	.394	.471	295	95	18	1	8	8	34	16	.292	.367	.413	1881	549	96	9	38	38	216	161
Leadoff	.350	.414	.500	100	35	6	0	3	3	11	8	.314	.374	.450	636	200	31	2	17	17	60	51
Runners On Base	.328	.391	.478	299	98	21	3	6	90	37	16	.318	.390	.439	1520	484	91	13	22	415	196	99
Scoring Position	.336	.424	.480	152	51	9	2	3	73	30	10	.306	.401	.422	864	264	50	9	11	369	157	70
Late and Close	.453	.529	.709	86	39	7	0	5	24	16	5	.332	.429	.444	552	183	22	2	12	82	94	39

MIKE GREENWELL — BL/TR — age 31 — BOS OF134, DH10

9-YEAR TOTALS (1985–1993)

1993	BA	OBA	SA	AB	H	2B	3B	HR	RBI	BB	SO	BA	OBA	SA	AB	H	2B	3B	HR	RBI	BB	SO
Total	.315	.379	.480	540	170	38	6	13	72	54	46	.307	.375	.466	3520	1082	205	32	97	561	366	276
vs. Left	.304	.362	.466	161	49	7	2	5	26	11	14	.293	.340	.413	1071	314	51	7	21	157	62	90
vs. Right	.319	.387	.485	379	121	31	4	8	46	43	32	.314	.390	.490	2449	768	154	25	76	404	304	186
at Home	.332	.401	.522	247	82	21	4	6	38	27	18	.318	.387	.490	1721	547	126	19	44	297	190	120
on Road	.300	.361	.444	293	88	17	2	7	34	27	28	.297	.363	.444	1799	535	79	13	53	264	176	156
on Grass	.307	.377	.466	440	135	30	5	10	52	48	36	.307	.377	.462	2965	910	181	25	76	465	320	224
on Turf	.350	.389	.540	100	35	8	1	3	20	6	10	.310	.365	.492	555	172	24	7	21	96	46	52
Day Games	.342	.407	.480	196	67	10	4	3	31	20	16	.320	.391	.477	1205	386	84	12	27	200	130	94
Night Games	.299	.363	.480	344	103	28	2	10	41	34	30	.301	.366	.461	2315	696	121	20	70	361	236	182
April	.306	.366	.529	85	26	7	3	2	18	7	8	.281	.373	.442	462	130	22	5	14	64	57	42
May	.316	.355	.404	57	18	5	0	0	6	4	3	.279	.358	.397	551	154	28	2	11	86	67	44
June	.289	.369	.464	97	28	5	0	4	17	13	11	.323	.377	.476	657	212	34	2	21	124	55	52
July	.270	.383	.461	89	24	6	1	3	13	15	11	.307	.377	.478	577	177	35	5	18	79	64	43
August	.307	.340	.386	101	31	8	0	0	5	4	4	.324	.385	.477	589	191	41	8	11	95	59	39
Sept-Oct	.387	.443	.595	111	43	7	2	4	13	11	9	.319	.377	.510	684	218	45	10	22	113	64	56
Bases Empty	.296	.346	.438	304	90	23	4	4	4	20	28	.302	.366	.464	1756	531	109	18	46	46	159	133
Leadoff	.280	.313	.402	107	30	7	3	0	0	4	8	.297	.346	.468	730	217	49	8	20	20	52	51
Runners On Base	.339	.420	.534	236	80	15	2	9	68	34	18	.312	.384	.469	1764	551	96	14	51	515	207	143
Scoring Position	.355	.449	.579	121	43	8	2	5	58	22	8	.297	.385	.445	1017	302	54	11	25	445	155	87
Late and Close	.386	.457	.530	83	32	3	0	3	17	10	7	.314	.392	.477	539	169	28	6	16	86	65	53

KEN GRIFFEY — BL/TL — age 25 — SEA OF139, DH19, 1B1

1993	BA	OBA	SA	AB	H	2B	3B	HR	RBI	BB	SO	BA	OBA	SA	AB	H	2B	3B	HR	RBI	BB	SO
Total	.309	.408	.617	582	180	38	3	45	109	96	91	.303	.375	.520	2747	832	170	15	132	453	318	404
vs. Left	.318	.394	.569	211	67	14	0	13	36	24	38	.308	.371	.501	880	271	54	1	38	131	81	167
vs. Right	.305	.416	.644	371	113	24	3	32	73	72	53	.300	.377	.529	1867	561	116	14	94	322	237	237
at Home	.332	.455	.646	274	91	21	1	21	60	59	46	.315	.394	.553	1356	427	96	7	71	247	175	187
on Road	.289	.363	.591	308	89	17	2	24	49	37	45	.291	.356	.487	1391	405	74	8	61	206	143	217
on Grass	.277	.347	.583	235	65	10	1	20	39	26	37	.292	.358	.490	1075	314	51	6	50	170	112	167
on Turf	.331	.446	.640	347	115	28	2	25	70	70	54	.310	.386	.539	1672	518	119	9	82	283	206	237
Day Games	.299	.412	.659	167	50	7	1	17	35	31	28	.306	.380	.523	759	232	38	5	39	119	90	127
Night Games	.313	.407	.600	415	130	31	2	28	74	65	63	.302	.373	.519	1988	600	132	10	93	334	228	277
April	.280	.388	.598	82	23	5	0	7	18	14	21	.309	.376	.508	392	121	19	1	19	62	44	65
May	.288	.372	.471	104	30	8	1	3	12	14	12	.306	.370	.535	490	150	33	2	25	73	51	70
June	.353	.427	.716	102	36	7	0	10	22	13	12	.284	.369	.493	426	121	29	0	20	65	57	60
July	.330	.403	.698	106	35	5	2	10	26	13	19	.332	.390	.568	470	156	31	4	24	90	46	72
August	.333	.479	.747	75	25	4	0	9	13	20	12	.318	.400	.577	444	141	31	3	26	72	59	64
Sept-Oct	.274	.393	.513	113	31	9	0	6	18	22	15	.272	.350	.446	525	143	27	5	18	91	61	73
Bases Empty	.318	.399	.646	333	106	22	0	29	29	40	50	.296	.357	.514	1501	444	88	7	75	75	134	209
Leadoff	.304	.336	.640	125	38	9	0	11	11	5	19	.281	.321	.493	556	156	26	4	28	28	31	66
Runners On Base	.297	.419	.578	249	74	16	3	16	80	56	41	.311	.395	.527	1246	388	82	8	57	378	184	195
Scoring Position	.239	.407	.458	142	34	6	2	7	58	45	31	.303	.414	.499	702	213	43	5	28	305	148	131
Late and Close	.305	.412	.474	95	29	5	1	3	15	17	19	.274	.373	.432	424	116	19	3	14	60	67	92

MARQUIS GRISSOM — BR/TR — age 27 — MON OF157

1993	BA	OBA	SA	AB	H	2B	3B	HR	RBI	BB	SO	BA	OBA	SA	AB	H	2B	3B	HR	RBI	BB	SO
Total	.298	.351	.438	630	188	27	2	19	95	52	76	.277	.329	.400	2203	610	105	19	43	231	167	307
vs. Left	.307	.362	.495	192	59	13	1	7	28	16	24	.276	.336	.420	830	229	50	8	18	87	74	118
vs. Right	.295	.346	.413	438	129	14	1	12	67	36	52	.277	.324	.388	1373	381	55	11	25	144	93	189
at Home	.319	.366	.450	307	98	13	0	9	50	23	32	.284	.335	.410	1039	295	51	7	22	117	78	143
on Road	.279	.336	.427	323	90	14	2	10	45	29	44	.271	.323	.392	1164	315	54	12	21	114	89	164
on Grass	.272	.336	.429	191	52	10	1	6	26	18	28	.264	.314	.364	629	166	24	6	9	58	44	96
on Turf	.310	.357	.442	439	136	17	1	13	69	34	48	.282	.334	.415	1574	444	81	13	34	173	123	211
Day Games	.273	.317	.402	194	53	6	2	5	26	13	28	.250	.303	.372	667	167	24	6	15	73	50	118
Night Games	.310	.365	.454	436	135	21	0	14	69	39	48	.288	.340	.413	1536	443	81	13	28	158	117	189
April	.294	.362	.471	85	25	3	0	4	17	9	10	.264	.323	.417	288	76	18	1	8	40	25	39
May	.326	.376	.478	92	30	6	1	2	17	7	11	.291	.339	.413	378	110	16	3	8	38	26	57
June	.276	.336	.467	105	29	6	1	4	13	10	13	.287	.355	.404	324	93	20	3	4	32	34	42
July	.224	.298	.318	107	24	4	0	2	13	10	17	.235	.291	.328	378	89	12	4	5	41	27	60
August	.325	.372	.427	117	38	3	0	3	18	10	14	.272	.317	.422	360	98	17	5	9	38	25	47
Sept-Oct	.339	.364	.476	124	42	5	0	4	17	6	11	.303	.345	.419	475	144	22	3	9	42	30	62
Bases Empty	.321	.373	.457	346	111	12	1	11	11	28	43	.276	.326	.406	1295	358	59	14	27	27	91	185
Leadoff	.356	.397	.473	146	52	6	1	3	3	10	14	.299	.348	.434	548	164	27	7	11	11	40	78
Runners On Base	.271	.324	.415	284	77	15	1	8	84	24	33	.278	.332	.392	908	252	46	5	16	204	76	122
Scoring Position	.263	.313	.425	186	49	10	1	6	77	16	18	.276	.340	.407	555	153	30	2	13	186	58	77
Late and Close	.347	.398	.459	98	34	8	0	1	21	9	18	.257	.313	.358	397	102	15	2	7	53	33	65

OZZIE GUILLEN — BL/TR — age 30 — CHA SS133

1993	BA	OBA	SA	AB	H	2B	3B	HR	RBI	BB	SO	BA	OBA	SA	AB	H	2B	3B	HR	RBI	BB	SO
Total	.280	.292	.374	457	128	23	4	4	50	10	41	.267	.288	.337	4298	1149	166	46	14	388	134	349
vs. Left	.231	.241	.292	130	30	4	2	0	6	2	11	.239	.256	.281	1317	315	35	7	2	105	31	132
vs. Right	.300	.312	.407	327	98	19	2	4	44	8	30	.280	.302	.362	2981	834	131	39	12	283	103	217
at Home	.297	.309	.396	212	63	10	1	3	22	5	19	.275	.296	.349	2080	571	74	27	9	201	73	164
on Road	.265	.277	.355	245	65	13	3	1	28	5	22	.261	.280	.326	2218	578	92	19	5	187	61	185
on Grass	.278	.290	.368	378	105	18	2	4	40	8	29	.265	.287	.336	3659	971	142	39	13	329	116	297
on Turf	.291	.301	.405	79	23	5	2	0	10	2	12	.279	.296	.343	639	178	24	7	1	59	18	52
Day Games	.277	.296	.377	130	36	5	1	2	19	4	7	.274	.298	.344	1176	322	45	14	3	108	43	89
Night Games	.281	.290	.373	327	92	18	3	2	31	6	34	.265	.284	.335	3122	827	121	32	11	280	91	260
April	.200	.230	.243	70	14	1	1	0	8	3	4	.246	.277	.304	589	145	22	6	0	48	27	46
May	.278	.293	.389	54	15	3	0	1	8	2	4	.276	.302	.341	731	202	22	8	1	50	28	61
June	.310	.322	.379	87	27	4	1	0	7	2	6	.263	.275	.320	734	193	27	6	1	69	13	54
July	.301	.318	.482	83	25	6	0	3	13	2	11	.289	.307	.364	720	208	33	6	3	81	20	58
August	.247	.240	.342	73	18	5	1	0	6	0	11	.264	.281	.345	754	199	33	8	4	66	20	58
Sept-Oct	.322	.330	.389	90	29	4	1	0	8	1	5	.262	.285	.343	770	202	29	12	3	74	26	69
Bases Empty	.272	.294	.345	261	71	15	2	0	0	8	23	.253	.278	.315	2522	638	93	24	5	5	82	241
Leadoff	.293	.320	.333	99	29	4	0	0	0	4	6	.257	.282	.307	1061	273	41	6	0	0	37	109
Runners On Base	.291	.289	.413	196	57	8	2	4	50	2	18	.288	.302	.369	1776	511	73	22	9	383	52	108
Scoring Position	.304	.300	.393	112	34	3	2	1	42	2	12	.295	.317	.383	1029	304	41	17	5	364	48	65
Late and Close	.273	.296	.312	77	21	3	0	0	8	3	11	.283	.313	.346	789	223	27	7	3	79	37	70

RICKY GUTIERREZ — BR/TR — age 24 — SD SS117, 2B6, OF5, 3B4

1993	BA	OBA	SA	AB	H	2B	3B	HR	RBI	BB	SO		BA	OBA	SA	AB	H	2B	3B	HR	RBI	BB	SO
Total	.251	.334	.331	438	110	10	5	5	26	50	97		.251	.334	.331	438	110	10	5	5	26	50	97
vs. Left	.277	.365	.365	159	44	3	1	3	12	22	32		.277	.365	.365	159	44	3	1	3	12	22	32
vs. Right	.237	.316	.312	279	66	7	4	2	14	28	65		.237	.316	.312	279	66	7	4	2	14	28	65
at Home	.257	.335	.339	230	59	2	1	5	16	24	58		.257	.335	.339	230	59	2	1	5	16	24	58
on Road	.245	.333	.322	208	51	8	4	0	10	26	39		.245	.333	.322	208	51	8	4	0	10	26	39
on Grass	.263	.346	.341	346	91	8	2	5	23	39	81		.263	.346	.341	346	91	8	2	5	23	39	81
on Turf	.207	.288	.293	92	19	2	3	0	3	11	16		.207	.288	.293	92	19	2	3	0	3	11	16
Day Games	.240	.338	.352	125	30	3	1	3	10	17	26		.240	.338	.352	125	30	3	1	3	10	17	26
Night Games	.256	.332	.323	313	80	7	4	2	16	33	71		.256	.332	.323	313	80	7	4	2	16	33	71
April	.364	.447	.364	33	12	0	0	0	1	4	9		.364	.447	.364	33	12	0	0	0	1	4	9
May	.229	.308	.257	35	8	1	0	0	0	4	3		.229	.308	.257	35	8	1	0	0	0	4	3
June	.284	.330	.352	88	25	1	1	1	7	6	25		.284	.330	.352	88	25	1	1	1	7	6	25
July	.263	.376	.434	99	26	3	4	2	8	18	21		.263	.376	.434	99	26	3	4	2	8	18	21
August	.239	.336	.293	92	22	5	0	0	3	12	15		.239	.336	.293	92	22	5	0	0	3	12	15
Sept-Oct	.187	.253	.253	91	17	0	0	2	7	6	24		.187	.253	.253	91	17	0	0	2	7	6	24
Bases Empty	.254	.337	.342	272	69	9	3	3	3	30	61		.254	.337	.342	272	69	9	3	3	3	30	61
Leadoff	.281	.360	.364	121	34	3	2	1	1	12	30		.281	.360	.364	121	34	3	2	1	1	12	30
Runners On Base	.247	.330	.313	166	41	1	2	2	23	20	36		.247	.330	.313	166	41	1	2	2	23	20	36
Scoring Position	.210	.322	.230	100	21	0	1	0	17	17	20		.210	.322	.230	100	21	0	1	0	17	17	20
Late and Close	.321	.424	.359	78	25	1	1	0	4	13	23		.321	.424	.359	78	25	1	1	0	4	13	23

1-YEAR TOTALS (1993)

TONY GWYNN — BL/TL — age 34 — SD OF121

1993	BA	OBA	SA	AB	H	2B	3B	HR	RBI	BB	SO		BA	OBA	SA	AB	H	2B	3B	HR	RBI	BB	SO
Total	.358	.398	.497	489	175	41	3	7	59	36	19		.332	.385	.443	5696	1890	292	74	64	596	505	273
vs. Left	.359	.393	.490	192	69	14	1	3	20	11	6		.317	.367	.410	2131	676	82	22	24	213	163	109
vs. Right	.357	.401	.502	297	106	27	2	4	39	25	13		.341	.396	.462	3565	1214	210	52	40	383	342	164
at Home	.382	.421	.524	254	97	20	2	4	32	20	14		.338	.394	.456	2781	941	135	42	36	275	260	145
on Road	.332	.373	.468	235	78	21	1	3	27	16	5		.326	.377	.430	2915	949	157	32	28	321	245	128
on Grass	.380	.422	.518	371	141	32	2	5	49	31	16		.331	.386	.440	4176	1381	207	55	46	411	382	206
on Turf	.288	.320	.432	118	34	9	1	2	10	5	3		.335	.383	.451	1520	509	85	19	18	185	123	67
Day Games	.341	.379	.515	167	57	12	1	5	21	10	6		.309	.366	.415	1766	545	83	21	21	186	165	91
Night Games	.366	.407	.488	322	118	29	2	2	38	26	13		.342	.394	.455	3930	1345	209	53	43	410	340	182
April	.295	.330	.400	95	28	5	1	1	8	6	3		.330	.378	.457	863	285	47	13	12	69	69	45
May	.342	.385	.414	111	38	8	0	0	8	8	3		.325	.390	.453	950	309	56	16	11	103	99	39
June	.286	.344	.482	56	16	6	1	1	9	5	7		.343	.398	.467	1036	355	53	17	14	131	101	51
July	.381	.420	.581	105	40	10	1	3	16	7	4		.317	.362	.423	1021	324	46	10	14	107	73	59
August	.448	.487	.600	105	47	10	0	2	14	10	2		.354	.402	.448	1079	382	58	8	9	107	88	49
Sept-Oct	.353	.333	.471	17	6	2	0	0	4	0	0		.315	.375	.400	747	235	32	10	4	79	75	30
Bases Empty	.343	.385	.471	289	99	21	2	4	4	19	15		.319	.361	.425	3377	1076	158	40	40	40	215	173
Leadoff	.328	.389	.462	119	39	6	2	2	2	11	7		.333	.370	.439	1146	382	45	17	14	14	63	53
Runners On Base	.380	.415	.535	200	76	20	1	3	55	17	4		.351	.418	.469	2319	814	134	34	24	556	290	100
Scoring Position	.372	.440	.547	86	32	10	1	1	49	16	4		.338	.436	.457	1196	404	69	20	11	490	237	68
Late and Close	.371	.416	.539	89	33	9	0	2	18	8	2		.339	.406	.444	953	323	45	8	13	113	112	54

10-YEAR TOTALS (1984–1993)

DARRYL HAMILTON — BL/TR — age 30 — MIL OF129, DH1

1993	BA	OBA	SA	AB	H	2B	3B	HR	RBI	BB	SO		BA	OBA	SA	AB	H	2B	3B	HR	RBI	BB	SO
Total	.310	.367	.406	520	161	21	1	9	48	45	62		.297	.353	.384	1654	492	64	14	17	196	144	163
vs. Left	.264	.316	.308	182	48	3	1	1	10	13	25		.244	.302	.295	397	97	11	3	1	35	31	49
vs. Right	.334	.394	.459	338	113	18	0	8	38	32	37		.314	.369	.412	1257	395	53	11	16	161	113	114
at Home	.317	.388	.416	262	83	9	1	5	28	30	30		.303	.369	.397	796	241	33	9	8	94	85	78
on Road	.302	.345	.395	258	78	12	0	4	20	15	32		.293	.338	.372	858	251	31	5	9	102	59	85
on Grass	.319	.380	.414	423	135	14	1	8	42	39	55		.295	.351	.379	1355	400	52	10	14	163	118	141
on Turf	.268	.311	.371	97	26	7	0	1	6	6	7		.308	.362	.405	299	92	12	4	3	33	26	22
Day Games	.278	.322	.366	194	54	6	1	3	15	12	22		.275	.330	.357	560	154	18	5	6	64	45	45
Night Games	.328	.393	.429	326	107	15	0	6	33	33	40		.309	.365	.398	1094	338	46	9	11	132	99	118
April	.346	.393	.359	78	27	1	0	0	7	5	8		.279	.350	.324	179	50	3	1	1	20	19	20
May	.304	.385	.411	56	17	3	0	1	3	8	6		.267	.326	.359	131	35	6	0	2	10	12	12
June	.314	.357	.390	105	33	5	0	1	11	7	11		.329	.371	.402	286	94	14	2	1	37	20	25
July	.327	.377	.439	98	32	5	0	2	8	8	12		.287	.342	.399	376	108	21	3	5	40	33	45
August	.296	.355	.469	98	29	3	1	4	12	7	13		.305	.355	.410	344	105	13	4	5	50	26	27
Sept-Oct	.271	.347	.353	85	23	4	0	1	7	10	12		.296	.361	.367	338	100	7	4	3	39	34	34
Bases Empty	.320	.364	.451	319	102	13	1	9	9	21	41		.285	.338	.384	956	272	40	8	13	13	76	107
Leadoff	.329	.366	.480	173	57	9	1	5	5	9	23		.288	.330	.399	416	120	22	3	6	6	25	46
Runners On Base	.294	.373	.333	201	59	8	0	0	39	24	21		.315	.373	.384	698	220	24	6	4	183	68	56
Scoring Position	.315	.425	.351	111	35	4	0	0	35	20	16		.319	.384	.392	423	135	14	4	3	174	49	41
Late and Close	.349	.413	.470	83	29	5	1	1	9	9	10		.352	.421	.447	253	89	12	3	2	31	31	29

5-YEAR TOTALS (1988–1993)

BRIAN HARPER — BR/TR — age 35 — MIN C134, DH7

1993	BA	OBA	SA	AB	H	2B	3B	HR	RBI	BB	SO	BA	OBA	SA	AB	H	2B	3B	HR	RBI	BB	SO
Total	.304	.347	.425	530	161	26	1	12	73	29	29	.301	.336	.421	2720	818	166	6	50	371	121	149
vs. Left	.333	.373	.545	123	41	9	1	5	25	8	9	.286	.327	.424	860	246	59	3	18	118	53	55
vs. Right	.295	.339	.388	407	120	17	0	7	48	21	20	.308	.340	.420	1860	572	107	3	32	253	68	94
at Home	.325	.374	.471	255	83	17	1	6	42	19	13	.309	.345	.422	1319	407	82	5	19	177	69	70
on Road	.284	.322	.382	275	78	9	0	6	31	10	16	.293	.327	.421	1401	411	84	1	31	194	52	79
on Grass	.275	.317	.368	204	56	7	0	4	20	9	13	.284	.320	.412	1034	294	60	0	24	147	45	65
on Turf	.322	.366	.460	326	105	19	1	8	53	20	16	.311	.345	.427	1686	524	106	6	26	224	76	84
Day Games	.321	.379	.459	159	51	11	1	3	25	12	7	.312	.351	.445	751	234	54	2	14	122	38	39
Night Games	.296	.333	.410	371	110	15	0	9	48	17	22	.297	.330	.412	1969	584	112	4	36	249	83	110
April	.319	.347	.391	69	22	5	0	0	8	3	2	.303	.348	.431	290	88	19	0	6	40	16	9
May	.299	.344	.448	87	26	4	0	3	16	4	6	.294	.330	.428	425	125	30	0	9	79	20	27
June	.326	.379	.500	86	28	3	0	4	12	5	4	.309	.350	.420	457	141	25	1	8	51	22	29
July	.298	.323	.447	94	28	5	0	3	17	2	7	.310	.335	.414	493	153	30	0	7	64	16	24
August	.330	.381	.447	103	34	6	0	2	12	9	3	.307	.333	.456	540	166	32	3	14	80	19	25
Sept-Oct	.253	.307	.308	91	23	3	1	0	8	6	7	.282	.324	.383	515	145	30	2	6	57	28	35
Bases Empty	.288	.326	.438	313	90	18	1	9	9	14	17	.291	.325	.415	1449	421	88	3	29	29	53	73
Leadoff	.299	.324	.485	134	40	8	1	5	5	4	5	.309	.339	.463	596	184	42	1	16	16	20	18
Runners On Base	.327	.376	.406	217	71	8	0	3	64	15	12	.312	.348	.428	1271	397	78	3	21	342	68	76
Scoring Position	.358	.417	.418	134	48	5	0	1	56	13	8	.307	.351	.407	739	227	42	1	10	302	52	46
Late and Close	.306	.346	.439	98	30	4	0	3	14	7	9	.306	.341	.428	451	138	17	1	12	72	23	26

10-YEAR TOTALS (1984–1993)

BILLY HATCHER — BR/TR — age 34 — BOS OF130, 2B2

1993	BA	OBA	SA	AB	H	2B	3B	HR	RBI	BB	SO	BA	OBA	SA	AB	H	2B	3B	HR	RBI	BB	SO
Total	.287	.336	.400	508	146	24	3	9	57	28	46	.266	.315	.366	4029	1072	195	28	51	368	249	447
vs. Left	.232	.269	.304	138	32	7	0	1	14	7	11	.264	.308	.361	1445	382	63	11	18	130	92	151
vs. Right	.308	.360	.435	370	114	17	3	8	43	21	35	.267	.319	.370	2584	690	132	17	33	238	157	296
at Home	.295	.344	.418	261	77	13	2	5	35	16	23	.265	.318	.360	1998	530	100	15	20	181	137	221
on Road	.279	.327	.381	247	69	11	1	4	22	12	23	.267	.312	.372	2031	542	95	13	31	187	112	226
on Grass	.286	.338	.409	440	126	21	3	9	54	26	41	.263	.311	.374	1764	464	76	13	31	177	107	188
on Turf	.294	.324	.338	68	20	3	0	0	3	2	5	.268	.318	.361	2265	608	119	15	20	191	142	259
Day Games	.294	.370	.412	160	47	11	1	2	24	14	13	.266	.324	.397	1287	342	79	9	24	147	93	119
Night Games	.284	.319	.394	348	99	13	2	7	33	14	33	.266	.311	.352	2742	730	116	19	27	221	156	328
April	.226	.284	.274	62	14	3	0	0	3	4	6	.275	.315	.373	502	138	20	4	7	48	26	70
May	.375	.407	.490	104	39	4	1	2	13	5	8	.302	.349	.381	609	184	28	4	4	54	37	65
June	.271	.340	.427	96	26	6	0	3	14	7	8	.277	.327	.416	762	211	45	8	15	77	51	93
July	.361	.400	.536	97	35	8	0	3	20	5	8	.271	.322	.357	683	185	41	0	6	63	46	79
August	.227	.283	.330	97	22	3	2	1	7	6	10	.259	.311	.380	719	186	39	6	12	69	47	71
Sept-Oct	.192	.222	.192	52	10	0	0	0	0	1	6	.223	.273	.296	754	168	22	6	7	57	42	69
Bases Empty	.268	.313	.351	299	80	12	2	3	3	15	25	.259	.307	.360	2514	651	126	16	32	32	140	282
Leadoff	.254	.283	.344	122	31	4	2	1	1	4	11	.261	.316	.354	1136	297	59	8	10	10	74	136
Runners On Base	.316	.366	.469	209	66	12	1	6	54	13	21	.278	.329	.377	1515	421	69	12	19	336	109	165
Scoring Position	.336	.385	.504	119	40	6	1	4	48	10	11	.272	.331	.369	914	249	42	8	10	305	84	107
Late and Close	.338	.378	.515	68	23	4	1	2	11	3	7	.291	.341	.402	659	192	35	7	8	80	44	94

10-YEAR TOTALS (1984–1993)

CHARLIE HAYES — BR/TR — age 29 — COL 3B154, SS1

1993	BA	OBA	SA	AB	H	2B	3B	HR	RBI	BB	SO	BA	OBA	SA	AB	H	2B	3B	HR	RBI	BB	SO
Total	.305	.355	.522	573	175	45	2	25	98	43	82	.263	.300	.409	2418	636	122	6	73	317	126	401
vs. Left	.338	.367	.542	142	48	14	0	5	21	6	21	.272	.303	.412	791	215	48	0	21	97	34	118
vs. Right	.295	.351	.515	431	127	31	2	20	77	37	61	.259	.298	.407	1627	421	74	6	52	220	92	283
at Home	.338	.387	.601	296	100	23	2	17	66	24	36	.263	.301	.412	1232	324	66	5	36	180	67	196
on Road	.271	.319	.437	277	75	22	0	8	32	19	46	.263	.298	.406	1186	312	56	1	37	137	59	205
on Grass	.304	.355	.523	438	133	32	2	20	78	34	61	.268	.310	.443	1210	324	60	4	48	174	73	200
on Turf	.311	.354	.519	135	42	13	0	5	20	9	21	.258	.289	.375	1208	312	62	2	25	143	53	201
Day Games	.280	.329	.461	193	54	12	1	7	29	14	32	.254	.289	.400	708	180	35	4	20	80	35	123
Night Games	.318	.368	.553	380	121	33	1	18	69	29	50	.267	.304	.413	1710	456	87	2	53	237	91	278
April	.317	.359	.561	82	26	5	0	5	18	6	4	.282	.310	.415	301	85	13	0	9	46	12	37
May	.240	.302	.404	104	25	8	0	3	13	9	18	.239	.285	.393	389	93	19	1	13	41	25	69
June	.381	.449	.595	84	32	6	0	4	18	10	14	.290	.338	.429	352	102	17	1	10	47	25	67
July	.330	.343	.560	100	33	1	0	5	16	2	16	.240	.272	.395	413	99	17	1	5	60	18	78
August	.226	.255	.398	93	21	7	0	3	9	4	13	.252	.275	.398	523	132	32	1	14	57	17	75
Sept-Oct	.345	.415	.618	110	38	13	1	5	24	12	17	.284	.329	.430	440	125	24	2	12	66	29	75
Bases Empty	.303	.356	.502	317	96	28	1	11	11	22	50	.259	.297	.403	1353	350	67	4	40	40	68	236
Leadoff	.301	.326	.571	133	40	15	0	7	7	5	18	.269	.294	.466	562	151	35	2	24	24	20	83
Runners On Base	.309	.353	.547	256	79	17	1	14	87	21	32	.269	.304	.417	1065	286	55	2	33	277	58	165
Scoring Position	.318	.374	.601	148	47	12	0	10	77	17	23	.262	.303	.417	592	155	30	1	20	238	41	103
Late and Close	.319	.378	.472	72	23	8	0	1	13	7	13	.274	.310	.421	413	113	23	1	12	49	21	82

6-YEAR TOTALS (1988–1993)

DAVE HENDERSON — BR/TR — age 36 — OAK OF76, DH28

1993	BA	OBA	SA	AB	H	2B	3B	HR	RBI	BB	SO
Total	.220	.275	.427	382	84	19	0	20	53	32	113
vs. Left	.225	.291	.500	142	32	6	0	11	29	14	36
vs. Right	.217	.265	.383	240	52	13	0	9	24	18	77
at Home	.194	.239	.336	211	41	9	0	7	27	14	47
on Road	.251	.318	.538	171	43	10	0	13	26	18	66
on Grass	.206	.257	.390	344	71	15	0	16	46	26	105
on Turf	.342	.432	.763	38	13	4	0	4	7	6	8
Day Games	.181	.234	.381	155	28	7	0	8	18	12	56
Night Games	.247	.303	.458	227	56	12	0	12	35	20	57
April	.179	.283	.333	39	7	0	0	2	6	6	16
May	.238	.273	.500	84	20	4	0	6	8	4	20
June	.000	.105	.000	16	0	0	0	0	1	2	5
July	.216	.274	.432	74	16	4	0	4	13	7	29
August	.202	.247	.326	89	18	5	0	2	10	6	26
Sept-Oct	.287	.341	.587	80	23	6	0	6	15	7	17
Bases Empty	.249	.318	.533	197	49	11	0	15	15	20	53
Leadoff	.241	.326	.557	79	19	7	0	6	6	10	24
Runners On Base	.189	.229	.314	185	35	8	0	5	38	12	60
Scoring Position	.161	.209	.277	112	18	4	0	3	33	9	43
Late and Close	.216	.286	.338	74	16	3	0	2	8	8	22

10-YEAR TOTALS (1984–1993)

	BA	OBA	SA	AB	H	2B	3B	HR	RBI	BB	SO
Total	.261	.324	.439	3998	1042	228	10	155	560	369	892
vs. Left	.293	.353	.510	1209	354	79	3	59	188	110	213
vs. Right	.247	.311	.408	2789	688	149	7	96	372	259	679
at Home	.266	.327	.449	2057	548	108	6	85	300	183	454
on Road	.255	.320	.429	1941	494	120	4	70	260	186	438
on Grass	.256	.319	.428	2864	733	155	4	110	396	263	657
on Turf	.272	.337	.466	1134	309	73	6	45	164	106	235
Day Games	.264	.325	.459	1362	359	76	2	62	208	128	303
Night Games	.259	.323	.429	2636	683	152	8	93	352	241	589
April	.259	.344	.453	537	139	23	3	25	74	70	131
May	.269	.318	.471	715	192	39	2	34	106	49	142
June	.243	.316	.428	680	165	41	2	27	96	71	153
July	.266	.321	.429	708	188	37	2	25	95	59	160
August	.268	.323	.430	682	183	45	1	21	89	53	146
Sept-Oct	.259	.325	.425	676	175	43	0	23	100	67	160
Bases Empty	.261	.330	.463	2160	563	123	5	101	101	211	464
Leadoff	.284	.337	.505	848	241	60	2	41	41	64	166
Runners On Base	.261	.316	.411	1838	479	105	5	54	459	158	428
Scoring Position	.261	.327	.395	1064	278	58	3	26	382	114	266
Late and Close	.255	.311	.430	642	164	24	2	28	80	52	149

RICKEY HENDERSON — BR/TL — age 36 — OAK/TOR OF118, DH16

1993	BA	OBA	SA	AB	H	2B	3B	HR	RBI	BB	SO
Total	.289	.432	.474	481	139	22	2	21	59	120	65
vs. Left	.315	.461	.623	130	41	4	0	12	16	35	23
vs. Right	.279	.421	.419	351	98	18	2	9	43	85	42
at Home	.283	.422	.458	251	71	12	1	10	26	60	39
on Road	.296	.442	.491	230	68	10	1	11	33	60	26
on Grass	.315	.458	.524	336	106	17	1	17	43	88	41
on Turf	.228	.369	.359	145	33	5	1	4	16	32	24
Day Games	.292	.459	.443	185	54	10	0	6	15	55	26
Night Games	.287	.414	.493	296	85	12	2	15	44	65	39
April	.286	.444	.492	63	18	4	0	3	11	17	5
May	.309	.478	.485	68	21	4	1	2	8	21	18
June	.313	.472	.469	96	30	3	0	4	13	29	11
July	.385	.477	.736	91	35	8	0	8	15	18	12
August	.208	.374	.286	77	16	1	1	1	4	20	12
Sept-Oct	.221	.340	.349	86	19	2	0	3	8	15	7
Bases Empty	.301	.438	.527	296	89	13	0	18	18	69	39
Leadoff	.324	.459	.589	185	60	7	0	14	14	45	32
Runners On Base	.270	.423	.389	185	50	9	2	3	41	51	26
Scoring Position	.241	.407	.384	112	27	5	1	3	39	33	20
Late and Close	.243	.367	.419	74	18	3	2	2	11	15	13

10-YEAR TOTALS (1984–1993)

	BA	OBA	SA	AB	H	2B	3B	HR	RBI	BB	SO
Total	.290	.409	.465	4946	1436	249	31	185	571	972	655
vs. Left	.303	.425	.520	1494	452	86	10	73	163	317	198
vs. Right	.285	.402	.442	3452	984	163	21	112	408	655	457
at Home	.286	.410	.456	2361	676	119	16	83	262	486	304
on Road	.294	.407	.474	2585	760	130	15	102	309	486	351
on Grass	.289	.408	.463	4075	1177	203	25	152	468	808	533
on Turf	.297	.410	.478	871	259	46	6	33	103	164	122
Day Games	.290	.416	.454	1626	471	83	5	58	185	346	219
Night Games	.291	.405	.471	3320	965	166	26	127	386	626	436
April	.293	.401	.474	685	201	39	5	25	90	123	90
May	.291	.417	.461	896	261	50	6	30	96	186	128
June	.326	.443	.503	778	254	37	5	30	101	163	92
July	.312	.423	.514	815	254	49	4	36	106	155	97
August	.261	.373	.411	820	214	30	3	29	87	143	110
Sept-Oct	.265	.396	.438	952	252	44	8	35	91	202	138
Bases Empty	.292	.403	.478	3254	951	178	22	128	128	576	429
Leadoff	.295	.403	.501	2040	602	112	18	91	91	358	264
Runners On Base	.287	.419	.440	1692	485	71	9	57	443	396	226
Scoring Position	.250	.406	.387	1010	253	34	4	32	368	276	158
Late and Close	.312	.434	.505	705	220	33	8	29	124	156	98

CHRIS HOILES — BR/TR — age 29 — BAL C124, DH2

1993	BA	OBA	SA	AB	H	2B	3B	HR	RBI	BB	SO
Total	.310	.416	.585	419	130	28	0	29	82	69	94
vs. Left	.318	.442	.618	110	35	9	0	8	25	25	22
vs. Right	.307	.406	.573	309	95	19	0	21	57	44	72
at Home	.322	.433	.620	205	66	13	0	16	46	38	46
on Road	.299	.399	.551	214	64	15	0	13	36	31	48
on Grass	.320	.419	.596	359	115	24	0	25	74	58	81
on Turf	.250	.400	.517	60	15	4	0	4	8	11	13
Day Games	.274	.406	.607	84	23	4	0	8	15	17	27
Night Games	.319	.419	.579	335	107	24	0	21	67	52	67
April	.220	.333	.373	59	13	3	0	2	4	8	18
May	.287	.402	.563	80	23	7	0	5	12	14	26
June	.350	.429	.675	80	28	5	0	7	18	11	13
July	.301	.426	.530	83	25	4	0	5	20	15	12
August	.269	.333	.423	26	7	1	0	1	3	3	6
Sept-Oct	.374	.482	.758	91	34	8	0	9	25	18	19
Bases Empty	.292	.401	.542	236	69	14	0	15	15	39	50
Leadoff	.307	.402	.533	75	23	5	0	4	4	12	20
Runners On Base	.333	.434	.639	183	61	14	0	14	67	30	44
Scoring Position	.280	.409	.500	100	28	4	0	6	46	21	27
Late and Close	.260	.349	.493	73	19	5	0	4	14	7	20

5-YEAR TOTALS (1989–1993)

	BA	OBA	SA	AB	H	2B	3B	HR	RBI	BB	SO
Total	.272	.365	.484	1142	311	57	1	61	160	159	230
vs. Left	.267	.366	.469	341	91	15	0	18	38	54	52
vs. Right	.275	.365	.491	801	220	42	1	43	122	105	178
at Home	.278	.374	.489	558	155	28	0	30	81	82	106
on Road	.267	.357	.479	584	156	29	1	31	79	77	124
on Grass	.277	.368	.498	962	266	46	1	55	138	135	193
on Turf	.250	.351	.411	180	45	11	0	6	22	24	37
Day Games	.248	.340	.504	266	66	11	0	19	39	36	66
Night Games	.280	.373	.478	876	245	46	1	42	121	123	164
April	.244	.337	.425	160	39	8	0	7	15	20	39
May	.272	.405	.502	213	58	11	1	12	27	47	48
June	.274	.358	.512	201	55	9	0	13	34	26	35
July	.304	.385	.506	158	48	8	0	8	30	18	24
August	.236	.291	.354	161	38	7	0	4	14	13	34
Sept-Oct	.293	.384	.554	249	73	14	0	17	40	35	50
Bases Empty	.282	.373	.526	642	181	29	1	42	42	88	121
Leadoff	.275	.354	.538	247	68	12	1	17	17	30	50
Runners On Base	.260	.356	.430	500	130	28	0	19	118	71	109
Scoring Position	.237	.360	.409	257	61	11	0	11	95	50	66
Late and Close	.225	.304	.461	191	43	6	0	13	36	19	50

DAVE HOLLINS — BB/TR — age 28 — PHI 3B143

1993	BA	OBA	SA	AB	H	2B	3B	HR	RBI	BB	SO		4-YEAR TOTALS (1990–1993) BA	OBA	SA	AB	H	2B	3B	HR	RBI	BB	SO
Total	.273	.372	.442	543	148	30	4	18	93	85	109		.267	.362	.451	1394	372	68	10	56	222	188	273
vs. Left	.323	.369	.549	195	63	14	3	8	34	13	33		.320	.379	.584	531	170	31	8	31	96	43	98
vs. Right	.244	.373	.382	348	85	16	1	10	59	72	76		.234	.353	.368	863	202	37	2	25	126	145	175
at Home	.271	.378	.431	262	71	13	1	9	39	44	49		.259	.371	.453	671	174	38	4	28	101	106	131
on Road	.274	.366	.452	281	77	17	3	9	54	41	60		.274	.353	.448	723	198	30	6	28	121	82	142
on Grass	.303	.397	.497	185	56	14	2	6	38	28	35		.290	.373	.491	411	119	21	4	18	81	48	84
on Turf	.257	.359	.413	358	92	16	2	12	55	57	74		.257	.358	.433	983	253	47	6	38	141	140	189
Day Games	.284	.395	.432	148	42	10	0	4	23	27	36		.283	.381	.492	378	107	21	2	18	67	54	82
Night Games	.268	.363	.446	395	106	20	4	14	70	58	73		.261	.355	.435	1016	265	47	8	38	155	134	191
April	.282	.374	.424	85	24	6	0	2	17	13	21		.237	.353	.360	186	44	8	0	5	33	28	42
May	.317	.408	.587	104	33	8	1	6	26	15	20		.301	.403	.539	206	62	15	2	10	38	32	39
June	.189	.347	.324	37	7	2	0	1	5	10	11		.237	.322	.399	173	41	5	1	7	21	23	35
July	.241	.315	.348	112	27	2	2	2	13	11	17		.270	.355	.477	281	76	12	5	12	47	29	57
August	.295	.417	.495	95	28	7	0	4	15	18	20		.268	.379	.459	220	59	12	0	10	32	36	45
Sept-Oct	.264	.362	.409	110	29	5	1	3	17	18	20		.274	.356	.445	328	90	16	2	12	51	40	55
Bases Empty	.252	.342	.405	242	61	11	1	8	8	32	47		.244	.333	.408	710	173	35	5	24	24	83	146
Leadoff	.244	.326	.285	123	30	2	0	1	1	14	28		.239	.320	.312	285	68	12	0	3	3	29	68
Runners On Base	.289	.395	.472	301	87	19	3	10	85	53	62		.291	.391	.494	684	199	33	5	32	198	105	127
Scoring Position	.294	.412	.476	170	50	14	1	5	70	37	40		.279	.399	.446	401	112	24	2	13	152	80	78
Late and Close	.232	.323	.390	82	19	2	1	3	16	11	24		.216	.312	.362	232	50	6	2	8	35	27	56

KENT HRBEK — BL/TR — age 34 — MIN 1B115, DH2

1993	BA	OBA	SA	AB	H	2B	3B	HR	RBI	BB	SO		10-YEAR TOTALS (1984–1993) BA	OBA	SA	AB	H	2B	3B	HR	RBI	BB	SO
Total	.242	.357	.467	392	95	11	1	25	83	71	57		.280	.369	.484	4804	1346	234	9	243	850	685	610
vs. Left	.224	.352	.397	58	13	1	0	3	14	12	12		.265	.343	.409	1314	348	50	1	46	215	155	217
vs. Right	.246	.358	.479	334	82	10	1	22	69	59	45		.286	.379	.513	3490	998	184	8	197	635	530	393
at Home	.249	.364	.482	193	48	7	1	12	45	35	28		.296	.384	.522	2424	718	130	8	134	502	352	305
on Road	.236	.350	.452	199	47	4	0	13	38	36	29		.264	.354	.446	2380	628	104	1	109	348	333	305
on Grass	.257	.369	.536	140	36	3	0	12	33	26	17		.268	.357	.465	1788	479	83	0	90	280	249	225
on Turf	.234	.350	.429	252	59	8	1	13	50	45	40		.287	.376	.496	3016	867	151	9	153	570	436	385
Day Games	.250	.363	.466	148	37	5	0	9	32	28	20		.278	.364	.475	1470	409	75	2	70	252	202	178
Night Games	.238	.353	.467	244	58	6	1	16	51	43	37		.281	.372	.489	3334	937	159	7	173	598	483	432
April	.303	.395	.530	66	20	4	1	3	14	10	9		.274	.375	.462	656	180	38	2	27	117	102	78
May	.219	.366	.469	64	14	1	0	5	13	16	10		.277	.370	.494	808	224	35	1	46	141	123	90
June	.129	.206	.226	31	4	0	0	1	2	3	5		.304	.388	.510	733	223	42	2	35	124	99	95
July	.240	.330	.413	75	18	1	0	4	17	10	10		.265	.356	.483	873	231	35	0	52	165	121	110
August	.221	.339	.400	95	21	2	0	5	17	17	16		.282	.360	.485	980	276	41	1	52	171	128	138
Sept-Oct	.295	.434	.689	61	18	3	0	7	20	15	7		.281	.372	.469	754	212	43	3	31	132	112	99
Bases Empty	.224	.327	.413	196	44	7	0	10	10	29	23		.278	.357	.485	2490	691	139	4	123	123	295	314
Leadoff	.219	.312	.417	96	21	4	0	5	5	13	12		.271	.347	.482	1076	292	58	2	55	55	120	128
Runners On Base	.260	.384	.520	196	51	4	1	15	73	42	34		.283	.381	.484	2314	655	95	5	120	727	390	296
Scoring Position	.206	.354	.405	126	26	2	1	7	55	31	23		.265	.385	.450	1289	342	61	3	57	577	276	180
Late and Close	.333	.459	.417	60	20	5	0	0	5	14	3		.299	.392	.460	708	212	33	0	27	107	111	87

TIM HULETT — BR/TR — age 34 — BAL 3B75, SS8, 2B4, DH2

1993	BA	OBA	SA	AB	H	2B	3B	HR	RBI	BB	SO		9-YEAR TOTALS (1984–1993) BA	OBA	SA	AB	H	2B	3B	HR	RBI	BB	SO
Total	.300	.361	.381	260	78	15	0	2	23	23	56		.250	.298	.374	2020	505	88	12	46	205	133	411
vs. Left	.288	.324	.346	104	30	6	0	0	7	6	18		.254	.301	.401	778	198	31	7	23	83	53	146
vs. Right	.308	.384	.404	156	48	9	0	2	16	17	38		.247	.296	.357	1242	307	57	5	23	122	80	265
at Home	.333	.393	.452	126	42	9	0	2	9	13	28		.257	.310	.382	948	244	40	9	20	85	72	198
on Road	.269	.331	.313	134	36	6	0	0	14	10	28		.243	.287	.367	1072	261	48	3	26	120	61	213
on Grass	.301	.365	.384	216	65	12	0	2	17	21	46		.251	.301	.381	1696	426	67	12	43	169	117	346
on Turf	.295	.340	.364	44	13	3	0	0	6	2	10		.244	.282	.336	324	79	21	0	3	36	16	65
Day Games	.291	.337	.329	79	23	3	0	0	6	5	16		.278	.322	.405	558	155	30	4	11	63	36	108
Night Games	.304	.371	.403	181	55	12	0	2	17	18	40		.239	.289	.362	1462	350	58	8	35	142	97	303
April	.391	.417	.522	23	9	3	0	0	2	1	4		.262	.302	.366	191	50	8	0	4	24	11	43
May	.276	.300	.310	29	8	1	0	0	1	1	7		.278	.313	.460	363	101	18	6	12	46	16	60
June	.263	.364	.316	19	5	1	0	0	1	3	3		.233	.292	.328	378	88	18	3	4	26	32	71
July	.342	.375	.447	76	26	8	0	0	5	2	13		.265	.316	.403	325	86	14	2	9	36	22	68
August	.289	.371	.373	83	24	1	0	2	11	11	19		.231	.293	.330	385	89	11	0	9	35	34	85
Sept-Oct	.200	.314	.233	30	6	1	0	0	3	5	10		.241	.276	.360	378	91	19	1	8	38	18	84
Bases Empty	.323	.375	.414	133	43	9	0	1	1	9	25		.253	.300	.399	1139	288	50	9	33	33	71	214
Leadoff	.358	.424	.434	53	19	4	0	0	0	6	11		.238	.277	.371	453	108	19	4	11	11	23	90
Runners On Base	.276	.347	.346	127	35	6	0	1	22	14	31		.246	.295	.341	881	217	38	3	13	172	62	197
Scoring Position	.271	.346	.386	70	19	5	0	1	22	9	14		.251	.302	.356	486	122	26	2	7	156	41	121
Late and Close	.190	.250	.214	42	8	1	0	0	2	4	15		.205	.243	.292	342	70	7	1	7	30	18	83

DAVID HULSE — BL/TL — age 26 — TEX OF112, DH2

1993	BA	OBA	SA	AB	H	2B	3B	HR	RBI	BB	SO
Total	.290	.333	.369	407	118	9	10	1	29	26	57
vs. Left	.257	.350	.343	35	9	1	1	0	5	4	7
vs. Right	.293	.331	.371	372	109	8	9	1	24	22	50
at Home	.276	.313	.362	199	55	5	6	0	15	11	29
on Road	.303	.351	.375	208	63	4	4	1	14	15	28
on Grass	.301	.343	.379	356	107	9	8	1	29	23	52
on Turf	.216	.259	.294	51	11	0	2	0	0	3	5
Day Games	.348	.397	.470	115	40	3	4	1	7	9	13
Night Games	.267	.306	.329	292	78	6	6	0	22	17	44
April	.184	.273	.237	38	7	0	1	0	1	5	9
May	.308	.333	.423	104	32	4	4	0	4	4	9
June	.300	.356	.375	80	24	2	2	0	7	7	11
July	.282	.325	.385	78	22	2	3	0	5	5	10
August	.308	.339	.327	52	16	1	0	0	5	2	8
Sept-Oct	.309	.345	.364	55	17	0	0	1	7	3	10
Bases Empty	.291	.339	.393	275	80	7	9	1	1	19	38
Leadoff	.272	.321	.331	151	41	5	2	0	0	11	19
Runners On Base	.288	.319	.318	132	38	2	1	0	28	7	19
Scoring Position	.304	.352	.342	79	24	1	1	0	27	7	8
Late and Close	.375	.388	.500	48	18	2	2	0	6	1	3

2-YEAR TOTALS (1992–1993)	BA	OBA	SA	AB	H	2B	3B	HR	RBI	BB	SO
Total	.293	.331	.365	499	146	13	10	1	31	29	75
vs. Left	.268	.339	.339	56	15	2	1	0	6	5	12
vs. Right	.296	.330	.368	443	131	11	9	1	25	24	63
at Home	.285	.315	.364	242	69	7	6	0	16	11	37
on Road	.300	.347	.366	257	77	6	4	1	15	18	38
on Grass	.298	.337	.371	429	128	12	8	1	30	25	66
on Turf	.257	.297	.329	70	18	1	2	0	1	4	9
Day Games	.370	.411	.479	146	54	5	4	1	8	10	16
Night Games	.261	.298	.317	353	92	8	6	0	23	19	59
April	.184	.273	.237	38	7	0	1	0	1	5	9
May	.308	.333	.423	104	32	4	4	0	4	4	9
June	.300	.356	.375	80	24	2	2	0	7	7	11
July	.282	.325	.385	78	22	2	3	0	5	5	10
August	.284	.325	.297	74	21	1	0	0	6	4	14
Sept-Oct	.320	.341	.376	125	40	4	0	1	8	4	22
Bases Empty	.290	.333	.381	341	99	10	9	1	1	21	50
Leadoff	.288	.330	.351	191	55	8	2	0	0	12	25
Runners On Base	.297	.327	.329	158	47	3	1	0	30	8	25
Scoring Position	.272	.324	.304	92	25	1	1	0	29	8	13
Late and Close	.339	.349	.452	62	21	3	2	0	6	1	7

TODD HUNDLEY — BB/TR — age 25 — NYN C123

1993	BA	OBA	SA	AB	H	2B	3B	HR	RBI	BB	SO
Total	.228	.269	.357	417	95	17	2	11	53	23	62
vs. Left	.259	.344	.296	54	14	2	0	0	5	5	14
vs. Right	.223	.257	.366	363	81	15	2	11	48	18	48
at Home	.258	.294	.392	209	54	13	0	5	27	9	22
on Road	.197	.244	.322	208	41	4	2	6	26	14	40
on Grass	.233	.277	.368	326	76	15	1	9	45	19	42
on Turf	.209	.240	.319	91	19	2	1	2	8	4	20
Day Games	.248	.286	.393	145	36	9	0	4	16	7	16
Night Games	.217	.260	.338	272	59	8	2	7	37	16	46
April	.226	.317	.491	53	12	3	1	3	11	5	12
May	.243	.274	.357	70	17	2	0	2	8	3	11
June	.192	.229	.321	78	15	2	1	2	8	4	13
July	.173	.238	.240	75	13	2	0	1	7	7	7
August	.215	.246	.308	65	14	3	0	1	7	3	10
Sept-Oct	.316	.325	.461	76	24	5	0	2	12	1	9
Bases Empty	.197	.237	.336	244	48	11	1	7	7	12	39
Leadoff	.233	.258	.419	86	20	4	0	4	4	2	9
Runners On Base	.272	.312	.387	173	47	6	1	4	46	11	23
Scoring Position	.276	.333	.400	105	29	2	1	3	43	10	16
Late and Close	.179	.255	.298	84	15	2	1	2	12	9	16

4-YEAR TOTALS (1990–1993)	BA	OBA	SA	AB	H	2B	3B	HR	RBI	BB	SO
Total	.213	.261	.327	902	192	40	3	19	94	54	170
vs. Left	.198	.263	.290	207	41	7	0	4	18	14	63
vs. Right	.217	.260	.338	695	151	33	3	15	76	40	107
at Home	.233	.282	.342	442	103	22	1	8	48	26	71
on Road	.193	.241	.313	460	89	18	2	11	46	28	99
on Grass	.217	.269	.330	658	143	31	2	13	71	42	113
on Turf	.201	.239	.320	244	49	9	1	6	23	12	57
Day Games	.223	.272	.345	287	64	14	0	7	26	17	54
Night Games	.208	.256	.319	615	128	26	3	12	68	37	116
April	.194	.279	.409	93	18	3	1	5	13	8	22
May	.196	.261	.291	148	29	5	0	3	13	11	28
June	.197	.224	.372	137	27	7	1	5	21	5	23
July	.212	.262	.305	151	32	8	0	2	11	11	24
August	.219	.265	.299	137	30	8	0	1	8	8	30
Sept-Oct	.237	.271	.322	236	56	9	1	3	28	11	43
Bases Empty	.190	.229	.307	537	102	25	1	12	12	24	107
Leadoff	.196	.225	.322	214	42	9	0	6	6	7	34
Runners On Base	.247	.305	.356	365	90	15	2	7	82	30	63
Scoring Position	.227	.303	.341	220	50	6	2	5	77	23	46
Late and Close	.219	.290	.332	187	41	10	1	3	18	17	39

PETE INCAVIGLIA — BR/TR — age 30 — PHI OF97

1993	BA	OBA	SA	AB	H	2B	3B	HR	RBI	BB	SO
Total	.274	.318	.530	368	101	16	3	24	89	21	82
vs. Left	.278	.318	.586	162	45	7	2	13	42	9	34
vs. Right	.272	.319	.485	206	56	9	1	11	47	12	48
at Home	.278	.324	.551	205	57	7	2	15	47	12	47
on Road	.270	.311	.503	163	44	9	1	9	42	9	35
on Grass	.281	.308	.583	96	27	6	1	7	28	4	18
on Turf	.272	.322	.511	272	74	10	2	17	61	17	64
Day Games	.236	.243	.445	110	26	3	1	6	25	2	30
Night Games	.291	.348	.566	258	75	13	2	18	64	19	52
April	.261	.292	.457	46	12	0	0	3	14	1	15
May	.294	.315	.662	68	20	6	2	5	18	2	12
June	.273	.314	.506	77	21	3	0	5	21	4	20
July	.173	.232	.327	52	9	2	0	2	5	2	14
August	.368	.449	.765	68	25	3	0	8	21	10	12
Sept-Oct	.246	.262	.368	57	14	2	1	1	10	2	9
Bases Empty	.263	.312	.527	186	49	11	1	12	12	10	31
Leadoff	.304	.353	.633	79	24	8	0	6	6	5	8
Runners On Base	.286	.325	.533	182	52	5	2	12	77	11	51
Scoring Position	.304	.338	.520	125	38	4	1	7	66	11	35
Late and Close	.154	.227	.215	65	10	0	0	1	12	7	17

8-YEAR TOTALS (1986–1993)	BA	OBA	SA	AB	H	2B	3B	HR	RBI	BB	SO
Total	.249	.313	.454	3503	873	170	18	170	558	301	1061
vs. Left	.271	.336	.508	1214	329	66	9	68	209	114	341
vs. Right	.238	.300	.425	2289	544	104	9	102	349	187	720
at Home	.261	.329	.480	1758	458	85	8	95	302	167	538
on Road	.238	.296	.427	1745	415	85	10	75	256	134	523
on Grass	.250	.316	.458	2524	630	125	12	126	401	235	773
on Turf	.248	.303	.441	979	243	45	6	44	157	66	288
Day Games	.227	.294	.413	803	182	26	5	38	126	74	257
Night Games	.256	.318	.466	2700	691	144	13	132	432	227	804
April	.238	.294	.433	526	125	20	1	27	87	37	177
May	.268	.330	.499	669	179	44	6	33	113	58	195
June	.249	.303	.433	607	151	29	4	25	93	44	186
July	.258	.324	.486	593	153	35	2	32	102	56	174
August	.236	.310	.411	601	142	17	2	28	82	58	186
Sept-Oct	.243	.309	.452	507	123	25	3	25	81	48	143
Bases Empty	.253	.317	.470	1821	460	99	10	92	92	151	531
Leadoff	.262	.324	.481	782	205	50	2	39	39	63	209
Runners On Base	.246	.308	.436	1682	413	71	8	78	466	150	530
Scoring Position	.241	.312	.422	955	230	45	4	40	372	102	311
Late and Close	.218	.285	.380	579	126	32	1	20	88	55	189

JOHN JAHA — BR/TR — age 28 — MIL 1B150, 2B1, 3B1   2-YEAR TOTALS (1992–1993)

1993	BA	OBA	SA	AB	H	2B	3B	HR	RBI	BB	SO	BA	OBA	SA	AB	H	2B	3B	HR	RBI	BB	SO
Total	.264	.337	.416	515	136	21	0	19	70	51	109	.256	.328	.394	648	166	24	1	21	80	63	139
vs. Left	.233	.296	.372	172	40	6	0	6	26	15	36	.220	.290	.349	218	48	7	0	7	31	21	46
vs. Right	.280	.357	.437	343	96	15	0	13	44	36	73	.274	.347	.416	430	118	17	1	14	49	42	93
at Home	.264	.325	.362	254	67	10	0	5	36	22	56	.252	.309	.349	341	86	13	1	6	41	26	80
on Road	.264	.349	.467	261	69	11	0	14	34	29	53	.261	.348	.443	307	80	11	0	15	39	37	59
on Grass	.260	.329	.389	427	111	16	0	13	57	41	93	.251	.318	.371	550	138	19	1	15	67	51	122
on Turf	.284	.376	.545	88	25	5	0	6	13	10	16	.286	.381	.520	98	28	5	0	6	13	12	17
Day Games	.216	.294	.300	190	41	7	0	3	21	17	41	.196	.268	.289	235	46	10	0	4	25	20	55
Night Games	.292	.362	.483	325	95	14	0	16	49	34	68	.291	.361	.453	413	120	14	1	17	55	43	84
April	.217	.304	.233	60	13	1	0	0	4	5	10	.217	.304	.233	60	13	1	0	0	4	5	10
May	.273	.326	.409	88	24	3	0	3	12	6	23	.273	.326	.409	88	24	3	0	3	12	6	23
June	.221	.295	.326	95	21	4	0	2	5	9	21	.221	.295	.326	95	21	4	0	2	5	9	21
July	.270	.329	.351	74	20	6	0	0	10	6	14	.256	.301	.333	129	33	7	0	1	16	7	26
August	.287	.350	.556	108	31	5	0	8	20	11	22	.275	.339	.491	167	46	7	1	9	23	17	36
Sept-Oct	.300	.402	.522	90	27	2	0	6	19	14	19	.266	.382	.450	109	29	2	0	6	20	19	23
Bases Empty	.230	.293	.403	313	72	12	0	14	14	23	70	.224	.282	.385	397	89	14	1	16	16	27	89
Leadoff	.254	.314	.476	126	32	7	0	7	7	10	25	.245	.302	.453	159	39	7	1	8	8	12	32
Runners On Base	.317	.401	.436	202	64	9	0	5	56	28	39	.307	.393	.406	251	77	10	0	5	64	36	50
Scoring Position	.308	.408	.408	120	37	6	0	2	47	22	26	.293	.398	.381	147	43	7	0	2	55	29	33
Late and Close	.312	.390	.441	93	29	3	0	3	9	9	18	.313	.394	.420	112	35	3	0	3	10	11	23

GREGG JEFFERIES — BB/TR — age 27 — SL 1B140, 2B1   7-YEAR TOTALS (1987–1993)

1993	BA	OBA	SA	AB	H	2B	3B	HR	RBI	BB	SO	BA	OBA	SA	AB	H	2B	3B	HR	RBI	BB	SO
Total	.342	.408	.485	544	186	24	3	16	83	62	32	.290	.346	.426	2861	830	156	15	68	363	245	195
vs. Left	.351	.394	.568	148	52	8	0	8	29	9	6	.282	.324	.433	935	264	55	4	26	118	54	64
vs. Right	.338	.414	.455	396	134	16	3	8	54	53	26	.294	.357	.423	1926	566	101	11	42	245	191	131
at Home	.341	.417	.518	249	85	10	2	10	43	31	19	.309	.374	.463	1392	430	84	10	37	186	142	93
on Road	.342	.401	.458	295	101	14	1	6	40	31	13	.272	.319	.391	1469	400	72	5	31	177	103	102
on Grass	.349	.415	.476	189	66	10	1	4	25	22	8	.297	.349	.435	1703	505	103	6	40	200	137	107
on Turf	.338	.405	.490	355	120	14	2	12	58	40	24	.281	.342	.415	1158	325	53	9	28	163	108	88
Day Games	.341	.398	.483	176	60	11	1	4	27	17	12	.297	.349	.426	933	277	59	6	17	111	70	65
Night Games	.342	.413	.486	368	126	13	2	12	56	45	20	.287	.345	.426	1928	553	97	9	51	252	175	130
April	.262	.310	.438	80	21	0	1	4	13	6	6	.220	.288	.331	354	78	22	1	5	38	32	31
May	.260	.343	.344	96	25	2	0	2	13	11	9	.282	.318	.405	447	126	28	0	9	55	22	35
June	.444	.465	.685	108	48	10	2	4	16	5	4	.337	.387	.518	469	158	31	3	16	69	39	22
July	.367	.425	.456	79	29	1	0	2	12	8	5	.304	.361	.451	450	137	19	4	13	69	40	32
August	.350	.443	.538	80	28	6	0	3	9	15	3	.297	.359	.420	481	143	27	4	8	50	46	32
Sept-Oct	.347	.445	.426	101	35	5	0	1	20	17	5	.285	.348	.415	660	188	29	3	17	82	66	43
Bases Empty	.338	.391	.509	275	93	17	3	8	8	23	17	.289	.343	.439	1612	466	95	7	44	44	123	110
Leadoff	.321	.375	.494	81	26	8	0	2	2	6	4	.286	.339	.449	623	178	38	2	20	20	47	38
Runners On Base	.346	.425	.461	269	93	7	0	8	75	39	15	.291	.350	.411	1249	364	61	8	24	319	122	85
Scoring Position	.384	.469	.507	146	56	6	0	4	66	26	10	.295	.364	.408	711	210	34	5	12	279	88	55
Late and Close	.402	.465	.506	87	35	3	0	2	12	11	3	.286	.348	.367	479	137	18	0	7	54	45	29

REGGIE JEFFERSON — BB/TL — age 26 — CLE DH88, 1B15   3-YEAR TOTALS (1991–1993)

1993	BA	OBA	SA	AB	H	2B	3B	HR	RBI	BB	SO	BA	OBA	SA	AB	H	2B	3B	HR	RBI	BB	SO
Total	.249	.310	.372	366	91	11	2	10	34	28	78	.252	.300	.377	563	142	20	4	14	53	33	119
vs. Left	.196	.283	.262	107	21	4	0	1	9	9	26	.199	.267	.291	151	30	6	1	2	15	10	40
vs. Right	.270	.321	.408	259	70	7	2	9	25	19	52	.272	.312	.408	412	112	14	3	12	38	23	79
at Home	.250	.314	.349	172	43	3	1	4	14	14	39	.242	.292	.351	285	69	8	1	7	22	18	61
on Road	.247	.307	.392	194	48	8	1	6	20	14	39	.263	.308	.403	278	73	12	3	7	31	15	58
on Grass	.265	.330	.396	313	83	10	2	9	31	26	63	.264	.314	.393	488	129	19	4	12	48	30	97
on Turf	.151	.182	.226	53	8	1	0	1	3	2	15	.173	.205	.267	75	13	1	0	2	5	3	22
Day Games	.270	.306	.409	115	31	6	1	3	15	6	24	.266	.301	.412	177	47	9	1	5	23	9	37
Night Games	.239	.312	.355	251	60	5	1	7	19	22	54	.246	.299	.360	386	95	11	3	9	30	24	82
April	.291	.333	.481	79	23	4	1	3	9	5	23	.291	.333	.481	79	23	4	1	3	9	5	23
May	.169	.242	.186	59	10	1	0	0	2	5	9	.169	.247	.231	65	11	1	0	1	3	6	11
June	.300	.356	.475	80	24	2	0	4	9	6	15	.296	.352	.469	81	24	2	0	4	9	6	15
July	.120	.170	.200	50	6	1	0	0	3	2	12	.158	.185	.225	120	19	2	0	2	6	3	31
August	.277	.326	.398	83	23	2	1	2	9	5	17	.277	.326	.398	83	23	2	1	2	9	5	17
Sept-Oct	.333	.524	.400	15	5	1	0	0	2	5	2	.311	.356	.452	135	42	9	2	2	17	6	22
Bases Empty	.244	.288	.390	213	52	9	2	6	6	10	46	.263	.290	.407	339	89	16	3	9	9	10	73
Leadoff	.207	.250	.310	87	18	3	0	2	2	5	16	.250	.277	.338	136	34	6	0	2	2	5	27
Runners On Base	.255	.339	.346	153	39	2	0	4	28	18	32	.237	.313	.330	224	53	4	1	5	44	23	46
Scoring Position	.209	.324	.337	86	18	2	0	3	26	14	19	.215	.311	.354	130	28	4	1	4	42	17	30
Late and Close	.246	.333	.377	61	15	2	0	2	5	7	9	.284	.352	.389	95	27	4	0	2	9	8	13

HOWARD JOHNSON — BB/TR — age 34 — NYN 3B67

1993	BA	OBA	SA	AB	H	2B	3B	HR	RBI	BB	SO		10-YEAR TOTALS (1984–1993) BA	OBA	SA	AB	H	2B	3B	HR	RBI	BB	SO
Total	.238	.354	.379	235	56	8	2	7	26	43	43		.251	.340	.454	4323	1085	228	19	204	679	595	894
vs. Left	.162	.269	.206	68	11	3	0	0	2	10	12		.232	.324	.410	1388	322	62	4	59	193	192	323
vs. Right	.269	.386	.449	167	45	5	2	7	24	33	31		.260	.348	.475	2935	763	166	15	145	486	403	571
at Home	.207	.313	.319	116	24	4	0	3	12	18	25		.240	.332	.430	2079	499	95	9	94	318	291	436
on Road	.269	.390	.437	119	32	4	2	4	14	25	18		.261	.348	.476	2244	586	133	10	110	361	304	458
on Grass	.242	.367	.360	186	45	8	1	4	20	38	34		.251	.342	.448	3086	774	155	15	141	475	436	621
on Turf	.224	.296	.449	49	11	0	1	3	6	5	9		.251	.335	.470	1237	311	73	4	63	204	159	273
Day Games	.202	.333	.374	99	20	4	2	3	12	20	18		.260	.349	.466	1501	391	86	5	71	251	212	292
Night Games	.265	.369	.382	136	36	4	0	4	14	23	25		.246	.335	.448	2822	694	142	14	133	428	383	602
April	.225	.367	.380	71	16	2	0	3	11	17	13		.231	.332	.405	580	134	23	0	26	96	90	128
May	.250	.355	.363	80	20	4	1	1	9	13	18		.238	.334	.417	774	184	38	4	31	115	115	169
June	.267	.313	.467	30	8	1	1	1	2	2	5		.273	.343	.524	761	208	46	5	45	124	83	153
July	.222	.354	.352	54	12	1	0	2	4	11	7		.257	.349	.455	828	213	45	1	39	129	122	149
August	.000	.000	.000	0	0	0	0	0	0	0	0		.255	.353	.468	686	175	34	5	34	99	103	139
Sept-Oct	.000	.000	.000	0	0	0	0	0	0	0	0		.246	.325	.444	694	171	42	4	29	116	82	156
Bases Empty	.231	.338	.392	130	30	4	1	5	5	21	21		.244	.324	.453	2414	590	112	13	122	122	276	478
Leadoff	.258	.343	.468	62	16	2	1	3	3	8	10		.263	.326	.507	1021	269	50	5	63	63	91	195
Runners On Base	.248	.372	.362	105	26	4	1	2	21	22	22		.259	.358	.455	1909	495	116	6	82	557	319	416
Scoring Position	.250	.388	.308	52	13	1	1	0	16	13	14		.264	.388	.465	1054	278	69	1	47	469	242	239
Late and Close	.298	.370	.319	47	14	1	0	0	5	6	12		.258	.355	.469	748	193	35	3	39	130	115	188

LANCE JOHNSON — BL/TL — age 31 — CHA OF146

1993	BA	OBA	SA	AB	H	2B	3B	HR	RBI	BB	SO		7-YEAR TOTALS (1987–1993) BA	OBA	SA	AB	H	2B	3B	HR	RBI	BB	SO
Total	.311	.354	.396	540	168	18	14	0	47	36	33		.281	.321	.356	2599	731	79	52	4	223	156	210
vs. Left	.272	.318	.333	147	40	5	2	0	9	10	16		.267	.308	.315	711	190	16	9	0	56	42	87
vs. Right	.326	.368	.420	393	128	13	12	0	38	26	17		.287	.326	.372	1888	541	63	43	4	167	114	123
at Home	.320	.369	.386	259	83	5	6	0	19	20	14		.278	.320	.348	1273	354	33	25	2	105	82	94
on Road	.302	.340	.406	281	85	13	8	0	28	16	19		.284	.322	.364	1326	377	46	27	2	118	74	116
on Grass	.302	.345	.372	444	134	13	9	0	31	29	25		.281	.320	.350	2139	600	57	40	4	171	127	172
on Turf	.354	.398	.510	96	34	5	5	0	16	7	8		.285	.327	.385	460	131	22	12	0	52	29	38
Day Games	.264	.319	.351	174	46	5	5	0	11	14	15		.272	.318	.343	738	201	22	15	0	57	51	71
Night Games	.333	.371	.418	366	122	13	9	0	36	22	18		.285	.323	.362	1861	530	57	37	4	166	105	139
April	.337	.360	.410	83	28	4	1	0	11	3	7		.264	.291	.313	345	91	11	3	0	27	13	34
May	.306	.352	.378	98	30	1	3	0	7	7	9		.267	.307	.308	409	109	8	3	1	27	24	38
June	.272	.330	.326	92	25	1	2	0	5	8	3		.284	.322	.354	373	106	12	7	0	31	23	25
July	.320	.364	.460	100	32	4	5	0	7	7	8		.292	.326	.377	411	120	8	12	1	38	21	34
August	.333	.375	.411	90	30	5	1	0	11	6	2		.281	.323	.374	470	132	16	11	2	50	30	32
Sept-Oct	.299	.341	.390	77	23	3	2	0	6	5	4		.293	.343	.387	591	173	24	16	0	50	45	47
Bases Empty	.290	.333	.371	310	90	9	8	0	0	20	23		.276	.317	.351	1537	424	46	30	3	3	92	136
Leadoff	.328	.366	.379	116	38	2	2	0	0	7	5		.277	.314	.354	667	185	19	13	2	2	36	46
Runners On Base	.339	.382	.430	230	78	9	6	0	47	16	10		.289	.328	.364	1062	307	33	22	1	220	64	74
Scoring Position	.364	.395	.500	118	43	6	5	0	45	6	4		.299	.345	.393	595	178	21	16	1	212	45	41
Late and Close	.274	.337	.393	84	23	4	3	0	9	8	6		.237	.293	.297	438	104	10	8	0	36	34	49

FELIX JOSE — BB/TR — age 29 — KC OF144, DH1

1993	BA	OBA	SA	AB	H	2B	3B	HR	RBI	BB	SO		6-YEAR TOTALS (1988–1993) BA	OBA	SA	AB	H	2B	3B	HR	RBI	BB	SO
Total	.253	.303	.349	499	126	24	3	6	43	36	95		.278	.330	.399	2065	575	105	13	39	253	154	403
vs. Left	.094	.134	.109	64	6	1	0	0	4	3	15		.300	.350	.421	634	190	37	5	10	87	49	126
vs. Right	.276	.327	.384	435	120	23	3	6	39	33	80		.269	.321	.389	1431	385	68	8	29	166	105	277
at Home	.269	.327	.370	238	64	16	1	2	24	21	34		.275	.332	.406	1019	280	52	8	22	141	85	186
on Road	.238	.281	.330	261	62	8	2	4	19	15	61		.282	.328	.391	1046	295	53	5	17	112	69	217
on Grass	.250	.287	.343	204	51	6	2	3	16	10	51		.270	.311	.366	869	235	39	4	12	94	47	186
on Turf	.254	.314	.353	295	75	18	1	3	27	26	44		.284	.343	.422	1196	340	66	9	27	159	107	217
Day Games	.269	.320	.338	160	43	6	1	1	15	12	26		.267	.313	.384	656	175	30	4	13	88	44	125
Night Games	.245	.295	.354	339	83	18	2	5	28	24	69		.284	.337	.405	1409	400	75	9	26	165	110	278
April	.224	.297	.328	67	15	4	0	1	7	7	12		.286	.350	.450	220	63	17	2	5	31	21	33
May	.294	.330	.329	85	25	3	0	0	8	4	14		.301	.364	.407	349	105	15	2	6	52	34	70
June	.298	.340	.447	94	28	7	2	1	11	6	14		.281	.318	.397	360	101	24	3	4	45	20	64
July	.190	.247	.228	79	15	1	1	0	3	6	14		.252	.308	.348	345	87	13	1	6	30	26	76
August	.239	.295	.364	88	21	5	0	2	6	7	20		.283	.329	.370	389	110	19	0	5	34	24	84
Sept-Oct	.256	.301	.372	86	22	4	0	2	8	6	21		.271	.319	.435	402	109	17	5	13	61	29	76
Bases Empty	.250	.297	.337	312	78	17	2	2	2	20	69		.269	.320	.377	1155	311	58	5	19	19	83	239
Leadoff	.257	.321	.333	171	44	9	2	0	0	15	34		.288	.336	.388	538	155	32	2	6	6	38	100
Runners On Base	.257	.312	.369	187	48	7	1	4	41	16	26		.290	.342	.425	910	264	47	8	20	234	71	164
Scoring Position	.245	.325	.343	102	25	4	0	2	34	13	17		.293	.358	.426	535	157	33	4	10	206	55	110
Late and Close	.210	.273	.284	81	17	3	0	1	5	7	15		.284	.344	.414	348	99	16	1	9	41	31	83

WALLY JOYNER — BL/TL — age 32 — KC 1B140

8-YEAR TOTALS (1986–1993)

1993	BA	OBA	SA	AB	H	2B	3B	HR	RBI	BB	SO	BA	OBA	SA	AB	H	2B	3B	HR	RBI	BB	SO
Total	.292	.375	.467	497	145	36	3	15	65	66	67	.286	.353	.447	4277	1224	241	16	138	649	444	448
vs. Left	.259	.340	.367	166	43	12	0	2	20	18	21	.258	.313	.377	1464	377	75	2	32	205	109	174
vs. Right	.308	.392	.517	331	102	24	3	13	45	48	46	.301	.373	.483	2813	847	166	14	106	444	335	274
at Home	.320	.389	.488	256	82	25	3	4	35	29	28	.278	.345	.433	2118	589	118	9	64	301	220	210
on Road	.261	.360	.444	241	63	11	0	11	30	37	39	.294	.361	.460	2159	635	123	7	74	348	224	238
on Grass	.263	.361	.452	186	49	8	0	9	25	29	29	.278	.346	.441	3132	871	157	10	111	477	331	322
on Turf	.309	.384	.476	311	96	28	3	6	40	37	38	.308	.372	.463	1145	353	84	6	27	172	113	126
Day Games	.253	.345	.407	150	38	10	2	3	16	22	22	.281	.359	.474	1134	319	66	4	48	179	134	139
Night Games	.308	.388	.493	347	107	26	1	12	49	44	45	.288	.351	.437	3143	905	175	12	90	470	310	309
April	.266	.389	.354	79	21	7	0	0	3	16	6	.281	.359	.427	647	182	43	0	17	79	79	64
May	.322	.423	.575	87	28	4	0	6	18	15	15	.310	.377	.514	741	230	33	2	38	135	78	77
June	.282	.342	.379	103	29	7	0	1	7	9	14	.282	.340	.415	804	227	47	3	18	121	74	92
July	.376	.443	.710	93	35	9	2	6	26	12	11	.307	.366	.488	735	226	49	6	24	136	68	79
August	.243	.295	.351	111	27	7	1	1	7	8	16	.265	.336	.434	733	194	38	4	26	103	78	71
Sept-Oct	.208	.367	.417	24	5	2	0	1	4	6	5	.267	.340	.394	617	165	31	1	15	75	67	65
Bases Empty	.288	.355	.496	278	80	23	1	11	11	27	32	.272	.331	.438	2349	638	130	8	82	82	197	232
Leadoff	.312	.353	.600	125	39	10	1	8	8	7	9	.267	.318	.446	924	247	48	3	37	37	67	79
Runners On Base	.297	.398	.429	219	65	13	2	4	54	39	35	.304	.378	.457	1928	586	111	8	56	567	247	216
Scoring Position	.279	.395	.403	129	36	8	1	2	46	27	24	.300	.390	.460	1115	335	69	5	33	495	185	129
Late and Close	.325	.440	.494	83	27	5	0	3	14	16	15	.274	.351	.418	705	193	38	2	20	104	84	74

DAVID JUSTICE — BL/TL — age 28 — ATL OF157

5-YEAR TOTALS (1989–1993)

1993	BA	OBA	SA	AB	H	2B	3B	HR	RBI	BB	SO	BA	OBA	SA	AB	H	2B	3B	HR	RBI	BB	SO
Total	.270	.357	.515	585	158	15	4	40	120	78	90	.270	.364	.496	1955	527	85	12	111	360	289	357
vs. Left	.294	.362	.508	177	52	5	0	11	36	18	27	.299	.366	.506	632	189	28	2	33	124	66	102
vs. Right	.260	.354	.517	408	106	10	4	29	84	60	63	.255	.363	.491	1323	338	57	10	78	236	223	255
at Home	.272	.348	.486	290	79	6	1	18	57	32	40	.271	.362	.516	972	263	48	7	59	183	141	183
on Road	.268	.365	.542	295	79	9	3	22	63	46	50	.269	.365	.475	983	264	37	5	52	177	148	174
on Grass	.273	.351	.536	461	126	11	4	34	98	54	71	.276	.364	.519	1462	403	65	12	89	275	204	276
on Turf	.258	.377	.435	124	32	4	0	6	22	24	19	.252	.362	.426	493	124	20	0	22	85	85	81
Day Games	.357	.452	.688	157	56	6	2	14	38	28	22	.279	.389	.522	531	148	16	4	35	106	99	77
Night Games	.238	.320	.451	428	102	9	2	26	82	50	68	.266	.354	.486	1424	379	69	8	76	254	190	280
April	.157	.272	.326	89	14	3	0	4	11	13	21	.168	.269	.303	185	31	7	0	6	21	25	48
May	.282	.330	.573	103	29	4	1	8	22	6	14	.292	.369	.509	373	109	22	1	19	71	42	63
June	.236	.317	.393	89	21	0	1	4	12	11	12	.247	.347	.429	336	83	11	4	14	53	52	64
July	.357	.453	.643	98	35	4	0	8	27	18	8	.289	.381	.487	263	76	11	1	13	43	40	40
August	.277	.370	.628	94	26	0	0	11	24	14	13	.282	.361	.580	355	100	15	2	29	76	44	62
Sept-Oct	.295	.380	.500	112	33	4	2	5	24	16	22	.289	.401	.553	443	128	19	4	30	96	86	80
Bases Empty	.247	.315	.481	312	77	7	3	20	20	30	44	.234	.315	.446	1050	246	40	7	56	56	118	200
Leadoff	.270	.313	.454	141	38	5	0	7	7	8	15	.230	.292	.423	487	112	21	2	23	23	41	94
Runners On Base	.297	.401	.553	273	81	8	1	20	100	48	46	.310	.416	.554	905	281	45	5	55	304	171	157
Scoring Position	.288	.410	.518	170	49	3	0	12	78	36	30	.294	.425	.534	541	159	28	3	32	246	131	105
Late and Close	.242	.343	.516	91	22	0	2	7	15	13	18	.253	.345	.473	296	75	11	3	16	46	41	70

RON KARKOVICE — BR/TR — age 31 — CHA C127

8-YEAR TOTALS (1986–1993)

1993	BA	OBA	SA	AB	H	2B	3B	HR	RBI	BB	SO	BA	OBA	SA	AB	H	2B	3B	HR	RBI	BB	SO
Total	.228	.287	.424	403	92	17	1	20	54	29	126	.227	.288	.384	1574	357	72	4	56	199	123	472
vs. Left	.198	.281	.413	121	24	5	0	7	18	12	39	.219	.286	.384	575	126	28	2	21	80	52	180
vs. Right	.241	.290	.429	282	68	12	1	13	36	17	87	.231	.289	.384	999	231	44	2	35	119	71	292
at Home	.217	.261	.360	189	41	9	0	6	20	9	51	.210	.266	.320	753	158	37	2	14	68	53	218
on Road	.238	.310	.481	214	51	8	1	14	34	20	75	.242	.308	.443	821	199	35	2	42	131	70	254
on Grass	.235	.291	.440	332	78	14	0	18	44	21	100	.230	.290	.384	1306	300	57	3	46	163	100	387
on Turf	.197	.272	.352	71	14	3	1	2	10	8	26	.213	.279	.388	268	57	15	1	10	36	23	85
Day Games	.218	.274	.395	124	27	5	1	5	16	8	47	.226	.278	.377	541	122	30	2	16	72	35	188
Night Games	.233	.293	.437	279	65	12	0	15	38	21	79	.227	.293	.388	1033	235	42	2	40	127	88	284
April	.217	.294	.367	60	13	3	0	2	10	7	20	.220	.294	.314	191	42	6	0	4	24	20	58
May	.234	.274	.416	77	18	5	0	3	9	4	18	.196	.263	.313	291	57	10	0	8	34	25	77
June	.373	.407	.824	51	19	3	1	6	13	2	15	.236	.289	.454	229	54	9	1	13	28	13	71
July	.167	.231	.217	60	10	0	0	1	3	4	18	.228	.279	.366	246	56	16	0	6	22	15	64
August	.209	.250	.419	86	18	3	0	5	12	4	29	.245	.298	.436	298	73	17	2	12	49	21	95
Sept-Oct	.203	.304	.377	69	14	3	0	3	7	8	26	.235	.304	.408	319	75	14	1	13	42	29	107
Bases Empty	.236	.283	.418	225	53	8	0	11	11	11	76	.226	.283	.375	891	201	44	1	29	29	61	268
Leadoff	.336	.365	.609	110	37	6	0	8	8	5	31	.281	.320	.464	384	108	25	0	15	15	20	101
Runners On Base	.219	.292	.433	178	39	9	1	9	43	18	50	.228	.295	.397	683	156	28	3	27	170	62	204
Scoring Position	.185	.282	.337	92	17	5	0	3	29	13	28	.221	.313	.349	384	85	14	1	11	133	52	124
Late and Close	.156	.169	.313	64	10	2	1	2	5	0	25	.219	.273	.312	247	54	9	1	4	14	16	78

ERIC KARROS — BR/TR — age 27 — LA 1B157

1993	BA	OBA	SA	AB	H	2B	3B	HR	RBI	BB	SO		BA	OBA	SA	AB	H	2B	3B	HR	RBI	BB	SO
Total	.247	.287	.409	619	153	27	2	23	80	34	82		.250	.293	.413	1178	294	58	3	43	169	72	191
vs. Left	.312	.343	.494	170	53	14	1	5	27	8	20		.285	.326	.450	393	112	24	1	13	59	25	50
vs. Right	.223	.267	.376	449	100	13	1	18	53	26	62		.232	.277	.395	785	182	34	2	30	110	47	141
at Home	.231	.279	.403	303	70	11	1	13	42	20	33		.243	.298	.398	560	136	26	2	19	78	44	81
on Road	.263	.295	.415	316	83	16	1	10	38	14	49		.256	.289	.427	618	158	32	1	24	91	28	110
on Grass	.242	.283	.416	476	115	22	2	19	62	27	64		.249	.296	.418	876	218	46	3	32	125	58	141
on Turf	.266	.300	.385	143	38	5	0	4	18	7	18		.252	.284	.401	302	76	12	0	11	44	14	50
Day Games	.280	.327	.467	182	51	12	2	6	24	12	31		.267	.306	.423	371	99	21	2	11	49	20	68
Night Games	.233	.271	.384	437	102	15	0	17	56	22	51		.242	.288	.409	807	195	37	1	32	120	52	123
April	.230	.284	.333	87	20	3	0	2	13	7	12		.246	.293	.385	122	30	5	0	4	19	9	17
May	.302	.350	.438	96	29	5	1	2	4	7	13		.286	.327	.468	154	44	8	1	6	16	10	26
June	.308	.333	.481	104	32	6	0	4	12	3	14		.290	.320	.443	210	61	11	0	7	21	9	34
July	.210	.252	.362	105	22	7	0	3	14	5	9		.228	.267	.411	224	51	12	1	9	34	9	27
August	.204	.241	.427	103	21	2	0	7	19	5	15		.215	.271	.407	209	45	10	0	10	40	16	37
Sept-Oct	.234	.271	.403	124	29	4	1	5	18	7	19		.243	.292	.378	259	63	12	1	7	39	19	50
Bases Empty	.255	.292	.444	322	82	15	2	14	14	17	40		.257	.293	.433	614	158	29	2	25	25	30	92
Leadoff	.276	.299	.513	152	42	7	1	9	9	5	20		.288	.312	.474	285	82	15	1	12	12	10	34
Runners On Base	.239	.282	.370	297	71	12	0	9	66	17	42		.241	.293	.392	564	136	29	1	18	144	42	99
Scoring Position	.254	.311	.429	177	45	7	0	8	63	15	27		.244	.313	.403	352	86	18	1	12	129	37	62
Late and Close	.182	.227	.306	121	22	3	0	4	9	6	19		.213	.269	.367	221	47	10	0	8	26	16	43

3-YEAR TOTALS (1991–1993)

PAT KELLY — BR/TR — age 27 — NYA 2B125

1993	BA	OBA	SA	AB	H	2B	3B	HR	RBI	BB	SO		BA	OBA	SA	AB	H	2B	3B	HR	RBI	BB	SO
Total	.273	.317	.389	406	111	24	1	7	51	24	68		.250	.303	.370	1022	255	58	7	17	101	64	192
vs. Left	.283	.333	.400	145	41	8	0	3	17	9	20		.260	.307	.374	358	93	18	1	7	31	22	58
vs. Right	.268	.309	.383	261	70	16	1	4	34	15	48		.244	.301	.367	664	162	40	6	10	70	42	134
at Home	.263	.319	.387	186	49	9	1	4	19	13	26		.246	.308	.375	512	126	26	5	10	48	39	91
on Road	.282	.316	.391	220	62	15	0	3	32	11	42		.253	.299	.365	510	129	32	2	7	53	25	101
on Grass	.270	.316	.376	348	94	17	1	6	40	20	55		.250	.309	.367	864	216	46	5	15	84	57	159
on Turf	.293	.328	.466	58	17	7	0	1	11	4	13		.247	.274	.386	158	39	12	2	2	17	7	33
Day Games	.293	.351	.421	133	39	9	1	2	25	11	22		.254	.318	.404	319	81	19	4	7	45	24	68
Night Games	.264	.300	.374	273	72	15	0	5	26	13	46		.248	.296	.354	703	174	39	3	10	56	40	124
April	.246	.270	.391	69	17	4	0	2	9	3	8		.232	.291	.354	99	23	6	0	2	9	8	17
May	.264	.303	.375	72	19	2	0	2	8	3	9		.253	.321	.418	170	43	12	2	4	22	11	35
June	.287	.359	.412	80	23	7	0	1	15	8	16		.246	.302	.364	187	46	8	1	4	20	11	37
July	.310	.355	.451	71	22	2	1	2	9	4	12		.244	.290	.364	225	55	11	2	4	22	13	41
August	.212	.269	.271	85	18	5	0	0	6	6	16		.254	.304	.352	236	60	10	2	3	22	16	41
Sept-Oct	.414	.400	.552	29	12	4	0	0	4	0	7		.267	.316	.371	105	28	11	0	0	6	5	21
Bases Empty	.272	.317	.394	213	58	11	0	5	5	13	25		.262	.318	.392	577	151	32	5	11	11	38	94
Leadoff	.264	.319	.414	87	23	4	0	3	3	7	11		.278	.326	.390	223	62	13	0	4	4	15	34
Runners On Base	.275	.318	.383	193	53	13	1	2	46	11	43		.234	.285	.342	445	104	26	2	6	90	26	98
Scoring Position	.274	.321	.385	117	32	10	0	1	41	7	32		.230	.298	.317	243	56	15	0	2	75	19	67
Late and Close	.333	.368	.429	63	21	6	0	0	8	4	13		.265	.316	.387	155	41	14	1	1	17	11	30

3-YEAR TOTALS (1991–1993)

BOBBY KELLY — BR/TR — age 30 — CIN OF77

1993	BA	OBA	SA	AB	H	2B	3B	HR	RBI	BB	SO		BA	OBA	SA	AB	H	2B	3B	HR	RBI	BB	SO
Total	.319	.354	.475	320	102	17	3	9	35	17	43		.285	.335	.420	2597	739	127	15	65	293	185	483
vs. Left	.250	.280	.427	96	24	6	1	3	8	3	12		.296	.353	.440	852	252	42	3	25	96	74	146
vs. Right	.348	.384	.496	224	78	11	2	6	27	14	31		.279	.326	.410	1745	487	85	12	40	197	111	337
at Home	.296	.337	.421	152	45	3	2	4	20	9	24		.291	.342	.421	1278	372	65	7	29	144	94	216
on Road	.339	.369	.524	168	57	14	1	5	15	8	19		.278	.327	.419	1319	367	62	8	36	149	91	267
on Grass	.350	.381	.590	100	35	10	1	4	11	5	11		.283	.336	.421	1999	565	103	9	52	223	150	370
on Turf	.305	.342	.423	220	67	7	2	5	24	12	32		.291	.331	.416	598	174	24	6	13	70	35	113
Day Games	.326	.361	.522	92	30	5	2	3	12	4	8		.300	.346	.450	783	235	41	5	22	107	53	138
Night Games	.316	.351	.456	228	72	12	1	6	23	13	35		.278	.330	.407	1814	504	86	10	43	186	132	345
April	.272	.298	.420	81	22	2	2	2	7	3	12		.304	.347	.421	404	123	21	4	6	50	26	72
May	.328	.371	.467	122	40	8	0	3	9	9	12		.289	.337	.426	519	150	26	3	13	54	37	96
June	.339	.373	.495	109	37	6	1	3	18	5	17		.273	.311	.412	495	135	19	4	14	53	23	101
July	.375	.375	.875	8	3	1	0	1	1	0	2		.299	.351	.444	331	99	19	1	9	45	26	61
August	.000	.000	.000	0	0	0	0	0	0	0	0		.294	.356	.446	408	120	24	1	12	40	36	79
Sept-Oct	.000	.000	.000	0	0	0	0	0	0	0	0		.255	.315	.380	440	112	18	2	11	51	37	74
Bases Empty	.315	.340	.533	184	58	12	2	8	8	6	30		.282	.334	.431	1537	433	70	8	48	48	110	312
Leadoff	.360	.368	.600	75	27	7	1	3	3	1	8		.283	.321	.454	672	190	41	4	22	22	32	131
Runners On Base	.324	.371	.397	136	44	5	1	1	27	11	13		.289	.336	.404	1060	306	57	7	17	245	75	171
Scoring Position	.278	.355	.342	79	22	2	0	1	26	10	7		.272	.333	.384	599	163	30	2	11	218	56	104
Late and Close	.256	.292	.279	43	11	1	0	0	5	2	5		.265	.322	.409	438	116	17	2	14	62	35	92

7-YEAR TOTALS (1987–1993)

JEFF KENT — BR/TR — age 26 — NYN 2B127, 3B12, SS2   2-YEAR TOTALS (1992–1993)

1993	BA	OBA	SA	AB	H	2B	3B	HR	RBI	BB	SO	BA	OBA	SA	AB	H	2B	3B	HR	RBI	BB	SO
Total	.270	.320	.446	496	134	24	0	21	80	30	88	.258	.317	.439	801	207	45	2	32	130	57	164
vs. Left	.230	.277	.291	148	34	9	0	0	11	10	22	.225	.282	.321	240	54	14	0	3	25	20	42
vs. Right	.287	.338	.511	348	100	15	0	21	69	20	66	.273	.331	.490	561	153	31	2	29	105	37	122
at Home	.275	.319	.437	247	68	13	0	9	41	13	44	.261	.319	.425	414	108	27	1	13	61	31	83
on Road	.265	.320	.454	249	66	11	0	12	39	17	44	.256	.315	.455	387	99	18	1	19	69	26	81
on Grass	.266	.316	.442	398	106	19	0	17	66	24	71	.266	.317	.454	542	144	26	2	24	95	32	112
on Turf	.286	.333	.459	98	28	5	0	4	14	6	17	.243	.316	.409	259	63	19	0	8	35	25	52
Day Games	.269	.330	.480	175	47	10	0	9	22	12	32	.230	.287	.415	270	62	17	0	11	28	18	57
Night Games	.271	.314	.427	321	87	14	0	12	58	18	56	.273	.332	.452	531	145	28	2	21	102	39	107
April	.213	.290	.295	61	13	2	0	1	5	5	19	.225	.319	.363	80	18	5	0	2	8	9	24
May	.257	.316	.443	70	18	7	0	2	9	4	13	.262	.330	.450	80	21	9	0	2	10	6	15
June	.231	.244	.372	78	18	2	0	3	13	0	11	.245	.301	.410	139	34	6	1	5	22	8	25
July	.323	.359	.552	96	31	6	0	6	19	6	15	.267	.313	.460	161	43	7	0	8	33	11	31
August	.330	.393	.505	97	32	5	0	4	14	10	13	.291	.343	.500	158	46	7	1	8	26	11	31
Sept-Oct	.234	.287	.436	94	22	4	0	5	20	5	17	.246	.303	.421	183	45	11	0	7	31	12	38
Bases Empty	.250	.298	.404	280	70	16	0	9	9	14	46	.248	.312	.405	435	108	26	0	14	14	33	85
Leadoff	.284	.305	.412	102	29	7	0	2	2	2	15	.302	.333	.456	169	51	14	0	4	4	7	32
Runners On Base	.296	.347	.500	216	64	8	0	12	71	16	42	.270	.323	.481	366	99	19	2	18	116	24	79
Scoring Position	.317	.381	.533	120	38	5	0	7	59	13	24	.290	.357	.538	210	61	12	2	12	101	20	45
Late and Close	.208	.252	.347	101	21	2	0	4	12	6	27	.242	.285	.450	149	36	7	0	8	24	7	41

JEFF KING — BR/TR — age 30 — PIT 3B156, 2B2, SS2   5-YEAR TOTALS (1989–1993)

1993	BA	OBA	SA	AB	H	2B	3B	HR	RBI	BB	SO	BA	OBA	SA	AB	H	2B	3B	HR	RBI	BB	SO
Total	.295	.356	.406	611	180	35	3	9	98	59	54	.252	.306	.389	1786	450	87	10	46	253	141	209
vs. Left	.324	.383	.463	188	61	12	1	4	34	18	13	.263	.321	.416	778	205	45	7	20	114	69	74
vs. Right	.281	.345	.381	423	119	23	2	5	64	41	41	.243	.295	.368	1008	245	42	3	26	139	72	135
at Home	.306	.366	.428	297	91	18	3	4	60	30	25	.260	.312	.407	905	235	46	6	25	147	71	99
on Road	.283	.347	.385	314	89	17	0	5	38	29	29	.244	.300	.371	881	215	41	4	21	106	70	110
on Grass	.230	.305	.291	196	45	9	0	1	20	21	22	.234	.296	.339	478	112	24	1	8	54	43	67
on Turf	.325	.381	.460	415	135	26	3	8	78	38	32	.258	.310	.407	1308	338	63	9	38	199	98	142
Day Games	.293	.350	.427	164	48	14	1	2	31	16	8	.264	.314	.404	507	134	28	2	13	79	39	52
Night Games	.295	.359	.398	447	132	21	2	7	67	43	46	.247	.303	.383	1279	316	59	8	33	174	102	157
April	.261	.356	.307	88	23	4	0	0	7	13	8	.227	.314	.296	247	56	5	3	2	23	31	29
May	.216	.261	.324	102	22	5	0	2	18	5	9	.223	.261	.364	264	59	13	0	8	35	13	28
June	.362	.409	.514	105	38	5	1	3	17	9	13	.254	.311	.390	272	69	10	3	7	36	21	35
July	.320	.393	.427	103	33	5	0	2	18	11	6	.286	.353	.429	245	70	14	0	7	37	24	22
August	.301	.345	.447	103	31	8	2	1	22	8	7	.265	.298	.446	359	95	23	3	12	62	20	44
Sept-Oct	.300	.368	.400	110	33	8	0	1	16	13	11	.253	.305	.388	399	101	22	1	10	60	32	51
Bases Empty	.300	.361	.413	303	91	20	1	4	4	28	30	.261	.312	.414	949	248	52	3	29	29	67	101
Leadoff	.333	.377	.468	171	57	14	0	3	3	11	10	.281	.312	.444	448	126	28	0	15	15	19	34
Runners On Base	.289	.351	.399	308	89	15	2	5	94	31	24	.241	.300	.361	837	202	35	7	17	224	74	108
Scoring Position	.303	.383	.427	178	54	12	2	2	86	25	13	.254	.319	.365	515	131	22	7	7	194	54	70
Late and Close	.257	.339	.295	105	27	4	0	0	11	11	15	.218	.286	.313	316	69	10	1	6	37	27	42

WAYNE KIRBY — BL/TR — age 30 — CLE OF123, DH5   3-YEAR TOTALS (1991–1993)

1993	BA	OBA	SA	AB	H	2B	3B	HR	RBI	BB	SO	BA	OBA	SA	AB	H	2B	3B	HR	RBI	BB	SO
Total	.269	.323	.371	458	123	19	5	6	60	37	58	.260	.315	.362	519	135	22	5	7	66	42	66
vs. Left	.231	.320	.278	108	25	3	1	0	9	12	21	.214	.298	.256	117	25	3	1	0	10	12	25
vs. Right	.280	.325	.400	350	98	16	4	6	51	25	37	.274	.320	.393	402	110	19	4	7	56	30	41
at Home	.289	.342	.409	232	67	10	3	4	29	19	29	.269	.322	.380	271	73	12	3	4	31	21	35
on Road	.248	.304	.332	226	56	9	2	2	31	18	29	.250	.308	.343	248	62	10	2	3	35	21	31
on Grass	.267	.326	.374	393	105	14	5	6	51	34	50	.257	.315	.356	452	116	17	5	6	56	39	58
on Turf	.277	.309	.354	65	18	5	0	0	9	3	8	.284	.314	.403	67	19	5	0	1	10	3	8
Day Games	.242	.295	.356	149	36	5	3	2	24	11	17	.228	.292	.333	171	39	6	3	2	25	15	19
Night Games	.282	.337	.379	309	87	14	2	4	36	26	41	.276	.327	.376	348	96	16	2	5	41	27	47
April	.000	.000	.000	0	0	0	0	0	0	0	0	.000	.000	.000	0	0	0	0	0	0	0	0
May	.333	.345	.395	81	27	3	0	0	10	2	8	.333	.345	.395	81	27	3	1	0	10	2	8
June	.273	.343	.409	88	24	6	0	2	12	10	12	.273	.343	.409	88	24	6	0	2	12	10	12
July	.256	.319	.402	82	21	4	1	2	14	8	7	.256	.319	.402	82	21	4	1	2	14	8	7
August	.250	.319	.375	104	26	1	3	2	15	9	15	.250	.319	.375	104	26	1	3	2	15	9	15
Sept-Oct	.243	.297	.291	103	25	5	0	0	9	8	16	.226	.281	.293	164	37	8	0	1	15	13	24
Bases Empty	.241	.304	.296	253	61	9	1	1	1	20	34	.236	.299	.295	288	68	9	1	2	2	23	40
Leadoff	.179	.250	.200	95	17	2	0	0	0	8	13	.173	.252	.192	104	18	2	0	0	0	10	16
Runners On Base	.302	.346	.463	205	62	10	4	5	59	17	24	.290	.335	.446	231	67	13	4	5	64	19	26
Scoring Position	.300	.343	.492	120	36	5	3	4	53	11	16	.293	.340	.481	133	39	7	3	4	58	13	17
Late and Close	.231	.307	.323	65	15	4	1	0	8	8	14	.202	.281	.310	84	17	4	1	1	10	10	17

CHUCK KNOBLAUCH — BR/TR — age 26 — MIN 2B148, SS6, OF1

3-YEAR TOTALS (1991–1993)

1993	BA	OBA	SA	AB	H	2B	3B	HR	RBI	BB	SO		BA	OBA	SA	AB	H	2B	3B	HR	RBI	BB	SO
Total	.277	.354	.346	602	167	27	4	2	41	65	44		.285	.364	.351	1767	504	70	16	5	147	212	144
vs. Left	.269	.321	.327	156	42	9	0	0	10	10	13		.278	.349	.353	428	119	23	3	1	25	42	34
vs. Right	.280	.365	.352	446	125	18	4	2	31	55	31		.288	.368	.351	1339	385	47	13	4	122	170	110
at Home	.298	.369	.362	312	93	12	1	2	22	33	21		.304	.382	.365	888	270	29	8	3	71	112	62
on Road	.255	.337	.328	290	74	15	3	0	19	32	23		.266	.344	.338	879	234	41	8	2	76	100	82
on Grass	.265	.346	.332	223	59	11	2	0	15	25	15		.275	.347	.335	677	186	30	4	1	56	72	53
on Turf	.285	.358	.354	379	108	16	2	2	26	40	29		.292	.374	.361	1090	318	40	12	4	91	140	91
Day Games	.312	.391	.387	186	58	9	1	1	15	22	11		.310	.391	.385	535	166	23	7	1	52	69	43
Night Games	.262	.337	.327	416	109	18	3	1	26	43	33		.274	.351	.337	1232	338	47	9	4	95	143	101
April	.197	.344	.250	76	15	4	0	0	4	16	9		.273	.359	.333	231	63	7	2	1	21	32	25
May	.348	.430	.435	92	32	6	1	0	10	10	8		.317	.401	.399	281	89	19	2	0	28	37	23
June	.236	.293	.264	106	25	1	1	0	6	9	5		.258	.349	.299	291	75	6	3	0	24	40	14
July	.313	.371	.406	96	30	6	0	1	8	8	3		.288	.350	.377	292	84	15	4	1	26	29	20
August	.306	.387	.417	108	33	7	1	1	7	14	8		.293	.353	.369	328	96	15	2	2	21	30	36
Sept-Oct	.258	.308	.298	124	32	3	1	0	6	8	11		.282	.369	.331	344	97	8	3	1	27	44	26
Bases Empty	.277	.339	.347	375	104	14	3	2	2	33	29		.284	.358	.355	1084	308	42	10	5	5	115	85
Leadoff	.245	.296	.276	192	47	4	1	0	0	13	15		.286	.353	.344	489	140	16	3	2	2	44	39
Runners On Base	.278	.376	.344	227	63	13	1	0	39	32	15		.287	.372	.346	683	196	28	6	0	142	97	59
Scoring Position	.262	.351	.333	126	33	7	1	0	37	15	10		.276	.360	.341	387	107	13	6	0	135	57	40
Late and Close	.236	.333	.270	89	21	3	0	0	7	14	7		.260	.334	.305	262	68	10	1	0	26	30	22

CHAD KREUTER — BB/TR — age 30 — DET C112, DH2, 1B1

6-YEAR TOTALS (1988–1993)

1993	BA	OBA	SA	AB	H	2B	3B	HR	RBI	BB	SO		BA	OBA	SA	AB	H	2B	3B	HR	RBI	BB	SO
Total	.286	.371	.484	374	107	23	3	15	51	49	92		.243	.335	.387	799	194	38	4	23	83	111	193
vs. Left	.209	.313	.382	110	23	4	0	5	17	17	32		.187	.310	.344	241	45	11	0	9	30	44	62
vs. Right	.318	.395	.527	264	84	19	3	10	34	32	60		.267	.346	.405	558	149	27	4	14	53	67	131
at Home	.283	.354	.485	198	56	11	1	9	27	21	53		.246	.341	.391	386	95	15	1	13	41	57	102
on Road	.290	.388	.483	176	51	12	2	6	24	28	39		.240	.328	.383	413	99	23	3	10	42	54	91
on Grass	.291	.371	.487	306	89	20	2	12	42	38	75		.243	.336	.379	671	163	31	3	18	72	95	166
on Turf	.265	.367	.471	68	18	3	1	3	9	11	17		.242	.326	.430	128	31	7	1	5	11	16	27
Day Games	.318	.395	.490	151	48	9	1	5	24	17	31		.283	.374	.430	251	71	12	2	7	29	34	53
Night Games	.265	.354	.480	223	59	14	2	10	27	32	61		.224	.317	.367	548	123	26	2	16	54	77	140
April	.431	.492	.765	51	22	6	1	3	10	6	7		.261	.346	.457	92	24	7	1	3	12	12	17
May	.324	.407	.465	71	23	4	0	2	8	10	16		.270	.349	.400	115	31	6	0	3	10	14	27
June	.250	.316	.389	72	18	6	2	0	2	7	14		.227	.298	.350	163	37	10	2	2	10	17	31
July	.149	.237	.313	67	10	2	0	3	7	8	21		.167	.284	.268	138	23	5	0	3	8	23	40
August	.276	.400	.466	58	16	2	0	3	13	11	17		.270	.369	.410	122	33	2	0	5	18	18	34
Sept-Oct	.327	.406	.600	55	18	3	0	4	11	7	17		.272	.370	.456	169	46	8	1	7	25	27	44
Bases Empty	.313	.391	.507	211	66	13	2	8	8	26	49		.261	.353	.403	472	123	21	2	14	14	66	111
Leadoff	.293	.356	.476	82	24	2	2	3	3	8	16		.233	.322	.375	176	41	6	2	5	5	23	39
Runners On Base	.252	.346	.454	163	41	10	1	7	43	23	43		.217	.310	.364	327	71	17	2	9	69	45	82
Scoring Position	.219	.339	.427	96	21	6	1	4	35	18	26		.212	.313	.392	189	40	12	2	6	61	30	48
Late and Close	.279	.380	.443	61	17	7	0	1	8	10	19		.279	.386	.378	111	31	8	0	1	10	20	32

JOHN KRUK — BL/TL — age 33 — PHI 1B144

8-YEAR TOTALS (1986–1993)

1993	BA	OBA	SA	AB	H	2B	3B	HR	RBI	BB	SO		BA	OBA	SA	AB	H	2B	3B	HR	RBI	BB	SO
Total	.316	.430	.475	535	169	33	5	14	85	111	87		.300	.397	.450	3483	1044	175	34	93	531	581	617
vs. Left	.292	.377	.416	185	54	6	1	5	30	27	39		.275	.353	.379	1129	311	44	8	19	163	143	237
vs. Right	.329	.456	.506	350	115	27	4	9	55	84	48		.311	.416	.483	2354	733	131	26	74	368	438	380
at Home	.327	.441	.506	257	84	14	4	8	47	54	34		.302	.405	.458	1693	511	90	15	48	280	304	284
on Road	.306	.420	.446	278	85	19	1	6	38	57	53		.298	.389	.442	1790	533	85	19	45	251	277	333
on Grass	.313	.410	.441	179	56	8	0	5	25	30	33		.283	.388	.432	1510	428	60	7	50	221	267	307
on Turf	.317	.440	.492	356	113	25	5	9	60	81	54		.312	.403	.463	1973	616	115	27	43	310	314	310
Day Games	.321	.419	.527	131	42	5	2	6	24	23	23		.293	.387	.453	981	287	45	11	30	140	154	184
Night Games	.314	.433	.458	404	127	28	3	8	61	88	64		.303	.401	.448	2502	757	130	23	63	391	427	433
April	.343	.459	.657	70	24	7	0	5	15	15	9		.297	.383	.455	451	134	19	2	16	79	65	69
May	.385	.517	.462	91	35	2	0	0	16	27	12		.328	.436	.474	540	177	32	4	13	86	110	101
June	.304	.439	.457	92	28	6	1	2	13	22	16		.295	.397	.427	604	178	29	9	11	89	104	95
July	.365	.491	.494	85	31	3	1	2	13	21	14		.297	.418	.461	482	143	25	3	16	68	103	92
August	.263	.333	.444	99	26	4	1	4	12	11	17		.298	.390	.454	711	212	33	6	22	106	111	118
Sept-Oct	.255	.348	.388	98	25	6	2	1	16	15	19		.288	.365	.435	695	200	37	10	15	103	88	142
Bases Empty	.303	.405	.471	274	83	19	3	7	7	47	45		.290	.378	.432	1855	538	90	15	48	48	263	329
Leadoff	.432	.514	.684	95	41	10	1	4	4	16	12		.320	.393	.465	802	257	45	4	21	21	96	122
Runners On Base	.330	.455	.479	261	86	14	2	7	78	64	42		.311	.416	.469	1628	506	85	19	45	483	318	288
Scoring Position	.279	.436	.418	165	46	10	2	3	68	50	29		.284	.415	.424	962	273	47	8	24	414	241	194
Late and Close	.329	.468	.541	85	28	4	1	4	18	23	14		.307	.421	.430	593	182	21	5	14	92	120	114

RAY LANKFORD — BL/TL — age 27 — SL OF121

1993	BA	OBA	SA	AB	H	2B	3B	HR	RBI	BB	SO
Total	.238	.366	.346	407	97	17	3	7	45	81	111
vs. Left	.207	.357	.233	116	24	1	1	0	7	26	38
vs. Right	.251	.370	.392	291	73	16	2	7	38	55	73
at Home	.249	.375	.396	197	49	9	1	6	26	40	46
on Road	.229	.358	.300	210	48	8	2	1	19	41	65
on Grass	.200	.315	.250	140	28	4	0	1	9	23	42
on Turf	.258	.392	.397	267	69	13	3	6	36	58	69
Day Games	.199	.306	.279	136	27	7	2	0	12	22	50
Night Games	.258	.395	.380	271	70	10	1	7	33	59	61
April	.230	.329	.311	74	17	1	1	1	7	11	14
May	.308	.429	.374	91	28	1	1	1	15	20	27
June	.261	.407	.377	69	18	5	0	1	7	15	24
July	.229	.383	.354	48	11	4	1	0	5	11	12
August	.185	.346	.369	65	12	3	0	3	6	16	16
Sept-Oct	.183	.271	.283	60	11	3	0	1	5	8	18
Bases Empty	.227	.345	.352	216	49	9	3	4	4	38	58
Leadoff	.294	.379	.500	102	30	6	3	3	3	13	23
Runners On Base	.251	.389	.340	191	48	8	0	3	41	43	53
Scoring Position	.246	.399	.357	126	31	5	0	3	41	33	37
Late and Close	.205	.318	.356	73	15	4	2	1	1	12	22

4-YEAR TOTALS (1990–1993)

	BA	OBA	SA	AB	H	2B	3B	HR	RBI	BB	SO
	.265	.346	.417	1697	450	90	25	39	212	207	399
	.243	.330	.343	597	145	26	11	4	66	73	159
	.277	.355	.456	1100	305	64	14	35	146	134	240
	.268	.348	.441	837	224	40	15	25	119	105	178
	.263	.344	.393	860	226	50	10	14	93	102	221
	.264	.340	.390	474	125	29	5	7	54	54	118
	.266	.348	.427	1223	325	61	20	32	158	153	281
	.225	.313	.374	489	110	28	9	9	54	63	128
	.281	.360	.434	1208	340	62	16	30	158	144	271
	.252	.348	.349	218	55	4	4	3	14	29	40
	.287	.359	.384	289	83	12	2	4	38	33	65
	.261	.356	.409	264	69	15	6	4	32	37	64
	.287	.361	.462	223	64	18	3	5	31	26	56
	.238	.305	.390	323	77	18	5	7	41	31	84
	.268	.353	.482	380	102	23	5	16	56	51	90
	.247	.314	.381	980	242	48	10	21	21	93	235
	.265	.319	.408	476	126	18	7	12	12	37	112
	.290	.387	.466	717	208	42	15	18	191	114	164
	.289	.392	.471	454	131	25	11	12	172	80	111
	.257	.346	.387	315	81	12	4	7	34	41	88

MIKE LANSING — BR/TR — age 26 — MON 3B81, SS51, 2B25

1993	BA	OBA	SA	AB	H	2B	3B	HR	RBI	BB	SO
Total	.287	.352	.369	491	141	29	1	3	45	46	56
vs. Left	.247	.315	.307	150	37	6	0	1	12	15	20
vs. Right	.305	.369	.396	341	104	23	1	2	33	31	36
at Home	.261	.331	.337	261	68	15	1	1	23	25	28
on Road	.317	.376	.404	230	73	14	0	2	22	21	28
on Grass	.349	.384	.457	129	45	8	0	2	14	8	16
on Turf	.265	.342	.337	362	96	21	1	1	31	38	40
Day Games	.309	.360	.438	162	50	12	0	3	14	12	23
Night Games	.277	.349	.334	329	91	17	1	0	31	34	33
April	.342	.375	.539	76	26	6	0	3	15	4	9
May	.278	.371	.356	90	25	5	1	0	4	11	10
June	.203	.270	.253	79	16	4	0	0	6	7	8
July	.297	.388	.351	74	22	4	0	0	3	11	10
August	.273	.319	.307	88	24	3	0	0	7	5	9
Sept-Oct	.333	.391	.417	84	28	7	0	0	10	8	10
Bases Empty	.281	.334	.351	285	80	15	1	1	1	21	29
Leadoff	.297	.339	.378	111	33	7	1	0	0	7	10
Runners On Base	.296	.376	.393	206	61	14	0	2	44	25	27
Scoring Position	.270	.361	.393	122	33	9	0	2	41	18	19
Late and Close	.298	.368	.357	84	25	5	0	0	6	10	11

1-YEAR TOTALS (1993)

	BA	OBA	SA	AB	H	2B	3B	HR	RBI	BB	SO
	.287	.352	.369	491	141	29	1	3	45	46	56
	.247	.315	.307	150	37	6	0	1	12	15	20
	.305	.369	.396	341	104	23	1	2	33	31	36
	.261	.331	.337	261	68	15	1	1	23	25	28
	.317	.376	.404	230	73	14	0	2	22	21	28
	.349	.384	.457	129	45	8	0	2	14	8	16
	.265	.342	.337	362	96	21	1	1	31	38	40
	.309	.360	.438	162	50	12	0	3	14	12	23
	.277	.349	.334	329	91	17	1	0	31	34	33
	.342	.375	.539	76	26	6	0	3	15	4	9
	.278	.371	.356	90	25	5	1	0	4	11	10
	.203	.270	.253	79	16	4	0	0	6	7	8
	.297	.388	.351	74	22	4	0	0	3	11	10
	.273	.319	.307	88	24	3	0	0	7	5	9
	.333	.391	.417	84	28	7	0	0	10	8	10
	.281	.334	.351	285	80	15	1	1	1	21	29
	.297	.339	.378	111	33	7	1	0	0	7	10
	.296	.376	.393	206	61	14	0	2	44	25	27
	.270	.361	.393	122	33	9	0	2	41	18	19
	.298	.368	.357	84	25	5	0	0	6	10	11

BARRY LARKIN — BR/TR — age 30 — CIN SS99

1993	BA	OBA	SA	AB	H	2B	3B	HR	RBI	BB	SO
Total	.315	.394	.445	384	121	20	3	8	51	51	33
vs. Left	.358	.448	.579	95	34	9	0	4	21	17	7
vs. Right	.301	.375	.401	289	87	11	3	4	30	34	26
at Home	.292	.379	.400	195	57	7	1	4	27	27	20
on Road	.339	.409	.492	189	64	13	2	4	24	24	13
on Grass	.327	.407	.535	101	33	8	2	3	15	15	8
on Turf	.311	.389	.413	283	88	12	1	5	36	36	25
Day Games	.306	.398	.577	111	34	5	2	7	22	19	6
Night Games	.319	.392	.392	273	87	15	1	1	29	32	27
April	.305	.400	.366	82	25	3	1	0	8	12	5
May	.342	.417	.486	111	38	7	0	3	20	15	8
June	.287	.354	.396	101	29	3	1	2	11	11	13
July	.329	.395	.513	76	25	5	0	3	11	9	4
August	.286	.444	.571	14	4	2	1	0	1	4	3
Sept-Oct	.000	.000	.000	0	0	0	0	0	0	0	0
Bases Empty	.286	.349	.403	196	56	9	1	4	4	18	17
Leadoff	.311	.323	.443	61	19	3	1	1	1	4	4
Runners On Base	.346	.438	.489	188	65	11	2	4	47	33	16
Scoring Position	.321	.446	.413	109	35	4	0	2	40	27	8
Late and Close	.286	.385	.321	56	16	0	1	0	4	9	9

8-YEAR TOTALS (1986–1993)

	BA	OBA	SA	AB	H	2B	3B	HR	RBI	BB	SO
	.298	.359	.432	3506	1045	170	33	78	419	324	324
	.326	.405	.515	1080	352	68	14	36	153	146	69
	.286	.338	.395	2426	693	102	19	42	266	178	255
	.296	.361	.445	1759	520	82	14	51	251	177	171
	.301	.357	.419	1747	525	88	19	27	168	147	153
	.292	.345	.411	1002	293	53	9	16	97	76	92
	.300	.365	.440	2504	752	117	24	62	322	248	232
	.291	.362	.420	1070	311	41	8	27	127	117	103
	.301	.358	.438	2436	734	129	25	51	292	207	221
	.291	.356	.410	444	129	13	5	10	53	39	42
	.312	.367	.436	597	186	29	6	11	77	51	52
	.301	.363	.452	675	203	32	2	22	95	66	70
	.299	.369	.449	568	170	38	4	13	50	57	51
	.278	.340	.404	623	173	32	10	9	65	59	57
	.307	.360	.436	599	184	26	6	13	79	52	52
	.279	.333	.411	2094	585	98	15	49	49	147	196
	.282	.334	.415	862	243	35	7	22	22	59	80
	.326	.396	.464	1412	460	72	18	29	370	177	128
	.310	.392	.440	844	262	35	10	18	335	129	81
	.306	.370	.391	555	170	18	7	5	63	56	63

MANUEL LEE — BB/TR — age 29 — TEX SS72, DH1

9-YEAR TOTALS (1985–1993)

1993	BA	OBA	SA	AB	H	2B	3B	HR	RBI	BB	SO		BA	OBA	SA	AB	H	2B	3B	HR	RBI	BB	SO
Total	.220	.300	.259	205	45	3	1	1	12	22	39		.251	.303	.318	2357	592	70	18	17	211	180	465
vs. Left	.233	.298	.256	43	10	1	0	0	1	3	8		.270	.315	.365	833	225	34	9	9	89	54	142
vs. Right	.216	.301	.259	162	35	2	1	1	11	19	31		.241	.297	.292	1524	367	36	9	8	122	126	323
at Home	.263	.352	.316	76	20	2	1	0	6	11	15		.250	.309	.320	1112	278	35	11	7	98	99	217
on Road	.194	.268	.225	129	25	1	0	1	6	11	24		.252	.298	.316	1245	314	35	7	10	113	81	248
on Grass	.230	.312	.261	165	38	3	1	0	9	18	31		264	.311	.326	1039	274	28	8	7	98	72	195
on Turf	.175	.250	.250	40	7	0	0	1	3	4	8		.241	.297	.311	1318	318	42	10	10	113	108	270
Day Games	.278	.365	.296	54	15	1	0	0	4	6	7		.249	.301	.323	742	185	19	6	8	66	55	139
Night Games	.199	.275	.245	151	30	2	1	1	8	16	32		.252	.304	.315	1615	407	51	12	9	145	125	326
April	.206	.308	.206	34	7	0	0	0	2	4	3		.247	.319	.290	324	80	12	1	0	26	34	67
May	.128	.186	.128	39	5	0	0	0	1	3	7		.241	.289	.370	257	62	3	3	8	25	17	53
June	.000	.000	.000	0	0	0	0	0	0	0	0		.277	.318	.345	440	122	16	4	2	45	28	81
July	.056	.105	.056	18	1	0	0	0	0	1	6		.219	.268	.255	420	92	10	1	1	34	29	91
August	.217	.280	.239	46	10	1	0	0	3	4	10		.253	.294	.320	490	124	13	4	4	46	30	98
Sept-Oct	.324	.418	.426	68	22	2	1	1	6	10	13		.263	.329	.338	426	112	16	5	2	35	42	75
Bases Empty	.227	.292	.252	119	27	3	0	0	0	11	23		.248	.306	.310	1365	339	37	7	11	11	113	267
Leadoff	.244	.326	.268	41	10	1	0	0	0	5	6		.258	.318	.323	530	137	18	2	4	4	46	110
Runners On Base	.209	.310	.267	86	18	0	1	1	12	11	16		.255	.300	.329	992	253	33	11	6	200	67	198
Scoring Position	.235	.344	.235	51	12	0	0	0	9	8	9		.268	.309	.348	578	155	20	7	4	191	40	118
Late and Close	.217	.280	.217	23	5	0	0	0	0	2	5		.228	.296	.257	404	92	5	2	1	33	39	84

MARK LEMKE — BB/TR — age 29 — ATL 2B150

6-YEAR TOTALS (1988–1993)

1993	BA	OBA	SA	AB	H	2B	3B	HR	RBI	BB	SO		BA	OBA	SA	AB	H	2B	3B	HR	RBI	BB	SO
Total	.252	.335	.341	493	124	19	2	7	49	65	50		.234	.309	.315	1541	361	56	9	17	131	174	150
vs. Left	.309	.382	.482	139	43	5	2	5	14	17	6		.262	.324	.389	550	144	24	5	12	59	53	34
vs. Right	.229	.317	.285	354	81	14	0	2	35	48	44		.219	.302	.274	991	217	32	4	5	72	121	116
at Home	.256	.338	.341	246	63	8	2	3	27	31	22		.243	.314	.330	779	189	32	3	10	72	83	69
on Road	.247	.332	.340	247	61	11	0	4	22	34	28		.226	.305	.301	762	172	24	6	7	59	91	81
on Grass	.235	.325	.329	371	87	13	2	6	37	52	36		.238	.316	.323	1143	272	41	7	14	101	135	107
on Turf	.303	.368	.377	122	37	6	0	1	12	13	14		.224	.290	.294	398	89	15	2	3	30	39	43
Day Games	.229	.341	.307	140	32	4	2	1	15	25	17		.252	.331	.316	433	109	16	3	2	38	55	42
Night Games	.261	.332	.354	353	92	15	0	6	34	40	33		.227	.301	.315	1108	252	40	6	15	93	119	108
April	.222	.346	.333	63	14	1	0	2	7	13	8		.217	.300	.293	157	34	6	0	2	14	20	21
May	.323	.394	.516	93	30	5	2	3	9	11	13		.252	.326	.364	258	65	11	3	4	17	30	27
June	.230	.309	.310	87	20	4	0	1	9	10	3		.236	.318	.319	191	45	6	2	2	15	23	13
July	.297	.371	.385	91	27	5	0	1	10	12	7		.248	.332	.326	218	54	9	1	2	27	29	16
August	.225	.290	.270	89	20	4	0	0	10	9	12		.263	.323	.332	289	76	8	0	4	26	27	34
Sept-Oct	.186	.287	.186	70	13	0	0	0	4	10	7		.203	.278	.276	428	87	16	3	3	32	45	39
Bases Empty	.238	.302	.333	282	67	10	1	5	5	26	30		.220	.286	.310	888	195	32	3	14	14	82	93
Leadoff	.203	.266	.288	118	24	5	1	1	1	10	16		.214	.275	.310	355	76	13	3	5	5	30	37
Runners On Base	.270	.375	.351	211	57	9	1	2	44	39	20		.254	.340	.323	653	166	24	6	3	117	92	57
Scoring Position	.246	.375	.331	118	29	7	0	1	41	28	8		.244	.341	.328	381	93	18	4	2	112	63	31
Late and Close	.236	.313	.393	89	21	2	0	4	10	10	13		.234	.308	.322	286	67	6	2	5	30	32	34

DARREN LEWIS — BR/TR — age 27 — SFOF131

4-YEAR TOTALS (1990–1993)

1993	BA	OBA	SA	AB	H	2B	3B	HR	RBI	BB	SO		BA	OBA	SA	AB	H	2B	3B	HR	RBI	BB	SO
Total	.253	.302	.324	522	132	17	7	2	48	30	40		.245	.314	.303	1099	269	30	11	4	82	102	120
vs. Left	.267	.321	.343	172	46	7	3	0	15	13	16		.255	.327	.329	380	97	14	4	2	26	39	41
vs. Right	.246	.292	.314	350	86	10	4	2	33	17	24		.239	.308	.289	719	172	16	7	2	56	63	79
at Home	.256	.302	.344	250	64	12	2	2	26	14	15		.226	.299	.281	531	120	16	2	3	40	50	49
on Road	.250	.301	.305	272	68	5	5	0	22	16	25		.262	.329	.324	568	149	14	9	1	42	52	71
on Grass	.257	.307	.341	393	101	15	6	2	39	23	26		.235	.309	.297	799	188	23	7	4	60	77	78
on Turf	.240	.285	.271	129	31	2	1	0	9	7	14		.270	.329	.320	300	81	7	4	0	22	25	42
Day Games	.246	.296	.322	264	65	8	3	2	29	15	17		.242	.310	.292	513	124	10	5	2	46	46	49
Night Games	.260	.308	.326	258	67	9	4	0	19	15	23		.247	.318	.312	586	145	20	6	2	36	56	71
April	.238	.290	.365	63	15	4	2	0	3	5	8		.286	.355	.364	154	44	6	3	0	9	17	22
May	.250	.302	.389	108	27	4	4	1	15	6	8		.215	.269	.292	195	42	4	4	1	19	12	22
June	.265	.336	.304	102	27	4	0	0	3	9	6		.235	.308	.294	153	36	6	0	1	7	14	14
July	.300	.336	.355	110	33	3	0	1	15	4	10		.301	.366	.366	183	55	7	1	1	20	16	21
August	.269	.296	.269	26	7	0	0	0	2	1	1		.259	.329	.315	143	37	1	2	1	10	14	14
Sept-Oct	.204	.244	.239	113	23	2	1	0	10	5	7		.203	.285	.232	271	55	6	1	0	17	29	27
Bases Empty	.223	.289	.280	336	75	13	3	0	0	25	30		.226	.307	.282	726	164	21	7	2	2	77	89
Leadoff	.245	.314	.298	188	46	6	2	0	0	15	14		.243	.328	.301	408	99	8	5	2	2	48	48
Runners On Base	.306	.326	.403	186	57	4	4	2	48	5	10		.282	.329	.343	373	105	9	4	2	80	25	31
Scoring Position	.319	.333	.422	116	37	2	2	2	45	2	7		.275	.326	.335	236	65	4	2	2	76	17	27
Late and Close	.197	.254	.242	66	13	1	1	0	4	4	9		.231	.310	.282	156	36	4	2	0	12	16	26

JOSE LIND — BR/TR — age 30 — KC 2B136

1993	BA	OBA	SA	AB	H	2B	3B	HR	RBI	BB	SO		BA	OBA	SA	AB	H	2B	3B	HR	RBI	BB	SO
Total	.248	.271	.288	431	107	13	2	0	37	13	36		.254	.295	.315	3247	824	124	25	8	286	193	324
vs. Left	.257	.270	.333	105	27	6	1	0	8	2	10		.255	.302	.327	1147	292	51	10	4	94	85	120
vs. Right	.245	.271	.273	326	80	7	1	0	29	11	26		.253	.290	.308	2100	532	73	15	4	192	108	204
at Home	.246	.267	.295	207	51	6	2	0	24	6	16		.258	.299	.327	1632	421	65	15	6	173	101	157
on Road	.250	.274	.281	224	56	7	0	0	13	7	20		.250	.291	.302	1615	403	59	10	2	113	92	167
on Grass	.222	.250	.244	180	40	4	0	0	7	7	15		.231	.269	.262	904	209	23	1	1	51	45	91
on Turf	.267	.285	.319	251	67	9	2	0	30	6	21		.262	.305	.335	2343	615	101	24	7	235	148	233
Day Games	.273	.302	.311	132	36	3	1	0	7	5	18		.246	.292	.302	910	224	30	9	1	75	57	119
Night Games	.237	.256	.278	299	71	10	1	0	30	8	18		.257	.296	.320	2337	600	94	16	7	211	136	205
April	.297	.328	.391	64	19	4	1	0	10	2	3		.239	.280	.295	440	105	15	2	2	38	26	37
May	.160	.160	.173	75	12	1	0	0	5	0	8		.261	.293	.327	517	135	23	4	1	62	23	49
June	.344	.375	.393	61	21	3	0	0	3	3	6		.271	.318	.338	536	145	23	2	3	50	39	57
July	.264	.274	.319	72	19	2	1	0	6	1	7		.243	.278	.307	527	128	18	5	2	35	25	51
August	.205	.242	.216	88	18	1	0	0	6	4	7		.214	.264	.261	590	126	20	4	0	41	42	67
Sept-Oct	.254	.273	.282	71	18	2	0	0	7	3	5		.290	.329	.355	637	185	25	8	0	60	38	63
Bases Empty	.224	.257	.252	250	56	7	0	0	0	10	24		.245	.281	.304	1802	441	73	8	6	6	88	177
Leadoff	.220	.254	.248	109	24	3	0	0	0	4	13		.237	.268	.295	638	151	25	3	2	2	6	61
Runners On Base	.282	.289	.337	181	51	6	2	0	37	3	12		.265	.311	.328	1445	383	51	17	2	280	105	147
Scoring Position	.267	.269	.327	101	27	2	2	0	34	2	8		.264	.325	.337	813	215	30	13	1	263	85	81
Late and Close	.167	.197	.167	72	12	0	0	0	6	3	5		.255	.296	.297	580	148	17	2	1	45	35	60

7-YEAR TOTALS (1987–1993) (right-hand columns)

PAT LISTACH — BB/TR — age 27 — MIL SS95, OF6

1993	BA	OBA	SA	AB	H	2B	3B	HR	RBI	BB	SO		BA	OBA	SA	AB	H	2B	3B	HR	RBI	BB	SO
Total	.244	.319	.317	356	87	15	1	3	30	37	70		.273	.339	.337	935	255	34	7	4	77	92	194
vs. Left	.279	.343	.395	129	36	7	1	2	14	12	21		.314	.363	.426	277	87	14	4	3	32	20	46
vs. Right	.225	.306	.273	227	51	8	0	1	16	25	49		.255	.329	.299	658	168	20	3	1	45	72	148
at Home	.247	.338	.287	174	43	7	0	0	16	23	29		.249	.320	.290	441	110	16	1	0	42	45	82
on Road	.242	.299	.346	182	44	8	1	3	14	14	41		.294	.356	.379	494	145	18	6	4	35	47	112
on Grass	.233	.315	.291	292	68	12	1	1	21	33	56		.268	.334	.321	775	208	29	3	2	58	74	153
on Turf	.297	.338	.438	64	19	3	0	2	9	4	14		.294	.365	.412	160	47	5	4	2	19	18	41
Day Games	.243	.335	.322	152	37	6	0	2	15	20	30		.274	.358	.330	336	92	13	0	2	32	43	71
Night Games	.245	.306	.314	204	50	9	1	1	15	17	40		.272	.328	.341	599	163	21	7	2	45	49	123
April	.237	.338	.254	59	14	1	0	0	2	7	10		.276	.364	.322	87	24	2	1	0	3	10	13
May	.210	.265	.295	105	22	4	1	1	3	8	28		.257	.319	.319	210	54	6	2	1	10	19	45
June	.000	.000	.000	1	0	0	0	0	0	0	0		.238	.269	.267	101	24	1	1	0	9	5	28
July	.170	.250	.191	47	8	1	0	0	1	5	12		.275	.366	.353	153	42	6	3	0	12	22	39
August	.279	.364	.385	104	29	8	0	1	16	15	15		.295	.357	.368	220	65	13	0	1	26	21	34
Sept-Oct	.350	.395	.450	40	14	0	0	1	8	2	5		.280	.344	.354	164	46	6	0	2	17	15	35
Bases Empty	.228	.319	.301	219	50	8	1	2	2	27	38		.262	.336	.323	572	150	18	4	3	3	62	107
Leadoff	.237	.302	.356	118	28	6	1	2	2	10	21		.265	.337	.351	313	83	10	4	3	3	33	56
Runners On Base	.270	.320	.343	137	37	7	0	1	28	10	32		.289	.343	.358	363	105	16	3	1	74	30	87
Scoring Position	.250	.316	.333	84	21	4	0	1	28	8	25		.259	.327	.320	228	59	9	1	1	69	23	63
Late and Close	.277	.319	.323	65	18	3	0	0	10	4	11		.318	.369	.383	154	49	8	1	0	22	13	28

2-YEAR TOTALS (1992–1993) (right-hand columns)

KENNY LOFTON — BL/TL — age 27 — CLE OF146

1993	BA	OBA	SA	AB	H	2B	3B	HR	RBI	BB	SO		BA	OBA	SA	AB	H	2B	3B	HR	RBI	BB	SO
Total	.325	.408	.408	569	185	28	8	1	42	81	83		.299	.377	.376	1219	364	44	16	6	84	154	156
vs. Left	.292	.388	.349	195	57	9	1	0	15	30	36		.318	.413	.374	337	107	15	2	0	27	53	59
vs. Right	.342	.418	.439	374	128	19	7	1	27	51	47		.291	.363	.376	882	257	29	14	6	57	101	97
at Home	.313	.414	.410	278	87	12	6	1	15	49	44		.295	.386	.382	589	174	19	10	4	37	87	80
on Road	.337	.401	.405	291	98	16	2	0	27	32	39		.302	.369	.370	630	190	25	6	2	47	67	76
on Grass	.328	.415	.422	467	153	25	8	1	35	71	70		.301	.384	.390	989	298	38	16	6	75	133	120
on Turf	.314	.372	.343	102	32	3	0	0	7	10	13		.287	.345	.313	230	66	6	0	0	9	21	36
Day Games	.327	.407	.382	199	65	7	2	0	16	29	28		.303	.394	.358	413	125	12	4	1	26	62	52
Night Games	.324	.408	.422	370	120	21	6	1	26	52	55		.297	.368	.385	806	239	32	12	5	58	92	104
April	.313	.398	.438	80	25	4	3	0	6	12	12		.269	.363	.345	145	39	5	3	0	9	21	17
May	.373	.443	.392	102	38	2	0	0	7	12	13		.336	.399	.379	211	71	4	1	1	18	21	20
June	.275	.362	.441	102	28	6	4	1	10	14	18		.261	.338	.377	199	52	8	6	1	14	23	23
July	.291	.364	.359	103	30	7	0	0	8	13	9		.269	.342	.360	197	53	10	1	2	14	22	17
August	.333	.408	.411	90	30	5	1	0	8	12	18		.337	.423	.473	184	62	9	5	2	18	28	30
Sept-Oct	.370	.473	.413	92	34	4	0	0	3	18	13		.307	.390	.336	283	87	8	0	0	11	39	49
Bases Empty	.339	.420	.431	378	128	23	6	0	0	53	56		.302	.382	.377	815	246	34	9	3	3	104	108
Leadoff	.326	.409	.419	227	74	11	5	0	0	32	36		.287	.374	.360	492	141	16	7	2	2	68	74
Runners On Base	.298	.384	.361	191	57	5	2	1	42	28	27		.292	.369	.374	404	118	10	7	3	81	50	48
Scoring Position	.282	.371	.330	103	29	2	0	1	39	16	14		.297	.366	.378	222	66	3	3	3	76	26	28
Late and Close	.281	.381	.326	89	25	4	0	0	7	14	14		.260	.356	.304	204	53	6	0	1	12	29	25

3-YEAR TOTALS (1991–1993) (right-hand columns)

TOREY LOVULLO — BB/TR — age 29 — CAL 2B91, 3B14, SS9, OF2, 1B1

1993	BA	OBA	SA	AB	H	2B	3B	HR	RBI	BB	SO		4-YEAR TOTALS (1988–1993) BA	OBA	SA	AB	H	2B	3B	HR	RBI	BB	SO
Total	.251	.318	.354	367	92	20	0	6	30	36	49		.226	.300	.323	526	119	25	1	8	38	56	78
vs. Left	.286	.352	.365	63	18	2	0	1	7	6	3		.215	.287	.290	107	23	2	0	2	11	11	10
vs. Right	.243	.310	.352	304	74	18	0	5	23	30	46		.229	.303	.332	419	96	23	1	6	27	45	68
at Home	.243	.318	.364	173	42	9	0	4	16	20	20		.233	.308	.335	236	55	12	0	4	17	27	28
on Road	.258	.318	.345	194	50	11	0	2	14	16	29		.221	.293	.314	290	64	13	1	4	21	29	50
on Grass	.250	.323	.354	280	70	14	0	5	24	30	38		.231	.307	.325	415	96	19	1	6	30	46	63
on Turf	.253	.301	.356	87	22	6	0	1	6	6	11		.207	.273	.315	111	23	6	0	2	8	10	15
Day Games	.248	.307	.352	125	31	10	0	1	8	11	15		.205	.283	.277	195	40	11	0	1	11	22	29
Night Games	.252	.323	.355	242	61	10	0	5	22	25	34		.239	.310	.350	331	79	14	1	7	27	34	49
April	.267	.313	.533	15	4	1	0	1	3	1	2		.143	.266	.231	91	13	2	0	2	7	16	24
May	.328	.379	.508	61	20	8	0	1	6	4	10		.253	.309	.391	87	22	9	0	1	6	6	13
June	.272	.333	.346	81	22	3	0	1	9	8	9		.272	.333	.346	81	22	3	0	1	9	8	9
July	.202	.284	.214	84	17	1	0	0	4	10	8		.202	.284	.214	84	17	1	0	0	4	10	8
August	.229	.250	.343	35	8	4	0	0	1	1	3		.229	.250	.343	35	8	4	0	0	1	1	3
Sept-Oct	.231	.320	.363	91	21	3	0	3	7	12	17		.250	.319	.385	148	37	6	1	4	11	15	21
Bases Empty	.239	.312	.345	197	47	12	0	3	3	20	29		.231	.301	.331	290	67	15	1	4		28	46
Leadoff	.211	.276	.256	90	19	4	0	0	0	8	18		.213	.278	.279	122	26	5	0	1	1	11	23
Runners On Base	.265	.324	.365	170	45	8	0	3	27	16	20		.220	.299	.314	236	52	10	0	4	34	28	32
Scoring Position	.239	.310	.352	88	21	4	0	2	25	10	11		.190	.297	.273	121	23	4	0	2	30	20	18
Late and Close	.274	.360	.411	73	20	1	0	3	16	10	8		.225	.315	.324	111	25	2	0	3	19	15	14

MIKE MACFARLANE — BR/TR — age 30 — KC C114

1993	BA	OBA	SA	AB	H	2B	3B	HR	RBI	BB	SO		7-YEAR TOTALS (1987–1993) BA	OBA	SA	AB	H	2B	3B	HR	RBI	BB	SO
Total	.273	.360	.497	388	106	27	0	20	67	40	83		.255	.321	.431	1844	471	119	9	62	262	142	359
vs. Left	.233	.337	.373	150	35	9	0	4	19	20	34		.249	.310	.409	700	174	45	5	19	77	50	135
vs. Right	.298	.375	.576	238	71	18	0	16	48	20	49		.260	.328	.444	1144	297	74	4	43	185	92	224
at Home	.284	.374	.487	197	56	19	0	7	35	23	37		.266	.334	.436	871	232	67	6	23	123	68	145
on Road	.262	.344	.508	191	50	8	0	13	32	17	46		.246	.310	.425	973	239	52	3	39	139	74	214
on Grass	.268	.356	.503	153	41	6	0	10	27	16	32		.251	.318	.428	764	192	39	3	30	120	62	155
on Turf	.277	.362	.494	235	65	21	0	10	40	24	51		.258	.324	.432	1080	279	80	6	32	142	80	204
Day Games	.314	.403	.569	102	32	8	0	6	20	12	19		.274	.348	.463	438	120	30	1	17	64	41	91
Night Games	.259	.344	.472	286	74	19	0	14	47	28	64		.250	.313	.420	1406	351	89	8	45	198	101	268
April	.233	.242	.333	30	7	0	0	1	4	1	8		.287	.353	.426	209	60	21	1	2	22	18	46
May	.338	.419	.708	65	22	6	0	6	20	5	8		.246	.319	.453	386	95	25	2	17	62	31	74
June	.246	.365	.478	69	17	4	0	4	14	9	16		.246	.296	.382	398	98	21	3	9	51	23	71
July	.240	.310	.400	75	18	3	0	3	9	5	21		.263	.327	.446	323	85	20	0	13	54	25	67
August	.256	.366	.488	86	22	8	0	5	9	12	20		.254	.327	.485	260	66	15	0	15	43	24	57
Sept-Oct	.317	.397	.508	63	20	6	0	2	11	8	10		.250	.325	.403	268	67	17	3	6	30	21	44
Bases Empty	.280	.364	.512	211	59	16	0	11	11	20	50		.251	.312	.441	1032	259	70	6	38	38	70	222
Leadoff	.276	.356	.543	105	29	7	0	7	7	10	26		.244	.304	.458	467	114	28	3	22	22	30	97
Runners On Base	.266	.355	.480	177	47	11	0	9	56	20	33		.261	.333	.417	812	212	49	3	24	224	72	137
Scoring Position	.293	.385	.500	116	34	9	0	5	48	14	22		.249	.333	.396	490	122	29	2	13	190	53	89
Late and Close	.277	.344	.518	83	23	5	0	5	14	7	19		.245	.324	.425	339	83	17	4	12	46	31	78

SHANE MACK — BR/TR — age 31 — MIN OF128

1993	BA	OBA	SA	AB	H	2B	3B	HR	RBI	BB	SO		6-YEAR TOTALS (1987–1993) BA	OBA	SA	AB	H	2B	3B	HR	RBI	BB	SO
Total	.276	.335	.412	503	139	30	4	10	61	41	76		.295	.361	.444	2215	653	112	25	56	291	200	398
vs. Left	.288	.317	.424	118	34	8	1	2	16	4	11		.310	.370	.504	716	222	45	11	24	121	59	106
vs. Right	.273	.340	.408	385	105	22	3	8	45	37	65		.288	.357	.415	1499	431	67	14	32	170	141	292
at Home	.289	.350	.436	218	63	17	3	3	25	19	36		.301	.370	.473	1019	307	61	21	24	142	99	193
on Road	.267	.323	.393	285	76	13	1	7	36	22	40		.289	.353	.419	1196	346	51	4	32	149	101	205
on Grass	.286	.347	.429	217	62	13	0	6	29	19	31		.293	.361	.433	1021	299	51	4	28	135	95	182
on Turf	.269	.325	.399	286	77	17	4	4	32	22	45		.296	.361	.453	1194	354	61	21	28	156	105	216
Day Games	.215	.251	.372	172	37	10	1	5	26	8	27		.291	.356	.453	735	214	39	7	22	108	64	113
Night Games	.308	.376	.432	331	102	20	3	5	35	33	49		.297	.363	.439	1480	439	73	18	34	183	136	285
April	.213	.250	.275	80	17	5	0	0	10	3	11		.246	.309	.389	211	52	12	3	4	24	13	37
May	.220	.245	.340	50	11	3	0	1	9	1	3		.297	.366	.425	320	95	13	2	8	47	30	46
June	.242	.355	.473	91	22	3	3	4	14	15	16		.255	.332	.422	431	110	22	4	14	61	46	80
July	.392	.447	.578	102	40	10	0	3	14	11	13		.339	.406	.519	428	145	24	7	13	55	48	81
August	.264	.308	.336	125	33	4	1	1	11	7	23		.299	.352	.434	438	131	20	6	9	56	31	86
Sept-Oct	.291	.339	.436	55	16	5	0	1	3	4	10		.310	.377	.442	387	120	21	3	8	48	32	68
Bases Empty	.262	.315	.353	309	81	13	3	3	3	21	45		.285	.349	.422	1291	368	61	3	30	30	110	231
Leadoff	.296	.327	.327	162	39	5	0	3	3	8	22		.296	.353	.447	611	181	28	5	18	18	45	96
Runners On Base	.299	.364	.505	194	58	17	1	7	58	20	31		.308	.377	.474	924	285	51	12	26	261	90	167
Scoring Position	.327	.395	.558	104	34	7	1	5	51	12	12		.297	.376	.463	516	153	28	8	14	224	61	95
Late and Close	.235	.303	.432	81	19	7	0	3	12	8	13		.251	.312	.355	346	87	16	1	6	41	31	69

DAVE MAGADAN — BL/TR — age 32 — FLO/SEA 3B90, 1B43, DH2

1993	BA	OBA	SA	AB	H	2B	3B	HR	RBI	BB	SO	8-YEAR TOTALS (1986–1993) BA	OBA	SA	AB	H	2B	3B	HR	RBI	BB	SO
Total	.273	.378	.356	455	124	23	0	5	50	80	63	.289	.389	.380	2543	734	133	11	26	304	427	312
vs. Left	.237	.333	.297	118	28	7	0	0	18	19	22	.272	.359	.331	786	214	30	2	4	99	107	105
vs. Right	.285	.394	.377	337	96	16	0	5	32	61	41	.296	.401	.402	1757	520	103	9	22	205	320	207
at Home	.286	.424	.403	206	59	15	0	3	28	51	23	.296	.402	.391	1228	363	62	5	15	163	229	142
on Road	.261	.336	.317	249	65	8	0	2	22	29	40	.282	.375	.370	1315	371	71	6	11	141	198	170
on Grass	.278	.388	.379	248	69	10	0	5	28	46	37	.291	.388	.377	1707	496	76	6	20	208	282	213
on Turf	.266	.366	.329	207	55	13	0	0	22	34	26	.285	.390	.386	836	238	57	5	6	96	145	99
Day Games	.226	.348	.263	137	31	5	0	0	12	26	20	.269	.374	.359	854	230	42	4	9	92	149	109
Night Games	.292	.392	.396	318	93	18	0	5	38	54	43	.298	.396	.391	1689	504	91	7	17	212	278	203
April	.320	.457	.413	75	24	4	0	1	10	18	10	.283	.401	.371	283	80	14	1	3	29	57	46
May	.244	.371	.346	78	19	5	0	1	8	17	8	.286	.378	.376	426	122	19	2	5	44	65	59
June	.310	.378	.414	87	27	3	0	2	12	10	13	.305	.408	.422	524	160	28	3	9	73	92	54
July	.286	.381	.357	70	20	5	0	0	10	12	8	.297	.391	.387	519	154	30	1	5	65	84	48
August	.227	.333	.273	66	15	3	0	0	4	11	11	.268	.370	.316	437	117	19	1	0	46	72	54
Sept-Oct	.241	.341	.316	79	19	3	0	1	6	12	13	.285	.381	.401	354	101	23	3	4	47	57	51
Bases Empty	.274	.381	.363	237	65	15	0	2	2	40	28	.266	.372	.359	1411	376	75	7	14	14	229	173
Leadoff	.256	.351	.354	82	21	8	0	0	0	12	6	.269	.373	.355	502	135	26	1	5	5	81	56
Runners On Base	.271	.375	.349	218	59	8	0	3	48	40	35	.316	.409	.406	1132	358	58	4	12	290	198	139
Scoring Position	.238	.364	.300	130	31	5	0	1	43	29	23	.300	.406	.390	657	197	33	1	8	266	138	88
Late and Close	.253	.345	.373	75	19	3	0	2	14	11	13	.268	.378	.355	425	114	14	1	7	55	72	64

KIRT MANWARING — BR/TR — age 29 — SFC130

1993	BA	OBA	SA	AB	H	2B	3B	HR	RBI	BB	SO	7-YEAR TOTALS (1987–1993) BA	OBA	SA	AB	H	2B	3B	HR	RBI	BB	SO
Total	.275	.345	.350	432	119	15	1	5	49	41	76	.246	.305	.317	1295	318	45	9	10	128	92	193
vs. Left	.315	.379	.390	146	46	5	0	2	18	14	32	.274	.326	.338	521	143	17	5	2	44	36	78
vs. Right	.255	.328	.329	286	73	10	1	3	31	27	44	.226	.292	.304	774	175	28	4	8	84	56	115
at Home	.270	.327	.354	189	51	7	0	3	19	14	32	.247	.290	.321	608	150	25	4	4	63	30	83
on Road	.280	.359	.346	243	68	8	1	2	30	27	44	.245	.318	.314	687	168	20	5	6	65	62	110
on Grass	.268	.341	.350	317	85	11	0	5	34	31	59	.252	.304	.325	966	243	34	5	9	97	59	144
on Turf	.296	.357	.348	115	34	4	1	0	15	10	17	.228	.309	.295	329	75	11	4	1	31	33	49
Day Games	.264	.344	.373	201	53	8	1	4	21	24	36	.252	.310	.342	567	143	19	4	6	63	40	79
Night Games	.286	.346	.329	231	66	7	0	1	28	17	40	.240	.302	.298	728	175	26	5	2	65	52	114
April	.288	.348	.407	59	17	2	1	1	10	4	7	.267	.323	.333	150	40	3	2	1	17	9	17
May	.306	.411	.339	62	19	2	0	0	5	10	10	.285	.386	.351	151	43	6	2	0	14	22	20
June	.239	.282	.284	67	16	3	0	0	4	3	13	.258	.302	.321	240	62	8	2	1	19	13	39
July	.377	.448	.494	77	29	3	0	2	14	9	9	.267	.325	.343	210	56	6	2	2	27	16	28
August	.184	.245	.287	87	16	3	0	2	10	6	20	.212	.264	.306	288	61	13	1	4	32	17	49
Sept-Oct	.275	.344	.300	80	22	2	0	0	6	9	17	.219	.278	.277	256	56	9	0	2	19	15	40
Bases Empty	.271	.341	.347	225	61	3	1	4	4	23	41	.234	.292	.311	755	177	21	5	9	9	53	122
Leadoff	.316	.381	.377	114	36	1	1	1	1	11	17	.262	.328	.341	305	80	8	2	4	4	24	40
Runners On Base	.280	.349	.353	207	58	12	0	1	45	18	35	.261	.324	.326	540	141	24	4	1	119	39	71
Scoring Position	.303	.392	.377	122	37	9	0	0	40	15	21	.271	.345	.345	328	89	18	3	0	111	32	44
Late and Close	.164	.190	.246	61	10	3	0	0	5	2	18	.214	.270	.291	196	42	7	1	2	19	14	36

ALBERT MARTIN — BL/TL — age 27 — PIT OF136

1993	BA	OBA	SA	AB	H	2B	3B	HR	RBI	BB	SO	2-YEAR TOTALS (1992–1993) BA	OBA	SA	AB	H	2B	3B	HR	RBI	BB	SO
Total	.281	.338	.481	480	135	26	8	18	64	42	122	.278	.334	.478	492	137	26	9	18	66	42	127
vs. Left	.191	.277	.303	89	17	5	1	1	8	11	27	.187	.272	.297	91	17	5	1	1	8	11	28
vs. Right	.302	.353	.522	391	118	21	7	17	56	31	95	.299	.349	.519	401	120	21	8	17	58	31	99
at Home	.273	.337	.538	253	69	12	5	15	44	25	72	.271	.335	.531	258	70	12	5	15	45	25	74
on Road	.291	.340	.419	227	66	14	3	3	20	17	50	.286	.333	.419	234	67	14	4	3	21	17	53
on Grass	.320	.365	.444	153	49	11	1	2	14	12	28	.313	.354	.444	160	50	11	2	2	15	12	31
on Turf	.263	.326	.498	327	86	15	7	16	50	30	94	.262	.324	.494	332	87	15	7	16	51	30	96
Day Games	.242	.287	.417	120	29	7	1	4	17	8	29	.238	.279	.415	130	31	7	2	4	19	8	32
Night Games	.294	.355	.503	360	106	19	7	14	47	34	93	.293	.353	.500	362	106	19	7	14	47	34	95
April	.260	.267	.452	73	19	5	3	1	5	1	17	.260	.267	.452	73	19	5	3	1	5	1	17
May	.207	.254	.328	58	12	2	1	1	3	4	13	.207	.254	.328	58	12	2	1	1	3	4	13
June	.284	.356	.519	81	23	5	1	4	7	9	19	.284	.356	.519	81	23	5	1	4	7	9	19
July	.289	.366	.344	90	26	5	0	0	8	10	30	.283	.359	.337	92	26	5	0	0	8	10	32
August	.337	.396	.565	92	31	4	1	5	16	9	18	.337	.396	.565	92	31	4	1	5	16	9	18
Sept-Oct	.279	.344	.628	86	24	5	2	7	25	9	25	.271	.327	.604	96	26	5	3	7	25	9	28
Bases Empty	.266	.313	.481	293	78	18	6	11	11	19	74	.266	.312	.485	297	79	18	7	11	11	19	75
Leadoff	.268	.322	.435	138	37	8	6	1	1	11	35	.268	.322	.435	138	37	8	6	1	1	11	35
Runners On Base	.305	.376	.481	187	57	8	2	7	53	23	48	.297	.365	.467	195	58	8	2	7	55	23	52
Scoring Position	.291	.377	.455	110	32	5	2	3	42	17	32	.284	.365	.440	116	33	5	2	3	44	17	35
Late and Close	.346	.388	.551	78	27	4	0	4	10	6	24	.325	.367	.518	83	27	4	0	4	10	6	27

TINO MARTINEZ — BL/TR — age 27 — SEA 1B103, DH6

1993	BA	OBA	SA	AB	H	2B	3B	HR	RBI	BB	SO	4-YEAR TOTALS (1990–1993) BA	OBA	SA	AB	H	2B	3B	HR	RBI	BB	SO
Total	.265	.343	.456	408	108	25	1	17	60	45	56	.252	.321	.411	1048	264	50	3	37	140	107	166
vs. Left	.250	.322	.439	132	33	8	1	5	17	10	22	.244	.305	.399	283	69	15	1	9	38	22	53
vs. Right	.272	.352	.464	276	75	17	0	12	43	35	34	.255	.328	.416	765	195	35	2	28	102	85	113
at Home	.238	.330	.430	193	46	10	0	9	26	23	22	.246	.321	.425	499	123	23	0	22	72	53	68
on Road	.288	.354	.479	215	62	15	1	8	34	22	34	.257	.322	.399	549	141	27	3	15	68	54	98
on Grass	.281	.335	.478	178	50	11	0	8	25	14	28	.275	.332	.435	425	117	21	1	15	53	37	73
on Turf	.252	.348	.439	230	58	14	1	9	35	31	28	.236	.314	.395	623	147	29	2	22	87	70	93
Day Games	.301	.356	.617	133	40	9	0	11	28	11	13	.253	.311	.438	324	82	13	1	15	47	29	56
Night Games	.247	.337	.378	275	68	16	1	6	32	34	43	.251	.326	.399	724	182	37	2	22	93	78	110
April	.160	.308	.360	75	12	3	0	4	9	15	9	.219	.314	.423	137	30	5	1	7	18	18	18
May	.306	.387	.509	108	33	4	0	6	15	13	18	.294	.369	.465	187	55	11	0	7	25	21	30
June	.292	.364	.510	96	28	10	1	3	15	11	12	.268	.325	.454	183	49	12	2	6	32	16	22
July	.303	.343	.495	99	30	7	0	4	18	5	12	.244	.302	.384	164	40	8	0	5	22	13	26
August	.167	.194	.200	30	5	1	0	0	3	1	5	.245	.290	.364	184	45	7	0	5	23	13	30
Sept-Oct	.000	.000	.000	0	0	0	0	0	0	0	0	.233	.321	.378	193	45	7	0	7	20	26	40
Bases Empty	.262	.327	.435	237	62	14	0	9	9	20	31	.256	.313	.435	593	152	28	0	26	26	45	92
Leadoff	.258	.294	.423	97	25	4	0	4	4	5	13	.273	.306	.419	253	69	13	0	8	8	11	37
Runners On Base	.269	.363	.485	171	46	11	1	8	51	25	25	.246	.331	.380	455	112	22	3	11	114	62	74
Scoring Position	.253	.362	.505	95	24	6	0	6	45	17	18	.231	.331	.400	255	59	12	2	9	107	43	50
Late and Close	.284	.372	.543	81	23	6	0	5	17	12	14	.286	.357	.461	206	59	12	0	8	32	22	41

DAVE MARTINEZ — BL/TL — age 30 — SFOF73

1993	BA	OBA	SA	AB	H	2B	3B	HR	RBI	BB	SO	8-YEAR TOTALS (1986–1993) BA	OBA	SA	AB	H	2B	3B	HR	RBI	BB	SO
Total	.241	.317	.361	241	58	10	0	5	27	27	39	.267	.325	.381	2796	746	111	38	44	255	241	464
vs. Left	.259	.394	.407	27	7	2	1	0	1	6	5	.232	.307	.320	366	85	14	3	4	35	37	98
vs. Right	.238	.306	.355	214	51	10	0	5	26	21	34	.272	.328	.390	2430	661	97	35	40	220	204	366
at Home	.197	.254	.274	117	23	4	1	1	4	9	19	.255	.313	.363	1365	348	49	18	21	108	114	208
on Road	.282	.373	.444	124	35	8	0	4	23	18	20	.278	.337	.398	1431	398	62	20	23	147	127	256
on Grass	.222	.293	.304	171	38	6	1	2	13	17	28	.263	.328	.378	1240	326	45	19	20	105	119	234
on Turf	.286	.375	.500	70	20	6	0	3	14	10	11	.270	.323	.383	1556	420	66	19	24	150	122	230
Day Games	.260	.331	.407	123	32	7	1	3	17	13	20	.260	.330	.390	1183	307	44	16	26	116	122	219
Night Games	.220	.303	.314	118	26	5	0	2	10	14	19	.272	.322	.374	1613	439	67	22	18	139	119	245
April	.163	.250	.209	43	7	2	0	0	4	5	6	.225	.294	.301	342	77	11	3	3	37	32	44
May	.000	.000	.000	0	0	0	0	0	0	0	0	.258	.331	.335	361	93	12	5	2	38	42	67
June	.286	.348	.548	42	12	2	0	3	6	4	9	.289	.339	.445	546	158	26	10	13	58	42	84
July	.234	.308	.298	47	11	3	0	0	4	5	11	.274	.325	.386	503	138	17	3	11	30	36	87
August	.264	.346	.403	72	19	2	1	2	8	9	11	.273	.331	.393	542	148	24	7	9	51	46	94
Sept-Oct	.243	.317	.324	37	9	3	0	0	5	4	2	.263	.321	.380	502	132	21	10	6	41	43	88
Bases Empty	.225	.281	.373	142	32	7	1	4	4	11	24	.267	.317	.390	1749	467	65	24	34	34	125	279
Leadoff	.220	.270	.339	59	13	4	0	1	1	4	8	.262	.312	.365	776	203	28	8	12	12	54	117
Runners On Base	.263	.365	.343	99	26	5	0	1	23	16	15	.266	.338	.366	1047	279	46	14	10	221	116	185
Scoring Position	.281	.395	.391	64	18	4	0	1	23	12	12	.262	.347	.367	640	168	31	9	6	205	87	122
Late and Close	.250	.415	.375	32	8	1	0	1	4	9	5	.211	.286	.281	455	96	14	6	2	40	47	98

DON MATTINGLY — BL/TL — age 33 — NYA 1B130, DH5

1993	BA	OBA	SA	AB	H	2B	3B	HR	RBI	BB	SO	10-YEAR TOTALS (1984–1993) BA	OBA	SA	AB	H	2B	3B	HR	RBI	BB	SO
Total	.291	.364	.445	530	154	27	2	17	86	61	42	.311	.359	.483	5882	1827	375	13	205	966	467	353
vs. Left	.264	.344	.388	201	53	10	0	5	34	23	19	.300	.346	.461	2106	631	145	4	62	386	152	147
vs. Right	.307	.377	.480	329	101	17	2	12	52	38	23	.317	.366	.496	3776	1196	230	9	143	580	315	206
at Home	.303	.386	.481	241	73	15	2	8	40	32	17	.316	.366	.512	2809	887	173	4	123	508	236	167
on Road	.280	.345	.415	289	81	12	0	9	46	29	25	.306	.352	.458	3073	940	202	9	82	458	231	186
on Grass	.296	.375	.445	456	135	22	2	14	71	57	38	.311	.361	.485	4941	1537	304	8	179	816	409	301
on Turf	.257	.295	.446	74	19	5	0	3	15	4	4	.308	.347	.477	941	290	71	5	26	150	58	52
Day Games	.317	.394	.519	183	58	11	1	8	31	23	14	.323	.379	.499	1886	609	130	5	64	306	180	105
Night Games	.277	.348	.406	347	96	16	1	9	55	38	28	.305	.349	.476	3996	1218	245	8	141	660	287	248
April	.233	.289	.289	90	21	5	0	0	7	7	9	.268	.335	.382	777	208	56	3	9	101	81	52
May	.314	.375	.471	51	16	2	0	2	5	4	5	.322	.375	.508	982	316	64	1	39	172	87	63
June	.333	.395	.487	78	26	3	0	3	11	8	3	.313	.353	.462	962	301	46	2	31	142	66	48
July	.362	.414	.600	105	38	8	1	5	25	9	8	.324	.362	.519	1014	329	77	3	38	170	64	57
August	.265	.368	.469	98	26	3	1	5	26	17	8	.312	.362	.504	1002	313	63	3	41	177	79	55
Sept-Oct	.250	.347	.361	108	27	6	0	2	12	16	9	.314	.360	.500	1145	360	69	1	47	204	90	78
Bases Empty	.234	.306	.392	273	64	11	1	10	10	27	27	.298	.339	.468	3144	936	196	11	106	106	183	202
Leadoff	.217	.265	.348	92	20	4	1	2	2	6	7	.291	.322	.471	1060	308	66	4	39	39	45	55
Runners On Base	.350	.424	.502	257	90	16	1	7	76	34	15	.325	.380	.501	2738	891	179	2	99	860	284	151
Scoring Position	.368	.471	.528	125	46	6	1	4	67	27	8	.324	.396	.503	1496	485	103	1	54	739	225	94
Late and Close	.307	.342	.440	75	23	4	0	2	17	4	5	.298	.367	.473	899	268	48	2	35	168	98	52

DERRICK MAY — BL/TR — age 26 — CHN OF122 | 4-YEAR TOTALS (1990–1993)

1993	BA	OBA	SA	AB	H	2B	3B	HR	RBI	BB	SO	BA	OBA	SA	AB	H	2B	3B	HR	RBI	BB	SO
Total	.295	.336	.422	465	137	25	2	10	77	31	41	.281	.319	.398	899	253	41	2	20	136	49	89
vs. Left	.247	.266	.438	89	22	3	1	4	22	2	13	.251	.286	.398	171	43	5	1	6	32	7	26
vs. Right	.306	.352	.418	376	115	22	1	6	55	29	28	.288	.326	.398	728	210	36	1	14	104	42	63
at Home	.319	.360	.427	248	79	16	1	3	40	16	26	.303	.343	.410	495	150	27	1	8	79	30	47
on Road	.267	.309	.415	217	58	9	1	7	37	15	15	.255	.289	.384	404	103	14	1	12	57	19	42
on Grass	.288	.327	.396	361	104	20	2	5	56	22	33	.290	.330	.394	672	195	33	2	11	102	40	63
on Turf	.317	.365	.510	104	33	5	0	5	21	9	8	.256	.285	.410	227	58	8	0	9	34	9	26
Day Games	.323	.368	.431	248	80	13	1	4	39	18	22	.285	.330	.381	499	142	22	1	8	75	34	50
Night Games	.263	.299	.410	217	57	12	1	6	38	13	19	.278	.304	.420	400	111	19	1	12	61	15	39
April	.345	.400	.517	58	20	1	0	3	14	5	5	.304	.372	.449	69	21	1	0	3	15	7	6
May	.286	.330	.385	91	26	6	0	1	15	6	10	.264	.306	.338	148	39	8	0	1	17	9	18
June	.274	.297	.432	95	26	6	0	3	12	4	4	.291	.312	.448	165	48	8	0	6	26	6	11
July	.337	.391	.455	101	34	6	0	2	18	9	8	.295	.348	.411	129	38	6	0	3	20	11	12
August	.295	.320	.400	95	28	5	1	1	16	5	8	.303	.342	.400	175	53	9	1	2	26	9	18
Sept-Oct	.120	.185	.240	25	3	1	1	0	2	2	6	.254	.276	.376	213	54	9	1	5	32	7	24
Bases Empty	.263	.303	.342	228	60	9	0	3	3	12	18	.256	.296	.328	464	119	15	0	6	6	24	42
Leadoff	.287	.322	.400	115	33	4	0	3	3	5	6	.266	.305	.364	214	57	6	0	5	5	11	13
Runners On Base	.325	.366	.498	237	77	16	2	7	74	19	23	.308	.343	.474	435	134	26	2	14	130	25	47
Scoring Position	.326	.374	.533	135	44	11	1	5	67	14	17	.309	.355	.508	246	76	17	1	10	116	20	32
Late and Close	.301	.310	.422	83	25	4	0	2	16	2	9	.267	.288	.410	161	43	5	0	6	29	5	18

DAVID MCCARTY — BR/TL — age 25 — MIN OF67, 1B36, DH2 | 1-YEAR TOTALS (1993)

1993	BA	OBA	SA	AB	H	2B	3B	HR	RBI	BB	SO	BA	OBA	SA	AB	H	2B	3B	HR	RBI	BB	SO
Total	.214	.257	.286	350	75	15	2	2	21	19	80	.214	.257	.286	350	75	15	2	2	21	19	80
vs. Left	.206	.248	.252	107	22	3	1	0	3	5	22	.206	.248	.252	107	22	3	1	0	3	5	22
vs. Right	.218	.261	.300	243	53	12	1	2	18	14	58	.218	.261	.300	243	53	12	1	2	18	14	58
at Home	.223	.279	.325	166	37	9	1	2	8	12	37	.223	.279	.325	166	37	9	1	2	8	12	37
on Road	.207	.236	.250	184	38	6	1	0	13	7	43	.207	.236	.250	184	38	6	1	0	13	7	43
on Grass	.210	.244	.242	157	33	3	1	0	9	7	34	.210	.244	.242	157	33	3	1	0	9	7	34
on Turf	.218	.267	.321	193	42	12	1	2	12	12	46	.218	.267	.321	193	42	12	1	2	12	12	46
Day Games	.218	.252	.336	110	24	8	1	1	10	5	24	.218	.252	.336	110	24	8	1	1	10	5	24
Night Games	.213	.259	.262	240	51	7	1	1	11	14	56	.213	.259	.262	240	51	7	1	1	11	14	56
April	.000	.000	.000	0	0	0	0	0	0	0	0	.000	.000	.000	0	0	0	0	0	0	0	0
May	.353	.365	.510	51	18	6	1	0	5	1	11	.353	.365	.510	51	18	6	1	0	5	1	11
June	.229	.289	.271	70	16	0	0	1	2	5	16	.229	.289	.271	70	16	0	0	1	2	5	16
July	.203	.217	.237	59	12	2	0	0	3	1	12	.203	.217	.237	59	12	2	0	0	3	1	12
August	.115	.194	.180	61	7	2	1	0	0	6	19	.115	.194	.180	61	7	2	1	0	0	6	19
Sept-Oct	.202	.243	.275	109	22	5	0	1	11	6	22	.202	.243	.275	109	22	5	0	1	11	6	22
Bases Empty	.232	.279	.308	185	43	6	1	2	2	11	40	.232	.279	.308	185	43	6	1	2	2	11	40
Leadoff	.206	.229	.279	68	14	3	1	0	0	2	13	.206	.229	.279	68	14	3	1	0	0	2	13
Runners On Base	.194	.231	.261	165	32	9	1	0	19	8	40	.194	.231	.261	165	32	9	1	0	19	8	40
Scoring Position	.213	.250	.262	80	17	4	0	0	18	4	22	.213	.250	.262	80	17	4	0	0	18	4	22
Late and Close	.232	.243	.275	69	16	3	0	0	2	1	15	.232	.243	.275	69	16	3	0	0	2	1	15

WILLIE MCGEE — BB/TR — age 36 — SFOF126 | 10-YEAR TOTALS (1984–1993)

1993	BA	OBA	SA	AB	H	2B	3B	HR	RBI	BB	SO	BA	OBA	SA	AB	H	2B	3B	HR	RBI	BB	SO
Total	.301	.353	.389	475	143	28	1	4	46	38	67	.300	.340	.406	5121	1535	252	68	52	554	315	789
vs. Left	.319	.349	.403	144	46	9	0	1	13	7	21	.295	.326	.429	1737	512	86	27	31	212	83	330
vs. Right	.293	.354	.384	331	97	19	1	3	33	31	46	.302	.347	.394	3384	1023	166	41	21	342	232	459
at Home	.318	.374	.382	217	69	12	1	0	14	19	31	.305	.342	.409	2490	760	122	34	23	260	144	362
on Road	.287	.335	.395	258	74	16	0	4	32	19	36	.295	.338	.403	2631	775	130	34	29	294	171	427
on Grass	.306	.354	.389	373	114	23	1	2	36	28	48	.296	.340	.388	2101	622	106	18	17	215	141	319
on Turf	.284	.348	.392	102	29	5	0	2	10	10	19	.302	.340	.419	3020	913	146	50	35	339	174	470
Day Games	.274	.323	.374	219	60	11	1	3	19	16	32	.318	.355	.433	1838	584	85	32	21	214	108	266
Night Games	.324	.377	.402	256	83	17	0	1	27	22	35	.290	.331	.391	3283	951	167	36	31	340	207	523
April	.266	.310	.309	94	25	4	0	0	5	6	17	.289	.332	.385	672	194	24	10	7	71	44	120
May	.375	.419	.500	96	36	7	1	1	8	8	9	.287	.328	.390	1020	293	48	15	9	111	61	149
June	.344	.397	.459	61	21	7	0	0	7	6	7	.321	.365	.417	894	287	45	13	5	98	67	130
July	.455	.500	.636	33	15	3	0	0	7	3	3	.319	.350	.459	697	222	45	7	13	79	33	113
August	.235	.278	.324	102	24	3	0	2	16	5	14	.294	.333	.401	895	263	41	11	11	116	50	128
Sept-Oct	.247	.323	.292	89	22	4	0	0	3	10	17	.293	.334	.392	943	276	49	12	7	79	60	149
Bases Empty	.285	.321	.377	284	81	17	0	3	3	15	48	.296	.329	.398	2968	878	147	35	29	29	139	471
Leadoff	.288	.331	.344	125	36	7	0	0	0	8	21	.286	.320	.373	1173	336	55	13	7	7	55	188
Runners On Base	.325	.396	.408	191	62	11	1	1	43	23	19	.305	.355	.417	2153	657	105	33	23	525	176	318
Scoring Position	.300	.394	.392	120	36	6	1	1	42	19	10	.296	.356	.405	1354	401	70	21	12	476	136	211
Late and Close	.400	.438	.493	75	30	4	0	1	9	5	10	.293	.332	.383	887	260	40	8	8	111	53	160

FRED McGRIFF — BL/TL — age 31 — SD/ATL 1B149

1993	BA	OBA	SA	AB	H	2B	3B	HR	RBI	BB	SO	8-YEAR TOTALS (1986–1993) BA	OBA	SA	AB	H	2B	3B	HR	RBI	BB	SO
Total	.291	.375	.549	557	162	29	2	37	101	76	106	.281	.389	.532	3560	1001	178	15	228	616	629	844
vs. Left	.274	.354	.448	201	55	9	1	8	30	25	38	.261	.349	.446	1207	315	45	8	54	198	162	319
vs. Right	.301	.386	.607	356	107	20	1	29	71	51	68	.292	.408	.576	2353	686	133	7	174	418	467	525
at Home	.282	.387	.498	255	72	10	0	15	47	44	47	.276	.396	.528	1694	468	84	5	111	301	334	377
on Road	.298	.364	.593	302	90	19	2	22	54	32	59	.286	.382	.535	1866	533	94	10	117	315	295	467
on Grass	.290	.368	.520	417	121	19	1	25	71	53	80	.285	.388	.522	1992	567	97	6	121	334	340	472
on Turf	.293	.394	.636	140	41	10	1	12	30	23	26	.277	.390	.545	1568	434	81	9	107	282	289	372
Day Games	.304	.372	.573	171	52	10	0	12	27	19	33	.270	.374	.501	1066	288	60	3	60	168	176	236
Night Games	.285	.376	.539	386	110	19	2	25	74	57	73	.286	.395	.545	2494	713	118	12	168	448	453	608
April	.190	.293	.342	79	15	3	0	3	7	11	22	.280	.404	.499	483	135	21	2	27	73	99	132
May	.308	.387	.529	104	32	2	0	7	18	14	18	.294	.389	.535	620	182	35	2	37	105	96	139
June	.262	.374	.536	84	22	3	1	6	11	15	11	.263	.384	.515	548	144	26	2	36	97	107	124
July	.412	.430	.863	80	33	7	1	9	22	4	9	.300	.388	.613	587	176	27	2	51	119	87	137
August	.272	.321	.505	103	28	6	0	6	18	8	21	.273	.377	.560	659	180	33	6	48	117	113	175
Sept-Oct	.299	.432	.542	107	32	8	0	6	25	24	25	.278	.393	.466	663	184	36	1	29	105	127	137
Bases Empty	.287	.352	.574	289	83	18	1	21	21	29	60	.286	.377	.551	1976	565	104	7	135	135	282	459
Leadoff	.310	.351	.570	158	49	9	1	10	10	10	25	.296	.374	.548	919	272	52	6	56	56	113	195
Runners On Base	.295	.398	.522	268	79	11	1	16	80	47	46	.275	.403	.508	1584	436	74	8	93	481	347	385
Scoring Position	.269	.393	.462	145	39	8	1	6	59	32	30	.257	.413	.453	878	226	42	5	40	356	247	239
Late and Close	.309	.406	.617	81	25	4	0	7	17	13	20	.266	.387	.454	537	143	34	2	21	73	106	147

MARK McLEMORE — BB/TR — age 30 — BAL OF124, 2B25, 3B4, DH1

1993	BA	OBA	SA	AB	H	2B	3B	HR	RBI	BB	SO	8-YEAR TOTALS (1986–1993) BA	OBA	SA	AB	H	2B	3B	HR	RBI	BB	SO
Total	.284	.353	.368	581	165	27	5	4	72	64	92	.248	.317	.317	1703	422	64	13	9	174	176	267
vs. Left	.216	.270	.253	162	35	4	1	0	12	12	24	.228	.285	.278	496	113	16	3	1	45	40	71
vs. Right	.310	.383	.413	419	130	23	4	4	60	52	68	.256	.329	.332	1207	309	48	10	8	129	136	196
at Home	.314	.377	.399	293	92	13	3	2	39	31	47	.251	.321	.324	829	208	29	7	6	88	89	127
on Road	.253	.328	.337	288	73	14	2	2	33	33	45	.245	.312	.309	874	214	35	6	3	86	87	140
on Grass	.268	.340	.342	488	131	21	3	3	59	55	80	.242	.312	.309	1380	334	50	9	8	141	144	215
on Turf	.366	.422	.505	93	34	6	2	1	13	9	12	.272	.336	.350	323	88	14	4	1	33	32	52
Day Games	.261	.335	.373	161	42	10	1	2	13	18	34	.251	.316	.347	510	128	23	7	4	51	50	91
Night Games	.293	.360	.367	420	123	17	4	2	59	46	58	.246	.317	.303	1193	294	41	6	5	123	126	176
April	.311	.367	.444	45	14	3	0	1	10	4	10	.236	.318	.305	377	89	14	3	2	41	44	70
May	.281	.331	.342	114	32	5	1	0	8	9	22	.239	.303	.292	373	89	16	2	0	28	36	51
June	.308	.404	.404	104	32	5	1	1	18	13	16	.258	.331	.323	229	59	8	2	1	29	25	43
July	.303	.353	.404	109	33	7	2	0	13	9	9	.272	.322	.366	235	64	11	4	1	30	19	27
August	.295	.360	.420	112	33	6	1	2	14	12	18	.280	.344	.401	232	65	9	2	5	25	23	32
Sept-Oct	.216	.330	.227	97	21	1	0	0	9	17	17	.218	.294	.241	257	56	6	0	0	21	29	44
Bases Empty	.288	.349	.372	333	96	13	3	3	3	31	56	.252	.315	.319	957	241	32	7	6	6	88	152
Leadoff	.216	.298	.255	102	22	1	0	1	1	12	22	.221	.306	.275	367	81	10	2	2	2	44	63
Runners On Base	.278	.358	.363	248	69	14	2	1	69	33	36	.243	.318	.314	746	181	32	6	3	168	88	115
Scoring Position	.303	.385	.388	152	46	11	1	0	66	23	22	.259	.333	.325	455	118	22	4	0	158	56	78
Late and Close	.264	.340	.356	87	23	3	1	1	9	10	20	.264	.338	.313	307	81	5	2	2	34	35	57

BRIAN McRAE — BB/TR — age 27 — KC OF153

1993	BA	OBA	SA	AB	H	2B	3B	HR	RBI	BB	SO	4-YEAR TOTALS (1990–1993) BA	OBA	SA	AB	H	2B	3B	HR	RBI	BB	SO
Total	.282	.325	.413	627	177	28	9	12	69	37	105	.260	.302	.370	1957	508	87	26	26	208	112	321
vs. Left	.322	.340	.477	199	64	8	4	5	26	3	23	.295	.325	.423	638	188	33	8	11	78	25	73
vs. Right	.264	.318	.383	428	113	20	5	7	43	34	82	.243	.291	.345	1319	320	54	18	15	130	87	248
at Home	.287	.322	.408	321	92	14	5	5	39	13	48	.271	.313	.389	977	265	48	17	11	117	55	159
on Road	.278	.328	.418	306	85	14	4	7	30	24	57	.248	.290	.352	980	243	39	9	15	91	57	162
on Grass	.274	.318	.371	237	65	7	2	4	19	16	40	.250	.286	.330	743	186	23	6	8	63	38	118
on Turf	.287	.329	.438	390	112	21	7	8	50	21	65	.265	.311	.395	1214	322	64	20	18	145	74	203
Day Games	.317	.379	.489	180	57	8	4	5	21	15	29	.242	.289	.373	528	128	18	9	11	59	32	89
Night Games	.268	.302	.383	447	120	20	5	7	48	22	76	.266	.306	.369	1429	380	69	17	15	149	80	232
April	.283	.333	.413	92	26	5	2	1	8	7	17	.214	.255	.323	220	47	9	3	3	22	13	37
May	.330	.370	.400	100	33	5	1	0	7	6	10	.272	.331	.374	305	83	14	4	3	33	27	43
June	.310	.347	.448	116	36	6	2	2	16	7	16	.287	.322	.391	327	94	15	5	3	37	18	51
July	.309	.361	.500	110	34	5	2	4	10	7	26	.281	.333	.401	324	91	13	4	6	32	21	55
August	.250	.281	.370	108	27	2	1	3	17	4	17	.259	.293	.365	359	93	13	5	5	41	16	51
Sept-Oct	.208	.252	.337	101	21	5	1	2	11	6	19	.237	.270	.358	422	100	23	5	6	43	17	84
Bases Empty	.296	.340	.416	392	116	21	4	6	6	24	61	.265	.308	.366	1208	320	63	13	11	11	68	188
Leadoff	.351	.385	.480	148	52	10	3	1	1	8	21	.291	.322	.397	557	162	37	8	2	2	23	82
Runners On Base	.260	.300	.409	235	61	7	5	6	63	13	44	.251	.291	.378	749	188	24	13	15	197	44	133
Scoring Position	.272	.325	.456	147	40	4	4	5	59	11	25	.264	.310	.398	447	118	12	9	10	175	32	83
Late and Close	.300	.336	.473	110	33	6	2	3	15	6	15	.265	.314	.381	328	87	14	6	4	39	24	47

KEVIN MCREYNOLDS — BR/TR — age 35 — KC OF104, DH1

	1993 BA	OBA	SA	AB	H	2B	3B	HR	RBI	BB	SO	10-YR BA	OBA	SA	AB	H	2B	3B	HR	RBI	BB	SO
Total	.245	.316	.425	351	86	22	4	11	42	37	56	.267	.329	.452	5103	1362	270	32	203	772	490	644
vs. Left	.222	.333	.349	126	28	8	1	2	12	22	18	.278	.352	.476	1743	484	97	15	73	251	205	188
vs. Right	.258	.306	.467	225	58	14	3	9	30	15	38	.261	.317	.439	3360	878	173	17	130	521	285	456
at Home	.284	.340	.515	194	55	15	3	8	26	16	21	.268	.330	.453	2515	675	124	16	103	367	240	308
on Road	.197	.289	.312	157	31	7	1	3	16	21	35	.265	.329	.450	2588	687	146	16	100	405	250	336
on Grass	.246	.323	.398	118	29	7	1	3	14	14	25	.264	.323	.452	3417	903	165	19	146	514	310	443
on Turf	.245	.313	.438	233	57	15	3	8	28	23	31	.272	.341	.451	1686	459	105	13	57	258	180	201
Day Games	.246	.297	.475	118	29	8	2	5	18	8	21	.260	.319	.452	1676	435	82	12	72	262	145	240
Night Games	.245	.326	.399	233	57	14	2	6	24	29	35	.270	.334	.452	3427	927	188	20	131	510	345	404
April	.262	.340	.548	42	11	4	1	2	6	5	4	.262	.324	.440	638	167	27	3	27	89	62	84
May	.250	.348	.400	20	5	3	0	0	0	3	5	.271	.342	.446	850	230	50	3	31	128	93	95
June	.192	.263	.288	52	10	2	0	1	5	5	12	.273	.339	.455	915	250	53	7	33	139	93	112
July	.262	.340	.417	84	22	5	1	2	11	11	6	.260	.336	.441	937	244	63	5	32	145	111	117
August	.234	.322	.429	77	18	3	0	4	10	9	13	.260	.307	.449	847	220	27	5	41	130	63	110
Sept-Oct	.263	.296	.461	76	20	5	2	2	10	4	16	.274	.324	.476	916	251	50	7	39	141	68	126
Bases Empty	.246	.300	.479	211	52	16	3	9	9	16	33	.263	.317	.456	2861	752	147	20	122	122	221	344
Leadoff	.191	.250	.315	89	17	8	0	1	1	7	17	.260	.316	.446	1156	300	61	11	44	44	92	131
Runners On Base	.243	.339	.343	140	34	6	1	2	33	21	23	.272	.344	.446	2242	610	123	12	81	650	269	300
Scoring Position	.274	.373	.333	84	23	2	0	1	30	15	17	.279	.362	.453	1356	379	66	8	51	563	204	196
Late and Close	.263	.317	.421	76	20	5	2	1	10	6	12	.262	.321	.433	944	247	43	4	37	150	85	141

PAT MEARES — BR/TR — age 26 — MIN SS111

	1993 BA	OBA	SA	AB	H	2B	3B	HR	RBI	BB	SO	1-YR BA	OBA	SA	AB	H	2B	3B	HR	RBI	BB	SO
Total	.251	.266	.309	346	87	14	3	0	33	7	52	.251	.266	.309	346	87	14	3	0	33	7	52
vs. Left	.242	.267	.253	95	23	1	0	0	4	4	15	.242	.267	.253	95	23	1	0	0	4	4	15
vs. Right	.255	.266	.331	251	64	13	3	0	29	3	37	.255	.266	.331	251	64	13	3	0	29	3	37
at Home	.287	.313	.338	157	45	8	0	0	16	6	19	.287	.313	.338	157	45	8	0	0	16	6	19
on Road	.222	.225	.286	189	42	6	3	0	17	1	33	.222	.225	.286	189	42	6	3	0	17	1	33
on Grass	.235	.239	.314	153	36	6	3	0	15	1	24	.235	.239	.314	153	36	6	3	0	15	1	24
on Turf	.264	.287	.306	193	51	8	0	0	18	6	28	.264	.287	.306	193	51	8	0	0	18	6	28
Day Games	.275	.272	.363	102	28	5	2	0	6	0	19	.275	.272	.363	102	28	5	2	0	6	0	19
Night Games	.242	.264	.287	244	59	9	1	0	27	7	33	.242	.264	.287	244	59	9	1	0	27	7	33
April	.000	.000	.000	0	0	0	0	0	0	0	0	.000	.000	.000	0	0	0	0	0	0	0	0
May	.278	.298	.352	54	15	2	1	0	4	2	11	.278	.298	.352	54	15	2	1	0	4	2	11
June	.342	.358	.430	79	27	5	1	0	7	1	11	.342	.358	.430	79	27	5	1	0	7	1	11
July	.250	.264	.321	84	21	4	1	0	9	2	18	.250	.264	.321	84	21	4	1	0	9	2	18
August	.188	.200	.217	69	13	2	0	0	4	1	8	.188	.200	.217	69	13	2	0	0	4	1	8
Sept-Oct	.183	.194	.200	60	11	1	0	0	9	1	4	.183	.194	.200	60	11	1	0	0	9	1	4
Bases Empty	.273	.293	.316	209	57	9	0	0	0	5	32	.273	.293	.316	209	57	9	0	0	0	5	32
Leadoff	.256	.273	.291	86	22	4	0	0	0	2	10	.256	.273	.291	86	22	4	0	0	0	2	10
Runners On Base	.219	.225	.299	137	30	5	3	0	33	2	20	.219	.225	.299	137	30	5	3	0	33	2	20
Scoring Position	.261	.270	.362	69	18	3	2	0	31	2	13	.261	.270	.362	69	18	3	2	0	31	2	13
Late and Close	.373	.373	.529	51	19	6	1	0	7	0	9	.373	.373	.529	51	19	6	1	0	7	0	9

ORLANDO MERCED — BB/TR — age 28 — PIT OF109, 1B42

	1993 BA	OBA	SA	AB	H	2B	3B	HR	RBI	BB	SO	4-YR BA	OBA	SA	AB	H	2B	3B	HR	RBI	BB	SO
Total	.313	.414	.443	447	140	26	4	8	70	77	64	.278	.372	.407	1287	358	72	11	24	180	194	217
vs. Left	.297	.386	.405	111	33	6	3	0	14	16	17	.238	.328	.316	256	61	12	4	0	27	33	43
vs. Right	.318	.423	.455	336	107	20	1	8	56	61	47	.288	.383	.430	1031	297	60	7	24	153	161	174
at Home	.298	.401	.415	205	61	13	1	3	20	35	27	.268	.371	.403	608	163	38	4	12	67	100	100
on Road	.326	.425	.467	242	79	13	3	5	50	42	37	.287	.373	.411	679	195	34	7	12	113	94	117
on Grass	.314	.410	.455	156	49	6	2	4	36	26	22	.286	.361	.399	378	108	16	3	7	65	46	64
on Turf	.313	.416	.436	291	91	20	2	4	34	51	42	.275	.377	.410	909	250	56	8	17	115	148	153
Day Games	.320	.424	.459	122	39	7	2	2	18	22	24	.304	.401	.451	355	108	21	5	7	63	58	65
Night Games	.311	.410	.437	325	101	19	2	6	52	55	40	.268	.361	.391	932	250	51	6	17	117	136	152
April	.343	.443	.388	67	23	3	0	0	10	12	14	.292	.422	.338	130	38	4	1	0	18	29	26
May	.380	.476	.535	71	27	2	0	3	15	13	12	.335	.425	.524	212	71	17	1	7	34	33	38
June	.329	.434	.463	82	27	5	0	2	15	15	4	.250	.332	.386	228	57	12	2	5	30	28	30
July	.366	.430	.549	71	26	8	1	1	11	8	11	.298	.371	.441	238	71	15	2	5	33	28	41
August	.250	.353	.380	100	25	7	0	2	14	16	12	.248	.346	.350	254	63	15	1	3	36	39	44
Sept-Oct	.214	.357	.339	56	12	1	0	3	5	13	11	.258	.364	.387	225	58	9	4	4	29	37	38
Bases Empty	.307	.410	.410	212	65	14	1	2	2	36	39	.259	.358	.365	713	185	41	5	8	8	108	134
Leadoff	.357	.465	.512	84	30	5	1	2	2	16	17	.272	.370	.382	353	96	20	5	3	3	54	65
Runners On Base	.319	.417	.472	235	75	12	3	6	68	41	25	.301	.390	.460	574	173	31	6	16	172	86	83
Scoring Position	.326	.457	.486	138	45	8	1	4	58	35	19	.312	.414	.499	359	112	23	4	12	157	67	57
Late and Close	.321	.411	.449	78	25	4	0	2	12	12	14	.262	.366	.412	233	61	17	0	6	38	39	49

KEVIN MITCHELL — BR/TR — age 32 — CIN OF87

1993	BA	OBA	SA	AB	H	2B	3B	HR	RBI	BB	SO	BA	OBA	SA	AB	H	2B	3B	HR	RBI	BB	SO
Total	.341	.385	.601	323	110	21	3	19	64	25	48	.282	.354	.515	3432	969	183	23	190	612	377	590
vs. Left	.394	.424	.745	94	37	7	1	8	16	5	7	.305	.383	.562	1145	349	72	5	71	208	149	151
vs. Right	.319	.370	.541	229	73	14	2	11	48	20	41	.271	.339	.491	2287	620	111	18	119	404	228	439
at Home	.349	.386	.613	186	65	15	2	10	35	13	26	.291	.359	.517	1727	503	106	16	84	316	186	281
on Road	.328	.384	.584	137	45	6	1	9	29	12	22	.273	.349	.513	1705	466	77	7	106	296	191	309
on Grass	.323	.387	.594	96	31	3	1	7	19	10	18	.280	.354	.509	2233	626	112	18	121	399	251	406
on Turf	.348	.385	.604	227	79	18	2	12	45	15	30	.286	.354	.526	1199	343	71	5	69	213	126	184
Day Games	.362	.404	.648	105	38	6	0	8	21	8	15	.288	.366	.519	1309	377	80	6	70	225	160	228
Night Games	.330	.377	.578	218	72	15	3	11	43	17	33	.279	.347	.513	2123	592	103	17	120	387	217	362
April	.357	.378	.548	42	15	2	0	2	10	2	1	.285	.342	.503	523	149	31	4	25	94	49	87
May	.333	.379	.538	93	31	5	1	4	19	8	16	.264	.343	.487	622	164	29	7	32	100	75	104
June	.421	.457	.737	76	32	7	1	5	16	5	9	.331	.398	.595	553	183	43	2	33	108	63	64
July	.318	.375	.682	44	14	4	0	4	11	3	7	.277	.348	.550	611	169	32	0	45	131	65	118
August	.269	.333	.522	67	18	3	1	4	8	7	14	.290	.364	.512	676	196	30	4	34	112	75	134
Sept-Oct	.000	.000	.000	1	0	0	0	0	0	0	1	.242	.321	.427	447	108	18	1	21	67	50	83
Bases Empty	.361	.395	.677	158	57	7	2	13	13	9	19	.282	.346	.539	1757	495	87	16	111	111	159	289
Leadoff	.325	.366	.649	77	25	2	1	7	7	5	7	.272	.330	.544	772	210	35	8	53	53	63	128
Runners On Base	.321	.376	.527	165	53	14	1	6	51	16	29	.283	.362	.490	1675	474	96	7	79	501	218	301
Scoring Position	.330	.387	.544	103	34	11	1	3	45	12	24	.276	.375	.472	980	270	59	4	42	408	170	188
Late and Close	.283	.346	.609	46	13	3	0	4	14	5	6	.259	.337	.462	548	142	21	0	30	88	64	113

PAUL MOLITOR — BR/TR — age 38 — TOR DH137, 1B23

1993	BA	OBA	SA	AB	H	2B	3B	HR	RBI	BB	SO	BA	OBA	SA	AB	H	2B	3B	HR	RBI	BB	SO
Total	.332	.402	.509	636	211	37	5	22	111	77	71	.314	.382	.466	5076	1593	295	55	122	620	564	607
vs. Left	.363	.446	.585	171	62	13	2	7	32	26	23	.326	.398	.494	1390	453	87	13	40	166	169	144
vs. Right	.320	.385	.482	465	149	24	3	15	79	51	48	.309	.376	.455	3686	1140	208	42	82	454	395	463
at Home	.364	.431	.573	316	115	23	2	13	68	37	30	.323	.392	.483	2436	787	144	28	63	332	283	274
on Road	.300	.374	.447	320	96	14	3	9	43	40	41	.305	.372	.450	2640	806	151	27	59	288	281	333
on Grass	.325	.399	.494	249	81	11	2	9	40	33	28	.313	.384	.462	3960	1240	223	43	94	473	458	461
on Turf	.336	.404	.519	387	130	26	3	13	71	44	43	.316	.376	.478	1116	353	72	12	28	147	106	146
Day Games	.302	.391	.460	215	65	10	3	6	30	31	25	.316	.390	.461	1589	502	95	11	38	187	195	197
Night Games	.347	.408	.534	421	146	27	2	16	81	46	46	.313	.378	.468	3487	1091	200	44	84	433	369	410
April	.292	.388	.416	89	26	3	1	2	13	14	10	.310	.383	.443	652	202	39	3	14	80	78	82
May	.374	.442	.539	115	43	2	1	5	22	13	8	.312	.378	.463	818	255	38	10	22	94	89	85
June	.284	.363	.422	109	31	9	0	2	16	14	11	.318	.393	.487	748	238	52	7	20	95	93	90
July	.347	.435	.571	98	34	4	0	6	17	15	13	.312	.377	.453	799	249	39	10	18	91	81	95
August	.355	.419	.555	110	39	9	2	3	24	14	18	.318	.386	.479	995	316	61	11	26	142	114	127
Sept-Oct	.330	.363	.539	115	38	10	1	4	19	7	11	.313	.376	.463	1064	333	66	14	22	118	109	128
Bases Empty	.332	.393	.537	322	107	18	3	14	14	32	39	.302	.363	.460	3212	970	189	40	80	80	297	392
Leadoff	.375	.450	.635	96	36	8	1	9	5	13	13	.310	.366	.478	1736	538	98	26	47	47	149	204
Runners On Base	.331	.411	.481	314	104	19	2	8	97	45	32	.334	.413	.475	1864	623	106	15	42	540	267	215
Scoring Position	.384	.468	.542	190	73	13	1	5	88	34	15	.348	.437	.490	1114	388	67	8	25	485	197	139
Late and Close	.411	.486	.544	90	37	6	0	2	21	15	12	.331	.410	.475	707	234	39	3	19	110	98	93

MICKEY MORANDINI — BL/TR — age 28 — PHI 2B111

1993	BA	OBA	SA	AB	H	2B	3B	HR	RBI	BB	SO	BA	OBA	SA	AB	H	2B	3B	HR	RBI	BB	SO
Total	.247	.309	.355	425	105	19	9	3	33	34	73	.253	.308	.340	1251	317	42	21	8	86	94	201
vs. Left	.212	.284	.303	99	21	2	2	1	6	9	10	.197	.248	.250	300	59	4	3	2	17	20	45
vs. Right	.258	.317	.371	326	84	17	7	2	27	25	63	.271	.326	.368	951	258	38	18	6	69	74	156
at Home	.262	.311	.360	225	59	10	3	2	19	15	33	.261	.310	.352	640	167	20	10	6	48	44	100
on Road	.230	.306	.350	200	46	9	6	1	14	19	40	.245	.306	.327	611	150	22	11	2	38	50	101
on Grass	.202	.267	.298	124	25	6	3	0	8	10	22	.273	.321	.361	341	93	15	6	1	29	24	51
on Turf	.266	.326	.379	301	80	13	6	3	25	24	51	.246	.303	.332	910	224	27	15	7	57	70	150
Day Games	.256	.326	.360	125	32	4	3	1	15	12	24	.270	.326	.352	330	89	12	6	1	27	27	51
Night Games	.243	.302	.353	300	73	15	6	2	18	22	49	.248	.301	.336	921	228	30	15	7	59	67	150
April	.222	.291	.361	72	16	5	1	1	3	7	14	.288	.339	.405	153	44	6	3	2	8	12	29
May	.211	.245	.278	90	19	4	1	0	5	4	14	.232	.288	.289	190	44	6	1	1	14	14	34
June	.287	.337	.415	94	27	4	4	0	7	5	22	.235	.299	.337	243	57	10	6	1	21	21	44
July	.198	.284	.275	91	18	1	0	2	10	10	10	.243	.300	.326	230	56	7	3	2	20	18	30
August	.323	.400	.548	31	10	1	3	0	5	4	5	.254	.317	.354	130	33	3	5	0	7	11	17
Sept-Oct	.319	.385	.404	47	15	4	0	0	3	4	8	.272	.314	.344	305	83	10	3	2	16	18	47
Bases Empty	.274	.320	.380	234	64	12	5	1	1	14	40	.265	.311	.346	743	197	29	11	6	3	46	117
Leadoff	.325	.379	.400	80	26	2	2	0	0	7	11	.284	.338	.347	285	81	9	3	1	1	22	40
Runners On Base	.215	.296	.325	191	41	7	4	2	32	20	33	.236	.303	.331	508	120	13	10	5	83	48	84
Scoring Position	.223	.339	.330	103	23	2	3	1	28	16	17	.238	.323	.331	281	67	3	7	3	74	35	54
Late and Close	.174	.237	.362	69	12	3	2	2	9	5	12	.248	.310	.343	210	52	8	3	2	16	18	31

HAL MORRIS — BL/TL — age 29 — CIN 1B98

1993	BA	OBA	SA	AB	H	2B	3B	HR	RBI	BB	SO
Total	.317	.371	.420	379	120	18	0	7	49	34	51
vs. Left	.244	.305	.291	86	21	4	0	0	8	7	20
vs. Right	.338	.390	.457	293	99	14	0	7	41	27	31
at Home	.321	.376	.418	184	59	12	0	2	20	17	23
on Road	.313	.366	.421	195	61	6	0	5	29	17	28
on Grass	.303	.358	.420	119	36	2	0	4	20	12	22
on Turf	.323	.376	.419	260	84	16	0	3	29	22	29
Day Games	.396	.475	.594	96	38	4	0	5	19	16	12
Night Games	.290	.330	.360	283	82	14	0	2	30	18	39
April	.000	.000	.000	0	0	0	0	0	0	0	0
May	.000	.000	.000	0	0	0	0	0	0	0	0
June	.284	.307	.296	81	23	1	0	0	8	4	10
July	.305	.377	.400	95	29	6	0	1	9	10	13
August	.330	.387	.470	100	33	5	0	3	17	9	14
Sept-Oct	.340	.397	.485	103	35	6	0	3	15	11	14
Bases Empty	.315	.373	.435	216	68	11	0	5	5	18	27
Leadoff	.308	.349	.423	78	24	3	0	2	2	5	12
Runners On Base	.319	.368	.399	163	52	7	0	2	44	16	24
Scoring Position	.280	.350	.360	100	28	5	0	1	40	14	18
Late and Close	.283	.338	.383	60	17	3	0	1	5	5	13

6-YEAR TOTALS (1988–1993)

	BA	OBA	SA	AB	H	2B	3B	HR	RBI	BB	SO
	.307	.364	.438	1599	491	94	7	34	201	147	210
vs. Left	.240	.299	.301	412	99	17	1	2	36	33	92
vs. Right	.330	.386	.486	1187	392	77	6	32	165	114	118
at Home	.307	.360	.451	788	242	56	3	17	104	67	100
on Road	.307	.368	.427	811	249	38	4	17	97	80	110
on Grass	.290	.351	.412	486	141	23	3	10	61	48	77
on Turf	.314	.370	.450	1113	350	71	4	24	140	99	133
Day Games	.298	.367	.469	503	150	34	2	16	73	55	59
Night Games	.311	.363	.424	1096	341	60	5	18	128	92	151
April	.307	.336	.465	101	31	8	1	2	12	4	14
May	.311	.376	.444	151	47	10	2	2	26	16	17
June	.309	.356	.400	265	82	13	1	3	38	21	36
July	.330	.393	.476	355	117	21	2	9	41	39	44
August	.293	.338	.442	335	98	20	0	10	40	23	45
Sept-Oct	.296	.366	.418	392	116	22	1	8	44	44	54
Bases Empty	.313	.367	.472	888	278	54	6	25	25	70	106
Leadoff	.309	.347	.433	330	102	17	3	6	6	19	44
Runners On Base	.300	.361	.397	711	213	40	1	9	176	77	104
Scoring Position	.298	.377	.399	419	125	25	1	5	160	63	65
Late and Close	.276	.330	.391	261	72	15	3	3	17	19	50

EDDIE MURRAY — BB/TR — age 38 — NYN 1B154

1993	BA	OBA	SA	AB	H	2B	3B	HR	RBI	BB	SO
Total	.285	.325	.467	610	174	28	1	27	100	40	61
vs. Left	.311	.355	.497	183	57	10	0	8	25	13	17
vs. Right	.274	.312	.454	427	117	18	1	19	75	27	44
at Home	.290	.320	.475	314	91	11	1	15	52	16	33
on Road	.280	.329	.459	296	83	17	0	12	48	24	28
on Grass	.288	.324	.478	483	139	21	1	23	85	30	50
on Turf	.276	.328	.425	127	35	7	0	4	15	10	11
Day Games	.295	.326	.530	217	64	12	0	13	48	12	25
Night Games	.280	.324	.433	393	110	16	1	14	52	28	36
April	.296	.367	.469	81	24	2	0	4	15	9	15
May	.256	.271	.356	90	23	6	0	1	10	3	9
June	.250	.284	.410	100	25	4	0	4	17	6	14
July	.333	.354	.552	105	35	5	0	6	26	5	8
August	.210	.236	.403	119	25	6	1	5	11	4	7
Sept-Oct	.365	.430	.591	115	42	5	0	7	21	13	8
Bases Empty	.270	.314	.418	359	97	18	1	11	11	23	36
Leadoff	.250	.281	.379	116	29	3	0	4	4	5	12
Runners On Base	.307	.339	.538	251	77	10	0	16	89	17	25
Scoring Position	.319	.365	.578	135	43	8	0	9	74	15	15
Late and Close	.265	.312	.441	102	27	4	1	4	14	7	15

10-YEAR TOTALS (1984–1993)

	BA	OBA	SA	AB	H	2B	3B	HR	RBI	BB	SO
	.285	.364	.466	5776	1645	282	18	243	965	747	720
vs. Left	.261	.333	.419	1978	517	100	4	68	298	219	239
vs. Right	.297	.379	.491	3798	1128	182	14	175	667	528	481
at Home	.286	.370	.460	2838	811	118	10	119	471	385	365
on Road	.284	.358	.472	2938	834	164	8	124	494	362	355
on Grass	.288	.369	.476	4584	1320	214	10	210	785	612	576
on Turf	.273	.344	.426	1192	325	68	8	33	180	135	144
Day Games	.283	.359	.472	1680	476	80	3	77	289	206	212
Night Games	.285	.366	.464	4096	1169	202	15	166	676	541	508
April	.261	.340	.428	762	199	38	1	29	137	94	105
May	.299	.381	.480	929	278	49	4	37	172	134	112
June	.254	.335	.417	1001	254	51	2	36	151	130	142
July	.278	.352	.496	924	257	43	1	52	175	110	122
August	.304	.377	.476	1049	319	40	7	42	164	125	112
Sept-Oct	.304	.388	.491	1111	338	61	3	47	166	154	127
Bases Empty	.270	.341	.423	3064	828	129	8	108	108	326	390
Leadoff	.268	.329	.418	1446	387	57	5	50	50	130	171
Runners On Base	.301	.388	.514	2712	817	153	10	135	857	421	330
Scoring Position	.299	.412	.535	1395	417	86	6	77	713	309	200
Late and Close	.274	.368	.462	901	247	44	4	39	167	139	137

GREG MYERS — BL/TR — age 28 — CAL C97, DH2

1993	BA	OBA	SA	AB	H	2B	3B	HR	RBI	BB	SO
Total	.255	.298	.362	290	74	10	0	7	40	17	47
vs. Left	.375	.400	.500	24	9	3	0	0	4	0	4
vs. Right	.244	.289	.350	266	65	7	0	7	36	17	43
at Home	.266	.296	.392	143	38	6	0	4	22	7	26
on Road	.245	.300	.333	147	36	4	0	3	18	10	21
on Grass	.239	.280	.357	238	57	10	0	6	30	14	41
on Turf	.327	.379	.385	52	17	0	0	1	10	3	6
Day Games	.268	.318	.305	82	22	3	0	0	5	5	16
Night Games	.250	.290	.385	208	52	7	0	7	35	12	31
April	.179	.233	.321	28	5	1	0	1	3	2	5
May	.260	.327	.380	50	13	3	0	1	4	5	7
June	.255	.327	.404	47	12	1	0	2	7	5	6
July	.311	.311	.410	61	19	3	0	1	8	0	11
August	.245	.309	.306	49	12	0	0	1	9	4	9
Sept-Oct	.236	.254	.327	55	13	2	0	1	9	1	9
Bases Empty	.242	.279	.395	157	38	6	0	6	6	8	25
Leadoff	.183	.197	.283	60	11	3	0	1	1	1	8
Runners On Base	.271	.320	.323	133	36	4	0	1	34	9	22
Scoring Position	.267	.313	.326	86	23	2	0	1	32	6	14
Late and Close	.241	.293	.333	54	13	2	0	1	6	3	6

6-YEAR TOTALS (1987–1993)

	BA	OBA	SA	AB	H	2B	3B	HR	RBI	BB	SO
	.243	.289	.358	980	238	48	1	21	112	67	148
vs. Left	.222	.265	.300	90	20	4	0	1	9	5	17
vs. Right	.245	.292	.364	890	218	44	1	20	103	62	131
at Home	.258	.309	.391	466	120	26	0	12	61	38	74
on Road	.230	.271	.329	514	118	22	1	9	51	29	74
on Grass	.223	.264	.332	497	111	19	1	11	50	29	83
on Turf	.263	.315	.385	483	127	29	0	10	62	38	65
Day Games	.244	.294	.336	271	66	13	0	4	28	19	46
Night Games	.243	.288	.367	709	172	35	1	17	84	48	102
April	.248	.307	.384	125	31	5	0	4	17	12	14
May	.261	.338	.396	134	35	12	0	2	13	16	18
June	.255	.300	.390	200	51	9	0	6	23	13	26
July	.226	.242	.325	212	48	13	1	2	25	6	38
August	.269	.305	.379	145	39	4	0	4	15	7	27
Sept-Oct	.207	.267	.293	164	34	5	0	3	19	13	25
Bases Empty	.253	.297	.390	521	132	29	0	14	14	32	81
Leadoff	.276	.306	.454	185	51	18	0	5	5	8	23
Runners On Base	.231	.281	.322	459	106	19	1	7	98	35	67
Scoring Position	.219	.271	.328	274	60	10	1	6	92	23	42
Late and Close	.272	.320	.380	158	43	11	0	2	15	10	22

TROY NEEL — BL/TR — age 29 — OAK DH85, 1B34

1993	BA	OBA	SA	AB	H	2B	3B	HR	RBI	BB	SO
Total	.290	.367	.473	427	124	21	0	19	63	49	101
vs. Left	.357	.427	.541	98	35	6	0	4	15	10	22
vs. Right	.271	.349	.453	329	89	15	0	15	48	39	79
at Home	.312	.388	.513	199	62	7	0	11	32	21	51
on Road	.272	.349	.439	228	62	14	0	8	31	28	50
on Grass	.281	.359	.446	363	102	15	0	15	51	41	89
on Turf	.344	.411	.625	64	22	6	0	4	12	8	12
Day Games	.298	.363	.470	181	54	7	0	8	31	19	43
Night Games	.285	.370	.476	246	70	14	0	11	32	30	58
April	.260	.315	.440	50	13	3	0	2	4	4	11
May	.149	.227	.269	67	10	2	0	2	9	7	16
June	.371	.410	.629	35	13	3	0	2	7	3	9
July	.333	.414	.552	87	29	4	0	5	19	12	20
August	.318	.412	.534	88	28	4	0	5	14	13	23
Sept-Oct	.310	.389	.450	100	31	5	0	3	10	10	22
Bases Empty	.321	.390	.563	240	77	16	0	14	14	24	56
Leadoff	.389	.450	.713	108	42	8	0	9	9	12	21
Runners On Base	.251	.340	.358	187	47	5	0	5	49	25	45
Scoring Position	.235	.348	.391	115	27	3	0	5	48	20	29
Late and Close	.266	.373	.438	64	17	5	0	2	13	11	16

2-YEAR TOTALS (1992–1993)

BA	OBA	SA	AB	H	2B	3B	HR	RBI	BB	SO
.287	.364	.475	480	138	24	0	22	72	54	116
.359	.426	.563	103	37	6	0	5	17	10	23
.268	.347	.451	377	101	18	0	17	55	44	93
.312	.383	.532	218	68	9	0	13	39	21	56
.267	.349	.427	262	70	15	0	9	33	33	60
.278	.354	.457	403	112	18	0	18	60	43	99
.338	.416	.571	77	26	6	0	4	12	11	17
.301	.367	.485	206	62	8	0	10	36	21	50
.277	.362	.467	274	76	16	0	12	36	33	66
.260	.315	.440	50	13	3	0	2	4	4	11
.141	.215	.254	71	10	2	0	2	9	7	18
.368	.405	.605	38	14	3	0	2	7	3	9
.324	.409	.532	111	36	5	0	6	21	15	26
.318	.412	.534	88	28	4	0	5	14	13	23
.303	.380	.484	122	37	7	0	5	17	12	29
.307	.383	.528	267	82	17	0	14	14	29	66
.365	.434	.670	115	42	8	0	9	9	14	24
.263	.340	.408	213	56	7	0	8	58	25	50
.230	.336	.389	126	29	5	0	5	51	20	32
.250	.354	.412	68	17	5	0	2	13	11	18

DAVE NILSSON — BL/TR — age 25 — MIL C91, 1B4, DH4

1993	BA	OBA	SA	AB	H	2B	3B	HR	RBI	BB	SO
Total	.257	.336	.375	296	76	10	2	7	40	37	36
vs. Left	.272	.358	.457	81	22	5	2	2	19	12	15
vs. Right	.251	.328	.344	215	54	5	0	5	21	25	21
at Home	.274	.344	.433	164	45	9	1	5	26	19	19
on Road	.235	.327	.303	132	31	1	1	2	14	18	17
on Grass	.262	.341	.391	271	71	10	2	7	39	34	33
on Turf	.200	.286	.200	25	5	0	0	0	1	3	3
Day Games	.253	.298	.358	95	24	4	0	2	14	7	12
Night Games	.259	.353	.383	201	52	6	2	5	26	30	24
April	.172	.226	.276	29	5	0	0	1	2	2	1
May	.160	.160	.200	25	4	1	0	0	0	0	2
June	.143	.217	.143	21	3	0	0	0	1	2	4
July	.308	.395	.400	65	20	1	1	1	12	10	9
August	.293	.355	.451	82	24	5	1	2	13	9	10
Sept-Oct	.270	.386	.432	74	20	3	0	3	12	14	10
Bases Empty	.268	.339	.376	157	42	5	0	4	4	17	23
Leadoff	.297	.375	.375	64	19	2	0	1	1	8	5
Runners On Base	.245	.333	.374	139	34	5	2	3	36	20	13
Scoring Position	.262	.380	.400	80	21	3	1	2	33	17	3
Late and Close	.245	.302	.265	49	12	1	0	0	5	4	6

2-YEAR TOTALS (1992–1993)

BA	OBA	SA	AB	H	2B	3B	HR	RBI	BB	SO
.248	.325	.367	460	114	18	2	11	65	54	54
.259	.339	.417	108	28	7	2	2	26	14	18
.244	.321	.352	352	86	11	0	9	39	40	36
.265	.352	.402	219	58	10	1	6	30	31	26
.232	.299	.336	241	56	8	1	5	35	23	28
.250	.330	.369	404	101	14	2	10	57	50	50
.232	.283	.357	56	13	4	0	1	8	4	4
.257	.321	.372	148	38	8	0	3	21	15	19
.244	.327	.365	312	76	10	2	8	44	39	35
.172	.226	.276	29	5	0	0	1	2	2	1
.191	.224	.298	47	9	2	0	1	6	2	5
.198	.232	.286	91	18	2	0	2	10	4	12
.274	.365	.356	73	20	1	1	1	12	11	10
.269	.352	.409	93	25	5	1	2	13	13	12
.291	.396	.449	127	37	8	0	4	22	22	14
.255	.324	.362	235	60	7	0	6	6	24	33
.243	.310	.330	103	25	3	0	2	2	10	9
.240	.326	.373	225	54	11	2	5	59	30	21
.252	.357	.392	143	36	9	1	3	54	25	9
.216	.275	.230	74	16	1	0	0	7	6	8

OTIS NIXON — BB/TR — age 35 — ATL OF116

1993	BA	OBA	SA	AB	H	2B	3B	HR	RBI	BB	SO
Total	.269	.351	.315	461	124	12	3	1	24	61	63
vs. Left	.263	.335	.316	152	40	1	2	1	6	17	21
vs. Right	.272	.359	.314	309	84	11	1	0	18	44	42
at Home	.287	.379	.361	216	62	9	2	1	12	34	22
on Road	.253	.325	.273	245	62	3	1	0	12	27	41
on Grass	.279	.365	.325	351	98	9	2	1	17	50	46
on Turf	.236	.282	.282	110	26	3	1	0	7	11	17
Day Games	.267	.351	.280	150	40	2	0	0	5	20	23
Night Games	.270	.351	.331	311	84	10	3	1	19	41	40
April	.247	.346	.270	89	22	2	0	0	9	14	13
May	.240	.330	.281	96	23	4	0	0	5	14	11
June	.227	.292	.227	22	5	0	0	0	0	2	4
July	.224	.281	.362	58	13	3	1	1	3	5	7
August	.289	.325	.289	76	22	0	0	0	1	4	15
Sept-Oct	.325	.427	.383	120	39	3	2	0	6	22	13
Bases Empty	.297	.381	.348	310	92	7	3	1	1	42	45
Leadoff	.281	.370	.327	199	56	4	1	1	1	28	31
Runners On Base	.212	.291	.245	151	32	5	0	0	23	19	18
Scoring Position	.196	.291	.216	97	19	2	0	0	22	15	10
Late and Close	.230	.341	.270	74	17	3	0	0	5	13	14

10-YEAR TOTALS (1984–1993)

BA	OBA	SA	AB	H	2B	3B	HR	RBI	BB	SO
.260	.332	.306	2443	635	65	13	7	147	268	322
.264	.330	.324	935	247	27	7	5	63	93	103
.257	.333	.294	1508	388	38	6	2	84	175	219
.267	.348	.316	1189	317	36	7	3	71	150	142
.254	.316	.296	1254	318	29	6	4	76	118	180
.271	.341	.315	1451	393	40	3	6	83	159	194
.244	.319	.292	992	242	25	10	1	64	109	128
.268	.328	.318	796	213	22	6	2	60	73	114
.256	.334	.300	1647	422	43	7	5	87	195	208
.222	.305	.250	284	63	6	1	0	22	35	36
.285	.354	.320	375	107	11	1	0	17	42	44
.246	.321	.291	358	88	6	2	2	25	38	43
.266	.329	.331	447	119	19	2	2	22	43	50
.253	.309	.297	495	125	10	3	2	31	41	81
.275	.363	.324	484	133	13	4	1	30	69	68
.271	.352	.312	1643	446	41	7	4	4	202	229
.278	.358	.323	968	269	27	4	3	3	120	140
.236	.291	.292	800	189	24	6	3	143	66	93
.236	.296	.291	492	116	18	3	1	134	47	63
.290	.367	.339	428	124	14	2	1	32	53	68

JOSE OFFERMAN — BB/TR — age 26 — LA SS158

1993	BA	OBA	SA	AB	H	2B	3B	HR	RBI	BB	SO	4-YR (1990–1993) BA	OBA	SA	AB	H	2B	3B	HR	RBI	BB	SO
Total	.269	.346	.331	590	159	21	6	1	62	71	75	.254	.334	.316	1295	329	43	14	3	102	157	219
vs. Left	.250	.327	.326	184	46	7	2	1	19	21	18	.260	.329	.321	461	120	16	3	2	30	48	60
vs. Right	.278	.354	.333	406	113	14	4	0	43	50	57	.251	.336	.313	834	209	27	11	1	72	109	159
at Home	.326	.409	.382	288	94	13	0	1	27	40	34	.285	.370	.357	667	190	29	5	3	51	89	101
on Road	.215	.284	.281	302	65	8	6	0	35	31	41	.221	.295	.272	628	139	14	9	0	51	68	118
on Grass	.283	.364	.336	459	130	17	2	1	49	60	55	.259	.340	.315	997	258	33	7	3	84	124	156
on Turf	.221	.281	.313	131	29	4	4	0	13	11	20	.238	.313	.319	298	71	10	7	0	18	33	63
Day Games	.280	.342	.343	175	49	7	2	0	21	18	25	.264	.333	.328	387	102	12	5	1	30	42	65
Night Games	.265	.347	.325	415	110	14	4	1	41	53	50	.250	.334	.311	908	227	31	9	2	72	115	154
April	.215	.287	.215	79	17	0	0	0	5	7	13	.216	.286	.261	153	33	3	2	0	9	14	27
May	.358	.431	.474	95	34	5	3	0	14	13	13	.300	.390	.375	200	60	7	4	0	19	30	35
June	.232	.319	.283	99	23	3	1	0	8	13	16	.258	.333	.321	190	49	6	3	0	13	22	31
July	.295	.322	.348	112	33	6	0	0	15	6	16	.269	.316	.326	227	61	11	1	0	18	17	43
August	.277	.370	.327	101	28	3	1	0	12	16	8	.267	.362	.338	281	75	8	3	2	24	42	46
Sept-Oct	.231	.336	.317	104	24	4	1	1	8	16	9	.209	.300	.262	244	51	8	1	1	19	32	37
Bases Empty	.269	.341	.344	334	90	14	4	1	1	34	48	.256	.327	.326	772	198	27	9	3	3	78	134
Leadoff	.266	.344	.339	109	29	3	1	1	1	13	16	.258	.332	.329	325	84	9	4	2	2	36	54
Runners On Base	.270	.352	.313	256	69	7	2	0	61	37	27	.250	.343	.300	523	131	16	5	0	99	79	85
Scoring Position	.308	.408	.356	146	45	3	2	0	60	30	17	.281	.400	.331	278	78	6	4	0	95	62	45
Late and Close	.218	.320	.218	101	22	0	0	0	12	17	13	.220	.291	.233	232	51	1	1	0	18	25	41

JOHN OLERUD — BL/TL — age 26 — TOR 1B137, DH20

1993	BA	OBA	SA	AB	H	2B	3B	HR	RBI	BB	SO	5-YR (1989–1993) BA	OBA	SA	AB	H	2B	3B	HR	RBI	BB	SO
Total	.363	.473	.599	551	200	54	2	24	107	114	65	.297	.398	.488	1829	544	127	4	71	289	309	286
vs. Left	.291	.413	.424	172	50	11	0	4	28	34	23	.277	.402	.427	426	118	23	1	13	74	88	77
vs. Right	.396	.500	.678	379	150	43	2	20	79	80	42	.304	.397	.506	1403	426	104	3	58	215	221	209
at Home	.346	.464	.550	269	93	24	2	9	48	56	28	.292	.399	.472	920	269	64	4	31	141	160	137
on Road	.379	.481	.645	282	107	30	0	15	59	58	37	.303	.396	.504	909	275	63	0	40	148	149	149
on Grass	.400	.509	.689	225	90	23	0	14	48	50	28	.320	.422	.547	697	223	53	0	35	121	127	111
on Turf	.337	.448	.537	326	110	31	2	10	59	64	37	.284	.383	.451	1132	321	74	4	36	168	182	175
Day Games	.380	.498	.641	184	70	18	0	10	37	42	20	.294	.410	.474	572	168	40	0	21	94	112	91
Night Games	.354	.460	.578	367	130	36	2	14	70	72	45	.299	.392	.494	1257	376	87	4	50	195	197	195
April	.450	.527	.650	80	36	7	0	3	18	13	7	.316	.425	.488	256	81	17	0	9	37	48	31
May	.348	.470	.652	92	32	8	1	6	16	21	10	.244	.361	.419	308	75	14	2	12	40	56	58
June	.427	.525	.760	96	41	17	0	5	30	22	8	.343	.420	.599	329	113	31	1	17	74	48	48
July	.389	.491	.700	90	35	10	0	6	19	18	11	.352	.431	.574	310	109	24	0	15	42	41	43
August	.310	.421	.460	100	31	4	1	3	14	19	17	.269	.370	.439	312	84	18	1	11	53	52	49
Sept-Oct	.269	.414	.387	93	25	8	0	1	10	21	12	.261	.386	.401	314	82	23	0	7	43	64	57
Bases Empty	.367	.454	.627	319	117	36	1	15	15	47	35	.301	.395	.508	1007	303	73	2	44	44	148	156
Leadoff	.389	.458	.682	157	61	22	0	8	8	19	24	.343	.424	.614	414	142	44	1	22	22	56	69
Runners On Base	.358	.495	.560	232	83	18	1	9	92	67	30	.293	.402	.462	822	241	54	2	27	245	161	130
Scoring Position	.371	.532	.543	140	52	13	1	3	76	54	19	.283	.425	.425	463	131	31	1	11	196	129	82
Late and Close	.308	.455	.474	78	24	4	0	3	12	22	16	.307	.408	.485	309	95	22	0	11	54	55	61

JOE OLIVER — BR/TR — age 29 — CIN C133, 1B12, OF1

1993	BA	OBA	SA	AB	H	2B	3B	HR	RBI	BB	SO	5-YR (1989–1993) BA	OBA	SA	AB	H	2B	3B	HR	RBI	BB	SO
Total	.239	.276	.384	482	115	28	0	14	75	27	91	.245	.293	.379	1751	429	95	1	46	248	123	322
vs. Left	.291	.338	.507	134	39	11	0	6	25	10	17	.288	.344	.455	699	201	45	0	24	117	63	114
vs. Right	.218	.251	.336	348	76	17	0	8	50	17	74	.217	.259	.329	1052	228	50	1	22	131	60	208
at Home	.250	.283	.414	232	58	17	0	7	38	12	41	.246	.293	.396	873	215	56	0	25	130	60	157
on Road	.228	.269	.356	250	57	11	0	7	37	15	50	.244	.294	.362	878	214	39	1	21	118	63	165
on Grass	.188	.229	.326	144	27	8	0	4	23	8	29	.232	.268	.371	512	119	27	1	14	78	26	100
on Turf	.260	.295	.408	338	88	20	0	10	52	19	62	.250	.304	.383	1239	310	68	0	32	170	97	222
Day Games	.237	.290	.386	114	27	8	0	3	25	8	18	.268	.319	.387	452	121	30	0	8	71	34	82
Night Games	.239	.271	.383	368	88	20	0	11	50	19	73	.237	.284	.376	1299	308	65	1	38	177	89	240
April	.262	.314	.412	80	21	6	0	2	13	6	13	.234	.303	.347	222	52	14	0	3	25	22	39
May	.213	.265	.383	94	20	7	0	3	16	6	19	.221	.300	.373	271	60	14	0	9	36	28	53
June	.214	.244	.329	70	15	5	0	1	8	4	12	.229	.283	.340	253	58	13	0	5	28	21	46
July	.302	.315	.442	86	26	3	0	3	14	2	17	.271	.307	.397	325	88	17	0	8	47	19	57
August	.200	.256	.400	75	15	6	0	3	15	6	13	.248	.285	.429	343	85	20	0	14	67	19	67
Sept-Oct	.234	.256	.325	77	18	1	0	2	9	3	17	.255	.285	.368	337	86	17	0	7	43	14	60
Bases Empty	.220	.264	.327	254	56	12	0	5	5	14	55	.241	.280	.349	952	229	47	1	18	18	49	182
Leadoff	.233	.303	.278	90	21	4	0	0	0	8	16	.240	.278	.357	387	93	21	0	8	8	18	73
Runners On Base	.259	.288	.447	228	59	16	0	9	70	13	36	.250	.309	.416	799	200	48	0	28	230	74	140
Scoring Position	.277	.301	.459	148	41	9	0	6	63	9	26	.249	.325	.425	478	119	30	0	18	203	61	91
Late and Close	.269	.298	.436	78	21	4	0	3	16	4	10	.260	.312	.365	285	74	15	0	5	33	23	45

GREG OLSON — BR/TR — age 34 — ATL C81

1993	BA	OBA	SA	AB	H	2B	3B	HR	RBI	BB	SO		BA	OBA	SA	AB	H	2B	3B	HR	RBI	BB	SO
Total	.225	.304	.309	262	59	10	0	4	24	29	27		.242	.317	.342	1275	309	61	3	20	131	137	157
vs. Left	.237	.282	.361	97	23	3	0	3	15	6	5		.278	.329	.415	468	130	25	3	11	67	37	50
vs. Right	.218	.316	.279	165	36	7	0	1	9	23	22		.222	.311	.300	807	179	36	0	9	64	100	107
at Home	.198	.277	.302	126	25	4	0	3	13	14	15		.258	.320	.369	616	159	27	1	13	76	60	64
on Road	.250	.329	.316	136	34	6	0	1	11	15	12		.228	.315	.317	659	150	34	2	7	55	77	93
on Grass	.220	.300	.312	205	45	7	0	4	20	24	21		.244	.315	.344	932	227	42	2	16	96	99	108
on Turf	.246	.317	.298	57	14	3	0	0	4	5	6		.239	.324	.335	343	82	19	1	4	35	38	49
Day Games	.210	.304	.284	81	17	3	0	1	6	11	10		.265	.331	.366	396	105	17	1	7	41	38	56
Night Games	.232	.303	.320	181	42	7	0	3	18	18	17		.232	.311	.331	879	204	44	2	13	90	99	101
April	.212	.317	.269	52	11	0	0	1	3	8	2		.273	.363	.344	128	35	6	0	1	7	18	16
May	.182	.250	.227	66	12	3	0	0	3	6	8		.234	.305	.342	231	54	7	0	6	28	21	31
June	.250	.306	.321	56	14	4	0	0	7	5	8		.260	.329	.370	265	69	14	0	5	29	27	26
July	.213	.288	.298	47	10	1	0	1	4	5	4		.221	.303	.328	235	52	9	2	4	22	28	29
August	.313	.313	.750	16	5	1	0	2	6	0	3		.283	.342	.420	205	58	14	1	4	32	19	28
Sept-Oct	.280	.419	.320	25	7	1	0	0	1	5	2		.194	.282	.246	211	41	11	0	0	13	24	27
Bases Empty	.255	.341	.297	145	37	6	0	0	0	18	11		.233	.303	.323	743	173	33	2	10	10	71	91
Leadoff	.190	.239	.222	63	12	2	0	0	0	4	2		.225	.293	.312	311	70	15	0	4	4	29	28
Runners On Base	.188	.256	.325	117	22	4	0	4	24	11	16		.256	.337	.368	532	136	28	1	10	121	66	66
Scoring Position	.200	.258	.317	60	12	1	0	2	18	5	11		.227	.328	.318	308	70	10	0	6	98	50	50
Late and Close	.190	.300	.286	42	8	1	0	1	4	7	6		.202	.298	.298	218	44	9	0	4	24	30	32

5-YEAR TOTALS (1989–1993)

PAUL O'NEILL — BL/TL — age 31 — NYA OF138, DH2

1993	BA	OBA	SA	AB	H	2B	3B	HR	RBI	BB	SO		BA	OBA	SA	AB	H	2B	3B	HR	RBI	BB	SO
Total	.311	.367	.504	498	155	34	1	20	75	44	69		.268	.341	.443	3116	834	181	8	116	486	350	525
vs. Left	.230	.279	.319	135	31	6	0	2	15	9	29		.217	.272	.325	869	189	44	2	15	118	65	229
vs. Right	.342	.400	.573	363	124	28	1	18	60	35	40		.287	.367	.488	2247	645	137	6	101	368	285	296
at Home	.325	.377	.498	249	81	17	1	8	39	20	32		.281	.353	.481	1557	437	93	3	71	259	171	245
on Road	.297	.358	.510	249	74	17	0	12	36	24	37		.255	.330	.404	1559	397	88	5	45	227	179	280
on Grass	.319	.378	.500	420	134	29	1	15	61	39	61		.289	.359	.454	1189	344	70	6	38	172	130	202
on Turf	.269	.310	.526	78	21	5	0	5	14	5	8		.254	.331	.435	1927	490	111	2	78	314	220	323
Day Games	.307	.364	.512	166	51	11	1	7	25	15	23		.264	.333	.442	1017	268	63	4	37	156	111	167
Night Games	.313	.369	.500	332	104	23	0	13	50	29	46		.270	.345	.443	2099	566	118	4	79	330	239	358
April	.296	.328	.444	54	16	3	1	1	10	3	8		.285	.358	.451	397	113	25	1	13	62	46	72
May	.340	.387	.515	103	35	9	0	3	11	8	9		.270	.345	.442	548	148	31	0	21	92	60	92
June	.343	.374	.608	102	35	6	0	7	18	5	11		.281	.356	.510	565	159	31	1	32	101	63	77
July	.313	.389	.530	83	26	9	0	3	13	10	17		.256	.332	.400	500	128	28	1	14	63	56	90
August	.260	.363	.364	77	20	2	0	2	14	12	13		.267	.356	.445	465	124	29	0	18	76	67	89
Sept-Oct	.291	.341	.506	79	23	5	0	4	9	6	11		.253	.312	.410	641	162	37	5	18	92	58	105
Bases Empty	.333	.389	.599	252	84	16	0	17	17	22	32		.263	.322	.447	1645	433	99	3	66	66	137	293
Leadoff	.276	.330	.480	98	27	2	0	6	6	7	15		.250	.307	.449	691	173	31	2	34	34	53	114
Runners On Base	.289	.346	.407	246	71	18	1	3	58	22	37		.273	.361	.437	1471	401	82	5	50	420	213	232
Scoring Position	.262	.340	.340	141	37	11	0	0	48	17	26		.261	.376	.408	880	230	53	2	24	350	172	152
Late and Close	.355	.425	.597	62	22	6	0	3	17	9	9		.247	.348	.396	503	124	31	1	14	78	78	101

9-YEAR TOTALS (1985–1993)

JOE ORSULAK — BL/TL — age 32 — NYN OF114, 1B4

1993	BA	OBA	SA	AB	H	2B	3B	HR	RBI	BB	SO		BA	OBA	SA	AB	H	2B	3B	HR	RBI	BB	SO
Total	.284	.331	.399	409	116	15	4	8	35	28	25		.279	.331	.383	3334	931	146	33	45	299	249	290
vs. Left	.357	.364	.429	42	15	1	1	0	7	1	5		.245	.293	.290	538	132	16	4	0	46	33	58
vs. Right	.275	.327	.395	367	101	14	3	8	28	27	20		.286	.338	.401	2796	799	130	29	45	253	216	232
at Home	.285	.350	.413	179	51	8	0	5	12	19	5		.281	.338	.385	1575	443	63	17	22	139	134	126
on Road	.283	.315	.387	230	65	7	4	3	23	9	20		.277	.324	.382	1759	488	83	16	23	160	115	164
on Grass	.280	.335	.390	300	84	11	2	6	25	25	14		.281	.337	.390	2247	631	103	13	39	216	184	189
on Turf	.294	.319	.422	109	32	4	2	2	10	3	11		.276	.318	.369	1087	300	43	20	6	83	65	101
Day Games	.230	.316	.296	135	31	1	1	2	9	16	13		.266	.326	.364	932	248	43	6	12	69	78	90
Night Games	.310	.339	.449	274	85	14	3	6	26	12	12		.284	.333	.391	2402	683	103	27	33	230	171	200
April	.282	.300	.308	39	11	1	0	0	2	1	3		.268	.317	.374	406	109	25	3	4	35	27	43
May	.292	.338	.389	72	21	1	0	2	6	4	5		.268	.333	.368	492	132	19	3	8	52	42	46
June	.313	.365	.463	67	21	4	0	2	8	5	3		.278	.330	.352	627	174	24	4	5	60	47	46
July	.292	.347	.446	65	19	4	0	2	6	6	2		.299	.339	.423	591	177	30	8	9	48	39	43
August	.300	.325	.475	80	24	4	2	2	7	3	5		.300	.345	.431	620	186	34	7	11	62	43	54
Sept-Oct	.233	.305	.291	86	20	1	2	0	6	9	7		.256	.318	.346	598	153	14	8	8	42	51	58
Bases Empty	.288	.333	.443	264	76	11	3	8	8	17	17		.293	.338	.410	2031	595	96	26	30	30	128	175
Leadoff	.304	.349	.480	102	31	7	1	3	3	6	4		.302	.350	.426	877	265	49	9	14	14	58	71
Runners On Base	.276	.327	.317	145	40	4	1	0	27	11	8		.258	.321	.342	1303	336	50	7	15	269	121	115
Scoring Position	.289	.344	.337	83	24	2	1	0	27	7	5		.260	.347	.356	711	185	31	5	9	250	97	64
Late and Close	.282	.341	.359	78	22	3	0	1	7	6	3		.262	.332	.346	564	148	21	4	6	52	56	46

9-YEAR TOTALS (1984–1993)

JUNIOR ORTIZ — BR/TR — age 35 — CLE C95

1993	BA	OBA	SA	AB	H	2B	3B	HR	RBI	BB	SO	10-YEAR TOTALS (1984–1993) BA	OBA	SA	AB	H	2B	3B	HR	RBI	BB	SO
Total	.221	.267	.273	249	55	13	0	0	20	11	26	.256	.308	.309	1610	412	63	4	5	165	111	174
vs. Left	.192	.231	.263	99	19	7	0	0	10	3	12	.259	.314	.318	672	174	30	2	2	69	51	70
vs. Right	.240	.290	.280	150	36	6	0	0	10	8	14	.254	.304	.303	938	238	33	2	3	96	60	104
at Home	.205	.260	.248	117	24	5	0	0	10	6	11	.279	.340	.328	777	217	29	3	1	99	65	76
on Road	.235	.273	.295	132	31	8	0	0	10	5	15	.234	.278	.292	833	195	34	1	4	66	46	98
on Grass	.231	.278	.279	208	48	10	0	0	18	9	19	.253	.302	.295	766	194	26	0	2	61	44	75
on Turf	.171	.209	.244	41	7	3	0	0	2	2	7	.258	.314	.322	844	218	37	4	3	104	67	99
Day Games	.197	.264	.242	66	13	3	0	0	3	3	6	.243	.297	.297	572	139	18	2	3	54	37	64
Night Games	.230	.268	.284	183	42	10	0	0	17	8	20	.263	.314	.316	1038	273	45	2	2	111	74	110
April	.125	.176	.125	16	2	0	0	0	0	0	2	.208	.289	.255	192	40	1	1	2	24	22	17
May	.211	.224	.298	57	12	5	0	0	6	1	7	.234	.280	.300	320	75	21	0	0	30	18	35
June	.226	.268	.302	53	12	4	0	0	6	2	4	.298	.338	.375	272	81	14	2	1	32	14	27
July	.268	.312	.296	71	19	2	0	0	7	4	8	.278	.321	.327	327	91	11	1	1	39	20	38
August	.250	.348	.300	20	5	1	0	0	0	3	2	.246	.316	.276	228	56	7	0	0	17	22	26
Sept-Oct	.156	.229	.188	32	5	1	0	0	1	1	3	.255	.303	.299	271	69	9	0	1	23	15	31
Bases Empty	.201	.241	.240	154	31	6	0	0	0	5	17	.234	.282	.289	915	214	36	1	4	4	53	100
Leadoff	.200	.246	.215	65	13	1	0	0	0	2	8	.234	.290	.294	364	85	14	1	2	2	25	39
Runners On Base	.253	.308	.326	95	24	7	0	0	20	6	9	.285	.341	.337	695	198	27	3	1	161	58	74
Scoring Position	.268	.344	.357	56	15	5	0	0	19	6	3	.288	.353	.346	416	120	19	1	1	156	45	48
Late and Close	.222	.276	.259	27	6	1	0	0	3	2	2	.240	.275	.289	242	58	9	0	1	18	10	30

SPIKE OWEN — BB/TR — age 33 — NYA SS96, DH2

1993	BA	OBA	SA	AB	H	2B	3B	HR	RBI	BB	SO	10-YEAR TOTALS (1984–1993) BA	OBA	SA	AB	H	2B	3B	HR	RBI	BB	SO
Total	.234	.294	.311	334	78	16	2	2	20	29	30	.246	.324	.343	4138	1018	178	51	40	353	478	436
vs. Left	.248	.290	.328	137	34	6	1	1	8	8	14	.274	.336	.399	1431	392	89	15	20	138	134	160
vs. Right	.223	.297	.299	197	44	10	1	1	12	21	16	.231	.317	.313	2707	626	89	36	20	215	344	276
at Home	.210	.256	.280	157	33	6	1	1	9	10	17	.245	.324	.347	1965	481	87	25	21	178	232	212
on Road	.254	.327	.339	177	45	10	1	1	11	19	13	.247	.324	.339	2173	537	91	26	19	175	246	224
on Grass	.241	.300	.313	278	67	12	1	2	17	24	26	.240	.319	.326	1947	468	73	21	17	165	228	202
on Turf	.196	.262	.304	56	11	4	1	0	3	5	4	.251	.327	.358	2191	550	105	30	23	188	250	234
Day Games	.304	.368	.422	102	31	4	1	2	10	11	10	.262	.335	.380	1265	332	59	18	18	123	142	148
Night Games	.203	.260	.263	232	47	12	1	0	10	18	20	.239	.319	.326	2873	686	119	33	22	230	336	288
April	.296	.367	.338	71	21	3	0	0	3	8	7	.245	.316	.347	599	147	30	8	5	44	64	60
May	.234	.301	.330	94	22	6	0	1	8	9	10	.235	.333	.358	695	163	30	10	12	65	102	84
June	.257	.345	.365	74	19	3	1	1	5	10	6	.264	.349	.390	849	224	51	13	10	81	110	73
July	.164	.188	.213	61	10	1	1	0	2	2	4	.256	.326	.330	622	159	23	7	3	49	66	61
August	.211	.211	.316	19	4	2	0	0	0	0	2	.232	.305	.295	685	159	23	4	4	63	74	85
Sept-Oct	.133	.133	.200	15	2	1	0	0	2	0	1	.241	.305	.324	688	166	21	9	6	51	62	73
Bases Empty	.268	.335	.363	190	51	11	2	1	1	19	15	.244	.316	.339	2450	597	107	24	26	26	255	260
Leadoff	.314	.377	.471	70	22	6	1	1	1	7	9	.242	.319	.341	962	233	44	12	9	9	106	94
Runners On Base	.188	.239	.243	144	27	5	0	1	19	10	15	.249	.334	.348	1688	421	71	27	14	327	223	176
Scoring Position	.190	.250	.274	84	16	4	0	1	19	7	10	.244	.348	.326	955	233	36	12	6	282	163	111
Late and Close	.200	.294	.311	45	9	3	1	0	0	6	4	.237	.321	.332	687	163	24	7	9	57	86	87

MIKE PAGLIARULO — BL/TR — age 34 — MIN/BAL 3B107, 1B4

1993	BA	OBA	SA	AB	H	2B	3B	HR	RBI	BB	SO	10-YEAR TOTALS (1984–1993) BA	OBA	SA	AB	H	2B	3B	HR	RBI	BB	SO
Total	.303	.357	.465	370	112	25	4	9	44	26	49	.242	.307	.410	3660	886	190	18	130	478	328	736
vs. Left	.417	.462	.472	36	15	2	0	0	2	2	4	.217	.287	.335	720	156	30	2	17	87	64	200
vs. Right	.290	.346	.464	334	97	23	4	9	42	24	45	.248	.312	.429	2940	730	160	16	113	391	264	536
at Home	.343	.393	.550	169	58	14	3	5	23	12	22	.244	.315	.416	1728	421	77	11	66	247	170	376
on Road	.269	.327	.393	201	54	11	1	4	21	14	27	.241	.300	.406	1932	465	113	7	64	231	158	360
on Grass	.293	.349	.460	215	63	13	1	7	31	15	22	.235	.304	.412	2695	633	131	14	106	361	255	542
on Turf	.316	.369	.471	155	49	12	3	2	13	11	27	.262	.316	.406	965	253	59	4	24	117	73	194
Day Games	.342	.403	.425	120	41	10	0	0	8	9	17	.238	.315	.390	1155	275	56	3	38	134	118	239
Night Games	.284	.335	.484	250	71	15	4	9	36	17	32	.244	.304	.420	2505	611	134	15	92	344	210	497
April	.269	.296	.442	52	14	1	4	0	5	2	3	.201	.281	.344	413	83	16	5	11	53	44	84
May	.328	.371	.517	58	19	5	0	2	6	4	10	.248	.322	.426	577	143	36	2	21	78	60	109
June	.273	.351	.485	33	9	4	0	1	7	3	2	.249	.311	.424	606	151	38	1	22	77	53	120
July	.282	.346	.338	71	20	4	0	0	1	4	14	.285	.350	.465	604	172	34	3	23	80	55	115
August	.333	.397	.536	69	23	5	0	3	13	7	12	.238	.293	.420	747	178	31	6	31	98	57	159
Sept-Oct	.310	.362	.483	87	27	6	0	3	12	6	8	.223	.286	.367	713	159	35	1	22	92	59	149
Bases Empty	.278	.333	.407	194	54	17	1	2	2	12	28	.226	.287	.389	2043	462	107	12	67	67	155	419
Leadoff	.270	.349	.338	74	20	5	0	0	0	6	10	.219	.286	.377	817	179	32	5	29	29	70	163
Runners On Base	.330	.383	.528	176	58	8	3	7	42	14	21	.262	.332	.438	1617	424	83	6	63	411	173	317
Scoring Position	.303	.358	.556	99	30	4	0	7	39	8	14	.246	.331	.412	900	221	41	2	35	335	121	196
Late and Close	.279	.328	.328	61	17	3	0	0	2	4	9	.230	.303	.356	562	129	24	1	15	57	59	128

TOM PAGNOZZI — BR/TR — age 32 — SL C92

1993

	BA	OBA	SA	AB	H	2B	3B	HR	RBI	BB	SO
Total	.258	.296	.373	330	85	15	1	7	41	19	30
vs. Left	.280	.313	.387	75	21	2	0	2	12	5	4
vs. Right	.251	.290	.369	255	64	13	1	5	29	14	26
at Home	.238	.287	.315	143	34	6	1	1	16	10	10
on Road	.273	.303	.417	187	51	9	0	6	25	9	20
on Grass	.347	.376	.500	124	43	7	0	4	21	7	7
on Turf	.204	.248	.296	206	42	8	1	3	20	12	23
Day Games	.294	.316	.440	109	32	4	0	4	18	3	8
Night Games	.240	.286	.339	221	53	11	1	3	23	16	22
April	.164	.235	.230	61	10	1	0	1	4	6	3
May	.211	.286	.474	19	4	2	0	1	3	2	0
June	.353	.361	.588	34	12	0	1	2	9	1	4
July	.268	.293	.310	71	19	3	0	0	5	3	10
August	.250	.272	.409	88	22	5	0	3	12	2	5
Sept-Oct	.316	.365	.386	57	18	4	0	0	8	5	8
Bases Empty	.266	.290	.412	177	47	8	0	6	6	5	16
Leadoff	.347	.355	.467	75	26	6	0	1	1	1	4
Runners On Base	.248	.302	.327	153	38	7	1	1	35	14	14
Scoring Position	.250	.310	.330	100	25	3	1	1	34	11	7
Late and Close	.213	.242	.279	61	13	1	0	1	8	2	4

7-YEAR TOTALS (1987–1993)

	BA	OBA	SA	AB	H	2B	3B	HR	RBI	BB	SO
Total	.255	.301	.349	1817	464	92	9	20	192	118	258
vs. Left	.252	.305	.359	701	177	33	3	12	79	55	112
vs. Right	.257	.299	.342	1116	287	59	6	8	113	63	146
at Home	.245	.305	.336	837	205	36	5	10	82	68	112
on Road	.264	.298	.360	980	259	56	4	10	110	50	146
on Grass	.291	.322	.399	509	148	34	3	5	69	25	68
on Turf	.242	.293	.330	1308	316	58	6	15	123	93	190
Day Games	.263	.308	.374	578	152	31	3	9	81	39	72
Night Games	.252	.298	.337	1239	312	61	6	11	111	79	186
April	.234	.274	.302	235	55	8	1	2	19	14	25
May	.264	.326	.377	273	72	15	2	4	35	23	36
June	.250	.289	.373	284	71	13	2	6	36	16	43
July	.259	.313	.350	294	76	12	3	3	33	23	44
August	.226	.263	.321	371	84	24	1	3	31	19	53
Sept-Oct	.294	.339	.367	360	106	20	0	2	38	23	57
Bases Empty	.251	.292	.349	999	251	50	3	14	14	52	124
Leadoff	.241	.281	.325	415	100	19	2	4	4	22	52
Runners On Base	.260	.312	.348	818	213	42	6	6	178	66	134
Scoring Position	.253	.318	.343	498	126	25	4	4	162	53	87
Late and Close	.205	.249	.257	370	76	10	0	3	33	19	66

RAFAEL PALMEIRO — BL/TL — age 30 — TEX 1B160

1993

	BA	OBA	SA	AB	H	2B	3B	HR	RBI	BB	SO
Total	.295	.371	.554	597	176	40	2	37	105	73	85
vs. Left	.268	.323	.356	149	40	7	0	2	18	12	24
vs. Right	.304	.387	.621	448	136	33	2	35	87	61	61
at Home	.282	.360	.578	294	83	19	1	22	58	36	42
on Road	.307	.382	.531	303	93	21	1	15	47	37	43
on Grass	.290	.370	.552	511	148	34	2	32	90	66	72
on Turf	.326	.381	.570	86	28	6	0	5	15	7	13
Day Games	.292	.386	.500	154	45	12	1	6	28	25	21
Night Games	.296	.366	.573	443	131	28	1	31	77	48	64
April	.183	.242	.280	82	15	3	1	1	8	7	7
May	.286	.339	.524	105	30	5	1	6	17	9	14
June	.348	.396	.609	92	32	6	0	6	14	7	15
July	.426	.484	.852	108	46	13	0	11	34	14	10
August	.257	.385	.545	101	26	5	0	8	16	18	18
Sept-Oct	.248	.349	.459	109	27	8	0	5	16	18	21
Bases Empty	.296	.352	.553	351	104	27	0	21	21	25	47
Leadoff	.368	.408	.684	133	49	15	0	9	9	7	14
Runners On Base	.293	.396	.557	246	72	13	2	16	84	48	38
Scoring Position	.266	.435	.452	124	33	7	2	4	57	44	19
Late and Close	.292	.376	.583	72	21	3	0	6	15	11	14

8-YEAR TOTALS (1986–1993)

	BA	OBA	SA	AB	H	2B	3B	HR	RBI	BB	SO
Total	.296	.360	.472	3867	1144	234	25	132	526	378	413
vs. Left	.286	.338	.424	1072	307	51	9	26	145	79	121
vs. Right	.299	.369	.490	2795	837	183	16	106	381	299	292
at Home	.290	.361	.473	1863	540	101	17	69	263	204	207
on Road	.301	.360	.470	2004	604	133	8	63	263	174	206
on Grass	.293	.359	.468	3131	916	165	24	112	445	319	337
on Turf	.310	.365	.488	736	228	69	1	20	81	59	76
Day Games	.290	.352	.453	1156	335	73	7	34	167	111	114
Night Games	.298	.364	.480	2711	809	161	18	98	359	267	299
April	.279	.345	.448	466	130	32	4	13	67	46	48
May	.327	.380	.488	640	209	41	4	18	82	54	60
June	.291	.347	.440	670	195	39	2	19	82	52	71
July	.318	.372	.526	642	204	31	5	31	103	55	59
August	.274	.346	.442	712	195	39	6	23	87	75	90
Sept-Oct	.286	.369	.482	737	211	52	4	28	105	96	85
Bases Empty	.298	.352	.474	2185	652	135	10	76	76	161	231
Leadoff	.309	.356	.517	745	230	51	4	32	32	48	70
Runners On Base	.293	.371	.469	1682	492	99	15	56	450	217	182
Scoring Position	.267	.376	.402	920	246	54	8	18	352	175	115
Late and Close	.270	.329	.444	603	163	31	4	22	75	54	77

DEAN PALMER — BR/TR — age 26 — TEX 3B148, SS1

1993

	BA	OBA	SA	AB	H	2B	3B	HR	RBI	BB	SO
Total	.245	.321	.503	519	127	31	2	33	96	53	154
vs. Left	.257	.367	.475	101	26	4	0	6	17	15	32
vs. Right	.242	.310	.510	418	101	27	2	27	79	38	122
at Home	.246	.329	.437	252	62	12	0	12	32	28	78
on Road	.243	.314	.566	267	65	19	2	21	64	25	76
on Grass	.257	.335	.517	443	114	27	2	28	80	47	129
on Turf	.171	.238	.421	76	13	4	0	5	16	6	25
Day Games	.287	.349	.618	157	45	13	0	13	41	14	42
Night Games	.227	.310	.453	362	82	18	2	20	55	39	112
April	.286	.370	.686	70	20	7	0	7	15	8	13
May	.210	.297	.448	105	22	7	0	6	18	13	42
June	.213	.307	.440	75	16	6	1	3	12	11	22
July	.247	.311	.452	93	23	2	1	5	20	5	26
August	.253	.324	.527	91	23	4	0	7	19	8	27
Sept-Oct	.271	.333	.506	85	23	5	0	5	12	8	24
Bases Empty	.226	.312	.442	274	62	15	1	14	14	29	85
Leadoff	.349	.403	.716	109	38	8	0	10	10	10	24
Runners On Base	.265	.332	.571	245	65	16	1	19	82	24	69
Scoring Position	.206	.308	.404	141	29	8	1	6	55	21	41
Late and Close	.167	.278	.372	78	13	4	0	4	9	12	28

4-YEAR TOTALS (1989–1993)

	BA	OBA	SA	AB	H	2B	3B	HR	RBI	BB	SO
Total	.225	.306	.445	1347	303	67	4	74	206	147	418
vs. Left	.250	.340	.503	336	84	16	0	23	53	44	108
vs. Right	.217	.295	.426	1011	219	51	4	51	153	103	310
at Home	.223	.319	.406	641	143	28	1	29	78	82	205
on Road	.227	.294	.482	706	160	39	3	45	128	65	213
on Grass	.223	.308	.430	1136	253	55	3	58	160	131	349
on Turf	.237	.293	.531	211	50	12	1	16	46	16	69
Day Games	.250	.316	.503	360	90	26	1	21	66	33	112
Night Games	.216	.303	.425	987	213	41	3	53	140	114	306
April	.267	.366	.575	146	39	9	0	12	28	22	39
May	.214	.276	.427	206	44	17	0	9	30	16	76
June	.255	.345	.468	188	48	11	1	9	39	27	50
July	.221	.288	.438	249	55	10	1	14	32	21	77
Sept-Oct	.195	.278	.401	302	59	14	0	16	38	34	107
Bases Empty	.215	.300	.406	759	163	40	3	33	33	84	245
Leadoff	.283	.360	.547	307	87	22	1	19	19	35	78
Runners On Base	.238	.314	.497	588	140	27	1	41	173	63	173
Scoring Position	.200	.297	.382	325	65	12	1	15	118	44	101
Late and Close	.213	.308	.457	221	47	10	1	14	32	31	73

CRAIG PAQUETTE — BR/TR — age 25 — OAK 3B104, OF1, DH1 — 1-YEAR TOTALS (1993)

1993	BA	OBA	SA	AB	H	2B	3B	HR	RBI	BB	SO		BA	OBA	SA	AB	H	2B	3B	HR	RBI	BB	SO
Total	.219	.245	.382	393	86	20	4	12	46	14	108		.219	.245	.382	393	86	20	4	12	46	14	108
vs. Left	.228	.276	.397	136	31	4	2	5	15	9	43		.228	.276	.397	136	31	4	2	5	15	9	43
vs. Right	.214	.228	.374	257	55	16	2	7	31	5	65		.214	.228	.374	257	55	16	2	7	31	5	65
at Home	.229	.264	.424	170	39	5	2	8	14	8	56		.229	.264	.424	170	39	5	2	8	14	8	56
on Road	.211	.230	.350	223	47	15	2	4	32	6	52		.211	.230	.350	223	47	15	2	4	32	6	52
on Grass	.219	.246	.368	302	66	14	2	9	24	11	84		.219	.246	.368	302	66	14	2	9	24	11	84
on Turf	.220	.242	.429	91	20	6	2	3	22	3	24		.220	.242	.429	91	20	6	2	3	22	3	24
Day Games	.207	.232	.372	145	30	7	1	5	11	5	42		.207	.232	.372	145	30	7	1	5	11	5	42
Night Games	.226	.253	.387	248	56	13	3	7	35	9	66		.226	.253	.387	248	56	13	3	7	35	9	66
April	.000	.000	.000	0	0	0	0	0	0	0	0		.000	.000	.000	0	0	0	0	0	0	0	0
May	.000	.000	.000	0	0	0	0	0	0	0	0		.000	.000	.000	0	0	0	0	0	0	0	0
June	.292	.296	.521	96	28	8	1	4	19	1	28		.292	.296	.521	96	28	8	1	4	19	1	28
July	.220	.245	.308	91	20	5	0	1	6	3	20		.220	.245	.308	91	20	5	0	1	6	3	20
August	.181	.232	.400	105	19	4	2	5	13	7	33		.181	.232	.400	105	19	4	2	5	13	7	33
Sept-Oct	.188	.212	.297	101	19	3	1	2	8	3	27		.188	.212	.297	101	19	3	1	2	8	3	27
Bases Empty	.204	.232	.370	216	44	12	3	6	6	8	61		.204	.232	.370	216	44	12	3	6	6	8	61
Leadoff	.216	.242	.364	88	19	3	2	2	2	3	21		.216	.242	.364	88	19	3	2	2	2	3	21
Runners On Base	.237	.261	.395	177	42	8	1	6	40	6	47		.237	.261	.395	177	42	8	1	6	40	6	47
Scoring Position	.229	.261	.410	105	24	5	1	4	35	5	31		.229	.261	.410	105	24	5	1	4	35	5	31
Late and Close	.238	.250	.444	63	15	4	0	3	12	1	23		.238	.250	.444	63	15	4	0	3	12	1	23

TONY PENA — BR/TR — age 37 — BOS C125, DH1 — 10-YEAR TOTALS (1984–1993)

1993	BA	OBA	SA	AB	H	2B	3B	HR	RBI	BB	SO		BA	OBA	SA	AB	H	2B	3B	HR	RBI	BB	SO
Total	.181	.246	.257	304	55	11	0	4	19	25	46		.252	.306	.351	4584	1154	207	17	71	483	351	593
vs. Left	.253	.264	.373	83	21	4	0	2	6	2	10		.289	.338	.415	1403	405	66	3	35	158	105	139
vs. Right	.154	.239	.213	221	34	7	0	2	13	23	36		.235	.291	.323	3181	749	141	14	36	325	246	454
at Home	.155	.227	.232	155	24	6	0	2	12	14	23		.251	.310	.346	2277	572	106	10	30	233	191	279
on Road	.208	.265	.282	149	31	5	0	2	7	11	23		.252	.301	.355	2307	582	101	7	41	250	160	314
on Grass	.160	.235	.234	256	41	7	0	4	18	24	39		.235	.295	.320	2163	509	95	7	25	227	179	314
on Turf	.292	.306	.375	48	14	4	0	0	1	1	7		.266	.316	.378	2421	645	112	10	46	256	172	279
Day Games	.173	.235	.245	110	19	1	0	1	2	9	19		.255	.315	.346	1371	349	68	5	16	150	118	186
Night Games	.186	.251	.263	194	36	6	0	1	17	16	27		.251	.302	.353	3213	805	139	12	55	333	233	407
April	.180	.176	.200	50	9	1	0	0	1	0	5		.255	.292	.371	591	151	29	0	13	47	30	78
May	.167	.265	.217	60	10	3	0	0	2	8	10		.242	.292	.346	785	190	32	4	14	86	49	109
June	.188	.264	.292	48	9	2	0	1	3	6	9		.267	.317	.365	832	222	38	7	10	99	63	111
July	.155	.246	.259	58	9	3	0	1	3	6	10		.238	.304	.327	810	193	35	2	11	66	75	97
August	.204	.250	.265	49	10	0	0	1	5	3	5		.247	.308	.329	781	193	27	2	11	93	69	103
Sept-Oct	.205	.267	.333	39	8	2	0	1	5	3	7		.261	.317	.371	785	205	46	2	12	92	65	95
Bases Empty	.196	.258	.279	179	35	6	0	3	3	14	27		.250	.307	.362	2494	624	121	11	45	45	195	352
Leadoff	.171	.237	.171	70	12	0	0	0	0	6	6		.253	.309	.366	1040	263	51	5	19	19	82	133
Runners On Base	.160	.229	.224	125	20	5	0	1	16	11	19		.254	.304	.338	2090	530	86	6	26	438	156	241
Scoring Position	.143	.232	.214	70	10	3	0	1	16	8	13		.246	.313	.328	1218	300	49	3	15	398	126	154
Late and Close	.258	.324	.355	31	8	3	0	0	0	3	6		.244	.298	.328	873	213	35	4	10	81	67	120

GERONIMO PENA — BB/TR — age 27 — SL 2B64 — 4-YEAR TOTALS (1990–1993)

1993	BA	OBA	SA	AB	H	2B	3B	HR	RBI	BB	SO		BA	OBA	SA	AB	H	2B	3B	HR	RBI	BB	SO
Total	.256	.330	.406	254	65	19	2	5	30	25	71		.266	.344	.418	687	183	41	6	17	80	71	167
vs. Left	.333	.385	.527	93	31	9	0	3	14	9	19		.320	.388	.511	266	85	19	1	10	38	26	56
vs. Right	.211	.298	.335	161	34	10	2	2	16	16	52		.233	.315	.359	421	98	22	5	7	42	45	111
at Home	.306	.385	.454	108	33	10	0	2	14	11	25		.274	.366	.418	318	87	19	3	7	30	40	71
on Road	.219	.288	.370	146	32	9	2	3	16	14	46		.260	.324	.417	369	96	22	3	10	50	31	96
on Grass	.230	.290	.389	113	26	8	2	2	14	10	34		.286	.330	.451	213	61	14	3	5	33	16	58
on Turf	.277	.360	.418	141	39	11	0	3	16	15	37		.257	.349	.403	474	122	27	3	12	47	55	109
Day Games	.237	.277	.395	76	18	6	0	2	11	4	21		.266	.302	.462	199	53	14	2	7	32	11	52
Night Games	.264	.351	.410	178	47	13	2	3	19	21	50		.266	.359	.400	488	130	27	4	10	48	60	115
April	.243	.345	.338	74	18	4	0	1	6	11	20		.239	.358	.352	88	21	4	0	2	7	14	24
May	.239	.327	.326	46	11	4	0	0	4	6	10		.270	.324	.390	100	27	7	1	1	8	8	20
June	.295	.348	.475	61	18	6	1	1	8	4	18		.276	.349	.429	170	47	15	1	3	21	16	39
July	.167	.214	.167	12	2	0	0	0	1	0	4		.167	.213	.381	42	7	1	1	2	7	2	17
August	.000	.000	.000	0	0	0	0	0	0	0	0		.250	.293	.472	36	9	2	0	2	5	2	8
Sept-Oct	.262	.318	.525	61	16	5	1	3	11	4	19		.287	.370	.442	251	72	12	3	7	32	29	59
Bases Empty	.255	.328	.401	157	40	12	1	3	3	15	39		.271	.354	.432	424	115	26	3	12	12	47	95
Leadoff	.210	.304	.395	81	17	9	0	2	2	10	25		.268	.353	.469	213	57	14	1	9	9	27	49
Runners On Base	.258	.333	.412	97	25	7	1	2	27	10	32		.259	.328	.395	263	68	15	3	5	68	24	72
Scoring Position	.250	.329	.467	60	15	5	1	2	27	6	21		.247	.320	.376	170	42	10	3	2	61	15	51
Late and Close	.283	.365	.457	46	13	3	1	1	6	6	17		.254	.325	.384	138	35	10	1	2	12	12	35

TERRY PENDLETON — BB/TR — age 34 — ATL 3B161 / 10-YEAR TOTALS (1984–1993)

1993	BA	OBA	SA	AB	H	2B	3B	HR	RBI	BB	SO		BA	OBA	SA	AB	H	2B	3B	HR	RBI	BB	SO
Total	.272	.311	.408	633	172	33	1	17	84	36	97		.273	.319	.394	5292	1446	261	34	104	717	368	664
vs. Left	.297	.326	.429	175	52	9	1	4	27	9	20		.290	.326	.408	1759	510	98	11	29	253	103	147
vs. Right	.262	.305	.400	458	120	24	0	13	57	27	77		.265	.315	.388	3533	936	163	23	75	464	265	517
at Home	.281	.314	.435	310	87	19	1	9	46	18	47		.280	.325	.421	2646	740	147	23	60	381	186	309
on Road	.263	.307	.381	323	85	14	0	8	38	18	50		.267	.312	.368	2646	706	114	11	44	336	182	355
on Grass	.276	.316	.412	485	134	25	1	13	67	29	71		.288	.331	.426	2237	644	110	7	62	319	154	289
on Turf	.257	.293	.392	148	38	8	0	4	17	7	26		.263	.309	.371	3055	802	151	27	42	398	214	375
Day Games	.262	.293	.387	168	44	4	1	5	22	9	30		.290	.335	.412	1696	491	73	6	41	239	120	218
Night Games	.275	.317	.415	465	128	29	0	12	62	27	67		.266	.311	.386	3596	955	188	28	63	478	248	446
April	.158	.234	.248	101	16	3	0	2	7	10	20		.236	.295	.328	673	159	38	0	8	73	59	96
May	.279	.291	.356	104	29	8	0	0	14	3	11		.293	.339	.414	840	246	48	3	16	129	66	89
June	.324	.336	.451	102	33	4	0	3	11	1	13		.267	.310	.387	778	208	31	4	18	102	47	106
July	.291	.336	.445	110	32	8	0	3	15	7	12		.277	.310	.394	941	261	45	4	19	124	47	117
August	.293	.330	.384	99	29	3	0	2	12	6	21		.259	.309	.382	1069	277	47	9	22	154	80	138
Sept-Oct	.282	.333	.538	117	33	7	1	7	25	9	20		.298	.342	.442	991	295	52	14	21	135	69	118
Bases Empty	.275	.313	.410	327	90	17	0	9	9	17	54		.269	.310	.390	2811	755	136	16	58	58	165	349
Leadoff	.230	.263	.345	113	26	4	0	3	3	5	20		.292	.327	.415	1043	305	59	9	17	17	53	119
Runners On Base	.268	.308	.405	306	82	16	1	8	75	19	43		.279	.328	.399	2481	691	125	18	46	659	203	315
Scoring Position	.229	.281	.341	170	39	7	0	4	60	14	24		.286	.342	.419	1500	429	80	16	29	602	152	200
Late and Close	.276	.354	.402	87	24	5	0	2	10	11	18		.261	.323	.379	877	229	46	6	15	99	81	143

EDUARDO PEREZ — BR/TR — age 25 — CAL 3B45, DH3 / 1-YEAR TOTALS (1993)

1993	BA	OBA	SA	AB	H	2B	3B	HR	RBI	BB	SO		BA	OBA	SA	AB	H	2B	3B	HR	RBI	BB	SO
Total	.250	.292	.372	180	45	6	2	4	30	9	39		.250	.292	.372	180	45	6	2	4	30	9	39
vs. Left	.268	.318	.366	41	11	2	1	0	9	2	8		.268	.318	.366	41	11	2	1	0	9	2	8
vs. Right	.245	.284	.374	139	34	4	1	4	21	7	31		.245	.284	.374	139	34	4	1	4	21	7	31
at Home	.183	.236	.317	82	15	1	2	2	13	5	15		.183	.236	.317	82	15	1	2	2	13	5	15
on Road	.306	.340	.418	98	30	5	0	2	17	4	24		.306	.340	.418	98	30	5	0	2	17	4	24
on Grass	.223	.261	.338	148	33	4	2	3	22	6	31		.223	.261	.338	148	33	4	2	3	22	6	31
on Turf	.375	.429	.531	32	12	2	0	1	8	3	8		.375	.429	.531	32	12	2	0	1	8	3	8
Day Games	.349	.396	.442	43	15	1	0	1	9	3	8		.349	.396	.442	43	15	1	0	1	9	3	8
Night Games	.219	.257	.350	137	30	5	2	3	21	6	31		.219	.257	.350	137	30	5	2	3	21	6	31
April	.000	.000	.000	0	0	0	0	0	0	0	0		.000	.000	.000	0	0	0	0	0	0	0	0
May	.000	.000	.000	0	0	0	0	0	0	0	0		.000	.000	.000	0	0	0	0	0	0	0	0
June	.000	.000	.000	0	0	0	0	0	0	0	0		.000	.000	.000	0	0	0	0	0	0	0	0
July	.300	.333	.650	20	6	1	0	2	5	1	1		.300	.333	.650	20	6	1	0	2	5	1	1
August	.245	.292	.349	106	26	3	1	2	16	6	24		.245	.292	.349	106	26	3	1	2	16	6	24
Sept-Oct	.241	.276	.315	54	13	2	1	0	9	2	14		.241	.276	.315	54	13	2	1	0	9	2	14
Bases Empty	.211	.257	.263	95	20	2	0	0	1	6	22		.211	.257	.263	95	20	2	0	0	1	6	22
Leadoff	.211	.250	.263	38	8	0	0	0	0	2	10		.211	.250	.263	38	8	0	0	0	0	2	10
Runners On Base	.294	.330	.494	85	25	4	2	3	29	3	17		.294	.330	.494	85	25	4	2	3	29	3	17
Scoring Position	.300	.333	.600	50	15	2	2	3	28	2	13		.300	.333	.600	50	15	2	2	3	28	2	13
Late and Close	.257	.297	.400	35	9	2	0	1	6	1	7		.257	.297	.400	35	9	2	0	1	6	1	7

TONY PHILLIPS — BB/TR — age 35 — DET OF108, 2B51, DH4, 3B1 / 10-YEAR TOTALS (1984–1993)

1993	BA	OBA	SA	AB	H	2B	3B	HR	RBI	BB	SO		BA	OBA	SA	AB	H	2B	3B	HR	RBI	BB	SO
Total	.313	.443	.398	566	177	27	0	7	57	132	102		.267	.368	.376	4404	1178	203	32	71	464	706	769
vs. Left	.316	.444	.380	171	54	8	0	1	10	40	28		.296	.402	.423	1384	410	66	13	28	150	244	181
vs. Right	.311	.443	.405	395	123	19	0	6	47	92	74		.254	.352	.355	3020	768	137	19	43	314	462	588
at Home	.309	.452	.391	256	79	12	0	3	23	67	56		.263	.371	.363	2131	560	88	10	35	231	368	389
on Road	.316	.436	.403	310	98	15	0	4	34	65	46		.272	.366	.389	2273	618	115	22	36	233	338	380
on Grass	.314	.444	.388	472	148	23	0	4	40	109	87		.266	.367	.367	3706	985	162	23	56	381	597	653
on Turf	.309	.442	.447	94	29	4	0	3	17	23	15		.277	.374	.426	698	193	41	9	15	83	109	116
Day Games	.309	.447	.412	194	60	11	0	3	26	50	32		.255	.353	.345	1520	388	61	9	19	157	234	271
Night Games	.315	.441	.390	372	117	16	0	4	31	82	70		.274	.376	.393	2884	790	142	23	52	307	472	498
April	.348	.464	.438	89	31	2	0	2	13	20	12		.278	.390	.367	626	174	24	4	8	54	114	109
May	.287	.427	.372	94	27	5	0	1	14	23	20		.266	.371	.388	758	202	33	7	15	101	124	128
June	.274	.412	.379	95	26	7	0	1	9	23	17		.237	.349	.345	748	177	32	5	13	79	130	134
July	.337	.485	.436	101	34	7	0	1	9	29	22		.281	.385	.401	750	211	47	5	11	79	128	129
August	.286	.423	.337	98	28	2	0	1	8	22	16		.260	.358	.355	681	177	26	6	9	61	105	119
Sept-Oct	.348	.448	.427	89	31	4	0	1	4	15	15		.282	.360	.396	841	237	41	5	15	90	105	150
Bases Empty	.329	.448	.426	371	122	21	0	5	5	78	61		.258	.359	.362	2760	711	121	16	45	45	429	490
Leadoff	.311	.432	.400	225	70	11	0	3	3	48	42		.263	.366	.361	1461	384	64	5	23	23	233	253
Runners On Base	.282	.435	.344	195	55	6	0	2	52	54	41		.284	.382	.401	1644	467	82	16	26	419	277	279
Scoring Position	.301	.446	.391	133	40	6	0	2	52	36	28		.287	.385	.406	963	276	49	12	14	375	173	164
Late and Close	.275	.419	.377	69	19	4	0	1	9	17	19		.255	.370	.393	651	166	38	5	14	83	119	134

MIKE PIAZZA — BR/TR — age 26 — LA C146, 1B1

1993	BA	OBA	SA	AB	H	2B	3B	HR	RBI	BB	SO	2-YEAR TOTALS (1992–1993) BA	OBA	SA	AB	H	2B	3B	HR	RBI	BB	SO
Total	.318	.370	.561	547	174	24	2	35	112	46	86	.308	.361	.534	616	190	27	2	36	119	50	98
vs. Left	.324	.377	.655	142	46	8	0	13	36	13	19	.314	.366	.599	172	54	10	0	13	40	15	24
vs. Right	.316	.368	.528	405	128	16	2	22	76	33	67	.306	.359	.509	444	136	17	2	23	79	35	74
at Home	.313	.370	.584	281	88	11	1	21	63	25	48	.311	.367	.575	299	93	11	1	22	67	26	51
on Road	.323	.371	.538	266	86	13	1	14	49	21	38	.306	.355	.495	317	97	16	1	14	52	24	47
on Grass	.319	.369	.577	430	137	19	1	30	94	34	69	.313	.364	.560	470	147	21	1	31	99	37	76
on Turf	.316	.377	.504	117	37	5	1	5	18	12	17	.295	.350	.452	146	43	6	1	5	20	13	22
Day Games	.364	.414	.649	151	55	10	0	11	31	14	22	.346	.394	.598	179	62	12	0	11	31	15	28
Night Games	.301	.353	.528	396	119	14	2	24	81	32	64	.293	.347	.508	437	128	15	2	25	88	35	70
April	.307	.354	.520	75	23	4	0	4	13	6	17	.307	.354	.520	75	23	4	0	4	13	6	17
May	.344	.385	.500	96	33	3	0	4	19	5	18	.344	.385	.500	96	33	3	0	4	19	5	18
June	.302	.333	.583	96	29	4	1	7	20	5	15	.302	.333	.583	96	29	4	1	7	20	5	15
July	.290	.347	.538	93	27	3	1	6	15	8	12	.290	.347	.538	93	27	3	1	6	15	8	12
August	.333	.402	.631	84	28	4	0	7	18	10	8	.333	.402	.631	84	28	4	0	7	18	10	8
Sept-Oct	.330	.397	.592	103	34	6	0	7	27	12	16	.291	.353	.483	172	50	9	0	8	34	16	28
Bases Empty	.308	.357	.590	312	96	15	2	23	23	22	54	.303	.347	.561	353	107	18	2	23	23	22	62
Leadoff	.377	.423	.746	114	43	6	0	12	12	7	15	.359	.400	.679	131	47	6	0	12	12	7	19
Runners On Base	.332	.387	.523	235	78	9	0	12	89	24	32	.316	.378	.498	263	83	9	0	13	96	28	36
Scoring Position	.320	.376	.456	147	47	2	0	6	71	16	22	.305	.365	.443	167	51	2	0	7	78	18	24
Late and Close	.237	.288	.361	97	23	4	1	2	6	7	18	.234	.292	.351	111	26	5	1	2	8	8	19

PHIL PLANTIER — BL/TR — age 25 — SD OF134

1993	BA	OBA	SA	AB	H	2B	3B	HR	RBI	BB	SO	4-YEAR TOTALS (1990–1993) BA	OBA	SA	AB	H	2B	3B	HR	RBI	BB	SO
Total	.240	.335	.509	462	111	20	1	34	100	61	124	.255	.347	.467	974	248	47	2	52	168	132	251
vs. Left	.185	.277	.378	119	22	2	0	7	21	13	39	.191	.275	.349	215	41	4	0	10	35	23	72
vs. Right	.259	.354	.554	343	89	18	1	27	79	48	85	.273	.367	.501	759	207	43	2	42	133	109	179
at Home	.224	.307	.464	237	53	7	1	16	47	27	62	.252	.330	.455	516	130	20	2	27	91	59	126
on Road	.258	.362	.556	225	58	13	0	18	53	34	62	.258	.365	.480	458	118	27	0	25	77	73	125
on Grass	.215	.304	.436	367	79	13	1	22	71	43	97	.243	.335	.433	820	199	35	2	39	134	110	210
on Turf	.337	.447	.789	95	32	7	0	12	29	18	27	.318	.408	.649	154	49	12	0	13	34	22	41
Day Games	.303	.389	.671	152	46	8	0	16	47	21	32	.274	.367	.531	354	97	14	1	25	78	51	83
Night Games	.210	.308	.429	310	65	12	1	18	53	40	92	.244	.336	.431	620	151	33	1	27	90	81	168
April	.260	.296	.500	50	13	3	0	3	8	3	13	.248	.315	.419	117	29	8	0	4	17	11	31
May	.232	.323	.482	56	13	5	0	3	13	5	16	.200	.303	.362	130	26	12	0	3	15	17	33
June	.267	.320	.522	90	24	3	1	6	15	7	23	.257	.321	.479	167	43	5	1	10	30	16	44
July	.211	.287	.433	90	19	2	0	6	14	10	24	.266	.328	.412	177	47	5	0	7	19	16	42
August	.298	.433	.726	84	25	3	0	11	30	18	15	.294	.430	.600	160	47	5	1	14	40	35	33
Sept-Oct	.185	.325	.391	92	17	4	0	5	20	18	33	.251	.357	.493	223	56	12	0	14	47	37	68
Bases Empty	.194	.298	.407	248	48	8	0	15	15	31	69	.231	.323	.422	510	118	19	0	26	26	61	132
Leadoff	.173	.277	.306	98	17	4	0	3	3	11	26	.224	.310	.373	201	45	9	0	7	7	22	52
Runners On Base	.294	.376	.626	214	63	12	1	19	85	30	55	.280	.372	.517	464	130	28	2	26	142	71	119
Scoring Position	.272	.370	.618	136	37	9	1	12	70	24	40	.250	.367	.507	276	69	19	2	16	119	55	74
Late and Close	.205	.286	.409	88	18	0	0	6	8	10	28	.225	.321	.377	191	43	5	0	8	22	27	68

LUIS POLONIA — BL/TL — age 30 — CAL OF141, DH4

1993	BA	OBA	SA	AB	H	2B	3B	HR	RBI	BB	SO	7-YEAR TOTALS (1987–1993) BA	OBA	SA	AB	H	2B	3B	HR	RBI	BB	SO
Total	.271	.328	.326	576	156	17	6	1	32	48	53	.294	.342	.369	3317	974	113	47	14	274	248	382
vs. Left	.232	.248	.241	112	26	1	0	0	7	3	10	.245	.286	.291	642	157	16	7	0	48	37	100
vs. Right	.280	.346	.347	464	130	16	6	1	25	45	43	.305	.355	.387	2675	817	97	40	14	226	211	282
at Home	.229	.282	.271	288	66	6	3	0	16	20	23	.290	.342	.363	1632	473	57	22	6	138	125	183
on Road	.313	.372	.382	288	90	11	3	1	16	28	30	.297	.342	.374	1685	501	56	25	8	136	123	199
on Grass	.262	.319	.310	478	125	13	5	0	24	39	41	.290	.340	.362	2790	808	92	39	11	228	213	306
on Turf	.316	.370	.408	98	31	4	1	1	8	9	12	.315	.354	.402	527	166	21	8	3	46	35	76
Day Games	.306	.369	.371	170	52	9	1	0	5	16	19	.308	.359	.392	1042	321	52	13	3	78	81	133
Night Games	.256	.310	.308	406	104	8	5	1	27	32	34	.287	.334	.358	2275	653	61	34	11	196	167	249
April	.289	.313	.368	76	22	2	2	0	7	3	7	.282	.339	.350	326	92	7	6	1	33	29	24
May	.257	.333	.343	105	27	4	1	0	3	12	15	.300	.345	.400	523	157	18	11	4	41	37	67
June	.218	.277	.241	87	19	2	0	0	2	6	8	.286	.334	.334	580	166	17	4	1	48	42	63
July	.274	.299	.319	113	31	3	1	0	6	4	6	.304	.338	.384	658	200	25	8	4	53	33	77
August	.341	.415	.415	82	28	4	1	0	6	10	6	.289	.339	.377	608	176	22	11	3	60	47	69
Sept-Oct	.257	.331	.292	113	29	2	1	0	8	13	11	.294	.356	.360	622	183	24	7	1	39	60	82
Bases Empty	.255	.307	.312	385	98	11	4	1	1	27	36	.287	.341	.360	2117	608	71	31	7	7	166	258
Leadoff	.257	.313	.306	245	63	8	2	0	1	19	20	.283	.341	.359	1244	352	46	17	5	5	107	159
Runners On Base	.304	.367	.356	191	58	6	2	0	31	21	17	.305	.344	.384	1200	366	42	16	7	267	82	124
Scoring Position	.336	.388	.395	119	40	5	1	0	30	12	11	.320	.358	.398	722	231	27	10	3	249	55	85
Late and Close	.253	.311	.316	95	24	2	2	0	6	8	11	.284	.321	.345	490	139	16	4	2	37	27	70

KIRBY PUCKETT — BR/TR — age 33 — MIN OF139, DH17

	BA	OBA	SA	AB	H	2B	3B	HR	RBI	BB	SO	BA	OBA	SA	AB	H	2B	3B	HR	RBI	BB	SO
1993												**10-YEAR TOTALS (1984–1993)**										
Total	.296	.349	.474	622	184	39	3	22	89	47	93	.318	.358	.469	6267	1996	343	54	164	873	366	829
vs. Left	.295	.371	.518	139	41	8	1	7	20	18	19	.337	.378	.512	1681	566	98	22	51	228	115	207
vs. Right	.296	.343	.462	483	143	31	2	15	69	29	74	.312	.351	.453	4586	1430	245	32	113	645	251	622
at Home	.322	.392	.522	320	103	22	3	12	53	32	44	.346	.387	.513	3180	1100	195	36	88	476	196	422
on Road	.268	.302	.424	302	81	17	0	10	36	15	49	.290	.328	.424	3087	896	148	18	76	397	170	407
on Grass	.291	.321	.426	230	67	13	0	6	28	10	36	.297	.334	.428	2351	698	113	12	57	312	129	321
on Turf	.298	.365	.503	392	117	26	3	16	61	37	57	.331	.372	.494	3916	1298	230	42	107	561	237	508
Day Games	.297	.364	.520	202	60	12	0	11	26	17	32	.318	.366	.481	1911	607	110	14	58	260	129	267
Night Games	.295	.342	.452	420	124	27	3	11	63	30	61	.319	.355	.464	4356	1389	233	40	106	613	237	562
April	.295	.385	.500	78	23	4	0	4	14	9	15	.325	.371	.529	753	245	45	9	30	116	50	98
May	.250	.314	.385	96	24	2	1	3	12	9	11	.336	.372	.509	1067	358	55	11	36	173	60	115
June	.321	.348	.491	106	34	9	0	3	18	5	13	.315	.350	.454	1103	347	62	10	24	144	55	129
July	.287	.345	.417	108	31	11	0	1	11	9	9	.309	.352	.440	1063	328	60	10	20	138	70	143
August	.322	.350	.539	115	37	8	1	5	17	4	23	.316	.354	.457	1104	349	59	6	28	139	59	178
Sept-Oct	.294	.359	.504	119	35	5	1	5	17	11	22	.314	.354	.446	1177	369	62	8	26	163	72	166
Bases Empty	.301	.331	.472	326	98	22	2	10	10	14	47	.314	.347	.461	3547	1112	192	25	94	94	159	463
Leadoff	.319	.336	.500	116	37	11	2	2	2	3	19	.326	.361	.460	1542	502	83	10	35	35	73	183
Runners On Base	.291	.368	.476	296	86	17	1	12	79	33	46	.325	.372	.479	2720	884	151	29	70	779	207	366
Scoring Position	.262	.369	.463	160	42	12	1	6	65	26	27	.319	.374	.474	1563	499	91	17	39	673	152	247
Late and Close	.358	.398	.474	95	34	6	1	1	12	7	15	.313	.361	.464	880	275	41	10	24	132	63	135

TIM RAINES — BB/TR — age 35 — CHA OF112

	BA	OBA	SA	AB	H	2B	3B	HR	RBI	BB	SO	BA	OBA	SA	AB	H	2B	3B	HR	RBI	BB	SO
1993												**10-YEAR TOTALS (1984–1993)**										
Total	.306	.401	.480	415	127	16	4	16	54	64	35	.301	.391	.437	5285	1592	254	77	104	558	780	527
vs. Left	.348	.439	.473	112	39	5	0	3	18	19	9	.301	.377	.424	1609	484	64	18	33	189	199	151
vs. Right	.290	.386	.482	303	88	11	4	13	36	45	26	.301	.397	.443	3676	1108	190	59	71	369	581	376
at Home	.291	.378	.434	196	57	5	1	7	25	26	15	.302	.392	.435	2546	769	119	38	48	262	375	247
on Road	.320	.421	.521	219	70	11	3	9	29	38	20	.300	.390	.440	2739	823	135	39	56	296	405	280
on Grass	.313	.401	.472	345	108	11	4	12	42	50	28	.302	.394	.427	2364	713	100	26	48	247	361	240
on Turf	.271	.400	.514	70	19	5	0	4	12	14	7	.301	.389	.446	2921	879	154	51	56	311	419	287
Day Games	.306	.412	.414	111	34	2	2	1	7	19	7	.301	.401	.443	1582	476	73	31	30	164	271	170
Night Games	.306	.397	.503	304	93	11	2	15	47	45	26	.301	.387	.435	3703	1116	181	46	74	394	509	357
April	.250	.400	.750	12	3	0	0	2	5	2	2	.269	.358	.391	616	166	28	10	9	72	88	56
May	.321	.424	.464	28	9	1	0	1	2	5	0	.308	.415	.470	907	279	42	18	23	102	162	107
June	.306	.452	.528	72	22	4	0	4	10	20	4	.304	.390	.433	877	267	54	7	15	107	128	83
July	.323	.380	.545	99	32	2	4	4	15	8	6	.291	.369	.415	881	256	31	14	17	87	107	84
August	.292	.372	.434	106	31	3	0	4	15	14	13	.307	.397	.452	1054	324	56	12	24	112	159	111
Sept-Oct	.306	.404	.398	98	30	6	0	1	7	15	10	.316	.403	.445	950	300	43	16	16	78	136	86
Bases Empty	.297	.377	.476	273	81	10	3	11	11	32	24	.297	.372	.436	3438	1021	177	51	66	66	393	342
Leadoff	.318	.397	.534	176	56	7	2	9	9	20	11	.297	.370	.440	1843	548	91	33	35	35	196	183
Runners On Base	.324	.443	.486	142	46	6	1	5	43	32	11	.309	.423	.441	1847	571	77	26	38	492	387	185
Scoring Position	.325	.471	.442	77	25	3	0	2	36	23	5	.310	.456	.429	1066	330	43	15	18	430	317	114
Late and Close	.361	.480	.459	61	22	3	0	1	6	14	3	.319	.423	.443	926	295	40	7	19	117	170	92

JODY REED — BR/TR — age 32 — LA 2B132

	BA	OBA	SA	AB	H	2B	3B	HR	RBI	BB	SO	BA	OBA	SA	AB	H	2B	3B	HR	RBI	BB	SO
1993												**7-YEAR TOTALS (1987–1993)**										
Total	.276	.333	.346	445	123	21	2	2	31	38	40	.279	.355	.368	3103	866	201	9	19	258	357	267
vs. Left	.325	.381	.390	123	40	8	0	0	7	11	9	.288	.362	.372	860	248	62	2	2	62	102	67
vs. Right	.258	.314	.329	322	83	13	2	2	24	27	31	.276	.352	.366	2243	618	139	7	17	196	255	200
at Home	.292	.357	.348	233	68	13	0	0	19	23	19	.286	.365	.384	1597	457	120	2	11	147	192	145
on Road	.259	.306	.344	212	55	8	2	2	12	15	21	.272	.344	.351	1506	409	81	7	8	111	165	122
on Grass	.295	.357	.365	353	104	17	1	2	26	34	35	.283	.360	.375	2659	752	176	6	19	236	317	226
on Turf	.207	.235	.272	92	19	4	1	0	5	4	5	.257	.322	.327	444	114	25	3	0	22	40	41
Day Games	.239	.307	.304	138	33	4	1	1	5	14	14	.277	.358	.360	1045	289	68	2	5	88	132	85
Night Games	.293	.344	.365	307	90	17	1	1	26	24	26	.280	.353	.372	2058	577	133	7	14	170	225	182
April	.225	.279	.250	80	18	2	0	0	3	5	8	.224	.307	.287	366	82	14	0	3	25	42	35
May	.306	.368	.424	85	26	3	2	1	12	9	4	.305	.368	.408	537	164	39	5	2	49	54	45
June	.364	.417	.477	44	16	2	0	1	5	4	5	.257	.330	.351	459	118	34	0	3	37	51	43
July	.278	.339	.333	54	15	3	0	0	4	5	7	.304	.375	.408	529	161	43	0	4	49	62	50
August	.227	.266	.284	88	20	5	0	0	3	5	7	.271	.339	.354	584	158	35	1	4	41	59	47
Sept-Oct	.298	.362	.362	94	28	6	0	0	4	10	9	.291	.385	.373	628	183	36	3	3	57	89	47
Bases Empty	.240	.277	.299	254	61	12	0	1	1	13	26	.263	.328	.348	1806	475	110	4	12	12	166	159
Leadoff	.241	.286	.286	112	27	5	0	0	0	7	15	.268	.336	.348	784	210	52	1	3	3	79	66
Runners On Base	.325	.400	.408	191	62	9	2	1	30	25	14	.301	.390	.396	1297	391	91	5	7	246	191	108
Scoring Position	.317	.422	.356	104	33	4	0	0	26	20	9	.279	.389	.348	692	193	41	2	1	225	130	63
Late and Close	.253	.300	.313	83	21	5	0	0	5	7	9	.260	.344	.318	488	127	25	0	1	47	62	49

KEVIN REIMER — BL/TR — age 30 — MIL DH83, OF37

1993	BA	OBA	SA	AB	H	2B	3B	HR	RBI	BB	SO		6-YEAR TOTALS (1988–1993) BA	OBA	SA	AB	H	2B	3B	HR	RBI	BB	SO
Total	.249	.303	.394	437	109	22	1	13	60	30	72		.258	.320	.430	1455	376	85	4	52	204	115	297
vs. Left	.208	.277	.283	106	22	5	0	1	15	8	18		.222	.303	.314	239	53	10	0	4	27	22	59
vs. Right	.263	.311	.429	331	87	17	1	12	45	22	54		.266	.324	.452	1216	323	75	4	48	177	93	238
at Home	.240	.310	.406	217	52	10	1	8	27	18	37		.264	.332	.471	694	183	45	3	31	111	58	158
on Road	.259	.295	.382	220	57	12	0	5	33	12	35		.254	.309	.392	761	193	40	1	21	93	57	139
on Grass	.257	.313	.424	354	91	18	1	13	51	25	62		.261	.324	.445	1190	310	68	4	48	180	96	251
on Turf	.217	.256	.265	83	18	4	0	0	9	5	10		.249	.302	.358	265	66	17	0	4	24	19	46
Day Games	.213	.277	.378	127	27	6	0	5	23	11	26		.259	.328	.462	351	91	20	0	17	58	33	77
Night Games	.265	.313	.400	310	82	16	1	8	37	19	46		.258	.318	.419	1104	285	65	4	35	146	82	220
April	.327	.362	.577	52	17	2	1	3	12	3	5		.308	.355	.521	169	52	13	1	7	30	12	27
May	.240	.255	.423	104	25	4	0	5	22	2	20		.266	.296	.417	271	72	17	0	8	43	11	55
June	.265	.327	.388	98	26	3	0	3	13	9	18		.262	.328	.408	267	70	10	1	9	41	24	48
July	.203	.267	.342	79	16	5	0	2	6	6	14		.261	.335	.440	234	61	21	0	7	23	21	51
August	.262	.314	.363	80	21	8	0	0	5	6	12		.264	.329	.470	296	78	17	1	14	43	23	63
Sept-Oct	.167	.333	.167	24	4	0	0	0	2	4	3		.197	.286	.335	218	43	7	1	7	24	24	53
Bases Empty	.253	.308	.397	229	58	9	0	8	8	15	45		.256	.306	.426	767	196	45	1	28	28	47	156
Leadoff	.273	.371	.364	77	21	4	0	1	1	10	14		.264	.332	.444	284	75	19	1	10	10	23	56
Runners On Base	.245	.297	.389	208	51	13	1	5	52	15	27		.262	.335	.433	688	180	40	3	24	176	68	141
Scoring Position	.218	.286	.327	110	24	4	1	2	41	11	14		.236	.323	.390	382	90	17	3	12	142	47	93
Late and Close	.225	.296	.310	71	16	3	0	1	5	8	16		.283	.357	.442	251	71	17	1	7	29	29	58

HAROLD REYNOLDS — BB/TR — age 34 — BAL 2B141

1993	BA	OBA	SA	AB	H	2B	3B	HR	RBI	BB	SO		10-YEAR TOTALS (1984–1993) BA	OBA	SA	AB	H	2B	3B	HR	RBI	BB	SO
Total	.252	.343	.334	485	122	20	4	4	47	66	47		.260	.329	.344	4516	1173	216	51	21	339	455	390
vs. Left	.179	.213	.209	134	24	4	0	0	12	6	17		.266	.320	.339	1304	347	65	6	6	108	104	98
vs. Right	.279	.387	.382	351	98	16	4	4	35	60	30		.257	.333	.346	3212	826	151	45	15	231	351	292
at Home	.249	.331	.345	261	65	13	3	2	24	32	28		.263	.336	.356	2248	592	112	32	11	165	237	182
on Road	.254	.356	.321	224	57	7	1	2	23	34	19		.256	.322	.332	2268	581	104	19	10	174	218	208
on Grass	.251	.333	.333	426	107	18	4	3	39	52	41		.251	.318	.326	2016	506	89	18	9	163	197	183
on Turf	.254	.408	.339	59	15	2	0	1	8	14	6		.267	.338	.358	2500	667	127	33	12	176	258	207
Day Games	.283	.343	.346	127	36	5	0	1	15	12	16		.254	.324	.338	1179	300	54	16	4	94	120	130
Night Games	.240	.343	.330	358	86	15	4	3	32	54	31		.262	.331	.346	3337	873	162	35	17	245	335	260
April	.228	.297	.298	57	13	2	1	0	5	5	6		.246	.298	.338	589	145	23	11	3	54	43	43
May	.253	.339	.360	95	24	2	0	0	6	13	9		.281	.344	.360	764	215	43	7	1	62	78	67
June	.295	.374	.379	95	28	8	0	1	7	11	7		.251	.332	.324	765	192	38	6	2	40	84	66
July	.244	.351	.308	78	19	2	0	1	5	13	7		.255	.332	.328	816	208	29	8	5	68	93	65
August	.215	.330	.342	79	17	1	0	3	13	14	9		.258	.333	.343	792	204	47	6	3	50	86	68
Sept-Oct	.259	.348	.395	81	21	5	3	0	11	10	9		.265	.327	.370	790	209	36	13	7	65	71	81
Bases Empty	.242	.333	.322	264	64	8	2	3	3	34	22		.251	.328	.336	2774	697	122	39	12	12	297	247
Leadoff	.229	.303	.328	131	30	5	1	2	2	13	9		.243	.323	.324	1384	337	64	19	3	3	150	124
Runners On Base	.262	.354	.348	221	58	12	2	1	44	32	25		.273	.331	.356	1742	476	94	12	9	327	158	143
Scoring Position	.319	.417	.448	116	37	10	1	1	43	23	13		.281	.346	.376	949	267	56	8	6	306	107	82
Late and Close	.355	.425	.447	76	27	4	0	1	7	10	8		.277	.344	.356	668	185	30	4	5	72	70	85

CAL RIPKEN — BR/TR — age 34 — BAL SS162

1993	BA	OBA	SA	AB	H	2B	3B	HR	RBI	BB	SO		10-YEAR TOTALS (1984–1993) BA	OBA	SA	AB	H	2B	3B	HR	RBI	BB	SO
Total	.257	.329	.420	641	165	26	3	24	90	65	58		.273	.346	.448	6283	1713	316	30	242	907	712	655
vs. Left	.282	.355	.441	177	50	7	0	7	31	21	18		.283	.360	.482	1810	513	112	10	76	245	224	162
vs. Right	.248	.318	.412	464	115	19	3	17	59	44	40		.268	.341	.434	4473	1200	204	20	166	662	488	493
at Home	.273	.360	.437	311	85	7	1	14	53	40	28		.261	.339	.435	3054	797	136	11	125	451	362	337
on Road	.242	.297	.403	330	80	19	2	10	37	25	30		.284	.353	.460	3229	916	180	19	117	456	350	318
on Grass	.263	.337	.433	540	142	21	1	23	80	57	49		.268	.343	.441	5309	1423	249	24	207	757	605	568
on Turf	.228	.282	.347	101	23	5	2	1	10	8	9		.298	.367	.487	974	290	67	6	35	150	107	87
Day Games	.270	.348	.448	174	47	8	1	7	27	20	12		.282	.356	.468	1727	487	76	7	77	264	197	192
Night Games	.253	.321	.409	467	118	18	2	17	63	45	46		.269	.343	.441	4556	1226	240	23	165	643	515	463
April	.239	.316	.420	88	21	4	3	2	11	10	8		.280	.373	.487	797	223	45	9	34	142	115	89
May	.200	.318	.327	110	22	5	0	3	11	17	8		.262	.349	.464	1034	271	53	6	48	143	135	120
June	.248	.320	.404	109	27	5	0	4	17	11	9		.293	.363	.437	1089	319	55	3	32	141	120	100
July	.235	.319	.469	98	23	2	0	7	19	13	11		.273	.351	.458	1044	285	49	3	46	169	126	102
August	.324	.366	.532	111	36	2	0	7	22	8	8		.272	.334	.438	1113	303	53	6	40	166	108	118
Sept-Oct	.288	.331	.376	125	36	8	0	1	10	6	14		.259	.318	.419	1206	312	61	3	42	146	108	126
Bases Empty	.225	.279	.381	360	81	10	2	14	14	23	37		.269	.335	.442	3470	932	165	13	137	137	326	366
Leadoff	.264	.312	.486	144	38	5	0	9	9	10	12		.289	.342	.487	1221	353	59	3	59	59	91	112
Runners On Base	.299	.387	.470	281	84	16	1	10	76	42	21		.278	.360	.455	2813	781	151	17	105	770	386	289
Scoring Position	.262	.393	.490	149	39	8	1	8	66	35	13		.275	.380	.457	1521	418	75	8	62	645	291	172
Late and Close	.239	.374	.413	92	22	4	0	4	14	19	8		.285	.366	.460	920	262	48	4	35	140	119	107

HENRY RODRIGUEZ — BL/TL — age 27 — LA OF48, 1B13

1993	BA	OBA	SA	AB	H	2B	3B	HR	RBI	BB	SO	2-YEAR TOTALS (1992–1993) BA	OBA	SA	AB	H	2B	3B	HR	RBI	BB	SO
Total	.222	.266	.415	176	39	10	0	8	23	11	39	.220	.262	.376	322	71	17	0	11	37	19	69
vs. Left	.000	.000	.000	6	0	0	0	0	0	0	3	.286	.318	.286	21	6	0	0	0	1	1	8
vs. Right	.229	.275	.429	170	39	10	0	8	23	11	36	.216	.259	.382	301	65	17	0	11	36	18	61
at Home	.237	.288	.443	97	23	5	0	5	14	7	24	.244	.290	.406	180	44	8	0	7	23	12	41
on Road	.203	.238	.380	79	16	5	0	3	9	4	15	.190	.227	.338	142	27	9	0	4	14	7	28
on Grass	.228	.279	.449	136	31	6	0	8	19	10	28	.222	.264	.381	252	56	10	0	10	28	15	52
on Turf	.200	.220	.300	40	8	4	0	0	4	1	11	.214	.257	.357	70	15	7	0	1	9	4	17
Day Games	.242	.309	.403	62	15	4	0	2	6	6	15	.216	.266	.363	102	22	6	0	3	9	7	23
Night Games	.211	.242	.421	114	24	6	0	6	17	5	24	.223	.261	.382	220	49	11	0	8	28	12	46
April	.000	.000	.000	0	0	0	0	0	0	0	0	.000	.000	.000	0	0	0	0	0	0	0	0
May	.000	.125	.000	0	0	0	0	0	0	1	3	.000	.125	.000	7	0	0	0	0	0	1	3
June	.308	.308	.538	13	4	0	0	1	3	0	4	.211	.224	.368	57	12	3	0	2	6	1	9
July	.273	.289	.477	44	12	3	0	2	6	1	6	.252	.289	.417	127	32	6	0	5	19	7	27
August	.204	.250	.367	49	10	2	0	2	8	3	11	.195	.256	.339	118	23	8	0	3	9	10	26
Sept-Oct	.206	.271	.429	63	13	5	0	3	6	6	15											
Bases Empty	.216	.238	.363	102	22	9	0	2	2	3	26	.201	.239	.318	179	36	12	0	3	3	9	40
Leadoff	.256	.304	.465	43	11	6	0	1	1	3	12	.183	.239	.293	82	15	6	0	1	1	6	22
Runners On Base	.230	.301	.486	74	17	1	0	6	21	8	13	.245	.290	.448	143	35	5	0	8	34	10	29
Scoring Position	.184	.241	.388	49	9	1	0	3	15	4	11	.174	.220	.304	92	16	3	0	3	23	6	26
Late and Close	.211	.231	.289	38	8	3	0	0	1	1	8	.200	.224	.277	65	13	5	0	0	3	2	14

IVAN RODRIGUEZ — BR/TR — age 23 — TEX C134, DH1

1993	BA	OBA	SA	AB	H	2B	3B	HR	RBI	BB	SO	3-YEAR TOTALS (1991–1993) BA	OBA	SA	AB	H	2B	3B	HR	RBI	BB	SO
Total	.273	.315	.412	473	129	28	4	10	66	29	70	.266	.301	.379	1173	312	60	5	21	130	58	185
vs. Left	.278	.325	.389	108	30	6	0	2	16	9	18	.268	.307	.377	284	76	16	0	5	34	18	41
vs. Right	.271	.312	.419	365	99	22	4	8	50	20	52	.265	.299	.380	889	236	44	5	16	96	40	144
at Home	.244	.286	.417	242	59	15	3	7	36	15	36	.240	.272	.374	588	141	29	4	14	73	27	104
on Road	.303	.345	.407	231	70	13	1	3	30	14	34	.292	.329	.385	585	171	31	1	7	57	31	81
on Grass	.266	.308	.405	402	107	24	4	8	58	24	60	.263	.294	.375	975	256	49	5	17	111	44	157
on Turf	.310	.355	.451	71	22	4	0	2	8	5	10	.283	.332	.399	198	56	11	0	4	19	14	28
Day Games	.385	.413	.530	117	45	15	2	2	18	6	13	.329	.359	.457	258	85	17	2	4	31	12	32
Night Games	.236	.284	.374	356	84	21	2	8	48	23	57	.248	.284	.357	915	227	43	3	17	99	46	153
April	.349	.425	.492	63	22	6	0	1	19	8	9	.331	.385	.459	133	44	11	0	2	27	11	18
May	.303	.320	.424	99	30	6	3	0	7	2	12	.280	.307	.412	182	51	6	3	4	20	7	31
June	.216	.244	.365	74	16	2	0	3	9	3	13	.269	.297	.423	130	35	5	0	5	17	6	21
July	.269	.342	.418	67	18	4	0	2	8	7	10	.259	.304	.362	224	58	12	1	3	18	14	33
August	.279	.312	.488	86	24	9	0	3	17	5	8	.258	.280	.373	260	67	18	0	4	31	9	36
Sept-Oct	.226	.264	.298	84	19	1	1	1	6	4	18	.234	.267	.311	244	57	8	1	3	17	11	46
Bases Empty	.287	.322	.425	254	73	17	3	4	4	13	33	.271	.300	.382	650	176	34	4	10	10	26	98
Leadoff	.320	.347	.505	97	31	10	1	2	2	4	11	.293	.326	.439	246	72	16	1	6	6	11	26
Runners On Base	.256	.308	.397	219	56	11	1	6	62	16	37	.260	.302	.377	523	136	26	1	11	120	32	87
Scoring Position	.270	.324	.405	126	34	8	0	3	52	10	24	.269	.317	.384	279	75	14	0	6	103	21	54
Late and Close	.318	.343	.439	66	21	1	2	1	10	3	11	.297	.332	.359	195	58	11	0	2	20	11	31

CHRIS SABO — BR/TR — age 32 — CIN 3B148

1993	BA	OBA	SA	AB	H	2B	3B	HR	RBI	BB	SO	6-YEAR TOTALS (1988–1993) BA	OBA	SA	AB	H	2B	3B	HR	RBI	BB	SO
Total	.259	.315	.440	552	143	33	2	21	82	43	105	.270	.327	.449	2887	780	186	13	101	357	232	381
vs. Left	.252	.333	.407	135	34	9	0	4	20	16	21	.300	.367	.498	928	278	65	4	37	122	94	101
vs. Right	.261	.309	.451	417	109	24	2	17	62	27	84	.256	.307	.425	1959	502	121	9	64	235	138	280
at Home	.281	.346	.498	263	74	19	1	12	47	27	52	.286	.347	.499	1402	401	103	6	61	194	127	176
on Road	.239	.286	.388	289	69	14	1	9	35	16	53	.255	.308	.401	1485	379	83	7	40	163	105	205
on Grass	.239	.281	.372	180	43	3	0	7	24	8	32	.254	.304	.398	894	227	44	2	27	101	58	121
on Turf	.269	.331	.473	372	100	30	2	14	58	35	73	.277	.337	.471	1993	553	142	11	74	256	174	260
Day Games	.295	.359	.511	176	52	12	1	8	26	17	34	.277	.327	.453	2020	559	129	9	70	259	144	264
Night Games	.242	.295	.407	376	91	21	1	13	56	26	71											
April	.221	.258	.419	86	19	5	0	4	14	3	11	.253	.314	.429	415	105	28	0	15	42	34	45
May	.243	.287	.374	107	26	5	0	3	18	5	15	.260	.317	.429	576	150	33	2	20	77	46	75
June	.308	.351	.385	52	16	1	0	1	7	3	7	.317	.378	.540	543	172	41	7	22	77	50	71
July	.337	.417	.545	101	34	9	0	4	16	15	21	.255	.320	.409	440	112	27	1	13	54	41	59
August	.250	.309	.480	100	25	7	2	4	16	9	27	.277	.318	.462	481	133	32	3	17	52	27	66
Sept-Oct	.217	.272	.415	106	23	6	0	5	11	8	24	.250	.306	.405	432	108	25	0	14	55	34	65
Bases Empty	.246	.303	.423	293	72	17	1	11	11	20	54	.273	.326	.466	1671	456	112	11	63	63	121	213
Leadoff	.264	.343	.464	125	33	10	0	5	5	11	18	.278	.344	.476	731	203	45	2	32	32	67	77
Runners On Base	.274	.329	.459	259	71	16	1	10	71	23	51	.266	.327	.424	1216	324	74	2	38	294	111	168
Scoring Position	.257	.329	.500	140	36	11	1	7	63	17	31	.261	.342	.445	705	184	45	2	27	264	90	103
Late and Close	.221	.277	.372	86	19	5	1	2	6	6	17	.245	.314	.393	445	109	20	2	14	48	43	64

TIM SALMON — BR/TR — age 26 — CAL OF140, DH1 — 2-YEAR TOTALS (1992–1993)

1993	BA	OBA	SA	AB	H	2B	3B	HR	RBI	BB	SO	BA	OBA	SA	AB	H	2B	3B	HR	RBI	BB	SO
Total	.283	.382	.536	515	146	35	1	31	95	82	135	.269	.369	.500	594	160	36	1	33	101	93	158
vs. Left	.230	.368	.434	122	28	2	1	7	24	25	31	.230	.369	.437	135	31	2	1	8	26	28	35
vs. Right	.300	.386	.567	393	118	33	0	24	71	57	104	.281	.369	.519	459	129	34	0	25	75	65	123
at Home	.314	.406	.636	258	81	14	0	23	58	41	62	.303	.401	.603	290	88	15	0	24	60	48	72
on Road	.253	.358	.436	257	65	21	1	8	37	41	73	.237	.339	.401	304	72	21	1	9	41	45	86
on Grass	.291	.387	.567	446	130	28	1	31	90	70	113	.274	.372	.522	525	144	29	1	33	96	81	136
on Turf	.232	.349	.333	69	16	7	0	0	5	12	22	.232	.349	.333	69	16	7	0	0	5	12	22
Day Games	.297	.357	.473	165	49	11	0	6	24	17	41	.295	.351	.480	173	51	11	0	7	27	17	43
Night Games	.277	.393	.566	350	97	24	1	25	71	65	94	.259	.376	.508	421	109	25	1	26	74	76	115
April	.254	.392	.559	59	15	3	0	5	14	14	12	.254	.392	.559	59	15	3	0	5	14	14	12
May	.294	.388	.471	102	30	6	0	4	18	16	30	.294	.388	.471	102	30	6	0	4	18	16	30
June	.273	.380	.523	88	24	7	0	5	15	16	22	.273	.380	.523	88	24	7	0	5	15	16	22
July	.283	.384	.594	106	30	6	0	9	24	17	26	.283	.384	.594	106	30	6	0	9	24	17	26
August	.250	.320	.482	112	28	6	1	6	15	11	30	.238	.309	.435	147	35	6	1	7	20	14	40
Sept-Oct	.396	.491	.667	48	19	7	0	2	9	8	15	.283	.394	.467	92	26	8	0	3	10	16	28
Bases Empty	.266	.361	.511	282	75	16	1	17	17	39	78	.254	.343	.483	331	84	17	1	19	19	41	88
Leadoff	.313	.364	.536	112	35	7	0	6	6	8	27	.295	.345	.508	132	39	7	0	7	7	9	34
Runners On Base	.305	.406	.567	233	71	19	0	14	78	43	57	.289	.399	.521	263	76	19	0	14	82	52	70
Scoring Position	.282	.414	.542	131	37	10	0	8	64	33	37	.272	.417	.497	151	41	10	0	8	68	42	44
Late and Close	.286	.384	.476	84	24	4	0	4	10	12	27	.252	.355	.437	103	26	4	0	5	12	15	32

JUAN SAMUEL — BR/TR — age 34 — CIN 2B70, 1B6, 3B4, OF3 — 10-YEAR TOTALS (1984–1993)

1993	BA	OBA	SA	AB	H	2B	3B	HR	RBI	BB	SO	BA	OBA	SA	AB	H	2B	3B	HR	RBI	BB	SO
Total	.230	.298	.345	261	60	10	4	4	26	23	53	.258	.311	.411	5342	1380	252	87	130	594	365	1244
vs. Left	.265	.339	.418	98	26	4	4	1	9	10	21	.260	.314	.420	1747	454	88	27	46	192	127	393
vs. Right	.209	.272	.301	163	34	6	0	3	17	13	32	.258	.310	.407	3595	926	164	60	84	402	238	851
at Home	.224	.310	.316	98	22	2	2	1	9	12	18	.258	.319	.418	2575	664	127	47	64	302	205	587
on Road	.233	.290	.362	163	38	8	2	3	17	11	35	.259	.304	.404	2767	716	125	40	66	292	160	657
on Grass	.248	.301	.371	105	26	5	1	2	13	6	23	.258	.309	.388	2166	558	81	24	51	232	145	524
on Turf	.218	.295	.327	156	34	5	3	2	13	17	30	.259	.312	.427	3176	822	171	63	79	362	220	720
Day Games	.224	.306	.400	85	19	3	2	2	13	8	12	.267	.319	.441	1586	424	79	31	45	187	111	346
Night Games	.233	.293	.318	176	41	7	1	2	13	15	41	.255	.308	.398	3756	956	173	56	85	407	254	898
April	.105	.190	.263	19	2	0	0	1	1	2	8	.259	.317	.387	622	161	28	11	10	59	49	153
May	.286	.286	.381	21	6	0	1	0	3	0	2	.265	.312	.416	853	226	35	11	24	94	53	197
June	.176	.200	.294	34	6	1	0	1	2	1	12	.264	.317	.417	939	248	41	14	25	116	67	224
July	.273	.344	.436	55	15	2	2	1	7	5	10	.268	.322	.448	927	248	44	18	29	120	63	202
August	.204	.317	.259	54	11	3	0	0	3	9	9	.237	.295	.370	980	232	46	17	17	104	76	243
Sept-Oct	.256	.318	.372	78	20	4	1	0	10	6	12	.260	.308	.421	1021	265	58	16	25	101	57	225
Bases Empty	.207	.257	.305	164	34	4	3	2	2	9	35	.253	.304	.397	3211	811	156	46	72	72	213	759
Leadoff	.194	.237	.292	72	14	1	3	0	0	3	18	.250	.309	.405	1480	370	72	25	36	36	111	328
Runners On Base	.268	.360	.412	97	26	6	1	2	24	14	18	.267	.321	.432	2131	569	96	41	58	522	152	485
Scoring Position	.348	.475	.565	46	16	2	1	2	24	12	4	.264	.329	.438	1266	334	52	29	37	461	117	296
Late and Close	.273	.347	.364	44	12	1	0	1	6	5	11	.264	.330	.413	836	221	37	12	21	114	76	219

REY SANCHEZ — BR/TR — age 27 — CHN SS98 — 3-YEAR TOTALS (1991–1993)

1993	BA	OBA	SA	AB	H	2B	3B	HR	RBI	BB	SO	BA	OBA	SA	AB	H	2B	3B	HR	RBI	BB	SO
Total	.282	.316	.326	344	97	11	2	0	28	15	22	.268	.306	.330	622	167	25	5	1	49	29	42
vs. Left	.297	.314	.305	118	35	1	0	0	8	3	5	.284	.320	.341	229	65	9	2	0	17	12	10
vs. Right	.274	.317	.336	226	62	10	2	0	20	12	17	.260	.298	.323	393	102	16	3	1	32	17	32
at Home	.308	.345	.365	159	49	7	1	0	18	8	11	.293	.327	.368	307	90	16	2	1	30	14	25
on Road	.259	.291	.292	185	48	4	1	0	10	7	11	.244	.285	.292	315	77	9	3	0	19	15	17
on Grass	.304	.330	.354	263	80	9	2	0	24	9	19	.277	.304	.343	470	130	22	3	1	37	17	35
on Turf	.210	.273	.235	81	17	2	0	0	4	6	3	.243	.310	.289	152	37	3	2	0	12	12	7
Day Games	.272	.307	.307	202	55	7	0	0	22	9	12	.273	.305	.331	344	94	13	2	1	34	14	23
Night Games	.296	.329	.352	142	42	4	2	0	6	6	10	.263	.307	.327	278	73	12	3	0	15	15	19
April	.256	.273	.267	86	22	1	0	0	6	2	5	.232	.247	.242	95	22	1	0	0	6	2	6
May	.344	.364	.375	32	11	1	0	0	2	1	4	.308	.317	.385	39	12	1	1	0	3	1	5
June	.395	.419	.500	86	34	5	2	0	10	4	4	.358	.380	.478	134	48	8	4	0	18	5	7
July	.250	.327	.318	44	11	3	0	0	4	5	3	.235	.303	.288	132	31	7	0	0	8	10	8
August	.195	.244	.208	77	15	1	0	0	4	3	5	.257	.294	.323	167	43	8	0	1	10	7	11
Sept-Oct	.211	.211	.211	19	4	0	0	0	2	0	1	.200	.254	.200	55	11	0	0	0	4	4	5
Bases Empty	.263	.287	.306	232	61	8	1	0	0	6	11	.263	.295	.323	403	106	17	2	1	1	14	23
Leadoff	.260	.294	.298	104	27	2	1	0	0	4	5	.263	.307	.321	190	50	6	1	1	1	9	10
Runners On Base	.321	.371	.366	112	36	3	1	0	28	9	11	.279	.325	.342	219	61	8	3	0	48	15	19
Scoring Position	.339	.414	.424	59	20	3	1	0	28	8	6	.297	.359	.387	111	33	6	2	0	46	11	9
Late and Close	.273	.284	.273	66	18	0	0	0	4	0	6	.236	.280	.244	123	29	1	0	0	7	5	9

RYNE SANDBERG — BR/TR — age 35 — CHN 2B115

1993	BA	OBA	SA	AB	H	2B	3B	HR	RBI	BB	SO
Total	.309	.359	.412	456	141	20	0	9	45	37	62
vs. Left	.385	.427	.459	109	42	5	0	1	7	8	11
vs. Right	.285	.339	.398	347	99	15	0	8	38	29	51
at Home	.296	.352	.399	243	72	10	0	5	30	22	34
on Road	.324	.368	.427	213	69	10	0	4	15	15	28
on Grass	.304	.352	.393	349	106	13	0	6	37	27	43
on Turf	.327	.381	.477	107	35	7	0	3	8	10	19
Day Games	.290	.335	.373	241	70	8	0	4	28	18	37
Night Games	.330	.387	.456	215	71	12	0	5	17	19	25
April	.000	.400	.000	3	0	0	0	0	0	2	2
May	.274	.336	.400	95	26	3	0	3	12	11	16
June	.341	.365	.407	91	31	3	0	1	11	3	9
July	.280	.322	.439	107	30	8	0	3	12	7	18
August	.348	.402	.446	112	39	5	0	2	7	9	10
Sept-Oct	.313	.377	.333	48	15	1	0	0	3	5	7
Bases Empty	.332	.385	.484	244	81	13	0	8	8	19	33
Leadoff	.351	.392	.459	74	26	5	0	1	1	5	7
Runners On Base	.283	.331	.330	212	60	7	0	1	37	18	29
Scoring Position	.282	.344	.330	103	29	5	0	0	34	13	15
Late and Close	.250	.333	.279	68	17	2	0	0	2	8	14

10-YEAR TOTALS (1984–1993)

	BA	OBA	SA	AB	H	2B	3B	HR	RBI	BB	SO
	.296	.357	.478	5887	1742	282	58	225	780	569	840
	.313	.384	.483	1661	520	98	16	51	188	196	200
	.289	.346	.476	4226	1222	184	42	174	592	373	640
	.309	.370	.520	2938	907	148	40	131	450	299	420
	.283	.343	.436	2949	835	134	18	94	330	270	420
	.301	.361	.497	4200	1266	198	49	175	600	402	589
	.282	.347	.432	1687	476	84	9	50	180	167	251
	.306	.365	.495	3453	1055	169	39	136	473	332	478
	.282	.346	.454	2434	687	113	19	89	307	237	362
	.236	.299	.367	719	170	36	5	16	73	64	97
	.318	.376	.518	1059	337	58	11	44	147	103	154
	.312	.369	.536	982	306	47	13	49	153	88	122
	.286	.348	.444	955	273	41	10	30	112	94	134
	.301	.362	.474	1116	336	44	7	45	135	108	167
	.303	.367	.495	1056	320	56	12	41	160	112	166
	.290	.346	.477	3458	1004	172	28	139	139	284	496
	.296	.350	.540	1125	333	67	12	61	61	93	164
	.304	.371	.480	2429	738	110	30	86	641	285	344
	.284	.367	.445	1325	376	51	20	41	513	201	208
	.284	.354	.435	940	267	29	13	29	135	104	164

REGGIE SANDERS — BR/TR — age 27 — CIN OF137

1993	BA	OBA	SA	AB	H	2B	3B	HR	RBI	BB	SO
Total	.274	.343	.444	496	136	16	4	20	83	51	118
vs. Left	.310	.366	.496	129	40	6	0	6	22	12	24
vs. Right	.262	.335	.425	367	96	10	4	14	61	39	94
at Home	.287	.357	.447	237	68	12	1	8	43	25	58
on Road	.263	.330	.440	259	68	4	3	12	40	26	60
on Grass	.261	.344	.472	161	42	3	2	9	28	20	34
on Turf	.281	.342	.430	335	94	13	2	11	55	31	84
Day Games	.270	.324	.428	152	41	5	2	5	33	14	34
Night Games	.276	.351	.451	344	95	11	2	15	50	37	84
April	.240	.294	.373	75	18	2	1	2	8	6	21
May	.308	.404	.538	91	28	3	0	6	15	15	19
June	.239	.311	.359	92	22	2	0	3	14	8	23
July	.278	.330	.456	90	25	4	0	4	19	6	16
August	.311	.386	.492	61	19	3	1	2	14	8	13
Sept-Oct	.276	.333	.448	87	24	2	2	3	13	8	26
Bases Empty	.281	.333	.479	242	68	7	1	13	13	16	58
Leadoff	.258	.333	.449	89	23	3	1	4	4	10	24
Runners On Base	.268	.351	.409	254	68	9	3	7	70	35	60
Scoring Position	.322	.414	.503	149	48	6	3	5	65	27	40
Late and Close	.243	.341	.386	70	17	2	1	2	9	10	21

3-YEAR TOTALS (1991–1993)

	BA	OBA	SA	AB	H	2B	3B	HR	RBI	BB	SO
	.269	.343	.444	921	248	42	10	33	122	99	225
	.303	.369	.516	320	97	21	4	13	41	31	57
	.251	.329	.406	601	151	21	6	20	81	68	168
	.260	.347	.428	453	118	26	4	14	65	57	112
	.278	.338	.459	468	130	16	6	19	57	42	113
	.263	.329	.450	300	79	9	4	13	38	28	62
	.272	.349	.441	621	169	33	6	20	84	71	163
	.260	.334	.422	289	75	17	3	8	46	34	74
	.274	.347	.454	632	173	25	7	25	76	65	151
	.277	.329	.439	148	41	6	3	6	14	12	37
	.310	.406	.504	129	40	7	0	6	22	21	28
	.237	.300	.376	173	41	7	1	5	22	14	44
	.288	.339	.483	118	34	7	2	4	19	8	25
	.273	.372	.497	161	44	8	2	8	22	24	38
	.250	.322	.401	192	48	7	2	6	23	20	53
	.283	.345	.492	492	139	25	6	22	22	43	113
	.236	.320	.379	195	46	8	1	6	6	24	51
	.254	.341	.389	429	109	17	4	11	100	56	112
	.271	.364	.410	251	68	9	4	6	87	38	77
	.271	.360	.421	140	38	7	1	4	18	19	44

BENITO SANTIAGO — BR/TR — age 29 — FLO C136, OF1

1993	BA	OBA	SA	AB	H	2B	3B	HR	RBI	BB	SO
Total	.230	.291	.380	469	108	19	6	13	50	37	88
vs. Left	.276	.355	.488	123	34	8	3	4	15	15	15
vs. Right	.214	.268	.341	346	74	11	3	9	35	22	73
at Home	.227	.291	.386	233	53	11	4	6	29	18	52
on Road	.233	.292	.373	236	55	8	2	7	21	19	36
on Grass	.216	.281	.352	361	78	14	4	9	39	30	72
on Turf	.278	.325	.472	108	30	5	2	4	11	7	16
Day Games	.270	.356	.338	74	20	2	0	1	6	11	13
Night Games	.223	.278	.387	395	88	17	6	12	44	26	75
April	.253	.322	.418	79	20	4	0	3	9	8	17
May	.189	.257	.278	90	17	5	0	1	10	8	17
June	.281	.354	.472	89	25	3	4	2	13	7	17
July	.183	.236	.293	82	15	3	0	2	7	6	20
August	.230	.264	.356	87	20	3	1	2	4	4	11
Sept-Oct	.262	.333	.548	42	11	1	1	3	9	4	6
Bases Empty	.237	.291	.393	262	62	11	3	8	8	19	63
Leadoff	.265	.324	.480	102	27	3	2	5	5	8	24
Runners On Base	.222	.292	.362	207	46	8	3	5	42	18	25
Scoring Position	.223	.295	.364	121	27	5	3	2	36	13	12
Late and Close	.148	.202	.250	88	13	3	0	2	5	5	26

8-YEAR TOTALS (1986–1993)

	BA	OBA	SA	AB	H	2B	3B	HR	RBI	BB	SO
	.259	.297	.403	3341	866	143	21	98	425	176	604
	.284	.326	.459	1034	294	54	8	37	142	66	175
	.248	.284	.377	2307	572	89	13	61	283	110	429
	.260	.296	.406	1678	437	72	13	49	220	85	303
	.258	.298	.399	1663	429	71	8	49	205	91	301
	.262	.300	.413	2479	650	100	16	81	335	129	458
	.251	.290	.371	862	216	43	5	17	90	47	146
	.286	.337	.419	744	213	28	4	21	93	56	126
	.251	.285	.398	2597	653	115	17	77	332	120	478
	.274	.300	.421	544	149	22	2	18	68	20	88
	.229	.263	.330	634	145	24	2	12	73	29	115
	.275	.324	.406	458	126	18	6	10	59	30	100
	.264	.312	.398	440	116	25	2	10	49	30	84
	.257	.296	.422	614	158	23	6	22	72	34	97
	.264	.300	.441	651	172	31	3	26	104	33	120
	.269	.307	.414	1813	488	81	11	53	53	89	352
	.270	.309	.401	730	197	30	3	20	20	37	145
	.247	.285	.389	1528	378	62	10	45	372	87	252
	.242	.284	.381	898	217	38	8	25	318	63	168
	.288	.326	.433	619	178	25	4	19	77	34	125

DAVID SEGUI — BB/TL — age 28 — BAL 1B144, DH1 — 4-YEAR TOTALS (1990–1993)

1993	BA	OBA	SA	AB	H	2B	3B	HR	RBI	BB	SO		BA	OBA	SA	AB	H	2B	3B	HR	RBI	BB	SO
Total	.273	.351	.400	450	123	27	0	10	60	58	53		.263	.330	.360	974	256	50	0	15	114	101	110
vs. Left	.292	.364	.444	144	42	7	0	5	15	17	18		.281	.333	.389	360	101	18	0	7	42	29	45
vs. Right	.265	.345	.379	306	81	20	0	5	45	41	35		.252	.328	.344	614	155	32	0	8	72	72	65
at Home	.280	.357	.436	236	66	19	0	6	36	31	29		.258	.324	.367	496	128	27	0	9	67	51	63
on Road	.266	.344	.360	214	57	8	0	4	24	27	24		.268	.336	.354	478	128	23	0	6	47	50	47
on Grass	.277	.352	.411	404	112	24	0	10	57	51	46		.266	.334	.362	836	222	42	0	13	100	90	95
on Turf	.239	.340	.304	46	11	3	0	0	3	7	7		.246	.302	.348	138	34	8	0	2	14	11	15
Day Games	.268	.343	.374	123	33	7	0	2	15	15	15		.252	.329	.320	278	70	13	0	2	26	33	31
Night Games	.275	.354	.410	327	90	20	0	8	45	43	38		.267	.330	.376	696	186	37	0	13	88	68	79
April	.292	.433	.333	24	7	1	0	0	4	6	5		.246	.350	.304	69	17	4	0	0	8	11	8
May	.270	.360	.446	74	20	7	0	2	10	11	6		.237	.308	.358	190	45	14	0	3	23	19	17
June	.403	.444	.558	77	31	6	0	2	16	9	6		.328	.377	.435	177	58	10	0	3	26	17	16
July	.275	.343	.429	91	25	5	0	3	9	10	11		.268	.323	.399	153	41	8	0	4	15	13	18
August	.242	.343	.308	91	22	3	0	1	4	14	14		.256	.337	.293	164	42	3	0	1	12	20	22
Sept-Oct	.194	.252	.312	93	18	5	0	2	17	8	11		.240	.303	.344	221	53	11	0	4	30	21	29
Bases Empty	.261	.357	.415	241	63	13	0	8	8	36	26		.260	.333	.366	519	135	25	0	10	10	57	54
Leadoff	.286	.364	.448	105	30	5	0	4	4	13	8		.295	.351	.414	220	65	11	0	5	5	19	17
Runners On Base	.287	.343	.383	209	60	14	0	2	52	22	27		.266	.326	.354	455	121	25	0	5	104	44	56
Scoring Position	.299	.343	.368	117	35	8	0	0	46	12	18		.280	.338	.354	257	72	13	0	2	95	27	35
Late and Close	.152	.233	.241	79	12	1	0	2	10	9	13		.210	.295	.313	176	37	3	0	5	23	22	25

KEVIN SEITZER — BR/TR — age 32 — OAK/MIL 3B79, 1B31, DH6, OF4, 2B3, SS1, P1 — 8-YEAR TOTALS (1986–1993)

1993	BA	OBA	SA	AB	H	2B	3B	HR	RBI	BB	SO		BA	OBA	SA	AB	H	2B	3B	HR	RBI	BB	SO
Total	.269	.338	.396	417	112	16	2	11	57	44	48		.288	.369	.390	3706	1067	179	27	49	393	470	418
vs. Left	.280	.356	.399	143	40	5	0	4	25	17	12		.298	.388	.426	1067	318	57	13	18	118	157	105
vs. Right	.263	.328	.394	274	72	11	2	7	32	27	36		.284	.361	.376	2639	749	122	14	31	275	313	313
at Home	.266	.363	.386	207	55	7	0	6	27	30	18		.302	.385	.418	1829	553	97	17	27	210	241	180
on Road	.271	.311	.405	210	57	9	2	5	30	14	30		.274	.353	.363	1877	514	82	10	22	183	229	238
on Grass	.274	.343	.416	358	98	14	2	11	51	37	37		.264	.344	.353	1874	494	73	10	25	190	224	208
on Turf	.237	.309	.271	59	14	2	0	0	6	7	11		.313	.395	.428	1832	573	106	17	24	203	246	210
Day Games	.277	.350	.420	188	52	9	0	6	31	22	25		.287	.381	.390	1070	307	54	7	14	128	157	128
Night Games	.262	.327	.376	229	60	7	2	5	26	22	23		.288	.364	.391	2636	760	125	20	35	265	313	290
April	.226	.281	.434	53	12	2	0	3	4	4	5		.281	.343	.393	506	142	24	6	7	61	47	49
May	.233	.307	.291	103	24	2	2	0	12	11	14		.290	.377	.378	614	178	30	3	6	63	82	78
June	.275	.341	.377	69	19	4	0	1	11	8	10		.294	.365	.389	676	199	30	5	8	65	78	62
July	.313	.389	.375	32	10	2	0	0	0	4	4		.285	.367	.391	594	169	34	4	7	56	77	75
August	.288	.391	.507	73	21	1	0	5	21	12	7		.285	.375	.397	575	164	25	3	11	77	82	66
Sept-Oct	.299	.337	.425	87	26	5	0	2	9	5	8		.290	.379	.395	741	215	36	6	10	71	104	88
Bases Empty	.236	.306	.362	229	54	8	0	7	7	21	31		.281	.356	.384	2228	626	102	14	33	33	247	262
Leadoff	.178	.253	.300	90	16	2	0	3	3	9	15		.265	.334	.364	879	233	38	5	13	13	81	106
Runners On Base	.309	.375	.436	188	58	8	2	4	50	23	17		.298	.387	.401	1478	441	77	13	16	360	223	156
Scoring Position	.269	.347	.433	104	28	3	1	4	47	15	11		.286	.400	.389	870	249	50	9	7	324	176	103
Late and Close	.282	.304	.424	85	24	6	0	2	12	4	15		.294	.363	.380	574	169	35	1	4	78	65	78

SCOTT SERVAIS — BR/TR — age 27 — HOU C82 — 3-YEAR TOTALS (1991–1993)

1993	BA	OBA	SA	AB	H	2B	3B	HR	RBI	BB	SO		BA	OBA	SA	AB	H	2B	3B	HR	RBI	BB	SO
Total	.244	.313	.415	258	63	11	0	11	32	22	45		.236	.300	.348	500	118	23	0	11	53	37	78
vs. Left	.297	.357	.522	138	41	10	0	7	24	12	21		.269	.325	.403	290	78	18	0	7	40	21	37
vs. Right	.183	.261	.292	120	22	1	0	4	8	10	24		.190	.266	.271	210	40	5	0	4	13	16	41
at Home	.246	.311	.433	134	33	10	0	5	19	10	20		.239	.298	.358	243	58	14	0	5	27	17	36
on Road	.242	.314	.395	124	30	1	0	6	13	12	25		.233	.302	.339	257	60	9	0	6	26	20	42
on Grass	.260	.348	.377	77	20	0	0	3	6	10	15		.235	.318	.327	153	36	5	0	3	16	16	24
on Turf	.238	.296	.431	181	43	11	0	8	26	12	30		.236	.292	.357	347	82	18	0	8	37	21	54
Day Games	.313	.367	.450	80	25	5	0	2	12	6	15		.256	.323	.337	172	44	8	0	2	18	14	24
Night Games	.213	.288	.399	178	38	6	0	9	20	16	30		.226	.288	.354	328	74	15	0	9	35	23	54
April	.474	.455	.684	19	9	1	0	1	4	1	2		.273	.277	.364	44	12	1	0	1	5	1	5
May	.220	.273	.390	41	9	1	0	2	3	3	7		.276	.329	.434	76	21	6	0	2	5	3	12
June	.295	.360	.500	78	23	4	0	4	12	7	11		.248	.313	.385	117	29	4	0	4	16	9	17
July	.200	.282	.300	70	14	4	0	1	8	4	14		.174	.259	.240	121	21	5	0	1	10	9	20
August	.147	.256	.441	34	5	1	0	3	3	5	7		.149	.219	.299	67	10	1	0	3	7	6	8
Sept-Oct	.188	.263	.188	16	3	0	0	0	2	2	4		.333	.400	.413	75	25	6	0	0	10	9	16
Bases Empty	.241	.310	.437	158	38	7	0	8	8	12	29		.233	.294	.368	288	67	15	0	8	8	19	46
Leadoff	.263	.300	.421	57	15	3	0	2	2	2	12		.246	.271	.377	114	28	9	0	2	2	3	20
Runners On Base	.250	.316	.380	100	25	4	0	3	24	10	16		.241	.308	.321	212	51	8	0	3	45	18	32
Scoring Position	.258	.347	.371	62	16	1	0	2	21	9	11		.238	.327	.317	126	30	4	0	2	42	15	19
Late and Close	.286	.286	.429	42	12	3	0	1	4	0	5		.216	.258	.318	88	19	6	0	1	5	4	12

GARY SHEFFIELD — BR/TR — age 26 — SD/FLO 3B133

1993	BA	OBA	SA	AB	H	2B	3B	HR	RBI	BB	SO
Total	.294	.361	.476	494	145	20	5	20	73	47	64
vs. Left	.326	.400	.444	135	44	4	0	4	23	16	10
vs. Right	.281	.346	.487	359	101	16	5	16	50	31	54
at Home	.315	.382	.506	241	76	12	2	10	40	24	24
on Road	.273	.340	.447	253	69	8	3	10	33	23	40
on Grass	.318	.383	.510	384	122	16	5	16	61	38	48
on Turf	.209	.281	.355	110	23	4	0	4	12	9	16
Day Games	.316	.386	.535	114	36	4	3	5	21	11	13
Night Games	.287	.353	.458	380	109	16	2	15	52	36	51
April	.286	.330	.488	84	24	2	0	5	13	6	11
May	.245	.318	.408	98	24	5	1	3	12	10	10
June	.354	.388	.521	96	34	5	1	3	14	4	9
July	.287	.370	.538	80	23	6	1	4	13	11	12
August	.292	.356	.449	89	26	2	0	4	16	6	12
Sept-Oct	.298	.433	.447	47	14	0	2	1	5	10	10
Bases Empty	.312	.360	.447	266	83	11	2	7	7	16	31
Leadoff	.284	.318	.402	102	29	7	1	1	1	3	10
Runners On Base	.272	.362	.509	228	62	9	3	13	66	31	33
Scoring Position	.263	.372	.430	114	30	1	3	4	44	22	16
Late and Close	.326	.429	.535	86	28	2	2	4	18	15	14

6-YEAR TOTALS (1988–1993)

	BA	OBA	SA	AB	H	2B	3B	HR	RBI	BB	SO
	.285	.345	.451	2161	615	115	11	74	305	192	200
	.304	.367	.484	638	194	35	4	24	99	65	49
	.276	.336	.437	1523	421	80	7	50	206	127	151
	.300	.367	.487	1072	322	65	6	41	148	108	98
	.269	.324	.415	1089	293	50	5	33	157	84	102
	.296	.359	.478	1714	507	96	11	65	240	162	162
	.242	.291	.345	447	108	19	0	9	65	30	38
	.266	.324	.423	665	177	34	5	20	88	57	58
	.293	.355	.463	1496	438	81	6	54	217	135	142
	.282	.350	.453	373	105	24	2	12	51	40	35
	.291	.348	.446	399	116	19	2	13	56	34	37
	.283	.330	.429	413	117	25	1	11	64	29	42
	.294	.353	.472	377	111	28	3	11	50	31	21
	.290	.347	.490	290	84	10	0	16	54	24	32
	.265	.344	.421	309	82	9	3	11	30	34	33
	.275	.333	.432	1182	325	71	5	35	35	91	108
	.275	.321	.417	403	111	23	2	10	10	23	29
	.296	.359	.473	979	290	44	6	39	270	101	92
	.283	.357	.446	520	147	22	6	17	216	71	56
	.340	.415	.514	321	109	12	4	12	56	41	30

RUBEN SIERRA — BB/TR — age 29 — OAK OF133, DH25

1993	BA	OBA	SA	AB	H	2B	3B	HR	RBI	BB	SO
Total	.233	.288	.390	630	147	23	5	22	101	52	97
vs. Left	.231	.297	.392	199	46	8	0	8	32	20	29
vs. Right	.234	.283	.390	431	101	15	5	14	69	32	68
at Home	.222	.280	.353	306	68	9	2	9	49	26	58
on Road	.244	.295	.426	324	79	14	3	13	52	26	39
on Grass	.242	.290	.405	516	125	19	4	19	84	38	80
on Turf	.193	.277	.325	114	22	4	1	3	17	14	17
Day Games	.225	.277	.345	267	60	8	3	6	33	20	44
Night Games	.240	.295	.424	363	87	15	2	16	68	32	53
April	.296	.316	.563	71	21	7	0	4	15	3	9
May	.200	.240	.333	120	24	5	1	3	22	7	18
June	.255	.331	.396	106	27	3	0	4	13	12	15
July	.306	.361	.500	108	33	4	1	5	23	11	12
August	.190	.242	.267	116	22	2	2	1	6	8	26
Sept-Oct	.183	.252	.358	109	20	2	1	5	22	11	17
Bases Empty	.218	.255	.343	321	70	14	4	6	6	16	51
Leadoff	.239	.271	.363	113	27	6	1	2	2	5	13
Runners On Base	.249	.318	.440	309	77	9	1	16	95	36	46
Scoring Position	.243	.338	.462	173	42	5	0	11	83	30	26
Late and Close	.252	.363	.398	103	26	1	1	4	19	19	16

8-YEAR TOTALS (1986–1993)

	BA	OBA	SA	AB	H	2B	3B	HR	RBI	BB	SO
	.274	.320	.459	4774	1307	253	49	178	774	350	694
	.296	.334	.486	1508	446	94	11	57	253	100	165
	.264	.313	.447	3266	861	159	38	121	521	250	529
	.273	.317	.477	2324	634	118	28	100	410	162	374
	.275	.322	.442	2450	673	135	21	78	364	188	320
	.270	.315	.455	3948	1065	203	37	151	652	281	575
	.293	.344	.481	826	242	50	12	27	122	69	119
	.256	.307	.413	1121	287	59	6	35	179	90	156
	.279	.324	.473	3653	1020	194	43	143	595	260	538
	.273	.321	.490	524	143	37	4	23	96	40	86
	.284	.330	.448	754	214	36	8	24	122	54	113
	.290	.343	.484	884	256	57	11	31	131	72	128
	.259	.298	.458	793	205	39	10	33	134	50	112
	.267	.307	.446	893	238	45	11	31	128	59	139
	.271	.319	.441	926	251	39	5	36	163	75	116
	.257	.300	.432	2447	630	126	30	80	80	143	381
	.266	.308	.442	1006	268	56	11	33	33	58	128
	.291	.339	.488	2327	677	127	19	98	694	207	313
	.283	.338	.489	1299	368	65	14	58	587	143	195
	.266	.331	.432	760	202	29	8	27	119	77	113

DON SLAUGHT — BR/TR — age 36 — PIT C105

1993	BA	OBA	SA	AB	H	2B	3B	HR	RBI	BB	SO
Total	.300	.356	.440	377	113	19	2	10	55	29	56
vs. Left	.333	.374	.458	120	40	5	2	2	13	6	14
vs. Right	.284	.347	.432	257	73	14	0	8	42	23	42
at Home	.284	.333	.388	183	52	12	2	1	20	13	28
on Road	.314	.377	.490	194	61	7	0	9	35	16	28
on Grass	.319	.382	.471	119	38	6	0	4	19	11	19
on Turf	.291	.344	.426	258	75	13	2	6	36	18	37
Day Games	.261	.347	.489	88	23	6	2	4	18	10	12
Night Games	.311	.359	.426	289	90	11	2	6	37	19	44
April	.383	.464	.467	60	23	3	1	0	10	7	8
May	.274	.303	.329	73	20	1	0	1	5	3	9
June	.261	.325	.435	69	18	3	0	3	10	5	12
July	.296	.358	.507	71	21	4	1	3	15	7	14
August	.279	.324	.441	68	19	8	0	1	9	4	10
Sept-Oct	.333	.385	.500	36	12	0	0	2	6	3	3
Bases Empty	.246	.298	.366	191	47	9	1	4	4	11	33
Leadoff	.307	.381	.507	75	23	4	1	3	3	7	15
Runners On Base	.355	.412	.516	186	66	10	1	6	51	18	23
Scoring Position	.350	.415	.450	100	35	4	0	2	38	12	14
Late and Close	.321	.396	.469	81	26	3	0	3	12	10	11

10-YEAR TOTALS (1984–1993)

	BA	OBA	SA	AB	H	2B	3B	HR	RBI	BB	SO
	.279	.333	.423	3056	854	193	24	66	370	228	455
	.294	.350	.448	1296	381	86	13	29	160	109	195
	.269	.321	.405	1760	473	107	11	37	210	119	260
	.292	.344	.443	1532	448	115	14	29	180	118	216
	.266	.322	.404	1524	406	78	10	37	190	110	239
	.277	.327	.431	1778	493	106	9	50	216	119	275
	.282	.342	.412	1278	361	87	15	16	154	109	180
	.271	.336	.428	743	201	46	7	19	102	71	112
	.282	.333	.422	2313	653	147	17	47	268	157	343
	.317	.366	.497	489	155	30	5	16	74	35	74
	.264	.329	.406	535	141	28	6	12	64	47	69
	.293	.342	.413	458	134	33	2	6	48	33	70
	.264	.320	.420	459	121	32	5	10	56	36	77
	.259	.312	.385	548	142	32	2	9	64	39	84
	.284	.334	.423	567	161	32	4	13	64	38	81
	.277	.330	.446	1708	473	118	16	46	46	115	266
	.294	.348	.464	700	206	56	6	17	17	49	92
	.283	.338	.395	1348	381	75	8	20	324	113	189
	.270	.335	.358	769	208	43	3	6	274	81	122
	.288	.349	.429	553	159	26	5	14	79	46	90

DWIGHT SMITH — BL/TR — age 31 — CHN OF89

1993	BA	OBA	SA	AB	H	2B	3B	HR	RBI	BB	SO	BA	OBA	SA	AB	H	2B	3B	HR	RBI	BB	SO
Total	.300	.355	.494	310	93	17	5	11	35	25	51	.285	.341	.433	1327	378	68	16	32	159	108	220
vs. Left	.364	.462	.636	11	4	3	0	0	3	0	3	.228	.288	.386	101	23	5	1	3	15	6	29
vs. Right	.298	.351	.488	299	89	14	5	11	32	25	48	.290	.345	.436	1226	355	63	15	29	144	102	191
at Home	.377	.440	.637	146	55	12	4	6	21	16	22	.315	.374	.488	629	198	36	8	19	90	57	95
on Road	.232	.274	.366	164	38	5	1	5	14	9	29	.258	.311	.383	698	180	32	8	13	69	51	125
on Grass	.311	.379	.519	241	75	13	5	9	30	25	36	.301	.356	.454	928	279	45	11	25	110	77	142
on Turf	.261	.261	.406	69	18	4	0	2	5	0	15	.248	.306	.383	399	99	23	5	7	49	31	78
Day Games	.296	.355	.454	152	45	8	2	4	16	13	26	.294	.351	.432	701	206	34	9	15	87	59	106
Night Games	.304	.355	.532	158	48	9	3	7	19	12	25	.275	.329	.433	626	172	34	7	17	72	49	114
April	.400	.462	.743	35	14	4	1	2	2	4	7	.264	.343	.440	125	33	9	2	3	9	14	22
May	.325	.345	.575	80	26	4	2	4	10	2	10	.316	.351	.490	263	83	15	5	7	29	13	39
June	.218	.266	.310	87	19	2	0	2	8	5	12	.267	.324	.400	300	80	14	1	8	34	25	49
July	.444	.400	.667	9	4	0	1	0	3	0	1	.288	.329	.464	153	44	11	2	4	20	9	22
August	.319	.407	.553	47	15	2	0	3	3	7	6	.258	.301	.394	221	57	7	1	7	29	14	45
Sept-Oct	.288	.383	.423	52	15	5	1	0	9	7	15	.306	.386	.423	265	81	12	5	3	38	33	43
Bases Empty	.302	.362	.500	212	64	10	4	8	8	17	35	.271	.328	.430	781	212	34	12	22	22	61	118
Leadoff	.326	.378	.530	132	43	8	2	5	5	10	18	.264	.318	.442	364	96	21	4	12	12	27	54
Runners On Base	.296	.339	.480	98	29	7	1	3	27	8	16	.304	.359	.436	546	166	34	4	10	137	47	102
Scoring Position	.241	.309	.397	58	14	4	1	1	23	7	11	.293	.356	.414	314	92	19	2	5	118	33	66
Late and Close	.279	.333	.372	43	12	1	0	1	7	4	8	.250	.297	.369	252	63	11	2	5	29	16	44

OZZIE SMITH — BB/TR — age 40 — SL SS134

1993	BA	OBA	SA	AB	H	2B	3B	HR	RBI	BB	SO	BA	OBA	SA	AB	H	2B	3B	HR	RBI	BB	SO
Total	.288	.337	.356	545	157	22	6	1	53	43	18	.279	.358	.349	5356	1494	251	37	17	512	664	308
vs. Left	.320	.354	.413	150	48	9	1	1	16	9	4	.279	.361	.371	1952	544	120	8	15	183	257	119
vs. Right	.276	.331	.334	395	109	13	5	0	37	34	14	.279	.356	.336	3404	950	131	29	2	329	407	189
at Home	.299	.357	.375	288	86	11	4	1	29	28	9	.289	.370	.361	2672	771	129	19	9	268	347	152
on Road	.276	.314	.335	257	71	11	2	0	24	15	9	.269	.345	.337	2684	723	122	18	8	244	317	156
on Grass	.313	.346	.382	144	45	8	1	0	18	9	3	.269	.335	.335	1421	382	71	10	1	128	144	85
on Turf	.279	.334	.347	401	112	14	5	1	35	34	15	.283	.366	.354	3935	1112	180	27	16	384	520	223
Day Games	.295	.335	.389	149	44	7	2	1	20	11	4	.289	.358	.366	1671	483	83	12	7	171	182	83
Night Games	.285	.338	.343	396	113	15	4	0	33	32	14	.274	.357	.342	3685	1011	168	25	10	341	482	225
April	.274	.311	.333	84	23	1	2	0	10	5	5	.255	.344	.309	663	169	19	4	3	66	94	40
May	.253	.308	.326	95	24	2	1	1	9	7	2	.284	.359	.356	975	277	51	5	3	93	112	48
June	.309	.364	.412	97	30	8	1	0	15	9	2	.285	.366	.354	923	263	46	6	2	113	121	51
July	.311	.345	.359	103	32	5	0	0	6	6	4	.295	.366	.364	857	253	43	5	2	73	94	52
August	.283	.330	.315	92	26	1	1	0	4	7	3	.258	.337	.324	941	243	37	8	3	73	113	59
Sept-Oct	.297	.365	.392	74	22	5	1	0	9	9	2	.290	.369	.375	997	289	55	9	4	94	130	58
Bases Empty	.276	.347	.323	297	82	10	2	0	0	32	9	.271	.349	.339	3163	856	154	17	9	9	376	202
Leadoff	.269	.346	.301	93	25	1	1	0	0	11	4	.284	.377	.360	1027	292	56	8	2	2	151	51
Runners On Base	.302	.326	.395	248	75	12	4	1	53	11	9	.291	.369	.364	2193	638	97	20	8	503	288	106
Scoring Position	.307	.338	.401	137	42	9	2	0	47	9	6	.272	.371	.338	1359	370	56	9	5	461	232	76
Late and Close	.323	.347	.441	93	30	5	3	0	13	4	4	.273	.359	.350	920	251	35	12	4	114	127	53

J. T. SNOW — BB/TL — age 26 — CAL 1B129

1993	BA	OBA	SA	AB	H	2B	3B	HR	RBI	BB	SO	BA	OBA	SA	AB	H	2B	3B	HR	RBI	BB	SO
Total	.241	.328	.408	419	101	18	2	16	57	55	88	.238	.329	.402	433	103	19	2	16	59	60	93
vs. Left	.218	.306	.345	87	19	3	1	2	10	10	18	.211	.297	.333	90	19	3	1	2	10	10	19
vs. Right	.247	.333	.425	332	82	15	1	14	47	45	70	.245	.338	.420	343	84	16	1	14	49	50	74
at Home	.286	.359	.475	196	56	6	1	10	35	24	38	.282	.368	.475	202	57	7	1	10	35	29	41
on Road	.202	.301	.345	223	45	12	1	6	22	31	50	.199	.296	.338	231	46	12	1	6	24	31	52
on Grass	.246	.325	.422	358	88	14	2	15	53	44	74	.245	.331	.420	367	90	15	2	15	55	49	78
on Turf	.213	.342	.328	61	13	4	0	1	4	11	14	.197	.321	.303	66	13	4	0	1	4	11	15
Day Games	.210	.291	.391	138	29	5	1	6	17	16	33	.204	.294	.381	147	30	6	1	6	17	19	36
Night Games	.256	.346	.416	281	72	13	1	10	40	39	55	.255	.347	.413	286	73	13	1	10	42	41	57
April	.343	.389	.687	67	23	1	2	6	17	4	11	.343	.389	.687	67	23	1	2	6	17	4	11
May	.124	.252	.270	89	11	1	0	4	11	15	21	.124	.252	.270	89	11	1	0	4	11	15	21
June	.292	.379	.361	72	21	5	0	0	11	12	10	.292	.379	.361	72	21	5	0	0	11	12	10
July	.159	.254	.254	63	10	3	0	1	4	8	20	.159	.254	.254	63	10	3	0	1	4	8	20
August	.222	.344	.407	27	6	2	0	1	2	5	5	.222	.344	.407	27	6	2	0	1	2	5	5
Sept-Oct	.297	.363	.475	101	30	6	0	4	12	11	21	.278	.364	.443	115	32	7	0	4	14	16	26
Bases Empty	.233	.331	.400	245	57	9	1	10	10	34	52	.229	.334	.395	253	58	10	1	10	10	38	55
Leadoff	.200	.304	.463	80	16	1	1	6	6	11	15	.207	.316	.476	82	17	1	1	6	6	15	18
Runners On Base	.253	.323	.420	174	44	9	1	6	47	21	36	.250	.322	.411	180	45	9	1	6	49	22	38
Scoring Position	.216	.287	.381	97	21	4	0	4	39	12	21	.214	.287	.369	103	22	4	0	4	41	13	23
Late and Close	.219	.350	.281	64	14	2	1	0	7	14	17	.209	.345	.269	67	14	2	1	0	7	15	20

CORY SNYDER — BR/TR — age 32 — LA OF115, 3B23, 1B12, SS2

1993	BA	OBA	SA	AB	H	2B	3B	HR	RBI	BB	SO		8-YEAR TOTALS (1986–1993) BA	OBA	SA	AB	H	2B	3B	HR	RBI	BB	SO
Total	.266	.331	.397	516	137	33	1	11	56	47	147		.247	.291	.426	3503	866	172	13	143	469	212	945
vs. Left	.265	.333	.397	151	40	11	0	3	13	15	36		.259	.308	.449	1128	292	66	2	48	152	80	291
vs. Right	.266	.330	.397	365	97	22	1	8	43	32	111		.242	.282	.416	2375	574	106	11	95	317	132	654
at Home	.266	.335	.379	256	68	14	0	5	26	24	71		.242	.288	.410	1685	407	86	3	64	217	109	447
on Road	.265	.327	.415	260	69	19	1	6	30	23	76		.252	.293	.441	1818	459	86	10	79	252	103	498
on Grass	.269	.333	.395	387	104	26	1	7	43	34	109		.251	.293	.432	2871	721	140	11	119	385	170	741
on Turf	.256	.324	.403	129	33	7	0	4	13	13	38		.229	.278	.400	632	145	32	2	24	84	42	204
Day Games	.276	.304	.421	152	42	11	1	3	18	6	40		.236	.272	.402	1124	265	47	4	44	149	56	304
Night Games	.261	.341	.387	364	95	22	0	8	38	41	107		.253	.299	.438	2379	601	125	9	99	320	156	641
April	.200	.333	.267	15	3	1	0	0	1	3	5		.266	.317	.454	394	105	21	1	17	62	29	106
May	.321	.409	.457	81	26	5	0	2	14	10	26		.213	.263	.362	553	118	23	1	19	70	34	159
June	.320	.394	.515	97	31	7	0	4	12	10	28		.286	.320	.533	658	188	41	4	38	109	33	167
July	.197	.221	.299	117	23	10	1	0	11	4	32		.244	.277	.393	656	160	35	3	19	82	31	172
August	.276	.343	.408	98	27	7	0	2	9	10	27		.236	.282	.419	656	155	28	4	28	77	43	175
Sept-Oct	.250	.314	.361	108	27	3	0	3	9	10	29		.239	.290	.392	586	140	24	0	22	69	42	166
Bases Empty	.255	.313	.389	298	76	19	0	7	7	23	78		.246	.286	.435	1952	481	92	9	86	86	103	509
Leadoff	.182	.224	.291	110	20	6	0	2	2	6	35		.237	.270	.430	844	200	37	3	40	40	37	222
Runners On Base	.280	.355	.408	218	61	14	1	4	49	24	69		.248	.297	.415	1551	385	80	4	57	383	109	436
Scoring Position	.260	.347	.366	131	34	9	1	1	41	18	45		.234	.292	.367	890	208	46	2	23	304	80	277
Late and Close	.267	.353	.389	90	24	6	1	1	13	11	30		.237	.280	.425	612	145	32	4	25	83	36	173

PAUL SORRENTO — BL/TR — age 29 — CLE 1B144, OF3, DH1

1993	BA	OBA	SA	AB	H	2B	3B	HR	RBI	BB	SO		5-YEAR TOTALS (1989–1993) BA	OBA	SA	AB	H	2B	3B	HR	RBI	BB	SO
Total	.257	.340	.434	463	119	26	1	18	65	58	121		.256	.334	.433	1110	284	56	3	45	152	130	256
vs. Left	.241	.305	.333	87	21	2	0	2	11	7	31		.218	.296	.310	142	31	4	0	3	17	15	51
vs. Right	.261	.347	.457	376	98	24	1	16	54	51	90		.261	.339	.451	968	253	52	3	42	135	115	205
at Home	.281	.389	.452	217	61	13	0	8	29	38	54		.279	.365	.467	544	152	31	1	23	73	73	121
on Road	.236	.293	.419	246	58	13	1	10	36	20	67		.233	.303	.401	566	132	25	2	22	79	57	135
on Grass	.274	.363	.439	383	105	22	1	13	51	53	96		.270	.350	.451	838	226	44	3	34	115	104	188
on Turf	.175	.221	.412	80	14	4	0	5	14	5	25		.213	.281	.379	272	58	12	0	11	37	26	68
Day Games	.272	.353	.525	162	44	9	1	10	21	21	49		.271	.346	.485	388	105	15	1	22	55	46	84
Night Games	.249	.332	.385	301	75	17	0	8	44	37	72		.248	.327	.406	722	179	41	2	23	97	84	172
April	.278	.329	.557	79	22	7	0	5	14	6	22		.245	.299	.405	163	40	8	0	6	21	12	42
May	.282	.402	.606	71	20	5	0	6	13	15	18		.250	.361	.529	140	35	6	0	11	28	25	38
June	.235	.311	.333	81	19	2	0	2	11	9	23		.287	.357	.415	164	47	6	0	5	18	18	34
July	.152	.197	.212	66	10	1	0	1	8	4	21		.239	.301	.395	205	49	9	1	7	26	19	49
August	.267	.360	.442	86	23	6	0	3	12	12	18		.261	.340	.460	176	46	11	0	8	25	20	34
Sept-Oct	.313	.404	.438	80	25	5	1	1	7	12	19		.256	.344	.424	262	67	16	2	8	34	36	59
Bases Empty	.258	.327	.440	252	65	19	0	9	9	25	63		.272	.345	.464	617	168	37	0	27	27	67	148
Leadoff	.308	.345	.533	107	33	12	0	4	4	5	23		.312	.365	.530	253	79	19	0	12	12	19	50
Runners On Base	.256	.353	.427	211	54	7	1	9	56	33	58		.235	.319	.396	493	116	19	3	18	125	63	108
Scoring Position	.226	.359	.365	115	26	4	0	4	43	26	34		.211	.315	.364	280	59	11	1	10	102	46	65
Late and Close	.306	.354	.431	72	22	3	0	1	12	6	22		.293	.359	.495	198	58	11	1	9	37	22	50

SAMMY SOSA — BR/TR — age 26 — CHN OF158

1993	BA	OBA	SA	AB	H	2B	3B	HR	RBI	BB	SO		5-YEAR TOTALS (1989–1993) BA	OBA	SA	AB	H	2B	3B	HR	RBI	BB	SO
Total	.261	.309	.485	598	156	25	5	33	93	38	135		.243	.291	.413	1891	459	76	18	70	234	115	493
vs. Left	.287	.344	.567	150	43	8	2	10	33	13	33		.273	.328	.471	664	181	35	5	29	95	56	169
vs. Right	.252	.297	.458	448	113	17	3	23	60	25	102		.227	.270	.381	1227	278	41	13	41	139	59	324
at Home	.272	.323	.557	298	81	14	1	23	57	21	61		.253	.309	.461	892	226	42	10	41	118	66	229
on Road	.250	.295	.413	300	75	11	4	10	36	17	74		.233	.274	.370	999	233	34	8	29	116	49	264
on Grass	.282	.336	.533	458	129	21	2	30	80	34	102		.244	.297	.421	1514	370	63	14	59	186	101	397
on Turf	.193	.215	.329	140	27	4	3	3	13	4	33		.236	.267	.379	377	89	13	4	11	48	14	96
Day Games	.246	.300	.495	321	79	8	3	22	52	23	77		.226	.280	.415	709	160	26	6	32	90	45	190
Night Games	.278	.320	.473	277	77	17	2	11	41	15	58		.253	.298	.412	1182	299	50	12	38	144	70	303
April	.229	.256	.446	83	19	4	1	4	11	3	19		.237	.287	.401	274	65	10	4	9	29	18	70
May	.284	.327	.495	95	27	5	0	5	15	6	21		.247	.288	.384	393	97	13	1	9	39	21	109
June	.277	.330	.545	101	28	2	2	7	20	7	21		.255	.295	.464	364	93	12	8	16	50	17	89
July	.252	.277	.430	107	27	5	1	4	13	4	17		.226	.252	.398	279	63	18	3	8	35	10	65
August	.270	.341	.559	111	30	5	0	9	18	10	28		.255	.324	.442	278	71	10	0	14	40	25	71
Sept-Oct	.248	.309	.426	101	25	4	1	4	16	8	29		.231	.297	.386	303	70	13	2	10	41	24	89
Bases Empty	.269	.307	.486	331	89	12	3	18	18	15	72		.240	.285	.396	1105	265	41	9	38	38	60	287
Leadoff	.277	.305	.500	148	41	7	1	8	8	5	28		.233	.279	.386	523	122	19	5	17	17	27	129
Runners On Base	.251	.312	.483	267	67	13	2	15	75	23	63		.247	.298	.436	786	194	35	9	32	196	55	206
Scoring Position	.213	.286	.341	164	35	7	1	4	50	16	39		.228	.287	.391	470	107	22	5	15	154	39	125
Late and Close	.214	.264	.282	103	22	1	0	2	8	7	29		.218	.275	.314	331	72	10	2	6	21	24	88

BILL SPIERS — BL/TR — age 28 — MIL 2B104, OF7, SS4

1993	BA	OBA	SA	AB	H	2B	3B	HR	RBI	BB	SO
Total	.238	.302	.303	340	81	8	4	2	36	29	51
vs. Left	.176	.273	.235	68	12	2	1	0	4	7	17
vs. Right	.254	.310	.320	272	69	6	3	2	32	22	34
at Home	.277	.344	.367	166	46	5	2	2	25	18	23
on Road	.201	.262	.241	174	35	3	2	0	11	11	28
on Grass	.257	.325	.318	280	72	7	2	2	30	26	42
on Turf	.150	.197	.233	60	9	1	2	0	6	3	9
Day Games	.233	.324	.289	90	21	1	2	0	6	12	13
Night Games	.240	.295	.308	250	60	7	2	2	30	17	38
April	.245	.315	.286	49	12	0	1	0	4	5	8
May	.244	.312	.293	82	20	2	1	0	8	7	15
June	.198	.275	.247	81	16	2	1	0	8	9	10
July	.263	.300	.386	57	15	2	1	1	10	2	8
August	.349	.370	.465	43	15	2	0	1	3	2	6
Sept-Oct	.107	.242	.107	28	3	0	0	0	3	4	4
Bases Empty	.244	.295	.316	193	47	4	2	2	2	11	35
Leadoff	.284	.342	.403	67	19	0	1	2	2	4	11
Runners On Base	.231	.312	.286	147	34	4	2	0	34	18	16
Scoring Position	.245	.306	.287	94	23	2	1	0	33	10	13
Late and Close	.250	.311	.304	56	14	1	1	0	6	4	7

5-YEAR TOTALS (1989–1993)

	BA	OBA	SA	AB	H	2B	3B	HR	RBI	BB	SO
	.256	.305	.342	1478	379	47	16	16	161	101	218
	.224	.285	.292	339	76	8	3	3	33	26	66
	.266	.311	.357	1139	303	39	13	13	128	75	152
	.283	.333	.369	707	200	27	8	6	89	55	106
	.232	.279	.318	771	179	20	8	10	72	46	112
	.269	.317	.357	1256	338	41	14	14	142	86	188
	.185	.236	.257	222	41	6	2	2	19	15	30
	.255	.306	.349	467	119	19	5	5	46	35	75
	.257	.304	.339	1011	260	28	11	11	115	66	143
	.242	.313	.356	132	32	1	1	4	19	14	21
	.225	.288	.278	227	51	10	1	0	17	18	41
	.247	.310	.324	259	64	11	3	1	23	23	35
	.265	.289	.350	257	68	6	2	4	34	10	41
	.268	.319	.341	287	77	9	3	2	35	22	36
	.275	.309	.392	316	87	10	6	5	33	14	44
	.251	.294	.325	873	219	24	7	9	9	48	132
	.226	.264	.302	371	84	13	3	3	3	16	50
	.264	.319	.367	605	160	23	9	7	152	53	86
	.276	.326	.397	373	103	16	7	5	146	34	58
	.281	.331	.349	249	70	6	4	1	30	18	38

ED SPRAGUE — BR/TR — age 27 — TOR 3B150

1993	BA	OBA	SA	AB	H	2B	3B	HR	RBI	BB	SO
Total	.260	.310	.386	546	142	31	1	12	73	32	85
vs. Left	.247	.304	.363	146	36	11	0	2	11	12	20
vs. Right	.265	.312	.395	400	106	20	1	10	62	20	65
at Home	.291	.328	.463	268	78	20	1	8	46	14	41
on Road	.230	.293	.313	278	64	11	0	4	27	18	44
on Grass	.242	.309	.336	211	51	8	0	4	20	16	27
on Turf	.272	.310	.418	335	91	23	1	8	53	16	58
Day Games	.310	.343	.529	187	58	14	0	9	44	9	23
Night Games	.234	.293	.312	359	84	17	1	3	29	23	62
April	.244	.264	.390	82	20	6	0	2	17	3	17
May	.282	.340	.459	85	24	3	0	4	13	6	14
June	.260	.319	.404	104	27	6	0	3	14	4	21
July	.250	.286	.350	100	25	5	1	1	5	5	18
August	.250	.291	.333	96	24	5	0	1	14	6	7
Sept-Oct	.278	.360	.392	79	22	6	0	1	10	8	8
Bases Empty	.279	.321	.446	276	77	17	1	9	9	15	41
Leadoff	.280	.313	.480	125	35	7	0	6	6	5	18
Runners On Base	.241	.299	.326	270	65	14	0	3	64	17	44
Scoring Position	.225	.294	.308	169	38	11	0	1	60	14	31
Late and Close	.257	.303	.300	70	18	1	1	0	9	2	18

3-YEAR TOTALS (1991–1993)

	BA	OBA	SA	AB	H	2B	3B	HR	RBI	BB	SO
	.262	.319	.385	753	197	40	1	17	100	54	135
	.260	.326	.382	246	64	15	0	5	25	23	44
	.262	.316	.387	507	133	25	1	12	75	31	91
	.282	.322	.444	369	104	22	1	12	60	19	62
	.242	.317	.328	384	93	18	0	5	40	35	73
	.258	.337	.358	302	78	15	0	5	32	31	51
	.264	.307	.404	451	119	25	1	12	68	23	84
	.293	.337	.484	246	72	17	0	10	53	16	44
	.247	.311	.337	507	125	23	1	7	47	38	91
	.244	.264	.390	82	20	6	0	2	17	3	17
	.321	.396	.489	131	42	7	0	5	22	13	24
	.247	.297	.361	166	41	7	0	4	20	6	40
	.244	.284	.362	127	31	7	1	2	7	7	22
	.267	.315	.356	135	36	6	0	2	19	10	17
	.241	.341	.357	112	27	7	0	2	15	15	15
	.269	.323	.405	398	107	22	1	10	10	29	71
	.254	.305	.429	177	45	10	0	7	7	11	30
	.254	.315	.363	355	90	18	0	7	90	25	64
	.240	.311	.330	221	53	14	0	2	79	20	42
	.250	.327	.326	92	23	2	1	1	14	8	23

MIKE STANLEY — BR/TR — age 31 — NYA C122, DH2

1993	BA	OBA	SA	AB	H	2B	3B	HR	RBI	BB	SO
Total	.305	.389	.534	423	129	17	1	26	84	57	85
vs. Left	.307	.415	.596	166	51	6	0	14	38	30	27
vs. Right	.304	.371	.494	257	78	11	1	12	46	27	58
at Home	.312	.408	.608	199	62	8	0	17	56	30	34
on Road	.299	.372	.469	224	67	9	1	9	28	27	51
on Grass	.300	.391	.518	363	109	14	1	21	70	52	70
on Turf	.333	.379	.633	60	20	3	0	5	14	5	15
Day Games	.357	.468	.603	126	45	4	0	9	30	25	21
Night Games	.283	.352	.505	297	84	13	1	17	54	32	64
April	.250	.333	.344	32	8	0	0	1	5	4	4
May	.382	.456	.605	76	29	8	0	3	12	12	19
June	.271	.347	.506	85	23	2	0	6	18	10	19
July	.378	.452	.756	82	31	2	1	9	27	8	13
August	.194	.289	.333	72	14	1	0	4	9	9	14
Sept-Oct	.316	.415	.526	76	24	4	0	4	13	14	16
Bases Empty	.295	.375	.488	244	72	8	0	13	13	28	49
Leadoff	.315	.373	.509	108	34	3	0	6	6	9	25
Runners On Base	.318	.407	.598	179	57	9	1	13	71	29	36
Scoring Position	.308	.431	.596	104	32	6	0	8	60	25	22
Late and Close	.369	.432	.508	65	24	3	0	2	10	7	12

8-YEAR TOTALS (1986–1993)

	BA	OBA	SA	AB	H	2B	3B	HR	RBI	BB	SO
	.265	.361	.409	1583	420	67	5	50	231	237	345
	.275	.378	.436	825	227	37	3	30	117	137	164
	.255	.343	.379	758	193	30	2	20	114	100	181
	.288	.382	.450	791	228	37	2	29	148	117	157
	.242	.341	.367	792	192	30	3	21	83	120	188
	.267	.363	.409	1319	352	54	4	42	201	196	280
	.258	.356	.405	264	68	13	1	8	30	41	65
	.270	.395	.454	366	99	9	2	18	65	74	85
	.264	.351	.395	1217	321	58	3	32	166	163	260
	.227	.348	.288	132	30	2	0	2	15	24	28
	.258	.354	.431	248	64	14	1	9	35	39	56
	.246	.325	.350	354	87	10	0	9	45	42	83
	.321	.397	.555	274	88	15	2	15	61	31	51
	.261	.361	.375	253	66	12	1	5	30	41	57
	.264	.382	.407	322	85	14	1	10	45	60	70
	.257	.350	.388	891	229	31	1	28	28	120	192
	.264	.350	.406	382	101	12	0	14	14	46	82
	.276	.376	.435	692	191	36	4	22	203	117	153
	.268	.387	.420	395	106	19	1	13	176	84	88
	.273	.372	.412	238	65	10	1	7	40	38	56

TERRY STEINBACH — BR/TR — age 32 — OAK C86, 1B15, DH6

1993	BA	OBA	SA	AB	H	2B	3B	HR	RBI	BB	SO	8-YEAR TOTALS (1986–1993) BA	OBA	SA	AB	H	2B	3B	HR	RBI	BB	SO
Total	.285	.333	.416	389	111	19	1	10	43	25	65	.274	.327	.401	2872	786	133	10	71	373	207	437
vs. Left	.296	.350	.500	108	32	4	0	6	13	9	19	.291	.343	.447	881	256	43	4	29	116	68	115
vs. Right	.281	.326	.384	281	79	15	1	4	30	16	46	.266	.319	.381	1991	530	90	6	42	257	139	322
at Home	.326	.377	.489	184	60	13	1	5	26	13	31	.270	.325	.382	1368	370	59	3	29	175	105	188
on Road	.249	.292	.351	205	51	6	0	5	17	12	34	.277	.328	.419	1504	416	74	7	42	198	102	249
on Grass	.280	.328	.414	321	90	14	1	9	37	20	52	.273	.328	.400	2395	655	105	6	62	315	181	347
on Turf	.309	.351	.426	68	21	5	0	1	6	5	13	.275	.322	.407	477	131	28	4	9	58	26	90
Day Games	.241	.296	.367	166	40	7	1	4	22	11	28	.277	.323	.403	1074	297	55	3	25	150	69	164
Night Games	.318	.360	.453	223	71	12	0	6	21	14	37	.272	.329	.400	1798	489	78	7	46	223	138	273
April	.300	.338	.457	70	21	5	0	2	8	4	5	.261	.327	.389	383	100	23	1	8	48	34	62
May	.315	.371	.438	89	28	5	0	2	11	7	11	.292	.343	.428	463	135	20	2	13	57	33	65
June	.271	.317	.385	96	26	6	1	1	8	7	25	.277	.326	.413	537	149	23	4	14	61	36	88
July	.279	.311	.384	86	24	0	0	3	12	4	15	.305	.339	.451	501	153	30	2	13	78	25	71
August	.250	.321	.438	48	12	3	0	2	4	3	9	.247	.307	.349	518	128	23	0	10	62	39	79
Sept-Oct	.000	.000	.000	0	0	0	0	0	0	0	0	.257	.321	.374	470	121	14	1	13	67	40	72
Bases Empty	.306	.336	.425	219	67	11	0	5	5	9	36	.269	.323	.394	1580	425	67	5	40	40	111	243
Leadoff	.299	.320	.423	97	29	6	0	2	2	3	15	.261	.319	.373	617	161	28	1	13	13	47	92
Runners On Base	.259	.328	.406	170	44	8	1	5	38	16	29	.279	.331	.410	1292	361	66	5	31	333	96	194
Scoring Position	.196	.288	.351	97	19	4	1	3	33	12	19	.273	.337	.407	703	192	34	3	18	295	71	109
Late and Close	.209	.284	.299	67	14	3	0	1	8	6	11	.234	.298	.306	461	108	12	0	7	57	37	78

KEVIN STOCKER — BB/TR — age 24 — PHI SS70

1993	BA	OBA	SA	AB	H	2B	3B	HR	RBI	BB	SO	1-YEAR TOTALS (1993) BA	OBA	SA	AB	H	2B	3B	HR	RBI	BB	SO
Total	.324	.409	.417	259	84	12	3	2	31	30	43	.324	.409	.417	259	84	12	3	2	31	30	43
vs. Left	.395	.479	.457	81	32	5	0	0	7	13	9	.395	.479	.457	81	32	5	0	0	7	13	9
vs. Right	.292	.377	.399	178	52	7	3	2	24	17	34	.292	.377	.399	178	52	7	3	2	24	17	34
at Home	.302	.395	.373	126	38	4	1	1	10	15	24	.302	.395	.373	126	38	4	1	1	10	15	24
on Road	.346	.424	.459	133	46	8	2	1	21	15	19	.346	.424	.459	133	46	8	2	1	21	15	19
on Grass	.342	.432	.474	76	26	5	1	1	13	11	12	.342	.432	.474	76	26	5	1	1	13	11	12
on Turf	.317	.400	.393	183	58	7	2	1	18	19	31	.317	.400	.393	183	58	7	2	1	18	19	31
Day Games	.384	.446	.425	73	28	3	0	0	4	9	12	.384	.446	.425	73	28	3	0	0	4	9	12
Night Games	.301	.395	.414	186	56	9	3	2	27	21	31	.301	.395	.414	186	56	9	3	2	27	21	31
April	.000	.000	.000	0	0	0	0	0	0	0	0	.000	.000	.000	0	0	0	0	0	0	0	0
May	.000	.000	.000	0	0	0	0	0	0	0	0	.000	.000	.000	0	0	0	0	0	0	0	0
June	.000	.000	.000	0	0	0	0	0	0	0	0	.000	.000	.000	0	0	0	0	0	0	0	0
July	.385	.467	.519	52	20	2	1	1	6	8	10	.385	.467	.519	52	20	2	1	1	6	8	10
August	.324	.393	.438	105	34	5	2	1	16	8	16	.324	.393	.438	105	34	5	2	1	16	8	16
Sept-Oct	.294	.397	.343	102	30	5	0	0	9	14	17	.294	.397	.343	102	30	5	0	0	9	14	17
Bases Empty	.376	.432	.474	133	50	8	1	1	1	11	23	.376	.432	.474	133	50	8	1	1	1	11	23
Leadoff	.397	.478	.466	58	23	4	0	0	0	8	9	.397	.478	.466	58	23	4	0	0	0	8	9
Runners On Base	.270	.388	.357	126	34	4	2	1	30	19	20	.270	.388	.357	126	34	4	2	1	30	19	20
Scoring Position	.229	.402	.329	70	16	2	1	1	28	16	13	.229	.402	.329	70	16	2	1	1	28	16	13
Late and Close	.292	.358	.375	48	14	2	1	0	8	3	5	.292	.358	.375	48	14	2	1	0	8	3	5

DOUG STRANGE — BB/TR — age 30 — TEX 2B135, 3B9, SS1

1993	BA	OBA	SA	AB	H	2B	3B	HR	RBI	BB	SO	4-YEAR TOTALS (1989–1993) BA	OBA	SA	AB	H	2B	3B	HR	RBI	BB	SO
Total	.256	.318	.360	484	124	29	0	7	60	43	69	.236	.301	.318	783	185	35	1	9	80	70	121
vs. Left	.248	.282	.303	109	27	6	0	0	13	6	19	.229	.275	.269	175	40	7	0	0	14	12	29
vs. Right	.259	.329	.376	375	97	23	0	7	47	37	50	.238	.309	.332	608	145	28	1	9	66	58	92
at Home	.296	.358	.420	257	76	20	0	4	37	23	34	.258	.329	.353	414	107	24	0	5	50	40	60
on Road	.211	.273	.291	227	48	9	0	3	23	20	35	.211	.269	.279	369	78	11	1	4	30	30	61
on Grass	.279	.344	.386	402	112	25	0	6	54	39	58	.247	.317	.332	647	160	29	1	8	72	63	101
on Turf	.146	.186	.232	82	12	4	0	1	6	4	11	.184	.224	.250	136	25	6	0	1	8	7	20
Day Games	.182	.252	.223	121	22	5	0	0	12	11	18	.180	.258	.224	228	41	7	0	1	19	23	40
Night Games	.281	.341	.405	363	102	24	0	7	48	32	51	.259	.320	.357	555	144	28	1	8	61	47	81
April	.280	.296	.480	25	7	2	0	1	4	0	6	.286	.323	.464	28	8	2	0	1	4	1	6
May	.278	.329	.392	79	22	6	0	1	11	5	6	.231	.290	.322	143	33	7	0	2	16	11	15
June	.281	.327	.375	96	27	3	0	2	11	7	14	.277	.333	.366	101	28	3	0	2	11	9	14
July	.198	.282	.231	91	18	3	0	0	9	10	11	.196	.253	.225	138	27	4	0	0	11	10	20
August	.215	.280	.336	107	23	7	0	2	12	10	21	.212	.270	.299	184	39	8	1	2	17	15	35
Sept-Oct	.314	.392	.442	86	27	8	0	1	13	11	11	.265	.352	.354	189	50	11	0	2	21	24	31
Bases Empty	.272	.334	.358	265	72	14	0	3	3	23	40	.244	.306	.321	442	108	19	0	5	5	36	75
Leadoff	.321	.372	.438	112	36	7	0	2	2	9	19	.291	.349	.391	179	52	9	0	3	3	16	30
Runners On Base	.237	.299	.361	219	52	15	0	4	57	20	29	.226	.296	.314	341	77	16	1	4	75	34	46
Scoring Position	.270	.347	.429	126	34	11	0	3	52	16	18	.262	.342	.382	191	50	12	1	3	70	24	28
Late and Close	.329	.400	.471	70	23	4	0	2	10	9	7	.252	.322	.341	135	34	4	1	2	14	14	16

B.J. SURHOFF — BL/TR — age 30 — MIL 3B121, OF24, 1B8, C3, DH1

1993	BA	OBA	SA	AB	H	2B	3B	HR	RBI	BB	SO		BA	OBA	SA	AB	H	2B	3B	HR	RBI	BB	SO
Total	.274	.318	.391	552	151	38	3	7	79	36	47		.269	.315	.362	3336	897	157	19	39	431	240	266
vs. Left	.274	.328	.403	186	51	13	1	3	33	14	15		.273	.321	.374	802	219	34	4	13	121	56	78
vs. Right	.273	.312	.385	366	100	25	2	4	46	22	32		.268	.314	.359	2534	678	123	15	26	310	184	188
at Home	.289	.325	.422	263	76	19	2	4	40	15	25		.274	.327	.376	1628	446	74	10	24	223	133	130
on Road	.260	.311	.363	289	75	19	1	3	39	21	22		.264	.304	.350	1708	451	83	9	15	208	107	136
on Grass	.270	.319	.393	466	126	33	3	6	64	33	42		.271	.320	.368	2853	774	136	16	36	366	213	223
on Turf	.291	.311	.384	86	25	5	0	1	15	3	5		.255	.288	.329	483	123	21	3	3	65	27	43
Day Games	.277	.345	.380	184	51	14	1	1	25	20	15		.261	.317	.342	1046	273	45	5	10	131	89	94
Night Games	.272	.303	.397	368	100	24	2	6	54	16	32		.272	.315	.372	2290	624	112	14	29	300	151	172
April	.203	.288	.254	59	12	3	0	0	7	7	9		.199	.254	.285	397	79	11	1	7	52	32	46
May	.162	.221	.200	80	13	3	0	0	7	6	8		.244	.287	.315	504	123	19	1	5	57	33	41
June	.275	.312	.333	102	28	4	1	0	11	4	8		.288	.324	.386	619	178	32	4	7	73	33	46
July	.347	.365	.535	101	35	9	2	2	14	3	10		.285	.319	.377	576	164	28	5	5	68	31	38
August	.290	.353	.439	107	31	7	0	3	22	11	6		.280	.341	.371	596	167	30	3	6	79	56	51
Sept-Oct	.311	.333	.485	103	32	12	0	2	18	5	6		.289	.339	.404	644	186	37	5	9	102	55	44
Bases Empty	.267	.305	.392	329	88	21	1	6	6	16	24		.251	.298	.344	1900	477	87	6	26	26	122	158
Leadoff	.281	.326	.438	121	34	7	0	4	4	6	10		.248	.287	.345	715	177	32	1	12	12	38	51
Runners On Base	.283	.335	.390	223	63	17	2	1	73	20	23		.292	.338	.386	1436	420	70	13	13	405	118	108
Scoring Position	.338	.389	.492	130	44	13	2	1	71	14	16		.299	.349	.418	840	251	44	10	12	384	87	72
Late and Close	.253	.300	.297	91	23	4	0	0	10	7	9		.256	.308	.336	559	143	22	1	7	79	46	60

7-YEAR TOTALS (1987–1993)

DANNY TARTABULL — BR/TR — age 32 — NYA DH88, OF50

1993	BA	OBA	SA	AB	H	2B	3B	HR	RBI	BB	SO		BA	OBA	SA	AB	H	2B	3B	HR	RBI	BB	SO
Total	.250	.363	.503	513	128	33	2	31	102	92	156		.280	.375	.510	3853	1078	226	18	208	722	591	1037
vs. Left	.200	.341	.394	175	35	11	1	7	23	38	50		.284	.407	.513	1118	318	72	5	58	191	235	278
vs. Right	.275	.375	.559	338	93	22	1	24	79	54	106		.278	.361	.508	2735	760	154	13	150	531	356	759
at Home	.210	.343	.410	229	48	13	0	11	42	47	70		.275	.375	.493	1844	508	101	11	93	324	297	474
on Road	.282	.381	.577	284	80	20	2	20	60	45	86		.284	.375	.525	2009	570	125	7	115	398	294	563
on Grass	.230	.337	.485	439	101	26	1	28	89	71	137		.274	.374	.510	1940	532	115	5	111	395	311	560
on Turf	.365	.505	.608	74	27	7	1	3	13	21	19		.285	.376	.509	1913	546	111	13	97	327	280	477
Day Games	.225	.345	.473	182	41	13	1	10	38	35	58		.264	.361	.485	1059	280	61	4	55	201	162	305
Night Games	.263	.373	.520	331	87	20	1	21	64	57	98		.286	.380	.519	2794	798	165	14	153	521	429	732
April	.247	.378	.493	73	18	4	1	4	13	16	22		.285	.375	.464	491	140	33	2	17	84	72	136
May	.183	.303	.378	82	15	7	0	3	13	15	32		.249	.344	.459	606	151	26	4	31	97	87	171
June	.260	.339	.560	50	13	3	0	4	11	6	15		.299	.386	.527	603	180	31	1	35	108	88	149
July	.340	.430	.701	97	33	5	0	10	27	16	22		.276	.363	.536	617	170	35	3	40	130	85	167
August	.229	.336	.514	105	24	9	0	7	20	17	29		.275	.376	.529	726	200	48	2	44	146	120	206
Sept-Oct	.236	.377	.387	106	25	5	1	3	18	22	36		.293	.398	.525	810	237	53	6	41	157	139	208
Bases Empty	.226	.328	.521	257	58	15	2	19	19	38	74		.266	.358	.492	2005	534	111	10	107	107	281	550
Leadoff	.230	.297	.556	126	29	8	0	11	11	12	36		.264	.343	.493	942	249	59	6	48	48	111	248
Runners On Base	.273	.397	.484	256	70	18	0	12	83	54	82		.294	.393	.529	1848	544	115	8	101	615	310	487
Scoring Position	.286	.429	.514	140	40	8	0	8	73	38	46		.289	.404	.527	1082	313	69	7	58	510	223	305
Late and Close	.348	.483	.609	69	24	9	0	3	13	18	14		.298	.387	.520	615	183	45	4	28	115	90	161

10-YEAR TOTALS (1984–1993)

EDDIE TAUBENSEE — BL/TR — age 26 — HOU C90

1993	BA	OBA	SA	AB	H	2B	3B	HR	RBI	BB	SO		BA	OBA	SA	AB	H	2B	3B	HR	RBI	BB	SO
Total	.250	.299	.389	288	72	11	1	9	42	21	44		.237	.298	.350	651	154	28	2	14	78	57	138
vs. Left	.200	.216	.280	50	10	1	0	1	6	1	9		.234	.293	.355	107	25	4	0	3	11	8	23
vs. Right	.261	.315	.412	238	62	10	1	8	36	20	35		.237	.299	.349	544	129	24	2	11	67	49	115
at Home	.243	.297	.397	136	33	7	1	4	17	11	19		.237	.304	.354	333	79	19	1	6	36	32	67
on Road	.257	.301	.382	152	39	4	0	5	25	10	25		.236	.292	.346	318	75	9	1	8	42	25	71
on Grass	.245	.290	.372	94	23	3	0	3	14	6	12		.225	.280	.321	249	56	7	1	5	32	19	55
on Turf	.253	.303	.397	194	49	8	1	6	28	15	32		.244	.309	.368	402	98	21	1	9	46	38	83
Day Games	.224	.295	.435	85	19	3	0	5	12	9	14		.217	.289	.383	180	39	9	0	7	25	25	40
Night Games	.261	.301	.369	203	53	8	1	4	30	12	30		.244	.302	.338	471	115	19	2	7	53	38	98
April	.200	.237	.382	55	11	2	1	2	10	3	7		.206	.268	.324	102	21	4	1	2	12	9	24
May	.245	.351	.327	49	12	1	0	1	4	8	9		.176	.272	.235	119	21	4	0	1	8	16	23
June	.385	.429	.385	13	5	0	0	0	6	1	1		.179	.256	.205	39	7	1	0	0	10	4	12
July	.353	.389	.676	34	12	2	0	3	7	2	5		.382	.408	.632	68	26	5	0	4	11	3	10
August	.217	.257	.377	69	15	2	0	3	7	4	13		.211	.266	.401	142	30	6	0	7	17	9	35
Sept-Oct	.250	.282	.309	68	17	4	0	0	8	3	9		.271	.327	.326	181	49	8	1	0	20	16	34
Bases Empty	.276	.314	.400	145	40	6	0	4	4	8	24		.245	.293	.352	355	87	15	1	7	7	24	86
Leadoff	.361	.391	.541	61	22	5	0	3	3	3	4		.310	.359	.451	142	44	6	1	4	4	11	24
Runners On Base	.224	.285	.378	143	32	5	1	5	38	13	20		.226	.304	.348	296	67	13	1	7	71	33	52
Scoring Position	.216	.297	.295	88	19	2	1	1	27	11	14		.216	.316	.273	176	38	5	1	1	53	27	38
Late and Close	.234	.265	.362	47	11	3	0	1	3	2	8		.205	.258	.295	112	23	4	0	2	11	8	26

3-YEAR TOTALS (1991–1993)

MICKEY TETTLETON — BB/TR — age 34 — DET 1B59, C56, OF55, DH4

1993	BA	OBA	SA	AB	H	2B	3B	HR	RBI	BB	SO
Total	.245	.372	.492	522	128	25	4	32	110	109	139
vs. Left	.260	.408	.520	123	32	9	1	7	28	32	28
vs. Right	.241	.360	.484	399	96	16	3	25	82	77	111
at Home	.230	.360	.480	256	59	14	1	16	52	54	68
on Road	.259	.384	.504	266	69	11	3	16	58	55	71
on Grass	.252	.374	.501	445	112	22	4	27	93	89	114
on Turf	.208	.364	.442	77	16	3	0	5	17	20	25
Day Games	.255	.373	.489	188	48	12	1	10	39	36	48
Night Games	.240	.371	.494	334	80	13	3	22	71	73	91
April	.185	.375	.462	65	12	3	0	5	19	21	17
May	.258	.337	.484	93	24	5	2	4	19	11	27
June	.271	.343	.635	96	26	2	0	11	25	11	22
July	.218	.341	.465	101	22	7	0	6	15	20	30
August	.253	.395	.440	91	23	3	1	4	21	22	22
Sept-Oct	.276	.450	.447	76	21	5	1	2	11	24	21
Bases Empty	.211	.329	.432	294	62	14	0	17	17	52	85
Leadoff	.248	.349	.544	149	37	8	0	12	12	23	36
Runners On Base	.289	.423	.570	228	66	11	4	15	93	57	54
Scoring Position	.311	.470	.568	132	41	4	3	8	77	45	31
Late and Close	.320	.422	.547	75	24	0	1	5	19	14	17

10-YEAR TOTALS (1984–1993)

	BA	OBA	SA	AB	H	2B	3B	HR	RBI	BB	SO
	.242	.363	.441	3395	821	146	12	169	516	647	950
	.246	.350	.467	1044	257	55	1	58	166	171	286
	.240	.368	.430	2351	564	91	11	111	350	476	664
	.256	.378	.473	1669	427	75	9	90	264	333	465
	.228	.348	.410	1726	394	71	3	79	252	314	485
	.248	.368	.459	2839	704	123	12	151	453	544	792
	.210	.335	.349	556	117	23	0	18	63	103	158
	.255	.360	.441	1101	281	49	4	49	156	199	322
	.235	.360	.442	2294	540	97	8	120	360	448	628
	.193	.326	.383	394	76	18	0	19	66	80	119
	.255	.350	.464	541	138	20	3	29	93	79	137
	.270	.383	.531	637	172	29	4	43	119	118	170
	.242	.361	.417	657	159	29	1	28	80	124	198
	.227	.366	.398	538	122	19	2	23	78	119	138
	.245	.374	.430	628	154	31	2	27	80	127	188
	.243	.344	.450	1924	468	87	8	98	98	287	535
	.253	.347	.477	853	216	42	4	47	47	118	215
	.240	.385	.430	1471	353	59	4	71	418	360	415
	.224	.397	.424	838	188	32	3	43	353	255	251
	.242	.344	.426	549	133	12	1	29	81	84	160

TIM TEUFEL — BR/TR — age 36 — SD 2B52, 3B9, 1B8

1993	BA	OBA	SA	AB	H	2B	3B	HR	RBI	BB	SO
Total	.250	.338	.430	200	50	11	2	7	31	27	39
vs. Left	.286	.381	.519	133	38	9	2	6	23	21	22
vs. Right	.179	.247	.254	67	12	2	0	1	8	6	17
at Home	.273	.360	.495	99	27	5	1	5	17	14	20
on Road	.228	.316	.366	101	23	6	1	2	14	13	19
on Grass	.281	.369	.473	146	41	8	1	6	26	21	26
on Turf	.167	.250	.315	54	9	3	1	1	5	6	13
Day Games	.271	.323	.593	59	16	2	1	5	11	5	16
Night Games	.241	.344	.362	141	34	9	1	2	20	22	23
April	.359	.432	.795	39	14	3	1	4	10	5	8
May	.167	.286	.200	30	5	1	0	0	4	5	7
June	.167	.257	.267	30	5	0	0	1	4	4	4
July	.275	.383	.350	40	11	3	0	0	6	7	8
August	.280	.345	.500	50	14	3	1	2	6	5	8
Sept-Oct	.091	.167	.182	11	1	1	0	0	1	1	4
Bases Empty	.187	.275	.336	107	20	5	1	3	3	13	23
Leadoff	.108	.214	.216	37	4	1	0	1	1	5	10
Runners On Base	.323	.407	.538	93	30	6	1	4	28	14	16
Scoring Position	.310	.423	.357	42	13	2	0	0	15	9	9
Late and Close	.233	.343	.367	30	7	1	0	1	6	5	10

10-YEAR TOTALS (1984–1993)

	BA	OBA	SA	AB	H	2B	3B	HR	RBI	BB	SO
	.252	.336	.400	3034	765	178	11	83	373	385	523
	.265	.354	.427	1451	385	96	5	43	183	202	203
	.240	.320	.375	1583	380	82	6	40	190	183	320
	.251	.333	.396	1454	365	81	5	40	188	181	239
	.253	.339	.404	1580	400	97	6	43	185	204	284
	.246	.335	.374	1773	436	98	3	41	203	240	318
	.261	.339	.437	1261	329	80	8	42	170	145	205
	.263	.335	.443	999	263	66	3	36	149	109	175
	.247	.337	.379	2035	502	112	8	47	224	276	348
	.256	.350	.377	422	108	23	2	8	58	59	59
	.263	.352	.392	487	128	20	2	13	62	68	97
	.270	.345	.413	477	129	33	1	11	67	54	68
	.251	.338	.369	499	125	27	1	10	50	67	84
	.264	.351	.449	535	141	32	2	21	67	75	95
	.218	.292	.396	614	134	43	3	20	69	62	120
	.244	.330	.390	1688	412	95	7	46	46	206	302
	.264	.333	.440	613	162	34	1	24	24	60	89
	.262	.344	.412	1346	353	83	4	37	327	179	221
	.242	.344	.386	772	187	46	1	21	273	133	145
	.236	.341	.360	542	128	25	0	14	67	87	96

FRANK THOMAS — BR/TR — age 26 — CHA 1B150, DH4

1993	BA	OBA	SA	AB	H	2B	3B	HR	RBI	BB	SO
Total	.317	.426	.607	549	174	36	0	41	128	112	54
vs. Left	.311	.419	.649	151	47	9	0	14	38	33	14
vs. Right	.319	.429	.590	398	127	27	0	27	90	79	40
at Home	.326	.432	.681	279	91	21	0	26	66	54	24
on Road	.307	.420	.530	270	83	15	0	15	62	58	30
on Grass	.318	.423	.609	466	148	31	0	35	108	90	44
on Turf	.313	.444	.590	83	26	5	0	6	20	22	10
Day Games	.285	.397	.521	165	47	12	0	9	34	32	22
Night Games	.331	.438	.643	384	127	24	0	32	94	80	32
April	.269	.362	.474	78	21	7	0	3	21	12	12
May	.290	.393	.527	93	27	5	0	5	16	17	14
June	.350	.456	.631	103	36	5	0	8	23	21	8
July	.345	.496	.770	87	30	4	0	11	25	27	5
August	.333	.413	.696	102	34	7	0	10	26	16	8
Sept-Oct	.302	.422	.512	86	26	6	0	4	17	19	7
Bases Empty	.321	.406	.573	293	94	17	0	19	19	42	25
Leadoff	.345	.390	.582	110	38	5	0	7	7	8	11
Runners On Base	.313	.446	.645	256	80	19	0	22	109	70	29
Scoring Position	.297	.436	.614	158	47	8	0	14	91	48	17
Late and Close	.304	.456	.580	69	21	4	0	5	20	19	5

4-YEAR TOTALS (1990–1993)

	BA	OBA	SA	AB	H	2B	3B	HR	RBI	BB	SO
	.321	.441	.561	1872	600	124	7	104	383	416	308
	.357	.471	.652	532	190	39	2	38	111	124	78
	.306	.429	.525	1340	410	85	5	66	272	292	230
	.334	.461	.619	911	304	64	5	62	194	220	153
	.308	.421	.506	961	296	60	2	42	189	196	155
	.328	.450	.579	1560	512	105	7	91	331	354	255
	.282	.395	.468	312	88	19	0	13	52	62	53
	.308	.428	.552	504	155	37	1	28	106	111	84
	.325	.445	.564	1368	445	87	6	76	277	305	224
	.265	.389	.456	204	54	14	2	7	41	42	40
	.316	.449	.560	275	87	19	0	16	62	70	50
	.313	.435	.539	310	97	17	1	17	64	67	50
	.340	.471	.639	285	97	16	0	23	58	72	32
	.346	.453	.629	399	138	27	4	26	88	81	54
	.318	.433	.509	399	127	31	0	15	70	84	82
	.314	.426	.558	979	307	61	2	58	58	188	156
	.322	.420	.590	354	114	27	1	22	22	58	59
	.328	.456	.564	893	293	63	5	46	325	228	152
	.320	.451	.543	532	170	32	3	27	274	148	94
	.303	.430	.517	300	91	18	2	14	72	66	58

JIM THOME — BL/TR — age 24 — CLE 3B47

1993	BA	OBA	SA	AB	H	2B	3B	HR	RBI	BB	SO
Total	.266	.385	.474	154	41	11	0	7	22	29	36
vs. Left	.302	.456	.558	43	13	5	0	2	11	11	4
vs. Right	.252	.356	.441	111	28	6	0	5	11	18	32
at Home	.247	.350	.494	81	20	5	0	5	15	12	15
on Road	.288	.424	.452	73	21	6	0	2	7	17	21
on Grass	.260	.379	.496	123	32	8	0	7	19	22	26
on Turf	.290	.410	.387	31	9	3	0	0	3	7	10
Day Games	.235	.385	.451	51	12	2	0	3	8	11	12
Night Games	.282	.386	.485	103	29	9	0	4	14	18	24
April	.000	.000	.000	0	0	0	0	0	0	0	0
May	.000	.000	.000	0	0	0	0	0	0	0	0
June	.000	.000	.000	0	0	0	0	0	0	0	0
July	.000	.000	.000	0	0	0	0	0	0	0	0
August	.300	.377	.517	60	18	7	0	2	7	7	13
Sept-Oct	.245	.390	.447	94	23	4	0	5	15	22	23
Bases Empty	.276	.411	.540	87	24	5	0	6	6	17	22
Leadoff	.237	.341	.316	38	9	0	0	1	1	6	14
Runners On Base	.254	.353	.388	67	17	6	0	1	16	12	14
Scoring Position	.243	.377	.324	37	9	3	0	0	14	11	10
Late and Close	.321	.394	.536	28	9	3	0	1	5	3	5

3-YEAR TOTALS (1991–1993)

	BA	OBA	SA	AB	H	2B	3B	HR	RBI	BB	SO
Total	.244	.330	.390	369	90	18	3	10	43	44	86
vs. Left	.221	.330	.364	77	17	5	0	2	11	11	17
vs. Right	.250	.330	.397	292	73	13	3	8	32	33	69
at Home	.237	.321	.391	215	51	9	3	6	25	23	44
on Road	.253	.343	.390	154	39	9	0	4	18	21	42
on Grass	.237	.322	.385	325	77	15	3	9	37	36	71
on Turf	.295	.389	.432	44	13	3	0	1	6	8	15
Day Games	.226	.341	.377	106	24	7	0	3	13	16	19
Night Games	.251	.326	.395	263	66	11	3	7	30	28	67
April	.000	.000	.000	0	0	0	0	0	0	0	0
May	.125	.125	.125	8	1	0	0	0	0	0	4
June	.231	.286	.538	13	3	1	0	1	3	1	2
July	.228	.318	.333	57	13	1	1	1	4	7	20
August	.253	.321	.394	99	25	8	0	2	12	9	21
Sept-Oct	.250	.348	.406	192	48	8	2	6	24	27	39
Bases Empty	.249	.345	.424	205	51	10	1	8	8	25	45
Leadoff	.247	.304	.329	85	21	2	1	1	1	7	21
Runners On Base	.238	.313	.348	164	39	8	2	2	35	19	41
Scoring Position	.216	.327	.318	88	19	5	2	0	31	17	27
Late and Close	.192	.241	.370	73	14	5	1	2	9	4	20

ROBBY THOMPSON — BR/TR — age 32 — SF2B128

1993	BA	OBA	SA	AB	H	2B	3B	HR	RBI	BB	SO
Total	.312	.375	.496	494	154	30	2	19	65	45	97
vs. Left	.352	.409	.538	145	51	12	0	5	20	14	21
vs. Right	.295	.361	.479	349	103	18	2	14	45	31	76
at Home	.309	.389	.561	223	69	13	2	13	31	26	43
on Road	.314	.362	.443	271	85	17	0	6	34	19	54
on Grass	.329	.388	.547	386	127	26	2	18	51	35	74
on Turf	.250	.325	.315	108	27	4	0	1	14	10	23
Day Games	.332	.394	.536	235	78	13	1	11	38	22	41
Night Games	.293	.357	.459	259	76	17	1	8	27	23	56
April	.250	.296	.297	64	16	3	0	0	11	5	11
May	.320	.368	.515	103	33	8	0	4	12	7	22
June	.398	.443	.612	98	39	6	0	5	15	8	16
July	.250	.294	.333	48	12	2	1	0	3	3	11
August	.394	.464	.727	99	39	7	1	8	18	11	16
Sept-Oct	.183	.302	.305	82	15	4	0	2	6	11	21
Bases Empty	.279	.337	.493	290	81	13	2	15	15	21	58
Leadoff	.329	.394	.659	85	28	7	0	7	7	7	17
Runners On Base	.358	.426	.500	204	73	17	0	4	50	24	39
Scoring Position	.304	.381	.408	125	38	10	0	1	41	17	29
Late and Close	.239	.263	.366	71	17	4	1	1	7	2	19

8-YEAR TOTALS (1986–1993)

	BA	OBA	SA	AB	H	2B	3B	HR	RBI	BB	SO
Total	.265	.334	.415	3920	1037	204	36	104	407	358	810
vs. Left	.300	.369	.472	1272	382	90	15	33	139	128	222
vs. Right	.247	.317	.387	2648	655	114	21	71	268	230	588
at Home	.278	.355	.454	1908	530	109	22	61	224	201	378
on Road	.252	.313	.377	2012	507	95	14	43	183	157	432
on Grass	.275	.346	.437	2927	804	159	29	86	324	286	588
on Turf	.235	.296	.348	993	233	45	7	18	83	72	222
Day Games	.282	.356	.452	1644	463	93	20	49	199	165	330
Night Games	.252	.317	.388	2276	574	111	16	55	208	193	480
April	.254	.329	.372	575	146	28	5	10	60	62	118
May	.304	.363	.480	619	188	39	5	20	68	51	120
June	.261	.340	.414	683	178	33	6	20	77	71	141
July	.250	.310	.390	661	165	31	7	16	65	47	142
August	.284	.343	.449	779	221	46	7	23	78	63	151
Sept-Oct	.231	.315	.370	603	139	27	6	15	59	64	138
Bases Empty	.260	.325	.419	2367	615	124	21	70	70	199	512
Leadoff	.271	.339	.451	842	228	55	8	27	27	72	170
Runners On Base	.272	.346	.408	1553	422	80	15	34	337	159	298
Scoring Position	.247	.338	.373	866	214	39	5	20	281	112	198
Late and Close	.247	.308	.363	659	163	32	4	12	76	51	142

RYAN THOMPSON — BR/TR — age 27 — NYN OF76

1993	BA	OBA	SA	AB	H	2B	3B	HR	RBI	BB	SO
Total	.250	.302	.444	288	72	19	2	11	26	19	81
vs. Left	.217	.258	.293	92	20	4	0	1	2	3	28
vs. Right	.265	.322	.515	196	52	15	2	10	24	16	53
at Home	.259	.310	.437	135	35	7	1	5	16	8	39
on Road	.242	.295	.451	153	37	12	1	6	10	11	42
on Grass	.254	.312	.463	201	51	10	1	10	23	15	61
on Turf	.241	.280	.402	87	21	9	1	1	3	4	20
Day Games	.305	.377	.611	95	29	7	2	6	10	10	22
Night Games	.223	.263	.363	193	43	12	1	5	16	9	59
April	.125	.167	.200	40	5	1	1	0	1	2	13
May	.000	.000	.000	0	0	0	0	0	0	0	0
June	.000	.000	.000	0	0	0	0	0	0	0	0
July	.286	.318	.524	21	6	2	0	1	2	1	4
August	.252	.314	.459	111	28	6	1	5	12	8	24
Sept-Oct	.284	.333	.500	116	33	10	0	5	11	8	40
Bases Empty	.282	.322	.489	188	53	12	0	9	9	10	45
Leadoff	.245	.295	.388	98	24	5	0	3	3	6	23
Runners On Base	.190	.268	.360	100	19	7	2	2	17	9	36
Scoring Position	.155	.254	.362	58	9	4	1	2	16	6	25
Late and Close	.277	.327	.574	47	13	2	0	4	6	3	18

2-YEAR TOTALS (1992–1993)

	BA	OBA	SA	AB	H	2B	3B	HR	RBI	BB	SO
Total	.242	.294	.429	396	96	26	3	14	36	27	105
vs. Left	.217	.279	.302	129	28	8	0	1	2	9	32
vs. Right	.255	.302	.491	267	68	18	3	13	34	18	73
at Home	.261	.321	.456	180	47	9	1	8	24	14	49
on Road	.227	.272	.407	216	49	17	2	6	12	13	56
on Grass	.251	.313	.467	255	64	12	2	13	31	21	72
on Turf	.227	.260	.362	141	32	14	1	1	5	6	33
Day Games	.271	.344	.517	118	32	7	2	6	12	12	26
Night Games	.230	.273	.392	278	64	19	1	8	24	15	79
April	.125	.167	.200	40	5	1	1	0	1	2	13
May	.000	.000	.000	0	0	0	0	0	0	0	0
June	.000	.000	.000	0	0	0	0	0	0	0	0
July	.286	.318	.524	21	6	2	0	1	2	1	4
August	.252	.314	.459	111	28	6	1	5	12	8	24
Sept-Oct	.254	.305	.446	224	57	17	1	8	21	16	64
Bases Empty	.265	.305	.471	257	68	18	1	11	11	14	58
Leadoff	.235	.283	.397	136	32	8	1	4	4	8	27
Runners On Base	.201	.276	.353	139	28	8	2	3	25	13	47
Scoring Position	.157	.258	.337	83	13	4	1	3	23	10	33
Late and Close	.265	.338	.529	68	18	3	0	5	8	7	23

ALAN TRAMMELL — BR/TR — age 36 — DET SS63, 3B35, OF8, DH6

1993

	BA	OBA	SA	AB	H	2B	3B	HR	RBI	BB	SO
Total	.329	.388	.496	401	132	25	3	12	60	38	38
vs. Left	.289	.386	.504	135	39	8	0	7	21	21	13
vs. Right	.350	.389	.492	266	93	17	3	5	39	17	25
at Home	.330	.396	.498	203	67	12	2	6	28	21	19
on Road	.328	.380	.495	198	65	13	1	6	32	17	19
on Grass	.317	.377	.482	338	107	20	3	10	46	32	33
on Turf	.397	.449	.571	63	25	5	0	2	14	6	5
Day Games	.331	.396	.563	142	47	7	1	8	25	16	16
Night Games	.328	.384	.459	259	85	18	2	4	35	22	22
April	.200	.333	.367	30	6	2	0	1	6	6	2
May	.323	.373	.419	62	20	1	1	1	8	5	5
June	.324	.378	.471	68	22	7	0	1	10	5	5
July	.312	.349	.403	77	24	4	0	1	7	5	11
August	.405	.457	.631	84	34	6	2	3	18	9	7
Sept-Oct	.325	.393	.575	80	26	5	0	5	11	8	8
Bases Empty	.314	.372	.495	204	64	13	3	6	6	19	21
Leadoff	.309	.378	.519	81	25	6	1	3	3	9	7
Runners On Base	.345	.405	.497	197	68	12	0	6	54	19	17
Scoring Position	.316	.374	.453	117	37	4	0	4	48	11	13
Late and Close	.245	.298	.264	53	13	1	0	0	7	3	7

10-YEAR TOTALS (1984–1993)

	BA	OBA	SA	AB	H	2B	3B	HR	RBI	BB	SO
	.293	.359	.445	4682	1371	255	31	132	633	479	464
vs. Left	.297	.370	.478	1548	460	94	9	56	213	181	129
vs. Right	.291	.353	.429	3134	911	161	22	76	420	298	335
at Home	.297	.367	.444	2324	690	120	13	65	343	250	207
on Road	.289	.351	.447	2358	681	135	18	67	290	229	257
on Grass	.289	.357	.441	3956	1145	210	25	113	539	414	389
on Turf	.311	.368	.468	726	226	45	6	19	94	65	75
Day Games	.294	.365	.455	1507	443	87	12	44	200	162	154
Night Games	.292	.356	.440	3175	928	168	19	88	433	317	310
April	.290	.365	.462	676	196	43	8	19	96	77	64
May	.293	.358	.406	874	256	42	3	17	99	91	84
June	.290	.346	.435	840	244	38	4	25	114	71	85
July	.268	.347	.391	660	177	37	4	12	70	77	72
August	.305	.359	.491	903	275	51	9	33	150	79	85
Sept-Oct	.306	.381	.481	729	223	44	3	26	104	84	74
Bases Empty	.286	.348	.451	2528	723	130	23	80	80	227	252
Leadoff	.299	.343	.483	891	266	43	8	35	35	60	70
Runners On Base	.301	.372	.439	2154	648	125	8	52	553	252	212
Scoring Position	.296	.374	.431	1199	355	64	4	30	487	169	127
Late and Close	.295	.373	.403	689	203	30	0	15	112	82	77

JOHN VALENTIN — BR/TR — age 27 — BOS SS144

1993

	BA	OBA	SA	AB	H	2B	3B	HR	RBI	BB	SO
Total	.278	.346	.447	468	130	40	3	11	66	49	77
vs. Left	.248	.319	.419	129	32	11	1	3	10	13	20
vs. Right	.289	.356	.457	339	98	29	2	8	56	36	57
at Home	.293	.376	.483	242	71	23	1	7	39	31	47
on Road	.261	.313	.407	226	59	17	2	4	27	18	30
on Grass	.291	.361	.463	395	115	34	2	10	57	43	68
on Turf	.205	.262	.356	73	15	6	1	1	9	6	9
Day Games	.287	.362	.431	167	48	14	2	2	26	20	29
Night Games	.272	.337	.455	301	82	26	1	9	40	29	48
April	.143	.194	.464	28	4	0	0	3	7	2	4
May	.258	.317	.333	93	24	5	1	0	8	8	19
June	.256	.333	.385	78	20	4	0	2	14	9	14
July	.273	.323	.420	88	24	11	1	0	9	7	13
August	.311	.374	.544	90	28	10	1	3	11	9	15
Sept-Oct	.330	.425	.538	91	30	10	0	3	17	14	12
Bases Empty	.260	.330	.435	269	70	22	2	7	7	27	42
Leadoff	.267	.374	.457	105	28	9	1	3	3	17	12
Runners On Base	.302	.367	.462	199	60	18	1	4	59	22	35
Scoring Position	.301	.371	.415	123	37	9	1	1	49	15	21
Late and Close	.253	.326	.557	79	20	9	0	5	15	8	18

2-YEAR TOTALS (1992–1993)

	BA	OBA	SA	AB	H	2B	3B	HR	RBI	BB	SO
	.277	.347	.441	653	181	53	3	16	91	69	94
vs. Left	.241	.333	.414	162	39	14	1	4	13	21	22
vs. Right	.289	.352	.450	491	142	39	2	12	78	48	72
at Home	.281	.363	.447	331	93	29	1	8	48	41	55
on Road	.273	.331	.435	322	88	24	2	8	43	28	39
on Grass	.282	.353	.444	563	159	45	2	14	80	60	85
on Turf	.244	.310	.422	90	22	8	1	2	11	9	9
Day Games	.311	.391	.473	222	69	20	2	4	37	29	34
Night Games	.260	.324	.425	431	112	33	1	12	54	40	60
April	.143	.194	.464	28	4	0	0	3	7	2	4
May	.258	.317	.333	93	24	5	1	0	8	8	19
June	.256	.333	.385	78	20	4	0	2	14	9	14
July	.260	.313	.390	100	26	11	1	0	10	8	15
August	.284	.349	.485	169	48	17	1	5	18	17	22
Sept-Oct	.319	.407	.503	185	59	16	0	6	34	25	20
Bases Empty	.266	.335	.448	368	98	30	2	11	11	36	52
Leadoff	.278	.363	.444	151	42	11	1	4	4	18	15
Runners On Base	.291	.363	.432	285	83	23	1	5	80	33	42
Scoring Position	.291	.374	.402	179	52	12	1	2	70	25	27
Late and Close	.241	.312	.491	112	27	10	0	6	18	11	22

DAVE VALLE — BR/TR — age 34 — SEA C135

1993

	BA	OBA	SA	AB	H	2B	3B	HR	RBI	BB	SO
Total	.258	.354	.395	423	109	19	0	13	63	48	56
vs. Left	.280	.370	.458	118	33	6	0	5	17	13	12
vs. Right	.249	.347	.370	305	76	13	0	8	46	35	44
at Home	.265	.340	.365	219	58	10	0	4	34	17	34
on Road	.250	.368	.426	204	51	9	0	9	29	31	22
on Grass	.280	.399	.490	157	44	6	0	9	27	27	19
on Turf	.244	.326	.338	266	65	13	0	4	36	21	37
Day Games	.292	.387	.521	96	28	7	0	5	10	11	11
Night Games	.248	.344	.358	327	81	12	0	8	53	37	45
April	.258	.351	.387	62	16	2	0	2	11	9	10
May	.266	.385	.354	79	21	1	0	2	5	11	9
June	.254	.356	.397	63	16	3	0	2	9	6	6
July	.259	.348	.517	58	15	3	0	4	10	4	10
August	.221	.316	.324	68	15	4	0	1	10	9	7
Sept-Oct	.280	.356	.409	93	26	6	0	2	18	9	14
Bases Empty	.260	.372	.411	219	57	9	0	8	8	31	30
Leadoff	.326	.423	.528	89	29	6	0	4	4	13	7
Runners On Base	.255	.333	.377	204	52	10	0	5	55	17	26
Scoring Position	.265	.348	.393	117	31	6	0	3	49	13	20
Late and Close	.267	.341	.373	75	20	2	0	2	15	6	9

10-YEAR TOTALS (1984–1993)

	BA	OBA	SA	AB	H	2B	3B	HR	RBI	BB	SO
	.235	.311	.371	2502	588	104	10	72	318	225	356
vs. Left	.261	.330	.426	890	232	37	4	34	123	81	110
vs. Right	.221	.301	.341	1612	356	67	6	38	195	144	246
at Home	.234	.307	.362	1289	302	64	4	31	161	108	183
on Road	.236	.316	.380	1213	286	40	6	41	157	117	173
on Grass	.241	.318	.396	939	226	30	4	36	133	93	144
on Turf	.232	.307	.356	1563	362	74	6	36	185	132	212
Day Games	.227	.303	.369	607	138	25	2	19	62	54	89
Night Games	.237	.314	.372	1895	450	79	8	53	256	171	267
April	.227	.301	.373	418	95	11	1	16	55	38	69
May	.251	.340	.387	367	92	17	3	9	48	42	43
June	.239	.321	.405	331	79	16	3	11	37	30	45
July	.212	.271	.376	391	83	18	2	14	51	22	51
August	.236	.316	.345	386	91	15	0	9	39	41	53
Sept-Oct	.243	.318	.355	609	148	27	1	13	88	52	95
Bases Empty	.225	.308	.370	1387	312	57	6	44	44	136	203
Leadoff	.236	.315	.400	563	133	28	2	20	20	49	70
Runners On Base	.248	.315	.372	1115	276	47	4	28	274	89	153
Scoring Position	.253	.318	.393	671	170	35	4	17	248	54	101
Late and Close	.224	.295	.346	419	94	12	3	11	54	30	62

ANDY VANSLYKE — BL/TR — age 34 — PIT OF78   10-YEAR TOTALS (1984–1993)

1993	BA	OBA	SA	AB	H	2B	3B	HR	RBI	BB	SO	BA	OBA	SA	AB	H	2B	3B	HR	RBI	BB	SO
Total	.310	.357	.449	323	100	13	4	8	50	24	40	.279	.351	.457	4751	1327	249	81	144	700	536	871
vs. Left	.308	.347	.376	117	36	3	1	1	14	7	14	.239	.306	.363	1566	374	71	29	22	202	151	327
vs. Right	.311	.362	.490	206	64	10	3	7	36	17	26	.299	.374	.503	3185	953	178	52	122	498	385	544
at Home	.255	.297	.412	153	39	7	1	5	26	9	22	.271	.348	.453	2307	625	121	43	71	357	281	408
on Road	.359	.410	.482	170	61	6	3	3	24	15	18	.287	.355	.460	2444	702	128	38	73	343	255	463
on Grass	.368	.420	.520	125	46	6	2	3	22	11	14	.296	.363	.478	1313	389	58	20	47	184	140	239
on Turf	.273	.316	.404	198	54	7	2	5	28	13	26	.273	.347	.449	3438	938	191	61	97	516	396	632
Day Games	.300	.387	.400	70	21	1	0	2	7	9	10	.286	.353	.473	1487	425	81	22	51	220	164	264
Night Games	.312	.348	.462	253	79	12	4	6	43	15	30	.276	.351	.449	3264	902	168	59	93	480	372	607
April	.267	.327	.400	90	24	4	1	2	17	8	11	.263	.353	.415	593	156	28	10	14	92	84	109
May	.362	.425	.571	105	38	7	3	3	17	11	16	.306	.383	.483	804	246	39	14	25	130	101	137
June	.340	.340	.404	47	16	0	0	1	5	1	6	.275	.342	.439	845	232	43	18	20	111	88	171
July	.000	.000	.000	0	0	0	0	0	0	0	0	.256	.338	.450	738	189	34	17	25	103	94	136
August	.000	.000	.000	4	0	0	0	0	0	0	1	.287	.349	.491	788	226	46	8	33	129	74	141
Sept-Oct	.286	.321	.390	77	22	2	0	2	11	4	6	.283	.344	.454	983	278	59	14	27	135	95	177
Bases Empty	.278	.325	.367	158	44	6	1	2	2	10	16	.270	.340	.433	2586	699	131	30	77	77	260	478
Leadoff	.154	.195	.154	39	6	0	0	0	0	2	4	.269	.331	.450	918	247	61	9	29	29	81	164
Runners On Base	.339	.386	.527	165	56	7	3	6	48	14	24	.290	.365	.485	2165	628	118	51	67	623	276	393
Scoring Position	.341	.412	.553	85	29	2	2	4	39	12	14	.285	.374	.455	1255	358	61	31	30	504	203	250
Late and Close	.274	.328	.403	62	17	2	0	2	8	5	8	.267	.335	.426	842	225	37	11	25	121	92	195

GREG VAUGHN — BR/TR — age 29 — MIL OF94, DH58   5-YEAR TOTALS (1989–1993)

1993	BA	OBA	SA	AB	H	2B	3B	HR	RBI	BB	SO	BA	OBA	SA	AB	H	2B	3B	HR	RBI	BB	SO
Total	.267	.369	.482	569	152	28	2	30	97	89	118	.243	.325	.446	2107	512	99	11	102	357	257	480
vs. Left	.319	.443	.518	166	53	10	1	7	22	37	29	.251	.352	.432	574	144	30	4	22	84	93	117
vs. Right	.246	.336	.467	403	99	18	1	23	75	52	89	.240	.315	.451	1533	368	69	7	80	273	164	363
at Home	.284	.389	.469	271	77	12	1	12	47	46	52	.246	.335	.447	1014	249	49	4	49	180	138	222
on Road	.252	.350	.493	298	75	16	1	18	50	43	66	.241	.316	.445	1093	263	50	7	53	177	119	258
on Grass	.250	.348	.444	484	121	21	2	23	77	72	100	.242	.323	.447	1815	440	83	9	90	312	218	407
on Turf	.365	.481	.694	85	31	7	0	7	20	17	18	.247	.343	.438	292	72	16	2	12	45	39	73
Day Games	.275	.402	.490	200	55	12	2	9	29	39	44	.250	.350	.467	651	163	29	5	34	117	100	149
Night Games	.263	.350	.477	369	97	16	0	21	68	50	74	.240	.314	.436	1456	349	70	6	68	240	157	331
April	.292	.432	.554	65	19	3	1	4	11	16	13	.277	.379	.549	224	62	15	2	14	43	37	50
May	.290	.395	.550	100	29	2	0	8	25	17	23	.227	.327	.445	330	75	13	1	19	62	49	78
June	.279	.310	.495	111	31	9	0	5	23	5	24	.241	.296	.440	332	80	20	2	14	66	25	72
July	.290	.337	.484	93	27	7	1	3	14	5	17	.234	.287	.417	367	86	17	4	14	51	26	97
August	.252	.410	.486	111	28	5	0	7	16	29	16	.232	.336	.412	379	88	12	1	18	51	60	78
Sept-Oct	.202	.330	.326	89	18	2	0	3	8	17	25	.255	.337	.451	475	121	22	1	23	84	60	105
Bases Empty	.234	.333	.492	295	69	12	2	20	20	39	63	.219	.297	.423	1149	252	48	9	56	56	121	260
Leadoff	.228	.309	.515	136	31	8	2	9	9	14	23	.221	.295	.455	534	118	25	5	30	30	53	100
Runners On Base	.303	.405	.471	274	83	16	0	10	77	50	55	.271	.358	.473	958	260	51	2	46	301	136	220
Scoring Position	.297	.432	.459	148	44	9	0	5	65	38	26	.284	.380	.493	566	161	32	1	28	257	99	139
Late and Close	.226	.339	.333	93	21	4	0	2	12	16	24	.211	.306	.339	327	69	9	0	11	47	45	79

MO VAUGHN — BL/TR — age 27 — BOS 1B131, DH19   3-YEAR TOTALS (1991–1993)

1993	BA	OBA	SA	AB	H	2B	3B	HR	RBI	BB	SO	BA	OBA	SA	AB	H	2B	3B	HR	RBI	BB	SO
Total	.297	.390	.525	539	160	34	1	29	101	79	130	.270	.360	.455	1113	300	62	3	46	190	152	240
vs. Left	.268	.351	.543	164	44	9	0	12	39	16	48	.239	.321	.475	276	66	14	0	17	60	28	73
vs. Right	.309	.407	.517	375	116	25	1	17	62	63	82	.280	.372	.448	837	234	48	3	29	130	124	167
at Home	.332	.418	.563	277	92	23	1	13	56	39	63	.306	.393	.503	579	177	42	3	22	109	81	121
on Road	.260	.361	.485	262	68	11	0	16	45	40	67	.230	.324	.403	534	123	20	0	24	81	71	119
on Grass	.300	.399	.533	454	136	29	1	25	87	72	108	.272	.364	.456	965	262	55	3	39	166	135	203
on Turf	.282	.340	.482	85	24	5	0	4	14	7	22	.257	.333	.446	148	38	7	0	7	24	17	37
Day Games	.340	.413	.580	200	68	15	0	11	51	26	42	.298	.395	.484	403	120	24	0	17	80	65	78
Night Games	.271	.377	.493	339	92	19	1	18	50	53	88	.254	.339	.438	710	180	38	3	29	110	87	162
April	.412	.474	.735	68	28	10	0	4	16	9	10	.325	.421	.573	117	38	11	0	6	23	21	25
May	.288	.383	.423	104	30	3	1	3	15	15	23	.267	.389	.383	120	32	3	1	3	19	23	30
June	.250	.385	.432	88	22	7	0	3	13	17	24	.268	.383	.457	127	34	9	0	5	18	22	28
July	.362	.439	.754	69	25	3	0	8	27	9	15	.273	.354	.493	227	62	9	1	13	53	28	46
August	.256	.349	.411	90	23	5	0	3	8	13	24	.263	.346	.415	236	62	12	0	8	31	30	40
Sept-Oct	.267	.355	.517	120	32	6	0	8	22	16	34	.252	.326	.437	286	72	18	1	11	46	28	71
Bases Empty	.288	.357	.505	309	89	20	1	15	15	28	79	.252	.330	.432	607	153	30	2	25	25	62	131
Leadoff	.289	.333	.520	152	44	12	1	7	7	10	40	.252	.329	.457	278	70	19	1	12	12	31	59
Runners On Base	.309	.430	.552	230	71	14	0	14	86	51	51	.291	.393	.482	506	147	32	1	21	165	90	109
Scoring Position	.351	.484	.627	134	47	7	0	10	78	39	32	.311	.427	.529	293	91	19	0	15	150	68	74
Late and Close	.262	.326	.500	84	22	3	1	5	12	7	19	.242	.314	.382	186	45	4	2	6	24	18	45

ROBIN VENTURA — BL/TR — age 27 — CHA 3B155, 1B4

1993	BA	OBA	SA	AB	H	2B	3B	HR	RBI	BB	SO	5-YEAR BA	OBA	SA	AB	H	2B	3B	HR	RBI	BB	SO
Total	.262	.379	.433	554	145	27	1	22	94	105	82	.269	.362	.407	2290	615	110	4	66	348	341	279
vs. Left	.267	.361	.420	176	47	12	0	5	29	26	42	.253	.351	.354	711	180	32	2	12	89	108	132
vs. Right	.259	.387	.439	378	98	15	1	17	65	79	40	.275	.367	.430	1579	435	78	2	54	259	233	147
at Home	.248	.386	.437	254	63	12	0	12	50	59	40	.275	.373	.424	1104	304	49	2	37	186	176	134
on Road	.273	.372	.430	300	82	15	1	10	44	46	42	.262	.351	.390	1186	311	61	2	29	162	165	145
on Grass	.252	.382	.422	453	114	20	0	19	84	96	64	.267	.362	.410	1936	517	91	3	60	313	292	235
on Turf	.307	.364	.485	101	31	7	1	3	10	9	18	.277	.361	.387	354	98	19	1	6	35	49	44
Day Games	.251	.355	.409	171	43	6	0	7	24	28	31	.284	.369	.428	617	175	30	1	19	83	88	92
Night Games	.266	.389	.444	383	102	21	1	15	70	77	51	.263	.359	.399	1673	440	80	3	47	265	253	187
April	.289	.415	.408	76	22	3	0	2	6	17	8	.272	.397	.407	246	67	13	1	6	29	51	28
May	.265	.421	.566	83	22	2	1	7	21	23	17	.238	.344	.367	357	85	11	1	11	48	59	54
June	.202	.288	.346	104	21	3	0	4	13	13	23	.291	.371	.416	406	118	19	1	10	52	53	58
July	.240	.365	.406	96	23	4	0	4	19	18	9	.263	.335	.439	426	112	18	0	19	71	45	39
August	.283	.380	.435	92	26	8	0	2	14	13	10	.275	.356	.419	375	103	22	1	10	69	49	39
Sept-Oct	.301	.413	.456	103	31	7	0	3	21	21	15	.271	.376	.390	480	130	27	1	10	79	84	61
Bases Empty	.252	.369	.428	290	73	13	1	12	12	53	47	.244	.339	.374	1293	316	55	4	35	35	181	169
Leadoff	.223	.343	.405	121	27	5	1	5	5	22	23	.223	.310	.357	462	103	19	2	13	13	57	61
Runners On Base	.273	.389	.439	264	72	14	0	10	82	52	35	.300	.390	.448	997	299	55	0	31	313	160	110
Scoring Position	.273	.420	.416	161	44	11	0	4	68	43	21	.305	.412	.437	593	181	33	0	15	264	123	74
Late and Close	.289	.368	.446	83	24	4	0	3	12	11	12	.267	.340	.389	375	100	17	1	9	54	43	48

JOSE VIZCAINO — BB/TR — age 26 — CHN SS81, 3B44, 2B34

1993	BA	OBA	SA	AB	H	2B	3B	HR	RBI	BB	SO	5-YEAR BA	OBA	SA	AB	H	2B	3B	HR	RBI	BB	SO
Total	.287	.340	.358	551	158	19	4	4	54	46	71	.265	.309	.330	1042	276	35	9	5	83	69	133
vs. Left	.297	.364	.328	128	38	4	0	0	8	14	15	.264	.316	.311	273	72	7	3	0	16	22	30
vs. Right	.284	.333	.366	423	120	15	4	4	46	32	56	.265	.306	.337	769	204	28	6	5	67	47	103
at Home	.338	.384	.399	278	94	10	2	1	26	23	34	.292	.333	.350	520	152	19	4	1	40	35	64
on Road	.234	.296	.315	273	64	9	2	3	28	23	37	.238	.285	.310	522	124	16	5	4	43	34	69
on Grass	.307	.355	.383	423	130	17	3	3	47	34	55	.279	.320	.346	811	226	29	7	4	70	52	100
on Turf	.219	.289	.273	128	28	2	1	1	7	12	16	.216	.272	.273	231	50	6	2	1	13	17	33
Day Games	.314	.363	.375	293	92	11	2	1	25	24	34	.273	.313	.333	565	154	21	5	1	43	36	77
Night Games	.256	.315	.337	258	66	8	2	3	29	22	37	.256	.304	.327	477	122	14	4	4	40	33	56
April	.347	.383	.440	75	26	2	1	1	13	5	9	.286	.322	.352	105	30	2	1	1	15	7	12
May	.372	.416	.383	94	35	1	0	0	5	6	6	.300	.344	.333	180	54	2	2	0	7	11	14
June	.253	.286	.354	99	25	6	2	0	3	5	17	.244	.278	.315	238	58	13	2	0	10	12	37
July	.230	.327	.333	87	20	4	1	1	15	13	12	.246	.311	.342	199	49	12	2	1	21	19	29
August	.210	.273	.235	81	17	2	0	0	5	7	12	.244	.287	.298	168	41	2	2	1	17	10	23
Sept-Oct	.304	.354	.391	115	35	4	0	2	13	10	15	.289	.329	.355	152	44	4	0	2	13	10	18
Bases Empty	.276	.342	.329	337	93	11	2	1	1	33	46	.250	.299	.308	665	166	23	5	2	2	46	91
Leadoff	.310	.387	.381	126	39	4	1	1	1	16	10	.250	.311	.325	280	70	9	3	2	2	25	32
Runners On Base	.304	.336	.402	214	65	8	2	3	53	13	25	.292	.326	.369	377	110	12	4	3	81	23	42
Scoring Position	.280	.344	.402	107	30	4	0	3	48	13	9	.261	.322	.335	203	53	6	0	3	74	22	23
Late and Close	.244	.298	.279	86	21	0	0	1	11	6	16	.234	.284	.277	184	43	5	0	1	19	13	26

OMAR VIZQUEL — BB/TR — age 27 — SEA SS155, DH2

1993	BA	OBA	SA	AB	H	2B	3B	HR	RBI	BB	SO	5-YEAR BA	OBA	SA	AB	H	2B	3B	HR	RBI	BB	SO
Total	.255	.319	.298	560	143	14	2	2	31	50	71	.252	.309	.303	2111	531	60	15	6	131	173	208
vs. Left	.197	.264	.242	132	26	6	0	0	6	11	16	.215	.264	.266	507	109	20	0	2	36	33	39
vs. Right	.273	.336	.315	428	117	8	2	2	25	39	55	.263	.323	.314	1604	422	40	15	4	95	140	169
at Home	.266	.333	.303	274	73	7	0	1	14	27	29	.258	.313	.320	1024	264	37	9	3	68	82	111
on Road	.245	.306	.294	286	70	7	2	1	17	23	42	.246	.305	.286	1087	267	23	6	3	63	91	97
on Grass	.222	.273	.243	230	51	5	0	0	10	15	39	.243	.294	.271	841	204	17	2	1	44	61	77
on Turf	.279	.351	.336	330	92	9	2	2	21	35	32	.257	.319	.324	1270	327	43	13	5	87	112	131
Day Games	.245	.307	.282	163	40	6	0	0	7	14	18	.258	.322	.307	600	155	20	3	1	41	55	54
Night Games	.259	.324	.305	397	103	8	2	2	24	36	53	.249	.304	.301	1511	376	40	12	5	90	118	154
April	.225	.340	.275	80	18	1	0	0	8	14	11	.191	.278	.226	199	38	2	1	1	13	24	17
May	.309	.353	.318	110	34	1	0	0	5	8	13	.277	.320	.329	292	81	5	5	0	22	20	28
June	.333	.405	.384	99	33	3	1	0	5	11	14	.291	.363	.341	337	98	15	1	0	16	38	36
July	.267	.324	.356	101	27	6	0	1	4	8	16	.293	.338	.377	427	125	20	2	4	30	39	39
August	.128	.160	.128	78	10	0	0	0	2	3	9	.204	.252	.234	411	84	5	2	1	21	26	46
Sept-Oct	.228	.287	.283	92	21	3	1	0	7	6	8	.236	.298	.283	445	105	13	4	0	29	37	42
Bases Empty	.252	.322	.294	326	82	9	1	1	1	33	41	.246	.309	.299	1242	306	33	10	4	4	110	130
Leadoff	.268	.367	.320	153	41	5	0	1	1	24	26	.267	.340	.334	554	148	18	5	3	3	61	70
Runners On Base	.261	.315	.303	234	61	5	1	1	30	17	30	.259	.308	.308	869	225	27	5	2	127	63	78
Scoring Position	.227	.291	.288	132	30	3	1	1	29	11	18	.245	.297	.301	502	123	14	4	2	122	39	47
Late and Close	.267	.351	.277	101	27	1	0	0	5	11	10	.252	.308	.305	357	90	11	4	0	13	27	29

LARRY WALKER — BL/TR — age 28 — MON OF132, 1B4

1993	BA	OBA	SA	AB	H	2B	3B	HR	RBI	BB	SO	5-YEAR TOTALS (1989–1993) BA	OBA	SA	AB	H	2B	3B	HR	RBI	BB	SO
Total	.265	.371	.469	490	130	24	5	22	86	80	76	.273	.349	.462	1971	539	103	14	80	298	217	400
vs. Left	.238	.336	.400	185	44	5	2	7	27	24	28	.267	.332	.441	674	180	28	4	27	112	55	136
vs. Right	.282	.391	.511	305	86	19	3	15	59	56	48	.277	.358	.473	1297	359	75	10	53	186	162	264
at Home	.307	.410	.560	241	74	18	2	13	56	41	36	.278	.357	.480	918	255	52	7	40	154	104	188
on Road	.225	.333	.382	249	56	6	3	9	30	39	40	.270	.342	.445	1053	284	51	7	40	144	113	212
on Grass	.213	.321	.348	141	30	1	3	4	17	23	23	.277	.355	.475	570	158	20	6	27	90	69	118
on Turf	.287	.391	.519	349	100	23	2	18	69	57	53	.272	.347	.456	1401	381	83	8	53	208	148	282
Day Games	.255	.349	.476	145	37	3	1	9	22	18	27	.243	.327	.428	584	142	21	6	25	86	66	136
Night Games	.270	.380	.467	345	93	21	4	13	64	62	49	.286	.359	.476	1387	397	82	8	55	212	151	264
April	.364	.463	.745	55	20	4	1	5	13	10	10	.262	.346	.476	252	66	17	2	11	36	30	60
May	.238	.340	.357	84	20	4	0	2	11	11	13	.260	.340	.432	315	82	14	2	12	40	37	63
June	.262	.355	.477	65	17	5	0	3	13	8	12	.268	.351	.489	276	74	16	0	15	49	34	61
July	.261	.376	.413	92	24	3	1	3	8	17	14	.250	.310	.422	308	77	8	3	13	41	26	72
August	.252	.347	.417	103	26	6	1	3	24	17	14	.307	.374	.491	397	122	27	2	14	66	41	63
Sept-Oct	.253	.376	.516	91	23	2	2	6	17	17	13	.279	.361	.459	423	118	21	5	15	66	49	81
Bases Empty	.248	.323	.476	254	63	13	0	15	15	26	43	.270	.334	.468	1077	291	58	7	47	47	92	236
Leadoff	.234	.312	.427	124	29	6	0	6	6	14	22	.283	.337	.498	484	137	27	4	23	23	.37	100
Runners On Base	.284	.417	.462	236	67	11	5	7	71	54	33	.277	.366	.454	894	248	45	7	33	251	125	164
Scoring Position	.254	.420	.401	142	36	7	4	2	58	42	27	.262	.376	.412	541	142	29	5	14	203	104	116
Late and Close	.235	.361	.383	81	19	2	2	2	7	15	11	.260	.355	.422	365	95	15	4	12	42	51	76

TIM WALLACH — BR/TR — age 37 — LA 3B130, 1B1

1993	BA	OBA	SA	AB	H	2B	3B	HR	RBI	BB	SO	10-YEAR TOTALS (1984–1993) BA	OBA	SA	AB	H	2B	3B	HR	RBI	BB	SO
Total	.222	.271	.342	477	106	19	1	12	62	32	70	.255	.312	.407	5606	1432	306	25	164	785	439	860
vs. Left	.194	.223	.338	139	27	5	0	5	21	6	23	.258	.318	.420	1676	432	103	8	51	228	147	219
vs. Right	.234	.290	.343	338	79	14	1	7	41	26	47	.254	.310	.401	3930	1000	203	17	113	557	292	641
at Home	.253	.297	.346	217	55	8	0	4	28	12	30	.263	.326	.407	2659	700	157	16	64	376	232	402
on Road	.196	.249	.338	260	51	11	1	8	34	20	40	.248	.299	.407	2947	732	149	9	100	409	207	458
on Grass	.230	.280	.346	361	83	13	1	9	48	25	55	.248	.298	.406	1767	439	76	5	64	248	120	288
on Turf	.198	.242	.328	116	23	6	0	3	14	7	15	.259	.319	.407	3839	993	230	20	100	537	319	572
Day Games	.195	.257	.361	133	26	4	0	6	12	10	25	.262	.315	.438	1758	460	97	6	67	258	129	291
Night Games	.233	.276	.334	344	80	15	1	6	50	22	45	.253	.311	.392	3848	972	209	19	97	527	310	569
April	.190	.239	.333	84	16	4	1	2	6	6	10	.269	.321	.422	766	206	50	2	21	95	57	106
May	.273	.318	.434	99	27	4	0	4	22	8	18	.265	.318	.438	998	264	62	6	33	151	69	152
June	.154	.188	.282	78	12	4	0	2	11	3	8	.266	.337	.420	973	259	65	5	25	149	98	135
July	.250	.328	.423	52	13	3	0	2	8	5	8	.252	.313	.426	922	232	49	5	34	144	81	154
August	.288	.329	.425	73	21	4	0	2	11	5	7	.260	.309	.389	997	259	41	5	26	129	67	147
Sept-Oct	.187	.237	.187	91	17	0	0	0	4	5	19	.223	.277	.347	950	212	39	2	25	117	67	166
Bases Empty	.197	.243	.348	279	55	10	1	10	10	15	45	.250	.293	.401	3142	785	164	15	94	94	178	491
Leadoff	.208	.250	.368	125	26	6	1	4	4	6	14	.276	.314	.444	1389	383	91	7	43	43	70	190
Runners On Base	.258	.307	.333	198	51	9	0	2	52	17	25	.263	.335	.414	2464	647	142	10	70	691	261	369
Scoring Position	.240	.287	.326	129	31	8	0	1	50	11	18	.260	.347	.411	1541	401	93	7	42	601	208	243
Late and Close	.174	.283	.279	86	15	3	0	2	9	12	13	.244	.322	.380	1037	253	49	1	30	136	111	165

WALT WEISS — BB/TR — age 31 — FLO SS153

1993	BA	OBA	SA	AB	H	2B	3B	HR	RBI	BB	SO	7-YEAR TOTALS (1987–1993) BA	OBA	SA	AB	H	2B	3B	HR	RBI	BB	SO
Total	.266	.367	.308	500	133	14	2	1	39	79	73	.250	.329	.307	2108	528	74	9	9	169	238	276
vs. Left	.234	.353	.281	128	30	6	0	0	11	23	19	.219	.282	.266	515	113	20	2	0	37	45	50
vs. Right	.277	.372	.317	372	103	8	2	1	28	56	54	.261	.343	.320	1593	415	54	7	9	132	193	226
at Home	.250	.362	.283	244	61	6	1	0	19	44	37	.228	.310	.272	1045	238	31	3	3	71	120	155
on Road	.281	.372	.332	256	72	8	1	1	20	35	36	.273	.347	.341	1063	290	43	6	6	98	118	121
on Grass	.264	.373	.309	382	101	12	1	1	28	66	57	.251	.331	.309	1740	436	63	7	8	130	199	231
on Turf	.271	.348	.305	118	32	2	1	0	11	13	16	.250	.320	.299	368	92	11	2	1	39	39	45
Day Games	.262	.374	.330	103	27	5	1	0	10	18	19	.238	.322	.293	745	177	26	3	3	60	88	106
Night Games	.267	.365	.302	397	106	9	1	1	29	61	54	.258	.332	.315	1363	351	48	6	6	109	150	170
April	.254	.378	.284	67	17	0	0	0	8	13	11	.246	.315	.333	285	70	11	1	4	29	29	31
May	.333	.423	.417	84	28	5	1	0	6	12	10	.260	.341	.315	365	95	15	1	1	27	43	43
June	.278	.337	.322	90	25	1	0	1	5	8	10	.265	.326	.320	362	96	10	2	2	25	30	42
July	.188	.268	.224	85	16	3	0	0	9	9	15	.217	.289	.266	346	75	10	2	1	33	35	45
August	.299	.408	.333	87	26	3	0	0	6	16	13	.267	.346	.329	374	100	14	3	1	27	44	57
Sept-Oct	.241	.385	.264	87	21	2	0	0	5	21	14	.245	.349	.282	376	92	14	0	0	28	57	58
Bases Empty	.242	.351	.281	281	68	8	0	1	1	47	42	.240	.325	.299	1179	283	51	2	5	5	140	160
Leadoff	.215	.317	.248	121	26	4	0	0	0	18	26	.247	.323	.297	502	124	23	1	0	0	50	76
Runners On Base	.297	.388	.342	219	65	6	2	0	38	32	31	.264	.333	.316	929	245	23	7	4	164	98	116
Scoring Position	.299	.440	.355	107	32	4	1	0	37	28	15	.228	.325	.281	509	116	13	4	2	155	78	67
Late and Close	.255	.370	.274	106	27	2	0	0	8	20	16	.243	.332	.279	337	82	8	2	0	28	46	47

LOU WHITAKER — BL/TR — age 37 — DET 2B110

1993

	BA	OBA	SA	AB	H	2B	3B	HR	RBI	BB	SO
Total	.290	.412	.449	383	111	32	1	9	67	78	46
vs. Left	.122	.254	.143	49	6	1	0	0	8	7	10
vs. Right	.314	.434	.494	334	105	31	1	9	59	71	36
at Home	.269	.388	.440	193	52	18	0	5	35	36	20
on Road	.311	.435	.458	190	59	14	1	4	32	42	26
on Grass	.272	.398	.416	320	87	25	0	7	52	66	37
on Turf	.381	.481	.619	63	24	7	1	2	15	12	9
Day Games	.225	.368	.297	138	31	10	0	0	9	30	15
Night Games	.327	.436	.535	245	80	22	1	9	58	48	31
April	.353	.493	.588	51	18	6	0	2	16	12	7
May	.247	.320	.353	85	21	4	1	1	11	10	11
June	.394	.506	.690	71	28	9	0	4	13	17	5
July	.226	.349	.340	53	12	3	0	1	8	10	6
August	.288	.468	.373	59	17	5	0	0	9	20	6
Sept-Oct	.234	.338	.359	64	15	5	0	1	10	9	11
Bases Empty	.292	.442	.433	171	50	15	0	3	3	44	17
Leadoff	.286	.407	.429	49	14	1	0	2	2	10	6
Runners On Base	.288	.385	.462	212	61	17	1	6	64	34	29
Scoring Position	.289	.375	.500	114	33	9	0	5	56	17	12
Late and Close	.271	.357	.424	59	16	3	0	2	14	8	7

10-YEAR TOTALS (1984–1993)

	BA	OBA	SA	AB	H	2B	3B	HR	RBI	BB	SO
Total	.271	.364	.441	5045	1367	263	29	179	677	754	625
vs. Left	.219	.309	.321	1256	275	44	9	22	143	161	230
vs. Right	.288	.382	.481	3789	1092	219	20	157	534	593	395
at Home	.272	.373	.459	2432	661	128	12	101	353	398	301
on Road	.270	.356	.424	2613	706	135	17	78	324	356	324
on Grass	.268	.364	.437	4238	1136	206	24	154	575	656	516
on Turf	.286	.363	.462	807	231	57	5	25	102	98	109
Day Games	.262	.361	.426	1544	405	83	5	53	200	245	193
Night Games	.275	.365	.448	3501	962	180	24	126	477	509	432
April	.277	.384	.446	621	172	30	3	23	82	109	72
May	.269	.358	.439	907	244	38	4	36	117	126	119
June	.279	.370	.453	943	263	51	7	33	117	143	120
July	.292	.370	.459	832	243	49	6	26	104	106	93
August	.271	.380	.465	918	249	51	5	39	156	165	115
Sept-Oct	.238	.324	.381	824	196	44	4	22	101	105	106
Bases Empty	.269	.359	.425	2967	798	166	18	87	87	411	359
Leadoff	.279	.358	.425	1452	405	73	11	39	39	175	166
Runners On Base	.274	.370	.464	2078	569	97	11	92	590	343	266
Scoring Position	.265	.369	.443	1134	301	53	5	46	474	213	145
Late and Close	.264	.369	.418	751	198	33	1	27	112	129	116

DEVON WHITE — BB/TR — age 32 — TOR OF145

1993

	BA	OBA	SA	AB	H	2B	3B	HR	RBI	BB	SO
Total	.273	.341	.438	598	163	42	6	15	52	57	127
vs. Left	.254	.324	.395	185	47	15	1	3	16	15	37
vs. Right	.281	.349	.458	413	116	27	5	12	36	42	90
at Home	.290	.361	.498	307	89	24	5	10	31	30	62
on Road	.254	.321	.375	291	74	18	1	5	21	27	65
on Grass	.250	.304	.364	236	59	13	1	4	17	18	51
on Turf	.287	.365	.486	362	104	29	5	11	35	39	76
Day Games	.341	.408	.605	205	70	15	3	11	25	21	42
Night Games	.237	.307	.351	393	93	27	3	4	27	36	85
April	.385	.439	.500	52	20	1	1	1	4	5	11
May	.290	.333	.516	124	36	13	0	5	13	7	26
June	.265	.333	.487	117	31	10	2	4	9	12	25
July	.183	.296	.269	93	17	3	1	1	7	10	19
August	.279	.341	.467	122	34	10	2	3	9	11	24
Sept-Oct	.278	.356	.367	90	25	5	0	1	10	12	22
Bases Empty	.279	.340	.453	384	107	26	4	11	11	32	83
Leadoff	.309	.359	.551	207	64	15	1	11	11	13	36
Runners On Base	.262	.343	.411	214	56	16	2	4	41	25	44
Scoring Position	.256	.353	.419	117	30	8	1	3	37	16	27
Late and Close	.247	.360	.397	73	18	4	2	1	8	11	20

9-YEAR TOTALS (1985–1993)

	BA	OBA	SA	AB	H	2B	3B	HR	RBI	BB	SO
Total	.256	.310	.406	4113	1054	199	47	108	413	303	870
vs. Left	.252	.306	.407	1274	321	64	10	38	123	91	236
vs. Right	.258	.312	.406	2839	733	135	37	70	290	212	634
at Home	.258	.313	.421	2024	523	108	30	54	211	151	427
on Road	.254	.307	.392	2089	531	91	17	54	202	152	443
on Grass	.247	.297	.386	2585	639	110	23	68	257	175	555
on Turf	.272	.333	.440	1528	415	89	24	40	156	128	315
Day Games	.279	.332	.438	1226	342	74	14	31	115	89	275
Night Games	.247	.301	.393	2887	712	125	33	77	298	214	595
April	.276	.332	.447	557	154	31	8	16	68	40	111
May	.258	.315	.416	671	173	40	9	16	65	53	131
June	.266	.317	.443	695	185	34	10	23	71	50	155
July	.248	.299	.368	693	172	26	6	15	75	45	146
August	.243	.297	.414	773	188	37	10	25	76	58	163
Sept-Oct	.251	.308	.359	724	182	31	4	13	58	57	164
Bases Empty	.266	.313	.427	2493	663	128	29	72	72	155	530
Leadoff	.291	.331	.470	1237	360	67	13	43	43	65	238
Runners On Base	.241	.306	.374	1620	391	71	18	36	341	148	340
Scoring Position	.228	.298	.349	931	212	40	8	19	294	94	220
Late and Close	.247	.320	.374	653	161	26	6	15	73	66	161

MARK WHITEN — BB/TR — age 28 — SL OF148

1993

	BA	OBA	SA	AB	H	2B	3B	HR	RBI	BB	SO
Total	.253	.323	.423	562	142	13	4	25	99	58	110
vs. Left	.231	.296	.394	160	37	2	0	8	26	15	22
vs. Right	.261	.333	.435	402	105	11	4	17	73	43	88
at Home	.237	.302	.397	262	62	6	0	12	52	24	54
on Road	.267	.340	.447	300	80	7	4	13	47	34	56
on Grass	.254	.342	.399	193	49	6	2	6	25	26	42
on Turf	.252	.312	.436	369	93	7	2	19	74	32	68
Day Games	.260	.338	.399	173	45	6	0	6	33	22	32
Night Games	.249	.315	.434	389	97	7	4	19	66	36	78
April	.253	.330	.460	87	22	1	1	5	12	10	20
May	.242	.299	.293	99	24	2	0	1	16	8	17
June	.238	.313	.396	101	24	2	1	4	15	10	23
July	.323	.410	.692	65	21	2	2	6	19	11	11
August	.207	.250	.293	92	19	2	0	2	10	6	17
Sept-Oct	.271	.348	.483	118	32	4	0	7	27	13	22
Bases Empty	.234	.291	.376	303	71	7	3	10	10	24	58
Leadoff	.248	.299	.365	137	34	5	1	3	3	10	27
Runners On Base	.274	.358	.479	259	71	6	1	15	89	34	52
Scoring Position	.266	.357	.450	169	45	5	1	8	74	24	36
Late and Close	.204	.298	.316	98	20	2	0	3	14	14	24

4-YEAR TOTALS (1990–1993)

	BA	OBA	SA	AB	H	2B	3B	HR	RBI	BB	SO
Total	.252	.324	.391	1565	394	51	16	45	194	167	311
vs. Left	.260	.337	.410	434	113	17	3	14	48	50	78
vs. Right	.248	.319	.384	1131	281	34	13	31	146	117	233
at Home	.251	.321	.400	748	188	26	8	23	96	74	155
on Road	.252	.327	.383	817	206	25	8	22	98	93	156
on Grass	.257	.334	.382	947	243	36	10	21	97	111	186
on Turf	.244	.308	.405	618	151	15	6	24	97	56	125
Day Games	.251	.328	.357	479	120	18	3	9	55	57	99
Night Games	.252	.323	.406	1086	274	33	13	36	139	110	212
April	.276	.333	.434	228	63	3	3	9	38	21	54
May	.251	.332	.353	255	64	11	3	3	28	30	55
June	.217	.299	.343	198	43	6	2	5	19	22	45
July	.260	.330	.451	304	79	12	5	12	42	30	52
August	.244	.311	.380	308	75	14	2	8	32	32	56
Sept-Oct	.257	.336	.371	272	70	5	1	8	35	32	49
Bases Empty	.252	.312	.389	893	225	30	10	24	24	74	172
Leadoff	.269	.317	.407	391	105	16	4	10	10	25	76
Runners On Base	.251	.339	.394	672	169	21	6	21	170	93	139
Scoring Position	.239	.341	.365	394	94	13	2	11	142	66	88
Late and Close	.219	.313	.339	283	62	8	1	8	33	39	60

DARRELL WHITMORE — BL/TR — age 26 — FLO OF69

1993	BA	OBA	SA	AB	H	2B	3B	HR	RBI	BB	SO
Total	.204	.249	.300	250	51	8	2	4	19	10	72
vs. Left	.128	.209	.205	39	5	3	0	0	2	1	16
vs. Right	.218	.257	.318	211	46	5	2	4	17	9	56
at Home	.227	.271	.326	132	30	2	1	3	13	5	42
on Road	.178	.224	.271	118	21	6	1	1	6	5	30
on Grass	.197	.243	.288	198	39	5	2	3	14	7	58
on Turf	.231	.273	.346	52	12	3	0	1	5	3	14
Day Games	.167	.216	.250	48	8	2	1	0	7	2	10
Night Games	.213	.257	.312	202	43	6	1	4	12	8	62
April	.000	.000	.000	0	0	0	0	0	0	0	0
May	.000	.000	.000	0	0	0	0	0	0	0	0
June	.190	.190	.333	21	4	1	1	0	1	0	10
July	.256	.318	.410	78	20	4	1	2	6	6	22
August	.162	.183	.275	80	13	3	0	2	7	2	21
Sept-Oct	.197	.260	.197	71	14	0	0	0	5	2	19
Bases Empty	.189	.227	.287	143	27	5	0	3	3	5	45
Leadoff	.164	.203	.311	61	10	3	0	2	2	2	24
Runners On Base	.224	.278	.318	107	24	3	2	1	16	5	27
Scoring Position	.161	.203	.179	56	9	1	0	0	12	1	18
Late and Close	.262	.340	.333	42	11	3	0	0	5	4	10

1-YEAR TOTALS (1993)

	BA	OBA	SA	AB	H	2B	3B	HR	RBI	BB	SO
	.204	.249	.300	250	51	8	2	4	19	10	72
	.128	.209	.205	39	5	3	0	0	2	1	16
	.218	.257	.318	211	46	5	2	4	17	9	56
	.227	.271	.326	132	30	2	1	3	13	5	42
	.178	.224	.271	118	21	6	1	1	6	5	30
	.197	.243	.288	198	39	5	2	3	14	7	58
	.231	.273	.346	52	12	3	0	1	5	3	14
	.167	.216	.250	48	8	2	1	0	7	2	10
	.213	.257	.312	202	43	6	1	4	12	8	62
	.000	.000	.000	0	0	0	0	0	0	0	0
	.000	.000	.000	0	0	0	0	0	0	0	0
	.190	.190	.333	21	4	1	1	0	1	0	10
	.256	.318	.410	78	20	4	1	2	6	6	22
	.162	.183	.275	80	13	3	0	2	7	2	21
	.197	.260	.197	71	14	0	0	0	5	2	19
	.189	.227	.287	143	27	5	0	3	3	5	45
	.164	.203	.311	61	10	3	0	2	2	2	24
	.224	.278	.318	107	24	3	2	1	16	5	27
	.161	.203	.179	56	9	1	0	0	12	1	18
	.262	.340	.333	42	11	3	0	0	5	4	10

RICK WILKINS — BL/TR — age 27 — CHN C133

1993	BA	OBA	SA	AB	H	2B	3B	HR	RBI	BB	SO
Total	.303	.376	.561	446	135	23	1	30	73	50	99
vs. Left	.224	.325	.403	67	15	3	0	3	10	8	22
vs. Right	.317	.385	.588	379	120	20	1	27	63	42	77
at Home	.256	.317	.429	238	61	11	0	10	31	19	61
on Road	.356	.440	.712	208	74	12	1	20	42	31	38
on Grass	.292	.361	.555	353	103	18	0	25	62	35	84
on Turf	.344	.431	.581	93	32	5	1	5	11	15	15
Day Games	.220	.284	.398	236	52	12	0	10	21	20	60
Night Games	.395	.473	.743	210	83	11	1	20	52	30	39
April	.122	.234	.195	41	5	0	0	1	2	6	6
May	.299	.357	.545	77	23	4	0	5	6	7	23
June	.414	.485	.793	87	36	7	1	8	20	11	15
July	.256	.340	.488	86	22	2	0	6	15	10	19
August	.286	.330	.548	84	24	1	0	5	16	6	21
Sept-Oct	.352	.439	.606	71	25	3	0	5	14	10	15
Bases Empty	.289	.339	.583	266	77	13	1	21	21	18	62
Leadoff	.235	.284	.412	102	24	3	0	5	5	6	28
Runners On Base	.322	.425	.528	180	58	10	0	9	52	32	37
Scoring Position	.283	.427	.487	113	32	5	0	6	43	28	32
Late and Close	.282	.371	.551	78	22	3	0	6	14	11	19

3-YEAR TOTALS (1991–1993)

	BA	OBA	SA	AB	H	2B	3B	HR	RBI	BB	SO
	.275	.352	.474	893	246	41	2	44	117	97	208
	.245	.331	.368	155	38	7	0	4	16	16	46
	.282	.356	.496	738	208	34	2	40	101	81	162
	.240	.312	.379	470	113	20	0	15	49	44	116
	.314	.394	.579	423	133	21	2	29	68	53	92
	.267	.339	.458	681	182	31	0	33	92	68	162
	.302	.392	.524	212	64	10	2	11	25	29	46
	.219	.288	.359	485	106	18	1	16	45	45	118
	.343	.424	.610	408	140	23	1	28	72	52	90
	.137	.241	.196	51	7	0	0	1	2	7	8
	.299	.357	.545	77	23	4	0	5	6	7	23
	.368	.432	.687	163	60	11	1	13	36	15	32
	.255	.318	.426	216	55	7	0	10	24	18	52
	.233	.314	.362	210	49	9	0	6	23	23	55
	.295	.392	.517	176	52	10	1	9	26	27	38
	.285	.342	.516	519	148	25	1	31	31	39	119
	.246	.300	.357	207	51	8	0	5	5	12	55
	.262	.364	.414	374	98	16	1	13	86	58	89
	.263	.409	.459	209	55	9	1	10	76	50	55
	.272	.364	.480	173	47	9	0	9	23	24	44

BERNIE WILLIAMS — BB/TR — age 26 — NYA OF139

1993	BA	OBA	SA	AB	H	2B	3B	HR	RBI	BB	SO
Total	.268	.333	.400	567	152	31	4	12	68	53	106
vs. Left	.325	.402	.503	191	62	13	0	7	29	26	33
vs. Right	.239	.297	.348	376	90	18	4	5	39	27	73
at Home	.266	.339	.395	256	68	14	2	5	32	28	40
on Road	.270	.328	.405	311	84	17	2	7	36	25	66
on Grass	.279	.346	.414	476	133	28	3	10	62	46	80
on Turf	.209	.265	.330	91	19	3	1	2	6	7	26
Day Games	.256	.317	.382	199	51	14	1	3	16	17	37
Night Games	.274	.342	.410	368	101	17	3	9	52	36	69
April	.264	.356	.425	87	23	6	1	2	12	12	17
May	.220	.316	.280	50	11	1	1	0	3	6	12
June	.255	.294	.480	102	26	4	2	5	20	6	20
July	.280	.358	.421	107	30	6	0	3	15	13	13
August	.349	.385	.459	109	38	9	0	1	11	6	22
Sept-Oct	.214	.285	.286	112	24	5	0	1	7	10	22
Bases Empty	.252	.329	.407	322	81	21	4	7	7	34	68
Leadoff	.259	.309	.458	166	43	11	2	6	6	10	30
Runners On Base	.290	.340	.392	245	71	10	0	5	61	19	38
Scoring Position	.270	.327	.405	148	40	8	0	4	58	14	20
Late and Close	.262	.326	.381	84	22	1	0	3	10	8	21

3-YEAR TOTALS (1991–1993)

	BA	OBA	SA	AB	H	2B	3B	HR	RBI	BB	SO
	.262	.339	.388	1148	301	64	10	20	128	130	199
	.285	.371	.435	379	108	25	1	10	51	53	55
	.251	.322	.364	769	193	39	9	10	77	77	144
	.271	.353	.397	549	149	32	5	9	64	68	82
	.254	.326	.379	599	152	32	5	11	64	62	117
	.268	.345	.395	973	261	54	9	17	116	111	153
	.229	.304	.349	175	40	10	1	3	12	19	46
	.285	.349	.406	379	108	28	3	4	45	36	69
	.251	.334	.378	769	193	36	7	16	83	94	130
	.261	.349	.413	92	24	6	1	2	12	12	19
	.220	.316	.280	50	11	1	1	0	3	6	12
	.255	.294	.480	102	26	4	2	5	20	6	20
	.270	.370	.421	178	48	10	1	5	26	28	27
	.276	.354	.401	359	99	25	1	6	37	42	63
	.253	.320	.341	367	93	18	4	2	30	36	58
	.246	.332	.381	679	167	39	7	13	13	83	123
	.252	.328	.383	373	94	19	3	8	8	40	62
	.286	.348	.397	469	134	25	3	7	115	47	76
	.276	.340	.391	279	77	16	2	4	105	30	42
	.232	.307	.324	185	43	6	1	3	23	19	45

MATT WILLIAMS — BR/TR — age 29 — SF3B144

1993	BA	OBA	SA	AB	H	2B	3B	HR	RBI	BB	SO		7-YEAR TOTALS (1987–1993) BA	OBA	SA	AB	H	2B	3B	HR	RBI	BB	SO
Total	.294	.325	.561	579	170	33	4	38	110	27	80		.251	.295	.467	3007	756	130	20	159	486	170	636
vs. Left	.328	.363	.683	186	61	11	2	17	42	11	19		.265	.313	.520	942	250	38	5	64	169	65	171
vs. Right	.277	.306	.504	393	109	22	2	21	68	16	61		.245	.287	.442	2065	506	92	15	95	317	105	465
at Home	.293	.330	.571	287	84	17	3	19	61	15	42		.256	.297	.492	1501	384	67	13	87	257	81	310
on Road	.295	.319	.551	292	86	16	1	19	49	12	38		.247	.293	.442	1506	372	63	7	72	229	89	326
on Grass	.296	.330	.540	452	134	24	4	26	81	22	63		.259	.297	.471	2292	593	102	15	118	367	116	474
on Turf	.283	.306	.638	127	36	9	0	12	29	5	17		.228	.288	.453	715	163	28	5	41	119	54	162
Day Games	.302	.332	.614	298	90	16	1	25	61	14	44		.269	.304	.525	1307	351	61	8	86	241	63	266
Night Games	.285	.317	.505	281	80	17	3	13	49	13	36		.238	.288	.422	1700	405	69	12	73	245	107	370
April	.330	.396	.660	94	31	7	0	8	18	11	11		.238	.289	.435	441	105	15	3	22	73	30	101
May	.284	.308	.526	116	33	5	1	7	25	3	22		.245	.289	.436	507	124	20	4	23	78	30	101
June	.250	.247	.538	80	20	5	0	6	21	0	13		.247	.277	.463	477	118	23	1	26	86	19	105
July	.293	.338	.500	58	17	3	0	3	10	3	6		.277	.334	.504	361	100	14	4	20	60	25	80
August	.312	.342	.486	109	34	8	1	3	11	5	15		.248	.286	.472	589	146	29	5	31	77	29	124
Sept-Oct	.287	.310	.631	122	35	5	2	11	25	5	13		.258	.304	.489	632	163	29	3	37	112	37	125
Bases Empty	.286	.309	.576	304	87	21	2	21	21	8	44		.248	.285	.467	1645	408	70	13	88	88	72	352
Leadoff	.324	.342	.710	145	47	14	0	14	14	4	16		.270	.311	.530	704	190	31	7	46	46	37	125
Runners On Base	.302	.341	.545	275	83	12	2	17	89	19	36		.256	.307	.466	1362	348	60	7	71	398	98	284
Scoring Position	.323	.352	.587	155	50	9	1	10	74	12	19		.250	.314	.452	792	198	32	4	40	321	78	181
Late and Close	.262	.289	.548	84	22	1	1	7	16	4	12		.213	.267	.375	475	101	17	3	18	62	30	109

DAVE WINFIELD — BR/TR — age 43 — MIN DH105, OF31, 1B5

1993	BA	OBA	SA	AB	H	2B	3B	HR	RBI	BB	SO		9-YEAR TOTALS (1984–1993) BA	OBA	SA	AB	H	2B	3B	HR	RBI	BB	SO
Total	.271	.325	.442	547	148	27	2	21	76	45	106		.285	.355	.477	5072	1446	266	29	217	869	562	842
vs. Left	.292	.345	.460	137	40	9	1	4	19	11	21		.297	.386	.524	1533	456	83	14	79	283	229	208
vs. Right	.263	.318	.437	410	108	18	1	17	57	34	85		.280	.341	.457	3539	990	183	15	138	586	333	634
at Home	.255	.313	.439	278	71	13	1	12	47	24	60		.285	.360	.479	2435	694	118	12	110	422	296	387
on Road	.286	.338	.446	269	77	14	1	9	29	21	46		.285	.350	.476	2637	752	148	17	107	447	266	455
on Grass	.301	.357	.445	209	63	10	1	6	22	18	32		.283	.355	.471	3767	1067	199	21	156	621	428	607
on Turf	.251	.305	.441	338	85	17	1	15	54	27	74		.290	.355	.494	1305	379	67	8	61	248	134	235
Day Games	.228	.293	.389	167	38	7	1	6	18	16	40		.286	.357	.461	1543	442	66	9	62	255	175	259
Night Games	.289	.339	.466	380	110	20	1	15	58	29	66		.284	.354	.484	3529	1004	200	20	155	614	387	583
April	.230	.269	.432	74	17	3	0	4	16	4	19		.298	.374	.499	601	179	28	3	29	109	76	109
May	.276	.330	.437	87	24	5	0	3	12	7	17		.263	.329	.473	858	226	46	7	40	141	86	137
June	.220	.264	.280	82	18	0	1	1	6	5	19		.311	.378	.519	867	270	51	6	39	156	94	137
July	.355	.410	.710	107	38	9	1	9	25	10	17		.290	.359	.499	851	247	48	5	40	146	90	128
August	.239	.298	.319	113	27	3	0	2	6	10	19		.278	.354	.448	920	256	43	4	35	145	108	160
Sept-Oct	.286	.351	.440	84	24	7	0	2	11	9	15		.275	.344	.439	975	268	50	4	34	172	108	171
Bases Empty	.282	.325	.429	301	85	16	2	8	8	19	55		.275	.339	.461	2654	731	144	9	110	110	251	472
Leadoff	.272	.316	.392	125	34	7	1	2	2	8	21		.278	.345	.443	1167	325	66	3	40	40	114	192
Runners On Base	.256	.325	.459	246	63	11	0	13	68	26	51		.296	.371	.495	2418	715	122	20	107	759	311	370
Scoring Position	.220	.300	.399	168	37	6	0	8	55	20	35		.301	.388	.502	1414	426	73	11	63	645	223	221
Late and Close	.242	.300	.363	91	22	3	1	2	10	8	17		.268	.336	.435	773	207	30	3	31	118	82	147

ERIC YOUNG — BR/TR — age 27 — COL 2B79, OF52

1993	BA	OBA	SA	AB	H	2B	3B	HR	RBI	BB	SO		2-YEAR TOTALS (1992–1993) BA	OBA	SA	AB	H	2B	3B	HR	RBI	BB	SO
Total	.269	.355	.353	490	132	16	8	3	42	63	41		.267	.344	.339	622	166	17	8	4	53	71	50
vs. Left	.289	.372	.375	128	37	5	3	0	13	16	12		.284	.350	.356	194	55	5	3	1	19	19	16
vs. Right	.262	.349	.345	362	95	11	5	3	29	47	29		.259	.341	.332	428	111	12	5	3	34	52	34
at Home	.303	.401	.420	238	72	5	7	3	33	41	14		.293	.382	.388	294	86	5	7	3	39	44	18
on Road	.238	.307	.290	252	60	11	1	0	9	22	27		.244	.307	.296	328	80	12	1	1	14	27	32
on Grass	.279	.373	.374	358	100	11	7	3	35	53	26		.279	.363	.362	448	125	11	7	4	44	58	32
on Turf	.242	.301	.295	132	32	5	1	0	7	10	15		.236	.293	.282	174	41	6	1	0	9	13	18
Day Games	.295	.380	.410	173	51	5	3	3	14	22	16		.288	.368	.382	212	61	5	3	3	15	25	20
Night Games	.256	.341	.322	317	81	11	5	0	28	41	25		.256	.331	.317	410	105	12	5	1	38	46	30
April	.259	.365	.370	81	21	2	2	1	8	13	5		.259	.365	.370	81	21	2	2	1	8	13	5
May	.255	.308	.340	106	27	3	3	0	7	7	7		.255	.308	.340	106	27	3	3	0	7	7	7
June	.265	.359	.279	68	18	1	0	0	7	10	9		.265	.359	.279	68	18	1	0	0	7	10	9
July	.272	.330	.359	92	25	6	1	0	6	8	8		.270	.330	.350	100	27	6	1	0	7	9	9
August	.169	.300	.220	59	10	1	1	0	1	10	5		.165	.248	.189	127	21	1	1	0	5	13	9
Sept-Oct	.369	.460	.500	84	31	3	1	2	13	15	7		.371	.444	.479	140	52	4	1	3	19	19	11
Bases Empty	.247	.330	.333	348	86	11	5	3	3	41	31		.236	.313	.315	416	98	11	5	4	4	45	35
Leadoff	.252	.333	.350	206	52	6	4	2	2	23	17		.240	.319	.326	233	56	6	4	2	2	25	18
Runners On Base	.324	.412	.401	142	46	5	3	0	39	22	10		.330	.403	.388	206	68	6	3	0	49	26	15
Scoring Position	.307	.414	.409	88	27	3	3	0	39	17	7		.318	.406	.388	129	41	3	3	0	48	20	10
Late and Close	.333	.405	.435	69	23	3	2	0	6	9	6		.352	.417	.429	91	32	3	2	0	8	11	7

KEVIN YOUNG — BR/TR — age 25 — PIT 1B135, 3B6

1993	BA	OBA	SA	AB	H	2B	3B	HR	RBI	BB	SO	2-YEAR TOTALS (1992–1993) BA	OBA	SA	AB	H	2B	3B	HR	RBI	BB	SO
Total	.236	.300	.343	449	106	24	3	6	47	36	82	.241	.307	.346	456	110	24	3	6	51	38	82
vs. Left	.237	.303	.355	169	40	11	0	3	14	16	31	.235	.305	.353	170	40	11	0	3	14	17	31
vs. Right	.236	.298	.336	280	66	13	3	3	33	20	51	.245	.307	.343	286	70	13	3	3	37	21	51
at Home	.240	.317	.384	229	55	13	1	6	35	24	38	.242	.318	.385	231	56	13	1	6	36	24	38
on Road	.232	.282	.300	220	51	11	2	0	12	12	44	.240	.294	.307	225	54	11	2	0	15	14	44
on Grass	.228	.279	.299	127	29	5	2	0	8	6	22	.238	.297	.308	130	31	5	2	0	11	8	22
on Turf	.239	.309	.360	322	77	19	1	6	39	30	60	.242	.311	.362	326	79	19	1	6	40	30	60
Day Games	.198	.257	.267	131	26	4	1	1	9	9	27	.217	.281	.283	138	30	4	1	1	13	14	27
Night Games	.252	.318	.374	318	80	20	2	5	38	27	55	.252	.318	.374	318	80	20	2	5	38	27	55
April	.239	.321	.328	67	16	1	1	1	13	7	14	.239	.321	.328	67	16	1	1	1	13	7	14
May	.194	.306	.375	72	14	2	1	3	8	8	8	.194	.306	.375	72	14	2	1	3	8	8	8
June	.244	.291	.308	78	19	5	0	0	7	5	14	.244	.291	.308	78	19	5	0	0	7	5	14
July	.230	.313	.287	87	20	5	0	0	6	10	22	.236	.317	.292	89	21	5	0	0	6	10	22
August	.243	.280	.300	70	17	4	0	0	5	3	11	.243	.280	.300	70	17	4	0	0	5	3	11
Sept-Oct	.267	.287	.467	75	20	7	1	2	8	3	13	.287	.322	.475	80	23	7	1	2	12	5	13
Bases Empty	.214	.252	.335	257	55	15	2	4	4	10	47	.215	.253	.335	260	56	15	2	4	4	10	47
Leadoff	.240	.290	.330	100	24	3	0	2	2	5	17	.238	.287	.327	101	24	3	0	2	2	5	17
Runners On Base	.266	.356	.354	192	51	9	1	2	43	26	35	.276	.368	.362	196	54	9	1	2	47	28	35
Scoring Position	.193	.291	.277	119	23	4	0	2	40	19	27	.213	.309	.295	122	26	4	0	2	44	20	27
Late and Close	.217	.296	.337	83	18	4	0	2	14	9	17	.214	.293	.333	84	18	4	0	2	14	9	17

ROBIN YOUNT — BR/TR — age 39 — MIL OF114, 1B7, DH6

1993	BA	OBA	SA	AB	H	2B	3B	HR	RBI	BB	SO	10-YEAR TOTALS (1984–1993) BA	OBA	SA	AB	H	2B	3B	HR	RBI	BB	SO
Total	.258	.326	.379	454	117	25	3	8	51	44	93	.287	.356	.434	5583	1601	287	61	138	771	609	766
vs. Left	.262	.362	.369	122	32	5	1	2	14	19	23	.284	.367	.427	1555	442	76	16	38	203	212	213
vs. Right	.256	.313	.383	332	85	20	2	6	37	25	70	.288	.352	.437	4028	1159	211	45	100	568	397	553
at Home	.256	.344	.333	234	60	9	3	1	25	31	44	.288	.359	.447	2762	796	136	37	76	414	307	368
on Road	.259	.305	.427	220	57	16	0	7	26	13	49	.285	.354	.422	2821	805	151	24	62	357	302	398
on Grass	.242	.314	.348	376	91	16	3	6	42	38	76	.286	.357	.435	4732	1355	224	52	125	671	524	647
on Turf	.333	.388	.526	78	26	9	0	2	9	6	17	.289	.353	.430	851	246	63	9	13	100	85	119
Day Games	.338	.391	.496	139	47	9	2	3	27	12	28	.298	.361	.470	1774	529	94	18	58	271	177	245
Night Games	.222	.297	.327	315	70	16	1	5	24	32	65	.281	.354	.418	3809	1072	193	43	80	500	432	521
April	.245	.304	.286	49	12	2	0	0	4	4	15	.280	.353	.412	731	205	30	9	16	88	78	101
May	.308	.373	.481	52	16	3	0	2	7	5	10	.297	.362	.457	923	274	46	6	30	126	94	122
June	.244	.315	.402	82	20	4	0	3	10	7	17	.285	.360	.424	987	281	59	9	20	131	119	140
July	.301	.353	.409	93	28	4	0	2	12	8	12	.296	.365	.462	939	278	55	16	23	128	102	126
August	.196	.277	.308	107	21	5	2	1	10	11	21	.269	.342	.390	1065	287	47	12	19	142	121	140
Sept-Oct	.282	.358	.408	71	20	7	1	0	8	9	18	.294	.358	.463	938	276	50	9	30	156	95	137
Bases Empty	.270	.333	.429	252	68	16	0	8	8	23	53	.271	.338	.415	3068	830	157	29	76	76	298	425
Leadoff	.281	.340	.393	89	25	4	0	2	2	8	16	.272	.324	.408	1181	321	62	12	25	25	85	151
Runners On Base	.243	.318	.317	202	49	9	3	0	43	21	40	.307	.378	.458	2515	771	130	32	62	695	311	341
Scoring Position	.236	.328	.336	110	26	5	3	0	40	15	22	.300	.382	.443	1451	435	77	22	29	598	226	219
Late and Close	.233	.301	.233	73	17	0	0	0	8	8	18	.286	.364	.395	807	231	33	5	15	118	104	125

TODD ZEILE — BR/TR — age 29 — SL 3B153

1993	BA	OBA	SA	AB	H	2B	3B	HR	RBI	BB	SO	5-YEAR TOTALS (1989–1993) BA	OBA	SA	AB	H	2B	3B	HR	RBI	BB	SO
Total	.277	.352	.433	571	158	36	1	17	103	70	76	.265	.347	.402	2152	571	118	12	51	297	276	331
vs. Left	.271	.355	.429	133	36	7	1	4	24	18	19	.283	.368	.417	715	202	40	4	16	99	96	106
vs. Right	.279	.352	.434	438	122	29	0	13	79	52	57	.257	.337	.395	1437	369	78	8	35	198	180	225
at Home	.304	.376	.454	280	85	18	0	8	49	35	35	.274	.360	.417	1057	290	58	6	27	158	143	147
on Road	.251	.329	.412	291	73	18	1	9	54	35	41	.257	.335	.388	1095	281	60	6	24	139	133	184
on Grass	.249	.338	.434	173	43	11	0	7	39	24	22	.253	.330	.389	589	149	37	2	13	75	70	103
on Turf	.289	.359	.432	398	115	25	1	10	64	46	54	.270	.353	.408	1563	422	81	10	38	222	206	228
Day Games	.329	.423	.484	161	53	14	1	3	29	27	25	.293	.380	.449	583	171	38	4	15	86	87	96
Night Games	.256	.323	.412	410	105	22	0	14	74	43	51	.255	.334	.385	1569	400	80	8	36	211	189	235
April	.286	.365	.345	84	24	5	0	0	8	11	7	.279	.360	.415	287	80	15	3	6	39	38	40
May	.213	.275	.319	94	20	7	0	1	12	8	11	.229	.313	.331	350	80	22	1	4	39	44	64
June	.247	.299	.348	89	22	6	0	1	15	7	9	.252	.324	.379	369	93	20	3	7	43	40	45
July	.363	.417	.667	102	37	8	1	7	30	11	19	.290	.363	.474	365	106	18	2	15	61	43	58
August	.287	.376	.417	108	31	5	0	3	16	16	20	.291	.351	.403	357	104	12	2	8	46	34	56
Sept-Oct	.255	.366	.468	94	24	5	0	5	22	17	10	.255	.368	.410	424	108	31	1	11	69	77	68
Bases Empty	.278	.338	.420	288	80	18	1	7	7	26	37	.264	.337	.411	1161	307	56	9	32	32	123	182
Leadoff	.300	.341	.500	130	39	10	0	5	5	8	17	.293	.359	.467	522	153	29	1	20	20	53	78
Runners On Base	.276	.366	.445	283	78	18	0	10	96	44	39	.266	.358	.393	991	264	62	3	19	265	153	149
Scoring Position	.270	.382	.444	189	51	14	0	7	85	38	25	.244	.361	.360	630	154	38	1	11	230	126	108
Late and Close	.229	.306	.323	96	22	6	0	1	14	11	17	.233	.320	.309	404	94	16	3	3	33	52	76

PITCHERS

JIM ABBOTT — BL/TL — age 27 — NYA SP32 FIN/GB

1993	G	IP	H	BB	SO	SB	CS	W	L	SV	ERA
Total	32	214.0	221	73	95	16	6	11	14	0	4.37
at Home	15	112.1	94	30	55	6	3	8	6	0	3.12
on Road	17	101.2	127	43	40	10	3	3	8	0	5.75
on Grass	25	170.1	163	58	81	10	4	9	11	0	4.02
on Turf	7	43.2	58	15	14	6	2	2	3	0	5.77
Day Games	12	80.2	70	35	40	7	2	6	4	0	4.24
Night Games	20	133.1	151	38	55	9	4	5	10	0	4.45
April	5	36.1	39	6	15	3	1	1	4	0	3.72
May	6	38.2	39	15	20	2	1	3	1	0	4.89
June	4	26.0	24	12	12	2	0	1	2	0	4.15
July	5	34.1	30	13	16	1	1	3	1	0	3.41
August	6	40.0	49	11	19	4	2	1	3	0	5.18
Sept-Oct	6	38.2	40	16	13	4	1	2	3	0	4.66

5-YEAR TOTALS (1989–1993)

	G	IP	H	BB	SO	SB	CS	W	L	SV	ERA
Total	157	1061.0	1087	360	603	85	45	58	66	0	3.66
at Home	77	534.0	549	159	296	40	27	27	33	0	3.64
on Road	80	527.0	538	201	307	45	18	31	33	0	3.69
on Grass	129	876.1	878	291	503	63	37	47	52	0	3.57
on Turf	28	184.2	209	69	100	22	8	11	14	0	4.09
Day Games	45	298.2	289	100	182	23	15	21	19	0	3.31
Night Games	112	762.1	798	260	421	62	30	37	47	0	3.80
April	21	136.1	154	41	72	14	8	3	14	0	3.89
May	29	187.2	178	75	104	12	10	14	9	0	3.79
June	25	170.0	169	63	98	12	5	9	9	0	3.97
July	24	170.1	164	39	107	10	7	11	9	0	2.75
August	29	190.2	209	70	110	18	6	12	11	0	4.06
Sept-Oct	29	206.0	213	72	112	19	9	9	14	0	3.54

	BA	OBA	SA	AB	H	2B	3B	HR	RBI	BB	SO
Total	.271	.332	.400	814	221	39	0	22	104	73	95
vs. Left	.294	.376	.363	102	30	7	0	0	7	12	8
vs. Right	.268	.326	.406	712	191	32	0	22	97	61	87
Bases Empty	.251	.316	.350	474	119	23	0	8	8	43	55
Leadoff	.261	.333	.394	203	53	12	0	5	5	22	19
Runners On Base	.300	.355	.471	340	102	16	0	14	96	30	40
Scoring Position	.302	.361	.484	182	55	9	0	8	82	19	26
Late and Close	.355	.388	.468	62	22	4	0	1	9	4	5

	BA	OBA	SA	AB	H	2B	3B	HR	RBI	BB	SO
Total	.269	.330	.372	4040	1087	164	11	77	414	360	603
vs. Left	.302	.370	.412	605	183	38	2	8	73	63	92
vs. Right	.263	.323	.365	3435	904	126	9	69	341	297	511
Bases Empty	.266	.328	.364	2342	624	99	5	40	40	201	338
Leadoff	.277	.333	.388	1026	284	48	3	20	20	83	132
Runners On Base	.273	.334	.383	1698	463	65	6	37	374	159	265
Scoring Position	.263	.340	.378	895	235	35	4	20	332	114	156
Late and Close	.319	.370	.420	357	114	10	1	8	43	29	41

RICK AGUILERA — BR/TR — age 33 — MIN RP65 FIN/FB

1993	G	IP	H	BB	SO	SB	CS	W	L	SV	ERA
Total	65	72.1	60	14	59	5	1	4	3	34	3.11
at Home	30	36.1	25	2	28	1	0	2	1	15	2.97
on Road	35	36.0	35	12	31	4	0	2	2	19	3.25
on Grass	30	30.0	29	12	26	3	0	2	2	16	3.60
on Turf	35	42.1	31	2	33	2	1	2	1	18	2.76
Day Games	26	29.0	23	6	31	2	0	1	1	13	3.10
Night Games	39	43.1	37	8	28	3	0	3	2	21	3.12
April	9	10.0	8	3	10	0	0	0	0	5	3.60
May	12	12.1	13	5	20	2	0	1	0	7	2.92
June	13	13.0	2	1	10	1	0	0	0	10	0.00
July	10	9.1	13	3	7	0	0	2	2	5	5.79
August	8	10.0	6	1	5	2	0	0	1	1	2.70
Sept-Oct	13	17.2	18	1	17	0	1	0	3	6	4.08

9-YEAR TOTALS (1985–1993)

	G	IP	H	BB	SO	SB	CS	W	L	SV	ERA
Total	373	822.0	764	234	641	60	21	55	49	156	3.27
at Home	187	404.0	353	102	340	26	9	28	18	74	3.10
on Road	186	418.0	411	132	301	34	12	27	31	82	3.44
on Grass	181	460.0	423	123	360	31	14	33	27	70	3.17
on Turf	192	362.0	341	111	281	29	7	22	22	86	3.41
Day Games	144	307.1	275	90	242	23	10	21	16	51	3.13
Night Games	229	514.2	489	144	399	37	11	34	33	105	3.36
April	48	98.1	107	28	91	6	3	3	8	18	4.48
May	65	117.2	108	39	111	10	3	5	7	35	2.83
June	70	99.1	82	42	80	12	1	6	6	35	3.08
July	65	146.1	135	40	107	9	6	11	11	25	3.01
August	54	159.1	150	34	112	10	5	10	10	18	3.67
Sept-Oct	71	201.0	182	51	140	13	3	20	7	25	2.91

	BA	OBA	SA	AB	H	2B	3B	HR	RBI	BB	SO
Total	.223	.263	.379	269	60	11	2	9	31	14	59
vs. Left	.200	.247	.324	145	29	5	2	3	13	8	30
vs. Right	.250	.282	.444	124	31	6	0	6	18	6	29
Bases Empty	.194	.230	.318	170	33	6	0	5	5	7	42
Leadoff	.156	.182	.234	64	10	2	0	1	1	2	12
Runners On Base	.273	.318	.485	99	27	5	2	4	26	7	17
Scoring Position	.263	.328	.386	57	15	4	0	1	17	6	12
Late and Close	.250	.294	.417	168	42	8	1	6	24	10	32

	BA	OBA	SA	AB	H	2B	3B	HR	RBI	BB	SO
Total	.246	.302	.372	3106	764	145	20	69	339	234	641
vs. Left	.250	.312	.357	1556	389	65	15	24	148	135	297
vs. Right	.242	.291	.387	1550	375	80	5	45	191	99	344
Bases Empty	.243	.294	.361	1765	429	81	11	35	35	114	368
Leadoff	.238	.291	.360	735	175	37	3	13	13	47	150
Runners On Base	.250	.312	.387	1341	335	64	9	34	304	120	273
Scoring Position	.238	.313	.362	790	188	34	5	18	251	90	179
Late and Close	.227	.291	.334	933	212	31	3	21	120	83	217

WILSON ALVAREZ — BL/TL — age 24 — CHA SP31 POW/FB

1993	G	IP	H	BB	SO	SB	CS	W	L	SV	ERA
Total	31	207.2	168	122	155	21	17	15	8	0	2.95
at Home	16	106.2	89	69	86	8	8	7	5	0	3.38
on Road	15	101.0	79	53	69	13	9	8	3	0	2.50
on Grass	28	191.2	155	110	150	18	16	13	8	0	2.96
on Turf	3	16.0	13	12	5	3	1	2	0	0	2.81
Day Games	9	55.0	48	35	34	9	3	3	3	0	4.09
Night Games	22	152.2	120	87	121	12	14	12	5	0	2.53
April	3	19.0	18	9	14	2	1	1	0	0	2.37
May	6	42.0	35	30	31	6	2	4	2	0	3.64
June	6	43.1	37	20	36	3	4	2	2	0	3.12
July	6	36.0	33	30	16	4	1	2	0	0	3.75
August	4	23.2	22	13	26	2	2	2	2	0	4.18
Sept-Oct	6	43.2	23	20	32	4	5	4	0	0	1.03

4-YEAR TOTALS (1989–1993)

	G	IP	H	BB	SO	SB	CS	W	L	SV	ERA
Total	76	364.1	321	218	253	30	29	23	14	1	3.73
at Home	34	171.1	152	110	122	12	15	10	8	0	4.04
on Road	42	193.0	169	108	131	18	14	13	6	1	3.45
on Grass	64	316.0	276	187	226	26	27	19	12	1	3.87
on Turf	12	48.1	45	31	27	4	2	4	2	0	2.79
Day Games	22	104.1	88	67	70	12	8	6	5	0	3.62
Night Games	54	260.0	233	151	183	18	21	17	9	1	3.77
April	7	28.0	21	11	21	2	1	1	0	1	1.61
May	10	52.2	48	43	39	7	4	4	2	0	3.76
June	13	55.2	54	29	42	4	7	2	5	0	4.20
July	12	60.1	56	44	25	5	5	3	4	0	4.18
August	16	60.0	64	31	50	4	5	4	4	0	4.95
Sept-Oct	18	107.2	78	60	76	8	7	9	0	0	3.09

	BA	OBA	SA	AB	H	2B	3B	HR	RBI	BB	SO
Total	.230	.344	.329	729	168	28	1	14	66	122	155
vs. Left	.258	.432	.315	89	23	2	0	1	9	25	20
vs. Right	.227	.330	.331	640	145	26	1	13	57	97	135
Bases Empty	.246	.361	.354	418	103	19	1	8	8	72	97
Leadoff	.251	.335	.377	191	48	4	1	6	6	23	43
Runners On Base	.209	.321	.296	311	65	9	0	6	58	50	58
Scoring Position	.206	.361	.306	160	33	7	0	3	50	40	36
Late and Close	.215	.373	.277	65	14	1	0	1	6	15	6

	BA	OBA	SA	AB	H	2B	3B	HR	RBI	BB	SO
Total	.244	.354	.368	1315	321	48	2	37	145	218	253
vs. Left	.237	.384	.293	198	47	3	0	1	20	46	42
vs. Right	.245	.348	.381	1117	274	40	2	36	125	172	211
Bases Empty	.254	.358	.388	753	191	31	2	22	22	119	157
Leadoff	.258	.343	.402	333	86	10	1	12	12	42	64
Runners On Base	.231	.349	.342	562	130	17	0	15	123	99	96
Scoring Position	.223	.352	.351	305	68	12	0	9	108	63	62
Late and Close	.273	.407	.354	99	27	2	0	2	11	19	9

KEVIN APPIER — BR/TR — age 27 — KC SP34 POW/FB

5-YEAR TOTALS (1989–1993)

1993	G	IP	H	BB	SO	SB	CS	W	L	SV	ERA		G	IP	H	BB	SO	SB	CS	W	L	SV	ERA
Total	34	238.2	183	81	186	11	8	18	8	0	2.56		136	862.0	768	276	631	55	28	59	38	0	2.95
at Home	17	116.2	84	39	90	2	6	8	5	0	2.39		64	407.1	344	120	307	23	16	29	20	0	2.76
on Road	17	122.0	99	42	96	9	2	10	3	0	2.73		72	454.2	424	156	324	32	12	30	18	0	3.13
on Grass	14	98.0	84	35	83	6	2	8	3	0	2.94		60	370.1	351	132	275	23	11	25	16	0	3.18
on Turf	20	140.2	99	46	103	5	6	10	5	0	2.30		76	491.2	417	144	356	32	17	34	22	0	2.78
Day Games	14	93.2	81	31	76	6	4	6	4	0	2.59		43	257.1	242	100	198	18	11	18	13	0	2.76
Night Games	20	145.0	102	50	110	5	4	12	4	0	2.54		93	604.2	526	176	433	37	17	41	25	0	3.04
April	6	41.1	37	16	34	1	0	2	3	0	3.70		17	100.1	87	37	74	5	3	3	8	0	2.96
May	5	35.2	38	16	28	4	1	3	1	0	3.28		24	139.2	140	45	88	6	4	10	4	0	3.09
June	6	44.1	30	12	33	0	1	4	0	0	2.23		28	171.2	158	54	116	11	3	11	8	0	3.57
July	5	29.2	17	9	30	3	1	2	1	0	2.43		23	155.2	127	41	131	11	6	13	3	0	2.78
August	6	43.2	36	11	25	1	3	3	1	0	2.89		23	157.2	134	49	115	12	7	14	6	0	2.80
Sept-Oct	6	44.0	25	17	36	2	2	4	2	0	1.02		21	137.0	122	50	107	10	5	8	9	0	2.43

	BA	OBA	SA	AB	H	2B	3B	HR	RBI	BB	SO		BA	OBA	SA	AB	H	2B	3B	HR	RBI	BB	SO
Total	.212	.279	.292	863	183	39	3	8	63	81	186		.237	.297	.331	3237	768	139	11	47	274	276	631
vs. Left	.239	.311	.321	439	105	19	1	5	37	47	83		.247	.316	.357	1567	387	69	7	30	156	166	262
vs. Right	.184	.245	.262	424	78	20	2	3	26	34	103		.228	.279	.305	1670	381	70	4	17	118	110	369
Bases Empty	.193	.260	.269	539	104	21	1	6	6	49	120		.228	.292	.316	1916	437	75	8	26	26	166	375
Leadoff	.165	.237	.228	224	37	8	0	2	2	21	45		.222	.286	.317	818	182	36	4	11	11	72	151
Runners On Base	.244	.309	.330	324	79	18	2	2	57	32	66		.251	.305	.351	1321	331	64	3	21	248	110	256
Scoring Position	.213	.282	.287	178	38	9	2	0	50	19	38		.222	.292	.304	721	160	32	3	7	209	78	157
Late and Close	.248	.320	.312	109	27	4	0	1	10	11	16		.205	.271	.273	341	70	9	1	4	28	30	55

JACK ARMSTRONG — BR/TR — age 29 — FLO SP33, RP3 FIN/GB

6-YEAR TOTALS (1988–1993)

1993	G	IP	H	BB	SO	SB	CS	W	L	SV	ERA		G	IP	H	BB	SO	SB	CS	W	L	SV	ERA
Total	36	196.1	210	78	118	18	3	9	17	0	4.49		150	776.2	798	317	503	81	29	40	64	0	4.59
at Home	20	118.0	125	42	80	10	1	5	13	0	4.73		76	382.2	395	160	260	34	12	24	34	0	5.08
on Road	16	78.1	85	36	38	8	2	4	4	0	4.14		74	394.0	403	157	243	47	17	16	30	0	4.11
on Grass	28	154.1	164	59	92	14	2	7	15	0	4.61		82	425.0	448	167	265	37	17	19	37	0	4.53
on Turf	8	42.0	46	19	26	4	1	2	2	0	4.07		68	351.2	350	150	238	44	12	21	27	0	4.66
Day Games	8	46.2	38	18	35	4	1	4	3	0	3.09		40	213.0	197	88	165	31	7	16	16	0	3.72
Night Games	28	149.2	172	60	83	14	2	5	14	0	4.93		110	563.2	601	229	338	50	22	24	48	0	4.92
April	5	32.1	33	11	30	2	0	2	2	0	3.62		16	99.0	94	30	74	8	3	7	6	0	3.27
May	6	39.2	38	12	23	7	1	2	2	0	4.08		26	162.2	149	63	95	13	5	10	9	0	3.76
June	6	31.2	32	9	16	3	0	1	5	0	4.83		25	138.1	147	62	99	19	7	5	15	0	5.07
July	5	27.2	33	9	16	2	0	2	1	0	4.88		29	146.1	165	50	92	16	6	8	14	0	5.54
August	6	35.0	41	21	18	1	2	0	4	0	5.40		20	91.0	102	53	48	4	6	3	10	0	6.03
Sept-Oct	8	30.0	33	16	15	3	0	2	3	0	4.20		34	139.1	141	59	95	21	2	7	10	0	4.07

	BA	OBA	SA	AB	H	2B	3B	HR	RBI	BB	SO		BA	OBA	SA	AB	H	2B	3B	HR	RBI	BB	SO
Total	.271	.339	.443	776	210	35	6	29	98	78	118		.266	.336	.426	3004	798	142	22	99	393	317	503
vs. Left	.284	.369	.505	422	120	23	2	22	60	57	58		.277	.361	.450	1604	444	81	13	57	226	213	214
vs. Right	.254	.300	.370	354	90	12	4	7	38	21	60		.253	.305	.399	1400	354	61	9	42	167	104	289
Bases Empty	.275	.339	.445	454	125	15	4	18	18	40	69		.249	.322	.399	1768	440	78	11	55	55	180	310
Leadoff	.270	.313	.403	196	53	3	1	7	7	10	32		.259	.321	.422	749	194	32	3	28	28	62	136
Runners On Base	.264	.338	.441	322	85	20	2	11	80	38	49		.290	.355	.466	1236	358	64	11	44	338	137	193
Scoring Position	.227	.333	.344	163	37	7	0	4	56	29	22		.273	.352	.433	700	191	31	6	23	274	100	116
Late and Close	.280	.357	.320	50	14	2	0	0	2	6	7		.260	.329	.349	146	38	5	4	0	9	14	25

RENE AROCHA — BR/TR — age 28 — SL SP29, RP3 FIN/GB

1-YEAR TOTALS (1993)

1993	G	IP	H	BB	SO	SB	CS	W	L	SV	ERA		G	IP	H	BB	SO	SB	CS	W	L	SV	ERA
Total	32	188.0	197	31	96	14	9	11	8	0	3.78		32	188.0	197	31	96	14	9	11	8	0	3.78
at Home	17	99.2	101	14	57	6	4	6	3	0	3.43		17	99.2	101	14	57	6	4	6	3	0	3.43
on Road	15	88.1	96	17	39	8	5	5	5	0	4.18		15	88.1	96	17	39	8	5	5	5	0	4.18
on Grass	11	62.2	66	13	25	4	4	3	0	0	4.16		11	62.2	66	13	25	4	4	3	0	0	4.16
on Turf	21	125.1	131	18	71	10	5	7	5	0	3.59		21	125.1	131	18	71	10	5	7	5	0	3.59
Day Games	11	60.2	61	8	35	5	5	2	5	0	4.30		11	60.2	61	8	35	5	5	2	5	0	4.30
Night Games	21	127.1	136	23	61	9	4	9	3	0	3.53		21	127.1	136	23	61	9	4	9	3	0	3.53
April	3	21.2	15	1	11	3	0	3	0	0	1.66		3	21.2	15	1	11	3	0	3	0	0	1.66
May	5	24.2	20	4	15	1	0	1	0	0	3.28		5	24.2	20	4	15	1	0	1	0	0	3.28
June	6	28.1	33	5	12	2	2	0	2	0	4.45		6	28.1	33	5	12	2	2	0	2	0	4.45
July	6	36.1	44	3	21	2	2	2	1	0	3.96		6	36.1	44	3	21	2	2	2	1	0	3.96
August	6	41.2	46	6	15	4	3	2	2	0	4.10		6	41.2	46	6	15	4	3	2	2	0	4.10
Sept-Oct	7	35.1	39	12	22	2	2	4	1	0	4.33		7	35.1	39	12	22	2	2	4	1	0	4.33

	BA	OBA	SA	AB	H	2B	3B	HR	RBI	BB	SO		BA	OBA	SA	AB	H	2B	3B	HR	RBI	BB	SO
Total	.271	.302	.422	727	197	36	7	20	83	31	96		.271	.302	.422	727	197	36	7	20	83	31	96
vs. Left	.312	.347	.462	353	110	16	5	9	44	19	35		.312	.347	.462	353	110	16	5	9	44	19	35
vs. Right	.233	.258	.385	374	87	20	2	11	39	12	61		.233	.258	.385	374	87	20	2	11	39	12	61
Bases Empty	.263	.285	.410	456	120	22	6	11	11	14	59		.263	.285	.410	456	120	22	6	11	11	14	59
Leadoff	.257	.279	.366	191	49	9	3	2	2	6	22		.257	.279	.366	191	49	9	3	2	2	6	22
Runners On Base	.284	.328	.443	271	77	14	1	9	72	17	37		.284	.328	.443	271	77	14	1	9	72	17	37
Scoring Position	.274	.344	.427	164	45	8	1	5	61	17	22		.274	.344	.427	164	45	8	1	5	61	17	22
Late and Close	.229	.240	.354	48	11	1	1	2	4	1	6		.229	.240	.354	48	11	1	1	2	4	1	6

ANDY ASHBY — BR/TR — age 27 — COL/SD SP21, RP11 POW/GB

1993

1993	G	IP	H	BB	SO	SB	CS	W	L	SV	ERA
Total	32	123.0	168	56	77	11	1	3	10	1	6.80
at Home	16	66.0	80	30	44	5	1	2	3	0	6.00
on Road	16	57.0	88	26	33	6	0	1	7	1	7.74
on Grass	24	92.0	119	40	52	7	1	2	6	0	5.97
on Turf	8	31.0	49	16	25	4	0	1	4	1	9.29
Day Games	15	68.1	89	26	42	4	0	1	8	0	5.93
Night Games	17	54.2	79	30	35	7	1	2	2	1	7.90
April	4	23.0	28	12	14	1	0	0	2	0	3.13
May	9	20.1	30	10	12	2	0	0	1	1	8.85
June	7	10.2	31	10	7	0	0	0	1	0	19.41
July	1	6.0	8	5	4	0	0	0	1	0	9.00
August	5	31.2	35	10	20	1	1	2	3	0	4.26
Sept-Oct	6	31.1	36	9	20	3	0	1	2	0	6.03

3-YEAR TOTALS (1991–1993)

	G	IP	H	BB	SO	SB	CS	W	L	SV	ERA
	50	202.0	251	96	127	15	4	5	18	1	6.77
	26	113.1	126	50	76	9	3	3	7	0	6.11
	24	88.2	125	46	51	6	1	2	11	1	7.61
	28	109.1	139	49	64	7	3	3	6	0	5.93
	22	92.2	112	47	63	8	2	2	12	1	7.77
	20	87.2	114	32	58	4	1	1	10	0	6.67
	30	114.1	137	64	69	11	3	4	8	1	6.85
	7	38.2	42	14	26	2	1	1	2	0	3.49
	9	20.1	30	10	12	2	0	0	1	1	8.85
	7	19.2	39	13	16	4	0	0	3	0	14.19
	1	6.0	8	5	4	0	0	0	1	0	9.00
	9	46.0	53	23	27	3	1	2	6	0	5.67
	15	71.1	79	31	42	4	2	2	5	0	6.43

	BA	OBA	SA	AB	H	2B	3B	HR	RBI	BB	SO
Total	.333	.399	.516	504	168	29	3	19	90	56	77
vs. Left	.307	.380	.423	274	84	7	2	7	41	31	35
vs. Right	.365	.422	.626	230	84	22	1	12	49	25	42
Bases Empty	.316	.384	.530	253	80	13	1	13	13	26	35
Leadoff	.416	.480	.735	113	47	10	1	8	8	12	11
Runners On Base	.351	.414	.502	251	88	16	2	6	77	30	42
Scoring Position	.367	.443	.557	158	58	14	2	4	73	25	25
Late and Close	.208	.269	.208	24	5	0	0	0	0	2	3

3-year totals:

	BA	OBA	SA	AB	H	2B	3B	HR	RBI	BB	SO
	.310	.384	.494	809	251	45	7	30	141	96	127
vs. Left	.296	.372	.436	452	134	13	4	14	70	54	59
vs. Right	.328	.398	.569	357	117	32	3	16	71	42	68
Bases Empty	.292	.370	.496	421	123	21	4	19	19	48	67
Leadoff	.357	.433	.643	185	66	12	4	11	11	23	28
Runners On Base	.330	.398	.492	388	128	24	3	11	122	48	60
Scoring Position	.342	.418	.534	234	80	18	3	7	112	36	36
Late and Close	.222	.300	.333	27	6	0	0	2	3	3	3

PEDRO ASTACIO — BR/TR — age 25 — LA SP31 FIN/GB

1993

1993	G	IP	H	BB	SO	SB	CS	W	L	SV	ERA
Total	31	186.1	165	68	122	19	12	14	9	0	3.57
at Home	16	97.0	94	38	62	11	7	6	3	0	3.34
on Road	15	89.1	71	30	60	8	5	8	6	0	3.83
on Grass	22	132.1	127	49	83	17	9	8	7	0	3.81
on Turf	9	54.0	38	19	39	2	3	6	2	0	3.00
Day Games	8	45.1	39	17	27	4	5	4	2	0	3.38
Night Games	23	141.0	126	51	95	15	7	10	7	0	3.64
April	4	24.0	21	11	14	2	2	1	2	0	3.00
May	5	25.1	32	7	15	5	2	2	1	0	4.97
June	6	36.2	34	9	15	2	3	1	1	0	4.17
July	5	26.0	28	16	17	6	1	1	2	0	6.92
August	5	27.0	20	13	20	0	3	3	1	0	2.67
Sept-Oct	6	47.1	30	12	41	4	2	4	2	0	1.33

2-YEAR TOTALS (1992–1993)

	G	IP	H	BB	SO	SB	CS	W	L	SV	ERA
	42	268.1	245	88	165	24	15	19	14	0	3.09
	22	145.1	141	48	84	15	8	9	6	0	2.79
	20	123.0	104	40	81	9	7	10	8	0	3.44
	30	192.1	189	64	111	21	10	12	11	0	3.32
	12	76.0	56	24	54	3	5	7	3	0	2.49
	12	70.1	73	23	46	5	7	4	2	0	3.33
	30	198.0	172	65	119	19	8	15	9	0	3.00
	4	24.0	21	11	14	2	2	1	2	0	3.00
	5	25.1	32	7	15	5	2	2	1	0	4.97
	6	36.2	34	9	15	2	3	1	1	0	4.17
	7	42.0	40	22	29	8	1	2	3	0	4.93
	8	49.0	43	17	29	1	4	4	2	0	2.02
	12	91.1	75	22	63	6	4	7	5	0	1.87

	BA	OBA	SA	AB	H	2B	3B	HR	RBI	BB	SO
Total	.239	.309	.353	689	165	32	2	14	63	68	122
vs. Left	.240	.304	.355	392	94	18	0	9	40	37	66
vs. Right	.239	.315	.350	297	71	14	2	5	23	31	56
Bases Empty	.249	.312	.366	429	107	25	2	7	7	36	71
Leadoff	.258	.322	.418	182	47	15	1	4	4	15	29
Runners On Base	.223	.305	.331	260	58	7	0	7	56	32	51
Scoring Position	.239	.319	.348	138	33	3	0	4	49	19	33
Late and Close	.294	.342	.441	34	10	2	0	1	3	3	5

2-year totals:

	BA	OBA	SA	AB	H	2B	3B	HR	RBI	BB	SO
	.244	.307	.337	1003	245	40	4	15	81	88	165
vs. Left	.241	.308	.337	572	138	21	2	10	47	55	83
vs. Right	.248	.306	.336	431	107	19	2	5	34	33	82
Bases Empty	.254	.313	.354	602	153	30	3	8	8	48	94
Leadoff	.241	.311	.370	257	62	16	1	5	5	24	41
Runners On Base	.229	.297	.312	401	92	10	1	7	73	40	71
Scoring Position	.234	.312	.311	209	49	4	0	4	64	26	44
Late and Close	.316	.349	.474	57	18	3	0	2	5	4	7

STEVE AVERY — BL/TL — age 24 — ATL SP35 FIN/FB

1993

1993	G	IP	H	BB	SO	SB	CS	W	L	SV	ERA
Total	35	223.1	216	43	125	32	14	18	6	0	2.94
at Home	18	116.2	120	17	59	14	7	9	2	0	2.85
on Road	17	106.2	96	26	66	18	7	9	4	0	3.04
on Grass	28	185.1	180	29	96	21	10	14	4	0	2.72
on Turf	7	38.0	36	14	29	11	4	4	2	0	4.03
Day Games	11	76.2	67	13	48	11	2	7	2	0	2.00
Night Games	24	146.2	149	30	77	21	12	11	4	0	3.44
April	5	36.0	34	6	18	4	1	1	2	0	2.75
May	6	35.2	37	9	22	5	1	2	1	0	3.53
June	6	41.2	38	4	23	8	4	4	0	0	2.16
July	5	25.1	37	6	14	3	2	1	1	0	4.26
August	6	44.2	34	9	19	5	3	4	1	0	2.22
Sept-Oct	7	40.0	36	9	29	7	2	3	2	0	3.38

4-YEAR TOTALS (1990–1993)

	G	IP	H	BB	SO	SB	CS	W	L	SV	ERA
	126	766.1	742	224	466	115	47	50	36	0	3.49
	63	389.1	392	106	229	55	28	27	15	0	3.19
	63	377.0	350	118	237	60	19	23	21	0	3.80
	94	587.1	559	160	336	80	39	40	24	0	3.11
	32	179.0	183	64	130	35	8	10	12	0	4.73
	38	231.2	215	60	150	35	14	17	10	0	3.34
	88	534.2	527	164	316	80	33	33	26	0	3.55
	13	84.1	73	24	43	14	4	4	5	0	2.88
	19	117.2	116	46	74	18	6	10	4	0	3.37
	20	123.1	126	33	70	20	9	9	5	0	3.28
	24	146.1	135	48	78	21	12	8	6	0	3.51
	24	146.2	158	42	98	22	12	11	9	0	3.93
	26	148.0	134	31	103	20	4	8	7	0	3.65

	BA	OBA	SA	AB	H	2B	3B	HR	RBI	BB	SO
Total	.261	.295	.362	827	216	35	3	14	74	43	125
vs. Left	.245	.299	.329	143	35	6	0	2	12	11	32
vs. Right	.265	.294	.368	684	181	29	3	12	62	32	93
Bases Empty	.254	.288	.356	531	135	24	3	8	8	25	86
Leadoff	.255	.284	.400	220	56	13	2	5	5	9	33
Runners On Base	.274	.307	.372	296	81	11	0	6	66	18	39
Scoring Position	.245	.288	.331	163	40	5	0	3	57	13	24
Late and Close	.263	.300	.368	95	25	4	0	2	6	5	14

4-year totals:

	BA	OBA	SA	AB	H	2B	3B	HR	RBI	BB	SO
	.256	.309	.368	2894	742	124	16	56	300	224	466
vs. Left	.231	.295	.319	523	121	16	3	8	52	48	122
vs. Right	.262	.312	.379	2371	621	108	13	48	248	176	344
Bases Empty	.242	.296	.348	1768	428	80	10	29	29	131	278
Leadoff	.266	.317	.405	749	199	41	6	17	17	55	114
Runners On Base	.279	.328	.401	1126	314	44	6	27	271	93	188
Scoring Position	.255	.315	.352	662	169	26	1	12	229	69	126
Late and Close	.260	.312	.337	258	67	9	1	3	26	20	34

WILLIE BANKS — BR/TR — age 25 — MIN SP30, RP1 POW/GB

1993	G	IP	H	BB	SO	SB	CS	W	L	SV	ERA		G	IP	H	BB	SO	SB	CS	W	L	SV	ERA
Total	31	171.1	186	78	138	6	6	11	12	0	4.04		52	259.2	287	127	191	16	10	16	17	0	4.61
at Home	19	106.0	111	47	81	5	3	7	7	0	3.65		28	146.1	152	68	108	11	5	8	10	0	3.87
on Road	12	65.1	75	31	57	1	3	4	5	0	4.68		24	113.1	135	59	83	5	5	8	7	0	5.56
on Grass	8	42.1	52	25	38	1	1	2	4	0	5.10		19	87.0	105	51	64	5	3	6	6	0	5.69
on Turf	23	129.0	134	53	100	5	5	9	8	0	3.70		33	172.2	182	76	127	11	7	10	11	0	4.07
Day Games	11	62.0	74	30	51	1	4	1	6	0	4.65		16	84.2	92	44	61	1	5	4	6	0	4.15
Night Games	20	109.1	112	48	87	5	2	10	6	0	3.70		36	175.0	195	83	130	15	5	12	11	0	4.83
April	4	23.2	25	10	21	1	3	2	1	0	2.66		4	23.2	25	10	21	1	3	2	1	0	2.66
May	5	22.0	31	9	14	3	0	2	1	0	5.73		5	22.0	31	9	14	3	0	2	1	0	5.73
June	5	26.2	29	13	22	0	1	1	2	0	5.40		10	53.0	62	23	35	3	4	3	3	0	5.43
July	5	28.0	24	10	17	0	1	2	3	0	3.54		12	64.0	57	27	35	3	2	4	6	0	3.66
August	6	38.0	40	14	35	0	0	1	2	0	3.55		13	60.1	69	33	55	4	0	2	3	0	5.82
Sept-Oct	6	33.0	37	22	29	2	1	3	3	0	3.82		8	36.2	43	25	31	2	1	3	3	0	3.68

	BA	OBA	SA	AB	H	2B	3B	HR	RBI	BB	SO		BA	OBA	SA	AB	H	2B	3B	HR	RBI	BB	SO
Total	.280	.356	.417	665	186	38	1	17	70	78	138		.282	.362	.415	1016	287	55	4	24	123	127	191
vs. Left	.292	.360	.427	391	114	21	1	10	36	43	79		.293	.360	.421	563	165	29	2	13	60	61	108
vs. Right	.263	.350	.401	274	72	17	0	7	34	35	59		.269	.364	.408	453	122	26	2	11	63	66	83
Bases Empty	.294	.370	.437	364	107	22	0	10	10	44	69		.294	.377	.426	545	160	28	1	14	14	72	88
Leadoff	.285	.372	.424	158	45	7	0	5	5	22	22		.275	.360	.392	240	66	10	0	6	6	32	33
Runners On Base	.262	.339	.392	301	79	16	1	7	60	34	69		.270	.345	.403	471	127	27	3	10	109	55	103
Scoring Position	.241	.347	.380	158	38	7	0	5	54	26	39		.255	.345	.396	255	65	13	1	7	96	38	57
Late and Close	.250	.368	.344	32	8	3	0	0	2	5	8		.256	.347	.395	43	11	3	0	1	3	5	9

3-YEAR TOTALS (1991–1993)

ROD BECK — BR/TR — age 26 — SF RP76 POW/FB

1993	G	IP	H	BB	SO	SB	CS	W	L	SV	ERA		G	IP	H	BB	SO	SB	CS	W	L	SV	ERA
Total	76	79.1	57	13	86	1	0	3	1	48	2.16		172	223.2	172	41	211	5	7	7	5	66	2.37
at Home	38	39.0	27	8	42	0	0	3	0	21	1.62		84	108.1	88	16	108	1	6	5	4	31	2.33
on Road	38	40.1	30	5	44	1	0	0	1	27	2.68		88	115.1	84	25	103	4	1	2	1	35	2.42
on Grass	60	63.0	42	12	67	1	0	3	0	39	1.71		126	161.1	125	27	159	3	6	5	4	55	2.06
on Turf	16	16.1	15	1	19	0	0	0	1	9	3.86		46	62.1	47	14	52	2	1	2	1	11	3.18
Day Games	41	43.1	31	8	51	0	0	1	0	27	1.66		81	97.2	73	17	108	3	2	2	1	35	2.03
Night Games	35	36.0	26	5	35	1	0	2	1	21	2.75		91	126.0	99	24	103	2	5	5	4	31	2.64
April	14	15.1	9	2	20	0	0	2	1	7	2.35		22	32.1	17	5	36	0	1	2	1	8	1.11
May	11	11.0	7	1	12	0	0	0	0	6	0.82		27	35.0	34	3	38	1	0	1	1	7	4.37
June	11	10.2	10	2	15	1	0	0	0	8	0.84		20	23.0	21	5	24	1	1	0	2	12	1.57
July	11	12.1	7	1	13	0	0	0	0	7	1.46		28	36.2	26	4	43	1	3	1	1	12	1.72
August	13	13.0	12	5	12	0	0	0	0	8	4.15		34	41.1	31	14	31	1	1	0	0	12	2.18
Sept-Oct	16	17.0	12	2	14	0	0	1	0	10	2.65		41	55.1	43	10	39	1	1	4	0	15	2.77

	BA	OBA	SA	AB	H	2B	3B	HR	RBI	BB	SO		BA	OBA	SA	AB	H	2B	3B	HR	RBI	BB	SO
Total	.201	.241	.335	284	57	5	0	11	26	13	86		.214	.255	.322	805	172	24	3	19	77	41	211
vs. Left	.180	.231	.304	161	29	2	0	6	13	11	56		.202	.245	.328	430	87	14	2	12	36	23	122
vs. Right	.228	.254	.374	123	28	3	0	5	13	2	30		.227	.266	.315	375	85	10	1	7	41	18	89
Bases Empty	.228	.273	.364	162	37	4	0	6	6	7	50		.218	.252	.343	467	102	12	2	14	14	17	125
Leadoff	.219	.275	.281	64	14	1	0	1	1	3	15		.229	.264	.309	188	43	3	0	4	4	6	39
Runners On Base	.164	.198	.295	122	20	1	0	5	20	6	36		.207	.259	.293	338	70	12	1	5	63	24	86
Scoring Position	.138	.197	.241	58	8	0	0	2	13	5	23		.216	.276	.291	199	43	7	1	2	55	18	57
Late and Close	.165	.227	.227	176	29	2	0	3	16	12	59		.185	.231	.261	395	73	10	1	6	33	22	112

3-YEAR TOTALS (1991–1993)

TIM BELCHER — BR/TR — age 33 — CIN/CHA SP33, RP1 FIN/FB

1993	G	IP	H	BB	SO	SB	CS	W	L	SV	ERA		G	IP	H	BB	SO	SB	CS	W	L	SV	ERA
Total	34	208.2	198	74	135	11	8	12	11	0	4.44		207	1242.1	1079	415	917	82	63	77	63	5	3.40
at Home	19	114.0	119	42	74	9	6	8	4	0	4.74		105	667.0	578	202	504	46	34	52	26	2	3.08
on Road	15	94.2	79	32	61	2	2	4	7	0	4.09		102	575.1	501	213	413	36	29	25	37	3	3.79
on Grass	15	96.2	84	29	50	1	6	4	7	0	3.26		127	770.0	657	230	558	49	40	47	35	3	2.91
on Turf	19	112.0	114	45	85	10	2	8	4	0	5.46		80	472.1	422	185	359	33	23	30	28	2	4.21
Day Games	8	41.0	51	13	23	2	2	2	3	0	5.71		67	344.0	338	125	249	26	20	19	21	1	4.03
Night Games	26	167.2	147	61	112	9	6	10	8	0	4.13		140	898.1	741	290	668	56	43	58	42	4	3.17
April	5	28.2	33	11	14	1	0	1	3	0	5.65		30	182.1	157	49	139	11	3	9	12	1	3.55
May	5	32.2	20	14	29	1	1	1	1	0	2.20		31	200.2	164	79	160	19	14	13	10	0	3.27
June	6	44.1	40	5	25	5	0	4	1	0	3.05		38	215.0	196	74	153	18	11	12	11	2	3.43
July	6	31.1	41	17	33	2	2	3	1	0	7.76		39	206.2	200	78	146	13	10	15	10	2	3.92
August	5	33.2	30	11	19	0	2	3	2	0	4.28		32	204.2	186	69	148	11	11	12	10	0	3.69
Sept-Oct	7	38.0	34	16	15	2	3	0	3	0	4.50		37	233.0	176	66	171	10	14	16	10	0	2.67

	BA	OBA	SA	AB	H	2B	3B	HR	RBI	BB	SO		BA	OBA	SA	AB	H	2B	3B	HR	RBI	BB	SO
Total	.250	.319	.381	792	198	33	7	19	90	74	135		.234	.299	.343	4612	1079	170	28	93	448	415	917
vs. Left	.258	.341	.379	396	102	18	3	8	50	48	53		.249	.321	.350	2526	628	100	15	42	229	267	465
vs. Right	.242	.296	.384	396	96	15	4	11	40	26	82		.216	.271	.336	2086	451	70	13	51	219	148	452
Bases Empty	.220	.290	.335	481	106	18	2	11	11	45	88		.222	.281	.323	2841	630	97	11	56	56	228	556
Leadoff	.208	.294	.340	197	41	9	1	5	5	23	32		.225	.288	.338	1184	266	39	7	27	27	101	194
Runners On Base	.296	.363	.453	311	92	15	5	8	79	29	47		.254	.325	.377	1771	449	73	17	37	392	187	361
Scoring Position	.280	.343	.417	175	49	10	1	4	64	16	32		.251	.323	.386	974	244	46	10	22	343	112	219
Late and Close	.356	.396	.422	45	16	1	1	0	4	3	4		.253	.316	.339	454	115	20	2	5	35	43	75

7-YEAR TOTALS (1987–1993)

STAN BELINDA — BR/TR — age 28 — PIT/KC RP63 POW/FB

1993	G	IP	H	BB	SO	SB	CS	W	L	SV	ERA		5-YEAR TOTALS (1989–1993) G	IP	H	BB	SO	SB	CS	W	L	SV	ERA
Total	63	69.2	65	17	55	17	2	4	2	19	3.88		245	288.0	234	112	248	51	7	20	16	61	3.59
at Home	30	34.2	34	7	27	10	2	4	1	8	4.67		116	142.0	125	47	120	25	4	9	6	31	3.49
on Road	33	35.0	31	10	28	7	0	0	1	11	3.09		129	146.0	109	65	128	26	3	11	10	30	3.70
on Grass	21	22.1	19	3	16	5	0	0	1	8	3.63		68	75.1	58	31	60	11	3	4	6	15	4.18
on Turf	42	47.1	46	14	39	12	2	4	1	11	3.99		177	212.2	176	81	188	40	4	16	10	46	3.39
Day Games	23	27.1	28	9	29	11	1	1	0	5	3.62		72	86.0	83	41	78	25	4	4	6	19	4.81
Night Games	40	42.1	37	8	26	6	1	3	2	14	4.04		173	202.0	151	71	170	26	3	16	10	42	3.07
April	9	10.0	7	1	9	1	0	0	0	5	2.70		21	26.2	14	8	27	2	1	1	1	12	3.04
May	11	14.1	13	4	13	8	0	1	0	5	3.14		38	45.1	41	18	40	12	1	5	2	9	4.76
June	10	10.0	6	2	1	3	0	2	0	4	1.80		44	45.2	28	17	37	10	0	5	2	13	1.18
July	10	8.0	9	4	7	1	0	0	1	5	7.88		45	52.0	41	28	43	5	2	2	4	13	4.67
August	15	16.2	12	1	16	1	2	1	1	0	3.24		51	61.0	49	21	57	7	2	1	4	8	3.39
Sept-Oct	8	10.2	18	5	9	3	0	0	0	0	5.91		46	57.1	61	20	44	15	1	6	3	6	4.08

	BA	OBA	SA	AB	H	2B	3B	HR	RBI	BB	SO		BA	OBA	SA	AB	H	2B	3B	HR	RBI	BB	SO
Total	.247	.296	.373	263	65	11	2	6	39	17	55		.223	.299	.354	1050	234	38	8	28	147	112	248
vs. Left	.303	.362	.504	119	36	5	2	5	18	10	21		.227	.309	.362	484	110	19	2	14	57	56	96
vs. Right	.201	.240	.264	144	29	6	0	1	21	7	34		.219	.290	.348	566	124	19	6	14	90	56	152
Bases Empty	.226	.275	.376	133	30	7	2	3	3	8	31		.198	.275	.316	572	113	20	6	12	12	56	152
Leadoff	.269	.345	.538	52	14	3	1	3	3	5	7		.200	.267	.361	230	46	10	3	7	7	20	61
Runners On Base	.269	.317	.369	130	35	4	0	3	36	9	24		.253	.326	.400	478	121	18	2	16	135	56	96
Scoring Position	.295	.360	.436	78	23	2	0	3	36	8	14		.243	.332	.409	313	76	9	2	13	125	46	65
Late and Close	.226	.258	.356	146	33	8	1	3	24	6	30		.215	.290	.345	638	137	28	5	15	91	66	147

ANDY BENES — BR/TR — age 27 — SD SP34 POW/FB

1993	G	IP	H	BB	SO	SB	CS	W	L	SV	ERA		5-YEAR TOTALS (1989–1993) G	IP	H	BB	SO	SB	CS	W	L	SV	ERA
Total	34	230.2	200	86	179	21	7	15	15	0	3.78		143	944.0	852	306	721	77	35	59	54	0	3.44
at Home	15	103.2	87	33	93	10	4	6	7	0	3.47		70	459.2	441	148	384	39	20	28	24	0	3.72
on Road	19	127.0	113	53	86	11	3	9	8	0	4.04		73	484.1	411	158	337	38	15	31	30	0	3.18
on Grass	24	164.2	137	59	143	17	6	12	10	0	3.39		105	692.0	634	218	549	56	27	44	36	0	3.38
on Turf	10	66.0	63	27	36	4	1	3	5	0	4.77		38	252.0	218	88	172	21	8	15	18	0	3.61
Day Games	8	55.0	44	17	55	6	3	5	2	0	2.78		39	262.0	221	75	232	23	13	21	8	0	2.47
Night Games	26	175.2	156	69	124	15	4	10	13	0	4.10		104	682.0	631	231	489	54	22	38	46	0	3.81
April	5	36.1	29	11	24	2	0	4	1	0	2.72		18	114.1	108	38	103	7	3	8	7	0	3.62
May	6	43.1	36	9	34	4	2	1	2	0	2.70		23	159.1	140	42	116	15	7	11	9	0	3.39
June	6	41.2	30	13	38	4	0	1	3	0	2.38		24	160.2	147	54	118	17	5	5	9	0	3.42
July	5	37.1	24	12	30	2	3	3	1	0	2.89		19	132.1	115	39	98	11	5	7	8	0	2.92
August	6	35.1	42	21	26	3	2	3	3	0	7.90		27	165.0	148	66	111	14	7	15	8	0	4.64
Sept-Oct	6	36.2	39	20	27	6	0	1	5	0	4.66		32	212.1	194	67	175	13	8	13	13	0	2.80

	BA	OBA	SA	AB	H	2B	3B	HR	RBI	BB	SO		BA	OBA	SA	AB	H	2B	3B	HR	RBI	BB	SO
Total	.232	.303	.371	862	200	37	7	23	90	86	179		.241	.302	.367	3538	852	134	29	85	341	306	721
vs. Left	.242	.327	.374	433	105	17	5	10	39	52	69		.247	.314	.373	1999	493	72	21	46	193	192	363
vs. Right	.221	.278	.368	429	95	20	2	13	51	34	110		.233	.286	.360	1539	359	62	8	39	148	114	358
Bases Empty	.233	.294	.382	523	122	24	6	14	14	43	118		.236	.293	.367	2162	510	78	22	54	54	168	443
Leadoff	.246	.302	.411	224	55	11	1	8	8	17	52		.249	.302	.400	916	228	30	9	30	30	65	168
Runners On Base	.230	.315	.354	339	78	13	1	9	76	43	61		.249	.316	.367	1376	342	56	7	31	287	138	278
Scoring Position	.221	.339	.374	190	42	9	1	6	68	35	34		.230	.312	.341	766	176	33	5	14	244	95	165
Late and Close	.301	.379	.398	83	25	5	0	1	9	10	15		.283	.348	.393	318	90	13	2	6	30	32	61

JASON BERE — BR/TR — age 23 — CHA SP24 POW/FB

1993	G	IP	H	BB	SO	SB	CS	W	L	SV	ERA		1-YEAR TOTALS (1993) G	IP	H	BB	SO	SB	CS	W	L	SV	ERA
Total	24	142.2	109	81	129	9	8	12	5	0	3.47		24	142.2	109	81	129	9	8	12	5	0	3.47
at Home	12	69.2	44	39	64	6	4	6	3	0	2.84		12	69.2	44	39	64	6	4	6	3	0	2.84
on Road	12	73.0	65	42	65	3	4	6	2	0	4.07		12	73.0	65	42	65	3	4	6	2	0	4.07
on Grass	22	129.2	98	74	117	8	7	11	5	0	3.33		22	129.2	98	74	117	8	7	11	5	0	3.33
on Turf	2	13.0	11	7	12	1	1	1	0	0	4.85		2	13.0	11	7	12	1	1	1	0	0	4.85
Day Games	8	51.0	39	26	38	7	4	4	2	0	2.82		8	51.0	39	26	38	7	4	4	2	0	2.82
Night Games	16	91.2	70	55	91	2	4	8	3	0	3.83		16	91.2	70	55	91	2	4	8	3	0	3.83
April	0	0.0	0	0	0	0	0	0	0	0	0.00		0	0.0	0	0	0	0	0	0	0	0	0.00
May	1	6.0	5	4	4	1	0	0	1	0	7.50		1	6.0	5	4	4	1	0	0	1	0	7.50
June	6	36.1	30	27	34	2	2	3	1	0	4.21		6	36.1	30	27	34	2	2	3	1	0	4.21
July	5	26.0	24	14	19	2	2	2	1	0	4.50		5	26.0	24	14	19	2	2	2	1	0	4.50
August	6	33.2	21	21	27	2	1	2	1	0	2.94		6	33.2	21	21	27	2	1	2	1	0	2.94
Sept-Oct	6	40.2	29	15	45	2	1	6	0	0	1.99		6	40.2	29	15	45	2	1	6	0	0	1.99

	BA	OBA	SA	AB	H	2B	3B	HR	RBI	BB	SO		BA	OBA	SA	AB	H	2B	3B	HR	RBI	BB	SO
Total	.210	.322	.311	518	109	14	1	12	50	81	129		.210	.322	.311	518	109	14	1	12	50	81	129
vs. Left	.212	.348	.261	264	56	7	0	2	18	54	51		.212	.348	.261	264	56	7	0	2	18	54	51
vs. Right	.209	.293	.362	254	53	7	1	10	32	27	78		.209	.293	.362	254	53	7	1	10	32	27	78
Bases Empty	.215	.340	.315	279	60	7	0	7	7	51	75		.215	.340	.315	279	60	7	0	7	7	51	75
Leadoff	.258	.399	.408	120	31	3	0	5	5	27	29		.258	.399	.408	120	31	3	0	5	5	27	29
Runners On Base	.205	.299	.305	239	49	7	1	5	43	30	54		.205	.299	.305	239	49	7	1	5	43	30	54
Scoring Position	.179	.309	.223	112	20	2	0	1	31	22	30		.179	.309	.223	112	20	2	0	1	31	22	30
Late and Close	.412	.474	.471	17	7	1	0	0	3	2	2		.412	.474	.471	17	7	1	0	0	3	2	2

RICKY BONES — BR/TR — age 25 — MIL SP31, RP1 FIN/FB

1993	G	IP	H	BB	SO	SB	CS	W	L	SV	ERA
Total	32	203.2	222	63	63	20	5	11	11	0	4.86
at Home	11	72.0	83	22	20	7	2	4	6	0	4.75
on Road	21	131.2	139	41	43	13	3	7	5	0	4.92
on Grass	25	150.2	182	50	48	17	5	6	11	0	5.56
on Turf	7	53.0	40	13	15	3	0	5	0	0	2.89
Day Games	11	64.2	86	23	19	10	4	4	5	0	5.98
Night Games	21	139.0	136	40	44	10	1	7	6	0	4.34
April	3	14.2	24	7	10	1	1	1	1	0	6.75
May	5	23.2	25	9	8	9	0	1	1	0	5.32
June	6	42.0	34	6	11	2	0	2	3	0	3.86
July	6	40.1	46	16	7	2	2	2	2	0	4.46
August	6	45.0	47	13	15	6	1	3	2	0	4.40
Sept-Oct	6	38.0	46	12	12	0	1	2	2	0	5.92

3-YEAR TOTALS (1991-1993)	G	IP	H	BB	SO	SB	CS	W	L	SV	ERA
	74	421.0	448	129	159	36	8	24	27	0	4.75
at Home	34	205.0	205	57	81	16	4	13	13	0	4.13
on Road	40	216.0	243	72	78	20	4	11	14	0	5.33
on Grass	60	328.0	362	105	134	33	7	17	23	0	4.97
on Turf	14	93.0	86	24	25	3	1	7	4	0	3.97
Day Games	26	149.0	163	46	60	14	4	9	10	0	4.83
Night Games	48	272.0	285	83	99	22	4	15	17	0	4.70
April	8	37.1	41	11	21	2	1	2	1	0	4.10
May	10	52.1	50	18	22	11	1	1	3	0	5.33
June	11	71.1	66	18	18	4	0	5	5	0	4.67
July	11	68.0	87	23	18	7	3	4	5	0	4.90
August	16	98.0	94	29	45	11	2	5	7	0	4.22
Sept-Oct	18	94.0	110	30	35	1	1	7	6	0	5.17

	BA	OBA	SA	AB	H	2B	3B	HR	RBI	BB	SO
Total	.278	.334	.461	800	222	41	11	28	100	63	63
vs. Left	.256	.303	.433	390	100	21	6	12	46	27	12
vs. Right	.298	.363	.488	410	122	20	5	16	54	36	51
Bases Empty	.263	.315	.474	494	130	30	7	20	20	34	37
Leadoff	.277	.317	.490	206	57	18	4	6	6	12	14
Runners On Base	.301	.363	.441	306	92	11	4	8	80	29	26
Scoring Position	.265	.336	.425	181	48	5	3	6	72	19	19
Late and Close	.196	.213	.239	46	9	2	0	0	1	1	8

	BA	OBA	SA	AB	H	2B	3B	HR	RBI	BB	SO
Total	.271	.327	.442	1653	448	75	17	58	204	129	159
vs. Left	.262	.313	.416	808	212	37	9	23	87	59	47
vs. Right	.279	.341	.467	845	236	38	8	35	117	70	112
Bases Empty	.259	.316	.445	1019	264	51	12	38	38	75	92
Leadoff	.255	.311	.446	419	107	29	6	13	13	30	32
Runners On Base	.290	.346	.438	634	184	24	5	20	166	54	67
Scoring Position	.262	.332	.409	347	91	10	4	11	141	38	43
Late and Close	.195	.222	.310	87	17	4	0	2	3	3	13

CHRIS BOSIO — BR/TR — age 31 — SEA SP24, RP5 POW/GB

1993	G	IP	H	BB	SO	SB	CS	W	L	SV	ERA
Total	29	164.1	138	59	119	8	6	9	9	1	3.45
at Home	17	94.2	68	31	65	2	2	6	6	1	2.95
on Road	12	69.2	70	28	54	6	4	3	3	0	4.13
on Grass	9	51.0	52	22	44	2	3	2	3	0	3.88
on Turf	20	113.1	86	37	75	6	3	7	6	1	3.26
Day Games	9	50.1	49	19	47	5	3	0	5	0	5.19
Night Games	20	114.0	89	40	72	3	3	9	4	1	2.68
April	5	33.2	24	10	29	1	2	2	1	0	2.67
May	1	3.0	1	1	3	0	0	0	0	0	0.00
June	3	11.1	14	7	11	1	1	0	2	0	5.56
July	8	29.0	33	9	20	1	0	2	2	1	6.21
August	6	45.0	35	19	28	4	3	3	2	0	3.40
Sept-Oct	6	42.1	31	13	28	1	0	2	2	0	1.91

8-YEAR TOTALS (1986-1993)	G	IP	H	BB	SO	SB	CS	W	L	SV	ERA
	241	1354.1	1322	348	868	94	30	76	71	9	3.71
at Home	122	712.0	689	176	456	49	19	40	37	4	3.56
on Road	119	642.1	633	172	412	45	11	36	34	5	3.87
on Grass	194	1102.1	1087	278	707	76	26	62	56	8	3.71
on Turf	47	252.0	235	70	161	18	4	14	15	1	3.71
Day Games	79	436.1	410	114	302	27	10	20	24	5	3.51
Night Games	162	918.0	912	234	566	67	20	56	47	4	3.80
April	38	227.2	180	56	143	11	5	20	6	1	2.41
May	40	229.1	252	45	142	21	3	8	16	0	3.89
June	41	203.1	213	60	124	14	4	6	13	1	4.69
July	38	222.1	239	61	143	15	4	14	13	1	3.89
August	42	249.2	244	72	177	21	9	13	13	1	3.97
Sept-Oct	42	222.0	194	54	139	12	5	15	10	5	3.49

	BA	OBA	SA	AB	H	2B	3B	HR	RBI	BB	SO
Total	.229	.303	.352	602	138	24	4	14	59	59	119
vs. Left	.260	.339	.402	296	77	10	4	8	33	35	50
vs. Right	.199	.266	.304	306	61	14	0	6	26	24	69
Bases Empty	.225	.292	.332	373	84	14	1	8	8	33	77
Leadoff	.266	.326	.373	158	42	5	0	4	4	14	27
Runners On Base	.236	.319	.384	229	54	10	3	6	51	26	42
Scoring Position	.211	.289	.366	123	26	6	2	3	43	13	24
Late and Close	.356	.397	.610	59	21	6	0	4	9	4	10

	BA	OBA	SA	AB	H	2B	3B	HR	RBI	BB	SO
Total	.255	.304	.375	5186	1322	210	26	121	546	348	868
vs. Left	.263	.313	.389	2695	709	108	18	65	286	193	368
vs. Right	.246	.293	.361	2491	613	102	8	56	260	155	500
Bases Empty	.243	.289	.357	3116	756	113	15	71	71	191	530
Leadoff	.255	.297	.370	1318	336	52	8	28	28	77	201
Runners On Base	.273	.325	.403	2070	566	97	11	50	475	157	338
Scoring Position	.256	.312	.381	1135	290	54	7	25	405	101	201
Late and Close	.247	.295	.338	580	143	20	3	9	42	40	84

KENT BOTTENFIELD — BB/TR — age 26 — MON/COL SP25, RP12 FIN/FB

1993	G	IP	H	BB	SO	SB	CS	W	L	SV	ERA
Total	37	159.2	179	71	63	16	6	5	10	0	5.07
at Home	18	76.2	93	35	27	9	1	2	3	0	5.28
on Road	19	83.0	86	36	36	7	5	3	7	0	4.88
on Grass	16	78.2	91	34	31	10	3	3	6	0	5.72
on Turf	21	81.0	88	37	32	6	3	2	4	0	4.44
Day Games	15	68.0	80	24	31	9	2	0	3	0	5.69
Night Games	22	91.2	99	47	32	7	4	5	7	0	4.61
April	4	23.1	24	8	5	3	0	1	2	0	4.24
May	9	20.1	19	14	9	2	0	0	1	0	4.43
June	7	28.2	32	7	15	1	1	1	1	0	2.51
July	6	28.1	37	15	9	6	1	1	3	0	6.99
August	5	30.2	35	12	7	1	1	1	2	0	6.16
Sept-Oct	6	28.1	32	15	18	3	3	1	1	0	5.72

2-YEAR TOTALS (1992-1993)	G	IP	H	BB	SO	SB	CS	W	L	SV	ERA
	47	192.0	205	82	77	19	6	6	12	1	4.59
at Home	23	91.1	107	38	38	11	1	2	4	0	5.03
on Road	24	100.2	98	44	39	8	5	4	8	1	4.20
on Grass	20	95.1	101	41	34	11	3	4	6	1	4.81
on Turf	27	96.2	104	41	43	8	3	2	6	0	4.38
Day Games	19	85.2	91	27	37	11	2	1	3	1	4.52
Night Games	28	106.1	114	55	40	8	4	5	9	0	4.66
April	4	23.1	24	8	5	3	0	1	2	0	4.24
May	9	20.1	19	14	9	2	0	0	1	0	4.43
June	7	28.2	32	7	15	1	1	1	1	0	2.51
July	7	33.0	38	20	10	6	1	1	3	0	6.00
August	5	30.2	35	12	7	1	1	1	2	0	6.16
Sept-Oct	15	56.0	57	21	31	6	3	2	3	1	4.18

	BA	OBA	SA	AB	H	2B	3B	HR	RBI	BB	SO
Total	.294	.372	.480	608	179	35	4	24	90	71	63
vs. Left	.325	.405	.514	286	93	19	1	11	33	38	22
vs. Right	.267	.341	.450	322	86	16	2	13	57	33	41
Bases Empty	.269	.354	.469	335	90	17	1	16	16	41	34
Leadoff	.363	.443	.568	146	53	9	0	7	7	18	14
Runners On Base	.326	.394	.495	273	89	18	2	8	74	30	29
Scoring Position	.293	.377	.459	181	53	13	1	5	67	25	23
Late and Close	.300	.378	.500	40	12	2	0	2	6	4	3

	BA	OBA	SA	AB	H	2B	3B	HR	RBI	BB	SO
Total	.282	.357	.451	728	205	40	4	25	99	82	77
vs. Left	.302	.382	.477	348	105	21	2	12	40	45	28
vs. Right	.263	.334	.426	380	100	19	2	13	59	37	49
Bases Empty	.269	.350	.450	402	108	21	2	16	16	47	44
Leadoff	.350	.422	.554	177	62	13	1	7	7	19	17
Runners On Base	.298	.367	.451	326	97	19	2	9	83	35	33
Scoring Position	.274	.360	.429	212	58	13	1	6	75	30	25
Late and Close	.286	.364	.490	49	14	2	1	2	7	5	5

RYAN BOWEN — BR/TR — age 26 — FLO SP27 POW/GB

1993	G	IP	H	BB	SO	SB	CS	W	L	SV	ERA
Total	27	156.2	156	87	98	15	7	8	12	0	4.42
at Home	15	88.2	95	40	61	9	4	4	7	0	4.47
on Road	12	68.0	61	47	37	6	3	4	5	0	4.37
on Grass	21	127.1	120	65	86	14	6	6	8	0	3.75
on Turf	6	29.1	36	22	12	1	1	2	4	0	7.36
Day Games	4	22.0	22	16	16	2	1	2	0	0	2.86
Night Games	23	134.2	134	71	82	13	6	6	12	0	4.68
April	5	31.0	25	22	21	6	0	2	2	0	2.61
May	5	33.1	27	19	19	2	2	1	3	0	3.78
June	6	34.2	42	17	23	1	4	1	3	0	6.49
July	5	29.0	32	10	16	3	1	2	2	0	3.41
August	5	27.1	27	18	19	3	0	2	1	0	4.94
Sept-Oct	1	1.1	3	1	0	0	0	0	1	0	20.25

	BA	OBA	SA	AB	H	2B	3B	HR	RBI	BB	SO
Total	.263	.358	.375	594	156	28	3	11	68	87	98
vs. Left	.278	.372	.377	302	84	13	1	5	35	46	46
vs. Right	.247	.342	.373	292	72	15	2	6	33	41	52
Bases Empty	.274	.377	.426	317	87	19	1	9	9	50	49
Leadoff	.259	.335	.435	147	38	8	0	6	6	16	21
Runners On Base	.249	.335	.318	277	69	9	2	2	59	37	49
Scoring Position	.228	.328	.287	167	38	4	0	2	55	26	30
Late and Close	.209	.320	.279	43	9	3	0	0	3	7	4

3-YEAR TOTALS (1991–1993)

	G	IP	H	BB	SO	SB	CS	W	L	SV	ERA
	52	262.0	277	153	169	32	12	14	23	0	5.46
at Home	28	152.1	161	74	98	16	5	7	13	0	4.79
on Road	24	109.2	116	79	71	16	7	7	10	0	6.40
on Grass	30	157.1	158	90	110	20	9	9	11	0	4.52
on Turf	22	104.2	119	63	59	12	3	5	12	0	6.88
Day Games	10	50.0	56	34	36	9	2	5	3	0	4.50
Night Games	42	212.0	221	119	133	23	10	9	20	0	5.69
April	9	42.0	40	29	25	7	0	2	4	0	4.93
May	7	38.1	37	24	24	2	2	1	5	0	5.17
June	6	34.2	42	17	23	1	4	1	3	0	6.49
July	7	39.0	42	18	22	6	1	3	3	0	4.38
August	11	58.0	59	31	48	7	2	4	2	0	5.12
Sept-Oct	12	50.0	57	34	33	9	3	3	6	0	6.66

	BA	OBA	SA	AB	H	2B	3B	HR	RBI	BB	SO
	.274	.371	.400	1010	277	50	4	23	137	153	169
vs. Left	.297	.391	.405	538	160	27	2	9	79	84	82
vs. Right	.248	.348	.394	472	117	23	2	14	58	69	87
Bases Empty	.282	.383	.407	535	151	29	1	12	12	82	75
Leadoff	.273	.365	.413	242	66	13	0	7	7	32	34
Runners On Base	.265	.358	.392	475	126	21	3	11	125	71	94
Scoring Position	.236	.342	.360	292	69	12	0	8	112	51	63
Late and Close	.231	.333	.308	52	12	4	0	0	3	8	5

DOUG BROCAIL — BL/TR — age 27 — SD SP24 FIN/FB

1993	G	IP	H	BB	SO	SB	CS	W	L	SV	ERA
Total	24	128.1	143	42	70	10	4	4	13	0	4.56
at Home	11	61.2	67	17	36	5	2	2	5	0	4.67
on Road	13	66.2	76	25	34	5	2	2	8	0	4.45
on Grass	19	101.1	118	37	54	8	4	3	11	0	5.24
on Turf	5	27.0	25	5	16	2	0	1	2	0	2.00
Day Games	9	42.0	51	15	25	3	1	1	5	0	5.36
Night Games	15	86.1	92	27	45	7	3	3	8	0	4.17
April	0	0.0	0	0	0	0	0	0	0	0	0.00
May	0	0.0	0	0	0	0	0	0	0	0	0.00
June	6	37.0	38	7	26	3	0	2	3	0	3.65
July	6	29.0	35	12	16	1	1	0	4	0	5.28
August	6	31.0	34	12	13	3	3	1	3	0	4.65
Sept-Oct	6	31.1	36	11	15	3	0	1	3	0	4.88

	BA	OBA	SA	AB	H	2B	3B	HR	RBI	BB	SO
Total	.283	.338	.443	506	143	25	4	16	65	42	70
vs. Left	.295	.369	.459	244	72	12	2	8	36	30	30
vs. Right	.271	.306	.427	262	71	13	2	8	29	12	40
Bases Empty	.285	.338	.447	291	83	17	0	10	10	22	38
Leadoff	.254	.293	.381	126	32	10	0	2	2	7	15
Runners On Base	.279	.337	.437	215	60	8	4	6	55	20	32
Scoring Position	.206	.280	.357	126	26	4	3	4	47	13	16
Late and Close	.250	.278	.438	16	4	1	1	0	3	1	1

2-YEAR TOTALS (1992–1993)

	G	IP	H	BB	SO	SB	CS	W	L	SV	ERA
	27	142.1	160	47	85	10	4	4	13	0	4.74
at Home	11	61.2	67	17	36	5	2	2	5	0	4.67
on Road	16	80.2	93	30	49	5	2	2	8	0	4.80
on Grass	21	110.0	130	41	62	8	4	3	11	0	5.40
on Turf	6	32.1	30	6	23	2	0	1	2	0	2.51
Day Games	10	47.0	57	16	29	3	1	1	5	0	5.36
Night Games	17	95.1	103	31	56	7	3	3	8	0	4.44
April	0	0.0	0	0	0	0	0	0	0	0	0.00
May	0	0.0	0	0	0	0	0	0	0	0	0.00
June	6	37.0	38	7	26	3	0	2	3	0	3.65
July	6	29.0	35	12	16	1	1	0	4	0	5.28
August	6	31.0	34	12	13	3	3	1	3	0	4.65
Sept-Oct	9	45.1	53	16	30	3	0	1	3	0	5.36

	BA	OBA	SA	AB	H	2B	3B	HR	RBI	BB	SO
	.284	.339	.448	563	160	30	4	18	73	47	85
vs. Left	.296	.368	.461	280	83	15	2	9	40	33	39
vs. Right	.272	.309	.435	283	77	15	2	9	33	14	46
Bases Empty	.284	.333	.437	327	93	20	0	10	10	23	45
Leadoff	.262	.297	.390	141	37	12	0	2	2	7	17
Runners On Base	.284	.347	.462	236	67	10	4	8	63	24	40
Scoring Position	.218	.296	.387	142	31	6	3	4	53	16	23
Late and Close	.250	.278	.438	16	4	1	1	0	3	1	1

KEVIN BROWN — BR/TR — age 29 — TEX SP34 FIN/GB

1993	G	IP	H	BB	SO	SB	CS	W	L	SV	ERA
Total	34	233.0	228	74	142	10	10	15	12	0	3.59
at Home	17	124.1	104	34	94	6	4	9	5	0	2.46
on Road	17	108.2	124	40	48	4	6	6	7	0	4.89
on Grass	31	214.1	203	71	136	10	8	13	11	0	3.40
on Turf	3	18.2	25	3	6	0	2	2	1	0	5.79
Day Games	11	67.0	71	21	31	4	3	6	3	0	4.03
Night Games	23	166.0	157	53	111	6	7	9	9	0	3.42
April	4	31.2	28	7	23	1	2	2	1	0	1.14
May	6	50.0	37	9	24	2	2	2	2	0	2.52
June	5	29.2	36	13	15	2	4	2	3	0	5.46
July	6	34.2	42	18	24	4	1	2	1	0	6.23
August	6	39.1	50	16	26	1	0	2	4	0	5.26
Sept-Oct	7	47.2	35	11	29	0	1	5	1	0	1.89

	BA	OBA	SA	AB	H	2B	3B	HR	RBI	BB	SO
Total	.252	.319	.353	903	228	41	4	14	87	74	142
vs. Left	.253	.324	.358	509	129	22	2	9	51	50	74
vs. Right	.251	.312	.348	394	99	19	2	5	36	24	68
Bases Empty	.250	.303	.353	533	133	25	3	8	8	35	91
Leadoff	.218	.267	.302	225	49	10	0	3	3	14	45
Runners On Base	.257	.340	.354	370	95	16	1	6	79	39	51
Scoring Position	.239	.331	.325	209	50	7	1	3	67	21	33
Late and Close	.197	.242	.361	61	12	4	0	2	4	2	11

7-YEAR TOTALS (1986–1993)

	G	IP	H	BB	SO	SB	CS	W	L	SV	ERA
	161	1108.2	1104	378	619	40	45	71	55	0	3.65
at Home	77	543.1	517	174	329	21	27	37	22	0	3.06
on Road	84	565.1	587	204	290	19	18	34	33	0	4.22
on Grass	134	928.0	912	321	527	32	38	59	47	0	3.57
on Turf	27	180.2	192	57	92	8	7	12	8	0	4.08
Day Games	41	257.2	280	107	122	14	9	14	14	0	4.51
Night Games	120	851.0	824	271	497	26	36	57	41	0	3.39
April	21	145.0	131	51	83	7	7	13	4	0	3.23
May	28	199.2	190	67	93	8	9	12	10	0	3.52
June	28	205.1	172	66	109	4	9	15	10	0	3.11
July	28	195.2	198	70	116	7	5	10	11	0	4.14
August	27	179.1	215	69	103	6	7	9	11	0	4.07
Sept-Oct	29	183.2	198	55	115	8	8	12	9	0	3.82

	BA	OBA	SA	AB	H	2B	3B	HR	RBI	BB	SO
Total	.260	.325	.356	4250	1104	187	11	67	440	378	619
vs. Left	.259	.327	.361	2150	556	102	5	36	216	216	298
vs. Right	.261	.323	.351	2100	548	85	6	31	224	162	321
Bases Empty	.255	.318	.351	2416	615	110	8	36	36	204	364
Leadoff	.248	.305	.327	1062	263	48	3	10	10	81	164
Runners On Base	.267	.333	.363	1834	489	77	3	31	404	174	255
Scoring Position	.258	.336	.357	1015	262	40	3	18	356	116	157
Late and Close	.277	.336	.431	462	128	23	3	14	59	40	57

TOM BROWNING — BL/TL — age 34 — CIN SP20, RP1 FIN/FB

1993 / 10-YEAR TOTALS (1984–1993)

1993	G	IP	H	BB	SO	SB	CS	W	L	SV	ERA		G	IP	H	BB	SO	SB	CS	W	L	SV	ERA
Total	21	114.0	159	20	53	5	7	7	7	0	4.74		293	1870.2	1884	493	975	122	69	120	87	0	3.91
at Home	8	50.2	61	9	28	3	2	4	2	0	2.84		144	923.0	919	256	470	60	41	62	44	0	4.14
on Road	13	63.1	98	11	25	2	5	3	5	0	6.25		149	947.2	965	237	505	62	28	58	43	0	3.68
on Grass	8	42.0	58	7	12	0	2	3	1	0	4.29		92	600.1	604	139	310	34	13	34	22	0	3.42
on Turf	13	72.0	101	13	41	5	5	4	6	0	5.00		201	1270.1	1280	354	665	88	56	86	65	0	4.14
Day Games	7	41.2	58	6	17	0	2	3	2	0	4.75		106	656.2	703	185	346	51	23	44	33	0	4.04
Night Games	14	72.1	101	14	36	5	5	4	5	0	4.73		187	1214.0	1181	308	629	71	46	76	54	0	3.84
April	3	14.0	28	2	9	2	0	1	2	0	9.64		42	254.0	254	54	135	13	14	16	12	0	4.07
May	6	33.1	48	12	17	3	3	2	2	0	4.86		52	313.2	348	101	156	27	11	17	24	0	4.65
June	5	26.0	32	3	13	0	2	2	0	0	3.46		50	307.0	300	98	162	25	16	23	8	0	3.61
July	5	28.0	37	2	11	0	2	2	3	0	4.82		49	319.2	326	59	159	12	13	19	17	0	3.94
August	2	12.2	14	1	3	0	0	0	1	0	1.42		47	320.2	299	89	161	15	5	21	12	0	3.45
Sept-Oct	0	0.0	0	0	0	0	0	0	0	0	0.00		53	355.2	357	92	202	30	10	24	14	0	3.80

	BA	OBA	SA	AB	H	2B	3B	HR	RBI	BB	SO		BA	OBA	SA	AB	H	2B	3B	HR	RBI	BB	SO
Total	.333	.359	.506	478	159	32	3	15	58	20	53		.263	.310	.418	7177	1884	368	34	226	795	493	975
vs. Left	.244	.302	.372	78	19	4	0	2	6	7	10		.253	.319	.397	1225	310	61	5	35	144	120	224
vs. Right	.350	.371	.533	400	140	28	3	13	52	13	43		.264	.308	.422	5952	1574	307	29	191	651	373	751
Bases Empty	.365	.386	.561	255	93	21	1	9	9	8	33		.260	.306	.414	4422	1151	203	16	148	148	267	630
Leadoff	.385	.400	.564	117	45	10	1	3	3	2	16		.266	.307	.423	1837	488	82	9	63	63	98	251
Runners On Base	.296	.329	.444	223	66	11	2	6	49	12	20		.266	.317	.424	2755	733	165	18	78	647	226	345
Scoring Position	.298	.349	.465	114	34	5	1	4	40	10	12		.273	.344	.432	1401	383	86	11	38	532	177	191
Late and Close	.200	.273	.200	10	2	0	0	0	0	1	0		.238	.290	.352	542	129	26	0	12	45	40	72

JOHN BURKETT — BR/TR — age 30 — SF SP34 FIN/GB

1993 / 5-YEAR TOTALS (1987–1993)

1993	G	IP	H	BB	SO	SB	CS	W	L	SV	ERA		G	IP	H	BB	SO	SB	CS	W	L	SV	ERA
Total	34	231.2	224	40	145	14	14	22	7	0	3.65		138	838.0	849	209	506	66	44	61	34	1	3.87
at Home	16	121.2	104	12	87	5	7	9	3	0	2.66		66	441.0	401	89	287	29	20	31	13	0	3.33
on Road	18	110.0	120	28	58	9	7	13	4	0	4.75		72	397.0	448	120	219	37	24	30	21	1	4.47
on Grass	25	174.1	164	28	118	9	11	15	5	0	3.56		102	630.1	615	149	390	46	29	45	24	1	3.63
on Turf	9	57.1	60	12	27	5	3	7	2	0	3.92		36	207.2	234	60	116	20	15	16	10	0	4.59
Day Games	17	122.1	118	25	78	8	7	9	4	0	3.24		63	396.0	387	102	234	30	24	30	16	0	3.32
Night Games	17	109.1	106	15	67	6	7	13	3	0	4.12		75	442.0	462	107	272	36	20	31	18	1	4.36
April	5	34.1	26	6	23	0	2	5	0	0	2.62		16	102.1	93	27	63	3	9	10	3	0	3.61
May	6	41.1	40	9	24	2	1	2	1	0	3.92		23	144.0	144	41	86	16	11	8	3	0	3.69
June	6	43.1	38	3	28	2	3	5	1	0	2.70		24	147.2	133	38	89	8	9	10	7	0	3.23
July	5	34.0	36	9	21	1	2	3	2	0	3.44		23	145.1	148	36	85	11	4	10	5	0	3.47
August	6	37.2	48	5	26	3	5	3	2	0	6.21		23	139.0	158	27	76	16	8	11	8	0	4.99
Sept-Oct	6	41.0	36	8	23	3	1	4	1	0	3.07		29	159.2	173	40	107	12	3	12	8	1	4.17

	BA	OBA	SA	AB	H	2B	3B	HR	RBI	BB	SO		BA	OBA	SA	AB	H	2B	3B	HR	RBI	BB	SO
Total	.255	.294	.366	879	224	30	7	18	90	40	145		.264	.312	.380	3222	849	130	18	70	355	209	506
vs. Left	.282	.318	.386	464	131	16	4	8	51	22	72		.282	.327	.412	1862	525	86	12	44	222	124	266
vs. Right	.224	.269	.345	415	93	14	3	10	39	18	73		.238	.293	.337	1360	324	44	6	26	133	85	240
Bases Empty	.240	.276	.319	551	132	20	3	6	6	23	98		.254	.299	.355	1905	483	68	6	38	38	108	314
Leadoff	.243	.284	.322	230	56	11	2	1	1	10	40		.270	.311	.371	819	221	35	3	14	14	44	120
Runners On Base	.280	.324	.445	328	92	10	4	12	84	17	47		.278	.331	.416	1317	366	62	12	32	317	101	192
Scoring Position	.282	.340	.441	170	48	2	2	7	68	13	31		.285	.349	.420	715	204	26	8	18	269	72	125
Late and Close	.258	.290	.394	66	17	3	2	2	7	2	11		.268	.310	.411	209	56	9	0	7	27	12	28

TOM CANDIOTTI — BR/TR — age 37 — LA SP32, RP1 POW/FB

1993 / 9-YEAR TOTALS (1984–1993)

1993	G	IP	H	BB	SO	SB	CS	W	L	SV	ERA		G	IP	H	BB	SO	SB	CS	W	L	SV	ERA
Total	33	213.2	192	71	155	25	6	8	10	0	3.12		268	1766.1	1656	579	1164	193	64	99	99	0	3.40
at Home	16	115.2	90	33	84	14	4	5	3	0	1.95		136	939.2	865	272	626	96	35	58	43	0	3.11
on Road	17	98.0	102	38	71	11	2	3	7	0	4.50		132	826.2	791	307	538	97	29	41	56	0	3.73
on Grass	23	155.0	133	49	114	18	4	6	5	0	2.44		212	1405.1	1302	444	908	142	48	82	76	0	3.32
on Turf	10	58.2	59	22	41	7	2	2	5	0	4.91		56	361.0	354	135	256	51	16	17	23	0	3.71
Day Games	10	62.2	46	29	50	7	0	3	3	0	2.87		83	551.1	537	175	373	51	25	33	32	0	3.64
Night Games	23	151.0	146	42	105	18	6	5	7	0	3.22		185	1215.0	1119	404	791	142	39	66	67	0	3.30
April	4	22.0	24	13	16	3	1	0	3	0	6.55		34	224.0	211	87	168	21	9	16	11	0	3.66
May	6	41.1	39	12	32	9	1	3	1	0	2.61		43	296.0	287	95	201	40	9	19	16	0	3.34
June	6	35.0	24	11	33	3	3	0	1	0	1.80		48	299.2	295	110	208	36	21	12	22	0	3.60
July	6	42.1	26	13	29	2	0	3	0	0	1.49		46	307.2	267	91	194	24	9	18	14	0	3.01
August	5	37.0	33	7	26	3	1	2	0	0	1.46		42	295.2	247	88	179	27	10	20	11	0	2.74
Sept-Oct	7	36.0	46	15	19	5	0	0	5	0	6.50		55	343.1	349	108	214	45	6	14	25	0	4.04

	BA	OBA	SA	AB	H	2B	3B	HR	RBI	BB	SO		BA	OBA	SA	AB	H	2B	3B	HR	RBI	BB	SO
Total	.241	.305	.338	797	192	33	4	12	75	71	155		.248	.309	.359	6685	1656	273	33	136	660	579	1164
vs. Left	.230	.302	.310	413	95	14	2	5	37	44	75		.249	.314	.351	3501	873	122	26	61	329	339	518
vs. Right	.253	.307	.367	384	97	19	2	7	38	27	80		.246	.304	.368	3184	783	151	7	75	331	240	646
Bases Empty	.222	.285	.316	478	106	15	3	8	8	37	94		.250	.304	.368	4006	1002	176	19	86	86	288	719
Leadoff	.220	.269	.298	205	45	7	0	3	3	13	39		.245	.292	.357	1711	419	80	6	33	33	108	312
Runners On Base	.270	.333	.370	319	86	18	1	4	67	34	61		.244	.317	.347	2679	654	97	14	50	574	291	445
Scoring Position	.236	.324	.330	182	43	5	2	1	60	27	39		.245	.333	.359	1546	378	58	10	33	525	220	265
Late and Close	.155	.226	.196	97	15	2	2	1		9	17		.241	.315	.339	697	168	25	5	11	57	73	111

FRANK CASTILLO — BR/TR — age 25 — CHN SP25, RP4 FIN/FB

1993	G	IP	H	BB	SO	SB	CS	W	L	SV	ERA
Total	29	141.1	162	39	84	7	12	5	8	0	4.84
at Home	13	71.1	79	20	46	2	5	2	4	0	4.54
on Road	16	70.0	83	19	38	5	7	3	4	0	5.14
on Grass	21	109.0	122	27	74	3	9	2	8	0	4.54
on Turf	8	32.1	40	12	10	4	3	3	0	0	5.85
Day Games	15	83.1	83	25	49	1	6	3	4	0	3.78
Night Games	14	58.0	79	14	35	6	6	2	4	0	6.36
April	4	20.0	22	10	9	1	2	0	1	0	4.50
May	5	27.0	26	9	20	2	1	1	1	0	2.33
June	5	23.1	37	4	13	0	0	1	3	0	8.10
July	5	31.0	29	7	18	0	5	3	1	0	3.19
August	6	32.0	38	6	19	3	3	0	2	0	5.63
Sept-Oct	4	8.0	10	3	5	1	1	0	0	0	7.88

3-YEAR TOTALS (1991–1993)

	G	IP	H	BB	SO	SB	CS	W	L	SV	ERA
	80	458.1	448	135	292	32	25	21	26	0	4.10
	40	243.1	227	69	171	15	11	11	14	0	3.92
	40	215.0	221	66	121	17	14	10	12	0	4.31
	57	332.2	321	96	231	20	18	15	22	0	4.03
	23	125.2	127	39	61	12	7	6	4	0	4.30
	41	245.0	220	75	160	12	14	13	13	0	3.71
	39	213.1	228	60	132	20	11	8	13	0	4.56
	8	44.2	38	16	28	2	4	0	3	0	4.03
	10	58.1	52	18	44	3	3	4	3	0	2.16
	12	70.0	79	19	37	5	1	4	5	0	5.14
	17	107.0	104	29	68	7	7	6	4	0	3.45
	15	89.2	81	21	49	9	6	4	5	0	4.22
	18	88.2	94	32	66	6	4	3	6	0	5.28

	BA	OBA	SA	AB	H	2B	3B	HR	RBI	BB	SO
Total	.293	.348	.474	553	162	28	6	20	75	39	84
vs. Left	.287	.350	.507	268	77	13	2	14	45	25	37
vs. Right	.298	.345	.442	285	85	15	4	6	30	14	47
Bases Empty	.287	.334	.467	321	92	17	4	11	11	16	48
Leadoff	.329	.377	.521	140	46	9	3	4	4	8	16
Runners On Base	.302	.365	.483	232	70	11	2	9	64	23	36
Scoring Position	.288	.363	.489	139	40	5	1	7	56	16	25
Late and Close	.310	.355	.552	29	9	2	1	1	4	1	4

	BA	OBA	SA	AB	H	2B	3B	HR	RBI	BB	SO
	.256	.313	.399	1748	448	93	12	44	188	135	292
	.259	.327	.405	992	257	45	5	30	116	101	160
	.253	.294	.390	756	191	48	7	14	72	34	132
	.245	.290	.389	1079	264	57	9	27	27	58	188
	.258	.315	.416	449	116	26	6	11	11	32	65
	.275	.348	.414	669	184	36	3	17	161	77	104
	.268	.367	.407	388	104	17	2	11	142	64	60
	.306	.361	.413	121	37	5	1	2	12	10	21

NORM CHARLTON — BB/TL — age 31 — SEA RP34 POW/GB

1993	G	IP	H	BB	SO	SB	CS	W	L	SV	ERA
Total	34	34.2	22	17	48	3	0	1	3	18	2.34
at Home	17	20.0	8	5	32	2	0	1	1	10	0.90
on Road	17	14.2	14	12	16	1	0	0	2	8	4.30
on Grass	13	10.2	12	11	11	1	0	0	2	4	5.06
on Turf	21	24.0	10	6	37	2	0	1	1	14	1.13
Day Games	10	11.2	5	6	15	2	0	1	2	4	1.54
Night Games	24	23.0	17	11	33	1	0	0	1	14	2.74
April	7	6.2	3	2	10	1	0	0	1	3	2.70
May	11	11.2	10	5	17	1	0	0	0	6	2.31
June	10	10.2	6	6	11	0	0	0	0	7	2.53
July	4	4.0	3	3	8	1	0	0	2	1	2.25
August	2	1.2	0	1	2	0	0	0	0	1	0.00
Sept-Oct	0	0.0	0	0	0	0	0	0	0	0	0.00

6-YEAR TOTALS (1988–1993)

	G	IP	H	BB	SO	SB	CS	W	L	SV	ERA
	272	535.1	451	207	469	59	22	32	27	47	2.96
	133	259.0	218	97	214	31	7	14	12	25	2.95
	139	276.1	233	110	255	28	15	18	15	22	2.96
	81	146.2	117	66	125	16	8	14	10	12	2.52
	191	388.2	334	141	344	43	14	18	17	35	3.13
	87	171.2	151	59	159	26	6	10	11	12	3.04
	185	363.2	300	148	310	33	16	22	16	35	2.92
	39	69.2	48	32	71	5	4	2	3	10	2.58
	53	81.1	82	30	74	7	3	7	4	11	3.76
	48	72.2	60	26	63	9	2	7	0	14	3.22
	38	72.2	60	23	61	6	5	3	8	8	2.60
	47	119.0	96	48	96	16	2	5	4	3	2.57
	47	120.0	105	48	104	16	6	8	8	1	3.08

	BA	OBA	SA	AB	H	2B	3B	HR	RBI	BB	SO
Total	.179	.277	.301	123	22	3	0	4	20	17	48
vs. Left	.095	.269	.095	21	2	0	0	0	3	5	9
vs. Right	.196	.278	.343	102	20	3	0	4	17	12	39
Bases Empty	.151	.235	.233	73	11	3	0	1	1	8	32
Leadoff	.133	.161	.200	30	4	2	0	0	0	1	14
Runners On Base	.220	.333	.400	50	11	0	0	3	19	9	16
Scoring Position	.265	.366	.441	34	9	0	0	2	17	6	12
Late and Close	.181	.289	.313	83	15	2	0	3	17	13	35

	BA	OBA	SA	AB	H	2B	3B	HR	RBI	BB	SO
	.231	.308	.338	1956	451	76	10	38	210	207	469
	.217	.322	.314	414	90	15	2	7	57	54	97
	.234	.304	.344	1542	361	61	8	31	153	153	372
	.217	.292	.321	1135	246	44	7	20	20	109	279
	.245	.315	.362	481	118	26	3	8	8	46	104
	.250	.329	.362	821	205	32	3	18	190	98	190
	.239	.325	.346	503	120	20	2	10	165	69	128
	.220	.306	.332	645	142	25	4	13	77	78	195

MARK CLARK — BR/TR — age 26 — CLE SP15, RP11 FIN/FB

1993	G	IP	H	BB	SO	SB	CS	W	L	SV	ERA
Total	26	109.1	119	25	57	8	10	7	5	0	4.28
at Home	13	57.2	56	14	26	2	6	3	4	0	3.43
on Road	13	51.2	63	11	31	6	4	4	1	0	5.23
on Grass	21	96.0	96	21	51	7	7	6	5	0	3.66
on Turf	5	13.1	23	4	6	1	3	1	0	0	8.77
Day Games	9	49.2	54	9	29	6	3	5	1	0	3.44
Night Games	17	59.2	65	16	28	2	7	2	4	0	4.98
April	5	20.2	23	2	11	1	2	1	2	0	6.10
May	10	20.0	31	6	8	5	1	1	0	0	6.75
June	3	16.1	20	3	8	0	4	2	1	0	3.31
July	3	14.2	19	7	9	0	3	1	1	0	5.52
August	0	0.0	0	0	0	0	0	0	0	0	0.00
Sept-Oct	5	37.2	26	7	21	2	0	3	1	0	1.91

3-YEAR TOTALS (1991–1993)

	G	IP	H	BB	SO	SB	CS	W	L	SV	ERA
	53	245.0	253	72	114	30	13	11	16	0	4.33
	26	121.1	116	36	48	13	7	5	11	0	4.15
	27	123.2	137	36	66	17	6	6	5	0	4.51
	29	139.1	132	35	70	12	9	8	7	0	3.42
	24	105.2	121	37	44	18	4	3	9	0	5.54
	18	95.0	93	26	47	14	5	6	4	0	3.69
	35	150.0	160	46	67	16	8	5	12	0	4.74
	5	20.2	23	2	11	1	2	1	2	0	6.10
	10	20.0	31	6	8	5	1	1	0	0	6.75
	9	45.0	48	12	17	4	4	5	4	0	4.20
	9	54.2	51	18	24	7	5	3	4	0	3.13
	4	22.2	17	8	9	4	0	1	2	0	5.16
	17	82.0	83	26	45	9	1	4	5	0	3.95

	BA	OBA	SA	AB	H	2B	3B	HR	RBI	BB	SO
Total	.279	.320	.469	426	119	21	3	18	53	25	57
vs. Left	.335	.365	.524	191	64	10	1	8	24	8	23
vs. Right	.234	.285	.426	235	55	11	2	10	29	17	34
Bases Empty	.283	.314	.517	265	75	11	3	15	15	11	32
Leadoff	.255	.288	.406	106	27	6	1	4	4	4	12
Runners On Base	.273	.330	.391	161	44	10	0	3	38	14	25
Scoring Position	.263	.330	.389	95	25	6	0	2	34	10	15
Late and Close	.125	.125	.188	16	2	0	0	0	0	5	2

	BA	OBA	SA	AB	H	2B	3B	HR	RBI	BB	SO
	.267	.317	.430	946	253	41	7	33	108	72	114
	.289	.340	.443	499	144	23	3	16	58	40	58
	.244	.292	.416	447	109	18	4	17	50	32	56
	.275	.317	.457	582	160	23	4	25	25	35	63
	.245	.287	.380	237	58	9	1	7	7	13	28
	.255	.318	.387	364	93	18	3	8	83	37	51
	.244	.318	.395	205	50	12	2	5	73	26	32
	.280	.308	.380	50	14	3	1	0	5	2	3

ROGER CLEMENS — BR/TR — age 32 — BOS SP29 POW/GB

1993	G	IP	H	BB	SO	SB	CS	W	L	SV	ERA
Total	29	191.2	175	67	160	16	7	11	14	0	4.46
at Home	16	105.0	106	38	92	7	3	6	8	0	5.14
on Road	13	86.2	69	29	68	9	4	5	6	0	3.63
on Grass	24	162.1	154	53	148	13	6	8	12	0	4.66
on Turf	5	29.1	21	14	12	3	1	3	2	0	3.38
Day Games	11	76.0	71	26	71	7	2	4	6	0	4.74
Night Games	18	115.2	104	41	89	9	5	7	8	0	4.28
April	5	38.1	28	10	29	2	3	3	1	0	1.64
May	6	42.2	34	16	48	4	2	3	3	0	3.80
June	4	23.0	26	6	21	2	0	1	2	0	6.65
July	4	29.0	25	6	23	2	1	2	1	0	2.17
August	6	33.1	38	15	22	0	1	1	4	0	7.02
Sept-Oct	4	25.1	24	14	17	6	0	1	3	0	7.11

10-YEAR TOTALS (1984–1993)

	G	IP	H	BB	SO	SB	CS	W	L	SV	ERA
Total	302	2222.2	1878	619	2033	185	108	163	86	0	2.94
at Home	153	1123.2	989	299	1059	92	48	79	45	0	3.12
on Road	149	1099.0	889	320	974	93	60	84	41	0	2.76
on Grass	257	1883.2	1625	527	1781	153	89	134	75	0	3.05
on Turf	45	339.0	253	92	252	32	19	29	11	0	2.31
Day Games	99	734.1	582	197	684	56	36	55	24	0	2.46
Night Games	203	1488.1	1296	422	1349	129	72	108	62	0	3.17
April	43	332.1	228	85	334	29	17	28	9	0	1.92
May	56	433.1	338	119	395	37	26	33	16	0	3.12
June	51	357.0	352	97	317	26	9	24	17	0	3.43
July	53	386.2	340	105	334	35	18	25	15	0	2.84
August	56	393.0	345	124	366	32	22	29	15	0	3.32
Sept-Oct	43	320.1	275	89	287	26	16	24	14	0	2.87

	BA	OBA	SA	AB	H	2B	3B	HR	RBI	BB	SO
Total	.244	.315	.372	718	175	31	5	17	91	67	160
vs. Left	.260	.346	.381	404	105	19	3	8	44	51	84
vs. Right	.223	.273	.360	314	70	12	2	9	47	16	76
Bases Empty	.223	.286	.336	440	98	19	2	9	9	36	96
Leadoff	.239	.308	.306	180	43	6	0	2	2	17	41
Runners On Base	.277	.358	.428	278	77	12	3	8	82	31	64
Scoring Position	.278	.383	.411	151	42	8	0	4	68	24	34
Late and Close	.159	.221	.222	63	10	1	0	1	2	5	17

	BA	OBA	SA	AB	H	2B	3B	HR	RBI	BB	SO
Total	.228	.285	.331	8253	1878	337	41	145	704	619	2033
vs. Left	.238	.299	.333	4483	1065	208	24	57	366	377	992
vs. Right	.216	.268	.329	3770	813	129	17	88	338	242	1041
Bases Empty	.226	.278	.326	5068	1147	206	20	87	87	325	1261
Leadoff	.235	.284	.324	2136	502	82	7	31	31	133	514
Runners On Base	.230	.297	.338	3185	731	131	21	58	617	294	772
Scoring Position	.217	.294	.310	1762	383	67	11	25	518	193	447
Late and Close	.215	.280	.304	939	202	30	4	15	60	80	235

DAVID CONE — BL/TR — age 31 — KC SP34 POW/FB

1993	G	IP	H	BB	SO	SB	CS	W	L	SV	ERA
Total	34	254.0	205	114	191	32	13	11	14	0	3.33
at Home	17	126.2	116	65	86	25	7	4	6	0	4.05
on Road	17	127.1	89	49	105	7	6	7	8	0	2.62
on Grass	13	99.2	72	36	82	4	5	5	7	0	2.71
on Turf	21	154.1	133	78	109	28	8	6	7	0	3.73
Day Games	8	59.0	39	22	53	5	2	2	4	0	2.90
Night Games	26	195.0	166	92	138	27	11	9	10	0	3.46
April	5	35.2	34	15	26	7	6	0	4	0	3.79
May	6	46.0	25	25	39	3	0	3	1	0	2.15
June	5	36.0	33	17	24	1	2	2	3	0	4.75
July	6	45.2	36	21	30	5	2	2	2	0	3.15
August	6	43.2	44	15	36	5	1	3	1	0	3.50
Sept-Oct	6	47.0	33	21	36	4	2	1	3	0	3.06

8-YEAR TOTALS (1986–1993)

	G	IP	H	BB	SO	SB	CS	W	L	SV	ERA
Total	235	1521.0	1264	574	1418	196	80	95	65	1	3.15
at Home	113	759.2	648	285	713	104	43	46	31	0	3.28
on Road	122	761.1	616	289	705	92	37	49	34	1	3.01
on Grass	139	943.2	780	319	926	100	51	62	44	0	3.08
on Turf	96	577.1	484	255	492	96	29	33	21	1	3.26
Day Games	81	494.2	433	168	463	66	38	32	24	1	3.38
Night Games	154	1026.1	831	406	955	130	42	63	41	0	3.03
April	35	187.1	180	91	164	30	17	8	12	0	4.23
May	37	256.0	196	93	229	28	15	18	8	0	2.60
June	39	221.1	195	76	208	39	5	12	9	0	3.62
July	34	248.2	193	97	240	32	10	18	6	0	3.08
August	39	272.1	243	86	246	33	16	18	13	0	3.17
Sept-Oct	54	335.1	257	131	331	34	17	21	17	1	2.68

	BA	OBA	SA	AB	H	2B	3B	HR	RBI	BB	SO
Total	.223	.312	.343	920	205	43	4	20	89	114	191
vs. Left	.227	.319	.355	498	113	16	3	14	52	65	80
vs. Right	.218	.304	.329	422	92	27	1	6	37	49	111
Bases Empty	.225	.316	.358	542	122	26	2	14	14	65	111
Leadoff	.253	.319	.439	237	60	13	2	9	9	19	44
Runners On Base	.220	.308	.323	378	83	17	2	6	75	49	80
Scoring Position	.178	.287	.236	225	40	7	0	2	60	36	55
Late and Close	.307	.386	.471	140	43	9	1	4	17	17	18

	BA	OBA	SA	AB	H	2B	3B	HR	RBI	BB	SO
Total	.226	.300	.340	5603	1264	213	47	112	518	574	1418
vs. Left	.237	.318	.362	3138	744	131	32	66	290	359	645
vs. Right	.211	.277	.312	2465	520	82	15	46	228	215	773
Bases Empty	.226	.298	.340	3339	756	132	27	64	64	313	828
Leadoff	.242	.302	.375	1432	346	50	15	37	37	111	318
Runners On Base	.224	.303	.341	2264	508	81	20	48	454	261	590
Scoring Position	.200	.298	.309	1332	266	41	10	28	385	194	385
Late and Close	.247	.313	.369	639	158	21	9	13	55	62	142

STEVE COOKE — BR/TL — age 24 — PIT SP32 FIN/FB

1993	G	IP	H	BB	SO	SB	CS	W	L	SV	ERA
Total	32	210.2	207	59	132	22	9	10	10	0	3.89
at Home	16	104.0	105	30	55	13	4	5	5	0	4.41
on Road	16	106.2	102	29	77	9	5	5	5	0	3.38
on Grass	11	74.1	65	21	55	6	3	4	2	0	2.54
on Turf	21	136.1	142	38	77	16	6	6	8	0	4.62
Day Games	11	71.2	80	16	46	8	3	4	4	0	4.40
Night Games	21	139.0	127	43	86	14	6	6	6	0	3.63
April	4	23.2	25	9	11	4	0	0	1	0	4.56
May	6	43.1	38	12	29	7	2	3	1	0	3.12
June	5	37.2	28	12	30	1	1	2	1	0	2.87
July	5	30.2	32	11	18	7	2	2	3	0	4.99
August	6	37.2	49	5	22	1	3	3	2	0	4.78
Sept-Oct	6	37.2	35	10	22	2	1	2	2	0	3.58

2-YEAR TOTALS (1992–1993)

	G	IP	H	BB	SO	SB	CS	W	L	SV	ERA
Total	43	233.2	229	63	142	22	9	12	10	1	3.85
at Home	20	117.2	117	33	61	13	4	6	5	0	4.05
on Road	23	116.0	112	30	81	9	5	6	5	1	3.65
on Grass	17	82.2	75	22	58	6	3	5	2	1	3.05
on Turf	26	151.0	154	41	84	16	6	7	8	0	4.29
Day Games	15	78.2	89	18	48	8	3	4	4	1	4.46
Night Games	28	155.0	140	45	94	14	6	8	6	0	3.54
April	4	23.2	25	9	11	4	0	0	1	0	4.56
May	6	43.1	38	12	29	7	2	3	1	0	3.12
June	5	37.2	28	12	30	1	1	2	1	0	2.87
July	6	32.2	38	11	19	7	2	2	3	0	5.79
August	10	44.2	59	6	24	1	3	4	2	0	5.04
Sept-Oct	12	51.2	41	13	29	2	1	3	2	1	2.61

	BA	OBA	SA	AB	H	2B	3B	HR	RBI	BB	SO
Total	.258	.310	.428	801	207	58	6	22	94	59	132
vs. Left	.265	.325	.404	136	36	7	3	2	20	12	25
vs. Right	.257	.306	.433	665	171	51	3	20	74	47	107
Bases Empty	.260	.316	.433	480	125	40	2	13	13	36	71
Leadoff	.265	.323	.515	200	53	21	1	9	9	16	26
Runners On Base	.255	.300	.421	321	82	18	4	9	81	23	61
Scoring Position	.258	.324	.419	186	48	14	2	4	67	21	39
Late and Close	.261	.282	.464	69	18	5	1	2	7	2	11

	BA	OBA	SA	AB	H	2B	3B	HR	RBI	BB	SO
Total	.258	.307	.425	888	229	64	6	24	101	63	142
vs. Left	.258	.310	.384	159	41	8	3	2	21	12	28
vs. Right	.258	.307	.433	729	188	56	3	22	80	51	114
Bases Empty	.258	.311	.430	535	138	43	2	15	15	38	78
Leadoff	.248	.304	.473	222	55	21	1	9	9	17	29
Runners On Base	.258	.302	.416	353	91	21	4	9	86	25	64
Scoring Position	.257	.325	.411	202	52	15	2	4	71	23	41
Late and Close	.233	.258	.389	90	21	6	1	2	7	3	12

RHEAL CORMIER — BL/TL — age 27 — SL SP21, RP17 FIN/GB

1993	G	IP	H	BB	SO	SB	CS	W	L	SV	ERA	3-YEAR TOTALS (1991–1993) G	IP	H	BB	SO	SB	CS	W	L	SV	ERA
Total	38	145.1	163	27	75	3	2	7	6	0	4.33	80	399.0	431	68	230	15	9	21	21	0	3.99
at Home	15	66.1	56	8	33	0	2	4	1	0	2.17	37	198.2	211	30	97	10	4	15	7	0	3.40
on Road	23	79.0	107	19	42	3	0	3	5	0	6.15	43	200.1	220	38	133	5	5	6	14	0	4.58
on Grass	11	48.0	57	11	26	2	0	2	3	0	4.69	23	119.2	127	23	77	4	3	3	9	0	4.06
on Turf	27	97.1	106	16	49	1	2	5	3	0	4.16	57	279.1	304	45	153	11	6	18	12	0	3.96
Day Games	12	50.2	67	6	22	0	2	2	1	0	4.44	27	143.0	160	18	77	5	3	9	5	0	3.52
Night Games	26	94.2	96	21	53	3	0	5	5	0	4.08	53	256.0	271	50	153	10	6	12	16	0	4.25
April	5	28.2	33	3	16	0	2	1	2	0	3.14	8	46.2	54	13	31	3	2	1	5	0	5.52
May	11	28.2	26	4	12	1	0	0	1	0	6.20	17	58.2	64	10	28	2	1	1	3	0	4.26
June	5	20.1	25	7	10	0	0	3	1	0	6.20	10	44.1	51	10	21	4	1	4	2	0	4.96
July	9	17.1	29	4	11	1	0	0	2	0	6.23	14	45.1	67	6	30	3	0	2	4	0	2.96
August	3	19.0	20	3	4	0	0	0	0	0	4.26	13	85.0	74	15	39	2	2	4	3	0	3.40
Sept-Oct	5	31.1	30	6	22	0	0	2	0	0	3.45	18	119.0	121	14	81	1	3	9	3	0	3.40

	BA	OBA	SA	AB	H	2B	3B	HR	RBI	BB	SO	BA	OBA	SA	AB	H	2B	3B	HR	RBI	BB	SO
Total	.284	.319	.456	574	163	39	3	18	70	27	75	.276	.309	.415	1561	431	89	7	38	167	68	230
vs. Left	.207	.248	.290	145	30	3	0	3	10	8	23	.231	.267	.314	325	75	13	1	4	24	14	58
vs. Right	.310	.342	.513	429	133	36	3	15	60	19	52	.288	.320	.442	1236	356	76	6	34	143	54	172
Bases Empty	.293	.326	.466	328	96	28	1	9	9	15	50	.270	.301	.394	928	251	57	2	18	18	35	153
Leadoff	.368	.393	.569	144	53	14	0	5	5	5	23	.302	.331	.456	397	120	31	0	10	10	14	64
Runners On Base	.272	.309	.443	246	67	11	2	9	61	12	25	.284	.320	.445	633	180	32	5	20	149	33	77
Scoring Position	.239	.304	.408	142	34	5	2	5	50	12	15	.253	.308	.415	359	91	19	3	11	125	28	50
Late and Close	.289	.373	.422	45	13	6	0	0	5	5	6	.348	.397	.473	112	39	8	0	2	14	8	13

RON DARLING — BR/TR — age 34 — OAK SP29, RP2 FIN/FB

1993	G	IP	H	BB	SO	SB	CS	W	L	SV	ERA	10-YEAR TOTALS (1984–1993) G	IP	H	BB	SO	SB	CS	W	L	SV	ERA
Total	31	178.0	198	72	95	14	11	5	9	0	5.16	331	2060.2	1927	784	1390	211	93	121	95	0	3.73
at Home	16	94.2	94	38	60	8	8	3	6	0	4.75	163	1071.2	957	359	743	96	51	70	45	0	3.36
on Road	15	83.1	104	34	35	6	3	2	3	0	5.62	168	989.0	970	425	647	115	42	51	50	0	4.12
on Grass	26	144.0	157	60	79	13	11	4	8	0	5.06	245	1540.1	1431	560	1067	141	67	94	69	0	3.70
on Turf	5	34.0	41	12	16	1	0	1	1	0	5.56	86	520.1	496	224	323	70	26	27	26	0	3.79
Day Games	12	72.1	70	37	45	6	8	1	5	0	4.35	113	692.2	638	284	443	72	33	38	37	0	3.73
Night Games	19	105.2	128	35	50	8	8	3	4	0	5.71	218	1368.0	1289	500	947	139	60	83	58	0	3.72
April	3	13.0	10	7	6	3	2	0	1	0	5.54	43	245.1	247	101	157	37	9	11	13	0	3.74
May	6	29.0	33	13	14	6	0	0	2	0	6.83	54	341.1	298	123	243	30	15	20	13	0	3.80
June	5	31.2	41	10	17	1	2	1	0	0	5.68	55	340.2	324	127	224	26	17	21	14	0	3.53
July	7	35.1	45	19	10	0	3	3	3	0	4.58	61	385.0	377	148	242	38	24	26	18	0	3.72
August	6	43.0	44	13	24	1	1	1	3	0	3.77	59	384.2	374	151	268	31	17	24	17	0	3.72
Sept-Oct	4	26.0	25	10	20	3	3	0	2	0	5.54	59	363.2	307	134	256	49	11	19	20	0	3.44

	BA	OBA	SA	AB	H	2B	3B	HR	RBI	BB	SO	BA	OBA	SA	AB	H	2B	3B	HR	RBI	BB	SO
Total	.281	.349	.441	705	198	39	4	22	97	72	95	.249	.319	.387	7747	1927	349	52	205	847	784	1390
vs. Left	.275	.350	.442	346	95	16	3	12	48	40	41	.250	.320	.378	4100	1026	187	31	91	419	426	707
vs. Right	.287	.348	.440	359	103	23	1	10	49	32	54	.247	.318	.397	3647	901	162	21	114	428	358	683
Bases Empty	.291	.342	.438	409	119	27	3	9	9	29	58	.250	.316	.389	4629	1157	204	30	126	126	417	826
Leadoff	.279	.306	.425	179	50	10	2	4	4	6	23	.253	.309	.380	1973	500	70	12	52	52	144	357
Runners On Base	.267	.357	.446	296	79	12	1	13	88	43	37	.247	.324	.384	3118	770	145	22	79	721	367	564
Scoring Position	.268	.374	.440	168	45	8	0	1	73	31	23	.239	.331	.374	1785	427	80	14	44	619	263	349
Late and Close	.259	.310	.333	27	7	1	0	0	2	2	5	.236	.317	.345	649	153	26	3	13	54	72	110

DANNY DARWIN — BR/TR — age 39 — BOS SP34 FIN/FB

1993	G	IP	H	BB	SO	SB	CS	W	L	SV	ERA	10-YEAR TOTALS (1984–1993) G	IP	H	BB	SO	SB	CS	W	L	SV	ERA
Total	34	229.1	196	49	130	11	5	15	11	0	3.26	403	1756.2	1658	461	1139	168	53	93	97	17	3.48
at Home	15	101.1	93	18	61	3	3	8	3	0	3.38	200	853.0	827	236	583	87	26	44	46	8	3.36
on Road	19	128.0	103	31	69	8	2	7	8	0	3.16	203	903.2	831	225	556	81	27	49	51	9	3.61
on Grass	31	212.2	170	44	120	8	4	15	9	0	2.88	231	1116.1	1056	284	714	86	33	58	67	9	3.56
on Turf	3	16.2	26	5	10	3	1	0	2	0	8.10	172	640.1	602	177	425	82	20	35	30	8	3.35
Day Games	11	70.0	59	23	45	2	4	7	2	0	3.33	126	527.1	499	151	383	47	24	30	33	4	3.57
Night Games	23	159.1	137	26	85	9	1	8	9	0	3.33	277	1229.1	1159	310	756	121	29	63	64	13	3.45
April	4	18.2	27	5	3	2	1	0	4	0	8.20	56	217.2	204	55	133	23	11	6	10	1	3.51
May	6	40.2	24	6	26	1	0	5	0	0	1.33	72	273.2	265	73	161	27	4	16	12	2	3.45
June	6	40.2	34	10	19	1	1	2	3	0	2.88	79	326.0	337	82	206	30	13	17	23	5	4.09
July	5	36.0	35	7	19	2	0	1	1	0	3.25	66	330.2	287	89	216	27	7	17	17	4	3.13
August	6	44.1	24	10	26	1	1	4	1	0	2.23	60	308.2	285	77	225	30	9	17	16	0	3.24
Sept-Oct	7	49.0	43	11	37	2	2	2	0	0	4.22	70	300.0	280	85	198	31	9	14	19	5	3.48

	BA	OBA	SA	AB	H	2B	3B	HR	RBI	BB	SO	BA	OBA	SA	AB	H	2B	3B	HR	RBI	BB	SO
Total	.230	.272	.399	852	196	45	3	31	83	49	130	.248	.299	.386	6678	1658	300	37	182	716	461	1139
vs. Left	.255	.300	.450	467	119	28	3	19	52	32	51	.271	.328	.423	3475	942	189	26	96	387	294	510
vs. Right	.200	.237	.338	385	77	17	0	12	31	17	79	.224	.265	.346	3203	716	111	11	86	329	167	629
Bases Empty	.233	.268	.410	563	131	33	2	21	21	24	78	.240	.287	.384	4021	965	194	18	117	117	240	687
Leadoff	.273	.297	.468	231	63	19	1	8	8	8	29	.253	.292	.399	1670	422	86	7	48	48	87	271
Runners On Base	.225	.279	.377	289	65	12	1	10	62	25	52	.261	.315	.388	2657	693	106	19	65	599	221	452
Scoring Position	.219	.287	.356	160	35	6	1	5	50	19	31	.247	.308	.364	1552	383	62	12	32	504	156	279
Late and Close	.256	.294	.449	78	20	5	1	5	10	7	10	.242	.299	.371	1089	263	42	6	29	109	88	197

JIM DESHAIES — BL/TL — age 34 — MIN/SF SP31, RP1 FIN/FB

1993	G	IP	H	BB	SO	SB	CS	W	L	SV	ERA
Total	32	184.1	183	57	85	8	18	13	15	0	4.39
at Home	15	89.2	84	22	41	1	8	8	6	0	3.81
on Road	17	94.2	99	35	44	7	10	5	9	0	4.94
on Grass	14	73.0	83	31	35	5	8	3	8	0	5.42
on Turf	18	111.1	100	26	50	3	10	10	7	0	3.72
Day Games	13	77.2	76	19	43	5	8	6	5	0	3.82
Night Games	19	106.2	107	38	42	3	10	7	10	0	4.81
April	5	34.1	29	11	13	3	6	4	1	0	2.36
May	6	30.2	34	8	19	2	3	2	3	0	6.16
June	5	32.1	28	12	10	1	3	3	1	0	3.34
July	6	34.1	39	13	20	0	2	2	3	0	6.55
August	5	35.2	29	7	18	2	1	0	5	0	3.79
Sept-Oct	5	17.0	24	6	5	0	3	2	2	0	4.24

10-YEAR TOTALS (1984–1993)

	G	IP	H	BB	SO	SB	CS	W	L	SV	ERA
	230	1389.2	1249	520	867	148	93	78	82	0	3.78
at Home	111	699.0	587	243	432	71	42	43	32	0	3.27
on Road	119	690.2	662	277	435	77	51	35	50	0	4.29
on Grass	78	453.0	452	179	285	41	32	22	35	0	4.49
on Turf	152	936.2	797	341	582	107	61	56	47	0	3.43
Day Games	65	379.1	364	124	240	41	27	22	23	0	4.03
Night Games	165	1010.1	885	396	627	107	66	56	59	0	3.68
April	28	175.0	140	68	102	18	12	11	7	0	2.93
May	37	220.2	197	89	120	28	15	14	12	0	4.53
June	38	237.1	219	93	130	22	13	16	10	0	3.72
July	39	234.1	210	89	171	20	18	11	16	0	4.22
August	44	272.2	255	105	179	35	17	11	23	0	4.06
Sept-Oct	44	249.2	228	76	165	25	18	15	14	0	3.03

	BA	OBA	SA	AB	H	2B	3B	HR	RBI	BB	SO
Total	.264	.323	.444	694	183	39	4	26	81	57	85
vs. Left	.230	.309	.352	122	28	4	1	3	6	10	13
vs. Right	.271	.326	.463	572	155	35	3	23	75	47	72
Bases Empty	.254	.313	.433	441	112	21	2	18	18	33	52
Leadoff	.260	.306	.448	181	47	8	1	8	8	11	18
Runners On Base	.281	.339	.462	253	71	18	2	8	63	24	33
Scoring Position	.266	.322	.398	128	34	9	1	2	47	13	19
Late and Close	.200	.293	.314	35	7	1	0	1	2	4	6

	BA	OBA	SA	AB	H	2B	3B	HR	RBI	BB	SO
Total	.243	.312	.390	5146	1249	252	34	146	532	520	867
vs. Left	.269	.362	.417	847	228	46	8	21	81	120	135
vs. Right	.237	.302	.385	4299	1021	206	26	125	451	400	732
Bases Empty	.240	.309	.386	3167	761	146	19	92	92	298	507
Leadoff	.245	.309	.399	1326	325	64	7	42	42	117	195
Runners On Base	.247	.317	.397	1979	488	106	15	54	440	222	360
Scoring Position	.232	.319	.364	1103	256	57	7	25	355	160	232
Late and Close	.216	.277	.293	352	76	8	2	5	19	30	50

ROB DIBBLE — BL/TR — age 30 — CIN RP45 POW/FB

1993	G	IP	H	BB	SO	SB	CS	W	L	SV	ERA
Total	45	41.2	34	42	49	13	1	1	4	19	6.48
at Home	21	20.2	18	24	21	5	1	0	0	9	8.71
on Road	24	21.0	16	18	28	8	1	1	4	10	4.29
on Grass	14	13.1	10	10	16	3	1	1	2	7	3.38
on Turf	31	28.1	24	32	33	10	1	0	2	12	7.94
Day Games	15	13.2	9	17	16	3	0	1	0	8	4.61
Night Games	30	28.0	25	25	33	10	2	0	4	11	7.39
April	6	6.0	5	8	2	2	0	0	0	3	7.50
May	2	2.0	0	4	1	0	0	0	0	0	0.00
June	10	10.2	5	7	14	1	1	1	0	4	1.69
July	10	8.2	2	8	9	0	0	0	0	7	0.00
August	10	8.2	10	7	10	3	1	0	2	4	7.27
Sept-Oct	7	5.2	12	8	7	1	0	0	2	0	25.41

6-YEAR TOTALS (1988–1993)

	G	IP	H	BB	SO	SB	CS	W	L	SV	ERA
	354	450.2	316	192	619	85	16	26	23	88	2.74
at Home	175	222.1	159	103	306	45	10	12	9	49	2.91
on Road	179	228.1	157	89	313	40	6	14	14	39	2.56
on Grass	109	142.2	105	52	185	19	4	7	9	22	2.78
on Turf	245	308.0	211	140	434	66	12	19	14	66	2.72
Day Games	102	135.2	91	65	185	26	3	11	4	24	2.65
Night Games	252	315.0	225	127	434	59	13	15	19	64	2.77
April	45	51.0	39	26	73	12	1	4	0	14	2.47
May	48	58.0	39	28	91	13	1	3	3	14	2.33
June	66	84.2	46	36	123	17	3	4	5	21	2.23
July	56	73.2	51	38	79	14	5	3	3	11	2.69
August	72	102.1	76	38	144	22	5	7	7	14	2.81
Sept-Oct	67	81.0	65	26	109	7	1	5	5	14	3.67

	BA	OBA	SA	AB	H	2B	3B	HR	RBI	BB	SO
Total	.225	.400	.424	151	34	2	2	8	33	42	49
vs. Left	.250	.481	.486	72	18	2	0	5	15	31	19
vs. Right	.203	.308	.367	79	16	0	2	3	18	11	30
Bases Empty	.250	.414	.441	68	17	1	0	4	4	17	20
Leadoff	.185	.405	.222	27	5	1	0	0	0	9	6
Runners On Base	.205	.389	.410	83	17	1	2	4	29	25	29
Scoring Position	.222	.417	.407	54	12	0	2	2	25	18	20
Late and Close	.225	.425	.438	89	20	2	1	5	25	30	24

	BA	OBA	SA	AB	H	2B	3B	HR	RBI	BB	SO
Total	.197	.284	.289	1601	316	51	10	25	184	192	619
vs. Left	.196	.306	.287	812	159	30	4	12	84	130	328
vs. Right	.199	.260	.290	789	157	21	6	13	100	62	291
Bases Empty	.191	.275	.276	836	160	25	5	12	12	91	342
Leadoff	.190	.273	.269	342	65	13	1	4	4	37	131
Runners On Base	.204	.294	.302	765	156	26	5	13	172	101	277
Scoring Position	.189	.282	.281	549	104	17	3	9	160	76	210
Late and Close	.213	.296	.310	980	209	31	5	18	133	114	372

JOHN DOHERTY — BR/TR — age 27 — DET SP31, RP1 FIN/GB

1993	G	IP	H	BB	SO	SB	CS	W	L	SV	ERA
Total	32	184.2	205	48	63	7	12	14	11	0	4.44
at Home	17	96.1	110	31	36	4	8	6	6	0	4.76
on Road	15	88.1	95	17	27	3	4	8	5	0	4.08
on Grass	28	163.2	183	47	58	5	9	12	10	0	4.67
on Turf	4	21.0	22	1	5	2	3	2	1	0	2.57
Day Games	15	71.1	94	24	20	5	5	4	8	0	6.18
Night Games	17	113.1	111	24	43	2	7	10	3	0	3.34
April	5	34.2	30	7	9	2	3	3	1	0	2.08
May	4	23.0	28	7	12	2	4	1	1	0	5.09
June	4	22.2	21	9	8	1	2	3	1	0	3.18
July	7	35.2	48	3	11	2	3	2	3	0	6.06
August	6	29.2	31	13	10	1	1	2	4	0	6.07
Sept-Oct	6	39.0	47	5	13	1	0	3	1	0	4.15

2-YEAR TOTALS (1992–1993)

	G	IP	H	BB	SO	SB	CS	W	L	SV	ERA
	79	300.2	336	73	100	11	16	21	15	3	4.22
at Home	42	152.2	175	46	57	7	11	11	7	1	4.42
on Road	37	148.0	161	27	43	4	5	10	8	2	4.01
on Grass	68	261.0	296	68	90	9	13	18	14	3	4.41
on Turf	11	39.2	40	5	10	2	3	3	1	0	2.95
Day Games	31	107.0	122	32	34	6	6	6	10	1	4.79
Night Games	48	193.2	214	41	66	5	10	15	5	2	3.90
April	12	47.2	43	8	11	0	2	3	1	1	2.27
May	15	42.0	46	19	15	2	4	3	2	0	4.93
June	9	27.1	28	11	9	1	2	3	1	0	3.29
July	20	53.2	64	7	21	2	4	2	5	0	5.53
August	11	60.1	68	15	16	2	4	4	5	0	4.18
Sept-Oct	12	69.2	87	13	28	4	2	6	2	0	4.52

	BA	OBA	SA	AB	H	2B	3B	HR	RBI	BB	SO
Total	.286	.333	.423	718	205	34	4	19	88	48	63
vs. Left	.310	.349	.469	384	119	19	3	12	42	24	35
vs. Right	.257	.315	.371	334	86	15	1	7	46	24	28
Bases Empty	.277	.313	.408	441	122	18	2	12	12	20	41
Leadoff	.259	.301	.357	185	48	6	1	4	4	9	23
Runners On Base	.300	.363	.448	277	83	16	2	7	76	28	22
Scoring Position	.324	.402	.547	148	48	19	2	7	73	20	14
Late and Close	.333	.356	.439	57	19	3	0	1	1	4	4

	BA	OBA	SA	AB	H	2B	3B	HR	RBI	BB	SO
Total	.286	.331	.393	1175	336	47	5	23	139	73	100
vs. Left	.286	.321	.406	584	167	25	3	13	68	32	52
vs. Right	.286	.341	.381	591	169	22	2	10	71	41	48
Bases Empty	.279	.313	.379	700	195	25	3	13	13	30	69
Leadoff	.264	.300	.342	295	78	7	2	4	4	12	34
Runners On Base	.297	.356	.415	475	141	22	2	10	126	43	31
Scoring Position	.307	.378	.455	264	81	11	2	8	117	31	21
Late and Close	.362	.393	.448	116	42	4	0	4	13	5	9

JOHN DOPSON — BL/TR — age 31 — BOS SP28, RP6 FIN/GB

1993	G	IP	H	BB	SO	SB	CS	W	L	SV	ERA
Total	34	155.2	170	59	89	11	5	7	11	0	4.97
at Home	19	85.1	91	33	46	3	1	5	3	0	4.64
on Road	15	70.1	79	26	43	8	4	2	8	0	5.37
on Grass	30	141.0	148	51	82	10	5	7	8	0	4.60
on Turf	4	14.2	22	8	7	1	0	0	3	0	8.59
Day Games	14	57.0	69	22	30	4	2	3	5	0	5.37
Night Games	20	98.2	101	37	59	7	3	4	6	0	4.74
April	5	30.1	24	8	28	2	1	2	1	0	3.26
May	6	33.0	39	12	18	1	2	1	3	0	3.82
June	5	28.0	26	12	19	0	1	0	1	0	4.50
July	5	23.1	22	11	13	4	0	1	0	0	6.56
August	6	19.0	29	9	6	2	0	0	4	0	6.16
Sept-Oct	7	22.0	30	7	5	2	1	0	2	0	6.95

7-YEAR TOTALS (1985–1993)

G	IP	H	BB	SO	SB	CS	W	L	SV	ERA
123	666.2	685	238	353	92	25	29	43	0	4.10
68	374.1	383	134	195	49	15	17	20	0	3.68
55	292.1	302	104	158	43	10	12	23	0	4.65
91	479.0	494	175	247	61	17	25	27	0	4.28
32	187.2	191	63	106	31	8	4	16	0	3.64
44	211.1	230	85	99	30	5	14	11	0	4.26
79	455.1	455	153	254	62	20	15	32	0	4.03
13	76.2	53	26	63	13	4	4	2	0	2.47
19	113.0	113	40	53	7	3	6	9	0	3.74
23	134.0	135	48	70	14	6	9	7	0	4.16
20	114.1	128	37	58	19	5	5	2	0	3.70
20	100.0	111	47	47	16	3	1	10	0	4.41
28	128.2	145	40	62	23	4	4	13	0	5.46

	BA	OBA	SA	AB	H	2B	3B	HR	RBI	BB	SO
Total	.281	.343	.437	604	170	34	6	16	77	59	89
vs. Left	.303	.366	.476	307	93	16	5	9	45	31	37
vs. Right	.259	.319	.397	297	77	18	1	7	32	28	52
Bases Empty	.281	.329	.452	363	102	20	3	12	12	26	56
Leadoff	.293	.343	.522	157	46	14	2	6	6	12	24
Runners On Base	.282	.363	.415	241	68	14	3	4	65	33	33
Scoring Position	.275	.376	.370	138	38	5	1	2	55	26	19
Late and Close	.400	.455	.750	20	8	2	1	1	4	2	3

BA	OBA	SA	AB	H	2B	3B	HR	RBI	BB	SO
.266	.327	.400	2578	685	114	14	68	289	238	353
.271	.335	.391	1273	345	48	9	29	135	127	148
.261	.319	.408	1305	340	66	5	39	154	111	205
.268	.330	.408	1521	408	64	8	44	44	136	225
.261	.328	.410	652	170	33	5	18	18	65	95
.262	.324	.389	1057	277	50	6	24	245	102	128
.255	.329	.366	615	157	26	3	12	209	74	83
.342	.374	.521	146	50	10	2	4	18	8	13

DOUG DRABEK — BR/TR — age 32 — HOU SP34 FIN/GB

1993	G	IP	H	BB	SO	SB	CS	W	L	SV	ERA
Total	34	237.2	242	60	157	28	7	9	18	0	3.79
at Home	19	142.1	136	35	100	18	4	5	8	0	3.04
on Road	15	95.1	106	25	57	10	3	4	10	0	4.91
on Grass	10	60.1	81	19	33	6	2	4	5	0	5.82
on Turf	24	177.1	161	41	124	22	5	5	13	0	3.10
Day Games	12	86.2	90	19	67	12	5	4	5	0	3.32
Night Games	22	151.0	152	41	90	16	6	4	14	0	4.05
April	5	41.0	28	8	31	5	1	2	3	0	1.98
May	6	43.2	48	9	25	7	1	3	2	0	3.71
June	6	41.0	41	10	19	3	2	1	3	0	4.17
July	6	40.2	40	12	29	5	1	1	4	0	3.98
August	5	32.2	35	10	29	8	0	0	3	0	4.13
Sept-Oct	6	38.2	50	11	24	7	2	2	3	0	4.89

8-YEAR TOTALS (1986–1993)

G	IP	H	BB	SO	SB	CS	W	L	SV	ERA
260	1732.0	1595	447	1053	146	79	108	88	0	3.21
126	884.1	791	210	586	73	40	56	38	0	2.81
134	847.2	804	237	467	73	39	52	50	0	3.62
86	493.1	514	156	261	38	21	27	36	0	4.51
174	1238.2	1081	291	792	108	58	81	52	0	2.69
77	498.2	455	125	299	45	17	33	23	0	3.09
183	1233.1	1140	322	754	101	62	75	65	0	3.25
34	231.0	197	57	133	25	9	15	15	0	2.88
36	248.1	224	68	141	27	12	12	13	0	3.23
47	280.2	282	84	169	23	17	10	16	0	3.98
46	306.2	276	90	182	20	15	22	16	0	3.40
48	333.2	303	77	217	29	11	22	14	0	2.78
49	331.2	313	71	211	22	15	27	14	0	3.01

	BA	OBA	SA	AB	H	2B	3B	HR	RBI	BB	SO
Total	.267	.312	.381	906	242	41	4	18	97	60	157
vs. Left	.288	.337	.427	459	132	25	3	11	59	35	60
vs. Right	.246	.287	.333	447	110	16	1	7	38	25	97
Bases Empty	.246	.278	.346	558	137	20	3	10	10	24	90
Leadoff	.239	.279	.321	234	56	3	2	4	4	13	33
Runners On Base	.302	.363	.437	348	105	21	1	8	87	36	67
Scoring Position	.274	.367	.428	208	57	9	1	7	77	33	46
Late and Close	.248	.296	.308	117	29	1	0	2	8	7	30

BA	OBA	SA	AB	H	2B	3B	HR	RBI	BB	SO
.246	.296	.366	6474	1595	274	36	143	597	447	1053
.264	.319	.389	3540	936	167	21	77	346	288	465
.225	.268	.339	2934	659	107	15	66	251	159	588
.241	.287	.360	4049	977	162	22	91	91	254	679
.255	.298	.369	1688	430	67	9	36	36	101	265
.255	.310	.377	2425	618	112	14	52	506	193	374
.238	.309	.357	1363	324	53	8	31	434	151	233
.240	.307	.323	662	159	19	0	12	41	62	110

DENNIS ECKERSLEY — BR/TR — age 40 — OAK RP64 POW/FB

1993	G	IP	H	BB	SO	SB	CS	W	L	SV	ERA
Total	64	67.0	67	13	80	12	2	1	4	36	4.16
at Home	36	38.0	31	8	53	8	2	0	3	19	3.08
on Road	28	29.0	36	5	27	4	0	1	1	17	5.59
on Grass	53	55.2	54	12	72	11	2	1	4	28	3.88
on Turf	11	11.1	13	1	8	1	0	1	0	8	5.56
Day Games	28	28.1	20	3	31	4	1	1	2	17	2.22
Night Games	36	38.2	47	10	49	8	1	1	2	19	5.59
April	9	8.2	10	4	12	4	0	0	1	2	5.19
May	12	11.0	11	2	10	3	0	1	1	7	4.91
June	10	11.2	11	1	13	0	1	0	1	7	3.09
July	10	11.2	8	1	16	0	0	0	0	7	3.09
August	12	13.2	16	4	14	3	1	0	1	6	3.29
Sept-Oct	11	10.1	12	1	9	2	0	0	2	7	6.10

10-YEAR TOTALS (1984–1993)

G	IP	H	BB	SO	SB	CS	W	L	SV	ERA
519	1137.2	1007	179	939	109	32	63	51	272	3.13
262	551.1	463	95	524	59	20	45	24	129	3.05
257	586.1	544	84	415	50	12	18	27	143	3.21
420	849.1	742	130	757	78	28	53	38	221	3.10
99	288.1	265	49	182	31	4	10	13	51	3.22
234	586.0	497	101	504	50	21	37	24	109	3.01
285	551.2	510	78	435	59	11	26	27	163	3.26
76	182.2	151	26	146	15	6	9	8	42	3.10
87	208.0	208	26	164	18	7	13	10	44	3.98
78	185.1	161	37	132	17	4	7	8	43	3.30
82	180.1	134	26	168	11	5	9	7	41	2.50
92	180.2	174	34	149	22	5	12	6	52	2.54
104	200.2	179	30	180	25	5	13	12	50	3.23

	BA	OBA	SA	AB	H	2B	3B	HR	RBI	BB	SO
Total	.261	.299	.405	257	67	8	4	7	43	13	80
vs. Left	.326	.367	.543	129	42	7	3	5	34	9	25
vs. Right	.195	.230	.266	128	25	1	1	2	9	4	55
Bases Empty	.228	.261	.353	136	31	1	2	4	4	5	43
Leadoff	.259	.286	.389	54	14	0	1	2	2	1	12
Runners On Base	.298	.341	.463	121	36	7	2	3	39	8	37
Scoring Position	.307	.357	.413	75	23	3	1	1	31	6	24
Late and Close	.262	.301	.421	195	51	7	3	6	39	10	62

BA	OBA	SA	AB	H	2B	3B	HR	RBI	BB	SO
.236	.267	.365	4276	1007	198	23	103	445	179	939
.262	.299	.405	2156	565	117	15	54	256	115	324
.208	.235	.324	2120	442	81	8	49	189	64	615
.240	.265	.363	2603	625	122	14	57	57	75	589
.249	.267	.376	1044	260	52	6	23	22	22	209
.228	.272	.367	1673	382	76	9	46	388	104	350
.226	.280	.350	993	224	48	5	22	329	82	223
.202	.231	.314	1527	308	50	8	35	174	57	428

CAL ELDRED — BR/TR — age 27 — MIL SP36 POW/FB

3-YEAR TOTALS (1991–1993)

1993	G	IP	H	BB	SO	SB	CS	W	L	SV	ERA		G	IP	H	BB	SO	SB	CS	W	L	SV	ERA
Total	36	258.0	232	91	180	21	9	16	16	0	4.01		53	374.1	328	120	252	32	14	29	18	0	3.44
at Home	19	148.2	118	37	97	9	8	11	6	0	2.91		29	217.1	171	57	132	15	9	19	6	0	2.48
on Road	17	109.1	114	54	83	12	1	5	10	0	5.52		24	157.0	157	63	120	17	5	10	12	0	4.76
on Grass	33	239.1	211	80	163	17	8	16	14	0	3.80		48	341.2	294	108	225	28	13	27	16	0	3.29
on Turf	3	18.2	21	11	17	4	1	0	2	0	6.75		5	32.2	34	12	27	4	1	2	2	0	4.96
Day Games	12	84.2	78	25	58	3	0	6	4	0	4.36		19	130.1	114	41	89	11	4	10	6	0	3.87
Night Games	24	173.1	154	66	122	18	9	10	12	0	3.84		34	244.0	214	79	163	21	10	19	12	0	3.21
April	5	31.1	23	10	26	1	0	3	2	0	3.73		5	31.1	23	10	26	1	0	3	2	0	3.73
May	6	41.2	46	10	29	3	3	3	3	0	3.67		6	41.2	46	10	29	3	3	3	3	0	3.67
June	6	44.0	39	13	21	7	1	3	3	0	3.48		6	44.0	39	13	21	0	1	3	3	0	3.48
July	7	46.2	49	20	33	7	2	2	3	0	5.40		10	64.1	70	26	43	11	4	3	4	0	4.90
August	6	48.1	41	19	36	8	0	4	1	0	3.54		10	78.0	58	27	51	8	1	8	1	0	2.42
Sept-Oct	6	46.0	34	19	35	2	3	1	4	0	4.11		16	115.0	92	34	82	9	5	9	5	0	3.13

	BA	OBA	SA	AB	H	2B	3B	HR	RBI	BB	SO		BA	OBA	SA	AB	H	2B	3B	HR	RBI	BB	SO
Total	.239	.308	.401	969	232	47	7	32	110	91	180		.234	.297	.371	1403	328	58	10	38	131	120	252
vs. Left	.245	.320	.393	507	124	27	6	12	53	52	75		.231	.302	.354	697	161	29	6	15	59	64	103
vs. Right	.234	.294	.411	462	108	20	1	20	57	39	105		.237	.293	.387	706	167	29	4	23	72	56	149
Bases Empty	.243	.302	.404	602	146	33	5	18	18	45	104		.243	.302	.385	868	211	40	7	23	23	65	139
Leadoff	.236	.293	.356	250	59	14	2	4	4	17	48		.236	.293	.341	364	86	14	3	6	6	26	67
Runners On Base	.234	.317	.398	367	86	14	2	14	92	46	76		.219	.290	.348	535	117	18	3	15	108	55	113
Scoring Position	.212	.304	.363	212	45	6	1	8	77	31	47		.196	.275	.307	296	58	7	1	8	89	35	67
Late and Close	.239	.286	.450	109	26	3	1	6	15	7	13		.233	.275	.409	159	37	4	3	6	18	8	25

SCOTT ERICKSON — BR/TR — age 26 — MIN SP34 FIN/GB

4-YEAR TOTALS (1990–1993)

1993	G	IP	H	BB	SO	SB	CS	W	L	SV	ERA		G	IP	H	BB	SO	SB	CS	W	L	SV	ERA
Total	34	218.2	266	71	116	27	4	8	19	0	5.19		117	747.2	760	276	378	60	24	49	43	0	3.78
at Home	19	127.1	150	43	80	16	1	4	11	0	5.30		65	426.0	453	132	232	37	8	29	22	0	4.01
on Road	15	91.1	116	28	36	11	3	4	8	0	5.03		52	321.2	307	144	146	23	16	20	21	0	3.47
on Grass	10	60.0	75	21	20	6	2	3	4	0	4.65		39	245.1	220	116	106	15	13	18	12	0	2.90
on Turf	24	158.2	191	50	96	21	2	5	15	0	5.39		78	502.1	540	160	272	45	11	31	31	0	4.21
Day Games	9	61.0	76	10	37	9	1	2	7	0	5.31		45	303.2	295	92	154	25	11	22	16	0	3.20
Night Games	25	157.2	190	61	79	18	3	6	12	0	5.14		72	444.0	465	184	224	35	13	27	27	0	4.18
April	3	15.0	21	6	7	1	2	0	3	0	9.60		12	76.0	77	31	31	6	8	2	8	0	4.74
May	6	40.2	34	9	22	3	0	2	3	0	4.20		17	115.0	101	32	69	5	2	10	4	0	3.21
June	7	43.2	58	17	25	2	0	2	3	0	5.98		20	132.0	137	50	76	6	0	11	6	0	3.82
July	6	38.0	47	17	18	4	1	2	3	0	4.74		21	122.0	134	54	53	8	3	6	6	0	3.91
August	6	43.0	57	9	21	7	1	2	4	0	4.60		22	131.0	156	45	61	12	5	7	12	0	4.74
Sept-Oct	6	38.1	49	13	23	10	0	0	3	0	4.70		25	171.2	155	64	88	23	6	13	7	0	2.88

	BA	OBA	SA	AB	H	2B	3B	HR	RBI	BB	SO		BA	OBA	SA	AB	H	2B	3B	HR	RBI	BB	SO
Total	.305	.359	.431	872	266	43	8	17	119	71	116		.268	.336	.387	2837	760	127	20	57	313	276	378
vs. Left	.342	.392	.481	474	162	31	7	7	57	44	55		.288	.353	.407	1525	439	76	14	26	161	157	152
vs. Right	.261	.320	.372	398	104	12	1	10	62	27	61		.245	.316	.364	1312	321	51	6	31	152	119	226
Bases Empty	.299	.360	.439	462	138	27	4	10	10	40	69		.269	.344	.395	1584	426	80	10	33	33	164	221
Leadoff	.338	.390	.502	213	72	11	1	5	5	16	28		.279	.347	.426	706	197	46	2	18	18	66	93
Runners On Base	.312	.359	.422	410	128	16	4	7	109	31	47		.267	.326	.377	1253	334	47	10	24	280	112	157
Scoring Position	.315	.369	.448	248	78	11	2	6	102	24	34		.260	.331	.375	696	181	23	6	15	249	82	105
Late and Close	.333	.416	.409	66	22	5	0	0	8	8	9		.290	.358	.429	238	69	12	3	5	26	24	31

STEVE FARR — BR/TR — age 38 — NYA RP49 POW/FB

10-YEAR TOTALS (1984–1993)

1993	G	IP	H	BB	SO	SB	CS	W	L	SV	ERA		G	IP	H	BB	SO	SB	CS	W	L	SV	ERA
Total	49	47.0	44	28	39	4	1	2	2	25	4.21		479	796.0	710	316	648	57	39	46	44	128	3.17
at Home	23	20.2	20	14	15	2	0	0	2	14	5.23		250	427.1	361	166	348	29	14	31	17	76	2.93
on Road	26	26.1	24	14	24	2	1	2	0	11	3.42		229	368.2	349	150	300	28	25	15	27	52	3.44
on Grass	39	37.2	40	24	29	2	1	1	2	21	5.02		264	424.0	390	173	330	32	19	15	32	83	3.69
on Turf	10	9.1	4	4	10	2	0	1	0	4	0.96		215	372.0	320	143	318	25	20	31	12	45	2.56
Day Games	17	16.2	16	5	13	4	1	0	0	7	4.86		130	225.2	214	91	194	22	12	11	15	30	3.71
Night Games	32	30.1	28	23	26	0	1	1	2	18	3.86		349	570.1	496	225	454	35	27	35	29	98	2.95
April	9	7.1	10	3	7	0	0	0	1	5	7.36		57	80.1	82	34	72	9	3	2	5	16	4.37
May	9	10.0	6	6	11	0	1	1	1	6	1.80		89	149.1	114	53	135	10	10	10	8	21	2.11
June	9	9.2	7	7	0	0	0	0	0	7	2.79		84	137.0	108	50	113	9	11	5	5	29	2.69
July	9	8.2	8	3	8	2	0	0	0	3	4.15		83	135.0	127	57	108	11	4	10	9	18	3.20
August	8	7.0	6	3	3	0	0	1	0	4	2.57		87	147.0	150	55	101	9	5	7	10	23	4.41
Sept-Oct	5	4.1	7	5	3	2	0	0	0	0	10.38		79	147.1	129	67	119	9	6	12	7	21	2.75

	BA	OBA	SA	AB	H	2B	3B	HR	RBI	BB	SO		BA	OBA	SA	AB	H	2B	3B	HR	RBI	BB	SO
Total	.253	.356	.471	174	44	10	2	8	36	28	39		.240	.318	.361	2953	710	127	17	65	362	316	648
vs. Left	.292	.393	.500	72	21	4	1	3	12	11	9		.246	.336	.360	1392	343	58	11	26	153	179	258
vs. Right	.225	.331	.451	102	23	6	1	5	24	17	30		.235	.301	.362	1561	367	69	6	39	209	137	390
Bases Empty	.202	.292	.383	94	19	3	1	4	4	11	24		.246	.316	.374	1601	394	78	9	36	36	147	345
Leadoff	.200	.263	.229	35	7	1	0	0	0	3	7		.251	.315	.391	677	170	39	4	16	16	58	125
Runners On Base	.313	.422	.575	80	25	7	1	4	32	17	15		.234	.320	.346	1352	316	49	8	29	326	169	303
Scoring Position	.327	.443	.635	52	17	4	0	3	30	13	13		.230	.335	.340	791	182	25	4	18	288	126	197
Late and Close	.224	.327	.336	125	28	6	1	2	22	20	30		.241	.322	.345	1072	258	37	3	23	144	123	244

JEFF FASSERO — BL/TL — age 31 — MON RP41, SP15 POW/GB

1993	G	IP	H	BB	SO	SB	CS	W	L	SV	ERA
Total	56	149.2	119	54	140	12	4	12	5	1	2.29
at Home	26	67.2	47	27	64	7	1	7	1	1	2.00
on Road	30	82.0	72	27	76	5	3	5	4	0	2.52
on Grass	16	51.0	40	15	53	3	1	3	3	0	1.76
on Turf	40	98.2	79	39	87	9	3	9	2	1	2.55
Day Games	19	39.2	38	17	33	3	2	1	3	0	3.63
Night Games	37	110.0	81	37	107	9	2	11	2	1	1.80
April	10	9.0	10	7	3	1	0	1	0	0	6.00
May	13	19.1	9	4	20	1	0	3	1	0	0.93
June	15	21.0	16	13	19	0	0	1	0	1	2.14
July	6	25.0	20	8	27	2	2	1	0	0	0.72
August	6	41.0	32	12	35	5	1	4	2	0	2.20
Sept-Oct	6	34.1	32	10	36	3	1	2	2	0	3.41

3-YEAR TOTALS (1991–1993)

	G	IP	H	BB	SO	SB	CS	W	L	SV	ERA
	177	290.2	239	105	245	27	7	22	17	10	2.48
	88	136.2	105	61	114	14	2	15	6	4	2.63
	89	154.0	134	44	131	13	5	7	11	6	2.34
	42	82.0	71	21	71	8	3	3	6	4	1.98
	135	208.2	168	84	174	19	4	19	11	6	2.67
	57	82.0	79	31	67	8	5	3	8	2	3.40
	120	208.2	160	74	178	19	2	19	9	8	2.11
	21	26.1	24	15	12	2	0	1	1	0	4.44
	26	36.2	22	11	35	3	1	5	3	0	1.96
	38	51.2	34	22	44	2	0	3	2	4	1.74
	28	51.2	43	18	48	8	4	2	1	2	1.92
	32	66.1	58	20	55	8	1	6	5	2	1.90
	32	58.0	58	19	51	4	1	5	5	2	3.72

	BA	OBA	SA	AB	H	2B	3B	HR	RBI	BB	SO
Total	.216	.284	.290	551	119	18	1	7	49	54	140
vs. Left	.184	.275	.246	114	21	4	0	1	14	15	28
vs. Right	.224	.287	.302	437	98	14	1	6	35	39	112
Bases Empty	.207	.264	.266	334	69	12	1	2	2	26	86
Leadoff	.208	.250	.236	144	30	4	0	0	0	8	34
Runners On Base	.230	.313	.327	217	50	6	0	5	47	28	54
Scoring Position	.239	.336	.282	117	28	2	0	1	36	19	35
Late and Close	.237	.324	.290	93	22	2	0	1	11	12	23

	BA	OBA	SA	AB	H	2B	3B	HR	RBI	BB	SO
	.222	.292	.297	1075	239	37	8	9	101	105	245
	.227	.294	.300	277	63	8	3	2	37	26	71
	.221	.291	.296	798	176	29	5	7	64	79	174
	.215	.274	.277	600	129	25	3	2	2	48	136
	.234	.283	.287	265	62	10	2	0	0	18	55
	.232	.313	.322	475	110	12	5	7	99	57	109
	.231	.325	.298	295	68	7	2	3	84	43	75
	.228	.308	.285	368	84	9	3	2	41	41	76

ALEX FERNANDEZ — BR/TR — age 25 — CHA SP34 FIN/FB

1993	G	IP	H	BB	SO	SB	CS	W	L	SV	ERA
Total	34	247.1	221	67	169	5	11	18	9	0	3.13
at Home	16	119.2	99	30	79	4	3	9	4	0	2.79
on Road	18	128.0	122	37	90	1	8	9	5	0	3.45
on Grass	26	184.0	167	49	127	5	8	14	8	0	3.38
on Turf	8	63.1	54	18	42	0	3	4	1	0	2.42
Day Games	12	83.2	75	26	62	0	5	5	5	0	3.98
Night Games	22	163.2	146	41	107	5	6	13	4	0	2.69
April	5	37.1	23	8	28	2	2	3	2	0	2.17
May	5	34.1	33	10	25	0	2	2	1	0	3.93
June	6	46.1	39	20	33	2	2	4	1	0	2.72
July	6	44.1	36	15	30	1	2	4	1	0	3.25
August	6	42.2	39	6	25	0	1	4	1	0	3.38
Sept-Oct	6	42.1	51	8	28	0	4	2	3	0	3.40

4-YEAR TOTALS (1990–1993)

	G	IP	H	BB	SO	SB	CS	W	L	SV	ERA
	110	714.1	695	239	470	36	30	40	38	0	3.88
	54	353.1	318	112	216	14	12	20	19	0	3.82
	56	361.0	377	127	254	22	18	20	19	0	3.94
	91	575.0	563	192	379	30	25	31	36	0	4.15
	19	139.1	132	47	91	6	5	9	2	0	2.78
	27	171.2	173	60	130	5	9	8	7	0	4.77
	83	542.2	522	179	340	31	21	32	26	0	3.60
	14	81.2	78	34	63	10	3	6	6	0	4.41
	15	101.0	91	41	68	4	3	3	6	0	3.92
	17	115.1	107	43	79	8	7	6	6	0	4.06
	15	94.0	86	27	56	3	3	6	1	0	3.64
	24	147.0	135	35	90	3	5	9	8	0	4.41
	25	175.1	176	59	114	8	9	10	11	0	3.18

	BA	OBA	SA	AB	H	2B	3B	HR	RBI	BB	SO
Total	.240	.295	.381	919	221	40	4	27	85	67	169
vs. Left	.261	.313	.430	437	114	27	1	15	41	34	81
vs. Right	.222	.280	.336	482	107	13	3	12	44	33	88
Bases Empty	.244	.305	.399	554	135	26	3	18	18	44	98
Leadoff	.255	.311	.430	235	60	16	2	7	7	18	35
Runners On Base	.236	.281	.353	365	86	14	1	9	67	23	71
Scoring Position	.215	.286	.294	177	38	8	0	2	49	19	38
Late and Close	.258	.303	.430	93	24	7	0	3	8	6	16

	BA	OBA	SA	AB	H	2B	3B	HR	RBI	BB	SO
	.256	.319	.387	2710	695	113	15	70	291	239	470
	.257	.317	.390	1294	333	69	5	31	134	112	219
	.256	.321	.383	1416	362	44	10	39	157	127	251
	.246	.310	.384	1595	392	66	10	46	46	135	271
	.251	.319	.380	681	171	33	5	15	15	63	101
	.272	.332	.387	1115	303	47	5	24	245	104	199
	.255	.334	.352	580	148	24	1	10	205	74	110
	.237	.283	.353	249	59	8	0	7	18	16	43

CHUCK FINLEY — BL/TL — age 32 — CAL SP35 POW/FB

1993	G	IP	H	BB	SO	SB	CS	W	L	SV	ERA
Total	35	251.1	243	82	187	21	9	16	14	0	3.15
at Home	16	122.2	106	32	104	8	4	8	5	0	2.79
on Road	19	128.2	137	50	83	13	5	8	9	0	3.50
on Grass	29	207.2	199	65	160	20	7	13	11	0	3.12
on Turf	6	43.2	44	17	27	1	2	3	3	0	3.30
Day Games	12	82.0	94	28	63	13	3	4	6	0	3.73
Night Games	23	169.1	149	54	124	8	6	12	8	0	2.87
April	5	36.1	28	18	29	3	2	2	1	0	3.47
May	6	39.2	45	13	30	3	2	3	3	0	2.72
June	5	37.2	33	6	27	3	1	4	1	0	1.91
July	7	46.2	52	13	37	5	2	3	3	0	4.63
August	5	37.0	31	12	31	2	2	2	2	0	2.43
Sept-Oct	7	54.0	54	20	33	5	2	2	4	0	3.33

8-YEAR TOTALS (1986–1993)

	G	IP	H	BB	SO	SB	CS	W	L	SV	ERA
	252	1450.0	1374	592	1026	112	88	89	76	0	3.40
	127	760.2	689	282	580	54	56	47	36	0	3.10
	125	689.1	685	310	446	58	32	42	40	0	3.73
	216	1232.2	1177	504	914	99	77	70	68	0	3.45
	36	217.1	197	88	112	13	11	19	8	0	3.15
	67	385.1	383	176	274	39	18	21	25	0	3.64
	185	1064.2	991	416	752	73	70	68	51	0	3.31
	31	184.1	143	76	125	16	10	15	10	0	2.78
	40	224.0	243	96	165	19	11	16	12	0	3.94
	44	253.2	251	91	191	19	19	16	15	0	3.51
	47	259.1	257	93	197	23	15	16	9	0	3.82
	43	245.2	221	102	163	19	16	14	14	0	3.11
	47	283.0	259	134	185	16	17	14	16	0	3.15

	BA	OBA	SA	AB	H	2B	3B	HR	RBI	BB	SO
Total	.253	.314	.364	959	243	38	1	22	93	82	187
vs. Left	.313	.381	.414	128	40	7	0	2	10	14	22
vs. Right	.244	.303	.356	831	203	31	1	20	83	68	165
Bases Empty	.258	.316	.373	555	143	23	1	13	13	45	116
Leadoff	.290	.342	.408	238	69	10	0	6	6	18	50
Runners On Base	.248	.312	.351	404	100	15	0	9	80	37	71
Scoring Position	.240	.313	.351	225	54	6	0	6	74	23	44
Late and Close	.245	.306	.275	102	25	3	0	0	5	9	20

	BA	OBA	SA	AB	H	2B	3B	HR	RBI	BB	SO
	.254	.329	.374	5408	1374	238	20	123	541	592	1026
	.276	.345	.357	892	246	43	1	9	77	91	141
	.250	.326	.377	4516	1128	195	19	114	464	501	885
	.257	.334	.384	3136	807	133	11	81	81	344	588
	.261	.328	.373	1371	358	55	6	29	29	126	238
	.250	.322	.359	2272	567	105	9	42	460	248	438
	.246	.330	.354	1223	301	57	6	21	402	166	249
	.256	.328	.360	645	165	29	1	12	53	69	125

DAVE FLEMING — BL/TL — age 25 — SEA SP26 FIN/FB · 3-YEAR TOTALS (1991–1993)

1993	G	IP	H	BB	SO	SB	CS	W	L	SV	ERA	G	IP	H	BB	SO	SB	CS	W	L	SV	ERA
Total	26	167.1	189	67	75	8	12	12	5	0	4.36	68	413.1	433	130	198	27	27	30	15	0	3.92
at Home	12	72.1	89	29	35	3	2	5	1	0	4.48	32	193.1	203	59	94	7	10	13	6	0	3.72
on Road	14	95.0	100	38	40	5	10	7	4	0	4.26	36	220.0	230	71	104	20	17	17	9	0	4.09
on Grass	9	61.2	66	26	28	3	3	4	3	0	4.52	26	153.2	165	49	78	12	8	12	6	0	4.28
on Turf	17	105.2	123	41	47	5	9	8	2	0	4.26	42	259.2	268	81	120	15	19	18	9	0	3.71
Day Games	8	51.1	58	23	26	4	4	4	0	0	3.33	19	107.0	134	40	55	13	7	6	5	0	4.71
Night Games	18	116.0	131	44	49	4	8	8	5	0	4.81	49	306.1	299	90	143	14	20	24	10	0	3.64
April	0	0.0	0	0	0	0	0	0	0	0	0.00	4	20.2	25	9	15	2	1	2	1	0	6.53
May	2	8.1	14	4	6	1	2	0	0	0	8.64	8	51.2	52	24	22	4	3	5	0	0	2.96
June	6	43.0	34	14	15	0	3	3	1	0	2.51	12	82.0	74	24	35	6	6	6	3	0	2.85
July	6	39.1	52	10	13	2	2	3	0	0	5.49	11	79.0	85	13	29	2	4	5	1	0	3.99
August	5	33.0	39	18	21	4	2	3	1	0	4.64	15	84.2	81	26	49	6	6	6	3	0	3.51
Sept-Oct	7	43.2	50	21	20	1	3	3	3	0	4.12	18	95.1	116	34	48	7	7	6	7	0	5.10

	BA	OBA	SA	AB	H	2B	3B	HR	RBI	BB	SO	BA	OBA	SA	AB	H	2B	3B	HR	RBI	BB	SO
Total	.290	.357	.419	652	189	35	2	15	75	67	75	.271	.329	.397	1596	433	94	7	31	169	130	198
vs. Left	.273	.308	.455	121	33	6	2	4	20	5	13	.262	.313	.413	271	71	17	3	6	34	17	37
vs. Right	.294	.368	.411	531	156	29	0	11	55	62	62	.273	.333	.394	1325	362	77	4	25	135	113	161
Bases Empty	.295	.349	.424	370	109	19	1	9	9	28	43	.274	.323	.400	930	255	55	4	18	18	61	111
Leadoff	.313	.371	.429	163	51	7	0	4	4	14	21	.283	.337	.405	400	113	23	1	8	8	30	49
Runners On Base	.284	.367	.411	282	80	16	1	6	66	39	32	.267	.338	.393	666	178	39	3	13	151	69	87
Scoring Position	.230	.342	.368	152	35	7	1	4	59	29	22	.239	.320	.353	380	91	19	3	6	128	45	51
Late and Close	.327	.377	.469	49	16	4	0	1	5	4	2	.283	.336	.433	127	36	8	1	3	10	10	12

JOHN FRANCO — BL/TL — age 34 — NYN RP35 POW/GB · 10-YEAR TOTALS (1984–1993)

1993	G	IP	H	BB	SO	SB	CS	W	L	SV	ERA	G	IP	H	BB	SO	SB	CS	W	L	SV	ERA
Total	35	36.1	46	19	29	4	0	4	3	10	5.20	566	720.1	658	279	517	38	35	62	47	236	2.62
at Home	15	16.1	14	7	11	1	0	1	0	6	3.31	296	384.2	344	130	256	19	19	35	19	126	2.50
on Road	20	20.0	32	12	18	3	0	3	3	4	6.75	270	335.2	314	149	261	19	16	27	28	110	2.76
on Grass	26	27.2	27	14	20	2	0	2	2	8	3.58	238	282.0	257	110	215	17	11	23	20	108	2.49
on Turf	9	8.2	19	5	9	2	0	2	1	2	10.38	328	438.1	401	169	302	21	24	39	27	128	2.71
Day Games	15	14.1	13	5	10	1	0	0	2	4	3.14	187	233.1	202	93	180	12	12	20	16	73	2.78
Night Games	20	22.0	33	14	19	3	0	4	1	6	6.55	379	487.0	456	186	337	26	23	42	31	163	2.55
April	2	2.0	2	0	1	0	0	0	0	0	4.50	65	82.1	44	28	51	1	3	3	3	33	1.42
May	6	6.1	5	3	4	0	0	2	0	1	0.00	88	120.2	107	55	91	6	6	12	7	36	2.09
June	8	7.2	7	7	2	0	0	0	0	0	2.35	110	133.2	132	54	84	7	6	14	10	35	2.49
July	7	9.0	10	3	9	1	0	1	0	5	5.00	93	125.1	100	41	93	4	9	12	4	45	2.44
August	4	4.0	6	2	5	0	0	0	0	2	4.50	107	139.2	136	48	98	9	5	11	6	44	2.13
Sept-Oct	8	7.1	16	4	8	3	0	1	3	1	13.50	103	118.2	139	53	100	11	6	10	17	43	4.93

	BA	OBA	SA	AB	H	2B	3B	HR	RBI	BB	SO	BA	OBA	SA	AB	H	2B	3B	HR	RBI	BB	SO
Total	.313	.393	.463	147	46	4	0	6	28	19	29	.246	.317	.329	2676	658	83	10	40	299	279	517
vs. Left	.317	.378	.488	41	13	1	0	2	9	4	10	.227	.289	.291	563	128	15	3	5	70	48	110
vs. Right	.311	.398	.453	106	33	3	0	4	19	15	19	.251	.324	.339	2113	530	68	7	35	229	231	407
Bases Empty	.296	.375	.437	71	21	1	0	3	3	9	18	.242	.303	.325	1399	338	40	5	22	22	121	268
Leadoff	.300	.364	.333	30	9	1	0	0	0	3	7	.247	.293	.339	607	150	19	2	11	11	38	92
Runners On Base	.329	.409	.487	76	25	3	0	3	25	10	11	.251	.331	.334	1277	320	43	5	18	277	158	249
Scoring Position	.311	.429	.422	45	14	2	0	1	21	9	4	.237	.346	.316	754	179	29	3	8	247	130	152
Late and Close	.322	.434	.460	87	28	3	0	3	18	17	16	.240	.312	.320	1973	474	57	8	28	227	206	380

STEVE FREY — BR/TL — age 31 — CAL RP55 FIN/FB · 5-YEAR TOTALS (1989–1993)

1993	G	IP	H	BB	SO	SB	CS	W	L	SV	ERA	G	IP	H	BB	SO	SB	CS	W	L	SV	ERA
Total	55	48.1	41	26	22	3	1	2	3	13	2.98	208	210.1	196	111	111	17	8	17	10	27	3.51
at Home	32	31.0	26	16	15	2	1	2	2	7	2.61	108	106.2	96	49	57	11	4	9	4	16	2.70
on Road	23	17.1	15	10	7	1	0	0	1	6	3.63	100	103.2	100	62	54	6	4	8	6	11	4.34
on Grass	47	42.0	38	22	19	3	1	2	3	9	3.00	116	109.0	104	60	49	7	4	8	8	15	4.13
on Turf	8	6.1	3	4	3	0	0	0	0	4	2.84	92	101.1	92	51	62	10	4	11	2	12	2.84
Day Games	10	11.0	7	7	7	1	0	0	1	2	1.64	65	67.2	66	34	43	8	2	5	3	9	3.59
Night Games	45	37.1	34	19	15	2	1	2	2	11	3.38	143	142.2	130	77	68	9	6	12	7	18	3.47
April	5	3.2	4	2	2	1	0	0	0	1	4.91	32	35.2	26	17	19	5	2	2	1	5	3.28
May	15	11.1	8	7	5	0	0	0	0	1	1.59	50	48.2	41	27	29	6	2	2	1	3	2.77
June	9	8.0	9	4	3	1	0	0	1	5	1.13	28	28.2	29	14	15	1	0	4	1	7	2.51
July	10	9.2	8	7	2	1	0	1	1	1	0.93	37	33.0	35	22	14	3	0	5	2	1	3.00
August	10	9.0	10	5	5	0	1	0	2	1	8.00	31	30.1	42	17	15	0	4	2	5	4	7.42
Sept-Oct	6	6.2	2	1	1	0	0	0	0	2	2.70	30	34.0	23	14	19	2	0	2	0	7	2.65

	BA	OBA	SA	AB	H	2B	3B	HR	RBI	BB	SO	BA	OBA	SA	AB	H	2B	3B	HR	RBI	BB	SO
Total	.230	.337	.303	178	41	8	1	1	26	26	22	.250	.345	.364	784	196	31	2	18	98	111	111
vs. Left	.231	.406	.346	52	12	4	1	0	6	13	8	.245	.355	.394	249	61	11	1	8	39	39	50
vs. Right	.230	.302	.286	126	29	4	0	1	20	13	14	.252	.340	.350	535	135	20	1	10	59	72	61
Bases Empty	.278	.366	.417	72	20	5	1	1	9	9	11	.244	.348	.396	369	90	16	2	12	12	54	58
Leadoff	.235	.333	.324	34	8	0	0	0	0	5	6	.251	.346	.389	167	42	6	1	5	5	21	24
Runners On Base	.198	.317	.226	106	21	3	0	0	25	17	11	.255	.342	.335	415	106	15	0	6	86	57	53
Scoring Position	.230	.341	.243	74	17	0	0	0	23	12	8	.230	.335	.276	257	59	6	0	2	74	44	34
Late and Close	.214	.344	.282	103	22	4	0	1	18	20	12	.229	.341	.319	376	86	13	0	7	38	65	50

TOM GLAVINE — BL/TL — age 28 — ATL SP36 FIN/FB

1993	G	IP	H	BB	SO	SB	CS	W	L	SV	ERA
Total	36	239.1	236	90	120	9	5	22	6	0	3.20
at Home	20	135.2	136	51	63	7	3	13	3	0	3.18
on Road	16	103.2	100	39	57	2	2	9	3	0	3.21
on Grass	27	175.1	193	67	93	8	5	15	5	0	3.70
on Turf	9	64.0	43	23	27	1	0	7	1	0	1.83
Day Games	8	51.0	56	20	28	3	1	5	1	0	4.06
Night Games	28	188.1	180	70	92	6	4	17	5	0	2.96
April	5	32.0	24	22	7	2	0	3	0	0	2.81
May	6	41.1	35	14	24	2	1	4	1	0	3.27
June	5	38.0	42	13	15	1	3	2	2	0	2.61
July	7	45.1	40	17	20	1	1	4	1	0	2.58
August	6	35.1	40	16	23	0	0	3	1	0	5.09
Sept-Oct	7	47.1	55	8	31	3	0	6	1	0	3.04

7-YEAR TOTALS (1987–1993)

G	IP	H	BB	SO	SB	CS	W	L	SV	ERA
208	1357.0	1294	443	764	92	59	95	66	0	3.53
105	690.2	674	207	364	35	33	51	32	0	3.57
103	666.1	620	236	400	57	26	44	34	0	3.48
147	955.2	956	286	533	43	42	68	45	0	3.64
61	401.1	338	157	231	49	17	27	21	0	3.27
57	348.2	370	134	221	17	13	24	20	0	4.44
151	1008.1	924	309	543	75	46	71	46	0	3.21
27	184.1	160	53	99	9	5	12	8	0	2.93
35	223.0	195	77	133	24	7	19	8	0	3.43
34	231.2	236	66	133	6	11	15	12	0	3.61
32	217.2	200	63	133	14	12	15	7	0	3.02
40	239.0	258	90	130	18	14	15	18	0	4.48
40	261.1	245	94	146	21	10	19	13	0	3.51

	BA	OBA	SA	AB	H	2B	3B	HR	RBI	BB	SO
Total	.259	.327	.376	910	236	50	4	16	77	90	120
vs. Left	.271	.349	.349	166	45	10	0	1	14	20	29
vs. Right	.257	.322	.382	744	191	40	4	15	63	70	91
Bases Empty	.273	.330	.398	523	143	26	3	11	11	43	70
Leadoff	.281	.328	.446	231	65	12	1	8	8	16	29
Runners On Base	.240	.323	.346	387	93	24	1	5	66	47	50
Scoring Position	.225	.329	.335	200	45	14	1	2	57	32	29
Late and Close	.209	.273	.297	91	19	2	0	2	5	8	13

BA	OBA	SA	AB	H	2B	3B	HR	RBI	BB	SO
.252	.312	.363	5132	1294	235	26	94	506	443	764
.255	.334	.342	925	236	37	5	11	83	107	174
.251	.307	.368	4207	1058	198	21	83	423	336	590
.245	.293	.361	3106	761	134	13	67	67	200	470
.254	.299	.371	1319	335	65	6	26	26	76	182
.263	.340	.366	2026	533	101	13	27	439	243	294
.260	.363	.363	1104	287	56	8	14	392	190	177
.253	.301	.362	483	122	25	2	8	41	34	64

DWIGHT GOODEN — BR/TR — age 30 — NYN SP29 FIN/GB

1993	G	IP	H	BB	SO	SB	CS	W	L	SV	ERA
Total	29	208.2	188	61	149	28	10	12	15	0	3.45
at Home	19	139.0	117	38	94	19	8	8	10	0	2.78
on Road	10	69.2	71	23	55	9	2	4	5	0	4.78
on Grass	25	185.0	161	55	131	26	8	11	13	0	3.11
on Turf	4	23.2	27	6	18	2	2	1	2	0	6.08
Day Games	11	85.0	65	35	52	10	6	6	5	0	2.54
Night Games	18	123.2	123	26	97	18	4	6	10	0	4.08
April	5	37.0	25	14	14	7	1	2	3	0	2.68
May	6	49.2	44	15	29	8	3	3	1	0	2.72
June	5	35.0	35	12	27	3	1	2	3	0	3.86
July	6	46.0	46	11	41	6	0	3	3	0	3.72
August	7	41.0	38	9	38	4	5	2	5	0	4.39
Sept-Oct	0	0.0	0	0	0	0	0	0	0	0	0.00

10-YEAR TOTALS (1984–1993)

G	IP	H	BB	SO	SB	CS	W	L	SV	ERA
298	2128.1	1852	636	1835	355	100	154	81	1	3.04
155	1132.0	919	335	989	169	63	89	38	0	2.74
143	996.1	933	301	846	186	37	65	43	1	3.37
220	1601.0	1359	478	1386	236	78	125	53	1	2.85
78	527.1	493	158	449	119	22	29	28	0	3.60
103	696.2	655	226	560	126	35	48	33	1	3.57
195	1431.2	1197	410	1275	229	65	106	48	0	2.78
43	305.0	219	95	254	54	12	25	9	0	2.45
52	371.2	349	114	331	64	16	23	19	0	3.37
57	415.0	364	142	325	77	17	28	16	0	3.34
46	328.2	290	96	270	47	15	27	11	0	2.85
53	354.0	345	101	319	52	21	26	14	0	3.64
47	354.0	285	88	336	61	19	25	12	1	2.42

	BA	OBA	SA	AB	H	2B	3B	HR	RBI	BB	SO
Total	.242	.302	.357	778	188	34	4	16	81	61	149
vs. Left	.247	.307	.366	396	98	18	1	9	37	34	70
vs. Right	.236	.296	.348	382	90	16	3	7	44	27	79
Bases Empty	.237	.293	.365	468	111	20	2	12	12	33	93
Leadoff	.253	.313	.371	194	49	12	1	3	3	16	37
Runners On Base	.248	.314	.345	310	77	14	2	4	69	28	56
Scoring Position	.217	.291	.315	203	44	9	1	3	64	19	41
Late and Close	.200	.292	.318	85	17	4	0	2	5	10	16

BA	OBA	SA	AB	H	2B	3B	HR	RBI	BB	SO
.234	.293	.328	7912	1852	308	48	114	710	636	1835
.234	.298	.320	4387	1026	171	23	54	359	398	919
.234	.286	.338	3525	826	137	25	60	351	238	916
.234	.295	.332	4669	1092	192	30	69	69	383	1065
.243	.304	.354	1994	485	88	14	35	35	164	428
.234	.289	.323	3243	760	116	18	45	641	253	770
.223	.291	.305	1961	438	65	10	25	573	193	515
.224	.282	.297	929	208	21	1	15	69	75	230

TOM GORDON — BR/TR — age 27 — KC RP34, SP14 POW/GB

1993	G	IP	H	BB	SO	SB	CS	W	L	SV	ERA
Total	48	155.2	125	77	143	15	9	12	6	1	3.58
at Home	23	72.0	45	31	64	1	5	6	1	1	2.38
on Road	25	83.2	80	46	79	14	4	6	5	0	4.63
on Grass	22	75.1	69	35	71	12	4	5	5	0	4.42
on Turf	26	80.1	56	42	72	3	5	7	1	1	2.80
Day Games	15	58.2	52	30	51	6	3	7	2	0	3.99
Night Games	33	97.0	73	47	92	9	6	5	4	1	3.34
April	8	15.1	11	18	15	2	3	1	0	0	5.87
May	11	17.2	15	7	20	5	1	2	1	1	4.58
June	10	17.2	13	6	16	0	0	1	1	0	2.55
July	7	23.1	16	13	22	1	1	2	0	0	2.70
August	6	38.2	34	16	36	3	4	2	4	0	4.19
Sept-Oct	6	43.0	36	17	34	4	0	4	0	0	2.72

6-YEAR TOTALS (1988–1993)

G	IP	H	BB	SO	SB	CS	W	L	SV	ERA
219	805.1	700	411	754	49	39	56	52	3	3.87
113	421.1	342	197	383	18	21	31	24	2	3.35
106	384.0	358	214	371	31	18	25	28	1	4.43
81	284.0	283	152	276	25	17	15	23	1	4.82
138	521.1	417	259	478	24	22	41	29	2	3.35
63	250.2	226	116	230	12	18	20	18	0	3.52
156	554.2	474	295	524	37	21	36	34	3	4.02
31	104.2	87	51	112	7	5	7	7	0	3.01
38	127.1	103	67	110	7	2	9	7	1	4.31
37	106.0	97	56	107	5	1	9	7	0	4.08
34	133.2	123	80	124	8	7	9	10	0	4.04
31	167.0	132	64	159	5	11	15	9	1	2.86
48	166.2	158	93	142	17	6	9	12	0	4.81

	BA	OBA	SA	AB	H	2B	3B	HR	RBI	BB	SO
Total	.223	.315	.340	561	125	27	3	11	64	77	143
vs. Left	.229	.320	.341	293	67	11	2	6	30	41	71
vs. Right	.216	.309	.340	268	58	16	1	5	34	36	72
Bases Empty	.223	.314	.327	318	71	16	1	5	5	41	80
Leadoff	.230	.311	.356	135	31	6	1	5	5	16	28
Runners On Base	.222	.316	.358	243	54	11	2	6	59	36	63
Scoring Position	.221	.326	.342	149	33	7	1	3	51	26	45
Late and Close	.273	.354	.466	88	24	6	1	3	18	11	26

BA	OBA	SA	AB	H	2B	3B	HR	RBI	BB	SO
.235	.328	.355	2982	700	118	24	64	352	411	754
.244	.336	.342	1499	366	53	12	23	160	211	345
.225	.320	.368	1483	334	65	12	41	192	200	409
.235	.326	.362	1651	388	69	13	38	38	217	414
.225	.313	.349	710	160	31	6	15	15	89	174
.234	.331	.346	1331	312	49	11	26	314	194	340
.247	.343	.374	788	195	34	9	16	282	120	230
.242	.337	.359	499	121	22	3	10	60	67	155

JIM GOTT — BR/TR — age 35 — LA RP62 POW/FB

1993 | 10-YEAR TOTALS (1984–1993)

1993	G	IP	H	BB	SO	SB	CS	W	L	SV	ERA	G	IP	H	BB	SO	SB	CS	W	L	SV	ERA
Total	62	77.2	71	17	67	4	2	4	8	25	2.32	428	739.2	668	300	586	45	29	35	43	86	3.36
at Home	31	42.1	44	10	39	3	1	2	4	12	3.19	211	390.0	315	150	333	24	18	19	18	43	2.82
on Road	31	35.1	27	7	28	1	1	2	4	13	1.27	217	349.2	353	150	253	21	11	16	25	43	3.96
on Grass	50	63.0	62	17	51	3	2	3	7	19	2.71	256	443.2	396	200	346	23	18	18	25	37	3.14
on Turf	12	14.2	9	0	16	1	0	1	1	6	0.61	172	296.0	272	100	240	22	11	17	18	49	3.68
Day Games	14	18.0	9	5	17	0	0	3	1	6	0.50	134	301.2	273	127	221	15	10	15	13	23	3.37
Night Games	48	59.2	62	12	50	4	2	1	7	19	2.87	294	438.0	395	173	365	30	19	20	30	63	3.35
April	8	12.1	8	7	9	0	1	0	0	2	0.00	54	92.1	87	48	69	3	2	3	3	8	4.00
May	11	14.2	14	2	14	0	0	2	1	4	3.07	61	132.0	111	45	99	9	5	6	4	8	2.86
June	15	16.0	16	3	13	1	0	0	4	7	3.94	75	130.2	129	63	105	9	6	7	13	10	3.99
July	12	16.1	13	1	15	1	0	2	0	5	1.65	75	138.1	122	52	111	6	8	5	8	16	3.12
August	10	13.1	14	3	11	2	1	0	2	6	2.03	89	141.2	110	56	107	14	4	9	9	25	2.73
Sept-Oct	6	5.0	6	1	5	0	0	0	1	1	3.60	74	104.2	109	36	95	4	5	5	6	19	3.78

	BA	OBA	SA	AB	H	2B	3B	HR	RBI	BB	SO	BA	OBA	SA	AB	H	2B	3B	HR	RBI	BB	SO
Total	.248	.291	.339	286	71	8	0	6	30	17	67	.242	.317	.347	2755	668	105	17	50	299	300	586
vs. Left	.222	.264	.346	153	34	4	0	5	18	9	41	.244	.332	.358	1374	335	54	11	27	148	181	293
vs. Right	.278	.322	.331	133	37	4	0	1	12	8	26	.241	.302	.337	1381	333	51	6	23	151	119	293
Bases Empty	.236	.259	.317	161	38	7	0	2	2	5	37	.234	.303	.336	1529	358	62	8	26	26	143	328
Leadoff	.242	.265	.348	66	16	4	0	1	1	2	11	.256	.326	.377	652	167	33	2	14	14	64	125
Runners On Base	.264	.329	.368	125	33	1	0	4	28	12	30	.253	.334	.361	1226	310	43	9	24	273	157	258
Scoring Position	.260	.341	.384	73	19	0	0	3	26	10	15	.231	.335	.335	749	173	23	8	13	240	127	168
Late and Close	.272	.315	.384	224	61	7	0	6	30	15	53	.248	.328	.351	961	238	30	3	21	125	114	224

JOE GRAHE — BR/TR — age 27 — CAL RP45 FIN/GB

1993 | 4-YEAR TOTALS (1990–1993)

1993	G	IP	H	BB	SO	SB	CS	W	L	SV	ERA	G	IP	H	BB	SO	SB	CS	W	L	SV	ERA
Total	45	56.2	54	25	31	4	0	4	1	11	2.86	117	267.2	274	120	135	23	11	15	18	32	3.97
at Home	21	28.0	27	9	17	1	0	3	1	7	3.54	58	136.0	138	55	67	12	5	7	10	21	4.24
on Road	24	28.2	27	16	14	3	0	1	0	4	2.20	59	131.2	136	65	68	11	6	8	8	11	3.69
on Grass	39	51.1	47	19	29	2	0	4	1	10	2.45	102	248.0	250	104	127	20	11	14	17	31	3.74
on Turf	6	5.1	7	6	2	2	0	0	0	1	6.75	15	19.2	24	16	8	3	0	1	1	1	6.86
Day Games	16	20.1	13	11	15	0	0	2	0	5	1.77	39	81.1	81	32	42	6	3	6	4	13	3.43
Night Games	29	36.1	41	14	16	4	0	2	1	6	3.47	78	186.1	193	88	93	17	8	9	14	19	4.20
April	5	9.2	12	3	7	0	0	1	1	2	2.79	10	38.2	46	18	19	3	2	3	3	2	6.05
May	11	11.2	7	7	6	2	0	1	0	4	4.63	13	22.1	18	14	11	2	1	1	1	4	3.63
June	2	1.1	3	0	0	0	0	0	0	0	0.00	15	28.0	28	9	22	1	0	1	1	1	3.86
July	6	7.2	9	3	4	1	0	1	0	0	3.52	18	26.1	25	10	10	1	1	2	0	8	2.39
August	11	14.1	12	6	7	1	0	0	0	0	2.51	31	76.1	83	34	34	11	5	3	8	6	4.01
Sept-Oct	10	12.0	11	6	7	0	0	0	0	5	1.50	30	76.0	74	35	39	5	2	5	5	9	3.55

	BA	OBA	SA	AB	H	2B	3B	HR	RBI	BB	SO	BA	OBA	SA	AB	H	2B	3B	HR	RBI	BB	SO
Total	.251	.331	.367	215	54	8	1	5	33	25	31	.267	.349	.373	1027	274	52	6	15	137	120	135
vs. Left	.329	.404	.443	79	26	6	0	1	5	10	9	.313	.383	.430	460	144	30	3	6	55	48	55
vs. Right	.206	.288	.324	136	28	2	1	4	28	15	22	.229	.323	.326	567	130	22	3	9	82	72	80
Bases Empty	.221	.302	.288	104	23	4	0	1	1	11	14	.246	.317	.335	544	134	24	0	8	8	52	75
Leadoff	.186	.239	.209	43	8	1	0	0	0	2	6	.245	.319	.308	237	58	12	0	1	1	22	29
Runners On Base	.279	.357	.441	111	31	4	1	4	32	14	17	.290	.383	.416	483	140	28	6	7	129	68	60
Scoring Position	.266	.367	.375	64	17	2	1	2	25	11	8	.274	.389	.411	285	78	19	4	4	114	53	39
Late and Close	.228	.318	.348	92	21	5	0	2	13	12	18	.208	.299	.297	279	58	10	0	5	27	35	39

TOMMY GREENE — BR/TR — age 27 — PHI SP30, RP1 POW/FB

1993 | 5-YEAR TOTALS (1989–1993)

1993	G	IP	H	BB	SO	SB	CS	W	L	SV	ERA	G	IP	H	BB	SO	SB	CS	W	L	SV	ERA
Total	31	200.0	175	62	167	18	5	16	4	0	3.42	99	549.2	499	194	398	52	21	36	19	0	3.82
at Home	17	114.1	87	37	99	7	3	10	0	0	2.99	51	295.2	248	103	230	25	10	21	6	0	3.26
on Road	14	85.2	88	25	68	11	2	6	4	0	3.99	48	254.0	251	91	168	27	11	15	13	0	4.46
on Grass	8	53.2	51	12	40	5	1	4	1	0	2.52	27	135.0	130	48	86	15	5	8	4	0	4.13
on Turf	23	146.1	124	50	127	13	4	12	3	0	3.75	72	414.2	369	146	312	37	16	28	15	0	3.71
Day Games	6	36.1	28	12	28	2	1	4	0	0	2.97	24	134.2	101	58	103	10	5	12	5	0	3.74
Night Games	25	163.2	147	50	139	16	4	12	4	0	3.52	75	415.0	398	136	295	42	16	24	14	0	3.84
April	5	29.1	19	8	28	2	0	2	0	0	2.45	18	79.1	70	36	54	10	1	4	1	0	4.65
May	5	43.1	28	8	35	1	1	5	0	0	1.45	12	79.2	44	23	68	5	3	9	0	0	1.36
June	6	29.2	41	13	26	6	1	2	1	0	6.98	15	81.0	91	28	63	10	2	4	3	0	5.00
July	5	30.2	28	10	22	1	1	3	1	0	3.52	11	66.2	60	25	46	6	3	5	2	0	3.78
August	4	22.0	30	7	18	4	1	0	0	0	5.32	13	71.2	82	26	52	6	4	2	4	0	4.90
Sept-Oct	6	45.0	30	16	38	4	2	4	1	0	2.60	30	171.1	152	56	115	15	8	12	7	0	3.57

	BA	OBA	SA	AB	H	2B	3B	HR	RBI	BB	SO	BA	OBA	SA	AB	H	2B	3B	HR	RBI	BB	SO
Total	.233	.291	.340	751	175	36	4	12	70	62	167	.242	.306	.372	2066	499	99	12	49	222	194	398
vs. Left	.235	.314	.327	358	84	16	1	5	34	42	75	.269	.346	.409	1092	294	56	4	27	125	132	189
vs. Right	.232	.269	.351	393	91	20	3	7	36	20	92	.210	.258	.331	974	205	43	4	22	97	62	209
Bases Empty	.229	.282	.344	459	105	20	3	9	9	32	103	.233	.297	.363	1255	293	53	5	33	33	109	259
Leadoff	.247	.291	.392	194	48	11	1	5	5	12	40	.235	.299	.358	519	122	24	2	12	12	46	103
Runners On Base	.240	.304	.332	292	70	16	1	3	61	30	64	.254	.318	.387	811	206	46	7	16	189	85	139
Scoring Position	.244	.327	.345	164	40	12	1	1	56	24	38	.261	.332	.394	452	118	29	5	7	160	59	87
Late and Close	.234	.280	.426	47	11	4	0	2	1	9	5	.225	.285	.350	120	27	9	0	2	15	10	23

KEVIN GROSS — BR/TR — age 33 — LA SP32, RP1 POW/GB

10-YEAR TOTALS (1984–1993)

1993	G	IP	H	BB	SO	SB	CS	W	L	SV	ERA		G	IP	H	BB	SO	SB	CS	W	L	SV	ERA
Total	33	202.1	224	74	150	18	10	13	13	0	4.14		361	1896.0	1875	749	1333	262	96	107	121	4	3.94
at Home	17	109.1	98	35	75	8	8	8	5	0	3.29		180	981.2	908	360	715	126	53	60	58	1	3.63
on Road	16	93.0	126	39	75	10	2	5	8	0	5.13		181	914.1	967	389	618	136	43	47	63	3	4.26
on Grass	27	169.2	181	61	122	16	10	12	8	0	3.77		152	758.2	803	295	544	102	39	43	52	3	4.24
on Turf	6	32.2	43	13	28	2	0	1	5	0	6.06		209	1137.1	1072	454	789	160	57	64	69	1	3.74
Day Games	8	51.1	54	19	38	3	5	3	1	0	4.03		116	602.2	574	227	429	73	35	35	34	1	3.70
Night Games	25	151.0	170	55	112	15	5	10	12	0	4.17		245	1293.1	1301	522	904	189	61	72	87	3	4.04
April	6	27.0	32	15	20	2	3	2	2	0	6.67		51	242.0	244	100	178	38	14	12	20	0	3.83
May	5	32.2	37	11	27	5	1	2	2	0	3.86		62	331.1	317	111	244	43	18	25	15	0	3.48
June	5	35.1	28	8	31	4	1	2	2	0	1.78		58	346.1	341	120	238	53	16	21	20	2	3.98
July	5	30.2	43	13	21	4	2	1	3	0	5.28		58	311.2	307	143	189	38	15	14	23	1	4.04
August	6	33.2	45	16	21	0	3	2	3	0	5.35		67	325.1	340	138	233	43	18	18	22	0	4.40
Sept-Oct	6	43.0	39	11	30	3	0	4	1	0	2.93		65	339.1	326	137	251	47	15	17	21	1	3.87

	BA	OBA	SA	AB	H	2B	3B	HR	RBI	BB	SO		BA	OBA	SA	AB	H	2B	3B	HR	RBI	BB	SO
Total	.282	.344	.379	795	224	26	3	15	95	74	150		.259	.332	.380	7228	1875	285	61	156	797	749	1333
vs. Left	.277	.363	.360	394	109	10	1	7	45	54	74		.270	.357	.399	3945	1064	176	42	83	452	519	696
vs. Right	.287	.325	.397	401	115	16	2	8	50	20	76		.247	.301	.359	3283	811	109	19	73	345	230	637
Bases Empty	.282	.349	.408	426	120	14	2	12	12	40	80		.258	.328	.393	4121	1062	156	28	115	115	391	778
Leadoff	.287	.368	.399	188	54	7	1	4	4	22	34		.268	.338	.417	1791	480	77	15	53	53	171	322
Runners On Base	.282	.339	.344	369	104	12	1	3	83	34	70		.262	.337	.364	3107	813	129	33	41	682	358	555
Scoring Position	.278	.350	.346	205	57	6	1	2	80	26	45		.259	.346	.367	1847	478	74	22	27	625	260	375
Late and Close	.282	.396	.359	39	11	3	0	0	4	8	5		.286	.356	.395	709	203	30	4	13	77	72	132

BILL GULLICKSON — BR/TR — age 35 — DET SP28 FIN/FB

8-YEAR TOTALS (1984–1993)

1993	G	IP	H	BB	SO	SB	CS	W	L	SV	ERA		G	IP	H	BB	SO	SB	CS	W	L	SV	ERA
Total	28	159.1	186	44	70	13	5	13	9	0	5.37		262	1666.1	1771	393	704	159	65	112	91	0	4.06
at Home	17	95.0	112	25	38	7	4	7	7	0	5.02		139	904.0	945	199	394	80	32	66	44	0	4.00
on Road	11	64.1	74	19	32	6	1	6	2	0	5.88		123	762.1	826	194	310	79	33	46	47	0	4.12
on Grass	24	133.0	162	36	57	12	5	10	9	0	5.68		129	801.1	885	192	319	72	33	50	49	0	4.53
on Turf	4	26.1	24	8	13	1	0	3	0	0	3.76		133	865.0	886	201	385	87	32	62	42	0	3.62
Day Games	10	55.0	64	16	24	2	1	5	3	0	5.24		92	570.0	628	141	230	50	25	40	30	0	4.29
Night Games	18	104.1	122	28	46	11	4	8	6	0	5.43		170	1096.1	1143	252	474	109	40	72	61	0	3.93
April	0	0.0	0	0	0	0	0	0	0	0	0.00		29	168.2	177	44	69	16	10	12	10	0	4.11
May	4	19.1	23	7	9	3	1	2	1	0	6.05		46	287.1	308	65	125	35	15	22	15	0	3.95
June	6	38.2	49	10	14	2	1	2	3	0	5.12		41	272.0	290	64	113	26	9	16	14	0	3.74
July	5	25.2	32	12	12	0	1	2	2	0	6.66		44	284.0	308	76	111	18	8	19	15	0	4.34
August	7	50.1	40	10	22	3	2	6	0	0	2.68		50	343.2	316	65	151	29	13	27	14	0	2.99
Sept-Oct	6	25.1	42	5	13	5	0	1	3	0	9.24		52	310.2	372	79	135	35	10	16	23	0	5.33

	BA	OBA	SA	AB	H	2B	3B	HR	RBI	BB	SO		BA	OBA	SA	AB	H	2B	3B	HR	RBI	BB	SO
Total	.291	.336	.496	639	186	37	5	28	91	44	70		.274	.314	.434	6465	1771	326	48	205	753	393	704
vs. Left	.329	.373	.554	316	104	24	4	13	52	23	25		.284	.330	.448	3418	970	182	29	107	388	242	287
vs. Right	.254	.300	.440	323	82	13	1	15	39	21	45		.263	.296	.419	3047	801	144	19	98	365	151	417
Bases Empty	.299	.342	.527	374	112	19	3	20	20	23	38		.272	.311	.438	3966	1080	197	26	136	136	212	457
Leadoff	.283	.325	.459	159	45	11	1	5	5	10	17		.275	.314	.423	1651	454	81	11	47	47	90	179
Runners On Base	.279	.329	.453	265	74	18	2	8	71	21	32		.277	.319	.429	2499	691	129	22	69	617	181	247
Scoring Position	.271	.331	.414	140	38	9	1	3	53	14	16		.267	.323	.409	1398	373	74	10	35	508	141	145
Late and Close	.333	.389	.576	33	11	2	0	2	4	3	4		.274	.325	.391	522	143	21	2	12	45	40	50

JOSE GUZMAN — BR/TR — age 31 — CHN SP30 POW/GB

7-YEAR TOTALS (1985–1993)

1993	G	IP	H	BB	SO	SB	CS	W	L	SV	ERA		G	IP	H	BB	SO	SB	CS	W	L	SV	ERA
Total	30	191.0	188	74	163	19	10	12	10	0	4.34		189	1204.2	1171	469	878	123	52	78	72	0	3.97
at Home	18	114.2	112	40	99	8	5	8	5	0	4.32		99	627.1	615	222	451	60	26	43	38	0	3.97
on Road	12	76.1	76	34	64	11	5	4	5	0	4.36		90	577.1	556	247	427	63	26	35	34	0	3.96
on Grass	23	148.2	146	48	131	12	6	10	6	0	4.30		158	1013.2	982	378	728	96	41	68	59	0	3.86
on Turf	7	42.1	42	26	32	7	4	2	4	0	4.46		31	191.0	189	91	150	27	11	10	13	0	4.52
Day Games	13	86.1	70	31	74	5	4	7	4	0	2.71		39	251.2	231	106	205	22	10	15	13	0	3.29
Night Games	17	104.2	118	43	89	14	6	5	6	0	5.68		150	953.0	940	363	673	101	42	63	59	0	4.15
April	5	32.0	24	16	19	4	3	3	2	0	2.81		23	143.0	123	42	88	14	7	10	10	0	3.27
May	6	32.0	37	11	29	3	1	1	2	0	5.63		31	189.2	209	83	141	20	11	9	11	0	4.46
June	6	38.2	41	15	32	5	2	3	2	0	4.66		35	235.0	226	84	172	23	10	18	13	0	4.17
July	5	32.2	26	12	30	2	2	2	1	0	3.31		32	204.0	203	85	146	25	7	11	13	0	3.75
August	6	42.1	43	16	39	5	1	2	2	0	4.25		35	204.0	209	81	159	21	8	14	10	0	4.15
Sept-Oct	2	13.1	17	4	14	0	1	1	1	0	6.75		33	229.0	201	94	172	20	9	16	15	0	3.81

	BA	OBA	SA	AB	H	2B	3B	HR	RBI	BB	SO		BA	OBA	SA	AB	H	2B	3B	HR	RBI	BB	SO
Total	.258	.327	.428	729	188	39	5	25	83	74	163		.255	.326	.397	4584	1171	238	14	128	480	469	878
vs. Left	.273	.345	.475	396	108	24	4	16	49	44	76		.258	.326	.401	2306	595	130	7	62	255	233	388
vs. Right	.240	.305	.372	333	80	15	1	9	34	30	87		.253	.325	.393	2278	576	108	7	66	225	236	490
Bases Empty	.241	.301	.410	456	110	25	2	16	16	37	99		.254	.321	.400	2739	695	149	6	80	80	261	545
Leadoff	.220	.283	.379	182	40	9	1	6	6	15	35		.245	.308	.390	1161	285	69	3	31	31	100	214
Runners On Base	.286	.367	.458	273	78	14	3	9	67	37	64		.258	.332	.393	1845	476	89	8	48	400	208	333
Scoring Position	.274	.358	.451	164	45	8	3	5	56	24	42		.233	.321	.347	1050	245	42	7	21	329	145	209
Late and Close	.225	.333	.275	40	9	2	0	0	3	6	7		.251	.320	.350	394	99	17	2	6	27	39	66

JUAN GUZMAN — BR/TR — age 28 — TOR SP33 POW/FB

3-YEAR TOTALS (1991–1993)

1993	G	IP	H	BB	SO	SB	CS	W	L	SV	ERA	G	IP	H	BB	SO	SB	CS	W	L	SV	ERA
Total	33	221.0	211	110	194	25	17	14	3	0	3.99	84	540.1	444	248	482	63	31	40	11	0	3.28
at Home	15	99.2	102	43	89	11	9	7	1	0	3.43	39	247.1	216	107	226	32	17	19	4	0	3.35
on Road	18	121.1	109	67	105	14	8	7	2	0	4.45	45	293.0	228	141	256	31	14	21	7	0	3.23
on Grass	14	91.1	83	52	80	11	8	5	2	0	4.83	33	213.1	165	107	190	23	13	15	5	0	3.33
on Turf	19	129.2	128	58	114	14	9	9	1	0	3.40	51	327.0	279	141	292	40	18	25	6	0	3.25
Day Games	13	85.1	88	44	74	11	4	7	0	0	4.11	33	203.2	177	102	182	25	14	15	4	0	3.36
Night Games	20	135.2	123	66	120	14	13	7	3	0	3.91	51	336.2	267	146	300	38	17	25	7	0	3.23
April	5	31.1	34	17	28	4	2	3	0	0	4.60	10	66.0	57	34	67	8	4	6	0	0	3.14
May	6	34.2	37	19	27	4	5	1	0	0	5.71	11	71.2	60	31	53	11	5	4	0	0	3.77
June	5	35.2	29	16	35	4	3	3	1	0	3.79	14	93.0	69	36	84	7	7	9	4	0	3.19
July	6	39.0	45	23	34	10	3	0	2	0	3.46	16	100.0	87	49	95	25	5	3	3	0	2.70
August	5	35.0	30	16	38	0	1	3	0	0	3.60	13	78.0	65	41	80	4	1	5	1	0	4.04
Sept-Oct	6	45.1	36	19	32	3	3	4	0	0	3.18	20	131.2	106	57	103	8	9	13	3	0	3.14

	BA	OBA	SA	AB	H	2B	3B	HR	RBI	BB	SO	BA	OBA	SA	AB	H	2B	3B	HR	RBI	BB	SO
Total	.252	.338	.358	836	211	35	1	17	85	110	194	.224	.310	.308	1985	444	72	4	29	178	248	482
vs. Left	.282	.372	.379	419	118	18	1	7	40	63	71	.238	.327	.301	980	233	31	2	9	71	133	178
vs. Right	.223	.304	.336	417	93	17	0	10	45	47	123	.210	.293	.314	1005	211	41	2	20	107	115	304
Bases Empty	.255	.337	.340	467	119	19	0	7	7	57	108	.222	.311	.292	1135	252	40	0	13	13	141	280
Leadoff	.230	.330	.295	200	46	7	0	2	2	29	42	.220	.312	.287	492	108	15	0	6	6	63	107
Runners On Base	.249	.339	.379	369	92	16	1	10	78	53	86	.226	.309	.329	850	192	32	4	16	165	107	202
Scoring Position	.226	.321	.307	199	45	7	0	3	58	31	55	.210	.304	.293	471	99	14	2	7	133	70	125
Late and Close	.250	.358	.279	68	17	2	0	0	4	12	9	.194	.312	.229	144	28	2	0	1	9	25	30

CHRIS HAMMOND — BL/TL — age 28 — FLO SP32 FIN/GB

4-YEAR TOTALS (1990–1993)

1993	G	IP	H	BB	SO	SB	CS	W	L	SV	ERA	G	IP	H	BB	SO	SB	CS	W	L	SV	ERA
Total	32	191.0	207	66	108	5	6	11	12	0	4.66	83	449.1	461	181	241	21	14	25	31	0	4.43
at Home	14	80.2	95	24	52	1	3	5	5	0	4.91	41	216.0	230	88	123	14	9	13	13	0	4.54
on Road	18	110.1	112	42	56	4	3	6	7	0	4.49	42	233.1	231	93	118	7	5	12	18	0	4.32
on Grass	24	142.0	157	44	81	3	5	9	8	0	4.50	33	186.2	203	62	105	5	6	11	11	0	4.44
on Turf	8	49.0	50	22	27	2	1	2	4	0	5.14	50	262.2	258	119	136	16	8	14	20	0	4.42
Day Games	8	51.2	50	16	28	0	2	4	2	0	3.48	27	145.1	134	49	75	7	6	10	8	0	3.59
Night Games	24	139.1	157	50	80	5	4	7	10	0	5.10	56	304.0	327	132	166	14	8	15	23	0	4.83
April	5	25.0	30	11	9	1	1	0	3	0	5.04	13	72.1	68	26	38	4	3	5	4	0	3.36
May	5	31.1	24	13	17	1	0	3	1	0	4.88	14	76.2	62	36	35	4	0	5	5	0	4.58
June	6	42.2	48	11	22	0	1	6	0	0	2.53	17	100.0	106	44	49	4	3	10	4	0	3.87
July	5	28.2	32	12	11	0	1	1	2	0	4.71	16	78.1	94	36	40	4	3	2	6	0	4.94
August	5	27.1	39	7	21	1	1	0	3	0	8.23	13	66.2	83	23	40	2	2	2	8	0	6.34
Sept-Oct	6	36.0	34	12	28	2	2	1	3	0	4.00	10	55.1	48	16	39	3	3	1	4	0	3.58

	BA	OBA	SA	AB	H	2B	3B	HR	RBI	BB	SO	BA	OBA	SA	AB	H	2B	3B	HR	RBI	BB	SO
Total	.277	.336	.406	747	207	30	6	18	92	66	108	.268	.339	.392	1719	461	70	16	37	203	181	241
vs. Left	.265	.374	.417	132	35	7	2	3	10	22	23	.256	.351	.419	360	92	14	6	11	41	51	58
vs. Right	.280	.327	.403	615	172	23	4	15	82	44	85	.272	.336	.385	1359	369	56	10	26	162	130	183
Bases Empty	.228	.290	.324	438	100	12	3	8	8	37	68	.233	.303	.328	1027	239	33	10	15	15	100	159
Leadoff	.254	.317	.351	185	47	2	2	4	4	17	20	.245	.310	.356	436	107	11	5	9	9	40	51
Runners On Base	.346	.400	.521	309	107	18	3	10	84	29	40	.321	.391	.487	692	222	37	6	22	188	81	82
Scoring Position	.344	.395	.473	186	64	8	2	4	64	17	28	.321	.404	.451	390	125	17	5	8	147	57	57
Late and Close	.275	.326	.425	40	11	3	0	1	5	3	10	.311	.393	.486	74	23	5	1	2	7	10	11

CHRIS HANEY — BL/TL — age 26 — KC SP23 FIN/FB

3-YEAR TOTALS (1991–1993)

1993	G	IP	H	BB	SO	SB	CS	W	L	SV	ERA	G	IP	H	BB	SO	SB	CS	W	L	SV	ERA
Total	23	124.0	141	53	65	7	4	9	9	0	6.02	55	288.2	310	122	170	24	14	16	22	0	5.05
at Home	13	69.1	85	21	30	4	1	3	7	0	6.36	29	156.2	170	48	83	8	5	8	13	0	5.11
on Road	10	54.2	56	32	35	3	3	6	2	0	5.60	26	132.0	140	74	87	16	9	8	9	0	4.98
on Grass	7	40.0	35	23	26	2	2	4	1	0	5.40	14	74.1	77	41	43	4	6	5	4	0	4.96
on Turf	16	84.0	106	30	39	5	2	5	8	0	6.32	41	214.1	233	81	127	20	8	11	18	0	5.08
Day Games	8	45.1	52	22	22	3	2	3	1	0	6.15	14	78.0	81	40	42	12	3	5	3	0	4.96
Night Games	15	78.2	89	31	43	4	2	6	8	0	5.95	41	210.2	229	82	128	12	11	11	19	0	5.08
April	0	0.0	0	0	0	0	0	0	0	0	0.00	4	20.0	20	5	12	3	0	2	1	0	4.50
May	2	14.0	13	5	4	1	1	2	0	0	3.21	6	29.2	32	9	17	3	2	2	2	0	5.16
June	6	32.2	35	10	22	1	1	2	1	0	6.61	9	45.0	46	15	32	2	2	3	3	0	6.20
July	6	33.2	35	12	21	2	0	3	2	0	5.35	9	50.0	57	19	28	2	1	4	4	0	4.68
August	5	32.2	30	14	13	1	1	2	3	0	3.03	12	71.0	64	37	37	3	3	4	3	0	3.30
Sept-Oct	4	11.0	28	12	5	2	1	0	3	0	18.82	15	73.0	91	37	44	10	6	2	9	0	6.41

	BA	OBA	SA	AB	H	2B	3B	HR	RBI	BB	SO	BA	OBA	SA	AB	H	2B	3B	HR	RBI	BB	SO
Total	.286	.356	.424	493	141	25	2	13	76	53	65	.274	.346	.424	1132	310	66	7	30	159	122	170
vs. Left	.277	.362	.349	83	23	3	0	1	14	10	5	.244	.336	.364	209	51	10	3	3	32	25	33
vs. Right	.288	.355	.439	410	118	22	2	12	62	43	60	.281	.348	.438	923	259	56	4	27	127	97	137
Bases Empty	.256	.316	.404	285	73	15	0	9	9	25	36	.260	.330	.406	645	168	37	3	17	17	63	96
Leadoff	.258	.308	.444	124	32	3	0	5	5	9	13	.261	.329	.413	276	72	15	0	9	9	26	38
Runners On Base	.327	.407	.452	208	68	10	2	4	67	28	29	.292	.365	.448	487	142	29	4	13	142	59	74
Scoring Position	.344	.436	.508	122	42	7	2	3	64	20	17	.297	.388	.448	279	83	16	4	6	126	44	42
Late and Close	.316	.316	.526	19	6	1	0	1	4	0	1	.250	.273	.469	32	8	1	0	2	5	1	4

ERIK HANSON — BR/TR — age 29 — SEA SP30, RP1 POW/GB

1993	G	IP	H	BB	SO	SB	CS	W	L	SV	ERA
Total	31	215.0	215	60	163	15	13	11	12	0	3.47
at Home	17	119.1	115	26	99	11	6	6	5	0	2.79
on Road	14	95.2	100	34	64	4	7	5	7	0	4.33
on Grass	12	80.2	89	29	54	4	5	4	7	0	4.69
on Turf	19	134.1	126	31	109	11	8	7	5	0	2.75
Day Games	7	51.2	50	12	37	4	2	4	2	0	2.96
Night Games	24	163.1	165	48	126	11	11	7	10	0	3.64
April	5	35.1	31	13	28	0	1	3	0	0	1.53
May	6	47.1	44	4	44	2	4	2	2	0	2.28
June	5	32.0	43	16	21	3	5	0	4	0	6.19
July	6	40.2	40	9	22	2	2	3	2	0	3.54
August	5	34.2	32	10	28	2	1	2	3	0	4.41
Sept-Oct	4	25.0	25	8	20	6	0	1	1	0	3.60

6-YEAR TOTALS (1988–1993)

	G	IP	H	BB	SO	SB	CS	W	L	SV	ERA
	145	967.1	949	285	740	64	44	56	54	0	3.69
	74	489.0	503	127	390	38	18	28	26	0	3.79
	71	478.1	446	158	350	26	26	28	28	0	3.59
	58	388.0	354	132	294	21	22	22	23	0	3.57
	87	579.1	595	153	446	43	22	34	31	0	3.78
	38	239.2	239	74	168	20	11	14	12	0	3.45
	107	727.2	710	211	572	44	33	42	42	0	3.77
	24	156.2	146	56	125	7	7	10	6	0	2.99
	26	166.2	178	48	136	11	12	9	12	0	4.05
	19	131.2	140	48	93	8	10	7	11	0	4.31
	23	155.1	146	38	106	7	4	11	9	0	3.65
	22	143.2	144	39	107	11	4	5	8	0	4.64
	31	213.1	195	56	173	20	7	14	8	0	2.95

	BA	OBA	SA	AB	H	2B	3B	HR	RBI	BB	SO
Total	.263	.315	.402	819	215	49	7	17	79	60	163
vs. Left	.231	.285	.327	425	98	23	3	4	33	33	94
vs. Right	.297	.348	.482	394	117	26	4	13	46	27	69
Bases Empty	.257	.304	.403	506	130	37	5	9	9	32	105
Leadoff	.245	.293	.365	208	51	15	2	2	2	14	39
Runners On Base	.272	.333	.399	313	85	12	2	8	70	28	58
Scoring Position	.253	.320	.423	194	49	7	1	8	69	19	39
Late and Close	.325	.389	.650	80	26	7	2	5	12	8	14

BA	OBA	SA	AB	H	2B	3B	HR	RBI	BB	SO
.258	.313	.379	3681	949	180	24	73	373	285	740
.231	.284	.334	1906	441	89	13	27	181	140	399
.286	.343	.428	1775	508	91	11	46	192	145	341
.245	.295	.361	2263	555	105	14	43	43	151	466
.227	.272	.336	949	215	46	5	16	16	57	189
.278	.340	.408	1418	394	75	10	30	330	134	274
.262	.333	.410	786	206	38	9	20	292	88	170
.254	.312	.402	331	84	17	4	8	33	28	74

MIKE HARKEY — BR/TR — age 28 — CHN SP28 FIN/FB

1993	G	IP	H	BB	SO	SB	CS	W	L	SV	ERA
Total	28	157.1	187	43	67	7	6	10	10	0	5.26
at Home	14	79.2	93	24	38	3	4	4	6	0	4.86
on Road	14	77.2	94	19	29	4	2	6	4	0	5.68
on Grass	23	131.1	154	34	60	6	6	9	7	0	4.73
on Turf	5	26.0	33	9	7	1	0	1	3	0	7.96
Day Games	17	97.1	114	29	46	5	4	5	7	0	5.18
Night Games	11	60.0	73	14	21	2	2	5	3	0	5.40
April	3	20.1	19	8	11	2	0	3	0	0	1.77
May	6	30.2	46	9	7	1	2	2	2	0	6.46
June	2	10.0	10	4	7	0	0	0	0	0	5.40
July	5	30.0	32	4	15	1	0	2	3	0	5.10
August	6	35.1	45	9	12	2	4	1	2	0	5.60
Sept-Oct	6	31.0	35	9	15	1	0	2	3	0	6.10

5-YEAR TOTALS (1988–1993)

	G	IP	H	BB	SO	SB	CS	W	L	SV	ERA
	71	422.1	428	138	215	23	20	26	21	0	3.92
	34	215.1	225	68	109	9	15	11	10	0	3.47
	37	207.0	203	70	106	14	5	15	11	0	4.39
	51	317.2	318	90	159	16	17	21	12	0	3.54
	20	104.2	110	48	56	7	3	5	9	0	5.07
	44	273.1	268	85	143	14	16	16	12	0	3.72
	27	149.0	160	53	72	9	4	10	9	0	4.29
	10	56.1	49	21	37	5	0	5	3	0	3.20
	12	64.1	89	22	27	3	3	2	2	0	5.88
	6	39.0	33	13	21	1	0	0	2	0	3.46
	13	76.2	80	19	41	3	2	7	5	0	3.99
	17	108.2	102	32	50	6	10	7	3	0	3.40
	13	77.1	75	31	39	5	5	2	6	0	3.72

	BA	OBA	SA	AB	H	2B	3B	HR	RBI	BB	SO
Total	.305	.349	.451	614	187	23	8	17	86	43	67
vs. Left	.279	.337	.420	305	85	10	4	9	46	27	37
vs. Right	.330	.361	.482	309	102	13	5	8	40	16	30
Bases Empty	.277	.322	.428	376	104	10	4	13	13	24	41
Leadoff	.275	.310	.438	160	44	2	0	8	8	7	16
Runners On Base	.349	.390	.487	238	83	13	4	4	73	19	26
Scoring Position	.359	.403	.511	131	47	3	3	2	65	14	15
Late and Close	.375	.476	.375	16	6	0	0	0	2	4	4

BA	OBA	SA	AB	H	2B	3B	HR	RBI	BB	SO
.265	.325	.401	1617	428	69	19	38	182	138	215
.254	.318	.384	898	228	39	9	20	99	85	121
.278	.333	.423	719	200	30	10	18	83	53	94
.259	.308	.414	989	256	41	11	30	30	65	133
.249	.299	.411	418	104	12	4	16	16	25	59
.274	.349	.382	628	172	28	8	8	152	73	82
.263	.356	.366	361	95	18	5	3	134	56	50
.269	.361	.409	93	25	3	2	2	11	14	8

PETE HARNISCH — BB/TR — age 28 — HOU SP33 POW/FB

1993	G	IP	H	BB	SO	SB	CS	W	L	SV	ERA
Total	33	217.2	171	79	185	15	6	16	9	0	2.98
at Home	18	128.2	92	38	117	11	3	9	5	0	2.52
on Road	15	89.0	79	41	68	4	3	7	4	0	3.64
on Grass	8	49.2	35	19	41	3	3	4	2	0	2.54
on Turf	25	168.0	136	60	144	12	3	12	7	0	3.11
Day Games	10	61.2	49	26	47	7	2	5	2	0	3.06
Night Games	23	156.0	122	53	138	8	4	11	7	0	2.94
April	5	30.0	22	19	21	5	0	2	0	0	3.30
May	6	38.2	34	10	35	3	2	3	2	0	3.26
June	5	28.2	33	7	32	3	0	1	3	0	5.02
July	6	41.2	31	16	36	2	1	4	2	0	3.24
August	6	40.0	28	14	29	0	2	2	1	0	2.47
Sept-Oct	5	38.2	23	13	32	2	1	4	1	0	1.16

6-YEAR TOTALS (1988–1993)

	G	IP	H	BB	SO	SB	CS	W	L	SV	ERA
	151	946.0	821	385	723	103	28	53	50	0	3.56
	77	509.1	399	162	415	52	14	33	20	0	2.99
	74	436.2	422	223	308	51	14	20	30	0	4.23
	68	407.2	364	197	300	44	15	25	25	0	3.66
	83	538.1	457	188	423	59	13	28	25	0	3.48
	36	216.1	193	98	169	21	12	11	11	0	3.74
	115	729.2	628	287	554	82	16	42	39	0	3.50
	20	122.2	96	64	84	13	1	6	4	0	2.79
	24	154.1	134	51	108	17	7	9	9	0	3.91
	22	138.1	123	53	116	20	4	6	10	0	3.58
	27	167.0	155	66	119	21	6	9	8	0	4.20
	30	190.0	168	86	156	14	6	8	11	0	3.27
	28	173.2	145	65	140	18	4	15	8	0	3.47

	BA	OBA	SA	AB	H	2B	3B	HR	RBI	BB	SO
Total	.214	.289	.340	798	171	32	4	20	75	79	185
vs. Left	.238	.327	.375	429	102	12	4	13	38	55	87
vs. Right	.187	.241	.298	369	69	20	0	7	37	24	98
Bases Empty	.205	.282	.337	484	99	16	3	14	14	48	119
Leadoff	.207	.271	.374	203	42	3	2	9	9	17	47
Runners On Base	.229	.299	.344	314	72	16	1	6	61	31	66
Scoring Position	.224	.295	.333	183	41	12	1	2	52	20	41
Late and Close	.167	.231	.333	48	8	2	0	2	4	4	14

BA	OBA	SA	AB	H	2B	3B	HR	RBI	BB	SO
.232	.309	.357	3536	821	155	24	80	347	385	723
.248	.332	.381	1986	493	86	20	46	193	240	347
.212	.280	.327	1550	328	69	4	34	154	145	376
.223	.301	.349	2089	465	80	17	50	50	219	439
.229	.300	.358	900	206	35	6	23	23	86	176
.246	.321	.370	1447	356	75	7	30	297	166	284
.229	.321	.348	831	190	46	4	15	255	125	176
.195	.282	.323	257	50	9	3	6	18	32	53

GREG A. HARRIS — BB/TR — age 39 — BOS RP80 POW/GB — 10-YEAR TOTALS (1984–1993)

1993	G	IP	H	BB	SO	SB	CS	W	L	SV	ERA	G	IP	H	BB	SO	SB	CS	W	L	SV	ERA
Total	80	112.1	95	60	103	5	4	6	7	8	3.77	569	1206.2	1057	542	925	81	47	64	71	50	3.39
at Home	39	54.2	53	30	45	1	1	3	5	5	4.77	281	599.2	538	259	465	39	15	37	33	28	3.63
on Road	41	57.2	42	30	58	4	3	3	2	3	2.81	288	607.0	519	283	460	42	32	27	38	22	3.16
on Grass	65	93.1	78	46	81	4	3	5	7	8	3.66	411	898.2	780	385	701	52	34	52	48	44	3.44
on Turf	15	19.0	17	14	22	1	1	1	0	0	4.26	158	308.0	277	157	224	29	13	12	23	6	3.27
Day Games	28	40.0	29	21	46	2	2	0	4	2	4.50	169	333.2	263	175	284	26	14	19	18	13	3.10
Night Games	52	72.1	66	39	57	3	2	6	3	6	3.36	400	873.0	794	367	641	55	33	45	53	37	3.51
April	9	14.0	10	7	9	2	1	0	0	0	2.57	70	137.1	107	65	106	9	5	8	9	3	3.15
May	16	19.1	14	10	21	2	1	1	0	0	1.86	104	203.1	176	84	157	12	12	6	15	10	3.19
June	14	20.1	14	12	16	0	0	3	2	2	3.98	101	212.1	188	93	155	10	3	13	11	13	3.48
July	12	19.1	11	7	19	1	1	3	0	2	1.40	93	221.0	195	88	149	14	9	13	14	6	2.77
August	14	18.1	16	10	18	0	1	0	1	0	3.93	103	231.1	182	98	206	16	10	16	7	4	3.00
Sept-Oct	15	21.0	30	14	20	0	0	0	3	4	8.14	98	201.1	209	114	152	20	8	15	14	14	4.83

	BA	OBA	SA	AB	H	2B	3B	HR	RBI	BB	SO	BA	OBA	SA	AB	H	2B	3B	HR	RBI	BB	SO
Total	.232	.341	.329	410	95	15	2	7	54	60	103	.237	.323	.356	4455	1057	194	26	94	516	542	925
vs. Left	.253	.353	.348	198	50	9	2	2	29	31	44	.229	.318	.335	2094	479	88	16	34	232	269	400
vs. Right	.212	.329	.311	212	45	6	0	5	25	29	59	.245	.328	.374	2361	578	106	10	60	284	273	525
Bases Empty	.206	.306	.284	194	40	9	0	2	2	23	49	.228	.311	.345	2432	554	107	14	50	50	267	516
Leadoff	.216	.258	.307	88	19	5	0	1	1	3	21	.219	.301	.337	1026	225	45	5	22	22	105	194
Runners On Base	.255	.370	.370	216	55	6	2	5	52	37	54	.249	.337	.369	2023	503	87	12	44	466	275	409
Scoring Position	.219	.348	.315	146	32	3	1	3	46	27	40	.233	.342	.336	1198	279	48	6	21	393	208	253
Late and Close	.260	.356	.355	231	60	11	1	3	33	29	59	.228	.321	.339	1278	291	45	8	27	153	164	278

GREG W. HARRIS — BR/TR — age 31 — SD/COL SP35 FIN/FB — 6-YEAR TOTALS (1988–1993)

1993	G	IP	H	BB	SO	SB	CS	W	L	SV	ERA	G	IP	H	BB	SO	SB	CS	W	L	SV	ERA
Total	35	225.1	239	69	123	22	10	11	17	0	4.59	207	746.2	679	235	502	70	30	42	47	15	3.30
at Home	18	120.0	121	33	66	8	7	6	7	0	3.68	98	380.1	335	113	267	30	17	24	20	4	2.77
on Road	17	105.1	118	36	57	14	3	5	10	0	5.64	109	366.1	344	122	235	40	13	18	27	11	3.86
on Grass	27	179.2	181	52	102	14	8	9	12	0	4.06	150	559.0	489	167	382	42	24	33	31	10	2.87
on Turf	8	45.2	58	17	21	8	2	2	5	0	6.70	57	187.2	190	68	120	28	6	9	16	5	4.60
Day Games	11	69.2	74	25	38	2	2	5	4	0	3.62	65	238.2	203	88	153	24	11	19	14	5	2.98
Night Games	24	155.2	165	44	85	20	8	6	13	0	5.03	142	508.0	476	147	349	46	19	23	33	10	3.45
April	5	31.0	33	8	14	2	1	1	4	0	5.23	26	101.1	86	20	60	10	3	5	6	0	2.84
May	6	40.2	42	12	24	6	2	2	2	0	3.32	36	112.1	105	45	86	15	4	7	5	1	3.69
June	6	43.2	47	11	27	6	2	2	2	0	3.50	31	84.1	78	34	62	10	6	5	5	1	3.09
July	6	40.2	37	9	20	3	1	3	2	0	3.76	31	116.2	109	34	69	8	5	5	10	1	3.86
August	6	37.1	42	12	25	4	1	1	4	0	6.27	36	144.2	134	44	102	10	7	8	9	2	3.61
Sept-Oct	6	32.0	38	17	13	1	3	0	0	0	6.19	47	187.1	167	58	123	17	5	12	10	5	2.83

	BA	OBA	SA	AB	H	2B	3B	HR	RBI	BB	SO	BA	OBA	SA	AB	H	2B	3B	HR	RBI	BB	SO
Total	.271	.328	.455	881	239	45	9	33	116	69	123	.242	.303	.373	2804	679	112	14	76	297	235	502
vs. Left	.271	.330	.432	465	126	19	4	16	60	40	64	.256	.314	.382	1604	410	59	7	43	172	137	259
vs. Right	.272	.325	.481	416	113	26	5	17	56	29	59	.224	.287	.363	1200	269	53	7	33	125	98	243
Bases Empty	.276	.317	.463	536	148	26	4	22	22	30	72	.243	.288	.376	1729	420	73	5	49	49	102	312
Leadoff	.281	.308	.522	228	64	8	1	15	15	8	32	.239	.280	.388	712	170	32	1	24	24	38	133
Runners On Base	.264	.344	.443	345	91	19	5	11	94	39	51	.241	.325	.369	1075	259	39	9	27	248	133	190
Scoring Position	.255	.361	.407	204	52	12	2	5	76	32	28	.226	.336	.338	625	141	23	4	13	208	106	121
Late and Close	.292	.333	.492	65	19	2	1	3	11	4	4	.212	.298	.285	613	130	18	3	7	57	73	122

GENE HARRIS — BR/TR — age 30 — SD RP59 POW/GB — 5-YEAR TOTALS (1989–1993)

1993	G	IP	H	BB	SO	SB	CS	W	L	SV	ERA	G	IP	H	BB	SO	SB	CS	W	L	SV	ERA
Total	59	59.1	57	37	39	10	0	6	6	23	3.03	135	194.1	189	117	138	25	3	9	15	25	4.40
at Home	30	32.1	27	14	20	3	0	5	3	8	2.78	65	105.2	91	55	71	10	1	8	5	9	3.75
on Road	29	27.0	30	23	19	7	0	1	3	15	3.33	70	88.2	98	62	67	15	2	1	10	16	5.18
on Grass	47	49.2	41	25	33	4	0	6	4	17	2.36	73	84.1	86	45	69	9	0	6	8	18	4.27
on Turf	12	9.2	16	12	6	6	0	0	2	6	6.52	62	110.0	103	72	69	16	3	3	7	7	4.50
Day Games	20	20.0	22	10	12	4	0	2	3	10	4.50	42	62.1	64	30	43	11	2	3	5	11	4.62
Night Games	39	39.1	35	27	27	6	0	4	3	13	2.29	93	132.0	125	87	95	14	1	6	10	14	4.30
April	8	8.2	5	6	9	0	0	1	0	5	3.12	29	39.2	27	26	31	1	1	2	1	5	3.86
May	9	9.2	7	4	2	0	0	0	0	3	1.86	21	28.0	25	19	17	2	0	2	1	3	6.43
June	12	12.1	11	2	12	1	0	1	1	2	2.92	28	54.2	50	20	44	8	1	1	3	5	3.46
July	11	9.2	15	12	6	5	0	0	0	4	5.59	20	26.2	48	17	17	7	1	1	7	4	8.10
August	11	11.2	9	6	5	4	0	1	0	4	0.77	18	18.2	16	15	11	5	0	2	1	4	2.89
Sept-Oct	8	7.1	10	7	5	0	0	0	1	1	4.91	19	26.2	23	16	18	2	0	1	2	4	2.36

	BA	OBA	SA	AB	H	2B	3B	HR	RBI	BB	SO	BA	OBA	SA	AB	H	2B	3B	HR	RBI	BB	SO
Total	.256	.361	.323	223	57	4	1	3	26	37	39	.259	.360	.380	731	189	31	5	16	103	117	138
vs. Left	.265	.371	.319	113	30	3	0	1	10	18	18	.263	.379	.371	342	90	20	1	5	39	63	51
vs. Right	.245	.351	.327	110	27	1	1	2	16	19	21	.254	.344	.388	389	99	11	4	11	64	54	87
Bases Empty	.240	.319	.375	104	25	3	1	3	3	12	14	.255	.347	.413	361	92	16	4	11	11	49	68
Leadoff	.250	.308	.333	48	12	1	0	1	1	4	4	.286	.372	.460	161	46	10	3	4	4	22	22
Runners On Base	.269	.395	.277	119	32	1	0	0	23	25	25	.262	.373	.349	370	97	15	1	5	92	68	70
Scoring Position	.268	.398	.280	82	22	1	0	0	23	19	18	.254	.371	.335	248	63	9	1	5	85	50	49
Late and Close	.261	.373	.335	161	42	1	1	3	20	29	29	.277	.397	.397	242	67	4	2	7	34	47	48

BRYAN HARVEY — BR/TR — age 31 — FLO RP59 POW/FB

1993	G	IP	H	BB	SO	SB	CS	W	L	SV	ERA		G	IP	H	BB	SO	SB	CS	W	L	SV	ERA
												7-YEAR TOTALS (1987–1993)												
Total	59	69.0	45	13	73	15	0	1	5	45	1.70		309	376.2	264	139	438	49	5	17	25	171	2.34
at Home	32	40.2	23	9	43	9	0	1	1	24	1.11		160	206.2	151	75	230	27	1	11	11	84	2.31
on Road	27	28.1	22	4	30	6	0	0	4	21	2.54		149	170.0	113	64	208	22	4	6	14	87	2.38
on Grass	49	59.0	39	12	64	14	0	1	4	38	1.68		267	329.0	227	124	384	47	4	14	21	147	2.46
on Turf	10	10.0	6	1	9	1	0	0	1	7	1.80		42	47.2	37	15	54	2	1	3	4	24	1.51
Day Games	16	19.1	13	4	20	4	0	1	1	12	1.86		78	100.1	72	34	117	14	1	3	4	44	1.97
Night Games	43	49.2	32	9	53	11	0	1	4	33	1.63		231	276.1	192	105	321	35	4	14	21	127	2.48
April	9	9.1	12	2	10	3	0	0	1	7	3.86		46	54.0	41	21	63	7	1	3	3	23	2.00
May	11	14.0	8	1	21	2	0	1	0	8	0.00		62	84.2	62	26	91	9	1	4	5	29	2.13
June	9	11.0	3	2	12	0	0	0	0	7	1.64		53	62.0	36	27	77	7	0	0	3	31	2.03
July	11	10.2	11	3	10	3	0	0	2	8	3.38		47	55.2	51	22	58	9	1	6	7	23	3.72
August	11	14.2	8	3	9	7	0	0	1	9	1.23		46	62.2	32	16	80	10	1	2	2	30	0.86
Sept-Oct	8	9.1	3	2	11	0	0	0	1	6	0.96		55	57.2	42	27	69	7	1	2	5	35	3.59

	BA	OBA	SA	AB	H	2B	3B	HR	RBI	BB	SO		BA	OBA	SA	AB	H	2B	3B	HR	RBI	BB	SO
Total	.186	.222	.240	242	45	1	0	4	21	13	73		.195	.268	.283	1351	264	29	3	28	138	139	438
vs. Left	.132	.191	.140	121	16	1	0	0	5	9	43		.170	.252	.252	702	119	18	2	12	70	80	246
vs. Right	.240	.254	.339	121	29	0	0	4	16	4	30		.223	.285	.317	649	145	11	1	16	68	59	192
Bases Empty	.195	.243	.242	128	25	0	0	2	2	8	36		.208	.266	.307	687	143	11	0	19	19	53	216
Leadoff	.273	.298	.327	55	15	0	0	1	1	2	12		.228	.290	.344	276	63	8	0	8	8	23	79
Runners On Base	.175	.200	.237	114	20	1	0	2	19	5	37		.182	.270	.259	664	121	18	3	9	119	86	222
Scoring Position	.169	.203	.220	59	10	0	0	1	16	4	18		.158	.274	.246	411	65	9	3	7	112	72	145
Late and Close	.174	.213	.222	207	36	1	0	3	19	12	64		.196	.271	.281	966	189	18	2	20	116	104	326

TOM HENKE — BR/TR — age 37 — TEX RP66 POW/GB

1993	G	IP	H	BB	SO	SB	CS	W	L	SV	ERA		G	IP	H	BB	SO	SB	CS	W	L	SV	ERA
													10-YEAR TOTALS (1984–1993)												
Total	66	74.1	55	27	79	3	2	5	5	40	2.91		537	665.2	502	213	748	42	13	35	35	259	2.68
at Home	38	44.1	28	5	50	1	1	1	5	27	1.62		273	331.0	240	91	368	25	6	23	9	130	2.42
on Road	28	30.0	27	22	29	2	1	0	4	13	4.80		264	334.2	262	122	380	17	7	12	26	129	2.93
on Grass	58	67.1	50	21	73	2	2	5	5	34	2.67		256	317.2	247	104	359	17	8	16	21	125	2.66
on Turf	8	7.0	5	6	6	1	0	0	0	6	5.14		281	348.0	255	109	389	25	5	19	14	134	2.69
Day Games	19	20.1	20	11	17	1	0	1	1	9	5.75		168	201.1	170	81	212	20	2	9	9	63	3.00
Night Games	47	54.0	35	16	62	2	2	5	4	31	1.83		369	464.1	332	132	536	22	11	26	26	196	2.54
April	8	9.0	3	2	10	0	1	0	0	4	0.00		67	67.2	56	30	70	2	2	5	5	24	3.33
May	13	15.2	14	6	20	0	1	3	1	5	2.30		76	100.2	67	39	110	4	2	8	6	27	2.77
June	11	10.1	9	4	10	1	0	0	1	6	5.23		86	101.2	76	36	111	9	3	5	3	45	2.66
July	10	10.0	11	3	16	2	0	0	1	7	5.40		90	112.2	74	35	128	12	2	5	6	51	2.64
August	11	14.0	5	2	17	0	1	1	1	9	1.93		105	145.1	105	26	173	6	3	6	5	59	2.11
Sept-Oct	13	15.1	13	10	13	1	0	1	1	9	2.93		113	137.2	124	47	156	9	1	6	10	53	2.94

	BA	OBA	SA	AB	H	2B	3B	HR	RBI	BB	SO		BA	OBA	SA	AB	H	2B	3B	HR	RBI	BB	SO
Total	.205	.278	.306	268	55	6	0	7	30	27	79		.208	.272	.323	2412	502	94	9	55	278	213	748
vs. Left	.205	.289	.303	132	27	4	0	3	14	16	36		.211	.283	.323	1231	260	46	4	28	144	127	366
vs. Right	.206	.267	.309	136	28	2	0	4	16	11	43		.205	.259	.323	1181	242	48	5	27	134	86	382
Bases Empty	.188	.238	.260	154	29	2	0	3	3	10	43		.202	.251	.299	1352	273	54	4	23	23	85	425
Leadoff	.197	.222	.295	61	12	0	0	2	2	2	15		.214	.258	.317	542	116	19	2	11	11	30	152
Runners On Base	.228	.326	.368	114	26	4	0	4	27	17	36		.216	.296	.354	1060	229	40	5	32	255	128	323
Scoring Position	.215	.325	.385	65	14	2	0	3	24	11	18		.218	.309	.360	652	142	23	5	20	225	97	201
Late and Close	.210	.290	.327	205	43	6	0	6	24	23	62		.206	.270	.337	1595	329	65	6	44	217	142	528

MIKE HENNEMAN — BR/TR — age 33 — DET RP63 POW/GB

1993	G	IP	H	BB	SO	SB	CS	W	L	SV	ERA		G	IP	H	BB	SO	SB	CS	W	L	SV	ERA
													7-YEAR TOTALS (1987–1993)												
Total	63	71.2	69	32	58	0	0	5	3	24	2.64		432	605.2	557	224	429	22	10	56	30	128	3.00
at Home	27	31.2	26	15	27	0	0	3	1	7	3.41		222	314.2	257	96	243	10	6	38	11	62	2.80
on Road	36	40.0	43	17	31	0	0	2	2	17	2.03		210	291.0	300	128	186	12	4	18	19	66	3.22
on Grass	50	56.1	44	23	47	0	0	5	1	20	2.40		366	519.2	470	186	375	19	8	53	22	105	2.91
on Turf	13	15.1	25	9	11	0	0	0	2	4	3.52		66	86.0	87	38	54	3	2	3	8	23	3.56
Day Games	20	19.2	16	12	14	0	0	2	1	7	1.83		129	178.2	177	73	107	9	3	18	10	37	3.38
Night Games	43	52.0	53	20	44	0	0	3	2	17	2.94		303	427.0	380	151	322	13	7	38	20	91	2.85
April	10	10.2	11	5	7	0	0	0	0	5	1.69		55	65.1	54	37	59	1	2	2	1	24	2.48
May	13	14.1	10	8	9	0	0	1	0	5	1.26		71	99.0	82	37	59	2	4	10	8	23	2.82
June	11	10.1	9	4	10	0	0	0	1	2	2.61		82	110.0	95	47	82	5	1	8	4	21	2.86
July	10	15.1	15	4	10	0	0	1	0	5	2.35		76	111.2	113	48	82	5	1	16	8	19	4.35
August	11	12.0	16	4	12	0	0	1	2	4	4.50		74	110.2	116	34	82	4	2	9	5	21	2.36
Sept-Oct	8	9.0	8	7	10	0	0	0	0	3	4.00		74	109.0	97	33	81	5	0	11	4	20	2.89

	BA	OBA	SA	AB	H	2B	3B	HR	RBI	BB	SO		BA	OBA	SA	AB	H	2B	3B	HR	RBI	BB	SO
Total	.251	.331	.356	275	69	11	3	4	31	32	58		.246	.315	.342	2266	557	89	12	35	251	224	429
vs. Left	.287	.376	.442	129	37	7	2	3	21	19	19		.261	.346	.368	1011	264	52	7	14	107	131	154
vs. Right	.219	.290	.281	146	32	4	1	1	10	13	39		.233	.289	.321	1255	293	37	5	21	144	93	275
Bases Empty	.275	.331	.433	120	33	6	2	3	3	10	23		.251	.304	.347	1170	294	44	7	18	18	82	217
Leadoff	.333	.404	.569	51	17	2	2	2	2	6	8		.244	.292	.343	495	121	16	6	7	7	31	82
Runners On Base	.232	.331	.297	155	36	5	1	1	28	22	35		.240	.326	.337	1096	263	45	5	17	233	142	212
Scoring Position	.214	.313	.286	98	21	2	1	1	28	14	22		.216	.320	.306	661	143	24	4	9	209	109	146
Late and Close	.271	.353	.370	181	49	7	1	3	25	22	36		.243	.318	.333	1329	323	48	4	21	150	144	260

DOUG HENRY — BR/TR — age 31 — MIL RP54 POW/GB

1993

1993	G	IP	H	BB	SO	SB	CS	W	L	SV	ERA
Total	54	55.0	67	25	38	4	0	4	4	17	5.56
at Home	30	30.0	40	14	21	3	0	3	2	7	7.20
on Road	24	25.0	27	11	17	1	0	1	2	10	3.60
on Grass	48	48.2	58	21	36	4	0	4	3	15	5.55
on Turf	6	6.1	9	4	2	0	0	0	1	2	5.68
Day Games	24	24.2	30	12	15	2	0	2	1	5	6.20
Night Games	30	30.1	37	13	23	2	0	2	3	12	5.04
April	9	9.0	13	6	4	1	0	0	0	5	10.00
May	11	12.0	12	3	8	0	0	0	0	4	1.50
June	11	9.0	8	1	10	0	0	0	2	5	2.00
July	8	8.1	8	5	4	1	0	2	1	3	6.48
August	10	11.2	17	8	10	1	0	2	1	0	6.94
Sept-Oct	5	5.0	9	2	2	1	0	0	0	0	9.00

	BA	OBA	SA	AB	H	2B	3B	HR	RBI	BB	SO
Total	.300	.373	.471	223	67	13	2	7	38	25	38
vs. Left	.314	.393	.431	102	32	4	1	2	13	13	20
vs. Right	.289	.355	.504	121	35	9	1	5	25	12	18
Bases Empty	.346	.393	.529	104	36	8	1	3	3	6	13
Leadoff	.348	.400	.500	46	16	4	0	2	1	3	5
Runners On Base	.261	.357	.420	119	31	5	1	4	35	19	25
Scoring Position	.247	.352	.356	73	18	2	0	2	29	14	17
Late and Close	.310	.373	.500	126	39	8	2	4	25	13	25

3-YEAR TOTALS (1991–1993)

	G	IP	H	BB	SO	SB	CS	W	L	SV	ERA
Total	154	156.0	147	63	118	9	4	7	9	61	3.87
at Home	82	83.1	76	31	69	6	1	4	3	33	3.89
on Road	72	72.2	71	32	49	3	3	3	6	28	3.84
on Grass	135	136.0	120	50	107	8	4	7	7	55	3.38
on Turf	19	20.0	27	13	11	1	0	0	2	6	7.20
Day Games	56	57.2	50	24	37	2	1	2	1	22	3.59
Night Games	98	98.1	97	39	81	7	3	5	8	39	4.03
April	17	17.0	27	9	8	1	1	0	0	9	7.94
May	23	23.2	18	9	16	1	0	1	1	7	1.90
June	23	22.2	14	5	23	1	1	0	2	11	1.19
July	25	24.2	24	11	17	3	1	3	1	10	4.74
August	36	41.1	43	22	34	2	0	3	3	10	5.44
Sept-Oct	30	26.2	21	7	20	1	1	0	2	14	2.03

	BA	OBA	SA	AB	H	2B	3B	HR	RBI	BB	SO
Total	.248	.319	.388	593	147	33	4	14	85	63	118
vs. Left	.231	.322	.325	268	62	14	1	3	28	37	51
vs. Right	.262	.317	.440	325	85	19	3	11	57	26	67
Bases Empty	.243	.289	.365	329	80	20	1	6	6	19	66
Leadoff	.221	.277	.351	131	29	8	0	3		9	26
Runners On Base	.254	.353	.417	264	67	13	3	8	79	44	52
Scoring Position	.278	.387	.449	158	44	7	1	6	70	33	31
Late and Close	.246	.320	.363	342	84	19	3	5	52	39	80

PAT HENTGEN — BR/TR — age 26 — TOR SP32, RP2 FIN/FB

1993

1993	G	IP	H	BB	SO	SB	CS	W	L	SV	ERA
Total	34	216.1	215	74	122	16	6	19	9	0	3.87
at Home	18	111.1	116	38	56	12	3	7	6	0	4.77
on Road	16	105.0	99	36	66	4	3	12	3	0	2.91
on Grass	14	89.0	92	31	58	4	2	10	3	0	3.13
on Turf	20	127.1	123	43	64	12	4	9	6	0	4.38
Day Games	11	65.2	64	24	37	9	2	8	2	0	4.39
Night Games	23	150.2	151	50	85	7	4	11	7	0	3.64
April	5	28.2	18	11	15	3	2	3	1	0	2.20
May	6	36.0	35	13	25	3	0	3	0	0	3.25
June	6	36.2	38	12	16	0	1	5	0	0	3.44
July	5	32.0	34	11	16	5	0	1	3	0	6.19
August	6	45.1	45	14	19	3	2	4	2	0	3.77
Sept-Oct	6	37.2	45	13	31	2	1	3	3	0	4.30

	BA	OBA	SA	AB	H	2B	3B	HR	RBI	BB	SO
Total	.258	.322	.414	834	215	35	7	27	91	74	122
vs. Left	.285	.339	.430	421	120	20	4	11	45	32	47
vs. Right	.230	.305	.397	413	95	15	3	16	46	42	75
Bases Empty	.263	.335	.451	472	124	24	7	17	17	46	67
Leadoff	.280	.354	.510	200	56	9	5	9	9	19	28
Runners On Base	.251	.305	.365	362	91	11	0	10	74	28	55
Scoring Position	.225	.276	.335	200	45	4	0	6	64	15	35
Late and Close	.258	.370	.355	62	16	3	0	1	2	10	8

3-YEAR TOTALS (1991–1993)

	G	IP	H	BB	SO	SB	CS	W	L	SV	ERA
Total	65	274.0	269	109	164	22	6	24	11	0	4.11
at Home	35	143.0	147	59	80	14	3	10	7	0	4.78
on Road	30	131.0	122	50	84	8	3	14	4	0	3.37
on Grass	25	105.1	110	43	70	6	2	10	4	0	3.84
on Turf	40	168.2	159	66	94	16	4	14	7	0	4.27
Day Games	23	83.0	80	35	51	11	2	10	3	0	4.77
Night Games	42	191.0	189	74	113	11	4	14	8	0	3.82
April	14	41.1	31	18	28	4	2	5	1	0	2.83
May	11	44.1	41	16	32	5	0	4	1	0	3.45
June	10	45.1	47	16	20	1	1	7	0	0	3.57
July	11	45.2	47	24	24	6	0	1	5	0	6.11
August	9	51.1	52	19	25	3	2	4	2	0	4.38
Sept-Oct	10	46.0	51	16	35	3	1	3	2	0	4.11

	BA	OBA	SA	AB	H	2B	3B	HR	RBI	BB	SO
Total	.256	.329	.417	1051	269	48	8	35	116	109	164
vs. Left	.280	.350	.424	514	144	25	5	13	53	52	60
vs. Right	.233	.310	.410	537	125	23	3	22	63	57	104
Bases Empty	.271	.348	.471	590	160	33	8	23	23	63	92
Leadoff	.265	.343	.466	253	67	14	5	9	9	25	39
Runners On Base	.236	.304	.347	461	109	15	0	12	93	46	72
Scoring Position	.213	.294	.311	254	54	7	0	6	78	31	43
Late and Close	.247	.361	.382	89	22	4	1	2	6	16	15

JEREMY HERNANDEZ — BR/TR — age 28 — SD/CLE RP70 FIN/GB

1993

1993	G	IP	H	BB	SO	SB	CS	W	L	SV	ERA
Total	70	111.2	116	34	70	4	6	6	7	8	3.63
at Home	40	64.0	68	18	35	0	4	5	3	5	3.66
on Road	30	47.2	48	16	35	4	2	1	4	3	3.59
on Grass	57	91.0	93	28	51	3	5	5	4	8	3.56
on Turf	13	20.2	23	6	19	1	1	1	3	0	3.92
Day Games	19	40.0	35	11	20	0	2	2	2	2	4.05
Night Games	51	71.2	81	23	50	4	4	4	5	6	3.39
April	9	15.0	22	2	7	0	0	0	2	0	6.00
May	12	19.1	19	5	18	1	2	0	0	0	3.72
June	14	25.0	13	5	12	1	2	1	1	4	1.08
July	11	14.0	16	5	7	0	0	1	0	3	5.14
August	12	22.1	23	4	16	0	1	2	0	1	2.82
Sept-Oct	12	16.0	23	13	11	2	1	2	3	0	5.06

	BA	OBA	SA	AB	H	2B	3B	HR	RBI	BB	SO
Total	.274	.324	.428	423	116	15	4	14	58	34	70
vs. Left	.282	.346	.447	188	53	7	0	8	25	20	27
vs. Right	.268	.306	.413	235	63	8	4	6	33	14	43
Bases Empty	.263	.313	.431	232	61	5	2	10	10	17	37
Leadoff	.286	.327	.449	98	28	1	0	5	5	6	15
Runners On Base	.288	.336	.424	191	55	10	2	4	48	17	33
Scoring Position	.347	.395	.515	101	35	4	2	3	45	12	15
Late and Close	.254	.310	.411	185	47	8	0	7	23	16	30

3-YEAR TOTALS (1991–1993)

	G	IP	H	BB	SO	SB	CS	W	L	SV	ERA
Total	105	162.2	163	50	104	7	7	7	11	11	3.43
at Home	62	97.2	103	30	57	2	5	5	6	7	3.50
on Road	43	65.0	60	20	47	5	2	2	5	4	3.32
on Grass	87	137.2	132	44	80	5	6	6	7	11	3.20
on Turf	18	25.0	31	6	24	2	1	1	4	0	4.68
Day Games	30	55.1	48	15	34	2	2	3	2	2	3.90
Night Games	75	107.1	115	35	70	5	5	4	9	9	3.19
April	17	27.2	39	7	20	1	1	0	3	0	6.18
May	16	26.2	24	7	20	2	2	0	0	0	3.38
June	14	25.0	13	5	12	1	2	1	1	4	1.08
July	11	14.0	16	5	7	0	0	1	0	3	5.14
August	14	25.1	25	4	16	0	1	2	0	1	2.49
Sept-Oct	33	44.0	46	22	29	3	1	3	6	3	3.07

	BA	OBA	SA	AB	H	2B	3B	HR	RBI	BB	SO
Total	.268	.319	.406	608	163	20	5	18	75	50	104
vs. Left	.270	.336	.415	282	76	8	0	11	36	32	44
vs. Right	.267	.304	.399	326	87	12	5	7	39	18	60
Bases Empty	.266	.310	.427	342	91	10	3	13	13	22	53
Leadoff	.276	.314	.407	145	40	4	0	5	5	8	20
Runners On Base	.271	.330	.380	266	72	10	2	5	62	28	51
Scoring Position	.315	.381	.434	143	45	4	2	3	57	21	25
Late and Close	.275	.330	.410	251	69	10	0	8	28	22	38

ROBERTO HERNANDEZ — BR/TR — age 30 — CHA RP70 POW/GB

3-YEAR TOTALS (1991–1993)

1993	G	IP	H	BB	SO	SB	CS	W	L	SV	ERA		G	IP	H	BB	SO	SB	CS	W	L	SV	ERA
Total	70	78.2	66	20	71	2	4	3	4	38	2.29		122	164.2	129	47	145	8	8	11	7	50	2.51
at Home	36	39.0	37	7	31	0	3	2	3	18	2.77		64	88.2	67	17	77	2	5	8	4	24	1.73
on Road	34	39.2	29	13	40	2	1	1	1	20	1.82		58	76.0	62	30	68	6	3	3	3	26	3.43
on Grass	58	64.0	54	17	61	2	3	2	4	30	2.53		106	142.1	109	43	129	7	7	10	6	40	2.47
on Turf	12	14.2	12	3	10	0	1	1	0	8	1.23		16	22.1	20	4	16	1	1	1	1	10	2.82
Day Games	22	23.0	25	4	21	0	2	1	0	11	1.96		36	44.0	43	10	43	1	3	3	1	13	2.86
Night Games	48	55.2	41	16	50	2	2	2	4	27	2.43		86	120.2	86	37	102	7	5	8	6	37	2.39
April	8	9.1	3	6	9	1	0	0	0	3	1.93		12	12.2	4	12	11	1	0	0	0	3	2.84
May	11	12.1	13	3	14	0	2	1	1	5	2.92		12	15.1	13	3	17	0	2	1	1	5	2.35
June	12	14.1	14	3	12	0	0	0	2	6	3.14		16	23.1	18	6	22	1	0	2	2	6	2.70
July	13	12.0	9	3	8	0	1	0	1	8	1.50		25	27.1	25	9	22	2	3	1	3	9	1.98
August	13	13.1	5	0	9	0	0	0	0	8	0.68		23	31.0	12	2	29	1	1	2	0	12	0.58
Sept-Oct	13	17.1	22	5	19	1	1	2	0	8	3.12		34	55.0	57	15	44	3	2	5	1	15	3.76

	BA	OBA	SA	AB	H	2B	3B	HR	RBI	BB	SO		BA	OBA	SA	AB	H	2B	3B	HR	RBI	BB	SO
Total	.228	.276	.324	290	66	6	2	6	33	20	71		.214	.274	.311	602	129	21	2	11	69	47	145
vs. Left	.231	.311	.308	117	27	3	0	4	13	14	33		.210	.290	.300	257	54	11	0	4	33	29	74
vs. Right	.225	.250	.335	173	39	3	2	4	20	6	38		.217	.261	.319	345	75	10	2	7	36	18	71
Bases Empty	.210	.257	.299	157	33	3	1	3	3	3	40		.188	.244	.277	336	63	10	1	6	6	25	87
Leadoff	.177	.227	.242	62	11	1	0	1	1	4	18		.164	.222	.276	134	22	3	0	4	4	10	35
Runners On Base	.248	.297	.353	133	33	3	1	3	30	10	31		.248	.310	.353	266	66	11	1	5	63	22	58
Scoring Position	.230	.298	.270	74	17	1	1	0	23	8	13		.237	.311	.314	156	37	4	1	2	55	16	26
Late and Close	.218	.281	.339	174	38	2	2	5	24	16	44		.205	.272	.314	341	70	12	2	7	44	29	83

OREL HERSHISER — BR/TR — age 36 — LA SP33 FIN/GB

10-YEAR TOTALS (1984–1993)

1993	G	IP	H	BB	SO	SB	CS	W	L	SV	ERA		G	IP	H	BB	SO	SB	CS	W	L	SV	ERA
Total	33	215.2	201	72	141	10	10	12	14	0	3.59		314	2012.2	1781	605	1366	133	66	128	96	4	2.95
at Home	16	99.1	88	38	70	4	6	4	8	0	3.17		159	1047.2	896	304	714	73	43	70	45	0	2.64
on Road	17	116.1	113	34	71	6	4	8	6	0	3.95		155	965.0	885	301	652	60	23	58	51	4	3.28
on Grass	27	181.1	153	56	121	7	10	12	10	0	3.13		233	1522.2	1316	431	1028	95	50	103	65	2	2.79
on Turf	6	34.1	48	16	20	3	0	0	4	0	6.03		81	490.0	465	174	338	38	16	25	31	2	3.43
Day Games	13	83.0	89	29	54	3	5	5	8	0	4.66		110	672.2	632	184	426	49	23	38	34	2	3.22
Night Games	20	132.2	112	43	87	7	5	7	6	0	2.92		204	1340.0	1149	421	940	84	43	90	62	2	2.81
April	5	36.2	30	12	20	0	0	3	2	0	2.70		49	290.2	243	94	194	11	8	23	12	0	2.72
May	5	26.2	25	11	25	1	2	2	2	0	5.06		49	281.2	262	93	230	22	13	17	13	2	3.20
June	6	41.1	44	17	27	1	3	1	3	0	3.92		56	359.0	325	115	245	28	11	22	17	2	3.03
July	5	35.0	34	11	17	1	2	2	2	0	2.57		51	327.2	292	101	220	29	7	23	15	2	3.08
August	6	38.0	35	11	27	3	2	2	3	0	4.50		53	354.2	328	103	230	20	12	18	19	0	3.27
Sept-Oct	6	38.0	33	10	25	4	1	2	2	0	3.08		56	399.0	331	99	247	23	15	25	20	0	2.46

	BA	OBA	SA	AB	H	2B	3B	HR	RBI	BB	SO		BA	OBA	SA	AB	H	2B	3B	HR	RBI	BB	SO
Total	.246	.311	.375	817	201	42	6	17	95	72	141		.236	.296	.329	7539	1781	296	37	110	662	605	1366
vs. Left	.241	.319	.351	436	105	25	4	5	44	51	69		.251	.317	.350	4083	1023	174	27	59	369	394	613
vs. Right	.252	.302	.402	381	96	17	2	12	51	21	72		.219	.271	.305	3456	758	122	10	51	293	211	753
Bases Empty	.217	.271	.347	502	109	24	1	13	13	32	89		.234	.283	.331	4555	1066	179	21	74	74	281	814
Leadoff	.240	.295	.385	208	50	7	1	7	7	7	33		.250	.295	.355	1942	485	75	8	38	38	113	339
Runners On Base	.292	.371	.419	315	92	18	5	4	82	40	52		.240	.315	.326	2984	715	117	16	36	588	324	552
Scoring Position	.296	.392	.447	206	61	14	4	3	76	33	34		.228	.327	.319	1697	387	64	11	23	538	253	372
Late and Close	.219	.345	.342	73	16	6	0	1	8	13	15		.233	.315	.339	900	210	36	7	15	83	102	160

GREG HIBBARD — BL/TL — age 30 — CHN SP31 FIN/GB

5-YEAR TOTALS (1989–1993)

1993	G	IP	H	BB	SO	SB	CS	W	L	SV	ERA		G	IP	H	BB	SO	SB	CS	W	L	SV	ERA
Total	31	191.0	209	47	82	2	10	15	11	0	3.96		150	909.1	936	257	369	37	38	56	45	1	3.82
at Home	17	102.0	104	25	40	1	4	7	6	0	4.24		77	480.1	453	139	186	18	21	30	22	1	3.41
on Road	14	89.0	105	22	42	1	6	8	5	0	3.64		73	429.0	483	118	183	19	17	26	23	0	4.28
on Grass	24	141.1	157	31	61	1	8	11	8	0	4.27		124	757.1	760	210	306	29	33	47	35	1	3.70
on Turf	7	49.2	52	16	21	1	2	4	3	0	3.08		26	152.0	176	47	63	8	5	9	10	0	4.44
Day Games	16	92.1	102	22	38	0	3	5	7	0	4.78		46	275.2	282	73	120	7	9	17	14	0	4.47
Night Games	15	98.2	107	25	44	2	7	10	4	0	3.19		104	633.2	654	184	249	30	29	39	31	1	3.54
April	5	29.1	32	9	7	0	1	1	2	0	5.83		16	105.2	91	35	38	4	6	9	3	0	3.32
May	5	35.2	30	5	15	0	2	2	2	0	2.52		25	159.1	156	45	63	8	7	8	9	0	3.62
June	3	16.2	15	4	5	1	1	2	1	0	2.70		25	155.2	171	35	57	10	5	8	8	0	3.87
July	6	29.2	37	10	18	0	1	3	1	0	4.55		27	151.1	158	48	74	5	4	7	7	0	4.46
August	6	40.0	39	10	14	0	2	2	4	0	3.38		28	169.2	171	52	61	2	7	13	1	0	3.71
Sept-Oct	6	39.2	56	9	23	1	4	5	1	0	4.54		29	167.2	189	42	76	8	9	14	5	0	3.81

	BA	OBA	SA	AB	H	2B	3B	HR	RBI	BB	SO		BA	OBA	SA	AB	H	2B	3B	HR	RBI	BB	SO
Total	.286	.327	.446	731	209	54	3	19	84	47	82		.270	.321	.395	3464	936	166	21	75	370	257	369
vs. Left	.274	.338	.436	117	32	4	0	5	18	10	17		.253	.314	.360	483	122	17	1	11	60	37	63
vs. Right	.288	.325	.448	614	177	50	3	14	66	37	65		.273	.323	.401	2981	814	149	20	64	310	220	306
Bases Empty	.292	.338	.438	438	128	30	2	10	10	27	52		.262	.317	.377	2089	548	87	10	44	44	154	232
Leadoff	.328	.368	.497	189	62	16	2	4	4	9	19		.254	.303	.373	905	230	40	7	18	18	58	89
Runners On Base	.276	.313	.457	293	81	24	1	9	74	20	30		.282	.329	.423	1375	388	79	11	31	326	103	137
Scoring Position	.303	.352	.480	152	46	15	0	4	61	17	19		.287	.341	.441	710	204	51	8	14	278	68	74
Late and Close	.205	.262	.333	39	8	2	0	1	3	3	4		.257	.314	.353	292	75	13	0	5	16	21	29

BRYAN HICKERSON — BL/TL — age 31 — SF RP32, SP15 FIN/FB

1993	G	IP	H	BB	SO	SB	CS	W	L	SV	ERA
Total	47	120.1	137	39	69	4	6	7	5	0	4.26
at Home	23	63.0	63	15	40	2	4	4	3	0	4.00
on Road	24	57.1	74	24	29	2	2	3	2	0	4.55
on Grass	37	91.2	99	25	54	4	5	4	5	0	4.12
on Turf	10	28.2	38	14	15	0	1	3	0	0	4.71
Day Games	23	59.2	70	21	36	2	4	3	3	0	4.98
Night Games	24	60.2	67	18	33	2	2	4	2	0	3.56
April	9	11.1	19	6	5	0	0	0	0	0	9.53
May	11	12.1	8	5	6	2	1	0	1	0	1.46
June	9	20.2	19	6	9	0	1	0	0	0	3.48
July	5	28.0	34	8	13	1	0	4	1	0	5.79
August	6	25.0	31	7	18	1	1	1	3	0	3.60
Sept-Oct	7	23.0	26	7	18	1	4	1	0	0	2.74

3-YEAR TOTALS (1991–1993)

G	IP	H	BB	SO	SB	CS	W	L	SV	ERA
125	257.2	264	77	180	11	16	14	10	0	3.74
60	125.2	119	26	96	6	7	7	7	0	3.94
65	132.0	145	51	84	5	9	7	3	0	3.55
92	189.0	192	48	133	8	11	8	10	0	3.71
33	68.2	72	29	47	3	5	6	0	0	3.80
52	116.2	115	33	81	5	7	5	6	0	4.09
73	141.0	149	44	99	6	9	9	4	0	3.45
19	21.0	26	9	15	0	1	1	1	0	5.57
22	28.0	22	9	18	3	3	1	1	0	2.57
18	33.1	30	10	20	0	0	1	0	0	3.78
18	48.0	46	10	28	1	1	6	1	0	4.13
26	62.2	68	17	50	4	2	3	5	0	4.02
22	64.2	72	22	49	3	9	2	2	0	3.06

	BA	OBA	SA	AB	H	2B	3B	HR	RBI	BB	SO
Total	.291	.344	.430	470	137	21	1	14	51	39	69
vs. Left	.241	.274	.278	108	26	1	0	1	10	6	16
vs. Right	.307	.365	.475	362	111	20	1	13	41	33	53
Bases Empty	.298	.356	.460	265	79	14	1	9	9	23	50
Leadoff	.339	.386	.576	118	40	11	1	5	5	9	19
Runners On Base	.283	.329	.390	205	58	7	0	5	42	16	19
Scoring Position	.291	.336	.379	103	30	6	0	1	34	9	11
Late and Close	.250	.300	.250	64	16	0	0	0	3	5	6

BA	OBA	SA	AB	H	2B	3B	HR	RBI	BB	SO
.270	.322	.400	977	264	51	2	24	102	77	180
.237	.277	.296	257	61	7	1	2	20	16	41
.282	.338	.438	720	203	44	1	22	82	61	139
.274	.330	.419	559	153	35	2	14	14	45	120
.286	.333	.452	241	69	17	1	7	7	17	46
.266	.312	.376	418	111	16	0	10	88	32	60
.262	.308	.364	225	59	11	0	4	74	19	36
.235	.293	.321	187	44	7	0	3	18	17	35

KEN HILL — BR/TR — age 29 — MON SP28 FIN/GB

1993	G	IP	H	BB	SO	SB	CS	W	L	SV	ERA
Total	28	183.2	163	74	90	21	8	9	7	0	3.23
at Home	15	101.0	89	39	40	13	5	4	4	0	3.12
on Road	13	82.2	74	35	50	8	3	5	3	0	3.38
on Grass	7	41.1	42	13	25	1	1	2	3	0	4.14
on Turf	21	142.1	121	61	65	20	7	7	4	0	2.97
Day Games	7	52.1	40	16	20	5	2	3	2	0	2.58
Night Games	21	131.1	123	58	70	16	6	6	5	0	3.49
April	5	40.0	23	12	23	6	2	4	0	0	1.80
May	5	34.1	28	15	14	3	1	2	2	0	3.15
June	4	25.1	24	13	8	1	3	1	0	0	3.20
July	3	18.2	15	7	13	0	0	1	0	0	2.41
August	6	35.1	37	16	18	3	2	1	3	0	3.31
Sept-Oct	5	30.0	36	11	14	6	2	1	2	0	5.70

6-YEAR TOTALS (1988–1993)

G	IP	H	BB	SO	SB	CS	W	L	SV	ERA
145	872.1	778	354	537	98	41	48	48	0	3.53
67	408.0	369	169	226	49	24	20	21	0	3.55
78	464.1	409	185	311	49	17	28	27	0	3.51
38	238.0	201	78	159	19	9	14	13	0	3.25
107	634.1	577	276	378	79	32	34	35	0	3.63
47	303.1	249	108	191	40	14	17	17	0	2.94
98	569.0	529	246	346	58	27	31	31	0	3.84
20	124.0	99	40	63	13	7	9	4	0	2.47
22	143.1	120	58	91	16	10	8	4	0	3.14
21	127.0	117	58	72	16	7	8	7	0	3.33
21	126.0	105	56	88	5	4	9	5	0	3.93
25	145.1	141	61	93	18	5	7	13	0	3.78
36	206.2	196	81	130	30	8	7	15	0	4.14

	BA	OBA	SA	AB	H	2B	3B	HR	RBI	BB	SO
Total	.238	.315	.336	684	163	42	2	7	68	74	90
vs. Left	.234	.322	.343	376	88	25	2	4	34	49	42
vs. Right	.244	.307	.328	308	75	17	0	3	34	25	48
Bases Empty	.242	.313	.343	388	94	22	1	5	5	37	47
Leadoff	.246	.309	.354	175	43	14	1	1	1	14	13
Runners On Base	.233	.318	.328	296	69	20	1	2	63	37	43
Scoring Position	.220	.310	.319	182	40	12	0	2	57	26	24
Late and Close	.236	.246	.400	55	13	6	0	1	4	1	7

BA	OBA	SA	AB	H	2B	3B	HR	RBI	BB	SO
.240	.316	.348	3246	778	152	24	51	329	354	537
.242	.327	.345	1815	440	79	16	25	167	227	271
.236	.302	.353	1431	338	73	8	26	162	127	266
.237	.315	.347	1860	441	86	11	32	32	198	303
.236	.316	.357	812	192	38	6	16	16	86	114
.243	.317	.351	1386	337	66	13	19	297	156	234
.237	.327	.348	818	194	37	6	14	265	120	145
.295	.362	.464	237	70	10	3	8	29	23	39

ERIC HILLMAN — BL/TL — age 28 — NYN SP22, RP5 FIN/GB

1993	G	IP	H	BB	SO	SB	CS	W	L	SV	ERA
Total	27	145.0	173	24	60	11	8	2	9	0	3.97
at Home	11	66.1	78	12	30	6	3	1	4	0	4.21
on Road	16	78.2	95	12	30	5	5	1	5	0	3.78
on Grass	18	100.1	117	13	42	8	5	2	6	0	3.95
on Turf	9	44.2	56	11	18	3	3	0	3	0	4.03
Day Games	9	49.2	62	6	23	3	3	1	2	0	4.53
Night Games	18	95.1	111	18	37	8	5	1	7	0	3.68
April	0	0.0	0	0	0	0	0	0	0	0	0.00
May	5	25.1	36	9	9	3	1	0	2	0	5.33
June	5	7.0	11	1	3	1	0	0	1	0	5.14
July	5	34.2	34	0	15	1	1	1	2	0	2.86
August	6	40.2	43	9	20	4	5	0	2	0	3.76
Sept-Oct	6	37.1	49	5	13	2	1	0	2	0	4.10

2-YEAR TOTALS (1992–1993)

G	IP	H	BB	SO	SB	CS	W	L	SV	ERA
38	197.1	240	34	76	15	13	4	11	0	4.33
16	95.2	114	13	41	7	6	2	5	0	4.14
22	101.2	126	21	35	8	7	2	6	0	4.51
26	141.0	165	17	56	10	10	4	7	0	4.02
12	56.1	75	17	20	5	3	0	4	0	5.11
12	65.2	82	12	27	5	5	2	3	0	5.48
26	131.2	158	22	49	7	8	2	8	0	3.76
0	0.0	0	0	0	0	0	0	0	0	0.00
7	28.1	43	11	10	3	2	0	2	0	5.72
5	7.0	11	1	3	1	0	0	1	0	5.14
5	34.2	34	0	15	1	1	1	2	0	2.86
9	64.0	66	11	28	6	7	2	2	0	3.66
12	63.1	86	11	20	4	3	1	4	0	5.12

	BA	OBA	SA	AB	H	2B	3B	HR	RBI	BB	SO
Total	.299	.326	.427	579	173	28	5	12	72	24	60
vs. Left	.280	.326	.360	125	35	3	2	1	16	8	18
vs. Right	.304	.326	.445	454	138	25	3	11	56	16	42
Bases Empty	.270	.303	.394	322	87	20	1	6	6	13	35
Leadoff	.324	.359	.503	145	47	9	1	5	5	5	8
Runners On Base	.335	.354	.467	257	86	8	4	6	66	11	25
Scoring Position	.338	.357	.432	148	50	4	2	2	55	8	14
Late and Close	.415	.412	.554	65	27	3	0	2	10	1	7

BA	OBA	SA	AB	H	2B	3B	HR	RBI	BB	SO
.304	.333	.447	790	240	38	6	21	101	34	76
.284	.331	.358	162	46	5	2	1	16	10	24
.309	.333	.470	628	194	33	4	20	85	24	52
.286	.318	.433	448	128	26	2	12	12	17	45
.340	.372	.528	197	67	12	2	7	7	6	11
.327	.352	.465	342	112	12	4	9	89	17	31
.335	.361	.450	191	64	6	2	4	76	12	18
.387	.392	.507	75	29	3	0	2	10	1	10

TREVOR HOFFMAN — BR/TR — age 27 — FLO/SD RP67 POW/FB

1993 / 1-YEAR TOTALS (1993)

1993	G	IP	H	BB	SO	SB	CS	W	L	SV	ERA	G	IP	H	BB	SO	SB	CS	W	L	SV	ERA
Total	67	90.0	80	39	79	7	1	4	6	5	3.90	67	90.0	80	39	79	7	1	4	6	5	3.90
at Home	34	45.0	45	15	36	4	1	2	3	1	3.40	34	45.0	45	15	36	4	1	2	3	1	3.40
on Road	33	45.0	35	24	43	3	0	2	3	4	4.40	33	45.0	35	24	43	3	0	2	3	4	4.40
on Grass	51	68.2	57	25	59	5	1	2	3	4	3.28	51	68.2	57	25	59	5	1	2	3	4	3.28
on Turf	16	21.1	23	14	20	2	0	2	3	1	5.91	16	21.1	23	14	20	2	0	2	3	1	5.91
Day Games	25	36.1	21	17	34	3	0	0	3	2	2.97	25	36.1	21	17	34	3	0	0	3	2	2.97
Night Games	42	53.2	59	22	45	4	1	4	3	3	4.53	42	53.2	59	22	45	4	1	4	3	3	4.53
April	10	11.2	6	7	7	0	0	1	0	1	3.09	10	11.2	6	7	7	0	0	1	0	1	3.09
May	10	13.0	13	9	9	1	0	1	1	0	4.15	10	13.0	13	9	9	1	0	1	1	0	4.15
June	11	14.0	16	4	11	0	0	1	1	1	5.79	11	14.0	16	4	11	0	0	1	1	1	5.79
July	10	14.2	11	10	19	2	0	1	1	0	3.68	10	14.2	11	10	19	2	0	1	1	0	3.68
August	14	18.2	17	5	13	3	0	0	2	2	3.38	14	18.2	17	5	13	3	0	0	2	2	3.38
Sept-Oct	12	18.0	17	4	20	1	1	1	1	1	3.50	12	18.0	17	4	20	1	1	1	1	1	3.50

	BA	OBA	SA	AB	H	2B	3B	HR	RBI	BB	SO	BA	OBA	SA	AB	H	2B	3B	HR	RBI	BB	SO
Total	.234	.310	.392	342	80	16	4	10	40	39	79	.234	.310	.392	342	80	16	4	10	40	39	79
vs. Left	.220	.330	.390	159	35	3	3	6	23	27	38	.220	.330	.390	159	35	3	3	6	23	27	38
vs. Right	.246	.291	.393	183	45	13	1	4	17	12	41	.246	.291	.393	183	45	13	1	4	17	12	41
Bases Empty	.250	.330	.451	184	46	8	4	7	7	21	37	.250	.330	.451	184	46	8	4	7	7	21	37
Leadoff	.287	.345	.512	80	23	5	2	3	3	6	13	.287	.345	.512	80	23	5	2	3	3	6	13
Runners On Base	.215	.287	.323	158	34	8	0	3	33	18	42	.215	.287	.323	158	34	8	0	3	33	18	42
Scoring Position	.182	.277	.263	99	18	2	0	2	28	15	28	.182	.277	.263	99	18	2	0	2	28	15	28
Late and Close	.228	.317	.347	193	44	10	2	3	20	25	43	.228	.317	.347	193	44	10	2	3	20	25	43

DARREN HOLMES — BR/TR — age 28 — COL RP62 POW/GB

1993 / 4-YEAR TOTALS (1990–1993)

1993	G	IP	H	BB	SO	SB	CS	W	L	SV	ERA	G	IP	H	BB	SO	SB	CS	W	L	SV	ERA
Total	62	66.2	56	20	60	3	2	3	3	25	4.05	157	202.2	196	69	169	12	8	8	12	34	4.09
at Home	35	36.2	36	14	37	1	1	3	2	13	5.65	83	106.0	114	34	92	5	5	6	6	17	5.01
on Road	27	30.0	20	6	23	2	1	0	1	12	2.10	74	96.2	82	35	77	7	3	2	6	17	3.07
on Grass	50	51.1	46	17	48	3	1	3	3	20	5.08	126	158.1	165	57	133	10	6	8	11	25	4.89
on Turf	12	15.1	10	3	12	0	1	0	0	5	0.59	31	44.1	31	12	36	2	2	0	1	9	1.22
Day Games	21	20.0	20	4	22	0	0	0	1	10	5.40	55	73.2	75	22	65	3	1	1	4	13	3.91
Night Games	41	46.2	36	16	38	3	2	3	2	15	3.47	102	129.0	121	47	104	9	7	7	8	21	4.19
April	7	5.1	12	7	6	0	0	0	2	1	18.56	13	20.1	24	12	20	1	1	1	3	1	6.64
May	10	8.2	8	3	7	1	0	0	1	2	5.19	23	33.1	36	9	27	2	1	2	2	4	2.70
June	8	10.1	7	2	9	1	0	0	0	2	2.61	27	32.0	34	10	24	1	0	0	2	2	4.50
July	13	14.2	12	2	14	0	1	1	0	5	4.30	28	31.2	36	9	26	1	2	2	2	6	8.24
August	12	13.1	8	4	12	1	0	0	0	9	1.35	25	31.1	24	8	26	1	1	0	1	11	2.30
Sept-Oct	12	14.1	9	2	12	0	1	2	0	6	1.26	41	54.0	42	21	46	6	3	3	2	10	2.33

	BA	OBA	SA	AB	H	2B	3B	HR	RBI	BB	SO	BA	OBA	SA	AB	H	2B	3B	HR	RBI	BB	SO
Total	.222	.285	.345	252	56	9	2	6	30	20	60	.253	.316	.362	776	196	33	5	14	98	69	169
vs. Left	.228	.305	.316	136	31	5	2	1	13	13	22	.250	.317	.333	384	96	19	2	3	39	35	69
vs. Right	.216	.260	.379	116	25	4	0	5	17	7	38	.255	.315	.390	392	100	14	3	11	59	34	100
Bases Empty	.212	.261	.298	151	32	3	2	2	2	8	31	.249	.289	.333	406	101	13	3	5	5	21	80
Leadoff	.217	.266	.233	60	13	1	0	0	0	2	13	.314	.355	.419	172	54	7	1	3	3	9	31
Runners On Base	.238	.319	.416	101	24	6	0	4	28	12	29	.257	.343	.395	370	95	20	2	9	93	48	89
Scoring Position	.218	.328	.345	55	12	4	0	1	22	9	15	.228	.331	.356	219	50	11	1	5	81	35	57
Late and Close	.214	.278	.352	145	31	6	1	4	18	13	34	.230	.289	.353	317	73	12	3	7	36	26	62

CHARLIE HOUGH — BR/TR — age 46 — FLO SP34 FIN/FB

1993 / 10-YEAR TOTALS (1984–1993)

1993	G	IP	H	BB	SO	SB	CS	W	L	SV	ERA	G	IP	H	BB	SO	SB	CS	W	L	SV	ERA
Total	34	204.1	202	71	126	19	14	9	16	0	4.27	331	2265.1	1973	961	1365	229	87	127	132	0	3.81
at Home	18	114.0	105	45	69	17	5	5	6	0	4.18	162	1127.0	1003	453	695	122	45	70	61	0	3.83
on Road	16	90.1	97	26	57	2	9	4	10	0	4.38	169	1138.1	970	508	670	107	42	57	71	0	3.80
on Grass	24	154.1	141	54	95	17	11	8	9	0	3.73	265	1829.0	1568	767	1125	181	73	111	98	0	3.72
on Turf	10	50.0	61	17	31	2	3	1	7	0	5.94	66	436.1	405	194	240	48	14	16	34	0	4.21
Day Games	7	45.0	39	16	26	6	5	2	2	0	2.60	76	524.1	426	231	305	48	27	24	25	0	3.38
Night Games	27	159.1	163	55	100	13	9	7	14	0	4.74	255	1741.0	1547	730	1060	181	60	103	107	0	3.94
April	5	31.1	32	7	22	2	1	2	2	0	3.73	40	258.1	230	118	166	22	13	11	14	0	4.08
May	6	34.1	40	10	20	6	0	0	4	0	6.55	56	351.1	344	147	198	39	10	21	23	0	4.66
June	5	32.2	28	15	24	3	2	1	2	0	2.48	60	461.2	329	194	272	29	18	28	20	0	2.73
July	6	36.1	30	8	15	1	5	2	3	0	3.47	54	380.2	318	168	237	34	14	16	29	0	3.85
August	6	35.1	41	13	23	1	3	3	3	0	5.09	61	407.0	391	185	253	44	17	29	24	0	4.42
Sept-Oct	6	34.1	31	18	22	6	2	1	2	0	4.19	60	406.1	361	149	239	61	15	22	22	0	3.50

	BA	OBA	SA	AB	H	2B	3B	HR	RBI	BB	SO	BA	OBA	SA	AB	H	2B	3B	HR	RBI	BB	SO
Total	.259	.325	.395	779	202	42	2	20	91	71	126	.234	.317	.374	8438	1973	343	46	249	954	961	1365
vs. Left	.251	.311	.387	382	96	17	1	11	42	34	56	.237	.319	.363	4121	977	149	26	106	456	475	633
vs. Right	.267	.338	.403	397	106	25	1	9	49	37	70	.231	.315	.384	4317	996	194	20	143	498	486	732
Bases Empty	.258	.319	.378	466	120	26	0	10	10	38	83	.230	.306	.377	5165	1189	224	23	162	162	514	837
Leadoff	.254	.316	.345	197	50	9	0	3	3	16	33	.231	.294	.372	2174	502	93	11	64	64	174	324
Runners On Base	.262	.333	.422	313	82	16	2	10	81	33	43	.240	.332	.370	3273	784	119	23	87	792	447	528
Scoring Position	.237	.324	.321	190	45	8	1	2	61	25	27	.232	.340	.348	1901	441	61	12	45	681	321	353
Late and Close	.292	.329	.354	65	19	1	0	1	6	1	7	.233	.312	.352	960	224	33	3	25	88	104	164

JEFF INNIS — BR/TR — age 32 — NYN RP67 FIN/GB

1993

1993	G	IP	H	BB	SO	SB	CS	W	L	SV	ERA
Total	67	76.2	81	38	36	9	3	2	3	3	4.11
at Home	33	41.0	40	21	18	3	1	1	0	1	3.51
on Road	34	35.2	41	17	18	6	2	1	3	2	4.79
on Grass	49	59.1	66	31	28	6	2	2	2	1	4.70
on Turf	18	17.1	15	7	8	3	1	0	1	2	2.08
Day Games	23	28.1	30	9	14	4	1	1	1	0	4.45
Night Games	44	48.1	51	29	22	5	2	1	2	3	3.91
April	9	11.2	12	2	5	0	0	0	1	0	3.86
May	13	13.1	19	7	4	0	2	0	1	1	4.72
June	11	10.0	10	5	7	1	0	0	0	0	5.40
July	11	10.0	16	7	7	2	0	1	0	0	7.20
August	12	14.0	8	5	6	3	0	0	1	2	1.93
Sept-Oct	11	17.2	16	12	7	3	1	1	0	0	3.06

	BA	OBA	SA	AB	H	2B	3B	HR	RBI	BB	SO
Total	.278	.372	.392	291	81	16	1	5	36	38	36
vs. Left	.296	.409	.357	115	34	4	0	1	12	19	11
vs. Right	.267	.347	.415	176	47	12	1	4	24	19	25
Bases Empty	.305	.380	.433	141	43	9	0	3	3	14	15
Leadoff	.297	.375	.406	64	19	4	0	1	1	6	9
Runners On Base	.253	.365	.353	150	38	7	1	2	33	24	21
Scoring Position	.274	.417	.400	95	26	6	0	2	32	21	13
Late and Close	.236	.340	.360	89	21	2	0	3	9	13	12

7-YEAR TOTALS (1987–1993)

	G	IP	H	BB	SO	SB	CS	W	L	SV	ERA
Total	288	360.0	337	121	192	47	14	10	20	5	3.05
at Home	148	187.2	159	64	102	17	5	6	11	3	2.59
on Road	140	172.1	178	57	90	30	9	4	9	2	3.55
on Grass	208	260.2	243	89	141	28	7	8	14	3	3.18
on Turf	80	99.1	94	32	51	19	7	2	6	2	2.72
Day Games	98	122.0	125	35	73	20	6	3	8	0	3.54
Night Games	190	238.0	212	86	119	27	8	7	12	5	2.80
April	30	36.0	37	11	25	9	0	3	5	0	4.25
May	40	47.2	49	17	20	5	4	1	2	1	3.02
June	58	69.2	65	21	45	10	2	2	3	1	2.84
July	56	78.1	74	24	39	5	3	2	5	1	3.45
August	56	61.1	55	19	37	11	0	0	2	2	2.79
Sept-Oct	48	67.0	57	29	26	7	5	2	3	0	2.42

	BA	OBA	SA	AB	H	2B	3B	HR	RBI	BB	SO
Total	.253	.319	.352	1332	337	52	7	22	144	121	192
vs. Left	.290	.372	.407	551	160	27	2	11	70	68	55
vs. Right	.227	.279	.314	781	177	25	5	11	74	53	137
Bases Empty	.262	.308	.383	729	191	29	4	17	17	42	107
Leadoff	.283	.331	.388	304	86	12	1	6	6	20	51
Runners On Base	.242	.332	.315	603	146	23	3	5	127	79	85
Scoring Position	.224	.334	.290	393	88	13	2	3	119	66	62
Late and Close	.277	.358	.398	440	122	18	4	9	54	51	60

DANNY JACKSON — BR/TL — age 32 — PHI SP32 FIN/GB

1993

1993	G	IP	H	BB	SO	SB	CS	W	L	SV	ERA
Total	32	210.1	214	80	120	15	7	12	11	0	3.77
at Home	16	109.2	119	32	67	8	2	8	5	0	3.86
on Road	16	100.2	95	48	53	7	5	4	6	0	3.67
on Grass	10	66.2	59	32	34	5	3	4	4	0	2.84
on Turf	22	143.2	155	48	86	10	4	8	7	0	4.20
Day Games	10	61.0	59	31	36	8	3	3	3	0	4.13
Night Games	22	149.1	155	49	84	7	4	9	8	0	3.62
April	5	33.1	32	12	19	4	2	2	0	0	3.51
May	5	34.0	30	10	18	2	1	2	2	0	3.97
June	6	43.1	38	17	18	0	2	3	2	0	2.91
July	6	40.0	49	20	30	4	1	2	4	0	4.72
August	4	26.2	25	7	16	1	0	2	1	0	1.35
Sept-Oct	6	33.0	40	14	19	4	1	1	2	0	5.73

	BA	OBA	SA	AB	H	2B	3B	HR	RBI	BB	SO
Total	.263	.329	.370	813	214	39	6	12	87	80	120
vs. Left	.296	.379	.415	142	42	5	0	4	19	16	23
vs. Right	.256	.319	.361	671	172	34	6	8	68	64	97
Bases Empty	.258	.333	.370	438	113	24	2	7	7	45	62
Leadoff	.228	.303	.365	197	45	13	1	4	4	19	25
Runners On Base	.269	.325	.371	375	101	15	4	5	80	35	58
Scoring Position	.268	.332	.397	209	56	10	4	5	75	24	36
Late and Close	.316	.400	.500	38	12	4	0	1	6	6	2

10-YEAR TOTALS (1984–1993)

	G	IP	H	BB	SO	SB	CS	W	L	SV	ERA
Total	275	1669.2	1650	672	976	109	70	92	102	1	3.77
at Home	138	850.2	835	325	480	48	26	51	42	1	3.55
on Road	137	819.0	815	347	496	61	44	41	60	0	4.00
on Grass	111	675.1	668	286	406	41	41	34	43	0	3.70
on Turf	164	994.1	982	386	570	68	29	58	59	1	3.82
Day Games	93	502.0	537	233	304	37	32	21	37	1	4.61
Night Games	182	1167.2	1113	439	672	72	38	71	65	0	3.41
April	41	229.2	237	117	110	17	13	7	17	0	4.31
May	46	271.0	269	110	172	15	12	13	18	0	3.85
June	47	301.0	304	132	177	20	19	22	18	0	4.07
July	42	264.2	232	96	165	19	9	17	15	1	2.89
August	42	266.1	247	88	171	15	7	18	13	0	3.55
Sept-Oct	57	337.0	361	129	181	23	10	15	21	0	3.95

	BA	OBA	SA	AB	H	2B	3B	HR	RBI	BB	SO
Total	.260	.332	.365	6355	1650	279	52	95	693	672	976
vs. Left	.269	.344	.366	1121	302	43	10	15	128	124	227
vs. Right	.258	.329	.365	5234	1348	236	42	80	565	548	749
Bases Empty	.248	.324	.350	3558	884	154	32	48	48	379	561
Leadoff	.247	.333	.352	1550	383	69	14	22	22	189	235
Runners On Base	.274	.341	.383	2797	766	125	20	47	645	293	415
Scoring Position	.270	.340	.378	1625	438	78	10	26	576	185	260
Late and Close	.260	.319	.385	600	156	26	5	13	61	51	94

RANDY JOHNSON — BR/TL — age 31 — SEA SP34, RP1 POW/FB

1993

1993	G	IP	H	BB	SO	SB	CS	W	L	SV	ERA
Total	35	255.1	185	99	308	28	12	19	8	1	3.24
at Home	20	151.0	102	53	193	14	5	11	3	1	2.86
on Road	15	104.1	83	46	115	14	7	8	5	0	3.80
on Grass	11	70.1	59	42	79	12	7	5	4	0	4.86
on Turf	24	185.0	126	57	229	16	5	14	4	1	2.63
Day Games	10	79.2	56	34	98	11	6	5	2	0	3.05
Night Games	25	175.2	129	65	210	17	6	14	6	1	3.33
April	5	39.1	33	15	44	2	3	3	1	0	2.97
May	6	44.0	29	18	48	6	4	3	2	0	2.45
June	6	46.1	31	19	65	8	2	4	1	0	3.11
July	5	29.1	28	16	30	4	1	0	3	0	7.36
August	7	44.1	36	16	54	5	1	4	1	0	3.45
Sept-Oct	6	52.0	28	15	67	3	1	5	0	1	1.73

	BA	OBA	SA	AB	H	2B	3B	HR	RBI	BB	SO
Total	.203	.290	.322	913	185	37	4	22	88	99	52
vs. Left	.183	.256	.239	71	13	4	0	0	6	4	27
vs. Right	.204	.293	.329	842	172	33	3	22	82	95	25
Bases Empty	.189	.276	.323	566	107	24	2	16	16	57	185
Leadoff	.199	.297	.338	231	46	13	2	5	5	26	69
Runners On Base	.225	.312	.320	347	78	13	1	6	72	42	133
Scoring Position	.244	.325	.341	205	50	9	1	3	65	26	170
Late and Close	.159	.266	.290	107	17	5	0	3	16	14	50

6-YEAR TOTALS (1988–1993)

	G	IP	H	BB	SO	SB	CS	W	L	SV	ERA
Total	165	1073.1	834	618	1126	152	51	68	56	1	3.78
at Home	84	563.1	401	301	614	65	28	37	24	1	3.29
on Road	81	510.0	433	317	512	87	23	31	32	0	4.32
on Grass	61	390.0	322	257	394	70	21	26	22	0	4.41
on Turf	104	683.1	512	361	732	82	30	42	34	1	3.42
Day Games	43	274.2	218	168	303	49	14	18	11	0	4.26
Night Games	122	798.2	616	450	823	103	37	50	45	1	3.62
April	22	139.0	117	74	130	13	10	10	7	0	3.76
May	28	170.0	131	120	175	29	10	8	13	0	4.39
June	23	151.1	102	99	165	19	6	14	4	0	3.27
July	28	187.0	155	116	184	33	4	8	14	0	3.99
August	30	201.1	153	97	214	32	10	16	8	0	3.58
Sept-Oct	34	224.2	176	112	258	26	11	12	10	0	3.69

	BA	OBA	SA	AB	H	2B	3B	HR	RBI	BB	SO
Total	.215	.328	.335	3871	834	161	13	92	432	618	870
vs. Left	.196	.284	.271	409	80	16	0	5	47	46	115
vs. Right	.218	.333	.343	3462	754	145	13	87	385	572	755
Bases Empty	.206	.323	.332	2214	456	88	10	57	57	352	635
Leadoff	.228	.347	.357	953	217	45	6	22	22	160	264
Runners On Base	.228	.335	.339	1657	378	73	3	35	375	266	235
Scoring Position	.225	.336	.330	996	224	44	2	19	331	173	65
Late and Close	.186	.304	.283	360	67	12	1	7	33	57	131

DOUG JONES — BR/TR — age 37 — HOU RP71 FIN/GB

1993	G	IP	H	BB	SO	SB	CS	W	L	SV	ERA
Total	71	85.1	102	21	66	2	0	4	10	26	4.54
at Home	30	36.0	43	8	25	0	0	3	4	8	5.00
on Road	41	49.1	59	13	41	2	0	1	6	18	4.20
on Grass	28	33.2	47	8	25	2	0	1	5	12	5.61
on Turf	43	51.2	55	13	41	0	0	3	5	14	3.83
Day Games	29	36.0	33	7	25	1	0	2	4	11	3.00
Night Games	42	49.1	69	14	41	1	0	2	6	15	5.66
April	11	15.2	11	2	15	0	0	1	0	4	1.72
May	14	17.2	20	3	12	0	0	1	4	7	4.58
June	10	12.2	27	3	8	1	0	1	2	2	9.95
July	13	12.2	13	6	10	1	0	0	2	5	4.26
August	13	16.2	13	3	11	0	0	1	2	5	2.16
Sept-Oct	10	10.0	18	4	10	0	0	0	0	3	6.30

8-YEAR TOTALS (1986–1993)

	G	IP	H	BB	SO	SB	CS	W	L	SV	ERA
Total	423	618.0	615	136	498	17	7	41	50	190	3.03
at Home	219	316.2	323	70	252	5	5	26	26	84	3.52
on Road	204	301.1	292	66	246	12	2	15	24	106	2.51
on Grass	281	421.2	437	90	334	11	4	28	35	130	3.20
on Turf	142	196.1	178	46	164	6	3	13	15	60	2.66
Day Games	139	191.1	172	41	144	2	2	9	12	70	2.45
Night Games	284	426.2	443	95	354	15	5	32	38	120	3.29
April	59	80.2	79	20	81	2	2	3	5	30	2.45
May	70	92.0	88	17	65	2	0	6	11	37	3.72
June	61	76.1	88	15	57	2	0	6	8	27	3.89
July	74	108.2	89	29	84	4	0	9	10	27	2.73
August	72	106.2	93	22	78	1	2	4	9	35	2.78
Sept-Oct	87	153.2	178	33	133	6	3	13	7	34	2.87

	BA	OBA	SA	AB	H	2B	3B	HR	RBI	BB	SO
Total	.298	.344	.392	342	102	11	0	7	50	21	66
vs. Left	.273	.335	.339	165	45	5	0	2	21	12	25
vs. Right	.322	.353	.441	177	57	6	0	5	29	9	41
Bases Empty	.254	.292	.303	185	47	6	0	1	1	9	36
Leadoff	.278	.313	.342	79	22	2	0	1	1	4	16
Runners On Base	.350	.401	.497	157	55	5	0	6	49	12	30
Scoring Position	.359	.427	.500	92	33	4	0	3	43	10	20
Late and Close	.318	.374	.421	195	62	5	0	5	35	16	34

	BA	OBA	SA	AB	H	2B	3B	HR	RBI	BB	SO
Total	.259	.303	.350	2376	615	98	10	33	295	136	498
vs. Left	.253	.299	.348	1235	312	54	5	18	149	79	215
vs. Right	.266	.307	.352	1141	303	44	5	15	146	57	283
Bases Empty	.260	.295	.338	1182	307	53	2	12	12	51	244
Leadoff	.261	.297	.338	506	132	24	0	5	5	23	101
Runners On Base	.258	.309	.362	1194	308	45	8	21	283	85	254
Scoring Position	.263	.320	.378	716	188	32	6	13	261	61	157
Late and Close	.265	.311	.359	1539	408	66	8	21	198	93	319

SCOTT KAMIENIECKI — BR/TR — age 30 — NYA SP20, RP10 FIN/GB

1993	G	IP	H	BB	SO	SB	CS	W	L	SV	ERA
Total	30	154.1	163	59	72	7	10	10	7	1	4.08
at Home	18	103.0	104	36	56	4	6	8	2	0	3.84
on Road	12	51.1	59	23	16	3	4	2	5	1	4.56
on Grass	28	144.2	151	56	70	7	9	9	6	1	3.98
on Turf	2	9.2	12	3	2	0	1	1	1	0	5.59
Day Games	8	47.0	34	15	21	6	1	4	0	1	2.68
Night Games	22	107.1	129	44	51	1	9	6	7	0	4.70
April	4	15.2	14	8	3	3	0	0	0	1	2.30
May	7	14.1	16	8	8	1	3	0	1	0	5.65
June	5	29.1	31	10	10	1	1	2	1	0	5.22
July	5	35.2	37	9	22	0	4	4	1	0	3.28
August	4	29.2	23	10	10	1	2	3	1	0	2.73
Sept-Oct	5	29.2	42	14	19	1	0	1	3	0	5.46

3-YEAR TOTALS (1991–1993)

	G	IP	H	BB	SO	SB	CS	W	L	SV	ERA
Total	67	397.2	410	155	194	40	18	20	25	1	4.19
at Home	37	225.1	223	83	117	16	11	16	8	0	3.91
on Road	30	172.1	187	72	77	24	7	4	17	1	4.54
on Grass	62	367.0	374	145	180	38	17	18	23	1	4.17
on Turf	5	30.2	36	10	14	2	1	2	2	0	4.40
Day Games	19	119.1	109	44	54	15	3	6	5	1	3.92
Night Games	48	278.1	301	111	140	25	15	14	20	0	4.30
April	4	15.2	14	8	3	3	0	0	0	1	2.30
May	13	56.2	55	26	24	7	4	1	3	0	3.97
June	13	78.2	90	30	38	7	3	4	5	0	5.03
July	15	101.2	101	30	54	10	5	7	6	0	3.90
August	11	74.0	66	30	31	8	6	5	5	0	3.89
Sept-Oct	11	71.0	84	31	44	5	0	3	6	0	4.56

	BA	OBA	SA	AB	H	2B	3B	HR	RBI	BB	SO
Total	.277	.343	.423	589	163	25	5	17	71	59	72
vs. Left	.284	.348	.450	282	80	14	4	9	32	28	38
vs. Right	.270	.338	.397	307	83	11	2	8	39	31	34
Bases Empty	.265	.330	.402	343	91	13	2	10	10	32	47
Leadoff	.288	.346	.418	146	42	4	0	5	5	13	18
Runners On Base	.293	.361	.451	246	72	12	3	7	61	27	25
Scoring Position	.311	.399	.451	122	38	5	0	4	51	20	12
Late and Close	.290	.436	.387	31	9	0	1	0	3	8	5

	BA	OBA	SA	AB	H	2B	3B	HR	RBI	BB	SO
Total	.270	.340	.407	1517	410	75	9	38	175	155	194
vs. Left	.279	.346	.423	735	205	37	6	19	80	76	102
vs. Right	.262	.335	.391	782	205	38	3	19	95	79	92
Bases Empty	.269	.329	.407	889	239	40	4	25	25	75	113
Leadoff	.285	.338	.426	383	109	15	0	13	13	29	50
Runners On Base	.272	.354	.406	628	171	35	5	13	150	80	81
Scoring Position	.278	.372	.403	352	98	18	1	8	131	58	50
Late and Close	.349	.445	.514	109	38	7	1	3	17	18	13

JIMMY KEY — BR/TL — age 33 — NYA SP34 FIN/GB

1993	G	IP	H	BB	SO	SB	CS	W	L	SV	ERA
Total	34	236.2	219	43	173	15	6	18	6	0	3.00
at Home	14	104.2	89	17	80	10	4	8	2	0	2.75
on Road	20	132.0	130	26	93	5	2	10	4	0	3.20
on Grass	30	212.0	189	36	152	12	5	16	5	0	2.84
on Turf	4	24.2	30	7	21	3	1	2	1	0	4.38
Day Games	9	62.0	68	8	46	2	2	3	2	0	4.35
Night Games	25	174.2	151	35	127	13	4	15	4	0	2.52
April	5	38.2	22	5	24	1	0	3	0	0	0.93
May	6	44.2	39	4	40	6	3	2	2	0	2.82
June	6	38.0	39	9	28	4	1	5	0	0	3.08
July	6	43.2	41	6	25	1	1	2	2	0	3.50
August	5	32.0	40	5	22	2	1	3	1	0	5.06
Sept-Oct	6	39.2	38	14	34	1	0	3	1	0	2.95

10-YEAR TOTALS (1984–1993)

	G	IP	H	BB	SO	SB	CS	W	L	SV	ERA
Total	351	1932.1	1843	447	1117	80	52	134	87	10	3.37
at Home	180	1009.0	966	234	587	45	29	68	47	3	3.44
on Road	171	923.1	877	213	530	35	23	66	40	7	3.29
on Grass	151	860.2	797	201	513	38	23	61	36	5	3.18
on Turf	200	1071.2	1046	246	604	42	29	73	51	5	3.53
Day Games	116	650.1	639	147	378	27	20	40	35	1	3.65
Night Games	235	1282.0	1204	300	739	53	32	94	52	9	3.23
April	46	252.0	222	58	139	7	7	20	9	1	3.36
May	61	310.0	289	72	184	19	12	21	14	3	3.63
June	55	309.0	293	68	184	15	9	19	15	0	2.80
July	61	363.0	363	77	188	8	10	21	19	0	3.62
August	59	306.2	317	72	172	18	10	24	18	3	3.87
Sept-Oct	69	391.2	359	100	250	13	4	29	12	3	3.01

	BA	OBA	SA	AB	H	2B	3B	HR	RBI	BB	SO
Total	.246	.279	.382	889	219	35	4	26	81	43	173
vs. Left	.260	.292	.420	131	34	3	0	6	13	6	26
vs. Right	.244	.277	.376	758	185	32	4	20	68	37	147
Bases Empty	.257	.288	.419	568	146	29	3	19	19	24	101
Leadoff	.250	.278	.422	232	58	11	1	9	9	8	40
Runners On Base	.227	.264	.318	321	73	6	1	7	62	19	72
Scoring Position	.225	.267	.308	169	38	3	1	3	53	13	40
Late and Close	.268	.276	.482	56	15	3	0	3	8	1	7

	BA	OBA	SA	AB	H	2B	3B	HR	RBI	BB	SO
Total	.251	.294	.388	7336	1843	357	36	191	719	447	1117
vs. Left	.232	.276	.330	1286	298	42	6	24	114	73	251
vs. Right	.255	.298	.400	6050	1545	315	30	167	605	374	866
Bases Empty	.244	.285	.376	4577	1118	219	22	114	114	245	707
Leadoff	.245	.276	.383	1909	467	92	10	51	51	77	273
Runners On Base	.263	.309	.407	2759	725	138	14	77	605	202	410
Scoring Position	.250	.312	.385	1441	360	70	10	35	490	148	223
Late and Close	.269	.321	.409	711	191	25	3	23	87	55	97

DARRYL KILE — BR/TR — age 26 — HOU SP26, RP6 POW/FB · 3-YEAR TOTALS (1991–1993)

1993	G	IP	H	BB	SO	SB	CS	W	L	SV	ERA	G	IP	H	BB	SO	SB	CS	W	L	SV	ERA
Total	32	171.2	152	69	141	9	5	15	8	0	3.51	91	450.2	420	216	331	27	11	27	29	0	3.69
at Home	16	92.0	66	32	83	5	1	9	4	0	2.35	45	233.1	195	113	183	15	3	16	14	0	3.01
on Road	16	79.2	86	37	58	4	4	6	4	0	4.86	46	217.1	225	103	148	12	8	11	15	0	4.43
on Grass	11	56.0	56	27	39	3	3	4	3	0	4.98	28	138.1	129	64	95	7	5	6	8	0	4.29
on Turf	21	115.2	96	42	102	6	2	11	5	0	2.80	63	312.1	291	152	236	20	6	21	21	0	3.43
Day Games	5	32.1	24	10	29	4	1	2	2	0	1.95	21	102.2	94	49	75	9	2	3	10	0	3.77
Night Games	27	139.1	128	59	112	5	4	13	6	0	3.88	70	348.0	326	167	256	18	9	24	19	0	3.67
April	4	10.0	7	7	7	0	0	1	0	0	3.60	16	57.2	47	29	45	2	0	3	3	0	3.75
May	6	22.1	17	10	14	0	2	2	1	0	3.22	17	57.2	62	38	29	4	5	2	4	0	4.37
June	5	31.0	26	11	23	1	1	5	0	0	1.16	14	74.1	58	40	46	4	2	7	2	0	2.18
July	6	36.0	39	11	31	2	1	3	2	0	4.50	12	61.2	69	22	53	4	2	5	6	0	4.23
August	5	34.0	28	13	29	2	1	3	2	0	4.24	15	89.0	89	39	66	4	1	5	7	0	4.45
Sept-Oct	6	38.1	35	17	37	4	0	1	3	0	3.99	17	110.1	95	48	92	9	1	5	7	0	3.43

	BA	OBA	SA	AB	H	2B	3B	HR	RBI	BB	SO	BA	OBA	SA	AB	H	2B	3B	HR	RBI	BB	SO
Total	.239	.324	.341	637	152	21	4	12	66	69	141	.247	.338	.373	1698	420	75	15	36	185	216	331
vs. Left	.236	.326	.345	330	78	8	2	8	36	44	59	.251	.351	.378	944	237	42	9	20	104	146	168
vs. Right	.241	.322	.336	307	74	13	2	4	30	25	82	.243	.321	.366	754	183	33	6	16	81	70	163
Bases Empty	.240	.334	.351	362	87	11	4	7	7	42	88	.247	.345	.383	915	226	43	9	21	21	125	199
Leadoff	.228	.279	.395	167	38	6	2	6	6	11	34	.250	.330	.430	416	104	22	7	13	13	48	89
Runners On Base	.236	.311	.327	275	65	10	0	5	59	27	53	.248	.329	.361	783	194	32	6	15	164	91	132
Scoring Position	.245	.317	.324	139	34	5	0	2	49	16	27	.223	.318	.330	457	102	18	9	9	139	68	86
Late and Close	.294	.333	.382	34	10	0	0	1	3	2	12	.264	.343	.414	87	23	3	2	2	10	11	21

TOM KRAMER — BB/TR — age 26 — CLE RP23, SP16 POW/FB · 2-YEAR TOTALS (1991–1993)

1993	G	IP	H	BB	SO	SB	CS	W	L	SV	ERA	G	IP	H	BB	SO	SB	CS	W	L	SV	ERA
Total	39	121.0	126	59	71	6	7	7	3	0	4.02	43	125.2	136	65	75	6	7	7	3	0	4.51
at Home	15	55.0	53	28	41	4	5	3	1	0	4.42	16	56.2	59	29	41	4	5	3	1	0	5.08
on Road	24	66.0	73	31	30	2	2	4	2	0	3.68	27	69.0	77	36	34	2	2	4	2	0	4.04
on Grass	32	101.2	104	49	60	6	7	5	1	0	3.81	36	106.1	114	55	64	6	7	5	1	0	4.40
on Turf	7	19.1	22	10	11	0	0	2	2	0	5.12	7	19.1	22	10	11	0	0	2	2	0	5.12
Day Games	13	40.2	47	26	25	0	3	2	1	0	3.54	15	43.1	54	28	26	0	3	2	1	0	4.36
Night Games	26	80.1	79	33	46	6	4	5	2	0	4.26	28	82.1	82	37	49	6	4	5	2	0	4.59
April	10	13.1	15	6	10	0	0	0	1	0	4.05	10	13.1	15	6	10	0	0	0	1	0	4.05
May	8	28.1	18	10	21	2	3	1	1	0	2.86	8	28.1	18	10	21	2	3	1	1	0	2.86
June	6	29.2	32	13	18	3	2	2	0	0	4.55	6	29.2	32	13	18	3	2	2	0	0	4.55
July	4	20.2	21	4	8	1	1	1	0	0	3.05	4	20.2	21	4	8	1	1	1	0	0	3.05
August	6	20.2	22	20	9	0	1	2	1	0	5.66	6	20.2	22	20	9	0	1	2	1	0	5.66
Sept-Oct	5	8.1	18	6	5	0	0	1	0	0	4.32	9	13.0	28	12	9	0	0	1	0	0	9.00

	BA	OBA	SA	AB	H	2B	3B	HR	RBI	BB	SO	BA	OBA	SA	AB	H	2B	3B	HR	RBI	BB	SO
Total	.269	.352	.450	469	126	24	2	19	61	59	71	.278	.361	.467	490	136	27	3	20	72	65	75
vs. Left	.236	.328	.399	233	55	8	0	10	32	31	28	.246	.338	.414	244	60	9	1	10	38	34	29
vs. Right	.301	.375	.500	236	71	16	2	9	29	28	43	.309	.384	.520	246	76	18	2	10	34	31	46
Bases Empty	.290	.363	.484	252	73	16	0	11	11	28	41	.294	.366	.500	262	77	18	0	12	12	29	43
Leadoff	.321	.410	.519	106	34	9	0	4	4	15	12	.318	.405	.518	110	35	10	0	4	4	15	13
Runners On Base	.244	.339	.410	217	53	8	2	8	50	31	30	.259	.356	.430	228	59	9	3	8	60	36	32
Scoring Position	.220	.348	.354	127	28	3	1	4	40	25	22	.235	.363	.382	136	32	4	2	4	50	29	24
Late and Close	.194	.356	.333	36	7	2	0	1	3	8	4	.194	.383	.333	36	7	2	0	1	4	10	4

MARK LANGSTON — BR/TL — age 34 — CAL SP35 POW/FB · 10-YEAR TOTALS (1984–1993)

1993	G	IP	H	BB	SO	SB	CS	W	L	SV	ERA	G	IP	H	BB	SO	SB	CS	W	L	SV	ERA
Total	35	256.1	220	85	196	10	12	16	11	0	3.20	334	2329.0	2037	1027	2000	166	117	144	126	0	3.69
at Home	18	135.1	118	43	112	7	7	9	5	0	3.66	166	1187.1	1034	490	1071	92	58	72	60	0	3.88
on Road	17	121.0	102	42	84	3	5	7	6	0	2.68	168	1141.2	1003	537	929	74	59	72	66	0	3.48
on Grass	30	220.1	182	72	175	9	10	15	8	0	3.19	196	1355.0	1186	585	1110	87	70	85	72	0	3.58
on Turf	5	36.0	38	13	21	1	2	1	3	0	3.25	138	974.0	851	442	890	79	47	59	54	0	3.83
Day Games	9	59.2	57	18	49	3	3	4	3	0	3.02	94	604.2	573	283	552	53	33	34	38	0	4.29
Night Games	26	196.2	163	67	147	7	9	12	8	0	3.25	240	1724.1	1464	744	1448	113	84	110	88	0	3.48
April	5	36.0	24	12	36	2	2	3	0	0	2.50	47	312.2	291	138	262	26	17	17	17	0	4.03
May	6	44.0	36	14	36	3	2	2	1	0	2.25	58	417.1	361	173	335	22	23	27	19	0	3.56
June	6	43.2	41	16	30	1	4	1	1	0	3.09	53	375.0	329	153	336	30	16	28	19	0	3.26
July	5	39.0	35	12	22	3	2	1	3	0	3.69	53	366.2	328	152	313	28	18	17	25	0	4.30
August	6	44.1	33	17	35	0	3	4	1	0	2.44	60	410.2	350	213	326	20	18	28	20	0	3.73
Sept-Oct	7	49.1	51	14	37	1	2	2	5	0	4.93	63	446.2	378	198	428	40	25	26	26	0	3.39

	BA	OBA	SA	AB	H	2B	3B	HR	RBI	BB	SO	BA	OBA	SA	AB	H	2B	3B	HR	RBI	BB	SO
Total	.234	.295	.347	942	220	39	1	22	89	85	196	.237	.319	.371	8596	2037	383	49	225	929	1027	2000
vs. Left	.178	.235	.244	135	24	3	0	2	11	10	28	.195	.276	.291	1308	255	46	7	22	114	139	323
vs. Right	.243	.306	.364	807	196	36	1	20	78	75	168	.245	.327	.386	7288	1782	337	42	203	815	888	1677
Bases Empty	.216	.293	.336	569	123	23	0	15	15	61	134	.227	.320	.362	5038	1146	206	25	141	141	663	1202
Leadoff	.238	.308	.368	239	57	13	0	6	6	23	58	.229	.318	.358	2148	491	91	9	56	56	273	493
Runners On Base	.260	.299	.365	373	97	16	1	7	74	24	62	.250	.319	.384	3558	891	177	24	84	788	364	798
Scoring Position	.272	.310	.382	191	52	12	0	3	64	14	33	.259	.333	.404	1896	492	103	15	47	690	228	451
Late and Close	.230	.301	.309	139	32	2	0	3	9	14	23	.248	.321	.370	1021	253	44	3	25	99	112	217

TIM LEARY — BR/TR — age 36 — SEA SP27, RP6 FIN/GB

10-YEAR TOTALS (1984–1993)

1993	G	IP	H	BB	SO	SB	CS	W	L	SV	ERA	G	IP	H	BB	SO	SB	CS	W	L	SV	ERA
Total	33	169.1	202	58	68	10	9	11	9	0	5.05	283	1457.2	1528	519	867	143	60	76	103	1	4.32
at Home	14	67.0	82	22	25	6	4	5	3	0	4.97	136	703.0	734	252	427	83	34	35	51	0	4.20
on Road	19	102.1	120	36	43	4	5	6	6	0	5.10	147	754.2	794	267	440	60	26	41	52	1	4.44
on Grass	15	82.0	91	29	35	2	5	6	4	0	4.61	194	985.0	1033	362	604	93	49	51	72	1	4.27
on Turf	18	87.1	111	29	33	8	4	5	5	0	5.46	89	472.2	495	157	263	50	11	25	31	0	4.44
Day Games	13	62.2	77	21	19	3	2	4	3	0	5.89	85	429.1	477	170	249	49	22	21	32	0	5.03
Night Games	20	106.2	125	37	49	7	7	7	6	0	4.56	198	1028.1	1051	349	618	94	38	55	71	1	4.03
April	6	13.1	17	8	9	0	1	0	1	0	7.43	41	203.1	194	65	143	18	8	12	9	0	3.81
May	6	40.0	40	11	14	3	1	3	1	0	3.83	56	288.2	292	107	174	39	15	13	20	0	4.24
June	5	31.1	35	4	9	1	1	3	1	0	4.02	51	285.0	296	80	139	20	8	14	19	0	4.23
July	4	20.1	25	8	7	0	0	2	1	0	5.31	41	188.2	225	77	109	20	8	12	17	0	5.39
August	6	24.0	38	12	7	2	2	0	3	0	9.75	47	223.2	236	94	138	15	13	13	17	0	4.51
Sept-Oct	6	40.1	47	15	22	4	4	3	2	0	3.35	47	268.1	285	96	164	31	8	12	21	1	3.99

	BA	OBA	SA	AB	H	2B	3B	HR	RBI	BB	SO	BA	OBA	SA	AB	H	2B	3B	HR	RBI	BB	SO
Total	.300	.362	.470	674	202	38	7	21	86	58	68	.272	.337	.408	5616	1528	263	36	143	644	519	867
vs. Left	.338	.399	.521	340	115	29	3	9	37	33	31	.282	.351	.426	2838	801	148	22	72	322	298	386
vs. Right	.260	.323	.419	334	87	9	4	12	49	25	37	.262	.323	.390	2778	727	115	14	71	322	221	481
Bases Empty	.302	.354	.503	384	116	23	3	16	16	28	39	.265	.324	.407	3279	868	151	21	91	91	262	513
Leadoff	.317	.374	.509	167	53	7	2	7	7	15	19	.280	.341	.441	1399	392	62	11	47	47	118	187
Runners On Base	.297	.371	.428	290	86	15	4	5	70	30	29	.282	.355	.410	2337	660	112	15	52	553	257	354
Scoring Position	.266	.373	.405	173	46	10	1	4	63	25	16	.258	.353	.388	1332	344	63	10	30	483	201	229
Late and Close	.371	.488	.657	35	13	0	2	2	5	8	5	.272	.353	.374	489	133	17	3	9	44	58	84

CHARLIE LEIBRANDT — BR/TL — age 38 — TEX SP26 FIN/FB

10-YEAR TOTALS (1984–1993)

1993	G	IP	H	BB	SO	SB	CS	W	L	SV	ERA	G	IP	H	BB	SO	SB	CS	W	L	SV	ERA
Total	26	150.1	169	45	89	19	5	9	10	0	4.55	312	1992.1	2030	537	1015	175	84	124	102	0	3.60
at Home	12	68.1	79	25	40	7	3	1	6	0	4.74	145	932.2	985	233	432	75	49	60	45	0	3.53
on Road	14	82.0	90	20	49	12	2	8	4	0	4.39	167	1059.2	1045	304	583	100	35	64	57	0	3.66
on Grass	21	124.0	135	38	77	14	3	7	7	0	4.14	168	1071.2	1069	293	570	104	39	64	61	0	3.63
on Turf	5	26.1	34	7	12	5	2	2	3	0	6.49	144	920.2	961	244	445	71	45	60	41	0	3.57
Day Games	6	35.2	40	6	19	5	2	4	2	0	5.05	86	526.0	543	141	263	64	29	35	29	0	3.59
Night Games	20	114.2	129	39	70	14	3	5	8	0	4.40	226	1466.1	1487	396	752	111	55	89	73	0	3.60
April	5	31.1	32	8	16	4	0	3	1	0	2.59	40	262.2	248	90	133	24	10	20	12	0	2.91
May	6	43.2	37	4	30	4	2	3	1	0	2.47	46	300.1	304	65	143	32	20	14	18	0	3.81
June	5	27.1	38	15	15	3	2	1	2	0	6.59	56	381.1	384	101	174	30	21	21	20	0	3.38
July	6	34.2	39	10	17	7	1	2	3	0	5.19	56	347.0	377	104	174	35	13	20	20	0	4.28
August	2	5.0	13	4	6	0	0	0	2	0	19.80	53	337.1	349	78	191	21	9	24	16	0	3.71
Sept-Oct	2	8.1	10	4	5	1	0	0	1	0	4.32	61	363.2	368	99	200	33	11	25	16	0	3.42

	BA	OBA	SA	AB	H	2B	3B	HR	RBI	BB	SO	BA	OBA	SA	AB	H	2B	3B	HR	RBI	BB	SO
Total	.284	.336	.440	595	169	40	4	15	73	45	89	.264	.313	.386	7683	2030	388	44	153	786	537	1015
vs. Left	.384	.418	.581	86	33	9	1	2	12	4	10	.268	.312	.366	1479	397	65	8	21	154	85	187
vs. Right	.267	.323	.417	509	136	31	3	13	61	41	79	.263	.313	.391	6204	1633	323	36	132	632	452	828
Bases Empty	.302	.339	.448	344	104	22	2	8	8	16	49	.266	.306	.386	4619	1230	231	25	91	91	249	597
Leadoff	.311	.354	.457	151	47	14	1	2	2	8	24	.262	.298	.385	1967	516	102	11	39	39	92	215
Runners On Base	.259	.333	.430	251	65	18	2	7	65	29	40	.261	.323	.385	3064	800	157	19	62	695	288	418
Scoring Position	.272	.367	.457	151	41	12	2	4	57	24	20	.250	.324	.367	1740	435	83	14	31	602	205	236
Late and Close	.344	.364	.531	32	11	3	0	1	3	1	3	.240	.302	.339	670	161	28	4	10	46	58	83

DEREK LILLIQUIST — BL/TL — age 28 — CLE RP54, SP2 FIN/FB

5-YEAR TOTALS (1989–1993)

1993	G	IP	H	BB	SO	SB	CS	W	L	SV	ERA	G	IP	H	BB	SO	SB	CS	W	L	SV	ERA
Total	56	64.0	64	19	40	2	0	4	4	10	2.25	193	427.2	466	117	236	24	12	22	30	16	3.94
at Home	29	30.1	30	10	11	1	0	3	3	6	2.67	102	223.0	235	55	120	7	4	12	17	11	3.63
on Road	27	33.2	34	9	29	1	0	1	1	4	1.87	91	204.2	231	62	116	17	8	10	13	5	4.27
on Grass	51	56.1	59	16	36	2	0	3	4	9	2.56	162	341.0	370	87	192	15	7	15	26	15	4.04
on Turf	5	7.2	5	3	4	0	0	0	0	1	0.00	31	86.2	96	30	44	9	5	7	4	1	3.53
Day Games	16	21.0	20	2	15	1	0	1	1	4	3.00	62	118.1	132	35	73	9	3	7	8	7	4.56
Night Games	40	43.0	44	17	25	1	0	3	3	6	1.88	131	309.1	334	82	163	15	9	15	22	9	3.70
April	8	8.2	6	0	8	0	0	0	0	3	2.08	26	60.0	66	15	38	5	2	1	4	5	4.50
May	11	11.1	6	3	7	0	0	1	1	3	1.59	36	98.2	84	26	46	4	2	7	8	3	3.10
June	9	7.1	5	2	4	0	0	0	0	2	0.00	30	53.0	68	14	27	2	1	4	3	2	5.09
July	12	9.2	11	4	6	1	0	0	0	1	0.93	33	56.1	70	20	33	4	1	2	2	3	4.31
August	7	17.0	22	5	8	1	0	0	1	1	3.71	31	71.2	86	24	34	4	5	3	3	3	3.89
Sept-Oct	9	10.0	14	5	7	0	0	2	2	0	3.60	37	88.0	92	18	58	5	1	5	8	1	3.58

	BA	OBA	SA	AB	H	2B	3B	HR	RBI	BB	SO	BA	OBA	SA	AB	H	2B	3B	HR	RBI	BB	SO
Total	.264	.318	.384	242	64	12	1	5	22	19	40	.280	.327	.419	1666	466	89	4	45	184	117	236
vs. Left	.266	.294	.297	64	17	0	1	0	6	2	13	.267	.310	.384	367	98	15	2	8	40	20	81
vs. Right	.264	.327	.416	178	47	12	0	5	16	17	27	.283	.332	.429	1299	368	74	2	37	144	97	155
Bases Empty	.268	.323	.423	123	33	5	1	4	4	9	26	.264	.310	.413	958	253	51	4	28	28	56	151
Leadoff	.291	.316	.491	55	16	2	0	3	3	2	12	.254	.303	.411	401	102	19	1	14	14	25	66
Runners On Base	.261	.313	.345	119	31	7	0	1	18	10	14	.301	.351	.427	708	213	38	0	17	156	61	85
Scoring Position	.227	.286	.307	75	17	3	0	1	18	7	9	.273	.340	.402	410	112	23	0	10	135	48	56
Late and Close	.281	.341	.342	114	32	4	0	1	14	11	18	.270	.331	.363	311	84	14	0	5	32	30	58

ROB MACDONALD — BL/TL — age 29 — DET RP68 POW/FB

1993	G	IP	H	BB	SO	SB	CS	W	L	SV	ERA	4-YEAR TOTALS (1990–1993) G	IP	H	BB	SO	SB	CS	W	L	SV	ERA
Total	68	65.2	67	33	39	2	3	3	3	3	5.35	144	169.0	168	76	89	12	7	7	6	3	4.21
at Home	38	37.0	39	24	22	1	1	3	2	2	6.81	77	92.1	105	45	46	8	4	4	3	2	5.07
on Road	30	28.2	28	9	17	1	2	0	1	1	3.45	67	76.2	63	31	43	4	3	3	3	1	3.17
on Grass	55	53.2	53	29	31	2	2	3	2	2	5.37	81	88.0	78	44	49	5	3	5	3	2	4.30
on Turf	13	12.0	14	4	8	0	1	0	1	1	5.25	63	81.0	90	32	40	7	4	2	3	1	4.11
Day Games	30	29.0	29	10	15	1	1	1	0	1	6.52	57	67.2	56	24	32	6	1	3	1	1	4.12
Night Games	38	36.2	38	23	24	1	2	2	3	2	4.42	87	101.1	112	52	57	6	6	4	5	2	4.26
April	10	9.2	9	2	3	1	0	1	0	0	2.79	19	23.1	18	3	12	1	0	2	0	0	2.31
May	13	14.0	11	6	9	0	2	2	2	1	3.21	22	26.2	23	15	16	3	2	2	2	1	3.04
June	11	8.2	9	4	4	0	0	0	0	2	5.19	29	40.2	37	15	21	3	1	1	0	2	3.54
July	14	13.2	18	11	7	0	0	0	1	0	7.90	23	24.2	31	21	14	0	1	1	2	0	6.93
August	8	10.0	11	4	10	0	1	0	0	0	7.20	26	34.0	40	13	15	2	3	1	0	0	5.03
Sept-Oct	12	9.2	9	6	6	1	0	0	0	0	5.59	25	19.2	19	9	11	3	0	0	2	0	4.58

	BA	OBA	SA	AB	H	2B	3B	HR	RBI	BB	SO	BA	OBA	SA	AB	H	2B	3B	HR	RBI	BB	SO
Total	.268	.349	.444	250	67	16	2	8	48	33	39	.261	.337	.407	643	168	35	4	17	106	76	89
vs. Left	.225	.317	.416	89	20	4	2	3	12	12	21	.234	.311	.359	231	54	10	2	5	34	26	44
vs. Right	.292	.367	.460	161	47	12	0	5	36	21	18	.277	.352	.434	412	114	25	2	12	72	50	45
Bases Empty	.285	.362	.415	123	35	6	2	2	2	15	22	.253	.321	.380	332	84	15	3	7	7	32	44
Leadoff	.255	.345	.294	51	13	2	0	0	0	7	8	.217	.275	.326	138	30	3	0	4	4	11	14
Runners On Base	.252	.338	.472	127	32	10	0	6	46	18	17	.270	.354	.437	311	84	20	1	10	99	44	45
Scoring Position	.253	.351	.453	75	19	6	0	3	37	13	8	.294	.383	.460	187	55	13	0	6	85	31	24
Late and Close	.281	.353	.449	89	25	5	2	2	17	10	15	.244	.327	.389	180	44	7	2	5	32	22	31

GREG MADDUX — BR/TR — age 28 — ATL SP36 FIN/GB

1993	G	IP	H	BB	SO	SB	CS	W	L	SV	ERA	8-YEAR TOTALS (1986–1993) G	IP	H	BB	SO	SB	CS	W	L	SV	ERA
Total	36	267.0	228	52	197	27	6	20	10	0	2.36	248	1709.0	1580	507	1135	159	58	115	85	0	3.19
at Home	16	123.1	97	27	93	12	3	8	4	0	2.19	118	833.0	760	254	569	63	33	54	38	0	3.18
on Road	20	143.2	131	25	104	15	3	12	6	0	2.51	130	876.0	820	253	566	96	25	61	47	0	3.21
on Grass	27	202.0	168	41	148	20	3	16	6	0	2.41	176	1206.2	1100	375	809	100	39	83	59	0	3.24
on Turf	9	65.0	60	11	49	7	3	4	4	0	2.22	72	502.1	480	132	326	59	19	32	26	0	3.06
Day Games	9	66.0	61	17	48	5	1	5	2	0	1.91	125	840.1	831	273	566	75	33	54	45	0	3.44
Night Games	27	201.0	167	35	149	22	5	15	8	0	2.51	123	868.2	749	234	569	84	25	61	40	0	2.95
April	6	43.2	40	9	31	4	1	2	2	0	3.09	33	223.1	205	66	135	15	5	16	11	0	3.30
May	6	46.0	33	11	40	7	2	3	2	0	2.35	41	293.1	239	84	202	28	10	18	17	0	2.98
June	5	36.2	35	7	21	3	0	2	2	0	2.70	41	283.1	244	97	191	34	7	15	16	0	3.21
July	7	48.1	48	8	37	8	1	5	2	0	3.17	42	288.2	279	80	183	34	15	23	9	0	3.34
August	6	47.0	36	6	29	4	1	4	1	0	1.53	42	292.1	270	95	185	23	14	20	12	0	3.05
Sept-Oct	6	45.1	36	11	39	1	1	4	1	0	1.39	49	328.0	343	85	239	25	7	23	20	0	3.29

	BA	OBA	SA	AB	H	2B	3B	HR	RBI	BB	SO	BA	OBA	SA	AB	H	2B	3B	HR	RBI	BB	SO
Total	.232	.273	.317	984	228	38	2	14	75	52	197	.246	.305	.342	6414	1580	264	32	96	611	507	1135
vs. Left	.235	.280	.304	520	122	19	1	5	36	33	97	.262	.329	.360	3622	949	157	22	51	363	348	593
vs. Right	.228	.264	.332	464	106	19	1	9	39	19	100	.226	.274	.320	2792	631	107	10	45	248	159	542
Bases Empty	.240	.280	.346	592	142	26	2	11	11	29	124	.236	.291	.324	3799	896	146	14	53	53	267	724
Leadoff	.285	.325	.398	256	73	12	1	5	5	12	47	.251	.303	.345	1638	411	60	8	26	26	106	288
Runners On Base	.219	.262	.273	392	86	12	0	3	64	23	73	.262	.325	.370	2615	684	118	18	43	558	240	411
Scoring Position	.210	.271	.262	233	49	6	0	2	57	20	42	.251	.333	.347	1517	381	59	13	20	485	186	264
Late and Close	.207	.270	.341	135	28	6	0	4	10	11	33	.241	.310	.321	739	178	20	3	11	61	72	137

MIKE MADDUX — BL/TR — age 33 — NYN RP58 POW/GB

1993	G	IP	H	BB	SO	SB	CS	W	L	SV	ERA	8-YEAR TOTALS (1986–1993) G	IP	H	BB	SO	SB	CS	W	L	SV	ERA
Total	58	75.0	67	27	57	9	3	3	8	5	3.60	247	501.1	488	169	330	64	31	22	26	16	3.72
at Home	27	35.1	36	7	27	6	2	3	3	1	3.31	124	246.2	238	65	172	31	17	18	9	4	3.39
on Road	31	39.2	31	20	30	3	1	0	5	4	3.86	123	254.2	250	104	158	33	14	4	17	12	4.03
on Grass	43	52.0	56	21	38	8	2	3	6	2	4.33	155	274.1	265	101	174	37	17	12	14	12	3.74
on Turf	15	23.0	11	6	19	1	1	0	2	3	1.96	92	227.0	223	68	156	27	14	10	12	4	3.69
Day Games	21	25.1	14	7	19	3	1	1	1	1	1.07	77	174.0	153	57	109	21	11	7	6	3	3.57
Night Games	37	49.2	53	20	38	6	2	2	7	4	4.89	170	327.1	335	112	221	43	20	15	20	13	3.79
April	10	11.1	6	5	3	0	0	0	1	2	2.38	34	57.2	51	17	39	1	2	4	2	4	3.12
May	10	14.2	12	6	6	1	1	3	0	0	4.30	50	86.1	82	28	59	11	8	0	5	0	3.54
June	9	15.0	20	5	10	2	1	0	1	1	6.60	40	84.0	92	26	50	15	3	2	6	5	5.25
July	8	10.0	8	4	6	1	0	1	0	0	0.90	32	63.0	65	22	36	11	4	2	2	1	2.86
August	9	10.2	9	0	9	2	1	3	0	1	0.84	38	102.1	105	37	65	16	8	9	5	2	4.22
Sept-Oct	12	13.1	12	7	12	1	0	0	2	1	4.72	53	108.0	93	39	81	10	6	5	6	4	3.00

	BA	OBA	SA	AB	H	2B	3B	HR	RBI	BB	SO	BA	OBA	SA	AB	H	2B	3B	HR	RBI	BB	SO
Total	.243	.313	.344	276	67	13	3	3	38	27	57	.258	.322	.355	1889	488	85	8	27	215	169	330
vs. Left	.264	.351	.392	125	33	8	1	2	21	17	24	.264	.335	.354	979	258	45	4	12	108	103	160
vs. Right	.225	.279	.305	151	34	5	2	1	17	10	33	.253	.306	.355	910	230	40	4	15	107	66	170
Bases Empty	.236	.301	.321	140	33	6	3	1	1	10	27	.254	.308	.340	1046	266	45	6	11	11	72	182
Leadoff	.258	.333	.339	62	16	3	1	0	0	6	7	.282	.344	.412	451	127	26	3	9	9	37	67
Runners On Base	.250	.325	.368	136	34	7	0	3	38	17	30	.263	.337	.372	843	222	40	2	16	204	97	148
Scoring Position	.228	.330	.293	92	21	6	0	0	31	16	24	.252	.346	.361	523	132	31	1	8	180	81	101
Late and Close	.283	.358	.417	127	36	7	2	2	25	15	24	.255	.325	.331	408	104	15	2	4	54	42	71

JOE MAGRANE — BR/TL — age 30 — SL/CAL SP28, RP2 FIN/FB

6-YEAR TOTALS (1987–1993)

1993	G	IP	H	BB	SO	SB	CS	W	L	SV	ERA	G	IP	H	BB	SO	SB	CS	W	L	SV	ERA
Total	30	164.0	175	58	62	22	13	11	12	0	4.66	151	969.0	922	315	510	105	54	54	56	0	3.38
at Home	13	70.0	73	24	21	8	6	5	4	0	4.50	75	486.1	468	149	236	44	31	24	27	0	3.33
on Road	17	94.0	102	34	41	14	7	6	8	0	4.79	76	482.2	454	166	274	61	23	30	29	0	3.43
on Grass	11	69.1	72	20	28	9	6	6	3	0	4.15	37	235.0	219	72	144	27	11	16	9	0	3.29
on Turf	19	94.2	103	38	34	13	7	5	9	0	5.04	114	734.0	703	243	366	78	43	38	47	0	3.41
Day Games	7	37.2	43	9	16	4	3	4	1	0	4.30	41	248.0	261	74	142	22	14	20	8	0	3.77
Night Games	23	126.1	132	49	46	18	10	7	11	0	4.77	110	721.0	661	241	368	83	40	34	48	0	3.25
April	4	26.1	25	6	5	3	3	1	2	0	3.76	17	94.0	106	28	47	10	8	4	8	0	5.17
May	5	30.0	33	11	13	6	1	1	3	0	4.50	22	147.0	132	44	72	19	5	7	8	0	2.94
June	6	40.0	33	9	15	1	3	5	1	0	2.47	24	167.2	150	52	89	15	13	13	9	0	3.11
July	5	18.0	31	9	5	2	0	1	3	0	11.50	27	168.2	168	58	97	13	5	8	9	0	3.68
August	4	11.1	15	7	4	3	2	0	2	0	7.15	27	178.2	149	55	85	21	10	11	13	0	3.07
Sept-Oct	6	38.1	38	16	20	7	4	3	1	0	3.76	34	213.0	217	78	120	27	13	11	9	0	3.13

	BA	OBA	SA	AB	H	2B	3B	HR	RBI	BB	SO	BA	OBA	SA	AB	H	2B	3B	HR	RBI	BB	SO
Total	.280	.341	.435	625	175	36	2	19	83	58	62	.253	.316	.357	3643	922	171	28	51	335	315	510
vs. Left	.277	.387	.415	94	26	2	1	3	10	15	11	.238	.322	.329	596	142	21	6	7	56	68	109
vs. Right	.281	.332	.439	531	149	34	1	16	73	43	51	.256	.314	.363	3047	780	150	22	44	279	247	401
Bases Empty	.274	.347	.429	361	99	19	2	11	11	37	36	.250	.310	.354	2165	541	104	14	31	31	164	301
Leadoff	.294	.365	.399	153	45	7	0	3	3	17	11	.254	.311	.342	925	235	36	6	11	11	71	125
Runners On Base	.288	.333	.443	264	76	17	0	8	72	21	26	.258	.324	.363	1478	381	67	14	20	304	151	209
Scoring Position	.272	.324	.443	158	43	12	0	5	65	16	23	.241	.323	.338	876	211	41	7	10	270	116	142
Late and Close	.209	.271	.209	43	9	0	0	0	1	4	2	.261	.321	.342	357	93	12	4	3	30	30	45

DENNIS MARTINEZ — BR/TR — age 39 — MON SP34, RP1 FIN/GB

10-YEAR TOTALS (1984–1993)

1993	G	IP	H	BB	SO	SB	CS	W	L	SV	ERA	G	IP	H	BB	SO	SB	CS	W	L	SV	ERA
Total	35	224.2	211	64	138	49	6	15	9	1	3.85	310	1937.1	1798	509	1120	223	68	119	92	1	3.41
at Home	18	110.1	105	31	71	25	2	9	2	1	3.51	149	952.0	867	238	561	105	31	58	45	1	3.35
on Road	17	114.1	106	33	67	24	4	6	7	0	4.17	161	985.1	931	271	559	118	37	61	47	0	3.47
on Grass	11	72.0	68	19	43	19	2	4	6	0	4.75	123	672.0	690	189	373	81	21	39	41	0	4.14
on Turf	24	152.2	143	45	95	30	4	11	3	1	3.42	187	1265.1	1108	320	747	142	47	80	51	1	3.02
Day Games	15	85.1	87	29	56	23	2	4	5	1	4.96	92	544.1	539	148	337	77	18	28	36	1	3.87
Night Games	20	139.1	124	35	82	26	4	11	4	0	3.17	218	1393.0	1259	361	783	146	50	91	56	0	3.23
April	6	30.2	33	8	20	10	2	1	4	0	4.70	45	249.0	215	71	143	34	10	13	15	0	2.96
May	5	35.0	34	12	15	6	1	2	1	0	3.60	45	268.0	271	72	146	21	10	17	14	0	3.32
June	6	45.2	34	13	29	12	0	5	0	0	2.17	55	363.2	310	112	196	52	11	25	10	0	2.87
July	7	39.1	39	6	22	6	1	2	2	1	4.35	56	356.0	358	78	213	36	12	24	15	0	3.97
August	5	32.0	37	12	20	5	1	2	1	0	6.47	56	375.1	341	82	221	36	16	24	18	0	3.33
Sept-Oct	6	42.0	34	13	32	10	1	0	1	0	2.79	53	325.1	303	94	201	44	9	16	20	0	3.90

	BA	OBA	SA	AB	H	2B	3B	HR	RBI	BB	SO	BA	OBA	SA	AB	H	2B	3B	HR	RBI	BB	SO
Total	.246	.306	.407	856	211	38	9	27	92	64	138	.245	.299	.377	7330	1798	315	53	181	725	509	1120
vs. Left	.249	.312	.403	434	108	18	5	13	45	38	61	.242	.298	.363	4135	999	170	29	91	390	336	632
vs. Right	.244	.300	.410	422	103	20	4	14	47	26	77	.250	.299	.395	3195	799	145	24	90	335	173	488
Bases Empty	.279	.319	.447	517	144	24	6	17	17	28	75	.248	.291	.379	4565	1133	200	35	109	109	247	673
Leadoff	.303	.348	.486	218	66	12	2	8	8	14	28	.254	.292	.395	1902	484	85	16	50	50	91	259
Runners On Base	.198	.287	.345	339	67	14	3	10	75	36	63	.241	.310	.373	2765	665	115	18	72	616	262	447
Scoring Position	.174	.306	.319	207	36	8	2	6	61	34	47	.230	.314	.355	1633	375	58	10	42	518	198	307
Late and Close	.286	.324	.386	70	20	2	1	1	8	4	12	.237	.284	.365	747	177	27	6	19	73	41	102

RAMON MARTINEZ — BR/TR — age 26 — LA SP32 POW/FB

6-YEAR TOTALS (1988–1993)

1993	G	IP	H	BB	SO	SB	CS	W	L	SV	ERA	G	IP	H	BB	SO	SB	CS	W	L	SV	ERA
Total	32	211.2	202	104	127	16	11	10	12	0	3.44	147	951.1	830	372	713	80	53	62	49	0	3.35
at Home	17	111.0	118	48	64	12	5	5	8	0	4.14	78	513.1	437	209	411	49	37	33	27	0	3.42
on Road	15	100.2	84	56	63	4	6	5	4	0	2.68	69	438.0	393	163	302	31	16	29	22	0	3.27
on Grass	26	165.2	172	83	102	15	10	6	11	0	3.86	114	742.1	644	290	558	60	46	47	38	0	3.33
on Turf	6	46.0	30	21	25	1	1	4	1	0	1.96	33	209.0	186	82	155	20	7	15	11	0	3.40
Day Games	9	62.1	46	30	44	2	3	4	4	0	2.17	47	300.2	244	119	228	23	21	20	17	0	2.87
Night Games	23	149.1	156	74	83	14	5	7	8	0	3.98	100	650.2	586	253	485	57	32	42	32	0	3.57
April	5	31.2	23	22	24	4	3	2	3	0	3.13	18	118.1	91	47	86	14	9	7	5	0	2.81
May	5	37.0	36	12	21	3	2	2	2	0	2.68	22	147.1	140	55	121	17	10	13	4	0	3.36
June	5	32.1	30	14	18	2	2	2	1	0	3.62	22	152.1	132	56	123	8	13	10	6	0	2.72
July	6	43.1	40	25	19	2	2	2	2	0	3.12	25	169.2	143	65	112	18	4	13	8	0	3.02
August	5	38.0	39	19	23	5	0	1	3	0	2.37	31	202.1	188	72	142	12	8	9	16	0	3.78
Sept-Oct	6	29.1	34	19	22	0	1	1	3	0	6.44	29	161.1	136	77	129	11	9	10	10	0	4.13

	BA	OBA	SA	AB	H	2B	3B	HR	RBI	BB	SO	BA	OBA	SA	AB	H	2B	3B	HR	RBI	BB	SO
Total	.255	.342	.366	793	202	31	6	15	77	104	127	.234	.310	.351	3547	830	147	18	77	350	372	713
vs. Left	.246	.362	.372	414	102	19	3	9	41	76	68	.243	.338	.368	1952	475	92	10	44	198	272	366
vs. Right	.264	.319	.359	379	100	12	3	6	36	28	59	.223	.273	.329	1595	355	55	8	33	152	100	347
Bases Empty	.270	.351	.401	441	119	18	5	10	10	52	70	.228	.304	.353	2093	478	92	12	48	48	211	442
Leadoff	.287	.377	.431	195	56	9	3	4	4	26	30	.247	.327	.392	882	218	39	7	25	25	95	172
Runners On Base	.236	.332	.321	352	83	13	1	5	67	52	57	.242	.319	.348	1454	352	55	6	29	302	161	271
Scoring Position	.183	.297	.254	197	36	9	1	2	57	33	33	.222	.308	.320	834	183	33	3	14	258	101	167
Late and Close	.254	.306	.358	67	17	1	0	2	2	4	12	.205	.271	.286	322	66	11	0	5	16	27	65

BEN McDONALD — BR/TR — age 27 — BAL SP34 POW/GB

1993	G	IP	H	BB	SO	SB	CS	W	L	SV	ERA		5-YEAR TOTALS (1989–1993) G	IP	H	BB	SO	SB	CS	W	L	SV	ERA
Total	34	220.1	185	86	171	19	11	13	14	0	3.39		117	699.2	620	242	482	64	24	41	40	0	3.82
at Home	19	132.1	106	43	104	12	8	10	4	0	2.72		63	401.2	359	115	272	37	18	21	19	0	3.59
on Road	15	88.0	79	43	67	7	3	3	10	0	4.40		54	298.0	261	127	210	27	6	20	21	0	4.14
on Grass	30	203.1	162	73	158	15	11	13	10	0	3.05		104	633.1	544	215	431	58	24	36	34	0	3.64
on Turf	4	17.0	23	13	13	4	0	0	4	0	7.41		13	66.1	76	27	51	6	0	5	6	0	5.56
Day Games	6	35.1	38	15	24	6	2	0	5	0	4.58		29	156.2	157	60	105	18	7	5	13	0	4.65
Night Games	28	185.0	147	71	147	13	9	13	9	0	3.16		88	543.0	463	182	377	46	17	36	27	0	3.58
April	5	26.1	33	15	17	4	5	2	2	0	4.44		11	57.0	66	31	40	9	5	4	3	0	5.05
May	5	30.2	28	6	21	0	1	0	3	0	4.70		16	97.0	83	26	67	4	3	6	7	0	4.73
June	6	37.1	29	18	29	1	0	2	2	0	1.69		12	74.1	67	27	55	3	0	3	5	0	3.87
July	6	42.0	28	14	33	6	2	4	2	0	2.57		27	156.0	131	44	112	13	6	12	6	0	3.23
August	5	33.2	38	13	25	3	3	1	2	0	4.81		22	145.2	154	53	85	16	6	6	11	0	4.32
Sept-Oct	7	50.1	29	20	46	5	0	4	3	0	3.04		29	169.2	119	61	123	19	4	10	8	0	2.97

	BA	OBA	SA	AB	H	2B	3B	HR	RBI	BB	SO		BA	OBA	SA	AB	H	2B	3B	HR	RBI	BB	SO
Total	.228	.304	.342	812	185	32	5	17	76	86	171		.237	.303	.377	2615	620	113	13	76	277	242	482
vs. Left	.232	.309	.329	431	100	17	5	5	37	48	91		.221	.294	.338	1321	292	51	8	29	118	138	254
vs. Right	.223	.299	.357	381	85	15	0	12	39	38	80		.253	.313	.418	1294	328	62	5	47	159	104	228
Bases Empty	.205	.272	.304	516	106	17	2	10	10	45	120		.218	.281	.348	1658	362	65	6	46	46	136	322
Leadoff	.224	.297	.355	214	48	9	2	5	5	21	44		.221	.281	.376	680	150	33	5	21	21	53	123
Runners On Base	.267	.358	.409	296	79	15	3	7	66	41	51		.270	.340	.428	957	258	48	7	30	231	106	160
Scoring Position	.230	.348	.364	165	38	6	2	4	56	30	26		.253	.339	.411	521	132	24	5	16	191	74	93
Late and Close	.287	.329	.350	80	23	2	0	1	5	5	15		.244	.297	.411	246	60	11	0	10	29	18	40

JACK McDOWELL — BR/TR — age 28 — CHA SP34 FIN/FB

1993	G	IP	H	BB	SO	SB	CS	W	L	SV	ERA		6-YEAR TOTALS (1987–1993) G	IP	H	BB	SO	SB	CS	W	L	SV	ERA
Total	34	256.2	261	69	158	10	15	22	10	0	3.37		166	1162.2	1072	377	791	100	56	81	49	0	3.46
at Home	18	131.0	154	32	70	7	10	9	7	0	4.19		90	626.0	580	200	418	58	30	42	25	0	3.45
on Road	16	125.2	107	37	88	3	5	13	3	0	2.51		76	536.2	492	177	373	42	26	39	24	0	3.47
on Grass	29	219.2	229	54	129	9	13	18	9	0	3.56		145	1014.1	927	330	700	85	48	71	42	0	3.49
on Turf	5	37.0	32	15	29	1	2	4	1	0	2.19		21	148.1	145	47	91	15	8	10	7	0	3.28
Day Games	10	73.0	70	21	57	2	5	6	4	0	3.45		50	353.0	310	123	246	27	18	25	15	0	3.59
Night Games	24	183.2	191	48	101	8	10	16	6	0	3.33		116	809.2	762	254	545	73	38	56	34	0	3.40
April	5	35.1	41	14	17	0	2	5	0	0	4.33		24	153.2	138	51	105	10	7	16	4	0	4.10
May	6	47.2	46	11	30	2	4	2	4	0	4.15		26	173.2	183	60	126	18	10	6	14	0	4.72
June	5	36.1	37	10	18	2	5	5	0	0	2.97		28	200.2	167	70	127	26	12	18	3	0	2.65
July	6	44.2	48	13	29	1	0	4	2	0	3.83		27	198.1	190	56	135	15	8	13	8	0	3.49
August	6	51.2	52	10	38	5	3	4	1	0	1.74		31	230.0	207	72	152	18	9	16	9	0	2.78
Sept-Oct	6	41.0	37	11	26	0	1	2	3	0	3.51		30	206.1	187	68	146	13	10	12	11	0	3.45

	BA	OBA	SA	AB	H	2B	3B	HR	RBI	BB	SO		BA	OBA	SA	AB	H	2B	3B	HR	RBI	BB	SO
Total	.266	.314	.379	981	261	43	4	20	93	69	158		.246	.308	.367	4364	1072	195	27	93	423	377	791
vs. Left	.259	.302	.354	491	127	21	1	8	41	32	80		.249	.311	.366	2227	555	93	14	46	203	195	377
vs. Right	.273	.326	.404	490	134	22	3	12	52	37	78		.242	.305	.368	2137	517	102	13	47	220	182	414
Bases Empty	.279	.326	.395	567	158	26	2	12	12	37	92		.244	.305	.357	2636	643	110	19	50	50	216	488
Leadoff	.283	.324	.425	247	70	14	0	7	7	13	36		.243	.295	.364	1125	273	54	7	23	23	76	204
Runners On Base	.249	.299	.357	414	103	17	2	8	81	32	66		.248	.312	.381	1728	429	85	8	43	373	161	303
Scoring Position	.239	.294	.320	222	53	8	2	2	65	20	39		.235	.313	.369	944	222	47	5	23	306	112	191
Late and Close	.244	.284	.362	127	31	3	0	4	11	6	20		.232	.287	.339	448	104	20	2	8	38	33	91

GREG McMICHAEL — BR/TR — age 28 — ATL RP74 POW/GB

1993	G	IP	H	BB	SO	SB	CS	W	L	SV	ERA		1-YEAR TOTALS (1993) G	IP	H	BB	SO	SB	CS	W	L	SV	ERA
Total	74	91.2	68	29	89	5	2	2	3	19	2.06		74	91.2	68	29	89	5	2	2	3	19	2.06
at Home	36	44.2	35	10	38	3	1	0	2	8	1.61		36	44.2	35	10	38	3	1	0	2	8	1.61
on Road	38	47.0	33	19	51	2	1	2	1	11	2.49		38	47.0	33	19	51	2	1	2	1	11	2.49
on Grass	57	73.0	55	18	71	5	2	2	2	15	1.73		57	73.0	55	18	71	5	2	2	2	15	1.73
on Turf	17	18.2	13	11	18	0	0	0	1	4	3.38		17	18.2	13	11	18	0	0	0	1	4	3.38
Day Games	23	29.0	23	11	26	2	0	1	1	6	3.41		23	29.0	23	11	26	2	0	1	1	6	3.41
Night Games	51	62.2	45	18	63	3	2	1	2	13	1.44		51	62.2	45	18	63	3	2	1	2	13	1.44
April	8	14.0	10	4	11	3	0	0	1	0	3.86		8	14.0	10	4	11	3	0	0	1	0	3.86
May	10	13.2	17	7	15	0	1	1	0	1	1.98		10	13.2	17	7	15	0	1	1	0	1	1.98
June	11	14.2	4	5	14	0	1	0	0	0	2.45		11	14.2	4	5	14	0	1	0	0	0	2.45
July	17	16.0	12	3	23	0	0	0	0	2	1.69		17	16.0	12	3	23	0	0	0	0	2	1.69
August	14	14.1	10	3	14	1	0	0	0	9	0.63		14	14.1	10	3	14	1	0	0	0	9	0.63
Sept-Oct	14	19.0	15	7	12	1	0	1	0	8	1.89		14	19.0	15	7	12	1	0	1	0	8	1.89

	BA	OBA	SA	AB	H	2B	3B	HR	RBI	BB	SO		BA	OBA	SA	AB	H	2B	3B	HR	RBI	BB	SO
Total	.206	.269	.261	330	68	7	1	3	23	29	89		.206	.269	.261	330	68	7	1	3	23	29	89
vs. Left	.194	.269	.252	155	30	4	1	1	12	16	37		.194	.269	.252	155	30	4	1	1	12	16	37
vs. Right	.217	.268	.269	175	38	3	0	2	11	13	52		.217	.268	.269	175	38	3	0	2	11	13	52
Bases Empty	.200	.269	.279	190	38	6	0	3	3	18	55		.200	.269	.279	190	38	6	0	3	3	18	55
Leadoff	.213	.284	.325	80	17	3	0	2	2	8	29		.213	.284	.325	80	17	3	0	2	2	8	29
Runners On Base	.214	.268	.236	140	30	1	1	0	20	11	34		.214	.268	.236	140	30	1	1	0	20	11	34
Scoring Position	.222	.278	.235	81	18	1	1	0	19	7	24		.222	.278	.235	81	18	1	1	0	19	7	24
Late and Close	.237	.289	.290	186	44	4	0	2	13	14	42		.237	.289	.290	186	44	4	0	2	13	14	42

JOSE MESA — BR/TR — age 28 — CLE SP33, RP1 FIN/FB

1993	G	IP	H	BB	SO	SB	CS	W	L	SV	ERA
Total	34	208.2	232	62	118	12	14	10	12	0	4.92
at Home	16	101.0	113	32	55	6	4	7	5	0	4.63
on Road	18	107.2	119	30	63	6	10	3	7	0	5.18
on Grass	29	179.0	194	54	98	8	10	10	10	0	4.83
on Turf	5	29.2	38	8	20	4	4	0	2	0	5.46
Day Games	11	56.1	72	25	35	4	8	2	6	0	6.39
Night Games	23	152.1	160	37	83	8	6	8	6	0	4.37
April	4	25.1	24	5	16	2	3	1	1	0	3.91
May	7	41.0	38	12	27	3	3	4	2	0	2.85
June	6	38.1	36	15	16	1	1	2	2	0	4.23
July	6	34.1	43	10	22	2	2	2	2	0	5.50
August	6	40.0	48	12	21	1	4	0	3	0	5.85
Sept-Oct	5	29.2	43	8	16	3	1	1	2	0	7.58

5-YEAR TOTALS (1987–1993)

	G	IP	H	BB	SO	SB	CS	W	L	SV	ERA
	98	571.0	627	236	285	40	29	27	40	0	5.03
	48	274.0	293	120	134	22	7	13	21	0	4.96
	50	297.0	334	116	151	18	22	14	19	0	5.09
	81	471.0	504	201	235	30	21	22	33	0	5.01
	17	100.0	123	35	50	10	8	5	7	0	5.13
	33	181.2	216	73	97	16	13	5	17	0	5.65
	65	389.1	411	163	188	24	16	22	23	0	4.74
	11	69.0	69	19	42	7	5	3	6	0	3.52
	19	109.1	115	49	50	10	5	8	7	0	4.36
	15	79.1	94	31	29	6	4	3	8	0	6.35
	10	57.1	63	19	31	3	4	3	3	0	4.08
	15	96.2	100	39	50	4	6	2	5	0	5.40
	28	159.1	186	79	83	10	5	8	11	0	5.59

	BA	OBA	SA	AB	H	2B	3B	HR	RBI	BB	SO
Total	.286	.339	.414	810	232	34	3	21	96	62	118
vs. Left	.304	.363	.392	372	113	12	0	7	42	34	43
vs. Right	.272	.318	.432	438	119	22	3	14	54	28	75
Bases Empty	.283	.339	.407	459	130	22	1	11	11	37	66
Leadoff	.298	.348	.439	205	61	11	0	6	6	15	29
Runners On Base	.291	.338	.422	351	102	12	2	10	85	25	52
Scoring Position	.268	.328	.379	198	53	8	1	4	71	19	31
Late and Close	.278	.333	.361	72	20	3	0	1	8	6	10

	BA	OBA	SA	AB	H	2B	3B	HR	RBI	BB	SO
	.283	.353	.416	2219	627	117	7	55	270	236	285
	.298	.366	.411	1120	334	52	1	24	129	120	115
	.267	.338	.421	1099	293	65	6	31	141	116	170
	.270	.345	.396	1256	339	66	3	29	29	137	156
	.290	.349	.439	563	163	33	0	17	17	49	67
	.299	.363	.441	963	288	51	4	26	241	99	129
	.297	.368	.449	539	160	31	3	15	212	68	73
	.277	.344	.385	148	41	7	0	3	14	15	16

BLAS MINOR — BR/TR — age 28 — PIT RP65 POW/GB

1993	G	IP	H	BB	SO	SB	CS	W	L	SV	ERA
Total	65	94.1	94	26	84	5	4	8	6	2	4.10
at Home	37	49.2	51	15	44	2	1	5	3	1	4.35
on Road	28	44.2	43	11	40	3	3	3	3	1	3.83
on Grass	18	29.0	24	8	28	0	2	2	3	1	2.79
on Turf	47	65.1	70	18	56	5	2	6	3	1	4.68
Day Games	18	25.0	25	4	20	2	2	3	2	0	3.60
Night Games	47	69.1	69	22	64	3	2	5	4	2	4.28
April	11	14.1	8	2	15	0	0	3	0	0	1.26
May	11	14.0	17	6	14	0	1	1	2	0	6.43
June	12	20.2	22	5	15	1	1	0	1	2	3.92
July	13	20.0	20	6	16	1	0	2	1	0	4.05
August	10	12.0	17	4	12	1	1	1	1	0	8.25
Sept-Oct	8	13.1	10	3	12	2	1	1	1	0	1.35

2-YEAR TOTALS (1992–1993)

	G	IP	H	BB	SO	SB	CS	W	L	SV	ERA
	66	96.1	97	26	84	5	4	8	6	2	4.11
	37	49.2	51	15	44	2	1	5	3	1	4.35
	29	46.2	46	11	40	3	3	3	3	1	3.86
	19	31.0	27	8	28	0	2	2	3	1	2.90
	47	65.1	70	18	56	5	2	6	3	1	4.68
	19	27.0	28	4	20	2	2	3	2	0	3.67
	47	69.1	69	22	64	3	2	5	4	2	4.28
	11	14.1	8	2	15	0	0	3	0	0	1.26
	11	14.0	17	6	14	0	1	1	2	0	6.43
	12	20.2	22	5	15	1	1	0	1	2	3.92
	14	22.0	23	6	16	1	0	2	1	0	4.09
	10	12.0	17	4	12	1	1	1	1	0	8.25
	8	13.1	10	3	12	2	1	1	1	0	1.35

	BA	OBA	SA	AB	H	2B	3B	HR	RBI	BB	SO
Total	.263	.316	.385	358	94	12	4	8	43	26	84
vs. Left	.284	.348	.454	141	40	5	2	5	23	15	26
vs. Right	.249	.295	.341	217	54	7	2	3	20	11	58
Bases Empty	.239	.291	.376	205	49	7	3	5	5	13	50
Leadoff	.214	.258	.321	84	18	3	3	0	0	5	20
Runners On Base	.294	.349	.399	153	45	5	1	3	38	13	34
Scoring Position	.319	.376	.415	94	30	3	0	2	34	10	27
Late and Close	.228	.281	.309	123	28	2	1	2	11	9	31

	BA	OBA	SA	AB	H	2B	3B	HR	RBI	BB	SO
	.264	.317	.392	367	97	13	5	8	43	26	84
	.287	.350	.455	143	41	5	2	5	23	15	26
	.250	.295	.353	224	56	8	3	3	20	11	58
	.249	.299	.397	209	52	8	4	5	5	13	50
	.221	.264	.337	86	19	4	3	0	0	5	20
	.285	.339	.386	158	45	5	1	3	38	13	34
	.306	.363	.398	98	30	3	0	2	34	10	27
	.228	.281	.309	123	28	2	1	2	-11	9	31

JEFF MONTGOMERY — BR/TR — age 32 — KC RP69 FIN/FB

1993	G	IP	H	BB	SO	SB	CS	W	L	SV	ERA
Total	69	87.1	65	23	66	7	1	7	5	45	2.27
at Home	33	43.1	30	8	29	4	0	5	4	16	2.49
on Road	36	44.0	35	15	37	3	1	2	1	29	2.05
on Grass	28	33.1	27	13	27	2	1	2	1	22	2.16
on Turf	41	54.0	38	10	39	5	0	5	4	23	2.33
Day Games	21	25.2	22	11	23	2	1	2	2	14	2.45
Night Games	48	61.2	43	12	43	5	0	5	3	31	2.19
April	10	13.0	10	3	10	0	0	1	0	6	2.08
May	14	18.1	16	7	12	2	1	1	1	10	2.95
June	10	13.0	7	1	11	3	0	0	0	7	0.69
July	10	13.2	7	1	11	1	0	1	0	8	0.66
August	14	16.0	12	7	12	1	0	0	3	10	3.38
Sept-Oct	11	13.1	13	4	10	1	0	2	0	4	3.38

7-YEAR TOTALS (1987–1993)

	G	IP	H	BB	SO	SB	CS	W	L	SV	ERA
	396	528.1	435	176	460	46	16	34	27	160	2.52
	210	282.1	235	69	251	16	11	26	16	79	2.20
	186	246.0	200	107	209	30	5	8	11	81	2.89
	137	188.2	151	84	155	22	4	8	10	60	2.86
	259	339.2	284	92	305	24	12	26	17	100	2.33
	106	147.0	122	56	135	20	7	10	9	39	2.76
	290	381.1	313	120	325	26	9	24	18	121	2.43
	45	60.1	53	13	52	5	3	5	6	13	2.39
	58	85.2	64	26	77	9	2	8	5	24	2.63
	66	89.2	79	25	81	2	2	0	3	29	2.81
	70	106.1	76	37	91	9	4	6	3	32	1.52
	81	98.0	78	43	90	5	3	8	6	36	3.03
	76	88.1	85	32	69	10	2	7	4	26	2.85

	BA	OBA	SA	AB	H	2B	3B	HR	RBI	BB	SO
Total	.206	.263	.291	316	65	14	2	3	29	23	66
vs. Left	.234	.297	.329	158	37	8	2	1	17	13	24
vs. Right	.177	.229	.253	158	28	6	0	2	12	10	42
Bases Empty	.214	.253	.295	173	37	8	0	2	2	9	40
Leadoff	.257	.276	.324	74	19	5	0	0	0	2	14
Runners On Base	.196	.275	.287	143	28	6	2	1	27	14	26
Scoring Position	.189	.260	.300	90	17	3	2	1	25	11	15
Late and Close	.210	.271	.276	257	54	9	1	2	27	21	53

	BA	OBA	SA	AB	H	2B	3B	HR	RBI	BB	SO
	.223	.291	.317	1955	435	79	6	31	211	176	460
	.244	.317	.350	943	230	44	4	16	111	97	165
	.203	.266	.286	1012	205	35	2	15	100	79	295
	.226	.291	.329	1029	233	49	3	17	17	86	236
	.223	.287	.322	435	97	22	0	7	7	36	103
	.218	.291	.302	926	202	30	3	14	194	90	224
	.211	.294	.295	569	120	18	3	8	175	65	141
	.233	.297	.328	1235	288	49	4	20	153	108	284

MIKE MOORE — BR/TR — age 35 — DET SP36 FIN/GB

10-YEAR TOTALS (1984–1993)

1993	G	IP	H	BB	SO	SB	CS	W	L	SV	ERA	G	IP	H	BB	SO	SB	CS	W	L	SV	ERA
Total	36	213.2	227	89	89	23	8	13	9	0	5.22	350	2272.1	2238	860	1360	139	94	132	129	2	4.06
at Home	15	91.1	88	36	41	7	3	6	4	0	5.12	175	1150.2	1087	430	692	63	45	72	54	2	3.64
on Road	21	122.1	139	53	48	16	5	7	5	0	5.30	175	1121.2	1151	430	668	76	49	60	75	0	4.49
on Grass	30	177.2	185	75	76	20	5	11	8	0	5.17	212	1365.2	1324	532	798	94	58	86	79	0	4.03
on Turf	6	36.0	42	14	13	3	3	2	1	0	5.50	138	906.2	914	328	562	45	36	46	50	2	4.09
Day Games	11	66.1	67	27	33	2	5	5	2	0	5.29	114	744.0	717	270	469	47	33	50	43	0	3.88
Night Games	25	147.1	160	62	56	21	3	8	7	0	5.19	236	1528.1	1521	590	891	92	61	82	86	2	4.14
April	6	31.2	36	18	11	7	1	2	1	0	6.25	50	326.2	319	149	177	22	16	20	13	0	3.99
May	5	29.1	28	14	10	2	3	1	0	0	4.60	55	339.1	331	157	188	28	15	18	25	0	4.43
June	6	33.0	36	15	12	2	0	2	4	0	7.64	60	352.1	360	136	195	23	11	17	25	1	4.62
July	6	31.1	42	7	16	3	1	2	0	0	5.74	58	367.2	388	121	217	10	19	21	23	0	4.46
August	6	47.2	36	16	22	4	0	4	1	0	2.45	62	446.1	412	133	307	24	14	26	21	1	3.21
Sept-Oct	7	40.2	49	19	18	5	3	2	3	0	5.75	65	440.0	428	164	276	32	19	30	22	0	3.89

	BA	OBA	SA	AB	H	2B	3B	HR	RBI	BB	SO	BA	OBA	SA	AB	H	2B	3B	HR	RBI	BB	SO
Total	.271	.340	.453	838	227	40	4	35	119	89	89	.258	.326	.389	8658	2238	410	45	209	976	860	1360
vs. Left	.271	.345	.439	428	116	19	4	15	54	48	35	.259	.330	.377	4660	1206	220	28	91	495	494	640
vs. Right	.271	.335	.468	410	111	21	0	20	65	41	54	.258	.323	.403	3998	1032	190	17	118	481	366	720
Bases Empty	.270	.333	.418	481	130	24	1	15	15	42	49	.251	.316	.379	5120	1283	240	26	121	121	460	860
Leadoff	.290	.363	.445	200	58	10	0	7	7	23	17	.251	.313	.384	2193	550	102	13	55	55	187	352
Runners On Base	.272	.350	.501	357	97	16	3	20	104	47	40	.270	.341	.403	3538	955	170	19	88	855	400	500
Scoring Position	.245	.338	.455	200	49	10	1	10	80	32	22	.264	.348	.392	1974	521	101	11	43	733	279	280
Late and Close	.176	.222	.265	34	6	0	0	1	1	2	5	.251	.319	.377	762	191	39	3	17	70	72	117

MIKE MORGAN — BR/TR — age 35 — CHN SP32 FIN/GB

9-YEAR TOTALS (1985–1993)

1993	G	IP	H	BB	SO	SB	CS	W	L	SV	ERA	G	IP	H	BB	SO	SB	CS	W	L	SV	ERA
Total	32	207.2	206	74	111	17	14	10	15	0	4.03	268	1548.1	1521	474	784	105	72	84	100	3	3.67
at Home	15	104.0	97	32	60	6	8	5	6	0	3.12	132	822.0	779	224	423	53	38	41	47	2	3.37
on Road	17	103.2	109	42	51	11	6	5	9	0	4.95	136	726.1	742	250	361	52	34	43	53	1	4.01
on Grass	24	158.0	159	48	85	7	10	8	10	0	3.99	166	976.1	897	272	488	54	45	53	51	3	3.12
on Turf	8	49.2	47	26	26	10	4	2	5	0	4.17	102	572.0	624	202	296	51	27	31	49	0	4.61
Day Games	19	130.0	120	44	68	8	6	5	9	0	3.05	89	562.1	510	180	285	31	23	35	30	2	2.83
Night Games	13	77.2	86	30	43	9	8	5	6	0	5.68	179	986.0	1011	294	499	74	49	49	70	1	4.15
April	5	31.0	30	17	14	2	2	1	4	0	4.65	42	230.2	206	71	98	8	9	11	20	1	3.86
May	5	33.2	31	10	12	2	1	2	2	0	2.94	49	287.1	265	93	173	15	14	21	14	1	3.26
June	4	28.1	31	10	16	4	1	2	2	0	4.45	39	262.2	266	61	122	17	10	13	15	0	3.08
July	6	39.0	35	10	22	4	3	2	2	0	2.77	47	245.2	256	93	111	24	9	14	18	1	4.07
August	6	38.2	52	13	25	3	3	1	3	0	5.12	48	270.0	289	82	144	19	15	10	20	0	3.77
Sept-Oct	6	37.0	27	14	22	1	4	2	2	0	4.38	43	252.0	239	74	136	22	15	15	13	0	4.11

	BA	OBA	SA	AB	H	2B	3B	HR	RBI	BB	SO	BA	OBA	SA	AB	H	2B	3B	HR	RBI	BB	SO
Total	.262	.329	.372	786	206	31	5	15	87	74	111	.259	.316	.376	5871	1521	250	33	123	608	474	784
vs. Left	.245	.330	.351	424	104	16	4	7	41	51	62	.266	.330	.385	3196	851	145	19	66	324	302	410
vs. Right	.282	.328	.395	362	102	15	1	8	46	23	49	.250	.298	.364	2675	670	105	14	57	284	172	374
Bases Empty	.248	.310	.345	467	116	18	3	8	7	38	64	.251	.303	.367	3525	886	142	21	74	74	244	484
Leadoff	.271	.329	.372	199	54	7	2	3	3	15	30	.248	.304	.357	1482	368	53	9	30	30	111	190
Runners On Base	.282	.355	.411	319	90	13	2	8	80	36	47	.271	.335	.390	2346	635	108	12	49	534	230	300
Scoring Position	.289	.378	.412	187	54	7	2	4	70	27	26	.256	.341	.367	1318	338	64	8	22	459	175	202
Late and Close	.300	.333	.450	60	18	3	0	2	5	3	7	.275	.328	.385	444	122	17	4	8	39	34	50

JACK MORRIS — BR/TR — age 39 — TOR SP27 POW/GB

10-YEAR TOTALS (1984–1993)

1993	G	IP	H	BB	SO	SB	CS	W	L	SV	ERA	G	IP	H	BB	SO	SB	CS	W	L	SV	ERA
Total	27	152.2	189	65	103	17	10	7	12	0	6.19	329	2325.1	2171	848	1612	255	88	156	116	0	3.92
at Home	14	76.0	102	36	59	10	5	3	6	0	7.34	165	1156.0	1087	398	779	134	45	79	53	0	3.96
on Road	13	76.2	87	29	44	7	5	4	6	0	5.05	164	1169.1	1084	450	833	121	43	77	63	0	3.89
on Grass	8	42.1	52	17	20	6	3	3	4	0	6.17	236	1668.1	1544	626	1156	168	59	109	92	0	3.88
on Turf	19	110.1	137	48	83	11	7	4	8	0	6.20	93	657.0	627	222	456	87	29	47	24	0	4.03
Day Games	7	38.1	43	16	28	7	1	4	3	0	5.40	107	761.1	701	264	519	91	29	58	34	0	3.68
Night Games	20	114.1	146	49	75	10	9	3	9	0	6.45	222	1564.0	1470	584	1093	164	59	98	82	0	4.05
April	5	22.2	43	14	15	3	0	1	3	0	11.51	52	366.0	375	149	272	46	10	24	23	0	4.45
May	4	22.0	28	9	13	5	3	2	2	0	7.36	55	382.1	342	159	271	45	29	23	22	0	4.03
June	5	30.1	29	8	20	5	2	0	2	0	5.04	51	347.1	346	119	215	37	11	32	11	0	4.30
July	5	29.2	31	12	24	2	5	0	3	0	4.85	49	343.2	326	97	247	37	17	18	21	0	3.74
August	6	34.2	41	17	24	1	0	2	1	0	4.41	60	415.2	381	158	278	41	10	29	19	0	4.07
Sept-Oct	2	13.1	17	5	7	1	2	2	0	0	5.40	62	470.1	401	166	329	49	11	30	20	0	3.16

	BA	OBA	SA	AB	H	2B	3B	HR	RBI	BB	SO	BA	OBA	SA	AB	H	2B	3B	HR	RBI	BB	SO
Total	.302	.368	.458	625	189	31	6	18	98	65	103	.246	.313	.381	8824	2171	348	56	243	994	848	1612
vs. Left	.318	.385	.480	321	102	17	4	9	50	37	41	.254	.326	.391	4583	1164	177	37	126	543	497	773
vs. Right	.286	.350	.434	304	87	14	2	9	48	28	62	.237	.299	.369	4241	1007	171	19	117	451	351	839
Bases Empty	.264	.346	.399	326	86	15	4	7	7	39	57	.238	.306	.376	5231	1244	214	33	147	147	494	988
Leadoff	.273	.350	.385	143	39	5	1	3	3	16	25	.243	.304	.399	2200	535	89	17	73	73	188	389
Runners On Base	.344	.393	.522	299	103	16	2	11	91	26	46	.258	.323	.388	3593	927	134	23	96	847	354	624
Scoring Position	.331	.381	.514	175	58	10	2	6	78	17	33	.253	.332	.389	2002	506	81	13	55	725	255	406
Late and Close	.256	.302	.436	39	10	1	0	3	6	3	7	.246	.303	.375	1018	250	38	2	30	115	86	179

JAMIE MOYER — BL/TL — age 32 — BAL SP25 FIN/GB

1993	G	IP	H	BB	SO	SB	CS	W	L	SV	ERA		G	IP	H	BB	SO	SB	CS	W	L	SV	ERA
Total	25	152.0	154	38	90	5	6	12	9	0	3.43		166	852.0	920	320	525	89	51	46	63	0	4.36
at Home	12	67.1	73	24	45	1	2	3	5	0	4.68		84	456.1	485	175	302	37	29	20	28	0	4.40
on Road	13	84.2	81	14	45	4	4	9	4	0	2.44		82	395.2	435	145	223	52	22	26	35	0	4.32
on Grass	22	127.2	135	37	73	5	5	9	9	0	3.95		120	630.0	679	239	385	55	40	32	46	0	4.34
on Turf	3	24.1	19	1	17	0	1	3	0	0	0.74		46	222.0	241	81	140	34	11	14	17	0	4.42
Day Games	9	55.1	64	9	38	2	4	5	3	0	4.39		69	387.2	426	154	238	36	28	20	23	0	4.64
Night Games	16	96.2	90	29	52	3	2	7	6	0	2.89		97	464.1	494	166	287	53	23	26	40	0	4.13
April	0	0.0	0	0	0	0	0	0	0	0	0.00		23	112.1	114	44	76	11	11	6	8	0	3.93
May	3	15.2	26	1	7	0	1	0	3	0	5.74		31	139.2	143	65	80	23	11	4	17	0	4.58
June	5	27.2	29	15	11	2	1	3	0	0	3.58		26	126.2	128	45	84	15	4	9	4	0	4.19
July	6	36.0	31	7	21	0	0	4	2	0	3.50		27	145.1	152	51	93	18	11	8	7	0	3.90
August	6	38.0	31	8	28	2	1	3	1	0	3.08		28	170.2	180	67	95	12	5	9	14	0	5.01
Sept-Oct	5	34.2	37	7	23	1	3	2	3	0	2.60		31	157.1	203	48	97	10	9	10	13	0	4.35

	BA	OBA	SA	AB	H	2B	3B	HR	RBI	BB	SO		BA	OBA	SA	AB	H	2B	3B	HR	RBI	BB	SO
Total	.265	.316	.376	582	154	30	1	11	53	38	90		.279	.345	.421	3292	920	164	16	90	399	320	525
vs. Left	.304	.377	.471	102	31	8	0	3	9	10	13		.259	.338	.421	525	136	27	2	18	65	58	81
vs. Right	.256	.302	.356	480	123	22	1	8	44	28	77		.283	.347	.421	2767	784	137	14	72	334	262	444
Bases Empty	.253	.289	.360	375	95	17	1	7	7	15	53		.276	.337	.415	1909	527	92	9	52	52	160	312
Leadoff	.228	.252	.316	158	36	5	0	3	3	3	26		.288	.343	.431	833	240	38	6	23	23	60	136
Runners On Base	.285	.361	.406	207	59	13	0	4	46	23	37		.284	.356	.429	1383	393	72	7	38	347	160	213
Scoring Position	.245	.333	.391	110	27	7	0	3	40	14	22		.271	.356	.407	786	213	39	4	20	292	113	127
Late and Close	.394	.412	.545	33	13	2	0	1	5	1	3		.294	.373	.502	231	68	13	1	11	37	28	24

7-YEAR TOTALS (1986–1993) (right-hand columns above)

TERRY MULHOLLAND — BR/TL — age 31 — PHI SP28, RP1 FIN/GB

1993	G	IP	H	BB	SO	SB	CS	W	L	SV	ERA		G	IP	H	BB	SO	SB	CS	W	L	SV	ERA
Total	29	191.0	177	40	116	1	5	12	9	0	3.25		177	1048.2	1045	255	569	24	24	57	58	0	3.76
at Home	14	92.0	88	19	73	1	4	6	4	0	3.62		88	562.1	517	135	318	8	12	34	23	0	3.25
on Road	15	99.0	89	21	43	0	1	6	5	0	2.91		89	486.1	528	120	251	16	12	23	35	0	4.35
on Grass	9	61.2	61	13	27	0	0	4	5	0	3.65		62	325.1	358	90	176	8	7	16	29	0	4.40
on Turf	20	129.1	116	27	89	1	5	8	4	0	3.06		115	723.1	687	165	393	16	17	41	29	0	3.47
Day Games	10	69.0	55	17	33	1	2	4	4	0	2.87		56	320.0	325	86	183	10	8	16	23	0	4.13
Night Games	19	122.0	122	23	83	0	3	8	5	0	3.47		121	728.2	720	169	386	14	16	41	35	0	3.59
April	5	36.0	30	7	22	1	0	2	3	0	3.00		19	119.0	121	34	61	7	1	5	8	0	4.31
May	5	35.0	30	10	16	0	3	4	1	0	2.83		28	165.1	158	39	74	2	8	15	5	0	3.10
June	5	39.1	36	6	31	0	1	3	1	0	2.06		31	155.2	164	46	95	4	5	7	12	0	4.51
July	5	32.2	34	9	19	0	0	1	3	0	4.41		36	242.2	231	39	130	7	5	11	14	0	2.89
August	5	34.0	38	5	22	0	0	1	1	0	4.76		32	196.1	209	49	119	1	0	10	9	0	4.13
Sept-Oct	4	14.0	9	3	5	0	1	1	0	0	1.93		31	169.2	162	48	90	3	5	9	10	0	4.14

	BA	OBA	SA	AB	H	2B	3B	HR	RBI	BB	SO		BA	OBA	SA	AB	H	2B	3B	HR	RBI	BB	SO
Total	.241	.282	.380	734	177	38	2	20	73	40	116		.260	.305	.380	4021	1045	208	21	78	427	255	569
vs. Left	.212	.265	.343	137	29	7	1	3	16	10	17		.235	.281	.358	707	166	29	5	16	81	46	104
vs. Right	.248	.285	.389	597	148	31	1	17	57	30	99		.265	.310	.385	3314	879	179	16	62	346	209	465
Bases Empty	.235	.272	.367	455	107	22	1	12	12	20	81		.253	.293	.369	2401	608	122	13	43	43	124	343
Leadoff	.233	.289	.378	180	42	5	0	7	7	11	40		.272	.316	.395	1020	277	53	5	21	21	59	146
Runners On Base	.251	.297	.401	279	70	16	1	8	61	20	35		.270	.321	.398	1620	437	86	8	35	384	131	226
Scoring Position	.266	.301	.462	143	38	11	1	5	53	9	16		.285	.338	.432	875	249	54	6	21	342	82	119
Late and Close	.292	.326	.449	89	26	8	0	2	13	5	13		.288	.314	.456	410	118	32	5	9	46	13	54

7-YEAR TOTALS (1986–1993) (right-hand columns above)

MIKE MUSSINA — BR/TR — age 26 — BAL SP25 FIN/FB

1993	G	IP	H	BB	SO	SB	CS	W	L	SV	ERA		G	IP	H	BB	SO	SB	CS	W	L	SV	ERA
Total	25	167.2	163	44	117	3	6	14	6	0	4.46		69	496.1	452	113	299	16	19	36	16	0	3.25
at Home	12	74.1	77	21	50	1	3	5	2	0	4.72		33	232.2	213	51	146	6	10	15	6	0	3.33
on Road	13	93.1	86	23	67	2	3	9	4	0	4.24		36	263.2	239	62	153	10	9	21	10	0	3.17
on Grass	22	143.1	149	39	107	2	5	11	6	0	4.83		59	421.0	377	96	273	13	18	30	14	0	3.19
on Turf	3	24.1	14	5	10	1	1	3	0	0	2.22		10	75.1	75	17	26	3	1	6	2	0	3.58
Day Games	9	69.1	57	16	55	1	3	7	1	0	3.38		21	152.2	133	39	91	5	8	11	5	0	3.01
Night Games	16	98.1	106	28	62	2	3	7	5	0	5.22		48	343.2	319	74	208	11	11	25	11	0	3.35
April	5	40.1	31	8	20	1	4	3	1	0	3.12		9	70.2	58	16	30	2	5	6	1	0	2.80
May	5	43.2	35	10	35	0	1	4	1	0	2.68		10	73.1	59	14	49	1	2	6	2	0	2.82
June	4	21.2	29	6	21	1	0	2	1	0	7.48		10	66.1	62	14	45	3	1	5	3	0	3.80
July	4	21.2	30	8	15	0	0	2	1	0	7.48		10	63.0	74	14	38	1	1	4	2	0	4.57
August	3	22.2	17	6	15	1	1	2	1	0	2.78		15	104.2	102	31	70	5	3	7	6	0	3.70
Sept-Oct	3	17.2	21	6	11	0	0	1	1	0	6.62		15	118.1	97	24	67	4	7	8	2	0	2.36

	BA	OBA	SA	AB	H	2B	3B	HR	RBI	BB	SO		BA	OBA	SA	AB	H	2B	3B	HR	RBI	BB	SO
Total	.256	.306	.410	636	163	34	2	20	78	44	117		.245	.289	.371	1846	452	87	8	43	172	113	299
vs. Left	.256	.308	.352	281	72	13	1	4	32	21	55		.231	.282	.307	885	204	38	3	8	66	64	148
vs. Right	.256	.304	.456	355	91	21	1	16	46	23	62		.258	.295	.429	961	248	49	5	35	106	49	151
Bases Empty	.253	.307	.411	387	98	21	2	12	12	28	76		.247	.297	.370	1150	284	59	4	25	25	78	196
Leadoff	.274	.316	.482	164	45	11	1	7	7	10	32		.248	.288	.376	487	121	25	2	11	11	26	87
Runners On Base	.261	.304	.410	249	65	13	0	8	66	16	41		.241	.275	.371	696	168	28	4	18	147	35	103
Scoring Position	.298	.356	.496	131	39	8	1	6	61	14	22		.239	.284	.372	339	81	17	2	8	121	25	47
Late and Close	.212	.281	.231	52	11	1	0	0	4	5	6		.244	.293	.330	176	43	9	0	2	15	13	16

3-YEAR TOTALS (1991–1993) (right-hand columns above)

RANDY MYERS — BL/TL — age 32 — CHN RP73 POW/FB

1993 / 9-YEAR TOTALS (1985–1993)

1993	G	IP	H	BB	SO	SB	CS	W	L	SV	ERA		G	IP	H	BB	SO	SB	CS	W	L	SV	ERA
Total	73	75.1	65	26	86	1	1	2	4	53	3.11		448	613.2	503	275	622	21	23	32	42	184	3.07
at Home	36	37.0	35	17	40	0	0	1	2	25	3.16		238	321.0	253	146	312	11	11	19	13	99	2.92
on Road	37	38.1	30	9	46	1	1	1	2	28	3.05		210	292.2	250	129	310	10	12	13	29	85	3.23
on Grass	56	56.1	51	21	66	1	1	2	4	39	3.20		269	342.2	270	139	357	10	10	19	19	118	2.92
on Turf	17	19.0	14	5	20	0	0	0	0	14	2.84		179	271.0	233	136	265	11	13	13	23	66	3.25
Day Games	38	39.0	37	17	42	0	0	1	2	27	3.46		163	203.1	174	103	216	9	7	7	11	63	3.45
Night Games	35	36.1	28	9	44	1	1	1	2	26	2.72		285	410.1	329	172	406	12	16	25	31	121	2.87
April	10	9.2	3	5	12	0	0	0	0	6	0.00		57	65.2	58	37	78	5	3	4	4	27	3.56
May	12	12.2	12	6	15	0	0	0	1	9	3.55		73	86.0	65	36	95	3	7	8	3	30	2.83
June	11	12.1	10	1	16	1	1	1	0	9	1.46		78	107.0	83	46	107	6	4	9	9	23	2.52
July	12	11.2	14	5	10	0	0	0	1	8	6.94		76	108.2	92	47	93	2	3	2	8	31	3.56
August	11	11.2	12	6	12	1	0	1	0	5	4.63		78	114.2	101	52	107	3	3	2	11	33	2.83
Sept-Oct	17	17.1	14	3	21	0	0	0	0	16	2.08		86	131.2	104	57	142	2	3	7	7	40	3.21

	BA	OBA	SA	AB	H	2B	3B	HR	RBI	BB	SO		BA	OBA	SA	AB	H	2B	3B	HR	RBI	BB	SO
Total	.230	.295	.364	283	65	15	1	7	28	26	86		.226	.310	.333	2228	503	81	13	44	252	275	622
vs. Left	.178	.302	.289	45	8	0	1	1	2	8	17		.212	.319	.324	513	109	18	6	9	53	83	188
vs. Right	.239	.293	.378	238	57	15	0	6	26	18	69		.230	.307	.336	1715	394	63	7	35	199	192	434
Bases Empty	.252	.321	.449	147	37	12	1	5	5	15	46		.236	.316	.362	1137	268	48	6	28	28	132	321
Leadoff	.246	.313	.361	61	15	5	1	0	0	6	16		.240	.315	.374	484	116	21	4	12	12	52	138
Runners On Base	.206	.267	.272	136	28	3	0	2	23	11	40		.215	.304	.302	1091	235	33	7	16	224	143	301
Scoring Position	.205	.294	.301	73	15	1	0	2	21	9	23		.204	.300	.290	648	132	18	4	10	201	96	192
Late and Close	.245	.313	.375	192	47	10	0	5	22	19	53		.220	.305	.323	1330	293	45	5	27	157	165	376

CHRIS NABHOLZ — BL/TL — age 27 — MON SP21, RP5 POW/FB

1993 / 4-YEAR TOTALS (1990–1993)

1993	G	IP	H	BB	SO	SB	CS	W	L	SV	ERA		G	IP	H	BB	SO	SB	CS	W	L	SV	ERA
Total	26	116.2	100	63	74	15	9	9	8	0	4.09		93	535.1	453	226	356	60	29	34	29	0	3.51
at Home	15	73.0	52	35	45	6	6	6	2	0	2.71		47	286.2	212	115	183	27	17	17	16	0	3.01
on Road	11	43.2	48	28	29	9	3	3	6	0	6.39		46	248.2	241	111	173	33	12	17	13	0	4.09
on Grass	6	28.1	25	16	16	8	2	2	3	0	4.13		21	120.2	114	52	78	19	5	7	9	0	4.40
on Turf	20	88.1	75	47	58	7	7	7	5	0	4.08		72	414.2	339	174	278	41	24	27	20	0	3.26
Day Games	6	29.0	29	17	19	4	3	1	2	0	3.10		24	150.0	116	62	96	12	8	10	6	0	3.12
Night Games	20	87.2	71	46	55	11	6	8	6	0	4.41		69	385.1	337	164	260	48	21	24	23	0	3.67
April	5	23.2	29	14	18	5	2	1	2	0	5.70		14	76.2	78	40	49	15	7	7	7	0	4.58
May	4	14.2	18	14	11	2	2	2	2	0	6.75		13	70.0	58	38	54	8	3	6	4	0	4.63
June	4	15.0	12	12	10	2	0	1	1	0	7.20		14	71.2	69	37	59	11	3	3	4	0	4.52
July	5	36.0	26	11	15	5	1	2	2	0	2.50		10	68.2	59	22	32	7	3	3	3	0	3.01
August	2	12.0	8	4	6	0	1	1	1	0	3.00		17	110.2	82	38	62	10	5	7	6	0	3.09
Sept-Oct	6	15.1	7	8	14	1	3	2	0	0	0.59		25	137.2	107	51	100	9	8	13	5	0	2.42

	BA	OBA	SA	AB	H	2B	3B	HR	RBI	BB	SO		BA	OBA	SA	AB	H	2B	3B	HR	RBI	BB	SO
Total	.236	.343	.348	423	100	18	1	9	47	63	74		.232	.315	.338	1956	453	90	13	31	180	226	356
vs. Left	.243	.354	.343	70	17	2	1	1	3	10	17		.231	.323	.348	342	79	11	4	7	28	42	90
vs. Right	.235	.341	.348	353	83	16	0	8	44	53	57		.232	.313	.336	1614	374	79	9	24	152	184	266
Bases Empty	.254	.364	.353	232	59	12	1	3	3	39	38		.233	.321	.343	1141	266	51	10	18	18	140	207
Leadoff	.260	.398	.360	100	26	7	0	1	1	22	18		.246	.338	.377	496	122	25	5	10	10	66	95
Runners On Base	.215	.319	.340	191	41	6	0	6	44	24	36		.229	.305	.333	815	187	39	3	13	162	86	149
Scoring Position	.250	.359	.442	104	26	5	0	5	42	17	21		.245	.333	.351	425	104	25	1	6	143	58	85
Late and Close	.240	.321	.240	25	6	0	0	0	0	3	7		.214	.324	.256	117	25	2	1	0	4	18	16

JAIME NAVARRO — BR/TR — age 27 — MIL SP34, RP1 FIN/FB

1993 / 5-YEAR TOTALS (1989–1993)

1993	G	IP	H	BB	SO	SB	CS	W	L	SV	ERA		G	IP	H	BB	SO	SB	CS	W	L	SV	ERA
Total	35	214.1	254	73	114	23	6	11	12	0	5.33		154	953.1	1010	283	459	86	33	58	50	1	4.08
at Home	16	98.1	112	38	55	12	2	5	5	0	5.03		74	460.1	473	141	230	43	15	33	20	1	3.79
on Road	19	116.0	142	35	59	11	4	6	7	0	5.59		80	493.0	537	142	229	43	18	25	30	0	4.34
on Grass	28	168.2	190	65	94	18	3	8	10	0	5.34		125	775.0	792	245	370	70	26	46	38	1	3.87
on Turf	7	45.2	64	8	20	5	3	3	2	0	5.32		29	178.1	218	38	89	16	7	12	12	0	5.00
Day Games	12	76.2	88	25	38	15	3	5	3	0	4.70		55	321.0	334	96	158	34	9	22	16	0	3.67
Night Games	23	137.2	166	48	76	8	3	6	9	0	5.69		99	632.1	676	187	301	52	24	36	34	1	4.28
April	5	28.0	31	13	18	4	2	0	2	0	6.11		17	93.2	117	37	45	9	5	2	4	0	5.48
May	5	34.0	38	10	12	4	1	3	1	0	3.18		21	142.1	156	29	60	13	2	11	9	0	3.86
June	5	46.2	45	16	23	2	3	0	2	0	4.24		23	157.2	155	57	74	22	6	10	6	0	3.94
July	5	28.2	43	9	7	2	1	1	4	0	8.16		29	154.0	155	46	67	12	6	6	11	1	3.80
August	7	39.2	54	14	26	6	1	2	1	0	6.35		32	186.1	200	52	102	14	8	14	12	0	4.69
Sept-Oct	6	37.1	43	11	28	4	1	3	3	0	4.82		32	219.1	227	62	111	16	6	15	11	0	3.41

	BA	OBA	SA	AB	H	2B	3B	HR	RBI	BB	SO		BA	OBA	SA	AB	H	2B	3B	HR	RBI	BB	SO
Total	.300	.356	.440	848	254	38	9	21	121	73	114		.273	.326	.387	3698	1010	160	25	70	407	283	459
vs. Left	.317	.367	.475	448	142	20	9	11	66	38	60		.284	.335	.400	1878	533	80	15	36	211	154	221
vs. Right	.280	.344	.400	400	112	18	0	10	55	35	54		.262	.316	.373	1820	477	80	10	34	196	129	238
Bases Empty	.283	.336	.419	494	140	21	5	12	12	34	68		.264	.315	.378	2184	576	92	16	42	42	149	280
Leadoff	.281	.341	.424	210	59	11	2	5	5	17	26		.251	.305	.364	931	234	38	5	19	19	65	115
Runners On Base	.322	.382	.469	354	114	17	4	9	109	39	46		.287	.341	.399	1514	434	68	9	28	365	134	179
Scoring Position	.285	.350	.425	207	59	15	3	4	94	27	37		.268	.329	.373	847	227	42	4	13	319	91	114
Late and Close	.300	.383	.450	40	12	3	1	0	1	3	5		.291	.333	.427	309	90	15	3	7	32	21	33

EDWIN NUNEZ — BR/TR — age 31 — OAK RP56 POW/GB

1993	G	IP	H	BB	SO	SB	CS	W	L	SV	ERA
Total	56	75.2	89	29	58	5	3	3	6	1	3.81
at Home	26	29.2	35	13	24	3	2	1	2	1	3.64
on Road	30	46.0	54	16	34	2	1	2	4	0	3.91
on Grass	44	56.2	71	24	45	3	3	1	5	1	4.61
on Turf	12	19.0	18	5	13	2	0	2	1	0	1.42
Day Games	23	25.2	43	15	25	1	3	1	1	1	6.31
Night Games	33	50.0	46	14	33	4	0	2	5	0	2.52
April	9	8.2	9	6	8	0	1	0	0	0	3.12
May	9	15.1	21	3	8	1	2	1	2	0	4.11
June	10	15.0	12	4	10	0	2	0	1	0	1.20
July	9	12.2	14	4	16	0	0	0	2	1	3.55
August	11	11.0	22	9	7	3	0	0	1	0	11.45
Sept-Oct	8	13.0	11	3	9	1	0	0	0	0	0.69

10-YEAR TOTALS (1984–1993)

	G	IP	H	BB	SO	SB	CS	W	L	SV	ERA
	390	565.0	564	232	431	40	17	27	30	54	3.95
	195	285.0	281	119	231	22	10	15	14	30	3.92
	195	280.0	283	113	200	18	7	12	16	24	3.99
	235	343.2	356	155	265	21	12	13	18	29	4.19
	155	221.1	208	77	166	19	5	14	12	25	3.58
	101	135.1	155	54	116	8	7	8	9	10	4.52
	289	429.2	409	178	315	32	10	19	21	44	3.77
	57	78.0	72	36	64	8	3	4	4	11	3.92
	50	67.0	77	31	38	6	3	4	4	5	4.16
	62	113.2	94	41	79	6	3	6	6	10	3.09
	66	100.0	96	34	78	3	5	6	6	5	3.06
	79	108.2	112	48	85	5	1	3	3	15	4.56
	76	97.2	113	42	86	12	2	4	7	8	5.07

	BA	OBA	SA	AB	H	2B	3B	HR	RBI	BB	SO
Total	.298	.369	.395	299	89	17	3	2	43	29	58
vs. Left	.265	.320	.346	136	36	9	1	0	15	12	28
vs. Right	.325	.409	.436	163	53	8	2	2	28	17	30
Bases Empty	.347	.428	.455	121	42	11	1	0	0	15	25
Leadoff	.311	.391	.459	61	19	7	1	0	0	7	15
Runners On Base	.264	.328	.354	178	47	6	2	2	43	14	33
Scoring Position	.284	.350	.413	109	31	4	2	2	43	10	21
Late and Close	.323	.385	.443	167	54	10	2	2	25	16	31

	BA	OBA	SA	AB	H	2B	3B	HR	RBI	BB	SO
	.261	.334	.411	2160	564	108	15	62	326	232	431
	.253	.332	.413	963	244	47	7	31	147	118	187
	.267	.335	.409	1197	320	61	8	31	179	114	244
	.248	.317	.400	1099	273	59	6	32	32	104	231
	.252	.323	.394	457	115	26	3	11	11	44	93
	.274	.350	.422	1061	291	49	9	30	294	128	200
	.278	.360	.431	666	185	28	7	20	266	94	136
	.291	.363	.472	808	235	44	6	30	151	97	140

GREGG OLSON — BR/TR — age 28 — BAL RP50 POW/GB

1993	G	IP	H	BB	SO	SB	CS	W	L	SV	ERA
Total	50	45.0	37	18	44	1	1	0	2	29	1.60
at Home	25	23.0	17	10	30	0	0	0	2	16	1.96
on Road	25	22.0	20	8	14	1	1	0	0	13	1.23
on Grass	40	35.1	28	15	36	0	0	0	2	27	1.53
on Turf	10	9.2	9	3	8	1	1	0	0	2	1.86
Day Games	11	11.1	12	7	9	0	1	0	1	6	2.38
Night Games	39	33.2	25	11	35	1	0	0	1	23	1.34
April	11	12.1	14	4	10	0	0	0	1	5	2.19
May	9	9.1	7	5	10	1	0	0	0	5	1.93
June	12	10.2	4	3	10	0	0	0	0	11	0.00
July	11	9.2	10	2	12	0	1	0	1	5	2.79
August	4	3.0	2	3	2	0	0	0	0	3	0.00
Sept-Oct	1	0.0	0	1	0	0	0	0	0	0	0.00

6-YEAR TOTALS (1988–1993)

	G	IP	H	BB	SO	SB	CS	W	L	SV	ERA
	320	350.1	281	158	347	54	5	17	21	160	2.26
	160	171.2	119	84	188	33	1	12	4	71	1.94
	160	178.2	162	74	159	21	4	5	17	89	2.57
	262	285.1	200	128	288	45	3	14	12	140	1.89
	58	65.0	81	30	59	9	2	3	9	20	3.88
	83	96.1	94	45	86	14	3	2	11	42	3.74
	237	254.0	187	113	261	40	2	15	10	118	1.70
	42	55.2	47	21	43	6	2	3	2	16	1.94
	56	67.0	46	31	74	7	2	2	2	27	1.48
	57	59.1	38	21	64	11	0	4	4	40	2.28
	57	57.2	59	31	65	5	1	1	7	29	3.12
	50	49.1	44	24	39	10	0	2	2	25	2.92
	58	61.1	47	30	62	15	0	5	4	23	2.05

	BA	OBA	SA	AB	H	2B	3B	HR	RBI	BB	SO
Total	.223	.296	.295	166	37	9	0	1	23	18	44
vs. Left	.212	.281	.294	85	18	4	0	1	13	9	24
vs. Right	.235	.311	.296	81	19	5	0	0	10	9	20
Bases Empty	.216	.301	.297	74	16	6	0	0	0	9	19
Leadoff	.290	.371	.323	31	9	1	0	0	0	4	8
Runners On Base	.228	.291	.293	92	21	3	0	1	23	9	25
Scoring Position	.237	.329	.339	59	14	3	0	1	23	9	18
Late and Close	.236	.304	.317	123	29	7	0	1	23	13	34

	BA	OBA	SA	AB	H	2B	3B	HR	RBI	BB	SO
	.220	.306	.281	1279	281	42	3	10	126	158	347
	.190	.282	.229	641	122	16	0	3	55	80	170
	.249	.331	.332	638	159	26	3	7	71	78	177
	.228	.301	.307	618	141	27	2	6	6	61	165
	.202	.283	.288	257	52	6	2	4	4	27	65
	.212	.311	.256	661	140	15	1	4	120	97	182
	.205	.324	.248	420	86	10	1	2	115	77	127
	.222	.311	.287	893	198	28	3	8	105	116	243

JESSE OROSCO — BR/TL — age 37 — MIL RP57 POW/GB

1993	G	IP	H	BB	SO	SB	CS	W	L	SV	ERA
Total	57	56.2	47	17	67	2	5	3	5	8	3.18
at Home	29	29.1	30	11	39	2	1	0	5	5	4.60
on Road	28	27.1	17	6	28	0	4	3	0	3	1.65
on Grass	50	48.1	43	17	57	2	5	2	5	7	3.54
on Turf	7	8.1	4	0	10	0	0	1	0	1	1.08
Day Games	23	19.0	14	3	18	0	1	0	2	3	3.32
Night Games	34	37.2	33	14	49	2	4	3	3	5	3.11
April	6	3.1	6	1	4	0	1	0	1	1	8.10
May	12	10.2	8	2	13	0	0	1	0	1	3.38
June	11	9.1	10	2	11	2	0	0	0	0	4.82
July	7	5.0	5	3	4	0	0	1	0	1	3.60
August	10	14.0	6	3	18	0	0	0	1	3	1.29
Sept-Oct	11	14.1	12	6	17	0	1	2	3	2	2.51

10-YEAR TOTALS (1984–1993)

	G	IP	H	BB	SO	SB	CS	W	L	SV	ERA
	572	661.0	551	272	613	57	20	48	43	108	3.04
	272	333.1	292	123	324	22	10	24	26	47	3.02
	300	327.2	259	149	289	35	10	24	17	61	3.05
	432	501.1	433	204	472	39	17	37	36	73	3.30
	140	159.2	118	68	141	18	3	11	7	35	2.20
	193	216.1	192	83	192	15	7	19	13	38	3.37
	379	444.2	359	189	421	42	13	29	30	70	2.87
	66	69.1	45	39	65	5	3	3	5	20	2.08
	102	113.2	101	41	114	10	3	11	10	20	3.56
	99	110.2	108	54	102	14	2	3	9	11	4.07
	102	117.0	101	48	97	14	0	9	4	20	3.00
	103	125.0	98	35	114	2	4	7	6	19	2.59
	100	125.1	98	55	121	12	8	15	9	18	2.66

	BA	OBA	SA	AB	H	2B	3B	HR	RBI	BB	SO
Total	.224	.289	.305	210	47	9	1	2	24	17	67
vs. Left	.313	.353	.438	64	20	5	0	1	8	3	15
vs. Right	.185	.262	.247	146	27	4	1	1	16	14	52
Bases Empty	.223	.286	.301	103	23	5	0	1	1	6	37
Leadoff	.302	.348	.442	43	13	3	0	1	1	3	10
Runners On Base	.224	.292	.308	107	24	4	1	1	23	11	30
Scoring Position	.220	.304	.305	59	13	2	0	1	20	8	15
Late and Close	.203	.275	.301	143	29	7	0	1	17	12	48

	BA	OBA	SA	AB	H	2B	3B	HR	RBI	BB	SO
	.226	.305	.336	2437	551	90	7	55	301	272	613
	.221	.283	.289	674	149	22	0	8	74	60	183
	.228	.313	.355	1763	402	68	7	47	227	212	430
	.243	.318	.369	1179	286	54	4	29	29	123	293
	.259	.338	.411	494	128	22	1	17	17	56	110
	.211	.293	.306	1258	265	36	3	26	272	149	320
	.201	.304	.283	762	153	20	2	13	240	118	205
	.224	.308	.327	1512	338	58	3	31	189	179	385

DONOVAN OSBORNE — BB/TL — age 25 — SL SP26 FIN/FB — 2-YEAR TOTALS (1992–1993)

1993	G	IP	H	BB	SO	SB	CS	W	L	SV	ERA		G	IP	H	BB	SO	SB	CS	W	L	SV	ERA
Total	26	155.2	153	47	83	4	5	10	7	0	3.76		60	334.2	346	85	187	19	8	21	16	0	3.76
at Home	13	86.1	85	20	46	2	2	7	3	0	2.50		29	165.1	169	37	95	11	2	12	6	0	2.94
on Road	13	69.1	68	27	37	2	3	3	4	0	5.32		31	169.1	177	48	92	8	6	9	10	0	4.57
on Grass	9	44.1	47	18	26	2	2	2	3	0	5.68		18	97.1	104	27	53	5	3	6	6	0	4.72
on Turf	17	111.1	106	29	57	2	3	8	4	0	2.99		42	237.1	242	58	134	14	5	15	10	0	3.38
Day Games	8	53.1	45	17	32	1	2	3	2	0	3.38		20	109.2	111	29	71	8	2	5	5	0	3.94
Night Games	18	102.1	108	30	51	3	3	7	5	0	3.96		40	225.0	235	56	116	11	6	16	11	0	3.68
April	5	29.1	24	11	13	0	1	1	0	0	3.38		9	50.1	41	16	22	0	2	3	0	0	2.68
May	5	31.1	34	11	15	1	0	1	2	0	2.87		11	75.2	73	17	41	4	1	4	4	0	2.85
June	6	39.0	42	8	24	2	2	4	1	0	4.15		11	69.1	74	16	40	4	3	4	3	0	4.02
July	5	29.1	25	9	16	1	1	3	1	0	4.91		12	54.1	62	16	35	6	1	5	3	0	5.96
August	5	26.2	28	8	15	0	1	1	3	0	3.38		11	50.0	50	11	35	2	1	3	4	0	3.42
Sept-Oct	0	0.0	0	0	0	0	0	0	0	0	0.00		6	35.0	46	9	14	3	0	2	2	0	3.86

	BA	OBA	SA	AB	H	2B	3B	HR	RBI	BB	SO		BA	OBA	SA	AB	H	2B	3B	HR	RBI	BB	SO
Total	.257	.318	.410	595	153	27	5	18	61	47	83		.267	.315	.407	1298	346	66	10	32	137	85	187
vs. Left	.203	.260	.297	118	24	5	0	2	10	9	16		.268	.309	.390	269	72	18	0	5	33	17	39
vs. Right	.270	.332	.438	477	129	22	5	16	51	38	67		.266	.316	.411	1029	274	48	10	27	104	68	148
Bases Empty	.249	.290	.412	381	95	21	4	11	11	21	59		.249	.284	.396	803	200	43	6	21	21	37	127
Leadoff	.258	.303	.400	155	40	8	1	4	4	9	17		.259	.305	.401	332	86	21	1	8	8	20	39
Runners On Base	.271	.363	.407	214	58	6	1	7	50	26	24		.295	.362	.424	495	146	23	4	11	116	48	60
Scoring Position	.261	.353	.412	119	31	3	0	5	44	15	14		.283	.346	.407	290	82	11	2	7	101	28	42
Late and Close	.220	.238	.341	41	9	3	1	0	3	1	3		.229	.250	.352	105	24	8	1	1	7	3	13

BOB PATTERSON — BR/TL — age 35 — TEX RP52 POW/FB — 8-YEAR TOTALS (1985–1993)

1993	G	IP	H	BB	SO	SB	CS	W	L	SV	ERA		G	IP	H	BB	SO	SB	CS	W	L	SV	ERA
Total	52	52.2	59	11	46	3	2	2	4	1	4.78		262	387.2	407	108	284	13	19	27	25	18	4.29
at Home	25	22.0	32	5	18	0	2	1	2	0	6.14		130	215.0	222	64	157	6	11	16	11	9	4.52
on Road	27	30.2	27	6	28	3	0	1	2	1	3.82		132	172.2	185	44	127	7	8	11	14	9	4.01
on Grass	44	43.2	48	10	36	1	2	2	4	1	4.95		106	137.2	166	38	107	1	8	7	10	6	4.90
on Turf	8	9.0	11	1	10	2	0	0	0	0	4.00		156	250.0	241	70	177	12	11	20	15	12	3.96
Day Games	15	16.0	17	4	13	1	0	0	1	1	4.50		83	115.2	126	29	79	4	4	7	9	7	4.44
Night Games	37	36.2	42	7	33	2	2	2	3	0	4.91		179	272.0	281	79	205	9	15	20	16	11	4.24
April	8	11.0	15	1	10	0	1	1	1	0	4.09		39	67.1	69	21	46	2	3	6	6	0	4.28
May	7	6.1	10	3	3	1	0	1	0	0	8.53		40	54.1	73	17	44	2	1	2	3	2	6.29
June	10	8.1	8	2	12	1	1	0	1	0	1.08		38	53.0	48	13	34	3	1	4	2	4	2.38
July	9	9.2	12	4	7	1	1	0	1	1	7.45		42	56.2	50	14	48	1	5	4	2	6	3.49
August	10	12.0	8	0	6	0	0	0	0	0	3.00		40	47.2	45	15	32	2	5	2	4	2	3.21
Sept-Oct	8	5.1	6	1	8	0	0	0	1	0	6.75		63	108.2	122	28	80	3	4	9	8	4	5.13

	BA	OBA	SA	AB	H	2B	3B	HR	RBI	BB	SO		BA	OBA	SA	AB	H	2B	3B	HR	RBI	BB	SO
Total	.282	.318	.450	209	59	9	1	8	33	11	46		.272	.321	.419	1495	407	78	9	41	210	108	284
vs. Left	.250	.267	.347	72	18	4	0	1	9	2	18		.227	.283	.330	436	99	21	3	6	53	34	108
vs. Right	.299	.345	.504	137	41	5	1	7	24	9	28		.291	.336	.455	1059	308	57	6	35	157	74	176
Bases Empty	.259	.301	.414	116	30	7	1	3	3	6	27		.255	.303	.395	831	212	53	6	17	17	53	165
Leadoff	.349	.378	.488	43	15	4	0	0	0	2	7		.319	.361	.491	348	111	27	3	9	9	21	63
Runners On Base	.312	.340	.495	93	29	2	0	5	30	5	19		.294	.342	.449	664	195	25	3	24	193	55	119
Scoring Position	.346	.368	.538	52	18	1	0	3	26	3	11		.305	.364	.506	387	118	19	1	19	178	43	67
Late and Close	.293	.339	.448	58	17	0	0	3	11	4	15		.264	.323	.420	398	105	18	1	14	57	35	89

ROGER PAVLIK — BB/TR — age 27 — TEX SP26 POW/FB — 2-YEAR TOTALS (1992–1993)

1993	G	IP	H	BB	SO	SB	CS	W	L	SV	ERA		G	IP	H	BB	SO	SB	CS	W	L	SV	ERA
Total	26	166.1	151	80	131	15	6	12	6	0	3.41		39	228.1	217	114	176	18	14	16	10	0	3.63
at Home	14	92.1	70	42	77	9	3	7	2	0	2.73		20	114.1	101	55	95	11	4	9	4	0	3.54
on Road	12	74.0	81	38	54	6	3	5	4	0	4.26		19	114.0	116	59	81	7	10	7	6	0	3.71
on Grass	21	133.1	117	63	108	12	4	10	4	0	3.38		33	190.0	173	94	148	15	9	14	7	0	3.51
on Turf	5	33.0	34	17	23	3	2	2	2	0	3.55		6	38.1	44	20	28	3	5	2	3	0	4.23
Day Games	5	30.2	32	18	25	2	1	4	1	0	3.23		8	53.0	46	27	39	2	3	6	1	0	2.21
Night Games	21	135.2	119	62	106	13	5	8	5	0	3.45		31	175.1	171	87	137	16	11	10	9	0	4.06
April	0	0.0	0	0	0	0	0	0	0	0	0.00		0	0.0	0	0	0	0	0	0	0	0	0.00
May	2	12.2	11	7	10	2	0	1	1	0	2.84		5	22.1	20	19	17	3	2	1	1	0	3.63
June	6	39.0	36	22	29	5	2	2	3	0	4.62		6	39.0	36	22	29	5	2	2	3	0	4.62
July	5	26.2	39	10	24	3	2	3	1	0	5.06		5	26.2	39	10	24	3	2	3	1	0	5.06
August	6	44.0	39	15	39	2	0	3	1	0	2.66		11	67.0	66	23	56	3	4	5	3	0	3.49
Sept-Oct	7	44.0	26	26	29	3	2	3	0	0	2.25		12	73.1	56	40	50	4	4	5	2	0	2.70

	BA	OBA	SA	AB	H	2B	3B	HR	RBI	BB	SO		BA	OBA	SA	AB	H	2B	3B	HR	RBI	BB	SO
Total	.245	.334	.382	617	151	25	3	18	56	80	131		.254	.346	.382	853	217	32	7	21	79	114	176
vs. Left	.228	.324	.353	329	75	13	2	8	23	46	71		.240	.332	.353	462	111	17	4	9	39	64	97
vs. Right	.264	.347	.417	288	76	12	1	10	33	34	60		.271	.361	.417	391	106	15	3	12	40	50	79
Bases Empty	.246	.331	.405	370	91	17	3	12	12	45	79		.261	.352	.409	494	129	24	5	13	13	66	100
Leadoff	.237	.324	.391	156	37	7	1	5	5	19	32		.255	.355	.387	212	54	9	2	5	5	32	39
Runners On Base	.243	.339	.348	247	60	8	0	6	44	35	52		.245	.337	.345	359	88	8	2	8	66	48	76
Scoring Position	.223	.321	.360	139	31	4	0	5	41	22	32		.245	.338	.359	192	47	4	0	6	59	29	44
Late and Close	.227	.300	.318	44	10	1	0	1	4	5	13		.250	.352	.350	60	15	3	0	1	5	10	16

MELIDO PEREZ — BR/TR — age 28 — NYA SP25 POW/FB

1993

1993	G	IP	H	BB	SO	SB	CS	W	L	SV	ERA
Total	25	163.0	173	64	148	11	6	6	14	0	5.19
at Home	14	83.1	98	34	75	3	2	3	9	0	6.26
on Road	11	79.2	75	30	73	8	4	3	5	0	4.07
on Grass	23	146.2	162	62	137	10	4	6	14	0	5.58
on Turf	2	16.1	11	2	11	1	2	0	0	0	1.65
Day Games	8	42.1	63	11	33	0	2	3	4	0	7.23
Night Games	17	120.2	110	53	115	11	4	3	10	0	4.48
April	3	22.0	13	8	22	2	1	1	1	0	2.05
May	6	46.0	41	17	39	3	3	2	3	0	4.11
June	5	35.0	45	15	35	4	1	0	3	0	5.66
July	5	28.0	34	11	20	1	0	1	3	0	6.75
August	5	27.0	31	12	28	1	0	1	4	0	6.67
Sept-Oct	1	5.0	9	1	4	1	0	0	1	0	9.00

7-YEAR TOTALS (1987–1993)

	G	IP	H	BB	SO	SB	CS	W	L	SV	ERA
Total	208	1134.0	1064	462	939	88	64	64	76	1	4.10
at Home	97	506.0	501	204	408	40	29	26	33	0	4.46
on Road	111	628.0	563	258	531	48	35	38	43	1	3.80
on Grass	170	933.0	868	384	775	72	48	54	61	1	4.11
on Turf	38	201.0	196	78	164	16	16	10	15	0	4.03
Day Games	54	309.0	312	135	244	21	19	21	18	0	4.34
Night Games	154	825.0	752	327	695	67	45	43	58	1	4.00
April	22	130.2	111	59	120	15	8	6	8	0	3.72
May	35	223.1	199	104	184	15	10	14	14	0	4.11
June	39	202.2	205	83	153	13	13	12	15	0	4.40
July	33	181.0	166	69	127	13	13	14	9	0	3.88
August	39	198.2	202	72	176	17	12	6	17	0	4.53
Sept-Oct	40	197.2	181	75	179	15	8	12	13	1	3.78

1993 Batting against

	BA	OBA	SA	AB	H	2B	3B	HR	RBI	BB	SO
Total	.267	.333	.431	647	173	34	3	22	86	64	148
vs. Left	.277	.352	.407	339	94	15	1	9	38	40	81
vs. Right	.256	.312	.458	308	79	19	2	13	48	24	67
Bases Empty	.236	.308	.378	373	88	19	2	10	10	39	88
Leadoff	.264	.320	.396	159	42	7	1	4	4	13	27
Runners On Base	.310	.368	.504	274	85	15	1	12	76	25	60
Scoring Position	.347	.402	.599	147	51	16	1	9	69	14	32
Late and Close	.232	.293	.290	69	16	4	0	0	4	6	12

7-YEAR TOTALS (1987–1993) Batting against

	BA	OBA	SA	AB	H	2B	3B	HR	RBI	BB	SO
Total	.248	.322	.388	4283	1064	179	33	118	495	462	939
vs. Left	.250	.325	.385	2172	542	91	22	53	239	247	469
vs. Right	.247	.318	.392	2111	522	88	11	65	256	215	470
Bases Empty	.240	.316	.381	2508	603	103	15	73	73	271	562
Leadoff	.261	.332	.398	1067	278	45	9	28	28	111	211
Runners On Base	.260	.329	.399	1775	461	76	18	45	422	191	377
Scoring Position	.263	.334	.399	977	257	38	7	27	364	113	223
Late and Close	.244	.312	.370	451	110	20	2	11	41	44	100

MIKE PEREZ — BR/TR — age 30 — SL RP65 POW/FB

1993

1993	G	IP	H	BB	SO	SB	CS	W	L	SV	ERA
Total	65	72.2	65	20	58	8	2	7	2	7	2.48
at Home	30	37.1	32	9	27	4	0	7	0	3	2.65
on Road	35	35.1	33	11	31	4	2	0	2	4	2.29
on Grass	24	26.0	22	9	26	3	2	0	1	2	2.42
on Turf	41	46.2	43	11	32	5	0	7	1	5	2.51
Day Games	26	25.1	27	8	21	2	1	3	1	3	4.26
Night Games	39	47.1	38	12	37	6	1	4	1	4	1.52
April	12	16.1	18	4	16	2	2	2	1	0	3.31
May	14	16.1	12	4	14	2	0	2	1	2	1.65
June	14	13.1	8	8	11	3	0	0	0	1	2.03
July	3	1.1	4	0	0	0	0	0	0	0	0.00
August	7	8.0	6	1	7	0	0	1	0	0	1.13
Sept-Oct	15	17.1	17	3	10	1	0	2	0	4	3.63

4-YEAR TOTALS (1990–1993)

	G	IP	H	BB	SO	SB	CS	W	L	SV	ERA
Total	169	196.1	166	62	116	17	5	17	7	8	2.57
at Home	77	99.2	78	26	53	6	1	13	3	4	2.08
on Road	92	96.2	88	36	63	11	4	4	4	4	3.07
on Grass	49	52.2	47	21	41	5	2	4	2	2	2.56
on Turf	120	143.2	119	41	75	12	3	13	5	6	2.57
Day Games	60	70.1	64	23	45	6	1	6	2	3	3.84
Night Games	109	126.0	102	39	71	11	4	11	5	5	1.86
April	31	48.1	43	12	32	4	2	4	2	0	2.42
May	31	32.2	31	11	24	1	1	4	2	2	3.03
June	30	29.1	19	14	21	3	0	1	1	1	2.15
July	14	16.0	17	5	6	3	1	1	1	1	1.13
August	19	23.0	17	11	11	2	1	2	1	1	1.96
Sept-Oct	44	47.0	39	9	22	3	0	5	0	5	3.45

1993 Batting against

	BA	OBA	SA	AB	H	2B	3B	HR	RBI	BB	SO
Total	.244	.295	.342	266	65	8	3	4	27	20	58
vs. Left	.270	.325	.374	115	31	4	1	2	13	10	21
vs. Right	.225	.271	.318	151	34	4	2	2	14	10	37
Bases Empty	.242	.278	.329	161	39	4	2	2	2	8	34
Leadoff	.209	.264	.313	67	14	2	1	1	1	5	12
Runners On Base	.248	.317	.362	105	26	4	1	2	25	12	24
Scoring Position	.262	.321	.354	65	17	3	0	1	22	8	15
Late and Close	.234	.277	.359	145	34	2	2	4	15	9	33

4-YEAR TOTALS (1990–1993) Batting against

	BA	OBA	SA	AB	H	2B	3B	HR	RBI	BB	SO
Total	.232	.292	.319	715	166	23	6	9	67	62	116
vs. Left	.261	.334	.348	322	84	12	2	4	34	37	45
vs. Right	.209	.256	.295	393	82	11	4	5	33	25	71
Bases Empty	.225	.265	.321	436	98	14	5	6	6	23	73
Leadoff	.217	.254	.328	180	39	4	2	4	4	8	21
Runners On Base	.244	.329	.315	279	68	9	1	3	61	39	43
Scoring Position	.242	.346	.315	165	40	6	0	2	57	31	25
Late and Close	.238	.313	.347	340	81	8	4	7	32	37	55

HIPOLITO PICHARDO — BR/TR — age 25 — KC SP25, RP5 FIN/GB

1993

1993	G	IP	H	BB	SO	SB	CS	W	L	SV	ERA
Total	30	165.0	183	53	70	8	7	7	8	0	4.04
at Home	17	90.0	105	26	38	2	4	4	4	0	3.90
on Road	13	75.0	78	27	32	6	3	3	4	0	4.20
on Grass	8	44.0	45	16	15	6	2	2	1	0	4.09
on Turf	22	121.0	138	37	55	2	5	5	7	0	4.02
Day Games	10	49.1	53	15	26	0	2	2	3	0	4.01
Night Games	20	115.2	130	38	44	8	5	5	5	0	4.05
April	5	27.1	30	7	16	0	0	1	1	0	4.28
May	5	31.2	37	14	16	1	2	2	1	0	4.26
June	5	31.2	31	17	13	3	3	1	1	0	4.55
July	6	34.2	44	5	12	1	1	1	3	0	4.67
August	3	16.2	16	7	7	1	1	1	0	0	2.70
Sept-Oct	6	23.0	25	3	6	3	0	0	2	0	2.74

2-YEAR TOTALS (1992–1993)

	G	IP	H	BB	SO	SB	CS	W	L	SV	ERA
Total	61	308.2	331	102	129	19	10	16	14	0	3.99
at Home	33	165.1	180	42	68	7	4	9	6	0	3.92
on Road	28	143.1	151	60	61	12	6	7	8	0	4.08
on Grass	20	100.1	106	44	39	11	4	5	5	0	4.13
on Turf	41	208.1	225	58	90	8	6	11	9	0	3.93
Day Games	19	85.0	103	27	38	3	3	4	4	0	4.98
Night Games	42	223.2	228	75	91	16	7	12	10	0	3.62
April	7	31.0	34	8	18	0	0	1	1	0	4.65
May	13	57.1	59	21	23	1	3	3	3	0	3.92
June	10	60.2	60	28	26	4	3	3	3	0	3.71
July	11	68.1	72	13	25	5	1	3	4	0	3.42
August	9	45.2	51	17	17	6	2	4	1	0	4.73
Sept-Oct	11	45.2	55	15	20	3	0	2	2	0	4.14

1993 Batting against

	BA	OBA	SA	AB	H	2B	3B	HR	RBI	BB	SO
Total	.282	.338	.398	650	183	46	0	10	76	53	70
vs. Left	.299	.354	.408	331	99	21	0	5	43	30	24
vs. Right	.263	.320	.389	319	84	25	0	5	33	23	46
Bases Empty	.299	.359	.428	341	102	26	0	6	6	28	33
Leadoff	.269	.325	.410	156	42	10	0	4	4	13	14
Runners On Base	.262	.314	.366	309	81	20	0	4	70	25	37
Scoring Position	.281	.346	.388	178	50	13	0	2	63	21	27
Late and Close	.257	.316	.400	35	9	2	0	1	3	3	4

2-YEAR TOTALS (1992–1993) Batting against

	BA	OBA	SA	AB	H	2B	3B	HR	RBI	BB	SO
Total	.275	.333	.390	1204	331	77	2	19	131	102	129
vs. Left	.294	.350	.407	575	169	39	1	8	68	53	45
vs. Right	.258	.316	.374	629	162	38	1	11	63	49	84
Bases Empty	.273	.341	.391	640	175	43	1	10	10	59	70
Leadoff	.278	.350	.406	288	80	20	1	5	5	30	31
Runners On Base	.277	.323	.388	564	156	34	1	9	121	43	59
Scoring Position	.283	.338	.393	318	90	20	0	5	108	32	43
Late and Close	.273	.333	.386	44	12	2	0	1	3	4	4

ERIC PLUNK — BR/TR — age 31 — CLE RP70 POW/FB · 8-YEAR TOTALS (1986–1993)

1993	G	IP	H	BB	SO	SB	CS	W	L	SV	ERA		G	IP	H	BB	SO	SB	CS	W	L	SV	ERA
Total	70	71.0	61	30	77	6	1	4	5	15	2.79		375	724.2	634	440	650	88	35	44	40	27	3.94
at Home	35	36.0	28	8	37	2	1	3	1	7	2.25		175	356.2	316	222	310	36	18	28	15	14	4.14
on Road	35	35.0	33	22	40	4	0	1	4	8	3.34		200	368.0	318	218	340	52	17	16	25	13	3.74
on Grass	58	59.0	52	22	64	6	1	4	4	11	3.20		317	620.0	541	371	557	74	32	38	34	22	4.04
on Turf	12	12.0	9	8	13	0	0	0	1	4	0.75		58	104.2	93	69	93	14	3	6	6	5	3.35
Day Games	21	21.2	19	10	30	2	0	1	2	4	1.66		122	233.0	184	164	216	26	9	20	13	8	3.28
Night Games	49	49.1	42	20	47	4	1	3	3	11	3.28		253	491.2	450	276	434	62	26	24	27	19	4.25
April	10	10.2	13	5	14	2	0	1	2	0	4.22		45	77.2	83	55	67	15	4	5	5	1	4.17
May	12	12.0	8	5	17	1	0	0	0	3	1.50		69	124.2	104	70	109	18	7	3	5	5	3.75
June	11	11.0	7	2	11	2	0	2	0	4	2.45		64	113.2	89	75	111	13	5	8	5	5	4.43
July	11	8.1	10	7	4	1	0	1	1	3	3.24		55	102.1	98	70	75	5	5	8	7	5	3.87
August	13	14.0	9	5	16	0	0	0	2	3	4.50		65	138.2	110	80	132	11	6	8	7	7	3.89
Sept-Oct	13	15.0	14	6	15	0	0	0	0	2	1.20		77	167.2	150	90	156	26	8	12	11	4	3.70

	BA	OBA	SA	AB	H	2B	3B	HR	RBI	BB	SO		BA	OBA	SA	AB	H	2B	3B	HR	RBI	BB	SO
Total	.226	.301	.352	270	61	17	1	5	32	30	77		.236	.344	.365	2685	634	101	14	72	355	440	650
vs. Left	.240	.336	.394	104	25	8	1	2	9	15	25		.249	.359	.377	1255	313	48	11	30	137	218	282
vs. Right	.217	.279	.325	166	36	9	0	3	23	15	52		.224	.330	.354	1430	321	53	3	42	218	222	368
Bases Empty	.238	.294	.413	126	30	11	1	3	3	10	30		.240	.347	.373	1404	337	53	11	37	37	226	320
Leadoff	.250	.316	.404	52	13	5	0	1	1	5	10		.237	.330	.365	616	146	23	4	16	16	83	137
Runners On Base	.215	.307	.299	144	31	6	0	2	29	20	47		.232	.340	.356	1281	297	48	3	35	318	214	330
Scoring Position	.200	.283	.295	105	21	4	0	2	28	13	32		.228	.350	.345	800	182	33	2	19	280	158	220
Late and Close	.261	.342	.410	161	42	10	1	4	23	21	40		.232	.330	.357	712	165	20	3	21	96	105	160

MARK PORTUGAL — BR/TR — age 32 — HOU SP33 FIN/GB · 9-YEAR TOTALS (1985–1993)

1993	G	IP	H	BB	SO	SB	CS	W	L	SV	ERA		G	IP	H	BB	SO	SB	CS	W	L	SV	ERA
Total	33	208.0	194	77	131	14	4	18	4	0	2.77		207	1020.2	965	386	673	79	41	63	49	5	3.76
at Home	15	95.0	97	30	72	5	1	10	1	0	2.37		102	492.2	468	174	350	37	20	36	17	3	3.14
on Road	18	113.0	97	47	59	9	3	8	3	0	3.11		105	528.0	497	212	323	42	21	27	32	2	4.33
on Grass	12	76.1	63	35	40	7	2	4	2	0	3.18		77	368.0	367	147	227	30	11	16	25	2	4.62
on Turf	21	131.2	131	42	91	7	2	14	2	0	2.53		130	652.2	598	239	446	49	30	47	24	3	3.27
Day Games	9	58.0	53	19	32	4	2	6	1	0	2.33		70	356.1	340	143	229	27	16	22	20	4	3.89
Night Games	24	150.0	141	58	99	10	2	12	3	0	2.94		137	664.1	625	243	444	52	25	41	29	1	3.68
April	5	31.2	31	7	14	1	1	2	2	0	3.69		26	126.1	135	45	78	14	6	8	10	1	4.70
May	5	28.1	25	15	18	3	0	2	0	0	1.91		37	181.0	183	73	111	18	8	8	9	0	4.33
June	5	29.0	28	16	22	6	0	1	1	0	4.66		33	179.0	160	67	122	16	6	5	10	0	4.07
July	6	37.2	47	10	27	2	1	4	1	0	2.39		32	144.2	146	51	104	4	3	11	5	2	3.11
August	6	37.0	34	18	19	0	2	4	0	0	2.92		30	174.0	164	71	117	13	8	14	3	0	3.16
Sept-Oct	6	44.1	29	11	31	2	0	5	0	0	1.62		49	215.2	177	79	141	14	10	17	12	2	3.38

	BA	OBA	SA	AB	H	2B	3B	HR	RBI	BB	SO		BA	OBA	SA	AB	H	2B	3B	HR	RBI	BB	SO
Total	.248	.318	.323	781	194	26	1	10	63	77	131		.252	.322	.380	3822	965	162	11	101	405	386	673
vs. Left	.234	.305	.294	411	96	11	1	4	30	42	71		.239	.315	.361	2098	501	84	10	51	217	234	408
vs. Right	.265	.332	.354	370	98	15	0	6	33	35	60		.269	.330	.403	1724	464	78	1	50	188	152	265
Bases Empty	.240	.313	.302	454	109	16	0	4	4	47	74		.257	.325	.382	2233	573	97	7	56	56	219	388
Leadoff	.253	.327	.313	198	50	9	0	1	1	22	30		.281	.355	.429	957	269	40	6	30	30	107	155
Runners On Base	.260	.325	.352	327	85	10	1	6	59	30	57		.247	.318	.378	1589	392	65	4	45	349	167	285
Scoring Position	.265	.349	.361	166	44	5	1	3	51	21	34		.250	.330	.386	859	215	36	3	25	296	109	162
Late and Close	.319	.353	.426	47	15	1	0	1	4	3	7		.305	.366	.442	321	98	14	0	10	32	31	46

TIM PUGH — BR/TR — age 27 — CIN SP27, RP4 FIN/GB · 2-YEAR TOTALS (1992–1993)

1993	G	IP	H	BB	SO	SB	CS	W	L	SV	ERA		G	IP	H	BB	SO	SB	CS	W	L	SV	ERA
Total	31	164.1	200	59	94	19	7	10	15	0	5.26		38	209.2	247	72	112	20	8	14	17	0	4.68
at Home	14	79.1	89	28	44	9	3	6	5	0	4.76		19	108.2	127	38	55	11	3	8	7	0	4.47
on Road	17	85.0	111	31	50	9	4	4	10	0	5.72		19	101.0	120	34	57	9	5	6	10	0	4.90
on Grass	12	62.2	75	22	40	4	4	3	6	0	5.17		14	78.2	84	25	47	4	5	5	6	0	4.23
on Turf	19	101.2	125	37	54	15	3	7	9	0	5.31		24	131.0	163	47	65	16	3	9	11	0	4.95
Day Games	12	60.1	73	17	40	6	1	3	6	0	6.12		14	73.1	88	21	48	6	1	4	6	0	5.40
Night Games	19	104.0	127	42	54	13	6	7	9	0	4.76		24	136.1	159	51	64	14	7	10	11	0	4.29
April	5	26.0	25	6	13	1	2	2	1	0	2.77		5	26.0	25	6	13	1	2	2	1	0	2.77
May	5	29.0	41	14	12	2	1	1	4	0	6.52		5	29.0	41	14	12	2	1	1	4	0	6.52
June	6	23.1	35	5	14	9	0	0	4	0	6.94		6	23.1	35	5	14	9	0	0	4	0	6.94
July	5	33.0	36	6	18	2	1	3	1	0	3.55		5	33.0	36	6	18	2	1	3	1	0	3.55
August	6	29.0	40	14	18	1	1	2	3	0	7.76		6	29.0	40	14	18	1	1	2	3	0	7.76
Sept-Oct	4	24.0	23	14	19	4	0	2	2	0	4.13		11	69.1	70	27	37	5	1	6	4	0	3.12

	BA	OBA	SA	AB	H	2B	3B	HR	RBI	BB	SO		BA	OBA	SA	AB	H	2B	3B	HR	RBI	BB	SO
Total	.303	.363	.437	661	200	20	6	19	92	59	94		.297	.357	.430	831	247	31	6	21	104	72	112
vs. Left	.348	.410	.529	325	113	15	4	12	55	35	40		.333	.401	.499	411	137	20	6	12	58	47	48
vs. Right	.259	.317	.348	336	87	5	2	7	37	24	54		.262	.311	.362	420	110	11	2	9	46	25	64
Bases Empty	.270	.332	.392	378	102	16	3	8	8	32	56		.283	.342	.411	470	133	22	4	10	10	39	64
Leadoff	.267	.314	.410	161	43	7	2	4	4	10	25		.294	.339	.441	204	60	11	2	5	5	13	27
Runners On Base	.346	.404	.498	283	98	4	3	11	84	27	38		.316	.375	.454	361	114	9	4	11	94	33	48
Scoring Position	.327	.384	.463	162	53	3	2	5	70	17	21		.302	.367	.427	199	60	6	2	5	79	22	25
Late and Close	.318	.348	.318	22	7	0	0	0	1	1	6		.303	.361	.394	33	10	1	0	1	2	3	8

SCOTT RADINSKY — BL/TL — age 26 — CHA RP73 POW/FB

1993	G	IP	H	BB	SO	SB	CS	W	L	SV	ERA
Total	73	54.2	61	19	44	2	0	8	2	4	4.28
at Home	36	30.0	35	11	26	1	0	3	2	2	5.70
on Road	37	24.2	26	8	18	1	0	5	0	2	2.55
on Grass	59	46.0	53	16	39	1	0	7	2	3	4.30
on Turf	14	8.2	8	3	5	1	0	1	0	1	4.15
Day Games	22	19.2	20	5	16	0	0	5	0	1	2.29
Night Games	51	35.0	41	14	28	2	0	3	2	3	5.40
April	9	11.1	10	4	8	0	0	0	0	0	3.18
May	11	8.0	15	2	5	1	0	2	0	0	10.13
June	16	8.1	10	3	10	0	0	0	0	0	2.16
July	12	8.1	2	1	5	0	0	4	0	0	1.08
August	13	9.1	10	5	8	0	0	0	2	1	5.79
Sept-Oct	12	9.1	14	4	8	1	0	2	0	0	3.86

4-YEAR TOTALS (1990–1993)

	G	IP	H	BB	SO	SB	CS	W	L	SV	ERA
	270	237.2	215	112	187	6	3	22	15	31	3.33
	135	128.1	109	47	110	4	1	9	7	20	3.02
	135	109.1	106	65	77	2	2	13	8	11	3.70
	223	199.1	173	90	166	5	2	18	11	28	2.98
	47	38.1	42	22	21	1	1	4	4	3	5.17
	81	78.2	79	35	60	2	2	10	5	9	3.20
	189	159.0	136	77	127	4	1	12	10	22	3.40
	33	30.2	25	12	26	0	0	2	2	2	2.05
	48	47.1	39	21	42	2	0	8	1	2	3.61
	50	40.1	31	18	32	1	0	1	4	6	2.68
	52	43.0	39	21	40	1	0	6	3	7	3.77
	42	39.2	37	17	26	0	1	2	3	10	2.72
	45	36.2	44	23	21	2	2	3	2	4	4.91

	BA	OBA	SA	AB	H	2B	3B	HR	RBI	BB	SO
Total	.268	.327	.333	228	61	6	0	3	27	19	44
vs. Left	.239	.287	.261	88	21	2	0	0	7	6	29
vs. Right	.286	.351	.379	140	40	4	0	3	20	13	15
Bases Empty	.279	.310	.333	111	31	3	0	1	1	5	18
Leadoff	.224	.240	.224	49	11	0	0	0	0	1	8
Runners On Base	.256	.341	.333	117	30	3	0	2	26	14	26
Scoring Position	.280	.349	.373	75	21	1	0	2	26	7	19
Late and Close	.239	.295	.283	113	27	2	0	1	7	9	20

	BA	OBA	SA	AB	H	2B	3B	HR	RBI	BB	SO
	.238	.324	.317	902	215	32	3	11	112	112	187
	.204	.264	.289	294	60	6	2	5	34	23	91
	.255	.352	.331	608	155	26	1	6	78	89	96
	.255	.325	.335	415	106	13	1	6	6	40	78
	.242	.320	.319	182	44	5	0	3	3	19	35
	.224	.323	.302	487	109	19	2	5	106	72	109
	.210	.318	.282	309	65	9	2	3	96	50	80
	.216	.306	.292	504	109	18	1	6	48	63	98

JEFF REARDON — BR/TR — age 39 — CIN RP58 FIN/FB

1993	G	IP	H	BB	SO	SB	CS	W	L	SV	ERA
Total	58	61.2	66	10	35	6	1	4	6	8	4.09
at Home	29	29.2	27	8	20	2	1	4	3	5	3.34
on Road	29	32.0	39	2	15	4	0	0	3	3	4.78
on Grass	17	18.1	22	0	6	0	0	0	1	1	5.40
on Turf	41	43.1	44	10	29	6	1	4	5	7	3.53
Day Games	16	16.1	14	2	7	1	0	1	1	1	3.86
Night Games	42	45.1	52	8	28	5	1	3	5	7	4.17
April	7	8.0	10	1	3	0	0	0	0	2	3.38
May	10	9.0	10	2	5	1	0	1	0	4	3.00
June	12	11.1	8	0	4	2	1	1	1	0	1.59
July	12	13.1	12	3	12	0	0	0	3	2	3.38
August	9	11.1	9	1	6	0	0	1	0	0	0.79
Sept-Oct	8	8.2	17	3	5	3	0	1	2	0	14.54

10-YEAR TOTALS (1984–1993)

	G	IP	H	BB	SO	SB	CS	W	L	SV	ERA
	606	720.1	653	197	549	64	10	46	55	302	3.49
	317	372.2	337	108	288	35	6	34	31	161	3.53
	289	347.2	316	89	261	29	4	12	24	141	3.44
	277	316.0	286	78	235	21	4	19	17	137	3.50
	329	404.1	367	119	314	43	6	27	38	165	3.47
	203	239.2	217	66	165	17	4	14	19	88	3.64
	403	480.2	436	131	384	47	6	32	36	214	3.41
	80	104.2	83	38	65	8	2	5	6	38	2.58
	114	137.0	110	30	109	14	0	9	7	62	3.02
	108	128.0	112	29	104	13	1	9	9	54	3.45
	98	108.1	118	29	84	10	3	3	11	45	4.24
	102	121.1	115	44	95	10	3	7	14	55	4.30
	104	121.0	115	27	92	9	1	13	8	48	3.35

	BA	OBA	SA	AB	H	2B	3B	HR	RBI	BB	SO
Total	.270	.308	.398	244	66	15	2	4	29	10	35
vs. Left	.297	.351	.390	118	35	9	1	0	11	8	10
vs. Right	.246	.265	.405	126	31	6	1	4	18	2	25
Bases Empty	.231	.259	.313	134	31	5	0	2	2	4	15
Leadoff	.135	.167	.212	52	7	1	0	1	1	1	8
Runners On Base	.318	.363	.500	110	35	10	2	2	27	6	20
Scoring Position	.227	.262	.373	75	17	6	1	1	24	3	15
Late and Close	.303	.325	.455	145	44	8	1	4	20	4	21

	BA	OBA	SA	AB	H	2B	3B	HR	RBI	BB	SO
	.240	.294	.374	2721	653	119	9	76	363	197	549
	.261	.325	.402	1387	362	59	5	42	194	126	212
	.218	.262	.346	1334	291	60	4	34	169	71	337
	.229	.274	.361	1472	337	60	4	42	42	84	285
	.181	.231	.295	570	103	22	2	13	13	32	117
	.253	.317	.390	1249	316	59	5	34	321	113	264
	.243	.318	.385	811	197	37	3	24	291	91	178
	.244	.301	.380	2006	489	78	8	60	307	155	411

STEVE REED — BR/TR — age 28 — COL RP64 FIN/GB

1993	G	IP	H	BB	SO	SB	CS	W	L	SV	ERA
Total	64	84.1	80	30	51	8	7	9	5	3	4.48
at Home	39	50.2	58	18	24	6	3	7	3	1	6.39
on Road	25	33.2	22	12	27	2	4	2	2	2	1.60
on Grass	54	71.2	75	25	38	7	6	9	4	2	4.90
on Turf	10	12.2	5	5	13	1	1	0	1	1	2.13
Day Games	21	23.2	29	10	20	0	1	2	2	2	6.85
Night Games	43	60.2	51	20	31	8	6	7	3	1	3.56
April	8	9.1	12	4	4	1	0	1	0	0	8.68
May	3	2.2	6	3	2	0	0	0	0	0	16.88
June	8	12.0	9	2	6	0	1	2	0	0	1.50
July	15	21.2	25	7	14	4	4	2	2	1	4.57
August	13	18.0	15	7	10	3	0	2	0	2	2.50
Sept-Oct	17	20.2	13	7	15	0	2	2	1	0	4.35

2-YEAR TOTALS (1992–1993)

	G	IP	H	BB	SO	SB	CS	W	L	SV	ERA
	82	100.0	93	33	62	9	7	10	5	3	4.14
	45	58.1	63	20	31	7	3	7	3	1	5.86
	37	41.2	30	13	31	2	4	3	2	2	1.73
	65	84.0	85	27	48	8	6	9	4	2	4.50
	17	16.0	8	6	14	1	1	1	1	1	2.25
	25	26.1	32	11	22	1	1	2	2	2	6.15
	57	73.2	61	22	40	8	6	8	3	1	3.42
	8	9.1	12	4	4	1	0	1	0	0	8.68
	3	2.2	6	3	2	0	0	0	0	0	16.88
	8	12.0	9	2	6	0	1	2	0	0	1.50
	15	21.2	25	7	14	4	4	2	2	1	4.57
	14	18.1	15	7	10	3	0	2	0	2	2.45
	34	36.0	26	10	26	1	2	3	1	0	3.50

	BA	OBA	SA	AB	H	2B	3B	HR	RBI	BB	SO
Total	.259	.328	.440	309	80	13	2	13	43	30	51
vs. Left	.336	.410	.607	122	41	8	2	7	21	13	16
vs. Right	.209	.272	.332	187	39	5	0	6	22	17	35
Bases Empty	.250	.302	.425	200	50	7	2	8	8	14	35
Leadoff	.263	.325	.434	76	20	4	0	3	3	6	15
Runners On Base	.275	.369	.468	109	30	6	0	5	35	16	16
Scoring Position	.304	.400	.493	69	21	2	0	2	30	12	8
Late and Close	.180	.265	.300	100	18	4	1	2	10	11	17

	BA	OBA	SA	AB	H	2B	3B	HR	RBI	BB	SO
	.253	.319	.432	368	93	17	2	15	55	33	62
	.326	.395	.576	144	47	11	2	7	26	14	19
	.205	.268	.339	224	46	6	0	8	29	19	43
	.244	.298	.404	225	55	8	2	8	8	16	40
	.238	.312	.393	84	20	4	0	3	3	8	17
	.266	.349	.476	143	38	9	0	7	47	17	22
	.298	.378	.532	94	28	7	0	5	42	13	13
	.202	.289	.336	119	24	5	1	3	14	13	19

ARMANDO REYNOSO — BR/TR — age 28 — COL SP30 FIN/FB

1993	G	IP	H	BB	SO	SB	CS	W	L	SV	ERA
Total	30	189.0	206	63	117	11	5	12	11	0	4.00
at Home	14	88.2	103	28	51	3	0	7	3	0	4.36
on Road	16	100.1	103	35	66	8	5	5	8	0	3.68
on Grass	24	152.2	170	47	96	7	3	11	8	0	4.01
on Turf	6	36.1	36	16	21	4	2	1	3	0	3.96
Day Games	11	66.0	74	23	44	3	2	5	5	0	3.55
Night Games	19	123.0	132	40	73	8	3	7	6	0	4.24
April	1	9.0	6	2	4	0	0	1	0	0	1.00
May	6	43.1	49	13	30	1	2	2	2	0	3.32
June	5	35.2	32	14	23	3	0	2	1	0	3.53
July	6	37.2	38	9	21	2	2	2	3	0	4.06
August	6	33.2	41	15	20	3	0	2	3	0	4.28
Sept-Oct	6	29.2	40	10	18	2	1	3	2	0	6.07

3-YEAR TOTALS (1991–1993)

	G	IP	H	BB	SO	SB	CS	W	L	SV	ERA
	39	220.0	243	75	129	12	7	15	12	1	4.25
	19	102.1	116	33	56	4	0	8	3	1	4.22
	20	117.2	127	42	73	8	7	7	9	0	4.28
	31	178.1	197	55	107	8	5	14	8	1	3.99
	8	41.2	46	20	22	4	2	1	4	0	5.40
	13	77.0	84	28	49	3	3	7	5	0	3.51
	26	143.0	159	47	80	9	4	8	7	1	4.66
	1	9.0	6	2	4	0	0	1	0	0	1.00
	6	43.1	49	13	30	1	2	2	2	0	3.32
	5	35.2	32	14	23	3	0	2	1	0	3.53
	6	37.2	38	9	21	2	2	2	3	0	4.06
	12	61.0	74	27	32	4	2	5	4	0	5.31
	9	33.1	44	10	19	2	1	3	2	1	5.40

	BA	OBA	SA	AB	H	2B	3B	HR	RBI	BB	SO
Total	.277	.337	.439	745	206	35	10	22	91	63	117
vs. Left	.275	.340	.452	378	104	23	7	10	47	32	64
vs. Right	.278	.333	.425	367	102	12	3	12	44	31	53
Bases Empty	.289	.339	.500	418	121	20	7	18	18	27	66
Leadoff	.321	.356	.587	184	59	12	5	9	9	10	24
Runners On Base	.260	.335	.361	327	85	15	3	4	73	36	51
Scoring Position	.226	.316	.317	208	47	10	3	1	64	28	35
Late and Close	.256	.370	.436	39	10	4	0	1	6	6	7

	BA	OBA	SA	AB	H	2B	3B	HR	RBI	BB	SO
	.283	.346	.460	860	243	43	13	28	113	75	129
	.286	.353	.497	433	124	29	10	14	59	37	70
	.279	.340	.424	427	119	14	3	14	54	38	59
	.294	.352	.515	480	141	22	9	22	22	35	75
	.324	.372	.610	210	68	14	5	12	12	15	29
	.268	.339	.392	380	102	21	4	6	91	40	54
	.245	.333	.365	233	57	13	3	3	80	32	37
	.256	.360	.488	43	11	4	0	2	7	6	9

JOSE RIJO — BR/TR — age 29 — CIN SP36 POW/GB

1993	G	IP	H	BB	SO	SB	CS	W	L	SV	ERA
Total	36	257.1	218	62	227	22	10	14	9	0	2.48
at Home	19	135.0	117	38	117	9	6	8	6	0	2.60
on Road	17	122.1	101	24	110	13	4	6	3	0	2.35
on Grass	10	74.1	57	8	69	7	4	3	3	0	2.06
on Turf	26	183.0	161	54	158	15	6	11	6	0	2.66
Day Games	9	68.0	55	16	47	5	1	6	2	0	2.25
Night Games	27	189.1	163	46	180	17	9	8	7	0	2.57
April	5	35.0	25	8	30	2	1	2	1	0	2.31
May	6	40.2	36	11	32	1	2	4	0	0	3.32
June	6	42.2	38	7	38	5	1	0	2	0	3.80
July	7	53.0	46	12	49	6	5	3	2	0	1.87
August	6	42.0	37	13	40	6	0	3	2	0	1.50
Sept-Oct	6	44.0	36	11	38	2	1	2	2	0	2.25

10-YEAR TOTALS (1984–1993)

	G	IP	H	BB	SO	SB	CS	W	L	SV	ERA
	292	1544.1	1349	560	1323	149	60	97	77	3	3.13
	137	741.0	625	287	663	78	33	47	33	1	3.06
	155	803.1	724	273	660	71	27	50	44	2	3.19
	133	673.1	607	259	564	65	27	38	39	3	3.27
	159	871.0	742	301	759	84	33	59	38	0	3.02
	97	484.2	409	177	420	46	17	31	23	0	2.86
	195	1059.2	940	383	903	103	43	66	54	3	3.25
	51	216.2	191	89	200	22	13	9	13	1	3.49
	56	262.0	226	108	220	27	10	18	6	0	3.06
	58	270.2	254	88	240	28	9	13	21	2	4.16
	36	233.2	207	75	196	21	13	16	10	2	2.43
	43	264.0	228	103	222	29	7	17	16	0	3.24
	48	297.1	243	97	245	22	8	24	11	0	2.45

	BA	OBA	SA	AB	H	2B	3B	HR	RBI	BB	SO
Total	.230	.278	.342	949	218	32	9	19	73	62	227
vs. Left	.241	.296	.359	523	126	20	6	10	48	40	112
vs. Right	.216	.254	.322	426	92	12	3	9	25	22	115
Bases Empty	.253	.289	.401	589	149	21	6	18	18	28	134
Leadoff	.264	.301	.411	246	65	8	2	8	8	12	51
Runners On Base	.192	.259	.247	360	69	11	3	1	55	34	93
Scoring Position	.187	.273	.246	203	38	7	2	0	51	25	58
Late and Close	.200	.231	.267	75	15	2	0	1	4	3	17

	BA	OBA	SA	AB	H	2B	3B	HR	RBI	BB	SO
	.235	.304	.348	5729	1349	238	39	110	544	560	1323
	.253	.334	.378	3145	795	144	27	65	335	384	688
	.214	.266	.312	2584	554	94	12	45	209	176	635
	.237	.297	.365	3435	814	156	21	81	81	286	757
	.239	.303	.381	1442	344	61	8	43	43	127	298
	.233	.314	.323	2294	535	82	18	29	463	274	566
	.233	.324	.308	1347	314	48	10	11	407	192	373
	.250	.327	.379	523	131	18	5	13	52	58	114

BEN RIVERA — BR/TR — age 25 — PHI SP28, RP2 POW/FB

1993	G	IP	H	BB	SO	SB	CS	W	L	SV	ERA
Total	30	163.0	175	85	123	15	3	13	9	0	5.02
at Home	16	80.0	90	38	71	8	2	4	6	0	5.74
on Road	14	83.0	85	47	52	7	1	9	3	0	4.34
on Grass	8	51.2	50	31	22	4	1	6	2	0	3.48
on Turf	22	111.1	125	54	101	11	2	7	7	0	5.74
Day Games	8	43.0	44	18	34	4	1	3	4	0	5.02
Night Games	22	120.0	131	67	89	11	2	10	5	0	5.03
April	3	11.0	14	12	12	0	0	1	1	0	6.55
May	5	30.0	35	18	11	4	0	2	1	0	3.60
June	6	39.0	39	11	34	3	0	5	1	0	3.69
July	4	20.0	26	14	17	1	2	1	3	0	9.45
August	6	34.1	35	12	23	2	1	3	1	0	4.72
Sept-Oct	6	28.2	26	18	26	5	0	1	2	0	5.02

2-YEAR TOTALS (1992–1993)

	G	IP	H	BB	SO	SB	CS	W	L	SV	ERA
	58	280.1	274	130	200	30	7	20	13	0	4.21
	28	133.2	129	61	106	10	3	9	6	0	4.24
	30	146.2	145	69	94	20	4	11	7	0	4.17
	19	85.1	87	38	46	9	1	7	3	0	3.80
	39	195.0	187	92	154	21	6	13	10	0	4.38
	17	81.2	74	34	59	14	2	5	6	0	4.30
	41	198.2	200	96	141	16	5	15	7	0	4.17
	6	16.0	19	18	14	1	0	1	1	0	6.19
	10	40.1	51	20	20	5	2	2	2	0	3.79
	12	53.0	52	20	44	3	0	5	1	0	3.57
	6	22.2	29	14	19	3	2	1	3	0	8.34
	12	76.2	65	24	51	9	1	7	3	0	3.64
	12	71.2	58	29	52	9	2	4	3	0	3.77

	BA	OBA	SA	AB	H	2B	3B	HR	RBI	BB	SO
Total	.273	.361	.409	641	175	19	10	16	83	85	123
vs. Left	.301	.384	.446	316	95	13	6	7	45	43	52
vs. Right	.246	.339	.372	325	80	6	4	9	38	42	71
Bases Empty	.270	.352	.396	341	92	6	5	9	9	41	72
Leadoff	.255	.308	.363	157	40	2	3	3	3	11	31
Runners On Base	.277	.371	.423	300	83	13	5	7	74	44	51
Scoring Position	.222	.336	.358	176	39	6	3	4	63	30	38
Late and Close	.250	.250	.375	24	6	0	0	1	2	0	3

	BA	OBA	SA	AB	H	2B	3B	HR	RBI	BB	SO
	.256	.340	.388	1072	274	37	15	25	125	130	200
	.272	.355	.406	566	154	25	9	11	69	70	84
	.237	.323	.368	506	120	12	6	14	56	60	116
	.257	.333	.394	592	152	16	10	15	15	64	116
	.253	.310	.377	265	67	5	5	6	6	20	51
	.254	.347	.381	480	122	21	5	10	110	66	84
	.228	.339	.349	281	64	10	3	6	95	46	58
	.240	.309	.420	50	12	1	1	2	5	4	6

KEVIN ROGERS — BB/TL — age 26 — SF RP64 POW/GB

1993	G	IP	H	BB	SO	SB	CS	W	L	SV	ERA
Total	64	80.2	71	28	62	6	2	2	2	0	2.68
at Home	30	42.1	37	18	32	5	1	1	0	0	2.55
on Road	34	38.1	34	10	30	1	1	1	2	0	2.82
on Grass	50	66.0	57	22	52	6	1	2	1	0	2.18
on Turf	14	14.2	14	6	10	0	1	0	1	0	4.91
Day Games	37	47.0	44	16	36	5	2	2	1	0	2.49
Night Games	27	33.2	27	12	26	1	0	0	1	0	2.94
April	10	17.1	15	15	12	3	1	0	1	0	4.67
May	11	15.0	10	0	14	2	1	0	0	0	0.60
June	9	10.2	10	3	8	1	0	0	1	0	2.53
July	10	13.1	12	2	8	0	0	0	0	0	3.38
August	10	10.1	9	3	11	0	0	2	0	0	0.87
Sept-Oct	14	14.0	15	5	9	0	0	0	0	0	3.21

2-YEAR TOTALS (1992–1993)

	G	IP	H	BB	SO	SB	CS	W	L	SV	ERA
Total	70	114.2	108	41	88	7	4	2	4	0	3.14
at Home	33	59.1	58	25	46	5	2	1	1	0	3.19
on Road	37	55.1	50	16	42	2	2	1	3	0	3.09
on Grass	53	83.0	78	29	66	6	2	2	2	0	2.71
on Turf	17	31.2	30	12	22	1	2	0	2	0	4.26
Day Games	39	60.0	52	20	46	6	2	2	1	0	2.25
Night Games	31	54.2	56	21	42	1	2	0	3	0	4.12
April	10	17.1	15	15	12	3	1	0	1	0	4.67
May	11	15.0	10	0	14	2	1	0	0	0	0.60
June	9	10.2	10	3	8	1	0	0	1	0	2.53
July	10	13.1	12	2	8	0	0	0	0	0	3.38
August	10	10.1	9	3	11	0	0	2	0	0	0.87
Sept-Oct	20	48.0	52	18	35	1	2	0	2	0	3.94

	BA	OBA	SA	AB	H	2B	3B	HR	RBI	BB	SO
Total	.236	.308	.299	301	71	10	0	3	25	28	62
vs. Left	.230	.323	.253	87	20	2	0	0	7	9	26
vs. Right	.238	.302	.318	214	51	8	0	3	18	19	36
Bases Empty	.265	.335	.344	151	40	6	0	2	2	14	32
Leadoff	.250	.320	.265	68	17	1	0	0	0	6	18
Runners On Base	.207	.281	.253	150	31	4	0	1	23	14	30
Scoring Position	.270	.375	.338	74	20	2	0	1	21	11	16
Late and Close	.306	.363	.396	134	41	6	0	2	14	12	24

	BA	OBA	SA	AB	H	2B	3B	HR	RBI	BB	SO
Total	.249	.321	.326	433	108	12	0	7	39	41	88
vs. Left	.241	.315	.259	112	27	2	0	0	10	9	30
vs. Right	.252	.323	.349	321	81	10	0	7	29	32	58
Bases Empty	.254	.336	.364	228	58	7	0	6	6	25	50
Leadoff	.228	.297	.267	101	23	1	0	1	1	9	25
Runners On Base	.244	.304	.283	205	50	5	0	1	33	16	38
Scoring Position	.330	.407	.388	103	34	3	0	1	31	12	23
Late and Close	.309	.364	.403	139	43	7	0	2	15	12	24

KENNY ROGERS — BL/TL — age 30 — TEX SP33, RP2 FIN/FB

1993	G	IP	H	BB	SO	SB	CS	W	L	SV	ERA
Total	35	208.1	210	71	140	4	11	16	10	0	4.10
at Home	17	93.2	100	32	64	4	4	9	4	0	5.00
on Road	18	114.2	110	39	76	0	7	7	6	0	3.38
on Grass	31	177.1	182	64	119	4	8	14	9	0	4.52
on Turf	4	31.0	28	7	21	0	3	2	1	0	1.74
Day Games	7	37.1	48	11	24	1	1	2	3	0	6.75
Night Games	28	171.0	162	60	116	3	10	14	7	0	3.53
April	6	28.2	15	11	21	0	3	2	1	0	2.51
May	5	19.1	32	13	16	1	1	1	3	0	11.17
June	6	38.0	42	15	27	0	2	2	2	0	4.97
July	5	31.1	37	8	23	2	2	3	0	0	3.16
August	7	48.0	43	16	29	0	1	6	1	0	3.19
Sept-Oct	6	43.0	41	8	24	1	2	2	3	0	2.93

5-YEAR TOTALS (1989–1993)

	G	IP	H	BB	SO	SB	CS	W	L	SV	ERA
Total	321	568.0	564	242	420	16	24	42	36	28	3.90
at Home	170	283.1	285	124	209	12	6	28	17	14	4.03
on Road	151	284.2	279	118	211	4	18	14	19	14	3.76
on Grass	270	479.1	473	210	360	16	14	37	30	26	4.02
on Turf	51	88.2	91	32	60	0	10	5	6	2	3.25
Day Games	59	94.1	108	45	71	2	7	6	8	7	5.06
Night Games	262	473.2	456	197	349	14	17	36	28	21	3.67
April	36	71.1	69	31	52	2	6	4	5	2	4.42
May	54	103.0	120	59	76	7	5	7	6	1	5.50
June	54	96.1	109	44	70	1	4	3	8	8	4.76
July	56	84.1	82	29	78	3	2	7	3	8	3.20
August	64	107.2	93	42	75	1	4	11	5	3	3.01
Sept-Oct	57	105.1	91	37	69	2	3	10	9	6	2.65

	BA	OBA	SA	AB	H	2B	3B	HR	RBI	BB	SO
Total	.263	.325	.406	798	210	46	7	18	91	71	140
vs. Left	.222	.271	.333	90	20	6	2	0	6	5	20
vs. Right	.268	.331	.415	708	190	40	5	18	85	66	120
Bases Empty	.234	.291	.377	483	113	27	3	12	12	36	88
Leadoff	.254	.318	.433	201	51	13	1	7	7	19	29
Runners On Base	.308	.374	.451	315	97	19	4	6	79	35	52
Scoring Position	.277	.353	.429	191	53	9	1	6	72	24	37
Late and Close	.179	.220	.179	39	7	0	0	0	2	2	8

	BA	OBA	SA	AB	H	2B	3B	HR	RBI	BB	SO
Total	.260	.336	.393	2167	564	119	14	47	290	242	420
vs. Left	.220	.296	.320	459	101	25	3	5	55	43	101
vs. Right	.271	.347	.413	1708	463	94	11	42	235	199	319
Bases Empty	.246	.313	.378	1132	279	60	7	25	25	103	221
Leadoff	.249	.317	.366	478	119	25	2	9	9	47	80
Runners On Base	.275	.361	.410	1035	285	59	7	22	265	139	199
Scoring Position	.270	.370	.427	640	173	34	3	20	252	105	134
Late and Close	.242	.323	.357	650	157	35	2	12	91	76	140

MEL ROJAS — BR/TR — age 28 — MON RP66 FIN/FB

1993	G	IP	H	BB	SO	SB	CS	W	L	SV	ERA
Total	66	88.1	80	30	48	8	1	5	8	10	2.95
at Home	31	44.0	28	16	21	4	1	4	3	4	3.07
on Road	35	44.1	52	14	27	4	0	1	5	6	2.84
on Grass	18	26.0	27	6	17	1	0	1	1	3	2.42
on Turf	48	62.1	53	24	31	7	1	4	7	7	3.18
Day Games	20	25.2	25	15	12	4	0	1	4	3	3.86
Night Games	46	62.2	55	15	36	4	1	4	4	7	2.59
April	10	9.0	11	4	6	2	0	0	1	5	5.00
May	14	18.1	21	7	21	5	1	0	2	1	3.44
June	11	17.0	12	8	5	1	1	2	3	0	3.71
July	8	12.2	13	3	11	0	0	1	1	2	2.84
August	10	18.2	10	5	15	3	0	0	1	2	0.96
Sept-Oct	13	12.2	13	3	6	1	0	1	0	0	2.84

4-YEAR TOTALS (1990–1993)

	G	IP	H	BB	SO	SB	CS	W	L	SV	ERA
Total	194	277.0	227	101	181	29	7	18	13	27	2.63
at Home	92	127.1	96	41	81	16	3	10	5	10	2.90
on Road	102	149.2	131	60	100	13	4	8	8	17	2.41
on Grass	50	73.1	63	27	49	3	3	5	3	11	2.70
on Turf	144	203.2	164	74	132	26	4	13	10	16	2.61
Day Games	55	76.0	62	28	44	8	1	7	4	9	2.84
Night Games	139	201.0	165	73	137	21	6	11	9	21	2.55
April	19	24.0	30	13	13	3	1	0	2	5	4.50
May	27	36.0	31	14	19	3	0	2	2	2	2.00
June	24	34.0	25	12	15	3	2	2	3	2	2.65
July	25	39.1	36	7	31	4	1	3	3	6	2.06
August	49	77.1	49	28	61	9	2	4	3	6	2.21
Sept-Oct	50	66.1	56	27	42	7	1	7	0	6	3.12

	BA	OBA	SA	AB	H	2B	3B	HR	RBI	BB	SO
Total	.242	.308	.382	330	80	24	2	6	49	30	48
vs. Left	.270	.338	.427	185	50	13	2	4	28	21	26
vs. Right	.207	.269	.324	145	30	11	0	2	21	9	22
Bases Empty	.263	.314	.411	175	46	12	1	4	4	11	27
Leadoff	.312	.354	.455	77	24	5	0	2	2	5	7
Runners On Base	.219	.302	.348	155	34	12	1	2	45	19	21
Scoring Position	.245	.350	.418	98	24	9	1	2	43	17	15
Late and Close	.239	.307	.386	184	44	11	2	4	18	18	28

	BA	OBA	SA	AB	H	2B	3B	HR	RBI	BB	SO
Total	.223	.297	.342	1016	227	55	7	17	111	101	181
vs. Left	.230	.310	.354	565	130	30	5	10	64	69	95
vs. Right	.215	.279	.326	451	97	25	2	7	47	32	86
Bases Empty	.268	.326	.409	518	139	35	4	10	10	41	96
Leadoff	.305	.364	.456	226	69	16	3	4	4	21	37
Runners On Base	.177	.268	.271	498	88	20	3	7	101	60	85
Scoring Position	.184	.299	.286	315	58	14	3	4	92	51	60
Late and Close	.223	.305	.316	452	101	16	4	6	43	52	80

BRUCE RUFFIN — BB/TL — age 31 — COL RP47, SP12 POW/GB

1993

	G	IP	H	BB	SO	SB	CS	W	L	SV	ERA
Total	59	139.2	145	69	126	14	9	6	5	2	3.87
at Home	29	80.1	79	44	75	8	7	3	3	1	3.81
on Road	30	59.1	66	25	51	6	2	3	2	1	3.94
on Grass	45	109.1	115	59	101	13	7	3	5	1	4.28
on Turf	14	30.1	30	10	25	1	2	3	0	1	2.37
Day Games	24	57.2	63	27	54	4	4	5	2	1	3.28
Night Games	35	82.0	82	42	72	10	5	1	3	1	4.28
April	4	19.0	29	13	16	2	2	1	1	0	6.16
May	6	19.0	22	11	11	0	1	0	0	0	3.32
June	7	27.2	39	12	27	3	1	1	2	0	6.51
July	11	25.2	22	13	19	2	1	0	0	0	4.21
August	14	20.2	11	9	16	2	2	1	1	0	1.31
Sept-Oct	17	27.2	22	11	37	5	2	2	0	2	1.63

8-YEAR TOTALS (1986–1993)

	G	IP	H	BB	SO	SB	CS	W	L	SV	ERA
Total	282	1086.2	1191	469	650	81	50	49	69	5	4.26
at Home	147	582.2	626	256	355	39	31	32	33	3	4.14
on Road	135	504.0	565	213	295	42	19	17	36	2	4.39
on Grass	117	374.1	413	179	257	30	16	13	27	1	4.69
on Turf	165	712.1	778	290	393	51	34	36	42	4	4.03
Day Games	90	326.0	356	135	198	23	15	14	19	3	4.14
Night Games	192	760.2	835	334	452	58	35	35	50	2	4.31
April	24	107.0	144	49	61	7	10	6	8	0	5.55
May	32	133.1	151	62	69	6	3	6	11	0	4.86
June	45	187.1	218	67	117	12	8	7	9	1	4.61
July	57	248.1	246	109	133	16	11	15	13	2	3.59
August	64	204.2	210	100	130	25	6	7	18	0	4.53
Sept-Oct	60	206.0	222	82	140	15	12	8	10	2	3.41

	BA	OBA	SA	AB	H	2B	3B	HR	RBI	BB	SO
Total	.269	.350	.380	539	145	24	3	10	65	69	126
vs. Left	.233	.360	.350	120	28	5	0	3	13	25	28
vs. Right	.279	.347	.389	419	117	19	3	7	52	44	98
Bases Empty	.266	.334	.355	282	75	12	2	3	3	29	71
Leadoff	.281	.356	.380	121	34	5	2	1	1	14	28
Runners On Base	.272	.366	.409	257	70	12	1	7	62	40	55
Scoring Position	.237	.353	.309	152	36	5	0	2	51	29	36
Late and Close	.182	.260	.227	66	12	0	0	1	4	7	17

	BA	OBA	SA	AB	H	2B	3B	HR	RBI	BB	SO
Total	.282	.353	.405	4216	1191	231	27	77	524	469	650
vs. Left	.250	.346	.339	821	205	35	4	10	106	123	157
vs. Right	.290	.355	.421	3395	986	196	23	67	418	346	493
Bases Empty	.279	.345	.400	2304	643	122	17	41	41	227	365
Leadoff	.285	.361	.405	1004	286	56	10	15	15	115	150
Runners On Base	.287	.362	.411	1912	548	109	10	36	483	242	285
Scoring Position	.292	.379	.422	1064	311	65	5	21	431	167	159
Late and Close	.270	.356	.360	392	106	20	0	5	39	52	60

JEFF RUSSELL — BR/TR — age 33 — BOS RP51 POW/FB

1993

	G	IP	H	BB	SO	SB	CS	W	L	SV	ERA
Total	51	46.2	39	14	45	1	1	1	4	33	2.70
at Home	25	22.2	21	8	19	1	0	0	1	15	1.99
on Road	26	24.0	18	6	26	0	1	1	3	18	3.38
on Grass	41	36.1	33	10	36	1	1	0	3	26	2.72
on Turf	10	10.1	6	4	9	0	0	1	1	7	2.61
Day Games	22	20.0	18	7	17	0	0	1	2	13	2.70
Night Games	29	26.2	21	7	28	1	1	0	2	20	2.70
April	7	7.0	3	0	6	0	0	0	0	4	1.29
May	9	9.0	4	1	9	0	0	0	0	8	2.00
June	10	8.0	9	2	10	0	0	0	1	4	2.25
July	14	13.0	13	4	14	0	1	0	1	11	4.15
August	8	8.1	8	4	6	1	0	1	0	6	2.16
Sept-Oct	3	1.1	2	3	0	0	0	0	0	0	6.75

10-YEAR TOTALS (1984–1993)

	G	IP	H	BB	SO	SB	CS	W	L	SV	ERA
Total	445	902.0	870	345	581	85	29	47	59	146	3.79
at Home	224	452.0	431	155	282	48	17	21	23	82	3.74
on Road	221	450.0	439	190	299	37	12	26	36	64	3.84
on Grass	361	678.0	638	257	444	60	23	32	41	127	3.57
on Turf	84	224.0	232	88	137	25	6	15	18	19	4.46
Day Games	115	204.2	200	87	143	18	5	17	37	37	3.87
Night Games	330	697.1	670	258	438	67	24	32	42	109	3.77
April	54	82.1	68	27	56	6	2	5	5	24	2.19
May	81	136.2	134	43	87	9	3	8	8	31	3.49
June	65	161.2	146	62	104	17	6	7	9	23	3.28
July	80	150.2	146	57	101	12	4	9	11	27	3.64
August	87	200.0	206	89	120	19	4	9	18	23	4.95
Sept-Oct	78	170.2	170	67	113	22	10	9	8	18	4.06

	BA	OBA	SA	AB	H	2B	3B	HR	RBI	BB	SO
Total	.231	.287	.314	169	39	11	0	1	23	14	45
vs. Left	.261	.293	.359	92	24	9	0	0	11	4	20
vs. Right	.195	.281	.260	77	15	2	0	1	12	10	25
Bases Empty	.168	.218	.242	95	16	7	0	0	0	6	35
Leadoff	.231	.250	.385	39	9	6	0	0	0	1	10
Runners On Base	.311	.368	.405	74	23	4	0	1	23	8	10
Scoring Position	.304	.368	.326	46	14	1	0	0	20	6	7
Late and Close	.210	.261	.290	124	26	1	0	1	17	10	34

	BA	OBA	SA	AB	H	2B	3B	HR	RBI	BB	SO
Total	.254	.324	.376	3422	870	155	11	80	465	345	581
vs. Left	.273	.347	.399	1636	447	86	4	37	236	186	252
vs. Right	.237	.302	.356	1786	423	69	7	43	229	159	329
Bases Empty	.237	.304	.345	1835	434	78	5	37	37	164	331
Leadoff	.237	.294	.342	764	181	28	2	16	16	58	125
Runners On Base	.275	.347	.412	1587	436	77	6	43	428	181	250
Scoring Position	.263	.345	.381	992	261	49	4	20	371	133	171
Late and Close	.219	.296	.318	1110	243	49	2	19	148	121	235

SCOTT SANDERSON — BR/TR — age 38 — CAL/SF SP29, RP3 FIN/FB

1993

	G	IP	H	BB	SO	SB	CS	W	L	SV	ERA
Total	32	184.0	201	34	102	7	6	11	13	0	4.21
at Home	15	85.1	89	18	50	1	2	5	5	0	4.85
on Road	17	98.2	112	16	52	6	4	6	8	0	3.65
on Grass	26	148.2	162	30	84	7	4	9	10	0	4.54
on Turf	6	35.1	39	4	18	0	2	2	3	0	2.80
Day Games	14	79.0	73	12	50	2	2	5	5	0	3.30
Night Games	18	105.0	128	22	52	5	4	6	8	0	4.89
April	4	27.0	19	8	19	0	0	3	0	0	3.00
May	6	43.1	40	4	22	2	1	4	2	0	2.70
June	6	35.2	51	10	16	0	2	0	4	0	6.06
July	5	29.1	43	3	9	3	1	0	3	0	6.44
August	5	23.0	26	3	13	1	1	2	1	0	4.30
Sept-Oct	6	25.2	22	4	23	1	1	2	1	0	2.81

10-YEAR TOTALS (1984–1993)

	G	IP	H	BB	SO	SB	CS	W	L	SV	ERA
Total	293	1529.1	1555	365	942	112	64	98	87	3	4.01
at Home	139	724.1	730	183	460	52	27	45	43	1	4.17
on Road	154	805.0	825	182	482	60	37	53	44	2	3.86
on Grass	228	1215.2	1243	290	770	81	51	80	69	2	4.01
on Turf	65	313.2	312	75	172	31	13	18	18	1	4.02
Day Games	140	720.2	689	185	491	53	29	40	41	1	3.81
Night Games	153	808.2	866	180	451	59	35	58	46	2	4.18
April	34	203.1	199	48	114	14	10	16	8	0	3.90
May	51	310.2	297	64	199	18	12	24	8	0	3.30
June	42	254.0	268	68	153	19	14	12	23	0	4.11
July	51	263.2	287	53	157	17	15	13	18	2	4.68
August	54	270.2	275	77	180	24	10	17	15	0	4.26
Sept-Oct	61	227.0	229	55	139	20	5	16	15	1	3.89

	BA	OBA	SA	AB	H	2B	3B	HR	RBI	BB	SO
Total	.280	.314	.448	718	201	34	3	27	89	34	102
vs. Left	.272	.318	.461	356	97	14	1	17	47	24	55
vs. Right	.287	.310	.436	362	104	20	2	10	42	10	47
Bases Empty	.265	.293	.432	449	119	25	1	16	16	14	62
Leadoff	.295	.321	.437	183	54	11	0	5	5	5	20
Runners On Base	.305	.346	.476	269	82	9	2	11	73	20	40
Scoring Position	.284	.339	.447	141	40	3	1	6	61	15	22
Late and Close	.429	.444	.571	35	15	2	0	1	5	1	1

	BA	OBA	SA	AB	H	2B	3B	HR	RBI	BB	SO
Total	.264	.307	.424	5893	1555	290	53	183	675	365	942
vs. Left	.265	.315	.429	3146	835	146	32	102	359	233	449
vs. Right	.262	.297	.418	2747	720	144	21	81	316	132	493
Bases Empty	.261	.300	.421	3627	948	185	31	111	111	189	576
Leadoff	.273	.307	.422	1515	414	79	16	38	38	67	207
Runners On Base	.268	.316	.429	2266	607	105	22	72	564	176	366
Scoring Position	.265	.324	.417	1216	322	57	13	34	463	130	214
Late and Close	.256	.310	.367	360	92	7	3	9	30	28	51

CURT SCHILLING — BR/TR — age 28 — PHI SP34 POW/FB

1993												6-YEAR TOTALS (1988–1993)										
	G	IP	H	BB	SO	SB	CS	W	L	SV	ERA	G	IP	H	BB	SO	SB	CS	W	L	SV	ERA
Total	34	235.1	234	57	186	11	11	16	7	0	4.02	176	606.2	548	187	446	25	23	34	29	13	3.43
at Home	16	113.0	111	28	100	8	3	9	4	0	3.90	92	334.2	297	108	252	19	12	21	16	5	3.33
on Road	18	122.1	123	29	86	3	8	7	3	0	4.12	84	272.0	251	79	194	6	11	13	13	8	3.54
on Grass	10	73.1	68	15	52	1	4	4	1	0	3.44	76	200.0	187	70	140	6	7	9	9	6	3.69
on Turf	24	162.0	166	42	134	10	7	12	6	0	4.28	100	406.2	361	117	306	19	16	25	20	7	3.30
Day Games	12	73.1	86	18	61	8	2	5	4	0	5.77	45	162.1	169	49	129	11	4	6	11	4	4.60
Night Games	22	162.0	148	39	125	3	9	11	3	0	3.22	131	444.1	379	138	317	14	19	28	18	9	3.00
April	5	39.0	31	9	26	0	1	4	1	0	2.54	24	67.1	52	22	55	0	2	6	3	4	2.81
May	6	48.0	37	12	34	2	4	2	0	0	3.00	26	92.2	80	29	75	6	5	4	4	3	3.21
June	5	29.1	32	6	18	1	2	2	2	0	5.52	20	83.2	76	21	59	2	4	7	6	1	3.76
July	6	34.0	47	10	26	3	0	1	3	0	6.62	21	89.0	94	17	62	3	2	5	4	1	3.94
August	6	42.2	44	11	42	1	2	2	0	0	4.01	36	124.2	110	51	95	5	4	4	3	1	2.96
Sept-Oct	6	42.1	43	9	40	4	2	5	1	0	3.40	49	149.1	136	47	100	9	6	8	9	3	3.74

	BA	OBA	SA	AB	H	2B	3B	HR	RBI	BB	SO	BA	OBA	SA	AB	H	2B	3B	HR	RBI	BB	SO
Total	.259	.303	.392	905	234	40	6	23	100	57	186	.241	.297	.353	2278	548	100	15	42	243	187	446
vs. Left	.257	.307	.398	495	127	23	4	13	59	37	106	.240	.303	.360	1210	290	53	10	24	122	114	234
vs. Right	.261	.298	.385	410	107	17	2	10	41	20	80	.242	.290	.346	1068	258	47	5	18	121	73	212
Bases Empty	.243	.282	.382	571	139	23	4	16	16	30	115	.230	.280	.338	1366	314	56	7	26	26	94	257
Leadoff	.261	.298	.417	230	60	14	2	6	6	11	44	.242	.289	.354	567	137	23	4	11	11	37	97
Runners On Base	.284	.337	.410	334	95	17	2	7	84	27	71	.257	.321	.375	912	234	44	8	16	217	93	189
Scoring Position	.311	.368	.475	177	55	10	2	5	77	19	43	.263	.341	.385	499	131	27	5	8	191	69	123
Late and Close	.260	.301	.404	104	27	4	1	3	14	6	20	.250	.313	.378	392	98	16	5	8	54	37	84

LEE SMITH — BR/TR — age 37 — SL/NYA RP63 POW/FB

1993												10-YEAR TOTALS (1984–1993)										
	G	IP	H	BB	SO	SB	CS	W	L	SV	ERA	G	IP	H	BB	SO	SB	CS	W	L	SV	ERA
Total	63	58.0	53	14	60	12	2	2	4	46	3.88	654	816.0	719	294	852	112	29	56	57	354	3.06
at Home	31	28.0	27	6	31	5	1	1	3	23	4.18	352	452.0	414	142	489	64	16	39	31	177	3.23
on Road	32	30.0	26	8	29	7	1	1	1	23	3.60	302	364.0	305	152	363	48	13	17	26	177	2.84
on Grass	26	24.2	22	7	24	7	1	0	0	21	2.55	380	496.0	423	183	527	58	19	37	26	200	2.99
on Turf	37	33.1	31	7	36	5	1	2	4	25	4.86	274	320.0	296	111	325	54	10	19	31	154	3.15
Day Games	24	19.2	13	7	19	5	0	2	1	15	3.66	319	419.1	373	151	459	56	16	36	29	158	3.39
Night Games	39	38.1	40	7	41	7	2	0	3	31	3.99	335	396.2	346	143	393	56	13	20	28	196	2.70
April	11	10.0	5	3	10	3	0	0	0	10	0.90	84	107.1	85	44	128	14	5	9	9	50	2.43
May	8	7.2	6	3	9	0	0	2	1	4	5.87	106	134.1	117	42	135	17	4	14	9	50	3.55
June	15	14.2	17	1	11	1	1	0	0	15	4.30	122	155.2	144	66	156	18	8	6	11	61	3.47
July	12	10.1	11	0	13	1	0	0	1	7	6.97	112	150.2	125	43	164	11	3	13	7	67	2.93
August	9	7.1	10	2	6	3	1	0	2	7	4.91	116	136.2	126	42	126	24	6	10	10	64	2.44
Sept-Oct	8	8.0	4	5	11	4	0	0	0	3	0.00	114	131.1	122	57	143	28	3	4	11	62	3.36

	BA	OBA	SA	AB	H	2B	3B	HR	RBI	BB	SO	BA	OBA	SA	AB	H	2B	3B	HR	RBI	BB	SO
Total	.239	.280	.455	222	53	9	3	11	29	14	60	.235	.301	.349	3056	719	117	22	62	357	294	852
vs. Left	.227	.277	.420	119	27	3	1	6	14	9	30	.244	.324	.361	1671	407	68	12	35	206	204	451
vs. Right	.252	.284	.495	103	26	6	2	5	15	5	30	.225	.272	.334	1385	312	49	10	27	151	90	401
Bases Empty	.256	.289	.473	129	33	7	3	5	5	6	30	.236	.292	.351	1570	370	62	13	31	31	124	425
Leadoff	.245	.288	.449	49	12	4	0	2	2	3	10	.236	.289	.373	656	155	29	5	17	17	47	156
Runners On Base	.215	.269	.430	93	20	2	0	6	24	8	30	.235	.309	.347	1486	349	55	9	31	326	170	427
Scoring Position	.172	.239	.379	58	10	0	0	4	19	6	25	.216	.303	.323	951	205	34	7	18	286	129	297
Late and Close	.254	.289	.497	169	43	4	2	11	27	9	43	.238	.304	.356	2360	561	91	14	53	314	230	666

JOHN SMOLTZ — BR/TR — age 27 — ATL SP35 POW/FB

1993												6-YEAR TOTALS (1988–1993)										
	G	IP	H	BB	SO	SB	CS	W	L	SV	ERA	G	IP	H	BB	SO	SB	CS	W	L	SV	ERA
Total	35	243.2	208	100	208	12	5	15	11	0	3.62	181	1223.1	1060	452	946	88	41	72	65	0	3.52
at Home	15	101.0	92	44	88	5	1	4	5	0	3.92	87	599.0	514	202	462	36	21	34	30	0	3.46
on Road	20	142.2	116	56	120	7	4	11	6	0	3.41	94	624.1	546	250	484	52	20	38	35	0	3.59
on Grass	27	190.0	152	77	160	7	4	12	9	0	3.36	134	915.0	776	326	688	63	28	54	46	0	3.50
on Turf	8	53.2	56	23	48	5	1	3	2	0	4.53	47	308.1	284	126	258	25	13	18	19	0	3.59
Day Games	11	78.0	70	37	76	3	1	3	5	0	3.12	48	345.0	274	113	290	23	7	20	18	0	2.95
Night Games	24	165.2	138	63	132	9	4	12	6	0	3.86	133	878.1	786	339	656	65	34	52	47	0	3.75
April	5	37.2	29	16	35	2	2	2	2	0	2.15	24	153.2	139	64	124	10	8	8	11	0	3.57
May	6	37.1	40	18	21	4	0	2	3	0	5.54	29	207.1	172	75	156	13	8	13	10	0	3.52
June	6	44.0	26	20	47	0	2	3	3	0	2.25	29	196.2	176	72	174	18	9	11	10	0	3.71
July	6	34.0	32	18	35	4	0	2	1	0	3.71	30	211.1	163	74	152	15	4	14	8	0	3.19
August	6	43.1	36	9	27	0	0	4	1	0	3.95	36	242.2	210	87	183	20	8	17	13	0	3.63
Sept-Oct	7	47.1	45	19	43	2	1	2	2	0	4.18	33	211.2	200	80	157	12	4	9	10	0	3.53

	BA	OBA	SA	AB	H	2B	3B	HR	RBI	BB	SO	BA	OBA	SA	AB	H	2B	3B	HR	RBI	BB	SO
Total	.230	.309	.369	905	208	45	6	23	93	100	208	.233	.303	.355	4549	1060	198	28	101	455	452	946
vs. Left	.261	.346	.412	459	120	29	5	10	51	55	72	.260	.336	.381	2605	676	123	23	49	260	297	422
vs. Right	.197	.271	.325	446	88	16	1	13	42	45	136	.198	.257	.322	1944	384	75	5	52	195	155	524
Bases Empty	.236	.304	.368	535	126	30	1	13	13	50	115	.229	.295	.347	2715	623	123	12	57	57	243	565
Leadoff	.259	.315	.422	232	60	15	1	7	7	19	45	.237	.298	.351	1159	275	49	7	23	23	97	229
Runners On Base	.222	.316	.370	370	82	15	5	10	80	50	93	.238	.314	.369	1834	437	75	16	44	398	209	381
Scoring Position	.232	.358	.401	207	48	11	3	6	69	42	60	.231	.332	.369	1003	232	40	13	24	340	163	250
Late and Close	.330	.421	.513	115	38	8	2	3	15	17	20	.231	.299	.361	471	109	25	3	10	44	44	96

MIKE STANTON — BL/TL — age 27 — ATL RP63 POW/FB

1993

1993	G	IP	H	BB	SO	SB	CS	W	L	SV	ERA
Total	63	52.0	51	29	43	5	1	4	6	27	4.67
at Home	31	28.0	22	17	27	4	0	4	3	14	2.25
on Road	32	24.0	29	12	16	1	1	0	3	13	7.50
on Grass	47	39.1	40	22	37	5	0	4	5	21	4.35
on Turf	16	12.2	11	7	6	0	1	0	1	6	5.68
Day Games	15	11.1	17	3	5	1	0	1	2	8	9.53
Night Games	48	40.2	34	26	38	4	1	3	4	19	3.32
April	13	10.1	9	5	6	0	0	1	1	8	3.48
May	12	10.2	10	3	8	0	0	0	0	10	3.38
June	7	7.0	5	4	7	1	0	2	1	3	2.57
July	12	9.2	10	6	8	1	1	1	1	6	5.59
August	10	6.2	9	9	10	2	0	0	2	0	12.15
Sept-Oct	9	7.2	8	2	4	1	0	0	1	0	2.35

5-YEAR TOTALS (1989–1993)

	G	IP	H	BB	SO	SB	CS	W	L	SV	ERA
	229	224.2	205	82	175	18	4	14	19	51	3.97
	109	117.0	102	36	88	10	2	7	7	25	3.15
	120	107.2	103	46	87	8	2	7	12	26	4.85
	166	166.2	151	58	123	15	2	10	15	39	3.83
	63	58.0	54	24	52	3	2	4	4	12	4.34
	61	56.1	52	20	44	8	2	3	4	12	5.27
	168	168.1	153	62	131	10	2	11	15	39	3.53
	37	32.0	35	16	22	2	1	1	5	11	5.91
	33	30.0	30	7	32	4	0	1	1	13	6.00
	31	28.0	25	10	23	2	0	5	4	5	4.50
	30	30.1	18	16	20	3	2	2	2	7	3.26
	41	43.0	34	20	36	2	0	0	2	7	3.56
	57	61.1	63	13	54	5	1	5	5	8	2.35

	BA	OBA	SA	AB	H	2B	3B	HR	RBI	BB	SO
Total	.255	.346	.370	200	51	11	0	4	33	29	43
vs. Left	.218	.357	.309	55	12	2	0	1	9	13	15
vs. Right	.269	.342	.393	145	39	9	0	3	24	16	28
Bases Empty	.224	.333	.337	98	22	5	0	2	2	16	18
Leadoff	.200	.333	.275	40	8	3	0	0	0	8	7
Runners On Base	.284	.359	.402	102	29	6	0	2	31	13	25
Scoring Position	.300	.389	.433	60	18	5	0	2	28	10	12
Late and Close	.277	.371	.423	130	36	7	0	4	29	20	30

	BA	OBA	SA	AB	H	2B	3B	HR	RBI	BB	SO
Total	.243	.312	.352	843	205	33	4	17	117	82	175
vs. Left	.215	.313	.316	256	55	6	1	6	29	36	73
vs. Right	.256	.311	.368	587	150	27	3	11	88	46	102
Bases Empty	.241	.300	.341	440	106	17	0	9	9	34	86
Leadoff	.261	.319	.346	188	49	10	0	2	2	15	39
Runners On Base	.246	.325	.365	403	99	16	4	8	108	48	89
Scoring Position	.255	.336	.376	255	65	10	3	5	99	32	58
Late and Close	.243	.315	.351	515	125	21	4	9	78	52	105

DAVE STEWART — BR/TR — age 37 — TOR SP26 POW/FB

1993

1993	G	IP	H	BB	SO	SB	CS	W	L	SV	ERA
Total	26	162.0	146	72	96	13	12	12	8	0	4.44
at Home	13	85.1	69	35	56	8	4	6	4	0	4.01
on Road	13	76.2	77	37	40	5	8	6	4	0	4.93
on Grass	10	56.1	60	26	25	4	6	5	3	0	5.27
on Turf	16	105.2	86	46	71	9	6	7	5	0	4.00
Day Games	8	53.2	38	18	34	4	4	6	2	0	3.35
Night Games	18	108.1	108	54	62	8	8	6	6	0	4.98
April	0	0.0	0	0	0	0	0	0	0	0	0.00
May	4	17.1	18	11	9	2	3	2	1	0	7.27
June	6	41.2	38	17	29	3	4	1	2	0	3.89
July	5	31.2	39	13	16	0	1	3	2	0	5.40
August	6	39.0	27	19	21	4	2	2	3	0	4.62
Sept-Oct	5	32.1	24	12	21	4	2	4	0	0	2.51

10-YEAR TOTALS (1984–1993)

	G	IP	H	BB	SO	SB	CS	W	L	SV	ERA
	353	2088.2	1952	820	1384	171	76	135	99	4	3.84
	180	1094.1	963	397	754	99	40	68	45	1	3.43
	173	994.1	989	423	630	72	36	67	54	3	4.29
	276	1670.0	1539	646	1113	138	59	107	76	4	3.70
	77	418.2	413	174	271	33	17	28	23	0	4.39
	119	750.2	665	263	517	56	25	56	35	1	3.33
	234	1338.0	1287	557	867	115	51	79	64	3	4.12
	50	275.0	264	119	157	29	10	22	14	2	4.09
	54	292.1	277	125	180	20	13	20	14	1	3.91
	65	364.0	335	144	242	35	17	18	19	1	4.33
	60	349.0	336	129	232	24	6	23	14	0	3.87
	61	403.0	356	147	281	28	16	26	19	0	3.62
	63	405.1	384	156	292	35	14	26	19	0	3.38

	BA	OBA	SA	AB	H	2B	3B	HR	RBI	BB	SO
Total	.242	.325	.419	604	146	30	4	23	82	72	96
vs. Left	.246	.334	.413	264	65	16	2	8	34	36	43
vs. Right	.238	.317	.424	340	81	14	2	15	48	36	53
Bases Empty	.233	.324	.413	356	83	17	4	13	13	44	52
Leadoff	.219	.317	.377	146	32	9	1	4	4	20	20
Runners On Base	.254	.325	.427	248	63	13	0	10	69	28	44
Scoring Position	.262	.358	.397	126	33	8	0	3	53	21	20
Late and Close	.250	.240	.500	24	6	1	0	0	2	5	4

	BA	OBA	SA	AB	H	2B	3B	HR	RBI	BB	SO
Total	.247	.319	.384	7890	1952	365	49	204	883	820	1384
vs. Left	.252	.328	.382	4026	1013	188	24	96	463	474	649
vs. Right	.243	.310	.386	3864	939	177	25	108	420	346	735
Bases Empty	.245	.315	.384	4644	1140	208	32	124	124	439	815
Leadoff	.244	.309	.390	1977	482	94	14	56	56	178	340
Runners On Base	.250	.326	.383	3246	812	157	17	80	759	381	569
Scoring Position	.232	.312	.358	1874	435	88	12	41	651	237	346
Late and Close	.243	.327	.363	741	180	28	2	19	71	96	120

TODD STOTTLEMYRE — BL/TR — age 29 — TOR SP28, RP2 FIN/FB

1993

1993	G	IP	H	BB	SO	SB	CS	W	L	SV	ERA
Total	30	176.2	204	69	98	24	7	11	12	0	4.84
at Home	15	92.2	91	36	57	15	3	6	5	0	4.18
on Road	15	84.0	113	33	41	9	4	5	7	0	5.57
on Grass	12	63.0	88	30	26	6	3	4	5	0	5.86
on Turf	18	113.2	116	39	72	18	4	7	7	0	4.28
Day Games	10	64.2	60	25	37	12	1	5	2	0	3.90
Night Games	20	112.0	144	44	61	12	6	6	10	0	5.38
April	5	35.1	44	10	18	3	2	3	2	0	4.33
May	4	18.0	25	10	13	2	1	1	2	0	5.00
June	4	16.0	19	4	13	0	1	0	1	0	3.94
July	5	33.1	35	13	15	3	1	0	2	0	5.13
August	6	34.1	44	13	14	9	3	3	2	0	5.77
Sept-Oct	6	39.2	37	19	14	6	0	3	3	0	4.54

6-YEAR TOTALS (1988–1993)

	G	IP	H	BB	SO	SB	CS	W	L	SV	ERA
	180	998.1	1033	366	557	119	36	62	63	0	4.41
	87	512.0	527	174	287	58	15	34	28	0	4.38
	93	486.1	506	192	270	61	21	28	35	0	4.44
	68	366.1	369	141	204	45	14	22	24	0	4.13
	112	632.0	664	225	353	74	22	40	39	0	4.57
	58	314.2	331	126	177	41	9	15	23	0	4.86
	122	683.2	702	240	380	78	27	47	40	0	4.20
	32	154.2	162	73	93	27	9	11	10	0	4.71
	29	155.2	158	60	101	25	3	7	14	0	4.74
	27	164.1	169	44	73	8	4	12	7	0	3.40
	28	149.2	168	67	90	16	5	6	10	0	5.17
	29	183.2	187	56	95	20	8	12	10	0	4.17
	35	190.1	189	66	105	23	7	14	12	0	4.40

	BA	OBA	SA	AB	H	2B	3B	HR	RBI	BB	SO
Total	.292	.353	.424	698	204	45	7	11	92	69	98
vs. Left	.305	.375	.452	374	114	28	3	7	50	45	48
vs. Right	.278	.328	.392	324	90	17	4	4	42	24	50
Bases Empty	.299	.356	.440	361	108	24	6	5	5	31	51
Leadoff	.357	.403	.524	168	60	13	3	3	3	12	26
Runners On Base	.285	.351	.407	337	96	21	1	6	87	38	47
Scoring Position	.275	.361	.430	200	55	14	1	5	81	32	27
Late and Close	.200	.259	.240	25	5	1	0	0	2	1	2

	BA	OBA	SA	AB	H	2B	3B	HR	RBI	BB	SO
Total	.269	.335	.405	3845	1033	186	25	96	469	366	557
vs. Left	.294	.361	.433	1894	557	100	13	46	226	196	204
vs. Right	.244	.310	.377	1951	476	86	12	50	243	170	353
Bases Empty	.268	.332	.398	2180	584	112	15	47	47	185	312
Leadoff	.304	.357	.445	955	290	46	7	25	25	71	134
Runners On Base	.270	.340	.414	1665	449	74	10	49	422	181	245
Scoring Position	.269	.354	.416	924	249	52	4	25	355	131	134
Late and Close	.257	.316	.339	230	59	11	1	2	18	19	39

RICK SUTCLIFFE — BL/TR — age 38 — BAL SP28, RP1 FIN/FB

1993

1993	G	IP	H	BB	SO	SB	CS	W	L	SV	ERA
Total	29	166.0	212	74	80	17	8	10	10	0	5.75
at Home	16	100.0	121	32	48	7	5	6	6	0	4.50
on Road	13	66.0	91	42	32	10	3	4	4	0	7.64
on Grass	24	137.2	179	54	68	13	8	8	8	0	5.36
on Turf	5	28.1	33	20	12	4	0	2	2	0	7.62
Day Games	5	24.2	36	9	11	7	4	1	2	0	6.20
Night Games	24	141.1	176	65	69	10	4	9	8	0	5.67
April	5	33.1	36	21	19	1	2	2	2	0	5.13
May	6	37.1	39	16	16	6	3	3	0	0	4.10
June	5	33.0	41	14	16	5	2	3	1	0	5.18
July	5	23.2	35	9	14	1	0	0	3	0	7.61
August	5	22.0	34	11	7	3	1	1	3	0	7.77
Sept-Oct	3	16.2	27	3	8	1	0	1	1	0	6.48

10-YEAR TOTALS (1984–1993)

	G	IP	H	BB	SO	SB	CS	W	L	SV	ERA
Total	273	1765.0	1760	675	1156	206	67	112	95	0	4.10
at Home	136	886.2	865	344	595	90	38	55	43	0	3.95
on Road	137	878.1	895	331	561	116	29	57	52	0	4.26
on Grass	199	1276.0	1286	495	828	141	53	78	67	0	4.15
on Turf	74	489.0	474	180	328	65	14	34	28	0	3.98
Day Games	144	924.1	912	353	661	110	44	51	53	0	3.93
Night Games	129	840.2	848	322	495	96	23	61	42	0	4.29
April	46	323.0	302	126	209	31	15	21	18	0	3.62
May	49	301.0	302	123	182	50	13	20	15	0	4.75
June	43	295.1	286	116	196	32	11	21	16	0	3.78
July	39	248.2	262	90	172	21	6	15	17	0	4.02
August	48	308.1	301	126	192	36	10	18	12	0	3.68
Sept-Oct	48	288.2	307	94	205	36	12	17	17	0	4.83

	BA	OBA	SA	AB	H	2B	3B	HR	RBI	BB	SO
Total	.314	.385	.496	676	212	44	5	23	102	74	80
vs. Left	.308	.387	.479	338	104	19	3	11	43	42	33
vs. Right	.320	.382	.512	338	108	25	2	12	59	32	47
Bases Empty	.303	.372	.454	370	112	23	3	9	9	38	41
Leadoff	.289	.362	.440	159	46	9	0	5	5	17	17
Runners On Base	.327	.399	.546	306	100	21	2	14	93	36	39
Scoring Position	.337	.431	.589	163	55	12	1	9	77	28	20
Late and Close	.303	.361	.394	33	10	0	0	1	3	3	3

	BA	OBA	SA	AB	H	2B	3B	HR	RBI	BB	SO
Total	.262	.329	.394	6719	1760	314	55	155	739	675	1156
vs. Left	.263	.335	.398	3619	953	184	33	79	376	398	597
vs. Right	.260	.322	.390	3100	807	130	22	76	363	277	559
Bases Empty	.256	.315	.385	3994	1023	180	33	89	89	329	684
Leadoff	.272	.325	.410	1718	468	85	19	38	38	128	271
Runners On Base	.270	.349	.408	2725	737	134	22	66	650	346	472
Scoring Position	.258	.361	.402	1534	396	69	13	42	569	275	307
Late and Close	.272	.332	.386	578	157	25	4	11	56	53	95

BILL SWIFT — BR/TR — age 33 — SF SP34 FIN/GB

1993

1993	G	IP	H	BB	SO	SB	CS	W	L	SV	ERA
Total	34	232.2	195	55	157	12	11	21	8	0	2.82
at Home	16	111.0	86	29	75	6	4	11	4	0	2.35
on Road	18	121.2	109	26	82	6	7	10	4	0	3.25
on Grass	27	184.1	157	48	124	8	10	16	8	0	3.03
on Turf	7	48.1	38	7	33	4	1	5	0	0	2.05
Day Games	20	136.0	118	31	91	6	6	13	5	0	3.31
Night Games	14	96.2	77	24	66	6	5	8	3	0	2.14
April	5	31.0	23	6	19	3	0	2	1	0	2.90
May	5	35.2	33	11	20	1	3	4	1	0	3.03
June	6	44.0	31	8	32	2	3	4	2	0	2.66
July	6	39.0	36	10	32	1	2	5	1	0	2.08
August	6	38.2	40	8	26	2	2	2	2	0	4.42
Sept-Oct	6	44.1	32	12	28	3	1	4	1	0	2.03

8-YEAR TOTALS (1985–1993)

	G	IP	H	BB	SO	SB	CS	W	L	SV	ERA
Total	317	1156.1	1166	351	526	54	41	61	52	25	3.52
at Home	155	579.2	574	179	256	30	16	31	25	10	3.29
on Road	162	576.2	592	172	270	24	25	30	27	15	3.75
on Grass	146	582.2	568	185	301	22	29	33	28	14	3.54
on Turf	171	573.2	598	166	225	32	12	28	24	11	3.50
Day Games	102	422.2	418	108	195	19	15	30	18	7	3.26
Night Games	215	733.2	748	243	331	35	26	31	34	18	3.67
April	33	130.0	128	44	66	8	2	7	1	1	2.84
May	54	201.1	208	59	96	8	8	14	8	5	3.75
June	51	206.1	210	58	81	13	13	11	9	1	3.97
July	48	203.0	217	61	93	5	6	13	13	4	3.55
August	55	209.1	210	70	84	9	5	5	11	4	3.53
Sept-Oct	76	206.1	193	59	106	11	7	11	10	10	3.23

	BA	OBA	SA	AB	H	2B	3B	HR	RBI	BB	SO
Total	.226	.277	.326	861	195	30	1	18	72	55	157
vs. Left	.268	.331	.387	470	126	20	0	12	47	42	64
vs. Right	.176	.208	.253	391	69	10	1	6	25	13	93
Bases Empty	.227	.275	.328	534	121	13	1	13	13	32	103
Leadoff	.188	.243	.220	223	42	4	0	1	1	13	41
Runners On Base	.226	.280	.324	327	74	17	0	5	59	23	54
Scoring Position	.218	.292	.315	165	36	10	0	2	50	17	34
Late and Close	.216	.247	.311	74	16	4	0	1	6	3	11

	BA	OBA	SA	AB	H	2B	3B	HR	RBI	BB	SO
Total	.265	.323	.356	4403	1166	184	17	61	470	351	526
vs. Left	.295	.359	.405	2272	671	117	8	39	261	215	205
vs. Right	.232	.285	.303	2131	495	67	9	22	209	136	321
Bases Empty	.258	.315	.342	2467	636	92	7	34	34	180	313
Leadoff	.250	.301	.320	1082	271	38	2	11	11	69	136
Runners On Base	.274	.334	.373	1936	530	92	10	27	436	171	213
Scoring Position	.258	.340	.349	1080	279	48	7	12	384	132	136
Late and Close	.247	.302	.332	608	150	17	1	11	52	43	76

GREG SWINDELL — BR/TL — age 29 — HOU SP30, RP1 FIN/FB

1993

1993	G	IP	H	BB	SO	SB	CS	W	L	SV	ERA
Total	31	190.1	215	40	124	16	11	12	13	0	4.16
at Home	14	82.2	98	17	48	6	5	3	9	0	4.90
on Road	17	107.2	117	23	76	10	6	9	4	0	3.59
on Grass	11	66.1	77	15	52	7	4	3	4	0	4.34
on Turf	20	124.0	138	25	72	9	7	5	12	0	4.06
Day Games	13	74.0	91	15	45	7	5	6	5	0	5.35
Night Games	18	116.1	124	25	79	9	6	6	8	0	3.40
April	5	38.0	35	4	19	0	1	4	1	0	3.08
May	6	30.1	44	9	25	6	2	1	4	0	7.71
June	6	37.2	41	9	16	2	2	1	1	0	3.82
July	2	8.0	12	3	4	1	3	0	1	0	6.75
August	6	37.1	35	5	30	4	2	4	2	0	2.41
Sept-Oct	6	39.0	48	10	30	3	2	3	2	0	3.92

8-YEAR TOTALS (1986–1993)

	G	IP	H	BB	SO	SB	CS	W	L	SV	ERA
Total	215	1447.0	1484	307	1018	85	78	84	76	0	3.68
at Home	107	746.0	732	151	504	39	39	44	37	0	3.39
on Road	108	701.0	752	156	514	46	39	40	39	0	3.98
on Grass	150	1018.0	1035	216	743	55	56	64	47	0	3.64
on Turf	65	429.0	449	91	275	30	22	20	29	0	3.76
Day Games	67	462.1	489	80	337	22	25	31	24	0	3.58
Night Games	148	984.2	995	227	681	63	53	53	52	0	3.72
April	34	231.2	217	47	161	9	11	15	10	0	3.46
May	40	281.2	279	61	202	17	16	12	12	0	3.42
June	39	257.2	299	62	169	17	20	11	14	0	4.30
July	29	199.2	183	40	146	10	11	13	11	0	3.11
August	32	211.2	228	42	152	15	10	15	15	0	3.44
Sept-Oct	41	264.2	278	55	188	17	10	14	14	0	4.15

	BA	OBA	SA	AB	H	2B	3B	HR	RBI	BB	SO
Total	.283	.318	.455	761	215	43	8	24	90	40	124
vs. Left	.315	.353	.520	127	40	11	3	3	11	8	19
vs. Right	.276	.311	.442	634	175	32	5	21	79	32	105
Bases Empty	.281	.313	.447	445	125	28	5	12	12	20	70
Leadoff	.270	.308	.481	185	50	15	3	6	6	9	27
Runners On Base	.285	.324	.465	316	90	15	3	12	78	20	54
Scoring Position	.259	.303	.422	185	48	7	3	0	65	13	29
Late and Close	.327	.340	.388	49	16	3	0	0	3	1	14

	BA	OBA	SA	AB	H	2B	3B	HR	RBI	BB	SO
Total	.266	.303	.403	5584	1484	255	36	147	583	307	1018
vs. Left	.269	.304	.393	941	253	51	6	18	95	48	155
vs. Right	.265	.303	.405	4643	1231	204	30	129	488	259	863
Bases Empty	.258	.295	.392	3453	891	157	23	87	87	171	658
Leadoff	.259	.291	.428	1442	373	76	15	46	46	58	268
Runners On Base	.278	.317	.421	2131	593	98	13	60	496	136	360
Scoring Position	.271	.319	.403	1154	313	51	7	29	413	98	211
Late and Close	.286	.325	.404	577	165	29	3	11	52	34	107

FRANK TANANA — BL/TL — age 41 — NYN/NYA SP32 FIN/FB

1993

	G	IP	H	BB	SO	SB	CS	W	L	SV	ERA
Total	32	202.2	216	55	116	15	6	7	17	0	4.35
at Home	15	99.1	112	25	64	11	4	3	8	0	4.62
on Road	17	103.1	104	30	52	4	2	4	9	0	4.09
on Grass	22	144.0	158	38	89	15	5	5	11	0	4.25
on Turf	10	58.2	58	17	27	0	1	2	6	0	4.60
Day Games	12	78.1	76	23	40	3	3	3	8	0	3.91
Night Games	20	124.1	140	32	76	12	3	4	9	0	4.63
April	3	21.0	22	8	10	5	1	2	0	0	1.71
May	6	32.2	44	16	21	2	1	1	3	0	5.79
June	6	33.2	43	10	23	2	2	1	4	0	5.35
July	5	34.2	30	7	15	4	2	1	3	0	4.67
August	6	44.0	38	5	23	1	0	1	3	0	3.68
Sept-Oct	6	36.2	39	9	24	1	0	1	4	0	4.17

10-YEAR TOTALS (1984–1993)

	G	IP	H	BB	SO	SB	CS	W	L	SV	ERA
Total	330	2078.0	2117	686	1268	155	86	120	121	1	4.06
at Home	169	1066.2	1081	351	678	74	45	64	62	0	4.23
on Road	161	1011.1	1036	335	590	81	41	56	59	1	3.89
on Grass	286	1803.1	1830	593	1127	142	75	111	101	1	4.02
on Turf	44	274.2	287	93	141	13	11	9	20	0	4.33
Day Games	103	652.2	670	226	380	58	23	37	44	0	4.07
Night Games	227	1425.1	1447	460	888	97	63	83	77	1	4.06
April	44	276.1	297	98	151	25	18	19	15	0	4.27
May	57	339.1	361	126	200	36	13	19	22	0	4.80
June	56	379.2	364	134	245	21	20	25	19	0	3.56
July	52	326.1	325	110	200	23	8	15	20	0	3.94
August	59	361.0	385	96	202	26	9	23	19	1	4.19
Sept-Oct	62	395.1	385	122	270	24	18	19	26	0	3.76

Batting Against — 1993

	BA	OBA	SA	AB	H	2B	3B	HR	RBI	BB	SO
Total	.273	.326	.441	792	216	41	4	28	95	55	116
vs. Left	.245	.292	.371	159	39	8	0	4	11	10	35
vs. Right	.280	.334	.458	633	177	33	4	24	84	45	81
Bases Empty	.270	.301	.440	500	135	28	3	17	17	19	69
Leadoff	.243	.257	.398	206	50	8	0	8	8	3	23
Runners On Base	.277	.364	.442	292	81	13	1	11	78	36	47
Scoring Position	.265	.373	.422	166	44	6	1	6	62	29	32
Late and Close	.383	.408	.553	47	18	2	0	2	4	2	6

Batting Against — 10-Year Totals

	BA	OBA	SA	AB	H	2B	3B	HR	RBI	BB	SO
Total	.264	.324	.417	8012	2117	366	47	255	938	686	1268
vs. Left	.249	.301	.375	1363	340	61	7	32	135	95	249
vs. Right	.267	.328	.426	6649	1777	305	40	223	803	591	1019
Bases Empty	.262	.313	.421	4859	1273	232	28	162	162	323	751
Leadoff	.257	.297	.410	2048	526	96	8	67	67	107	311
Runners On Base	.268	.340	.411	3153	844	134	19	93	776	363	517
Scoring Position	.256	.349	.388	1705	437	64	11	46	647	272	314
Late and Close	.275	.354	.439	586	161	28	4	20	63	72	77

KEVIN TAPANI — BR/TR — age 30 — MIN SP35, RP1 FIN/GB

1993

	G	IP	H	BB	SO	SB	CS	W	L	SV	ERA
Total	36	225.2	243	57	150	42	13	12	15	0	4.43
at Home	14	98.1	102	28	66	19	5	3	9	0	4.39
on Road	22	127.1	141	29	84	23	8	9	6	0	4.45
on Grass	16	92.1	99	24	65	16	6	8	4	0	4.19
on Turf	20	133.1	144	33	85	26	7	4	11	0	4.59
Day Games	14	86.1	85	18	64	13	5	6	5	0	3.23
Night Games	22	139.1	158	39	86	29	8	6	10	0	5.17
April	5	28.2	34	10	17	5	2	0	3	0	7.85
May	7	41.0	50	11	30	6	2	6	0	0	3.95
June	5	30.0	40	12	21	8	5	1	3	0	6.00
July	7	34.2	40	6	20	5	2	2	2	0	5.45
August	5	37.2	32	8	24	4	0	2	2	0	3.11
Sept-Oct	7	53.2	47	10	38	14	2	5	2	0	2.35

5-YEAR TOTALS (1989–1993)

	G	IP	H	BB	SO	SB	CS	W	L	SV	ERA
Total	140	889.0	897	186	547	100	36	58	45	0	3.83
at Home	67	450.1	458	100	286	48	17	33	22	0	3.56
on Road	73	438.2	439	86	261	52	19	25	23	0	4.10
on Grass	53	312.1	311	63	190	35	14	22	15	0	3.98
on Turf	87	576.2	586	123	357	65	22	36	30	0	3.75
Day Games	42	262.0	255	50	174	26	10	19	10	0	3.23
Night Games	98	627.0	642	136	373	74	26	39	35	0	4.08
April	17	105.0	108	26	69	11	5	5	7	0	4.46
May	25	153.0	181	35	111	15	5	10	12	0	4.65
June	22	149.1	148	24	90	15	12	9	7	0	3.68
July	28	156.1	157	28	77	16	5	12	3	0	3.51
August	19	137.0	116	33	75	11	5	9	6	0	3.42
Sept-Oct	29	188.1	187	40	125	32	4	13	10	0	3.49

Batting Against — 1993

	BA	OBA	SA	AB	H	2B	3B	HR	RBI	BB	SO
Total	.272	.318	.419	893	243	56	6	21	106	57	150
vs. Left	.280	.320	.432	525	147	34	5	12	64	32	91
vs. Right	.261	.317	.399	368	96	22	1	9	42	25	59
Bases Empty	.270	.315	.415	523	141	30	2	14	14	31	90
Leadoff	.284	.324	.449	225	64	7	1	7	7	11	47
Runners On Base	.276	.323	.424	370	102	26	4	7	92	26	60
Scoring Position	.266	.320	.399	233	62	17	1	4	80	19	43
Late and Close	.264	.321	.389	72	19	6	0	1	8	6	7

Batting Against — 5-Year Totals

	BA	OBA	SA	AB	H	2B	3B	HR	RBI	BB	SO
Total	.262	.301	.399	3424	897	192	24	76	354	186	547
vs. Left	.268	.304	.413	1886	506	113	20	40	202	101	301
vs. Right	.254	.296	.381	1538	391	79	4	36	152	85	246
Bases Empty	.256	.296	.400	2122	544	116	13	54	54	110	358
Leadoff	.258	.291	.431	886	229	52	10	27	27	37	148
Runners On Base	.271	.308	.397	1302	353	76	11	22	300	76	189
Scoring Position	.266	.306	.380	764	203	42	6	11	259	53	124
Late and Close	.263	.316	.387	266	70	14	2	5	27	21	37

BOB TEWKSBURY — BR/TR — age 34 — SL SP32 FIN/GB

1993

	G	IP	H	BB	SO	SB	CS	W	L	SV	ERA
Total	32	213.2	258	20	97	21	6	17	10	0	3.83
at Home	19	131.2	150	10	57	9	2	11	7	0	3.35
on Road	13	82.0	108	10	40	12	4	6	3	0	4.61
on Grass	7	44.0	59	3	27	5	3	5	1	0	3.68
on Turf	25	169.2	199	17	70	16	3	12	9	0	3.87
Day Games	11	81.2	90	1	44	10	2	7	3	0	3.09
Night Games	21	132.0	168	19	53	11	4	10	7	0	4.30
April	4	23.2	34	1	11	1	1	1	3	0	3.80
May.	6	44.0	48	2	18	3	8	3	2	0	3.68
June	5	31.0	40	3	16	3	1	4	1	0	4.65
July	6	42.0	44	4	23	2	1	2	1	0	3.43
August	6	42.2	54	7	15	2	1	4	1	0	3.59
Sept-Oct	5	30.1	38	3	14	5	2	3	2	0	4.15

8-YEAR TOTALS (1986–1993)

	G	IP	H	BB	SO	SB	CS	W	L	SV	ERA
Total	169	998.0	1086	156	402	50	29	65	49	1	3.35
at Home	84	521.2	524	71	209	21	16	36	21	0	2.95
on Road	85	476.1	562	85	193	29	13	29	28	1	3.80
on Grass	63	371.1	430	70	155	14	11	23	21	0	3.56
on Turf	106	626.2	656	86	247	36	18	42	28	1	3.23
Day Games	58	348.0	369	58	145	19	8	22	21	0	3.47
Night Games	111	650.0	717	98	257	31	21	43	28	0	3.30
April	26	123.0	146	19	52	7	4	7	6	1	3.88
May.	23	138.0	154	17	51	11	5	10	5	0	3.46
June	28	184.1	189	24	68	8	2	15	5	0	2.69
July	30	182.2	203	37	90	7	8	7	16	0	3.40
August	27	166.0	179	20	54	6	2	13	6	0	3.04
Sept-Oct	35	204.0	215	39	87	11	8	13	11	0	3.79

Batting Against — 1993

	BA	OBA	SA	AB	H	2B	3B	HR	RBI	BB	SO
Total	.301	.318	.412	857	258	42	4	15	87	20	97
vs. Left	.313	.326	.418	431	135	19	4	6	41	10	47
vs. Right	.289	.311	.406	426	123	23	0	9	46	10	50
Bases Empty	.310	.324	.419	496	154	21	0	11	11	8	55
Leadoff	.325	.347	.439	212	69	9	0	5	5	5	17
Runners On Base	.288	.311	.402	361	104	21	4	4	76	12	42
Scoring Position	.239	.271	.325	197	47	6	4	1	65	8	34
Late and Close	.313	.338	.391	64	19	6	0	0	6	2	5

Batting Against — 8-Year Totals

	BA	OBA	SA	AB	H	2B	3B	HR	RBI	BB	SO
Total	.280	.308	.396	3883	1086	197	26	67	380	156	402
vs. Left	.279	.306	.388	2125	592	103	15	33	191	91	195
vs. Right	.281	.312	.405	1758	494	94	11	34	189	65	207
Bases Empty	.278	.306	.401	2349	654	127	14	44	44	78	253
Leadoff	.276	.303	.390	997	275	51	6	17	17	32	104
Runners On Base	.282	.313	.388	1534	432	70	12	23	336	78	149
Scoring Position	.268	.304	.372	862	231	35	8	13	299	57	87
Late and Close	.264	.306	.396	265	70	13	2	6	20	16	24

MATT TURNER — BR/TR — age 27 — FLO RP55 POW/FB

1993

	G	IP	H	BB	SO	SB	CS	W	L	SV	ERA
Total	55	68.0	55	26	59	1	2	4	5	0	2.91
at Home	31	40.1	31	15	34	1	0	2	2	0	3.12
on Road	24	27.2	24	11	25	0	2	2	3	0	2.60
on Grass	46	57.0	47	23	51	1	2	3	4	0	3.32
on Turf	9	11.0	8	3	8	0	0	1	1	0	0.82
Day Games	12	13.0	10	4	8	0	1	2	1	0	1.38
Night Games	43	55.0	45	22	51	1	1	2	4	0	3.27
April	2	3.2	1	1	4	0	0	0	0	0	0.00
May	4	5.0	4	1	2	0	0	0	0	0	0.00
June	8	11.1	5	3	16	0	1	0	1	0	1.59
July	14	18.0	20	6	14	0	2	0	2	0	4.50
August	14	17.0	15	9	10	1	0	2	1	0	3.18
Sept-Oct	13	13.0	10	6	13	0	0	1	1	0	3.46

	BA	OBA	SA	AB	H	2B	3B	HR	RBI	BB	SO
Total	.227	.300	.364	242	55	10	1	7	33	26	59
vs. Left	.254	.344	.412	114	29	7	1	3	16	16	23
vs. Right	.203	.261	.320	128	26	3	0	4	17	10	36
Bases Empty	.225	.296	.362	138	31	5	1	4	4	14	38
Leadoff	.190	.230	.293	58	11	1	1	1	1	3	18
Runners On Base	.231	.306	.365	104	24	5	0	3	29	12	21
Scoring Position	.262	.355	.361	61	16	3	0	1	25	11	14
Late and Close	.253	.337	.373	150	38	7	1	3	20	19	35

1-YEAR TOTALS (1993)

G	IP	H	BB	SO	SB	CS	W	L	SV	ERA
55	68.0	55	26	59	1	2	4	5	0	2.91
31	40.1	31	15	34	1	0	2	2	0	3.12
24	27.2	24	11	25	0	2	2	3	0	2.60
46	57.0	47	23	51	1	2	3	4	0	3.32
9	11.0	8	3	8	0	0	1	1	0	0.82
12	13.0	10	4	8	0	1	2	1	0	1.38
43	55.0	45	22	51	1	1	2	4	0	3.27
2	3.2	1	1	4	0	0	0	0	0	0.00
4	5.0	4	1	2	0	0	0	0	0	0.00
8	11.1	5	3	16	0	1	0	1	0	1.59
14	18.0	20	6	14	0	2	0	2	0	4.50
14	17.0	15	9	10	1	0	2	1	0	3.18
13	13.0	10	6	13	0	0	1	1	0	3.46

BA	OBA	SA	AB	H	2B	3B	HR	RBI	BB	SO
.227	.300	.364	242	55	10	1	7	33	26	59
.254	.344	.412	114	29	7	1	3	16	16	23
.203	.261	.320	128	26	3	0	4	17	10	36
.225	.296	.362	138	31	5	1	4	4	14	38
.190	.230	.293	58	11	1	1	1	1	3	18
.231	.306	.365	104	24	5	0	3	29	12	21
.262	.355	.361	61	16	3	0	1	25	11	14
.253	.337	.373	150	38	7	1	3	20	19	35

FERNANDO VALENZUELA — BL/TL — age 34 — BAL SP31, RP1 FIN/FB

1993

	G	IP	H	BB	SO	SB	CS	W	L	SV	ERA
Total	32	178.2	179	79	78	1	14	8	10	0	4.94
at Home	15	88.0	89	33	37	4	5	5	3	0	4.40
on Road	17	90.2	90	46	41	6	9	3	7	0	5.46
on Grass	26	139.1	152	65	64	9	11	7	10	0	5.68
on Turf	6	39.1	27	14	14	1	3	1	0	0	2.29
Day Games	8	45.1	44	23	18	6	4	3	3	0	4.76
Night Games	24	133.1	135	56	60	4	10	5	7	0	4.99
April	3	7.1	11	3	3	0	1	0	2	0	11.05
May	6	40.2	34	16	21	5	3	1	3	0	3.54
June	6	38.0	33	18	16	3	4	2	2	0	3.79
July	5	40.1	24	14	13	0	3	3	0	0	1.56
August	6	20.0	39	11	10	2	0	0	2	0	13.95
Sept-Oct	6	32.1	38	17	15	0	3	2	1	0	5.29

	BA	OBA	SA	AB	H	2B	3B	HR	RBI	BB	SO
Total	.266	.343	.429	674	179	44	6	18	87	79	78
vs. Left	.283	.379	.483	120	34	10	1	4	19	19	22
vs. Right	.262	.335	.417	554	145	34	5	14	68	60	56
Bases Empty	.240	.324	.393	392	94	29	2	9	9	47	50
Leadoff	.271	.325	.463	177	48	14	1	6	6	14	14
Runners On Base	.301	.368	.479	282	85	15	4	9	78	32	28
Scoring Position	.321	.380	.503	165	53	11	2	5	67	18	18
Late and Close	.235	.366	.294	34	8	2	0	0	3	7	1

9-YEAR TOTALS (1984–1993)

G	IP	H	BB	SO	SB	CS	W	L	SV	ERA
258	1782.0	1652	749	1258	131	96	100	98	1	3.64
127	895.2	813	349	615	55	48	48	44	1	3.32
131	886.1	839	400	643	76	48	52	54	0	3.96
194	1336.0	1236	559	958	88	73	76	73	1	3.60
64	446.0	416	190	300	43	23	24	25	0	3.75
77	521.1	501	207	380	51	28	26	32	1	3.95
181	1260.2	1151	542	878	80	68	74	66	0	3.51
38	261.2	230	90	195	12	22	14	16	0	2.75
43	303.1	268	139	217	27	16	16	17	0	3.62
48	322.2	319	139	219	29	17	20	19	0	3.90
44	312.2	276	125	200	15	15	18	17	0	3.48
41	282.2	274	124	222	21	13	18	17	0	4.14
44	299.0	285	132	205	27	13	14	12	1	3.82

BA	OBA	SA	AB	H	2B	3B	HR	RBI	BB	SO
.247	.322	.361	6685	1652	316	24	133	703	749	1258
.260	.324	.385	1203	313	63	6	25	123	117	243
.244	.322	.356	5482	1339	253	18	108	580	632	1015
.232	.309	.339	3840	889	181	10	70	70	420	797
.232	.297	.325	1671	387	79	4	23	23	154	340
.268	.341	.392	2845	763	135	14	63	633	329	461
.251	.339	.350	1639	411	64	6	29	532	237	296
.238	.317	.310	772	184	32	1	7	76	91	134

TODD VANPOPPEL — BR/TR — age 23 — OAK SP16 POW/FB

1993

	G	IP	H	BB	SO	SB	CS	W	L	SV	ERA
Total	16	84.0	76	62	47	5	5	6	6	0	5.04
at Home	6	32.0	28	25	18	1	3	3	2	0	5.91
on Road	10	52.0	48	37	29	4	2	3	4	0	4.50
on Grass	13	67.1	61	53	33	3	4	4	6	0	5.48
on Turf	3	16.2	15	9	14	2	1	2	0	0	3.24
Day Games	4	18.2	17	18	11	1	1	2	2	0	5.79
Night Games	12	65.1	59	44	36	4	4	4	4	0	4.82
April	0	0.0	0	0	0	0	0	0	0	0	0.00
May	0	0.0	0	0	0	0	0	0	0	0	0.00
June	0	0.0	0	0	0	0	0	0	0	0	0.00
July	4	15.2	13	17	5	2	1	0	3	0	7.47
August	6	31.2	23	25	15	1	2	4	2	0	3.69
Sept-Oct	6	36.2	40	20	27	2	2	2	1	0	5.15

	BA	OBA	SA	AB	H	2B	3B	HR	RBI	BB	SO
Total	.243	.369	.406	313	76	17	2	10	45	62	47
vs. Left	.242	.382	.406	165	40	8	2	5	29	37	25
vs. Right	.243	.354	.405	148	36	9	0	5	16	25	22
Bases Empty	.206	.353	.297	175	36	7	0	3	3	39	26
Leadoff	.164	.322	.233	73	12	2	0	1	1	17	8
Runners On Base	.290	.390	.543	138	40	10	2	7	42	23	21
Scoring Position	.268	.386	.535	71	19	6	2	3	30	14	16
Late and Close	.375	.375	.500	8	3	1	0	0	0	0	0

2-YEAR TOTALS (1991–1993)

G	IP	H	BB	SO	SB	CS	W	L	SV	ERA
17	88.2	83	64	53	6	6	6	6	0	5.28
7	36.2	35	27	24	2	4	3	2	0	6.38
10	52.0	48	37	29	4	2	3	4	0	4.50
14	72.0	68	55	39	4	5	4	6	0	5.75
3	16.2	15	9	14	2	1	2	0	0	3.24
5	23.1	24	20	17	2	2	2	2	0	6.56
12	65.1	59	44	36	4	4	4	4	0	4.82
0	0.0	0	0	0	0	0	0	0	0	0.00
0	0.0	0	0	0	0	0	0	0	0	0.00
0	0.0	0	0	0	0	0	0	0	0	0.00
4	15.2	13	17	5	2	1	0	3	0	7.47
6	31.2	23	25	15	1	2	4	2	0	3.69
7	41.1	47	22	33	3	3	2	1	0	5.66

BA	OBA	SA	AB	H	2B	3B	HR	RBI	BB	SO
.250	.373	.419	332	83	17	3	11	50	64	53
.253	.385	.416	178	45	8	3	5	31	38	28
.247	.357	.422	154	38	9	0	6	19	26	25
.204	.351	.290	186	38	7	0	3	3	41	31
.167	.316	.231	78	13	2	0	1	1	17	9
.308	.401	.582	146	45	10	3	8	47	23	22
.293	.402	.613	75	22	6	3	4	35	14	16
.375	.375	.500	8	3	1	0	0	0	0	0

FRANK VIOLA — BL/TL — age 34 — BOS SP29 FIN/GB

1993	G	IP	H	BB	SO	SB	CS	W	L	SV	ERA
Total	29	183.2	180	72	91	11	11	11	8	0	3.14
at Home	14	91.2	93	30	48	3	6	5	3	0	2.26
on Road	15	92.0	87	42	43	8	5	6	5	0	4.01
on Grass	24	150.1	151	55	77	9	10	8	7	0	3.17
on Turf	5	33.1	29	17	14	2	1	3	1	0	2.97
Day Games	10	66.1	64	23	31	3	4	5	0	0	2.17
Night Games	19	117.1	116	49	60	8	7	6	8	0	3.68
April	5	36.2	31	7	15	3	4	4	1	0	1.47
May	5	30.1	32	17	16	1	1	0	3	0	4.45
June	5	29.2	33	12	18	1	1	0	3	0	4.55
July	6	35.1	47	20	18	3	4	2	1	0	4.58
August	5	33.0	23	11	13	1	0	4	0	0	1.64
Sept-Oct	3	18.2	14	5	11	1	1	0	0	0	1.93

10-YEAR TOTALS (1984–1993)

	G	IP	H	BB	SO	SB	CS	W	L	SV	ERA
	349	2424.2	2336	693	1602	108	106	163	120	0	3.42
	169	1207.1	1173	313	837	50	56	87	51	0	3.23
	180	1217.1	1163	380	765	58	50	76	69	0	3.62
	197	1330.1	1298	386	837	65	59	89	73	0	3.48
	152	1094.1	1038	307	765	43	47	74	47	0	3.36
	116	814.2	762	208	528	30	37	57	38	0	3.12
	233	1610.0	1574	485	1074	78	69	106	82	0	3.58
	50	352.2	321	101	236	17	20	23	17	0	3.09
	57	389.0	394	103	261	15	18	27	21	0	3.72
	57	399.0	396	109	254	24	20	28	17	0	3.27
	59	419.2	371	140	258	22	17	29	18	0	3.15
	63	433.0	435	123	276	14	15	27	28	0	3.72
	63	431.1	419	117	317	16	16	29	19	0	3.53

	BA	OBA	SA	AB	H	2B	3B	HR	RBI	BB	SO
Total	.259	.331	.372	694	180	32	5	12	63	72	91
vs. Left	.272	.341	.404	114	31	8	2	1	8	13	11
vs. Right	.257	.329	.366	580	149	24	3	11	55	59	80
Bases Empty	.273	.345	.412	400	109	15	4	11	11	42	64
Leadoff	.249	.330	.422	173	43	3	3	7	7	21	29
Runners On Base	.241	.313	.316	294	71	17	1	1	52	30	27
Scoring Position	.209	.297	.281	153	32	6	1	1	49	20	14
Late and Close	.210	.246	.226	62	13	1	0	0	0	3	9

	BA	OBA	SA	AB	H	2B	3B	HR	RBI	BB	SO
	.253	.306	.379	9227	2336	406	39	227	904	693	1602
	.256	.307	.382	1627	416	84	8	35	162	110	269
	.253	.306	.379	7600	1920	322	31	192	742	583	1333
	.253	.306	.380	5534	1398	235	28	138	138	408	967
	.247	.299	.382	2344	580	97	13	64	64	169	390
	.254	.307	.379	3693	938	171	11	89	766	285	635
	.251	.310	.377	1905	479	82	7	48	647	178	359
	.232	.281	.330	915	212	25	4	19	70	61	127

PAUL WAGNER — BR/TR — age 27 — PIT RP27, SP17 POW/FB

1993	G	IP	H	BB	SO	SB	CS	W	L	SV	ERA
Total	44	141.1	143	42	114	18	7	8	8	2	4.27
at Home	21	62.2	67	10	55	7	1	4	4	0	4.31
on Road	23	78.2	76	32	59	11	6	4	4	2	4.23
on Grass	17	56.1	50	24	48	5	5	2	1	0	3.20
on Turf	27	85.0	93	18	66	13	2	6	7	0	4.98
Day Games	10	33.2	34	9	34	4	2	1	2	0	5.35
Night Games	34	107.2	109	33	80	14	5	7	6	2	3.93
April	13	15.0	17	4	18	0	2	0	0	0	4.20
May	10	12.1	14	6	10	2	0	1	2	0	6.57
June	6	36.2	34	9	26	2	3	2	2	0	3.68
July	5	24.1	28	7	13	6	1	2	2	0	6.29
August	5	18.1	21	10	19	4	0	0	0	0	4.91
Sept-Oct	5	34.2	29	6	28	1	1	3	2	0	2.34

2-YEAR TOTALS (1992–1993)

	G	IP	H	BB	SO	SB	CS	W	L	SV	ERA
	50	154.1	152	47	119	18	8	10	8	2	3.97
	23	65.1	70	11	56	7	1	4	4	0	4.13
	27	89.0	82	36	63	11	7	6	4	2	3.84
	19	64.1	55	26	50	5	5	3	1	2	2.94
	31	90.0	97	21	69	13	3	7	7	0	4.70
	13	40.0	40	10	36	4	2	1	2	0	4.72
	37	114.1	112	37	83	14	6	9	6	2	3.70
	13	15.0	17	4	18	0	2	0	0	0	4.20
	10	12.1	14	6	10	2	0	1	2	0	6.57
	6	36.2	34	9	26	2	3	2	2	0	3.68
	6	28.1	32	8	14	6	1	2	2	0	5.72
	5	18.1	21	10	19	4	0	0	0	0	4.91
	10	43.2	34	10	32	4	2	5	2	0	1.85

	BA	OBA	SA	AB	H	2B	3B	HR	RBI	BB	SO
Total	.263	.314	.392	543	143	21	2	15	65	42	114
vs. Left	.296	.351	.437	270	80	13	2	7	35	25	49
vs. Right	.231	.276	.348	273	63	8	0	8	30	17	65
Bases Empty	.274	.330	.420	307	84	14	2	9	9	26	64
Leadoff	.259	.301	.356	135	35	5	1	2	2	8	22
Runners On Base	.250	.292	.356	236	59	7	0	6	56	16	50
Scoring Position	.254	.295	.391	138	35	4	0	5	52	10	30
Late and Close	.333	.371	.471	87	29	3	0	3	18	7	19

	BA	OBA	SA	AB	H	2B	3B	HR	RBI	BB	SO
	.258	.310	.381	590	152	24	2	15	66	47	119
	.294	.354	.429	289	85	14	2	7	36	29	51
	.223	.266	.336	301	67	10	0	8	30	18	68
	.270	.331	.414	333	90	17	2	9	9	30	67
	.245	.288	.340	147	36	6	1	2	2	9	24
	.241	.284	.339	257	62	7	0	6	57	17	52
	.237	.276	.362	152	36	4	0	5	53	10	30
	.322	.360	.456	90	29	3	0	3	18	7	19

TIM WAKEFIELD — BR/TR — age 28 — PIT SP20, RP4 POW/FB

1993	G	IP	H	BB	SO	SB	CS	W	L	SV	ERA
Total	24	128.1	145	75	59	8	5	6	11	0	5.61
at Home	12	74.1	63	48	36	6	4	4	3	0	3.15
on Road	12	54.0	82	27	23	2	1	2	8	0	9.00
on Grass	7	35.2	56	19	10	1	0	1	6	0	8.33
on Turf	17	92.2	89	56	49	7	5	5	5	0	4.56
Day Games	5	31.0	25	10	10	2	1	1	2	0	2.90
Night Games	19	97.1	120	65	49	6	3	5	9	0	6.47
April	5	39.0	32	35	18	1	2	3	2	0	4.38
May	6	33.1	50	19	12	5	2	3	0	0	7.02
June	6	13.0	17	2	7	0	1	0	2	0	7.62
July	2	9.2	13	5	6	0	0	0	1	0	10.24
August	0	0.0	0	0	0	0	0	0	0	0	0.00
Sept-Oct	5	33.1	33	14	16	2	1	2	3	0	3.51

2-YEAR TOTALS (1992–1993)

	G	IP	H	BB	SO	SB	CS	W	L	SV	ERA
	37	220.1	221	110	110	12	14	14	12	0	4.17
	18	117.1	105	67	62	8	7	9	3	0	2.76
	19	103.0	116	43	48	4	7	5	9	0	5.77
	12	70.2	78	32	27	2	5	4	7	0	5.35
	25	149.2	143	78	83	10	9	10	5	0	3.61
	10	61.1	51	16	22	4	5	4	2	0	2.93
	27	159.0	170	94	88	8	9	10	10	0	4.64
	5	39.0	32	35	18	1	2	3	2	0	4.38
	6	33.1	50	19	12	5	2	3	0	0	7.02
	6	13.0	17	2	7	0	1	0	2	0	7.62
	3	18.2	19	10	16	0	1	1	1	0	5.30
	5	40.0	31	17	22	3	5	3	1	0	2.47
	12	76.1	72	27	35	3	4	6	3	0	2.83

	BA	OBA	SA	AB	H	2B	3B	HR	RBI	BB	SO
Total	.291	.390	.456	498	145	34	3	14	75	75	59
vs. Left	.279	.417	.438	208	58	14	2	5	37	45	26
vs. Right	.300	.369	.469	290	87	20	1	9	38	30	33
Bases Empty	.267	.364	.435	262	70	15	1	9	9	38	36
Leadoff	.259	.358	.448	116	30	2	1	6	6	17	16
Runners On Base	.318	.418	.479	236	75	19	2	5	66	37	23
Scoring Position	.309	.423	.489	139	43	12	2	3	60	26	13
Late and Close	.232	.323	.429	56	13	2	0	3	5	7	6

	BA	OBA	SA	AB	H	2B	3B	HR	RBI	BB	SO
	.268	.357	.398	825	221	46	5	17	100	110	110
	.246	.361	.354	410	101	20	3	6	49	70	61
	.289	.354	.441	415	120	26	2	11	51	40	49
	.255	.340	.374	455	116	22	1	10	10	57	65
	.260	.348	.380	200	52	4	1	6	6	26	28
	.284	.377	.427	370	105	24	4	7	90	53	45
	.265	.379	.433	215	57	16	4	4	82	39	30
	.219	.280	.342	114	25	5	0	3	9	9	12

BOB WALK — BR/TR — age 38 — PIT SP32 FIN/GB

1993	G	IP	H	BB	SO	SB	CS	W	L	SV	ERA
Total	32	187.0	214	70	80	19	6	13	14	0	5.68
at Home	17	101.0	115	32	40	9	3	9	6	0	5.35
on Road	15	86.0	99	38	40	10	3	4	8	0	6.07
on Grass	9	51.0	59	22	20	7	2	3	5	0	6.00
on Turf	23	136.0	155	48	60	12	4	10	9	0	5.56
Day Games	10	53.1	69	25	28	9	3	3	4	0	7.26
Night Games	22	133.2	145	45	52	10	3	10	10	0	5.05
April	5	31.1	35	9	20	2	1	2	2	0	5.17
May	5	32.2	38	10	7	3	1	4	1	0	4.41
June	6	38.2	36	13	13	1	1	3	5	0	5.12
July	5	29.1	38	10	18	2	1	2	3	0	5.22
August	6	30.2	36	12	14	8	1	1	4	0	7.92
Sept-Oct	5	24.1	31	16	8	3	1	1	2	0	6.66

10-YEAR TOTALS (1984–1993)

	G	IP	H	BB	SO	SB	CS	W	L	SV	ERA
Total	278	1303.0	1281	451	650	122	57	82	61	5	3.83
at Home	141	660.1	643	208	337	64	27	46	30	3	3.65
on Road	137	642.2	638	243	313	58	30	36	31	2	4.02
on Grass	68	313.1	307	117	142	30	19	19	17	1	3.94
on Turf	210	989.2	974	334	508	92	38	63	44	4	3.80
Day Games	82	365.2	360	131	194	36	15	24	15	3	4.09
Night Games	196	937.1	921	320	456	86	42	58	46	2	3.74
April	39	182.2	171	63	108	18	12	10	9	1	3.35
May	48	203.1	188	74	92	15	10	16	9	0	3.67
June	46	204.0	193	79	100	18	7	14	7	2	4.10
July	44	218.1	229	67	107	19	10	12	14	0	3.87
August	46	252.1	250	85	109	30	13	17	13	2	3.92
Sept-Oct	55	242.1	250	83	134	22	5	13	9	0	3.97

	BA	OBA	SA	AB	H	2B	3B	HR	RBI	BB	SO
Total (1993)	.294	.356	.452	728	214	36	5	23	108	70	80
vs. Left	.275	.348	.449	385	106	25	3	12	56	45	44
vs. Right	.315	.365	.455	343	108	11	2	11	52	25	36
Bases Empty	.274	.335	.416	423	116	20	2	12	12	37	46
Leadoff	.274	.326	.419	179	49	6	1	6	6	14	14
Runners On Base	.321	.383	.502	305	98	16	3	11	96	33	34
Scoring Position	.315	.382	.511	178	56	8	3	7	85	24	24
Late and Close	.378	.417	.556	45	17	1	2	1	11	3	3
Total (career)	.259	.323	.385	4954	1281	232	33	110	549	451	650
vs. Left	.269	.338	.397	2700	726	136	24	54	280	279	298
vs. Right	.246	.304	.371	2254	555	96	9	56	269	172	352
Bases Empty	.250	.311	.368	2939	734	132	21	58	58	241	364
Leadoff	.255	.307	.378	1253	320	49	9	29	29	89	138
Runners On Base	.271	.339	.410	2015	547	100	12	52	491	210	286
Scoring Position	.265	.345	.413	1185	314	63	11	30	432	154	179
Late and Close	.291	.359	.430	412	120	20	2	11	54	42	44

DUANE WARD — BR/TR — age 30 — TOR RP71 POW/GB

1993	G	IP	H	BB	SO	SB	CS	W	L	SV	ERA
Total	71	71.2	49	25	97	3	0	2	3	45	2.13
at Home	33	33.0	25	14	45	2	0	1	2	21	2.73
on Road	38	38.2	24	11	52	1	0	1	1	24	1.63
on Grass	32	32.2	20	11	42	1	0	1	1	21	1.38
on Turf	39	39.0	29	14	55	2	0	1	2	24	2.77
Day Games	23	23.1	13	5	34	1	0	0	1	15	1.16
Night Games	48	48.1	36	20	63	2	0	2	2	30	2.61
April	10	9.0	5	1	12	0	0	0	0	8	2.00
May	13	14.0	8	8	19	2	0	0	2	7	2.57
June	12	12.1	6	2	13	0	0	0	0	7	1.46
July	10	10.1	5	4	21	0	0	0	0	6	1.74
August	12	11.1	12	3	14	0	0	0	0	10	1.59
Sept-Oct	14	14.2	10	7	18	1	0	0	1	7	3.07

8-YEAR TOTALS (1986–1993)

	G	IP	H	BB	SO	SB	CS	W	L	SV	ERA
Total	458	664.0	540	281	676	65	24	32	36	121	3.20
at Home	231	342.1	268	135	357	30	10	19	19	62	3.00
on Road	227	321.2	272	146	319	35	14	13	17	59	3.41
on Grass	180	251.2	210	118	246	24	11	11	15	44	3.50
on Turf	278	412.1	330	163	430	41	13	21	21	77	3.01
Day Games	151	220.2	161	98	242	25	8	16	12	40	3.02
Night Games	307	443.1	379	183	434	40	16	16	24	81	3.29
April	70	86.0	77	33	91	12	5	2	9	20	3.45
May	77	108.2	95	67	103	16	2	9	7	22	3.06
June	77	128.1	98	53	118	12	2	9	5	18	3.44
July	66	108.2	96	32	122	7	1	6	5	19	2.90
August	72	107.2	95	32	104	7	8	7	5	20	3.18
Sept-Oct	96	124.2	79	64	138	11	6	4	6	22	3.18

	BA	OBA	SA	AB	H	2B	3B	HR	RBI	BB	SO
Total (1993)	.193	.266	.264	254	49	6	0	4	24	25	97
vs. Left	.211	.310	.285	123	26	3	0	2	11	18	47
vs. Right	.176	.221	.244	131	23	3	0	2	13	7	50
Bases Empty	.166	.239	.248	145	24	3	0	3	3	13	57
Leadoff	.177	.215	.274	62	11	3	0	1	1	3	22
Runners On Base	.229	.301	.284	109	25	3	0	1	21	12	40
Scoring Position	.243	.313	.300	70	17	1	0	1	21	8	28
Late and Close	.156	.237	.208	154	24	2	0	2	19	17	64
Total (career)	.225	.307	.307	2401	540	80	11	32	268	281	676
vs. Left	.229	.335	.336	1075	246	41	4	22	127	174	319
vs. Right	.222	.283	.284	1326	294	39	7	10	141	107	357
Bases Empty	.212	.286	.293	1291	274	48	4	16	16	130	395
Leadoff	.213	.295	.290	541	115	20	2	6	6	63	159
Runners On Base	.240	.329	.324	1110	266	32	7	16	252	151	281
Scoring Position	.242	.336	.335	708	171	16	4	14	241	107	188
Late and Close	.218	.301	.301	1302	284	37	7	19	154	156	387

BILL WEGMAN — BR/TR — age 32 — MIL SP18, RP2 FIN/GB

1993	G	IP	H	BB	SO	SB	CS	W	L	SV	ERA
Total	20	120.2	135	34	50	10	7	4	14	0	4.48
at Home	9	62.2	70	15	27	7	2	3	6	0	3.88
on Road	11	58.0	65	19	23	3	5	1	8	0	5.12
on Grass	17	99.0	114	26	45	10	6	4	11	0	4.73
on Turf	3	21.2	21	8	5	0	1	0	3	0	3.32
Day Games	11	68.0	84	15	35	8	5	3	7	0	4.63
Night Games	9	52.2	51	19	15	2	2	1	7	0	4.27
April	5	37.1	41	9	20	6	4	2	3	0	3.62
May	6	44.1	40	13	17	1	2	2	2	0	3.05
June	6	34.2	42	10	11	2	1	0	6	0	5.71
July	1	2.0	9	1	1	1	0	0	1	0	22.50
August	0	0.0	0	0	0	0	0	0	0	0	0.00
Sept-Oct	2	2.1	3	1	1	0	0	0	0	0	11.57

9-YEAR TOTALS (1985–1993)

	G	IP	H	BB	SO	SB	CS	W	L	SV	ERA
Total	206	1296.2	1338	305	587	85	46	68	79	0	4.07
at Home	109	717.2	722	149	326	56	23	38	33	0	3.65
on Road	97	579.0	616	156	261	29	23	30	46	0	4.59
on Grass	177	1128.2	1151	262	510	77	38	59	63	0	3.94
on Turf	29	168.0	187	43	77	8	8	9	16	0	4.93
Day Games	72	445.2	500	102	198	35	16	23	27	0	4.02
Night Games	134	851.0	838	203	389	50	30	45	52	0	4.09
April	30	206.0	197	59	82	22	11	9	12	0	3.32
May	45	264.0	288	64	121	13	11	13	23	0	4.67
June	34	207.2	220	52	93	12	5	11	13	0	4.55
July	30	207.1	217	35	91	12	9	12	13	0	3.73
August	29	178.0	202	36	87	14	5	7	10	0	4.60
Sept-Oct	38	233.2	214	59	113	12	5	17	8	0	3.50

	BA	OBA	SA	AB	H	2B	3B	HR	RBI	BB	SO
Total (1993)	.291	.335	.472	464	135	35	5	13	61	34	50
vs. Left	.326	.358	.493	221	72	14	4	5	28	13	18
vs. Right	.259	.313	.453	243	63	21	1	8	33	21	32
Bases Empty	.300	.355	.485	270	81	23	3	7	7	22	27
Leadoff	.364	.414	.644	118	43	11	2	6	6	9	10
Runners On Base	.278	.307	.454	194	54	12	2	6	54	12	23
Scoring Position	.268	.301	.411	112	30	7	0	3	44	10	13
Late and Close	.465	.519	.558	43	20	4	0	0	7	7	2
Total (career)	.266	.310	.421	5026	1338	255	23	159	570	305	587
vs. Left	.259	.302	.399	2588	670	119	12	73	280	164	232
vs. Right	.274	.319	.445	2438	668	136	11	86	290	141	355
Bases Empty	.260	.304	.417	3115	811	159	15	100	100	171	368
Leadoff	.267	.303	.455	1291	345	57	7	57	57	61	135
Runners On Base	.276	.320	.427	1911	527	96	8	59	470	134	219
Scoring Position	.279	.322	.420	1037	289	49	4	30	394	82	123
Late and Close	.295	.344	.447	447	132	28	2	12	51	31	58

BOB WELCH — BR/TR — age 38 — OAK SP28, RP2 FIN/FB — 10-YEAR TOTALS (1984–1993)

1993	G	IP	H	BB	SO	SB	CS	W	L	SV	ERA	G	IP	H	BB	SO	SB	CS	W	L	SV	ERA
Total	30	166.2	208	56	63	8	12	9	11	0	5.29	311	2036.1	1947	660	1234	145	102	142	93	0	3.52
at Home	15	85.0	117	25	36	2	5	5	6	0	5.61	159	1087.1	1018	295	691	68	59	81	45	0	3.09
on Road	15	81.2	91	31	27	6	7	4	5	0	4.96	152	949.0	929	365	543	77	43	61	48	0	4.01
on Grass	27	151.1	192	48	61	7	12	9	10	0	5.23	251	1672.1	1573	513	1028	114	89	122	68	0	3.28
on Turf	3	15.1	16	8	2	1	0	0	1	0	5.87	60	364.0	374	147	206	31	13	20	25	0	4.60
Day Games	13	71.0	98	24	36	2	4	4	6	0	6.08	115	758.0	712	250	468	53	31	59	31	0	3.36
Night Games	17	95.2	110	32	27	6	8	5	5	0	4.70	196	1278.1	1235	410	766	92	71	83	62	0	3.61
April	5	27.0	33	5	8	2	1	2	2	0	5.00	42	291.1	247	87	167	18	14	22	13	0	2.53
May	6	35.1	45	13	16	3	3	2	2	0	4.58	50	331.0	330	115	191	26	7	22	16	0	3.92
June	5	34.2	41	9	9	2	1	1	2	0	4.15	53	344.0	354	114	182	27	18	23	15	0	3.85
July	6	28.1	37	10	11	0	3	3	1	0	5.40	55	348.0	340	103	232	22	24	23	16	0	3.52
August	4	20.2	21	8	14	1	2	1	0	0	5.23	55	369.0	344	121	254	25	22	29	15	0	3.37
Sept-Oct	4	20.2	31	11	5	0	2	0	4	0	8.71	56	353.0	332	120	208	27	17	23	18	0	3.80

	BA	OBA	SA	AB	H	2B	3B	HR	RBI	BB	SO	BA	OBA	SA	AB	H	2B	3B	HR	RBI	BB	SO
Total	.310	.368	.491	670	208	36	5	25	91	56	63	.252	.314	.382	7717	1947	341	52	186	763	660	1234
vs. Left	.309	.362	.477	369	114	23	3	11	50	30	34	.252	.316	.368	4040	1018	178	35	74	364	373	571
vs. Right	.312	.375	.508	301	94	13	2	14	41	26	29	.253	.313	.398	3677	929	163	17	112	399	287	663
Bases Empty	.321	.376	.514	383	123	17	3	17	17	32	31	.255	.307	.390	4695	1197	212	34	118	118	329	694
Leadoff	.284	.313	.450	169	48	8	1	6	6	7	15	.250	.297	.384	1983	496	89	9	53	53	128	268
Runners On Base	.296	.357	.460	287	85	19	2	8	74	24	32	.248	.325	.370	3022	750	129	18	68	645	331	540
Scoring Position	.295	.365	.463	149	44	9	2	4	62	14	14	.254	.339	.373	1696	431	75	14	33	550	222	342
Late and Close	.348	.348	.348	23	8	0	0	0	1	0	1	.238	.288	.341	680	162	22	3	14	58	45	95

DAVID WELLS — BL/TL — age 31 — DET SP30, RP2 FIN/FB — 7-YEAR TOTALS (1987–1993)

1993	G	IP	H	BB	SO	SB	CS	W	L	SV	ERA	G	IP	H	BB	SO	SB	CS	W	L	SV	ERA
Total	32	187.0	183	42	139	14	10	11	9	0	4.19	269	874.1	842	243	588	64	47	58	46	13	3.87
at Home	16	108.1	90	18	78	5	9	8	3	0	2.74	133	431.0	394	110	283	27	27	29	19	6	3.30
on Road	16	78.2	93	24	61	9	1	3	6	0	6.18	136	443.1	448	133	305	37	20	29	27	7	4.43
on Grass	26	157.1	145	32	109	11	10	11	7	0	3.78	122	447.1	434	124	316	36	24	32	24	6	4.10
on Turf	6	29.2	38	10	30	3	0	0	2	0	6.37	147	427.0	408	119	272	28	23	26	22	7	3.63
Day Games	13	77.0	79	20	54	9	3	3	4	0	4.79	88	259.1	260	82	156	28	14	15	15	2	4.72
Night Games	19	110.0	104	22	85	5	7	8	5	0	3.76	181	615.0	582	161	432	36	33	43	31	11	3.51
April	5	30.2	20	5	16	0	2	4	0	0	1.47	42	116.0	95	32	74	12	6	9	7	3	3.57
May	6	44.0	29	10	35	5	2	2	1	0	2.45	57	153.2	110	45	123	15	9	11	4	4	2.28
June	6	38.0	42	11	33	5	2	3	2	0	5.68	47	171.1	177	55	135	11	7	11	9	4	4.15
July	6	29.1	41	10	23	2	1	1	4	0	8.28	34	160.2	158	40	90	12	11	12	9	0	4.31
August	3	8.1	10	0	8	0	1	0	0	0	2.16	28	114.0	147	40	58	10	7	5	10	0	6.32
Sept-Oct	6	36.2	41	6	24	2	2	1	2	0	4.17	61	158.2	155	31	108	4	7	10	7	2	3.12

	BA	OBA	SA	AB	H	2B	3B	HR	RBI	BB	SO	BA	OBA	SA	AB	H	2B	3B	HR	RBI	BB	SO
Total	.254	.300	.416	721	183	33	3	26	78	42	139	.253	.306	.404	3327	842	175	18	97	366	243	588
vs. Left	.250	.328	.361	108	27	4	1	2	7	9	20	.254	.316	.368	631	160	31	4	11	64	45	87
vs. Right	.254	.295	.426	613	156	29	2	24	71	33	119	.253	.304	.412	2696	682	144	14	86	302	198	501
Bases Empty	.259	.300	.397	448	116	19	2	13	13	20	84	.253	.304	.390	1972	499	100	7	52	52	131	364
Leadoff	.283	.309	.412	187	53	12	0	4	4	6	34	.261	.309	.388	816	213	40	2	20	20	55	151
Runners On Base	.245	.301	.447	273	67	14	1	13	65	22	55	.253	.310	.424	1355	343	75	11	45	314	112	224
Scoring Position	.223	.306	.388	139	31	8	0	5	46	17	37	.245	.327	.395	734	180	47	6	17	245	91	136
Late and Close	.390	.431	.678	59	23	6	1	3	9	5	6	.272	.330	.430	639	174	31	5	20	71	56	129

JOHN WETTELAND — BR/TR — age 28 — MON RP70 POW/FB — 5-YEAR TOTALS (1989–1993)

1993	G	IP	H	BB	SO	SB	CS	W	L	SV	ERA	G	IP	H	BB	SO	SB	CS	W	L	SV	ERA
Total	70	85.1	58	28	113	13	2	9	3	43	1.37	196	323.1	252	118	353	43	11	21	19	81	2.95
at Home	38	43.2	31	10	57	6	1	6	1	22	1.44	104	154.0	123	46	167	22	5	14	9	44	3.04
on Road	32	41.2	27	18	56	7	1	3	2	21	1.30	92	169.1	129	72	186	21	6	7	10	37	2.87
on Grass	18	24.1	19	7	35	3	0	1	1	12	1.48	75	158.2	131	54	153	14	7	10	11	20	3.06
on Turf	52	61.0	39	21	78	10	2	8	2	31	1.33	121	164.2	121	64	200	29	4	11	8	61	2.84
Day Games	19	23.2	18	8	31	5	0	3	1	9	2.66	58	95.2	88	32	104	15	5	6	6	19	4.33
Night Games	51	61.2	40	20	82	8	2	6	2	34	0.88	138	227.2	164	86	249	28	6	15	13	62	2.37
April	3	3.1	6	2	1	0	0	0	0	1	2.70	17	19.1	30	7	20	3	0	1	3	4	6.98
May	15	17.1	11	3	21	2	0	2	0	7	2.08	32	45.0	41	16	54	6	1	2	2	12	4.60
June	12	17.2	9	10	21	2	0	1	0	8	0.51	37	64.0	39	24	67	8	2	3	1	13	1.97
July	13	16.1	13	4	24	3	1	1	1	6	2.76	34	55.0	41	17	60	10	3	7	4	16	2.29
August	12	15.2	15	6	22	4	0	1	0	9	1.15	30	60.0	47	28	65	9	3	4	6	16	2.55
Sept-Oct	15	15.0	4	3	22	2	1	1	0	12	0.00	46	80.0	54	26	87	7	2	4	3	20	2.59

	BA	OBA	SA	AB	H	2B	3B	HR	RBI	BB	SO	BA	OBA	SA	AB	H	2B	3B	HR	RBI	BB	SO
Total	.188	.260	.276	308	58	10	4	3	23	28	113	.214	.290	.317	1178	252	40	6	23	132	118	353
vs. Left	.175	.254	.266	177	31	4	1	3	15	18	69	.210	.287	.304	649	136	19	3	12	68	66	201
vs. Right	.206	.268	.290	131	27	5	3	0	8	10	44	.219	.294	.333	529	116	21	3	11	64	52	152
Bases Empty	.212	.283	.311	151	32	3	3	2	2	14	48	.214	.291	.317	622	133	15	5	13	13	64	181
Leadoff	.213	.304	.393	61	13	2	1	1	1	8	25	.242	.319	.415	265	64	9	5	9	9	30	82
Runners On Base	.166	.237	.242	157	26	7	1	1	21	14	65	.214	.289	.317	556	119	25	1	10	119	54	172
Scoring Position	.149	.230	.198	101	15	5	0	0	16	11	49	.231	.319	.354	342	79	18	0	8	108	45	109
Late and Close	.183	.254	.272	268	49	9	3	3	21	24	94	.213	.290	.319	564	120	17	5	11	60	58	182

WALLY WHITEHURST — BR/TR — age 30 — SD SP19, RP2 FIN/FB

1993	G	IP	H	BB	SO	SB	CS	W	L	SV	ERA	5-YEAR TOTALS (1989–1993) G	IP	H	BB	SO	SB	CS	W	L	SV	ERA
Total	21	105.2	109	30	57	3	7	4	7	0	3.83	148	415.2	430	102	269	26	21	15	29	3	3.83
at Home	10	46.0	49	12	25	1	2	1	5	0	4.11	73	196.0	193	47	129	15	6	7	16	1	3.58
on Road	11	59.2	60	18	32	2	5	3	2	0	3.62	75	219.2	237	55	140	11	15	8	13	2	4.06
on Grass	17	82.0	89	27	45	3	7	3	6	0	4.50	103	304.1	315	76	205	19	17	11	22	3	3.93
on Turf	4	23.2	20	3	12	0	0	1	1	0	1.52	45	111.1	115	26	64	7	4	4	7	0	3.56
Day Games	7	30.2	36	9	14	2	5	1	3	0	4.11	48	110.1	136	29	72	5	8	2	10	1	4.81
Night Games	14	75.0	73	21	43	1	2	3	4	0	3.72	100	305.1	294	73	197	21	13	13	19	2	3.48
April	0	0.0	0	0	0	0	0	0	0	0	0.00	17	36.1	34	5	15	1	3	1	3	0	3.47
May	5	27.0	31	9	18	0	1	0	3	0	5.00	28	73.2	73	20	62	2	3	2	4	2	3.42
June	6	33.0	29	12	17	3	3	2	2	0	1.91	25	89.0	87	28	54	7	5	4	5	0	2.73
July	5	31.2	32	7	11	0	1	1	1	0	4.83	23	95.2	96	18	51	9	3	3	7	0	4.61
August	2	9.0	12	0	7	0	0	1	0	0	3.00	20	55.2	68	13	34	4	2	2	5	0	4.53
Sept-Oct	3	5.0	5	2	4	0	2	0	1	0	5.40	35	65.1	72	18	53	3	5	3	5	1	4.27

	BA	OBA	SA	AB	H	2B	3B	HR	RBI	BB	SO	BA	OBA	SA	AB	H	2B	3B	HR	RBI	BB	SO
Total	.276	.326	.425	395	109	20	3	11	44	30	57	.269	.315	.399	1597	430	79	13	34	189	102	269
vs. Left	.277	.346	.436	188	52	8	2	6	23	22	23	.271	.324	.403	813	220	43	7	17	90	64	143
vs. Right	.275	.306	.415	207	57	12	1	5	21	8	34	.268	.305	.394	784	210	36	6	17	99	38	126
Bases Empty	.283	.324	.430	244	69	12	3	6	6	14	42	.265	.303	.384	932	247	44	8	17	17	46	156
Leadoff	.294	.333	.529	102	30	7	1	5	5	5	15	.276	.311	.441	395	109	22	5	11	11	18	48
Runners On Base	.265	.328	.417	151	40	8	0	5	38	16	15	.275	.330	.420	665	183	35	5	17	172	56	113
Scoring Position	.272	.368	.407	81	22	5	0	2	31	15	11	.271	.344	.394	391	106	16	4	8	142	46	78
Late and Close	.176	.250	.294	17	3	0	1	0	1	2	1	.276	.327	.368	185	51	9	1	2	24	12	24

BOB WICKMAN — BR/TR — age 25 — NYA RP22, SP19 FIN/GB

1993	G	IP	H	BB	SO	SB	CS	W	L	SV	ERA	2-YEAR TOTALS (1992–1993) G	IP	H	BB	SO	SB	CS	W	L	SV	ERA
Total	41	140.0	156	69	70	20	9	14	4	4	4.63	49	190.1	207	89	91	28	10	20	5	4	4.49
at Home	21	68.2	56	29	38	4	5	9	0	1	2.75	25	91.2	81	35	46	7	5	11	1	1	3.34
on Road	20	71.1	100	40	32	16	4	5	4	3	6.43	24	98.2	126	54	45	21	5	9	4	3	5.56
on Grass	36	121.1	129	54	63	15	7	13	2	4	4.01	42	157.1	167	67	78	20	7	17	3	4	4.00
on Turf	5	18.2	27	15	7	5	2	1	2	0	8.68	7	33.0	40	22	13	8	3	3	2	0	6.82
Day Games	16	58.1	55	33	30	9	3	9	1	1	3.39	18	71.2	69	36	35	11	3	11	1	1	3.39
Night Games	25	81.2	101	36	40	11	6	5	3	3	5.51	31	118.2	138	53	56	17	7	9	4	3	5.16
April	3	19.0	18	11	6	5	0	2	0	0	4.74	3	19.0	18	11	6	5	0	2	0	0	4.74
May	6	39.0	40	21	17	5	5	4	0	0	3.46	6	39.0	40	21	17	5	5	4	0	0	3.46
June	5	25.2	37	10	12	3	1	2	1	0	5.26	5	25.2	37	10	12	3	1	2	1	0	5.26
July	6	22.1	24	12	12	2	0	2	2	0	5.64	6	22.1	24	12	12	2	0	2	2	0	5.64
August	10	22.1	19	8	15	5	2	0	1	4	3.22	12	36.1	30	13	22	8	3	1	1	1	3.47
Sept-Oct	11	11.2	18	7	8	0	1	4	0	0	7.71	17	48.0	58	22	22	5	1	9	1	0	5.06

	BA	OBA	SA	AB	H	2B	3B	HR	RBI	BB	SO	BA	OBA	SA	AB	H	2B	3B	HR	RBI	BB	SO
Total	.284	.368	.425	550	156	31	4	13	76	69	70	.281	.362	.415	737	207	40	7	15	99	89	91
vs. Left	.279	.374	.426	244	68	18	0	6	34	36	29	.279	.366	.426	333	93	22	3	7	47	46	37
vs. Right	.288	.363	.425	306	88	13	4	7	42	33	41	.282	.358	.406	404	114	18	4	8	52	43	54
Bases Empty	.302	.375	.443	291	88	15	1	8	8	32	34	.301	.384	.435	386	116	18	2	10	10	48	48
Leadoff	.301	.349	.456	136	41	9	0	4	4	10	12	.287	.348	.409	181	52	10	0	4	4	16	19
Runners On Base	.263	.360	.405	259	68	16	3	5	68	37	36	.259	.338	.393	351	91	22	5	5	89	41	43
Scoring Position	.270	.385	.474	152	41	10	3	5	66	26	25	.257	.349	.447	206	53	14	5	5	86	28	28
Late and Close	.344	.394	.525	61	21	3	1	2	12	3	7	.351	.415	.514	74	26	4	1	2	15	6	7

MITCH WILLIAMS — BL/TL — age 30 — PHI RP65 POW/FB

1993	G	IP	H	BB	SO	SB	CS	W	L	SV	ERA	8-YEAR TOTALS (1986–1993) G	IP	H	BB	SO	SB	CS	W	L	SV	ERA
Total	65	62.0	56	44	60	9	0	3	7	43	3.34	567	654.0	492	493	620	58	29	43	51	186	3.40
at Home	32	28.0	26	16	27	3	0	1	3	19	4.18	285	331.0	268	255	318	25	14	27	21	87	3.62
on Road	33	34.0	30	28	33	6	0	2	4	24	2.65	282	323.0	224	238	302	33	15	16	30	99	3.18
on Grass	17	18.2	17	13	15	2	0	2	0	14	2.41	337	395.2	301	310	357	23	22	24	26	87	3.53
on Turf	48	43.1	39	31	45	7	0	1	7	29	3.74	230	258.1	191	183	263	35	7	19	25	99	3.21
Day Games	18	17.2	20	14	18	2	0	1	3	12	3.57	182	188.0	163	150	164	21	5	11	13	61	3.64
Night Games	47	44.1	36	30	42	7	0	2	4	31	3.25	385	466.0	329	343	456	37	24	32	38	125	3.30
April	12	12.0	11	4	13	0	0	1	0	10	3.00	82	89.0	69	56	83	8	7	6	6	36	2.93
May	7	6.1	8	4	4	2	0	0	2	4	5.68	90	99.2	68	79	109	8	4	4	8	26	3.34
June	10	8.2	7	4	9	0	0	0	1	9	2.08	93	106.2	76	75	112	9	0	4	7	33	2.87
July	13	13.0	7	9	7	0	0	1	0	5	2.08	88	104.2	81	79	86	5	5	4	5	27	3.18
August	10	10.1	12	11	13	3	0	1	1	8	4.35	110	135.2	96	106	123	18	5	15	8	33	3.12
Sept-Oct	13	11.2	11	12	14	4	0	0	3	7	3.86	104	118.1	102	98	107	10	8	6	17	31	4.79

	BA	OBA	SA	AB	H	2B	3B	HR	RBI	BB	SO	BA	OBA	SA	AB	H	2B	3B	HR	RBI	BB	SO
Total	.245	.368	.323	229	56	9	0	3	29	44	60	.213	.359	.322	2311	492	99	14	42	310	493	620
vs. Left	.250	.340	.250	40	10	0	0	0	4	5	12	.205	.342	.292	600	123	24	2	8	85	109	180
vs. Right	.243	.374	.339	189	46	9	0	3	25	39	48	.216	.365	.333	1711	369	75	12	34	225	384	440
Bases Empty	.252	.375	.327	107	27	5	0	1	1	20	24	.214	.365	.314	1035	222	41	4	18	18	223	253
Leadoff	.229	.373	.333	48	11	2	0	1	1	10	13	.200	.356	.291	450	90	11	0	10	10	97	109
Runners On Base	.238	.362	.320	122	29	4	0	2	28	24	36	.212	.354	.329	1276	270	58	10	24	292	270	367
Scoring Position	.221	.340	.286	77	17	2	0	1	26	14	20	.199	.350	.308	814	162	30	7	15	260	187	232
Late and Close	.260	.392	.320	169	44	6	0	2	25	37	46	.216	.352	.313	1450	313	57	6	24	196	287	398

CARL WILLIS — BL/TR — age 34 — MIN RP53 POW/GB

7-YEAR TOTALS (1984–1993)

1993	G	IP	H	BB	SO	SB	CS	W	L	SV	ERA		G	IP	H	BB	SO	SB	CS	W	L	SV	ERA
Total	53	58.0	56	17	44	4	1	3	0	5	3.10		215	330.0	331	98	185	20	10	20	12	10	3.76
at Home	26	27.0	29	8	19	0	1	1	0	1	5.00		110	176.1	182	45	99	8	7	14	7	3	4.39
on Road	27	31.0	27	9	25	4	0	2	0	4	1.45		105	153.2	149	53	86	12	3	6	5	7	3.05
on Grass	22	26.0	24	9	21	4	0	2	0	2	1.73		87	135.1	135	45	78	9	4	6	5	4	3.39
on Turf	31	32.0	32	8	23	0	1	1	0	3	4.22		128	194.2	196	53	107	11	6	14	7	6	4.02
Day Games	18	13.1	18	8	9	0	0	0	0	2	5.40		66	90.0	100	36	43	6	3	4	1	4	4.70
Night Games	35	44.2	38	9	35	4	1	3	0	3	2.42		149	240.0	231	62	142	14	7	16	11	6	3.41
April	0	0.0	0	0	0	0	0	0	0	0	0.00		16	23.0	28	7	10	3	2	2	1	1	5.09
May	7	5.0	11	3	4	0	0	0	0	0	16.20		29	34.2	46	12	17	0	0	1	1	1	7.01
June	11	8.0	10	3	8	0	0	1	0	1	2.25		39	55.1	57	14	29	4	1	3	2	2	3.58
July	11	15.0	14	1	10	1	0	1	0	1	3.60		44	70.0	65	19	37	1	4	8	4	1	3.21
August	9	13.2	9	1	10	1	1	1	0	2	0.66		41	82.0	82	23	42	7	1	3	3	3	3.51
Sept-Oct	15	16.1	12	9	12	2	0	0	0	1	1.10		46	65.0	53	23	50	5	2	3	1	2	2.63

	BA	OBA	SA	AB	H	2B	3B	HR	RBI	BB	SO		BA	OBA	SA	AB	H	2B	3B	HR	RBI	BB	SO
Total	.259	.312	.389	216	56	20	1	2	39	17	44		.265	.317	.393	1248	331	73	10	22	180	98	185
vs. Left	.295	.367	.455	88	26	8	0	2	16	10	15		.286	.347	.406	503	144	28	4	8	66	47	61
vs. Right	.234	.272	.344	128	30	12	1	0	23	7	29		.251	.296	.384	745	187	45	6	14	114	51	124
Bases Empty	.250	.290	.386	88	22	6	0	2	2	5	18		.269	.313	.388	644	173	28	5	13	13	40	105
Leadoff	.368	.429	.526	38	14	3	0	1	1	4	6		.304	.362	.435	276	84	13	4	5	5	24	36
Runners On Base	.266	.326	.391	128	34	14	1	0	37	12	26		.262	.320	.397	604	158	45	5	9	167	58	80
Scoring Position	.286	.365	.429	84	24	10	1	0	35	11	19		.271	.346	.397	365	99	31	3	3	147	48	58
Late and Close	.224	.297	.308	107	24	9	0	0	11	11	24		.262	.322	.381	370	97	22	2	6	34	33	55

TREVOR WILSON — BL/TL — age 28 — SF SP18, RP4 FIN/GB

6-YEAR TOTALS (1988–1993)

1993	G	IP	H	BB	SO	SB	CS	W	L	SV	ERA		G	IP	H	BB	SO	SB	CS	W	L	SV	ERA
Total	22	110.0	110	40	57	4	4	7	5	0	3.60		137	637.2	575	262	387	22	32	38	42	0	3.88
at Home	11	62.0	61	26	32	2	4	4	2	0	2.76		68	371.0	318	149	213	11	20	22	21	0	3.27
on Road	11	48.0	49	14	25	2	0	3	3	0	4.69		69	266.2	257	113	174	11	12	16	21	0	4.72
on Grass	16	84.2	75	32	46	2	4	6	3	0	2.76		103	494.1	432	188	290	13	22	30	31	0	3.57
on Turf	6	25.1	35	8	11	2	0	1	2	0	6.39		34	143.1	143	74	97	9	10	8	11	0	4.96
Day Games	9	34.2	30	22	23	1	3	3	1	0	2.60		54	258.2	228	104	177	7	11	19	13	0	3.48
Night Games	13	75.1	80	18	34	3	1	4	4	0	4.06		83	379.0	347	158	210	15	21	19	29	0	4.16
April	5	29.0	33	18	12	0	4	0	2	0	4.66		17	60.2	67	34	34	0	6	1	5	0	4.75
May	4	25.1	19	8	14	1	0	2	1	0	2.84		19	89.2	70	38	55	5	4	6	6	0	3.61
June	5	32.0	34	7	19	3	0	3	1	0	3.38		28	149.1	134	56	87	9	8	11	8	0	3.44
July	1	3.2	3	0	2	0	0	0	0	0	2.45		25	129.2	114	59	83	6	9	7	10	0	4.16
August	3	16.0	16	5	8	0	0	2	1	0	3.94		21	116.2	110	42	71	1	3	8	8	0	4.09
Sept-Oct	4	4.0	5	2	2	0	0	0	0	0	2.25		27	91.2	80	33	57	1	2	5	5	0	3.63

	BA	OBA	SA	AB	H	2B	3B	HR	RBI	BB	SO		BA	OBA	SA	AB	H	2B	3B	HR	RBI	BB	SO
Total	.275	.347	.380	400	110	14	2	8	41	40	57		.247	.326	.366	2332	575	94	13	53	257	262	387
vs. Left	.179	.231	.262	84	15	4	0	1	6	4	12		.206	.288	.281	480	99	14	2	6	49	49	99
vs. Right	.301	.377	.411	316	95	10	2	7	35	36	45		.257	.336	.388	1852	476	80	11	47	208	213	288
Bases Empty	.288	.376	.400	215	62	8	2	4	4	26	36		.235	.325	.337	1328	312	51	5	25	25	167	234
Leadoff	.317	.395	.416	101	32	5	1	1	1	12	19		.243	.337	.321	580	141	21	3	6	6	78	98
Runners On Base	.259	.314	.357	185	48	6	0	4	37	14	21		.262	.327	.404	1004	263	43	8	28	232	95	153
Scoring Position	.279	.337	.395	86	24	1	0	3	31	8	11		.282	.361	.451	514	145	22	4	19	203	66	80
Late and Close	.273	.333	.273	22	6	0	0	0	1	1	.0		.212	.295	.274	179	38	8	0	1	8	18	34

BOBBY WITT — BR/TR — age 30 — OAK SP33, RP2 FIN/FB

8-YEAR TOTALS (1986–1993)

1993	G	IP	H	BB	SO	SB	CS	W	L	SV	ERA		G	IP	H	BB	SO	SB	CS	W	L	SV	ERA
Total	35	220.0	226	91	131	19	9	14	13	0	4.21		226	1393.1	1250	887	1207	230	48	83	86	0	4.52
at Home	17	125.1	108	53	79	11	4	7	6	0	3.30		111	716.1	625	429	598	118	28	40	40	0	3.93
on Road	18	94.2	118	38	52	8	5	7	7	0	5.42		115	677.0	625	458	609	112	20	43	46	0	5.13
on Grass	31	193.2	206	82	112	15	8	11	12	0	4.46		196	1203.0	1092	776	1040	205	44	70	75	0	4.58
on Turf	4	26.1	20	9	19	4	1	3	1	0	2.39		30	190.1	158	111	167	25	4	13	11	0	4.11
Day Games	15	96.0	104	44	57	10	4	5	8	0	4.78		61	373.0	347	260	326	72	15	18	28	0	4.73
Night Games	20	124.0	122	47	74	9	5	9	5	0	3.77		165	1020.1	903	627	881	158	33	65	58	0	4.44
April	4	26.2	22	11	13	1	2	1	0	0	3.04		32	191.0	165	143	164	35	7	9	12	0	4.38
May	6	39.2	43	20	21	4	2	4	2	0	4.31		39	236.2	227	164	179	34	9	13	20	0	5.48
June	6	35.0	38	16	22	5	3	2	3	0	4.11		31	183.1	175	117	148	42	8	12	13	0	4.61
July	7	32.0	47	7	25	1	0	1	4	0	7.31		36	225.0	190	117	206	30	8	16	12	0	4.00
August	6	40.1	41	22	16	2	0	1	3	0	4.24		45	283.1	253	191	250	40	9	14	10	0	4.76
Sept-Oct	6	46.1	35	15	34	6	2	5	1	0	2.72		43	274.0	240	155	260	49	7	19	11	0	3.88

	BA	OBA	SA	AB	H	2B	3B	HR	RBI	BB	SO		BA	OBA	SA	AB	H	2B	3B	HR	RBI	BB	SO
Total	.269	.340	.392	839	226	47	4	16	96	91	131		.242	.352	.353	5171	1250	219	23	103	629	887	1207
vs. Left	.279	.350	.418	426	119	32	2	7	47	45	56		.244	.362	.355	2565	626	116	17	45	319	481	557
vs. Right	.259	.330	.366	413	107	15	1	9	49	46	75		.239	.341	.350	2606	624	103	6	58	310	406	650
Bases Empty	.259	.335	.372	468	121	24	1	9	9	53	67		.232	.348	.344	2814	654	111	7	63	63	492	652
Leadoff	.310	.375	.429	210	65	13	0	4	4	21	27		.253	.362	.380	1254	317	54	3	33	33	211	280
Runners On Base	.283	.346	.418	371	105	23	3	7	87	38	64		.253	.355	.363	2357	596	108	16	40	566	395	555
Scoring Position	.267	.332	.417	206	55	12	2	5	79	24	40		.247	.357	.354	1369	338	67	8	21	504	260	355
Late and Close	.231	.278	.308	91	21	4	0	1	5	6	18		.219	.329	.301	438	96	13	4	5	31	69	103

Part 2

Non-Regular Players' Situational Statistics

In this part are situational breakdowns for every major-league player who was not a regular in 1993. Players are listed alphabetically, separated into batters and pitchers.

Each player's statistics follow the same format. The first line gives the player's name, how he bats and throws, and his age, effective for the 1994 season. It also lists the team he played for and the positions he played in 1993.

On the left-hand side of the page are the player's situational statistics for 1993 for the most important breakdowns (vs. left/vs. right, home/road, runners on base and for the second half). On the right-hand side of the page are the player's situational statistics totals from 1984–1993. If a player played in the majors every year from 1984 to 1993, it will show "10-Year Totals." If he played in the majors for only part of that period, the header will list the actual number of years he played and the first year he played. For example, a player who played in 1989, 1990, and 1993 would have "3-Year Totals" listed.

Non-regular players who made their major-league debuts in 1993 are listed separately at the end of the batter and pitchers, respectively, since their career totals are identical to their 1993 statistics.

There were 203 players who first played in the majors in 1993. Twelve batters (Brad Ausmus, Tim Bogar, Frank Bolick, Brent Gates, Ricky Gutierrez, Mike Lansing, David McCarty, Pat Meares, Craig Paquette, Eduardo Perez, Kevin Stocker, Darrell Whitmore) and five pitchers (Rene Arocha, Jason Bere, Trevor Hoffman, Greg McMichael, Matt Turner) can be found in Part 1 with the regulars.

Abbreviations used in Part 2 are the same as in Part 1. The situational categories shown for non-regulars are the same as for regulars, except that statistics for July, August, and September–October are combined into a "Second Half" line. Since the All-Star break occurs at different times each season, separating the two halves of the season at July 1st allows for more consistency. It is also closer to the actual midpoint of the season in most years than the All-Star break is.

BATTERS

MIKE ALDRETE — BL/TL — age 33 — OAK 1B59, OF20, DH6

1993	BA	OBA	SA	AB	H	2B	3B	HR	RBI	BB	SO
vs. Left	.138	.265	.345	29	4	0	0	2	4	5	6
vs. Right	.283	.365	.456	226	64	13	1	8	29	29	39
at Home	.233	.311	.361	133	31	2	0	5	13	15	28
on Road	.303	.397	.533	122	37	11	1	5	20	19	17
Runners On Base	.353	.421	.618	102	36	6	0	7	30	12	10
Second Half	.267	.356	.456	195	52	8	1	9	28	27	34

7-YEAR TOTALS (1986–1993)

	BA	OBA	SA	AB	H	2B	3B	HR	RBI	BB	SO
vs. Left	.247	.310	.354	243	60	11	3	3	20	24	46
vs. Right	.272	.373	.379	1469	399	74	6	24	189	237	250
at Home	.261	.372	.370	828	216	30	6	16	90	146	146
on Road	.275	.357	.381	884	243	55	3	11	119	115	150
Runners On Base	.301	.397	.422	740	223	42	4	13	195	121	119
Second Half	.269	.371	.390	1091	294	53	8	21	145	178	183

MANNY ALEXANDER — BR/TR — age 23 — BAL

1993	BA	OBA	SA	AB	H	2B	3B	HR	RBI	BB	SO
vs. Left	.000	.000	.000	0	0	0	0	0	0	0	0
vs. Right	.000	.000	.000	0	0	0	0	0	0	0	0
at Home	.000	.000	.000	0	0	0	0	0	0	0	0
on Road	.000	.000	.000	0	0	0	0	0	0	0	0
Runners On Base	.000	.000	.000	0	0	0	0	0	0	0	0
Second Half	.000	.000	.000	0	0	0	0	0	0	0	0

2-YEAR TOTALS (1992–1993)

	BA	OBA	SA	AB	H	2B	3B	HR	RBI	BB	SO
vs. Left	.000	.000	.000	0	0	0	0	0	0	0	0
vs. Right	.200	.200	.200	5	1	0	0	0	0	0	3
at Home	.000	.000	.000	0	0	0	0	0	0	0	0
on Road	.200	.200	.200	5	1	0	0	0	0	0	3
Runners On Base	.333	.333	.333	3	1	0	0	0	0	0	2
Second Half	.200	.200	.200	5	1	0	0	0	0	0	3

ANDY ALLANSON — BR/TR — age 33 — SF C8, 1B2

1993	BA	OBA	SA	AB	H	2B	3B	HR	RBI	BB	SO
vs. Left	.167	.231	.167	12	2	0	0	0	0	1	0
vs. Right	.167	.167	.250	12	2	1	0	0	2	0	2
at Home	.083	.154	.167	12	1	1	0	0	2	1	1
on Road	.250	.250	.250	12	3	0	0	0	0	0	1
Runners On Base	.273	.333	.364	11	3	1	0	0	2	1	1
Second Half	.133	.133	.133	15	2	0	0	0	0	0	2

7-YEAR TOTALS (1986–1993)

	BA	OBA	SA	AB	H	2B	3B	HR	RBI	BB	SO
vs. Left	.257	.294	.313	463	119	22	2	0	35	25	71
vs. Right	.238	.282	.308	941	224	23	2	13	95	55	140
at Home	.236	.285	.301	681	161	19	2	7	73	45	93
on Road	.252	.287	.318	723	182	26	2	6	57	35	118
Runners On Base	.258	.301	.337	605	156	24	3	6	123	38	98
Second Half	.250	.293	.304	727	182	19	1	6	62	46	122

SANDY ALOMAR — BR/TR — age 28 — CLE C64

1993	BA	OBA	SA	AB	H	2B	3B	HR	RBI	BB	SO
vs. Left	.283	.318	.383	60	17	1	1	1	9	3	9
vs. Right	.265	.318	.400	155	41	6	0	5	23	8	19
at Home	.293	.337	.446	92	27	5	0	3	16	5	11
on Road	.252	.303	.358	123	31	2	1	3	16	6	17
Runners On Base	.330	.377	.460	100	33	5	1	2	28	7	18
Second Half	.321	.347	.472	159	51	7	1	5	28	4	17

6-YEAR TOTALS (1988–1993)

	BA	OBA	SA	AB	H	2B	3B	HR	RBI	BB	SO
vs. Left	.287	.337	.365	282	81	11	1	3	31	21	32
vs. Right	.255	.296	.365	881	225	48	2	15	106	39	102
at Home	.278	.324	.383	564	157	29	0	10	67	36	61
on Road	.249	.289	.349	599	149	30	3	8	70	24	73
Runners On Base	.262	.310	.356	522	137	29	1	6	125	32	61
Second Half	.291	.330	.418	595	173	38	1	12	82	29	50

RUBEN AMARO — BB/TR — age 29 — PHI OF16

1993	BA	OBA	SA	AB	H	2B	3B	HR	RBI	BB	SO
vs. Left	.500	.563	.821	28	14	2	2	1	5	4	1
vs. Right	.100	.174	.100	20	2	0	0	0	1	2	4
at Home	.067	.125	.067	15	1	0	0	0	0	1	2
on Road	.455	.513	.727	33	15	2	2	1	6	5	3
Runners On Base	.350	.417	.600	20	7	0	1	1	6	3	0
Second Half	.148	.226	.148	27	4	0	0	0	2	3	3

3-YEAR TOTALS (1991–1993)

	BA	OBA	SA	AB	H	2B	3B	HR	RBI	BB	SO
vs. Left	.285	.373	.441	186	53	10	5	3	22	23	15
vs. Right	.193	.271	.305	259	50	8	3	5	20	23	47
at Home	.200	.282	.358	190	38	7	4	5	17	18	30
on Road	.255	.338	.365	255	65	11	4	3	25	28	32
Runners On Base	.225	.305	.342	187	42	7	3	3	37	21	26
Second Half	.234	.293	.347	239	56	8	5	3	19	16	29

ALEX ARIAS — BR/TR — age 27 — FLO 2B30, 3B22, SS18

1993	BA	OBA	SA	AB	H	2B	3B	HR	RBI	BB	SO
vs. Left	.284	.366	.309	81	23	2	0	0	8	9	4
vs. Right	.262	.333	.327	168	44	3	1	2	12	18	14
at Home	.276	.356	.314	105	29	1	0	1	8	11	8
on Road	.264	.335	.326	144	38	4	1	1	12	16	10
Runners On Base	.286	.365	.316	98	28	3	0	0	18	12	3
Second Half	.250	.322	.287	108	27	1	0	1	8	12	9

2-YEAR TOTALS (1992–1993)

	BA	OBA	SA	AB	H	2B	3B	HR	RBI	BB	SO
vs. Left	.295	.370	.344	122	36	6	0	0	10	13	7
vs. Right	.265	.344	.323	226	60	5	1	2	17	25	24
at Home	.262	.330	.306	160	42	4	0	1	13	14	16
on Road	.287	.372	.351	188	54	7	1	1	14	24	15
Runners On Base	.284	.362	.319	141	40	5	0	0	25	15	4
Second Half	.271	.348	.319	207	56	7	0	1	15	23	22

BILLY ASHLEY — BR/TR — age 24 — LA OF11

1993	BA	OBA	SA	AB	H	2B	3B	HR	RBI	BB	SO
vs. Left	.200	.273	.200	10	2	0	0	0	0	1	4
vs. Right	.259	.286	.259	27	7	0	0	0	0	1	7
at Home	.368	.400	.368	19	7	0	0	0	0	1	2
on Road	.111	.158	.111	18	2	0	0	0	0	1	9
Runners On Base	.235	.278	.235	17	4	0	0	0	0	1	5
Second Half	.243	.282	.243	37	9	0	0	0	0	2	11

2-YEAR TOTALS (1992–1993)

	BA	OBA	SA	AB	H	2B	3B	HR	RBI	BB	SO
vs. Left	.300	.333	.500	40	12	2	0	2	4	2	10
vs. Right	.196	.237	.228	92	18	3	0	0	2	5	35
at Home	.316	.350	.456	57	18	2	0	2	3	3	13
on Road	.160	.203	.200	75	12	3	0	0	3	4	32
Runners On Base	.200	.245	.240	50	10	2	0	0	6	3	18
Second Half	.227	.266	.311	132	30	5	0	2	6	7	45

WALLY BACKMAN — BB/TR — age 35 — SEA 3B9, 2B1

1993	BA	OBA	SA	AB	H	2B	3B	HR	RBI	BB	SO
vs. Left	.000	.000	.000	0	0	0	0	0	0	0	0
vs. Right	.138	.167	.138	29	4	0	0	0	0	1	8
at Home	.188	.188	.188	16	3	0	0	0	0	0	3
on Road	.077	.143	.077	13	1	0	0	0	0	1	5
Runners On Base	.077	.143	.077	13	1	0	0	0	0	1	5
Second Half	.000	.000	.000	0	0	0	0	0	0	0	0

10-YEAR TOTALS (1984–1993)

	BA	OBA	SA	AB	H	2B	3B	HR	RBI	BB	SO
vs. Left	.170	.264	.207	401	68	11	2	0	33	50	73
vs. Right	.293	.359	.359	2412	707	111	13	7	173	255	331
at Home	.288	.361	.348	1366	393	64	8	1	104	158	183
on Road	.264	.330	.326	1447	382	58	7	6	102	147	221
Runners On Base	.290	.369	.346	1021	296	41	5	2	201	136	152
Second Half	.279	.353	.347	1411	394	66	9	4	109	165	203

KEVIN BAEZ — BR/TR — age 27 — NYN SS52

1993	BA	OBA	SA	AB	H	2B	3B	HR	RBI	BB	SO
vs. Left	.180	.226	.280	50	9	5	0	0	4	3	8
vs. Right	.184	.279	.237	76	14	4	0	0	3	10	9
at Home	.143	.169	.190	63	9	3	0	0	3	2	10
on Road	.222	.338	.317	63	14	6	0	0	4	11	7
Runners On Base	.190	.277	.214	42	8	1	0	0	7	5	10
Second Half	.185	.265	.261	119	22	9	0	0	5	13	16

3-YEAR TOTALS (1990–1993)

	BA	OBA	SA	AB	H	2B	3B	HR	RBI	BB	SO
vs. Left	.175	.212	.270	63	11	6	0	0	4	3	8
vs. Right	.182	.265	.227	88	16	4	0	0	3	10	9
at Home	.145	.169	.188	69	10	3	0	0	3	2	10
on Road	.207	.301	.293	82	17	7	0	0	4	11	7
Runners On Base	.163	.241	.184	49	8	1	0	0	7	5	10
Second Half	.184	.253	.255	141	26	10	0	0	5	13	16

STEVE BALBONI — BR/TR — age 37 — TEX DH2

1993	BA	OBA	SA	AB	H	2B	3B	HR	RBI	BB	SO
vs. Left	.000	.000	.000	0	0	0	0	0	0	0	0
vs. Right	.600	.600	.600	5	3	0	0	0	0	0	2
at Home	.600	.600	.600	5	3	0	0	0	0	0	2
on Road	.000	.000	.000	0	0	0	0	0	0	0	0
Runners On Base	.000	.000	.000	1	0	0	0	0	0	0	1
Second Half	.600	.600	.600	5	3	0	0	0	0	0	2

8-YEAR TOTALS (1984–1993)

BA	OBA	SA	AB	H	2B	3B	HR	RBI	BB	SO
.232	.315	.468	1072	249	42	2	69	170	128	297
.229	.283	.450	1849	423	80	7	105	300	130	498
.224	.286	.438	1433	321	72	5	75	224	121	390
.236	.302	.474	1488	351	50	4	99	246	137	405
.244	.302	.462	1354	331	66	5	73	369	115	337
.236	.301	.487	1573	372	66	8	104	275	139	432

SKEETER BARNES — BR/TR — age 37 — DET 1B27, OF18, 3B13, DH13, 2B10, SS2

1993	BA	OBA	SA	AB	H	2B	3B	HR	RBI	BB	SO
vs. Left	.278	.327	.392	97	27	6	1	1	19	8	14
vs. Right	.286	.304	.365	63	18	2	0	1	8	3	5
at Home	.262	.291	.400	80	21	3	1	2	12	4	7
on Road	.300	.344	.363	80	24	5	0	0	15	7	12
Runners On Base	.282	.333	.353	85	24	4	1	0	25	9	9
Second Half	.297	.327	.386	101	30	6	0	1	19	6	13

7-YEAR TOTALS (1984–1993)

BA	OBA	SA	AB	H	2B	3B	HR	RBI	BB	SO
.254	.298	.391	343	87	18	4	7	51	22	45
.273	.308	.398	216	59	12	0	5	24	12	24
.260	.296	.411	258	67	12	3	7	37	14	31
.262	.307	.379	301	79	18	1	5	38	20	38
.287	.327	.410	251	72	8	4	5	68	19	32
.272	.313	.390	397	108	24	1	7	49	25	55

KEVIN BASS — BB/TR — age 35 — HOU OF64

1993	BA	OBA	SA	AB	H	2B	3B	HR	RBI	BB	SO
vs. Left	.225	.303	.412	80	18	9	0	2	15	9	13
vs. Right	.315	.389	.396	149	47	9	0	1	22	17	18
at Home	.270	.336	.400	100	27	7	0	2	20	9	17
on Road	.295	.377	.403	129	38	11	0	1	17	17	14
Runners On Base	.327	.397	.500	104	34	12	0	2	36	11	17
Second Half	.313	.408	.435	131	41	10	0	2	22	21	17

10-YEAR TOTALS (1984–1993)

BA	OBA	SA	AB	H	2B	3B	HR	RBI	BB	SO
.277	.314	.474	1554	430	109	10	59	231	71	218
.272	.334	.388	2559	697	105	26	46	294	227	344
.276	.332	.412	2038	562	103	14	49	268	161	296
.272	.321	.428	2075	565	111	22	56	257	137	266
.279	.348	.422	1759	491	96	12	44	464	185	260
.282	.337	.431	2117	596	109	20	56	274	165	300

KIM BATISTE — BR/TR — age 26 — PHI 3B58, SS24

1993	BA	OBA	SA	AB	H	2B	3B	HR	RBI	BB	SO
vs. Left	.349	.356	.698	43	15	1	1	4	11	1	9
vs. Right	.257	.276	.336	113	29	6	0	1	18	2	20
at Home	.300	.300	.400	80	24	5	0	1	15	0	13
on Road	.263	.296	.474	76	20	2	1	4	14	3	16
Runners On Base	.290	.306	.493	69	20	3	1	3	27	2	14
Second Half	.280	.294	.400	50	14	3	0	1	10	1	6

3-YEAR TOTALS (1991–1993)

BA	OBA	SA	AB	H	2B	3B	HR	RBI	BB	SO
.266	.278	.398	128	34	3	1	4	16	3	21
.230	.251	.304	191	44	8	0	2	24	5	34
.255	.266	.333	153	39	9	0	1	18	3	27
.235	.259	.349	166	39	2	1	5	22	5	28
.238	.261	.364	143	34	4	1	4	38	6	22
.260	.278	.338	77	20	3	0	1	11	2	14

BILL BEAN — BL/TL — age 30 — SD OF54, 1B12

1993	BA	OBA	SA	AB	H	2B	3B	HR	RBI	BB	SO
vs. Left	.200	.188	.267	15	3	1	0	0	2	0	2
vs. Right	.265	.293	.407	162	43	8	0	5	30	6	27
at Home	.268	.295	.451	82	22	3	0	4	17	3	13
on Road	.253	.275	.347	95	24	6	0	1	15	3	16
Runners On Base	.333	.338	.606	66	22	6	0	4	31	2	10
Second Half	.268	.294	.425	127	34	5	0	5	28	5	19

4-YEAR TOTALS (1987–1993)

BA	OBA	SA	AB	H	2B	3B	HR	RBI	BB	SO
.190	.182	.238	21	4	1	0	0	2	0	3
.238	.282	.337	315	75	14	1	5	37	17	52
.253	.297	.384	146	37	5	1	4	20	9	27
.221	.260	.289	190	42	10	0	1	19	8	28
.284	.308	.433	134	38	8	0	4	38	6	22
.239	.274	.364	209	50	.9	1	5	31	9	31

JUAN BELL — BR/TR — age 26 — PHI/MIL SS62, 2B47, OF3, DH2

1993	BA	OBA	SA	AB	H	2B	3B	HR	RBI	BB	SO
vs. Left	.271	.344	.375	144	39	6	0	3	13	14	28
vs. Right	.198	.289	.285	207	41	6	3	2	23	27	48
at Home	.275	.369	.389	193	53	10	3	2	19	29	41
on Road	.171	.237	.241	158	27	2	0	3	17	12	35
Runners On Base	.241	.327	.297	145	35	5	0	1	32	18	34
Second Half	.222	.310	.307	212	47	4	1	4	24	27	49

5-YEAR TOTALS (1989–1993)

BA	OBA	SA	AB	H	2B	3B	HR	RBI	BB	SO
.220	.287	.290	255	56	9	0	3	16	21	57
.197	.267	.282	458	90	15	6	4	43	46	101
.225	.308	.324	373	84	16	6	3	34	45	82
.182	.235	.241	340	62	8	0	4	25	22	76
.213	.304	.284	296	63	11	2	2	54	39	65
.202	.273	.279	520	105	14	4	6	44	51	117

RAFAEL BELLIARD — BR/TR — age 33 — ATL SS58, 2B24

1993	BA	OBA	SA	AB	H	2B	3B	HR	RBI	BB	SO
vs. Left	.118	.167	.118	17	2	0	0	0	2	1	3
vs. Right	.258	.324	.339	62	16	5	0	0	4	3	10
at Home	.184	.244	.211	38	7	1	0	0	0	2	3
on Road	.268	.333	.366	41	11	4	0	0	6	2	10
Runners On Base	.195	.267	.268	41	8	3	0	0	6	2	6
Second Half	.245	.288	.327	49	12	4	0	0	3	2	9

10-YEAR TOTALS (1984–1993)

BA	OBA	SA	AB	H	2B	3B	HR	RBI	BB	SO
.226	.280	.255	522	118	7	4	0	33	36	79
.222	.282	.261	1243	276	29	8	1	86	89	207
.211	.274	.247	837	177	14	8	0	57	62	120
.234	.288	.269	928	217	22	4	1	62	63	166
.236	.293	.280	763	180	17	7	1	119	53	106
.220	.280	.260	755	166	18	6	0	45	56	127

FREDDIE BENAVIDES — BR/TR — age 28 — COL SS48, 2B19, 3B5, 1B1

1993	BA	OBA	SA	AB	H	2B	3B	HR	RBI	BB	SO
vs. Left	.356	.367	.492	59	21	3	1	1	5	1	4
vs. Right	.260	.281	.370	154	40	7	2	2	21	5	23
at Home	.387	.406	.591	93	36	6	2	3	21	3	11
on Road	.208	.226	.258	120	25	4	1	0	5	3	16
Runners On Base	.342	.370	.447	76	26	1	2	1	24	4	9
Second Half	.316	.336	.471	136	43	6	3	3	18	4	18

3-YEAR TOTALS (1991–1993)

BA	OBA	SA	AB	H	2B	3B	HR	RBI	BB	SO
.293	.337	.401	167	49	10	1	2	20	9	21
.248	.267	.330	282	70	11	3	2	26	8	55
.309	.333	.448	194	60	11	2	4	28	6	32
.231	.264	.286	255	59	10	2	0	18	11	44
.301	.340	.393	183	55	7	2	2	44	11	32
.280	.313	.386	246	69	11	3	3	27	11	40

MIKE BENJAMIN — BR/TR — age 29 — SF 2B23, SS23, 3B16

1993	BA	OBA	SA	AB	H	2B	3B	HR	RBI	BB	SO
vs. Left	.316	.333	.658	38	12	4	0	3	8	1	2
vs. Right	.157	.242	.213	108	17	3	0	1	8	8	21
at Home	.197	.250	.380	71	14	4	0	3	10	5	13
on Road	.200	.277	.280	75	15	3	0	1	6	4	10
Runners On Base	.270	.352	.540	63	17	6	0	4	16	7	5
Second Half	.235	.316	.353	51	12	3	0	1	6	3	9

5-YEAR TOTALS (1989–1993)

BA	OBA	SA	AB	H	2B	3B	HR	RBI	BB	SO
.233	.277	.421	133	31	6	2	5	12	8	17
.145	.208	.227	256	37	9	0	4	18	15	58
.172	.225	.301	186	32	7	1	5	15	13	38
.177	.236	.286	203	36	8	1	4	15	10	37
.174	.253	.323	155	27	9	1	4	25	14	24
.191	.244	.307	251	48	10	2	5	17	14	50

TODD BENZINGER — BB/TR — age 31 — SF 1B40, OF7, 3B1

1993

	BA	OBA	SA	AB	H	2B	3B	HR	RBI	BB	SO
vs. Left	.486	.512	.730	37	18	1	1	2	11	4	5
vs. Right	.236	.280	.379	140	33	6	1	4	15	9	30
at Home	.194	.218	.222	72	14	2	0	0	6	3	16
on Road	.352	.409	.610	105	37	5	2	6	20	10	19
Runners On Base	.207	.277	.354	82	17	3	0	3	23	9	17
Second Half	.313	.363	.545	112	35	6	1	6	20	10	23

7-YEAR TOTALS (1987–1993)

BA	OBA	SA	AB	H	2B	3B	HR	RBI	BB	SO
.270	.302	.373	893	241	38	3	16	114	48	99
.248	.299	.390	1625	403	84	13	40	229	114	366
.265	.310	.399	1237	328	75	9	24	162	81	201
.247	.291	.369	1281	316	47	7	32	181	81	264
.236	.289	.374	1142	270	60	8	27	314	91	223
.261	.303	.404	1474	385	73	10	39	206	86	273

GERONIMO BERROA — BR/TR — age 29 — FLO OF9

1993

	BA	OBA	SA	AB	H	2B	3B	HR	RBI	BB	SO
vs. Left	.188	.278	.188	16	3	0	0	0	0	2	5
vs. Right	.056	.056	.111	18	1	1	0	0	0	0	2
at Home	.136	.208	.182	22	3	1	0	0	0	2	6
on Road	.083	.083	.083	12	1	0	0	0	0	0	1
Runners On Base	.000	.053	.000	18	0	0	0	0	0	1	5
Second Half	.000	.000	.000	0	0	0	0	0	0	0	0

4-YEAR TOTALS (1989–1993)

BA	OBA	SA	AB	H	2B	3B	HR	RBI	BB	SO
.262	.320	.333	141	37	4	0	2	8	11	31
.146	.163	.188	48	7	2	0	0	1	1	10
.222	.257	.278	108	24	3	0	1	4	5	24
.247	.315	.321	81	20	3	0	1	5	7	17
.172	.226	.207	87	15	3	0	0	7	5	20
.194	.275	.226	62	12	2	0	0	0	6	16

RAFAEL BOURNIGAL — BR/TR — age 28 — LA 2B4, SS4

1993

	BA	OBA	SA	AB	H	2B	3B	HR	RBI	BB	SO
vs. Left	.500	.500	.500	4	2	0	0	0	0	0	0
vs. Right	.500	.500	.571	14	7	1	0	0	3	0	2
at Home	.625	.625	.750	8	5	1	0	0	1	0	0
on Road	.400	.400	.400	10	4	0	0	0	2	0	2
Runners On Base	.667	.667	.667	6	4	0	0	0	3	0	1
Second Half	.500	.500	.556	18	9	1	0	0	3	0	2

2-YEAR TOTALS (1992–1993)

BA	OBA	SA	AB	H	2B	3B	HR	RBI	BB	SO
.250	.308	.250	12	3	0	0	0	0	1	2
.346	.370	.423	26	9	2	0	0	3	0	2
.556	.556	.667	9	5	1	0	0	1	0	1
.241	.290	.276	29	7	1	0	0	2	1	3
.333	.385	.333	12	4	0	0	0	3	0	1
.316	.350	.368	38	12	2	0	0	3	1	4

SID BREAM — BL/TL — age 34 — ATL 1B90

1993

	BA	OBA	SA	AB	H	2B	3B	HR	RBI	BB	SO
vs. Left	.276	.290	.379	29	8	3	0	0	5	1	7
vs. Right	.258	.337	.419	248	64	11	1	9	30	30	36
at Home	.232	.309	.392	125	29	5	0	5	9	14	15
on Road	.283	.351	.434	152	43	9	1	4	26	17	28
Runners On Base	.261	.331	.426	115	30	5	1	4	30	13	16
Second Half	.288	.368	.470	66	19	3	0	3	11	9	7

10-YEAR TOTALS (1984–1993)

BA	OBA	SA	AB	H	2B	3B	HR	RBI	BB	SO
.233	.275	.378	712	166	43	3	18	99	44	124
.271	.351	.433	2324	630	143	9	72	347	298	315
.262	.333	.428	1435	376	97	6	43	214	157	187
.262	.336	.413	1601	420	89	6	47	232	185	252
.278	.362	.443	1376	383	93	5	41	397	197	194
.256	.326	.395	1533	393	90	3	39	234	167	209

ROD BREWER — BL/TL — age 28 — SL OF33, 1B32, P1

1993

	BA	OBA	SA	AB	H	2B	3B	HR	RBI	BB	SO
vs. Left	.267	.353	.333	15	4	1	0	0	0	2	3
vs. Right	.288	.360	.386	132	38	7	0	2	20	15	23
at Home	.324	.386	.365	74	24	3	0	0	5	7	11
on Road	.247	.333	.397	73	18	5	0	2	15	10	15
Runners On Base	.246	.375	.333	57	14	5	0	0	18	12	12
Second Half	.321	.409	.457	81	26	5	0	2	10	11	15

4-YEAR TOTALS (1990–1993)

BA	OBA	SA	AB	H	2B	3B	HR	RBI	BB	SO
.271	.300	.333	48	13	3	0	0	5	2	9
.279	.343	.354	240	67	12	0	2	28	23	38
.288	.344	.338	139	40	7	0	0	10	11	22
.268	.329	.362	149	40	8	0	2	23	14	25
.280	.367	.344	125	35	8	0	0	31	17	20
.288	.348	.369	222	64	12	0	2	23	19	36

GREG BRILEY — BL/TR — age 29 — FLO OF67

1993

	BA	OBA	SA	AB	H	2B	3B	HR	RBI	BB	SO
vs. Left	.214	.214	.429	14	3	0	0	1	3	0	4
vs. Right	.192	.253	.269	156	30	6	0	2	9	12	38
at Home	.165	.234	.247	85	14	1	0	2	7	8	25
on Road	.224	.267	.318	85	19	5	0	1	5	4	17
Runners On Base	.203	.259	.311	74	15	2	0	2	11	6	16
Second Half	.134	.203	.149	67	9	1	0	0	2	6	17

6-YEAR TOTALS (1988–1993)

BA	OBA	SA	AB	H	2B	3B	HR	RBI	BB	SO
.243	.300	.351	148	36	6	2	2	22	11	35
.254	.311	.374	1370	348	69	7	27	113	113	225
.232	.294	.335	719	167	26	3	14	64	64	118
.272	.324	.404	799	217	49	6	15	71	60	142
.244	.303	.361	620	151	30	5	11	117	59	108
.262	.330	.387	778	204	36	8	15	69	79	127

BERNARDO BRITO — BR/TR — age 31 — MIN OF10, DH7

1993

	BA	OBA	SA	AB	H	2B	3B	HR	RBI	BB	SO
vs. Left	.333	.353	.758	33	11	2	0	4	9	1	9
vs. Right	.095	.095	.095	21	2	0	0	0	0	0	11
at Home	.176	.222	.294	17	3	2	0	0	1	1	7
on Road	.270	.270	.595	37	10	0	0	4	8	0	13
Runners On Base	.227	.261	.682	22	5	0	0	3	8	1	8
Second Half	.241	.255	.500	54	13	2	0	4	9	1	20

2-YEAR TOTALS (1992–1993)

BA	OBA	SA	AB	H	2B	3B	HR	RBI	BB	SO
.325	.333	.700	40	13	3	0	4	11	1	11
.071	.071	.071	28	2	0	0	0	0	0	13
.174	.208	.304	23	4	3	0	0	2	1	8
.244	.239	.511	45	11	0	0	4	9	0	16
.207	.226	.586	29	6	2	0	3	10	1	10
.221	.229	.441	68	15	3	0	4	11	1	24

HUBIE BROOKS — BR/TR — age 38 — KC OF40, DH9, 1B3

1993

	BA	OBA	SA	AB	H	2B	3B	HR	RBI	BB	SO
vs. Left	.327	.368	.445	110	36	10	0	1	13	7	12
vs. Right	.207	.266	.241	58	12	2	0	0	11	4	15
at Home	.286	.330	.381	84	24	8	0	0	13	5	12
on Road	.286	.333	.369	84	24	4	0	1	11	6	15
Runners On Base	.307	.361	.420	88	27	7	0	1	24	7	13
Second Half	.298	.348	.440	84	25	9	0	1	16	7	14

10-YEAR TOTALS (1984–1993)

BA	OBA	SA	AB	H	2B	3B	HR	RBI	BB	SO
.291	.349	.471	1424	414	93	7	50	230	125	206
.261	.303	.401	3007	785	133	15	86	434	180	542
.281	.332	.429	2153	604	121	11	59	331	164	361
.261	.305	.418	2278	595	105	11	77	333	141	387
.277	.336	.417	2047	568	108	12	51	579	190	370
.265	.310	.408	2192	580	122	8	59	330	145	359

SCOTT BROSIUS — BR/TR — age 28 — OAK OF46, 1B11, 3B10, SS6, DH2

1993

	BA	OBA	SA	AB	H	2B	3B	HR	RBI	BB	SO
vs. Left	.210	.261	.370	81	17	4	0	3	11	5	14
vs. Right	.273	.317	.402	132	36	6	1	3	14	9	23
at Home	.208	.274	.321	106	22	3	0	3	10	10	15
on Road	.290	.319	.458	107	31	7	1	3	15	4	22
Runners On Base	.225	.283	.382	89	20	6	0	4	23	8	17
Second Half	.287	.329	.441	143	41	8	1	4	22	9	21

3-YEAR TOTALS (1991–1993)

BA	OBA	SA	AB	H	2B	3B	HR	RBI	BB	SO
.225	.284	.403	129	29	5	0	6	19	10	21
.247	.281	.381	239	59	12	1	6	23	10	40
.201	.254	.328	174	35	7	0	5	16	12	23
.273	.307	.443	194	53	10	1	7	26	8	38
.223	.277	.363	157	35	4	0	6	36	12	26
.265	.309	.439	264	70	14	1	10	37	15	40

JARVIS BROWN — BR/TR — age 27 — SD OF43

1993	BA	OBA	SA	AB	H	2B	3B	HR	RBI	BB	SO
vs. Left	.263	.349	.395	38	10	3	1	0	1	5	9
vs. Right	.221	.330	.305	95	21	6	1	0	7	10	17
at Home	.148	.217	.241	54	8	3	1	0	1	3	13
on Road	.291	.411	.392	79	23	6	1	0	7	12	13
Runners On Base	.250	.340	.425	40	10	5	1	0	8	4	10
Second Half	.233	.335	.331	133	31	9	2	0	8	15	26

3-YEAR TOTALS (1991–1993)

	BA	OBA	SA	AB	H	2B	3B	HR	RBI	BB	SO
	.200	.286	.300	50	10	3	1	0	1	6	10
	.222	.321	.281	135	30	6	1	0	7	13	28
	.159	.224	.232	69	11	3	1	0	1	3	19
	.250	.360	.319	116	29	6	1	0	7	16	19
	.246	.343	.368	57	14	5	1	0	8	7	14
	.229	.320	.306	170	39	9	2	0	8	17	34

JERRY BROWNE — BB/TR — age 28 — OAK OF56, 3B13, 2B3, 1B2

1993	BA	OBA	SA	AB	H	2B	3B	HR	RBI	BB	SO
vs. Left	.267	.302	.350	60	16	2	0	1	3	3	4
vs. Right	.245	.308	.315	200	49	11	0	1	16	19	13
at Home	.321	.372	.393	112	36	5	0	1	8	9	9
on Road	.196	.258	.270	148	29	8	0	1	11	13	8
Runners On Base	.231	.274	.269	104	24	4	0	0	17	7	10
Second Half	.241	.294	.325	228	55	13	0	2	15	18	14

8-YEAR TOTALS (1986–1993)

	BA	OBA	SA	AB	H	2B	3B	HR	RBI	BB	SO
	.278	.347	.363	695	193	29	9	4	67	75	59
	.267	.345	.345	1982	529	85	12	15	174	241	224
	.297	.373	.378	1347	400	61	12	8	123	162	133
	.242	.317	.320	1330	322	53	9	11	118	154	150
	.276	.355	.349	963	266	38	7	6	228	131	89
	.285	.364	.381	1452	414	79	9	14	134	184	151

J. T. BRUETT — BL/TL — age 27 — MIN OF13

1993	BA	OBA	SA	AB	H	2B	3B	HR	RBI	BB	SO
vs. Left	.000	.000	.000	2	0	0	0	0	0	0	1
vs. Right	.278	.350	.389	18	5	2	0	0	1	1	3
at Home	.333	.385	.500	12	4	2	0	0	1	0	2
on Road	.125	.222	.125	8	1	0	0	0	0	1	2
Runners On Base	.286	.444	.429	7	2	1	0	0	1	1	1
Second Half	.000	.000	.000	0	0	0	0	0	0	0	0

2-YEAR TOTALS (1992–1993)

	BA	OBA	SA	AB	H	2B	3B	HR	RBI	BB	SO
	.125	.222	.125	8	1	0	0	0	1	1	1
	.261	.323	.330	88	23	6	0	0	2	6	15
	.318	.400	.432	44	14	5	0	0	2	4	8
	.192	.236	.212	52	10	1	0	0	1	3	8
	.207	.303	.310	29	6	3	0	0	3	3	3
	.309	.345	.382	55	17	4	0	0	1	2	9

JACOB BRUMFIELD — BR/TR — age 29 — CIN OF96, 2B4

1993	BA	OBA	SA	AB	H	2B	3B	HR	RBI	BB	SO
vs. Left	.303	.340	.449	89	27	7	0	2	5	5	9
vs. Right	.251	.312	.404	183	46	10	3	4	18	16	38
at Home	.217	.264	.300	120	26	7	0	1	8	8	23
on Road	.309	.365	.513	152	47	10	3	5	15	13	24
Runners On Base	.263	.333	.389	95	25	7	1	1	18	10	18
Second Half	.267	.307	.429	240	64	15	3	6	21	14	40

2-YEAR TOTALS (1992–1993)

	BA	OBA	SA	AB	H	2B	3B	HR	RBI	BB	SO
	.266	.310	.385	109	29	7	0	2	7	6	12
	.249	.310	.394	193	48	10	3	4	18	17	39
	.206	.257	.286	126	26	7	0	1	8	9	24
	.290	.347	.466	176	51	10	3	5	17	14	27
	.250	.333	.365	104	26	7	1	1	20	12	20
	.267	.307	.429	240	64	15	3	6	21	14	40

MIKE BRUMLEY — BB/TR — age 31 — HOU 3B1, SS1, OF1

1993	BA	OBA	SA	AB	H	2B	3B	HR	RBI	BB	SO
vs. Left	.000	.000	.000	2	0	0	0	0	0	0	1
vs. Right	.375	.444	.375	8	3	0	0	0	2	1	2
at Home	.000	.000	.000	3	0	0	0	0	0	0	1
on Road	.429	.500	.429	7	3	0	0	0	2	1	2
Runners On Base	.600	.600	.600	5	3	0	0	0	2	0	1
Second Half	.300	.364	.300	10	3	0	0	0	2	1	3

6-YEAR TOTALS (1987–1993)

	BA	OBA	SA	AB	H	2B	3B	HR	RBI	BB	SO
	.236	.276	.292	161	38	4	1	1	9	9	31
	.200	.263	.269	431	86	13	7	1	25	36	91
	.207	.254	.278	299	62	10	4	1	20	18	61
	.212	.280	.273	293	62	7	4	1	14	27	61
	.202	.246	.267	258	52	9	1	2	34	15	56
	.216	.270	.262	320	69	10	1	1	18	23	75

TOM BRUNANSKY — BR/TR — age 34 — MIL OF71, DH6

1993	BA	OBA	SA	AB	H	2B	3B	HR	RBI	BB	SO
vs. Left	.178	.284	.347	101	18	4	2	3	14	15	23
vs. Right	.187	.248	.301	123	23	3	1	3	15	10	36
at Home	.180	.261	.310	100	18	3	2	2	17	11	29
on Road	.185	.268	.331	124	23	4	1	4	12	14	30
Runners On Base	.187	.269	.308	107	20	4	0	3	26	12	28
Second Half	.164	.233	.327	55	9	4	0	3	8	5	13

10-YEAR TOTALS (1984–1993)

	BA	OBA	SA	AB	H	2B	3B	HR	RBI	BB	SO
	.248	.331	.452	1636	405	86	10	76	256	217	224
	.245	.323	.418	3410	836	154	16	134	494	389	700
	.264	.340	.462	2478	653	139	18	106	418	297	431
	.229	.311	.396	2568	588	101	8	104	332	309	493
	.246	.330	.420	2394	588	120	11	92	632	321	460
	.237	.312	.417	2617	621	122	13	107	373	288	482

SCOTT BULLETT — BB/TL — age 26 — PIT OF19

1993	BA	OBA	SA	AB	H	2B	3B	HR	RBI	BB	SO
vs. Left	.100	.182	.100	10	1	0	0	0	0	1	2
vs. Right	.222	.250	.311	45	10	0	2	0	4	2	13
at Home	.192	.250	.269	26	5	0	1	0	0	2	7
on Road	.207	.226	.276	29	6	0	1	0	4	1	8
Runners On Base	.115	.143	.192	26	3	0	1	0	4	1	8
Second Half	.200	.237	.273	55	11	0	2	0	4	3	15

2-YEAR TOTALS (1991–1993)

	BA	OBA	SA	AB	H	2B	3B	HR	RBI	BB	SO
	.100	.182	.100	10	1	0	0	0	0	1	2
	.204	.245	.286	49	10	0	2	0	4	2	16
	.185	.241	.259	27	5	0	1	0	0	2	7
	.188	.229	.250	32	6	0	1	0	4	1	11
	.111	.138	.185	27	3	0	1	0	4	1	8
	.186	.234	.254	59	11	0	2	0	4	3	18

RANDY BUSH — BL/TL — age 36 — MIN DH5, 1B4, OF1

1993	BA	OBA	SA	AB	H	2B	3B	HR	RBI	BB	SO
vs. Left	.000	.000	.000	1	0	0	0	0	0	0	0
vs. Right	.159	.275	.205	44	7	2	0	0	3	7	13
at Home	.200	.333	.250	20	4	1	0	0	2	4	4
on Road	.120	.214	.160	25	3	1	0	0	1	3	9
Runners On Base	.174	.296	.174	23	4	0	0	0	3	4	4
Second Half	.000	.000	.000	0	0	0	0	0	0	0	0

10-YEAR TOTALS (1984–1993)

	BA	OBA	SA	AB	H	2B	3B	HR	RBI	BB	SO
	.159	.253	.256	82	13	6	1	0	7	10	24
	.254	.340	.417	2471	628	118	21	81	332	296	402
	.258	.356	.441	1230	317	66	14	44	180	169	203
	.245	.318	.385	1323	324	58	8	37	159	137	223
	.270	.362	.433	1135	306	52	11	37	295	173	174
	.263	.347	.404	1409	371	64	10	38	166	166	250

FRANCISCO CABRERA — BR/TR — age 28 — ATL 1B12, C2

1993	BA	OBA	SA	AB	H	2B	3B	HR	RBI	BB	SO
vs. Left	.280	.368	.580	50	14	3	0	4	10	7	13
vs. Right	.182	.206	.182	33	6	0	0	0	1	1	8
at Home	.250	.304	.346	52	13	2	0	1	8	4	15
on Road	.226	.314	.548	31	7	1	0	3	3	4	6
Runners On Base	.158	.256	.342	38	6	1	0	1	8	5	11
Second Half	.143	.200	.286	28	4	1	0	1	5	2	11

5-YEAR TOTALS (1989–1993)

	BA	OBA	SA	AB	H	2B	3B	HR	RBI	BB	SO
	.261	.296	.479	238	62	11	1	13	43	13	40
	.239	.289	.398	113	27	6	0	4	19	8	29
	.263	.300	.429	198	52	12	0	7	37	11	42
	.242	.287	.484	153	37	1	1	10	25	10	27
	.260	.306	.456	169	44	10	1	7	52	12	35
	.247	.285	.468	231	57	13	1	12	45	13	48

IVAN CALDERON — BR/TR — age 32 — BOS/CHA OF47, DH25

1993	BA	OBA	SA	AB	H	2B	3B	HR	RBI	BB	SO
vs. Left	.127	.188	.159	63	8	2	0	0	2	5	8
vs. Right	.239	.304	.324	176	42	8	2	1	20	16	25
at Home	.191	.258	.292	89	17	5	2	0	12	8	11
on Road	.220	.283	.273	150	33	5	0	1	10	13	22
Runners On Base	.223	.276	.286	112	25	5	1	0	21	8	11
Second Half	.169	.194	.220	59	10	3	0	0	6	2	10

10-YEAR TOTALS (1984–1993)

BA	OBA	SA	AB	H	2B	3B	HR	RBI	BB	SO
.292	.361	.495	1090	318	73	10	43	142	119	165
.262	.318	.415	2222	583	127	15	61	302	187	391
.272	.336	.438	1561	424	93	16	45	216	154	254
.272	.330	.445	1751	477	107	9	59	228	152	302
.269	.326	.431	1507	405	85	12	45	385	141	245
.274	.334	.437	1493	409	86	14	43	185	138	244

CASEY CANDAELE — BB/TR — age 33 — HOU 2B19, OF17, SS14, 3B4

1993	BA	OBA	SA	AB	H	2B	3B	HR	RBI	BB	SO
vs. Left	.268	.333	.366	41	11	1	0	1	2	4	4
vs. Right	.225	.279	.313	80	18	7	0	0	5	6	10
at Home	.196	.262	.250	56	11	3	0	0	3	5	5
on Road	.277	.329	.400	65	18	5	0	1	4	5	9
Runners On Base	.200	.234	.289	45	9	4	0	0	6	2	6
Second Half	.235	.278	.338	68	16	4	0	1	5	4	8

7-YEAR TOTALS (1986–1993)

BA	OBA	SA	AB	H	2B	3B	HR	RBI	BB	SO
.288	.343	.381	670	193	37	5	5	46	56	56
.227	.289	.303	1194	271	46	15	5	85	103	145
.253	.318	.341	957	242	40	16	4	77	89	105
.245	.298	.321	907	222	43	4	6	54	70	96
.255	.309	.324	701	179	28	7	2	123	57	78
.261	.315	.344	943	246	43	10	5	74	74	101

OZZIE CANSECO — BR/TR — age 30 — SL OF5

1993	BA	OBA	SA	AB	H	2B	3B	HR	RBI	BB	SO
vs. Left	.222	.222	.222	9	2	0	0	0	0	0	2
vs. Right	.125	.222	.125	8	1	0	0	0	0	1	1
at Home	.000	.143	.000	6	0	0	0	0	0	1	1
on Road	.273	.273	.273	11	3	0	0	0	0	0	2
Runners On Base	.143	.143	.143	7	1	0	0	0	0	0	3
Second Half	.000	.000	.000	0	0	0	0	0	0	0	0

3-YEAR TOTALS (1990–1993)

BA	OBA	SA	AB	H	2B	3B	HR	RBI	BB	SO
.226	.314	.323	31	7	3	0	0	2	4	9
.176	.282	.265	34	6	3	0	0	2	5	8
.167	.271	.238	42	7	3	0	0	2	6	13
.261	.346	.391	23	6	3	0	0	2	3	4
.156	.182	.188	32	5	1	0	0	4	1	10
.208	.321	.333	48	10	6	0	0	4	8	14

MARK CARREON — BR/TL — age 31 — SF OF41, 1B3

1993	BA	OBA	SA	AB	H	2B	3B	HR	RBI	BB	SO
vs. Left	.350	.409	.610	100	35	8	0	6	25	11	14
vs. Right	.280	.296	.400	50	14	1	1	1	8	2	2
at Home	.280	.344	.451	82	23	6	1	2	12	8	10
on Road	.382	.408	.647	68	26	3	0	5	21	5	6
Runners On Base	.387	.427	.680	75	29	5	1	5	31	8	5
Second Half	.282	.321	.538	78	22	6	1	4	19	5	7

7-YEAR TOTALS (1987–1993)

BA	OBA	SA	AB	H	2B	3B	HR	RBI	BB	SO
.261	.311	.429	578	151	25	0	24	75	40	71
.274	.324	.407	504	138	21	2	14	64	37	76
.249	.310	.387	543	135	26	2	15	59	44	79
.286	.325	.451	539	154	20	0	23	80	33	68
.286	.333	.417	504	144	22	1	14	115	35	62
.261	.310	.392	587	153	27	1	16	75	41	66

MATIAS CARRILLO — BL/TL — age 31 — FLO OF16

1993	BA	OBA	SA	AB	H	2B	3B	HR	RBI	BB	SO
vs. Left	.400	.500	.400	5	2	0	0	0	0	1	1
vs. Right	.240	.255	.360	50	12	6	0	0	3	0	6
at Home	.310	.333	.414	29	9	3	0	0	3	1	5
on Road	.192	.222	.308	26	5	3	0	0	0	0	2
Runners On Base	.241	.290	.310	29	7	2	0	0	3	1	1
Second Half	.255	.281	.364	55	14	6	0	0	3	1	7

2-YEAR TOTALS (1991–1993)

BA	OBA	SA	AB	H	2B	3B	HR	RBI	BB	SO
.400	.500	.400	5	2	0	0	0	0	1	1
.240	.255	.360	50	12	6	0	0	3	0	6
.310	.333	.414	29	9	3	0	0	3	1	5
.192	.222	.308	26	5	3	0	0	0	0	2
.241	.290	.310	29	7	2	0	0	3	1	1
.255	.281	.364	55	14	6	0	0	3	1	7

WES CHAMBERLAIN — BR/TR — age 28 — PHI OF76

1993	BA	OBA	SA	AB	H	2B	3B	HR	RBI	BB	SO
vs. Left	.328	.374	.612	134	44	9	1	9	25	10	23
vs. Right	.240	.270	.387	150	36	11	1	3	20	7	28
at Home	.310	.335	.488	168	52	13	1	5	30	6	25
on Road	.241	.300	.500	116	28	7	1	7	15	11	26
Runners On Base	.274	.324	.492	124	34	8	2	5	38	10	20
Second Half	.297	.331	.478	138	41	8	1	5	25	7	31

4-YEAR TOTALS (1990–1993)

BA	OBA	SA	AB	H	2B	3B	HR	RBI	BB	SO
.288	.339	.511	403	116	26	2	20	68	31	63
.239	.275	.385	585	140	31	3	16	72	28	125
.284	.317	.445	550	156	34	2	17	81	26	97
.228	.283	.425	438	100	23	3	19	59	33	91
.262	.308	.457	455	119	21	4	20	124	30	82
.254	.302	.423	646	164	32	4	23	99	44	132

CRAIG COLBERT — BR/TR — age 29 — SF C10, 2B2, 3B1

1993	BA	OBA	SA	AB	H	2B	3B	HR	RBI	BB	SO
vs. Left	.136	.174	.227	22	3	2	0	0	2	1	6
vs. Right	.200	.294	.400	15	3	0	0	1	3	2	7
at Home	.100	.143	.250	20	2	0	0	1	3	1	7
on Road	.235	.316	.353	17	4	2	0	0	2	2	6
Runners On Base	.250	.294	.500	16	4	0	0	1	5	1	7
Second Half	.000	.000	.000	1	0	0	0	0	0	0	0

2-YEAR TOTALS (1992–1993)

BA	OBA	SA	AB	H	2B	3B	HR	RBI	BB	SO
.205	.241	.321	78	16	4	1	1	12	4	9
.224	.287	.318	85	19	3	1	1	9	8	26
.221	.262	.338	77	17	4	1	1	11	5	15
.209	.269	.302	86	18	3	1	1	10	7	20
.222	.261	.358	81	18	3	1	2	21	5	21
.238	.283	.352	105	25	5	2	1	13	7	16

GREG COLBRUNN — BR/TR — age 25 — MON 1B61

1993	BA	OBA	SA	AB	H	2B	3B	HR	RBI	BB	SO
vs. Left	.324	.333	.541	74	24	4	0	4	17	2	14
vs. Right	.190	.235	.253	79	15	5	0	0	6	4	19
at Home	.233	.275	.384	73	17	5	0	2	14	4	12
on Road	.275	.289	.400	80	22	4	0	2	9	2	21
Runners On Base	.246	.290	.459	61	15	4	0	3	22	4	15
Second Half	.231	.286	.308	13	3	1	0	0	0	0	1

2-YEAR TOTALS (1992–1993)

BA	OBA	SA	AB	H	2B	3B	HR	RBI	BB	SO
.274	.286	.418	146	40	6	0	5	26	4	28
.251	.291	.331	175	44	11	0	1	15	8	39
.262	.292	.381	160	42	10	0	3	22	7	26
.261	.285	.360	161	42	7	0	3	19	5	41
.265	.302	.394	132	35	8	0	3	38	8	29
.265	.294	.348	181	48	9	0	2	18	6	35

DARNELL COLES — BR/TR — age 32 — TOR OF44, 3B16, 1B1, DH1

1993	BA	OBA	SA	AB	H	2B	3B	HR	RBI	BB	SO
vs. Left	.213	.310	.230	61	13	1	0	0	5	8	9
vs. Right	.271	.324	.436	133	36	8	1	4	21	8	20
at Home	.300	.376	.467	90	27	4	1	3	16	9	15
on Road	.212	.270	.288	104	22	5	0	1	10	7	14
Runners On Base	.261	.330	.420	88	23	4	1	3	25	8	12
Second Half	.268	.321	.392	97	26	6	0	2	13	4	18

10-YEAR TOTALS (1984–1993)

BA	OBA	SA	AB	H	2B	3B	HR	RBI	BB	SO
.245	.313	.384	971	238	52	4	25	128	97	127
.247	.304	.385	1525	377	69	9	41	201	107	255
.262	.328	.416	1208	316	54	5	41	182	110	181
.232	.288	.355	1288	299	67	8	25	147	94	201
.245	.302	.385	1088	267	59	3	29	292	90	153
.251	.315	.400	1308	328	59	5	42	182	113	202

TIM COSTO — BR/TR — age 25 — CIN OF26, 1B2, 3B2

2-YEAR TOTALS (1992–1993)

1993	BA	OBA	SA	AB	H	2B	3B	HR	RBI	BB	SO		BA	OBA	SA	AB	H	2B	3B	HR	RBI	BB	SO
vs. Left	.316	.333	.526	38	12	2	0	2	7	1	1		.288	.321	.462	52	15	3	0	2	8	3	3
vs. Right	.167	.200	.267	60	10	3	0	1	5	3	16		.183	.233	.268	82	15	4	0	1	6	6	20
at Home	.179	.233	.232	56	10	3	0	0	4	4	9		.171	.242	.232	82	14	5	0	0	5	8	13
on Road	.286	.273	.548	42	12	2	0	3	8	0	8		.308	.309	.519	52	16	2	0	3	9	1	10
Runners On Base	.256	.279	.410	39	10	3	0	1	10	2	7		.236	.274	.364	55	13	4	0	1	12	4	10
Second Half	.227	.252	.371	97	22	5	0	3	12	4	17		.226	.269	.346	133	30	7	0	3	14	9	23

HENRY COTTO — BR/TR — age 33 — SEA/FLO OF80, DH15

10-YEAR TOTALS (1984–1993)

1993	BA	OBA	SA	AB	H	2B	3B	HR	RBI	BB	SO		BA	OBA	SA	AB	H	2B	3B	HR	RBI	BB	SO
vs. Left	.282	.301	.356	149	42	5	0	2	12	5	27		.275	.312	.382	1161	319	44	6	23	118	62	184
vs. Right	.198	.215	.330	91	18	3	0	3	9	0	13		.246	.285	.356	1017	250	43	3	21	92	45	168
at Home	.259	.279	.336	116	30	6	0	1	10	3	21		.263	.307	.374	1054	277	43	4	22	111	60	159
on Road	.242	.260	.355	124	30	2	0	4	11	2	19		.260	.292	.367	1124	292	44	5	22	99	47	193
Runners On Base	.248	.264	.327	101	25	2	0	2	18	3	21		.277	.318	.403	901	250	33	7	22	188	52	141
Second Half	.303	.319	.424	132	40	7	0	3	14	3	18		.253	.291	.366	1091	276	50	5	21	104	52	170

MILT CUYLER — BB/TR — age 26 — DET OF80

4-YEAR TOTALS (1990–1993)

1993	BA	OBA	SA	AB	H	2B	3B	HR	RBI	BB	SO		BA	OBA	SA	AB	H	2B	3B	HR	RBI	BB	SO
vs. Left	.182	.241	.234	77	14	2	1	0	8	6	14		.256	.315	.327	297	76	11	2	2	27	22	44
vs. Right	.227	.291	.349	172	39	9	6	0	11	13	39		.237	.301	.326	769	182	29	14	4	61	64	173
at Home	.220	.286	.299	127	28	4	3	0	11	10	21		.223	.306	.285	515	115	14	6	2	37	53	95
on Road	.205	.265	.328	122	25	7	4	0	8	9	32		.260	.303	.365	551	143	26	10	4	51	33	122
Runners On Base	.259	.320	.371	116	30	5	4	0	19	9	24		.229	.285	.322	463	106	19	9	3	85	31	97
Second Half	.211	.348	.289	38	8	3	0	0	1	7	9		.253	.333	.319	430	109	18	5	0	29	48	95

DOUG DASCENZO — BB/TL — age 30 — TEX OF68, DH2

6-YEAR TOTALS (1988–1993)

1993	BA	OBA	SA	AB	H	2B	3B	HR	RBI	BB	SO		BA	OBA	SA	AB	H	2B	3B	HR	RBI	BB	SO
vs. Left	.237	.233	.288	59	14	3	0	0	5	0	7		.262	.297	.318	531	139	25	1	1	50	28	37
vs. Right	.172	.242	.287	87	15	2	1	2	5	8	15		.215	.292	.283	685	147	17	9	4	40	74	78
at Home	.215	.261	.308	65	14	4	1	0	3	4	9		.244	.303	.315	626	153	25	8	1	44	52	59
on Road	.185	.221	.272	81	15	1	0	2	7	4	13		.225	.284	.281	590	133	17	2	4	46	50	56
Runners On Base	.218	.254	.273	55	12	1	1	0	8	3	8		.250	.304	.300	436	109	8	4	2	87	36	37
Second Half	.278	.316	.306	36	10	1	0	0	3	2	4		.250	.314	.308	652	163	23	6	1	46	62	57

JACK DAUGHERTY — BB/TL — age 34 — HOU/CIN OF17, 1B3

6-YEAR TOTALS (1987–1993)

1993	BA	OBA	SA	AB	H	2B	3B	HR	RBI	BB	SO		BA	OBA	SA	AB	H	2B	3B	HR	RBI	BB	SO
vs. Left	.600	.600	.600	5	3	0	0	0	1	0	1		.259	.323	.337	166	43	6	2	1	17	15	39
vs. Right	.193	.319	.333	57	11	2	0	2	8	11	14		.255	.322	.369	593	151	33	4	9	70	61	93
at Home	.297	.386	.514	37	11	2	0	2	8	6	7		.275	.343	.405	393	108	19	4	8	45	40	62
on Road	.120	.267	.120	25	3	0	0	0	1	5	8		.235	.299	.317	366	86	20	2	2	42	36	70
Runners On Base	.250	.406	.417	24	6	1	0	1	8	7	7		.237	.299	.356	320	76	19	2	5	82	31	59
Second Half	.220	.338	.356	59	13	2	0	2	9	11	15		.271	.342	.404	468	127	22	5	10	57	51	89

GLENN DAVIS — BR/TR — age 33 — BAL 1B22, DH7

10-YEAR TOTALS (1984–1993)

1993	BA	OBA	SA	AB	H	2B	3B	HR	RBI	BB	SO		BA	OBA	SA	AB	H	2B	3B	HR	RBI	BB	SO
vs. Left	.222	.282	.222	36	8	0	0	0	1	3	10		.257	.341	.499	1206	310	61	3	75	211	142	172
vs. Right	.156	.205	.234	77	12	3	0	1	8	4	19		.261	.328	.452	2513	655	116	10	115	392	228	441
at Home	.157	.214	.235	51	8	1	0	1	3	3	17		.279	.347	.471	1850	516	96	8	81	280	176	304
on Road	.194	.242	.226	62	12	2	0	0	6	4	12		.240	.318	.464	1869	449	81	5	109	323	194	309
Runners On Base	.122	.170	.143	49	6	1	0	0	8	3	12		.259	.351	.466	1696	440	85	5	85	498	238	276
Second Half	.000	.000	.000	0	0	0	0	0	0	0	0		.264	.343	.467	2033	537	102	8	98	328	221	320

BUTCH DAVIS — BR/TR — age 36 — TEX OF44, DH11

6-YEAR TOTALS (1984–1993)

1993	BA	OBA	SA	AB	H	2B	3B	HR	RBI	BB	SO		BA	OBA	SA	AB	H	2B	3B	HR	RBI	BB	SO
vs. Left	.255	.305	.473	55	14	2	2	2	8	3	11		.184	.220	.316	158	29	5	2	4	15	7	31
vs. Right	.240	.255	.385	104	25	8	2	1	12	2	17		.224	.267	.340	156	35	11	2	1	17	9	30
at Home	.265	.296	.412	68	18	4	3	0	10	3	11		.250	.297	.368	144	36	8	3	1	18	10	20
on Road	.231	.255	.418	91	21	6	1	3	10	2	17		.165	.197	.294	170	28	8	1	4	14	6	41
Runners On Base	.323	.373	.548	62	20	3	4	1	18	4	7		.243	.291	.368	136	33	6	4	1	28	9	19
Second Half	.265	.286	.412	68	18	5	1	1	9	1	12		.231	.254	.355	121	28	7	1	2	12	3	29

STEVE DECKER — BR/TR — age 29 — FLO C5

4-YEAR TOTALS (1990–1993)

1993	BA	OBA	SA	AB	H	2B	3B	HR	RBI	BB	SO		BA	OBA	SA	AB	H	2B	3B	HR	RBI	BB	SO
vs. Left	.000	.273	.000	7	0	0	0	0	1	3	1		.217	.250	.349	129	28	3	1	4	16	7	17
vs. Right	.000	.000	.000	8	0	0	0	0	0	0	2		.199	.275	.287	216	43	7	0	4	18	19	44
at Home	.000	.400	.000	3	0	0	0	0	0	2	2		.212	.279	.345	165	35	5	1	5	23	14	26
on Road	.000	.071	.000	12	0	0	0	0	1	1	1		.200	.254	.278	180	36	5	0	3	11	12	38
Runners On Base	.000	.250	.000	8	0	0	0	0	1	3	3		.212	.279	.305	151	32	6	1	2	28	14	32
Second Half	.000	.000	.000	0	0	0	0	0	0	0	0		.217	.278	.311	161	35	4	1	3	15	12	25

DREW DENSON — BB/TR — age 29 — CHA 1B3

2-YEAR TOTALS (1989–1993)

1993	BA	OBA	SA	AB	H	2B	3B	HR	RBI	BB	SO		BA	OBA	SA	AB	H	2B	3B	HR	RBI	BB	SO
vs. Left	.000	.000	.000	2	0	0	0	0	0	0	1		.167	.250	.222	18	3	1	0	0	0	2	4
vs. Right	.333	.333	.333	3	1	0	0	0	0	0	1		.304	.333	.304	23	7	0	0	0	5	1	7
at Home	.000	.000	.000	3	0	0	0	0	0	0	2		.294	.368	.294	17	5	0	0	0	4	2	8
on Road	.500	.500	.500	2	1	0	0	0	0	0	0		.208	.240	.250	24	5	1	0	0	1	1	3
Runners On Base	.333	.333	.333	3	1	0	0	0	0	0	2		.304	.333	.348	23	7	1	0	0	5	1	4
Second Half	.200	.200	.200	5	1	0	0	0	0	0	2		.244	.295	.268	41	10	1	0	0	5	3	11

ALEX DIAZ — BB/TR — age 26 — MIL OF28, DH1

1993	BA	OBA	SA	AB	H	2B	3B	HR	RBI	BB	SO
vs. Left	.382	.382	.441	34	13	2	0	0	0	0	6
vs. Right	.257	.257	.257	35	9	0	0	0	1	0	6
at Home	.300	.300	.300	30	9	0	0	0	0	0	5
on Road	.333	.333	.385	39	13	2	0	0	1	0	7
Runners On Base	.207	.207	.207	29	6	0	0	0	1	0	6
Second Half	.364	.364	.382	55	20	1	0	0	1	0	9

2-YEAR TOTALS (1992–1993)

	BA	OBA	SA	AB	H	2B	3B	HR	RBI	BB	SO
vs. Left	.371	.371	.429	35	13	2	0	0	0	0	6
vs. Right	.233	.233	.233	43	10	0	0	0	2	0	6
at Home	.281	.281	.281	32	9	0	0	0	0	0	5
on Road	.304	.304	.348	46	14	2	0	0	2	0	7
Runners On Base	.206	.206	.206	34	7	0	0	0	2	0	6
Second Half	.328	.328	.344	64	21	1	0	0	2	0	9

MARIO DIAZ — BR/TR — age 32 — TEX SS57, 3B12, 1B1

1993	BA	OBA	SA	AB	H	2B	3B	HR	RBI	BB	SO
vs. Left	.333	.375	.471	51	17	4	0	1	6	4	4
vs. Right	.253	.270	.325	154	39	6	1	1	18	4	9
at Home	.238	.268	.286	105	25	2	0	1	9	4	7
on Road	.310	.327	.440	100	31	8	1	1	15	4	6
Runners On Base	.284	.292	.330	88	25	4	0	0	22	2	4
Second Half	.277	.306	.361	166	46	9	1	1	18	8	11

7-YEAR TOTALS (1987–1993)

	BA	OBA	SA	AB	H	2B	3B	HR	RBI	BB	SO
vs. Left	.254	.304	.313	240	61	11	0	1	25	18	23
vs. Right	.249	.278	.320	369	92	13	2	3	42	16	29
at Home	.226	.270	.285	288	65	9	1	2	24	18	24
on Road	.274	.305	.346	321	88	15	1	2	43	16	28
Runners On Base	.264	.290	.312	269	71	10	0	1	64	12	17
Second Half	.248	.281	.305	436	108	18	2	1	44	22	44

CHRIS DONNELS — BL/TR — age 28 — HOU 3B31, 1B23, 2B1

1993	BA	OBA	SA	AB	H	2B	3B	HR	RBI	BB	SO
vs. Left	.242	.359	.364	33	8	2	1	0	1	6	3
vs. Right	.260	.319	.397	146	38	12	1	2	23	13	30
at Home	.200	.273	.271	70	14	5	0	0	8	7	13
on Road	.294	.361	.468	109	32	9	2	2	16	12	20
Runners On Base	.286	.353	.418	91	26	6	0	2	24	10	18
Second Half	.268	.338	.420	138	37	11	2	2	20	15	21

3-YEAR TOTALS (1991–1993)

	BA	OBA	SA	AB	H	2B	3B	HR	RBI	BB	SO
vs. Left	.242	.337	.308	91	22	4	1	0	4	13	18
vs. Right	.218	.304	.299	298	65	16	1	2	31	37	59
at Home	.179	.253	.220	173	31	7	0	0	13	17	39
on Road	.259	.356	.366	216	56	13	2	2	22	33	38
Runners On Base	.249	.332	.335	173	43	9	0	2	35	22	34
Second Half	.228	.310	.308	325	74	16	2	2	28	39	59

BILL DORAN — BB/TR — age 36 — MIL 2B17, 1B4

1993	BA	OBA	SA	AB	H	2B	3B	HR	RBI	BB	SO
vs. Left	.200	.267	.275	40	8	3	0	0	5	4	1
vs. Right	.250	.318	.300	20	5	1	0	0	1	2	2
at Home	.185	.267	.222	27	5	1	0	0	1	3	0
on Road	.242	.297	.333	33	8	3	0	0	5	3	3
Runners On Base	.360	.414	.440	25	9	2	0	0	6	3	0
Second Half	.308	.308	.308	13	4	0	0	0	1	0	0

10-YEAR TOTALS (1984–1993)

	BA	OBA	SA	AB	H	2B	3B	HR	RBI	BB	SO
vs. Left	.272	.371	.387	1513	412	73	7	29	152	241	153
vs. Right	.262	.344	.370	2986	782	132	25	47	299	378	369
at Home	.270	.367	.385	2169	586	104	20	35	225	337	235
on Road	.261	.339	.367	2330	608	101	12	41	226	282	287
Runners On Base	.282	.369	.389	1685	476	85	7	27	402	247	169
Second Half	.263	.353	.371	2327	612	111	19	34	211	324	283

BRIAN DORSETT — BR/TR — age 33 — CIN C18, 1B3

1993	BA	OBA	SA	AB	H	2B	3B	HR	RBI	BB	SO
vs. Left	.333	.385	.542	24	8	2	0	1	4	2	6
vs. Right	.205	.225	.333	39	8	0	1	0	8	1	8
at Home	.276	.300	.517	29	8	1	0	2	7	1	4
on Road	.235	.278	.324	34	8	3	0	0	5	2	10
Runners On Base	.407	.429	.741	27	11	3	0	2	12	1	4
Second Half	.254	.288	.413	63	16	4	0	2	12	3	14

6-YEAR TOTALS (1987–1993)

	BA	OBA	SA	AB	H	2B	3B	HR	RBI	BB	SO
vs. Left	.228	.267	.333	57	13	3	0	1	5	2	9
vs. Right	.216	.255	.320	97	21	4	0	2	17	5	23
at Home	.284	.321	.459	74	21	4	0	3	13	3	9
on Road	.162	.202	.200	80	13	3	0	0	9	4	23
Runners On Base	.311	.329	.486	74	23	4	0	3	22	2	11
Second Half	.231	.272	.343	143	33	7	0	2	21	7	29

ROB DUCEY — BL/TR — age 29 — TEX OF26

1993	BA	OBA	SA	AB	H	2B	3B	HR	RBI	BB	SO
vs. Left	.182	.167	.364	11	2	0	1	0	1	0	4
vs. Right	.297	.376	.514	74	22	6	2	2	8	10	13
at Home	.348	.400	.609	46	16	4	1	2	4	4	9
on Road	.205	.298	.359	39	8	2	2	0	5	6	8
Runners On Base	.258	.359	.419	31	8	3	1	0	7	6	8
Second Half	.282	.351	.494	85	24	6	3	2	9	10	17

7-YEAR TOTALS (1987–1993)

	BA	OBA	SA	AB	H	2B	3B	HR	RBI	BB	SO
vs. Left	.257	.315	.386	101	26	3	2	2	12	9	32
vs. Right	.240	.314	.342	363	87	23	4	2	29	41	90
at Home	.251	.327	.359	251	63	12	3	3	22	29	63
on Road	.235	.298	.343	213	50	14	3	1	19	21	59
Runners On Base	.250	.332	.345	200	50	12	2	1	38	27	55
Second Half	.262	.324	.391	343	90	22	5	4	32	33	81

SHAWON DUNSTON — BR/TR — age 31 — CHN SS2

1993	BA	OBA	SA	AB	H	2B	3B	HR	RBI	BB	SO
vs. Left	.429	.429	.714	7	3	2	0	0	2	0	0
vs. Right	.333	.333	.333	3	1	0	0	0	0	0	1
at Home	.667	.667	1.000	3	2	1	0	0	1	0	0
on Road	.286	.286	.429	7	2	1	0	0	1	0	1
Runners On Base	.500	.500	.750	4	2	1	0	0	2	0	1
Second Half	.400	.400	.600	10	4	2	0	0	2	0	1

9-YEAR TOTALS (1985–1993)

	BA	OBA	SA	AB	H	2B	3B	HR	RBI	BB	SO
vs. Left	.263	.285	.419	998	262	44	14	28	117	33	140
vs. Right	.258	.291	.385	2345	605	115	24	45	227	104	443
at Home	.274	.306	.416	1657	454	84	19	38	175	71	285
on Road	.245	.272	.374	1686	413	75	19	35	169	69	298
Runners On Base	.259	.292	.399	1330	344	68	16	29	300	67	211
Second Half	.254	.282	.376	1676	426	71	23	29	162	66	286

DAMION EASLEY — BR/TR — age 25 — CAL 2B54, 3B14, DH1

1993	BA	OBA	SA	AB	H	2B	3B	HR	RBI	BB	SO
vs. Left	.361	.418	.500	72	26	4	0	1	3	5	9
vs. Right	.291	.380	.373	158	46	6	2	1	19	23	26
at Home	.302	.381	.388	129	39	7	2	0	12	15	21
on Road	.327	.405	.446	101	33	6	0	2	10	13	14
Runners On Base	.310	.393	.410	100	31	6	1	1	21	12	19
Second Half	.327	.441	.382	55	18	3	0	0	4	11	6

2-YEAR TOTALS (1992–1993)

	BA	OBA	SA	AB	H	2B	3B	HR	RBI	BB	SO
vs. Left	.333	.385	.435	108	36	8	0	1	6	7	15
vs. Right	.275	.350	.348	273	75	10	2	2	28	29	46
at Home	.291	.364	.372	196	57	9	2	1	18	19	32
on Road	.292	.354	.373	185	54	9	0	2	16	17	29
Runners On Base	.283	.354	.365	159	45	5	1	2	33	15	31
Second Half	.277	.346	.330	206	57	8	0	1	16	19	32

ALVARO ESPINOZA — BR/TR — age 32 — CLE 3B99, SS35, 2B2

1993	BA	OBA	SA	AB	H	2B	3B	HR	RBI	BB	SO
vs. Left	.345	.364	.478	113	39	9	0	2	12	4	13
vs. Right	.227	.248	.307	150	34	6	0	2	15	4	23
at Home	.218	.244	.331	124	27	5	0	3	14	4	17
on Road	.331	.347	.424	139	46	10	0	1	13	4	19
Runners On Base	.308	.324	.413	104	32	8	0	1	24	4	13
Second Half	.255	.285	.331	157	40	9	0	1	10	7	22

7-YEAR TOTALS (1985–1993)

	BA	OBA	SA	AB	H	2B	3B	HR	RBI	BB	SO
vs. Left	.315	.346	.384	607	191	28	1	4	50	29	53
vs. Right	.228	.249	.293	1179	269	48	4	7	81	27	173
at Home	.246	.272	.312	900	221	37	4	5	64	29	102
on Road	.270	.293	.336	886	239	39	1	6	67	27	124
Runners On Base	.287	.307	.347	701	201	34	1	2	122	20	78
Second Half	.258	.282	.320	1036	267	44	3	5	72	29	138

CECIL ESPY — BB/TR — age 31 — CIN OF18

1993	BA	OBA	SA	AB	H	2B	3B	HR	RBI	BB	SO
vs. Left	.231	.267	.231	13	3	0	0	0	1	1	2
vs. Right	.234	.393	.277	47	11	2	0	0	4	13	11
at Home	.278	.440	.333	18	5	1	0	0	3	6	3
on Road	.214	.333	.238	42	9	1	0	0	2	8	10
Runners On Base	.214	.314	.286	28	6	2	0	0	5	5	9
Second Half	.000	.000	.000	0	0	0	0	0	0	0	0

7-YEAR TOTALS (1987–1993)

	BA	OBA	SA	AB	H	2B	3B	HR	RBI	BB	SO
	.243	.294	.338	272	66	9	1	5	26	21	52
	.244	.303	.315	965	235	33	15	2	81	82	223
	.269	.316	.367	594	160	19	12	5	60	42	131
	.219	.288	.277	643	141	23	4	2	47	61	144
	.247	.291	.316	494	122	16	3	4	104	34	116
	.237	.294	.319	621	147	22	10	3	56	50	143

PAUL FARIES — BR/TR — age 29 — SF 2B7, SS4, 3B1

1993	BA	OBA	SA	AB	H	2B	3B	HR	RBI	BB	SO
vs. Left	.154	.214	.231	13	2	1	0	0	0	1	0
vs. Right	.261	.250	.391	23	6	1	1	0	4	0	4
at Home	.118	.167	.176	17	2	1	0	0	0	1	1
on Road	.316	.300	.474	19	6	1	1	0	4	0	3
Runners On Base	.227	.250	.364	22	5	1	1	0	4	1	4
Second Half	.222	.237	.333	36	8	2	1	0	4	1	4

4-YEAR TOTALS (1990–1993)

	BA	OBA	SA	AB	H	2B	3B	HR	RBI	BB	SO
	.266	.314	.342	79	21	6	0	0	4	6	4
	.163	.250	.200	135	22	1	2	0	10	14	30
	.221	.265	.312	77	17	5	1	0	6	4	9
	.190	.277	.219	137	26	2	1	0	8	16	25
	.247	.327	.333	93	23	4	2	0	14	10	12
	.208	.261	.257	144	30	5	1	0	9	10	21

MONTY FARISS — BR/TR — age 27 — FLO OF8

1993	BA	OBA	SA	AB	H	2B	3B	HR	RBI	BB	SO
vs. Left	.158	.304	.316	19	3	1	1	0	2	4	9
vs. Right	.200	.273	.300	10	2	1	0	0	0	1	4
at Home	.250	.438	.333	12	3	1	0	0	1	4	5
on Road	.118	.167	.294	17	2	1	1	0	1	1	8
Runners On Base	.154	.353	.308	13	2	0	1	0	2	4	7
Second Half	.000	.000	.000	0	0	0	0	0	0	0	0

3-YEAR TOTALS (1991–1993)

	BA	OBA	SA	AB	H	2B	3B	HR	RBI	BB	SO
	.197	.309	.308	117	23	2	1	3	16	18	47
	.239	.314	.358	109	26	8	1	1	13	11	28
	.255	.336	.330	106	27	5	0	1	14	13	34
	.183	.290	.333	120	22	5	2	3	15	16	41
	.221	.331	.375	104	23	6	2	2	27	15	34
	.222	.297	.335	167	37	8	1	3	21	17	50

JUNIOR FELIX — BB/TR — age 27 — FLO OF52

1993	BA	OBA	SA	AB	H	2B	3B	HR	RBI	BB	SO
vs. Left	.250	.271	.485	68	17	4	0	4	11	2	11
vs. Right	.233	.277	.356	146	34	7	1	3	11	8	39
at Home	.277	.348	.446	83	23	3	1	3	7	8	23
on Road	.214	.226	.366	131	28	8	0	4	15	2	27
Runners On Base	.242	.274	.451	91	22	4	0	5	20	3	23
Second Half	.000	.000	.000	0	0	0	0	0	0	0	0

5-YEAR TOTALS (1989–1993)

	BA	OBA	SA	AB	H	2B	3B	HR	RBI	BB	SO
	.236	.284	.408	522	123	26	5	18	75	35	138
	.265	.317	.389	1309	347	54	18	24	156	97	295
	.257	.319	.400	874	225	30	16	21	95	74	195
	.256	.297	.389	957	245	50	7	21	136	58	238
	.272	.316	.404	773	210	32	8	18	207	51	164
	.234	.286	.355	761	178	29	12	13	82	55	188

CARLTON FISK — BR/TR — age 47 — CHA C25

1993	BA	OBA	SA	AB	H	2B	3B	HR	RBI	BB	SO
vs. Left	.290	.290	.387	31	9	0	0	1	3	0	3
vs. Right	.045	.154	.045	22	1	0	0	0	1	2	8
at Home	.133	.212	.133	30	4	0	0	0	2	2	7
on Road	.261	.250	.391	23	6	0	0	1	2	0	4
Runners On Base	.160	.185	.160	25	4	0	0	0	3	1	6
Second Half	.000	.000	.000	0	0	0	0	0	0	0	0

10-YEAR TOTALS (1984–1993)

	BA	OBA	SA	AB	H	2B	3B	HR	RBI	BB	SO
	.259	.326	.455	1278	331	62	3	61	204	123	189
	.247	.319	.429	2316	571	97	4	106	362	208	424
	.247	.321	.418	1770	438	85	3	70	265	179	290
	.254	.322	.459	1824	464	74	4	97	301	152	323
	.255	.333	.434	1635	417	77	4	69	468	179	274
	.259	.328	.468	2035	527	102	4	105	338	188	318

JOHN FLAHERTY — BR/TR — age 27 — BOS C13

1993	BA	OBA	SA	AB	H	2B	3B	HR	RBI	BB	SO
vs. Left	.286	.375	.571	7	2	2	0	0	2	1	2
vs. Right	.056	.150	.056	18	1	0	0	0	0	1	4
at Home	.095	.208	.143	21	2	1	0	0	0	2	5
on Road	.250	.250	.500	4	1	1	0	0	2	0	1
Runners On Base	.071	.188	.143	14	1	1	0	0	2	1	4
Second Half	.120	.214	.200	25	3	2	0	0	2	2	6

2-YEAR TOTALS (1992–1993)

	BA	OBA	SA	AB	H	2B	3B	HR	RBI	BB	SO
	.222	.276	.333	27	6	3	0	0	2	2	2
	.156	.203	.172	64	10	1	0	0	2	3	11
	.175	.226	.211	57	10	2	0	0	2	3	10
	.176	.222	.235	34	6	2	0	0	2	2	3
	.132	.209	.158	38	5	1	0	0	4	3	6
	.196	.262	.250	56	11	3	0	0	2	4	10

TOM FOLEY — BL/TR — age 35 — PIT 2B35, 1B12, 3B7, SS6

1993	BA	OBA	SA	AB	H	2B	3B	HR	RBI	BB	SO
vs. Left	.417	.417	.500	12	5	1	0	0	1	0	1
vs. Right	.242	.279	.357	182	44	10	1	3	21	11	25
at Home	.272	.299	.395	81	22	5	1	1	12	4	8
on Road	.239	.279	.345	113	27	6	0	2	10	7	18
Runners On Base	.218	.250	.345	87	19	5	0	2	21	5	16
Second Half	.269	.303	.394	104	28	7	0	2	8	5	14

10-YEAR TOTALS (1984–1993)

	BA	OBA	SA	AB	H	2B	3B	HR	RBI	BB	SO
	.228	.263	.259	263	60	6	1	0	16	13	54
	.248	.308	.356	2200	546	115	18	29	221	191	294
	.248	.306	.361	1181	293	63	11	16	107	100	162
	.244	.300	.332	1282	313	58	8	13	130	104	186
	.244	.307	.352	1020	249	48	10	14	222	101	153
	.254	.306	.357	1462	371	74	7	21	128	109	200

ERIC FOX — BB/TL — age 31 — OAK OF26, DH2

1993	BA	OBA	SA	AB	H	2B	3B	HR	RBI	BB	SO
vs. Left	.125	.176	.313	16	2	0	0	1	4	1	3
vs. Right	.150	.171	.175	40	6	1	0	0	1	1	4
at Home	.148	.207	.296	27	4	1	0	1	4	2	3
on Road	.138	.138	.138	29	4	0	0	0	1	0	4
Runners On Base	.043	.043	.174	23	1	0	0	1	5	0	2
Second Half	.000	.000	.000	0	0	0	0	0	0	0	0

2-YEAR TOTALS (1992–1993)

	BA	OBA	SA	AB	H	2B	3B	HR	RBI	BB	SO
	.184	.244	.289	38	7	1	0	1	5	3	9
	.217	.270	.329	161	35	5	2	3	13	12	27
	.223	.286	.320	103	23	5	1	1	7	9	17
	.198	.243	.323	96	19	1	1	3	11	6	19
	.186	.253	.314	86	16	1	2	2	16	8	18
	.238	.299	.364	143	34	5	2	3	13	13	29

DAVE GALLAGHER — BR/TR — age 34 — NYN OF72, 1B9

1993	BA	OBA	SA	AB	H	2B	3B	HR	RBI	BB	SO
vs. Left	.259	.312	.420	143	37	7	2	4	15	11	13
vs. Right	.310	.397	.500	58	18	5	0	2	13	9	5
at Home	.240	.315	.370	100	24	6	2	1	5	11	11
on Road	.307	.360	.515	101	31	6	0	5	23	9	7
Runners On Base	.289	.362	.446	83	24	5	1	4	24	10	6
Second Half	.248	.319	.410	105	26	3	1	4	13	11	11

7-YEAR TOTALS (1987–1993)

	BA	OBA	SA	AB	H	2B	3B	HR	RBI	BB	SO
	.267	.323	.343	827	221	34	7	5	74	69	87
	.276	.332	.363	929	256	48	3	9	90	78	126
	.263	.324	.338	862	227	40	6	4	70	79	94
	.280	.332	.369	894	250	42	4	10	94	68	119
	.270	.331	.346	682	184	26	7	4	154	66	80
	.266	.321	.345	1012	269	49	5	7	92	79	133

BOB GEREN — BR/TR — age 33 — SD C49, 1B1, 3B1

1993	BA	OBA	SA	AB	H	2B	3B	HR	RBI	BB	SO
vs. Left	.280	.325	.467	75	21	5	0	3	5	5	10
vs. Right	.143	.231	.157	70	10	1	0	0	1	8	18
at Home	.203	.253	.284	74	15	3	0	1	1	5	15
on Road	.225	.304	.352	71	16	3	0	2	5	8	13
Runners On Base	.114	.184	.129	70	8	1	0	0	3	6	17
Second Half	.219	.265	.406	32	7	3	0	1	2	2	4

5-YEAR TOTALS (1988–1993)

BA	OBA	SA	AB	H	2B	3B	HR	RBI	BB	SO
.262	.311	.393	366	96	15	0	11	36	24	65
.206	.258	.308	399	82	6	1	11	40	25	114
.221	.260	.326	411	91	13	0	10	33	20	99
.246	.309	.376	354	87	8	1	12	43	29	80
.230	.273	.351	339	78	11	0	10	64	20	74
.238	.288	.357	403	96	10	1	12	46	26	88

JERRY GOFF — BL/TR — age 30 — PIT C14

1993	BA	OBA	SA	AB	H	2B	3B	HR	RBI	BB	SO
vs. Left	.333	.333	.333	3	1	0	0	0	1	0	2
vs. Right	.294	.429	.529	34	10	2	0	2	5	8	7
at Home	.346	.452	.654	26	9	2	0	2	5	5	5
on Road	.182	.357	.182	11	2	0	0	0	1	3	4
Runners On Base	.455	.647	.636	11	5	2	0	0	4	6	1
Second Half	.297	.422	.514	37	11	2	0	2	6	8	9

3-YEAR TOTALS (1990–1993)

BA	OBA	SA	AB	H	2B	3B	HR	RBI	BB	SO
.143	.143	.143	14	2	0	0	0	1	0	6
.248	.374	.372	145	36	3	0	5	12	29	42
.256	.396	.354	82	21	2	0	2	8	19	22
.221	.310	.351	77	17	1	0	3	5	10	26
.291	.458	.345	55	16	3	0	0	8	17	15
.250	.361	.364	132	33	3	0	4	12	23	34

LEO GOMEZ — BR/TR — age 28 — BAL 3B70, DH1

1993	BA	OBA	SA	AB	H	2B	3B	HR	RBI	BB	SO
vs. Left	.224	.303	.358	67	15	3	0	2	6	7	16
vs. Right	.186	.293	.345	177	33	4	0	8	19	25	44
at Home	.200	.296	.409	110	22	2	0	7	15	13	27
on Road	.194	.295	.299	134	26	5	0	3	10	19	33
Runners On Base	.183	.289	.287	115	21	3	0	3	18	15	29
Second Half	.071	.176	.071	14	1	0	0	0	1	2	2

4-YEAR TOTALS (1990–1993)

BA	OBA	SA	AB	H	2B	3B	HR	RBI	BB	SO
.234	.331	.399	303	71	14	0	12	39	44	54
.240	.324	.396	839	201	34	2	31	96	99	173
.238	.327	.395	559	133	24	2	20	63	71	101
.238	.324	.398	583	139	24	0	23	72	72	126
.222	.309	.355	535	119	17	0	18	110	66	105
.229	.306	.405	576	132	24	1	25	72	63	112

RENE GONZALES — BR/TR — age 34 — CAL 3B79, 1B31, SS5, 2B4, P1

1993	BA	OBA	SA	AB	H	2B	3B	HR	RBI	BB	SO
vs. Left	.295	.388	.402	112	33	9	0	1	8	16	14
vs. Right	.229	.326	.278	223	51	8	0	1	23	33	31
at Home	.230	.320	.303	178	41	10	0	1	16	23	23
on Road	.274	.375	.338	157	43	7	0	1	15	26	22
Runners On Base	.248	.349	.305	141	35	2	0	2	31	22	21
Second Half	.259	.332	.335	170	44	10	0	1	15	19	20

9-YEAR TOTALS (1984–1993)

BA	OBA	SA	AB	H	2B	3B	HR	RBI	BB	SO
.257	.348	.347	435	112	20	2	5	40	57	65
.228	.297	.295	969	221	33	1	10	82	89	147
.245	.326	.345	686	168	34	1	11	63	77	103
.230	.301	.279	718	165	19	2	4	59	69	109
.239	.324	.312	565	135	17	3	6	113	68	86
.240	.304	.289	705	169	25	2	2	47	61	109

TOM GOODWIN — BL/TR — age 26 — LA OF12

1993	BA	OBA	SA	AB	H	2B	3B	HR	RBI	BB	SO
vs. Left	.000	.000	.000	1	0	0	0	0	0	0	0
vs. Right	.313	.353	.375	16	5	1	0	0	1	1	4
at Home	.286	.286	.286	7	2	0	0	0	1	0	1
on Road	.300	.364	.400	10	3	1	0	0	0	1	3
Runners On Base	.333	.333	.333	6	2	0	0	0	1	0	2
Second Half	.333	.375	.400	15	5	1	0	0	1	1	3

3-YEAR TOTALS (1991–1993)

BA	OBA	SA	AB	H	2B	3B	HR	RBI	BB	SO
.182	.182	.182	11	2	0	0	0	0	0	1
.244	.301	.291	86	21	2	1	0	4	7	13
.255	.271	.255	47	12	0	0	0	1	1	5
.220	.304	.300	50	11	2	1	0	3	6	9
.200	.216	.220	50	10	1	0	0	4	1	4
.237	.290	.280	93	22	2	1	0	3	7	13

CRAIG GREBECK — BR/TR — age 30 — CHA SS46, 2B16, 3B14

1993	BA	OBA	SA	AB	H	2B	3B	HR	RBI	BB	SO
vs. Left	.222	.289	.248	117	26	3	0	0	6	11	16
vs. Right	.233	.364	.301	73	17	2	0	1	6	15	10
at Home	.274	.358	.311	106	29	4	0	0	8	14	14
on Road	.167	.271	.214	84	14	1	0	1	4	12	12
Runners On Base	.260	.374	.299	77	20	3	0	0	11	14	9
Second Half	.225	.328	.270	111	25	5	0	0	7	17	14

4-YEAR TOTALS (1990–1993)

BA	OBA	SA	AB	H	2B	3B	HR	RBI	BB	SO
.244	.316	.350	406	99	22	3	5	40	43	64
.251	.349	.365	414	104	23	3	6	47	59	60
.264	.347	.374	406	107	23	2	6	49	53	59
.232	.318	.341	414	96	22	4	5	38	49	65
.267	.354	.407	329	88	25	3	5	81	44	47
.263	.365	.381	415	109	24	5	5	49	64	68

WILLIE GREENE — BL/TR — age 23 — CIN SS10, 3B5

1993	BA	OBA	SA	AB	H	2B	3B	HR	RBI	BB	SO
vs. Left	.063	.059	.250	16	1	0	0	1	2	0	10
vs. Right	.206	.250	.382	34	7	1	1	1	3	2	9
at Home	.147	.143	.324	34	5	0	0	2	4	0	15
on Road	.188	.278	.375	16	3	1	1	0	1	2	4
Runners On Base	.059	.105	.176	17	1	0	0	1	3	1	8
Second Half	.147	.194	.324	34	5	1	1	1	2	2	14

2-YEAR TOTALS (1992–1993)

BA	OBA	SA	AB	H	2B	3B	HR	RBI	BB	SO
.182	.208	.295	44	8	0	1	1	6	2	17
.253	.321	.444	99	25	6	2	3	12	10	25
.226	.277	.376	93	21	2	0	4	10	7	31
.240	.304	.440	50	12	4	3	0	8	5	11
.270	.314	.492	63	17	5	3	1	15	5	17
.236	.300	.402	127	30	6	3	3	15	12	37

TOMMY GREGG — BL/TL — age 31 — CIN OF4

1993	BA	OBA	SA	AB	H	2B	3B	HR	RBI	BB	SO
vs. Left	.000	.000	.000	0	0	0	0	0	0	0	0
vs. Right	.167	.154	.167	12	2	0	0	0	0	0	0
at Home	.167	.143	.167	6	1	0	0	0	0	0	0
on Road	.167	.167	.167	6	1	0	0	0	0	0	0
Runners On Base	.250	.200	.250	4	1	0	0	0	0	0	0
Second Half	.167	.154	.167	12	2	0	0	0	0	0	0

7-YEAR TOTALS (1987–1993)

BA	OBA	SA	AB	H	2B	3B	HR	RBI	BB	SO
.174	.248	.185	92	16	1	0	0	2	9	31
.254	.306	.383	613	156	33	2	14	66	45	92
.246	.290	.353	357	88	18	1	6	40	22	55
.241	.306	.362	348	84	16	1	8	28	32	68
.251	.321	.361	291	73	9	1	7	61	31	45
.253	.297	.385	467	118	22	2	12	50	31	90

ALFREDO GRIFFIN — BB/TR — age 37 — TOR SS20, 2B11, 3B6

1993	BA	OBA	SA	AB	H	2B	3B	HR	RBI	BB	SO
vs. Left	.148	.148	.148	27	4	0	0	0	1	0	6
vs. Right	.235	.268	.279	68	16	3	0	0	2	3	7
at Home	.261	.292	.304	46	12	2	0	0	3	2	4
on Road	.163	.180	.184	49	8	1	0	0	0	1	9
Runners On Base	.214	.233	.262	42	9	2	0	0	3	1	5
Second Half	.159	.178	.182	44	7	1	0	0	2	1	9

10-YEAR TOTALS (1984–1993)

BA	OBA	SA	AB	H	2B	3B	HR	RBI	BB	SO
.253	.292	.301	1350	342	33	10	4	105	73	144
.245	.280	.311	2648	649	101	20	11	231	130	265
.236	.273	.283	1929	456	57	10	4	154	100	195
.259	.294	.331	2069	535	77	20	11	182	103	214
.269	.298	.334	1615	435	45	19	7	328	75	149
.240	.275	.294	2116	507	65	15	7	161	103	224

KELLY GRUBER — BR/TR — age 32 — CAL 3B17, OF1, DH1

1993	BA	OBA	SA	AB	H	2B	3B	HR	RBI	BB	SO
vs. Left	.304	.304	.478	23	7	1	0	1	5	0	4
vs. Right	.262	.311	.452	42	11	2	0	2	4	2	7
at Home	.158	.273	.316	19	3	0	0	1	2	2	3
on Road	.326	.326	.522	46	15	3	0	2	7	0	8
Runners On Base	.296	.345	.444	27	8	1	0	1	7	2	6
Second Half	.000	.000	.000	0	0	0	0	0	0	0	0

10-YEAR TOTALS (1984–1993)

BA	OBA	SA	AB	H	2B	3B	HR	RBI	BB	SO
.266	.308	.443	987	263	50	11	34	135	63	163
.256	.306	.427	2172	555	98	13	83	308	134	341
.263	.309	.440	1558	409	63	15	61	226	94	259
.255	.305	.425	1601	409	85	9	56	217	103	245
.281	.327	.460	1383	389	69	14	50	376	97	201
.239	.284	.391	1614	386	66	13	51	212	91	253

CHRIS GWYNN — BL/TL — age 30 — KC OF83, DH5, 1B1

1993	BA	OBA	SA	AB	H	2B	3B	HR	RBI	BB	SO
vs. Left	.176	.176	.235	17	3	1	0	0	2	0	2
vs. Right	.307	.364	.396	270	83	13	4	1	23	24	32
at Home	.333	.385	.447	132	44	9	3	0	15	11	15
on Road	.271	.327	.335	155	42	5	1	1	10	13	19
Runners On Base	.270	.350	.320	122	33	4	1	0	24	16	17
Second Half	.282	.361	.359	131	37	4	3	0	3	16	19

7-YEAR TOTALS (1987–1993)

BA	OBA	SA	AB	H	2B	3B	HR	RBI	BB	SO
.181	.213	.278	72	13	2	1	1	8	3	16
.286	.326	.396	690	197	27	8	11	77	45	97
.294	.331	.391	330	97	13	5	3	31	19	45
.262	.305	.380	432	113	16	4	9	54	29	68
.266	.322	.361	327	87	9	2	6	79	31	53
.261	.306	.369	352	92	9	4	7	33	24	56

CHIP HALE — BL/TR — age 30 — MIN 2B21, 3B19, DH19, 1B1, SS1

1993	BA	OBA	SA	AB	H	2B	3B	HR	RBI	BB	SO
vs. Left	.143	.333	.143	7	1	0	0	0	1	1	2
vs. Right	.341	.411	.436	179	61	6	1	3	26	17	15
at Home	.353	.466	.447	85	30	3	1	1	13	15	8
on Road	.317	.352	.406	101	32	3	0	2	14	3	9
Runners On Base	.333	.424	.429	84	28	3	1	1	25	11	9
Second Half	.333	.427	.407	123	41	3	0	2	19	15	12

3-YEAR TOTALS (1989–1993)

BA	OBA	SA	AB	H	2B	3B	HR	RBI	BB	SO
.111	.200	.167	18	2	1	0	0	1	1	4
.312	.366	.392	237	74	8	1	3	32	18	20
.303	.390	.378	119	36	4	1	1	17	16	12
.294	.319	.375	136	40	5	0	2	16	3	12
.304	.371	.384	112	34	4	1	1	31	12	11
.286	.350	.349	192	55	6	0	2	25	16	19

DAVE HANSEN — BL/TR — age 26 — LA 3B18

1993	BA	OBA	SA	AB	H	2B	3B	HR	RBI	BB	SO
vs. Left	.000	.000	.000	2	0	0	0	0	0	0	1
vs. Right	.369	.472	.515	103	38	3	0	4	30	21	12
at Home	.375	.492	.500	48	18	0	0	2	13	11	3
on Road	.351	.441	.509	57	20	3	0	2	17	10	10
Runners On Base	.492	.569	.695	59	29	3	0	3	29	12	9
Second Half	.375	.480	.525	80	30	3	0	3	22	17	9

4-YEAR TOTALS (1990–1993)

BA	OBA	SA	AB	H	2B	3B	HR	RBI	BB	SO
.182	.233	.236	55	10	3	0	0	1	4	12
.258	.335	.363	454	117	15	0	11	57	53	65
.261	.336	.318	264	69	6	0	3	25	29	34
.237	.313	.384	245	58	12	0	8	33	28	43
.268	.346	.380	213	57	9	0	5	52	27	33
.266	.332	.350	357	95	12	0	6	41	36	58

DONALD HARRIS — BR/TR — age 27 — TEX OF38, DH3

1993	BA	OBA	SA	AB	H	2B	3B	HR	RBI	BB	SO
vs. Left	.225	.295	.225	40	9	0	0	0	4	3	7
vs. Right	.167	.205	.306	36	6	2	0	1	4	2	11
at Home	.159	.224	.250	44	7	1	0	1	4	3	9
on Road	.250	.294	.281	32	8	1	0	0	4	2	9
Runners On Base	.233	.273	.300	30	7	2	0	0	7	2	9
Second Half	.197	.253	.263	76	15	2	0	1	8	5	18

3-YEAR TOTALS (1991–1993)

BA	OBA	SA	AB	H	2B	3B	HR	RBI	BB	SO
.246	.303	.262	61	15	1	0	0	5	4	18
.161	.186	.304	56	9	2	0	2	6	2	18
.125	.169	.181	72	9	1	0	1	5	3	23
.333	.375	.444	45	15	2	0	1	6	3	13
.212	.250	.308	52	11	2	0	1	10	3	18
.205	.248	.282	117	24	3	0	2	11	6	36

LENNY HARRIS — BL/TR — age 30 — LA 2B35, 3B17, SS3, OF2

1993	BA	OBA	SA	AB	H	2B	3B	HR	RBI	BB	SO
vs. Left	.333	.333	.400	15	5	1	0	0	1	0	1
vs. Right	.228	.300	.317	145	33	5	1	2	10	15	14
at Home	.284	.314	.343	67	19	4	0	0	3	3	7
on Road	.204	.295	.312	93	19	2	1	2	8	12	8
Runners On Base	.288	.364	.339	59	17	1	1	0	9	7	6
Second Half	.226	.293	.333	84	19	3	0	2	6	8	7

6-YEAR TOTALS (1988–1993)

BA	OBA	SA	AB	H	2B	3B	HR	RBI	BB	SO
.223	.285	.255	251	56	3	1	1	19	16	29
.284	.335	.349	1494	425	57	6	9	123	114	110
.274	.321	.322	855	234	29	3	2	62	57	68
.278	.334	.348	890	247	31	4	8	80	73	71
.287	.336	.358	698	200	24	4	6	138	51	60
.269	.324	.332	973	262	36	2	7	84	74	72

BILL HASELMAN — BR/TR — age 28 — SEA C49, DH4, OF2

1993	BA	OBA	SA	AB	H	2B	3B	HR	RBI	BB	SO
vs. Left	.280	.302	.420	50	14	4	0	1	8	2	3
vs. Right	.241	.323	.425	87	21	4	0	4	8	10	16
at Home	.254	.333	.444	63	16	3	0	3	10	8	11
on Road	.257	.300	.405	74	19	5	0	2	6	4	8
Runners On Base	.228	.281	.333	57	13	4	0	1	12	5	9
Second Half	.258	.290	.364	66	17	4	0	1	5	3	6

3-YEAR TOTALS (1990–1993)

BA	OBA	SA	AB	H	2B	3B	HR	RBI	BB	SO
.284	.310	.388	67	19	4	0	1	11	3	6
.225	.298	.382	102	23	4	0	4	8	10	25
.237	.303	.387	80	19	3	0	3	11	8	16
.258	.302	.382	89	23	5	0	2	8	5	15
.214	.269	.300	70	15	3	0	1	15	6	14
.245	.275	.316	98	24	4	0	1	8	4	18

SCOTT HEMOND — BR/TR — age 29 — OAK C75, OF6, DH3, 1B1, 2B1

1993	BA	OBA	SA	AB	H	2B	3B	HR	RBI	BB	SO
vs. Left	.299	.409	.468	77	23	7	0	2	7	15	25
vs. Right	.232	.384	.384	138	32	9	0	4	19	17	30
at Home	.247	.365	.392	97	24	5	0	3	9	18	23
on Road	.263	.343	.432	118	31	11	0	3	17	14	32
Runners On Base	.261	.365	.489	88	23	8	0	4	24	15	22
Second Half	.276	.377	.466	163	45	13	0	6	23	26	37

5-YEAR TOTALS (1989–1993)

BA	OBA	SA	AB	H	2B	3B	HR	RBI	BB	SO
.270	.363	.391	115	31	8	0	2	9	18	37
.227	.306	.352	176	40	10	0	4	20	19	43
.238	.333	.354	130	31	6	0	3	12	19	36
.248	.326	.379	161	40	12	0	3	17	18	44
.250	.333	.417	120	30	8	0	4	27	16	33
.261	.346	.415	207	54	14	0	6	25	27	54

CARLOS HERNANDEZ — BR/TR — age 27 — LA C43

1993	BA	OBA	SA	AB	H	2B	3B	HR	RBI	BB	SO
vs. Left	.267	.290	.400	30	8	1	0	1	1	1	3
vs. Right	.246	.257	.348	69	17	4	0	1	6	1	8
at Home	.205	.205	.333	39	8	2	0	1	2	0	4
on Road	.283	.306	.383	60	17	3	0	1	5	2	7
Runners On Base	.244	.262	.268	41	10	1	0	0	5	1	5
Second Half	.262	.273	.354	65	17	3	1	1	6	1	5

4-YEAR TOTALS (1990–1993)

BA	OBA	SA	AB	H	2B	3B	HR	RBI	BB	SO
.285	.325	.399	158	45	6	0	4	12	8	14
.216	.253	.270	148	32	5	0	1	14	5	25
.241	.300	.324	145	35	6	0	2	11	10	17
.261	.281	.348	161	42	5	0	3	15	3	22
.252	.296	.317	123	31	2	0	2	23	5	11
.243	.279	.346	185	45	7	0	4	20	8	26

CESAR HERNANDEZ — BR/TR — age 28 — CIN OF23

2-YEAR TOTALS (1992–1993)

1993	BA	OBA	SA	AB	H	2B	3B	HR	RBI	BB	SO		BA	OBA	SA	AB	H	2B	3B	HR	RBI	BB	SO
vs. Left	.000	.091	.000	10	0	0	0	0	0	1	4		.271	.286	.354	48	13	4	0	0	2	1	10
vs. Right	.143	.143	.143	14	2	0	0	0	1	0	4		.111	.111	.111	27	3	0	0	0	3	0	8
at Home	.000	.000	.000	5	0	0	0	0	0	0	2		.258	.258	.323	31	8	2	0	0	2	0	5
on Road	.105	.150	.105	19	2	0	0	0	1	1	6		.182	.200	.227	44	8	2	0	0	3	1	13
Runners On Base	.000	.167	.000	5	0	0	0	0	1	1	1		.194	.219	.226	31	6	1	0	0	5	1	9
Second Half	.000	.000	.000	0	0	0	0	0	0	0	0		.275	.275	.353	51	14	4	0	0	4	0	10

GLENALLEN HILL — BR/TR — age 29 — CLE/CHN OF60, DH18

5-YEAR TOTALS (1989–1993)

1993	BA	OBA	SA	AB	H	2B	3B	HR	RBI	BB	SO		BA	OBA	SA	AB	H	2B	3B	HR	RBI	BB	SO
vs. Left	.275	.317	.562	153	42	6	1	12	33	11	36		.259	.314	.491	528	137	25	5	29	80	42	111
vs. Right	.250	.293	.426	108	27	8	1	3	14	6	35		.241	.287	.406	635	153	24	3	25	80	39	161
at Home	.229	.279	.458	96	22	5	1	5	20	6	27		.254	.305	.440	543	138	28	2	23	74	37	113
on Road	.285	.324	.533	165	47	9	1	10	27	11	44		.245	.294	.448	620	152	21	6	31	86	44	159
Runners On Base	.276	.314	.488	127	35	4	1	7	39	9	30		.262	.314	.426	516	135	19	3	20	126	43	113
Second Half	.285	.337	.576	151	43	8	0	12	33	12	44		.255	.309	.464	666	170	25	3	36	100	52	163

SAM HORN — BL/TL — age 31 — CLE DH11

7-YEAR TOTALS (1987–1993)

1993	BA	OBA	SA	AB	H	2B	3B	HR	RBI	BB	SO		BA	OBA	SA	AB	H	2B	3B	HR	RBI	BB	SO
vs. Left	.000	.200	.000	4	0	0	0	0	0	1	1		.152	.247	.329	79	12	2	0	4	10	8	35
vs. Right	.517	.516	.966	29	15	1	0	4	8	0	4		.249	.336	.483	952	237	47	1	58	169	123	282
at Home	.563	.611	1.000	16	9	1	0	2	3	1	3		.251	.351	.481	522	131	22	1	32	88	77	158
on Road	.353	.333	.706	17	6	0	0	2	5	0	2		.232	.306	.462	509	118	27	0	30	91	54	159
Runners On Base	.412	.389	.588	17	7	0	0	1	5	0	3		.246	.344	.477	491	121	26	0	29	146	72	141
Second Half	.455	.472	.848	33	15	1	0	4	8	1	5		.254	.332	.520	564	143	24	0	42	110	64	164

STEVE HOSEY — BR/TR — age 25 — SF OF1

2-YEAR TOTALS (1992–1993)

1993	BA	OBA	SA	AB	H	2B	3B	HR	RBI	BB	SO		BA	OBA	SA	AB	H	2B	3B	HR	RBI	BB	SO
vs. Left	.500	.667	1.000	2	1	1	0	0	1	1	1		.290	.303	.419	31	9	1	0	1	4	1	9
vs. Right	.000	.000	.000	0	0	0	0	0	0	0	0		.222	.214	.259	27	6	1	0	0	3	0	7
at Home	.500	.667	1.000	2	1	1	0	0	1	1	1		.368	.400	.632	19	7	2	0	1	3	1	5
on Road	.000	.000	.000	0	0	0	0	0	0	0	0		.205	.195	.205	39	8	0	0	0	4	0	11
Runners On Base	.500	.500	1.000	2	1	1	0	0	1	0	1		.240	.222	.320	25	6	2	0	0	6	0	7
Second Half	.500	.667	1.000	2	1	1	0	0	1	1	1		.259	.262	.345	58	15	2	0	1	7	1	16

WAYNE HOUSIE — BB/TR — age 29 — NYN OF2

2-YEAR TOTALS (1991–1993)

1993	BA	OBA	SA	AB	H	2B	3B	HR	RBI	BB	SO		BA	OBA	SA	AB	H	2B	3B	HR	RBI	BB	SO
vs. Left	.250	.250	.250	4	1	0	0	0	1	0	0		.333	.333	.500	6	2	1	0	0	1	0	0
vs. Right	.167	.231	.250	12	2	1	0	0	0	1	1		.167	.250	.222	18	3	1	0	0	0	2	4
at Home	.125	.222	.125	8	1	0	0	0	0	1	1		.143	.250	.214	14	2	1	0	0	0	2	3
on Road	.250	.250	.375	8	2	1	0	0	1	0	0		.300	.300	.400	10	3	1	0	0	1	0	1
Runners On Base	.167	.286	.167	6	1	0	0	0	1	1	1		.300	.364	.400	10	3	1	0	0	1	1	2
Second Half	.000	.000	.000	0	0	0	0	0	0	0	0		.250	.333	.375	8	2	1	0	0	0	1	3

CHRIS HOWARD — BR/TR — age 28 — SEA C4

2-YEAR TOTALS (1991–1993)

1993	BA	OBA	SA	AB	H	2B	3B	HR	RBI	BB	SO		BA	OBA	SA	AB	H	2B	3B	HR	RBI	BB	SO
vs. Left	.000	.000	.000	0	0	0	0	0	0	0	0		.200	.333	.400	5	1	1	0	0	0	1	1
vs. Right	.000	.000	.000	1	0	0	0	0	0	0	0		.000	.000	.000	2	0	0	0	0	0	0	1
at Home	.000	.000	.000	1	0	0	0	0	0	0	0		.000	.200	.000	4	0	0	0	0	0	1	1
on Road	.000	.000	.000	0	0	0	0	0	0	0	0		.333	.333	.667	3	1	1	0	0	0	0	1
Runners On Base	.000	.000	.000	1	0	0	0	0	0	0	0		.000	.000	.000	3	0	0	0	0	0	0	2
Second Half	.000	.000	.000	1	0	0	0	0	0	0	0		.143	.250	.286	7	1	1	0	0	0	1	2

DAVID HOWARD — BB/TR — age 27 — KC 2B7, SS3, 3B2, OF1

3-YEAR TOTALS (1991–1993)

1993	BA	OBA	SA	AB	H	2B	3B	HR	RBI	BB	SO		BA	OBA	SA	AB	H	2B	3B	HR	RBI	BB	SO
vs. Left	.000	.000	.000	0	0	0	0	0	0	0	0		.217	.255	.276	152	33	4	1	1	12	8	27
vs. Right	.333	.370	.417	24	8	0	1	0	2	2	5		.229	.283	.278	327	75	9	2	1	25	25	66
at Home	.385	.400	.538	13	5	0	1	0	2	1	2		.231	.289	.283	251	58	6	2	1	23	22	51
on Road	.273	.333	.273	11	3	0	0	0	0	1	3		.219	.257	.272	228	50	7	1	1	14	11	42
Runners On Base	.143	.222	.143	7	1	0	0	0	2	1	3		.236	.277	.292	195	46	5	0	2	37	13	32
Second Half	.000	.500	.000	1	0	0	0	0	0	1	1		.242	.286	.300	393	95	13	2	2	31	25	75

THOMAS HOWARD — BB/TR — age 30 — CLE/CIN OF84, DH7

4-YEAR TOTALS (1990–1993)

1993	BA	OBA	SA	AB	H	2B	3B	HR	RBI	BB	SO		BA	OBA	SA	AB	H	2B	3B	HR	RBI	BB	SO
vs. Left	.156	.213	.193	109	17	1	0	1	8	9	34		.226	.275	.296	257	58	4	1	4	21	19	66
vs. Right	.305	.350	.486	210	64	14	3	6	28	15	29		.274	.315	.382	748	205	40	7	9	69	46	125
at Home	.252	.321	.413	143	36	6	1	5	17	16	23		.263	.313	.372	486	128	15	4	10	49	36	89
on Road	.256	.285	.364	176	45	9	2	2	19	8	40		.260	.297	.349	519	135	29	4	3	41	29	102
Runners On Base	.224	.278	.336	134	30	4	1	3	32	12	28		.267	.315	.361	404	108	14	3	6	83	32	86
Second Half	.266	.324	.431	188	50	10	3	5	18	17	35		.259	.308	.378	564	146	27	5	10	51	41	120

DANN HOWITT — BL/TR — age 30 — SEA OF29, DH2

5-YEAR TOTALS (1989–1993)

1993	BA	OBA	SA	AB	H	2B	3B	HR	RBI	BB	SO		BA	OBA	SA	AB	H	2B	3B	HR	RBI	BB	SO
vs. Left	.000	.000	.000	3	0	0	0	0	0	0	2		.000	.059	.000	16	0	0	0	0	0	1	7
vs. Right	.219	.260	.370	73	16	3	1	2	8	4	16		.198	.247	.335	212	42	8	3	5	22	15	46
at Home	.094	.094	.188	32	3	0	0	1	5	0	6		.135	.168	.216	111	15	3	0	2	14	5	21
on Road	.295	.354	.477	44	13	3	1	1	3	4	12		.231	.295	.402	117	27	5	3	3	8	11	32
Runners On Base	.212	.235	.424	33	7	1	0	2	8	1	4		.165	.183	.320	97	16	2	2	3	20	3	20
Second Half	.211	.250	.355	76	16	3	1	2	8	4	18		.191	.232	.330	188	36	8	3	4	20	11	50

MIKE HUFF — BR/TR — age 31 — CHA OF43

4-YEAR TOTALS (1989–1993)

1993	BA	OBA	SA	AB	H	2B	3B	HR	RBI	BB	SO		BA	OBA	SA	AB	H	2B	3B	HR	RBI	BB	SO
vs. Left	.188	.278	.438	16	3	1	0	1	1	2	5		.225	.312	.340	244	55	11	1	5	19	28	44
vs. Right	.179	.342	.214	28	5	1	0	0	5	7	10		.235	.356	.284	183	43	7	1	0	22	31	49
at Home	.182	.310	.227	22	4	1	0	0	5	4	5		.226	.328	.307	212	48	10	2	1	20	27	46
on Road	.182	.333	.364	22	4	1	0	1	1	5	10		.233	.335	.326	215	50	8	0	4	21	32	47
Runners On Base	.364	.500	.455	11	4	1	0	0	5	5	2		.258	.365	.313	163	42	7	1	0	36	28	33
Second Half	.136	.296	.136	22	3	0	0	0	0	4	9		.212	.309	.291	189	40	7	1	2	19	22	44

KEITH HUGHES — BL/TL — age 31 — CIN OF2

4-YEAR TOTALS (1987–1993)

1993	BA	OBA	SA	AB	H	2B	3B	HR	RBI	BB	SO		BA	OBA	SA	AB	H	2B	3B	HR	RBI	BB	SO
vs. Left	.000	.000	.000	0	0	0	0	0	0	0	0		.263	.318	.368	19	5	1	0	2	2	2	5
vs. Right	.000	.000	.000	4	0	0	0	0	0	0	0		.198	.283	.275	182	36	6	1	2	22	21	39
at Home	.000	.000	.000	0	0	0	0	0	0	0	0		.194	.292	.286	98	19	4	1	1	11	14	20
on Road	.000	.000	.000	4	0	0	0	0	0	0	0		.214	.281	.282	103	22	2	1	1	13	9	24
Runners On Base	.000	.000	.000	1	0	0	0	0	0	0	0		.250	.313	.352	88	22	4	1	1	23	8	20
Second Half	.000	.000	.000	0	0	0	0	0	0	0	0		.218	.288	.257	101	22	2	1	0	8	9	20

MIKE HUMPHREYS — BR/TR — age 27 — NYA OF21, DH3

3-YEAR TOTALS (1991–1993)

1993	BA	OBA	SA	AB	H	2B	3B	HR	RBI	BB	SO		BA	OBA	SA	AB	H	2B	3B	HR	RBI	BB	SO
vs. Left	.115	.226	.269	26	3	2	1	0	2	4	10		.154	.286	.231	52	8	2	1	0	5	10	15
vs. Right	.333	.333	.667	9	3	0	0	1	4	0	1		.212	.278	.303	33	7	0	0	1	4	3	4
at Home	.095	.200	.238	21	2	0	0	1	5	3	8		.160	.259	.220	50	8	0	0	1	8	7	11
on Road	.286	.333	.571	14	4	2	1	0	1	1	3		.200	.317	.314	35	7	2	1	0	1	6	8
Runners On Base	.250	.231	.667	12	3	0	1	1	6	0	5		.263	.356	.395	38	10	0	1	1	9	6	8
Second Half	.143	.250	.143	7	1	0	0	0	0	1	1		.180	.317	.180	50	9	0	0	0	3	10	8

BRIAN HUNTER — BR/TL — age 26 — ATL 1B29, OF2

3-YEAR TOTALS (1991–1993)

1993	BA	OBA	SA	AB	H	2B	3B	HR	RBI	BB	SO		BA	OBA	SA	AB	H	2B	3B	HR	RBI	BB	SO
vs. Left	.161	.183	.250	56	9	3	1	0	6	2	11		.253	.295	.479	332	84	17	2	18	60	24	51
vs. Right	.083	.080	.083	24	2	0	0	0	2	0	4		.202	.249	.370	257	52	15	2	8	39	16	62
at Home	.152	.143	.196	46	7	2	0	0	6	0	9		.259	.315	.483	294	76	14	2	16	62	27	55
on Road	.118	.167	.206	34	4	1	1	0	2	2	6		.203	.233	.380	295	60	18	2	10	37	13	58
Runners On Base	.121	.135	.182	33	4	2	0	0	8	1	6		.251	.287	.451	255	64	20	2	9	82	17	46
Second Half	.172	.167	.207	29	5	1	0	0	2	0	4		.234	.284	.417	372	87	21	1	15	60	27	70

JEFF HUSON — BL/TR — age 30 — TEX SS12, 2B5, 3B2

6-YEAR TOTALS (1988–1993)

1993	BA	OBA	SA	AB	H	2B	3B	HR	RBI	BB	SO		BA	OBA	SA	AB	H	2B	3B	HR	RBI	BB	SO
vs. Left	.222	.222	.556	9	2	1	1	0	1	0	2		.211	.284	.286	133	28	5	1	1	9	13	28
vs. Right	.111	.111	.111	36	4	0	0	0	1	0	8		.236	.317	.303	1010	238	37	8	5	76	123	120
at Home	.050	.050	.050	20	1	0	0	0	0	0	4		.215	.299	.268	568	122	19	4	1	40	67	82
on Road	.200	.200	.320	25	5	1	1	0	2	0	6		.250	.328	.334	575	144	23	5	5	45	69	66
Runners On Base	.143	.143	.190	21	3	1	0	0	2	0	5		.227	.305	.303	458	104	14	6	3	82	54	64
Second Half	.083	.083	.083	24	2	0	0	0	0	0	4		.215	.296	.270	599	129	17	2	4	48	70	73

DARRIN JACKSON — BR/TR — age 32 — TOR/NYN OF72

8-YEAR TOTALS (1985–1993)

1993	BA	OBA	SA	AB	H	2B	3B	HR	RBI	BB	SO		BA	OBA	SA	AB	H	2B	3B	HR	RBI	BB	SO
vs. Left	.250	.273	.357	84	21	3	0	2	8	3	20		.252	.292	.435	703	177	30	6	29	87	41	117
vs. Right	.190	.220	.291	179	34	6	0	4	18	7	55		.241	.276	.368	993	239	36	3	28	107	45	219
at Home	.230	.255	.363	135	31	6	0	4	14	5	35		.263	.298	.432	817	215	32	5	32	103	38	150
on Road	.188	.218	.258	128	24	3	0	2	12	5	40		.229	.268	.362	879	201	34	4	25	91	48	186
Runners On Base	.204	.242	.292	113	23	7	0	1	21	6	32		.239	.290	.360	678	162	28	3	16	153	48	123
Second Half	.233	.244	.256	43	10	1	0	0	4	1	10		.252	.288	.408	873	220	34	3	32	106	42	164

BO JACKSON — BR/TR — age 32 — CHA OF47, DH36

7-YEAR TOTALS (1986–1993)

1993	BA	OBA	SA	AB	H	2B	3B	HR	RBI	BB	SO		BA	OBA	SA	AB	H	2B	3B	HR	RBI	BB	SO
vs. Left	.203	.264	.414	133	27	1	0	9	22	11	50		.247	.318	.477	687	170	19	5	43	114	68	255
vs. Right	.258	.311	.450	151	39	8	0	7	23	12	56		.247	.301	.468	1505	372	60	9	85	258	112	514
at Home	.228	.277	.448	145	33	5	0	9	25	10	49		.271	.328	.507	1077	292	56	9	60	198	90	335
on Road	.237	.301	.417	139	33	4	0	7	20	13	57		.224	.285	.437	1115	250	23	5	68	174	90	434
Runners On Base	.269	.324	.492	130	35	2	0	9	38	11	46		.246	.314	.468	1006	247	31	8	59	303	100	356
Second Half	.229	.268	.447	179	41	6	0	11	35	10	63		.224	.284	.450	1139	255	37	8	68	205	93	412

DION JAMES — BL/TL — age 32 — NYA OF103, 1B1, DH1

8-YEAR TOTALS (1984–1993)

1993	BA	OBA	SA	AB	H	2B	3B	HR	RBI	BB	SO		BA	OBA	SA	AB	H	2B	3B	HR	RBI	BB	SO
vs. Left	.231	.310	.269	26	6	1	0	0	4	3	2		.252	.363	.348	290	73	18	2	2	29	48	43
vs. Right	.341	.397	.483	317	108	20	2	7	32	28	29		.296	.368	.405	2178	644	118	18	28	210	247	245
at Home	.359	.394	.519	181	65	12	1	5	16	11	14		.297	.375	.415	1180	351	68	13	15	119	145	131
on Road	.302	.386	.407	162	49	9	1	2	20	20	17		.284	.359	.383	1288	366	68	7	15	120	150	157
Runners On Base	.335	.402	.413	155	52	8	2	0	29	18	11		.308	.386	.412	1006	310	51	10	11	220	132	114
Second Half	.354	.412	.471	206	73	12	0	4	16	19	15		.309	.376	.421	1290	398	66	11	19	134	138	130

CHRIS JAMES — BR/TR — age 32 — HOU/TEX OF41

8-YEAR TOTALS (1986–1993)

1993	BA	OBA	SA	AB	H	2B	3B	HR	RBI	BB	SO		BA	OBA	SA	AB	H	2B	3B	HR	RBI	BB	SO
vs. Left	.246	.311	.551	118	29	10	1	8	19	12	27		.265	.311	.449	1023	271	52	8	40	148	70	157
vs. Right	.357	.449	.452	42	15	1	0	1	7	6	13		.259	.300	.386	1802	467	81	12	41	211	96	281
at Home	.277	.333	.662	65	18	5	1	6	14	5	15		.274	.317	.433	1349	369	67	11	42	194	82	190
on Road	.274	.358	.432	95	26	6	0	3	12	13	25		.250	.292	.396	1476	369	66	9	39	165	84	248
Runners On Base	.319	.402	.551	69	22	5	1	3	20	10	19		.258	.302	.389	1297	335	56	9	32	310	84	215
Second Half	.289	.362	.542	83	24	4	1	5	16	10	22		.270	.310	.427	1565	422	76	15	47	203	90	230

STAN JAVIER — BB/TR — age 29 — CAL OF64, 1B12, 2B2, DH1

1993	BA	OBA	SA	AB	H	2B	3B	HR	RBI	BB	SO
vs. Left	.271	.357	.376	85	23	4	1	1	8	12	10
vs. Right	.303	.365	.421	152	46	6	3	2	20	15	23
at Home	.318	.396	.375	88	28	3	1	0	10	12	15
on Road	.275	.341	.423	149	41	7	3	3	18	15	18
Runners On Base	.286	.330	.439	98	28	4	4	1	26	8	19
Second Half	.333	.401	.469	147	49	7	2	3	21	17	21

9-YEAR TOTALS (1984–1993)

BA	OBA	SA	AB	H	2B	3B	HR	RBI	BB	SO
.237	.307	.311	758	180	25	8	5	53	74	120
.259	.334	.338	1277	331	51	13	8	122	144	222
.258	.340	.319	945	244	33	6	4	82	118	153
.245	.309	.337	1090	267	43	15	9	93	100	189
.253	.325	.331	853	216	32	11	4	166	94	139
.252	.327	.316	1008	254	35	6	6	82	111	172

DOUG JENNINGS — BL/TL — age 30 — CHN 1B10

1993	BA	OBA	SA	AB	H	2B	3B	HR	RBI	BB	SO
vs. Left	.250	.250	.250	4	1	0	0	0	1	0	0
vs. Right	.250	.321	.479	48	12	3	1	2	7	3	10
at Home	.269	.321	.577	26	7	2	0	2	5	2	6
on Road	.231	.310	.346	26	6	1	1	0	3	1	4
Runners On Base	.313	.450	.688	16	5	1	1	1	7	3	3
Second Half	.314	.400	.514	35	11	2	1	1	5	3	6

5-YEAR TOTALS (1988–1993)

BA	OBA	SA	AB	H	2B	3B	HR	RBI	BB	SO
.222	.222	.333	18	4	0	1	0	1	0	2
.201	.306	.316	304	61	16	2	5	36	43	88
.175	.290	.271	166	29	7	0	3	14	26	50
.231	.315	.365	156	36	9	3	2	23	17	40
.182	.296	.295	132	24	7	1	2	34	21	40
.220	.304	.330	200	44	9	2	3	21	21	48

CHRIS JONES — BR/TR — age 29 — COL OF70

1993	BA	OBA	SA	AB	H	2B	3B	HR	RBI	BB	SO
vs. Left	.299	.313	.474	97	29	7	2	2	13	2	22
vs. Right	.250	.298	.429	112	28	4	2	4	18	8	26
at Home	.260	.304	.423	104	27	5	3	2	15	7	18
on Road	.286	.306	.476	105	30	6	1	4	16	3	30
Runners On Base	.275	.299	.500	102	28	5	0	6	31	4	20
Second Half	.268	.304	.416	149	40	8	4	2	20	8	34

3-YEAR TOTALS (1991–1993)

BA	OBA	SA	AB	H	2B	3B	HR	RBI	BB	SO
.265	.293	.392	189	50	9	3	3	20	8	56
.262	.304	.442	172	45	5	4	6	21	11	44
.249	.301	.370	181	45	7	3	3	19	14	47
.278	.296	.461	180	50	7	4	6	22	5	53
.259	.287	.443	158	41	6	1	7	39	7	34
.234	.259	.374	222	52	9	5	4	23	8	61

TIM JONES — BL/TR — age 32 — SL SS21, 2B7

1993	BA	OBA	SA	AB	H	2B	3B	HR	RBI	BB	SO
vs. Left	.143	.143	.143	7	1	0	0	0	0	0	1
vs. Right	.278	.391	.389	54	15	6	0	0	1	9	7
at Home	.400	.471	.600	15	6	3	0	0	1	2	4
on Road	.217	.333	.283	46	10	3	0	0	0	7	4
Runners On Base	.263	.300	.368	19	5	2	0	0	1	1	1
Second Half	.262	.366	.361	61	16	6	0	0	1	9	8

6-YEAR TOTALS (1988–1993)

BA	OBA	SA	AB	H	2B	3B	HR	RBI	BB	SO
.209	.272	.264	91	19	5	0	0	9	8	15
.239	.307	.302	394	94	20	1	1	19	37	66
.216	.278	.284	194	42	10	0	1	11	17	33
.244	.315	.302	291	71	15	1	0	17	28	48
.244	.309	.305	197	48	10	1	0	27	19	29
.259	.325	.331	293	76	16	1	1	17	27	51

BRIAN JORDAN — BR/TR — age 27 — SL OF65

1993	BA	OBA	SA	AB	H	2B	3B	HR	RBI	BB	SO
vs. Left	.365	.412	.825	63	23	4	2	7	18	5	7
vs. Right	.287	.328	.431	160	46	6	4	3	26	7	28
at Home	.299	.342	.504	137	41	6	5	4	27	7	20
on Road	.326	.366	.605	86	28	4	1	6	17	5	15
Runners On Base	.318	.372	.533	107	34	4	2	5	39	8	16
Second Half	.339	.377	.619	168	57	9	4	10	39	8	29

2-YEAR TOTALS (1992–1993)

BA	OBA	SA	AB	H	2B	3B	HR	RBI	BB	SO
.291	.348	.630	127	37	6	2	11	28	11	21
.249	.286	.391	289	72	13	8	4	38	11	62
.276	.323	.493	217	60	12	7	7	43	12	39
.246	.284	.432	199	49	7	3	8	23	10	44
.268	.322	.464	194	52	6	4	8	59	13	39
.315	.355	.555	200	63	10	4	10	39	10	35

RICKY JORDAN — BR/TR — age 29 — PHI 1B33

1993	BA	OBA	SA	AB	H	2B	3B	HR	RBI	BB	SO
vs. Left	.275	.329	.391	69	19	0	1	2	7	6	13
vs. Right	.300	.319	.444	90	27	4	0	3	11	2	19
at Home	.317	.352	.476	82	26	2	1	3	13	5	16
on Road	.260	.293	.364	77	20	2	0	2	5	3	16
Runners On Base	.293	.310	.402	82	24	3	0	2	15	3	14
Second Half	.304	.324	.431	102	31	2	1	3	14	4	18

6-YEAR TOTALS (1988–1993)

BA	OBA	SA	AB	H	2B	3B	HR	RBI	BB	SO
.314	.350	.477	727	228	48	4	21	105	43	85
.261	.282	.383	1129	295	54	4	25	158	27	180
.290	.310	.429	909	264	43	4	25	144	26	133
.273	.308	.411	947	259	59	4	21	119	44	132
.280	.311	.431	908	254	51	4	26	243	44	136
.295	.315	.440	1108	327	59	6	30	166	30	159

TERRY JORGENSEN — BR/TR — age 28 — MIN 3B45, 1B9, SS6

1993	BA	OBA	SA	AB	H	2B	3B	HR	RBI	BB	SO
vs. Left	.273	.342	.364	66	18	3	0	1	6	7	7
vs. Right	.186	.211	.233	86	16	4	0	0	6	3	14
at Home	.247	.293	.294	85	21	4	0	0	7	6	12
on Road	.194	.239	.284	67	13	3	0	1	5	4	9
Runners On Base	.257	.321	.343	70	18	0	0	1	12	7	8
Second Half	.239	.284	.318	88	21	4	0	1	8	6	11

3-YEAR TOTALS (1989–1993)

BA	OBA	SA	AB	H	2B	3B	HR	RBI	BB	SO
.268	.336	.339	112	30	5	0	1	9	11	15
.215	.250	.248	121	26	4	0	0	10	6	22
.264	.314	.312	125	33	6	0	0	9	10	21
.213	.267	.269	108	23	3	0	1	10	7	16
.256	.321	.316	117	30	4	0	1	19	12	17
.254	.308	.308	169	43	6	0	1	15	13	27

RYAN KLESKO — BL/TL — age 23 — ATL 1B3, OF2

1993	BA	OBA	SA	AB	H	2B	3B	HR	RBI	BB	SO
vs. Left	.000	.500	.000	1	0	0	0	0	0	1	1
vs. Right	.375	.444	.813	16	6	1	0	2	5	2	3
at Home	.500	.500	1.200	10	5	1	0	2	5	0	1
on Road	.143	.400	.143	7	1	0	0	0	0	3	3
Runners On Base	.500	.600	1.000	8	4	1	0	1	4	2	0
Second Half	.500	.571	1.167	6	3	1	0	1	4	1	1

2-YEAR TOTALS (1992–1993)

BA	OBA	SA	AB	H	2B	3B	HR	RBI	BB	SO
.000	.333	.000	2	0	0	0	0	0	1	2
.207	.281	.448	29	6	1	0	2	6	2	7
.250	.286	.600	20	5	1	0	2	6	0	5
.091	.286	.091	11	1	0	0	0	0	3	4
.211	.286	.421	19	4	1	0	1	5	2	4
.150	.227	.350	20	3	1	0	1	5	1	6

RANDY KNORR — BR/TR — age 26 — TOR C39

1993	BA	OBA	SA	AB	H	2B	3B	HR	RBI	BB	SO
vs. Left	.229	.308	.400	35	8	1	1	1	7	4	10
vs. Right	.258	.310	.455	66	17	2	1	3	13	5	19
at Home	.186	.222	.372	43	8	0	1	2	6	2	11
on Road	.293	.369	.483	58	17	3	1	2	14	7	18
Runners On Base	.314	.375	.627	51	16	2	1	3	19	5	14
Second Half	.333	.391	.540	63	21	3	2	2	15	6	16

3-YEAR TOTALS (1991–1993)

BA	OBA	SA	AB	H	2B	3B	HR	RBI	BB	SO
.256	.333	.465	43	11	1	1	2	9	5	11
.244	.298	.410	78	19	2	1	3	13	6	24
.200	.245	.360	50	10	0	1	2	7	3	13
.282	.354	.479	71	20	3	1	3	15	8	22
.328	.391	.603	58	19	3	2	3	20	6	16
.313	.374	.506	83	26	3	2	3	17	8	22

KEVIN KOSLOFSKI — BL/TR — age 28 — KC OF13

1993

	BA	OBA	SA	AB	H	2B	3B	HR	RBI	BB	SO
vs. Left	.250	.250	.250	4	1	0	0	0	0	0	2
vs. Right	.273	.407	.409	22	6	0	0	1	2	4	3
at Home	.313	.450	.313	16	5	0	0	0	1	3	1
on Road	.200	.273	.500	10	2	0	0	1	1	1	4
Runners On Base	.273	.333	.273	11	3	0	0	0	1	1	1
Second Half	.269	.387	.385	26	7	0	0	1	2	4	5

2-YEAR TOTALS (1992–1993)

	BA	OBA	SA	AB	H	2B	3B	HR	RBI	BB	SO
vs. Left	.389	.500	.389	18	7	0	0	0	1	4	5
vs. Right	.234	.301	.348	141	33	0	2	4	14	12	23
at Home	.214	.297	.265	98	21	0	1	1	9	10	18
on Road	.311	.373	.492	61	19	0	1	3	6	6	10
Runners On Base	.276	.325	.276	76	21	0	0	0	11	6	13
Second Half	.242	.320	.346	153	37	0	2	4	14	16	27

STEVE LAKE — BR/TR — age 37 — CHN C41

1993

	BA	OBA	SA	AB	H	2B	3B	HR	RBI	BB	SO
vs. Left	.192	.222	.359	78	15	4	0	3	6	3	10
vs. Right	.286	.302	.476	42	12	2	0	2	7	1	9
at Home	.163	.196	.265	49	8	2	0	1	4	2	8
on Road	.268	.288	.493	71	19	4	0	4	9	2	11
Runners On Base	.214	.254	.304	56	12	2	0	1	9	3	6
Second Half	.243	.274	.457	70	17	3	0	4	10	3	9

10-YEAR TOTALS (1984–1993)

	BA	OBA	SA	AB	H	2B	3B	HR	RBI	BB	SO
vs. Left	.250	.280	.345	585	146	22	2	10	56	24	73
vs. Right	.218	.250	.305	455	99	15	2	7	46	17	80
at Home	.239	.267	.330	473	113	18	2	7	43	17	65
on Road	.233	.267	.326	567	132	19	2	10	59	24	88
Runners On Base	.257	.300	.333	459	118	16	2	5	90	28	62
Second Half	.229	.263	.331	462	106	16	2	9	53	20	77

TIM LAKER — BR/TR — age 25 — MON C43

1993

	BA	OBA	SA	AB	H	2B	3B	HR	RBI	BB	SO
vs. Left	.227	.222	.250	44	10	1	0	0	6	0	7
vs. Right	.167	.222	.238	42	7	1	1	0	1	2	9
at Home	.204	.220	.224	49	10	1	0	0	4	1	9
on Road	.189	.225	.270	37	7	1	1	0	3	1	7
Runners On Base	.194	.211	.250	36	7	2	0	0	7	1	8
Second Half	.400	.455	.500	10	4	1	0	0	3	1	0

2-YEAR TOTALS (1992–1993)

	BA	OBA	SA	AB	H	2B	3B	HR	RBI	BB	SO
vs. Left	.230	.238	.262	61	14	2	0	0	7	1	11
vs. Right	.183	.227	.254	71	13	3	1	0	4	3	19
at Home	.216	.237	.257	74	16	3	0	0	6	2	15
on Road	.190	.226	.259	58	11	2	1	0	5	2	15
Runners On Base	.167	.193	.204	54	9	2	0	0	11	2	14
Second Half	.250	.288	.321	56	14	4	0	0	7	3	14

TOM LAMPKIN — BL/TR — age 30 — MIL C60, OF3, DH1

1993

	BA	OBA	SA	AB	H	2B	3B	HR	RBI	BB	SO
vs. Left	.114	.205	.257	35	4	2	0	1	5	4	6
vs. Right	.220	.299	.339	127	28	6	0	3	20	16	20
at Home	.178	.256	.260	73	13	3	0	1	7	8	13
on Road	.213	.298	.371	89	19	5	0	3	18	12	13
Runners On Base	.305	.400	.627	59	18	7	0	4	25	12	11
Second Half	.196	.273	.330	97	19	4	0	3	13	11	16

5-YEAR TOTALS (1988–1993)

	BA	OBA	SA	AB	H	2B	3B	HR	RBI	BB	SO
vs. Left	.152	.220	.261	46	7	2	0	1	7	4	10
vs. Right	.209	.290	.306	258	54	9	2	4	25	30	35
at Home	.219	.283	.318	151	33	5	2	2	13	13	23
on Road	.183	.277	.281	153	28	6	0	3	19	21	22
Runners On Base	.265	.362	.436	117	31	8	0	4	31	19	19
Second Half	.201	.290	.309	194	39	5	2	4	17	24	27

CED LANDRUM — BL/TR — age 31 — NYN OF3

1993

	BA	OBA	SA	AB	H	2B	3B	HR	RBI	BB	SO
vs. Left	.000	.000	.000	0	0	0	0	0	0	0	0
vs. Right	.263	.263	.316	19	5	1	0	0	1	0	5
at Home	.200	.200	.300	10	2	1	0	0	0	0	3
on Road	.333	.333	.333	9	3	0	0	0	1	0	2
Runners On Base	.333	.333	.333	6	2	0	0	0	1	0	2
Second Half	.263	.263	.316	19	5	1	0	0	1	0	5

2-YEAR TOTALS (1991–1993)

	BA	OBA	SA	AB	H	2B	3B	HR	RBI	BB	SO
vs. Left	.385	.467	.538	13	5	0	1	0	2	2	4
vs. Right	.217	.280	.250	92	20	3	0	0	5	8	19
at Home	.208	.276	.245	53	11	2	0	0	1	5	14
on Road	.269	.333	.327	52	14	1	1	0	6	5	9
Runners On Base	.310	.375	.379	29	9	2	0	0	7	3	6
Second Half	.244	.322	.308	78	19	3	1	0	5	9	19

GENE LARKIN — BB/TR — age 32 — MIN OF28, 1B18, DH3, 3B2

1993

	BA	OBA	SA	AB	H	2B	3B	HR	RBI	BB	SO
vs. Left	.263	.310	.316	38	10	2	0	0	3	2	1
vs. Right	.264	.372	.358	106	28	5	1	1	16	19	15
at Home	.235	.330	.333	81	19	3	1	1	13	12	7
on Road	.302	.392	.365	63	19	4	0	0	6	9	9
Runners On Base	.281	.383	.375	64	18	3	0	1	19	12	5
Second Half	.226	.306	.355	31	7	1	0	1	6	3	4

7-YEAR TOTALS (1987–1993)

	BA	OBA	SA	AB	H	2B	3B	HR	RBI	BB	SO
vs. Left	.293	.367	.400	685	201	48	5	5	80	74	68
vs. Right	.255	.340	.364	1636	417	83	7	27	187	194	209
at Home	.277	.357	.394	1169	324	68	6	19	151	139	120
on Road	.255	.339	.354	1152	294	63	6	13	116	129	157
Runners On Base	.260	.342	.365	1104	287	59	6	15	250	133	138
Second Half	.263	.345	.376	1136	299	61	8	17	119	135	122

MIKE LAVALLIERE — BL/TR — age 34 — PIT/CHA C38

1993

	BA	OBA	SA	AB	H	2B	3B	HR	RBI	BB	SO
vs. Left	.357	.357	.429	14	5	1	0	0	2	0	2
vs. Right	.239	.266	.250	88	21	1	0	0	6	4	12
at Home	.246	.279	.281	57	14	2	0	0	4	3	6
on Road	.267	.277	.267	45	12	0	0	0	4	1	8
Runners On Base	.255	.260	.255	47	12	0	0	0	8	1	8
Second Half	.230	.253	.243	74	17	1	0	0	5	3	12

10-YEAR TOTALS (1984–1993)

	BA	OBA	SA	AB	H	2B	3B	HR	RBI	BB	SO
vs. Left	.235	.323	.314	379	89	17	2	3	53	46	69
vs. Right	.275	.358	.344	1857	511	82	3	13	198	246	145
at Home	.281	.368	.348	1105	310	44	3	8	132	155	100
on Road	.256	.336	.330	1131	290	55	2	8	119	137	114
Runners On Base	.270	.376	.351	943	255	40	3	10	245	170	95
Second Half	.269	.345	.342	1315	354	59	2	11	140	151	138

SCOTT LEIUS — BR/TR — age 29 — MIN SS9

1993

	BA	OBA	SA	AB	H	2B	3B	HR	RBI	BB	SO
vs. Left	.000	.000	.000	1	0	0	0	0	0	0	0
vs. Right	.176	.238	.176	17	3	0	0	0	2	2	4
at Home	.333	.385	.333	9	3	0	0	0	2	2	1
on Road	.000	.000	.000	9	0	0	0	0	0	0	3
Runners On Base	.143	.111	.143	7	1	0	0	0	2	0	1
Second Half	.000	.000	.000	0	0	0	0	0	0	0	0

4-YEAR TOTALS (1990–1993)

	BA	OBA	SA	AB	H	2B	3B	HR	RBI	BB	SO
vs. Left	.305	.398	.408	262	80	11	2	4	27	41	31
vs. Right	.226	.277	.306	389	88	15	2	4	34	27	71
at Home	.294	.364	.384	333	98	12	3	4	39	37	47
on Road	.220	.289	.308	318	70	14	1	4	22	31	55
Runners On Base	.231	.299	.280	286	66	9	1	1	54	29	50
Second Half	.255	.335	.352	321	82	14	1	3	31	38	51

MARK LEONARD — BL/TR — age 30 — BAL OF4, DH3

1993

	BA	OBA	SA	AB	H	2B	3B	HR	RBI	BB	SO
vs. Left	.000	.000	.000	0	0	0	0	0	0	0	0
vs. Right	.067	.190	.133	15	1	1	0	0	3	3	7
at Home	.091	.214	.182	11	1	1	0	0	1	2	5
on Road	.000	.143	.000	4	0	0	0	0	2	1	2
Runners On Base	.091	.133	.182	11	1	1	0	0	3	1	5
Second Half	.000	.000	.000	0	0	0	0	0	0	0	0

4-YEAR TOTALS (1990–1993)

	BA	OBA	SA	AB	H	2B	3B	HR	RBI	BB	SO
vs. Left	.152	.222	.182	33	5	1	0	0	1	3	11
vs. Right	.234	.320	.383	256	60	15	1	7	34	31	60
at Home	.189	.283	.315	127	24	7	0	3	17	17	32
on Road	.253	.330	.395	162	41	9	1	4	18	17	39
Runners On Base	.227	.294	.383	141	32	8	1	4	32	14	40
Second Half	.227	.330	.369	198	45	10	0	6	21	27	47

JESSE LEVIS — BL/TR — age 26 — CLE C29

1993	BA	OBA	SA	AB	H	2B	3B	HR	RBI	BB	SO		2-YEAR TOTALS (1992–1993) BA	OBA	SA	AB	H	2B	3B	HR	RBI	BB	SO
vs. Left	.125	.222	.125	8	1	0	0	0	0	1	2		.300	.364	.400	10	3	1	0	0	1	1	2
vs. Right	.182	.193	.218	55	10	2	0	0	4	1	8		.208	.214	.292	96	20	5	0	1	6	1	13
at Home	.156	.170	.178	45	7	1	0	0	2	1	6		.152	.162	.182	66	10	2	0	0	2	1	9
on Road	.222	.263	.278	18	4	1	0	0	2	1	4		.325	.341	.500	40	13	4	0	1	5	1	6
Runners On Base	.107	.161	.143	28	3	1	0	0	4	2	3		.171	.205	.220	41	7	2	0	0	6	2	5
Second Half	.273	.304	.318	22	6	1	0	0	3	1	4		.259	.273	.370	54	14	3	0	1	5	1	9

MARK LEWIS — BR/TR — age 25 — CLE SS13

1993	BA	OBA	SA	AB	H	2B	3B	HR	RBI	BB	SO		3-YEAR TOTALS (1991–1993) BA	OBA	SA	AB	H	2B	3B	HR	RBI	BB	SO
vs. Left	.235	.235	.353	17	4	2	0	0	3	0	3		.279	.318	.383	201	56	15	0	2	20	13	28
vs. Right	.257	.257	.343	35	9	0	0	1	2	0	4		.258	.291	.322	578	149	23	1	4	45	27	93
at Home	.219	.219	.344	32	7	1	0	1	4	0	4		.272	.305	.352	386	105	20	1	3	36	20	51
on Road	.300	.300	.350	20	6	1	0	0	1	0	3		.254	.292	.323	393	100	18	0	3	29	20	70
Runners On Base	.160	.160	.280	25	4	0	0	1	5	0	3		.277	.307	.338	343	95	15	0	2	61	18	50
Second Half	.250	.250	.346	52	13	2	0	1	5	0	7		.258	.294	.342	333	86	17	1	3	23	16	58

JIM LEYRITZ — BR/TR — age 31 — NYA 1B29, OF28, DH21, C12

1993	BA	OBA	SA	AB	H	2B	3B	HR	RBI	BB	SO		4-YEAR TOTALS (1990–1993) BA	OBA	SA	AB	H	2B	3B	HR	RBI	BB	SO
vs. Left	.289	.398	.470	149	43	9	0	6	22	25	35		.274	.375	.437	391	107	23	1	13	51	55	73
vs. Right	.336	.426	.600	110	37	5	0	8	31	12	24		.260	.338	.393	392	102	13	0	13	57	36	74
at Home	.350	.462	.556	117	41	6	0	6	23	21	20		.283	.383	.422	374	106	20	1	10	48	51	63
on Road	.275	.364	.500	142	39	8	0	8	30	16	39		.252	.332	.408	409	103	16	0	16	60	40	84
Runners On Base	.299	.423	.535	127	38	6	0	8	47	22	29		.254	.362	.413	334	85	14	0	13	95	49	66
Second Half	.270	.354	.461	115	31	7	0	5	20	14	26		.244	.329	.360	464	113	22	1	10	53	47	90

JIM LINDEMAN — BR/TR — age 32 — HOU 1B9

1993	BA	OBA	SA	AB	H	2B	3B	HR	RBI	BB	SO		8-YEAR TOTALS (1986–1993) BA	OBA	SA	AB	H	2B	3B	HR	RBI	BB	SO
vs. Left	.222	.222	.222	9	2	0	0	0	0	0	3		.240	.297	.358	321	77	11	0	9	43	28	83
vs. Right	.429	.429	.643	14	6	3	0	0	0	0	4		.234	.268	.372	218	51	15	0	5	26	8	55
at Home	.000	.000	.000	0	0	0	0	0	0	0	0		.229	.278	.332	253	58	11	0	5	35	17	73
on Road	.348	.348	.478	23	8	3	0	0	0	0	7		.245	.292	.392	286	70	15	0	9	34	19	65
Runners On Base	.200	.200	.200	10	2	0	0	0	0	0	4		.235	.277	.300	260	61	8	0	3	58	18	65
Second Half	.348	.348	.478	23	8	3	0	0	0	0	7		.244	.298	.349	295	72	13	0	6	31	21	70

DOUG LINDSEY — BR/TR — age 27 — PHI/CHA C4

1993	BA	OBA	SA	AB	H	2B	3B	HR	RBI	BB	SO		2-YEAR TOTALS (1991–1993) BA	OBA	SA	AB	H	2B	3B	HR	RBI	BB	SO
vs. Left	.000	.000	.000	0	0	0	0	0	0	0	0		.000	.000	.000	0	0	0	0	0	0	0	0
vs. Right	.333	.333	.333	3	1	0	0	0	0	0	1		.167	.167	.167	6	1	0	0	0	0	0	4
at Home	.000	.000	.000	0	0	0	0	0	0	0	0		.000	.000	.000	3	0	0	0	0	0	0	3
on Road	.333	.333	.333	3	1	0	0	0	0	0	1		.333	.333	.333	3	1	0	0	0	0	0	1
Runners On Base	.000	.000	.000	1	0	0	0	0	0	0	0		.000	.000	.000	2	0	0	0	0	0	0	1
Second Half	.000	.000	.000	1	0	0	0	0	0	0	0		.000	.000	.000	4	0	0	0	0	0	0	3

NELSON LIRIANO — BB/TR — age 30 — COL SS35, 2B16, 3B1

1993	BA	OBA	SA	AB	H	2B	3B	HR	RBI	BB	SO		6-YEAR TOTALS (1987–1993) BA	OBA	SA	AB	H	2B	3B	HR	RBI	BB	SO
vs. Left	.212	.257	.242	33	7	1	0	0	4	2	8		.235	.303	.313	345	81	12	3	3	40	34	68
vs. Right	.331	.407	.475	118	39	5	3	2	11	16	14		.269	.329	.371	1035	278	44	16	10	90	92	113
at Home	.330	.388	.443	88	29	4	3	0	13	9	13		.270	.337	.378	696	188	30	15	5	79	71	101
on Road	.270	.361	.397	63	17	2	0	2	2	9	9		.250	.307	.335	684	171	26	4	8	51	55	80
Runners On Base	.265	.351	.327	49	13	1	1	0	13	7	3		.267	.329	.355	561	150	17	10	4	121	55	75
Second Half	.346	.407	.531	81	28	6	3	1	9	9	11		.268	.341	.380	732	196	33	14	7	73	81	100

GREG LITTON — BR/TR — age 30 — SEA OF22, 2B17, 1B13, DH12, 3B7, SS5

1993	BA	OBA	SA	AB	H	2B	3B	HR	RBI	BB	SO		5-YEAR TOTALS (1989–1993) BA	OBA	SA	AB	H	2B	3B	HR	RBI	BB	SO
vs. Left	.308	.379	.481	104	32	12	0	2	15	12	14		.271	.314	.428	435	118	30	4	10	57	27	72
vs. Right	.286	.346	.400	70	20	5	0	1	10	6	16		.212	.281	.280	353	75	13	1	3	39	31	90
at Home	.307	.380	.534	88	27	11	0	3	20	11	18		.284	.341	.455	356	101	27	5	8	55	30	76
on Road	.291	.351	.360	86	25	6	0	0	5	7	12		.213	.263	.285	432	92	16	0	5	41	28	86
Runners On Base	.299	.360	.468	77	23	10	0	1	23	7	12		.247	.292	.362	356	88	25	2	4	87	21	70
Second Half	.305	.386	.492	128	39	15	0	3	20	16	21		.256	.308	.382	453	116	29	2	8	60	33	87

SCOTT LIVINGSTONE — BL/TR — age 29 — DET 3B62, DH32

1993	BA	OBA	SA	AB	H	2B	3B	HR	RBI	BB	SO		3-YEAR TOTALS (1991–1993) BA	OBA	SA	AB	H	2B	3B	HR	RBI	BB	SO
vs. Left	.261	.320	.261	23	6	0	0	0	3	2	2		.300	.360	.412	80	24	3	0	2	11	8	11
vs. Right	.295	.329	.367	281	83	10	2	2	36	17	30		.287	.322	.365	705	202	33	2	6	85	42	82
at Home	.286	.322	.342	161	46	2	2	1	23	9	14		.266	.310	.340	379	101	12	2	4	54	26	45
on Road	.301	.335	.378	143	43	8	0	1	16	10	18		.308	.342	.397	406	125	24	0	4	42	24	48
Runners On Base	.286	.315	.327	147	42	4	1	0	37	9	14		.289	.326	.345	357	103	12	1	2	90	25	39
Second Half	.310	.338	.397	126	39	4	2	1	19	7	14		.286	.320	.385	493	141	24	2	7	67	28	57

JAVY LOPEZ — BR/TR — age 24 — ATL C7

1993	BA	OBA	SA	AB	H	2B	3B	HR	RBI	BB	SO		2-YEAR TOTALS (1992–1993) BA	OBA	SA	AB	H	2B	3B	HR	RBI	BB	SO
vs. Left	.500	.500	.500	2	1	0	0	0	0	0	0		.375	.375	.500	8	3	1	0	0	0	0	0
vs. Right	.357	.400	.786	14	5	1	1	1	2	0	2		.375	.400	.667	24	9	2	1	1	4	0	3
at Home	.222	.222	.444	9	2	1	0	1	0	0	2		.333	.333	.500	24	8	2	1	0	2	0	3
on Road	.571	.625	1.143	7	4	0	1	1	2	1	0		.500	.556	1.000	8	4	1	0	1	2	0	0
Runners On Base	.333	.333	.833	6	2	0	0	1	2	0	1		.364	.364	.727	11	4	1	0	1	4	0	1
Second Half	.375	.412	.750	16	6	1	1	1	2	0	2		.375	.394	.625	32	12	3	1	1	4	0	3

STEVE LYONS — BL/TR — age 34 — BOS OF10, 2B9, C1, 1B1, 3B1, DH1

9-YEAR TOTALS (1985–1993)

1993	BA	OBA	SA	AB	H	2B	3B	HR	RBI	BB	SO		BA	OBA	SA	AB	H	2B	3B	HR	RBI	BB	SO
vs. Left	.111	.200	.111	9	1	0	0	0	0	1	1		.239	.281	.320	410	98	8	5	5	43	26	92
vs. Right	.143	.200	.214	14	2	1	0	0	0	1	4		.255	.306	.345	1752	447	92	12	14	153	130	272
at Home	.083	.154	.167	12	1	1	0	0	0	1	2		.241	.291	.326	1081	261	45	11	8	95	76	166
on Road	.182	.250	.182	11	2	0	0	0	0	1	3		.263	.311	.355	1081	284	55	6	11	101	80	198
Runners On Base	.000	.111	.000	8	0	0	0	0	0	1	2		.256	.301	.345	937	240	38	9	9	186	69	149
Second Half	.125	.125	.125	8	1	0	0	0	0	0	3		.252	.293	.340	1346	339	66	13	9	123	79	241

KEVIN MAAS — BL/TL — age 29 — NYA DH31, 1B17

4-YEAR TOTALS (1990–1993)

1993	BA	OBA	SA	AB	H	2B	3B	HR	RBI	BB	SO		BA	OBA	SA	AB	H	2B	3B	HR	RBI	BB	SO
vs. Left	.300	.333	.350	20	6	1	0	0	0	1	3		.208	.307	.357	322	67	9	0	13	43	44	101
vs. Right	.191	.314	.420	131	25	3	0	9	25	23	29		.241	.341	.453	869	209	30	1	51	121	131	198
at Home	.189	.286	.486	74	14	1	0	7	18	9	15		.211	.314	.422	573	121	19	0	34	85	83	136
on Road	.221	.344	.338	77	17	3	0	2	7	15	17		.251	.348	.432	618	155	20	1	30	79	92	163
Runners On Base	.266	.368	.531	64	17	2	0	5	21	10	13		.211	.334	.373	502	106	18	0	21	121	93	130
Second Half	.200	.200	.300	10	2	1	0	0	0	0	0		.220	.312	.406	618	136	19	0	32	80	80	171

MIKE MAKSUDIAN — BL/TR — age 28 — MIN 1B4, 3B1

2-YEAR TOTALS (1992–1993)

1993	BA	OBA	SA	AB	H	2B	3B	HR	RBI	BB	SO		BA	OBA	SA	AB	H	2B	3B	HR	RBI	BB	SO
vs. Left	.000	.000	.000	0	0	0	0	0	0	0	0		.000	.000	.000	0	0	0	0	0	0	0	0
vs. Right	.167	.353	.250	12	2	1	0	0	2	4	2		.133	.300	.200	15	2	1	0	0	2	4	2
at Home	.000	.000	.000	3	0	0	0	0	1	0	0		.000	.000	.000	5	0	0	0	0	1	0	0
on Road	.222	.462	.333	9	2	1	0	0	1	4	2		.200	.429	.300	10	2	1	0	0	1	4	2
Runners On Base	.200	.375	.400	5	1	1	0	0	2	2	0		.167	.333	.333	6	1	1	0	0	2	2	0
Second Half	.000	.000	.000	0	0	0	0	0	0	0	0		.000	.000	.000	3	0	0	0	0	0	0	0

CANDY MALDONADO — BR/TR — age 34 — CHN/CLE OF67, DH2

10-YEAR TOTALS (1984–1993)

1993	BA	OBA	SA	AB	H	2B	3B	HR	RBI	BB	SO		BA	OBA	SA	AB	H	2B	3B	HR	RBI	BB	SO
vs. Left	.257	.333	.448	105	27	5	0	5	20	12	24		.269	.337	.425	1433	386	75	5	46	207	148	241
vs. Right	.164	.246	.259	116	19	2	0	3	15	12	34		.249	.311	.424	2313	575	130	10	85	364	186	521
at Home	.238	.289	.419	105	25	4	0	5	20	8	31		.239	.295	.393	1796	429	83	5	61	271	136	396
on Road	.181	.286	.284	116	21	3	0	3	15	16	27		.273	.344	.453	1950	532	122	10	70	300	198	366
Runners On Base	.228	.324	.407	123	28	4	0	6	33	17	34		.272	.347	.445	1756	478	108	12	57	497	198	358
Second Half	.233	.295	.400	120	28	5	0	5	22	11	30		.254	.319	.421	2042	518	100	10	74	319	187	436

JEFF MANTO — BR/TR — age 30 — PHI 3B6, SS1

3-YEAR TOTALS (1990–1993)

1993	BA	OBA	SA	AB	H	2B	3B	HR	RBI	BB	SO		BA	OBA	SA	AB	H	2B	3B	HR	RBI	BB	SO
vs. Left	.125	.125	.125	8	1	0	0	0	0	0	1		.225	.344	.275	80	18	4	0	0	8	15	14
vs. Right	.000	.091	.000	10	0	0	0	0	0	0	2		.190	.311	.345	142	27	8	1	4	19	20	29
at Home	.000	.000	.000	4	0	0	0	0	0	0	0		.215	.351	.331	121	26	9	1	1	16	24	25
on Road	.071	.133	.071	14	1	0	0	0	0	0	2		.188	.287	.307	101	19	3	0	3	11	11	18
Runners On Base	.000	.111	.000	8	0	0	0	0	0	0	1		.228	.347	.337	101	23	8	0	1	24	16	12
Second Half	.000	.167	.000	5	0	0	0	0	0	0	1		.223	.347	.355	166	37	11	1	3	21	29	34

CARLOS MARTINEZ — BR/TR — age 30 — CLE 3B35, 1B22, DH19

6-YEAR TOTALS (1988–1993)

1993	BA	OBA	SA	AB	H	2B	3B	HR	RBI	BB	SO		BA	OBA	SA	AB	H	2B	3B	HR	RBI	BB	SO
vs. Left	.276	.336	.371	116	32	5	0	2	12	12	14		.268	.300	.374	597	160	24	3	11	62	31	81
vs. Right	.219	.260	.315	146	32	5	0	3	19	8	15		.256	.290	.357	827	212	38	3	13	90	37	121
at Home	.246	.302	.322	118	29	3	0	2	14	10	14		.269	.304	.367	694	187	27	4	11	81	36	101
on Road	.243	.288	.354	144	35	7	0	3	17	10	15		.253	.285	.360	730	185	35	2	13	71	32	101
Runners On Base	.225	.275	.310	129	29	2	0	3	29	10	18		.245	.278	.319	661	162	22	3	7	135	34	99
Second Half	.200	.303	.309	55	11	3	0	1	8	9	6		.273	.303	.378	884	241	40	4	15	92	41	126

DOMINGO MARTINEZ — BR/TR — age 27 — TOR 1B7, 3B1

2-YEAR TOTALS (1992–1993)

1993	BA	OBA	SA	AB	H	2B	3B	HR	RBI	BB	SO		BA	OBA	SA	AB	H	2B	3B	HR	RBI	BB	SO
vs. Left	.500	.500	1.000	6	3	0	0	1	3	0	2		.583	.583	1.083	12	7	0	0	2	6	0	2
vs. Right	.125	.222	.125	8	1	0	0	0	0	1	5		.200	.273	.200	10	2	0	0	0	0	1	6
at Home	.000	.000	.000	1	0	0	0	0	0	0	0		.571	.571	1.000	7	4	0	0	1	3	0	1
on Road	.308	.357	.538	13	4	0	0	1	3	1	7		.333	.375	.533	15	5	0	0	1	3	1	7
Runners On Base	.250	.333	.250	8	2	0	0	0	2	1	5		.357	.400	.571	14	5	0	0	1	5	1	6
Second Half	.300	.364	.600	10	3	0	0	1	3	1	4		.444	.474	.778	18	8	0	0	2	6	1	5

EDGAR MARTINEZ — BR/TR — age 31 — SEA DH24, 3B16

7-YEAR TOTALS (1987–1993)

1993	BA	OBA	SA	AB	H	2B	3B	HR	RBI	BB	SO		BA	OBA	SA	AB	H	2B	3B	HR	RBI	BB	SO
vs. Left	.111	.298	.139	36	4	1	0	0	3	10	3		.319	.405	.466	580	185	44	1	13	68	84	60
vs. Right	.283	.393	.465	99	28	6	0	4	10	18	16		.300	.385	.452	1360	408	85	7	36	149	179	192
at Home	.228	.371	.316	57	13	2	0	1	5	13	4		.299	.391	.456	919	275	67	4	23	101	133	119
on Road	.244	.362	.423	78	19	5	0	3	8	15	15		.311	.392	.456	1021	318	62	4	26	116	130	133
Runners On Base	.288	.456	.407	59	17	4	0	1	10	19	4		.283	.384	.412	826	234	38	1	22	190	134	91
Second Half	.257	.396	.432	74	19	4	0	3	7	17	9		.312	.395	.461	985	307	75	3	22	109	133	115

CHITO MARTINEZ — BL/TL — age 29 — BAL OF5, DH2

3-YEAR TOTALS (1991–1993)

1993	BA	OBA	SA	AB	H	2B	3B	HR	RBI	BB	SO		BA	OBA	SA	AB	H	2B	3B	HR	RBI	BB	SO
vs. Left	.000	.000	.000	2	0	0	0	0	0	0	0		.257	.312	.429	70	18	3	0	3	10	5	23
vs. Right	.000	.235	.000	13	0	0	0	0	0	4	4		.259	.333	.448	359	93	19	2	15	48	41	79
at Home	.000	.200	.000	8	0	0	0	0	0	2	3		.282	.359	.484	213	60	13	0	10	33	27	50
on Road	.000	.222	.000	7	0	0	0	0	0	2	1		.236	.300	.407	216	51	9	2	8	25	19	52
Runners On Base	.000	.273	.000	8	0	0	0	0	0	3	3		.263	.329	.463	190	50	7	2	9	49	21	48
Second Half	.000	.000	.000	0	0	0	0	0	0	0	0		.281	.332	.480	331	93	19	1	15	43	26	81

BRENT MAYNE — BL/TR — age 26 — KC C68, DH1

1993	BA	OBA	SA	AB	H	2B	3B	HR	RBI	BB	SO	4-YEAR TOTALS (1990–1993) BA	OBA	SA	AB	H	2B	3B	HR	RBI	BB	SO
vs. Left	.211	.250	.211	19	4	0	0	0	1	1	6	.143	.208	.143	63	9	0	0	0	5	6	17
vs. Right	.258	.324	.349	186	48	9	1	2	21	17	25	.254	.310	.327	599	152	27	1	5	67	49	85
at Home	.320	.371	.371	97	31	3	1	0	9	7	12	.272	.322	.335	346	94	14	1	2	37	26	48
on Road	.194	.269	.306	108	21	6	0	2	13	11	19	.212	.276	.282	316	67	13	0	3	35	29	54
Runners On Base	.311	.380	.367	90	28	3	1	0	20	10	16	.291	.353	.377	302	88	15	1	3	70	32	53
Second Half	.213	.300	.281	89	19	3	0	1	10	10	11	.225	.287	.292	418	94	16	0	4	48	37	64

LLOYD MCCLENDON — BR/TR — age 35 — PIT OF61, 1B6

1993	BA	OBA	SA	AB	H	2B	3B	HR	RBI	BB	SO	7-YEAR TOTALS (1987–1993) BA	OBA	SA	AB	H	2B	3B	HR	RBI	BB	SO
vs. Left	.254	.335	.338	142	36	10	1	0	14	18	12	.266	.346	.396	740	197	38	2	18	93	93	96
vs. Right	.103	.200	.282	39	4	1	0	2	5	5	5	.202	.292	.344	372	75	12	1	13	49	46	58
at Home	.182	.264	.260	77	14	3	0	1	9	9	6	.230	.311	.358	522	120	20	1	15	71	61	72
on Road	.250	.336	.375	104	26	8	1	1	10	14	11	.258	.343	.397	590	152	30	2	16	71	78	82
Runners On Base	.204	.296	.280	93	19	5	1	0	17	13	7	.229	.311	.347	550	126	22	2	13	124	67	72
Second Half	.270	.365	.404	89	24	7	1	1	10	14	5	.247	.335	.402	518	128	26	3	16	65	67	66

TERRY MCGRIFF — BR/TR — age 31 — FLO C3

1993	BA	OBA	SA	AB	H	2B	3B	HR	RBI	BB	SO	5-YEAR TOTALS (1987–1993) BA	OBA	SA	AB	H	2B	3B	HR	RBI	BB	SO
vs. Left	.000	.143	.000	6	0	0	0	0	0	1	1	.220	.309	.305	59	13	2	0	1	3	8	15
vs. Right	.000	.000	.000	1	0	0	0	0	0	0	0	.190	.262	.255	153	29	4	0	2	14	15	39
at Home	.000	.125	.000	7	0	0	0	0	0	1	2	.235	.319	.333	102	24	4	0	2	8	13	29
on Road	.000	.000	.000	0	0	0	0	0	0	0	0	.164	.233	.209	110	18	2	0	1	9	10	25
Runners On Base	.000	.000	.000	4	0	0	0	0	0	0	2	.233	.300	.322	90	21	2	0	2	16	9	18
Second Half	.000	.125	.000	7	0	0	0	0	0	1	2	.198	.264	.279	111	22	3	0	2	13	10	20

MARK MCGWIRE — BR/TR — age 31 — OAK 1B25

1993	BA	OBA	SA	AB	H	2B	3B	HR	RBI	BB	SO	8-YEAR TOTALS (1986–1993) BA	OBA	SA	AB	H	2B	3B	HR	RBI	BB	SO
vs. Left	.455	.556	1.000	22	10	3	0	3	12	4	3	.262	.377	.549	869	228	43	1	68	197	166	163
vs. Right	.290	.438	.629	62	18	3	0	6	12	17	16	.245	.353	.494	2337	572	91	4	161	435	382	553
at Home	.341	.491	.756	41	14	2	0	5	15	12	9	.238	.358	.485	1548	369	66	2	104	295	283	356
on Road	.326	.442	.698	43	14	4	0	4	9	9	10	.260	.361	.531	1658	431	68	3	125	337	265	360
Runners On Base	.275	.464	.575	40	11	3	0	3	18	14	8	.263	.373	.523	1450	381	63	4	102	505	272	329
Second Half	.000	.500	.000	1	0	0	0	0	0	1	0	.248	.351	.485	1649	409	73	1	105	309	256	368

TIM MCINTOSH — BR/TR — age 29 — MIL/MON OF7, C6

1993	BA	OBA	SA	AB	H	2B	3B	HR	RBI	BB	SO	4-YEAR TOTALS (1990–1993) BA	OBA	SA	AB	H	2B	3B	HR	RBI	BB	SO
vs. Left	.154	.154	.231	13	2	1	0	0	2	0	6	.207	.242	.362	58	12	3	0	2	8	2	12
vs. Right	.000	.000	.000	8	0	0	0	0	0	0	1	.161	.190	.196	56	9	2	0	0	2	1	10
at Home	.071	.071	.071	14	1	0	0	0	0	0	7	.160	.222	.300	50	8	1	0	2	5	3	18
on Road	.143	.143	.286	7	1	1	0	0	2	0	0	.203	.212	.266	64	13	4	0	0	5	0	4
Runners On Base	.091	.091	.182	11	1	1	0	0	2	0	4	.163	.176	.204	49	8	2	0	0	8	1	10
Second Half	.000	.000	.000								2	.195	.233	.415	41	8	3	0	2	3	2	13

JEFF MCKNIGHT — BB/TR — age 31 — NYN SS29, 2B15, 1B10, 3B9, C1

1993	BA	OBA	SA	AB	H	2B	3B	HR	RBI	BB	SO	5-YEAR TOTALS (1989–1993) BA	OBA	SA	AB	H	2B	3B	HR	RBI	BB	SO
vs. Left	.171	.237	.171	35	6	0	0	0	1	2	7	.244	.291	.261	119	29	2	0	0	10	7	15
vs. Right	.279	.331	.364	129	36	3	1	2	12	11	24	.236	.284	.337	258	61	7	2	5	22	17	49
at Home	.259	.312	.365	85	22	1	1	2	9	7	17	.250	.286	.354	192	48	4	2	4	21	10	31
on Road	.253	.310	.278	79	20	2	0	0	4	6	14	.227	.287	.270	185	42	5	0	1	11	14	33
Runners On Base	.254	.307	.358	67	17	1	0	2	13	5	12	.244	.283	.351	168	41	6	0	4	31	9	28
Second Half	.283	.308	.354	113	32	3	1	1	7	5	21	.256	.288	.344	273	70	8	2	4	24	12	46

JIM MCNAMARA — BL/TR — age 29 — SF C4

1993	BA	OBA	SA	AB	H	2B	3B	HR	RBI	BB	SO	2-YEAR TOTALS (1992–1993) BA	OBA	SA	AB	H	2B	3B	HR	RBI	BB	SO
vs. Left	.500	.500	.500	2	1	0	0	0	1	0	1	.250	.250	.250	8	2	0	0	0	1	0	3
vs. Right	.000	.000	.000	5	0	0	0	0	0	0	0	.205	.266	.260	73	15	1	0	1	9	6	23
at Home	.000	.000	.000	4	0	0	0	0	0	0	0	.239	.271	.304	46	11	0	0	1	8	2	12
on Road	.333	.333	.333	3	1	0	0	0	1	0	1	.171	.256	.200	35	6	1	0	0	2	4	14
Runners On Base	.250	.250	.250	4	1	0	0	0	1	0	1	.333	.409	.436	39	13	1	0	1	10	5	9
Second Half	.143	.143	.143	7	1	0	0	0	1	0	1	.143	.143	.143	7	1	0	0	0	1	0	1

BOB MELVIN — BR/TR — age 33 — BOS C76, 1B1

1993	BA	OBA	SA	AB	H	2B	3B	HR	RBI	BB	SO	9-YEAR TOTALS (1985–1993) BA	OBA	SA	AB	H	2B	3B	HR	RBI	BB	SO
vs. Left	.250	.302	.375	40	10	2	0	1	4	3	7	.284	.326	.409	797	226	48	2	16	91	53	112
vs. Right	.213	.236	.294	136	29	5	0	2	19	4	37	.198	.227	.286	1124	223	37	4	18	117	44	275
at Home	.237	.265	.329	76	18	4	0	1	14	3	22	.219	.248	.316	905	198	36	2	16	101	38	190
on Road	.210	.240	.300	100	21	3	0	2	9	4	22	.247	.286	.356	1016	251	49	4	18	107	59	197
Runners On Base	.267	.310	.367	90	24	0	0	2	22	6	22	.267	.300	.375	846	226	41	4	14	188	47	159
Second Half	.186	.202	.291	86	16	3	0	2	10	2	22	.219	.253	.316	970	212	37	5	16	101	49	192

HENRY MERCEDES — BR/TR — age 25 — OAK C18, DH1

1993	BA	OBA	SA	AB	H	2B	3B	HR	RBI	BB	SO	2-YEAR TOTALS (1992–1993) BA	OBA	SA	AB	H	2B	3B	HR	RBI	BB	SO
vs. Left	.304	.304	.348	23	7	1	0	0	0	0	6	.360	.360	.400	25	9	1	0	0	0	0	6
vs. Right	.125	.222	.167	24	3	1	0	0	3	2	9	.185	.267	.296	27	5	1	1	0	3	2	10
at Home	.250	.250	.313	16	4	1	0	0	0	0	7	.350	.350	.500	20	7	1	0	0	1	0	8
on Road	.194	.265	.226	31	6	1	0	0	3	2	8	.219	.286	.250	32	7	1	1	0	3	2	8
Runners On Base	.308	.357	.385	13	4	1	0	0	3	1	3	.357	.400	.571	14	5	1	0	0	4	1	3
Second Half	.213	.260	.255	47	10	2	0	0	3	2	15	.255	.296	.333	51	13	2	1	0	4	2	16

LUIS MERCEDES — BR/TR — age 26 — BAL/SF OF13, DH2

1993	BA	OBA	SA	AB	H	2B	3B	HR	RBI	BB	SO
vs. Left	.241	.313	.310	29	7	2	0	0	0	3	4
vs. Right	.200	.360	.300	20	4	0	1	0	3	3	3
at Home	.192	.276	.231	26	5	1	0	0	0	1	1
on Road	.261	.393	.391	23	6	1	1	0	3	5	6
Runners On Base	.250	.308	.375	24	6	1	1	0	3	2	4
Second Half	.200	.200	.600	5	1	0	1	0	3	0	2

3-YEAR TOTALS (1991–1993)

BA	OBA	SA	AB	H	2B	3B	HR	RBI	BB	SO
.204	.275	.245	98	20	4	0	0	4	9	16
.164	.303	.236	55	9	2	1	0	5	9	9
.173	.262	.240	75	13	5	0	0	3	6	6
.205	.308	.244	78	16	1	1	0	6	12	19
.190	.268	.254	63	12	2	1	0	9	7	10
.202	.265	.270	89	18	4	1	0	9	7	15

MATT MERULLO — BL/TR — age 29 — CHA DH6

1993	BA	OBA	SA	AB	H	2B	3B	HR	RBI	BB	SO
vs. Left	.000	.000	.000	0	0	0	0	0	0	0	0
vs. Right	.050	.050	.050	20	1	0	0	0	0	0	1
at Home	.000	.000	.000	13	0	0	0	0	0	0	0
on Road	.143	.143	.143	7	1	0	0	0	0	0	1
Runners On Base	.111	.111	.111	9	1	0	0	0	0	0	0
Second Half	.050	.050	.050	20	1	0	0	0	0	0	1

4-YEAR TOTALS (1989–1993)

BA	OBA	SA	AB	H	2B	3B	HR	RBI	BB	SO
.222	.333	.389	18	4	0	0	1	2	3	2
.205	.239	.278	273	56	3	1	5	30	13	39
.193	.229	.253	166	32	2	1	2	17	9	24
.224	.267	.328	125	28	1	0	4	15	7	17
.234	.293	.270	137	32	2	0	1	27	13	14
.125	.182	.208	72	9	0	0	2	6	6	9

HENSLEY MEULENS — BR/TR — age 27 — NYA OF24, 1B3, 3B1

1993	BA	OBA	SA	AB	H	2B	3B	HR	RBI	BB	SO
vs. Left	.159	.275	.250	44	7	1	0	1	1	7	16
vs. Right	.222	.300	.778	9	2	0	1	1	4	1	3
at Home	.120	.241	.280	25	3	1	0	1	1	4	7
on Road	.214	.313	.393	28	6	0	1	1	4	4	12
Runners On Base	.111	.250	.185	27	3	0	1	0	3	5	8
Second Half	.143	.217	.286	21	3	0	0	1	1	2	9

5-YEAR TOTALS (1989–1993)

BA	OBA	SA	AB	H	2B	3B	HR	RBI	BB	SO
.229	.296	.357	258	59	10	1	7	25	21	80
.211	.282	.327	199	42	6	1	5	21	17	69
.228	.287	.367	259	59	12	0	8	24	19	80
.212	.293	.313	198	42	4	2	4	22	19	69
.235	.311	.350	183	43	5	2	4	38	17	55
.219	.297	.346	283	62	12	0	8	26	25	88

KEITH MILLER — BR/TR — age 31 — KC 3B21, DH6, OF4, 2B3

1993	BA	OBA	SA	AB	H	2B	3B	HR	RBI	BB	SO
vs. Left	.071	.212	.071	28	2	0	0	0	0	5	8
vs. Right	.200	.235	.237	80	16	3	0	0	3	3	11
at Home	.162	.215	.176	74	12	1	0	0	2	4	12
on Road	.176	.256	.235	34	6	2	0	0	1	4	7
Runners On Base	.140	.170	.160	50	7	1	0	0	3	1	13
Second Half	.179	.303	.179	28	5	0	0	0	0	5	9

7-YEAR TOTALS (1987–1993)

BA	OBA	SA	AB	H	2B	3B	HR	RBI	BB	SO
.258	.316	.347	554	143	32	4	3	32	46	95
.265	.330	.356	742	197	35	4	8	57	52	103
.258	.329	.336	648	167	28	4	5	44	58	86
.267	.320	.367	648	173	39	4	6	45	40	112
.265	.327	.352	452	120	27	3	2	80	33	72
.257	.322	.335	731	188	33	3	6	51	57	115

JOE MILLETTE — BR/TR — age 28 — PHI SS7, 3B3

1993	BA	OBA	SA	AB	H	2B	3B	HR	RBI	BB	SO
vs. Left	.000	.000	.000	5	0	0	0	0	0	0	0
vs. Right	.400	.500	.400	5	2	0	0	0	2	1	2
at Home	.143	.250	.143	7	1	0	0	0	1	1	1
on Road	.333	.333	.333	3	1	0	0	0	1	0	1
Runners On Base	.250	.400	.250	4	1	0	0	0	2	1	0
Second Half	.000	.000	.000	0	0	0	0	0	0	0	0

2-YEAR TOTALS (1992–1993)

BA	OBA	SA	AB	H	2B	3B	HR	RBI	BB	SO
.100	.156	.100	30	3	0	0	0	1	2	2
.259	.328	.259	58	15	0	0	0	3	4	10
.237	.308	.237	59	14	0	0	0	3	4	10
.138	.194	.138	29	4	0	0	0	1	2	2
.122	.234	.122	41	5	0	0	0	4	5	6
.205	.271	.205	78	16	0	0	0	2	5	10

RANDY MILLIGAN — BR/TR — age 33 — CIN/CLE 1B79, OF9, DH1

1993	BA	OBA	SA	AB	H	2B	3B	HR	RBI	BB	SO
vs. Left	.383	.484	.586	133	51	13	1	4	21	26	17
vs. Right	.223	.370	.297	148	33	5	0	2	15	34	36
at Home	.308	.465	.477	130	40	7	0	5	19	38	30
on Road	.291	.382	.397	151	44	11	1	1	17	22	23
Runners On Base	.306	.406	.388	121	37	7	0	1	31	20	25
Second Half	.348	.487	.494	89	31	10	0	1	13	25	16

7-YEAR TOTALS (1987–1993)

BA	OBA	SA	AB	H	2B	3B	HR	RBI	BB	SO
.276	.413	.469	706	195	44	4	28	102	163	132
.255	.382	.399	1330	339	60	6	40	170	270	278
.250	.403	.418	987	247	44	4	38	132	251	193
.274	.382	.428	1049	287	60	6	30	140	182	217
.267	.384	.392	929	248	47	3	21	225	176	188
.254	.383	.397	945	240	45	6	26	112	198	181

PEDRO MUNOZ — BR/TR — age 26 — MIN OF102

1993	BA	OBA	SA	AB	H	2B	3B	HR	RBI	BB	SO
vs. Left	.255	.321	.461	102	26	3	0	6	19	9	26
vs. Right	.223	.281	.362	224	50	8	1	7	19	16	71
at Home	.196	.274	.280	168	33	6	1	2	12	16	55
on Road	.272	.315	.513	158	43	5	0	11	26	9	42
Runners On Base	.286	.349	.406	133	38	4	0	4	29	12	43
Second Half	.212	.272	.340	156	33	5	0	5	23	11	47

4-YEAR TOTALS (1990–1993)

BA	OBA	SA	AB	H	2B	3B	HR	RBI	BB	SO
.289	.330	.474	291	84	12	3	12	58	19	62
.247	.286	.383	676	167	26	3	20	82	34	172
.247	.296	.396	470	116	22	3	14	65	31	118
.272	.302	.425	497	135	16	3	18	75	22	116
.283	.328	.448	420	119	17	2	16	124	28	97
.242	.279	.370	508	123	18	4	13	71	24	126

DALE MURPHY — BR/TR — age 38 — COL OF13

1993	BA	OBA	SA	AB	H	2B	3B	HR	RBI	BB	SO
vs. Left	.143	.235	.179	28	4	1	0	0	6	4	8
vs. Right	.143	.200	.143	14	2	0	0	0	1	1	7
at Home	.130	.259	.174	23	3	1	0	0	4	4	7
on Road	.158	.182	.158	19	3	0	0	0	3	1	8
Runners On Base	.174	.276	.217	23	4	1	0	0	7	4	6
Second Half	.000	.000	.000	0	0	0	0	0	0	0	0

10-YEAR TOTALS (1984–1993)

BA	OBA	SA	AB	H	2B	3B	HR	RBI	BB	SO
.289	.401	.518	1478	427	74	9	82	239	283	285
.248	.318	.442	3302	820	155	15	152	500	330	785
.276	.369	.488	2362	651	116	10	122	394	349	487
.246	.320	.444	2418	596	113	14	112	345	264	583
.265	.365	.476	2151	569	96	7	115	620	350	490
.261	.342	.466	2463	642	118	14	120	390	301	539

TIM NAEHRING — BR/TR — age 27 — BOS 2B15, DH10, 3B9, SS4

1993	BA	OBA	SA	AB	H	2B	3B	HR	RBI	BB	SO
vs. Left	.395	.447	.488	43	17	4	0	0	4	4	6
vs. Right	.298	.341	.405	84	25	6	0	1	13	6	20
at Home	.311	.366	.392	74	23	6	0	0	10	7	18
on Road	.358	.393	.491	53	19	4	0	1	7	3	8
Runners On Base	.367	.418	.469	49	18	5	0	0	16	5	6
Second Half	.331	.377	.433	127	42	10	0	1	17	10	26

4-YEAR TOTALS (1990–1993)

BA	OBA	SA	AB	H	2B	3B	HR	RBI	BB	SO
.301	.364	.423	156	47	10	0	3	20	14	28
.226	.294	.306	297	67	15	0	3	26	28	59
.239	.322	.321	209	50	11	0	2	21	26	49
.262	.314	.369	244	64	14	0	4	25	16	38
.289	.356	.399	173	50	13	0	2	42	19	22
.289	.346	.396	308	89	21	0	4	38	28	54

ROB NATAL — BR/TR — age 29 — FLO C38

1993	BA	OBA	SA	AB	H	2B	3B	HR	RBI	BB	SO
vs. Left	.219	.265	.250	32	7	1	0	0	1	2	5
vs. Right	.212	.277	.306	85	18	3	1	1	5	4	17
at Home	.177	.268	.242	62	11	2	1	0	2	4	14
on Road	.255	.281	.345	55	14	2	0	1	4	2	8
Runners On Base	.228	.286	.298	57	13	2	1	0	5	3	12
Second Half	.236	.299	.321	106	25	4	1	1	6	6	17

2-YEAR TOTALS (1992–1993)

	BA	OBA	SA	AB	H	2B	3B	HR	RBI	BB	SO
	.194	.256	.222	36	7	1	0	0	1	3	6
	.207	.271	.299	87	18	3	1	1	5	4	17
	.162	.247	.221	68	11	2	1	0	2	4	15
	.255	.293	.345	55	14	2	0	1	4	3	8
	.217	.284	.283	60	13	2	1	0	5	4	12
	.223	.290	.304	112	25	4	1	1	6	7	18

WARREN NEWSON — BL/TL — age 30 — CHA DH10, OF5

1993	BA	OBA	SA	AB	H	2B	3B	HR	RBI	BB	SO
vs. Left	.667	.800	.667	3	2	0	0	0	0	2	0
vs. Right	.270	.386	.432	37	10	0	0	2	6	7	12
at Home	.320	.433	.560	25	8	0	0	2	5	5	8
on Road	.267	.421	.267	15	4	0	0	0	1	4	4
Runners On Base	.400	.591	.400	15	6	0	0	0	4	7	4
Second Half	.300	.429	.450	40	12	0	0	2	6	9	12

3-YEAR TOTALS (1991–1993)

	BA	OBA	SA	AB	H	2B	3B	HR	RBI	BB	SO
	.286	.500	.286	14	4	0	0	0	0	6	5
	.262	.401	.361	294	77	8	0	7	42	68	79
	.248	.385	.338	157	39	2	0	4	24	35	38
	.278	.426	.377	151	42	6	0	3	18	39	46
	.288	.441	.345	139	40	5	0	1	36	38	41
	.267	.415	.386	202	54	6	0	6	30	51	58

MELVIN NIEVES — BB/TR — age 23 — SD OF15

1993	BA	OBA	SA	AB	H	2B	3B	HR	RBI	BB	SO
vs. Left	.167	.167	.667	6	1	0	0	1	1	0	4
vs. Right	.195	.267	.268	41	8	0	0	1	2	3	17
at Home	.231	.268	.385	39	9	0	0	2	3	1	18
on Road	.000	.200	.000	8	0	0	0	0	0	2	3
Runners On Base	.133	.188	.133	15	2	0	0	0	1	1	7
Second Half	.191	.255	.319	47	9	0	0	2	3	3	21

2-YEAR TOTALS (1992–1993)

	BA	OBA	SA	AB	H	2B	3B	HR	RBI	BB	SO
	.182	.250	.455	11	2	0	0	1	1	1	7
	.200	.267	.273	55	11	1	0	1	3	4	21
	.214	.267	.339	56	12	1	0	2	4	3	25
	.100	.250	.100	10	1	0	0	0	0	2	3
	.182	.217	.182	22	4	0	0	0	2	1	10
	.197	.264	.303	66	13	1	0	2	4	5	28

MATT NOKES — BL/TR — age 31 — NYA C56, DH11

1993	BA	OBA	SA	AB	H	2B	3B	HR	RBI	BB	SO
vs. Left	.100	.129	.300	30	3	0	0	2	3	0	6
vs. Right	.273	.329	.444	187	51	4	0	8	32	16	25
at Home	.245	.294	.402	102	25	4	0	4	14	6	10
on Road	.252	.310	.443	115	29	4	0	6	21	10	21
Runners On Base	.245	.327	.436	94	23	3	0	5	30	11	19
Second Half	.221	.303	.325	77	17	2	0	2	12	10	14

9-YEAR TOTALS (1985–1993)

	BA	OBA	SA	AB	H	2B	3B	HR	RBI	BB	SO
	.219	.271	.412	398	87	11	0	22	68	24	84
	.263	.318	.446	2197	577	80	4	105	329	167	280
	.265	.321	.470	1204	319	33	2	70	205	92	174
	.248	.302	.416	1391	345	58	2	57	192	99	190
	.264	.322	.445	1214	321	39	0	60	330	101	191
	.251	.313	.427	1315	330	47	2	60	193	108	180

CHARLIE O'BRIEN — BR/TR — age 34 — NYN C65

1993	BA	OBA	SA	AB	H	2B	3B	HR	RBI	BB	SO
vs. Left	.271	.310	.364	118	32	8	0	1	13	7	5
vs. Right	.229	.316	.400	70	16	3	0	3	10	7	9
at Home	.200	.250	.247	85	17	1	0	1	4	4	9
on Road	.301	.363	.485	103	31	10	0	3	19	10	5
Runners On Base	.275	.354	.377	69	19	4	0	1	20	9	3
Second Half	.274	.333	.436	117	32	7	0	4	16	9	7

8-YEAR TOTALS (1985–1993)

	BA	OBA	SA	AB	H	2B	3B	HR	RBI	BB	SO
	.216	.278	.324	550	119	34	2	7	45	42	55
	.211	.303	.313	527	111	25	1	9	70	58	70
	.204	.286	.307	486	99	19	2	9	45	51	48
	.222	.294	.328	591	131	40	1	7	70	49	77
	.249	.329	.371	445	111	29	2	7	106	47	46
	.223	.297	.335	663	148	35	0	13	78	58	76

PETE O'BRIEN — BL/TL — age 36 — SEA DH52, 1B9, OF1

1993	BA	OBA	SA	AB	H	2B	3B	HR	RBI	BB	SO
vs. Left	.200	.286	.200	25	5	0	0	0	0	3	4
vs. Right	.265	.341	.416	185	49	7	0	7	27	23	17
at Home	.222	.310	.283	99	22	3	0	1	13	13	11
on Road	.288	.357	.486	111	32	4	0	6	14	13	10
Runners On Base	.232	.339	.347	95	22	2	0	3	23	17	13
Second Half	.200	.310	.200	25	5	0	0	0	1	4	3

10-YEAR TOTALS (1984–1993)

	BA	OBA	SA	AB	H	2B	3B	HR	RBI	BB	SO
	.246	.311	.345	1390	342	61	2	24	173	134	199
	.272	.350	.442	3456	939	165	13	133	496	443	295
	.271	.347	.421	2345	635	124	6	72	362	291	232
	.258	.332	.408	2501	646	102	9	85	307	286	262
	.267	.352	.405	2147	573	102	9	59	571	317	213
	.264	.340	.401	2456	648	110	8	70	333	299	260

JOSE OQUENDO — BB/TR — age 31 — SL SS22, 2B16

1993	BA	OBA	SA	AB	H	2B	3B	HR	RBI	BB	SO
vs. Left	.125	.160	.125	24	3	0	0	0	0	1	2
vs. Right	.245	.377	.245	49	12	0	0	0	4	11	6
at Home	.192	.250	.192	26	5	0	0	0	1	2	2
on Road	.213	.345	.213	47	10	0	0	0	3	10	6
Runners On Base	.241	.281	.241	29	7	0	0	0	4	2	1
Second Half	.115	.200	.115	26	3	0	0	0	2	3	2

9-YEAR TOTALS (1984–1993)

	BA	OBA	SA	AB	H	2B	3B	HR	RBI	BB	SO
	.258	.342	.345	948	245	40	6	10	86	125	96
	.270	.366	.318	1577	426	47	13	1	125	248	183
	.273	.360	.335	1233	336	40	11	5	102	174	128
	.259	.355	.322	1292	335	47	8	6	109	199	151
	.281	.372	.341	1033	290	33	7	5	205	167	109
	.274	.364	.345	1232	338	46	10	7	112	181	143

JOHN ORTON — BR/TR — age 29 — CAL C35, OF1

1993	BA	OBA	SA	AB	H	2B	3B	HR	RBI	BB	SO
vs. Left	.054	.146	.054	37	2	0	0	0	0	4	9
vs. Right	.276	.323	.414	58	16	5	0	1	4	3	15
at Home	.136	.208	.182	44	6	2	0	0	1	3	13
on Road	.235	.291	.353	51	12	3	0	1	3	4	11
Runners On Base	.167	.239	.190	42	7	1	0	0	3	3	9
Second Half	.000	.143	.000	6	0	0	0	0	0	1	2

5-YEAR TOTALS (1989–1993)

	BA	OBA	SA	AB	H	2B	3B	HR	RBI	BB	SO
	.143	.221	.193	119	17	3	0	1	7	10	36
	.223	.284	.309	282	63	15	0	3	22	21	85
	.172	.226	.222	198	34	7	0	1	12	12	62
	.227	.302	.325	203	46	11	0	3	17	19	59
	.218	.291	.285	165	36	8	0	1	26	12	48
	.202	.279	.287	178	36	9	0	2	18	17	57

ERIK PAPPAS — BR/TR — age 28 — SL C63, OF16, 1B2

1993	BA	OBA	SA	AB	H	2B	3B	HR	RBI	BB	SO
vs. Left	.319	.434	.406	69	22	3	0	1	9	14	13
vs. Right	.258	.339	.314	159	41	9	0	0	19	21	22
at Home	.216	.292	.276	116	25	4	0	1	15	13	19
on Road	.339	.441	.411	112	38	8	0	0	13	22	16
Runners On Base	.277	.359	.357	112	31	6	0	1	28	16	22
Second Half	.238	.333	.300	130	31	8	0	0	13	19	27

2-YEAR TOTALS (1991–1993)

	BA	OBA	SA	AB	H	2B	3B	HR	RBI	BB	SO
	.291	.404	.367	79	23	3	0	1	10	15	16
	.259	.337	.313	166	43	9	0	0	20	21	24
	.220	.295	.280	118	26	4	0	1	15	13	19
	.315	.414	.378	127	40	8	0	0	15	23	21
	.284	.363	.362	116	33	6	0	1	30	16	23
	.238	.333	.300	130	31	8	0	0	13	19	27

MARK PARENT — BR/TR — age 33 — BAL C21, DH1

1993	BA	OBA	SA	AB	H	2B	3B	HR	RBI	BB	SO
vs. Left	.364	.391	.682	22	8	1	0	2	6	1	4
vs. Right	.188	.229	.406	32	6	1	0	2	6	2	10
at Home	.310	.344	.483	29	9	2	0	1	8	2	11
on Road	.200	.231	.560	25	5	0	0	3	4	1	3
Runners On Base	.281	.294	.531	32	9	2	0	2	10	1	7
Second Half	.259	.293	.519	54	14	2	0	4	12	3	14

8-YEAR TOTALS (1986–1993)

BA	OBA	SA	AB	H	2B	3B	HR	RBI	BB	SO
.246	.310	.418	232	57	10	0	10	27	22	43
.177	.211	.314	344	61	11	0	12	43	15	77
.224	.261	.411	246	55	10	0	12	36	14	62
.191	.244	.315	330	63	11	0	10	34	23	58
.189	.242	.313	259	49	8	0	8	56	20	56
.215	.262	.390	354	76	14	0	16	49	23	70

RICK PARKER — BR/TR — age 31 — HOU OF16, 2B1, SS1

1993	BA	OBA	SA	AB	H	2B	3B	HR	RBI	BB	SO
vs. Left	.375	.429	.469	32	12	3	0	0	4	3	4
vs. Right	.231	.231	.231	13	3	0	0	0	0	0	4
at Home	.438	.526	.438	16	7	0	0	0	3	3	2
on Road	.276	.276	.379	29	8	3	0	0	1	0	6
Runners On Base	.412	.444	.471	17	7	1	0	0	4	1	4
Second Half	.407	.429	.481	27	11	2	0	0	3	1	5

3-YEAR TOTALS (1990–1993)

BA	OBA	SA	AB	H	2B	3B	HR	RBI	BB	SO
.287	.349	.400	115	33	7	0	2	14	11	16
.176	.236	.196	51	9	1	0	0	5	3	12
.250	.320	.250	68	17	0	0	0	5	7	11
.255	.311	.398	98	25	8	0	2	14	7	17
.286	.345	.390	77	22	5	0	1	18	7	12
.241	.313	.276	58	14	2	0	0	4	6	11

DEREK PARKS — BR/TR — age 26 — MIN C7

1993	BA	OBA	SA	AB	H	2B	3B	HR	RBI	BB	SO
vs. Left	.143	.250	.143	7	1	0	0	0	1	1	1
vs. Right	.231	.231	.231	13	3	0	0	0	0	0	1
at Home	.231	.231	.231	13	3	0	0	0	1	0	2
on Road	.143	.250	.143	7	1	0	0	0	0	1	1
Runners On Base	.125	.222	.125	8	1	0	0	0	1	1	2
Second Half	.200	.238	.200	20	4	0	0	0	1	1	2

2-YEAR TOTALS (1992–1993)

BA	OBA	SA	AB	H	2B	3B	HR	RBI	BB	SO
.250	.357	.250	12	3	0	0	0	1	2	1
.214	.267	.214	14	3	0	0	0	0	0	2
.333	.375	.333	15	5	0	0	0	1	1	2
.091	.231	.091	11	1	0	0	0	0	1	1
.091	.231	.091	11	1	0	0	0	1	2	2
.231	.310	.231	26	6	0	0	0	1	2	3

LANCE PARRISH — BR/TR — age 38 — CLE C10

1993	BA	OBA	SA	AB	H	2B	3B	HR	RBI	BB	SO
vs. Left	.000	.000	.000	5	0	0	0	0	0	0	2
vs. Right	.267	.421	.533	15	4	1	0	1	2	4	3
at Home	.200	.429	.800	5	1	0	0	1	2	2	0
on Road	.200	.294	.267	15	3	1	0	0	0	2	5
Runners On Base	.111	.273	.444	9	1	0	0	1	2	2	2
Second Half	.000	.000	.000	0	0	0	0	0	0	0	0

10-YEAR TOTALS (1984–1993)

BA	OBA	SA	AB	H	2B	3B	HR	RBI	BB	SO
.265	.341	.449	1225	325	38	5	59	175	146	224
.234	.294	.415	2719	635	101	3	129	416	219	669
.253	.316	.432	1950	494	78	5	87	292	177	416
.234	.302	.419	1994	466	61	3	101	299	188	477
.253	.321	.438	1860	471	71	4	88	491	188	411
.233	.300	.414	1955	456	66	4	93	270	182	469

DAN PASQUA — BL/TL — age 33 — CHA OF37, 1B32, DH6

1993	BA	OBA	SA	AB	H	2B	3B	HR	RBI	BB	SO
vs. Left	.400	.500	1.100	10	4	1	0	2	4	2	4
vs. Right	.193	.290	.313	166	32	9	1	3	16	24	47
at Home	.263	.380	.395	76	20	4	0	2	10	15	26
on Road	.160	.239	.330	100	16	6	1	3	10	11	25
Runners On Base	.203	.313	.418	79	16	2	0	5	20	14	19
Second Half	.218	.317	.391	87	19	1	1	2	7	13	21

9-YEAR TOTALS (1985–1993)

BA	OBA	SA	AB	H	2B	3B	HR	RBI	BB	SO
.192	.275	.321	386	74	15	1	11	50	39	110
.253	.341	.457	2211	559	112	14	104	336	296	523
.259	.352	.453	1251	324	57	9	56	178	181	301
.230	.311	.422	1346	309	70	6	59	208	154	332
.246	.351	.433	1185	291	54	9	50	321	199	301
.246	.329	.443	1514	373	76	9	68	225	182	352

JOHN PATTERSON — BB/TR — age 27 — SF

1993	BA	OBA	SA	AB	H	2B	3B	HR	RBI	BB	SO
vs. Left	.200	.200	.200	5	1	0	0	0	1	0	1
vs. Right	.182	.182	.455	11	2	0	0	1	1	0	4
at Home	.200	.200	.200	10	2	0	0	0	1	0	3
on Road	.167	.167	.667	6	1	0	0	1	1	0	2
Runners On Base	.125	.125	.125	8	1	0	0	0	1	0	3
Second Half	.188	.188	.375	16	3	0	0	1	2	0	5

2-YEAR TOTALS (1992–1993)

BA	OBA	SA	AB	H	2B	3B	HR	RBI	BB	SO
.233	.258	.267	30	7	1	0	0	2	1	7
.169	.213	.225	89	15	0	1	1	4	4	22
.190	.217	.241	58	11	1	1	0	3	2	12
.180	.231	.230	61	11	0	0	1	3	3	17
.182	.200	.227	44	8	0	1	0	5	1	13
.178	.213	.233	90	16	0	1	1	5	4	21

BILL PECOTA — BR/TR — age 34 — ATL 3B23, 2B4, OF1

1993	BA	OBA	SA	AB	H	2B	3B	HR	RBI	BB	SO
vs. Left	.412	.429	.529	34	14	2	1	0	5	1	1
vs. Right	.214	.241	.214	28	6	0	0	0	0	1	4
at Home	.258	.303	.290	31	8	1	0	0	2	2	1
on Road	.387	.387	.484	31	12	1	1	0	3	0	4
Runners On Base	.375	.375	.542	24	9	2	1	0	5	0	1
Second Half	.375	.394	.469	32	12	1	1	0	2	1	0

8-YEAR TOTALS (1986–1993)

BA	OBA	SA	AB	H	2B	3B	HR	RBI	BB	SO
.284	.353	.405	524	149	33	3	8	54	55	60
.232	.306	.329	891	207	34	8	12	78	89	140
.253	.331	.357	656	166	32	6	8	71	72	83
.250	.317	.357	759	190	35	5	12	61	72	117
.241	.332	.343	572	138	23	7	7	119	77	76
.245	.322	.350	1035	254	49	10	13	88	111	142

DAN PELTIER — BL/TL — age 26 — TEX OF55, 1B5

1993	BA	OBA	SA	AB	H	2B	3B	HR	RBI	BB	SO
vs. Left	.125	.222	.125	8	1	0	0	0	1	1	1
vs. Right	.276	.358	.355	152	42	7	1	1	16	19	26
at Home	.314	.379	.395	86	27	4	0	1	10	8	12
on Road	.216	.322	.284	74	16	3	1	0	7	12	15
Runners On Base	.247	.340	.358	81	20	4	1	0	17	11	18
Second Half	.227	.313	.286	119	27	5	1	0	8	14	19

2-YEAR TOTALS (1992–1993)

BA	OBA	SA	AB	H	2B	3B	HR	RBI	BB	SO
.111	.200	.111	9	1	0	0	0	1	1	2
.263	.337	.331	175	46	7	1	1	18	19	28
.307	.371	.386	88	27	4	0	1	10	8	13
.208	.294	.260	96	20	3	1	0	9	12	17
.228	.314	.326	92	21	4	1	1	19	11	19
.231	.309	.284	134	31	5	1	0	10	14	22

WILL PENNYFEATHER — BR/TR — age 26 — PIT OF17

1993	BA	OBA	SA	AB	H	2B	3B	HR	RBI	BB	SO
vs. Left	.150	.150	.200	20	3	1	0	0	1	0	2
vs. Right	.286	.286	.286	14	4	0	0	0	1	0	4
at Home	.176	.176	.235	17	3	1	0	0	2	0	2
on Road	.235	.235	.235	17	4	0	0	0	0	0	4
Runners On Base	.200	.200	.300	10	2	1	0	0	2	0	3
Second Half	.364	.364	.364	11	4	0	0	0	1	0	2

2-YEAR TOTALS (1992–1993)

BA	OBA	SA	AB	H	2B	3B	HR	RBI	BB	SO
.125	.125	.167	24	3	1	0	0	1	0	2
.316	.316	.316	19	6	0	0	0	1	0	4
.158	.158	.211	19	3	1	0	0	2	0	2
.250	.250	.250	24	6	0	0	0	0	0	4
.214	.214	.286	14	3	1	0	0	1	0	3
.333	.333	.333	15	5	0	0	0	1	0	2

GERALD PERRY — BL/TR — age 34 — SL 1B15, OF1

1993	BA	OBA	SA	AB	H	2B	3B	HR	RBI	BB	SO		BA	OBA	SA	AB	H	2B	3B	HR	RBI	BB	SO
vs. Left	.250	.400	.250	8	2	0	0	0	0	2	1		.253	.300	.362	829	210	33	3	17	95	54	117
vs. Right	.344	.443	.533	90	31	5	0	4	16	16	22		.269	.343	.379	2120	570	104	8	38	271	248	229
at Home	.281	.452	.594	32	9	1	0	3	6	10	7		.271	.339	.381	1489	404	78	7	24	199	158	162
on Road	.364	.432	.470	66	24	4	0	1	10	8	16		.258	.323	.367	1460	376	59	4	31	167	144	184
Runners On Base	.353	.476	.490	51	18	4	0	1	13	12	10		.288	.358	.407	1363	393	76	7	24	335	166	158
Second Half	.338	.442	.492	65	22	4	0	2	10	12	18		.264	.330	.383	1433	379	73	5	29	172	145	182

GENO PETRALLI — BL/TR — age 35 — TEX C39, DH2, 2B1, 3B1

1993	BA	OBA	SA	AB	H	2B	3B	HR	RBI	BB	SO		BA	OBA	SA	AB	H	2B	3B	HR	RBI	BB	SO
vs. Left	.267	.353	.333	15	4	1	0	0	0	2	1		.193	.279	.207	150	29	2	0	0	9	19	30
vs. Right	.237	.348	.297	118	28	4	0	1	13	20	16		.272	.348	.373	1676	456	79	9	24	182	192	226
at Home	.185	.267	.259	54	10	1	0	1	3	6	10		.247	.334	.320	849	210	32	3	8	73	106	130
on Road	.278	.400	.329	79	22	4	0	0	10	16	7		.281	.350	.393	977	275	49	6	16	118	105	126
Runners On Base	.238	.360	.270	63	15	2	0	0	12	12	8		.258	.347	.340	799	206	35	5	7	174	114	104
Second Half	.218	.333	.264	87	19	4	0	0	8	15	13		.273	.346	.362	999	273	40	5	13	103	112	147

GUS POLIDOR — BR/TR — age 33 — FLO 2B1, 3B1

1993	BA	OBA	SA	AB	H	2B	3B	HR	RBI	BB	SO		BA	OBA	SA	AB	H	2B	3B	HR	RBI	BB	SO
vs. Left	.500	.500	1.000	2	1	1	0	0	0	0	0		.199	.243	.252	206	41	8	0	1	14	10	25
vs. Right	.000	.000	.000	4	0	0	0	0	0	0	2		.215	.224	.259	228	49	7	0	1	21	2	22
at Home	.250	.250	.500	4	1	1	0	0	0	0	1		.253	.276	.287	174	44	6	0	0	18	5	20
on Road	.000	.000	.000	2	0	0	0	0	0	0	1		.177	.204	.235	260	46	9	0	2	17	7	27
Runners On Base	.000	.000	.000	0	0	0	0	0	0	0	0		.249	.276	.277	177	44	5	0	0	33	5	23
Second Half	.167	.167	.333	6	1	1	0	0	0	0	2		.221	.248	.272	290	64	9	0	2	23	9	25

TODD PRATT — BR/TR — age 27 — PHI C26

1993	BA	OBA	SA	AB	H	2B	3B	HR	RBI	BB	SO		BA	OBA	SA	AB	H	2B	3B	HR	RBI	BB	SO
vs. Left	.400	.464	1.040	25	10	4	0	4	9	2	4		.345	.406	.690	58	20	5	0	5	17	5	11
vs. Right	.242	.273	.323	62	15	2	0	1	4	3	15		.240	.275	.347	75	18	2	0	2	6	4	20
at Home	.256	.289	.605	43	11	3	0	4	8	1	10		.286	.333	.586	70	20	3	0	6	17	4	16
on Road	.318	.367	.455	44	14	3	0	1	5	4	9		.286	.333	.397	63	18	4	0	1	6	5	15
Runners On Base	.257	.325	.514	35	9	3	0	2	10	3	11		.258	.319	.452	62	16	3	0	2	13	5	17
Second Half	.333	.381	.614	57	19	4	0	4	10	4	14		.311	.363	.534	103	32	5	0	6	20	8	26

TOM PRINCE — BR/TR — age 30 — PIT C59

1993	BA	OBA	SA	AB	H	2B	3B	HR	RBI	BB	SO		BA	OBA	SA	AB	H	2B	3B	HR	RBI	BB	SO
vs. Left	.229	.280	.343	70	16	8	0	0	4	4	9		.186	.256	.287	188	35	13	0	2	13	17	32
vs. Right	.174	.268	.284	109	19	6	0	2	20	9	29		.168	.256	.257	214	36	13	0	2	31	20	49
at Home	.165	.239	.304	79	13	5	0	2	13	7	18		.157	.247	.252	159	25	9	0	2	20	19	33
on Road	.220	.298	.310	100	22	9	0	0	11	6	20		.189	.262	.284	243	46	17	0	3	24	18	48
Runners On Base	.273	.337	.442	77	21	7	0	0	24	5	16		.212	.283	.341	179	38	14	0	3	43	16	34
Second Half	.204	.281	.333	108	22	11	0	0	12	8	28		.197	.274	.310	239	47	18	0	3	24	21	49

HARVEY PULLIAM — BR/TR — age 27 — KC OF26

1993	BA	OBA	SA	AB	H	2B	3B	HR	RBI	BB	SO		BA	OBA	SA	AB	H	2B	3B	HR	RBI	BB	SO
vs. Left	.333	.362	.511	45	15	5	0	1	6	1	9		.304	.353	.544	79	24	7	0	4	10	5	19
vs. Right	.059	.111	.059	17	1	0	0	0	0	1	5		.095	.136	.095	21	2	0	0	0	0	1	7
at Home	.310	.355	.414	29	9	3	0	0	2	2	4		.269	.333	.462	52	14	4	0	2	5	5	10
on Road	.212	.235	.364	33	7	2	0	1	4	0	10		.250	.280	.438	48	12	3	0	2	5	1	16
Runners On Base	.381	.435	.619	21	8	2	0	1	6	1	5		.313	.405	.563	32	10	2	0	3	8	4	9
Second Half	.000	.000	.000	0	0	0	0	0	0	0	0		.273	.333	.576	33	9	1	0	3	4	3	9

CARLOS QUINTANA — BR/TR — age 29 — BOS 1B53, OF51

1993	BA	OBA	SA	AB	H	2B	3B	HR	RBI	BB	SO		BA	OBA	SA	AB	H	2B	3B	HR	RBI	BB	SO
vs. Left	.250	.342	.260	104	26	1	0	0	9	15	18		.319	.394	.417	477	152	23	0	8	65	59	66
vs. Right	.241	.303	.276	199	48	4	0	1	10	16	34		.254	.326	.333	899	228	36	1	11	100	94	141
at Home	.264	.329	.291	148	39	4	0	0	10	15	23		.284	.361	.347	651	185	26	0	5	72	77	93
on Road	.226	.305	.252	155	35	1	0	0	9	16	29		.269	.339	.375	725	195	33	1	14	93	76	114
Runners On Base	.207	.291	.228	145	30	3	0	0	18	16	28		.265	.335	.362	668	177	33	1	10	156	72	91
Second Half	.170	.267	.198	106	18	3	0	0	7	13	22		.256	.339	.347	723	185	34	1	10	96	92	113

RANDY READY — BR/TR — age 34 — MON 2B28, 1B13, 3B3

1993	BA	OBA	SA	AB	H	2B	3B	HR	RBI	BB	SO		BA	OBA	SA	AB	H	2B	3B	HR	RBI	BB	SO
vs. Left	.186	.255	.209	43	8	1	0	0	4	4	2		.269	.374	.418	1029	277	61	10	24	129	176	120
vs. Right	.286	.414	.418	91	26	7	1	1	6	19	6		.242	.336	.346	973	235	42	9	14	101	133	141
at Home	.209	.329	.313	67	14	5	1	0	5	12	5		.254	.361	.380	970	246	49	10	18	115	163	128
on Road	.299	.405	.388	67	20	3	0	1	5	11	3		.258	.350	.386	1032	266	54	9	20	115	146	133
Runners On Base	.230	.382	.311	61	14	5	0	0	9	15	4		.267	.370	.386	868	232	39	11	14	206	147	120
Second Half	.254	.367	.351	134	34	8	1	1	10	23	8		.254	.357	.395	1099	279	53	15	24	132	177	139

JEFF REBOULET — BR/TR — age 30 — MIN SS62, 3B35, 2B11, OF3, DH1

1993	BA	OBA	SA	AB	H	2B	3B	HR	RBI	BB	SO		BA	OBA	SA	AB	H	2B	3B	HR	RBI	BB	SO
vs. Left	.290	.380	.344	93	27	1	0	0	5	13	13		.275	.376	.325	120	33	6	0	0	7	18	19
vs. Right	.238	.341	.279	147	35	3	0	1	10	22	24		.214	.322	.280	257	55	9	0	1	24	40	44
at Home	.183	.264	.198	126	23	2	0	0	2	12	24		.210	.313	.265	181	38	5	1	1	13	24	33
on Road	.342	.449	.421	114	39	6	0	1	13	23	13		.255	.364	.321	196	50	10	0	1	18	34	30
Runners On Base	.219	.339	.281	96	21	3	0	1	15	16	10		.242	.357	.320	153	37	7	1	1	30	26	20
Second Half	.326	.417	.388	129	42	5	0	1	12	20	17		.266	.366	.335	218	58	9	0	2	19	34	34

GARY REDUS — BR/TR — age 38 — TEX OF61, 1B5, 2B1, DH1

1993	BA	OBA	SA	AB	H	2B	3B	HR	RBI	BB	SO
vs. Left	.302	.358	.500	86	26	7	2	2	10	8	12
vs. Right	.279	.346	.434	136	38	5	2	4	21	15	23
at Home	.275	.339	.385	109	30	2	2	2	18	11	14
on Road	.301	.362	.531	113	34	10	2	4	13	12	21
Runners On Base	.303	.368	.475	99	30	6	1	3	28	12	13
Second Half	.309	.374	.493	152	47	10	3	4	23	17	23

10-YEAR TOTALS (1984–1993)

BA	OBA	SA	AB	H	2B	3B	HR	RBI	BB	SO
.263	.357	.425	1481	389	85	25	35	138	224	252
.245	.327	.392	1463	358	74	15	37	154	177	298
.265	.357	.422	1503	399	90	22	34	169	217	269
.241	.326	.393	1441	348	69	18	38	123	184	281
.240	.332	.378	995	239	43	11	24	244	149	205
.253	.340	.419	1687	427	91	24	47	179	228	318

JEFF REED — BL/TR — age 32 — SF C37

1993	BA	OBA	SA	AB	H	2B	3B	HR	RBI	BB	SO
vs. Left	.375	.500	1.125	8	3	0	0	2	2	2	2
vs. Right	.252	.333	.387	111	28	3	0	4	10	14	20
at Home	.274	.308	.493	73	20	1	0	5	9	4	9
on Road	.239	.397	.348	46	11	2	0	1	3	12	13
Runners On Base	.220	.355	.280	50	11	0	0	1	7	11	15
Second Half	.289	.372	.342	38	11	2	0	0	2	5	3

10-YEAR TOTALS (1984–1993)

BA	OBA	SA	AB	H	2B	3B	HR	RBI	BB	SO
.225	.322	.355	169	38	10	0	4	24	22	36
.236	.302	.319	1375	325	56	6	15	107	134	189
.228	.295	.333	741	169	36	3	12	66	73	114
.242	.313	.313	803	194	30	3	7	65	83	111
.220	.313	.293	617	136	15	3	8	120	87	100
.243	.310	.321	816	198	38	4	6	64	83	108

RICH RENTERIA — BR/TR — age 33 — FLO 2B45, 3B25, OF1

1993	BA	OBA	SA	AB	H	2B	3B	HR	RBI	BB	SO
vs. Left	.211	.255	.295	95	20	3	1	1	12	6	13
vs. Right	.280	.346	.345	168	47	6	1	1	18	15	18
at Home	.292	.358	.396	144	42	5	2	2	20	14	19
on Road	.210	.258	.244	119	25	4	0	0	10	7	12
Runners On Base	.292	.341	.372	113	33	4	1	1	29	8	12
Second Half	.230	.286	.280	161	37	6	1	0	12	11	19

4-YEAR TOTALS (1986–1993)

BA	OBA	SA	AB	H	2B	3B	HR	RBI	BB	SO
.221	.255	.329	149	33	11	1	1	17	7	21
.250	.309	.313	224	56	9	1	1	20	17	24
.254	.310	.349	209	53	10	2	2	26	16	27
.220	.259	.280	164	36	10	0	0	11	8	18
.253	.298	.325	166	42	7	1	1	36	10	21
.231	.283	.283	173	40	7	1	0	13	11	23

KARL RHODES — BL/TL — age 26 — HOU/CHN OF18

1993	BA	OBA	SA	AB	H	2B	3B	HR	RBI	BB	SO
vs. Left	.250	.500	1.000	8	2	0	0	2	3	4	3
vs. Right	.283	.377	.435	46	13	2	1	1	4	7	6
at Home	.250	.429	.375	16	4	0	1	0	3	5	2
on Road	.289	.386	.579	38	11	2	0	3	4	6	7
Runners On Base	.438	.609	.750	16	7	0	1	1	5	7	0
Second Half	.288	.413	.538	52	15	2	1	3	7	11	9

4-YEAR TOTALS (1990–1993)

BA	OBA	SA	AB	H	2B	3B	HR	RBI	BB	SO
.189	.283	.340	53	10	2	0	2	7	7	14
.242	.333	.348	227	55	9	3	3	15	31	35
.233	.340	.301	133	31	5	2	0	10	22	19
.231	.309	.388	147	34	6	1	5	12	24	30
.212	.311	.279	104	22	2	1	1	18	16	16
.261	.368	.435	138	36	8	2	4	10	24	21

JEFF RICHARDSON — BR/TR — age 29 — BOS 2B8, SS5, 3B1

1993	BA	OBA	SA	AB	H	2B	3B	HR	RBI	BB	SO
vs. Left	.000	.000	.000	1	0	0	0	0	0	0	0
vs. Right	.217	.250	.304	23	5	2	0	0	2	1	3
at Home	.154	.214	.308	13	2	2	0	0	1	1	3
on Road	.273	.273	.273	11	3	0	0	0	1	0	0
Runners On Base	.333	.333	.556	9	3	2	0	0	0	0	0
Second Half	.000	.000	.000	0	0	0	0	0	0	0	0

3-YEAR TOTALS (1989–1993)

BA	OBA	SA	AB	H	2B	3B	HR	RBI	BB	SO
.196	.281	.333	51	10	1	0	2	5	6	8
.167	.211	.216	102	17	5	0	0	8	5	21
.133	.207	.205	83	11	3	0	1	5	7	17
.229	.270	.314	70	16	3	0	1	8	4	12
.214	.253	.300	70	15	3	0	1	12	3	12
.168	.234	.248	125	21	4	0	2	11	10	23

ERNIE RILES — BL/TR — age 34 — BOS 2B20, DH15, 3B11, 1B1

1993	BA	OBA	SA	AB	H	2B	3B	HR	RBI	BB	SO
vs. Left	.167	.333	.667	6	1	0	0	1	2	2	3
vs. Right	.190	.289	.336	137	26	8	0	4	18	18	37
at Home	.220	.324	.390	59	13	4	0	2	9	9	17
on Road	.167	.268	.321	84	14	4	0	3	11	11	23
Runners On Base	.157	.295	.243	70	11	3	0	1	16	14	19
Second Half	.125	.271	.313	48	6	0	0	3	7	8	13

9-YEAR TOTALS (1985–1993)

BA	OBA	SA	AB	H	2B	3B	HR	RBI	BB	SO
.211	.278	.297	431	91	9	5	6	41	39	94
.263	.328	.379	2073	546	83	15	42	243	205	315
.275	.348	.403	1197	329	51	12	26	137	136	187
.236	.293	.330	1307	308	41	8	22	147	108	222
.261	.335	.369	1082	282	32	5	25	261	128	166
.250	.315	.353	1437	359	46	9	28	160	139	224

BILLY RIPKEN — BR/TR — age 30 — TEX 2B34, SS18, 3B1

1993	BA	OBA	SA	AB	H	2B	3B	HR	RBI	BB	SO
vs. Left	.222	.280	.267	45	10	2	0	0	3	4	7
vs. Right	.172	.265	.195	87	15	2	0	0	8	7	12
at Home	.192	.306	.212	52	10	1	0	0	8	7	7
on Road	.188	.244	.225	80	15	3	0	0	3	4	12
Runners On Base	.193	.266	.228	57	11	2	0	0	11	3	9
Second Half	.167	.211	.278	18	3	2	0	0	1	1	2

7-YEAR TOTALS (1987–1993)

BA	OBA	SA	AB	H	2B	3B	HR	RBI	BB	SO
.267	.317	.330	772	206	38	1	3	57	58	81
.227	.278	.294	1447	329	58	4	10	122	90	177
.243	.299	.305	1068	260	45	3	5	90	78	121
.239	.285	.314	1151	275	51	2	6	89	70	137
.254	.294	.314	904	230	36	0	6	172	46	91
.261	.311	.326	1158	302	49	3	7	95	83	130

LUIS RIVERA — BR/TR — age 30 — BOS 2B27, SS27, DH7, 3B2

1993	BA	OBA	SA	AB	H	2B	3B	HR	RBI	BB	SO
vs. Left	.239	.286	.304	46	11	3	0	0	0	3	12
vs. Right	.190	.266	.310	84	16	5	1	1	7	8	24
at Home	.241	.281	.352	54	13	4	0	2	5	3	15
on Road	.184	.267	.276	76	14	5	1	0	2	8	21
Runners On Base	.163	.236	.245	49	8	1	0	1	7	4	16
Second Half	.206	.250	.353	34	7	2	0	1	3	2	13

8-YEAR TOTALS (1986–1993)

BA	OBA	SA	AB	H	2B	3B	HR	RBI	BB	SO
.235	.286	.348	695	163	41	4	10	68	49	140
.230	.290	.320	1375	316	67	6	15	126	110	266
.237	.292	.344	1024	243	58	3	15	114	75	188
.226	.286	.315	1046	236	50	7	10	80	84	218
.236	.292	.336	914	216	51	5	10	179	75	174
.227	.282	.332	1155	262	65	7	14	111	84	235

BIP ROBERTS — BB/TR — age 31 — CIN 2B64, OF11, 3B3, SS1

1993	BA	OBA	SA	AB	H	2B	3B	HR	RBI	BB	SO
vs. Left	.179	.258	.238	84	15	5	0	0	5	8	10
vs. Right	.264	.358	.317	208	55	8	0	1	13	30	36
at Home	.221	.313	.250	140	31	4	0	0	12	17	21
on Road	.257	.347	.336	152	39	9	0	1	6	21	25
Runners On Base	.194	.268	.259	108	21	5	1	0	1	10	18
Second Half	.156	.289	.188	32	5	1	0	0	0	6	12

7-YEAR TOTALS (1986–1993)

BA	OBA	SA	AB	H	2B	3B	HR	RBI	BB	SO
.266	.324	.366	864	230	41	6	11	63	69	104
.307	.383	.397	1519	466	75	16	10	113	187	208
.290	.356	.384	1186	344	53	11	12	92	114	152
.294	.369	.388	1197	352	63	11	9	84	142	160
.303	.356	.440	745	226	46	10	12	167	65	91
.312	.380	.413	1106	345	55	6	15	85	122	136

RICO ROSSY — BR/TR — age 30 — KC 2B24, 3B16, SS11

1993	BA	OBA	SA	AB	H	2B	3B	HR	RBI	BB	SO
vs. Left	.333	.400	.667	27	9	3	0	2	6	2	3
vs. Right	.169	.258	.186	59	10	1	0	0	6	7	8
at Home	.298	.375	.456	57	17	3	0	2	12	7	6
on Road	.069	.156	.103	29	2	1	0	0	0	2	5
Runners On Base	.244	.326	.268	41	10	1	0	0	10	5	6
Second Half	.186	.284	.271	59	11	2	0	1	6	7	8

3-YEAR TOTALS (1991–1993)

	BA	OBA	SA	AB	H	2B	3B	HR	RBI	BB	SO
	.247	.344	.429	77	19	8	0	2	12	11	8
	.201	.287	.258	159	32	4	1	1	12	18	24
	.265	.346	.389	113	30	6	1	2	17	14	18
	.171	.270	.244	123	21	6	0	1	7	15	14
	.239	.328	.303	109	26	5	1	0	21	15	13
	.227	.299	.299	97	22	4	0	1	10	9	13

RICH ROWLAND — BR/TR — age 27 — DET C17, DH3

1993	BA	OBA	SA	AB	H	2B	3B	HR	RBI	BB	SO
vs. Left	.229	.289	.314	35	8	3	0	0	4	3	10
vs. Right	.182	.308	.182	11	2	0	0	0	0	2	6
at Home	.278	.316	.333	18	5	1	0	0	2	1	7
on Road	.179	.281	.250	28	5	2	0	0	2	4	9
Runners On Base	.227	.320	.318	22	5	2	0	0	4	3	6
Second Half	.217	.294	.283	46	10	3	0	0	4	5	16

4-YEAR TOTALS (1990–1993)

	BA	OBA	SA	AB	H	2B	3B	HR	RBI	BB	SO
	.241	.318	.310	58	14	4	0	0	5	7	13
	.120	.241	.120	25	3	0	0	0	0	4	12
	.276	.333	.310	29	8	1	0	0	3	3	9
	.167	.274	.222	54	9	3	0	0	2	8	16
	.162	.256	.216	37	6	2	0	0	5	5	10
	.205	.295	.253	83	17	4	0	0	5	11	25

STAN ROYER — BR/TR — age 27 — SL 3B10, 1B2

1993	BA	OBA	SA	AB	H	2B	3B	HR	RBI	BB	SO
vs. Left	.294	.368	.294	17	5	0	0	0	3	2	7
vs. Right	.310	.310	.483	29	9	2	0	1	5	0	7
at Home	.050	.136	.050	20	1	0	0	0	0	2	9
on Road	.500	.500	.692	26	13	2	0	1	8	0	5
Runners On Base	.412	.444	.471	17	7	1	0	0	7	1	4
Second Half	.324	.359	.459	37	12	2	0	1	8	2	10

3-YEAR TOTALS (1991–1993)

	BA	OBA	SA	AB	H	2B	3B	HR	RBI	BB	SO
	.333	.361	.364	33	11	1	0	0	7	2	9
	.292	.313	.492	65	19	4	0	3	11	2	11
	.149	.200	.234	47	7	1	0	1	4	3	12
	.451	.453	.647	51	23	4	0	2	14	1	8
	.386	.417	.568	44	17	2	0	2	17	3	6
	.315	.340	.472	89	28	5	0	3	18	4	16

JOHN RUSSELL — BR/TR — age 33 — TEX C11, 1B1, 3B1, OF1

1993	BA	OBA	SA	AB	H	2B	3B	HR	RBI	BB	SO
vs. Left	.300	.364	.400	10	3	1	0	0	2	1	3
vs. Right	.167	.231	.417	12	2	0	0	1	1	1	7
at Home	.333	.429	.583	12	4	0	0	1	2	2	6
on Road	.100	.100	.200	10	1	0	0	0	1	0	4
Runners On Base	.250	.333	.313	16	4	1	0	0	2	2	8
Second Half	.167	.231	.250	12	2	1	0	0	2	1	5

10-YEAR TOTALS (1984–1993)

	BA	OBA	SA	AB	H	2B	3B	HR	RBI	BB	SO
	.223	.290	.348	511	114	26	1	12	51	45	155
	.227	.276	.391	576	131	24	2	22	78	39	200
	.251	.306	.419	546	137	29	3	19	76	43	179
	.200	.258	.322	541	108	21	0	15	53	41	176
	.259	.314	.395	501	130	25	2	13	108	41	144
	.234	.285	.378	698	163	32	3	21	85	50	219

DEION SANDERS — BL/TL — age 27 — ATL OF60

1993	BA	OBA	SA	AB	H	2B	3B	HR	RBI	BB	SO
vs. Left	.143	.167	.143	35	5	0	0	0	2	0	8
vs. Right	.295	.342	.498	237	70	18	6	6	26	16	34
at Home	.289	.319	.459	135	39	12	4	1	11	6	19
on Road	.263	.322	.445	137	36	6	2	5	17	10	23
Runners On Base	.301	.355	.470	83	25	7	2	1	23	7	12
Second Half	.328	.379	.555	128	42	4	5	5	18	11	13

5-YEAR TOTALS (1989–1993)

	BA	OBA	SA	AB	H	2B	3B	HR	RBI	BB	SO
	.191	.232	.328	131	25	2	5	2	9	6	37
	.266	.320	.440	734	195	27	19	21	76	56	115
	.249	.309	.398	410	102	14	10	9	40	34	75
	.259	.305	.446	455	118	15	14	14	45	28	77
	.275	.353	.420	295	81	11	7	6	68	36	56
	.267	.313	.454	337	90	9	9	12	43	21	57

NELSON SANTOVENIA — BR/TR — age 33 — KC C4

1993	BA	OBA	SA	AB	H	2B	3B	HR	RBI	BB	SO
vs. Left	.000	.500	.000	1	0	0	0	0	0	1	0
vs. Right	.143	.143	.143	7	1	0	0	0	0	0	2
at Home	.000	.000	.000	0	0	0	0	0	0	0	0
on Road	.167	.286	.167	6	1	0	0	0	0	1	2
Runners On Base	.200	.200	.200	5	1	0	0	0	0	0	1
Second Half	.125	.222	.125	8	1	0	0	0	0	1	2

7-YEAR TOTALS (1987–1993)

	BA	OBA	SA	AB	H	2B	3B	HR	RBI	BB	SO
	.250	.305	.389	296	74	13	2	8	40	24	41
	.224	.268	.352	588	132	29	2	14	76	35	125
	.276	.322	.455	413	114	25	2	15	72	30	65
	.195	.244	.285	471	92	17	2	7	44	29	101
	.260	.300	.396	407	106	19	3	10	104	29	67
	.223	.262	.354	494	110	21	4	12	64	28	88

MACKEY SASSER — BL/TR — age 32 — SEA OF37, DH19, C4, 1B1

1993	BA	OBA	SA	AB	H	2B	3B	HR	RBI	BB	SO
vs. Left	.286	.286	.286	7	2	0	0	0	1	0	0
vs. Right	.215	.274	.309	181	39	10	2	1	20	15	30
at Home	.225	.302	.314	102	23	7	1	0	11	11	15
on Road	.209	.239	.302	86	18	3	1	1	10	4	15
Runners On Base	.253	.303	.402	87	22	6	2	1	21	8	13
Second Half	.196	.283	.315	92	18	6	1	1	11	11	16

7-YEAR TOTALS (1987–1993)

	BA	OBA	SA	AB	H	2B	3B	HR	RBI	BB	SO
	.200	.229	.276	145	29	8	0	1	13	6	23
	.280	.311	.397	1014	284	60	7	15	143	49	81
	.267	.303	.387	592	158	39	4	8	87	33	54
	.273	.298	.377	567	155	29	3	8	69	22	50
	.287	.323	.419	544	156	32	5	10	150	37	52
	.263	.288	.378	695	183	42	4	10	97	27	66

STEVE SAX — BR/TR — age 34 — CHA OF32, DH21, 2B1

1993	BA	OBA	SA	AB	H	2B	3B	HR	RBI	BB	SO
vs. Left	.239	.282	.299	67	16	4	0	0	5	4	3
vs. Right	.231	.286	.308	52	12	1	0	1	3	4	3
at Home	.250	.286	.333	60	15	2	0	1	4	3	4
on Road	.220	.281	.271	59	13	3	0	0	4	5	2
Runners On Base	.196	.245	.239	46	9	2	0	0	5	3	3
Second Half	.239	.280	.268	71	17	2	0	0	5	4	3

10-YEAR TOTALS (1984–1993)

	BA	OBA	SA	AB	H	2B	3B	HR	RBI	BB	SO
	.292	.348	.386	1800	525	104	7	17	137	160	104
	.276	.328	.346	3736	1030	131	27	26	315	282	338
	.274	.330	.347	2711	742	115	14	20	212	227	208
	.288	.339	.369	2825	813	120	20	23	240	215	234
	.281	.344	.353	1926	541	66	15	14	423	194	165
	.284	.333	.364	3016	857	140	18	22	239	215	236

STEVE SCARSONE — BR/TR — age 28 — SF 2B20, 3B8, 1B6

1993	BA	OBA	SA	AB	H	2B	3B	HR	RBI	BB	SO
vs. Left	.256	.286	.359	39	10	4	0	0	3	1	11
vs. Right	.250	.273	.422	64	16	5	0	2	12	2	21
at Home	.244	.255	.400	45	11	4	0	1	8	1	13
on Road	.259	.295	.397	58	15	5	0	1	7	3	19
Runners On Base	.333	.325	.641	39	13	6	0	2	15	0	9
Second Half	.252	.278	.398	103	26	9	0	2	15	4	32

2-YEAR TOTALS (1992–1993)

	BA	OBA	SA	AB	H	2B	3B	HR	RBI	BB	SO
	.218	.241	.291	55	12	4	0	0	3	2	20
	.244	.280	.385	78	19	5	0	2	12	4	24
	.212	.222	.346	52	11	4	0	1	8	1	15
	.247	.291	.346	81	20	5	0	1	7	5	29
	.302	.309	.528	53	16	6	0	2	15	1	15
	.242	.270	.367	120	29	9	0	2	15	5	38

DICK SCHOFIELD — BR/TR — age 32 — TOR SS36

1993	BA	OBA	SA	AB	H	2B	3B	HR	RBI	BB	SO
vs. Left	.171	.293	.171	35	6	0	0	0	1	6	8
vs. Right	.200	.294	.267	75	15	1	2	0	4	10	17
at Home	.255	.388	.345	55	14	1	2	0	5	12	16
on Road	.127	.186	.127	55	7	0	0	0	0	4	9
Runners On Base	.200	.294	.222	45	9	1	0	0	5	6	11
Second Half	.100	.182	.100	20	2	0	0	0	0	2	2

10-YEAR TOTALS (1984–1993)

BA	OBA	SA	AB	H	2B	3B	HR	RBI	BB	SO
.239	.325	.333	1303	311	46	13	17	92	155	180
.223	.296	.304	2571	574	75	18	32	244	245	428
.223	.300	.301	1928	430	49	15	24	168	198	306
.234	.311	.326	1946	455	72	16	25	148	202	302
.231	.326	.316	1559	360	54	12	18	285	206	250
.236	.314	.318	1967	465	59	18	22	153	210	299

MIKE SHARPERSON — BR/TR — age 33 — LA 2B17, 3B6, SS3, 1B1, OF1

1993	BA	OBA	SA	AB	H	2B	3B	HR	RBI	BB	SO
vs. Left	.253	.277	.380	79	20	4	0	2	9	2	15
vs. Right	.273	.429	.273	11	3	0	0	0	1	3	2
at Home	.243	.293	.324	37	9	0	0	1	3	2	7
on Road	.264	.304	.396	53	14	4	0	1	7	3	10
Runners On Base	.211	.295	.316	38	8	1	0	1	9	4	9
Second Half	.327	.353	.449	49	16	3	0	1	6	1	9

7-YEAR TOTALS (1987–1993)

BA	OBA	SA	AB	H	2B	3B	HR	RBI	BB	SO
.303	.369	.397	716	217	37	3	8	72	76	87
.250	.338	.321	480	120	24	2	2	49	63	65
.293	.361	.368	581	170	25	2	5	59	62	76
.272	.353	.364	615	167	36	3	5	62	77	76
.290	.368	.374	545	158	26	4	4	115	69	69
.279	.352	.370	667	186	34	3	7	60	74	89

DANNY SHEAFFER — BR/TR — age 33 — COL C65, 1B7, OF2, 3B1

1993	BA	OBA	SA	AB	H	2B	3B	HR	RBI	BB	SO
vs. Left	.396	.400	.500	48	19	2	0	1	7	1	1
vs. Right	.244	.271	.351	168	41	7	1	3	25	7	14
at Home	.295	.302	.418	122	36	7	1	2	22	2	9
on Road	.255	.295	.340	94	24	2	0	2	10	6	6
Runners On Base	.255	.290	.309	94	24	2	0	1	29	6	9
Second Half	.303	.333	.403	119	36	4	1	2	23	7	8

3-YEAR TOTALS (1987–1993)

BA	OBA	SA	AB	H	2B	3B	HR	RBI	BB	SO
.286	.307	.357	84	24	3	0	1	9	3	6
.210	.232	.308	214	45	7	1	4	28	7	25
.248	.260	.349	149	37	7	1	2	23	3	12
.215	.247	.295	149	32	3	0	3	15	7	19
.221	.252	.265	136	30	3	0	1	33	7	19
.255	.287	.333	153	39	4	1	2	24	8	13

LARRY SHEETS — BL/TR — age 35 — SEA DH5, OF1

1993	BA	OBA	SA	AB	H	2B	3B	HR	RBI	BB	SO
vs. Left	.000	.000	.000	0	0	0	0	0	0	0	0
vs. Right	.118	.250	.176	17	2	1	0	0	1	2	1
at Home	.000	.300	.000	7	0	0	0	0	0	2	1
on Road	.200	.200	.300	10	2	1	0	0	1	0	0
Runners On Base	.200	.200	.300	10	2	1	0	0	1	0	1
Second Half	.118	.250	.176	17	2	1	0	0	1	2	1

8-YEAR TOTALS (1984–1993)

BA	OBA	SA	AB	H	2B	3B	HR	RBI	BB	SO
.231	.301	.354	359	83	8	0	12	41	32	71
.272	.324	.452	1925	524	90	5	82	298	143	280
.263	.317	.441	1135	298	49	2	50	186	89	183
.269	.324	.432	1149	309	49	3	44	153	86	168
.273	.322	.463	1040	284	45	3	49	294	80	155
.265	.312	.432	1167	309	47	2	48	160	76	188

TOMMY SHIELDS — BL/TR — age 30 — CHN 2B7, 3B7, 1B1, OF1

1993	BA	OBA	SA	AB	H	2B	3B	HR	RBI	BB	SO
vs. Left	.188	.235	.188	16	3	0	0	0	0	1	6
vs. Right	.167	.211	.222	18	3	1	0	0	1	1	4
at Home	.375	.375	.375	8	3	0	0	0	0	0	2
on Road	.115	.179	.154	26	3	1	0	0	1	2	8
Runners On Base	.235	.316	.294	17	4	1	0	0	1	2	4
Second Half	.273	.333	.364	11	3	1	0	0	1	1	2

2-YEAR TOTALS (1992–1993)

BA	OBA	SA	AB	H	2B	3B	HR	RBI	BB	SO
.188	.235	.188	16	3	0	0	0	0	1	6
.167	.211	.222	18	3	1	0	0	1	1	4
.375	.375	.375	8	3	0	0	0	0	0	2
.115	.179	.154	26	3	1	0	0	1	2	8
.235	.316	.294	17	4	1	0	0	1	2	4
.273	.333	.364	11	3	1	0	0	1	1	2

CRAIG SHIPLEY — BR/TR — age 31 — SD SS38, 3B37, 2B12, OF5

1993	BA	OBA	SA	AB	H	2B	3B	HR	RBI	BB	SO
vs. Left	.229	.282	.292	96	22	3	0	1	7	7	10
vs. Right	.239	.270	.351	134	32	6	0	3	15	3	21
at Home	.222	.270	.315	108	24	4	0	2	11	6	8
on Road	.246	.279	.336	122	30	5	0	2	11	4	23
Runners On Base	.222	.273	.321	81	18	2	0	2	20	6	7
Second Half	.241	.305	.343	108	26	2	0	3	11	7	17

6-YEAR TOTALS (1986–1993)

BA	OBA	SA	AB	H	2B	3B	HR	RBI	BB	SO
.252	.291	.317	202	51	7	0	2	12	11	25
.229	.253	.304	293	67	13	0	3	29	5	53
.219	.251	.279	233	51	8	0	2	20	8	34
.256	.285	.336	262	67	12	0	3	21	8	44
.222	.262	.289	194	43	7	0	4	38	9	23
.249	.287	.325	305	76	11	0	4	23	11	51

TERRY SHUMPERT — BR/TR — age 28 — KC 2B8

1993	BA	OBA	SA	AB	H	2B	3B	HR	RBI	BB	SO
vs. Left	.000	.000	.000	1	0	0	0	0	0	0	0
vs. Right	.111	.273	.111	9	1	0	0	0	0	2	2
at Home	.000	.000	.000	2	0	0	0	0	0	0	1
on Road	.125	.300	.125	8	1	0	0	0	0	2	1
Runners On Base	.000	.500	.000	1	0	0	0	0	0	1	0
Second Half	.100	.250	.100	10	1	0	0	0	0	2	2

4-YEAR TOTALS (1990–1993)

BA	OBA	SA	AB	H	2B	3B	HR	RBI	BB	SO
.231	.281	.338	195	45	12	0	3	21	10	32
.203	.259	.301	369	75	15	6	3	32	27	79
.206	.256	.298	272	56	12	5	1	23	15	50
.219	.276	.329	292	64	15	1	5	30	22	61
.216	.262	.303	241	52	11	2	2	49	14	46
.207	.284	.297	232	48	11	2	2	19	20	47

DAVE SILVESTRI — BR/TR — age 27 — NYA SS4, 3B3

1993	BA	OBA	SA	AB	H	2B	3B	HR	RBI	BB	SO
vs. Left	.444	.583	.778	9	4	0	0	1	3	3	1
vs. Right	.167	.286	.250	12	2	1	0	0	1	2	2
at Home	.214	.389	.286	14	3	1	0	0	1	4	3
on Road	.429	.500	.857	7	3	0	0	1	3	1	0
Runners On Base	.286	.412	.500	14	4	0	0	1	4	3	1
Second Half	.000	.000	.000	0	0	0	0	0	0	0	0

2-YEAR TOTALS (1992–1993)

BA	OBA	SA	AB	H	2B	3B	HR	RBI	BB	SO
.375	.474	.688	16	6	0	0	1	4	3	2
.222	.300	.389	18	4	1	0	0	1	2	4
.263	.391	.421	19	5	1	0	0	1	4	4
.333	.375	.667	15	5	0	0	1	4	1	2
.333	.429	.611	15	6	0	0	1	5	3	2
.333	.333	.667	6	2	0	0	0	0	0	1

LONNIE SMITH — BR/TR — age 39 — PIT/BAL OF64, DH5

1993	BA	OBA	SA	AB	H	2B	3B	HR	RBI	BB	SO
vs. Left	.303	.426	.455	132	40	3	1	5	20	28	30
vs. Right	.242	.412	.440	91	22	3	3	3	7	23	22
at Home	.313	.447	.525	99	31	1	1	6	13	23	26
on Road	.250	.399	.387	124	31	5	3	2	14	28	26
Runners On Base	.250	.409	.352	88	22	2	2	1	20	22	19
Second Half	.292	.445	.522	113	33	6	1	6	15	28	31

10-YEAR TOTALS (1984–1993)

BA	OBA	SA	AB	H	2B	3B	HR	RBI	BB	SO
.293	.380	.447	1285	377	75	16	30	140	176	213
.267	.359	.394	2234	596	99	22	47	242	282	417
.288	.378	.430	1709	492	90	21	37	198	232	298
.266	.356	.397	1810	481	84	17	40	184	226	332
.291	.388	.432	1306	380	72	23	22	327	201	233
.285	.368	.421	2145	611	118	15	48	228	256	381

LUIS SOJO — BR/TR — age 28 — TOR 2B8, SS8, 3B3   4-YEAR TOTALS (1990–1993)

1993	BA	OBA	SA	AB	H	2B	3B	HR	RBI	BB	SO	BA	OBA	SA	AB	H	2B	3B	HR	RBI	BB	SO
vs. Left	.071	.235	.143	14	1	1	0	0	2	3	0	.247	.291	.301	259	64	12	1	0	15	16	19
vs. Right	.212	.229	.242	33	7	1	0	0	4	1	2	.260	.291	.357	600	156	19	3	11	63	21	38
at Home	.130	.259	.130	23	3	0	0	0	3	4	2	.245	.287	.298	400	98	12	0	3	36	23	21
on Road	.208	.200	.292	24	5	2	0	0	3	0	0	.266	.294	.377	459	122	19	4	8	42	14	36
Runners On Base	.190	.250	.238	21	4	1	0	0	6	2	1	.269	.294	.339	386	104	13	3	3	70	12	22
Second Half	.000	.000	.000	0	0	0	0	0	0	0	0	.266	.301	.355	597	159	20	3	9	55	27	44

TIM SPEHR — BR/TR — age 28 — MON C49   2-YEAR TOTALS (1991–1993)

1993	BA	OBA	SA	AB	H	2B	3B	HR	RBI	BB	SO	BA	OBA	SA	AB	H	2B	3B	HR	RBI	BB	SO
vs. Left	.245	.310	.396	53	13	5	0	1	5	4	7	.229	.312	.427	96	22	7	0	4	15	10	18
vs. Right	.206	.237	.324	34	7	1	0	1	5	2	13	.185	.236	.292	65	12	4	0	1	9	5	20
at Home	.244	.295	.317	41	10	3	0	0	2	3	9	.227	.338	.348	66	15	5	0	1	12	11	15
on Road	.217	.269	.413	46	10	3	0	2	8	3	11	.200	.240	.389	95	19	6	0	4	12	4	23
Runners On Base	.171	.262	.286	35	6	1	0	1	9	4	7	.139	.235	.264	72	10	3	0	2	21	9	15
Second Half	.350	.366	.500	40	14	3	0	1	4	1	9	.246	.310	.421	114	28	8	0	4	18	10	27

MATT STAIRS — BL/TR — age 26 — MON OF1   2-YEAR TOTALS (1992–1993)

1993	BA	OBA	SA	AB	H	2B	3B	HR	RBI	BB	SO	BA	OBA	SA	AB	H	2B	3B	HR	RBI	BB	SO
vs. Left	.500	.500	1.000	2	1	1	0	0	1	0	1	.250	.500	.500	4	1	1	0	0	1	2	1
vs. Right	.333	.333	.333	6	2	0	0	0	1	0	0	.206	.300	.265	34	7	2	0	0	6	5	7
at Home	.500	.500	1.000	2	1	1	0	0	1	0	1	.182	.357	.273	11	2	1	0	0	1	3	3
on Road	.333	.333	.333	6	2	0	0	0	1	0	0	.222	.313	.296	27	6	2	0	0	6	4	5
Runners On Base	.400	.400	.600	5	2	1	0	0	2	0	1	.300	.400	.450	20	6	3	0	0	7	4	4
Second Half	.000	.000	.000	0	0	0	0	0	0	0	0	.000	.000	.000	0	0	0	0	0	0	0	0

ANDY STANKIEWICZ — BR/TR — age 30 — NYA 2B6, 3B4, SS1, DH1   2-YEAR TOTALS (1992–1993)

1993	BA	OBA	SA	AB	H	2B	3B	HR	RBI	BB	SO	BA	OBA	SA	AB	H	2B	3B	HR	RBI	BB	SO
vs. Left	.000	.167	.000	5	0	0	0	0	0	1	0	.262	.329	.312	141	37	5	1	0	10	11	11
vs. Right	.000	.000	.000	4	0	0	0	0	0	0	0	.261	.334	.354	268	70	17	1	2	15	28	32
at Home	.000	.111	.000	8	0	0	0	0	0	1	1	.284	.345	.381	215	61	13	1	2	15	20	19
on Road	.000	.000	.000	1	0	0	0	0	0	0	0	.237	.320	.294	194	46	9	1	0	10	19	24
Runners On Base	.000	.000	.000	1	0	0	0	0	0	0	1	.270	.327	.358	137	37	10	1	0	23	10	17
Second Half	.000	.167	.000	5	0	0	0	0	0	1	0	.229	.291	.273	227	52	8	1	0	10	18	20

KURT STILLWELL — BB/TR — age 29 — SD/CAL SS37, 2B18, 3B3   8-YEAR TOTALS (1986–1993)

1993	BA	OBA	SA	AB	H	2B	3B	HR	RBI	BB	SO	BA	OBA	SA	AB	H	2B	3B	HR	RBI	BB	SO
vs. Left	.160	.276	.160	25	4	0	0	0	0	3	5	.238	.309	.319	802	191	30	10	5	83	78	116
vs. Right	.242	.292	.325	157	38	6	2	1	14	12	28	.252	.310	.360	2246	567	117	20	28	223	186	328
at Home	.250	.326	.333	84	21	4	0	1	9	9	16	.245	.309	.349	1479	363	74	17	15	160	135	223
on Road	.214	.257	.276	98	21	2	2	0	5	6	17	.252	.310	.349	1569	395	73	13	18	146	129	221
Runners On Base	.200	.279	.227	75	15	2	0	0	13	9	10	.278	.330	.390	1290	358	63	14	18	291	109	173
Second Half	.227	.277	.307	75	17	2	2	0	5	6	13	.239	.296	.338	1428	341	67	16	14	143	113	190

DARRYL STRAWBERRY — BL/TL — age 32 — LA OF29   10-YEAR TOTALS (1984–1993)

1993	BA	OBA	SA	AB	H	2B	3B	HR	RBI	BB	SO	BA	OBA	SA	AB	H	2B	3B	HR	RBI	BB	SO
vs. Left	.143	.367	.190	21	3	1	0	0	1	8	5	.241	.318	.449	1665	401	63	8	89	295	186	439
vs. Right	.139	.233	.342	79	11	1	0	5	11	8	14	.272	.382	.545	2579	701	141	19	175	501	457	572
at Home	.158	.227	.421	38	6	1	0	3	7	3	6	.266	.359	.527	2017	536	99	14	133	414	293	471
on Road	.129	.289	.242	62	8	1	0	2	5	13	13	.254	.356	.489	2227	566	105	13	131	382	350	540
Runners On Base	.106	.279	.234	47	5	0	0	2	9	12	10	.278	.387	.534	2022	562	93	13	133	665	378	484
Second Half	.000	.000	.000	0	0	0	0	0	0	0	0	.262	.355	.514	2352	617	109	17	150	474	336	577

WILLIAM SUERO — BR/TR — age 28 — MIL 2B8, 3B1   2-YEAR TOTALS (1992–1993)

1993	BA	OBA	SA	AB	H	2B	3B	HR	RBI	BB	SO	BA	OBA	SA	AB	H	2B	3B	HR	RBI	BB	SO
vs. Left	.364	.417	.364	11	4	0	0	0	0	1	1	.318	.400	.364	22	7	1	0	0	0	3	2
vs. Right	.000	.000	.000	3	0	0	0	0	0	0	2	.000	.111	.000	8	0	0	0	0	0	0	2
at Home	.333	.429	.333	6	2	0	0	0	0	1	2	.182	.357	.182	11	2	0	0	0	0	2	2
on Road	.250	.250	.250	8	2	0	0	0	0	0	1	.263	.300	.316	19	5	1	0	0	0	1	2
Runners On Base	.167	.286	.167	6	1	0	0	0	0	1	2	.071	.235	.071	14	1	0	0	0	0	2	3
Second Half	1.000	1.000	1.000	1	1	0	0	0	0	0	0	1.000	1.000	1.000	1	1	0	0	0	0	0	0

DALE SVEUM — BB/TR — age 31 — OAK 1B14, 3B7, 2B4, DH2, SS1, OF1   7-YEAR TOTALS (1986–1993)

1993	BA	OBA	SA	AB	H	2B	3B	HR	RBI	BB	SO	BA	OBA	SA	AB	H	2B	3B	HR	RBI	BB	SO
vs. Left	.133	.278	.133	15	2	0	0	0	1	3	5	.250	.318	.408	708	177	38	7	20	91	71	182
vs. Right	.188	.325	.344	64	12	2	1	2	5	13	16	.226	.285	.348	1322	299	57	4	32	179	110	333
at Home	.074	.194	.074	27	2	0	0	0	0	4	7	.234	.301	.352	1019	238	49	6	20	122	99	247
on Road	.231	.375	.423	52	12	2	1	2	6	12	14	.235	.292	.386	1011	238	46	5	32	148	82	268
Runners On Base	.258	.378	.387	31	8	2	1	0	4	6	7	.262	.317	.425	890	233	57	8	24	242	78	210
Second Half	.000	.000	.000	0	0	0	0	0	0	0	0	.246	.305	.392	1001	246	52	5	28	137	86	223

JEFF TACKETT — BR/TR — age 29 — BAL C38, P1   3-YEAR TOTALS (1991–1993)

1993	BA	OBA	SA	AB	H	2B	3B	HR	RBI	BB	SO	BA	OBA	SA	AB	H	2B	3B	HR	RBI	BB	SO
vs. Left	.263	.364	.263	19	5	0	0	0	2	3	6	.284	.376	.459	74	21	1	0	4	9	10	11
vs. Right	.147	.253	.191	68	10	3	0	0	7	10	22	.190	.268	.265	200	38	10	1	1	24	22	47
at Home	.227	.352	.227	44	10	3	0	0	8	9	16	.239	.307	.403	134	32	8	1	4	24	14	28
on Road	.116	.191	.116	43	5	0	0	0	1	4	12	.193	.287	.236	140	27	3	0	1	9	18	30
Runners On Base	.190	.327	.238	42	8	2	0	0	9	9	14	.216	.313	.296	125	27	7	1	0	29	20	27
Second Half	.114	.205	.114	35	4	0	0	0	4	4	10	.192	.277	.246	167	32	7	1	0	16	20	32

JIM TATUM — BR/TR — age 27 — COL 1B12, 3B6, OF3

2-YEAR TOTALS (1992–1993)

1993	BA	OBA	SA	AB	H	2B	3B	HR	RBI	BB	SO	BA	OBA	SA	AB	H	2B	3B	HR	RBI	BB	SO
vs. Left	.250	.294	.406	32	8	2	0	1	5	1	8	.250	.289	.389	36	9	2	0	1	5	1	9
vs. Right	.182	.222	.227	66	12	3	0	0	7	4	19	.171	.221	.214	70	12	3	0	0	7	5	20
at Home	.148	.203	.222	54	8	4	0	0	5	3	11	.153	.215	.220	59	9	4	0	0	5	4	13
on Road	.273	.298	.364	44	12	1	0	1	7	2	16	.255	.280	.340	47	12	1	0	1	7	2	16
Runners On Base	.213	.220	.362	47	10	4	0	1	12	1	14	.200	.222	.340	50	10	4	0	1	12	2	16
Second Half	.211	.273	.289	38	8	3	0	0	5	4	14	.196	.264	.261	46	9	3	0	0	5	5	16

MILT THOMPSON — BL/TR — age 35 — PHI OF106

10-YEAR TOTALS (1984–1993)

1993	BA	OBA	SA	AB	H	2B	3B	HR	RBI	BB	SO	BA	OBA	SA	AB	H	2B	3B	HR	RBI	BB	SO
vs. Left	.175	.250	.175	57	10	0	0	0	2	6	9	.223	.271	.290	668	149	29	5	2	48	40	143
vs. Right	.279	.359	.385	283	79	14	2	4	42	34	48	.293	.356	.402	2654	778	109	32	39	253	251	412
at Home	.252	.341	.346	159	40	7	1	2	19	22	25	.284	.344	.398	1650	469	73	27	20	166	149	262
on Road	.271	.342	.354	181	49	7	1	2	25	18	32	.274	.334	.362	1672	458	65	10	21	135	142	293
Runners On Base	.279	.376	.382	165	46	9	1	2	42	27	28	.293	.363	.388	1295	379	50	19	12	272	143	222
Second Half	.277	.348	.399	188	52	10	2	3	19	20	31	.290	.344	.389	1862	540	82	17	23	158	147	315

DICKIE THON — BR/TR — age 36 — MIL SS28, 3B25, 2B22, DH14

10-YEAR TOTALS (1984–1993)

1993	BA	OBA	SA	AB	H	2B	3B	HR	RBI	BB	SO	BA	OBA	SA	AB	H	2B	3B	HR	RBI	BB	SO
vs. Left	.270	.336	.320	122	33	3	0	1	15	13	21	.267	.332	.375	1339	357	51	11	24	130	135	200
vs. Right	.268	.311	.341	123	33	7	1	0	18	9	18	.249	.292	.346	1577	392	62	10	24	164	98	286
at Home	.280	.333	.322	118	33	5	0	0	14	10	19	.251	.306	.344	1424	358	50	11	20	144	115	242
on Road	.260	.315	.339	127	33	5	1	1	19	12	20	.262	.315	.374	1492	391	63	10	28	150	118	244
Runners On Base	.324	.380	.378	111	36	4	1	0	32	13	12	.256	.316	.367	1233	316	52	11	21	267	117	198
Second Half	.213	.286	.270	89	19	2	0	1	5	9	14	.271	.317	.390	1417	384	59	10	30	145	96	220

GARY THURMAN — BR/TR — age 30 — DET OF53, DH9

7-YEAR TOTALS (1987–1993)

1993	BA	OBA	SA	AB	H	2B	3B	HR	RBI	BB	SO	BA	OBA	SA	AB	H	2B	3B	HR	RBI	BB	SO
vs. Left	.276	.328	.345	58	16	2	1	0	8	5	15	.256	.302	.329	434	111	19	5	1	38	29	89
vs. Right	.097	.243	.161	31	3	0	0	0	5	6	15	.222	.291	.255	333	74	6	1	1	23	31	95
at Home	.200	.267	.309	55	11	2	2	0	8	5	17	.213	.270	.274	380	81	14	3	1	27	28	84
on Road	.235	.341	.235	34	8	0	0	0	5	6	13	.269	.323	.320	387	104	11	3	1	34	32	100
Runners On Base	.267	.358	.356	45	12	0	2	0	13	7	15	.268	.318	.316	313	84	7	4	0	59	24	74
Second Half	.196	.269	.283	46	9	2	1	0	5	5	15	.255	.311	.306	474	121	17	2	1	33	38	114

RON TINGLEY — BR/TR — age 35 — CAL C58

6-YEAR TOTALS (1988–1993)

1993	BA	OBA	SA	AB	H	2B	3B	HR	RBI	BB	SO	BA	OBA	SA	AB	H	2B	3B	HR	RBI	BB	SO
vs. Left	.167	.233	.204	54	9	2	0	0	7	5	14	.188	.243	.271	133	25	5	0	2	13	9	35
vs. Right	.250	.341	.389	36	9	5	0	0	5	4	8	.201	.288	.297	229	46	11	1	3	22	25	65
at Home	.196	.288	.261	46	9	3	0	0	4	5	8	.234	.328	.357	171	40	10	1	3	22	22	41
on Road	.205	.265	.295	44	9	4	0	0	8	4	14	.162	.218	.225	191	31	6	0	2	13	12	59
Runners On Base	.265	.333	.382	34	9	4	0	0	12	3	6	.177	.233	.286	147	26	8	1	2	32	9	36
Second Half	.217	.262	.283	60	13	4	0	0	8	3	13	.203	.281	.281	217	44	9	1	2	19	21	63

JEFF TREADWAY — BL/TR — age 31 — CLE 3B42, 2B19, DH4

7-YEAR TOTALS (1987–1993)

1993	BA	OBA	SA	AB	H	2B	3B	HR	RBI	BB	SO	BA	OBA	SA	AB	H	2B	3B	HR	RBI	BB	SO
vs. Left	.105	.227	.105	19	2	0	0	0	0	2	2	.236	.293	.303	314	74	7	1	4	33	23	36
vs. Right	.322	.359	.431	202	65	14	1	2	27	12	19	.292	.334	.404	1671	488	91	12	24	157	107	136
at Home	.265	.290	.314	102	27	3	1	0	13	4	10	.277	.327	.372	960	266	43	6	12	92	67	72
on Road	.336	.394	.479	119	40	11	0	2	14	10	11	.289	.328	.403	1025	296	55	7	16	98	63	100
Runners On Base	.348	.386	.478	92	32	7	1	1	26	6	10	.302	.351	.416	781	236	42	7	11	173	66	60
Second Half	.305	.342	.448	105	32	7	1	2	19	7	12	.270	.315	.373	1028	278	48	6	15	101	68	90

EDDIE TUCKER — BR/TR — age 28 — HOU C8

2-YEAR TOTALS (1992–1993)

1993	BA	OBA	SA	AB	H	2B	3B	HR	RBI	BB	SO	BA	OBA	SA	AB	H	2B	3B	HR	RBI	BB	SO
vs. Left	.250	.333	.250	8	2	0	0	0	1	1	2	.148	.258	.148	27	4	0	0	0	3	3	7
vs. Right	.167	.211	.222	18	3	1	0	0	2	1	1	.143	.192	.184	49	7	2	0	0	3	2	9
at Home	.400	.400	.400	5	2	0	0	0	0	0	1	.214	.333	.214	28	6	2	0	0	2	3	8
on Road	.143	.217	.190	21	3	1	0	0	3	2	2	.104	.140	.146	48	5	2	0	0	6	2	8
Runners On Base	.125	.300	.250	8	1	1	0	0	3	2	0	.120	.267	.200	25	3	2	0	0	6	4	4
Second Half	.192	.250	.231	26	5	1	0	0	3	2	3	.149	.184	.191	47	7	2	0	0	4	2	10

JOSE URIBE — BB/TR — age 35 — HOU SS41

10-YEAR TOTALS (1984–1993)

1993	BA	OBA	SA	AB	H	2B	3B	HR	RBI	BB	SO	BA	OBA	SA	AB	H	2B	3B	HR	RBI	BB	SO
vs. Left	.294	.400	.353	17	5	1	0	0	2	2	1	.252	.306	.336	946	238	38	6	10	87	73	127
vs. Right	.222	.333	.222	36	8	0	0	0	1	6	4	.236	.297	.304	2118	500	61	28	9	132	183	298
at Home	.333	.444	.333	15	5	0	0	0	0	3	2	.243	.304	.317	1466	356	56	14	8	94	129	199
on Road	.211	.318	.237	38	8	1	0	0	3	5	3	.239	.296	.312	1598	382	43	20	11	125	127	226
Runners On Base	.167	.375	.222	18	3	1	0	0	3	5	4	.258	.334	.333	1257	324	41	16	7	207	144	159
Second Half	.276	.382	.310	29	8	1	0	0	3	4	3	.239	.302	.309	1645	393	56	15	10	119	148	232

JOSE VALENTIN — BB/TR — age 25 — MIL SS19

2-YEAR TOTALS (1992–1993)

1993	BA	OBA	SA	AB	H	2B	3B	HR	RBI	BB	SO	BA	OBA	SA	AB	H	2B	3B	HR	RBI	BB	SO
vs. Left	.263	.333	.368	19	5	0	1	0	1	1	6	.263	.333	.368	19	5	0	1	0	1	1	6
vs. Right	.235	.350	.412	34	8	1	1	1	6	6	10	.216	.318	.378	37	8	1	1	1	7	6	10
at Home	.333	.391	.667	21	7	0	2	1	5	5	4	.333	.391	.667	21	7	0	2	1	5	5	4
on Road	.188	.316	.237	32	6	1	0	0	2	2	12	.171	.286	.200	35	6	1	0	0	3	6	12
Runners On Base	.292	.370	.458	24	7	1	0	1	7	3	5	.280	.345	.440	25	7	1	0	1	8	3	5
Second Half	.245	.344	.396	53	13	1	2	1	7	7	16	.232	.323	.375	56	13	1	2	1	8	7	16

JOHN VANDERWAL — BL/TL — age 28 — MON 1B42, OF38

1993	BA	OBA	SA	AB	H	2B	3B	HR	RBI	BB	SO
vs. Left	.118	.286	.176	17	2	1	0	0	0	4	1
vs. Right	.242	.323	.389	198	48	6	4	5	30	23	29
at Home	.241	.355	.329	79	19	4	0	1	11	13	7
on Road	.228	.298	.397	136	31	3	4	4	19	14	23
Runners On Base	.253	.336	.414	99	25	4	3	2	27	13	15
Second Half	.194	.308	.320	103	20	5	1	2	12	17	16

3-YEAR TOTALS (1991–1993)

	BA	OBA	SA	AB	H	2B	3B	HR	RBI	BB	SO
	.161	.232	.177	62	10	1	0	0	2	6	15
	.244	.318	.389	427	104	18	7	10	56	46	69
	.247	.341	.357	182	45	9	1	3	23	25	24
	.225	.286	.307	307	69	10	6	7	35	27	60
	.244	.320	.372	242	59	12	5	3	51	28	48
	.218	.288	.339	289	63	12	4	5	29	29	51

GARY VARSHO — BL/TR — age 33 — CIN OF22

1993	BA	OBA	SA	AB	H	2B	3B	HR	RBI	BB	SO
vs. Left	.400	.400	.400	5	2	0	0	0	0	0	2
vs. Right	.222	.297	.356	90	20	6	0	2	11	9	17
at Home	.179	.273	.308	39	7	2	0	1	2	5	9
on Road	.268	.323	.393	56	15	4	0	1	9	4	10
Runners On Base	.156	.235	.244	45	7	1	0	1	10	4	8
Second Half	.188	.235	.333	48	9	1	0	1	3	3	7

6-YEAR TOTALS (1988–1993)

	BA	OBA	SA	AB	H	2B	3B	HR	RBI	BB	SO
	.184	.205	.316	38	7	2	0	1	4	0	10
	.244	.295	.363	614	150	32	7	9	64	44	100
	.230	.278	.356	326	75	16	5	5	32	20	47
	.252	.302	.365	326	82	18	2	5	36	24	63
	.244	.307	.411	270	66	15	3	8	66	24	46
	.244	.283	.368	361	88	17	2	8	40	20	55

RANDY VELARDE — BR/TR — age 32 — NYA OF50, SS26, 3B16, DH1

1993	BA	OBA	SA	AB	H	2B	3B	HR	RBI	BB	SO
vs. Left	.345	.402	.595	116	40	7	2	6	13	10	15
vs. Right	.255	.317	.336	110	28	6	0	1	11	8	24
at Home	.313	.365	.487	115	36	8	0	4	13	9	19
on Road	.288	.355	.450	111	32	5	2	3	11	9	20
Runners On Base	.266	.359	.367	109	29	3	1	2	19	14	20
Second Half	.328	.352	.500	134	44	7	2	4	13	5	22

7-YEAR TOTALS (1987–1993)

	BA	OBA	SA	AB	H	2B	3B	HR	RBI	BB	SO
	.291	.355	.443	461	134	26	4	12	46	42	84
	.238	.300	.348	827	197	38	4	15	82	67	173
	.272	.338	.381	617	168	33	2	10	70	55	109
	.243	.302	.383	671	163	31	6	17	58	54	148
	.244	.317	.360	528	129	22	3	11	112	53	106
	.272	.329	.406	860	234	46	6	19	94	72	166

GUILLERMO VELASQUEZ — BL/TR — age 26 — SD 1B38, OF6

1993	BA	OBA	SA	AB	H	2B	3B	HR	RBI	BB	SO
vs. Left	.143	.143	.357	14	2	0	0	1	2	0	8
vs. Right	.217	.287	.279	129	28	2	0	2	18	13	27
at Home	.242	.346	.303	66	16	1	0	1	11	11	15
on Road	.182	.203	.273	77	14	1	0	2	9	2	20
Runners On Base	.284	.364	.343	67	19	1	0	1	18	9	17
Second Half	.223	.287	.321	112	25	2	0	3	11	10	28

2-YEAR TOTALS (1992–1993)

	BA	OBA	SA	AB	H	2B	3B	HR	RBI	BB	SO
	.150	.150	.300	20	3	0	0	1	2	0	9
	.233	.298	.308	146	34	2	0	3	23	14	33
	.254	.349	.352	71	18	1	0	2	13	11	17
	.200	.224	.274	95	19	1	0	2	12	3	25
	.287	.356	.375	80	23	1	0	2	23	9	21
	.237	.295	.341	135	32	2	0	4	16	11	35

HECTOR VILLANUEVA — BR/TR — age 30 — SL C17

1993	BA	OBA	SA	AB	H	2B	3B	HR	RBI	BB	SO
vs. Left	.167	.167	.667	12	2	0	0	2	5	0	4
vs. Right	.140	.213	.233	43	6	1	0	1	4	4	13
at Home	.185	.267	.407	27	5	0	0	2	3	3	7
on Road	.107	.138	.250	28	3	1	0	1	6	1	10
Runners On Base	.174	.240	.478	23	4	1	0	2	8	2	5
Second Half	.000	.000	.000	0	0	0	0	0	0	0	0

4-YEAR TOTALS (1990–1993)

	BA	OBA	SA	AB	H	2B	3B	HR	RBI	BB	SO
	.240	.317	.489	221	53	9	2	14	40	25	45
	.222	.270	.401	252	56	12	0	11	32	15	53
	.256	.320	.508	242	62	8	1	17	46	21	49
	.203	.264	.372	231	47	13	1	8	26	19	49
	.222	.286	.498	207	46	7	1	16	63	17	40
	.293	.347	.527	184	54	11	1	10	28	15	41

JACK VOIGT — BR/TR — age 28 — BAL OF43, DH9, 1B5, 3B3

1993	BA	OBA	SA	AB	H	2B	3B	HR	RBI	BB	SO
vs. Left	.352	.410	.637	91	32	8	0	6	19	9	15
vs. Right	.213	.377	.295	61	13	3	1	0	4	16	18
at Home	.314	.416	.558	86	27	6	0	5	14	15	19
on Road	.273	.368	.424	66	18	5	1	1	9	10	14
Runners On Base	.284	.363	.420	81	23	5	0	2	19	10	14
Second Half	.309	.411	.564	110	34	11	1	5	17	19	25

2-YEAR TOTALS (1992–1993)

	BA	OBA	SA	AB	H	2B	3B	HR	RBI	BB	SO
	.352	.410	.637	91	32	8	0	6	19	9	15
	.213	.377	.295	61	13	3	1	0	4	16	18
	.314	.416	.558	86	27	6	0	5	14	15	19
	.273	.368	.424	66	18	5	1	1	9	10	14
	.284	.363	.420	81	23	5	0	2	19	10	14
	.309	.411	.564	110	34	11	1	5	17	19	25

JIM WALEWANDER — BB/TR — age 32 — CAL SS6, DH3, 2B2

1993	BA	OBA	SA	AB	H	2B	3B	HR	RBI	BB	SO
vs. Left	.500	.500	.500	2	1	0	0	0	2	1	0
vs. Right	.000	.400	.000	6	0	0	0	0	1	4	1
at Home	.500	.667	.500	2	1	0	0	0	3	3	0
on Road	.000	.250	.000	6	0	0	0	0	0	2	1
Runners On Base	.143	.364	.143	7	1	0	0	0	1	2	0
Second Half	.125	.429	.125	8	1	0	0	0	3	5	1

4-YEAR TOTALS (1987–1993)

	BA	OBA	SA	AB	H	2B	3B	HR	RBI	BB	SO
	.235	.279	.265	102	24	3	0	0	8	7	9
	.199	.285	.277	141	28	6	1	1	6	17	25
	.222	.291	.296	135	30	5	1	1	8	14	18
	.204	.271	.241	108	22	4	0	0	6	10	16
	.163	.229	.204	98	16	1	0	1	14	9	16
	.190	.272	.243	189	36	5	1	1	12	22	24

CHICO WALKER — BB/TR — age 37 — NYN 2B24, 3B23, OF15

1993	BA	OBA	SA	AB	H	2B	3B	HR	RBI	BB	SO
vs. Left	.319	.347	.514	72	23	6	1	2	11	3	4
vs. Right	.177	.234	.248	141	25	1	1	3	8	11	25
at Home	.208	.245	.260	96	20	2	0	1	5	5	9
on Road	.239	.291	.402	117	28	5	1	4	14	9	20
Runners On Base	.242	.300	.384	99	24	3	1	3	17	9	14
Second Half	.231	.277	.347	121	28	3	1	3	11	8	16

8-YEAR TOTALS (1984–1993)

	BA	OBA	SA	AB	H	2B	3B	HR	RBI	BB	SO
	.272	.308	.373	327	89	14	2	5	38	19	44
	.234	.302	.311	811	190	23	3	11	70	83	156
	.252	.312	.316	544	137	16	2	5	51	52	91
	.239	.296	.340	594	142	21	3	11	57	50	109
	.262	.335	.358	458	120	11	3	9	101	57	86
	.268	.327	.367	664	178	23	5	11	70	62	110

DAN WALTERS — BR/TR — age 28 — SD C26

1993	BA	OBA	SA	AB	H	2B	3B	HR	RBI	BB	SO
vs. Left	.324	.390	.405	37	12	3	0	0	5	4	2
vs. Right	.123	.164	.175	57	7	0	0	1	5	3	11
at Home	.222	.263	.333	54	12	3	0	1	6	3	8
on Road	.175	.244	.175	40	7	0	0	0	4	4	5
Runners On Base	.182	.282	.242	33	6	2	0	0	9	5	5
Second Half	.000	.000	.000	0	0	0	0	0	0	0	0

2-YEAR TOTALS (1992–1993)

	BA	OBA	SA	AB	H	2B	3B	HR	RBI	BB	SO
	.286	.317	.388	98	28	7	0	1	13	5	11
	.206	.262	.326	175	36	7	1	4	19	12	30
	.250	.297	.417	144	36	10	1	4	18	9	18
	.217	.244	.271	129	28	4	0	1	14	8	23
	.189	.244	.252	111	21	5	1	0	27	9	21
	.232	.275	.389	95	22	6	0	3	8	5	16

JEROME WALTON — BR/TR — age 29 — CAL DH4, OF1

1993	BA	OBA	SA	AB	H	2B	3B	HR	RBI	BB	SO		BA	OBA	SA	AB	H	2B	3B	HR	RBI	BB	SO
vs. Left	.000	.500	.000	1	0	0	0	0	0	1	1		.256	.329	.333	450	115	18	4	3	38	46	78
vs. Right	.000	.000	.000	1	0	0	0	0	0	0	1		.259	.321	.349	744	193	34	3	9	47	60	139
at Home	.000	.000	.000	0	0	0	0	0	0	0	0		.277	.336	.373	571	158	21	5	8	39	50	88
on Road	.000	.333	.000	2	0	0	0	0	0	1	2		.241	.313	.316	623	150	31	2	4	46	56	129
Runners On Base	.000	.000	.000	1	0	0	0	0	0	0	1		.256	.325	.317	375	96	15	4	0	73	36	72
Second Half	.000	.000	.000	0	0	0	0	0	0	0	0		.262	.319	.348	584	153	21	4	7	50	46	104

TURNER WARD — BB/TR — age 29 — TOR OF65, 1B1

1993	BA	OBA	SA	AB	H	2B	3B	HR	RBI	BB	SO		BA	OBA	SA	AB	H	2B	3B	HR	RBI	BB	SO
vs. Left	.367	.424	.600	30	11	2	1	1	6	3	5		.341	.407	.476	82	28	6	1	1	12	9	10
vs. Right	.153	.259	.248	137	21	2	1	3	22	20	21		.209	.290	.315	273	57	10	2	5	36	32	46
at Home	.132	.212	.276	76	10	1	2	2	10	7	13		.170	.243	.275	153	26	6	2	2	13	14	29
on Road	.242	.345	.341	91	22	3	0	2	18	16	13		.292	.371	.411	202	59	10	1	4	35	27	27
Runners On Base	.205	.305	.385	78	16	3	1	3	27	12	13		.262	.338	.413	172	45	10	2	4	46	21	31
Second Half	.169	.244	.234	77	13	3	1	0	14	9	12		.260	.326	.364	154	40	6	2	2	29	17	24

LENNY WEBSTER — BR/TR — age 29 — MIN C45, DH1

1993	BA	OBA	SA	AB	H	2B	3B	HR	RBI	BB	SO		BA	OBA	SA	AB	H	2B	3B	HR	RBI	BB	SO
vs. Left	.267	.353	.300	30	8	1	0	0	4	4	2		.299	.382	.403	77	23	5	0	1	13	11	7
vs. Right	.171	.241	.224	76	13	1	0	1	4	7	6		.237	.301	.357	207	49	11	1	4	17	19	25
at Home	.172	.232	.234	64	11	1	0	1	4	5	7		.239	.286	.356	163	39	8	1	3	17	11	21
on Road	.238	.333	.262	42	10	1	0	0	4	6	1		.273	.371	.388	121	33	8	0	2	13	19	11
Runners On Base	.190	.261	.214	42	8	1	0	0	7	4	5		.250	.331	.367	120	30	8	0	2	27	15	17
Second Half	.176	.288	.176	51	9	0	0	0	5	8	4		.285	.370	.397	151	43	10	1	2	17	17	18

MITCH WEBSTER — BB/TL — age 35 — LA OF56

1993	BA	OBA	SA	AB	H	2B	3B	HR	RBI	BB	SO		BA	OBA	SA	AB	H	2B	3B	HR	RBI	BB	SO
vs. Left	.275	.292	.391	69	19	4	2	0	6	2	8		.287	.335	.440	1229	353	64	14	32	144	85	174
vs. Right	.223	.293	.301	103	23	2	0	2	8	9	16		.251	.329	.379	2039	512	81	40	33	183	227	377
at Home	.221	.279	.299	77	17	1	1	1	6	6	12		.254	.326	.380	1567	398	62	26	28	165	161	244
on Road	.263	.304	.368	95	25	5	1	1	8	5	12		.275	.336	.422	1701	467	83	28	37	162	151	307
Runners On Base	.225	.270	.313	80	18	2	1	1	13	5	16		.268	.338	.395	1364	365	58	19	26	288	149	225
Second Half	.203	.250	.328	64	13	3	1	1	5	3	8		.272	.332	.429	1715	467	79	32	42	189	148	291

ERIC WEDGE — BR/TR — age 26 — COL C1

1993	BA	OBA	SA	AB	H	2B	3B	HR	RBI	BB	SO		BA	OBA	SA	AB	H	2B	3B	HR	RBI	BB	SO
vs. Left	.000	.000	.000	2	0	0	0	0	0	0	2		.289	.372	.632	38	11	1	0	4	8	5	10
vs. Right	.222	.222	.222	9	2	0	0	0	1	0	2		.214	.340	.310	42	9	1	0	1	4	8	12
at Home	.222	.222	.222	9	2	0	0	0	1	0	2		.295	.380	.500	44	13	0	0	3	8	6	14
on Road	.000	.000	.000	2	0	0	0	0	0	0	2		.194	.326	.417	36	7	2	0	2	4	7	8
Runners On Base	.333	.333	.333	3	1	0	0	0	1	0	1		.357	.486	.714	28	10	1	0	3	10	7	6
Second Half	.182	.182	.182	11	2	0	0	0	1	0	4		.250	.355	.463	80	20	2	0	5	12	13	22

JOHN WEHNER — BR/TR — age 27 — PIT OF13, 2B3, 3B3

1993	BA	OBA	SA	AB	H	2B	3B	HR	RBI	BB	SO		BA	OBA	SA	AB	H	2B	3B	HR	RBI	BB	SO
vs. Left	.050	.240	.050	20	1	0	0	0	0	5	6		.227	.293	.273	128	29	6	0	0	4	12	22
vs. Right	.267	.313	.267	15	4	0	0	0	0	1	4		.250	.315	.301	136	34	7	0	0	7	13	27
at Home	.000	.045	.000	21	0	0	0	0	0	1	7		.241	.274	.304	112	27	7	0	0	7	5	21
on Road	.357	.526	.357	14	5	0	0	0	0	5	3		.237	.326	.276	152	36	6	0	0	4	20	28
Runners On Base	.143	.250	.143	21	3	0	0	0	0	3	6		.197	.277	.231	117	23	4	0	0	11	13	27
Second Half	.067	.176	.067	15	1	0	0	0	0	2	2		.250	.304	.305	220	55	12	0	0	11	17	38

CURTIS WILKERSON — BB/TR — age 33 — KC 2B10, SS4

1993	BA	OBA	SA	AB	H	2B	3B	HR	RBI	BB	SO		BA	OBA	SA	AB	H	2B	3B	HR	RBI	BB	SO
vs. Left	.000	.000	.000	7	0	0	0	0	0	0	1		.235	.294	.298	540	127	19	3	3	40	44	85
vs. Right	.190	.227	.190	21	4	0	0	0	0	1	5		.249	.285	.308	1877	467	59	19	5	138	92	313
at Home	.100	.182	.100	10	1	0	0	0	0	1	2		.254	.296	.322	1162	295	37	12	6	97	65	180
on Road	.167	.167	.167	18	3	0	0	0	0	0	4		.238	.279	.292	1255	299	41	10	2	81	71	218
Runners On Base	.100	.100	.100	10	1	0	0	0	0	0	1		.238	.287	.294	949	226	21	13	2	172	66	143
Second Half	.000	.000	.000	0	0	0	0	0	0	0	0		.240	.284	.300	1202	288	37	10	5	90	72	190

GERALD WILLIAMS — BR/TR — age 28 — NYA OF37

1993	BA	OBA	SA	AB	H	2B	3B	HR	RBI	BB	SO		BA	OBA	SA	AB	H	2B	3B	HR	RBI	BB	SO
vs. Left	.139	.179	.194	36	5	0	1	0	2	1	6		.200	.226	.380	50	10	1	1	2	6	1	8
vs. Right	.161	.188	.355	31	5	2	2	0	4	0	8		.182	.200	.409	44	8	3	2	1	6	0	9
at Home	.108	.132	.216	37	4	0	2	0	2	1	8		.163	.180	.388	49	8	1	2	2	5	1	9
on Road	.200	.242	.333	30	6	2	1	0	4	0	6		.222	.250	.400	45	10	3	1	1	7	0	8
Runners On Base	.091	.114	.212	33	3	0	2	0	6	0	4		.152	.167	.326	46	7	1	2	1	10	0	5
Second Half	.071	.129	.071	28	2	0	0	0	1	0	6		.182	.207	.382	55	10	2	0	3	7	0	9

CRAIG WILSON — BR/TR — age 30 — KC 3B15, 2B1, OF1

1993	BA	OBA	SA	AB	H	2B	3B	HR	RBI	BB	SO		BA	OBA	SA	AB	H	2B	3B	HR	RBI	BB	SO
vs. Left	.250	.357	.500	12	3	0	0	1	2	2	1		.260	.316	.302	192	50	5	0	1	26	18	29
vs. Right	.270	.357	.297	37	10	1	0	0	1	5	5		.241	.299	.276	170	41	6	0	0	11	14	21
at Home	.192	.300	.308	26	5	0	0	1	3	4	1		.215	.291	.267	191	41	7	0	1	19	21	27
on Road	.348	.423	.391	23	8	1	0	0	0	3	5		.292	.328	.316	171	50	4	0	0	18	11	23
Runners On Base	.250	.348	.400	20	5	1	0	1	3	3	3		.229	.282	.276	192	44	6	0	1	37	16	33
Second Half	.222	.344	.370	27	6	1	0	1	2	5	3		.239	.297	.274	226	54	5	0	1	18	20	31

DAN WILSON — BR/TR — age 25 — CIN C35

1993	BA	OBA	SA	AB	H	2B	3B	HR	RBI	BB	SO
vs. Left	.167	.211	.167	18	3	0	0	0	1	1	3
vs. Right	.241	.328	.293	58	14	3	0	0	7	8	13
at Home	.280	.333	.320	50	14	2	0	0	5	4	7
on Road	.115	.250	.154	26	3	1	0	0	3	5	9
Runners On Base	.189	.295	.243	37	7	2	0	0	8	6	7
Second Half	.214	.241	.250	28	6	1	0	0	4	1	5

2-YEAR TOTALS (1992–1993)

BA	OBA	SA	AB	H	2B	3B	HR	RBI	BB	SO
.267	.290	.300	30	8	1	0	0	4	1	7
.254	.349	.296	71	18	3	0	0	7	11	17
.279	.338	.324	68	19	3	0	0	7	6	13
.212	.325	.242	33	7	1	0	0	4	6	11
.220	.310	.280	50	11	3	0	0	11	7	11
.283	.333	.321	53	15	2	0	0	7	4	13

GLENN WILSON — BR/TR — age 36 — PIT OF5

1993	BA	OBA	SA	AB	H	2B	3B	HR	RBI	BB	SO
vs. Left	.167	.167	.167	12	2	0	0	0	0	0	7
vs. Right	.000	.000	.000	2	0	0	0	0	0	0	2
at Home	.000	.000	.000	5	0	0	0	0	0	0	4
on Road	.222	.222	.222	9	2	0	0	0	0	0	5
Runners On Base	.000	.000	.000	6	0	0	0	0	0	0	5
Second Half	.000	.000	.000	0	0	0	0	0	0	0	0

8-YEAR TOTALS (1984–1993)

BA	OBA	SA	AB	H	2B	3B	HR	RBI	BB	SO
.272	.313	.405	1119	304	75	1	24	143	71	154
.256	.300	.384	2207	565	94	18	51	279	142	388
.271	.320	.406	1587	430	92	9	35	228	120	240
.252	.289	.377	1739	439	77	10	40	194	93	302
.251	.291	.378	1489	374	71	8	34	381	91	250
.264	.306	.380	1666	439	90	7	30	205	108	254

WILLIE WILSON — BB/TR — age 39 — CHN OF82

1993	BA	OBA	SA	AB	H	2B	3B	HR	RBI	BB	SO
vs. Left	.235	.257	.275	102	24	4	0	0	4	3	12
vs. Right	.277	.336	.412	119	33	7	3	1	7	8	28
at Home	.289	.331	.395	114	33	6	3	0	4	6	21
on Road	.224	.270	.299	107	24	5	0	1	7	5	19
Runners On Base	.227	.288	.242	66	15	1	0	0	10	4	8
Second Half	.275	.337	.396	91	25	4	2	1	6	8	18

10-YEAR TOTALS (1984–1993)

BA	OBA	SA	AB	H	2B	3B	HR	RBI	BB	SO
.276	.308	.367	1410	389	66	19	8	114	69	255
.270	.320	.363	3169	857	108	66	18	245	204	469
.283	.329	.379	2297	651	84	54	9	179	145	334
.261	.304	.350	2282	595	90	31	17	180	128	390
.284	.327	.373	1733	493	75	29	7	340	106	255
.278	.320	.372	2411	671	94	47	13	195	135	384

TED WOOD — BL/TL — age 27 — MON OF8

1993	BA	OBA	SA	AB	H	2B	3B	HR	RBI	BB	SO
vs. Left	.000	.500	.000	1	0	0	0	0	0	1	0
vs. Right	.200	.259	.240	25	5	1	0	0	3	2	3
at Home	.200	.238	.200	20	4	0	0	0	0	1	2
on Road	.167	.375	.333	6	1	1	0	0	3	2	1
Runners On Base	.300	.417	.400	10	3	1	0	0	3	2	1
Second Half	.000	.000	.000	0	0	0	0	0	0	0	0

3-YEAR TOTALS (1991–1993)

BA	OBA	SA	AB	H	2B	3B	HR	RBI	BB	SO
.353	.421	.353	17	6	0	0	0	0	1	2
.152	.235	.217	92	14	3	0	1	7	10	27
.207	.281	.224	58	12	1	0	0	3	5	14
.157	.246	.255	51	8	2	0	1	4	6	15
.231	.362	.256	39	9	1	0	0	4	8	15
.181	.261	.241	83	15	2	0	1	4	8	26

TRACY WOODSON — BR/TR — age 32 — SL 3B28, 1B11

1993	BA	OBA	SA	AB	H	2B	3B	HR	RBI	BB	SO
vs. Left	.208	.218	.245	53	11	2	0	0	2	1	10
vs. Right	.208	.208	.208	24	5	0	0	0	0	0	4
at Home	.237	.250	.263	38	9	1	0	0	1	1	10
on Road	.179	.179	.205	39	7	1	0	0	1	0	4
Runners On Base	.192	.185	.192	26	5	0	0	0	2	0	6
Second Half	.194	.194	.226	31	6	1	0	0	0	0	7

5-YEAR TOTALS (1987–1993)

BA	OBA	SA	AB	H	2B	3B	HR	RBI	BB	SO
.256	.288	.350	223	57	12	0	3	22	10	33
.240	.272	.311	283	68	10	2	2	28	10	45
.223	.262	.298	215	48	7	0	3	18	10	33
.265	.292	.351	291	77	15	2	2	32	10	45
.261	.300	.353	184	48	9	1	2	47	10	32
.259	.287	.338	355	92	14	1	4	40	12	52

RICK WRONA — BR/TR — age 31 — CHA C4

1993	BA	OBA	SA	AB	H	2B	3B	HR	RBI	BB	SO
vs. Left	.333	.333	.333	3	1	0	0	0	0	0	1
vs. Right	.000	.000	.000	5	0	0	0	0	1	0	3
at Home	.333	.333	.333	3	1	0	0	0	0	0	1
on Road	.000	.000	.000	5	0	0	0	0	1	0	3
Runners On Base	.333	.333	.333	3	1	0	0	0	1	0	1
Second Half	.200	.200	.200	5	1	0	0	0	0	0	2

5-YEAR TOTALS (1988–1993)

BA	OBA	SA	AB	H	2B	3B	HR	RBI	BB	SO
.212	.257	.227	66	14	1	0	0	1	4	17
.239	.242	.337	92	22	1	1	2	14	0	23
.195	.218	.207	82	16	1	0	0	4	3	19
.263	.282	.382	76	20	1	1	2	11	1	21
.275	.288	.362	69	19	1	1	1	14	2	16
.273	.283	.386	88	24	2	1	2	11	1	23

ERIC YELDING — BR/TR — age 29 — CHN 2B32, 3B7, SS1, OF1

1993	BA	OBA	SA	AB	H	2B	3B	HR	RBI	BB	SO
vs. Left	.313	.371	.375	32	10	2	0	0	1	3	3
vs. Right	.158	.238	.263	76	12	3	1	1	9	8	19
at Home	.192	.250	.288	52	10	2	0	1	3	4	11
on Road	.214	.302	.304	56	12	3	1	0	7	7	11
Runners On Base	.167	.245	.271	48	8	3	1	0	9	5	6
Second Half	.171	.267	.263	76	13	5	1	0	9	10	20

5-YEAR TOTALS (1989–1993)

BA	OBA	SA	AB	H	2B	3B	HR	RBI	BB	SO
.280	.326	.329	410	115	12	4	0	26	30	58
.218	.268	.269	583	127	15	3	3	41	40	119
.235	.286	.270	477	112	6	4	1	27	36	85
.252	.298	.316	516	130	21	3	2	40	34	92
.249	.283	.302	354	88	9	5	0	64	20	42
.231	.285	.282	489	113	16	3	1	32	38	97

GERALD YOUNG — BB/TR — age 30 — COL OF11

1993	BA	OBA	SA	AB	H	2B	3B	HR	RBI	BB	SO
vs. Left	.000	.000	.000	3	0	0	0	0	0	0	0
vs. Right	.063	.250	.063	16	1	0	0	0	1	4	1
at Home	.083	.313	.083	12	1	0	0	0	1	4	1
on Road	.000	.000	.000	7	0	0	0	0	0	0	0
Runners On Base	.000	.111	.000	8	0	0	0	0	1	1	0
Second Half	.000	.000	.000	0	0	0	0	0	0	0	0

7-YEAR TOTALS (1987–1993)

BA	OBA	SA	AB	H	2B	3B	HR	RBI	BB	SO
.267	.340	.330	619	165	22	4	3	41	68	76
.232	.322	.283	1155	268	33	13	0	69	156	129
.252	.332	.310	914	230	30	10	1	57	110	97
.236	.324	.288	860	203	25	7	2	53	114	108
.270	.363	.327	563	152	22	5	0	107	87	58
.258	.338	.313	1023	264	29	12	1	64	124	119

BOB ZUPCIC — BR/TR — age 28 — BOS OF122, DH5

1993	BA	OBA	SA	AB	H	2B	3B	HR	RBI	BB	SO
vs. Left	.216	.303	.381	97	21	6	2	2	6	11	14
vs. Right	.254	.311	.349	189	48	18	0	0	20	16	40
at Home	.279	.337	.422	154	43	17	1	1	17	13	30
on Road	.197	.275	.288	132	26	7	1	1	9	14	24
Runners On Base	.274	.350	.406	106	29	12	1	0	24	13	20
Second Half	.213	.266	.320	169	36	13	1	1	16	13	30

3-YEAR TOTALS (1991–1993)

BA	OBA	SA	AB	H	2B	3B	HR	RBI	BB	SO
.257	.330	.365	241	62	14	3	2	23	25	29
.258	.303	.346	462	119	29	0	4	49	28	91
.270	.321	.402	356	96	28	2	5	44	24	65
.245	.303	.303	347	85	15	1	1	28	29	55
.298	.344	.408	272	81	20	2	2	68	20	46
.239	.291	.320	485	116	23	2	4	51	34	80

1993 DEBUT BATTERS

KURT ABBOTT — BR/TR — age 26 — OAK OF13, SS6, 2B2

1993	BA	OBA	SA	AB	H	2B	3B	HR	RBI	BB	SO
vs. Left	.231	.259	.462	26	6	0	0	2	3	1	9
vs. Right	.257	.297	.371	35	9	1	0	1	6	2	11
at Home	.087	.125	.087	23	2	0	0	0	1	1	7
on Road	.342	.375	.605	38	13	1	0	3	8	2	13
Runners On Base	.313	.333	.500	32	10	0	0	2	8	1	11
Second Half	.246	.281	.410	61	15	1	0	3	9	3	20

MARCOS ARMAS — BR/TR — age 25 — OAK 1B12, DH2, OF1

1993	BA	OBA	SA	AB	H	2B	3B	HR	RBI	BB	SO
vs. Left	.235	.278	.471	17	4	1	0	1	1	0	7
vs. Right	.143	.200	.214	14	2	1	0	0	1	1	5
at Home	.200	.231	.360	25	5	1	0	1	1	1	10
on Road	.167	.286	.333	6	1	1	0	0	0	0	2
Runners On Base	.118	.118	.118	17	2	0	0	0	0	0	8
Second Half	.211	.286	.263	19	4	1	0	0	0	1	7

RICH AUDE — BR/TR — age 23 — PIT 1B7, OF1

1993	BA	OBA	SA	AB	H	2B	3B	HR	RBI	BB	SO
vs. Left	.214	.214	.286	14	3	1	0	0	4	0	3
vs. Right	.000	.077	.000	12	0	0	0	0	0	1	4
at Home	.059	.111	.059	17	1	0	0	0	1	1	5
on Road	.222	.222	.333	9	2	1	0	0	3	0	2
Runners On Base	.214	.267	.286	14	3	1	0	0	4	1	2
Second Half	.115	.148	.154	26	3	1	0	0	4	1	7

DANNY BAUTISTA — BR/TR — age 22 — DET OF16

1993	BA	OBA	SA	AB	H	2B	3B	HR	RBI	BB	SO
vs. Left	.167	.167	.333	18	3	0	0	1	2	0	2
vs. Right	.372	.378	.442	43	16	3	0	0	7	1	8
at Home	.231	.259	.269	26	6	1	0	0	0	1	5
on Road	.371	.361	.514	35	13	2	0	1	9	0	5
Runners On Base	.296	.286	.333	27	8	1	0	0	8	0	7
Second Half	.311	.317	.410	61	19	3	0	1	9	1	10

RICH BECKER — BB/TR — age 22 — MIN OF3

1993	BA	OBA	SA	AB	H	2B	3B	HR	RBI	BB	SO
vs. Left	.333	.500	.667	3	1	1	0	0	0	1	2
vs. Right	.250	.625	.500	4	1	1	0	0	0	4	2
at Home	.000	.000	.000	0	0	0	0	0	0	0	0
on Road	.286	.583	.571	7	2	2	0	0	0	5	4
Runners On Base	.333	.600	.667	3	1	1	0	0	0	2	1
Second Half	.286	.583	.571	7	2	2	0	0	0	5	4

GREG BLOSSER — BL/TL — age 23 — BOS OF9, DH1

1993	BA	OBA	SA	AB	H	2B	3B	HR	RBI	BB	SO
vs. Left	.000	.000	.000	0	0	0	0	0	0	0	0
vs. Right	.071	.133	.107	28	2	1	0	0	1	2	7
at Home	.077	.143	.154	13	1	1	0	0	0	1	3
on Road	.067	.125	.067	15	1	0	0	0	1	1	4
Runners On Base	.000	.100	.000	9	0	0	0	0	0	1	2
Second Half	.071	.133	.107	28	2	1	0	0	1	2	7

JERRY BROOKS — BR/TR — age 27 — LA OF2

1993	BA	OBA	SA	AB	H	2B	3B	HR	RBI	BB	SO
vs. Left	.000	.000	.000	3	0	0	0	0	0	0	1
vs. Right	.333	.333	1.000	6	2	1	0	1	1	0	1
at Home	.000	.000	.000	5	0	0	0	0	0	0	2
on Road	.500	.500	1.500	4	2	1	0	1	1	0	0
Runners On Base	.250	.250	.500	4	1	1	0	0	0	0	0
Second Half	.222	.222	.667	9	2	1	0	1	1	0	2

DAMON BUFORD — BR/TR — age 24 — BAL OF30, DH17

1993	BA	OBA	SA	AB	H	2B	3B	HR	RBI	BB	SO
vs. Left	.217	.250	.348	23	5	3	0	0	1	0	8
vs. Right	.232	.338	.375	56	13	2	0	2	8	9	11
at Home	.125	.243	.156	32	4	1	0	0	1	4	10
on Road	.298	.365	.511	47	14	4	0	2	8	5	9
Runners On Base	.344	.432	.438	32	11	3	0	0	7	4	8
Second Half	.200	.238	.300	20	4	2	0	0	2	1	6

JEROMY BURNITZ — BL/TR — age 25 — NYN OF79

1993	BA	OBA	SA	AB	H	2B	3B	HR	RBI	BB	SO
vs. Left	.242	.324	.485	33	8	1	2	1	3	4	6
vs. Right	.243	.341	.474	230	56	9	4	12	35	34	60
at Home	.255	.325	.475	141	36	5	4	6	17	15	33
on Road	.230	.354	.475	122	28	5	2	7	21	23	33
Runners On Base	.282	.353	.513	117	33	3	6	31	14	24	
Second Half	.244	.340	.472	246	60	8	6	12	36	37	61

ROB BUTLER — BL/TL — age 24 — TOR OF16

1993	BA	OBA	SA	AB	H	2B	3B	HR	RBI	BB	SO
vs. Left	.294	.400	.412	17	5	2	0	0	1	2	4
vs. Right	.258	.361	.323	31	8	2	0	0	1	5	8
at Home	.333	.385	.500	12	4	2	0	0	1	1	4
on Road	.250	.372	.306	36	9	2	0	0	1	6	8
Runners On Base	.118	.167	.118	17	2	0	0	0	2	0	6
Second Half	.294	.455	.412	17	5	2	0	0	1	5	4

JIM BYRD — BR/TR — age 26 — BOS

1993	BA	OBA	SA	AB	H	2B	3B	HR	RBI	BB	SO
vs. Left	.000	.000	.000	0	0	0	0	0	0	0	0
vs. Right	.000	.000	.000	0	0	0	0	0	0	0	0
at Home	.000	.000	.000	0	0	0	0	0	0	0	0
on Road	.000	.000	.000	0	0	0	0	0	0	0	0
Runners On Base	.000	.000	.000	0	0	0	0	0	0	0	0
Second Half	.000	.000	.000	0	0	0	0	0	0	0	0

WILLIE CANATE — BR/TR — age 23 — TOR OF31, DH1

1993	BA	OBA	SA	AB	H	2B	3B	HR	RBI	BB	SO
vs. Left	.222	.250	.222	18	4	0	0	0	1	1	9
vs. Right	.207	.343	.310	29	6	0	0	1	2	5	6
at Home	.174	.269	.304	23	4	0	0	1	2	2	5
on Road	.250	.345	.250	24	6	0	0	0	1	4	10
Runners On Base	.158	.261	.158	19	3	0	0	0	2	2	5
Second Half	.250	.354	.325	40	10	0	0	1	3	6	12

RAMON CARABALLO — BB/TR — age 25 — ATL 2B5

1993	BA	OBA	SA	AB	H	2B	3B	HR	RBI	BB	SO
vs. Left	.000	.000	.000	0	0	0	0	0	0	0	0
vs. Right	.000	.000	.000	0	0	0	0	0	0	0	0
at Home	.000	.000	.000	0	0	0	0	0	0	0	0
on Road	.000	.000	.000	0	0	0	0	0	0	0	0
Runners On Base	.000	.000	.000	0	0	0	0	0	0	0	0
Second Half	.000	.000	.000	0	0	0	0	0	0	0	0

PAUL CAREY — BL/TR — age 26 — BAL 1B9, DH5

1993	BA	OBA	SA	AB	H	2B	3B	HR	RBI	BB	SO
vs. Left	.000	.000	.000	2	0	0	0	0	0	0	1
vs. Right	.222	.300	.244	45	10	1	0	0	3	5	13
at Home	.267	.389	.267	15	4	0	0	0	3	3	7
on Road	.188	.235	.219	32	6	1	0	0	3	2	7
Runners On Base	.250	.280	.292	24	6	1	0	0	3	1	5
Second Half	.200	.250	.200	15	3	0	0	0	1	1	5

PEDRO CASTELLANO — BR/TR — age 24 — COL 3B13, 1B10, SS5, 2B4

1993	BA	OBA	SA	AB	H	2B	3B	HR	RBI	BB	SO
vs. Left	.333	.455	.333	9	3	0	0	0	1	2	3
vs. Right	.161	.235	.339	62	10	2	0	3	6	3	13
at Home	.175	.233	.275	40	7	1	0	1	4	3	10
on Road	.194	.306	.419	31	6	1	0	2	3	5	6
Runners On Base	.212	.257	.303	33	7	1	0	1	5	2	8
Second Half	.184	.279	.447	38	7	1	0	3	5	5	7

DOMINGO CEDENO — BB/TR — age 26 — TOR SS10, 2B5

1993	BA	OBA	SA	AB	H	2B	3B	HR	RBI	BB	SO
vs. Left	.273	.273	.273	11	3	0	0	0	1	0	3
vs. Right	.143	.162	.143	35	5	0	0	0	6	1	7
at Home	.118	.167	.118	17	2	0	0	0	0	1	4
on Road	.207	.200	.207	29	6	0	0	0	7	0	6
Runners On Base	.294	.316	.294	17	5	0	0	0	7	1	4
Second Half	.100	.091	.100	10	1	0	0	0	0	0	

ROD CORREIA — BR/TR — age 27 — CAL SS40, 2B11, DH6, 3B3

1993	BA	OBA	SA	AB	H	2B	3B	HR	RBI	BB	SO
vs. Left	.326	.396	.395	43	14	3	0	0	0	4	4
vs. Right	.235	.278	.259	85	20	2	0	0	9	2	16
at Home	.267	.313	.300	60	16	2	0	0	4	2	9
on Road	.265	.324	.309	68	18	3	0	0	5	4	11
Runners On Base	.255	.321	.275	51	13	2	0	0	9	3	8
Second Half	.258	.313	.298	124	32	5	0	0	7	6	19

TRIPP CROMER — BR/TR — age 27 — SL SS9

1993	BA	OBA	SA	AB	H	2B	3B	HR	RBI	BB	SO
vs. Left	.182	.250	.182	11	2	0	0	0	0	1	1
vs. Right	.000	.000	.000	12	0	0	0	0	0	0	5
at Home	.000	.000	.000	2	0	0	0	0	0	0	0
on Road	.095	.136	.095	21	2	0	0	0	0	1	6
Runners On Base	.111	.200	.111	9	1	0	0	0	0	1	2
Second Half	.087	.125	.087	23	2	0	0	0	0	1	6

MIDRE CUMMINGS — BB/TR — age 23 — PIT OF11

1993	BA	OBA	SA	AB	H	2B	3B	HR	RBI	BB	SO
vs. Left	.077	.077	.077	13	1	0	0	0	0	0	4
vs. Right	.130	.250	.174	23	3	1	0	0	3	4	5
at Home	.118	.273	.118	17	2	0	0	0	1	4	4
on Road	.105	.105	.158	19	2	1	0	0	2	0	5
Runners On Base	.091	.160	.136	22	2	1	0	0	3	2	6
Second Half	.111	.195	.139	36	4	1	0	0	3	4	9

CARLOS DELGADO — BL/TR — age 22 — TOR C1, DH1

1993	BA	OBA	SA	AB	H	2B	3B	HR	RBI	BB	SO
vs. Left	.000	.000	.000	0	0	0	0	0	0	0	0
vs. Right	.000	.500	.000	1	0	0	0	0	0	1	0
at Home	.000	.000	.000	0	0	0	0	0	0	0	0
on Road	.000	.500	.000	1	0	0	0	0	0	1	0
Runners On Base	.000	.000	.000	1	0	0	0	0	0	0	0
Second Half	.000	.500	.000	1	0	0	0	0	0	1	0

JIM EDMONDS — BL/TL — age 24 — CAL OF17

1993	BA	OBA	SA	AB	H	2B	3B	HR	RBI	BB	SO
vs. Left	.222	.300	.222	9	2	0	0	0	0	0	4
vs. Right	.250	.264	.365	52	13	4	1	0	4	1	12
at Home	.257	.278	.343	35	9	1	1	0	3	1	10
on Road	.231	.259	.346	26	6	3	0	0	1	1	6
Runners On Base	.259	.286	.407	27	7	2	1	0	4	1	9
Second Half	.246	.270	.344	61	15	4	1	0	4	2	16

CARL EVERETT — BB/TR — age 24 — FLO OF8

1993	BA	OBA	SA	AB	H	2B	3B	HR	RBI	BB	SO
vs. Left	.000	.000	.000	5	0	0	0	0	0	0	1
vs. Right	.143	.200	.143	14	2	0	0	0	0	1	8
at Home	.000	.200	.000	4	0	0	0	0	0	1	3
on Road	.133	.133	.133	15	2	0	0	0	0	0	6
Runners On Base	.000	.200	.000	4	0	0	0	0	0	1	0
Second Half	.105	.150	.105	19	2	0	0	0	0	1	9

RIKKERT FANEYTE — BR/TR — age 25 — SF OF6

1993	BA	OBA	SA	AB	H	2B	3B	HR	RBI	BB	SO
vs. Left	.222	.222	.222	9	2	0	0	0	0	0	2
vs. Right	.000	.250	.000	6	0	0	0	0	0	2	2
at Home	.000	.000	.000	2	0	0	0	0	0	0	1
on Road	.154	.267	.154	13	2	0	0	0	0	2	3
Runners On Base	.333	.333	.333	6	2	0	0	0	0	0	2
Second Half	.133	.235	.133	15	2	0	0	0	0	2	4

CLIFF FLOYD — BL/TL — age 22 — MON 1B10

1993	BA	OBA	SA	AB	H	2B	3B	HR	RBI	BB	SO
vs. Left	.000	.000	.000	2	0	0	0	0	0	0	0
vs. Right	.241	.241	.345	29	7	0	0	1	2	0	9
at Home	.154	.154	.154	13	2	0	0	0	0	0	6
on Road	.278	.278	.444	18	5	0	0	1	2	0	3
Runners On Base	.500	.500	1.000	6	3	0	0	1	2	0	2
Second Half	.226	.226	.323	31	7	0	0	1	2	0	9

LOU FRAZIER — BB/TR — age 28 — MON OF60, 1B8, 2B1

1993	BA	OBA	SA	AB	H	2B	3B	HR	RBI	BB	SO
vs. Left	.295	.338	.377	61	18	2	0	1	4	4	9
vs. Right	.281	.340	.336	128	36	5	1	0	12	12	15
at Home	.350	.387	.437	103	36	4	1	1	12	7	11
on Road	.209	.284	.244	86	18	3	0	0	4	9	13
Runners On Base	.325	.368	.363	80	26	3	0	0	15	6	9
Second Half	.258	.293	.301	93	24	2	1	0	9	5	16

JAY GAINER — BL/TL — age 28 — COL 1B7

1993	BA	OBA	SA	AB	H	2B	3B	HR	RBI	BB	SO
vs. Left	.000	.250	.000	3	0	0	0	0	0	1	1
vs. Right	.184	.244	.421	38	7	0	0	3	6	3	11
at Home	.143	.143	.571	7	1	0	0	1	4	0	4
on Road	.176	.263	.353	34	6	0	0	2	2	4	8
Runners On Base	.063	.118	.250	16	1	0	0	1	4	1	6
Second Half	.167	.167	.667	12	2	0	0	2	5	0	6

BENJI GIL — BR/TR — age 22 — TEX SS22

1993	BA	OBA	SA	AB	H	2B	3B	HR	RBI	BB	SO
vs. Left	.222	.300	.222	9	2	0	0	0	0	1	4
vs. Right	.104	.173	.104	48	5	0	0	0	2	4	18
at Home	.098	.119	.098	41	4	0	0	0	2	1	15
on Road	.188	.350	.188	16	3	0	0	0	0	4	7
Runners On Base	.148	.233	.148	27	4	0	0	0	2	3	10
Second Half	.000	.000	.000	0	0	0	0	0	0	0	0

CHRIS GOMEZ — BR/TR — age 23 — DET SS29, 2B17, DH1

1993	BA	OBA	SA	AB	H	2B	3B	HR	RBI	BB	SO
vs. Left	.154	.214	.212	52	8	1	1	0	3	4	5
vs. Right	.316	.366	.395	76	24	6	0	0	8	5	12
at Home	.196	.262	.286	56	11	3	1	0	5	4	6
on Road	.292	.338	.347	72	21	4	0	0	6	5	11
Runners On Base	.351	.403	.474	57	20	5	1	0	11	4	10
Second Half	.250	.304	.320	128	32	7	1	0	11	9	17

LARRY GONZALES — BR/TR — age 27 — CAL C2

1993	BA	OBA	SA	AB	H	2B	3B	HR	RBI	BB	SO
vs. Left	.500	.667	.500	2	1	0	0	0	1	1	0
vs. Right	.000	.000	.000	0	0	0	0	0	0	0	0
at Home	.500	.667	.500	2	1	0	0	0	1	1	0
on Road	.000	.000	.000	0	0	0	0	0	0	0	0
Runners On Base	.500	.667	.500	2	1	0	0	0	1	1	0
Second Half	.000	.000	.000	0	0	0	0	0	0	0	0

KEITH GORDON — BR/TR — age 25 — CIN OF2

1993	BA	OBA	SA	AB	H	2B	3B	HR	RBI	BB	SO
vs. Left	.000	.000	.000	1	0	0	0	0	0	0	0
vs. Right	.200	.200	.200	5	1	0	0	0	0	0	2
at Home	.000	.000	.000	0	0	0	0	0	0	0	0
on Road	.167	.167	.167	6	1	0	0	0	0	0	2
Runners On Base	.000	.000	.000	3	0	0	0	0	0	0	0
Second Half	.167	.167	.167	6	1	0	0	0	0	0	2

SHAWN GREEN — BL/TL — age 22 — TOR OF2, DH1

1993	BA	OBA	SA	AB	H	2B	3B	HR	RBI	BB	SO
vs. Left	.000	.000	.000	1	0	0	0	0	0	0	0
vs. Right	.000	.000	.000	5	0	0	0	0	0	0	1
at Home	.000	.000	.000	0	0	0	0	0	0	0	0
on Road	.000	.000	.000	6	0	0	0	0	0	0	1
Runners On Base	.000	.000	.000	3	0	0	0	0	0	0	0
Second Half	.000	.000	.000	6	0	0	0	0	0	0	1

BOB HAMELIN — BL/TL — age 27 — KC 1B15

1993	BA	OBA	SA	AB	H	2B	3B	HR	RBI	BB	SO
vs. Left	.400	.400	.400	5	2	0	0	0	2	0	2
vs. Right	.205	.300	.409	44	9	3	0	2	3	6	13
at Home	.235	.350	.471	17	4	1	0	1	2	3	3
on Road	.219	.286	.375	32	7	2	0	1	3	3	12
Runners On Base	.111	.238	.111	18	2	0	0	0	3	3	6
Second Half	.224	.309	.408	49	11	3	0	2	5	6	15

JEFFREY HAMMONDS — BR/TR — age 23 — BAL OF23, DH8

1993	BA	OBA	SA	AB	H	2B	3B	HR	RBI	BB	SO
vs. Left	.279	.273	.488	43	12	3	0	2	7	0	7
vs. Right	.323	.338	.452	62	20	5	0	1	12	2	9
at Home	.277	.284	.415	65	18	3	0	2	9	1	10
on Road	.350	.357	.550	40	14	5	0	1	10	1	6
Runners On Base	.388	.385	.592	49	19	4	0	2	18	1	5
Second Half	.280	.282	.439	82	23	7	0	2	15	1	12

ERIC HELFAND — BL/TR — age 25 — OAK C5

1993	BA	OBA	SA	AB	H	2B	3B	HR	RBI	BB	SO
vs. Left	1.000	1.000	1.000	1	1	0	0	0	0	0	0
vs. Right	.167	.167	.167	12	2	0	0	0	1	0	1
at Home	.200	.200	.200	5	1	0	0	0	1	0	1
on Road	.250	.250	.250	8	2	0	0	0	0	0	0
Runners On Base	.600	.600	.600	5	3	0	0	0	1	0	0
Second Half	.231	.231	.231	13	3	0	0	0	1	0	1

PHIL HIATT — BR/TR — age 25 — KC 3B70, DH9

1993	BA	OBA	SA	AB	H	2B	3B	HR	RBI	BB	SO
vs. Left	.250	.307	.387	80	20	5	0	2	12	7	28
vs. Right	.203	.274	.354	158	32	7	1	5	24	9	54
at Home	.260	.304	.417	127	33	8	0	4	21	6	43
on Road	.171	.264	.306	111	19	4	1	3	15	10	39
Runners On Base	.263	.338	.500	114	30	10	1	5	34	10	36
Second Half	.207	.258	.293	58	12	2	0	1	5	3	19

KEVIN HIGGINS — BL/TR — age 27 — SD C59, 3B4, 1B3, OF3, 2B1

1993	BA	OBA	SA	AB	H	2B	3B	HR	RBI	BB	SO
vs. Left	.250	.250	.250	16	4	0	0	0	2	0	2
vs. Right	.218	.297	.255	165	36	4	1	0	11	16	15
at Home	.228	.297	.272	92	21	2	1	0	3	6	9
on Road	.213	.290	.236	89	19	2	0	0	10	10	8
Runners On Base	.195	.272	.232	82	16	3	0	0	13	7	10
Second Half	.187	.248	.234	107	20	3	1	0	7	7	13

DENNIS HOCKING — BB/TR — age 24 — MIN SS12, 2B1

1993	BA	OBA	SA	AB	H	2B	3B	HR	RBI	BB	SO
vs. Left	.167	.286	.167	6	1	0	0	0	0	1	0
vs. Right	.133	.257	.167	30	4	1	0	0	0	5	8
at Home	.091	.200	.091	22	2	0	0	0	0	3	5
on Road	.214	.353	.286	14	3	1	0	0	0	3	3
Runners On Base	.000	.143	.000	12	0	0	0	0	0	2	2
Second Half	.139	.262	.167	36	5	1	0	0	0	6	8

BUTCH HUSKEY — BR/TR — age 23 — NYN 3B13

1993	BA	OBA	SA	AB	H	2B	3B	HR	RBI	BB	SO
vs. Left	.067	.067	.067	15	1	0	0	0	0	0	4
vs. Right	.192	.207	.231	26	5	1	0	0	3	1	9
at Home	.136	.160	.136	22	3	0	0	0	2	1	6
on Road	.158	.158	.211	19	3	1	0	0	1	0	7
Runners On Base	.222	.238	.278	18	4	1	0	0	3	1	4
Second Half	.146	.159	.171	41	6	1	0	0	3	1	13

ERIK JOHNSON — BR/TR — age 29 — SF 2B2, 3B1, SS1

1993	BA	OBA	SA	AB	H	2B	3B	HR	RBI	BB	SO
vs. Left	.500	.500	1.000	2	1	1	0	0	0	0	0
vs. Right	.333	.333	.667	3	1	1	0	0	0	0	1
at Home	.000	.000	.000	1	0	0	0	0	0	0	0
on Road	.500	.500	1.000	4	2	2	0	0	0	0	1
Runners On Base	.000	.000	.000	2	0	0	0	0	0	0	1
Second Half	.400	.400	.800	5	2	2	0	0	0	0	1

CHIPPER JONES — BB/TR — age 22 — ATL SS3

1993	BA	OBA	SA	AB	H	2B	3B	HR	RBI	BB	SO
vs. Left	1.000	1.000	1.000	1	1	0	0	0	0	1	0
vs. Right	.500	.500	.500	2	1	0	0	0	0	0	1
at Home	.500	.500	.500	2	1	0	0	0	0	0	1
on Road	1.000	1.000	2.000	1	1	1	0	0	0	1	0
Runners On Base	.000	.000	.000	1	0	0	0	0	0	0	0
Second Half	.667	.750	1.000	3	2	1	0	0	0	1	1

KEITH KESSINGER — BB/TR — age 27 — CIN SS11

1993	BA	OBA	SA	AB	H	2B	3B	HR	RBI	BB	SO
vs. Left	.600	.600	.800	5	3	1	0	0	0	0	1
vs. Right	.182	.296	.318	22	4	0	0	1	3	4	3
at Home	.278	.316	.500	18	5	1	0	1	2	1	4
on Road	.222	.385	.222	9	2	0	0	0	1	3	0
Runners On Base	.182	.286	.182	11	2	0	0	0	2	2	2
Second Half	.259	.344	.407	27	7	1	0	1	3	4	4

JOE KMAK — BR/TR — age 31 — MIL C50

1993	BA	OBA	SA	AB	H	2B	3B	HR	RBI	BB	SO
vs. Left	.221	.303	.250	68	15	2	0	0	3	7	8
vs. Right	.214	.340	.286	42	9	3	0	0	4	7	5
at Home	.213	.315	.255	47	10	2	0	0	3	6	6
on Road	.222	.319	.270	63	14	3	0	0	4	8	7
Runners On Base	.289	.400	.395	38	11	4	0	0	7	6	4
Second Half	.143	.400	.143	7	1	0	0	0	0	3	1

BRIAN KOELLING — BR/TR — age 25 — CIN 2B3, SS2

1993	BA	OBA	SA	AB	H	2B	3B	HR	RBI	BB	SO
vs. Left	.125	.125	.125	8	1	0	0	0	0	0	0
vs. Right	.000	.125	.000	7	0	0	0	0	0	0	2
at Home	.000	.000	.000	7	0	0	0	0	0	0	1
on Road	.125	.222	.125	8	1	0	0	0	0	0	1
Runners On Base	.000	.000	.000	5	0	0	0	0	0	0	0
Second Half	.067	.125	.067	15	1	0	0	0	0	0	2

DEREK LEE — BL/TR — age 28 — MIN OF13

1993	BA	OBA	SA	AB	H	2B	3B	HR	RBI	BB	SO
vs. Left	.000	.000	.000	0	0	0	0	0	0	0	0
vs. Right	.152	.176	.182	33	5	1	0	0	4	1	4
at Home	.167	.200	.167	24	4	0	0	0	1	1	3
on Road	.111	.111	.222	9	1	1	0	0	3	0	1
Runners On Base	.200	.200	.267	15	3	1	0	0	4	0	1
Second Half	.115	.148	.154	26	3	1	0	0	3	1	2

TONY LONGMIRE — BL/TR — age 26 — PHI OF2

1993	BA	OBA	SA	AB	H	2B	3B	HR	RBI	BB	SO
vs. Left	.000	.000	.000	0	0	0	0	0	0	0	0
vs. Right	.231	.231	.231	13	3	0	0	0	1	0	1
at Home	.200	.200	.200	5	1	0	0	0	0	0	0
on Road	.250	.250	.250	8	2	0	0	0	1	0	1
Runners On Base	.400	.400	.400	5	2	0	0	0	1	0	0
Second Half	.231	.231	.231	13	3	0	0	0	1	0	1

LUIS LOPEZ — BB/TR — age 24 — SD 2B15

1993	BA	OBA	SA	AB	H	2B	3B	HR	RBI	BB	SO
vs. Left	.111	.100	.111	9	1	0	0	0	0	1	2
vs. Right	.118	.118	.147	34	4	1	0	0	0	0	6
at Home	.107	.103	.143	28	3	1	0	0	1	0	7
on Road	.133	.133	.133	15	2	0	0	0	0	0	1
Runners On Base	.176	.167	.176	17	3	0	0	0	1	0	3
Second Half	.116	.114	.140	43	5	1	0	0	1	0	8

MITCH LYDEN — BR/TR — age 30 — FLO C2

1993	BA	OBA	SA	AB	H	2B	3B	HR	RBI	BB	SO
vs. Left	.500	.500	.500	4	2	0	0	0	0	0	0
vs. Right	.167	.167	.667	6	1	0	0	1	1	0	1
at Home	.250	.250	.250	4	1	0	0	0	0	0	3
on Road	.333	.333	.833	6	2	0	0	1	1	0	0
Runners On Base	.200	.200	.200	5	1	0	0	0	0	0	2
Second Half	.250	.250	.250	4	1	0	0	0	0	0	3

SCOTT LYDY — BR/TR — age 26 — OAK OF38, DH2

1993	BA	OBA	SA	AB	H	2B	3B	HR	RBI	BB	SO
vs. Left	.213	.260	.255	47	10	2	0	0	2	2	20
vs. Right	.236	.311	.400	55	13	3	0	2	5	6	19
at Home	.286	.362	.405	42	12	2	0	1	3	5	12
on Road	.183	.234	.283	60	11	3	0	1	4	3	27
Runners On Base	.190	.292	.286	42	8	1	0	1	6	5	16
Second Half	.235	.293	.341	85	20	3	0	2	6	6	31

LONNIE MACLIN — BL/TL — age 27 — SL OF5

1993	BA	OBA	SA	AB	H	2B	3B	HR	RBI	BB	SO
vs. Left	.000	.000	.000	0	0	0	0	0	0	0	0
vs. Right	.077	.071	.077	13	1	0	0	0	0	1	5
at Home	.000	.000	.000	3	0	0	0	0	0	0	2
on Road	.100	.091	.100	10	1	0	0	0	0	1	3
Runners On Base	.000	.000	.000	4	0	0	0	0	0	1	1
Second Half	.077	.071	.077	13	1	0	0	0	0	1	5

ORESTE MARRERO — BL/TL — age 25 — MON 1B32

1993	BA	OBA	SA	AB	H	2B	3B	HR	RBI	BB	SO
vs. Left	.300	.364	.300	10	3	0	0	0	0	1	4
vs. Right	.197	.321	.338	71	14	5	1	1	4	13	12
at Home	.250	.362	.400	40	10	3	0	1	2	7	3
on Road	.171	.292	.268	41	7	2	1	0	2	7	13
Runners On Base	.206	.386	.353	34	7	2	0	1	4	10	9
Second Half	.210	.326	.333	81	17	5	1	1	4	14	16

NORBERTO MARTIN — BR/TR — age 28 — CHA 2B5, DH1

1993	BA	OBA	SA	AB	H	2B	3B	HR	RBI	BB	SO
vs. Left	.000	.000	.000	1	0	0	0	0	0	0	0
vs. Right	.385	.429	.385	13	5	0	0	0	2	1	1
at Home	.400	.400	.400	10	4	0	0	0	2	0	0
on Road	.250	.400	.250	4	1	0	0	0	0	1	1
Runners On Base	.400	.400	.400	5	2	0	0	0	2	0	1
Second Half	.357	.400	.357	14	5	0	0	0	2	1	1

JEFF MCNEELY — BR/TR — age 25 — BOS OF13, DH3

1993	BA	OBA	SA	AB	H	2B	3B	HR	RBI	BB	SO
vs. Left	.200	.273	.200	10	2	0	0	0	1	1	1
vs. Right	.333	.455	.444	27	9	1	1	0	0	6	8
at Home	.375	.500	.500	24	9	1	1	0	0	6	5
on Road	.154	.214	.154	13	2	0	0	0	0	1	4
Runners On Base	.200	.333	.200	10	2	0	0	0	1	2	4
Second Half	.297	.409	.378	37	11	1	1	0	1	7	9

ROBERTO MEJIA — BR/TR — age 22 — COL 2B65

1993	BA	OBA	SA	AB	H	2B	3B	HR	RBI	BB	SO
vs. Left	.306	.352	.633	49	15	4	3	2	9	4	10
vs. Right	.211	.253	.339	180	38	10	2	3	11	9	53
at Home	.274	.333	.491	106	29	6	3	3	14	9	26
on Road	.195	.220	.325	123	24	8	1	2	6	4	37
Runners On Base	.200	.258	.341	85	17	5	2	1	16	6	22
Second Half	.231	.275	.402	229	53	14	5	5	20	13	63

MATT MIESKE — BR/TR — age 26 — MIL OF22

1993	BA	OBA	SA	AB	H	2B	3B	HR	RBI	BB	SO
vs. Left	.261	.320	.522	23	6	0	0	2	4	2	4
vs. Right	.229	.270	.314	35	8	0	0	1	3	2	10
at Home	.200	.200	.350	20	4	0	0	1	2	0	2
on Road	.263	.333	.421	38	10	0	0	2	5	4	12
Runners On Base	.368	.400	.526	19	7	0	0	1	5	1	2
Second Half	.290	.371	.387	31	9	0	0	1	4	4	11

RAUL MONDESI — BR/TR — age 23 — LA OF40

1993	BA	OBA	SA	AB	H	2B	3B	HR	RBI	BB	SO
vs. Left	.315	.339	.519	54	17	3	1	2	5	2	7
vs. Right	.250	.294	.438	32	8	0	0	2	5	2	9
at Home	.302	.318	.488	43	13	2	0	2	3	1	8
on Road	.279	.326	.488	43	12	1	1	2	7	3	8
Runners On Base	.209	.244	.465	43	9	0	1	3	9	2	6
Second Half	.291	.322	.488	86	25	3	1	4	10	4	16

CHARLIE MONTOYO — BR/TR — age 29 — MON 2B3

1993	BA	OBA	SA	AB	H	2B	3B	HR	RBI	BB	SO
vs. Left	.500	.500	.750	4	2	1	0	0	3	0	0
vs. Right	.000	.000	.000	1	0	0	0	0	0	0	0
at Home	.500	.500	.500	2	1	0	0	0	1	0	0
on Road	.333	.333	.667	3	1	1	0	0	2	0	0
Runners On Base	.500	.500	.750	4	2	1	0	0	3	0	0
Second Half	.400	.400	.600	5	2	1	0	0	3	0	0

TITO NAVARRO — BB/TR — age 24 — NYN SS2

1993	BA	OBA	SA	AB	H	2B	3B	HR	RBI	BB	SO
vs. Left	.000	.000	.000	4	0	0	0	0	0	0	0
vs. Right	.077	.077	.077	13	1	0	0	0	1	0	4
at Home	.000	.000	.000	7	0	0	0	0	0	0	1
on Road	.100	.100	.100	10	1	0	0	0	1	0	3
Runners On Base	.167	.167	.167	6	1	0	0	0	1	0	1
Second Half	.059	.059	.059	17	1	0	0	0	1	0	4

MARC NEWFIELD — BR/TR — age 22 — SEA DH15, OF5

1993	BA	OBA	SA	AB	H	2B	3B	HR	RBI	BB	SO
vs. Left	.259	.300	.444	27	7	2	0	1	5	2	4
vs. Right	.205	.225	.231	39	8	1	0	0	2	0	4
at Home	.209	.239	.326	43	9	2	0	1	5	2	5
on Road	.261	.292	.304	23	6	1	0	0	2	0	3
Runners On Base	.214	.258	.286	28	6	2	0	0	6	1	3
Second Half	.227	.257	.318	66	15	3	0	1	7	2	8

SHERMAN OBANDO — BR/TR — age 24 — BAL DH21, OF8

1993	BA	OBA	SA	AB	H	2B	3B	HR	RBI	BB	SO
vs. Left	.295	.340	.477	44	13	2	0	2	10	3	11
vs. Right	.250	.280	.313	48	12	0	0	1	5	1	15
at Home	.245	.288	.388	49	12	1	0	2	8	2	13
on Road	.302	.333	.395	43	13	1	0	1	7	2	13
Runners On Base	.386	.400	.500	44	17	2	0	1	13	1	12
Second Half	.167	.200	.458	24	4	1	0	2	6	1	8

TROY O'LEARY — BL/TL — age 25 — MIL OF19

1993	BA	OBA	SA	AB	H	2B	3B	HR	RBI	BB	SO
vs. Left	.111	.273	.111	9	1	0	0	0	0	2	2
vs. Right	.344	.400	.438	32	11	3	0	0	3	3	7
at Home	.217	.280	.217	23	5	0	0	0	1	2	6
on Road	.389	.476	.556	18	7	3	0	0	2	3	3
Runners On Base	.188	.235	.250	16	3	1	0	0	3	1	4
Second Half	.282	.364	.359	39	11	3	0	0	3	5	9

LUIS ORTIZ — BR/TR — age 24 — BOS 3B5, DH3

1993	BA	OBA	SA	AB	H	2B	3B	HR	RBI	BB	SO
vs. Left	.500	.500	.500	6	3	0	0	0	1	0	1
vs. Right	.000	.000	.000	6	0	0	0	0	0	0	1
at Home	.273	.273	.273	11	3	0	0	0	1	0	2
on Road	.000	.000	.000	1	0	0	0	0	0	0	0
Runners On Base	.286	.286	.286	7	2	0	0	0	1	0	1
Second Half	.250	.250	.250	12	3	0	0	0	1	0	2

J OWENS — BR/TR — age 25 — COL C32

1993	BA	OBA	SA	AB	H	2B	3B	HR	RBI	BB	SO
vs. Left	.217	.280	.391	23	5	1	0	1	2	2	4
vs. Right	.206	.275	.365	63	13	4	0	2	4	4	26
at Home	.326	.392	.543	46	15	4	0	2	5	4	12
on Road	.075	.140	.175	40	3	1	0	1	1	2	18
Runners On Base	.208	.345	.208	24	5	0	0	0	3	5	11
Second Half	.143	.213	.304	56	8	3	0	2	2	3	18

J. R. PHILLIPS — BL/TL — age 24 — SF 1B5

1993	BA	OBA	SA	AB	H	2B	3B	HR	RBI	BB	SO
vs. Left	.000	.000	.000	2	0	0	0	0	0	0	1
vs. Right	.357	.357	.786	14	5	1	1	1	4	0	4
at Home	.333	.333	.444	9	3	1	0	0	1	0	2
on Road	.286	.286	1.000	7	2	0	1	1	3	0	3
Runners On Base	.375	.375	.875	8	3	1	0	1	4	0	4
Second Half	.313	.313	.688	16	5	1	1	1	4	0	5

GREG PIRKL — BR/TR — age 24 — SEA 1B5, DH2

1993	BA	OBA	SA	AB	H	2B	3B	HR	RBI	BB	SO
vs. Left	.214	.214	.429	14	3	0	0	1	4	0	1
vs. Right	.111	.111	.111	9	1	0	0	0	0	0	3
at Home	.200	.200	.350	20	4	0	0	1	4	0	3
on Road	.000	.000	.000	3	0	0	0	0	0	0	1
Runners On Base	.182	.182	.455	11	2	0	0	1	4	0	1
Second Half	.174	.174	.304	23	4	0	0	1	4	0	4

SCOTT POSE — BL/TR — age 27 — FLO OF10

1993	BA	OBA	SA	AB	H	2B	3B	HR	RBI	BB	SO
vs. Left	.167	.167	.167	6	1	0	0	0	0	0	0
vs. Right	.200	.243	.257	35	7	2	0	0	3	2	4
at Home	.276	.323	.345	29	8	2	0	0	3	2	3
on Road	.000	.000	.000	12	0	0	0	0	0	0	1
Runners On Base	.118	.167	.118	17	2	0	0	0	3	1	2
Second Half	.000	.000	.000	0	0	0	0	0	0	0	0

CURTIS PRIDE — BL/TR — age 26 — MON OF2

1993	BA	OBA	SA	AB	H	2B	3B	HR	RBI	BB	SO
vs. Left	.000	.000	.000	0	0	0	0	0	0	0	0
vs. Right	.444	.444	1.111	9	4	1	1	1	5	0	3
at Home	.600	.600	1.200	5	3	1	1	0	3	0	1
on Road	.250	.250	1.000	4	1	0	1	0	2	0	2
Runners On Base	.500	.500	1.250	8	4	1	1	1	5	0	2
Second Half	.444	.444	1.111	9	4	1	1	1	5	0	3

MANNY RAMIREZ — BR/TR — age 22 — CLE DH20, OF1

1993	BA	OBA	SA	AB	H	2B	3B	HR	RBI	BB	SO
vs. Left	.115	.115	.231	26	3	0	0	1	1	0	5
vs. Right	.222	.276	.370	27	6	1	0	1	4	2	3
at Home	.194	.242	.194	31	6	0	0	0	2	2	5
on Road	.136	.136	.455	22	3	1	0	2	3	0	3
Runners On Base	.188	.212	.281	32	6	0	0	1	4	1	5
Second Half	.170	.200	.302	53	9	1	0	2	5	2	8

KEVIN ROBERSON — BB/TR — age 26 — CHN OF51

1993	BA	OBA	SA	AB	H	2B	3B	HR	RBI	BB	SO
vs. Left	.156	.169	.266	64	10	1	0	2	6	1	14
vs. Right	.207	.292	.431	116	24	3	1	7	21	11	34
at Home	.159	.245	.307	88	14	1	0	4	11	8	26
on Road	.217	.258	.435	92	20	3	1	5	16	4	22
Runners On Base	.225	.287	.500	80	18	2	1	6	24	6	21
Second Half	.189	.251	.372	180	34	4	1	9	27	12	48

MARC RONAN — BL/TR — age 25 — SL C6

1993	BA	OBA	SA	AB	H	2B	3B	HR	RBI	BB	SO
vs. Left	.000	.000	.000	1	0	0	0	0	0	0	1
vs. Right	.091	.091	.091	11	1	0	0	0	0	0	4
at Home	.333	.333	.333	3	1	0	0	0	0	0	2
on Road	.000	.000	.000	9	0	0	0	0	0	0	3
Runners On Base	.000	.000	.000	6	0	0	0	0	0	0	3
Second Half	.083	.083	.083	12	1	0	0	0	0	0	5

DOUG SAUNDERS — BR/TR — age 25 — NYN 2B22, 3B4, SS1

1993	BA	OBA	SA	AB	H	2B	3B	HR	RBI	BB	SO
vs. Left	.217	.250	.261	23	5	1	0	0	0	1	0
vs. Right	.205	.239	.227	44	9	1	0	0	0	2	4
at Home	.292	.370	.333	24	7	1	0	0	0	3	1
on Road	.163	.163	.186	43	7	1	0	0	0	0	3
Runners On Base	.087	.160	.087	23	2	0	0	0	0	2	2
Second Half	.150	.190	.250	20	3	2	0	0	0	1	2

JON SHAVE — BR/TR — age 27 — TEX SS9, 2B8

1993	BA	OBA	SA	AB	H	2B	3B	HR	RBI	BB	SO
vs. Left	.545	.545	.636	11	6	1	0	0	3	0	1
vs. Right	.250	.237	.278	36	9	1	0	0	4	0	7
at Home	.091	.083	.091	11	1	0	0	0	1	0	1
on Road	.389	.378	.444	36	14	2	0	0	6	0	7
Runners On Base	.471	.421	.588	17	8	2	0	0	7	0	1
Second Half	.364	.364	.424	33	12	2	0	0	4	0	7

BEN SHELTON — BR/TL — age 25 — PIT OF6, 1B2

1993	BA	OBA	SA	AB	H	2B	3B	HR	RBI	BB	SO
vs. Left	.200	.333	.300	10	2	1	0	0	3	2	1
vs. Right	.286	.333	.714	14	4	0	0	2	4	1	2
at Home	.286	.375	.714	14	4	0	0	2	5	2	2
on Road	.200	.273	.300	10	2	1	0	0	2	1	1
Runners On Base	.300	.364	.400	10	3	0	0	0	5	1	1
Second Half	.200	.200	.500	10	2	0	0	1	1	0	1

DARRELL SHERMAN — BL/TL — age 27 — SD OF26

1993	BA	OBA	SA	AB	H	2B	3B	HR	RBI	BB	SO
vs. Left	.091	.167	.091	11	1	0	0	0	0	1	1
vs. Right	.250	.344	.269	52	13	1	0	0	2	5	7
at Home	.278	.350	.278	36	10	0	0	0	0	2	4
on Road	.148	.273	.185	27	4	1	0	0	2	4	4
Runners On Base	.200	.381	.200	15	3	0	0	0	2	3	1
Second Half	.000	.000	.000	0	0	0	0	0	0	0	0

JOE SIDDALL — BL/TR — age 27 — MON C15, 1B1, OF1

1993	BA	OBA	SA	AB	H	2B	3B	HR	RBI	BB	SO
vs. Left	.143	.143	.143	7	1	0	0	0	0	0	3
vs. Right	.077	.143	.154	13	1	1	0	0	1	1	2
at Home	.143	.200	.214	14	2	1	0	0	1	1	1
on Road	.000	.000	.000	6	0	0	0	0	0	0	4
Runners On Base	.400	.500	.600	5	2	1	0	0	1	1	2
Second Half	.100	.143	.150	20	2	1	0	0	1	1	5

SCOTT STAHOVIAK — BL/TR — age 24 — MIN 3B19

1993	BA	OBA	SA	AB	H	2B	3B	HR	RBI	BB	SO
vs. Left	.333	.333	.667	3	1	1	0	0	0	0	1
vs. Right	.185	.228	.241	54	10	3	0	0	1	3	21
at Home	.212	.212	.303	33	7	3	0	0	1	0	12
on Road	.167	.259	.208	24	4	1	0	0	0	3	10
Runners On Base	.115	.115	.115	26	3	0	0	0	1	0	11
Second Half	.193	.233	.263	57	11	4	0	0	1	3	22

DAVE STATON — BR/TR — age 26 — SD 1B12

1993	BA	OBA	SA	AB	H	2B	3B	HR	RBI	BB	SO
vs. Left	.286	.286	.429	7	2	1	0	0	0	0	3
vs. Right	.257	.333	.743	35	9	1	0	5	9	3	9
at Home	.261	.320	.696	23	6	1	0	3	7	1	5
on Road	.263	.333	.684	19	5	2	0	2	2	2	7
Runners On Base	.300	.417	.700	10	3	1	0	1	5	2	1
Second Half	.262	.326	.690	42	11	3	0	5	9	3	12

TONY TARASCO — BL/TR — age 24 — ATL OF12

1993	BA	OBA	SA	AB	H	2B	3B	HR	RBI	BB	SO
vs. Left	.500	.500	.667	6	3	1	0	0	1	0	0
vs. Right	.172	.194	.207	29	5	1	0	0	1	0	5
at Home	.318	.348	.364	22	7	1	0	0	0	0	2
on Road	.077	.071	.154	13	1	1	0	0	2	0	3
Runners On Base	.200	.235	.267	15	3	1	0	0	1	0	1
Second Half	.200	.190	.300	20	4	2	0	0	2	0	1

LEE TINSLEY — BB/TR — age 25 — SEA OF6, DH2

1993	BA	OBA	SA	AB	H	2B	3B	HR	RBI	BB	SO
vs. Left	.000	.167	.000	5	0	0	0	0	0	1	2
vs. Right	.214	.267	.500	14	3	1	0	1	2	1	7
at Home	.200	.429	.200	5	1	0	0	0	0	2	3
on Road	.143	.143	.429	14	2	1	0	1	2	0	6
Runners On Base	.100	.250	.400	10	1	0	0	1	2	2	4
Second Half	.182	.182	.545	11	2	1	0	1	2	0	4

ANDY TOMBERLIN — BL/TL — age 28 — PIT OF7

1993	BA	OBA	SA	AB	H	2B	3B	HR	RBI	BB	SO
vs. Left	.167	.167	.167	6	1	0	0	0	0	0	4
vs. Right	.306	.359	.444	36	11	0	0	1	5	2	10
at Home	.280	.308	.280	25	7	0	0	0	2	1	8
on Road	.294	.368	.588	17	5	0	1	1	3	1	6
Runners On Base	.208	.240	.292	24	5	0	1	0	4	1	11
Second Half	.286	.333	.405	42	12	0	1	1	5	2	14

GREG TUBBS — BR/TR — age 32 — CIN OF21

1993	BA	OBA	SA	AB	H	2B	3B	HR	RBI	BB	SO
vs. Left	.048	.130	.048	21	1	0	0	0	0	2	5
vs. Right	.263	.451	.342	38	10	0	0	1	2	12	5
at Home	.200	.349	.286	35	7	0	0	1	2	8	6
on Road	.167	.355	.167	24	4	0	0	0	0	6	4
Runners On Base	.133	.278	.133	15	2	0	0	0	0	3	2
Second Half	.186	.351	.237	59	11	0	0	1	2	14	10

BRIAN TURANG — BR/TR — age 27 — SEA OF38, 3B2, 2B1, DH1

1993	BA	OBA	SA	AB	H	2B	3B	HR	RBI	BB	SO
vs. Left	.302	.371	.397	63	19	1	0	0	5	7	3
vs. Right	.208	.315	.299	77	16	5	1	0	2	10	17
at Home	.247	.322	.333	81	20	7	0	0	3	8	9
on Road	.254	.362	.356	59	15	4	1	0	4	9	11
Runners On Base	.245	.373	.327	49	12	4	1	0	7	8	3
Second Half	.250	.340	.343	140	35	11	1	0	7	17	20

CHRIS TURNER — BR/TR — age 25 — CAL C25

1993	BA	OBA	SA	AB	H	2B	3B	HR	RBI	BB	SO
vs. Left	.500	.647	.667	12	6	2	0	0	2	5	3
vs. Right	.238	.290	.333	63	15	3	0	1	11	4	13
at Home	.294	.368	.324	34	10	1	0	0	3	4	10
on Road	.268	.354	.439	41	11	4	0	1	10	5	6
Runners On Base	.375	.417	.563	32	12	3	0	1	13	3	5
Second Half	.280	.360	.387	75	21	5	0	1	13	9	16

TY VANBURKLEO — BL/TL — age 31 — CAL 1B12

1993	BA	OBA	SA	AB	H	2B	3B	HR	RBI	BB	SO
vs. Left	.333	.333	.667	3	1	1	0	0	0	0	1
vs. Right	.133	.278	.300	30	4	2	0	1	1	6	8
at Home	.095	.269	.286	21	2	1	0	1	1	5	6
on Road	.250	.308	.417	12	3	2	0	0	0	1	3
Runners On Base	.154	.267	.308	13	2	2	0	0	0	2	4
Second Half	.152	.282	.333	33	5	3	0	1	1	6	9

FERNANDO VINA — BL/TR — age 25 — SEA 2B16, SS4, DH2

1993	BA	OBA	SA	AB	H	2B	3B	HR	RBI	BB	SO
vs. Left	.000	.000	.000	2	0	0	0	0	0	0	0
vs. Right	.233	.340	.279	43	10	2	0	0	0	4	3
at Home	.226	.294	.290	31	7	2	0	0	0	2	3
on Road	.214	.389	.214	14	3	0	0	0	0	2	0
Runners On Base	.190	.320	.190	21	4	0	0	0	0	2	2
Second Half	.000	.000	.000	0	0	0	0	0	0	0	0

MATT WALBECK — BB/TR — age 25 — CHN C11

1993	BA	OBA	SA	AB	H	2B	3B	HR	RBI	BB	SO
vs. Left	.091	.167	.091	11	1	0	0	0	2	1	0
vs. Right	.263	.263	.526	19	5	2	0	1	4	0	6
at Home	.333	.375	.600	15	5	1	0	1	5	1	2
on Road	.067	.067	.133	15	1	1	0	0	1	0	4
Runners On Base	.417	.417	.833	12	5	2	0	1	6	0	2
Second Half	.067	.125	.133	15	1	1	0	0	1	1	5

DERRICK WHITE — BR/TR — age 25 — MON 1B17

1993	BA	OBA	SA	AB	H	2B	3B	HR	RBI	BB	SO
vs. Left	.348	.400	.696	23	8	2	0	2	3	1	6
vs. Right	.115	.148	.154	26	3	1	0	0	1	1	6
at Home	.250	.250	.500	16	4	1	0	1	1	0	7
on Road	.212	.278	.364	33	7	2	0	1	3	2	5
Runners On Base	.125	.192	.167	24	3	1	0	0	2	2	7
Second Half	.224	.269	.408	49	11	3	0	2	4	2	12

RONDELL WHITE — BR/TR — age 22 — MON OF21

1993	BA	OBA	SA	AB	H	2B	3B	HR	RBI	BB	SO
vs. Left	.296	.345	.556	27	8	1	0	2	8	2	6
vs. Right	.239	.308	.326	46	11	2	1	0	7	5	10
at Home	.200	.294	.400	30	6	1	1	1	8	4	8
on Road	.302	.340	.419	43	13	2	0	1	7	3	8
Runners On Base	.317	.356	.488	41	13	2	1	1	14	3	5
Second Half	.260	.321	.411	73	19	3	1	2	15	7	16

NIGEL WILSON — BL/TL — age 24 — FLO OF3

1993	BA	OBA	SA	AB	H	2B	3B	HR	RBI	BB	SO
vs. Left	.000	.000	.000	2	0	0	0	0	0	0	2
vs. Right	.000	.000	.000	14	0	0	0	0	0	0	9
at Home	.000	.000	.000	2	0	0	0	0	0	0	2
on Road	.000	.000	.000	14	0	0	0	0	0	0	9
Runners On Base	.000	.000	.000	8	0	0	0	0	0	0	4
Second Half	.000	.000	.000	16	0	0	0	0	0	0	11

TONY WOMACK — BL/TR — age 25 — PIT SS6

1993	BA	OBA	SA	AB	H	2B	3B	HR	RBI	BB	SO
vs. Left	.000	.000	.000	5	0	0	0	0	0	0	1
vs. Right	.105	.227	.105	19	2	0	0	0	0	3	2
at Home	.111	.238	.111	18	2	0	0	0	0	3	3
on Road	.000	.000	.000	6	0	0	0	0	0	0	0
Runners On Base	.000	.000	.000	8	0	0	0	0	0	0	2
Second Half	.083	.185	.083	24	2	0	0	0	0	3	3

EDUARDO ZAMBRANO — BR/TR — age 28 — CHN OF4, 1B2

1993	BA	OBA	SA	AB	H	2B	3B	HR	RBI	BB	SO
vs. Left	.167	.167	.167	6	1	0	0	0	0	0	0
vs. Right	.364	.417	.364	11	4	0	0	0	2	1	3
at Home	.286	.286	.286	7	2	0	0	0	1	0	0
on Road	.300	.364	.300	10	3	0	0	0	1	1	3
Runners On Base	.300	.364	.300	10	3	0	0	0	2	1	2
Second Half	.294	.333	.294	17	5	0	0	0	2	1	3

PITCHERS

PAUL ABBOTT — BR/TR — age 27 — CLE SP5 FIN/GB

1993	G	IP	H	BB	SO	SB	CS	W	L	SV	ERA
at Home	3	9.2	7	7	5	1	0	0	0	0	3.72
on Road	2	8.2	12	4	2	2	0	0	1	0	9.35
Second Half	1	4.0	5	2	1	2	0	0	0	0	9.00

	BA	OBA	SA	AB	H	2B	3B	HR	RBI	BB	SO
Total	.260	.357	.562	73	19	5	1	5	13	11	7
vs. Left	.244	.367	.415	41	10	2	1	1	5	8	5
vs. Right	.281	.343	.750	32	9	3	0	4	8	3	2
Runners On Base	.286	.429	.571	28	8	2	0	2	10	7	3

4-YEAR TOTALS (1990-1993)

G	IP	H	BB	SO	SB	CS	W	L	SV	ERA
15	45.0	38	27	38	8	0	2	2	0	4.20
18	66.1	68	53	50	13	3	1	5	0	5.97
25	78.0	75	60	66	17	2	1	6	0	5.65

BA	OBA	SA	AB	H	2B	3B	HR	RBI	BB	SO
.258	.378	.426	411	106	26	5	11	63	80	88
.219	.373	.323	201	44	5	2	4	27	50	48
.295	.383	.524	210	62	21	3	7	36	30	40
.246	.360	.429	203	50	8	4	7	59	39	39

JUAN AGOSTO — BL/TL — age 36 — HOU RP6 FIN/GB

1993	G	IP	H	BB	SO	SB	CS	W	L	SV	ERA
at Home	3	2.2	3	0	1	0	0	0	0	0	0.00
on Road	3	3.1	5	0	2	1	0	0	0	0	10.80
Second Half	0	0.0	0	0	0	0	0	0	0	0	0.00

	BA	OBA	SA	AB	H	2B	3B	HR	RBI	BB	SO
Total	.308	.308	.462	26	8	1	0	1	6	0	3
vs. Left	.333	.333	.667	12	4	1	0	1	3	0	1
vs. Right	.286	.286	.286	14	4	0	0	0	3	0	2
Runners On Base	.375	.375	.563	16	6	0	0	1	6	0	2

10-YEAR TOTALS (1984-1993)

G	IP	H	BB	SO	SB	CS	W	L	SV	ERA
256	314.2	302	131	159	27	5	24	14	14	3.49
245	262.1	284	106	115	31	4	14	17	8	4.49
248	282.1	275	115	131	30	3	18	16	15	3.79

BA	OBA	SA	AB	H	2B	3B	HR	RBI	BB	SO
.270	.346	.364	2172	586	90	17	27	306	237	274
.229	.314	.298	759	174	29	4	5	106	78	129
.292	.363	.400	1413	412	61	13	22	200	159	145
.280	.365	.391	1064	298	45	11	17	296	136	139

SCOTT ALDRED — BL/TL — age 26 — COL/MON RP8 POW/FB

1993	G	IP	H	BB	SO	SB	CS	W	L	SV	ERA
at Home	5	7.0	14	6	6	0	1	1	0	0	14.14
on Road	3	5.0	5	4	3	2	0	0	0	0	1.80
Second Half	0	0.0	0	0	0	0	0	0	0	0	0.00

	BA	OBA	SA	AB	H	2B	3B	HR	RBI	BB	SO
Total	.365	.476	.577	52	19	5	0	2	14	10	9
vs. Left	.429	.556	.857	7	3	0	0	1	4	2	2
vs. Right	.356	.463	.533	45	16	5	0	1	10	8	7
Runners On Base	.343	.452	.600	35	12	3	0	2	14	7	5

4-YEAR TOTALS (1990-1993)

G	IP	H	BB	SO	SB	CS	W	L	SV	ERA
20	78.1	95	44	49	8	4	3	8	0	7.24
19	70.1	75	39	36	9	3	4	6	0	4.73
19	80.0	81	46	46	9	2	4	8	0	4.95

BA	OBA	SA	AB	H	2B	3B	HR	RBI	BB	SO
.293	.383	.471	580	170	30	2	23	92	83	85
.293	.364	.444	99	29	3	0	4	19	11	10
.293	.387	.476	481	141	27	2	19	73	72	75
.263	.364	.420	274	72	11	1	10	79	45	41

LARRY ANDERSEN — BR/TR — age 41 — PHI RP64 POW/FB

1993	G	IP	H	BB	SO	SB	CS	W	L	SV	ERA
at Home	32	31.2	28	12	33	2	1	1	0	0	1.14
on Road	32	30.0	26	9	34	2	0	2	2	0	4.80
Second Half	38	38.1	35	13	43	2	0	0	1	0	3.52

	BA	OBA	SA	AB	H	2B	3B	HR	RBI	BB	SO
Total	.233	.299	.332	232	54	5	3	4	26	21	67
vs. Left	.291	.330	.395	86	25	1	1	2	14	4	23
vs. Right	.199	.282	.295	146	29	4	2	2	12	17	44
Runners On Base	.221	.283	.298	104	23	1	2	1	23	9	33

10-YEAR TOTALS (1984-1993)

G	IP	H	BB	SO	SB	CS	W	L	SV	ERA
284	389.2	333	106	342	51	16	22	11	20	2.01
266	362.2	351	125	284	43	10	13	22	23	3.55
290	403.0	366	123	355	56	13	14	19	29	2.93

BA	OBA	SA	AB	H	2B	3B	HR	RBI	BB	SO
.243	.300	.325	2812	684	94	20	32	331	231	626
.270	.341	.355	1325	358	47	7	17	168	142	233
.219	.262	.299	1487	326	47	13	15	163	89	393
.245	.311	.323	1300	318	42	12	12	311	132	286

LUIS AQUINO — BR/TR — age 30 — FLO RP25, SP13 FIN/GB

1993	G	IP	H	BB	SO	SB	CS	W	L	SV	ERA
at Home	21	44.2	48	21	33	4	2	3	3	0	2.62
on Road	17	66.0	67	19	34	6	3	3	5	0	3.95
Second Half	23	36.0	39	17	26	3	1	2	3	0	4.25

	BA	OBA	SA	AB	H	2B	3B	HR	RBI	BB	SO
Total	.276	.345	.384	417	115	23	2	6	37	40	67
vs. Left	.257	.320	.371	237	61	10	1	5	16	21	34
vs. Right	.300	.376	.400	180	54	13	1	1	21	19	33
Runners On Base	.259	.354	.341	170	44	11	0	1	32	25	28

7-YEAR TOTALS (1986-1993)

G	IP	H	BB	SO	SB	CS	W	L	SV	ERA
77	277.1	264	92	126	14	13	15	10	1	2.92
82	308.0	338	97	144	18	10	14	18	2	4.18
94	360.1	379	115	152	17	14	19	19	2	3.65

BA	OBA	SA	AB	H	2B	3B	HR	RBI	BB	SO
.269	.328	.379	2242	602	118	11	36	245	189	270
.276	.338	.392	1101	304	59	9	17	113	105	134
.261	.318	.366	1141	298	59	2	19	132	84	136
.275	.340	.394	972	267	51	4	19	228	96	108

PAUL ASSENMACHER — BL/TL — age 34 — CHN/NYA RP72 POW/GB

1993	G	IP	H	BB	SO	SB	CS	W	L	SV	ERA
at Home	43	32.1	29	11	29	3	1	2	1	0	3.34
on Road	29	23.2	25	11	16	1	0	2	2	0	3.42
Second Half	35	25.2	19	10	21	1	0	2	2	0	2.81

	BA	OBA	SA	AB	H	2B	3B	HR	RBI	BB	SO
Total	.257	.330	.371	210	54	9	0	5	26	22	45
vs. Left	.242	.317	.385	91	22	1	0	4	14	9	24
vs. Right	.269	.341	.361	119	32	8	0	1	12	13	21
Runners On Base	.278	.358	.402	97	27	3	0	3	24	12	19

8-YEAR TOTALS (1986-1993)

G	IP	H	BB	SO	SB	CS	W	L	SV	ERA
289	332.1	303	106	316	28	10	28	16	26	3.39
242	276.1	263	119	253	17	13	13	16	21	3.48
254	311.1	296	102	301	18	7	27	16	24	3.30

BA	OBA	SA	AB	H	2B	3B	HR	RBI	BB	SO
.248	.316	.366	2286	566	93	12	51	294	225	569
.226	.291	.316	775	175	25	3	13	99	65	220
.259	.329	.391	1511	391	68	9	38	195	160	349
.247	.333	.355	1083	267	45	6	20	263	139	277

JIM AUSTIN — BR/TR — age 31 — MIL RP31 FIN/FB

1993	G	IP	H	BB	SO	SB	CS	W	L	SV	ERA
at Home	18	21.1	13	6	10	0	1	1	1	0	2.53
on Road	13	11.2	15	7	5	0	0	0	1	0	6.17
Second Half	7	8.2	10	2	3	0	0	0	0	0	3.12

	BA	OBA	SA	AB	H	2B	3B	HR	RBI	BB	SO
Total	.230	.309	.336	122	28	4	0	3	13	13	15
vs. Left	.297	.316	.432	37	11	2	0	1	4	1	3
vs. Right	.200	.306	.294	85	17	2	0	2	9	12	12
Runners On Base	.193	.324	.263	57	11	1	0	1	11	10	8

3-YEAR TOTALS (1991-1993)

G	IP	H	BB	SO	SB	CS	W	L	SV	ERA
45	57.1	37	25	30	2	3	3	2	0	2.20
38	42.2	37	31	18	0	2	3	2	0	4.22
36	50.1	38	28	23	1	3	4	0	0	2.86

BA	OBA	SA	AB	H	2B	3B	HR	RBI	BB	SO
.211	.329	.306	350	74	15	0	6	36	56	48
.242	.357	.318	132	32	7	0	1	13	20	12
.193	.311	.298	218	42	8	0	5	23	36	36
.202	.333	.292	178	36	7	0	3	33	32	26

BOBBY AYALA — BR/TR — age 25 — CIN RP34, SP9 POW/GB

1993	G	IP	H	BB	SO	SB	CS	W	L	SV	ERA
at Home	23	57.1	61	21	38	1	0	4	7	1	5.02
on Road	20	40.2	45	24	27	8	1	3	3	2	6.42
Second Half	24	64.2	82	30	49	5	1	4	7	0	6.96

	BA	OBA	SA	AB	H	2B	3B	HR	RBI	BB	SO
Total	.274	.358	.447	387	106	15	2	16	66	45	65
vs. Left	.273	.371	.426	183	50	8	1	6	21	26	35
vs. Right	.275	.346	.466	204	56	7	1	10	45	19	30
Runners On Base	.284	.385	.494	176	50	5	1	10	60	28	27

2-YEAR TOTALS (1992-1993)

G	IP	H	BB	SO	SB	CS	W	L	SV	ERA
26	76.0	81	27	55	2	2	6	7	1	4.74
22	51.0	58	31	33	9	2	3	4	2	6.18
29	93.2	115	43	72	7	4	6	8	0	6.15

BA	OBA	SA	AB	H	2B	3B	HR	RBI	BB	SO
.279	.362	.440	498	139	25	2	17	78	58	88
.276	.370	.415	246	68	14	1	6	28	34	49
.282	.355	.464	252	71	11	1	11	50	24	39
.293	.385	.484	225	66	11	1	10	71	33	39

BOB AYRAULT — BR/TR — age 28 — PHI/SEA RP24 POW/FB

1993	G	IP	H	BB	SO	SB	CS	W	L	SV	ERA
at Home	14	16.0	11	7	9	2	0	2	0	0	2.81
on Road	10	14.0	25	9	6	2	0	1	1	0	8.36
Second Half	9	13.2	12	6	4	0	0	1	0	0	3.29

	BA	OBA	SA	AB	H	2B	3B	HR	RBI	BB	SO
Total	.303	.384	.445	119	36	7	2	2	26	16	15
vs. Left	.317	.420	.390	41	13	3	0	0	4	8	2
vs. Right	.295	.364	.474	78	23	4	2	2	22	8	13
Runners On Base	.309	.402	.471	68	21	4	2	1	25	11	8

2-YEAR TOTALS (1992-1993)

G	IP	H	BB	SO	SB	CS	W	L	SV	ERA
27	34.0	24	16	21	3	0	3	1	0	2.65
27	39.1	44	17	21	4	0	2	2	0	5.26
29	40.1	34	17	22	2	0	3	1	0	3.35

BA	OBA	SA	AB	H	2B	3B	HR	RBI	BB	SO
.250	.330	.360	272	68	16	4	2	46	33	42
.275	.350	.350	120	33	7	1	0	14	15	15
.230	.314	.368	152	35	9	3	2	32	18	27
.254	.347	.394	142	36	9	4	1	45	21	21

JEFF BALLARD — BL/TL — age 31 — PIT RP20, SP5 FIN/GB

1993	G	IP	H	BB	SO	SB	CS	W	L	SV	ERA
at Home	15	32.1	38	11	10	2	0	0	1	0	4.18
on Road	10	21.1	32	4	6	0	1	4	0	0	5.91
Second Half	25	53.2	70	15	16	2	1	4	1	0	4.86

	BA	OBA	SA	AB	H	2B	3B	HR	RBI	BB	SO
Total	.332	.380	.450	211	70	12	2	3	25	15	16
vs. Left	.328	.382	.377	61	20	3	0	0	6	6	8
vs. Right	.333	.379	.480	150	50	9	2	3	19	9	8
Runners On Base	.326	.375	.463	95	31	6	2	1	23	7	6

6-YEAR TOTALS (1987-1993)

G	IP	H	BB	SO	SB	CS	W	L	SV	ERA
85	377.1	439	110	126	32	18	17	29	0	4.44
84	371.2	443	109	107	14	17	23	23	0	4.87
107	396.1	465	116	117	28	16	20	25	0	4.66

BA	OBA	SA	AB	H	2B	3B	HR	RBI	BB	SO
.297	.347	.453	2969	882	172	15	87	372	219	233
.279	.334	.440	552	154	21	2	14	62	44	83
.301	.350	.465	2417	728	151	13	73	310	175	150
.298	.359	.464	1220	363	68	6	41	326	118	100

SCOTT BANKHEAD — BR/TR — age 31 — BOS RP40 POW/FB

1993	G	IP	H	BB	SO	SB	CS	W	L	SV	ERA
at Home	20	31.0	31	14	26	2	1	0	0	0	3.19
on Road	20	33.1	28	15	21	1	1	2	1	0	3.78
Second Half	21	30.1	30	18	25	3	1	1	0	0	4.15

	BA	OBA	SA	AB	H	2B	3B	HR	RBI	BB	SO
Total	.250	.327	.386	236	59	11	0	7	32	29	47
vs. Left	.269	.353	.385	104	28	6	0	2	13	14	19
vs. Right	.235	.307	.386	132	31	5	0	5	19	15	28
Runners On Base	.280	.367	.420	100	28	5	0	3	28	16	21

8-YEAR TOTALS (1986-1993)

G	IP	H	BB	SO	SB	CS	W	L	SV	ERA
113	404.1	405	122	282	33	11	26	21	0	4.34
107	420.0	393	139	287	32	11	27	24	1	3.81
115	410.2	409	138	279	29	13	24	23	0	4.32

BA	OBA	SA	AB	H	2B	3B	HR	RBI	BB	SO
.253	.310	.415	3155	798	159	30	97	360	261	569
.258	.315	.417	1634	422	91	17	45	186	139	277
.247	.305	.412	1521	376	68	13	52	174	122	292
.273	.339	.434	1211	331	64	13	35	298	131	231

BRIAN BARNES — BL/TL — age 27 — MON RP44, SP8 POW/FB

1993	G	IP	H	BB	SO	SB	CS	W	L	SV	ERA
at Home	24	53.1	54	20	34	1	0	1	2	3	4.05
on Road	28	46.2	51	28	26	7	3	1	4	0	4.82
Second Half	27	37.2	42	18	28	2	0	0	3	0	5.26

	BA	OBA	SA	AB	H	2B	3B	HR	RBI	BB	SO
Total	.274	.353	.420	383	105	23	3	9	57	48	60
vs. Left	.352	.453	.534	88	31	8	1	2	16	17	12
vs. Right	.251	.320	.386	295	74	15	2	7	41	31	48
Runners On Base	.259	.341	.407	189	49	11	1	5	53	25	26

4-YEAR TOTALS (1990-1993)

G	IP	H	BB	SO	SB	CS	W	L	SV	ERA
49	195.2	159	80	146	24	5	7	10	3	3.45
56	192.1	183	105	119	22	13	7	11	0	4.26
68	256.1	214	120	179	28	11	11	14	0	3.58

BA	OBA	SA	AB	H	2B	3B	HR	RBI	BB	SO
.239	.328	.370	1431	342	65	7	36	165	185	265
.273	.385	.455	275	75	17	3	9	39	48	47
.231	.314	.349	1156	267	48	4	27	126	137	218
.250	.343	.402	600	150	29	4	18	147	87	112

JOSE BAUTISTA — BR/TR — age 30 — CHN RP51, SP7 FIN/GB

1993	G	IP	H	BB	SO	SB	CS	W	L	SV	ERA
at Home	31	54.1	45	16	29	2	1	5	0	1	2.32
on Road	27	57.1	60	11	34	3	1	5	3	1	3.30
Second Half	36	67.0	63	16	37	3	0	8	1	2	2.82

	BA	OBA	SA	AB	H	2B	3B	HR	RBI	BB	SO
Total	.250	.301	.383	420	105	19	2	11	47	27	63
vs. Left	.232	.311	.324	185	43	8	0	3	19	19	25
vs. Right	.264	.293	.430	235	62	11	2	8	28	8	38
Runners On Base	.239	.289	.350	180	43	5	0	5	41	13	32

5-YEAR TOTALS (1988-1993)

G	IP	H	BB	SO	SB	CS	W	L	SV	ERA
70	207.1	203	51	91	23	4	11	10	1	4.04
63	186.0	198	48	96	18	7	9	13	1	4.45
70	189.0	180	43	89	17	4	12	10	2	3.62

BA	OBA	SA	AB	H	2B	3B	HR	RBI	BB	SO
.263	.313	.430	1522	401	65	13	54	200	99	187
.267	.323	.440	727	194	34	7	26	90	54	78
.260	.304	.420	795	207	31	6	28	110	45	109
.275	.318	.486	622	171	26	3	33	179	39	82

STEVE BEDROSIAN — BR/TR — age 37 — ATL RP49 FIN/FB

1993	G	IP	H	BB	SO	SB	CS	W	L	SV	ERA
at Home	28	27.1	22	5	20	3	2	2	1	0	1.32
on Road	21	22.1	12	9	13	3	0	3	1	0	2.01
Second Half	30	32.2	23	6	24	4	2	5	0	0	1.38

	BA	OBA	SA	AB	H	2B	3B	HR	RBI	BB	SO
Total	.194	.256	.303	175	34	7	0	4	24	14	33
vs. Left	.203	.256	.311	74	15	2	0	2	12	5	16
vs. Right	.188	.257	.297	101	19	5	0	2	12	9	17
Runners On Base	.188	.266	.237	80	15	4	0	0	20	9	17

9-YEAR TOTALS (1984-1993)

G	IP	H	BB	SO	SB	CS	W	L	SV	ERA
259	426.1	375	160	314	54	13	30	26	75	3.36
249	408.2	353	205	296	68	7	27	31	79	3.41
266	438.0	386	182	324	59	11	31	26	83	3.60

BA	OBA	SA	AB	H	2B	3B	HR	RBI	BB	SO
.234	.315	.360	3114	728	117	12	84	364	365	610
.252	.345	.410	1608	405	67	8	57	216	232	289
.214	.280	.307	1506	323	50	4	27	148	133	321
.239	.330	.354	1412	337	52	6	33	313	198	269

ERIC BELL — BL/TL — age 31 — HOU RP10 FIN/FB

1993	G	IP	H	BB	SO	SB	CS	W	L	SV	ERA
at Home	8	6.2	10	1	1	0	0	0	1	0	6.75
on Road	2	0.2	0	1	1	2	0	0	0	0	0.00
Second Half	0	0.0	0	0	0	0	0	0	0	0	0.00

	BA	OBA	SA	AB	H	2B	3B	HR	RBI	BB	SO
Total	.313	.353	.344	32	10	1	0	0	5	2	2
vs. Left	.500	.556	.500	8	4	0	0	0	0	1	1
vs. Right	.250	.280	.292	24	6	1	0	0	5	1	1
Runners On Base	.333	.364	.381	21	7	1	0	0	5	1	1

6-YEAR TOTALS (1985-1993)

G	IP	H	BB	SO	SB	CS	W	L	SV	ERA
33	108.0	115	51	69	10	3	5	10	0	5.67
35	126.2	123	61	83	12	7	10	8	0	4.76
34	141.2	129	55	95	12	6	9	10	0	4.57

BA	OBA	SA	AB	H	2B	3B	HR	RBI	BB	SO
.264	.346	.458	902	238	53	4	38	128	112	152
.263	.347	.413	167	44	7	0	6	22	21	21
.264	.346	.468	735	194	46	4	32	106	91	131
.302	.391	.497	358	108	21	2	15	105	54	58

MIKE BIELECKI — BR/TR — age 35 — CLE SP13 FIN/FB

1993	G	IP	H	BB	SO	SB	CS	W	L	SV	ERA
at Home	8	44.2	53	12	21	4	1	3	1	0	4.23
on Road	5	24.0	37	11	17	10	0	1	4	0	9.00
Second Half	0	0.0	0	0	0	0	0	0	0	0	0.00

	BA	OBA	SA	AB	H	2B	3B	HR	RBI	BB	SO
Total	.310	.363	.455	290	90	18	0	8	36	23	38
vs. Left	.312	.372	.447	141	44	7	0	4	20	14	22
vs. Right	.309	.354	.463	149	46	11	0	4	16	9	16
Runners On Base	.286	.362	.376	133	38	3	0	3	31	16	18

10-YEAR TOTALS (1984-1993)

G	IP	H	BB	SO	SB	CS	W	L	SV	ERA
103	520.1	510	198	315	40	30	29	29	0	4.06
113	475.2	499	201	274	53	17	28	28	1	4.30
106	484.2	478	175	273	43	21	28	24	1	4.05

BA	OBA	SA	AB	H	2B	3B	HR	RBI	BB	SO
.265	.334	.402	3814	1009	195	41	82	429	399	589
.269	.340	.406	2109	568	108	20	47	229	232	289
.259	.326	.396	1705	441	87	21	35	200	167	300
.264	.342	.387	1619	427	73	18	30	377	202	277

BUD BLACK — BL/TL — age 37 — SF SP16 FIN/FB

1993	G	IP	H	BB	SO	SB	CS	W	L	SV	ERA
at Home	7	38.2	43	16	21	4	3	4	2	0	3.96
on Road	9	55.0	46	17	24	5	5	4	0	0	3.27
Second Half	4	21.2	27	5	6	1	1	1	1	0	4.98

	BA	OBA	SA	AB	H	2B	3B	HR	RBI	BB	SO
Total	.256	.321	.409	347	89	10	2	13	36	33	45
vs. Left	.294	.333	.392	51	15	2	0	1	4	3	2
vs. Right	.250	.319	.412	296	74	8	2	12	32	30	43
Runners On Base	.220	.299	.378	127	28	2	0	6	29	15	21

10-YEAR TOTALS (1984-1993)

G	IP	H	BB	SO	SB	CS	W	L	SV	ERA
169	901.2	844	245	459	57	46	58	47	7	3.38
160	799.1	768	266	420	49	35	41	52	4	4.06
165	867.2	852	240	461	65	34	46	58	8	3.87

BA	OBA	SA	AB	H	2B	3B	HR	RBI	BB	SO
.250	.307	.382	6451	1612	257	42	171	664	511	879
.233	.288	.349	1335	311	39	7	34	139	102	178
.254	.312	.391	5116	1301	218	35	137	525	409	701
.249	.319	.386	2498	621	89	14	75	568	254	368

WILLIE BLAIR — BR/TR — age 29 — COL RP28, SP18 FIN/FB

1993	G	IP	H	BB	SO	SB	CS	W	L	SV	ERA
at Home	21	54.1	80	18	27	3	3	2	3	0	5.96
on Road	25	91.2	104	24	57	5	4	7	0	0	4.03
Second Half	17	67.1	89	21	34	3	0	5	0	0	4.41

	BA	OBA	SA	AB	H	2B	3B	HR	RBI	BB	SO
Total	.306	.350	.476	601	184	30	6	20	90	42	84
vs. Left	.282	.336	.442	308	87	17	4	8	47	26	44
vs. Right	.331	.365	.512	293	97	13	2	12	43	16	40
Runners On Base	.282	.334	.484	277	78	12	4	12	82	25	34

4-YEAR TOTALS (1990-1993)

G	IP	H	BB	SO	SB	CS	W	L	SV	ERA
60	145.2	175	53	86	9	5	9	8	0	4.76
53	183.2	207	52	102	11	6	7	17	0	4.56
62	181.0	205	56	96	7	4	13	12	0	4.48

BA	OBA	SA	AB	H	2B	3B	HR	RBI	BB	SO
.290	.342	.445	1316	382	69	13	36	195	105	188
.280	.339	.420	664	186	37	7	14	89	60	94
.301	.345	.469	652	196	32	6	22	106	45	94
.310	.355	.501	581	180	33	9	20	179	49	71

MIKE BODDICKER — BR/TR — age 37 — MIL SP10 FIN/GB

1993	G	IP	H	BB	SO	SB	CS	W	L	SV	ERA
at Home	7	35.1	47	13	14	3	2	3	2	0	5.09
on Road	3	18.2	30	2	10	3	1	0	3	0	6.75
Second Half	0	0.0	0	0	0	0	0	0	0	0	0.00

	BA	OBA	SA	AB	H	2B	3B	HR	RBI	BB	SO
Total	.338	.387	.478	228	77	10	2	6	33	15	24
vs. Left	.392	.429	.592	130	51	6	1	6	20	7	9
vs. Right	.265	.333	.327	98	26	4	1	0	13	8	15
Runners On Base	.375	.416	.500	104	39	2	1	3	30	6	12

10-YEAR TOTALS (1984-1993)

G	IP	H	BB	SO	SB	CS	W	L	SV	ERA
152	971.0	975	319	603	99	42	61	56	0	3.78
153	935.0	929	331	581	115	29	56	51	3	4.00
147	930.2	971	297	595	112	35	58	52	1	3.91

BA	OBA	SA	AB	H	2B	3B	HR	RBI	BB	SO
.261	.327	.388	7285	1904	325	44	171	788	650	1184
.272	.335	.402	3914	1066	181	27	91	434	339	475
.249	.318	.373	3371	838	144	17	80	354	311	709
.260	.328	.382	3068	797	123	17	73	690	289	521

JOE BOEVER — BR/TR — age 34 — OAK/DET RP61 POW/FB

1993	G	IP	H	BB	SO	SB	CS	W	L	SV	ERA
at Home	30	47.2	50	18	27	2	2	5	2	1	3.21
on Road	31	54.2	51	26	36	2	1	1	2	2	3.95
Second Half	34	49.0	49	22	33	1	4	2	4	1	4.22

	BA	OBA	SA	AB	H	2B	3B	HR	RBI	BB	SO
Total	.260	.336	.401	389	101	22	3	9	55	44	63
vs. Left	.291	.365	.442	172	50	12	1	4	30	21	20
vs. Right	.235	.312	.369	217	51	10	2	5	25	23	43
Runners On Base	.235	.354	.371	170	40	9	1	4	50	31	35

9-YEAR TOTALS (1985-1993)

G	IP	H	BB	SO	SB	CS	W	L	SV	ERA
213	313.0	285	125	223	28	15	14	16	17	2.96
184	246.1	241	131	192	30	8	6	18	24	4.06
232	313.1	302	127	231	30	12	10	19	21	3.36

BA	OBA	SA	AB	H	2B	3B	HR	RBI	BB	SO
.250	.331	.366	2103	526	88	12	44	265	256	415
.247	.344	.339	1008	249	40	7	13	125	151	195
.253	.319	.391	1095	277	48	5	31	140	105	220
.234	.332	.326	1000	234	42	7	12	233	150	213

BRIAN BOHANON — BL/TL — age 26 — TEX RP28, SP8 FIN/GB

1993	G	IP	H	BB	SO	SB	CS	W	L	SV	ERA
at Home	20	51.2	57	23	26	4	4	4	2	0	4.35
on Road	16	41.0	50	23	19	4	3	0	2	0	5.27
Second Half	18	56.1	73	28	29	7	2	1	3	0	5.59

	BA	OBA	SA	AB	H	2B	3B	HR	RBI	BB	SO
Total	.296	.377	.429	361	107	22	1	8	53	46	45
vs. Left	.326	.434	.427	89	29	3	0	2	19	15	11
vs. Right	.287	.358	.430	272	78	19	1	6	34	31	34
Runners On Base	.278	.351	.428	180	50	13	1	4	49	22	27

4-YEAR TOTALS (1990-1993)

G	IP	H	BB	SO	SB	CS	W	L	SV	ERA
39	117.2	136	58	60	9	8	6	7	0	5.20
37	116.0	134	54	63	5	4	3	4	0	5.51
43	151.0	179	68	87	12	3	6	7	0	5.25

BA	OBA	SA	AB	H	2B	3B	HR	RBI	BB	SO
.291	.367	.432	928	270	48	4	25	147	112	123
.280	.367	.368	182	51	5	1	3	39	24	23
.294	.368	.448	746	219	43	3	22	108	88	100
.301	.372	.467	435	131	25	4	13	135	54	61

TOM BOLTON — BL/TL — age 32 — DET RP35, SP8 POW/GB

7-YEAR TOTALS (1987-1993)

1993	G	IP	H	BB	SO	SB	CS	W	L	SV	ERA
at Home	20	51.2	56	20	42	2	4	3	1	0	4.01
on Road	23	51.0	57	25	24	5	1	3	5	0	4.94
Second Half	23	63.2	67	27	42	7	3	5	3	0	3.82
	85	264.1	297	101	171	13	10	18	11	1	4.15
	102	252.2	288	130	153	19	6	12	21	0	4.92
	115	343.2	372	151	203	23	12	21	22	1	4.37

	BA	OBA	SA	AB	H	2B	3B	HR	RBI	BB	SO
Total	.282	.363	.384	401	113	22	2	5	55	45	66
vs. Left	.266	.361	.383	94	25	5	0	2	13	12	20
vs. Right	.287	.363	.384	307	88	17	2	3	42	33	46
Runners On Base	.280	.373	.410	200	56	12	1	4	54	27	35
	.288	.362	.410	2033	585	98	11	43	265	231	324
	.271	.343	.374	521	141	25	4	7	73	54	99
	.294	.369	.423	1512	444	73	7	36	192	177	225
	.294	.376	.427	954	280	52	6	21	243	125	153

PEDRO BORBON — BR/TL — age 27 — ATL RP3 POW/GB

2-YEAR TOTALS (1992-1993)

1993	G	IP	H	BB	SO	SB	CS	W	L	SV	ERA
at Home	3	1.2	3	3	2	0	0	0	0	0	21.60
on Road	0	0.0	0	0	0	0	0	0	0	0	0.00
Second Half	3	1.2	3	3	2	0	0	0	0	0	21.60
	5	3.0	5	4	3	0	0	0	1	0	15.00
	0	0.0	0	0	0	0	0	0	0	0	0.00
	5	3.0	5	4	3	0	0	0	1	0	15.00

	BA	OBA	SA	AB	H	2B	3B	HR	RBI	BB	SO
Total	.429	.600	.571	7	3	1	0	0	1	3	2
vs. Left	.000	.600	.000	2	0	0	0	0	0	3	1
vs. Right	.600	.600	.800	5	3	1	0	0	1	0	1
Runners On Base	.200	.500	.200	5	1	0	0	0	1	3	2
	.385	.529	.538	13	5	2	0	0	2	4	3
	.167	.444	.333	6	1	1	0	0	0	3	2
	.571	.625	.714	7	4	1	0	0	2	1	1
	.250	.500	.250	8	2	0	0	0	2	4	3

SHAWN BOSKIE — BR/TR — age 27 — CHN RP37, SP2 FIN/GB

4-YEAR TOTALS (1990-1993)

1993	G	IP	H	BB	SO	SB	CS	W	L	SV	ERA
at Home	22	39.2	33	14	23	4	1	4	1	0	2.72
on Road	17	26.0	30	7	16	0	0	1	2	0	4.50
Second Half	36	53.0	47	16	30	4	0	4	2	0	2.72
	60	204.0	224	80	92	8	5	12	14	0	4.50
	45	180.0	184	60	97	8	5	7	15	0	4.45
	65	171.1	186	65	80	8	3	8	13	0	4.31

	BA	OBA	SA	AB	H	2B	3B	HR	RBI	BB	SO
Total	.258	.333	.406	244	63	11	2	7	28	21	39
vs. Left	.218	.306	.336	110	24	4	0	3	9	12	18
vs. Right	.291	.356	.463	134	39	7	2	4	19	9	21
Runners On Base	.241	.338	.384	112	27	6	2	2	23	12	23
	.278	.345	.438	1466	408	85	10	43	176	140	189
	.290	.372	.467	810	235	52	8	25	102	107	95
	.264	.309	.402	656	173	33	2	18	74	33	94
	.277	.350	.435	621	172	32	6	18	151	68	72

DENIS BOUCHER — BR/TL — age 26 — MON SP5 FIN/FB

3-YEAR TOTALS (1991-1993)

1993	G	IP	H	BB	SO	SB	CS	W	L	SV	ERA
at Home	4	22.2	18	3	11	0	1	2	1	0	1.99
on Road	1	5.2	6	0	3	1	1	1	0	0	1.59
Second Half	5	28.1	24	3	14	1	2	3	1	0	1.91
	12	56.1	73	17	25	1	2	2	4	0	6.23
	13	71.0	73	30	35	3	2	4	6	0	4.44
	10	50.0	58	10	25	3	2	4	4	0	4.68

	BA	OBA	SA	AB	H	2B	3B	HR	RBI	BB	SO
Total	.229	.243	.333	105	24	4	2	1	7	3	14
vs. Left	.263	.273	.474	19	5	2	1	0	4	1	4
vs. Right	.221	.236	.302	86	19	2	1	1	3	2	10
Runners On Base	.176	.205	.235	34	6	2	0	0	6	2	6
	.290	.349	.496	504	146	30	4	22	70	47	60
	.325	.393	.532	77	25	8	1	2	8	10	7
	.283	.341	.489	427	121	22	3	20	62	37	53
	.300	.348	.507	217	65	12	0	11	59	17	27

JEFF BRANTLEY — BR/TR — age 31 — SF RP41, SP12 POW/FB

6-YEAR TOTALS (1988-1993)

1993	G	IP	H	BB	SO	SB	CS	W	L	SV	ERA
at Home	27	60.1	51	20	41	1	0	3	2	0	3.58
on Road	26	53.1	61	26	35	0	5	2	4	0	5.06
Second Half	35	45.1	32	18	39	0	2	1	1	0	3.97
	139	242.0	206	97	190	17	3	17	8	19	2.83
	160	263.1	251	122	194	26	12	12	12	23	3.62
	158	256.1	226	108	224	28	8	16	9	21	3.41

	BA	OBA	SA	AB	H	2B	3B	HR	RBI	BB	SO
Total	.259	.336	.439	433	112	15	3	19	49	46	76
vs. Left	.285	.374	.511	221	63	13	2	11	26	33	30
vs. Right	.231	.295	.363	212	49	2	1	8	23	13	46
Runners On Base	.282	.349	.406	170	48	3	3	4	34	19	28
	.244	.327	.365	1876	457	68	5	50	205	219	384
	.249	.343	.366	1003	250	44	2	23	93	146	186
	.237	.307	.364	873	207	24	3	27	112	73	198
	.243	.331	.339	855	208	24	5	16	171	112	167

WILLIAM BRENNAN — BR/TR — age 31 — CHN RP7, SP1 POW/GB

2-YEAR TOTALS (1988-1993)

1993	G	IP	H	BB	SO	SB	CS	W	L	SV	ERA
at Home	3	4.2	3	3	2	0	2	1	0	0	1.93
on Road	5	10.1	13	5	9	1	1	1	1	0	5.23
Second Half	8	15.0	16	8	11	1	3	2	1	0	4.20
	4	7.1	7	4	6	0	2	1	0	0	6.14
	8	17.0	22	10	12	3	2	1	2	0	4.76
	12	24.1	29	14	18	3	4	2	2	0	5.18

	BA	OBA	SA	AB	H	2B	3B	HR	RBI	BB	SO
Total	.291	.385	.436	55	16	2	0	2	10	8	11
vs. Left	.333	.459	.567	30	10	1	0	2	5	7	7
vs. Right	.240	.286	.280	25	6	1	0	0	5	1	4
Runners On Base	.240	.355	.400	25	6	1	0	1	9	4	5
	.312	.404	.419	93	29	4	0	2	15	14	18
	.364	.462	.509	55	20	2	0	2	9	10	12
	.237	.318	.289	38	9	2	0	0	6	4	6
	.292	.386	.396	48	14	2	0	1	14	7	8

BRAD BRINK — BR/TR — age 29 — PHI RP2 POW/FB

2-YEAR TOTALS (1992-1993)

1993	G	IP	H	BB	SO	SB	CS	W	L	SV	ERA
at Home	1	2.0	2	0	3	0	0	0	0	0	4.50
on Road	1	4.0	1	3	5	0	0	0	1	0	2.25
Second Half	2	6.0	3	3	8	0	0	0	1	0	3.00
	5	25.0	34	6	12	1	1	0	3	0	4.68
	5	22.1	22	10	12	2	1	0	1	0	3.22
	4	13.0	11	7	9	0	0	0	1	0	2.77

	BA	OBA	SA	AB	H	2B	3B	HR	RBI	BB	SO
Total	.143	.250	.333	21	3	1	0	1	2	3	8
vs. Left	.133	.235	.200	15	2	0	0	0	1	2	5
vs. Right	.167	.286	.667	6	1	1	0	1	1	1	3
Runners On Base	.111	.200	.111	9	1	0	0	0	1	1	3
	.290	.348	.404	193	56	9	2	3	25	16	24
	.265	.317	.368	117	31	4	1	2	14	9	11
	.329	.393	.461	76	25	5	1	1	11	7	13
	.301	.376	.398	83	25	2	0	2	24	9	7

JOHN BRISCOE — BR/TR — age 27 — OAK RP17 POW/GB

1993 / 3-YEAR TOTALS (1991-1993)

1993	G	IP	H	BB	SO	SB	CS	W	L	SV	ERA		G	IP	H	BB	SO	SB	CS	W	L	SV	ERA
at Home	6	11.1	7	10	14	0	1	0	1	0	4.76		11	19.1	22	19	19	0	2	0	0	0	7.91
on Road	11	13.1	19	16	10	0	1	1	0	0	10.80		19	26.1	28	26	18	0	1	1	1	0	7.18
Second Half	17	24.2	26	26	24	0	2	1	0	0	8.03		17	24.2	26	26	24	0	2	1	0	0	8.03

	BA	OBA	SA	AB	H	2B	3B	HR	RBI	BB	SO		BA	OBA	SA	AB	H	2B	3B	HR	RBI	BB	SO
Total	.277	.426	.404	94	26	6	0	2	16	26	24		.286	.426	.434	175	50	11	0	5	35	45	37
vs. Left	.405	.527	.500	42	17	4	0	0	9	12	9		.359	.495	.423	78	28	5	0	0	15	22	15
vs. Right	.173	.343	.327	52	9	2	0	2	7	14	15		.227	.369	.443	97	22	6	0	5	20	23	22
Runners On Base	.291	.423	.418	55	16	4	0	1	15	14	12		.302	.417	.425	106	32	7	0	2	32	23	17

TERRY BROSS — BR/TR — age 28 — SF RP2 FIN/FB

1993 / 2-YEAR TOTALS (1991-1993)

1993	G	IP	H	BB	SO	SB	CS	W	L	SV	ERA		G	IP	H	BB	SO	SB	CS	W	L	SV	ERA
at Home	2	2.0	3	1	1	0	0	0	0	0	9.00		8	10.0	10	3	6	0	0	0	0	0	3.60
on Road	0	0.0	0	0	0	0	0	0	0	0	0.00		1	0.0	0	1	0	0	0	0	0	0	0.00
Second Half	2	2.0	3	1	1	0	0	0	0	0	9.00		10	12.0	10	4	6	0	0	0	0	0	3.00

	BA	OBA	SA	AB	H	2B	3B	HR	RBI	BB	SO		BA	OBA	SA	AB	H	2B	3B	HR	RBI	BB	SO
Total	.333	.400	.667	9	3	0	0	1	6	1	1		.227	.292	.386	44	10	1	0	2	8	4	6
vs. Left	.333	.500	.333	3	1	0	0	0	1	1	1		.158	.238	.158	19	3	0	0	0	1	2	4
vs. Right	.333	.333	.833	6	2	0	0	1	5	0	0		.280	.333	.560	25	7	1	0	2	7	2	2
Runners On Base	.375	.375	.750	8	3	0	0	1	6	0	3		.261	.261	.522	23	6	0	0	2	8	0	3

JIM BULLINGER — BR/TR — age 29 — CHN RP15 POW/GB

1993 / 2-YEAR TOTALS (1992-1993)

1993	G	IP	H	BB	SO	SB	CS	W	L	SV	ERA		G	IP	H	BB	SO	SB	CS	W	L	SV	ERA
at Home	6	6.2	6	4	1	1	0	1	0	0	5.40		27	61.0	49	35	24	7	1	3	6	4	3.69
on Road	9	10.0	12	5	9	0	1	0	0	1	3.60		27	40.2	41	28	22	2	2	0	2	4	5.98
Second Half	7	8.1	7	3	2	0	0	0	0	1	1.08		31	77.0	66	46	32	7	2	2	8	1	4.32

	BA	OBA	SA	AB	H	2B	3B	HR	RBI	BB	SO		BA	OBA	SA	AB	H	2B	3B	HR	RBI	BB	SO
Total	.277	.360	.431	65	18	5	1	1	8	9	10		.241	.352	.390	374	90	14	6	10	52	63	46
vs. Left	.360	.485	.600	25	9	3	0	1	6	7	3		.231	.363	.426	195	45	7	5	7	33	40	20
vs. Right	.225	.262	.325	40	9	2	1	0	2	2	7		.251	.340	.352	179	45	7	1	3	19	23	26
Runners On Base	.300	.389	.400	30	9	3	0	0	7	5	4		.288	.401	.466	163	47	7	2	6	48	33	18

DAVE BURBA — BR/TR — age 28 — SF RP49, SP5 POW/FB

1993 / 4-YEAR TOTALS (1990-1993)

1993	G	IP	H	BB	SO	SB	CS	W	L	SV	ERA		G	IP	H	BB	SO	SB	CS	W	L	SV	ERA
at Home	30	58.1	53	22	54	5	1	5	1	0	3.39		55	112.2	101	44	83	8	2	7	4	1	3.36
on Road	24	37.0	42	15	34	5	2	5	2	0	5.59		50	98.0	116	40	72	8	3	7	8	0	5.60
Second Half	27	50.0	46	24	50	4	2	5	1	0	4.14		50	92.1	92	43	75	5	2	7	3	0	4.00

	BA	OBA	SA	AB	H	2B	3B	HR	RBI	BB	SO		BA	OBA	SA	AB	H	2B	3B	HR	RBI	BB	SO
Total	.265	.336	.421	359	95	12	1	14	53	37	88		.269	.340	.413	807	217	34	5	24	114	84	155
vs. Left	.318	.379	.464	151	48	4	0	6	24	14	25		.308	.371	.435	370	114	18	1	9	46	35	50
vs. Right	.226	.305	.389	208	47	8	1	8	29	23	63		.236	.313	.394	437	103	16	4	15	68	49	105
Runners On Base	.286	.376	.474	154	44	6	1	7	46	23	41		.282	.379	.435	347	98	19	2	10	100	55	75

TODD BURNS — BR/TR — age 31 — TEX/SL RP44, SP5 FIN/FB

1993 / 6-YEAR TOTALS (1988-1993)

1993	G	IP	H	BB	SO	SB	CS	W	L	SV	ERA		G	IP	H	BB	SO	SB	CS	W	L	SV	ERA
at Home	21	39.0	31	13	13	0	1	0	2	0	3.92		99	249.1	197	75	123	5	11	13	6	8	2.53
on Road	28	56.2	64	28	32	3	2	0	6	0	5.88		104	240.1	242	100	130	9	12	8	17	5	4.46
Second Half	31	42.2	39	18	18	0	1	0	4	0	5.06		126	286.2	264	105	145	7	9	13	15	8	3.67

	BA	OBA	SA	AB	H	2B	3B	HR	RBI	BB	SO		BA	OBA	SA	AB	H	2B	3B	HR	RBI	BB	SO
Total	.260	.333	.456	366	95	20	5	14	60	41	45		.241	.308	.378	1822	439	90	15	43	207	175	253
vs. Left	.230	.305	.403	139	32	10	1	4	19	14	16		.227	.302	.348	807	183	38	9	14	64	83	97
vs. Right	.278	.350	.489	227	63	10	4	10	41	27	29		.252	.312	.401	1015	256	52	6	29	143	92	156
Runners On Base	.270	.343	.391	174	47	11	2	2	48	22	20		.232	.296	.354	802	186	39	7	15	179	78	107

MIKE BUTCHER — BR/TR — age 29 — CAL RP23 POW/FB

1993 / 2-YEAR TOTALS (1992-1993)

1993	G	IP	H	BB	SO	SB	CS	W	L	SV	ERA		G	IP	H	BB	SO	SB	CS	W	L	SV	ERA
at Home	10	13.0	10	7	7	2	0	1	0	3	3.46		18	28.2	27	13	18	3	0	1	1	3	2.51
on Road	13	15.1	11	8	17	2	0	0	0	5	2.35		24	27.1	23	15	30	4	0	2	1	5	3.62
Second Half	21	26.2	18	12	24	4	0	1	0	8	1.69		40	54.1	47	25	48	7	0	3	2	8	2.48

	BA	OBA	SA	AB	H	2B	3B	HR	RBI	BB	SO		BA	OBA	SA	AB	H	2B	3B	HR	RBI	BB	SO
Total	.204	.309	.301	103	21	4	0	2	15	15	24		.235	.331	.333	213	50	6	0	5	30	28	48
vs. Left	.186	.300	.302	43	8	2	0	1	3	5	13		.230	.352	.338	74	17	2	0	2	10	11	22
vs. Right	.217	.315	.300	60	13	2	0	1	12	10	11		.237	.319	.331	139	33	4	0	3	20	17	26
Runners On Base	.250	.333	.385	52	13	1	0	2	15	8	8		.216	.313	.320	125	27	1	0	4	29	17	28

GREG CADARET — BL/TL — age 32 — CIN/KC RP47 POW/GB

1993 / 7-YEAR TOTALS (1987-1993)

1993	G	IP	H	BB	SO	SB	CS	W	L	SV	ERA		G	IP	H	BB	SO	SB	CS	W	L	SV	ERA
at Home	26	27.2	29	10	12	2	2	1	2	1	2.60		175	335.1	311	173	251	22	22	22	12	3	3.44
on Road	21	20.1	25	20	13	1	2	0	0	0	6.64		173	290.2	304	171	207	25	20	14	17	8	4.52
Second Half	17	20.1	21	11	5	2	2	1	1	0	3.54		187	349.1	347	181	269	17	21	25	14	9	3.99

	BA	OBA	SA	AB	H	2B	3B	HR	RBI	BB	SO		BA	OBA	SA	AB	H	2B	3B	HR	RBI	BB	SO
Total	.293	.398	.386	184	54	6	0	3	30	30	25		.262	.357	.378	2344	615	111	11	46	304	344	458
vs. Left	.333	.408	.365	63	21	2	0	0	8	7	6		.245	.331	.324	682	167	25	1	9	74	84	119
vs. Right	.273	.393	.397	121	33	4	0	3	22	23	19		.270	.367	.400	1662	448	86	10	37	230	260	339
Runners on Base	.319	.418	.447	94	30	6	0	2	29	16	9		.267	.364	.379	1147	306	52	7	21	279	185	219

KEVIN CAMPBELL — BR/TR — age 30 — OAK RP11 POW/FB

1993	G	IP	H	BB	SO	SB	CS	W	L	SV	ERA
at Home	4	5.2	4	3	5	0	0	0	0	0	4.76
on Road	7	10.1	16	8	4	0	2	0	0	0	8.71
Second Half	11	16.0	20	11	9	0	2	0	0	0	7.31

	BA	OBA	SA	AB	H	2B	3B	HR	RBI	BB	SO
Total	.313	.416	.438	64	20	5	0	1	12	11	9
vs. Left	.417	.517	.458	24	10	1	0	0	3	5	4
vs. Right	.250	.354	.425	40	10	4	0	1	9	6	5
Runners On Base	.343	.442	.486	35	12	2	0	1	12	7	4

3-YEAR TOTALS (1991-1993)

G	IP	H	BB	SO	SB	CS	W	L	SV	ERA
27	51.0	41	28	35	3	2	1	1	0	3.35
30	53.0	58	42	28	0	5	2	2	1	6.45
46	77.2	74	56	51	1	4	1	2	1	4.87

BA	OBA	SA	AB	H	2B	3B	HR	RBI	BB	SO
.254	.369	.380	389	99	20	1	9	51	70	63
.258	.399	.356	163	42	7	0	3	16	39	29
.252	.345	.398	226	57	13	1	6	35	31	34
.278	.381	.385	187	52	8	0	4	46	33	28

JOHN CANDELARIA — BL/TL — age 41 — PIT RP24 POW/FB

1993	G	IP	H	BB	SO	SB	CS	W	L	SV	ERA
at Home	11	11.1	12	8	7	1	1	0	3	1	8.74
on Road	13	8.1	13	1	10	0	0	0	0	0	7.56
Second Half	2	0.2	1	0	1	0	0	0	0	0	0.00

	BA	OBA	SA	AB	H	2B	3B	HR	RBI	BB	SO
Total	.313	.385	.500	80	25	5	2	2	18	9	17
vs. Left	.290	.333	.355	31	9	2	0	0	4	1	12
vs. Right	.327	.414	.592	49	16	3	2	2	14	8	5
Runners On Base	.341	.404	.610	41	14	4	2	1	17	5	7

10-YEAR TOTALS (1984-1993)

G	IP	H	BB	SO	SB	CS	W	L	SV	ERA
172	494.0	491	115	407	12	22	34	30	16	3.95
177	417.2	406	98	304	15	15	33	23	9	3.32
170	481.2	462	121	381	15	18	37	28	8	3.59

BA	OBA	SA	AB	H	2B	3B	HR	RBI	BB	SO
.258	.300	.415	3473	897	168	37	101	421	213	711
.209	.247	.292	681	142	22	4	9	61	37	225
.270	.313	.445	2792	755	146	33	92	360	176	486
.264	.309	.432	1396	369	63	18	45	365	110	311

CRIS CARPENTER — BR/TR — age 29 — FLO/TEX RP56 POW/FB

1993	G	IP	H	BB	SO	SB	CS	W	L	SV	ERA
at Home	29	38.2	39	15	33	3	0	3	1	1	4.19
on Road	27	30.2	25	10	20	2	1	1	1	0	2.64
Second Half	32	41.1	38	15	34	1	1	4	1	1	3.27

	BA	OBA	SA	AB	H	2B	3B	HR	RBI	BB	SO
Total	.248	.320	.372	258	64	13	2	5	34	25	53
vs. Left	.333	.400	.532	111	37	11	1	3	20	14	13
vs. Right	.184	.255	.252	147	27	2	1	2	14	11	40
Runners On Base	.240	.325	.333	129	31	9	0	1	30	15	31

6-YEAR TOTALS (1988-1993)

G	IP	H	BB	SO	SB	CS	W	L	SV	ERA
113	172.1	165	56	108	15	7	10	7	2	4.13
123	174.2	152	53	103	15	6	15	10	0	3.14
103	132.0	123	43	90	7	5	11	5	1	3.55

BA	OBA	SA	AB	H	2B	3B	HR	RBI	BB	SO
.244	.305	.383	1297	317	68	11	30	171	109	211
.274	.339	.426	631	173	44	5	14	90	65	81
.216	.271	.342	666	144	24	6	16	81	44	130
.256	.329	.396	579	148	35	5	12	153	64	92

CHUCK CARY — BL/TL — age 34 — CHA RP16 FIN/GB

1993	G	IP	H	BB	SO	SB	CS	W	L	SV	ERA
at Home	12	14.2	13	9	7	0	2	1	0	0	3.68
on Road	4	6.0	9	2	3	0	0	0	0	0	9.00
Second Half	13	17.0	15	9	9	0	2	1	0	0	3.71

	BA	OBA	SA	AB	H	2B	3B	HR	RBI	BB	SO
Total	.286	.379	.429	77	22	6	1	1	17	11	10
vs. Left	.276	.389	.379	29	8	3	0	0	6	3	3
vs. Right	.292	.373	.458	48	14	3	1	1	11	8	7
Runners On Base	.349	.407	.512	43	15	4	0	1	17	6	4

8-YEAR TOTALS (1985-1993)

G	IP	H	BB	SO	SB	CS	W	L	SV	ERA
71	229.0	203	77	180	18	9	9	9	2	3.54
63	181.1	187	81	142	15	7	5	17	1	4.96
78	238.0	209	78	196	14	11	9	14	3	3.63

BA	OBA	SA	AB	H	2B	3B	HR	RBI	BB	SO
.250	.319	.415	1562	390	87	11	50	215	158	322
.265	.339	.408	343	91	18	2	9	54	34	65
.245	.314	.418	1219	299	69	9	41	161	124	257
.279	.347	.462	639	178	30	3	27	192	72	121

LARRY CASIAN — BR/TL — age 29 — MIN RP54 FIN/FB

1993	G	IP	H	BB	SO	SB	CS	W	L	SV	ERA
at Home	25	23.2	24	8	8	1	0	2	0	0	4.18
on Road	29	33.0	35	6	23	0	0	3	3	1	2.18
Second Half	38	42.1	40	11	21	1	0	4	2	1	3.83

	BA	OBA	SA	AB	H	2B	3B	HR	RBI	BB	SO
Total	.268	.311	.336	220	59	12	0	1	24	14	31
vs. Left	.289	.296	.382	76	22	4	0	1	13	1	12
vs. Right	.257	.318	.313	144	37	8	0	0	11	13	19
Runners On Base	.283	.319	.368	106	30	6	0	1	24	6	10

4-YEAR TOTALS (1990-1993)

G	IP	H	BB	SO	SB	CS	W	L	SV	ERA
43	54.1	66	14	20	1	0	4	1	0	4.97
37	49.2	54	12	30	0	0	4	3	1	2.54
49	71.1	73	16	34	1	0	7	3	1	3.53

BA	OBA	SA	AB	H	2B	3B	HR	RBI	BB	SO
.292	.334	.414	411	120	29	0	7	46	26	50
.238	.248	.310	126	30	6	0	1	16	2	22
.316	.371	.460	285	90	23	0	6	30	24	28
.270	.312	.390	200	54	12	0	4	43	13	16

TONY CASTILLO — BL/TL — age 31 — TOR RP51 FIN/GB

1993	G	IP	H	BB	SO	SB	CS	W	L	SV	ERA
at Home	26	29.1	27	15	15	3	1	3	2	0	4.91
on Road	25	21.1	17	7	13	1	0	0	0	0	1.27
Second Half	29	26.0	25	11	17	2	1	2	2	0	4.15

	BA	OBA	SA	AB	H	2B	3B	HR	RBI	BB	SO
Total	.242	.320	.352	182	44	4	2	4	23	22	28
vs. Left	.213	.222	.311	61	13	1	1	1	9	1	7
vs. Right	.256	.364	.372	121	31	3	1	3	14	21	21
Runners On Base	.239	.314	.326	92	22	2	0	2	21	11	13

5-YEAR TOTALS (1988-1993)

G	IP	H	BB	SO	SB	CS	W	L	SV	ERA
75	97.2	110	35	68	14	3	5	3	1	4.42
88	104.0	108	34	71	12	3	7	3	1	3.38
103	125.0	133	40	85	17	5	8	4	1	3.53

BA	OBA	SA	AB	H	2B	3B	HR	RBI	BB	SO
.280	.335	.383	779	218	31	2	15	115	69	139
.247	.276	.345	235	58	9	1	4	36	10	50
.294	.359	.399	544	160	22	1	11	79	59	89
.278	.336	.379	396	110	16	0	8	108	40	77

MIKE CHRISTOPHER — BR/TR — age 31 — CLE RP9 FIN/FB

1993	G	IP	H	BB	SO	SB	CS	W	L	SV	ERA
at Home	5	7.2	8	2	6	1	0	0	0	0	3.52
on Road	4	4.0	6	0	2	0	0	0	0	0	4.50
Second Half	2	2.1	2	1	0	1	0	0	0	0	3.86

	BA	OBA	SA	AB	H	2B	3B	HR	RBI	BB	SO
Total	.286	.314	.490	49	14	1	0	2	6	2	8
vs. Left	.391	.417	.696	23	9	1	0	2	2	1	3
vs. Right	.192	.222	.308	26	5	0	0	1	4	1	5
Runners On Base	.160	.222	.160	25	4	0	0	0	3	2	4

3-YEAR TOTALS (1991-1993)

G	IP	H	BB	SO	SB	CS	W	L	SV	ERA
8	15.0	16	6	10	2	0	0	0	0	4.20
14	18.2	17	9	13	1	2	0	0	0	1.93
10	15.0	10	10	10	3	0	0	0	0	1.80

BA	OBA	SA	AB	H	2B	3B	HR	RBI	BB	SO
.258	.333	.453	128	33	4	0	5	15	15	23
.298	.389	.511	47	14	2	1	2	4	7	7
.235	.300	.420	81	19	4	1	3	11	8	16
.176	.235	.243	74	13	2	0	1	11	6	11

DENNIS COOK — BL/TL — age 32 — CLE RP19, SP6 FIN/FB

1993	G	IP	H	BB	SO	SB	CS	W	L	SV	ERA
at Home	12	25.2	28	5	19	1	1	3	3	0	4.56
on Road	13	28.1	34	11	15	0	4	2	2	0	6.67
Second Half	5	5.0	7	0	2	0	1	0	1	0	3.60

6-YEAR TOTALS (1988-1993)	G	IP	H	BB	SO	SB	CS	W	L	SV	ERA
	75	299.0	259	88	172	17	12	18	12	1	3.46
	76	229.2	245	90	110	16	16	11	13	0	4.39
	92	301.2	285	105	163	21	15	15	14	1	3.70

	BA	OBA	SA	AB	H	2B	3B	HR	RBI	BB	SO
Total	.295	.348	.543	210	62	17	4	9	33	16	34
vs. Left	.259	.276	.444	54	14	4	0	2	10	2	10
vs. Right	.308	.372	.577	156	48	13	4	7	23	14	24
Runners On Base	.348	.420	.594	69	24	6	1	3	27	9	9

	BA	OBA	SA	AB	H	2B	3B	HR	RBI	BB	SO
	.253	.314	.432	1995	504	100	13	77	249	178	282
	.254	.310	.427	382	97	18	3	14	57	31	52
	.252	.314	.433	1613	407	82	10	63	192	147	230
	.276	.355	.465	699	193	38	5	28	200	93	94

MIKE COOK — BR/TR — age 31 — BAL RP2 POW/FB

1993	G	IP	H	BB	SO	SB	CS	W	L	SV	ERA
at Home	2	3.0	1	2	3	0	0	0	0	0	0.00
on Road	0	0.0	0	0	0	0	0	0	0	0	0.00
Second Half	2	3.0	1	2	3	0	0	0	0	0	0.00

5-YEAR TOTALS (1986-1993)	G	IP	H	BB	SO	SB	CS	W	L	SV	ERA
	20	36.1	36	26	25	4	3	1	2	0	5.70
	21	35.0	38	19	28	4	1	0	4	0	5.40
	18	25.2	28	14	18	2	1	0	3	0	5.61

	BA	OBA	SA	AB	H	2B	3B	HR	RBI	BB	SO
Total	.091	.231	.091	11	1	0	0	0	2	2	3
vs. Left	.200	.333	.200	5	1	0	0	0	0	1	1
vs. Right	.000	.143	.000	6	0	0	0	0	2	1	2
Runners On Base	.000	.125	.000	7	0	0	0	0	2	1	2

	BA	OBA	SA	AB	H	2B	3B	HR	RBI	BB	SO
	.270	.375	.434	274	74	10	1	11	52	45	53
	.285	.385	.423	123	35	5	0	4	23	20	17
	.258	.367	.444	151	39	5	1	7	29	25	36
	.289	.413	.537	121	35	4	1	8	49	27	25

JIM CORSI — BR/TR — age 33 — FLO RP15 FIN/GB

1993	G	IP	H	BB	SO	SB	CS	W	L	SV	ERA
at Home	7	11.1	11	6	5	1	0	0	0	0	3.18
on Road	8	9.0	17	4	2	1	0	0	2	0	11.00
Second Half	2	1.0	5	2	0	0	0	0	1	0	54.00

5-YEAR TOTALS (1988-1993)	G	IP	H	BB	SO	SB	CS	W	L	SV	ERA
	59	97.0	85	29	55	16	6	5	5	0	3.43
	68	104.2	109	38	55	5	3	0	7	0	2.92
	83	127.0	120	41	77	15	7	4	6	0	3.05

	BA	OBA	SA	AB	H	2B	3B	HR	RBI	BB	SO
Total	.337	.404	.422	83	28	2	1	1	13	10	7
vs. Left	.354	.415	.438	48	17	2	1	0	7	5	3
vs. Right	.314	.390	.400	35	11	0	0	1	6	5	4
Runners On Base	.348	.426	.478	46	16	1	1	1	13	7	4

	BA	OBA	SA	AB	H	2B	3B	HR	RBI	BB	SO
	.259	.317	.345	748	194	20	4	12	90	67	110
	.277	.334	.369	358	99	11	2	6	36	31	46
	.244	.302	.323	390	95	9	2	6	54	36	64
	.261	.316	.384	341	89	12	3	8	86	32	46

DANNY COX — BR/TR — age 35 — TOR RP44 POW/GB

1993	G	IP	H	BB	SO	SB	CS	W	L	SV	ERA
at Home	20	42.0	36	16	44	3	2	3	1	0	3.21
on Road	24	41.2	37	13	40	4	1	4	5	2	3.02
Second Half	20	32.2	35	13	33	4	1	2	3	1	4.13

8-YEAR TOTALS (1984-1993)	G	IP	H	BB	SO	SB	CS	W	L	SV	ERA
	120	633.2	606	178	337	29	22	38	29	2	3.27
	112	517.2	530	191	298	48	29	31	36	3	3.91
	123	597.1	589	179	323	43	25	36	37	4	3.44

	BA	OBA	SA	AB	H	2B	3B	HR	RBI	BB	SO
Total	.230	.293	.343	318	73	12	0	8	32	29	84
vs. Left	.255	.344	.431	137	35	9	0	5	19	19	34
vs. Right	.210	.251	.276	181	38	3	0	3	13	10	50
Runners On Base	.252	.354	.374	123	31	3	0	4	28	20	31

	BA	OBA	SA	AB	H	2B	3B	HR	RBI	BB	SO
	.262	.320	.389	4341	1136	216	30	92	454	369	635
	.280	.345	.423	2142	600	121	17	50	246	218	241
	.244	.295	.356	2199	536	95	13	42	208	151	394
	.267	.321	.389	1786	476	86	14	35	397	153	264

CHUCK CRIM — BR/TR — age 33 — CAL RP11 FIN/GB

1993	G	IP	H	BB	SO	SB	CS	W	L	SV	ERA
at Home	7	8.0	10	2	5	2	0	2	0	0	7.88
on Road	4	7.1	7	3	5	1	0	0	2	0	3.68
Second Half	0	0.0	0	0	0	0	0	0	0	0	0.00

7-YEAR TOTALS (1987-1993)	G	IP	H	BB	SO	SB	CS	W	L	SV	ERA
	207	325.2	342	85	145	32	11	24	17	24	3.76
	193	306.1	320	100	146	16	6	18	22	19	3.76
	199	314.0	324	81	157	24	9	23	13	27	3.01

	BA	OBA	SA	AB	H	2B	3B	HR	RBI	BB	SO
Total	.298	.369	.439	57	17	2	0	2	10	5	10
vs. Left	.308	.379	.423	26	8	0	0	1	4	1	4
vs. Right	.290	.361	.452	31	9	2	0	1	6	4	6
Runners On Base	.320	.400	.640	25	8	2	0	2	10	3	6

	BA	OBA	SA	AB	H	2B	3B	HR	RBI	BB	SO
	.272	.325	.392	2436	662	87	10	62	332	185	291
	.270	.331	.389	1045	282	38	1	28	133	93	122
	.273	.321	.395	1391	380	49	9	34	199	92	169
	.283	.349	.391	1126	319	33	5	26	296	114	136

STORM DAVIS — BR/TR — age 33 — OAK/DET RP35, SP8 POW/GB

1993	G	IP	H	BB	SO	SB	CS	W	L	SV	ERA
at Home	24	63.2	65	22	46	8	2	1	4	3	4.52
on Road	19	34.1	28	26	27	7	1	1	4	1	6.03
Second Half	27	42.1	31	16	40	5	1	0	2	4	2.98

10-YEAR TOTALS (1984-1993)	G	IP	H	BB	SO	SB	CS	W	L	SV	ERA
	177	765.1	791	273	449	50	28	49	43	5	3.95
	167	666.1	689	288	370	45	29	41	38	6	4.35
	170	668.2	700	251	395	44	18	52	30	7	3.98

	BA	OBA	SA	AB	H	2B	3B	HR	RBI	BB	SO
Total	.250	.338	.387	372	93	18	3	9	53	48	73
vs. Left	.233	.348	.330	176	41	8	0	3	26	32	38
vs. Right	.265	.329	.439	196	52	10	3	6	27	16	35
Runners On Base	.246	.361	.329	167	41	5	0	3	47	30	31

	BA	OBA	SA	AB	H	2B	3B	HR	RBI	BB	SO
	.269	.336	.387	5504	1480	247	35	111	643	561	819
	.273	.352	.391	2755	751	131	19	52	333	351	444
	.265	.319	.383	2749	729	116	16	59	310	210	375
	.275	.346	.384	2423	667	103	13	45	577	276	364

MARK DAVIS — BL/TL — age 34 — PHI/SD RP60 POW/GB

1993	G	IP	H	BB	SO	SB	CS	W	L	SV	ERA
at Home	32	37.0	37	23	39	4	2	1	3	2	4.14
on Road	28	32.2	42	21	31	4	0	0	2	2	4.41
Second Half	36	38.2	46	22	43	7	2	0	3	4	3.96

10-YEAR TOTALS (1984-1993)	G	IP	H	BB	SO	SB	CS	W	L	SV	ERA
	268	472.1	427	212	435	36	24	28	32	48	3.66
	286	479.0	454	225	426	45	14	16	43	48	4.30
	291	490.2	440	215	434	45	17	22	36	48	3.98

	BA	OBA	SA	AB	H	2B	3B	HR	RBI	BB	SO
Total	.285	.384	.458	277	79	12	3	10	44	44	70
vs. Left	.253	.343	.463	95	24	3	1	5	15	13	29
vs. Right	.302	.405	.456	182	55	9	2	5	29	31	41
Runners On Base	.259	.355	.373	158	41	5	2	3	37	23	41

	BA	OBA	SA	AB	H	2B	3B	HR	RBI	BB	SO
	.248	.331	.385	3557	881	152	18	100	490	437	861
	.218	.294	.332	850	185	30	5	19	112	85	236
	.257	.342	.402	2707	696	122	13	81	378	352	625
	.256	.345	.397	1686	431	70	11	49	439	241	394

KEN DAYLEY — BL/TL — age 35 — TOR RP2 POW/GB

1993	G	IP	H	BB	SO	SB	CS	W	L	SV	ERA
at Home	1	0.0	0	1	0	0	0	0	0	0	0.00
on Road	1	0.2	0	3	2	0	0	0	0	0	0.00
Second Half	0	0.0	0	0	0	0	0	0	0	0	0.00

	BA	OBA	SA	AB	H	2B	3B	HR	RBI	BB	SO
Total	.333	.714	.667	3	1	1	0	0	0	4	2
vs. Left	.000	.333	.000	2	0	0	0	0	0	1	2
vs. Right	1.000	1.000	2.000	1	1	1	0	0	0	3	0
Runners On Base	.000	.600	.000	2	0	0	0	0	0	3	2

9-YEAR TOTALS (1984-1993)

	G	IP	H	BB	SO	SB	CS	W	L	SV	ERA
	177	208.0	218	73	146	12	7	13	13	22	3.20
	164	189.1	167	89	155	16	4	10	18	17	3.42
	178	201.0	161	86	168	13	7	14	17	19	2.87

	BA	OBA	SA	AB	H	2B	3B	HR	RBI	BB	SO
	.257	.330	.364	1498	385	73	12	21	201	162	301
	.267	.332	.351	487	130	22	2	5	64	47	113
	.252	.328	.370	1011	255	51	10	16	137	115	188
	.281	.360	.388	743	209	42	5	9	189	95	129

JOSE DELEON — BR/TR — age 34 — PHI/CHA RP32, SP3 POW/FB

1993	G	IP	H	BB	SO	SB	CS	W	L	SV	ERA
at Home	19	34.1	28	17	24	1	3	1	0	0	2.62
on Road	16	23.0	16	13	16	4	5	2	0	0	3.52
Second Half	17	29.2	23	12	20	1	4	0	0	0	2.12

	BA	OBA	SA	AB	H	2B	3B	HR	RBI	BB	SO
Total	.218	.333	.366	202	44	7	1	7	23	30	40
vs. Left	.261	.378	.446	92	24	6	1	3	10	15	16
vs. Right	.182	.295	.300	110	20	1	0	4	13	15	24
Runners On Base	.229	.359	.398	83	19	2	0	4	20	16	16

10-YEAR TOTALS (1984-1993)

	G	IP	H	BB	SO	SB	CS	W	L	SV	ERA
	161	869.1	704	355	727	89	51	37	58	2	3.70
	152	777.1	662	373	617	98	42	34	52	2	3.83
	157	839.2	678	354	671	95	47	31	56	3	3.66

	BA	OBA	SA	AB	H	2B	3B	HR	RBI	BB	SO
	.226	.312	.348	6036	1366	255	43	131	626	728	1344
	.258	.352	.391	3212	829	151	31	71	372	466	530
	.190	.265	.299	2824	537	104	12	60	254	262	814
	.240	.320	.360	2468	593	105	17	52	547	298	544

RICH DELUCIA — BR/TR — age 30 — SEA RP29, SP1 POW/FB

1993	G	IP	H	BB	SO	SB	CS	W	L	SV	ERA
at Home	18	22.0	25	12	28	2	2	2	2	0	5.32
on Road	12	20.2	21	11	20	0	0	1	4	0	3.92
Second Half	4	5.1	10	1	4	1	0	1	1	0	3.38

	BA	OBA	SA	AB	H	2B	3B	HR	RBI	BB	SO
Total	.272	.361	.408	169	46	6	1	5	29	23	48
vs. Left	.338	.425	.554	74	25	5	1	3	16	12	14
vs. Right	.221	.308	.295	95	21	1	0	2	13	11	34
Runners On Base	.326	.404	.512	86	28	2	1	4	28	11	27

4-YEAR TOTALS (1990-1993)

	G	IP	H	BB	SO	SB	CS	W	L	SV	ERA
	50	171.2	180	62	117	9	6	13	8	1	4.72
	47	172.2	172	83	115	2	8	6	19	0	4.90
	44	172.0	168	57	100	2	7	8	13	1	4.50

	BA	OBA	SA	AB	H	2B	3B	HR	RBI	BB	SO
	.266	.338	.447	1321	352	71	7	51	184	145	232
	.297	.382	.461	616	183	32	6	19	79	88	74
	.240	.298	.434	705	169	39	1	32	105	57	158
	.287	.371	.471	526	151	31	3	20	153	75	96

MARK DEWEY — BR/TR — age 29 — PIT RP21 FIN/GB

1993	G	IP	H	BB	SO	SB	CS	W	L	SV	ERA
at Home	8	10.2	6	1	9	1	0	1	0	1	1.69
on Road	13	16.0	8	9	5	1	0	0	2	6	2.81
Second Half	21	26.2	14	10	14	2	0	1	2	7	2.36

	BA	OBA	SA	AB	H	2B	3B	HR	RBI	BB	SO
Total	.157	.257	.236	89	14	5	1	0	12	10	14
vs. Left	.194	.295	.250	36	7	2	0	0	7	6	5
vs. Right	.132	.230	.226	53	7	3	1	0	5	4	9
Runners On Base	.174	.281	.304	46	8	4	1	0	12	7	5

3-YEAR TOTALS (1990-1993)

	G	IP	H	BB	SO	SB	CS	W	L	SV	ERA
	25	38.0	31	6	20	1	2	2	1	1	1.66
	30	44.2	42	19	29	4	2	1	2	6	4.63
	50	73.0	62	22	47	5	3	3	3	7	2.84

	BA	OBA	SA	AB	H	2B	3B	HR	RBI	BB	SO
	.239	.300	.330	306	73	13	3	3	37	25	49
	.261	.318	.344	157	41	6	2	1	16	14	13
	.215	.280	.315	149	32	7	1	2	21	11	36
	.247	.319	.384	146	36	9	1	3	37	16	24

FRANK DIPINO — BL/TL — age 38 — KC RP11 FIN/GB

1993	G	IP	H	BB	SO	SB	CS	W	L	SV	ERA
at Home	6	10.1	12	3	2	0	0	0	0	0	4.35
on Road	5	5.1	9	3	3	0	0	1	1	0	11.81
Second Half	5	8.1	14	1	4	0	0	0	0	0	8.64

	BA	OBA	SA	AB	H	2B	3B	HR	RBI	BB	SO
Total	.328	.392	.578	64	21	8	1	2	12	6	5
vs. Left	.333	.467	.583	12	4	3	0	0	3	2	1
vs. Right	.327	.373	.577	52	17	5	1	2	9	4	4
Runners On Base	.344	.361	.594	32	11	3	1	0	11	1	1

9-YEAR TOTALS (1984-1993)

	G	IP	H	BB	SO	SB	CS	W	L	SV	ERA
	233	306.2	277	119	211	24	8	19	17	17	3.43
	220	291.1	312	116	210	12	13	11	15	19	4.36
	242	332.0	339	120	249	15	8	18	14	16	3.96

	BA	OBA	SA	AB	H	2B	3B	HR	RBI	BB	SO
	.261	.329	.386	2259	589	108	12	50	341	235	421
	.235	.287	.316	737	173	29	2	9	105	56	149
	.273	.348	.419	1522	416	79	10	41	236	179	272
	.274	.343	.414	1093	300	61	8	25	316	126	199

KELLY DOWNS — BR/TR — age 34 — OAK RP30, SP12 POW/FB

1993	G	IP	H	BB	SO	SB	CS	W	L	SV	ERA
at Home	23	68.1	68	32	42	8	1	3	3	3	4.35
on Road	19	51.1	67	28	24	5	3	2	7	0	7.36
Second Half	21	67.2	72	21	37	7	2	3	8	0	5.05

	BA	OBA	SA	AB	H	2B	3B	HR	RBI	BB	SO
Total	.287	.368	.419	470	135	20	0	14	69	60	66
vs. Left	.320	.417	.444	225	72	7	0	7	32	38	20
vs. Right	.257	.320	.396	245	63	13	0	7	37	22	46
Runners On Base	.295	.386	.449	227	67	11	0	8	63	36	32

8-YEAR TOTALS (1986-1993)

	G	IP	H	BB	SO	SB	CS	W	L	SV	ERA
	116	479.0	404	184	309	39	14	32	19	1	3.51
	121	484.2	508	189	289	50	21	25	34	0	4.20
	143	572.2	528	210	354	53	16	36	31	1	3.60

	BA	OBA	SA	AB	H	2B	3B	HR	RBI	BB	SO
	.250	.321	.362	3650	912	172	9	73	404	373	598
	.261	.332	.365	1956	510	94	8	31	208	209	263
	.237	.308	.359	1694	402	78	1	42	196	164	335
	.255	.334	.386	1569	400	86	4	37	368	190	256

BRIAN DRAHMAN — BR/TR — age 28 — CHA RP5 FIN/FB

1993	G	IP	H	BB	SO	SB	CS	W	L	SV	ERA
at Home	1	1.0	0	0	1	0	0	0	0	0	0.00
on Road	4	4.1	7	2	2	0	0	0	0	0	0.00
Second Half	5	5.1	7	2	3	0	0	0	0	1	1.29

	BA	OBA	SA	AB	H	2B	3B	HR	RBI	BB	SO
Total	.333	.391	.381	21	7	1	0	0	1	2	3
vs. Left	.333	.400	.333	9	3	0	0	0	1	1	0
vs. Right	.333	.385	.417	12	4	1	0	0	1	1	3
Runners On Base	.364	.417	.364	11	4	0	0	0	1	1	2

3-YEAR TOTALS (1991-1993)

	G	IP	H	BB	SO	SB	CS	W	L	SV	ERA
	15	15.0	15	8	10	0	1	2	2	0	5.40
	23	28.0	19	9	12	1	0	1	0	1	1.29
	24	28.0	20	10	13	1	1	2	1	1	1.29

	BA	OBA	SA	AB	H	2B	3B	HR	RBI	BB	SO
	.217	.291	.338	157	34	5	1	4	24	17	22
	.222	.283	.426	54	12	3	1	2	9	5	2
	.214	.296	.291	103	22	2	0	2	15	12	20
	.230	.333	.351	74	17	3	0	2	22	12	11

TOM EDENS — BR/TR — age 33 — HOU RP38 FIN/GB

1993	G	IP	H	BB	SO	SB	CS	W	L	SV	ERA
at Home	17	20.0	19	6	7	3	0	0	0	0	3.15
on Road	21	29.0	28	13	14	1	1	1	1	0	3.10
Second Half	24	34.2	25	11	15	2	1	1	0	0	2.86

	BA	OBA	SA	AB	H	2B	3B	HR	RBI	BB	SO
Total	.263	.332	.374	179	47	6	1	4	26	19	21
vs. Left	.267	.375	.373	75	20	3	1	1	8	13	10
vs. Right	.260	.297	.375	104	27	3	0	3	18	6	11
Runners On Base	.278	.363	.392	79	22	3	0	2	24	11	4

5-YEAR TOTALS (1987-1993)

G	IP	H	BB	SO	SB	CS	W	L	SV	ERA
64	115.1	123	45	65	20	6	8	5	2	4.76
71	140.0	127	57	76	10	8	5	6	3	2.89
84	170.2	162	65	93	18	8	8	10	3	3.96

BA	OBA	SA	AB	H	2B	3B	HR	RBI	BB	SO
.260	.333	.368	963	250	37	8	17	114	102	141
.271	.339	.384	406	110	14	7	6	44	41	67
.251	.329	.355	557	140	23	1	11	70	61	74
.257	.345	.344	439	113	14	3	6	103	55	58

MARK EICHHORN — BR/TR — age 34 — TOR RP54 FIN/GB

1993	G	IP	H	BB	SO	SB	CS	W	L	SV	ERA
at Home	29	42.2	45	16	33	6	3	2	1	0	3.38
on Road	25	30.0	31	6	14	2	0	1	0	0	1.80
Second Half	25	23.2	22	10	10	1	2	1	1	0	1.90

	BA	OBA	SA	AB	H	2B	3B	HR	RBI	BB	SO
Total	.272	.330	.373	279	76	15	2	3	45	22	47
vs. Left	.326	.382	.417	132	43	4	1	2	19	10	17
vs. Right	.224	.284	.333	147	33	11	1	1	26	12	30
Runners On Base	.284	.380	.381	134	38	11	1	0	42	20	27

8-YEAR TOTALS (1986-1993)

G	IP	H	BB	SO	SB	CS	W	L	SV	ERA
242	383.1	358	106	297	43	18	23	17	12	2.96
247	363.0	329	120	268	40	8	18	16	19	2.83
253	362.0	343	123	277	41	12	21	15	9	3.31

BA	OBA	SA	AB	H	2B	3B	HR	RBI	BB	SO
.247	.309	.348	2777	687	124	16	41	358	226	565
.292	.357	.412	1216	355	60	10	22	169	114	192
.213	.271	.298	1561	332	64	6	19	189	112	373
.255	.339	.355	1311	334	64	7	18	335	159	280

DAVE EILAND — BR/TR — age 28 — SD SP9, RP1 FIN/GB

1993	G	IP	H	BB	SO	SB	CS	W	L	SV	ERA
at Home	4	19.2	25	8	6	3	2	0	1	0	5.49
on Road	6	28.2	33	9	8	5	1	0	2	0	5.02
Second Half	0	0.0	0	0	0	0	0	0	0	0	0.00

	BA	OBA	SA	AB	H	2B	3B	HR	RBI	BB	SO
Total	.297	.353	.431	195	58	11	0	5	29	17	14
vs. Left	.311	.376	.369	103	32	6	0	0	15	12	6
vs. Right	.283	.327	.500	92	26	5	0	5	14	5	8
Runners On Base	.298	.358	.351	94	28	5	0	0	24	10	5

6-YEAR TOTALS (1988-1993)

G	IP	H	BB	SO	SB	CS	W	L	SV	ERA
27	120.0	143	36	48	10	4	4	6	0	5.55
22	105.1	125	31	28	13	4	1	8	0	4.87
21	90.0	114	21	36	7	1	3	5	0	5.60

BA	OBA	SA	AB	H	2B	3B	HR	RBI	BB	SO
.296	.348	.473	905	268	53	10	29	134	67	76
.306	.357	.483	493	151	29	8	14	69	40	28
.284	.336	.461	412	117	24	2	15	65	27	48
.314	.364	.491	385	121	25	8	9	114	30	31

HECTOR FAJARDO — BR/TR — age 24 — TEX RP1 POW/FB

1993	G	IP	H	BB	SO	SB	CS	W	L	SV	ERA
at Home	1	0.2	0	0	1	0	0	0	0	0	0.00
on Road	0	0.0	0	0	0	0	0	0	0	0	0.00
Second Half	1	0.2	0	0	1	0	0	0	0	0	0.00

	BA	OBA	SA	AB	H	2B	3B	HR	RBI	BB	SO
Total	.000	.000	.000	2	0	0	0	0	0	0	1
vs. Left	.000	.000	.000	0	0	0	0	0	0	0	0
vs. Right	.000	.000	.000	2	0	0	0	0	0	0	1
Runners On Base	.000	.000	.000	0	0	0	0	0	0	0	1

2-YEAR TOTALS (1991-1993)

G	IP	H	BB	SO	SB	CS	W	L	SV	ERA
5	12.0	21	10	16	6	2	0	1	0	9.00
2	14.0	14	1	8	1	0	0	1	0	4.50
7	26.0	35	11	24	7	2	0	2	0	6.58

BA	OBA	SA	AB	H	2B	3B	HR	RBI	BB	SO
.330	.388	.462	106	35	6	1	2	10	11	24
.298	.370	.404	47	14	3	1	0	3	6	11
.356	.403	.508	59	21	3	0	2	7	5	13
.236	.318	.291	55	13	0	0	1	9	7	18

JOHN FARRELL — BR/TR — age 32 — CAL SP17, RP4 FIN/FB

1993	G	IP	H	BB	SO	SB	CS	W	L	SV	ERA
at Home	9	39.1	53	24	24	7	2	2	6	0	8.69
on Road	12	51.1	57	20	21	7	1	1	6	0	6.31
Second Half	9	31.0	41	11	16	2	0	1	4	0	7.84

	BA	OBA	SA	AB	H	2B	3B	HR	RBI	BB	SO
Total	.301	.385	.556	365	110	23	2	22	70	44	45
vs. Left	.323	.412	.577	189	61	16	1	10	34	28	22
vs. Right	.278	.355	.534	176	49	7	1	12	36	16	23
Runners On Base	.311	.399	.615	161	50	8	1	13	61	22	25

5-YEAR TOTALS (1987-1993)

G	IP	H	BB	SO	SB	CS	W	L	SV	ERA
51	312.1	329	112	150	24	13	17	20	0	4.50
59	362.1	369	125	191	24	11	18	22	0	4.30
53	317.1	333	104	181	21	11	17	17	0	4.25

BA	OBA	SA	AB	H	2B	3B	HR	RBI	BB	SO
.267	.333	.408	2615	698	131	17	68	304	237	341
.267	.341	.399	1395	373	74	13	28	157	153	163
.266	.323	.418	1220	325	57	4	40	147	84	178
.278	.343	.413	1105	307	51	4	30	266	105	158

SID FERNANDEZ — BL/TL — age 32 — NYN SP18 FIN/FB

1993	G	IP	H	BB	SO	SB	CS	W	L	SV	ERA
at Home	8	58.1	40	14	49	3	0	2	2	0	3.24
on Road	10	61.1	42	22	32	10	4	3	4	0	2.64
Second Half	13	91.1	55	30	57	12	2	4	6	0	2.56

	BA	OBA	SA	AB	H	2B	3B	HR	RBI	BB	SO
Total	.192	.260	.338	426	82	11	0	17	38	36	81
vs. Left	.185	.298	.284	81	15	2	0	2	5	12	16
vs. Right	.194	.250	.351	345	67	9	0	15	33	24	65
Runners On Base	.211	.315	.325	123	26	2	0	4	25	17	27

10-YEAR TOTALS (1984-1993)

G	IP	H	BB	SO	SB	CS	W	L	SV	ERA
124	821.2	531	291	825	89	25	58	31	1	2.52
131	763.0	636	305	624	108	29	40	47	0	3.81
152	961.2	703	342	870	107	29	57	48	1	3.06

BA	OBA	SA	AB	H	2B	3B	HR	RBI	BB	SO
.204	.281	.331	5719	1167	231	41	138	525	596	1449
.210	.291	.322	906	190	41	8	15	79	99	271
.203	.279	.333	4813	977	190	33	123	446	497	1178
.213	.297	.347	2066	441	90	16	51	438	251	484

MIKE FETTERS — BR/TR — age 30 — MIL RP45 FIN/GB

1993	G	IP	H	BB	SO	SB	CS	W	L	SV	ERA
at Home	26	36.1	34	11	15	2	6	2	1	0	2.97
on Road	19	23.0	25	11	8	4	1	1	2	0	3.91
Second Half	19	32.1	33	10	15	3	2	1	2	0	2.78

	BA	OBA	SA	AB	H	2B	3B	HR	RBI	BB	SO
Total	.278	.344	.392	212	59	6	3	4	42	22	23
vs. Left	.233	.317	.367	90	21	0	3	2	16	12	10
vs. Right	.311	.365	.410	122	38	6	0	2	26	10	13
Runners On Base	.289	.338	.421	114	33	3	3	2	40	9	9

5-YEAR TOTALS (1989-1993)

G	IP	H	BB	SO	SB	CS	W	L	SV	ERA
71	108.2	98	38	51	9	7	6	3	2	2.73
70	129.0	134	57	78	13	10	5	7	1	4.19
86	156.2	160	65	93	14	11	7	8	2	3.62

BA	OBA	SA	AB	H	2B	3B	HR	RBI	BB	SO
.265	.344	.378	874	232	27	6	21	137	95	129
.277	.357	.412	379	105	10	4	11	63	46	43
.257	.335	.352	495	127	17	0	10	74	49	86
.279	.358	.400	430	120	11	4	11	127	49	61

TONY FOSSAS — BL/TL — age 37 — BOS RP71 POW/FB

1993	G	IP	H	BB	SO	SB	CS	W	L	SV	ERA
at Home	36	22.0	17	9	21	0	0	1	1	0	3.68
on Road	35	18.0	21	6	18	3	0	0	0	0	7.00
Second Half	44	25.0	23	9	24	1	0	1	1	0	5.76

	BA	OBA	SA	AB	H	2B	3B	HR	RBI	BB	SO
Total	.242	.314	.363	157	38	7	0	4	20	15	39
vs. Left	.132	.211	.162	68	9	2	0	0	7	5	21
vs. Right	.326	.394	.517	89	29	5	0	4	13	10	18
Runners On Base	.272	.341	.370	81	22	5	0	1	17	8	19

6-YEAR TOTALS (1988-1993)

G	IP	H	BB	SO	SB	CS	W	L	SV	ERA
145	121.2	112	47	87	9	3	5	3	3	3.03
138	101.0	118	44	66	7	3	4	7	1	5.35
163	125.0	128	53	89	11	4	6	5	3	4.10

BA	OBA	SA	AB	H	2B	3B	HR	RBI	BB	SO
.268	.341	.385	858	230	42	5	16	144	91	153
.193	.264	.262	336	65	11	0	4	48	28	92
.316	.390	.464	522	165	31	5	12	96	63	61
.284	.356	.390	490	139	26	1	8	136	56	92

STEVE FOSTER — BR/TR — age 28 — CIN RP17 FIN/FB

1993	G	IP	H	BB	SO	SB	CS	W	L	SV	ERA
at Home	9	13.1	10	3	8	0	0	1	0	0	1.35
on Road	8	12.1	13	2	8	0	0	1	2	0	2.19
Second Half	0	0.0	0	0	0	0	0	0	0	0	0.00

	BA	OBA	SA	AB	H	2B	3B	HR	RBI	BB	SO
Total	.235	.279	.316	98	23	3	1	1	10	5	16
vs. Left	.209	.261	.326	43	9	2	0	1	3	3	12
vs. Right	.255	.293	.309	55	14	1	1	0	7	2	4
Runners On Base	.256	.304	.326	43	11	1	1	0	9	3	5

3-YEAR TOTALS (1991-1993)

G	IP	H	BB	SO	SB	CS	W	L	SV	ERA
30	44.2	33	9	27	1	0	1	0	1	1.01
29	45.0	49	13	34	0	1	2	3	1	3.80
37	52.0	41	10	37	1	1	0	1	2	2.08

BA	OBA	SA	AB	H	2B	3B	HR	RBI	BB	SO
.244	.291	.357	336	82	12	4	6	32	22	61
.259	.302	.392	158	41	5	2	4	15	10	24
.230	.281	.326	178	41	7	2	2	17	12	37
.221	.280	.295	149	33	4	2	1	17	13	27

MARVIN FREEMAN — BR/TR — age 31 — ATL RP21 POW/GB

1993	G	IP	H	BB	SO	SB	CS	W	L	SV	ERA
at Home	10	10.0	20	9	10	3	0	0	0	0	14.40
on Road	11	13.2	4	1	15	0	3	2	0	0	0.00
Second Half	10	10.2	7	1	14	0	1	1	0	0	2.53

	BA	OBA	SA	AB	H	2B	3B	HR	RBI	BB	SO
Total	.261	.340	.370	92	24	5	1	1	16	10	25
vs. Left	.286	.429	.500	28	8	1	1	1	7	7	3
vs. Right	.250	.294	.313	64	16	4	0	0	9	3	22
Runners On Base	.364	.429	.568	44	16	4	1	1	16	5	8

7-YEAR TOTALS (1986-1993)

G	IP	H	BB	SO	SB	CS	W	L	SV	ERA
78	126.1	118	62	92	11	6	5	5	3	4.56
75	128.1	108	65	91	22	11	10	5	2	3.86
89	162.2	134	82	120	24	9	12	6	2	3.93

BA	OBA	SA	AB	H	2B	3B	HR	RBI	BB	SO
.238	.332	.340	951	226	34	6	17	131	127	183
.262	.379	.376	458	120	15	5	9	67	86	60
.215	.285	.306	493	106	19	1	8	64	41	123
.264	.353	.369	436	115	24	3	7	121	56	86

TODD FROHWIRTH — BR/TR — age 32 — BAL RP70 FIN/GB

1993	G	IP	H	BB	SO	SB	CS	W	L	SV	ERA
at Home	37	57.1	51	24	30	7	3	6	1	1	3.92
on Road	33	39.0	40	20	20	9	1	0	6	2	3.69
Second Half	36	51.0	58	21	25	9	3	2	3	1	4.94

	BA	OBA	SA	AB	H	2B	3B	HR	RBI	BB	SO
Total	.256	.342	.349	355	91	10	1	7	46	44	50
vs. Left	.270	.373	.417	115	31	3	1	4	18	18	9
vs. Right	.250	.326	.317	240	60	7	0	3	28	26	41
Runners On Base	.262	.348	.349	195	51	5	0	4	43	25	24

7-YEAR TOTALS (1987-1993)

G	IP	H	BB	SO	SB	CS	W	L	SV	ERA
135	218.0	184	66	138	25	8	14	3	4	2.85
123	167.1	155	85	107	23	5	6	13	6	3.17
151	245.0	214	78	151	27	10	11	8	6	3.09

BA	OBA	SA	AB	H	2B	3B	HR	RBI	BB	SO
.240	.317	.326	1412	339	51	7	19	182	151	245
.273	.367	.380	521	142	22	5	8	74	74	61
.221	.286	.295	891	197	29	2	11	108	77	184
.250	.339	.341	689	172	27	3	10	173	90	113

RICH GARCES — BR/TR — age 23 — MIN RP3 POW/GB

1993	G	IP	H	BB	SO	SB	CS	W	L	SV	ERA
at Home	1	1.0	0	1	1	0	0	0	0	0	0.00
on Road	2	3.0	4	1	2	0	0	0	0	0	0.00
Second Half	0	0.0	0	0	0	0	0	0	0	0	0.00

	BA	OBA	SA	AB	H	2B	3B	HR	RBI	BB	SO
Total	.250	.333	.250	16	4	0	0	0	1	2	3
vs. Left	.500	.556	.500	8	4	0	0	0	1	1	1
vs. Right	.000	.111	.000	8	0	0	0	0	0	1	2
Runners On Base	.111	.200	.111	9	1	0	0	0	1	1	2

2-YEAR TOTALS (1990-1993)

G	IP	H	BB	SO	SB	CS	W	L	SV	ERA
5	6.0	3	4	1	1	0	0	0	2	0.00
3	3.2	5	2	3	2	0	0	0	0	2.45
5	5.2	4	4	1	3	0	0	0	2	1.59

BA	OBA	SA	AB	H	2B	3B	HR	RBI	BB	SO
.222	.333	.222	36	8	0	0	0	2	6	4
.333	.440	.333	21	7	0	0	0	1	4	1
.067	.176	.067	15	1	0	0	0	1	2	3
.143	.182	.143	21	3	0	0	0	2	1	3

MIKE GARDINER — BB/TR — age 29 — MON/DET RP32, SP2 POW/FB

1993	G	IP	H	BB	SO	SB	CS	W	L	SV	ERA
at Home	18	28.0	29	18	14	4	1	1	3	0	4.50
on Road	16	21.1	23	8	11	0	1	1	0	0	5.48
Second Half	14	16.0	20	10	4	2	0	1	1	0	6.75

	BA	OBA	SA	AB	H	2B	3B	HR	RBI	BB	SO
Total	.271	.356	.391	192	52	10	2	3	28	26	25
vs. Left	.258	.340	.398	93	24	5	1	2	14	11	14
vs. Right	.283	.371	.384	99	28	5	1	1	14	15	11
Runners On Base	.230	.355	.330	100	23	4	0	2	27	21	15

4-YEAR TOTALS (1990-1993)

G	IP	H	BB	SO	SB	CS	W	L	SV	ERA
43	162.2	178	74	94	10	3	7	11	0	4.98
46	160.0	162	62	107	8	7	8	14	0	5.12
48	167.2	187	71	94	14	6	8	13	0	5.53

BA	OBA	SA	AB	H	2B	3B	HR	RBI	BB	SO
.270	.341	.413	1259	340	54	12	34	170	136	201
.264	.329	.388	587	155	27	8	10	66	58	95
.275	.351	.435	672	185	27	4	24	104	78	106
.298	.371	.465	561	167	23	7	19	155	68	80

MARK GARDNER — BR/TR — age 32 — KC SP16, RP1 FIN/FB

1993	G	IP	H	BB	SO	SB	CS	W	L	SV	ERA
at Home	7	40.0	47	13	18	4	3	4	2	0	6.30
on Road	10	51.2	45	23	36	7	1	1	4	0	6.10
Second Half	2	6.0	8	5	3	3	0	0	1	0	10.50

	BA	OBA	SA	AB	H	2B	3B	HR	RBI	BB	SO
Total	.272	.343	.512	338	92	26	2	17	58	36	54
vs. Left	.311	.376	.512	164	51	10	1	7	24	18	20
vs. Right	.236	.312	.511	174	41	16	1	10	34	18	34
Runners On Base	.316	.406	.553	114	36	13	1	4	45	19	16

5-YEAR TOTALS (1989-1993)

G	IP	H	BB	SO	SB	CS	W	L	SV	ERA
53	299.2	270	106	238	33	18	18	15	0	3.66
58	319.0	295	137	211	39	28	14	24	0	4.88
54	298.0	262	120	224	39	20	15	19	0	4.41

BA	OBA	SA	AB	H	2B	3B	HR	RBI	BB	SO
.246	.323	.387	2297	565	107	13	64	275	243	449
.250	.330	.383	1326	332	58	11	32	150	156	229
.240	.312	.393	971	233	49	2	32	125	87	220
.289	.374	.445	870	251	50	7	24	235	115	165

PAUL GIBSON — BL/TR — age 34 — NYN/NYA RP28 POW/FB

1993	G	IP	H	BB	SO	SB	CS	W	L	SV	ERA
at Home	13	21.1	19	5	18	3	0	1	1	0	3.80
on Road	15	22.2	26	6	19	2	0	2	0	0	3.18
Second Half	19	34.1	31	8	25	5	0	2	0	0	3.15

6-YEAR TOTALS (1988-1993)

	G	IP	H	BB	SO	SB	CS	W	L	SV	ERA
	138	278.2	253	107	192	23	10	13	9	6	3.23
	147	244.2	285	112	129	24	11	8	14	5	4.89
	145	271.2	278	111	154	27	9	10	11	4	4.11

	BA	OBA	SA	AB	H	2B	3B	HR	RBI	BB	SO
Total	.265	.304	.418	170	45	9	1	5	30	11	37
vs. Left	.200	.250	.308	65	13	4	0	1	10	5	14
vs. Right	.305	.339	.486	105	32	5	1	4	20	6	23
Runners On Base	.301	.322	.458	83	25	5	1	2	27	4	19
	.269	.341	.408	2003	538	104	14	49	278	219	321
	.275	.336	.420	612	168	25	5	18	101	60	77
	.266	.343	.403	1391	370	79	9	31	177	159	244
	.268	.341	.408	975	261	48	10	23	252	114	148

RICH GOSSAGE — BR/TR — age 43 — OAK RP39 POW/FB

1993	G	IP	H	BB	SO	SB	CS	W	L	SV	ERA
at Home	17	22.1	21	14	17	2	1	3	1	1	4.03
on Road	22	25.1	28	12	23	0	1	4	0	1	4.97
Second Half	18	20.0	29	8	21	3	0	0	2	0	6.75

9-YEAR TOTALS (1984-1993)

	G	IP	H	BB	SO	SB	CS	W	L	SV	ERA
	194	253.1	222	81	193	19	9	25	13	56	2.81
	204	272.0	243	118	203	31	13	15	21	47	3.71
	181	230.1	230	78	177	26	7	22	21	41	3.79

	BA	OBA	SA	AB	H	2B	3B	HR	RBI	BB	SO
Total	.266	.357	.446	184	49	9	3	6	34	26	40
vs. Left	.246	.384	.319	69	17	5	0	0	9	15	14
vs. Right	.278	.339	.522	115	32	4	3	6	25	11	26
Runners On Base	.318	.386	.511	88	28	3	1	4	32	10	20
	.240	.312	.352	1938	465	74	13	39	269	199	396
	.250	.333	.358	899	225	41	7	14	118	117	160
	.231	.293	.346	1039	240	33	6	25	151	82	236
	.262	.333	.393	926	243	35	7	24	254	103	170

MAURO GOZZO — BR/TR — age 28 — NYN RP10 FIN/FB

1993	G	IP	H	BB	SO	SB	CS	W	L	SV	ERA
at Home	5	8.0	6	3	2	1	0	0	1	0	1.13
on Road	5	6.0	5	2	4	0	0	0	0	1	4.50
Second Half	10	14.0	11	5	6	1	0	0	1	1	2.57

5-YEAR TOTALS (1989-1993)

	G	IP	H	BB	SO	SB	CS	W	L	SV	ERA
	14	31.1	37	15	11	1	0	2	2	0	7.18
	11	23.2	27	8	11	2	0	2	0	1	4.18
	25	55.0	64	23	22	3	0	4	2	1	5.89

	BA	OBA	SA	AB	H	2B	3B	HR	RBI	BB	SO
Total	.212	.281	.288	52	11	1	0	1	4	5	6
vs. Left	.300	.382	.433	30	9	1	0	1	4	4	2
vs. Right	.091	.130	.091	22	2	0	0	0	0	1	4
Runners On Base	.174	.208	.304	23	4	0	0	1	4	1	2
	.296	.362	.440	216	64	17	1	4	31	23	22
	.347	.405	.490	98	34	8	0	2	17	11	8
	.254	.326	.398	118	30	9	1	2	14	12	14
	.307	.339	.491	114	35	9	0	4	31	6	8

MARK GRANT — BR/TR — age 31 — HOU/COL RP20 FIN/GB

1993	G	IP	H	BB	SO	SB	CS	W	L	SV	ERA
at Home	10	11.1	15	10	9	0	1	0	1	1	9.53
on Road	10	14.0	19	1	5	1	0	0	0	0	5.79
Second Half	6	7.0	9	1	4	0	0	0	0	0	10.29

8-YEAR TOTALS (1984-1993)

	G	IP	H	BB	SO	SB	CS	W	L	SV	ERA
	115	306.0	317	119	199	22	17	11	14	5	4.59
	118	332.2	359	116	183	21	14	11	18	3	4.06
	134	385.2	415	139	229	26	18	17	19	6	4.41

	BA	OBA	SA	AB	H	2B	3B	HR	RBI	BB	SO
Total	.337	.395	.535	101	34	8	0	4	22	11	14
vs. Left	.395	.442	.447	38	15	0	0	0	6	4	6
vs. Right	.302	.366	.587	63	19	6	0	4	16	7	8
Runners On Base	.354	.431	.542	48	17	3	0	2	20	8	7
	.277	.341	.431	2441	676	132	14	72	325	235	382
	.276	.345	.406	1246	344	69	9	25	133	132	176
	.278	.336	.457	1195	332	63	5	47	192	103	206
	.286	.355	.462	1067	305	58	5	40	293	120	158

MARK GRATER — BR/TR — age 30 — DET RP6 POW/FB

1993	G	IP	H	BB	SO	SB	CS	W	L	SV	ERA
at Home	3	3.2	4	3	1	0	0	0	0	0	2.45
on Road	3	1.1	2	1	3	0	0	0	0	0	13.50
Second Half	0	0.0	0	0	0	0	0	0	0	0	0.00

2-YEAR TOTALS (1991-1993)

	G	IP	H	BB	SO	SB	CS	W	L	SV	ERA
	4	4.1	4	3	1	0	0	0	0	0	2.08
	5	3.2	7	3	3	0	1	0	0	0	4.91
	0	0.0	0	0	0	0	0	0	0	0	0.00

	BA	OBA	SA	AB	H	2B	3B	HR	RBI	BB	SO
Total	.286	.400	.286	21	6	0	0	0	6	4	4
vs. Left	.429	.500	.429	7	3	0	0	0	2	1	0
vs. Right	.214	.353	.214	14	3	0	0	0	4	3	4
Runners On Base	.333	.467	.333	12	4	0	0	0	6	3	2
	.324	.425	.324	34	11	0	0	0	7	6	4
	.375	.444	.375	16	6	0	0	0	2	2	0
	.278	.409	.278	18	5	0	0	0	5	4	4
	.286	.400	.286	21	6	0	0	0	7	4	2

JASON GRIMSLEY — BR/TR — age 27 — CLE SP6, RP4 POW/GB

1993	G	IP	H	BB	SO	SB	CS	W	L	SV	ERA
at Home	5	20.0	29	9	13	1	0	1	3	0	7.65
on Road	5	22.1	23	11	14	6	1	2	1	0	3.22
Second Half	10	42.1	52	20	27	7	1	3	4	0	5.31

4-YEAR TOTALS (1989-1993)

	G	IP	H	BB	SO	SB	CS	W	L	SV	ERA
	16	78.2	76	49	51	9	0	2	8	0	5.03
	21	100.1	96	74	66	17	7	6	8	0	4.22
	25	118.0	118	82	75	12	6	7	9	0	4.42

	BA	OBA	SA	AB	H	2B	3B	HR	RBI	BB	SO
Total	.302	.378	.390	172	52	6	0	3	18	20	27
vs. Left	.281	.361	.375	64	18	3	0	1	6	8	10
vs. Right	.315	.388	.398	108	34	3	0	2	12	12	17
Runners On Base	.312	.398	.390	77	24	3	0	1	16	10	11
	.256	.374	.357	673	172	28	5	10	65	123	117
	.246	.376	.343	362	89	14	3	5	32	74	65
	.267	.371	.373	311	83	14	2	5	33	49	52
	.244	.385	.332	307	75	10	4	3	58	67	54

BUDDY GROOM — BL/TL — age 29 — DET RP16, SP3 FIN/FB

1993	G	IP	H	BB	SO	SB	CS	W	L	SV	ERA
at Home	9	16.1	24	6	10	1	2	0	0	0	5.51
on Road	10	20.1	24	7	5	3	0	0	2	0	6.64
Second Half	10	19.0	26	8	9	4	0	0	2	0	8.05

2-YEAR TOTALS (1992-1993)

	G	IP	H	BB	SO	SB	CS	W	L	SV	ERA
	15	35.1	56	16	18	1	3	0	3	0	6.11
	16	40.0	40	19	12	3	1	0	4	1	5.85
	19	40.1	58	19	16	4	2	0	5	1	7.59

	BA	OBA	SA	AB	H	2B	3B	HR	RBI	BB	SO
Total	.322	.375	.483	149	48	12	0	4	23	13	15
vs. Left	.273	.313	.477	44	12	3	0	2	5	3	5
vs. Right	.343	.400	.486	105	36	9	0	2	18	10	10
Runners On Base	.323	.395	.468	62	20	6	0	1	20	9	7
	.321	.389	.488	299	96	22	2	8	47	35	30
	.307	.365	.453	75	23	3	1	2	10	8	10
	.326	.397	.500	224	73	19	1	6	37	27	20
	.361	.450	.521	119	43	11	1	2	41	23	12

KIP GROSS — BR/TR — age 30 — LA RP10 POW/FB

1993	G	IP	H	BB	SO	SB	CS	W	L	SV	ERA
at Home	6	8.0	6	3	7	1	1	0	0	0	1.13
on Road	4	7.0	7	1	5	1	0	0	0	0	0.00
Second Half	10	15.0	13	4	12	2	1	0	0	0	0.60

	BA	OBA	SA	AB	H	2B	3B	HR	RBI	BB	SO
Total	.236	.288	.273	55	13	2	0	0	2	4	12
vs. Left	.208	.269	.208	24	5	0	0	0	1	2	8
vs. Right	.258	.303	.323	31	8	2	0	0	1	2	4
Runners On Base	.217	.280	.261	23	5	1	0	0	2	2	4

4-YEAR TOTALS (1990-1993)

G	IP	H	BB	SO	SB	CS	W	L	SV	ERA
27	57.1	68	26	30	6	4	2	4	0	4.24
33	73.1	76	30	39	7	2	5	1	0	2.58
46	107.1	118	41	61	10	4	6	5	0	3.35

BA	OBA	SA	AB	H	2B	3B	HR	RBI	BB	SO
.283	.352	.381	509	144	19	2	9	57	56	69
.293	.370	.392	263	77	6	1	6	32	33	40
.272	.332	.370	246	67	13	1	3	25	23	29
.300	.376	.422	230	69	11	1	5	53	30	28

MARK GUBICZA — BR/TR — age 32 — KC RP43, SP6 POW/GB

1993	G	IP	H	BB	SO	SB	CS	W	L	SV	ERA
at Home	30	61.0	75	27	49	6	1	4	4	2	5.02
on Road	19	43.1	53	16	31	5	1	1	4	0	4.15
Second Half	27	41.0	53	19	36	2	1	5	2	2	3.95

	BA	OBA	SA	AB	H	2B	3B	HR	RBI	BB	SO
Total	.307	.370	.393	417	128	24	3	2	62	43	80
vs. Left	.311	.382	.411	190	59	12	2	1	33	23	33
vs. Right	.304	.359	.379	227	69	12	1	1	29	20	47
Runners On Base	.300	.363	.419	217	65	14	3	2	62	23	44

10-YEAR TOTALS (1984-1993)

G	IP	H	BB	SO	SB	CS	W	L	SV	ERA
170	976.2	926	343	622	93	26	62	52	2	3.51
138	779.1	788	318	549	58	40	47	48	0	4.18
155	841.2	832	304	577	68	40	56	44	2	3.87

BA	OBA	SA	AB	H	2B	3B	HR	RBI	BB	SO
.257	.325	.362	6664	1714	299	50	99	706	661	1171
.258	.334	.366	3464	895	150	29	55	356	388	553
.256	.315	.357	3200	819	149	21	44	350	273	618
.262	.326	.363	2886	755	114	24	44	651	286	513

LEE GUETTERMAN — BL/TL — age 36 — SL RP40 FIN/GB

1993	G	IP	H	BB	SO	SB	CS	W	L	SV	ERA
at Home	19	21.2	16	5	12	0	0	3	1	0	2.49
on Road	21	24.1	25	11	7	5	0	2	1	1	3.33
Second Half	39	43.2	40	15	19	5	0	3	3	1	3.09

	BA	OBA	SA	AB	H	2B	3B	HR	RBI	BB	SO
Total	.240	.309	.327	171	41	4	4	1	25	16	19
vs. Left	.234	.345	.298	47	11	0	0	1	4	7	7
vs. Right	.242	.294	.339	124	30	4	4	0	21	9	12
Runners On Base	.253	.346	.330	91	23	3	2	0	24	13	9

9-YEAR TOTALS (1984-1993)

G	IP	H	BB	SO	SB	CS	W	L	SV	ERA
201	346.1	375	108	160	17	7	27	15	14	4.47
184	283.2	310	93	110	27	5	11	19	10	4.03
228	360.1	403	120	156	25	11	24	25	12	4.65

BA	OBA	SA	AB	H	2B	3B	HR	RBI	BB	SO
.281	.336	.406	2434	685	107	21	51	334	201	270
.244	.314	.331	668	163	24	5	8	73	63	87
.296	.344	.434	1766	522	83	16	43	261	138	183
.280	.347	.415	1167	327	55	12	26	309	128	126

MARK GUTHRIE — BB/TR — age 29 — MIN RP22 POW/FB

1993	G	IP	H	BB	SO	SB	CS	W	L	SV	ERA
at Home	12	12.1	14	10	8	2	0	1	1	0	5.11
on Road	10	8.2	6	6	7	2	3	1	0	0	4.15
Second Half	0	0.0	0	0	0	0	0	0	0	0	0.00

	BA	OBA	SA	AB	H	2B	3B	HR	RBI	BB	SO
Total	.267	.387	.400	75	20	4	0	2	15	16	15
vs. Left	.148	.233	.185	27	4	1	0	0	2	3	6
vs. Right	.333	.460	.521	48	16	3	0	2	13	13	9
Runners On Base	.250	.364	.364	44	11	2	0	1	14	9	8

5-YEAR TOTALS (1989-1993)

G	IP	H	BB	SO	SB	CS	W	L	SV	ERA
74	194.0	204	68	168	16	11	8	10	4	4.04
80	202.0	211	72	134	25	17	12	12	3	3.79
85	246.1	244	67	185	16	17	10	13	6	3.18

BA	OBA	SA	AB	H	2B	3B	HR	RBI	BB	SO
.274	.334	.397	1515	415	68	7	35	169	140	302
.285	.322	.387	344	98	12	1	7	36	20	60
.271	.337	.401	1171	317	56	6	28	133	120	242
.249	.311	.365	679	169	23	4	16	150	65	146

DAVE HAAS — BR/TR — age 29 — DET RP20 FIN/GB

1993	G	IP	H	BB	SO	SB	CS	W	L	SV	ERA
at Home	11	15.0	26	4	12	0	0	1	2	0	7.20
on Road	9	13.0	19	4	11	0	0	0	0	0	4.85
Second Half	0	0.0	0	0	0	0	0	0	0	0	0.00

	BA	OBA	SA	AB	H	2B	3B	HR	RBI	BB	SO
Total	.375	.411	.633	120	45	4	0	9	22	8	17
vs. Left	.426	.471	.574	47	20	1	0	2	6	4	7
vs. Right	.342	.372	.671	73	25	3	0	7	16	4	10
Runners On Base	.317	.373	.467	60	19	3	0	2	15	6	10

3-YEAR TOTALS (1991-1993)

G	IP	H	BB	SO	SB	CS	W	L	SV	ERA
23	53.1	66	20	29	1	1	3	3	0	5.06
20	47.0	55	16	23	1	1	4	2	0	4.60
23	72.1	76	28	35	1	2	6	3	0	4.35

BA	OBA	SA	AB	H	2B	3B	HR	RBI	BB	SO
.303	.361	.479	399	121	14	1	18	59	36	52
.318	.373	.435	170	54	5	0	5	16	15	19
.293	.353	.511	229	67	9	1	13	43	21	33
.283	.346	.398	191	54	5	1	5	46	19	25

JOHN HABYAN — BR/TR — age 31 — NYA/KC RP48 POW/GB

1993	G	IP	H	BB	SO	SB	CS	W	L	SV	ERA
at Home	22	28.1	19	4	20	2	0	2	0	1	2.54
on Road	26	28.0	40	16	19	4	0	0	1	0	5.79
Second Half	19	20.1	24	5	16	3	0	1	0	0	4.43

	BA	OBA	SA	AB	H	2B	3B	HR	RBI	BB	SO
Total	.272	.331	.429	217	59	12	2	6	32	20	39
vs. Left	.244	.282	.462	78	19	4	2	3	13	5	11
vs. Right	.288	.357	.410	139	40	8	0	3	19	15	28
Runners On Base	.315	.377	.509	108	34	6	0	5	31	12	21

8-YEAR TOTALS (1985-1993)

G	IP	H	BB	SO	SB	CS	W	L	SV	ERA
103	199.0	200	49	115	15	5	15	8	6	3.71
115	188.2	185	76	126	19	3	5	11	5	3.91
116	227.0	232	67	144	15	6	11	12	8	4.04

BA	OBA	SA	AB	H	2B	3B	HR	RBI	BB	SO
.261	.320	.411	1473	385	75	14	39	194	125	241
.275	.329	.426	662	182	35	10	15	77	56	74
.250	.312	.398	811	203	40	4	24	117	69	167
.270	.343	.432	644	174	38	9	16	171	74	105

MIKE HARTLEY — BR/TR — age 33 — MIN RP53 POW/FB

1993	G	IP	H	BB	SO	SB	CS	W	L	SV	ERA
at Home	28	45.0	51	18	34	7	1	1	2	1	4.60
on Road	25	36.0	35	18	23	4	3	0	0	3	3.25
Second Half	24	37.0	45	14	24	3	1	0	2	1	3.16

	BA	OBA	SA	AB	H	2B	3B	HR	RBI	BB	SO
Total	.281	.363	.395	306	86	23	0	4	44	36	57
vs. Left	.248	.325	.358	137	34	9	0	2	16	17	22
vs. Right	.308	.394	.426	169	52	14	0	2	28	19	35
Runners On Base	.291	.366	.405	158	46	15	0	1	41	22	26

5-YEAR TOTALS (1989-1993)

G	IP	H	BB	SO	SB	CS	W	L	SV	ERA
99	160.0	142	62	148	25	4	11	5	2	3.38
95	144.2	132	74	105	21	4	7	8	2	3.92
101	169.1	148	67	135	27	4	12	9	1	3.40

BA	OBA	SA	AB	H	2B	3B	HR	RBI	BB	SO
.240	.328	.371	1140	274	54	7	27	144	136	253
.233	.327	.339	566	132	23	5	9	53	79	111
.247	.329	.402	574	142	31	2	18	91	57	142
.249	.336	.400	527	131	31	5	13	130	70	115

HILLY HATHAWAY — BL/TL — age 25 — CAL SP11 FIN/GB

1993	G	IP	H	BB	SO	SB	CS	W	L	SV	ERA
at Home	6	34.1	41	19	6	6	3	2	2	0	4.72
on Road	5	23.0	30	7	5	1	0	2	1	0	5.48
Second Half	9	46.1	59	20	9	6	3	3	3	0	4.47

	BA	OBA	SA	AB	H	2B	3B	HR	RBI	BB	SO
Total	.326	.405	.459	218	71	11	0	6	32	26	11
vs. Left	.268	.362	.341	41	11	3	0	0	4	4	2
vs. Right	.339	.415	.486	177	60	8	0	6	28	22	9
Runners On Base	.231	.317	.352	108	25	4	0	3	29	14	4

2-YEAR TOTALS (1992-1993)

G	IP	H	BB	SO	SB	CS	W	L	SV	ERA
8	40.0	49	22	7	6	3	2	2	0	5.18
5	23.0	30	7	5	1	0	2	1	0	5.48
11	52.0	67	23	10	6	3	3	3	0	4.85

BA	OBA	SA	AB	H	2B	3B	HR	RBI	BB	SO
.326	.404	.463	242	79	12	0	7	37	29	12
.289	.385	.422	45	13	3	0	1	5	5	2
.335	.408	.472	197	66	9	0	6	32	24	10
.246	.331	.364	118	29	5	0	3	33	16	4

NEAL HEATON — BL/TL — age 34 — NYA RP18 FIN/GB

1993	G	IP	H	BB	SO	SB	CS	W	L	SV	ERA
at Home	8	12.1	15	5	6	0	0	1	0	0	5.84
on Road	10	14.2	19	6	9	2	0	0	0	0	6.14
Second Half	0	0.0	0	0	0	0	0	0	0	0	0.00

	BA	OBA	SA	AB	H	2B	3B	HR	RBI	BB	SO
Total	.301	.375	.504	113	34	5	0	6	28	11	15
vs. Left	.250	.385	.281	32	8	1	0	0	6	4	6
vs. Right	.321	.371	.593	81	26	4	0	6	22	7	9
Runners On Base	.350	.420	.517	60	21	4	0	2	24	7	6

10-YEAR TOTALS (1984-1993)

G	IP	H	BB	SO	SB	CS	W	L	SV	ERA
162	690.1	710	232	325	52	36	37	39	1	3.83
173	636.1	690	232	285	76	26	32	48	2	4.96
157	609.0	674	211	313	59	29	29	47	2	4.39

BA	OBA	SA	AB	H	2B	3B	HR	RBI	BB	SO
.274	.336	.425	5102	1400	259	29	151	632	464	610
.264	.320	.404	1032	272	53	7	26	125	82	157
.277	.340	.431	4070	1128	206	22	125	507	382	453
.275	.342	.423	2111	580	113	12	59	540	226	253

DWAYNE HENRY — BR/TR — age 32 — CIN/SEA RP33, SP1 POW/FB

1993	G	IP	H	BB	SO	SB	CS	W	L	SV	ERA
at Home	18	32.1	33	25	21	2	1	2	2	0	6.12
on Road	16	26.1	29	14	16	1	1	0	0	2	6.84
Second Half	11	13.1	13	10	16	2	0	0	0	1	7.43

	BA	OBA	SA	AB	H	2B	3B	HR	RBI	BB	SO
Total	.273	.379	.458	227	62	16	4	6	46	39	37
vs. Left	.281	.420	.506	89	25	6	4	2	21	21	12
vs. Right	.268	.350	.428	138	37	10	0	4	25	18	25
Runners On Base	.272	.375	.456	125	34	9	1	4	44	22	24

10-YEAR TOTALS (1984-1993)

G	IP	H	BB	SO	SB	CS	W	L	SV	ERA
128	175.1	147	106	155	13	6	11	7	5	4.41
118	150.2	140	100	111	11	5	2	8	4	4.84
132	170.1	149	99	168	9	2	6	10	6	4.28

BA	OBA	SA	AB	H	2B	3B	HR	RBI	BB	SO
.239	.351	.374	1202	287	61	12	26	198	206	266
.235	.366	.386	549	129	30	10	11	88	113	118
.242	.338	.364	653	158	31	2	15	110	93	148
.276	.384	.423	591	163	36	6	13	185	107	116

BUTCH HENRY — BL/TL — age 26 — COL/MON SP16, RP14 FIN/GB

1993	G	IP	H	BB	SO	SB	CS	W	L	SV	ERA
at Home	16	48.1	77	12	19	3	1	1	4	0	7.45
on Road	14	54.2	58	16	28	6	3	2	5	0	4.94
Second Half	13	25.2	34	5	14	3	1	1	2	0	6.31

	BA	OBA	SA	AB	H	2B	3B	HR	RBI	BB	SO
Total	.317	.356	.491	426	135	25	2	15	69	28	47
vs. Left	.340	.380	.530	100	34	11	1	2	16	7	10
vs. Right	.310	.348	.479	326	101	14	1	13	53	21	37
Runners On Base	.339	.380	.503	183	62	10	1	6	60	15	22

2-YEAR TOTALS (1992-1993)

G	IP	H	BB	SO	SB	CS	W	L	SV	ERA
30	136.1	168	31	70	10	4	4	7	0	4.75
28	132.1	152	38	73	9	7	5	11	0	4.90
26	110.2	125	19	66	8	5	5	5	0	3.82

BA	OBA	SA	AB	H	2B	3B	HR	RBI	BB	SO
.298	.337	.456	1075	320	63	7	31	138	69	143
.315	.363	.461	241	76	21	1	4	29	19	24
.293	.330	.454	834	244	42	6	27	109	50	119
.292	.337	.444	439	128	22	3	13	120	36	57

GIL HEREDIA — BR/TR — age 29 — MON RP11, SP9 FIN/GB

1993	G	IP	H	BB	SO	SB	CS	W	L	SV	ERA
at Home	8	20.0	30	7	12	1	0	2	1	0	5.85
on Road	12	37.1	36	7	28	6	0	2	1	2	2.89
Second Half	15	39.0	38	11	29	2	0	3	0	2	2.54

	BA	OBA	SA	AB	H	2B	3B	HR	RBI	BB	SO
Total	.293	.339	.396	225	66	9	1	4	22	14	40
vs. Left	.242	.301	.347	124	30	5	1	2	14	11	20
vs. Right	.356	.387	.455	101	36	4	0	2	8	3	20
Runners On Base	.271	.343	.354	96	26	3	1	1	19	10	23

3-YEAR TOTALS (1991-1993)

G	IP	H	BB	SO	SB	CS	W	L	SV	ERA
23	65.2	66	19	34	5	3	3	5	0	4.80
24	69.1	71	22	41	9	2	3	2	2	3.25
29	86.2	77	22	49	6	3	3	2	2	2.91

BA	OBA	SA	AB	H	2B	3B	HR	RBI	BB	SO
.272	.328	.391	504	137	20	2	12	60	41	75
.263	.321	.367	278	73	10	2	5	38	25	38
.283	.337	.420	226	64	10	0	7	22	16	37
.302	.372	.392	189	57	7	2	2	50	22	32

XAVIER HERNANDEZ — BL/TR — age 29 — HOU RP72 POW/FB

1993	G	IP	H	BB	SO	SB	CS	W	L	SV	ERA
at Home	37	50.0	35	16	54	5	2	1	2	5	2.88
on Road	35	46.2	40	12	47	4	0	3	3	4	2.31
Second Half	36	52.0	38	13	60	4	0	2	3	6	1.90

	BA	OBA	SA	AB	H	2B	3B	HR	RBI	BB	SO
Total	.212	.269	.322	354	75	19	1	6	43	28	101
vs. Left	.220	.293	.381	168	37	7	1	6	22	17	52
vs. Right	.204	.247	.269	186	38	12	0	0	21	11	49
Runners On Base	.222	.296	.335	158	35	10	1	2	39	17	40

5-YEAR TOTALS (1989-1993)

G	IP	H	BB	SO	SB	CS	W	L	SV	ERA
106	177.1	129	53	143	16	6	10	6	11	2.54
116	178.1	178	81	140	19	5	8	8	4	4.09
115	168.1	131	58	152	15	3	10	6	13	2.57

BA	OBA	SA	AB	H	2B	3B	HR	RBI	BB	SO
.230	.302	.340	1333	307	57	4	27	154	134	283
.236	.328	.345	658	155	25	4	13	72	89	141
.225	.276	.335	675	152	32	0	14	82	45	142
.236	.314	.359	610	144	25	4	14	141	70	130

JOE HESKETH — BR/TL — age 35 — BOS RP23, SP5 POW/GB

1993	G	IP	H	BB	SO	SB	CS	W	L	SV	ERA
at Home	12	29.0	27	15	18	0	0	2	1	1	2.17
on Road	16	24.1	35	14	16	4	2	1	3	0	8.51
Second Half	10	14.1	11	7	6	0	1	0	1	1	1.88

	BA	OBA	SA	AB	H	2B	3B	HR	RBI	BB	SO
Total	.294	.376	.422	211	62	15	0	4	33	29	34
vs. Left	.206	.267	.294	68	14	3	0	1	8	6	12
vs. Right	.336	.425	.483	143	48	12	0	3	25	23	22
Runners On Base	.279	.369	.385	104	29	5	0	2	31	16	19

10-YEAR TOTALS (1984-1993)

G	IP	H	BB	SO	SB	CS	W	L	SV	ERA
154	417.0	423	171	331	30	14	27	18	9	3.56
160	430.2	407	161	311	44	16	25	24	12	3.87
158	429.2	413	155	323	32	14	27	22	12	3.27

BA	OBA	SA	AB	H	2B	3B	HR	RBI	BB	SO
.258	.327	.397	3213	830	187	15	76	365	332	642
.236	.312	.335	662	156	26	2	12	86	71	153
.264	.331	.413	2551	674	161	13	64	279	261	489
.254	.330	.388	1373	349	80	7	30	319	165	291

TEDDY HIGUERA — BB/TL — age 36 — MIL SP8 POW/FB

1993	G	IP	H	BB	SO	SB	CS	W	L	SV	ERA
at Home	5	17.1	20	10	15	2	1	1	2	0	4.67
on Road	3	12.2	23	6	12	1	0	0	1	0	10.66
Second Half	8	30.0	43	16	27	3	1	1	3	0	7.20

	BA	OBA	SA	AB	H	2B	3B	HR	RBI	BB	SO
Total	.333	.408	.581	129	43	16	2	4	23	16	27
vs. Left	.154	.200	.231	13	2	1	0	0	1	1	5
vs. Right	.353	.432	.621	116	41	15	2	4	22	15	22
Runners On Base	.367	.451	.700	60	22	9	1	3	22	10	8

8-YEAR TOTALS (1985-1993)

G	IP	H	BB	SO	SB	CS	W	L	SV	ERA
103	707.1	601	207	573	52	22	55	24	0	3.17
93	614.0	587	200	473	41	24	38	35	0	3.80
105	744.0	681	224	579	54	26	57	30	0	3.36

BA	OBA	SA	AB	H	2B	3B	HR	RBI	BB	SO
.240	.298	.364	4949	1188	225	18	118	493	407	1046
.236	.277	.345	855	202	36	3	17	83	47	199
.241	.302	.368	4094	986	189	15	101	410	360	847
.260	.310	.379	1940	504	104	5	39	414	155	377

MILT HILL — BR/TR — age 29 — CIN RP19 POW/FB

1993	G	IP	H	BB	SO	SB	CS	W	L	SV	ERA
at Home	9	15.2	17	2	11	1	2	2	0	1	3.45
on Road	10	13.0	17	7	12	1	0	0	0	0	8.31
Second Half	0	0.0	0	0	0	0	0	0	0	0	0.00

	BA	OBA	SA	AB	H	2B	3B	HR	RBI	BB	SO
Total	.301	.344	.513	113	34	7	1	5	21	9	23
vs. Left	.250	.302	.438	48	12	1	1	2	7	4	8
vs. Right	.338	.375	.569	65	22	6	0	3	14	5	15
Runners On Base	.304	.364	.478	46	14	5	0	1	17	6	14

3-YEAR TOTALS (1991-1993)

G	IP	H	BB	SO	SB	CS	W	L	SV	ERA
34	54.2	47	13	27	5	4	2	1	1	2.80
21	27.1	38	9	26	2	1	2	0	0	7.24
34	50.0	49	12	30	5	4	1	1	1	3.78

BA	OBA	SA	AB	H	2B	3B	HR	RBI	BB	SO
.278	.321	.425	306	85	18	3	7	45	22	53
.213	.286	.309	136	29	5	1	2	14	15	23
.329	.352	.518	170	56	13	2	5	31	7	30
.287	.329	.441	136	39	11	2	2	40	12	27

SHAWN HILLEGAS — BR/TR — age 30 — OAK SP11, RP7 FIN/FB

1993	G	IP	H	BB	SO	SB	CS	W	L	SV	ERA
at Home	8	29.0	38	13	17	2	2	3	1	0	4.97
on Road	10	31.2	40	20	12	0	2	0	5	0	8.81
Second Half	5	11.0	15	3	6	0	0	1	0	0	4.09

	BA	OBA	SA	AB	H	2B	3B	HR	RBI	BB	SO
Total	.317	.404	.504	246	78	14	4	8	43	33	29
vs. Left	.326	.391	.551	138	45	10	3	5	23	15	10
vs. Right	.306	.419	.444	108	33	4	1	3	20	18	19
Runners On Base	.327	.433	.509	110	36	6	1	4	39	20	11

7-YEAR TOTALS (1987-1993)

G	IP	H	BB	SO	SB	CS	W	L	SV	ERA
95	274.0	264	117	189	26	15	15	15	6	4.01
86	241.1	257	121	143	18	12	9	23	4	5.30
113	318.0	314	138	209	34	14	15	21	4	4.27

BA	OBA	SA	AB	H	2B	3B	HR	RBI	BB	SO
.264	.344	.408	1975	521	86	18	54	264	238	332
.289	.376	.424	989	286	44	10	23	131	140	146
.238	.310	.391	986	235	42	8	31	133	98	186
.277	.360	.414	864	239	42	4	23	233	116	149

STERLING HITCHCOCK — BL/TL — age 23 — NYA SP6 POW/FB

1993	G	IP	H	BB	SO	SB	CS	W	L	SV	ERA
at Home	3	16.1	14	8	17	2	1	0	1	0	4.41
on Road	3	14.2	18	6	9	1	1	1	1	0	4.91
Second Half	6	31.0	32	14	26	3	2	1	2	0	4.65

	BA	OBA	SA	AB	H	2B	3B	HR	RBI	BB	SO
Total	.271	.348	.432	118	32	7	0	4	17	14	26
vs. Left	.273	.393	.273	22	6	0	0	0	3	5	3
vs. Right	.271	.336	.469	96	26	7	0	4	14	9	23
Runners On Base	.294	.345	.529	51	15	3	0	3	16	4	11

2-YEAR TOTALS (1992-1993)

G	IP	H	BB	SO	SB	CS	W	L	SV	ERA
6	29.1	37	14	23	3	2	0	3	0	6.14
3	14.2	18	6	9	1	1	1	1	0	4.91
9	44.0	55	20	32	4	3	1	4	0	5.73

BA	OBA	SA	AB	H	2B	3B	HR	RBI	BB	SO
.307	.379	.475	179	55	12	0	6	29	20	32
.286	.417	.357	28	8	2	0	0	4	6	4
.311	.371	.497	151	47	10	0	6	25	14	28
.325	.383	.590	83	27	7	0	5	28	8	15

RICK HONEYCUTT — BL/TL — age 42 — OAK RP52 FIN/GB

1993	G	IP	H	BB	SO	SB	CS	W	L	SV	ERA
at Home	26	21.0	13	8	12	2	3	0	2	1	2.14
on Road	26	20.2	17	12	9	0	0	1	2	0	3.48
Second Half	26	20.0	14	10	10	1	1	1	2	0	2.25

	BA	OBA	SA	AB	H	2B	3B	HR	RBI	BB	SO
Total	.211	.305	.296	142	30	4	1	2	14	20	21
vs. Left	.241	.317	.352	54	13	1	1	1	8	6	6
vs. Right	.193	.298	.261	88	17	3	0	1	14	14	15
Runners On Base	.209	.305	.343	67	14	3	0	2	14	11	13

10-YEAR TOTALS (1984-1993)

G	IP	H	BB	SO	SB	CS	W	L	SV	ERA
226	515.0	464	138	292	31	22	24	30	17	2.74
231	459.1	462	183	269	28	24	19	34	14	4.02
253	459.1	477	176	243	29	19	20	36	14	4.08

BA	OBA	SA	AB	H	2B	3B	HR	RBI	BB	SO
.251	.312	.361	3690	926	176	22	62	382	321	561
.205	.258	.298	868	178	28	7	13	100	58	165
.265	.328	.380	2822	748	148	15	49	282	263	396
.260	.334	.386	1564	407	85	9	31	351	179	248

VINCE HORSMAN — BR/TL — age 27 — OAK RP40 POW/GB

1993	G	IP	H	BB	SO	SB	CS	W	L	SV	ERA
at Home	19	12.1	15	7	10	0	1	0	0	0	7.30
on Road	21	12.2	10	8	7	1	1	1	0	0	3.55
Second Half	33	21.2	24	14	16	1	1	2	0	0	5.40

	BA	OBA	SA	AB	H	2B	3B	HR	RBI	BB	SO
Total	.255	.371	.337	98	25	2	0	2	16	15	17
vs. Left	.298	.411	.319	47	14	1	0	0	4	8	7
vs. Right	.216	.333	.353	51	11	1	0	2	12	7	10
Runners On Base	.292	.460	.458	48	14	2	0	2	16	13	9

3-YEAR TOTALS (1991-1993)

G	IP	H	BB	SO	SB	CS	W	L	SV	ERA
57	41.0	38	21	20	0	1	1	1	0	4.39
45	31.1	28	18	17	2	2	3	0	1	2.01
65	41.1	39	28	23	2	2	2	1	0	3.92

BA	OBA	SA	AB	H	2B	3B	HR	RBI	BB	SO
.249	.351	.328	265	66	6	0	5	35	39	37
.240	.351	.272	125	30	1	0	1	17	21	16
.257	.350	.379	140	36	5	0	4	18	18	21
.248	.387	.357	129	32	2	0	4	34	28	20

STEVE HOWE — BL/TL — age 36 — NYA RP51 FIN/GB

1993	G	IP	H	BB	SO	SB	CS	W	L	SV	ERA
at Home	18	17.1	25	3	4	1	0	1	2	1	5.71
on Road	33	33.1	33	7	15	0	1	2	3	3	4.59
Second Half	32	32.2	35	5	13	0	1	1	2	2	3.03

	BA	OBA	SA	AB	H	2B	3B	HR	RBI	BB	SO
Total	.297	.338	.462	195	58	11	0	7	31	10	19
vs. Left	.238	.284	.302	63	15	1	0	1	6	3	9
vs. Right	.326	.364	.538	132	43	10	0	6	25	7	10
Runners On Base	.304	.340	.489	92	28	5	0	4	28	6	8

5-YEAR TOTALS (1985-1993)

G	IP	H	BB	SO	SB	CS	W	L	SV	ERA
75	96.2	99	17	51	4	3	9	5	7	3.72
89	96.2	98	23	54	2	1	6	8	10	4.00
85	100.1	113	22	54	3	3	7	9	4	4.04

BA	OBA	SA	AB	H	2B	3B	HR	RBI	BB	SO
.266	.309	.370	741	197	33	1	14	102	40	105
.240	.279	.306	229	55	7	1	2	22	8	35
.277	.322	.398	512	142	26	0	12	80	32	70
.313	.353	.449	352	110	19	1	9	97	25	44

JAY HOWELL — BR/TR — age 39 — ATL RP54 FIN/FB

1993	G	IP	H	BB	SO	SB	CS	W	L	SV	ERA
at Home	35	39.2	33	9	25	4	5	2	1	0	1.82
on Road	19	18.2	15	7	12	1	0	1	2	0	3.38
Second Half	30	33.0	26	11	27	4	5	2	1	0	2.18

	BA	OBA	SA	AB	H	2B	3B	HR	RBI	BB	SO
Total	.229	.278	.300	210	48	6	0	3	23	16	37
vs. Left	.233	.263	.256	90	21	2	0	0	6	4	16
vs. Right	.225	.289	.333	120	27	4	0	3	17	12	21
Runners On Base	.269	.322	.359	78	21	4	0	1	21	8	15

10-YEAR TOTALS (1984-1993)

G	IP	H	BB	SO	SB	CS	W	L	SV	ERA
253	363.0	303	100	307	31	13	35	20	75	2.31
235	302.2	273	117	244	21	7	14	24	78	3.09
254	338.1	285	101	282	26	11	27	19	79	2.74

BA	OBA	SA	AB	H	2B	3B	HR	RBI	BB	SO
.233	.296	.321	2469	576	88	10	36	260	217	551
.231	.299	.311	1273	294	50	5	14	122	121	282
.236	.292	.331	1196	282	38	5	22	138	96	269
.243	.314	.320	1119	272	36	7	12	236	121	253

BRUCE HURST — BL/TL — age 36 — SD/COL SP5 POW/FB

1993	G	IP	H	BB	SO	SB	CS	W	L	SV	ERA
at Home	4	10.0	9	4	7	0	0	0	2	0	5.40
on Road	1	3.0	6	2	2	3	1	0	0	0	15.00
Second Half	3	8.2	6	3	6	0	0	0	1	0	5.19

	BA	OBA	SA	AB	H	2B	3B	HR	RBI	BB	SO
Total	.283	.356	.358	53	15	1	0	1	11	6	9
vs. Left	.200	.333	.200	5	1	0	0	0	2	1	1
vs. Right	.292	.358	.375	48	14	1	0	1	9	5	8
Runners On Base	.360	.407	.360	25	9	0	0	0	10	2	5

10-YEAR TOTALS (1984-1993)

G	IP	H	BB	SO	SB	CS	W	L	SV	ERA
156	1081.1	1015	319	849	51	40	73	43	0	3.57
137	916.0	931	275	621	72	42	51	48	0	3.73
150	1017.2	996	309	740	58	38	63	46	0	3.73

BA	OBA	SA	AB	H	2B	3B	HR	RBI	BB	SO
.256	.310	.390	7609	1946	354	24	207	762	594	1470
.257	.318	.391	1275	328	62	3	34	147	110	263
.255	.308	.390	6334	1618	292	21	173	615	484	1207
.262	.309	.394	3066	802	172	10	71	626	218	575

MIKE IGNASIAK — BB/TR — age 28 — MIL RP27 POW/FB

1993	G	IP	H	BB	SO	SB	CS	W	L	SV	ERA
at Home	16	24.0	15	14	19	1	1	0	0	0	2.63
on Road	11	13.0	17	7	9	0	2	1	1	0	5.54
Second Half	21	29.2	24	16	24	1	2	1	1	0	3.34

	BA	OBA	SA	AB	H	2B	3B	HR	RBI	BB	SO
Total	.241	.350	.331	133	32	4	1	2	20	21	28
vs. Left	.318	.456	.432	44	14	2	0	1	9	11	4
vs. Right	.202	.290	.281	89	18	2	1	1	11	10	24
Runners On Base	.254	.333	.380	71	18	3	0	2	20	8	13

2-YEAR TOTALS (1991-1993)

G	IP	H	BB	SO	SB	CS	W	L	SV	ERA
17	29.0	17	17	25	2	1	0	1	0	3.10
14	20.2	22	12	13	1	3	1	1	0	5.66
25	42.1	31	24	34	3	2	3	2	0	4.04

BA	OBA	SA	AB	H	2B	3B	HR	RBI	BB	SO
.222	.337	.335	176	39	4	2	4	26	29	38
.266	.422	.391	64	17	2	0	2	11	17	5
.196	.280	.304	112	22	2	2	2	15	12	33
.239	.317	.424	92	22	3	1	4	26	10	17

MIKE JACKSON — BR/TR — age 30 — SF RP81 POW/FB

1993	G	IP	H	BB	SO	SB	CS	W	L	SV	ERA
at Home	38	33.1	33	12	33	1	1	3	4	1	4.32
on Road	43	44.0	25	12	37	0	0	3	2	0	2.05
Second Half	37	35.1	34	13	36	1	0	2	4	0	3.82

	BA	OBA	SA	AB	H	2B	3B	HR	RBI	BB	SO
Total	.204	.272	.313	284	58	8	1	7	39	24	70
vs. Left	.246	.317	.365	126	31	4	1	3	21	13	23
vs. Right	.171	.236	.272	158	27	4	0	4	18	11	47
Runners On Base	.220	.291	.386	132	29	7	1	6	38	13	31

8-YEAR TOTALS (1986-1993)

G	IP	H	BB	SO	SB	CS	W	L	SV	ERA
229	323.0	239	138	283	38	6	21	18	13	3.37
245	323.2	278	154	276	31	11	16	29	19	3.67
255	314.1	270	158	284	34	6	16	28	9	3.78

BA	OBA	SA	AB	H	2B	3B	HR	RBI	BB	SO
.220	.310	.346	2352	517	91	8	63	325	292	559
.254	.359	.397	1044	265	52	5	29	154	168	168
.193	.269	.305	1308	252	39	3	34	171	124	391
.228	.333	.360	1100	251	48	5	29	291	172	265

DAVE JOHNSON — BR/TR — age 35 — DET RP6 POW/FB

1993	G	IP	H	BB	SO	SB	CS	W	L	SV	ERA
at Home	5	6.1	10	5	6	0	0	1	1	0	15.63
on Road	1	2.0	3	0	1	0	0	0	0	0	4.50
Second Half	2	2.0	5	2	1	0	0	0	0	0	27.00

	BA	OBA	SA	AB	H	2B	3B	HR	RBI	BB	SO
Total	.342	.435	.605	38	13	1	0	3	13	5	7
vs. Left	.421	.520	.895	19	8	0	0	3	10	5	3
vs. Right	.263	.333	.316	19	5	1	0	0	3	0	4
Runners On Base	.360	.414	.720	25	9	0	0	3	13	4	4

5-YEAR TOTALS (1987-1993)

G	IP	H	BB	SO	SB	CS	W	L	SV	ERA
40	193.0	225	56	82	2	7	11	14	0	4.80
37	175.0	214	46	61	2	6	11	11	0	5.45
45	233.2	263	68	96	4	12	13	17	0	4.93

BA	OBA	SA	AB	H	2B	3B	HR	RBI	BB	SO
.298	.347	.493	1471	439	81	8	63	199	102	143
.334	.384	.549	734	245	50	6	32	107	63	54
.263	.309	.437	737	194	31	2	31	92	39	89
.294	.349	.469	588	173	22	3	25	161	46	54

JEFF JOHNSON — BR/TL — age 28 — NYA SP2 FIN/FB

1993	G	IP	H	BB	SO	SB	CS	W	L	SV	ERA
at Home	0	0.0	0	0	0	0	0	0	0	0	0.00
on Road	2	2.2	12	2	1	0	0	0	2	0	30.38
Second Half	0	0.0	0	0	0	0	0	0	0	0	0.00

	BA	OBA	SA	AB	H	2B	3B	HR	RBI	BB	SO
Total	.600	.636	.900	20	12	3	0	1	9	2	0
vs. Left	.250	.400	.500	4	1	0	0	0	0	1	0
vs. Right	.688	.706	1.000	16	11	2	0	1	9	1	0
Runners On Base	.750	.769	1.000	12	9	3	0	0	8	1	0

3-YEAR TOTALS (1991-1993)

G	IP	H	BB	SO	SB	CS	W	L	SV	ERA
17	95.1	121	20	38	5	2	3	8	0	5.85
21	87.0	118	38	38	18	5	5	8	0	7.24
21	105.1	139	28	55	15	4	5	8	0	6.66

BA	OBA	SA	AB	H	2B	3B	HR	RBI	BB	SO
.320	.372	.473	748	239	41	7	20	125	58	76
.263	.355	.400	95	25	5	1	2	15	11	11
.328	.375	.484	653	214	36	6	18	110	47	65
.354	.408	.546	339	120	25	5	10	115	32	36

JOEL JOHNSTON — BR/TR — age 27 — PIT RP33 FIN/FB

1993	G	IP	H	BB	SO	SB	CS	W	L	SV	ERA
at Home	20	36.2	28	13	23	1	1	2	4	2	3.93
on Road	13	16.2	10	6	8	1	0	0	0	0	2.16
Second Half	33	53.1	38	19	31	2	1	2	4	2	3.38

	BA	OBA	SA	AB	H	2B	3B	HR	RBI	BB	SO
Total	.203	.277	.380	187	38	10	1	7	18	19	31
vs. Left	.227	.318	.453	75	17	5	0	4	10	10	9
vs. Right	.188	.248	.330	112	21	5	1	3	8	9	22
Runners On Base	.271	.377	.424	59	16	6	0	1	12	10	9

3-YEAR TOTALS (1991-1993)

G	IP	H	BB	SO	SB	CS	W	L	SV	ERA
27	48.0	34	16	33	1	1	2	4	2	3.56
24	30.1	16	14	19	2	1	1	0	0	1.78
46	75.2	47	28	52	3	2	3	4	2	2.50

BA	OBA	SA	AB	H	2B	3B	HR	RBI	BB	SO
.183	.264	.330	273	50	11	1	9	22	30	52
.189	.268	.351	111	21	6	0	4	10	12	15
.179	.261	.315	162	29	5	1	5	12	18	37
.206	.325	.330	97	20	6	0	2	15	17	20

BARRY JONES — BR/TR — age 31 — CHA RP6 POW/GB

1993	G	IP	H	BB	SO	SB	CS	W	L	SV	ERA
at Home	5	6.0	11	3	6	1	0	0	0	0	7.50
on Road	1	1.1	3	0	1	0	1	0	1	0	13.50
Second Half	0	0.0	0	0	0	0	0	0	0	0	0.00

8-YEAR TOTALS (1986-1993)

G	IP	H	BB	SO	SB	CS	W	L	SV	ERA
179	229.1	230	97	130	23	10	20	13	9	3.65
169	203.2	185	96	120	13	6	13	20	14	3.67
190	228.1	209	114	138	21	10	12	18	15	3.55

	BA	OBA	SA	AB	H	2B	3B	HR	RBI	BB	SO
Total	.412	.459	.618	34	14	1	0	2	9	3	7
vs. Left	.636	.667	1.182	11	7	0	0	2	5	1	2
vs. Right	.304	.360	.348	23	7	1	0	0	4	2	5
Runners On Base	.421	.450	.632	19	8	1	0	1	8	1	6

BA	OBA	SA	AB	H	2B	3B	HR	RBI	BB	SO
.260	.338	.372	1596	415	63	10	32	237	193	250
.286	.369	.398	703	201	30	5	13	104	97	77
.240	.313	.352	893	214	33	5	19	133	96	173
.287	.368	.417	780	224	34	8	17	222	109	115

JIMMY JONES — BR/TR — age 30 — MON SP6, RP6 FIN/GB

1993	G	IP	H	BB	SO	SB	CS	W	L	SV	ERA
at Home	4	18.0	15	5	9	2	0	2	0	0	4.50
on Road	8	21.2	32	4	12	3	0	2	1	0	7.89
Second Half	1	2.0	5	0	0	0	0	0	0	0	13.50

8-YEAR TOTALS (1986-1993)

G	IP	H	BB	SO	SB	CS	W	L	SV	ERA
81	405.2	401	130	209	41	14	22	19	0	3.73
72	349.1	408	109	167	37	12	21	20	0	5.31
78	374.2	410	121	188	36	11	21	20	0	4.32

	BA	OBA	SA	AB	H	2B	3B	HR	RBI	BB	SO
Total	.285	.322	.467	165	47	12	0	6	27	9	21
vs. Left	.321	.376	.564	78	25	7	0	4	15	7	6
vs. Right	.253	.270	.379	87	22	5	0	2	12	2	15
Runners On Base	.413	.448	.730	63	26	5	0	5	26	4	4

BA	OBA	SA	AB	H	2B	3B	HR	RBI	BB	SO
.275	.331	.408	2943	809	135	21	72	372	239	376
.289	.350	.425	1624	470	77	15	38	189	151	194
.257	.307	.387	1319	339	58	6	34	183	88	182
.298	.355	.450	1221	364	64	10	34	334	112	151

JEFF JUDEN — BR/TR — age 23 — HOU RP2 POW/FB

1993	G	IP	H	BB	SO	SB	CS	W	L	SV	ERA
at Home	1	2.0	1	2	3	0	0	0	0	0	0.00
on Road	1	3.0	3	2	4	1	0	0	1	0	9.00
Second Half	2	5.0	4	4	7	1	0	0	1	0	5.40

2-YEAR TOTALS (1991-1993)

G	IP	H	BB	SO	SB	CS	W	L	SV	ERA
3	13.1	11	4	11	1	0	0	1	0	4.05
3	9.2	12	7	7	3	1	0	2	0	8.38
6	23.0	23	11	18	4	1	0	3	0	5.87

	BA	OBA	SA	AB	H	2B	3B	HR	RBI	BB	SO
Total	.222	.348	.444	18	4	1	0	1	3	4	7
vs. Left	.400	.538	.800	10	4	1	0	1	2	3	4
vs. Right	.000	.100	.000	8	0	0	0	0	1	1	3
Runners On Base	.250	.364	.375	8	2	1	0	0	2	2	5

BA	OBA	SA	AB	H	2B	3B	HR	RBI	BB	SO
.264	.333	.448	87	23	4	0	4	16	11	18
.261	.333	.478	46	12	1	0	3	6	6	12
.268	.333	.415	41	11	3	0	1	10	5	6
.361	.386	.528	36	13	3	0	1	13	4	8

JEFF KAISER — BR/TL — age 34 — CIN/NYN RP9 POW/FB

1993	G	IP	H	BB	SO	SB	CS	W	L	SV	ERA
at Home	2	2.0	2	2	1	1	0	0	0	0	13.50
on Road	7	6.0	8	3	8	3	1	0	0	0	6.00
Second Half	0	0.0	0	0	0	0	0	0	0	0	0.00

7-YEAR TOTALS (1985-1993)

G	IP	H	BB	SO	SB	CS	W	L	SV	ERA
25	24.2	26	20	18	4	1	0	2	1	8.03
25	27.1	42	26	20	3	1	0	0	1	10.21
22	17.2	26	16	15	2	0	0	2	2	11.72

	BA	OBA	SA	AB	H	2B	3B	HR	RBI	BB	SO
Total	.323	.405	.548	31	10	4	0	1	6	5	9
vs. Left	.357	.400	.714	14	5	2	0	1	3	1	4
vs. Right	.294	.409	.412	17	5	2	0	0	3	4	5
Runners On Base	.278	.364	.389	18	5	2	0	0	5	3	6

BA	OBA	SA	AB	H	2B	3B	HR	RBI	BB	SO
.318	.433	.565	214	68	13	2	12	65	46	38
.355	.484	.566	76	27	5	1	3	25	17	13
.297	.405	.565	138	41	8	1	9	40	29	25
.372	.483	.690	113	42	7	1	9	62	30	19

JOHN KIELY — BR/TR — age 30 — DET RP8 POW/GB

1993	G	IP	H	BB	SO	SB	CS	W	L	SV	ERA
at Home	3	3.1	3	6	2	0	0	0	0	0	10.80
on Road	5	8.1	10	7	3	0	0	0	2	0	6.48
Second Half	0	0.0	0	0	0	0	0	0	0	0	0.00

3-YEAR TOTALS (1991-1993)

G	IP	H	BB	SO	SB	CS	W	L	SV	ERA
21	31.1	26	20	10	1	0	3	0	0	2.01
33	42.0	44	30	14	1	1	1	3	0	5.79
41	51.2	49	33	15	2	1	3	3	0	3.66

	BA	OBA	SA	AB	H	2B	3B	HR	RBI	BB	SO
Total	.295	.466	.500	44	13	3	0	2	11	13	5
vs. Left	.154	.353	.385	13	2	0	0	1	3	4	0
vs. Right	.355	.512	.548	31	11	3	0	1	8	9	5
Runners On Base	.292	.500	.417	24	7	1	0	1	10	9	3

BA	OBA	SA	AB	H	2B	3B	HR	RBI	BB	SO
.260	.375	.368	269	70	17	0	4	43	50	24
.198	.333	.255	106	21	3	0	1	14	22	7
.301	.403	.442	163	49	14	0	3	29	28	17
.227	.356	.286	154	35	6	0	1	40	31	12

PAUL KILGUS — BL/TL — age 32 — SL RP21, SP1 FIN/FB

1993	G	IP	H	BB	SO	SB	CS	W	L	SV	ERA
at Home	9	6.1	5	3	4	3	0	0	0	0	1.42
on Road	13	22.1	13	5	17	1	2	1	0	1	0.40
Second Half	14	19.0	10	7	14	1	0	1	0	1	0.95

6-YEAR TOTALS (1987-1993)

G	IP	H	BB	SO	SB	CS	W	L	SV	ERA
80	287.1	293	94	125	18	10	10	17	1	4.32
83	258.0	253	96	126	14	11	11	17	3	4.05
76	263.1	262	95	129	13	12	8	17	2	4.44

	BA	OBA	SA	AB	H	2B	3B	HR	RBI	BB	SO
Total	.180	.248	.240	100	18	3	0	1	2	8	21
vs. Left	.160	.276	.360	25	4	2	0	1	1	3	8
vs. Right	.187	.237	.200	75	14	1	0	0	1	5	13
Runners On Base	.100	.200	.125	40	4	1	0	0	1	4	7

BA	OBA	SA	AB	H	2B	3B	HR	RBI	BB	SO
.259	.325	.393	2107	546	101	12	52	251	190	251
.235	.309	.378	447	105	19	3	13	64	39	65
.266	.329	.396	1660	441	82	9	39	187	151	186
.269	.330	.425	908	244	51	8	25	224	81	109

JOE KLINK — BL/TL — age 32 — FLO RP59 POW/GB

1993	G	IP	H	BB	SO	SB	CS	W	L	SV	ERA
at Home	32	20.0	14	13	11	4	0	0	0	0	4.05
on Road	27	17.2	23	11	9	1	3	0	2	0	6.11
Second Half	34	19.2	23	14	12	2	0	1	0	1	5.95

4-YEAR TOTALS (1987-1993)

G	IP	H	BB	SO	SB	CS	W	L	SV	ERA
89	83.0	73	27	47	10	0	4	1	1	3.14
84	79.1	95	47	45	2	5	5	5	2	5.45
92	77.1	81	38	45	6	2	5	2	1	4.42

	BA	OBA	SA	AB	H	2B	3B	HR	RBI	BB	SO
Total	.266	.367	.338	139	37	8	1	0	22	24	22
vs. Left	.216	.333	.243	74	16	2	0	0	6	13	12
vs. Right	.323	.405	.446	65	21	6	1	0	16	11	10
Runners On Base	.265	.360	.325	83	22	5	0	0	22	14	15

BA	OBA	SA	AB	H	2B	3B	HR	RBI	BB	SO
.271	.352	.370	619	168	28	3	9	78	74	92
.240	.321	.336	271	65	12	1	4	27	31	49
.296	.375	.397	348	103	16	2	5	51	43	43
.277	.373	.366	325	90	15	1	4	73	50	46

KURT KNUDSEN — BR/TR — age 27 — DET RP30 POW/FB

1993	G	IP	H	BB	SO	SB	CS	W	L	SV	ERA
at Home	11	15.1	18	6	10	1	2	0	1	1	5.28
on Road	19	22.1	23	10	19	1	1	3	1	1	4.43
Second Half	14	20.2	21	10	15	1	3	3	2	1	6.10

	BA	OBA	SA	AB	H	2B	3B	HR	RBI	BB	SO
Total	.281	.361	.500	146	41	5	0	9	28	16	29
vs. Left	.400	.483	.740	50	20	2	0	5	15	8	5
vs. Right	.219	.294	.375	96	21	3	0	4	13	8	24
Runners On Base	.324	.395	.603	68	22	4	0	5	24	8	11

2-YEAR TOTALS (1992-1993)

G	IP	H	BB	SO	SB	CS	W	L	SV	ERA
34	52.0	54	23	39	5	5	2	2	2	4.33
44	56.1	57	34	41	3	3	3	3	5	4.95
43	60.1	63	34	52	6	4	3	5	4	6.12

BA	OBA	SA	AB	H	2B	3B	HR	RBI	BB	SO
.270	.362	.450	411	111	18	1	18	71	57	80
.308	.398	.522	159	49	7	0	9	32	24	12
.246	.339	.405	252	62	11	1	9	39	33	68
.266	.375	.435	207	55	11	0	8	61	36	36

MARK KNUDSON — BR/TR — age 34 — COL RP4 POW/GB

1993	G	IP	H	BB	SO	SB	CS	W	L	SV	ERA
at Home	3	3.1	9	4	2	0	0	0	0	0	24.30
on Road	1	2.1	7	0	0	0	0	0	0	0	19.29
Second Half	0	0.0	0	0	0	0	0	0	0	0	0.00

	BA	OBA	SA	AB	H	2B	3B	HR	RBI	BB	SO
Total	.471	.538	.912	34	16	1	1	4	15	5	3
vs. Left	.364	.500	.818	11	4	0	1	1	4	3	2
vs. Right	.522	.560	.957	23	12	1	0	3	11	2	1
Runners On Base	.545	.600	.909	22	12	0	1	2	13	3	2

8-YEAR TOTALS (1985-1993)

G	IP	H	BB	SO	SB	CS	W	L	SV	ERA
61	235.2	295	67	100	20	13	12	15	0	5.16
60	246.1	268	61	95	12	10	12	14	0	4.31
69	291.2	334	70	116	18	13	16	20	0	4.63

BA	OBA	SA	AB	H	2B	3B	HR	RBI	BB	SO
.291	.334	.446	1938	563	92	13	61	252	128	195
.284	.328	.428	951	270	54	7	23	112	66	95
.297	.340	.463	987	293	38	6	38	140	62	100
.279	.329	.433	817	228	33	6	27	218	65	83

BILL KRUEGER — BL/TL — age 36 — DET RP25, SP7 POW/FB

1993	G	IP	H	BB	SO	SB	CS	W	L	SV	ERA
at Home	12	42.2	39	10	29	7	3	4	0	0	1.69
on Road	20	39.1	51	20	31	4	1	2	4	0	5.26
Second Half	10	31.0	25	11	33	5	1	1	1	0	2.90

	BA	OBA	SA	AB	H	2B	3B	HR	RBI	BB	SO
Total	.285	.351	.392	316	90	14	1	6	38	30	60
vs. Left	.292	.338	.458	72	21	3	0	3	14	5	8
vs. Right	.283	.355	.373	244	69	11	1	3	24	25	52
Runners On Base	.245	.341	.354	147	36	7	0	3	35	19	27

10-YEAR TOTALS (1984-1993)

G	IP	H	BB	SO	SB	CS	W	L	SV	ERA
116	512.2	532	200	280	72	20	31	26	2	4.04
132	483.2	551	208	238	53	18	25	29	2	4.50
119	490.0	547	202	268	82	23	21	27	3	4.67

BA	OBA	SA	AB	H	2B	3B	HR	RBI	BB	SO
.279	.348	.402	3877	1083	183	20	84	473	408	518
.279	.342	.390	777	217	34	5	14	102	72	106
.279	.349	.405	3100	866	149	15	70	371	336	412
.283	.357	.399	1736	491	90	12	29	418	213	238

LES LANCASTER — BR/TR — age 32 — SL RP50 FIN/FB

1993	G	IP	H	BB	SO	SB	CS	W	L	SV	ERA
at Home	23	25.0	25	10	17	1	2	0	0	0	5.04
on Road	27	36.1	31	11	19	2	1	4	1	0	1.49
Second Half	15	19.0	15	6	13	0	1	1	1	0	2.37

	BA	OBA	SA	AB	H	2B	3B	HR	RBI	BB	SO
Total	.242	.307	.377	231	56	14	1	5	35	21	36
vs. Left	.237	.321	.361	97	23	7	1	1	7	12	16
vs. Right	.246	.297	.388	134	33	7	0	4	28	9	20
Runners On Base	.261	.331	.423	111	29	4	1	4	34	11	16

7-YEAR TOTALS (1987-1993)

G	IP	H	BB	SO	SB	CS	W	L	SV	ERA
168	377.1	389	134	221	20	20	23	13	10	4.29
155	326.1	326	127	187	23	14	18	15	12	3.78
162	381.1	389	129	233	23	17	21	17	14	4.27

BA	OBA	SA	AB	H	2B	3B	HR	RBI	BB	SO
.265	.329	.390	2695	715	135	11	60	375	261	408
.280	.360	.399	1309	367	76	5	23	147	165	181
.251	.299	.382	1386	348	59	6	37	228	96	227
.272	.343	.409	1226	334	57	6	33	348	142	173

BILL LANDRUM — BR/TR — age 37 — CIN RP18 FIN/GB

1993	G	IP	H	BB	SO	SB	CS	W	L	SV	ERA
at Home	7	8.2	8	3	5	1	1	0	0	0	5.19
on Road	11	13.0	10	3	9	3	0	0	2	0	2.77
Second Half	0	0.0	0	0	0	0	0	0	0	0	0.00

	BA	OBA	SA	AB	H	2B	3B	HR	RBI	BB	SO
Total	.231	.286	.372	78	18	6	1	2	10	6	14
vs. Left	.225	.311	.375	40	9	4	1	0	2	5	8
vs. Right	.237	.256	.368	38	9	2	0	1	8	1	6
Runners On Base	.258	.324	.387	31	8	4	0	0	9	3	7

8-YEAR TOTALS (1986-1993)

G	IP	H	BB	SO	SB	CS	W	L	SV	ERA
135	179.1	181	58	105	20	9	10	6	28	3.76
133	182.0	179	66	113	20	7	8	9	30	3.02
127	165.1	184	69	103	17	8	8	9	22	4.19

BA	OBA	SA	AB	H	2B	3B	HR	RBI	BB	SO
.265	.325	.359	1361	360	48	13	18	165	124	218
.253	.321	.341	668	169	22	5	9	67	68	89
.276	.328	.375	693	191	26	8	9	98	56	129
.262	.339	.354	646	169	25	7	7	154	79	107

TIM LAYANA — BR/TR — age 30 — SF RP1 FIN/GB

1993	G	IP	H	BB	SO	SB	CS	W	L	SV	ERA
at Home	1	2.0	7	1	1	2	0	0	0	0	22.50
on Road	0	0.0	0	0	0	0	0	0	0	0	0.00
Second Half	1	2.0	7	1	1	2	0	0	0	0	22.50

	BA	OBA	SA	AB	H	2B	3B	HR	RBI	BB	SO
Total	.538	.571	.923	13	7	2	0	1	5	1	1
vs. Left	.800	.800	1.600	5	4	1	0	1	4	0	0
vs. Right	.375	.444	.500	8	3	1	0	0	1	1	1
Runners On Base	.444	.500	1.000	9	4	2	0	1	5	1	1

3-YEAR TOTALS (1990-1993)

G	IP	H	BB	SO	SB	CS	W	L	SV	ERA
40	57.1	60	29	31	12	3	4	2	1	5.49
38	45.1	41	27	37	4	3	1	3	1	3.38
52	66.0	60	36	45	12	4	2	5	1	5.05

BA	OBA	SA	AB	H	2B	3B	HR	RBI	BB	SO
.261	.355	.388	387	101	22	0	9	54	56	68
.286	.388	.434	175	50	14	0	4	30	29	28
.241	.326	.349	212	51	8	0	5	24	27	40
.243	.350	.368	185	45	8	0	5	50	30	30

TERRY LEACH — BR/TR — age 40 — CHA RP14 FIN/FB

1993	G	IP	H	BB	SO	SB	CS	W	L	SV	ERA
at Home	7	6.2	8	1	0	0	0	0	0	0	2.70
on Road	7	9.1	7	1	0	0	0	0	0	0	2.89
Second Half	0	0.0	0	0	0	0	0	0	0	0	0.00

	BA	OBA	SA	AB	H	2B	3B	HR	RBI	BB	SO
Total	.250	.281	.300	60	15	3	0	0	4	2	3
vs. Left	.227	.227	.227	22	5	0	0	0	1	0	2
vs. Right	.263	.310	.342	38	10	3	0	0	3	2	1
Runners On Base	.308	.345	.423	26	8	3	0	0	4	1	3

9-YEAR TOTALS (1985-1993)

G	IP	H	BB	SO	SB	CS	W	L	SV	ERA
157	281.0	279	62	135	35	7	12	2	4	3.04
177	338.1	337	105	150	40	16	23	23	3	3.22
168	340.0	350	106	166	46	15	23	19	4	3.26

BA	OBA	SA	AB	H	2B	3B	HR	RBI	BB	SO
.261	.311	.365	2359	616	118	12	34	266	167	285
.292	.349	.410	1019	298	65	8	13	114	90	75
.237	.282	.330	1340	318	53	4	21	152	77	210
.264	.324	.351	1040	275	49	7	9	241	93	130

CRAIG LEFFERTS — BL/TL — age 37 — TEX RP44, SP8 POW/FB

1993	G	IP	H	BB	SO	SB	CS	W	L	SV	ERA
at Home	21	32.2	37	13	24	1	2	1	3	0	5.51
on Road	31	50.2	65	15	34	3	2	2	6	0	6.39
Second Half	32	30.1	31	13	21	2	1	1	3	0	3.56

	BA	OBA	SA	AB	H	2B	3B	HR	RBI	BB	SO
Total	.304	.357	.499	335	102	10	2	17	59	28	58
vs. Left	.256	.312	.360	86	22	3	0	2	11	6	16
vs. Right	.321	.372	.546	249	80	7	2	15	48	22	42
Runners On Base	.367	.431	.583	139	51	4	1	8	50	17	21

10-YEAR TOTALS (1984-1993)

G	IP	H	BB	SO	SB	CS	W	L	SV	ERA
296	501.1	448	122	330	42	27	32	30	45	2.98
314	521.0	530	159	303	38	15	22	37	54	3.82
325	500.2	495	139	306	37	22	23	33	47	3.31

BA	OBA	SA	AB	H	2B	3B	HR	RBI	BB	SO
.255	.305	.386	3833	978	157	22	100	452	281	633
.227	.271	.322	918	208	25	6	17	107	55	195
.264	.315	.406	2915	770	132	16	83	345	226	438
.249	.310	.370	1704	424	60	15	39	391	161	296

AL LEITER — BL/TL — age 29 — TOR RP22, SP12 POW/GB

1993	G	IP	H	BB	SO	SB	CS	W	L	SV	ERA
at Home	20	58.2	61	29	35	4	2	5	2	0	4.30
on Road	14	46.1	32	27	31	3	3	4	4	2	3.88
Second Half	19	44.1	42	21	29	3	1	5	1	1	3.05

	BA	OBA	SA	AB	H	2B	3B	HR	RBI	BB	SO
Total	.240	.339	.314	388	93	5	0	8	44	56	66
vs. Left	.233	.316	.320	103	24	0	0	3	14	13	14
vs. Right	.242	.347	.312	285	69	5	0	5	30	43	52
Runners On Base	.254	.351	.294	177	45	1	0	2	38	25	31

7-YEAR TOTALS (1987-1993)

G	IP	H	BB	SO	SB	CS	W	L	SV	ERA
37	131.0	123	74	112	13	6	8	7	0	4.47
28	96.1	80	62	74	4	6	8	7	2	4.86
31	84.1	75	48	69	5	1	7	4	1	3.84

BA	OBA	SA	AB	H	2B	3B	HR	RBI	BB	SO
.240	.351	.339	847	203	25	1	19	99	136	186
.215	.319	.271	181	39	1	0	3	19	27	44
.246	.359	.357	666	164	24	1	16	80	109	142
.270	.359	.348	396	107	11	1	6	86	53	86

MARK LEITER — BR/TR — age 31 — DET RP14, SP13 POW/FB

1993	G	IP	H	BB	SO	SB	CS	W	L	SV	ERA
at Home	13	47.0	48	15	33	3	0	1	4	0	4.98
on Road	14	59.2	63	29	37	5	4	5	2	0	4.53
Second Half	8	21.0	30	5	13	0	1	0	2	0	6.86

	BA	OBA	SA	AB	H	2B	3B	HR	RBI	BB	SO
Total	.267	.338	.428	416	111	12	2	17	56	44	70
vs. Left	.268	.354	.437	213	57	5	2	9	26	28	29
vs. Right	.266	.320	.419	203	54	7	0	8	30	16	41
Runners On Base	.269	.366	.444	171	46	4	1	8	47	27	31

4-YEAR TOTALS (1990-1993)

G	IP	H	BB	SO	SB	CS	W	L	SV	ERA
58	203.0	204	80	156	12	5	10	10	1	4.57
50	176.2	181	66	113	12	15	14	9	0	4.48
49	191.2	201	50	128	8	7	11	10	0	4.60

BA	OBA	SA	AB	H	2B	3B	HR	RBI	BB	SO
.265	.334	.420	1451	385	57	13	47	188	146	269
.273	.353	.444	684	187	27	9	24	87	85	97
.258	.317	.398	767	198	30	4	23	101	61	172
.278	.351	.425	612	170	19	4	21	162	73	106

RICHIE LEWIS — BR/TR — age 28 — FLO RP57 POW/FB

1993	G	IP	H	BB	SO	SB	CS	W	L	SV	ERA
at Home	30	39.0	29	23	37	2	3	4	2	0	2.54
on Road	27	38.1	39	20	28	3	0	2	1	0	3.99
Second Half	33	40.1	41	25	32	3	2	2	3	0	4.24

	BA	OBA	SA	AB	H	2B	3B	HR	RBI	BB	SO
Total	.239	.336	.386	285	68	15	3	7	43	43	65
vs. Left	.256	.365	.421	133	34	8	1	4	28	23	28
vs. Right	.224	.310	.355	152	34	7	2	3	15	20	37
Runners On Base	.237	.360	.403	139	33	10	2	3	39	28	33

2-YEAR TOTALS (1992-1993)

G	IP	H	BB	SO	SB	CS	W	L	SV	ERA
31	41.1	37	24	38	5	3	4	3	0	3.48
28	42.2	44	26	31	3	0	3	1	0	4.22
35	47.0	54	32	36	6	2	3	4	0	5.17

BA	OBA	SA	AB	H	2B	3B	HR	RBI	BB	SO
.256	.354	.407	317	81	18	3	8	51	50	69
.267	.377	.425	146	39	9	1	4	31	26	28
.246	.333	.392	171	42	9	2	4	20	24	41
.265	.383	.426	155	41	12	2	3	46	32	36

SCOTT LEWIS — BR/TR — age 29 — CAL RP11, SP4 FIN/GB

1993	G	IP	H	BB	SO	SB	CS	W	L	SV	ERA
at Home	9	19.1	20	9	4	1	0	1	0	0	3.72
on Road	6	12.2	17	3	6	1	0	0	2	0	4.97
Second Half	3	3.0	2	0	1	0	0	0	0	0	0.00

	BA	OBA	SA	AB	H	2B	3B	HR	RBI	BB	SO
Total	.311	.364	.445	119	37	5	1	3	17	12	10
vs. Left	.317	.343	.467	60	19	1	1	2	8	4	4
vs. Right	.305	.384	.424	59	18	4	0	1	9	8	6
Runners On Base	.327	.365	.388	49	16	0	0	1	15	7	5

4-YEAR TOTALS (1990-1993)

G	IP	H	BB	SO	SB	CS	W	L	SV	ERA
30	82.2	91	29	34	7	6	6	4	0	4.35
24	64.1	73	20	40	2	1	3	4	0	5.32
26	56.1	50	10	33	4	3	6	1	0	2.88

BA	OBA	SA	AB	H	2B	3B	HR	RBI	BB	SO
.286	.343	.423	574	164	26	1	17	72	49	74
.256	.321	.356	281	72	11	1	5	31	27	28
.314	.364	.488	293	92	15	0	12	41	22	46
.312	.364	.423	234	73	8	0	6	61	23	31

DOUG LINTON — BR/TR — age 29 — TOR/CAL RP22, SP1 POW/FB

1993	G	IP	H	BB	SO	SB	CS	W	L	SV	ERA
at Home	12	28.1	31	17	17	2	2	1	1	0	6.04
on Road	11	8.1	15	6	6	1	0	0	0	0	11.88
Second Half	13	20.1	29	12	14	3	2	0	0	0	7.97

	BA	OBA	SA	AB	H	2B	3B	HR	RBI	BB	SO
Total	.305	.393	.550	151	46	9	2	8	33	23	23
vs. Left	.370	.463	.704	54	20	4	1	4	19	11	5
vs. Right	.268	.351	.464	97	26	5	1	4	14	12	18
Runners On Base	.345	.420	.607	84	29	5	1	5	30	13	12

2-YEAR TOTALS (1992-1993)

G	IP	H	BB	SO	SB	CS	W	L	SV	ERA
15	37.2	41	21	21	2	3	3	1	0	6.45
16	23.0	36	19	18	1	1	0	3	0	10.17
21	44.1	60	29	30	3	4	3	3	0	8.32

BA	OBA	SA	AB	H	2B	3B	HR	RBI	BB	SO
.312	.403	.543	247	77	14	2	13	52	40	39
.352	.456	.626	91	32	5	1	6	25	20	10
.288	.369	.494	156	45	9	1	7	27	20	29
.354	.442	.559	127	45	6	1	6	45	24	20

MIKE MAGNANTE — BL/TL — age 29 — KC SP6, RP1 FIN/FB

1993	G	IP	H	BB	SO	SB	CS	W	L	SV	ERA
at Home	4	20.1	18	6	9	0	2	1	0	0	1.77
on Road	3	15.0	19	5	7	0	2	0	2	0	7.20
Second Half	7	35.1	37	11	16	0	4	1	2	0	4.08

	BA	OBA	SA	AB	H	2B	3B	HR	RBI	BB	SO
Total	.282	.340	.420	131	37	5	2	3	15	11	16
vs. Left	.360	.407	.480	25	9	1	0	0	3	2	2
vs. Right	.264	.325	.406	106	28	4	1	3	12	9	14
Runners On Base	.294	.351	.510	51	15	1	2	3	14	5	7

3-YEAR TOTALS (1991-1993)

G	IP	H	BB	SO	SB	CS	W	L	SV	ERA
47	99.2	104	28	58	3	3	3	4	0	3.43
42	80.0	103	41	31	7	6	2	8	0	4.72
64	110.1	114	42	57	3	8	2	6	0	3.51

BA	OBA	SA	AB	H	2B	3B	HR	RBI	BB	SO
.298	.360	.413	695	207	37	5	11	90	69	89
.324	.389	.435	170	55	9	2	2	21	19	24
.290	.350	.406	525	152	28	3	9	69	50	65
.314	.375	.444	322	101	17	5	5	84	35	40

PAT MAHOMES — BR/TR — age 24 — MIN RP7, SP5 POW/FB

1993	G	IP	H	BB	SO	SB	CS	W	L	SV	ERA
at Home	7	15.2	20	7	12	1	1	1	2	0	9.77
on Road	5	21.2	27	9	11	4	2	2	3	0	6.23
Second Half	0	0.0	0	0	0	0	0	0	0	0	0.00

	BA	OBA	SA	AB	H	2B	3B	HR	RBI	BB	SO
Total	.309	.372	.586	152	47	10	4	8	31	16	23
vs. Left	.309	.374	.568	81	25	5	2	4	17	8	10
vs. Right	.310	.370	.606	71	22	5	2	4	14	8	13
Runners On Base	.329	.359	.571	70	23	4	2	3	26	5	12

2-YEAR TOTALS (1992-1993)

G	IP	H	BB	SO	SB	CS	W	L	SV	ERA
14	49.0	61	25	38	5	1	2	5	0	7.90
12	58.0	59	28	29	9	10	2	5	0	4.34
5	28.1	30	12	16	2	5	0	2	0	4.76

BA	OBA	SA	AB	H	2B	3B	HR	RBI	BB	SO
.290	.367	.493	414	120	29	8	13	70	53	67
.292	.362	.486	216	63	13	4	7	37	25	27
.288	.373	.500	198	57	16	4	6	33	28	40
.284	.344	.497	197	56	14	5	6	63	21	32

CARLOS MALDONADO — BB/TR — age 28 — MIL RP29 FIN/FB

1993	G	IP	H	BB	SO	SB	CS	W	L	SV	ERA
at Home	13	18.2	19	4	7	1	0	0	1	1	3.38
on Road	16	18.2	21	13	11	1	0	1	1	0	5.79
Second Half	17	22.1	25	5	10	2	0	1	1	1	3.63

	BA	OBA	SA	AB	H	2B	3B	HR	RBI	BB	SO
Total	.282	.350	.394	142	40	8	1	2	20	17	18
vs. Left	.327	.397	.462	52	17	1	0	2	12	8	6
vs. Right	.256	.320	.356	90	23	7	1	0	8	9	12
Runners On Base	.264	.352	.431	72	19	4	1	2	20	12	6

3-YEAR TOTALS (1990-1993)

G	IP	H	BB	SO	SB	CS	W	L	SV	ERA
18	25.0	30	10	10	1	0	0	1	1	5.40
20	26.0	30	20	18	2	0	2	1	0	5.88
24	33.0	43	16	20	3	0	1	1	1	5.73

BA	OBA	SA	AB	H	2B	3B	HR	RBI	BB	SO
.299	.381	.418	201	60	14	2	2	30	30	28
.346	.424	.481	81	28	3	1	2	18	14	10
.267	.350	.375	120	32	11	1	0	12	16	18
.299	.398	.477	107	32	9	2	2	30	21	12

JOSIAS MANZANILLO — BR/TR — age 27 — MIL/NYN RP15, SP1 POW/FB

1993	G	IP	H	BB	SO	SB	CS	W	L	SV	ERA
at Home	5	10.1	9	8	4	1	0	0	1	0	9.58
on Road	11	18.2	21	11	17	1	0	1	0	1	5.30
Second Half	6	12.0	8	9	11	1	0	0	0	0	3.00

	BA	OBA	SA	AB	H	2B	3B	HR	RBI	BB	SO
Total	.265	.372	.407	113	30	10	0	2	28	19	21
vs. Left	.277	.400	.340	47	13	3	0	0	11	11	9
vs. Right	.258	.351	.455	66	17	7	0	2	17	8	12
Runners On Base	.346	.479	.500	52	18	5	0	1	27	15	11

2-YEAR TOTALS (1991-1993)

G	IP	H	BB	SO	SB	CS	W	L	SV	ERA
6	11.1	11	9	5	1	0	0	1	0	10.32
11	18.2	21	11	17	1	0	1	0	1	5.30
7	13.0	10	12	12	1	0	0	0	0	4.15

BA	OBA	SA	AB	H	2B	3B	HR	RBI	BB	SO
.271	.386	.415	118	32	11	0	2	30	22	22
.286	.413	.367	49	14	4	0	0	11	12	9
.261	.366	.449	69	18	7	0	2	19	10	13
.351	.487	.509	57	20	6	0	1	29	17	12

PEDRO J. MARTINEZ — BR/TR — age 23 — LA RP63, SP2 POW/FB

1993	G	IP	H	BB	SO	SB	CS	W	L	SV	ERA
at Home	32	51.1	39	23	65	3	4	7	3	2	1.93
on Road	33	55.2	37	34	54	3	0	3	2	0	3.23
Second Half	36	59.0	45	30	73	2	1	2	5	3	2.59

	BA	OBA	SA	AB	H	2B	3B	HR	RBI	BB	SO
Total	.201	.309	.283	378	76	6	5	5	29	57	119
vs. Left	.227	.305	.309	220	50	3	3	3	18	25	63
vs. Right	.165	.313	.247	158	26	3	2	2	11	32	56
Runners On Base	.189	.267	.267	180	34	4	2	2	26	21	61

2-YEAR TOTALS (1992-1993)

G	IP	H	BB	SO	SB	CS	W	L	SV	ERA
33	53.1	41	24	66	3	4	7	3	2	1.86
34	61.2	41	34	61	3	0	3	3	0	3.21
38	67.0	51	31	81	2	2	5	4	1	2.55

BA	OBA	SA	AB	H	2B	3B	HR	RBI	BB	SO
.201	.303	.284	408	82	9	5	5	31	58	127
.226	.302	.311	235	53	5	3	3	20	26	65
.168	.305	.249	173	29	4	2	2	11	32	62
.189	.267	.268	190	36	5	2	2	28	22	63

ROGER MASON — BR/TR — age 36 — SD/PHI RP68 POW/FB

1993	G	IP	H	BB	SO	SB	CS	W	L	SV	ERA
at Home	36	60.1	59	17	43	3	4	4	6	0	4.18
on Road	32	39.1	31	17	28	2	1	1	6	0	3.89
Second Half	36	51.1	48	18	35	2	1	5	5	0	4.91

	BA	OBA	SA	AB	H	2B	3B	HR	RBI	BB	SO
Total	.244	.307	.366	369	90	13	1	10	51	34	71
vs. Left	.284	.351	.378	148	42	5	0	3	19	17	30
vs. Right	.217	.277	.357	221	48	8	1	7	32	17	41
Runners On Base	.270	.333	.350	163	44	5	1	2	43	18	28

8-YEAR TOTALS (1984-1993)

G	IP	H	BB	SO	SB	CS	W	L	SV	ERA
89	198.1	168	60	136	7	13	13	11	6	3.31
96	158.0	162	76	117	11	8	19	19	6	5.01
105	182.1	168	66	135	7	10	14	15	6	4.29

BA	OBA	SA	AB	H	2B	3B	HR	RBI	BB	SO
.248	.320	.382	1328	330	61	7	34	162	136	253
.267	.343	.387	648	173	29	5	13	69	80	117
.231	.297	.376	680	157	32	2	21	93	56	136
.256	.335	.380	577	148	24	4	13	141	73	115

TIM MAUSER — BR/TR — age 28 — PHI/SD RP36 POW/GB

1993	G	IP	H	BB	SO	SB	CS	W	L	SV	ERA
at Home	16	25.0	18	10	19	2	2	0	0	0	3.24
on Road	20	29.0	33	14	27	2	1	0	1	0	4.66
Second Half	29	41.2	38	17	36	3	3	0	1	0	3.24

	BA	OBA	SA	AB	H	2B	3B	HR	RBI	BB	SO
Total	.245	.325	.394	208	51	11	1	6	33	24	46
vs. Left	.202	.270	.327	104	21	4	0	3	13	10	26
vs. Right	.288	.378	.462	104	30	7	1	3	20	14	20
Runners On Base	.242	.350	.424	99	24	5	1	3	32	17	24

2-YEAR TOTALS (1991-1993)

G	IP	H	BB	SO	SB	CS	W	L	SV	ERA
19	35.2	36	13	25	2	2	0	0	0	4.54
20	29.0	33	14	27	2	1	0	1	0	4.66
32	52.1	56	20	42	3	3	0	1	0	4.13

BA	OBA	SA	AB	H	2B	3B	HR	RBI	BB	SO
.268	.339	.440	257	69	15	1	9	43	27	52
.246	.311	.393	122	30	6	0	4	17	12	26
.289	.364	.481	135	39	9	1	5	26	15	26
.258	.350	.444	124	32	5	1	6	40	18	27

MATT MAYSEY — BR/TR — age 27 — MIL RP23 POW/GB

1993	G	IP	H	BB	SO	SB	CS	W	L	SV	ERA
at Home	15	15.1	25	7	6	1	0	1	1	0	7.63
on Road	8	6.2	3	6	4	2	0	1	1	0	1.35
Second Half	23	22.0	28	13	10	3	0	1	2	0	5.73

	BA	OBA	SA	AB	H	2B	3B	HR	RBI	BB	SO
Total	.322	.408	.517	87	28	5	0	4	20	13	10
vs. Left	.306	.395	.444	36	11	2	0	1	9	6	5
vs. Right	.333	.417	.569	51	17	3	0	3	11	7	5
Runners On Base	.281	.348	.509	57	16	4	0	3	19	7	7

2-YEAR TOTALS (1992-1993)

G	IP	H	BB	SO	SB	CS	W	L	SV	ERA
15	15.1	25	7	6	1	0	1	1	0	7.63
10	9.0	7	6	5	2	1	0	1	1	2.00
25	24.1	32	13	11	3	1	1	2	1	5.55

BA	OBA	SA	AB	H	2B	3B	HR	RBI	BB	SO
.327	.409	.531	98	32	5	0	5	22	13	11
.326	.400	.442	43	14	2	0	1	10	6	5
.327	.415	.600	55	18	3	0	4	12	7	6
.286	.347	.492	63	18	4	0	3	20	7	7

KIRK McCASKILL — BR/TR — age 33 — CHA RP16, SP14 FIN/GB

1993	G	IP	H	BB	SO	SB	CS	W	L	SV	ERA
at Home	18	66.1	71	20	38	4	3	2	2	1	3.80
on Road	12	47.1	73	16	27	4	6	2	6	1	7.23
Second Half	18	53.0	60	17	35	1	2	2	1	2	4.42

	BA	OBA	SA	AB	H	2B	3B	HR	RBI	BB	SO
Total	.313	.362	.457	460	144	26	2	12	72	36	65
vs. Left	.350	.410	.545	200	70	14	2	7	35	21	19
vs. Right	.285	.324	.388	260	74	12	0	5	37	15	46
Runners On Base	.337	.388	.473	205	69	13	0	5	65	19	23

9-YEAR TOTALS (1985-1993)

G	IP	H	BB	SO	SB	CS	W	L	SV	ERA
128	783.2	737	258	454	21	31	48	41	1	3.62
128	760.0	791	321	434	34	34	46	54	1	4.41
140	818.2	819	308	444	33	31	50	50	2	4.24

BA	OBA	SA	AB	H	2B	3B	HR	RBI	BB	SO
.259	.327	.381	5889	1528	239	40	132	677	579	888
.274	.338	.406	3020	828	124	26	74	352	291	374
.244	.315	.354	2869	700	115	14	58	325	288	514
.280	.340	.412	2478	695	100	19	63	608	237	358

BOB McCLURE — BR/TL — age 42 — FLO RP14 POW/FB

1993	G	IP	H	BB	SO	SB	CS	W	L	SV	ERA
at Home	7	3.2	7	3	4	0	2	0	1	0	9.82
on Road	7	2.2	6	2	2	0	0	1	0	0	3.38
Second Half	0	0.0	0	0	0	0	0	0	0	0	0.00

	BA	OBA	SA	AB	H	2B	3B	HR	RBI	BB	SO
Total	.419	.500	.677	31	13	2	0	2	8	5	6
vs. Left	.450	.522	.700	20	9	2	0	1	5	3	3
vs. Right	.364	.462	.636	11	4	0	0	1	3	2	3
Runners On Base	.474	.545	.842	19	9	1	0	2	8	3	3

10-YEAR TOTALS (1984-1993)

G	IP	H	BB	SO	SB	CS	W	L	SV	ERA
206	275.1	293	106	161	11	12	21	10	8	3.76
210	263.1	253	98	161	12	6	11	14	13	3.96
229	309.1	310	111	185	17	11	17	13	11	3.58

BA	OBA	SA	AB	H	2B	3B	HR	RBI	BB	SO
.267	.333	.404	2048	546	100	17	49	285	204	322
.222	.291	.348	689	153	26	8	15	96	71	141
.289	.354	.432	1359	393	74	9	34	189	133	181
.271	.352	.423	956	259	46	9	27	263	128	173

ROGER McDOWELL — BR/TR — age 34 — LA RP54 FIN/GB

1993	G	IP	H	BB	SO	SB	CS	W	L	SV	ERA
at Home	24	33.0	40	15	12	1	4	2	1	0	2.45
on Road	30	35.0	36	15	15	7	2	3	2	2	2.06
Second Half	25	32.0	36	22	13	5	2	1	3	1	3.09

	BA	OBA	SA	AB	H	2B	3B	HR	RBI	BB	SO
Total	.288	.364	.360	264	76	9	2	2	32	30	27
vs. Left	.312	.399	.400	125	39	6	1	1	20	17	11
vs. Right	.266	.331	.324	139	37	3	1	1	12	13	16
Runners On Base	.259	.354	.374	139	36	6	2	2	32	19	17

9-YEAR TOTALS (1985-1993)

G	IP	H	BB	SO	SB	CS	W	L	SV	ERA
269	414.2	391	137	206	26	14	35	27	68	2.80
317	449.1	449	195	221	44	13	27	35	83	3.32
323	461.1	446	170	218	43	13	28	36	91	3.02

BA	OBA	SA	AB	H	2B	3B	HR	RBI	BB	SO
.258	.327	.335	3262	840	114	17	35	385	332	427
.272	.360	.363	1621	441	60	14	20	217	221	173
.243	.293	.307	1641	399	54	3	15	168	111	254
.261	.344	.345	1594	416	58	8	20	370	198	215

CHUCK McELROY — BL/TL — age 27 — CHN RP49 POW/FB

1993	G	IP	H	BB	SO	SB	CS	W	L	SV	ERA
at Home	25	26.1	31	17	10	1	1	1	1	0	5.47
on Road	24	21.0	20	8	21	3	1	1	1	0	3.43
Second Half	22	17.0	21	9	8	1	1	0	0	0	4.24

	BA	OBA	SA	AB	H	2B	3B	HR	RBI	BB	SO
Total	.280	.368	.396	182	51	9	0	4	23	25	31
vs. Left	.313	.416	.438	64	20	2	0	2	9	12	10
vs. Right	.263	.341	.373	118	31	7	0	2	14	13	21
Runners On Base	.303	.394	.449	89	27	7	0	2	21	13	12

5-YEAR TOTALS (1989-1993)

G	IP	H	BB	SO	SB	CS	W	L	SV	ERA
115	142.0	137	75	122	7	8	7	7	4	3.49
104	114.2	96	72	108	16	7	5	5	5	2.98
123	137.2	137	78	120	9	9	3	6	3	3.53

BA	OBA	SA	AB	H	2B	3B	HR	RBI	BB	SO
.247	.345	.361	944	233	49	4	17	121	147	230
.246	.338	.369	317	78	16	1	7	44	47	86
.247	.348	.357	627	155	33	3	10	77	100	144
.247	.351	.351	465	115	23	2	7	111	80	113

RUSTY MEACHAM — BR/TR — age 26 — KC RP15 FIN/FB

1993	G	IP	H	BB	SO	SB	CS	W	L	SV	ERA
at Home	12	16.2	24	2	12	1	0	2	1	0	5.94
on Road	3	4.1	7	1	4	0	0	0	1	0	4.15
Second Half	0	0.0	0	0	0	0	0	0	0	0	0.00

	BA	OBA	SA	AB	H	2B	3B	HR	RBI	BB	SO
Total	.326	.375	.474	95	31	6	1	2	19	5	13
vs. Left	.400	.432	.625	40	16	4	1	1	10	2	3
vs. Right	.273	.333	.364	55	15	2	0	1	9	3	10
Runners On Base	.347	.421	.449	49	17	3	1	0	17	4	7

3-YEAR TOTALS (1991-1993)

G	IP	H	BB	SO	SB	CS	W	L	SV	ERA
50	84.1	97	16	48	2	0	9	1	1	4.70
39	66.0	57	21	43	0	1	5	3	1	2.18
42	74.2	85	25	50	1	1	7	4	2	4.58

BA	OBA	SA	AB	H	2B	3B	HR	RBI	BB	SO
.264	.306	.384	584	154	29	4	11	82	37	91
.268	.320	.394	231	62	10	2	5	37	19	29
.261	.296	.377	353	92	19	2	6	45	18	62
.297	.344	.414	266	79	12	2	5	76	24	40

JOSE MELENDEZ — BR/TR — age 29 — BOS RP9 POW/FB

1993	G	IP	H	BB	SO	SB	CS	W	L	SV	ERA
at Home	5	11.2	5	2	11	0	0	2	0	0	0.77
on Road	4	4.1	5	3	3	0	0	0	1	0	6.23
Second Half	0	0.0	0	0	0	0	0	0	0	0	0.00

	BA	OBA	SA	AB	H	2B	3B	HR	RBI	BB	SO
Total	.179	.238	.393	56	10	2	2	2	11	5	14
vs. Left	.190	.333	.381	21	4	2	0	1	3	5	3
vs. Right	.171	.167	.400	35	6	2	0	2	8	0	11
Runners On Base	.200	.290	.560	25	5	1	1	2	11	4	5

4-YEAR TOTALS (1990-1993)

G	IP	H	BB	SO	SB	CS	W	L	SV	ERA
50	114.2	104	25	95	3	5	9	7	1	3.53
49	89.2	73	27	68	2	5	7	6	2	2.91
53	92.1	86	26	77	2	4	6	4	3	3.02

BA	OBA	SA	AB	H	2B	3B	HR	RBI	BB	SO
.234	.283	.374	757	177	28	3	24	92	52	163
.253	.319	.391	368	93	11	2	12	43	39	72
.216	.247	.357	389	84	17	1	12	49	13	91
.249	.299	.379	293	73	9	1	9	77	25	59

TONY MENENDEZ — BR/TR — age 29 — PIT RP14 FIN/FB

1993	G	IP	H	BB	SO	SB	CS	W	L	SV	ERA
at Home	7	12.0	15	2	6	0	0	1	0	0	3.75
on Road	7	9.0	5	2	11	0	1	0	0	0	2.00
Second Half	14	21.0	20	4	13	0	1	2	0	0	3.00

	BA	OBA	SA	AB	H	2B	3B	HR	RBI	BB	SO
Total	.256	.298	.462	78	20	4	0	4	8	4	13
vs. Left	.250	.273	.750	20	5	1	0	3	6	1	4
vs. Right	.259	.306	.362	58	15	3	0	1	3	3	9
Runners On Base	.212	.270	.394	33	7	0	0	2	6	3	5

2-YEAR TOTALS (1992-1993)

G	IP	H	BB	SO	SB	CS	W	L	SV	ERA
8	14.2	16	2	7	0	0	1	0	0	3.68
9	11.0	5	2	11	0	1	0	0	0	1.64
15	22.0	20	4	14	0	1	3	0	0	2.86

BA	OBA	SA	AB	H	2B	3B	HR	RBI	BB	SO
.226	.263	.430	93	21	4	0	5	9	4	18
.208	.231	.625	24	5	1	0	3	6	1	5
.232	.274	.362	69	16	3	0	2	3	3	13
.212	.270	.394	33	7	0	0	2	6	3	5

KENT MERCKER — BL/TL — age 26 — ATL RP37, SP6 POW/FB

1993	G	IP	H	BB	SO	SB	CS	W	L	SV	ERA
at Home	23	35.1	29	20	25	3	2	2	0	0	2.55
on Road	20	30.2	23	16	34	3	0	1	1	0	3.23
Second Half	18	44.0	31	21	36	5	2	1	1	0	2.66

	BA	OBA	SA	AB	H	2B	3B	HR	RBI	BB	SO
Total	.214	.320	.292	243	52	11	1	2	22	36	59
vs. Left	.211	.341	.268	71	15	4	0	0	6	14	21
vs. Right	.215	.311	.302	172	37	7	1	2	16	22	38
Runners On Base	.211	.289	.258	128	27	6	0	0	20	14	32

5-YEAR TOTALS (1989-1993)

G	IP	H	BB	SO	SB	CS	W	L	SV	ERA
97	136.1	114	70	102	14	6	11	4	14	3.23
87	124.0	96	66	111	20	2	4	9	5	3.05
104	167.2	139	90	125	23	6	7	10	13	3.54

BA	OBA	SA	AB	H	2B	3B	HR	RBI	BB	SO
.219	.320	.322	957	210	39	4	17	105	136	213
.226	.335	.301	266	60	11	0	3	24	45	71
.217	.314	.330	691	150	28	4	14	81	91	142
.238	.326	.329	450	107	17	0	8	96	58	100

BOB MILACKI — BR/TR — age 30 — CLE RP3, SP2 POW/FB

1993	G	IP	H	BB	SO	SB	CS	W	L	SV	ERA
at Home	3	7.2	8	7	4	0	0	1	0	0	2.35
on Road	2	8.1	11	4	3	1	0	0	1	0	4.32
Second Half	5	16.0	19	11	7	1	0	1	1	0	3.38

	BA	OBA	SA	AB	H	2B	3B	HR	RBI	BB	SO
Total	.302	.405	.508	63	19	2	1	3	7	11	7
vs. Left	.324	.452	.588	34	11	1	1	2	4	8	5
vs. Right	.276	.344	.414	29	8	1	0	1	3	3	2
Runners On Base	.219	.342	.219	32	7	0	0	0	4	6	5

6-YEAR TOTALS (1988-1993)

G	IP	H	BB	SO	SB	CS	W	L	SV	ERA
62	347.2	367	123	186	31	11	18	18	0	4.45
64	371.1	352	143	171	32	5	20	20	1	3.90
63	360.2	336	120	186	23	5	21	19	1	3.79

BA	OBA	SA	AB	H	2B	3B	HR	RBI	BB	SO
.261	.326	.403	2751	719	139	11	76	321	266	357
.255	.324	.380	1383	353	68	7	30	136	145	187
.268	.327	.426	1368	366	71	4	46	185	121	170
.268	.323	.405	1131	303	54	6	31	276	100	133

SAM MILITELLO — BR/TR — age 25 — NYA SP2, RP1 POW/FB

1993	G	IP	H	BB	SO	SB	CS	W	L	SV	ERA
at Home	1	1.2	1	1	0	0	0	0	0	0	10.80
on Road	2	7.2	9	6	5	1	0	1	1	0	5.87
Second Half	0	0.0	0	0	0	0	0	0	0	0	0.00

	BA	OBA	SA	AB	H	2B	3B	HR	RBI	BB	SO
Total	.270	.413	.432	37	10	3	0	1	6	7	5
vs. Left	.333	.364	.571	21	7	2	0	1	3	1	2
vs. Right	.188	.458	.250	16	3	1	0	0	3	6	3
Runners On Base	.238	.360	.381	21	5	3	0	0	5	3	3

2-YEAR TOTALS (1992-1993)

G	IP	H	BB	SO	SB	CS	W	L	SV	ERA
7	41.1	22	23	31	4	0	2	1	0	2.83
5	28.0	31	16	16	4	0	2	3	0	5.46
9	60.0	43	32	42	7	0	3	3	0	3.45

BA	OBA	SA	AB	H	2B	3B	HR	RBI	BB	SO
.205	.319	.349	258	53	16	0	7	26	39	47
.273	.354	.484	128	35	9	0	6	16	16	14
.138	.287	.215	130	18	7	0	1	10	23	33
.183	.290	.317	120	22	7	0	3	22	17	24

PAUL MILLER — BR/TR — age 29 — PIT SP2, RP1 FIN/FB

1993	G	IP	H	BB	SO	SB	CS	W	L	SV	ERA
at Home	2	6.1	10	0	0	0	0	0	0	0	7.11
on Road	1	3.2	5	2	2	1	0	0	0	0	2.45
Second Half	3	10.0	15	2	2	1	0	0	0	0	5.40

	BA	OBA	SA	AB	H	2B	3B	HR	RBI	BB	SO
Total	.349	.378	.558	43	15	3	0	2	6	2	2
vs. Left	.278	.278	.500	18	5	1	0	1	1	0	2
vs. Right	.400	.444	.600	25	10	2	0	1	5	2	0
Runners On Base	.316	.350	.368	19	6	1	0	0	6	1	1

3-YEAR TOTALS (1991-1993)

G	IP	H	BB	SO	SB	CS	W	L	SV	ERA
6	15.1	20	1	1	0	1	1	0	0	4.70
4	11.0	10	5	8	1	0	0	0	0	3.27
4	15.0	19	5	4	1	0	0	0	0	5.40

BA	OBA	SA	AB	H	2B	3B	HR	RBI	BB	SO
.288	.324	.442	104	30	10	0	2	12	6	9
.318	.362	.500	44	14	5	0	1	3	3	4
.267	.297	.400	60	16	5	0	1	9	3	5
.280	.302	.360	50	14	4	0	0	10	2	6

ALAN MILLS — BR/TR — age 28 — BAL RP45 POW/FB

1993	G	IP	H	BB	SO	SB	CS	W	L	SV	ERA
at Home	26	54.1	43	29	28	2	2	3	3	3	3.31
on Road	19	46.0	37	22	40	4	1	2	1	1	3.13
Second Half	22	47.2	39	24	32	3	1	4	1	4	3.21

	BA	OBA	SA	AB	H	2B	3B	HR	RBI	BB	SO
Total	.225	.324	.390	356	80	11	3	14	49	51	68
vs. Left	.269	.365	.410	134	36	1	1	5	17	20	16
vs. Right	.198	.299	.378	222	44	9	2	9	32	31	52
Runners On Base	.187	.282	.310	171	32	1	1	6	41	22	38

4-YEAR TOTALS (1990-1993)

G	IP	H	BB	SO	SB	CS	W	L	SV	ERA
63	134.1	115	70	74	12	4	8	9	5	3.08
59	127.1	107	76	89	13	4	9	5	1	3.32
66	141.1	124	85	91	13	5	10	8	6	3.95

BA	OBA	SA	AB	H	2B	3B	HR	RBI	BB	SO
.236	.338	.368	942	222	39	7	24	120	146	163
.269	.369	.386	420	113	18	2	9	46	66	50
.209	.313	.354	522	109	21	5	15	74	80	113
.211	.317	.318	469	99	12	4	10	106	75	96

GINO MINUTELLI — BL/TL — age 30 — SF RP9 POW/FB

1993	G	IP	H	BB	SO	SB	CS	W	L	SV	ERA
at Home	5	10.2	3	11	6	2	0	0	0	0	4.22
on Road	4	3.2	4	4	4	0	0	0	1	0	2.45
Second Half	4	8.2	3	8	4	0	0	0	0	0	5.19

	BA	OBA	SA	AB	H	2B	3B	HR	RBI	BB	SO
Total	.152	.349	.348	46	7	1	1	2	7	15	10
vs. Left	.091	.231	.091	11	1	0	0	0	0	2	3
vs. Right	.171	.380	.429	35	6	1	1	2	7	13	7
Runners On Base	.273	.379	.545	22	6	1	1	1	6	5	4

3-YEAR TOTALS (1990-1993)

G	IP	H	BB	SO	SB	CS	W	L	SV	ERA
17	28.2	24	24	19	3	0	0	1	0	3.77
10	12.0	13	11	12	1	0	0	2	0	9.00
21	34.0	32	26	24	1	0	0	2	0	5.82

BA	OBA	SA	AB	H	2B	3B	HR	RBI	BB	SO
.242	.378	.458	153	37	6	3	7	21	35	31
.263	.423	.474	38	10	3	1	1	5	12	9
.235	.362	.452	115	27	3	2	6	16	23	22
.286	.413	.500	70	20	2	3	3	17	17	16

DAVE MLICKI — BR/TR — age 26 — CLE SP3 FIN/FB

1993	G	IP	H	BB	SO	SB	CS	W	L	SV	ERA
at Home	3	13.1	11	6	7	2	2	0	0	0	3.38
on Road	0	0.0	0	0	0	0	0	0	0	0	0.00
Second Half	3	13.1	11	6	7	2	2	0	0	0	3.38

	BA	OBA	SA	AB	H	2B	3B	HR	RBI	BB	SO
Total	.220	.328	.400	50	11	3	0	2	5	6	7
vs. Left	.172	.294	.310	29	5	1	0	1	2	3	3
vs. Right	.286	.375	.524	21	6	2	0	1	3	3	4
Runners On Base	.200	.238	.400	20	4	1	0	1	4	1	1

2-YEAR TOTALS (1992-1993)

G	IP	H	BB	SO	SB	CS	W	L	SV	ERA
5	24.0	26	13	15	5	3	0	2	0	5.25
2	11.0	8	9	8	4	0	0	0	0	2.45
7	35.0	34	22	23	9	3	0	2	0	4.37

BA	OBA	SA	AB	H	2B	3B	HR	RBI	BB	SO
.258	.376	.432	132	34	6	1	5	13	22	23
.253	.371	.400	75	19	3	1	2	6	11	11
.263	.382	.474	57	15	3	0	3	7	11	12
.231	.306	.323	65	15	3	0	1	9	7	7

DENNIS MOELLER — BR/TL — age 27 — PIT RP10 POW/GB

1993	G	IP	H	BB	SO	SB	CS	W	L	SV	ERA
at Home	4	7.0	10	2	5	1	0	0	0	0	7.71
on Road	6	9.1	16	5	8	1	1	1	0	0	11.57
Second Half	0	0.0	0	0	0	0	0	0	0	0	0.00

	BA	OBA	SA	AB	H	2B	3B	HR	RBI	BB	SO
Total	.356	.420	.493	73	26	4	0	2	19	7	13
vs. Left	.348	.444	.478	23	8	0	0	1	7	3	2
vs. Right	.360	.407	.500	50	18	4	0	1	12	4	11
Runners On Base	.567	.639	.833	30	17	2	0	2	19	5	4

2-YEAR TOTALS (1992-1993)

G	IP	H	BB	SO	SB	CS	W	L	SV	ERA
6	13.0	15	5	7	1	0	0	0	0	4.15
9	21.1	35	13	12	3	1	1	3	0	10.97
5	18.0	24	11	6	2	0	0	3	0	7.00

BA	OBA	SA	AB	H	2B	3B	HR	RBI	BB	SO
.345	.413	.545	145	50	8	0	7	34	18	19
.379	.457	.586	29	11	0	0	2	11	4	2
.336	.402	.534	116	39	8	0	5	23	14	17
.433	.500	.683	60	26	3	0	4	31	10	6

RICH MONTELEONE — BR/TR — age 31 — NYA RP42 FIN/GB

1993	G	IP	H	BB	SO	SB	CS	W	L	SV	ERA
at Home	18	33.1	38	12	21	2	1	1	0	0	5.13
on Road	24	52.1	47	23	29	3	0	6	3	0	4.82
Second Half	21	33.0	41	17	21	2	0	2	1	0	6.55

	BA	OBA	SA	AB	H	2B	3B	HR	RBI	BB	SO
Total	.262	.329	.468	325	85	13	6	14	49	35	50
vs. Left	.271	.357	.549	133	36	4	3	9	22	19	22
vs. Right	.255	.308	.411	192	49	9	3	5	27	16	28
Runners On Base	.252	.337	.448	143	36	2	4	6	41	21	19

7-YEAR TOTALS (1987-1993)

G	IP	H	BB	SO	SB	CS	W	L	SV	ERA
75	136.1	130	42	87	6	5	7	5	0	3.89
75	147.1	140	59	99	5	5	12	6	0	3.97
86	150.1	160	51	100	5	6	8	6	0	4.61

BA	OBA	SA	AB	H	2B	3B	HR	RBI	BB	SO
.250	.313	.400	1081	270	47	11	31	149	101	186
.260	.325	.417	465	121	22	6	13	54	45	60
.242	.304	.386	616	149	25	5	18	95	56	126
.273	.352	.437	465	127	19	6	15	133	60	68

MIKE MUNOZ — BL/TL — age 29 — DET/COL RP29 POW/GB

1993	G	IP	H	BB	SO	SB	CS	W	L	SV	ERA
at Home	12	9.1	13	5	10	0	1	2	0	0	5.79
on Road	17	11.2	12	10	7	1	0	0	2	0	3.86
Second Half	21	18.0	21	9	16	1	1	2	1	0	4.50

	BA	OBA	SA	AB	H	2B	3B	HR	RBI	BB	SO
Total	.309	.408	.506	81	25	6	2	2	19	15	17
vs. Left	.316	.357	.553	38	12	3	0	2	7	3	8
vs. Right	.302	.446	.465	43	13	3	2	0	12	12	9
Runners On Base	.385	.509	.667	39	15	4	2	1	18	12	6

5-YEAR TOTALS (1989-1993)

G	IP	H	BB	SO	SB	CS	W	L	SV	ERA
48	39.1	50	19	28	1	4	2	2	0	5.03
63	47.1	44	31	20	3	0	1	3	2	4.18
62	47.2	52	21	28	2	3	2	2	2	4.72

BA	OBA	SA	AB	H	2B	3B	HR	RBI	BB	SO
.283	.372	.401	332	94	15	3	6	55	50	48
.254	.314	.348	138	35	7	0	2	19	13	21
.304	.410	.438	194	59	8	3	4	36	37	27
.259	.377	.351	174	45	9	2	1	50	36	22

ROB MURPHY — BL/TL — age 34 — SL RP73 FIN/FB

1993	G	IP	H	BB	SO	SB	CS	W	L	SV	ERA
at Home	35	32.0	37	8	19	2	1	2	2	1	4.22
on Road	38	32.2	36	12	22	1	0	3	5	0	5.51
Second Half	36	33.1	51	11	19	1	1	4	3	1	6.48

	BA	OBA	SA	AB	H	2B	3B	HR	RBI	BB	SO
Total	.290	.342	.429	252	73	7	2	8	28	20	41
vs. Left	.293	.326	.402	82	24	3	0	2	10	4	14
vs. Right	.288	.349	.441	170	49	4	2	6	18	16	27
Runners On Base	.275	.372	.382	102	28	2	0	3	23	16	18

9-YEAR TOTALS (1985-1993)

G	IP	H	BB	SO	SB	CS	W	L	SV	ERA
266	297.0	276	109	254	19	10	12	13	11	3.21
264	272.0	270	117	234	26	9	15	20	17	3.67
288	306.1	310	119	261	22	7	21	15	19	3.70

BA	OBA	SA	AB	H	2B	3B	HR	RBI	BB	SO
.255	.325	.372	2144	546	95	15	42	267	226	488
.235	.290	.311	689	162	29	1	7	71	52	151
.264	.341	.401	1455	384	66	14	35	196	174	337
.262	.342	.369	1018	267	42	11	15	240	128	243

JEFF MUTIS — BL/TL — age 28 — CLE SP13, RP4 FIN/GB

1993	G	IP	H	BB	SO	SB	CS	W	L	SV	ERA
at Home	7	41.1	41	14	16	4	2	3	1	0	3.70
on Road	10	39.2	52	19	13	2	1	0	5	0	7.94
Second Half	13	59.1	69	27	18	5	1	2	4	0	5.76

	BA	OBA	SA	AB	H	2B	3B	HR	RBI	BB	SO
Total	.289	.365	.475	322	93	16	1	14	52	33	29
vs. Left	.320	.363	.560	75	24	1	1	5	17	4	5
vs. Right	.279	.366	.449	247	69	15	0	9	35	29	24
Runners On Base	.358	.408	.540	137	49	8	1	5	43	10	12

3-YEAR TOTALS (1991-1993)

G	IP	H	BB	SO	SB	CS	W	L	SV	ERA
11	58.0	75	22	22	4	2	3	4	0	5.90
12	46.2	65	24	21	2	1	0	7	0	8.10
16	70.2	93	33	26	5	1	2	6	0	6.37

BA	OBA	SA	AB	H	2B	3B	HR	RBI	BB	SO
.321	.391	.530	436	140	24	5	19	75	46	43
.333	.375	.600	90	30	2	2	6	20	5	7
.318	.394	.512	346	110	22	3	13	55	41	36
.375	.432	.557	192	72	13	2	6	62	20	21

CHARLES NAGY — BL/TR — age 27 — CLE SP9 FIN/GB

1993	G	IP	H	BB	SO	SB	CS	W	L	SV	ERA
at Home	4	22.2	24	8	11	4	1	2	2	0	4.37
on Road	5	26.0	42	5	19	6	1	0	4	0	7.96
Second Half	1	3.0	4	3	2	0	0	0	1	0	6.00

	BA	OBA	SA	AB	H	2B	3B	HR	RBI	BB	SO
Total	.322	.367	.463	205	66	11	0	6	33	13	30
vs. Left	.288	.324	.385	104	30	4	0	2	14	6	14
vs. Right	.356	.409	.545	101	36	7	0	4	19	7	16
Runners On Base	.313	.368	.510	96	30	4	0	5	32	8	14

4-YEAR TOTALS (1990-1993)

G	IP	H	BB	SO	SB	CS	W	L	SV	ERA
41	288.2	289	76	182	24	14	18	14	0	3.27
43	269.0	308	81	152	23	12	13	21	0	4.65
43	283.2	303	83	171	19	13	17	16	0	4.19

BA	OBA	SA	AB	H	2B	3B	HR	RBI	BB	SO
.276	.326	.391	2161	597	106	12	39	230	157	334
.277	.326	.382	1094	303	48	8	17	115	82	162
.276	.326	.399	1067	294	58	4	22	115	75	172
.271	.326	.386	912	247	36	3	21	212	75	125

DENNY NEAGLE — BL/TL — age 26 — PIT RP43, SP7 POW/FB

1993	G	IP	H	BB	SO	SB	CS	W	L	SV	ERA
at Home	25	37.0	37	14	35	5	3	1	1	0	4.86
on Road	25	44.1	45	23	38	11	2	2	4	1	5.68
Second Half	26	31.0	26	11	26	2	0	1	2	1	4.94

	BA	OBA	SA	AB	H	2B	3B	HR	RBI	BB	SO
Total	.258	.340	.421	318	82	18	2	10	54	37	73
vs. Left	.223	.305	.383	94	21	4	1	3	18	10	29
vs. Right	.272	.354	.438	224	61	14	1	7	36	27	44
Runners On Base	.284	.370	.539	141	40	11	2	7	51	18	31

3-YEAR TOTALS (1991-1993)

G	IP	H	BB	SO	SB	CS	W	L	SV	ERA
58	93.2	111	42	87	10	6	2	7	0	5.28
54	94.0	80	45	77	22	3	5	5	3	4.31
64	88.2	85	42	77	8	1	2	5	2	4.06

BA	OBA	SA	AB	H	2B	3B	HR	RBI	BB	SO
.261	.342	.421	731	191	43	4	22	100	87	164
.227	.316	.372	207	47	13	1	5	33	25	61
.275	.352	.441	524	144	30	3	17	67	62	103
.278	.368	.466	313	87	22	2	11	89	45	74

JEFF NELSON — BR/TR — age 28 — SEA RP71 POW/GB

1993	G	IP	H	BB	SO	SB	CS	W	L	SV	ERA
at Home	36	35.1	29	16	38	6	1	3	0	1	3.57
on Road	35	24.2	28	18	23	4	0	2	3	0	5.47
Second Half	40	31.2	28	17	33	6	1	3	1	1	5.40

	BA	OBA	SA	AB	H	2B	3B	HR	RBI	BB	SO
Total	.258	.371	.362	221	57	8	0	5	49	34	61
vs. Left	.354	.484	.625	48	17	4	0	3	17	10	12
vs. Right	.231	.337	.289	173	40	4	0	2	32	.24	49
Runners On Base	.281	.415	.359	128	36	4	0	2	46	26	30

2-YEAR TOTALS (1992-1993)

G	IP	H	BB	SO	SB	CS	W	L	SV	ERA
66	77.0	63	30	61	7	3	4	2	6	3.51
71	64.0	65	48	46	7	1	2	8	1	4.22
75	77.2	64	44	62	10	2	4	6	7	3.94

BA	OBA	SA	AB	H	2B	3B	HR	RBI	BB	SO
.250	.361	.368	511	128	18	3	12	89	78	107
.308	.439	.468	156	48	8	1	5	27	35	30
.225	.324	.324	355	80	10	2	7	62	43	77
.255	.385	.340	282	72	10	1	4	81	57	53

GENE NELSON — BR/TR — age 34 — CAL/TEX RP52

1993	G	IP	H	BB	SO	SB	CS	W	L	SV	ERA
at Home	28	32.1	32	10	21	2	0	0	2	4	2.23
on Road	24	28.1	28	14	14	1	1	0	3	1	4.13
Second Half	24	32.0	42	11	16	1	0	0	5	2	4.78

	BA	OBA	SA	AB	H	2B	3B	HR	RBI	BB	SO
Total	.259	.328	.358	232	60	12	1	3	31	24	35
vs. Left	.324	.441	.500	74	24	4	1	1	13	17	4
vs. Right	.228	.266	.291	158	36	8	0	2	18	7	31
Runners On Base	.270	.333	.357	115	31	8	1	0	28	13	13

FIN/FB   10-YEAR TOTALS (1984-1993)

G	IP	H	BB	SO	SB	CS	W	L	SV	ERA
216	442.0	396	160	304	22	14	26	24	11	3.67
237	444.0	454	154	253	23	14	18	27	17	4.14
239	526.2	523	162	319	22	17	23	32	15	4.07

BA	OBA	SA	AB	H	2B	3B	HR	RBI	BB	SO
.253	.319	.401	3358	850	156	36	90	441	314	557
.266	.336	.410	1492	397	75	20	33	182	162	215
.243	.306	.395	1866	453	81	16	57	259	152	342
.249	.320	.386	1512	376	66	17	36	387	165	247

ROD NICHOLS — BR/TR — age 30 — LA RP4 FIN/FB

1993	G	IP	H	BB	SO	SB	CS	W	L	SV	ERA
at Home	0	0.0	0	0	0	0	0	0	0	0	0.00
on Road	4	6.1	9	2	3	0	0	0	1	0	5.68
Second Half	3	4.1	5	1	2	0	0	0	1	0	6.23

	BA	OBA	SA	AB	H	2B	3B	HR	RBI	BB	SO
Total	.360	.407	.560	25	9	2	0	1	7	2	3
vs. Left	.417	.462	.833	12	5	2	0	1	6	1	0
vs. Right	.308	.357	.308	13	4	0	0	0	1	1	3
Runners On Base	.417	.500	.750	12	5	1	0	1	7	2	2

6-YEAR TOTALS (1988-1993)

G	IP	H	BB	SO	SB	CS	W	L	SV	ERA
48	221.0	242	65	114	25	10	5	16	0	4.36
47	185.0	204	51	97	16	7	6	15	1	4.48
65	302.2	332	86	154	32	13	10	22	0	4.46

BA	OBA	SA	AB	H	2B	3B	HR	RBI	BB	SO
.279	.331	.410	1596	446	66	13	39	211	116	211
.299	.353	.436	752	225	37	6	18	106	59	87
.262	.312	.387	844	221	29	7	21	105	57	124
.282	.334	.426	699	197	28	8	19	191	58	90

DAVID NIED — BR/TR — age 26 — COL SP16 FIN/FB

1993	G	IP	H	BB	SO	SB	CS	W	L	SV	ERA
at Home	7	45.0	47	13	27	4	1	4	3	0	3.60
on Road	9	42.0	52	29	19	8	1	1	6	0	6.86
Second Half	5	22.0	23	10	11	0	1	2	2	0	3.68

	BA	OBA	SA	AB	H	2B	3B	HR	RBI	BB	SO
Total	.296	.369	.430	335	99	19	1	8	52	42	46
vs. Left	.314	.394	.467	169	53	11	0	5	21	25	19
vs. Right	.277	.342	.392	166	46	8	1	3	31	17	27
Runners On Base	.315	.394	.483	149	47	5	1	6	50	24	21

2-YEAR TOTALS (1992-1993)

G	IP	H	BB	SO	SB	CS	W	L	SV	ERA
10	56.0	51	14	40	9	1	5	3	0	3.21
12	54.0	58	33	25	9	1	3	6	0	5.50
11	45.0	33	15	30	2	1	5	2	0	2.40

BA	OBA	SA	AB	H	2B	3B	HR	RBI	BB	SO
.265	.336	.386	412	109	24	1	8	55	47	65
.289	.369	.431	211	61	15	0	5	24	29	24
.239	.300	.338	201	48	9	1	3	31	18	41
.285	.369	.430	172	49	5	1	6	53	27	26

JERRY NIELSEN — BL/TL — age 28 — CAL RP10 FIN/FB

1993	G	IP	H	BB	SO	SB	CS	W	L	SV	ERA
at Home	6	9.1	14	3	6	1	0	0	0	0	9.64
on Road	4	3.0	4	1	2	0	0	0	0	0	3.00
Second Half	2	3.1	4	1	2	0	0	0	0	0	10.80

	BA	OBA	SA	AB	H	2B	3B	HR	RBI	BB	SO
Total	.340	.377	.434	53	18	2	0	1	11	4	8
vs. Left	.320	.320	.400	25	8	2	0	0	4	0	3
vs. Right	.357	.417	.464	28	10	0	0	1	7	4	5
Runners On Base	.500	.464	.542	24	12	1	0	0	10	1	3

2-YEAR TOTALS (1992-1993)

G	IP	H	BB	SO	SB	CS	W	L	SV	ERA
15	19.1	20	11	12	1	1	1	0	0	6.05
15	12.2	15	11	8	2	1	0	0	0	5.68
22	23.0	21	19	14	2	2	1	0	0	5.48

BA	OBA	SA	AB	H	2B	3B	HR	RBI	BB	SO
.285	.387	.382	123	35	4	1	2	17	22	20
.298	.370	.426	47	14	3	0	1	7	6	7
.276	.396	.355	76	21	1	1	1	10	16	13
.290	.377	.339	62	18	3	0	0	15	11	10

RAFAEL NOVOA — BL/TL — age 27 — MIL RP8, SP7 FIN/FB

1993	G	IP	H	BB	SO	SB	CS	W	L	SV	ERA
at Home	7	26.1	32	13	8	2	0	0	0	0	4.78
on Road	8	29.2	26	9	9	1	1	0	2	0	4.25
Second Half	15	56.0	58	22	17	3	1	0	3	0	4.50

	BA	OBA	SA	AB	H	2B	3B	HR	RBI	BB	SO
Total	.267	.343	.429	217	58	14	0	7	33	22	17
vs. Left	.227	.271	.409	44	10	2	0	2	9	0	3
vs. Right	.277	.360	.434	173	48	12	0	5	24	22	14
Runners On Base	.232	.339	.404	99	23	5	0	4	30	16	7

2-YEAR TOTALS (1990-1993)

G	IP	H	BB	SO	SB	CS	W	L	SV	ERA
13	43.2	49	24	20	5	2	0	2	1	5.15
9	31.0	30	11	11	1	1	0	2	0	4.94
22	74.2	79	35	31	6	3	0	4	1	5.06

BA	OBA	SA	AB	H	2B	3B	HR	RBI	BB	SO
.271	.354	.430	291	79	14	1	10	47	35	31
.190	.250	.328	58	11	2	0	2	10	2	8
.292	.379	.455	233	68	12	1	8	37	33	23
.252	.354	.444	135	34	5	0	7	44	22	16

BOB OJEDA — BL/TL — age 37 — CLE SP7, RP2 POW/FB

1993	G	IP	H	BB	SO	SB	CS	W	L	SV	ERA
at Home	4	21.1	22	15	8	1	0	1	1	0	4.22
on Road	5	21.2	26	6	19	1	1	0	0	0	4.57
Second Half	9	43.0	48	21	27	2	1	2	1	0	4.40

	BA	OBA	SA	AB	H	2B	3B	HR	RBI	BB	SO
Total	.289	.363	.470	166	48	13	1	5	22	21	27
vs. Left	.278	.341	.472	36	10	2	0	1	5	4	7
vs. Right	.292	.369	.469	130	38	11	1	4	17	17	20
Runners On Base	.217	.299	.349	83	18	7	0	3	20	11	14

10-YEAR TOTALS (1984-1993)

G	IP	H	BB	SO	SB	CS	W	L	SV	ERA
138	784.1	754	253	498	76	49	46	38	0	3.30
143	752.2	711	276	441	82	47	46	44	1	3.59
144	793.1	745	254	491	70	42	46	42	0	3.41

BA	OBA	SA	AB	H	2B	3B	HR	RBI	BB	SO
.253	.315	.369	5794	1465	269	40	108	584	529	939
.226	.282	.327	1125	254	43	10	17	91	86	251
.259	.323	.379	4669	1211	226	30	91	493	443	688
.242	.312	.347	2403	582	99	19	38	514	257	407

OMAR OLIVARES — BR/TR — age 27 — SL RP49, SP9 FIN/GB

1993	G	IP	H	BB	SO	SB	CS	W	L	SV	ERA
at Home	27	63.0	73	26	37	2	2	2	3	1	4.71
on Road	31	55.2	61	28	26	10	3	3	0	0	3.56
Second Half	38	57.1	62	27	29	4	4	3	1	0	3.92

	BA	OBA	SA	AB	H	2B	3B	HR	RBI	BB	SO
Total	.288	.370	.423	466	134	29	2	10	66	54	63
vs. Left	.276	.361	.448	232	64	18	2	6	42	28	35
vs. Right	.299	.378	.397	234	70	11	0	4	24	26	28
Runners On Base	.280	.365	.393	239	67	11	2	4	60	30	35

4-YEAR TOTALS (1990-1993)

G	IP	H	BB	SO	SB	CS	W	L	SV	ERA
65	293.1	283	97	168	15	19	14	14	2	3.84
62	239.0	233	98	130	21	13	12	6	0	3.73
84	338.2	326	117	201	20	21	19	14	0	3.40

BA	OBA	SA	AB	H	2B	3B	HR	RBI	BB	SO
.259	.329	.384	1992	516	93	10	45	218	195	298
.260	.338	.391	1093	284	57	7	24	127	123	159
.258	.319	.375	899	232	36	3	21	91	72	139
.259	.329	.387	834	216	40	5	19	192	88	123

STEVE ONTIVEROS — BR/TR — age 33 — SEA RP14 POW/GB

1993	G	IP	H	BB	SO	SB	CS	W	L	SV	ERA
at Home	7	10.2	9	6	6	1	0	0	1	0	0.00
on Road	7	7.1	9	0	7	0	0	0	1	0	2.45
Second Half	14	18.0	18	6	13	1	0	0	2	0	1.00

	BA	OBA	SA	AB	H	2B	3B	HR	RBI	BB	SO
Total	.277	.338	.338	65	18	4	0	0	7	6	13
vs. Left	.226	.294	.258	31	7	1	0	0	0	3	9
vs. Right	.324	.378	.412	34	11	3	0	0	7	3	4
Runners On Base	.233	.343	.267	30	7	1	0	0	7	5	5

7-YEAR TOTALS (1985-1993)

G	IP	H	BB	SO	SB	CS	W	L	SV	ERA
77	213.1	174	69	133	16	5	9	13	9	3.16
78	198.0	202	70	115	12	1	9	7	10	4.18
85	209.0	192	67	114	11	3	7	13	12	3.75

BA	OBA	SA	AB	H	2B	3B	HR	RBI	BB	SO
.242	.306	.366	1552	376	60	6	40	175	139	248
.257	.334	.385	782	201	35	4	19	90	91	129
.227	.276	.347	770	175	25	2	21	85	48	119
.232	.298	.333	681	158	23	2	14	149	67	106

AL OSUNA — BR/TL — age 29 — HOU RP44 POW/FB

1993	G	IP	H	BB	SO	SB	CS	W	L	SV	ERA
at Home	17	9.0	7	4	7	0	0	1	0	1	3.00
on Road	27	16.1	10	9	14	0	0	0	1	1	3.31
Second Half	27	14.1	9	8	12	0	0	0	0	0	1.88

	BA	OBA	SA	AB	H	2B	3B	HR	RBI	BB	SO
Total	.200	.301	.318	85	17	1	0	3	10	13	21
vs. Left	.222	.400	.417	36	8	0	0	2	5	11	8
vs. Right	.184	.208	.245	49	9	0	0	1	5	2	13
Runners On Base	.214	.327	.310	42	9	1	0	1	8	9	8

4-YEAR TOTALS (1990-1993)

G	IP	H	BB	SO	SB	CS	W	L	SV	ERA
97	86.2	66	42	60	4	2	11	4	6	3.63
96	93.1	72	61	72	2	0	5	6	8	3.86
111	102.2	78	59	80	2	1	7	4	7	4.03

BA	OBA	SA	AB	H	2B	3B	HR	RBI	BB	SO
.217	.326	.342	635	138	24	2	17	78	103	132
.235	.340	.359	234	55	8	0	7	34	36	52
.207	.318	.332	401	83	16	2	10	44	67	80
.235	.337	.339	307	72	15	1	5	66	52	59

DAVE OTTO — BL/TL — age 30 — PIT RP20, SP8 FIN/GB

1993	G	IP	H	BB	SO	SB	CS	W	L	SV	ERA
at Home	13	30.1	39	14	16	7	2	0	1	0	2.97
on Road	15	37.2	46	14	14	1	0	3	3	0	6.69
Second Half	10	12.1	24	6	4	2	1	1	0	0	8.03

	BA	OBA	SA	AB	H	2B	3B	HR	RBI	BB	SO
Total	.317	.387	.485	268	85	14	2	9	34	28	30
vs. Left	.348	.423	.435	69	24	3	0	1	10	7	7
vs. Right	.307	.374	.503	199	61	11	2	8	24	21	23
Runners On Base	.269	.342	.362	130	35	3	0	3	28	12	11

7-YEAR TOTALS (1987-1993)

G	IP	H	BB	SO	SB	CS	W	L	SV	ERA
36	142.2	168	45	77	13	7	4	9	0	4.48
37	130.2	160	55	48	13	2	6	12	0	6.13
39	143.2	175	47	63	9	6	4	10	0	5.14

BA	OBA	SA	AB	H	2B	3B	HR	RBI	BB	SO
.306	.367	.445	1073	328	51	7	29	147	100	125
.323	.381	.396	217	70	10	0	2	33	18	17
.301	.364	.458	856	258	41	6	27	114	82	108
.302	.372	.448	480	145	15	2	17	135	54	54

DONN PALL — BR/TR — age 32 — CHA/PHI RP47 FIN/GB

1993	G	IP	H	BB	SO	SB	CS	W	L	SV	ERA
at Home	26	34.0	41	9	20	0	0	2	2	1	4.50
on Road	21	42.1	36	5	20	4	0	1	1	0	1.91
Second Half	27	37.2	46	7	19	1	0	1	1	0	3.58

	BA	OBA	SA	AB	H	2B	3B	HR	RBI	BB	SO
Total	.260	.297	.358	296	77	11	0	6	37	14	40
vs. Left	.258	.296	.351	151	39	8	0	2	18	8	18
vs. Right	.262	.299	.366	145	38	3	0	4	19	6	22
Runners On Base	.298	.336	.359	131	39	5	0	1	32	8	17

6-YEAR TOTALS (1988-1993)

G	IP	H	BB	SO	SB	CS	W	L	SV	ERA
135	204.2	212	55	121	19	5	12	7	6	3.91
128	207.1	195	57	99	13	4	10	12	4	2.91
136	228.1	244	64	121	17	5	13	11	6	3.86

BA	OBA	SA	AB	H	2B	3B	HR	RBI	BB	SO
.260	.316	.383	1565	407	66	5	39	204	112	220
.261	.317	.366	681	178	30	4	11	78	54	100
.259	.314	.397	884	229	36	1	28	126	58	120
.267	.326	.379	744	199	33	1	16	181	63	98

JEFF PARRETT — BR/TR — age 33 — COL RP34, SP6 POW/FB

1993	G	IP	H	BB	SO	SB	CS	W	L	SV	ERA
at Home	20	43.2	55	30	38	9	1	3	2	0	6.18
on Road	20	30.0	23	15	28	2	1	0	1	1	4.20
Second Half	6	19.0	19	10	17	0	1	1	1	0	5.68

	BA	OBA	SA	AB	H	2B	3B	HR	RBI	BB	SO
Total	.274	.371	.389	285	78	13	1	6	51	45	66
vs. Left	.295	.383	.362	149	44	7	0	1	28	21	35
vs. Right	.250	.358	.419	136	34	6	1	5	23	24	31
Runners On Base	.312	.417	.426	141	44	7	0	3	48	27	31

8-YEAR TOTALS (1986-1993)

G	IP	H	BB	SO	SB	CS	W	L	SV	ERA
190	315.0	288	163	245	33	10	25	17	13	4.06
191	266.2	249	123	236	32	15	24	16	9	3.65
167	265.1	242	126	226	23	11	28	16	10	3.70

BA	OBA	SA	AB	H	2B	3B	HR	RBI	BB	SO
.250	.336	.382	2152	537	101	16	51	305	286	481
.259	.357	.367	1074	278	48	10	16	156	167	219
.240	.314	.398	1078	259	53	6	35	149	119	262
.254	.349	.385	1014	258	44	11	22	276	157	225

KEN PATTERSON — BL/TL — age 30 — CAL RP46 POW/GB

1993	G	IP	H	BB	SO	SB	CS	W	L	SV	ERA
at Home	26	34.2	28	21	22	2	2	1	0	1	4.93
on Road	20	24.1	26	14	13	5	1	0	1	0	4.07
Second Half	26	31.0	22	16	25	5	2	1	0	1	2.32

	BA	OBA	SA	AB	H	2B	3B	HR	RBI	BB	SO
Total	.249	.352	.387	217	54	9	0	7	28	35	36
vs. Left	.273	.385	.442	77	21	4	0	3	13	14	10
vs. Right	.236	.333	.357	140	33	5	0	4	15	21	26
Runners On Base	.242	.372	.414	99	24	5	0	5	26	21	16

6-YEAR TOTALS (1988-1993)

G	IP	H	BB	SO	SB	CS	W	L	SV	ERA
112	161.1	145	81	101	11	6	6	4	4	4.02
111	155.2	145	85	81	14	8	8	4	1	3.76
125	164.0	148	77	101	10	8	8	5	4	3.24

BA	OBA	SA	AB	H	2B	3B	HR	RBI	BB	SO
.248	.341	.402	1168	290	48	9	38	172	166	182
.261	.356	.378	360	94	12	3	8	57	55	55
.243	.334	.413	808	196	36	6	30	115	111	127
.227	.328	.379	554	126	16	4	20	154	87	84

MARK PETKOVSEK — BR/TR — age 29 — PIT RP26 FIN/GB

1993	G	IP	H	BB	SO	SB	CS	W	L	SV	ERA
at Home	13	18.0	18	6	4	3	0	1	0	0	4.50
on Road	13	14.1	25	3	10	4	0	2	0	0	10.05
Second Half	17	20.1	29	6	8	5	0	2	0	0	8.85

	BA	OBA	SA	AB	H	2B	3B	HR	RBI	BB	SO
Total	.328	.369	.603	131	43	7	4	7	31	9	14
vs. Left	.409	.447	.705	44	18	3	2	2	8	3	6
vs. Right	.287	.330	.552	87	25	4	2	5	23	6	8
Runners On Base	.357	.410	.571	70	25	4	1	3	27	7	7

2-YEAR TOTALS (1991-1993)

G	IP	H	BB	SO	SB	CS	W	L	SV	ERA
16	22.2	29	6	7	3	0	1	0	0	6.75
14	19.0	35	5	13	5	0	2	1	0	10.89
17	20.1	29	6	8	5	0	2	0	0	8.85

BA	OBA	SA	AB	H	2B	3B	HR	RBI	BB	SO
.358	.397	.642	179	64	10	4	11	47	13	20
.431	.479	.769	65	28	6	2	4	15	6	6
.316	.350	.570	114	36	4	2	7	32	7	14
.409	.452	.656	93	38	6	1	5	41	9	8

DAN PLESAC — BL/TL — age 32 — CHN RP57 POW/FB

1993	G	IP	H	BB	SO	SB	CS	W	L	SV	ERA
at Home	28	32.1	40	13	29	0	0	1	0	0	5.85
on Road	29	30.1	34	8	18	3	2	1	0	0	3.56
Second Half	33	25.2	31	12	21	0	0	2	1	0	4.91

	BA	OBA	SA	AB	H	2B	3B	HR	RBI	BB	SO
Total	.298	.349	.472	248	74	9	2	10	44	21	47
vs. Left	.258	.305	.393	89	23	4	1	2	12	6	29
vs. Right	.321	.373	.516	159	51	5	1	8	32	15	18
Runners On Base	.318	.381	.527	110	35	3	1	6	40	13	18

8-YEAR TOTALS (1986-1993)

G	IP	H	BB	SO	SB	CS	W	L	SV	ERA
204	286.1	272	98	260	19	8	15	16	62	3.93
218	300.2	262	109	235	13	11	16	22	71	2.84
214	302.2	280	113	245	19	8	17	22	57	3.39

BA	OBA	SA	AB	H	2B	3B	HR	RBI	BB	SO
.244	.309	.368	2191	534	91	11	53	318	207	495
.232	.295	.362	508	118	20	5	12	86	45	135
.247	.313	.370	1683	416	71	6	41	232	162	360
.252	.313	.388	1092	275	50	6	29	294	102	233

JIM POOLE — BL/TL — age 28 — BAL RP55 FIN/FB

1993	G	IP	H	BB	SO	SB	CS	W	L	SV	ERA
at Home	30	27.2	18	11	15	1	0	2	0	0	2.28
on Road	25	22.2	12	10	14	1	1	0	1	2	1.99
Second Half	29	27.0	16	11	9	2	1	1	1	2	2.00

	BA	OBA	SA	AB	H	2B	3B	HR	RBI	BB	SO
Total	.175	.263	.240	171	30	5	0	2	20	21	29
vs. Left	.179	.235	.218	78	14	3	0	0	9	6	15
vs. Right	.172	.284	.258	93	16	2	0	2	11	15	14
Runners On Base	.167	.267	.233	90	15	3	0	1	19	13	16

4-YEAR TOTALS (1990-1993)

G	IP	H	BB	SO	SB	CS	W	L	SV	ERA
59	66.1	36	23	43	1	1	5	1	1	1.90
47	40.0	33	19	33	3	2	0	2	2	3.15
69	74.0	43	29	48	4	3	4	3	2	2.31

BA	OBA	SA	AB	H	2B	3B	HR	RBI	BB	SO
.186	.266	.265	370	69	11	0	6	46	42	76
.188	.220	.267	165	31	4	0	3	24	7	37
.185	.299	.263	205	38	7	0	3	22	35	39
.196	.285	.283	184	36	4	0	4	44	25	42

DENNIS POWELL — BR/TL — age 31 — SEA RP31, SP2 POW/GB

1993	G	IP	H	BB	SO	SB	CS	W	L	SV	ERA
at Home	19	25.1	23	8	18	1	3	0	0	0	4.26
on Road	14	22.1	19	16	14	3	0	0	0	0	4.03
Second Half	13	12.1	10	9	7	2	2	0	0	0	4.38

	BA	OBA	SA	AB	H	2B	3B	HR	RBI	BB	SO
Total	.255	.349	.424	165	42	7	0	7	23	24	32
vs. Left	.156	.214	.234	64	10	2	0	1	7	5	17
vs. Right	.317	.426	.545	101	32	5	0	6	16	19	15
Runners On Base	.281	.407	.469	64	18	3	0	6	19	14	9

8-YEAR TOTALS (1985-1993)

G	IP	H	BB	SO	SB	CS	W	L	SV	ERA
99	148.2	162	71	92	8	5	3	9	1	5.02
108	191.1	198	88	107	13	10	8	13	2	4.89
106	188.0	205	81	99	9	9	6	12	2	4.79

BA	OBA	SA	AB	H	2B	3B	HR	RBI	BB	SO
.279	.360	.419	1292	360	64	6	35	185	159	199
.229	.288	.344	407	93	16	2	9	65	32	83
.302	.391	.453	885	267	48	4	26	120	127	116
.273	.356	.405	619	169	35	4	13	163	78	82

TED POWER — BR/TR — age 39 — CLE/SEA RP45 FIN/FB

1993	G	IP	H	BB	SO	SB	CS	W	L	SV	ERA
at Home	25	19.1	27	8	8	0	1	0	1	8	6.98
on Road	20	26.0	30	9	19	1	0	2	3	5	4.15
Second Half	25	25.1	27	9	16	0	1	2	2	13	3.91

	BA	OBA	SA	AB	H	2B	3B	HR	RBI	BB	SO
Total	.310	.365	.429	184	57	11	1	3	29	17	27
vs. Left	.314	.392	.471	70	22	3	1	2	11	9	11
vs. Right	.307	.347	.404	114	35	8	0	1	18	8	16
Runners On Base	.292	.358	.396	106	31	6	0	1	27	12	16

10-YEAR TOTALS (1984-1993)

G	IP	H	BB	SO	SB	CS	W	L	SV	ERA
267	504.1	506	189	307	41	21	31	23	38	3.80
231	496.2	478	184	315	44	14	30	36	30	3.91
269	577.0	560	207	346	54	21	39	35	44	3.90

BA	OBA	SA	AB	H	2B	3B	HR	RBI	BB	SO
.260	.325	.385	3781	984	188	18	83	487	373	622
.273	.350	.405	1791	489	99	13	37	222	217	283
.249	.302	.368	1990	495	89	5	46	265	156	339
.261	.335	.392	1768	462	81	9	44	448	213	310

PAUL QUANTRILL — BL/TR — age 26 — BOS RP35, SP14 FIN/FB

1993	G	IP	H	BB	SO	SB	CS	W	L	SV	ERA
at Home	26	83.1	90	27	35	7	1	4	6	1	3.67
on Road	23	54.2	61	17	31	5	0	2	6	0	4.28
Second Half	26	66.2	75	28	30	7	1	3	7	1	4.86

	BA	OBA	SA	AB	H	2B	3B	HR	RBI	BB	SO
Total	.279	.334	.426	542	151	29	6	13	62	44	66
vs. Left	.273	.350	.445	245	67	15	3	7	24	27	29
vs. Right	.283	.320	.411	297	84	14	3	6	38	17	37
Runners On Base	.284	.371	.409	232	66	8	3	5	54	32	28

2-YEAR TOTALS (1992-1993)

G	IP	H	BB	SO	SB	CS	W	L	SV	ERA
42	116.0	131	33	48	9	2	5	7	2	3.34
34	71.1	75	26	42	6	1	3	8	0	3.66
53	116.0	130	43	54	10	3	5	10	2	3.72

BA	OBA	SA	AB	H	2B	3B	HR	RBI	BB	SO
.281	.335	.405	733	206	35	7	14	75	59	90
.270	.346	.418	318	86	18	4	7	29	34	40
.289	.327	.395	415	120	17	3	7	46	25	50
.296	.375	.395	324	96	11	3	5	66	42	36

PAT RAPP — BR/TR — age 27 — FLO SP16 FIN/GB

1993	G	IP	H	BB	SO	SB	CS	W	L	SV	ERA
at Home	7	42.2	49	19	28	0	3	4	1	0	4.64
on Road	9	51.1	52	20	29	3	3	0	7	0	3.51
Second Half	16	94.0	101	39	57	3	6	4	6	0	4.02

	BA	OBA	SA	AB	H	2B	3B	HR	RBI	BB	SO
Total	.281	.351	.421	359	101	21	4	7	44	39	57
vs. Left	.269	.363	.406	175	47	11	2	3	20	26	17
vs. Right	.293	.340	.435	184	54	10	2	4	24	13	40
Runners On Base	.275	.342	.401	167	46	10	2	3	40	18	30

2-YEAR TOTALS (1992-1993)

G	IP	H	BB	SO	SB	CS	W	L	SV	ERA
8	44.2	50	20	28	0	4	4	1	0	4.43
11	59.1	59	25	32	7	3	0	7	0	4.25
19	104.0	109	45	60	7	7	4	8	0	4.33

BA	OBA	SA	AB	H	2B	3B	HR	RBI	BB	SO
.277	.353	.417	393	109	24	5	7	51	45	60
.273	.370	.412	194	53	12	3	3	25	30	19
.281	.335	.422	199	56	12	2	4	26	15	41
.275	.346	.401	182	50	10	2	3	47	21	31

DENNIS RASMUSSEN — BL/TL — age 35 — KC RP5, SP4 FIN/FB

1993	G	IP	H	BB	SO	SB	CS	W	L	SV	ERA
at Home	3	14.2	18	7	4	0	4	1	0	0	6.14
on Road	6	14.1	22	7	8	1	0	0	2	0	8.79
Second Half	5	23.2	32	10	8	1	4	1	1	0	7.23

	BA	OBA	SA	AB	H	2B	3B	HR	RBI	BB	SO
Total	.328	.399	.516	122	40	7	2	4	22	14	12
vs. Left	.316	.333	.368	19	6	1	0	0	3	1	2
vs. Right	.330	.410	.544	103	34	6	2	4	19	13	10
Runners On Base	.356	.435	.576	59	21	2	1	3	21	9	8

10-YEAR TOTALS (1984-1993)

G	IP	H	BB	SO	SB	CS	W	L	SV	ERA
109	653.0	613	238	398	38	47	47	34	0	3.94
138	784.0	788	268	418	64	39	44	42	0	4.30
135	785.1	769	273	441	57	44	55	45	0	4.25

BA	OBA	SA	AB	H	2B	3B	HR	RBI	BB	SO
.257	.320	.408	5452	1401	239	37	171	620	506	816
.262	.318	.401	931	244	32	8	27	116	75	145
.256	.321	.410	4521	1157	207	29	144	504	431	671
.273	.332	.424	2132	583	90	13	68	517	198	330

RICK REED — BR/TR — age 30 — KC/TEX RP3 FIN/GB

1993	G	IP	H	BB	SO	SB	CS	W	L	SV	ERA
at Home	2	5.1	7	1	5	0	1	1	0	0	6.75
on Road	1	2.1	5	1	0	0	0	0	0	0	3.86
Second Half	3	7.2	12	2	5	0	1	1	0	0	5.87

	BA	OBA	SA	AB	H	2B	3B	HR	RBI	BB	SO
Total	.375	.444	.563	32	12	3	0	1	4	2	5
vs. Left	.222	.364	.333	9	2	1	0	0	2	1	1
vs. Right	.435	.480	.652	23	10	2	0	1	2	1	4
Runners On Base	.375	.412	.563	16	6	3	0	0	3	0	3

6-YEAR TOTALS (1988-1993)

G	IP	H	BB	SO	SB	CS	W	L	SV	ERA
26	111.2	123	20	53	14	2	4	6	0	3.87
27	121.0	136	28	70	9	3	4	8	1	4.98
42	186.2	215	40	95	22	4	6	11	0	4.82

BA	OBA	SA	AB	H	2B	3B	HR	RBI	BB	SO
.282	.322	.426	918	259	52	4	24	109	48	123
.237	.285	.375	459	109	27	3	10	56	31	59
.327	.359	.477	459	150	25	1	14	53	17	64
.306	.352	.460	363	111	28	2	8	93	23	45

SHANE REYNOLDS — BR/TR — age 26 — HOU RP4, SP1 POW/GB

1993	G	IP	H	BB	SO	SB	CS	W	L	SV	ERA
at Home	1	0.1	1	0	0	0	0	0	0	0	0.00
on Road	4	10.2	10	6	10	0	0	0	0	0	0.84
Second Half	5	11.0	11	6	10	0	0	0	0	0	0.82

	BA	OBA	SA	AB	H	2B	3B	HR	RBI	BB	SO
Total	.256	.347	.279	43	11	1	0	0	4	6	10
vs. Left	.292	.393	.292	24	7	0	0	0	2	4	5
vs. Right	.211	.286	.263	19	4	1	0	0	2	2	5
Runners On Base	.208	.345	.208	24	5	0	0	0	4	5	7

2-YEAR TOTALS (1992-1993)

G	IP	H	BB	SO	SB	CS	W	L	SV	ERA
3	7.0	15	3	3	4	0	0	1	0	11.57
10	29.1	38	9	17	2	1	1	2	0	3.68
13	36.1	53	12	20	6	1	1	3	0	5.20

BA	OBA	SA	AB	H	2B	3B	HR	RBI	BB	SO
.349	.394	.507	152	53	12	3	2	23	12	20
.379	.433	.552	87	33	8	2	1	15	9	11
.308	.338	.446	65	20	4	1	1	8	3	9
.284	.333	.409	88	25	6	1	1	22	7	13

ARTHUR LEE RHODES — BL/TL — age 25 — BAL SP17 POW/FB

1993	G	IP	H	BB	SO	SB	CS	W	L	SV	ERA
at Home	7	36.2	37	23	23	5	2	2	4	0	7.36
on Road	10	49.0	54	26	26	0	2	3	2	0	5.88
Second Half	11	60.2	54	37	31	1	1	4	4	0	5.34

	BA	OBA	SA	AB	H	2B	3B	HR	RBI	BB	SO
Total	.274	.366	.509	332	91	20	5	16	55	49	49
vs. Left	.300	.404	.475	40	12	4	0	1	5	7	2
vs. Right	.271	.361	.514	292	79	16	5	15	50	42	47
Runners On Base	.299	.385	.489	137	41	9	1	5	44	20	19

3-YEAR TOTALS (1991-1993)

G	IP	H	BB	SO	SB	CS	W	L	SV	ERA
20	109.1	110	59	83	9	7	6	9	0	5.84
20	106.2	115	51	66	7	3	6	5	0	5.15
34	191.0	188	98	131	12	7	11	12	0	4.99

BA	OBA	SA	AB	H	2B	3B	HR	RBI	BB	SO
.272	.356	.449	827	225	48	10	26	113	110	149
.255	.364	.330	94	24	4	0	1	8	16	15
.274	.355	.464	733	201	44	10	25	105	94	134
.301	.379	.460	346	104	22	3	9	96	47	63

DAVE RIGHETTI — BL/TL — age 36 — SF RP51 FIN/FB

1993	G	IP	H	BB	SO	SB	CS	W	L	SV	ERA
at Home	24	22.2	21	11	15	1	2	0	1	1	3.57
on Road	27	24.2	37	6	16	0	2	1	0	0	7.66
Second Half	24	20.1	31	5	15	0	0	0	0	1	8.85

	BA	OBA	SA	AB	H	2B	3B	HR	RBI	BB	SO
Total	.305	.365	.532	190	58	6	2	11	31	17	31
vs. Left	.288	.311	.576	59	17	3	1	4	12	2	11
vs. Right	.313	.388	.511	131	41	3	1	7	19	15	20
Runners On Base	.286	.323	.516	91	26	3	0	6	26	5	10

10-YEAR TOTALS (1984-1993)

G	IP	H	BB	SO	SB	CS	W	L	SV	ERA
304	415.0	353	143	349	25	11	29	20	128	2.67
302	396.1	413	188	286	19	13	17	33	123	4.04
319	420.1	385	147	346	17	7	19	28	142	2.95

BA	OBA	SA	AB	H	2B	3B	HR	RBI	BB	SO
.250	.324	.352	3059	766	111	13	58	385	331	635
.240	.316	.351	761	183	29	5	15	109	83	170
.254	.326	.352	2298	583	82	8	43	276	248	465
.263	.338	.366	1553	409	60	6	29	356	184	311

BILL RISLEY — BR/TR — age 27 — MON RP2 POW/FB

1993	G	IP	H	BB	SO	SB	CS	W	L	SV	ERA
at Home	1	1.0	1	1	1	0	0	0	0	0	0.00
on Road	1	2.0	1	1	1	0	0	0	0	0	9.00
Second Half	0	0.0	0	0	0	0	0	0	0	0	0.00

	BA	OBA	SA	AB	H	2B	3B	HR	RBI	BB	SO
Total	.200	.385	.500	10	2	0	0	1	2	2	2
vs. Left	.333	.500	.833	6	2	0	0	1	2	2	2
vs. Right	.000	.200	.000	4	0	0	0	0	0	0	0
Runners On Base	.400	.500	1.000	5	2	0	0	1	2	0	1

2-YEAR TOTALS (1992-1993)

G	IP	H	BB	SO	SB	CS	W	L	SV	ERA
1	1.0	1	1	1	0	0	0	0	0	0.00
2	7.0	5	2	3	2	0	1	0	0	3.86
1	5.0	4	1	2	2	0	1	0	0	1.80

BA	OBA	SA	AB	H	2B	3B	HR	RBI	BB	SO
.222	.323	.370	27	6	1	0	1	3	3	4
.250	.348	.400	20	5	1	0	1	3	3	3
.143	.250	.286	7	1	0	0	0	0	0	1
.214	.267	.429	14	3	0	0	1	3	0	2

RICH RODRIGUEZ — BL/TL — age 31 — SD/FLO RP70 FIN/GB

1993	G	IP	H	BB	SO	SB	CS	W	L	SV	ERA
at Home	34	36.0	37	16	22	2	1	2	1	2	3.50
on Road	36	40.0	36	17	21	3	1	0	3	1	4.05
Second Half	34	44.1	36	24	21	2	0	0	1	1	3.86

	BA	OBA	SA	AB	H	2B	3B	HR	RBI	BB	SO
Total	.251	.331	.395	291	73	10	1	10	40	33	43
vs. Left	.263	.348	.404	99	26	3	1	3	13	12	7
vs. Right	.245	.322	.391	192	47	7	0	7	27	21	36
Runners On Base	.271	.358	.444	133	36	5	0	6	36	17	18

4-YEAR TOTALS (1990-1993)

G	IP	H	BB	SO	SB	CS	W	L	SV	ERA
118	152.2	147	67	95	7	6	8	3	2	3.07
109	142.0	121	55	74	14	7	4	6	2	3.04
131	170.0	149	66	103	12	6	5	3	2	3.02

BA	OBA	SA	AB	H	2B	3B	HR	RBI	BB	SO
.246	.322	.359	1090	268	45	3	24	129	122	169
.238	.324	.342	365	87	12	1	8	45	46	53
.250	.321	.367	725	181	33	2	16	84	76	116
.250	.330	.359	513	128	24	1	10	115	63	68

SCOTT RUSKIN — BR/TL — age 31 — CIN RP4 POW/FB

1993	G	IP	H	BB	SO	SB	CS	W	L	SV	ERA
at Home	2	0.1	1	1	0	0	0	0	0	0	27.00
on Road	2	0.2	2	1	0	0	0	0	0	0	13.50
Second Half	4	1.0	3	2	0	0	0	0	0	0	18.00

	BA	OBA	SA	AB	H	2B	3B	HR	RBI	BB	SO
Total	.500	.625	1.167	6	3	1	0	1	4	2	0
vs. Left	.500	.500	2.000	2	1	0	0	1	1	0	0
vs. Right	.500	.667	.750	4	2	1	0	0	3	2	0
Runners On Base	.500	.667	.500	2	1	0	0	0	3	1	0

4-YEAR TOTALS (1990-1993)

G	IP	H	BB	SO	SB	CS	W	L	SV	ERA
89	96.0	86	41	71	16	6	7	4	4	2.34
103	97.2	105	49	75	16	2	4	5	4	5.53
103	105.2	109	52	82	15	3	5	5	1	4.17

BA	OBA	SA	AB	H	2B	3B	HR	RBI	BB	SO
.260	.343	.379	736	191	37	3	15	94	90	146
.273	.347	.378	275	75	12	1	5	38	32	67
.252	.341	.380	461	116	25	2	10	56	58	79
.284	.375	.431	341	97	18	1	10	89	48	63

KEN RYAN — BR/TR — age 26 — BOS RP47 POW/GB

1993	G	IP	H	BB	SO	SB	CS	W	L	SV	ERA
at Home	23	24.1	26	13	23	2	1	3	2	0	5.55
on Road	24	25.2	17	16	26	1	1	4	0	1	1.75
Second Half	26	27.2	21	16	33	1	1	6	2	1	3.58

	BA	OBA	SA	AB	H	2B	3B	HR	RBI	BB	SO
Total	.235	.342	.333	183	43	10	1	2	29	29	49
vs. Left	.235	.370	.309	81	19	6	0	1	11	18	29
vs. Right	.235	.319	.353	102	24	4	1	2	18	11	20
Runners On Base	.261	.374	.359	92	24	7	1	0	27	16	21

2-YEAR TOTALS (1992-1993)

G	IP	H	BB	SO	SB	CS	W	L	SV	ERA
27	28.0	27	14	25	2	1	3	2	1	4.82
27	29.0	20	20	29	1	1	4	0	1	3.10
33	34.2	25	21	38	1	1	6	2	2	4.15

BA	OBA	SA	AB	H	2B	3B	HR	RBI	BB	SO
.228	.339	.345	206	47	10	1	4	34	34	54
.216	.358	.284	88	19	6	0	1	11	20	31
.237	.324	.390	118	28	4	1	4	23	14	23
.260	.369	.375	104	27	7	1	1	31	18	22

NOLAN RYAN — BR/TR — age 47 — TEX SP13 POW/GB

1993	G	IP	H	BB	SO	SB	CS	W	L	SV	ERA
at Home	7	39.1	33	21	31	5	2	4	2	0	4.12
on Road	6	27.0	21	19	15	8	2	1	3	0	6.00
Second Half	10	52.1	35	32	36	13	4	4	3	0	4.99

	BA	OBA	SA	AB	H	2B	3B	HR	RBI	BB	SO
Total	.220	.329	.341	246	54	13	1	5	39	40	46
vs. Left	.188	.339	.278	133	25	4	1	2	20	30	22
vs. Right	.257	.315	.416	113	29	9	0	3	19	10	24
Runners On Base	.252	.339	.393	107	27	4	1	3	37	15	18

10-YEAR TOTALS (1984-1993)

G	IP	H	BB	SO	SB	CS	W	L	SV	ERA
161	1075.1	745	412	1197	162	39	67	46	0	3.03
130	790.1	655	360	840	147	39	38	51	0	3.81
158	1019.1	751	436	1115	168	36	55	53	0	3.28

BA	OBA	SA	AB	H	2B	3B	HR	RBI	BB	SO
.207	.291	.315	6773	1400	254	44	131	688	772	2037
.207	.296	.303	3476	720	109	30	55	320	440	966
.206	.287	.328	3297	680	145	14	76	368	332	1071
.232	.317	.349	2633	610	109	13	58	615	323	692

BRET SABERHAGEN — BR/TR — age 30 — NYN SP19 FIN/FB

1993	G	IP	H	BB	SO	SB	CS	W	L	SV	ERA
at Home	8	59.2	47	6	41	3	4	3	3	0	2.41
on Road	11	79.2	84	11	52	6	3	4	4	0	3.95
Second Half	4	30.1	26	5	14	2	0	3	0	0	3.56

	BA	OBA	SA	AB	H	2B	3B	HR	RBI	BB	SO
Total	.250	.275	.366	524	131	20	4	11	50	17	93
vs. Left	.264	.298	.412	250	66	8	4	7	29	11	49
vs. Right	.237	.253	.325	274	65	12	0	4	21	6	44
Runners On Base	.269	.295	.417	175	47	11	0	5	44	9	31

10-YEAR TOTALS (1984-1993)

G	IP	H	BB	SO	SB	CS	W	L	SV	ERA
140	969.2	880	166	643	51	38	58	40	1	2.99
148	927.2	886	209	623	36	32	62	50	0	3.49
139	874.0	820	171	615	44	37	59	39	1	3.37

BA	OBA	SA	AB	H	2B	3B	HR	RBI	BB	SO
.247	.286	.367	7150	1766	299	66	143	666	375	1266
.238	.284	.364	3762	895	140	41	84	356	244	744
.257	.288	.371	3388	871	159	25	59	310	131	522
.252	.295	.377	2678	674	131	26	51	574	177	451

BILL SAMPEN — BR/TR — age 31 — KC RP18 FIN/GB

1993	G	IP	H	BB	SO	SB	CS	W	L	SV	ERA
at Home	8	12.1	16	4	6	4	0	0	1	0	5.11
on Road	10	6.0	9	5	3	0	2	1	1	0	7.50
Second Half	3	5.0	11	2	2	1	0	0	1	0	9.00

	BA	OBA	SA	AB	H	2B	3B	HR	RBI	BB	SO
Total	.338	.437	.446	74	25	3	1	1	14	9	9
vs. Left	.514	.571	.649	37	19	2	0	1	9	3	4
vs. Right	.162	.311	.243	37	6	1	1	0	5	6	5
Runners On Base	.361	.465	.472	36	13	2	1	0	13	3	4

4-YEAR TOTALS (1990-1993)

G	IP	H	BB	SO	SB	CS	W	L	SV	ERA
81	130.1	139	55	89	22	6	11	8	0	3.25
91	153.2	159	65	78	28	9	13	12	2	3.87
75	132.2	150	50	72	29	7	11	13	1	3.66

BA	OBA	SA	AB	H	2B	3B	HR	RBI	BB	SO
.276	.352	.396	1080	298	47	4	25	145	120	167
.285	.371	.405	533	152	24	2	12	75	74	66
.267	.333	.388	547	146	23	2	13	70	46	101
.274	.347	.382	518	142	23	3	9	129	55	65

MO SANFORD — BR/TR — age 28 — COL SP6, RP5 POW/FB

1993	G	IP	H	BB	SO	SB	CS	W	L	SV	ERA
at Home	6	13.0	14	10	14	3	1	0	1	0	5.54
on Road	5	22.2	23	17	22	5	0	1	1	0	5.16
Second Half	11	35.2	37	27	36	8	1	1	2	0	5.30

	BA	OBA	SA	AB	H	2B	3B	HR	RBI	BB	SO
Total	.278	.395	.459	133	37	6	3	4	23	27	36
vs. Left	.349	.481	.571	63	22	4	2	2	14	17	13
vs. Right	.214	.309	.357	70	15	2	1	2	9	10	23
Runners On Base	.274	.360	.493	73	20	3	2	3	22	11	20

2-YEAR TOTALS (1991-1993)

G	IP	H	BB	SO	SB	CS	W	L	SV	ERA
9	28.0	26	19	32	4	1	0	2	0	5.79
7	35.2	30	23	35	8	0	2	2	0	3.79
16	63.2	56	42	67	12	1	2	4	0	4.66

BA	OBA	SA	AB	H	2B	3B	HR	RBI	BB	SO
.238	.354	.387	235	56	8	3	7	35	42	67
.281	.421	.446	121	34	4	2	4	20	30	26
.193	.273	.325	114	22	4	1	3	15	12	41
.265	.358	.436	117	31	4	2	4	32	18	37

BOB SCANLAN — BR/TR — age 28 — CHN RP70 FIN/GB

1993	G	IP	H	BB	SO	SB	CS	W	L	SV	ERA
at Home	36	35.2	39	15	23	3	2	2	4	0	5.80
on Road	34	39.2	40	13	21	2	2	2	1	0	3.40
Second Half	31	37.0	45	14	21	3	3	1		0	5.35

	BA	OBA	SA	AB	H	2B	3B	HR	RBI	BB	SO
Total	.278	.343	.444	284	79	25	2	6	48	28	44
vs. Left	.305	.368	.466	118	36	11	1	2	23	13	22
vs. Right	.259	.324	.428	166	43	14	1	4	25	15	22
Runners On Base	.277	.330	.471	155	43	13	1	1	47	14	19

3-YEAR TOTALS (1991-1993)

G	IP	H	BB	SO	SB	CS	W	L	SV	ERA
89	135.1	151	49	65	10	9	8	11	4	4.72
90	138.1	118	49	65	6	5	6	8	11	2.80
96	136.2	135	47	64	10	6	9	8	12	4.02

BA	OBA	SA	AB	H	2B	3B	HR	RBI	BB	SO
.261	.325	.375	1031	269	57	8	15	136	98	130
.260	.332	.382	503	131	30	5	7	70	54	62
.261	.319	.369	528	138	27	3	8	66	44	68
.267	.327	.394	505	135	27	5	9	130	49	62

MIKE SCHOOLER — BR/TR — age 32 — TEX RP17 POW/GB

1993	G	IP	H	BB	SO	SB	CS	W	L	SV	ERA
at Home	6	8.1	11	3	4	2	1	0	0	0	5.40
on Road	11	16.0	19	7	12	3	0	3	0	0	5.63
Second Half	13	18.1	24	10	11	2	0	3	0	0	6.38

	BA	OBA	SA	AB	H	2B	3B	HR	RBI	BB	SO
Total	.303	.367	.485	99	30	7	1	3	17	10	16
vs. Left	.382	.462	.559	34	13	1	1	1	8	5	4
vs. Right	.262	.314	.446	65	17	6	0	2	9	5	12
Runners On Base	.237	.286	.373	59	14	5	0	1	15	4	12

6-YEAR TOTALS (1988-1993)

G	IP	H	BB	SO	SB	CS	W	L	SV	ERA
136	150.2	143	42	129	17	4	7	14	54	3.29
124	141.0	140	61	119	18	2	8	15	44	3.70
147	169.1	174	58	149	20	5	12	20	46	3.99

BA	OBA	SA	AB	H	2B	3B	HR	RBI	BB	SO
.253	.316	.363	1120	283	41	4	23	159	103	248
.262	.343	.390	523	137	22	6	11	86	66	103
.245	.290	.340	597	146	19	1	12	73	37	145
.277	.337	.398	566	157	25	2	13	149	53	120

PETE SCHOUREK — BL/TL — age 25 — NYN RP23, SP18 FIN/FB

1993	G	IP	H	BB	SO	SB	CS	W	L	SV	ERA
at Home	20	62.2	89	19	32	5	1	1	8	0	6.46
on Road	21	65.2	79	26	40	5	3	4	4	0	5.48
Second Half	26	61.0	74	22	32	4	1	3	3	0	5.90

	BA	OBA	SA	AB	H	2B	3B	HR	RBI	BB	SO
Total	.319	.370	.486	527	168	41	4	13	83	45	72
vs. Left	.315	.368	.419	124	39	6	2	1	15	11	17
vs. Right	.320	.371	.506	403	129	35	2	12	68	34	55
Runners On Base	.361	.422	.594	219	79	24	3	7	77	27	34

3-YEAR TOTALS (1991-1993)

G	IP	H	BB	SO	SB	CS	W	L	SV	ERA
51	202.0	214	75	108	18	6	10	12	0	4.10
47	148.2	173	57	91	19	3	6	12	0	5.39
59	221.0	227	79	120	23	4	11	12	0	4.52

BA	OBA	SA	AB	H	2B	3B	HR	RBI	BB	SO
.280	.342	.425	1382	387	83	15	29	188	132	199
.280	.348	.390	354	99	14	5	5	41	40	49
.280	.340	.437	1028	288	69	10	24	147	92	150
.306	.376	.456	599	183	40	7	12	171	73	94

TIM SCOTT — BR/TR — age 28 — SD/MON RP56 POW/FB

1993	G	IP	H	BB	SO	SB	CS	W	L	SV	ERA
at Home	27	37.1	32	14	29	9	1	4	1	1	2.41
on Road	29	34.1	37	20	36	9	1	3	1	0	3.67
Second Half	29	32.0	29	16	34	8	1	5	1	1	2.81

	BA	OBA	SA	AB	H	2B	3B	HR	RBI	BB	SO
Total	.253	.342	.359	273	69	13	2	4	35	34	65
vs. Left	.178	.289	.217	129	23	2	0	1	13	20	39
vs. Right	.319	.390	.486	144	46	11	2	3	22	14	26
Runners On Base	.230	.323	.295	139	32	4	1	1	32	20	34

3-YEAR TOTALS (1991-1993)

G	IP	H	BB	SO	SB	CS	W	L	SV	ERA
44	58.0	51	23	48	12	2	8	2	1	3.41
48	52.1	59	32	48	12	2	3	1	0	4.30
56	62.1	60	32	59	12	2	8	2	1	3.75

BA	OBA	SA	AB	H	2B	3B	HR	RBI	BB	SO
.259	.349	.384	424	110	19	5	8	56	55	96
.206	.332	.309	194	40	4	2	4	25	37	56
.304	.365	.448	230	70	15	3	4	31	18	40
.256	.345	.374	203	52	9	3	3	51	28	47

SCOTT SCUDDER — BR/TR — age 26 — CLE SP1, RP1 POW/FB

1993	G	IP	H	BB	SO	SB	CS	W	L	SV	ERA
at Home	1	1.0	0	0	0	0	0	0	0	0	0.00
on Road	1	3.0	5	4	2	1	0	0	1	0	12.00
Second Half	0	0.0	0	0	0	0	0	0	0	0	0.00

	BA	OBA	SA	AB	H	2B	3B	HR	RBI	BB	SO
Total	.333	.500	.533	15	5	3	0	0	4	4	1
vs. Left	.250	.400	.500	8	2	2	0	0	2	2	0
vs. Right	.429	.600	.571	7	3	1	0	0	2	2	1
Runners On Base	.300	.417	.500	10	3	2	0	0	4	1	1

5-YEAR TOTALS (1989-1993)

G	IP	H	BB	SO	SB	CS	W	L	SV	ERA
51	194.0	214	94	120	17	9	10	17	0	5.10
45	192.1	181	112	106	36	10	11	17	1	4.49
54	216.0	220	116	132	26	12	10	21	0	5.17

BA	OBA	SA	AB	H	2B	3B	HR	RBI	BB	SO
.266	.358	.415	1486	395	75	10	42	189	206	226
.268	.360	.398	829	222	44	8	16	98	117	107
.263	.355	.435	657	173	31	2	26	91	89	119
.268	.365	.427	661	177	34	4	21	168	101	95

RUDY SEANEZ — BR/TR — age 26 — SD RP3 FIN/GB

1993	G	IP	H	BB	SO	SB	CS	W	L	SV	ERA
at Home	2	3.0	7	2	1	0	0	0	0	0	15.00
on Road	1	0.1	1	0	1	0	0	0	0	0	0.00
Second Half	3	3.1	8	2	1	0	0	0	0	0	13.50

	BA	OBA	SA	AB	H	2B	3B	HR	RBI	BB	SO
Total	.471	.526	.706	17	8	1	0	1	6	2	1
vs. Left	.500	.556	.625	8	4	0	0	0	3	1	0
vs. Right	.444	.500	.778	9	4	1	0	1	3	1	1
Runners On Base	.385	.429	.692	13	5	1	0	1	6	1	0

4-YEAR TOTALS (1989-1993)

G	IP	H	BB	SO	SB	CS	W	L	SV	ERA
18	21.1	25	23	20	5	0	0	0	0	10.13
19	19.1	16	15	19	2	1	2	1	0	4.19
25	26.2	32	25	25	4	0	1	0	0	9.11

BA	OBA	SA	AB	H	2B	3B	HR	RBI	BB	SO
.261	.402	.401	157	41	5	1	5	38	38	39
.338	.464	.446	65	22	2	1	1	18	16	6
.207	.357	.370	92	19	3	0	4	20	22	33
.262	.363	.408	103	27	4	1	3	36	17	23

FRANK SEMINARA — BR/TR — age 27 — SD RP11, SP7 FIN/GB

1993	G	IP	H	BB	SO	SB	CS	W	L	SV	ERA
at Home	11	25.2	38	11	14	1	3	1	3	0	5.61
on Road	7	20.2	15	10	2	0	0	2	0	0	3.05
Second Half	11	13.2	10	7	9	1	0	2	1	0	1.98

	BA	OBA	SA	AB	H	2B	3B	HR	RBI	BB	SO
Total	.294	.374	.450	180	53	7	3	5	27	21	22
vs. Left	.287	.368	.446	101	29	5	1	3	21	13	13
vs. Right	.304	.382	.456	79	24	2	2	2	6	8	9
Runners On Base	.237	.357	.350	80	19	4	1	1	23	16	11

2-YEAR TOTALS (1992-1993)

G	IP	H	BB	SO	SB	CS	W	L	SV	ERA
21	82.0	91	44	51	9	6	7	4	0	3.84
16	64.2	60	23	32	4	3	5	3	0	4.04
24	82.2	77	36	53	6	2	8	3	0	2.72

BA	OBA	SA	AB	H	2B	3B	HR	RBI	BB	SO
.270	.352	.379	560	151	19	6	10	65	67	83
.292	.382	.420	305	89	12	3	7	46	45	37
.243	.313	.329	255	62	7	3	3	19	22	46
.270	.366	.388	237	64	10	3	4	59	37	37

SCOTT SERVICE — BR/TR — age 27 — COL/CIN RP29 POW/FB

1993	G	IP	H	BB	SO	SB	CS	W	L	SV	ERA
at Home	12	20.0	25	5	17	1	0	0	0	2	4.95
on Road	17	26.0	19	11	26	1	2	2	2	0	3.81
Second Half	29	46.0	44	16	43	2	2	2	2	2	4.30

	BA	OBA	SA	AB	H	2B	3B	HR	RBI	BB	SO
Total	.254	.318	.445	173	44	7	4	6	23	16	43
vs. Left	.231	.357	.431	65	15	2	4	1	10	13	9
vs. Right	.269	.288	.454	108	29	5	0	5	13	3	34
Runners On Base	.243	.310	.378	74	18	4	0	2	19	8	18

3-YEAR TOTALS (1988-1993)

G	IP	H	BB	SO	SB	CS	W	L	SV	ERA
17	25.0	37	9	24	2	0	0	0	2	6.48
22	33.1	29	13	36	2	2	2	2	0	4.32
34	51.1	51	17	49	2	2	2	2	2	4.03

BA	OBA	SA	AB	H	2B	3B	HR	RBI	BB	SO
.287	.351	.461	230	66	9	5	7	35	22	60
.272	.383	.446	92	25	3	5	1	14	17	15
.297	.326	.471	138	41	6	0	6	21	5	45
.274	.333	.425	113	31	6	0	3	31	10	29

JEFF SHAW — BR/TR — age 28 — MON RP47, SP8 FIN/GB

1993	G	IP	H	BB	SO	SB	CS	W	L	SV	ERA
at Home	26	55.2	50	20	28	3	1	1	3	0	3.07
on Road	29	40.0	41	12	22	2	1	1	4	0	5.63
Second Half	35	43.0	43	14	23	2	0	1	4	0	4.40

	BA	OBA	SA	AB	H	2B	3B	HR	RBI	BB	SO
Total	.254	.326	.422	358	91	22	1	12	46	32	50
vs. Left	.312	.383	.497	173	54	11	0	7	23	20	18
vs. Right	.200	.271	.351	185	37	11	1	5	23	12	32
Runners On Base	.233	.294	.356	163	38	12	1	2	36	14	24

4-YEAR TOTALS (1990-1993)

G	IP	H	BB	SO	SB	CS	W	L	SV	ERA
49	139.0	141	45	64	5	5	3	10	1	4.27
49	85.1	102	38	45	6	1	2	7	0	5.06
67	127.1	142	46	65	6	1	3	10	0	4.31

BA	OBA	SA	AB	H	2B	3B	HR	RBI	BB	SO
.281	.348	.451	865	243	48	3	31	122	83	109
.319	.383	.482	407	130	22	1	14	53	43	39
.247	.317	.424	458	113	26	2	17	69	40	70
.251	.316	.381	407	102	21	1	10	101	40	55

KEITH SHEPHERD — BR/TR — age 26 — COL RP13, SP1 FIN/GB

1993	G	IP	H	BB	SO	SB	CS	W	L	SV	ERA
at Home	8	10.1	18	3	4	0	2	1	2	0	10.45
on Road	6	9.0	8	1	3	0	0	0	1	1	3.00
Second Half	5	4.0	14	2	1	0	1	0	1	0	18.00

	BA	OBA	SA	AB	H	2B	3B	HR	RBI	BB	SO
Total	.333	.369	.538	78	26	4	0	4	15	4	7
vs. Left	.286	.306	.286	35	10	0	0	0	2	1	3
vs. Right	.372	.417	.744	43	16	4	0	4	13	3	4
Runners On Base	.424	.412	.848	33	14	2	0	4	15	0	2

2-YEAR TOTALS (1992-1993)

G	IP	H	BB	SO	SB	CS	W	L	SV	ERA
13	20.2	28	6	9	1	5	2	2	1	6.53
13	20.2	17	4	8	2	0	0	2	2	3.48
17	26.0	33	8	11	3	4	1	2	2	5.54

BA	OBA	SA	AB	H	2B	3B	HR	RBI	BB	SO
.290	.329	.432	155	45	10	0	4	26	10	17
.272	.307	.309	81	22	3	0	0	9	5	7
.311	.354	.568	74	23	7	0	4	17	5	10
.314	.325	.543	70	22	4	0	4	26	3	6

HEATHCLIFF SLOCUMB — BR/TR — age 28 — CHN/CLE RP30 POW/FB

1993	G	IP	H	BB	SO	SB	CS	W	L	SV	ERA
at Home	18	21.2	22	10	15	1	0	1	0	0	2.49
on Road	12	16.1	13	10	7	3	0	3	1	0	6.06
Second Half	6	7.0	10	3	7	1	0	0	1	0	9.00

	BA	OBA	SA	AB	H	2B	3B	HR	RBI	BB	SO
Total	.250	.337	.336	140	35	4	0	3	25	20	22
vs. Left	.244	.375	.311	45	11	0	0	1	9	10	5
vs. Right	.253	.318	.347	95	24	3	0	2	16	10	17
Runners On Base	.240	.348	.333	75	18	1	0	2	24	14	16

3-YEAR TOTALS (1991-1993)

G	IP	H	BB	SO	SB	CS	W	L	SV	ERA
57	74.1	73	32	51	7	3	3	2	2	3.27
55	62.1	67	39	32	13	2	3	3	0	5.78
40	55.0	81	27	41	9	5	2	2	0	6.55

BA	OBA	SA	AB	H	2B	3B	HR	RBI	BB	SO
.271	.357	.358	517	140	16	1	9	84	71	83
.322	.412	.445	227	73	5	1	7	40	35	29
.231	.313	.290	290	67	11	0	2	44	36	54
.302	.387	.418	275	83	9	1	7	82	44	46

JOE SLUSARSKI — BR/TR — age 28 — OAK SP1, RP1 POW/FB

1993	G	IP	H	BB	SO	SB	CS	W	L	SV	ERA
at Home	0	0.0	0	0	0	0	0	0	0	0	0.00
on Road	2	8.2	9	11	1	0	0	0	0	0	5.19
Second Half	0	0.0	0	0	0	0	0	0	0	0	0.00

	BA	OBA	SA	AB	H	2B	3B	HR	RBI	BB	SO
Total	.300	.488	.433	30	9	1	0	1	5	11	1
vs. Left	.375	.524	.625	16	6	1	0	1	4	5	0
vs. Right	.214	.450	.214	14	3	0	0	0	1	6	1
Runners On Base	.231	.565	.538	13	3	1	0	1	5	10	0

3-YEAR TOTALS (1991-1993)

G	IP	H	BB	SO	SB	CS	W	L	SV	ERA
17	96.1	106	34	56	5	5	5	7	0	5.14
20	97.2	109	56	43	6	4	5	5	0	5.53
10	56.1	63	23	26	2	1	3	4	0	4.95

BA	OBA	SA	AB	H	2B	3B	HR	RBI	BB	SO
.284	.365	.466	756	215	35	6	30	98	90	99
.290	.350	.471	403	117	19	6	14	47	39	47
.278	.380	.459	353	98	16	1	16	51	51	52
.294	.385	.472	299	88	15	1	12	80	44	43

JOHN SMILEY — BL/TL — age 29 — CIN SP18 FIN/FB

1993	G	IP	H	BB	SO	SB	CS	W	L	SV	ERA
at Home	8	48.2	49	14	21	5	2	1	5	0	4.81
on Road	10	57.0	68	17	39	8	2	2	4	0	6.32
Second Half	1	4.2	11	2	1	1	0	0	0	0	11.57

	BA	OBA	SA	AB	H	2B	3B	HR	RBI	BB	SO
Total	.286	.337	.452	409	117	17	3	15	63	31	60
vs. Left	.275	.383	.412	51	14	2	1	1	7	9	5
vs. Right	.288	.330	.458	358	103	15	2	14	56	22	55
Runners On Base	.344	.404	.530	151	52	4	3	6	54	16	16

8-YEAR TOTALS (1986-1993)

G	IP	H	BB	SO	SB	CS	W	L	SV	ERA
123	600.1	516	182	373	64	32	42	31	2	3.18
125	600.1	594	144	384	65	24	37	29	2	4.18
127	600.0	553	166	364	56	29	38	33	2	3.62

BA	OBA	SA	AB	H	2B	3B	HR	RBI	BB	SO
.246	.297	.378	4512	1110	215	26	110	480	326	757
.227	.288	.339	746	169	28	10	12	73	65	125
.250	.299	.386	3766	941	187	16	98	407	261	632
.262	.312	.400	1720	450	75	14	45	415	136	266

BRYN SMITH — BR/TR — age 39 — COL RP6, SP5 FIN/GB

1993	G	IP	H	BB	SO	SB	CS	W	L	SV	ERA
at Home	6	23.1	31	5	7	2	1	1	3	0	4.63
on Road	5	6.1	16	6	2	2	0	1	1	0	22.74
Second Half	0	0.0	0	0	0	0	0	0	0	0	0.00

	BA	OBA	SA	AB	H	2B	3B	HR	RBI	BB	SO
Total	.362	.412	.454	130	47	4	1	2	22	11	9
vs. Left	.371	.392	.471	70	26	1	1	1	14	5	4
vs. Right	.350	.435	.433	60	21	2	0	1	8	6	5
Runners On Base	.366	.410	.423	71	26	1	0	1	21	7	6

10-YEAR TOTALS (1984-1993)

G	IP	H	BB	SO	SB	CS	W	L	SV	ERA
133	815.0	753	211	487	92	33	52	34	0	3.28
129	729.0	735	152	381	90	24	47	45	0	3.98
132	764.2	700	177	445	90	21	48	40	0	3.37

BA	OBA	SA	AB	H	2B	3B	HR	RBI	BB	SO
.253	.299	.371	5889	1488	241	47	121	620	363	868
.264	.310	.371	3232	854	138	31	48	345	210	404
.239	.285	.372	2657	634	103	16	73	275	153	464
.262	.310	.396	2333	611	107	18	57	556	158	356

PETE SMITH — BR/TR — age 28 — ATL SP14, RP6 FIN/FB

1993	G	IP	H	BB	SO	SB	CS	W	L	SV	ERA
at Home	12	54.1	57	21	29	6	5	3	7	0	4.31
on Road	8	36.1	35	15	24	2	3	1	1	0	4.46
Second Half	7	19.2	23	7	10	3	2	1	0	0	3.66

	BA	OBA	SA	AB	H	2B	3B	HR	RBI	BB	SO
Total	.270	.339	.469	341	92	17	3	15	39	36	53
vs. Left	.275	.348	.461	178	49	5	2	8	22	21	25
vs. Right	.264	.328	.479	163	43	12	1	7	17	15	28
Runners On Base	.221	.287	.420	131	29	5	0	7	31	12	26

7-YEAR TOTALS (1987-1993)

G	IP	H	BB	SO	SB	CS	W	L	SV	ERA
67	360.0	366	153	223	55	26	18	29	0	4.28
58	303.2	280	116	208	33	13	12	19	0	3.88
60	315.1	295	119	184	38	19	18	18	0	3.37

BA	OBA	SA	AB	H	2B	3B	HR	RBI	BB	SO
.257	.326	.390	2516	646	111	14	65	280	269	431
.278	.356	.411	1415	394	68	9	34	163	179	198
.229	.287	.361	1101	252	43	5	31	117	90	233
.266	.337	.410	989	263	45	8	27	242	115	162

ZANE SMITH — BL/TL — age 34 — PIT SP14 FIN/GB

1993	G	IP	H	BB	SO	SB	CS	W	L	SV	ERA
at Home	7	44.0	50	11	16	3	1	1	3	0	3.48
on Road	7	39.0	47	11	16	4	1	2	4	0	5.77
Second Half	11	65.2	79	16	25	3	1	3	5	0	4.80

	BA	OBA	SA	AB	H	2B	3B	HR	RBI	BB	SO
Total	.298	.343	.449	325	97	18	8	5	42	22	32
vs. Left	.211	.262	.246	57	12	2	0	0	4	4	8
vs. Right	.317	.360	.493	268	85	16	8	5	38	18	24
Runners On Base	.321	.368	.515	134	43	8	6	2	39	10	12

10-YEAR TOTALS (1984-1993)

G	IP	H	BB	SO	SB	CS	W	L	SV	ERA
149	824.2	844	253	482	88	23	43	41	2	3.46
146	743.2	726	252	378	87	33	35	52	1	3.73
153	742.2	724	237	397	71	30	39	40	3	3.62

BA	OBA	SA	AB	H	2B	3B	HR	RBI	BB	SO
.265	.324	.370	5918	1570	263	43	90	658	505	860
.218	.266	.277	952	208	25	5	7	92	61	220
.274	.335	.388	4966	1362	238	38	83	566	444	640
.274	.338	.392	2464	676	112	19	47	615	236	365

RUSS SPRINGER — BR/TR — age 26 — CAL SP9, RP5 POW/FB

1993	G	IP	H	BB	SO	SB	CS	W	L	SV	ERA
at Home	7	32.0	45	21	15	4	1	1	2	0	6.75
on Road	7	28.0	28	11	16	7	0	0	4	0	7.71
Second Half	6	36.2	39	23	16	5	1	1	3	0	6.14

	BA	OBA	SA	AB	H	2B	3B	HR	RBI	BB	SO
Total	.303	.390	.481	241	73	10	0	11	41	32	31
vs. Left	.301	.386	.455	123	37	4	0	5	16	15	20
vs. Right	.305	.394	.508	118	36	6	0	6	25	17	11
Runners On Base	.308	.379	.547	117	36	4	0	8	38	12	14

2-YEAR TOTALS (1992-1993)

G	IP	H	BB	SO	SB	CS	W	L	SV	ERA
14	40.2	56	25	20	4	1	1	2	0	7.08
14	35.1	35	17	23	10	0	0	4	0	6.88
18	48.1	51	29	26	8	1	1	3	0	5.77

BA	OBA	SA	AB	H	2B	3B	HR	RBI	BB	SO
.298	.389	.459	305	91	14	1	11	54	42	43
.304	.394	.446	148	45	4	1	5	21	19	27
.293	.385	.471	157	46	10	0	6	33	23	16
.316	.395	.529	155	49	7	1	8	51	18	20

DAVE STIEB — BR/TR — age 37 — CHA SP4 POW/GB

1993	G	IP	H	BB	SO	SB	CS	W	L	SV	ERA
at Home	3	16.1	19	11	10	2	0	1	2	0	6.06
on Road	1	6.0	8	3	1	1	0	1	0	0	6.00
Second Half	0	0.0	0	0	0	0	0	0	0	0	0.00

	BA	OBA	SA	AB	H	2B	3B	HR	RBI	BB	SO
Total	.300	.390	.367	90	27	1	1	1	15	14	11
vs. Left	.222	.357	.244	45	10	1	0	0	6	10	5
vs. Right	.378	.429	.489	45	17	0	1	1	9	4	6
Runners On Base	.364	.453	.432	44	16	1	1	0	14	8	5

10-YEAR TOTALS (1984-1993)

G	IP	H	BB	SO	SB	CS	W	L	SV	ERA
134	852.1	772	320	534	46	44	59	41	0	3.57
139	870.2	729	337	531	47	38	51	35	1	3.27
134	846.1	700	303	550	39	36	51	32	1	3.07

BA	OBA	SA	AB	H	2B	3B	HR	RBI	BB	SO
.236	.314	.354	6363	1501	265	35	138	638	657	1065
.244	.322	.363	3375	822	137	18	77	358	376	465
.227	.305	.343	2988	679	128	17	61	280	281	600
.254	.320	.358	2625	667	117	12	44	544	242	428

RUSS SWAN — BL/TL — age 30 — SEA RP23 POW/GB

1993	G	IP	H	BB	SO	SB	CS	W	L	SV	ERA
at Home	12	9.2	8	7	5	1	0	2	2	0	3.72
on Road	11	10.0	17	11	5	1	1	1	1	0	14.40
Second Half	2	1.1	3	2	0	0	0	0	0	0	20.25

	BA	OBA	SA	AB	H	2B	3B	HR	RBI	BB	SO
Total	.316	.455	.430	79	25	3	0	2	14	18	10
vs. Left	.231	.412	.269	26	6	1	0	0	5	7	3
vs. Right	.358	.477	.509	53	19	2	0	2	9	11	7
Runners On Base	.354	.475	.458	48	17	2	0	1	13	10	5

5-YEAR TOTALS (1989-1993)

G	IP	H	BB	SO	SB	CS	W	L	SV	ERA
74	111.1	140	44	55	8	0	5	11	4	5.42
82	147.1	129	73	51	10	5	9	10	7	4.03
74	104.0	108	49	40	8	2	5	10	7	4.67

BA	OBA	SA	AB	H	2B	3B	HR	RBI	BB	SO
.271	.348	.412	991	269	52	6	25	142	117	106
.203	.278	.233	266	54	5	0	1	27	27	33
.297	.374	.477	725	215	47	6	24	115	90	73
.279	.358	.440	473	132	27	5	13	130	59	55

SCOTT TAYLOR — BL/TL — age 27 — BOS RP16 POW/GB

1993	G	IP	H	BB	SO	SB	CS	W	L	SV	ERA
at Home	10	5.1	12	10	4	0	0	0	1	0	13.50
on Road	6	5.2	2	2	4	0	0	0	0	0	3.18
Second Half	16	11.0	14	12	8	0	0	0	1	0	8.18

	BA	OBA	SA	AB	H	2B	3B	HR	RBI	BB	SO
Total	.311	.466	.511	45	14	6	0	1	13	12	8
vs. Left	.313	.450	.625	16	5	2	0	1	5	4	3
vs. Right	.310	.474	.448	29	9	4	0	0	8	8	5
Runners On Base	.375	.559	.500	24	9	3	0	0	12	10	7

2-YEAR TOTALS (1992-1993)

G	IP	H	BB	SO	SB	CS	W	L	SV	ERA
13	19.0	23	14	10	0	1	1	2	0	7.11
7	6.2	4	2	5	0	0	0	0	0	4.05
20	25.2	27	16	15	0	1	1	2	0	6.31

BA	OBA	SA	AB	H	2B	3B	HR	RBI	BB	SO
.276	.383	.551	98	27	8	2	5	25	16	15
.300	.400	.633	30	9	2	1	2	8	5	5
.265	.375	.515	68	18	6	1	3	17	11	10
.341	.481	.634	41	14	4	1	2	22	11	11

ANTHONY TELFORD — BR/TR — age 28 — BAL RP3 FIN/FB

1993	G	IP	H	BB	SO	SB	CS	W	L	SV	ERA
at Home	1	2.0	0	1	1	1	0	0	0	0	0.00
on Road	2	5.1	9	0	5	0	0	0	0	0	13.50
Second Half	2	5.1	9	0	5	0	0	0	0	0	13.50

	BA	OBA	SA	AB	H	2B	3B	HR	RBI	BB	SO
Total	.344	.382	.656	32	11	1	0	3	8	1	6
vs. Left	.353	.389	.529	17	6	0	0	1	2	1	3
vs. Right	.333	.375	.800	15	5	1	0	2	6	0	3
Runners On Base	.308	.357	.615	13	4	1	0	1	6	0	2

3-YEAR TOTALS (1990-1993)

G	IP	H	BB	SO	SB	CS	W	L	SV	ERA
11	46.1	44	22	30	3	2	3	2	0	2.91
9	24.0	37	4	20	2	1	0	1	0	9.38
19	68.1	79	25	49	4	3	3	3	0	5.27

BA	OBA	SA	AB	H	2B	3B	HR	RBI	BB	SO
.289	.350	.450	280	81	15	0	10	40	26	50
.301	.338	.451	133	40	5	0	5	20	8	22
.279	.361	.449	147	41	10	0	5	20	18	28
.282	.338	.403	124	35	9	0	2	32	10	25

BOBBY THIGPEN — BR/TR — age 31 — CHA/PHI RP42 FIN/FB

1993	G	IP	H	BB	SO	SB	CS	W	L	SV	ERA
at Home	17	22.2	23	10	15	2	3	1	1	0	6.75
on Road	25	31.1	51	11	24	2	1	2	0	1	5.17
Second Half	27	35.0	50	13	19	2	4	3	1	0	6.69

	BA	OBA	SA	AB	H	2B	3B	HR	RBI	BB	SO
Total	.335	.401	.493	221	74	12	1	7	45	21	29
vs. Left	.330	.402	.528	106	35	7	1	4	22	13	14
vs. Right	.339	.400	.461	115	39	5	0	3	23	8	15
Runners On Base	.382	.429	.555	110	42	8	1	3	41	10	7

8-YEAR TOTALS (1986-1993)

G	IP	H	BB	SO	SB	CS	W	L	SV	ERA
227	297.2	291	116	207	17	8	21	16	96	3.36
214	263.1	234	117	165	15	4	10	18	105	3.35
243	319.1	306	119	214	21	9	18	18	111	3.27

BA	OBA	SA	AB	H	2B	3B	HR	RBI	BB	SO
.250	.329	.365	2096	525	64	8	53	293	233	372
.264	.349	.373	999	264	27	5	24	140	135	148
.238	.310	.356	1097	261	37	3	29	153	98	224
.248	.325	.361	1098	272	32	4	28	268	123	182

MIKE TIMLIN — BR/TR — age 28 — TOR RP54 POW/GB

1993

	G	IP	H	BB	SO	SB	CS	W	L	SV	ERA
at Home	31	30.1	34	14	30	5	0	2	1	0	4.15
on Road	23	25.1	29	13	19	4	0	2	1	1	5.33
Second Half	21	22.1	22	9	18	1	0	3	1	1	2.82

	BA	OBA	SA	AB	H	2B	3B	HR	RBI	BB	SO
Total	.284	.360	.405	222	63	6	0	7	36	27	49
vs. Left	.275	.356	.441	102	28	5	0	4	16	14	19
vs. Right	.292	.363	.375	120	35	1	0	3	20	13	30
Runners On Base	.276	.360	.371	116	32	5	0	2	31	16	22

3-YEAR TOTALS (1991-1993)

G	IP	H	BB	SO	SB	CS	W	L	SV	ERA
78	116.1	119	53	92	17	4	9	5	2	3.56
65	91.1	83	44	77	7	4	6	5	3	4.04
74	107.0	100	46	89	12	4	8	4	3	3.45

BA	OBA	SA	AB	H	2B	3B	HR	RBI	BB	SO
.255	.336	.330	792	201	18	1	13	117	97	169
.293	.385	.394	345	101	12	1	7	55	53	57
.226	.297	.280	447	101	6	0	6	62	44	112
.291	.383	.373	378	110	11	1	6	110	57	75

FREDDIE TOLIVER — BR/TR — age 33 — PIT RP12 FIN/GB

1993

	G	IP	H	BB	SO	SB	CS	W	L	SV	ERA
at Home	4	3.0	0	1	5	0	0	1	0	0	0.00
on Road	8	18.2	20	7	9	2	0	0	0	0	4.34
Second Half	2	3.1	2	2	1	0	0	0	0	0	2.70

	BA	OBA	SA	AB	H	2B	3B	HR	RBI	BB	SO
Total	.267	.341	.373	75	20	2	0	2	13	8	14
vs. Left	.286	.311	.381	42	12	1	0	1	7	1	9
vs. Right	.242	.372	.364	33	8	1	0	1	6	7	5
Runners On Base	.231	.327	.231	39	9	0	0	0	11	7	7

7-YEAR TOTALS (1984-1993)

G	IP	H	BB	SO	SB	CS	W	L	SV	ERA
35	127.0	144	66	91	14	8	5	5	0	5.03
43	143.1	144	70	88	12	7	5	11	1	4.46
55	192.0	194	102	130	14	11	8	10	1	4.36

BA	OBA	SA	AB	H	2B	3B	HR	RBI	BB	SO
.280	.365	.404	1029	288	55	5	21	131	136	179
.282	.369	.398	503	142	25	3	9	63	70	93
.278	.360	.411	526	146	30	2	12	68	66	86
.283	.368	.405	491	139	32	2	8	118	69	89

RANDY TOMLIN — BL/TL — age 28 — PIT SP18 FIN/GB

1993

	G	IP	H	BB	SO	SB	CS	W	L	SV	ERA
at Home	10	56.2	65	8	27	5	2	2	4	0	4.13
on Road	8	41.2	44	7	17	2	2	2	4	0	5.83
Second Half	9	47.2	60	8	16	1	3	2	5	0	5.29

	BA	OBA	SA	AB	H	2B	3B	HR	RBI	BB	SO
Total	.291	.320	.485	375	109	30	5	11	52	15	44
vs. Left	.315	.338	.507	73	23	7	2	1	13	2	10
vs. Right	.285	.316	.480	302	86	23	3	10	39	13	34
Runners On Base	.304	.338	.493	138	42	15	1	3	44	7	17

4-YEAR TOTALS (1990-1993)

G	IP	H	BB	SO	SB	CS	W	L	SV	ERA
50	309.2	302	50	173	20	18	16	14	0	2.94
46	250.0	265	73	107	27	12	14	14	0	4.00
58	351.2	361	70	177	25	20	15	16	0	3.38

BA	OBA	SA	AB	H	2B	3B	HR	RBI	BB	SO
.267	.310	.392	2125	567	120	19	36	210	123	280
.239	.294	.336	402	96	17	2	6	37	27	77
.273	.314	.405	1723	471	103	17	30	173	96	203
.272	.311	.401	863	235	54	9	13	187	47	119

RICKY TRLICEK — BR/TR — age 25 — LA RP41 FIN/GB

1993

	G	IP	H	BB	SO	SB	CS	W	L	SV	ERA
at Home	18	26.2	21	7	17	4	0	1	1	0	2.03
on Road	23	37.1	38	14	24	2	1	0	1	1	5.54
Second Half	20	33.0	30	10	23	3	1	1	1	1	3.27

	BA	OBA	SA	AB	H	2B	3B	HR	RBI	BB	SO
Total	.244	.309	.360	242	59	13	3	3	35	21	41
vs. Left	.314	.367	.432	118	37	4	1	1	20	9	14
vs. Right	.177	.255	.290	124	22	4	2	2	15	12	27
Runners On Base	.268	.338	.366	123	33	8	2	0	32	12	16

2-YEAR TOTALS (1992-1993)

G	IP	H	BB	SO	SB	CS	W	L	SV	ERA
19	27.2	21	7	17	4	0	1	1	0	1.95
24	38.0	40	16	25	2	1	0	1	1	5.92
20	33.0	30	10	23	3	1	1	1	1	3.27

BA	OBA	SA	AB	H	2B	3B	HR	RBI	BB	SO
.245	.314	.357	249	61	13	3	3	37	23	42
.308	.366	.425	120	37	9	1	1	20	10	15
.186	.266	.295	129	24	4	2	2	17	13	27
.273	.345	.367	128	35	8	2	0	34	13	17

MIKE TROMBLEY — BR/TR — age 27 — MIN RP34, SP10 POW/FB

1993

	G	IP	H	BB	SO	SB	CS	W	L	SV	ERA
at Home	23	61.0	60	10	48	1	4	2	4	2	4.28
on Road	21	53.1	71	31	37	6	2	4	2	0	5.57
Second Half	21	61.2	81	19	46	4	6	2	3	1	4.52

	BA	OBA	SA	AB	H	2B	3B	HR	RBI	BB	SO
Total	.290	.349	.490	451	131	33	6	15	73	41	85
vs. Left	.320	.396	.550	222	71	18	3	9	40	31	40
vs. Right	.262	.298	.432	229	60	15	3	6	33	10	45
Runners On Base	.304	.366	.490	204	62	11	3	7	65	24	43

2-YEAR TOTALS (1992-1993)

G	IP	H	BB	SO	SB	CS	W	L	SV	ERA
27	79.0	75	15	65	3	5	3	4	2	4.10
27	81.2	99	43	58	6	4	4	4	0	4.74
31	108.0	124	36	84	6	5	5	5	1	4.00

BA	OBA	SA	AB	H	2B	3B	HR	RBI	BB	SO
.278	.340	.466	625	174	45	6	20	91	58	123
.309	.387	.522	301	93	25	3	11	50	41	57
.250	.293	.414	324	81	20	3	9	41	17	66
.289	.352	.480	273	79	16	3	10	81	29	56

SERGIO VALDEZ — BR/TR — age 30 — MON RP4 FIN/GB

1993

	G	IP	H	BB	SO	SB	CS	W	L	SV	ERA
at Home	2	1.2	1	0	1	0	0	0	0	0	0.00
on Road	2	1.1	3	1	1	1	0	0	0	0	20.25
Second Half	0	0.0	0	0	0	0	0	0	0	0	0.00

	BA	OBA	SA	AB	H	2B	3B	HR	RBI	BB	SO
Total	.308	.357	.615	13	4	1	0	1	4	1	2
vs. Left	.429	.500	.571	7	3	1	0	0	2	1	0
vs. Right	.167	.167	.667	6	1	0	0	1	2	0	2
Runners On Base	.600	.600	1.400	5	3	1	0	1	4	0	0

6-YEAR TOTALS (1986-1993)

G	IP	H	BB	SO	SB	CS	W	L	SV	ERA
45	112.1	112	33	74	12	2	4	6	0	4.33
46	109.2	117	51	83	13	5	4	8	0	5.58
58	145.1	151	55	104	16	3	5	10	0	4.52

BA	OBA	SA	AB	H	2B	3B	HR	RBI	BB	SO
.266	.330	.429	862	229	47	2	30	123	84	157
.259	.341	.400	417	108	19	2	12	53	53	61
.272	.319	.456	445	121	28	0	18	70	31	96
.294	.354	.464	377	111	26	1	12	105	37	61

JULIO VALERA — BR/TR — age 26 — CAL RP14, SP5 FIN/GB

1993

	G	IP	H	BB	SO	SB	CS	W	L	SV	ERA
at Home	11	32.1	51	10	21	0	1	2	3	2	5.85
on Road	8	20.2	26	5	7	2	0	0	3	2	7.84
Second Half	0	0.0	0	0	0	0	0	0	0	0	0.00

	BA	OBA	SA	AB	H	2B	3B	HR	RBI	BB	SO
Total	.344	.388	.522	224	77	14	1	8	37	15	28
vs. Left	.396	.458	.585	106	42	6	1	4	20	12	8
vs. Right	.297	.320	.466	118	35	8	0	4	17	3	20
Runners On Base	.398	.438	.602	103	41	6	0	5	34	6	11

4-YEAR TOTALS (1990-1993)

G	IP	H	BB	SO	SB	CS	W	L	SV	ERA
28	141.1	148	40	80	7	6	9	6	2	3.31
26	114.2	138	50	68	10	1	3	12	2	5.89
19	114.2	135	42	64	5	3	5	5	2	4.24

BA	OBA	SA	AB	H	2B	3B	HR	RBI	BB	SO
.284	.345	.420	1006	286	57	4	24	116	90	148
.321	.380	.438	480	154	28	2	8	50	46	43
.251	.312	.405	526	132	29	2	16	66	44	105
.287	.354	.410	442	127	20	2	10	102	45	63

DAVE WAINHOUSE — BL/TR — age 27— SEA RP3 POW/FB

1993	G	IP	H	BB	SO	SB	CS	W	L	SV	ERA
at Home	2	1.1	2	1	1	2	0	0	0	0	0.00
on Road	1	1.0	5	4	1	0	0	0	0	0	63.00
Second Half	0	0.0	0	0	0	0	0	0	0	0	0.00

	BA	OBA	SA	AB	H	2B	3B	HR	RBI	BB	SO
Total	.500	.650	.786	14	7	1	0	1	9	5	2
vs. Left	.500	.571	1.000	6	3	0	0	1	5	1	2
vs. Right	.500	.692	.625	8	4	1	0	0	4	4	0
Runners On Base	.667	.769	1.111	9	6	1	0	1	9	4	1

2-YEAR TOTALS (1991-1993)

G	IP	H	BB	SO	SB	CS	W	L	SV	ERA
3	3.1	3	2	2	2	0	0	0	0	2.70
2	1.2	6	7	2	0	0	0	1	0	43.20
2	2.2	2	4	1	0	0	0	1	0	6.75

BA	OBA	SA	AB	H	2B	3B	HR	RBI	BB	SO
.391	.559	.565	23	9	1	0	1	11	9	3
.375	.545	.750	8	3	0	0	1	5	3	2
.400	.565	.467	15	6	1	0	0	6	6	1
.533	.636	.800	15	8	1	0	1	11	6	2

BRUCE WALTON — BR/TR — age 32 — MON RP4 FIN/GB

1993	G	IP	H	BB	SO	SB	CS	W	L	SV	ERA
at Home	2	3.0	4	1	0	0	0	0	0	0	6.00
on Road	2	2.2	7	2	0	0	0	0	0	0	13.50
Second Half	0	0.0	0	0	0	0	0	0	0	0	0.00

	BA	OBA	SA	AB	H	2B	3B	HR	RBI	BB	SO
Total	.407	.467	.556	27	11	1	0	1	5	3	0
vs. Left	.308	.308	.538	13	4	0	0	1	2	0	0
vs. Right	.500	.588	.571	14	7	1	0	0	3	3	0
Runners On Base	.375	.444	.375	16	6	0	0	0	4	2	0

3-YEAR TOTALS (1991-1993)

G	IP	H	BB	SO	SB	CS	W	L	SV	ERA
7	8.2	7	3	5	1	0	0	1	0	7.27
16	20.0	32	9	12	1	0	0	0	0	8.55
8	10.1	15	3	11	0	0	0	0	0	11.32

BA	OBA	SA	AB	H	2B	3B	HR	RBI	BB	SO
.325	.385	.508	120	39	7	0	5	24	12	17
.250	.298	.341	44	11	1	0	1	4	2	3
.368	.432	.605	76	28	6	0	4	20	10	14
.328	.357	.469	64	21	3	0	2	21	4	8

GARY WAYNE — BL/TL — age 32 — COL RP65 POW/FB

1993	G	IP	H	BB	SO	SB	CS	W	L	SV	ERA
at Home	32	34.0	48	14	33	1	0	0	1	0	7.15
on Road	33	28.1	20	12	16	2	1	5	2	1	2.54
Second Half	32	30.2	32	10	27	0	0	3	1	0	4.40

	BA	OBA	SA	AB	H	2B	3B	HR	RBI	BB	SO
Total	.276	.339	.480	246	68	14	6	8	46	26	49
vs. Left	.277	.319	.505	101	28	4	5	3	22	7	23
vs. Right	.276	.353	.462	145	40	10	1	5	24	19	26
Runners On Base	.255	.315	.393	145	37	4	5	2	40	16	28

5-YEAR TOTALS (1989-1993)

G	IP	H	BB	SO	SB	CS	W	L	SV	ERA
108	122.0	120	56	92	5	2	5	3	2	4.50
104	110.1	98	42	62	10	2	8	8	2	3.18
98	100.1	90	35	70	7	1	7	7	3	3.59

BA	OBA	SA	AB	H	2B	3B	HR	RBI	BB	SO
.249	.324	.401	876	218	53	10	20	137	98	154
.234	.294	.399	291	68	14	5	8	57	24	65
.256	.339	.402	585	150	39	5	12	80	74	89
.244	.318	.390	454	111	20	8	10	127	54	81

DAVE WEATHERS — BR/TR — age 25 — FLO RP8, SP6 POW/GB

1993	G	IP	H	BB	SO	SB	CS	W	L	SV	ERA
at Home	5	20.0	30	6	14	2	0	0	3	0	7.20
on Road	9	25.2	27	7	20	5	0	2	0	0	3.51
Second Half	14	45.2	57	13	34	7	0	2	3	0	5.12

	BA	OBA	SA	AB	H	2B	3B	HR	RBI	BB	SO
Total	.306	.355	.441	186	57	14	1	3	23	13	34
vs. Left	.309	.356	.464	97	30	10	1	1	7	7	15
vs. Right	.303	.354	.416	89	27	4	0	2	16	6	19
Runners On Base	.313	.394	.398	83	26	4	0	1	21	11	17

3-YEAR TOTALS (1991-1993)

G	IP	H	BB	SO	SB	CS	W	L	SV	ERA
13	26.1	38	16	18	2	0	0	3	0	6.84
18	37.1	39	16	32	9	1	3	0	0	4.10
31	63.2	77	32	50	11	1	3	3	0	5.23

BA	OBA	SA	AB	H	2B	3B	HR	RBI	BB	SO
.301	.384	.438	256	77	18	1	5	36	32	50
.317	.379	.483	120	38	12	1	2	9	12	21
.287	.387	.397	136	39	6	0	3	27	20	29
.305	.412	.391	128	39	5	0	2	33	23	24

DAVID WEST — BL/TL — age 30 — PHI RP76 POW/FB

1993	G	IP	H	BB	SO	SB	CS	W	L	SV	ERA
at Home	36	43.0	31	27	52	4	1	3	1	2	2.93
on Road	40	43.1	29	24	35	3	2	3	3	1	2.91
Second Half	44	46.2	27	30	46	4	2	5	2	1	2.51

	BA	OBA	SA	AB	H	2B	3B	HR	RBI	BB	SO
Total	.194	.316	.294	309	60	11	1	6	45	51	87
vs. Left	.193	.385	.313	83	16	2	1	2	12	23	25
vs. Right	.195	.287	.288	226	44	9	0	4	33	28	62
Runners On Base	.173	.330	.327	150	26	6	1	5	44	33	40

6-YEAR TOTALS (1988-1993)

G	IP	H	BB	SO	SB	CS	W	L	SV	ERA
72	183.1	177	102	169	9	5	9	13	2	5.99
80	218.2	202	111	134	7	6	13	11	1	3.99
100	274.1	264	150	203	11	7	18	16	1	5.28

BA	OBA	SA	AB	H	2B	3B	HR	RBI	BB	SO
.249	.343	.416	1525	379	84	8	52	231	213	303
.223	.350	.338	278	62	9	4	5	34	51	63
.254	.341	.434	1247	317	75	4	47	197	162	240
.270	.369	.482	662	179	38	3	32	211	102	135

MICKEY WESTON — BR/TR — age 33 — NYN RP4 FIN/GB

1993	G	IP	H	BB	SO	SB	CS	W	L	SV	ERA
at Home	3	5.1	9	1	1	1	0	0	0	0	5.06
on Road	1	0.1	2	0	1	0	0	0	0	0	54.00
Second Half	0	0.0	0	0	0	0	0	0	0	0	0.00

	BA	OBA	SA	AB	H	2B	3B	HR	RBI	BB	SO
Total	.393	.433	.429	28	11	1	0	0	5	1	2
vs. Left	.273	.333	.364	11	3	1	0	0	2	1	2
vs. Right	.471	.500	.471	17	8	0	0	0	3	0	0
Runners On Base	.333	.364	.333	21	7	0	0	0	5	1	1

5-YEAR TOTALS (1989-1993)

G	IP	H	BB	SO	SB	CS	W	L	SV	ERA
11	24.2	26	7	9	1	0	0	0	1	3.65
12	20.2	39	4	10	1	0	1	2	0	11.32
8	18.1	32	3	6	0	0	0	1	0	9.33

BA	OBA	SA	AB	H	2B	3B	HR	RBI	BB	SO
.340	.385	.518	191	65	8	1	8	38	11	19
.337	.394	.500	86	29	3	1	3	15	8	7
.343	.378	.533	105	36	5	0	5	23	3	12
.379	.422	.516	95	36	4	0	3	33	6	9

MATT WHITESIDE — BR/TR — age 27 — TEX RP60 FIN/GB

1993	G	IP	H	BB	SO	SB	CS	W	L	SV	ERA
at Home	28	39.0	35	11	19	1	3	1	1	0	3.23
on Road	32	34.0	43	12	20	3	3	1	0	1	5.56
Second Half	26	27.0	33	12	14	1	2	0	1	0	6.00

	BA	OBA	SA	AB	H	2B	3B	HR	RBI	BB	SO
Total	.281	.337	.399	278	78	10	1	7	33	23	39
vs. Left	.298	.355	.357	84	25	5	0	0	6	7	9
vs. Right	.273	.329	.418	194	53	5	1	7	27	16	30
Runners On Base	.262	.336	.369	130	34	6	1	2	28	15	19

2-YEAR TOTALS (1992-1993)

G	IP	H	BB	SO	SB	CS	W	L	SV	ERA
39	55.1	49	16	28	1	3	2	1	0	2.60
41	45.2	55	18	24	4	3	1	1	5	4.93
46	55.0	59	23	27	2	2	1	1	5	3.93

BA	OBA	SA	AB	H	2B	3B	HR	RBI	BB	SO
.271	.330	.380	384	104	16	1	8	43	34	52
.296	.356	.378	135	40	8	0	1	12	12	11
.257	.316	.382	249	64	8	1	7	31	22	41
.249	.335	.345	177	44	6	1	3	38	24	23

KEVIN WICKANDER — BL/TL — age 29 — CLE/CIN RP44 POW/FB

1993	G	IP	H	BB	SO	SB	CS	W	L	SV	ERA
at Home	23	20.0	32	15	13	0	0	0	0	0	8.10
on Road	21	14.0	15	7	10	3	1	1	0	0	3.21
Second Half	24	16.1	25	16	14	0	0	0	0	0	8.82

	BA	OBA	SA	AB	H	2B	3B	HR	RBI	BB	SO
Total	.324	.420	.559	145	47	6	2	8	33	22	23
vs. Left	.263	.408	.386	57	15	1	0	2	11	13	13
vs. Right	.364	.429	.670	88	32	5	2	6	22	9	10
Runners On Base	.321	.424	.564	78	25	3	2	4	29	13	18

4-YEAR TOTALS (1989-1993)

G	IP	H	BB	SO	SB	CS	W	L	SV	ERA
43	45.0	54	29	32	0	0	1	0	0	4.40
57	45.0	52	27	39	6	2	2	1	1	4.20
50	37.1	47	30	30	1	0	2	0	0	5.79

BA	OBA	SA	AB	H	2B	3B	HR	RBI	BB	SO
.299	.401	.438	354	106	14	4	9	54	56	71
.277	.416	.362	130	36	3	1	2	18	31	34
.313	.392	.482	224	70	11	3	7	36	25	37
.278	.387	.419	198	55	7	3	5	50	34	47

BRIAN WILLIAMS — BR/TR — age 25 — HOU RP37, SP5 POW/GB

1993	G	IP	H	BB	SO	SB	CS	W	L	SV	ERA
at Home	19	43.2	41	14	35	5	1	2	2	2	4.33
on Road	23	38.1	35	24	21	1	1	2	2	0	5.40
Second Half	16	39.1	40	20	28	3	0	3	2	0	5.03

	BA	OBA	SA	AB	H	2B	3B	HR	RBI	BB	SO
Total	.248	.335	.375	307	76	14	2	7	39	38	56
vs. Left	.241	.344	.368	133	32	5	0	4	15	19	32
vs. Right	.253	.328	.379	174	44	9	2	3	24	19	24
Runners On Base	.266	.341	.406	143	38	9	1	3	35	16	24

3-YEAR TOTALS (1991-1993)

G	IP	H	BB	SO	SB	CS	W	L	SV	ERA
27	90.1	89	38	61	7	4	5	5	2	4.18
33	100.0	90	46	53	7	3	6	6	1	4.41
31	126.2	130	58	78	8	4	7	9	0	4.69

BA	OBA	SA	AB	H	2B	3B	HR	RBI	BB	SO
.251	.332	.385	712	179	30	4	19	86	84	114
.255	.343	.378	381	97	13	2	10	44	50	63
.248	.320	.393	331	82	17	2	9	42	34	51
.248	.318	.387	323	80	13	1	10	77	34	50

MIKE WILLIAMS — BR/TR — age 25 — PHI RP13, SP4 POW/GB

1993	G	IP	H	BB	SO	SB	CS	W	L	SV	ERA
at Home	11	32.0	33	9	22	4	0	1	2	0	4.50
on Road	6	19.0	17	13	11	2	3	0	1	0	6.63
Second Half	16	48.0	47	20	31	6	3	1	3	0	4.88

	BA	OBA	SA	AB	H	2B	3B	HR	RBI	BB	SO
Total	.253	.327	.409	198	50	12	2	5	29	22	33
vs. Left	.234	.333	.436	94	22	5	1	4	13	14	12
vs. Right	.269	.321	.385	104	28	7	1	1	16	8	21
Runners On Base	.282	.378	.494	85	24	7	1	3	27	13	17

2-YEAR TOTALS (1992-1993)

G	IP	H	BB	SO	SB	CS	W	L	SV	ERA
14	46.2	50	15	25	5	1	1	3	0	5.40
8	33.0	29	14	13	2	3	1	1	0	5.18
20	72.0	70	26	34	7	3	2	3	0	4.88

BA	OBA	SA	AB	H	2B	3B	HR	RBI	BB	SO
.255	.318	.419	310	79	21	3	8	45	29	38
.240	.316	.443	167	40	12	2	6	26	19	15
.273	.320	.392	143	39	9	1	2	19	10	23
.280	.356	.500	132	37	12	1	5	42	16	19

MARK WILLIAMSON — BR/TR — age 35 — BAL RP47, SP1 FIN/GB

1993	G	IP	H	BB	SO	SB	CS	W	L	SV	ERA
at Home	21	34.0	44	9	9	0	1	5	1	0	4.76
on Road	27	54.0	62	16	36	3	3	2	4	0	5.00
Second Half	26	40.0	54	16	18	2	2	3	4	0	6.97

	BA	OBA	SA	AB	H	2B	3B	HR	RBI	BB	SO
Total	.304	.345	.418	349	106	25	0	5	47	25	45
vs. Left	.254	.313	.370	138	35	7	0	3	16	12	22
vs. Right	.336	.365	.450	211	71	18	0	2	31	13	23
Runners On Base	.346	.389	.453	159	55	11	0	2	44	15	22

7-YEAR TOTALS (1987-1993)

G	IP	H	BB	SO	SB	CS	W	L	SV	ERA
170	317.1	285	94	170	17	10	27	16	9	3.06
167	305.0	341	115	199	23	14	16	18	11	4.66
166	271.1	278	97	165	15	9	24	17	8	3.81

BA	OBA	SA	AB	H	2B	3B	HR	RBI	BB	SO
.265	.323	.392	2364	626	119	11	53	351	209	369
.254	.313	.373	1040	264	41	7	23	137	92	163
.273	.331	.406	1324	362	78	4	30	214	117	206
.294	.362	.428	1095	322	58	4	27	325	129	175

STEVE WILSON — BL/TL — age 30 — LA RP25 POW/GB

1993	G	IP	H	BB	SO	SB	CS	W	L	SV	ERA
at Home	14	17.2	20	5	14	1	0	1	0	1	4.08
on Road	11	8.0	10	9	9	4	1	0	0	0	5.63
Second Half	9	12.2	13	6	14	3	1	0	0	0	4.26

	BA	OBA	SA	AB	H	2B	3B	HR	RBI	BB	SO
Total	.288	.378	.413	104	30	5	3	2	14	14	23
vs. Left	.304	.396	.391	46	14	2	1	0	4	6	10
vs. Right	.276	.364	.431	58	16	3	0	2	10	8	13
Runners On Base	.306	.433	.531	49	15	3	1	2	14	11	9

6-YEAR TOTALS (1988-1993)

G	IP	H	BB	SO	SB	CS	W	L	SV	ERA
98	170.2	186	64	133	8	5	8	10	5	5.01
107	174.2	162	66	119	14	10	5	8	1	3.86
112	191.2	190	69	154	13	10	5	9	3	4.60

BA	OBA	SA	AB	H	2B	3B	HR	RBI	BB	SO
.262	.328	.405	1327	348	58	16	33	177	130	252
.251	.321	.365	406	102	14	7	6	55	41	90
.267	.331	.422	921	246	44	9	27	122	89	162
.265	.337	.422	599	159	30	11	14	158	68	112

MIKE WITT — BR/TR — age 34 — NYA SP9 POW/GB

1993	G	IP	H	BB	SO	SB	CS	W	L	SV	ERA
at Home	7	32.0	29	15	21	2	2	2	2	0	4.78
on Road	2	9.0	10	7	9	1	1	1	0	0	7.00
Second Half	0	0.0	0	0	0	0	0	0	0	0	0.00

	BA	OBA	SA	AB	H	2B	3B	HR	RBI	BB	SO
Total	.248	.352	.414	157	39	5	0	7	22	22	30
vs. Left	.213	.359	.320	75	16	2	0	2	11	16	10
vs. Right	.280	.344	.500	82	23	3	0	5	11	6	20
Runners On Base	.224	.298	.408	76	17	5	0	3	18	8	17

9-YEAR TOTALS (1984-1993)

G	IP	H	BB	SO	SB	CS	W	L	SV	ERA
120	851.1	765	258	574	34	30	51	44	1	3.41
123	794.2	828	286	562	43	33	43	43	0	4.24
119	846.2	831	248	567	40	35	49	42	3	3.88

BA	OBA	SA	AB	H	2B	3B	HR	RBI	BB	SO
.254	.314	.382	6270	1593	274	35	152	684	544	1136
.259	.320	.383	3428	888	147	18	81	354	306	542
.248	.307	.380	2842	705	127	17	71	330	238	594
.265	.327	.403	2514	665	111	16	68	600	247	431

MARK WOHLERS — BR/TR — age 24 — ATL RP46 POW/GB

1993	G	IP	H	BB	SO	SB	CS	W	L	SV	ERA
at Home	26	29.1	23	14	26	2	0	4	2	0	4.91
on Road	20	18.2	14	8	19	1	1	0	2	0	3.86
Second Half	37	38.1	29	19	32	1	0	4	2	0	4.70

	BA	OBA	SA	AB	H	2B	3B	HR	RBI	BB	SO
Total	.218	.309	.294	170	37	7	0	2	24	22	45
vs. Left	.225	.337	.282	71	16	1	0	1	9	12	18
vs. Right	.212	.288	.303	99	21	6	0	1	15	10	27
Runners On Base	.278	.356	.380	79	22	5	0	1	23	9	17

3-YEAR TOTALS (1991-1993)

G	IP	H	BB	SO	SB	CS	W	L	SV	ERA
47	56.1	42	27	39	6	0	5	3	3	3.83
48	46.2	40	22	36	5	1	5	2	3	3.28
77	87.1	69	41	58	8	1	8	4	3	3.30

BA	OBA	SA	AB	H	2B	3B	HR	RBI	BB	SO
.228	.325	.300	360	82	15	1	3	43	49	75
.244	.361	.311	164	40	3	1	2	15	30	35
.214	.293	.291	196	42	12	0	1	28	19	40
.250	.340	.333	180	45	12	0	1	41	23	37

TODD WORRELL — BR/TR — age 35 — LA RP35 POW/FB

1993	G	IP	H	BB	SO	SB	CS	W	L	SV	ERA
at Home	16	18.2	25	8	13	5	0	0	1	0	7.23
on Road	19	20.0	21	3	18	4	1	1	0	5	4.95
Second Half	28	32.0	33	10	25	6	1	1	0	4	5.06

	BA	OBA	SA	AB	H	2B	3B	HR	RBI	BB	SO
Total	.313	.348	.490	147	46	8	0	6	28	11	31
vs. Left	.313	.359	.538	80	25	6	0	4	18	8	19
vs. Right	.313	.333	.433	67	21	2	0	2	10	3	12
Runners On Base	.296	.325	.507	71	21	3	0	4	26	6	13

7-YEAR TOTALS (1985-1993)

G	IP	H	BB	SO	SB	CS	W	L	SV	ERA
197	240.2	187	87	194	30	7	20	19	61	2.77
186	223.2	204	91	202	31	4	14	15	73	2.94
215	254.1	212	86	220	34	4	19	13	78	2.94

BA	OBA	SA	AB	H	2B	3B	HR	RBI	BB	SO
.231	.301	.359	1695	391	81	8	40	199	178	396
.236	.321	.389	789	186	35	4	26	102	104	203
.226	.284	.332	906	205	46	4	14	97	74	193
.212	.296	.324	836	177	25	3	21	180	108	194

ANTHONY YOUNG — BR/TR — age 28 — NYN RP29, SP10 POW/GB

1993	G	IP	H	BB	SO	SB	CS	W	L	SV	ERA
at Home	20	60.0	66	26	40	9	2	1	10	1	4.65
on Road	19	40.1	37	16	22	6	0	0	6	2	2.45
Second Half	16	40.1	38	14	27	3	0	1	6	3	2.90

	BA	OBA	SA	AB	H	2B	3B	HR	RBI	BB	SO
Total	.265	.336	.363	388	103	12	1	8	60	42	62
vs. Left	.263	.353	.392	186	49	9	0	5	31	27	33
vs. Right	.267	.320	.337	202	54	3	1	3	29	15	29
Runners On Base	.289	.358	.390	187	54	7	0	4	56	22	25

3-YEAR TOTALS (1991-1993)

G	IP	H	BB	SO	SB	CS	W	L	SV	ERA
51	141.0	166	48	83	19	4	2	20	9	4.21
50	129.2	119	37	63	9	5	3	15	9	3.40
61	129.1	120	37	64	8	3	3	17	18	3.06

BA	OBA	SA	AB	H	2B	3B	HR	RBI	BB	SO
.273	.327	.392	1045	285	43	11	20	137	85	146
.298	.354	.436	557	166	28	8	11	76	51	74
.244	.295	.342	488	119	15	3	9	61	34	72
.297	.347	.437	458	136	20	4	12	129	39	50

PETE YOUNG — BR/TR — age 26 — MON RP4 FIN/FB

1993	G	IP	H	BB	SO	SB	CS	W	L	SV	ERA
at Home	3	4.1	4	0	3	0	0	1	0	0	4.15
on Road	1	1.0	0	0	0	0	0	0	0	0	0.00
Second Half	4	5.1	4	0	3	0	0	1	0	0	3.38

	BA	OBA	SA	AB	H	2B	3B	HR	RBI	BB	SO
Total	.211	.211	.421	19	4	1	0	2	2	0	3
vs. Left	.333	.333	.833	6	2	0	0	1	1	0	2
vs. Right	.154	.154	.231	13	2	1	0	0	1	0	1
Runners On Base	.333	.333	.667	3	1	1	0	0	1	0	0

2-YEAR TOTALS (1992-1993)

G	IP	H	BB	SO	SB	CS	W	L	SV	ERA
10	13.2	12	4	6	1	0	1	0	0	4.61
7	12.0	10	5	8	1	1	0	0	0	3.00
10	15.1	13	3	8	1	0	1	0	0	3.52

BA	OBA	SA	AB	H	2B	3B	HR	RBI	BB	SO
.239	.308	.380	92	22	6	2	1	16	9	14
.341	.431	.585	41	14	3	2	1	12	8	7
.157	.189	.216	51	8	3	0	0	4	1	7
.261	.333	.435	46	12	4	2	0	15	5	8

CLIFF YOUNG — BL/TL — age 30 — CLE RP14, SP7 FIN/GB

1993	G	IP	H	BB	SO	SB	CS	W	L	SV	ERA
at Home	9	33.2	33	7	19	3	0	2	0	1	2.41
on Road	12	26.2	41	11	12	1	4	1	3	0	7.43
Second Half	4	18.2	27	4	8	0	3	1	1	0	6.27

	BA	OBA	SA	AB	H	2B	3B	HR	RBI	BB	SO
Total	.298	.352	.456	248	74	12	0	9	38	18	31
vs. Left	.316	.339	.351	57	18	2	0	0	8	1	5
vs. Right	.293	.355	.487	191	56	10	0	9	30	17	26
Runners On Base	.286	.352	.411	112	32	2	0	4	33	11	15

3-YEAR TOTALS (1990-1993)

G	IP	H	BB	SO	SB	CS	W	L	SV	ERA
22	55.0	69	13	32	4	1	3	0	1	3.93
27	48.2	57	15	24	1	6	2	4	0	4.62
30	60.1	76	14	33	1	5	3	2	0	4.48

BA	OBA	SA	AB	H	2B	3B	HR	RBI	BB	SO
.302	.348	.456	417	126	20	1	14	67	28	56
.337	.365	.408	98	33	4	0	1	18	4	13
.292	.343	.470	319	93	16	1	13	49	24	43
.284	.328	.412	211	60	6	0	7	60	11	28

CURT YOUNG — BR/TL — age 34 — OAK SP3 FIN/GB

1993	G	IP	H	BB	SO	SB	CS	W	L	SV	ERA
at Home	2	10.2	8	5	2	2	1	1	1	0	3.38
on Road	1	4.0	6	1	2	0	0	0	0	0	6.75
Second Half	1	4.2	4	2	0	2	1	0	1	0	3.86

	BA	OBA	SA	AB	H	2B	3B	HR	RBI	BB	SO
Total	.241	.313	.517	58	14	1	0	5	6	6	4
vs. Left	.333	.385	.417	12	4	1	0	0	0	1	2
vs. Right	.217	.294	.543	46	10	0	0	5	6	5	2
Runners On Base	.167	.250	.333	18	3	0	0	1	2	2	1

10-YEAR TOTALS (1984-1993)

G	IP	H	BB	SO	SB	CS	W	L	SV	ERA
124	578.2	556	191	285	43	34	32	24	0	3.83
119	519.1	560	170	246	32	23	37	28	0	4.64
142	613.0	639	190	296	36	34	40	22	0	4.04

BA	OBA	SA	AB	H	2B	3B	HR	RBI	BB	SO
.264	.324	.423	4231	1116	205	16	146	495	361	531
.243	.291	.332	876	213	31	1	15	94	46	117
.269	.333	.447	3355	903	174	15	131	401	315	414
.274	.336	.426	1677	459	79	6	55	404	158	193

MATT YOUNG — BL/TL — age 36 — CLE RP14, SP8 POW/GB

1993	G	IP	H	BB	SO	SB	CS	W	L	SV	ERA
at Home	9	30.1	31	22	22	3	5	0	3	0	5.04
on Road	13	44.0	44	35	43	6	2	1	3	0	5.32
Second Half	9	22.0	20	22	24	1	2	0	1	0	4.09

	BA	OBA	SA	AB	H	2B	3B	HR	RBI	BB	SO
Total	.266	.394	.390	282	75	11	0	8	35	57	65
vs. Left	.236	.364	.291	55	13	0	0	1	6	10	17
vs. Right	.273	.401	.414	227	62	11	0	7	29	47	48
Runners On Base	.259	.395	.378	135	35	7	0	3	30	28	32

9-YEAR TOTALS (1984-1993)

G	IP	H	BB	SO	SB	CS	W	L	SV	ERA
149	549.1	530	250	412	42	28	30	37	14	3.88
151	436.1	499	236	315	38	23	14	43	11	5.63
156	484.2	501	223	374	30	22	17	38	13	4.36

BA	OBA	SA	AB	H	2B	3B	HR	RBI	BB	SO
.270	.355	.384	3810	1029	152	18	82	497	486	727
.232	.322	.298	724	168	20	2	8	82	85	178
.279	.363	.404	3086	861	132	16	74	415	401	549
.279	.366	.388	1795	500	75	8	35	450	240	346

1993 DEBUT PITCHERS

BRIAN ANDERSON — BL/TL — age 22 — CAL RP3, SP1 FIN/FB

1993	G	IP	H	BB	SO	SB	CS	W	L	SV	ERA
at Home	2	3.1	2	0	1	0	0	0	0	0	2.70
on Road	2	8.0	9	2	3	1	0	0	0	0	4.50
Second Half	4	11.1	11	2	4	1	0	0	0	0	3.97

	BA	OBA	SA	AB	H	2B	3B	HR	RBI	BB	SO
Total	.256	.289	.442	43	11	3	1	1	6	2	4
vs. Left	.167	.167	.167	6	1	0	0	0	0	1	0
vs. Right	.270	.308	.486	37	10	3	1	1	5	2	4
Runners On Base	.429	.500	.500	14	6	1	0	0	5	2	0

MIKE ANDERSON — BR/TR — age 28 — CIN RP3 POW/FB

1993	G	IP	H	BB	SO	SB	CS	W	L	SV	ERA
at Home	2	3.0	9	3	2	0	0	0	0	0	27.00
on Road	1	2.1	3	0	2	0	0	0	0	0	7.71
Second Half	3	5.1	12	3	4	0	0	0	0	0	18.56

	BA	OBA	SA	AB	H	2B	3B	HR	RBI	BB	SO
Total	.444	.500	.778	27	12	0	0	3	10	3	4
vs. Left	.500	.563	1.143	14	7	0	0	3	9	2	3
vs. Right	.385	.429	.385	13	5	0	0	0	1	1	1
Runners On Base	.538	.600	1.231	13	7	0	0	3	10	2	1

CORY BAILEY — BR/TR — age 23 — BOS RP11 POW/GB

1993	G	IP	H	BB	SO	SB	CS	W	L	SV	ERA
at Home	8	13.1	11	9	10	1	2	0	1	0	2.70
on Road	3	2.1	1	3	1	2	0	0	0	0	7.71
Second Half	11	15.2	12	12	11	3	2	0	1	0	3.45

	BA	OBA	SA	AB	H	2B	3B	HR	RBI	BB	SO
Total	.231	.369	.288	52	12	1	1	0	8	7	11
vs. Left	.375	.565	.563	16	6	1	1	0	4	7	1
vs. Right	.167	.262	.167	36	6	0	0	0	4	5	10
Runners On Base	.267	.378	.367	30	8	1	1	0	8	6	6

RICH BATCHELOR — BR/TR — age 27 — SL RP9 FIN/FB

1993	G	IP	H	BB	SO	SB	CS	W	L	SV	ERA
at Home	3	2.1	2	2	1	0	0	0	0	0	11.57
on Road	6	7.2	12	1	3	2	0	0	0	0	7.04
Second Half	9	10.0	14	3	4	2	0	0	0	0	8.10

	BA	OBA	SA	AB	H	2B	3B	HR	RBI	BB	SO
Total	.359	.386	.487	39	14	2	0	1	6	3	4
vs. Left	.368	.381	.579	19	7	0	0	1	5	1	2
vs. Right	.350	.391	.400	20	7	1	0	0	1	2	2
Runners On Base	.538	.529	.846	13	7	1	0	1	6	2	1

SEAN BERGMAN — BR/TR — age 24 — DET SP6, RP3 POW/GB

1993	G	IP	H	BB	SO	SB	CS	W	L	SV	ERA
at Home	4	23.0	26	14	12	0	0	0	3	0	5.87
on Road	5	16.2	21	9	7	4	0	1	1	0	5.40
Second Half	9	39.2	47	23	19	4	0	1	4	0	5.67

	BA	OBA	SA	AB	H	2B	3B	HR	RBI	BB	SO
Total	.294	.382	.450	160	47	3	2	6	27	23	19
vs. Left	.297	.395	.547	64	19	0	2	4	14	10	6
vs. Right	.292	.373	.385	96	28	3	0	2	13	13	13
Runners On Base	.287	.352	.475	80	23	2	2	3	24	8	10

RODNEY BOLTON — BR/TR — age 26 — CHA SP8, RP1 FIN/GB

1993	G	IP	H	BB	SO	SB	CS	W	L	SV	ERA
at Home	4	18.1	20	5	8	0	0	0	2	0	5.89
on Road	5	24.0	35	11	9	2	0	0	4	0	8.63
Second Half	5	22.0	22	7	13	0	0	2	2	0	6.14

	BA	OBA	SA	AB	H	2B	3B	HR	RBI	BB	SO
Total	.314	.367	.440	175	55	6	2	4	32	16	17
vs. Left	.337	.386	.457	92	31	4	2	1	19	8	8
vs. Right	.289	.347	.422	83	24	2	0	3	13	8	9
Runners On Base	.368	.416	.539	76	28	4	0	3	31	8	10

BILLY BREWER — BL/TL — age 26 — KC RP46 POW/FB

1993	G	IP	H	BB	SO	SB	CS	W	L	SV	ERA
at Home	25	20.1	16	9	10	1	1	1	2	0	3.10
on Road	21	18.2	15	11	18	4	1	1	0	0	3.86
Second Half	28	24.2	21	14	20	2	1	1	0	0	4.01

	BA	OBA	SA	AB	H	2B	3B	HR	RBI	BB	SO
Total	.230	.327	.407	135	31	4	1	6	16	20	28
vs. Left	.183	.286	.333	60	11	0	0	3	11	9	14
vs. Right	.267	.360	.467	75	20	4	1	3	5	11	14
Runners On Base	.116	.235	.188	69	8	0	0	1	11	11	17

JEFF BRONKEY — BR/TR — age 29 — TEX RP21 FIN/GB

1993	G	IP	H	BB	SO	SB	CS	W	L	SV	ERA
at Home	9	19.0	24	6	8	0	0	0	0	1	3.79
on Road	12	17.0	15	5	10	0	1	1	1	0	4.24
Second Half	8	13.1	15	5	3	0	0	1	0	0	4.72

	BA	OBA	SA	AB	H	2B	3B	HR	RBI	BB	SO
Total	.285	.338	.431	137	39	8	0	4	22	11	18
vs. Left	.283	.320	.370	46	13	1	0	1	7	3	7
vs. Right	.286	.347	.462	91	26	7	0	3	15	8	11
Runners On Base	.328	.394	.492	61	20	7	0	1	19	7	5

SCOTT BROW — BR/TR — age 25 — TOR SP3, RP3 FIN/GB

1993	G	IP	H	BB	SO	SB	CS	W	L	SV	ERA
at Home	4	11.0	14	6	3	2	0	0	1	0	5.73
on Road	2	7.0	5	4	4	0	0	1	0	0	6.43
Second Half	4	9.0	8	5	4	0	0	1	0	0	6.00

	BA	OBA	SA	AB	H	2B	3B	HR	RBI	BB	SO
Total	.275	.366	.391	69	19	2	0	2	12	10	7
vs. Left	.205	.319	.231	39	8	1	0	0	5	7	5
vs. Right	.367	.429	.600	30	11	1	0	2	7	3	2
Runners On Base	.394	.421	.545	33	13	2	0	1	11	3	1

GREG BRUMMETT — BR/TR — age 27 — SF/MIN SP13 FIN/FB

1993	G	IP	H	BB	SO	SB	CS	W	L	SV	ERA
at Home	7	40.1	45	17	15	4	1	2	2	0	4.69
on Road	6	32.1	37	11	15	8	0	2	2	0	5.57
Second Half	11	60.0	68	26	24	10	1	3	3	0	5.55

	BA	OBA	SA	AB	H	2B	3B	HR	RBI	BB	SO
Total	.297	.356	.475	276	82	9	2	12	40	28	30
vs. Left	.348	.427	.538	132	46	5	1	6	24	21	11
vs. Right	.250	.283	.417	144	36	4	1	6	16	7	19
Runners On Base	.284	.348	.474	116	33	2	1	6	34	14	13

ENRIQUE BURGOS — BL/TL — age 29 — KC RP5 POW/GB

1993	G	IP	H	BB	SO	SB	CS	W	L	SV	ERA
at Home	2	1.1	2	1	3	0	0	0	0	0	0.00
on Road	3	3.2	5	3	3	1	0	0	1	0	12.27
Second Half	5	5.0	5	6	6	1	0	0	1	0	9.00

	BA	OBA	SA	AB	H	2B	3B	HR	RBI	BB	SO
Total	.238	.429	.286	21	5	1	0	0	1	6	6
vs. Left	1.000	1.000	2.000	1	1	0	0	0	0	1	0
vs. Right	.200	.385	.200	20	4	0	0	0	1	5	6
Runners On Base	.077	.333	.077	13	1	0	0	0	4	4	6

CHRIS BUSHING — BR/TR — age 27 — CIN RP6 POW/GB

1993	G	IP	H	BB	SO	SB	CS	W	L	SV	ERA
at Home	3	2.0	7	1	0	0	0	0	0	0	18.00
on Road	3	2.1	2	4	2	0	0	0	0	0	7.71
Second Half	6	4.1	9	4	3	0	0	0	0	0	12.46

	BA	OBA	SA	AB	H	2B	3B	HR	RBI	BB	SO
Total	.450	.520	.850	20	9	3	1	1	6	4	3
vs. Left	.333	.444	1.000	6	2	1	0	1	2	2	0
vs. Right	.500	.563	.786	14	7	2	1	0	4	2	3
Runners On Base	.357	.444	.500	14	5	2	0	0	5	3	2

JIM CONVERSE — BL/TR — age 23 — SEA SP4 — POW/GB

1993	G	IP	H	BB	SO	SB	CS	W	L	SV	ERA
at Home	3	13.1	17	13	3	1	2	1	2	0	6.75
on Road	1	7.0	6	1	1	0	0	1	0	0	2.57
Second Half	1	0.0	0	0	0	0	0	0	0	0	0.00

	BA	OBA	SA	AB	H	2B	3B	HR	RBI	BB	SO
Total	.295	.398	.385	78	23	7	0	0	12	14	10
vs. Left	.326	.436	.435	46	15	5	0	0	5	9	5
vs. Right	.250	.342	.313	32	8	2	0	0	7	5	5
Runners On Base	.353	.477	.471	34	12	4	0	0	12	9	4

ANDY COOK — BR/TR — age 27 — NYA RP4 POW/GB

1993	G	IP	H	BB	SO	SB	CS	W	L	SV	ERA
at Home	2	3.1	3	1	2	0	0	0	0	1	8.10
on Road	2	2.0	1	0	2	0	0	0	0	0	0.00
Second Half	0	0.0	0	0	0	0	0	0	0	0	0.00

	BA	OBA	SA	AB	H	2B	3B	HR	RBI	BB	SO
Total	.200	.407	.400	20	4	1	0	1	0	2	4
vs. Left	.125	.462	.125	8	1	0	0	0	0	3	1
vs. Right	.250	.357	.583	12	3	1	0	1	0	1	3
Runners On Base	.083	.267	.083	12	1	0	0	0	0	3	4

JOHN CUMMINGS — BL/TL — age 25 — SEA SP8, RP2 FIN/GB

1993	G	IP	H	BB	SO	SB	CS	W	L	SV	ERA
at Home	5	21.1	30	9	8	0	1	0	3	0	8.86
on Road	5	25.0	29	7	11	2	3	0	3	0	3.60
Second Half	1	3.0	6	1	3	0	0	0	0	0	12.00

	BA	OBA	SA	AB	H	2B	3B	HR	RBI	BB	SO
Total	.316	.372	.449	187	59	7	0	6	30	16	19
vs. Left	.225	.326	.400	40	9	1	0	2	8	5	1
vs. Right	.340	.385	.463	147	50	6	0	4	22	11	18
Runners On Base	.345	.404	.529	87	30	4	0	4	28	9	11

OMAR DAAL — BL/TL — age 22 — LA RP47 POW/GB

1993	G	IP	H	BB	SO	SB	CS	W	L	SV	ERA
at Home	22	15.2	18	10	8	1	1	0	3	0	5.74
on Road	25	19.2	18	11	11	0	0	2	0	0	4.58
Second Half	25	22.2	27	13	11	1	1	1	2	0	6.35

	BA	OBA	SA	AB	H	2B	3B	HR	RBI	BB	SO
Total	.277	.373	.438	130	36	4	1	5	27	21	19
vs. Left	.230	.326	.338	74	17	2	0	2	16	11	12
vs. Right	.339	.433	.571	56	19	2	1	3	11	10	7
Runners On Base	.358	.438	.597	67	24	1	0	5	27	11	9

JOHN DESILVA — BR/TR — age 27 — DET/ LA RP4 POW/GB

1993	G	IP	H	BB	SO	SB	CS	W	L	SV	ERA
at Home	1	1.1	2	0	0	0	0	0	0	0	6.75
on Road	3	5.0	6	1	6	0	0	0	0	0	7.20
Second Half	4	6.1	8	1	6	0	0	0	0	0	7.11

	BA	OBA	SA	AB	H	2B	3B	HR	RBI	BB	SO
Total	.320	.333	.440	25	8	3	0	0	5	1	6
vs. Left	.125	.200	.125	8	1	0	0	0	1	1	1
vs. Right	.412	.412	.588	17	7	3	0	0	4	0	5
Runners On Base	.357	.333	.500	14	5	2	0	0	5	0	3

JERRY DIPOTO — BR/TR — age 26 — CLE RP46 POW/GB

1993	G	IP	H	BB	SO	SB	CS	W	L	SV	ERA
at Home	21	27.1	33	15	27	0	0	1	2	5	1.65
on Road	25	29.0	24	15	14	1	0	3	2	6	3.10
Second Half	44	55.1	50	30	41	1	0	4	4	11	1.95

	BA	OBA	SA	AB	H	2B	3B	HR	RBI	BB	SO
Total	.270	.361	.303	211	57	7	0	0	23	30	41
vs. Left	.274	.398	.274	84	23	0	0	0	5	18	12
vs. Right	.268	.333	.323	127	34	7	0	0	18	12	29
Runners On Base	.234	.324	.266	128	30	4	0	0	23	17	25

STEVE DIXON — BL/TL — age 25 — SL RP4 POW/GB

1993	G	IP	H	BB	SO	SB	CS	W	L	SV	ERA
at Home	1	0.0	0	1	0	0	0	0	0	0	0.00
on Road	3	2.2	7	4	2	0	0	0	0	0	33.75
Second Half	4	2.2	7	5	2	0	0	0	0	0	33.75

	BA	OBA	SA	AB	H	2B	3B	HR	RBI	BB	SO
Total	.538	.667	.923	13	7	2	0	1	7	5	2
vs. Left	.400	.625	.600	5	2	1	0	0	5	3	1
vs. Right	.625	.700	1.125	8	5	1	0	1	2	2	1
Runners On Base	.800	.875	1.200	5	4	2	0	0	6	3	0

MIKE DRAPER — BR/TR — age 28 — NYN RP28, SP1 FIN/FB

1993	G	IP	H	BB	SO	SB	CS	W	L	SV	ERA
at Home	16	26.2	32	12	11	2	1	0	0	0	3.38
on Road	13	15.2	21	2	5	5	0	1	1	0	5.74
Second Half	7	11.0	14	6	2	2	1	1	0	0	4.91

	BA	OBA	SA	AB	H	2B	3B	HR	RBI	BB	SO
Total	.327	.370	.457	162	53	13	1	2	26	14	16
vs. Left	.384	.447	.507	73	28	9	0	0	8	10	6
vs. Right	.281	.302	.416	89	25	4	1	2	18	4	10
Runners On Base	.326	.364	.488	86	28	6	1	2	26	8	6

STEVE DREYER — BR/TR — age 25 — TEX SP6, RP4 POW/GB

1993	G	IP	H	BB	SO	SB	CS	W	L	SV	ERA
at Home	5	26.2	24	10	17	0	2	3	1	0	3.38
on Road	5	14.1	24	10	6	2	0	0	2	0	10.05
Second Half	10	41.0	48	20	23	2	2	3	3	0	5.71

	BA	OBA	SA	AB	H	2B	3B	HR	RBI	BB	SO
Total	.291	.371	.479	165	48	10	0	7	19	20	23
vs. Left	.266	.389	.430	79	21	4	0	3	8	16	10
vs. Right	.314	.352	.523	86	27	6	0	4	11	4	13
Runners On Base	.264	.369	.472	72	19	3	0	4	16	11	11

MARK ETTLES — BR/TR — age 28 — SD RP14 FIN/FB

1993	G	IP	H	BB	SO	SB	CS	W	L	SV	ERA
at Home	7	8.0	9	2	4	0	0	0	0	0	5.63
on Road	7	10.0	14	2	5	0	0	1	0	0	7.20
Second Half	4	5.2	7	2	1	0	0	0	0	0	4.76

	BA	OBA	SA	AB	H	2B	3B	HR	RBI	BB	SO
Total	.307	.333	.507	75	23	1	0	4	21	4	9
vs. Left	.448	.485	.793	29	13	1	0	3	11	3	1
vs. Right	.217	.229	.326	46	10	0	0	1	10	1	8
Runners On Base	.382	.395	.676	34	13	1	0	3	20	2	3

HUCK FLENER — BB/TL — age 25 — TOR RP6 FIN/GB

1993	G	IP	H	BB	SO	SB	CS	W	L	SV	ERA
at Home	2	1.1	2	1	0	0	0	0	0	0	0.00
on Road	4	5.1	5	3	2	1	0	0	0	0	5.06
Second Half	6	6.2	7	4	2	1	0	0	0	0	4.05

	BA	OBA	SA	AB	H	2B	3B	HR	RBI	BB	SO
Total	.269	.367	.423	26	7	2	1	0	3	4	2
vs. Left	.267	.267	.400	15	4	2	0	0	2	0	1
vs. Right	.273	.467	.455	11	3	0	1	0	1	4	1
Runners On Base	.235	.316	.353	17	4	2	0	0	3	2	1

PAUL FLETCHER — BR/TR — age 27 — PHI RP1 FIN/FB

1993	G	IP	H	BB	SO	SB	CS	W	L	SV	ERA
at Home	1	0.1	0	0	0	0	0	0	0	0	0.00
on Road	0	0.0	0	0	0	0	0	0	0	0	0.00
Second Half	1	0.1	0	0	0	0	0	0	0	0	0.00

	BA	OBA	SA	AB	H	2B	3B	HR	RBI	BB	SO
Total	.000	.000	.000	1	0	0	0	0	0	0	0
vs. Left	.000	.000	.000	0	0	0	0	0	0	0	0
vs. Right	.000	.000	.000	1	0	0	0	0	0	0	0
Runners On Base	.000	.000	.000	0	0	0	0	0	0	0	0

KEVIN FOSTER — BR/TR — age 25 — PHI SP1, RP1 POW/FB

1993	G	IP	H	BB	SO	SB	CS	W	L	SV	ERA
at Home	1	2.2	4	3	3	0	0	0	0	0	10.13
on Road	1	4.0	9	4	3	2	0	0	1	0	18.00
Second Half	2	6.2	13	7	6	2	0	0	1	0	14.85

	BA	OBA	SA	AB	H	2B	3B	HR	RBI	BB	SO
Total	.394	.500	.758	33	13	3	0	3	10	7	6
vs. Left	.458	.567	.917	24	11	2	0	3	10	6	4
vs. Right	.222	.300	.333	9	2	1	0	0	0	1	2
Runners On Base	.381	.458	.619	21	8	2	0	1	8	3	4

SCOTT FREDRICKSON — BR/TR — age 27 — COL RP25 POW/GB

1993	G	IP	H	BB	SO	SB	CS	W	L	SV	ERA
at Home	16	18.2	17	11	16	1	1	0	1	0	5.79
on Road	9	10.1	16	6	4	0	1	1	0	0	6.97
Second Half	9	9.1	19	6	5	1	1	1	0	0	9.64

	BA	OBA	SA	AB	H	2B	3B	HR	RBI	BB	SO
Total	.287	.378	.417	115	33	4	1	3	20	17	20
vs. Left	.212	.339	.250	52	11	0	0	0	5	10	8
vs. Right	.349	.411	.556	63	22	4	0	3	15	7	12
Runners On Base	.290	.378	.355	62	18	2	1	0	17	9	9

GREG GOHR — BR/TR — age 27 — DET RP16 POW/FB

1993	G	IP	H	BB	SO	SB	CS	W	L	SV	ERA
at Home	10	13.1	11	5	13	0	0	0	0	0	2.70
on Road	6	9.1	15	9	10	1	0	0	0	0	10.61
Second Half	10	13.1	15	8	15	1	0	0	0	0	4.72

	BA	OBA	SA	AB	H	2B	3B	HR	RBI	BB	SO
Total	.289	.393	.411	90	26	4	2	1	15	14	23
vs. Left	.306	.405	.389	36	11	1	1	0	5	6	11
vs. Right	.278	.385	.426	54	15	3	1	1	10	8	12
Runners On Base	.326	.434	.465	43	14	1	1	1	15	8	12

PAT GOMEZ — BL/TL — age 26 — SD RP26, SP1 POW/GB

1993	G	IP	H	BB	SO	SB	CS	W	L	SV	ERA
at Home	12	12.2	14	8	13	0	2	1	1	0	2.84
on Road	15	19.0	21	11	13	0	1	0	1	0	6.63
Second Half	0	0.0	0	0	0	0	0	0	0	0	0.00

	BA	OBA	SA	AB	H	2B	3B	HR	RBI	BB	SO
Total	.294	.380	.412	119	35	6	1	2	18	19	26
vs. Left	.268	.256	.293	41	11	1	0	0	5	0	8
vs. Right	.308	.434	.474	78	24	5	1	2	13	19	18
Runners On Base	.344	.418	.469	64	22	2	0	2	18	11	14

JEFF GRANGER — BR/TL — age 23 — KC RP1 POW/GB

1993	G	IP	H	BB	SO	SB	CS	W	L	SV	ERA
at Home	0	0.0	0	0	0	0	0	0	0	0	0.00
on Road	1	1.0	3	2	1	0	0	0	0	0	27.00
Second Half	1	1.0	3	2	1	0	0	0	0	0	27.00

	BA	OBA	SA	AB	H	2B	3B	HR	RBI	BB	SO
Total	.500	.625	.500	6	3	0	0	0	3	2	1
vs. Left	1.000	1.000	1.000	1	1	0	0	0	0	0	0
vs. Right	.400	.571	.400	5	2	0	0	0	3	2	1
Runners On Base	.500	.571	.500	6	3	0	0	0	3	1	1

TYLER GREEN — BR/TR — age 24 — PHI SP2, RP1 POW/GB

1993	G	IP	H	BB	SO	SB	CS	W	L	SV	ERA
at Home	2	5.2	11	4	4	0	1	0	0	0	7.94
on Road	1	1.2	5	1	3	0	0	0	0	0	5.40
Second Half	2	6.1	14	3	6	0	1	0	0	0	5.68

	BA	OBA	SA	AB	H	2B	3B	HR	RBI	BB	SO
Total	.444	.512	.583	36	16	0	1	1	6	5	7
vs. Left	.462	.533	.692	13	6	0	0	1	4	2	4
vs. Right	.435	.500	.522	23	10	0	1	0	2	3	3
Runners On Base	.320	.370	.440	25	8	0	1	0	6	2	5

KENNY GREER — BR/TR — age 27 — NYN RP1 POW/FB

1993	G	IP	H	BB	SO	SB	CS	W	L	SV	ERA
at Home	1	1.0	0	0	2	0	0	1	0	0	0.00
on Road	0	0.0	0	0	0	0	0	0	0	0	0.00
Second Half	1	1.0	0	0	2	0	0	1	0	0	0.00

	BA	OBA	SA	AB	H	2B	3B	HR	RBI	BB	SO
Total	.000	.000	.000	3	0	0	0	0	0	0	2
vs. Left	.000	.000	.000	1	0	0	0	0	0	0	1
vs. Right	.000	.000	.000	2	0	0	0	0	0	0	1
Runners On Base	.000	.000	.000	0	0	0	0	0	0	0	0

EDDIE GUARDADO — BR/TL — age 24 — MIN SP16, RP3 FIN/FB

1993	G	IP	H	BB	SO	SB	CS	W	L	SV	ERA
at Home	9	43.2	64	15	21	6	3	1	3	0	6.39
on Road	10	51.0	59	21	25	6	2	2	5	0	6.00
Second Half	15	74.0	98	25	37	10	5	3	6	0	6.08

	BA	OBA	SA	AB	H	2B	3B	HR	RBI	BB	SO
Total	.319	.376	.535	385	123	34	5	13	64	36	46
vs. Left	.318	.348	.523	88	28	6	3	2	15	4	12
vs. Right	.320	.384	.539	297	95	28	2	11	49	32	34
Runners On Base	.369	.416	.581	160	59	14	4	4	55	15	17

MIKE HAMPTON — BR/TL — age 22 — SEA RP10, SP3 POW/FB

1993	G	IP	H	BB	SO	SB	CS	W	L	SV	ERA
at Home	6	10.0	21	8	5	1	0	1	2	0	12.60
on Road	7	7.0	9	3	3	0	1	1	1	1	5.14
Second Half	7	7.1	14	7	3	0	0	0	1	1	11.05

	BA	OBA	SA	AB	H	2B	3B	HR	RBI	BB	SO
Total	.368	.479	.592	76	28	6	1	3	17	17	8
vs. Left	.345	.367	.655	29	10	1	1	2	6	1	2
vs. Right	.383	.531	.553	47	18	5	0	1	11	16	6
Runners On Base	.425	.538	.625	40	17	3	1	1	15	11	4

BRAD HOLMAN — BR/TR — age 26 — SEA RP19 FIN/FB

1993	G	IP	H	BB	SO	SB	CS	W	L	SV	ERA
at Home	11	16.1	18	8	10	1	0	1	2	0	6.61
on Road	8	20.0	9	8	7	0	1	1	1	3	1.35
Second Half	19	36.1	27	16	17	1	0	1	3	3	3.72

	BA	OBA	SA	AB	H	2B	3B	HR	RBI	BB	SO
Total	.208	.318	.277	130	27	6	0	1	12	16	17
vs. Left	.208	.288	.283	53	11	1	0	1	5	6	6
vs. Right	.208	.337	.273	77	16	5	0	0	7	10	11
Runners On Base	.236	.382	.309	55	13	4	0	0	11	10	6

MARK HOLZEMER — BL/TL — age 25 — CAL SP4, RP1 FIN/FB

1993	G	IP	H	BB	SO	SB	CS	W	L	SV	ERA
at Home	2	13.0	16	6	4	1	1	0	1	0	6.92
on Road	3	10.1	18	7	6	1	0	0	2	0	11.32
Second Half	5	23.1	34	13	10	2	1	0	3	0	8.87

	BA	OBA	SA	AB	H	2B	3B	HR	RBI	BB	SO
Total	.340	.431	.480	100	34	8	0	2	23	13	10
vs. Left	.296	.457	.333	27	8	1	0	0	4	6	2
vs. Right	.356	.420	.534	73	26	7	0	2	19	7	8
Runners On Base	.367	.424	.533	60	22	4	0	2	23	5	6

JOHN HOPE — BR/TR — age 24 — PIT SP7 FIN/GB

1993	G	IP	H	BB	SO	SB	CS	W	L	SV	ERA
at Home	4	22.1	30	6	6	0	1	0	1	0	4.43
on Road	3	15.2	17	2	2	3	1	0	1	0	3.45
Second Half	7	38.0	47	8	8	3	2	0	2	0	4.03

	BA	OBA	SA	AB	H	2B	3B	HR	RBI	BB	SO
Total	.313	.354	.453	150	47	11	2	2	19	8	8
vs. Left	.303	.370	.333	66	20	2	0	0	7	7	3
vs. Right	.321	.341	.548	84	27	9	2	2	12	1	5
Runners On Base	.306	.346	.417	72	22	2	0	2	19	4	4

CHRIS HOWARD — BR/TL — age 29 — CHA RP3 POW/GB

1993	G	IP	H	BB	SO	SB	CS	W	L	SV	ERA
at Home	1	0.2	1	0	1	0	0	1	0	0	0.00
on Road	2	1.2	2	2	1	0	0	0	1	0	0.00
Second Half	3	2.1	2	3	1	0	1	1	1	0	0.00

	BA	OBA	SA	AB	H	2B	3B	HR	RBI	BB	SO
Total	.286	.500	.286	7	2	0	0	0	1	3	1
vs. Left	.250	.500	.250	4	1	0	0	0	2	2	0
vs. Right	.333	.500	.333	3	1	0	0	0	1	1	1
Runners On Base	.333	.500	.333	6	2	0	0	0	1	2	1

MARK HUTTON — BR/TR — age 24 — NYA SP4, RP3 POW/GB

1993	G	IP	H	BB	SO	SB	CS	W	L	SV	ERA
at Home	3	13.0	9	8	7	3	1	1	0	0	2.08
on Road	4	9.0	15	9	5	1	0	0	1	0	11.00
Second Half	7	22.0	24	17	12	4	1	1	1	0	5.73

	BA	OBA	SA	AB	H	2B	3B	HR	RBI	BB	SO
Total	.293	.412	.427	82	24	5	0	2	15	17	12
vs. Left	.298	.389	.426	47	14	3	0	1	6	7	5
vs. Right	.286	.438	.429	35	10	2	0	1	9	10	7
Runners On Base	.361	.457	.500	36	13	5	0	0	13	7	5

DOMINGO JEAN — BR/TR — age 25 — NYA SP6, RP4 FIN/GB

1993	G	IP	H	BB	SO	SB	CS	W	L	SV	ERA
at Home	4	19.0	13	8	6	1	0	1	0	0	2.37
on Road	6	21.1	24	11	14	1	0	0	1	0	6.33
Second Half	10	40.1	37	19	20	2	0	1	1	0	4.46

	BA	OBA	SA	AB	H	2B	3B	HR	RBI	BB	SO
Total	.237	.318	.442	156	37	7	2	7	19	19	20
vs. Left	.236	.300	.403	72	17	3	2	2	10	7	11
vs. Right	.238	.333	.476	84	20	4	0	5	9	12	9
Runners On Base	.298	.414	.553	47	14	1	1	3	15	10	5

MIGUEL JIMENEZ — BR/TR — age 25 — OAK SP4, RP1 POW/FB

1993	G	IP	H	BB	SO	SB	CS	W	L	SV	ERA
at Home	2	11.0	13	7	3	0	0	1	0	0	4.91
on Road	3	16.0	14	9	10	1	0	0	1	0	3.38
Second Half	5	27.0	27	16	13	1	0	1	1	0	4.00

	BA	OBA	SA	AB	H	2B	3B	HR	RBI	BB	SO
Total	.262	.367	.447	103	27	4	0	5	12	16	13
vs. Left	.304	.391	.446	56	17	2	0	2	6	8	4
vs. Right	.213	.339	.447	47	10	2	0	3	6	8	9
Runners On Base	.204	.291	.367	49	10	2	0	2	9	5	7

JOHN JOHNSTONE — BR/TR — age 26 — FLO RP7 POW/GB

1993	G	IP	H	BB	SO	SB	CS	W	L	SV	ERA
at Home	5	6.1	11	5	1	1	0	0	2	0	8.53
on Road	2	4.1	5	2	4	0	0	0	0	0	2.08
Second Half	7	10.2	16	7	5	1	0	0	2	0	5.91

	BA	OBA	SA	AB	H	2B	3B	HR	RBI	BB	SO
Total	.340	.426	.489	47	16	4	0	1	7	7	5
vs. Left	.348	.464	.565	23	8	2	0	1	5	5	1
vs. Right	.333	.385	.417	24	8	2	0	0	2	2	4
Runners On Base	.200	.333	.233	30	6	1	0	0	6	6	3

BOBBY JONES — BR/TR — age 24 — NYN SP9 FIN/FB

1993	G	IP	H	BB	SO	SB	CS	W	L	SV	ERA
at Home	4	28.0	27	14	20	2	1	0	3	0	3.54
on Road	5	33.2	34	8	15	1	1	2	1	0	3.74
Second Half	9	61.2	61	22	35	3	2	2	4	0	3.65

	BA	OBA	SA	AB	H	2B	3B	HR	RBI	BB	SO
Total	.262	.327	.425	233	61	18	1	6	27	22	35
vs. Left	.224	.317	.320	125	28	7	1	1	7	17	21
vs. Right	.306	.339	.546	108	33	11	0	5	20	5	14
Runners On Base	.240	.321	.344	96	23	4	0	1	23	11	14

TODD JONES — BL/TR — age 26 — HOU RP27 POW/GB

1993	G	IP	H	BB	SO	SB	CS	W	L	SV	ERA
at Home	12	19.0	10	6	14	1	1	1	1	1	1.42
on Road	15	18.1	18	9	11	1	2	0	1	1	4.91
Second Half	27	37.1	28	15	25	2	3	1	2	2	3.13

	BA	OBA	SA	AB	H	2B	3B	HR	RBI	BB	SO
Total	.214	.297	.336	131	28	4	0	4	10	15	25
vs. Left	.194	.282	.226	62	12	2	0	0	2	7	11
vs. Right	.232	.312	.435	69	16	2	0	4	8	8	14
Runners On Base	.289	.353	.444	45	13	1	0	2	8	4	5

STEVE KARSAY — BR/TR — age 22 — OAK SP8 FIN/FB

1993	G	IP	H	BB	SO	SB	CS	W	L	SV	ERA
at Home	4	27.1	27	8	16	2	1	1	2	0	3.62
on Road	4	21.2	22	8	17	3	1	2	1	0	4.57
Second Half	8	49.0	49	16	33	5	2	3	3	0	4.04

	BA	OBA	SA	AB	H	2B	3B	HR	RBI	BB	SO
Total	.258	.319	.384	190	49	8	2	4	22	16	33
vs. Left	.267	.330	.376	101	27	4	2	1	14	10	17
vs. Right	.247	.306	.393	89	22	4	0	3	8	6	16
Runners On Base	.262	.322	.425	80	21	2	1	3	21	6	11

MARK KIEFER — BR/TR — age 26 — MIL RP6 POW/FB

1993	G	IP	H	BB	SO	SB	CS	W	L	SV	ERA
at Home	2	2.1	1	1	3	0	0	0	0	0	0.00
on Road	4	7.0	2	4	4	1	0	0	0	1	0.00
Second Half	6	9.1	3	5	7	1	0	0	0	1	0.00

	BA	OBA	SA	AB	H	2B	3B	HR	RBI	BB	SO
Total	.097	.243	.097	31	3	0	0	0	3	5	7
vs. Left	.083	.214	.083	12	1	0	0	0	0	1	2
vs. Right	.105	.261	.105	19	2	0	0	0	3	4	5
Runners On Base	.071	.235	.071	14	1	0	0	0	3	3	2

KEVIN KING — BL/TL — age 25 — SEA RP13 POW/GB

1993	G	IP	H	BB	SO	SB	CS	W	L	SV	ERA
at Home	6	4.1	0	1	2	0	0	0	0	0	0.00
on Road	7	7.1	9	3	6	1	0	0	1	0	9.82
Second Half	13	11.2	9	4	8	1	0	0	1	0	6.17

	BA	OBA	SA	AB	H	2B	3B	HR	RBI	BB	SO
Total	.231	.304	.538	39	9	3	0	3	10	4	8
vs. Left	.286	.412	.643	14	4	1	0	1	4	2	3
vs. Right	.200	.241	.480	25	5	1	0	2	6	2	5
Runners On Base	.250	.320	.650	20	5	2	0	2	9	3	6

PHIL LEFTWICH — BR/TR — age 25 — CAL SP12 FIN/FB

1993	G	IP	H	BB	SO	SB	CS	W	L	SV	ERA
at Home	7	51.2	46	12	23	4	2	2	4	0	2.96
on Road	5	29.0	35	15	8	0		2	2	0	5.28
Second Half	12	80.2	81	27	31	4	4	4	6	0	3.79

	BA	OBA	SA	AB	H	2B	3B	HR	RBI	BB	SO
Total	.262	.326	.366	309	81	15	1	5	33	27	31
vs. Left	.248	.322	.325	157	39	4	1	2	19	17	10
vs. Right	.276	.331	.408	152	42	11	0	3	14	10	21
Runners On Base	.252	.354	.341	123	31	3	1	2	30	17	9

CURT LESKANIC — BR/TR — age 26 — COL RP10, SP8 FIN/FB

1993	G	IP	H	BB	SO	SB	CS	W	L	SV	ERA
at Home	9	30.0	30	13	19	0	0	1	1	0	4.20
on Road	9	27.0	29	14	11	0	1	0	4	0	6.67
Second Half	17	50.0	52	24	30	0	0	1	4	0	5.40

	BA	OBA	SA	AB	H	2B	3B	HR	RBI	BB	SO
Total	.266	.345	.401	222	59	9	0	7	37	27	30
vs. Left	.305	.381	.458	118	36	6	0	4	20	14	14
vs. Right	.221	.306	.337	104	23	3	0	3	17	13	16
Runners On Base	.290	.370	.480	100	29	4	0	5	35	15	8

GRAEME LLOYD — BL/TL — age 27 — MIL RP55 FIN/GB

1993	G	IP	H	BB	SO	SB	CS	W	L	SV	ERA
at Home	26	26.1	35	2	15	2	0	1	1	0	3.42
on Road	29	37.1	29	11	16	0	0	2	3	0	2.41
Second Half	23	22.0	27	4	9	0	0	1	4	0	4.09

	BA	OBA	SA	AB	H	2B	3B	HR	RBI	BB	SO
Total	.256	.299	.356	250	64	8	1	5	34	13	31
vs. Left	.203	.224	.311	74	15	2	0	2	11	1	11
vs. Right	.278	.328	.375	176	49	6	1	3	23	12	20
Runners On Base	.252	.299	.370	135	34	4	0	4	33	8	18

BRIAN LOONEY — BL/TL — age 25 — MON RP2, SP1 POW/FB

1993	G	IP	H	BB	SO	SB	CS	W	L	SV	ERA
at Home	1	1.2	0	3	0	0	0	0	0	0	0.00
on Road	2	4.1	8	2	4	0	0	0	0	0	4.15
Second Half	3	6.0	8	2	7	0	0	0	0	0	3.00

	BA	OBA	SA	AB	H	2B	3B	HR	RBI	BB	SO
Total	.308	.357	.385	26	8	2	0	0	0	2	7
vs. Left	.250	.250	.500	4	1	1	0	0	0	0	1
vs. Right	.318	.375	.364	22	7	1	0	0	2	2	6
Runners On Base	.333	.375	.400	15	5	1	0	0	2	1	3

ALBIE LOPEZ — BR/TR — age 23 — CLE SP9 POW/GB

1993	G	IP	H	BB	SO	SB	CS	W	L	SV	ERA
at Home	5	31.1	21	19	18	3	2	3	0	0	3.45
on Road	4	18.1	28	13	7	2	1	0	1	0	10.31
Second Half	9	49.2	49	32	25	5	3	3	1	0	5.98

	BA	OBA	SA	AB	H	2B	3B	HR	RBI	BB	SO
Total	.262	.371	.412	187	49	7	0	7	30	32	25
vs. Left	.271	.412	.385	96	26	2	0	3	11	22	11
vs. Right	.253	.324	.440	91	23	5	0	4	19	10	14
Runners On Base	.269	.355	.430	93	25	6	0	3	26	13	15

LARRY LUEBBERS — BR/TR — age 25 — CIN SP14 FIN/FB

1993	G	IP	H	BB	SO	SB	CS	W	L	SV	ERA
at Home	7	42.0	35	21	22	4	4	1	3	0	4.07
on Road	7	35.1	39	17	16	1	4	1	2	0	5.09
Second Half	14	77.1	74	38	38	5	8	2	5	0	4.54

	BA	OBA	SA	AB	H	2B	3B	HR	RBI	BB	SO
Total	.261	.345	.377	284	74	12	0	7	40	38	38
vs. Left	.267	.351	.404	146	39	5	0	5	24	21	16
vs. Right	.254	.338	.348	138	35	7	0	2	16	17	22
Runners On Base	.281	.370	.474	114	32	5	0	5	37	19	15

PEDRO A. MARTINEZ — BL/TL — age 26 — SD RP32 POW/FB

1993	G	IP	H	BB	SO	SB	CS	W	L	SV	ERA
at Home	17	23.1	10	8	24	1	0	3	0	0	1.54
on Road	15	13.2	13	5	8	2	2	0	1	0	3.95
Second Half	30	35.2	21	13	31	3	2	3	1	0	2.02

	BA	OBA	SA	AB	H	2B	3B	HR	RBI	BB	SO
Total	.172	.250	.299	134	23	5	0	4	11	13	32
vs. Left	.224	.296	.429	49	11	1	0	3	7	4	9
vs. Right	.141	.223	.224	85	12	4	0	1	4	9	23
Runners On Base	.159	.243	.270	63	10	1	0	2	9	7	15

KEVIN MCGEHEE — BR/TR — age 25 — BAL RP5 FIN/FB

1993	G	IP	H	BB	SO	SB	CS	W	L	SV	ERA
at Home	3	10.1	9	6	2	1	0	0	0	0	4.35
on Road	2	6.1	9	1	5	1	0	0	0	0	8.53
Second Half	5	16.2	18	7	7	2	0	0	0	0	5.94

	BA	OBA	SA	AB	H	2B	3B	HR	RBI	BB	SO
Total	.281	.365	.625	64	18	5	1	5	13	7	7
vs. Left	.150	.320	.350	20	3	1	0	1	2	4	2
vs. Right	.341	.388	.750	44	15	4	1	4	11	3	5
Runners On Base	.318	.429	.682	22	7	1	0	2	10	3	2

BRETT MERRIMAN — BR/TR — age 28 — MIN RP19 POW/GB

1993	G	IP	H	BB	SO	SB	CS	W	L	SV	ERA
at Home	11	19.1	24	15	12	0	0	1	0	0	8.38
on Road	8	7.2	12	8	2	0	1	0	1	0	12.91
Second Half	13	18.0	18	11	10	0	1	1	1	0	5.00

	BA	OBA	SA	AB	H	2B	3B	HR	RBI	BB	SO
Total	.343	.466	.543	105	36	10	1	3	27	23	14
vs. Left	.426	.548	.660	47	20	5	0	2	14	13	2
vs. Right	.276	.394	.448	58	16	5	1	1	13	10	12
Runners On Base	.397	.481	.635	63	25	9	0	2	26	10	8

DANNY MICELI — BR/TR — age 24 — PIT RP9 POW/FB

1993	G	IP	H	BB	SO	SB	CS	W	L	SV	ERA
at Home	6	3.2	1	1	3	0	0	0	0	0	0.00
on Road	3	1.2	5	2	1	2	0	0	0	0	16.20
Second Half	9	5.1	6	3	4	2	0	0	0	0	5.06

	BA	OBA	SA	AB	H	2B	3B	HR	RBI	BB	SO
Total	.273	.360	.364	22	6	2	0	0	3	3	4
vs. Left	.500	.625	.500	6	3	0	0	0	0	2	1
vs. Right	.188	.235	.313	16	3	2	0	0	3	1	3
Runners On Base	.308	.400	.462	13	4	2	0	0	3	2	3

NATE MINCHEY — BR/TR — age 25 — BOS SP5 FIN/GB

1993	G	IP	H	BB	SO	SB	CS	W	L	SV	ERA
at Home	2	11.2	14	4	7	0	1	0	1	0	4.63
on Road	3	21.1	21	4	11	1	0	1	1	0	2.95
Second Half	5	33.0	35	8	18	1	1	1	2	0	3.55

	BA	OBA	SA	AB	H	2B	3B	HR	RBI	BB	SO
Total	.265	.307	.455	132	35	8	1	5	14	8	18
vs. Left	.220	.292	.424	59	13	1	1	3	6	6	3
vs. Right	.301	.320	.479	73	22	7	0	2	8	2	15
Runners On Base	.229	.302	.417	48	11	4	1	1	10	5	9

DARREN OLIVER — BR/TL — age 24 — TEX RP2 POW/FB

1993	G	IP	H	BB	SO	SB	CS	W	L	SV	ERA
at Home	1	3.1	2	0	4	0	0	0	0	0	2.70
on Road	1	0.0	0	1	0	1	0	0	0	0	0.00
Second Half	2	3.1	2	1	4	1	0	0	0	0	2.70

	BA	OBA	SA	AB	H	2B	3B	HR	RBI	BB	SO
Total	.154	.214	.385	13	2	0	0	1	1	1	4
vs. Left	.167	.286	.167	6	1	0	0	0	0	1	3
vs. Right	.143	.143	.571	7	1	0	0	1	1	0	1
Runners On Base	.000	.333	.000	2	0	0	0	0	0	1	1

ANGEL MIRANDA — BL/TL — age 25 — MIL SP17, RP5 POW/FB

1993	G	IP	H	BB	SO	SB	CS	W	L	SV	ERA
at Home	12	70.1	63	26	52	5	2	3	2	0	3.07
on Road	10	49.2	37	26	36	5	1	1	3	0	3.62
Second Half	17	108.2	92	45	82	7	3	4	4	0	3.23

	BA	OBA	SA	AB	H	2B	3B	HR	RBI	BB	SO
Total	.226	.309	.373	442	100	23	3	12	44	52	88
vs. Left	.210	.330	.296	81	17	7	0	0	6	15	16
vs. Right	.230	.303	.391	361	83	16	3	12	38	37	72
Runners On Base	.235	.337	.428	166	39	10	2	6	38	26	36

MIKE OQUIST — BR/TR — age 26 — BAL RP5 POW/FB

1993	G	IP	H	BB	SO	SB	CS	W	L	SV	ERA
at Home	2	5.2	10	4	4	0	1	0	0	0	7.94
on Road	3	6.0	2	0	4	0	0	1	0	0	0.00
Second Half	5	11.2	12	4	8	0	1	0	0	0	3.86

	BA	OBA	SA	AB	H	2B	3B	HR	RBI	BB	SO
Total	.261	.320	.326	46	12	3	0	0	3	4	8
vs. Left	.267	.353	.267	15	4	0	0	0	2	2	0
vs. Right	.258	.303	.355	31	8	3	0	0	1	2	8
Runners On Base	.269	.296	.269	26	7	0	0	0	3	1	4

MIKE MOHLER — BR/TL — age 26 — OAK RP33, SP9 POW/FB

1993	G	IP	H	BB	SO	SB	CS	W	L	SV	ERA
at Home	20	28.1	28	16	25	4	2	0	3	0	5.40
on Road	22	36.0	29	28	17	4	1		3	0	5.75
Second Half	15	43.2	37	23	26	6	2	1	5	0	5.77

	BA	OBA	SA	AB	H	2B	3B	HR	RBI	BB	SO
Total	.241	.361	.414	237	57	11	0	10	43	44	42
vs. Left	.183	.310	.239	71	13	4	0	0	10	13	17
vs. Right	.265	.383	.488	166	44	7	0	10	33	31	25
Runners On Base	.261	.396	.513	115	30	5	0	8	41	26	23

LANCE PAINTER — BL/TL — age 27 — COL SP6, RP4 FIN/FB

1993	G	IP	H	BB	SO	SB	CS	W	L	SV	ERA
at Home	4	15.1	24	4	9	1	1	1	1	0	7.63
on Road	6	23.2	28	5	7	1	3	1	1	0	4.94
Second Half	7	24.1	26	4	9	3	2	2	0	0	2.96

	BA	OBA	SA	AB	H	2B	3B	HR	RBI	BB	SO
Total	.333	.370	.532	156	52	10	3	5	24	9	16
vs. Left	.226	.333	.452	31	7	0	2	1	6	5	4
vs. Right	.360	.380	.552	125	45	10	1	4	18	4	12
Runners On Base	.385	.420	.585	65	25	3	2	2	21	4	7

MARCUS MOORE — BB/TR — age 24 — COL RP27 POW/FB

1993	G	IP	H	BB	SO	SB	CS	W	L	SV	ERA
at Home	14	14.1	13	12	8	2	0	1	0	0	4.40
on Road	13	12.0	17	8	5	0	0	2	1	0	9.75
Second Half	27	26.1	30	20	13	2	0	3	1	0	6.84

	BA	OBA	SA	AB	H	2B	3B	HR	RBI	BB	SO
Total	.291	.398	.495	103	30	5	2	4	23	20	13
vs. Left	.265	.394	.449	49	13	1	1	2	12	12	9
vs. Right	.315	.403	.537	54	17	4	1	2	11	8	4
Runners On Base	.333	.391	.561	57	19	2	1	3	22	7	5

BRAD PENNINGTON — BL/TL — age 25 — BAL RP34 POW/FB

1993	G	IP	H	BB	SO	SB	CS	W	L	SV	ERA
at Home	18	18.0	23	16	19	3	1	1	1	3	8.00
on Road	16	15.0	11	9	20	0	0	2	1	1	4.80
Second Half	13	11.0	18	15	12	0	0	1	0	0	13.91

	BA	OBA	SA	AB	H	2B	3B	HR	RBI	BB	SO
Total	.266	.391	.477	128	34	4	1	7	35	25	39
vs. Left	.342	.419	.447	38	13	1	0	1	9	4	5
vs. Right	.233	.381	.489	90	21	3	1	6	26	21	34
Runners On Base	.277	.384	.458	83	23	4	1	3	31	15	25

BOBBY MUNOZ — BR/TR — age 26 — NYA RP38 POW/GB

1993	G	IP	H	BB	SO	SB	CS	W	L	SV	ERA
at Home	18	24.1	20	11	18	2	0	3	1	0	3.70
on Road	20	21.1	28	15	15	4	0	0	2	0	7.17
Second Half	24	27.2	36	17	16	4	0	1	3	0	7.16

	BA	OBA	SA	AB	H	2B	3B	HR	RBI	BB	SO
Total	.270	.357	.337	178	48	9	0	1	19	26	33
vs. Left	.207	.299	.259	58	12	3	0	0	4	8	10
vs. Right	.300	.386	.375	120	36	6	0	1	15	18	23
Runners On Base	.294	.411	.365	85	25	3	0	1	19	19	15

ERIK PLANTENBERG — BB/TL — age 26 — SEA RP20 POW/GB

1993	G	IP	H	BB	SO	SB	CS	W	L	SV	ERA
at Home	11	5.0	8	9	3	0	0	0	0	1	9.00
on Road	9	4.2	3	3	0	0	0	0	0	0	3.86
Second Half	20	9.2	11	12	3	0	0	0	1	0	6.52

	BA	OBA	SA	AB	H	2B	3B	HR	RBI	BB	SO
Total	.282	.462	.333	39	11	2	0	0	5	12	3
vs. Left	.211	.400	.263	19	4	1	0	0	3	5	2
vs. Right	.350	.519	.400	20	7	1	0	0	2	7	1
Runners On Base	.250	.417	.321	28	7	2	0	0	5	7	3

ROBB NEN — BR/TR — age 25 — TEX/ — FLO RP20, SP4 POW/GB

1993	G	IP	H	BB	SO	SB	CS	W	L	SV	ERA
at Home	15	38.2	42	25	28	3	1	2	0	0	6.28
on Road	9	17.1	21	21	11	2	1	0	1	0	7.79
Second Half	15	33.1	35	20	27	4	0	1	0	0	7.02

	BA	OBA	SA	AB	H	2B	3B	HR	RBI	BB	SO
Total	.283	.402	.457	223	63	17	2	6	39	46	39
vs. Left	.216	.339	.289	97	21	3	2	0	9	18	17
vs. Right	.333	.449	.587	126	42	14	0	6	30	28	22
Runners On Base	.316	.410	.453	117	37	10	0	2	35	20	15

ROSS POWELL — BL/TL — age 26 — CIN RP8, SP1 POW/FB

1993	G	IP	H	BB	SO	SB	CS	W	L	SV	ERA
at Home	5	7.1	5	2	8	1	0	0	1	0	2.45
on Road	4	9.0	8	4	9	1	1	0	2	0	6.00
Second Half	9	16.1	13	6	17	2	1	0	3	0	4.41

	BA	OBA	SA	AB	H	2B	3B	HR	RBI	BB	SO
Total	.224	.297	.328	58	13	1	1	1	4	6	17
vs. Left	.154	.267	.154	13	2	0	0	0	0	2	3
vs. Right	.244	.306	.378	45	11	1	1	1	4	4	14
Runners On Base	.227	.261	.364	22	5	0	0	1	4	1	2

JOHN O'DONOGHUE — BL/TL — age 25 — BAL RP10, SP1 POW/GB

1993	G	IP	H	BB	SO	SB	CS	W	L	SV	ERA
at Home	5	13.0	16	8	9	2	0	0	1	0	6.23
on Road	6	6.2	2	7	1	0	0	0	0	0	1.35
Second Half	10	13.0	13	6	13	3	0	0	0	0	2.77

	BA	OBA	SA	AB	H	2B	3B	HR	RBI	BB	SO
Total	.278	.367	.519	79	22	7	0	4	13	10	16
vs. Left	.217	.379	.261	23	5	1	0	0	2	5	4
vs. Right	.304	.361	.625	56	17	6	0	4	11	5	12
Runners On Base	.282	.317	.590	39	11	3	0	3	12	2	7

RICH ROBERTSON — BL/TL — age 26 — PIT RP9 FIN/GB

1993	G	IP	H	BB	SO	SB	CS	W	L	SV	ERA
at Home	4	5.0	8	3	2	0	0	0	1	0	9.00
on Road	5	4.0	7	1	3	0	0	0	0	0	2.25
Second Half	7	7.1	12	3	4	1	0	0	0	0	7.36

	BA	OBA	SA	AB	H	2B	3B	HR	RBI	BB	SO
Total	.385	.442	.462	39	15	3	0	0	4	4	5
vs. Left	.333	.444	.333	15	5	0	0	0	2	3	4
vs. Right	.417	.440	.542	24	10	3	0	0	2	1	1
Runners On Base	.375	.423	.417	24	9	0	0	0	4	2	3

JOHN ROPER — BR/TR — age 23 — CIN SP15, RP1 POW/GB

1993	G	IP	H	BB	SO	SB	CS	W	L	SV	ERA
at Home	9	48.1	46	20	34	7	4	2	4	0	4.84
on Road	7	31.2	46	16	20	3	0	0	1	0	6.82
Second Half	12	66.0	77	31	47	9	4	1	4	0	5.73

	BA	OBA	SA	AB	H	2B	3B	HR	RBI	BB	SO
Total	.295	.372	.462	312	92	14	4	10	44	36	54
vs. Left	.358	.429	.554	148	53	6	4	5	22	17	24
vs. Right	.238	.321	.378	164	39	8	0	5	22	19	30
Runners On Base	.310	.376	.552	145	45	9	1	8	42	15	17

KIRK RUETER — BL/TL — age 24 — MON SP14 FIN/FB

1993	G	IP	H	BB	SO	SB	CS	W	L	SV	ERA
at Home	6	38.1	37	11	16	2	3	4	0	0	2.82
on Road	8	47.1	48	7	15	2	4	4	0	0	2.66
Second Half	14	85.2	85	18	31	4	7	8	0	0	2.73

	BA	OBA	SA	AB	H	2B	3B	HR	RBI	BB	SO
Total	.264	.303	.373	322	85	20	0	5	30	18	31
vs. Left	.250	.280	.271	48	12	1	0	0	4	2	5
vs. Right	.266	.307	.391	274	73	19	0	5	26	16	26
Runners On Base	.287	.315	.393	122	35	10	0	1	26	5	16

SCOTT RUFFCORN — BR/TR — age 25 — CHA SP2, RP1 POW/GB

1993	G	IP	H	BB	SO	SB	CS	W	L	SV	ERA
at Home	1	4.1	4	3	1	0	0	0	1	0	8.31
on Road	2	5.2	5	7	1	5	0	0	1	0	7.94
Second Half	2	5.1	5	4	2	0	0	0	1	0	6.75

	BA	OBA	SA	AB	H	2B	3B	HR	RBI	BB	SO
Total	.265	.422	.500	34	9	2	0	2	10	10	2
vs. Left	.250	.455	.438	16	4	0	0	1	4	6	0
vs. Right	.278	.391	.556	18	5	2	0	1	6	4	2
Runners On Base	.300	.375	.650	20	6	1	0	2	10	3	1

JOHNNY RUFFIN — BR/TR — age 23 — CIN RP21 POW/FB

1993	G	IP	H	BB	SO	SB	CS	W	L	SV	ERA
at Home	11	19.1	18	5	15	3	0	0	0	1	1.86
on Road	10	18.1	18	6	15	1	0	2	1	1	5.40
Second Half	21	37.2	36	11	30	4	0	2	1	2	3.58

	BA	OBA	SA	AB	H	2B	3B	HR	RBI	BB	SO
Total	.247	.304	.432	146	36	7	4	4	20	11	30
vs. Left	.286	.329	.468	77	22	3	4	1	7	5	15
vs. Right	.203	.276	.391	69	14	4	0	3	13	6	15
Runners On Base	.270	.324	.524	63	17	3	2	3	19	4	15

ROGER SALKELD — BR/TR — age 23 — SEA SP2, RP1 POW/FB

1993	G	IP	H	BB	SO	SB	CS	W	L	SV	ERA
at Home	0	0.0	0	0	0	0	0	0	0	0	0.00
on Road	3	14.1	13	4	13	0	0	0	0	0	2.51
Second Half	3	14.1	13	4	13	0	0	0	0	0	2.51

	BA	OBA	SA	AB	H	2B	3B	HR	RBI	BB	SO
Total	.232	.295	.357	56	13	5	1	0	3	4	13
vs. Left	.300	.323	.467	30	9	3	1	0	2	1	5
vs. Right	.154	.267	.231	26	4	2	0	0	1	3	8
Runners On Base	.231	.286	.308	26	6	2	0	0	3	2	5

SCOTT SANDERS — BR/TR — age 25 — SD SP9 POW/GB

1993	G	IP	H	BB	SO	SB	CS	W	L	SV	ERA
at Home	5	27.0	30	12	17	2	2	2	1	0	4.33
on Road	4	25.1	24	11	20	2	1	1	2	0	3.91
Second Half	9	52.1	54	23	37	4	3	3	3	0	4.13

	BA	OBA	SA	AB	H	2B	3B	HR	RBI	BB	SO
Total	.265	.339	.363	204	54	6	1	4	29	23	37
vs. Left	.337	.447	.474	95	32	4	0	3	15	18	10
vs. Right	.202	.233	.266	109	22	2	1	1	14	5	27
Runners On Base	.313	.369	.404	99	31	3	0	2	27	10	17

JEFF SCHWARZ — BR/TR — age 30 — CHA RP41 POW/GB

1993	G	IP	H	BB	SO	SB	CS	W	L	SV	ERA
at Home	18	21.1	13	13	19	3	2	1	1	0	1.69
on Road	23	29.2	22	25	22	5	3	1	2	0	5.16
Second Half	19	21.0	18	21	17	0	4	1	2	0	5.14

	BA	OBA	SA	AB	H	2B	3B	HR	RBI	BB	SO
Total	.201	.349	.293	174	35	9	2	1	18	38	41
vs. Left	.216	.379	.338	74	16	4	1	1	9	19	19
vs. Right	.190	.325	.260	100	19	5	1	0	9	19	22
Runners On Base	.172	.316	.237	93	16	4	1	0	17	20	24

DARRYL SCOTT — BR/TR — age 26 — CAL RP16 POW/FB

1993	G	IP	H	BB	SO	SB	CS	W	L	SV	ERA
at Home	8	9.1	9	2	7	1	0	1	0	0	2.89
on Road	8	10.2	10	9	6	3	0	0	2	0	8.44
Second Half	10	11.1	10	5	5	3	0	1	2	0	5.56

	BA	OBA	SA	AB	H	2B	3B	HR	RBI	BB	SO
Total	.250	.344	.368	76	19	6	0	1	18	11	13
vs. Left	.171	.256	.257	35	6	3	0	0	5	4	6
vs. Right	.317	.412	.463	41	13	3	0	1	13	7	7
Runners On Base	.293	.380	.463	41	12	4	0	1	18	7	5

AARON SELE — BR/TR — age 24 — BOS SP18 POW/GB

1993	G	IP	H	BB	SO	SB	CS	W	L	SV	ERA
at Home	9	57.2	49	26	50	3	0	4	2	0	2.81
on Road	9	54.0	51	22	43	5	1	3	0	0	2.67
Second Half	16	99.0	91	41	79	8	1	6	2	0	2.91

	BA	OBA	SA	AB	H	2B	3B	HR	RBI	BB	SO
Total	.237	.322	.334	422	100	24	1	5	37	48	93
vs. Left	.227	.327	.310	216	49	12	0	2	16	33	43
vs. Right	.248	.316	.359	206	51	12	1	3	21	15	50
Runners On Base	.237	.316	.317	186	44	10	1	0	33	21	43

ZAK SHINALL — BR/TR — age 26 — SEA RP1 FIN/FB

1993	G	IP	H	BB	SO	SB	CS	W	L	SV	ERA
at Home	1	2.2	4	2	0	0	0	0	0	0	3.38
on Road	0	0.0	0	0	0	0	0	0	0	0	0.00
Second Half	0	0.0	0	0	0	0	0	0	0	0	0.00

	BA	OBA	SA	AB	H	2B	3B	HR	RBI	BB	SO
Total	.333	.429	.833	12	4	1	0	1	1	2	0
vs. Left	.250	.400	.750	4	1	0	1	0	0	1	0
vs. Right	.375	.444	.875	8	3	1	0	1	1	1	0
Runners On Base	.333	.429	.500	6	2	1	0	0	1	2	0

BRIAN SHOUSE — BL/TL — age 26 — PIT RP6 POW/GB

1993	G	IP	H	BB	SO	SB	CS	W	L	SV	ERA
at Home	2	1.1	3	0	1	0	0	0	0	0	13.50
on Road	4	2.2	4	2	2	0	0	0	0	0	6.75
Second Half	6	4.0	7	2	3	0	0	0	0	0	9.00

	BA	OBA	SA	AB	H	2B	3B	HR	RBI	BB	SO
Total	.368	.409	.579	19	7	1	0	1	3	2	3
vs. Left	.556	.500	1.000	9	5	1	0	1	3	0	2
vs. Right	.200	.333	.200	10	2	0	0	0	0	2	1
Runners On Base	.300	.273	.600	10	3	0	0	1	3	0	2

ROGER SMITHBERG — BR/TR — age 28 — OAK RP13 FIN/GB

1993	G	IP	H	BB	SO	SB	CS	W	L	SV	ERA
at Home	6	10.2	5	1	1	0	0	0	1	2	1.69
on Road	7	9.0	8	6	3	1	0	1	1	1	4.00
Second Half	13	19.2	13	7	4	1	0	1	2	3	2.75

	BA	OBA	SA	AB	H	2B	3B	HR	RBI	BB	SO
Total	.197	.284	.333	66	13	3	0	2	9	5	4
vs. Left	.231	.310	.462	26	6	0	0	2	4	3	1
vs. Right	.175	.267	.250	40	7	3	0	0	5	2	3
Runners On Base	.136	.321	.227	22	3	2	0	0	7	5	2

JERRY SPRADLIN — BB/TR — age 27 — CIN RP37 FIN/FB

1993	G	IP	H	BB	SO	SB	CS	W	L	SV	ERA
at Home	20	24.0	21	7	12	1	0	1	0	2	3.75
on Road	17	25.0	23	2	12	3	2	1	1	0	3.24
Second Half	37	49.0	44	9	24	4	2	2	1	2	3.49

	BA	OBA	SA	AB	H	2B	3B	HR	RBI	BB	SO
Total	.249	.279	.401	177	44	7	4	4	26	9	24
vs. Left	.261	.297	.551	69	18	2	3	4	14	4	10
vs. Right	.241	.267	.306	108	26	5	1	0	12	5	14
Runners On Base	.260	.266	.493	73	19	2	3	3	25	2	12

PAUL SWINGLE — BR/TR — age 28 — CAL RP9 POW/FB

1993	G	IP	H	BB	SO	SB	CS	W	L	SV	ERA
at Home	4	3.1	5	4	1	0	0	0	0	0	13.50
on Road	5	6.1	10	2	5	3	0	1	0	0	5.68
Second Half	9	9.2	15	6	6	3	0	1	0	0	8.38

	BA	OBA	SA	AB	H	2B	3B	HR	RBI	BB	SO
Total	.357	.429	.595	42	15	4	0	2	7	6	6
vs. Left	.286	.286	.714	14	4	0	0	2	2	0	3
vs. Right	.393	.486	.536	28	11	4	0	0	5	6	3
Runners On Base	.235	.417	.353	17	4	2	0	0	5	6	2

JULIAN TAVAREZ — BR/TR — age 21 — CLE SP7, RP1 FIN/GB

1993	G	IP	H	BB	SO	SB	CS	W	L	SV	ERA
at Home	3	14.2	19	2	4	1	0	1	0	0	4.30
on Road	5	22.1	34	11	15	1	2	1	2	0	8.06
Second Half	8	37.0	53	13	19	2	2	2	2	0	6.57

	BA	OBA	SA	AB	H	2B	3B	HR	RBI	BB	SO
Total	.340	.395	.526	156	53	8	0	7	26	13	19
vs. Left	.343	.397	.471	70	24	3	0	2	11	6	7
vs. Right	.337	.394	.570	86	29	5	0	5	15	7	12
Runners On Base	.338	.383	.595	74	25	4	0	5	24	6	8

KERRY TAYLOR — BR/TR — age 23 — SD RP29, SP7 POW/FB

1993	G	IP	H	BB	SO	SB	CS	W	L	SV	ERA
at Home	20	41.2	26	25	31	8	2	0	2	0	3.89
on Road	16	26.2	46	24	14	5	1	0	3	0	10.46
Second Half	21	31.1	38	20	22	1	1	0	0	0	5.17

	BA	OBA	SA	AB	H	2B	3B	HR	RBI	BB	SO
Total	.277	.396	.385	260	72	11	1	5	45	49	45
vs. Left	.308	.418	.453	117	36	6	1	3	20	23	15
vs. Right	.252	.377	.329	143	36	5	0	2	25	26	30
Runners On Base	.357	.468	.492	126	45	9	1	2	42	26	19

DAVE TELGHEDER — BR/TR — age 28 — NYN RP17, SP7 FIN/FB

1993	G	IP	H	BB	SO	SB	CS	W	L	SV	ERA
at Home	11	37.1	40	11	15	3	4	3	1	0	5.54
on Road	13	38.1	42	10	20	1	1	3	1	0	3.99
Second Half	18	60.2	71	17	29	4	4	4	2	0	5.04

	BA	OBA	SA	AB	H	2B	3B	HR	RBI	BB	SO
Total	.276	.331	.455	297	82	19	2	10	39	21	35
vs. Left	.281	.335	.451	153	43	12	1	4	17	12	19
vs. Right	.271	.327	.458	144	39	7	1	6	22	9	16
Runners On Base	.293	.343	.496	123	36	11	1	4	33	6	11

SALOMON TORRES — BR/TR — age 22 — SF SP8 POW/GB

1993	G	IP	H	BB	SO	SB	CS	W	L	SV	ERA
at Home	4	23.2	15	17	15	3	3	1	3	0	3.42
on Road	4	21.0	22	10	8	2	0	2	2	0	4.71
Second Half	8	44.2	37	27	23	5	3	3	5	0	4.03

	BA	OBA	SA	AB	H	2B	3B	HR	RBI	BB	SO
Total	.231	.344	.369	160	37	7	0	5	18	27	23
vs. Left	.169	.307	.337	83	14	2	0	4	11	17	12
vs. Right	.299	.386	.403	77	23	5	0	1	7	10	11
Runners On Base	.231	.354	.323	65	15	6	0	0	13	13	11

STEVE TRACHSEL — BR/TR — age 24 — CHN SP3 FIN/FB

1993	G	IP	H	BB	SO	SB	CS	W	L	SV	ERA
at Home	1	7.0	4	1	5	0	0	0	1	0	2.57
on Road	2	12.2	12	2	9	2	0	0	1	0	5.68
Second Half	3	19.2	16	3	14	2	0	0	2	0	4.58

	BA	OBA	SA	AB	H	2B	3B	HR	RBI	BB	SO
Total	.219	.247	.452	73	16	3	1	4	8	3	14
vs. Left	.150	.190	.250	40	6	1	0	1	2	2	8
vs. Right	.303	.314	.697	33	10	2	1	3	6	1	6
Runners On Base	.087	.154	.174	23	2	2	0	0	4	2	5

GEORGE TSAMIS — BR/TL — age 27 — MIN RP41 FIN/FB

1993	G	IP	H	BB	SO	SB	CS	W	L	SV	ERA
at Home	22	30.0	39	15	15	0	2	0	1	0	7.50
on Road	19	38.1	47	12	15	0	1	1	1	1	5.17
Second Half	28	41.2	62	18	18	0	1	0	1	1	7.34

	BA	OBA	SA	AB	H	2B	3B	HR	RBI	BB	SO
Total	.317	.378	.487	271	86	17	1	9	51	27	30
vs. Left	.344	.404	.533	90	31	5	0	4	22	6	9
vs. Right	.304	.365	.464	181	55	12	1	5	29	21	21
Runners On Base	.333	.397	.485	132	44	12	1	2	44	16	16

TOM URBANI — BL/TL — age 26 — SL SP9, RP9 FIN/GB

1993	G	IP	H	BB	SO	SB	CS	W	L	SV	ERA
at Home	9	34.1	47	14	15	0	6	0	3	0	5.50
on Road	9	27.2	26	12	18	1	0	1	0	0	3.58
Second Half	9	50.2	54	20	24	1	5	1	2	0	3.73

	BA	OBA	SA	AB	H	2B	3B	HR	RBI	BB	SO
Total	.296	.355	.433	247	73	16	3	4	35	26	33
vs. Left	.175	.292	.250	40	7	0	0	1	8	7	8
vs. Right	.319	.368	.469	207	66	16	3	3	27	19	25
Runners On Base	.302	.346	.414	116	35	5	1	2	33	11	17

ALLEN WATSON — BL/TL — age 24 — SL SP15, RP1 FIN/FB

1993	G	IP	H	BB	SO	SB	CS	W	L	SV	ERA
at Home	8	46.0	42	17	25	5	3	3	2	0	3.13
on Road	8	40.0	48	11	24	6	1	3	5	0	6.30
Second Half	16	86.0	90	28	49	11	4	6	7	0	4.60

	BA	OBA	SA	AB	H	2B	3B	HR	RBI	BB	SO
Total	.271	.330	.443	332	90	18	3	11	42	28	49
vs. Left	.240	.345	.320	50	12	1	0	1	5	8	7
vs. Right	.277	.327	.465	282	78	17	3	10	37	20	42
Runners On Base	.277	.333	.461	141	39	7	2	5	36	12	19

TURK WENDELL — BB/TR — age 27 — CHN SP4, RP3 FIN/GB

1993	G	IP	H	BB	SO	SB	CS	W	L	SV	ERA
at Home	3	5.1	9	3	2	1	0	0	1	0	8.44
on Road	4	17.1	15	5	13	0	0	1	1	0	3.12
Second Half	4	10.1	6	2	8	1	0	1	0	0	0.87

	BA	OBA	SA	AB	H	2B	3B	HR	RBI	BB	SO
Total	.273	.333	.318	88	24	4	0	0	7	8	15
vs. Left	.372	.426	.465	43	16	4	0	0	5	4	7
vs. Right	.178	.245	.178	45	8	0	0	0	2	4	8
Runners On Base	.289	.386	.342	38	11	2	0	0	7	6	7

BILL WERTZ — BR/TR — age 27 — CLE RP34 POW/FB

1993	G	IP	H	BB	SO	SB	CS	W	L	SV	ERA
at Home	18	30.2	27	17	24	0	0	0	3	0	5.28
on Road	16	29.0	27	15	29	1	0	2	0	0	1.86
Second Half	30	55.2	46	27	47	1	0	2	3	0	3.40

	BA	OBA	SA	AB	H	2B	3B	HR	RBI	BB	SO
Total	.238	.333	.344	227	54	9	0	5	28	32	53
vs. Left	.218	.319	.327	101	22	5	0	2	13	15	21
vs. Right	.254	.345	.357	126	32	4	0	3	15	17	32
Runners On Base	.264	.358	.387	106	28	7	0	2	25	15	25

WOODY WILLIAMS — BR/TR — age 28 — TOR RP30 POW/FB

1993	G	IP	H	BB	SO	SB	CS	W	L	SV	ERA
at Home	15	18.2	19	13	13	0	0	0	3	0	4.34
on Road	15	18.1	21	9	11	0	0	0	1	0	4.42
Second Half	16	16.2	13	12	10	0	0	0	1	0	5.40

	BA	OBA	SA	AB	H	2B	3B	HR	RBI	BB	SO
Total	.274	.371	.363	146	40	7	0	2	19	22	24
vs. Left	.246	.377	.281	57	14	2	0	0	4	12	7
vs. Right	.292	.366	.416	89	26	5	0	2	15	10	17
Runners On Base	.312	.407	.429	77	24	6	0	1	18	12	13

TIM WORRELL — BR/TR — age 27 — SD SP16, RP5 FIN/FB

1993	G	IP	H	BB	SO	SB	CS	W	L	SV	ERA
at Home	12	68.1	62	23	40	4	5	2	3	0	3.82
on Road	9	32.1	42	20	12	6	4	0	4	0	7.24
Second Half	19	91.1	93	40	47	8	9	2	6	0	4.83

	BA	OBA	SA	AB	H	2B	3B	HR	RBI	BB	SO
Total	.269	.338	.406	387	104	16	2	11	58	43	52
vs. Left	.272	.357	.387	191	52	5	1	5	26	27	20
vs. Right	.265	.318	.423	196	52	11	1	6	32	16	32
Runners On Base	.319	.383	.491	163	52	9	2	5	52	20	24

Part 3

Team and League Statistics

This part contains batting and pitching situational totals for the 1993 season for both leagues and for all 28 teams. The reports are presented in exactly the same fashion as for regular batters and pitchers.

Also included are the 1993 official batting, pitching, and fielding statistics totals for both leagues and all 28 teams as well as the final standings for both leagues.

Following the team batting and pitching totals are three other interesting team breakdowns.

The first report lists each team's batting statistics by Lineup Order, allowing you to see which slots in the batting order were carrying their weight and which were not.

The second report lists each team's batting statistics by Defensive Position, allowing you to see which positions were producing offensively and which were not.

The third report separates team pitching totals by Starting Pitching and Relief Pitching, allowing you to see how effective or ineffective each team's rotation and bullpen were.

Abbreviations used in these reports are the same as in Part 1 (for situational statistics) and Part 5 (for traditional statistics).

The Park Effects report details the influence of each current major-league stadium on the way the game is played. The report gives data for the 1993 season as well as for recent seasons. Armed with this information, one can better interpret player statistics by making adjustments for the substantial effects of venues like the Astrodome and Fenway Park. Be sure to check out the numbers for Mile High Stadium!

TEAM AND LEAGUE SITUATIONAL STATISTICS

AMERICAN LEAGUE BATTING

	BA	OBA	SA	AB	H	2B	3B	HR	RBI	BB	SO
Totals	.267	.337	.408	77506	20661	3861	427	2074	10063	8006	12952
vs. Left	.264	.333	.404	22350	5909	1116	95	605	2873	2339	3748
vs. Right	.267	.337	.409	55156	14752	2745	332	1469	7190	5667	9204
at Home	.272	.343	.417	37894	10311	1934	230	1038	5169	4094	6149
on Road	.261	.329	.398	39612	10350	1927	197	1036	4894	3912	6803
on Grass	.266	.336	.407	55102	14655	2578	279	1538	7173	5754	9182
on Turf	.268	.338	.410	22404	6006	1283	148	536	2890	2252	3770
Day Games	.268	.340	.412	25765	6900	1293	151	709	3400	2699	4437
Night Games	.266	.336	.405	51741	13761	2568	276	1365	6663	5307	8515
April	.265	.336	.402	10072	2667	509	62	249	1358	1048	1709
May	.262	.332	.399	13257	3473	612	84	345	1634	1338	2262
June	.267	.338	.414	12971	3466	668	74	361	1716	1350	2110
July	.278	.345	.430	12989	3609	678	67	389	1789	1273	2026
August	.263	.334	.404	13825	3638	677	70	379	1742	1434	2341
Sept-Oct	.265	.339	.397	14392	3808	717	70	351	1824	1563	2504
Bases Empty	.260	.328	.402	43344	11287	2179	231	1169	1169	3964	7304
Leadoff	.268	.331	.415	18539	4965	984	106	512	512	1627	2931
Runners on base	.274	.346	.415	34162	9374	1682	196	905	8894	4042	5648
Scoring Position	.270	.357	.411	19740	5335	971	119	526	7777	2890	3508
Late and Close	.265	.342	.385	12039	3188	535	57	265	1604	1387	2228

Cleveland Indians Batting

	BA	OBA	SA	AB	H	2B	3B	HR	RBI	BB	SO
Totals	.275	.335	.409	5619	1547	264	31	141	747	488	843
vs. Left	.270	.334	.392	1792	484	84	9	39	228	163	294
vs. Right	.278	.335	.416	3827	1063	180	22	102	519	325	549
at Home	.272	.338	.404	2667	726	106	19	69	366	264	384
on Road	.278	.331	.413	2952	821	158	12	72	381	224	459
on Grass	.276	.337	.412	4729	1303	215	29	124	633	426	701
on Turf	.274	.320	.391	890	244	49	2	17	114	62	142
Day Games	.277	.337	.415	1938	537	81	11	55	266	170	291
Night Games	.274	.333	.405	3681	1010	183	20	86	481	318	552
April	.284	.335	.443	779	221	42	5	24	103	56	138
May	.262	.315	.378	968	254	36	5	22	117	71	136
June	.267	.326	.419	886	237	46	8	24	123	74	128
July	.268	.330	.389	895	240	41	2	21	119	81	124
August	.290	.351	.426	1055	306	51	7	26	150	99	150
Sept-Oct	.279	.347	.403	1036	289	48	4	24	135	107	167
Bases Empty	.268	.325	.402	3139	840	165	14	76	76	239	466
Leadoff	.271	.327	.403	1339	363	73	10	28	28	102	188
Runners on base	.285	.346	.417	2480	707	99	17	65	671	249	377
Scoring Position	.281	.353	.424	1426	401	62	11	40	598	187	233
Late and Close	.286	.354	.410	878	251	39	2	22	135	91	138

Baltimore Orioles Batting

	BA	OBA	SA	AB	H	2B	3B	HR	RBI	BB	SO
Totals	.267	.346	.413	5508	1470	287	24	157	744	655	930
vs. Left	.268	.342	.406	1650	442	83	2	47	216	182	288
vs. Right	.266	.348	.416	3858	1028	204	22	110	528	473	642
at Home	.278	.360	.436	2722	757	148	11	87	414	348	469
on Road	.256	.332	.391	2786	713	139	13	70	330	307	461
on Grass	.266	.345	.413	4665	1241	238	18	137	638	555	772
on Turf	.272	.351	.415	843	229	49	6	20	106	100	158
Day Games	.266	.339	.410	1513	403	78	7	42	183	164	286
Night Games	.267	.349	.414	3995	1067	209	17	115	561	491	644
April	.258	.335	.380	740	191	43	7	11	85	80	138
May	.238	.326	.351	960	228	42	2	21	93	121	188
June	.279	.356	.438	927	259	59	2	28	133	110	141
July	.290	.358	.455	887	257	51	3	30	137	95	131
August	.268	.352	.426	964	258	39	3	36	147	131	157
Sept-Oct	.269	.347	.424	1030	277	53	7	31	149	118	175
Bases Empty	.254	.333	.403	3026	769	135	15	95	95	337	522
Leadoff	.259	.335	.423	1294	335	58	5	48	48	143	222
Runners on base	.282	.361	.426	2482	701	152	9	62	649	318	408
Scoring Position	.282	.366	.432	1431	404	91	6	37	573	213	254
Late and Close	.247	.333	.374	853	211	37	4	21	108	110	171

Detroit Tigers Batting

	BA	OBA	SA	AB	H	2B	3B	HR	RBI	BB	SO
Totals	.275	.362	.434	5620	1546	282	38	178	853	765	1122
vs. Left	.259	.357	.419	1555	403	74	6	54	239	236	292
vs. Right	.281	.365	.440	4065	1143	208	32	124	614	529	830
at Home	.273	.363	.452	2728	746	137	20	103	436	381	526
on Road	.277	.362	.417	2892	800	145	18	75	417	384	596
on Grass	.270	.358	.424	4695	1268	221	34	145	695	645	920
on Turf	.301	.383	.482	925	278	61	4	33	158	120	202
Day Games	.281	.368	.439	2093	588	112	16	62	315	282	413
Night Games	.272	.359	.431	3527	958	170	22	116	538	483	709
April	.298	.397	.484	768	229	46	5	29	160	127	160
May	.270	.356	.415	919	248	35	13	24	127	124	195
June	.249	.327	.427	971	242	49	5	38	137	115	182
July	.271	.352	.432	995	270	62	4	30	124	122	210
August	.290	.386	.442	994	288	47	7	30	178	153	187
Sept-Oct	.276	.361	.412	973	269	43	4	27	127	124	188
Bases Empty	.265	.354	.428	2909	772	151	16	97	97	385	588
Leadoff	.268	.355	.426	1265	339	58	8	42	42	165	248
Runners on base	.286	.371	.440	2711	774	131	22	81	756	380	534
Scoring Position	.278	.373	.436	1579	439	67	13	52	662	257	316
Late and Close	.281	.375	.422	720	202	31	4	21	122	108	163

Boston Red Sox Batting

	BA	OBA	SA	AB	H	2B	3B	HR	RBI	BB	SO
Totals	.264	.330	.395	5496	1451	319	29	114	644	508	871
vs. Left	.264	.324	.415	1512	399	82	10	42	188	120	229
vs. Right	.264	.333	.387	3984	1052	237	19	72	456	388	642
at Home	.281	.349	.420	2743	770	193	14	54	367	269	432
on Road	.247	.312	.369	2753	681	126	15	60	277	239	439
on Grass	.268	.336	.399	4624	1238	269	23	98	554	440	723
on Turf	.244	.303	.369	872	213	50	6	16	90	68	148
Day Games	.275	.343	.408	2075	570	122	13	43	265	203	338
Night Games	.258	.323	.387	3421	881	197	16	71	379	305	533
April	.261	.322	.382	733	191	40	5	13	87	62	107
May	.276	.338	.375	947	261	52	6	10	105	85	146
June	.255	.336	.388	885	226	47	3	21	109	99	146
July	.279	.347	.440	904	252	59	3	27	133	88	127
August	.245	.298	.369	918	225	60	6	14	76	62	141
Sept-Oct	.267	.338	.411	1109	296	61	6	29	134	112	204
Bases Empty	.259	.317	.388	3144	813	180	20	62	62	240	502
Leadoff	.256	.312	.392	1346	345	82	11	26	26	99	188
Runners on base	.271	.347	.404	2352	638	139	9	52	582	268	369
Scoring Position	.278	.364	.417	1354	376	79	7	32	525	192	222
Late and Close	.269	.333	.420	845	227	51	4	23	110	76	149

Milwaukee Brewers Batting

	BA	OBA	SA	AB	H	2B	3B	HR	RBI	BB	SO
Totals	.258	.328	.378	5525	1426	240	25	125	688	555	932
vs. Left	.256	.332	.371	1872	480	78	11	38	235	203	305
vs. Right	.259	.326	.382	3653	946	162	14	87	453	352	627
at Home	.268	.343	.381	2704	724	112	17	53	353	302	442
on Road	.249	.313	.376	2821	702	128	8	72	335	253	490
on Grass	.258	.328	.376	4645	1197	191	23	104	576	471	796
on Turf	.260	.328	.392	880	229	49	2	21	112	84	136
Day Games	.255	.331	.375	2048	523	84	13	45	270	223	350
Night Games	.259	.326	.381	3477	903	156	12	80	418	332	582
April	.257	.330	.335	650	167	19	4	8	76	67	105
May	.234	.293	.356	932	218	37	4	23	111	74	174
June	.255	.322	.364	976	249	44	4	18	116	93	168
July	.272	.329	.402	891	242	43	5	21	109	73	143
August	.267	.349	.420	1107	296	54	5	35	158	138	167
Sept-Oct	.262	.340	.375	969	254	43	3	20	118	110	175
Bases Empty	.246	.311	.376	3164	779	124	14	86	86	271	558
Leadoff	.258	.322	.390	1335	344	58	7	35	35	115	221
Runners on base	.274	.350	.382	2361	647	116	11	39	602	284	374
Scoring Position	.277	.368	.385	1370	380	66	9	21	540	214	231
Late and Close	.253	.325	.333	932	236	35	3	11	105	99	178

New York Yankees Batting

	BA	OBA	SA	AB	H	2B	3B	HR	RBI	BB	SO
Totals	.279	.353	.435	5615	1568	294	24	178	793	629	910
vs. Left	.266	.347	.419	1930	514	98	7	61	256	233	317
vs. Right	.286	.357	.444	3685	1054	196	17	117	537	396	593
at Home	.280	.357	.439	2674	750	139	10	88	374	309	395
on Road	.278	.350	.432	2941	818	155	14	90	419	320	515
on Grass	.279	.354	.430	4757	1328	244	17	147	668	535	759
on Turf	.280	.351	.463	858	240	50	7	31	125	94	151
Day Games	.293	.372	.468	1892	555	106	9	69	295	230	302
Night Games	.272	.344	.418	3723	1013	188	15	109	498	399	608
April	.275	.345	.420	738	203	38	3	21	101	79	119
May	.276	.354	.432	1041	287	62	4	31	145	120	174
June	.284	.356	.471	969	275	48	8	39	154	107	156
July	.301	.367	.482	923	278	45	4	38	144	91	137
August	.272	.350	.407	937	255	50	2	24	120	114	159
Sept-Oct	.268	.347	.399	1007	270	51	3	25	129	118	165
Bases Empty	.272	.344	.442	3054	830	167	13	109	109	317	481
Leadoff	.260	.326	.431	1306	340	69	5	48	48	121	215
Runners on base	.288	.364	.427	2561	738	127	11	69	684	312	429
Scoring Position	.274	.367	.423	1436	394	75	5	43	610	224	262
Late and Close	.291	.363	.423	784	228	40	2	20	118	88	142

Chicago White Sox Batting

	BA	OBA	SA	AB	H	2B	3B	HR	RBI	BB	SO
Totals	.265	.338	.411	5483	1454	228	44	162	731	604	834
vs. Left	.254	.326	.394	1674	425	64	6	53	209	182	280
vs. Right	.270	.344	.419	3809	1029	164	38	109	522	422	554
at Home	.270	.345	.419	2657	718	109	20	82	369	300	385
on Road	.260	.332	.404	2826	736	119	24	80	362	304	449
on Grass	.264	.338	.408	4611	1219	183	32	138	615	509	670
on Turf	.269	.339	.431	872	235	45	12	24	116	95	164
Day Games	.251	.325	.384	1632	410	63	15	41	208	179	265
Night Games	.271	.344	.423	3851	1044	165	29	121	523	425	569
April	.268	.342	.384	750	201	34	7	13	102	86	120
May	.259	.336	.426	842	218	29	8	32	116	102	129
June	.268	.340	.418	946	254	36	6	31	125	102	141
July	.279	.356	.454	917	256	36	11	34	138	107	123
August	.268	.327	.419	974	261	47	5	30	130	85	160
Sept-Oct	.250	.331	.370	1054	264	46	7	22	120	122	161
Bases Empty	.255	.324	.392	3119	795	123	27	84	84	301	507
Leadoff	.268	.331	.414	1320	354	50	10	41	41	118	195
Runners on base	.279	.356	.437	2364	659	105	17	78	647	303	327
Scoring Position	.271	.358	.422	1356	367	57	11	42	553	209	205
Late and Close	.259	.336	.370	789	204	34	6	14	101	93	130

Toronto Blue Jays Batting

	BA	OBA	SA	AB	H	2B	3B	HR	RBI	BB	SO
Totals	.279	.350	.436	5579	1556	317	42	159	796	588	861
vs. Left	.265	.338	.405	1587	421	90	9	38	204	166	257
vs. Right	.284	.355	.449	3992	1135	227	33	121	592	422	604
at Home	.285	.355	.464	2734	778	161	30	90	413	282	404
on Road	.273	.345	.409	2845	778	156	12	69	383	306	457
on Grass	.282	.354	.431	2246	634	117	10	66	318	246	334
on Turf	.277	.348	.440	3333	922	200	32	93	478	342	527
Day Games	.282	.354	.469	1869	527	107	13	72	291	199	313
Night Games	.277	.348	.420	3710	1029	210	29	87	505	389	548
April	.277	.342	.419	773	214	41	6	19	114	78	149
May	.284	.345	.476	979	278	48	7	42	141	86	138
June	.279	.355	.454	967	270	68	7	29	145	103	147
July	.268	.339	.405	885	237	46	6	21	114	91	141
August	.287	.355	.433	1004	288	54	9	25	136	105	155
Sept-Oct	.277	.362	.424	971	269	60	7	23	146	125	131
Bases Empty	.281	.345	.448	3040	854	175	19	98	98	278	463
Leadoff	.294	.356	.488	1309	385	77	6	55	55	117	181
Runners on base	.276	.356	.423	2539	702	142	23	61	698	310	398
Scoring Position	.287	.376	.434	1510	434	84	13	37	618	224	252
Late and Close	.280	.362	.410	785	220	32	8	18	120	96	150

Kansas City Royals Batting

	BA	OBA	SA	AB	H	2B	3B	HR	RBI	BB	SO
Totals	.263	.320	.397	5522	1455	294	35	125	641	428	936
vs. Left	.258	.316	.388	1561	403	94	8	31	189	121	259
vs. Right	.266	.321	.401	3961	1052	200	27	94	452	307	677
at Home	.283	.336	.419	2785	788	183	23	50	355	205	401
on Road	.244	.304	.375	2737	667	111	12	75	286	223	535
on Grass	.247	.304	.380	2118	524	77	9	62	229	166	399
on Turf	.274	.329	.408	3404	931	217	26	63	412	262	537
Day Games	.262	.321	.401	1681	441	83	15	40	206	134	300
Night Games	.264	.319	.396	3841	1014	211	20	85	435	294	636
April	.253	.309	.361	770	195	40	5	11	84	61	116
May	.270	.321	.391	879	237	43	5	18	103	57	137
June	.283	.337	.408	972	275	58	5	18	117	74	161
July	.283	.333	.446	958	271	56	11	26	129	66	156
August	.244	.303	.386	987	241	52	5	26	95	79	178
Sept-Oct	.247	.314	.384	956	236	45	4	26	113	91	188
Bases Empty	.262	.313	.402	3186	836	183	20	74	74	210	543
Leadoff	.279	.329	.417	1351	377	89	10	26	26	90	207
Runners on base	.265	.328	.391	2336	619	111	15	51	567	218	393
Scoring Position	.260	.334	.385	1364	355	69	10	27	490	162	260
Late and Close	.254	.318	.380	1033	262	43	5	26	123	93	194

California Angels Batting

	BA	OBA	SA	AB	H	2B	3B	HR	RBI	BB	SO
Totals	.260	.331	.380	5391	1399	259	24	114	644	564	930
vs. Left	.261	.336	.370	1332	348	61	6	24	149	142	216
vs. Right	.259	.330	.383	4059	1051	198	18	90	495	422	714
at Home	.264	.334	.390	2654	701	118	12	64	345	270	437
on Road	.255	.329	.370	2737	698	141	12	50	299	294	493
on Grass	.260	.332	.380	4452	1156	205	19	98	544	470	775
on Turf	.259	.330	.378	939	243	54	5	16	100	94	155
Day Games	.270	.339	.398	1630	440	90	4	36	203	167	294
Night Games	.255	.328	.372	3761	959	169	19	78	441	397	636
April	.266	.323	.415	612	163	27	5	18	87	51	104
May	.257	.350	.368	958	246	47	3	18	113	133	174
June	.250	.325	.374	891	223	50	3	18	113	99	137
July	.258	.325	.369	943	243	41	2	20	101	91	145
August	.266	.329	.371	956	254	47	3	16	105	86	179
Sept-Oct	.262	.331	.393	1031	270	47	8	24	125	104	191
Bases Empty	.250	.322	.366	3062	764	144	13	62	62	312	537
Leadoff	.241	.305	.339	1326	320	61	7	18	18	116	212
Runners on base	.273	.343	.398	2329	635	115	11	52	582	252	393
Scoring Position	.281	.359	.417	1338	376	68	6	34	516	175	246
Late and Close	.245	.333	.332	897	220	26	5	14	97	111	164

Minnesota Twins Batting

	BA	OBA	SA	AB	H	2B	3B	HR	RBI	BB	SO
Totals	.264	.327	.385	5601	1480	261	27	121	642	493	850
vs. Left	.275	.334	.404	1345	370	67	5	32	160	113	191
vs. Right	.261	.325	.379	4256	1110	194	22	89	482	380	659
at Home	.270	.337	.393	2768	746	141	17	56	330	265	423
on Road	.259	.318	.377	2833	734	120	10	65	312	228	427
on Grass	.269	.330	.389	2182	586	91	8	52	249	187	305
on Turf	.261	.326	.383	3419	894	170	19	69	393	306	545
Day Games	.260	.327	.388	1912	498	101	8	42	218	173	296
Night Games	.266	.327	.384	3689	982	160	19	79	424	320	554
April	.240	.309	.365	726	174	40	6	13	83	69	109
May	.278	.343	.405	869	242	42	4	20	110	79	128
June	.263	.324	.382	901	237	31	8	20	94	75	135
July	.279	.334	.414	939	262	57	2	22	113	68	118
August	.261	.320	.373	1085	283	42	4	24	116	91	182
Sept-Oct	.261	.331	.373	1081	282	49	3	22	126	111	178
Bases Empty	.263	.317	.374	3183	836	152	15	57	57	229	476
Leadoff	.263	.308	.371	1371	360	71	6	22	22	83	189
Runners on base	.266	.341	.401	2418	644	109	12	64	585	264	374
Scoring Position	.257	.343	.392	1378	354	60	6	38	506	182	230
Late and Close	.278	.344	.380	911	253	51	3	12	102	92	138

Oakland Athletics Batting

	BA	OBA	SA	AB	H	2B	3B	HR	RBI	BB	SO
Totals	.254	.330	.394	5543	1408	260	21	158	679	622	1048
vs. Left	.255	.338	.416	1653	422	75	2	62	206	201	343
vs. Right	.253	.327	.385	3890	986	185	19	96	473	421	705
at Home	.252	.331	.382	2675	674	105	5	78	313	309	533
on Road	.256	.329	.405	2868	734	155	16	80	366	313	515
on Grass	.249	.323	.386	4572	1138	193	15	135	531	490	856
on Turf	.278	.363	.430	971	270	67	6	23	148	132	192
Day Games	.235	.314	.353	2330	547	94	8	55	236	269	463
Night Games	.268	.342	.424	3213	861	166	13	103	443	353	585
April	.257	.337	.423	596	153	30	0	23	76	70	89
May	.237	.328	.370	961	228	44	6	24	114	128	195
June	.267	.353	.403	894	239	46	3	23	119	121	172
July	.272	.342	.413	980	267	38	2	32	130	107	174
August	.235	.303	.375	1014	238	44	7	28	99	95	214
Sept-Oct	.258	.323	.393	1098	283	58	3	28	141	101	204
Bases Empty	.252	.325	.396	3095	781	160	11	88	88	313	586
Leadoff	.261	.339	.426	1311	342	71	5	45	45	147	234
Runners on base	.256	.336	.391	2448	627	100	10	70	591	309	462
Scoring Position	.237	.338	.376	1410	334	58	6	42	518	233	296
Late and Close	.239	.335	.356	930	222	40	3	21	130	133	203

NATIONAL LEAGUE BATTING

	BA	OBA	SA	AB	H	2B	3B	HR	RBI	BB	SO
Totals	.264	.327	.399	77489	20427	3588	513	1956	9534	7104	13358
vs. Left	.272	.333	.413	22808	6209	1155	146	588	2843	2061	3655
vs. Right	.260	.322	.393	54681	14218	2433	367	1368	6691	5043	9703
at Home	.268	.332	.406	37813	10135	1755	257	981	4857	3565	6370
on Road	.259	.321	.392	39676	10292	1833	256	975	4677	3539	6988
on Grass	.260	.322	.391	44199	11475	1890	230	1156	5228	3992	7779
on Turf	.269	.333	.409	33290	8952	1698	283	800	4306	3112	5579
Day Games	.263	.327	.404	25761	6779	1208	172	688	3156	2355	4437
Night Games	.264	.327	.397	51728	13648	2380	341	1268	6378	4749	8921
April	.252	.323	.375	10705	2702	460	70	237	1246	1089	1809
May	.266	.331	.395	12867	3423	609	77	300	1597	1190	2113
June	.266	.324	.400	12881	3429	607	87	314	1550	1079	2237
July	.271	.331	.415	13182	3570	650	88	359	1693	1157	2220
August	.264	.327	.412	13528	3576	605	89	405	1691	1206	2320
Sept-Oct	.260	.327	.392	14326	3727	657	102	341	1757	1383	2659
Bases Empty	.258	.320	.393	44127	11385	2036	280	1123	1123	3494	7682
Leadoff	.267	.322	.407	18820	5026	925	137	479	479	1398	3048
Runners on base	.271	.336	.406	33362	9042	1552	233	833	8411	3610	5676
Scoring Position	.264	.349	.397	19652	5193	926	149	460	7306	2738	3634
Late and Close	.254	.325	.372	11994	3045	481	68	268	1502	1273	2347

Seattle Mariners Batting

	BA	OBA	SA	AB	H	2B	3B	HR	RBI	BB	SO
Totals	.260	.339	.406	5494	1429	272	24	161	681	624	901
vs. Left	.281	.356	.445	1670	470	105	6	52	231	179	252
vs. Right	.251	.332	.389	3824	959	167	18	109	450	445	649
at Home	.259	.350	.401	2698	699	141	10	74	353	356	445
on Road	.261	.328	.411	2796	730	131	14	87	328	268	456
on Grass	.259	.325	.419	2140	555	93	7	78	245	201	351
on Turf	.261	.347	.398	3354	874	179	17	83	436	423	550
Day Games	.266	.339	.438	1664	443	82	6	64	218	171	273
Night Games	.257	.339	.392	3830	986	190	18	97	463	453	628
April	.255	.348	.385	732	187	30	1	21	95	101	128
May	.273	.339	.413	1020	278	41	6	30	115	95	158
June	.270	.346	.420	911	246	49	5	26	110	102	145
July	.283	.357	.453	903	256	51	3	32	136	96	134
August	.224	.308	.377	861	193	40	4	28	91	104	152
Sept-Oct	.252	.334	.386	1067	269	61	5	24	134	126	184
Bases Empty	.261	.331	.408	3093	806	158	11	92	92	300	514
Leadoff	.271	.332	.418	1333	361	76	6	36	36	119	226
Runners on base	.259	.348	.404	2401	623	114	13	69	589	324	387
Scoring Position	.246	.350	.380	1370	337	62	7	36	498	233	238
Late and Close	.267	.352	.380	937	250	45	2	19	122	121	158

Chicago Cubs Batting

	BA	OBA	SA	AB	H	2B	3B	HR	RBI	BB	SO
Totals	.270	.325	.414	5627	1521	259	32	161	706	446	923
vs. Left	.276	.329	.416	1532	423	71	4	45	199	118	230
vs. Right	.268	.324	.413	4095	1098	188	28	116	507	328	693
at Home	.283	.338	.424	2769	784	131	16	76	366	223	453
on Road	.258	.313	.403	2858	737	128	16	85	340	223	470
on Grass	.276	.333	.421	4302	1189	210	23	122	559	356	711
on Turf	.251	.299	.389	1325	332	49	9	39	147	90	212
Day Games	.263	.318	.388	2945	775	118	13	75	333	231	482
Night Games	.278	.333	.441	2682	746	141	19	86	373	215	441
April	.258	.304	.388	760	196	31	4	20	88	50	118
May	.285	.327	.424	887	253	42	6	23	106	56	152
June	.277	.325	.426	974	270	47	7	28	122	67	131
July	.261	.321	.402	928	242	41	6	26	114	80	154
August	.262	.323	.400	1044	274	46	1	32	123	89	167
Sept-Oct	.277	.345	.435	1034	286	52	8	32	153	104	201
Bases Empty	.266	.316	.407	3219	855	142	15	94	94	217	548
Leadoff	.269	.317	.405	1357	365	59	6	38	38	87	206
Runners on base	.277	.337	.423	2408	666	117	17	67	612	229	375
Scoring Position	.268	.349	.408	1366	366	69	10	34	510	181	245
Late and Close	.272	.330	.396	890	242	27	4	25	127	74	181

Texas Rangers Batting

	BA	OBA	SA	AB	H	2B	3B	HR	RBI	BB	SO
Totals	.267	.329	.431	5510	1472	284	39	181	780	483	984
vs. Left	.270	.325	.412	1217	328	61	8	32	163	98	225
vs. Right	.266	.330	.437	4293	1144	223	31	149	617	385	759
at Home	.273	.334	.443	2685	734	141	22	90	381	234	473
on Road	.261	.323	.421	2825	738	143	17	91	399	249	511
on Grass	.272	.333	.437	4666	1268	241	35	154	678	413	821
on Turf	.242	.302	.398	844	204	43	4	27	102	70	163
Day Games	.281	.345	.444	1488	418	90	12	43	226	135	253
Night Games	.262	.323	.427	4022	1054	194	27	138	554	348	731
April	.252	.319	.423	705	178	39	3	25	105	61	127
May	.255	.301	.424	982	250	54	11	30	124	63	190
June	.267	.325	.422	875	234	37	7	28	121	76	151
July	.287	.354	.467	969	278	52	9	35	162	97	163
August	.260	.331	.432	969	252	50	3	37	141	92	160
Sept-Oct	.277	.337	.418	1010	280	52	6	26	127	94	193
Bases Empty	.259	.316	.411	3130	812	162	23	89	89	232	561
Leadoff	.300	.350	.478	1333	400	91	10	42	42	92	205
Runners on base	.277	.344	.458	2380	660	122	16	92	691	251	423
Scoring Position	.271	.349	.430	1418	384	73	9	45	570	185	263
Late and Close	.271	.339	.421	745	202	31	6	23	111	76	150

Florida Marlins Batting

	BA	OBA	SA	AB	H	2B	3B	HR	RBI	BB	SO
Totals	.248	.314	.346	5475	1356	197	31	94	542	498	1054
vs. Left	.256	.325	.367	1571	402	68	11	28	166	156	302
vs. Right	.244	.310	.338	3904	954	129	20	66	376	342	752
at Home	.251	.324	.348	2706	680	98	16	44	281	275	544
on Road	.244	.304	.345	2769	676	99	15	50	261	223	510
on Grass	.242	.314	.340	4140	1002	147	22	71	410	415	825
on Turf	.265	.313	.368	1335	354	50	9	23	132	83	229
Day Games	.247	.322	.336	1257	310	39	5	21	125	134	243
Night Games	.248	.311	.350	4218	1046	158	26	73	417	364	811
April	.244	.324	.329	763	186	27	4	10	74	89	145
May	.246	.326	.329	890	219	36	4	10	93	98	162
June	.267	.326	.403	925	247	36	12	22	106	80	184
July	.240	.289	.347	899	216	42	3	16	91	59	185
August	.265	.318	.382	979	259	29	4	26	99	70	167
Sept-Oct	.225	.302	.289	1019	229	27	4	10	79	102	211
Bases Empty	.244	.307	.335	3121	760	120	14	46	46	265	602
Leadoff	.239	.294	.334	1352	323	57	9	18	18	93	265
Runners on base	.253	.323	.362	2354	596	77	17	48	496	233	452
Scoring Position	.242	.331	.335	1326	321	41	8	22	424	178	272
Late and Close	.242	.327	.321	985	238	31	7	11	105	119	214

Montreal Expos Batting

	BA	OBA	SA	AB	H	2B	3B	HR	RBI	BB	SO
Totals	.257	.326	.386	5493	1410	270	36	122	682	542	860
vs. Left	.258	.328	.390	1723	444	86	11	40	203	168	264
vs. Right	.256	.325	.384	3770	966	184	25	82	479	374	596
at Home	.261	.334	.394	2640	689	139	13	62	349	281	403
on Road	.253	.319	.378	2853	721	131	23	60	333	261	457
on Grass	.243	.308	.358	1706	414	62	13	36	179	154	284
on Turf	.263	.334	.398	3787	996	208	23	86	503	388	576
Day Games	.254	.315	.380	1746	444	91	12	35	201	146	300
Night Games	.258	.331	.388	3747	966	179	24	87	481	396	560
April	.278	.346	.441	774	215	43	7	23	111	80	118
May	.256	.325	.369	910	233	49	3	16	102	82	143
June	.226	.301	.336	906	205	41	2	18	100	90	137
July	.269	.338	.388	936	252	36	6	21	111	95	151
August	.251	.319	.373	991	249	47	7	20	126	99	156
Sept-Oct	.262	.330	.414	976	256	54	11	24	132	96	155
Bases Empty	.256	.313	.383	3106	794	141	18	73	73	239	476
Leadoff	.270	.323	.400	1346	363	69	13	27	27	97	181
Runners on base	.258	.342	.389	2387	616	129	18	49	609	303	384
Scoring Position	.241	.339	.368	1521	366	84	10	30	537	237	261
Late and Close	.264	.343	.364	887	234	41	6	12	112	104	163

New York Mets Batting

	BA	OBA	SA	AB	H	2B	3B	HR	RBI	BB	SO
Totals	.248	.305	.390	5448	1350	228	37	158	632	448	879
vs. Left	.251	.302	.367	1601	402	76	10	30	158	115	226
vs. Right	.246	.307	.400	3847	948	152	27	128	474	333	653
at Home	.245	.297	.380	2668	653	102	17	75	306	196	424
on Road	.251	.313	.400	2780	697	126	20	83	326	252	455
on Grass	.250	.305	.392	4158	1040	160	28	125	496	327	674
on Turf	.240	.306	.384	1290	310	68	9	33	136	121	205
Day Games	.246	.312	.407	1949	480	88	12	67	233	181	310
Night Games	.249	.302	.381	3499	870	140	25	91	399	267	569
April	.229	.313	.346	690	158	24	6	15	84	82	118
May	.236	.294	.371	905	214	42	4	24	103	72	140
June	.257	.298	.381	930	239	37	6	22	97	53	145
July	.264	.324	.417	904	239	34	4	32	117	84	143
August	.243	.302	.417	971	236	43	12	34	117	80	143
Sept-Oct	.252	.304	.396	1048	264	48	5	31	114	77	190
Bases Empty	.241	.296	.384	3316	800	151	21	94	94	243	537
Leadoff	.258	.303	.416	1374	355	66	12	42	42	83	205
Runners on base	.258	.320	.399	2132	550	77	16	64	538	205	342
Scoring Position	.257	.332	.404	1189	305	44	13	35	467	148	212
Late and Close	.227	.292	.353	1008	229	36	8	25	113	95	195

Philadelphia Phillies Batting

	BA	OBA	SA	AB	H	2B	3B	HR	RBI	BB	SO
Totals	.274	.351	.426	5685	1555	297	51	156	811	665	1049
vs. Left	.280	.350	.453	1889	528	93	18	66	271	202	345
vs. Right	.271	.352	.413	3796	1027	204	33	90	540	463	704
at Home	.276	.353	.432	2793	771	143	26	80	407	322	499
on Road	.271	.349	.420	2892	784	154	25	76	404	343	550
on Grass	.266	.347	.401	1744	464	83	9	45	235	213	342
on Turf	.277	.353	.437	3941	1091	214	42	111	576	452	707
Day Games	.279	.352	.423	1575	440	76	11	43	226	175	319
Night Games	.271	.351	.427	4110	1115	221	40	113	585	490	730
April	.246	.337	.401	759	187	43	4	22	102	99	142
May	.271	.347	.440	936	254	58	5	30	153	110	170
June	.279	.356	.443	950	265	51	15	25	135	110	197
July	.279	.355	.411	1021	285	40	7	27	139	116	171
August	.287	.364	.484	963	276	54	14	36	150	112	182
Sept-Oct	.273	.345	.378	1056	288	51	6	16	132	118	187
Bases Empty	.277	.345	.431	2995	829	169	24	82	82	294	536
Leadoff	.298	.372	.458	1307	390	82	6	38	38	146	229
Runners on base	.270	.357	.420	2690	726	128	27	74	729	371	513
Scoring Position	.261	.364	.402	1633	426	76	16	41	632	278	326
Late and Close	.258	.346	.407	888	229	38	5	28	150	122	179

Pittsburgh Pirates Batting

	BA	OBA	SA	AB	H	2B	3B	HR	RBI	BB	SO
Totals	.267	.335	.393	5549	1482	267	50	110	664	536	972
vs. Left	.271	.339	.382	1756	475	98	14	23	182	176	280
vs. Right	.265	.333	.398	3793	1007	169	36	87	482	360	692
at Home	.260	.330	.398	2719	708	131	25	64	346	277	485
on Road	.273	.340	.388	2830	774	136	25	46	318	259	487
on Grass	.283	.347	.399	1759	498	82	14	31	208	162	290
on Turf	.260	.329	.390	3790	984	185	36	79	456	374	682
Day Games	.264	.331	.384	1536	405	79	11	28	172	146	251
Night Games	.268	.336	.396	4013	1077	188	39	82	492	390	721
April	.271	.336	.368	780	211	34	9	8	94	73	132
May	.259	.329	.394	895	232	42	11	19	113	87	156
June	.257	.323	.369	921	237	39	5	18	103	90	159
July	.268	.338	.384	947	254	53	6	15	100	94	185
August	.291	.352	.436	988	288	54	7	25	133	82	159
Sept-Oct	.255	.329	.397	1018	260	45	12	25	121	110	181
Bases Empty	.266	.327	.399	3079	818	156	30	65	65	252	560
Leadoff	.266	.332	.402	1330	354	66	12	30	30	117	221
Runners on base	.269	.344	.385	2470	664	111	20	45	599	284	412
Scoring Position	.262	.355	.372	1440	377	69	12	22	520	221	270
Late and Close	.266	.346	.372	987	263	37	5	19	121	117	209

St. Louis Cardinals Batting

	BA	OBA	SA	AB	H	2B	3B	HR	RBI	BB	SO
Totals	.272	.341	.395	5551	1508	262	34	118	724	588	882
vs. Left	.284	.347	.420	1477	419	65	7	41	202	144	209
vs. Right	.267	.339	.386	4074	1089	197	27	77	522	444	673
at Home	.279	.348	.406	2660	741	125	18	59	359	280	394
on Road	.265	.335	.385	2891	767	137	16	59	365	308	488
on Grass	.270	.340	.393	1791	484	93	8	37	232	191	308
on Turf	.272	.342	.396	3760	1024	169	26	81	492	397	574
Day Games	.278	.348	.401	1750	486	100	13	30	240	190	282
Night Games	.269	.338	.392	3801	1022	162	21	88	484	398	600
April	.245	.319	.344	773	189	18	7	15	82	87	127
May	.253	.322	.320	882	223	27	4	8	99	90	138
June	.297	.359	.449	930	276	63	8	21	141	89	146
July	.298	.358	.448	940	280	48	6	27	140	90	155
August	.259	.336	.387	964	250	44	5	23	114	112	133
Sept-Oct	.273	.348	.407	1062	290	62	4	24	148	120	183
Bases Empty	.263	.328	.381	3082	810	143	21	60	60	285	486
Leadoff	.275	.339	.407	1325	364	73	9	28	28	122	211
Runners on base	.283	.358	.412	2469	698	119	13	58	664	303	396
Scoring Position	.286	.375	.424	1501	430	78	10	36	599	233	258
Late and Close	.272	.352	.383	963	262	46	8	15	123	121	171

Atlanta Braves Batting

	BA	OBA	SA	AB	H	2B	3B	HR	RBI	BB	SO
Totals	.262	.331	.408	5515	1444	239	29	169	712	560	946
vs. Left	.273	.334	.423	1521	415	63	12	47	215	145	223
vs. Right	.258	.330	.402	3994	1029	176	17	122	497	415	723
at Home	.262	.331	.403	2693	705	116	15	78	340	279	432
on Road	.262	.331	.412	2822	739	123	14	91	372	281	514
on Grass	.256	.325	.398	4166	1067	170	22	126	508	417	714
on Turf	.279	.351	.442	1349	377	69	7	43	204	143	232
Day Games	.262	.336	.388	1501	394	50	11	39	173	165	274
Night Games	.262	.329	.415	4014	1050	189	18	130	539	395	672
April	.229	.314	.336	839	192	33	0	19	80	102	150
May	.264	.333	.413	900	238	49	5	25	112	89	147
June	.249	.306	.384	873	217	43	6	21	95	70	147
July	.279	.342	.462	959	268	41	7	40	142	92	139
August	.268	.329	.430	898	241	26	4	37	124	79	165
Sept-Oct	.275	.356	.411	1046	288	47	7	27	159	128	198
Bases Empty	.255	.321	.394	3126	796	124	16	93	93	285	554
Leadoff	.246	.306	.369	1327	327	47	7	34	34	109	206
Runners on base	.271	.344	.426	2389	648	115	13	76	619	275	392
Scoring Position	.257	.343	.406	1398	359	66	5	44	524	202	247
Late and Close	.248	.323	.404	876	217	34	5	31	116	96	167

Cincinnati Reds Batting

	BA	OBA	SA	AB	H	2B	3B	HR	RBI	BB	SO
Totals	.264	.324	.396	5517	1457	261	28	137	669	485	1025
vs. Left	.271	.326	.422	1534	415	89	7	43	184	124	263
vs. Right	.262	.323	.386	3983	1042	172	21	94	485	361	762
at Home	.265	.328	.401	2659	705	134	10	69	344	252	494
on Road	.263	.319	.392	2858	752	127	18	68	325	233	531
on Grass	.259	.321	.390	4188	1084	188	18	109	513	382	793
on Turf	.281	.332	.414	1329	373	73	10	28	156	103	232
Day Games	.276	.340	.435	1686	465	84	13	53	240	170	295
Night Games	.259	.316	.379	3831	992	177	15	84	429	315	730
April	.251	.321	.358	742	186	28	5	14	77	77	134
May	.281	.352	.414	973	273	51	2	25	134	105	170
June	.277	.323	.392	966	268	42	3	21	119	66	170
July	.279	.337	.442	955	266	56	5	30	126	82	172
August	.242	.305	.388	926	224	45	6	26	114	85	191
Sept-Oct	.251	.301	.373	955	240	39	7	21	99	70	188
Bases Empty	.260	.315	.396	3130	814	141	16	84	84	234	590
Leadoff	.270	.326	.415	1332	360	65	10	36	36	102	234
Runners on base	.269	.334	.396	2387	643	120	12	53	585	251	435
Scoring Position	.271	.346	.408	1400	379	71	8	35	530	188	271
Late and Close	.250	.318	.354	817	204	32	4	15	94	83	164

Los Angeles Dodgers Batting

	BA	OBA	SA	AB	H	2B	3B	HR	RBI	BB	SO
Totals	.261	.321	.383	5588	1458	234	28	130	639	492	937
vs. Left	.269	.324	.393	1613	434	79	8	35	184	136	244
vs. Right	.258	.320	.378	3975	1024	155	20	95	455	356	693
at Home	.275	.339	.391	2716	747	104	7	66	318	258	437
on Road	.248	.304	.374	2872	711	130	21	64	321	234	500
on Grass	.265	.328	.385	4303	1139	173	16	104	496	402	720
on Turf	.248	.299	.375	1285	319	61	12	26	143	90	217
Day Games	.257	.314	.398	1661	427	84	12	42	178	139	295
Night Games	.263	.324	.376	3927	1031	150	16	88	461	353	642
April	.227	.300	.311	761	173	24	2	12	68	78	128
May	.289	.346	.417	896	259	39	8	20	126	80	158
June	.269	.323	.401	905	243	37	4	25	111	72	168
July	.254	.305	.380	989	251	51	7	20	110	73	152
August	.260	.322	.397	931	242	42	4	26	104	81	141
Sept-Oct	.262	.327	.378	1106	290	41	3	27	120	108	190
Bases Empty	.254	.309	.386	3228	821	145	17	82	82	238	546
Leadoff	.267	.314	.422	1383	369	64	8	45	45	89	227
Runners on base	.270	.338	.378	2360	637	89	11	48	557	254	391
Scoring Position	.272	.351	.377	1410	383	49	9	27	497	192	258
Late and Close	.240	.314	.345	1063	255	40	6	20	107	112	198

Colorado Rockies Batting

	BA	OBA	SA	AB	H	2B	3B	HR	RBI	BB	SO
Totals	.273	.323	.422	5517	1507	278	59	142	704	388	944
vs. Left	.289	.332	.449	1282	370	78	17	31	170	79	216
vs. Right	.268	.321	.414	4235	1137	200	42	111	534	309	728
at Home	.306	.361	.482	2754	843	158	48	77	449	228	410
on Road	.240	.285	.362	2763	664	120	11	65	255	160	534
on Grass	.231	.275	.348	1707	395	69	5	40	147	96	330
on Turf	.292	.345	.455	3810	1112	209	54	102	557	292	614
Day Games	.265	.316	.424	1879	497	92	23	54	234	132	327
Night Games	.278	.327	.421	3638	1010	186	36	88	470	256	617
April	.274	.328	.407	734	201	34	8	16	97	59	99
May	.251	.308	.367	993	249	39	8	20	105	72	142
June	.298	.347	.453	853	254	51	6	23	126	64	172
July	.272	.310	.444	903	246	55	11	26	111	47	160
August	.248	.293	.383	1029	255	40	9	27	107	62	204
Sept-Oct	.300	.358	.483	1005	302	59	17	30	158	84	167
Bases Empty	.263	.312	.410	3251	855	160	38	81	81	206	567
Leadoff	.275	.314	.434	1371	377	76	17	36	36	70	221
Runners on base	.288	.339	.439	2266	652	118	21	61	623	182	377
Scoring Position	.284	.349	.449	1326	376	71	16	39	558	148	248
Late and Close	.279	.330	.434	768	214	42	7	21	121	59	133

San Diego Padres Batting

	BA	OBA	SA	AB	H	2B	3B	HR	RBI	BB	SO
Totals	.252	.312	.389	5503	1386	239	28	153	634	443	1046
vs. Left	.268	.328	.408	1692	453	79	6	49	202	150	287
vs. Right	.245	.305	.380	3811	933	160	22	104	432	293	759
at Home	.255	.316	.398	2748	701	105	14	87	322	223	526
on Road	.249	.308	.379	2755	685	134	14	66	312	220	520
on Grass	.257	.315	.396	4282	1102	180	20	124	493	335	803
on Turf	.233	.301	.365	1221	284	59	8	29	141	108	243
Day Games	.252	.311	.403	1781	449	81	8	57	205	134	321
Night Games	.252	.312	.382	3722	937	158	20	96	429	309	725
April	.251	.307	.397	760	191	33	3	24	82	58	151
May	.264	.327	.389	938	248	44	2	23	105	80	145
June	.246	.305	.357	947	233	33	6	20	85	75	179
July	.257	.319	.419	927	238	47	8	29	120	82	171
August	.283	.340	.445	963	273	48	3	34	133	76	164
Sept-Oct	.210	.273	.329	968	203	34	6	23	109	72	236
Bases Empty	.244	.300	.372	3238	789	134	15	84	84	229	626
Leadoff	.253	.307	.373	1354	342	63	8	28	28	92	240
Runners on base	.264	.328	.413	2265	597	105	13	69	550	214	420
Scoring Position	.256	.335	.392	1288	330	60	8	33	458	160	268
Late and Close	.234	.307	.347	997	233	30	1	27	119	94	228

Houston Astros Batting

	BA	OBA	SA	AB	H	2B	3B	HR	RBI	BB	SO
Totals	.267	.330	.409	5464	1459	288	37	138	656	497	911
vs. Left	.273	.343	.434	1819	497	109	11	54	249	183	284
vs. Right	.264	.324	.396	3645	962	179	26	84	407	314	627
at Home	.267	.332	.406	2625	700	142	19	62	332	244	436
on Road	.267	.329	.412	2839	759	146	18	76	324	253	475
on Grass	.263	.325	.413	1765	465	85	10	53	209	162	287
on Turf	.269	.332	.407	3699	994	203	27	85	447	335	624
Day Games	.264	.328	.414	1747	461	92	13	48	208	158	290
Night Games	.268	.331	.407	3717	998	196	24	90	448	339	621
April	.266	.333	.418	741	197	46	5	19	97	70	106
May	.273	.336	.436	912	249	48	4	31	118	84	136
June	.248	.306	.372	866	215	39	7	18	84	70	145
July	.274	.337	.418	971	266	55	8	23	129	85	152
August	.271	.338	.419	962	261	49	6	27	114	97	181
Sept-Oct	.268	.329	.391	1012	271	51	7	20	114	91	191
Bases Empty	.265	.325	.416	3107	824	163	19	89	89	254	513
Leadoff	.272	.324	.421	1331	362	64	12	37	37	95	203
Runners on base	.269	.336	.400	2357	635	125	18	49	567	243	398
Scoring Position	.262	.336	.389	1387	363	68	12	28	490	167	249
Late and Close	.260	.325	.385	865	225	47	2	19	94	77	145

San Francisco Giants Batting

	BA	OBA	SA	AB	H	2B	3B	HR	RBI	BB	SO
Totals	.276	.340	.427	5557	1534	269	33	168	759	516	930
vs. Left	.296	.354	.457	1798	532	101	10	56	258	165	282
vs. Right	.267	.333	.413	3759	1002	168	23	112	501	351	648
at Home	.266	.326	.416	2663	708	127	13	82	338	227	433
on Road	.285	.352	.437	2894	826	142	20	86	421	289	497
on Grass	.270	.334	.421	4188	1132	188	22	133	543	380	698
on Turf	.294	.358	.446	1369	402	81	11	35	216	136	232
Day Games	.271	.335	.436	2748	746	134	15	96	388	254	448
Night Games	.281	.344	.418	2809	788	135	18	72	371	262	482
April	.265	.332	.403	829	220	42	6	20	110	85	141
May	.294	.356	.444	950	279	43	11	26	128	85	154
June	.278	.338	.432	935	260	48	0	32	126	83	157
July	.296	.357	.451	903	267	51	4	27	143	78	130
August	.270	.332	.431	919	248	38	7	32	133	82	167
Sept-Oct	.255	.324	.402	1021	260	47	5	31	119	103	181
Bases Empty	.262	.323	.411	3129	820	147	16	96	96	253	541
Leadoff	.282	.336	.444	1331	375	74	8	42	42	96	199
Runners on base	.294	.361	.447	2428	714	122	17	72	663	263	389
Scoring Position	.281	.362	.421	1467	412	80	12	34	560	205	249
Late and Close	.252	.301	.398	811	204	33	4	26	95	57	152

AMERICAN LEAGUE PITCHING

	G	IP	H	BB	SO	SB	CS	W	L	S	ERA
Totals	7237	20222.1	20661	8006	12952	1549	872	1134	1134	593	4.32
at Home	3648	10400.1	10350	3912	6803	720	451	619	515	295	4.09
on Road	3589	9822.0	10311	4094	6149	829	421	515	619	298	4.59
on Grass	5176	14393.0	14655	5754	9182	1059	623	810	810	426	4.32
on Turf	2061	5829.1	6006	2252	3770	490	249	324	324	167	4.37
Day Games	2395	6707.1	6900	2699	4437	572	297	377	377	184	4.40
Night Games	4842	13515.0	13761	5307	8515	977	575	757	757	409	4.30
April	919	2643.1	2667	1048	1709	220	131	149	149	72	4.42
May	1244	3460.2	3473	1338	2262	307	187	193	193	104	4.09
June	1233	3390.1	3466	1350	2110	232	142	192	192	107	4.40
July	1208	3339.2	3609	1273	2026	240	143	189	189	104	4.69
August	1251	3628.1	3638	1434	2341	262	140	202	202	108	4.23
Sept-Oct	1382	3760.0	3808	1563	2504	288	129	209	209	98	4.23

	BA	OBA	SA	AB	H	2B	3B	HR	RBI	BB	SO
Totals	.267	.337	.408	77506	20661	3861	427	2074	10063	8006	12696
vs. Left	.275	.349	.413	31355	8625	1572	226	769	3984	3527	4695
vs. Right	.261	.329	.404	46151	12036	2289	201	1305	6079	4479	8001
Home	.273	.345	.416	37894	10350	1927	197	1036	4894	3912	6803
Road	.260	.328	.399	39612	10311	1934	230	1038	5169	4094	6149
Bases Empty	.260	.328	.402	43344	11287	2179	231	1169	1169	3964	7304
Leadoff	.268	.331	.415	18539	4965	984	106	512	512	1627	2931
Runners on Base	.274	.350	.415	34162	9374	1682	196	905	8894	4042	5648
Scoring Position	.270	.357	.411	19740	5335	971	119	526	7777	2890	3508
Late and Close	.265	.342	.385	12039	3188	535	57	265	1604	1387	2228

Baltimore Orioles Pitching

	G	IP	H	BB	SO	SB	CS	W	L	S	ERA
Totals	491	1442.2	1427	579	900	96	64	85	77	42	4.32
at Home	251	747.0	737	296	457	47	33	48	33	23	4.18
on Road	240	695.2	690	283	443	49	31	37	44	19	4.48
on Grass	426	1235.1	1227	495	783	81	55	75	63	37	4.31
on Turf	65	207.1	200	84	117	15	9	10	14	5	4.38
Day Games	130	389.2	401	155	260	38	26	20	24	9	4.41
Night Games	361	1053.0	1026	424	640	58	38	65	53	33	4.29
April	65	191.2	183	81	123	15	17	8	13	6	4.32
May	86	257.2	253	89	165	19	11	13	16	7	3.77
June	87	241.0	227	105	151	15	9	20	7	14	3.62
July	77	228.1	217	78	133	10	7	14	12	6	4.57
August	91	256.0	281	113	156	17	10	15	14	5	5.41
Sept-Oct	85	268.0	266	113	172	20	10	15	15	4	4.23

	BA	OBA	SA	AB	H	2B	3B	HR	RBI	BB	SO
Totals	.261	.333	.407	5473	1427	284	30	153	710	579	900
vs. Left	.262	.341	.388	1981	519	93	12	44	235	230	317
vs. Right	.260	.329	.419	3492	908	191	18	109	475	349	583
Home	.260	.331	.405	2832	737	140	14	81	354	296	457
Road	.261	.335	.410	2641	690	144	16	72	356	283	443
Bases Empty	.249	.320	.394	3096	771	165	18	83	83	304	518
Leadoff	.268	.336	.423	1312	352	69	7	40	40	127	197
Runners on Base	.276	.350	.424	2377	656	119	12	70	627	275	382
Scoring Position	.272	.363	.431	1370	372	68	6	46	551	208	231
Late and Close	.256	.334	.357	828	212	34	4	14	100	97	157

Boston Red Sox Pitching

	G	IP	H	BB	SO	SB	CS	W	L	S	ERA
Totals	551	1452.1	1379	552	997	92	44	80	82	44	3.80
at Home	279	750.0	739	286	516	33	20	43	38	22	3.74
on Road	272	702.1	640	266	481	59	24	37	44	22	3.87
on Grass	458	1229.2	1164	447	858	71	39	67	70	37	3.73
on Turf	93	222.2	215	105	139	21	5	13	12	7	4.20
Day Games	204	545.1	504	210	414	33	18	32	28	16	3.50
Night Games	347	907.0	875	342	583	59	26	48	54	28	3.99
April	65	194.0	169	62	118	15	11	13	9	4	3.20
May	95	249.0	222	90	191	14	7	14	14	8	3.11
June	86	237.0	233	81	167	8	4	11	16	6	3.95
July	90	241.1	226	83	169	15	9	20	7	14	3.62
August	89	244.1	232	99	155	14	4	11	16	7	3.68
Sept-Oct	126	286.2	297	137	197	26	9	11	20	5	4.96

	BA	OBA	SA	AB	H	2B	3B	HR	RBI	BB	SO
Totals	.252	.322	.384	5483	1379	281	33	127	650	552	997
vs. Left	.257	.334	.397	2476	636	137	22	55	286	287	410
vs. Right	.247	.312	.374	3007	743	144	11	72	364	265	587
Home	.260	.328	.385	2847	739	163	18	53	337	286	516
Road	.243	.315	.383	2636	640	118	15	74	313	266	481
Bases Empty	.244	.304	.385	3169	774	167	15	83	83	254	579
Leadoff	.252	.310	.405	1343	338	83	6	37	37	105	248
Runners on Base	.261	.345	.383	2314	605	114	18	44	567	298	418
Scoring Position	.254	.355	.370	1354	344	62	10	25	502	227	262
Late and Close	.249	.327	.355	912	227	45	5	14	110	103	209

Cleveland Indians Pitching

	G	IP	H	BB	SO	SB	CS	W	L	S	ERA
Totals	572	1445.2	1591	591	888	113	68	76	86	45	4.58
at Home	283	737.0	756	284	435	45	33	46	35	24	3.83
on Road	289	708.2	835	307	453	68	35	30	51	21	5.35
on Grass	481	1230.0	1323	496	752	94	57	69	69	38	4.44
on Turf	91	215.2	268	95	136	19	11	7	17	7	5.34
Day Games	187	496.1	572	213	311	43	26	25	31	13	4.95
Night Games	385	949.1	1019	378	577	70	42	51	55	32	4.38
April	83	192.1	235	52	136	20	8	7	15	3	5.57
May	96	249.1	277	94	156	30	18	12	17	7	4.76
June	94	238.0	225	95	135	18	12	17	10	10	3.63
July	96	229.0	251	97	132	14	13	12	14	8	4.72
August	101	266.0	296	133	155	12	10	14	14	8	4.97
Sept-Oct	102	271.0	307	120	174	19	7	14	16	9	4.02

	BA	OBA	SA	AB	H	2B	3B	HR	RBI	BB	SO
Totals	.281	.351	.434	5664	1591	278	21	182	759	591	888
vs. Left	.286	.359	.418	2241	640	86	8	65	287	251	319
vs. Right	.278	.345	.444	3423	951	192	13	117	472	340	569
Home	.266	.335	.401	2838	756	123	5	83	326	284	435
Road	.295	.366	.467	2826	835	155	16	99	433	307	453
Bases Empty	.284	.349	.455	3066	871	163	13	112	112	288	467
Leadoff	.285	.347	.458	1326	378	71	7	48	48	115	173
Runners on Base	.277	.352	.408	2598	720	115	8	70	647	303	421
Scoring Position	.282	.364	.419	1519	429	68	5	43	576	210	260
Late and Close	.274	.349	.390	942	258	42	2	21	123	107	149

Detroit Tigers Pitching

	G	IP	H	BB	SO	SB	CS	W	L	S	ERA
Totals	537	1436.2	1547	542	828	102	57	85	77	36	4.70
at Home	263	737.0	762	263	443	40	37	44	37	14	4.45
on Road	274	699.2	785	279	385	62	20	41	40	22	4.98
on Grass	445	1217.1	1287	464	714	87	49	72	65	31	4.69
on Turf	92	219.1	260	78	114	15	8	13	12	5	4.80
Day Games	207	535.0	594	212	298	39	26	31	30	13	5.18
Night Games	330	901.2	953	330	530	63	31	54	47	23	4.42
April	80	195.1	196	79	82	16	7	15	7	5	3.82
May	94	239.0	243	93	145	17	18	15	11	7	4.10
June	89	252.0	283	101	148	13	7	13	16	4	5.18
July	86	248.1	312	87	140	16	10	10	18	5	5.65
August	82	252.2	227	92	144	21	9	18	11	6	4.03
Sept-Oct	106	249.1	286	90	169	19	6	14	14	9	5.23

	BA	OBA	SA	AB	H	2B	3B	HR	RBI	BB	SO
Totals	.276	.342	.436	5605	1547	263	35	188	783	542	828
vs. Left	.290	.360	.467	2222	645	100	22	83	316	240	273
vs. Right	.267	.330	.416	3383	902	163	13	105	467	302	555
Home	.269	.333	.424	2837	762	116	14	99	383	263	443
Road	.284	.351	.448	2768	785	147	21	89	400	279	385
Bases Empty	.282	.335	.435	3142	885	141	20	100	100	230	452
Leadoff	.291	.344	.431	1335	389	59	8	37	37	103	192
Runners on Base	.269	.350	.438	2463	662	122	15	88	683	312	376
Scoring Position	.261	.361	.419	1378	359	63	7	47	567	232	222
Late and Close	.303	.377	.462	766	232	33	7	25	114	87	114

Milwaukee Brewers Pitching

	G	IP	H	BB	SO	SB	CS	W	L	S	ERA
Totals	515	1447.0	1511	522	810	115	51	69	93	29	4.47
at Home	264	741.0	764	247	425	57	28	38	43	13	4.09
on Road	251	706.0	747	275	385	58	23	31	50	16	4.86
on Grass	446	1229.1	1284	452	704	96	46	58	79	25	4.50
on Turf	69	217.2	227	70	106	19	5	11	14	4	4.26
Day Games	189	543.1	560	188	304	53	18	28	33	11	4.27
Night Games	326	903.2	951	334	506	62	33	41	60	18	4.58
April	66	174.0	192	68	109	16	9	9	11	6	5.53
May	89	248.2	261	79	133	24	11	13	14	5	3.47
June	95	250.2	243	75	108	11	7	10	19	5	4.38
July	82	227.0	246	84	100	22	8	9	17	4	5.04
August	86	291.2	303	110	187	30	8	16	16	4	4.17
Sept-Oct	97	255.0	266	106	173	12	8	12	16	5	4.62

	BA	OBA	SA	AB	H	2B	3B	HR	RBI	BB	SO
Totals	.271	.336	.422	5577	1511	290	48	153	758	522	810
vs. Left	.282	.341	.433	2373	669	118	30	60	317	213	277
vs. Right	.263	.331	.415	3204	842	172	18	93	441	309	533
Home	.268	.329	.404	2852	764	148	22	65	361	247	425
Road	.274	.342	.442	2725	747	142	26	88	397	275	385
Bases Empty	.268	.327	.418	3143	843	178	26	80	80	243	451
Leadoff	.283	.334	.440	1349	382	89	13	32	32	95	184
Runners on Base	.274	.346	.429	2434	668	112	22	73	678	279	359
Scoring Position	.256	.339	.397	1436	368	68	10	38	577	203	230
Late and Close	.270	.349	.396	889	240	43	6	19	117	107	148

New York Yankees Pitching

	G	IP	H	BB	SO	SB	CS	W	L	S	ERA
Totals	494	1438.1	1467	552	899	115	47	88	74	38	4.37
at Home	233	732.0	676	256	474	47	25	50	31	19	3.85
on Road	261	706.1	791	296	425	68	22	38	43	19	4.91
on Grass	410	1231.0	1227	480	787	94	38	77	61	33	4.24
on Turf	84	207.1	240	72	112	21	9	11	13	5	5.12
Day Games	172	493.1	485	197	299	44	14	36	19	10	4.34
Night Games	322	945.0	982	355	600	71	33	52	55	28	4.38
April	60	186.0	180	63	108	17	3	12	9	7	4.21
May	77	274.2	240	112	186	25	18	17	13	6	3.74
June	86	245.2	273	98	151	19	6	17	11	9	4.73
July	80	230.2	245	84	140	11	8	14	12	5	4.53
August	90	249.1	259	84	148	23	8	15	13	8	4.40
Sept-Oct	101	252.0	270	111	166	20	4	13	16	3	4.64

	BA	OBA	SA	AB	H	2B	3B	HR	RBI	BB	SO
Totals	.266	.333	.416	5522	1467	262	30	170	730	552	899
vs. Left	.263	.345	.408	1860	490	87	11	53	230	227	299
vs. Right	.267	.327	.421	3662	977	175	19	117	500	325	600
Home	.246	.313	.379	2743	676	89	10	85	326	256	474
Road	.285	.353	.453	2779	791	173	20	85	404	296	425
Bases Empty	.254	.319	.399	3148	800	148	15	93	93	283	513
Leadoff	.259	.320	.401	1325	343	61	5	39	39	116	191
Runners on Base	.281	.351	.439	2374	667	114	15	77	637	269	386
Scoring Position	.285	.365	.456	1331	379	63	9	49	556	187	231
Late and Close	.285	.359	.430	752	214	37	3	22	119	89	129

Toronto Blue Jays Pitching

	G	IP	H	BB	SO	SB	CS	W	L	S	ERA
Totals	506	1441.1	1441	620	1023	136	64	95	67	50	4.22
at Home	259	742.0	754	322	539	81	32	48	33	21	4.40
on Road	247	699.1	687	298	484	55	32	47	34	29	4.03
on Grass	207	546.2	549	240	369	42	26	39	24	25	4.17
on Turf	299	894.2	892	380	654	94	38	56	43	25	4.26
Day Games	161	485.0	447	207	363	53	14	38	16	17	3.86
Night Games	345	956.1	994	413	660	83	50	57	51	33	4.40
April	69	202.2	217	86	144	21	6	13	10	8	4.80
May	94	246.0	256	114	175	30	16	16	12	8	4.50
June	87	252.2	237	102	191	19	11	19	9	8	3.88
July	74	230.0	245	95	158	23	13	12	14	6	4.42
August	94	260.0	262	115	180	22	10	17	12	12	4.12
Sept-Oct	88	250.0	224	108	175	21	8	18	10	8	3.74

	BA	OBA	SA	AB	H	2B	3B	HR	RBI	BB	SO
Totals	.261	.336	.388	5527	1441	240	31	134	694	620	1023
vs. Left	.277	.353	.408	2591	718	128	17	59	322	311	405
vs. Right	.246	.321	.371	2936	723	112	14	75	372	309	618
Home	.264	.338	.411	2857	754	138	19	81	369	322	539
Road	.257	.333	.364	2670	687	102	12	53	325	298	484
Bases Empty	.251	.326	.383	3008	754	125	25	74	74	318	563
Leadoff	.258	.334	.392	1295	334	56	11	32	32	138	227
Runners on Base	.273	.347	.395	2519	687	115	6	60	620	302	460
Scoring Position	.265	.351	.385	1448	383	73	4	31	540	213	292
Late and Close	.231	.315	.335	810	187	30	0	18	93	102	173

California Angels Pitching

	G	IP	H	BB	SO	SB	CS	W	L	S	ERA
Totals	482	1430.1	1482	550	843	122	52	71	91	41	4.36
at Home	248	744.0	761	278	464	57	31	44	37	23	4.39
on Road	234	686.1	721	272	379	65	21	27	54	18	4.33
on Grass	398	1200.1	1226	449	735	104	45	63	72	36	4.30
on Turf	84	230.0	256	101	108	18	7	8	19	5	4.70
Day Games	140	420.1	441	173	262	50	16	20	28	11	4.33
Night Games	342	1010.0	1041	377	581	72	36	51	63	30	4.38
April	48	168.0	137	69	121	14	4	13	6	5	3.48
May	94	261.0	265	90	153	21	10	14	15	11	3.62
June	90	235.2	284	91	136	17	6	10	17	6	5.73
July	79	251.0	270	85	135	26	10	11	17	5	4.20
August	85	247.0	243	111	151	17	15	11	17	7	4.34
Sept-Oct	86	267.2	283	104	147	27	7	12	19	7	4.61

	BA	OBA	SA	AB	H	2B	3B	HR	RBI	BB	SO
Totals	.270	.339	.408	5488	1482	268	15	153	732	550	843
vs. Left	.283	.363	.427	1708	484	88	7	48	233	203	217
vs. Right	.264	.328	.399	3780	998	180	8	105	499	347	626
Home	.268	.335	.407	2841	761	134	4	84	376	278	464
Road	.272	.342	.410	2647	721	134	11	69	356	272	379
Bases Empty	.262	.330	.393	3048	798	164	8	73	73	283	511
Leadoff	.283	.347	.420	1305	369	76	2	33	33	116	214
Runners on Base	.280	.349	.427	2440	684	104	7	80	659	267	332
Scoring Position	.283	.358	.446	1387	393	62	4	52	588	182	200
Late and Close	.265	.348	.371	840	223	38	0	17	110	107	133

Chicago White Sox Pitching

	G	IP	H	BB	SO	SB	CS	W	L	S	ERA
Totals	484	1454.0	1398	566	974	82	82	94	68	48	3.72
at Home	246	737.0	705	283	492	36	42	45	36	22	3.70
on Road	238	717.0	693	283	482	46	40	49	32	26	3.74
on Grass	412	1234.1	1182	485	833	72	69	77	61	38	3.76
on Turf	72	219.2	216	81	141	10	13	17	7	10	3.52
Day Games	145	434.2	419	169	306	25	27	28	21	14	3.64
Night Games	339	1019.1	979	397	668	57	55	66	47	34	3.75
April	60	197.0	197	73	115	10	8	13	9	5	3.79
May	77	222.1	234	85	149	21	13	11	14	6	4.61
June	85	251.0	234	113	175	24	16	15	13	7	3.69
July	85	241.0	240	107	147	8	14	18	9	10	4.26
August	86	259.2	239	85	187	10	13	17	12	9	3.40
Sept-Oct	91	283.0	254	103	201	9	18	20	11	11	2.83

	BA	OBA	SA	AB	H	2B	3B	HR	RBI	BB	SO
Totals	.255	.328	.372	5472	1398	217	22	125	625	566	974
vs. Left	.264	.340	.378	2298	607	101	8	48	252	262	387
vs. Right	.249	.318	.367	3174	791	116	14	77	373	304	587
Home	.255	.325	.373	2770	705	93	12	70	312	283	492
Road	.256	.330	.371	2702	693	124	10	55	313	283	482
Bases Empty	.251	.326	.370	3063	769	120	14	72	72	318	559
Leadoff	.252	.323	.387	1318	332	53	7	37	37	130	221
Runners on Base	.261	.329	.374	2409	629	97	8	53	553	248	415
Scoring Position	.256	.337	.352	1311	335	50	5	22	470	175	239
Late and Close	.243	.312	.340	857	208	28	2	17	89	82	153

Kansas City Royals Pitching

	G	IP	H	BB	SO	SB	CS	W	L	S	ERA
Totals	465	1445.1	1379	571	985	119	71	84	78	48	4.04
at Home	244	747.1	728	270	471	56	38	43	38	19	3.94
on Road	221	698.0	651	301	514	63	33	41	40	29	4.15
on Grass	174	534.1	492	223	400	48	27	31	31	22	4.01
on Turf	291	911.0	887	348	585	71	44	53	47	26	4.06
Day Games	139	433.2	409	165	325	33	18	26	23	15	3.84
Night Games	326	1011.2	970	406	660	86	53	58	55	33	4.13
April	59	203.2	204	84	141	16	10	9	14	6	4.60
May	73	227.2	207	109	161	22	11	16	9	11	3.68
June	82	250.1	233	85	161	22	14	13	15	7	4.35
July	79	249.0	245	95	173	19	9	16	12	9	4.27
August	88	260.1	242	87	176	19	16	15	14	11	3.28
Sept-Oct	84	254.1	248	111	173	21	11	15	14	4	4.18

	BA	OBA	SA	AB	H	2B	3B	HR	RBI	BB	SO
Totals	.254	.327	.376	5436	1379	292	28	105	651	571	985
vs. Left	.266	.340	.385	2447	652	121	14	47	306	271	376
vs. Right	.243	.316	.368	2989	727	171	14	58	345	300	609
Home	.257	.324	.383	2833	728	172	19	49	328	270	471
Road	.250	.330	.368	2603	651	120	9	56	323	301	514
Bases Empty	.247	.318	.371	3075	761	162	8	67	67	300	554
Leadoff	.249	.311	.403	1330	331	77	4	40	40	112	209
Runners on Base	.262	.337	.382	2361	618	130	20	38	584	271	431
Scoring Position	.264	.350	.392	1399	369	79	17	22	526	198	285
Late and Close	.270	.342	.377	1020	275	47	6	17	134	106	184

Minnesota Twins Pitching

	G	IP	H	BB	SO	SB	CS	W	L	S	ERA
Totals	518	1444.1	1591	514	901	137	66	71	91	44	4.73
at Home	262	750.0	804	255	480	61	29	36	45	19	4.73
on Road	256	694.1	787	259	421	76	37	35	46	25	4.73
on Grass	204	534.1	608	219	327	57	28	28	34	19	4.75
on Turf	314	910.0	983	295	574	80	38	43	57	25	4.72
Day Games	182	497.2	536	165	340	41	28	24	32	18	4.50
Night Games	336	946.2	1055	349	561	96	38	47	59	26	4.85
April	69	193.0	216	98	125	20	17	8	14	6	6.06
May	88	218.0	234	72	145	24	9	12	13	8	4.87
June	86	235.2	255	86	141	16	11	12	15	11	4.66
July	85	233.2	279	74	130	14	10	11	16	8	5.01
August	81	281.0	277	68	177	22	12	13	17	4	3.52
Sept-Oct	109	283.0	330	116	183	41	7	15	16	7	4.74

	BA	OBA	SA	AB	H	2B	3B	HR	RBI	BB	SO
Totals	.283	.344	.438	5618	1591	349	39	148	781	514	901
vs. Left	.297	.357	.451	2553	759	158	23	63	341	242	398
vs. Right	.271	.334	.427	3065	832	191	16	85	440	272	503
Home	.277	.337	.429	2900	804	196	17	70	405	255	480
Road	.290	.353	.448	2718	787	153	22	78	376	259	421
Bases Empty	.274	.337	.433	3095	847	183	16	93	93	267	503
Leadoff	.278	.339	.443	1325	369	83	6	41	41	113	212
Runners on Base	.295	.354	.444	2523	744	166	23	55	688	247	398
Scoring Position	.291	.361	.436	1508	439	106	14	28	602	189	257
Late and Close	.262	.337	.381	790	207	46	3	14	108	85	131

Oakland Athletics Pitching

	G	IP	H	BB	SO	SB	CS	W	L	S	ERA
Totals	586	1452.1	1551	680	864	120	71	68	94	42	4.90
at Home	284	743.0	752	314	479	64	39	38	43	24	4.34
on Road	302	709.1	799	366	385	56	32	30	51	18	5.49
on Grass	487	1207.1	1315	572	717	103	65	52	84	33	5.08
on Turf	99	245.0	236	108	147	17	6	16	10	9	4.04
Day Games	256	631.0	694	306	398	54	31	24	47	18	5.06
Night Games	330	821.1	857	374	466	66	40	44	47	24	4.78
April	70	160.1	173	76	96	20	10	7	11	3	5.22
May	104	250.2	269	124	141	28	14	12	16	8	4.88
June	94	234.1	253	112	122	14	9	12	14	7	4.61
July	108	251.2	307	107	153	16	12	12	17	8	5.61
August	105	267.2	278	136	164	21	11	9	21	6	4.91
Sept-Oct	105	287.2	271	125	188	21	15	16	15	10	4.35

	BA	OBA	SA	AB	H	2B	3B	HR	RBI	BB	SO
Totals	.276	.356	.422	5623	1551	283	35	157	801	680	864
vs. Left	.288	.369	.431	2713	782	153	22	63	395	350	356
vs. Right	.264	.344	.415	2910	769	130	13	94	406	330	508
Home	.265	.341	.407	2835	752	137	15	78	368	314	479
Road	.287	.372	.438	2788	799	146	20	79	433	366	385
Bases Empty	.272	.345	.407	3053	830	152	19	74	74	322	449
Leadoff	.265	.327	.399	1334	354	64	12	30	30	119	178
Runners on Base	.281	.369	.441	2570	721	131	16	83	727	358	415
Scoring Position	.283	.380	.450	1464	415	71	10	51	628	242	241
Late and Close	.280	.357	.394	896	251	40	10	14	127	105	174

Seattle Mariners Pitching

	G	IP	H	BB	SO	SB	CS	W	L	S	ERA
Totals	515	1453.2	1421	605	1083	105	68	82	80	41	4.20
at Home	274	755.0	709	297	607	56	30	46	35	22	3.91
on Road	241	698.2	712	308	476	49	38	36	45	19	4.52
on Grass	190	535.2	544	257	369	35	28	26	36	13	4.57
on Turf	325	918.0	877	348	714	70	40	56	44	28	3.99
Day Games	144	429.2	433	191	336	40	19	22	26	8	4.63
Night Games	371	1024.0	988	414	747	65	49	60	54	33	4.03
April	64	198.1	193	91	165	12	11	11	11	4	4.27
May	92	262.2	243	97	208	18	17	14	15	6	3.77
June	85	240.2	242	110	173	19	14	13	14	7	4.26
July	90	231.0	251	88	134	16	8	13	13	7	5.03
August	86	235.1	239	103	191	22	8	14	13	11	4.97
Sept-Oct	98	285.2	253	116	212	18	10	17	14	6	3.21

	BA	OBA	SA	AB	H	2B	3B	HR	RBI	BB	SO
Totals	.259	.337	.395	5483	1421	276	31	135	697	605	827
vs. Left	.268	.343	.412	1902	510	108	20	42	240	208	324
vs. Right	.254	.334	.385	3581	911	168	11	93	457	397	503
Home	.251	.327	.383	2829	709	151	13	66	337	297	607
Road	.268	.349	.407	2654	712	125	18	69	360	308	476
Bases Empty	.248	.316	.386	3109	770	161	17	78	78	280	632
Leadoff	.261	.329	.397	1324	346	72	9	30	30	122	256
Runners on Base	.274	.364	.406	2374	651	115	14	57	619	325	451
Scoring Position	.266	.366	.403	1418	377	66	9	37	559	227	304
Late and Close	.262	.361	.409	924	242	39	5	29	154	137	215

Texas Rangers Pitching

	G	IP	H	BB	SO	SB	CS	W	L	S	ERA
Totals	521	1438.1	1476	562	957	95	67	86	76	45	4.28
at Home	258	738.0	703	261	521	40	34	50	31	30	3.73
on Road	263	700.1	773	301	436	55	33	36	45	15	4.86
on Grass	438	1227.1	1227	475	834	75	51	76	61	39	4.08
on Turf	83	211.0	249	87	123	20	16	10	15	6	5.46
Day Games	139	372.1	405	148	221	26	16	23	19	11	4.96
Night Games	382	1066.0	1071	414	736	69	51	63	57	34	4.04
April	61	187.0	175	66	126	8	10	11	10	4	3.13
May	85	254.0	269	90	154	14	14	14	14	6	4.54
June	87	225.2	244	96	151	17	16	10	16	6	4.99
July	97	247.2	275	109	182	30	12	17	11	9	4.76
August	87	257.1	260	98	170	12	6	17	12	10	4.13
Sept-Oct	104	266.2	253	103	174	14	9	17	13	10	3.95

	BA	OBA	SA	AB	H	2B	3B	HR	RBI	BB	SO
Totals	.267	.337	.405	5535	1476	278	29	144	692	562	957
vs. Left	.258	.338	.374	1990	514	94	10	39	224	232	337
vs. Right	.271	.336	.423	3545	962	184	19	105	468	330	620
Home	.251	.317	.385	2798	703	127	15	72	312	261	521
Road	.282	.356	.427	2737	773	151	14	72	380	301	436
Bases Empty	.260	.324	.402	3129	814	150	17	87	87	274	553
Leadoff	.264	.326	.414	1318	348	71	9	36	36	116	229
Runners on Base	.275	.352	.409	2406	662	128	12	57	605	288	404
Scoring Position	.263	.350	.401	1417	373	72	9	35	535	197	254
Late and Close	.261	.322	.400	813	212	33	4	24	106	73	159

NATIONAL LEAGUE PITCHING

	G	IP	H	BB	SO	SB	CS	W	L	S	ERA
Totals	7602	20284.2	20427	7104	13358	1714	789	1134	1134	599	4.04
at Home	3808	10418.0	10292	3539	6988	851	402	602	532	278	3.84
on Road	3794	9866.2	10135	3565	6370	863	387	532	602	321	4.26
on Grass	4303	11626.2	11475	3992	7779	917	477	648	648	349	3.85
on Turf	3299	8658.0	8952	3112	5579	797	312	486	486	250	4.31
Day Games	2577	6758.2	6779	2355	4437	557	279	379	379	214	3.99
Night Games	5025	13526.0	13648	4749	8921	1157	510	755	755	385	4.07
April	1049	2843.1	2702	1089	1809	260	105	158	158	95	3.75
May	1243	3363.0	3423	1190	2113	343	136	188	188	86	4.11
June	1224	3361.0	3429	1079	2237	277	129	190	190	101	4.04
July	1275	3422.2	3570	1157	2220	263	135	192	192	104	4.25
August	1315	3534.0	3576	1206	2320	272	140	196	196	108	4.08
Sept-Oct	1496	3760.2	3727	1383	2659	299	144	210	210	105	4.01

	BA	OBA	SA	AB	H	2B	3B	HR	RBI	BB	SO
Totals	.264	.327	.399	77489	20427	3588	513	1956	9534	7104	13358
vs. Left	.266	.339	.399	32329	8585	1436	244	797	3980	3582	5407
vs. Right	.262	.331	.399	45160	11842	2152	269	1159	5554	3522	7951
Home	.259	.327	.392	39676	10292	1833	256	975	4677	3539	6988
Road	.268	.338	.406	37813	10135	1755	257	981	4857	3565	6370
Bases Empty	.258	.326	.393	44127	11385	2036	280	1123	1123	3494	7682
Leadoff	.267	.322	.407	18820	5026	925	137	479	479	1398	3048
Runners on Base	.271	.341	.406	33362	9042	1552	233	833	8411	3610	5676
Scoring Position	.264	.348	.397	19652	5193	926	149	460	7306	2738	3634
Late and Close	.254	.325	.374	12805	3249	514	72	294	1597	1330	2499

Chicago Cubs Pitching

	G	IP	H	BB	SO	SB	CS	W	L	S	ERA
Totals	585	1449.2	1514	470	905	84	69	84	78	56	4.18
at Home	302	748.0	761	252	472	35	34	43	38	26	4.10
on Road	283	701.2	753	218	433	49	35	41	40	30	4.26
on Grass	456	1126.1	1163	357	722	52	53	67	57	42	4.04
on Turf	129	323.1	351	113	183	32	16	17	21	14	4.65
Day Games	311	785.0	790	255	477	35	35	42	45	28	3.89
Night Games	274	664.2	724	215	428	49	34	42	33	28	4.52
April	76	195.0	186	82	117	14	8	11	11	6	3.78
May	96	229.0	233	71	131	15	10	13	12	9	4.01
June	103	244.0	273	83	161	15	12	13	15	9	4.65
July	95	244.1	248	66	158	14	11	15	12	8	3.83
August	106	273.1	301	90	165	15	14	12	18	7	4.31
Sept-Oct	109	264.0	273	78	173	11	14	20	10	17	4.36

	BA	OBA	SA	AB	H	2B	3B	HR	RBI	BB	SO
Totals	.273	.332	.421	5545	1514	285	38	153	691	470	905
vs. Left	.266	.339	.417	2340	622	106	16	72	304	251	394
vs. Right	.278	.327	.424	3205	892	179	22	81	387	219	511
Home	.266	.327	.435	2857	761	155	23	94	355	252	472
Road	.280	.337	.406	2688	753	130	15	59	336	218	433
Bases Empty	.268	.322	.414	3206	858	162	22	88	88	233	520
Leadoff	.277	.330	.418	1344	372	67	12	33	33	93	188
Runners on Base	.280	.344	.430	2339	656	123	16	65	603	237	385
Scoring Position	.283	.360	.436	1344	380	68	12	38	522	178	233
Late and Close	.264	.334	.394	879	232	44	5	20	115	89	159

Florida Marlins Pitching

	G	IP	H	BB	SO	SB	CS	W	L	S	ERA
Totals	571	1440.1	1437	598	945	118	51	64	98	48	4.15
at Home	298	750.0	748	308	525	68	23	35	46	25	4.16
on Road	273	690.1	689	290	420	50	28	29	52	23	4.13
on Grass	443	1118.2	1089	456	763	95	35	54	70	41	3.92
on Turf	128	321.2	348	142	182	23	16	10	28	7	4.95
Day Games	131	328.0	298	133	216	26	16	16	21	12	3.18
Night Games	440	1112.1	1139	465	729	92	35	48	77	36	4.43
April	79	203.1	199	85	146	19	5	10	13	8	3.63
May	87	232.2	214	89	147	27	8	11	15	8	4.06
June	87	239.0	225	86	160	12	8	13	14	8	3.39
July	94	232.1	243	78	140	15	12	9	18	8	4.49
August	109	256.0	272	130	166	19	11	12	16	9	4.82
Sept-Oct	115	277.0	284	130	186	26	7	9	22	7	4.35

	BA	OBA	SA	AB	H	2B	3B	HR	RBI	BB	SO
Totals	.261	.334	.395	5501	1437	264	33	135	680	598	945
vs. Left	.259	.344	.398	2517	652	124	16	65	292	327	393
vs. Right	.263	.326	.392	2984	785	140	17	70	388	271	552
Home	.261	.334	.395	2861	748	137	15	72	349	308	525
Road	.261	.335	.394	2640	689	127	18	63	331	290	420
Bases Empty	.255	.324	.386	3061	781	136	19	76	76	296	525
Leadoff	.268	.326	.400	1331	357	53	10	34	34	107	214
Runners on Base	.269	.346	.405	2440	656	128	14	59	604	302	420
Scoring Position	.248	.343	.348	1473	365	65	7	23	493	228	266
Late and Close	.237	.321	.345	985	233	36	4	21	109	121	201

Montreal Expos Pitching

	G	IP	H	BB	SO	SB	CS	W	L	S	ERA
Totals	548	1456.2	1369	521	934	172	51	94	68	61	3.55
at Home	269	751.0	662	268	463	82	24	55	26	32	3.18
on Road	279	705.2	707	253	471	90	27	39	42	29	3.94
on Grass	162	427.0	407	133	294	50	17	24	25	18	3.56
on Turf	386	1029.2	962	388	640	122	34	70	43	43	3.54
Day Games	184	450.2	469	173	279	62	16	22	28	14	4.13
Night Games	364	1006.0	900	348	655	110	35	72	40	47	3.28
April	74	201.0	199	75	110	33	7	13	10	8	4.25
May	101	240.2	220	101	142	29	11	14	12	9	3.81
June	89	250.1	237	110	149	26	4	14	14	9	3.63
July	94	242.0	233	72	159	26	7	15	12	10	3.50
August	85	261.0	240	81	184	29	9	17	12	11	2.83
Sept-Oct	105	261.2	240	82	190	29	13	21	8	14	3.44

	BA	OBA	SA	AB	H	2B	3B	HR	RBI	BB	SO
Totals	.249	.317	.377	5501	1369	287	30	119	626	521	934
vs. Left	.257	.332	.398	2250	579	125	16	53	262	250	365
vs. Right	.243	.307	.362	3251	790	162	14	66	364	271	569
Home	.237	.307	.359	2796	662	159	17	50	288	268	463
Road	.261	.328	.395	2705	707	128	13	69	338	253	471
Bases Empty	.256	.318	.387	3102	795	160	20	69	69	258	498
Leadoff	.268	.330	.398	1337	358	79	10	25	25	116	198
Runners on Base	.239	.316	.363	2399	574	127	10	50	557	263	436
Scoring Position	.235	.330	.353	1474	346	77	5	29	487	214	302
Late and Close	.221	.294	.326	1001	221	42	6	17	90	100	222

New York Mets Pitching

	G	IP	H	BB	SO	SB	CS	W	L	S	ERA
Totals	459	1438.0	1483	434	867	143	56	59	103	22	4.05
at Home	221	739.0	746	220	454	75	31	28	53	9	3.95
on Road	238	699.0	737	214	413	68	25	31	50	13	4.16
on Grass	339	1112.2	1147	333	693	108	41	49	75	16	3.95
on Turf	120	325.1	336	101	174	35	15	10	28	6	4.40
Day Games	161	516.1	486	152	292	49	22	21	37	8	3.64
Night Games	298	921.2	997	282	575	94	34	38	66	14	4.28
April	58	187.2	189	55	94	21	8	8	13	3	3.69
May	84	238.2	272	87	155	31	10	9	18	2	4.03
June	81	237.0	264	70	157	21	11	6	21	1	4.75
July	72	243.2	264	58	141	23	6	12	16	6	4.36
August	81	257.2	237	63	161	26	14	11	18	7	4.12
Sept-Oct	83	273.1	257	101	159	21	7	13	17	3	3.36

	BA	OBA	SA	AB	H	2B	3B	HR	RBI	BB	SO
Totals	.269	.324	.404	5522	1483	275	29	139	700	434	867
vs. Left	.267	.336	.388	2026	541	99	12	41	234	207	347
vs. Right	.269	.317	.414	3496	942	176	17	98	466	227	520
Home	.264	.320	.396	2829	746	129	14	72	349	220	454
Road	.274	.329	.414	2693	737	146	15	67	351	214	413
Bases Empty	.256	.304	.389	3230	827	155	16	81	81	199	517
Leadoff	.257	.303	.389	1356	349	70	9	30	30	80	200
Runners on Base	.286	.352	.426	2292	656	120	13	58	619	235	350
Scoring Position	.282	.363	.409	1378	388	74	7	29	531	188	225
Late and Close	.292	.358	.431	870	254	42	2	25	138	88	136

Philadelphia Phillies Pitching

	G	IP	H	BB	SO	SB	CS	W	L	S	ERA
Totals	512	1472.2	1419	573	1117	101	49	97	65	46	3.97
at Home	257	755.0	725	268	629	51	21	52	29	21	3.89
on Road	255	717.2	694	305	488	50	28	45	36	25	4.05
on Grass	143	434.2	408	175	289	20	21	29	20	16	3.60
on Turf	369	1038.0	1011	398	828	81	28	68	45	30	4.12
Day Games	148	397.1	385	161	301	29	11	25	20	14	4.30
Night Games	364	1075.1	1034	412	816	72	38	72	45	32	3.84
April	75	205.0	173	86	165	14	7	17	5	11	3.25
May	68	241.0	224	93	155	14	10	17	10	5	3.55
June	82	249.0	242	82	187	13	6	18	10	9	3.90
July	93	262.0	278	106	183	13	11	14	14	5	4.50
August	90	245.1	249	88	202	17	7	16	11	8	4.37
Sept-Oct	104	270.1	253	118	225	30	8	15	15	8	4.06

	BA	OBA	SA	AB	H	2B	3B	HR	RBI	BB	SO
Totals	.252	.322	.378	5642	1419	247	39	129	673	573	1117
vs. Left	.260	.339	.391	2118	551	92	16	51	268	246	408
vs. Right	.246	.312	.370	3524	868	155	23	78	405	327	709
Home	.248	.314	.368	2920	725	140	20	57	335	268	629
Road	.255	.331	.388	2722	694	107	19	72	338	305	488
Bases Empty	.245	.310	.371	3195	784	136	19	76	76	280	637
Leadoff	.245	.308	.378	1352	331	67	7	33	33	114	270
Runners on Base	.260	.337	.386	2447	635	111	20	53	597	293	480
Scoring Position	.257	.345	.402	1430	367	72	14	36	541	204	301
Late and Close	.245	.336	.350	988	242	41	3	19	143	131	218

Pittsburgh Pirates Pitching

	G	IP	H	BB	SO	SB	CS	W	L	S	ERA
Totals	546	1445.2	1557	485	832	148	51	75	87	34	4.77
at Home	277	751.0	791	240	419	73	24	40	41	13	4.36
on Road	269	694.2	766	245	413	75	27	35	46	21	5.21
on Grass	164	434.1	461	143	267	31	17	25	25	16	4.83
on Turf	382	1011.1	1096	342	565	117	34	50	62	18	4.74
Day Games	148	399.2	426	113	240	43	18	22	23	10	4.57
Night Games	398	1046.0	1131	372	592	105	33	53	64	24	4.84
April	79	204.0	204	83	136	16	6	11	11	8	4.72
May	84	234.1	268	82	141	37	9	12	14	5	4.92
June	85	243.0	234	82	148	25	12	14	14	6	4.33
July	90	244.0	290	82	126	24	6	10	18	5	5.35
August	100	254.0	293	68	140	19	10	15	13	5	5.39
Sept-Oct	108	266.1	268	88	141	27	8	13	17	5	3.95

	BA	OBA	SA	AB	H	2B	3B	HR	RBI	BB	SO
Totals	.280	.339	.437	5567	1557	317	50	153	767	485	832
vs. Left	.283	.355	.434	1954	553	103	18	52	293	215	308
vs. Right	.278	.331	.439	3613	1004	214	32	101	474	270	524
Home	.276	.334	.423	2869	791	166	28	67	360	240	419
Road	.284	.345	.452	2698	766	151	22	86	407	245	413
Bases Empty	.270	.328	.428	3143	849	180	25	89	89	251	481
Leadoff	.273	.328	.445	1339	366	76	14	42	42	103	193
Runners on Base	.292	.354	.448	2424	708	137	25	64	678	234	351
Scoring Position	.295	.367	.461	1458	430	90	19	38	600	180	236
Late and Close	.255	.320	.401	912	233	45	8	24	131	84	153

St. Louis Cardinals Pitching

	G	IP	H	BB	SO	SB	CS	W	L	S	ERA
Totals	585	1453.0	1553	383	775	112	55	87	75	54	4.10
at Home	274	733.0	751	171	388	43	28	49	32	26	3.51
on Road	311	720.0	802	212	387	69	27	38	43	28	4.70
on Grass	191	446.0	480	124	249	35	16	26	24	18	4.36
on Turf	394	1007.0	1073	259	526	77	39	61	51	36	3.99
Day Games	190	455.0	489	101	264	41	21	31	20	20	4.05
Night Games	395	998.0	1064	282	511	71	34	56	55	34	4.12
April	80	211.1	209	55	121	22	11	13	10	11	3.41
May	86	233.1	231	62	122	21	2	12	14	6	3.63
June	98	239.0	254	51	129	17	10	20	7	16	3.84
July	102	237.2	294	67	127	16	9	14	13	8	5.49
August	98	260.2	284	67	119	18	10	13	16	8	4.25
Sept-Oct	121	271.0	281	81	157	18	13	15	15	5	3.92

	BA	OBA	SA	AB	H	2B	3B	HR	RBI	BB	SO
Totals	.276	.324	.422	5632	1553	282	44	152	693	383	775
vs. Left	.274	.326	.405	1972	540	87	15	47	235	149	276
vs. Right	.277	.322	.432	3660	1013	195	29	105	458	234	499
Home	.267	.311	.395	2815	751	143	20	59	303	171	388
Road	.285	.336	.450	2817	802	139	24	93	390	212	387
Bases Empty	.273	.313	.423	3273	895	175	26	87	87	174	458
Leadoff	.284	.325	.411	1374	390	71	7	30	30	78	165
Runners on Base	.279	.338	.422	2359	658	107	18	65	606	209	317
Scoring Position	.264	.339	.413	1403	370	58	13	42	536	166	224
Late and Close	.252	.305	.395	994	250	38	12	27	119	77	155

Atlanta Braves Pitching

	G	IP	H	BB	SO	SB	CS	W	L	S	ERA
Totals	515	1455.0	1297	480	1036	121	53	104	58	46	3.14
at Home	273	747.0	689	247	505	66	29	51	30	22	3.11
on Road	242	708.0	608	233	531	55	24	53	28	24	3.17
on Grass	393	1125.0	997	349	797	88	40	79	45	35	2.95
on Turf	122	330.0	300	131	239	33	13	25	13	11	3.76
Day Games	143	391.2	380	141	289	30	7	27	17	14	3.45
Night Games	372	1063.1	917	339	747	91	46	77	41	32	3.02
April	76	229.0	199	83	147	24	7	12	13	8	2.91
May	81	238.2	218	84	160	20	9	17	10	10	3.66
June	72	230.2	199	79	167	19	10	15	11	3	2.97
July	96	247.0	234	88	187	29	12	19	9	8	3.17
August	86	237.0	205	73	153	16	7	19	7	9	3.27
Sept-Oct	104	272.2	242	73	222	13	8	22	8	8	2.87

	BA	OBA	SA	AB	H	2B	3B	HR	RBI	BB	SO
Totals	.240	.303	.349	5394	1297	240	21	101	524	480	1036
vs. Left	.243	.316	.342	2012	488	85	10	32	196	214	382
vs. Right	.239	.295	.353	3382	809	155	11	69	328	266	654
Home	.246	.308	.354	2798	689	130	8	52	268	247	505
Road	.234	.298	.343	2596	608	110	13	49	256	233	531
Bases Empty	.242	.302	.357	3162	765	143	13	65	65	258	605
Leadoff	.256	.307	.396	1359	348	72	8	34	34	95	239
Runners on Base	.238	.305	.337	2232	532	97	8	36	459	222	431
Scoring Position	.233	.320	.330	1259	293	59	5	18	400	175	272
Late and Close	.244	.315	.352	989	241	40	2	21	106	102	207

Cincinnati Reds Pitching

	G	IP	H	BB	SO	SB	CS	W	L	S	ERA
Totals	537	1434.0	1510	508	996	134	56	73	89	37	4.51
at Home	267	730.0	747	266	497	64	29	41	40	21	4.33
on Road	270	704.0	763	242	499	70	27	32	49	16	4.70
on Grass	404	1112.1	1149	384	755	90	47	59	66	29	4.26
on Turf	133	321.2	361	124	241	44	9	14	23	8	5.40
Day Games	161	439.1	477	145	283	36	8	23	27	12	4.75
Night Games	376	994.2	1033	363	713	98	48	50	62	25	4.41
April	71	194.2	190	66	130	14	4	8	14	5	3.84
May	88	250.0	251	91	152	20	12	17	12	7	3.92
June	90	247.0	268	60	166	37	9	13	14	6	4.66
July	88	245.1	249	78	178	16	14	15	13	11	3.89
August	96	247.1	265	91	183	19	6	13	15	5	4.66
Sept-Oct	104	249.2	287	122	187	28	11	7	21	3	5.95

	BA	OBA	SA	AB	H	2B	3B	HR	RBI	BB	SO
Totals	.272	.336	.420	5549	1510	239	54	158	743	508	996
vs. Left	.277	.357	.429	2383	659	103	31	66	316	293	394
vs. Right	.269	.319	.413	3166	851	136	23	92	427	215	602
Home	.267	.332	.409	2797	747	113	20	81	365	266	497
Road	.277	.339	.432	2752	763	126	34	77	378	242	499
Bases Empty	.264	.320	.401	3164	835	138	24	83	83	239	582
Leadoff	.271	.327	.413	1332	361	61	10	36	36	99	221
Runners on Base	.283	.355	.445	2385	675	101	30	75	660	269	414
Scoring Position	.282	.362	.444	1422	401	64	16	45	573	189	260
Late and Close	.266	.340	.398	777	207	28	7	20	101	85	132

Colorado Rockies Pitching

	G	IP	H	BB	SO	SB	CS	W	L	S	ERA
Totals	615	1431.1	1664	609	913	119	56	67	95	35	5.44
at Home	322	733.0	907	320	483	60	28	39	42	16	5.87
on Road	293	698.1	757	289	430	59	28	28	53	19	4.99
on Grass	174	435.0	492	180	267	43	16	14	37	8	5.38
on Turf	441	996.1	1172	429	646	76	40	53	58	27	5.47
Day Games	216	495.1	564	214	325	42	14	23	34	13	5.18
Night Games	399	936.0	1100	395	588	77	42	44	61	22	5.58
April	75	192.0	219	92	116	22	4	8	14	1	4.78
May	110	258.2	343	119	164	27	10	7	22	4	7.03
June	89	218.2	271	85	136	16	8	11	14	5	5.89
July	105	236.0	286	88	145	14	12	10	17	6	5.91
August	108	266.2	276	122	161	27	6	14	16	11	4.29
Sept-Oct	128	259.1	269	103	191	13	16	17	12	8	4.72

	BA	OBA	SA	AB	H	2B	3B	HR	RBI	BB	SO
Totals	.294	.362	.458	5660	1664	280	54	181	913	609	913
vs. Left	.295	.371	.452	2464	728	121	33	66	383	297	375
vs. Right	.293	.355	.464	3196	936	159	21	115	530	312	538
Home	.308	.376	.490	2948	907	142	37	107	510	320	483
Road	.279	.347	.424	2712	757	138	17	74	403	289	430
Bases Empty	.280	.344	.440	3038	851	150	25	95	95	273	502
Leadoff	.294	.358	.473	1304	384	74	15	43	43	121	222
Runners on Base	.310	.383	.480	2622	813	130	29	86	818	336	411
Scoring Position	.293	.377	.449	1622	475	87	20	42	709	255	268
Late and Close	.270	.345	.416	730	197	28	8	21	113	85	135

Houston Astros Pitching

	G	IP	H	BB	SO	SB	CS	W	L	S	ERA
Totals	486	1441.1	1363	476	1056	110	42	85	77	42	3.49
at Home	229	734.0	664	213	570	59	19	44	37	17	3.11
on Road	257	707.1	699	263	486	51	23	41	40	25	3.88
on Grass	159	444.0	409	155	313	31	15	30	20	18	3.43
on Turf	327	997.1	954	321	743	79	27	55	57	24	3.52
Day Games	162	457.0	431	158	322	40	17	28	23	15	3.47
Night Games	324	984.1	932	318	734	70	25	57	54	27	3.50
April	58	197.0	162	58	130	15	5	14	8	6	3.06
May	87	242.2	239	80	173	26	10	13	14	7	3.60
June	85	224.2	249	74	148	19	4	11	15	8	4.61
July	89	260.2	247	89	200	18	8	16	13	7	3.38
August	84	251.2	213	82	189	16	8	15	13	8	3.00
Sept-Oct	83	264.2	253	93	216	16	7	16	14	6	3.33

	BA	OBA	SA	AB	H	2B	3B	HR	RBI	BB	SO
Totals	.251	.313	.366	5440	1363	226	25	117	590	476	1056
vs. Left	.254	.329	.371	2461	624	92	15	56	255	272	447
vs. Right	.248	.300	.361	2979	739	134	10	61	335	204	609
Home	.241	.299	.351	2751	664	110	12	56	268	213	570
Road	.260	.328	.381	2689	699	116	13	61	322	263	486
Bases Empty	.238	.299	.348	3146	750	122	17	63	63	251	630
Leadoff	.240	.294	.370	1342	322	49	10	35	35	99	260
Runners on Base	.267	.333	.390	2294	613	104	8	54	527	225	426
Scoring Position	.259	.338	.375	1326	344	60	6	27	452	168	264
Late and Close	.278	.341	.395	914	254	33	1	24	118	83	208

Los Angeles Dodgers Pitching

	G	IP	H	BB	SO	SB	CS	W	L	S	ERA
Totals	508	1472.2	1406	567	1043	129	66	81	81	36	3.50
at Home	246	747.0	703	273	530	68	41	41	40	15	3.17
on Road	262	725.2	703	294	513	61	25	40	41	21	3.84
on Grass	392	1155.1	1094	426	815	101	55	65	61	30	3.33
on Turf	116	317.1	312	141	228	28	11	16	20	6	4.14
Day Games	147	437.1	404	192	310	33	25	24	25	10	3.60
Night Games	361	1035.1	1002	375	733	96	41	57	56	26	3.46
April	74	204.0	185	106	136	16	12	8	15	5	3.71
May	82	233.1	228	73	170	28	9	18	8	5	3.36
June	80	240.0	227	82	170	18	15	14	13	7	3.45
July	84	256.1	241	105	168	20	9	14	13	7	3.58
August	83	247.2	245	96	177	19	13	12	15	6	3.09
Sept-Oct	105	291.1	280	105	222	28	8	15	17	6	3.80

	BA	OBA	SA	AB	H	2B	3B	HR	RBI	BB	SO
Totals	.254	.324	.361	5544	1406	223	33	103	613	567	1043
vs. Left	.252	.331	.358	2908	732	120	16	52	328	351	531
vs. Right	.256	.317	.366	2636	674	103	17	51	285	216	512
Home	.250	.317	.347	2811	703	107	11	48	296	273	530
Road	.257	.331	.376	2733	703	116	22	55	317	294	513
Bases Empty	.247	.314	.356	3128	773	125	18	60	60	279	588
Leadoff	.255	.319	.372	1351	345	63	8	26	26	115	238
Runners on Base	.262	.337	.368	2416	633	98	15	43	553	288	455
Scoring Position	.248	.340	.349	1417	351	59	11	21	488	215	295
Late and Close	.241	.318	.332	1035	249	35	3	18	112	116	231

San Diego Padres Pitching

	G	IP	H	BB	SO	SB	CS	W	L	S	ERA
Totals	559	1437.2	1470	558	957	142	68	61	101	32	4.23
at Home	289	752.0	725	258	527	64	40	34	47	12	3.79
on Road	270	685.2	745	300	430	78	28	27	54	20	4.70
on Grass	436	1131.0	1125	426	771	107	57	50	76	23	4.00
on Turf	123	306.2	345	132	186	35	11	11	25	9	5.05
Day Games	178	463.0	476	169	310	44	32	20	32	15	4.10
Night Games	381	974.2	994	389	647	98	36	41	69	17	4.28
April	84	202.2	196	78	119	14	9	10	12	7	3.91
May	93	243.0	258	87	150	35	15	10	18	3	4.48
June	92	249.0	258	74	184	26	8	9	19	4	3.80
July	84	239.1	236	110	155	22	11	11	16	7	4.36
August	96	241.0	242	97	152	20	15	12	15	6	4.11
Sept-Oct	110	262.2	280	112	197	25	10	9	21	5	4.63

	BA	OBA	SA	AB	H	2B	3B	HR	RBI	BB	SO
Totals	.266	.334	.404	5520	1470	238	40	148	716	558	957
vs. Left	.271	.347	.407	2643	716	100	20	73	350	315	402
vs. Right	.262	.321	.402	2877	754	138	20	75	366	243	555
Home	.253	.316	.391	2860	725	110	23	79	347	258	527
Road	.280	.352	.419	2660	745	128	17	69	369	300	430
Bases Empty	.265	.326	.420	3065	811	143	25	94	94	257	536
Leadoff	.287	.337	.455	1341	385	71	11	44	44	92	208
Runners on Base	.268	.344	.385	2455	659	95	15	54	622	301	421
Scoring Position	.264	.355	.382	1478	390	60	9	32	555	234	258
Late and Close	.279	.354	.399	838	234	35	7	17	101	96	154

San Francisco Giants Pitching

	G	IP	H	BB	SO	SB	CS	W	L	S	ERA
Totals	576	1456.2	1385	442	982	81	66	103	59	50	3.63
at Home	284	748.0	673	235	526	43	31	50	31	23	3.27
on Road	292	708.2	712	207	456	38	35	53	28	27	4.00
on Grass	447	1124.1	1054	351	784	66	47	77	47	39	3.56
on Turf	129	332.1	331	91	198	15	19	26	12	11	3.85
Day Games	297	743.0	704	248	529	47	37	55	27	29	3.61
Night Games	279	713.2	681	194	453	34	29	48	32	21	3.64
April	90	216.2	192	85	142	16	12	15	9	8	3.70
May	96	247.0	224	71	151	13	11	18	9	6	3.32
June	91	249.2	228	61	175	13	12	19	9	10	2.85
July	89	232.0	227	70	153	13	7	18	8	8	3.80
August	93	234.2	254	58	168	12	10	15	11	8	4.64
Sept-Oct	117	276.2	260	97	193	14	14	18	13	10	3.55

	BA	OBA	SA	AB	H	2B	3B	HR	RBI	BB	SO
Totals	.253	.313	.387	5472	1385	185	23	168	605	442	982
vs. Left	.263	.323	.400	2281	600	79	10	71	264	195	385
vs. Right	.246	.306	.379	3191	785	106	13	97	341	247	597
Home	.243	.304	.370	2764	673	92	8	81	284	235	526
Road	.263	.321	.405	2708	712	93	15	87	321	207	456
Bases Empty	.252	.312	.384	3214	811	111	11	97	97	246	603
Leadoff	.264	.315	.386	1358	358	52	6	34	34	86	232
Runners on Base	.254	.313	.392	2258	574	74	12	71	508	196	379
Scoring Position	.251	.330	.390	1168	293	33	5	40	419	144	230
Late and Close	.226	.287	.333	893	202	27	4	20	101	73	188

1993 AMERICAN LEAGUE TEAM STATISTICS (Final, unofficial; compiled by the MLB-IBM Baseball Information System)

BATTING

TEAM	AB	R	H	2B	3B	HR	RBI	SH	SF	HP	BB	IBB	SO	SB	CS	GDP	SHO	BA	SA	OBA
NEW YORK	5615	821	1568	294	24	178	793	22	50	43	629	47	910	39	35	149	4	.279	.435	.353
TORONTO	5579	847	1556	317	42	159	796	46	54	52	588	57	861	170	49	138	1	.279	.436	.350
CLEVELAND	5619	790	1547	264	31	141	747	39	72	49	488	57	843	159	55	131	10	.275	.409	.335
DETROIT	5620	899	1546	282	38	178	853	33	52	35	765	50	1122	104	63	101	2	.275	.434	.362
TEXAS	5510	835	1472	284	39	181	780	69	56	48	483	56	984	113	67	111	6	.267	.431	.329
BALTIMORE	5508	786	1470	287	24	157	744	49	56	41	655	52	930	73	54	131	11	.267	.413	.346
CHICAGO	5483	776	1454	228	44	162	731	72	61	33	604	52	834	106	57	126	14	.265	.411	.338
MINNESOTA	5601	693	1480	261	27	121	642	27	37	51	493	35	850	83	59	150	13	.264	.385	.327
BOSTON	5496	686	1451	319	29	114	644	80	49	62	508	69	871	73	38	146	8	.264	.395	.330
KANSAS CITY	5522	675	1455	294	35	125	641	48	51	52	428	50	936	100	75	107	7	.263	.397	.320
SEATTLE	5494	734	1429	272	24	161	681	63	51	56	624	73	901	91	68	132	9	.260	.406	.339
CALIFORNIA	5391	684	1399	259	24	114	644	50	46	38	564	39	930	169	100	129	8	.260	.380	.331
MILWAUKEE	5525	733	1426	240	25	125	688	57	45	40	555	52	932	138	93	117	4	.258	.378	.328
OAKLAND	5543	715	1408	260	21	158	679	46	49	33	622	45	1048	131	59	125	13	.254	.394	.330
TOTALS	77506	10674	20661	3861	427	2074	63	701	729	633	8006	734	12952	1549	872	1793	110	.267	.408	.337

PITCHING

TEAM	W	L	ERA	G	CG	SHO	REL	SV	IP	H	R	ER	HR	HB	BB	IBB	SO	WP	BK	O/BA
CHICAGO	94	68	3.70	162	16	11	322	48	1454.0	1398	664	598	125	40	566	36	974	51	7	.255
BOSTON	80	82	3.77	162	9	11	389	44	1452.1	1379	698	609	127	48	552	87	997	42	11	.252
KANSAS CITY	84	78	4.04	162	16	6	303	48	1445.1	1379	694	649	105	44	571	36	985	76	7	.254
SEATTLE	82	80	4.20	162	22	10	353	41	1453.2	1421	731	678	135	66	605	56	1083	57	6	.259
TORONTO	95	67	4.21	162	11	11	344	50	1441.1	1441	742	674	134	32	620	38	1023	83	8	.261
TEXAS	86	76	4.28	162	20	6	359	45	1438.1	1476	751	684	144	44	562	42	957	52	14	.267
BALTIMORE	85	77	4.31	162	21	10	329	42	1442.2	1427	745	691	153	38	579	50	900	41	2	.261
CALIFORNIA	71	91	4.34	162	26	6	320	41	1430.1	1482	770	690	153	51	550	35	843	55	7	.270
NEW YORK	88	74	4.35	162	11	13	332	38	1438.1	1467	761	695	170	29	552	58	899	33	5	.266
MILWAUKEE	69	93	4.45	162	26	6	353	29	1447.0	1511	792	716	153	60	522	58	810	45	7	.271
CLEVELAND	76	86	4.58	162	7	8	410	45	1445.2	1591	813	736	182	39	591	53	888	41	5	.281
DETROIT	85	77	4.65	162	11	7	375	36	1436.2	1547	837	742	188	48	542	92	828	68	5	.276
MINNESOTA	71	91	4.71	162	5	3	356	44	1444.1	1591	830	756	148	45	514	34	901	43	13	.283
OAKLAND	68	94	4.90	162	8	2	424	42	1452.1	1551	846	791	157	49	680	59	864	39	6	.276
TOTALS	1134	1134	4.32	1134	209	110	4969	593	20222.1	20661	10674	9709	2074	633	8006	734	12952	726	103	.267

FIELDING

TEAM	FA	G	PO	A	E	TC	DP	TP	PB
SEATTLE	.985	162	4361	1726	90	6177	173	0	13
KANSAS CITY	.984	162	4336	1709	97	6142	150	0	14
BALTIMORE	.984	162	4328	1789	100	6217	171	0	6
MINNESOTA	.984	162	4333	1755	100	6188	160	0	21
NEW YORK	.983	162	4315	1889	105	6309	166	0	7
TORONTO	.982	162	4324	1583	107	6014	144	0	6
OAKLAND	.982	162	4357	1627	111	6095	161	0	15
CHICAGO	.982	162	4362	1665	112	6139	153	0	15
CALIFORNIA	.980	162	4291	1694	120	6105	161	0	10
BOSTON	.980	162	4357	1692	122	6171	155	0	11
TEXAS	.979	162	4315	1779	132	6226	145	0	18
DETROIT	.979	162	4310	1777	132	6219	148	0	8
MILWAUKEE	.979	162	4341	1633	131	6105	148	0	12
CLEVELAND	.976	162	4337	1661	148	6146	174	0	9
TOTALS	.981	1134	60667	23979	1607	86253	2209	0	165

1993 NATIONAL LEAGUE TEAM STATISTICS (Final, unofficial; compiled by the MLB-IBM Baseball Information System)

BATTING

TEAM	AB	R	H	2B	3B	HR	RBI	SH	SF	HP	BB	IBB	SO	SB	CS	GDP	SHO	BA	SA	OBA
SAN FRANCISCO	5557	636	1534	269	33	168	759	102	50	46	516	88	930	120	65	121	5	.276	.427	.340
PHILADELPHIA	5685	740	1555	297	51	156	811	84	51	42	665	70	1049	91	32	107	2	.274	.426	.351
COLORADO	5517	967	1507	278	59	142	704	70	52	46	388	40	944	146	90	125	13	.273	.422	.323
ST. LOUIS	5551	744	1508	262	34	118	724	59	54	27	588	50	882	153	72	128	8	.272	.395	.341
CHICAGO	5627	739	1521	259	32	161	706	67	42	34	446	50	923	100	43	131	10	.270	.414	.325
PITTSBURGH	5549	806	1482	267	50	110	664	76	52	55	536	50	972	92	55	129	6	.267	.393	.335
HOUSTON	5464	630	1459	288	37	138	656	82	47	40	497	58	911	103	60	125	8	.267	.409	.330
CINCINNATI	5517	785	1457	261	28	137	669	63	66	32	485	42	1025	142	59	104	10	.264	.396	.324
ATLANTA	5515	559	1444	239	29	169	712	73	50	36	560	46	946	125	48	127	9	.262	.408	.331
LOS ANGELES	5588	662	1458	234	28	130	639	107	47	27	492	48	937	126	61	105	8	.261	.383	.321
MONTREAL	5493	682	1410	270	36	122	682	100	50	48	542	65	860	228	56	95	5	.257	.386	.326
SAN DIEGO	5503	772	1386	239	28	153	633	80	50	59	443	43	1046	92	41	111	8	.252	.389	.312
NEW YORK	5448	744	1350	228	37	158	632	89	43	24	448	43	879	79	50	108	4	.248	.390	.305
FLORIDA	5475	724	1356	197	31	94	542	58	43	51	498	39	1054	117	56	122	14	.248	.346	.314
TOTALS	77489	10190	20427	3588	513	1956	9533	110	701	567	7104	743	13358	1714	788	1638	110	.264	.399	.327

PITCHING

TEAM	W	L	ERA	G	CG	SHO	REL	SV	IP	H	R	ER	HR	HB	BB	IBB	SO	WP	BK	O/BA
ATLANTA	104	58	3.14	162	18	16	353	46	1455.0	1297	559	507	101	22	480	59	1036	46	9	.240
HOUSTON	85	77	3.49	162	18	14	324	42	1441.1	1363	630	559	117	41	476	52	1056	60	12	.251
LOS ANGELES	81	81	3.50	162	17	9	346	36	1472.2	1406	662	573	103	37	567	68	1043	47	20	.254
MONTREAL	94	68	3.55	163	8	7	385	61	1456.2	1369	682	574	119	47	521	38	934	46	12	.249
SAN FRANCISCO	103	59	3.61	162	4	9	414	50	1456.2	1385	636	585	168	50	442	46	982	33	18	.253
PHILADELPHIA	97	65	3.95	162	24	11	350	46	1472.2	1419	740	647	129	37	573	33	1117	74	7	.252
NEW YORK	59	103	4.05	162	16	8	297	22	1438.0	1483	744	647	139	50	434	61	867	32	14	.269
ST. LOUIS	87	75	4.09	162	5	7	423	54	1453.0	1553	744	660	152	43	383	50	775	40	7	.276
FLORIDA	64	98	4.13	162	4	5	409	48	1440.1	1437	724	661	135	32	598	58	945	85	20	.261
CHICAGO	84	78	4.18	163	8	5	422	56	1449.2	1514	739	673	153	43	470	61	905	43	21	.273
SAN DIEGO	61	101	4.23	162	8	6	397	32	1437.2	1470	772	675	148	34	558	72	957	57	14	.266
CINCINNATI	73	89	4.51	162	11	8	375	37	1434.0	1510	785	718	158	44	508	36	996	47	8	.272
PITTSBURGH	75	87	4.77	162	12	5	384	34	1445.2	1557	806	766	153	46	485	43	832	55	11	.280
COLORADO	67	95	5.41	162	9	0	453	35	1431.1	1664	967	860	181	41	609	66	913	82	22	.294
TOTALS	1134	1134	4.04	1135	162	110	5332	599	20284.2	20427	10190	9105	1956	567	7104	743	13358	747	195	.264

FIELDING

TEAM	FA	G	PO	A	E	TC	DP	TP	PB
SAN FRANCISCO	.984	162	4370	1733	101	6204	169	0	15
PITTSBURGH	.983	162	4337	1816	105	6258	161	1	19
ATLANTA	.983	162	4365	1769	108	6242	146	0	13
CHICAGO	.982	163	4349	1889	115	6353	162	0	14
CINCINNATI	.980	162	4302	1633	121	6056	133	0	12
FLORIDA	.980	162	4321	1703	125	6149	130	0	29
HOUSTON	.979	162	4324	1652	126	6102	141	0	7
LOS ANGELES	.979	162	4418	1838	133	6389	141	0	15
PHILADELPHIA	.977	162	4418	1536	141	6095	123	0	12
ST. LOUIS	.975	162	4359	1890	159	6408	157	1	14
NEW YORK	.975	162	4314	1781	156	6251	143	0	4
MONTREAL	.975	163	4370	1827	159	6356	144	2	14
SAN DIEGO	.974	162	4313	1616	160	6089	129	0	20
COLORADO	.973	162	4294	1760	167	6221	149	0	11
TOTALS	.978	1135	60854	24443	1876	87173	2028	4	199

TEAM BATTING BY LINEUP ORDER

AMERICAN LEAGUE

TEAM	POS	BA	OBA	SA	AB	R	H	2B	3B	HR	RBI	BB	SO
BALTIMORE	P1	.261	.359	.408	652	99	170	41	8	13	70	94	106
	P2	.271	.340	.360	663	89	180	30	7	5	75	70	98
	P3	.245	.317	.380	658	78	161	27	4	18	89	68	93
	P4	.265	.346	.440	623	102	165	25	0	28	99	81	87
	P5	.268	.343	.449	622	90	167	34	0	26	99	68	112
	P6	.277	.358	.449	603	102	167	29	0	25	83	70	136
	P7	.303	.386	.469	574	86	174	38	0	19	82	78	103
	P8	.286	.362	.432	563	72	161	39	2	13	76	67	84
	P9	.227	.302	.336	550	68	125	24	3	10	71	59	111
BOSTON	P1	.264	.323	.370	686	98	181	37	6	8	60	51	60
	P2	.307	.367	.434	657	103	202	34	5	13	65	57	71
	P3	.285	.350	.411	635	77	181	45	4	9	75	59	78
	P4	.279	.340	.460	637	87	178	35	1	26	103	52	106
	P5	.253	.345	.429	590	79	149	35	3	21	92	78	138
	P6	.267	.330	.396	604	77	161	37	1	13	77	57	94
	P7	.257	.336	.362	580	67	149	30	5	7	58	63	101
	P8	.234	.286	.339	573	48	134	34	1	8	65	42	109
	P9	.217	.285	.339	534	50	116	32	3	9	49	49	114
CLEVELAND	P1	.317	.398	.401	666	127	211	30	10	2	56	89	104
	P2	.267	.307	.375	688	98	184	29	3	13	95	42	91
	P3	.315	.351	.474	667	111	210	28	6	22	117	38	75
	P4	.290	.373	.551	610	97	177	36	3	39	133	81	99
	P5	.262	.355	.425	602	89	158	38	0	20	85	87	123
	P6	.236	.281	.365	631	72	149	20	2	19	67	38	128
	P7	.272	.328	.416	592	72	161	38	4	13	74	46	97
	P8	.263	.310	.338	594	68	156	20	2	7	57	38	57
	P9	.248	.294	.327	569	56	141	25	1	6	63	29	69
DETROIT	P1	.310	.433	.417	641	127	199	29	3	11	69	137	119
	P2	.278	.375	.445	647	120	180	46	1	20	107	98	83
	P3	.308	.384	.495	656	110	202	42	6	23	106	80	130
	P4	.271	.367	.468	630	99	171	26	1	32	129	95	140
	P5	.260	.355	.434	622	96	162	29	5	23	90	92	136
	P6	.265	.354	.492	620	98	164	28	7	33	120	88	159
	P7	.258	.338	.401	608	85	157	29	5	16	75	72	133
	P8	.284	.344	.413	603	88	171	30	3	14	88	57	111
	P9	.236	.294	.329	593	76	140	23	7	6	69	46	111
MILWAUKEE	P1	.281	.354	.368	672	99	189	27	2	9	61	73	108
	P2	.238	.294	.324	672	83	160	21	2	11	67	50	99
	P3	.280	.342	.422	651	89	182	40	1	17	93	60	97
	P4	.260	.364	.466	607	104	158	28	2	31	100	95	115
	P5	.277	.338	.418	617	86	171	38	5	13	90	56	105
	P6	.242	.302	.372	608	74	147	24	2	17	84	47	97
	P7	.242	.310	.333	582	62	141	18	1	11	79	58	116
	P8	.267	.335	.373	569	72	152	24	6	8	64	58	98
	P9	.230	.307	.325	547	64	126	20	4	8	50	58	97
NEW YORK	P1	.281	.354	.403	690	106	194	32	8	12	85	77	92
	P2	.291	.345	.393	685	106	199	38	1	10	68	58	88
	P3	.295	.372	.434	648	94	191	33	3	17	99	79	49
	P4	.247	.361	.483	611	98	151	35	2	35	120	105	174
	P5	.332	.396	.581	633	107	210	39	1	39	125	66	94
	P6	.263	.334	.395	617	80	162	28	0	18	78	63	111
	P7	.249	.336	.405	587	76	146	25	2	21	83	74	123
	P8	.280	.362	.436	571	87	160	28	5	17	67	72	94
	P9	.271	.316	.387	573	67	155	36	2	9	68	35	85
TORONTO	P1	.264	.358	.416	663	140	175	37	5	18	55	90	115
	P2	.282	.359	.433	656	118	185	39	6	16	82	79	103
	P3	.337	.413	.505	647	124	218	37	6	20	114	84	67
	P4	.257	.320	.499	649	101	167	36	5	37	129	56	123
	P5	.350	.461	.558	568	107	199	51	2	21	107	115	69
	P6	.282	.340	.447	618	76	174	34	7	18	91	51	97
	P7	.258	.300	.394	619	66	160	31	7	13	87	34	98
	P8	.244	.292	.349	599	62	146	28	1	11	73	37	85
	P9	.236	.289	.316	560	53	132	24	3	5	58	42	104
CALIFORNIA	P1	.266	.328	.325	668	87	178	22	7	1	42	61	67
	P2	.282	.355	.372	639	103	180	29	4	7	66	72	100
	P3	.276	.364	.511	616	108	170	36	2	35	106	85	149
	P4	.248	.328	.439	624	84	155	35	0	28	119	73	144
	P5	.244	.327	.358	587	66	143	20	1	15	79	70	111
	P6	.250	.310	.361	593	66	148	28	4	10	51	51	94
	P7	.257	.335	.357	560	63	144	33	1	7	52	65	105
	P8	.268	.330	.362	553	59	148	30	2	6	66	51	70
	P9	.241	.296	.327	551	48	133	26	3	5	63	36	90

TEAM	POS	BA	OBA	SA	AB	R	H	2B	3B	HR	RBI	BB	SO
CHICAGO	P1	.292	.376	.437	664	117	194	24	9	18	79	88	58
	P2	.272	.349	.345	640	102	174	16	11	3	55	70	68
	P3	.306	.417	.592	591	115	181	40	0	43	131	120	65
	P4	.233	.311	.369	634	78	148	28	2	18	92	70	93
	P5	.244	.326	.421	606	76	148	24	1	27	99	75	105
	P6	.250	.316	.434	604	84	151	29	5	24	90	59	150
	P7	.289	.350	.384	599	76	173	23	11	4	60	57	79
	P8	.226	.278	.367	575	68	130	19	1	20	67	37	158
	P9	.272	.303	.356	570	60	155	25	4	5	58	28	58
KANSAS CITY	P1	.275	.319	.395	691	96	190	44	6	9	51	41	124
	P2	.277	.335	.406	660	93	183	29	7	14	74	56	107
	P3	.273	.320	.450	653	88	178	38	3	24	86	47	79
	P4	.282	.360	.462	611	84	172	40	2	22	93	68	122
	P5	.242	.318	.386	598	74	145	34	5	14	70	57	108
	P6	.276	.326	.431	606	69	167	37	3	17	77	44	101
	P7	.258	.315	.412	578	69	149	35	3	16	83	45	113
	P8	.237	.284	.308	577	50	137	17	3	6	59	33	111
	P9	.245	.291	.308	548	52	134	20	3	3	48	37	71
MINNESOTA	P1	.274	.347	.351	680	94	186	33	4	4	49	68	73
	P2	.279	.353	.357	653	82	182	30	3	5	63	70	80
	P3	.293	.355	.488	651	98	191	39	5	26	98	58	101
	P4	.258	.336	.485	623	94	161	24	3	37	125	74	97
	P5	.277	.335	.416	628	72	174	31	1	18	82	50	89
	P6	.290	.340	.414	625	65	181	32	2	14	73	41	90
	P7	.217	.284	.294	586	61	127	16	1	9	45	51	131
	P8	.245	.292	.352	591	66	145	31	4	8	55	39	102
	P9	.236	.291	.294	564	61	133	25	4	0	52	42	87
OAKLAND	P1	.280	.396	.428	640	114	179	32	3	19	64	120	102
	P2	.278	.341	.392	669	78	186	34	0	14	74	63	97
	P3	.237	.295	.401	658	77	156	23	5	25	110	57	101
	P4	.276	.359	.481	616	100	170	25	1	33	101	80	146
	P5	.241	.302	.373	627	70	151	35	3	14	70	53	123
	P6	.277	.342	.445	611	76	169	36	2	21	80	61	111
	P7	.210	.271	.308	610	60	128	21	3	11	51	52	150
	P8	.231	.295	.344	584	71	135	29	2	11	64	51	118
	P9	.254	.363	.366	528	69	134	25	2	10	65	85	100
SEATTLE	P1	.259	.321	.320	688	80	178	29	5	1	48	60	96
	P2	.237	.291	.342	676	78	160	29	6	10	59	50	103
	P3	.300	.403	.603	609	120	183	36	2	48	113	102	96
	P4	.258	.359	.431	605	89	156	28	1	25	97	98	133
	P5	.280	.358	.445	614	83	172	32	3	21	93	75	105
	P6	.253	.337	.435	596	85	151	34	1	24	78	72	115
	P7	.238	.326	.333	579	57	138	32	4	5	51	71	102
	P8	.272	.354	.438	559	73	152	31	1	20	94	58	76
	P9	.245	.298	.322	568	69	139	21	1	7	48	38	75
TEXAS	P1	.271	.318	.387	693	109	188	26	15	8	60	50	106
	P2	.244	.301	.404	659	104	161	37	4	20	95	59	102
	P3	.295	.366	.547	634	117	187	42	2	38	118	67	125
	P4	.298	.349	.580	647	123	193	38	3	46	129	38	117
	P5	.276	.356	.446	597	104	165	33	4	20	83	70	112
	P6	.262	.321	.449	599	81	157	34	3	24	102	52	123
	P7	.264	.333	.422	576	75	152	34	3	17	81	56	114
	P8	.254	.323	.335	556	59	141	27	3	4	61	56	87
	P9	.233	.285	.286	549	63	128	13	2	4	51	35	98
AMERICAN LEAGUE TOTALS	P1	.278	.356	.387	9394	1493	2612	443	91	133	849	1099	1330
	P2	.272	.337	.384	9264	1357	2516	441	60	161	1045	894	1290
	P3	.289	.361	.478	8974	1406	2591	506	49	365	1455	1004	1305
	P4	.266	.348	.473	8727	1340	2322	439	26	437	1569	1066	1696
	P5	.272	.351	.438	8511	1199	2314	473	34	292	1264	1012	1530
	P6	.263	.328	.420	8535	1105	2248	430	39	277	1151	794	1606
	P7	.255	.325	.378	8230	975	2099	403	50	169	961	822	1565
	P8	.256	.318	.370	8067	943	2068	387	36	153	956	696	1360
	P9	.242	.301	.330	7804	856	1891	339	42	87	813	619	1270

NATIONAL LEAGUE

TEAM	POS	BA	OBA	SA	AB	R	H	2B	3B	HR	RBI	BB	SO
CHICAGO	P1	.275	.328	.387	695	104	191	29	5	13	49	51	89
	P2	.293	.339	.379	676	104	198	29	4	7	51	45	81
	P3	.321	.381	.453	647	86	208	32	4	15	102	67	52
	P4	.289	.338	.440	647	89	187	34	2	20	105	51	88
	P5	.262	.314	.440	638	89	167	35	5	23	99	44	118
	P6	.284	.345	.491	613	89	174	34	3	29	88	57	124
	P7	.235	.310	.402	587	76	138	22	2	24	81	57	125
	P8	.293	.349	.478	577	67	169	29	3	24	91	46	108
	P9	.163	.203	.238	547	34	89	15	4	6	40	28	138
FLORIDA	P1	.265	.323	.331	680	85	180	23	2	6	50	59	89
	P2	.274	.338	.379	654	86	179	29	2	12	66	60	106
	P3	.270	.343	.373	633	72	171	24	4	11	70	68	102
	P4	.276	.333	.431	627	71	173	25	6	20	100	51	123
	P5	.238	.316	.357	600	61	143	24	1	15	72	65	127
	P6	.233	.295	.344	605	57	141	19	6	12	61	48	129
	P7	.260	.327	.378	580	58	151	27	4	11	45	46	117
	P8	.255	.341	.318	548	49	140	18	2	4	46	70	83
	P9	.142	.190	.188	548	42	78	8	4	3	32	31	178
MONTREAL	P1	.307	.376	.419	681	116	209	24	8	12	64	76	88
	P2	.260	.346	.371	642	95	167	29	6	10	61	80	77
	P3	.285	.342	.423	653	97	186	30	3	18	98	55	83
	P4	.252	.356	.449	602	98	152	30	5	26	104	91	95
	P5	.240	.305	.360	622	79	149	36	3	11	84	55	84
	P6	.264	.329	.460	605	87	160	36	5	24	105	57	76
	P7	.254	.314	.358	587	59	149	32	4	7	64	51	96
	P8	.273	.335	.401	571	69	156	32	1	13	69	47	100
	P9	.155	.202	.204	530	32	82	21	1	1	33	30	161
NEW YORK	P1	.256	.295	.368	688	101	176	28	11	9	50	36	122
	P2	.262	.316	.394	649	86	170	27	4	17	64	53	73
	P3	.276	.319	.436	652	78	180	28	2	24	99	44	71
	P4	.260	.344	.501	601	102	156	28	3	37	96	83	105
	P5	.265	.342	.415	603	87	160	27	3	19	80	71	95
	P6	.274	.324	.430	603	67	165	27	2	21	83	43	104
	P7	.194	.259	.339	578	59	112	25	7	15	65	46	89
	P8	.242	.309	.362	553	58	134	28	1	12	60	50	90
	P9	.186	.220	.244	521	34	97	10	4	4	35	22	130
PHILADELPHIA	P1	.301	.416	.475	655	145	197	45	6	19	67	131	66
	P2	.282	.324	.422	721	108	203	43	11	12	91	41	122
	P3	.314	.415	.478	640	116	201	36	6	19	99	112	106
	P4	.268	.365	.429	630	116	169	36	4	19	105	95	131
	P5	.256	.377	.469	597	102	153	36	5	27	119	117	124
	P6	.297	.342	.502	650	97	193	35	7	28	133	44	95
	P7	.290	.340	.439	638	75	185	26	3	21	91	46	118
	P8	.271	.333	.380	606	73	164	29	8	7	72	46	108
	P9	.164	.213	.210	548	45	90	11	1	4	34	33	179
PITTSBURGH	P1	.261	.308	.392	702	103	183	24	10	16	58	43	100
	P2	.305	.385	.432	650	106	198	35	9	10	55	80	131
	P3	.287	.362	.413	649	90	186	27	5	15	84	75	116
	P4	.288	.367	.401	626	97	180	43	2	8	100	79	61
	P5	.292	.363	.443	610	89	178	24	7	18	103	70	91
	P6	.278	.346	.451	597	76	166	29	7	20	97	55	109
	P7	.254	.312	.349	602	42	153	26	5	7	69	45	112
	P8	.235	.299	.361	570	57	134	39	3	9	60	48	106
	P9	.192	.252	.274	543	47	104	20	2	7	38	41	146
ST.LOUIS	P1	.290	.359	.434	679	116	197	48	4	14	67	71	105
	P2	.279	.330	.348	675	87	188	24	7	3	62	54	43
	P3	.332	.397	.493	645	105	214	28	5	22	98	72	51
	P4	.277	.371	.427	613	102	170	31	2	19	106	91	113
	P5	.262	.340	.420	621	96	163	29	6	19	92	72	114
	P6	.280	.346	.416	608	72	170	22	5	17	103	61	104
	P7	.265	.346	.378	584	68	155	34	4	8	76	70	110
	P8	.231	.294	.340	580	63	134	28	1	11	71	55	83
	P9	.214	.270	.275	546	49	117	18	0	5	49	42	159
ATLANTA	P1	.270	.339	.357	675	107	182	23	9	6	44	74	94
	P2	.301	.397	.437	627	109	189	33	2	16	77	86	114
	P3	.270	.320	.413	663	108	179	22	2	23	103	51	109
	P4	.270	.354	.504	623	107	168	32	3	36	115	78	100
	P5	.275	.349	.519	618	104	170	30	5	37	108	71	111
	P6	.266	.318	.452	613	80	163	30	3	26	99	50	104
	P7	.244	.303	.363	603	57	147	28	4	12	65	50	91
	P8	.250	.329	.335	555	54	139	24	1	7	52	65	61
	P9	.199	.249	.264	538	41	107	17	0	6	49	35	162

TEAM	POS	BA	OBA	SA	AB	R	H	2B	3B	HR	RBI	BB	SO
CINCINNATI	P1	.250	.319	.363	684	99	171	36	7	9	40	68	103
	P2	.284	.334	.389	682	94	194	25	5	12	61	49	112
	P3	.298	.373	.429	631	91	188	32	3	15	88	79	87
	P4	.284	.338	.480	638	101	181	34	5	27	99	54	117
	P5	.273	.329	.434	622	97	170	33	2	21	92	48	112
	P6	.271	.331	.422	587	83	159	31	2	18	91	55	116
	P7	.267	.327	.438	573	68	153	25	2	23	98	51	121
	P8	.229	.287	.318	563	52	129	28	2	6	53	48	103
	P9	.209	.258	.274	537	37	112	17	0	6	47	33	154
COLORADO	P1	.255	.334	.343	651	101	166	23	11	4	51	76	71
	P2	.280	.336	.410	646	105	181	34	13	8	62	51	115
	P3	.294	.338	.489	656	112	193	47	3	25	105	36	113
	P4	.345	.383	.590	646	105	223	46	8	32	126	39	109
	P5	.291	.343	.488	623	92	181	35	5	26	105	46	97
	P6	.286	.333	.447	609	83	174	31	5	19	81	39	90
	P7	.232	.277	.316	585	47	136	23	4	6	67	35	87
	P8	.265	.303	.435	570	68	151	28	9	17	57	31	95
	P9	.192	.241	.245	531	45	102	11	1	5	50	35	167
HOUSTON	P1	.288	.372	.475	649	106	187	45	5	22	68	80	95
	P2	.264	.314	.380	671	97	177	21	12	11	58	45	85
	P3	.318	.385	.506	626	93	199	44	4	22	97	72	84
	P4	.266	.333	.402	627	98	167	29	4	16	82	63	110
	P5	.273	.334	.424	618	81	169	37	1	18	93	58	107
	P6	.268	.322	.427	609	73	163	39	5	16	87	44	103
	P7	.265	.327	.423	577	64	153	33	2	18	74	51	100
	P8	.268	.334	.370	568	61	152	20	4	10	62	56	96
	P9	.177	.223	.245	519	43	92	20	0	5	35	28	131
LOS ANGELES	P1	.298	.380	.374	657	87	196	22	11	2	49	85	78
	P2	.268	.339	.333	624	83	167	25	5	2	61	68	67
	P3	.241	.312	.389	643	88	155	29	3	20	91	66	126
	P4	.228	.293	.406	640	81	146	33	0	27	106	59	85
	P5	.264	.311	.457	641	88	169	30	5	28	96	43	113
	P6	.264	.314	.408	628	71	166	24	0	22	69	43	150
	P7	.279	.327	.423	617	68	172	30	1	19	64	44	100
	P8	.288	.352	.360	584	63	168	24	3	4	57	57	72
	P9	.215	.251	.278	554	46	119	17	0	6	46	27	146
SAN DIEGO	P1	.266	.347	.359	661	86	176	39	5	4	46	70	114
	P2	.260	.323	.351	666	101	173	25	6	8	53	60	95
	P3	.299	.343	.449	662	89	198	42	3	17	89	43	80
	P4	.265	.359	.502	600	103	159	23	1	39	107	84	115
	P5	.266	.310	.451	627	85	167	30	1	28	111	36	142
	P6	.241	.301	.401	601	53	145	18	6	22	81	45	143
	P7	.255	.304	.377	592	56	151	23	2	15	66	38	92
	P8	.237	.293	.362	569	60	135	21	4	14	49	45	108
	P9	.156	.194	.225	525	46	82	18	0	6	32	22	157
SAN FRANCISCO	P1	.252	.301	.313	707	99	178	21	5	4	53	44	75
	P2	.295	.356	.476	662	118	195	41	5	23	85	57	125
	P3	.287	.372	.461	635	112	182	35	2	24	98	84	97
	P4	.288	.327	.564	660	122	190	39	4	45	132	40	90
	P5	.337	.446	.626	570	125	192	39	6	38	114	114	85
	P6	.318	.365	.445	620	69	197	34	3	13	101	47	91
	P7	.286	.339	.394	594	56	170	27	5	9	74	44	95
	P8	.245	.314	.339	575	65	141	23	2	9	65	52	106
	P9	.167	.218	.206	534	42	89	10	1	3	37	34	166
NATIONAL LEAGUE TOTALS	P1	.274	.343	.384	9464	1455	2589	430	99	140	756	964	1289
	P2	.279	.341	.393	9245	1379	2579	420	91	151	907	829	1346
	P3	.292	.357	.443	9035	1337	2640	456	49	270	1321	924	1277
	P4	.276	.347	.466	8780	1392	2421	463	49	371	1483	958	1442
	P5	.271	.341	.449	8610	1275	2331	445	55	328	1368	910	1520
	P6	.273	.330	.436	8548	1057	2336	409	59	287	1279	688	1538
	P7	.256	.315	.384	8297	853	2125	381	49	195	999	674	1453
	P8	.256	.320	.369	7989	859	2046	371	44	147	864	716	1319
	P9	.181	.228	.241	7521	583	1360	213	18	67	557	441	2174

TEAM BATTING BY DEFENSIVE POSITION

AMERICAN LEAGUE

TEAM	POS	BA	OBA	SA	AB	R	H	2B	3B	HR	RBI	BB	SO
BALTIMORE	C	.285	.384	.524	550	94	157	32	0	33	103	82	131
	1B	.266	.336	.383	582	66	155	35	0	11	74	65	87
	2B	.243	.333	.324	581	73	141	24	4	5	56	77	59
	3B	.262	.340	.401	588	88	154	28	0	18	65	65	119
	SS	.262	.332	.423	646	87	169	26	3	24	90	65	59
	LF	.266	.367	.446	616	101	164	43	7	18	79	94	115
	CF	.242	.301	.380	652	87	158	34	4	16	87	53	124
	RF	.304	.372	.405	634	86	193	37	6	5	79	71	112
	DH	.280	.355	.455	617	93	173	27	0	27	104	75	107
	PH	.185	.328	.204	54	9	10	1	0	0	10	11	18
BOSTON	C	.192	.246	.274	500	35	96	20	0	7	42	34	95
	1B	.287	.370	.473	600	87	172	32	1	26	98	75	135
	2B	.264	.323	.363	644	93	170	37	6	5	52	53	67
	3B	.282	.355	.407	578	74	163	33	3	11	71	61	94
	SS	.271	.339	.430	547	59	148	45	3	12	71	56	100
	LF	.293	.359	.441	631	89	185	48	6	11	79	63	66
	CF	.280	.336	.391	632	90	177	30	5	10	63	44	72
	RF	.246	.325	.350	602	66	148	29	2	10	56	65	112
	DH	.265	.317	.428	635	77	168	35	3	21	94	41	100
	PH	.179	.270	.276	134	5	24	10	0	1	18	17	33
CLEVELAND	C	.236	.285	.322	534	52	126	23	1	7	58	28	65
	1B	.268	.352	.426	585	89	157	36	1	18	81	76	128
	2B	.311	.344	.470	662	111	206	30	6	21	121	34	73
	3B	.288	.348	.411	584	79	168	39	0	11	65	51	77
	SS	.263	.295	.327	590	58	155	19	2	5	57	24	34
	LF	.286	.363	.530	611	93	175	38	3	35	131	74	102
	CF	.314	.394	.397	663	126	208	31	9	2	54	89	103
	RF	.264	.316	.385	629	96	166	25	6	13	88	50	110
	DH	.251	.306	.409	618	70	155	17	3	25	72	48	118
	PH	.205	.275	.323	161	13	33	7	0	4	19	15	37
DETROIT	C	.269	.369	.465	579	87	156	33	4	24	89	92	146
	1B	.275	.366	.477	629	85	173	27	2	32	129	89	138
	2B	.297	.414	.423	610	108	181	45	1	10	87	121	81
	3B	.303	.369	.439	633	92	192	38	3	14	79	65	89
	SS	.303	.363	.473	634	104	192	33	6	21	103	61	103
	LF	.264	.352	.410	637	105	168	27	3	20	93	85	115
	CF	.252	.322	.411	604	98	152	24	12	16	78	58	122
	RF	.223	.329	.371	606	91	135	22	1	22	71	94	194
	DH	.284	.372	.435	616	97	175	27	6	18	103	89	119
	PH	.316	.393	.449	98	15	31	7	0	2	26	12	18
MILWAUKEE	C	.231	.316	.345	528	60	122	23	2	11	66	67	68
	1B	.274	.345	.426	577	84	158	28	0	20	78	57	116
	2B	.231	.300	.289	577	69	133	14	4	4	58	57	99
	3B	.271	.321	.389	632	70	171	36	3	11	93	46	61
	SS	.252	.328	.344	610	92	154	22	5	8	63	65	118
	LF	.279	.357	.455	624	95	174	34	2	24	94	75	99
	CF	.261	.315	.371	639	89	167	30	2	12	63	48	122
	RF	.276	.344	.388	616	74	170	21	3	14	72	62	107
	DH	.252	.329	.409	623	87	157	29	3	21	90	67	124
	PH	.193	.267	.239	109	9	21	3	1	0	12	11	20
NEW YORK	C	.288	.365	.487	587	85	169	22	1	31	103	69	102
	1B	.288	.374	.443	632	93	182	31	2	21	104	82	63
	2B	.262	.319	.383	554	75	145	32	1	11	69	44	99
	3B	.305	.384	.377	652	98	199	30	1	5	66	83	58
	SS	.268	.330	.372	589	70	158	31	3	8	60	56	73
	LF	.303	.363	.464	604	92	183	34	3	19	67	56	74
	CF	.273	.337	.418	660	82	180	39	9	13	82	59	119
	RF	.272	.353	.485	610	97	166	36	2	30	98	77	134
	DH	.253	.350	.487	612	96	155	33	1	36	124	89	157
	PH	.272	.355	.440	125	18	34	7	1	4	21	15	37
TORONTO	C	.253	.291	.383	588	49	149	33	2	13	75	30	94
	1B	.382	.483	.637	581	120	222	55	3	29	120	112	71
	2B	.310	.389	.465	641	111	199	36	6	17	99	81	77
	3B	.261	.311	.385	605	58	158	35	2	12	80	34	94
	SS	.264	.325	.359	587	71	155	22	11	4	65	54	64
	LF	.241	.331	.407	605	101	146	30	5	20	85	79	108
	CF	.274	.338	.432	672	124	184	46	6	16	64	61	147
	RF	.222	.289	.397	634	82	141	24	3	27	102	55	122
	DH	.308	.383	.471	639	116	197	36	4	20	101	80	77
	PH	.185	.267	.296	27	1	5	0	0	1	5	2	7
CALIFORNIA	C	.234	.295	.325	517	44	121	26	0	7	60	42	106
	1B	.246	.331	.397	562	73	138	30	2	17	67	73	107
	2B	.272	.333	.369	577	63	157	35	3	5	48	52	78
	3B	.256	.327	.352	583	60	149	22	2	10	69	60	96
	SS	.236	.283	.308	533	52	126	22	2	4	56	27	58

TEAM	POS	BA	OBA	SA	AB	R	H	2B	3B	HR	RBI	BB	SO
CALIFORNIA *continued*	LF	.267	.330	.325	659	85	176	21	7	1	43	61	63
	CF	.284	.359	.377	634	104	180	28	5	7	65	73	102
	RF	.285	.376	.517	600	102	171	38	1	33	102	87	151
	DH	.245	.326	.431	624	83	153	35	0	27	119	74	146
	PH	.272	.367	.417	103	11	28	2	2	3	15	15	24
CHICAGO	C	.230	.279	.381	557	66	128	19	1	21	67	34	152
	1B	.306	.415	.584	582	109	178	39	0	41	124	116	60
	2B	.268	.352	.347	637	104	171	18	13	2	57	75	69
	3B	.259	.375	.423	582	86	151	27	1	22	95	108	84
	SS	.270	.299	.355	560	58	151	25	4	5	55	26	56
	LF	.285	.377	.446	625	100	178	24	4	23	80	92	81
	CF	.295	.347	.389	627	87	185	22	14	3	55	49	53
	RF	.268	.335	.438	594	80	159	27	4	22	89	61	136
	DH	.214	.252	.365	654	69	140	27	3	22	103	33	127
	PH	.187	.299	.227	75	10	14	0	0	1	7	12	19
KANSAS CITY	C	.264	.343	.438	580	75	153	33	1	22	86	56	111
	1B	.291	.369	.470	598	92	174	44	3	19	76	75	96
	2B	.243	.273	.296	530	41	129	16	3	2	43	21	50
	3B	.228	.288	.381	578	66	132	27	2	19	77	36	161
	SS	.274	.317	.391	583	71	160	32	3	10	63	38	99
	LF	.266	.327	.416	587	73	156	33	8	13	63	53	83
	CF	.283	.331	.406	668	82	189	28	9	12	72	43	108
	RF	.263	.309	.369	628	78	165	37	3	8	59	42	113
	DH	.255	.304	.410	647	79	165	34	3	20	80	46	83
	PH	.260	.347	.346	127	15	33	11	0	0	23	18	33
MINNESOTA	C	.281	.330	.384	612	66	172	25	1	12	73	38	33
	1B	.234	.334	.408	578	77	135	18	1	27	99	88	95
	2B	.271	.349	.335	657	87	178	28	4	2	45	71	54
	3B	.272	.329	.371	563	66	153	31	5	5	38	43	91
	SS	.245	.288	.292	535	54	131	19	3	0	47	33	79
	LF	.234	.289	.378	606	69	142	29	5	16	77	43	139
	CF	.296	.353	.447	665	93	197	42	2	18	90	52	105
	RF	.274	.331	.440	614	81	168	28	4	22	75	52	121
	DH	.273	.329	.413	641	82	175	35	2	17	78	53	106
	PH	.222	.340	.311	135	11	30	6	0	2	20	21	29
OAKLAND	C	.269	.332	.389	581	69	156	35	1	11	64	52	116
	1B	.272	.365	.464	580	89	158	31	1	26	81	82	118
	2B	.273	.348	.369	623	77	170	32	2	8	74	72	93
	3B	.222	.270	.373	622	62	138	28	6	18	66	41	140
	SS	.257	.339	.324	571	65	147	22	2	4	54	63	62
	LF	.251	.359	.394	609	100	153	28	1	19	63	101	104
	CF	.236	.314	.382	594	66	140	26	2	19	73	69	130
	RF	.252	.310	.417	647	77	163	27	4	24	102	57	106
	DH	.257	.334	.427	630	87	162	27	1	26	86	73	161
	PH	.250	.330	.410	100	13	25	5	1	3	17	13	21
SEATTLE	C	.257	.344	.394	545	66	140	27	0	16	75	57	71
	1B	.264	.340	.435	605	74	160	38	1	21	89	67	85
	2B	.270	.330	.389	612	80	165	30	2	13	66	49	104
	3B	.266	.347	.413	579	75	154	34	3	15	67	71	129
	SS	.251	.313	.299	613	73	154	16	2	3	42	51	78
	LF	.224	.280	.312	626	60	140	27	8	4	49	47	96
	CF	.294	.384	.580	616	113	181	42	4	42	102	88	84
	RF	.269	.373	.457	595	94	160	28	3	26	98	100	146
	DH	.253	.344	.394	597	86	151	25	1	19	77	85	92
	PH	.267	.324	.382	131	11	35	6	0	3	26	13	24
TEXAS	C	.270	.326	.401	589	71	159	33	4	12	75	49	86
	1B	.292	.367	.545	613	124	179	40	2	37	107	73	87
	2B	.245	.308	.330	563	63	138	30	0	6	63	49	79
	3B	.239	.312	.471	594	96	142	35	2	33	102	57	159
	SS	.230	.283	.286	521	60	120	14	3	3	46	36	92
	LF	.303	.360	.594	636	114	193	37	5	46	129	44	117
	CF	.266	.315	.365	644	102	171	19	12	7	55	47	101
	RF	.265	.324	.429	615	81	163	36	7	17	87	53	117
	DH	.277	.343	.426	631	104	175	34	3	18	97	65	118
	PH	.315	.378	.454	108	13	34	7	1	2	21	11	28
AMERICAN LEAGUE TOTALS	P	.250	.250	.250	4	0	1	0	0	0	0	0	2
	C	.255	.324	.396	7847	919	2004	384	18	227	1036	730	1376
	1B	.282	.368	.469	8304	1262	2341	484	19	345	1327	1130	1386
	2B	.270	.339	.370	8468	1155	2283	407	55	111	938	856	1082
	3B	.266	.335	.399	8373	1070	2224	443	33	204	1033	821	1452
	SS	.261	.318	.358	8119	974	2120	348	52	111	872	655	1075
	LF	.269	.344	.430	8676	1277	2333	453	67	269	1132	967	1362
	CF	.275	.339	.410	8970	1343	2469	441	95	193	1003	833	1492
	RF	.263	.335	.417	8624	1185	2268	415	49	273	1178	926	1781
	DH	.262	.332	.426	8784	1226	2501	421	33	317	1328	918	1635
	PH	.240	.326	.349	1487	154	357	72	6	26	240	186	348

TEAM	POS	BA	OBA	SA	AB	R	H	2B	3B	HR	RBI	BB	SO
CHICAGO	P	.117	.141	.131	351	10	41	5	0	0	14	10	94
	C	.279	.344	.511	581	88	162	31	1	34	89	55	120
	1B	.323	.394	.466	631	89	204	40	4	14	100	77	36
	2B	.296	.346	.394	639	84	189	28	1	11	66	50	95
	3B	.262	.334	.413	600	71	157	32	4	17	79	63	111
	SS	.289	.332	.342	653	83	189	23	4	1	58	40	54
	LF	.282	.326	.435	650	80	183	34	3	20	113	43	90
	CF	.283	.332	.477	665	106	188	32	8	27	74	43	123
	RF	.242	.296	.428	621	86	150	23	3	29	80	43	140
	PH	.243	.306	.417	235	35	57	11	3	8	30	21	60
FLORIDA	P	.124	.161	.165	322	21	40	3	2	2	14	13	117
	C	.222	.283	.358	603	53	134	23	7	15	57	44	113
	1B	.255	.323	.409	623	69	159	21	3	23	95	62	143
	2B	.269	.337	.356	635	74	171	26	4	7	61	56	82
	3B	.300	.389	.428	601	68	180	23	3	16	81	86	76
	SS	.264	.360	.305	545	55	144	15	2	1	41	81	74
	LF	.278	.333	.378	627	72	174	27	3	10	77	51	147
	CF	.267	.323	.340	677	85	181	27	2	6	51	55	90
	RF	.229	.268	.356	632	65	145	30	4	14	54	28	146
	PH	.133	.224	.152	210	17	28	2	1	0	11	22	66
MONTREAL	P	.118	.159	.139	330	13	39	7	0	0	12	15	119
	C	.233	.289	.342	567	46	132	28	2	10	72	40	79
	1B	.225	.294	.357	608	78	137	27	4	15	69	56	116
	2B	.293	.386	.386	648	104	190	28	7	6	49	95	78
	3B	.260	.342	.406	599	87	156	37	4	14	67	73	102
	SS	.265	.327	.386	611	69	162	40	2	10	70	49	71
	LF	.289	.345	.467	630	95	182	33	8	21	110	51	78
	CF	.300	.352	.440	666	110	200	29	2	20	102	56	77
	RF	.257	.355	.435	604	97	155	30	6	22	93	90	88
	PH	.249	.301	.358	229	22	57	11	1	4	38	17	52
NEW YORK	P	.148	.184	.196	337	17	50	6	2	2	19	14	93
	C	.237	.281	.366	587	54	139	27	2	15	74	34	74
	1B	.286	.328	.468	650	82	186	29	1	29	105	45	68
	2B	.263	.313	.431	601	80	158	29	0	24	87	39	96
	3B	.252	.330	.422	588	70	148	19	3	25	80	73	102
	SS	.213	.290	.279	549	52	117	26	2	2	40	56	75
	LF	.265	.308	.372	667	101	177	24	13	7	49	43	89
	CF	.254	.313	.437	602	78	153	31	2	25	69	48	129
	RF	.247	.330	.459	595	107	147	29	8	27	83	75	106
	PH	.277	.328	.358	271	26	75	8	4	2	26	21	47
PHILADELPHIA	P	.130	.166	.163	368	23	48	6	0	2	17	15	144
	C	.263	.385	.492	590	98	155	40	4	29	116	120	128
	1B	.316	.417	.479	637	115	201	35	6	19	99	113	104
	2B	.260	.305	.377	693	90	180	36	12	7	67	39	123
	3B	.270	.357	.431	638	113	172	33	5	20	108	85	126
	SS	.288	.343	.403	618	89	178	31	5	10	86	43	105
	LF	.270	.332	.453	640	95	173	28	4	27	121	56	120
	CF	.299	.414	.472	655	145	196	44	6	19	67	131	67
	RF	.312	.356	.491	647	79	202	37	8	21	104	44	85
	PH	.253	.314	.328	198	23	50	7	1	2	26	19	46
PITTSBURGH	P	.154	.168	.194	350	16	54	9	1	1	16	3	99
	C	.261	.327	.391	575	51	150	32	2	13	81	47	103
	1B	.245	.317	.349	593	53	145	32	3	8	74	60	96
	2B	.265	.312	.385	660	88	175	30	5	13	57	39	83
	3B	.292	.350	.400	638	83	186	36	3	9	102	57	59
	SS	.297	.380	.422	647	107	192	33	9	10	53	81	129
	LF	.278	.365	.450	600	98	167	30	11	17	77	80	121
	CF	.289	.338	.442	647	83	187	24	9	19	98	48	121
	RF	.276	.360	.411	598	90	165	30	6	13	78	78	103
	PH	.252	.361	.393	242	32	61	11	1	7	28	43	59
ST.LOUIS	P	.186	.219	.217	345	19	64	11	0	0	21	15	115
	C	.255	.312	.362	580	57	148	27	1	11	72	50	75
	1B	.328	.395	.461	634	103	208	27	3	17	88	70	48
	2B	.267	.349	.386	611	84	163	39	5	8	71	73	120
	3B	.273	.342	.422	631	86	172	38	1	18	110	70	91
	SS	.277	.333	.339	654	84	181	26	6	1	55	56	32
	LF	.293	.347	.455	672	105	197	44	7	17	84	56	86
	CF	.274	.376	.450	595	100	163	25	7	22	99	94	140
	RF	.249	.326	.386	611	80	152	16	4	20	90	69	123
	PH	.278	.373	.375	216	29	60	9	0	4	34	35	52
ATLANTA	P	.165	.202	.187	364	16	60	8	0	0	21	17	127
	C	.243	.303	.365	597	48	145	28	3	13	67	49	90
	1B	.270	.340	.491	593	98	160	35	3	30	92	65	104
	2B	.253	.332	.340	550	55	139	23	2	7	54	67	60
	3B	.276	.314	.413	652	84	180	34	2	17	86	36	98

TEAM	POS	BA	OBA	SA	AB	R	H	2B	3B	HR	RBI	BB	SO
ATLANTA *continued*	SS	.300	.397	.430	619	111	186	31	2	15	74	87	111
	LF	.266	.335	.494	635	114	169	29	4	36	119	66	122
	CF	.270	.340	.358	673	107	182	23	9	6	44	74	94
	RF	.270	.355	.505	610	92	165	15	4	40	121	78	91
	PH	.264	.329	.391	220	24	58	13	0	5	34	21	48
CINCINNATI	P	.217	.237	.262	351	18	76	10	0	2	30	7	108
	C	.240	.282	.378	580	50	139	32	0	16	88	38	112
	1B	.296	.370	.408	615	76	182	28	1	13	73	72	94
	2B	.236	.305	.319	648	85	153	29	5	5	45	61	118
	3B	.258	.313	.426	624	95	161	35	2	22	88	49	120
	SS	.272	.336	.385	628	85	171	27	4	12	68	62	83
	LF	.298	.364	.481	620	87	185	38	6	21	95	68	98
	CF	.291	.339	.441	657	93	191	36	6	17	61	47	100
	RF	.273	.336	.449	593	101	162	18	4	26	95	55	138
	PH	.187	.279	.273	198	18	37	8	0	3	26	26	52
COLORADO	P	.132	.178	.169	296	14	39	3	1	2	21	17	108
	C	.270	.315	.385	600	69	162	27	6	10	64	36	86
	1B	.348	.384	.559	646	92	225	43	6	27	121	34	100
	2B	.248	.307	.365	630	93	156	27	13	7	56	52	108
	3B	.294	.347	.510	618	95	182	46	3	27	104	49	93
	SS	.271	.305	.402	594	70	161	21	9	13	55	30	75
	LF	.263	.327	.402	612	78	161	26	7	15	64	49	84
	CF	.266	.335	.387	617	94	164	33	6	10	73	63	108
	RF	.305	.346	.520	640	111	195	45	6	27	114	38	109
	PH	.234	.288	.322	261	29	61	7	2	4	32	20	72
HOUSTON	P	.141	.167	.189	334	22	47	7	0	3	18	10	97
	C	.247	.305	.397	559	51	138	22	1	20	77	44	86
	1B	.316	.381	.505	620	87	196	44	5	21	93	67	89
	2B	.285	.369	.472	648	104	185	45	5	22	68	79	97
	3B	.265	.326	.397	620	82	164	38	1	14	87	58	101
	SS	.275	.341	.393	575	76	158	27	4	11	59	56	105
	LF	.284	.344	.433	619	89	176	39	4	15	74	52	102
	CF	.271	.306	.389	669	79	181	20	13	11	64	33	89
	RF	.268	.352	.433	594	97	159	33	4	19	90	76	98
	PH	.246	.316	.330	224	24	55	13	0	2	25	22	47
LOS ANGELES	P	.199	.221	.234	342	24	68	9	0	1	19	9	107
	C	.313	.361	.541	630	84	197	29	2	37	119	48	92
	1B	.247	.289	.411	659	80	163	30	3	24	83	38	92
	2B	.276	.333	.358	576	69	159	26	3	5	46	50	51
	3B	.236	.289	.347	619	58	146	28	1	13	77	48	100
	SS	.268	.344	.328	615	78	165	22	6	1	65	73	80
	LF	.236	.295	.376	628	80	148	26	1	20	71	52	135
	CF	.299	.386	.382	646	86	193	23	11	3	52	89	76
	RF	.257	.328	.418	615	78	158	31	1	22	76	61	144
	PH	.233	.300	.315	257	23	60	9	0	4	29	24	60
SAN DIEGO	P	.107	.129	.142	309	16	33	8	0	1	11	7	117
	C	.235	.289	.330	561	51	132	22	2	9	40	39	82
	1B	.257	.323	.450	615	86	158	19	2	32	98	60	122
	2B	.262	.336	.372	600	71	157	30	9	6	46	65	98
	3B	.286	.332	.468	630	77	180	28	3	27	88	39	96
	SS	.240	.310	.330	630	94	151	20	5	9	45	59	117
	LF	.247	.332	.487	594	80	147	29	1	37	114	70	141
	CF	.242	.299	.384	623	82	151	25	3	19	77	36	145
	RF	.326	.367	.449	662	86	216	48	3	9	74	43	52
	PH	.220	.282	.300	277	28	61	10	0	4	41	24	75
SAN FRANCISCO	P	.171	.210	.190	357	28	61	4	0	1	24	17	126
	C	.271	.342	.365	564	58	153	21	1	10	65	56	98
	1B	.296	.368	.465	632	104	187	33	4	22	99	70	98
	2B	.285	.341	.458	646	104	184	40	3	22	82	50	131
	3B	.295	.331	.555	654	119	193	39	4	41	124	33	94
	SS	.272	.321	.358	595	58	162	23	5	6	72	41	97
	LF	.334	.455	.668	566	132	189	38	5	47	128	130	82
	CF	.246	.301	.321	688	104	169	24	8	4	67	47	65
	RF	.308	.360	.428	636	76	196	39	2	11	77	52	86
	PH	.179	.246	.280	218	19	39	8	1	4	21	20	53
NATIONAL LEAGUE TOTALS	P	.151	.182	.185	4756	257	720	96	6	17	257	169	1571
	C	.255	.317	.400	8174	858	2086	389	34	242	1081	700	1338
	1B	.287	.352	.449	8756	1212	2511	443	48	294	1289	889	1310
	2B	.269	.334	.386	8785	1185	2359	436	74	150	855	815	1340
	3B	.273	.336	.432	8712	1188	2377	466	39	280	1281	819	1369
	SS	.272	.338	.365	8533	1111	2317	365	65	102	841	814	1208
	LF	.277	.344	.452	8760	1306	2428	445	77	310	1296	867	1495
	CF	.275	.341	.408	9080	1352	2499	396	92	208	998	864	1424
	RF	.273	.338	.441	8658	1245	2367	424	63	300	1229	830	1509
	PH	.233	.304	.330	3256	349	759	127	14	53	401	335	789

TEAM AND LEAGUE STARTING PITCHING/RELIEF PITCHING STATISTICS

AMERICAN LEAGUE		G	IP	H	BB	SO	SB	CS	W	L	S	ERA
	SP	2268	13879.0	14287	5201	8432	1178	687	811	827	0	4.44
	RP	4974	6343.1	6374	2805	4520	371	185	323	307	593	4.10
BALTIMORE	SP	162	977.1	993	373	589	62	50	62	56	0	4.57
	RP	329	465.1	434	206	311	34	14	23	21	42	3.81
BOSTON	SP	162	1001.0	966	332	623	72	34	55	56	0	3.81
	RP	389	451.1	413	220	374	20	10	25	26	44	3.79
CLEVELAND	SP	162	884.1	1002	341	481	86	53	42	54	0	5.25
	RP	410	561.1	589	250	407	27	15	34	32	45	3.51
DETROIT	SP	162	940.1	1012	304	473	79	47	64	51	0	4.78
	RP	375	496.1	535	238	355	23	10	21	26	36	4.57
MILWAUKEE	SP	162	1036.0	1100	349	554	99	35	50	70	0	4.63
	RP	355	411.0	411	173	256	16	16	19	23	29	4.05
NEW YORK	SP	162	1011.2	1038	358	627	85	42	60	55	0	4.26
	RP	332	426.2	429	194	272	30	5	28	19	38	4.62
TORONTO	SP	162	999.1	1023	432	649	104	55	70	50	0	4.63
	RP	344	442.0	418	188	374	32	9	25	17	50	3.30
CALIFORNIA	SP	162	1039.1	1080	371	612	87	44	57	71	0	4.32
	RP	320	391.0	402	179	231	35	8	14	20	41	4.47
CHICAGO	SP	162	1067.1	1006	425	708	66	66	76	55	0	3.72
	RP	322	386.2	392	141	266	16	16	18	13	48	3.72
KANSAS CITY	SP	162	1040.0	979	404	682	79	55	59	55	0	4.03
	RP	303	405.1	400	167	303	40	16	25	23	48	4.06
MINNESOTA	SP	162	966.0	1086	338	581	115	51	50	78	0	4.92
	RP	356	478.1	505	176	320	22	15	21	13	44	4.35
OAKLAND	SP	162	904.0	987	415	476	87	49	41	63	0	5.19
	RP	425	548.1	564	265	388	33	22	27	31	42	4.43
SEATTLE	SP	162	1043.2	1023	381	754	81	58	62	54	0	3.99
	RP	355	410.0	398	224	329	24	10	20	26	41	4.74
TEXAS	SP	162	968.2	992	378	623	76	48	63	59	0	4.39
	RP	359	469.2	484	184	334	19	19	23	17	45	4.06

NATIONAL LEAGUE		G	IP	H	BB	SO	SB	CS	W	L	S	ERA
	SP	2270	13850.2	14193	4506	8502	1194	595	808	813	0	4.08
	RP	5332	6433.1	6234	2598	4856	520	192	326	321	599	3.98
CHICAGO	SP	163	981.1	1051	304	566	62	58	58	62	0	4.45
	RP	422	468.1	463	166	339	22	11	26	16	56	3.61
FLORIDA	SP	162	959.2	998	371	585	73	40	47	72	0	4.33
	RP	409	480.0	439	225	358	44	10	17	26	48	3.79
MONTREAL	SP	163	944.1	909	319	540	127	38	64	44	0	3.61
	RP	385	512.1	460	202	394	45	13	30	24	61	3.43
NEW YORK	SP	162	1064.1	1069	281	634	97	44	45	76	0	3.88
	RP	297	373.1	414	154	232	46	12	14	27	22	4.53
PHILADELPHIA	SP	162	1040.2	1027	346	749	66	38	69	42	0	3.95
	RP	350	432.0	392	227	368	35	11	28	23	46	4.00
PITTSBURGH	SP	162	954.0	1046	323	483	101	40	46	64	0	4.78
	RP	384	491.2	511	162	349	47	11	29	23	34	4.74
ST. LOUIS	SP	162	973.1	1051	226	475	72	37	61	49	0	4.03
	RP	423	479.2	502	156	301	40	17	26	26	54	4.24
ATLANTA	SP	162	1083.0	997	327	719	92	42	79	42	0	3.13
	RP	353	372.0	300	153	317	29	11	25	16	46	3.15
CINCINNATI	SP	162	969.0	1042	314	652	92	45	49	62	0	4.50
	RP	375	465.0	468	194	344	42	11	24	27	37	4.55
COLORADO	SP	162	878.2	1072	348	492	77	33	37	73	0	5.49
	RP	453	552.2	592	261	421	42	23	30	22	35	5.36
HOUSTON	SP	162	1049.1	997	339	764	86	32	72	53	0	3.48
	RP	324	392.0	366	137	292	24	10	13	24	42	3.51
LOS ANGELES	SP	162	1033.2	990	390	700	90	49	57	59	0	3.55
	RP	346	439.0	416	177	343	39	17	24	22	36	3.38
SAN DIEGO	SP	162	939.0	973	341	559	96	44	42	72	0	4.53
	RP	397	498.2	497	217	398	46	24	19	29	32	3.65
SAN FRANCISCO	SP	162	980.1	971	277	584	63	55	82	43	0	3.72
	RP	414	476.2	414	167	400	19	11	21	16	50	3.44

FINAL 1993 REGULAR SEASON STANDINGS

AMERICAN LEAGUE

EAST	WON	LOST	PCT.	G.B.	HOME	ROAD	vs EAST	vs WEST
Toronto	95	67	.586	—	48-33	47-34	50-28	45-39
New York	88	74	.543	7.0	50-31	38-43	44-34	44-40
Baltimore	85	77	.525	10.0	48-33	37-44	38-40	47-37
Detroit	85	77	.525	10.0	44-37	41-40	40-38	45-39
Boston	80	82	.494	15.0	43-38	37-44	32-46	48-36
Cleveland	76	86	.469	19.0	46-35	30-51	37-41	39-45
Milwaukee	69	93	.426	26.0	38-43	31-50	32-46	37-47

WEST	WON	LOST	PCT.	G.B.	HOME	ROAD	vs EAST	vs WEST
Chicago	94	68	.580	—	45-36	49-32	48-36	46-32
Texas	86	76	.531	8.0	50-31	36-45	49-35	37-41
Kansas City	84	78	.519	10.0	43-38	41-40	43-41	41-37
Seattle	82	80	.506	12.0	46-35	36-45	44-40	38-40
California	71	91	.438	23.0	44-37	27-54	36-48	35-43
Minnesota	71	91	.438	23.0	36-45	35-46	34-50	37-41
Oakland	68	94	.420	26.0	38-43	30-51	29-55	39-39

G.B. = Games Behind

NATIONAL LEAGUE

EAST	WON	LOST	PCT.	G.B.	HOME	ROAD	vs EAST	vs WEST
Philadelphia	97	65	.599	—	52-29	45-36	47-31	50-34
Montreal	94	68	.580	3.0	55-26	39-42	46-32	48-36
St. Louis	87	75	.537	10.0	49-32	38-43	42-36	45-39
Chicago	84	78	.519	13.0	43-38	41-40	39-39	45-39
Pittsburgh	75	87	.463	22.0	40-41	35-46	39-39	36-48
Florida	64	98	.395	33.0	35-46	29-52	30-48	34-50
New York	59	103	.364	38.0	28-53	31-50	30-48	29-55

WEST	WON	LOST	PCT.	G.B.	HOME	ROAD	vs EAST	vs WEST
Atlanta	104	58	.642	—	51-30	53-28	49-35	55-23
San Francisco	103	59	.636	1.0	50-31	53-28	50-34	53-25
Houston	85	77	.525	19.0	44-37	41-40	51-33	34-44
Los Angeles	81	81	.500	23.0	41-40	40-41	42-42	39-39
Cincinnati	73	89	.451	31.0	41-40	32-49	39-45	34-44
Colorado	67	95	.414	37.0	39-42	28-53	36-48	31-47
San Diego	61	101	.377	43.0	34-47	27-54	34-50	27-51

G.B. = Games Behind

1993 MAJOR LEAGUE ATTENDANCE (regular season games only)

AMERICAN LEAGUE

CLUB	HM TOT	HM AVG	HM DATES	HM GAMES	HIGH	DATE	1992 TOT	CHANGE	RD TOT	RD AVG	RD DATES
Toronto	4,057,947	50,098	81	81	50,533	4/09	4,028,318	29,629	2,549,438	31,475	81
Baltimore	3,644,965	45,562	80	81	46,834	8/02	3,567,819	77,146	2,192,041	27,062	81
Chicago	2,581,091	32,672	79	81	43,559	6/26	2,614,084	-32,993	2,571,904	31,752	81
Boston	2,422,021	30,275	80	81	34,923	4/18	2,468,570	-46,549	2,542,188	31,777	80
New York	2,416,942	30,212	80	81	56,704	4/12	1,748,733	668,209	2,603,321	32,140	81
Texas	2,244,616	28,413	79	81	41,339	7/17	2,170,693	73,923	2,401,702	30,791	78
Cleveland	2,177,908	27,224	80	81	73,290	4/05	1,224,274	953,634	2,216,265	27,703	80
California	2,057,460	25,401	81	81	60,326	9/17	2,065,444	-7,984	2,286,553	28,582	80
Seattle	2,052,638	25,341	81	81	56,120	4/06	1,651,398	401,240	2,307,636	28,489	81
Minnesota	2,048,673	25,292	81	81	51,617	4/06	2,482,428	-433,755	2,300,626	29,495	78
Oakland	2,035,025	25,760	79	81	43,627	7/04	2,428,038	-393,013	2,326,866	29,454	79
Detroit	1,971,421	24,339	81	81	49,674	4/13	1,423,963	547,458	2,387,180	30,605	78
Kansas City	1,934,578	24,182	80	81	40,329	7/04	1,867,689	66,889	2,378,568	29,365	81
Milwaukee	1,688,080	21,642	78	81	53,621	4/12	1,802,327	-114,247	2,269,077	28,013	81
Totals	33,333,365	29,762	1120	1134			31,543,778	1,789,587	33,333,365	29,762	1120

NATIONAL LEAGUE

CLUB	HM TOT	HM AVG	HM DATES	HM GAMES	HIGH	DATE	1992 TOT	CHANGE	RD TOT	RD AVG	RD DATES
Colorado	4,483,350	56,751	79	81	80,227	4/09	0	4,483,350	2,695,060	33,688	80
Atlanta	3,884,720	47,960	81	81	49,469	8/17	3,077,400	807,320	2,944,157	36,348	81
Los Angeles	3,170,393	39,141	81	81	54,667	6/30	2,473,266	697,127	2,663,857	33,298	80
Philadelphia	3,137,674	39,221	80	81	61,120	4/09	1,927,448	1,210,226	2,666,341	32,918	81
Florida	3,064,847	38,311	80	81	45,900	10/03	0	3,064,847	2,701,057	33,346	81
St. Louis	2,844,977	35,123	81	81	53,146	7/10	2,418,483	426,494	2,612,017	32,650	80
Chicago	2,653,763	33,172	80	82	39,763	7/31	2,126,720	527,043	2,592,790	32,410	80
San Francisco	2,606,354	32,177	81	81	56,689	4/12	1,561,987	1,044,367	2,773,307	34,666	80
Cincinnati	2,453,232	31,054	79	81	55,456	4/05	2,293,476	159,756	2,532,304	31,263	81
Houston	2,084,618	25,736	81	81	49,075	6/19	1,211,412	873,206	2,421,564	30,653	79
New York	1,873,183	23,711	79	81	53,134	4/05	1,779,534	93,649	2,660,514	33,256	80
Pittsburgh	1,650,593	20,894	79	81	44,103	4/06	1,772,292	-121,699	2,507,548	31,741	79
Montreal	1,641,437	20,265	81	81	51,539	4/13	1,669,857	28,420	2,620,012	32,346	81
San Diego	1,375,432	17,193	80	81	46,192	4/12	1,705,218	-329,786	2,534,045	32,077	79
Totals	36,924,573	32,910	1122	1135			24,017,093	12,907,480	36,924,573	32,910	1122

HM TOT / RD TOT = 1993 Total Home Attendance / 1993 Total Road Attendance
HM AVG / RD AVG = 1993 Average Home Attendance / 1993 Average Road Attendance
HM DATES / HM GAMES / RD DATES = Number of 1993 Home Dates / Number of 1993 Home Games / Number of 1993 Road Dates
1992 TOT = 1992 Total Home Attendance
CHANGE = Difference (+/-) between 1993 and 1992

PARK EFFECTS

This chart summarizes the effects of current ballparks upon the play of the game, showing the percentage changes in various important categories. Of course, by far the most important category is the first one: Runs. That's what the game hinges on, and comparing the difference between Candlestick and Wrigley, between the Coliseum and Fenway in recent years goes a long way toward explaining the home teams' and players' performances there.

The effects of each park are shown separately for the 1993 season; the average park effects for recent years are also shown. If there has been a major change in a ballpark, such as moving the fences in or out or changing the height of the outfield fences, data are shown only since that change. Note that the Skydome opened during the 1989 season (1989ms). Take a look at the astronomical results achieved at Mile High Stadium!

AMERICAN LEAGUE		R%	2B%	3B%	HR%	BB%	SO%	GDP%	BA%	OBA%	SA%
Oriole Park at Camden Yards (BAL)	1993	11.4	2.3	-13.3	18.8	9.7	2.9	3.5	4.6	4.1	5.7
	1992	-2.0	-14.2	3.5	13.0	-1.0	-4.7	-20.5	-4.7	-3.4	-2.5
Fenway Park (BOS)	1993	20.9	46.4	7.2	-19.6	10.4	3.5	33.3	10.6	8.3	7.5
	1984–1992	9.8	30.1	3.5	1.1	0.9	1.5	10.5	8.3	5.8	8.5
Cleveland Stadium (CLE)	1993	-14.2	-26.3	-13.8	-10.6	3.7	-9.7	-13.5	-5.6	-2.8	-7.9
	1992	16.6	15.0	-3.3	20.5	7.0	4.3	10.5	8.4	6.2	10.0
Tiger Stadium (DET)	1993	-0.2	-12.9	-12.3	23.7	-2.4	-0.7	-5.5	-2.7	-2.1	1.7
	1984–1992	-1.5	-14.5	-11.5	16.6	2.9	2.5	-7.8	-3.7	-1.7	-0.8
County Stadium (MIL)	1993	-2.2	-3.2	15.2	-25.8	4.5	-0.4	10.1	3.0	2.9	-3.5
	1985–1992	0.9	-0.1	0.7	-5.0	0.8	2.7	5.6	-0.1	0.0	-1.2
Yankee Stadium (NY)	1993	-13.6	-30.0	-40.7	-0.6	-7.8	-7.1	10.7	-5.9	-4.1	-7.1
	1988–1992	2.6	-2.0	-33.7	11.7	0.5	-2.0	-8.4	0.5	0.3	0.9
Skydome** (TOR)	1993	9.0	16.4	104.7	40.7	0.5	0.7	7.1	3.7	2.7	13.2
	1989ms–1992	1.5	5.7	21.3	13.2	2.8	-2.8	5.3	1.1	1.9	4.5
Anaheim Stadium (CAL)	1993	10.3	-7.9	-29.9	24.9	-2.7	3.8	-15.3	1.4	0.1	2.8
	1984–1992	-2.6	-14.8	-31.7	14.8	-4.6	-1.1	5.1	-2.2	-2.4	-1.4
Comiskey Park II (CHI)	1993	-0.3	-16.4	-5.4	13.1	-0.2	-5.3	2.8	1.9	1.8	2.4
	1991–1992	-5.5	-11.2	-12.2	3.5	-3.8	-6.1	15.8	0.3	-0.5	-0.4
Royals Stadium* (KC)	1993	12.7	54.2	100.5	-23.9	-8.9	-16.4	-4.7	9.8	4.6	8.4
	1984–1992	0.5	17.3	69.8	-32.2	-4.6	-10.6	-3.5	1.5	0.1	-1.5
Hubert H. Humphrey Metrodome** (MIN)	1993	9.1	23.9	6.8	-11.4	7.3	7.0	11.6	0.3	1.0	0.4
	1987–1992	8.0	15.7	56.2	-0.1	5.2	6.1	0.1	4.5	4.1	5.6
Oakland–Alameda County Coliseum (OAK)	1993	-13.9	-19.1	-43.9	-1.4	-7.7	12.9	-7.0	-4.0	-3.7	-5.8
	1986–1992	-11.7	-20.3	-29.4	-11.6	0.9	3.8	-1.0	-6.0	-3.5	-9.1
Kingdome** (SEA)	1993	-0.2	14.6	-27.6	-9.8	13.9	13.4	-10.3	-3.2	0.4	-3.7
	1993	-0.2	14.6	-27.6	-9.8	13.9	13.4	-10.3	-3.2	0.4	-3.7
Arlington Stadium (TEX)	1993	-8.6	-8.3	19.9	-0.1	-9.5	5.5	-10.2	-3.0	-3.6	-2.0
	1986–1992	0.5	-6.0	12.2	5.9	-2.3	4.9	9.9	2.0	1.1	1.7

NATIONAL LEAGUE		R%	2B%	3B%	HR%	BB%	SO%	GDP%	BA%	OBA%	SA%
Wrigley Field (CHI)	1993	6.1	10.0	24.8	17.1	6.9	1.7	16.9	2.7	2.8	6.9
	1988–1992	13.7	-2.3	14.3	27.0	-1.7	2.1	15.1	6.3	3.8	7.8
Joe Robbie Stadium (FLO)	1993	5.4	4.5	-5.6	3.2	14.1	15.4	-16.3	2.1	3.6	1.4
Stade Olympique** (MON)	1993	-5.2	17.0	-15.1	-11.6	8.6	-5.0	3.6	-2.8	-0.5	-2.1
	1991–1992	-1.4	9.3	8.5	-14.8	-3.6	0.3	14.9	-1.3	-1.2	-1.5
Shea Stadium (NY)	1993	-3.6	-14.6	-10.9	-1.5	-10.2	1.7	-4.7	-2.4	-3.2	-4.1
	1984–1992	-7.2	-8.0	-12.5	-6.8	-4.6	2.5	-14.4	-2.3	-2.1	-3.6
Veterans Stadium* (PHI)	1993	1.4	8.9	5.0	-6.9	-8.5	9.2	-11.6	0.0	-1.5	-0.8
	1984–1992	5.1	14.0	29.9	2.6	4.2	3.3	2.7	1.1	1.6	3.3
Three Rivers Stadium* (PIT)	1993	1.4	4.0	13.3	-0.3	3.1	0.9	2.8	-3.2	-2.4	-1.5
	1984–1992	-2.6	5.7	3.5	-7.8	5.5	0.7	3.8	-0.9	0.5	-1.0
Busch Stadium* (SL)	1993	-12.9	-2.4	-4.5	-21.9	-12.8	-10.1	-8.8	-0.4	-1.5	-3.6
	1992	3.0	-2.6	5.8	2.4	2.5	1.2	12.6	-0.8	0.0	-1.1
Atlanta–Fulton County Stadium (ATL)	1993	-1.3	6.1	-14.3	-6.6	2.8	-9.8	0.5	2.6	1.9	0.2
	1984–1992	14.9	9.2	-14.0	21.3	1.8	-5.2	12.5	6.7	4.5	7.5
Riverfront Stadium* (CIN)	1993	-1.5	-1.9	-41.8	3.9	9.6	-3.3	-5.0	-1.0	0.9	-1.0
	1984–1992	9.8	14.6	0.7	28.0	8.2	-2.8	-2.9	3.9	4.2	8.2
Mile High Stadium (COL)	1993	52.3	16.8	204.1	32.9	22.5	-6.9	55.0	18.7	17.1	24.2
Astrodome** (HOU)	1993	-6.7	-3.3	0.5	-13.4	-10.9	5.2	-8.2	-3.3	-3.5	-4.2
	1992	-12.1	-2.6	-6.2	-24.5	9.1	17.3	6.8	-4.0	-1.1	-8.3
Dodger Stadium (LA)	1993	-5.5	-13.7	-57.6	-3.7	1.1	-4.0	-5.6	4.5	3.8	-1.2
	1984–1992	-7.2	-21.8	-31.1	-16.2	-7.7	-1.4	-7.2	-0.5	-1.9	-6.8
San Diego–Jack Murphy Stadium (SD)	1993	-0.7	-17.4	19.9	23.5	-7.0	11.3	1.4	-3.2	-3.8	-0.5
	1984–1992	0.1	-12.1	2.3	27.2	3.3	7.3	-1.9	-1.4	-0.1	2.1
Candlestick Park (SF)	1993	-16.5	-6.3	-39.5	-5.3	-6.4	1.1	-3.4	-6.8	-6.1	-6.4
	1984–1992	-8.1	-4.0	-23.6	0.1	-5.8	-0.5	2.3	-3.1	-3.2	-3.0

*Artificial Turf
**Domed with Artificial Turf

Part 4

Special Reports

These special reports on Starting Pitching, Relief Pitching, Basestealing, Fielding, Injuries, and Park Effects give information that is not contained in the official statistics—and is very useful when analyzing player performance.

The Starting Pitching report includes all pitchers who had at least one game started in 1993. They are listed alphabetically by league; pitchers who played on more than one team are listed separately for each team for which they started a game. This report tells you how well each pitcher was supported by his offense, what his team's record was in the games he started, his endurance by innings, and his quality starts.

The Relief Pitching report includes all pitchers who had at least one relief appearance in 1993, listed alphabetically by league. This report tells you how often a pitcher was used in save situations, how effective he was, when he entered games, how many inherited runners he allowed to score, and how he did against the first batter he faced in each appearance.

Special introductions precede each of the Basestealing and Fielding reports, which explain exactly how the numbers are derived and how they are presented.

The Disabled List report shows all players who were injured badly enough in 1993 to require a stint on the major-league DL. Judgments about player consistency and durability are much more accurate when made with this information in hand.

STARTING PITCHING STATISTICS

SP	Starting Pitcher or Starting Pitching
R/GS	Run Support per Game Started
TM/W	Team Wins
TM/L	Team Losses
1I,2I,...,9I,XI	Endurance per Game Started (number of times pitcher left game in 1st inning, 2nd inning, ..., 9th inning, or extra innings)

RELIEF PITCHING STATISTICS

RP	Relief Pitcher or Relief Pitching
GR	Games in Relief
SVS	Games Entered in Save Situation
BSV	Blown Saves
SC%	Save Situation Conversion Percentage (SV/SVS)
SV%	Save Percentage [SV/(SV+BSV)]
<6I	Games Entered before 6th Inning
6I,7I,8I,9I	Games Entered in 6th, 7th, 8th, or 9th Innings
XI	Games Entered in Extra Innings
IR	Inherited Runners
IRS	Inherited Runners Scoring
IRP	Inherited Runners Scoring Percentage

FIELDING STATISTICS

G	Games at Position
PO	Putouts
A	Assists
E	Errors
TC	Total Chances (PO+A+E)
DP	Double Plays
TP	Triple Plays
FA	Fielding Average [(PO+A)/(TC)]
PB	Passed Balls

STARTING PITCHING REPORT

AMERICAN LEAGUE

	TEAM	GS	R/G	R/9	W	L	TW	TL	1-5I	6I	7I	8I	9-EI	QS	QS ERA
Jim Abbott	NYA	32	4.69	4.82	11	14	13	19	5	3	5	7	12	20	2.35
Paul Abbott	CLE	5	4.40	3.79	0	1	2	3	4	1	0	0	0	0	0.00
Wilson Alvarez	CHA	31	4.58	4.12	15	8	21	10	3	4	4	12	8	20	1.92
Brian Anderson	CAL	1	3.00	3.86	0	0	0	1	0	0	1	0	0	1	4.50
Kevin Appier	KC	34	4.44	4.35	18	8	23	11	2	1	8	11	12	29	2.04
Willie Banks	MIN	30	4.63	4.50	11	12	15	15	7	8	7	7	1	12	2.40
Tim Belcher	CHA	11	3.55	3.58	3	5	5	6	2	1	2	4	2	5	1.73
Jason Bere	CHA	24	5.75	5.68	12	5	14	10	3	3	10	6	2	16	2.01
Sean Bergman	DET	6	5.17	5.10	0	4	1	5	3	1	1	0	1	0	0.00
Mike Bielecki	CLE	13	5.23	5.79	4	5	5	8	3	6	4	0	0	2	2.13
Mike Boddicker	MIL	10	4.50	5.60	3	5	4	6	4	2	2	2	0	2	0.66
Brian Bohanon	TEX	8	4.75	4.03	1	3	4	4	4	3	1	0	0	0	0.00
Rod Bolton	CHA	8	3.50	2.25	1	6	2	6	3	3	0	2	0	1	1.29
Tom Bolton	DET	8	6.00	5.52	5	2	5	3	2	2	3	0	1	4	2.73
Ricky Bones	MIL	31	5.29	5.59	11	11	14	17	5	6	7	5	8	14	2.16
Chris Bosio	SEA	24	3.83	4.09	8	9	10	14	2	4	6	5	7	12	1.85
Kevin Brown	TEX	34	4.88	4.67	15	12	18	16	6	3	1	10	14	20	1.34
Scott Brow	TOR	3	8.00	9.56	1	1	1	2	1	0	2	0	0	0	0.00
Greg Brummett	MIN	5	7.00	5.67	2	1	4	1	1	2	1	1	0	2	2.84
Todd Burns	TEX	5	2.60	1.04	0	4	1	4	2	1	2	0	0	1	2.70
Mark Clark	CLE	15	4.53	4.94	7	5	7	8	4	1	6	0	4	8	1.56
Roger Clemens	BOS	29	3.24	3.53	11	14	12	17	3	3	7	9	7	14	1.36
David Cone	KC	34	2.97	2.84	11	14	16	18	0	3	2	17	12	24	2.17
Jim Converse	SEA	4	2.50	1.71	1	3	1	3	2	0	0	2	0	2	1.93
Dennis Cook	CLE	6	4.17	3.10	1	3	2	4	3	2	0	0	1	0	0.00
John Cummings	SEA	8	3.00	2.05	0	6	0	8	2	3	1	2	0	2	3.86
Ron Darling	OAK	29	5.21	3.94	5	9	15	14	7	4	7	7	4	12	2.29
Danny Darwin	BOS	34	4.35	4.31	15	11	19	15	3	3	8	14	6	23	1.84
Storm Davis	OAK	8	4.13	4.50	1	4	3	5	3	1	2	2	0	3	2.37
Rich Delucia	SEA	1	4.00	0.00	0	1	0	1	1	0	0	0	0	0	0.00
Jim Deshaies	MIN	27	4.04	4.06	11	13	13	14	3	7	6	9	2	15	2.40
John Doherty	DET	31	5.39	5.81	14	11	19	12	10	5	2	8	6	14	1.25
John Dopson	BOS	28	4.93	5.08	7	9	14	14	9	8	5	5	1	9	1.99
Kelly Downs	OAK	12	4.17	4.06	0	6	4	8	7	2	2	0	1	3	2.70
Steve Dreyer	TEX	6	6.50	7.59	3	3	3	3	2	2	1	0	1	2	2.51
Cal Eldred	MIL	36	4.56	4.69	16	16	19	17	6	0	7	7	16	21	2.14
Scott Erickson	MIN	34	4.38	4.76	8	19	13	21	5	4	10	9	6	12	2.35
John Farrell	CAL	17	3.82	3.89	3	11	3	14	8	1	6	2	0	5	1.89
Alex Fernandez	CHA	34	5.12	5.34	18	9	23	11	0	3	6	13	12	23	1.90
Chuck Finley	CAL	35	3.94	4.23	16	14	18	17	2	4	6	12	11	25	1.95
Dave Fleming	SEA	26	5.15	4.94	12	5	18	8	4	1	8	10	3	14	2.24
Mark Gardner	KC	16	4.06	5.12	4	6	5	11	4	4	3	5	0	5	2.60
Tom Gordon	KC	14	5.14	5.26	8	4	10	4	0	3	4	3	4	9	2.17
Jason Grimsley	CLE	6	2.50	2.37	2	2	4	2	0	2	3	1	0	3	2.33
Buddy Groom	DET	3	5.33	3.86	0	1	1	2	1	2	0	0	0	0	0.00
Eddie Guardado	MIN	16	4.13	4.35	3	8	6	10	4	4	4	4	0	5	3.18
Mark Gubicza	KC	6	4.33	3.00	0	4	2	4	2	0	3	1	0	2	3.55
Bill Gullickson	DET	28	5.71	6.88	13	9	15	13	8	6	4	5	5	11	2.28
Juan Guzman	TOR	33	6.15	5.92	14	3	23	10	2	5	5	15	6	20	2.01
Mike Hampton	SEA	3	4.33	5.14	0	3	0	3	3	0	0	0	0	0	0.00
Chris Haney	KC	23	4.83	5.29	9	9	12	11	7	5	4	5	2	8	1.94
Erik Hanson	SEA	30	4.13	4.39	11	11	14	16	5	0	6	8	11	22	1.72
Hilly Hathaway	CAL	11	4.82	5.75	4	3	6	5	2	2	5	2	0	6	2.65
Dwayne Henry	SEA	1	16.00	14.40	0	0	1	0	1	0	0	0	0	0	0.00
Pat Hentgen	TOR	32	5.72	5.68	19	8	22	10	4	2	11	7	8	16	1.73
Joe Hesketh	BOS	5	4.00	5.48	1	3	2	3	4	0	0	1	1	1	0.00
Teddy Higuera	MIL	8	5.50	6.19	1	3	3	5	5	2	1	0	0	0	0.00
Shawn Hillegas	OAK	11	5.00	4.32	2	5	5	6	4	4	3	0	0	2	0.71
Sterling Hitchcock	NYA	6	5.33	4.78	1	2	4	2	3	1	1	1	0	1	0.00
Mark Holzemer	CAL	4	4.00	4.70	0	3	1	3	1	1	1	1	0	0	0.00
Mark Hutton	NYA	4	6.25	6.86	1	1	2	2	3	0	0	0	0	1	1.12
Domingo Jean	NYA	6	4.83	4.38	1	1	5	1	1	1	3	1	0	3	2.84
Miguel Jimenez	OAK	4	5.75	5.88	1	0	3	1	2	0	1	2	1	3	1.42
Jeff Johnson	NYA	2	2.00	0.00	0	2	0	2	2	0	0	0	0	0	0.00
Randy Johnson	SEA	34	5.06	5.39	19	8	23	11	2	0	6	8	18	23	1.80
Scott Kamieniecki	NYA	20	4.45	4.95	10	6	12	8	4	1	5	4	6	11	1.98
Steve Karsay	OAK	8	4.13	4.59	3	3	4	4	1	2	2	3	0	4	2.73
Jimmy Key	NYA	34	5.79	5.76	18	6	24	10	1	2	11	12	8	25	2.06
Tom Kramer	CLE	16	5.75	5.55	5	2	11	5	5	5	4	1	1	6	2.18
Bill Krueger	DET	7	7.43	8.55	3	2	3	4	3	1	1	2	0	3	1.31

AMERICAN LEAGUE (continued)

	TEAM	GS	R/G	R/9	W	L	TW	TL	1–5I	6I	7I	8I	9–EI	QS	QS ERA
Mark Langston	CAL	35	3.54	3.83	16	11	19	16	2	3	3	12	15	23	1.81
Tim Leary	SEA	27	4.96	6.00	11	8	14	13	6	3	8	6	4	13	2.40
Craig Lefferts	TEX	8	5.13	4.07	1	5	1	7	5	0	3	0	0	1	4.50
Phil Leftwich	CAL	12	5.00	5.10	4	6	4	8	1	1	3	5	2	8	2.11
Charlie Leibrandt	TEX	26	5.42	5.64	9	10	15	11	7	3	3	9	2	12	2.26
Al Leiter	TOR	12	4.33	4.57	6	5	7	5	5	2	1	1	1	5	1.06
Mark Leiter	DET	13	4.54	5.22	5	4	6	7	3	1	5	2	2	6	1.90
Scott Lewis	CAL	4	5.75	5.32	1	1	3	1	0	3	1	0	0	0	0.00
Derek Lilliquist	CLE	2	6.00	0.82	0	0	2	0	2	0	0	0	0	0	0.00
Doug Linton	TOR	1	3.00	2.25	0	1	0	1	0	0	0	0	0	0	0.00
Albie Lopez	CLE	9	6.89	7.41	3	1	1	6	3	1	4	2	0	5	2.48
Mike Magnante	KC	6	2.83	3.25	1	2	2	4	1	2	2	1	0	3	2.37
Joe Magrane	CAL	8	5.00	5.65	3	2	4	4	2	0	2	3	1	5	1.80
Pat Mahomes	MIN	5	1.40	1.57	2	5	0	5	3	0	2	0	0	0	0.00
Josias Manzanillo	MIL	1	4.00	3.60	0	1	0	1	0	1	0	0	0	0	0.00
Kirk McCaskill	CHA	14	4.64	5.84	4	7	5	9	5	3	3	3	0	5	2.73
Ben McDonald	BAL	34	4.15	3.95	13	14	19	15	4	10	7	8	23	23	2.00
Jack McDowell	CHA	34	4.88	5.37	22	10	23	11	7	6	11	16	21	21	1.80
Jose Mesa	CLE	33	4.85	4.56	10	12	15	18	7	5	9	7	14	14	1.84
Bob Milacki	CLE	2	2.00	3.27	0	1	0	2	2	2	0	0	0	0	0.00
Sam Militello	NYA	2	5.00	5.00	1	1	1	1	0	1	3	0	1	3	1.71
Nate Minchey	BOS	5	5.20	5.56	1	2	1	4	0	3	0	5	5	11	2.06
Angel Miranda	MIL	17	4.35	4.42	4	5	7	10	2	3	2	5	0	0	0.00
David Mlicki	CLE	3	4.67	2.08	0	0	2	1	2	0	0	0	0	0	0.00
Mike Mohler	OAK	9	3.56	1.70	0	5	2	7	6	2	0	1	0	1	1.80
Mike Moore	DET	36	6.03	6.05	13	9	18	18	9	4	6	10	7	15	1.97
Jack Morris	TOR	27	4.22	4.50	7	12	11	16	6	5	5	7	6	8	1.55
Jamie Moyer	BAL	25	5.20	4.18	12	9	16	9	6	2	6	5	6	16	1.79
Mike Mussina	BAL	25	5.84	5.93	14	6	16	9	4	1	6	3	11	14	2.49
Jeff Mutis	CLE	13	4.08	4.56	3	6	6	7	3	5	4	0	1	3	1.29
Charles Nagy	CLE	9	5.33	6.30	2	6	3	6	3	1	2	3	0	2	2.35
Jaime Navarro	MIL	34	4.74	5.03	11	12	16	18	7	6	6	8	7	15	3.00
Robb Nen	TEX	3	8.33	10.38	1	1	2	1	2	0	1	0	0	1	2.70
Rafael Novoa	MIL	7	3.14	2.45	0	3	2	5	2	1	3	1	1	3	0.00
John O'Donoghue	BAL	1	5.00	4.50	0	1	0	1	0	0	1	0	0	0	2.95
Bobby Ojeda	CLE	7	5.00	4.50	2	1	3	4	1	3	3	0	0	3	2.00
Roger Pavlik	TEX	26	5.12	4.45	12	6	19	7	5	2	8	5	6	18	1.71
Melido Perez	NYA	25	3.36	3.36	6	14	8	17	2	4	6	6	8	8	2.11
Hipolito Pichardo	KC	25	4.28	4.75	7	7	13	12	1	8	7	3	0	8	0.00
Dennis Powell	SEA	2	3.00	1.80	0	0	0	2	1	1	0	0	0	0	2.11
Paul Quantrill	BOS	14	3.43	2.68	2	7	5	9	3	4	4	1	2	6	3.00
Dennis Rasmussen	KC	4	6.25	6.00	1	1	1	3	2	1	1	0	0	1	2.25
Arthur Lee Rhodes	BAL	17	4.59	4.95	5	6	6	11	6	6	3	0	2	2	2.37
Kenny Rogers	TEX	33	5.67	6.04	16	10	18	15	7	4	9	4	9	22	0.00
Scott Ruffcorn	CHA	2	3.00	2.00	0	2	0	2	2	0	0	0	0	0	1.09
Nolan Ryan	TEX	13	4.00	4.18	5	5	5	8	4	3	3	3	0	5	1.42
Roger Salkeld	SEA	2	2.50	2.25	0	0	1	1	1	0	1	0	0	1	2.48
Scott Sanderson	CAL	21	4.24	3.96	7	11	9	12	2	3	6	8	2	3	0.00
Scott Scudder	CLE	1	3.00	0.00	0	1	0	1	1	0	0	0	0	0	2.57
Aaron Sele	BOS	18	4.72	5.00	7	2	11	7	1	5	7	3	2	12	2.70
Joe Slusarski	OAK	1	3.00	1.29	0	0	1	0	0	1	1	0	1	1	3.18
Russell Springer	CAL	9	4.44	3.81	1	6	2	7	2	4	0	2	5	2	1.75
Dave Stewart	TOR	26	5.12	5.56	12	8	15	11	4	3	7	7	0	11	4.50
Dave Stieb	CHA	4	4.50	3.52	1	3	1	3	1	0	3	0	0	2	1.72
Todd Stottlemyre	TOR	28	4.82	4.95	11	12	15	13	4	7	5	6	6	9	2.42
Rick Sutcliffe	BAL	28	4.96	5.26	10	10	14	14	8	2	8	5	5	12	3.20
Frank Tanana	NYA	3	4.33	3.15	0	2	1	2	0	0	2	1	0	3	2.32
Kevin Tapani	MIN	35	4.09	3.94	12	15	16	19	7	2	8	9	9	20	2.51
Julian Tavarez	CLE	7	7.29	7.82	2	2	4	3	3	2	0	2	0	2	2.95
Mike Trombley	MIN	10	4.50	4.83	3	5	4	6	2	4	4	0	0	3	
Fernando Valenzuela	BAL	31	4.65	4.52	8	10	14	17	11	3	4	6	7	15	1.95
Julio Valera	CAL	5	6.60	6.84	2	3	2	3	2	1	2	0	0	1	1.50
Todd VanPoppel	OAK	16	5.63	5.60	6	6	8	8	5	5	4	1	1	4	2.36
Frank Viola	BOS	29	4.38	4.64	11	8	16	13	4	7	4	10	4	16	1.75
Bill Wegman	MIL	18	3.06	2.78	4	14	4	14	3	1	4	5	5	10	2.24
Bob Welch	OAK	28	3.75	3.67	8	11	8	20	5	7	10	4	2	12	2.84
Dave Wells	DET	30	4.97	4.98	11	9	17	13	4	5	5	9	5	17	2.44
Bob Wickman	NYA	19	7.26	6.28	8	4	13	6	5	7	3	0	6	6	0.75
Mark Williamson	BAL	1	3.00	0.00	0	0	0	1	1	0	0	0	0	0	0.00
Bobby Witt	OAK	33	3.85	4.17	14	13	14	19	6	5	5	7	3	18	2.22
Mike Witt	NYA	9	5.56	7.07	3	2	5	4	4	2	0	3	0	3	0.86
Curt Young	OAK	3	4.33	4.80	1	1	1	2	2	0	1	0	0	1	3.00
Cliff Young	CLE	7	3.86	2.77	1	2	1	3	2	3	1	2	1	3	2.08
Matt Young	CLE	8	3.88	4.17	0	4	1	7	3	0	2	0	0	1	1.50

	TEAM	GS	R/G	R/9	W	L	TW	TL	1–5I	6I	7I	8I	9–EI	QS	QS ERA
Luis Aquino	FLO	13	3.31	3.58	4	6	4	9	2	2	3	4	2	9	2.15
Jack Armstrong	FLO	33	3.15	3.34	8	17	10	23	7	5	9	9	3	17	2.25
Rene Arocha	SL	29	4.55	4.71	11	7	15	14	4	6	5	9	5	16	1.99
Andy Ashby	SD	12	4.83	5.92	3	6	5	7	2	3	3	3	1	5	2.91
Andy Ashby	COL	9	6.22	4.00	0	4	2	7	3	3	2	1	0	2	1.38
Pedro Astacio	LA	31	4.26	4.52	14	9	17	14	5	7	9	6	4	16	1.59
Steve Avery	ATL	35	4.71	4.87	18	6	28	7	6	3	9	8	9	25	1.78
Bobby Ayala	CIN	9	3.67	3.64	2	6	3	6	6	1	0	2	0	2	1.29
Jeff Ballard	PIT	5	5.80	5.67	1	1	3	2	2	1	1	0	1	2	2.45
Brian Barnes	MON	8	3.88	3.51	1	3	3	5	2	5	1	0	0	0	0.00
Jose Bautista	CHN	7	6.86	6.85	4	2	5	2	1	1	2	1	2	5	2.48
Tim Belcher	CIN	22	5.27	5.53	9	6	14	8	4	5	3	4	6	11	1.79
Andy Benes	SD	34	3.88	3.94	15	15	15	19	5	2	8	8	11	20	1.42
Buddy Black	SF	16	6.06	6.39	8	2	11	5	2	6	4	3	1	6	1.51
Willie Blair	COL	18	3.17	2.87	4	10	6	12	5	2	4	3	4	9	1.99
Shawn Boskie	CHN	2	6.00	5.73	1	1	1	1	0	2	0	0	0	0	0.00
Kent Bottenfield	MON	11	3.55	3.10	2	4	6	5	5	1	2	2	1	6	2.04
Kent Bottenfield	COL	14	4.71	3.73	3	5	8	6	4	3	6	0	1	5	3.66
Denis Boucher	MON	5	3.80	3.86	3	1	4	1	0	3	2	0	0	2	1.42
Ryan Bowen	FLO	27	4.19	3.97	8	12	12	15	6	6	6	6	3	13	1.72
Jeff Brantley	SF	12	5.00	5.29	3	5	6	6	5	2	3	2	0	4	2.81
William Brennan	CHN	1	0.00	0.00	0	1	0	1	0	1	0	0	0	0	0.00
Doug Brocail	SD	24	4.00	3.80	4	13	8	16	8	5	7	3	1	7	1.13
Tom Browning	CIN	20	4.55	5.06	7	7	11	9	3	5	8	4	0	11	2.90
Greg Brummett	SF	8	5.50	5.44	2	3	3	5	1	2	4	1	0	4	2.81
Dave Burba	SF	5	5.60	4.13	3	1	4	1	1	2	2	0	0	2	2.13
John Burkett	SF	34	5.44	5.28	22	7	25	9	3	3	8	9	11	24	2.25
Tom Candiotti	LA	32	2.94	2.36	8	10	16	16	4	5	3	7	13	22	1.56
Frank Castillo	CHN	25	4.28	4.75	5	8	13	11	8	4	4	8	1	13	1.89
Steve Cooke	PIT	32	4.69	4.68	10	10	18	14	3	3	13	5	8	20	2.29
Rheal Cormier	SL	21	5.05	5.05	6	5	9	12	5	5	4	5	2	11	1.73
Jose DeLeon	PHI	3	4.00	5.00	0	0	1	2	0	2	1	0	0	1	3.00
Jim Deshaies	SF	4	4.50	4.76	2	2	2	2	2	1	1	0	0	1	1.50
Doug Drabek	HOU	34	3.21	3.57	9	18	12	22	3	4	4	12	11	22	2.27
Mike Draper	NYN	1	10.00	9.00	0	0	1	0	1	0	0	0	0	0	0.00
Dave Eiland	SD	9	4.33	3.71	0	3	2	7	3	2	1	3	0	3	0.86
Jeff Fassero	MON	15	3.60	3.87	7	4	9	6	2	4	2	5	2	9	1.64
Sid Fernandez	NYN	18	3.72	3.30	5	6	6	12	1	4	2	6	5	12	2.34
Kevin Foster	PHI	1	1.00	1.80	0	1	0	1	1	0	0	0	0	0	0.00
Mike Gardiner	MON	2	6.50	13.50	1	1	1	1	1	1	0	0	0	0	0.00
Tom Glavine	ATL	36	5.50	5.48	22	6	27	9	5	2	8	9	12	28	1.87
Pat Gomez	SD	1	4.00	0.00	0	1	0	1	1	0	0	0	0	0	0.00
Dwight Gooden	NYN	29	4.07	4.44	12	15	12	17	3	1	2	10	13	18	1.80
Tommy Greene	PHI	30	6.00	6.86	16	4	23	7	6	4	3	7	10	17	1.64
Tyler Green	PHI	2	6.50	9.00	0	0	2	0	2	0	0	0	0	0	0.00
Kevin Gross	LA	32	5.09	5.66	13	12	14	18	4	6	10	5	7	16	1.92
Jose Guzman	CHN	30	5.37	5.04	12	10	17	13	1	16	6	3	16	2.59	
Chris Hammond	FLO	32	4.19	4.12	11	12	14	18	7	6	7	8	4	16	2.40
Mike Harkey	CHN	28	4.61	5.15	10	10	14	14	7	5	8	4	4	13	2.16
Pete Harnisch	HOU	33	4.64	5.00	16	9	19	14	5	3	7	9	9	24	1.73
Greg W. Harris	SD	22	4.36	4.30	10	9	11	11	4	0	3	10	5	13	2.04
Greg W. Harris	COL	13	3.69	2.77	1	8	5	8	4	1	5	2	1	5	3.21
Butch Henry	COL	15	4.33	4.33	2	8	3	12	6	3	4	1	1	5	2.31
Butch Henry	MON	1	6.00	9.00	1	0	1	0	0	1	0	0	0	0	0.00
Gil Heredia	MON	9	5.11	5.40	4	2	4	4	4	1	4	0	0	4	0.74
Orel Hershiser	LA	33	4.55	4.88	12	14	17	16	6	3	4	11	9	21	1.89
Greg Hibbard	CHN	31	4.68	4.59	15	11	18	13	6	4	8	8	5	16	1.55
Bryan Hickerson	SF	15	5.20	5.96	7	3	10	5	3	6	3	3	0	6	3.18
Eric Hillman	NYN	22	4.23	3.72	2	8	8	14	5	2	5	6	4	13	2.19
Ken Hill	MON	28	4.54	4.41	9	7	17	11	2	8	4	7	7	16	1.81
John Hope	PIT	7	5.29	2.93	0	2	1	6	1	4	1	1	0	2	2.77
Charlie Hough	FLO	34	3.00	3.03	9	16	14	20	6	4	10	12	2	21	2.26
Bruce Hurst	COL	3	5.67	10.13	0	1	2	1	3	0	0	0	0	0	0.00
Bruce Hurst	SD	2	5.50	3.60	0	1	0	2	2	0	0	0	0	0	0.00
Danny Jackson	PHI	32	5.13	5.33	12	11	16	16	4	2	11	10	5	22	2.42
Bobby Jones	NYN	9	4.22	2.91	2	4	4	5	0	2	3	2	2	6	1.81
Jimmy Jones	MON	6	8.00	6.60	3	1	4	2	2	2	1	1	0	2	3.46
Darryl Kile	HOU	26	5.19	6.16	14	8	16	10	6	3	3	9	5	14	1.50
Paul Kilgus	SL	1	1.00	1.50	0	0	0	1	0	1	0	0	0	0	0.00
Curt Leskanic	COL	8	3.75	2.44	1	4	3	5	3	3	1	0	0	2	0.00
Brian Looney	MON	1	5.00	2.25	0	0	1	0	0	1	0	0	0	0	0.00
Larry Luebbers	CIN	14	4.00	2.89	2	5	4	10	3	4	4	3	0	7	2.54

	TEAM	GS	R/G	R/9	W	L	TW	TL	1-5I	6I	7I	8I	9-EI	QS	QS ERA
Greg Maddux	ATL	36	4.03	4.11	20	10	22	14	2	2	6	9	17	29	1.83
Joe Magrane	SL	20	3.70	3.59	8	9	10	10	6	2	3	7	2	9	1.39
Dennis Martinez	MON	34	4.44	4.44	15	9	21	13	2	5	9	11	7	22	2.29
Pedro J. Martinez	LA	2	4.50	2.25	0	2	0	2	1	1	0	0	0	0	0.00
Ramon Martinez	LA	32	3.97	3.37	10	12	17	15	5	2	8	7	10	20	1.80
Kent Mercker	ATL	6	3.33	2.25	1	1	4	2	2	3	1	0	0	1	0.00
Paul Miller	PIT	2	4.50	2.25	0	0	1	1	2	0	0	0	0	0	0.00
Mike Morgan	CHN	32	3.31	3.26	10	15	13	19	3	4	7	13	5	19	2.10
Terry Mulholland	PHI	28	5.00	4.78	12	9	14	14	3	3	5	6	11	18	1.95
Chris Nabholz	MON	21	4.81	5.26	9	8	11	10	7	2	6	1	5	10	1.24
Denny Neagle	PIT	7	4.00	4.37	2	3	3	4	3	3	1	0	0	1	1.50
Robb Nen	FLO	1	7.00	7.50	1	0	1	0	0	0	1	0	0	1	1.50
David Nied	COL	16	4.69	5.23	5	9	5	11	4	6	2	2	2	3	2.62
Omar Olivares	SL	9	5.00	3.88	2	3	5	4	2	4	2	1	0	3	3.32
Donovan Osborne	SL	26	4.58	4.30	10	7	15	11	6	3	7	8	2	17	2.43
Dave Otto	PIT	8	4.13	4.50	2	3	3	5	2	1	2	2	1	4	2.00
Lance Painter	COL	6	6.17	5.35	2	2	4	2	2	2	0	1	1	1	1.00
Jeff Parrett	COL	6	6.33	6.26	2	1	3	3	3	1	2	0	0	2	1.42
Mark Portugal	HOU	33	4.94	4.75	18	4	21	12	3	8	9	8	5	21	1.94
Ross Powell	CIN	1	2.00	1.80	0	1	0	1	1	0	0	0	0	0	0.00
Tim Pugh	CIN	27	4.44	5.31	10	14	13	14	8	6	2	8	3	12	2.26
Pat Rapp	FLO	16	3.88	3.78	4	6	7	9	2	5	6	1	2	8	2.38
Armando Reynoso	COL	30	4.87	4.59	12	11	18	12	4	8	6	7	5	13	2.16
Shane Reynolds	HOU	1	4.00	9.00	0	0	0	1	1	0	0	0	0	0	0.00
Jose Rijo	CIN	36	3.94	4.02	14	9	17	19	0	2	4	20	10	28	1.68
Ben Rivera	PHI	28	6.43	6.66	13	9	16	12	6	6	7	5	4	11	2.07
John Roper	CIN	15	5.40	6.80	2	5	6	9	4	5	5	0	1	5	2.76
Kirk Rueter	MON	14	5.14	5.56	8	0	10	4	3	3	2	3	3	7	0.84
Bruce Ruffin	COL	12	5.83	6.33	3	4	4	8	6	3	2	1	0	3	0.44
Bret Saberhagen	NYN	19	4.42	4.41	7	7	8	11	0	2	3	6	8	12	2.06
Scott Sanderson	SF	8	4.88	4.00	4	2	5	3	1	4	3	0	0	13	1.00
Scott Sanders	SD	9	3.56	4.83	3	3	4	5	1	4	3	0	1	3	2.08
Mo Sanford	COL	6	4.33	3.94	1	2	2	4	3	2	0	1	0	1	1.29
Curt Schilling	PHI	34	4.82	4.83	16	7	22	12	3	3	8	8	12	23	2.48
Pete Schourek	NYN	18	4.56	4.50	5	11	5	13	6	2	4	2	4	6	1.58
Frank Seminara	SD	7	5.14	3.82	1	2	3	4	3	2	2	0	0	1	1.50
Jeff Shaw	MON	8	2.50	2.68	1	4	2	6	4	1	3	0	0	3	0.98
Keith Shepherd	COL	1	6.00	0.00	0	0	1	0	1	0	0	0	0	0	0.00
John Smiley	CIN	18	4.50	4.30	3	9	5	13	5	4	1	5	3	8	2.36
Bryn Smith	COL	5	4.20	4.68	1	4	1	4	2	2	0	1	0	1	0.00
Pete Smith	ATL	14	4.71	4.61	3	8	5	9	4	3	3	1	3	5	1.22
Zane Smith	PIT	14	3.79	2.90	3	7	5	9	3	3	3	2	3	7	2.28
John Smoltz	ATL	35	4.94	5.05	15	11	18	17	2	2	10	12	9	19	1.98
Bill Swift	SF	34	5.03	5.56	21	8	23	11	2	3	8	11	10	23	1.27
Greg Swindell	HOU	30	4.23	4.16	12	13	13	17	2	7	11	6	4	16	2.19
Frank Tanana	NYN	29	4.14	3.88	7	15	10	19	4	3	8	8	6	17	2.82
Kerry Taylor	SD	7	3.71	3.60	0	5	2	5	4	1	2	0	0	2	3.75
Dave Telgheder	NYN	7	5.71	6.19	5	2	5	2	1	2	0	1	3	4	2.61
Bob Tewksbury	SL	32	4.84	5.69	17	10	18	14	3	2	6	12	9	22	2.61
Randy Tomlin	PIT	18	3.83	4.33	4	8	8	10	6	2	5	2	3	9	2.43
Salomon Torres	SF	8	2.75	3.45	3	5	3	5	3	0	1	2	2	5	2.25
Steve Trachsel	CHN	3	3.33	2.57	0	2	1	2	0	1	0	2	0	2	3.07
Tom Urbani	SL	9	5.11	3.63	1	2	6	3	2	1	4	2	0	6	2.79
Paul Wagner	PIT	17	4.24	4.25	6	5	10	7	2	4	7	0	4	11	2.16
Tim Wakefield	PIT	20	3.90	4.18	5	11	7	13	6	2	4	2	6	8	2.18
Bob Walk	PIT	32	4.66	4.85	13	14	16	16	6	7	8	8	3	10	2.78
Allen Watson	SL	15	5.33	5.59	6	6	9	6	3	2	7	3	0	8	2.25
Dave Weathers	FLO	6	2.67	1.70	2	3	2	4	1	1	2	1	1	2	1.29
Turk Wendell	CHN	4	5.00	3.00	1	2	2	2	2	0	0	2	0	2	1.88
Wally Whitehurst	SD	19	3.63	3.06	4	7	6	13	5	5	5	3	1	7	1.93
Brian Williams	HOU	5	5.00	5.91	3	1	4	1	0	1	3	1	0	0	2.84
Mike Williams	PHI	4	5.75	3.68	0	1	3	1	0	4	0	0	0	0	0.00
Trevor Wilson	SF	18	3.67	3.63	7	5	11	7	4	5	2	5	2	8	1.73
Tim Worrell	SD	16	5.00	4.99	2	7	5	11	5	3	3	3	2	6	1.66
Anthony Young	NYN	10	2.00	1.61	0	8	0	10	0	2	4	2	2	6	2.47

RELIEF PITCHING REPORT

AMERICAN LEAGUE

Name	GR	SVS	SV	BS	SC%	SV%	<6I	6I	7I	8I	9I	XI	IR	IRS	IRP	BA	OBA
Aguilera, Rick	65	40	34	6	.850	.850	0	0	0	22	40	3	21	8	.381	.177	.200
Anderson, Brian	3	0	0	0	.000	.000	0	0	2	0	1	0	2	1	.500	1.000	1.000
Assenmacher, Paul	26	7	0	1	.000	.000	0	1	5	13	7	0	29	8	.276	.174	.240
Austin, Jim	31	6	0	2	.000	.000	3	2	9	12	4	1	26	8	.308	.261	.452
Ayrault, Bob	14	3	0	1	.000	.000	3	2	3	1	3	2	19	9	.474	.250	.231
Bailey, Cory	11	0	0	0	.000	.000	0	1	2	4	2	2	10	4	.400	.200	.273
Bankhead, Scott	40	11	0	2	.000	.000	11	13	7	6	2	1	28	11	.393	.333	.350
Banks, Willie	1	0	0	0	.000	.000	0	0	1	0	0	0	0	0	.000	.000	.000
Belcher, Tim	1	0	0	0	.000	.000	0	0	0	1	0	0	0	0	.000	.000	.000
Belinda, Stan	23	9	0	1	.000	.000	0	3	6	9	4	1	13	5	.385	.238	.304
Bergman, Sean	3	0	0	0	.000	.000	2	0	0	1	0	0	3	1	.333	.333	.333
Boever, Joe	61	20	3	2	.150	.600	11	11	19	13	6	1	36	15	.417	.268	.328
Bohanon, Brian	28	3	0	1	.000	.000	12	3	7	5	1	0	33	13	.394	.200	.286
Bolton, Rodney	1	0	0	0	.000	.000	1	0	0	0	0	0	2	0	.000	.000	1.000
Bolton, Tom	35	2	0	0	.000	.000	16	6	5	4	2	2	33	16	.485	.233	.314
Bones, Ricky	2	0	0	0	.000	.000	0	0	1	1	0	0	0	0	.000	.000	.000
Bosio, Chris	5	3	1	1	.333	.500	1	0	1	0	3	0	0	0	.000	.250	.400
Brewer, Billy	46	8	0	2	.000	.000	3	2	13	22	5	1	39	8	.205	.256	.370
Briscoe, John	17	0	0	0	.000	.000	5	1	2	4	3	2	9	2	.222	.091	.412
Bronkey, Jeff	21	5	1	2	.200	.333	7	2	4	5	1	2	24	10	.417	.316	.381
Brow, Scott	3	0	0	0	.000	.000	1	0	0	1	1	0	0	0	.000	.000	.333
Burgos, Enrique	5	1	0	0	.000	.000	0	1	1	1	2	0	2	1	.500	.500	.600
Burns, Todd	20	7	0	3	.000	.000	3	7	7	2	1	0	23	9	.391	.118	.250
Butcher, Mike	23	13	8	2	.615	.800	1	3	7	6	4	2	21	5	.238	.000	.130
Cadaret, Greg	13	1	0	0	.000	.000	2	2	4	2	3	0	4	1	.250	.250	.308
Campbell, Kevin	11	0	0	0	.000	.000	3	4	2	1	1	0	8	0	.000	.300	.364
Canseco, Jose	1	0	0	0	.000	.000	0	0	0	1	0	0	0	0	.000	.000	1.000
Carpenter, Cris	27	13	1	1	.077	.500	0	1	10	12	4	0	28	10	.357	.227	.346
Cary, Chuck	16	2	0	0	.000	.000	1	5	4	1	4	1	14	8	.571	.400	.562
Casian, Larry	54	21	1	2	.048	.333	3	7	20	20	3	1	47	16	.340	.167	.226
Castillo, Tony	51	16	0	1	.000	.000	3	3	18	18	7	2	45	15	.333	.217	.240
Charlton, Norm	34	22	18	3	.818	.857	0	0	1	2	28	3	13	9	.692	.194	.265
Christopher, Mike	9	1	0	0	.000	.000	1	1	4	2	1	0	4	0	.000	.333	.333
Clark, Mark	11	3	0	0	.000	.000	3	7	1	0	0	0	17	8	.471	.375	.545
Cook, Andy	4	0	0	0	.000	.000	1	0	0	2	1	0	1	0	.000	.000	.000
Cook, Dennis	19	4	0	2	.000	.000	6	4	5	4	0	0	13	5	.385	.278	.278
Cook, Mike	2	0	0	0	.000	.000	0	0	1	1	0	0	2	2	1.000	.000	.000
Cox, Danny	44	17	2	4	.118	.333	8	7	14	11	4	0	26	10	.385	.143	.182
Crim, Chuck	11	2	0	0	.000	.000	1	5	2	1	0	2	7	0	.000	.222	.300
Cummings, John	2	0	0	0	.000	.000	1	0	0	1	0	0	0	0	.000	.500	.500
Darling, Ron	2	0	0	0	.000	.000	2	0	0	0	0	0	0	0	.000	.500	.500
Davis, Chili	1	0	0	0	.000	.000	0	0	0	1	0	0	0	0	.000	.000	.000
Davis, Storm	35	9	4	1	.444	.800	8	6	6	10	5	0	28	6	.214	.194	.257
Dayley, Ken	2	0	0	0	.000	.000	1	0	1	0	0	0	2	0	.000	1.000	1.000
DeLeon, Jose	11	5	0	1	.000	.000	0	0	3	7	1	0	3	2	.667	.200	.273
DeLucia, Rich	29	11	0	4	.000	.000	1	3	9	8	8	0	26	12	.462	.370	.414
DeSilva, John	1	0	0	0	.000	.000	0	0	0	1	0	0	0	0	.000	1.000	1.000
DiPino, Frank	11	0	0	0	.000	.000	2	2	1	5	1	0	6	3	.500	.444	.545
DiPoto, Jerry	46	24	11	6	.458	.647	0	4	14	6	20	2	30	11	.367	.308	.413
Doherty, John	1	0	0	0	.000	.000	0	0	1	0	0	0	1	1	1.000	1.000	1.000
Dopson, John	6	1	0	0	.000	.000	0	1	2	1	0	2	7	2	.286	.200	.333
Downs, Kelly	30	5	0	1	.000	.000	10	7	4	4	4	1	26	3	.115	.154	.233
Drahman, Brian	5	1	1	0	1.000	1.000	0	1	1	0	2	1	2	1	.500	.000	.200
Dreyer, Steve	4	0	0	0	.000	.000	3	0	0	0	1	0	1	0	.000	.000	.500
Eckersley, Dennis	64	46	36	10	.783	.783	0	0	0	17	42	5	32	13	.406	.279	.297
Eichhorn, Mark	54	10	0	2	.000	.000	5	6	14	21	7	1	48	21	.438	.260	.283
Eldred, Cal	1	0	0	0	.000	.000	0	0	0	1	0	0	0	0	.000	.000	.000
Fajardo, Hector	1	0	0	0	.000	.000	0	0	0	0	1	0	1	0	.000	.000	.000
Farr, Steve	49	32	25	6	.781	.806	0	0	3	9	32	5	28	17	.607	.293	.408
Farrell, John	4	0	0	0	.000	.000	1	1	2	0	0	0	0	0	.000	.750	.750
Fetters, Mike	45	9	0	0	.000	.000	5	8	10	15	7	0	39	18	.462	.500	.578
Flener, Huck	6	3	0	0	.000	.000	0	1	2	2	1	0	3	0	.000	.500	.667
Fossas, Tony	71	18	0	2	.000	.000	1	3	12	35	17	3	60	15	.250	.200	.268
Frey, Steve	55	25	13	3	.520	.813	0	1	9	20	20	5	49	16	.327	.298	.389
Frohwirth, Todd	70	26	3	4	.115	.429	6	4	22	23	13	2	79	22	.278	.322	.429
Garces, Rich	3	0	0	0	.000	.000	0	1	0	2	0	0	1	0	.000	.333	.333
Gardiner, Mike	10	3	0	1	.000	.000	4	1	3	2	0	0	7	0	.000	.250	.400
Gardner, Mark	1	0	0	0	.000	.000	1	0	0	0	0	0	1	0	.000	.000	.000
Gibson, Paul	20	0	0	0	.000	.000	4	4	4	4	3	1	18	7	.389	.316	.300
Gohr, Greg	16	3	0	1	.000	.000	1	4	5	4	2	0	10	3	.300	.231	.375
Gonzales, Rene	1	0	0	0	.000	.000	0	0	0	0	1	0	0	0	.000	.000	.000
Gordon, Tom	34	8	1	5	.125	.167	4	10	9	6	5	0	23	11	.478	.250	.353

Name	GR	SVS	SV	BS	SC%	SV%	<6I	6I	7I	8I	9I	XI	IR	IRS	IRP	BA	OBA
Gossage, Rich	40	16	1	3	.062	.250	1	8	11	12	4	4	29	13	.448	.257	.350
Grahe, Joe	45	17	11	2	.647	.846	1	4	5	20	13	2	38	13	.342	.194	.318
Granger, Jeff	1	0	0	0	.000	.000	0	0	1	0	0	0	0	0	.000	.000	1.000
Grater, Mark	6	2	0	0	.000	.000	1	2	1	2	0	0	6	5	.833	.400	.500
Grimsley, Jason	4	1	0	0	.000	.000	1	2	0	0	0	1	1	0	.000	.000	.000
Groom, Buddy	17	1	0	0	.000	.000	4	0	7	2	3	1	4	2	.500	.375	.412
Guardado, Eddie	3	0	0	0	.000	.000	1	0	0	1	1	0	5	3	.600	.333	.333
Gubicza, Mark	43	13	2	1	.154	.667	5	9	10	13	3	3	33	17	.515	.342	.405
Guthrie, Mark	22	9	0	1	.000	.000	0	4	10	6	2	0	21	10	.476	.300	.364
Haas, David	20	6	0	0	.000	.000	3	5	3	8	0	1	17	6	.353	.400	.550
Habyan, John	48	10	1	2	.100	.333	4	7	9	17	8	3	33	10	.303	.302	.375
Hampton, Mike	10	3	1	0	.333	1.000	1	2	1	3	2	1	4	1	.250	.250	.400
Hanson, Erik	1	0	0	0	.000	.000	1	0	0	0	0	0	0	0	.000	.000	1.000
Harris, Greg A.	80	37	8	10	.216	.444	2	10	21	37	8	2	75	21	.280	.271	.338
Hartley, Mike	53	10	1	2	.100	.333	8	11	12	15	5	2	54	20	.370	.250	.385
Heaton, Neal	18	2	0	0	.000	.000	4	4	4	3	3	0	16	12	.750	.267	.389
Henke, Tom	67	48	40	7	.833	.851	0	0	0	18	45	4	36	9	.250	.297	.328
Henneman, Mike	63	33	24	5	.727	.828	0	0	3	22	38	0	42	11	.262	.281	.333
Henry, Doug	55	26	17	7	.654	.708	5	1	1	8	36	4	27	10	.370	.392	.436
Henry, Dwayne	30	3	2	0	.667	1.000	8	3	7	4	5	3	22	7	.318	.200	.300
Hentgen, Pat	2	0	0	0	.000	.000	1	0	1	0	0	0	4	3	.750	.000	.000
Hernandez, Jeremy	49	25	8	5	.320	.615	1	10	16	14	6	2	39	14	.359	.318	.388
Hernandez, Roberto	70	44	38	6	.864	.864	0	0	0	21	47	2	39	13	.333	.227	.271
Hesketh, Joe	23	2	1	0	.500	1.000	6	5	5	3	3	1	17	11	.647	.278	.381
Hillegas, Shawn	7	0	0	0	.000	.000	2	1	0	2	1	1	3	3	1.000	.286	.286
Holman, Brad	20	6	3	0	.500	1.000	5	0	3	6	5	1	23	5	.217	.125	.300
Holzemer, Mark	1	0	0	0	.000	.000	0	0	0	1	0	0	0	0	.000	1.000	1.000
Honeycutt, Rick	52	25	1	2	.040	.333	2	2	11	21	10	6	35	10	.286	.265	.294
Horsman, Vince	40	11	0	0	.000	.000	6	5	12	13	3	1	35	11	.314	.243	.300
Howard, Chris	3	0	0	0	.000	.000	1	0	1	0	1	0	2	1	.500	.333	.333
Howe, Steve	52	21	4	3	.190	.571	1	2	18	16	13	2	59	18	.305	.250	.300
Hutton, Mark	3	0	0	0	.000	.000	0	0	0	2	1	0	0	0	.000	1.000	1.000
Ignasiak, Mike	27	6	0	2	.000	.000	4	8	5	5	3	2	26	11	.423	.160	.185
Jean, Domingo	4	0	0	0	.000	.000	2	0	1	0	1	0	1	1	1.000	.250	.250
Jimenez, Miguel	1	0	0	0	.000	.000	1	0	0	0	0	0	0	0	.000	.000	.000
Johnson, Dave	6	0	0	0	.000	.000	0	2	1	1	1	1	4	1	.250	.000	.167
Johnson, Randy	2	2	1	0	.500	1.000	0	0	0	1	1	0	3	2	.667	.500	.500
Jones, Barry	6	1	0	0	.000	.000	1	0	2	2	0	1	2	2	1.000	.200	.333
Kamieniecki, Scott	10	2	1	0	.500	1.000	3	3	1	2	0	1	10	7	.700	.500	.500
Kiefer, Mark	6	2	1	1	.500	.500	0	1	2	1	2	0	6	3	.500	.250	.500
Kiely, John	8	0	0	0	.000	.000	0	2	0	3	2	1	6	2	.333	.250	.625
King, Kevin	13	6	0	1	.000	.000	1	0	2	8	1	1	15	6	.400	.400	.462
Knudsen, Kurt	30	11	2	2	.182	.500	2	8	8	9	2	1	27	12	.444	.423	.467
Kramer, Tommy	23	5	0	2	.000	.000	8	7	4	2	1	1	19	10	.526	.450	.522
Krueger, Bill	25	10	0	3	.000	.000	8	5	5	5	2	0	25	7	.280	.348	.400
Leach, Terry	14	4	1	0	.250	1.000	0	1	5	6	2	0	8	1	.125	.214	.214
Leary, Tim	7	1	0	1	.000	.000	0	1	2	2	2	0	4	0	.000	.333	.429
Lefferts, Craig	44	15	0	0	.000	.000	4	9	16	11	3	1	38	12	.316	.275	.326
Leiter, Al	22	7	2	1	.286	.667	7	2	6	5	1	1	22	5	.227	.118	.238
Leiter, Mark	14	2	0	1	.000	.000	6	1	5	1	1	0	18	5	.278	.182	.357
Lewis, Scott	11	4	0	0	.000	.000	0	2	5	3	1	0	11	6	.545	.300	.273
Lilliquist, Derek	54	25	10	3	.400	.769	1	0	5	22	22	4	42	10	.238	.283	.296
Linton, Doug	22	1	0	1	.000	.000	6	4	4	6	1	1	19	11	.579	.300	.364
Lloyd, Graeme	55	11	0	4	.000	.000	7	10	16	16	4	2	65	22	.338	.226	.236
MacDonald, Bob	69	25	3	4	.120	.429	4	3	15	26	18	3	56	21	.375	.155	.261
Magnante, Mike	1	0	0	0	.000	.000	0	0	0	0	0	0	0	0	.000	.000	.000
Mahomes, Pat	7	0	0	0	.000	.000	2	0	1	3	1	0	3	0	.000	.200	.429
Maldonado, Carlos	29	3	1	0	.333	1.000	2	5	9	4	6	3	17	6	.353	.321	.345
Manzanillo, Josias	9	2	1	1	.500	.500	3	0	1	3	1	1	7	4	.571	.500	.556
Maysey, Matt	23	4	1	1	.250	.500	3	2	3	7	6	2	18	8	.444	.353	.455
McCaskill, Kirk	16	4	2	0	.500	1.000	6	1	4	3	1	1	14	7	.500	.312	.312
McGehee, Kevin	5	0	0	0	.000	.000	3	2	0	0	0	0	7	2	.286	.250	.400
Meacham, Rusty	15	1	0	0	.000	.000	0	0	1	7	6	1	8	6	.750	.214	.267
Melendez, Jose	9	1	0	1	.000	.000	3	1	1	2	1	1	14	7	.500	.286	.222
Merriman, Brett	19	1	0	0	.000	.000	0	1	7	8	1	2	12	4	.333	.214	.368
Mesa, Jose	1	0	0	0	.000	.000	0	0	0	0	0	0	2	0	.000	.000	.000
Milacki, Bob	3	0	0	0	.000	.000	3	0	0	0	0	0	2	2	1.000	1.000	1.000
Militello, Sam	1	0	0	0	.000	.000	0	1	0	0	0	0	2	0	.000	.000	.000
Mills, Alan	46	12	4	3	.333	.571	15	4	7	12	6	2	53	23	.434	.231	.311
Miranda, Angel	5	0	0	0	.000	.000	2	1	0	1	1	0	5	1	.200	.250	.400
Mohler, Mike	33	4	0	1	.000	.000	5	8	7	10	3	0	38	14	.368	.208	.375
Monteleone, Rich	42	2	0	1	.000	.000	15	8	6	8	4	1	40	11	.275	.194	.262
Montgomery, Jeff	69	51	45	6	.882	.882	0	0	1	26	35	7	30	8	.267	.258	.290
Munoz, Bobby	38	12	0	2	.000	.000	1	3	17	12	5	0	33	7	.212	.172	.342
Munoz, Mike	8	1	0	0	.000	.000	2	1	1	1	2	1	7	4	.571	.200	.500
Mutis, Jeff	4	0	0	0	.000	.000	2	1	0	0	0	1	3	3	1.000	.500	.500

Name	GR	SVS	SV	BS	SC%	SV%	<6I	6I	7I	8I	9I	XI	IR	IRS	IRP	BA	OBA
Navarro, Jaime	1	0	0	0	.000	.000	1	0	0	0	0	0	0	0	.000	.000	.000
Nelson, Gene	52	20	5	3	.250	.625	0	4	18	16	10	4	40	12	.300	.306	.346
Nelson, Jeff	72	31	1	10	.032	.091	2	4	30	25	9	2	94	39	.415	.279	.361
Nen, Robb	6	0	0	0	.000	.000	2	0	1	2	1	0	4	1	.250	.333	.333
Nielsen, Jerry	10	2	0	0	.000	.000	2	1	1	6	0	0	3	2	.667	.375	.500
Novoa, Rafael	8	0	0	0	.000	.000	4	2	0	1	0	1	6	4	.667	.429	.500
Nunez, Edwin	56	21	1	3	.048	.250	2	7	18	20	6	3	43	15	.349	.300	.375
O'Donoghue, John	10	1	0	0	.000	.000	2	1	3	3	1	0	7	3	.429	.000	.000
Ojeda, Bob	2	0	0	0	.000	.000	2	0	0	0	0	0	1	1	1.000	.500	.500
Oliver, Darren	2	0	0	0	.000	.829	0	1	0	0	0	1	1	0	.000	.000	.500
Olson, Gregg	50	35	29	6	.829	.000	0	0	1	10	38	1	31	15	.484	.341	.449
Ontiveros, Steve	14	2	0	0	.000	.000	2	2	1	3	5	1	9	5	.556	.462	.500
Oquist, Mike	5	0	0	0	.000	.615	3	0	1	1	0	0	5	1	.200	.400	.400
Orosco, Jesse	58	26	8	5	.308	.000	0	1	6	27	19	5	41	11	.268	.255	.291
Pall, Donn	39	13	1	1	.077	.500	6	5	4	15	7	2	26	13	.500	.278	.297
Patterson, Bob	52	9	1	1	.111	.500	0	3	10	20	18	1	29	14	.483	.320	.346
Patterson, Ken	46	8	1	1	.125	.500	13	7	16	7	1	2	53	13	.245	.267	.283
Pennington, Brad	34	12	4	3	.333	.571	1	2	5	17	9	0	45	16	.356	.207	.324
Pichardo, Hipolito	5	1	0	0	.000	.000	1	2	2	0	0	0	4	2	.500	.400	.400
Plantenberg, Erik	20	9	1	0	.111	1.000	0	1	4	7	8	0	21	11	.524	.214	.450
Plunk, Eric	70	34	15	3	.441	.833	0	0	10	31	26	3	56	14	.250	.226	.294
Poole, Jim	55	22	2	1	.091	.667	3	6	19	18	9	0	65	22	.338	.235	.259
Powell, Dennis	31	15	0	0	.000	.000	3	2	10	11	4	1	30	14	.467	.240	.310
Power, Ted	45	25	13	3	.520	.813	1	3	6	17	18	0	42	15	.357	.333	.372
Quantrill, Paul	35	9	1	1	.111	.500	6	6	8	12	0	3	36	6	.167	.212	.229
Radinsky, Scott	73	23	4	1	.174	.800	0	0	13	38	19	3	50	16	.320	.221	.274
Rasmussen, Dennis	5	1	0	0	.000	.000	1	0	3	1	0	0	6	2	.333	.400	.400
Reed, Rick	3	0	0	0	.000	.000	2	1	0	0	0	0	1	1	1.000	.667	.667
Rogers, Kenny	2	1	0	0	.000	.000	0	0	0	2	0	0	0	0	.000	.000	.000
Ruffcorn, Scott	1	0	0	0	.000	.000	0	0	0	1	0	0	0	0	.000	.000	1.000
Russell, Jeff	51	38	33	4	.868	.892	0	0	1	6	41	3	24	10	.417	.277	.294
Ryan, Ken	47	7	1	3	.143	.250	1	3	7	15	16	5	41	18	.439	.175	.298
Salkeld, Roger	1	0	0	0	.000	.000	1	0	0	0	0	0	2	1	.500	.000	.000
Sampen, Bill	18	8	0	4	.000	.000	2	0	8	6	1	1	16	7	.438	.267	.353
Schooler, Mike	17	5	0	0	.000	.000	8	1	3	4	0	1	23	7	.304	.200	.250
Schwarz, Jeff	41	7	0	0	.000	.000	3	7	12	12	6	1	22	7	.318	.182	.341
Scott, Darryl	16	2	0	0	.000	.000	5	2	3	4	2	0	15	10	.667	.467	.500
Scudder, Scott	1	0	0	0	.000	.000	0	0	0	0	1	0	0	0	.000	.000	.000
Seitzer, Kevin	1	0	0	0	.000	.000	0	0	0	1	0	0	0	0	.000	.000	.000
Shinall, Zak	1	0	0	0	.000	.000	1	0	0	0	0	0	1	0	.000	1.000	1.000
Slocumb, Heathcliff	20	3	0	2	.000	.000	2	6	6	3	2	1	22	10	.455	.438	.500
Slusarski, Joe	1	0	0	0	.000	.000	1	0	0	0	0	0	2	2	1.000	1.000	1.000
Smith, Lee	8	3	3	0	1.000	1.000	0	0	0	3	5	0	4	1	.250	.143	.250
Smithberg, Roger	13	4	3	1	.750	.750	1	0	2	4	3	3	3	2	.667	.455	.538
Springer, Russ	5	1	0	0	.000	.000	1	0	0	2	2	0	0	0	.000	.600	.600
Stottlemyre, Todd	2	2	0	0	.000	.000	0	1	1	0	0	0	0	0	.000	.000	.000
Sutcliffe, Rick	1	0	0	0	.000	.000	0	0	1	0	0	0	0	0	.000	.000	.000
Swan, Russ	23	6	0	0	.000	.000	3	2	5	6	3	4	20	4	.200	.294	.478
Swingle, Paul	9	0	0	0	.000	.000	3	1	3	1	0	1	7	4	.571	.000	.222
Tackett, Jeff	1	0	0	0	.000	.000	0	0	0	1	0	0	0	0	.000	.000	.000
Tapani, Kevin	1	0	0	0	.000	.000	1	0	0	0	0	0	0	0	.000	.000	.000
Tavarez, Julian	1	0	0	0	.000	.000	0	0	1	0	0	0	1	0	.000	.000	.000
Taylor, Scott	16	2	0	0	.000	.000	1	1	4	8	1	1	19	10	.526	.417	.562
Telford, Anthony	3	0	0	0	.000	.000	1	0	1	1	0	0	2	0	.000	.000	.000
Thigpen, Bobby	25	3	1	1	.333	.500	2	6	6	5	6	0	14	7	.500	.381	.480
Timlin, Mike	54	14	1	3	.071	.250	1	3	6	24	16	4	32	14	.438	.222	.352
Trombley, Mike	34	14	2	3	.143	.400	9	10	9	5	0	1	29	11	.379	.250	.294
Tsamis, George	41	4	1	1	.250	.500	10	3	8	12	7	1	39	15	.385	.306	.390
Valenzuela, Fernando	1	0	0	0	.000	.000	0	0	1	0	0	0	0	0	.000	.000	.000
Valera, Julio	14	10	4	3	.400	.571	0	3	7	3	0	1	10	2	.200	.154	.214
Wainhouse, Dave	3	0	0	0	.000	.000	0	2	0	0	0	1	2	2	1.000	.333	.333
Ward, Duane	71	51	45	6	.882	.882	0	0	0	13	56	2	26	9	.346	.227	.282
Wegman, Bill	2	0	0	0	.000	.000	0	0	2	0	0	0	0	0	.000	.500	.500
Welch, Bob	2	0	0	0	.000	.000	2	0	0	0	0	0	0	0	.000	.500	.500
Wells, David	2	1	0	0	.000	.000	1	0	0	1	0	0	2	0	.000	1.000	1.000
Wertz, Bill	34	6	0	2	.000	.000	5	15	7	4	2	1	29	8	.276	.241	.353
Whiteside, Matt	60	20	1	4	.050	.200	7	13	18	19	3	0	59	18	.305	.185	.254
Wickander, Kevin	11	2	0	0	.000	.000	1	1	7	2	0	0	14	10	.714	.500	.545
Wickman, Bob	22	10	4	4	.400	.500	4	2	5	7	4	0	24	6	.250	.333	.429
Williams, Woody	30	8	0	2	.000	.000	4	5	5	10	5	1	20	11	.550	.280	.400
Williamson, Mark	47	14	0	2	.000	.000	11	10	9	11	3	3	43	11	.256	.267	.298
Willis, Carl	53	25	5	4	.200	.556	1	4	16	24	5	3	59	23	.390	.306	.358
Witt, Bobby	3	1	0	0	.000	.000	2	0	0	0	1	0	0	0	.000	.000	.000
Young, Cliff	14	2	1	1	.500	.500	5	5	2	2	0	0	23	10	.435	.333	.429
Young, Matt	14	0	0	0	.000	.000	11	0	1	1	0	1	13	4	.308	.455	.538

NATIONAL LEAGUE

Name	GR	SVS	SV	BS	SC%	SV%	<6I	6I	7I	8I	9I	XI	IR	IRS	IRP	BA	OBA
Agosto, Juan	6	1	0	0	.000	.000	1	0	1	2	2	0	4	4	1.000	.500	.500
Aldred, Scott	8	1	0	1	.000	.000	3	2	0	3	0	0	7	3	.429	.500	.500
Andersen, Larry	64	30	0	4	.000	.000	0	0	16	34	10	4	48	15	.312	.121	.203
Anderson, Mike	3	0	0	0	.000	.000	1	2	0	0	0	0	4	0	.000	.000	.333
Aquino, Luis	25	6	0	1	.000	.000	3	5	3	11	0	3	10	1	.100	.400	.520
Armstrong, Jack	3	0	0	0	.000	.000	0	0	0	2	1	0	0	0	.000	.000	.000
Arocha, Rene	3	0	0	0	.000	.000	1	1	1	0	0	0	0	0	.000	.000	.000
Ashby, Andy	11	1	1	0	1.000	1.000	2	2	2	2	2	1	4	4	1.000	.455	.455
Assenmacher, Paul	46	20	0	4	.000	.000	0	1	15	23	6	1	34	14	.412	.295	.326
Ayala, Bobby	34	11	3	2	.273	.600	5	12	6	6	1	4	23	6	.261	.161	.206
Ayrault, Bob	10	3	0	1	.000	.000	1	4	2	1	1	1	9	3	.333	.500	.600
Ballard, Jeff	20	3	0	0	.000	.000	3	4	8	4	1	0	7	1	.143	.278	.300
Barnes, Brian	44	7	3	2	.429	.600	6	10	15	7	4	2	32	14	.438	.286	.381
Batchelor, Richard	9	1	0	0	.000	.000	1	1	6	1	0	0	3	2	.667	.500	.556
Bautista, Jose	51	9	2	0	.222	1.000	8	8	12	12	9	2	38	16	.421	.250	.300
Beck, Rodney	76	52	48	4	.923	.923	0	0	0	13	58	5	35	7	.200	.159	.224
Bedrosian, Steve	49	5	0	0	.000	.000	13	5	12	9	5	5	36	16	.444	.225	.327
Belinda, Stan	40	22	19	3	.864	.864	0	0	0	10	26	4	16	3	.188	.270	.325
Bell, Eric	10	2	0	0	.000	.000	0	0	4	4	1	1	10	3	.300	.333	.400
Blair, Willie	28	5	0	0	.000	.000	7	6	4	8	2	1	18	9	.500	.182	.333
Borbon, Pedro	3	0	0	0	.000	.000	0	1	1	1	0	0	3	0	.000	.333	.333
Boskie, Shawn	37	11	1	3	.091	.250	5	8	8	12	2	2	28	6	.214	.257	.297
Bottenfield, Kent	12	0	0	0	.000	.000	6	2	1	2	0	1	5	1	.200	.222	.417
Brantley, Jeff	41	15	0	3	.000	.000	3	7	16	9	6	0	18	6	.333	.143	.250
Brennan, Bill	7	1	0	0	.000	.000	2	3	1	1	0	0	9	4	.444	.333	.429
Brewer, Rod	1	0	0	0	.000	.000	0	0	0	1	0	0	0	0	.000	.000	1.000
Brink, Brad	2	0	0	0	.000	.000	2	0	0	0	0	0	0	0	.000	1.000	1.000
Bross, Terry	2	0	0	0	.000	.000	0	1	0	0	1	0	4	4	1.000	1.000	1.000
Browning, Tom	1	0	0	0	.000	.000	0	0	1	0	0	0	0	0	.000	1.000	1.000
Bullinger, Jim	15	4	1	0	.250	1.000	0	3	4	5	3	0	7	0	.000	.167	.333
Burba, Dave	49	13	0	0	.000	.000	14	12	10	6	5	2	35	13	.371	.255	.286
Burns, Todd	24	9	0	2	.000	.000	2	2	8	7	4	1	22	9	.409	.318	.348
Bushing, Chris	6	0	0	0	.000	.000	1	2	1	2	0	0	4	1	.250	.400	.500
Cadaret, Greg	34	7	1	0	.143	1.000	1	2	6	15	6	4	17	5	.294	.240	.424
Candelaria, John	24	8	1	2	.125	.333	0	2	4	15	2	1	15	7	.467	.174	.208
Candiotti, Tom	1	0	0	0	.000	.000	0	1	0	0	0	0	0	0	.000	1.000	1.000
Carpenter, Cris	29	6	0	0	.000	.000	3	4	11	9	2	0	17	5	.294	.333	.345
Castillo, Frank	4	0	0	0	.000	.000	3	0	1	0	0	0	1	1	1.000	.000	.250
Cormier, Rheal	17	2	0	0	.000	.000	3	5	2	3	3	1	8	2	.250	.400	.471
Corsi, Jim	15	1	0	0	.000	.000	1	5	1	5	3	0	9	2	.222	.071	.071
Daal, Omar	47	9	0	1	.000	.000	5	7	9	15	8	3	48	16	.333	.275	.383
Davis, Mark	60	15	4	3	.267	.571	6	5	15	26	7	1	38	13	.342	.271	.417
DeLeon, Jose	21	5	0	1	.000	.000	2	5	5	5	2	2	10	2	.200	.231	.476
Deshaies, Jim	1	0	0	0	.000	.000	0	0	0	1	0	0	1	1	1.000	1.000	1.000
DeSilva, John	3	0	0	0	.000	.000	1	0	1	1	0	0	2	0	.000	.333	.333
Dewey, Mark	21	12	7	5	.583	.583	0	0	2	7	12	0	12	5	.417	.250	.286
Dibble, Rob	45	28	19	9	.679	.679	0	0	0	6	36	3	19	7	.368	.206	.400
Dixon, Steve	4	0	0	0	.000	.000	1	0	2	1	0	0	3	3	1.000	.000	.750
Draper, Mike	28	5	0	2	.000	.000	6	6	3	7	5	1	18	10	.556	.269	.286
Edens, Tom	38	4	0	1	.000	.000	7	7	4	11	8	1	27	10	.370	.212	.289
Eiland, Dave	1	0	0	0	.000	.000	1	0	0	0	0	0	0	0	.000	.000	.000
Ettles, Mark	14	1	0	0	.000	.000	2	1	3	6	1	1	9	5	.556	.214	.214
Fassero, Jeff	41	11	1	2	.091	.333	5	9	10	12	1	4	24	11	.458	.286	.341
Fletcher, Paul	1	0	0	0	.000	.000	1	0	0	0	0	0	1	0	.000	.000	.000
Foster, Kevin	1	0	0	0	.000	.000	0	0	1	0	0	0	0	0	.000	.000	.000
Foster, Steve	17	6	0	0	.000	.000	1	1	3	10	1	1	4	2	.500	.312	.353
Franco, John	35	17	10	7	.588	.588	0	0	0	9	23	3	12	6	.500	.222	.364
Fredrickson, Scott	25	2	0	0	.000	.000	6	3	6	5	4	1	20	6	.300	.316	.458
Freeman, Marvin	21	3	0	0	.000	.000	5	3	5	3	5	0	10	3	.300	.111	.200
Gardiner, Mike	22	3	0	1	.000	.000	11	3	5	1	1	1	20	4	.200	.118	.318
Gibson, Paul	8	2	0	1	.000	.000	1	2	3	0	1	1	12	7	.583	.714	.750
Gomez, Pat	26	2	0	0	.000	.000	5	6	7	5	3	0	21	12	.571	.286	.385
Gott, Jim	62	36	25	4	.694	.862	0	0	2	21	30	9	34	14	.412	.237	.274
Gozzo, Mauro	10	3	1	0	.333	1.000	0	1	2	3	2	2	0	0	.000	.111	.200
Grant, Mark	20	2	1	1	.500	.500	4	4	4	5	3	0	16	4	.250	.176	.320
Green, Tyler	1	0	0	0	.000	.000	0	0	0	0	1	0	0	0	.000	.000	1.000
Greene, Tommy	1	0	0	0	.000	.000	1	0	0	0	0	0	1	0	.000	.000	.000
Greer, Kenny	1	0	0	0	.000	.000	0	0	0	0	0	1	0	0	.000	.000	.000
Gross, Kevin	1	0	0	0	.000	.000	0	0	0	1	0	0	0	0	.000	.000	1.000
Gross, Kip	10	4	0	0	.000	.000	2	2	2	3	1	0	3	1	.333	.300	.300
Guetterman, Lee	40	9	1	3	.111	.250	3	3	14	10	6	4	30	14	.467	.342	.375
Harris, Gene	59	32	23	8	.719	.742	0	0	0	20	31	8	31	9	.290	.218	.254
Harvey, Bryan	59	49	45	4	.918	.918	0	0	0	16	39	4	28	9	.321	.263	.271
Henry, Butch	14	0	0	0	.000	.000	3	3	3	4	1	0	6	2	.333	.429	.429
Henry, Dwayne	3	0	0	0	.000	.000	2	0	0	0	1	0	0	0	.000	.333	.333

Name	GR	SVS	SV	BS	SC%	SV%	<6I	6I	7I	8I	9I	XI	IR	IRS	IRP	BA	OBA
Heredia, Gil	11	4	2	1	.500	.667	3	6	1	0	0	1	8	1	.125	.200	.200
Hernandez, Jeremy	21	0	0	0	.000	.000	2	7	3	5	2	2	11	5	.455	.429	.429
Hernandez, Xavier	72	40	9	8	.225	.529	0	6	21	34	10	1	48	14	.292	.242	.278
Hickerson, Bryan	32	8	0	0	.000	.000	6	6	8	6	4	2	11	4	.364	.226	.219
Hill, Milt	19	0	0	0	.000	.000	7	3	3	4	2	0	16	5	.312	.312	.316
Hillman, Eric	5	1	0	0	.000	.000	1	1	2	0	1	0	0	0	.000	.400	.400
Hoffman, Trevor	67	24	5	3	.208	.625	0	8	21	20	18	0	45	7	.156	.226	.269
Holmes, Darren	62	31	25	4	.806	.862	0	1	2	19	34	6	13	6	.462	.255	.339
Howell, Jay	54	11	0	3	.000	.000	3	3	8	21	15	4	25	11	.440	.196	.264
Innis, Jeff	67	13	3	2	.231	.600	2	8	17	21	17	2	34	10	.294	.242	.284
Jackson, Mike	81	41	1	5	.024	.167	0	6	16	44	11	4	58	17	.293	.227	.262
Johnston, Joel	33	8	2	1	.250	.000	2	3	6	13	6	3	14	2	.143	.258	.303
Johnstone, John	7	0	0	0	.000	.667	1	1	2	1	1	1	3	0	.000	.571	.571
Jones, Doug	71	35	26	8	.743	.765	1	0	3	19	43	5	20	9	.450	.324	.352
Jones, Jimmy	6	0	0	0	.000	.000	2	2	1	1	0	0	1	1	1.000	.333	.333
Jones, Todd	27	10	2	1	.200	.667	4	6	6	7	4	0	8	1	.125	.120	.154
Juden, Jeff	2	0	0	0	.000	.000	1	0	0	1	0	0	0	0	.000	.500	.500
Kaiser, Jeff	9	0	0	0	.000	.000	0	4	1	3	1	0	4	1	.250	.556	.556
Kile, Darryl	6	0	0	0	.000	.000	1	3	1	1	0	0	4	2	.500	.750	.833
Kilgus, Paul	21	8	1	0	.125	1.000	2	3	7	5	4	0	14	1	.071	.250	.286
Klink, Joe	59	11	0	0	.000	.000	3	7	19	21	6	3	56	18	.321	.269	.339
Knudson, Mark	4	0	0	0	.000	.000	1	0	1	1	1	0	4	2	.500	1.000	1.000
Lancaster, Lester	50	8	0	0	.000	.000	13	9	11	10	4	3	48	20	.417	.152	.220
Landrum, Bill	18	2	0	0	.000	.000	2	5	4	4	2	1	11	2	.182	.267	.389
Layana, Tim	1	0	0	0	.000	.000	1	0	0	0	0	0	1	0	.000	.000	.000
Leskanic, Curt	10	1	0	0	.000	.000	5	0	3	1	0	1	6	4	.667	.125	.300
Lewis, Richie	57	5	0	2	.000	.000	15	12	13	9	5	3	55	21	.382	.235	.316
Looney, Brian	2	0	0	0	.000	.000	0	1	0	1	0	0	3	0	.000	.000	.000
Maddux, Mike	58	14	5	6	.357	.455	4	4	16	17	16	1	36	12	.333	.250	.310
Magrane, Joe	2	0	0	0	.000	.000	0	0	0	0	1	1	0	0	.000	1.000	1.000
Manzanillo, Josias	6	0	0	0	.000	.000	1	3	0	2	0	0	4	3	.750	.000	.000
Martinez, Dennis	1	1	1	0	1.000	1.000	0	0	0	0	1	0	1	0	.000	.000	.000
Martinez, Pedro J.	63	20	2	1	.100	.000	5	7	21	14	12	4	33	7	.212	.196	.286
Martinez, Pedro A.	32	5	0	1	.000	.667	8	6	6	7	4	1	22	5	.227	.241	.312
Mason, Roger	68	13	0	3	.000	.000	9	11	14	18	10	6	41	14	.341	.262	.294
Mauser, Tim	36	3	0	0	.000	.000	7	4	12	8	4	1	34	14	.412	.281	.361
McClure, Bob	14	2	0	2	.000	.000	0	0	6	7	1	0	11	8	.727	.500	.571
McDowell, Roger	54	7	2	1	.286	.667	5	6	17	16	4	6	30	9	.300	.269	.296
McElroy, Chuck	49	5	0	0	.000	.000	12	8	10	14	3	2	23	11	.478	.381	.458
McMichael, Greg	74	37	19	2	.514	.905	3	4	13	20	32	2	22	6	.273	.227	.284
Menendez, Tony	14	0	0	0	.000	.000	6	0	5	3	0	0	10	1	.100	.231	.286
Mercker, Kent	37	8	0	3	.000	.000	4	6	10	5	10	2	20	8	.400	.097	.243
Miceli, Danny	9	0	0	0	.000	.000	3	0	4	1	0	1	8	1	.125	.143	.333
Miller, Paul	1	0	0	0	.000	.000	0	0	0	1	0	0	0	0	.000	1.000	1.000
Minor, Blas	65	9	1	1	.111	.500	15	9	18	12	5	6	37	18	.486	.241	.281
Minutelli, Gino	9	2	0	1	.000	.000	2	2	0	3	1	1	3	2	.667	.333	.556
Moeller, Dennis	10	0	0	0	.000	.000	1	2	2	2	1	2	2	2	1.000	.111	.111
Moore, Marcus	27	6	0	2	.000	.000	0	1	11	8	5	2	22	8	.364	.318	.407
Mulholland, Terry	1	0	0	0	.000	.000	0	1	0	0	0	0	0	0	.000	.000	.000
Munoz, Mike	21	3	0	2	.000	.000	2	1	8	4	6	0	14	6	.429	.167	.286
Murphy, Rob	73	31	1	3	.032	.250	1	0	9	41	17	5	33	5	.152	.239	.260
Myers, Randy	73	60	53	6	.883	.898	0	0	0	12	58	3	24	4	.167	.231	.315
Nabholz, Chris	5	1	0	0	.000	.000	0	1	1	1	2	0	2	0	.000	.500	.600
Neagle, Denny	43	8	1	0	.125	1.000	2	4	15	9	11	2	28	11	.393	.162	.279
Nen, Robb	14	0	0	0	.000	.000	7	4	1	0	2	0	7	3	.429	.500	.571
Nichols, Rod	4	1	0	1	.000	.000	1	1	0	0	1	1	4	3	.750	.333	.333
Olivares, Omar	49	9	1	4	.111	.200	7	10	16	10	6	0	38	19	.500	.372	.449
Osuna, Al	44	18	2	0	.111	1.000	0	4	9	25	5	1	44	12	.273	.194	.295
Otto, Dave	20	2	0	0	.000	.000	3	4	5	5	3	0	6	2	.333	.500	.550
Painter, Lance	4	0	0	0	.000	.000	2	0	0	1	0	1	2	0	.000	.250	.250
Pall, Donn	8	2	1	0	.500	1.000	2	2	2	2	0	0	8	2	.250	.429	.500
Parrett, Jeff	34	5	1	3	.200	.250	2	5	12	9	4	2	20	13	.650	.167	.265
Perez, Mike	65	24	7	3	.292	.700	0	2	11	28	18	6	22	7	.318	.237	.277
Petkovsek, Mark	26	0	0	0	.000	.000	8	6	3	6	3	0	19	8	.421	.300	.391
Plesac, Dan	57	15	0	2	.000	.000	8	5	13	25	4	2	38	21	.553	.308	.351
Powell, Ross	8	0	0	0	.000	.000	3	1	0	2	1	1	2	0	.000	.143	.250
Pugh, Tim	4	0	0	0	.000	.000	2	1	0	0	0	1	1	0	.000	.500	.500
Reardon, Jeff	58	23	8	4	.348	.667	0	2	5	27	23	1	28	1	.036	.200	.241
Reed, Steve	64	19	3	3	.158	.500	8	15	17	18	5	1	43	10	.233	.228	.286
Reynolds, Shane	4	0	0	0	.000	.000	3	1	0	0	0	0	4	1	.250	.250	.250
Righetti, Dave	51	13	1	2	.077	.333	2	5	14	16	12	2	23	9	.391	.292	.333
Risley, Bill	2	0	0	0	.000	.000	0	1	1	0	0	0	0	0	.000	.000	1.000
Rivera, Ben	2	0	0	0	.000	.000	1	0	1	0	1	0	0	0	.000	.000	.500
Robertson, Rich	9	2	0	1	.000	.000	1	3	3	1	1	0	2	1	.500	.500	.556
Rodriguez, Rich	70	21	3	4	.143	.429	4	6	17	29	10	4	51	16	.314	.266	.329

Name	GR	SVS	SV	BS	SC%	SV%	<6I	6I	7I	8I	9I	XI	IR	IRS	IRP	BA	OBA
Rogers, Kevin	64	22	0	2	.000	.000	2	8	21	16	14	3	41	11	.268	.267	.312
Rojas, Mel	66	36	10	9	.278	.526	0	9	21	23	9	4	37	19	.514	.321	.385
Roper, John	1	0	0	0	.000	.000	0	0	0	0	1	0	0	0	.000	.000	.000
Ruffin, Bruce	47	9	2	1	.222	.667	17	7	6	16	1	0	25	6	.240	.158	.304
Ruffin, Johnny	21	5	2	1	.400	.667	5	2	9	5	0	0	10	5	.500	.400	.429
Ruskin, Scott	4	0	0	0	.000	.000	1	0	0	2	0	1	6	4	.667	.333	.500
Sanderson, Scott	3	0	0	0	.000	.000	1	0	2	0	0	0	2	1	.500	.333	.333
Sanford, Mo	5	0	0	0	.000	.000	1	1	2	0	1	0	1	1	1.000	.400	.400
Scanlan, Bob	70	30	0	3	.000	.000	0	7	29	24	7	3	59	22	.373	.213	.275
Schourek, Pete	23	3	0	1	.000	.000	3	2	6	8	4	0	10	4	.400	.250	.261
Scott, Tim	56	9	1	3	.111	.250	8	11	11	14	9	3	31	17	.548	.220	.286
Seanez, Rudy	3	0	0	0	.000	.000	0	0	0	2	1	0	3	3	1.000	1.000	1.000
Seminara, Frank	11	2	0	1	.000	.000	2	4	4	1	0	0	8	3	.375	.182	.182
Service, Scott	29	6	2	0	.333	1.000	5	9	7	5	2	1	18	5	.278	.250	.321
Shaw, Jeff	47	7	0	1	.000	.000	9	10	8	11	8	1	32	8	.250	.103	.186
Shepherd, Keith	13	4	1	1	.250	.500	1	5	4	2	1	0	7	1	.143	.273	.385
Shouse, Brian	6	0	0	0	.000	.000	0	1	1	3	1	0	1	0	.000	.667	.667
Slocumb, Heathcliff	10	3	0	0	.000	.000	1	1	3	2	3	0	10	4	.400	.222	.300
Smith, Bryn	6	1	0	1	.000	.000	1	0	3	1	1	0	0	0	.000	.400	.500
Smith, Lee	55	51	43	7	.843	.860	0	0	0	7	44	4	21	4	.190	.200	.259
Smith, Pete	6	2	0	0	.000	.000	1	2	0	1	2	0	1	0	.000	.200	.333
Spradlin, Jerry	37	3	2	1	.667	.667	6	6	9	7	8	1	22	10	.455	.294	.324
Stanton, Mike	63	39	27	6	.692	.818	1	0	4	14	39	5	25	10	.400	.167	.286
Swindell, Greg	1	0	0	0	.000	.000	0	1	0	0	0	0	0	0	.000	1.000	1.000
Taylor, Kerry	29	0	0	0	.000	.000	11	5	3	4	6	0	16	7	.438	.292	.393
Telgheder, Dave	17	1	0	0	.000	.000	3	3	4	3	2	2	5	3	.600	.133	.235
Thigpen, Bobby	17	3	0	2	.000	.000	0	4	5	2	5	1	4	3	.750	.235	.235
Toliver, Fred	12	1	0	0	.000	.000	5	2	5	0	0	0	16	4	.250	.111	.250
Trlicek, Ricky	41	2	1	0	.500	1.000	10	7	9	8	3	4	37	12	.324	.225	.244
Turner, Matt	55	12	0	1	.000	.000	0	2	13	22	16	2	40	14	.350	.212	.222
Urbani, Tom	9	1	0	1	.000	.000	2	2	1	4	0	0	9	5	.556	.500	.444
Valdez, Sergio	4	0	0	0	.000	.000	2	0	1	0	0	1	3	1	.333	.333	.500
Wagner, Paul	27	11	2	3	.182	.400	2	4	8	7	5	1	21	11	.524	.417	.462
Wakefield, Tim	4	0	0	0	.000	.000	0	1	1	1	1	0	0	0	.000	.000	.000
Walton, Bruce	4	0	0	0	.000	.000	1	0	1	1	1	0	2	0	.000	.333	.500
Watson, Allen	1	1	0	1	.000	.000	0	1	0	0	0	0	0	0	.000	.000	.000
Wayne, Gary	65	8	1	2	.125	.333	4	9	16	18	13	5	57	23	.404	.309	.349
Weathers, David	8	0	0	0	.000	.000	2	3	1	2	0	0	5	2	.400	.500	.500
Wendell, Turk	3	0	0	0	.000	.000	2	0	0	0	1	0	2	1	.500	.333	.333
West, David	76	32	3	6	.094	.333	1	6	15	38	10	6	52	21	.404	.250	.368
Weston, Mickey	4	0	0	0	.000	.000	2	2	0	0	0	0	4	3	.750	.333	.500
Wetteland, John	70	49	43	6	.878	.878	0	0	1	28	36	5	32	5	.156	.203	.309
Whitehurst, Wally	2	0	0	0	.000	.000	0	1	0	1	0	0	0	0	.000	.500	.500
Wickander, Kevin	33	4	0	1	.000	.000	4	6	6	11	6	0	32	8	.250	.083	.312
Williams, Brian	37	8	3	3	.375	.500	3	7	12	11	4	0	22	7	.318	.294	.351
Williams, Mike	13	0	0	0	.000	.000	6	5	0	0	0	2	11	5	.455	.167	.231
Williams, Mitch	65	51	43	6	.843	.878	0	0	1	4	55	5	9	4	.444	.189	.338
Wilson, Steve	25	2	1	0	.500	1.000	7	5	4	7	2	0	25	8	.320	.273	.360
Wilson, Trevor	4	0	0	0	.000	.000	1	1	1	0	1	0	2	0	.000	.500	.500
Wohlers, Mark	46	12	0	0	.000	.000	0	1	14	23	7	1	21	8	.381	.125	.222
Worrell, Tim	5	1	0	0	.000	.000	2	1	2	0	0	0	2	1	.500	.000	.400
Worrell, Todd	35	12	5	3	.417	.625	0	0	2	13	19	1	13	3	.231	.226	.235
Young, Anthony	29	7	3	2	.429	.600	1	1	3	13	8	3	7	2	.286	.200	.286
Young, Pete	4	0	0	0	.000	.000	1	0	0	2	1	0	0	0	.000	.250	.250

The Basestealing Reports

These special reports are designed to give more insight into basestealing. They do so in two ways: first, by showing opportunities for basestealing; second, by showing the defensive aspects of basestealing. The reports are presented for pitchers and catchers (minimum 10 opposition stolen base attempts) and baserunners (minimum 10 stolen base attempts). Players are listed by team in each category.

Counting stolen base opportunities is almost as important as knowing the traditional stolen base success rate. (Imagine if you knew only how many base hits a player made, without knowing how many at-bats it took him to accumulate them!) Looking at how well pitchers and catchers defend against the steal is just as important as looking at how baserunners do offensively—they are mirror images of the same part of the game. The league averages and totals are given after the pitcher listings; note the large difference between the leagues in the frequency of basestealing attempts and the smaller difference in success rates.

Calculating stolen base opportunities defensively shows the effect pitchers and catchers have on their opponents' running game, both by preventing basestealing attempts as well as by throwing runners out. For pitchers and baserunners, individual success rates vary even more than they do for catchers. In each case, exactly the same things are being counted—an opportunity for a runner is also an opportunity "against" the pitcher and the catcher.

A stolen base opportunity (for second base) is defined as a plate appearance that occurs with first base occupied and second base not occupied, or an attempt to steal second even if it is occupied (i.e., part of a double steal). If Lenny Dykstra walks to lead off an inning, stays put while Mariano Duncan pops up and John Kruk strikes out, then steals second with Dave Hollins at bat with two out, he is charged with three opportunities: one each for being on first base with second base unoccupied during Duncan's, Kruk's, and Hollins's at-bats. The definition for opportunities to steal third base is analogous to that for stealing second base, but no opportunities are calculated for the rare attempts to steal home.

Once we know how many opportunities there were to steal a base, we calculate the **Attempt Percentage** for both second base and third base. "Attempts" are simply stolen bases plus caught stealings; attempt percentages (**A2%, A3%**) show the rate of attempts per 100 basestealing opportunities of second and third bases, respectively.

Shown after the attempt percentages are the actual totals of stolen bases and caught stealings of second base (**SB2, CS2**) and third base (**SB3, CS3**). Note that all caught stealings are counted here, whether they were initiated by the pitcher (e.g., scored "1-3-6") or the catcher (e.g., scored "2-6").

The next columns in each report show the **total stolen bases (SB)** and **caught stealings (CS)** for each runner or against each pitcher or catcher, including steals and caught stealings at home plate. (These are quite rare, with only a dozen or so successful steals of home in a typical season.) For baserunners, the last column shows the traditional stolen base percentage (**SB%**—stolen bases divided by attempts); for pitchers and catchers, the last column is their opponents' stolen base percentage (**OSB%**, calculated the same way). Obviously, the higher the SB% for runners, the better they were at theft on the base-paths. The lower the OSB% for pitchers and catchers, the better they were at foiling attempted larcenies.

All things considered, the most important stat for pitchers and catchers is the percentage of times opposing baserunners attempted to steal second base (A2%). Why? Because stealing second base puts a runner in scoring position, which is critical to his chances of scoring; stealing third base merely advances a runner who was already in scoring position. It's safe to say that managers would almost always gladly trade the certainty of keeping a runner at first—and keeping the double play in order—than take their chances on throwing the runner out at second.

BASESTEALING REPORTS

PITCHERS

AMERICAN LEAGUE

NAME	TM	A2%	SB2	CS2	A3%	SB3	CS3	OSB	OCS	SB%
Paul Abbott	CLE	17.6	3	0	0	0	0	3	0	100
Jim Abbott	NYA	8.8	14	5	2.1	2	1	16	6	72.7
Rick Aguilera	MIN	7	4	0	2.4	1	0	5	0	100
Wilson Alvarez	CHA	12.9	19	12	3.6	1	4	21	17	55.3
Brian Anderson	CAL	16.7	1	0	0	0	0	1	0	100
Kevin Appier	KC	8	10	6	1.4	1	1	11	8	57.9
Paul Assenmacher	NYA	5.9	1	0	0	0	0	1	0	100
Jim Austin	MIL	3	0	1	0	0	0	0	1	0
Bob Ayrault	SEA	0	0	0	0	0	0	0	0	0
Cory Bailey	BOS	25	3	2	0	0	0	3	2	60
Scott Bankhead	BOS	7	3	2	0	0	0	3	2	60
Willie Banks	MIN	6.2	6	6	0	0	0	6	6	50
Tim Belcher	CHA	7.1	0	5	0	0	0	0	5	0
Stan Belinda	KC	18.8	4	2	0	0	0	4	2	66.7
Jason Bere	CHA	7.9	8	6	2.2	1	1	9	8	52.9
Sean Bergman	DET	6.7	4	0	0	0	0	4	0	100
Mike Bielecki	CLE	16	12	1	3	2	0	14	1	93.3
Mike Boddicker	MIL	10.6	5	2	4.5	1	1	6	3	66.7
Joe Boever	DET	0	0	0	0	0	0	0	0	0
Joe Boever	OAK	4.9	3	1	3	1	1	4	3	57.1
Brian Bohanon	TEX	11.9	8	6	1.3	0	1	8	7	53.3
Rod Bolton	CHA	4.3	2	0	0	0	0	2	0	100
Tom Bolton	DET	7.9	5	5	2.4	2	0	7	5	58.3
Ricky Bones	MIL	11.8	17	5	2.2	3	0	20	5	80
Chris Bosio	SEA	9	7	6	1	1	0	8	6	57.1
Billy Brewer	KC	9.5	3	1	10.7	2	1	5	2	71.4
John Briscoe	OAK	5.3	0	2	0	0	0	0	2	0
Jeff Bronkey	TEX	2.9	0	1	0	0	0	0	1	0
Scott Brow	TOR	9.1	2	0	0	0	0	2	0	100
Kevin Brown	TEX	6.2	7	8	2.6	2	2	10	10	50
Greg Brummett	MIN	25	5	1	0	0	0	5	1	83.3
Enrique Burgos	KC	11.1	1	0	0	0	0	1	0	100
Todd Burns	TEX	5.3	2	2	2	1	0	3	2	60
Mike Butcher	CAL	9.7	3	0	4.8	1	0	4	0	100
Greg Cadaret	KC	11.1	1	1	11.1	0	1	1	2	33.3
Kevin Campbell	OAK	4.8	0	1	5.6	0	1	0	2	0
Jose Canseco	TEX	0	0	0	0	0	0	0	0	0
Cris Carpenter	TEX	2.5	0	1	0	0	0	0	1	0
Chuck Cary	CHA	4.3	0	1	5	0	1	0	2	0
Larry Casian	MIN	1.5	1	0	0	0	0	1	0	100
Tony Castillo	TOR	7.1	3	1	2.9	1	0	4	1	80
Norm Charlton	SEA	9.7	3	0	0	0	0	3	0	100
Mike Christopher	CLE	7.1	1	0	0	0	0	1	0	100
Mark Clark	CLE	16.7	8	8	3	0	2	8	10	44.4
Roger Clemens	BOS	11.5	14	7	1.8	2	0	16	7	69.6
David Cone	KC	16.7	30	12	1.7	2	1	32	13	71.1
Jim Converse	SEA	21.1	2	2	0	0	0	2	2	50
Mike Cook	BAL	0	0	0	0	0	0	0	0	0
Dennis Cook	CLE	9.1	0	4	6.2	1	1	1	5	16.7
Andy Cook	NYA	0	0	0	0	0	0	0	0	0
Danny Cox	TOR	13.9	7	3	0	0	0	7	3	70
Chuck Crim	CAL	18.8	3	0	0	0	0	3	0	100
John Cummings	SEA	10.5	2	4	0	0	0	2	4	33.3
Ron Darling	OAK	12	13	10	0.7	0	1	14	11	56
Danny Darwin	BOS	8.5	11	4	0	0	0	11	5	68.8
Chili Davis	CAL	0	0	0	0	0	0	0	0	0
Storm Davis	DET	13.3	3	1	4.8	1	0	4	1	80
Storm Davis	OAK	16.9	10	1	3.5	1	1	11	2	84.6
Ken Dayley	TOR	0	0	0	0	0	0	0	0	0
Jose DeLeon	CHA	0	0	0	0	0	0	0	0	0
Rich Delucia	SEA	8.5	2	2	0	0	0	2	2	50
Jim Deshaies	MIN	12.8	6	14	3.5	2	1	8	15	34.8
John DeSilva	DET	0	0	0	0	0	0	0	0	0
Frank DiPino	KC	0	0	0	0	0	0	0	0	0
Jerry DiPoto	CLE	1.4	1	0	0	0	0	1	0	100
John Doherty	DET	9.7	7	11	0	0	0	7	12	36.8
John Dopson	BOS	9.2	10	4	2	1	1	11	5	68.8
Kelly Downs	OAK	9.2	12	2	3.5	1	2	13	4	76.5
Brian Drahman	CHA	0	0	0	0	0	0	0	0	0
Steve Dreyer	TEX	6.1	2	1	3.2	0	1	2	2	50
Dennis Eckersley	OAK	16.9	10	2	4.7	2	0	12	2	85.7
Mark Eichhorn	TOR	14.1	7	2	3.3	1	1	8	3	72.7
Cal Eldred	MIL	12.1	20	8	1.3	1	1	21	9	70
Scott Erickson	MIN	11.4	25	4	1.1	2	0	27	4	87.1
Hector Fajardo	TEX	0	0	0	0	0	0	0	0	0
Steve Farr	NYA	11.4	4	1	0	0	0	4	1	80
John Farrell	CAL	14.6	13	2	2.6	1	1	14	3	82.4
Alex Fernandez	CHA	4.1	4	6	3.3	1	3	5	11	31.2
Mike Fetters	MIL	14.8	6	6	2.3	0	1	6	7	46.2
Chuck Finley	CAL	9.8	19	8	1.9	2	1	21	9	70
Dave Fleming	SEA	8.7	6	10	2.6	2	1	8	12	40
Huck Flener	TOR	9.1	1	0	0	0	0	1	0	100
Tony Fossas	BOS	3.8	2	0	2.9	1	0	3	0	100
Steve Frey	CAL	5.5	2	1	1.8	1	0	3	1	75
Todd Frohwirth	BAL	11.5	11	3	8	5	1	16	4	80
Rich Garces	MIN	0	0	0	0	0	0	0	0	0
Mike Gardiner	DET	5.9	1	0	0	0	0	1	0	100
Mark Gardner	KC	21.7	7	11	1.9	1	0	8	11	42.1
Paul Gibson	NYA	8.3	3	0	10.5	2	0	5	0	100
Greg Gohr	DET	4	1	0	0	0	0	1	0	100
Tom Gordon	KC	14.1	14	8	0.9	1	0	15	9	62.5
Rich Gossage	OAK	12.2	5	1	2.6	1	0	6	1	85.7
Joe Grahe	CAL	6	4	0	0	0	0	4	0	100
Jeff Granger	KC	0	0	0	0	0	0	0	0	0
Mark Grater	DET	0	0	0	0	0	0	0	0	0
Jason Grimsley	CLE	13.2	6	1	2.9	1	0	7	1	87.5
Buddy Groom	DET	9.3	2	2	6.5	2	0	4	2	66.7
Eddie Guardado	MIN	13.2	9	3	4.1	3	0	12	5	70.6
Mark Gubicza	KC	7.7	9	1	2.1	2	0	11	2	84.6
Bill Gullickson	DET	10.6	13	5	0	0	0	13	5	72.2
Mark Guthrie	MIN	16.7	3	2	8.7	1	1	4	3	57.1
Juan Guzman	TOR	13.9	24	14	1.2	1	1	25	17	59.5
David Haas	DET	3.7	1	0	0	0	0	1	0	100
John Habyan	KC	15.4	2	0	8.3	1	0	3	0	100
John Habyan	NYA	6.8	3	0	0	0	0	3	0	100
Mike Hampton	SEA	10.3	3	0	4.2	1	0	4	0	100
Chris Haney	KC	6.6	4	4	3.1	3	0	7	4	63.6
Erik Hanson	SEA	12.6	11	12	3.4	4	1	15	13	53.6
Greg Harris	BOS	6.2	4	4	0.9	1	0	5	4	55.6
Mike Hartley	MIN	14.8	9	4	2.4	2	0	11	4	73.3
Hilly Hathaway	CAL	13	7	3	0	0	0	7	3	70
Neal Heaton	NYA	2.9	1	0	0	0	0	2	0	100
Tom Henke	TEX	5.6	3	1	2	0	0	3	2	60
Mike Henneman	DET	0	0	0	0	0	0	0	0	0
Doug Henry	MIL	5.6	4	0	0	0	0	4	0	100
Dwayne Henry	SEA	7.4	3	2	0	0	0	3	2	60
Pat Hentgen	TOR	9.2	16	6	0	0	0	16	6	72.7
Roberto Hernandez	CHA	7.1	2	4	0	0	0	2	4	33.3
Jeremy Hernandez	CLE	4.8	2	2	2.4	1	0	3	4	42.9
Joe Hesketh	BOS	8.3	4	1	0	0	0	4	2	66.7
Teddy Higuera	MIL	13.3	3	1	0	0	0	3	1	75
Shawn Hillegas	OAK	7	1	4	2.2	1	0	2	4	33.3
Sterling Hitchcock	NYA	12.9	3	1	4	0	0	3	2	60
Brad Holman	SEA	2.9	1	0	0	0	0	1	0	100
Mark Holzemer	CAL	8.1	2	1	0	0	0	2	1	66.7
Rick Honeycutt	OAK	7	1	3	3.8	1	0	2	3	40
Vince Horsman	OAK	6.9	2	0	0	0	0	2	1	66.7
Chris Howard	CHA	0	0	0	14.3	0	1	0	1	0
Steve Howe	NYA	3.6	1	1	0	0	0	1	1	50
Mark Hutton	NYA	11.5	2	1	11.8	2	0	4	1	80
Mike Ignasiak	MIL	8.7	1	3	0	0	0	1	3	25

NAME	TM	A2%	SB2	CS2	A3%	SB3	CS3	OSB	OCS	SB%
Domingo Jean	NYA	6.2	2	0	0	0	0	2	0	100
Miguel Jimenez	OAK	5	1	1	0	0	0	1	1	50
Dave Johnson	DET	0	0	0	0	0	0	0	0	0
Jeff Johnson	NYA	25	1	1	0	0	0	1	1	50
Randy Johnson	SEA	14.2	21	11	4.6	6	1	28	12	70
Barry Jones	CHA	16.7	1	1	0	0	0	1	1	50
Scott Kamieniecki	NYA	9.1	7	9	1.2	0	1	7	10	41.2
Steve Karsay	OAK	12.3	5	2	0	0	0	5	2	71.4
Jimmy Key	NYA	6.3	10	3	5.6	4	3	15	6	71.4
Mark Kiefer	MIL	11.1	1	0	0	0	0	1	0	100
John Kiely	DET	0	0	0	0	0	0	0	0	0
Kevin King	SEA	7.7	1	0	0	0	0	1	0	100
Kurt Knudsen	DET	7	2	1	0	0	0	2	3	40
Tom Kramer	CLE	9.5	6	6	1.1	0	1	6	7	46.2
Bill Krueger	DET	12.1	9	4	3.1	2	0	11	4	73.3
Mark Langston	CAL	8.5	10	11	0.7	0	1	10	12	45.5
Terry Leach	CHA	0	0	0	0	0	0	0	0	0
Tim Leary	SEA	9.5	8	8	2.6	2	1	10	9	52.6
Craig Lefferts	TEX	6.7	3	3	3.6	1	1	4	4	50
Phil Leftwich	CAL	9.2	4	3	1.6	0	1	4	4	50
Charlie Leibrandt	TEX	12.7	15	5	3.5	4	0	19	5	79.2
Mark Leiter	DET	9.4	8	4	0	0	0	8	4	66.7
Al Leiter	TOR	8.4	6	5	1.6	1	0	7	5	58.3
Scott Lewis	CAL	5.7	1	1	0	0	0	1	1	50
Derek Lilliquist	CLE	2.9	2	0	0	0	0	2	0	100
Doug Linton	CAL	8.6	2	1	3.6	1	0	3	2	60
Doug Linton	TOR	0	0	0	0	0	0	0	0	0
Graeme Lloyd	MIL	1.3	1	0	1.9	1	0	2	0	100
Albie Lopez	CLE	11.3	5	2	2.6	0	1	5	3	62.5
Rob MacDonald	DET	6.8	2	3	0	0	0	2	3	40
Mike Magnante	KC	10.3	0	4	0	0	0	0	4	0
Joe Magrane	CAL	22.8	8	5	2.7	1	0	9	6	60
Pat Mahomes	MIN	17.1	5	2	2.8	0	1	5	3	62.5
Carlos Maldonado	MIL	5.4	2	0	0	0	0	2	0	100
Josias Manzanillo	MIL	8.3	1	0	0	0	0	1	0	100
Matt Maysey	MIL	8.3	3	0	0	0	0	3	0	100
Kirk McCaskill	CHA	11	7	8	2.5	1	1	8	9	47.1
Ben McDonald	BAL	13	16	10	2.5	2	1	19	11	63.3
Jack McDowell	CHA	8.7	10	15	0	0	0	10	15	40
Kevin McGehee	BAL	20	2	0	0	0	0	2	0	100
Rusty Meacham	KC	4.3	1	0	0	0	0	1	0	100
Jose Melendez	BOS	0	0	0	0	0	0	0	0	0
Brett Merriman	MIN	2.7	0	1	0	0	0	0	1	0
Jose Mesa	CLE	10.1	12	11	1.4	0	2	12	14	46.2
Bob Milacki	CLE	4.5	1	0	0	0	0	1	0	100
Sam Militello	NYA	7.1	1	0	0	0	0	1	0	100
Alan Mills	BAL	7.9	6	3	0	0	0	6	3	66.7
Nate Minchey	BOS	6.1	1	1	0	0	0	1	1	50
Angel Miranda	MIL	6.4	5	2	4.1	2	1	7	3	70
David Mlicki	CLE	28.6	2	2	0	0	0	2	2	50
Mike Mohler	OAK	10.3	6	3	3.6	2	0	8	3	72.7
Rich Monteleone	NYA	5.7	4	1	1.7	1	0	5	1	83.3
Jeff Montgomery	KC	8.9	7	1	0	0	0	7	1	87.5
Mike Moore	DET	11	20	6	3.3	3	2	23	8	74.2
Jack Morris	TOR	13.5	15	9	2.5	2	1	17	10	63
Jamie Moyer	BAL	6.7	3	6	2.2	2	0	5	6	45.5
Mike Munoz	DET	0	0	0	0	0	0	0	0	0
Bobby Munoz	NYA	8.6	5	0	2.4	1	0	6	0	100
Mike Mussina	BAL	5	3	5	1	0	1	3	6	33.3
Jeff Mutis	CLE	7.8	5	2	3.8	1	1	6	3	66.7
Charles Nagy	CLE	16.4	9	1	4.2	1	1	10	2	83.3
Jaime Navarro	MIL	10.6	21	4	1.9	2	2	23	6	79.3
Gene Nelson	CAL	4.3	3	0	0	0	0	3	1	75
Jeff Nelson	SEA	13.8	8	1	3.1	2	0	10	1	90.9
Gene Nelson	TEX	0	0	0	0	0	0	0	0	0
Robb Nen	TEX	6.7	1	1	3.8	0	1	1	2	33.3
Jerry Nielsen	CAL	0	0	0	7.7	1	0	1	0	100
Rafael Novoa	MIL	3.3	1	1	4.7	2	0	3	1	75
Ed Nunez	OAK	6.4	4	3	1.4	0	0	5	3	62.5
John O'Donoghue	BAL	15	3	0	0	0	0	3	0	100
Bobby Ojeda	CLE	6.1	2	1	0	0	0	2	1	66.7
Darren Oliver	TEX	100	1	0	0	0	0	1	0	100
Gregg Olson	BAL	4.3	1	1	0	0	0	1	1	50
Steve Ontiveros	SEA	9.1	1	0	1.1	0	0	1	1	100
Mike Oquist	BAL	9.1	0	1	0	0	0	0	1	0
Jesse Orosco	MIL	6.5	1	3	6.8	1	2	2	5	28.6

NAME	TM	A2%	SB2	CS2	A3%	SB3	CS3	OSB	OCS	SB%
Donn Pall	CHA	4.9	3	0	2.5	1	0	4	0	100
Ken Patterson	CAL	15.3	6	3	2.1	0	1	7	3	70
Bob Patterson	TEX	5.6	1	2	5.4	2	0	3	2	60
Roger Pavlik	TEX	12.3	15	5	0.9	0	1	15	6	71.4
Brad Pennington	BAL	7.3	2	1	2.1	1	0	3	1	75
Melido Perez	NYA	8.3	10	5	2.2	1	1	11	6	64.7
Hipolito Pichardo	KC	6.4	8	4	1.5	0	2	8	7	53.3
Erik Plantenberg	SEA	0	0	0	0	0	0	0	0	0
Eric Plunk	CLE	8.8	6	1	0	0	0	6	1	85.7
Jim Poole	BAL	3.4	2	0	2.8	0	1	2	1	66.7
Dennis Powell	SEA	10.6	3	2	2.9	1	0	4	3	57.1
Ted Power	CLE	5.9	1	0	0	0	0	1	0	100
Ted Power	SEA	3.8	0	1	0	0	0	0	1	0
Paul Quantrill	BOS	8.6	11	1	0.9	1	0	12	1	92.3
Scott Radinsky	CHA	1.4	1	0	2	1	0	2	0	100
Dennis Rasmussen	KC	13.2	1	4	0	0	0	1	4	20
Rick Reed	KC	0	0	0	0	0	0	0	0	0
Rick Reed	TEX	16.7	0	1	0	0	0	0	1	0
Arthur Rhodes	BAL	10.4	4	4	1.6	1	0	5	4	55.6
Kenny Rogers	TEX	8	4	11	0	0	0	4	11	26.7
Scott Ruffcorn	CHA	28.6	4	0	8.3	1	0	5	0	100
Jeff Russell	BOS	4.9	1	1	0	0	0	1	1	50
Ken Ryan	BOS	5.7	2	1	4	1	1	3	2	60
Nolan Ryan	TEX	25	13	4	0	0	0	13	4	76.5
Roger Salkeld	SEA	0	0	0	0	0	0	0	0	0
Bill Sampen	KC	17.9	3	2	6.2	1	0	4	2	66.7
Scott Sanderson	CAL	6.2	4	4	1.3	1	0	5	4	55.6
Mike Schooler	TEX	16.7	4	1	4.3	1	0	5	1	83.3
Jeff Schwarz	CHA	17.6	7	5	2.3	1	0	8	5	61.5
Darryl Scott	CAL	14.3	3	0	4.3	1	0	4	0	100
Scott Scudder	CLE	50	2	1	0	0	0	2	1	66.7
Aaron Sele	BOS	7.8	8	1	0	0	0	8	1	88.9
Zak Shinall	SEA	0	0	0	0	0	0	0	0	0
Heathcliff Slocumb	CLE	3.4	1	0	6.7	1	0	2	0	100
Joe Slusarski	OAK	0	0	0	0	0	0	0	0	0
Lee Smith	NYA	23.1	3	0	12.5	1	0	4	0	100
Roger Smithberg	OAK	6.2	1	0	0	0	0	1	0	100
Russell Springer	CAL	14.6	11	1	0	0	0	11	1	91.7
Dave Stewart	TOR	14.1	13	11	0	0	0	13	12	52
Dave Stieb	CHA	8.1	2	1	7.7	1	0	3	1	75
Todd Stottlemyre	TOR	12.8	21	6	2.8	3	1	24	7	77.4
Rick Sutcliffe	BAL	7.6	13	1	7.1	4	5	17	8	68
Russ Swan	SEA	0	0	0	5.3	1	0	1	1	50
Paul Swingle	CAL	27.3	3	0	0	0	0	3	0	100
Jeff Tackett	BAL	0	0	0	0	0	0	0	0	0
Frank Tanana	NYA	5.6	1	0	0	0	0	1	0	100
Kevin Tapani	MIN	22.2	40	11	2.3	2	2	42	13	76.4
Julian Tavarez	CLE	5.8	2	1	3.6	0	1	2	2	50
Scott Taylor	BOS	0	0	0	0	0	0	0	0	0
Anthony Telford	BAL	16.7	1	0	0	0	0	1	0	100
Bobby Thigpen	CHA	10.6	2	3	0	0	0	2	3	40
Mike Timlin	TOR	12.5	9	0	0	0	0	9	0	100
Mike Trombley	MIN	8.5	6	4	3.2	1	2	7	6	53.8
George Tsamis	MIN	4.1	0	3	1.7	1	0	4	0	0
Fernando Valenzuela	BAL	9.9	6	12	4.2	4	2	10	14	41.7
Julio Valera	CAL	4.9	2	1	0	0	0	2	1	66.7
Todd Van Poppel	OAK	9.5	4	5	1.6	1	0	5	5	50
Frank Viola	BOS	9	10	8	2.5	1	2	11	11	50
Dave Wainhouse	SEA	16.7	1	0	20	1	0	2	0	100
Duane Ward	TOR	3.2	2	0	2.1	1	0	3	0	100
Bill Wegman	MIL	10.5	6	6	5.5	4	1	10	7	58.8
Bob Welch	OAK	9.7	7	12	1	0	1	8	12	40
Dave Wells	DET	11.9	12	10	1.8	2	0	14	10	58.3
Bill Wertz	CLE	1.3	1	0	0	0	0	1	0	100
Matt Whiteside	TEX	11.7	3	6	1.8	1	0	4	6	40
Kevin Wickander	CLE	5.2	1	0	20	1	0	2	0	100
Bob Wickman	NYA	14.2	15	3	4.5	5	0	20	9	69
Woody Williams	TOR	0	0	0	0	0	0	0	0	0
Mark Williamson	BAL	7.4	3	4	0	0	0	3	4	42.9
Carl Willis	MIN	6.2	3	1	1.7	0	1	4	1	80
Mike Witt	NYA	11.1	3	3	0	0	0	3	3	50
Bobby Witt	OAK	7.9	11	8	5.6	8	1	19	9	67.9
Cliff Young	CLE	10.1	4	3	2.2	0	1	4	4	50
Matt Young	CLE	15.8	9	7	0	0	0	9	7	56.2
Curt Young	OAK	23.1	2	1	0	0	0	2	1	66.7

TEAM PITCHERS	TM	A2%	SB2	CS2	A3%	SB3	CS3	OSB	OCS	SB%
	BAL	8.7	76	51	2.9	19	11	96	64	60
	BOS	8.4	84	37	1.1	8	4	92	44	67.6
	CAL	10	111	45	1.4	11	4	122	52	70.1
	CHA	8.4	72	67	2.1	9	11	82	82	50
	CLE	9.7	104	54	1.8	9	11	113	68	62.4
	DET	8.9	90	52	1.4	12	2	102	57	64.2
	KC	11.2	105	61	1.9	14	6	119	71	62.6
	MIL	9.4	98	42	2.3	17	8	115	51	69.3
	MIN	11.6	122	56	2	15	8	137	66	67.5
	NYA	8.8	94	40	2.7	19	7	115	47	71
	OAK	9.5	98	62	2.6	21	7	120	71	62.8
	SEA	9.9	83	61	2.4	21	4	105	68	60.7
	TEX	9.4	82	59	1.9	12	3	95	67	58.6
	TOR	11.2	126	57	1.4	10	4	136	64	68
LEAGUE PITCHERS	AL	9.6	1345	744	2	197	95	1549	872	64

PITCHERS

NATIONAL LEAGUE

NAME	TM	A2%	SB2	CS2	A3%	SB3	CS3	OSB	OCS	SB%
Juan Agosto	HOU	20	1	0	0	0	0	1	0	100
Scott Aldred	COL	7.1	1	0	0	0	0	1	0	100
Scott Aldred	MON	12.5	1	0	12.5	0	1	1	1	50
Larry Andersen	PHI	8.6	4	1	0	0	0	4	1	80
Mike Anderson	CIN	0	0	0	0	0	0	0	0	0
Luis Aquino	FLO	12.6	10	3	2.4	0	2	10	5	66.7
Jack Armstrong	FLO	8.7	17	3	0.8	1	0	18	3	85.7
Rene Arocha	SL	14.5	13	9	0.8	1	0	14	9	60.9
Andy Ashby	COL	8.5	6	0	1.5	1	0	7	0	100
Andy Ashby	SD	7.4	4	1	0	0	0	4	1	80
Paul Assenmacher	CHN	10.3	3	1	0	0	0	3	1	75
Pedro Astacio	LA	14.4	17	10	3.3	2	2	19	12	61.3
Steve Avery	ATL	16.6	23	12	8.8	9	2	32	14	69.6
Bobby Ayala	CIN	7.3	6	1	1.9	2	0	9	1	90
Bob Ayrault	PHI	14.3	3	0	6.7	1	0	4	0	100
Jeff Ballard	PIT	3.4	1	1	2.8	1	0	2	1	66.7
Brian Barnes	MON	10.2	8	2	1	0	1	8	3	72.7
Rich Batchelor	SL	11.1	1	0	16.7	1	0	2	0	100
Jose Bautista	CHN	5.9	4	2	1.2	1	0	5	2	71.4
Rod Beck	SF	1.2	1	0	0	0	0	1	0	100
Steve Bedrosian	ATL	11.8	5	1	5.1	1	1	6	2	75
Tim Belcher	CIN	8.3	10	2	1.1	0	1	11	3	78.6
Stan Belinda	PIT	25.5	12	0	3.2	1	0	13	0	100
Eric Bell	HOU	10	1	0	8.3	1	0	2	0	100
Andy Benes	SD	11.4	19	7	1.3	2	0	21	7	75
Buddy Black	SF	15.2	6	8	5.8	3	1	9	8	52.9
Willie Blair	COL	6	7	3	1.8	1	1	8	4	66.7
Pedro Borbon	ATL	0	0	0	0	0	0	0	0	0
Shawn Boskie	CHN	7.2	4	1	0	0	0	4	1	80
Kent Bottenfield	COL	14	7	5	0	0	0	7	5	58.3
Kent Bottenfield	MON	9.8	7	1	2.7	2	0	9	1	90
Denis Boucher	MON	9.5	0	2	5.6	1	0	1	2	33.3
Ryan Bowen	FLO	10.3	13	6	2.8	2	1	15	7	68.2
Jeff Brantley	SF	5.4	1	5	0	0	0	1	5	16.7
William Brennan	CHN	16.7	1	2	10	0	1	1	3	25
Rod Brewer	SL	0	0	0	0	0	0	0	0	0
Brad Brink	PHI	0	0	0	0	0	0	0	0	0
Doug Brocail	SD	8.5	9	3	2.1	1	1	10	4	71.4
Terry Bross	SF	0	0	0	0	0	0	0	0	0
Tom Browning	CIN	5.7	3	5	3.6	2	1	5	7	41.7
Greg Brummett	SF	12.2	6	0	3.1	1	0	7	0	100
Jim Bullinger	CHN	14.3	1	1	0	0	0	1	1	50
Dave Burba	SF	10.9	8	2	4.4	2	1	10	3	76.9
John Burkett	SF	11.5	14	13	0	0	0	14	14	50
Todd Burns	SL	3.4	0	1	0	0	0	0	1	0
Chris Bushing	CIN	0	0	0	0	0	0	0	0	0
Greg Cadaret	CIN	7.7	2	1	0	0	0	2	1	66.7
John Candelaria	PIT	4.3	1	0	0	0	0	1	1	50
Tom Candiotti	LA	13.5	22	6	2.2	3	0	25	6	80.6
Cris Carpenter	FLO	13.9	5	0	0	0	0	5	0	100
Frank Castillo	CHN	11.2	6	10	3.1	1	2	7	12	36.8
Steve Cooke	PIT	12	14	9	5.4	8	0	22	9	71
Rheal Cormier	SL	3.7	3	2	0	0	0	3	2	60
Jim Corsi	FLO	6.1	2	0	0	0	0	2	0	100

NAME	TM	A2%	SB2	CS2	A3%	SB3	CS3	OSB	OCS	SB%
Omar Daal	LA	0	0	0	3	1	0	1	1	50
Mark Davis	PHI	2.4	1	0	0	0	0	1	0	100
Mark Davis	SD	14.6	5	2	4.9	2	0	7	2	77.8
Jose DeLeon	PHI	26.7	5	7	2.2	0	1	5	8	38.5
Jim Deshaies	SF	13	0	3	0	0	0	0	3	0
John DeSilva	LA	0	0	0	0	0	0	0	0	0
Mark Dewey	PIT	6.7	2	0	0	0	0	2	0	100
Rob Dibble	CIN	21.4	10	2	7.3	3	0	13	2	86.7
Steve Dixon	SL	0	0	0	0	0	0	0	0	0
Doug Drabek	HOU	15.3	27	5	1.2	0	2	28	7	80
Mike Draper	NYN	12.8	5	1	5	2	0	7	1	87.5
Tom Edens	HOU	6.8	2	1	4.4	2	0	4	1	80
Dave Eiland	SD	20.4	8	2	1.9	0	1	8	3	72.7
Mark Ettles	SD	0	0	0	0	0	0	0	0	0
Jeff Fassero	MON	8.5	9	3	4.5	3	1	12	4	75
Sid Fernandez	NYN	15.7	10	4	5.4	3	0	13	4	76.5
Paul Fletcher	PHI	0	0	0	0	0	0	0	0	0
Steve Foster	CIN	0	0	0	0	0	0	0	0	0
Kevin Foster	PHI	15.4	2	0	0	0	0	2	0	100
Johnny Franco	NYN	6.2	3	0	2.8	1	0	4	0	100
Scott Frederickson	COL	5.4	1	1	0	0	0	1	2	33.3
Marvin Freeman	ATL	21.4	3	3	0	0	0	3	3	50
Mike Gardiner	MON	7.1	2	1	2.9	1	0	3	2	60
Paul Gibson	NYN	0	0	0	0	0	0	0	0	0
Tom Glavine	ATL	4.4	7	4	1.4	2	0	9	5	64.3
Pat Gomez	SD	5.6	0	2	2.9	0	1	0	3	0
Dwight Gooden	NYN	17.2	25	8	3.4	3	2	28	10	73.7
Jim Gott	LA	7.3	4	2	0	0	0	4	2	66.7
Mauro Gozzo	NYN	7.1	1	0	0	0	0	1	0	100
Mark Grant	COL	0	0	0	0	0	0	0	0	0
Mark Grant	HOU	18.2	1	1	0	0	0	1	1	50
Tyler Green	PHI	0	0	0	7.1	0	1	0	1	0
Tommy Greene	PHI	11.6	17	5	0.7	1	0	18	5	78.3
Kevin Gross	LA	10.4	17	8	1.4	0	2	18	10	64.3
Kip Gross	LA	18.8	2	1	0	0	0	2	1	66.7
Lee Guetterman	SL	8.5	4	0	2.6	1	0	5	0	100
Jose Guzman	CHN	12.7	12	10	4.3	6	0	19	10	65.5
Chris Hammond	FLO	5.6	5	6	0	0	0	5	6	45.5
Mike Harkey	CHN	8	7	6	0	0	0	7	6	53.8
Pete Harnisch	HOU	9.7	14	5	1.4	1	1	15	6	71.4
Greg Harris	COL	9.2	4	3	3.6	1	1	5	4	55.6
Gene Harris	SD	12.5	9	0	1.8	1	0	10	0	100
Greg Harris	SD	14.4	16	4	2	0	2	17	6	73.9
Bryan Harvey	FLO	15.9	13	0	4.2	2	0	15	0	100
Dwayne Henry	CIN	0	0	0	0	0	0	0	0	0
Butch Henry	COL	6.9	4	3	4.5	3	0	7	3	70
Butch Henry	MON	18.2	1	1	7.1	1	0	2	1	66.7
Gil Heredia	MON	12.7	7	0	0	0	0	7	0	100
Xavier Hernandez	HOU	10.7	7	2	2.6	2	0	9	2	81.8
Jeremy Hernandez	SD	7.5	1	2	0	0	0	1	2	33.3
Orel Hershiser	LA	10.7	9	10	0.6	1	0	10	10	50
Greg Hibbard	CHN	6.3	2	10	0	0	0	2	10	16.7
Bryan Hickerson	SF	6.4	4	5	1.4	1	0	4	6	40
Milt Hill	CIN	14.8	2	2	0	0	0	2	2	50
Ken Hill	MON	16	20	8	0.7	1	0	21	8	72.4
Eric Hillman	NYN	7.1	7	4	7.9	4	4	11	8	57.9
Trevor Hoffman	FLO	3.6	1	0	0	0	0	1	0	100
Trevor Hoffman	SD	7.7	4	1	4.1	2	0	6	1	85.7
Darren Holmes	COL	7.9	3	2	0	0	0	3	2	60
John Hope	PIT	12.5	3	2	0	0	0	3	2	60
Charlie Hough	FLO	14.6	16	14	1.9	3	0	19	14	57.6
Jay Howell	ATL	15.1	4	4	4.9	1	1	5	5	50
Bruce Hurst	COL	0	0	0	0	0	0	0	0	0
Bruce Hurst	SD	16.7	1	1	25	2	0	3	1	75
Jeff Innis	NYN	11.5	8	3	1.3	1	0	9	3	75
Danny Jackson	PHI	7.1	12	5	3.4	3	2	15	7	68.2
Michael Jackson	SF	2.7	1	1	0	0	0	1	1	50
Joel Johnston	PIT	7.9	2	1	0	0	0	2	1	66.7
John Johnstone	FLO	0	0	0	8.3	1	0	1	0	100
Todd Jones	HOU	12.9	1	3	5.6	1	0	2	3	40
Doug Jones	HOU	2.1	2	0	0	0	0	2	0	100
Jimmy Jones	MON	15.6	5	0	0	0	0	5	0	100
Bobby Jones	NYN	9.3	3	2	0	0	0	3	2	60
Jeff Juden	HOU	33.3	1	0	0	0	0	1	0	100

NAME	TM	A2%	SB2	CS2	A3%	SB3	CS3	OSB	OCS	SB%
Jeff Kaiser	CIN	0	0	0	0	0	0	0	0	0
Jeff Kaiser	NYN	57.1	3	1	25	1	0	4	1	80
Darryl Kile	HOU	6.7	8	5	0	0	0	9	5	64.3
Paul Kilgus	SL	16.7	3	1	10.5	1	1	4	2	66.7
Joe Klink	FLO	10.8	4	0	9.1	1	3	5	3	62.5
Mark Knudson	COL	0	0	0	0	0	0	0	0	0
Lester Lancaster	SL	10.9	3	3	0	0	0	3	3	50
Bill Landrum	CIN	33.3	4	1	0	0	0	4	1	80
Tim Layana	SF	40	2	0	0	0	0	2	0	100
Curt Leskanic	COL	0	0	0	2.1	0	1	0	1	0
Richie Lewis	FLO	8.6	5	1	2.9	0	2	5	3	62.5
Brian Looney	MON	0	0	0	0	0	0	0	0	0
Larry Luebbers	CIN	15.3	5	8	0	0	0	5	8	38.5
Greg Maddux	ATL	12.2	23	6	2.2	4	0	27	6	81.8
Mike Maddux	NYN	13.5	8	2	2.7	1	1	9	3	75
Joe Magrane	SL	15.7	11	7	2.5	2	0	13	7	65
Josias Manzanillo	NYN	12.5	1	0	0	0	0	1	0	100
Ramon Martinez	LA	11	16	10	0.7	0	1	16	11	59.3
Pedro Martinez	LA	6.9	4	4	3.3	2	0	6	4	60
Dennis Martinez	MON	20.1	40	3	6.8	9	2	49	6	89.1
Pedro Martinez	SD	12.5	3	2	0	0	0	3	2	60
Roger Mason	PHI	6.2	2	1	0	0	0	2	1	66.7
Roger Mason	SD	10.9	3	3	2.7	0	1	3	4	42.9
Tim Mauser	PHI	6.2	1	0	0	0	0	1	0	100
Tim Mauser	SD	15	3	3	0	0	0	3	3	50
Bob McClure	FLO	10	0	1	14.3	0	1	0	2	0
Roger McDowell	LA	13.6	7	5	2.9	1	1	8	6	57.1
Chuck McElroy	CHN	10.7	4	2	0	0	0	4	2	66.7
Greg McMichael	ATL	7.1	4	2	1.8	1	0	5	2	71.4
Tony Menendez	PIT	0	0	0	7.1	0	1	0	1	0
Kent Mercker	ATL	8.2	5	2	2	1	0	6	2	75
Daniel Miceli	PIT	28.6	2	0	0	0	0	2	0	100
Paul Miller	PIT	7.7	1	0	0	0	0	1	0	100
Blas Minor	PIT	7.4	5	2	1.3	0	2	5	4	55.6
Gino Minutelli	SF	5.6	1	0	10	1	0	2	0	100
Dennis Moeller	PIT	11.8	1	1	6.7	1	0	2	1	66.7
Marcus Moore	COL	3.1	1	0	0	0	0	2	0	100
Mike Morgan	CHN	13.7	17	12	1.4	0	2	17	14	54.8
Terry Mulholland	PHI	3.4	1	5	0	0	0	1	5	16.7
Mike Munoz	COL	6.2	1	0	5	0	1	1	1	50
Rob Murphy	SL	6.2	3	1	0	0	0	3	1	75
Randy Myers	CHN	2.4	1	1	0	0	0	1	1	50
Chris Nabholz	MON	14.8	13	8	3.4	2	1	15	9	62.5
Denny Neagle	PIT	16.5	10	5	10	6	0	16	5	76.2
Robb Nen	FLO	7.3	3	0	3.6	1	0	4	0	100
Rod Nichols	LA	0	0	0	0	0	0	0	0	0
David Nied	COL	12.4	12	1	7.5	4	1	16	2	88.9
Omar Olivares	SL	11.7	12	4	0	0	0	12	5	70.6
Donovan Osborne	SL	6	4	4	1	0	1	4	5	44.4
Al Osuna	HOU	0	0	0	0	0	0	0	0	0
Dave Otto	PIT	7	5	1	5.5	3	0	8	2	80
Lance Painter	COL	13.5	1	4	3.8	1	0	2	4	33.3
Donn Pall	PHI	0	0	0	0	0	0	0	0	0
Jeff Parrett	COL	13.6	9	2	2.8	2	0	11	2	84.6
Mike Perez	SL	13.7	8	2	0	0	0	8	2	80
Mark Petkovsek	PIT	18.8	6	0	2.9	1	0	7	0	100
Dan Plesac	CHN	5.6	2	2	2.3	1	0	3	2	60
Mark Portugal	HOU	7.2	13	3	1.6	1	1	14	4	77.8
Ross Powell	CIN	21.4	2	1	0	0	0	2	1	66.7
Tim Pugh	CIN	12.3	17	6	1.7	2	0	19	7	73.1
Pat Rapp	FLO	7.9	3	5	1.2	0	1	3	6	33.3
Jeff Reardon	CIN	11.1	5	1	1.9	1	0	6	1	85.7
Steve Reed	COL	20.5	8	7	0	0	0	8	7	53.3
Shane Reynolds	HOU	0	0	0	0	0	0	0	0	0
Armando Reynoso	COL	6.4	10	3	0.7	1	0	11	5	68.8
Dave Righetti	SF	5.1	1	2	5.3	0	2	1	4	20
Jose Rijo	CIN	13.4	20	10	1.4	2	0	22	10	68.8
Bill Risley	MON	0	0	0	0	0	0	0	0	0
Ben Rivera	PHI	7.7	14	1	1.6	1	1	15	3	83.3
Rich Robertson	PIT	0	0	0	7.1	1	0	1	0	100
Rich Rodriguez	FLO	5	2	0	0	0	0	2	0	100
Rich Rodriguez	SD	12.1	2	2	4.8	1	0	3	2	60
Kevin Rogers	SF	6.2	4	2	3.4	2	0	6	2	75
Mel Rojas	MON	7.6	6	1	2.7	2	0	8	1	88.9
John Roper	CIN	13.6	10	4	0	0	0	10	4	71.4
Kirk Rueter	MON	13.7	3	7	1.9	1	0	4	7	36.4
Johnny Ruffin	CIN	8.1	3	0	4.2	1	0	4	0	100
Bruce Ruffin	COL	11.8	11	8	3.5	3	1	14	9	60.9
Bret Saberhagen	NYN	12.6	9	7	0	0	0	9	7	56.2
Scott Sanders	SD	11.8	4	4	0	0	0	4	4	50
Scott Sanderson	SF	9.8	2	2	0	0	0	2	2	50
Mo Sanford	COL	16.3	7	1	2.2	1	0	8	1	88.9
Bob Scanlan	CHN	6.9	2	4	4.5	3	0	5	4	55.6
Curt Schilling	PHI	9.1	11	10	0.8	0	1	11	11	50
Pete Schourek	NYN	9.1	9	3	1	1	0	10	4	71.4
Tim Scott	MON	24.2	7	1	3.1	1	0	8	1	88.9
Tim Scott	SD	23.9	10	1	0	0	0	10	1	90.9
Rudy Seanez	SD	0	0	0	0	0	0	0	0	0
Frank Seminara	SD	10.9	3	3	0	0	0	3	3	50
Scott Service	CIN	8.3	2	1	0	0	0	2	1	66.7
Scott Service	COL	0	0	0	0	0	0	0	0	0
Jeff Shaw	MON	7.2	5	2	0	0	0	5	2	71.4
Keith Shepherd	COL	7.1	0	0	0	0	0	0	2	0
Brian Shouse	PIT	0	0	0	0	0	0	0	0	0
Heathcliff Slocumb	CHN	15.4	2	0	0	0	0	2	0	100
John Smiley	CIN	13.3	11	3	3.9	2	1	13	4	76.5
Pete Smith	ATL	15.7	6	8	3.3	2	0	8	8	50
Bryn Smith	COL	9.1	3	1	3.4	1	0	4	1	80
Zane Smith	PIT	9.5	5	2	4	2	0	7	2	77.8
Lee Smith	SL	16.3	6	2	7.4	2	0	8	2	80
John Smoltz	ATL	5.7	10	4	1.9	2	1	12	5	70.6
Jerry Spradlin	CIN	9.1	3	1	3.2	1	0	4	2	66.7
Mike Stanton	ATL	7.6	5	0	2	0	1	5	1	83.3
Bill Swift	SF	10	11	11	0.9	1	0	12	11	52.2
Greg Swindell	HOU	11.6	13	9	2.4	3	0	16	11	59.3
Frank Tanana	NYN	6.9	7	5	5.5	6	1	14	6	70
Kerry Taylor	SD	13.3	10	1	5.6	3	1	13	3	81.2
Dave Telgheder	NYN	9.5	4	3	3.8	0	2	4	5	44.4
Bob Tewksbury	SL	11.2	20	6	0.7	1	0	21	6	77.8
Bobby Thigpen	PHI	8.7	1	1	7.1	1	0	2	1	66.7
Freddie Toliver	PIT	8	2	0	0	0	0	2	0	100
Randy Tomlin	PIT	8.9	3	4	5.8	4	0	7	4	63.6
Solomon Torres	SF	12.5	4	2	3	1	0	5	2	71.4
Steve Trachsel	CHN	12.5	2	0	0	0	0	2	0	100
Ricky Trlicek	LA	10.9	5	1	1.9	1	0	6	1	85.7
Matt Turner	FLO	3.1	1	1	2	0	1	1	2	33.3
Tom Urbani	SL	9.3	1	6	0	0	0	1	6	14.3
Sergio Valdez	MON	50	1	1	0	0	0	1	1	50
Paul Wagner	PIT	14.1	16	6	3.2	2	1	18	7	72
Tim Wakefield	PIT	7.9	7	5	0.9	1	0	8	5	61.5
Bob Walk	PIT	10.7	15	6	2.9	4	0	19	6	76
Bruce Walton	MON	0	0	0	0	0	0	0	0	0
Allen Watson	SL	10.1	7	2	6.8	3	2	11	4	73.3
Gary Wayne	COL	4.4	2	1	1.3	1	0	3	1	75
Dave Weathers	FLO	11.8	6	0	2.4	1	0	7	0	100
Turk Wendell	CHN	4.3	1	0	0	0	0	1	0	100
David West	PHI	8.1	4	3	1.4	1	0	5	3	62.5
Mickey Weston	NYN	9.1	1	0	0	0	0	1	0	100
John Wetteland	MON	13.1	11	2	2.5	2	0	13	2	86.7
Wally Whitehurst	SD	8.9	3	6	0	0	0	3	7	30
Kevin Wickander	CIN	3	1	0	0	0	0	1	1	50
Brian Williams	HOU	7.7	5	2	1.6	1	0	6	2	75
Mike Williams	PHI	15.1	6	2	0	0	0	6	3	66.7
Mitch Williams	PHI	7.6	6	0	5.1	3	0	9	0	100
Steve Wilson	LA	11.8	4	0	4.8	1	0	5	1	83.3
Trevor Wilson	SF	5.2	4	3	1.6	0	1	4	4	50
Mark Wohlers	ATL	6.1	3	0	0	0	0	3	0	100
Todd Worrell	LA	21.7	9	1	0	0	0	9	1	90
Tim Worrell	SD	16.7	9	9	1.5	1	0	10	9	52.6
Pete Young	MON	0	0	0	0	0	0	0	0	0
Anthony Young	NYN	12	13	1	3.7	2	1	15	2	88.2

TEAM PITCHERS	TM	A2%	SB2	CS2	A3%	SB3	CS3	OSB	OCS	SB%
	ATL	9.9	98	46	3	23	6	121	53	69.5
	CHN	9.2	71	64	1.7	12	5	84	69	54.9
	CIN	11.1	116	49	1.8	16	3	134	56	70.5
	COL	9	98	47	2.2	20	6	119	56	68
	FLO	9.6	106	40	2.1	12	11	118	51	69.8
	HOU	9.3	96	36	1.6	12	4	110	42	72.4
	LA	11.4	116	58	1.7	12	6	129	66	66.2
	MON	13.1	146	43	2.8	26	6	172	51	77.1
	NYN	11.3	117	44	3.4	25	11	143	56	71.9
	PHI	8.5	90	41	1.6	11	6	101	49	67.3
	PIT	10.6	113	45	3.5	35	3	148	51	74.4
	SD	11.9	126	59	2	15	7	142	68	67.6
	SF	8.5	70	59	1.8	11	5	81	65	55.5
	SL	10.5	99	50	1.5	12	4	112	55	67.1
LEAGUE PITCHERS	NL	10.2	1462	681	2.2	242	83	1714	788	68.5

CATCHERS

AMERICAN LEAGUE

NAME	TM	A2%	SB2	CS2	A3%	SB3	CS3	OSB	OCS	SB%
Sandy Alomar	CLE	7.9	36	13	1.9	5	3	41	16	71.9
Mike Blowers	SEA	0	0	0	0	0	0	0	0	0
Pat Borders	TOR	11.1	99	47	1.6	9	4	108	53	67.1
Carlos Delgado	TOR	0	0	0	0	0	0	0	0	0
Carlton Fisk	CHA	15.5	20	2	2	2	0	22	2	91.7
John Flaherty	BOS	16.2	8	5	1.5	1	0	9	5	64.3
Larry Gonzales	CAL	0	0	0	0	0	0	0	0	0
Brian Harper	MIN	12.5	101	47	2.2	13	7	114	55	67.5
Bill Haselman	SEA	11.6	27	9	3.8	8	1	35	10	77.8
Eric Helfand	OAK	14.3	3	2	0	0	0	3	2	60
Scott Hemond	OAK	9.1	38	24	3.5	12	3	50	27	64.9
Chris Hoiles	BAL	8.7	56	35	2.6	10	9	67	46	59.3
Chris Howard	SEA	66.7	2	0	0	0	0	2	0	100
Ron Karkovice	CHA	7.5	41	46	2.2	6	8	48	56	46.2
Joe Kmak	MIL	9.3	22	11	3.7	5	3	27	15	64.3
Randy Knorr	TOR	12.2	27	10	0.5	1	0	28	11	71.8
Chad Kreuter	DET	9	51	40	1.3	6	2	57	45	55.9
Tom Lampkin	MIL	10	26	12	1.1	2	1	28	13	68.3
Mike LaValliere	CHA	8.8	8	19	1.5	1	3	8	24	25
Jesse Levis	CLE	11.2	12	7	1	1	0	13	7	65
Jim Leyritz	NYA	8.7	3	1	3.7	1	0	4	1	80
Doug Lindsey	CHA	0	0	0	0	0	0	0	0	0
Steve Lyons	BOS	0	0	0	0	0	0	0	0	0
Mike Macfarlane	KC	11.2	60	47	1.9	10	3	70	53	56.9
Brent Mayne	KC	11.5	44	14	1.9	4	3	48	18	72.7
Tim McIntosh	MIL	0	0	0	0	0	0	0	0	0
Bob Melvin	BOS	7.3	27	7	1.5	4	1	31	8	79.5
Henry Mercedes	OAK	7.9	4	7	2.4	1	1	5	8	38.5
Greg Myers	CAL	11.3	62	23	1.5	5	2	67	27	71.3
Dave Nilsson	MIL	9.1	50	18	2.4	10	4	60	22	73.2
Matt Nokes	NYA	12.7	37	15	4.1	8	2	46	17	73
Junior Ortiz	CLE	9.8	45	30	1.5	2	6	47	39	54.7
John Orton	CAL	8.5	16	7	1.1	1	1	17	9	65.4
Mark Parent	BAL	2.8	4	0	2.9	3	1	7	1	87.5
Derek Parks	MIN	8.2	4	0	0	0	0	4	0	100
Lance Parrish	CLE	20.3	11	4	7	1	2	12	6	66.7
Tony Pena	BOS	8.2	49	25	0.9	3	3	52	31	62.7
Gene Petralli	TEX	12.6	26	14	2.1	4	1	30	15	66.7
Ivan Rodriguez	TEX	8.6	55	44	1.9	8	7	64	51	55.7
Rich Rowland	DET	8.1	7	3	2.9	2	0	9	3	75
John Russell	TEX	6.1	1	1	0	0	0	1	1	50
Nelson Santovenia	KC	4.8	1	0	0	0	0	1	0	100
Mackey Sasser	SEA	6.2	0	1	0	0	0	0	1	0
Mike Stanley	NYA	7.3	54	24	2.2	10	5	65	29	69.1
Terry Steinbach	OAK	9.8	53	29	1.9	8	3	62	34	64.6
B.J. Surhoff	MIL	9.1	0	1	0	0	0	0	1	0

NAME	TM	A2%	SB2	CS2	A3%	SB3	CS3	OSB	OCS	SB%
Jeff Tackett	BAL	11.6	16	16	4.3	6	1	22	17	56.4
Mickey Tettleton	DET	8.7	32	9	1.2	4	0	36	9	80
Ron Tingley	CAL	6.5	12	10	1.9	3	1	15	11	57.7
Chris Turner	CAL	13.1	21	5	1.3	2	0	23	5	82.1
Dave Valle	SEA	9.4	54	51	2	13	3	68	57	54.4
Lenny Webster	MIN	8.9	17	9	1.6	2	1	19	11	63.3
Rick Wrona	CHA	10.7	3	0	7.7	1	0	4	0	100
TEAM CATCHERS	BAL	8.7	76	51	2.9	19	11	96	64	60
	BOS	8.4	84	37	1.1	8	4	92	44	67.6
	CAL	10	111	45	1.4	11	4	122	52	70.1
	CHA	8.4	72	67	2.1	9	11	82	82	50
	CLE	9.7	104	54	1.8	9	11	113	68	62.4
	DET	8.9	90	52	1.4	12	2	102	57	64.2
	KC	11.2	105	61	1.9	14	6	119	71	62.6
	MIL	9.4	98	42	2.3	17	8	115	51	69.3
	MIN	11.6	122	56	2	15	8	137	66	67.5
	NYA	8.8	94	40	2.7	19	7	115	47	71
	OAK	9.5	98	62	2.6	21	7	120	71	62.8
	SEA	9.9	83	61	2.4	21	4	105	68	60.7
	TEX	9.4	82	59	1.9	12	8	95	67	58.6
	TOR	11.2	126	57	1.4	10	4	136	64	68
LEAGUE CATCHERS	AL	9.6	1345	744	2	197	95	1549	872	64

CATCHERS

NATIONAL LEAGUE

NAME	TM	A2%	SB2	CS2	A3%	SB3	CS3	OSB	OCS	SB%
Andy Allanson	SF	5.3	1	1	4.5	1	0	2	1	66.7
Brad Ausmus	SD	10.6	27	18	1.5	4	1	31	19	62
Damon Berryhill	ATL	9.8	49	26	2.9	13	2	62	28	68.9
Phil Clark	SD	8.8	2	1	0	0	0	2	1	66.7
Craig Colbert	SF	5.5	1	2	2.6	1	0	2	2	50
Darren Daulton	PHI	8.7	78	39	1.7	11	4	89	45	66.4
Steve Decker	FLO	14.7	4	1	0	0	0	4	1	80
Brian Dorsett	CIN	7.9	8	3	1	1	0	9	3	75
Darrin Fletcher	MON	11.9	85	21	2.5	14	3	99	26	79.2
Bob Geren	SD	13	33	15	3.3	6	3	39	19	67.2
Joe Girardi	COL	9.7	52	25	2.3	11	3	64	29	68.8
Jerry Goff	PIT	9.9	6	4	1.6	1	0	7	4	63.6
Carlos Hernandez	LA	9.6	17	5	2.8	4	1	21	7	75
Kevin Higgins	SD	11	38	15	1.8	4	1	43	16	72.9
Todd Hundley	NYN	11.6	82	27	3.2	18	5	101	33	75.4
Steve Lake	CHN	5.8	8	11	0.8	1	1	10	12	45.5
Tim Laker	MON	11.8	24	5	2.5	4	1	28	6	82.4
Mike LaValliere	PIT	9.1	1	0	0	0	0	1	0	100
Doug Lindsey	PHI	0	0	0	0	0	0	0	0	0
Javier Lopez	ATL	9.1	3	1	5	0	1	3	2	60
Mitch Lyden	FLO	10	1	0	0	0	0	1	0	100
Kirt Manwaring	SF	8.2	52	44	2	8	5	60	50	54.5
Terry McGriff	FLO	0	0	0	0	0	0	0	0	0
Tim McIntosh	MON	0	0	0	0	0	0	0	0	0
Jeff McKnight	NYN	0	0	0	0	0	0	0	0	0
Jim McNamara	SF	7.1	1	0	0	0	0	1	0	100
Bobby Natal	FLO	9.6	18	9	2.9	5	2	23	11	67.6
Charlie O'Brien	NYN	10.9	35	17	3.9	9	6	42	23	64.6
Joe Oliver	CIN	11.5	87	44	1.7	11	2	100	50	66.7
Greg Olson	ATL	10	46	19	3.1	10	3	56	23	70.9
Jayhawk Owens	COL	9.1	16	9	1.6	2	1	18	11	62.1
Tom Pagnozzi	SL	9.5	50	28	1.4	7	1	58	30	65.9
Erik Pappas	SL	11.1	33	17	1.8	4	3	37	20	64.9
Mike Piazza	LA	11.7	99	53	1.5	8	5	108	59	64.7
Todd Pratt	PHI	7.3	12	2	1.3	0	2	12	4	75
Tom Prince	PIT	11.3	42	14	3.7	12	3	54	17	76.1
Jeff Reed	SF	10.9	15	12	0.6	1	0	16	12	57.1
Marc Ronan	SL	0	0	0	0	0	0	0	0	0

NAME	TM	A2%	SB2	CS2	A3%	SB3	CS3	OSB	OCS	SB%
Benito Santiago	FLO	9.6	83	30	1.9	7	9	90	39	69.8
Scott Servais	HOU	10.1	48	15	2.1	7	2	56	18	75.7
Danny Sheaffer	COL	7.8	29	13	2.1	7	1	36	15	70.6
Joe Siddall	.MON	14.5	5	3	1.9	1	0	6	3	66.7
Don Slaught	PIT	10.3	64	27	3.7	22	1	86	30	74.1
Tim Spehr	MON	19.3	32	14	4.5	7	2	39	16	70.9
Ed Taubensee	HOU	8.8	46	19	1.1	4	2	51	22	69.9
Eddie Tucker	HOU	6.8	2	2	1.9	1	0	3	2	60
Hector Villanueva	SL	18.3	16	5	1.1	1	0	17	5	77.3
Matt Walbeck	CHN	13.1	7	1	2.3	1	0	8	1	88.9
Dan Walters	SD	14.8	26	10	1.4	1	2	27	13	67.5
Eric Wedge	COL	8.3	1	0	25	0	1	1	1	50
Rick Wilkins	CHN	10	56	52	1.9	10	4	66	56	54.1
Dan Wilson	CIN	11	21	2	3.2	4	1	25	3	89.3
TEAM CATCHERS	ATL	9.9	98	46	3	23	6	121	53	69.5
	CHN	9.2	71	64	1.7	12	5	84	69	54.9
	CIN	11.1	116	49	1.8	16	3	134	56	70.5
	COL	9	98	47	2.2	20	6	119	56	68
	FLO	9.6	106	40	2.1	12	11	118	51	69.8
	HOU	9.3	96	36	1.6	12	4	110	42	72.4
	LA	11.4	116	58	1.7	12	6	129	66	66.2
	MON	13.1	146	43	2.8	26	6	172	51	77.1
	NYN	11.3	117	44	3.4	25	11	143	56	71.9
	PHI	8.5	90	41	1.6	11	6	101	49	67.3
	PIT	10.6	113	45	3.5	35	3	148	51	74.4
	SD	11.9	126	59	2	15	7	142	68	67.6
	SF	8.5	70	59	1.8	11	5	81	65	55.5
	SL	10.5	99	50	1.5	12	4	112	55	67.1
LEAGUE CATCHERS	NL	10.2	1462	681	2.2	242	83	1714	788	68.5

RUNNERS

AMERICAN LEAGUE

NAME	TM	A2%	SB2	CS2	A3%	SB3	CS3	SB	CS	SB%
Kurt Abbott	OAK	12.5	2	0	0	0	0	2	0	100
Mike Aldrete	OAK	2.5	1	1	0	0	0	1	1	50
Manny Alexander	BAL	0	0	0	0	0	0	0	0	0
Sandy Alomar	CLE	6	3	0	4.2	0	1	3	1	75
Roberto Alomar	TOR	24.8	40	10	12.9	15	5	55	15	78.6
Rich Amaral	SEA	21.8	18	9	3.2	1	2	19	11	63.3
Brady Anderson	BAL	18.4	20	12	2.9	4	0	24	12	66.7
Marcos Armas	OAK	9.1	1	0	0	0	0	1	0	100
Wally Backman	SEA	0	0	0	0	0	0	0	0	0
Carlos Baerga	CLE	8.1	13	3	1.8	1	1	15	4	78.9
Harold Baines	BAL	0	0	0	0	0	0	0	0	0
Steve Balboni	TEX	0	0	0	0	0	0	0	0	0
Skeeter Barnes	DET	14.9	4	3	11.1	1	2	5	5	50
Daniel Bautista	DET	25	3	1	0	0	0	3	1	75
Rich Becker	MIN	40	1	1	0	0	0	1	1	50
George Bell	CHA	4.3	1	1	0	0	0	1	1	50
Juan Bell	MIL	12	5	6	1.7	1	0	6	6	50
Albert Belle	CLE	18.6	21	9	3.6	2	2	23	12	65.7
Lance Blankenship	OAK	18.9	12	5	1.7	1	0	13	5	72.2
Greg Blosser	BOS	20	1	0	0	0	0	1	0	100
Mike Blowers	SEA	6.7	1	5	0	0	0	1	5	16.7
Wade Boggs	NYA	0.5	0	1	0	0	0	0	1	0
Bret Boone	SEA	7.2	2	3	0	0	0	2	3	40
Pat Borders	TOR	3.5	2	2	0	0	0	2	2	50
Mike Bordick	OAK	10.4	9	9	1.7	1	1	10	10	50
George Brett	KC	9.8	7	5	0	0	0	7	5	58.3
Bernardo Brito	MIN	0	0	0	0	0	0	0	0	0
Hubie Brooks	KC	0	0	0	0	0	0	0	0	0
Scott Brosius	OAK	8	4	0	4.4	2	0	6	0	100
Kevin Brown	TEX	0	0	0	0	0	0	0	0	0
Jerry Browne	OAK	5.2	4	0	0	0	0	4	0	100
J.T. Bruett	MIN	0	0	0	0	0	0	0	0	0
Tom Brunansky	MIL	11.6	1	4	6.9	2	0	3	4	42.9
Damon Buford	BAL	12.5	2	2	0	0	0	2	2	50
Jay Buhner	SEA	3.6	2	4	1	0	0	2	5	28.6
Ellis Burks	CHA	8.7	5	7	1.2	0	0	6	9	40
Randy Bush	MIN	0	0	0	0	0	0	0	0	0
Rob Butler	TOR	14.8	2	2	0	0	0	2	2	50
Jim Byrd	BOS	0	0	0	0	0	0	0	0	0

NAME	TM	A2%	SB2	CS2	A3%	SB3	CS3	SB	CS	SB%
Ivan Calderon	BOS	8.1	3	2	0	0	0	4	2	66.7
Ivan Calderon	CHA	0	0	0	0	0	0	0	0	0
Willie Canate	TOR	10	1	1	0	0	0	1	1	50
Jose Canseco	TEX	16	6	2	6.8	0	3	6	6	50
Paul Carey	BAL	0	0	0	0	0	0	0	0	0
Joe Carter	TOR	7.9	6	3	1.9	2	0	8	3	72.7
Domingo Cedeno	TOR	11.1	1	0	0	0	0	1	0	100
Darnell Coles	TOR	0	0	0	4.9	1	1	1	1	50
Scott Cooper	BOS	3.9	4	2	1.2	1	0	5	2	71.4
Joey Cora	CHA	13.4	18	7	2.3	2	1	20	8	71.4
Rod Correia	CAL	8.5	1	3	5.4	1	1	2	4	33.3
Henry Cotto	SEA	24	4	2	17.6	1	2	5	4	55.6
Chad Curtis	CAL	25	38	20	10.6	10	4	48	24	66.7
Milt Cuyler	DET	21.3	11	2	4.2	2	0	13	2	86.7
Doug Dascenzo	TEX	3.2	1	0	3.2	1	0	2	0	100
Glenn Davis	BAL	4.3	0	1	0	0	0	0	1	0
Chili Davis	CAL	4.4	4	1	0	0	0	4	1	80
Eric Davis	DET	20	2	2	0	0	0	2	2	50
Butch Davis	TEX	14.8	3	1	0	0	0	3	1	75
Andre Dawson	BOS	3.5	2	1	0	0	0	2	1	66.7
Rob Deer	BOS	6.5	2	0	0	0	0	2	0	100
Rob Deer	DET	4.9	3	1	2.4	0	1	3	2	60
Carlos Delgado	TOR	0	0	0	0	0	0	0	0	0
Mike Devereaux	BAL	3.9	3	2	1.1	0	1	3	3	50
Alex Diaz	MIL	36.4	5	3	0	0	0	5	3	62.5
Mario Diaz	TEX	2	1	0	0	0	0	1	0	100
Gary DiSarcina	CAL	9.9	4	6	3.2	1	1	5	7	41.7
Bill Doran	MIL	7.7	1	0	0	0	0	1	0	100
Rob Ducey	TEX	17.9	2	3	0	0	0	2	3	40
Damion Easley	CAL	15.3	6	5	1.8	0	1	6	6	50
Jim Edmonds	CAL	15.4	2	0	0	0	0	2	0	0
Alvaro Espinoza	CLE	5.6	2	2	0	0	0	2	2	50
Mike Felder	SEA	24.4	14	7	5.1	1	2	15	9	62.5
Felix Fermin	CLE	6.2	3	5	1.4	1	0	4	5	44.4
Tony Fernandez	TOR	25	14	6	5.3	1	2	15	8	65.2
Cecil Fielder	DET	0.7	0	1	0	0	0	0	1	0
Carlton Fisk	CHA	7.7	0	1	0	0	0	0	1	0
John Flaherty	BOS	0	0	0	0	0	0	0	0	0
Scott Fletcher	BOS	10.3	13	2	2.7	3	1	16	3	84.2
Eric Fox	OAK	20	0	2	0	0	0	0	2	0
Julio Franco	TEX	8	8	3	0.9	1	0	9	3	75
Travis Fryman	DET	6.7	9	2	1.6	0	2	9	4	69.2
Gary Gaetti	CAL	33.3	1	0	0	0	0	1	0	100
Gary Gaetti	KC	3.1	0	2	2.4	0	1	0	3	0
Greg Gagne	KC	14.4	9	11	1.8	1	1	10	12	45.5
Mike Gallego	NYA	3.5	3	1	1.2	0	1	3	2	60
Brent Gates	OAK	5.4	7	2	0.9	0	1	7	3	70
Kirk Gibson	DET	14	11	5	7.9	4	1	15	6	71.4
Benji Gil	TEX	25	1	2	0	0	0	1	2	33.3
Dan Gladden	DET	16.7	8	5	0	0	0	8	5	61.5
Leo Gomez	BAL	1.8	0	1	0	0	0	0	1	0
Chris Gomez	DET	11.5	2	1	4.2	0	1	2	2	50
Larry Gonzales	CAL	0	0	0	0	0	0	0	0	0
Rene Gonzales	CAL	5.7	4	3	1.6	1	0	5	5	50
Juan Gonzalez	TEX	3.6	4	1	0	0	0	4	1	80
Craig Grebeck	CHA	5.2	1	2	0	0	0	1	2	33.3
Shawn Green	TOR	0	0	0	0	0	0	0	0	0
Mike Greenwell	BOS	4.9	5	3	1	0	1	5	4	55.6
Ken Griffey	SEA	13.8	14	9	2.5	3	0	17	9	65.4
Alfredo Griffin	TOR	0	0	0	0	0	0	0	0	0
Kelly Gruber	CAL	0	0	0	0	0	0	0	0	0
Ozzie Guillen	CHA	7.4	5	4	0	0	0	5	4	55.6
Chris Gwynn	KC	1	0	1	0	0	0	0	1	0
Chip Hale	MIN	4.2	2	1	0	0	0	2	1	66.7
Bob Hamelin	KC	0	0	0	0	0	0	0	0	0
Darryl Hamilton	MIL	16.7	18	11	4.5	3	2	21	13	61.8
Jeffrey Hammonds	BAL	12.5	3	5	1	0	0	4	0	100
Erik Hanson	SEA	0	0	0	0	0	0	0	0	0
Brian Harper	MIN	1.3	1	1	1.1	0	0	1	3	25
Donald Harris	TEX	4.5	1	0	0	0	0	1	0	0
Bill Haselman	SEA	10.3	2	1	0	0	0	2	1	66.7
Billy Hatcher	BOS	14.7	14	7	0	0	0	14	7	66.7
Eric Helfand	OAK	0	0	0	0	0	0	0	0	0
Scott Hemond	OAK	25.4	13	5	1.5	1	0	14	5	73.7
Dave Henderson	OAK	1.6	0	1	3.9	0	0	0	3	0
Rickey Henderson	OAK	17.4	20	5	13	11	1	31	6	83.8

NAME	TM	A2%	SB2	CS2	A3%	SB3	CS3	OSB	OCS	SB%
Rickey Henderson	TOR	29.9	18	2	8.9	4	0	22	2	91.7
Phil Hiatt	KC	15.9	5	2	3.1	1	0	6	3	66.7
Glenallen Hill	CLE	24.1	4	3	11.1	3	0	7	3	70
Denny Hocking	MIN	7.7	1	0	0	0	0	1	0	100
Chris Hoiles	BAL	1.5	1	1	0	0	0	1	1	50
Sam Horn	CLE	0	0	0	0	0	0	0	0	0
Thomas Howard	CLE	5.5	2	1	7.5	3	0	5	1	83.3
David Howard	KC	14.3	1	0	0	0	0	1	0	100
Dann Howitt	SEA	0	0	0	0	0	0	0	0	0
Kent Hrbek	MIN	5.5	4	2	.0	0	0	4	2	66.7
Mike Huff	CHA	7.7	1	0	0	0	0	1	0	100
Tim Hulett	BAL	2.5	0	2	2	1	0	1	2	33.3
David Hulse	TEX	25.4	28	7	3.3	1	2	29	9	76.3
Mike Humphreys	NYA	25	1	1	33.3	1	0	2	1	66.7
Jeff Huson	TEX	0	0	0	0	0	0	0	0	0
Bo Jackson	CHA	3.6	0	2	0	0	0	0	2	0
Darrin Jackson	TOR	7.1	0	2	0	0	0	0	2	0
John Jaha	MIL	14.6	11	7	3.2	2	1	13	9	59.1
Dion James	NYA	0	0	0	0	0	0	0	0	0
Chris James	TEX	0	0	0	0	0	0	0	0	0
Stan Javier	CAL	13.8	10	2	3.2	2	0	12	2	85.7
Reggie Jefferson	CLE	3.1	1	2	0	0	0	1	3	25
Lance Johnson	CHA	20.1	32	6	2.6	3	0	35	7	83.3
Terry Jorgensen	MIN	3.4	1	0	0	0	0	1	0	100
Felix Jose	KC	27.8	26	11	5.2	5	1	31	13	70.5
Wally Joyner	KC	9.2	4	9	0.9	1	0	5	9	35.7
Ron Karkovice	CHA	4.4	2	2	0	0	0	2	2	50
Pat Kelly	NYA	23.4	13	9	4.1	1	2	14	11	56
Wayne Kirby	CLE	12.1	13	4	6.1	4	1	17	5	77.3
Joe Kmak	MIL	21.2	5	2	4.5	1	0	6	2	75
Chuck Knoblauch	MIN	18.5	26	10	3.1	3	1	29	11	72.5
Randy Knorr	TOR	0	0	0	0	0	0	0	0	0
Kevin Koslofski	KC	10	0	1	0	0	0	0	1	0
Chad Kreuter	DET	2.8	2	1	0	0	0	2	1	66.7
Tom Lampkin	MIL	18.8	7	2	2.9	0	1	7	3	70
Gene Larkin	MIN	2.7	0	1	0	0	0	0	1	0
Mike LaValliere	CHA	3.8	0	1	0	0	0	0	1	0
Derek Lee	MIN	0	0	0	0	0	0	0	0	0
Manuel Lee	TEX	8.8	2	4	0	0	0	2	4	33.3
Scott Leius	MIN	0	0	0	0	0	0	0	0	0
Mark Leonard	BAL	0	0	0	0	0	0	0	0	0
Jesse Levis	CLE	0	0	0	0	0	0	0	0	0
Mark Lewis	CLE	15.4	2	0	8.3	1	0	3	0	100
Jim Leyritz	NYA	0	0	0	0	0	0	0	0	0
Jose Lind	KC	2.7	2	1	2.9	1	1	3	2	60
Pat Listach	MIL	21.2	16	8	4.3	2	1	18	9	66.7
Greg Litton	SEA	2	0	1	0	0	0	0	1	0
Scott Livingstone	DET	3.6	1	2	0	0	0	1	3	25
Kenny Lofton	CLE	29.9	61	11	7.6	9	3	70	14	83.3
Torri Lovullo	CAL	10.9	6	5	3	1	1	7	6	53.8
Scott Lydy	OAK	3.8	1	0	4.8	1	0	2	0	100
Steve Lyons	BOS	15.4	0	2	11.1	1	0	1	2	33.3
Kevin Maas	NYA	5.4	1	1	0	0	0	1	1	50
Mike Macfarlane	KC	6	2	4	1.4	0	0	2	5	28.6
Shane Mack	MIN	13.4	14	5	0.9	1	0	15	5	75
Dave Magadan	SEA	2.4	2	0	0	0	0	2	0	100
Mike Maksudian	MIN	0	0	0	0	0	0	0	0	0
Candy Maldonado	CLE	6.7	0	1	0	0	0	0	1	0
Paco Martin	CHA	0	0	0	0	0	0	0	0	0
Chito Martinez	BAL	0	0	0	0	0	0	0	0	0
Carlos Martinez	CLE	1.4	0	1	2.4	1	0	1	1	50
Edgar Martinez	SEA	0	0	0	0	0	0	0	0	0
Tino Martinez	SEA	1.9	0	2	1.4	0	1	0	3	0
Domingo Martinez	TOR	0	0	0	0	0	0	0	0	0
Don Mattingly	NYA	0	0	0	0	0	0	0	0	0
Brent Mayne	KC	10.2	3	2	0	0	0	3	2	60
David McCarty	MIN	10.5	2	6	0	0	0	2	6	25
Mark McGwire	OAK	4	0	1	0	0	0	0	1	0
Mark McLemore	BAL	17.9	19	14	2.3	2	1	21	15	58.3
Jeff McNeely	BOS	33.3	6	0	0	0	0	6	0	100
Brian McRae	KC	18.5	21	13	2.3	2	1	23	14	62.2
Kevin McReynolds	KC	3.3	2	1	0	0	0	2	2	50
Pat Meares	MIN	9.5	4	4	1.8	0	1	4	5	44.4
Bob Melvin	BOS	0	0	0	0	0	0	0	0	0
Luis Mercedes	BAL	20	1	1	0	0	0	1	1	50
Henry Mercedes	OAK	16.7	1	1	0	0	0	1	1	50
Hensley Meulens	NYA	8.3	0	1	0	0	0	0	1	0

NAME	TM	A2%	SB2	CS2	A3%	SB3	CS3	OSB	OCS	SB%
Matt Mieske	MIL	5	0	1	10	0	0	1	2	0
Keith Miller	KC	10.7	2	1	8.3	1	0	3	1	75
Randy Milligan	CLE	0	0	0	0	0	0	0	0	0
Paul Molitor	TOR	10.5	20	4	0.7	1	0	22	4	84.6
Pedro Munoz	MIN	5	1	2	0	0	0	1	2	33.3
Greg Myers	CAL	8.8	3	3	0	0	0	3	3	50
Tim Naehring	BOS	2.4	1	0	0	0	0	1	0	100
Troy Neel	OAK	5.9	3	5	0	0	0	3	5	37.5
Marc Newfield	SEA	6.7	0	1	0	0	0	0	1	0
Warren Newson	CHA	0	0	0	0	0	0	0	0	0
Dave Nilsson	MIL	11.5	3	6	0	0	0	3	6	33.3
Matt Nokes	NYA	0	0	0	0	0	0	0	0	0
Pete O'Brien	SEA	0	0	0	0	0	0	0	0	0
Troy O'Leary	MIL	0	0	0	0	0	0	0	0	0
Paul O'Neill	NYA	5.1	2	4	0	0	0	2	4	33.3
Sherman Obando	BAL	0	0	0	0	0	0	0	0	0
John Olerud	TOR	1	0	2	0	0	0	0	2	0
Luis Ortiz	BOS	0	0	0	0	0	0	0	0	0
Junior Ortiz	CLE	1.9	1	0	0	0	0	1	0	100
John Orton	CAL	16.7	1	2	0	0	0	1	2	33.3
Spike Owen	NYA	4.2	2	2	1.5	1	0	3	2	60
Mike Pagliarulo	BAL	0	0	0	0	0	0	0	0	0
Mike Pagliarulo	MIN	13.9	5	5	1.9	1	0	6	6	50
Rafael Palmeiro	TEX	12.6	18	2	4.2	4	1	22	3	88
Dean Palmer	TEX	16.7	11	10	0	0	0	11	10	52.4
Craig Paquette	OAK	9.8	4	1	1.7	0	1	4	2	66.7
Mark Parent	BAL	0	0	0	0	0	0	0	0	0
Derek Parks	MIN	0	0	0	0	0	0	0	0	0
Lance Parrish	CLE	20	1	0	0	0	0	1	0	100
Dan Pasqua	CHA	8.1	2	1	0	0	0	2	2	50
Dan Peltier	TEX	3.7	0	2	6.2	2	0	2	4	0
Tony Pena	BOS	6.5	1	3	0	0	0	1	3	25
Eduardo Perez	CAL	17.9	5	2	4.5	0	1	5	4	55.6
Gene Petralli	TEX	4.4	2	0	0	0	0	2	0	100
Tony Phillips	DET	8.3	13	10	2.2	3	1	16	11	59.3
Greg Pirkl	SEA	0	0	0	0	0	0	0	0	0
Luis Polonia	CAL	37	46	21	8.8	9	2	55	24	69.6
Kirby Puckett	MIN	9.9	8	6	0	0	0	8	6	57.1
Harvey Pulliam	KC	0	0	0	0	0	0	0	0	0
Carlos Quintana	BOS	0	0	0	0	0	0	1	0	100
Tim Raines	CHA	19.2	21	7	0	0	0	21	7	75
Manny Ramirez	CLE	0	0	0	0	0	0	0	0	0
Jeff Reboulet	MIN	10.5	4	5	1.5	1	0	5	5	50
Gary Redus	TEX	14	4	3	2.6	0	1	4	4	50
Kevin Reimer	MIL	7.6	5	3	1.5	0	1	5	4	55.6
Harold Reynolds	BAL	14	11	11	1.1	1	0	12	11	52.2
Jeff Richardson	BOS	0	0	0	0	0	0	0	0	0
Ernie Riles	BOS	10	1	2	0	0	0	1	3	25
Cal Ripken	BAL	3	1	4	0	0	0	1	4	20
Billy Ripken	TEX	5.9	0	2	0	0	0	0	2	0
Luis Rivera	BOS	5.7	0	2	4	1	0	1	2	33.3
Ivan Rodriguez	TEX	12	7	6	2.2	1	1	8	7	53.3
Rico Rossy	KC	0	0	0	0	0	0	0	0	0
Rich Rowland	DET	0	0	0	0	0	0	0	0	0
John Russell	TEX	0	0	0	0	0	0	0	0	0
Tim Salmon	CAL	4.7	4	4	3.4	1	2	5	6	45.5
Nelson Santovenia	KC	0	0	0	0	0	0	0	0	0
Mackey Sasser	SEA	2.6	1	0	0	0	0	1	0	100
Steve Sax	CHA	17.8	6	2	6.5	1	1	7	3	70
Dick Schofield	TOR	7.3	3	0	0	0	0	3	0	100
David Segui	BAL	1.4	2	0	1	0	1	2	1	66.7
Kevin Seitzer	MIL	6.2	3	0	0	0	0	3	0	100
Kevin Seitzer	OAK	14.1	3	7	2.2	1	0	4	7	36.4
Jon Shave	TEX	25	0	3	25	1	0	1	3	25
Larry Sheets	SEA	0	0	0	0	0	0	0	0	0
Terry Shumpert	KC	50	1	0	0	0	0	1	0	100
Ruben Sierra	OAK	19.1	22	4	4.1	3	1	25	5	83.3
Dave Silvestri	NYA	0	0	0	0	0	0	0	0	0
Lonnie Smith	BAL	0	0	0	0	0	0	0	0	0
J.T. Snow	CAL	2.6	3	0	0	0	0	3	0	100
Luis Sojo	TOR	0	0	0	0	0	0	0	0	0
Paul Sorrento	CLE	2.5	0	3	0	0	0	3	1	75
Bill Spiers	MIL	13.9	7	8	4.7	0	0	9	8	52.9
Ed Sprague	TOR	0.9	1	0	0	0	0	1	0	100
Scott Stahoviak	MIN	22.2	0	2	0	0	0	0	2	0
Andy Stankiewicz	NYA	0	0	0	0	0	0	0	0	0

NAME	TM	A2%	SB2	CS2	A3%	SB3	CS3	OSB	OCS	SB%
Mike Stanley	NYA	0.8	1	0	1.2	0	1	1	1	50
Terry Steinbach	OAK	4.5	3	2	0	0	0	3	3	50
Kurt Stillwell	CAL	14.3	2	0	0	0	0	2	0	100
Doug Strange	TEX	6.8	6	3	0	0	0	6	4	60
William Suero	MIL	0	0	0	0	0	0	0	1	0
B.J. Surhoff	MIL	7.4	5	6	6	6	1	12	9	57.1
Dale Sveum	OAK	0	0	0	0	0	0	0	0	0
Jeff Tackett	BAL	0	0	0	0	0	0	0	0	0
Dan Tartabull	NYA	0	0	0	0	0	0	0	0	0
Mickey Tettleton	DET	4.6	2	5	2.8	1	1	3	7	30
Frank Thomas	CHA	3.1	4	2	0	0	0	4	2	66.7
Jim Thome	CLE	3.5	2	0	0	0	0	2	1	66.7
Dickie Thon	MIL	13.1	5	3	2.8	1	0	6	5	54.5
Gary Thurman	DET	10	5	0	6.1	2	0	7	0	100
Ron Tingley	CAL	11.5	1	2	0	0	0	1	2	33.3
Lee Tinsley	SEA	0	0	0	0	0	0	0	0	0
Alan Trammell	DET	14	11	7	2.4	1	1	12	8	60
Jeff Treadway	CLE	3.5	1	1	0	0	0	1	1	50
Brian Turang	SEA	15	5	1	5.7	1	1	6	2	75
Chris Turner	CAL	7.4	1	1	0	0	0	1	1	50
John Valentin	BOS	6	3	4	0	0	0	3	4	42.9
Jose Valentin	MIL	7.1	1	0	0	0	0	1	0	100
Dave Valle	SEA	0	0	0	1.4	1	0	1	0	100
Ty VanBurkleo	CAL	11.1	1	0	0	0	0	1	0	100
Mo Vaughn	BOS	5.1	4	3	0	0	0	4	3	57.1
Greg Vaughn	MIL	9.8	10	4	0	0	0	10	7	58.8
Randy Velarde	NYA	8	2	2	0	0	0	2	2	50
Robin Ventura	CHA	3.7	1	6	0	0	0	1	6	14.3
Fernando Vina	SEA	33.3	6	0	0	0	0	6	0	100
Omar Vizquel	SEA	13.6	11	13	1.8	1	1	12	14	46.2
Jack Voigt	BAL	2	1	0	0	0	0	1	0	100
Jim Walewander	CAL	12.5	1	0	20	0	1	1	1	50
Jerome Walton	CAL	20	1	0	0	0	0	1	0	100
Turner Ward	TOR	14.6	3	3	0	0	0	3	3	50
Lenny Webster	MIN	2.6	1	0	0	0	0	1	0	100
Lou Whitaker	DET	3.8	3	3	0	0	0	3	3	50
Devon White	TOR	22.2	30	4	2.7	4	0	34	4	89.5
Curt Wilkerson	KC	33.3	2	0	0	0	0	2	0	100
Bernie Williams	NYA	11.3	8	9	0.9	1	0	9	9	50
Gerald Williams	NYA	7.7	1	0	0	0	0	2	0	100
Craig Wilson	KC	9.1	1	1	0	0	0	1	1	50
Dave Winfield	MIN	3.8	2	3	0	0	0	2	3	40
Robin Yount	MIL	7.2	7	2	2.2	2	0	9	2	81.8
Bob Zupcic	BOS	8.8	5	2	0	0	0	5	2	71.4
TEAM RUNNERS	BAL	7.3	64	51	1.1	9	3	73	54	57.5
	BOS	6.9	65	35	0.7	6	1	73	38	65.8
	CAL	14.2	143	82	4.1	26	14	169	100	62.8
	CHA	9.6	99	51	0.9	6	3	106	57	65
	CLE	10.8	133	43	3.1	25	8	159	55	74.3
	DET	8.2	90	51	2.1	14	10	104	63	62.3
	KC	10.7	88	65	1.7	12	6	100	75	57.1
	MIL	12.4	115	76	3	22	8	138	93	59.7
	MIN	8.8	77	54	0.9	6	3	83	59	58.5
	NYA	4.1	34	31	0.8	4	4	39	35	52.7
	OAK	10.4	110	51	2.6	21	7	131	59	68.9
	SEA	9.1	82	58	1.8	9	10	91	68	57.2
	TEX	11	104	55	1.8	9	10	113	67	62.8
	TOR	11.6	141	41	3.1	28	8	170	49	77.6
LEAGUE RUNNERS	AL	9.6	1345	744	2	197	95	1549	872	64

RUNNERS

NATIONAL LEAGUE

NAME	TM	A2%	SB2	CS2	A3%	SB3	CS3	SB	CS	SB%
Luis Alicea	SL	8.5	11	0	1.2	0	1	11	1	91.7
Andy Allanson	SF	0	0	0	0	0	0	0	0	0
Moises Alou	MON	18.8	16	6	1.4	1	0	17	6	73.9
Ruben Amaro	PHI	0	0	0	0	0	0	0	0	0
Larry Andersen	PHI	0	0	0	0	0	0	0	0	0
Eric Anthony	HOU	5	3	4	1.1	0	1	3	5	37.5
Luis Aquino	FLO	0	0	0	0	0	0	0	0	0
Alex Arias	FLO	2.1	1	1	0	0	0	1	1	50

NAME	TM	A2%	SB2	CS2	A3%	SB3	CS3	OSB	OCS	SB%
Jack Armstrong	FLO	0	0	0	0	0	0	0	0	0
Rene Arocha	SL	0	0	0	0	0	0	0	0	0
Andy Ashby	COL	0	0	0	0	0	0	0	0	0
Andy Ashby	SD	0	0	0	0	0	0	0	0	0
Billy Ashley	LA	0	0	0	0	0	0	0	0	0
Paul Assenmacher	CHN	0	0	0	0	0	0	0	0	0
Pedro Astacio	LA	0	0	0	0	0	0	0	0	0
Rich Aude	PIT	0	0	0	0	0	0	0	1	0
Brad Ausmus	SD	3.3	1	0	3.7	1	0	2	0	100
Steve Avery	ATL	0	0	0	0	0	0	0	0	0
Bobby Ayala	CIN	100	0	1	0	0	0	0	1	0
Kevin Baez	NYN	0	0	0	0	0	0	0	0	0
Jeff Bagwell	HOU	10.1	11	4	1	1	0	13	4	76.5
Jeff Ballard	PIT	0	0	0	0	0	0	0	0	0
Bret Barberie	FLO	4.5	2	4	0	0	0	2	4	33.3
Brian Barnes	MON	0	0	0	0	0	0	0	0	0
Kevin Bass	HOU	13.6	7	1	0	0	0	7	1	87.5
Kim Batiste	PHI	0	0	0	3.6	0	1	0	1	0
Jose Bautista	CHN	0	0	0	0	0	0	0	0	0
Bill Bean	SD	13.3	2	4	0	0	0	2	4	33.3
Tim Belcher	CIN	9.1	0	1	0	0	0	0	1	0
Juan Bell	PHI	5.3	0	1	0	0	0	0	1	0
Jay Bell	PIT	9.3	12	8	3.7	4	1	16	10	61.5
Derek Bell	SD	17.4	18	5	8.2	7	0	26	5	83.9
Rafael Belliard	ATL	0	0	0	0	0	0	0	0	0
Freddie Benavides	COL	6.2	3	1	0	0	0	3	2	60
Andy Benes	SD	0	0	0	0	0	0	0	0	0
Mike Benjamin	SF	0	0	0	0	0	0	0	0	0
Todd Benzinger	SF	0	0	0	0	0	0	0	0	0
Geronimo Berroa	FLO	0	0	0	0	0	0	0	0	0
Sean Berry	MON	14.1	11	2	1.6	1	0	12	2	85.7
Damon Berryhill	ATL	0	0	0	0	0	0	0	0	0
Dante Bichette	COL	13.7	10	8	3.2	3	0	14	8	63.6
Craig Biggio	HOU	13.1	10	13	5.8	5	3	15	17	46.9
Buddy Black	SF	0	0	0	0	0	0	0	0	0
Willie Blair	COL	0	0	0	0	0	0	0	0	0
Jeff Blauser	ATL	8.1	15	4	1.3	1	1	16	6	72.7
Tim Bogar	NYN	0	0	0	2.6	0	1	0	1	0
Frank Bolick	MON	2.4	1	0	0	0	0	1	0	100
Barry Bonds	SF	22.8	21	12	6.6	8	0	29	12	70.7
Bobby Bonilla	NYN	3.3	3	2	1.3	0	1	3	3	50
Shawn Boskie	CHN	0	0	0	0	0	0	0	0	0
Daryl Boston	COL	11.7	1	6	0	0	0	1	6	14.3
Kent Bottenfield	COL	0	0	0	20	1	0	1	0	100
Kent Bottenfield	MON	0	0	0	0	0	0	0	0	0
Denis Boucher	MON	0	0	0	0	0	0	0	0	0
Rafael Bournigal	LA	0	0	0	0	0	0	0	0	0
Ryan Bowen	FLO	0	0	0	0	0	0	0	0	0
Jeff Branson	CIN	4	3	1	1.4	1	0	4	1	80
Jeff Brantley	SF	0	0	0	0	0	0	0	0	0
Sid Bream	ATL	8	4	2	0	0	0	4	2	66.7
Rod Brewer	SL	2.3	1	0	0	0	0	1	0	100
Greg Briley	FLO	20.6	6	1	2.3	0	1	6	2	75
Doug Brocail	SD	33.3	2	0	0	0	0	2	0	100
Jerry Brooks	LA	0	0	0	0	0	0	0	0	0
Jarvis Brown	SD	12.8	3	3	0	0	0	3	3	50
Tom Browning	CIN	0	0	0	0	0	0	0	0	0
Jacob Brumfield	CIN	25.9	13	8	10.6	7	0	20	8	71.4
Mike Brumley	HOU	33.3	0	1	0	0	0	0	1	0
Steve Buechele	CHN	1.6	1	1	0	0	0	1	1	50
Scott Bullett	PIT	33.3	2	2	11.1	1	0	3	2	60
Dave Burba	SF	0	0	0	0	0	0	0	0	0
John Burkett	SF	0	0	0	0	0	0	0	0	0
Jeromy Burnitz	NYN	12.7	3	5	2.7	0	1	3	6	33.3
Todd Burns	SL	0	0	0	0	0	0	0	0	0
Brett Butler	LA	20.3	30	17	6.5	9	2	39	19	67.2
Francisco Cabrera	ATL	0	0	0	0	0	0	0	0	0
Ken Caminiti	HOU	7.7	6	5	2	2	0	8	5	61.5
Casey Candaele	HOU	12.5	2	3	0	0	0	2	3	40
Tom Candiotti	LA	0	0	0	0	0	0	0	0	0
Ozzie Canseco	SL	0	0	0	0	0	0	0	0	0
Ramon Caraballo	ATL	0	0	0	0	0	0	0	0	0
Chuck Carr	FLO	45.1	54	19	5.6	4	3	58	22	72.5
Mark Carreon	SF	2.2	1	0	0	0	0	1	0	100
Matias Carrillo	FLO	0	0	0	0	0	0	0	0	0
Pedro Castellano	COL	10.5	1	1	0	0	0	1	1	50
Vinny Castilla	COL	6.2	2	3	2.5	0	1	2	5	28.6
Frank Castillo	CHN	0	0	0	0	0	0	0	0	0

NAME	TM	A2%	SB2	CS2	A3%	SB3	CS3	OSB	OCS	SB%
Andujar Cedeno	HOU	10.2	8	7	1.1	1	0	9	7	56.2
Wes Chamberlain	PHI	5.5	2	1	0	0	0	2	1	66.7
Archi Cianfrocco	MON	0	0	0	0	0	0	0	0	0
Archi Cianfrocco	SD	3.2	2	0	0	0	0	2	0	100
Jerald Clark	COL	11.6	7	6	2.7	2	0	9	6	60
Dave Clark	PIT	1.4	1	0	0	0	0	1	0	100
Phil Clark	SD	3	2	0	0	0	0	2	0	100
Will Clark	SF	2.5	2	2	0	0	0	2	2	50
Royce Clayton	SF	12	10	9	1.9	1	1	11	10	52.4
Craig Colbert	SF	0	0	0	0	0	0	0	0	0
Greg Colbrunn	MON	14.3	4	2	0	0	0	4	2	66.7
Alex Cole	COL	30.9	23	11	14.5	7	2	30	13	69.8
Vince Coleman	NYN	39.8	33	10	10.1	5	3	38	13	74.5
Jeff Conine	FLO	1.6	1	2	1	1	0	2	2	50
Steve Cooke	PIT	0	0	0	0	0	0	0	0	0
Wil Cordero	MON	12.8	11	3	0.9	1	0	12	3	80
Rheal Cormier	SL	0	0	0	0	0	0	0	0	0
Tim Costo	CIN	0	0	0	0	0	0	0	0	0
Henry Cotto	FLO	31.4	11	1	3.4	0	1	11	1	91.7
Tripp Cromer	SL	0	0	0	0	0	0	0	0	0
Midre Cummings	PIT	0	0	0	0	0	0	0	0	0
Jack Daugherty	CIN	0	0	0	0	0	0	0	0	0
Jack Daugherty	HOU	0	0	0	0	0	0	0	0	0
Darren Daulton	PHI	2.1	3	0	1.6	2	0	5	0	100
Eric Davis	LA	32.5	25	2	13.8	8	3	33	5	86.8
Mark Davis	PHI	0	0	0	0	0	0	0	0	0
Steve Decker	FLO	0	0	0	0	0	0	0	0	0
Delino DeShields	MON	24.9	38	7	5.4	5	3	43	10	81.1
Orestes Destrade	FLO	1.5	0	2	0	0	0	0	2	0
Mark Dewey	PIT	0	0	0	0	0	0	0	0	0
Chris Donnels	HOU	5.4	2	0	0	0	0	2	0	100
Brian Dorsett	CIN	0	0	0	0	0	0	0	0	0
Doug Drabek	HOU	0	0	0	0	0	0	0	0	0
Mike Draper	NYN	0	0	0	0	0	0	0	0	0
Mariano Duncan	PHI	8.9	6	5	0	0	0	6	5	54.5
Shawon Dunston	CHN	0	0	0	0	0	0	0	0	0
Lenny Dykstra	PHI	17.8	33	10	3	4	2	37	12	75.5
Dave Eiland	SD	0	0	0	0	0	0	0	0	0
Jim Eisenreich	PHI	5.3	5	0	0	0	0	5	0	100
Cecil Espy	CIN	20	2	2	0	0	0	2	2	50
Carl Everett	FLO	20	1	0	0	0	0	1	0	100
Rikkert Faneyte	SF	0	0	0	0	0	0	0	0	0
Paul Faries	SF	28.6	2	0	0	0	0	2	0	100
Monty Fariss	FLO	0	0	0	0	0	0	0	0	0
Jeff Fassero	MON	0	0	0	0	0	0	0	0	0
Junior Felix	FLO	3.6	1	1	2.9	1	0	2	1	66.7
Sid Fernandez	NYN	0	0	0	0	0	0	0	0	0
Tony Fernandez	NYN	14.8	6	2	0	0	0	6	2	75
Steve Finley	HOU	12.1	16	4	4.1	3	1	19	6	76
Darrin Fletcher	MON	0	0	0	0	0	0	0	0	0
Cliff Floyd	MON	0	0	0	0	0	0	0	0	0
Tom Foley	PIT	0	0	0	0	0	0	0	0	0
Lou Frazier	MON	25.8	14	2	5.3	3	0	17	2	89.5
Jay Gainer	COL	20	1	1	0	0	0	1	1	50
Andres Galarraga	COL	3.1	2	2	0	0	0	2	4	33.3
Dave Gallagher	NYN	3.2	1	1	0	0	0	1	1	50
Ron Gant	ATL	21.4	24	9	2.3	2	0	26	9	74.3
Carlos Garcia	PIT	18.6	16	11	1.9	2	0	18	11	62.1
Mike Gardiner	MON	0	0	0	0	0	0	0	0	0
Jeff Gardner	SD	4.9	2	5	1.1	0	1	2	6	25
Bob Geren	SD	0	0	0	0	0	0	0	0	0
Bernard Gilkey	SL	15	14	10	0.8	1	0	15	10	60
Joe Girardi	COL	9.5	5	5	3.2	1	1	6	6	50
Tom Glavine	ATL	0	0	0	0	0	0	0	0	0
Jerry Goff	PIT	0	0	0	0	0	0	0	0	0
Luis Gonzalez	HOU	17.3	18	8	1.6	1	1	20	9	69
Dwight Gooden	NYN	0	0	0	0	0	0	0	0	0
Tom Goodwin	LA	17.6	1	2	0	0	0	1	2	33.3
Keith Gordon	CIN	0	0	0	0	0	0	0	0	0
Mark Grace	CHN	5.8	8	4	0	0	0	8	4	66.7
Willie Greene	CIN	0	0	0	0	0	0	0	0	0
Tommy Greene	PHI	0	0	0	0	0	0	0	0	0
Marquis Grissom	MON	26.7	42	6	9.9	11	4	53	10	84.1
Kevin Gross	LA	0	0	0	0	0	0	0	0	0
Lee Guetterman	SL	0	0	0	0	0	0	0	0	0
Ricky Gutierrez	SD	2.7	2	2	2.5	1	1	4	3	57.1
Jose Guzman	CHN	0	0	0	0	0	0	0	0	0
Tony Gwynn	SD	7.5	11	1	2.5	3	0	14	1	93.3
Chris Hammond	FLO	0	0	0	0	0	0	0	0	0
Dave Hansen	LA	0	0	0	6.7	0	1	0	1	0
Mike Harkey	CHN	0	0	0	0	0	0	0	0	0
Pete Harnisch	HOU	0	0	0	0	0	0	0	0	0
Lenny Harris	LA	6.7	3	0	2.8	0	1	3	1	75
Greg Harris	SD	0	0	0	0	0	0	0	0	0
Charlie Hayes	COL	9.5	8	5	2	2	0	11	6	64.7
Butch Henry	COL	0	0	0	0	0	0	0	0	0
Gil Heredia	MON	0	0	0	0	0	0	0	0	0
Cesar Hernandez	CIN	27.3	1	2	0	0	0	1	2	33.3
Carlos Hernandez	LA	0	0	0	0	0	0	0	0	0
Orel Hershiser	LA	4.5	0	1	0	0	0	0	1	0
Greg Hibbard	CHN	0	0	0	0	0	0	0	0	0
Bryan Hickerson	SF	0	0	0	0	0	0	0	0	0
Kevin Higgins	SD	1.9	0	1	0	0	0	0	1	0
Glenallen Hill	CHN	5.3	1	0	0	0	0	1	0	100
Ken Hill	MON	0	0	0	0	0	0	0	0	0
Eric Hillman	NYN	14.3	0	1	0	0	0	0	1	0
Dave Hollins	PHI	3.1	2	3	0	0	0	2	3	40
Steve Hosey	SF	0	0	0	0	0	0	0	0	0
Charlie Hough	FLO	0	0	0	0	0	0	0	0	0
Wayne Housie	NYN	0	0	0	0	0	0	0	0	0
Thomas Howard	CIN	28.6	5	5	3.8	0	1	5	6	45.5
Todd Hundley	NYN	2.7	1	1	0	0	0	1	1	50
Brian Hunter	ATL	0	0	0	0	0	0	0	0	0
Butch Huskey	NYN	0	0	0	0	0	0	0	0	0
Pete Incaviglia	PHI	2.5	1	1	0	0	0	1	1	50
Darrin Jackson	NYN	0	0	0	0	0	0	0	0	0
Danny Jackson	PHI	0	0	0	0	0	0	0	0	0
Michael Jackson	SF	0	0	0	0	0	0	0	0	0
Chris James	HOU	5.3	1	0	6.2	1	0	2	0	100
Gregg Jefferies	SL	27.9	41	7	4.4	5	2	46	9	83.6
Doug Jennings	CHN	0	0	0	0	0	0	0	0	0
Howard Johnson	NYN	12.7	4	4	4.9	2	0	6	4	60
Erik Johnson	SF	0	0	0	0	0	0	0	0	0
Joel Johnston	PIT	0	0	0	0	0	0	0	0	0
Chipper Jones	ATL	0	0	0	0	0	0	0	0	0
Chris Jones	COL	28.3	9	4	0	0	0	9	4	69.2
Jimmy Jones	MON	0	0	0	0	0	0	0	0	0
Bobby Jones	NYN	0	0	0	0	0	0	0	0	0
Tim Jones	SL	12.9	2	2	0	0	0	2	2	50
Ricky Jordan	PHI	0	0	0	0	0	0	0	0	0
Brian Jordan	SL	21.2	6	5	3.1	0	1	6	6	50
Dave Justice	ATL	5.3	3	5	0	0	0	3	5	37.5
Eric Karros	LA	0.8	0	1	0	0	0	0	1	0
Bobby Kelly	CIN	20.3	12	3	14.9	9	2	21	5	80.8
Jeff Kent	NYN	6.2	4	3	0	0	0	4	4	50
Keith Kessinger	CIN	0	0	0	0	0	0	0	0	0
Darryl Kile	HOU	0	0	0	0	0	0	0	0	0
Jeff King	PIT	6.3	6	5	1.9	2	1	8	6	57.1
Ryan Klesko	ATL	0	0	0	0	0	0	0	0	0
Brian Koelling	CIN	0	0	0	0	0	0	0	0	0
John Kruk	PHI	3.9	6	2	0	0	0	6	2	75
Steve Lake	CHN	0	0	0	0	0	0	0	0	0
Tim Laker	MON	9.5	2	0	0	0	0	2	0	100
Lester Lancaster	SL	0	0	0	0	0	0	0	0	0
Bill Landrum	CIN	0	0	0	0	0	0	0	0	0
Ced Landrum	NYN	0	0	0	0	0	0	0	0	0
Ray Lankford	SL	19.2	12	12	2.3	2	0	14	14	50
Mike Lansing	MON	15.7	20	4	2.3	2	1	23	5	82.1
Barry Larkin	CIN	10.3	11	1	4	3	0	14	1	93.3
Mike LaValliere	PIT	0	0	0	0	0	0	0	0	0
Mark Lemke	ATL	2.3	1	2	0	0	0	1	2	33.3
Curt Leskanic	COL	0	0	0	0	0	0	0	0	0
Darren Lewis	SF	34	35	14	9.4	11	1	46	15	75.4
Jim Lindeman	HOU	0	0	0	0	0	0	0	0	0
Doug Lindsey	PHI	0	0	0	0	0	0	0	0	0
Nelson Liriano	COL	17.9	6	4	0	0	0	6	4	60
Tony Longmire	PHI	0	0	0	0	0	0	0	0	0
Javier Lopez	ATL	0	0	0	0	0	0	0	0	0
Luis Lopez	SD	0	0	0	0	0	0	0	0	0
Larry Luebbers	CIN	0	0	0	0	0	0	0	0	0
Mitch Lyden	FLO	0	0	0	0	0	0	0	0	0

NAME	TM	A2%	SB2	CS2	A3%	SB3	CS3	OSB	OCS	SB%
Lonnie Maclin	SL	14.3	1	0	0	0	0	1	0	100
Greg Maddux	ATL	0	0	0	0	0	0	0	0	0
Dave Magadan	FLO	1.1	0	1	0	0	0	0	1	0
Joe Magrane	SL	0	0	0	0	0	0	0	0	0
Candy Maldonado	CHN	0	0	0	0	0	0	0	0	0
Jeff Manto	PHI	0	0	0	0	0	0	0	0	0
Kirt Manwaring	SF	2.8	1	3	0	0	0	1	3	25
Oreste Marrero	MON	11.1	1	1	0	0	0	1	3	25
Al Martin	PIT	15.3	12	7	5.4	4	1	16	9	64
Ramon Martinez	LA	0	0	0	0	0	0	0	0	0
Dennis Martinez	MON	0	0	0	0	0	0	0	0	0
Dave Martinez	SF	12	4	2	5.6	2	1	6	3	66.7
Roger Mason	PHI	0	0	0	0	0	0	0	0	0
Roger Mason	SD	0	0	0	0	0	0	0	0	0
Tim Mauser	PHI	0	0	0	0	0	0	0	0	0
Tim Mauser	SD	0	0	0	0	0	0	0	0	0
Derrick May	CHN	10.1	10	3	0	0	0	10	3	76.9
Lloyd McClendon	PIT	4.1	0	2	3.8	0	1	0	3	0
Roger McDowell	LA	0	0	0	0	0	0	0	0	0
Willie McGee	SF	13.3	10	8	1	0	1	10	9	52.6
Fred McGriff	ATL	1.4	1	0	0	0	0	1	0	100
Terry McGriff	FLO	0	0	0	0	0	0	0	0	0
Fred McGriff	SD	7.4	2	3	4.3	2	0	4	3	57.1
Tim McIntosh	MON	0	0	0	0	0	0	0	0	0
Jeff McKnight	NYN	0	0	0	0	0	0	0	0	0
Greg McMichael	ATL	0	0	0	0	0	0	0	0	0
Jim McNamara	SF	0	0	0	0	0	0	0	0	0
Roberto Mejia	COL	10	3	1	2.6	1	0	4	1	80
Orlando Merced	PIT	3	3	2	0	0	0	3	3	50
Luis Mercedes	SF	11.1	0	1	0	0	0	0	1	0
Joe Millette	PHI	0	0	0	0	0	0	0	0	0
Randy Milligan	CIN	2.3	0	2	0	0	0	0	2	0
Blas Minor	PIT	0	0	0	0	0	0	0	0	0
Kevin Mitchell	CIN	1.4	1	0	0	0	0	1	0	100
Raul Mondesi	LA	17.4	3	1	5	1	0	4	1	80
Charlie Montoyo	MON	0	0	0	0	0	0	0	0	0
Mickey Morandini	PHI	14.1	11	2	2.3	2	0	13	2	86.7
Mike Morgan	CHN	0	0	0	0	0	0	0	0	0
Hal Morris	CIN	3.1	2	2	0	0	0	2	2	50
Terry Mulholland	PHI	0	0	0	0	0	0	0	0	0
Dale Murphy	COL	0	0	0	0	0	0	0	0	0
Eddie Murray	NYN	1.9	1	2	1.1	1	0	2	2	50
Randy Myers	CHN	0	0	0	0	0	0	0	0	0
Chris Nabholz	MON	0	0	0	0	0	0	0	0	0
Bobby Natal	FLO	3.4	1	0	0	0	0	1	0	100
Tito Navarro	NYN	0	0	0	0	0	0	0	0	0
David Nied	COL	0	0	0	0	0	0	0	0	0
Melvin Nieves	SD	0	0	0	0	0	0	0	0	0
Otis Nixon	ATL	26.7	40	11	6.1	7	2	47	13	78.3
Charlie O'Brien	NYN	4.2	1	1	0	0	0	1	1	50
Jose Offerman	LA	20.9	28	13	1.8	2	0	30	13	69.8
Omar Olivares	SL	0	0	0	0	0	0	0	0	0
Joe Oliver	CIN	0	0	0	0	0	0	0	0	0
Greg Olson	ATL	1.4	1	0	0	0	0	1	0	100
Jose Oquendo	SL	0	0	0	0	0	0	0	0	0
Joe Orsulak	NYN	7.2	5	4	0	0	0	5	4	55.6
Donovan Osborne	SL	0	0	0	0	0	0	0	0	0
Dave Otto	PIT	0	0	0	0	0	0	0	0	0
Jayhawk Owens	COL	4.5	1	0	0	0	0	1	0	100
Tom Pagnozzi	SL	1.4	1	0	0	0	0	1	0	100
Lance Painter	COL	0	0	0	0	0	0	0	0	0
Erik Pappas	SL	3.4	1	2	2.4	0	1	1	3	25
Rich Parker	HOU	13.6	1	2	0	0	0	1	2	33.3
Jeff Parrett	COL	0	0	0	0	0	0	0	0	0
John Patterson	SF	25	0	1	0	0	0	0	1	0
Bill Pecota	ATL	5.9	1	1	0	0	0	1	1	50
Geronimo Pena	SL	20.3	9	5	7.8	4	0	13	5	72.2
Terry Pendleton	ATL	3.8	5	1	0	0	0	5	1	83.3
Will Pennyfeather	PIT	0	0	0	0	0	0	0	1	0
Mike Perez	SL	0	0	0	0	0	0	0	0	0
Gerald Perry	SL	6.7	1	1	0	0	0	1	1	50
J.R. Phillips	SF	0	0	0	0	0	0	0	0	0
Mike Piazza	LA	3.6	2	4	0.9	1	0	3	4	42.9
Phil Plantier	SD	5.8	3	4	0	0	0	4	4	50
Gus Polidor	FLO	0	0	0	0	0	0	0	0	0
Mark Portugal	HOU	0	0	0	0	0	0	0	0	0
Scott Pose	FLO	14.3	0	2	0	0	0	0	2	0
Todd Pratt	PHI	0	0	0	0	0	0	0	0	0
Curtis Pride	MON	100	1	0	0	0	0	1	0	100
Tom Prince	PIT	3.1	0	1	3.6	1	0	1	1	50
Tim Pugh	CIN	0	0	0	0	0	0	0	0	0
Pat Rapp	FLO	0	0	0	0	0	0	0	0	0
Randy Ready	MON	4.9	1	1	0	0	0	2	1	66.7
Jody Reed	LA	3.1	1	3	0	0	0	1	3	25
Jeff Reed	SF	2.5	0	1	0	0	0	0	1	0
Rich Renteria	FLO	1.4	0	1	1.8	0	1	0	2	0
Shane Reynolds	HOU	0	0	0	0	0	0	0	0	0
Armando Reynoso	COL	0	0	0	0	0	0	0	0	0
Karl Rhodes	CHN	11.8	2	0	0	0	0	2	0	100
Jose Rijo	CIN	0	0	0	0	0	0	0	0	0
Ben Rivera	PHI	0	0	0	0	0	0	0	0	0
Kevin Roberson	CHN	3.2	0	1	0	0	0	0	1	0
Bip Roberts	CIN	30.9	24	6	2.2	2	0	26	6	81.2
Henry Rodriguez	LA	3.7	1	0	0	0	0	1	0	100
Mel Rojas	MON	0	0	0	0	0	0	0	0	0
Marc Ronan	SL	0	0	0	0	0	0	0	0	0
John Roper	CIN	0	0	0	0	0	0	0	0	0
Stan Royer	SL	10	0	1	0	0	0	0	1	0
Kirk Rueter	MON	0	0	0	0	0	0	0	0	0
Bruce Ruffin	COL	0	0	0	0	0	0	0	0	0
Bret Saberhagen	NYN	0	0	0	0	0	0	0	0	0
Chris Sabo	CIN	6.5	5	3	2.2	1	1	6	4	60
Juan Samuel	CIN	17.1	7	5	4.4	2	2	9	7	56.2
Rey Sanchez	CHN	1.8	1	1	0	0	0	1	1	50
Ryne Sandberg	CHN	7.3	9	2	0	0	0	9	2	81.8
Deion Sanders	ATL	36.8	19	6	1.7	0	1	19	7	73.1
Reggie Sanders	CIN	23.4	23	7	7.7	4	3	27	10	73
Scott Sanders	SD	0	0	0	0	0	0	0	0	0
Scott Sanderson	SF	0	0	0	0	0	0	0	0	0
Mo Sanford	COL	0	0	0	0	0	0	0	0	0
Benito Santiago	FLO	12.1	7	7	5	3	0	10	7	58.8
Doug Saunders	NYN	0	0	0	0	0	0	0	0	0
Bob Scanlan	CHN	0	0	0	0	0	0	0	0	0
Steve Scarsone	SF	4.3	0	1	0	0	0	0	1	0
Curt Schilling	PHI	0	0	0	0	0	0	0	0	0
Pete Schourek	NYN	0	0	0	0	0	0	0	0	0
Frank Seminara	SD	0	0	0	0	0	0	0	0	0
Scott Servais	HOU	0	0	0	0	0	0	0	0	0
Mike Sharperson	LA	10	2	0	0	0	0	2	0	100
Jeff Shaw	MON	0	0	0	0	0	0	0	0	0
Danny Sheaffer	COL	8.6	2	3	0	0	0	2	3	40
Gary Sheffield	FLO	20.8	12	4	0	0	0	12	4	75
Gary Sheffield	SD	7.9	5	0	2.7	1	1	5	1	83.3
Ben Shelton	PIT	0	0	0	0	0	0	0	0	0
Darrell Sherman	SD	16.7	2	1	0	0	0	2	1	66.7
Tommy Shields	CHN	0	0	0	0	0	0	0	0	0
Craig Shipley	SD	17.5	8	2	8.9	4	0	12	3	80
Joe Siddall	MON	0	0	0	0	0	0	0	0	0
Don Slaught	PIT	2.2	1	1	1.3	1	0	2	1	66.7
John Smiley	CIN	0	0	0	0	0	0	0	0	0
Pete Smith	ATL	0	0	0	0	0	0	0	0	0
Dwight Smith	CHN	12.9	7	5	3.4	1	1	8	6	57.1
Bryn Smith	COL	50	1	0	0	0	0	1	0	100
Zane Smith	PIT	0	0	0	0	0	0	0	0	0
Lonnie Smith	PIT	15.9	9	4	0	0	0	9	4	69.2
Ozzie Smith	SL	12.7	14	8	5.4	7	0	21	8	72.4
John Smoltz	ATL	14.3	1	1	0	0	0	1	1	50
Cory Snyder	LA	3.1	3	1	1.3	1	0	4	1	80
Sammy Sosa	CHN	34.8	31	9	6.2	5	2	36	11	76.6
Tim Spehr	MON	8.3	2	0	0	0	0	2	0	100
Matt Stairs	MON	0	0	0	0	0	0	0	0	0
Dave Staton	SD	0	0	0	0	0	0	0	0	0
Kurt Stillwell	SD	20.6	4	3	0	0	0	4	3	57.1
Kevin Stocker	PHI	4.9	4	0	1.3	1	0	5	0	100
Darryl Strawberry	LA	5	1	0	0	0	0	1	0	100
Bill Swift	SF	0	0	0	0	0	0	0	0	0
Greg Swindell	HOU	0	0	0	0	0	0	0	0	0
Frank Tanana	NYN	7.7	0	1	0	0	0	0	1	0
Tony Tarasco	ATL	11.1	0	1	0	0	0	0	1	0
Jim Tatum	COL	0	0	0	0	0	0	0	0	0
Ed Taubensee	HOU	1.4	1	0	0	0	0	1	0	100
Dave Telgheder	NYN	0	0	0	0	0	0	0	0	0
Tim Teufel	SD	7.5	1	2	3.1	1	0	2	2	50
Bob Tewksbury	SL	0	0	0	0	0	0	0	0	0
Ryan Thompson	NYN	11.8	2	6	0	0	0	2	7	22.2
Milt Thompson	PHI	11.7	9	4	0	0	0	9	4	69.2

NAME	TM	A2%	SB2	CS2	A3%	SB3	CS3	OSB	OCS	SB%
Robbie Thompson	SF	8.2	9	3	2.2	1	1	10	4	71.4
Andy Tomberlin	PIT	0	0	0	0	0	0	0	0	0
Randy Tomlin	PIT	0	0	0	0	0	0	0	0	0
Salomon Torres	SF	0	0	0	0	0	0	0	0	0
Steve Trachsel	CHN	0	0	0	0	0	0	0	0	0
Ricky Trlicek	LA	0	0	0	0	0	0	0	0	0
Greg Tubbs	CIN	10.5	3	1	0	0	0	3	1	75
Eddie Tucker	HOU	0	0	0	0	0	0	0	0	0
Tom Urbani	SL	0	0	0	0	0	0	0	0	0
Jose Uribe	HOU	4.8	1	0	0	0	0	1	0	100
John VanderWal	MON	10.8	6	1	3	0	1	6	3	66.7
Andy Van Slyke	PIT	13	11	2	0	0	0	11	2	84.6
Gary Varsho	CIN	3.6	1	0	0	0	0	1	0	100
Guillermo Velasquez	SD	0	0	0	0	0	0	0	0	0
Hector Villanueva	SL	0	0	0	0	0	0	0	0	0
Jose Vizcaino	CHN	10.4	11	9	0.9	1	0	12	9	57.1
Paul Wagner	PIT	0	0	0	0	0	0	0	0	0
Tim Wakefield	PIT	0	0	0	0	0	0	0	0	0
Matt Walbeck	CHN	0	0	0	0	0	0	0	0	0
Bob Walk	PIT	0	0	0	0	0	0	0	0	0
Larry Walker	MON	21.6	24	3	6.9	4	3	29	7	80.6
Chico Walker	NYN	13	6	0	2.9	1	0	7	0	100
Tim Wallach	LA	0	0	0	2.8	0	2	0	2	0
Dan Walters	SD	0	0	0	0	0	0	0	0	0
Allen Watson	SL	0	0	0	0	0	0	0	0	0
Dave Weathers	FLO	0	0	0	0	0	0	0	0	0
Mitch Webster	LA	17.8	3	5	8.3	1	1	4	6	40
Eric Wedge	COL	0	0	0	0	0	0	0	0	0
John Wehner	PIT	0	0	0	0	0	0	0	0	0
Walt Weiss	FLO	5.2	6	3	1	1	0	7	3	70
Turk Wendell	CHN	0	0	0	0	0	0	0	0	0
David West	PHI	0	0	0	0	0	0	0	0	0
Rondell White	MON	13.6	1	2	0	0	0	1	2	33.3
Derrick White	MON	20	2	0	0	0	0	2	0	100
Wally Whitehurst	SD	0	0	0	0	0	0	0	0	0
Mark Whiten	SL	16.1	14	8	1.2	1	0	15	8	65.2
Darrell Whitmore	FLO	11.4	3	2	4.2	1	0	4	2	66.7

NAME	TM	A2%	SB2	CS2	A3%	SB3	CS3	OSB	OCS	SB%
Rick Wilkins	CHN	2.7	2	1	0	0	0	2	1	66.7
Brian Williams	HOU	0	0	0	0	0	0	0	0	0
Mike Williams	PHI	0	0	0	0	0	0	0	0	0
Matt Williams	SF	2.8	1	2	1.1	0	1	1	3	25
Willie Wilson	CHN	12.3	5	2	4.9	2	0	7	2	77.8
Dan Wilson	CIN	0	0	0	0	0	0	0	0	0
Nigel Wilson	FLO	0	0	0	0	0	0	0	0	0
Glenn Wilson	PIT	0	0	0	0	0	0	0	0	0
Trevor Wilson	SF	16.7	1	0	0	0	0	1	0	100
Tony Womack	PIT	20	2	0	0	0	0	2	0	100
Ted Wood	MON	0	0	0	0	0	0	0	0	0
Tracy Woodson	SL	0	0	0	0	0	0	0	0	0
Tim Worrell	SD	0	0	0	0	0	0	0	0	0
Eric Yelding	CHN	13.9	3	2	0	0	0	3	2	60
Gerald Young	COL	16.7	0	1	0	0	0	0	1	0
Eric Young	COL	30.2	34	15	9.2	8	2	42	19	68.9
Anthony Young	NYN	0	0	0	0	0	0	0	0	0
Kevin Young	PIT	4.1	2	2	0	0	0	2	2	50
Eddie Zambrano	CHN	0	0	0	0	0	0	0	0	0
Todd Zeile	SL	6.3	5	4	0	0	0	5	4	55.6
TEAM RUNNERS	ATL	10.4	115	43	1.3	10	4	125	48	72.3
	CHN	8.6	91	40	1.2	9	3	100	43	69.9
	CIN	11.1	115	50	3.4	27	9	142	59	70.6
	COL	13.7	119	77	3.3	25	6	146	90	61.9
	FLO	10.2	106	50	1.7	11	6	117	56	67.6
	HOU	9.4	87	52	1.9	14	6	103	60	63.2
	LA	10.2	103	50	3.2	23	10	126	61	67.4
	MON	16.1	197	40	3.4	28	12	228	56	80.3
	NYN	8.2	70	43	1.7	9	6	79	51	60.8
	PHI	7	82	29	1	9	3	91	32	74
	PIT	8.1	77	47	1.7	15	4	92	55	62.6
	SD	7.4	70	36	2.3	19	3	92	40	69.7
	SF	10.5	97	59	2.6	23	6	120	65	64.9
	SL	12.6	133	65	2.2	20	5	153	72	68
LEAGUE RUNNERS	NL	10.2	1462	681	2.2	242	83	1714	788	68.5

The Fielding Reports

The fielding reports combine four pieces of information for each player in an easy-to-read matrix. **Positions:** Players are listed alphabetically by team, showing all their positions played (including DH) on one line. **Games Started:** The first number in each column is the number of games the player started at that position. **Games Played:** The number after the slash is the total number of games the player played at that position. **Adjusted Fielding Range (AFR):** If a player played more than 10 games at a position, his AFR is shown after that position. (Range is not calculated for catchers, and it varies too much for small samples of less than 10 games.)

Adjusted Fielding Range is an accurate way of measuring a fielder's performance, since it is based on what really matters for fielders—their ability to position themselves to field batted balls and turn them into outs. Of course, there are many ways to do this: by catching fly balls or line drives; by fielding ground balls and making an unassisted putout; or by fielding grounders and throwing to another player. Only one player can get credit for a ball fielded on each play.

Infielders, especially, get putouts in various ways that have nothing to do with their range and everything to do with their position (e.g., receiving a throw at first base). Traditional ways of measuring fielding range are much less accurate, since they are based simply on putouts, assists or total chances, not on actual balls fielded. For outfielders, the problem with traditional fielding statistics is different, since putouts are clearly related to their range while assists equally clearly are not. Here the problem is that the official fielding statistics add all plays in left, center, and right fields together, giving one total for three different positions. The fielding reports that follow separate each player's defensive statistics in left field, center field, and right field, making meaningful comparisons possible. Note that an outfielder's total games (LF+CF+RF) will frequently be greater than his official games in the outfield, since he may have played more than one outfield position in some games (e.g., starting in center field and moving to right later in the game).

Calculating fielding range begins with crediting a "Ball Fielded" to each player when he is the first to handle a batted ball that results in an out. The player who catches a fly ball or who starts a ground out or double play gets credit for fielding that ball.

The second step is to get a more accurate measure of just how much time a player puts in at a fielding position. While the official fielding statistics tally "Games at Position," these can't be used to determine range accurately (because a player gets credit for one game at position whether he plays the whole game or only the ninth inning). Therefore, to determine the opportunities that a player has to field batted balls, we count the number of balls put into play by opposing batters when he is in the field. A "Ball in Play" is defined as a hit (except for home runs), an error, or an out.

In the third step, "Defensive Equivalent Games" (DEG) are computed for all players by counting the balls put into play while they are on the field and dividing by the league average of balls put into play per game. This compensates for pitching staffs that are above or below league average in hits allowed or strikeouts, thus affecting their fielders' opportunities. A player's fielding range is computed by dividing his balls fielded by his DEG. Then a final adjustment is made in order to get the Adjusted Fielding Range (AFR).

Players on different teams face different numbers of right- and left-handed batters due to the composition of their pitching staff. This can have a substantial effect on range calculations, for right-handed batters hit many more ground balls to shortstop and third base than left-handed batters do. (The converse is true for balls hit to the right side of the infield.) Therefore, each player's range is adjusted to reflect this.

A special report for catchers follows, showing the wild pitches (**WP**) and passed balls (**PB**) they allowed while behind the plate. Because there are relatively few wild pitches and even fewer passed balls, we compute the rates per 162 Games (**WP/162** and **PB/162**) for catchers, based on their defensive equivalent games. Balls put into play are not particularly relevant for catchers, so catchers' DEG are defined simply as their defensive innings behind the plate (**Innings**) divided by nine (**Inn/9**).

Another important aspect of a catcher's defense is his ability to shut down the opponent's running game. This aspect is included in the basestealing reports that precede the fielding reports.

FIELDING REPORT: AMERICAN LEAGUE

BALTIMORE	C	1B	AFR	2B	AFR	3B	AFR	SS	AFR	LF	AFR	CF	AFR	RF	AFR	DH
Manny Alexander	—	—		—		—		—								0/1
Brady Anderson	—	—		—		—		—		123/126	2.13	13/18	2.74	3/3		0/2
Harold Baines	—	—		—		—		—								110/116
Damon Buford	—	—		—		—		—		2/5		19/24	2.84	1/1		0/17
Paul Carey	—	8/9		—		—		—								4/5
Glenn Davis	—	22/22	1.92	—		—		—								7/7
Mike Devereaux	—	—		—		—		—				130/130	2.49			
Leo Gomez	—	—		—		67/70	2.59	—								1/1
Jeffrey Hammonds	—	—		—		—		—		14/14	2.06			8/10	2.18	5/8
Chris Hoiles	117/124	—		—		—		—								2/2
Tim Hulett	—	—		4/4		65/75	2.88	0/8								0/2
Mark Leonard	—	—		—		—		—		2/4						3/3
Chito Martinez	—	—		—		—		—						2/5		1/2
Mark McLemore	—	—		20/25	3.06	3/4		—						120/124	2.38	1/1
Luis Mercedes	—	—		—		—		—						7/8		0/2
Sherman Obando	—	—		—		—		—		0/1				5/7		20/21
Mike Pagliarulo*	—	3/4		—		27/28	2.34	—								
Mark Parent	15/21	—		—		—		—								0/1
Harold Reynolds	—	—		138/141	3.17	—		—								
Cal Ripken	—	—		—		—		162/162	3.33							
David Segui	—	127/144	2.07	—		—		—								0/1
Lonnie Smith	—	—		—		—		—		4/4						4/5
Jeff Tackett	30/3	—		—		—		—								
Jack Voigt	—	2/5		—		0/3		—		17/22	2.15			16/23	2.02	4/9

BOSTON	C	1B	AFR	2B	AFR	3B	AFR	SS	AFR	LF	AFR	CF	AFR	RF	AFR	DH
Greg Blosser	—	—		—		—		—		5/9		—		—		1/1
Jim Byrd	—	—		—		—		—		—		—		—		0/1
Ivan Calderon*	—	—		—		—		—		7/9		2/2		32/39	2.23	15/19
Scott Cooper	—	0/2		—		145/154	2.31	0/1		—		—		—		
Andre Dawson	—	—		—		—		—		—		—		20/20	2.57	97/97
Rob Deer*	—	—		—		—		—		—		—		34/36	2.40	2/2
John Flaherty	10/13	—		—		—		—		—		—		—		
Scott Fletcher	—	—		115/116	3.85	0/1		0/2		—		—		—		1/1
Mike Greenwell	—	—		—		—		—		130/134	2.1	—		—		9/10
Billy Hatcher	—	—		0/2		—		—		—		125/129	2.32	1/2		
Steve Lyons	0/1	0/1		2/9		0/1		—		—		1/6		0/4		0/1
Jeff McNeely	—	—		—		—		—		—		11/13	1.85	—		0/3
Bob Melvin	50/76	0/1		—		—		—		—		—		—		
Tim Naehring	—	—		10/15	2.87	8/9		2/4		—		—		—		10/10
Luis Ortiz	—	—		—		1/5		—		—		—		—		0/3
Tony Pena	102/125	—		—		—		—		—		—		—		0/1
Carlos Quintana	—	32/53	1.94	—		—		—		0/1		—		46/50	2.17	
Jeff Richardson	—	—		4/8		0/1		1/5		—		—		—		
Ernie Riles	—	0/1		13/20	3.79	6/11	1.89	—		—		—		—		8/15
Luis Rivera	—	—		18/27	3.41	2/2		21/27	2.82	—		—		—		0/7
John Valentin	—	—		—		—		138/144	3.64	—		—		—		
Mo Vaughn	—	130/131	1.89	—		—		—		—		—		—		19/19
Bob Zupcic	—	—		—		—		—		20/48	1.72	23/37	2.23	29/54	2.59	0/5

CLEVELAND	C	1B	AFR	2B	AFR	3B	AFR	SS	AFR	LF	AFR	CF	AFR	RF	AFR	DH
Sandy Alomar Jr.	55/64	—		—		—		—		—		—		—		4/4
Carlos Baerga	—	—		148/150	3.42	—		—		—		—		—		9/9
Albert Belle	—	—		—		—		—		149/150	2.21	—		—		9/9
Alvaro Espinoza	—	—		2/2		50/99	2.40	13/35	2.79	—		—		—		
Felix Fermin	—	—		—		—		137/140	2.93	—		—		—		
Glenallen Hill	—	—		—		—		—		8/9		—		23/30	1.86	17/18
Sam Horn	—	—		—		—		—		—		—		—		10/11
Thomas Howard	—	—		—		—		—		2/9		7/11	2.94	20/28	1.99	6/7
Reggie Jefferson	—	13/15	1.96	—		—		—		—		—		—		79/88
Wayne Kirby	—	—		—		—		—		2/2		12/15	2.65	98/113	2.35	0/5
Jesse Levis	16/29	—		—		—		—		—		—		—		
Mark Lewis	—	—		—		—		12/13	3.02	—		—		—		
Kenny Lofton	—	—		—		—		—		—		143/147	2.8	—		
Candy Maldonado	—	—		—		—		—		1/2		—		18/25	1.90	1/2
Carlos Martinez	—	19/22	1.65	—		33/35	2.07	—		—		—		—		19/19
Randy Milligan	—	11/18	1.50	—		—		—		—		—		—		1/1
Junior Ortiz	84/95	—		—		—		—		—		—		—		
Lance Parrish	7/10	—		—		—		—		—		—		—		
Manny Ramirez	—	—		—		—		—		—		—		1/1		12/20
Paul Sorrento	—	119/144	2.00	—		—		—		—		—		2/3		0/1
Jim Thome	—	—		—		45/47	2.22	—		—		—		—		
Jeff Treadway	—	—		12/19	3.86	34/42	2.31	—		—		—		—		4/4

DETROIT

Player	C	1B	AFR	2B	AFR	3B	AFR	SS	AFR	LF	AFR	CF	AFR	RF	AFR	DH
Skeeter Barnes	—	9/27	2.5	1/10	3.42	7/13	3.22	0/2		10/12	2.01	—		4/6		7/13
Danny Bautista	—	—		—		—		—		—		9/9		6/8		—
Milt Cuyler	—	—		—		—		—		—		67/80	2.93	—		—
Eric Davis	—	—		—		—		—		—		17/18	3.06	—		3/5
Rob Deer*	—	—		—		—		—		—		0/2		80/84	2.40	0/4
Cecil Fielder	—	118/119	1.68	—		—		—		—		—		—		35/36
Travis Fryman	—	—		—		68/69	2.25	81/81	3.32	—		—		—		1/1
Kirk Gibson	—	—		—		—		—		0/2		27/30	2.74	—		75/76
Dan Gladden	—	—		—		—		—		67/69	2.21	17/18	2.67	—		1/5
Chris Gomez	—	—		17/17	3.50	—		23/29	3.23	—		—		—		0/1
Chad Kreuter	99/112	0/1		—		—		—		—		—		—		0/2
Scott Livingstone	—	—		—		59/62	2.03	—		—		—		—		27/32
Tony Phillips	—	—		47/51	3.64	1/1		—		61/70	2.11	7/9		27/34	2.56	4/4
Rich Rowland	12/17	—		—		—		—		—		—		—		1/3
Mickey Tettleton	51/56	35/59	1.83	—		—		—		16/18	1.56	—		38/39	1.90	3/4
Gary Thurman	—	—		—		—		—		4/17	1.50	14/21	1.67	7/15	2.52	0/9
Alan Trammell	—	—		—		27/35	2.13	58/63	3.45	4/4		4/4		—		5/6
Lou Whitaker	—	—		97/110	3.64	—		—		—		—		—		—

MILWAUKEE

Player	C	1B	AFR	2B	AFR	3B	AFR	SS	AFR	LF	AFR	CF	AFR	RF	AFR	DH
Juan Bell	—	—		44/47	3.09	—		36/40	3.81	—		0/1		1/2		0/2
Ricky Bones	—	—		—		—		—		—		0/1		—		—
Tom Brunansky	—	—		—		—		—		—		—		56/71	2.45	3/6
Alex Diaz	—	—		—		—		—		1/4		7/12	3.07	7/13	1.96	0/1
Bill Doran	—	2/4		10/17	2.83	—		—		—		—		—		—
Darryl Hamilton	—	—		—		—		—		26/31	2.60	33/49	2.91	64/70	2.57	0/1
John Jaha	—	143/150	2.16	0/1		0/1		—		—		—		—		—
Joe Kmak	37/50	—		—		—		—		—		—		—		—
Tom Lampkin	40/60	—		—		—		—		—		—		0/1		0/1
Pat Listach	—	—		—		—		89/95	3.24	—		3/6		—		—
Tim McIntosh	0/1	—		—		—		—		—		—		—		—
Matt Mieske	—	—		—		—		—		0/1		8/9		12/12	1.88	—
Dave Nilsson	85/91	3/4		—		—		—		—		—		—		4/4
Troy O'Leary	—	—		—		—		—		8/15	2.90	—		3/5		—
Kevin Reimer	—	—		—		—		—		25/28	2.07	—		6/10	3.14	80/83
Kevin Seitzer*	—	6/7	1.78	0/1		30/33	2.28	1/1		—		—		1/1		2/3
Bill Spiers	—	—		92/104	2.84	—		1/4		1/2		0/2		0/4		—
William Suero	—	—		2/8		0/1		—		—		—		—		—
B.J. Surhoff	0/3	4/8		—		116/121	2.51	—		8/12	2.39	—		12/14	1.70	1/1
Dickie Thon	—	—		14/22	2.79	16/25	2.38	19/28	3.12	—		—		—		10/14
Jose Valentin	—	—		—		—		17/19	3.32	—		—		—		—
Greg Vaughn	—	—		—		—		—		93/94	2.27	—		—		58/58
Robin Yount	—	4/7		—		—		—		—		111/114	2.69	—		4/6

NEW YORK

Player	C	1B	AFR	2B	AFR	3B	AFR	SS	AFR	LF	AFR	CF	AFR	RF	AFR	DH
Wade Boggs	—	—		—		129/134	2.66	—		—		—		—		8/8
Mike Gallego	—	—		41/52	3.70	24/27	2.73	46/55	3.68	—		—		—		—
Mike Humphreys	—	—		—		—		—		2/11	1.84	1/5		4/7		0/3
Dion James	—	0/1		—		—		—		71/91	1.85	12/14	1.32	0/1		0/1
Pat Kelly	—	—		119/125	3.51	—		—		—		—		—		—
Jim Leyritz	3/12	24/29	2.36	—		—		—		5/6		—		21/23	1.71	19/21
Kevin Maas	—	11/17	1.96	—		—		—		—		—		—		29/31
Don Mattingly	—	126/130	2.04	—		—		—		—		—		—		5/5
Hensley Meulens	—	1/3		—		0/1		—		14/23	2.09	—		0/1		11/11
Matt Nokes	47/56	—		—		—		—		—		—		—		1/2
Paul O'Neill	—	—		—		—		—		40/46	1.70	—		81/103	1.82	1/2
Spike Owen	—	—		—		—		88/96	3.59	—		—		—		0/2
Dave Silvestri	—	—		—		3/3		4/4		—		—		—		—
Andy Stankiewicz	—	—		2/6		1/4		0/1		—		—		—		0/1
Mike Stanley	112/122	—		—		—		—		—		—		—		1/2
Danny Tartabull	—	—		—		—		—		—		—		49/50	1.76	88/88
Randy Velarde	—	—		—		5/16	3.34	24/26	3.01	30/48	2.22	2/2		—		0/1
Bernie Williams	—	—		—		—		—		—		139/139	2.67	—		—
Gerald Williams	—	—		—		—		—		0/10	0.73	8/17	3.09	7/12	1.12	—

TORONTO	C	1B	AFR	2B	AFR	3B	AFR	SS	AFR	LF	AFR	CF	AFR	RF	AFR	DH
Roberto Alomar	—	—		151/151	3.27	—		—		—		—		—		—
Pat Borders	134/138	—		—		—		—		—		—		—		—
Rob Butler	—	—		—		—		—		11/15	2.82	1/1		—		—
Willie Canate	—	—		—		—		—		4/17	2.01	4/6		2/9		0/1
Joe Carter	—	—		—		—		—		55/55	1.89	—		96/96	2.16	3/3
Domingo Cedeno	—	—		3/5		—		8/10	3.6	—		—		—		—
Darnell Coles	—	0/1		—		12/16	2.11	—		26/31	1.74	—		13/13	2.20	1/1
Carlos Delgado	0/1	—		—		—		—		—		—		—		0/1
Tony Fernandez	—	—		—		—		94/94	3.79	—		—		—		—
Shawn Green	—	—		—		—		—		—		—		0/2		1/1
Alfredo Griffin	—	—		5/11	3.23	0/6		18/20	2.80	—		—		—		—
Rickey Henderson*	—	—		—		—		—		44/44	2.09	—		—		—
Darrin Jackson	—	—		—		—		—		—		10/10	1.81	36/37	1.97	—
Randy Knorr	28/39	—		—		—		—		—		—		—		—
Domingo Martinez	—	2/7		—		0/1		—		—		—		—		—
Paul Molitor	—	23/23	2.35	—		—		—		—		—		—		137/137
John Olerud	—	137/137	2.04	—		—		—		—		—		—		20/20
Dick Schofield	—	—		—		—		34/36	3.81	—		—		—		—
Luis Sojo	—	—		3/8		0/3		8/8		—		—		—		—
Ed Sprague	—	—		—		150/150	2.41	—		—		—		—		—
Turner Ward	—	0/1		—		—		—		22/33	2.11	3/10	2.92	15/22	1.67	—
Devon White	—	—		—		—		—		—		144/145	2.90	—		—

CALIFORNIA	C	1B	AFR	2B	AFR	3B	AFR	SS	AFR	LF	AFR	CF	AFR	RF	AFR	DH
Rod Correia	—	—		10/11	3.76	0/3		33/40	3.99	—		—		—		0/6
Chad Curtis	—	—		0/3		—		—		—		150/151	2.80	—		—
Chili Davis	—	—		—		—		—		—		—		—		150/150
Gary DiSarcina	—	—		—		—		124/126	3.19	—		—		—		—
Damion Easley	—	—		54/54	2.79	14/14	2.60	—		—		—		—		0/1
Jim Edmonds	—	—		—		—		—		1/1		1/1		14/15	2.65	—
Gary Gaetti*	—	5/6	1.80	—		1/7		—		—		—		—		5/5
Larry Gonzales	0/2	—		—		—		—		—		—		—		—
Rene Gonzales	—	19/31	1.96	3/4		73/79	2.48	0/5		—		—		—		1/1
Kelly Gruber	—	—		—		17/17	3.20	—		—		—		—		—
Stan Javier	—	8/12	1.57	0/2		—		—		25/36	1.78	11/16	2.07	7/16	2.54	0/1
Torey Lovullo	—	0/1		79/91	2.95	12/14	3.14	0/9		—		—		0/2		—
Greg Myers	72/97	—		—		—		—		—		—		—		2/2
John Orton	33/35	—		—		—		—		0/1		—		—		—
Eduardo Perez	—	—		—		45/45	2.27	—		—		—		—		0/3
Luis Polonia	—	—		—		—		—		135/141	2.29	—		—		3/4
Tim Salmon	—	—		—		—		—		—		0/1		141/141	2.35	1/1
J.T. Snow	—	119/129	1.91	—		—		—		—		—		—		—
Kurt Stillwell	—	—		15/18	3.92	—		3/7		—		—		—		—
Ron Tingley	34/57	—		—		—		—		—		—		—		—
Chris Turner	23/25	—		—		—		—		—		—		—		—
Ty VanBurkleo	—	11/12	2.85	—		—		—		—		—		—		—
Jim Walewander	—	—		1/2		—		2/6		—		—		—		0/3
Jerome Walton	—	—		—		—		—		1/1		—		—		0/4

CHICAGO	C	1B	AFR	2B	AFR	3B	AFR	SS	AFR	LF	AFR	CF	AFR	RF	AFR	DH
George Bell	—	—		—		—		—		—		—		—		102/102
Ellis Burks	—	—		—		—		—		—		20/21	2.68	113/132	2.35	—
Ivan Calderon*	—	—		—		—		—		—		—		—		5/6
Joey Cora	—	—		145/151	3.37	1/3		—		—		—		—		—
Drew Denson	—	0/3		—		—		—		—		—		—		—
Carlton Fisk	13/25	—		—		—		—		—		—		—		—
Craig Grebeck	—	—		15/16	4.26	6/14	2.62	34/46	3.26	—		—		—		—
Ozzie Guillen	—	—		—		—		128/133	3.21	—		—		—		—
Mike Huff	—	—		—		—		—		0/31	2.66	6/8		0/7		—
Bo Jackson	—	—		—		—		—		27/28	2.59	—		18/19	1.79	32/36
Lance Johnson	—	—		—		—		—		—		136/146	3.14	—		—
Ron Karkovice	118/127	—		—		—		—		—		—		—		—
Mike LaValliere	29/37	—		—		—		—		—		—		—		—
Doug Lindsey	0/2	—		—		—		—		—		—		—		—
Norberto Martin	—	—		2/5		—		—		—		—		—		0/1
Matt Merullo	—	—		—		—		—		—		—		—		5/6
Warren Newson	—	—		—		—		—		1/2		—		1/3		7/10
Dan Pasqua	—	13/32	2.16	—		—		—		10/11	1.98	—		26/26	1.97	4/6
Tim Raines	—	—		—		—		—		102/112	2.04	—		—		3/21
Steve Sax	—	—		0/1		—		—		22/26	1.73	—		4/6		4/4
Frank Thomas	—	149/150	1.67	—		—		—		—		—		—		—
Robin Ventura	—	0/4		—		155/155	2.41	—		—		—		—		—
Rick Wrona	2/4	—		—		—		—		—		—		—		—

KANSAS CITY

	C	1B	AFR	2B	AFR	3B	AFR	SS	AFR	LF	AFR	CF	AFR	RF	AFR	DH
George Brett	—	—		—		—		—		—		—		—		139/140
Hubie Brooks	—	3/3		—		—		—		4/6		—		26/34	2.07	6/9
Gary Gaetti*	—	10/18	1.80	—		65/72	2.69	—		—		—		—		0/1
Greg Gagne	—	—		—		—		148/159	3.69	—		—		—		—
Chris Gwynn	—	1/1		—		—		—		61/66	2.21	—		12/19	2.32	5/5
Bob Hamelin	—	14/15	2.77	—		—		—		—		—		—		—
Phil Hiatt	—	—		—		67/70	2.54	—		—		—		—		4/9
David Howard	—	—		7/7		0/2		1/3		—		0/1		—		—
Felix Jose	—	—		—		—		—		—		8/10	2.29	113/136	2.01	1/1
Wally Joyner	—	134/140	2.14	—		—		—		—		—		—		—
Kevin Koslofski	—	—		—		—		—		2/3		4/4		0/7		—
Jose Lind	—	—		132/136	3.24	—		—		—		—		—		—
Mike MacFarlane	102/114	—		—		—		—		—		—		—		—
Brent Mayne	58/68	—		—		—		—		—		—		—		1/1
Brian McRae	—	—		—		—		—		—		150/153	2.69	—		1/1
Kevin McReynolds	—	—		—		—		—		89/104	2.09	—		—		1/1
Keith Miller	—	—		2/3		17/21	2.06	—		3/4		—		—		5/6
Harvey Pulliam	—	—		—		—		—		3/12	1.28	—		11/16	2.84	—
Rico Rossy	—	—		14/24	2.83	2/16	1.58	9/11	2.73	—		—		—		—
Nelson Santovenia	2/4	—		—		—		—		—		—		—		—
Terry Shumpert	—	—		3/8		—		—		—		—		—		—
Curtis Wilkerson	—	—		4/10	3.70	—		4/4		—		—		—		—
Craig Wilson	—	—		0/1		11/15	2.53	—		—		0/1		—		—

MINNESOTA

	C	1B	AFR	2B	AFR	3B	AFR	SS	AFR	LF	AFR	CF	AFR	RF	AFR	DH
Rich Becker	—	—		—		—		—		—		3/3		—		—
Bernardo Brito	—	—		—		—		—		4/10	1.78	—		—		5/7
J.T. Bruett	—	—		—		—		—		2/2		0/4		1/8		—
Randy Bush	—	1/4		—		—		—		—		—		0/1		5/5
Chip Hale	—	0/1		9/21	3.72	13/19	2.55	—		—		—		—		19/19
Brian Harper	129/134	—		—		—		—		—		—		—		7/7
Denny Hocking	—	—		1/1		—		8/12	2.27	—		—		—		—
Kent Hrbek	—	109/115	1.91	—		—		—		—		—		—		1/2
Terry Jorgensen	—	3/9		—		39/45	2.78	0/6		—		—		—		—
Chuck Knoblauch	—	—		147/148	3.09	—		1/6		—		0/1		—		—
Gene Larkin	—	12/18	1.95	—		0/2		—		4/4		—		18/25	1.45	3/3
Derek Lee	—	—		—		—		—		6/9		—		2/4		—
Scott Leius	—	—		—		—		7/9		—		—		—		—
Shane Mack	—	—		—		—		—		60/64	2.45	63/67	3.00	1/2		—
Mike Maksudian	—	4/4		—		0/1		—		—		—		—		—
David McCarty	—	29/36	2.34	—		—		—		30/38	2.42	2/2		29/34	1.60	0/2
Pat Meares	—	—		—		—		103/111	3.62	—		—		—		—
Pedro Munoz	—	—		—		—		—		55/64	2.11	—		38/41	1.46	—
Mike Pagliarulo*	—	—		—		71/79	2.34	—		—		—		—		—
Derek Parks	6/7	—		—		—		—		—		—		—		—
Kirby Puckett	—	—		—		—		—		1/1		94/95	2.34	44/47	2.13	17/17
Jeff Reboulet	—	—		5/11	2.39	25/34	3.15	43/62	3.45	0/1		0/2		—		0/1
Scott Stahoviak	—	—		—		14/19	2.83	—		—		—		—		—
Lenny Webster	27/45	—		—		—		—		—		—		—		1/1
Dave Winfield	—	4/5		—		—		—		—		—		29/31	2.10	104/105

OAKLAND

	C	1B	AFR	2B	AFR	3B	AFR	SS	AFR	LF	AFR	CF	AFR	RF	AFR	DH
Kurt Abbott	—	—		0/2		—		3/6		11/13	3.20	—		—		—
Mike Aldrete	—	52/59	1.76	—		—		—		14/17	2.36	—		1/3		5/6
Marcos Armas	—	6/12	2.04	—		—		—		—		—		1/1		0/2
Lance Blankenship	—	1/6		18/19	3.15	—		2/2		15/17	2.78	40/49	2.66	1/2		0/5
Mike Bordick	—	—		1/1		—		154/159	3.14	—		—		—		—
Scott Brosius	—	5/11	1.16	—		7/10	3.05	1/6		5/8		30/34	2.64	5/6		1/2
Jerry Browne	—	1/2		3/3		9/13	2.27	—		25/30	2.46	21/26	2.76	3/4		—
Eric Fox	—	—		—		—		—		2/5		10/18	3.21	0/3		0/2
Brent Gates	—	—		135/139	3.44	—		—		—		—		—		—
Eric Helfand	2/5	—		—		—		—		—		—		—		—
Scott Hemond	66/75	0/1		0/1		—		—		0/4		0/1		0/1		0/3
Dave Henderson	—	—		—		—		—		1/2		57/60	3.01	13/14	2.69	26/28
Rickey Henderson*	—	—		—		—		—		74/74	2.09	—		—		13/16
Scott Lydy	—	—		—		—		—		14/17	2.15	4/5		7/16	2.65	0/2
Mark McGwire	—	25/25	2.00	—		—		—		—		—		—		—
Henry Mercedes	12/18	—		—		—		—		—		—		—		0/1
Troy Neel	—	31/34	1.98	—		—		—		—		—		—		84/85
Craig Paquette	—	—		—		100/104	2.36	—		0/1		—		—		0/1
Kevin Seitzer*	—	18/24/	1.78	2/2		43/46	2.28	—		1/3		—		—		—
Ruben Sierra	—	—		—		—		—		—		—		131/133	2.29	25/25
Terry Steinbach	82/86	12/15	1.28	—		—		—		—		—		—		5/6
Dale Sveum	—	11/14	1.92	3/4		3/7		1/1		0/1		—		—		2/2

SEATTLE	C	1B	AFR	2B	AFR	3B	AFR	SS	AFR	LF	AFR	CF	AFR	RF	AFR	DH
Rich Amaral	—	0/3		72/77	3.53	10/19	2.94	9/14	3.81	—		—		—		6/9
Wally Backman	0/1	0/1		0/1		8/9		—								—
Mike Blowers	0/1	0/1		—		103/117	2.69	—		1/1		—		0/1		0/3
Bret Boone	—	—		69/74	3.02	—		—				—				1/1
Jay Buhner	—	—		—		—		—				—		146/148	1.87	9/10
Henry Cotto	—	—		—		—		—		14/23	2.50	7/9		1/4		3/15
Mike Felder	—	—		—		0/2		—		69/89	1.99	5/7		—		1/6
Ken Griffey Jr.	—	0/1		—		—		—		—		137/139	2.44			19/19
Bill Haselman	29/49	—		—		—		—				—		0/2		4/4
Chris Howard	0/4	—		—		—		—								—
Dann Howitt	—	—		—		—		—		10/16	1.94	1/6		5/12	3.14	1/2
Randy Johnson	—	—		—		—		—		0/1						—
Greg Litton	—	11/13	2.75	10/16	3.00	1/7		2/5		16/21	1.67	—		0/2		4/12
Dave Magadan	—	36/41	1.93	—		24/27	2.4	—								2/2
Edgar Martinez	—	—		—		16/16	0.98	—								24/24
Tino Martinez	—	105/105	2.17	—		—		—								4/6
Jeff Nelson	—	—		—		—		—		0/1						—
Marc Newfield	—	—		—		—		—		2/5						15/15
Pete O'Brien	—	5/7		—		—		—		0/1						51/52
Greg Pirkl	—	5/5		—		—		—								1/2
Mackey Sasser	0/5	0/1		—		—		—		24/26	1.62	—		9/11	2.10	13/19
Larry Sheets	—	—		—		—		—						1/1		3/5
Lee Tinsley	—	—		—		—		—		2/5		0/1		0/1		1/2
Brian Turang	—	—		0/1		0/1		—		24/26	2.19	12/14	2.13	0/1		0/1
Dave Valle	133/135	—		—		—		—		—						—
Fernando Vina	—	—		11/16	3.18	—		1/4		—						0/2
Omar Vizquel	—	—		—		—		150/155	3.65	—						0/2

TEXAS	C	1B	AFR	2B	AFR	3B	AFR	SS	AFR	LF	AFR	CF	AFR	RF	AFR	DH
Steve Balboni	—	—		—		—		—		—		—		—		1/2
Jose Canseco	—	—		—		—		—		—		—		48/49	1.93	9/9
Doug Dascenzo	—	—		—		—		—		6/16	2.18	19/35	2.34	4/25	2.48	0/2
Butch Davis	—	—		—		—		—		17/23	2.64	10/10	3.1	8/17	2.44	0/11
Mario Diaz	—	0/1		—		11/12	1.97	48/57	3.39			—		—		—
Rob Ducey	—	—		—		—		—		0/1		14/14	1.61	10/13	2.40	—
Julio Franco	—	—		—		—		—		—		—		—		140/140
Benji Gil	—	—		—		—		20/22	3.58							10/10
Juan Gonzalez	—	—		—		—		—		129/129	2.26	—		—		10/10
Donald Harris	—	—		—		—		—		1/1		15/27	2.10	3/11	1.44	0/3
David Hulse	—	—		—		—		—		—		96/112	2.57	—		0/2
Jeff Huson	—	—		2/5		1/2		9/12	3.31	—				—		—
Chris James	—	—		—		—		—		4/4		—		3/4		—
Manuel Lee	—	—		—		—		65/72	3.62	—						0/1
Rafael Palmeiro	—	158/160	2.12	—		—		—		—						—
Dean Palmer	—	—		—		144/148	2.14	0/1		—				—		—
Dan Peltier	—	0/5		—		—		—		1/2		—		50/54	1.72	—
Geno Petralli	30/39	—		0/1		0/1		—		—				—		1/2
Gary Redus	—	3/5		0/1		0/1		—		4/5		8/17	3.26	36/46	1.89	0/1
Billy Ripken	—	—		32/34	3.05	0/1		14/18	3.26	—		—		—		—
Ivan Rodriguez	130/134	—		—		—		—		—		—		—		1/1
John Russell	2/11	1/1		—		0/1		—		0/1		—		—		—
Jon Shave	—	—		6/8		—		6/9		—						—
Doug Strange	—	—		122/135	3.24	6/9		0/1		—		—		—		—

Players who played on two teams are indicated by an asterisk; their AFR is based on all their games at that position with both teams.

LEAGUE		1B	AFR	2B	AFR	3B	AFR	SS	AFR	LF	AFR	CF	AFR	RF	AFR
			1.98		3.30		2.44		3.39		2.15		2.68		2.14

FIELDING REPORT: NATIONAL LEAGUE

CHICAGO	C	1B	AFR	2B	AFR	3B	AFR	SS	AFR	LF	AFR	CF	AFR	RF	AFR
Steve Buechele	—	2/6		—		126/129	2.33	—		—		—		—	
Shawn Dunston	—	—		—		—		2/2		—		—		—	
Mark Grace	—	153/154	2.15	—		—		—		—		—		—	
Glenallen Hill	—	—		—		—		—		17/18	2.27	—		—	
Doug Jennings	—	6/11	1.90	—		—		—		—		—		—	
Steve Lake	38/41	—		—		—		—		—		—		—	
Candy Maldonado	—	—		—		—		—		20/29	1.86	—		10/15	1.61
Derrick May	—	—		—		—		—		112/121	1.95	—		1/2	
Karl Rhodes*	—	—		—		—		—		0/6		13/14	2.48	0/1	
Kevin Roberson	—	—		—		—		—		7/14	1.26	0/1		37/42	1.78
Rey Sanchez	—	—		—		—		82/98	4.04	—		—		—	
Ryne Sandberg	—	—		114/115	3.03	—		—		—		—		—	
Tommy Shields	—	0/1		2/7		4/7		—		0/1		—		—	
Dwight Smith	—	—		—		—		—		7/14	1.66	49/53	2.42	20/28	2.45
Sammy Sosa	—	—		—		—		—		—		61/70	2.42	92/114	2.08
Jose Vizcaino	—	—		27/34	2.99	29/44	2.54	79/81	3.72	—		—		—	
Matt Walbeck	7/11	—		—		—		—		—		—		—	
Rick Wilkins	118/133	—		—		—		—		—		—		—	
Willie Wilson	—	—		—		—		—		—		39/82	2.42	—	
Eric Yelding	—	—		20/32	3.93	4/7		0/1		—		1/1		—	
Eddie Zambrano	—	2/2		—		—		—		0/1		—		2/3	

FLORIDA	C	1B	AFR	2B	AFR	3B	AFR	SS	AFR	LF	AFR	CF	AFR	RF	AFR
Alex Arias	—	—		29/30	3.49	18/22	1.95	13/18	2.42	—		—		—	
Bret Barberie	—	—		96/97	3.19	—		—		—		—		—	
Geronimo Berroa	—	—		—		—		—		1/1		—		7/8	
Greg Briley	—	—		—		—		—		11/32	2.19	1/1		13/36	2.47
Matias Carrillo	—	—		—		—		—		2/4		2/5		5/9	
Chuck Carr	—	—		—		—		—		—		133/139	2.96	—	
Jeff Conine	—	11/43	3.14	—		—		—		143/147	1.79	—		—	
Henry Cotto	—	—		—		—		—		1/13	1.47	12/15	3.41	16/21	2.37
Steve Decker	4/5	—		—		—		—		—		—		—	
Orestes Destrade	—	151/152	2.02	—		—		—		—		—		—	
Carl Everett	—	—		—		—		—		—		3/8		—	
Monty Fariss	—	—		—		—		—		1/1		—		5/7	
Junior Felix	—	—		—		—		—		—		3/3		49/50	1.77
Mitch Lyden	1/2	—		—		—		—		—		—		—	
Dave Magadan	—	0/2		—		63/63	2.58	—		—		—		—	
Terry McGriff	2/3	—		—		—		—		—		—		—	
Bob Natal	30/38	—		—		—		—		—		—		—	
Gus Polidor	—	—		0/1		0/1		—		—		—		—	
Scott Pose	—	—		—		—		—		0/6		8/8		—	
Rich Renteria	—	—		37/45	3.25	15/25	2.47	—		0/1		—		—	
Benito Santiago	125/136	—		—		—		—		0/1		—		—	
Gary Sheffield*	—	—		—		66/66	2.19	—		—		—		—	
Walt Weiss	—	—		—		—		149/153	3.33	—		—		—	
Darrell Whitmore	—	—		—		—		—		0/1		—		67/69	2.19
Nigel Wilson	—	—		—		—		—		3/3		—		—	

MONTREAL	C	1B	AFR	2B	AFR	3B	AFR	SS	AFR	LF	AFR	CF	AFR	RF	AFR
Moises Alou	—	—		—		—		—		91/102	2.06	7/12	3.06	25/34	1.83
Sean Berry	—	—		—		73/96	2.58	—		—		—		—	
Frank Bolick	—	39/51	2.11	—		11/24	2.37	—		—		—		—	
Archi Cianfrocco*	—	3/11	2.16	—		—		—		—		—		—	
Greg Colbrunn	—	33/61	1.96	—		—		—		—		—		—	
Wil Cordero	—	—		—		2/2		129/134	3.20	—		—		—	
Delino DeShields	—	—		123/123	3.39	—		—		—		—		—	
Darrin Fletcher	105/127	—		—		—		—		—		—		—	
Cliff Floyd	—	7/10	1.95	—		—		—		—		—		—	
Lou Frazier	—	2/8		0/1		—		—		28/52	1.89	—		1/2	
Marquis Grissom	—	—		—		—		—		—		156/157	2.76	—	
Tim Laker	26/43	—		—		—		—		—		—		—	
Mike Lansing	—	—		15/25	2.92	74/81	2.89	34/51	3.67	—		—		—	
Oreste Marrero	—	21/32	1.72	—		—		—		—		—		—	
Tim McIntosh	0/5	—		—		—		—		1/2		—		0/6	
Charlie Montoyo	—	—		0/3		—		—		—		—		—	
Curtis Pride	—	—		—		—		—		0/2		—		—	
Randy Ready	—	10/13	2.34	25/28	3.69	3/3		—		—		—		—	
Joe Siddall	6/15	0/1		—		—		—		0/1		—		—	
Tim Spehr	26/49	—		—		—		—		—		—		—	
Matt Stairs	—	—		—		—		—		1/1		—		—	
John Vanderwal	—	31/42	2.04	—		—		—		19/27	1.44	0/2		4/10	1.83
Larry Walker	—	4/4		—		—		—		—		—		132/132	2.17
Derrick White	—	13/17	2.40	—		—		—		—		—		—	
Rondell White	—	—		—		—		—		18/19	1.86	0/5		—	
Ted Wood	—	—		—		—		—		5/8		—		1/1	

NATIONAL LEAGUE (continued)

NEW YORK	C	1B	AFR	2B	AFR	3B	AFR	SS	AFR	LF	AFR	CF	AFR	RF	AFR
Kevin Baez	—	—		—		—		38/52	3.19	—		—		—	
Tim Bogar	—	—		3/6		3/7		60/66	3.48	—		—		—	
Bobby Bonilla	—	4/6		—		50/52	2.47	—		—		—		83/85	1.71
Jeromy Burnitz	—	—		—		—		—		—		19/21	2.22	54/60	2.20
Vince Coleman	—	—		—		—		—		88/90	1.88	—		—	
Tony Fernandez	—	—		—		—		48/48	3.28	—		—		—	
Dave Gallagher	—	1/9		—		—		—		10/19	1.94	19/39	2.52	14/20	2.59
Wayne Housie	—	—		—		—		—		—		—		0/2	
Todd Hundley	105/123	—		—		—		—		—		—		—	
Butch Huskey	—	—		—		13/13	2.65	—		—		—		—	
Darrin Jackson	—	—		—		—		—		8/10	2.27	15/16	2.39	—	
Howard Johnson	—	—		—		67/68	2.38	—		—		—		—	
Jeff Kent	—	—		124/127	3.05	12/12	2.74	0/2		—		—		—	
Ced Landrum	—	—		—		—		—		—		0/3		—	
Jeff McKnight	0/1	2/10	1.94	7/15	3.89	2/9		14/29	3.74	—		—		—	
Eddie Murray	—	154/154	2.01	—		—		—		—		—		—	
Tito Navarro	—	—		—		—		2/2		—		—		—	
Charlie O'Brien	57/65	—		—		—		—		—		—		—	
Joe Orsulak	—	1/4		—		—		—		49/66	2.35	34/39	2.37	11/24	1.75
Doug Saunders	—	—		17/22	3.18	0/4		0/1		—		—		—	
Ryan Thompson	—	—		—		—		—		—		75/76	3.04	—	
Chico Walker	—	—		11/24	3.50	15/23	2.51	—		7/15	1.81	—		0/1	

PHILADELPHIA	C	1B	AFR	2B	AFR	3B	AFR	SS	AFR	LF	AFR	CF	AFR	RF	AFR
Ruben Amaro	—	—		—		—		—		2/3		2/8		5/6	
Kim Batiste	—	—		—		15/58	2.51	20/24	3.98	—		—		—	
Juan Bell	—	—		—		—		20/22	3.63	—		—		—	
Wes Chamberlain	—	—		—		—		—		—		—		73/76	2.15
Darren Daulton	143/146	—		—		—		—		—		—		—	
Mariano Duncan	—	—		61/65	3.41	—		49/59	3.21	—		—		—	
Lenny Dykstra	—	—		—		—		—		—		160/160	3.00	—	
Jim Eisenreich	—	0/1		—		—		—		1/2		0/3		77/132	2.37
Dave Hollins	—	—		—		143/143	1.98	—		—		—		—	
Pete Incaviglia	—	—		—		—		—		80/89	2.09	—		6/8	
Ricky Jordan	—	24/33	1.51	—		—		—		—		—		—	
John Kruk	—	138/144	2.04	—		—		—		—		—		—	
Doug Lindsey	0/2	—		—		—		—		—		—		—	
Tony Longmire	—	—		—		—		—		1/2		—		—	
Jeff Manto	—	—		—		4/6		0/1		—		—		—	
Joe Millette	—	—		—		0/3		3/7		—		—		—	
Mickey Morandini	—	—		101/111	3.39	—		—		—		—		—	
Todd Pratt	19/26	—		—		—		—		—		—		—	
Kevin Stocker	—	—		—		—		70/70	3.37	—		—		—	
Milt Thompson	—	—		—		—		—		78/101	2.08	0/4		1/1	

PITTSBURGH	C	1B	AFR	2B	AFR	3B	AFR	SS	AFR	LF	AFR	CF	AFR	RF	AFR
Rich Aude	—	5/7		—		—		—		0/1		—		—	
Jay Bell	—	—		—		—		153/154	3.66	—		—		—	
Scott Bullett	—	—		—		—		—		—		12/18	2.44	1/1	
Dave Clark	—	—		—		—		—		33/41	1.94	—		42/52	1.82
Midre Cummings	—	—		—		—		—		4/5		4/5		1/1	
Tom Foley	—	4/12	1.99	29/35	2.51	4/7		4/6		—		—		—	
Carlos Garcia	—	—		132/140	3.01	—		0/3		—		—		—	
Jerry Goff	12/14	—		—		—		—		—		—		—	
Jeff King	—	—		1/2		155/156	2.60	0/2		—		—		—	
Mike LaValliere	1/1	—		—		—		—		—		—		—	
Al Martin	—	—		—		—		—		62/81	2.09	58/63	2.25	0/6	
Lloyd McClendon	—	0/6		—		—		—		10/21	2.62	—		33/48	1.90
Orlando Merced	—	31/42	1.54	—		—		—		—		—		83/109	2.22
Will Pennyfeather	—	—		—		—		—		0/1		5/15	2.49	0/2	
Tom Prince	50/59	—		—		—		—		—		—		—	
Ben Shelton	—	1/2		—		—		—		5/6		—		—	
Don Slaught	99/105	—		—		—		—		—		—		—	
Lonnie Smith	—	—		—		—		—		42/58	2.22	2/3		—	
Andy Tomberlin	—	—		—		—		—		5/5		—		1/2	
Andy VanSlyke	—	—		—		—		—		—		76/78	2.63	—	
John Wehner	—	—		0/3		1/3		—		1/4		4/8		0/2	
Glenn Wilson	—	—		—		—		—		—		1/3		1/2	
Tony Womack	—	—		—		—		5/6		—		—		—	
Kevin Young	—	121/135	2.20	—		2/6		—		—		—		—	

ST. LOUIS	C	1B	AFR	2B	AFR	3B	AFR	SS	AFR	LF	AFR	CF	AFR	RF	AFR
Luis Alicea	—	—		87/96	3.27	0/1		—		3/4		—		—	
Rod Brewer	—	5/32	1.45	—		—		—		7/15	1.76	—		14/19	2.15
Ozzie Canseco	—	—		—		—		—		5/5		—		—	
Tripp Cromer	—	—		—		—		5/9		—		—		—	
Bernard Gilkey	—	3/3		—		—		—		130/132	1.69	—		2/3	
Gregg Jefferies	—	139/140	1.83	0/1		—		—		—		—		—	
Tim Jones	—	—		4/7		—		12/21	4.12	—		—		—	
Brian Jordan	—	—		—		—		—		15/22	2.16	32/37	2.34	8/11	2.86
Ray Lankford	—	—		—		—		—		—		112/121	2.72	—	
Lonnie Maclin	—	—		—		—		—		2/5		—		—	
Jose Oquendo	—	—		8/16	2.84	—		14/22	3.84	—		—		—	
Tom Pagnozzi	90/92	—		—		—		—		—		—		—	
Erik Pappas	53/63	1/2		—		—		—		0/1		—		10/15	3.07
Geronimo Peña	—	—		63/64	3.46	—		—		—		—		—	
Gerald Perry	—	7/15	1.35	—		—		—		—		—		0/1	
Marc Ronan	3/6	—		—		—		—		—		—		—	
Stan Royer	—	2/2		—		6/10	2.15	—		—		—		—	
Ozzie Smith	—	—		—		—		131/134	3.76	—		—		—	
Hector Villanueva	16/17	—		—		—		—		—		—		—	
Mark Whiten	—	—		—		—		—		0/1		18/22	2.66	128/137	1.97
Tracy Woodson	—	5/11	2	—		7/28	3.02	—		—		—		—	
Todd Zeile	—	—		—		149/153	2.26	—		—		—		—	

ATLANTA	C	1B	AFR	2B	AFR	3B	AFR	SS	AFR	LF	AFR	CF	AFR	RF	AFR
Rafael Belliard	—	—		13/24	4.13	—		3/58	4.07	—		—		—	
Damon Berryhill	85/105	—		—		—		—		—		—		—	
Jeff Blauser	—	—		—		—		159/161	3.25	—		—		—	
Sid Bream	—	69/90	2.03	—		—		—		—		—		—	
Francisco Cabrera	0/2	11/12	2.41	—		—		—		—		—		—	
Ramon Caraballo	—	—		0/5		—		—		—		—		—	
Ron Gant	—	—		—		—		—		155/155	1.87	—		—	
Brian Hunter	—	16/29	2.13	—		—		—		—		—		2/2	
Chipper Jones	—	—		—		—		0/3		—		—		—	
Dave Justice	—	—		—		—		—		—		—		157/157	2.12
Ryan Klesko	—	0/3		—		—		—		0/2		—		—	
Mark Lemke	—	—		148/150	3.34	—		—		—		—		—	
Javier Lopez	4/7	—		—		—		—		—		—		—	
Fred McGriff*	—	66/66	1.79	—		—		—		—		—		—	
Otis Nixon	—	—		—		—		—		—		111/115	2.86	0/2	
Greg Olson	73/81	—		—		—		—		—		—		—	
Bill Pecota	—	—		1/4		2/23	1.91	—		—		—		1/1	
Terry Pendleton	—	—		—		160/161	2.74	—		—		—		—	
Deion Sanders	—	—		—		—		—		4/5		51/55	2.65	—	
Tony Tarasco	—	—		—		—		—		3/4		—		2/8	

CINCINNATI	C	1B	AFR	2B	AFR	3B	AFR	SS	AFR	LF	AFR	CF	AFR	RF	AFR
Jeff Branson	—	1/1		36/45	3.09	8/14	2.21	46/59	3.45	—		—		—	
Jacob Brumfield	—	—		2/4		—		—		4/24	2.52	56/68	2.64	2/5	
Tim Costo	—	1/2		—		—		—		11/11	2.49	—		15/16	1.83
Jack Daugherty*	—	2/2		—		0/2		—		7/11	1.23	—		0/5	
Brian Dorsett	14/18	1/3		—		—		—		—		—		—	
Cecil Espy	—	—		—		—		—		11/18	1.99	—		0/1	
Keith Gordon	—	—		—		—		—		1/2		—		—	
Tommy Gregg	—	—		—		—		—		1/3		—		1/1	
Willie Greene	—	—		—		4/5		10/10	3.68	—		—		—	
Cesar Hernandez	—	—		—		—		—		0/17	5.30	3/7		—	
Thomas Howard	—	—		—		—		—		21/27	2.05	10/12	2.30	—	
Keith Hughes	—	—		—		—		—		0/2		—		—	
Roberto Kelly	—	—		—		—		—		—		77/78	2.65	—	
Keith Kessinger	—	—		—		—		7/11	3.44	—		—		—	
Brian Koelling	—	—		3/3		—		1/2		—		—		—	
Barry Larkin	—	—		—		—		98/99	3.35	—		—		—	
Randy Milligan	—	60/61	1.98	—		—		—		8/9		—		—	
Kevin Mitchell	—	—		—		—		—		85/86	1.97	—		2/2	
Hal Morris	—	94/98	2.06	—		—		—		—		—		—	
Joe Oliver	128/133	3/12	0.82	—		—		—		—		—		1/1	
Bip Roberts	—	—		63/65	3.69	2/3		0/1		5/12	2.36	1/1		—	
Chris Sabo	—	—		—		148/148	2.17	—		—		—		—	
Juan Samuel	—	0/6		58/70	3.01	0/4		—		0/2		—		1/1	
Reggie Sanders	—	—		—		—		—		—		4/4		133/135	2.32
Greg Tubbs	—	—		—		—		—		2/11	1.65	11/14	3.06	1/2	
Gary Varsho	—	—		—		—		—		6/13	1.64	—		6/9	
Dan Wilson	20/35	—		—		—		—		—		—		—	

COLORADO

	C	1B	AFR	2B	AFR	3B	AFR	SS	AFR	LF	AFR	CF	AFR	RF	AFR
Freddie Benavides	—	0/1		11/19	3.66	1/5		43/48	2.85	—					
Dante Bichette	—	—		—		—		—		—		9/9		125/134	2.15
Daryl Boston	—	—		—		—		—		39/41	1.73	22/30	2.08	8/9	
Pedro Castellano	—	3/10	3.22	4/4		8/13	1.95	1/5		—		—		—	
Vinny Castilla	—	—		—		—		92/104	3.13	—		—		—	
Jerald Clark	—	29/37	2.19	—		—		—		76/80	2.03	—		16/17	2.09
Alex Cole	—	—		—		—		—		—		85/93	2.49	—	
Jay Gainer	—	7/7		—		—		—		—		—		—	
Andres Galarraga	—	119/119	2.02	—		—		—		—		—		—	
Joe Girardi	80/84	—		—		—		—		—		—		—	
Charlie Hayes	—	—		—		151/154	2.48	0/1		—		—		—	
Chris Jones	—	—		—		—		—		6/16	1.57	38/52	2.38	1/4	
Nelson Liriano	—	—		11/16	2.66	0/1		26/35	2.71	—		—		—	
Roberto Mejia	—	—		62/65	3.37	—		—		—		—		—	
Dale Murphy	—	—		—		—		—		1/2		—		10/11	1.71
Jayhawk Owens	24/32	—		—		—		—		—		—		—	
Danny Sheaffer	57/65	0/7		—		0/1		—		0/2		—		—	
Jim Tatum	—	4/12	1.44	—		2/6		—		1/2		—		0/1	
Eric Wedge	1/1	—		—		—		—		—		—		—	
Eric Young	—	—		74/79	3.22	—		—		39/46	2.14	8/10	1.60	—	
Gerald Young	—	—		—		—		—		0/4		0/3		2/5	

HOUSTON

	C	1B	AFR	2B	AFR	3B	AFR	SS	AFR	LF	AFR	CF	AFR	RF	AFR
Eric Anthony	—	—		—		—		—		—		19/23	1.93	106/121	1.97
Jeff Bagwell	—	138/141	2.01	—		—		—		—		—		—	
Kevin Bass	—	—		—		—		—		4/12	1.65	1/2		38/51	1.72
Craig Biggio	—	—		155/155	3.37	—		—		—		—		—	
Mike Brumley	—	—		—		0/1		0/1		0/1		—		1/1	
Ken Caminiti	—	—		—		142/143	2.71	—		—		—		—	
Casey Candaele	—	—		7/19	2.30	0/4		3/14	3.31	1/4		5/12	3.50	0/2	
Andujar Cedeno	—	—		—		0/1		146/149	2.91	—		—		—	
Jack Daugherty*	—	0/1		—		—		—		—		—		0/1	
Chris Donnels	—	20/23	2.17	0/1		20/31	2.76	—		—		—		—	
Steve Finley	—	—		—		—		—		—		131/140	2.63	—	
Luis Gonzalez	—	—		—		—		—		142/149	2.55	—		—	
Chris James	—	—		—		—		—		15/16	2.72	—		17/18	2.27
Jim Lindeman	—	4/9		—		—		—		—		—		—	
Rick Parker	—	—		0/1		—		0/1		0/3		6/13	2.45	0/1	
Karl Rhodes*	—	—		—		—		—		0/1		0/2		0/1	
Scott Servais	75/82	—		—		—		—		—		—		—	
Ed Taubensee	80/90	—		—		—		—		—		—		—	
Eddie Tucker	7/8	—		—		—		—		—		—		—	
Jose Uribe	—	—		—		—		13/41	3.31	—		—		—	

LOS ANGELES

	C	1B	AFR	2B	AFR	3B	AFR	SS	AFR	LF	AFR	CF	AFR	RF	AFR
Billy Ashley	—	—		—		—		—		9/11	1.21	—		—	
Rafael Bournigal	—	—		0/4		—		4/4		—		—		—	
Jerry Brooks	—	—		—		—		—		—		—		0/2	
Brett Butler	—	—		—		—		—		—		154/155	2.35	—	
Eric Davis	—	—		—		—		—		92/101	2.13	3/3		—	
Tom Goodwin	—	—		—		—		—		0/6		1/4		0/2	
Dave Hansen	—	—		—		15/18	2.69	—		—		—		—	
Lenny Harris	—	—		24/35	3.83	2/17	2.06	0/3		—		—		—	
Carlos Hernandez	21/43	—		—		—		—		—		—		—	
Orel Hershiser	—	—		—		1/1		—		—		—		—	
Eric Karros	—	157/157	1.97	—		—		—		—		—		—	
Pedro Martinez	—	—		—		1/1		—		—		—		—	
Raul Mondesi	—	—		—		—		—		7/20	2.29	3/6		10/17	2.29
Jose Offerman	—	—		—		—		156/158	3.50	—		—		—	
Mike Piazza	141/146	0/1		—		—		—		—		—		—	
Jody Reed	—	—		129/132	3.44	—		—		—		—		—	
Henry Rodriguez	—	4/13	1.64	—		—		—		24/26	1.57	—		14/23	1.72
Mike Sharperson	—	0/1		9/17	2.78	1/6		2/3		—		—		0/1	
Cory Snyder	—	0/12	1.60	—		22/24	1.82	0/2		2/2		1/1		107/112	1.75
Darryl Strawberry	—	—		—		—		—		4/4		—		25/25	1.68
Tim Wallach	—	1/1		—		120/129	2.80	—		—		—		1/1	
Mitch Webster	—	—		—		—		—		24/32	2.12	0/2		5/27	2.24

NATIONAL LEAGUE (continued)

SAN DIEGO	C	1B	AFR	2B	AFR	3B	AFR	SS	AFR	LF	AFR	CF	AFR	RF	AFR
Brad Ausmus	47/49	—		—		—		—							
Billy Bean	—	5/12	1.33	—		—		—		0/11	0.99	12/17	2.66	17/32	2.00
Derek Bell	—	—		—		18/19	2.66	—		0/1		116/119	2.81	5/6	
Jarvis Brown	—	—		—		—		—		3/5		29/40	3.36	—	
Archi Cianfrocco*	—	18/31	2.16	—		61/64	1.99	—		—		—		—	
Phil Clark	1/11	18/24	2.44	—		4/5		—		18/22	3.06	—		9/15	1.95
Jeff Gardner	—	—		96/133	3.06	0/1		0/1		—		—		—	
Bob Geren	41/49	0/1		—		0/1		—		—		—		—	
Ricky Gutierrez	—	—		1/6		1/4		106/117	3.42	0/3		—		0/2	
Tony Gwynn	—	—		—		—		—		—		0/4		119/121	2.20
Kevin Higgins	47/59	0/3		0/1		0/4		—		0/1		—		0/2	
Luis Lopez	—	—		13/15	2.94	—		—		—		—		—	
Fred McGriff*	—	83/83	1.79	—		—		—		—		—		—	
Melvin Nieves	—	—		—		—		—		—		—		11/15	2.73
Phil Plantier	—	—		—		—		—		131/134	2.10	—		—	
Gary Sheffield*	—	—		—		66/67	2.19	—		—		—		—	
Darrell Sherman	—	—		—		—		—		8/24	2.73	3/6		0/1	
Craig Shipley	—	—		5/12	3.28	7/37	2.37	30/38	3.34	0/2		2/3		—	
Dave Staton	—	10/12	2.39	—		—		—		—		—		—	
Kurt Stillwell	—	—		—		0/3		26/30	2.90	—		—		—	
Tim Teufel	—	2/9		47/52	3.05	4/9		—		—		—		—	
Guillermo Velasquez	—	26/38	2.28	—		—		—		2/4		—		1/2	
Dan Walters	26/26	—		—		—		—		—		—		—	

SAN FRANCISCO	C	1B	AFR	2B	AFR	3B	AFR	SS	AFR	LF	AFR	CF	AFR	RF	AFR
Andy Allanson	4/8	0/2		—		—		—		—		—		—	
Mike Benjamin	—	—		17/23	3.82	14/16	2.86	9/23	4.14	—		—		—	
Todd Benzinger	—	27/40	1.98	—		0/1		—		4/7		—		—	
Barry Bonds	—	—		—		—		—		156/157	2.08	—		—	
Mark Carreon	—	2/3		—		—		—		2/9		4/5		21/30	1.76
Will Clark	—	129/129	2.19	—		—		—		—		—		—	
Royce Clayton	—	—		—		—		151/153	3.49	—		—		—	
Craig Colbert	7/10	—		0/2		1/1		—		—		—		—	
Rikkert Faneyte	—	—		—		—		—		0/1		3/5		—	
Paul Faries	—	—		6/7		0/1		2/4		—		—		—	
Steve Hosey	—	—		—		—		—		—		—		0/1	
Erik Johnson	—	—		0/2		0/1		0/1		—		—		—	
Darren Lewis	—	—		—		—		—		—		120/131	2.97	—	
Kirt Manwaring	126/130	—		—		—		—		—		—		—	
Dave Martinez	—	—		—		—		—		0/3		32/43	2.72	21/34	2.00
Willie McGee	—	—		—		—		—		—		—		120/126	1.99
Jim McNamara	1/4	—		—		—		—		—		—		—	
Luis Mercedes	—	—		—		—		—		0/1		3/3		0/1	
J.R. Phillips	—	3/5		—		—		—		—		—		—	
Jeff Reed	24/37	—		—		—		—		—		—		—	
Steve Scarsone	—	1/6		15/20	2.63	4/8		—		—		—		—	
Rob Thompson	—	—		124/128	3.39	—		—		—		—		—	
Matt Williams	—	—		—		143/144	2.51	—		—		—		—	

Players who played on two teams are indicated by an asterisk; their AFR is based on all their games at that position with both teams.

LEAGUE	1B	AFR	2B	AFR	3B	AFR	SS	AFR	LF	AFR	CF	AFR	RF	AFR
		2.02		3.27		2.46		3.42		2.02		2.68		2.07

CATCHER FIELDING REPORTS

AMERICAN LEAGUE

CATCHER	Innings	Inn/9	WP	WP/162	PB	PB/162
Alomar, Sandy	520.0	57.8	10	28.0	3	8.4
Blowers, Mike	1.0	0.1	0	0.0	0	0.0
Borders, Pat	1182.0	131.3	69	85.1	6	7.4
Delgado, Carlos	3.0	0.3	0	0.0	0	0.0
Fisk, Carlton	125.2	14.0	4	46.4	2	23.2
Flaherty, John	77.0	8.6	1	18.9	1	18.9
Gonzales, Larry	5.1	0.6	1	273.4	0	0.0
Harper, Brian	1125.2	125.1	33	42.7	18	23.3
Haselman, Bill	304.1	33.8	12	57.5	5	24.0
Helfand, Eric	25.0	2.8	2	116.6	0	0.0
Hemond, Scott	600.0	66.7	17	41.3	10	24.3
Hoiles, Chris	1040.0	115.6	26	36.4	2	2.8
Howard, Chris	5.0	0.6	0	0.0	0	0.0
Karkovice, Ron	1038.2	115.4	33	46.3	9	12.6
Kmak, Joe	316.1	35.1	5	23.0	4	18.4
Knorr, Randy	256.1	28.5	14	79.6	0	0.0
Kreuter, Chad	897.0	99.7	44	71.5	4	6.5
Lampkin, Tom	400.0	44.4	17	62.0	1	3.6
LaValliere, Mike	259.2	28.9	14	78.6	4	22.5
Levis, Jesse	155.2	17.3	4	37.5	1	9.4
Leyritz, Jim	37.0	4.1	0	0.0	0	0.0
Lindsey, Doug	5.0	0.6	0	0.0	0	0.0
Lyons, Steve	1.0	0.1	0	0.0	0	0.0
MacFarlane, Mike	917.1	101.9	53	84.2	9	14.3
Mayne, Brent	505.0	56.1	22	63.5	5	14.4
McIntosh, Tim	1.0	0.1	0	0.0	0	0.0
Melvin, Bob	459.0	51.0	10	31.8	5	15.9
Mercedes, Henry	119.0	13.2	6	73.5	1	12.3
Myers, Greg	646.1	71.8	19	42.9	5	11.3
Nilsson, Dave	719.0	79.9	23	46.6	7	14.2
Nokes, Matt	400.2	44.5	9	32.8	1	3.6
Ortiz, Junior	707.2	78.6	25	51.5	2	4.1
Orton, John	268.0	29.8	5	27.2	1	5.4
Parent, Mark	143.0	15.9	6	61.2	1	10.2
Parks, Derek	50.0	5.6	1	29.2	2	58.3
Parrish, Lance	62.1	6.9	2	46.8	3	70.2
Pena, Tony	915.1	101.7	31	49.4	5	8.0
Petralli, Geno	288.1	32.0	8	40.5	2	10.1
Rodriguez, Ivan	1117.0	124.1	42	54.8	14	18.3
Rowland, Rich	109.2	12.2	4	53.2	0	0.0
Russell, John	33.0	3.7	2	88.4	2	88.4
Santovenia, Nelson	23.0	2.6	1	63.4	2	126.8
Sasser, Mackey	11.0	1.2	0	0.0	0	0.0
Stanley, Mike	1000.2	111.2	24	35.0	6	8.7
Steinbach, Terry	708.1	78.7	14	28.8	4	8.2
Surhoff, B.J.	10.2	1.2	0	0.0	0	0.0
Tackett, Jeff	259.2	28.9	9	50.5	3	16.8
Tettleton, Mickey	430.0	47.8	20	67.8	4	13.6
Tingley, Ron	316.2	35.2	15	69.1	3	13.8
Turner, Chris	194.0	21.6	15	112.7	1	7.5
Valle, Dave	1132.1	125.8	45	57.9	8	10.3
Webster, Lenny	268.2	29.9	9	48.8	1	5.4
Wrona, Rick	25.0	2.8	0	0.0	0	0.0
League	**20222.1**	**2246.9**	**726**	**52.3**	**167**	**12.0**
BAL	1442.2	160.3	41	41.4	6	6.1
BOS	1452.1	161.4	42	42.2	11	11.0
CLE	1445.2	160.6	41	41.3	9	9.1
DET	1436.2	159.6	68	69.0	8	8.1
MIL	1447.0	160.8	45	45.3	12	12.1
NYA	1438.1	159.8	33	33.5	7	7.1
TOR	1441.1	160.1	83	84.0	6	6.1
CAL	1430.1	158.9	55	56.1	10	10.2
CHA	1454.0	161.6	51	51.1	15	15.0
KC	1445.1	160.6	76	76.7	16	16.1
MIN	1444.1	160.5	43	43.4	21	21.2
OAK	1452.1	161.4	39	39.2	15	15.1
SEA	1453.2	161.5	57	57.2	13	13.0
TEX	1438.1	159.8	52	52.7	18	18.2

NATIONAL LEAGUE

CATCHER	Innings	Inn/9	WP	WP/162	PB	PB/162
Allanson, Andy	45.2	5.1	2	63.9	0	0.0
Ausmus, Brad	402.1	44.7	15	54.4	2	7.2
Berryhill, Damon	774.0	86.0	23	43.3	6	11.3
Cabrera, Francisco	3.0	0.3	0	0.0	0	0.0
Clark, Phil	27.1	3.0	0	0.0	0	0.0
Colbert, Craig	63.2	7.1	0	0.0	0	0.0
Daulton, Darren	1278.0	142.0	64	73.0	12	13.7
Decker, Steve	33.1	3.7	0	0.0	0	0.0
Dorsett, Brian	127.1	14.1	4	45.8	0	0.0
Fletcher, Darrin	918.1	102.0	24	38.1	4	6.4
Geren, Bob	361.0	40.1	21	84.8	4	16.2
Girardi, Joe	707.2	78.6	42	86.5	2	4.1
Goff, Jerry	105.0	11.7	2	27.8	2	27.8
Hernandez, Carlos	229.1	25.5	15	95.4	1	6.4
Higgins, Kevin	412.1	45.8	17	60.1	10	35.4
Hundley, Todd	942.2	104.7	22	34.0	4	6.2
Lake, Steve	303.1	33.7	11	52.9	2	9.6
Laker, Tim	230.1	25.6	15	94.9	9	57.0
LaValliere, Mike	9.0	1.0	1	162.0	1	162.0
Lindsey, Doug	3.0	0.3	0	0.0	0	0.0
Lopez, Javier	37.0	4.1	1	39.4	1	39.4
Lyden, Mitch	11.1	1.3	0	0.0	0	0.0
Manwaring, Kirt	1090.2	121.2	20	26.7	11	14.7
McGriff, Terry	19.0	2.1	2	153.5	0	0.0
McIntosh, Tim	9.1	1.0	0	0.0	0	0.0
McKnight, Jeff	1.0	0.1	0	0.0	0	0.0
McNamara, Jim	17.0	1.9	0	0.0	0	0.0
Natal, Bob	281.2	31.3	23	119.1	6	31.1
O'Brien, Charlie	494.1	54.9	10	29.5	0	0.0
Oliver, Joe	1102.2	122.5	32	42.3	11	14.5
Olson, Greg	641.0	71.2	22	50.0	6	13.6
Owens, Jayhawk	221.2	24.6	13	85.5	3	19.7
Pagnozzi, Tom	787.0	87.4	24	44.5	9	16.7
Pappas, Erik	489.2	54.4	16	47.6	3	8.9
Piazza, Mike	1243.1	138.1	32	37.5	14	16.4
Pratt, Todd	191.2	21.3	10	76.1	0	0.0
Prince, Tom	457.0	50.8	18	57.4	6	19.1
Reed, Jeff	239.2	26.6	11	66.9	4	24.3
Ronan, Marc	33.0	3.7	0	0.0	1	44.2
Santiago, Benito	1095.0	121.7	60	79.9	23	30.6
Servais, Scott	653.2	72.6	20	44.6	4	8.9
Sheaffer, Danny	493.0	54.8	27	79.8	6	17.7
Siddall, Joe	57.0	6.3	2	51.2	1	25.6
Slaught, Don	874.2	97.2	34	56.7	10	16.7
Spehr, Tim	241.2	26.9	5	30.2	0	0.0
Taubensee, Ed	727.2	80.9	38	76.1	3	6.0
Tucker, Eddie	60.0	6.7	2	48.6	0	0.0
Villanueva, Hector	143.1	15.9	0	0.0	1	10.2
Walbeck, Matt	69.0	7.7	2	42.3	1	21.1
Walters, Dan	234.2	26.1	4	24.9	4	24.9
Wedge, Eric	9.0	1.0	0	0.0	0	0.0
Wilkins, Rick	1077.1	119.7	30	40.6	11	14.9
Wilson, Dan	204.0	22.7	11	78.6	1	7.1
League	**20284.2**	**2253.9**	**747**	**53.7**	**199**	**14.3**
CHN	1449.2	161.1	43	43.2	14	14.1
FLO	1440.1	160.0	85	86.0	29	29.4
MON	1456.2	161.9	46	46.0	14	14.0
NYN	1438.0	159.8	32	32.4	4	4.1
PHI	1472.2	163.6	74	73.3	12	11.9
PIT	1445.2	160.6	55	55.5	19	19.2
SL	1453.0	161.4	40	40.1	14	14.0
ATL	1455.0	161.7	46	46.1	13	13.0
CIN	1434.0	159.3	47	47.8	12	12.2
COL	1431.1	159.0	82	83.5	11	11.2
HOU	1441.1	160.1	60	60.7	7	7.1
LA	1472.2	163.6	47	46.5	15	14.9
SD	1437.2	159.7	57	57.8	20	20.3
SF	1456.2	161.9	33	33.0	15	15.0

1993 DISABLED LIST TIME, BY PLAYER

This alphabetical list shows every player who spent time on any major-league Disabled List during the 1993 season. The number after a player's name shows how many days he spent on the DL between Opening Day and the end of the regular season (including rehabilitation assignments to minor leagues). Players who were on the DL for the whole season are shown as being disabled for 182 days. If a player was disabled more than once during the season, the number of separate stays on the DL (not counting transfers from one DL to another) is shown in parentheses after his name.

Player	Team	DL Days
Abbott, Jim	NYA	15
Aldred, Scott	MON	119
Alomar, Sandy	CLE	98
Alou, Moises	MON	16
Amaral, Rich	SEA	15
Anderson, Brady	BAL	15
Andersen, Larry	PHI	19
Aquino, Luis	FLO	30
Arocha, Rene	SL	22
Austin, Jim	MIL	15
Backman, Wally	SEA	16
Baines, Harold	BAL	22
Barberie, Bret (2x)	FLO	68
Becker, Rich	MIN	21
Bell, George	CHA	41
Benavides, Freddie (2x)	COL	41
Benjamin, Mike	SF	29
Black, Buddy (3x)	SF	103
Blankenship, Lance	OAK	49
Boddicker, Mike (2x)	MIL-KC	60
Bogar, Tim	NYN	16
Bohanon, Brian	TEX	21
Bosio, Chris (2x)	SEA	48
Browne, Jerry	OAK	90
Brown, Kevin	TEX	6
Browning, Tom	CIN	58
Brunansky, Tom	MIL	60
Buechele, Steve	CHN	15
Butcher, Mike	CAL	71
Butler, Rob	TOR	70
Calderon, Ivan	BOS	19
Canate, Willie (2x)	CIN	40
Candaele, Casey	HOU	23
Candelaria, John	PIT	17
Canseco, Jose	TEX	102
Carr, Chuck	FLO	17
Cary, Chuck (2x)	CHA	127
Casian, Larry	MIN	44
Castilla, Vinny	COL	15
Chamberlain, Wes	PHI	18
Charlton, Norm (2x)	SEA	72
Clark, Mark	CLE	54
Clark, Will	SF	15
Clemens, Roger	BOS	27
Colbert, Craig	SF	79
Colbrunn, Greg (2x)	MON	100
Cormier, Rheal	SL	26
Corsi, Jim (2x)	FLO	115
Cuyler, Milt	DET	56
Davis, Butch	TEX	15
Davis, Glenn	BAL	91
Dawson, Andre	BOS	19
Decker, Steve	FLO	139
Deer, Rob	DET	15
DeJesus, Jose	PHI	120
Delucia, Rich	SEA	24
DeShields, Delino	MON	30
Devereaux, Mike	BAL	24
Diaz, Alex	MIL	119
Dibble, Rob (2x)	CIN	48
DiPino, Frank	KC	31
DiSarcina, Gary	CAL	38
Doherty, John	DET	15
Doran, Bill (2x)	MIL	45
Draper, Mike	NYN	52
Duncan, Mariano	PHI	15
Dunne, Mike	CHA	107
Dunston, Shawon	CHN	149
Easley, Damion (2x)	CAL	83
Edens, Tom	HOU	31
Embree, Alan (2x)	CLE	182
Erickson, Scott	MIN	13
Fajardo, Hector	TEX	148
Farr, Steve	NYA	17
Felder, Mike	SEA	20
Fernandez, Sid	NYN	89
Finley, Steve	HOU	19
Fleming, Dave	SEA	48
Fletcher, Scott	BOS	15
Foley, Tom	PIT	16
Foster, Steve (2x)	CIN	134
Franco, John (2x)	NYN	43
Freeman, Marvin	ATL	64
Frye, Jeff	TEX	182
Galarraga, Andres (2x)	COL	44
Gallego, Mike	NYA	15
Gardner, Mark	KC	51
Gilkey, Bernard	SL	15
Girardi, Joe	COL	67
Gladden, Dan	DET	50
Gomez, Leo	BAL	55
Gomez, Pat	SD	100
Gossage, Rich	OAK	26
Grahe, Joe	CAL	40
Grant, Mark (2x)	COL	34
Greenwell, Mike	BOS	15
Greene, Tommy	PHI	15
Greene, Willie	CIN	44
Griffin, Alfredo	TOR	25
Gruber, Kelly (2x)	CAL	152
Gullickson, Bill	DET	35
Guthrie, Mark	MIN	128
Haas, David	DET	112
Hamilton, Darryl	MIL	15
Hammonds, Jeffrey (2x)	BAL	30
Harkey, Mike (2x)	CHN	31
Hathaway, Hilly	CAL	24
Henderson, Dave	OAK	24
Henry, Dwayne	SEA	30
Hesketh, Joe	BOS	45
Hibbard, Greg	CHN	20
Higuera, Teddy	MIL	131
Hill, Ken	MON	21
Hoiles, Chris	BAL	21
Hollins, Dave	PHI	17
Hollins, Jessie	CHN	182
Holman, Brian	SEA	182
Holman, Brad	SEA	19
Honeycutt, Rick	OAK	39
Howard, David (2x)	KC	92
Howe, Steve	NYA	29
Hrbek, Kent	MIN	15
Hulse, David	TEX	18
Hunter, Brian	ATL	30
Hurst, Bruce (4x)	SD-COL	143
Huson, Jeff (3x)	TEX	122
Jackson, Darrin	NYN	44
Jackson, Michael	SF	16
Johnson, Dave	DET	115
Johnson, Howard (2x)	NYN	94
Jones, Jimmy (2x)	MON	34
Kaiser, Jeff	NYN	20
Karkovice, Ron	CHA	16
Kelly, Bobby	CIN	82
Kilgus, Paul	SL	69
Knudsen, Kurt	DET	31
Kramer, Tom	CLE	18
Krueger, Bill	DET	49
Lancaster, Lester	SL	58
Landrum, Bill	CIN	122
Lankford, Ray	SL	15
Larkin, Barry	CIN	60
Larkin, Gene (3x)	MIN	99
Leach, Terry (2x)	CHA	133
Lee, Manuel (2x)	TEX	80
Lefferts, Craig	TEX	15
Leibrandt, Charlie (2x)	TEX	36
Leiter, Al	TOR	15
Leiter, Mark	DET	28
Leius, Scott	MIN	165
Lewis, Darren	SF	15
Lewis, Scott	CAL	19
Listach, Pat	MIL	46
Lloyd, Graeme	MIL	15
Mack, Shane	MIN	15
Maksudian, Mike	MIN	13
Mallicoat, Rob	HOU	182
Manuel, Barry	TEX	76
Martinez, Dave	SF	35
Martinez, Edgar (3x)	SEA	126
Martinez, Tino	SEA	55
Mattingly, Don	NYA	27
Maurer, Rob	TEX	182
McCaskill, Kirk	CHA	15
McGee, Willie	SF	19
McGwire, Mark	OAK	112
McReynolds, Kevin	KC	23
Meacham, Rusty (2x)	KC	171
Melendez, Jose (2x)	BOS	147
Melvin, Bob	BOS	15
Miller, Keith (2x)	KC	94
Miranda, Angel	MIL	57
Mitchell, Kevin	CIN	15
Mlicki, David	CLE	121
Morgan, Mike	CHN	15
Morris, Hal	CIN	63
Morris, Jack	TOR	19
Munoz, Pedro	MIN	25
Mussina, Mike	BAL	29
Nabholz, Chris	MON	31
Naehring, Tim	BOS	88
Nagy, Charles	CLE	140
Natal, Bobby	FLO	21
Nen, Robb	TEX	35
Nied, David	COL	99
Nilsson, Dave (2x)	MIL	44
Nokes, Matt	NYA	16
Novoa, Rafael	MIL	15
Obando, Sherman (2x)	BAL	45
Ojeda, Bobby	CLE	124
Olivares, Omar	SL	16
Olson, Gregg	BAL	42
Olson, Greg	ATL	23
Oquendo, Jose	SL	56
Orton, John (2x)	CAL	84
Pagnozzi, Tom	SL	40
Parrett, Jeff	COL	67
Patterson, John	SF	149
Pena, Geronimo	SL	59
Perez, Melido	NYA	13
Perez, Mike	SL	40
Petralli, Gene	TEX	39
Pichardo, Hipolito	KC	18
Plantier, Phil	SD	15
Power, Ted (2x)	CLE	55
Pratt, Todd	PHI	29
Raines, Tim	CHA	42
Rasmussen, Dennis (2x)	KC	60
Redus, Gary	TEX	17
Reed, Darren	NYN	157
Reed, Jeff	SF	34
Reed, Jody	LA	29
Revenig, Todd	OAK	182
Rhodes, Arthur	BAL	78
Richardson, Jeff (2x)	BOS	127
Ripken, Billy (2x)	TEX	87
Ritz, Kevin	COL	182
Rivera, Luis (2x)	BOS	42
Roberts, Bip (2x)	CIN	76
Rojas, Mel	MON	15
Roper, John	CIN	30
Rossy, Rico	KC	15
Russell, Jeff	BOS	30
Ryan, Nolan (3x)	TEX	115
Saberhagen, Bret	NYN	62
Sabo, Chris	CIN	15
Sanders, Deion	ATL	15
Sandberg, Ryne	CHN	25
Sasser, Mackey	SEA	16
Scarsone, Steve	SF	57
Schofield, Dick	TOR	111
Schwarz, Jeff	CHA	15
Scioscia, Mike	SD	182
Scudder, Scott	CLE	43
Seanez, Rudy	COL	102
Shipley, Craig	SD	17
Skinner, Joel	CLE	182
Smiley, John	CIN	93
Smith, Bryn	COL	16
Smith, Dwight	CHN	28
Smith, Dan (2x)	TEX	76
Smith, Pete	ATL	38
Smith, Zane	PIT	72
Sojo, Luis	TOR	20
Springer, Russell	CAL	63
Steinbach, Terry	OAK	49
Stewart, Dave	TOR	38
Stieb, Dave	CHA	23
Stillwell, Kurt	SD	22
Stottlemyre, Todd	TOR	21
Strawberry, Darryl (2x)	LA	132
Sutcliffe, Rick	BAL	19
Swan, Russ	SEA	42
Swindell, Greg	HOU	20
Tartabull, Dan	NYA	21
Thompson, Robbie	SF	17
Thon, Dickie	MIL	16
Tomlin, Randy (2x)	PIT	80
Trammell, Alan	DET	12
Valera, Julio	CAL	102
Valentin, John	BOS	15
VanSlyke, Andy	PIT	73
Velarde, Randy	NYA	54
Wagner, Paul	PIT	16
Walker, Larry	MON	15
Wallach, Tim	LA	22
Ward, Turner	TOR	30
Wedge, Eric (2x)	COL	112
Wegman, Bill	MIL	69
Welch, Bob	OAK	16
Wells, Dave	DET	19
Wetteland, John	MON	18
Whitehurst, Wally (3x)	SD	88
Wickander, Kevin (2x)	CIN	35
Wilkerson, Curt	KC	140
Williams, Brian	HOU	15
Williams, Bernie	NYA	25
Willis, Carl	MIN	39
Williams, Matt	SF	16
Wilson, Trevor (3x)	SF	75
Witt, Mike (3x)	NYA	144
Woodson, Kerry	SEA	182
Worrell, Todd (2x)	LA	83
Young, Curt (2x)	OAK	110
Young, Cliff	CLE	70
Yount, Robin	MIL	17
Zosky, Eddie	TOR	128

Part 5 Career Records

This part includes year-by-year, career major-league batting and pitching information for all 1,104 players who played in the majors in 1993. Each team for every year is listed separately, and if a player played for more than one major-league team in the same season, a totals line for the year is also included.

The career records are separated into alphabetical batter and pitcher registers. Every official batting and pitching category is included. (Note that batting stats for pitchers are not shown in the batter register, nor are pitching stats for non-pitchers shown in the pitcher register.)

The minor league statistics in this section are provided by Howe Sportsdata International, the official statisticians for the minor leagues. For all players in this section, complete minor-league records are included back through the 1984 season. Prior to 1984, Howe Sportsdata's minor-league records are not completely computerized, so 1983 and earlier data are not available for some players.

The first line for each player lists his full name, followed by his "use" name in quotes. A player's use name is the name he is commonly called (if different from his given name). Matronymic surnames for Hispanic players are shown in parentheses. Shown after the player's name are how he bats and throws and his date of birth. The next entry on the name line for major-leaguers shows how many games they played at each position for their career.

The career statistics are organized so that similar types of stats are grouped together from left to right across the page:

- The first columns show the year, team, and league.
- The second group is usage—how often they played, pitched, and batted.
- Third are the ways players reach base. For batters, these show their base hits and walks; for pitchers, how many hits and walks they allowed. Hit batters are placed next to walks, since they have exactly the same effect.
- Next come ways of making outs—strikeouts, double plays, and sacrifices.
- Next are basestealing stats for batters and the pitcher statistics that advance baserunners (wild pitches and balks).
- The last group of categories is the most important, showing the results of all the others. For batters, their runs scored and driven in are shown, followed by their batting, on-base, and slugging averages. For pitchers, their runs allowed are shown, followed by wins, losses, saves, and earned-run averages.

American and National League-leading totals in all important batting and pitching categories are denoted with an asterisk. Career games at position are shown for all major-league batters. Draft or signing information is shown for each player at the end of his name line.

Draft information is given only for teams which signed a player. If a player was drafted earlier but didn't sign a contract, that information is not shown. The format for draft information shows the drafting team's abbreviation followed by the year of the draft. An asterisk after the year indicates a January draft (discontinued in 1987); otherwise, all drafts were held in June. "DOM" indicates special drafts of Dominican Republic players held in the late 1980s.

After the draft year are two numbers: the first is the round in which the player was selected, the second in the overall pick number of the selection. An "S" before the round number indicates the player was selected in a secondary draft (held for amateur players who had been previously drafted but not signed). If a player was signed as a non-drafted amateur free agent, the team which signed him and the date are shown. "MEX" indicates players signed out of the Mexican League. A few players were originally signed by independent minor-league clubs; their signing date is shown after the signing club abbreviation.

KEY TO ABBREVIATIONS

CAREER RECORDS
YR	Year
TM/LG	Team/League
CL	Classification (for Minor Leagues)

MINOR LEAGUE TEAMS

MINOR LEAGUE CLASSIFICATIONS
AAA	Triple-A
AA	Double-A
A+	Single-A (Advanced)
A	Single-A
A—	Single-A (Short Season)
R+	Rookie (Advanced)
R	Rookie

MINOR LEAGUES
AMA	American Association (Triple-A)
INT	International League (Triple-A)
PCL	Pacific Coast League (Triple-A)
MEX	Mexican League (Triple-A)
EAS	Eastern League (Double-A)
SOU	Southern League (Double-A)
TEX	Texas League (Double-A)
CAL	California League (Single-A, Advanced)
CAR	Carolina League (Single-A, Advanced)
FSL	Florida State League (Single-A, Advanced)
MID	Midwest League (Single-A)
SAL	South Atlantic League, a.k.a. "Sally League" (Single-A)
NYP	New York-Pennsylvania League (Single-A, Short Season)

NWL	Northwest League (Single-A, Short Season)
PIO	Pioneer League (Rookie, Advanced)
APP	Appalachian League (Rookie, Advanced)
GCL	Gulf Coast League (Rookie)
ARI	Arizona League (Rookie)

CITY/TEAM ABBREVIATIONS

American Association (AMA)
AMA	BUF	Buffalo
AMA	DEN	Denver
DM		Des Moines
AMA	EVA	Evansville
AMA	IND	Indianapolis
AMA	IOW	Iowa
AMA	LOU	Louisville
AMA	NAS	Nashville
NO		New Orleans
AMA	OC	Oklahoma City
AMA	OMA	Omaha
AMA	VAN	Vancouver
AMA	WIC	Wichita

Appalachian League (APP)
APP	BLU	Bluefield
APP	BRI	Bristol
APP	BUR	Burlington
APP	ELI	Elizabethton
APP	HUN	Huntington
APP	JC	Johnson City
APP	KIN	Kingsport
APP	MAR	Martinsville
APP	PAI	Paintsville
APP	PIK	Pikeville
APP	PRI	Princeton
APP	PUL	Pulaski
APP	WYT	Wytheville

Arizona League (ARI)
ARI	ANG	Angels
ARI	ATH	Athletics
ARI	BRE	Brewers
ARI	MAR	Mariners
ARI	RSM	Red Sox Mariners

California League (CAL)
CAL	BAK	Bakersfield
CAL	CV	Central Valley
CAL	FRE	Fresno
CAL	HD	High Desert
CAL	LOD	Lodi
CAL	MOD	Modesto
CAL	PS	Palm Springs
CAL	RC	Rancho Cucamonga
CAL	RED	Redwood
CAL	REN	Reno
CAL	RIV	Riverside
CAL	SAL	Salinas
CAL	SB	San Bernardino
CAL	SJ	San Jose
CAL	SC	Santa Clara
CAL	STO	Stockton
CAL	VEN	Ventura
CAL	VIS	Visalia

Carolina League (CAR)
CAR	ALE	Alexandria
CAR	DUR	Durham
CAR	FRE	Frederick
CAR	HAG	Hagerstown
CAR	KIN	Kinston
CAR	LYN	Lynchburg
CAR	PEN	Peninsula
CAR	PW	Prince William
CAR	SAL	Salem
CAR	WIN	Winston-Salem

Eastern League (EAS)
EAS	ALB	Albany
EAS	BIN	Binghamton
EAS	BOW	Bowie
EAS	BRI	Bristol
EAS	BUF	Buffalo
EAS	CAN	Canton-Akron
EAS	GF	Glens Falls
EAS	HAG	Hagerstown
EAS	HAR	Harrisburg
EAS	HOL	Holyoke
EAS	LON	London
EAS	LYN	Lynn
EAS	NAS	Nashua
EAS	NB	New Britain
EAS	PIT	Pittsfield
EAS	REA	Reading
EAS	VER	Vermont
EAS	WAT	Waterbury
EAS	WIL	Williamsport

Florida State League (FSL)
FSL	BC	Baseball City
FSL	CHA	Charlotte
FSL	CLE	Clearwater
FSL	DB	Daytona Beach
FSL	DUN	Dunedin
FSL	FM	Ft. Myers
FSL	FL	Ft. Lauderdale
FSL	LAK	Lakeland
FSL	MIA	Miami
FSL	MIR	Miracle
FSL	OSC	Osceola
FSL	SAR	Sarasota
FSL	SL	St. Lucie
FSL	SP	St. Petersburg
FSL	TAM	Tampa
FSL	VB	Vero Beach

KEY TO ABBREVIATIONS (continued)

FSL WH   Winter Haven
FSL WPB West Palm Beach

Gulf Coast League (GCL)
GCL AST Astros
GCL BJ   Blue Jays
GCL BRA Braves
GCL CUB Cubs
GCL DOD Dodgers
GCL EXP Expos
GCL IND Indians
GCL MAR Marlins
GCL MET Mets
GCL PHI Phillies
GCL PIR Pirates
GCL RAN Rangers
GCL RS   Red Sox
GCL RED Reds
GCL ROY Royals
GCL TWI Twins
GCL WS   White Sox
GCL YAN Yankees

International League (INT)
INT CHA Charlotte
INT CMB Columbus
INT MAI Maine
INT NOR Norfolk
INT OTT Ottawa
INT PAW Pawtucket
INT RIC Richmond
INT ROC Rochester
INT SCR Scranton-Wilkes-Barre
INT SYR Syracuse
INT TID Tidewater
INT TOL Toledo

Midwest League (MID)
MID APP Appleton
MID BEL Beloit
MID BUR Burlington
MID CR   Cedar Rapids
MID CLI Clinton
MID KC   Kane County
MID KEN Kenosha
MID MAD Madison
MID PEO Peoria
MID QC   Quad City
MID ROC Rockford
MID SB   South Bend
MID SPR Springfield
MID WAT Waterloo
MID WAU Wausau

Northwest League (NWL)
NWL BEL Bellingham
NWL BEN Bend
NWL BOI Boise
NWL EUG Eugene
NWL EVE Everett
NWL MED Medford
NWL SAL Salem
NWL SO   Southern Oregon
NWL SPO Spokane
NWL TRI Tri-Cities
NWL WW   Walla Walla
NWL YAK Yakima

New York–Pennsylvania League (NYP)
NYP AUB Auburn
NYP BAT Batavia
NYP ELM Elmira
NYP ERI Erie
NYP GEN Geneva
NYP HAM Hamilton
NYP JAM Jamestown
NYP LF   Little Falls
NYP NEW Newark
NYP NF   Niagara Falls
NYP ONE Oneonta
NYP PIT Pittsfield
NYP SC   St. Catherines
NYP UTI Utica
NYP WAT Watertown
NYP WEL Welland

Pacific Coast League (PCL)
PCL ALB Albuquerque
PCL CAL Calgary
PCL CS   Colorado Springs
PCL EDM Edmonton
PCL HAW Hawaii
PCL LV   Las Vegas
PCL PHO Phoenix
PCL POR Portland
PCL SLC Salt Lake City
PCL SJ   San Jose
PCL TAC Tacoma
PCL TUC Tucson
PCL VAN Vancouver

Pioneer League (PIO)
PIO BIL Billings
PIO BUT Butte
PIO CAL Calgary
PIO GC   Gate City
PIO GF   Great Falls
PIO HEL Helena
PIO IF   Idaho Falls
PIO MH   Medicine Hat
PIO POC Pocatello

South Atlantic League (SAL)
SAL ALB Albany
SAL AND Anderson
SAL ASH Asheville
SAL AUG Augusta
SAL CHS Charleston, SC
SAL CHW Charleston, WV
SAL COL Columbia
SAL CMB Columbus
SAL FAY Fayetteville
SAL FLO Florence
SAL GAS Gastonia
SAL GRE Greensboro
SAL GRN Greenwood
SAL MAC Macon
SAL MB   Myrtle Beach
SAL SAV Savannah
SAL SPA Spartanburg
SAL SUM Sumter

Southern League (SOU)
SOU BIR Birmingham
SOU CAR Carolina
SOU CHA Charlotte
SOU CHT Chattanooga
SOU CMB Columbus
SOU GRE Greenville
SOU HUN Huntsville
SOU JAC Jacksonville
SOU KNO Knoxville
SOU MEM Memphis
SOU NAS Nashville
SOU ORL Orlando

Texas League (TEX)
TEX AMA Amarillo
TEX ARK Arkansas
TEX BEA Beaumont
TEX EP   El Paso
TEX JAC Jackson
TEX MID Midland
TEX SA   San Antonio
TEX SHR Shreveport
TEX TUL Tulsa
TEX WIC Wichita

BATTER REGISTER

Abbott, Kurt Thomas — BR/TR — b.6/2/68 — POS OF-13, SS-6, 2B-2 — OAK89 15/400

YR	TM/LG	CL	G	TPA	AB	H	2B	3B	HR	TB	BB	IBB	HB	SO	GDP	SH	SF	SB	CS	R	RBI	BA	OBA	SA
89	SO/NWL	A-	5	11	10	1	0	0	0	1	0	0	0	3	0	0	1	1	0	2	1	.100	.091	.100
	ATH/ARI	R	36	169	155	42	5	3	0	53	8	2	2	40	2	0	4	0	1	27	25	.271	.308	.342
90	MAD/MID	A	104	423	362	84	18	0	0	102	47	1	5	74	10	5	4	21	9	38	28	.232	.325	.282
91	MOD/CAL	A+	58	252	216	55	8	2	3	76	29	0	1	55	2	2	4	6	3	36	25	.255	.340	.352
	HUN/SOU	AA	53	202	182	46	6	1	0	54	17	0	1	39	4	1	1	6	3	18	11	.253	.318	.297
92	TAC/PCL	AAA	11	46	39	6	1	0	0	7	4	0	1	9	0	2	0	1	0	2	1	.154	.250	.179
	HUN/SOU	AA	124	493	452	115	14	5	9	166	31	0	3	75	5	4	3	16	5	64	52	.254	.305	.367
93	TAC/PCL	AAA	133	522	480	153	36	11	.12	247	33	4	2	123	8	4	3	19	9	75	79	.319	.363	.515
	OAK/AL		20	67	61	15	1	0	3	25	3	0	0	20	3	3	0	2	0	11	9	.246	.281	.410

Aldrete, Michael Peter "Mike" — BL/TL — b.1/29/61 — POS OF-341, 1B-214, DH-13 — SF83 6/174

YR	TM/LG	CL	G	TPA	AB	H	2B	3B	HR	TB	BB	IBB	HB	SO	GDP	SH	SF	SB	CS	R	RBI	BA	OBA	SA
84	FRE/CAL	A+	136	572	457	155	28	3	12	225	109	5	1	77	5	1	4	14	5	89	72	.339	.464	.492
85	SHR/TEX	AA	127	541	441	147	32	1	15	226	94	9	0	57	11	2	4	16	7	80	77	.333	.447	.512
	PHO/PCL	AAA	3	8	8	1	1	0	0	2	0	0	0	3	0	0	0	0	0	0	1	.125	.125	.250
86	PHO/PCL	AAA	47	200	159	59	14	0	6	91	36	3	0	24	1	1	4	0	0	36	35	.371	.477	.572
	SF/NL		84	256	216	54	18	3	2	84	33	4	2	34	3	4	1	1	3	27	25	.250	.353	.389
87	SF/NL		126	406	357	116	18	2	9	165	43	5	0	50	6	4	2	6	0	50	51	.325	.396	.462
88	SF/NL		139	449	389	104	15	0	3	128	56	13	0	65	10	1	3	6	5	44	50	.267	.357	.329
89	IND/AMA	AAA	10	39	31	4	1	0	0	5	8	0	0	10	0	0	0	0	1	4	2	.129	.308	.161
	MON/NL		76	159	136	30	8	1	1	43	19	0	1	30	4	1	2	1	3	12	12	.221	.316	.316
90	MON/NL		96	200	161	39	7	1	1	51	37	2	1	31	2	1	1	2	2	22	18	.242	.385	.317
91	SD/NL		12	18	15	0	0	0	0	0	3	0	0	4	1	0	0	0	1	2	1	.000	.167	.000
	CS/PCL	AAA	23	84	76	22	5	0	0	27	8	1	0	17	2	0	0	0	0	4	8	.289	.357	.355
	CLE/AL		85	222	183	48	6	1	1	59	36	1	0	37	0	1	2	1	2	22	19	.262	.380	.322
	YEAR		97	240	198	48	6	1	1	59	39	1	0	41	1	1	2	1	3	24	20	.242	.364	.298
92	CS/PCL	AAA	128	536	463	149	42	2	8	219	65	8	3	113	7	1	4	1	0	69	84	.322	.406	.473
93	TAC/PCL	AAA	37	149	122	39	11	2	7	75	26	5	0	22	6	1	0	2	2	20	21	.320	.439	.615
	OAK/AL		95	292	255	68	13	1	10	113	34	2	0	45	7	0	0	1	1	40	33	.267	.353	.443
7 YR TOTALS			**713**	**2002**	**1712**	**459**	**85**	**9**	**27**	**643**	**261**	**27**	**4**	**296**	**33**	**14**	**11**	**17**	**17**	**219**	**209**	**.268**	**.364**	**.376**

Alexander, Manuel De Jesus "Manny" — BR/TR — b.3/20/71 — POS SS-3 — BAL 2/4/88

YR	TM/LG	CL	G	TPA	AB	H	2B	3B	HR	TB	BB	IBB	HB	SO	GDP	SH	SF	SB	CS	R	RBI	BA	OBA	SA
89	BLU/APP	R+	65	299	274	85	13	2	2	108	20	1	3	49	2	0	2	19	8	49	34	.310	.361	.394
90	WAU/MID	A	44	169	152	27	3	1	0	32	12	1	1	41	2	1	3	8	3	16	11	.178	.238	.211
91	FRE/CAR	A+	134	598	548	143	17	3	3	175	44	0	2	68	4	3	1	47	14	81	42	.261	.318	.319
	HAG/EAS	AA	3	12	9	3	1	0	0	4	1	0	1	3	0	0	1	0	0	3	2	.333	.417	.444
92	HAG/EAS	AA	127	538	499	129	23	8	2	174	25	0	6	62	10	4	4	43	12	69	41	.259	.300	.349
	ROC/INT	AAA	6	26	24	7	1	0	0	8	1	0	0	3	0	1	0	2	2	3	3	.292	.320	.333
	BAL/AL		4	5	5	1	0	0	0	1	0	0	0	3	0	0	0	0	0	1	0	.200	.200	.200
93	ROC/INT	AAA	120	500	471	115	23	8	6	172	22	0	4	60	11	2	1	19	7	55	51	.244	.283	.365
	BAL/AL		3	0	0	0	0	0	0	0	0	0	0	0	0	0	0	0	0	1	0	.000	.000	.000
2 YR TOTALS			**7**	**5**	**5**	**1**	**0**	**0**	**0**	**1**	**0**	**0**	**0**	**3**	**0**	**0**	**0**	**0**	**0**	**2**	**0**	**.200**	**.200**	**.200**

Alicea, Luis Rene — BB/TR — b.7/29/65 — POS 2B-273, SS-5, OF-4, 3B-3 — SL86 1/23

YR	TM/LG	CL	G	TPA	AB	H	2B	3B	HR	TB	BB	IBB	HB	SO	GDP	SH	SF	SB	CS	R	RBI	BA	OBA	SA
86	ERI/NYP	A-	47	201	163	46	6	1	3	63	37	2	1	20	0	0	0	27	4	40	18	.282	.418	.387
	ARK/TEX	AA	25	77	68	16	3	0	0	19	5	0	0	11	2	2	2	0	3	8	3	.235	.280	.279
87	ARK/TEX	AA	101	398	337	91	14	3	4	123	49	2	2	28	1	5	5	13	8	57	47	.270	.361	.365
	LOU/AMA	AAA	29	117	105	32	10	2	2	52	9	1	1	9	2	1	1	4	2	18	20	.305	.362	.495
88	LOU/AMA	AAA	49	209	191	53	11	6	1	79	11	1	1	21	1	5	3	8	4	21	21	.277	.316	.414
	STL/NL		93	330	297	63	10	4	1	84	25	4	2	32	12	4	2	1	1	20	24	.212	.276	.283
89	LOU/AMA	AAA	124	482	412	102	20	3	8	152	59	1	4	55	10	3	4	13	5	53	48	.248	.344	.369
90	SP/FSL	A+	29	121	95	22	1	4	0	31	20	2	5	14	1	0	1	9	2	14	12	.232	.388	.326
	ARK/TEX	AA	14	57	49	14	3	1	0	19	7	0	1	8	0	0	0	4	0	11	4	.286	.386	.388
	LOU/AMA	AAA	25	98	92	32	6	3	0	44	5	0	1	12	4	0	0	1	0	10	9	.348	.388	.478
91	LOU/AMA	AAA	31	132	112	44	6	3	4	68	14	1	2	8	2	2	2	5	4	26	19	.393	.462	.607
	STL/NL		56	76	68	13	3	0	0	16	6	0	0	19	0	0	0	1	5	0	11	5	.191	.276	.235
92	LOU/AMA	AAA	20	88	71	20	4	1	0	28	16	1	0	6	5	0	1	4	2	11	6	.282	.409	.394
	STL/NL		85	302	265	65	9	11	2	102	27	1	4	40	5	2	4	2	6	26	32	.245	.320	.385
93	STL/NL		115	421	362	101	19	3	3	135	47	2	4	54	9	1	7	11	1	50	46	.279	.362	.373
4 YR TOTALS			**349**	**1129**	**992**	**242**	**41**	**18**	**6**	**337**	**107**	**7**	**10**	**145**	**26**	**7**	**13**	**14**	**8**	**101**	**102**	**.244**	**.320**	**.340**

Allanson, Andrew Neal "Andy" — BR/TR — b.12/22/61 — POS C-466, 1B-4, DH-1 — CLE83 2/39

YR	TM/LG	CL	G	TPA	AB	H	2B	3B	HR	TB	BB	IBB	HB	SO	GDP	SH	SF	SB	CS	R	RBI	BA	OBA	SA
83	WAT/MID	A	17	57	50	10	0	0	0	10	7	0	0	10	1	0	0	1	1	4	0	.200	.298	.200
	BAT/NYP	A-	51	174	145	38	3	0	0	41	25	0	0	16	5	4	0	3	0	27	6	.262	.371	.283
84	WAT/MID	A	46	165	144	39	5	0	0	44	20	0	0	16	3	1	0	6	5	14	10	.271	.360	.306
	BUF/EAS	AA	39	127	111	28	4	0	0	32	15	0	0	18	3	1	0	1	0	12	11	.252	.341	.288
85	WAT/EAS	AA	120	487	420	131	17	1	0	150	52	1	3	25	13	8	4	22	9	69	47	.312	.388	.357
86	CLE/AL		101	323	293	66	7	3	1	82	14	0	1	36	7	11	4	10	5	30	29	.225	.260	.280
87	BUF/AMA	AAA	76	289	276	75	8	0	4	95	9	0	0	36	10	1	2	2	4	21	39	.272	.295	.344
	CLE/AL		50	172	154	41	6	0	1	56	9	0	0	30	2	4	5	1	1	17	16	.266	.298	.364
88	CLE/AL		133	474	434	114	11	0	5	140	25	2	8	63	6	8	4	5	9	44	50	.263	.305	.323
89	CLE/AL		111	359	323	75	9	1	3	95	23	2	4	47	7	6	3	4	4	30	17	.232	.289	.294

Allanson, Andrew Neal "Andy" (continued)

YR	TM/LG	CL	G	TPA	AB	H	2B	3B	HR	TB	BB	IBB	HB	SO	GDP	SH	SF	SB	CS	R	RBI	BA	OBA	SA
90	OC/AMA	AAA	13	47	40	4	0	0	0	4	6	0	0	7	2	1	0	0	0	3	4	.100	.217	.100
	SAL/CAL	A+	36	150	127	37	6	1	3	54	19	0	2	22	4	0	2	6	5	21	19	.291	.387	.425
91	DET/AL		60	160	151	35	10	0	1	48	7	0	0	31	3	2	0	0	1	10	16	.232	.266	.318
92	MIL/AL		9	28	25	8	1	0	0	9	1	0	0	2	1	2	0	3	1	6	0	.320	.346	.360
	DEN/AMA	AAA	72	294	266	79	16	3	4	113	23	0	1	29	4	3	1	9	4	42	31	.297	.354	.425
93	PHO/PCL	AAA	50	175	161	57	15	2	6	94	10	1	1	18	4	1	2	7	4	31	23	.354	.391	.584
	SF/NL		13	26	24	4	1	0	0	5	1	0	0	2	1	1	0	0	0	3	2	.167	.200	.208
7 YR TOTALS			477	1542	1404	343	45	4	13	435	80	4	8	211	27	34	16	23	17	140	130	.244	.286	.310

Alomar, Roberto — BB/TR — b.2/5/68 — POS 2B-897, SS-5, DH-1　　　SD 2/16/85

YR	TM/LG	CL	G	TPA	AB	H	2B	3B	HR	TB	BB	IBB	HB	SO	GDP	SH	SF	SB	CS	R	RBI	BA	OBA	SA
85	CHS/SAL	A	137	623	546	160	14	3	0	180	61	3	0	73	9	12	4	36	19	89	54	.293	.362	.330
86	REN/CAL	A+	90	404	356	123	16	4	4	159	32	2	3	38	7	6	7	14	8	53	49	.346	.397	.447
87	WIC/TEX	AA	130	595	536	171	41	4	12	256	49	5	2	74	9	1	7	43	15	88	68	.319	.374	.478
88	LV/PCL	AAA	9	41	37	10	1	0	2	17	1	0	0	4	0	2	1	3	0	5	14	.270	.282	.459
	SD/NL		143	611	545	145	24	6	9	208	47	5	3	83	15	16	0	24	6	84	41	.266	.328	.382
89	SD/NL		158	702	623	184	27	1	7	234	53	4	1	76	10	17	8	42	17	82	56	.295	.347	.376
90	SD/NL		147	646	586	168	27	5	6	223	48	1	2	72	16	5	5	24	7	80	60	.287	.340	.381
91	TOR/AL		161	719	637	188	41	11	9	278	57	3	4	86	16	5	16	53	11	88	69	.295	.354	.436
92	TOR/AL		152	671	571	177	27	8	8	244	87	5	5	52	8	6	5	49	9	105	76	.310	.405	.427
93	TOR/AL		153	683	589	192	35	6	17	290	80	5	5	67	13	4	5	55	15	109	93	.326	.408	.492
6 YR TOTALS			914	4032	3551	1054	181	37	56	1477	372	23	20	436	67	64	25	247	65	548	395	.297	.364	.416

Alomar, Santos Jr. "Sandy" — BR/TR — b.6/18/66 — POS C-333, DH-5　　　SD 10/21/83

YR	TM/LG	CL	G	TPA	AB	H	2B	3B	HR	TB	BB	IBB	HB	SO	GDP	SH	SF	SB	CS	R	RBI	BA	OBA	SA
84	SPO/NWL	A-	59	239	219	47	5	0	0	52	13	0	1	20	7	4	2	3	0	13	21	.215	.260	.237
85	CHS/SAL	A	100	393	352	73	7	0	3	89	31	1	3	30	9	5	2	3	1	38	43	.207	.276	.253
86	BEA/TEX	AA	100	367	346	83	15	1	4	112	15	1	1	35	16	2	3	2	6	36	27	.240	.271	.324
87	WIC/TEX	AA	103	411	375	115	19	1	8	160	21	1	5	37	12	3	7	1	5	50	65	.307	.346	.427
88	LV/PCL	AAA	93	374	337	100	9	5	16	167	28	5	4	35	11	1	4	1	3	59	71	.297	.354	.496
	SD/NL		1	1	1	0	0	0	0	0	0	0	0	0	1	0	0	0	0	0	0	.000	.000	.000
89	LV/PCL	AAA	131	572	523	160	33	8	13	248	42	5	2	58	23	2	3	3	1	88	101	.306	.358	.474
	SD/NL		7	22	19	4	1	0	1	8	3	1	0	3	1	0	0	0	0	1	6	.211	.318	.421
90	CLE/AL		132	483	445	129	26	2	9	186	25	2	2	46	10	5	0	4	1	60	66	.290	.326	.418
91	CLE/AL		51	199	184	40	9	0	0	49	8	1	4	24	4	2	1	0	0	10	7	.217	.264	.266
	CS/PCL	AAA	12	41	35	14	2	0	1	19	5	2	0	0	0	0	1	0	0	5	10	.400	.463	.543
92	CLE/AL		89	320	299	75	16	0	2	97	13	3	5	32	7	3	0	3	3	22	26	.251	.293	.324
93	CHW/INT	AAA	12	50	44	16	5	0	1	24	5	1	1	8	1	0	0	0	0	8	8	.364	.440	.545
	CLE/AL		64	237	215	58	7	1	6	85	11	0	6	28	3	1	4	3	1	24	32	.270	.318	.395
6 YR TOTALS			344	1262	1163	306	59	3	18	425	60	7	17	134	25	11	11	10	9	117	137	.263	.306	.365

Alou, Moises Rojas — BR/TR — b.7/3/66 — POS OF-243　　　PIT86* 1/2

YR	TM/LG	CL	G	TPA	AB	H	2B	3B	HR	TB	BB	IBB	HB	SO	GDP	SH	SF	SB	CS	R	RBI	BA	OBA	SA
86	WAT/NYP	A-	69	277	254	60	9	8	6	103	22	1	1	72	5	0	0	14	8	30	35	.236	.300	.406
87	MAC/SAL	A	4	10	8	1	0	0	0	1	2	0	0	4	0	0	0	0	0	1	0	.125	.300	.125
	WAT/NYP	A-	39	139	117	25	6	2	4	47	16	0	4	36	0	0	2	9	6	20	18	.214	.324	.402
88	AUG/SAL	A	105	421	358	112	23	8	7	166	51	4	5	84	5	0	7	24	12	58	62	.313	.399	.464
89	SAL/CAR	A+	86	361	321	97	29	2	14	172	35	2	3	69	6	0	2	12	5	50	53	.302	.374	.536
	HAR/EAS	AA	54	224	205	60	5	2	3	78	17	1	0	38	1	0	2	8	4	36	19	.293	.344	.380
90	HAR/EAS	AA	36	150	132	39	12	2	3	64	16	3	1	21	5	0	1	7	4	19	22	.295	.373	.485
	PIT/NL		2	5	5	1	0	0	0	1	0	0	0	0	1	0	0	0	0	0	0	.200	.200	.200
	BUF/AMA	AAA	75	309	271	74	4	6	5	105	30	0	2	43	8	2	4	9	4	38	31	.273	.345	.387
	IND/AMA	AAA	15	59	55	12	1	0	0	13	3	0	0	7	0	0	1	4	3	6	6	.218	.254	.236
	MON/NL		14	16	15	3	0	0	0	5	0	0	1	0	0	1	0	0	0	4	0	.200	.200	.333
	YEAR		16	21	20	4	0	1	0	6	0	0	1	0	3	1	0	0	0	4	0	.200	.200	.300
92	MON/NL		115	377	341	96	28	2	9	155	25	0	1	46	5	5	5	16	2	53	56	.282	.328	.455
93	MON/NL		136	535	482	138	29	6	18	233	38	9	5	53	9	3	3	17	6	70	85	.286	.340	.483
3 YR TOTALS			267	933	843	238	57	9	27	394	63	9	6	102	15	9	12	33	8	127	141	.282	.332	.467

Amaral, Richard Louis "Rich" — BR/TR — b.4/1/62 — POS 2B-83, 3B-38, SS-33, DH-11, 1B-6, OF-3　　　CHN83 2/34

YR	TM/LG	CL	G	TPA	AB	H	2B	3B	HR	TB	BB	IBB	HB	SO	GDP	SH	SF	SB	CS	R	RBI	BA	OBA	SA
83	GEN/NYP	A-	67	318	269	68	17	3	1	94	45	2	2	47	5	1	1	22	7	63	24	.253	.363	.349
84	QC/MID	A	34	144	119	25	1	0	0	26	24	0	0	29	0	1	0	12	0	21	7	.210	.343	.218
85	WIN/CAR	A+	124	495	428	116	15	5	3	150	59	1	2	68	11	5	1	26	7	62	36	.271	.361	.350
86	PIT/EAS	AA	114	405	355	89	12	0	0	101	39	1	1	65	5	5	0	25	8	43	24	.251	.330	.285
87	PIT/EAS	AA	104	368	315	80	8	5	0	98	43	2	1	50	1	5	1	28	6	45	28	.254	.348	.311
88	PIT/EAS	AA	122	489	422	117	15	4	4	152	56	1	2	53	2	5	5	54	5	66	47	.277	.360	.360
89	BIR/SOU	AA	122	533	432	123	15	4	4	162	88	2	2	66	6	7	4	57	14	90	48	.285	.405	.375
90	VAN/PCL	AAA	130	567	462	139	39	5	4	200	88	3	4	68	4	9	4	20	14	87	56	.301	.414	.433
91	CAL/PCL	AAA	86	409	347	120	26	2	3	159	53	2	3	37	6	3	0	30	7	79	36	.346	.433	.458
	SEA/AL		14	18	16	1	0	0	0	1	1	0	1	5	1	0	0	0	0	2	0	.063	.167	.063
92	CAL/PCL	AAA	106	475	403	128	21	8	0	165	69	7	2	53	2	2	0	53	16	79	21	.318	.414	.409
	SEA/AL		35	109	100	24	3	0	0	30	5	0	4	16	4	4	0	4	1	9	7	.240	.276	.300
93	SEA/AL		110	421	373	108	24	1	1	137	33	0	3	54	5	7	5	19	11	53	44	.290	.348	.367
3 YR TOTALS			159	548	489	133	27	1	2	168	39	0	4	75	10	11	5	23	13	64	51	.272	.328	.344

Amaro, Ruben Jr. — BB/TR — b.2/12/65 — POS OF-134, 2B-4, DH-1 — CAL87 13/291

YR	TM/LG	CL	G	TPA	AB	H	2B	3B	HR	TB	BB	IBB	HB	SO	GDP	SH	SF	SB	CS	R	RBI	BA	OBA	SA
87	SAL/NWL	A-	71	306	241	68	7	3	3	90	49	5	7	28	5	3	6	27	11	51	31	.282	.409	.373
88	MID/TEX	AA	13	36	31	4	1	0	0	5	4	0	1	5	1	0	0	4	0	5	2	.129	.250	.161
	PS/CAL	A+	115	537	417	111	13	3	4	142	105	2	8	61	13	5	2	44	20	96	50	.266	.421	.341
89	QC/MID	A	59	250	200	72	9	4	3	98	42	4	7	25	5	0	1	20	8	50	27	.360	.484	.490
	MID/TEX	AA	29	125	110	42	9	2	3	64	10	1	1	19	0	2	2	7	1	28	9	.382	.431	.582
90	MID/TEX	AA	57	266	224	80	15	6	4	119	29	1	9	23	4	2	2	10	8	50	38	.357	.447	.531
	EDM/PCL	AAA	82	373	318	92	15	4	3	124	40	2	7	43	4	5	3	32	14	53	32	.289	.378	.390
91	EDM/PCL	AAA	121	552	472	154	42	6	3	217	63	2	6	48	6	9	2	36	18	95	42	.326	.411	.460
	CAL/AL		10	26	23	5	1	0	0	6	3	1	0	3	1	0	0	0	0	0	2	.217	.308	.261
92	SCR/INT	AAA	18	77	68	20	4	1	1	29	9	3	0	6	0	0	0	2	2	8	10	.294	.377	.426
	PHI/NL		126	426	374	82	15	6	7	130	37	1	9	54	11	4	2	11	5	43	34	.219	.303	.348
93	SCR/INT	AAA	101	454	412	120	30	5	9	187	31	2	5	44	5	3	3	25	4	76	37	.291	.346	.454
	PHI/NL		25	58	48	16	2	2	1	25	6	0	0	5	1	3	1	0	0	7	6	.333	.400	.521
3 YR TOTALS			**161**	**510**	**445**	**103**	**18**	**8**	**8**	**161**	**46**	**2**	**9**	**62**	**13**	**7**	**3**	**11**	**5**	**50**	**42**	**.231**	**.314**	**.362**

Anderson, Brady Kevin — BL/TL — b.1/18/64 — POS OF-631, DH-23 — BOS85 10/257

YR	TM/LG	CL	G	TPA	AB	H	2B	3B	HR	TB	BB	IBB	HB	SO	GDP	SH	SF	SB	CS	R	RBI	BA	OBA	SA
85	ELM/NYP	A-	71	285	215	55	7	6	5	89	67	0	2	32	2	1	0	13	9	36	21	.256	.437	.414
86	WH/FSL	A+	126	543	417	133	19	11	12	210	107	5	6	47	2	7	6	44	19	86	87	.319	.459	.504
87	NB/EAS	AA	52	219	170	50	4	3	6	78	45	3	2	24	5	1	1	7	3	30	35	.294	.445	.459
	PAW/INT	AAA	23	95	79	30	4	0	2	40	16	3	0	8	0	0	0	2	1	18	8	.380	.484	.506
88	BOS/AL		41	172	148	34	5	3	0	45	15	0	4	35	2	4	1	4	2	14	12	.230	.315	.304
	PAW/INT	AAA	49	196	167	48	6	1	4	68	26	3	3	33	2	0	0	8	3	27	19	.287	.393	.407
	BAL/AL		53	192	177	35	8	1	1	48	8	0	0	40	1	7	0	6	4	17	9	.198	.232	.271
	YEAR		94	364	325	69	13	4	1	93	23	0	4	75	3	11	1	10	6	31	21	.212	.272	.286
89	ROC/INT	AAA	21	84	70	14	1	2	1	22	12	1	2	13	0	0	0	2	2	14	8	.200	.333	.314
	BAL/AL		94	317	266	55	12	2	4	83	43	6	3	45	4	5	0	16	4	44	16	.207	.324	.312
90	FRE/CAR	A+	2	8	7	3	1	0	0	4	1	0	0	1	0	0	0	2	0	2	3	.429	.500	.571
	HAG/EAS	AA	9	41	34	13	1	0	2	20	5	1	0	5	1	0	1	2	1	8	5	.382	.450	.588
	BAL/AL		89	279	234	54	5	2	3	72	31	2	5	46	4	4	5	15	2	24	24	.231	.327	.308
91	ROC/INT	AAA	7	33	26	10	3	0	0	13	7	0	0	4	0	0	0	4	1	5	2	.385	.515	.500
	BAL/AL		113	313	256	59	12	3	2	83	38	0	5	44	1	11	3	12	5	40	27	.230	.338	.324
92	BAL/AL		159	749	623	169	28	10	21	280	98	14	9	98	2	10	9	53	16	100	80	.271	.373	.449
93	BAL/AL		142	664	560	147	36	8	13	238	82	4	10	99	4	6	6	24	12	87	66	.262	.363	.425
6 YR TOTALS			**691**	**2686**	**2264**	**553**	**106**	**29**	**44**	**849**	**315**	**26**	**36**	**407**	**18**	**47**	**24**	**130**	**45**	**326**	**234**	**.244**	**.343**	**.375**

Anthony, Eric Todd — BL/TL — b.11/8/67 — POS OF-375 — HOU86 34/795

YR	TM/LG	CL	G	TPA	AB	H	2B	3B	HR	TB	BB	IBB	HB	SO	GDP	SH	SF	SB	CS	R	RBI	BA	OBA	SA
86	AST/GCL	R	13	18	12	3	0	0	0	3	5	0	1	5	1	0	0	1	0	2	0	.250	.500	.250
87	AST/GCL	R	60	245	216	57	11	6	10	110	26	3	2	58	4	0	1	2	2	38	46	.264	.347	.509
88	ASH/SAL	A	115	485	439	120	36	1	29	245	40	5	3	101	10	0	3	10	4	73	89	.273	.336	.558
89	CMB/SOU	AA	107	444	403	121	16	2	28	225	35	5	3	127	3	0	3	14	9	67	79	.300	.358	.558
	TUC/PCL	AAA	12	52	46	10	3	0	3	22	6	0	0	11	2	0	0	0	0	10	11	.217	.308	.478
	HOU/NL		25	70	61	11	2	0	4	25	9	2	0	16	1	0	0	0	0	7	7	.180	.286	.410
90	CMB/SOU	AA	4	15	12	2	0	0	1	5	3	0	0	4	0	0	0	0	0	2	3	.167	.333	.417
	TUC/PCL	AAA	40	182	161	46	10	2	6	78	17	0	1	41	4	0	3	8	3	28	26	.286	.352	.484
	HOU/NL		84	277	239	46	8	0	10	84	29	3	2	78	4	1	6	5	0	26	29	.192	.279	.351
91	HOU/NL		39	132	118	18	6	0	1	27	12	1	0	41	2	0	1	0	0	11	7	.153	.227	.229
	TUC/PCL	AAA	79	349	318	107	22	2	9	160	25	6	3	58	13	0	3	11	5	57	63	.336	.387	.503
92	HOU/NL		137	483	440	105	15	1	19	179	38	5	2	98	7	0	4	5	4	45	80	.239	.298	.407
93	HOU/NL		145	539	486	121	19	4	15	193	49	2	2	88	9	0	2	3	5	70	66	.249	.319	.397
5 YR TOTALS			**430**	**1501**	**1344**	**301**	**50**	**5**	**49**	**508**	**137**	**13**	**5**	**321**	**23**	**1**	**14**	**14**	**9**	**159**	**189**	**.224**	**.295**	**.378**

Arias, Alejandro "Alex" — BR/TR — b.11/20/67 — POS SS-48, 2B-30, 3B-22 — CHN87 2/62

YR	TM/LG	CL	G	TPA	AB	H	2B	3B	HR	TB	BB	IBB	HB	SO	GDP	SH	SF	SB	CS	R	RBI	BA	OBA	SA
87	WYT/APP	R+	61	262	233	69	7	0	0	76	27	0	1	29	2	0	1	16	6	41	24	.296	.370	.326
88	CHW/SAL	A	127	542	472	122	12	1	1	136	54	3	4	44	9	10	3	41	12	57	33	.258	.336	.288
89	PEO/MID	A	136	573	506	140	10	11	2	178	49	3	7	67	11	9	2	31	6	74	64	.277	.348	.352
90	CHA/SOU	AA	119	475	419	103	16	3	4	137	42	0	2	53	11	9	3	12	5	55	38	.246	.315	.327
91	CHA/SOU	AA	134	544	488	134	26	0	4	172	47	2	3	42	9	3	3	23	9	69	47	.275	.340	.352
92	IOW/AMA	AAA	106	466	409	114	23	3	5	158	44	1	6	27	4	7	0	14	3	52	40	.279	.357	.386
	CHI/NL		32	113	99	29	6	0	0	35	11	0	2	13	4	1	0	0	0	14	7	.293	.375	.354
93	FLO/NL		96	283	249	67	5	1	2	80	27	0	3	18	5	1	3	1	1	27	20	.269	.344	.321
2 YR TOTALS			**128**	**396**	**348**	**96**	**11**	**1**	**2**	**115**	**38**	**0**	**5**	**31**	**9**	**2**	**3**	**1**	**1**	**41**	**27**	**.276**	**.353**	**.330**

Armas, Marcos Rafael — BR/TR — b.8/5/69 — POS 1B-12, DH-2, OF-1 — OAK 12/15/87

YR	TM/LG	CL	G	TPA	AB	H	2B	3B	HR	TB	BB	IBB	HB	SO	GDP	SH	SF	SB	CS	R	RBI	BA	OBA	SA
88	ATH/ARI	R	17	63	58	17	2	1	0	21	5	0	0	17	2	0	0	0	0	14	10	.293	.349	.362
89	SO/NWL	A-	36	144	136	43	5	2	3	61	6	0	0	42	6	1	1	1	0	18	22	.316	.343	.449
90	MAD/MID	A	75	276	260	62	13	0	7	96	10	0	2	80	11	1	3	3	5	32	33	.238	.269	.369
91	MOD/CAL	A+	36	158	140	39	7	0	8	70	10	0	4	41	5	1	5	0	5	21	33	.279	.325	.500
	HUN/SOU	AA	81	329	305	69	16	1	8	111	18	1	4	89	11	2	4	2	1	40	53	.226	.266	.364
92	HUN/SOU	AA	132	559	509	144	30	6	17	237	41	4	3	133	11	0	6	9	1	83	84	.283	.336	.466
93	TAC/PCL	AAA	117	479	434	126	27	8	15	214	35	1	3	113	7	1	6	4	0	69	89	.290	.343	.493
	OAK/AL		15	33	31	6	1	0	1	11	1	0	1	12	0	0	0	0	0	7	1	.194	.242	.355

Ashley, Billy Manual — BR/TR — b.7/11/70 — POS OF-38   LA88 2/62

YR	TM/LG	CL	G	TPA	AB	H	2B	3B	HR	TB	BB	IBB	HB	SO	GDP	SH	SF	SB	CS	R	RBI	BA	OBA	SA
88	DOD/GCL	R	9	27	26	4	0	0	0	4	1	0	0	9	0	0	0	1	0	3	0	.154	.185	.154
89	DOD/GCL	R	48	184	160	38	6	2	1	51	19	1	2	42	4	0	3	9	1	23	19	.237	.321	.319
90	BAK/CAL	A+	99	363	331	72	13	1	9	114	25	1	3	135	5	3	1	17	3	48	40	.218	.278	.344
91	VB/FSL	A+	61	214	206	52	11	2	7	88	7	0	0	69	4	0	1	9	2	18	42	.252	.276	.427
92	ALB/PCL	AAA	25	101	95	20	7	0	2	33	6	0	0	42	2	0	0	1	0	11	10	.211	.257	.347
	SA/TEX	AA	101	404	380	106	23	4	24	203	16	3	6	111	9	0	2	13	7	60	66	.279	.317	.534
	LA/NL		29	100	95	21	5	0	2	32	5	0	0	34	2	0	0	0	0	6	6	.221	.260	.337
93	ALB/PCL	AAA	125	524	482	143	31	4	26	260	35	1	2	143	16	0	5	6	4	88	100	.297	.344	.539
	LA/NL		14	39	37	9	0	0	0	9	2	0	0	11	0	0	0	0	0	0	0	.243	.282	.243
2 YR TOTALS			**43**	**139**	**132**	**30**	**5**	**0**	**2**	**41**	**7**	**0**	**0**	**45**	**2**	**0**	**0**	**0**	**0**	**6**	**6**	**.227**	**.266**	**.311**

Aude, Richard Thomas "Rich" — BR/TR — b.7/13/71 — POS 1B-7, OF-1   PIT89 2/48

YR	TM/LG	CL	G	TPA	AB	H	2B	3B	HR	TB	BB	IBB	HB	SO	GDP	SH	SF	SB	CS	R	RBI	BA	OBA	SA
89	PIR/GCL	R	24	97	88	19	3	0	0	22	5	0	3	17	1	0	1	2	0	13	7	.216	.278	.250
90	AUG/SAL	A	128	527	475	111	23	1	6	154	41	1	7	133	12	0	4	4	1	48	61	.234	.302	.324
91	SAL/CAR	A+	103	402	366	97	12	2	3	122	27	5	9	72	7	0	0	4	0	45	43	.265	.331	.333
92	SAL/CAR	A+	122	506	447	128	26	4	9	189	50	2	8	79	10	0	1	11	2	63	63	.286	.368	.423
	CAR/SOU	AA	6	21	20	4	1	0	2	11	1	0	0	3	0	0	0	0	0	4	3	.200	.238	.550
93	BUF/AMA	AAA	21	76	64	24	9	0	4	45	10	0	1	15	1	0	0	1	1	17	16	.375	.461	.703
	CAR/SOU	AA	120	491	422	122	25	3	18	207	50	7	12	79	6	1	6	8	4	66	73	.289	.376	.491
	PIT/NL		13	27	26	3	1	0	0	4	1	0	0	7	0	0	0	0	0	1	4	.115	.148	.154

Ausmus, Bradley David "Brad" — BR/TR — b.4/14/69 — POS C-49   NYA87 46/1152

YR	TM/LG	CL	G	TPA	AB	H	2B	3B	HR	TB	BB	IBB	HB	SO	GDP	SH	SF	SB	CS	R	RBI	BA	OBA	SA
88	ONE/NYP	A-	2	4	4	1	0	0	0	1	0	0	0	2	1	0	0	0	0	0	0	.250	.250	.250
	YAN/GCL	R	43	151	133	34	2	0	0	36	11	1	2	25	4	4	1	5	2	22	15	.256	.320	.271
89	ONE/NYP	A-	52	189	165	43	6	0	1	52	22	0	0	28	2	2	0	6	4	29	18	.261	.348	.315
90	PW/CAR	A+	107	402	364	86	12	2	0	102	32	0	3	73	7	3	0	2	8	46	27	.236	.303	.280
91	PW/CAR	A+	63	258	230	70	14	3	2	96	24	3	0	37	2	1	3	17	6	28	30	.304	.366	.417
	ALB/EAS	AA	67	261	229	61	9	2	1	77	27	1	1	36	8	3	1	14	3	36	29	.266	.345	.336
92	ALB/EAS	AA	5	20	18	3	0	1	0	5	2	0	0	3	1	0	0	2	1	0	1	.167	.250	.278
	CMB/INT	AAA	111	410	364	88	14	3	2	114	40	0	1	56	14	3	2	19	5	48	35	.242	.317	.313
93	CS/PCL	AAA	76	274	241	65	10	4	2	89	27	1	1	41	6	2	3	10	6	31	33	.270	.342	.369
	SD/NL		49	166	160	41	8	1	5	66	6	0	0	28	2	0	0	2	0	18	12	.256	.283	.412

Backman, Walter Wayne "Wally" — BB/TR — b.9/22/59 — POS 2B-826, 3B-111, SS-18, DH-1   NYN77 1/26

YR	TM/LG	CL	G	TPA	AB	H	2B	3B	HR	TB	BB	IBB	HB	SO	GDP	SH	SF	SB	CS	R	RBI	BA	OBA	SA
80	NY/NL		27	110	93	30	1	1	0	33	11	1	1	14	3	4	1	2	3	12	9	.323	.396	.355
81	NY/NL		26	42	36	10	2	0	0	12	4	0	0	7	0	2	0	1	0	5	0	.278	.350	.333
82	NY/NL		96	312	261	71	13	2	3	97	49	1	0	47	6	2	0	8	7	37	22	.272	.387	.372
83	NY/NL		26	45	42	7	0	1	0	9	2	0	0	8	2	1	0	0	0	6	3	.167	.205	.214
84	NY/NL		128	499	436	122	19	2	1	148	56	2	0	63	13	5	1	32	9	68	26	.280	.360	.339
85	NY/NL		145	574	520	142	24	5	1	179	36	1	1	72	14	14	3	30	12	77	38	.273	.320	.344
86	NY/NL		124	440	387	124	18	2	1	149	36	1	0	32	3	14	3	13	7	67	27	.320	.376	.385
87	NY/NL		94	335	300	75	6	1	1	86	25	0	0	43	5	9	1	11	3	43	23	.250	.307	.287
88	NY/NL		99	347	294	89	12	0	0	101	41	1	1	49	6	9	2	9	5	44	17	.303	.388	.344
89	MIN/AL		87	337	299	69	9	2	1	85	32	0	1	45	4	1	1	1	1	33	26	.231	.306	.284
90	PIT/NL		104	361	315	92	21	3	2	125	42	1	1	53	5	0	3	6	3	62	28	.292	.374	.397
91	PHI/NL		94	220	185	45	12	0	0	57	30	1	0	30	2	3	3	3	2	20	15	.243	.344	.308
92	PHI/NL		42	55	48	13	1	0	0	14	6	1	0	9	3	1	0	1	0	6	6	.271	.352	.292
93	SEA/AL		10	31	29	4	0	0	0	4	1	0	0	8	0	1	0	0	0	2	0	.138	.167	.138
14 YR TOTALS			**1102**	**3708**	**3245**	**893**	**138**	**19**	**10**	**1099**	**371**	**9**	**5**	**480**	**55**	**68**	**19**	**117**	**52**	**482**	**240**	**.275**	**.349**	**.339**

Baerga, Carlos Obed — BB/TR — b.11/4/68 — POS 2B-393, 3B-139, SS-50, DH-5   SD 11/4/85

YR	TM/LG	CL	G	TPA	AB	H	2B	3B	HR	TB	BB	IBB	HB	SO	GDP	SH	SF	SB	CS	R	RBI	BA	OBA	SA
86	CHS/SAL	A	111	416	378	102	14	4	7	145	26	1	5	60	4	2	5	6	1	57	41	.270	.321	.384
87	CHS/SAL	A	134	573	515	157	23	9	7	219	38	7	12	107	10	6	2	26	21	83	50	.305	.365	.425
88	WIC/TEX	AA	122	487	444	121	28	1	12	187	31	2	9	83	8	0	3	4	4	67	65	.273	.331	.421
89	LV/PCL	AAA	132	562	520	143	28	2	10	205	30	5	5	98	10	0	6	6	4	63	74	.275	.319	.394
90	CS/PCL	AAA	12	55	50	19	2	1	1	26	5	2	0	4	4	0	0	1	0	11	11	.380	.436	.520
	CLE/AL		108	338	312	81	17	2	7	123	16	2	4	57	4	1	5	0	2	46	47	.260	.300	.394
91	CLE/AL		158	654	593	171	28	2	11	236	48	5	6	74	12	4	3	3	2	80	69	.288	.346	.398
92	CLE/AL		161	716	657	205	32	1	20	299	35	10	13	76	15	2	9	10	2	92	105	.312	.354	.455
93	CLE/AL		154	680	624	200	28	6	21	303	34	7	6	68	17	3	13	15	4	105	114	.321	.355	.486
4 YR TOTALS			**581**	**2388**	**2186**	**657**	**105**	**11**	**59**	**961**	**133**	**24**	**29**	**275**	**48**	**10**	**30**	**28**	**10**	**323**	**335**	**.301**	**.344**	**.440**

Baez, Kevin Richard — BR/TR — b.1/10/67 — POS SS-61   NYN88 8/182

YR	TM/LG	CL	G	TPA	AB	H	2B	3B	HR	TB	BB	IBB	HB	SO	GDP	SH	SF	SB	CS	R	RBI	BA	OBA	SA
88	LF/NYP	A-	70	257	218	58	7	1	1	70	32	1	2	30	3	2	3	7	3	23	19	.266	.361	.321
89	COL/SAL	A	123	502	426	108	25	4	1	150	58	3	6	53	5	9	3	11	9	59	44	.254	.349	.352
90	JAC/TEX	AA	106	379	326	76	11	0	2	93	38	4	2	44	7	11	2	3	4	29	29	.233	.315	.285
	NY/NL		5	12	12	2	1	0	0	3	0	0	0	2	0	0	0	0	0	1	0	.167	.167	.250
91	TID/INT	AAA	65	235	210	36	8	0	0	44	12	0	1	32	6	4	8	0	1	18	13	.171	.226	.210
92	TID/INT	AAA	109	379	352	83	16	1	2	107	13	1	4	57	9	5	5	1	1	30	33	.236	.267	.304
	NY/NL		6	13	13	2	0	0	0	2	0	0	0	1	0	0	0	0	0	0	0	.154	.154	.154

(continued)

Baez, Kevin Richard (continued)

YR	TM/LG	CL	G	TPA	AB	H	2B	3B	HR	TB	BB	IBB	HB	SO	GDP	SH	SF	SB	CS	R	RBI	BA	OBA	SA
93	NOR/INT	AAA	63	233	209	54	11	1	2	73	20	1	1	29	3	2	1	0	2	23	21	.258	.325	.349
	NY/NL		52	143	126	23	9	0	0	32	13	1	0	17	1	4	0	0	0	10	7	.183	.259	.254
3 YR TOTALS			**63**	**168**	**151**	**27**	**10**	**0**	**0**	**37**	**13**	**1**	**0**	**17**	**4**	**4**	**0**	**0**	**0**	**10**	**7**	**.179**	**.244**	**.245**

Bagwell, Jeffery Robert "Jeff" — BR/TR — b.5/27/68 — POS 1B-454   BOS89 6/110

YR	TM/LG	CL	G	TPA	AB	H	2B	3B	HR	TB	BB	IBB	HB	SO	GDP	SH	SF	SB	CS	R	RBI	BA	OBA	SA
89	RS/GCL	R	5	22	19	6	1	0	0	7	3	0	0	0	1	0	0	0	0	3	3	.316	.409	.368
	WH/FSL	A+	64	240	210	65	13	2	2	88	23	0	3	25	7	3	1	1	1	27	19	.310	.384	.419
90	NB/EAS	AA	136	569	481	160	34	7	4	220	73	12	6	57	15	3	6	5	7	63	61	.333	.422	.457
91	HOU/NL		156	650	554	163	26	4	15	242	75	5	13	116	12	1	7	7	4	79	82	.294	.387	.437
92	HOU/NL		162	697	586	160	34	6	18	260	84	13	12	97	17	2	13	10	6	87	96	.273	.368	.444
93	HOU/NL		142	609	535	171	37	4	20	276	62	6	3	73	20	0	9	13	4	76	88	.320	.388	.516
3 YR TOTALS			**460**	**1956**	**1675**	**494**	**97**	**14**	**53**	**778**	**221**	**24**	**28**	**286**	**49**	**3**	**29**	**30**	**14**	**242**	**266**	**.295**	**.380**	**.464**

Baines, Harold Douglass — BL/TL — b.3/15/59 — POS OF-1060, DH-868   CHA77 1/1

YR	TM/LG	CL	G	TPA	AB	H	2B	3B	HR	TB	BB	IBB	HB	SO	GDP	SH	SF	SB	CS	R	RBI	BA	OBA	SA
80	CHI/AL		141	518	491	125	23	6	13	199	19	7	1	65	15	2	5	2	4	55	49	.255	.281	.405
81	CHI/AL		82	296	280	80	11	7	10	135	12	4	2	41	6	0	2	6	2	42	41	.286	.318	.482
82	CHI/AL		161	668	608	165	29	8	25	285	49	10	0	95	12	2	9	10	3	89	105	.271	.321	.469
83	CHI/AL		156	655	596	167	33	2	20	264	49	13	1	85	15	3	6	7	5	76	99	.280	.333	.443
84	CHI/AL		147	629	569	173	28	10	29	308	54	12	1	75	12	1	5	1	2	72	94	.304	.361	*.541
85	CHI/AL		160	693	640	198	29	3	22	299	42	8	1	89	23	0	10	1	1	86	113	.309	.348	.467
86	CHI/AL		145	618	570	169	29	2	21	265	38	9	2	89	14	0	8	2	1	72	88	.296	.338	.465
87	CHI/AL		132	554	505	148	26	4	20	242	46	2	1	82	12	0	2	0	0	59	93	.293	.352	.479
88	CHI/AL		158	674	599	166	39	1	13	246	67	14	1	109	21	0	7	0	0	55	81	.277	.347	.411
89	CHI/AL		96	397	333	107	20	1	13	168	60	13	1	52	11	0	2	0	1	55	56	.321	.423	.505
	TEX/AL		50	186	172	49	9	0	3	67	13	0	0	27	4	0	1	0	2	18	16	.285	.333	.390
	YEAR		146	583	505	156	29	1	16	235	73	13	1	79	15	0	4	0	3	73	72	.309	.395	.465
90	TEX/AL		103	371	321	93	10	1	13	144	47	9	0	63	13	0	3	0	1	41	44	.290	.377	.449
	OAK/AL		32	118	94	25	5	0	3	39	20	1	0	17	4	0	4	0	2	11	21	.266	.381	.415
	YEAR		135	489	415	118	15	1	16	183	67	10	0	80	17	0	7	0	3	52	65	.284	.378	.441
91	OAK/AL		141	566	488	144	25	1	20	231	72	22	1	67	12	0	5	0	1	76	90	.295	.383	.473
92	OAK/AL		140	543	478	121	18	0	16	187	59	6	0	61	11	0	6	1	3	58	76	.253	.331	.391
93	BOW/EAS	AA	2	7	6	0	0	0	0	0	1	0	0	1	0	0	0	0	0	0	0	.000	.143	.000
	BAL/AL		118	480	416	130	22	0	20	212	57	9	0	52	14	1	6	0	0	64	78	.313	.390	.510
14 YR TOTALS			**1962**	**7966**	**7160**	**2060**	**356**	**46**	**261**	**3291**	**704**	**136**	**11**	**1069**	**199**	**9**	**82**	**30**	**28**	**929**	**1144**	**.288**	**.349**	**.460**

Balboni, Stephen Charles "Steve" — BR/TR — b.1/16/57 — POS 1B-630, DH-281   NYA78 4/52

YR	TM/LG	CL	G	TPA	AB	H	2B	3B	HR	TB	BB	IBB	HB	SO	GDP	SH	SF	SB	CS	R	RBI	BA	OBA	SA
81	NY/AL		4	8	7	2	1	0	1	5	1	0	0	4	0	0	0	0	0	2	2	.286	.375	.714
82	NY/AL		33	114	107	20	2	1	2	30	6	0	0	34	1	0	1	0	0	8	4	.187	.228	.280
83	NY/AL		32	95	86	20	2	0	5	37	8	0	0	23	2	0	1	0	0	8	17	.233	.295	.430
84	KC/AL		126	488	438	107	23	2	28	218	45	5	4	139	9	0	1	0	0	58	77	.244	.320	.498
85	KC/AL		160	662	600	146	28	2	36	286	52	4	5	166	14	0	5	1	1	74	88	.243	.307	.477
86	KC/AL		138	562	512	117	25	1	29	231	43	2	1	146	8	0	6	0	0	54	88	.229	.286	.451
87	KC/AL		121	425	386	80	11	1	24	165	34	1	2	111	9	0	3	0	0	44	60	.207	.273	.427
88	KC/AL		21	64	63	9	2	0	2	17	1	0	0	20	0	0	0	0	0	2	5	.143	.156	.270
	SEA/AL		97	376	350	88	15	1	21	168	23	2	1	67	8	0	2	0	1	44	61	.251	.298	.480
	YEAR		118	440	413	97	17	1	23	185	24	2	1	87	8	0	2	0	1	46	66	.235	.277	.448
89	NY/AL		110	334	300	71	12	2	17	138	25	5	3	67	10	0	6	0	0	33	59	.237	.296	.460
90	NY/AL		116	307	266	51	6	0	17	108	35	2	3	91	4	0	3	0	0	24	34	.192	.291	.406
91	OC/AMA	AAA	83	339	301	81	15	1	20	158	33	2	1	74	6	0	4	0	0	44	63	.269	.339	.525
92	OC/AMA	AAA	117	518	454	114	26	2	30	234	55	6	3	100	12	0	6	0	0	75	104	.251	.332	.515
93	OC/AMA	AAA	126	535	471	115	22	0	36	245	51	4	6	98	16	0	7	0	0	67	108	.244	.321	.520
	TEX/AL		2	5	5	3	0	0	0	3	0	0	0	0	0	0	0	0	0	0	0	.600	.600	.600
11 YR TOTALS			**960**	**3440**	**3120**	**714**	**127**	**11**	**181**	**1406**	**273**	**21**	**19**	**856**	**67**	**1**	**27**	**1**	**2**	**351**	**495**	**.229**	**.293**	**.451**

Barberie, Bret Edward — BB/TR — b.8/16/67 — POS 2B-133, 3B-73, SS-20, 1B-1   MON88 7/180

YR	TM/LG	CL	G	TPA	AB	H	2B	3B	HR	TB	BB	IBB	HB	SO	GDP	SH	SF	SB	CS	R	RBI	BA	OBA	SA
89	WPB/FSL	A+	124	540	457	122	16	4	4	158	64	7	10	39	9	5	4	10	4	63	34	.267	.366	.346
90	JAC/SOU	AA	133	537	431	112	18	3	7	157	86	5	11	64	3	4	5	20	7	71	56	.260	.392	.364
91	IND/AMA	AAA	71	283	218	68	10	4	10	116	59	2	3	47	5	1	2	10	5	45	48	.312	.461	.532
	MON/NL		57	162	136	48	12	2	2	70	20	2	2	22	4	1	0	0	0	16	18	.353	.435	.515
92	IND/AMA	AAA	10	44	43	17	3	0	3	29	1	0	0	9	1	0	0	0	0	4	8	.395	.409	.674
	MON/NL		111	343	285	66	11	0	1	80	47	3	8	62	4	1	2	9	5	26	24	.232	.354	.281
93	EDM/PCL	AAA	4	20	19	8	2	0	1	13	0	0	1	2	0	0	0	0	0	3	8	.421	.450	.684
	MAR/GCL	R	2	9	8	2	0	0	0	2	1	0	0	1	0	0	0	0	0	0	1	.250	.333	.250
	FLO/NL		99	423	375	104	16	2	5	139	33	2	7	58	7	1	5	2	4	45	33	.277	.344	.371
3 YR TOTALS			**267**	**928**	**796**	**218**	**39**	**4**	**8**	**289**	**100**	**7**	**17**	**142**	**15**	**7**	**8**	**11**	**9**	**87**	**75**	**.274**	**.364**	**.363**

Barnes, William Henry "Skeeter" — BR/TR — b.3/3/57 — POS 3B-92, OF-72, 1B-61, 2B-24, DH-23, SS-2   CIN78 16/407

YR	TM/LG	CL	G	TPA	AB	H	2B	3B	HR	TB	BB	IBB	HB	SO	GDP	SH	SF	SB	CS	R	RBI	BA	OBA	SA
78	BIL/PIO	R+	68	314	277	102	22	5	3	143	29	5	1	27	7	1	6	21	3	66	76	.368	.422	.516
79	NAS/SOU	AA	145	542	500	133	19	4	12	196	27	1	4	64	18	4	7	5	3	54	77	.266	.305	.392
80	WAT/EAS	AA	138	571	533	156	27	4	4	207	24	0	1	54	18	6	7	12	6	62	64	.293	.320	.388
81	WAT/EAS	AA	96	406	363	93	17	0	6	128	33	6	4	29	9	3	3	15	4	45	49	.256	.323	.353
	IND/AMA	AAA	36	129	118	31	6	1	1	42	9	4	1	10	6	1	0	1	1	10	11	.263	.320	.356

Barnes, William Henry "Skeeter" (continued)

YR	TM/LG	CL	G	TPA	AB	H	2B	3B	HR	TB	BB	IBB	HB	SO	GDP	SH	SF	SB	CS	R	RBI	BA	OBA	SA
82	IND/AMA	AAA	18	62	59	18	5	1	1	28	1	0	0	6	0	2	0	1	2	8	3	.305	.317	.475
	WAT/EAS	AA	112	470	418	128	24	6	12	200	44	5	1	32	6	5	2	31	9	67	72	.306	.372	.478
83	CIN/NL		15	43	34	7	0	0	1	10	7	0	2	3	0	0	0	2	2	5	4	.206	.372	.294
	IND/AMA	AAA	109	408	377	127	19	6	7	179	26	2	0	42	3	3	2	10	5	67	56	.337	.378	.475
84	WIC/AMA	AAA	92	393	360	118	23	4	14	191	26	3	1	30	13	1	5	24	5	59	67	.328	.370	.531
	CIN/NL		32	46	42	5	0	0	1	8	4	1	0	6	1	0	0	0	0	5	3	.119	.196	.190
85	DEN/AMA	AAA	12	49	41	9	2	0	1	15	6	1	1	7	3	1	0	2	3	6	8	.220	.333	.366
	MON/NL		19	26	26	4	1	0	0	5	0	0	0	2	1	0	0	0	0	0	0	.154	.154	.192
	IND/AMA	AAA	83	340	299	86	16	0	6	120	32	2	4	38	6	2	3	18	5	45	55	.288	.361	.401
86	JAC/SOU	AA	3	10	8	4	0	0	0	4	1	0	0	1	0	0	0	0	1	1	1	.500	.500	.500
	IND/AMA	AAA	85	338	300	80	18	5	1	123	26	2	2	28	5	4	3	16	10	40	40	.267	.332	.410
	POR/PCL	AAA	38	157	141	52	8	4	1	71	7	0	0	9	1	0	2	5	3	21	29	.369	.395	.504
87	STL/NL		4	4	4	1	0	0	1	4	0	0	0	0	0	0	0	0	0	1	3	.250	.250	1.000
	LOU/AMA	AAA	62	271	242	68	19	2	5	106	23	1	1	18	5	1	4	7	2	38	34	.281	.341	.438
	DEN/AMA	AAA	48	211	189	63	14	3	11	116	18	0	1	20	0	1	2	10	3	41	42	.333	.390	.614
88	BUF/AMA	AAA	21	51	51	11	1	0	2	18	0	0	0	7	0	0	0	0	1	4	5	.216	.216	.353
	NAS/AMA	AAA	101	354	328	85	15	0	4	112	17	0	3	40	7	3	3	15	3	43	34	.259	.299	.341
89	CIN/NL		5	3	3	0	0	0	0	0	0	0	0	0	0	0	0	0	0	1	0	.000	.000	.000
	NAS/AMA	AAA	124	522	472	143	39	3	6	206	32	2	5	59	7	5	8	15	6	57	55	.303	.348	.436
90	NAS/AMA	AAA	144	615	548	156	21	2	7	202	47	2	11	57	15	3	6	34	11	83	66	.285	.350	.369
91	TOL/INT	AAA	62	264	233	77	14	0	9	118	23	1	4	26	6	2	2	27	7	48	40	.330	.397	.506
	DET/AL		75	171	159	46	13	2	5	78	9	1	0	24	1	2	1	10	7	28	17	.289	.325	.491
92	DET/AL		95	181	165	45	8	1	3	64	10	1	2	18	4	2	3	2	1	27	25	.273	.318	.388
93	DET/AL		84	180	160	45	8	1	2	61	11	0	0	19	2	4	5	5	5	24	27	.281	.318	.381
8 YR TOTALS			**329**	**654**	**593**	**153**	**30**	**4**	**13**	**230**	**41**	**3**	**4**	**72**	**9**	**8**	**8**	**20**	**17**	**91**	**79**	**.258**	**.307**	**.388**

Bass, Kevin Charles — BB/TR — b.5/12/59 — POS OF-1167, DH-2   MIL77 2/29

YR	TM/LG	CL	G	TPA	AB	H	2B	3B	HR	TB	BB	IBB	HB	SO	GDP	SH	SF	SB	CS	R	RBI	BA	OBA	SA
82	MIL/AL		18	11	9	0	0	0	0	0	1	0	0	1	0	1	0	0	0	4	0	.000	.100	.000
	HOU/NL		12	24	24	1	0	0	0	1	0	0	0	8	1	0	0	0	0	2	1	.042	.042	.042
	YEAR		30	35	33	1	0	0	0	1	1	0	0	9	1	1	0	0	0	6	1	.030	.059	.030
83	HOU/NL		88	206	195	46	7	3	2	65	6	1	0	27	2	4	1	2	2	25	18	.236	.257	.333
84	HOU/NL		121	342	331	86	17	5	2	119	6	1	3	57	2	2	0	5	5	33	29	.260	.279	.360
85	HOU/NL		150	582	539	145	27	5	16	230	31	1	6	63	10	4	2	19	8	72	68	.269	.315	.427
86	HOU/NL		157	640	591	184	33	5	20	287	38	11	6	72	15	4	4	22	13	83	79	.311	.357	.486
87	HOU/NL		157	654	592	168	31	5	19	266	53	13	4	77	15	3	5	21	8	83	85	.284	.344	.449
88	HOU/NL		157	595	541	138	27	2	14	211	42	10	6	65	16	3	3	31	6	57	72	.255	.314	.390
89	TUC/PCL	AAA	6	19	17	5	1	0	0	6	1	0	0	2	0	1	0	0	0	1	2	.294	.316	.353
	HOU/NL		87	348	313	94	19	4	5	136	29	3	1	44	2	1	4	11	4	42	44	.300	.357	.435
90	SJ/CAL	A+	6	23	22	8	1	0	0	9	0	0	1	0	1	0	0	1	0	2	4	.364	.391	.409
	PHO/PCL	AAA	8	33	33	8	2	0	0	10	0	0	0	3	0	1	0	1	1	2	4	.242	.242	.303
	SF/NL		61	233	214	54	9	1	7	86	14	3	2	26	5	2	1	22	7	25	32	.252	.303	.402
91	SJ/CAL	A+	5	22	19	2	2	0	0	4	2	1	0	3	0	0	0	2	0	1	1	.105	.227	.211
	PHO/PCL	AAA	10	44	41	13	3	1	2	24	2	0	0	4	0	0	0	2	1	8	7	.317	.341	.585
	SF/NL		124	406	361	84	10	4	10	132	36	8	4	56	12	2	3	15	7	43	40	.233	.307	.366
92	SF/NL		89	285	265	71	11	3	7	109	16	1	1	53	6	1	2	7	7	25	30	.268	.310	.411
	NY/NL		46	145	137	37	12	2	2	59	7	2	0	17	2	1	1	7	2	15	9	.270	.303	.431
	YEAR		135	430	402	108	23	5	9	168	23	3	1	70	8	2	3	14	9	40	39	.269	.308	.418
93	HOU/NL		111	258	229	65	18	0	3	92	26	3	1	31	4	2	0	7	1	31	37	.284	.359	.402
12 YR TOTALS			**1378**	**4729**	**4341**	**1173**	**221**	**39**	**107**	**1793**	**305**	**57**	**34**	**597**	**92**	**23**	**26**	**141**	**62**	**540**	**544**	**.270**	**.321**	**.413**

Batiste, Kimothy Emil "Kim" — BR/TR — b.3/15/68 — POS SS-72, 3B-58   PHI87 2/78

YR	TM/LG	CL	G	TPA	AB	H	2B	3B	HR	TB	BB	IBB	HB	SO	GDP	SH	SF	SB	CS	R	RBI	BA	OBA	SA
87	UTI/NYP	A-	46	157	150	26	8	1	2	42	7	3	0	65	3	0	0	4	0	15	10	.173	.210	.280
88	SPA/SAL	A	122	451	430	107	19	6	6	156	14	1	1	101	13	5	1	16	9	51	52	.249	.274	.363
89	CLE/FSL	A+	114	418	385	90	12	4	3	119	17	1	4	67	7	11	1	13	7	36	33	.234	.273	.309
90	REA/EAS	AA	125	508	486	134	14	4	6	174	13	1	2	73	11	5	2	28	14	57	33	.276	.296	.358
91	SCR/INT	AAA	122	491	462	135	25	6	1	175	11	0	4	72	5	10	4	18	13	54	41	.292	.312	.379
	PHI/NL		10	28	27	6	0	0	0	6	1	1	0	5	0	0	0	0	0	2	1	.222	.250	.222
92	PHI/NL		44	145	136	28	4	0	1	35	4	1	0	18	7	2	3	0	0	9	10	.206	.224	.257
	SCR/INT	AAA	71	279	269	70	12	6	2	100	7	1	1	42	8	2	0	6	5	30	29	.260	.282	.372
93	PHI/NL		79	161	156	44	7	1	5	68	3	2	1	29	3	0	1	0	1	14	29	.282	.298	.436
3 YR TOTALS			**133**	**334**	**319**	**78**	**11**	**1**	**6**	**109**	**8**	**4**	**1**	**55**	**10**	**2**	**4**	**0**	**2**	**25**	**40**	**.245**	**.262**	**.342**

Bautista, Daniel "Danny" — BR/TR — b.5/24/72 — POS OF-16   DET 6/24/89

YR	TM/LG	CL	G	TPA	AB	H	2B	3B	HR	TB	BB	IBB	HB	SO	GDP	SH	SF	SB	CS	R	RBI	BA	OBA	SA
90	BRI/APP	R+	27	104	95	26	3	0	2	35	8	1	0	21	1	1	0	2	3	9	12	.274	.330	.368
91	FAY/SAL	A	69	263	234	45	6	4	1	62	21	1	1	65	8	4	3	7	7	21	30	.192	.259	.265
92	FAY/SAL	A	121	493	453	122	22	0	5	159	29	0	5	76	9	4	2	18	20	59	52	.269	.319	.351
93	LON/EAS	AA	117	468	424	121	21	1	6	162	32	1	2	69	8	4	6	28	12	55	48	.285	.334	.382
	DET/AL		17	63	61	19	3	0	1	25	1	0	0	10	1	0	0	3	1	6	9	.311	.317	.410

Bean, William Daro "Bill" — BL/TL — b.5/11/64 — POS OF-132, 1B-16, DH-1   DET86 4/99

YR	TM/LG	CL	G	TPA	AB	H	2B	3B	HR	TB	BB	IBB	HB	SO	GDP	SH	SF	SB	CS	R	RBI	BA	OBA	SA
86	GF/EAS	AA	80	324	279	77	10	3	8	117	36	2	4	27	6	2	3	3	3	43	49	.276	.363	.419
87	DET/AL		26	71	66	17	2	0	0	19	5	0	4	11	1	0	1	0	1	6	4	.258	.310	.288
	TOL/INT	AAA	104	408	357	98	18	2	8	144	38	3	7	52	6	3	3	14	11	51	43	.275	.353	.403

(continued)

Bean, William Daro "Bill" (continued)

YR	TM/LG	CL	G	TPA	AB	H	2B	3B	HR	TB	BB	IBB	HB	SO	GDP	SH	SF	SB	CS	R	RBI	BA	OBA	SA
88	TOL/INT	AAA	138	545	484	124	19	1	6	163	41	3	8	45	13	6	6	12	11	59	40	.256	.321	.337
	DET/AL		10	12	11	2	0	1	0	4	0	0	0	2	0	1	0	0	0	2	0	.182	.182	.364
89	DET/AL		9	14	11	0	0	0	0	0	2	0	1	3	0	0	0	0	0	0	0	.000	.214	.000
	TOL/INT	AAA	76	307	267	84	14	2	4	114	27	0	7	35	10	4	2	7	2	43	29	.315	.389	.427
	ALB/PCL	AAA	3	11	9	2	0	1	0	4	2	0	0	0	0	0	0	0	0	1	3	.222	.364	.444
	LA/NL		51	76	71	14	4	0	0	18	4	0	1	10	0	0	0	0	2	7	3	.197	.250	.254
	YEAR		60	90	82	14	4	0	0	18	6	0	2	13	0	0	0	0	2	7	3	.171	.244	.220
90	ALB/PCL	AAA	129	507	427	126	26	5	7	183	69	2	6	63	8	1	4	16	8	85	67	.295	.397	.429
91	ALB/PCL	AAA	103	289	259	77	22	6	2	117	23	3	3	32	5	2	2	7	7	35	35	.297	.359	.452
92	EDM/PCL	AAA	39	158	138	34	8	2	1	49	7	1	8	13	6	1	4	5	3	17	24	.246	.312	.355
93	LV/PCL	AAA	53	205	167	59	11	2	7	95	32	3	2	14	2	0	4	3	1	31	40	.353	.454	.569
	SD/NL		88	192	177	46	9	0	5	70	6	1	2	29	4	2	5	2	4	19	32	.260	.284	.395
4 YR TOTALS			**184**	**365**	**336**	**79**	**15**	**1**	**5**	**111**	**17**	**1**	**4**	**55**	**5**	**3**	**5**	**3**	**7**	**34**	**39**	**.235**	**.276**	**.330**

Becker, Richard Goodhard "Rich" — BB/TR — b.2/1/72 — POS OF-3   MIN90 6/85

YR	TM/LG	CL	G	TPA	AB	H	2B	3B	HR	TB	BB	IBB	HB	SO	GDP	SH	SF	SB	CS	R	RBI	BA	OBA	SA
90	ELI/APP	R+	56	255	194	56	5	1	6	81	53	0	3	54	3	5	0	18	2	54	24	.289	.448	.418
91	KEN/MID	A	130	573	494	132	38	3	13	215	72	3	2	108	7	1	4	19	4	100	53	.267	.360	.435
92	VIS/CAL	A+	136	631	506	160	37	2	15	246	114	2	4	122	5	1	6	29	13	118	82	.316	.441	.486
93	NAS/SOU	AA	138	618	516	148	25	4	15	232	94	5	3	117	10	2	3	29	7	93	66	.287	.398	.450
	MIN/AL		3	12	7	2	2	0	0	4	5	0	0	4	0	0	0	1	1	3	0	.286	.583	.571

Bell, Derek Nathaniel — BR/TR — b.12/11/68 — POS OF-194, 3B-19, DH-1   TOR87 2/49

YR	TM/LG	CL	G	TPA	AB	H	2B	3B	HR	TB	BB	IBB	HB	SO	GDP	SH	SF	SB	CS	R	RBI	BA	OBA	SA
87	SC/NYP	A-	74	302	273	72	11	3	10	119	18	1	6	60	5	2	3	12	4	46	42	.264	.320	.436
88	MB/SAL	A	91	377	352	121	29	5	12	196	15	3	6	67	9	0	4	18	6	55	60	.344	.377	.557
	KNO/SOU	AA	14	53	52	13	3	1	0	18	1	0	0	14	1	0	0	2	1	5	4	.250	.264	.346
89	KNO/SOU	AA	136	549	513	124	22	6	16	206	26	4	6	92	6	0	4	15	7	72	75	.242	.284	.402
90	SYR/INT	AAA	109	434	402	105	13	5	7	149	23	1	3	75	8	0	6	21	7	57	56	.261	.302	.371
91	SYR/INT	AAA	119	528	457	158	22	12	13	243	57	7	9	69	16	0	5	27	13	89	93	.346	.424	.532
	TOR/AL		18	35	28	4	0	0	0	4	6	0	1	5	0	0	0	3	2	5	1	.143	.314	.143
92	DUN/FSL	A+	7	30	25	6	2	0	0	8	4	0	1	4	1	0	1	3	0	7	4	.240	.333	.320
	TOR/AL		61	184	161	39	6	3	2	57	15	1	5	34	6	2	1	7	2	23	15	.242	.324	.354
93	SD/NL		150	585	542	142	19	1	21	226	23	5	12	122	7	0	8	26	5	73	72	.262	.303	.417
3 YR TOTALS			**229**	**804**	**731**	**185**	**25**	**4**	**23**	**287**	**44**	**6**	**18**	**161**	**13**	**2**	**9**	**36**	**9**	**101**	**88**	**.253**	**.308**	**.393**

Bell, Jay Stuart — BR/TR — b.12/11/65 — POS SS-816, DH-3, 2B-2   MIN84 1/8

YR	TM/LG	CL	G	TPA	AB	H	2B	3B	HR	TB	BB	IBB	HB	SO	GDP	SH	SF	SB	CS	R	RBI	BA	OBA	SA
84	ELI/APP	R+	66	290	245	54	12	1	6	86	42	0	1	50	5	0	2	4	2	43	30	.220	.334	.351
85	VIS/CAL	A+	106	432	376	106	16	6	9	161	41	0	4	73	6	0	4	10	6	56	59	.282	.353	.428
	WAT/EAS	AA	29	124	114	34	11	2	1	52	9	1	0	16	3	1	0	3	3	13	14	.298	.350	.456
86	WAT/EAS	AA	138	593	494	137	28	4	7	194	87	0	1	65	7	1	11	11	9	86	74	.277	.378	.393
	CLE/AL		5	16	14	5	2	0	1	10	2	0	0	3	0	0	0	0	0	3	4	.357	.438	.714
87	BUF/AMA	AAA	110	440	362	94	15	4	17	168	70	1	2	84	3	1	3	6	3	71	60	.260	.380	.464
	CLE/AL		38	137	125	27	9	1	2	44	8	0	1	31	0	1	0	2	0	14	13	.216	.269	.352
88	CS/PCL	AAA	49	209	181	50	12	2	7	87	26	0	1	27	8	0	1	3	1	35	24	.276	.368	.481
	CLE/AL		73	236	211	46	5	1	2	59	21	0	1	53	3	1	2	4	2	23	21	.218	.289	.280
89	BUF/AMA	AAA	86	344	298	85	15	3	10	136	38	1	3	55	6	3	2	12	5	49	54	.285	.370	.456
	PIT/NL		78	303	271	70	13	3	2	95	19	0	1	47	9	10	2	5	3	33	27	.258	.307	.351
90	PIT/NL		159	696	583	148	28	7	7	211	65	0	3	109	14	39	6	10	6	93	52	.254	.329	.362
91	PIT/NL		157	697	608	164	32	8	16	260	52	1	4	99	15	30	3	10	6	96	67	.270	.330	.428
92	PIT/NL		159	712	632	167	36	6	9	242	55	0	4	103	12	19	2	7	5	87	55	.264	.326	.383
93	PIT/NL		154	701	604	187	32	9	9	264	77	6	6	122	16	13	1	16	10	102	51	.310	.392	.437
8 YR TOTALS			**823**	**3498**	**3048**	**814**	**157**	**35**	**48**	**1185**	**299**	**7**	**20**	**567**	**69**	**115**	**16**	**54**	**32**	**451**	**290**	**.267**	**.335**	**.389**

Bell, Jorge Antonio "George" — BR/TR — b.10/21/59 — POS OF-1227, DH-339, 3B-8, 2B-1   PHI 6/23/78

YR	TM/LG	CL	G	TPA	AB	H	2B	3B	HR	TB	BB	IBB	HB	SO	GDP	SH	SF	SB	CS	R	RBI	BA	OBA	SA
81	TOR/AL		60	168	163	38	2	1	5	57	5	1	0	27	1	0	0	3		19	12	.233	.256	.350
83	TOR/AL		39	118	112	30	5	4	2	49	4	1	2	17	4	0	0	1	1	5	17	.268	.305	.438
84	TOR/AL		159	641	606	177	39	4	26	302	24	2	8	86	14	0	3	11	2	85	87	.292	.326	.498
85	TOR/AL		157	666	607	167	28	6	28	291	43	6	8	90	8	0	8	21	6	87	95	.275	.327	.479
86	TOR/AL		159	690	641	198	38	6	31	341	41	3	2	62	15	0	6	7	8	101	108	.309	.349	.532
87	TOR/AL		156	665	610	188	32	4	47	*369	39	9	7	75	17	0	9	5	1	111	*134	.308	.352	.605
88	TOR/AL		156	657	614	165	27	5	24	274	34	5	2	66	21	0	8	4	2	78	97	.269	.304	.446
89	TOR/AL		153	664	613	182	41	2	18	281	33	3	4	60	18	0	14	4	3	88	104	.297	.330	.458
90	TOR/AL		142	608	562	149	25	0	21	237	32	7	3	80	14	0	11	3	2	67	86	.265	.303	.422
91	CHI/AL		149	603	558	159	27	0	25	261	32	6	4	62	10	0	9	2	6	63	86	.285	.323	.468
92	CHI/AL		155	670	627	160	27	0	25	262	31	8	6	97	29	0	9	1	1	74	112	.255	.294	.418
93	SB/MID	A	2	9	8	1	0	0	0	1	0	0	0	0	0	0	0	0	0	1	0	.125	.222	.125
	CHI/AL		102	436	410	89	17	2	13	149	13	2	4	49	14	0	9	1	1	36	64	.217	.243	.363
12 YR TOTALS			**1587**	**6586**	**6123**	**1702**	**308**	**34**	**265**	**2873**	**333**	**49**		**771**	**165**	**0**	**83**	**67**	**36**	**814**	**1002**	**.278**	**.316**	**.469**

Bell, Juan — BR/TR — b.3/29/68 — POS 2B-126, SS-126, DH-11, OF-4   LA 9/1/84

YR	TM/LG	CL	G	TPA	AB	H	2B	3B	HR	TB	BB	IBB	HB	SO	GDP	SH	SF	SB	CS	R	RBI	BA	OBA	SA
85	DOD/GCL	R	42	121	106	17	0	0	0	17	12	0	1	20	1	2	0	2	1	11	8	.160	.252	.160
86	DOD/GCL	R	59	250	217	52	6	2	0	62	29	1	1	28	2	0	3	12	2	38	26	.240	.328	.286
87	BAK/CAL	A+	156	665	610	188	32	4	47	369	39	9	7	75	17	0	9	5	1	111	134	.308	.352	.605

Bell, Juan (continued)

YR	TM/LG	CL	G	TPA	AB	H	2B	3B	HR	TB	BB	IBB	HB	SO	GDP	SH	SF	SB	CS	R	RBI	BA	OBA	SA
88	SA/TEX	AA	61	237	215	60	4	2	5	83	16	2	2	37	3	3	1	11	3	37	21	.279	.333	.386
	ALB/PCL	AAA	73	283	257	77	9	3	8	116	16	1	1	70	3	6	3	7	10	42	45	.300	.339	.451
89	ROC/INT	AAA	116	454	408	107	15	6	2	140	39	0	1	92	8	2	4	17	10	50	32	.262	.325	.343
	BAL/AL		8	4	4	0	0	0	0	0	0	0	0	1	0	0	0	1	0	2	0	.000	.000	.000
90	ROC/INT	AAA	82	367	326	93	12	5	6	133	36	1	3	59	9	0	2	16	12	59	35	.285	.360	.408
	BAL/AL		5	2	2	0	0	0	0	0	0	0	0	1	0	0	0	0	0	1	0	.000	.000	.000
91	BAL/AL		100	223	209	36	9	2	1	52	8	0	0	51	1	4	2	0	0	26	15	.172	.201	.249
92	ROC/INT	AAA	39	157	138	27	6	3	2	45	14	0	0	40	3	2	3	2	4	21	14	.196	.265	.326
	OC/AMA	AAA	24	86	82	21	4	1	1	30	4	0	0	19	0	0	0	2	0	12	9	.256	.291	.366
	PHI/NL		46	168	147	30	3	1	1	38	18	5	1	29	1	0	2	5	0	12	8	.204	.292	.259
93	PHI/NL		24	73	65	13	6	1	0	21	5	0	1	12	0	2	0	0	0	5	7	.200	.268	.323
	MIL/AL		91	327	286	67	6	2	5	92	36	0	0	64	4	3	1	6	6	42	29	.234	.321	.322
	YEAR		115	400	351	80	12	3	5	113	41	0	1	76	4	5	1	6	7	47	36	.228	.311	.322
5 YR TOTALS			274	797	713	146	24	6	7	203	67	5	3	158	6	9	5	12	7	88	59	.205	.274	.285

Belle, Albert Jojuan — BR/TR — b.8/25/66 — POS OF-336, DH-164   CLE87 1/47

YR	TM/LG	CL	G	TPA	AB	H	2B	3B	HR	TB	BB	IBB	HB	SO	GDP	SH	SF	SB	CS	R	RBI	BA	OBA	SA
87	KIN/CAR	A+	10	45	37	12	2	0	3	23	8	0	0	16	1	0	0	0	1	5	9	.324	.444	.622
88	KIN/CAR	A+	41	171	153	46	16	0	8	86	18	1	0	45	4	0	0	2	0	21	39	.301	.374	.562
	WAT/MID	A	9	29	28	7	1	0	1	11	1	0	0	9	1	0	0	0	0	2	2	.250	.276	.393
89	CAN/EAS	AA	89	350	312	88	20	0	20	168	32	5	4	82	6	0	2	8	4	48	69	.282	.354	.538
	CLE/AL		62	234	218	49	8	4	7	86	12	0	2	55	4	0	2	2	2	22	37	.225	.269	.394
90	CLE/AL		9	25	23	4	0	0	1	7	1	0	0	6	1	0	0	0	0	1	3	.174	.208	.304
	CS/PCL	AAA	24	101	96	33	3	1	5	53	5	0	0	16	4	0	0	0	3	16	19	.344	.376	.552
	CAN/EAS	AA	9	35	32	8	1	0	0	9	3	1	0	7	2	0	0	0	0	4	3	.250	.314	.281
91	CS/PCL	AAA	16	66	61	20	3	2	2	33	2	0	1	8	1	0	2	1	1	9	16	.328	.348	.541
	CLE/AL		123	496	461	130	31	2	28	249	25	2	5	99	24	0	5	3	6	60	95	.282	.323	.540
92	CLE/AL		153	650	585	152	23	1	34	279	52	5	4	128	18	1	8	8	2	81	112	.260	.320	.477
93	CLE/AL		159	693	594	172	36	3	38	328	76	13	8	96	18	0	14	23	12	93	*129	.290	.370	.552
5 YR TOTALS			506	2098	1881	507	98	10	108	949	166	20	19	384	65	3	29	36	17	257	376	.270	.330	.505

Belliard, Rafael Leonidas — BR/TR — b.10/24/61 — POS SS-707, 2B-100, 3B-11   PIT 7/10/80

YR	TM/LG	CL	G	TPA	AB	H	2B	3B	HR	TB	BB	IBB	HB	SO	GDP	SH	SF	SB	CS	R	RBI	BA	OBA	SA
82	PIT/NL		9	2	2	1	0	0	0	1	0	0	0	0	0	0	0	1	0	3	0	.500	.500	.500
83	PIT/NL		4	1	1	0	0	0	0	0	0	0	0	1	0	0	0	0	0	1	0	.000	.000	.000
84	PIT/NL		20	22	22	5	0	0	0	5	0	0	0	1	0	0	0	4	1	3	0	.227	.227	.227
85	HAW/PCL	AAA	100	350	341	84	12	4	1	107	4	0	1	49	6	3	1	9	7	35	18	.246	.256	.314
	PIT/NL		17	20	20	4	0	0	0	4	0	0	0	5	0	0	0	0	0	1	1	.200	.200	.200
86	PIT/NL		117	350	309	72	5	3	0	81	26	6	3	54	8	11	1	12	2	33	31	.233	.298	.262
87	HAR/EAS	AA	37	153	145	49	5	2	0	58	6	0	0	16	2	2	0	7	5	24	9	.338	.364	.400
	PIT/NL		81	229	203	42	4	3	1	55	20	6	3	25	4	2	1	5	1	26	15	.207	.286	.271
88	PIT/NL		122	321	286	61	0	4	0	69	26	3	4	47	10	5	0	7	1	28	11	.213	.288	.241
89	PIT/NL		67	165	154	31	0	2	0	37	8	2	2	22	1	3	0	5	2	10	8	.214	.253	.240
90	PIT/NL		47	61	54	11	3	0	0	14	5	0	1	13	2	1	0	1	2	10	6	.204	.283	.259
91	ATL/NL		149	385	353	88	9	2	0	101	22	2	2	63	4	7	1	3	1	36	27	.249	.296	.286
92	ATL/NL		144	315	285	60	6	1	0	68	14	4	3	43	6	13	0	0	0	20	14	.211	.255	.239
93	ATL/NL		91	89	79	18	5	0	0	23	4	0	1	13	1	3	0	0	0	6	6	.228	.291	.291
12 YR TOTALS			868	1960	1768	395	36	12	1	458	125	23	19	287	36	45	3	38	11	177	119	.223	.281	.259

Benavides, Alfredo "Freddie" — BR/TR — b.4/7/66 — POS SS-102, 2B-59, 3B-6, 1B-1   CIN87 2/50

YR	TM/LG	CL	G	TPA	AB	H	2B	3B	HR	TB	BB	IBB	HB	SO	GDP	SH	SF	SB	CS	R	RBI	BA	OBA	SA
87	CR/MID	A	5	15	15	2	1	0	0	3	0	0	0	7	1	0	0	0	1	2	0	.133	.133	.200
88	CR/MID	A	88	359	314	70	9	2	1	86	35	3	2	75	7	4	4	18	7	38	32	.223	.301	.274
89	CHT/SOU	AA	88	313	284	71	14	3	0	91	22	0	2	46	2	2	3	1	4	25	27	.250	.305	.320
	NAS/AMA	AAA	31	101	94	16	4	0	1	23	6	0	0	24	1	1	0	0	0	9	12	.170	.220	.245
90	CHT/SOU	AA	55	215	197	51	10	1	1	66	11	0	2	25	4	3	2	4	2	20	28	.259	.302	.335
	NAS/AMA	AAA	77	286	266	56	7	3	2	75	12	3	3	50	4	4	1	3	1	30	20	.211	.252	.282
91	NAS/AMA	AAA	94	350	331	80	8	0	0	88	16	1	3	55	10	3	0	7	7	24	21	.242	.277	.266
	CIN/NL		24	67	63	18	1	0	0	19	1	1	1	15	1	1	1	0	0	11	3	.286	.303	.302
92	CIN/NL		74	186	173	40	10	1	1	55	10	1	0	34	3	2	0	0	0	14	17	.231	.277	.318
93	CS/PCL	AAA	5	17	16	7	1	0	0	8	1	0	0	0	0	0	0	0	2	3	2	.438	.471	.500
	COL/NL		74	223	213	61	10	3	3	86	6	1	0	27	4	3	1	3	2	20	26	.286	.305	.404
3 YR TOTALS			172	476	449	119	21	4	4	160	17	6	2	76	8	6	2	4	3	45	46	.265	.294	.356

Benjamin, Michael Paul "Mike" — BR/TR — b.11/22/65 — POS SS-136, 2B-23, 3B-19   SF87 3/74

YR	TM/LG	CL	G	TPA	AB	H	2B	3B	HR	TB	BB	IBB	HB	SO	GDP	SH	SF	SB	CS	R	RBI	BA	OBA	SA
87	FRE/CAL	A+	64	240	212	51	6	4	6	83	24	1	2	71	1	2	0	6	2	25	24	.241	.324	.392
88	SHR/TEX	AA	89	338	309	73	19	5	6	120	22	1	4	63	5	5	2	14	6	48	37	.236	.285	.388
	PHO/PCL	AAA	37	124	106	18	4	1	0	24	13	0	2	32	3	2	1	2	0	13	6	.170	.270	.226
89	PHO/PCL	AAA	113	401	363	94	17	6	2	132	18	0	6	82	6	12	3	10	4	44	36	.259	.303	.364
	SF/NL		14	6	6	1	0	0	0	1	0	0	0	1	0	0	0	0	0	6	0	.167	.167	.167
90	PHO/PCL	AAA	118	456	419	105	21	7	5	155	25	3	5	89	6	2	5	13	7	46	39	.251	.297	.370
	SF/NL		22	59	56	12	3	0	2	23	3	0	1	10	2	0	0	0	1	7	3	.214	.254	.411
91	PHO/PCL	AAA	64	253	226	46	13	2	6	81	20	3	4	67	5	1	4	3	2	34	31	.204	.270	.358
	SF/NL		54	120	106	13	3	0	2	22	7	2	1	26	1	3	0	1	0	12	8	.123	.188	.208
92	PHO/PCL	AAA	31	115	108	33	10	2	0	47	3	1	0	18	1	1	0	0	4	15	17	.306	.342	.435
	SF/NL		40	82	75	13	2	1	1	20	4	1	0	15	1	3	0	1	0	4	3	.173	.215	.267

(continued)

Benjamin, Michael Paul "Mike" (continued)

YR	TM/LG	CL	G	TPA	AB	H	2B	3B	HR	TB	BB	IBB	HB	SO	GDP	SH	SF	SB	CS	R	RBI	BA	OBA	SA
93	SJ/CAL	A+	2	10	8	0	0	0	0	0	1	0	1	0	0	0	0	0	0	1	0	.000	.200	.000
	SF/NL		63	165	146	29	7	0	4	48	9	2	4	23	3	6	0	0	0	22	16	.199	.264	.329
5 YR TOTALS			**193**	**432**	**389**	**68**	**15**	**2**	**9**	**114**	**23**	**6**	**6**	**75**	**7**	**12**	**2**	**5**	**0**	**51**	**30**	**.175**	**.231**	**.293**

Benzinger, Todd Eric — BB/TR — b.2/11/63 — POS 1B-518, OF-192, DH-2, 3B-1   BOS81 5/96

YR	TM/LG	CL	G	TPA	AB	H	2B	3B	HR	TB	BB	IBB	HB	SO	GDP	SH	SF	SB	CS	R	RBI	BA	OBA	SA
84	NB/EAS	AA	110	430	391	101	25	5	10	166	33	4	1	89	10	3	2	0	1	49	60	.258	.316	.425
85	PAW/INT	AAA	70	273	256	64	13	1	11	112	12	1	0	49	13	2	3	0	0	31	47	.250	.280	.438
86	PAW/INT	AAA	90	342	314	79	13	2	11	129	23	2	1	76	6	1	3	7	5	41	32	.252	.302	.411
87	PAW/INT	AAA	65	278	257	83	17	3	13	145	16	1	2	41	5	0	3	7	2	47	49	.323	.363	.564
	BOS/AL		73	253	223	62	11	1	8	99	22	3	2	41	5	3	5	3	4	36	43	.278	.344	.444
88	BOS/AL		120	436	405	103	28	1	13	172	22	4	1	80	8	6	2	2	3	47	70	.254	.293	.425
89	CIN/NL		161	686	628	154	28	3	17	239	44	13	2	120	5	4	8	3	7	79	76	.245	.293	.381
90	CIN/NL		118	408	376	95	14	2	5	128	19	4	4	69	3	2	7	2	4	35	46	.253	.291	.340
91	CIN/NL		51	136	123	23	3	2	1	33	10	2	0	20	2	1	2	2	0	7	11	.187	.244	.268
	KC/AL		78	315	293	86	15	3	2	113	17	2	3	46	5	1	1	2	6	29	40	.294	.338	.386
	YEAR		129	451	416	109	18	5	3	146	27	4	3	66	7	2	3	4	6	36	51	.262	.310	.351
92	LA/NL		121	313	293	70	16	2	4	102	15	1	0	54	6	0	5	2	4	24	31	.239	.272	.348
93	SF/NL		86	194	177	51	7	2	6	80	13	1	0	35	2	3	0	0	0	25	26	.288	.332	.452
7 YR TOTALS			**808**	**2741**	**2518**	**644**	**122**	**16**	**56**	**966**	**162**	**30**	**12**	**465**	**36**	**18**	**31**	**19**	**28**	**282**	**343**	**.256**	**.300**	**.384**

Berroa, Geronimo Emiliano Letta — BR/TR — b.3/18/65 — POS OF-49   TOR 9/4/83

YR	TM/LG	CL	G	TPA	AB	H	2B	3B	HR	TB	BB	IBB	HB	SO	GDP	SH	SF	SB	CS	R	RBI	BA	OBA	SA
84	BJ/GCL	R	62	251	235	59	16	1	3	86	12	2	2	34	1	0	2	2	3	31	34	.251	.291	.366
85	KIN/CAR	A+	19	48	43	8	0	0	1	11	4	0	0	10	0	0	1	0	1	4	4	.186	.250	.256
	MH/PIO	R+	54	223	201	69	22	2	6	113	18	0	3	40	4	0	1	6	3	39	45	.343	.404	.562
	FLO/SAL	A	19	74	66	21	2	0	3	32	6	0	1	13	0	1	1	0	1	7	20	.318	.370	.485
86	VEN/CAL	A+	128	511	459	137	22	5	21	232	38	2	5	92	3	1	8	12	9	76	73	.298	.353	.505
	KNO/SOU	AA	1	4	4	0	0	0	0	0	0	0	0	1	0	0	0	0	0	0	0	.000	.000	.000
87	KNO/SOU	AA	134	581	523	150	33	3	36	297	46	1	5	104	4	0	7	2	1	87	108	.287	.346	.568
88	SYR/INT	AAA	131	526	470	122	29	1	8	177	38	5	10	88	8	0	8	7	5	55	64	.260	.323	.377
89	ATL/NL		81	143	136	36	4	0	2	46	7	1	0	32	2	0	0	1	5	7	9	.265	.301	.338
90	RIC/INT	AAA	135	544	499	134	17	2	12	191	34	1	1	89	17	0	9	4	2	56	80	.269	.322	.383
	ATL/NL		7	5	4	0	0	0	0	0	1	0	0	1	0	0	0	0	0	0	0	.000	.200	.000
91	CS/PCL	AAA	125	519	478	154	31	7	18	253	35	2	2	88	10	1	3	2	1	81	91	.322	.369	.529
92	NAS/AMA	AAA	112	505	461	151	33	2	22	254	32	1	8	69	6	0	4	8	9	73	88	.328	.378	.551
	CIN/NL		13	18	15	4	1	0	0	5	2	0	1	1	1	0	2	0	0	2	0	.267	.389	.333
93	EDM/PCL	AAA	90	370	327	107	33	4	16	196	36	3	4	71	6	0	3	1	2	64	68	.327	.397	.599
	FLO/NL		14	36	34	4	1	0	0	5	2	0	0	7	2	0	0	0	0	3	0	.118	.167	.147
4 YR TOTALS			**115**	**202**	**189**	**44**	**6**	**0**	**2**	**56**	**12**	**2**	**1**	**41**	**5**	**0**	**0**	**0**	**2**	**12**	**9**	**.233**	**.282**	**.296**

Berry, Sean Robert — BR/TR — b.3/22/66 — POS 3B-154   KC86* S1/9

YR	TM/LG	CL	G	TPA	AB	H	2B	3B	HR	TB	BB	IBB	HB	SO	GDP	SH	SF	SB	CS	R	RBI	BA	OBA	SA
86	EUG/NWL	A-	65	290	238	76	20	2	5	115	44	0	5	73	2	1	2	10	1	53	44	.319	.433	.483
87	FM/FSL	A+	66	253	205	52	7	2	2	69	43	1	1	65	1	1	4	4	4	26	30	.254	.389	.337
88	BC/FSL	A+	94	343	304	71	6	4	4	97	31	1	2	62	3	3	3	24	11	34	30	.234	.306	.319
89	BC/FSL	A+	116	459	399	106	19	7	4	151	44	1	6	68	6	5	5	37	11	67	44	.266	.344	.378
90	MEM/SOU	AA	135	548	487	142	25	4	14	217	44	1	5	89	10	7	5	19	9	73	77	.292	.353	.446
	KC/AL		8	25	23	5	1	1	0	8	2	0	0	5	0	0	0	0	0	2	4	.217	.280	.348
91	OMA/AMA	AAA	103	424	368	97	21	9	11	169	48	2	1	70	3	0	5	8	6	62	54	.264	.349	.459
	KC/AL		31	66	60	8	3	0	0	11	5	0	1	23	1	0	0	1	0	5	1	.133	.212	.183
92	OMA/AMA	AAA	122	493	439	126	22	2	21	215	39	1	7	87	6	2	6	6	8	61	77	.287	.350	.490
	MON/NL		24	58	57	19	5	0	1	23	1	0	0	11	1	0	0	2	1	5	4	.333	.345	.404
93	MON/NL		122	351	299	78	15	2	14	139	41	6	2	70	4	1	5	6	12	50	49	.261	.348	.465
4 YR TOTALS			**185**	**500**	**439**	**110**	**20**	**3**	**15**	**181**	**49**	**6**	**3**	**109**	**6**	**1**	**6**	**14**	**3**	**62**	**58**	**.251**	**.326**	**.412**

Berryhill, Damon Scott — BB/TR — b.12/3/63 — POS C-443   CHN84* 1/4

YR	TM/LG	CL	G	TPA	AB	H	2B	3B	HR	TB	BB	IBB	HB	SO	GDP	SH	SF	SB	CS	R	RBI	BA	OBA	SA
84	QC/MID	A	62	235	217	60	14	0	0	74	16	0	1	44	3	1	0	4	4	30	31	.276	.329	.341
85	WIN/CAR	A+	117	430	386	90	25	1	9	144	32	3	1	90	6	4	7	4	4	31	50	.233	.289	.373
86	PIT/EAS	AA	112	391	345	71	13	1	6	104	37	3	1	54	8	1	7	2	5	33	35	.206	.279	.301
87	IOW/AMA	AAA	121	470	429	123	22	1	18	201	32	3	0	58	6	1	8	5	4	54	67	.287	.330	.469
	CHI/NL		12	31	28	5	1	0	0	6	3	0	0	5	1	0	0	0	1	2	1	.179	.258	.214
88	IOW/AMA	AAA	21	81	73	16	5	1	2	29	7	1	0	21	0	1	0	1	0	11	11	.219	.284	.397
	CHI/NL		95	332	309	80	19	1	7	122	17	5	0	56	11	2	1	0	1	19	38	.259	.295	.395
89	IOW/AMA	AAA	7	31	30	6	1	0	2	13	1	0	0	8	2	0	0	0	0	4	4	.200	.226	.433
	CHI/NL		91	361	334	86	13	0	5	114	16	4	2	54	13	4	2	0	1	37	41	.257	.291	.341
90	PEO/MID	A	7	30	26	10	2	0	3	21	3	1	0	7	0	0	0	0	0	10	8	.385	.467	.808
	IOW/AMA	AAA	22	83	79	17	0	0	3	27	4	1	0	18	1	0	0	0	0	8	6	.215	.253	.342
	CHI/NL		17	59	53	10	4	0	1	17	5	1	0	14	3	0	1	0	0	6	9	.189	.254	.321
91	IOW/AMA	AAA	26	111	97	32	5	1	8	62	12	0	0	25	2	0	2	0	0	20	24	.330	.396	.639
	CHI/NL		62	172	159	30	7	1	5	52	11	1	1	41	2	0	1	0	0	13	14	.189	.244	.327
	ATL/NL		1	1	1	0	0	0	0	0	0	0	0	1	0	0	0	0	0	0	0	.000	.000	.000
	YEAR		63	173	160	30	7	1	5	52	11	1	1	42	2	0	1	0	0	13	14	.188	.243	.325
92	ATL/NL		101	328	307	70	16	1	10	118	17	4	1	67	4	0	3	0	2	21	43	.228	.268	.384
93	ATL/NL		115	363	335	82	18	2	8	128	21	1	1	64	7	1	4	0	2	24	43	.245	.291	.382
7 YR TOTALS			**494**	**1647**	**1526**	**363**	**78**	**4**	**36**	**557**	**90**	**16**	**6**	**302**	**41**	**9**	**16**	**3**	**5**	**122**	**189**	**.238**	**.280**	**.365**

Bichette, Alphonse Dante "Dante" — BR/TR — b.11/18/63 — POS OF-531, DH-5, 3B-1   CAL84 17/424

YR	TM/LG	CL	G	TPA	AB	H	2B	3B	HR	TB	BB	IBB	HB	SO	GDP	SH	SF	SB	CS	R	RBI	BA	OBA	SA
84	SAL/NWL	A-	64	263	250	58	9	2	4	83	6	0	3	53	6	3	1	6	2	27	30	.232	.258	.332
85	QC/MID	A	137	582	547	145	28	4	11	214	25	1	3	89	11	0	7	25	11	58	78	.265	.297	.391
86	PS/CAL	A+	68	318	290	79	15	0	10	124	21	1	3	53	7	0	4	2	0	39	73	.272	.324	.428
	MID/TEX	AA	62	266	243	69	16	2	12	125	18	0	2	50	5	0	3	3	0	43	36	.284	.335	.514
87	EDM/PCL	AAA	92	392	360	108	20	3	13	173	26	4	4	68	8	0	2	3	3	54	50	.300	.352	.481
88	EDM/PCL	AAA	132	537	509	136	29	10	14	227	25	2	2	80	12	0	1	8	1	64	81	.267	.304	.446
	CAL/AL		21	50	46	12	2	0	0	14	0	0	0	7	0	0	4	0	0	1	8	.261	.240	.304
89	EDM/PCL	AAA	61	255	226	55	11	2	11	103	24	0	2	39	12	1	2	4	5	39	40	.243	.319	.456
	CAL/AL		48	146	138	29	7	0	3	45	6	0	0	24	3	0	2	3	0	13	15	.210	.240	.326
90	CAL/AL		109	371	349	89	15	1	15	151	16	1	0	79	9	1	2	5	2	40	53	.255	.292	.433
91	MIL/AL		134	475	445	106	18	3	15	175	22	4	1	107	9	1	6	14	8	53	59	.238	.272	.393
92	MIL/AL		112	411	387	111	27	2	5	157	16	3	3	74	13	0	3	18	7	37	41	.287	.318	.406
93	COL/NL		141	581	538	167	43	5	21	283	28	2	7	99	7	0	8	14	8	93	89	.310	.348	.526
6 YR TOTALS			**565**	**2034**	**1903**	**514**	**112**	**11**	**59**	**825**	**88**	**10**	**14**	**390**	**41**	**4**	**25**	**54**	**25**	**237**	**265**	**.270**	**.303**	**.434**

Biggio, Craig Alan — BR/TR — b.12/14/65 — POS C-427, 2B-319, OF-57   HOU87 1/22

YR	TM/LG	CL	G	TPA	AB	H	2B	3B	HR	TB	BB	IBB	HB	SO	GDP	SH	SF	SB	CS	R	RBI	BA	OBA	SA
87	ASH/SAL	A	64	260	216	81	17	2	9	129	39	0	2	33	5	1	2	31	10	59	49	.375	.471	.597
88	TUC/PCL	AAA	77	329	281	90	21	4	3	128	40	1	3	39	2	3	2	19	4	60	41	.320	.408	.456
	HOU/NL		50	131	123	26	6	1	3	43	7	2	0	29	1	1	0	6	1	14	5	.211	.254	.350
89	HOU/NL		134	509	443	114	21	2	13	178	49	8	6	64	7	6	5	21	3	64	60	.257	.336	.402
90	HOU/NL		150	621	555	153	24	2	4	193	53	1	3	79	11	9	1	25	11	53	42	.276	.342	.348
91	HOU/NL		149	609	546	161	23	4	4	204	53	3	2	71	2	5	3	19	6	79	46	.295	.358	.374
92	HOU/NL		162	721	613	170	32	3	6	226	94	9	7	95	5	5	2	38	15	96	39	.277	.378	.369
93	HOU/NL		155	706	610	175	41	5	21	289	77	7	10	93	10	4	5	15	17	98	64	.287	.373	.474
6 YR TOTALS			**800**	**3297**	**2890**	**799**	**147**	**17**	**51**	**1133**	**333**	**30**	**28**	**431**	**36**	**30**	**16**	**124**	**53**	**404**	**256**	**.276**	**.355**	**.392**

Blankenship, Lance Robert — BR/TR — b.12/6/63 — POS OF-198, 2B-190, 3B-42, DH-34, 1B-14, SS-2   OAK86 10/249

YR	TM/LG	CL	G	TPA	AB	H	2B	3B	HR	TB	BB	IBB	HB	SO	GDP	SH	SF	SB	CS	R	RBI	BA	OBA	SA
86	MED/NWL	A-	14	74	52	21	3	0	2	30	17	1	0	9	0	1	4	10	1	22	17	.404	.521	.577
	MOD/CAL	A+	55	217	171	50	5	3	6	79	41	0	4	39	2	1	0	15	5	47	25	.292	.440	.462
87	MOD/CAL	A+	22	98	84	23	9	2	0	36	12	1	1	29	0	1	0	12	3	14	17	.274	.371	.429
	HUN/SOU	AA	107	471	390	99	21	3	4	138	67	0	6	60	5	3	5	34	7	64	39	.254	.368	.354
88	TAC/PCL	AAA	131	545	437	116	21	8	9	180	96	0	2	74	10	0	4	40	12	84	52	.265	.397	.412
	OAK/AL		10	3	3	0	0	0	0	0	0	0	0	1	0	0	0	0	0	1	0	.000	.000	.000
89	TAC/PCL	AAA	25	121	98	29	8	2	2	47	19	0	1	15	4	2	1	5	3	25	9	.296	.412	.480
	OAK/AL		58	137	125	29	5	1	1	39	8	0	0	31	0	1	1	5	1	22	4	.232	.276	.312
90	TAC/PCL	AAA	24	108	93	24	7	1	1	36	14	0	1	16	2	0	0	7	3	18	9	.258	.361	.387
	OAK/AL		86	162	136	26	3	0	1	29	20	0	0	23	6	6	0	3	1	18	10	.191	.295	.213
91	TAC/PCL	AAA	30	136	109	32	7	1	0	42	22	0	2	27	2	2	3	9	1	19	11	.294	.412	.385
	OAK/AL		90	216	185	46	8	0	3	63	23	0	3	42	2	3	2	12	3	33	21	.249	.336	.341
92	TAC/PCL	AAA	5	22	19	3	0	0	1	6	2	0	0	7	0	0	1	0	0	3	5	.158	.227	.316
	OAK/AL		123	446	349	84	24	1	3	119	82	2	6	57	10	8	1	21	7	59	34	.241	.393	.341
93	OAK/AL		94	328	252	48	8	0	2	64	67	0	2	64	9	4	1	13	5	43	23	.190	.363	.254
6 YR TOTALS			**461**	**1292**	**1050**	**233**	**48**	**3**	**9**	**314**	**200**	**2**	**11**	**218**	**27**	**25**	**6**	**54**	**18**	**176**	**92**	**.222**	**.350**	**.299**

Blauser, Jeffrey Michael "Jeff" — BR/TR — b.11/8/65 — POS SS-533, 2B-115, 3B-106, OF-3   ATL84 S1/5

YR	TM/LG	CL	G	TPA	AB	H	2B	3B	HR	TB	BB	IBB	HB	SO	GDP	SH	SF	SB	CS	R	RBI	BA	OBA	SA
84	PUL/APP	R+	62	262	217	54	6	1	3	71	38	0	3	47	4	3	1	14	2	41	24	.249	.367	.327
85	SUM/SAL	A	125	520	422	99	19	0	5	133	82	1	9	94	3	2	1	36	6	74	49	.235	.367	.315
86	DUR/CAR	A+	123	544	447	128	27	3	13	200	81	2	7	92	5	2	7	12	9	94	52	.286	.399	.447
87	RIC/INT	AAA	33	127	113	20	1	0	1	24	11	2	0	24	1	1	3	3	2	11	12	.177	.244	.212
	GRE/SOU	AA	72	311	265	66	13	3	4	97	34	0	3	49	3	6	3	5	3	35	32	.249	.338	.366
	ATL/NL		51	187	165	40	6	3	2	58	18	1	3	34	4	1	0	7	3	11	15	.242	.328	.352
88	RIC/INT	AAA	69	300	271	77	19	1	5	113	19	3	5	53	3	3	2	6	5	40	23	.284	.340	.417
	ATL/NL		18	74	67	16	3	1	2	27	2	0	1	11	1	3	1	0	1	7	7	.239	.268	.403
89	ATL/NL		142	507	456	123	24	2	12	187	38	2	1	101	7	8	4	5	4	63	46	.270	.325	.410
90	ATL/NL		115	429	386	104	24	3	8	158	35	4	1	70	4	3	4	3	2	46	39	.269	.338	.409
91	ATL/NL		129	415	352	91	14	3	11	144	54	4	2	82	4	2	3	5	4	49	54	.259	.358	.409
92	ATL/NL		123	403	343	90	19	3	14	157	46	2	4	82	2	7	1	5	4	61	46	.262	.354	.458
93	ATL/NL		161	710	597	182	29	2	15	260	85	0	16	109	13	5	2	16	6	110	73	.305	.401	.436
7 YR TOTALS			**739**	**2725**	**2366**	**646**	**119**	**17**	**64**	**991**	**278**	**10**	**32**	**466**	**35**	**31**	**18**	**41**	**28**	**347**	**280**	**.273**	**.355**	**.419**

Blosser, Gregory Brent "Greg" — BL/TL — b.6/26/71 — POS OF-9, DH-1   BOS89 1/16

YR	TM/LG	CL	G	TPA	AB	H	2B	3B	HR	TB	BB	IBB	HB	SO	GDP	SH	SF	SB	CS	R	RBI	BA	OBA	SA
89	RS/GCL	R	40	174	146	42	7	3	2	61	25	1	1	19	7	0	2	3	0	17	20	.288	.391	.418
	WH/FSL	A+	28	104	94	24	1	1	2	33	8	0	1	14	1	0	1	1	0	6	14	.255	.317	.351
90	LYN/CAR	A+	119	504	447	126	23	1	18	205	55	3	1	99	13	0	1	5	4	63	62	.282	.361	.459
91	NB/EAS	AA	134	520	452	98	21	3	8	149	63	0	1	114	16	0	0	1	1	47	46	.217	.312	.330
92	NB/EAS	AA	129	502	434	105	23	4	22	202	64	0	3	122	1	0	1	2	2	59	71	.242	.339	.465
93	PAW/INT	AAA	130	543	478	109	22	6	23	204	58	5	2	139	4	0	2	6	3	66	66	.228	.312	.427
	BOS/AL		17	30	28	2	0	0	0	2	2	0	0	7	0	0	0	1	1	1	1	.071	.133	.107

Blowers, Michael Roy "Mike" — BR/TR — b.4/24/65 — POS 3B-218, DH-5, 1B-4, OF-2, C-1   MON86 10/252

YR	TM/LG	CL	G	TPA	AB	H	2B	3B	HR	TB	BB	IBB	HB	SO	GDP	SH	SF	SB	CS	R	RBI	BA	OBA	SA
86	JAM/NYP	A-	32	117	95	24	9	2	1	40	17	2	3	18	4	2	0	3	2	13	6	.253	.383	.421
	EXP/GCL	R	31	132	115	25	3	1	2	36	15	0	0	25	4	2	0	3	2	14	17	.217	.308	.313

(continued)

Blowers, Michael Roy "Mike" (continued)

YR	TM/LG	CL	G	TPA	AB	H	2B	3B	HR	TB	BB	IBB	HB	SO	GDP	SH	SF	SB	CS	R	RBI	BA	OBA	SA
87	WPB/FSL	A+	136	542	491	124	30	3	16	208	48	0	0	118	11	0	3	4	4	68	71	.253	.317	.424
88	JAC/SOU	AA	137	531	460	115	20	6	15	192	68	3	2	114	11	1	0	6	4	58	60	.250	.349	.417
89	IND/AMA	AAA	131	508	461	123	29	6	14	206	41	4	2	109	10	1	3	3	2	49	56	.267	.327	.447
	NY/AL		13	41	38	10	0	0	0	10	3	0	0	13	1	0	0	0	0	2	3	.263	.317	.263
90	CMB/INT	AAA	62	264	230	78	20	6	6	128	29	1	1	40	8	0	4	3	0	30	50	.339	.409	.557
	NY/AL		48	157	144	27	4	0	5	46	12	1	1	50	3	0	0	0	0	16	21	.188	.255	.319
91	NY/AL		15	40	35	7	0	0	1	10	4	0	0	3	1	1	0	0	0	3	1	.200	.282	.286
	CAL/PCL	AAA	90	379	329	95	20	2	9	146	40	1	3	74	12	1	6	3	1	56	59	.289	.365	.444
92	CAL/PCL	AAA	83	353	300	95	28	2	9	154	50	2	1	64	12	0	2	2	3	56	67	.317	.414	.513
	SEA/AL		31	80	73	14	3	0	1	20	6	0	0	20	3	1	0	0	0	7	2	.192	.253	.274
93	SEA/AL		127	429	379	106	23	3	15	180	44	3	2	98	12	3	1	1	5	55	57	.280	.357	.475
5 YR TOTALS			234	747	669	164	30	3	22	266	69	4	3	184	20	5	1	2	5	83	84	**.245**	**.318**	**.398**

Bogar, Timothy Paul "Tim" — BR/TR — b.10/28/66 — POS SS-66, 3B-7, 2B-6   NYN87 9/212

YR	TM/LG	CL	G	TPA	AB	H	2B	3B	HR	TB	BB	IBB	HB	SO	GDP	SH	SF	SB	CS	R	RBI	BA	OBA	SA
87	LF/NYP	A-	58	228	205	48	9	0	0	57	18	0	3	39	3	0	2	2	2	31	23	.234	.303	.278
88	COL/SAL	A	45	170	142	40	4	2	3	57	22	0	3	29	6	1	2	5	3	19	21	.282	.385	.401
	SL/FSL	A+	76	277	236	65	7	1	2	80	34	0	2	57	4	4	1	9	7	34	30	.275	.370	.339
89	JAC/TEX	AA	112	462	406	108	13	5	4	143	41	4	1	57	15	3	5	8	3	44	45	.266	.340	.352
90	TID/INT	AAA	33	130	117	19	2	0	0	21	8	0	1	22	4	4	0	1	1	10	4	.162	.222	.179
91	WIL/EAS	AA	63	271	243	61	12	2	2	83	20	0	2	44	5	2	4	13	8	33	25	.251	.309	.342
	TID/INT	AAA	65	245	218	56	11	0	1	70	20	0	3	35	8	4	2	1	0	23	23	.257	.320	.321
92	TID/INT	AAA	129	503	481	134	32	1	5	183	14	0	3	65	15	5	0	9	7	54	38	.279	.303	.380
93	NY/NL		78	224	205	50	13	0	3	72	14	2	1	29	2	1	1	0	1	19	25	.244	.300	.351

Boggs, Wade Anthony — BL/TR — b.6/15/58 — POS 3B-1654, 1B-50, DH-44, OF-1   BOS76 7/166

YR	TM/LG	CL	G	TPA	AB	H	2B	3B	HR	TB	BB	IBB	HB	SO	GDP	SH	SF	SB	CS	R	RBI	BA	OBA	SA
82	BOS/AL		104	381	338	118	14	1	5	149	35	4	0	21	9	4	4	1	0	51	44	.349	.406	.441
83	BOS/AL		153	685	582	210	44	7	5	283	92	2	1	36	15	3	7	3	3	100	74	*.361	*.444	.486
84	BOS/AL		158	726	625	203	31	4	6	260	89	6	0	44	13	8	4	3	2	109	55	.325	.407	.416
85	BOS/AL		161	758	653	*240	42	3	8	312	96	5	4	61	20	3	2	2	1	107	78	*.368	*.450	.478
86	BOS/AL		149	693	580	207	47	2	8	282	*105	14	0	44	11	4	4	0	0	107	71	*.357	*.453	.486
87	BOS/AL		147	667	551	200	40	6	24	324	105	19	2	48	13	0	4	1	3	108	89	*.363	*.461	.588
88	BOS/AL		155	719	584	214	*45	6	5	286	*125	18	0	34	23	0	5	2	3	*128	58	*.366	*.476	.490
89	BOS/AL		156	742	621	205	*51	7	3	279	107	19	1	51	19	0	7	2	6	*113	54	.330	*.430	.449
90	BOS/AL		155	713	619	187	44	5	6	259	87	19	1	68	14	0	6	0	0	89	63	.302	.386	.418
91	BOS/AL		144	641	546	181	42	2	8	251	89	25	0	32	16	0	4	1	2	93	51	.332	.421	.460
92	BOS/AL		143	598	514	133	22	4	7	184	74	4	1	31	10	0	8	1	2	62	50	.259	.353	.358
93	NY/AL		143	644	560	169	26	1	2	203	74	4	0	49	10	1	9	0	1	83	59	.302	.378	.363
12 YR TOTALS			1768	7967	6773	2267	448	48	87	3072	1078	154	22	519	173	24	70	16	28	1150	746	**.335**	**.424**	**.454**

Bolick, Frank Charles — BB/TR — b.6/28/66 — POS 1B-51, 3B-24   MIL87 10/227

YR	TM/LG	CL	G	TPA	AB	H	2B	3B	HR	TB	BB	IBB	HB	SO	GDP	SH	SF	SB	CS	R	RBI	BA	OBA	SA
87	HEL/PIO	R+	52	201	156	39	8	1	10	79	41	1	3	44	3	1	0	4	0	41	28	.250	.415	.506
88	BEL/MID	A	55	225	180	41	14	1	2	63	43	0	1	49	3	1	0	3	3	28	16	.228	.379	.350
	BRE/ARI	R	23	105	80	30	9	3	1	48	22	0	0	8	0	0	3	1	0	20	20	.375	.495	.600
	HEL/PIO	R+	40	167	131	39	10	1	10	81	32	2	1	31	2	1	1	5	1	35	28	.298	.434	.618
89	BEL/MID	A	88	354	299	90	23	0	9	140	47	5	6	52	3	1	0	5	3	44	41	.301	.404	.468
90	STO/CAL	A+	50	209	164	51	9	1	8	86	38	1	2	33	0	0	5	5	3	39	36	.311	.435	.524
	SB/CAL	A+	78	340	277	92	24	4	10	154	53	6	2	53	2	2	6	8	5	61	66	.332	.432	.556
91	JAC/SOU	AA	136	566	468	119	19	2	16	186	84	3	5	115	7	2	1	9	4	69	73	.254	.369	.397
92	JAC/SOU	AA	63	271	224	60	9	2	13	108	42	1	1	38	3	0	4	1	4	32	42	.268	.380	.482
	CAL/PCL	AAA	78	319	274	79	18	4	14	151	39	2	1	52	4	0	4	4	4	35	54	.288	.374	.551
93	OTT/INT	AAA	2	8	8	1	0	0	0	1	0	0	0	0	0	0	0	0	0	0	0	.125	.125	.125
	MON/NL		95	242	213	45	13	0	4	70	23	2	0	37	4	0	4	1	0	25	24	.211	.298	.329

Bonds, Barry Lamar — BL/TL — b.7/24/64 — POS OF-1143   PIT85 1/6

YR	TM/LG	CL	G	TPA	AB	H	2B	3B	HR	TB	BB	IBB	HB	SO	GDP	SH	SF	SB	CS	R	RBI	BA	OBA	SA
85	PW/CAR	A+	71	296	254	76	16	4	13	139	37	0	0	52	3	1	4	15	3	49	37	.299	.383	.547
86	HAW/PCL	AAA	44	186	148	46	7	2	7	78	33	0	2	31	1	0	3	16	5	30	37	.311	.435	.527
	PIT/NL		113	484	413	92	26	3	16	172	65	2	2	102	4	2	4	36	7	72	48	.223	.330	.416
87	PIT/NL		150	611	551	144	34	9	25	271	54	3	3	88	4	2	3	32	10	99	59	.261	.329	.492
88	PIT/NL		144	614	538	152	30	5	24	264	72	14	2	82	3	0	2	17	11	97	58	.283	.368	.491
89	PIT/NL		159	679	580	144	34	6	19	247	93	22	1	93	3	1	4	32	10	96	58	.248	.351	.426
90	PIT/NL		151	621	519	156	32	3	33	293	93	15	3	83	8	0	6	52	13	104	114	.301	.406	*.565
91	PIT/NL		153	634	510	149	28	5	25	262	107	25	0	73	8	0	13	43	13	95	116	.292	*.410	.514
92	PIT/NL		140	612	473	147	36	5	34	295	*127	32	2	69	9	0	7	39	8	*109	103	.311	*.456	*.624
93	SF/NL		159	674	539	181	38	4	*46	*365	126	43	2	79	11	0	7	29	12	129	*123	.336	*.458	*.677
8 YR TOTALS			1169	4929	4123	1165	258	40	222	2169	737	156	22	669	56	3	44	280	84	801	679	**.283**	**.391**	**.526**

Bonilla, Roberto Martin Antonio "Bobby" — BB/TR — b.2/23/63 — POS OF-600, 3B-541, 1B-67   PIT 7/11/81

YR	TM/LG	CL	G	TPA	AB	H	2B	3B	HR	TB	BB	IBB	HB	SO	GDP	SH	SF	SB	CS	R	RBI	BA	OBA	SA
84	NAS/EAS	AA	136	544	484	128	19	5	11	190	49	2	3	89	9	1	7	15	7	74	71	.264	.331	.393
85	PW/CAR	A+	39	147	130	34	4	1	3	49	16	2	0	29	5	0	1	5	1	15	11	.262	.340	.377
86	CHI/AL		75	271	234	63	10	2	2	83	33	2	1	49	4	2	1	4	1	11	26	.269	.361	.355
	PIT/NL		63	225	192	46	6	2	1	59	29	1	1	39	5	3	0	4	1	28	17	.240	.342	.307
	YEAR		138	496	426	109	16	4	3	142	62	3	2	88	9	5	1	8	2	55	43	.256	.352	.333

Bonilla, Roberto Martin Antonio "Bobby" (continued)

YR	TM/LG	CL	G	TPA	AB	H	2B	3B	HR	TB	BB	IBB	HB	SO	GDP	SH	SF	SB	CS	R	RBI	BA	OBA	SA
87	PIT/NL		141	515	466	140	33	3	15	224	39	4	2	64	8	0	8	3	5	58	77	.300	.351	.481
88	PIT/NL		159	681	584	160	32	7	24	278	85	19	4	82	4	0	8	3	5	87	100	.274	.366	.476
89	PIT/NL		163	698	616	173	37	10	24	302	76	20	1	93	10	0	5	8	8	96	86	.281	.358	.490
90	PIT/NL		160	686	625	175	39	7	32	324	45	9	1	103	11	0	15	4	3	112	120	.280	.322	.518
91	PIT/NL		157	680	577	174	*44	6	18	284	90	8	2	67	14	0	11	2	4	102	100	.302	.391	.492
92	NY/NL		128	506	438	109	23	0	19	189	66	10	1	73	11	0	1	4	3	62	70	.249	.348	.432
93	NY/NL		139	582	502	133	21	3	34	262	72	11	0	96	12	0	8	3	3	81	87	.265	.352	.522
8 YR TOTALS			**1185**	**4844**	**4234**	**1173**	**245**	**40**	**169**	**2005**	**535**	**84**	**13**	**666**	**79**	**5**	**57**	**35**	**36**	**653**	**683**	**.277**	**.356**	**.474**

Boone, Bret Robert — BR/TR — b.4/6/69 — POS 2B-106, 3B-6, DH-1   SEA90 5/134

YR	TM/LG	CL	G	TPA	AB	H	2B	3B	HR	TB	BB	IBB	HB	SO	GDP	SH	SF	SB	CS	R	RBI	BA	OBA	SA
90	PEN/CAR	A+	74	303	255	68	13	2	8	109	47	0	1	57	1	0	0	5	2	42	38	.267	.383	.427
91	JAC/SOU	AA	139	556	475	121	18	1	19	198	72	2	5	123	21	1	3	9	9	64	75	.255	.357	.417
92	CAL/PCL	AAA	118	511	439	138	26	5	13	213	60	7	5	88	12	1	6	17	12	73	73	.314	.398	.485
	SEA/AL		33	135	129	25	4	0	4	41	4	0	1	34	4	1	0	1	1	15	15	.194	.224	.318
93	CAL/PCL	AAA	71	309	274	91	18	3	8	139	28	0	1	58	7	0	6	3	8	48	56	.332	.388	.507
	SEA/AL		76	302	271	68	12	2	12	120	17	1	4	52	6	1	4	3	4	46	53	.251	.301	.443
2 YR TOTALS			**109**	**437**	**400**	**93**	**16**	**2**	**16**	**161**	**21**	**1**	**5**	**86**	**10**	**2**	**4**	**4**	**5**	**61**	**68**	**.233**	**.277**	**.403**

Borders, Patrick Lance "Pat" — BR/TR — b.5/14/63 — POS C-603, DH-26, 2B-1, 3B-1   TOR82 6/134

YR	TM/LG	CL	G	TPA	AB	H	2B	3B	HR	TB	BB	IBB	HB	SO	GDP	SH	SF	SB	CS	R	RBI	BA	OBA	SA
84	FLO/SAL	A	131	527	467	129	32	5	12	207	56	0	1	109	6	0	3	3	4	69	85	.276	.353	.443
85	KIN/CAR	A+	127	508	460	120	16	1	10	168	45	1	1	116	11	0	2	6	5	43	60	.261	.327	.365
86	FLO/SAL	A	16	42	40	15	7	0	3	31	2	0	0	9	0	0	0	0	0	8	9	.375	.405	.775
	KNO/SOU	AA	12	37	34	12	1	0	2	19	1	0	0	6	2	2	0	0	3	3	5	.353	.371	.559
	KIN/CAR	A+	49	186	174	57	10	0	6	85	10	0	1	42	5	0	1	0	0	24	26	.328	.366	.489
87	DUN/FSL	A+	3	11	11	4	0	0	0	4	0	0	0	3	0	0	0	0	0	0	1	.364	.364	.364
	KNO/SOU	AA	94	374	349	102	14	1	11	151	20	0	2	56	13	0	2	0	3	44	51	.292	.332	.433
88	SYR/INT	AAA	35	138	120	29	8	0	3	46	16	0	0	22	1	0	2	0	0	15	21	.242	.326	.383
	TOR/AL		56	160	154	42	6	3	5	69	3	0	0	24	5	1	2	2	0	22	21	.273	.285	.448
89	TOR/AL		94	256	241	62	11	1	3	84	11	2	1	45	7	1	3	0	1	22	29	.257	.290	.349
90	TOR/AL		125	368	346	99	24	2	15	172	18	2	0	57	17	1	3	0	1	36	49	.286	.319	.497
91	TOR/AL		105	312	291	71	17	0	5	103	11	1	1	45	8	6	3	0	0	22	36	.244	.271	.354
92	TOR/AL		138	521	480	116	26	2	13	185	33	3	2	75	11	1	5	1	1	47	53	.242	.290	.385
93	TOR/AL		138	520	488	124	30	0	9	181	20	2	0	66	18	1	3	2	2	38	55	.254	.285	.371
6 YR TOTALS			**656**	**2137**	**2000**	**514**	**114**	**8**	**50**	**794**	**96**	**10**	**6**	**312**	**66**	**18**	**17**	**5**	**5**	**180**	**243**	**.257**	**.291**	**.397**

Bordick, Michael Todd "Mike" — BR/TR — b.7/21/65 — POS SS-322, 2B-108, 3B-11   OAK 7/10/86

YR	TM/LG	CL	G	TPA	AB	H	2B	3B	HR	TB	BB	IBB	HB	SO	GDP	SH	SF	SB	CS	R	RBI	BA	OBA	SA
86	MED/NWL	A-	46	230	187	48	3	1	0	53	40	0	1	21	5	1	1	6	0	30	19	.257	.389	.283
87	MOD/CAL	A+	133	601	497	133	17	0	3	159	87	3	5	92	13	4	8	8	8	73	75	.268	.377	.320
88	HUN/SOU	AA	132	584	481	130	13	2	0	147	87	0	4	50	11	9	3	7	9	55	43	.270	.384	.306
89	TAC/PCL	AAA	136	569	487	117	17	1	1	139	58	0	7	51	14	15	2	4	9	49	30	.240	.329	.285
90	TAC/PCL	AAA	111	406	348	79	16	1	2	103	46	0	3	40	6	7	2	3	0	49	30	.227	.321	.296
	OAK/AL		25	15	14	1	0	0	0	1	1	0	0	4	0	0	0	0	0	0	0	.071	.133	.071
91	TAC/PCL	AAA	26	100	81	22	4	1	2	34	17	0	1	0	0	1	0	0	1	15	14	.272	.404	.420
	OAK/AL		90	265	235	56	5	1	0	63	14	0	3	37	3	12	1	3	4	21	21	.238	.289	.268
92	OAK/AL		154	572	504	151	19	4	3	187	40	2	9	59	10	14	5	12	6	62	48	.300	.358	.371
93	OAK/AL		159	633	546	136	21	2	3	170	60	2	11	58	10	10	6	10	10	60	48	.249	.332	.311
4 YR TOTALS			**428**	**1485**	**1299**	**344**	**45**	**7**	**6**	**421**	**115**	**4**	**23**	**158**	**22**	**36**	**12**	**25**	**20**	**143**	**117**	**.265**	**.333**	**.324**

Boston, Daryl Lamont — BL/TL — b.1/4/63 — POS OF-831, DH-26   CHA81 1/7

YR	TM/LG	CL	G	TPA	AB	H	2B	3B	HR	TB	BB	IBB	HB	SO	GDP	SH	SF	SB	CS	R	RBI	BA	OBA	SA
84	DEN/AMA	AAA	127	550	471	147	21	19	15	251	65	1	2	82	10	1	11	40	17	94	82	.312	.390	.533
	CHI/AL		35	87	83	14	3	1	0	19	4	0	0	20	0	0	0	6	0	8	3	.169	.207	.229
85	BUF/AMA	AAA	63	281	241	66	12	1	10	110	33	0	4	48	4	2	1	15	5	45	36	.274	.369	.456
	CHI/AL		95	248	232	53	13	1	3	77	14	1	0	44	3	1	1	8	5	20	15	.228	.271	.332
86	BUF/AMA	AAA	96	411	360	109	16	3	5	146	42	4	1	45	3	5	3	38	10	57	41	.303	.374	.406
	CHI/AL		56	224	199	53	11	5	4	85	21	3	0	33	4	1	3	9	5	29	22	.266	.335	.427
87	HAW/PCL	AAA	21	88	77	23	3	0	5	41	10	1	1	10	3	0	0	3	1	14	13	.299	.386	.532
	CHI/AL		103	369	337	87	21	2	10	142	25	2	0	68	5	3	3	12	6	51	29	.258	.307	.421
88	CHI/AL		105	305	281	61	12	2	15	122	21	5	0	44	5	2	1	9	3	37	31	.217	.271	.434
89	CHI/AL		101	247	218	55	3	4	5	81	24	3	0	31	1	4	1	7	2	34	23	.252	.325	.372
90	CHI/AL		5	1	1	0	0	0	0	0	0	0	0	0	0	0	0	0	0	0	0	.000	.000	.000
	NY/NL		115	396	366	100	21	2	12	161	28	4	2	50	7	0	0	18	7	65	45	.273	.328	.440
	YEAR		120	397	367	100	21	2	12	161	28	4	2	50	7	0	1	18	7	65	45	.272	.327	.439
91	NY/NL		137	286	255	70	16	4	4	106	30	4	2	42	2	0	1	15	4	40	21	.275	.350	.416
92	NY/NL		130	334	289	72	14	2	11	123	38	6	3	60	5	0	4	12	6	37	35	.249	.338	.426
93	COL/NL		124	320	291	76	15	2	14	135	26	1	2	57	5	0	1	6	0	46	40	.261	.325	.464
10 YR TOTALS			**1006**	**2817**	**2552**	**641**	**129**	**22**	**79**	**1051**	**231**	**23**	**7**	**449**	**37**	**14**	**13**	**98**	**49**	**367**	**264**	**.251**	**.314**	**.412**

Bournigal, Rafael Antonio — BR/TR — b.5/12/66 — POS SS-13, 2B-4   LA87 19/482

YR	TM/LG	CL	G	TPA	AB	H	2B	3B	HR	TB	BB	IBB	HB	SO	GDP	SH	SF	SB	CS	R	RBI	BA	OBA	SA
87	GF/PIO	R+	30	87	82	12	4	0	0	16	3	0	1	7	1	0	0	0	0	5	4	.146	.186	.195
88	SAL/NWL	A-	70	321	275	86	10	1	0	98	38	0	0	32	5	6	2	11	6	54	25	.313	.394	.356
89	VB/FSL	A+	132	528	484	128	11	1	1	144	33	0	3	21	19	5	3	18	13	74	37	.264	.314	.298
90	SA/TEX	AA	69	211	194	41	4	2	0	49	8	0	0	25	9	7	2	2	1	20	14	.211	.240	.253

(continued)

Bournigal, Rafael Antonio (continued)

YR	TM/LG	CL	G	TPA	AB	H	2B	3B	HR	TB	BB	IBB	HB	SO	GDP	SH	SF	SB	CS	R	RBI	BA	OBA	SA
91	VB/FSL	A+	20	69	66	16	2	0	0	18	1	0	0	3	1	1	1	2	1	6	3	.242	.250	.273
	SA/TEX	AA	16	69	65	21	2	0	0	23	2	0	0	7	2	1	1	2	3	6	9	.323	.338	.354
	ALB/PCL	AAA	66	241	215	63	5	5	0	78	14	1	0	13	3	8	4	4	1	34	29	.293	.330	.363
92	ALB/PCL	AAA	122	436	395	128	18	1	0	148	22	5	5	7	17	10	4	5	3	47	34	.324	.364	.375
	LA/NL		10	22	20	3	1	0	0	4	1	0	1	2	0	0	0	0	0	1	0	.150	.227	.200
93	ALB/PCL	AAA	134	510	465	129	25	0	4	166	29	1	3	18	11	8	5	3	5	75	55	.277	.321	.357
	LA/NL		8	18	18	9	1	0	0	10	0	0	0	2	0	0	0	0	0	0	3	.500	.500	.556
2 YR TOTALS			**18**	**40**	**38**	**12**	**2**	**0**	**0**	**14**	**1**	**0**	**1**	**4**	**0**	**0**	**0**	**0**	**0**	**1**	**3**	**.316**	**.350**	**.368**

Branson, Jeffery Glenn "Jeff" — BL/TR — b.1/26/67 — POS 2B-78, SS-60, 3B-22, 1B-1   CIN88 1/45

YR	TM/LG	CL	G	TPA	AB	H	2B	3B	HR	TB	BB	IBB	HB	SO	GDP	SH	SF	SB	CS	R	RBI	BA	OBA	SA
89	CR/MID	A	127	520	469	132	28	1	10	192	41	3	2	90	10	4	4	5	6	70	68	.281	.339	.409
90	CHT/SOU	AA	63	249	233	49	9	1	2	66	13	2	0	48	4	1	2	3	1	19	29	.210	.250	.283
	CR/MID	A	62	265	239	60	13	4	6	99	24	3	0	44	6	0	2	11	3	37	24	.251	.317	.414
91	CHT/SOU	AA	88	343	304	80	13	3	2	105	31	2	1	51	4	2	5	3	7	35	28	.263	.328	.345
	NAS/AMA	AAA	43	154	145	35	4	1	0	41	8	2	0	31	1	1	0	5	4	10	11	.241	.281	.283
92	NAS/AMA	AAA	36	133	123	40	6	3	0	64	9	1	0	19	1	1	1	0	3	18	12	.325	.371	.520
	CIN/NL		72	123	115	34	7	1	0	43	5	2	0	16	4	1	1	0	3	12	15	.296	.322	.374
93	CIN/NL		125	412	381	92	15	1	3	118	19	2	0	73	4	3	4	4	1	40	22	.241	.275	.310
2 YR TOTALS			**197**	**535**	**496**	**126**	**22**	**2**	**3**	**161**	**24**	**4**	**0**	**89**	**8**	**10**	**5**	**4**	**2**	**52**	**37**	**.254**	**.286**	**.325**

Bream, Sidney Eugene "Sid" — BL/TL — b.8/3/60 — POS 1B-944, OF-2   LA81 2/48

YR	TM/LG	CL	G	TPA	AB	H	2B	3B	HR	TB	BB	IBB	HB	SO	GDP	SH	SF	SB	CS	R	RBI	BA	OBA	SA
83	LA/NL		15	13	11	2	0	0	0	2	2	0	0	2	1	0	0	0	0	0	2	.182	.308	.182
84	ALB/PCL	AAA	114	506	429	147	25	4	20	240	67	7	1	62	8	1	8	2	2	82	90	.343	.426	.559
	LA/NL		27	58	49	9	3	0	0	12	6	2	0	9	1	1	2	1	0	2	6	.184	.263	.245
85	ALB/PCL	AAA	85	333	297	110	25	3	17	192	35	1	0	38	9	1	0	1	1	51	57	.370	.437	.646
	PIT/NL		26	108	95	27	7	0	3	43	11	2	0	14	4	1	1	0	2	14	15	.284	.355	.453
	LA/NL		24	63	53	7	0	0	3	16	7	3	0	10	0	2	1	0	0	4	6	.132	.230	.302
	YEAR		50	171	148	34	7	0	6	59	18	5	0	24	4	3	2	0	2	18	21	.230	.310	.399
86	PIT/NL		154	591	522	140	37	5	16	235	60	5	1	73	14	1	7	13	7	73	77	.268	.341	.450
87	PIT/NL		149	572	516	142	25	3	13	212	49	11	1	69	19	3	4	9	7	64	65	.275	.336	.411
88	PIT/NL		148	522	462	122	37	0	10	189	47	6	1	64	11	4	8	9	9	50	65	.264	.328	.409
89	PIT/NL		19	50	36	8	3	0	0	11	12	0	0	10	0	2	0	0	0	3	4	.222	.417	.306
90	PIT/NL		147	448	389	105	23	2	15	177	48	5	4	65	6	4	5	8	4	39	67	.270	.349	.455
91	ATL/NL		91	298	265	67	12	0	11	112	25	5	0	31	6	4	4	0	3	32	45	.253	.313	.423
92	ATL/NL		125	426	372	97	25	1	10	154	46	2	1	51	3	4	6	4	0	30	61	.261	.340	.414
93	ATL/NL		117	311	277	72	14	1	9	115	31	3	0	43	6	1	2	4	2	33	35	.260	.332	.415
11 YR TOTALS			**1042**	**3460**	**3047**	**798**	**186**	**12**	**90**	**1278**	**344**	**44**	**5**	**441**	**73**	**26**	**38**	**50**	**39**	**344**	**448**	**.262**	**.334**	**.419**

Brett, George Howard — BL/TR — b.5/15/53 — POS 3B-1692, DH-505, 1B-461, OF-36, SS-11   KC71 2/29

YR	TM/LG	CL	G	TPA	AB	H	2B	3B	HR	TB	BB	IBB	HB	SO	GDP	SH	SF	SB	CS	R	RBI	BA	OBA	SA
73	KC/AL		13	41	40	5	2	0	0	7	0	0	0	5	0	1	0	0	0	2	0	.125	.125	.175
74	KC/AL		133	486	457	129	21	5	2	166	21	3	0	38	9	6	2	8	5	49	47	.282	.313	.363
75	KC/AL		159	697	634	*195	35	*13	11	289	46	6	2	49	8	9	6	13	10	84	89	.308	.353	.456
76	KC/AL		159	705	645	*215	34	*14	7	*298	49	4	1	36	8	2	8	21	11	94	67	*.333	.377	.462
77	KC/AL		139	627	564	176	32	13	22	300	55	9	2	24	12	3	3	14	12	105	88	.312	.373	.532
78	KC/AL		128	558	510	150	*45	8	9	238	39	6	1	35	6	3	5	23	7	79	62	.294	.342	.467
79	KC/AL		154	701	645	*212	42	*20	23	363	51	14	0	36	8	1	4	17	10	119	107	.329	.376	.563
80	KC/AL		117	515	449	175	33	9	24	298	58	16	1	22	11	0	7	15	6	87	118	*.390	*.454	*.664
81	KC/AL		89	379	347	109	27	7	6	168	27	7	1	23	7	0	4	14	6	42	43	.314	.361	.484
82	KC/AL		144	629	552	166	32	9	21	279	71	14	1	51	12	0	5	6	1	101	82	.301	.378	.505
83	KC/AL		123	525	464	144	38	2	25	261	57	13	1	39	9	0	3	0	1	90	93	.310	.385	*.563
84	KC/AL		104	422	377	107	21	3	13	173	38	6	0	37	11	0	2	0	0	42	69	.284	.344	.459
85	KC/AL		155	665	550	184	38	5	30	322	103	31	3	49	12	0	9	9	1	108	112	.335	.436	*.585
86	KC/AL		124	529	441	128	28	4	16	212	80	18	4	45	6	0	4	1	2	70	73	.290	.401	.481
87	KC/AL		115	508	427	124	18	2	22	212	72	14	1	47	10	0	8	6	3	71	78	.290	.388	.496
88	KC/AL		157	681	589	180	42	3	24	300	82	15	2	51	15	0	4	7	14	90	103	.306	.389	.509
89	KC/AL		124	528	457	129	26	3	12	197	59	6	3	47	18	0	6	14	4	67	80	.282	.362	.431
90	KC/AL		142	607	544	179	*45	7	14	280	56	14	0	63	18	0	7	9	2	82	87	*.329	.387	.515
91	KC/AL		131	572	505	129	40	2	10	203	58	9	2	75	20	1	8	2	0	77	61	.255	.327	.402
92	KC/AL		152	637	592	169	35	5	7	235	35	6	3	69	15	0	4	8	6	55	61	.285	.330	.397
93	KC/AL		145	612	560	149	31	3	19	243	39	9	3	67	20	0	10	7	5	69	75	.266	.312	.434
21 YR TOTALS			**2707**	**11624**	**10349**	**3154**	**665**	**137**	**317**	**5044**	**1096**	**229**	**33**	**908**	**235**	**26**	**120**	**201**	**97**	**1583**	**1595**	**.305**	**.369**	**.487**

Brewer, Rodney Lee "Rod" — BL/TL — b.2/24/66 — POS 1B-83, OF-40, P-1   SL87 5/124

YR	TM/LG	CL	G	TPA	AB	H	2B	3B	HR	TB	BB	IBB	HB	SO	GDP	SH	SF	SB	CS	R	RBI	BA	OBA	SA
87	JC/APP	R+	67	279	238	60	11	2	10	105	36	5	3	40	4	0	2	2	2	33	42	.252	.355	.441
88	SPR/MID	A	133	530	457	136	25	2	8	189	63	7	5	52	22	1	4	6	4	57	64	.298	.386	.414
89	ARK/TEX	AA	128	526	470	130	25	2	8	189	46	3	7	46	8	1	3	2	3	71	93	.277	.348	.402
90	LOU/AMA	AAA	144	583	514	129	15	2	14	190	54	7	9	62	9	0	3	2	2	60	83	.251	.329	.370
	STL/NL		14	25	25	6	1	0	0	7	0	0	0	4	1	0	0	0	0	4	2	.240	.240	.280
91	LOU/AMA	AAA	104	424	382	86	21	1	8	133	35	1	0	57	10	0	1	4	1	39	52	.225	.300	.348
	STL/NL		19	13	13	1	0	0	0	1	0	0	0	3	0	0	0	0	0	0	1	.077	.077	.077
92	LOU/AMA	AAA	120	478	423	122	20	2	18	200	49	6	5	60	8	0	0	6	2	57	86	.288	.368	.473
	STL/NL		29	113	103	31	6	0	0	37	8	0	0	11	1	0	1	0	0	11	10	.301	.354	.359
93	STL/NL		110	169	147	42	8	0	2	56	12	2	2	26	6	2	3	1	1	15	20	.286	.359	.381
4 YR TOTALS			**172**	**320**	**288**	**80**	**15**	**0**	**2**	**101**	**25**	**5**	**2**	**47**	**7**	**2**	**3**	**1**	**1**	**30**	**33**	**.278**	**.336**	**.351**

Briley, Gregory "Greg" — BL/TR — b.5/24/65 — POS OF-457, DH-20, 2B-15, 3B-5   SEA86 S1/12

YR	TM/LG	CL	G	TPA	AB	H	2B	3B	HR	TB	BB	IBB	HB	SO	GDP	SH	SF	SB	CS	R	RBI	BA	OBA	SA
86	BEL/NWL	A-	63	278	218	65	12	4	7	106	50	1	3	29	1	0	7	26	5	52	46	.298	.424	.486
87	CHT/SOU	AA	137	592	539	148	21	5	7	200	41	0	2	58	10	2	8	34	14	81	61	.275	.324	.371
88	SEA/AL		13	42	36	9	2	0	1	14	5	1	0	6	0	0	1	0	1	6	4	.250	.333	.389
	CAL/PCL	AAA	112	497	445	139	29	9	11	219	40	5	3	51	2	2	7	27	10	74	66	.312	.368	.492
89	CAL/PCL	AAA	25	109	94	32	8	1	4	54	13	1	2	10	8	0	0	14	2	27	20	.340	.431	.574
	SEA/AL		115	444	394	105	22	4	13	174	39	1	5	82	9	1	5	11	5	52	52	.266	.336	.442
90	SEA/AL		125	380	337	83	18	2	5	120	37	0	1	48	6	1	4	16	4	40	29	.246	.319	.356
91	SEA/AL		139	412	381	99	17	3	2	128	27	0	0	51	7	1	3	23	11	39	26	.260	.307	.336
92	SEA/AL		86	207	200	55	10	0	5	80	4	0	1	31	4	0	2	9	2	18	12	.275	.290	.400
93	FLO/NL		120	185	170	33	6	0	2	48	12	0	1	42	5	1	1	12	7	17	12	.194	.250	.282
6 YR TOTALS			**598**	**1670**	**1518**	**384**	**75**	**9**	**29**	**564**	**124**	**2**	**8**	**260**	**31**	**4**	**16**	**65**	**25**	**172**	**135**	**.253**	**.310**	**.372**

Brito, Bernardo — BR/TR — b.12/4/63 — POS OF-13, DH-8   CLE 10/8/80

YR	TM/LG	CL	G	TPA	AB	H	2B	3B	HR	TB	BB	IBB	HB	SO	GDP	SH	SF	SB	CS	R	RBI	BA	OBA	SA
81	BAT/NYP	A-	12	33	29	6	0	0	0	6	2	0	1	9	1	1	0	0	0	1	2	.207	.281	.207
82	BAT/NYP	A-	41	136	123	29	2	0	4	43	8	0	2	34	3	1	2	1	0	10	15	.236	.289	.350
83	WAT/MID	A	35	132	119	24	4	0	4	40	10	1	1	40	2	1	1	3	1	13	17	.202	.267	.336
	BAT/NYP	A-	60	229	206	50	10	3	7	87	15	1	5	65	6	2	1	5	1	18	34	.243	.308	.422
84	BAT/NYP	A-	76	314	297	89	19	3	19	171	14	1	1	67	7	2	0	3	4	41	57	.300	.333	.576
85	WAT/MID	A	135	529	498	128	27	1	29	244	24	1	4	133	15	0	3	1	4	66	78	.257	.295	.490
86	WAT/EAS	AA	129	510	479	118	17	1	18	191	22	0	3	127	10	3	6	1	1	61	75	.246	.282	.399
87	WIL/EAS	AA	124	487	452	125	20	4	24	225	24	2	5	121	15	0	6	2	6	64	79	.277	.316	.498
88	ORL/SOU	AA	135	538	508	122	20	4	24	222	20	2	1	138	12	0	9	2	2	55	76	.240	.266	.437
89	POR/PCL	AAA	111	394	355	90	12	7	22	182	31	7	4	111	7	2	2	1	3	51	74	.254	.319	.513
90	POR/PCL	AAA	113	411	376	106	26	3	25	213	27	3	2	102	13	0	4	1	4	48	79	.282	.330	.566
91	POR/PCL	AAA	115	470	428	111	17	2	27	213	28	1	7	110	8	0	7	1	0	65	83	.259	.311	.498
92	POR/PCL	AAA	140	607	564	152	27	7	26	271	32	6	6	124	19	0	5	0	1	80	96	.270	.313	.480
	MIN/AL		8	15	14	2	1	0	0	3	0	0	0	4	1	0	1	0	0	1	2	.143	.133	.214
93	POR/PCL	AAA	85	355	319	108	18	3	20	192	26	5	4	65	8	0	5	0	1	64	72	.339	.389	.602
	MIN/AL		27	55	54	13	2	0	4	27	1	0	0	20	1	0	0	0	1	8	9	.241	.255	.500
2 YR TOTALS			**35**	**70**	**68**	**15**	**3**	**0**	**4**	**30**	**1**	**0**	**0**	**24**	**1**	**0**	**1**	**0**	**1**	**9**	**11**	**.221**	**.229**	**.441**

Brooks, Hubert "Hubie" — BR/TR — b.9/24/56 — POS OF-582, 3B-516, SS-371, DH-79, 1B-9, 2B-7   NYN78 1/3

YR	TM/LG	CL	G	TPA	AB	H	2B	3B	HR	TB	BB	IBB	HB	SO	GDP	SH	SF	SB	CS	R	RBI	BA	OBA	SA
80	NY/NL		24	89	81	25	2	1	1	32	5	0	2	9	1	1	0	1	1	8	10	.309	.364	.395
81	NY/NL		98	389	358	110	21	2	4	147	23	2	1	65	9	1	6	9	5	34	38	.307	.345	.411
82	NY/NL		126	498	457	114	21	2	2	145	28	5	5	76	11	3	5	6	3	40	40	.249	.297	.317
83	NY/NL		150	624	586	147	18	4	5	188	24	2	4	96	14	7	3	6	4	53	58	.251	.284	.321
84	NY/NL		153	613	561	159	23	2	16	234	48	15	2	79	17	0	2	6	5	61	73	.283	.341	.417
85	MON/NL		156	652	605	163	34	7	13	250	34	5	3	79	20	0	5	4	9	67	100	.269	.310	.413
86	MON/NL		80	338	306	104	18	5	14	174	25	3	2	60	11	0	5	4	2	50	58	.340	.388	.569
87	MON/NL		112	459	430	113	22	3	14	183	24	2	1	72	7	0	4	4	3	57	72	.263	.301	.426
88	MON/NL		151	628	588	164	35	2	20	263	35	3	1	108	21	0	4	7	3	61	90	.279	.318	.447
89	MON/NL		148	593	542	145	30	1	14	219	39	2	4	108	15	0	8	6	11	56	70	.268	.317	.404
90	LA/NL		153	618	568	151	28	1	20	241	33	10	6	108	13	0	11	2	5	74	91	.266	.307	.424
91	NY/NL		103	407	357	85	11	1	16	146	44	8	3	62	7	0	3	3	1	48	50	.238	.324	.409
92	EDM/PCL	AAA	8	29	24	7	2	1	1	14	1	0	2	2	0	0	0	2	0	2	11	.292	.345	.583
	CAL/AL		82	320	306	66	13	0	8	103	12	3	1	46	10	0	1	3	3	28	36	.216	.247	.337
93	KC/AL		75	181	168	48	12	0	1	63	11	1	1	27	5	0	1	0	1	14	24	.286	.331	.375
14 YR TOTALS			**1611**	**6409**	**5913**	**1594**	**288**	**31**	**148**	**2388**	**385**	**62**	**38**	**995**	**161**	**12**	**61**	**63**	**56**	**651**	**810**	**.270**	**.315**	**.404**

Brooks, Jerome Edward "Jerry" — BR/TR — b.3/23/67 — POS OF-2   LA88 11/296

YR	TM/LG	CL	G	TPA	AB	H	2B	3B	HR	TB	BB	IBB	HB	SO	GDP	SH	SF	SB	CS	R	RBI	BA	OBA	SA
88	GF/PIO	R+	68	322	285	99	21	3	8	150	24	0	4	25	9	0	9	7	4	63	60	.347	.394	.526
89	BAK/CAL	A+	141	604	565	164	39	1	16	253	25	0	6	79	10	0	8	9	6	70	87	.290	.323	.448
90	SA/TEX	AA	106	427	391	118	20	0	9	165	26	4	4	39	7	1	5	5	8	52	58	.302	.347	.422
91	ALB/PCL	AAA	125	469	429	126	20	7	13	199	29	5	6	49	14	1	4	4	3	64	82	.294	.344	.464
92	ALB/PCL	AAA	129	517	467	124	36	1	14	204	39	9	0	68	9	0	7	3	2	77	78	.266	.323	.437
93	ALB/PCL	AAA	116	454	421	145	28	1	11	214	21	2	2	44	11	0	7	3	4	67	71	.344	.373	.508
	LA/NL		9	9	9	2	1	0	1	6	0	0	0	6	0	0	0	0	0	2	1	.222	.222	.667

Brosius, Scott David — BR/TR — b.8/15/66 — POS OF-79, 3B-29, 2B-18, 1B-14, SS-7, DH-4   OAK87 19/511

YR	TM/LG	CL	G	TPA	AB	H	2B	3B	HR	TB	BB	IBB	HB	SO	GDP	SH	SF	SB	CS	R	RBI	BA	OBA	SA
87	MED/NWL	A-	65	289	255	73	18	1	3	102	26	0	3	36	7	1	7	5	2	34	49	.286	.344	.400
88	MAD/MID	A	132	571	504	153	28	2	9	212	56	1	3	67	7	4	4	13	12	82	58	.304	.374	.421
89	HUN/SOU	AA	128	536	461	125	22	2	7	172	58	3	5	62	11	6	6	4	6	68	60	.271	.355	.373
90	HUN/SOU	AA	142	645	547	162	39	2	23	274	81	2	1	81	8	7	9	12	3	94	88	.296	.382	.501
	TAC/PCL	AAA	3	8	7	1	0	1	0	3	1	0	0	3	0	0	0	0	0	2	0	.143	.250	.429
91	TAC/PCL	AAA	65	268	245	70	16	3	8	116	18	0	2	29	1	2	4	2	4	28	31	.286	.337	.473
	OAK/AL		36	72	68	16	5	0	2	27	3	0	0	11	2	1	1	0	1	9	13	.235	.268	.397
92	TAC/PCL	AAA	63	264	236	56	13	0	9	96	23	1	4	44	5	0	0	4	0	29	31	.237	.303	.407
	OAK/AL		38	93	87	19	2	0	4	33	3	1	2	13	0	0	1	3	0	13	13	.218	.258	.379
93	TAC/PCL	AAA	56	239	209	62	13	1	8	103	21	0	4	50	5	0	4	1	0	38	41	.297	.367	.493
	OAK/AL		70	233	213	53	10	1	6	83	14	0	1	37	6	0	2	6	1	26	25	.249	.296	.390
3 YR TOTALS			**144**	**398**	**368**	**88**	**17**	**1**	**12**	**143**	**20**	**1**	**3**	**61**	**8**	**4**	**3**	**12**	**1**	**48**	**42**	**.239**	**.282**	**.389**

Brown, Jarvis Ardel — BR/TR — b.3/26/67 — POS OF-106, DH-6   MIN86* 1/9

YR	TM/LG	CL	G	TPA	AB	H	2B	3B	HR	TB	BB	IBB	HB	SO	GDP	SH	SF	SB	CS	R	RBI	BA	OBA	SA
86	ELI/APP	R+	49	208	180	41	4	0	3	54	18	0	4	41	3	5	1	15	3	28	23	.228	.310	.300
87	ELI/APP	R+	67	314	258	63	9	1	1	77	48	1	5	50	3	3	0	30	2	52	15	.244	.373	.298
	KEN/MID	A	43	141	117	22	4	1	3	37	19	0	2	24	2	1	2	6	2	17	16	.188	.307	.316
88	KEN/MID	A	138	624	531	156	25	7	7	216	71	0	10	89	10	7	5	72	15	108	45	.294	.384	.407
89	VIS/CAL	A+	141	639	545	131	21	6	4	176	73	0	13	112	12	4	4	49	13	95	46	.240	.342	.323
90	ORL/SOU	AA	135	623	527	137	22	7	14	215	80	1	9	79	13	5	2	33	19	104	57	.260	.366	.408
91	POR/PCL	AAA	108	482	436	126	5	8	3	156	36	1	6	66	6	3	1	27	12	62	37	.289	.351	.358
	MIN/AL		38	40	37	8	0	0	0	8	2	0	0	8	0	1	0	7	1	10	0	.216	.256	.216
92	MIN/AL		35	18	15	1	0	0	0	1	2	0	1	4	0	0	0	2	2	8	0	.067	.222	.067
	POR/PCL	AAA	62	251	224	56	8	2	2	74	20	0	5	37	2	1	1	17	1	25	16	.250	.324	.330
93	LV/PCL	AAA	100	455	402	124	27	9	3	178	41	0	5	55	10	5	2	22	5	74	47	.308	.378	.443
	SD/NL		47	157	133	31	9	2	0	44	15	0	6	26	4	2	1	3	3	21	8	.233	.335	.331
3 YR TOTALS			120	215	185	40	9	2	0	53	19	0	7	38	4	3	1	12	6	39	8	.216	.311	.286

Browne, Jerome Austin "Jerry" — BB/TR — b.2/13/66 — POS 2B-567, OF-116, 3B-86, DH-12, 1B-2, SS-1   TEX 3/3/83

YR	TM/LG	CL	G	TPA	AB	H	2B	3B	HR	TB	BB	IBB	HB	SO	GDP	SH	SF	SB	CS	R	RBI	BA	OBA	SA
84	BUR/MID	A	127	501	420	99	10	1	0	111	71	0	1	76	7	7	2	31	8	70	18	.236	.346	.264
85	SAL/CAR	A+	122	545	460	123	18	4	3	158	82	2	1	62	8	1	1	24	16	69	58	.267	.379	.343
86	TUL/TEX	AA	128	559	491	149	15	7	2	184	62	1	0	61	10	5	1	39	11	82	57	.303	.381	.375
	TEX/AL		12	25	24	10	2	0	0	12	1	0	0	0	0	0	0	2	0	6	3	.417	.440	.500
87	TEX/AL		132	526	454	123	16	6	1	154	61	0	2	50	6	7	2	27	17	63	38	.271	.358	.339
88	OC/AMA	AAA	76	329	286	72	15	2	5	106	37	2	0	29	9	4	2	14	5	45	34	.252	.335	.371
	TEX/AL		73	243	214	49	9	2	0	65	25	0	0	32	5	3	1	7	5	26	17	.229	.308	.304
89	CLE/AL		153	685	598	179	31	4	5	233	68	0	1	64	9	14	4	14	6	83	45	.299	.370	.390
90	CLE/AL		140	610	513	137	26	5	6	191	72	1	2	46	12	5	12	11	6	92	50	.267	.353	.372
91	CLE/AL		107	334	290	66	5	2	1	78	27	0	1	46	12	5	4	2	4	28	29	.228	.292	.269
92	TAC/PCL	AAA	4	20	17	7	1	1	0	10	3	0	0	1	0	0	0	1	1	1	3	.412	.500	.588
	OAK/AL		111	390	324	93	12	2	3	118	40	0	4	40	7	16	6	3	3	43	40	.287	.366	.364
93	TAC/PCL	AAA	6	25	25	6	0	0	0	6	0	0	0	4	1	0	0	1	0	3	2	.240	.240	.240
	OAK/AL		76	286	260	65	13	0	2	84	22	0	0	17	9	2	2	4	0	27	19	.250	.306	.323
8 YR TOTALS			804	3099	2677	722	114	21	19	935	316	11	10	282	53	66	30	69	44	368	241	.270	.346	.349

Bruett, Joseph Timothy "J. T." — BL/TL — b.10/8/67 — POS OF-58, DH-3   MIN88 11/285

YR	TM/LG	CL	G	TPA	AB	H	2B	3B	HR	TB	BB	IBB	HB	SO	GDP	SH	SF	SB	CS	R	RBI	BA	OBA	SA
88	ELI/APP	R+	28	110	91	27	3	0	0	30	19	0	0	15	3	0	0	17	4	23	3	.297	.418	.330
	KEN/MID	A	3	13	10	2	0	0	0	2	3	0	0	0	0	0	0	1	1	2	0	.200	.385	.200
89	KEN/MID	A	120	537	445	119	9	1	3	139	89	2	0	64	6	2	1	61	27	82	29	.267	.389	.312
90	POR/PCL	AAA	10	46	34	8	2	0	0	10	11	0	0	4	0	0	1	2	1	8	3	.235	.413	.294
	VIS/CAL	A+	123	553	437	134	15	3	1	158	101	4	0	60	8	8	3	50	21	86	33	.307	.439	.362
91	POR/PCL	AAA	99	397	345	98	6	3	0	110	40	1	3	41	10	9	0	21	9	51	35	.284	.363	.319
92	POR/PCL	AAA	77	347	280	70	10	3	0	86	60	3	1	27	5	3	3	29	12	41	17	.250	.381	.307
	MIN/AL		56	84	76	19	4	0	0	23	6	1	0	12	0	1	0	6	3	7	2	.250	.313	.303
93	MIN/AL		17	22	20	5	2	0	0	7	1	0	0	0	0	0	0	0	0	2	1	.250	.318	.350
	POR/PCL	AAA	90	391	320	103	17	6	2	138	55	3	3	38	7	10	3	12	11	70	40	.322	.423	.431
2 YR TOTALS			73	106	96	24	6	0	0	30	7	1	2	16	1	1	0	6	3	9	3	.250	.314	.313

Brumfield, Jacob Donnell — BR/TR — b.5/27/65 — POS OF-112, 2B-4   CHN83 7/164

YR	TM/LG	CL	G	TPA	AB	H	2B	3B	HR	TB	BB	IBB	HB	SO	GDP	SH	SF	SB	CS	R	RBI	BA	OBA	SA
83	PIK/APP	R+	42	141	113	29	0	1	3	40	25	1	0	34	1	1	2	8	5	17	15	.257	.386	.354
86	FM/FSL	A+	12	43	41	13	3	1	1	21	2	0	0	11	0	0	0	1	1	3	5	.317	.349	.512
87	MEM/SOU	AA	9	43	39	13	3	2	1	23	3	0	0	8	0	1	0	0	1	7	6	.333	.381	.590
	FM/FSL	A+	114	425	379	93	14	10	6	145	45	2	0	78	12	1	0	43	14	56	34	.245	.325	.383
88	MEM/SOU	AA	128	499	433	98	15	5	6	141	52	0	1	104	2	8	5	47	7	70	28	.226	.308	.326
89	MEM/SOU	AA	104	407	346	79	14	2	1	100	53	0	3	74	1	4	3	28	12	43	25	.228	.336	.289
90	BC/FSL	A+	109	438	372	125	24	3	0	155	60	6	2	44	7	2	2	47	10	66	40	.336	.429	.417
	OMA/AMA	AAA	24	87	77	25	6	1	2	39	7	0	0	14	2	1	2	10	1	10	11	.325	.372	.506
91	OMA/AMA	AAA	111	436	397	106	14	2	6	143	33	0	2	64	9	2	2	36	16	62	43	.267	.323	.360
92	CIN/NL		24	33	30	4	0	0	0	4	2	1	1	4	0	0	0	6	2	6	2	.133	.212	.133
	NAS/AMA	AAA	56	239	208	59	10	2	5	90	26	0	2	35	1	3	0	22	11	32	19	.284	.369	.433
93	IND/AMA	AAA	33	136	126	41	14	1	4	69	6	0	0	14	1	1	0	11	0	23	19	.325	.358	.548
	CIN/NL		103	299	272	73	17	3	2	114	21	4	1	47	1	3	2	20	8	40	23	.268	.321	.419
2 YR TOTALS			127	332	302	77	17	3	6	118	23	5	1	51	1	3	2	26	8	46	25	.255	.310	.391

Brumley, Anthony Michael "Mike" — BB/TR — b.4/9/63 — POS SS-155, 2B-38, 3B-32, OF-11, DH-11   BOS83 2/33

YR	TM/LG	CL	G	TPA	AB	H	2B	3B	HR	TB	BB	IBB	HB	SO	GDP	SH	SF	SB	CS	R	RBI	BA	OBA	SA
83	WH/FSL	A+	44	177	153	48	6	4	1	65	16	0	3	31	2	2	3	4	3	25	18	.314	.383	.425
84	NB/EAS	AA	34	142	121	28	6	2	0	38	18	0	0	33	5	1	3	3	0	14	9	.231	.329	.314
	MID/TEX	AA	73	305	255	55	11	3	6	90	48	3	0	49	2	1	1	5	2	37	21	.216	.339	.353
85	PIT/EAS	AA	131	545	460	127	23	14	3	187	74	3	0	95	8	2	1	29	7	66	58	.276	.370	.407
86	IOW/AMA	AAA	139	530	458	103	21	5	10	164	63	3	0	102	5	4		35	14	74	44	.225	.316	.358
87	IOW/AMA	AAA	92	360	319	81	20	5	6	129	35	1	1	61	2	2	1	27	10	44	42	.254	.328	.404
	CHI/NL		39	117	104	21	2	2	1	30	10	1	1	30	2	1	1	7	1	8	9	.202	.276	.288
88	LV/PCL	AAA	113	486	425	134	16	7	3	173	56	2	0	84	6	3	2	41	14	77	41	.315	.393	.407
89	TOL/INT	AAA	8	30	26	6	1	2	0	11	0	0	0	11	0	0	0	0	0	4	1	.231	.333	.462
	DET/AL		92	230	212	42	5	1	0	54	14	0	1	45	4	3	3	11	0	33	11	.198	.255	.255
90	CAL/PCL	AAA	8	29	28	9	1	0	0	10	0	0	0	3	1	0	0	1	0	4	1	.321	.345	.357
	SEA/AL		62	162	147	33	5	4	0	46	10	0	0	22	5	1	1	2	0	19	7	.224	.272	.313

Brumley, Anthony Michael "Mike" (continued)

YR	TM/LG	CL	G	TPA	AB	H	2B	3B	HR	TB	BB	IBB	HB	SO	GDP	SH	SF	SB	CS	R	RBI	BA	OBA	SA
91	PAW/INT	AAA	32	134	108	29	2	2	4	47	24	1	1	21	2	1	0	8	4	25	16	.269	.406	.435
	BOS/AL		63	132	118	25	5	0	0	30	10	0	0	22	0	4	0	2	0	16	5	.212	.273	.254
92	BOS/AL		2	1	1	0	0	0	0	0	0	0	0	0	0	0	0	0	0	0	0	.000	.000	.000
	PAW/INT	AAA	101	412	365	96	16	5	4	134	37	0	1	76	12	3	6	14	6	50	41	.263	.328	.367
93	TUC/PCL	AAA	93	396	346	122	25	5	0	163	44	6	0	71	4	0	6	24	11	65	46	.353	.419	.471
	HOU/NL		8	11	10	3	0	0	0	3	1	0	0	3	0	0	0	0	1	1	2	.300	.364	.300
6 YR TOTALS			**266**	**653**	**592**	**124**	**17**	**8**	**2**	**163**	**45**	**1**	**2**	**122**	**11**	**12**	**2**	**19**	**6**	**77**	**34**	**.209**	**.267**	**.275**

Brunansky, Thomas Andrew "Tom" — BR/TR — b.8/20/60 — POS OF-1631, DH-56, 1B-29 CAL78 1/14

YR	TM/LG	CL	G	TPA	AB	H	2B	3B	HR	TB	BB	IBB	HB	SO	GDP	SH	SF	SB	CS	R	RBI	BA	OBA	SA
81	CAL/AL		11	41	33	5	0	0	3	14	8	0	0	10	0	0	2	0	1	0	7	6	.152	.317	.424
82	MIN/AL		127	545	463	126	30	1	20	218	71	0	8	101	12	1	2	1	2	77	46	.272	.377	.471
83	MIN/AL		151	611	542	123	24	5	28	241	61	4	4	95	13	1	3	2	5	70	82	.227	.308	.445
84	MIN/AL		155	628	567	144	21	0	32	261	57	2	0	94	15	0	4	4	5	75	85	.254	.320	.460
85	MIN/AL		157	651	567	137	28	4	27	254	71	7	0	86	12	0	13	5	3	71	90	.242	.320	.448
86	MIN/AL		157	655	593	152	28	1	23	251	53	4	1	98	15	1	7	12	4	69	75	.256	.315	.423
87	MIN/AL		155	614	532	138	22	2	32	260	74	5	4	104	12	0	4	11	11	83	85	.259	.352	.489
88	MIN/AL		14	56	49	9	1	0	1	13	7	0	0	11	0	0	0	1	2	5	6	.184	.286	.265
	STL/NL		143	613	523	128	22	4	22	224	79	6	4	82	17	1	6	16	6	69	79	.245	.345	.428
	YEAR		157	669	572	137	23	4	23	237	86	6	4	93	17	1	6	17	8	74	85	.240	.340	.414
89	STL/NL		158	622	556	133	29	3	20	228	59	3	2	107	10	0	5	5	9	67	85	.239	.312	.410
90	STL/NL		19	71	57	9	3	0	1	15	12	0	1	10	1	0	0	0	0	5	2	.158	.310	.263
	BOS/AL		129	526	461	123	24	5	15	202	54	7	3	105	12	0	8	5	10	61	71	.267	.342	.438
	YEAR		148	597	518	132	27	5	16	217	66	7	4	115	13	0	9	5	10	66	73	.255	.338	.419
91	BOS/AL		142	519	459	105	24	1	16	179	49	2	3	72	8	0	8	1	2	54	70	.229	.303	.390
92	BOS/AL		138	533	458	122	31	3	15	204	66	2	0	96	11	2	2	3	5	47	74	.266	.354	.445
93	MIL/AL		80	251	224	41	7	3	6	72	25	0	0	59	5	2	0	2	0	20	29	.183	.265	.321
13 YR TOTALS			**1736**	**6936**	**6084**	**1495**	**294**	**32**	**261**	**2636**	**746**	**42**	**30**	**1130**	**143**	**8**	**68**	**69**	**68**	**780**	**885**	**.246**	**.328**	**.433**

Buechele, Steven Bernard "Steve" — BR/TR — b.9/26/61 — POS 3B-1129, 2B-91, 1B-6, SS-5, OF-4, DH-1 TEX82 4/122

YR	TM/LG	CL	G	TPA	AB	H	2B	3B	HR	TB	BB	IBB	HB	SO	GDP	SH	SF	SB	CS	R	RBI	BA	OBA	SA
84	OC/AMA	AAA	131	499	447	118	25	3	7	170	36	3	4	71	14	7	5	7	2	48	59	.264	.321	.380
85	OC/AMA	AAA	89	389	350	104	20	7	9	165	33	2	4	62	11	0	2	6	3	56	64	.297	.362	.471
	TEX/AL		69	236	219	48	6	3	6	78	14	2	1	38	11	0	1	3	2	22	21	.219	.271	.356
86	TEX/AL		153	513	461	112	19	2	18	189	35	1	5	98	10	9	3	5	8	54	54	.243	.302	.410
87	TEX/AL		136	400	363	86	20	0	13	145	28	3	1	66	7	4	4	2	2	45	50	.237	.290	.399
88	TEX/AL		155	579	503	126	21	4	16	203	65	6	5	79	8	6	0	2	4	68	58	.250	.342	.404
89	TEX/AL		155	530	486	114	22	2	16	188	36	0	5	107	21	2	1	2	3	60	59	.235	.294	.387
90	OC/AMA	AAA	6	23	21	3	0	0	0	6	2	0	0	4	1	0	0	0	0	0	1	.143	.217	.286
	TEX/AL		91	289	251	54	10	0	7	85	27	1	2	63	5	7	2	1	0	30	30	.215	.294	.339
91	TEX/AL		121	472	416	111	17	2	18	186	39	4	5	69	11	10	2	0	4	58	66	.267	.335	.447
	PIT/NL		31	128	114	28	5	1	4	47	10	0	2	28	3	1	1	0	1	16	19	.246	.315	.412
	YEAR		152	600	530	139	22	3	22	233	49	4	7	97	14	11	3	0	5	74	85	.262	.331	.440
92	PIT/NL		80	325	285	71	14	1	8	111	34	4	2	61	5	2	2	0	2	27	43	.249	.331	.389
	CHI/NL		65	265	239	66	9	3	1	84	18	2	5	44	5	2	1	1	1	25	21	.276	.338	.351
	YEAR		145	590	524	137	23	4	9	195	52	6	7	105	10	4	3	1	3	52	64	.261	.334	.372
93	CHI/NL		133	520	460	125	27	2	15	201	48	5	5	87	12	4	3	1	1	53	65	.272	.345	.437
9 YR TOTALS			**1189**	**4257**	**3797**	**941**	**170**	**20**	**122**	**1517**	**354**	**28**	**39**	**740**	**98**	**47**	**20**	**16**	**28**	**458**	**486**	**.248**	**.317**	**.400**

Buford, Damon Jackson — BR/TR — b.6/12/70 — POS OF-30, DH-17 BAL90 11/283

YR	TM/LG	CL	G	TPA	AB	H	2B	3B	HR	TB	BB	IBB	HB	SO	GDP	SH	SF	SB	CS	R	RBI	BA	OBA	SA
90	WAU/MID	A	41	188	160	48	7	2	1	62	21	1	4	32	1	1	2	15	4	31	14	.300	.390	.387
91	FRE/CAR	A+	133	575	505	138	25	6	8	199	51	1	10	92	6	7	2	50	14	71	54	.273	.350	.394
92	HAG/EAS	AA	101	426	373	89	17	3	1	115	42	0	1	62	3	7	3	41	12	53	30	.239	.315	.308
	ROC/INT	AAA	45	173	155	44	10	2	1	61	14	0	1	23	5	2	1	23	4	29	12	.284	.345	.394
93	ROC/INT	AAA	27	124	116	33	6	1	1	44	7	0	0	16	0	1	0	10	2	24	4	.284	.325	.379
	BAL/AL		53	90	79	18	1	0	2	29	9	0	0	19	1	1	0	2	0	18	9	.228	.315	.367

Buhner, Jay Campbell — BR/TR — b.8/13/64 — POS OF-614, DH-20 PIT84* S2/36

YR	TM/LG	CL	G	TPA	AB	H	2B	3B	HR	TB	BB	IBB	HB	SO	GDP	SH	SF	SB	CS	R	RBI	BA	OBA	SA
84	WAT/NYP	A-	65	274	229	74	16	3	9	123	42	4	1	58	3	0	2	3	1	43	58	.323	.427	.537
85	FL/FSL	A+	117	481	409	121	18	10	11	192	65	4	2	76	12	1	4	6	4	65	76	.296	.392	.469
86	FL/FSL	A+	36	155	139	42	9	1	7	74	15	1	0	30	5	0	1	1	0	24	31	.302	.368	.532
87	CMB/INT	AAA	134	563	502	140	23	1	31	258	55	6	2	124	14	2	2	4	2	83	85	.279	.351	.514
	NY/AL		7	23	22	5	2	0	0	7	1	0	0	6	0	0	0	0	0	1	0	.227	.261	.318
88	NY/AL		25	76	69	13	0	0	3	22	3	0	0	25	1	0	1	0	0	8	13	.188	.250	.319
	CMB/INT	AAA	38	152	129	33	5	0	8	62	19	3	3	33	0	0	1	1	1	26	18	.256	.362	.481
	SEA/AL		60	223	192	43	13	1	10	88	25	1	3	68	4	1	3	1	1	28	25	.224	.320	.458
	YEAR		85	299	261	56	13	1	13	110	28	1	3	93	5	1	4	1	1	36	38	.215	.302	.421
89	CAL/PCL	AAA	56	243	196	61	12	1	11	108	44	1	0	56	1	1	3	4	4	27	45	.311	.432	.551
	SEA/AL		58	226	204	56	15	1	9	100	19	0	2	55	0	0	1	1	4	27	33	.275	.341	.490
90	CAL/PCL	AAA	13	42	34	7	1	0	2	14	7	0	0	11	0	0	1	0	0	6	5	.206	.333	.412
	SEA/AL		51	185	163	45	12	0	7	78	17	1	4	50	6	1	2	2	0	16	33	.276	.357	.479
91	SEA/AL		137	471	406	99	14	4	27	202	53	5	6	117	10	2	4	0	1	64	77	.244	.337	.498
92	SEA/AL		152	629	543	132	16	3	25	229	71	2	6	146	12	2	4	1	2	69	79	.243	.333	.422
93	SEA/AL		158	615	563	153	28	3	27	268	100	11	2	144	12	2	8	2	5	91	98	.272	.379	.476
7 YR TOTALS			**648**	**2508**	**2162**	**546**	**100**	**12**	**108**	**994**	**289**	**20**	**26**	**611**	**46**	**6**	**25**	**6**	**19**	**303**	**359**	**.253**	**.344**	**.460**

Bullett, Scott Douglas — BB/TL — b.12/25/68 — POS OF-22 PIT 6/20/88

YR	TM/LG	CL	G	TPA	AB	H	2B	3B	HR	TB	BB	IBB	HB	SO	GDP	SH	SF	SB	CS	R	RBI	BA	OBA	SA
88	PIR/GCL	R	21	70	61	11	1	0	0	12	7	1	0	9	0	1	1	2	5	6	8	.180	.261	.197
89	PIR/GCL	R	46	183	165	42	7	3	1	58	12	1	2	31	1	0	1	15	5	24	16	.255	.324	.352
90	WEL/NYP	A-	74	271	255	77	11	4	3	105	13	2	2	50	7	1	0	30	6	46	33	.302	.341	.412
91	AUG/SAL	A	95	415	384	109	22	6	1	146	27	2	2	79	1	1	1	48	17	61	36	.284	.333	.380
	SAL/CAR	A+	39	164	156	52	7	5	2	75	8	1	0	29	0	0	0	15	7	22	15	.333	.366	.481
	PIT/NL		11	5	4	0	0	0	0	0	0	0	0	3	0	0	0	0	1	2	0	.000	.200	.000
92	CAR/SOU	AA	132	565	518	140	20	5	8	194	28	5	10	98	7	2	7	29	21	59	45	.270	.316	.375
	BUF/AMA	AAA	3	10	10	4	0	2	0	8	0	0	0	2	0	0	0	0	0	1	0	.400	.400	.800
93	BUF/AMA	AAA	110	456	408	117	13	6	1	145	39	0	1	67	5	8	0	28	17	62	30	.287	.350	.355
	PIT/NL		23	59	55	11	0	2	0	15	3	0	0	15	1	0	1	3	2	2	4	.200	.237	.273
2 YR TOTALS			34	64	59	11	0	2	0	15	3	0	1	18	1	0	1	4	3	4	4	**.186**	**.234**	**.254**

Burks, Ellis Rena — BR/TR — b.9/11/64 — POS OF-847, DH-13 BOS83* 1/20

YR	TM/LG	CL	G	TPA	AB	H	2B	3B	HR	TB	BB	IBB	HB	SO	GDP	SH	SF	SB	CS	R	RBI	BA	OBA	SA
84	WH/FSL	A+	112	425	375	96	15	4	6	137	42	1	5	68	8	1	2	29	8	52	43	.256	.337	.365
85	NB/EAS	AA	133	527	476	121	25	7	10	190	42	0	3	85	5	2	4	17	14	66	61	.254	.316	.399
86	NB/EAS	AA	124	513	462	126	20	3	14	194	44	3	4	75	4	3	2	31	9	70	55	.273	.337	.420
87	PAW/INT	AAA	11	47	40	9	3	1	2	23	7	0	0	7	1	0	1	0	0	11	6	.225	.340	.575
	BOS/AL		133	606	558	152	30	2	20	246	41	0	2	98	4	4	0	27	6	94	59	.272	.324	.441
88	BOS/AL		144	615	540	159	37	5	18	260	62	1	3	89	8	4	6	25	9	93	92	.294	.367	.481
89	PAW/INT	AAA	5	23	21	3	1	0	0	4	2	0	0	3	2	0	0	0	0	4	0	.143	.217	.190
	BOS/AL		97	446	399	121	19	6	12	188	36	2	5	52	8	2	4	21	5	73	61	.303	.365	.471
90	BOS/AL		152	641	588	174	33	8	21	286	48	4	1	82	18	2	2	9	5	89	89	.296	.349	.486
91	BOS/AL		130	524	474	119	33	3	14	200	39	2	4	81	7	2	3	6	11	56	56	.251	.314	.422
92	BOS/AL		66	263	235	60	8	3	8	98	25	2	1	48	5	1	5	5	11	35	30	.255	.327	.417
93	CHI/AL		146	574	499	137	24	4	17	220	60	2	4	97	11	3	8	6	9	75	74	.275	.352	.441
7 YR TOTALS			868	3669	3293	922	184	31	110	1498	311	13	22	547	58	17	26	99	53	515	461	**.280**	**.344**	**.455**

Burnitz, Jeromy Neal — BL/TR — b.4/15/69 — POS OF-79 NYN90 1/17

YR	TM/LG	CL	G	TPA	AB	H	2B	3B	HR	TB	BB	IBB	HB	SO	GDP	SH	SF	SB	CS	R	RBI	BA	OBA	SA
90	PIT/NYP	A-	51	225	173	52	6	5	6	86	45	6	3	39	3	0	4	12	5	37	22	.301	.444	.497
	SL/FSL	A+	11	43	32	5	1	0	0	6	7	0	4	12	0	1	0	1	0	6	3	.156	.372	.188
91	WIL/EAS	AA	135	573	457	103	16	10	31	232	104	4	4	127	7	0	8	31	13	80	85	.225	.368	.508
92	TID/INT	AAA	121	486	445	108	21	3	8	159	33	2	3	84	7	2	3	30	7	56	40	.243	.298	.357
93	NOR/INT	AAA	65	285	255	58	15	3	8	103	25	2	2	53	6	0	3	10	7	33	44	.227	.298	.404
	NY/NL		86	306	263	64	10	6	13	125	38	2	4	66	2	2	2	3	7	49	38	.243	.339	.475

Bush, Robert Randall "Randy" — BL/TL — b.10/5/58 — POS OF-537, DH-341, 1B-79 MIN79 2/37

YR	TM/LG	CL	G	TPA	AB	H	2B	3B	HR	TB	BB	IBB	HB	SO	GDP	SH	SF	SB	CS	R	RBI	BA	OBA	SA
82	MIN/AL		55	131	119	29	6	1	4	49	8	0	3	28	1	0	1	0	0	13	13	.244	.305	.412
83	MIN/AL		124	415	373	93	24	3	11	156	34	8	2	51	7	0	1	0	1	43	56	.249	.323	.418
84	MIN/AL		113	356	311	69	17	1	11	121	31	6	4	60	1	0	1	0	1	46	43	.222	.292	.389
85	MIN/AL		97	265	234	56	13	3	10	105	24	1	1	30	7	0	5	1	2	26	35	.239	.321	.449
86	MIN/AL		130	402	357	96	19	7	7	150	39	2	2	63	7	1	1	5	3	50	45	.269	.347	.420
87	MIN/AL		122	349	293	74	10	2	11	121	43	5	1	49	6	5	5	10	3	46	46	.253	.349	.413
88	MIN/AL		136	466	394	103	20	3	14	171	58	14	9	49	8	0	5	8	6	51	51	.261	.365	.434
89	MIN/AL		141	444	391	103	17	4	14	170	48	6	3	73	16	0	2	5	1	60	54	.263	.347	.435
90	POR/PCL	AAA	3	12	9	2	0	0	0	2	3	1	0	0	0	0	0	0	0	2	1	.222	.417	.444
	MIN/AL		73	210	181	44	8	0	6	70	21	2	6	27	2	0	2	0	0	17	18	.243	.338	.387
91	MIN/AL		93	192	165	50	10	1	3	71	24	3	1	25	5	0	2	1	1	21	23	.303	.401	.485
92	MIN/AL		100	198	182	39	8	1	2	55	11	3	2	37	5	0	3	0	1	14	22	.214	.263	.302
93	MIN/AL		35	52	45	7	2	0	0	9	7	0	0	13	3	0	0	0	0	1	3	.156	.269	.200
12 YR TOTALS			1219	3480	3045	763	154	26	96	1257	348	51	49	505	64	6	32	33	29	388	409	**.251**	**.334**	**.413**

Butler, Brett Morgan — BL/TL — b.6/15/57 — POS OF-1795, DH-1 ATL79 22/573

YR	TM/LG	CL	G	TPA	AB	H	2B	3B	HR	TB	BB	IBB	HB	SO	GDP	SH	SF	SB	CS	R	RBI	BA	OBA	SA
81	ATL/NL		40	145	126	32	2	3	0	40	19	0	0	17	0	0	0	9	1	17	4	.254	.352	.317
82	ATL/NL		89	268	240	52	2	0	0	54	25	0	0	35	1	3	0	21	8	35	7	.217	.291	.225
83	ATL/NL		151	613	549	154	21	*13	5	216	54	3	2	56	5	3	5	39	23	84	37	.281	.344	.393
84	CLE/AL		159	709	602	162	25	9	3	214	86	1	4	62	6	11	6	52	22	108	49	.269	.361	.355
85	CLE/AL		152	666	591	184	28	14	5	255	63	2	1	42	8	8	3	47	20	106	50	.311	.377	.431
86	CLE/AL		161	683	587	163	17	*14	4	220	70	2	8	65	8	17	5	32	15	92	51	.278	.356	.375
87	CLE/AL		137	618	522	154	25	8	9	222	91	0	1	55	3	3	16	33	16	91	41	.295	.399	.425
88	SF/NL		157	679	568	163	27	9	6	226	97	4	2	64	2	8	2	43	20	*109	43	.287	.393	.398
89	SF/NL		154	672	594	168	22	4	4	210	59	2	0	69	4	13	3	31	16	100	36	.283	.349	.354
90	SF/NL		160	732	622	*192	20	9	3	239	90	7	4	62	3	7	7	51	19	108	44	.309	.397	.384
91	LA/NL		161	730	615	182	13	5	2	211	*108	4	1	79	3	4	2	38	28	*112	38	.296	.401	.343
92	LA/NL		157	676	553	171	14	11	3	216	95	2	3	67	4	24	4	41	21	86	39	.309	.413	.391
93	LA/NL		156	716	607	181	21	10	1	225	86	1	5	69	6	14	4	39	19	80	42	.298	.387	.371
13 YR TOTALS			1834	7907	6776	1958	237	109	45	2548	943	21	34	742	53	114	40	476	228	1128	481	**.289**	**.377**	**.376**

Butler, Robert Frank John "Rob" — BL/TL — b.4/10/70 — POS OF-16 TOR 9/24/90

YR	TM/LG	CL	G	TPA	AB	H	2B	3B	HR	TB	BB	IBB	HB	SO	GDP	SH	SF	SB	CS	R	RBI	BA	OBA	SA
91	SC/NYP	A-	76	342	311	105	16	5	7	152	20	5	0	21	2	6	3	33	15	71	45	.338	.378	.489
92	DUN/FSL	A+	92	418	391	140	13	7	4	179	22	5	2	36	2	3	1	19	14	67	41	.358	.394	.458
93	SYR/INT	AAA	55	231	208	59	11	6	1	77	15	3	0	29	6	0	3	7	5	30	14	.284	.338	.370
	TOR/AL		17	56	48	13	4	0	0	17	6	0	0	12	0	0	2	1	2	8	2	.271	.375	.354

Byrd, James Edward "Jim" — BR/TR — b.10/3/68 — POS SS BOS87 9/214

YR	TM/LG	CL	G	TPA	AB	H	2B	3B	HR	TB	BB	IBB	HB	SO	GDP	SH	SF	SB	CS	R	RBI	BA	OBA	SA
88	RSM/ARI	R	33	130	121	36	7	2	2	53	6	0	2	19	3	0	1	7	1	18	13	.298	.338	.438
89	WH/FSL	A+	126	487	447	88	17	2	3	118	25	0	4	104	13	11	1	22	10	42	25	.197	.246	.264
90	LYN/CAR	A+	131	569	511	115	20	1	8	161	38	0	15	139	14	1	4	24	11	59	45	.225	.296	.315
	NB/EAS	AA	2	5	5	1	1	0	0	2	0	0	0	1	1	0	0	0	0	1	0	.200	.200	.400
91	LYN/CAR	A+	52	223	206	49	10	0	1	62	13	0	3	50	6	0	1	10	3	29	18	.238	.291	.301
	NB/EAS	AA	79	328	292	70	9	1	0	81	28	0	1	53	12	5	2	14	10	28	15	.240	.307	.277
92	WH/FSL	A+	18	77	71	19	2	1	0	23	5	0	1	7	3	1	0	4	0	12	1	.268	.316	.324
	NB/EAS	AA	20	67	63	14	1	2	0	19	3	0	1	13	1	0	0	2	3	5	6	.222	.269	.302
	PAW/INT	AAA	72	261	246	55	5	1	2	68	7	0	4	48	5	4	0	2	3	27	18	.224	.257	.276
93	BOS/AL		2	0	0	0	0	0	0	0	0	0	0	0	0	0	0	0	0	0	0	.000	.000	.000
	PAW/INT	AAA	117	410	378	67	12	4	3	96	18	1	9	111	5	5	0	10	9	33	26	.177	.232	.254

Cabrera, Francisco — BR/TR — b.10/10/66 — POS 1B-76, C-24, DH-3 TOR 2/28/86

YR	TM/LG	CL	G	TPA	AB	H	2B	3B	HR	TB	BB	IBB	HB	SO	GDP	SH	SF	SB	CS	R	RBI	BA	OBA	SA
86	VEN/CAL	A+	6	12	12	2	1	0	0	3	0	0	0	4	0	0	0	1	0	2	3	.167	.167	.250
	SC/NYP	A-	68	268	246	73	13	2	6	108	16	1	4	48	6	1	1	7	4	31	35	.297	.348	.439
87	MB/SAL	A	129	498	449	124	27	1	14	195	40	6	3	82	12	0	6	4	2	61	72	.276	.335	.434
88	DUN/FSL	A	9	36	35	14	4	0	1	21	1	0	0	2	0	0	0	0	0	2	9	.400	.417	.600
	KNO/SOU	AA	119	464	429	122	19	1	20	203	26	2	2	75	13	2	5	4	3	59	54	.284	.325	.473
89	TOR/AL		3	13	12	2	1	0	0	3	1	0	0	3	0	0	0	0	0	1	0	.167	.231	.250
	SYR/INT	AAA	113	459	428	128	30	5	9	195	20	2	3	72	11	1	7	4	4	59	71	.299	.330	.456
	RIC/INT	AAA	3	7	6	2	1	0	0	3	0	0	0	0	0	0	0	0	0	0	1	.333	.286	.500
	ATL/NL		4	14	14	3	2	0	0	5	0	0	0	6	0	0	0	0	0	0	0	.214	.214	.357
	YEAR		7	27	26	5	3	0	0	8	1	0	0	6	0	0	0	0	0	1	0	.192	.222	.308
90	RIC/INT	AAA	35	142	132	30	3	1	7	56	7	0	1	23	3	0	2	2	0	12	20	.227	.268	.424
	ATL/NL		63	143	137	38	5	0	7	66	5	0	0	21	4	0	1	1	0	14	25	.277	.301	.482
91	RIC/INT	AAA	32	133	119	31	7	1	7	61	10	0	3	21	6	0	1	0	1	22	24	.261	.331	.513
	ATL/NL		44	102	95	23	6	0	4	41	6	0	0	20	5	0	1	1	1	7	23	.242	.284	.432
92	RIC/INT	AAA	81	319	301	82	11	0	9	120	17	2	0	49	6	0	1	0	1	30	35	.272	.310	.399
	ATL/NL		12	11	10	3	0	0	2	9	1	0	0	1	0	0	0	0	0	2	3	.300	.364	.900
93	ATL/NL		70	91	83	20	3	0	4	35	8	1	0	21	2	0	0	8	1	8	11	.241	.308	.422
5 YR TOTALS			**196**	**374**	**351**	**89**	**17**	**1**	**17**	**159**	**21**	**1**	**0**	**69**	**11**	**0**	**2**	**2**	**1**	**32**	**62**	**.254**	**.294**	**.453**

Calderon, Ivan — BR/TR — b.3/19/62 — POS OF-755, DH-103, 1B-34 SEA 7/30/79

YR	TM/LG	CL	G	TPA	AB	H	2B	3B	HR	TB	BB	IBB	HB	SO	GDP	SH	SF	SB	CS	R	RBI	BA	OBA	SA
84	SLC/PCL	AAA	66	281	255	93	7	9	4	130	21	1	1	32	4	1	3	18	6	61	45	.365	.411	.510
	SEA/AL		11	26	24	5	1	0	0	9	2	0	0	5	3	0	0	0	0	2	1	.208	.269	.375
85	SEA/AL		67	233	210	60	16	4	8	108	19	1	2	45	10	1	1	4	2	37	28	.286	.349	.514
86	SEA/AL		37	138	131	31	5	0	2	42	6	0	0	33	1	0	0	3	1	13	13	.237	.275	.321
	CAL/PCL	AAA	24	99	81	27	3	0	3	39	15	1	0	8	1	0	0	5	1	17	18	.333	.424	.481
	CHI/AL		13	36	33	10	2	1	0	14	3	1	0	6	0	0	0	0	0	3	2	.303	.361	.424
	YEAR		50	174	164	41	7	1	2	56	9	1	0	39	1	0	0	3	1	16	15	.250	.293	.341
	BUF/AMA	AAA	27	118	105	23	9	0	5	47	9	2	2	28	2	0	0	0	0	11	22	.219	.288	.448
87	CHI/AL		144	607	542	159	38	2	28	285	60	6	1	109	13	0	4	10	5	93	83	.293	.362	.526
88	CHI/AL		73	301	264	56	14	0	14	112	34	2	0	66	6	0	3	4	4	40	35	.212	.299	.424
89	CHI/AL		157	676	622	178	34	9	14	272	43	7	3	94	20	2	6	7	1	83	87	.286	.332	.437
90	CHI/AL		158	667	607	166	44	2	14	256	51	7	1	79	26	1	2	32	16	85	74	.273	.327	.422
91	MON/NL		134	537	470	141	22	3	19	226	53	4	3	64	7	1	10	31	16	69	75	.300	.368	.481
92	WPB/FSL	A+	9	32	26	3	0	0	0	3	4	0	1	6	1	0	0	0	0	2	2	.115	.219	.115
	MON/NL		48	186	170	45	14	2	0	72	14	1	1	22	4	0	1	2	2	19	24	.265	.323	.424
93	BOS/AL		73	239	213	47	8	2	0	62	21	1	0	28	10	2	4	2	2	25	19	.221	.291	.291
	CHI/AL		9	26	26	3	2	0	0	5	0	0	0	5	2	0	0	0	0	1	3	.115	.115	.192
	YEAR		82	265	239	50	10	2	0	67	21	1	0	33	12	2	4	2	2	26	22	.209	.274	.280
10 YR TOTALS			**924**	**3672**	**3312**	**901**	**200**	**25**	**104**	**1463**	**306**	**30**	**13**	**556**	**102**	**6**	**35**	**97**	**49**	**470**	**444**	**.272**	**.333**	**.442**

Caminiti, Kenneth Gene "Ken" — BB/TR — b.4/21/63 — POS 3B-822 HOU84 4/71

YR	TM/LG	CL	G	TPA	AB	H	2B	3B	HR	TB	BB	IBB	HB	SO	GDP	SH	SF	SB	CS	R	RBI	BA	OBA	SA
85	OSC/FSL	A+	126	527	468	133	26	9	4	189	51	5	1	54	13	1	6	14	4	83	73	.284	.352	.404
86	CMB/SOU	AA	137	582	513	154	29	3	12	225	56	6	1	78	13	2	10	5	3	82	81	.300	.364	.439
87	CMB/SOU	AA	95	407	375	122	25	2	15	196	25	4	0	58	8	0	7	11	5	66	69	.325	.361	.523
	HOU/NL		63	218	203	50	7	1	3	68	12	1	0	44	6	2	1	0	0	10	23	.246	.287	.335
88	TUC/PCL	AAA	109	457	416	113	24	7	6	166	29	4	3	54	14	1	8	13	5	54	66	.272	.318	.399
	HOU/NL		30	89	83	15	2	0	1	20	5	0	0	18	3	0	1	0	0	5	7	.181	.225	.241
89	HOU/NL		161	646	585	149	31	3	10	216	51	9	3	93	8	3	4	4	1	71	72	.255	.316	.369
90	HOU/NL		153	596	541	131	20	2	4	167	48	7	0	97	15	3	4	9	4	52	51	.242	.302	.309
91	HOU/NL		152	632	574	145	30	3	13	220	46	7	3	85	18	3	4	4	5	65	80	.253	.312	.383
92	HOU/NL		135	557	506	149	31	2	13	223	44	13	2	68	14	2	4	10	4	68	62	.294	.350	.441
93	HOU/NL		143	596	543	142	31	0	13	212	49	10	1	88	15	1	3	8	5	75	75	.262	.321	.390
7 YR TOTALS			**837**	**3334**	**3035**	**781**	**152**	**11**	**57**	**1126**	**255**	**47**	**9**	**493**	**79**	**14**	**21**	**35**	**19**	**346**	**370**	**.257**	**.315**	**.371**

Canate, Emisael William "Willie" — BR/TR — b.12/11/71 — POS OF-31, DH-1 CLE 6/22/89

YR	TM/LG	CL	G	TPA	AB	H	2B	3B	HR	TB	BB	IBB	HB	SO	GDP	SH	SF	SB	CS	R	RBI	BA	OBA	SA
89	IND/GCL	R	11	24	24	5	2	0	0	7	0	0	0	3	0	0	0	0	0	4	0	.208	.208	.292
90	WAT/NYP	A-	57	213	199	52	5	2	0	67	10	0	3	43	6	0	1	9	4	28	15	.261	.307	.337
91	KIN/CAR	A+	51	211	189	41	3	1	1	49	14	0	3	29	5	5	0	4	2	28	12	.217	.282	.259
	CMB/SAL	A	62	243	204	49	13	2	4	78	25	0	4	32	10	7	3	14	5	32	20	.240	.331	.382
92	CMB/SAL	A	133	603	528	167	37	8	2	235	56	3	10	66	3	0	8	25	9	110	63	.316	.388	.445

(continued)

Canate, Emisael William "Willie" (continued)

YR	TM/LG	CL	G	TPA	AB	H	2B	3B	HR	TB	BB	IBB	HB	SO	GDP	SH	SF	SB	CS	R	RBI	BA	OBA	SA
93	IND/AMA	AAA	3	5	5	0	0	0	0	0	0	0	0	1	0	0	0	0	0	0	0	.000	.000	.000
	KNO/SOU	AA	9	42	37	10	2	0	1	15	5	0	0	2	1	0	0	2	1	8	4	.270	.357	.405
	SYR/INT	AAA	7	29	24	6	0	0	2	12	5	0	0	3	1	0	0	0	2	3	5	.250	.379	.500
	TOR/AL		38	57	47	10	0	0	1	13	6	0	1	15	2	2	1	1	1	12	3	.213	.309	.277

Candaele, Casey Todd — BB/TR — b.1/12/61 — POS 2B-323, OF-194, SS-117, 3B-50, 1B-1   MON 8/15/82

YR	TM/LG	CL	G	TPA	AB	H	2B	3B	HR	TB	BB	IBB	HB	SO	GDP	SH	SF	SB	CS	R	RBI	BA	OBA	SA
84	JAC/SOU	AA	132	574	532	145	23	3	2	178	30	1	1	35	13	5	6	26	16	68	53	.273	.309	.335
85	IND/AMA	AAA	127	446	390	101	13	5	0	124	44	2	0	33	15	11	1	13	10	55	35	.259	.333	.318
86	IND/AMA	AAA	119	540	480	145	32	6	2	195	46	6	1	29	8	11	2	16	10	77	42	.302	.363	.406
	MON/NL		30	110	104	24	4	1	0	30	5	0	0	15	3	0	1	3	5	9	6	.231	.264	.288
87	MON/NL		138	495	449	122	23	4	1	156	38	3	2	28	5	4	2	7	10	62	23	.272	.330	.347
88	MON/NL		36	128	116	20	5	1	0	27	10	1	0	11	7	2	0	1	0	9	4	.172	.238	.233
	IND/AMA	AAA	60	259	239	63	11	6	2	92	12	0	0	20	5	1	7	5	1	23	36	.264	.291	.385
	TUC/PCL	AAA	17	70	66	17	3	0	0	20	4	0	0	6	5	0	0	4	2	8	5	.258	.300	.303
	HOU/NL		21	33	31	5	3	0	0	8	1	0	0	6	0	1	0	0	1	2	1	.161	.188	.258
	YEAR		57	161	147	25	8	1	0	35	11	1	0	17	7	3	0	1	1	11	5	.170	.228	.238
89	TUC/PCL	AAA	68	231	206	45	6	1	0	53	20	4	0	37	7	4	1	6	3	22	17	.218	.286	.257
90	TUC/PCL	AAA	7	33	28	6	1	0	0	7	3	1	1	2	2	1	1	1	2	2	2	.214	.313	.250
	HOU/NL		130	298	262	75	8	6	3	104	31	4	4	42	4	4	0	7	5	30	22	.286	.364	.397
91	HOU/NL		151	505	461	121	20	7	4	167	40	7	0	49	5	1	3	9	3	44	50	.262	.319	.362
92	HOU/NL		135	360	320	68	12	1	0	85	24	3	3	36	5	6	7	7	1	19	18	.213	.269	.266
93	TUC/PCL	AAA	6	30	27	8	1	0	0	9	3	1	0	2	2	0	0	1	2	4	4	.296	.367	.333
	HOU/NL		75	131	121	29	8	0	1	40	10	0	0	14	0	0	0	2	3	18	7	.240	.298	.331
7 YR TOTALS			**716**	**2060**	**1864**	**464**	**83**	**20**	**10**	**617**	**159**	**19**	**6**	**201**	**29**	**19**	**12**	**36**	**28**	**193**	**131**	**.249**	**.308**	**.331**

Canseco, Jose — BR/TR — b.7/2/64 — POS OF-869, DH-144, P-1   OAK82 14/392

YR	TM/LG	CL	G	TPA	AB	H	2B	3B	HR	TB	BB	IBB	HB	SO	GDP	SH	SF	SB	CS	R	RBI	BA	OBA	SA
84	MOD/CAL	A+	116	500	410	113	21	2	15	183	74	5	6	127	3	3	7	10	6	61	73	.276	.388	.446
85	HUN/SOU	AA	58	251	211	67	10	2	25	156	30	6	5	55	2	0	5	6	0	47	80	.318	.406	.739
	TAC/PCL	AAA	60	277	233	81	16	1	11	132	40	5	1	66	5	0	3	5	0	41	47	.348	.440	.567
	OAK/AL		29	100	96	29	3	0	5	47	4	0	0	31	1	0	0	1	1	16	13	.302	.330	.490
86	OAK/AL		157	682	600	144	29	1	33	274	65	1	8	175	12	0	9	15	7	85	117	.240	.318	.457
87	OAK/AL		159	691	630	162	35	3	31	296	50	2	2	157	16	0	9	15	3	81	113	.257	.310	.470
88	OAK/AL		158	705	610	187	34	0	*42	347	78	10	10	128	15	1	6	40	16	120	*124	.307	.391	*.569
89	HUN/SOU	AA	9	34	29	6	0	0	0	6	5	0	0	11	0	0	0	1	0	2	3	.207	.324	.207
	OAK/AL		65	258	227	61	9	1	17	123	23	4	2	69	4	0	4	6	1	40	57	.269	.333	.542
90	OAK/AL		131	563	481	132	14	2	37	261	72	8	5	158	9	0	5	19	10	83	101	.274	.371	.543
91	OAK/AL		154	665	572	152	32	1	*44	318	78	7	9	152	16	0	6	26	6	115	122	.266	.359	.556
92	OAK/AL		97	421	366	90	11	0	22	167	48	1	3	104	15	0	4	5	7	66	72	.246	.335	.456
	TEX/AL		22	91	73	17	4	0	4	33	15	1	3	24	1	0	0	0	0	8	15	.233	.385	.452
	YEAR		119	512	439	107	15	0	26	200	63	2	6	128	16	0	4	6	7	74	87	.244	.344	.456
93	TEX/AL		60	253	231	59	14	1	10	105	16	2	3	62	6	0	3	6	6	30	46	.255	.308	.455
9 YR TOTALS			**1032**	**4429**	**3886**	**1033**	**185**	**9**	**245**	**1971**	**449**	**36**	**45**	**1060**	**95**	**1**	**48**	**134**	**59**	**644**	**780**	**.266**	**.345**	**.507**

Canseco, Osvaldo "Ozzie" — BR/TR — b.7/2/64 — POS OF-15, DH-4   NYA83* 2/40

YR	TM/LG	CL	G	TPA	AB	H	2B	3B	HR	TB	BB	IBB	HB	SO	GDP	SH	SF	SB	CS	R	RBI	BA	OBA	SA
84	GRE/SAL	A	8	1	1	0	0	0	0	0	0	0	0	0	0	0	0	0	0	1	0	.000	.000	.000
85	YAN/GCL	R	20	41	39	7	1	0	1	12	2	0	0	18	0	0	0	0	0	2	5	.179	.220	.308
86	YAN/GCL	R	7	20	15	2	1	0	0	6	5	0	0	9	0	0	0	0	0	3	3	.133	.350	.400
	MAD/MID	A	42	153	128	20	1	1	3	32	22	0	0	47	2	0	3	1	1	17	17	.156	.275	.250
87	MAD/MID	A	92	378	309	82	12	1	11	135	67	3	1	104	6	0	1	6	7	64	54	.265	.397	.437
88	MAD/MID	A	99	419	359	98	17	7	12	165	49	3	3	84	8	1	7	15	8	63	68	.273	.359	.460
	HUN/SOU	AA	27	105	99	22	7	0	3	38	6	1	0	31	1	0	0	3	0	6	12	.222	.267	.384
89	HUN/SOU	AA	91	379	317	74	17	2	12	131	51	0	5	88	4	2	4	1	2	52	52	.233	.345	.413
90	OAK/AL		9	20	19	2	1	0	0	3	1	0	0	10	0	0	0	1	0	1	1	.105	.150	.158
	HUN/SOU	AA	97	383	325	73	21	0	20	154	47	2	7	103	5	2	2	2	2	50	67	.225	.333	.474
92	LOU/AMA	AAA	98	356	308	82	19	1	22	169	43	0	2	96	1	3	2	1	1	53	57	.266	.358	.549
	STL/NL		9	36	29	8	5	0	0	13	7	0	0	4	1	0	0	0	0	7	3	.276	.417	.448
93	LOU/AMA	AAA	44	170	154	37	6	1	13	84	15	4	0	59	3	0	1	0	0	20	33	.240	.306	.545
	STL/NL		6	18	17	3	0	0	0	3	1	0	0	3	0	0	0	0	0	0	0	.176	.222	.176
3 YR TOTALS			**24**	**74**	**65**	**13**	**6**	**0**	**0**	**19**	**9**	**0**	**0**	**17**	**1**	**0**	**0**	**0**	**0**	**8**	**4**	**.200**	**.297**	**.292**

Caraballo, Ramon — BB/TR — b.5/23/69 — POS 2B-5   ATL 4/10/88

YR	TM/LG	CL	G	TPA	AB	H	2B	3B	HR	TB	BB	IBB	HB	SO	GDP	SH	SF	SB	CS	R	RBI	BA	OBA	SA
89	BRA/GCL	R	20	89	77	19	3	1	1	27	10	0	0	14	0	1	1	5	4	9	10	.247	.330	.351
	SUM/SAL	A	45	193	171	45	10	5	1	68	16	0	2	38	5	1	3	9	4	22	32	.263	.328	.398
90	BUR/MID	A	102	450	390	113	18	14	7	180	49	2	7	68	4	2	2	41	20	83	55	.290	.377	.462
91	DUR/CAR	A+	120	490	444	111	13	8	6	158	38	1	3	91	5	2	3	53	23	73	52	.250	.312	.356
92	GRE/SOU	AA	24	108	93	29	4	4	1	44	14	0	0	13	1	0	1	10	6	15	8	.312	.398	.473
	RIC/INT	AAA	101	438	405	114	20	3	2	146	22	1	3	60	6	1	7	19	16	42	40	.281	.323	.360
93	RIC/INT	AAA	126	519	470	128	25	9	3	180	30	3	3	81	5	7	5	20	14	73	41	.272	.322	.383
	ATL/NL		6			0	0	0	0	0	0	0	0	0	0	0	0	0	0	0	0	.000	.000	.000

Carey, Paul Stephan — BL/TR — b.1/8/68 — POS 1B-9, DH-5   MIAN90 1/100

YR	TM/LG	CL	G	TPA	AB	H	2B	3B	HR	TB	BB	IBB	HB	SO	GDP	SH	SF	SB	CS	R	RBI	BA	OBA	SA
90	MIA/FSL	A+	49	199	153	50	5	3	4	73	43	1	2	39	2	0	1	4	3	23	20	.327	.477	.477

Carey, Paul Stephan (continued)

YR	TM/LG	CL	G	TPA	AB	H	2B	3B	HR	TB	BB	IBB	HB	SO	GDP	SH	SF	SB	CS	R	RBI	BA	OBA	SA
91	HAG/EAS	AA	114	452	373	94	29	1	12	161	68	8	4	109	11	2	5	5	4	63	65	.252	.369	.432
92	FRE/CAR	A+	41	167	136	41	6	0	9	74	28	5	2	22	2	0	1	0	1	24	26	.301	.425	.544
	ROC/INT	AAA	30	96	87	20	4	1	1	29	6	0	2	16	2	0	1	0	0	9	7	.230	.292	.333
	HAG/EAS	AA	48	181	163	44	8	0	4	64	15	5	2	37	4	0	1	3	2	17	18	.270	.337	.393
93	ROC/INT	AAA	96	398	325	101	20	4	12	165	65	11	5	92	10	1	2	0	0	63	50	.311	.431	.508
	BAL/AL		18	52	47	10	1	0	0	11	5	0	0	14	4	0	0	0	0	1	3	.213	.288	.234

Carr, Charles Lee Glenn "Chuck" — BB/TR — b.8/10/67 — POS OF-168   CIN86 9/228

YR	TM/LG	CL	G	TPA	AB	H	2B	3B	HR	TB	BB	IBB	HB	SO	GDP	SH	SF	SB	CS	R	RBI	BA	OBA	SA
86	RED/GCL	R	44	140	123	21	5	0	0	26	10	0	0	27	2	5	2	9	1	13	10	.171	.230	.211
87	BEL/NWL	A-	44	181	165	40	1	1	1	46	12	0	1	38	2	3	0	20	1	31	11	.242	.298	.279
88	WAU/MID	A	82	327	304	91	14	2	6	127	14	0	1	49	3	3	5	41	11	58	30	.299	.327	.418
	VER/EAS	AA	41	171	159	39	4	2	0	50	8	0	0	33	0	3	1	21	9	26	13	.245	.280	.314
89	JAC/TEX	AA	116	481	444	107	13	1	0	122	27	2	1	66	3	7	2	47	20	45	22	.241	.285	.275
90	TID/INT	AAA	20	87	81	21	5	1	0	28	4	0	0	12	0	0	2	6	4	13	8	.259	.287	.346
	NY/NL		4	2	2	0	0	0	0	0	0	0	0	2	0	0	0	1	0	0	0	.000	.000	.000
	JAC/TEX	AA	93	411	361	93	19	9	3	139	43	2	4	77	4	3	2	48	15	60	24	.258	.338	.385
91	TID/INT	AAA	64	266	246	48	6	1	1	59	18	0	1	37	3	1	0	27	8	34	11	.195	.253	.240
	NY/NL		12	11	11	2	0	0	0	2	0	0	0	2	0	0	0	1	0	1	1	.182	.182	.182
92	ARK/TEX	AA	28	119	111	29	5	1	1	39	8	1	0	23	2	0	0	8	2	17	6	.261	.311	.351
	LOU/AMA	AAA	96	411	377	116	11	9	3	154	31	0	3	60	4	0	0	53	10	68	28	.308	.365	.408
	STL/NL		22	76	64	14	3	0	0	17	9	0	0	6	0	3	0	10	2	8	3	.219	.315	.266
93	MAR/GCL	R	3	12	12	5	1	0	1	9	0	0	0	0	0	0	0	3	0	4	3	.417	.417	.750
	FLO/NL		142	613	551	147	19	2	4	182	49	0	2	74	6	7	4	*58	22	75	41	.267	.327	.330
4 YR TOTALS			**180**	**702**	**628**	**163**	**22**	**2**	**4**	**201**	**58**	**0**	**2**	**84**	**6**	**10**	**4**	**70**	**24**	**84**	**45**	**.260**	**.322**	**.320**

Carreon, Mark Steven — BR/TL — b.7/19/63 — POS OF-309, DH-13, 1B-3   NYN81 7/185

YR	TM/LG	CL	G	TPA	AB	H	2B	3B	HR	TB	BB	IBB	HB	SO	GDP	SH	SF	SB	CS	R	RBI	BA	OBA	SA
84	JAC/TEX	AA	119	490	435	122	14	3	1	145	38	1	5	24	10	7	5	12	8	64	43	.280	.342	.333
85	TID/INT	AAA	7	17	15	2	1	0	1	6	2	0	0	5	0	0	0	0	1	2	1	.133	.235	.400
	JAC/TEX	AA	123	547	447	140	23	4	6	191	87	3	6	32	8	3	4	23	6	96	51	.313	.428	.427
86	TID/INT	AAA	115	482	426	123	23	2	10	180	50	5	3	42	9	1	2	12	4	62	64	.289	.366	.423
87	TID/INT	AAA	133	563	525	164	41	5	10	245	34	2	0	48	16	0	4	31	6	83	89	.312	.352	.467
	NY/NL		9	13	12	3	0	0	0	3	1	0	0	1	0	0	0	0	1	0	1	.250	.308	.250
88	TID/INT	AAA	102	409	365	96	13	3	14	157	40	2	2	53	10	0	2	11	6	48	55	.263	.337	.430
	NY/NL		7	11	9	5	2	0	1	10	2	0	0	0	0	0	0	0	0	5	1	.556	.636	1.111
89	TID/INT	AAA	32	139	122	34	4	0	1	41	13	1	0	20	5	0	4	8	3	22	21	.279	.338	.336
	NY/NL		68	146	133	41	6	0	6	65	12	0	1	17	1	0	0	2	3	20	16	.308	.370	.489
90	NY/NL		82	205	188	47	12	0	10	89	15	0	2	29	1	0	0	1	1	30	26	.250	.312	.473
91	NY/NL		106	270	254	66	14	0	4	84	12	2	0	26	13	1	1	2	1	18	21	.260	.297	.331
92	DET/AL		101	364	336	78	11	1	10	121	22	2	1	57	12	1	4	3	1	34	41	.232	.278	.360
93	SF/NL		78	169	150	49	9	1	7	81	13	2	1	16	8	0	5	1	0	22	33	.327	.373	.540
7 YR TOTALS			**451**	**1178**	**1082**	**289**	**46**	**2**	**38**	**453**	**77**	**6**	**7**	**147**	**35**	**2**	**10**	**9**	**6**	**129**	**139**	**.267**	**.317**	**.419**

Carrillo, Matias — BL/TL — b.2/24/63 — POS OF-19   MEX 1982

YR	TM/LG	CL	G	TPA	AB	H	2B	3B	HR	TB	BB	IBB	HB	SO	GDP	SH	SF	SB	CS	R	RBI	BA	OBA	SA
86	NAS/EAS	AA	15	56	52	8	1	0	0	9	4	1	0	13	0	0	0	2	4	3	0	.154	.214	.173
87	SAL/CAR	A+	90	309	284	77	11	3	8	118	19	1	2	41	2	0	4	15	4	42	37	.271	.317	.415
88	EP/TEX	AA	106	428	396	118	17	2	12	175	26	1	0	81	10	2	4	11	11	76	55	.298	.338	.442
89	DEN/AMA	AAA	125	435	400	104	14	4	10	156	24	1	2	90	7	7	2	22	6	46	43	.260	.304	.390
90	DEN/AMA	AAA	21	78	75	20	6	2	2	36	2	0	0	16	2	0	1	0	2	15	10	.267	.282	.480
91	DEN/AMA	AAA	120	461	421	116	18	5	8	168	32	2	5	85	11	5	3	10	13	56	56	.276	.325	.399
	MIL/AL		3	0	0	0	0	0	0	0	0	0	0	0	0	0	0	0	0	0	0	.000	.000	.000
93	FLO/NL		24	58	55	14	6	0	0	20	1	0	1	7	5	1	0	0	0	4	3	.255	.281	.364
2 YR TOTALS			**27**	**58**	**55**	**14**	**6**	**0**	**0**	**20**	**1**	**0**	**1**	**7**	**5**	**1**	**0**	**0**	**0**	**4**	**3**	**.255**	**.281**	**.364**

Carter, Joseph Chris "Joe" — BR/TR — b.3/7/60 — POS OF-1259, 1B-201, DH-58, 2B-1, 3B-1   CHN81 1/2

YR	TM/LG	CL	G	TPA	AB	H	2B	3B	HR	TB	BB	IBB	HB	SO	GDP	SH	SF	SB	CS	R	RBI	BA	OBA	SA
83	CHI/NL		23	52	51	9	1	1	0	12	0	0	0	21	1	1	0	1	0	6	1	.176	.176	.235
84	IOW/AMA	AAA	61	273	248	77	12	7	14	145	20	5	3	31	4	0	2	11	6	45	67	.310	.366	.585
	CLE/AL		66	257	244	67	6	1	13	114	11	0	1	48	2	0	1	2	4	32	41	.275	.307	.467
85	CLE/AL		143	523	489	128	27	0	15	200	25	2	2	74	9	3	4	24	6	64	59	.262	.298	.409
86	CLE/AL		162	709	663	200	36	9	29	341	32	3	5	95	8	1	8	29	7	108	*121	.302	.335	.514
87	CLE/AL		149	629	588	155	27	2	32	282	27	6	9	105	8	1	4	31	6	83	106	.264	.304	.480
88	CLE/AL		157	670	621	168	36	6	27	297	35	6	8	82	6	1	6	27	5	85	98	.271	.314	.478
89	CLE/AL		162	705	651	158	32	4	35	303	39	8	8	112	6	1	5	13	6	84	105	.243	.292	.465
90	SD/NL		162	697	634	147	27	1	24	248	48	18	7	93	12	0	8	22	6	79	115	.232	.290	.391
91	TOR/AL		162	706	638	174	42	3	33	321	49	12	10	112	6	0	9	20	9	89	108	.273	.330	.503
92	TOR/AL		158	683	622	164	30	7	34	310	36	4	11	109	14	1	13	12	5	97	119	.264	.309	.498
93	TOR/AL		155	669	603	153	33	5	33	295	47	5	9	113	10	0	10	8	8	92	121	.254	.312	.489
11 YR TOTALS			**1499**	**6300**	**5804**	**1523**	**297**	**39**	**275**	**2723**	**349**	**64**	**69**	**964**	**82**	**10**	**68**	**189**	**56**	**819**	**994**	**.262**	**.309**	**.469**

Castellano, Pedro Orlando — BR/TR — b.3/11/70 — POS 3B-13, 1B-10, SS-5, 2B-4   CHN 4/14/88

YR	TM/LG	CL	G	TPA	AB	H	2B	3B	HR	TB	BB	IBB	HB	SO	GDP	SH	SF	SB	CS	R	RBI	BA	OBA	SA
89	WYT/APP	R+	66	297	244	76	17	4	9	128	46	2	3	44	9	1	3	5	2	55	42	.311	.422	.525
90	PEO/MID	A	117	490	417	115	27	4	2	156	63	2	3	73	9	3	4	7	1	61	44	.276	.372	.374
	WIN/CAR	A+	19	80	66	13	0	0	1	16	10	0	2	11	3	2	0	1	0	6	8	.197	.321	.242

(continued)

Castellano, Pedro Orlando (continued)

YR	TM/LG	CL	G	TPA	AB	H	2B	3B	HR	TB	BB	IBB	HB	SO	GDP	SH	SF	SB	CS	R	RBI	BA	OBA	SA
91	WIN/CAR	A+	129	541	459	139	25	3	10	200	72	4	3	97	13	2	5	11	10	59	87	.303	.397	.436
	CHA/SOU	AA	7	22	19	8	0	0	0	8	1	0	1	6	1	0	1	0	0	2	2	.421	.455	.421
92	IOW/AMA	AAA	74	280	238	59	14	4	2	87	32	0	1	42	6	8	1	2	2	25	20	.248	.338	.366
	CHA/SOU	AA	45	175	147	33	3	0	1	39	19	0	4	21	2	3	2	0	1	16	15	.224	.326	.265
93	CS/PCL	AAA	90	355	304	95	21	2	12	156	36	0	6	63	8	1	8	3	5	61	60	.313	.387	.513
	COL/NL		34	79	71	13	2	0	3	24	8	0	0	16	1	0	0	1	1	12	7	.183	.266	.338

Castilla, Vinicio "Vinny" — BR/TR — b.7/4/67 — POS SS-120, 3B-4   MEX 3/7/89

YR	TM/LG	CL	G	TPA	AB	H	2B	3B	HR	TB	BB	IBB	HB	SO	GDP	SH	SF	SB	CS	R	RBI	BA	OBA	SA
90	SUM/SAL	A	93	381	339	91	15	2	9	137	28	1	8	54	8	1	5	2	5	47	53	.268	.334	.404
	GRE/SOU	AA	46	186	170	40	5	1	4	59	13	3	2	23	7	0	1	4	4	20	16	.235	.296	.347
91	GRE/SOU	AA	66	276	259	70	17	3	7	114	9	1	2	35	4	2	4	0	1	34	44	.270	.296	.440
	RIC/INT	AAA	67	262	240	54	7	4	7	90	14	2	3	32	4	0	5	1	1	25	36	.225	.271	.375
	ATL/NL		12	6	5	1	0	0	0	1	0	0	0	2	0	1	0	0	0	1	0	.200	.200	.200
92	RIC/INT	AAA	127	483	449	113	29	1	7	165	21	1	4	68	19	3	6	1	1	49	44	.252	.287	.367
	ATL/NL		9	18	16	4	1	0	0	5	1	1	1	4	0	0	0	0	0	1	1	.250	.333	.313
93	COL/NL		105	357	337	86	9	7	9	136	13	4	2	45	10	0	5	2	5	36	30	.255	.283	.404
3 YR TOTALS			**126**	**381**	**358**	**91**	**10**	**7**	**9**	**142**	**14**	**5**	**3**	**51**	**10**	**1**	**5**	**2**	**5**	**38**	**31**	**.254**	**.284**	**.397**

Cedeno, Andujar — BR/TR — b.8/21/69 — POS SS-288, 3B-1   HOU 10/1/86

YR	TM/LG	CL	G	TPA	AB	H	2B	3B	HR	TB	BB	IBB	HB	SO	GDP	SH	SF	SB	CS	R	RBI	BA	OBA	SA
88	AST/GCL	R	46	181	165	47	5	2	1	59	11	0	1	34	1	0	4	10	4	25	20	.285	.326	.358
89	ASH/SAL	A	126	524	487	146	23	6	14	223	29	0	1	124	10	2	5	23	10	76	93	.300	.337	.458
90	CMB/SOU	AA	132	546	495	119	21	11	19	219	33	1	6	135	11	7	5	6	10	57	64	.240	.293	.442
	HOU/NL		7	8	8	0	0	0	0	0	0	0	0	5	0	0	0	0	0	0	0	.000	.000	.000
91	TUC/PCL	AAA	93	381	347	105	19	6	7	157	19	2	5	68	9	3	7	5	3	49	55	.303	.341	.452
	HOU/NL		67	264	251	61	13	2	9	105	9	1	1	74	3	1	0	4	3	27	36	.243	.270	.418
92	TUC/PCL	AAA	74	306	280	82	18	4	6	126	18	3	1	49	8	1	6	6	4	27	56	.293	.331	.450
	HOU/NL		71	237	220	38	13	2	2	61	14	2	3	71	1	0	2	0	0	15	13	.173	.232	.277
93	HOU/NL		149	565	505	143	24	4	11	208	48	9	3	97	17	4	5	9	7	69	56	.283	.346	.412
4 YR TOTALS			**294**	**1074**	**984**	**242**	**50**	**8**	**22**	**374**	**71**	**12**	**7**	**247**	**21**	**5**	**7**	**15**	**10**	**111**	**105**	**.246**	**.299**	**.380**

Cedeno, Domingo — BB/TR — b.11/4/68 — POS SS-10, 2B-5   TOR 9/4/87

YR	TM/LG	CL	G	TPA	AB	H	2B	3B	HR	TB	BB	IBB	HB	SO	GDP	SH	SF	SB	CS	R	RBI	BA	OBA	SA
89	MB/SAL	A	9	39	35	7	0	0	0	7	3	0	1	12	0	1	0	1	1	4	2	.200	.263	.200
	DUN/FSL	A+	9	31	28	6	0	1	0	8	3	0	1	6	0	1	0	0	1	3	1	.214	.290	.286
	MH/PIO	R+	53	224	194	45	6	4	1	62	23	0	3	65	0	3	1	6	3	28	20	.232	.321	.320
90	DUN/FSL	A+	124	555	493	109	12	10	7	162	48	2	2	127	6	4	8	6	4	64	61	.221	.289	.329
91	KNO/SOU	AA	100	379	336	75	7	6	1	97	29	1	1	81	2	12	1	11	6	39	26	.223	.286	.289
92	KNO/SOU	AA	106	366	337	76	7	7	2	103	18	0	4	88	6	7	0	8	9	31	21	.226	.273	.306
	SYR/INT	AAA	18	62	57	11	4	0	0	15	3	0	0	14	1	2	0	0	0	4	5	.193	.233	.263
93	SYR/INT	AAA	103	426	382	104	16	10	2	146	33	2	1	67	6	8	2	15	10	58	28	.272	.330	.382
	TOR/AL		15	50	46	8	0	0	0	8	1	0	1	10	2	2	1	0	0	5	7	.174	.188	.174

Chamberlain, Wesley Polk "Wes" — BR/TR — b.4/13/66 — POS OF-257   PIT87 4/86

YR	TM/LG	CL	G	TPA	AB	H	2B	3B	HR	TB	BB	IBB	HB	SO	GDP	SH	SF	SB	CS	R	RBI	BA	OBA	SA
87	WAT/NYP	A-	66	287	258	67	13	4	5	103	25	2	1	48	6	0	3	22	7	50	35	.260	.324	.399
88	AUG/SAL	A	27	121	107	36	7	2	1	50	11	0	1	11	4	2	0	1	3	22	17	.336	.403	.467
	SAL/CAR	A+	92	405	365	100	15	1	11	150	38	2	0	59	7	0	2	14	4	66	50	.274	.341	.411
89	HAR/EAS	AA	129	512	471	144	26	3	21	239	32	4	2	82	14	0	7	11	10	65	87	.306	.348	.507
90	BUF/AMA	AAA	123	465	416	104	24	4	6	150	34	0	8	58	19	2	5	14	20	43	52	.250	.315	.361
	PHI/NL		18	47	46	13	3	0	2	22	1	0	0	9	0	0	0	4	0	9	4	.283	.298	.478
91	SCR/INT	AAA	39	156	144	37	7	2	2	54	8	1	0	13	6	0	4	7	4	12	20	.257	.288	.375
	PHI/NL		101	417	383	92	16	3	13	153	31	2	0	73	6	0	3	9	4	51	50	.240	.300	.399
92	SCR/INT	AAA	34	143	127	42	6	2	4	64	11	0	2	21	2	1	3	2	2	16	26	.331	.387	.504
	PHI/NL		76	289	275	71	18	0	9	116	10	2	1	55	7	1	2	4	2	26	41	.258	.285	.422
93	PHI/NL		96	306	284	80	20	2	12	140	17	3	1	51	8	0	2	2	1	34	45	.282	.320	.493
4 YR TOTALS			**291**	**1059**	**988**	**256**	**57**	**5**	**36**	**431**	**59**	**5**	**4**	**188**	**23**	**2**	**6**	**19**	**5**	**120**	**140**	**.259**	**.302**	**.436**

Cianfrocco, Angelo Dominic "Archi" — BR/TR — b.10/6/66 — POS 1B-98, 3B-83, OF-5   MON87 7/122

YR	TM/LG	CL	G	TPA	AB	H	2B	3B	HR	TB	BB	IBB	HB	SO	GDP	SH	SF	SB	CS	R	RBI	BA	OBA	SA
87	JAM/NYP	A-	70	269	251	62	8	4	3	84	9	2	1	59	2	4	4	2	0	28	27	.247	.272	.335
88	ROC/MID	A	126	494	455	115	34	0	15	194	26	0	6	99	8	2	4	6	1	54	65	.253	.299	.426
89	JAC/SOU	AA	132	472	429	105	22	7	7	162	37	1	1	126	8	0	5	3	7	46	50	.245	.303	.378
90	JAC/SOU	AA	62	213	196	43	10	0	5	68	12	1	2	45	4	0	3	0	1	18	29	.219	.268	.347
91	HAR/EAS	AA	124	507	456	144	21	10	9	212	38	2	9	112	11	2	2	11	3	71	77	.316	.378	.465
92	MON/NL		86	247	232	56	5	2	6	83	11	0	1	66	2	1	4	2	3	25	30	.241	.276	.358
	IND/AMA	AAA	15	67	59	18	5	0	2	29	4	0	2	15	0	0	0	0	1	12	16	.305	.373	.559
93	OTT/INT	AAA	50	201	188	56	14	2	4	86	7	0	2	33	5	2	0	4	2	21	27	.298	.323	.457
	MON/NL		12	17	17	4	1	0	0	5	0	0	0	5	0	0	0	0	0	3	1	.235	.235	.471
	SD/NL		84	306	279	68	10	2	11	115	9	1	3	64	6	2	5	2	1	27	47	.244	.289	.412
	YEAR		96	323	296	72	11	2	12	123	17	1	3	69	9	2	5	2	1	30	48	.243	.287	.416
2 YR TOTALS			**182**	**570**	**528**	**128**	**16**	**4**	**18**	**206**	**28**	**1**	**4**	**135**	**11**	**3**	**7**	**5**	**0**	**55**	**78**	**.242**	**.282**	**.390**

Clark, David Earl "Dave" — BL/TR — b.9/3/62 — POS OF-206, DH-102   CLE83 1/11

YR	TM/LG	CL	G	TPA	AB	H	2B	3B	HR	TB	BB	IBB	HB	SO	GDP	SH	SF	SB	CS	R	RBI	BA	OBA	SA
84	WAT/MID	A	110	438	363	112	16	3	15	179	57	4	10	68	6	4	4	20	5	74	63	.309	.412	.493

Clark, David Earl "Dave" (continued)

YR	TM/LG	CL	G	TPA	AB	H	2B	3B	HR	TB	BB	IBB	HB	SO	GDP	SH	SF	SB	CS	R	RBI	BA	OBA	SA
	BUF/EAS	AA	17	68	56	10	1	0	3	20	9		1	13	1	0	2	1	1	12	10	.179	.294	.357
85	WAT/EAS	AA	132	555	463	140	24	7	12	214	86	8	1	79	11	1	4	27	12	75	64	.302	.410	.462
86	MAI/INT	AAA	106	414	355	99	17	2	19	177	52	5	3	70	8	2	2	6	5	56	58	.279	.374	.499
	CLE/AL		18	68	58	16	1	0	3	26	7	0	0	11	1	2	1	1	0	10	9	.276	.348	.448
87	BUF/AMA	AAA	108	481	420	143	22	3	30	261	52	7	3	62	13	1	5	14	11	83	80	.340	.412	.621
	CLE/AL		29	89	87	18	5	0	3	32	2	0	0	24	4	0	0	1	0	11	12	.207	.225	.368
88	CS/PCL	AAA	47	197	165	49	10	2	4	75	27	1	2	38	5	1	2	4	5	27	31	.297	.398	.455
	CLE/AL		63	174	156	41	4	1	3	56	17	2	0	28	8	0	1	0	2	11	18	.263	.333	.359
89	CLE/AL		102	285	253	60	12	0	8	96	30	5	0	63	7	1	1	0	2	21	29	.237	.317	.379
90	CHI/NL		84	181	171	47	4	2	5	70	8	1	0	40	4	0	2	7	1	22	20	.275	.304	.409
91	OMA/AMA	AAA	104	391	359	108	24	3	13	177	30	4	0	53	13	0	2	6	4	45	64	.301	.353	.493
	KC/AL		11	11	10	2	0	0	0	2	1	0	0	1	0	0	0	0	0	1	1	.200	.273	.200
92	BUF/AMA	AAA	78	292	253	77	17	6	11	139	34	4	2	51	4	2	1	6	4	43	55	.304	.390	.549
	PIT/NL		23	40	33	7	0	0	2	13	6	0	0	8	0	0	1	0	0	3	7	.212	.325	.394
93	PIT/NL		110	318	277	75	11	2	11	123	38	5	1	58	10	0	2	1	0	43	46	.271	.358	.444
8 YR TOTALS			**440**	**1166**	**1045**	**266**	**37**	**5**	**35**	**418**	**109**	**13**	**1**	**233**	**34**	**3**	**8**	**10**	**5**	**122**	**142**	**.255**	**.323**	**.400**

Clark, Jerald Dwayne — BR/TR — b.8/10/63 — POS OF-357, 1B-79   SD85 12/310

YR	TM/LG	CL	G	TPA	AB	H	2B	3B	HR	TB	BB	IBB	HB	SO	GDP	SH	SF	SB	CS	R	RBI	BA	OBA	SA
85	SPO/NWL	A-	73	328	283	92	24	3	2	128	34	0	4	38	7	1	6	9	4	45	50	.325	.398	.452
86	REN/CAL	A+	95	434	389	118	34	3	7	179	29	3	9	46	8	0	7	5	4	76	58	.303	.359	.460
	BEA/TEX	AA	16	65	56	18	4	1	0	24	5	0	3	9	2	1	0	1	2	9	6	.321	.406	.429
87	WIC/TEX	AA	132	584	531	165	36	8	18	271	40	6	7	82	11	0	6	2	5	86	95	.311	.363	.510
88	LV/PCL	AAA	107	438	408	123	27	7	9	191	17	2	9	66	7	2	2	6	2	65	67	.301	.342	.468
	SD/NL		6	15	15	3	1	0	0	4	0	0	0	4	0	0	0	0	0	0	3	.200	.200	.267
89	LV/PCL	AAA	107	467	419	131	27	4	22	232	38	3	5	81	11	0	5	5	2	84	83	.313	.373	.554
	SD/NL		17	44	41	8	2	0	1	13	3	0	0	9	0	0	0	1	0	5	7	.195	.250	.317
90	LV/PCL	AAA	40	168	161	49	7	4	12	100	5	0	0	35	1	0	2	0	2	30	32	.304	.321	.621
	SD/NL		53	107	101	27	4	1	5	48	5	0	0	24	3	0	1	0	0	12	11	.267	.299	.475
91	SD/NL		118	411	369	84	16	0	10	130	31	2	6	90	10	1	4	2	1	26	47	.228	.295	.352
92	SD/NL		146	526	496	120	22	6	12	190	22	3	4	97	7	1	3	3	0	45	58	.242	.278	.383
93	COL/NL		140	512	478	135	26	6	13	212	20	2	10	60	12	3	1	9	6	65	67	.282	.324	.444
6 YR TOTALS			**480**	**1615**	**1500**	**377**	**71**	**13**	**41**	**597**	**81**	**7**	**20**	**284**	**32**	**5**	**9**	**14**	**8**	**153**	**193**	**.251**	**.297**	**.398**

Clark, Phillip Benjamin "Phil" — BR/TR — b.5/6/68 — POS OF-49, 1B-24, C-11, DH-7, 3B-5   DET86 1/18

YR	TM/LG	CL	G	TPA	AB	H	2B	3B	HR	TB	BB	IBB	HB	SO	GDP	SH	SF	SB	CS	R	RBI	BA	OBA	SA
86	BRI/APP	R+	66	277	247	82	4	2	4	102	19	2	4	42	3	1	4	12	1	40	36	.332	.388	.413
87	FAY/SAL	A	135	582	542	160	26	9	8	228	25	0	6	43	16	1	8	25	9	83	79	.295	.329	.421
88	LAK/FSL	A+	109	437	403	120	17	4	9	172	15	2	10	43	9	2	7	16	7	60	66	.298	.333	.427
89	LON/EAS	AA	104	415	373	108	15	4	8	155	31	1	8	49	16	1	2	2	2	43	42	.290	.356	.416
90	TOL/INT	AAA	75	233	207	47	14	1	2	69	14	0	4	35	6	6	2	1	1	15	22	.227	.286	.333
91	TOL/INT	AAA	110	393	362	92	14	4	4	126	21	0	5	49	10	3	2	6	6	47	45	.254	.303	.348
92	TOL/INT	AAA	79	292	271	76	20	0	10	126	16	0	2	35	8	1	2	4	2	29	39	.280	.323	.465
	DET/AL		23	61	54	22	4	0	1	29	6	1	0	9	2	1	0	1	0	3	5	.407	.467	.537
93	SD/NL		102	256	240	75	17	0	9	119	8	2	5	31	2	1	2	2	0	33	33	.313	.345	.496
2 YR TOTALS			**125**	**317**	**294**	**97**	**21**	**0**	**10**	**148**	**14**	**3**	**5**	**40**	**4**	**2**	**2**	**3**	**0**	**36**	**38**	**.330**	**.368**	**.503**

Clark, William Nuschler "Will" — BL/TL — b.3/13/64 — POS 1B-1124   SF85 1/2

YR	TM/LG	CL	G	TPA	AB	H	2B	3B	HR	TB	BB	IBB	HB	SO	GDP	SH	SF	SB	CS	R	RBI	BA	OBA	SA
85	FRE/CAL	A+	65	289	217	67	14	0	10	111	62		2	46	4	3	5	11	2	41	48	.309	.458	.512
86	PHO/PCL	AAA	6	24	20	5	0	0	0	5	4	0	0	2	0	0	0	1	1	3	1	.250	.375	.250
	SF/NL		111	458	408	117	27	2	11	181	34	10	3	76	3	9	4	4	7	66	41	.287	.343	.444
87	SF/NL		150	588	529	163	29	5	35	307	49	11	5	98	2	3	2	5	17	89	91	.308	.371	.580
88	SF/NL		162	689	575	162	31	6	29	292	*100	27	4	129	6	0	10	9	1	102	*109	.282	.386	.508
89	SF/NL		159	675	588	196	38	9	23	321	74	14	5	103	6	0	8	8	3	*104	111	.333	.407	.546
90	SF/NL		154	678	600	177	25	5	19	269	62	9	3	97	7	0	13	8	2	91	95	.295	.357	.448
91	SF/NL		148	622	565	170	32	7	29	*303	51	12	2	91	5	0	4	4	2	84	116	.301	.359	*.536
92	SF/NL		144	601	513	154	40	1	16	244	73	23	4	82	5	0	11	12	5	69	73	.300	.384	.476
93	SF/NL		132	567	491	139	27	2	14	212	63	6	6	81	10	1	6	2	2	82	73	.283	.367	.432
8 YR TOTALS			**1160**	**4878**	**4269**	**1278**	**249**	**37**	**176**	**2129**	**506**	**112**	**32**	**744**	**47**	**13**	**58**	**52**	**41**	**687**	**709**	**.299**	**.373**	**.499**

Clayton, Royce Spencer — BR/TR — b.1/2/70 — POS SS-255, 3B-1   SF88 1/15

YR	TM/LG	CL	G	TPA	AB	H	2B	3B	HR	TB	BB	IBB	HB	SO	GDP	SH	SF	SB	CS	R	RBI	BA	OBA	SA
88	EVE/NWL	A-	60	245	212	55	4	0	3	68	27	0	3	54	8	1	2	10	4	35	29	.259	.348	.321
89	CLI/MID	A	104	437	385	91	13	3	0	110	39	0	4	101	4	5	5	28	16	39	24	.236	.309	.286
	SJ/CAL	A+	28	106	92	11	2	0	0	13	13	0	1	27	5	0	0	10	1	5	4	.120	.236	.141
90	SJ/CAL	A+	123	536	460	123	15	0	7	179	68	0	4	98	13	0	4	33	15	80	71	.267	.364	.389
91	SHR/TEX	AA	126	557	485	136	22	8	5	189	61	0	3	104	11	3	5	36	10	84	68	.280	.361	.390
	SF/NL		9	27	26	3	1	0	0	4	1	0	0	6	0	0	0	0	0	0	2	.115	.148	.154
92	PHO/PCL	AAA	48	212	192	46	6	2	3	65	17	0	0	25	0	2	1	15	6	30	18	.240	.300	.339
	SF/NL		98	352	321	72	7	4	4	99	26	3	0	63	11	3	2	8	11	31	24	.224	.281	.308
93	SF/NL		153	607	549	155	21	5	6	204	38	2	5	91	16	8	7	11	10	54	70	.282	.331	.372
3 YR TOTALS			**260**	**986**	**896**	**230**	**29**	**9**	**10**	**307**	**65**	**5**	**5**	**160**	**28**	**11**	**9**	**19**	**14**	**85**	**96**	**.257**	**.308**	**.343**

Colbert, Craig Charles — BR/TR — b.2/13/65 — POS C-45, 3B-10, 2B-4   SF86 20/500

YR	TM/LG	CL	G	TPA	AB	H	2B	3B	HR	TB	BB	IBB	HB	SO	GDP	SH	SF	SB	CS	R	RBI	BA	OBA	SA
86	CLI/MID	A	72	290	263	60	12	0	1	75	23	1	3	53	7	0	1	4	1	26	17	.228	.297	.285

(continued)

Colbert, Craig Charles (continued)

YR	TM/LG	CL	G	TPA	AB	H	2B	3B	HR	TB	BB	IBB	HB	SO	GDP	SH	SF	SB	CS	R	RBI	BA	OBA	SA
87	FRE/CAL	A+	115	422	388	95	12	4	6	133	22	2	4	89	11	3	5	5	5	41	51	.245	.289	.343
88	CLI/MID	A	124	501	455	106	19	2	11	162	41	0	1	100	4	2	2	8	9	56	64	.233	.297	.356
89	SHR/TEX	AA	106	390	363	94	19	3	7	140	23	5	0	67	11	2	2	3	7	47	34	.259	.302	.386
90	PHO/PCL	AAA	111	437	400	112	22	2	8	162	31	3	3	80	8	1	2	4	5	41	47	.280	.335	.405
91	PHO/PCL	AAA	42	154	142	35	6	2	2	51	11	2	0	38	7	0	1	0	1	9	13	.246	.299	.359
92	PHO/PCL	AAA	36	148	140	45	8	1	1	58	3	3	0	16	4	2	2	0	1	16	12	.321	.336	.414
	SF/NL		49	139	126	29	5	2	1	41	9	0	0	22	8	2	2	1	0	10	16	.230	.277	.325
93	PHO/PCL	AAA	13	47	45	10	2	1	1	17	0	0	1	11	1	0	1	0	0	5	7	.222	.234	.378
	SF/NL		23	40	37	6	2	0	1	11	3	1	0	13	0	0	0	0	0	2	5	.162	.225	.297
	2 YR TOTALS		72	179	163	35	7	2	2	52	12	1	0	35	8	2	2	1	0	12	21	**.215**	**.266**	**.319**

Colbrunn, Gregory Joseph "Greg" — BR/TR — b.7/26/69 — POS 1B-108   MON87 8/148

YR	TM/LG	CL	G	TPA	AB	H	2B	3B	HR	TB	BB	IBB	HB	SO	GDP	SH	SF	SB	CS	R	RBI	BA	OBA	SA
88	ROC/MID	A	115	455	417	111	18	2	7	154	22	2	11	60	5	2	3	5	3	55	46	.266	.318	.369
89	WPB/FSL	A+	59	238	228	54	8	0	0	62	6	1	2	29	5	0	2	3	1	20	25	.237	.261	.272
	JAC/SOU	AA	55	194	178	49	11	1	3	71	13	0	2	33	9	0	1	0	1	21	18	.275	.330	.399
90	JAC/SOU	AA	125	511	458	138	29	1	13	208	38	4	6	78	8	3	6	1	2	57	76	.301	.358	.454
92	IND/AMA	AAA	57	228	216	66	19	1	11	120	7	2	3	41	7	0	2	1	0	32	48	.306	.333	.556
	MON/NL		52	180	168	45	9	0	2	59	6	1	2	34	1	0	4	3	2	12	18	.268	.294	.351
93	WPB/FSL	A+	8	35	31	12	2	1	1	19	4	0	0	1	2	0	0	0	0	6	5	.387	.457	.613
	OTT/INT	AAA	6	24	22	6	1	0	0	7	1	0	0	2	1	0	1	0	0	4	8	.273	.292	.318
	MON/NL		70	164	153	39	9	0	4	60	6	1	1	33	1	1	3	4	2	15	23	.255	.282	.392
	2 YR TOTALS		122	344	321	84	17	0	6	119	12	2	3	67	2	1	7	7	4	27	41	**.262**	**.289**	**.371**

Cole, Alexander "Alex" — BL/TL — b.8/17/65 — POS OF-336, DH-11   SL85* 2/43

YR	TM/LG	CL	G	TPA	AB	H	2B	3B	HR	TB	BB	IBB	HB	SO	GDP	SH	SF	SB	CS	R	RBI	BA	OBA	SA
85	JC/APP	R+	66	264	232	61	5	1	1	71	30	0	1	27	4	0	1	46	8	60	13	.263	.348	.306
86	SP/FSL	A+	74	345	286	98	9	1	0	109	54	1	2	37	2	2	1	56	22	76	26	.343	.449	.381
	LOU/AMA	AAA	63	219	200	50	2	4	1	63	17	0	1	30	3	0	1	24	13	25	16	.250	.311	.315
87	ARK/TEX	AA	125	527	477	122	12	4	2	148	44	5	0	55	3	5	1	68	29	68	27	.256	.318	.310
88	LOU/AMA	AAA	120	442	392	91	7	8	0	114	42	1	1	59	2	6	1	40	15	44	24	.232	.307	.291
89	SP/FSL	A+	8	35	32	6	0	0	0	6	3	0	1	7	1	0	0	4	1	2	1	.188	.257	.188
	LOU/AMA	AAA	127	532	455	128	5	5	2	149	71	1	1	76	3	4	1	47	19	75	29	.281	.379	.327
90	LV/PCL	AAA	90	399	341	99	7	4	1	114	47	0	1	62	4	8	1	32	15	58	28	.290	.376	.334
	CS/PCL	AAA	14	57	49	21	2	0	0	23	8	0	0	7	1	0	0	6	4	13	3	.429	.509	.469
	CLE/AL		63	256	227	68	5	4	0	81	28	0	0	38	2	0	0	40	9	43	13	.300	.379	.357
91	CS/PCL	AAA	8	37	32	6	1	0	0	8	4	0	1	3	0	0	0	3	2	3	3	.188	.297	.250
	CLE/AL		122	452	387	114	17	3	0	137	58	2	1	47	8	4	2	27	17	58	21	.295	.386	.354
92	CLE/AL		41	109	97	20	1	0	0	21	10	0	1	21	2	0	1	9	2	11	5	.206	.284	.216
	PIT/NL		64	225	205	57	3	7	0	74	18	1	0	46	2	1	1	7	4	33	10	.278	.335	.361
	YEAR		105	334	302	77	4	7	0	95	28	1	1	67	4	1	2	16	6	44	15	.255	.318	.315
93	COL/NL		126	399	348	89	9	4	0	106	43	3	2	58	6	4	2	30	13	50	24	.256	.339	.305
	4 YR TOTALS		416	1441	1264	348	35	18	0	419	157	6	5	210	20	9	6	113	45	195	73	**.275**	**.356**	**.331**

Coleman, Vincent Maurice "Vince" — BB/TR — b.9/22/61 — POS OF-1082   SL82 10/257

YR	TM/LG	CL	G	TPA	AB	H	2B	3B	HR	TB	BB	IBB	HB	SO	GDP	SH	SF	SB	CS	R	RBI	BA	OBA	SA
84	LOU/AMA	AAA	152	671	608	156	21	7	4	203	55	1	5	112	7	2	1	101	36	97	48	.257	.323	.334
85	LOU/AMA	AAA	5	22	21	3	0	0	0	3	0	0	0	2	0	1	0	0	0	1	0	.143	.143	.143
	STL/NL		151	692	636	170	20	10	1	213	50	1	0	115	3	5	1	*110	25	107	40	.267	.320	.335
86	STL/NL		154	670	600	139	13	8	0	168	60	0	2	98	4	3	3	*107	14	94	29	.232	.301	.280
87	STL/NL		151	702	623	180	14	10	3	223	70	0	3	126	7	5	1	*109	22	121	43	.289	.363	.358
88	STL/NL		153	679	616	160	20	10	3	209	49	4	1	111	4	8	5	*81	27	77	38	.260	.313	.339
89	STL/NL		145	624	563	143	21	9	2	188	50	0	2	90	4	7	2	*65	10	94	28	.254	.316	.334
90	STL/NL		124	539	497	145	18	9	6	199	35	1	2	88	6	4	1	*77	17	73	39	.292	.340	.400
91	NY/NL		72	318	278	71	7	5	1	91	39	0	0	47	3	1	0	37	14	45	17	.255	.347	.327
92	SL/FSL	A+	6	24	22	8	0	0	0	8	2	0	0	6	0	0	0	4	2	4	2	.364	.417	.364
	NY/NL		71	261	229	63	11	1	2	82	27	3	2	41	1	2	1	24	9	37	21	.275	.355	.358
93	NY/NL		92	399	373	104	14	8	2	140	21	1	0	58	2	3	2	38	13	64	25	.279	.316	.375
	9 YR TOTALS		1113	4884	4415	1175	138	70	20	1513	401	10	12	774	34	38	18	648	151	712	280	**.266**	**.328**	**.343**

Coles, Darnell — BR/TR — b.6/2/62 — POS 3B-334, OF-315, DH-66, 1B-56, SS-18   SEA80 1/6

YR	TM/LG	CL	G	TPA	AB	H	2B	3B	HR	TB	BB	IBB	HB	SO	GDP	SH	SF	SB	CS	R	RBI	BA	OBA	SA
83	SEA/AL		27	100	92	26	7	0	1	36	7	0	0	12	8	1	0	0	3	9	6	.283	.333	.391
84	SLC/PCL	AAA	69	304	242	77	22	3	14	147	48	2	2	41	4	6	6	7	2	57	68	.318	.426	.607
	SEA/AL		48	165	143	23	3	1	0	28	17	0	2	26	5	3	0	2	1	15	6	.161	.259	.196
85	SEA/AL		27	71	59	14	4	0	1	21	9	0	1	17	0	0	2	1	1	8	5	.237	.338	.356
	CAL/PCL	AAA	31	118	97	31	8	0	4	51	17	0	2	15	2	1	1	2	1	16	24	.320	.427	.526
86	DET/AL		142	587	521	142	30	2	20	236	45	3	6	84	8	7	8	6	2	67	86	.273	.333	.453
87	TOL/INT	AAA	10	41	37	12	5	0	1	20	4	1	0	2	0	0	0	0	2	7	7	.324	.390	.541
	DET/AL		53	169	149	27	5	1	4	46	15	1	2	23	1	2	1	0	1	14	15	.181	.263	.309
	PIT/NL		40	144	119	27	8	0	3	53	19	2	1	20	4	2	1	3	3	20	24	.227	.333	.445
	YEAR		93	313	268	54	13	1	7	99	34	3	3	43	5	4	3	3	4	34	39	.201	.295	.369
88	PIT/NL		68	241	211	49	13	1	5	79	20	1	1	44	3	3	2	2	1	20	15	.232	.299	.374
	SEA/AL		55	221	195	57	10	1	10	99	17	0	4	26	5	3	2	3	2	32	34	.292	.356	.508
	YEAR		123	462	406	106	23	2	15	178	37	1	5	67	8	6	4	5	3	52	49	.261	.326	.438
89	SEA/AL		146	573	535	135	21	3	10	192	27	1	6	61	13	2	3	5	4	54	59	.252	.294	.359
90	SEA/AL		37	113	107	23	5	1	2	36	4	1	1	17	1	1	0	1	0	9	16	.215	.248	.336

Coles, Darnell (continued)

YR	TM/LG	CL	G	TPA	AB	H	2B	3B	HR	TB	BB	IBB	HB	SO	GDP	SH	SF	SB	CS	R	RBI	BA	OBA	SA
	DET/AL		52	122	108	22	2	0	1	27	12	1	0	21	3	1	1	0	4	13	4	.204	.281	.250
	YEAR		89	235	215	45	7	1	3	63	16	2	1	38	4	1	2	0	4	22	20	.209	.265	.293
91	SF/NL		11	14	14	3	0	0	0	3	0	0	0	2	1	0	0	0	0	1	0	.214	.214	.214
	PHO/PCL	AAA	83	365	328	95	23	2	6	140	27	2	6	43	10	1	3	0	0	43	65	.290	.352	.427
92	NAS/AMA	AAA	22	92	81	24	5	0	6	47	8	0	2	13	1	0	1	1	0	19	16	.296	.370	.580
	CIN/NL		55	149	141	44	11	2	3	68	3	0	0	15	1	3	2	1	0	16	18	.312	.322	.482
93	TOR/AL		64	217	194	49	9	1	4	72	16	1	4	29	3	1	2	1	1	26	26	.253	.319	.371
11 YR TOTALS			**825**	**2886**	**2588**	**641**	**128**	**13**	**67**	**996**	**211**	**11**	**30**	**394**	**55**	**25**	**32**	**20**	**23**	**304**	**335**	**.248**	**.308**	**.385**

Conine, Jeffrey Guy "Jeff" — BR/TR — b.6/27/66 — POS OF-170, 1B-56   KC87 58/1226

YR	TM/LG	CL	G	TPA	AB	H	2B	3B	HR	TB	BB	IBB	HB	SO	GDP	SH	SF	SB	CS	R	RBI	BA	OBA	SA
88	BC/FSL	A+	118	470	415	113	23	9	10	184	46	1	0	77	6	5	4	26	12	63	59	.272	.342	.443
89	BC/FSL	A+	113	471	425	116	12	7	14	184	40	2	3	91	14	0	3	32	13	68	60	.273	.338	.433
90	MEM/SOU	AA	137	590	487	156	37	8	15	254	94	6	1	88	10	0	8	21	6	89	95	.320	.425	.522
	KC/AL		9	22	20	5	2	0	0	7	2	0	0	5	1	0	0	0	0	3	2	.250	.318	.350
91	OMA/AMA	AAA	51	198	171	44	9	1	3	64	26	2	1	39	3	0	0	0	6	23	15	.257	.359	.374
92	OMA/AMA	AAA	110	461	397	120	24	5	20	214	54	5	2	67	6	2	6	4	5	69	72	.302	.383	.539
	KC/AL		28	99	91	23	5	2	0	32	8	1	0	23	1	0	0	0	0	10	9	.253	.313	.352
93	FLO/NL		162	658	595	174	24	3	12	240	52	2	5	135	14	0	6	2	2	75	79	.292	.351	.403
3 YR TOTALS			**199**	**779**	**706**	**202**	**31**	**5**	**12**	**279**	**62**	**3**	**5**	**163**	**16**	**0**	**6**	**2**	**2**	**88**	**90**	**.286**	**.345**	**.395**

Cooper, Scott Kendrick — BL/TR — b.10/13/67 — POS 3B-214, 1B-64, SS-2, DH-2, 2B-1   BOS86 2/69

YR	TM/LG	CL	G	TPA	AB	H	2B	3B	HR	TB	BB	IBB	HB	SO	GDP	SH	SF	SB	CS	R	RBI	BA	OBA	SA
86	ELM/NYP	A-	51	215	191	55	9	0	9	91	19	2	0	32	6	1	4	1	4	23	43	.288	.346	.476
87	GRE/SAL	A	119	436	370	93	21	2	15	163	58	7	2	69	5	0	6	1	0	52	63	.251	.351	.441
88	LYN/CAR	A+	130	563	497	148	45	7	9	234	58	0	2	74	11	2	4	0	0	90	73	.298	.371	.471
89	NB/EAS	AA	124	492	421	104	24	2	7	153	55	2	6	84	5	5	5	1	1	50	39	.247	.339	.363
90	PAW/INT	AAA	124	486	433	115	17	1	12	170	39	3	7	75	9	4	3	2	3	56	44	.266	.334	.393
	BOS/AL		2	1	1	0	0	0	0	0	0	0	0	1	0	0	0	0	0	0	0	.000	.000	.000
91	PAW/INT	AAA	137	550	483	134	21	2	15	204	50	11	7	58	14	4	6	3	5	55	72	.277	.350	.422
	BOS/AL		14	37	35	16	4	2	0	24	2	0	0	4	0	0	0	0	0	6	7	.457	.486	.686
92	BOS/AL		123	378	337	93	21	0	5	129	37	0	0	33	5	2	2	1	1	34	33	.276	.346	.383
93	BOS/AL		156	596	526	147	29	3	9	209	58	15	5	81	8	4	3	5	2	67	63	.279	.355	.397
4 YR TOTALS			**295**	**1012**	**899**	**256**	**54**	**5**	**14**	**362**	**97**	**15**	**5**	**117**	**13**	**6**	**5**	**6**	**3**	**107**	**103**	**.285**	**.356**	**.403**

Cora, Jose Manuel "Joey" — BB/TR — b.5/14/65 — POS 2B-341, SS-45, DH-20, 3B-10, C-1   SD85 1/23

YR	TM/LG	CL	G	TPA	AB	H	2B	3B	HR	TB	BB	IBB	HB	SO	GDP	SH	SF	SB	CS	R	RBI	BA	OBA	SA
85	SPO/NWL	A-	43	210	170	55	11	2	3	79	27	0	8	24	4	4	1	13	2	48	26	.324	.437	.465
86	BEA/TEX	AA	81	371	315	96	5	5	3	120	47	3	3	28	6	3	3	24	11	54	41	.305	.397	.381
87	LV/PCL	AAA	81	363	293	81	9	1	1	95	62	2	2	39	5	5	1	12	7	50	24	.276	.405	.324
	SD/NL		77	276	241	57	7	2	0	68	28	1	1	26	4	5	1	15	11	23	13	.237	.317	.282
88	LV/PCL	AAA	127	517	460	136	15	3	3	166	44	3	2	19	6	6	5	31	7	73	55	.296	.356	.361
89	LV/PCL	AAA	119	562	507	157	25	4	0	190	42	3	8	31	4	4	1	40	15	79	37	.310	.371	.375
	SD/NL		12	20	19	6	1	0	0	7	1	0	0	0	0	0	0	1	0	5	1	.316	.350	.368
90	LV/PCL	AAA	51	249	211	74	13	9	0	105	29	2	4	16	2	1	4	15	7	41	24	.351	.431	.498
	SD/NL		51	106	100	27	3	0	0	30	6	1	0	9	1	0	0	8	3	12	2	.270	.311	.300
91	SB/MID	A	1	5	5	1	0	0	0	1	0	0	0	1	0	0	0	0	0	1	0	.200	.200	.200
	CHI/AL		100	264	228	55	2	3	0	63	20	0	5	21	1	8	3	11	6	37	18	.241	.313	.276
92	CHI/AL		68	153	122	30	7	1	0	39	22	1	4	13	2	2	3	10	3	27	9	.246	.371	.320
93	CHI/AL		153	678	579	155	15	13	2	202	67	0	9	63	14	19	4	20	8	95	51	.268	.351	.349
6 YR TOTALS			**461**	**1497**	**1289**	**330**	**35**	**19**	**2**	**409**	**144**	**3**	**19**	**132**	**22**	**34**	**11**	**65**	**31**	**199**	**94**	**.256**	**.337**	**.317**

Cordero, Wilfredo "Wil" — BR/TR — b.10/3/71 — POS SS-169, 2B-9, 3B-2   MON 5/25/88

YR	TM/LG	CL	G	TPA	AB	H	2B	3B	HR	TB	BB	IBB	HB	SO	GDP	SH	SF	SB	CS	R	RBI	BA	OBA	SA
88	JAM/NYP	A-	52	211	190	49	3	0	2	58	15	0	4	44	2	0	2	3	3	18	22	.258	.322	.305
89	WPB/FSL	A+	78	328	289	80	12	2	6	114	33	2	3	58	6	1	2	5	5	37	29	.277	.355	.394
	JAC/SOU	AA	39	137	121	26	6	1	3	43	12	0	0	33	3	3	1	1	2	9	17	.215	.284	.355
90	JAC/SOU	AA	131	509	444	104	18	4	7	151	56	0	5	122	5	3	1	9	4	63	40	.234	.326	.340
91	IND/AMA	AAA	98	391	360	94	16	4	11	151	26	2	0	89	4	0	2	9	2	48	52	.261	.315	.419
92	IND/AMA	AAA	52	230	204	64	11	1	6	95	24	2	0	54	7	1	1	6	7	32	27	.314	.384	.466
	MON/NL		45	137	126	38	4	1	2	50	9	0	1	31	3	1	0	0	0	17	8	.302	.353	.397
93	MON/NL		138	521	475	118	32	2	10	184	34	8	7	60	12	4	1	12	3	56	58	.248	.308	.387
2 YR TOTALS			**183**	**658**	**601**	**156**	**36**	**3**	**12**	**234**	**43**	**8**	**8**	**91**	**15**	**5**	**1**	**12**	**3**	**73**	**66**	**.260**	**.317**	**.389**

Correia, Ronald Douglas "Rod" — BR/TR — b.9/13/67 — POS SS-40, 2B-11, DH-6, 3B-3   OAK88 16/385

YR	TM/LG	CL	G	TPA	AB	H	2B	3B	HR	TB	BB	IBB	HB	SO	GDP	SH	SF	SB	CS	R	RBI	BA	OBA	SA
88	SO/NWL	A-	56	230	207	52	7	3	1	68	18	0	3	42	9	1	1	6	1	23	19	.251	.319	.329
89	MOD/CAL	A+	107	390	339	71	9	3	0	86	34	0	12	64	10	4	1	7	7	31	26	.209	.303	.254
90	MOD/CAL	A+	87	278	246	60	6	3	0	72	22	0	4	41	6	5	1	4	6	27	16	.244	.315	.293
91	MOD/CAL	A+	5	22	19	5	0	0	0	5	2	0	1	0	1	1	0	1	0	8	3	.263	.333	.263
	TAC/PCL	AAA	17	64	56	14	0	0	1	17	4	0	1	6	1	3	0	0	0	9	7	.250	.311	.304
	HUN/SOU	AA	87	336	290	64	10	1	1	79	31	0	6	50	11	8	1	2	4	25	22	.221	.308	.272
92	MID/TEX	AA	123	529	482	140	23	1	6	183	28	2	8	75	14	5	6	20	11	73	56	.290	.336	.380
93	VAN/PCL	AAA	60	231	207	56	10	4	4	86	15	1	1	25	5	3	5	11	4	43	28	.271	.316	.415
	CAL/AL		64	143	128	34	5	0	0	39	6	0	4	20	1	5	0	2	4	12	9	.266	.319	.305

Costo, Timothy Roger "Tim" — BR/TR — b.2/16/69 — POS OF-26, 1B-14, 3B-2 CLE90 1/8

YR	TM/LG	CL	G	TPA	AB	H	2B	3B	HR	TB	BB	IBB	HB	SO	GDP	SH	SF	SB	CS	R	RBI	BA	OBA	SA
90	KIN/CAR	A+	56	243	206	65	13	1	4	92	23	0	6	47	3	0	8	4	0	34	42	.316	.387	.447
91	CAN/EAS	AA	52	213	192	52	10	3.	1	71	15	0	0	44	10	0	6	2	1	28	24	.271	.315	.370
	CHT/SOU	AA	85	319	293	82	19	3	5	122	20	0	4	65	5	0	2	11	5	31	29	.280	.332	.416
92	CHT/SOU	AA	121	486	424	102	18	2	28	208	48	1	11	128	10	0	1	24	5	63	71	.241	.332	.491
	CIN/NL		12	42	36	8	2	0	0	10	5	0	0	6	4	0	1	0	0	3	2	.222	.310	.278
93	IND/AMA	AAA	106	391	362	118	30	2	11	185	22	1	5	60	5	1	3	2	2	49	57	.326	.372	.511
	CIN/NL		31	104	98	22	5	0	3	36	4	0	0	17	1	0	2	0	0	13	12	.224	.250	.367
2 YR TOTALS			43	146	134	30	7	0	3	46	9	0	0	23	5	0	3	0	0	16	14	**.224**	**.267**	**.343**

Cotto, Henry — BR/TR — b.1/5/61 — POS OF-760, DH-32 CHN 6/7/80

YR	TM/LG	CL	G	TPA	AB	H	2B	3B	HR	TB	BB	IBB	HB	SO	GDP	SH	SF	SB	CS	R	RBI	BA	OBA	SA
84	IOW/AMA	AAA	8	33	30	6	2	0	0	8	2	0	1	3	2	0	0	1	2	3	0	.200	.273	.267
	CHI/NL		105	160	146	40	5	0	0	45	10	2	1	23	1	3	0	9	3	24	8	.274	.325	.308
85	CMB/INT	AAA	75	297	272	70	16	2	7	111	19	0	2	61	4	1	3	10	4	38	36	.257	.307	.408
	NY/AL		34	60	56	17	1	0	1	21	3	0	0	12	1	1	0	1	1	4	6	.304	.339	.375
86	CMB/INT	AAA	97	384	359	89	17	6	7	139	19	1	4	53	10	1	1	16	6	45	48	.248	.292	.387
	NY/AL		35	83	80	17	3	0	1	23	2	0	0	17	0	0	0	3	0	11	6	.213	.229	.287
87	CMB/INT	AAA	34	141	129	39	13	2	3	65	10	0	1	16	3	0	1	14	2	26	20	.302	.355	.504
	NY/AL		68	156	149	35	10	0	5	60	6	0	1	35	7	0	0	4	2	21	20	.235	.269	.403
88	SEA/AL		133	418	386	100	18	1	8	144	23	0	1	53	8	4	3	27	3	50	33	.259	.302	.373
89	SEA/AL		100	310	295	78	11	2	9	120	12	3	3	44	4	0	0	10	4	44	33	.264	.300	.407
90	SEA/AL		127	390	355	92	14	3	4	124	22	2	4	52	13	6	3	21	3	40	33	.259	.307	.349
91	SEA/AL		66	192	177	54	6	2	6	82	10	0	2	27	7	2	1	16	3	35	23	.305	.347	.463
92	SEA/AL		108	313	294	76	11	1	5	104	14	3	1	49	2	3	1	23	2	42	27	.259	.294	.354
93	SEA/AL		54	109	105	20	1	0	2	27	2	0	1	22	0	1	0	5	4	10	7	.190	.213	.257
	FLO/NL		54	142	135	40	7	0	3	56	3	0	1	18	3	1	2	11	1	15	14	.296	.312	.415
	YEAR		108	251	240	60	8	0	5	83	5	0	2	40	3	2	2	16	5	25	21	.250	.269	.346
10 YR TOTALS			884	2333	2178	569	87	9	44	806	107	10	16	352	49	21	11	130	26	296	210	**.261**	**.299**	**.370**

Cromer, Roy Bunyan "Tripp" — BR/TR — b.11/21/67 — POS SS-9 SL89 3/66

YR	TM/LG	CL	G	TPA	AB	H	2B	3B	HR	TB	BB	IBB	HB	SO	GDP	SH	SF	SB	CS	R	RBI	BA	OBA	SA
89	HAM/NYP	A-	35	158	137	36	6	3	0	48	17	0	1	30	5	2	1	4	4	18	6	.263	.346	.350
90	SP/FSL	A+	121	467	408	88	12	5	5	125	46	0	5	78	11	3	5	7	12	53	38	.216	.300	.306
91	SP/FSL	A+	43	151	137	28	3	1	0	33	9	0	1	17	8	3	1	0	0	11	10	.204	.257	.241
	ARK/TEX	AA	73	250	227	52	12	1	1	69	15	1	3	37	8	2	3	0	1	28	18	.229	.282	.304
92	ARK/TEX	AA	110	371	339	81	16	6	7	130	22	1	4	82	9	4	2	4	6	30	29	.239	.292	.383
	LOU/AMA	AAA	6	27	25	5	1	1	1	11	1	0	0	6	0	0	1	0	0	5	7	.200	.222	.440
93	LOU/AMA	AAA	86	328	309	85	8	4	11	134	15	3	2	60	10	2	0	1	3	39	33	.275	.313	.434
	STL/NL		10	24	23	2	0	0	0	2	1	0	0	6	0	0	0	0	0	1	0	.087	.125	.087

Cummings, Midre Almeric — BB/TR — b.10/14/71 — POS OF-11 MIN90 2/29

YR	TM/LG	CL	G	TPA	AB	H	2B	3B	HR	TB	BB	IBB	HB	SO	GDP	SH	SF	SB	CS	R	RBI	BA	OBA	SA
90	TWI/GCL	R	47	196	177	56	3	4	5	82	13	1	2	32	1	0	4	14	7	28	28	.316	.362	.463
91	KEN/MID	A	106	416	382	123	20	4	4	163	22	2	6	66	7	4	2	28	10	59	54	.322	.367	.427
92	SAL/CAR	A+	113	462	420	128	20	5	14	200	35	2	4	67	2	0	3	23	9	55	75	.305	.361	.476
93	CAR/SOU	AA	63	254	237	70	17	2	6	109	14	1	1	23	3	2	0	5	3	33	26	.295	.337	.460
	BUF/AMA	AAA	60	256	232	64	9	1	9	105	22	4	0	45	2	0	2	5	1	36	21	.276	.336	.453
	PIT/NL		13	41	36	4	1	0	0	5	0	0	0	9	1	0	1	0	0	5	3	.111	.195	.139

Curtis, Chad David — BR/TR — b.11/6/68 — POS OF-286, 2B-3, DH-1 CAL89 45/1157

YR	TM/LG	CL	G	TPA	AB	H	2B	3B	HR	TB	BB	IBB	HB	SO	GDP	SH	SF	SB	CS	R	RBI	BA	OBA	SA
89	ANG/ARI	R	32	141	122	37	4	4	3	58	14	0	2	20	3	1	2	17	2	30	20	.303	.379	.475
	QC/MID	A	23	86	78	19	3	0	2	28	6	0	0	17	1	1	1	7	5	7	11	.244	.294	.359
90	QC/MID	A	135	568	492	151	28	1	14	223	57	3	12	78	8	4	3	64	22	87	65	.307	.390	.453
91	EDM/PCL	AAA	115	493	431	136	28	7	9	205	51	2	4	56	9	4	4	46	11	81	61	.316	.389	.476
92	CAL/AL		139	507	441	114	16	2	10	164	51	2	4	71	10	5	4	43	18	59	46	.259	.341	.372
93	CAL/AL		152	671	583	166	25	3	6	215	70	2	6	89	16	7	7	48	24	94	59	.285	.361	.369
2 YR TOTALS			291	1178	1024	280	41	5	16	379	121	4	10	160	26	12	11	91	42	153	105	**.273**	**.352**	**.370**

Cuyler, Milton "Milt" — BB/TR — b.10/7/68 — POS OF-337 DET86 2/46

YR	TM/LG	CL	G	TPA	AB	H	2B	3B	HR	TB	BB	IBB	HB	SO	GDP	SH	SF	SB	CS	R	RBI	BA	OBA	SA
86	BRI/APP	R+	45	196	174	40	3	5	1	56	15	0	2	35	1	2	0	12	4	24	11	.230	.309	.322
87	FAY/SAL	A	94	426	366	107	8	4	2	129	34	4	7	78	3	17	2	27	13	65	34	.292	.362	.352
88	LAK/FSL	A+	132	573	483	143	11	3	2	166	71	2	4	83	3	14	1	50	25	100	32	.296	.390	.344
89	TOL/INT	AAA	24	95	83	14	3	2	0	21	8	0	0	27	1	3	1	4	1	4	6	.169	.239	.253
	LON/EAS	AA	98	421	366	96	8	7	7	139	47	2	4	74	2	4	0	32	5	69	34	.262	.353	.380
90	TOL/INT	AAA	124	535	461	119	11	8	2	152	60	1	5	77	6	7	2	52	14	77	42	.258	.348	.330
	DET/AL		19	59	51	13	3	1	0	18	5	0	0	10	1	2	1	1	2	8	8	.255	.316	.353
91	DET/AL		154	546	475	122	15	7	3	160	52	0	5	92	4	12	2	41	10	77	33	.257	.335	.337
92	DET/AL		89	313	291	70	11	1	3	92	10	0	4	62	4	8	0	8	5	39	28	.241	.275	.316
93	DET/AL		82	276	249	53	11	7	0	78	19	0	3	53	2	4	1	13	2	46	19	.213	.276	.313
4 YR TOTALS			344	1194	1066	258	40	16	6	348	86	0	12	217	11	26	4	63	19	170	88	**.242**	**.305**	**.326**

Dascenzo, Douglas Craig "Doug" — BB/TL — b.6/30/64 — POS OF-448, P-4, DH-2 CHN85 13/312

YR	TM/LG	CL	G	TPA	AB	H	2B	3B	HR	TB	BB	IBB	HB	SO	GDP	SH	SF	SB	CS	R	RBI	BA	OBA	SA
85	GEN/NYP	A-	70	320	252	84	15	1	3	110	61	4	2	20	1	1	4	33	9	59	23	.333	.461	.437
86	WIN/CAR	A+	138	627	545	178	29	11	6	247	63	5	2	44	9	12	5	57	13	107	83	.327	.395	.453

Dascenzo, Douglas Craig "Doug" (continued)

YR	TM/LG	CL	G	TPA	AB	H	2B	3B	HR	TB	BB	IBB	HB	SO	GDP	SH	SF	SB	CS	R	RBI	BA	OBA	SA
87	PIT/EAS	AA	134	582	496	152	32	6	3	205	73	5	1	38	5	7	5	36	7	84	56	.306	.393	.413
88	IOW/AMA	AAA	132	556	505	149	22	5	6	199	37	4	2	41	7	7	5	30	14	73	49	.295	.342	.394
	CHI/NL		26	85	75	16	3	0	0	19	9	1	0	4	2	1	0	6	1	9	4	.213	.298	.253
89	IOW/AMA	AAA	111	493	431	121	18	4	4	159	51	3	0	41	7	9	2	34	21	59	33	.281	.355	.369
	CHI/NL		47	157	139	23	1	0	1	27	13	0	0	13	2	3	2	6	3	20	12	.165	.234	.194
90	CHI/NL		113	271	241	61	9	5	1	83	21	2	1	18	3	5	3	15	6	27	26	.253	.312	.344
91	CHI/NL		118	272	239	61	11	0	1	75	24	2	2	26	3	6	1	14	7	40	18	.255	.327	.314
92	CHI/NL		139	409	376	96	13	4	0	117	27	2	0	32	3	4	2	6	8	37	20	.255	.304	.311
93	OC/AMA	AAA	38	176	157	39	8	2	1	54	16	0	0	16	7	2	1	6	5	21	13	.248	.316	.344
	TEX/AL		76	158	146	29	5	1	2	42	8	0	0	22	1	3	1	2	0	20	10	.199	.239	.288
6 YR TOTALS			**519**	**1352**	**1216**	**286**	**42**	**10**	**5**	**363**	**102**	**7**	**3**	**115**	**14**	**22**	**9**	**49**	**25**	**153**	**90**	**.235**	**.294**	**.299**

Daugherty, John Michael "Jack" — BB/TL — b.7/3/60 — POS OF-127, 1B-76, DH-43 — OAK 10/9/82

YR	TM/LG	CL	G	TPA	AB	H	2B	3B	HR	TB	BB	IBB	HB	SO	GDP	SH	SF	SB	CS	R	RBI	BA	OBA	SA
84	HEL/PIO	R+	66	315	259	104	26	2	15	179	52	10	2	48	2	0	2	16	3	77	82	.402	.502	.691
85	WPB/FSL	A+	133	561	481	152	25	3	10	213	75	11	0	58	14	0	5	33	6	76	87	.316	.405	.443
86	JAC/SOU	AA	138	595	502	159	37	4	4	216	79	1	4	58	14	7	3	15	6	87	63	.317	.412	.430
87	IND/AMA	AAA	117	469	420	131	35	3	7	193	42	5	1	54	12	2	4	11	0	65	50	.312	.373	.460
	MON/NL		11	12	10	1	1	0	0	2	0	0	0	3	0	2	0	0	0	1	1	.100	.100	.200
88	IND/AMA	AAA	137	552	481	137	33	2	6	192	56	4	1	50	14	7	7	18	6	82	67	.285	.356	.399
89	OC/AMA	AAA	82	355	311	78	15	3	3	108	39	5	0	35	9	2	3	2	2	28	32	.251	.331	.347
	TEX/AL		52	121	106	32	4	2	1	43	11	0	1	21	1	0	3	2	1	15	10	.302	.364	.406
90	TEX/AL		125	339	310	93	20	2	6	135	22	0	2	49	4	2	3	0	0	36	47	.300	.347	.435
91	OC/AMA	AAA	22	85	77	11	2	0	0	13	8	2	0	14	1	0	0	4	0	4	4	.143	.224	.169
	TEX/AL		58	167	144	28	3	2	1	38	16	1	0	23	2	4	3	1	0	8	11	.194	.270	.264
92	OC/AMA	AAA	9	21	18	5	2	0	0	7	3	0	0	3	1	0	0	0	0	3	2	.278	.381	.389
	TEX/AL		59	146	127	26	9	0	0	35	16	1	1	21	3	0	2	2	1	13	9	.205	.295	.276
93	TUC/PCL	AAA	42	172	141	55	9	2	2	74	26	2	3	12	1	0	2	1	0	23	29	.390	.488	.525
	HOU/NL		4	3	3	1	0	0	0	1	0	0	0	0	0	0	0	0	0	0	0	.333	.333	.333
	CIN/NL		46	71	59	13	2	0	2	21	11	0	0	15	0	0	1	0	0	7	9	.220	.338	.356
	YEAR		50	74	62	14	2	0	2	22	11	0	0	15	0	0	1	0	0	7	9	.226	.338	.355
6 YR TOTALS			**355**	**859**	**759**	**194**	**39**	**6**	**10**	**275**	**76**	**2**	**4**	**132**	**10**	**8**	**12**	**5**	**2**	**80**	**87**	**.256**	**.322**	**.362**

Daulton, Darren Arthur — BL/TR — b.1/3/62 — POS C-802, 1B-2 — PHI80 25/629

YR	TM/LG	CL	G	TPA	AB	H	2B	3B	HR	TB	BB	IBB	HB	SO	GDP	SH	SF	SB	CS	R	RBI	BA	OBA	SA
83	PHI/NL		2	4	3	1	0	0	0	1	1	0	0	1	0	0	0	0	0	1	0	.333	.500	.333
84	POR/PCL	AAA	80	313	252	75	19	4	7	123	57	3	0	49	4	3	1	3	3	45	38	.298	.426	.488
85	POR/PCL	AAA	23	82	64	19	5	3	2	36	16	0	1	13	1	0	1	6	1	13	10	.297	.439	.563
	PHI/NL		36	119	103	21	3	1	4	38	16	0	0	37	1	0	0	3	0	14	11	.204	.311	.369
86	PHI/NL		49	181	138	31	4	0	8	59	38	3	1	41	1	2	2	2	3	18	21	.225	.391	.428
87	CLE/FSL	A+	9	27	22	5	3	0	1	11	4	0	0	3	1	0	1	0	0	1	5	.227	.333	.500
	MAI/INT	AAA	20	87	70	15	1	1	3	27	16	0	0	15	5	0	1	5	0	9	10	.214	.356	.386
	PHI/NL		53	150	129	25	6	0	3	40	16	1	0	37	0	4	1	0	1	10	13	.194	.281	.310
88	PHI/NL		58	163	144	30	6	0	1	39	17	1	0	26	2	2	0	2	2	13	12	.208	.288	.271
89	PHI/NL		131	424	368	74	12	2	8	114	52	8	2	58	4	1	2	2	1	29	44	.201	.303	.310
90	PHI/NL		143	540	459	123	30	1	12	191	72	9	2	72	6	3	4	7	1	62	57	.268	.367	.416
91	SCR/INT	AAA	2	9	9	2	0	0	1	5	0	0	0	0	0	0	0	0	0	1	1	.222	.222	.556
	REA/EAS	AA	1	5	4	1	0	0	0	1	1	0	0	0	0	0	0	0	0	1	1	.250	.400	.250
	PHI/NL		89	335	285	56	12	0	12	104	41	4	2	66	4	2	5	5	0	36	42	.196	.297	.365
92	PHI/NL		145	585	485	131	32	5	27	254	88	11	6	103	3	0	6	11	2	80	*109	.270	.385	.524
93	PHI/NL		147	637	510	131	35	4	24	246	117	12	2	111	2	0	8	5	0	90	105	.257	.392	.482
10 YR TOTALS			**853**	**3138**	**2624**	**623**	**140**	**13**	**99**	**1086**	**458**	**49**	**15**	**552**	**23**	**12**	**29**	**37**	**8**	**353**	**414**	**.237**	**.351**	**.414**

Davis, Charles Theodore "Chili" — BB/TR — b.1/17/60 — POS OF-1182, DH-494, 1B-1, P-1 — SF77 11/270

YR	TM/LG	CL	G	TPA	AB	H	2B	3B	HR	TB	BB	IBB	HB	SO	GDP	SH	SF	SB	CS	R	RBI	BA	OBA	SA
81	SF/NL		8	16	15	2	0	0	0	2	1	0	0	2	1	0	0	0	2	1	0	.133	.188	.133
82	SF/NL		154	701	641	167	27	6	19	263	45	2	2	115	13	7	6	24	13	86	76	.261	.308	.410
83	SF/NL		137	553	486	113	21	2	11	171	55	6	0	108	9	3	9	10	12	54	59	.233	.305	.352
84	SF/NL		137	546	499	157	21	6	21	253	42	6	1	74	13	2	2	12	8	87	81	.315	.368	.507
85	SF/NL		136	551	481	130	25	2	13	198	62	12	0	74	16	1	7	15	7	53	56	.270	.349	.412
86	SF/NL		153	618	526	146	28	3	13	219	84	23	1	96	11	2	6	16	13	71	70	.278	.375	.416
87	SF/NL		149	578	500	125	22	1	24	221	72	15	2	109	8	0	4	16	9	80	76	.250	.344	.442
88	CAL/AL		158	667	600	161	29	3	21	259	56	14	0	118	13	1	10	9	10	81	93	.268	.326	.432
89	CAL/AL		154	630	560	152	24	1	22	244	61	12	0	109	21	3	6	3	0	81	90	.271	.340	.436
90	CAL/AL		113	476	412	109	17	1	12	164	61	4	0	89	14	0	3	1	2	58	58	.265	.357	.398
91	MIN/AL		153	634	534	148	34	1	29	271	95	13	1	117	9	0	4	5	3	84	93	.277	.385	.507
92	MIN/AL		138	529	444	128	27	2	12	195	73	11	3	76	11	0	9	4	5	63	66	.288	.386	.439
93	CAL/AL		153	645	573	139	32	0	27	252	71	12	1	135	18	0	4	4	1	74	112	.243	.327	.440
13 YR TOTALS			**1743**	**7144**	**6271**	**1677**	**307**	**28**	**224**	**2712**	**778**	**130**	**11**	**1222**	**157**	**19**	**65**	**121**	**86**	**873**	**930**	**.267**	**.346**	**.432**

Davis, Eric Keith — BR/TR — b.5/29/62 — POS OF-1000, DH-5 — CIN80 10/201

YR	TM/LG	CL	G	TPA	AB	H	2B	3B	HR	TB	BB	IBB	HB	SO	GDP	SH	SF	SB	CS	R	RBI	BA	OBA	SA
84	WIC/AMA	AAA	52	223	194	61	9	5	14	122	25	1	2	55	2	1	1	27	10	42	34	.314	.396	.629
	CIN/NL		57	200	174	39	10	1	10	81	24	0	1	48	1	0	1	10	2	33	30	.224	.320	.466
85	DEN/AMA	AAA	64	239	206	57	10	2	15	116	29	1	0	67	2	0	3	35	5	48	38	.277	.364	.563
	CIN/NL		56	131	122	30	3	3	8	63	7	0	0	39	1	0	2	16	3	26	18	.246	.287	.516
86	CIN/NL		132	487	415	115	15	3	27	217	68	5	1	100	6	0	3	80	11	97	71	.277	.378	.523

(continued)

Davis, Eric Keith (continued)

YR	TM/LG	CL	G	TPA	AB	H	2B	3B	HR	TB	BB	IBB	HB	SO	GDP	SH	SF	SB	CS	R	RBI	BA	OBA	SA
87	CIN/NL		129	562	474	139	23	4	37	281	84	8	1	134	6	0	3	50	6	120	100	.293	.399	.593
88	CIN/NL		135	543	472	129	18	3	26	231	65	10	3	124	11	0	3	35	3	81	93	.273	.363	.489
89	CIN/NL		131	542	462	130	14	2	34	250	68	12	1	116	16	0	11	21	7	74	101	.281	.367	.541
90	CIN/NL		127	518	453	118	26	2	24	220	60	6	2	100	7	0	3	21	3	84	86	.260	.347	.486
91	CIN/NL		89	340	285	67	10	0	11	110	48	5	5	92	4	0	2	14	2	39	33	.235	.353	.386
92	LA/NL		76	308	267	61	8	1	5	86	36	2	3	71	9	0	2	19	1	21	32	.228	.325	.322
93	LA/NL		108	422	376	88	17	0	14	147	41	6	1	88	8	0	4	33	5	57	53	.234	.308	.391
	DET/AL		23	89	75	19	1	1	6	40	14	1	0	18	4	0	0	2	2	14	15	.253	.371	.533
	YEAR		131	511	451	107	18	1	20	187	55	7	1	106	12	0	4	35	7	71	68	.237	.319	.415
10 YR TOTALS			**1063**	**4142**	**3575**	**935**	**145**	**20**	**202**	**1726**	**515**	**55**	**18**	**930**	**73**	**2**	**32**	**301**	**45**	**646**	**632**	**.262**	**.355**	**.483**

Davis, Glenn Earle — BR/TR — b.3/28/61 — POS 1B-870, DH-122, OF-9   HOU81* S1/5

YR	TM/LG	CL	G	TPA	AB	H	2B	3B	HR	TB	BB	IBB	HB	SO	GDP	SH	SF	SB	CS	R	RBI	BA	OBA	SA
84	TUC/PCL	AAA	131	535	471	140	28	7	16	230	49	3	5	88	14	1	9	3	2	66	94	.297	.363	.488
	HOU/NL		18	68	61	13	5	0	2	24	4	0	0	12	0	2	1	0	0	6	8	.213	.258	.393
85	TUC/PCL	AAA	60	239	220	67	24	2	5	110	13	3	3	23	7	0	3	1	0	22	35	.305	.347	.500
	HOU/NL		100	390	350	95	11	0	20	166	27	6	7	68	12	2	4	0	0	51	64	.271	.332	.474
86	HOU/NL		158	654	574	152	32	3	31	283	64	6	9	72	11	0	7	3	1	91	101	.265	.344	.493
87	HOU/NL		151	635	578	145	35	2	27	265	47	10	5	84	16	0	5	4	1	70	93	.251	.310	.458
88	HOU/NL		152	634	561	152	26	0	30	268	53	20	11	77	11	0	9	4	3	78	99	.271	.341	.478
89	HOU/NL		158	663	581	156	26	1	34	286	69	17	7	123	9	0	6	4	2	87	89	.269	.350	.492
90	CMB/SOU	AA	12	40	37	11	0	0	1	14	2	0	1	9	0	0	0	1	0	3	8	.297	.350	.378
	HOU/NL		93	381	327	82	15	4	22	171	46	17	8	54	5	0	0	8	3	44	64	.251	.357	.523
91	HAG/EAS	AA	7	26	24	6	1	0	1	10	1	0	0	2	1	0	1	0	0	4	3	.250	.269	.417
	BAL/AL		49	199	176	40	9	1	10	81	16	0	5	29	2	0	2	4	0	29	28	.227	.307	.460
92	BAL/AL		106	442	398	110	15	2	13	168	37	2	2	65	12	1	4	1	0	46	48	.276	.338	.422
93	BAL/AL		30	123	113	20	3	0	1	26	7	0	1	29	2	1	1	0	1	8	9	.177	.230	.230
	FRE/CAR	A+	3	12	11	3	1	0	0	4	1	0	0	3	0	0	0	0	0	1	2	.273	.333	.364
	ROC/INT	AAA	7	26	24	6	1	1	0	9	2	0	0	8	0	0	0	0	0	2	3	.250	.308	.375
	BOW/EAS	AA	2	7	6	2	1	0	1	6	1	0	0	1	0	0	0	0	0	2	1	.333	.429	1.000
10 YR TOTALS			**1015**	**4189**	**3719**	**965**	**177**	**13**	**190**	**1738**	**370**	**78**	**55**	**613**	**80**	**6**	**39**	**28**	**11**	**510**	**603**	**.259**	**.332**	**.467**

Davis, Wallace McArthur "Butch" — BR/TR — b.6/19/58 — POS OF-126, DH-15   KC80 13/302

YR	TM/LG	CL	G	TPA	AB	H	2B	3B	HR	TB	BB	IBB	HB	SO	GDP	SH	SF	SB	CS	R	RBI	BA	OBA	SA
80	ROY/GCL	R	61	270	235	74	17	4	2	105	29	2	1	36	4	0	5	31	4	46	35	.315	.385	.447
81	FM/FSL	A+	126	527	464	139	17	10	13	215	54	2	3	99	8	1	5	44	3	89	70	.300	.373	.463
82	JAC/SOU	AA	122	505	450	115	18	4	10	171	46	1	3	101	6	3	3	17	9	64	57	.256	.327	.380
83	JAC/SOU	AA	90	375	331	105	15	7	14	176	36	2	0	78	9	2	6	29	7	51	63	.317	.378	.532
	OMA/AMA	AAA	46	191	171	54	10	3	5	85	18	0	1	36	4	1	0	13	5	27	21	.316	.384	.497
	KC/AL		33	130	122	42	2	6	2	62	4	0	0	19	3	2	2	4	3	13	18	.344	.359	.508
84	KC/AL		41	128	116	17	3	0	2	26	10	0	0	19	2	0	2	4	3	11	12	.147	.211	.224
	OMA/AMA	AAA	83	342	314	102	15	5	7	148	24	4	1	56	9	2	1	9	7	45	43	.325	.374	.471
85	OMA/AMA	AAA	109	436	403	106	26	10	6	170	26	0	1	89	6	3	3	15	6	58	34	.263	.307	.422
87	PIT/NL		7	8	7	1	1	0	0	2	1	0	0	3	0	0	0	0	0	3	0	.143	.250	.286
	VAN/PCL	AAA	111	454	424	115	17	7	7	167	22	1	1	73	6	1	6	22	6	58	57	.271	.305	.394
88	ROC/INT	AAA	8	31	28	4	0	0	0	8	0	0	0	2	0	1	0	0	0	4	0	.143	.200	.286
	CHA/SOU	AA	101	440	412	124	23	7	13	200	24	2	1	40	12	2	1	17	5	62	82	.301	.340	.485
	BAL/AL		13	25	25	6	1	0	0	7	0	0	0	8	2	0	0	1	0	2	0	.240	.240	.280
89	ROC/INT	AAA	127	520	479	145	29	9	10	222	28	4	6	57	12	2	5	19	8	81	64	.303	.346	.463
	BAL/AL		5	6	6	1	1	0	0	2	0	0	0	3	0	0	0	0	0	1	0	.167	.167	.333
90	ALB/PCL	AAA	124	519	480	164	31	9	10	243	24	5	4	53	18	0	11	25	14	87	85	.342	.370	.506
91	LA/NL		1	1	1	0	0	0	0	0	0	0	0	0	0	0	0	0	0	0	0	.000	.000	.000
	ALB/PCL	AAA	91	306	284	89	19	10	7	149	18	6	2	51	5	0	2	12	5	55	44	.313	.356	.525
92	SYR/INT	AAA	134	592	550	154	31	9	9	230	33	4	2	77	20	2	5	19	6	67	74	.280	.320	.418
	LV/PCL	AAA	1	1	1	0	0	0	0	1	0	0	0	0	0	0	0	0	0	0	0	1.000	1.000	1.000
93	TEX/AL		62	170	159	39	10	4	3	66	5	1	1	28	0	5	0	3	1	24	20	.245	.273	.415
7 YR TOTALS			**162**	**468**	**436**	**106**	**18**	**10**	**7**	**165**	**20**	**1**	**1**	**80**	**7**	**7**	**4**	**12**	**7**	**54**	**50**	**.243**	**.275**	**.378**

Dawson, Andre Fernando — BR/TR — b.7/10/54 — POS OF-2258, DH-97   MON75 11/250

YR	TM/LG	CL	G	TPA	AB	H	2B	3B	HR	TB	BB	IBB	HB	SO	GDP	SH	SF	SB	CS	R	RBI	BA	OBA	SA
76	MON/NL		24	92	85	20	4	1	0	26	5	1	0	13	0	2	0	1	2	9	7	.235	.278	.306
77	MON/NL		139	566	525	148	26	9	19	249	34	4	2	93	6	1	4	21	7	64	65	.282	.326	.474
78	MON/NL		157	660	609	154	24	8	25	269	30	3	12	128	7	4	5	28	11	84	72	.253	.299	.442
79	MON/NL		155	684	639	176	24	12	25	299	27	5	6	115	10	8	4	35	10	90	92	.275	.309	.468
80	MON/NL		151	638	577	178	41	7	17	284	44	7	6	69	9	1	10	34	9	96	87	.308	.358	.492
81	MON/NL		103	441	394	119	21	3	24	218	35	14	7	50	6	0	5	26	4	71	64	.302	.365	.553
82	MON/NL		148	660	608	183	37	7	23	303	34	4	8	96	8	4	6	39	10	107	83	.301	.343	.498
83	MON/NL		159	698	633	*189	36	10	32	*341	38	12	9	81	14	0	18	25	11	104	113	.299	.338	.539
84	MON/NL		138	583	533	132	23	6	17	218	41	2	2	80	12	1	6	13	5	73	86	.248	.301	.409
85	MON/NL		139	570	529	135	27	2	23	235	29	8	4	92	12	1	7	13	4	65	91	.255	.295	.444
86	MON/NL		130	546	496	141	32	2	20	237	37	11	6	79	13	1	6	18	12	65	78	.284	.338	.478
87	CHI/NL		153	662	621	178	24	2	*49	*353	32	7	7	103	15	0	2	11	3	90	*137	.287	.328	.568
88	CHI/NL		157	640	591	179	31	8	24	298	37	12	4	73	13	1	7	12	4	78	79	.303	.344	.504
89	CHI/NL		118	459	416	105	18	6	21	198	35	13	1	62	16	0	7	8	2	62	77	.252	.307	.476
90	CHI/NL		147	581	529	164	28	5	27	283	42	21	2	65	12	0	8	16	2	72	100	.310	.358	.535
91	CHI/NL		149	596	563	153	21	4	31	275	22	3	5	80	10	0	6	4	5	69	104	.272	.302	.488
92	CHI/NL		143	582	542	150	27	2	22	247	30	8	4	70	13	0	6	6	2	60	90	.277	.316	.456

Dawson, Andre Fernando (continued)

YR	TM/LG	CL	G	TPA	AB	H	2B	3B	HR	TB	BB	IBB	HB	SO	GDP	SH	SF	SB	CS	R	RBI	BA	OBA	SA
93	BOS/AL		121	498	461	126	29	1	13	196	17	4	13	49	18	0	7	2	1	44	67	.273	.313	.425
18 YR TOTALS			2431	10156	9351	2630	473	95	412	4529	569	139	98	1398	194	24	114	312	107	1303	1492	**.281**	**.325**	**.484**

Decker, Steven Michael "Steve" — BR/TR — b.10/25/65 — POS C-113 SF88 23/542

YR	TM/LG	CL	G	TPA	AB	H	2B	3B	HR	TB	BB	IBB	HB	SO	GDP	SH	SF	SB	CS	R	RBI	BA	OBA	SA
88	EVE/NWL	A-	13	53	42	22	2	0	2	30	7	0	1	5	1	0	3	0	0	11	13	.524	.566	.714
	SJ/CAL	A+	47	198	175	56	9	0	4	77	21	1	1	21	4	1	0	0	2	31	34	.320	.396	.440
89	SJ/CAL	A+	64	274	225	65	12	0	3	86	44	3	0	36	9	0	5	8	5	27	46	.289	.398	.382
	SHR/TEX	AA	44	155	142	46	8	0	1	57	11	0	0	24	5	1	1	0	3	19	18	.324	.370	.401
90	SHR/TEX	AA	116	452	403	118	22	1	15	187	39	1	3	64	11	0	7	3	7	52	80	.293	.354	.464
	SF/NL		15	56	54	16	2	0	3	27	1	0	0	10	1	0	0	0	0	5	8	.296	.309	.500
91	PHO/PCL	AAA	31	125	111	28	5	1	6	53	13	0	1	29	1	0	0	0	0	20	14	.252	.336	.477
	SF/NL		79	258	233	48	7	1	5	72	16	1	3	44	7	2	4	0	1	11	24	.206	.262	.309
92	PHO/PCL	AAA	125	509	450	127	22	2	8	177	47	2	3	64	19	0	9	2	4	50	74	.282	.348	.393
	SF/NL		15	50	43	7	1	0	0	8	6	0	1	7	0	0	0	0	0	3	1	.163	.280	.186
93	FLO/NL		8	19	15	0	0	0	0	0	3	0	0	3	2	0	0	0	0	0	1	.000	.158	.000
4 YR TOTALS			117	383	345	71	10	1	8	107	26	1	4	64	10	3	5	0	1	19	34	**.206**	**.266**	**.310**

Deer, Robert George "Rob" — BR/TR — b.9/29/60 — POS OF-1035, 1B-47, DH-21 SF78 4/85

YR	TM/LG	CL	G	TPA	AB	H	2B	3B	HR	TB	BB	IBB	HB	SO	GDP	SH	SF	SB	CS	R	RBI	BA	OBA	SA
84	PHO/PCL	AAA	133	551	449	102	21	1	31	218	96	4	2	175	7	2	2	9	3	88	69	.227	.364	.486
	SF/NL		13	32	24	4	0	0	3	13	7	0	1	10	0	0	0	1	1	5	3	.167	.375	.542
85	SF/NL		78	187	162	30	5	1	8	61	23	0	0	71	0	0	2	0	1	22	20	.185	.283	.377
86	MIL/AL		134	546	466	108	17	3	33	230	72	3	3	179	4	2	3	5	2	75	86	.232	.336	.494
87	MIL/AL		134	566	474	113	15	2	28	216	86	6	5	186	4	0	1	12	4	71	80	.238	.360	.456
88	MIL/AL		135	555	492	124	24	2	23	217	51	4	7	153	4	0	5	9	5	71	85	.252	.328	.441
89	MIL/AL		130	532	466	98	18	2	26	198	60	5	4	158	8	0	2	4	8	72	65	.210	.305	.425
90	MIL/AL		134	511	440	92	15	1	27	190	64	6	4	147	9	0	3	2	3	57	69	.209	.313	.432
91	DET/AL		134	539	448	80	14	2	25	173	89	1	0	175	3	0	2	1	3	64	64	.179	.314	.386
92	DET/AL		110	448	393	97	20	1	32	215	51	1	3	131	8	0	1	4	2	66	64	.247	.337	.547
93	DET/AL		90	367	323	70	11	0	14	123	38	1	3	120	4	0	3	3	2	48	39	.217	.302	.381
	BOS/AL		38	165	143	28	6	1	7	57	20	0	2	49	2	0	0	2	0	18	16	.196	.303	.399
	YEAR		128	532	466	98	17	1	21	180	58	1	5	169	6	0	3	5	2	66	55	.210	.303	.386
10 YR TOTALS			1130	4448	3831	844	145	13	226	1693	561	27	32	1379	37	2	22	43	31	569	591	**.220**	**.323**	**.442**

Delgado, Carlos Juan — BL/TR — b.6/25/72 — POS C-1, DH-1 TOR 10/9/88

YR	TM/LG	CL	G	TPA	AB	H	2B	3B	HR	TB	BB	IBB	HB	SO	GDP	SH	SF	SB	CS	R	RBI	BA	OBA	SA
89	SC/NYP	A-	31	113	89	16	5	0	0	21	23	1	0	39	4	0	1	0	0	9	11	.180	.345	.236
90	SC/NYP	A-	67	273	228	64	13	0	6	95	35	2	5	65	2	1	4	2	8	30	39	.281	.382	.417
91	MB/SAL	A	132	528	441	126	18	2	18	202	75	2	8	97	7	1	3	9	10	72	70	.286	.397	.458
	SYR/INT	AAA	1	3	3	0	0	0	0	0	0	0	0	2	0	0	0	0	0	0	0	.000	.000	.000
92	DUN/FSL	A+	133	552	485	157	30	2	30	281	59	11	6	91	8	0	2	2	5	83	100	.324	.402	.579
93	KNO/SOU	AA	140	581	468	142	28	0	25	245	102	18	6	98	11	0	5	10	3	91	102	.303	.430	.524
	TOR/AL		2	2	1	0	0	0	0	0	0	0	0	1	0	0	0	0	0	0	0	.000	.500	.000

Denson, Andrew "Drew" — BB/TR — b.11/16/65 — POS 1B-15 ATL84 1/19

YR	TM/LG	CL	G	TPA	AB	H	2B	3B	HR	TB	BB	IBB	HB	SO	GDP	SH	SF	SB	CS	R	RBI	BA	OBA	SA
84	BRA/GCL	R	62	260	239	77	20	3	10	133	17	0	3	41	8	0	1	5	2	43	45	.322	.373	.556
85	SUM/SAL	A	111	444	383	115	18	4	14	183	53	3	4	76	16	0	4	5	3	59	74	.300	.387	.478
86	DUR/CAR	A+	72	259	231	54	6	3	4	78	25	0	2	46	10	1	0	6	1	31	23	.234	.314	.338
87	GRE/SOU	AA	128	494	447	98	23	1	14	165	33	1	11	95	15	1	2	1	7	54	55	.219	.288	.369
88	GRE/SOU	AA	140	572	507	136	26	4	13	209	44	1	14	116	11	3	4	11	9	85	78	.268	.341	.412
89	RIC/INT	AAA	138	523	463	118	32	0	9	177	42	2	12	116	4	1	5	0	1	50	59	.255	.330	.382
	ATL/NL		12	39	36	9	1	0	0	10	3	0	0	9	0	0	0	1	0	1	5	.250	.308	.278
90	RIC/INT	AAA	90	333	295	68	4	1	7	95	26	3	7	57	10	1	0	1	0	25	29	.231	.309	.322
92	VAN/PCL	AAA	105	383	340	94	7	3	13	146	36	3	7	58	12	0	1	0	0	43	70	.276	.358	.429
93	NAS/AMA	AAA	136	590	513	144	36	0	24	252	46	7	23	98	22	0	8	0	0	82	103	.281	.361	.491
	CHI/AL		4	5	5	1	0	0	0	1	0	0	0	2	0	0	0	0	0	0	0	.200	.200	.200
2 YR TOTALS			16	44	41	10	1	0	0	11	3	0	0	11	0	0	0	1	0	1	5	**.244**	**.295**	**.268**

DeShields, Delino Lamont — BL/TR — b.1/15/69 — POS 2B-533 MON87 1/12

YR	TM/LG	CL	G	TPA	AB	H	2B	3B	HR	TB	BB	IBB	HB	SO	GDP	SH	SF	SB	CS	R	RBI	BA	OBA	SA
87	EXP/GCL	R	31	134	111	24	5	2	1	36	21	0	2	30	0	0	0	16	5	17	4	.216	.351	.324
	JAM/NYP	A-	34	124	96	21	1	2	1	29	24	1	1	28	0	2	1	14	4	16	5	.219	.377	.302
88	ROC/MID	A	129	562	460	116	26	6	12	190	95	3	2	110	4	2	3	59	18	97	46	.252	.380	.413
89	JAC/SOU	AA	93	391	307	83	10	6	3	114	76	0	1	89	3	4	3	37	12	55	35	.270	.413	.371
	IND/AMA	AAA	47	198	181	47	8	4	2	69	16	0	0	53	0	1	0	16	7	29	14	.260	.320	.381
90	MON/NL		129	572	499	144	28	6	4	196	66	3	4	96	10		3	42	22	69	45	.289	.375	.393
91	MON/NL		151	673	563	134	15	4	10	187	95	2	2	151	6	8	5	56	23	83	51	.238	.347	.332
92	MON/NL		135	599	530	155	19	8	7	211	54	4	3	108	10	9	3	46	15	82	56	.292	.359	.398
93	MON/NL		123	562	481	142	17	7	2	179	72	3	3	64	6	4	2	43	10	75	29	.295	.389	.372
4 YR TOTALS			538	2406	2073	575	79	25	23	773	287	12	12	419	32	22	12	187	70	309	181	**.277**	**.367**	**.373**

Devereaux, Michael "Mike" — BR/TR — b.4/10/63 — POS OF-694, DH-8 LA85 6/116

YR	TM/LG	CL	G	TPA	AB	H	2B	3B	HR	TB	BB	IBB	HB	SO	GDP	SH	SF	SB	CS	R	RBI	BA	OBA	SA
85	GF/PIO	R+	70	329	289	103	17	10	4	152	32	1	2	29	6	0	6	40	9	73	67	.356	.416	.526
86	SA/TEX	AA	115	497	431	130	22	2	10	186	58	2	3	47	6	1	4	31	8	69	53	.302	.385	.432

(continued)

Devereaux, Michael "Mike" (continued)

YR	TM/LG	CL	G	TPA	AB	H	2B	3B	HR	TB	BB	IBB	HB	SO	GDP	SH	SF	SB	CS	R	RBI	BA	OBA	SA
87	SA/TEX	AA	135	624	562	169	28	9	26	293	48	8	2	65	8	1	11	33	18	90	91	.301	.352	.521
	ALB/PCL	AAA	3	11	11	3	1	0	1	7	0	0	0	2	0	0	0	1	0	2	1	.273	.273	.636
	LA/NL		19	58	54	12	3	0	0	15	3	0	0	10	0	1	0	3	1	7	4	.222	.263	.278
88	ALB/PCL	AAA	109	477	423	144	26	4	13	217	44	2	2	46	7	1	7	33	9	88	76	.340	.399	.513
	LA/NL		30	45	43	5	1	0	0	6	2	0	0	10	0	0	0	0	1	4	2	.116	.156	.140
89	BAL/AL		122	434	391	104	14	3	8	148	36	0	0	60	7	2	3	22	11	55	46	.266	.329	.379
90	FRE/CAR	A+	2	9	8	4	0	0	1	7	1	0	0	2	0	0	0	1	0	3	3	.500	.556	.875
	HAG/EAS	AA	4	20	20	5	3	0	0	8	0	0	0	1	2	0	0	0	1	4	3	.250	.250	.400
	BAL/AL		108	403	367	88	18	1	12	144	28	0	0	48	10	4	4	13	12	48	49	.240	.291	.392
91	BAL/AL		149	668	608	158	27	10	19	262	47	2	2	115	13	7	4	16	9	82	59	.260	.313	.431
92	BAL/AL		156	710	653	180	29	11	24	303	44	1	4	94	14	0	9	10	8	76	107	.276	.321	.464
93	BOW/EAS	AA	2	7	7	2	1	0	0	3	0	0	0	2	1	0	0	0	0	1	2	.286	.286	.429
	BAL/AL		131	577	527	132	31	3	14	211	43	0	1	99	13	2	4	3	3	72	75	.250	.306	.400
7 YR TOTALS			**715**	**2895**	**2643**	**679**	**123**	**28**	**77**	**1089**	**203**	**3**	**9**	**436**	**57**	**16**	**24**	**67**	**45**	**344**	**342**	**.257**	**.309**	**.412**

Diaz, Alexis "Alex" — BB/TR — b.10/5/68 — POS OF-39, DH-3   NYN 8/24/86

YR	TM/LG	CL	G	TPA	AB	H	2B	3B	HR	TB	BB	IBB	HB	SO	GDP	SH	SF	SB	CS	R	RBI	BA	OBA	SA
87	KIN/APP	R+	54	234	212	56	9	1	0	67	16	0	1	31	4	4	1	34	9	29	13	.264	.317	.316
	LF/NYP	A-	12	49	47	16	4	1	0	22	2	0	0	3	1	0	0	2	2	7	8	.340	.367	.468
88	COL/SAL	A	123	515	481	126	14	11	0	162	21	3	2	49	4	9	2	28	8	82	37	.262	.294	.337
	SL/FSL	A+	3	8	6	0	0	0	0	0	0	0	0	1	0	1	0	0	0	2	1	.000	.250	.000
89	SL/FSL	A+	102	447	416	106	11	10	1	140	20	3	3	38	8	5	3	43	16	54	33	.255	.292	.337
	JAC/TEX	AA	23	98	95	26	5	1	2	39	3	0	0	11	1	0	0	3	4	11	9	.274	.296	.411
90	TID/INT	AAA	124	479	437	112	15	2	1	134	30	4	7	39	7	7	4	23	13	55	36	.256	.303	.307
91	IND/AMA	AAA	108	403	370	90	14	4	1	115	27	2	1	46	6	3	2	17	3	48	21	.243	.295	.311
92	DEN/AMA	AAA	106	494	455	122	17	4	1	150	24	0	5	36	12	5	5	42	12	67	41	.268	.309	.330
	MIL/AL		22	9	9	1	0	0	0	1	0	0	0	0	0	0	0	3	2	5	1	.111	.111	.111
93	NO/AMA	AAA	16	59	55	16	2	0	0	18	3	1	0	6	1	1	0	7	0	8	5	.291	.328	.327
	MIL/AL		32	72	69	22	2	0	0	24	0	0	0	12	3	3	0	5	3	9	1	.319	.319	.348
2 YR TOTALS			**54**	**81**	**78**	**23**	**2**	**0**	**0**	**25**	**0**	**0**	**0**	**12**	**3**	**3**	**0**	**8**	**5**	**14**	**2**	**.295**	**.295**	**.321**

Diaz, Mario Rafael — BR/TR — b.1/10/62 — POS SS-216, 2B-42, 3B-25, 1B-2, DH-1   SEA 12/21/78

YR	TM/LG	CL	G	TPA	AB	H	2B	3B	HR	TB	BB	IBB	HB	SO	GDP	SH	SF	SB	CS	R	RBI	BA	OBA	SA
79	BEL/NWL	A-	32	105	96	19	2	0	1	24	5	0	1	17	2	3	0	0	3	12	5	.198	.245	.250
80	WAU/MID	A	110	375	349	63	5	0	3	77	19	0	1	37	17	4	2	5	6	28	21	.181	.224	.221
81	LYN/EAS	AA	106	344	314	63	8	1	1	76	16	0	1	42	16	7	6	1	1	16	22	.201	.237	.242
82	SLC/PCL	AAA	5	20	19	7	1	0	0	8	0	0	1	1	0	1	0	1	0	2	2	.368	.368	.421
	LYN/EAS	AA	53	188	162	35	7	1	1	47	19	0	1	24	3	5	1	2	1	19	13	.216	.301	.290
83	BAK/CAL	A+	51	185	171	41	5	1	0	48	10	0	0	26	4	4	0	3	1	23	10	.240	.282	.281
	CHT/SOU	AA	33	116	111	30	6	5	2	52	5	0	0	15	5	0	0	0	1	18	13	.270	.302	.468
84	CHT/SOU	AA	108	361	322	67	7	1	1	79	21	0	0	18	14	13	5	6	5	23	19	.208	.253	.245
85	CHT/SOU	AA	115	442	400	101	6	7	0	121	21	2	1	20	15	14	7	3	4	38	38	.253	.285	.303
86	CAL/PCL	AAA	109	401	379	107	17	6	1	139	13	2	0	29	13	5	4	1	5	40	41	.282	.303	.367
87	CAL/PCL	AAA	108	407	376	106	17	3	4	141	19	2	1	25	13	10	1	1	5	52	52	.282	.317	.375
	SEA/AL		11	23	23	7	0	1	0	9	0	0	0	4	0	0	0	0	0	4	3	.304	.304	.391
88	CAL/PCL	AAA	46	180	164	54	18	0	1	75	9	0	3	10	5	1	3	1	2	16	30	.329	.369	.457
	SEA/AL		28	76	72	22	5	0	0	27	3	0	0	5	3	0	1	0	0	6	9	.306	.329	.375
89	CAL/PCL	AAA	37	137	127	43	8	1	2	59	8	0	1	7	2	0	1	1	4	22	9	.339	.380	.465
	SEA/AL		52	86	74	10	0	0	1	13	7	0	0	7	2	5	0	0	0	9	7	.135	.210	.176
90	CAL/PCL	AAA	32	108	105	35	5	1	1	45	1	0	1	8	4	0	1	1	0	10	19	.333	.343	.429
	NY/NL		16	23	22	3	1	0	0	4	0	0	0	3	0	0	0	0	1	0	1	.136	.130	.182
	TID/INT	AAA	29	111	104	33	8	0	1	44	6	0	0	6	3	0	0	0	2	15	9	.317	.360	.423
91	TEX/AL		96	202	182	48	7	0	1	58	15	0	0	18	5	4	1	0	1	24	22	.264	.318	.319
92	CAL/PCL	AAA	18	54	52	14	4	0	0	18	0	0	0	6	3	1	1	1	1	8	11	.269	.264	.346
	OC/AMA	AAA	43	171	167	56	11	0	3	76	2	1	0	12	7	0	2	4	0	24	20	.335	.339	.455
	TEX/AL		19	33	31	7	0	0	0	8	1	1	0	2	1	0	1	0	0	2	1	.226	.250	.258
93	OC/AMA	AAA	48	188	177	58	12	2	3	83	7	0	1	15	7	1	2	3	0	24	20	.328	.353	.469
	TEX/AL		71	226	205	56	10	1	2	74	8	0	1	13	6	7	5	1	0	24	24	.273	.297	.361
7 YR TOTALS			**293**	**669**	**609**	**153**	**24**	**2**	**4**	**193**	**34**	**1**	**1**	**52**	**18**	**17**	**8**	**1**	**2**	**69**	**67**	**.251**	**.288**	**.317**

Disarcina, Gary Thomas — BR/TR — b.11/19/67 — POS SS-308, 2B-10, 3B-2   CAL88 5/143

YR	TM/LG	CL	G	TPA	AB	H	2B	3B	HR	TB	BB	IBB	HB	SO	GDP	SH	SF	SB	CS	R	RBI	BA	OBA	SA
88	BEN/NWL	A-	71	332	295	90	11	5	2	117	27	1	2	34	6	4	4	7	4	40	39	.305	.363	.397
89	MID/TEX	AA	126	481	441	126	18	7	4	170	24	3	4	54	17	7	5	11	6	65	54	.286	.325	.385
	CAL/AL		2	0	0	0	0	0	0	0	0	0	0	0	0	0	0	0	0	0	0	.000	.000	.000
90	EDM/PCL	AAA	97	366	330	70	12	2	4	98	25	0	4	46	6	5	2	5	3	46	37	.212	.274	.297
	CAL/AL		18	61	57	8	1	0	0	11	3	0	0	4	0	0	0	0	0	8	0	.140	.183	.193
91	EDM/PCL	AAA	119	435	390	121	21	4	4	162	29	1	9	32	13	4	3	16	5	61	58	.310	.369	.415
	CAL/AL		18	64	57	12	2	0	0	14	3	0	2	4	0	2	0	0	0	5	3	.211	.274	.246
92	CAL/AL		157	553	518	128	19	0	3	156	20	1	5	50	15	5	5	9	7	48	42	.247	.283	.301
93	CAL/AL		126	445	416	99	20	0	3	130	15	1	3	38	13	5	3	5	7	44	45	.238	.273	.313
5 YR TOTALS			**321**	**1123**	**1048**	**247**	**42**	**2**	**6**	**311**	**41**	**0**	**15**	**102**	**31**	**13**	**6**	**15**	**14**	**105**	**90**	**.236**	**.273**	**.297**

Distrade, Orestes — BB/TR — b.5/8/62 — POS 1B-163, DH-2   NYA 5/17/81

YR	TM/LG	CL	G	TPA	AB	H	2B	3B	HR	TB	BB	IBB	HB	SO	GDP	SH	SF	SB	CS	R	RBI	BA	OBA	SA
84	FL/FSL	A+	95	381	308	68	14	2	12	122	64	8	2	82	5	1	6	3	4	40	57	.221	.353	.396
	NAS/SOU	AA	35	137	121	29	6	0	6	53	15	0	0	36	3	1	1	0	1	15	12	.240	.321	.438

Distrade, Orestes (continued)

YR	TM/LG	CL	G	TPA	AB	H	2B	3B	HR	TB	BB	IBB	HB	SO	GDP	SH	SF	SB	CS	R	RBI	BA	OBA	SA
85	ALB/EAS	AA	136	564	471	119	24	5	23	222	86	8	1	129	5	0	6	9	4	82	72	.253	.365	.471
86	CMB/INT	AAA	98	402	359	99	21	4	19	185	40	5	0	88	6	0	3	1	4	59	56	.276	.346	.515
87	CMB/INT	AAA	135	552	465	119	26	3	25	226	79	9	5	118	18	0	3	0	2	76	81	.256	.368	.486
	NY/AL		9	24	19	5	0	0	0	5	5	0	0	5	1	0	0	1	0	5	1	.263	.417	.263
88	BUF/AMA	AAA	77	318	273	74	16	1	12	128	44	7	0	67	3	0	1	2	2	37	42	.271	.371	.469
	PIT/NL		36	53	47	7	1	0	1	11	5	0	0	17	0	0	1	0	0	2	3	.149	.226	.234
89	BUF/AMA	AAA	33	118	100	23	6	0	1	32	13	2	3	13	0	1	1	0	1	8	17	.230	.333	.320
93	FLO/NL		153	637	569	145	20	3	20	231	58	8	3	130	17	1	6	0	2	61	87	.255	.324	.406
3 YR TOTALS			**198**	**714**	**635**	**157**	**21**	**3**	**21**	**247**	**68**	**8**	**3**	**152**	**18**	**1**	**7**	**0**	**2**	**68**	**91**	**.247**	**.320**	**.389**

Donnels, Chris Barton — BL/TR — b.4/21/66 — POS 3B-71, 1B-38, 2B-13 — NYN87 1/24

YR	TM/LG	CL	G	TPA	AB	H	2B	3B	HR	TB	BB	IBB	HB	SO	GDP	SH	SF	SB	CS	R	RBI	BA	OBA	SA
87	KIN/APP	R+	26	106	86	26	4	0	3	39	17	1	1	17	1	0	2	4	1	18	16	.302	.415	.453
	COL/SAL	A	41	162	136	35	7	0	2	48	24	1	1	27	1	0	1	3	1	20	17	.257	.370	.353
88	SL/FSL	A+	65	235	198	43	14	2	3	70	32	1	1	53	4	2	1	4	3	25	22	.217	.330	.354
	COL/SAL	A	42	167	133	32	6	0	2	44	30	2	1	25	3	2	1	5	0	19	13	.241	.382	.331
89	SL/FSL	A+	117	480	386	121	23	1	17	197	83	15	6	65	5	2	3	18	4	70	78	.313	.439	.510
90	JAC/TEX	AA	130	543	419	114	24	0	12	174	111	5	1	80	12	5	7	10	8	66	63	.272	.420	.415
91	TID/INT	AAA	84	353	287	87	19	2	8	134	62	3	1	56	13	0	3	1	4	45	56	.303	.425	.467
	NY/NL		37	104	89	20	2	0	0	22	14	1	0	19	0	1	0	1	1	7	5	.225	.330	.247
92	TID/INT	AAA	81	342	279	84	15	3	5	120	58	1	0	45	8	3	2	12	1	35	32	.301	.419	.430
	NY/NL		45	139	121	21	4	0	0	25	17	0	0	25	1	1	0	1	0	8	6	.174	.275	.207
93	HOU/NL		88	199	179	46	14	2	2	70	19	0	0	33	6	0	1	2	0	18	24	.257	.327	.391
3 YR TOTALS			**170**	**442**	**389**	**87**	**20**	**2**	**2**	**117**	**50**	**1**	**0**	**77**	**7**	**2**	**1**	**4**	**1**	**33**	**35**	**.224**	**.311**	**.301**

Doran, William Donald "Bill" — BB/TR — b.5/28/58 — POS 2B-1359, 1B-33, SS-16, OF-6, 3B-4 — HOU79 6/138

YR	TM/LG	CL	G	TPA	AB	H	2B	3B	HR	TB	BB	IBB	HB	SO	GDP	SH	SF	SB	CS	R	RBI	BA	OBA	SA
82	HOU/NL		26	102	97	27	3	0	0	30	4	0	0	11	0	0	0	1	5	0	11	6	.278	.304	.309
83	HOU/NL		154	629	535	145	12	7	8	195	86	11	0	67	6	7	1	12	12	70	39	.271	.371	.364
84	HOU/NL		147	626	548	143	18	11	4	195	66	7	2	69	6	7	3	21	12	92	41	.261	.341	.356
85	HOU/NL		148	657	578	166	31	6	14	251	71	6	0	69	10	3	5	23	15	84	59	.287	.362	.434
86	HOU/NL		145	642	550	152	29	3	6	205	81	7	2	57	10	4	5	42	19	92	37	.276	.368	.373
87	HOU/NL		162	719	625	177	23	3	16	254	82	3	3	64	11	2	5	31	11	82	79	.283	.365	.406
88	HOU/NL		132	552	480	119	18	1	7	160	65	3	1	60	7	4	2	17	4	66	53	.248	.338	.333
89	HOU/NL		142	574	507	111	25	2	8	164	59	2	2	63	8	3	3	22	3	65	58	.219	.301	.323
90	HOU/NL		109	421	344	99	21	2	6	142	71	2	1	53	2	1	5	18	9	49	32	.288	.405	.413
	CIN/NL		17	67	59	22	8	0	1	33	8	1	0	5	1	0	0	5	0	10	5	.373	.448	.559
	YEAR		126	488	403	121	29	2	7	175	79	2	1	58	3	1	5	23	9	59	37	.300	.411	.434
91	CIN/NL		111	410	361	101	12	2	6	135	46	1	0	39	4	0	3	5	4	51	35	.280	.359	.374
92	CIN/NL		132	456	387	91	16	2	8	135	64	9	0	40	11	3	2	7	4	48	47	.235	.342	.349
93	STO/CAL	A+	1	3	2	1	0	0	0	1	1	0	0	0	0	0	0	0	0	0	0	.500	.667	.500
	EP/TEX	AA	5	14	11	4	1	0	0	5	3	1	0	2	0	0	0	0	0	3	0	.364	.500	.455
	MIL/AL		28	67	60	13	4	0	0	17	6	1	0	3	3	0	1	1	0	7	6	.217	.284	.283
12 YR TOTALS			**1453**	**5922**	**5131**	**1366**	**220**	**39**	**84**	**1916**	**709**	**52**	**10**	**600**	**79**	**34**	**38**	**209**	**93**	**727**	**497**	**.266**	**.354**	**.373**

Dorsett, Brian Richard — BR/TR — b.4/9/61 — POS C-46, DH-5, 1B-5 — OAK83 10/241

YR	TM/LG	CL	G	TPA	AB	H	2B	3B	HR	TB	BB	IBB	HB	SO	GDP	SH	SF	SB	CS	R	RBI	BA	OBA	SA
83	MED/NWL	A-	14	53	48	13	2	1	1	20	5	0	0	5	1	0	0	0	0	11	10	.271	.340	.417
	MAD/MID	A	58	223	204	52	7	0	3	68	17	1	0	35	4	0	2	2	1	16	27	.255	.309	.333
84	MOD/CAL	A+	99	407	375	99	19	0	8	142	23	1	2	93	7	0	7	0	1	39	52	.264	.305	.379
85	MAD/MID	A	40	178	161	43	11	0	2	60	12	1	0	23	5	1	2	0	2	15	30	.267	.322	.373
	HUN/SOU	AA	88	354	313	84	18	3	11	141	38	1	0	61	11	3	0	0	0	38	43	.268	.348	.450
86	TAC/PCL	AAA	117	460	426	111	33	1	10	176	26	1	3	82	16	0	5	0	0	49	51	.261	.304	.413
87	TAC/PCL	AAA	78	324	282	66	14	1	6	100	33	3	3	50	12	1	5	0	0	31	39	.234	.316	.355
	BUF/AMA	AAA	26	90	86	22	5	1	4	41	3	1	0	21	2	0	1	0	0	9	14	.256	.278	.477
	CLE/AL		5	12	11	3	0	0	1	6	0	0	0	3	0	0	1	0	0	2	3	.273	.333	.545
88	EDM/PCL	AAA	53	194	163	43	7	0	11	83	28	0	0	29	1	2	1	2	0	21	32	.264	.368	.509
	CAL/AL		7	12	11	1	0	0	0	1	1	0	0	5	0	0	0	0	0	0	2	.091	.167	.091
89	CMB/INT	AAA	110	431	388	97	21	1	17	171	31	2	5	87	10	2	5	2	2	45	62	.250	.310	.441
	NY/AL		8	23	22	8	1	0	0	9	1	0	0	3	0	0	0	0	0	3	4	.364	.391	.409
90	CMB/INT	AAA	114	473	415	113	28	0	14	185	49	6	5	71	12	1	3	1	1	44	67	.272	.354	.446
	NY/AL		14	37	35	5	2	0	0	7	2	0	0	4	2	0	0	0	0	2	0	.143	.189	.200
91	SD/NL		11	12	12	1	0	0	0	1	0	0	0	0	0	0	0	0	0	0	1	.083	.083	.083
	LV/PCL	AAA	62	234	215	66	13	1	13	120	17	0	1	43	2	0	1	0	0	36	38	.307	.359	.558
	BUF/AMA	AAA	29	116	103	28	6	0	2	40	8	1	1	19	1	0	4	0	0	17	18	.272	.319	.388
92	BUF/AMA	AAA	131	543	492	142	35	0	21	240	38	4	6	68	12	2	5	1	0	69	102	.289	.344	.488
93	IND/AMA	AAA	77	314	278	83	27	0	18	164	28	2	3	53	4	0	5	0	0	38	57	.299	.363	.590
	CIN/NL		25	66	63	16	4	0	2	26	3	0	0	14	1	0	0	0	0	7	12	.254	.288	.413
6 YR TOTALS			**70**	**162**	**154**	**34**	**7**	**0**	**3**	**50**	**7**	**0**	**1**	**32**	**3**	**0**	**0**	**0**	**0**	**14**	**22**	**.221**	**.259**	**.325**

Ducey, Robert Thomas "Rob" — BL/TR — b.5/24/65 — POS OF-191, DH-10 — TOR 5/16/84

YR	TM/LG	CL	G	TPA	AB	H	2B	3B	HR	TB	BB	IBB	HB	SO	GDP	SH	SF	SB	CS	R	RBI	BA	OBA	SA
84	MH/PIO	R+	63	279	235	71	10	3	12	123	41	0	1	61	4	1	1	13	6	49	49	.302	.406	.523
85	FLO/SAL	A	134	589	529	133	22	2	13	198	49	2	1	103	3	3	7	12	4	78	86	.251	.312	.374
86	VEN/CAL	A+	47	203	178	60	11	3	12	113	21	2	1	24	3	1	2	17	5	36	38	.337	.406	.635
	KNO/SOU	AA	88	377	344	106	22	3	11	167	29	3	0	59	2	4	0	5	7	49	58	.308	.358	.485
87	SYR/INT	AAA	100	428	359	102	14	10	10	166	61	5	3	88	6	0	5	7	7	62	60	.284	.388	.462

(continued)

Ducey, Robert Thomas "Rob" (continued)

YR	TM/LG	CL	G	TPA	AB	H	2B	3B	HR	TB	BB	IBB	HB	SO	GDP	SH	SF	SB	CS	R	RBI	BA	OBA	SA
	TOR/AL		34	57	48	9	1	0	1	13	8	0	0	10	0	0	1	2	0	12	6	.188	.298	.271
88	SYR/INT	AAA	90	369	317	81	14	4	7	124	43	0	3	81	3	2	4	7	6	40	42	.256	.346	.391
	TOR/AL		27	63	54	17	4	1	0	23	5	0	0	7	1	2	2	1	0	15	6	.315	.361	.426
89	SYR/INT	AAA	10	40	29	3	0	1	0	5	10	0	0	13	0	0	1	0	0	0	3	.103	.325	.172
	TOR/AL		41	86	76	16	4	0	0	20	9	1	0	25	2	1	0	2	1	5	7	.211	.294	.263
90	SYR/INT	AAA	127	504	438	117	32	7	7	184	60	6	4	87	10	1	1	14	9	53	47	.267	.360	.420
	TOR/AL		19	62	53	16	5	0	0	21	7	0	1	15	0	0	1	1	1	7	7	.302	.387	.396
91	SYR/INT	AAA	72	323	266	78	10	3	8	118	51	4	0	58	1	4	2	5	7	53	40	.293	.404	.444
	TOR/AL		39	75	68	16	2	2	1	25	6	0	0	26	1	1	0	2	0	8	4	.235	.297	.368
92	TOR/AL		23	21	21	1	1	0	0	2	0	0	0	10	0	0	0	0	0	3	0	.048	.048	.095
	CAL/AL		31	65	59	14	3	0	0	17	5	0	0	12	1	0	1	2	3	4	2	.237	.292	.288
	YEAR		54	86	80	15	4	0	0	19	5	0	0	22	1	0	1	2	3	7	2	.188	.233	.237
93	OC/AMA	AAA	105	440	389	118	17	10	17	206	46	2	2	97	5	0	4	17	9	68	56	.303	.375	.530
	TEX/AL		27	99	85	24	6	3	2	42	10	2	0	17	1	2	2	2	3	15	9	.282	.351	.494
7 YR TOTALS			241	528	464	113	26	6	4	163	50	3	1	122	6	6	7	12	9	69	41	.244	.314	.351

Duncan, Mariano — BR/TR — b.3/13/63 — POS SS-501, 2B-333, OF-82, 3B-4   LA 1/17/82

YR	TM/LG	CL	G	TPA	AB	H	2B	3B	HR	TB	BB	IBB	HB	SO	GDP	SH	SF	SB	CS	R	RBI	BA	OBA	SA
84	SA/TEX	AA	125	554	502	127	14	11	2	169	41	0	5	110	8	4	2	41	13	80	44	.253	.315	.337
85	LA/NL		142	620	562	137	24	6	6	191	38	4	3	113	9	13	4	38	8	74	39	.244	.293	.340
86	LA/NL		109	445	407	93	7	0	8	124	30	1	2	78	6	5	1	48	13	47	30	.229	.284	.305
87	ALB/PCL	AAA	6	24	22	6	0	0	0	6	2	0	0	5	0	0	0	3	0	6	0	.273	.333	.273
	LA/NL		76	287	261	56	8	1	6	84	17	1	2	62	4	6	1	11	1	31	18	.215	.267	.322
88	ALB/PCL	AAA	56	250	227	65	4	8	0	85	10	0	0	40	0	2	3	33	7	48	25	.286	.335	.374
89	LA/NL		49	87	84	21	5	1	0	28	0	0	2	15	1	1	0	3	3	9	8	.250	.267	.333
	CIN/NL		45	186	174	43	10	1	3	64	8	0	3	36	2	1	0	6	2	23	13	.247	.292	.368
	YEAR		94	273	258	64	15	2	3	92	8	0	5	51	3	2	0	9	5	32	21	.248	.284	.357
90	CIN/NL		125	471	435	133	22	*11	10	207	24	4	4	67	10	4	4	13	7	67	55	.306	.345	.476
91	CIN/NL		100	356	333	86	7	4	12	137	12	0	3	57	0	5	3	5	4	46	40	.258	.288	.411
92	PHI/NL		142	605	574	153	40	3	8	223	17	2	5	108	15	5	4	23	3	71	50	.267	.292	.389
93	PHI/NL		124	518	496	140	26	4	11	207	12	0	4	88	13	4	2	6	5	68	73	.282	.304	.417
8 YR TOTALS			912	3575	3326	862	149	31	64	1265	158	10	28	624	60	44	19	153	46	436	326	.259	.297	.380

Dunston, Shawon Donnell — BR/TR — b.3/21/63 — POS SS-911   CHN82 1/1

YR	TM/LG	CL	G	TPA	AB	H	2B	3B	HR	TB	BB	IBB	HB	SO	GDP	SH	SF	SB	CS	R	RBI	BA	OBA	SA
84	MID/TEX	AA	73	318	298	98	13	3	3	126	11	2	3	38	9	2	4	11	8	44	34	.329	.354	.423
	IOW/AMA	AAA	61	217	210	49	11	1	7	83	6	3	0	40	4	2	1	9	3	25	27	.233	.247	.395
85	IOW/AMA	AAA	73	284	272	73	9	6	2	100	5	0	1	49	5	1	5	17	12	24	28	.268	.283	.368
	CHI/NL		74	272	250	65	12	4	4	97	19	3	0	42	3	1	2	11	3	40	18	.260	.310	.388
86	CHI/NL		150	611	581	145	37	3	17	239	21	5	3	114	5	4	2	13	11	66	68	.250	.278	.411
87	IOW/AMA	AAA	5	19	19	8	1	0	0	9	0	0	0	3	0	0	0	1	1	1	2	.421	.421	.474
	CHI/NL		95	359	346	85	18	3	5	124	10	1	1	68	6	0	2	12	3	40	22	.246	.267	.358
88	CHI/NL		155	599	575	143	23	6	9	205	16	8	2	108	6	4	2	30	9	69	56	.249	.271	.357
89	CHI/NL		138	512	471	131	20	6	9	190	30	15	1	86	7	6	4	19	11	52	60	.278	.320	.403
90	CHI/NL		146	573	545	143	22	8	17	232	15	1	3	87	9	4	6	25	5	73	66	.262	.283	.426
91	CHI/NL		142	534	492	128	22	7	12	200	23	5	4	64	9	4	11	21	6	59	50	.260	.292	.407
92	CHI/NL		18	76	73	23	3	1	0	28	1	0	0	13	0	1	2	2	0	8	2	.315	.342	.384
93	CHI/NL		7	10	10	4	2	0	0	6	0	0	0	0	0	0	0	0	0	3	2	.400	.400	.600
9 YR TOTALS			925	3546	3343	867	159	38	73	1321	137	38	14	583	45	23	29	133	51	410	344	.259	.289	.395

Dykstra, Leonard Kyle "Lenny" — BL/TL — b.2/10/63 — POS OF-1039   NYN81 12/315

YR	TM/LG	CL	G	TPA	AB	H	2B	3B	HR	TB	BB	IBB	HB	SO	GDP	SH	SF	SB	CS	R	RBI	BA	OBA	SA
84	JAC/TEX	AA	131	581	501	138	25	7	6	195	73	6	5	45	6	1	1	53	17	100	52	.275	.372	.389
85	TID/INT	AAA	58	264	229	71	8	6	1	94	31	0	1	20	2	1	2	26	6	44	25	.310	.392	.410
	NY/NL		83	273	236	60	9	3	1	78	30	0	1	24	4	4	2	15	2	40	19	.254	.338	.331
86	NY/NL		147	498	431	127	27	7	8	192	58	1	0	55	4	7	2	31	7	77	45	.295	.377	.445
87	NY/NL		132	479	431	123	37	3	10	196	40	3	4	67	1	4	0	27	7	86	43	.285	.352	.455
88	NY/NL		126	466	429	116	19	3	8	165	30	2	2	43	3	2	2	30	6	57	33	.270	.321	.385
89	NY/NL		56	192	159	43	12	1	3	66	23	0	2	15	4	1	4	13	1	27	13	.270	.362	.415
	PHI/NL		90	392	352	78	20	3	4	116	37	1	1	38	5	1	1	17	11	39	19	.222	.297	.330
	YEAR		146	584	511	121	32	4	7	182	60	1	3	53	7	5	5	30	12	66	32	.237	.318	.356
90	PHI/NL		149	691	590	*192	35	3	9	260	89	14	7	48	5	2	3	33	5	106	60	.325	.418	.441
91	PHI/NL		63	284	246	73	13	5	3	105	37	1	1	20	1	0	0	24	4	48	12	.297	.391	.427
92	PHI/NL		85	392	345	104	18	0	6	140	40	4	3	32	1	0	4	30	5	53	39	.301	.375	.406
93	PHI/NL		161	773	637	*194	44	6	19	307	*129	9	2	64	8	0	5	37	12	*143	66	.305	.420	.482
9 YR TOTALS			1092	4440	3856	1110	234	34	71	1625	513	35	24	406	34	24	23	257	62	676	349	.288	.373	.421

Easley, Jacinto Damion "Damion" — BR/TR — b.11/11/69 — POS 3B-59, 2B-54, SS-3, DH-1   CAL88 30/767

YR	TM/LG	CL	G	TPA	AB	H	2B	3B	HR	TB	BB	IBB	HB	SO	GDP	SH	SF	SB	CS	R	RBI	BA	OBA	SA
89	BEN/NWL	A-	36	160	131	39	5	1	4	58	25	0	4	21	1	0	0	9	4	34	21	.298	.425	.443
90	QC/MID	A	103	417	365	100	19	3	10	155	41	0	8	60	7	1	2	25	8	59	56	.274	.358	.425
91	MID/TEX	AA	127	525	452	115	24	5	6	167	58	2	7	67	12	6	2	23	9	73	57	.254	.347	.369
92	EDM/PCL	AAA	108	474	429	124	18	3	3	157	31	0	5	44	13	3	6	26	10	61	44	.289	.340	.366
	CAL/AL		47	165	151	39	5	0	1	47	14	0	3	26	2	1	2	9	5	14	12	.258	.307	.311
93	CAL/AL		73	264	230	72	13	2	2	95	28	2	2	35	5	1	2	6	6	33	22	.313	.392	.413
2 YR TOTALS			120	429	381	111	18	2	3	142	36	2	6	61	7	3	3	15	11	47	34	.291	.359	.373

Edmonds, James Patrick "Jim" — BL/TL — b.6/27/70 — POS OF-17 CAL88 6/169

YR	TM/LG	CL	G	TPA	AB	H	2B	3B	HR	TB	BB	IBB	HB	SO	GDP	SH	SF	SB	CS	R	RBI	BA	OBA	SA
88	BEN/NWL	A-	35	143	122	27	4	0	0	31	20	0	0	44	2	0	1	4	0	23	13	.221	.329	.254
89	QC/MID	A	31	99	92	24	4	0	1	31	7	0	0	34	3	0	0	1	0	11	4	.261	.313	.337
90	PS/CAL	A+	91	346	314	92	18	6	3	131	27	3	2	75	10	1	2	5	2	36	56	.293	.351	.417
91	PS/CAL	A+	60	231	187	55	15	1	2	78	40	3	0	57	2	3	1	2	2	28	27	.294	.417	.417
92	MID/TEX	AA	70	289	246	77	15	2	8	120	41	1	1	83	8	1	0	3	4	42	32	.313	.413	.488
	EDM/PCL	AAA	50	212	194	58	15	2	6	95	14	2	0	55	2	2	2	3	1	37	36	.299	.343	.490
93	VAN/PCL	AAA	95	403	356	112	28	4	9	175	41	4	0	81	5	2	4	6	8	59	74	.315	.382	.492
	CAL/AL		18	63	61	15	4	1	0	21	2	1	0	16	1	0	0	0	2	5	4	.246	.270	.344

Eisenreich, James Michael "Jim" — BL/TL — b.4/18/59 — POS OF-690, DH-66, 1B-16 MIN80 16

YR	TM/LG	CL	G	TPA	AB	H	2B	3B	HR	TB	BB	IBB	HB	SO	GDP	SH	SF	SB	CS	R	RBI	BA	OBA	SA
82	MIN/AL		34	111	99	30	6	0	2	42	11	0	0	13	1	0	0	0	0	10	9	.303	.378	.424
83	MIN/AL		2	8	7	2	1	0	0	3	1	0	0	1	0	0	0	0	0	1	0	.286	.375	.429
84	MIN/AL		12	36	32	7	1	0	0	8	2	1	0	4	1	0	2	2	0	1	3	.219	.250	.250
87	MEM/SOU	AA	70	324	275	105	36	10	11	194	47	3	0	44	8	0	2	13	4	60	57	.382	.469	.705
	KC/AL		44	115	105	25	8	2	4	49	7	2	0	13	2	0	3	1	1	10	21	.238	.278	.467
88	OMA/AMA	AAA	36	156	142	41	8	3	4	67	9	0	0	20	1	0	4	9	1	28	14	.289	.327	.472
	KC/AL		82	214	202	44	8	1	1	57	6	1	0	31	2	2	4	9	3	26	19	.218	.236	.282
89	KC/AL		134	519	475	139	33	7	9	213	37	9	0	44	8	3	4	27	8	64	59	.293	.341	.448
90	KC/AL		142	545	496	139	29	7	5	197	42	2	1	51	7	2	4	12	14	61	51	.280	.335	.397
91	KC/AL		135	405	375	113	22	3	2	147	20	1	1	35	10	3	6	5	3	47	47	.301	.333	.392
92	KC/AL		113	380	353	95	13	3	2	120	24	4	0	36	6	0	3	11	6	31	28	.269	.313	.340
93	PHI/NL		153	394	362	115	17	4	7	161	26	5	1	36	6	3	2	5	0	51	54	.318	.363	.445
10 YR TOTALS			**851**	**2727**	**2506**	**709**	**138**	**27**	**32**	**997**	**176**	**25**	**4**	**264**	**43**	**13**	**28**	**72**	**35**	**302**	**291**	**.283**	**.328**	**.398**

Espinoza, Alvaro Alberto — BR/TR — b.2/19/62 — POS SS-529, 3B-101, 2B-23, P-1 HOU 10/30/78

YR	TM/LG	CL	G	TPA	AB	H	2B	3B	HR	TB	BB	IBB	HB	SO	GDP	SH	SF	SB	CS	R	RBI	BA	OBA	SA
84	TOL/INT	AAA	104	368	344	80	12	5	0	102	3	0	3	49	13	16	2	3	1	22	30	.233	.244	.297
	MIN/AL		1	0	0	0	0	0	0	0	0	0	0	0	0	0	0	0	0	0	0	.000	.000	.000
85	TOL/INT	AAA	82	293	266	61	11	0	1	75	14	0	3	30	10	8	2	1	3	24	33	.229	.274	.282
	MIN/AL		32	62	57	15	2	0	0	17	1	0	1	9	2	3	0	0	1	5	9	.263	.288	.298
86	TOL/INT	AAA	73	267	253	71	8	1	2	87	6	1	0	30	3	7	1	1	1	18	27	.281	.296	.344
	MIN/AL		37	45	42	9	1	0	0	10	1	0	0	10	0	2	0	0	1	4	1	.214	.233	.238
87	POR/PCL	AAA	91	309	291	80	3	2	4	99	12	1	2	37	12	4	0	2	1	28	28	.275	.308	.340
88	NY/AL		3	3	3	0	0	0	0	0	0	0	0	0	0	0	0	0	0	0	0	.000	.000	.000
	CMB/INT	AAA	119	456	435	107	10	5	2	133	7	1	3	53	11	9	2	4	3	42	30	.246	.262	.306
89	NY/AL		146	544	503	142	23	1	0	167	14	1	1	60	14	14	3	3	3	51	41	.282	.301	.332
90	NY/AL		150	472	438	98	12	2	2	120	16	0	5	54	13	11	2	1	2	31	20	.224	.258	.274
91	NY/AL		148	509	480	123	23	2	5	165	16	0	2	57	10	9	2	4	1	51	33	.256	.282	.344
92	CS/PCL	AAA	122	515	483	145	36	6	9	220	21	0	4	55	15	4	3	2	5	64	79	.300	.333	.455
93	CLE/AL		129	283	263	73	15	0	4	100	8	0	1	36	7	8	3	2	2	34	27	.278	.298	.380
8 YR TOTALS			**646**	**1918**	**1786**	**460**	**76**	**5**	**11**	**579**	**56**	**1**	**10**	**226**	**46**	**56**	**10**	**10**	**10**	**176**	**131**	**.258**	**.282**	**.324**

Espy, Cecil Edward — BB/TR — b.1/20/63 — POS OF-428, DH-19, SS-3, C-2, 2B-2, 1B-1 CHA80 1/8

YR	TM/LG	CL	G	TPA	AB	H	2B	3B	HR	TB	BB	IBB	HB	SO	GDP	SH	SF	SB	CS	R	RBI	BA	OBA	SA
80	WSO/GCL	R	58	243	212	58	7	3	0	71	26	1	0	38	5	2	3	23	6	33	26	.274	.349	.335
81	WSO/GCL	R	43	158	142	40	3	1	0	45	11	1	1	13	4	3	1	9	4	24	16	.282	.335	.317
	APP/MID	A	72	312	273	55	2	2	1	64	30	2	1	54	2	8	0	11	3	37	19	.201	.283	.234
82	VB/FSL	A+	131	585	523	166	14	7	1	197	58	4	0	70	4	3	0	74	15	100	34	.317	.387	.377
83	SA/TEX	AA	133	611	564	151	16	11	4	201	39	2	1	77	11	3	4	51	16	88	38	.268	.314	.356
	LA/NL		20	12	11	3	1	0	0	4	1	0	0	2	0	0	0	0	0	4	1	.273	.333	.364
84	SA/TEX	AA	133	602	535	146	19	8	8	205	54	5	1	75	11	5	7	48	16	99	60	.273	.337	.383
85	SA/TEX	AA	124	517	461	129	24	3	5	174	47	1	1	59	10	4	3	20	17	64	49	.280	.347	.377
86	HAW/PCL	AAA	106	412	384	101	19	3	4	138	24	1	0	83	6	3	1	41	13	49	38	.263	.306	.359
87	OC/AMA	AAA	118	482	443	134	18	6	1	167	31	2	1	66	8	4	4	46	14	76	37	.302	.347	.377
	TEX/AL		14	9	8	0	0	0	0	0	1	0	0	3	1	0	0	4	2	1	0	.000	.111	.000
88	TEX/AL		123	376	347	86	17	6	2	121	20	1	1	83	2	5	0	33	10	46	39	.248	.288	.349
89	TEX/AL		142	527	475	122	12	7	3	157	38	2	2	99	11	10	2	45	20	65	31	.257	.313	.331
90	TEX/AL		52	82	71	9	0	0	0	9	10	0	0	20	1	1	0	5	0	10	1	.127	.235	.127
	OC/AMA	AAA	34	147	126	34	4	2	1	45	16	0	0	29	0	1	4	10	3	15	20	.270	.342	.365
91	BUF/AMA	AAA	102	442	398	124	27	10	2	177	36	1	0	65	2	4	4	22	10	69	43	.312	.365	.445
	PIT/NL		43	92	82	20	4	0	1	27	5	0	0	17	0	3	2	4	0	7	11	.244	.281	.329
92	PIT/NL		112	211	194	50	7	3	1	66	15	2	0	40	3	1	1	9	3	21	20	.258	.310	.340
93	IND/AMA	AAA	25	89	83	19	3	0	0	22	6	0	0	16	3	0	0	3	0	10	7	.229	.281	.265
	CIN/NL		40	76	60	14	2	0	0	16	14	0	0	13	2	2	0	2	1	6	5	.233	.368	.267
8 YR TOTALS			**546**	**1385**	**1248**	**304**	**43**	**16**	**7**	**400**	**104**	**5**	**3**	**277**	**11**	**20**	**10**	**103**	**40**	**160**	**108**	**.244**	**.301**	**.321**

Everett, Carl Edward — BB/TR — b.6/3/70 — POS OF-8 NYA90 1/10

YR	TM/LG	CL	G	TPA	AB	H	2B	3B	HR	TB	BB	IBB	HB	SO	GDP	SH	SF	SB	CS	R	RBI	BA	OBA	SA
90	YAN/GCL	R	48	209	185	48	8	5	1	69	15	0	6	38	1	2	1	15	2	28	14	.259	.333	.373
91	GRE/SAL	A	123	553	468	127	18	0	4	157	57	2	23	122	1	2	3	28	19	96	40	.271	.376	.335
92	FL/FSL	A+	46	203	183	42	8	2	2	60	12	1	4	40	1	4	0	11	3	30	9	.230	.291	.328
	PW/CAR	A+	6	27	22	7	0	0	4	19	5	0	0	4	0	0	0	1	0	7	9	.318	.444	.864
93	HD/CAL	A+	59	282	253	73	12	6	10	127	22	0	6	73	3	0	1	24	9	48	52	.289	.358	.502
	EDM/PCL	AAA	35	158	136	42	13	4	6	81	19	0	2	45	1	0	0	12	1	28	16	.309	.401	.596
	FLO/NL		11	20	19	2	0	0	0	2	1	0	0	9	0	0	0	1	0	0	0	.105	.150	.105

Faneyte, Rikkert — BR/TR — b.5/31/69 — POS OF-6　　　　　SF90 19/446

YR	TM/LG	CL	G	TPA	AB	H	2B	3B	HR	TB	BB	IBB	HB	SO	GDP	SH	SF	SB	CS	R	RBI	BA	OBA	SA
91	CLI/MID	A	107	461	384	98	14	7	6	144	61	1	9	106	8	3	4	18	11	73	52	.255	.367	.375
92	SJ/CAL	A+	94	428	342	90	13	2	9	134	73	3	6	65	7	4	3	17	9	69	43	.263	.399	.392
93	PHO/PCL	AAA	115	479	426	133	23	2	11	193	40	1	8	72	8	2	3	15	9	71	71	.312	.379	.453
	SF/NL		7	17	15	2	0	0	0	2	2	0	0	4	0	0	0	0	0	2	0	.133	.235	.133

Faries, Paul Tyrrell — BR/TR — b.2/20/65 — POS 2B-54, SS-17, 3B-16　　　　　SD87 23/588

YR	TM/LG	CL	G	TPA	AB	H	2B	3B	HR	TB	BB	IBB	HB	SO	GDP	SH	SF	SB	CS	R	RBI	BA	OBA	SA
87	SPO/NWL	A-	74	330	280	86	9	3	0	101	36	0	5	25	7	4	5	30	9	67	27	.307	.390	.361
88	RIV/CAL	A+	141	673	579	183	39	4	2	236	72	1	8	79	14	7	7	65	30	108	77	.316	.395	.408
89	WIC/TEX	AA	130	565	513	136	25	8	6	195	47	0	2	52	13	2	1	41	13	79	52	.265	.329	.380
90	LV/PCL	AAA	137	641	552	172	29	3	5	222	75	1	6	60	16	7	1	48	15	109	64	.312	.399	.402
	SD/NL		14	45	37	7	1	0	0	8	4	0	0	7	0	2	1	0	1	4	2	.189	.279	.216
91	HD/CAL	A+	10	46	42	13	2	2	0	19	2	1	0	3	2	1	1	1	0	6	5	.310	.333	.452
	LV/PCL	AAA	20	90	75	23	2	1	1	30	12	0	1	5	2	2	1	7	3	16	12	.307	.398	.400
	SD/NL		57	149	130	23	3	1	0	28	14	0	1	21	5	4	0	3	1	13	7	.177	.262	.215
92	LV/PCL	AAA	125	506	457	134	15	6	1	164	40	1	3	53	13	4	2	28	9	77	40	.293	.353	.359
	SD/NL		10	12	11	5	1	0	0	6	1	0	0	2	0	0	0	0	0	3	1	.455	.500	.545
93	PHO/PCL	AAA	78	354	327	99	14	5	2	129	22	1	1	30	8	3	1	18	11	56	32	.303	.348	.394
	SF/NL		15	39	36	8	2	1	0	12	1	0	0	4	1	1	1	2	0	6	4	.222	.237	.333
4 YR TOTALS			96	245	214	43	7	2	0	54	20	0	2	34	6	7	2	5	2	26	14	.201	.273	.252

Fariss, Monty Ted — BR/TR — b.10/13/67 — POS OF-65, 2B-21, DH-8, 1B-1　　　　　TEX88 1/6

YR	TM/LG	CL	G	TPA	AB	H	2B	3B	HR	TB	BB	IBB	HB	SO	GDP	SH	SF	SB	CS	R	RBI	BA	OBA	SA
88	BUT/PIO	R+	17	77	53	21	1	0	4	34	20	2	2	7	1	0	2	2	0	16	22	.396	.558	.642
	TUL/TEX	AA	49	189	165	37	6	6	3	64	22	0	0	39	2	1	1	2	0	21	31	.224	.314	.388
89	TUL/TEX	AA	132	575	497	135	27	2	5	181	64	0	0	112	13	8	6	12	6	72	52	.272	.351	.364
90	TUL/TEX	AA	71	282	244	73	15	6	7	121	36	0	0	60	9	1	0	8	5	45	34	.299	.391	.496
	OC/AMA	AAA	62	261	225	68	12	3	4	98	34	0	0	48	7	0	2	1	1	30	31	.302	.391	.436
91	OC/AMA	AAA	137	590	494	134	31	6	13	222	91	1	0	143	11	3	2	5	7	84	73	.271	.383	.449
	TEX/AL		19	38	31	8	1	0	1	12	7	0	0	11	0	0	0	0	0	6	6	.258	.395	.387
92	OC/AMA	AAA	49	219	187	56	13	3	9	102	31	1	0	42	5	0	1	5	4	28	38	.299	.397	.545
	TEX/AL		67	187	166	36	7	1	3	54	17	0	2	51	3	2	0	0	2	13	21	.217	.297	.325
93	EDM/PCL	AAA	74	302	254	65	11	4	6	102	43	0	2	74	3	1	2	1	5	32	37	.256	.365	.402
	FLO/NL		18	34	29	5	2	1	0	9	5	0	0	13	2	0	0	0	0	3	2	.172	.294	.310
3 YR TOTALS			104	259	226	49	10	2	4	75	29	0	2	75	5	2	0	0	2	22	29	.217	.311	.332

Felder, Michael Otis "Mike" — BB/TR — b.11/18/61 — POS OF-692, DH-38, 2B-17, 3B-6　　　　　MIL81* 3/74

YR	TM/LG	CL	G	TPA	AB	H	2B	3B	HR	TB	BB	IBB	HB	SO	GDP	SH	SF	SB	CS	R	RBI	BA	OBA	SA
84	EP/TEX	AA	122	571	496	144	19	2	9	194	63	2	1	57	4	2	9	58	16	98	72	.290	.366	.391
85	VAN/PCL	AAA	137	628	563	177	16	11	2	221	55	1	2	70	14	3	5	61	12	91	43	.314	.374	.393
	MIL/AL		15	62	56	11	1	0	0	12	5	0	0	6	2	1	0	4	1	8	0	.196	.262	.214
86	EP/TEX	AA	8	38	31	14	3	0	0	17	5	1	1	3	1	1	1	7	0	10	2	.452	.514	.548
	MIL/AL		44	174	155	37	2	4	1	50	13	1	1	16	2	1	5	16	2	24	13	.239	.289	.323
	VAN/PCL	AAA	39	173	153	40	3	4	1	54	17	2	0	15	2	0	3	4	3	21	15	.261	.329	.353
87	DEN/AMA	AAA	27	130	113	41	6	2	2	57	14	0	1	6	0	1	1	17	1	26	20	.363	.434	.504
	MIL/AL		108	328	289	77	5	7	2	102	28	0	0	23	3	9	2	34	8	48	31	.266	.329	.353
88	DEN/AMA	AAA	20	84	78	21	4	1	0	27	5	0	0	10	2	0	1	8	1	10	5	.269	.310	.346
	MIL/AL		50	85	81	14	1	0	0	15	0	0	0	11	1	3	0	9	1	14	5	.173	.183	.185
89	MIL/AL		117	345	315	76	11	3	3	102	23	2	0	38	4	7	0	26	5	50	23	.241	.293	.324
90	MIL/AL		121	272	237	65	7	2	3	85	22	0	0	17	0	8	5	20	9	38	27	.274	.330	.359
91	SF/NL		132	383	348	92	10	6	0	114	30	2	1	31	1	4	0	21	6	51	18	.264	.325	.328
92	SF/NL		145	351	322	92	13	3	4	123	21	2	0	29	3	3	3	14	4	44	23	.286	.330	.382
93	SEA/AL		109	374	342	72	7	5	1	92	22	2	2	34	2	7	1	15	9	31	20	.211	.262	.269
9 YR TOTALS			841	2374	2145	536	57	30	14	695	164	8	6	205	18	43	16	158	46	308	160	.250	.303	.324

Felix, Junior Francisco — BB/TR — b.10/3/67 — POS OF-477, DH-11　　　　　TOR 9/15/85

YR	TM/LG	CL	G	TPA	AB	H	2B	3B	HR	TB	BB	IBB	HB	SO	GDP	SH	SF	SB	CS	R	RBI	BA	OBA	SA
86	MH/PIO	R+	67	304	263	75	9	3	4	102	35	1	6	84	4	0	0	37	9	57	28	.285	.382	.388
87	MB/SAL	A	124	523	466	135	15	6	12	204	43	8	10	124	2	2	2	64	28	70	51	.290	.361	.438
88	KNO/SOU	AA	93	386	360	91	16	5	3	126	20	2	3	82	4	2	1	40	16	52	25	.253	.297	.350
89	SYR/INT	AAA	21	98	87	24	4	2	1	35	9	0	0	18	2	1	1	13	3	17	10	.276	.340	.402
	TOR/AL		110	454	415	107	14	8	9	164	33	2	3	101	5	0	3	18	12	62	46	.258	.315	.395
90	TOR/AL		127	517	463	122	23	7	15	204	45	0	2	99	4	2	5	13	8	73	65	.263	.328	.441
91	PS/CAL	A+	18	80	64	23	3	0	2	32	16	1	0	11	2	0	0	8	2	12	10	.359	.488	.500
	CAL/AL		66	246	230	65	10	2	2	85	11	0	3	55	5	0	2	7	5	32	26	.283	.321	.370
92	CAL/AL		139	558	509	125	22	5	9	184	33	1	2	128	9	5	4	8	6	63	72	.246	.289	.361
93	EDM/PCL	AAA	7	35	31	11	2	0	0	13	4	0	0	6	0	0	0	1	0	7	5	.355	.429	.419
	FLO/NL		57	225	214	51	11	1	7	85	10	1	0	50	6	0	0	2	1	25	22	.238	.276	.397
5 YR TOTALS			499	2000	1831	470	80	23	42	722	132	8	11	433	29	7	19	48	34	255	231	.257	.308	.394

Fermin, Felix Jose — BR/TR — b.10/9/63 — POS SS-690, 3B-17, 2B-10, 1B-2　　　　　PIT 6/11/83

YR	TM/LG	CL	G	TPA	AB	H	2B	3B	HR	TB	BB	IBB	HB	SO	GDP	SH	SF	SB	CS	R	RBI	BA	OBA	SA
84	PW/CAR	A+	119	423	382	94	13	1	0	109	29	1	0	32	13	5	2	32	10	34	41	.246	.306	.285
85	NAS/EAS	AA	137	495	443	100	11	3	0	114	37	0	3	30	14	10	2	29	15	32	27	.226	.289	.257
86	PW/CAR	A+	84	355	322	90	10	1	0	102	25	0	4	19	4	3	1	40	12	58	26	.280	.338	.317
	HAW/PCL	AAA	39	133	125	32	5	0	0	37	7	0	0	13	3	1	0	11	1	13	9	.256	.295	.296
87	HAR/EAS	AA	100	438	399	107	9	5	0	126	27	1	0	22	12	7	3	22	13	62	35	.268	.316	.316

Fermin, Felix Jose (continued)

YR	TM/LG	CL	G	TPA	AB	H	2B	3B	HR	TB	BB	IBB	HB	SO	GDP	SH	SF	SB	CS	R	RBI	BA	OBA	SA
	PIT/NL		23	75	68	17	0	0	0	17	4	1	1	9	3	2	0	0	0	6	4	.250	.301	.250
88	BUF/AMA	AAA	87	375	352	92	11	1	0	105	17	0	1	18	15	4	1	8	6	38	31	.261	.296	.298
	PIT/NL		43	100	87	24	0	2	0	28	8	1	3	10	3	1	1	3	1	9	2	.276	.354	.322
89	CLE/AL		156	562	484	115	9	1	0	126	41	0	4	27	15	32	1	6	4	50	21	.238	.302	.260
90	CLE/AL		148	458	414	106	13	2	1	126	26	0	0	22	13	13	5	3	3	47	40	.256	.297	.304
91	CS/PCL	AAA	2	8	8	2	0	0	0	2	0	0	0	0	0	0	0	0	0	1	1	.250	.250	.250
	CLE/AL		129	469	424	111	13	2	0	128	26	0	3	27	17	13	3	5	4	30	31	.262	.307	.302
92	CLE/AL		79	245	215	58	7	2	0	69	18	1	1	10	7	9	2	0	0	27	13	.270	.326	.321
93	CLE/AL		140	514	480	126	16	2	2	152	24	1	4	14	12	5	1	4	5	48	45	.262	.303	.317
7 YR TOTALS			**718**	**2423**	**2172**	**557**	**58**	**11**	**3**	**646**	**147**	**4**	**16**	**119**	**70**	**75**	**13**	**21**	**17**	**217**	**156**	**.256**	**.307**	**.297**

Fernandez, Octavio Antonio "Tony" — BB/TR — b.6/30/62 — POS SS-1451, 3B-10, DH-2   TOR 4/24/79

YR	TM/LG	CL	G	TPA	AB	H	2B	3B	HR	TB	BB	IBB	HB	SO	GDP	SH	SF	SB	CS	R	RBI	BA	OBA	SA
83	TOR/AL		15	38	34	9	1	1	0	12	2	0	1	2	1	1	0	0	1	5	2	.265	.324	.353
84	SYR/INT	AAA	26	109	94	24	1	0	0	25	13	0	0	9	4	1	1	1	3	12	6	.255	.343	.266
	TOR/AL		88	254	233	63	5	3	3	83	17	0	0	15	3	2	2	5	7	29	19	.270	.317	.356
85	TOR/AL		161	618	564	163	31	10	2	220	43	2	2	41	12	7	2	13	6	71	51	.289	.340	.390
86	TOR/AL		163	727	687	213	33	9	10	294	27	0	4	52	8	5	4	25	12	91	65	.310	.338	.428
87	TOR/AL		146	642	578	186	29	8	5	246	51	3	5	48	14	4	4	32	12	90	67	.322	.379	.426
88	TOR/AL		154	704	648	186	41	4	5	250	45	3	4	65	9	3	4	15	5	76	70	.287	.335	.386
89	TOR/AL		140	617	573	147	25	9	11	223	29	1	3	51	9	2	10	22	6	64	64	.257	.291	.389
90	TOR/AL		161	721	635	175	27	*17	4	248	71	4	7	70	17	2	6	26	13	84	66	.276	.352	.391
91	SD/NL		145	621	558	152	27	5	4	201	55	4	0	74	12	7	1	23	9	81	38	.272	.337	.360
92	SD/NL		155	694	622	171	32	4	4	223	56	4	4	62	6	9	3	20	20	84	37	.275	.337	.359
93	NY/NL		48	204	173	39	5	2	1	51	25	0	1	19	3	3	2	6	2	20	14	.225	.323	.295
	TOR/AL		94	390	353	108	18	9	4	156	31	3	0	26	13	5	1	15	8	45	50	.306	.361	.442
	YEAR		142	594	526	147	23	11	5	207	56	3	1	45	16	8	3	21	10	65	64	.279	.348	.394
11 YR TOTALS			**1470**	**6230**	**5658**	**1612**	**274**	**81**	**53**	**2207**	**452**	**20**	**31**	**525**	**107**	**50**	**39**	**202**	**101**	**740**	**543**	**.285**	**.339**	**.390**

Fielder, Cecil Grant — BR/TR — b.9/21/63 — POS 1B-563, DH-263, 3B-7, 2B-2, OF-1   KC82 S4/67

YR	TM/LG	CL	G	TPA	AB	H	2B	3B	HR	TB	BB	IBB	HB	SO	GDP	SH	SF	SB	CS	R	RBI	BA	OBA	SA
84	KIN/CAR	A+	61	255	222	63	12	1	19	134	28	7	1	44	8	1	3	2	1	42	49	.284	.362	.604
	KNO/SOU	AA	64	262	236	60	12	2	9	103	22	3	1	48	6	0	3	0	1	33	44	.254	.317	.436
85	KNO/SOU	AA	96	414	361	106	26	2	18	190	45	3	3	83	5	0	5	0	0	52	81	.294	.372	.526
	TOR/AL		30	81	74	23	4	0	4	39	6	0	0	16	2	0	1	0	0	6	16	.311	.358	.527
86	SYR/INT	AAA	88	363	325	91	13	3	18	164	32	3	3	91	11	0	3	0	0	47	68	.280	.347	.505
	TOR/AL		34	90	83	13	2	0	4	27	6	0	0	27	3	0	0	0	0	7	13	.157	.222	.325
87	TOR/AL		82	197	175	47	7	1	14	98	20	2	1	48	6	0	1	0	1	30	32	.269	.345	.560
88	TOR/AL		74	190	174	40	6	1	9	75	14	0	1	53	6	0	1	0	1	24	23	.230	.289	.431
90	DET/AL		159	673	573	159	25	1	*51	*339	90	11	5	182	15	0	5	0	1	104	*132	.277	.377	*.592
91	DET/AL		162	712	624	163	25	0	*44	320	78	12	6	151	17	0	4	0	0	102	*133	.261	.347	.513
92	DET/AL		155	676	594	145	22	0	35	272	73	8	2	151	14	0	7	0	0	80	*124	.244	.325	.458
93	DET/AL		154	672	573	153	23	0	30	266	90	15	4	125	22	0	5	0	1	80	117	.267	.368	.464
8 YR TOTALS			**850**	**3291**	**2870**	**743**	**114**	**3**	**191**	**1436**	**377**	**48**	**20**	**753**	**85**	**0**	**24**	**0**	**4**	**433**	**590**	**.259**	**.346**	**.500**

Finley, Steven Allen "Steve" — BL/TL — b.3/12/65 — POS OF-662, DH-5   BAL87 14/325

YR	TM/LG	CL	G	TPA	AB	H	2B	3B	HR	TB	BB	IBB	HB	SO	GDP	SH	SF	SB	CS	R	RBI	BA	OBA	SA
87	NEW/NYP	A-	54	249	222	65	13	2	3	91	22	0	2	24	4	1	0	26	5	40	33	.293	.359	.410
	HAG/CAR	A+	15	66	65	22	3	2	1	32	1	0	0	6	2	0	0	7	2	9	5	.338	.348	.492
88	HAG/CAR	A+	8	32	28	6	2	0	0	8	4	0	0	3	2	0	0	4	0	2	3	.214	.313	.286
	CHA/SOU	AA	10	45	40	12	4	2	1	23	4	0	1	3	1	0	0	2	0	7	6	.300	.378	.575
	ROC/INT	AAA	120	494	456	143	19	7	5	191	28	5	0	55	4	8	2	20	11	61	54	.314	.352	.419
89	ROC/INT	AAA	7	26	25	4	0	0	0	4	1	0	0	5	0	0	0	3	0	2	2	.160	.192	.160
	HAG/EAS	AA	11	53	48	20	3	1	0	25	4	0	0	5	0	0	1	4	0	11	7	.417	.453	.521
	BAL/AL		81	241	217	54	5	2	2	69	15	1	1	30	3	6	3	17	3	35	25	.249	.298	.318
90	BAL/AL		142	513	464	119	16	4	3	152	32	3	3	53	8	10	6	22	9	46	37	.256	.304	.328
91	HOU/NL		159	656	596	170	28	10	8	242	42	5	2	65	8	10	3	34	18	84	54	.285	.331	.406
92	HOU/NL		162	686	607	177	29	13	5	247	58	6	3	63	10	16	2	44	9	84	55	.292	.355	.407
93	HOU/NL		142	585	545	145	15	*13	8	210	28	1	3	65	8	4	3	19	6	69	44	.266	.304	.385
5 YR TOTALS			**686**	**2681**	**2429**	**665**	**93**	**42**	**26**	**920**	**175**	**16**	**11**	**276**	**37**	**48**	**18**	**136**	**45**	**318**	**215**	**.274**	**.323**	**.379**

Fisk, Carlton Ernest — BR/TR — b.12/26/47 — POS C-2229, DH-166, OF-41, 1B-27, 3B-4   BOS67* 1/2

YR	TM/LG	CL	G	TPA	AB	H	2B	3B	HR	TB	BB	IBB	HB	SO	GDP	SH	SF	SB	CS	R	RBI	BA	OBA	SA
69	BOS/AL		2	5	5	0	0	0	0	0	0	0	0	2	0	0	0	0	0	0	0	.000	.000	.000
71	BOS/AL		14	49	48	15	2	1	2	25	1	0	0	10	1	0	0	0	0	7	6	.313	.327	.521
72	BOS/AL		131	514	457	134	28	*9	22	246	52	6	4	83	11	1	0	5	5	74	61	.293	.370	.538
73	BOS/AL		135	558	508	125	21	0	26	224	37	2	10	99	11	1	2	7	2	65	71	.246	.309	.441
74	BOS/AL		52	216	187	56	12	1	11	103	24	2	2	23	5	2	1	5	1	36	26	.299	.383	.551
75	BOS/AL		79	294	263	87	14	4	10	139	27	4	2	32	7	0	2	4	3	47	52	.331	.395	.529
76	BOS/AL		134	557	487	124	17	5	17	202	56	5	3	71	11	3	5	12	5	76	58	.255	.336	.415
77	BOS/AL		152	632	536	169	26	3	26	279	75	8	9	85	9	2	10	7	6	106	102	.315	.402	.521
78	BOS/AL		157	658	571	162	39	5	20	271	71	6	7	83	10	3	6	7	7	94	88	.284	.366	.475
79	BOS/AL		91	340	320	87	23	2	10	144	10	0	6	38	9	1	3	3	3	49	42	.272	.304	.450
80	BOS/AL		131	530	478	138	25	3	18	223	36	6	13	62	12	0	3	11	5	73	62	.289	.353	.467
81	CHI/AL		96	394	338	89	12	0	7	122	38	3	12	37	9	1	3	3	2	44	45	.263	.354	.361
82	CHI/AL		135	536	476	127	17	3	14	192	46	7	6	60	12	4	4	17	2	66	65	.267	.336	.403
83	CHI/AL		138	545	488	141	26	4	26	253	46	3	6	88	8	2	3	9	6	85	86	.289	.355	.518

(continued)

Fisk, Carlton Ernest (continued)

YR	TM/LG	CL	G	TPA	AB	H	2B	3B	HR	TB	BB	IBB	HB	SO	GDP	SH	SF	SB	CS	R	RBI	BA	OBA	SA
84	CHI/AL		102	395	359	83	20	1	21	168	26	4	5	60	7	1	4	6	0	54	43	.231	.289	.468
85	CHI/AL		153	620	543	129	23	1	37	265	52	12	17	81	9	2	6	17	9	85	107	.238	.320	.488
86	CHI/AL		125	491	457	101	11	0	14	154	22	2	6	92	10	0	6	2	4	42	63	.221	.263	.337
87	CHI/AL		135	508	454	116	22	1	23	209	39	8	8	72	9	1	6	1	4	68	71	.256	.321	.460
88	CHI/AL		76	298	253	70	8	1	19	137	37	9	5	40	6	1	2	0	0	37	50	.277	.377	.542
89	CHI/AL		103	419	375	110	25	2	13	178	36	8	3	60	15	0	5	1	0	47	68	.293	.356	.475
90	CHI/AL		137	521	452	129	21	0	18	204	61	8	7	73	12	0	1	7	2	65	65	.285	.378	.451
91	CHI/AL		134	501	460	111	25	0	18	190	32	4	7	86	19	0	2	1	2	42	74	.241	.299	.413
92	SB/MID	A	1	3	2	1	0	0	1	4	1	0	0	0	0	0	0	0	0	1	3	.500	.667	2.000
	SAR/FSL	A+	7	29	25	3	1	0	1	7	3	0	1	6	1	0	0	1	0	3	2	.120	.241	.280
	CHI/AL		62	214	188	43	4	1	3	58	23	5	1	38	2	0	2	3	0	12	21	.229	.313	.309
93	CHI/AL		25	58	53	10	0	0	1	13	2	0	1	11	0	1	1	0	1	4	2	.189	.228	.245
24 YR TOTALS			**2499**	**9853**	**8756**	**2356**	**421**	**47**	**376**	**3999**	**849**	**105**	**143**	**1386**	**204**	**26**	**79**	**128**	**58**	**1276**	**1330**	**.269**	**.341**	**.457**

Flaherty, John Timothy — BR/TR — b.10/21/67 — POS C-47   BOS88 25/641

YR	TM/LG	CL	G	TPA	AB	H	2B	3B	HR	TB	BB	IBB	HB	SO	GDP	SH	SF	SB	CS	R	RBI	BA	OBA	SA
88	ELM/NYP	A-	46	180	162	38	3	0	3	50	12	0	2	23	5	3	1	2	1	17	16	.235	.294	.309
89	WH/FSL	A+	95	361	334	87	14	2	4	117	20	1	3	44	19	2	2	1	0	31	28	.260	.306	.350
90	LYN/CAR	A+	1	5	4	0	0	0	0	0	0	0	0	1	0	0	1	0	0	0	0	.000	.000	.000
	PAW/INT	AAA	99	347	317	72	18	0	4	102	24	0	2	43	11	0	2	2	1	35	32	.227	.284	.322
91	PAW/INT	AAA	45	175	156	29	7	0	3	45	15	0	0	14	1	4	0	0	1	18	13	.186	.257	.288
	NB/EAS	AA	67	259	225	65	9	0	3	83	31	1	1	22	5	0	0	0	2	27	18	.289	.375	.369
92	PAW/INT	AAA	31	111	104	26	3	0	0	29	5	0	1	8	6	1	0	0	0	11	7	.250	.291	.279
	BOS/AL		35	71	66	13	2	0	0	15	3	0	1	7	0	1	1	0	0	3	2	.197	.229	.227
93	PAW/INT	AAA	105	400	365	99	22	0	6	139	26	1	5	41	9	2	2	3	1	29	35	.271	.327	.381
	BOS/AL		13	29	25	3	2	0	0	5	2	0	1	6	0	1	0	0	0	3	2	.120	.214	.200
2 YR TOTALS			**48**	**100**	**91**	**16**	**4**	**0**	**0**	**20**	**5**	**0**	**1**	**13**	**0**	**2**	**1**	**0**	**0**	**6**	**4**	**.176**	**.224**	**.220**

Fletcher, Darrin Glen — BL/TR — b.10/3/66 — POS C-253   LA87 6/144

YR	TM/LG	CL	G	TPA	AB	H	2B	3B	HR	TB	BB	IBB	HB	SO	GDP	SH	SF	SB	CS	R	RBI	BA	OBA	SA
87	VB/FSL	A+	43	151	124	33	7	0	0	40	22	3	1	12	6	0	4	0	2	13	15	.266	.371	.323
88	SA/TEX	AA	89	307	279	58	8	0	1	69	17	5	3	42	6	6	2	2	6	19	20	.208	.259	.247
89	ALB/PCL	AAA	100	355	315	86	16	1	5	119	30	0	2	38	12	2	6	1	5	34	44	.273	.334	.378
	LA/NL		5	9	8	4	0	0	1	7	1	0	0	0	0	0	0	0	0	1	2	.500	.556	.875
90	ALB/PCL	AAA	105	404	350	102	23	1	13	166	40	6	5	37	11	3	6	1	1	58	65	.291	.367	.474
	LA/NL		2	1	1	0	0	0	0	0	0	0	0	1	0	0	0	0	0	0	0	.000	.000	.000
	PHI/NL		9	23	22	3	1	0	0	4	1	0	0	5	0	0	0	0	0	3	1	.136	.174	.182
	YEAR		11	24	23	3	1	0	0	4	1	0	0	6	0	0	0	0	0	3	1	.130	.167	.174
91	SCR/INT	AAA	90	339	306	87	13	1	8	126	23	4	3	29	7	1	6	1	3	39	50	.284	.334	.412
	PHI/NL		46	142	136	31	8	0	1	42	5	0	0	15	2	1	0	0	0	5	12	.228	.255	.309
92	IND/AMA	AAA	13	53	51	13	2	0	1	18	2	0	0	10	0	0	0	0	0	2	9	.255	.283	.353
	MON/NL		83	244	222	54	10	2	2	74	14	3	2	28	8	2	4	0	2	13	26	.243	.289	.333
93	MON/NL		133	445	396	101	20	1	9	150	34	2	6	40	7	5	4	0	0	33	60	.255	.320	.379
5 YR TOTALS			**278**	**864**	**785**	**193**	**39**	**3**	**13**	**277**	**55**	**5**	**8**	**89**	**17**	**8**	**8**	**0**	**3**	**55**	**101**	**.246**	**.299**	**.353**

Fletcher, Scott Brian — BR/TR — b.7/30/58 — POS SS-836, 2B-613, 3B-84, DH-6   CHN79 S1/6

YR	TM/LG	CL	G	TPA	AB	H	2B	3B	HR	TB	BB	IBB	HB	SO	GDP	SH	SF	SB	CS	R	RBI	BA	OBA	SA
81	CHI/NL		19	48	46	10	4	0	0	14	2	0	0	4	0	0	0	0	0	6	1	.217	.250	.304
82	CHI/NL		11	28	24	4	0	0	0	4	4	0	0	5	0	0	1	0	1	4	1	.167	.286	.167
83	CHI/AL		114	302	262	62	16	5	3	97	29	0	2	22	8	7	2	5	1	42	31	.237	.315	.370
84	CHI/AL		149	521	456	114	13	3	3	142	46	2	8	46	5	9	2	10	4	46	35	.250	.328	.311
85	CHI/AL		119	348	301	77	8	1	2	93	35	0	0	47	9	11	1	5	5	38	31	.256	.332	.309
86	TEX/AL		147	594	530	159	34	5	3	212	47	0	4	59	10	10	3	24	11	82	50	.300	.360	.400
87	TEX/AL		156	668	588	169	28	4	5	220	61	3	5	66	14	12	2	13	12	82	63	.287	.358	.374
88	TEX/AL		140	609	515	142	19	4	0	169	62	1	12	34	13	15	5	8	5	59	47	.276	.364	.328
89	TEX/AL		83	358	314	75	14	1	0	91	38	1	2	41	8	2	2	1	0	47	22	.239	.323	.290
	CHI/AL		59	271	232	63	11	1	1	79	26	0	1	19	4	9	3	1	1	30	21	.272	.344	.341
	YEAR		142	629	546	138	25	2	1	170	64	1	3	60	12	11	5	2	1	77	43	.253	.332	.311
90	CHI/AL		151	573	509	123	18	3	4	159	45	0	3	60	10	11	5	1	3	54	56	.242	.304	.312
91	CHI/AL		90	277	248	51	10	1	1	66	17	0	3	26	3	6	3	0	2	14	28	.206	.262	.266
92	MIL/AL		123	433	386	106	18	3	3	139	30	1	7	33	4	6	3	17	10	53	51	.275	.335	.360
93	BOS/AL		121	531	480	137	31	5	5	193	37	1	5	35	12	6	3	16	3	81	45	.285	.341	.402
13 YR TOTALS			**1482**	**5561**	**4891**	**1292**	**224**	**36**	**30**	**1678**	**479**	**12**	**52**	**500**	**100**	**104**	**35**	**90**	**57**	**638**	**482**	**.264**	**.334**	**.343**

Floyd, Cornelius Clifford "Cliff" — BL/TL — b.12/5/72 — POS 1B-10   MON91 1/14

YR	TM/LG	CL	G	TPA	AB	H	2B	3B	HR	TB	BB	IBB	HB	SO	GDP	SH	SF	SB	CS	R	RBI	BA	OBA	SA
91	EXP/GCL	R	56	240	214	56	9	3	6	89	19	1	5	37	3	1	1	13	3	35	30	.262	.335	.416
92	ALB/SAL	A	134	573	516	157	24	16	16	261	45	9	9	75	4	0	3	32	11	83	97	.304	.368	.506
	WPB/FSL	A+	1	5	4	0	0	0	0	0	0	0	0	1	0	0	1	0	0	0	1	.000	.000	.000
93	HAR/EAS	AA	101	441	380	125	17	4	26	228	54	12	5	71	8	0	2	31	10	82	101	.329	.417	.600
	OTT/INT	AAA	32	143	125	30	2	2	2	42	16	3	1	34	1	0	1	2	2	12	18	.240	.329	.336
	MON/NL		10	31	31	7	0	0	1	10	0	0	0	9	0	0	0	0	0	3	2	.226	.226	.323

Foley, Thomas Michael "Tom" — BL/TR — b.9/9/59 — POS SS-455, 2B-365, 3B-76, 1B-56, P-1, OF-1   CIN77 7/180

YR	TM/LG	CL	G	TPA	AB	H	2B	3B	HR	TB	BB	IBB	HB	SO	GDP	SH	SF	SB	CS	R	RBI	BA	OBA	SA
83	CIN/NL		68	113	98	20	4	1	0	26	13	2	0	17	1	2	0	1	0	7	9	.204	.297	.265
84	CIN/NL		106	304	277	70	8	3	5	99	24	7	0	36	2	1	2	3	2	26	27	.253	.310	.357

Foley, Thomas Michael "Tom" (continued)

YR	TM/LG	CL	G	TPA	AB	H	2B	3B	HR	TB	BB	IBB	HB	SO	GDP	SH	SF	SB	CS	R	RBI	BA	OBA	SA
85	CIN/NL		43	98	92	18	5	1	0	25	6	1	0	16	0	0	0	1	0	7	6	.196	.245	.272
	PHI/NL		46	171	158	42	8	0	3	59	13	7	0	18	2	0	0	1	3	17	17	.266	.322	.373
	YEAR		89	269	250	60	13	1	3	84	19	8	0	34	2	0	0	2	3	24	23	.240	.294	.336
86	REA/EAS	AA	3	12	11	2	2	0	0	4	1	0	0	0	0	0	0	0	0	2	0	.182	.250	.364
	PHI/NL		39	72	61	18	2	1	0	22	10	1	0	11	1	0	1	2	0	8	5	.295	.389	.361
	MON/NL		64	227	202	52	13	2	1	72	20	5	0	26	3	2	3	8	3	18	18	.257	.320	.356
	YEAR		103	299	263	70	15	3	1	94	30	6	0	37	4	2	4	10	3	26	23	.266	.337	.357
87	MON/NL		106	293	280	82	18	3	5	121	11	0	1	40	6	1	0	6	10	35	28	.293	.322	.432
88	MON/NL		127	411	377	100	21	3	5	142	30	10	1	49	11	0	3	2	7	33	43	.265	.319	.377
89	MON/NL		122	431	375	86	19	2	7	130	45	4	4	53	2	4	4	2	7	34	39	.229	.314	.347
90	MON/NL		73	178	164	35	2	1	0	39	12	2	0	22	4	1	1	0	1	11	12	.213	.266	.238
91	MON/NL		86	187	168	35	11	1	0	48	14	4	1	30	4	1	3	2	0	12	15	.208	.269	.286
92	MON/NL		72	129	115	20	3	1	0	25	8	2	1	21	6	3	2	3	0	7	5	.174	.230	.217
93	PIT/NL		86	211	194	49	11	1	3	71	11	1	0	26	4	2	4	0	0	18	22	.253	.287	.366
11 YR TOTALS			**1038**	**2825**	**2561**	**627**	**125**	**20**	**29**	**879**	**217**	**46**	**7**	**365**	**46**	**17**	**23**	**31**	**29**	**233**	**246**	**.245**	**.303**	**.343**

Fox, Eric Hollis — BB/TL — b.8/15/63 — POS OF-69, DH-6   SEA86* S1/5

YR	TM/LG	CL	G	TPA	AB	H	2B	3B	HR	TB	BB	IBB	HB	SO	GDP	SH	SF	SB	CS	R	RBI	BA	OBA	SA
86	SAL/CAL	A+	133	609	526	137	17	3	5	175	69	7	1	78	2	9	4	41	27	80	42	.260	.345	.333
87	CHT/SOU	AA	134	574	523	139	28	10	8	211	40	5	2	93	2	4	5	22	10	76	54	.266	.318	.403
88	VER/EAS	AA	129	530	478	120	20	6	3	161	39	3	7	69	1	7	4	33	12	55	39	.251	.308	.337
89	HUN/SOU	AA	139	583	498	125	10	5	15	190	72	1	0	85	2	11	4	49	15	84	51	.251	.344	.382
90	TAC/PCL	AAA	62	248	221	61	9	2	4	86	20	0	0	34	2	5	2	8	8	37	34	.276	.333	.389
91	TAC/PCL	AAA	127	594	522	141	24	8	4	193	57	4	2	82	6	9	4	17	11	85	52	.270	.342	.370
92	HUN/SOU	AA	59	270	240	65	16	2	5	100	27	4	0	43	0	3	3	16	5	42	14	.271	.341	.417
	TAC/PCL	AAA	37	141	121	24	3	1	1	32	16	1	0	25	2	2	2	5	0	16	7	.198	.288	.264
	OAK/AL		51	163	143	34	5	2	3	52	13	0	0	29	1	6	1	3	4	24	13	.238	.299	.364
93	OAK/AL		29	61	56	8	1	0	1	12	2	0	0	7	0	3	0	0	2	5	5	.143	.172	.214
	TAC/PCL	AAA	92	369	317	99	14	5	11	156	41	3	7	48	4	7	3	18	8	49	52	.312	.390	.492
2 YR TOTALS			**80**	**224**	**199**	**42**	**6**	**2**	**4**	**64**	**15**	**0**	**0**	**36**	**1**	**9**	**1**	**3**	**6**	**29**	**18**	**.211**	**.265**	**.322**

Franco, Julio Cesar — BR/TR — b.8/23/58 — POS SS-715, 2B-628, DH-182, OF-4, 3B-2   PHI 6/23/78

YR	TM/LG	CL	G	TPA	AB	H	2B	3B	HR	TB	BB	IBB	HB	SO	GDP	SH	SF	SB	CS	R	RBI	BA	OBA	SA
82	PHI/NL		16	32	29	8	1	0	0	9	2	1	0	4	1	1	0	0	2	3	3	.276	.323	.310
83	CLE/AL		149	598	560	153	24	8	8	217	27	1	2	50	21	3	6	32	12	68	80	.273	.306	.387
84	CLE/AL		160	718	658	188	22	5	3	229	43	1	6	68	23	1	10	19	10	82	79	.286	.331	.348
85	CLE/AL		160	703	636	183	33	4	6	242	54	2	4	74	26	0	9	13	9	97	90	.288	.343	.381
86	CLE/AL		149	636	599	183	30	5	10	253	32	1	0	66	28	0	5	10	7	80	74	.306	.338	.422
87	CLE/AL		128	560	495	158	24	3	8	212	57	2	2	56	23	0	5	32	9	86	52	.319	.389	.428
88	CLE/AL		152	676	613	186	23	6	10	251	56	4	2	72	17	1	4	25	11	88	54	.303	.361	.409
89	TEX/AL		150	621	548	173	31	5	13	253	66	11	1	69	27	0	6	21	3	80	92	.316	.386	.462
90	TEX/AL		157	670	582	172	27	1	11	234	82	3	2	83	12	2	2	31	10	96	69	.296	.383	.402
91	TEX/AL		146	659	589	201	27	3	15	279	65	8	3	78	13	0	2	36	9	108	78	*.341	.408	.474
92	TEX/AL		35	123	107	25	7	0	2	38	15	2	0	17	3	1	0	1	1	19	8	.234	.328	.355
93	TEX/AL		144	607	532	154	31	3	14	233	62	4	1	95	16	5	7	9	3	85	84	.289	.360	.438
12 YR TOTALS			**1546**	**6603**	**5948**	**1784**	**280**	**43**	**100**	**2450**	**561**	**40**	**24**	**732**	**210**	**14**	**56**	**229**	**86**	**892**	**763**	**.300**	**.360**	**.412**

Frazier, Arthur Louis "Lou" — BB/TR — b.1/26/66 — POS OF-60, 1B-8, 2B-1   HOU86 S1/5

YR	TM/LG	CL	G	TPA	AB	H	2B	3B	HR	TB	BB	IBB	HB	SO	GDP	SH	SF	SB	CS	R	RBI	BA	OBA	SA
86	AST/GCL	R	51	215	178	51	7	2	1	65	32	0	1	25	3	3	1	17	8	39	23	.287	.396	.365
87	ASH/SAL	A	108	476	399	103	9	2	1	119	68	1	2	89	3	4	3	75	24	83	33	.258	.367	.298
88	OSC/FSL	A+	130	568	468	110	11	3	0	127	90	5	4	104	9	5	1	87	16	79	34	.235	.362	.271
89	CMB/SOU	AA	135	541	460	106	10	1	4	130	76	2	2	101	7	2	2	43	14	65	31	.230	.340	.283
90	LON/EAS	AA	81	271	242	53	4	1	0	59	27	0	0	52	5	1	1	20	3	29	15	.219	.296	.244
91	LON/EAS	AA	122	521	439	105	9	4	3	131	77	6	1	87	8	3	1	42	17	69	40	.239	.353	.298
92	LON/EAS	AA	129	576	477	120	16	3	0	142	95	1	0	107	3	2	2	58	23	85	34	.252	.375	.298
93	MON/NL		112	211	189	54	7	1	1	66	16	0	0	24	3	5	1	17	2	27	16	.286	.340	.349

Fryman, David Travis "Travis" — BR/TR — b.3/25/69 — POS SS-306, 3B-228, DH-2   DET87 3/30

YR	TM/LG	CL	G	TPA	AB	H	2B	3B	HR	TB	BB	IBB	HB	SO	GDP	SH	SF	SB	CS	R	RBI	BA	OBA	SA
87	BRI/APP	R+	67	273	248	58	12	0	1	73	22	0	1	40	12	0	2	5	2	25	20	.234	.297	.294
88	FAY/SAL	A	123	458	411	96	17	4	0	121	24	0	10	83	6	8	5	18	5	44	47	.234	.289	.294
89	LON/EAS	AA	118	459	426	113	30	1	9	172	19	0	8	78	5	2	4	5	3	52	56	.265	.306	.404
90	TOL/INT	AAA	87	351	327	84	22	2	10	140	17	0	2	59	9	2	3	4	7	38	53	.257	.295	.428
	DET/AL		66	251	232	69	11	1	9	109	17	3	1	51	3	1	0	3	3	32	27	.297	.348	.470
91	DET/AL		149	612	557	144	36	3	21	249	40	1	6	149	12	1	6	12	5	65	91	.259	.309	.447
92	DET/AL		161	721	659	175	31	4	20	274	45	1	6	144	13	5	6	4	9	87	96	.266	.316	.416
93	DET/AL		151	695	607	182	37	5	22	295	77	1	4	128	8	1	6	9	4	98	97	.300	.379	.486
4 YR TOTALS			**527**	**2279**	**2055**	**570**	**115**	**13**	**72**	**927**	**179**	**2**	**14**	**472**	**37**	**13**	**18**	**32**	**16**	**282**	**311**	**.277**	**.337**	**.451**

Gaetti, Gary Joseph — BR/TR — b.8/19/58 — POS 3B-1609, 1B-73, DH-37, SS-13, OF-13, 2B-1   MIN79 S1/11

YR	TM/LG	CL	G	TPA	AB	H	2B	3B	HR	TB	BB	IBB	HB	SO	GDP	SH	SF	SB	CS	R	RBI	BA	OBA	SA
81	MIN/AL		9	26	26	5	0	0	2	11	0	0	0	6	0	0	0	0	0	4	3	.192	.192	.423
82	MIN/AL		145	565	508	117	25	4	25	225	37	2	3	107	16	4	13	0	4	59	84	.230	.280	.443
83	MIN/AL		157	650	584	143	30	3	21	242	54	2	4	121	18	0	8	7	1	81	78	.245	.309	.414
84	MIN/AL		162	644	588	154	29	4	5	206	44	1	4	81	9	3	5	11	5	55	65	.262	.315	.350
85	MIN/AL		160	608	560	138	31	0	20	229	37	3	7	89	15	3	1	13	5	71	63	.246	.301	.409

(continued)

Gaetti, Gary Joseph (continued)

YR	TM/LG	CL	G	TPA	AB	H	2B	3B	HR	TB	BB	IBB	HB	SO	GDP	SH	SF	SB	CS	R	RBI	BA	OBA	SA
86	MIN/AL		157	661	596	171	34	1	34	309	52	4	6	108	18	1	6	14	15	91	108	.287	.347	.518
87	MIN/AL		154	628	584	150	36	2	31	283	37	7	3	92	25	1	3	10	7	95	109	.257	.303	.485
88	MIN/AL		133	516	468	141	29	2	28	258	36	5	5	85	10	1	6	7	4	66	88	.301	.353	.551
89	MIN/AL		130	536	498	125	11	4	19	201	25	5	3	87	12	1	9	6	2	63	75	.251	.286	.404
90	MIN/AL		154	625	577	132	27	5	16	217	36	1	3	101	22	1	8	6	1	61	85	.229	.274	.376
91	CAL/AL		152	634	586	144	22	1	18	222	33	3	8	104	13	2	5	5	5	58	66	.246	.293	.379
92	CAL/AL		130	486	456	103	13	2	12	156	21	4	6	79	9	0	3	3	1	41	48	.226	.267	.342
93	CAL/AL		20	56	50	9	2	0	0	11	5	0	0	12	3	1	1	0	0	3	4	.180	.250	.220
	KC/AL		82	313	281	72	18	1	14	134	16	0	8	75	2	2	6	0	3	37	46	.256	.309	.477
	YEAR		102	369	331	81	20	1	14	145	21	0	8	87	5	2	7	1	3	40	50	.245	.300	.438
13 YR TOTALS			1745	6948	6362	1604	307	29	245	2704	433	37	60	1147	173	19	74	83	53	785	922	.252	.303	.425

Gagne, Gregory Carpenter "Greg" — BR/TR — b.11/12/61 — POS SS-1271, DH-9, OF-8, 2B-6, 3B-1   NYA79 5/129

YR	TM/LG	CL	G	TPA	AB	H	2B	3B	HR	TB	BB	IBB	HB	SO	GDP	SH	SF	SB	CS	R	RBI	BA	OBA	SA
83	MIN/AL		10	29	27	3	1	0	0	4	0	0	0	6	0	0	0	2	0	2	3	.111	.103	.148
84	TOL/INT	AAA	70	274	236	66	7	2	9	104	34	2	1	52	6	2	1	2	3	31	27	.280	.371	.441
	MIN/AL		2	1	1	0	0	0	0	0	0	0	0	0	0	0	0	0	0	0	0	.000	.000	.000
85	MIN/AL		114	322	293	66	15	3	2	93	20	0	3	57	5	3	3	10	4	37	23	.225	.279	.317
86	MIN/AL		156	524	472	118	22	6	12	188	30	0	6	108	4	13	3	12	10	63	54	.250	.301	.398
87	MIN/AL		137	478	437	116	28	7	10	188	25	0	4	84	3	10	2	6	6	68	40	.265	.310	.430
88	MIN/AL		149	507	461	109	20	6	14	183	27	2	7	110	13	11	1	15	7	70	48	.236	.288	.397
89	MIN/AL		149	491	460	125	29	7	9	195	17	0	2	80	10	7	5	11	4	69	48	.272	.298	.424
90	MIN/AL		138	423	388	91	22	3	7	140	24	0	1	76	5	8	2	8	8	38	38	.235	.280	.361
91	MIN/AL		139	447	408	108	23	3	8	161	26	0	3	127	15	5	5	11	9	52	42	.265	.310	.395
92	MIN/AL		146	473	439	108	23	0	7	152	19	0	2	83	11	12	1	6	7	53	39	.246	.280	.346
93	KC/AL		159	581	540	151	32	3	10	219	33	1	0	93	7	4	4	10	12	66	57	.280	.319	.406
11 YR TOTALS			1299	4276	3926	995	215	38	79	1523	221	3	28	769	73	73	28	89	67	518	392	.253	.296	.388

Gainer, Johnathan Keith "Jay" — BL/TL — b.10/8/66 — POS 1B-7   SD90 24/655

YR	TM/LG	CL	G	TPA	AB	H	2B	3B	HR	TB	BB	IBB	HB	SO	GDP	SH	SF	SB	CS	R	RBI	BA	OBA	SA
90	SPO/NWL	A-	74	322	281	100	21	0	10	151	31	3	5	49	4	1	4	4	4	41	54	.356	.424	.537
91	HD/CAL	A+	127	570	499	131	17	0	32	244	52	3	0	105	8	0	16	4	3	83	120	.263	.326	.489
92	WIC/TEX	AA	105	429	376	98	12	1	23	181	46	6	0	101	6	1	6	4	2	57	67	.261	.336	.481
93	CS/PCL	AAA	86	321	293	86	11	3	10	133	22	2	1	70	6	1	4	4	2	51	74	.294	.341	.454
	COL/NL		23	45	41	7	0	0	3	16	4	0	0	12	0	0	0	1	1	4	6	.171	.244	.390

Galarraga, Andres Jose — BR/TR — b.6/18/61 — POS 1B-1042   MON 1/19/79

YR	TM/LG	CL	G	TPA	AB	H	2B	3B	HR	TB	BB	IBB	HB	SO	GDP	SH	SF	SB	CS	R	RBI	BA	OBA	SA
84	JAC/SOU	AA	143	606	533	154	28	4	27	271	59	10	9	122	10	1	4	2	8	81	87	.289	.367	.508
85	IND/AMA	AAA	121	494	439	118	15	8	25	224	45	4	7	103	12	0	3	3	0	75	87	.269	.344	.510
	MON/NL		24	79	75	14	1	0	2	21	3	0	1	18	0	0	0	1	2	9	4	.187	.228	.280
86	MON/NL		105	356	321	87	13	0	10	130	30	5	3	79	8	1	1	6	5	39	42	.271	.338	.405
87	MON/NL		147	606	551	168	40	3	13	253	41	13	10	127	11	0	4	7	10	72	90	.305	.361	.459
88	MON/NL		157	661	609	*184	*42	8	29	*329	39	9	10	153	12	0	3	13	4	99	92	.302	.352	.540
89	MON/NL		152	636	572	147	30	1	23	248	48	10	13	158	12	0	3	12	5	76	85	.257	.327	.434
90	MON/NL		155	628	579	148	29	0	20	237	40	8	4	169	14	0	5	10	1	65	87	.256	.306	.409
91	MON/NL		107	400	375	82	13	2	9	126	23	5	2	86	6	0	0	5	6	34	33	.219	.268	.336
92	LOU/AMA	AAA	11	35	34	6	0	1	2	14	0	0	0	1	0	0	0	0	0	3	3	.176	.200	.412
	STL/NL		95	347	325	79	14	2	10	127	11	0	8	69	8	0	3	5	4	38	39	.243	.282	.391
93	COL/NL		120	506	470	174	35	4	22	283	24	12	6	73	9	0	0	6	2	71	98	*.370	.403	.602
9 YR TOTALS			1062	4219	3877	1083	217	20	138	1754	259	62	57	932	80	1	25	61	41	503	570	.279	.332	.452

Gallagher, David Thomas "Dave" — BR/TR — b.9/20/60 — POS OF-561, DH-11, 1B-9   CLE80 S1/8

YR	TM/LG	CL	G	TPA	AB	H	2B	3B	HR	TB	BB	IBB	HB	SO	GDP	SH	SF	SB	CS	R	RBI	BA	OBA	SA
84	MAI/INT	AAA	116	451	380	94	19	5	6	141	49	0	3	42	9	10	9	4	1	49	49	.247	.331	.371
85	MAI/INT	AAA	132	575	488	118	22	3	9	173	65	0	3	38	12	11	8	16	8	71	55	.242	.330	.355
86	MAI/INT	AAA	132	553	497	145	23	5	8	202	41	1	1	41	7	12	2	19	12	59	44	.292	.346	.406
87	CLE/AL		15	39	36	4	1	1	0	7	2	0	0	5	1	1	0	2	0	2	1	.111	.158	.194
	BUF/AMA	AAA	12	60	46	12	4	0	0	16	11	0	0	3	2	1	2	1	0	10	6	.261	.390	.348
	CAL/PCL	AAA	75	316	268	82	27	2	3	122	37	1	0	36	10	8	3	12	4	45	46	.306	.386	.455
88	VAN/PCL	AAA	34	147	131	44	8	1	4	66	12	0	1	21	1	4	1	5	4	23	27	.336	.390	.504
	CHI/AL		101	384	347	105	15	3	5	141	29	3	0	40	8	6	2	5	4	59	31	.303	.354	.406
89	CHI/AL		161	667	601	160	22	2	1	189	46	1	2	79	9	16	2	5	6	74	46	.266	.320	.314
90	CHI/AL		45	84	75	21	3	1	0	26	3	0	1	9	3	5	0	1	0	5	5	.280	.316	.347
	BAL/AL		23	58	51	11	1	0	0	12	4	0	0	3	0	2	1	1	2	7	2	.216	.268	.235
	YEAR		68	142	126	32	4	1	0	38	7	0	1	12	3	7	1	2	2	12	7	.254	.296	.302
91	CAL/AL		90	306	270	79	17	0	1	99	24	0	6	43	6	10	0	2	2	32	30	.293	.355	.367
92	TID/INT	AAA	3	15	12	3	0	0	0	3	3	0	0	0	0	0	0	0	1	1	0	.250	.400	.250
	NY/NL		98	205	175	42	11	1	1	58	19	0	1	16	7	3	7	4	5	20	21	.240	.307	.331
93	NY/NL		99	229	201	55	12	2	6	89	20	1	0	18	7	1	1	1	1	34	28	.274	.338	.443
7 YR TOTALS			632	1972	1756	477	82	10	14	621	147	5	6	213	41	50	13	20	22	233	164	.272	.328	.354

Gallego, Michael Anthony "Mike" — BR/TR — b.10/31/60 — POS 2B-526, SS-337, 3B-111, DH-2, OF-1   OAK81 2/33

YR	TM/LG	CL	G	TPA	AB	H	2B	3B	HR	TB	BB	IBB	HB	SO	GDP	SH	SF	SB	CS	R	RBI	BA	OBA	SA
84	TAC/PCL	AAA	101	324	288	70	8	1	0	80	27	0	0	39	7	7	2	7	5	29	18	.243	.306	.278
85	MOD/CAL	A+	6	27	25	5	1	0	0	6	2	0	0	8	1	0	0	1	1	1	2	.200	.259	.240
	OAK/AL		76	93	77	16	5	1	1	26	12	0	0	14	2	2	1	1	1	13	9	.208	.319	.338

Gallego, Michael Anthony "Mike" (continued)

YR	TM/LG	CL	G	TPA	AB	H	2B	3B	HR	TB	BB	IBB	HB	SO	GDP	SH	SF	SB	CS	R	RBI	BA	OBA	SA
86	TAC/PCL	AAA	132	505	443	122	16	5	4	160	39	0	8	58	9	8	7	3	3	58	46	.275	.340	.361
	OAK/AL		20	40	37	10	2	0	0	12	1	0	0	6	0	2	0	0	2	2	4	.270	.289	.324
87	TAC/PCL	AAA	10	51	41	11	0	2	0	15	10	0	0	7	1	0	0	1	1	6	6	.268	.412	.366
	OAK/AL		72	143	124	31	6	0	2	43	12	0	1	21	5	5	1	0	1	18	14	.250	.319	.347
88	OAK/AL		129	320	277	58	8	0	2	72	34	0	1	53	6	8	0	2	3	38	20	.209	.298	.260
89	OAK/AL		133	409	357	90	14	2	3	117	35	0	4	43	10	8	3	7	5	45	30	.252	.327	.328
90	OAK/AL		140	447	389	80	13	2	3	106	35	0	4	50	13	17	2	5	5	36	34	.206	.277	.272
91	OAK/AL		159	567	482	119	15	4	12	178	67	3	5	84	8	10	3	6	9	67	49	.247	.343	.369
92	FL/FSL	A+	3	11	10	2	1	0	0	3	1	0	0	4	0	0	0	1	0	0	2	.200	.273	.300
	NY/AL		53	201	173	44	7	1	3	62	20	0	4	22	5	3	1	0	1	24	14	.254	.343	.358
93	NY/AL		119	465	403	114	20	1	10	166	50	0	4	65	16	3	5	3	2	63	54	.283	.364	.412
9 YR TOTALS			**901**	**2685**	**2319**	**562**	**90**	**11**	**36**	**782**	**266**	**3**	**26**	**358**	**65**	**58**	**16**	**24**	**29**	**306**	**228**	**.242**	**.325**	**.337**

Gant, Ronald Edwin "Ron" — BR/TR — b.3/2/65 — POS OF-610, 2B-142, 3B-75   ATL83 4/100

YR	TM/LG	CL	G	TPA	AB	H	2B	3B	HR	TB	BB	IBB	HB	SO	GDP	SH	SF	SB	CS	R	RBI	BA	OBA	SA
84	AND/SAL	A	105	395	359	85	14	6	3	120	29	0	1	65	6	0	6	13	5	44	38	.237	.291	.334
85	SUM/SAL	A	102	341	305	78	14	4	7	121	33	2	2	59	8	1	0	19	10	46	37	.256	.332	.397
86	DUR/CAR	A+	137	601	512	142	31	10	26	271	78	0	3	85	12	2	6	35	9	108	102	.277	.372	.529
87	GRE/SOU	AA	140	598	527	130	27	3	14	205	59	0	2	92	8	3	7	24	4	78	82	.247	.321	.389
	ATL/NL		21	86	83	22	4	0	2	32	1	0	0	11	3	1	1	4	2	9	9	.265	.271	.386
88	RIC/INT	AAA	12	48	45	14	2	2	0	20	2	0	0	10	0	0	1	1	1	3	4	.311	.333	.444
	ATL/NL		146	618	563	146	28	8	19	247	46	4	3	118	7	2	4	19	10	85	60	.259	.317	.439
89	SUM/SAL	A	12	50	39	15	4	1	1	24	11	2	0	3	0	0	0	4	2	13	5	.385	.520	.615
	RIC/INT	AAA	63	255	225	59	13	2	11	109	29	1	0	42	6	0	1	7	2	42	27	.262	.345	.484
	ATL/NL		75	285	260	46	8	3	9	87	20	0	1	63	0	2	2	9	6	26	25	.177	.237	.335
90	ATL/NL		152	631	575	174	34	3	32	310	50	0	1	86	8	1	4	33	16	107	84	.303	.357	.539
91	ATL/NL		154	642	561	141	35	3	32	278	71	8	5	104	6	0	5	34	15	101	105	.251	.338	.496
92	ATL/NL		153	602	544	141	22	6	17	226	45	5	7	101	10	0	6	32	10	74	80	.259	.321	.415
93	ATL/NL		157	682	606	166	27	4	36	309	67	2	2	117	14	0	7	26	9	113	117	.274	.345	.510
7 YR TOTALS			**858**	**3546**	**3192**	**836**	**158**	**27**	**147**	**1489**	**300**	**19**	**19**	**600**	**48**	**6**	**29**	**157**	**68**	**515**	**480**	**.262**	**.326**	**.466**

Garcia, Carlos Jesus — BR/TR — b.10/15/67 — POS 2B-155, SS-23, 3B-2   PIT 1/9/87

YR	TM/LG	CL	G	TPA	AB	H	2B	3B	HR	TB	BB	IBB	HB	SO	GDP	SH	SF	SB	CS	R	RBI	BA	OBA	SA
87	MAC/SAL	A	110	406	373	95	14	3	3	124	23	2	6	80	6	2	2	20	10	44	38	.255	.307	.332
88	AUG/SAL	A	73	295	269	78	13	2	1	98	22	0	1	46	5	2	1	11	6	32	45	.290	.345	.364
	SAL/CAR	A+	62	250	236	65	9	3	1	83	10	0	1	32	9	0	3	8	2	21	28	.275	.304	.352
89	SAL/CAR	A+	81	332	304	86	12	4	7	127	18	0	1	51	3	1	5	19	6	45	49	.283	.326	.418
	HAR/EAS	AA	54	197	188	53	5	5	3	77	8	0	0	36	4	0	1	6	4	28	25	.282	.310	.410
90	HAR/EAS	AA	65	263	242	67	11	2	5	97	16	0	3	36	6	1	1	12	1	36	25	.277	.328	.401
	BUF/AMA	AAA	63	218	197	52	10	0	5	77	16	0	2	41	5	1	2	7	4	23	18	.264	.323	.391
	PIT/NL		4	4	4	2	0	0	0	2	0	0	0	2	0	0	0	0	0	1	0	.500	.500	.500
91	BUF/AMA	AAA	127	512	463	123	21	6	6	177	33	5	7	78	6	6	3	30	7	62	60	.266	.322	.382
	PIT/NL		12	25	24	6	0	2	0	10	1	0	0	6	0	1	0	0	0	2	1	.250	.280	.417
92	BUF/AMA	AAA	113	463	426	129	28	9	13	214	24	2	4	64	7	1	4	21	7	73	70	.303	.342	.502
	PIT/NL		22	42	39	8	1	0	0	9	0	0	0	9	1	2	0	0	0	4	4	.205	.195	.231
93	PIT/NL		141	597	546	147	25	5	12	218	31	2	9	67	9	6	5	18	11	77	47	.269	.316	.399
4 YR TOTALS			**179**	**668**	**613**	**163**	**26**	**7**	**12**	**239**	**32**	**2**	**9**	**86**	**11**	**7**	**7**	**18**	**11**	**84**	**52**	**.266**	**.309**	**.390**

Gardner, Jeffrey Scott "Jeff" — BL/TR — b.2/4/64 — POS 2B-147, SS-9, 3B-1   NYN 8/28/84

YR	TM/LG	CL	G	TPA	AB	H	2B	3B	HR	TB	BB	IBB	HB	SO	GDP	SH	SF	SB	CS	R	RBI	BA	OBA	SA
85	COL/SAL	A	123	559	401	118	9	1	0	129	142	1	5	40	9	10	1	31	5	80	50	.294	.483	.322
86	LYN/CAR	A+	111	430	334	91	11	2	1	109	81	3	4	33	10	8	3	6	4	59	39	.272	.417	.326
87	JAC/TEX	AA	119	467	399	109	10	3	0	125	58	1	3	55	7	5	2	1	5	55	30	.273	.368	.313
88	JAC/TEX	AA	134	517	432	109	15	2	0	128	69	7	1	52	6	14	1	13	8	46	33	.252	.356	.296
	TID/INT	AAA	2	9	8	3	1	1	0	6	1	0	0	1	0	0	0	0	0	3	2	.375	.444	.750
89	TID/INT	AAA	101	301	269	75	11	0	0	86	25	1	0	27	7	4	3	0	0	28	24	.279	.337	.320
90	TID/INT	AAA	138	553	463	125	11	1	0	138	84	3	1	33	12	4	1	3	5	55	33	.270	.383	.298
91	TID/INT	AAA	136	603	504	147	23	4	1	181	84	4	3	48	8	7	5	6	5	73	56	.292	.393	.359
	NY/NL		13	42	37	6	0	0	0	6	4	0	0	6	0	0	1	0	0	3	1	.162	.238	.162
92	LV/PCL	AAA	120	517	439	147	30	4	2	190	67	6	2	48	7	7	2	7	2	82	51	.335	.424	.433
	SD/NL		15	20	19	2	0	0	0	2	1	0	0	8	0	0	0	0	0	1	0	.105	.150	.105
93	SD/NL		140	452	404	106	21	7	1	144	45	0	1	69	11	3	1	2	6	53	24	.262	.337	.356
3 YR TOTALS			**168**	**514**	**460**	**114**	**21**	**7**	**1**	**152**	**50**	**0**	**1**	**83**	**11**	**3**	**2**	**2**	**6**	**56**	**25**	**.248**	**.322**	**.330**

Gates, Brent Robert — BB/TR — b.3/14/70 — POS 2B-139   OAK91 1/26

YR	TM/LG	CL	G	TPA	AB	H	2B	3B	HR	TB	BB	IBB	HB	SO	GDP	SH	SF	SB	CS	R	RBI	BA	OBA	SA
91	SO/NWL	A-	58	258	219	63	11	0	3	83	30	2	2	33	5	5	2	8	2	41	26	.288	.375	.379
	MAD/MID	A	4	15	12	4	2	0	0	6	3	0	0	4	0	0	0	0	0	4	1	.333	.467	.500
92	MOD/CAL	A+	133	603	505	162	39	2	10	235	85	9	2	60	9	2	9	9	7	94	88	.321	.414	.465
93	HUN/SOU	AA	12	53	45	15	4	0	1	22	7	0	0	9	3	1	0	0	0	7	11	.333	.423	.489
	TAC/PCL	AAA	12	49	44	15	7	0	1	25	4	1	1	6	0	0	0	2	0	7	4	.341	.408	.568
	OAK/AL		139	609	535	155	29	2	7	209	56	4	4	75	17	6	8	7	3	64	69	.290	.357	.391

Geren, Robert Peter "Bob" — BR/TR — b.9/22/61 — POS C-289, DH-3, 1B-1, 3B-1   SD79 2/24

YR	TM/LG	CL	G	TPA	AB	H	2B	3B	HR	TB	BB	IBB	HB	SO	GDP	SH	SF	SB	CS	R	RBI	BA	OBA	SA
84	ARK/TEX	AA	86	331	292	72	12	0	15	129	34	1	1	69	10	3	1	1	0	39	40	.247	.326	.442
	LOU/AMA	AAA	15	45	40	7	1	0	0	8	5	0	0	8	1	0	0	0	0	3	3	.175	.267	.200

(continued)

Geren, Robert Peter "Bob" (continued)

YR	TM/LG	CL	G	TPA	AB	H	2B	3B	HR	TB	BB	IBB	HB	SO	GDP	SH	SF	SB	CS	R	RBI	BA	OBA	SA
85	LOU/AMA	AAA	5	14	14	5	2	0	1	10	0	0	0	1	0	0	0	0	0	2	3	.357	.357	.714
	ARK/TEX	AA	103	359	315	71	18	1	5	106	31	2	1	74	10	7	5	3	1	38	40	.225	.293	.337
86	ALB/EAS	AA	11	33	27	4	1	0	0	5	6	0	0	12	0	0	0	1	0	3	0	.148	.303	.185
	CMB/INT	AAA	68	229	205	52	15	3	7	94	21	0	2	60	8	1	0	1	2	24	25	.254	.329	.459
87	CMB/INT	AAA	5	21	20	3	0	0	1	6	0	0	0	9	0	1	0	0	0	1	3	.150	.150	.300
	ALB/EAS	AA	78	245	213	47	7	2	11	91	21	2	2	42	6	4	5	1	1	33	31	.221	.290	.427
88	CMB/INT	AAA	95	363	321	87	13	2	8	128	33	0	1	69	10	4	4	0	0	37	35	.271	.337	.399
	NY/AL		10	12	10	1	0	0	0	1	2	0	0	3	0	0	0	0	0	0	0	.100	.250	.100
89	CMB/INT	AAA	27	104	95	24	4	1	2	36	5	0	1	25	2	2	1	1	0	11	13	.253	.294	.379
	NY/AL		65	225	205	59	5	1	9	93	12	0	1	44	10	6	1	0	0	26	27	.288	.329	.454
90	NY/AL		110	303	277	59	7	0	8	90	13	1	5	73	7	6	2	0	0	21	31	.213	.259	.325
91	NY/AL		64	140	128	28	3	0	2	37	9	0	1	31	5	3	0	0	1	7	12	.219	.270	.289
92	WH/FSL	A+	7	24	23	7	0	0	1	10	1	1	0	5	0	0	0	0	0	3	2	.304	.333	.435
	PAW/INT	AAA	66	230	213	44	7	0	9	78	17	3	0	53	5	0	0	0	2	28	25	.207	.265	.366
93	SD/NL		58	162	145	31	6	0	3	46	13	4	0	28	4	4	0	0	0	8	6	.214	.278	.317
5 YR TOTALS			307	842	765	178	21	1	22	267	49	5	6	179	26	19	3	0	1	62	76	.233	.283	.349

Gibson, Kirk Harold — BL/TL — b.5/28/57 — POS OF-1200, DH-208   DET78 1/12

YR	TM/LG	CL	G	TPA	AB	H	2B	3B	HR	TB	BB	IBB	HB	SO	GDP	SH	SF	SB	CS	R	RBI	BA	OBA	SA
79	DET/AL		12	39	38	9	3	0	1	15	1	0	0	3	0	0	0	3	3	3	4	.237	.256	.395
80	DET/AL		51	189	175	46	2	1	9	77	10	0	1	45	0	1	2	4	7	23	16	.263	.303	.440
81	DET/AL		83	313	290	95	11	3	9	139	18	1	2	64	9	1	2	17	5	41	40	.328	.369	.479
82	DET/AL		69	294	266	74	16	2	8	118	25	2	1	41	2	1	1	9	7	34	35	.278	.341	.444
83	DET/AL		128	467	401	91	12	9	15	166	53	3	4	96	2	5	4	14	3	60	51	.227	.320	.414
84	DET/AL		149	611	531	150	23	10	27	274	63	6	8	103	4	3	6	29	9	92	91	.282	.363	.516
85	DET/AL		154	670	581	167	37	5	29	301	71	16	5	137	5	3	10	30	4	96	97	.287	.364	.518
86	DET/AL		119	521	441	118	11	2	28	217	68	4	7	107	8	1	4	34	6	84	86	.268	.371	.492
87	TOL/INT	AAA	6	21	17	4	0	0	0	4	4	0	0	3	0	0	0	1	0	2	3	.235	.381	.235
	DET/AL		128	568	487	135	25	3	24	238	71	8	5	117	5	1	4	26	7	95	79	.277	.372	.489
88	LA/NL		150	632	542	157	28	1	25	262	73	14	3	120	8	3	7	31	4	106	76	.290	.377	.483
89	LA/NL		71	292	253	54	8	2	9	93	35	5	2	55	5	0	2	12	3	35	28	.213	.312	.368
90	ALB/PCL	AAA	5	18	14	6	2	0	1	11	4	2	0	3	1	0	0	1	0	6	4	.429	.556	.786
	LA/NL		89	359	315	82	20	0	8	126	39	0	3	65	4	0	2	26	2	59	38	.260	.345	.400
91	KC/AL		132	540	462	109	17	6	16	186	69	3	6	103	9	1	2	18	4	81	55	.236	.341	.403
92	PIT/NL		16	60	56	11	0	0	2	17	3	0	1	12	1	1	0	3	1	6	5	.196	.237	.304
93	DET/AL		116	454	403	105	18	6	13	174	44	4	4	87	2	0	3	15	6	62	62	.261	.337	.432
15 YR TOTALS			1467	6009	5241	1403	231	50	223	2403	643	66	55	1155	64	21	49	271	71	877	763	.268	.351	.459

Gil, Romar Benjamin "Benji" — BR/TR — b.10/6/72 — POS SS-22   TEX91 1/19

YR	TM/LG	CL	G	TPA	AB	H	2B	3B	HR	TB	BB	IBB	HB	SO	GDP	SH	SF	SB	CS	R	RBI	BA	OBA	SA
91	BUT/PIO	R+	32	144	129	37	4	3	2	53	14	1	0	36	0	0	1	9	3	25	15	.287	.354	.411
92	GAS/SAL	A	132	542	482	132	21	1	9	182	50	0	3	106	16	3	4	26	13	75	55	.274	.343	.378
93	TEX/AL		22	66	57	7	0	0	0	7	5	0	0	22	0	4	0	1	2	3	2	.123	.194	.123
	TUL/TEX	AA	101	387	342	94	9	1	17	156	35	2	7	89	9	0	3	20	12	45	59	.275	.351	.456

Gilkey, Otis Bernard "Bernard" — BR/TR — b.9/24/66 — POS OF-337, 1B-3   SL 8/22/84

YR	TM/LG	CL	G	TPA	AB	H	2B	3B	HR	TB	BB	IBB	HB	SO	GDP	SH	SF	SB	CS	R	RBI	BA	OBA	SA
85	ERI/NYP	A-	77	358	294	60	9	1	7	92	55	1	3	57	4	4	2	34	10	57	27	.204	.333	.313
86	SAV/SAL	A	105	466	374	88	15	4	6	129	84	1	2	57	6	3	2	32	15	64	36	.235	.376	.345
87	SPR/MID	A	46	207	162	37	5	0	0	42	39	1	2	28	3	2	2	18	5	30	9	.228	.380	.259
88	SPR/MID	A	125	564	491	120	18	7	6	170	65	1	4	53	10	2	2	56	18	84	36	.244	.336	.346
89	ARK/TEX	AA	131	585	500	139	25	3	6	188	70	2	2	54	9	8	5	53	22	104	57	.278	.366	.376
90	LOU/AMA	AAA	132	578	499	147	26	8	3	198	75	3	2	49	11	1	1	45	33	83	46	.295	.388	.397
	STL/NL		18	72	64	19	5	2	1	31	8	0	0	5	1	0	1	6	1	11	3	.297	.375	.484
91	LOU/AMA	AAA	11	47	41	6	2	0	0	8	6	0	0	10	0	0	0	1	3	5	2	.146	.255	.195
	STL/NL		81	311	268	58	7	2	5	84	39	0	1	33	14	1	2	14	8	28	20	.216	.316	.313
92	STL/NL		131	431	384	116	19	4	7	164	39	1	1	52	5	3	4	18	12	56	43	.302	.364	.427
93	STL/NL		137	622	557	170	40	5	16	268	56	2	4	66	16	0	5	15	10	99	70	.305	.370	.481
4 YR TOTALS			367	1436	1273	363	71	13	29	547	142	3	6	156	36	4	11	53	31	194	136	.285	.357	.430

Girardi, Joseph Elliott "Joe" — BR/TR — b.10/14/64 — POS C-383   CHN86 5/116

YR	TM/LG	CL	G	TPA	AB	H	2B	3B	HR	TB	BB	IBB	HB	SO	GDP	SH	SF	SB	CS	R	RBI	BA	OBA	SA
86	PEO/MID	A	68	255	230	71	13	1	3	95	17	1	3	36	8	2	3	6	3	36	28	.309	.360	.413
87	WIN/CAR	A+	99	402	364	102	9	8	8	151	33	2	2	64	11	2	1	9	2	51	46	.280	.343	.415
88	PIT/EAS	AA	104	393	357	97	14	1	7	134	29	2	2	51	10	2	7	4	7	44	41	.272	.330	.375
89	IOW/AMA	AAA	32	115	110	27	4	2	2	41	5	0	0	19	0	0	0	3	1	12	11	.245	.278	.373
	CHI/NL		59	172	157	39	10	0	1	52	11	5	2	26	4	1	1	2	2	15	14	.248	.304	.331
90	CHI/NL		133	447	419	113	24	2	1	144	17	11	3	50	13	4	4	8	3	36	38	.270	.300	.344
91	IOW/AMA	AAA	12	41	36	8	2	0	0	9	4	0	0	8	1	0	1	0	0	3	4	.222	.300	.250
	CHI/NL		21	54	47	9	2	0	0	11	6	1	0	6	1	1	0	0	0	3	6	.191	.283	.234
92	CHI/NL		91	291	270	73	3	1	1	81	19	3	1	38	8	0	1	0	2	19	12	.270	.320	.300
93	CS/PCL	AAA	8	31	31	15	1	1	1	21	0	0	0	3	0	0	0	1	0	6	6	.484	.484	.677
	COL/NL		86	350	310	90	14	5	3	123	24	0	3	41	6	12	1	6	6	35	31	.290	.346	.397
5 YR TOTALS			390	1314	1203	324	53	8	6	411	77	20	9	161	31	18	7	16	12	108	101	.269	.316	.342

Gladden, Clinton Daniel "Dan" — BR/TR — b.7/7/57 — POS OF-1137, DH-15, P-2, 2B-1, 3B-1   SF 6/17/79

YR	TM/LG	CL	G	TPA	AB	H	2B	3B	HR	TB	BB	IBB	HB	SO	GDP	SH	SF	SB	CS	R	RBI	BA	OBA	SA
83	SF/NL		18	72	63	14	2	0	1	19	5	0	0	11	3	3	1	4	3	6	9	.222	.275	.302
84	PHO/PCL	AAA	59	280	234	93	11	7	3	127	45	2	0	23	4	0	1	32	11	70	27	.397	.493	.543
	SF/NL		86	384	342	120	17	2	4	153	33	2	2	37	3	6	1	31	16	71	31	.351	.410	.447
85	SF/NL		142	561	502	122	15	8	7	174	40	1	7	78	10	10	2	32	15	64	41	.243	.307	.347
86	PHO/PCL	AAA	7	29	27	9	4	0	0	13	2	0	0	2	0	0	0	0	0	5	0	.333	.379	.481
	SF/NL		102	402	351	97	16	1	4	127	39	3	5	59	5	7	0	27	10	55	29	.276	.357	.362
87	MIN/AL		121	482	438	109	21	2	8	158	38	2	3	72	8	1	2	25	9	69	38	.249	.312	.361
88	MIN/AL		141	633	576	155	32	6	11	232	46	4	4	74	9	2	5	28	8	91	62	.269	.325	.403
89	MIN/AL		121	501	461	136	23	3	8	189	23	3	5	53	6	5	7	23	7	69	46	.295	.331	.410
90	MIN/AL		136	571	534	147	27	6	5	201	26	2	6	67	17	1	4	25	9	64	40	.275	.314	.376
91	MIN/AL		126	511	461	114	14	9	6	164	36	1	5	60	13	5	4	15	9	65	52	.247	.306	.356
92	DET/AL		113	459	417	106	20	1	7	149	30	0	2	64	10	5	5	4	2	57	42	.254	.304	.357
93	TOL/INT	AAA	7	29	28	11	1	0	1	15	0	0	0	6	1	1	0	1	0	6	7	.393	.393	.536
	DET/AL		91	386	356	95	16	2	13	154	21	0	3	50	14	4	2	8	5	52	56	.267	.312	.433
11 YR TOTALS			**1197**	**4962**	**4501**	**1215**	**203**	**40**	**74**	**1720**	**337**	**18**	**42**	**625**	**98**	**49**	**33**	**222**	**93**	**663**	**446**	**.270**	**.324**	**.382**

Goff, Jerry Leroy — BL/TR — b.4/12/64 — POS C-52, 1B-3, 3B-3   SEA86 3/63

YR	TM/LG	CL	G	TPA	AB	H	2B	3B	HR	TB	BB	IBB	HB	SO	GDP	SH	SF	SB	CS	R	RBI	BA	OBA	SA
86	BEL/NWL	A-	54	218	168	32	7	2	7	64	42	1	4	55	4	1	3	4	3	26	25	.190	.359	.381
87	WAU/MID	A	109	412	336	78	17	2	13	138	65	3	8	87	4	1	2	4	7	51	47	.232	.367	.411
88	SB/CAL	A+	65	273	215	62	11	0	13	112	53	6	3	59	0	0	2	2	3	38	43	.288	.432	.521
	VER/EAS	AA	63	222	195	41	7	1	7	71	23	1	4	58	1	0	0	2	3	27	23	.210	.306	.364
89	WIL/EAS	AA	33	134	119	22	5	0	3	36	14	2	1	42	3	0	0	1	1	9	8	.185	.276	.303
	CAL/PCL	AAA	76	282	253	59	16	0	11	108	23	1	3	62	4	1	2	1	0	40	50	.233	.302	.427
90	IND/AMA	AAA	39	167	143	41	10	2	5	70	24	3	0	33	1	0	0	3	1	23	26	.287	.389	.490
	MON/NL		52	141	119	27	1	0	3	37	21	4	0	36	0	1	0	0	0	14	7	.227	.343	.311
91	IND/AMA	AAA	57	216	191	48	10	2	9	89	22	2	3	51	5	0	0	2	0	32	37	.251	.338	.466
92	MON/NL		3	3	3	0	0	0	0	0	0	0	0	3	0	0	0	0	0	0	0	.000	.000	.000
	IND/AMA	AAA	94	352	314	75	17	1	14	136	32	3	2	97	2	1	0	3	0	37	39	.239	.311	.433
93	BUF/AMA	AAA	104	425	362	91	27	3	14	166	55	4	1	82	0	7	1	1	1	52	69	.251	.346	.459
	PIT/NL		14	46	37	11	2	0	2	19	8	1	0	9	0	1	0	0	0	5	6	.297	.422	.514
3 YR TOTALS			**69**	**190**	**159**	**38**	**3**	**0**	**5**	**56**	**29**	**5**	**0**	**48**	**0**	**2**	**0**	**0**	**0**	**19**	**13**	**.239**	**.356**	**.352**

Gomez, Chris Cory — BR/TR — b.6/16/71 — POS SS-29, 2B-17, DH-1   DET92 3/84

YR	TM/LG	CL	G	TPA	AB	H	2B	3B	HR	TB	BB	IBB	HB	SO	GDP	SH	SF	SB	CS	R	RBI	BA	OBA	SA
92	LON/EAS	AA	64	243	220	59	13	2	1	79	20	0	3	34	11	0	0	1	3	20	19	.268	.337	.359
93	TOL/INT	AAA	87	311	277	68	12	2	0	84	23	0	3	37	4	6	2	6	2	29	20	.245	.308	.303
	DET/AL		46	141	128	32	7	1	0	41	9	0	1	17	2	3	0	2	2	11	11	.250	.304	.320

Gomez, Leonardo "Leo" — BR/TR — b.3/2/66 — POS 3B-324, DH-11, 1B-3   BAL 12/13/85

YR	TM/LG	CL	G	TPA	AB	H	2B	3B	HR	TB	BB	IBB	HB	SO	GDP	SH	SF	SB	CS	R	RBI	BA	OBA	SA
86	BLU/APP	R+	27	117	88	31	7	1	7	61	25	0	1	27	1	0	3	1	0	23	28	.352	.487	.693
87	HAG/CAR	A+	131	574	466	152	38	2	19	251	95	3	2	85	8	1	10	6	2	94	110	.326	.435	.539
88	CHA/SOU	AA	24	99	89	26	5	0	1	34	10	0	0	17	2	0	0	1	2	6	10	.292	.364	.382
89	HAG/EAS	AA	134	547	448	126	23	3	18	209	89	6	5	102	8	0	5	2	2	71	78	.281	.402	.467
90	ROC/INT	AAA	131	532	430	119	26	4	26	231	89	4	6	89	11	0	7	2	2	97	97	.277	.402	.537
	BAL/AL		12	48	39	9	0	0	0	9	8	0	0	7	2	1	0	0	0	3	1	.231	.362	.231
91	ROC/INT	AAA	28	119	101	26	6	0	6	50	16	0	2	18	1	0	0	1	0	13	19	.257	.370	.495
	BAL/AL		118	445	391	91	17	2	16	160	40	4	8	82	11	5	7	1	1	40	45	.233	.302	.409
92	BAL/AL		137	552	468	124	24	0	17	199	63	4	8	78	14	5	8	2	3	62	64	.265	.356	.425
93	ROC/INT	AAA	4	18	15	3	1	0	0	4	3	0	0	4	1	0	0	0	0	3	1	.200	.333	.267
	BAL/AL		71	284	244	48	7	0	10	85	32	1	3	60	2	3	2	0	1	30	25	.197	.295	.348
4 YR TOTALS			**338**	**1329**	**1142**	**272**	**48**	**2**	**43**	**453**	**143**	**5**	**13**	**227**	**29**	**14**	**17**	**3**	**5**	**135**	**135**	**.238**	**.325**	**.397**

Gonzales, Lawrence Christopher "Larry" — BR/TR — b.3/28/67 — POS C-2   CAL88 21/559

YR	TM/LG	CL	G	TPA	AB	H	2B	3B	HR	TB	BB	IBB	HB	SO	GDP	SH	SF	SB	CS	R	RBI	BA	OBA	SA
88	PS/CAL	A+	35	124	100	20	0	0	0	20	22	0	1	25	2	1	0	0	0	11	11	.200	.350	.200
89	QC/MID	A	69	241	195	38	3	1	6	61	39	1	4	34	3	1	2	2	5	24	20	.195	.339	.313
90	QC/MID	A	99	357	309	95	16	1	8	137	36	1	8	56	9	2	2	2	1	44	75	.307	.392	.443
91	EDM/PCL	AAA	2	4	3	0	0	0	0	0	1	0	0	1	0	0	0	0	0	0	0	.000	.250	.000
	MID/TEX	AA	78	294	257	82	13	0	4	107	22	0	6	33	9	3	6	2	2	27	56	.319	.378	.416
92	EDM/PCL	AAA	80	290	241	79	10	0	3	98	38	0	4	24	10	3	3	0	1	37	47	.328	.422	.407
93	CAL/AL		2	3	2	1	0	0	0	1	1	0	0	0	0	0	0	0	0	0	1	.500	.667	.500
	VAN/PCL	AAA	81	300	264	69	9	0	2	84	26	2	2	28	9	5	3	5	1	30	27	.261	.329	.318

Gonzales, Rene Adrian — BR/TR — b.9/3/60 — POS 3B-305, 2B-174, SS-95, 1B-47, OF-2, P-1   MON82 4/123

YR	TM/LG	CL	G	TPA	AB	H	2B	3B	HR	TB	BB	IBB	HB	SO	GDP	SH	SF	SB	CS	R	RBI	BA	OBA	SA
84	IND/AMA	AAA	114	395	359	84	12	2	2	106	20	0	2	33	9	10	4	10	4	41	32	.234	.275	.295
	MON/NL		29	33	30	7	1	0	0	8	2	0	1	5	0	0	0	0	0	3	2	.233	.303	.267
85	IND/AMA	AAA	130	367	340	77	11	1	0	90	22	0	0	49	4	4	1	3	5	21	25	.226	.273	.265
86	IND/AMA	AAA	116	449	395	108	14	2	3	135	41	0	2	47	7	4	7	8	6	57	43	.273	.342	.342
	MON/NL		11	28	26	3	0	0	0	3	2	0	0	7	0	0	0	0	0	1	0	.115	.179	.115
87	ROC/INT	AAA	42	192	170	51	9	3	0	66	13	2	1	17	7	4	4	2	2	20	24	.300	.346	.388
	BAL/AL		37	65	60	16	2	1	1	23	4	0	0	11	2	2	0	1	0	14	7	.267	.302	.383
88	BAL/AL		92	260	237	51	6	0	2	63	13	0	4	32	5	7	2	2	3	13	15	.215	.263	.266
89	BAL/AL		71	185	166	36	4	0	1	43	12	0	0	30	6	6	1	6	3	16	11	.217	.268	.259
90	BAL/AL		67	121	103	22	3	1	0	30	12	0	0	14	3	6	0	1	1	13	12	.214	.296	.291

(continued)

Gonzales, Rene Adrian (continued)

YR	TM/LG	CL	G	TPA	AB	H	2B	3B	HR	TB	BB	IBB	HB	SO	GDP	SH	SF	SB	CS	R	RBI	BA	OBA	SA
91	TOR/AL		71	141	118	23	3	0	1	29	12	0	4	22	5	6	1	0	0	16	6	.195	.289	.246
92	CAL/AL		104	380	329	91	17	1	7	131	41	1	4	46	17	5	1	7	4	47	38	.277	.363	.398
93	CAL/AL		118	389	335	84	17	0	2	107	49	2	1	45	12	2	5	5	5	34	31	.251	.346	.319
9 YR TOTALS			**600**	**1602**	**1404**	**333**	**53**	**3**	**15**	**437**	**146**	**3**	**13**	**212**	**50**	**32**	**7**	**21**	**16**	**159**	**122**	**.237**	**.313**	**.311**

Gonzalez, Juan Alberto — BR/TR — b.10/20/69 — POS OF-453, DH-27   TEX 5/30/86

YR	TM/LG	CL	G	TPA	AB	H	2B	3B	HR	TB	BB	IBB	HB	SO	GDP	SH	SF	SB	CS	R	RBI	BA	OBA	SA
86	RAN/GCL	R	60	259	233	56	4	1	0	62	21	0	1	57	9	1	3	7	5	24	36	.240	.302	.266
87	GAS/SAL	A	127	549	509	135	21	2	14	202	30	2	5	92	14	1	4	9	4	69	74	.265	.310	.397
88	CHA/FSL	A+	77	308	277	71	14	3	8	115	25	3	4	64	7	0	2	5	2	25	43	.256	.325	.415
89	TUL/TEX	AA	133	547	502	147	30	7	21	254	31	3	9	98	8	1	4	1	8	73	85	.293	.342	.506
	TEX/AL		24	68	60	9	3	0	1	15	6	0	0	17	4	2	0	0	0	6	7	.150	.227	.250
90	OC/AMA	AAA	128	537	496	128	29	4	29	252	32	2	1	109	11	0	8	2	2	78	101	.258	.300	.508
	TEX/AL		25	95	90	26	1	1	4	47	2	0	2	18	2	0	1	0	1	11	12	.289	.316	.522
91	TEX/AL		142	595	545	144	34	1	27	261	42	7	5	118	10	0	3	4	4	78	102	.264	.321	.479
92	TEX/AL		155	632	584	152	24	2	*43	309	35	1	5	143	16	0	8	0	1	77	109	.260	.304	.529
93	TEX/AL		140	587	536	166	33	1	*46	339	37	7	13	99	12	0	1	4	1	105	118	.310	.368	*.632
5 YR TOTALS			**486**	**1977**	**1815**	**497**	**101**	**5**	**121**	**971**	**122**	**15**	**25**	**395**	**44**	**2**	**13**	**8**	**7**	**277**	**348**	**.274**	**.326**	**.535**

Gonzalez, Luis Emilio — BL/TR — b.9/3/67 — POS OF-393, 3B-4, 1B-2   HOU88 5/90

YR	TM/LG	CL	G	TPA	AB	H	2B	3B	HR	TB	BB	IBB	HB	SO	GDP	SH	SF	SB	CS	R	RBI	BA	OBA	SA
88	AUB/NYP	A-	39	176	157	49	10	3	5	80	12	1	1	19	1	1	5	2	0	32	27	.312	.354	.510
	ASH/SAL	A	31	129	115	29	7	1	2	44	12	0	2	17	4	0	0	2	3	13	14	.252	.333	.383
89	OSC/FSL	A+	86	333	287	82	16	7	6	130	37	5	4	49	3	1	4	2	1	46	38	.286	.370	.453
90	CMB/SOU	AA	138	568	495	131	30	6	24	245	54	9	6	100	6	1	12	27	9	86	89	.265	.337	.495
	HOU/NL		12	23	21	4	2	0	0	6	2	1	0	5	0	0	0	0	0	1	0	.190	.261	.286
91	HOU/NL		137	526	473	120	28	9	13	205	40	4	8	101	9	1	4	10	7	51	69	.254	.320	.433
92	TUC/PCL	AAA	13	51	44	19	4	2	1	30	5	2	1	7	0	0	0	1	1	11	9	.432	.490	.682
	HOU/NL		122	416	387	94	19	3	10	149	24	3	2	52	6	1	2	7	7	40	55	.243	.289	.385
93	HOU/NL		154	610	540	162	34	3	15	247	47	7	10	83	9	3	10	20	9	82	72	.300	.361	.457
4 YR TOTALS			**425**	**1575**	**1421**	**380**	**83**	**15**	**38**	**607**	**113**	**15**	**20**	**241**	**24**	**5**	**16**	**37**	**23**	**174**	**196**	**.267**	**.327**	**.427**

Goodwin, Thomas Jones "Tom" — BL/TR — b.7/27/68 — POS OF-62   LA89 2/22

YR	TM/LG	CL	G	TPA	AB	H	2B	3B	HR	TB	BB	IBB	HB	SO	GDP	SH	SF	SB	CS	R	RBI	BA	OBA	SA
89	GF/PIO	R+	63	273	240	74	12	3	2	98	28	1	2	30	3	1	2	60	8	55	33	.308	.382	.408
90	BAK/CAL	A+	32	146	134	39	6	2	0	49	11	0	0	22	0	1	0	22	4	24	13	.291	.345	.366
	SA/TEX	AA	102	478	428	119	15	4	0	142	38	2	1	72	3	8	3	60	11	76	28	.278	.336	.332
91	ALB/PCL	AAA	132	583	509	139	19	4	1	169	59	0	1	83	5	10	3	48	23	84	45	.273	.349	.332
	LA/NL		16	7	7	1	0	0	0	1	0	0	0	0	0	0	0	1	1	3	0	.143	.143	.143
92	ALB/PCL	AAA	82	366	319	96	10	4	2	120	37	2	1	47	3	6	3	27	10	48	28	.301	.372	.376
	LA/NL		57	79	73	17	1	1	0	20	6	0	0	10	0	0	0	7	3	15	3	.233	.291	.274
93	ALB/PCL	AAA	85	330	289	75	5	5	1	93	30	2	2	51	1	5	4	21	5	48	28	.260	.329	.322
	LA/NL		30	18	17	5	1	0	0	6	1	0	0	4	1	0	0	1	2	6	1	.294	.333	.353
3 YR TOTALS			**103**	**104**	**97**	**23**	**2**	**1**	**0**	**27**	**7**	**0**	**0**	**14**	**1**	**0**	**0**	**9**	**6**	**24**	**4**	**.237**	**.288**	**.278**

Gordon, Keith Bradley — BR/TR — b.1/22/69 — POS OF-2   CIN90 2/47

YR	TM/LG	CL	G	TPA	AB	H	2B	3B	HR	TB	BB	IBB	HB	SO	GDP	SH	SF	SB	CS	R	RBI	BA	OBA	SA
90	BIL/PIO	R+	49	184	154	36	5	1	1	46	24	1	3	51	2	2	1	6	4	21	14	.234	.346	.299
91	CHW/SAL	A	123	451	388	104	14	10	8	162	50	2	5	135	5	7	1	25	9	63	46	.268	.358	.418
92	CR/MID	A	114	426	375	94	19	3	12	155	43	2	1	135	5	1	4	21	10	59	63	.251	.329	.413
93	CIN/NL		3	6	6	1	0	0	0	1	0	0	0	2	0	0	0	0	0	0	0	.167	.167	.167
	CHT/SOU	AA	116	444	419	122	26	3	14	196	19	0	4	132	15	0	2	13	17	69	59	.291	.327	.468

Grace, Mark Eugene — BL/TL — b.6/28/64 — POS 1B-899   CHN85 25/624

YR	TM/LG	CL	G	TPA	AB	H	2B	3B	HR	TB	BB	IBB	HB	SO	GDP	SH	SF	SB	CS	R	RBI	BA	OBA	SA
86	PEO/MID	A	126	537	465	159	30	4	15	242	60	6	4	28	11	2	6	6	5	81	95	.342	.417	.520
87	PIT/EAS	AA	123	513	453	151	29	8	17	247	48	11	2	24	3	3	7	5	5	81	101	.333	.394	.545
88	IOW/AMA	AAA	21	83	67	17	4	0	0	21	13	1	0	4	0	0	1	0	1	11	14	.254	.361	.313
	CHI/NL		134	550	486	144	23	4	7	196	60	3	0	43	12	0	4	3	3	65	57	.296	.371	.403
89	CHI/NL		142	596	510	160	28	3	13	233	80	13	0	42	13	3	3	14	7	74	79	.314	.405	.457
90	CHI/NL		157	662	589	182	32	1	9	243	59	5	5	54	10	1	8	15	6	72	82	.309	.372	.413
91	CHI/NL		160	703	619	169	28	5	8	231	70	7	3	53	6	4	7	3	4	87	58	.273	.346	.373
92	CHI/NL		158	689	603	185	37	5	9	259	72	8	4	36	14	2	8	6	1	72	79	.307	.380	.430
93	CHI/NL		155	676	594	193	39	4	14	282	71	14	4	32	25	1	9	8	2	86	98	.325	.393	.475
6 YR TOTALS			**906**	**3876**	**3401**	**1033**	**187**	**22**	**60**	**1444**	**412**	**52**	**13**	**260**	**80**	**11**	**39**	**49**	**25**	**456**	**453**	**.304**	**.377**	**.425**

Grebeck, Craig Allen — BR/TR — b.12/29/64 — POS SS-173, 3B-105, 2B-58, OF-2, DH-1   CHA 8/13/86

YR	TM/LG	CL	G	TPA	AB	H	2B	3B	HR	TB	BB	IBB	HB	SO	GDP	SH	SF	SB	CS	R	RBI	BA	OBA	SA
87	PEN/CAR	A+	104	422	378	106	22	3	15	179	37	0	1	62	8	2	4	3	6	63	67	.280	.343	.474
88	BIR/SOU	AA	133	527	450	126	21	1	9	176	65	3	2	72	10	7	3	5	7	57	53	.280	.371	.391
89	BIR/SOU	AA	143	618	533	153	25	4	5	201	63	4	4	77	15	11	7	14	15	85	80	.287	.362	.377
90	VAN/PCL	AAA	12	47	41	8	0	0	1	11	6	0	0	7	2	0	0	0	0	8	3	.195	.298	.268
	CHI/AL		59	135	119	20	3	1	1	28	8	0	5	24	2	3	0	1	0	7	9	.168	.227	.235
91	CHI/AL		107	268	224	63	16	3	6	103	38	0	1	40	3	4	1	1	1	37	31	.281	.386	.460
92	CHI/AL		88	333	287	77	21	2	3	111	30	0	3	34	5	10	3	0	0	24	35	.268	.341	.387
93	CHI/AL		72	223	190	43	5	0	1	51	26	0	0	26	9	7	0	1	7	25	12	.226	.319	.268
4 YR TOTALS			**326**	**959**	**820**	**203**	**45**	**6**	**11**	**293**	**102**	**0**	**6**	**124**	**19**	**24**	**7**	**2**	**8**	**93**	**87**	**.248**	**.333**	**.357**

Green, Shawn David — BL/TL — b.11/10/72 — POS OF-2, DH-1 TOR91 1/16

YR	TM/LG	CL	G	TPA	AB	H	2B	3B	HR	TB	BB	IBB	HB	SO	GDP	SH	SF	SB	CS	R	RBI	BA	OBA	SA
92	DUN/FSL	A+	114	462	417	114	21	3	1	144	28	0	4	66	9	5	8	22	9	44	49	.273	.319	.345
93	KNO/SOU	AA	99	398	360	102	14	2	4	132	26	2	5	72	6	6	1	4	9	40	34	.283	.339	.367
	TOR/AL		3	6	6	0	0	0	0	0	0	0	0	1	0	0	0	0	0	0	0	.000	.000	.000

Greene, Willie Louis — BL/TR — b.9/23/71 — POS 3B-30, SS-10 PIT89 1/18

YR	TM/LG	CL	G	TPA	AB	H	2B	3B	HR	TB	BB	IBB	HB	SO	GDP	SH	SF	SB	CS	R	RBI	BA	OBA	SA
89	PIR/GCL	R	23	96	86	24	3	3	5	48	9	1	0	6	0	0	0	4	3	17	11	.279	.354	.558
	PRI/APP	R+	39	147	136	44	6	4	2	64	9	1	2	29	0	0	0	4	4	22	24	.324	.374	.471
90	AUG/SAL	A	86	361	291	75	12	4	11	128	61	3	3	58	5	1	5	7	5	59	47	.258	.386	.440
	SAL/CAR	A+	17	69	60	11	1	1	3	23	7	1	1	18	1	0	0	1	0	9	9	.183	.275	.383
	ROC/MID	A	11	41	35	14	3	0	0	17	6	0	0	7	0	0	0	2	1	4	2	.400	.488	.486
91	WPB/FSL	A+	99	379	322	70	9	3	12	121	50	2	3	93	3	1	3	10	7	46	43	.217	.325	.376
92	CR/MID	A	34	142	120	34	8	2	12	82	18	0	2	27	3	0	2	3	4	26	40	.283	.380	.683
	CHT/SOU	AA	96	404	349	97	19	2	15	165	46	3	3	90	8	1	5	9	9	47	66	.278	.362	.473
	CIN/NL		29	104	93	25	5	2	2	40	10	0	0	23	1	0	1	0	2	10	13	.269	.337	.430
93	IND/AMA	AAA	98	397	341	91	19	0	22	176	51	2	1	83	6	5	2	2	4	62	58	.267	.362	.516
	CIN/NL		15	53	50	8	1	1	2	17	2	0	0	19	1	0	1	0	0	7	5	.160	.189	.340
2 YR TOTALS			44	157	143	33	6	3	4	57	12	0	0	42	2	0	2	0	2	17	18	.231	.287	.399

Greenwell, Michael Lewis "Mike" — BL/TR — b.7/18/63 — POS OF-886, DH-51, C-1 BOS82 6/72

YR	TM/LG	CL	G	TPA	AB	H	2B	3B	HR	TB	BB	IBB	HB	SO	GDP	SH	SF	SB	CS	R	RBI	BA	OBA	SA
84	WIN/CAR	A+	130	527	454	139	23	6	16	222	56	4	15	40	10	1	1	9	5	70	84	.306	.399	.489
85	PAW/INT	AAA	117	467	418	107	21	1	13	169	38	2	6	45	6	1	4	3	4	47	52	.256	.324	.404
	BOS/AL		17	34	31	10	1	0	4	23	3	1	0	4	0	0	0	1	0	7	8	.323	.382	.742
86	PAW/INT	AAA	89	372	320	96	21	1	18	173	43	4	2	45	6	1	7	6	2	62	59	.300	.379	.541
	BOS/AL		31	40	35	11	2	0	0	13	5	0	0	7	1	0	0	0	0	4	4	.314	.400	.371
87	BOS/AL		125	456	412	135	31	6	19	235	35	1	1	40	6	0	3	5	4	71	89	.328	.386	.570
88	BOS/AL		158	693	590	192	39	8	22	313	87	18	9	38	11	1	7	16	8	86	119	.325	.416	.531
89	BOS/AL		145	641	578	178	36	0	14	256	56	15	3	44	21	0	4	13	5	87	95	.308	.370	.443
90	BOS/AL		159	682	610	181	30	6	14	265	65	12	4	43	19	0	3	8	7	71	73	.297	.367	.434
91	BOS/AL		147	598	544	163	26	6	9	228	43	6	3	35	11	0	7	15	5	76	83	.300	.350	.419
92	BOS/AL		49	202	180	42	2	0	2	50	18	1	1	19	8	0	2	2	3	16	18	.233	.307	.278
93	BOS/AL		146	603	540	170	38	6	13	259	54	12	4	46	17	2	3	5	4	77	72	.315	.379	.480
9 YR TOTALS			977	3949	3520	1082	205	32	97	1642	366	66	31	276	95	3	29	65	36	495	561	.307	.375	.466

Gregg, William Thomas "Tommy" — BL/TL — b.7/29/63 — POS OF-112, 1B-100 PIT85 7/164

YR	TM/LG	CL	G	TPA	AB	H	2B	3B	HR	TB	BB	IBB	HB	SO	GDP	SH	SF	SB	CS	R	RBI	BA	OBA	SA
85	MAC/SAL	A	72	309	259	81	14	2	1	102	49	6	1	38	6	1	0	16	7	43	18	.313	.422	.394
86	NAS/EAS	AA	126	497	421	113	13	4	1	137	66	3	3	48	12	6	1	11	8	55	29	.268	.371	.325
87	HAR/EAS	AA	133	550	461	171	22	9	10	241	84	14	1	47	9	4	3	35	10	99	82	.371	.465	.523
	PIT/NL		10	8	8	2	1	0	0	3	0	0	0	2	2	0	0	0	0	3	0	.250	.250	.375
88	PIT/NL		14	17	15	3	1	0	1	7	1	0	0	4	0	0	1	0	0	4	3	.200	.235	.467
	BUF/AMA	AAA	72	282	252	74	12	0	6	104	25	0	1	26	3	0	4	7	9	34	27	.294	.355	.413
	ATL/NL		11	31	29	10	3	0	1	16	2	1	0	6	1	0	0	0	0	1	4	.345	.387	.552
	YEAR		25	48	44	13	4	0	2	23	3	1	0	10	1	0	1	0	0	5	7	.295	.333	.523
89	ATL/NL		102	298	276	67	8	0	6	93	18	2	0	45	4	3	1	3	3	24	23	.243	.288	.337
90	ATL/NL		124	261	239	63	13	1	5	93	20	1	1	39	1	0	0	0	0	18	32	.264	.322	.389
91	RIC/INT	AAA	3	14	13	6	2	0	0	9	1	0	0	2	0	0	0	2	1	3	4	.462	.500	.692
	ATL/NL		72	120	107	20	3	0	1	26	12	1	0	24	1	0	1	0	2	17	12	.187	.275	.243
92	RIC/INT	AAA	39	145	125	36	9	2	0	49	19	1	0	27	2	0	0	3	1	17	12	.288	.386	.392
	ATL/NL		18	20	19	5	0	0	1	8	1	0	0	7	1	0	0	1	1	1	1	.263	.300	.421
93	CIN/NL		10	13	12	2	0	0	0	2	0	0	0	0	0	0	1	0	0	1	1	.167	.154	.167
	IND/AMA	AAA	71	227	198	63	12	5	7	106	26	3	1	28	3	1	1	3	5	34	30	.318	.398	.535
7 YR TOTALS			361	768	705	172	34	2	14	252	54	9	3	123	10	3	4	10	10	65	68	.244	.298	.357

Griffey, George Kenneth Jr. "Ken" — BL/TL — b.11/21/69 — POS OF-706, DH-25, 1B-1 SEA87 1/1

YR	TM/LG	CL	G	TPA	AB	H	2B	3B	HR	TB	BB	IBB	HB	SO	GDP	SH	SF	SB	CS	R	RBI	BA	OBA	SA
87	BEL/NWL	A-	54	228	182	57	9	1	14	110	44	3	0	42	2	1	1	13	6	43	40	.313	.445	.604
88	SB/CAL	A+	58	256	219	74	13	3	11	126	34	5	2	39	3	1	0	32	9	50	42	.338	.431	.575
	VER/EAS	AA	17	68	61	17	5	1	2	30	4	0	0	12	3	0	2	0	0	10	10	.279	.353	.492
89	SEA/AL		127	506	455	120	23	0	16	191	44	8	2	83	4	1	4	16	7	61	61	.264	.329	.420
90	SEA/AL		155	666	597	179	28	7	22	287	63	12	2	81	12	0	6	16	11	91	80	.300	.366	.481
91	SEA/AL		154	633	548	179	42	1	22	289	71	21	1	82	10	4	9	18	6	76	100	.327	.399	.527
92	SEA/AL		142	617	565	174	39	4	27	302	44	15	5	67	15	0	3	10	5	83	103	.308	.361	.535
93	SEA/AL		156	691	582	180	38	3	45	*359	96	25	6	91	14	0	7	17	9	113	109	.309	.408	.617
5 YR TOTALS			734	3113	2747	832	170	15	132	1428	318	81	16	404	55	5	27	77	38	424	453	.303	.375	.520

Griffin, Alfredo Claudino — BB/TR — b.10/6/57 — POS SS-1861, 2B-55, DH-11, 3B-10 CLE 8/22/73

YR	TM/LG	CL	G	TPA	AB	H	2B	3B	HR	TB	BB	IBB	HB	SO	GDP	SH	SF	SB	CS	R	RBI	BA	OBA	SA
76	CLE/AL		12	4	4	1	0	0	0	1	0	0	0	2	0	0	0	0	1	0	0	.250	.250	.250
77	CLE/AL		14	44	41	6	1	0	0	7	3	0	0	5	1	0	0	2	2	5	3	.146	.205	.171
78	CLE/AL		5	6	4	2	1	0	0	3	2	0	0	0	0	0	0	0	0	0	0	.500	.667	.750
79	TOR/AL		153	689	624	179	22	10	2	227	40	2	5	59	10	16	4	21	16	81	31	.287	.333	.364
80	TOR/AL		155	696	653	166	26	*15	2	228	24	2	4	58	7	11	5	18	23	63	41	.254	.283	.349
81	TOR/AL		101	414	388	81	19	6	0	112	17	1	0	38	6	6	3	8	12	30	21	.209	.243	.289
82	TOR/AL		162	576	539	130	20	8	1	169	22	0	3	44	5	11	4	10	8	57	48	.241	.269	.314
83	TOR/AL		162	572	528	132	22	9	4	184	27	0	3	44	5	11	3	8	11	62	47	.250	.289	.348

(continued)

Griffin, Alfredo Claudino (continued)

YR	TM/LG	CL	G	TPA	AB	H	2B	3B	HR	TB	BB	IBB	HB	SO	GDP	SH	SF	SB	CS	R	RBI	BA	OBA	SA
84	TOR/AL		140	441	419	101	8	2	4	125	4	0	1	33	5	13	4	11	3	53	30	.241	.248	.298
85	OAK/AL		162	646	614	166	18	7	2	204	20	1	0	50	6	5	7	24	9	75	64	.270	.290	.332
86	OAK/AL		162	649	594	169	23	6	4	216	35	6	2	52	5	12	6	33	16	74	51	.285	.323	.364
87	OAK/AL		144	539	494	130	23	5	3	172	28	2	4	41	9	10	3	26	13	69	60	.263	.306	.348
88	LA/NL		95	354	316	63	8	3	1	80	24	7	2	30	3	11	1	7	5	39	27	.199	.259	.253
89	LA/NL		136	547	506	125	27	2	0	156	29	2	0	57	5	11	1	10	7	49	29	.247	.287	.308
90	LA/NL		141	502	461	97	11	3	1	117	29	11	2	65	5	6	4	6	3	38	35	.210	.258	.254
91	LA/NL		109	385	350	85	6	2	0	95	22	5	1	49	5	7	5	5	4	27	27	.243	.286	.271
92	TOR/AL		63	164	150	35	7	0	0	42	9	0	0	19	3	3	2	3	1	21	10	.233	.273	.280
93	TOR/AL		46	102	95	20	3	0	0	23	3	0	0	13	3	4	0	0	0	15	3	.211	.235	.242
18 YR TOTALS			**1962**	**7330**	**6780**	**1688**	**245**	**78**	**24**	**2161**	**338**	**37**	**25**	**664**	**85**	**136**	**51**	**192**	**134**	**759**	**527**	**.249**	**.285**	**.319**

Grissom, Marquis Deon — BR/TR — b.4/17/67 — POS OF-562
MON88 4/76

YR	TM/LG	CL	G	TPA	AB	H	2B	3B	HR	TB	BB	IBB	HB	SO	GDP	SH	SF	SB	CS	R	RBI	BA	OBA	SA
88	JAM/NYP	A-	74	335	291	94	14	7	8	146	35	2	2	39	2	2	5	23	7	69	39	.323	.393	.502
89	JAC/SOU	AA	78	313	278	83	15	4	3	115	24	1	7	31	1	1	3	24	6	43	31	.299	.365	.414
	IND/AMA	AAA	49	202	187	52	10	4	2	76	14	0	0	23	2	0	1	16	4	28	21	.278	.327	.406
	MON/NL		26	87	74	19	2	0	1	24	12	0	0	21	1	1	0	1	1	16	2	.257	.360	.324
90	IND/AMA	AAA	5	22	22	4	0	0	2	10	0	0	0	5	0	0	0	1	0	3	3	.182	.182	.455
	MON/NL		98	320	288	74	14	2	3	101	27	2	0	40	3	4	1	22	2	42	29	.257	.320	.351
91	MON/NL		148	597	558	149	23	9	6	208	34	0	1	89	8	4	0	*76	17	73	39	.267	.310	.373
92	MON/NL		159	707	653	180	39	6	14	273	42	6	5	81	12	3	4	*78	13	99	66	.276	.322	.418
93	MON/NL		157	693	630	188	27	2	19	276	52	6	3	76	9	0	8	53	10	104	95	.298	.351	.438
5 YR TOTALS			**588**	**2404**	**2203**	**610**	**105**	**19**	**43**	**882**	**167**	**14**	**9**	**307**	**33**	**12**	**13**	**230**	**42**	**334**	**231**	**.277**	**.329**	**.400**

Gruber, Kelly Wayne — BR/TR — b.2/26/62 — POS 3B-846, OF-38, SS-29, 2B-29, DH-21
CLE80 1/10

YR	TM/LG	CL	G	TPA	AB	H	2B	3B	HR	TB	BB	IBB	HB	SO	GDP	SH	SF	SB	CS	R	RBI	BA	OBA	SA
84	SYR/INT	AAA	97	373	342	92	12	2	21	171	23	0	7	67	6	0	1	12	2	53	55	.269	.327	.500
	TOR/AL		15	16	16	1	0	0	1	4	0	0	0	5	1	0	0	0	0	1	2	.063	.063	.250
85	SYR/INT	AAA	121	514	473	118	16	5	21	207	28	2	7	92	17	1	5	20	8	71	69	.249	.298	.438
	TOR/AL		5	13	13	3	0	0	0	3	0	0	0	3	0	0	0	0	0	0	1	.231	.231	.231
86	TOR/AL		87	152	143	28	4	1	5	49	5	0	0	27	4	2	2	2	2	20	15	.196	.220	.343
87	TOR/AL		138	368	341	80	14	3	12	136	17	2	7	70	11	1	2	12	2	50	36	.235	.283	.399
88	TOR/AL		158	623	569	158	33	5	16	249	38	1	7	92	20	5	4	23	5	75	81	.278	.328	.438
89	TOR/AL		135	583	545	158	24	4	18	244	30	0	3	60	13	0	5	10	5	83	73	.290	.328	.448
90	TOR/AL		150	662	592	162	36	6	31	303	48	2	8	94	14	1	13	14	2	92	118	.274	.330	.512
91	TOR/AL		113	474	429	108	18	2	20	190	31	5	6	70	7	3	5	12	7	58	65	.252	.308	.443
92	TOR/AL		120	481	446	102	16	3	11	157	26	2	4	72	14	0	7	7	4	42	43	.229	.275	.352
93	PS/CAL	A+	5	10	9	2	0	0	0	2	1	0	0	2	0	0	0	0	0	0	1	.222	.300	.222
	VAN/PCL	AAA	8	26	24	11	1	0	1	15	1	0	0	2	1	0	1	0	0	4	5	.458	.462	.625
	CAL/AL		18	70	65	18	3	0	3	30	2	0	1	11	2	2	0	0	0	10	9	.277	.309	.462
10 YR TOTALS			**939**	**3442**	**3159**	**818**	**148**	**24**	**117**	**1365**	**197**	**13**	**36**	**504**	**86**	**15**	**35**	**80**	**33**	**431**	**443**	**.259**	**.307**	**.432**

Guillen, Oswaldo Jose "Ozzie" — BL/TR — b.1/20/64 — POS SS-1220, DH-1
SD 12/17/80

YR	TM/LG	CL	G	TPA	AB	H	2B	3B	HR	TB	BB	IBB	HB	SO	GDP	SH	SF	SB	CS	R	RBI	BA	OBA	SA
85	CHI/AL		150	513	491	134	21	9	1	176	12	1	1	36	5	8	1	7	4	71	33	.273	.291	.358
86	CHI/AL		159	577	547	137	19	4	2	170	12	1	1	52	14	12	5	8	4	58	47	.250	.265	.311
87	CHI/AL		149	604	560	156	22	7	2	198	22	2	1	52	10	13	8	25	8	64	51	.279	.303	.354
88	CHI/AL		156	606	566	148	16	7	0	178	25	3	2	40	14	10	3	25	13	58	39	.261	.294	.314
89	CHI/AL		155	626	597	151	20	8	1	190	15	3	0	48	8	11	3	36	17	63	54	.253	.270	.318
90	CHI/AL		160	563	516	144	21	4	1	176	26	8	1	37	6	15	5	13	17	61	58	.279	.312	.341
91	CHI/AL		154	555	524	143	20	3	3	178	11	1	0	38	7	13	7	21	15	52	49	.273	.284	.340
92	CHI/AL		12	43	40	8	4	0	0	12	1	0	0	5	1	1	1	1	0	5	7	.200	.214	.300
93	CHI/AL		134	486	457	128	23	4	4	171	10	0	0	41	6	13	6	5	4	44	50	.280	.292	.374
9 YR TOTALS			**1229**	**4573**	**4298**	**1149**	**166**	**46**	**14**	**1449**	**134**	**19**	**6**	**349**	**71**	**96**	**39**	**141**	**82**	**476**	**388**	**.267**	**.288**	**.337**

Gutierrez, Ricardo "Ricky" — BR/TR — b.5/23/70 — POS SS-117, 2B-6, OF-5, 3B-4
BAL88 2/30

YR	TM/LG	CL	G	TPA	AB	H	2B	3B	HR	TB	BB	IBB	HB	SO	GDP	SH	SF	SB	CS	R	RBI	BA	OBA	SA
88	BLU/APP	R+	62	263	208	51	8	2	2	69	44	0	5	40	4	2	4	5	3	35	19	.245	.383	.332
89	FRE/CAR	A+	127	504	456	106	16	2	3	135	39	2	3	86	12	1	5	15	10	48	41	.232	.294	.296
90	HAG/EAS	AA	20	69	64	15	0	1	0	17	3	0	0	8	2	1	1	2	0	4	6	.234	.265	.266
	FRE/CAR	A+	112	481	425	117	16	4	1	144	38	0	6	59	11	9	3	12	6	54	44	.275	.341	.339
91	HAG/EAS	AA	84	356	292	69	6	4	0	83	57	0	2	52	6	3	2	11	0	47	30	.236	.363	.284
	ROC/INT	AAA	49	185	157	48	5	3	0	59	24	1	0	27	3	3	1	4	1	23	15	.306	.396	.376
92	ROC/INT	AAA	125	492	431	109	9	3	0	124	53	2	0	77	12	3	5	14	12	54	41	.253	.331	.288
	LV/PCL		3	8	6	1	0	0	0	1	1	0	0	2	0	0	0	0	0	0	1	.167	.250	.167
93	LV/PCL	AAA	5	24	24	10	4	0	0	14	0	0	0	4	0	0	0	1	0	4	4	.417	.417	.583
	SD/NL		133	495	438	110	10	5	5	145	50	2	0	97	7	1	5	4	3	76	26	.251	.334	.331

Gwynn, Anthony Keith "Tony" — BL/TL — b.5/9/60 — POS OF-1570
SD81 4/58

YR	TM/LG	CL	G	TPA	AB	H	2B	3B	HR	TB	BB	IBB	HB	SO	GDP	SH	SF	SB	CS	R	RBI	BA	OBA	SA
82	SD/NL		54	209	190	55	12	2	1	74	14	0	0	16	5	4	1	8	3	33	17	.289	.337	.389
83	SD/NL		86	334	304	94	12	2	1	113	23	5	0	21	9	4	2	7	4	34	37	.309	.355	.372
84	SD/NL		158	675	606	*213	21	10	5	269	59	13	2	23	15	6	2	33	18	88	71	*.351	.410	.444
85	SD/NL		154	671	622	197	29	5	6	254	45	4	2	33	17	1	1	14	11	90	46	.317	.364	.408
86	SD/NL		160	701	642	*211	33	7	14	300	52	11	3	35	20	2	2	37	9	*107	59	.329	.381	.467
87	SD/NL		157	680	589	*218	36	13	7	301	82	26	3	35	13	2	4	56	12	119	54	*.370	.447	.511

Gwynn, Anthony Keith "Tony" (continued)

YR	TM/LG	CL	G	TPA	AB	H	2B	3B	HR	TB	BB	IBB	HB	SO	GDP	SH	SF	SB	CS	R	RBI	BA	OBA	SA
88	SD/NL		133	578	521	163	22	5	7	216	51	13	0	40	11	4	2	26	11	64	70	*.313	.373	.415
89	SD/NL		158	679	604	*203	27	7	4	256	56	16	1	30	12	11	7	40	16	82	62	*.336	.389	.424
90	SD/NL		141	629	573	177	29	10	4	238	44	20	1	23	13	7	4	17	8	79	72	.309	.357	.415
91	SD/NL		134	569	530	168	27	11	4	229	34	8	0	19	11	0	5	8	8	69	62	.317	.355	.432
92	SD/NL		128	569	520	165	27	3	6	216	46	12	0	16	12	0	3	3	6	77	41	.317	.371	.415
93	SD/NL		122	534	489	175	41	3	7	243	36	11	3	19	18	1	7	14	1	70	59	.358	.398	.497
12 YR TOTALS			1585	6828	6190	2039	316	78	66	2709	542	139	13	310	156	42	41	263	107	912	650	**.329**	**.382**	**.438**

Gwynn, Christopher Karlton "Chris" — BL/TL — b.10/13/64 — POS OF-220, DH-7, 1B-1 LA85 1/10

YR	TM/LG	CL	G	TPA	AB	H	2B	3B	HR	TB	BB	IBB	HB	SO	GDP	SH	SF	SB	CS	R	RBI	BA	OBA	SA
85	VB/FSL	A+	52	199	179	46	8	6	0	66	16	0	2	34	4	1	1	2	2	19	17	.257	.323	.369
86	SA/TEX	AA	111	427	401	115	22	1	6	157	16	7	3	44	8	1	6	2	2	46	67	.287	.315	.392
87	ALB/PCL	AAA	110	400	362	101	12	3	5	134	36	5	1	38	5	1	0	5	7	54	41	.279	.346	.370
	LA/NL		17	34	32	7	1	0	0	8	1	0	0	7	0	1	0	0	0	2	2	.219	.242	.250
88	ALB/PCL	AAA	112	465	411	123	22	10	5	180	39	6	2	39	4	4	9	1	2	57	61	.299	.356	.438
	LA/NL		12	12	11	2	0	0	0	2	1	0	0	0	0	0	0	0	0	1	0	.182	.250	.182
89	LA/NL		32	73	68	16	4	1	0	22	2	0	0	9	1	1	1	0		8	7	.235	.254	.324
	ALB/PCL	AAA	26	100	89	29	9	1	0	40	7	0	2	7	1	1	3	1		14	12	.326	.384	.449
90	LA/NL		101	151	141	40	2	1	5	59	7	2	0	28	2	0	3	0	1	19	22	.284	.311	.418
91	LA/NL		94	154	139	35	5	1	5	57	10	1	1	23	5	1	3	1	0	18	22	.252	.301	.410
92	KC/AL		34	90	84	24	3	2	1	34	3	0	0	10	1		2	0	0	10	7	.286	.303	.405
93	KC/AL		103	316	287	86	14	4	1	111	24	5	1	34	7	2	2	0	1	36	25	.300	.354	.387
7 YR TOTALS			393	830	762	210	29	9	12	293	48	8	2	113	16	7	11	2	2	94	85	**.276**	**.316**	**.385**

Hale, Walter William "Chip" — BL/TR — b.12/2/64 — POS 2B-38, 3B-28, DH-21, 1B-1, SS-1 MIN87 17/425

YR	TM/LG	CL	G	TPA	AB	H	2B	3B	HR	TB	BB	IBB	HB	SO	GDP	SH	SF	SB	CS	R	RBI	BA	OBA	SA
87	KEN/MID	A	87	383	339	117	12	7	7	164	33	4	4	26	4	0	7	3	3	65	65	.345	.402	.484
88	ORL/SOU	AA	133	557	482	126	20	1	11	181	64	3	3	31	12	5	3	8	3	62	65	.261	.350	.376
89	POR/PCL	AAA	108	454	411	112	16	9	2	152	35	2	1	55	11	5	2	3	2	49	34	.273	.330	.370
	MIN/AL		28	71	67	14	3	0	0	17	1	0	0	6	0	1	2	0	0	6	4	.209	.214	.254
90	MIN/AL		1	4	2	0	0	0	0	0	0	0	0	0	0	0	0	0	2	0	2	.000	.000	.000
	POR/PCL	AAA	130	562	479	134	24	2	3	171	68	3	1	57	16	7	7	6	6	71	40	.280	.366	.357
91	POR/PCL	AAA	110	409	352	85	16	3	1	110	47	4	0	22	5	5	5	3	3	45	37	.241	.327	.313
92	POR/PCL	AAA	132	557	474	135	25	8	1	179	73	11	3	45	7	4	6	3	3	77	53	.285	.376	.378
93	POR/PCL	AAA	55	236	211	59	15	3	1	83	21	1	0	13	6	3	1	2	1	25	27	.333	.408	.425
	MIN/AL		69	213	186	62	6	1	3	79	18	0	6	17	3	3	5	2	1	31	33	.298	.354	.376
3 YR TOTALS			98	288	255	76	9	1	3	96	19	0	6	24	3	3	5	2	1	31	33	**.298**	**.354**	**.376**

Hamelin, Robert James "Bob" — BL/TL — b.11/29/67 — POS 1B-15 KC88 2/48

YR	TM/LG	CL	G	TPA	AB	H	2B	3B	HR	TB	BB	IBB	HB	SO	GDP	SH	SF	SB	CS	R	RBI	BA	OBA	SA
88	EUG/NWL	A-	70	304	235	70	19	1	17	142	56	4	5	67	7	0	8	9	1	42	61	.298	.431	.604
89	MEM/SOU	AA	68	269	211	65	12	5	16	135	52	7	5	52	2	0	1	3	6	45	47	.308	.454	.640
90	OMA/AMA	AAA	90	340	271	63	11	2	8	102	62	5	4	78	1	1	2	2	2	31	30	.232	.381	.376
91	OMA/AMA	AAA	37	148	127	24	3	1	4	41	16	0	0	32	4	1	4	0	0	13	19	.189	.272	.323
92	BC/FSL	A+	11	46	44	12	0	1	1	17	2	0	0	11	0	0	0	0	0	7	6	.273	.304	.386
	MEM/SOU	AA	35	146	120	40	8	0	6	66	26	2	0	17	2	0	0	0	1	23	22	.333	.452	.550
	OMA/AMA	AAA	27	112	95	19	3	1	5	39	14	0	0	15	1	0	3	8	3	9	15	.200	.295	.411
93	OMA/AMA	AAA	137	575	479	124	19	3	29	236	82	9	5	94	8	0	9	8	3	77	84	.259	.367	.493
	KC/AL		16	55	49	11	3	0	2	20	6	0	0	15	2	0	0	0	0	2	5	.224	.309	.408

Hamilton, Darryl Quinn — BL/TR — b.12/3/64 — POS OF-479, DH-13 MIL86 11/269

YR	TM/LG	CL	G	TPA	AB	H	2B	3B	HR	TB	BB	IBB	HB	SO	GDP	SH	SF	SB	CS	R	RBI	BA	OBA	SA
86	HEL/PIO	R+	65	302	248	97	12	6	0	121	51	1	1	18	3	1	1	34	8	72	35	.391	.495	.488
87	STO/CAL	A+	125	586	494	162	17	6	8	215	74	9	6	59	2	5	7	43	12	102	61	.328	.417	.435
88	DEN/AMA	AAA	72	323	277	90	11	4	0	109	39	0	1	28	4	1	1	23	7	55	32	.325	.404	.394
	MIL/AL		44	117	103	19	4	0	1	26	12	0	1	9	2	0	1	7	3	14	11	.184	.274	.252
89	DEN/AMA	AAA	129	554	497	142	24	2	2	180	42	3	5	58	13	5	5	20	13	72	40	.286	.344	.362
90	MIL/AL		89	168	156	46	5	0	1	54	9	0	1	12	2	3	0	10	3	27	18	.295	.333	.346
91	MIL/AL		122	448	405	126	15	6	1	156	33	1	3	38	10	3	16	41	6	64	57	.311	.361	.385
92	MIL/AL		128	527	470	140	19	7	5	188	45	0	1	42	10	4	7	41	10	67	62	.298	.356	.400
93	MIL/AL		135	573	520	161	21	1	9	211	45	5	3	62	9	4	1	21	13	74	48	.310	.367	.406
5 YR TOTALS			518	1833	1654	492	64	14	17	635	144	7	5	163	33	18	12	95	39	246	196	**.297**	**.353**	**.384**

Hammonds, Jeffrey Bryan — BR/TR — b.3/5/71 — POS OF-23, DH-8 BAL92 1/4

YR	TM/LG	CL	G	TPA	AB	H	2B	3B	HR	TB	BB	IBB	HB	SO	GDP	SH	SF	SB	CS	R	RBI	BA	OBA	SA
93	ROC/INT	AAA	36	161	151	47	9	1	5	73	5	0	2	27	1	1	2	6	3	25	23	.311	.338	.483
	BOW/EAS	AA	24	105	92	26	3	0	3	38	9	0	2	18	1	1	1	4	3	13	10	.283	.356	.413
	BAL/AL		33	110	105	32	8	0	3	49	2	1	0	16	3	1	1	4	0	10	19	.305	.312	.467

Hansen, David Andrew "Dave" — BL/TR — b.11/24/68 — POS 3B-149, SS-1 LA86 2/47

YR	TM/LG	CL	G	TPA	AB	H	2B	3B	HR	TB	BB	IBB	HB	SO	GDP	SH	SF	SB	CS	R	RBI	BA	OBA	SA
86	GF/PIO	R+	61	232	204	61	7	3	1	77	27	0	0	28	6	1	0	9	3	39	36	.299	.381	.377
87	BAK/CAL	A+	132	508	432	113	22	1	3	146	65	1	4	61	11	6	1	6	5	68	38	.262	.363	.338
88	VB/FSL	A+	135	582	512	149	28	6	3	210	56	6	4	46	11	5	2	4	2	68	81	.291	.360	.410
89	SA/TEX	AA	121	521	464	138	21	4	6	185	50	3	6	44	18	0	5	3	2	72	52	.297	.365	.399
	ALB/PCL	AAA	6	32	30	8	1	0	2	15	2	0	0	3	0	0	0	0		6	10	.267	.313	.500
90	ALB/PCL	AAA	135	589	487	154	20	3	11	213	90	4	3	54	12	0	9	9	4	90	92	.316	.419	.437

(continued)

Hansen, David Andrew "Dave" (continued)

YR	TM/LG	CL	G	TPA	AB	H	2B	3B	HR	TB	BB	IBB	HB	SO	GDP	SH	SF	SB	CS	R	RBI	BA	OBA	SA
	LA/NL		5	7	7	1	0	0	0	1	0	0	0	3	0	0	0	0	0	0	1	.143	.143	.143
91	ALB/PCL	AAA	68	310	254	77	11	1	5	105	49	3	0	33	7	0	7	4	3	42	40	.303	.406	.413
	LA/NL		53	58	56	15	4	0	1	22	2	0	0	12	2	0	0	1	0	3	5	.268	.293	.393
92	LA/NL		132	378	341	73	11	0	6	102	34	3	1	49	9	0	2	0	2	30	22	.214	.286	.299
93	LA/NL		84	127	105	38	3	0	4	53	21	3	0	13	0	0	1	0	1	13	30	.362	.465	.505
4 YR TOTALS			**274**	**570**	**509**	**127**	**18**	**0**	**11**	**178**	**57**	**6**	**1**	**77**	**11**	**0**	**3**	**1**	**3**	**46**	**58**	**.250**	**.325**	**.350**

Harper, Brian David — BR/TR — b.10/16/59 — POS C-661, OF-111, DH-60, 3B-13, 1B-9   CAL77 4/85

YR	TM/LG	CL	G	TPA	AB	H	2B	3B	HR	TB	BB	IBB	HB	SO	GDP	SH	SF	SB	CS	R	RBI	BA	OBA	SA
79	CAL/AL		1	2	2	0	0	0	0	0	0	0	0	1	0	0	0	0	0	0	0	.000	.000	.000
81	CAL/AL		4	12	11	3	0	0	0	3	0	0	0	0	0	0	1	0	0	1	1	.273	.250	.273
82	PIT/NL		20	31	29	8	1	0	2	15	1	1	0	4	1	1	0	0	0	4	4	.276	.300	.517
83	PIT/NL		61	140	131	29	4	1	7	56	7	0	1	15	3	2	4	0	0	16	20	.221	.232	.427
84	PIT/NL		46	121	112	29	4	0	2	39	5	0	2	11	4	1	0	0	0	4	11	.259	.300	.348
85	STL/NL		43	55	52	13	4	0	0	17	2	0	0	3	2	0	1	0	0	5	8	.250	.273	.327
86	DET/AL		19	41	36	5	1	0	0	6	3	0	0	3	1	1	1	0	0	2	3	.139	.200	.167
	NAS/AMA	AAA	95	351	317	83	11	1	11	129	26	1	2	27	9	1	5	3	8	41	45	.262	.317	.407
87	SJ/CAL	A+	8	32	29	9	0	0	3	18	2	0	0	0	0	0	1	0	0	5	8	.310	.344	.621
	TAC/PCL	AAA	94	371	323	100	17	0	9	144	28	7	4	23	13	4	12	1	2	41	62	.310	.360	.446
	OAK/AL		11	19	17	4	1	0	0	5	0	0	0	4	1	1	1	0	0	1	3	.235	.222	.294
88	POR/PCL	AAA	46	191	170	60	10	1	13	111	14	3	3	7	6	0	4	2	0	34	42	.353	.403	.653
	MIN/AL		60	182	166	49	11	0	3	71	10	1	3	12	12	2	1	0	3	15	20	.295	.344	.428
89	MIN/AL		126	412	385	125	24	0	8	173	13	3	6	16	11	4	4	2	4	43	57	.325	.353	.449
90	MIN/AL		134	509	479	141	42	3	6	207	19	2	7	27	20	0	4	3	2	61	54	.294	.328	.432
91	MIN/AL		123	469	441	137	28	1	10	197	14	3	6	22	14	2	6	1	2	54	69	.311	.336	.447
92	MIN/AL		140	546	502	154	25	0	9	206	26	7	7	22	15	1	10	0	1	58	73	.307	.343	.410
93	MIN/AL		147	573	530	161	26	1	12	225	29	9	9	29	15	0	5	1	3	52	73	.304	.347	.425
14 YR TOTALS			**935**	**3112**	**2893**	**858**	**171**	**7**	**59**	**1220**	**124**	**26**	**41**	**169**	**99**	**15**	**39**	**8**	**15**	**316**	**396**	**.297**	**.330**	**.422**

Harris, Donald — BR/TR — b.11/12/67 — POS OF-74, DH-6   TEX89 1/5

YR	TM/LG	CL	G	TPA	AB	H	2B	3B	HR	TB	BB	IBB	HB	SO	GDP	SH	SF	SB	CS	R	RBI	BA	OBA	SA
89	BUT/PIO	R+	65	285	264	75	7	8	6	116	12	0	6	54	6	0	3	14	4	50	37	.284	.326	.439
90	TUL/TEX	AA	64	226	213	34	5	1	1	44	7	0	3	69	6	3	0	7	3	16	15	.160	.197	.207
	GAS/SAL	A	58	241	221	46	10	0	3	65	14	0	4	63	2	4	0	15	8	27	13	.208	.262	.294
91	TUL/TEX	AA	130	492	450	102	17	8	11	168	26	1	7	118	12	7	2	9	8	47	53	.227	.278	.373
	TEX/AL		18	9	8	3	0	0	1	6	1	0	0	3	0	0	0	1	0	4	2	.375	.444	.750
92	TUL/TEX	AA	83	323	303	77	15	2	11	129	9	1	7	85	11	3	1	4	3	39	39	.254	.291	.426
	TEX/AL		24	33	33	6	1	0	0	7	0	0	0	15	0	0	0	0	0	3	1	.182	.182	.212
93	OC/AMA	AAA	96	403	367	93	13	9	6	142	23	0	4	89	5	4	5	4	4	48	40	.253	.301	.387
	TEX/AL		40	86	76	15	2	0	1	20	5	0	3	18	0	3	1	0	1	10	8	.197	.253	.263
3 YR TOTALS			**82**	**128**	**117**	**24**	**3**	**0**	**2**	**33**	**6**	**0**	**3**	**36**	**0**	**3**	**1**	**2**	**1**	**17**	**11**	**.205**	**.248**	**.282**

Harris, Leonard Anthony "Lenny" — BL/TR — b.10/28/64 — POS 3B-291, 2B-239, SS-52, OF-41   CIN83 5/108

YR	TM/LG	CL	G	TPA	AB	H	2B	3B	HR	TB	BB	IBB	HB	SO	GDP	SH	SF	SB	CS	R	RBI	BA	OBA	SA
84	CR/MID	A	132	521	468	115	15	3	6	154	42	4	3	59	14	2	6	31	10	52	53	.246	.308	.329
85	TAM/FSL	A+	132	549	499	129	11	8	3	165	37	2	1	57	9	5	7	15	8	66	51	.259	.307	.331
86	VER/EAS	AA	119	492	450	114	17	2	10	165	29	4	6	38	9	1	6	36	10	68	52	.253	.303	.367
87	NAS/AMA	AAA	120	439	403	100	12	3	2	124	27	4	5	43	10	2	2	30	12	45	31	.248	.302	.308
88	GF/EAS	AA	17	75	65	22	5	1	1	32	9	0	0	6	1	1	0	6	3	9	7	.338	.419	.492
	NAS/AMA	AAA	107	446	422	117	20	2	0	141	22	2	0	36	13	2	0	45	22	46	35	.277	.313	.334
	CIN/NL		16	51	43	16	1	0	0	17	5	0	0	4	0	1	2	4	1	7	8	.372	.420	.395
89	NAS/AMA	AAA	8	34	34	9	2	0	3	20	0	0	0	5	0	0	0	0	2	6	6	.265	.265	.588
	CIN/NL		61	199	188	42	4	0	2	52	9	0	0	20	5	1	0	10	6	17	11	.223	.263	.277
	LA/NL		54	159	147	37	6	1	1	48	11	0	0	13	9	0	1	4	0	19	15	.252	.308	.327
	YEAR		115	358	335	79	10	1	3	100	20	0	0	33	14	1	1	14	6	36	26	.236	.283	.299
90	LA/NL		137	465	431	131	16	4	2	161	29	2	1	31	8	3	1	15	10	61	29	.304	.348	.374
91	LA/NL		145	485	429	123	16	1	3	150	37	4	5	32	16	12	2	12	3	59	38	.287	.349	.350
92	LA/NL		135	380	347	94	11	0	0	105	24	3	1	24	10	6	2	19	7	28	30	.271	.318	.303
93	LA/NL		107	176	160	38	6	1	2	52	15	4	0	15	4	1	0	3	1	20	11	.237	.303	.325
6 YR TOTALS			**655**	**1915**	**1745**	**481**	**60**	**7**	**10**	**585**	**130**	**14**	**9**	**139**	**52**	**24**	**7**	**67**	**31**	**211**	**142**	**.276**	**.328**	**.335**

Haselman, William Joseph "Bill" — BR/TR — b.5/25/66 — POS C-55, DH-7, OF-4   TEX87 2/23

YR	TM/LG	CL	G	TPA	AB	H	2B	3B	HR	TB	BB	IBB	HB	SO	GDP	SH	SF	SB	CS	R	RBI	BA	OBA	SA
87	GAS/SAL	A	61	256	235	72	13	1	8	111	19	0	1	46	3	0	1	1	2	35	33	.306	.359	.472
88	CHA/FSL	A+	122	504	453	111	17	2	10	162	45	3	3	99	10	1	2	8	5	56	54	.245	.316	.358
89	TUL/TEX	AA	107	398	352	95	17	2	7	137	40	0	3	88	7	1	2	5	10	38	36	.270	.348	.389
90	TUL/TEX	AA	120	485	430	137	39	2	18	234	44	1	6	96	11	2	3	3	7	68	80	.319	.387	.544
	TEX/AL		7	14	13	2	0	0	0	2	1	0	0	4	0	1	0	0	0	3	0	.154	.214	.154
91	OC/AMA	AAA	126	509	442	113	22	6	9	166	61	1	1	89	14	1	4	10	7	57	60	.256	.344	.376
92	OC/AMA	AAA	17	71	58	14	5	0	1	22	13	0	0	12	2	0	0	1	0	8	9	.241	.380	.379
	CAL/PCL	AAA	88	349	302	77	14	2	19	152	41	4	2	89	9	1	3	3	3	49	53	.255	.345	.503
	SEA/AL		8	19	19	5	0	0	0	5	0	0	0	7	0	0	0	1	0	1	0	.263	.263	.263
93	SEA/AL		58	154	137	35	8	0	5	58	12	0	1	19	5	2	2	2	1	21	16	.255	.316	.423
3 YR TOTALS			**73**	**187**	**169**	**42**	**8**	**0**	**5**	**65**	**13**	**0**	**1**	**31**	**6**	**2**	**2**	**2**	**1**	**22**	**19**	**.249**	**.303**	**.385**

Hatcher, William Augustus "Billy" — BR/TR — b.10/4/60 — POS OF-1055, 2B-2   CHN81* 6/131

YR	TM/LG	CL	G	TPA	AB	H	2B	3B	HR	TB	BB	IBB	HB	SO	GDP	SH	SF	SB	CS	R	RBI	BA	OBA	SA
84	IOW/AMA	AAA	150	659	595	164	27	18	9	254	51	4	9	54	8	1	3	56	18	96	59	.276	.340	.427
	CHI/NL		8	10	9	1	0	0	0	1	1	1	0	0	0	0	0	2	0	1	0	.111	.200	.111
85	IOW/AMA	AAA	67	309	279	78	14	5	5	117	24	0	2	40	5	2	2	17	11	39	19	.280	.339	.419
	CHI/NL		53	178	163	40	12	1	2	60	8	0	3	12	9	2	2	4	4	24	10	.245	.290	.368
86	HOU/NL		127	453	419	108	15	4	6	149	22	1	5	52	3	5	1	38	14	55	36	.258	.302	.356
87	HOU/NL		141	627	564	167	28	3	11	234	42	1	9	70	11	7	5	53	9	96	63	.296	.352	.415
88	HOU/NL		145	591	530	142	25	4	7	196	37	4	8	56	6	8	8	32	13	79	52	.268	.321	.370
89	HOU/NL		108	433	395	90	15	3	3	120	30	2	1	53	3	3	4	22	6	49	44	.228	.281	.304
	PIT/NL		27	87	86	21	4	0	1	28	0	0	1	9	1	0	0	2	1	10	7	.244	.253	.326
	YEAR		135	520	481	111	19	3	4	148	30	2	2	62	4	3	4	24	7	59	51	.231	.277	.308
90	CIN/NL		139	545	504	139	28	5	5	192	33	5	6	42	4	1	1	30	10	68	25	.276	.327	.381
91	CIN/NL		138	482	442	116	25	4	4	159	26	4	7	55	9	4	3	11	9	45	41	.262	.312	.360
92	CIN/NL		43	102	94	27	3	0	2	36	5	0	0	11	2	0	3	0	2	10	10	.287	.314	.383
	BOS/AL		75	342	315	75	16	2	1	98	17	1	3	41	9	6	4	14	6	37	23	.238	.283	.311
	YEAR		118	444	409	102	19	2	3	134	22	1	3	52	11	6	4	14	8	47	33	.249	.290	.328
93	BOS/AL		136	562	508	146	24	3	9	203	28	4	11	46	14	11	4	14	7	71	57	.287	.336	.400
10 YR TOTALS			**1140**	**4412**	**4029**	**1072**	**195**	**28**	**51**	**1476**	**249**	**23**	**54**	**447**	**71**	**48**	**32**	**210**	**81**	**545**	**368**	**.266**	**.315**	**.366**

Hayes, Charles Dewayne "Charlie" — BR/TR — b.5/29/65 — POS 3B-665, 1B-8, OF-4, SS-3, 2B-1   SF83 3/96

YR	TM/LG	CL	G	TPA	AB	H	2B	3B	HR	TB	BB	IBB	HB	SO	GDP	SH	SF	SB	CS	R	RBI	BA	OBA	SA
84	CLI/MID	A	116	435	392	96	17	2	2	123	34	1	1	110	7	5	3	4	1	41	51	.245	.305	.314
85	FRE/CAL	A+	131	534	467	132	17	2	4	165	56	0	2	95	9	1	4	7	8	73	68	.283	.364	.353
86	SHR/TEX	AA	121	472	434	107	23	2	5	149	28	3	2	83	11	1	4	1	4	52	45	.247	.293	.343
87	SHR/TEX	AA	128	524	487	148	33	3	14	229	26	6	3	76	12	1	7	5	9	66	75	.304	.338	.470
88	PHO/PCL	AAA	131	533	492	151	26	4	7	206	34	1	0	91	19	2	5	4	4	71	71	.307	.348	.419
	SF/NL		7	11	11	1	0	0	0	1	0	0	0	3	0	0	0	0	0	0	0	.091	.091	.091
89	SF/NL		3	5	5	1	0	0	0	1	0	0	0	1	0	0	0	0	0	0	0	.200	.200	.200
	PHO/PCL	AAA	61	246	229	65	15	1	7	103	15	1	0	48	2	0	2	5	0	25	27	.284	.325	.450
	SCR/INT	AAA	7	28	27	11	3	1	1	19	0	1	0	3	0	0	0	0	0	4	3	.407	.429	.704
	PHI/NL		84	315	299	77	15	1	8	118	11	1	0	49	6	2	3	3	1	26	43	.258	.281	.395
	YEAR		87	320	304	78	15	1	8	119	11	1	0	50	6	2	3	3	1	26	43	.257	.280	.391
90	PHI/NL		152	597	561	145	20	0	10	195	28	3	2	91	12	0	6	4	4	56	57	.258	.293	.348
91	PHI/NL		142	480	460	106	23	1	12	167	16	3	1	75	13	2	1	3	3	34	53	.230	.257	.363
92	NY/AL		142	549	509	131	19	2	18	208	28	0	3	100	12	3	6	3	3	52	66	.257	.297	.409
93	COL/NL		157	630	573	175	*45	2	25	299	43	6	5	82	25	1	8	11	6	89	98	.305	.355	.522
6 YR TOTALS			**687**	**2587**	**2418**	**636**	**122**	**6**	**73**	**989**	**126**	**13**	**11**	**401**	**68**	**8**	**24**	**24**	**19**	**257**	**317**	**.263**	**.300**	**.409**

Helfand, Eric James — BL/TR — b.3/25/69 — POS C-5   OAK90 6/65

YR	TM/LG	CL	G	TPA	AB	H	2B	3B	HR	TB	BB	IBB	HB	SO	GDP	SH	SF	SB	CS	R	RBI	BA	OBA	SA
90	SO/NWL	A-	57	235	207	59	12	0	2	77	20	1	7	49	2	0	1	4	1	29	39	.285	.366	.372
91	MOD/CAL	A+	67	285	242	62	15	1	7	100	37	2	2	56	6	2	2	0	1	35	38	.256	.357	.413
92	MOD/CAL	A+	72	306	249	72	15	0	10	117	47	4	6	46	5	1	3	0	1	40	44	.289	.410	.470
	HUN/SOU	AA	37	120	114	26	7	0	2	39	5	0	1	32	4	0	0	0	0	13	9	.228	.267	.342
93	HUN/SOU	AA	100	363	302	69	15	2	10	118	43	2	8	78	5	3	7	1	1	38	48	.228	.333	.391
	OAK/AL		8	13	13	3	0	0	0	3	0	0	0	5	0	0	0	0	0	1	1	.231	.231	.231

Hemond, Scott Mathew — BR/TR — b.11/18/65 — POS C-92, DH-15, 3B-12, OF-10, 2B-9, SS-4, 1B-1   OAK86 1/12

YR	TM/LG	CL	G	TPA	AB	H	2B	3B	HR	TB	BB	IBB	HB	SO	GDP	SH	SF	SB	CS	R	RBI	BA	OBA	SA
86	MAD/MID	A	22	91	85	26	2	0	2	34	5	0	0	19	0	0	1	2	1	9	13	.306	.341	.400
87	MAD/MID	A	90	386	343	99	21	4	8	152	40	1	1	79	10	0	2	27	12	60	52	.289	.363	.443
	HUN/SOU	AA	33	115	110	20	3	1	1	28	4	0	0	30	3	1	0	5	1	10	8	.182	.211	.255
88	HUN/SOU	AA	133	541	482	106	22	4	9	163	48	1	3	114	7	1	7	29	8	51	53	.220	.291	.338
89	HUN/SOU	AA	132	578	490	130	26	6	5	183	62	0	7	77	11	13	6	45	17	89	62	.265	.352	.373
	OAK/AL		4	0	0	0	0	0	0	0	0	0	0	0	0	0	0	0	0	2	0	.000	.000	.000
90	OAK/AL		7	13	13	2	0	0	0	2	0	0	0	5	0	0	0	0	0	0	1	.154	.154	.154
	TAC/PCL	AAA	72	249	218	53	11	0	8	88	24	3	1	52	7	3	0	10	5	32	35	.243	.317	.404
91	TAC/PCL	AAA	92	379	327	89	19	5	3	127	39	1	7	69	11	5	1	11	8	50	31	.272	.361	.388
	OAK/AL		23	24	23	5	0	0	0	5	0	0	0	7	0	0	1	0	1	4	0	.217	.250	.217
92	OAK/AL		17	30	27	6	1	0	0	7	2	0	0	7	2	0	1	0	1	3	1	.222	.300	.259
	HUN/SOU	AA	9	31	27	9	0	0	0	9	4	0	0	8	0	0	0	2	0	3	2	.333	.419	.333
	TAC/PCL	AAA	8	38	33	8	0	0	1	11	5	0	0	6	1	0	0	3	1	6	3	.242	.342	.333
	CHI/AL		8	15	13	3	1	0	0	4	2	0	0	6	0	0	0	1	0	1	1	.231	.267	.308
	YEAR		25	45	40	9	2	0	0	11	4	0	0	13	2	0	1	1	0	4	2	.225	.289	.275
93	OAK/AL		91	255	215	55	16	0	6	89	32	0	1	55	5	4	2	14	5	31	26	.256	.353	.414
5 YR TOTALS			**150**	**337**	**291**	**71**	**18**	**0**	**6**	**107**	**37**	**0**	**1**	**80**	**4**	**6**	**2**	**16**	**7**	**45**	**29**	**.244**	**.329**	**.368**

Henderson, David Lee "Dave" — BR/TR — b.7/21/58 — POS OF-1348, DH-83, 2B-1   SEA77 1/26

YR	TM/LG	CL	G	TPA	AB	H	2B	3B	HR	TB	BB	IBB	HB	SO	GDP	SH	SF	SB	CS	R	RBI	BA	OBA	SA
81	SEA/AL		59	145	126	21	3	0	6	42	16	1	1	24	4	1	1	2	1	17	13	.167	.264	.333
82	SEA/AL		104	362	324	82	17	1	14	143	36	2	0	67	5	1	2	2	5	47	48	.253	.327	.441
83	SEA/AL		137	521	484	130	24	5	17	215	28	3	1	93	6	3	6	9	3	50	55	.269	.306	.444
84	SEA/AL		112	374	350	98	23	0	14	163	19	0	2	56	4	1	1	5	5	42	43	.280	.320	.466
85	SEA/AL		139	556	502	121	28	2	14	195	48	1	3	104	11	1	2	6	1	70	68	.241	.310	.388
86	SEA/AL		103	378	337	93	19	4	14	162	37	4	0	95	5	1	3	2	2	51	44	.276	.350	.481
	BOS/AL		36	54	51	10	3	0	1	16	2	0	0	15	1	0	1	0	0	8	3	.196	.226	.314
	YEAR		139	432	388	103	22	4	15	178	39	4	0	110	6	1	4	2	2	59	47	.265	.335	.459
87	BOS/AL		75	209	184	43	10	0	8	77	22	0	0	48	3	1	2	0	1	30	25	.234	.313	.418

(continued)

Henderson, David Lee "Dave" (continued)

YR	TM/LG	CL	G	TPA	AB	H	2B	3B	HR	TB	BB	IBB	HB	SO	GDP	SH	SF	SB	CS	R	RBI	BA	OBA	SA
	SF/NL		15	29	21	5	2	0	0	7	8	0	0	5	0	0	0	2	0	2	1	.238	.448	.333
	YEAR		90	238	205	48	12	0	8	84	30	0	0	53	3	0	3	3	1	32	26	.234	.329	.410
88	OAK/AL		146	570	507	154	38	1	24	266	47	1	4	92	14	5	7	2	4	100	94	.304	.363	.525
89	OAK/AL		152	643	579	145	24	3	15	220	54	1	3	131	13	1	6	8	5	77	80	.250	.315	.380
90	OAK/AL		127	494	450	122	28	0	20	210	40	1	1	105	5	1	2	3	1	65	63	.271	.331	.467
91	OAK/AL		150	637	572	158	33	0	25	266	58	3	4	113	9	1	2	6	6	86	85	.276	.346	.465
92	TAC/PCL	AAA	3	11	11	2	0	0	0	2	0	0	0	3	0	0	0	0	0	0	1	.182	.182	.182
	MOD/CAL	A+	3	13	13	4	1	0	1	8	0	0	0	3	0	0	0	0	0	3	2	.308	.308	.615
	OAK/AL		20	65	63	9	1	0	0	10	2	0	0	16	0	0	0	0	0	1	2	.143	.169	.159
93	TAC/PCL	AAA	3	12	11	2	1	0	0	3	0	0	0	2	0	0	1	0	0	1	2	.182	.167	.273
	OAK/AL		107	422	382	84	19	0	20	163	32	0	0	113	11	0	8	0	3	37	53	.220	.275	.427
13 YR TOTALS			**1482**	**5459**	**4932**	**1275**	**272**	**16**	**192**	**2155**	**449**	**18**	**21**	**1077**	**80**	**18**	**39**	**48**	**38**	**683**	**677**	**.259**	**.321**	**.437**

Henderson, Rickey Henley — BR/TL — b.12/25/58 — POS OF-1880, DH-89   OAK76 4/96

YR	TM/LG	CL	G	TPA	AB	H	2B	3B	HR	TB	BB	IBB	HB	SO	GDP	SH	SF	SB	CS	R	RBI	BA	OBA	SA
79	OAK/AL		89	398	351	96	13	3	1	118	34	0	2	39	4	8	3	33	11	49	26	.274	.338	.336
80	OAK/AL		158	722	591	179	22	4	9	236	117	7	5	54	6	6	3	*100	26	111	53	.303	.420	.399
81	OAK/AL		108	493	423	*135	18	7	6	185	64	4	2	68	7	0	4	*56	22	*89	35	.319	.408	.437
82	OAK/AL		149	656	536	143	24	4	10	205	*116	1	2	94	5	0	2	*130	42	119	51	.267	.398	.382
83	OAK/AL		145	622	513	150	25	7	9	216	*103	8	4	80	11	1	1	*108	19	105	48	.292	.414	.421
84	OAK/AL		142	597	502	147	27	4	16	230	86	1	5	81	7	1	3	*66	18	113	58	.293	.399	.458
85	FL/FSL	A+	3	11	6	1	0	1	0	3	5	0	0	2	0	0	0	1	1	5	3	.167	.545	.500
	NY/AL		143	654	547	172	28	5	24	282	99	1	3	65	8	0	5	*80	10	*146	72	.314	.419	.516
86	NY/AL		153	701	608	160	31	5	28	285	89	2	2	81	12	0	2	*87	18	*130	74	.263	.358	.469
87	NY/AL		95	440	358	104	17	3	17	178	80	1	2	52	10	0	0	41	8	78	37	.291	.423	.497
88	NY/AL		140	647	554	169	30	2	6	221	82	1	3	54	4	0	6	*93	13	118	50	.305	.394	.399
89	NY/AL		65	293	235	58	13	1	3	82	56	0	1	29	0	0	1	25	8	41	22	.247	.392	.349
	OAK/AL		85	381	306	90	13	2	9	134	70	5	2	39	8	0	3	52	6	72	35	.294	.425	.438
	YEAR		150	674	541	148	26	3	12	216	*126	5	3	68	8	0	4	*77	14	*113	57	.274	.411	.399
90	OAK/AL		136	594	489	159	33	3	28	282	97	2	4	60	13	2	2	*65	10	*119	61	.325	*.439	.577
91	OAK/AL		134	578	470	126	17	1	18	199	98	7	7	73	7	0	3	*58	18	105	57	.268	.400	.423
92	OAK/AL		117	500	396	112	18	3	15	181	95	5	6	56	5	0	3	48	11	77	46	.283	.426	.457
93	OAK/AL		90	407	318	104	19	1	17	176	85	6	2	46	8	0	2	31	6	77	47	.327	.469	.553
	TOR/AL		44	203	163	35	3	1	4	52	35	1	2	19	1	1	2	22	2	37	12	.215	.356	.319
	YEAR		134	610	481	139	22	2	21	228	120	7	4	65	9	1	4	53	8	114	59	.289	.432	.474
15 YR TOTALS			**1993**	**8886**	**7360**	**2139**	**351**	**56**	**220**	**3262**	**1406**	**52**	**54**	**990**	**118**	**21**	**45**	**1095**	**248**	**1586**	**784**	**.291**	**.406**	**.443**

Hernandez, Carlos Alberto — BR/TR — b.5/24/67 — POS C-129, 3B-1   LA 10/10/84

YR	TM/LG	CL	G	TPA	AB	H	2B	3B	HR	TB	BB	IBB	HB	SO	GDP	SH	SF	SB	CS	R	RBI	BA	OBA	SA
85	DOD/GCL	R	22	52	49	12	1	0	0	13	3	0	0	8	4	0	0	0	0	3	6	.245	.288	.265
86	DOD/GCL	R	57	214	205	64	7	0	1	74	5	2	2	18	7	1	1	1	2	19	31	.312	.333	.361
87	BAK/CAL	A+	48	182	162	37	6	1	3	54	14	0	3	23	6	1	2	4	4	22	22	.228	.298	.333
88	BAK/CAL	A+	92	357	333	103	15	2	5	137	16	2	1	39	18	3	4	1	4	37	52	.309	.339	.411
	ALB/PCL	AAA	3	8	8	1	0	0	0	1	0	0	0	1	0	0	0	0	0	0	1	.125	.125	.125
89	SA/TEX	AA	99	393	370	111	16	3	8	157	12	0	4	46	12	1	5	2	3	37	41	.300	.332	.424
	ALB/PCL	AAA	4	16	14	3	0	0	0	3	2	0	1	1	1	0	0	0	0	1	1	.214	.313	.214
90	ALB/PCL	AAA	52	155	143	45	8	1	0	55	8	1	1	25	5	0	3	2	2	11	16	.315	.348	.385
	LA/NL		10	20	20	4	1	0	0	5	0	0	0	4	0	0	0	0	0	2	1	.200	.200	.250
91	ALB/PCL	AAA	95	372	345	119	24	2	8	171	24	5	1	36	10	0	2	5	5	60	44	.345	.387	.496
	LA/NL		15	16	14	3	1	0	0	4	0	0	1	5	2	0	1	0	0	1	1	.214	.250	.286
92	LA/NL		69	190	173	45	4	0	3	58	11	1	4	21	8	0	2	0	1	11	17	.260	.316	.335
93	LA/NL		50	102	99	25	5	0	2	36	2	0	0	11	0	1	0	0	0	6	7	.253	.267	.364
4 YR TOTALS			**144**	**328**	**306**	**77**	**11**	**0**	**5**	**103**	**13**	**1**	**5**	**39**	**10**	**1**	**3**	**1**	**1**	**20**	**26**	**.252**	**.291**	**.337**

Hernandez, Cesar Dario — BR/TR — b.9/28/66 — POS OF-41   MON85 1/1

YR	TM/LG	CL	G	TPA	AB	H	2B	3B	HR	TB	BB	IBB	HB	SO	GDP	SH	SF	SB	CS	R	RBI	BA	OBA	SA
86	BUR/MID	A	38	118	104	26	11	0	1	40	7	0	4	24	2	1	2	7	0	12	12	.250	.316	.385
87	WPB/FSL	A+	32	112	106	25	3	1	2	36	4	0	0	29	1	0	1	6	1	14	6	.236	.268	.340
88	ROC/MID	A	117	442	411	101	20	4	19	186	25	1	4	109	11	1	1	28	8	71	60	.246	.295	.453
89	WPB/FSL	A+	42	174	158	45	8	3	1	62	8	1	5	32	2	1	2	16	4	16	15	.285	.335	.392
	JAC/SOU	AA	81	245	222	47	9	1	3	67	22	2	0	60	3	1	0	11	4	25	13	.212	.283	.302
90	JAC/SOU	AA	118	425	393	94	21	7	10	159	18	3	1	75	4	1	6	17	11	58	50	.239	.281	.405
91	HAR/EAS	AA	128	458	418	106	15	2	13	164	25	2	8	106	7	1	6	34	10	58	52	.254	.304	.392
92	NAS/AMA	AAA	1	2	2	2	0	0	0	2	0	0	0	0	0	0	0	0	1	0	0	1.000	1.000	1.000
	CHT/SOU	AA	93	353	328	91	24	4	3	132	19	1	4	65	5	2	0	12	9	50	27	.277	.325	.402
	CIN/NL		34	51	51	14	4	0	0	18	0	0	0	10	1	0	0	4	0	6	4	.275	.275	.353
93	CIN/NL		27	26	24	2	0	0	0	2	1	0	0	9	0	0	2	0	5	3	1	.083	.120	.083
	IND/AMA	AAA	84	287	272	70	12	4	5	105	9	0	3	63	2	1	2	5	7	30	22	.257	.287	.386
2 YR TOTALS			**61**	**77**	**75**	**16**	**4**	**0**	**0**	**20**	**1**	**0**	**0**	**18**	**1**	**1**	**2**	**4**	**3**	**9**	**5**	**.213**	**.224**	**.267**

Hiatt, Philip Farrell "Phil" — BR/TR — b.5/1/69 — POS 3B-70, DH-9   KC90 6/234

YR	TM/LG	CL	G	TPA	AB	H	2B	3B	HR	TB	BB	IBB	HB	SO	GDP	SH	SF	SB	CS	R	RBI	BA	OBA	SA
90	EUG/NWL	A-	73	312	289	85	18	5	2	119	17	1	1	70	1	1	4	15	4	33	44	.294	.331	.412
91	BC/FSL	A+	81	343	315	94	21	6	2	142	22	4	3	70	8	1	2	28	14	41	33	.298	.348	.451
	MEM/SOU	AA	56	224	206	47	7	1	6	74	9	0	3	63	3	0	6	6	2	29	33	.228	.263	.359
92	MEM/SOU	AA	129	521	487	119	20	5	27	230	25	1	5	157	11	1	3	5	10	71	83	.244	.287	.472
	OMA/AMA	AAA	5	16	14	3	0	0	2	9	2	0	0	3	0	0	1	0	0	3	4	.214	.313	.643

Hiatt, Philip Farrell "Phil" (continued)

YR	TM/LG	CL	G	TPA	AB	H	2B	3B	HR	TB	BB	IBB	HB	SO	GDP	SH	SF	SB	CS	R	RBI	BA	OBA	SA
93	OMA/AMA	AAA	12	56	51	12	2	1	3	23	4	0	1	20	0	0	0	0	0	8	10	.235	.304	.451
	KC/AL		81	263	238	52	12	1	7	87	16	0	7	82	8	0	2	6	3	30	36	.218	.285	.366

Higgins, Kevin Wayne — BL/TR — b.1/22/67 — POS C-59, 3B-4, 1B-3, OF-3, 2B-1   SD89 11/312

YR	TM/LG	CL	G	TPA	AB	H	2B	3B	HR	TB	BB	IBB	HB	SO	GDP	SH	SF	SB	CS	R	RBI	BA	OBA	SA
89	SPO/NWL	A-	71	340	295	98	9	3	3	119	30	1	5	13	8	1	9	2	4	54	52	.332	.392	.403
90	LV/PCL	AAA	9	32	26	7	1	1	0	10	4	0	1	3	1	0	1	0	1	4	3	.269	.375	.385
	RIV/CAL	A+	49	208	176	53	5	1	2	66	27	3	2	15	6	2	1	0	1	27	18	.301	.398	.375
	WIC/TEX	AA	52	209	187	67	7	1	1	79	16	3	1	8	6	1	4	5	0	24	23	.358	.404	.422
91	LV/PCL	AAA	130	465	403	116	12	4	3	145	47	5	2	38	13	10	3	2	2	53	45	.288	.363	.360
92	LV/PCL	AAA	124	411	355	90	12	3	0	108	41	2	3	31	10	5	7	6	4	49	40	.254	.330	.304
93	LV/PCL	AAA	40	162	142	51	8	0	1	62	18	0	1	8	3	1	1	0	1	22	22	.359	.429	.437
	SD/NL		71	202	181	40	4	1	0	46	16	1	0	3	17	1	1	0	1	17	13	.221	.294	.254

Hill, Glenallen — BR/TR — b.3/22/65 — POS OF-241, DH-92   TOR83 9/219

YR	TM/LG	CL	G	TPA	AB	H	2B	3B	HR	TB	BB	IBB	HB	SO	GDP	SH	SF	SB	CS	R	RBI	BA	OBA	SA
83	MH/PIO	R+	46	153	133	34	3	4	.6	63	17	0	1	49	3	2	0	4	4	26	27	.256	.344	.474
84	FLO/SAL	A	129	512	440	105	19	5	16	182	63	3	3	150	6	0	6	30	15	75	64	.239	.334	.414
85	KIN/CAR	A+	131	530	466	98	13	6	20	171	57	0	1	211	7	2	4	42	15	57	56	.210	.295	.367
86	KNO/SOU	AA	141	623	570	159	23	6	31	287	39	3	1	153	10	0	13	18	18	87	96	.279	.319	.504
87	SYR/INT	AAA	137	568	536	126	25	6	16	211	25	1	1	152	10	1	5	22	9	65	77	.235	.268	.394
88	SYR/INT	AAA	51	192	172	40	7	0	4	59	15	3	2	59	2	0	3	7	2	21	19	.233	.297	.343
	KNO/SOU	AA	79	302	269	71	13	2	12	124	28	1	0	75	4	0	4	21	7	37	38	.264	.334	.461
89	SYR/INT	AAA	125	529	483	155	31	15	21	279	34	0	5	107	4	3	0	21	7	86	72	.321	.369	.578
	TOR/AL		19	55	52	15	0	0	1	18	3	0	0	12	0	0	0	2	1	4	7	.288	.327	.346
90	TOR/AL		84	278	260	60	11	3	12	113	18	0	0	62	5	0	0	5	2	47	32	.231	.281	.435
91	TOR/AL		35	108	99	25	5	2	3	43	7	0	0	24	2	0	2	2	2	14	11	.253	.296	.434
	CLE/AL		37	140	122	32	3	0	5	50	16	0	0	30	5	1	1	4	4	15	14	.262	.345	.410
	YEAR		72	248	221	57	8	2	8	93	23	0	0	54	7	1	3	6	6	29	25	.258	.324	.421
92	CAN/EAS	AA	3	12	9	1	1	0	0	2	3	0	0	4	0	0	0	0	0	1	1	.111	.333	.222
	CLE/AL		102	394	369	89	16	1	18	161	20	0	4	73	11	0	1	9	6	38	49	.241	.287	.436
93	CLE/AL		66	191	174	39	7	2	5	65	11	1	1	50	3	1	4	7	3	19	25	.224	.268	.374
	CHI/NL		31	93	87	30	7	0	10	67	6	0	0	21	1	0	0	1	0	14	22	.345	.387	.770
	YEAR		97	284	261	69	14	2	15	132	17	1	1	71	4	1	4	8	3	33	47	.264	.307	.506
5 YR TOTALS			**374**	**1259**	**1163**	**290**	**49**	**8**	**54**	**517**	**81**	**1**	**5**	**272**	**27**	**2**	**8**	**33**	**17**	**151**	**160**	**.249**	**.299**	**.445**

Hocking, Dennis Lee — BB/TR — b.4/2/70 — POS SS-12, 2B-1   MIN89 52/1314

YR	TM/LG	CL	G	TPA	AB	H	2B	3B	HR	TB	BB	IBB	HB	SO	GDP	SH	SF	SB	CS	R	RBI	BA	OBA	SA
90	ELI/APP	R+	54	250	201	59	6	2	6	87	40	1	6	26	6	1	2	14	4	45	30	.294	.422	.433
91	KEN/MID	A	125	522	432	110	17	8	2	149	77	4	6	69	6	3	4	22	10	72	36	.255	.372	.345
92	VIS/CAL	A+	135	634	550	182	34	9	7	255	72	1	8	77	7	2	2	38	18	117	81	.331	.415	.464
93	NAS/SOU	AA	107	452	409	109	9	4	8	150	34	0	0	66	12	3	2	15	5	54	50	.267	.327	.367
	MIN/AL		15	42	36	5	1	0	0	6	6	0	0	8	1	0	0	1	0	7	0	.139	.262	.167

Hoiles, Christopher Allen "Chris" — BR/TR — b.3/20/65 — POS C-318, DH-26, 1B-8   DET86 19/489

YR	TM/LG	CL	G	TPA	AB	H	2B	3B	HR	TB	BB	IBB	HB	SO	GDP	SH	SF	SB	CS	R	RBI	BA	OBA	SA
86	BRI/APP	R+	68	286	253	81	19	2	13	143	30	3	1	20	9	0	2	10	1	42	57	.320	.392	.565
87	GF/EAS	AA	108	425	380	105	12	0	13	156	35	4	3	37	10	4	3	1	5	47	53	.276	.340	.411
88	TOL/INT	AAA	22	73	69	11	1	0	2	18	2	0	2	12	4	0	0	1	0	4	6	.159	.205	.261
	GF/EAS	AA	103	423	360	102	21	3	17	180	50	4	7	57	5	3	3	4	3	67	73	.283	.379	.500
89	ROC/INT	AAA	96	363	322	79	19	1	10	130	31	1	4	58	10	2	4	1	2	41	51	.245	.316	.404
	BAL/AL		6	10	9	1	0	0	0	2	1	0	0	4	0	0	0	0	0	0	1	.111	.200	.222
90	ROC/INT	AAA	74	294	247	86	20	1	18	162	44	4	1	47	7	1	1	4	2	52	56	.348	.447	.656
	BAL/AL		23	68	63	12	3	0	1	18	5	1	0	12	0	0	0	0	0	7	6	.190	.250	.286
91	BAL/AL		107	372	341	83	15	0	11	131	29	1	1	61	11	0	3	0	0	36	31	.243	.304	.384
92	HAG/EAS	AA	7	26	24	11	1	0	1	15	2	0	0	5	0	0	0	0	0	7	5	.458	.500	.625
	BAL/AL		96	371	310	85	10	1	20	157	55	2	2	60	8	3	1	0	1	49	40	.274	.384	.506
93	BAL/AL		126	503	419	130	28	0	29	245	69	4	9	94	10	3	3	1	1	80	82	.310	.416	.585
5 YR TOTALS			**358**	**1324**	**1142**	**311**	**57**	**1**	**61**	**553**	**159**	**8**	**12**	**230**	**29**	**4**	**7**	**1**	**5**	**172**	**160**	**.272**	**.365**	**.484**

Hollins, David Michael "Dave" — BB/TR — b.5/25/66 — POS 3B-365, 1B-8   SD87 6/146

YR	TM/LG	CL	G	TPA	AB	H	2B	3B	HR	TB	BB	IBB	HB	SO	GDP	SH	SF	SB	CS	R	RBI	BA	OBA	SA
87	SPO/NWL	A-	75	340	278	86	14	4	2	114	53	7	2	36	3	3	4	20	5	52	44	.309	.418	.410
88	RIV/CAL	A+	139	608	516	157	32	1	9	218	82	2	1	67	15	0	9	13	11	90	92	.304	.395	.422
89	WIC/TEX	AA	131	538	459	126	29	4	9	190	63	4	5	88	4	1	10	8	3	69	79	.275	.361	.414
90	PHI/NL		72	127	114	21	0	0	5	36	10	3	1	28	1	0	2	0	0	14	15	.184	.252	.316
91	SCR/INT	AAA	72	278	229	61	11	6	8	108	43	3	4	43	7	0	2	4	1	37	35	.266	.388	.472
	PHI/NL		56	172	151	45	10	2	6	77	17	1	3	26	2	0	1	1	1	18	21	.298	.378	.510
92	PHI/NL		156	685	586	158	28	4	27	275	76	4	19	110	8	0	4	9	6	104	93	.270	.369	.469
93	PHI/NL		143	640	543	148	30	4	18	240	85	5	5	109	15	0	7	2	2	104	93	.273	.372	.442
4 YR TOTALS			**427**	**1624**	**1394**	**372**	**68**	**10**	**56**	**628**	**188**	**13**	**28**	**273**	**26**	**0**	**14**	**12**	**10**	**240**	**222**	**.267**	**.362**	**.451**

Horn, Samuel Lee "Sam" — BL/TL — b.11/2/63 — POS DH-292, 1B-12   BOS82 1/16

YR	TM/LG	CL	G	TPA	AB	H	2B	3B	HR	TB	BB	IBB	HB	SO	GDP	SH	SF	SB	CS	R	RBI	BA	OBA	SA
84	WIN/CAR	A+	127	487	403	126	22	3	21	217	76	5	4	107	3	1	3	5	4	67	89	.313	.424	.538
85	NB/EAS	AA	134	535	457	129	32	0	11	194	64	14	4	107	5	1	9	4	6	64	82	.282	.369	.425
86	PAW/INT	AAA	20	82	77	15	2	0	3	26	5	1	0	23	1	0	0	.0	0	8	14	.195	.244	.338

(continued)

Horn, Samuel Lee "Sam" (continued)

YR	TM/LG	CL	G	TPA	AB	H	2B	3B	HR	TB	BB	IBB	HB	SO	GDP	SH	SF	SB	CS	R	RBI	BA	OBA	SA
	NB/EAS	AA	100	400	345	85	13	0	8	122	49	4	1	80	6	0	5	1	0	41	46	.246	.338	.354
87	PAW/INT	AAA	94	373	333	107	19	0	30	216	33	3	5	88	9	0	2	0	0	57	84	.321	.389	.649
	BOS/AL		46	177	158	44	7	0	14	93	17	0	5	55	5	0	0	0	0	31	34	.278	.356	.589
88	BOS/AL		24	73	61	9	0	0	2	15	11	3	0	20	1	0	1	0	0	8	8	.148	.274	.246
	PAW/INT	AAA	83	324	279	65	10	0	10	105	44	10	0	82	9	0	1	0	0	33	31	.233	.336	.376
89	PAW/INT	AAA	51	187	164	38	9	1	8	73	20	2	0	46	4	0	3	0	3	15	27	.232	.310	.445
	BOS/AL		33	62	54	8	2	0	0	10	8	1	0	16	4	0	0	0	0	1	4	.148	.258	.185
90	HAG/EAS	AA	7	29	23	6	2	0	1	11	6	1	0	5	0	0	0	0	0	2	3	.261	.414	.478
	ROC/INT	AAA	17	67	58	24	3	0	9	54	9	1	0	13	1	0	0	0	1	16	26	.414	.493	.931
	BAL/AL		79	280	246	61	13	0	14	116	32	1	0	62	8	0	2	0	0	30	45	.248	.332	.472
91	BAL/AL		121	362	317	74	16	0	23	159	41	4	3	99	10	0	1	0	0	45	61	.233	.326	.502
92	BAL/AL		63	185	162	38	10	1	5	65	21	2	1	60	8	0	1	0	0	13	19	.235	.324	.401
93	CHW/INT	AAA	122	471	402	108	17	1	38	241	60	8	2	131	10	0	7	1	0	62	96	.269	.361	.600
	CLE/AL		12	36	33	15	1	0	4	28	1	0	1	5	1	0	0	0	0	8	8	.455	.472	.848
7 YR TOTALS			378	1175	1031	249	49	1	62	486	131	11	7	317	37	0	6	0	1	132	179	**.242**	**.329**	**.471**

Hosey, Steven Bernard "Steve" — BR/TR — b.4/2/69 — POS OF-19   SF89 1/14

YR	TM/LG	CL	G	TPA	AB	H	2B	3B	HR	TB	BB	IBB	HB	SO	GDP	SH	SF	SB	CS	R	RBI	BA	OBA	SA
89	EVE/NWL	A-	73	327	288	83	14	3	13	142	27	2	10	84	3	0	2	15	3	44	59	.288	.367	.493
90	SJ/CAL	A+	139	560	479	111	13	6	16	184	71	2	4	139	1	1	4	16	17	85	78	.232	.335	.384
91	SHR/TEX	AA	126	480	409	120	21	5	17	202	56	5	6	88	7	1	4	26	11	79	74	.293	.383	.384
92	PHO/PCL	AAA	125	512	462	132	28	7	10	204	39	4	6	98	11	0	5	15	15	64	65	.286	.346	.442
	SF/NL		21	58	56	14	1	0	1	18	0	0	0	15	1	0	1	1	1	6	6	.250	.241	.321
93	PHO/PCL	AAA	129	529	455	133	40	4	16	229	66	5	3	129	7	0	5	16	10	70	85	.292	.382	.503
	SF/NL		3	3	2	1	0	0	0	2	0	0	0	0	0	0	0	0	0	0	1	.500	.667	1.000
2 YR TOTALS			24	61	58	15	2	0	1	20	1	0	0	16	1	0	1	1	1	6	7	**.259**	**.262**	**.345**

Housie, Wayne Tyrone — BB/TR — b.5/20/65 — POS OF-6, DH-2   DET86* 8/199

YR	TM/LG	CL	G	TPA	AB	H	2B	3B	HR	TB	BB	IBB	HB	SO	GDP	SH	SF	SB	CS	R	RBI	BA	OBA	SA
86	GAS/SAL	A	90	388	336	87	10	6	2	115	43	0	4	85	4	4	1	38	13	55	29	.259	.349	.342
87	LAK/FSL	A+	125	512	458	118	12	7	1	147	39	2	3	74	7	6	6	26	11	58	45	.258	.316	.321
88	GF/EAS	AA	63	240	202	38	4	2	1	49	28	1	3	34	2	5	2	9	5	26	16	.188	.294	.243
	LAK/FSL	A+	55	231	212	57	11	3	0	74	13	0	3	40	1	2	1	24	5	31	23	.269	.319	.349
89	LON/EAS	AA	127	496	434	103	17	2	5	139	52	3	4	90	5	3	3	23	14	56	28	.237	.323	.320
90	SAL/CAL	A+	92	401	367	99	20	6	3	146	22	1	5	72	5	5	3	27	11	51	49	.270	.316	.398
	NB/EAS	AA	30	125	113	31	8	3	1	48	6	0	1	33	0	5	1	7	2	13	12	.274	.317	.425
91	NB/EAS	AA	113	508	444	123	24	2	6	169	55	2	3	86	5	6	0	43	14	58	26	.277	.361	.381
	PAW/INT	AAA	21	86	79	26	9	0	2	41	6	0	1	20	0	0	0	2	2	14	8	.329	.384	.519
	BOS/AL		11	10	8	2	1	0	0	3	1	0	0	3	1	1	0	1	0	2	0	.250	.333	.375
92	PAW/INT	AAA	134	502	456	100	22	5	2	138	32	1	3	102	7	10	2	20	6	53	28	.219	.274	.303
93	NOR/INT	AAA	16	72	67	14	0	0	1	17	3	0	1	13	2	1	1	7	0	5	5	.209	.239	.254
	NO/AMA	AAA	64	136	113	31	6	1	0	39	18	0	1	21	2	4	0	6	2	22	7	.274	.379	.345
	NY/NL		18	17	16	3	1	0	0	4	1	0	0	4	1	0	0	0	0	2	1	.188	.235	.250
2 YR TOTALS			29	27	24	5	2	0	0	7	2	0	0	4	1	1	0	1	0	4	1	**.208**	**.269**	**.292**

Howard, Christopher Hugh "Chris" — BR/TR — b.2/27/66 — POS C-13   NYA 6/16/86

YR	TM/LG	CL	G	TPA	AB	H	2B	3B	HR	TB	BB	IBB	HB	SO	GDP	SH	SF	SB	CS	R	RBI	BA	OBA	SA
88	BEL/NWL	A-	2	10	9	3	0	0	1	6	1	0	0	2	0	0	0	0	0	3	3	.333	.400	.667
	WAU/MID	A	61	209	187	45	10	1	7	78	18	0	3	60	4	0	1	1	3	20	20	.241	.316	.417
89	WAU/MID	A	36	140	125	30	8	0	4	50	13	0	1	35	2	0	1	1	3	13	32	.240	.314	.400
	WIL/EAS	AA	86	331	296	75	13	0	9	115	28	1	3	79	10	2	0	1	1	30	36	.253	.328	.389
90	WIL/EAS	AA	118	449	401	95	19	1	5	131	37	1	3	91	16	4	4	3	1	48	49	.237	.303	.327
91	CAL/PCL	AAA	82	315	293	72	12	1	8	110	16	1	1	56	10	3	3	2	2	32	36	.246	.288	.375
	SEA/AL		9	7	6	1	1	0	0	2	0	0	0	2	0	0	0	0	0	1	0	.167	.286	.333
92	CAL/PCL	AAA	97	343	319	76	16	0	8	116	14	0	5	73	9	3	2	5	7	29	45	.238	.279	.364
93	CAL/PCL	AAA	94	366	331	106	23	0	6	147	23	1	7	62	4	3	2	3	7	40	55	.320	.371	.444
	SEA/AL		4	1	1	0	0	0	0	0	0	0	0	0	0	0	0	0	0	0	0	.000	.000	.000
2 YR TOTALS			13	8	7	1	1	0	0	2	0	0	0	2	0	0	0	0	0	1	0	**.143**	**.250**	**.286**

Howard, David Wayne — BB/TR — b.2/26/67 — POS SS-140, 2B-33, OF-4, 3B-3, DH-1   KC86 25/774

YR	TM/LG	CL	G	TPA	AB	H	2B	3B	HR	TB	BB	IBB	HB	SO	GDP	SH	SF	SB	CS	R	RBI	BA	OBA	SA
87	FM/FSL	A+	89	326	289	56	9	4	1	76	30	0	0	68	3	7	0	11	10	26	19	.194	.270	.263
88	APP/MID	A	110	402	368	82	9	4	1	102	25	0	2	80	1	4	3	7	5	48	22	.223	.274	.277
89	BC/FSL	A+	83	296	267	63	7	3	3	85	23	1	1	44	1	3	2	12	2	36	30	.236	.297	.318
90	MEM/SOU	AA	116	440	384	96	14	4	5	129	39	2	8	74	6	10	6	15	4	41	44	.250	.316	.336
91	OMA/AMA	AAA	14	51	41	5	0	0	0	5	7	0	1	11	0	2	1	1	1	2	2	.122	.265	.122
	KC/AL		94	264	236	51	7	0	1	61	16	0	1	45	1	9	2	3	2	20	17	.216	.267	.258
92	BC/FSL	A+	3	11	9	4	1	0	0	5	2	0	0	3	0	0	0	0	0	3	0	.444	.545	.556
	OMA/AMA	AAA	19	75	68	8	1	0	0	9	5	0	0	8	1	2	0	5	0	3	5	.118	.151	.132
	KC/AL		74	244	219	49	6	2	1	62	15	0	1	43	3	5	0	3	4	19	18	.224	.271	.283
93	OMA/AMA	AAA	47	172	157	40	4	0	1	52	7	0	1	20	1	4	0	5	2	15	18	.255	.286	.331
	KC/AL		15	29	24	8	1	0	0	10	2	0	0	5	0	0	0	5	2	5	2	.333	.370	.417
3 YR TOTALS			183	537	479	108	13	3	2	133	33	0	1	93	4	19	5	7	6	44	37	**.225**	**.274**	**.278**

Howard, Thomas Sylvester — BB/TR — b.12/11/64 — POS OF-280, DH-9   SD86 1/11

YR	TM/LG	CL	G	TPA	AB	H	2B	3B	HR	TB	BB	IBB	HB	SO	GDP	SH	SF	SB	CS	R	RBI	BA	OBA	SA
86	SPO/NWL	A-	13	59	55	23	3	3	2	38	3	0	1	9	0	0	0	2	1	16	17	.418	.458	.691

Howard, Thomas Sylvester (continued) — SD86 1/11

YR	TM/LG	CL	G	TPA	AB	H	2B	3B	HR	TB	BB	IBB	HB	SO	GDP	SH	SF	SB	CS	R	RBI	BA	OBA	SA
	REN/CAL	A+	61	261	223	57	7	3	10	100	34	1	0	49	3	1	0	3	10	1	35	39	.256	.350	.448
87	WIC/TEX	AA	113	447	401	133	27	4	14	210	36	9	1	0	72	8	8	1	26	8	72	60	.332	.387	.524
88	LV/PCL	AAA	44	181	167	42	9	1	0	53	12	2	1	0	31	5	1	0	3	4	29	15	.251	.306	.317
	WIC/TEX	AA	29	116	103	31	9	2	0	44	13	0	0	0	14	3	0	0	6	3	15	16	.301	.379	.427
89	LV/PCL	AAA	80	337	303	91	18	3	3	124	30	1	0	0	56	6	3	1	22	11	45	31	.300	.362	.409
90	SD/NL		20	45	44	12	2	0	0	14	0	0	0	0	11	1	1	0	0	1	4	0	.273	.273	.318
	LV/PCL	AAA	89	393	341	112	26	8	5	169	44	5	0	0	63	5	4	4	27	5	58	51	.328	.401	.496
91	LV/PCL	AAA	25	107	94	29	3	1	2	40	10	3	0	0	16	1	1	2	11	5	22	16	.309	.368	.426
	SD/NL		106	309	281	70	12	3	4	100	24	4	1	0	57	4	2	1	10	7	30	22	.249	.309	.356
92	SD/NL		5	4	3	1	0	0	0	1	0	0	0	0	0	0	0	0	0	1	0	0	.333	.333	.333
	CLE/AL		117	387	358	99	15	2	2	124	17	1	0	0	60	4	10	2	15	8	36	32	.277	.308	.346
	YEAR		122	391	361	100	15	2	2	125	17	1	0	0	60	4	11	2	15	8	37	32	.277	.308	.346
93	CLE/AL		74	194	178	42	7	0	3	58	12	1	0	0	42	5	0	4	5	1	26	23	.236	.278	.326
	CIN/NL		38	154	141	39	8	3	4	65	12	0	0	0	21	4	0	1	5	6	22	13	.277	.331	.461
	YEAR		112	348	319	81	15	3	7	123	24	0	0	0	63	9	0	5	10	7	48	36	.254	.302	.386
4 YR TOTALS			**360**	**1093**	**1005**	**263**	**44**	**8**	**13**	**362**	**65**	**5**	**1**		**191**	**18**	**14**	**8**	**35**	**23**	**119**	**90**	**.262**	**.305**	**.360**

Howitt, Dann Paul John — BL/TR — b.2/13/64 — POS OF-91, 1B-11, DH-3, 3B-1 — OAK86 18/457

YR	TM/LG	CL	G	TPA	AB	H	2B	3B	HR	TB	BB	IBB	HB	SO	GDP	SH	SF	SB	CS	R	RBI	BA	OBA	SA
86	MED/NWL	A-	66	260	208	66	9	2	6	97	49	3	1	37	7	1	1	5	1	36	37	.317	.448	.466
87	MOD/CAL	A+	109	405	336	70	11	2	8	109	59	1	4	110	8	3	3	7	9	44	42	.208	.331	.324
88	MOD/CAL	A+	132	565	480	121	20	2	18	199	81	3	2	106	9	0	2	11	5	75	86	.252	.361	.415
	TAC/PCL	AAA	4	15	15	2	1	0	0	3	0	0	0	4	0	0	0	0	0	1	0	.133	.133	.200
89	HUN/SOU	AA	138	588	509	143	28	2	26	253	68	7	3	107	6	2	6	2	1	78	111	.281	.365	.497
	OAK/AL		3	3	3	0	0	0	0	0	0	0	0	2	0	0	0	0	0	0	0	.000	.000	.000
90	TAC/PCL	AAA	118	481	437	116	30	1	11	181	38	3	0	95	16	0	4	4	4	58	69	.265	.324	.414
	OAK/AL		14	25	22	3	0	1	0	5	3	0	0	12	0	0	0	0	0	3	1	.136	.240	.227
91	TAC/PCL	AAA	122	506	449	120	28	6	14	202	49	2	2	92	14	0	1	5	2	58	73	.267	.339	.450
	OAK/AL		21	44	42	7	1	0	1	11	1	0	0	12	1	0	0	0	0	5	3	.167	.182	.262
92	TAC/PCL	AAA	43	170	140	41	13	1	1	59	23	0	2	20	3	0	5	5	3	25	27	.293	.388	.421
	OAK/AL		22	54	48	6	0	0	1	9	5	1	0	4	4	1	0	0	0	1	2	.125	.208	.188
	CAL/PCL	AAA	50	194	178	54	9	5	6	91	12	1	1	38	7	2	1	4	0	29	33	.303	.349	.511
	SEA/AL		13	43	37	10	4	1	1	19	3	0	0	5	2	3	1	1	1	6	8	.270	.302	.514
	YEAR		35	97	85	16	4	1	2	28	8	1	0	9	6	1	3	1	1	7	10	.188	.250	.329
93	CAL/PCL	AAA	95	381	333	93	20	1	21	178	39	2	1	67	4	1	7	7	5	57	77	.279	.350	.535
	SEA/AL		32	80	76	16	3	1	2	27	4	0	0	18	0	0	0	0	0	6	8	.211	.250	.355
5 YR TOTALS			**105**	**249**	**228**	**42**	**8**	**3**	**5**	**71**	**16**	**1**	**0**	**53**	**7**	**1**	**4**	**1**	**1**	**21**	**22**	**.184**	**.234**	**.311**

Hrbek, Kent Alan — BL/TR — b.5/21/60 — POS 1B-1537, DH-102, 3B-1 — MIN78 17/432

YR	TM/LG	CL	G	TPA	AB	H	2B	3B	HR	TB	BB	IBB	HB	SO	GDP	SH	SF	SB	CS	R	RBI	BA	OBA	SA
81	MIN/AL		24	73	67	16	5	0	1	24	5	1	1	9	0	0	0	0	0	5	7	.239	.301	.358
82	MIN/AL		140	591	532	160	21	4	23	258	54	12	0	80	17	1	4	3	1	82	92	.301	.363	.485
83	MIN/AL		141	582	515	153	41	5	16	252	57	5	3	71	12	0	7	4	6	75	84	.297	.366	.489
84	MIN/AL		149	635	559	174	31	3	27	292	65	15	4	87	17	1	6	1	1	80	107	.311	.383	.522
85	MIN/AL		158	666	593	165	31	2	21	263	67	12	2	87	12	0	4	1	1	78	93	.278	.351	.444
86	MIN/AL		149	634	550	147	27	1	29	263	71	9	6	81	15	0	7	2	2	85	91	.267	.353	.478
87	MIN/AL		143	566	477	136	20	1	34	260	84	12	0	60	13	0	5	5	2	85	90	.285	.389	.545
88	MIN/AL		143	586	510	159	31	0	25	265	67	7	0	54	9	2	7	0	3	75	76	.312	.387	.520
89	MIN/AL		109	434	375	102	17	0	25	194	53	4	1	35	6	1	4	3	0	59	84	.272	.360	.517
90	MIN/AL		143	578	492	141	26	0	22	233	69	8	7	45	17	2	8	5	2	61	79	.287	.377	.474
91	MIN/AL		132	534	462	131	20	1	20	213	67	4	0	48	15	3	4	5	4	72	89	.284	.373	.461
92	MIN/AL		112	470	394	96	20	0	15	161	71	9	0	56	12	3	2	3	2	52	58	.244	.357	.409
93	MIN/AL		123	471	392	95	11	1	25	183	71	6	1	57	12	3	4	4	2	60	83	.242	.357	.467
13 YR TOTALS			**1666**	**6820**	**5918**	**1675**	**301**	**18**	**283**	**2861**	**801**	**104**	**25**	**770**	**157**	**15**	**61**	**37**	**26**	**869**	**1033**	**.283**	**.368**	**.483**

Huff, Michael Kale "Mike" — BR/TR — b.8/11/63 — POS OF-204, 2B-4, DH-3 — LA85 17/510

YR	TM/LG	CL	G	TPA	AB	H	2B	3B	HR	TB	BB	IBB	HB	SO	GDP	SH	SF	SB	CS	R	RBI	BA	OBA	SA
85	GF/PIO	R+	70	310	247	78	6	6	0	96	56	0	4	44	3	2	1	28	6	70	35	.316	.448	.389
86	VB/FSL	A+	113	439	362	106	6	8	2	134	67	1	5	67	10	3	2	28	13	73	32	.293	.408	.370
87	SA/TEX	AA	31	149	135	42	5	1	3	58	9	0	3	21	3	2	1	23	8	28	18	.311	.367	.430
88	SA/TEX	AA	102	443	395	120	18	10	2	164	37	2	5	55	3	5	1	34	10	68	40	.304	.370	.415
	ALB/PCL	AAA	2	4	4	1	1	0	0	2	0	0	0	0	0	0	0	0	0	0	0	.250	.250	.500
89	LA/NL		12	30	25	5	1	0	1	9	3	0	1	6	0	1	0	0	0	4	2	.200	.310	.360
	ALB/PCL	AAA	115	520	471	150	29	7	10	223	38	0	2	75	6	4	5	32	10	75	78	.318	.368	.473
90	ALB/PCL	AAA	138	575	474	154	28	11	7	225	82	5	3	68	11	6	10	27	13	99	84	.325	.420	.475
91	CLE/AL		51	179	146	35	6	1	3	49	25	0	4	30	2	3	1	11	2	28	10	.240	.364	.336
	CHI/AL		51	115	97	26	4	1	0	35	12	2	2	18	5	3	1	3	2	14	15	.268	.357	.361
	YEAR		102	294	243	61	10	2	3	84	37	2	6	48	7	6	2	14	4	42	25	.251	.361	.346
92	VAN/PCL	AAA	1	5	4	1	1	0	0	1	1	0	0	1	0	0	0	0	0	1	0	.250	.400	.250
	SB/MID	A	12	51	40	15	2	1	1	22	11	1	0	7	0	2	0	3	3	13	8	.375	.510	.550
	CHI/AL		60	130	115	24	5	0	0	29	10	1	1	24	2	2	0	3	3	13	8	.209	.273	.252
93	NAS/AMA	AAA	92	417	344	101	12	6	6	149	64	4	1	63	4	1	2	18	6	65	32	.294	.411	.433
	CHI/AL		43	57	44	8	2	0	1	13	9	0	1	15	0	1	1	0	1	4	6	.182	.321	.295
4 YR TOTALS			**217**	**511**	**427**	**98**	**18**	**2**	**5**	**135**	**59**	**3**	**9**	**93**	**9**	**10**	**6**	**16**	**7**	**63**	**41**	**.230**	**.331**	**.316**

(continued)

Hughes, Keith Wills — BL/TL — b.9/12/63 — POS OF-57, DH-1   PHI 8/24/81

YR	TM/LG	CL	G	TPA	AB	H	2B	3B	HR	TB	BB	IBB	HB	SO	GDP	SH	SF	SB	CS	R	RBI	BA	OBA	SA
82	BEN/NWL	A-	55	213	179	46	10	2	3	69	30	1	1	42	2	1	2	2	0	29	26	.257	.363	.385
83	SPA/SAL	A	131	562	484	159	31	4	15	243	67	5	4	83	8	2	5	16	1	80	90	.329	.411	.502
84	REA/EAS	AA	70	263	230	60	7	5	2	83	31	2	0	43	6	0	2	1	0	35	20	.261	.346	.361
	NAS/SOU	AA	21	60	50	9	0	0	0	9	10	0	0	14	0	0	0	0	0	6	5	.180	.317	.180
85	CMB/INT	AAA	18	56	54	16	4	0	3	29	2	0	0	11	0	0	0	0	2	7	8	.296	.321	.537
	ALB/EAS	AA	104	416	361	97	22	5	10	159	51	3	3	73	4	0	1	4	4	53	54	.269	.363	.440
86	ALB/EAS	AA	94	361	323	99	21	3	7	147	32	2	3	53	8	2	3	6	8	44	37	.307	.368	.455
	CMB/INT	AAA	2	8	8	1	0	0	0	1	0	0	0	2	1	0	0	0	0	0	0	.125	.125	.125
87	NY/AL		4	4	4	0	0	0	0	0	0	0	0	2	0	0	0	0	0	0	0	.000	.000	.000
	CMB/INT	AAA	40	153	139	41	7	4	5	71	13	0	0	24	4	0	0	1	0	21	20	.295	.353	.511
	MAI/INT	AAA	50	205	177	52	8	0	12	96	24	2	3	34	5	0	1	4	2	27	37	.294	.385	.542
	PHI/NL		37	84	76	20	2	0	0	22	7	0	1	11	1	0	0	0	0	8	10	.263	.333	.289
	YEAR		41	88	80	20	2	0	0	22	7	0	1	13	1	0	0	0	0	8	10	.250	.318	.275
88	ROC/INT	AAA	77	323	274	74	13	2	7	112	43	5	2	57	2	0	4	11	3	44	49	.270	.368	.409
	BAL/AL		41	126	108	21	4	2	2	35	16	1	0	27	3	0	2	1	0	10	14	.194	.294	.324
89	ROC/INT	AAA	83	332	285	78	20	4	2	112	44	3	1	47	3	0	2	4	5	44	43	.274	.370	.393
90	TID/INT	AAA	117	444	379	117	24	5	10	181	57	7	4	58	9	0	4	7	4	77	53	.309	.401	.478
	NY/NL		8	9	9	0	0	0	0	0	0	0	0	4	0	0	0	0	0	0	0	.000	.000	.000
91	CMB/INT	AAA	130	495	424	115	18	8	3	173	60	2	3	74	1	0	8	6	7	64	66	.271	.360	.408
92	POR/PCL	AAA	89	247	221	60	11	3	5	92	25	2	0	39	3	0	1	6	4	37	26	.271	.344	.416
93	CIN/NL		3	4	4	0	0	0	0	0	0	0	0	0	0	0	0	0	0	0	0	.000	.000	.000
	IND/AMA	AAA	82	328	283	81	28	3	13	156	41	2	2	61	1	1	1	5	0	55	42	.286	.379	.551
4 YR TOTALS			**93**	**227**	**201**	**41**	**6**	**2**	**2**	**57**	**23**	**1**	**1**	**44**	**4**	**0**	**2**	**1**	**0**	**18**	**24**	**.204**	**.286**	**.284**

Hulett, Timothy Craig "Tim" — BR/TR — b.1/12/60 — POS 3B-445, 2B-190, DH-38, SS-14, OF-1   CHA 5/28/80

YR	TM/LG	CL	G	TPA	AB	H	2B	3B	HR	TB	BB	IBB	HB	SO	GDP	SH	SF	SB	CS	R	RBI	BA	OBA	SA
80	GF/EAS	AA	6	26	23	4	0	0	0	4	3	0	0	5	0	0	0	0	1	2	0	.174	.269	.174
	DM/AMA	AAA	3	8	8	2	0	0	0	2	0	0	0	0	1	0	0	0	0	1	0	.250	.250	.250
81	GF/EAS	AA	134	511	437	99	27	1	10	158	66	2	3	87	4	1	4	0	3	59	55	.227	.329	.362
82	GF/EAS	AA	140	641	536	145	28	5	22	249	95	1	3	135	10	1	6	1	8	113	87	.271	.380	.465
83	DEN/AMA	AAA	133	551	477	130	19	4	21	220	61	3	2	64	20	2	9	5	3	77	88	.273	.352	.461
	CHI/AL		6	5	5	1	0	0	0	1	0	0	0	0	0	0	0	1	0	0	0	.200	.200	.200
84	CHI/AL		8	8	7	0	0	0	0	0	1	0	0	4	0	0	0	1	0	1	0	.000	.125	.000
	DEN/AMA	AAA	139	554	475	125	32	6	16	217	67	3	0	88	5	3	9	3	4	72	80	.263	.348	.457
85	CHI/AL		141	436	395	106	19	4	5	148	30	1	4	81	8	4	3	6	4	52	37	.268	.324	.375
86	CHI/AL		150	552	520	120	16	5	17	197	21	0	1	91	11	6	4	4	1	53	44	.231	.260	.379
87	CHI/AL		68	257	240	52	10	0	7	83	10	1	0	41	6	5	0	2	2	20	28	.217	.246	.346
	HAW/PCL	AAA	42	170	157	37	5	2	1	49	9	0	0	28	7	1	3	4	1	13	24	.236	.272	.312
88	IND/AMA	AAA	126	471	427	100	29	2	7	154	34	1	0	106	11	1	9	2	0	36	59	.234	.285	.361
89	ROC/INT	AAA	122	514	461	129	32	12	3	194	38	1	9	81	9	1	5	2	5	61	50	.280	.343	.421
	BAL/AL		33	109	97	27	5	0	3	41	10	0	0	17	3	1	0	1	0	12	18	.278	.343	.423
90	ROC/INT	AAA	14	55	43	16	2	1	2	26	11	0	0	7	2	1	0	1	0	10	4	.372	.500	.605
	BAL/AL		53	169	153	39	7	1	3	57	15	0	0	41	2	1	0	1	0	16	16	.255	.321	.373
91	BAL/AL		79	221	206	42	9	0	2	72	13	0	1	49	3	1	0	0	1	29	18	.204	.255	.350
92	BAL/AL		57	153	142	41	7	2	2	58	10	1	1	31	7	0	0	0	0	11	21	.289	.340	.408
93	BAL/AL		85	289	260	78	15	0	2	99	23	1	1	56	5	1	2	1	2	40	23	.300	.361	.381
10 YR TOTALS			**680**	**2199**	**2025**	**506**	**88**	**12**	**46**	**756**	**133**	**4**	**10**	**411**	**45**	**19**	**12**	**14**	**11**	**234**	**205**	**.250**	**.298**	**.373**

Hulse, David Lindsey — BL/TL — b.2/25/68 — POS OF-143, DH-3   TEX90 13/360

YR	TM/LG	CL	G	TPA	AB	H	2B	3B	HR	TB	BB	IBB	HB	SO	GDP	SH	SF	SB	CS	R	RBI	BA	OBA	SA
90	BUT/PIO	R+	64	286	257	92	12	2	2	114	25	1	2	30	4	2	0	24	6	54	36	.358	.419	.444
91	CHA/FSL	A+	88	353	310	86	4	5	0	100	36	2	1	74	4	6	0	44	7	41	17	.277	.354	.323
92	TUL/TEX	AA	88	378	354	101	14	3	3	130	20	2	3	86	2	1	0	17	10	40	20	.285	.329	.367
	OC/AMA	AAA	8	33	30	7	1	1	0	10	1	0	1	4	0	1	0	2	2	7	3	.233	.281	.333
	TEX/AL		32	97	92	28	4	0	0	32	3	0	0	18	0	2	0	3	1	14	7	.304	.326	.348
93	TEX/AL		114	441	407	118	9	10	1	150	26	1	1	57	9	5	2	29	9	71	29	.290	.333	.369
2 YR TOTALS			**146**	**538**	**499**	**146**	**13**	**10**	**1**	**182**	**29**	**1**	**1**	**75**	**9**	**7**	**2**	**32**	**10**	**85**	**31**	**.293**	**.331**	**.365**

Humphreys, Michael Butler "Mike" — BR/TR — b.4/10/67 — POS OF-32, DH-11, 3B-6   SD88 15/370

YR	TM/LG	CL	G	TPA	AB	H	2B	3B	HR	TB	BB	IBB	HB	SO	GDP	SH	SF	SB	CS	R	RBI	BA	OBA	SA
88	SPO/NWL	A-	76	353	303	93	16	5	6	137	46	1	0	57	9	0	4	21	4	67	59	.307	.394	.452
89	RIV/CAL	A+	117	507	420	121	26	1	13	188	72	4	7	79	9	3	5	23	10	77	66	.288	.397	.448
90	WIC/TEX	AA	116	499	421	116	21	4	17	196	67	4	5	79	6	2	4	38	9	92	79	.276	.378	.466
	LV/PCL	AAA	12	49	42	10	1	0	2	17	4	0	1	11	4	2	0	1	0	7	6	.238	.319	.405
91	CMB/INT	AAA	117	486	413	117	23	5	9	177	63	2	3	62	10	1	6	34	9	71	53	.283	.377	.429
	NY/AL		25	50	40	8	0	0	0	8	9	0	0	7	0	1	0	2	0	9	3	.200	.347	.200
92	NY/AL		4	10	10	1	0	0	0	1	0	0	0	1	2	0	0	0	0	0	0	.100	.100	.100
	CMB/INT	AAA	114	476	408	115	18	6	6	163	59	0	1	70	9	3	5	37	13	83	46	.282	.370	.400
93	CMB/INT	AAA	92	389	330	95	16	2	6	133	52	2	3	57	6	2	2	18	15	59	42	.288	.388	.403
	NY/AL		25	40	35	6	1	0	0	13	4	0	0	11	0	0	0	2	1	6	6	.171	.250	.371
3 YR TOTALS			**54**	**100**	**85**	**15**	**2**	**1**	**0**	**22**	**13**	**0**	**0**	**19**	**2**	**1**	**1**	**4**	**1**	**15**	**9**	**.176**	**.283**	**.259**

Hundley, Todd Randolph — BB/TR — b.5/27/69 — POS C-300   NYN87 2/39

YR	TM/LG	CL	G	TPA	AB	H	2B	3B	HR	TB	BB	IBB	HB	SO	GDP	SH	SF	SB	CS	R	RBI	BA	OBA	SA
87	LF/NYP	A-	34	118	103	15	4	0	1	22	12	2	3	27	2	0	0	0	0	12	10	.146	.254	.214
88	LF/NYP	A-	52	199	176	33	8	0	2	47	16	1	4	31	2	2	1	1	1	23	18	.188	.269	.267
	SL/FSL	A+	1	3	1	0	0	0	0	0	2	0	0	0	0	0	0	0	0	0	0	.000	.667	.000

Hundley, Todd Randolph (continued)

YR	TM/LG	CL	G	TPA	AB	H	2B	3B	HR	TB	BB	IBB	HB	SO	GDP	SH	SF	SB	CS	R	RBI	BA	OBA	SA
89	COL/SAL	A	125	507	439	118	23	4	11	182	54	10	8	67	20	1	5	6	3	67	66	.269	.356	.415
90	JAC/TEX	AA	81	317	279	74	12	2	1	93	34	3	1	44	5	0	3	5	3	27	35	.265	.344	.333
	NY/NL		36	74	67	14	6	0	0	20	6	0	0	18	1	1	0	0	0	8	2	.209	.274	.299
91	TID/INT	AAA	125	519	454	124	24	4	14	198	51	2	2	95	12	4	8	1	2	62	66	.273	.344	.436
	NY/NL		21	69	60	8	0	1	1	13	6	0	1	14	3	1	1	0	0	5	7	.133	.221	.217
92	NY/NL		123	390	358	75	17	0	7	113	19	4	4	76	8	7	2	3	2	32	32	.209	.256	.316
93	NY/NL		130	448	417	95	17	2	11	149	23	7	2	62	10	2	4	1	1	40	53	.228	.269	.357
4 YR TOTALS			**310**	**981**	**902**	**192**	**40**	**3**	**19**	**295**	**54**	**11**	**7**	**170**	**22**	**11**	**7**	**4**	**1**	**85**	**94**	**.213**	**.261**	**.327**

Hunter, Brian Ronald — BR/TL — b.3/4/68 — POS 1B-206, OF-14   ATL87 8/194

YR	TM/LG	CL	G	TPA	AB	H	2B	3B	HR	TB	BB	IBB	HB	SO	GDP	SH	SF	SB	CS	R	RBI	BA	OBA	SA
87	PUL/APP	R+	65	275	251	58	10	2	8	96	18	0	5	47	7	0	1	3	2	38	30	.231	.295	.382
88	BUR/MID	A	117	478	417	108	17	0	22	191	45	2	8	90	7	1	7	7	2	58	71	.259	.338	.458
	DUR/CAR	A+	13	56	49	17	3	0	3	29	7	0	0	8	0	0	0	2	0	13	9	.347	.429	.592
89	GRE/SOU	AA	124	501	451	114	19	2	19	194	33	2	7	61	4	1	9	5	4	57	82	.253	.308	.430
90	RIC/INT	AAA	43	157	137	27	4	0	5	46	18	0	0	37	0	0	1	2	1	13	16	.197	.288	.336
	GRE/SOU	AA	88	370	320	77	13	1	14	134	43	1	3	62	6	0	4	3	4	45	55	.241	.332	.419
91	RIC/INT	AAA	48	198	181	47	7	0	10	84	11	1	1	24	6	2	3	3	2	28	30	.260	.301	.464
	ATL/NL		97	291	271	68	16	1	12	122	17	0	1	48	6	2	0	0	2	32	50	.251	.296	.450
92	ATL/NL		102	268	238	57	13	2	14	116	21	3	0	50	2	1	8	1	2	34	41	.239	.292	.487
93	RIC/INT	AAA	30	112	99	24	7	0	6	49	10	0	3	21	2	0	0	4	2	16	26	.242	.330	.495
	ATL/NL		37	85	80	11	3	1	0	16	2	1	0	15	1	0	3	0	0	4	8	.138	.153	.200
3 YR TOTALS			**236**	**644**	**589**	**136**	**32**	**4**	**26**	**254**	**40**	**4**	**1**	**113**	**9**	**1**	**13**	**1**	**4**	**70**	**99**	**.231**	**.275**	**.431**

Huskey, Robert Leon "Butch" — BR/TR — b.11/10/71 — POS 3B-13   NYN89 7/190

YR	TM/LG	CL	G	TPA	AB	H	2B	3B	HR	TB	BB	IBB	HB	SO	GDP	SH	SF	SB	CS	R	RBI	BA	OBA	SA
89	MET/GCL	R	54	205	190	50	14	2	6	86	14	0	1	36	2	0	0	4	1	27	34	.263	.317	.453
90	KIN/APP	R+	72	310	279	75	13	0	14	130	24	1	2	74	5	0	5	7	3	39	53	.269	.326	.466
91	COL/SAL	A	134	558	492	141	27	5	26	256	54	5	4	89	12	1	7	22	10	88	99	.287	.357	.520
92	SL/FSL	A+	134	532	493	125	17	1	18	198	33	6	1	74	5	0	5	7	3	65	75	.254	.299	.402
93	BIN/EAS	AA	139	584	526	132	23	1	25	232	48	3	2	102	14	0	8	11	2	72	98	.251	.312	.441
	NY/NL		13	44	41	6	1	0	0	7	1	1	0	13	0	0	2	0	0	2	3	.146	.159	.171

Huson, Jeffrey Kent "Jeff" — BL/TR — b.8/15/64 — POS SS-364, 2B-77, 3B-41, OF-3, DH-1   MON 8/18/85

YR	TM/LG	CL	G	TPA	AB	H	2B	3B	HR	TB	BB	IBB	HB	SO	GDP	SH	SF	SB	CS	R	RBI	BA	OBA	SA
86	BUR/MID	A	133	540	457	132	19	1	16	201	76	4	2	68	13	2	3	32	6	85	72	.289	.390	.440
	JAC/SOU	AA	1	4	4	0	0	0	0	0	0	0	0	0	0	0	0	0	0	0	0	.000	.000	.000
87	WPB/FSL	A+	131	520	455	130	15	4	1	156	50	4	1	30	9	6	8	33	9	54	53	.286	.352	.343
88	JAC/SOU	AA	128	546	471	117	18	1	0	137	59	3	3	45	15	10	3	56	13	72	34	.248	.334	.291
	MON/NL		20	46	42	13	2	0	0	15	4	2	0	3	0	0	0	2	1	7	3	.310	.370	.357
89	IND/AMA	AAA	102	433	378	115	17	4	3	149	50	1	1	26	10	2	2	30	17	70	35	.304	.385	.394
	MON/NL		32	83	74	12	5	0	0	17	6	3	0	6	6	3	0	3	0	1	2	.162	.225	.230
90	TEX/AL		145	454	396	95	12	2	0	111	46	0	2	54	8	7	3	12	4	57	28	.240	.320	.280
91	OC/AMA	AAA	2	6	6	3	1	0	0	4	0	0	0	0	0	0	0	0	0	3	0	.500	.500	.667
	TEX/AL		119	317	268	57	8	3	2	77	39	0	0	32	6	9	1	8	3	36	26	.213	.312	.287
92	TEX/AL		123	374	318	83	14	3	4	115	41	2	1	43	7	6	6	18	6	49	24	.261	.342	.362
93	OC/AMA	AAA	24	89	76	22	5	0	1	30	13	0	0	10	2	0	0	3	2	11	10	.289	.393	.395
	TEX/AL		23	46	45	6	1	1	0	9	0	0	0	10	0	1	0	0	2	3	2	.133	.133	.200
6 YR TOTALS			**462**	**1320**	**1143**	**266**	**42**	**9**	**6**	**344**	**136**	**7**	**3**	**148**	**29**	**28**	**10**	**43**	**14**	**153**	**85**	**.233**	**.313**	**.301**

Incaviglia, Peter Joseph "Pete" — BR/TR — b.4/2/64 — POS OF-858, DH-111   MON85 1/8

YR	TM/LG	CL	G	TPA	AB	H	2B	3B	HR	TB	BB	IBB	HB	SO	GDP	SH	SF	SB	CS	R	RBI	BA	OBA	SA
86	TEX/AL		153	606	540	135	21	2	30	250	55	2	4	185	9	0	7	3	2	82	88	.250	.320	.463
87	TEX/AL		139	563	509	138	26	4	27	253	48	1	1	168	8	0	5	9	3	85	80	.271	.332	.497
88	TEX/AL		116	467	418	104	19	3	22	195	39	3	7	153	6	0	1	6	4	59	54	.249	.321	.467
89	TEX/AL		133	495	453	107	27	4	21	205	32	0	4	136	12	0	4	5	7	48	81	.236	.293	.453
90	TEX/AL		153	587	529	123	27	0	24	222	45	0	9	146	18	0	4	3	4	59	85	.233	.302	.420
91	DET/AL		97	377	337	72	12	1	11	119	36	0	1	92	6	2	1	1	3	38	38	.214	.290	.353
92	HOU/NL		113	379	349	93	22	1	11	150	25	2	3	99	6	0	2	2	2	31	44	.266	.319	.430
93	PHI/NL		116	402	368	101	16	3	24	195	21	1	6	82	9	0	7	1	1	60	89	.274	.318	.530
8 YR TOTALS			**1020**	**3876**	**3503**	**873**	**170**	**18**	**170**	**1589**	**301**	**14**	**37**	**1061**	**74**	**1**	**34**	**30**	**26**	**462**	**559**	**.249**	**.313**	**.454**

Jackson, Darrin Jay — BR/TR — b.8/22/62 — POS OF-508, P-1   CHN81 3/28

YR	TM/LG	CL	G	TPA	AB	H	2B	3B	HR	TB	BB	IBB	HB	SO	GDP	SH	SF	SB	CS	R	RBI	BA	OBA	SA
81	CUB/GCL	R	62	244	210	39	5	0	1	47	28	0	1	53	5	3	2	18	4	29	15	.186	.282	.224
82	QC/MID	A	132	590	529	146	23	5	5	194	47	0	4	106	6	3	7	58	17	86	48	.276	.338	.367
83	SAL/CAL	A+	129	564	509	126	18	5	6	172	38	0	4	111	4	9	4	36	12	70	54	.248	.303	.338
84	MID/TEX	AA	132	555	496	134	18	2	15	201	49	2	7	103	7	6	2	13	8	63	54	.270	.337	.405
85	IOW/AMA	AAA	10	43	40	7	2	1	0	11	3	0	0	10	0	0	0	1	0	5	3	.175	.233	.275
	CHI/NL		5	11	11	1	0	0	0	1	0	0	0	3	0	0	0	0	0	0	0	.091	.091	.091
	PIT/EAS	AA	91	367	325	82	10	3	1	103	34	3	0	64	2	5	3	8	7	38	30	.252	.320	.317
86	PIT/EAS	AA	137	574	520	139	28	2	15	216	43	1	1	115	6	2	8	42	16	82	64	.267	.320	.415
87	IOW/AMA	AAA	132	510	474	130	32	5	23	241	26	3	2	110	6	5	3	13	10	81	81	.274	.313	.508
	CHI/NL		7	5	5	4	2	0	0	6	0	0	0	0	0	0	0	1	0	2	0	.800	.800	1.000
88	CHI/NL		100	197	188	50	11	3	6	85	5	1	1	28	3	2	1	4	1	29	20	.266	.287	.452
89	IOW/AMA	AAA	30	129	120	31	4	1	7	58	7	2	2	22	3	0	0	4	0	18	17	.258	.310	.483
	CHI/NL		45	89	83	19	4	0	1	26	6	1	0	17	1	0	0	1	1	7	8	.229	.281	.313

(continued)

Jackson, Darrin Jay (continued)

YR	TM/LG	CL	G	TPA	AB	H	2B	3B	HR	TB	BB	IBB	HB	SO	GDP	SH	SF	SB	CS	R	RBI	BA	OBA	SA
	SD/NL		25	96	87	18	3	0	3	30	7	4	0	17	1	0	2	0	2	10	12	.207	.260	.345
	YEAR		70	185	170	37	7	0	4	56	13	5	0	34	2	0	2	1	4	17	20	.218	.270	.329
90	LV/PCL	AAA	29	109	98	27	4	0	5	46	9	0	0	21	5	0	2	3	0	14	15	.276	.330	.469
	SD/NL		58	120	113	29	3	0	3	41	5	1	0	24	1	1	1	3	0	10	9	.257	.286	.363
91	SD/NL		122	394	359	94	12	1	21	171	27	2	2	66	5	3	3	5	3	51	49	.262	.315	.476
92	SD/NL		155	628	587	146	23	5	17	230	26	4	4	106	21	6	5	14	3	72	70	.249	.283	.392
93	TOR/AL		46	189	176	38	8	0	5	61	8	0	0	53	9	5	0	0	0	15	19	.216	.250	.347
	NY/NL		31	91	87	17	1	0	1	21	2	0	0	22	0	1	0	0	2	4	7	.195	.211	.241
	YEAR		77	280	263	55	9	0	6	82	10	0	0	75	9	6	1	0	2	19	26	.209	.237	.312
8 YR TOTALS			**594**	**1820**	**1696**	**416**	**66**	**9**	**57**	**671**	**86**	**13**	**7**	**336**	**41**	**18**	**13**	**27**	**13**	**200**	**194**	**.245**	**.282**	**.396**

Jackson, Vincent Edward "Bo" — BR/TR — b.11/30/62 — POS OF-511, DH-95   KC86 4/105

YR	TM/LG	CL	G	TPA	AB	H	2B	3B	HR	TB	BB	IBB	HB	SO	GDP	SH	SF	SB	CS	R	RBI	BA	OBA	SA
86	MEM/SOU	AA	53	212	184	51	9	3	7	87	22	0	5	81		0	1	3	6	30	25	.277	.368	.473
	KC/AL		25	91	82	17	2	1	2	27	7	0	2	34	1	0	0	3	1	9	9	.207	.286	.329
87	KC/AL		116	434	396	93	17	2	22	180	30	0	5	158	3	1	2	10	4	46	53	.235	.296	.455
88	KC/AL		124	468	439	108	16	4	25	207	25	6	1	146	6	1	2	27	6	63	68	.246	.287	.472
89	KC/AL		135	561	515	132	15	6	32	255	39	8	3	172	10	0	4	26	9	86	105	.256	.310	.495
90	KC/AL		111	456	405	110	16	1	28	212	44	2	2	128	10	0	5	15	9	74	78	.272	.342	.523
91	SAR/FSL	A+	2	7	6	2	0	0	0	2	0	0	0	0	0	0	0	1	0	1	2	.333	.286	.333
	BIR/SOU	AA	4	17	13	4	0	0	0	4	4	0	0	2	0	0	0	1	0	2	0	.308	.471	.308
	CHI/AL		23	84	71	16	4	0	3	29	12	1	0	25	3	0	0	1	1	8	14	.225	.333	.408
93	CHI/AL		85	308	284	66	9	0	16	123	23	1	0	106	5	0	0	0	2	32	45	.232	.289	.433
7 YR TOTALS			**619**	**2402**	**2192**	**542**	**79**	**14**	**128**	**1033**	**180**	**18**	**13**	**769**	**38**	**2**	**15**	**81**	**32**	**318**	**372**	**.247**	**.306**	**.471**

Jaha, John Emil — BR/TR — b.5/27/66 — POS 1B-188, DH-8, OF-1, 2B-1, 3B-1   MIL84 14/358

YR	TM/LG	CL	G	TPA	AB	H	2B	3B	HR	TB	BB	IBB	HB	SO	GDP	SH	SF	SB	CS	R	RBI	BA	OBA	SA
85	HEL/PIO	R+	24	83	68	18	3	0	2	27	14	0	0	23	0	0	1	4	0	13	14	.265	.386	.397
86	TRI/NWL	A-	73	335	258	82	13	2	15	144	70	4	5	75	2	0	2	9	4	65	67	.318	.469	.558
87	BEL/MID	A	122	487	376	101	22	0	7	144	102	0	4	86	11	2	3	10	5	68	47	.269	.427	.383
88	STO/CAL	A+	99	376	302	77	14	6	8	127	69	0	2	85	10	2	1	10	6	58	54	.255	.396	.421
89	STO/CAL	A+	140	611	479	140	26	5	25	251	112	6	5	115	15	2	13	8	11	83	91	.292	.422	.524
90	STO/CAL	A+	26	104	84	22	5	0	4	39	18	0	0	25	1	0	0	2	0	12	19	.262	.404	.464
91	EP/TEX	AA	130	578	486	167	38	4	30	301	78	6	8	101	9	1	5	12	6	121	134	.344	.438	.619
92	DEN/AMA	AAA	79	333	274	88	18	2	18	164	50	2	1	60	3	1	2	6	4	61	69	.321	.434	.599
	MIL/AL		47	152	133	30	3	1	2	41	12	1	2	30	1	1	4	10	0	17	10	.226	.291	.308
93	MIL/AL		153	582	515	136	21	0	19	214	51	4	8	109	6	4	4	13	9	78	70	.264	.337	.416
2 YR TOTALS			**200**	**734**	**648**	**166**	**24**	**1**	**21**	**255**	**63**	**5**	**10**	**139**	**7**	**5**	**8**	**23**	**9**	**95**	**80**	**.256**	**.328**	**.394**

James, Dion — BL/TL — b.11/9/62 — POS OF-649, DH-48, 1B-46   MIL80 1/25

YR	TM/LG	CL	G	TPA	AB	H	2B	3B	HR	TB	BB	IBB	HB	SO	GDP	SH	SF	SB	CS	R	RBI	BA	OBA	SA
83	MIL/AL		11	22	20	2	0	0	0	2	2	0	0	2	0	0	0	1	0	1	1	.100	.182	.100
84	MIL/AL		128	431	387	114	19	5	1	146	32	1	0	41	7	6	3	10	10	52	30	.295	.351	.377
85	VAN/PCL	AAA	10	41	37	4	2	0	0	6	4	0	0	6	1	0	0	0	0	2	5	.108	.195	.162
	MIL/AL		18	55	49	11	1	0	0	12	6	0	0	6	0	0	0	0	0	5	3	.224	.309	.245
86	VAN/PCL	AAA	130	561	485	137	25	6	6	192	61	0	3	66	13	6	6	30	17	85	55	.282	.362	.396
87	ATL/NL		134	574	494	154	37	6	10	233	70	2	2	63	6	5	3	10	8	80	61	.312	.397	.472
88	ATL/NL		132	449	386	99	17	5	3	135	58	5	1	59	12	1	2	9	9	46	30	.256	.353	.350
89	ATL/NL		63	200	170	44	7	0	1	54	25	2	1	23	4	3	1	2	3	15	11	.259	.355	.318
	CLE/AL		71	271	245	75	11	0	4	98	24	4	0	26	5	2	1	2	4	26	29	.306	.368	.400
	YEAR		134	471	415	119	18	0	5	152	49	6	1	49	9	5	1	4	7	41	40	.287	.363	.366
90	CLE/AL		87	280	248	68	15	2	1	90	27	3	1	23	6	3	1	5	3	28	22	.274	.347	.363
92	NY/AL		67	170	145	38	6	0	3	55	22	0	1	15	5	1	0	1	0	24	17	.262	.359	.379
93	NY/AL		115	378	343	114	21	2	7	160	31	1	2	31	1	1	0	1	0	62	36	.332	.390	.466
9 YR TOTALS			**826**	**2830**	**2487**	**719**	**136**	**20**	**30**	**985**	**297**	**18**	**11**	**289**	**50**	**22**	**13**	**38**	**37**	**339**	**240**	**.289**	**.366**	**.396**

James, Donald Chris "Chris" — BR/TR — b.10/4/62 — POS OF-507, DH-184, 3B-48, 1B-15   PHI 10/30/81

YR	TM/LG	CL	G	TPA	AB	H	2B	3B	HR	TB	BB	IBB	HB	SO	GDP	SH	SF	SB	CS	R	RBI	BA	OBA	SA
84	REA/EAS	AA	128	507	457	117	19	12	8	184	40	1	3	74	12	3	4	19	5	66	57	.256	.317	.403
85	POR/PCL	AAA	135	555	507	160	35	8	11	244	33	1	7	72	12	5	3	23	10	78	73	.316	.364	.481
86	POR/PCL	AAA	69	288	266	64	6	2	12	110	17	1	0	45	9	3	2	3	6	30	41	.241	.284	.414
	PHI/NL		16	48	46	13	3	0	1	19	1	0	0	13	1	0	0	0	0	5	5	.283	.298	.413
87	MAI/INT	AAA	13	45	40	9	2	1	0	13	3	1	0	9	0	0	2	0	0	5	3	.225	.267	.325
	PHI/NL		115	391	358	105	20	6	17	188	27	0	2	67	4	1	3	3	1	48	54	.293	.344	.525
88	PHI/NL		150	605	566	137	24	1	19	220	31	2	3	73	15	0	5	7	4	57	66	.242	.283	.389
89	PHI/NL		45	185	179	37	4	0	2	47	4	0	0	23	6	1	1	3	1	14	19	.207	.223	.263
	SD/NL		87	331	303	80	13	2	11	130	22	2	1	45	16	0	1	2	1	41	46	.264	.314	.429
	YEAR		132	516	482	117	17	2	13	177	26	2	1	68	22	1	2	5	2	55	65	.243	.281	.367
90	CLE/AL		140	569	528	158	32	4	12	234	31	4	4	71	11	3	3	5	2	62	70	.299	.341	.443
91	CLE/AL		115	463	437	104	16	2	5	139	18	2	4	61	9	2	2	3	4	31	41	.238	.273	.318
92	SF/NL		111	267	248	60	14	4	5	93	14	2	2	45	2	1	2	0	2	25	32	.242	.285	.375
93	HOU/NL		65	148	129	33	10	1	6	63	15	2	1	34	2	1	0	2	0	19	19	.256	.333	.488
	TEX/AL		8	34	31	11	1	0	3	21	3	0	0	6	0	0	2	0	0	5	7	.355	.412	.677
	YEAR		73	182	160	44	11	1	9	84	18	2	1	40	2	1	2	2	0	24	26	.275	.348	.525
8 YR TOTALS			**852**	**3041**	**2825**	**738**	**133**	**20**	**81**	**1154**	**166**	**14**	**17**	**438**	**64**	**12**	**21**	**26**	**17**	**307**	**359**	**.261**	**.304**	**.408**

Javier, Stanley Julian Antonio "Stan" — BB/TR — b.9/1/65 — POS OF-683, 1B-25, DH-8, 2B-3   SL 3/26/81

YR	TM/LG	CL	G	TPA	AB	H	2B	3B	HR	TB	BB	IBB	HB	SO	GDP	SH	SF	SB	CS	R	RBI	BA	OBA	SA
84	NY/AL		7	7	7	1	0	0	0	1	0	0	0	1	0	0	0	0	0	1	0	.143	.143	.143
	NAS/SOU	AA	76	304	262	76	17	4	7	122	39	1	1	57	3	1	1	17	5	40	38	.290	.383	.466
	CMB/INT	AAA	32	114	99	22	3	1	0	27	12	1	0	26	3	1	2	1	1	12	7	.222	.301	.273
85	HUN/SOU	AA	140	613	486	138	22	8	9	203	112	6	5	92	8	4	6	61	15	105	64	.284	.419	.418
86	TAC/PCL	AAA	69	302	248	81	16	2	4	113	47	2	2	46	2	0	5	18	8	50	51	.327	.430	.456
	OAK/AL		59	131	114	23	8	0	0	31	16	0	1	27	2	0	0	8	0	13	8	.202	.305	.272
87	TAC/PCL	AAA	15	55	51	11	2	0	0	13	4	0	0	12	2	0	0	3	1	6	2	.216	.273	.255
	OAK/AL		81	176	151	28	3	1	2	39	19	3	0	33	2	6	0	3	2	22	9	.185	.276	.258
88	OAK/AL		125	440	397	102	13	3	2	127	32	1	2	63	13	6	0	20	1	49	35	.257	.313	.320
89	OAK/AL		112	348	310	77	12	3	1	98	31	1	1	45	4	4	2	12	2	42	28	.248	.317	.316
90	OAK/AL		19	36	33	8	0	2	0	12	3	0	0	6	0	0	0	0	0	4	3	.242	.306	.364
	LA/NL		104	321	276	84	9	4	3	110	37	2	0	44	6	6	2	15	7	56	24	.304	.384	.399
	YEAR		123	357	309	92	9	6	3	122	40	2	0	50	6	6	2	15	7	60	27	.298	.376	.395
91	LA/NL		121	197	176	36	5	3	1	50	16	0	0	36	4	3	2	7	1	21	11	.205	.268	.284
92	LA/NL		56	66	58	11	3	0	1	17	6	2	1	11	0	1	0	3	0	6	5	.190	.277	.293
	PHI/NL		74	313	276	72	14	1	0	88	31	0	2	43	4	2	2	17	1	36	24	.261	.338	.319
	YEAR		130	379	334	83	17	1	1	105	37	2	3	54	4	3	2	18	3	42	29	.249	.327	.314
93	CAL/AL		92	269	237	69	10	4	3	96	27	1	1	33	7	1	3	12	2	33	28	.291	.362	.405
9 YR TOTALS			**850**	**2304**	**2035**	**511**	**77**	**21**	**13**	**669**	**218**	**10**	**8**	**342**	**44**	**29**	**14**	**95**	**18**	**283**	**175**	**.251**	**.324**	**.329**

Jefferies, Gregory Scott "Gregg" — BB/TR — b.8/1/67 — POS 2B-330, 3B-271, 1B-140, DH-1   NYN85 1/20

YR	TM/LG	CL	G	TPA	AB	H	2B	3B	HR	TB	BB	IBB	HB	SO	GDP	SH	SF	SB	CS	R	RBI	BA	OBA	SA
85	KIN/APP	R+	47	182	166	57	18	2	3	88	14	2	1	16	1	0	1	21	1	27	29	.343	.396	.530
	COL/SAL	A	20	68	64	18	2	2	1	27	4	0	0	4	1	0	0	7	0	7	12	.281	.324	.422
86	COL/SAL	A	25	122	112	38	6	1	5	61	9	0	0	10	1	0	1	13	1	29	24	.339	.385	.545
	LYN/CAR	A+	95	430	390	138	25	9	11	214	33	3	2	29	6	0	5	43	8	66	80	.354	.402	.549
	JAC/TEX	AA	5	21	19	8	1	1	0	11	2	1	0	2	0	0	0	1	0	1	7	.421	.476	.579
87	JAC/TEX	AA	134	570	510	187	48	5	20	305	49	18	5	43	12	0	6	26	10	81	101	.367	.423	.598
	NY/NL		6	6	6	3	1	0	0	4	0	0	0	0	0	0	0	0	0	0	2	.500	.500	.667
88	TID/INT	AAA	132	543	504	142	28	4	7	199	32	10	1	34	12	0	6	32	6	62	61	.282	.322	.395
	NY/NL		29	118	109	35	8	2	6	65	8	0	0	10	1	0	1	5	1	19	17	.321	.364	.596
89	NY/NL		141	559	508	131	28	2	12	199	39	8	5	46	16	2	5	21	5	72	56	.258	.314	.392
90	NY/NL		153	659	604	171	*40	3	15	262	46	2	5	40	12	0	4	11	5	96	68	.283	.337	.434
91	NY/NL		136	539	486	132	19	2	9	182	47	2	2	38	12	1	3	26	5	59	62	.272	.336	.374
92	KC/AL		152	657	604	172	36	3	10	244	43	4	1	29	24	0	4	19	9	66	75	.285	.329	.404
93	STL/NL		142	612	544	186	24	3	16	264	62	7	2	32	15	0	4	46	3	89	83	.342	.408	.485
7 YR TOTALS			**759**	**3150**	**2861**	**830**	**156**	**15**	**68**	**1220**	**245**	**23**	**15**	**195**	**80**	**3**	**26**	**128**	**32**	**401**	**363**	**.290**	**.346**	**.426**

Jefferson, Reginald Jirod "Reggie" — BB/TL — b.9/25/68 — POS DH-95, 1B-58   CIN86 3/72

YR	TM/LG	CL	G	TPA	AB	H	2B	3B	HR	TB	BB	IBB	HB	SO	GDP	SH	SF	SB	CS	R	RBI	BA	OBA	SA
86	RED/GCL	R	59	237	208	54	4	5	3	77	24	1	2	40	3	1	2	10	9	28	33	.260	.339	.370
87	CR/MID	A	15	58	54	12	5	0	3	26	1	0	3	12	2	0	0	1	1	9	11	.222	.276	.481
	BIL/PIO	R+	8	27	22	8	1	0	1	12	4	1	1	2	1	0	0	1	0	10	9	.364	.481	.545
88	CR/MID	A	135	575	517	149	26	2	18	233	40	6	13	89	12	0	5	2	1	76	90	.288	.351	.451
89	CHT/SOU	AA	135	541	487	140	19	3	17	216	43	5	7	73	11	0	4	2	3	66	80	.287	.351	.444
90	NAS/AMA	AAA	37	141	126	34	11	2	5	64	14	1	1	30	3	0	0	1	0	24	23	.270	.348	.508
91	NAS/AMA	AAA	28	117	103	33	1	3	4	47	10	1	4	22	3	0	0	3	1	15	20	.320	.402	.456
	CIN/NL		5	8	7	1	0	0	0	1	1	0	0	0	0	0	0	0	0	1	1	.143	.250	.571
	CAN/EAS	AA	6	26	25	7	1	0	0	8	0	0	0	5	2	0	0	0	0	2	4	.280	.308	.320
	CS/PCL	AAA	39	155	136	42	11	0	3	62	16	1	1	28	1	0	2	0	0	29	21	.309	.381	.456
	CLE/AL		26	105	101	20	3	0	2	29	3	0	1	24	1	0	0	1	0	10	12	.198	.219	.287
	YEAR		31	113	108	21	3	0	3	33	4	0	1	24	1	0	1	1	0	11	13	.194	.221	.306
92	CS/PCL	AAA	57	249	218	68	11	4	11	120	29	3	0	50	7	0	2	1	0	49	44	.312	.390	.550
	CLE/AL		24	91	89	30	6	2	1	43	1	0	1	17	2	0	0	0	0	8	6	.337	.352	.483
93	CLE/AL		113	403	366	91	11	2	10	136	28	7	5	78	7	3	1	1	3	35	34	.249	.310	.372
3 YR TOTALS			**168**	**607**	**563**	**142**	**20**	**4**	**14**	**212**	**33**	**7**	**6**	**119**	**10**	**3**	**2**	**1**	**3**	**54**	**53**	**.252**	**.300**	**.377**

Jennings, James Douglas "Doug" — BL/TL — b.9/30/64 — POS OF-77, 1B-28, DH-10   CAL84* 2/31

YR	TM/LG	CL	G	TPA	AB	H	2B	3B	HR	TB	BB	IBB	HB	SO	GDP	SH	SF	SB	CS	R	RBI	BA	OBA	SA
84	SAL/NWL	A-	52	221	173	45	7	1	1	57	40	1	3	45	2	1	4	12	12	29	17	.260	.400	.329
85	QC/MID	A	95	394	319	81	17	7	5	127	62	1	5	76	7	2	6	10	8	50	54	.254	.378	.398
86	PS/CAL	A+	129	566	429	136	31	9	17	236	117	7	10	103	6	2	8	7	11	95	89	.317	.466	.550
87	MID/TEX	AA	126	577	464	157	33	1	30	282	94	11	13	136	8	2	4	7	3	106	104	.338	.459	.608
88	TAC/PCL	AAA	16	71	49	16	1	0	0	17	18	1	2	13	1	2	0	5	1	12	9	.327	.522	.347
	OAK/AL		71	128	101	21	6	0	1	30	21	1	2	28	1	1	3	0	1	9	15	.208	.346	.297
89	TAC/PCL	AAA	137	616	497	136	35	5	11	214	93	4	16	95	9	2	8	10	12	99	64	.274	.399	.431
	OAK/AL		4	4	4	0	0	0	0	0	0	0	0	2	0	0	0	0	0	0	0	.000	.000	.000
90	TAC/PCL	AAA	60	245	208	72	19	1	6	111	31	4	2	36	1	1	3	4	2	32	30	.346	.430	.534
	OAK/AL		64	180	156	30	2	2	2	47	17	0	2	48	1	0	2	2	2	19	14	.192	.275	.301
91	OAK/AL		8	11	9	1	0	0	0	1	2	0	0	2	0	0	0	0	0	1	1	.111	.273	.111
	TAC/PCL	AAA	95	400	332	89	17	2	3	119	47	1	11	65	6	1	9	5	1	43	44	.268	.368	.358
92	ROC/INT	AAA	119	477	396	109	23	5	14	184	68	5	9	80	10	3	1	4	4	70	76	.275	.390	.465
93	IOW/AMA	AAA	65	263	228	67	20	1	7	110	29	2	4	64	5	0	2	3	4	38	37	.294	.380	.482
	CHI/NL		42	57	52	13	3	1	2	24	3	0	0	10	0	0	2	0	0	8	8	.250	.316	.462
5 YR TOTALS			**189**	**380**	**322**	**65**	**16**	**3**	**5**	**102**	**43**	**1**	**6**	**90**	**3**	**3**	**6**	**0**	**5**	**36**	**37**	**.202**	**.302**	**.317**

(continued)

Johnson, Erik Anthony — BR/TR — b.10/11/65 — POS 2B-2, 3B-1, SS-1 — SF87 18/464

YR	TM/LG	CL	G	TPA	AB	H	2B	3B	HR	TB	BB	IBB	HB	SO	GDP	SH	SF	SB	CS	R	RBI	BA	OBA	SA
87	POC/PIO	R+	43	145	129	34	7	0	4	53	13	0	0	21	1	3	0	6	2	19	12	.264	.331	.411
	SHR/TEX	AA	9	21	21	2	1	0	0	3	0	0	0	5	0	0	0	0	1	1	3	.095	.095	.143
88	CLI/MID	A	90	359	322	72	12	3	5	105	28	3	3	39	6	4	2	4	7	29	38	.224	.290	.326
	SJ/CAL	A+	44	181	160	40	3	1	1	48	18	0	2	29	5	1	0	4	2	25	16	.250	.333	.300
89	SHR/TEX	AA	87	278	246	56	5	4	3	78	23	3	1	37	10	4	4	3	2	28	29	.228	.292	.317
90	PHO/PCL	AAA	2	4	3	0	0	0	0	0	0	1	0	0	1	1	0	0	0	0	0	.000	.250	.000
	SHR/TEX	AA	91	298	270	60	6	0	1	69	22	3	3	38	3	3	0	6	6	35	15	.222	.288	.256
91	PHO/PCL	AAA	16	38	34	11	1	1	0	14	3	1	0	5	0	0	1	0	0	6	4	.324	.368	.412
	SHR/TEX	AA	58	167	146	32	7	0	2	45	16	4	1	20	3	4	0	6	2	27	20	.219	.301	.308
92	PHO/PCL	AAA	90	257	229	55	5	1	0	62	20	2	2	38	9	5	1	8	10	24	19	.240	.306	.271
93	PHO/PCL	AAA	101	398	363	90	8	5	0	108	29	2	1	51	13	2	3	3	9	33	33	.248	.303	.298
	SF/NL		4	5	5	2	0	0	0	4	0	0	0	0	0	0	0	0	0	1	0	.400	.400	.800

Johnson, Howard Michael — BB/TR — b.11/29/60 — POS 3B-997, SS-272, OF-142, DH-16, 1B-1 — DET79* S1/12

YR	TM/LG	CL	G	TPA	AB	H	2B	3B	HR	TB	BB	IBB	HB	SO	GDP	SH	SF	SB	CS	R	RBI	BA	OBA	SA
82	DET/AL		54	173	155	49	5	0	4	66	16	1	1	30	3	1	0	7	4	23	14	.316	.384	.426
83	DET/AL		27	74	66	14	0	0	3	23	7	0	1	10	1	0	0	0	0	11	5	.212	.297	.348
84	DET/AL		116	402	355	88	14	1	12	140	40	1	1	67	6	4	2	10	6	43	50	.248	.324	.394
85	NY/NL		126	428	389	94	18	4	11	153	34	10	0	78	6	1	4	6	4	38	46	.242	.300	.393
86	NY/NL		88	253	220	54	14	0	10	98	31	8	1	64	2	1	0	8	1	30	39	.245	.341	.445
87	NY/NL		157	645	554	147	22	1	36	279	83	18	5	113	4	0	3	32	10	93	99	.265	.364	.504
88	NY/NL		148	594	495	114	21	1	24	209	86	25	3	104	6	2	8	23	7	85	68	.230	.343	.422
89	NY/NL		153	655	571	164	41	3	36	319	77	8	1	126	4	0	6	41	8	*104	101	.287	.369	.559
90	NY/NL		154	668	590	144	37	3	23	256	69	12	0	100	7	0	9	34	8	89	90	.244	.319	.434
91	NY/NL		156	658	564	146	34	4	*38	302	78	12	1	120	4	1	15	30	16	108	*117	.259	.342	.535
92	NY/NL		100	410	350	78	19	0	7	118	55	5	2	79	7	0	3	22	5	48	43	.223	.329	.337
93	NY/NL		72	280	235	56	8	2	7	89	43	3	0	43	3	0	2	6	4	32	26	.238	.354	.379
12 YR TOTALS			1351	5240	4544	1148	233	19	211	2052	619	103	16	934	57	9	52	219	73	704	698	.253	.341	.452

Johnson, Kenneth Lance "Lance" — BL/TL — b.7/6/63 — POS OF-709, DH-3 — SL84 6/139

YR	TM/LG	CL	G	TPA	AB	H	2B	3B	HR	TB	BB	IBB	HB	SO	GDP	SH	SF	SB	CS	R	RBI	BA	OBA	SA
84	ERI/NYP	A-	71	332	283	96	7	5	1	116	45	0	0	20	6	1	3	29	10	63	28	.339	.426	.410
85	SP/FSL	A+	129	566	497	134	17	10	2	177	58	5	2	39	7	2	9	33	19	68	55	.270	.340	.356
86	ARK/TEX	AA	127	510	445	128	24	6	2	170	59	2	1	57	6	3	2	49	15	82	33	.288	.371	.382
87	LOU/AMA	AAA	116	531	477	159	21	11	5	217	49	7	0	45	9	3	2	42	16	89	50	.333	.394	.455
	STL/NL		33	63	59	13	2	1	0	17	4	1	0	6	2	0	0	6	1	4	7	.220	.270	.288
88	VAN/PCL	AAA	100	460	411	126	12	6	2	156	42	4	0	52	7	2	5	49	16	71	36	.307	.367	.380
	CHI/AL		33	132	124	23	4	1	0	29	6	0	0	11	1	2	0	6	2	11	6	.185	.223	.234
89	VAN/PCL	AAA	106	458	408	124	11	7	0	149	46	0	0	36	2	0	4	33	18	69	28	.304	.371	.365
	CHI/AL		50	199	180	54	8	2	0	66	17	0	1	24	1	2	0	16	3	28	16	.300	.360	.367
90	CHI/AL		151	587	541	154	18	9	1	193	33	2	1	45	12	8	5	36	22	76	51	.285	.325	.357
91	CHI/AL		159	624	588	161	14	*13	0	201	26	2	1	58	14	6	3	26	11	72	49	.274	.304	.342
92	CHI/AL		157	611	567	158	15	*12	3	206	34	4	1	33	20	4	5	41	14	67	47	.279	.318	.363
93	CHI/AL		147	579	540	168	18	*14	0	214	36	1	0	33	10	3	0	35	7	75	47	.311	.354	.396
7 YR TOTALS			730	2795	2599	731	79	52	4	926	156	10	3	210	60	25	12	166	60	333	223	.281	.321	.356

Jones, Christopher Carlos "Chris" — BR/TR — b.12/16/65 — POS OF-139 — CIN84 3/59

YR	TM/LG	CL	G	TPA	AB	H	2B	3B	HR	TB	BB	IBB	HB	SO	GDP	SH	SF	SB	CS	R	RBI	BA	OBA	SA
84	BIL/PIO	R+	21	76	73	11	2	0	2	19	2	0	0	24	0	0	1	4	0	8	13	.151	.171	.260
85	BIL/PIO	R+	63	262	240	62	12	5	4	96	19	0	1	72	3	1	1	13	0	43	33	.258	.314	.400
86	CR/MID	A	128	500	473	117	13	9	20	208	20	1	3	126	7	0	4	23	17	65	78	.247	.280	.440
87	VER/EAS	AA	113	415	383	88	11	4	10	137	23	4	4	99	12	2	3	13	10	50	39	.230	.278	.358
88	CHT/SOU	AA	116	448	410	111	20	7	4	157	29	1	1	102	4	0	4	11	9	50	61	.271	.317	.383
89	NAS/AMA	AAA	21	50	49	8	1	0	2	15	0	1	0	16	0	1	0	2	0	8	5	.163	.163	.306
	CHT/SOU	AA	103	405	378	95	18	2	10	147	23	1	3	68	13	0	1	10	2	47	54	.251	.299	.389
90	NAS/AMA	AAA	134	467	436	114	23	3	10	173	23	3	2	86	18	5	1	12	8	53	52	.261	.301	.397
91	NAS/AMA	AAA	73	289	267	65	5	4	9	105	19	1	1	65	6	0	1	10	5	29	33	.243	.298	.393
	CIN/NL		52	92	89	26	2	1	2	37	2	0	0	31	2	0	1	2	1	14	6	.292	.304	.416
92	HOU/NL		54	73	63	12	2	1	1	19	7	0	0	21	1	3	0	2	0	7	4	.190	.271	.302
	TUC/PCL	AAA	45	191	170	55	9	8	3	89	18	2	0	34	7	1	2	7	1	25	28	.324	.384	.524
93	CS/PCL	AAA	46	193	168	47	5	5	12	98	19	2	2	47	2	0	2	9	4	41	40	.280	.352	.583
	COL/NL		86	225	209	57	11	4	6	94	10	1	0	48	6	5	5	9	4	29	31	.273	.305	.450
3 YR TOTALS			192	390	361	95	14	7	9	150	19	1	0	100	9	8	6	14	5	50	41	.263	.298	.416

Jones, Larry Wayne "Chipper" — BB/TR — b.4/24/72 — POS SS-3 — ATL90 1/1

YR	TM/LG	CL	G	TPA	AB	H	2B	3B	HR	TB	BB	IBB	HB	SO	GDP	SH	SF	SB	CS	R	RBI	BA	OBA	SA
90	BRA/GCL	R	44	164	140	32	1	1	1	38	14	1	6	25	3	2	2	5	3	20	18	.229	.321	.271
91	MAC/SAL	A	136	556	473	154	24	11	15	245	69	4	3	70	1	6	10	40	9	104	98	.326	.407	.518
92	DUR/CAR	A+	70	301	264	73	22	1	4	109	31	1	2	34	5	1	3	10	8	43	31	.277	.353	.413
	GRE/SOU	AA	67	285	266	92	17	11	9	158	11	1	0	32	5	4	4	14	1	43	42	.346	.367	.594
93	RIC/INT	AAA	139	603	536	174	31	12	13	268	57	5	1	70	8	3	6	23	7	97	89	.325	.387	.500
	ATL/NL		8	4	3	2	1	0	0	3	1	0	0	1	0	0	1	0	0	2	0	.667	.750	1.000

Jones, William Timothy "Tim" — BL/TR — b.12/1/62 — POS SS-119, 2B-78, 3B-14, OF-2, C-1, P-1 — SL85 3/46

YR	TM/LG	CL	G	TPA	AB	H	2B	3B	HR	TB	BB	IBB	HB	SO	GDP	SH	SF	SB	CS	R	RBI	BA	OBA	SA
85	JC/APP	R+	68	267	235	75	10	1	3	96	27	0	0	19	1	0	5	28	6	33	48	.319	.382	.409
86	SP/FSL	A+	39	176	142	36	3	2	0	43	30	0	1	8	3	0	5	8	6	19	27	.254	.381	.303

Jones, William Timothy "Tim" (continued)

YR	TM/LG	CL	G	TPA	AB	H	2B	3B	HR	TB	BB	IBB	HB	SO	GDP	SH	SF	SB	CS	R	RBI	BA	OBA	SA
	ARK/TEX	AA	96	333	284	76	15	1	2	99	42	2	2	32	7	3	2	7	5	36	27	.268	.364	.349
87	ARK/TEX	AA	61	213	176	58	12	0	3	79	29	4	2	16	3	3	3	16	10	23	26	.330	.424	.449
	LOU/AMA	AAA	73	307	276	78	14	3	4	110	29	1	0	27	4	2	0	11	3	48	43	.283	.351	.399
88	LOU/AMA	AAA	103	415	370	95	21	2	6	138	36	3	3	56	5	5	1	39	12	63	38	.257	.327	.373
	STL/NL		31	56	52	14	0	0	0	14	4	0	0	10	1	0	0	4	1	2	3	.269	.321	.269
89	STL/NL		42	86	75	22	6	0	0	28	7	1	1	8	2	1	2	1	0	11	7	.293	.353	.373
90	STL/NL		67	145	128	28	7	1	1	40	12	1	1	20	1	4	0	3	4	9	12	.219	.291	.313
91	LOU/AMA	AAA	86	349	306	78	9	1	5	104	36	1	0	59	2	4	3	19	5	34	29	.255	.330	.340
	STL/NL		16	27	24	4	2	0	0	6	2	1	0	6	0	0	1	0	1	1	2	.167	.222	.250
92	STL/NL		67	158	145	29	4	0	0	33	11	1	0	29	1	2	0	5	2	9	3	.200	.256	.228
93	LOU/AMA	AAA	101	460	408	118	22	10	5	175	44	1	2	67	4	2	4	13	8	72	46	.289	.358	.429
	STL/NL		29	73	61	16	6	0	0	22	9	0	1	8	0	2	0	2	2	13	1	.262	.366	.361
6 YR TOTALS			**252**	**545**	**485**	**113**	**25**	**1**	**1**	**143**	**45**	**4**	**3**	**81**	**5**	**9**	**3**	**15**	**10**	**45**	**28**	**.233**	**.300**	**.295**

Jordan, Brian O'Neal — BR/TR — b.3/29/67 — POS OF-118

SL88 3/29

YR	TM/LG	CL	G	TPA	AB	H	2B	3B	HR	TB	BB	IBB	HB	SO	GDP	SH	SF	SB	CS	R	RBI	BA	OBA	SA
88	HAM/NYP	A-	19	81	71	22	3	1	4	39	6	1	3	15	0	1	0	3	3	12	12	.310	.387	.549
89	SP/FSL	A+	11	45	43	15	4	1	2	27	0	0	2	8	1	0	0	0	2	7	11	.349	.378	.628
90	ARK/TEX	AA	16	51	50	8	1	0	0	9	0	0	1	11	1	0	0	0	2	4	0	.160	.176	.180
	SP/FSL	A+	9	32	30	5	0	1	0	7	2	0	0	11	0	0	0	0	2	3	1	.167	.219	.233
91	LOU/AMA	AAA	61	238	212	56	11	4	4	87	17	1	8	41	5	1	0	10	3	35	24	.264	.342	.410
92	STL/NL		55	204	193	40	9	4	5	72	10	1	0	48	6	0	0	7	2	17	22	.207	.250	.373
	LOU/AMA	AAA	43	169	155	45	3	1	4	62	8	1	4	21	1	0	2	13	2	23	16	.290	.337	.400
93	LOU/AMA	AAA	38	165	144	54	13	2	5	86	16	0	3	17	3	0	2	9	4	24	35	.375	.442	.597
	STL/NL		67	242	223	69	10	6	10	121	12	0	4	35	6	0	3	6	6	33	44	.309	.351	.543
2 YR TOTALS			**122**	**446**	**416**	**109**	**19**	**10**	**15**	**193**	**22**	**1**	**5**	**83**	**12**	**0**	**3**	**13**	**8**	**50**	**66**	**.262**	**.305**	**.464**

Jordan, Paul Scott "Ricky" — BR/TR — b.5/26/65 — POS 1B-452, OF-11

PHI83 1/22

YR	TM/LG	CL	G	TPA	AB	H	2B	3B	HR	TB	BB	IBB	HB	SO	GDP	SH	SF	SB	CS	R	RBI	BA	OBA	SA
84	SPA/SAL	A	128	531	490	143	23	4	10	204	32	2	4	63	14	0	5	8	2	72	76	.292	.337	.416
85	CLE/FSL	A+	139	560	528	146	22	8	7	205	25	3	1	59	10	2	4	26	8	60	62	.277	.308	.388
86	REA/EAS	AA	133	507	478	131	19	3	2	162	21	3	3	44	5	1	4	17	7	44	60	.274	.306	.339
87	REA/EAS	AA	132	515	475	151	28	3	16	233	28	4	3	22	18	0	9	15	9	78	95	.318	.353	.491
88	MAI/INT	AAA	87	345	338	104	23	1	7	150	6	0	0	30	15	0	1	1	0	42	36	.308	.319	.444
	PHI/NL		69	281	273	84	15	1	11	134	7	2	0	39	5	0	1	1	1	41	43	.308	.324	.491
89	PHI/NL		144	559	523	149	22	3	12	213	23	5	5	62	19	0	8	4	3	63	75	.285	.317	.407
90	SCR/INT	AAA	27	111	104	29	1	0	2	36	5	0	1	18	6	0	1	0	0	8	11	.279	.315	.346
	PHI/NL		92	346	324	78	21	0	5	114	13	6	5	39	9	0	4	2	0	32	44	.241	.277	.352
91	PHI/NL		101	322	301	82	21	3	9	136	14	2	2	49	11	0	5	0	2	38	49	.272	.304	.452
92	SCR/INT	AAA	4	20	19	5	0	0	0	5	1	0	0	2	0	0	0	0	0	1	2	.263	.300	.263
	PHI/NL		94	284	276	84	19	0	4	115	5	0	0	44	8	0	3	3	0	33	34	.304	.313	.417
93	PHI/NL		90	170	159	46	4	1	5	67	8	1	1	32	2	0	2	0	0	21	18	.289	.324	.421
6 YR TOTALS			**590**	**1962**	**1856**	**523**	**102**	**8**	**46**	**779**	**70**	**16**	**13**	**265**	**54**	**0**	**23**	**10**	**6**	**228**	**263**	**.282**	**.309**	**.420**

Jorgensen, Terry Allen — BR/TR — b.9/2/66 — POS 3B-63, 1B-22, SS-8

MIN87 2/35

YR	TM/LG	CL	G	TPA	AB	H	2B	3B	HR	TB	BB	IBB	HB	SO	GDP	SH	SF	SB	CS	R	RBI	BA	OBA	SA
87	KEN/MID	A	67	275	254	80	17	0	7	118	18	0	2	43	7	0	1	1	0	37	33	.315	.364	.465
88	ORL/SOU	AA	135	526	472	116	27	4	3	160	40	3	6	62	11	2	6	4	1	53	43	.246	.309	.339
89	ORL/SOU	AA	135	604	514	135	27	5	13	211	76	4	5	78	6	0	9	1	1	84	101	.263	.358	.411
	MIN/AL		10	27	23	4	1	0	0	5	4	0	0	5	1	0	0	0	0	1	2	.174	.296	.217
90	POR/PCL	AAA	123	489	440	114	28	3	10	178	44	2	0	83	11	1	4	0	4	43	50	.259	.324	.405
91	POR/PCL	AAA	126	518	456	136	29	2	11	198	54	1	4	41	22	2	2	1	0	74	59	.298	.376	.434
92	POR/PCL	AAA	135	571	505	149	32	2	14	227	54	3	4	58	22	3	5	2	0	78	71	.295	.364	.450
	MIN/AL		22	63	58	18	1	0	0	19	3	0	1	11	4	0	1	1	2	5	5	.310	.349	.328
93	POR/PCL	AAA	61	259	238	73	18	2	4	107	19	2	1	28	11	1	0	1	0	37	44	.307	.360	.450
	MIN/AL		59	163	152	34	7	0	1	44	10	0	0	21	7	0	1	1	0	15	12	.224	.270	.289
3 YR TOTALS			**91**	**253**	**233**	**56**	**9**	**0**	**1**	**68**	**17**	**0**	**1**	**37**	**12**	**0**	**2**	**2**	**2**	**21**	**19**	**.240**	**.292**	**.292**

Jose, Domingo Felix Andujar "Felix" — BB/TR — b.5/2/65 — POS OF-564, DH-8

OAK 1/3/84

YR	TM/LG	CL	G	TPA	AB	H	2B	3B	HR	TB	BB	IBB	HB	SO	GDP	SH	SF	SB	CS	R	RBI	BA	OBA	SA
84	IF/PIO	R+	45	173	152	33	6	0	1	42	18	1	1	37	4	0	2	5	1	16	18	.217	.301	.276
85	MAD/MID	A	117	450	409	89	13	3	3	117	33	2	5	82	8	1	2	6	6	46	33	.218	.283	.286
86	MOD/CAL	A+	127	559	516	147	22	8	14	227	36	5	2	89	5	3	2	14	9	77	77	.285	.333	.440
87	HUN/SOU	AA	91	330	296	67	11	1	5	95	28	1	1	61	11	1	3	3	3	29	42	.226	.295	.321
88	TAC/PCL	AAA	134	568	508	161	29	5	12	236	53	9	1	77	10	2	4	16	8	72	83	.317	.380	.465
	OAK/AL		8	6	6	2	1	0	0	3	0	0	0	1	0	0	0	0	0	2	1	.333	.333	.500
89	TAC/PCL	AAA	104	434	387	111	26	0	14	179	41	8	3	82	14	0	2	11	7	59	63	.287	.358	.463
	OAK/AL		20	61	57	11	2	0	0	13	4	0	0	13	2	0	0	0	0	3	5	.193	.246	.228
90	OAK/AL		101	365	341	90	12	0	8	126	16	0	5	65	8	2	1	8	2	42	39	.264	.306	.370
	STL/NL		25	93	85	23	4	1	3	38	8	0	0	16	1	0	0	4	4	12	13	.271	.333	.447
	YEAR		126	458	426	113	16	1	11	164	24	0	5	81	9	2	1	12	6	54	52	.265	.311	.385
91	STL/NL		154	625	568	173	40	6	8	249	50	8	2	113	12	0	5	20	12	69	77	.305	.360	.438
92	LOU/AMA	AAA	2	8	7	1	0	0	0	1	0	0	0	0	0	0	1	0	0	0	0	.143	.250	.143
	SP/FSL	A+	6	19	18	8	1	0	0	11	1	0	0	0	0	0	0	2	1	2	2	.444	.474	.611
	STL/NL		131	551	509	150	22	3	14	220	40	8	0	100	9	0	1	28	12	62	75	.295	.347	.432
93	KC/AL		149	539	499	126	24	3	6	174	36	5	0	95	5	1	4	31	13	64	43	.253	.303	.349
6 YR TOTALS			**588**	**2240**	**2065**	**575**	**105**	**13**	**39**	**823**	**154**	**21**	**9**	**403**	**37**	**3**	**9**	**92**	**44**	**254**	**253**	**.278**	**.330**	**.399**

Joyner, Wallace Keith "Wally" — BL/TL — b.6/16/62 — POS 1B-1125, DH-4 — CAL83 3/67

YR	TM/LG	CL	G	TPA	AB	H	2B	3B	HR	TB	BB	IBB	HB	SO	GDP	SH	SF	SB	CS	R	RBI	BA	OBA	SA
84	WAT/EAS	AA	134	548	467	148	24	7	12	222	67	8	1	60	8	5	8	0	5	81	72	.317	.398	.475
85	EDM/PCL	AAA	126	545	477	135	29	5	12	210	60	2	2	64	9	3	3	2	2	68	73	.283	.363	.440
86	CAL/AL		154	674	593	172	27	3	22	271	57	8	2	58	11	10	12	5	2	82	100	.290	.348	.457
87	CAL/AL		149	653	564	161	33	1	34	298	72	12	5	64	14	2	10	8	2	100	117	.285	.366	.528
88	CAL/AL		158	663	597	176	31	2	13	250	55	14	5	51	16	0	6	8	2	81	85	.295	.356	.419
89	CAL/AL		159	654	593	167	30	2	16	249	46	7	6	58	15	1	8	3	2	78	79	.282	.335	.420
90	CAL/AL		83	358	310	83	15	0	8	122	41	4	1	34	10	1	5	2	1	35	41	.268	.350	.394
91	CAL/AL		143	611	551	166	34	3	21	269	52	4	1	66	11	2	5	2	0	79	96	.301	.360	.488
92	KC/AL		149	633	572	154	36	2	9	221	55	4	4	50	19	0	2	11	5	66	66	.269	.336	.386
93	KC/AL		141	573	497	145	36	3	15	232	66	13	3	67	6	2	5	5	9	83	65	.292	.375	.467
8 YR TOTALS			1136	4819	4277	1224	242	16	138	1912	444	66	27	448	102	18	53	44	23	604	649	.286	.353	.447

Justice, David Christopher — BL/TL — b.4/14/66 — POS OF-480, 1B-69 — ATL85 3/94

YR	TM/LG	CL	G	TPA	AB	H	2B	3B	HR	TB	BB	IBB	HB	SO	GDP	SH	SF	SB	CS	R	RBI	BA	OBA	SA
85	PUL/APP	R+	66	249	204	50	8	5	10	88	40	0	0	30	5	0	5	0	1	39	46	.245	.361	.431
86	SUM/SAL	A	61	280	220	66	16	0	10	112	48	2	5	28	7	0	7	10	2	48	61	.300	.425	.509
	DUR/CAR	A+	67	284	229	64	9	1	12	111	46	5	7	24	4	1	2	4	4	47	44	.279	.413	.485
87	GRE/SOU	AA	93	405	348	79	12	4	6	117	53	6	0	48	9	1	3	3	2	38	40	.227	.327	.336
88	RIC/INT	AAA	70	275	227	46	9	1	8	81	39	9	0	55	3	2	4	4	3	27	28	.203	.311	.357
	GRE/SOU	AA	58	237	198	55	13	1	9	97	36	4	2	43	6	0	1	6	2	34	37	.278	.392	.490
89	RIC/INT	AAA	115	457	391	102	24	3	12	168	59	4	3	66	4	1	3	12	8	47	58	.261	.360	.430
	ATL/NL		16	56	51	12	3	0	1	18	3	1	1	9	1	0	1	2	1	7	3	.235	.291	.353
90	RIC/INT	AAA	12	52	45	16	5	1	2	29	7	2	0	6	0	0	0	0	0	7	7	.356	.442	.644
	ATL/NL		127	504	439	124	23	2	28	235	64	4	0	92	4	0	1	11	6	76	78	.282	.373	.535
91	MAC/SAL	A	3	13	10	2	0	0	2	8	2	1	0	1	0	0	1	0	0	2	5	.200	.308	.800
	ATL/NL		109	469	396	109	25	1	21	199	65	9	3	81	4	0	5	8	6	67	87	.275	.377	.503
92	ATL/NL		144	571	484	124	19	5	21	216	79	8	2	85	1	0	6	2	4	78	72	.256	.359	.446
93	ATL/NL		157	670	585	158	15	4	40	301	78	12	3	90	9	0	4	3	5	90	120	.270	.357	.515
5 YR TOTALS			553	2270	1955	527	85	12	111	969	289	34	9	357	17	1	16	26	24	318	360	.270	.364	.496

Karkovice, Ronald Joseph "Ron" — BR/TR — b.8/8/63 — POS C-567, DH-5, OF-2 — CHA82 1/14

YR	TM/LG	CL	G	TPA	AB	H	2B	3B	HR	TB	BB	IBB	HB	SO	GDP	SH	SF	SB	CS	R	RBI	BA	OBA	SA
84	DEN/AMA	AAA	31	99	86	19	1	0	2	26	8	0	1	25	4	1	3	1	0	7	10	.221	.286	.302
	GF/EAS	AA	88	287	260	56	9	1	13	106	25	1	1	102	2	1	0	3	1	37	39	.215	.287	.408
85	GF/EAS	AA	99	375	324	70	9	3	11	118	49	1	2	105	1	0	0	6	2	37	37	.216	.323	.364
86	BIR/SOU	AA	97	395	319	90	13	1	20	165	61	3	4	109	3	2	9	2	2	63	53	.282	.394	.517
	CHI/AL		37	109	97	24	7	0	4	43	9	0	1	37	3	1	1	1	0	13	13	.247	.315	.443
87	CHI/AL		39	95	85	6	0	0	2	12	7	0	2	40	2	1	0	3	0	7	7	.071	.160	.141
	HAW/PCL	AAA	34	112	104	19	3	0	4	34	8	0	0	37	4	0	0	3	0	15	11	.183	.241	.327
88	CHI/AL		46	126	115	20	4	0	3	33	7	0	1	30	1	3	0	4	2	10	9	.174	.228	.287
	VAN/PCL	AAA	39	129	116	29	10	0	2	45	8	0	1	26	2	3	1	2	0	12	13	.250	.302	.388
89	CHI/AL		71	203	182	48	7	3	2	70	10	0	2	56	0	1	2	0	2	21	24	.264	.306	.385
90	CHI/AL		68	208	183	45	10	0	6	73	16	1	1	52	1	7	1	2	0	30	20	.246	.308	.399
91	CHI/AL		75	193	167	41	13	0	5	69	15	1	1	42	2	9	1	0	0	25	22	.246	.310	.413
92	CHI/AL		123	381	342	81	12	1	13	134	30	1	3	89	3	4	2	10	4	39	50	.237	.302	.392
93	CHI/AL		128	453	403	92	17	1	20	171	29	1	6	126	12	11	4	2	2	60	54	.228	.287	.424
8 YR TOTALS			587	1768	1574	357	72	4	56	605	123	4	17	472	24	43	11	22	8	205	199	.227	.288	.384

Karros, Eric Peter — BR/TR — b.11/4/67 — POS 1B-310 — LA88 5/140

YR	TM/LG	CL	G	TPA	AB	H	2B	3B	HR	TB	BB	IBB	HB	SO	GDP	SH	SF	SB	CS	R	RBI	BA	OBA	SA
88	GF/PIO	R+	66	307	268	98	12	1	12	148	32	0	3	35	7	0	4	9	2	68	55	.366	.433	.552
89	BAK/CAL	A+	142	614	545	165	40	1	15	252	63	3	2	99	15	0	4	18	7	86	86	.303	.375	.462
90	SA/TEX	AA	131	579	509	179	45	2	18	282	57	5	6	79	18	1	6	8	9	91	78	.352	.419	.554
91	ALB/PCL	AAA	132	557	488	154	33	8	22	269	58	8	6	80	6	0	5	3	2	88	101	.316	.391	.551
	LA/NL		14	15	14	1	1	0	0	2	1	0	0	6	0	0	0	0	0	0	1	.071	.133	.143
92	LA/NL		149	589	545	140	30	1	20	232	37	3	2	103	15	0	5	2	4	63	88	.257	.304	.426
93	LA/NL		158	658	619	153	27	2	23	253	34	1	2	82	17	0	3	0	1	74	80	.247	.287	.409
3 YR TOTALS			321	1262	1178	294	58	3	43	487	72	4	4	191	32	0	8	2	5	137	169	.250	.293	.413

Kelly, Patrick Franklin "Pat" — BR/TR — b.10/14/67 — POS 2B-245, 3B-80, DH-1 — NYA88 6/235

YR	TM/LG	CL	G	TPA	AB	H	2B	3B	HR	TB	BB	IBB	HB	SO	GDP	SH	SF	SB	CS	R	RBI	BA	OBA	SA
88	ONE/NYP	A-	71	307	280	92	11	6	2	121	16	0	5	45	0	5	1	25	6	49	34	.329	.374	.432
89	PW/CAR	A+	124	487	436	116	21	7	3	160	32	1	8	79	3	4	7	31	9	61	45	.266	.323	.367
90	ALB/EAS	AA	126	470	418	113	19	6	8	168	37	1	6	79	7	5	4	32	14	67	44	.270	.335	.402
91	CMB/INT	AAA	31	126	116	39	9	2	3	61	9	1	0	16	2	1	0	8	2	27	19	.336	.384	.526
	NY/AL		96	322	298	72	12	4	3	101	15	0	5	52	5	2	2	12	1	35	23	.242	.287	.339
92	ALB/EAS	AA	2	9	6	0	0	0	0	0	2	0	0	1	0	0	0	0	0	1	0	.000	.250	.000
	NY/AL		106	362	318	72	22	2	7	119	25	1	10	72	6	6	3	8	5	38	27	.226	.301	.374
93	NY/AL		127	451	406	111	24	1	7	158	24	0	5	68	9	10	6	14	11	49	51	.273	.317	.389
3 YR TOTALS			329	1135	1022	255	58	7	17	378	64	1	20	192	20	18	11	34	17	122	101	.250	.303	.370

Kelly, Roberto Conrado "Bobby" — BR/TR — b.10/1/64 — POS OF-692, DH-6 — NYA 2/21/82

YR	TM/LG	CL	G	TPA	AB	H	2B	3B	HR	TB	BB	IBB	HB	SO	GDP	SH	SF	SB	CS	R	RBI	BA	OBA	SA
84	GRE/SAL	A	111	423	361	86	13	2	1	106	57	0	1	49	1	1	3	42	10	68	26	.238	.341	.294
85	FL/FSL	A+	114	487	417	103	4	13	3	142	58	1	3	70	6	3	6	49	14	86	38	.247	.339	.341
86	ALB/EAS	AA	86	334	299	87	11	4	2	112	29	0	0	63	6	1	5	10	5	42	43	.291	.348	.375
87	CMB/INT	AAA	118	516	471	131	19	8	13	205	33	0	3	116	5	1	8	51	10	77	62	.278	.324	.435

Kelly, Roberto Conrado "Bobby" (continued)

YR	TM/LG	CL	G	TPA	AB	H	2B	3B	HR	TB	BB	IBB	HB	SO	GDP	SH	SF	SB	CS	R	RBI	BA	OBA	SA
	NY/AL		23	59	52	14	3	0	1	20	5	0	0	15	0	1	1	9	3	12	7	.269	.328	.385
88	CMB/INT	AAA	30	128	120	40	8	1	3	59	6	1	1	29	3	1	0	11	3	25	16	.333	.370	.492
	NY/AL		38	84	77	19	4	1	1	28	3	0	0	15	0	3	1	5	2	9	7	.247	.272	.364
89	NY/AL		137	496	441	133	18	3	9	184	41	3	6	89	9	8	0	35	12	65	48	.302	.369	.417
90	NY/AL		162	686	641	183	32	4	15	268	33	0	4	148	7	4	4	42	17	85	61	.285	.323	.418
91	NY/AL		126	543	486	130	22	2	20	216	45	2	5	77	14	2	5	32	9	68	69	.267	.333	.444
92	NY/AL		152	632	580	158	31	2	10	223	41	4	4	96	19	1	6	28	5	81	66	.272	.322	.384
93	CIN/NL		78	342	320	102	17	3	9	152	17	0	2	43	10	0	3	21	5	44	35	.319	.354	.475
7 YR TOTALS			716	2842	2597	739	127	15	65	1091	185	9	21	483	59	19	20	172	53	364	293	**.285**	**.335**	**.420**

Kent, Jeffrey Franklin "Jeff" — BR/TR — b.3/7/68 — POS 2B-178, 3B-62, 1B-3, SS-3   TOR89 21/523

YR	TM/LG	CL	G	TPA	AB	H	2B	3B	HR	TB	BB	IBB	HB	SO	GDP	SH	SF	SB	CS	R	RBI	BA	OBA	SA
89	SC/NYP	A-	73	311	268	60	14	1	13	115	33	2	6	81	2	0	4	5	1	34	37	.224	.318	.429
90	DUN/FSL	A+	132	512	447	124	32	2	16	208	53	5	6	98	4	3	3	17	7	72	60	.277	.360	.465
91	KNO/SOU	AA	139	540	445	114	34	1	12	186	80	2	10	104	3	2	3	25	6	68	61	.256	.379	.418
92	TOR/AL		65	222	192	46	13	1	8	85	20	0	6	47	3	0	4	2	1	36	35	.240	.324	.443
	NY/NL		37	121	113	27	8	1	3	46	7	0	1	29	2	0	0	0	2	16	15	.239	.289	.407
	YEAR		102	343	305	73	21	2	11	131	27	0	7	76	5	0	4	2	3	52	50	.239	.312	.430
93	NY/NL		140	544	496	134	24	0	21	221	30	2	8	88	11	6	4	4	4	65	80	.270	.320	.446
2 YR TOTALS			242	887	801	207	45	2	32	352	57	2	15	164	16	6	8	6	7	117	130	**.258**	**.317**	**.439**

Kessinger, Robert Keith "Keith" — BB/TR — b.2/19/67 — POS SS-11   BAL89 37/921

YR	TM/LG	CL	G	TPA	AB	H	2B	3B	HR	TB	BB	IBB	HB	SO	GDP	SH	SF	SB	CS	R	RBI	BA	OBA	SA
89	BLU/APP	R+	28	110	99	27	4	0	2	37	8	0	1	12	1	2	0	1	0	17	9	.273	.333	.374
90	WAU/MID	A	37	143	134	29	8	0	0	37	6	0	3	23	2	0	0	1	1	17	9	.216	.266	.276
	FRE/CAR	A+	64	173	145	22	4	0	0	26	20	0	3	36	2	5	0	0	0	18	8	.152	.268	.179
91	FRE/CAR	A+	26	65	56	10	3	0	0	13	8	0	0	12	3	1	0	2	0	5	4	.179	.281	.232
	CR/MID	A	59	238	206	42	5	0	1	50	23	1	3	46	3	5	1	0	1	15	15	.204	.292	.243
92	CR/MID	A	95	351	308	73	15	1	4	102	36	2	1	57	7	5	1	2	0	41	38	.237	.318	.331
93	CHT/SOU	AA	56	190	161	50	9	0	3	68	24	2	0	18	4	5	0	0	3	24	28	.311	.400	.422
	IND/AMA	AAA	35	136	120	34	9	0	2	49	14	4	1	14	0	1	0	0	0	17	15	.283	.363	.408
	CIN/NL		11	32	27	7	1	0	1	11	4	0	1	4	0	1	0	0	0	4	3	.259	.344	.407

King, Jeffrey Wayne "Jeff" — BR/TR — b.12/26/64 — POS 3B-390, 1B-79, 2B-41, SS-9, OF-1   PIT86 1/1

YR	TM/LG	CL	G	TPA	AB	H	2B	3B	HR	TB	BB	IBB	HB	SO	GDP	SH	SF	SB	CS	R	RBI	BA	OBA	SA
86	PW/CAR	A+	37	152	132	31	4	1	6	55	19	2	1	34	4	0	0	1	1	18	20	.235	.336	.417
87	SAL/CAR	A+	90	374	310	86	9	1	26	175	61	2	1	88	7	0	2	6	2	68	71	.277	.396	.565
	HAR/EAS	AA	26	108	100	24	7	0	2	37	4	0	0	27	2	0	4	0	1	12	25	.240	.259	.370
88	HAR/EAS	AA	117	467	411	105	21	1	14	170	46	3	0	87	5	2	8	5	4	49	66	.255	.325	.414
89	BUF/AMA	AAA	51	189	169	43	5	2	6	70	13	0	0	22	5	2	5	1	1	26	29	.254	.299	.414
	PIT/NL		75	243	215	42	13	3	5	76	20	1	2	34	3	2	4	4	2	31	19	.195	.266	.353
90	PIT/NL		127	402	371	91	17	1	14	152	21	1	1	50	12	2	7	3	3	46	53	.245	.283	.410
91	PIT/NL		33	125	109	26	1	1	4	41	14	3	1	15	3	0	1	0	0	16	18	.239	.328	.376
	BUF/AMA	AAA	9	24	18	4	1	1	0	7	6	0	0	3	0	0	0	1	0	3	2	.222	.417	.389
92	BUF/AMA	AAA	7	31	29	10	2	0	2	18	2	0	0	2	0	0	0	1	0	6	5	.345	.387	.621
	PIT/NL		130	522	480	111	21	2	14	178	27	3	2	56	8	8	5	4	6	56	65	.231	.272	.371
93	PIT/NL		158	683	611	180	35	3	9	248	59	4	4	54	17	1	8	8	6	82	98	.295	.356	.406
5 YR TOTALS			523	1975	1786	450	87	10	46	695	141	12	10	209	43	13	25	22	18	231	253	**.252**	**.306**	**.389**

Kirby, Wayne Leonard — BL/TR — b.1/22/64 — POS OF-146, DH-9   LA83* 13/291

YR	TM/LG	CL	G	TPA	AB	H	2B	3B	HR	TB	BB	IBB	HB	SO	GDP	SH	SF	SB	CS	R	RBI	BA	OBA	SA
83	DOD/GCL	R	60	256	216	63	7	1	0	72	34	0	1	19	3	4	1	23	8	43	13	.292	.389	.333
84	VB/FSL	A+	76	258	224	61	6	3	0	73	21	2	6	30	3	5	2	11	9	39	21	.272	.348	.326
	GF/PIO	R+	20	98	84	26	2	2	1	35	12	2	0	9	2	1	1	19	3	19	11	.310	.392	.417
	BAK/CAL	A+	23	91	84	23	3	0	0	26	4	0	0	5	0	2	1	8	3	14	10	.274	.303	.310
85	VB/FSL	A+	122	488	437	123	9	3	0	138	41	1	3	41	3	4	3	31	14	70	28	.281	.345	.316
86	VB/FSL	A+	114	429	387	101	9	4	2	124	37	3	0	30	5	2	2	28	17	60	31	.261	.326	.320
87	SA/TEX	AA	24	87	80	19	4	2	1	27	4	0	0	3	0	3	0	6	4	7	9	.237	.274	.338
	BAK/CAL	A+	105	475	416	112	14	3	0	132	49	1	5	41	3	5	2	56	21	77	34	.269	.349	.317
88	BAK/CAL	A+	12	58	47	13	0	1	0	15	11	0	0	4	0	0	0	9	2	12	4	.277	.414	.319
	SA/TEX	AA	100	369	334	80	9	2	0	93	21	2	2	42	5	10	1	26	10	50	21	.240	.290	.278
89	SA/TEX	AA	44	162	140	30	3	1	0	35	18	0	1	17	4	2	1	11	6	14	7	.214	.306	.250
	ALB/PCL	AAA	79	343	310	106	18	4	2	140	26	1	1	27	2	5	1	29	14	62	30	.342	.393	.452
90	ALB/PCL	AAA	119	380	342	95	14	5	0	119	28	1	3	36	2	4	3	29	14	56	30	.278	.335	.348
91	CS/PCL	AAA	118	429	385	113	14	4	1	138	34	2	2	36	3	5	3	29	14	66	39	.294	.351	.358
	CLE/AL		21	47	43	9	2	0	0	11	2	0	0	6	2	1	1	1	2	4	5	.209	.239	.256
92	CS/PCL	AAA	123	514	470	162	18	16	11	245	36	4	4	28	7	4	4	51	20	101	74	.345	.392	.521
	CLE/AL		21	21	18	3	1	0	0	7	3	0	0	2	0	0	0	1	1	9	1	.167	.286	.389
93	CHW/INT	AAA	17	79	76	22	1	2	3	41	3	0	0	10	1	0	0	6	1	10	7	.289	.316	.539
	CLE/AL		131	511	458	123	19	5	6	170	37	2	3	58	8	7	6	17	5	71	60	.269	.323	.371
3 YR TOTALS			173	579	519	135	22	5	7	188	42	2	3	66	11	8	7	18	10	84	66	**.260**	**.315**	**.362**

Klesko, Ryan Anthony — BL/TL — b.6/12/71 — POS 1B-8, OF-2   ATL89 6/116

YR	TM/LG	CL	G	TPA	AB	H	2B	3B	HR	TB	BB	IBB	HB	SO	GDP	SH	SF	SB	CS	R	RBI	BA	OBA	SA
89	BRA/GCL	R	17	64	57	23	5	4	1	39	6	2	0	6	2	0	1	4	3	14	16	.404	.453	.684
	SUM/SAL	A	25	103	90	26	6	1	0	35	11	1	0	14	5	1	1	0	1	17	12	.289	.363	.389
90	SUM/SAL	A	63	268	231	85	15	1	10	132	31	5	1	30	6	0	5	13	1	41	38	.368	.437	.571

(continued)

Klesko, Ryan Anthony (continued)

YR	TM/LG	CL	G	TPA	AB	H	2B	3B	HR	TB	BB	IBB	HB	SO	GDP	SH	SF	SB	CS	R	RBI	BA	OBA	SA
	DUR/CAR	A+	77	332	292	80	16	1	7	119	32	4	2	53	8	0	6	10	5	40	47	.274	.343	.408
91	GRE/SOU	AA	126	506	419	122	22	3	14	192	75	14	6	60	5	3	3	14	17	64	67	.291	.404	.458
92	RIC/INT	AAA	123	466	418	105	22	2	17	182	41	6	4	72	14	1	2	3	5	63	59	.251	.323	.435
	ATL/NL		13	15	14	0	0	0	0	0	0	0	1	5	0	0	0	0	0	0	1	.000	.067	.000
93	RIC/INT	AAA	98	396	343	94	14	2	22	178	47	4	2	69	8	0	4	4	3	59	74	.274	.361	.519
	ATL/NL		22	20	17	6	1	0	2	13	3	1	0	4	0	0	0	0	0	3	5	.353	.450	.765
2 YR TOTALS			**35**	**35**	**31**	**6**	**1**	**0**	**2**	**13**	**3**	**1**	**1**	**9**	**0**	**0**	**0**	**0**	**0**	**3**	**6**	**.194**	**.286**	**.419**

Kmak, Joseph Robert "Joe" — BR/TR — b.5/3/63 — POS C-50   SF85 10/238

YR	TM/LG	CL	G	TPA	AB	H	2B	3B	HR	TB	BB	IBB	HB	SO	GDP	SH	SF	SB	CS	R	RBI	BA	OBA	SA
85	EVE/NWL	A-	40	154	129	40	10	1	1	55	20	0	3	23	3	0	2	0	1	21	14	.310	.409	.426
86	FRE/CAL	A+	60	182	163	44	5	0	1	52	15	0	3	38	6	0	1	3	2	23	9	.270	.341	.319
87	FRE/CAL	A+	48	175	154	34	8	0	0	42	15	0	3	32	3	3	0	1	2	18	12	.221	.302	.273
	SHR/TEX	AA	15	45	41	8	0	1	0	10	3	0	1	4	1	0	0	0	0	5	3	.195	.267	.244
88	SHR/TEX	AA	71	195	178	40	5	2	1	52	11	2	4	19	3	1	1	0	0	16	14	.225	.284	.292
89	REN/CAL	A+	78	294	248	68	10	5	4	100	40	1	5	41	9	0	1	8	4	39	34	.274	.384	.403
90	EP/TEX	AA	35	123	109	31	3	2	2	44	7	0	2	22	2	3	2	0	0	8	11	.284	.333	.404
	DEN/AMA	AAA	28	107	95	22	3	0	1	28	4	0	3	16	3	5	0	2	1	12	10	.232	.284	.295
91	DEN/AMA	AAA	100	336	295	70	17	2	1	94	28	0	5	45	6	7	1	7	3	34	33	.237	.313	.319
92	DEN/AMA	AAA	67	254	225	70	11	4	3	98	19	0	3	39	5	5	2	6	3	27	31	.311	.369	.436
93	MIL/AL		51	127	110	24	5	0	0	29	14	0	2	13	2	1	0	0	0	9	7	.218	.317	.264
	NO/AMA	AAA	24	84	76	23	3	2	1	33	8	0	0	14	1	0	0	1	0	9	13	.303	.369	.434

Knoblauch, Edward Charles "Chuck" — BR/TR — b.7/7/68 — POS 2B-450, SS-9, DH-1, OF-1   MIN89 1/25

YR	TM/LG	CL	G	TPA	AB	H	2B	3B	HR	TB	BB	IBB	HB	SO	GDP	SH	SF	SB	CS	R	RBI	BA	OBA	SA
89	KEN/MID	A	51	231	196	56	13	1	2	77	32	0	1	23	5	1	1	9	7	29	19	.286	.387	.393
	VIS/CAL	A+	18	86	77	28	10	0	0	38	6	0	1	11	0	1	1	4	0	20	21	.364	.412	.494
90	ORL/SOU	AA	118	509	432	125	23	6	2	166	63	0	9	31	13	2	3	23	7	74	53	.289	.389	.384
91	MIN/AL		151	634	565	159	24	6	1	198	59	0	4	40	8	1	5	25	5	78	50	.281	.351	.350
92	MIN/AL		155	707	600	178	19	6	2	215	88	1	5	60	8	2	12	34	13	104	56	.297	.384	.358
93	MIN/AL		153	685	602	167	27	4	2	208	65	1	9	44	11	4	5	29	11	82	41	.277	.354	.346
3 YR TOTALS			**459**	**2026**	**1767**	**504**	**70**	**16**	**5**	**621**	**212**	**2**	**18**	**144**	**27**	**7**	**22**	**88**	**29**	**264**	**147**	**.285**	**.364**	**.351**

Knorr, Randy Duane — BR/TR — b.11/12/68 — POS C-50   TOR86 10/263

YR	TM/LG	CL	G	TPA	AB	H	2B	3B	HR	TB	BB	IBB	HB	SO	GDP	SH	SF	SB	CS	R	RBI	BA	OBA	SA
86	MH/PIO	R+	55	238	215	58	13	0	4	83	17	0	0	53	6	3	3	0	0	21	32	.270	.319	.386
87	MH/PIO	R+	26	115	106	31	7	0	10	68	5	3	1	26	1	0	3	0	0	21	24	.292	.322	.642
	MB/SAL	A	46	137	129	34	4	0	6	56	6	0	1	46	1	0	2	0	0	17	21	.264	.292	.434
88	MB/SAL	A	117	416	364	85	13	0	9	125	41	0	0	91	7	4	7	0	1	43	42	.234	.310	.343
89	DUN/FSL	A+	33	130	122	32	6	0	6	56	6	0	2	21	0	0	2	0	2	13	23	.262	.292	.459
90	KNO/SOU	AA	116	435	392	108	12	1	13	161	31	2	2	83	7	4	6	0	3	51	64	.276	.327	.411
91	KNO/SOU	AA	24	86	74	13	4	0	0	17	10	1	1	18	0	1	1	2	0	7	4	.176	.279	.230
	SYR/INT	AAA	91	372	342	89	20	0	5	124	23	3	3	58	17	0	4	1	0	29	44	.260	.309	.363
	TOR/AL		3	2	1	0	0	0	0	0	1	0	0	1	0	0	0	0	0	0	0	.000	.500	.000
92	SYR/INT	AAA	61	248	228	62	13	1	11	110	17	1	0	38	5	0	3	1	0	27	27	.272	.319	.482
	TOR/AL		8	20	19	5	0	0	1	8	1	1	0	5	0	0	0	0	0	1	2	.263	.300	.421
93	TOR/AL		39	112	101	25	3	2	4	44	9	0	0	29	2	2	0	0	0	11	20	.248	.309	.436
3 YR TOTALS			**50**	**134**	**121**	**30**	**3**	**2**	**5**	**52**	**11**	**1**	**0**	**35**	**2**	**2**	**0**	**0**	**0**	**12**	**22**	**.248**	**.311**	**.430**

Koelling, Brian Wayne — BR/TR — b.6/11/69 — POS 2B-3, SS-2   CIN91 14/379

YR	TM/LG	CL	G	TPA	AB	H	2B	3B	HR	TB	BB	IBB	HB	SO	GDP	SH	SF	SB	CS	R	RBI	BA	OBA	SA
91	BIL/PIO	R+	22	100	85	30	7	1	2	45	14	0	1	23	0	0	0	6	2	17	13	.353	.450	.529
	CR/MID	A	35	165	147	38	6	0	1	47	14	0	3	39	0	0	1	22	6	27	12	.259	.333	.320
92	CR/MID	A	129	521	460	121	18	7	5	168	49	0	1	137	3	9	2	47	16	81	43	.263	.334	.365
93	CHT/SOU	AA	110	471	430	119	17	6	4	160	32	1	2	105	2	4	3	34	13	64	47	.277	.328	.372
	IND/AMA	AAA	2	10	9	2	0	0	0	2	0	0	1	1	0	0	0	0	1	1	0	.222	.300	.222
	CIN/NL		7	16	15	1	0	0	0	1	0	0	0	6	0	0	1	0	0	2	0	.067	.125	.067

Koslofski, Kevin Craig — BL/TR — b.9/24/66 — POS OF-65   KC84 20/512

YR	TM/LG	CL	G	TPA	AB	H	2B	3B	HR	TB	BB	IBB	HB	SO	GDP	SH	SF	SB	CS	R	RBI	BA	OBA	SA
84	EUG/NWL	A-	53	182	155	29	2	2	1	38	25	0	0	37	3	1	1	10	2	23	10	.187	.298	.245
85	ROY/GCL	R	33	125	108	27	4	2	0	35	12	0	3	19	1	2	0	7	2	17	11	.250	.341	.324
86	FM/FSL	A+	103	391	331	84	13	5	0	107	47	2	2	59	6	7	4	12	6	44	29	.254	.346	.323
87	FM/FSL	A+	109	388	330	80	12	3	0	98	46	3	6	64	4	3	2	25	9	46	25	.242	.345	.297
88	BC/FSL	A+	108	422	368	97	7	8	3	129	44	5	4	71	4	4	2	32	11	52	30	.264	.347	.351
89	BC/FSL	A+	116	407	343	89	10	3	4	117	51	2	5	57	9	5	3	41	14	65	33	.259	.361	.341
90	MEM/SOU	AA	118	433	367	78	11	5	3	108	54	1	2	89	4	7	3	12	7	52	32	.213	.315	.294
91	MEM/SOU	AA	81	332	287	93	15	3	7	135	33	3	4	56	2	4	4	44	13	41	39	.324	.396	.470
	OMA/AMA	AAA	25	113	94	28	3	2	2	41	15	0	1	21	1	1	4	3	0	13	19	.298	.396	.436
92	OMA/AMA	AAA	78	311	280	87	12	5	4	121	21	3	2	47	2	7	1	8	3	29	32	.311	.362	.432
	KC/AL		55	150	133	33	0	2	3	46	12	0	1	23	2	3	1	2	1	20	13	.248	.313	.346
93	OMA/AMA	AAA	111	445	395	109	22	5	5	162	43	3	2	73	9	4	2	15	7	58	45	.276	.348	.410
	KC/AL		15	32	26	7	0	0	1	10	4	0	1	5	1	1	0	0	1	4	2	.269	.387	.385
2 YR TOTALS			**70**	**182**	**159**	**40**	**0**	**2**	**4**	**56**	**16**	**0**	**2**	**28**	**3**	**4**	**1**	**2**	**2**	**24**	**15**	**.252**	**.326**	**.352**

Kreuter, Chadden Michael "Chad" — BB/TR — b.8/26/64 — POS C-296, DH-4, 1B-1   TEX85 4/109

YR	TM/LG	CL	G	TPA	AB	H	2B	3B	HR	TB	BB	IBB	HB	SO	GDP	SH	SF	SB	CS	R	RBI	BA	OBA	SA
85	BUR/MID	A	69	246	199	53	9	0	4	74	38	0	1	48	4	5	3	3	2	25	26	.266	.382	.372
86	SAL/CAR	A+	125	465	387	85	21	2	6	128	67	2	3	82	14	4	4	5	5	55	49	.220	.336	.331
87	CHA/FSL	A+	85	316	281	61	18	1	9	108	31	2	1	32	5	2	1	1	1	36	40	.217	.296	.384
88	TUL/TEX	AA	108	422	358	95	24	6	3	140	55	1	2	66	12	2	5	2	2	46	51	.265	.362	.391
	TEX/AL		16	58	51	14	2	1	1	21	7	0	0	13	1	0	0	0	0	3	5	.275	.362	.412
89	OC/AMA	AAA	26	102	87	22	3	0	0	25	13	0	0	11	2	1	1	1	1	10	6	.253	.347	.287
	TEX/AL		87	192	158	24	3	0	5	42	27	0	0	40	4	6	1	0	1	16	9	.152	.274	.266
90	OC/AMA	AAA	92	347	291	65	17	1	7	105	52	0	2	80	8	2	0	0	3	41	35	.223	.345	.361
	TEX/AL		22	32	22	1	1	0	0	2	8	0	0	9	0	1	1	0	0	2	2	.045	.290	.091
91	TEX/AL		3	4	4	0	0	0	0	0	0	0	0	1	0	0	0	0	0	0	0	.000	.000	.000
	OC/AMA	AAA	24	89	70	19	6	0	1	28	18	0	0	16	4	0	1	2	0	14	12	.271	.416	.400
	TUL/TEX	AA	42	158	128	30	5	1	2	43	29	4	1	23	4	3	0	1	0	23	10	.234	.380	.336
92	DET/AL		67	215	190	48	9	0	2	63	20	1	0	38	8	3	2	1	0	22	16	.253	.321	.332
93	DET/AL		119	431	374	107	23	3	15	181	49	4	3	92	5	2	3	2	1	59	51	.286	.371	.484
6 YR TOTALS			**314**	**932**	**799**	**194**	**38**	**4**	**23**	**309**	**111**	**5**	**3**	**193**	**18**	**12**	**7**	**2**	**3**	**102**	**83**	**.243**	**.335**	**.387**

Kruk, John Martin — BL/TL — b.2/9/61 — POS 1B-608, OF-431   SD81 S3/62

YR	TM/LG	CL	G	TPA	AB	H	2B	3B	HR	TB	BB	IBB	HB	SO	GDP	SH	SF	SB	CS	R	RBI	BA	OBA	SA
84	LV/PCL	AAA	115	392	340	111	25	6	11	181	45	4	1	37	8	2	4	2	6	56	57	.326	.403	.532
85	LV/PCL	AAA	123	493	422	148	29	4	7	206	67	12	1	48	13	0	3	2	4	61	59	.351	.438	.488
86	LV/PCL	AAA	6	32	28	13	3	1	0	18	4	2	0	5	0	0	0	0	0	6	9	.464	.531	.643
	SD/NL		122	327	278	86	16	2	4	118	45	0	0	58	11	2	2	2	4	33	38	.309	.403	.424
87	SD/NL		138	527	447	140	14	2	20	218	73	15	3	93	6	3	4	18	10	72	91	.313	.406	.488
88	SD/NL		120	466	378	91	17	1	9	137	80	12	0	68	7	3	5	5	3	54	44	.241	.369	.362
89	SD/NL		31	94	76	14	0	0	3	23	17	0	0	14	5	1	0	0	0	7	6	.184	.333	.303
	PHI/NL		81	312	281	93	13	6	5	133	27	2	0	39	5	1	3	3	0	46	38	.331	.386	.473
	YEAR		112	406	357	107	13	6	8	156	44	2	0	53	10	2	3	3	0	53	44	.300	.374	.437
90	PHI/NL		142	515	443	129	25	8	7	191	69	16	0	70	11	2	1	10	5	52	67	.291	.386	.431
91	PHI/NL		152	615	538	158	27	6	21	260	67	16	1	100	11	0	5	7	4	84	92	.294	.367	.483
92	PHI/NL		144	607	507	164	30	4	10	232	92	8	1	88	11	0	3	3	5	86	70	.323	.423	.458
93	PHI/NL		150	651	535	169	33	5	14	254	111	10	0	87	11	0	5	6	2	100	85	.316	.430	.475
8 YR TOTALS			**1080**	**4114**	**3483**	**1044**	**175**	**34**	**93**	**1566**	**581**	**79**	**2**	**617**	**78**	**12**	**36**	**54**	**29**	**534**	**531**	**.300**	**.397**	**.450**

Lake, Steven Michael "Steve" — BR/TR — b.3/14/57 — POS C-424   BAL75 3/71

YR	TM/LG	CL	G	TPA	AB	H	2B	3B	HR	TB	BB	IBB	HB	SO	GDP	SH	SF	SB	CS	R	RBI	BA	OBA	SA
83	CHI/NL		38	88	85	22	4	1	1	31	2	2	1	6	4	0	0	0	0	9	7	.259	.284	.365
84	MID/TEX	AA	9	26	25	4	0	0	0	4	0	0	1	5	1	0	0	0	0	2	1	.160	.192	.160
	CHI/NL		25	57	54	12	4	0	2	22	0	0	1	7	0	1	1	0	0	4	7	.222	.232	.407
85	CHI/NL		58	128	119	18	2	0	1	23	3	1	1	21	3	4	1	1	0	5	11	.151	.177	.193
86	IOW/AMA	AAA	17	52	49	10	4	0	0	14	0	0	2	13	1	1	0	0	0	3	2	.204	.235	.286
	CHI/NL		10	21	19	8	1	0	0	9	1	1	0	2	1	1	0	0	0	4	4	.421	.450	.474
	LOU/AMA	AAA	16	51	49	14	2	0	0	16	2	0	0	1	0	1	0	1	0	2	11	.286	.314	.327
	STL/NL		26	51	49	12	1	0	2	19	2	0	0	5	2	0	0	0	0	4	10	.245	.275	.388
	YEAR		36	72	68	20	2	0	2	28	3	1	0	7	3	1	0	0	0	8	14	.294	.324	.412
87	STL/NL		74	195	179	45	7	2	2	62	10	4	0	18	2	5	1	0	0	19	19	.251	.289	.346
88	STL/NL		36	59	54	15	3	0	1	21	3	0	2	15	0	0	0	0	0	5	4	.278	.339	.389
89	PHI/NL		58	169	155	39	4	2	2	52	12	4	0	20	6	1	0	0	0	9	14	.252	.304	.335
90	PHI/NL		29	84	80	20	2	0	0	22	3	1	0	12	1	0	0	0	0	4	6	.250	.286	.275
91	PHI/NL		58	164	158	36	4	1	1	45	2	1	0	26	5	4	0	0	0	12	11	.228	.237	.285
92	PHI/NL		20	55	53	13	1	0	1	18	1	0	0	10	1	0	1	0	0	3	2	.245	.255	.340
93	CHI/NL		44	126	120	27	6	0	5	48	4	3	0	19	8	2	0	0	0	11	13	.225	.250	.400
11 YR TOTALS			**476**	**1197**	**1125**	**267**	**41**	**5**	**18**	**372**	**43**	**17**	**6**	**159**	**33**	**18**	**5**	**1**	**0**	**89**	**108**	**.237**	**.268**	**.331**

Laker, Timothy John "Tim" — BR/TR — b.11/27/69 — POS C-71   MON88 7/154

YR	TM/LG	CL	G	TPA	AB	H	2B	3B	HR	TB	BB	IBB	HB	SO	GDP	SH	SF	SB	CS	R	RBI	BA	OBA	SA
88	JAM/NYP	A-	47	163	152	34	9	0	0	43	8	0	0	30	4	2	1	2	1	14	17	.224	.261	.283
89	ROC/MID	A	14	51	48	11	1	1	0	14	3	0	0	6	1	0	1	0	0	4	4	.229	.275	.292
	JAM/NYP	A-	58	237	216	48	9	1	2	65	16	1	2	40	4	0	3	8	4	25	24	.222	.278	.301
90	ROC/MID	A	120	467	425	94	18	3	7	139	32	1	1	83	9	1	4	6	3	46	57	.221	.273	.327
	WPB/FSL	A+	2	3	3	0	0	0	0	0	0	0	0	0	0	0	0	0	0	0	0	.000	.000	.000
91	HAR/EAS	AA	11	38	35	10	1	0	1	14	2	1	0	6	1	0	0	1	0	4	5	.286	.342	.400
	WPB/FSL	A+	100	361	333	77	15	2	5	111	22	0	2	51	8	0	4	10	3	35	33	.231	.280	.333
92	HAR/EAS	AA	117	458	409	99	19	3	15	169	39	2	5	89	10	0	5	3	1	55	68	.242	.312	.413
	MON/NL		28	48	46	10	3	0	0	13	2	0	0	14	1	0	0	1	1	8	4	.217	.250	.283
93	OTT/INT	AAA	56	227	204	47	10	0	4	69	21	0	0	41	10	0	1	3	2	26	23	.230	.304	.338
	MON/NL		43	93	86	17	2	1	0	21	4	0	1	16	2	0	0	3	1	3	7	.198	.222	.244
2 YR TOTALS			**71**	**141**	**132**	**27**	**5**	**1**	**0**	**34**	**4**	**0**	**1**	**30**	**3**	**3**	**0**	**3**	**1**	**11**	**11**	**.205**	**.232**	**.258**

Lampkin, Thomas Michael "Tom" — BL/TR — b.3/4/64 — POS C-101, OF-4, DH-1   CLE86 11/265

YR	TM/LG	CL	G	TPA	AB	H	2B	3B	HR	TB	BB	IBB	HB	SO	GDP	SH	SF	SB	CS	R	RBI	BA	OBA	SA
86	BAT/NYP	A-	63	223	190	49	5	1	1	59	31	3	0	14	4	1	1	4	3	24	20	.258	.360	.311
87	WAT/MID	A	118	441	398	106	19	2	7	150	34	2	2	41	7	1	6	3	5	49	55	.266	.323	.377
88	WIL/EAS	AA	80	291	263	71	10	0	3	90	25	1	3	20	6	0	0	1	2	38	23	.270	.340	.342
	CS/PCL	AAA	34	119	107	30	6	0	2	35	7	2	2	12	3	1	0	0	1	14	7	.280	.347	.327
	CLE/AL		4	5	4	0	0	0	0	0	1	0	0	1	0	0	0	0	0	0	0	.000	.200	.000
89	CS/PCL	AAA	63	224	209	67	10	3	4	95	10	1	2	18	5	2	1	4	2	26	32	.321	.356	.455
90	CS/PCL	AAA	69	221	199	44	7	5	1	64	19	0	2	19	2	0	1	2	2	32	18	.221	.294	.322

(continued)

Lampkin, Thomas Michael "Tom" (continued)

YR	TM/LG	CL	G	TPA	AB	H	2B	3B	HR	TB	BB	IBB	HB	SO	GDP	SH	SF	SB	CS	R	RBI	BA	OBA	SA
	LV/PCL	AAA	1	2	2	1	0	0	0	1	0	0	0	1	0	0	0	0	0	0	0	.500	.500	.500
	SD/NL		26	67	63	14	0	1	1	19	4	1	0	9	2	0	0	0	1	4	4	.222	.269	.302
91	LV/PCL	AAA	45	177	164	52	11	1	2	71	10	1	2	19	4	0	1	2	1	25	29	.317	.362	.433
	SD/NL		38	61	58	11	3	1	0	16	3	0	0	9	0	0	0	0	0	4	3	.190	.230	.276
92	LV/PCL	AAA	108	403	340	104	17	4	3	138	53	7	6	27	12	1	3	15	8	45	48	.306	.405	.406
	SD/NL		9	24	17	4	0	0	0	4	6	0	1	1	0	0	0	2	0	3	0	.235	.458	.235
93	NO/AMA	AAA	25	102	80	26	5	0	2	37	18	2	3	4	2	1	0	5	4	18	10	.325	.465	.463
	MIL/AL		73	188	162	32	8	0	4	52	20	3	0	26	2	2	4	7	3	22	25	.198	.280	.321
5 YR TOTALS			**150**	**345**	**304**	**61**	**11**	**2**	**5**	**91**	**34**	**4**	**1**	**45**	**5**	**2**	**4**	**9**	**4**	**33**	**32**	**.201**	**.280**	**.299**

Landrum, Cedric Bernard "Ced" — BL/TR — b.9/3/63 — POS OF-47   CHN 11/9/85

YR	TM/LG	CL	G	TPA	AB	H	2B	3B	HR	TB	BB	IBB	HB	SO	GDP	SH	SF	SB	CS	R	RBI	BA	OBA	SA
86	GEN/NYP	A-	64	263	213	67	6	2	3	86	40	1	3	33	1	4	3	49	10	51	16	.315	.425	.404
87	WIN/CAR	A+	126	547	458	129	13	7	4	168	78	3	6	50	6	1	4	79	18	82	49	.282	.390	.367
88	PIT/EAS	AA	128	522	445	109	15	8	1	143	55	2	8	63	4	10	4	69	17	82	39	.245	.336	.321
89	CHA/SOU	AA	123	421	361	92	11	2	6	125	48	0	5	54	5	5	2	45	9	72	37	.255	.349	.346
90	IOW/AMA	AAA	123	424	372	110	10	4	0	128	43	1	1	63	5	5	3	46	17	71	24	.296	.368	.344
91	IOW/AMA	AAA	38	138	131	44	8	2	1	59	5	0	2	21	2	2	0	13	3	14	11	.336	.360	.450
	CHI/NL		56	99	86	20	2	1	0	24	10	0	2	18	2	3	0	27	5	28	6	.233	.313	.279
92	IOW/AMA	AAA	8	25	20	6	0	0	0	6	4	0	1	1	0	0	0	1	1	4	0	.300	.440	.300
	DEN/AMA	AAA	43	163	144	45	7	0	1	55	13	0	0	16	1	4	2	15	9	20	19	.313	.365	.382
93	POR/PCL	AAA	4	4	4	0	0	0	0	0	0	0	0	0	0	0	0	0	0	0	0	.000	.000	.000
	NOR/INT	AAA	69	298	275	80	13	5	5	118	19	2	1	30	5	3	0	16	6	39	29	.291	.339	.429
	NY/NL		22	20	19	5	1	0	0	6	0	0	0	5	0	1	0	0	0	2	1	.263	.263	.316
2 YR TOTALS			**78**	**119**	**105**	**25**	**3**	**1**	**0**	**30**	**10**	**0**	**0**	**23**	**2**	**4**	**0**	**27**	**5**	**30**	**7**	**.238**	**.304**	**.286**

Lankford, Raymond Lewis "Ray" — BL/TL — b.6/5/67 — POS OF-458   SL87 3/72

YR	TM/LG	CL	G	TPA	AB	H	2B	3B	HR	TB	BB	IBB	HB	SO	GDP	SH	SF	SB	CS	R	RBI	BA	OBA	SA
87	JC/APP	R+	66	278	253	78	17	4	3	112	19	1	5	43	5	0	1	14	11	45	32	.308	.367	.443
88	SPR/MID	A	135	605	532	151	26	16	11	242	60	2	10	92	4	1	2	33	17	90	66	.284	.366	.455
89	ARK/TEX	AA	134	574	498	158	28	12	11	243	65	6	4	57	7	0	7	38	10	98	98	.317	.395	.488
90	LOU/AMA	AAA	132	552	473	123	25	8	10	194	72	9	5	81	9	0	2	30	7	61	72	.260	.362	.410
	STL/NL		39	139	126	36	10	1	3	57	13	0	0	27	1	0	0	8	2	12	12	.286	.353	.452
91	STL/NL		151	615	566	142	23	*15	9	222	41	1	1	114	4	4	3	44	20	83	69	.251	.301	.392
92	STL/NL		153	682	598	175	40	6	20	287	72	6	5	147	5	2	5	42	24	87	86	.293	.371	.480
93	STL/NL		127	495	407	97	17	3	7	141	81	7	3	111	5	1	3	14	14	64	45	.238	.366	.346
4 YR TOTALS			**470**	**1931**	**1697**	**450**	**90**	**25**	**39**	**707**	**207**	**14**	**9**	**399**	**15**	**7**	**11**	**108**	**60**	**246**	**212**	**.265**	**.346**	**.417**

Lansing, Michael Thomas "Mike" — BR/TR — b.4/3/68 — POS 3B-81, SS-51, 2B-25   MIA90 3/155

YR	TM/LG	CL	G	TPA	AB	H	2B	3B	HR	TB	BB	IBB	HB	SO	GDP	SH	SF	SB	CS	R	RBI	BA	OBA	SA
90	MIA/FSL	A+	61	240	207	50	5	2	2	65	29	0	1	35	3	3	0	15	5	20	11	.242	.338	.314
91	MIA/FSL	A+	104	435	384	110	20	7	6	162	40	1	4	75	3	1	6	29	14	54	55	.286	.355	.422
92	HAR/EAS	AA	128	543	483	135	20	6	6	185	52	3	4	64	15	1	3	46	9	66	54	.280	.352	.383
93	MON/NL		141	555	491	141	29	1	3	181	46	2	5	56	16	10	3	23	5	64	45	.287	.352	.369

Larkin, Barry Louis — BR/TR — b.4/28/64 — POS SS-899, 2B-3   CIN85 1/4

YR	TM/LG	CL	G	TPA	AB	H	2B	3B	HR	TB	BB	IBB	HB	SO	GDP	SH	SF	SB	CS	R	RBI	BA	OBA	SA
85	VER/EAS	AA	72	288	255	68	13	2	1	88	23	1	3	21	13	4	3	12	1	42	31	.267	.331	.345
86	DEN/AMA	AAA	103	457	413	136	31	10	10	217	31	1	2	43	1	4	7	19	6	67	51	.329	.373	.525
	CIN/NL		41	169	159	45	4	3	3	64	9	1	0	21	2	0	1	8	0	27	19	.283	.320	.403
87	CIN/NL		125	488	439	107	16	2	12	163	36	3	5	52	8	5	3	21	6	64	43	.244	.306	.371
88	CIN/NL		151	652	588	174	32	5	12	252	41	8	3	24	7	10	5	40	7	91	56	.296	.347	.429
89	NAS/AMA	AAA	2	5	5	5	1	0	0	6	0	0	0	0	0	0	0	0	0	2	0	1.000	1.000	1.200
	CIN/NL		97	357	325	111	14	4	4	145	20	5	2	23	7	2	8	10	5	47	36	.342	.375	.446
90	CIN/NL		158	681	614	185	25	6	7	243	49	3	7	49	14	7	4	30	5	85	67	.301	.358	.396
91	CIN/NL		123	527	464	140	27	4	20	235	55	1	5	64	7	3	2	24	4	88	69	.302	.378	.506
92	CIN/NL		140	609	533	162	32	6	12	242	63	8	4	58	13	2	7	15	4	76	78	.304	.377	.454
93	CIN/NL		100	440	384	121	20	3	8	171	51	6	1	33	13	1	3	14	1	57	51	.315	.394	.445
8 YR TOTALS			**935**	**3923**	**3506**	**1045**	**170**	**33**	**78**	**1515**	**324**	**30**	**30**	**324**	**71**	**30**	**33**	**162**	**34**	**535**	**419**	**.298**	**.359**	**.432**

Larkin, Eugene Thomas "Gene" — BB/TR — b.10/24/62 — POS 1B-293, DH-221, OF-197, 3B-3, 2B-1 MIN84 20/504

YR	TM/LG	CL	G	TPA	AB	H	2B	3B	HR	TB	BB	IBB	HB	SO	GDP	SH	SF	SB	CS	R	RBI	BA	OBA	SA
84	ELI/APP	R+	57	227	193	63	13	1	6	96	29	1	2	18	2	0	3	1	1	29	37	.326	.414	.497
85	VIS/CAL	A+	142	625	528	161	25	3	13	231	81	5	2	61	8	0	14	0	0	90	106	.305	.390	.438
86	ORL/SOU	AA	142	632	529	170	29	6	15	256	84	2	5	50	9	1	13	1	0	85	104	.321	.410	.484
87	POR/PCL	AAA	35	150	129	39	9	0	1	51	20	0	1	11	3	0	0	0	0	17	14	.302	.400	.395
	MIN/AL		85	262	233	62	11	2	4	89	25	3	2	31	4	0	2	1	4	23	28	.266	.340	.382
88	MIN/AL		149	594	505	135	30	2	8	193	68	8	15	55	12	1	5	5	2	56	70	.267	.368	.382
89	MIN/AL		136	520	446	119	25	1	6	164	54	6	7	57	13	5	6	5	2	61	46	.267	.353	.368
90	MIN/AL		119	457	401	108	26	4	5	157	42	2	5	55	6	1	5	3	2	46	42	.269	.343	.392
91	MIN/AL		98	291	255	73	14	1	2	95	30	3	3	21	9	3	2	2	3	34	19	.286	.361	.373
92	MIN/AL		115	373	337	83	18	1	6	121	28	6	4	43	7	0	4	1	2	38	42	.246	.308	.359
93	MIN/AL		56	173	144	38	7	1	2	50	21	3	2	16	5	2	0	1	1	17	19	.264	.357	.347
7 YR TOTALS			**758**	**2670**	**2321**	**618**	**131**	**12**	**32**	**869**	**268**	**31**	**38**	**278**	**56**	**16**	**27**	**23**	**17**	**275**	**266**	**.266**	**.348**	**.374**

LaValliere, Michael Eugene "Mike" — BL/TR — b.8/18/60 — POS C-747, 3B-1 — PHI 7/12/81

YR	TM/LG	CL	G	TPA	AB	H	2B	3B	HR	TB	BB	IBB	HB	SO	GDP	SH	SF	SB	CS	R	RBI	BA	OBA	SA
84	REA/EAS	AA	55	189	147	37	6	6	6	61	36	3	1	15	2	3	2	0	1	19	22	.252	.398	.415
	POR/PCL	AAA	37	140	122	38	6	3	5	65	15	1	1	11	4	1	1	0	0	20	21	.311	.388	.533
	PHI/NL		6	9	7	0	0	0	0	0	2	0	0	2	0	0	0	0	0	0	0	.000	.222	.000
85	STL/NL		12	44	34	5	1	0	0	6	7	0	0	3	2	0	3	0	0	2	6	.147	.273	.176
	LOU/AMA	AAA	83	289	231	47	12	1	4	73	48	2	1	20	9	3	6	0	1	19	26	.203	.336	.316
86	STL/NL		110	350	303	71	10	2	3	94	36	5	1	37	7	10	0	0	1	18	30	.234	.318	.310
87	PIT/NL		121	390	340	102	19	0	1	124	43	9	1	32	4	3	3	0	0	33	36	.300	.377	.365
88	PIT/NL		120	409	352	92	18	0	2	116	50	10	2	34	8	1	4	3	2	24	47	.261	.353	.330
89	BUF/AMA	AAA	7	22	18	2	0	0	0	2	3	0	0	4	1	0	1	0	0	0	1	.111	.227	.111
	PIT/NL		68	223	190	60	10	0	2	76	29	7	0	24	4	4	0	0	2	15	23	.316	.406	.400
90	PIT/NL		96	330	279	72	15	0	3	96	44	8	2	20	6	4	1	0	3	27	31	.258	.362	.344
91	PIT/NL		108	377	336	97	11	2	3	121	33	4	2	27	10	1	5	2	1	25	41	.289	.351	.360
92	PIT/NL		95	343	293	75	13	1	2	96	44	14	1	21	8	0	5	0	3	22	29	.256	.350	.328
93	SAR/FSL	A+	32	131	108	33	2	0	0	35	19	1	1	5	4	0	3	2	0	6	14	.306	.405	.324
	PIT/NL		1	5	5	1	0	0	0	1	0	0	0	0	0	0	0	0	0	0	0	.200	.200	.200
	CHI/AL		37	110	97	25	2	0	0	27	4	0	0	14	1	7	2	0	1	6	8	.258	.282	.278
	YEAR		38	115	102	26	2	0	0	28	4	0	0	14	1	7	2	0	1	6	8	.255	.278	.275
10 YR TOTALS			**774**	**2590**	**2236**	**600**	**99**	**5**	**16**	**757**	**292**	**57**	**9**	**214**	**50**	**30**	**23**	**5**	**13**	**172**	**251**	**.268**	**.352**	**.339**

Lee, Derek Gerald — BL/TR — b.7/28/66 — POS OF-13 — CHA88 42/1078

YR	TM/LG	CL	G	TPA	AB	H	2B	3B	HR	TB	BB	IBB	HB	SO	GDP	SH	SF	SB	CS	R	RBI	BA	OBA	SA
88	UTI/NYP	A-	76	312	252	86	7	5	2	109	50	5	3	48	2	3	4	54	15	51	47	.341	.450	.433
89	SB/MID	A	125	550	448	128	24	7	11	199	87	4	9	83	5	4	2	45	26	89	48	.286	.410	.444
90	BIR/SOU	AA	126	496	411	105	21	3	7	153	71	5	6	93	8	3	5	14	10	68	75	.255	.369	.372
91	BIR/SOU	AA	45	207	154	50	10	2	5	79	46	5	6	23	1	0	1	9	7	36	16	.325	.493	.513
	VAN/PCL	AAA	87	359	318	94	28	5	6	150	35	2	2	62	2	3	1	4	3	54	44	.296	.368	.472
92	VAN/PCL	AAA	115	449	381	104	20	6	7	157	56	7	6	65	11	4	2	17	7	58	50	.273	.373	.412
93	MIN/AL		15	34	33	5	1	0	0	6	1	0	0	4	0	0	0	0	0	3	4	.152	.176	.182
	POR/PCL	AAA	106	453	381	120	30	7	10	194	60	2	4	51	10	4	4	16	5	79	80	.315	.410	.509

Lee, Manuel Lora — BB/TR — b.6/17/65 — POS SS-437, 2B-344, 3B-32, DH-25, OF-1 — NYN 5/10/82

YR	TM/LG	CL	G	TPA	AB	H	2B	3B	HR	TB	BB	IBB	HB	SO	GDP	SH	SF	SB	CS	R	RBI	BA	OBA	SA
84	COL/SAL	A	102	411	346	114	12	5	2	142	60	2	0	42	5	1	4	24	6	84	33	.329	.424	.410
85	TOR/AL		64	43	40	8	0	0	0	8	2	0	0	9	2	1	0	1	4	9	0	.200	.238	.200
86	KNO/SOU	AA	41	179	158	43	1	2	0	48	20	1	0	29	1	0	1	8	4	21	11	.272	.352	.304
	SYR/INT	AAA	76	260	236	58	6	1	1	69	21	0	0	39	5	3	0	7	9	34	19	.246	.307	.292
	TOR/AL		35	85	78	16	0	1	1	21	4	0	0	10	5	2	1	0	1	8	7	.205	.241	.269
87	SYR/INT	AAA	74	274	251	71	9	5	3	99	18	0	0	50	3	2	2	2	2	25	26	.283	.328	.394
	TOR/AL		56	129	121	31	2	3	1	42	6	0	0	13	1	1	1	2	1	14	11	.256	.289	.347
88	TOR/AL		116	415	381	111	16	3	2	139	26	1	0	64	13	4	4	3	2	38	38	.291	.333	.365
89	TOR/AL		99	322	300	78	9	2	3	100	20	1	0	64	8	1	1	4	2	27	34	.260	.305	.333
90	TOR/AL		117	421	391	95	12	4	6	133	26	1	0	90	10	3	1	3	1	45	41	.243	.288	.340
91	TOR/AL		138	485	445	104	18	3	0	128	24	0	2	107	11	10	4	7	2	41	29	.234	.274	.288
92	TOR/AL		128	457	396	104	10	1	3	125	50	0	0	73	8	8	3	6	2	49	39	.263	.343	.316
93	TEX/AL		73	239	205	45	3	1	1	53	22	3	2	39	2	9	1	2	4	31	12	.220	.300	.259
9 YR TOTALS			**826**	**2596**	**2357**	**592**	**70**	**18**	**17**	**749**	**180**	**5**	**4**	**465**	**59**	**37**	**18**	**28**	**19**	**262**	**211**	**.251**	**.303**	**.318**

Leius, Scott Thomas — BR/TR — b.9/24/65 — POS 3B-205, SS-50, OF-2 — MIN86 13/325

YR	TM/LG	CL	G	TPA	AB	H	2B	3B	HR	TB	BB	IBB	HB	SO	GDP	SH	SF	SB	CS	R	RBI	BA	OBA	SA
86	ELI/APP	R+	61	269	237	66	14	1	4	94	26	0	3	45	6	1	1	5	0	37	23	.278	.356	.397
87	KEN/MID	A	126	476	414	99	16	4	8	147	50	0	3	88	2	5	4	6	4	65	51	.239	.323	.355
88	VIS/CAL	A+	93	362	308	73	14	4	3	104	42	0	3	50	11	8	1	3	1	44	46	.237	.333	.338
89	ORL/SOU	AA	99	389	346	105	22	2	4	143	38	0	1	74	4	3	2	3	2	49	45	.303	.370	.413
90	POR/PCL	AAA	103	392	353	81	13	5	2	110	35	0	0	66	8	4	0	5	3	34	23	.229	.299	.312
	MIN/AL		14	28	25	6	1	0	1	10	2	0	0	2	2	1	0	0	0	4	4	.240	.296	.400
91	MIN/AL		109	235	199	57	7	2	5	83	30	1	0	35	4	5	1	5	5	35	20	.286	.378	.417
92	MIN/AL		129	449	409	102	18	2	2	130	34	0	1	61	10	5	0	6	5	50	35	.249	.309	.318
93	MIN/AL		10	22	18	3	0	0	0	3	2	0	0	4	1	0	2	0	0	4	2	.167	.227	.167
4 YR TOTALS			**262**	**734**	**651**	**168**	**26**	**4**	**8**	**226**	**68**	**1**	**1**	**102**	**17**	**11**	**3**	**11**	**10**	**93**	**61**	**.258**	**.328**	**.347**

Lemke, Mark Alan — BB/TR — b.8/13/65 — POS 2B-479, 3B-73, SS-1 — ATL83 27/677

YR	TM/LG	CL	G	TPA	AB	H	2B	3B	HR	TB	BB	IBB	HB	SO	GDP	SH	SF	SB	CS	R	RBI	BA	OBA	SA
83	BRA/GCL	R	53	244	209	55	6	0	0	61	30	0	0	19	4	3	2	10	4	37	19	.263	.353	.292
84	AND/SAL	A	42	138	121	18	2	0	0	20	14	0	1	14	6	0	2	3	1	18	5	.149	.239	.165
	BRA/GCL	R	63	280	243	67	11	0	3	87	29	0	2	14	1	2	4	2	2	41	32	.276	.353	.358
85	SUM/SAL	A	90	274	231	50	6	0	0	56	34	2	6	31	9	1	2	1	2	25	20	.216	.331	.242
86	SUM/SAL	A	126	551	448	122	24	2	18	204	87	3	7	31	9	5	4	11	7	99	66	.272	.396	.455
87	DUR/CAR	A+	127	559	489	143	28	3	20	237	54	3	5	45	10	4	7	10	7	75	68	.292	.364	.485
	GRE/SOU	AA	6	27	26	6	0	0	0	6	0	0	1	4	0	1	0	0	0	0	4	.231	.231	.231
88	GRE/SOU	AA	143	628	567	153	30	4	16	239	52	5	2	92	8	1	6	18	2	81	80	.270	.330	.422
	ATL/NL		16	64	58	13	4	0	0	17	4	0	0	5	1	2	0	0	0	8	2	.224	.274	.293
89	RIC/INT	AAA	146	595	518	143	22	7	5	194	66	8	0	45	12	5	5	7	4	69	61	.276	.354	.375
	ATL/NL		14	60	55	10	2	1	2	20	5	0	0	7	0	0	0	0	4	10	.182	.250	.364
90	BRA/GCL	R	4	13	11	4	0	0	1	7	1	0	0	0	3	0	1	0	0	2	5	.364	.385	.636
	ATL/NL		102	266	239	54	13	0	0	67	21	3	0	22	6	4	2	0	1	22	21	.226	.286	.280
91	ATL/NL		136	308	269	63	11	2	2	84	29	2	0	27	9	6	4	1	2	36	23	.234	.305	.312
92	ATL/NL		155	491	427	97	7	4	6	130	50	11	0	39	9	12	2	0	3	38	26	.227	.307	.304

(continued)

Lemke, Mark Alan (continued)

YR	TM/LG	CL	G	TPA	AB	H	2B	3B	HR	TB	BB	IBB	HB	SO	GDP	SH	SF	SB	CS	R	RBI	BA	OBA	SA
93	ATL/NL		151	569	493	124	19	2	7	168	65	13	0	50	21		6	1	2	52	49	.252	.335	.341
6 YR TOTALS			574	1758	1541	361	56	9	17	486	174	29	0	150	47	29	14	2	11	160	131	**.234**	**.309**	**.315**

Leonard, Mark David — BL/TR — b.8/14/64 — POS OF-82, DH-3   SF86 29/709

YR	TM/LG	CL	G	TPA	AB	H	2B	3B	HR	TB	BB	IBB	HB	SO	GDP	SH	SF	SB	CS	R	RBI	BA	OBA	SA
86	EVE/NWL	A-	2	11	8	1	0	0	0	1	2	0	0	2	0	0	1	0	0	0	2	.125	.273	.125
	TRI/NWL	A-	36	146	120	32	6	0	4	50	25	0	1	19	7	0	0	4	2	21	15	.267	.397	.417
87	CLI/MID	A	128	492	413	132	31	2	15	212	71	3	5	61	7	0	3	5	8	57	80	.320	.423	.513
88	SJ/CAL	A+	142	644	510	176	50	6	15	283	118	13	5	82	10	0	11	11	6	102	118	.345	.464	.555
89	SHR/TEX	AA	63	258	219	68	15	3	10	119	33	8	3	40	7	0	3	1	5	29	52	.311	.403	.543
	PHO/PCL	AAA	27	88	78	21	4	0	0	25	9	1	0	15	3	0	1	1	1	7	6	.269	.341	.321
90	PHO/PCL	AAA	109	474	390	130	22	2	19	213	76	1	4	81	7	0	4	6	3	76	82	.333	.443	.546
	SF/NL		11	20	17	3	1	0	1	7	3	0	0	8	0	0	0	0	0	3	2	.176	.300	.412
91	PHO/PCL	AAA	41	169	146	37	7	0	8	68	21	1	0	29	5	0	2	1	0	27	25	.253	.343	.466
	SF/NL		64	145	129	31	7	1	2	46	12	1	1	25	3	1	2	0	1	14	14	.240	.306	.357
92	PHO/PCL	AAA	39	165	139	47	4	1	5	68	21	1	3	29	1	0	2	1	0	17	25	.338	.430	.489
	SF/NL		55	148	128	30	7	0	4	49	16	1	3	31	3	0	1	0	1	13	16	.234	.331	.383
93	BAL/AL		10	21	15	1	1	0	0	2	3	0	1	7	0	0	3	0	0	1	3	.067	.190	.133
	ROC/INT	AAA	97	406	330	91	23	1	17	167	60	4	10	81	4	0	6	0	1	57	58	.276	.397	.506
4 YR TOTALS			140	334	289	65	16	1	7	104	34	1	4	71	6	1	6	0	2	31	35	**.225**	**.309**	**.360**

Levis, Jesse — BL/TR — b.4/14/68 — POS C-50, DH-1   CLE89 3/98

YR	TM/LG	CL	G	TPA	AB	H	2B	3B	HR	TB	BB	IBB	HB	SO	GDP	SH	SF	SB	CS	R	RBI	BA	OBA	SA
89	CS/PCL	AAA	1	1	1	0	0	0	0	0	0	0	0	0	0	0	0	0	0	0	0	.000	.000	.000
	BUR/APP	R+	27	106	93	32	4	0	4	48	10	3	2	7	2	0	1	1	0	11	16	.344	.415	.516
	KIN/CAR	A+	27	101	87	26	6	0	2	38	12	0	2	15	3	0	0	1	0	11	11	.299	.396	.437
90	KIN/CAR	A+	107	458	382	113	18	3	7	158	64	1	5	42	5	1	6	4	1	63	64	.296	.398	.414
91	CAN/EAS	AA	115	428	382	101	17	3	6	142	40	5	0	36	11	4	2	2	5	31	45	.264	.333	.372
92	CS/PCL	AAA	87	296	253	92	20	1	6	132	37	0	1	25	9	3	2	1	3	39	44	.364	.444	.522
	CLE/AL		28	43	43	12	4	0	1	19	0	0	0	5	1	0	0	0	0	2	3	.279	.279	.442
93	CLE/AL		31	67	63	11	2	0	0	13	2	0	0	10	0	1	1	0	0	7	4	.175	.197	.206
	CHW/INT	AAA	47	148	129	32	6	1	2	46	15	1	1	12	7	1	2	0	0	10	20	.248	.327	.357
2 YR TOTALS			59	110	106	23	6	0	1	32	2	0	0	15	1	1	1	0	0	9	7	**.217**	**.229**	**.302**

Lewis, Darren Joel — BR/TR — b.8/28/67 — POS OF-316, DH-2   OAK88 19/463

YR	TM/LG	CL	G	TPA	AB	H	2B	3B	HR	TB	BB	IBB	HB	SO	GDP	SH	SF	SB	CS	R	RBI	BA	OBA	SA
88	ATH/ARI	R	5	24	15	5	3	0	0	8	6	0	1	5	1	1	1	4	0	8	4	.333	.522	.533
	MAD/MID	A	60	256	199	49	4	1	0	55	46	0	4	37	3	4	3	21	10	38	11	.246	.393	.276
89	MOD/CAL	A+	129	579	503	150	23	5	4	195	59	0	11	84	4	2	4	27	22	74	39	.298	.381	.388
	HUN/SOU	AA	9	36	31	10	1	1	1	16	2	0	1	6	1	2	0	1	1	7	7	.323	.382	.516
90	HUN/SOU	AA	71	330	284	84	11	3	3	110	36	3	7	28	8	0	3	21	7	52	23	.296	.385	.387
	TAC/PCL	AAA	60	270	247	72	5	2	2	87	16	0	1	35	2	4	2	16	6	32	26	.291	.335	.352
	OAK/AL		25	46	35	8	0	0	0	8	7	0	1	4	2	3	0	2	0	4	1	.229	.372	.229
91	PHO/PCL	AAA	81	367	315	107	12	10	0	145	41	1	2	36	11	4	6	32	10	63	52	.340	.413	.460
	SF/NL		72	267	222	55	5	3	1	69	36	0	2	30	1	7	0	13	7	41	15	.248	.358	.311
92	PHO/PCL	AAA	42	173	158	36	5	2	0	45	11	0	2	15	8	2	0	9	6	22	6	.228	.287	.285
	SF/NL		100	362	320	74	8	1	1	87	29	0	1	46	3	10	2	28	6	38	18	.231	.295	.272
93	SF/NL		136	572	522	132	17	7	2	169	30	0	7	40	4	12	1	46	15	84	48	.253	.302	.324
4 YR TOTALS			333	1247	1099	269	30	11	4	333	102	0	11	120	10	32	3	89	30	167	82	**.245**	**.314**	**.303**

Lewis, Mark David — BR/TR — b.11/30/69 — POS SS-170, 2B-50, 3B-1   CLE88 1/2

YR	TM/LG	CL	G	TPA	AB	H	2B	3B	HR	TB	BB	IBB	HB	SO	GDP	SH	SF	SB	CS	R	RBI	BA	OBA	SA
88	BUR/APP	R+	61	262	227	60	13	1	7	96	25	0	5	44	2	0	5	14	6	39	43	.264	.344	.423
89	KIN/CAR	A+	93	393	349	94	16	3	1	119	34	4	2	50	7	3	5	17	9	50	32	.269	.333	.341
	CAN/EAS	AA	7	26	25	5	1	0	0	6	1	0	0	3	1	0	0	0	0	4	1	.200	.231	.240
90	CAN/EAS	AA	102	424	390	106	19	3	10	161	23	3	4	49	10	2	5	8	7	55	60	.272	.315	.413
	CS/PCL	AAA	34	135	124	38	8	1	1	51	9	0	0	13	4	1	1	3	2	16	21	.306	.351	.411
91	CS/PCL	AAA	46	203	179	50	10	3	2	72	18	0	2	23	4	0	6	3	1	29	31	.279	.335	.402
	CLE/AL		84	336	314	83	15	1	0	100	15	0	0	45	12	2	5	2	2	29	30	.264	.293	.318
92	CLE/AL		122	446	413	109	21	0	5	145	25	1	3	69	12	1	4	4	5	44	30	.264	.308	.351
93	CHW/INT	AAA	126	554	507	144	30	4	17	233	34	2		76	19	8	3	9	5	93	67	.284	.330	.460
	CLE/AL		14	53	52	13	2	0	1	18	0	0		7	1	1	0	3	0	6	5	.250	.250	.346
3 YR TOTALS			220	835	779	205	38	1	6	263	40	1	3	121	25	4	9	9	7	79	65	**.263**	**.298**	**.338**

Leyritz, James Joseph "Jim" — BR/TR — b.12/27/63 — POS 3B-89, DH-53, C-46, OF-44, 1B-34, 2B-1   NYA 8/24/85

YR	TM/LG	CL	G	TPA	AB	H	2B	3B	HR	TB	BB	IBB	HB	SO	GDP	SH	SF	SB	CS	R	RBI	BA	OBA	SA
86	FL/FSL	A+	12	39	34	10	1	1	0	13	4	1		5	1	0	0	0	0	3	1	.294	.385	.382
	ONE/NYP	A-	23	101	91	33	3	1	4	50	5	1	0	10	0	2	3	1	0	12	15	.363	.384	.549
87	FL/FSL	A+	102	429	374	115	22	0	6	155	38	1	6	54	8	7	4	2	1	48	51	.307	.377	.414
88	ALB/EAS	AA	112	436	382	92	18	3	5	131	43	5	6	60	8	3	2	3	3	40	50	.241	.326	.343
89	ALB/EAS	AA	114	456	375	118	18	2	10	170	65	5	9	51	8	2	5	2	1	53	66	.315	.423	.453
90	CMB/INT	AAA	59	247	204	59	11	0	8	96	37	1	3	33	6	2	1	4	2	36	32	.289	.404	.471
	NY/AL		92	339	303	78	13	1	5	108	27	1	7	51	11	1	2	3	3	28	25	.257	.331	.356
91	CMB/INT	AAA	79	320	270	72	24	1	11	131	38	1	9	50	5	1	3	2	1	50	48	.267	.370	.485
	NY/AL		32	91	77	14	3	0	0	17	13	0	0	15	0	1	0	0	1	8	4	.182	.300	.221
92	NY/AL		63	167	144	37	6	0	7	64	14	1	6	22	2	0	0	1	6	17	26	.257	.341	.444
93	NY/AL		95	305	259	80	14	0	14	136	37	3	8	59	12	0	1	0	0	43	53	.309	.410	.525
4 YR TOTALS			282	902	783	209	36	1	26	325	91	5	21	147	25	2	5	2	5	96	108	**.267**	**.357**	**.415**

Lind, Jose "Jose" — BR/TR — b.5/1/64 — POS 2B-910   PIT 12/10/82

YR	TM/LG	CL	G	TPA	AB	H	2B	3B	HR	TB	BB	IBB	HB	SO	GDP	SH	SF	SB	CS	R	RBI	BA	OBA	SA
84	MAC/SAL	A	121	430	396	82	5	2	0	91	29	3	0	48	9	2	3	17	7	39	30	.207	.259	.230
85	PW/CAR	A+	105	409	377	104	9	4	0	121	32	1	0	42	9	0	0	11	7	42	28	.276	.333	.321
86	NAS/EAS	AA	134	568	520	137	18	5	1	168	43	5	1	28	17	2	2	29	12	58	33	.263	.320	.323
87	VAN/PCL	AAA	128	575	533	143	16	3	3	174	35	0	3	52	14	3	1	21	9	75	30	.268	.316	.326
	PIT/NL		35	157	143	46	8	4	0	62	8	1	0	12	5	6	0	2	1	21	11	.322	.358	.434
88	PIT/NL		154	668	611	160	24	4	2	198	42	0	0	75	11	12	3	15	4	82	49	.262	.308	.324
89	PIT/NL		153	637	578	134	21	3	2	167	39	7	2	64	13	13	5	15	1	52	48	.232	.280	.289
90	PIT/NL		152	561	514	134	28	5	1	175	35	19	1	52	20	4	7	8	0	46	48	.261	.305	.340
91	PIT/NL		150	545	502	133	16	6	3	170	30	10	2	56	20	5	6	7	4	53	54	.265	.306	.339
92	PIT/NL		135	506	468	110	14	4	0	126	26	12	1	29	14	7	4	3	1	38	39	.235	.275	.269
93	KC/AL		136	464	431	107	13	2	0	124	13	0	2	36	7	13	5	3	2	33	37	.248	.271	.288
7 YR TOTALS			915	3538	3247	824	124	25	8	1022	193	49	8	324	90	60	30	53	13	325	286	**.254**	**.295**	**.315**

Lindeman, James William "Jim" — BR/TR — b.1/10/62 — POS OF-107, 1B-93, DH-10, 3B-1   SL83 1/24

YR	TM/LG	CL	G	TPA	AB	H	2B	3B	HR	TB	BB	IBB	HB	SO	GDP	SH	SF	SB	CS	R	RBI	BA	OBA	SA
83	SP/FSL	A+	70	264	232	64	13	1	8	103	27	2	0	51	6	3	2	9	2	45	37	.276	.349	.444
84	SPR/MID	A	94	407	354	96	15	2	18	169	47	2	3	81	6	2	1	6	3	69	66	.271	.360	.477
	ARK/TEX	AA	40	151	137	26	4	3	0	36	10	0	1	34	2	2	1	3	1	14	13	.190	.248	.263
85	ARK/TEX	AA	128	502	450	127	30	6	10	199	41	1	6	82	13	2	3	11	13	54	63	.282	.348	.442
86	LOU/AMA	AAA	139	556	509	128	38	5	20	236	39	2	4	97	9	0	4	9	6	82	96	.251	.308	.464
	STL/NL		19	58	55	14	1	0	1	18	2	0	0	10	2	0	1	1	1	7	6	.255	.276	.327
87	LOU/AMA	AAA	20	86	78	24	3	1	4	41	8	1	0	15	1	0	0	0	0	11	10	.308	.372	.526
	STL/NL		75	227	207	43	13	0	8	80	11	0	3	56	4	2	4	3	1	20	28	.208	.253	.386
88	LOU/AMA	AAA	73	298	261	66	18	4	2	98	33	2	2	59	5	0	2	2	0	32	30	.253	.339	.375
	STL/NL		17	46	43	9	1	0	2	16	2	0	0	9	1	0	1	0	0	3	7	.209	.244	.372
89	LOU/AMA	AAA	29	123	109	33	8	1	5	58	14	2	0	17	5	0	0	0	0	18	20	.303	.382	.532
	STL/NL		73	50	45	5	1	0	0	6	3	0	0	18	2	1	1	0	0	8	2	.111	.163	.133
90	DET/AL		12	34	32	7	1	0	2	14	2	0	0	13	0	0	0			5	8	.219	.265	.438
	TOL/INT	AAA	109	410	374	85	17	2	12	142	26	2	6	83	16	1	3	2	0	48	50	.227	.286	.380
91	SCR/INT	AAA	11	45	40	11	1	1	2	20	5	0	0	6	1	0	0	0	0	7	7	.275	.356	.500
	PHI/NL		65	111	95	32	6	0	0	37	13	1	0	14	1	2	1	0	0	13	12	.337	.413	.389
92	SCR/INT	AAA	15	61	53	16	0	1	0	18	7	1	1	11	2	0	0	0	0	5	8	.302	.393	.340
	PHI/NL		29	42	39	10	1	0	1	14	3	0	0	11	1	0	0	0	0	6	6	.256	.310	.359
93	TUC/PCL	AAA	101	443	390	141	28	7	12	219	41	4	5	68	9	0	7	5	0	72	88	.362	.422	.562
	HOU/NL		9	23	23	8	3	0	0	11	0	0	0	7	0	0	0	0	0	2	0	.348	.348	.478
8 YR TOTALS			299	591	539	128	26	0	14	196	36	1	3	138	11	6	7	4	3	64	69	**.237**	**.285**	**.364**

Lindsey, Michael Douglas "Doug" — BR/TR — b.9/22/67 — POS C-5   PHI87 5/156

YR	TM/LG	CL	G	TPA	AB	H	2B	3B	HR	TB	BB	IBB	HB	SO	GDP	SH	SF	SB	CS	R	RBI	BA	OBA	SA
87	UTI/NYP	A-	52	195	169	41	7	0	1	51	22	2	1	34	2	0	3	1	3	23	25	.243	.328	.302
88	SPA/SAL	A	90	362	324	76	19	0	4	107	29	1	4	68	5	2	3	4	2	29	46	.235	.303	.330
89	SPA/SAL	A	39	161	136	31	7	0	3	47	23	2	0	31	7	1	1	2	2	14	17	.228	.338	.346
	CLE/FSL	A+	36	125	118	23	3	0	0	26	5	0	0	18	4	0	2	0	0	8	9	.195	.224	.220
90	REA/EAS	AA	107	359	323	56	11	0	1	70	26	1	1	78	10	6	3	2	1	16	32	.173	.235	.217
91	REA/EAS	AA	94	344	313	81	13	0	1	97	21	0	2	49	12	4	4	1	0	26	34	.259	.306	.310
	PHI/NL		1	3	3	0	0	0	0	0	0	0	0	3	0	0	0	0	0	0	0	.000	.000	.000
92	SCR/INT	AAA	87	315	274	57	9	0	4	78	37	4	1	66	11	1	2	0	0	28	27	.208	.303	.285
93	SCR/INT	AAA	38	126	121	21	4	1	2	33	5	0	0	24	6	0	0	0	0	9	7	.174	.206	.273
	PHI/NL		2	2	2	1	0	0	0	1	0	0	0	1	0	0	0	0	0	0	0	.500	.500	.500
	CHI/AL		2	1	1	0	0	0	0	0	0	0	0	0	0	0	0	0	0	0	0	.000	.000	.000
	YEAR		4	3	3	1	0	0	0	1	0	0	0	1	0	0	0	0	0	0	0	.333	.333	.333
2 YR TOTALS			5	6	6	1	0	0	0	1	0	0	0	4	0	0	0	0	0	0	0	**.167**	**.167**	**.167**

Liriano, Nelson Arturo — BB/TR — b.6/3/64 — POS 2B-364, SS-36, DH-18, 3B-2   TOR 11/1/82

YR	TM/LG	CL	G	TPA	AB	H	2B	3B	HR	TB	BB	IBB	HB	SO	GDP	SH	SF	SB	CS	R	RBI	BA	OBA	SA
84	KIN/CAR	A+	132	571	512	126	22	4	5	171	46	4	4	86	13	7	2	10	9	68	50	.246	.312	.334
85	KIN/CAR	A+	134	496	451	130	23	1	6	173	39	1	2	55	11	4	0	25	11	68	36	.288	.348	.384
86	KNO/SOU	AA	135	617	557	159	25	15	7	235	48	2	3	63	11	4	5	35	14	88	59	.285	.343	.422
87	SYR/INT	AAA	130	588	531	133	19	10	10	202	44	3	2	76	5	5	6	36	10	72	55	.250	.307	.380
	TOR/AL		37	176	158	38	6	2	2	54	16	2	0	22	3	2	0	13	2	29	10	.241	.310	.342
88	SYR/INT	AAA	8	33	31	6	1	1	0	9	2	0	0	4	1	0	0	2	1	2	1	.194	.242	.290
	TOR/AL		99	295	276	73	6	2	3	92	11	0	2	40	4	5	1	12	5	36	23	.264	.297	.333
89	TOR/AL		132	478	418	110	26	3	5	157	43	1	10	51	10	10	5	16	7	51	53	.263	.331	.376
90	TOR/AL		50	189	170	36	7	2	1	50	16	1	1	20	5	1	1	3	5	16	15	.212	.282	.294
	MIN/AL		53	211	185	47	5	7	0	66	22	0	3	23	3	3	1	5	2	30	13	.254	.332	.357
	YEAR		103	400	355	83	12	9	1	116	38	1	4	44	8	4	2	8	7	46	28	.234	.308	.327
91	KC/AL		10	23	22	9	0	0	0	9	0	0	0	2	0	1	0	1	0	5	1	.409	.409	.409
	OMA/AMA	AAA	86	331	292	80	16	9	2	120	31	3	2	39	8	3	3	6	8	50	36	.274	.345	.411
92	CS/PCL	AAA	106	420	361	110	19	9	5	162	48	4	1	50	6	3	7	20	8	73	52	.305	.381	.449
93	CV/CAL	A+	6	28	22	8	0	2	0	12	6	0	0	0	0	0	0	2	0	3	4	.364	.500	.545
	CS/PCL	AAA	79	331	293	105	23	6	6	158	32	1	1	34	11	2	3	9	13	48	46	.358	.419	.539
	COL/NL		48	175	151	46	6	3	2	64	18	2	0	22	6	5	1	1	4	28	15	.305	.376	.424
6 YR TOTALS			429	1547	1380	359	56	19	13	492	126	4	5	181	31	27	9	55	26	195	130	**.260**	**.322**	**.357**

Listach, Patrick Alan "Pat" — BB/TR — b.9/12/67 — POS SS-243, OF-7, 2B-1   MIL88 5/133

YR	TM/LG	CL	G	TPA	AB	H	2B	3B	HR	TB	BB	IBB	HB	SO	GDP	SH	SF	SB	CS	R	RBI	BA	OBA	SA
88	BEL/MID	A	53	230	200	48	5	1	1	58	18	0	6	20	6	4	1	20	9	40	18	.240	.319	.290

Listach, Patrick Alan "Pat" (continued)

YR	TM/LG	CL	G	TPA	AB	H	2B	3B	HR	TB	BB	IBB	HB	SO	GDP	SH	SF	SB	CS	R	RBI	BA	OBA	SA
89	STO/CAL	A+	132	550	480	110	11	4	2	135	58	1	4	106	10	7	1	37	19	73	34	.229	.317	.281
90	STO/CAL	A+	139	618	503	137	21	6	2	176	105	2	6	122	8	3	1	78	28	116	39	.272	.403	.350
91	EP/TEX	AA	49	218	186	47	5	2	0	56	25	0	5	56	3	2	0	14	2	40	13	.253	.356	.301
	DEN/AMA	AAA	89	338	286	72	10	4	1	93	45	1	0	66	2	3	4	23	8	51	31	.252	.349	.325
92	MIL/AL		149	649	579	168	19	6	1	202	55	0	1	124	3	12	2	54	18	93	47	.290	.352	.349
93	BEL/MID	A	4	14	12	3	0	0	0	3	1	0	1	2	0	0	0	2	0	2	1	.250	.357	.250
	MIL/AL		98	403	356	87	15	1	3	113	37	0	3	70	7	5	2	18	9	50	30	.244	.319	.317
2 YR TOTALS			**247**	**1052**	**935**	**255**	**34**	**7**	**4**	**315**	**92**	**0**	**4**	**194**	**10**	**17**	**4**	**72**	**27**	**143**	**77**	**.273**	**.339**	**.337**

Litton, Jon Gregory "Greg" — BR/TR — b.7/13/64 — POS 2B-96, OF-91, 3B-67, 1B-36, SS-33, DH-12, C-3, P-1SF84*   1/10

YR	TM/LG	CL	G	TPA	AB	H	2B	3B	HR	TB	BB	IBB	HB	SO	GDP	SH	SF	SB	CS	R	RBI	BA	OBA	SA
84	EVE/NWL	A-	62	271	243	57	12	2	4	85	27	0	1	47	4	0	0	2	1	29	26	.235	.314	.350
85	FRE/CAL	A+	141	626	564	150	33	7	12	233	50	0	3	86	8	2	7	8	4	88	103	.266	.325	.413
86	SHR/TEX	AA	131	518	455	112	30	3	10	178	52	4	4	77	13	5	2	1	2	46	55	.246	.327	.391
87	SHR/TEX	AA	72	282	254	66	6	3	8	102	22	2	2	51	2	2	2	2	4	34	33	.260	.321	.402
	PHO/PCL	AAA	60	228	203	44	8	2	1	59	18	1	2	40	5	2	3	0	1	24	22	.217	.283	.291
88	SHR/TEX	AA	116	482	432	120	35	5	11	198	37	2	5	84	8	1	7	2	2	58	64	.278	.337	.458
89	PHO/PCL	AAA	30	99	89	16	4	2	2	30	8	0	0	24	3	0	2	1	3	6	6	.180	.242	.337
	SF/NL		71	155	143	36	5	3	4	59	7	0	1	29	3	4	0	0	2	12	17	.252	.291	.413
90	PHO/PCL	AAA	6	25	22	6	1	0	0	7	2	0	1	7	0	0	1	0	0	3	4	.273	.320	.318
	SF/NL		93	220	204	50	9	1	1	64	11	0	1	45	5	2	2	1	0	17	24	.245	.284	.314
91	PHO/PCL	AAA	8	35	27	11	1	0	4	24	8	0	0	5	0	0	0	0	0	9	9	.407	.543	.889
	SF/NL		59	143	127	23	7	1	1	35	11	0	1	25	2	3	1	0	0	13	15	.181	.250	.276
92	PHO/PCL	AAA	25	95	85	26	7	0	4	45	8	1	0	21	2	1	1	0	1	14	19	.306	.362	.529
	SF/NL		68	154	140	32	5	0	4	49	11	0	0	33	2	3	0	0	1	9	15	.229	.285	.350
93	CAL/PCL	AAA	49	198	170	54	16	3	6	94	25	0	1	36	3	0	2	3	1	35	27	.318	.404	.553
	SEA/AL		72	199	174	52	17	0	3	78	18	2	1	30	6	5	1	0	1	25	25	.299	.366	.448
5 YR TOTALS			**363**	**871**	**788**	**193**	**43**	**5**	**13**	**285**	**58**	**2**	**4**	**162**	**18**	**17**	**4**	**1**	**6**	**76**	**96**	**.245**	**.299**	**.362**

Livingstone, Scott Louis — BL/TR — b.7/15/65 — POS 3B-217, DH-32   DET88 2/56

YR	TM/LG	CL	G	TPA	AB	H	2B	3B	HR	TB	BB	IBB	HB	SO	GDP	SH	SF	SB	CS	R	RBI	BA	OBA	SA
88	LAK/FSL	A+	53	198	180	51	8	1	2	67	11	3	3	25	3	2	1	1	1	28	25	.283	.332	.372
89	LON/EAS	AA	124	512	452	98	18	1	14	160	52	4	4	67	4	0	6	1	1	46	71	.217	.297	.354
90	TOL/INT	AAA	103	369	345	94	19	0	6	131	22	0	1	40	7	0	1	1	5	44	36	.272	.317	.380
91	TOL/INT	AAA	92	382	331	100	13	3	3	128	40	3	2	52	9	3	6	2	1	48	62	.302	.375	.387
	DET/AL		44	139	127	37	5	0	2	48	10	0	0	25	0	1	1	2	1	19	11	.291	.341	.378
92	DET/AL		117	382	354	100	21	0	4	133	21	1	0	36	8	3	4	1	3	43	46	.282	.319	.376
93	DET/AL		98	330	304	89	10	2	2	109	19	1	0	32	4	1	6	1	3	39	39	.293	.328	.359
3 YR TOTALS			**259**	**851**	**785**	**226**	**36**	**2**	**8**	**290**	**50**	**2**	**0**	**93**	**12**	**5**	**11**	**4**	**7**	**101**	**96**	**.288**	**.326**	**.369**

Lofton, Kenneth "Kenny" — BL/TL — b.5/31/67 — POS OF-309   HOU88 18/428

YR	TM/LG	CL	G	TPA	AB	H	2B	3B	HR	TB	BB	IBB	HB	SO	GDP	SH	SF	SB	CS	R	RBI	BA	OBA	SA
88	AUB/NYP	A-	48	207	187	40	6	1	1	51	19	0	0	51	3	1	0	26	4	23	14	.214	.286	.273
89	AUB/NYP	A-	34	129	110	29	3	1	0	34	14	0	0	30	1	1	4	26	5	21	8	.264	.336	.309
	ASH/SAL	A	22	97	82	27	2	0	1	32	12	0	1	10	1	2	0	14	6	14	9	.329	.421	.390
90	OSC/FSL	A+	124	556	481	159	15	5	2	190	61	2	3	77	4	8	3	62	16	98	35	.331	.407	.395
91	TUC/PCL	AAA	130	607	545	168	19	17	2	227	52	5	0	95	2	8	2	40	23	93	50	.308	.367	.417
	HOU/NL		20	79	74	15	1	0	0	16	5	0	0	19	0	0	0	2	1	9	0	.203	.253	.216
92	CLE/AL		148	651	576	164	15	8	5	210	68	3	2	54	7	4	1	*66	12	96	42	.285	.362	.365
93	CLE/AL		148	657	569	185	28	8	1	232	81	6	1	83	8	2	4	*70	14	116	42	.325	.408	.408
3 YR TOTALS			**316**	**1387**	**1219**	**364**	**44**	**16**	**6**	**458**	**154**	**9**	**3**	**156**	**15**	**6**	**5**	**138**	**27**	**221**	**84**	**.299**	**.377**	**.376**

Longmire, Anthony Eugene "Tony" — BL/TR — b.8/12/68 — POS OF-2   PIT86 8/186

YR	TM/LG	CL	G	TPA	AB	H	2B	3B	HR	TB	BB	IBB	HB	SO	GDP	SH	SF	SB	CS	R	RBI	BA	OBA	SA
86	PIR/GCL	R	15	44	40	11	2	1	0	15	2	0	1	2	2	0	1	1	2	6	6	.275	.318	.375
87	MAC/SAL	A	127	500	445	117	15	4	5	155	41	6	5	73	8	3	6	18	7	63	62	.263	.328	.348
88	HAR/EAS	AA	32	104	94	14	2	2	0	20	9	0	1	12	3	0	0	1	0	7	4	.149	.231	.213
	SAL/CAR	A+	64	256	218	60	12	2	11	109	36	1	1	44	5	1	0	4	3	46	40	.275	.380	.500
89	PIR/GCL	R	2	6	5	0	0	0	0	0	1	0	0	1	0	0	0	0	0	0	0	.000	.167	.000
	SAL/CAR	A+	14	63	62	20	3	1	1	28	1	0	0	13	1	0	0	1	0	8	6	.323	.333	.452
	HAR/EAS	AA	37	141	127	37	7	0	3	53	12	0	1	21	2	1	0	1	0	15	22	.291	.357	.417
90	HAR/EAS	AA	24	99	91	27	6	0	1	36	7	0	0	11	3	0	1	0	0	9	13	.297	.343	.396
91	SCR/INT	AAA	36	120	111	29	3	2	0	36	8	1	0	20	4	1	0	4	4	11	9	.261	.311	.324
	REA/EAS	AA	85	362	323	93	22	1	9	144	32	6	2	45	9	1	4	10	7	43	56	.288	.352	.446
93	SCR/INT	AAA	120	499	447	136	36	4	6	198	41	6	4	71	6	4	4	12	4	63	67	.304	.364	.443
	PHI/NL		11	13	13	3	0	0	0	3	0	0	0	1	0	0	0	0	0	1	1	.231	.231	.231

Lopez, Javier Torres "Javy" — BR/TR — b.11/5/70 — POS C-16   ATL 11/6/87

YR	TM/LG	CL	G	TPA	AB	H	2B	3B	HR	TB	BB	IBB	HB	SO	GDP	SH	SF	SB	CS	R	RBI	BA	OBA	SA
88	BRA/GCL	R	31	99	94	18	4	0	1	25	3	0	0	19	0	1	1	0	0	8	9	.191	.214	.266
89	PUL/APP	R+	51	162	153	40	8	1	3	59	5	0	1	35	8	0	3	2	3	27	27	.261	.284	.386
90	BUR/MID	A	116	445	422	112	17	3	11	168	14	2	5	84	10	4	0	0	2	48	55	.265	.297	.398
91	DUR/CAR	A+	113	415	384	94	14	2	11	145	25	4	3	88	10	0	3	10	3	43	51	.245	.294	.378
92	GRE/SOU	AA	115	474	442	142	28	3	16	224	24	1	5	47	8	1	2	7	3	63	60	.321	.362	.507
	ATL/NL		9	16	16	6	2	0	0	8	0	0	0	1	0	0	0	0	0	3	2	.375	.375	.500
93	RIC/INT	AAA	100	401	380	116	23	2	17	194	12	1	6	53	8	0	1	0	6	56	74	.305	.334	.511
	ATL/NL		8	17	16	6	1	0	1	10	0	0	1	2	0	0	0	0	0	1	2	.375	.412	.750
2 YR TOTALS			**17**	**33**	**32**	**12**	**3**	**1**	**1**	**20**	**0**	**0**	**1**	**3**	**0**	**0**	**0**	**0**	**0**	**4**	**4**	**.375**	**.394**	**.625**

Lopez, Luis Manuel — BB/TR — b.9/4/70 — POS 2B-15 SD 9/9/87

YR	TM/LG	CL	G	TPA	AB	H	2B	3B	HR	TB	BB	IBB	HB	SO	GDP	SH	SF	SB	CS	R	RBI	BA	OBA	SA
88	SPO/NWL	A-	70	338	312	95	13	1	0	110	18	0	4	59	7		2	14	5	50	35	.304	.348	.353
89	CHS/SAL	A	127	489	460	102	15	1	1	122	17	0	2	85	9	7	3	12	9	50	29	.222	.251	.265
90	RIV/CAL	A+	14	50	46	17	3	1	0	25	3	2	0	3	1	1	0	4	2	5	4	.370	.408	.543
91	WIC/TEX	AA	125	486	452	121	17	1	1	143	18	3	8	70	8	4	4	6	8	43	41	.268	.305	.316
92	LV/PCL	AAA	120	427	395	92	8	8	1	119	19	1	3	65	12	7	3	6	4	44	31	.233	.271	.301
93	LV/PCL	AAA	131	539	491	150	36	6	6	216	27	3	5	62	7	13	3	8	0	52	58	.305	.346	.440
	SD/NL		17	44	43	5	1	0	0	6	0	0	0	8	0	0	1	0	0	1	1	.116	.114	.140

Lovullo, Salvatore Anthony "Torey" — BB/TR — b.7/25/65 — POS 2B-100, 3B-50, 1B-19, SS-9, OF-2 DET87 7/131

YR	TM/LG	CL	G	TPA	AB	H	2B	3B	HR	TB	BB	IBB	HB	SO	GDP	SH	SF	SB	CS	R	RBI	BA	OBA	SA
87	FAY/SAL	A	55	233	191	49	13	0	8	86	37	4	2	30	3	2	1	6	0	34	32	.257	.381	.450
	LAK/FSL	A+	18	73	60	16	3	0	1	22	10	0	0	8	0	0	3	0	0	11	16	.267	.356	.367
88	GF/EAS	AA	78	313	270	74	17	1	9	120	36	3	1	44	5	0	6	2	0	37	50	.274	.355	.444
	TOL/INT	AAA	57	194	177	41	8	1	5	66	9	0	0	24	1	7	1	2	1	18	20	.232	.267	.373
	DET/AL		12	23	21	8	1	1	1	14	1	0	0	2	1	1	0	0	0	2	2	.381	.409	.667
89	DET/AL		29	104	87	10	2	0	1	15	14	0	1	20	3	1	2	0	0	8	4	.115	.233	.172
	TOL/INT	AAA	112	465	409	94	23	2	10	151	44	10	1	57	10	7	4	2	1	48	52	.230	.303	.369
90	TOL/INT	AAA	141	557	486	131	38	1	14	213	61	6	4	74	12	2	4	4	1	71	58	.270	.353	.438
91	CMB/INT	AAA	106	462	395	107	24	5	10	171	59	4	1	54	10	2	6	4	4	74	75	.271	.361	.433
	NY/AL		22	59	51	9	2	0	0	11	5	1	0	7	0	3	0	0	0	0	2	.176	.250	.216
92	CMB/INT	AAA	131	543	468	138	33	5	19	238	64	4	3	65	8	2	6	9	4	69	89	.295	.379	.509
93	CAL/AL		116	409	367	92	20	0	6	130	36	1	1	49	8	3	2	2	6	42	30	.251	.318	.354
4 YR TOTALS			**179**	**595**	**526**	**119**	**25**	**1**	**8**	**170**	**56**	**2**	**1**	**78**	**12**	**8**	**4**	**7**	**6**	**52**	**38**	**.226**	**.300**	**.323**

Lyden, Mitchell Scott "Mitch" — BR/TR — b.12/14/64 — POS C-2 NYA83 4/93

YR	TM/LG	CL	G	TPA	AB	H	2B	3B	HR	TB	BB	IBB	HB	SO	GDP	SH	SF	SB	CS	R	RBI	BA	OBA	SA
83	ONE/NYP	A-	47	146	128	19	1	0	0	20	12	0	2	36	3	2	2	3	0	14	7	.148	.229	.156
84	GRE/SAL	A	14	33	32	7	1	0	1	11	1	1	0	9	3	0	0	0	0	3	2	.219	.242	.344
	YAN/GCL	R	54	220	200	47	4	0	1	54	13	1	4	36	3	1	2	3	1	21	21	.235	.292	.270
85	FL/FSL	A+	116	438	400	102	21	0	10	155	27	0	5	93	15	1	5	1	2	43	58	.255	.307	.387
86	YAN/GCL	R	17	58	50	17	7	0	3	33	7	0	0	7	1	0	1	0	0	8	16	.340	.414	.660
	ALB/EAS	AA	46	167	159	48	14	1	8	88	4	1	2	39	5	0	2	0	1	19	29	.302	.323	.553
	CMB/INT	AAA	2	8	7	0	0	0	0	0	1	0	0	1	0	0	0	0	0	0	0	.000	.125	.000
87	CMB/INT	AAA	29	109	100	22	3	0	0	25	4	0	1	22	7	1	3	1	0	7	8	.220	.250	.250
	ALB/EAS	AA	71	248	233	59	12	2	8	99	11	0	2	47	4	1	1	0	0	25	36	.253	.291	.425
88	PW/CAR	A+	67	259	234	66	12	2	17	133	19	3	4	59	5	0	2	1	0	42	47	.282	.344	.568
	ALB/EAS	AA	20	84	78	32	7	1	8	65	5	1	0	15	3	0	1	0	2	16	21	.410	.440	.833
89	ALB/EAS	AA	53	196	181	43	2	0	6	63	12	3	2	51	5	1	0	1	0	24	21	.238	.292	.348
	PW/CAR	A+	30	122	105	29	2	1	7	54	8	0	8	26	0	1	1	0	0	17	28	.276	.369	.514
90	ALB/EAS	AA	85	348	311	92	22	1	17	167	24	1	9	67	13	0	4	1	0	55	63	.296	.359	.537
	CMB/INT	AAA	41	159	147	33	8	0	7	62	7	0	0	34	9	0	1	0	0	18	20	.224	.277	.422
91	TOL/INT	AAA	101	362	340	76	11	2	18	145	15	4	0	108	12	0	7	0	0	34	55	.224	.251	.426
92	TID/INT	AAA	91	318	299	77	13	0	14	132	12	0	3	95	11	0	4	0	0	34	52	.258	.289	.441
93	EDM/PCL	AAA	50	167	160	49	15	1	8	90	5	0	0	34	2	1	2	1	1	34	31	.306	.323	.563
	FLO/NL		6	10	10	3	0	0	1	6	0	0	0	3	0	0	0	0	0	2	1	.300	.300	.600

Lydy, Donald Scott "Scott" — BR/TR — b.10/26/68 — POS OF-38, DH-2 OAK89 1/56

YR	TM/LG	CL	G	TPA	AB	H	2B	3B	HR	TB	BB	IBB	HB	SO	GDP	SH	SF	SB	CS	R	RBI	BA	OBA	SA
89	SO/NWL	A-	67	271	230	48	11	2	3	72	31	0	3	72	7	3	4	8	5	37	28	.209	.306	.313
90	MAD/MID	A	54	202	174	33	6	2	4	55	25	1	1	62	1	0	2	7	5	33	19	.190	.292	.316
	ATH/ARI	R	18	60	50	17	6	0	2	29	10	0	1	14	1	0	0	0	0	8	11	.340	.450	.580
91	MAD/MID	A	127	539	464	120	26	2	12	186	66	5	5	109	10	0	4	24	9	64	69	.259	.354	.401
92	REN/CAL	A+	33	150	124	49	13	2	2	72	26	2	0	30	1	0	0	4	4	29	27	.395	.500	.581
	HUN/SOU	AA	109	462	387	118	20	3	9	171	67	5	4	95	4	0	4	16	5	64	65	.305	.409	.442
93	TAC/PCL	AAA	95	397	341	100	22	6	9	161	50	3	1	87	8	2	0	12	4	70	41	.293	.382	.472
	OAK/AL		41	111	102	23	5	0	2	34	8	0	1	39	1	0	0	2	0	11	7	.225	.288	.333

Lyons, Stephen John "Steve" — BL/TR — b.6/3/60 — POS OF-334, 3B-229, 2B-118, 1B-115, DH-24, SS-6, C-4, P-2 BOS81 1/19

YR	TM/LG	CL	G	TPA	AB	H	2B	3B	HR	TB	BB	IBB	HB	SO	GDP	SH	SF	SB	CS	R	RBI	BA	OBA	SA
84	PAW/INT	AAA	131	520	444	119	21	2	17	195	66	3	1	71	9	3	6	35	14	80	62	.268	.360	.439
85	BOS/AL		133	409	371	98	14	3	5	133	32	0	1	64	2	2	3	12	9	52	30	.264	.322	.358
86	BOS/AL		59	139	124	31	7	2	1	45	12	2	0	23	3	1	2	2	3	20	14	.250	.312	.363
	BUF/AMA	AAA	20	92	74	22	5	1	3	38	16	1	1	14	1	1	0	5	1	18	8	.297	.429	.514
	CHI/AL		42	136	123	25	2	1	0	29	7	0	1	24	1	3	2	2	3	10	6	.203	.248	.236
	YEAR		101	275	247	56	9	3	1	74	19	2	1	47	4	4	4	4	6	30	20	.227	.280	.300
87	HAW/PCL	AAA	47	192	167	48	11	0	2	65	22	1	1	27	7	1	7	5	7	26	16	.287	.372	.389
	CHI/AL		76	210	193	54	11	1	1	70	12	0	0	37	4	1	1	0	3	26	19	.280	.320	.363
88	CHI/AL		146	526	472	127	28	3	5	176	32	1	1	59	6	15	6	1	2	59	45	.269	.313	.373
89	CHI/AL		140	494	443	117	21	3	2	150	35	3	1	68	3	12	3	9	5	51	50	.264	.317	.339
90	CHI/AL		94	163	146	28	6	1	1	39	10	1	1	41	1	4	2	1	0	22	11	.192	.245	.267
91	BOS/AL		87	227	212	51	10	1	4	75	11	2	0	35	1	1	3	1	1	15	17	.241	.277	.354
92	ATL/NL		11	14	14	1	0	0	0	3	0	0	0	4	1	0	0	0	0	0	0	.071	.071	.214
	MON/NL		16	15	13	3	2	0	0	3	0	0	0	4	0	0	0	0	0	0	1	.231	.286	.231
	PAW/INT	AAA	37	144	135	35	14	1	2	59	8	2	1	50	2	2	1	0	0	14	12	.259	.306	.437
	BOS/AL		21	30	28	7	1	0	0	9	2	0	0	10	1	0	0	0	0	3	2	.250	.300	.321
	YEAR		48	59	55	11	4	0	0	15	3	0	0	16	0	0	0	3	1	5	4	.200	.241	.273
93	PAW/INT	AAA	67	226	197	42	6	0	4	60	26	3	0	50	2	2	1	0	0	24	18	.213	.304	.305

(continued)

Lyons, Stephen John "Steve" (continued)

YR	TM/LG	CL	G	TPA	AB	H	2B	3B	HR	TB	BB	IBB	HB	SO	GDP	SH	SF	SB	CS	R	RBI	BA	OBA	SA
	BOS/AL		28	25	23	3	1	0	0	4	2	0	0	5	0	0	0	1	2	4	0	.130	.200	.174
9 YR TOTALS			853	2388	2162	545	100	17	19	736	156	9	5	364	23	45	20	42	32	264	196	.252	.301	.340

Maas, Kevin Christian — BL/TL — b.1/20/65 — POS DH-220, 1B-132   NYA86 23/572

YR	TM/LG	CL	G	TPA	AB	H	2B	3B	HR	TB	BB	IBB	HB	SO	GDP	SH	SF	SB	CS	R	RBI	BA	OBA	SA
86	ONE/NYP	A-	28	109	101	36	10	0	0	46	7	1	0	9	1	0	1	5	1	14	18	.356	.394	.455
87	FL/FSL	A+	116	502	439	122	28	4	11	191	53	4	2	108	5	0	8	14	4	77	73	.278	.353	.435
88	PW/CAR	A+	29	133	108	32	7	0	12	75	17	1	4	28	0	0	4	3	1	24	35	.296	.398	.694
	ALB/EAS	AA	109	445	372	98	14	3	16	166	64	4	4	103	5	3	2	5	1	66	55	.263	.376	.446
89	CMB/INT	AAA	83	336	291	93	23	2	6	138	40	0	1	73	3	0	4	2	3	42	45	.320	.399	.474
90	CMB/INT	AAA	57	228	194	55	15	2	13	113	34	1	0	45	5	0	0	2	2	37	38	.284	.390	.582
	NY/AL		79	300	254	64	9	0	21	136	43	10	3	76	2	0	0	1	2	42	41	.252	.367	.535
91	NY/AL		148	592	500	110	14	1	23	195	83	3	4	128	4	0	5	5	1	69	63	.220	.333	.390
92	NY/AL		98	315	286	71	12	0	11	116	25	4	0	63	1	0	4	3	1	35	35	.248	.305	.406
93	CMB/INT	AAA	28	125	104	29	6	0	4	47	19	2	1	22	1	0	1	0	1	14	18	.279	.392	.452
	NY/AL		59	177	151	31	4	0	9	62	24	2	1	32	2	0	1	1	1	20	25	.205	.316	.411
4 YR TOTALS			384	1384	1191	276	39	1	64	509	175	19	8	299	9	0	10	10	5	166	164	.232	.332	.427

Macfarlane, Michael Andrew "Mike" — BR/TR — b.4/12/64 — POS C-534, DH-26   KC85 4/97

YR	TM/LG	CL	G	TPA	AB	H	2B	3B	HR	TB	BB	IBB	HB	SO	GDP	SH	SF	SB	CS	R	RBI	BA	OBA	SA
85	MEM/SOU	AA	65	243	223	60	15	4	8	107	11	0	5	30	6	2	2	0	0	29	39	.269	.315	.480
86	MEM/SOU	AA	40	154	141	34	7	2	12	81	10	0	2	26	7	0	1	0	0	26	29	.241	.299	.574
87	KC/AL		8	21	19	4	1	0	0	5	2	0	0	2	1	0	0	0	0	0	3	.211	.286	.263
	OMA/AMA	AAA	87	330	302	79	25	1	13	145	22	1	6	50	7	0	0	0	0	53	50	.262	.324	.480
88	KC/AL		70	236	211	56	15	0	4	83	21	2	1	37	5	1	2	0	0	25	26	.265	.332	.393
	OMA/AMA	AAA	21	83	76	18	7	2	2	35	4	0	2	15	1	1	0	0	1	8	8	.237	.293	.461
89	KC/AL		69	167	157	35	6	0	2	47	7	0	2	27	8	0	1	0	0	13	19	.223	.263	.299
90	KC/AL		124	439	400	102	24	4	6	152	25	2	7	69	9	1	6	1	0	37	58	.255	.306	.380
91	KC/AL		84	295	267	74	18	2	13	135	17	0	6	52	4	1	4	1	0	34	41	.277	.330	.506
92	KC/AL		129	450	402	94	28	3	17	179	30	2	15	89	8	1	2	1	5	51	48	.234	.310	.445
93	KC/AL		117	451	388	106	27	0	20	193	40	2	16	83	8	1	6	2	5	55	67	.273	.360	.497
7 YR TOTALS			601	2059	1844	471	119	9	62	794	142	8	47	359	43	5	21	5	10	215	262	.255	.321	.431

Mack, Shane Lee — BR/TR — b.12/7/63 — POS OF-678, DH-5   SD84 1/11

YR	TM/LG	CL	G	TPA	AB	H	2B	3B	HR	TB	BB	IBB	HB	SO	GDP	SH	SF	SB	CS	R	RBI	BA	OBA	SA
85	BEA/TEX	AA	125	479	430	112	23	3	6	159	38	2	3	89	11	7	1	12	5	59	55	.260	.324	.370
86	BEA/TEX	AA	115	485	452	127	26	3	15	204	21	2	2	79	10	2	3	14	9	61	68	.281	.321	.451
	LV/PCL	AAA	19	72	69	25	1	6	0	38	2	0	1	13	0	0	3	3	4	13	6	.362	.389	.551
87	LV/PCL	AAA	39	173	152	51	11	1	5	79	19	0	1	32	2	0	1	13	0	38	26	.336	.410	.520
	SD/NL		105	267	238	57	11	3	4	86	18	0	3	47	11	6	2	4	6	28	25	.239	.299	.361
88	SD/NL		56	140	119	29	3	0	0	32	14	0	3	21	2	3	1	5	1	13	12	.244	.336	.269
	LV/PCL	AAA	55	230	196	68	7	1	10	107	29	4	3	44	3	0	2	7	1	43	40	.347	.435	.546
89	LV/PCL	AAA	24	96	80	18	3	1	1	26	14	0	1	19	1	0	1	4	2	10	8	.225	.344	.325
90	MIN/AL		125	353	313	102	10	4	8	144	29	1	5	69	7	6	0	13	4	50	44	.326	.392	.460
91	MIN/AL		143	489	442	137	27	8	18	234	34	1	6	79	11	2	5	13	9	79	74	.310	.363	.529
92	MIN/AL		156	692	600	189	31	6	16	280	64	1	15	106	8	11	2	26	14	101	75	.315	.394	.467
93	MIN/AL		128	553	503	139	30	4	10	207	41	1	4	76	13	3	2	15	5	66	61	.276	.335	.412
6 YR TOTALS			713	2494	2215	653	112	25	56	983	200	4	36	398	52	31	12	76	39	337	291	.295	.361	.444

Maclin, Lonnie Lee — BL/TL — b.2/17/67 — POS OF-5   SL86 S3/63

YR	TM/LG	CL	G	TPA	AB	H	2B	3B	HR	TB	BB	IBB	HB	SO	GDP	SH	SF	SB	CS	R	RBI	BA	OBA	SA
87	JC/APP	R+	62	255	229	69	6	1	3	86	24	0	1	32	2	0	1	22	5	45	22	.301	.369	.376
88	SP/FSL	A+	51	197	175	33	3	1	3	47	18	1	2	41	2	2	0	9	7	22	12	.189	.272	.269
	SAV/SAL	A	46	133	119	28	3	0	0	31	12	1	0	19	3	0	2	8	4	10	9	.235	.301	.261
89	SPR/MID	A	103	343	315	78	10	3	3	103	21	0	4	56	3	4	1	18	14	33	34	.248	.298	.327
90	SP/FSL	A+	31	131	119	46	6	3	2	64	11	0	0	12	4	0	1	6	2	18	17	.387	.435	.538
	ARK/TEX	AA	74	290	264	82	14	5	2	112	19	1	0	35	4	5	2	11	7	32	25	.311	.354	.424
	LOU/AMA	AAA	17	68	58	18	3	2	0	25	9	0	1	11	1	1	1	4	1	9	6	.310	.388	.431
91	LOU/AMA	AAA	84	346	327	94	12	2	4	122	16	0	0	50	5	2	1	19	12	35	37	.287	.320	.373
92	LOU/AMA	AAA	111	328	290	94	17	3	1	120	22	1	5	31	1	4	7	4	7	29	38	.324	.373	.414
93	LOU/AMA	AAA	62	238	220	61	10	3	4	89	16	2	0	48	4	0	0	4	4	29	18	.277	.332	.405
	STL/NL		12	14	13	1	0	0	0	1	0	0	0	5	0	0	1	1	0	2	1	.077	.071	.077

Magadan, David Joseph "Dave" — BL/TR — b.9/30/62 — POS 1B-460, 3B-328, DH-2   NYN83 4/32

YR	TM/LG	CL	G	TPA	AB	H	2B	3B	HR	TB	BB	IBB	HB	SO	GDP	SH	SF	SB	CS	R	RBI	BA	OBA	SA
84	LYN/CAR	A+	112	486	371	130	22	4	0	160	104	10	6	43	12	0	5	2	1	78	62	.350	.494	.431
85	JAC/TEX	AA	134	582	466	144	22	0	0	166	106	2	4	57	16	4	1	0	3	84	76	.309	.441	.356
86	TID/INT	AAA	133	571	473	147	33	6	1	195	84	5	3	45	10	2	2	2	2	68	64	.311	.411	.412
	NY/NL		10	21	18	8	0	0	0	8	3	0	0	1	1	0	0	0	0	3	3	.444	.524	.444
87	NY/NL		85	216	192	61	13	1	3	85	22	2	0	22	5	1	1	0	0	21	24	.318	.386	.443
88	NY/NL		112	380	314	87	15	0	1	105	60	4	1	39	9	1	3	0	1	39	35	.277	.393	.334
89	NY/NL		127	429	374	107	22	3	4	147	49	6	1	37	2	1	4	1	0	47	41	.286	.367	.393
90	NY/NL		144	541	451	148	28	6	6	206	74	4	2	55	11	4	10	2	1	74	72	.328	*.417	.457
91	NY/NL		124	517	418	108	23	0	4	143	83	3	2	50	5	7	7	1	1	58	51	.258	.378	.342
92	NY/NL		99	379	321	91	9	1	3	111	56	3	0	44	6	2	0	1	0	33	28	.283	.390	.346
93	FLO/NL		66	275	227	65	12	0	4	89	44	4	1	30	3	0	3	0	1	22	29	.286	.400	.392
	SEA/AL		71	269	228	59	11	0	1	73	36	3	0	33	9	2	3	2	0	27	21	.259	.356	.320

Magadan, David Joseph "Dave" (continued)

YR	TM/LG	CL	G	TPA	AB	H	2B	3B	HR	TB	BB	IBB	HB	SO	GDP	SH	SF	SB	CS	R	RBI	BA	OBA	SA
	YEAR		137	544	455	124	23	0	5	162	80	7	1	63	12	2	6	2	1	49	50	.273	.378	.356
8 YR TOTALS			838	3027	2543	734	133	11	26	967	427	29	8	311	51	18	31	7	4	324	304	.289	.389	.380

Maksudian, Michael Bryant "Mike" — BL/TR — b.5/28/66 — POS 1B-5, 3B-1   CHA 7/13/87

YR	TM/LG	CL	G	TPA	AB	H	2B	3B	HR	TB	BB	IBB	HB	SO	GDP	SH	SF	SB	CS	R	RBI	BA	OBA	SA
87	WS/GCL	R	34	131	109	38	11	3	1	58	19	4	1	13	2	0	2	7	2	23	28	.349	.443	.532
88	SB/MID	A	102	431	366	111	26	3	4	155	60	9	3	59	1	0	2	5	3	51	50	.303	.404	.423
	TAM/FSL	A+	1	3	3	2	1	0	0	3	0	0	0	1	0	0	0	0	0	1	2	.667	.667	1.000
	SL/FSL	A+	13	51	42	9	2	1	0	13	8	0	0	6	1	0	1	0	0	7	1	.214	.333	.310
89	MIA/FSL	A+	83	318	288	90	18	4	9	143	28	2	0	42	11	0	2	6	4	36	42	.313	.371	.497
90	KNO/SOU	AA	121	475	422	121	22	5	8	177	50	6	2	66	9	0	1	6	4	51	55	.287	.364	.419
91	SYR/INT	AAA	31	108	97	32	6	3	1	47	10	0	0	17	2	1	0	0	0	13	13	.330	.393	.485
	KNO/SOU	AA	71	273	231	59	12	3	5	92	37	5	0	43	3	0	5	2	2	32	35	.255	.352	.398
92	SYR/INT	AAA	101	373	339	95	17	1	13	153	32	6	1	63	7	0	1	4	1	38	58	.280	.343	.451
	TOR/AL		3	3	3	0	0	0	0	0	0	0	0	0	0	0	0	0	0	0	0	.000	.000	.000
93	MIN/AL		5	17	12	2	1	0	0	3	4	0	0	2	1	0	1	0	0	2	2	.167	.353	.250
	POR/PCL	AAA	76	313	264	83	16	7	10	143	45	3	0	51	1	0	4	5	1	57	49	.314	.409	.542
2 YR TOTALS			8	20	15	2	1	0	0	3	4	0	0	2	1	0	1	0	0	2	2	.133	.300	.200

Maldonado, Candido "Candy" — BR/TR — b.9/5/60 — POS OF-1141, DH-35, 3B-5   LA 6/6/78

YR	TM/LG	CL	G	TPA	AB	H	2B	3B	HR	TB	BB	IBB	HB	SO	GDP	SH	SF	SB	CS	R	RBI	BA	OBA	SA
81	LA/NL		11	12	12	1	0	0	0	1	0	0	0	5	0	0	0	0	0	0	0	.083	.083	.083
82	LA/NL		6	5	4	0	0	0	0	0	1	1	0	2	0	0	0	0	0	0	0	.000	.200	.000
83	LA/NL		42	68	62	12	1	1	1	18	5	0	0	14	1	1	0	0	0	5	6	.194	.254	.290
84	LA/NL		116	278	254	68	14	0	5	97	19	0	1	29	6	1	3	0	3	25	28	.268	.318	.382
85	LA/NL		121	235	213	48	7	1	5	72	19	4	0	40	3	2	1	1	1	20	19	.225	.288	.338
86	SF/NL		133	432	405	102	31	3	18	193	20	4	3	77	12	0	4	4	4	49	85	.252	.289	.477
87	SF/NL		118	489	442	129	28	4	20	225	34	4	6	78	9	0	7	8	8	69	85	.292	.346	.509
88	SF/NL		142	552	499	127	23	1	12	188	37	1	7	89	13	3	6	6	5	53	68	.255	.311	.377
89	SF/NL		129	389	345	75	23	0	9	125	37	4	3	69	8	1	3	4	1	39	41	.217	.296	.362
90	CLE/AL		155	651	590	161	32	2	22	263	49	4	5	134	13	0	7	3	5	76	95	.273	.330	.446
91	MIL/AL		34	125	111	23	6	0	5	44	13	0	0	23	4	0	1	1	0	11	20	.207	.288	.396
	TOR/AL		52	208	177	49	9	0	7	79	23	4	6	53	4	0	2	3	0	26	28	.277	.375	.446
	YEAR		86	333	288	72	15	0	12	123	36	4	6	76	8	0	3	4	0	37	48	.250	.342	.427
92	TOR/AL		137	560	489	133	25	4	20	226	59	3	7	112	13	2	3	2	2	64	66	.272	.357	.462
93	CHI/NL		70	154	140	26	5	0	3	40	11	0	1	40	3	0	0	0	0	8	15	.186	.260	.286
	CLE/AL		28	94	81	20	2	0	5	37	11	2	0	18	2	1	1	0	1	11	20	.247	.333	.457
	YEAR		98	248	221	46	7	0	8	77	24	2	1	58	5	1	1	0	1	19	35	.208	.287	.348
13 YR TOTALS			1294	4252	3824	974	206	16	132	1608	340	31	39	783	91	11	38	32	30	456	576	.255	.319	.421

Manto, Jeffrey Paul "Jeff" — BR/TR — b.8/23/64 — POS 3B-43, 1B-39, C-5, OF-1, SS-1   CAL85 16/355

YR	TM/LG	CL	G	TPA	AB	H	2B	3B	HR	TB	BB	IBB	HB	SO	GDP	SH	SF	SB	CS	R	RBI	BA	OBA	SA
85	QC/MID	A	74	282	233	46	5	2	11	88	40	0	5	74	7	1	3	3	1	34	34	.197	.324	.378
86	QC/MID	A	73	283	239	59	13	0	8	96	37	0	4	70	2	1	2	2	1	31	49	.247	.355	.402
87	PS/CAL	A+	112	497	375	96	21	4	7	146	102	1	8	85	7	5	7	8	2	61	63	.256	.419	.389
88	MID/TEX	AA	120	485	408	123	23	3	24	224	62	5	8	76	17	3	4	7	5	88	101	.301	.400	.549
89	EDM/PCL	AAA	127	515	408	113	25	3	23	213	91	5	9	81	12	3	4	4	4	89	67	.277	.416	.522
90	CS/PCL	AAA	96	407	316	94	27	1	18	177	78	2	9	65	9	1	3	10	3	73	82	.297	.446	.560
	CLE/AL		30	97	76	17	5	1	2	30	21	1	0	18	0	0	0	1	0	12	14	.224	.392	.395
91	CS/PCL	AAA	43	192	153	49	16	0	6	83	33	2	3	24	3	0	3	1	0	36	36	.320	.443	.542
	CLE/AL		47	148	128	27	7	0	2	40	14	0	4	30	3	1	2	0	0	15	13	.211	.306	.313
92	RIC/INT	AAA	127	521	450	131	24	1	13	196	57	4	7	63	8	0	7	1	2	65	68	.291	.374	.436
93	SCR/INT	AAA	106	454	388	112	30	1	17	195	55	3	5	58	9	0	6	4	1	62	88	.289	.379	.503
	PHI/NL		8	19	18	1	0	0	0	1	0	0	0	7	1	0	1	0	0	0	0	.056	.105	.056
3 YR TOTALS			85	264	222	45	12	1	4	71	35	1	5	43	3	1	1	2	1	27	27	.203	.323	.320

Manwaring, Kirt Dean — BR/TR — b.7/15/65 — POS C-440   SF86 2/31

YR	TM/LG	CL	G	TPA	AB	H	2B	3B	HR	TB	BB	IBB	HB	SO	GDP	SH	SF	SB	CS	R	RBI	BA	OBA	SA
86	CLI/MID	A	49	167	147	36	7	1	2	51	14	1	1	26	0	4	1	1	2	18	16	.245	.313	.347
87	SHR/TEX	AA	98	336	307	82	13	2	2	105	19	2	8	33	6	2	0	1	0	27	22	.267	.326	.342
	SF/NL		6	8	7	1	0	0	0	1	0	0	1	1	1	0	0	0	0	0	0	.143	.250	.143
88	PHO/PCL	AAA	81	293	273	77	12	2	2	99	14	1	3	32	9	1	2	3	4	29	35	.282	.322	.363
	SF/NL		40	123	116	29	7	0	1	39	2	0	3	21	1	1	1	0	1	12	15	.250	.279	.336
89	SF/NL		85	223	200	42	4	2	0	50	11	1	4	28	5	7	1	2	1	14	18	.210	.264	.250
90	PHO/PCL	AAA	74	274	247	58	10	2	3	81	24	1	3	34	4	0	0	0	3	20	14	.235	.310	.328
	SF/NL		8	13	13	2	0	1	0	4	0	0	0	1	0	0	0	0	1	0	1	.154	.154	.308
91	PHO/PCL	AAA	24	90	81	18	0	0	4	30	8	0	0	15	2	0	1	0	0	8	14	.222	.289	.370
	SJ/CAL	A+	1	4	3	0	0	0	0	0	1	0	0	1	0	0	0	0	0	0	0	.000	.250	.000
	SF/NL		67	199	178	40	9	0	0	49	9	0	3	22	2	7	2	1	1	16	19	.225	.271	.275
92	SF/NL		109	389	349	85	10	5	4	117	29	0	5	42	12	6	0	2	1	24	26	.244	.311	.335
93	SF/NL		130	486	432	119	15	1	5	151	41	13	6	76	14	5	2	1	2	48	49	.275	.345	.350
7 YR TOTALS			445	1441	1295	318	45	9	10	411	92	14	22	193	35	26	6	6	7	114	128	.246	.305	.317

Marrero, Oreste Vilato — BL/TL — b.10/31/69 — POS 1B-32   MIL 9/29/86

YR	TM/LG	CL	G	TPA	AB	H	2B	3B	HR	TB	BB	IBB	HB	SO	GDP	SH	SF	SB	CS	R	RBI	BA	OBA	SA
87	HEL/PIO	R+	51	174	154	50	8	2	7	83	18	3	1	31	1	1	1	0	2	1	30	34	.325	.399	.539
88	BEL/MID	A	19	55	52	9	2	0	1	14	3	0	0	16	0	0	0	0	1	5	7	.173	.218	.269

(continued)

Marrero, Oreste Vilato (continued)

YR	TM/LG	CL	G	TPA	AB	H	2B	3B	HR	TB	BB	IBB	HB	SO	GDP	SH	SF	SB	CS	R	RBI	BA	OBA	SA
	HEL/PIO	R+	67	284	240	85	15	0	16	148	42	2	0	48	4	1	1	3	4	52	44	.354	.449	.617
89	BEL/MID	A	14	44	40	5	1	0	0	6	3	0	0	20	0	0	1	2	0	1	3	.125	.182	.150
	BRE/ARI	R	10	47	44	18	0	1	3	29	2	0	0	5	0	0	1	2	2	13	16	.409	.426	.659
	BOI/NWL	A-	54	237	203	56	8	1	11	99	30	3	0	60	3	0	4	1	2	38	43	.276	.363	.488
90	BEL/MID	A	119	446	400	110	25	1	16	185	45	3	0	107	12	0	1	8	4	59	55	.275	.348	.463
91	STO/CAL	A+	123	503	438	110	15	2	13	168	57	8	0	98	5	1	7	4	5	63	61	.251	.333	.384
92	EP/TEX	AA	18	59	54	10	2	1	1	17	4	0	0	13	0	0	1	1	0	8	8	.185	.237	.315
	STO/CAL	A+	76	290	243	67	17	0	7	105	44	6	1	49	0	1	1	1	2	35	51	.276	.388	.432
93	HAR/EAS	AA	85	284	255	85	18	1	10	135	22	2	0	46	2	3	4	3	3	39	49	.333	.381	.529
	MON/NL		32	95	81	17	5	1	1	27	14	0	0	16	0	0	0	1	3	10	4	.210	.326	.333

Martin, Albert Lee — BL/TL — b.11/24/67 — POS OF-143   ATL85 7/198

YR	TM/LG	CL	G	TPA	AB	H	2B	3B	HR	TB	BB	IBB	HB	SO	GDP	SH	SF	SB	CS	R	RBI	BA	OBA	SA
85	BRA/GCL	R	40	160	138	32	3	0	0	35	19	2	2	36	4	0	1	1	4	16	9	.232	.331	.254
86	SUM/SAL	A	44	179	156	38	5	0	1	46	23	1	0	36	6	0	0	6	2	23	24	.244	.341	.295
	IF/PIO	R+	63	264	242	80	17	6	4	121	20	0	2	53	1	0	0	11	2	39	44	.331	.386	.500
87	SUM/SAL	A	117	426	375	95	18	5	12	159	44	5	2	69	5	1	4	27	8	59	64	.253	.332	.424
88	BUR/MID	A	123	524	480	134	21	3	7	182	30	1	4	88	6	5	5	40	12	69	42	.279	.324	.379
89	DUR/CAR	A+	128	497	457	124	26	3	9	183	34	0	3	107	6	0	3	27	14	84	48	.271	.324	.400
90	GRE/SOU	AA	133	505	455	110	17	4	11	168	43	4	3	101	9	0	3	19	12	64	50	.242	.310	.369
91	GRE/SOU	AA	86	343	301	73	13	3	7	113	32	1	8	84	2	1	1	19	7	38	38	.243	.330	.375
	RIC/INT	AAA	44	159	151	42	11	1	5	70	7	0	1	33	0	0	0	11	2	20	18	.278	.314	.464
92	BUF/AMA	AAA	125	469	420	128	16	15	20	234	35	4	6	93	1	3	5	20	5	85	59	.305	.363	.557
	PIT/NL		12	13	12	2	0	1	0	4	0	0	1	5	0	0	0	0	0	1	2	.167	.154	.333
93	PIT/NL		143	528	480	135	26	8	18	231	42	5	1	122	5	2	3	16	9	85	64	.281	.338	.481
2 YR TOTALS			155	541	492	137	26	9	18	235	42	5	1	127	5	2	4	16	9	86	66	.278	.334	.478

Martin, Norberto Edonal — BR/TR — b.12/10/66 — POS 2B-5, DH-1   CHA 3/27/84

YR	TM/LG	CL	G	TPA	AB	H	2B	3B	HR	TB	BB	IBB	HB	SO	GDP	SH	SF	SB	CS	R	RBI	BA	OBA	SA
84	WS/GCL	R	56	235	205	56	8	2	1	71	21	0	4	31	3	1	4	18	5	36	30	.273	.346	.346
85	APP/MID	A	30	108	96	19	2	0	0	21	9	0	0	23	1	3	0	2	2	15	5	.198	.267	.219
	NF/NYP	A-	60	230	217	55	9	0	1	67	7	0	1	41	2	5	0	6	4	22	13	.253	.280	.309
86	APP/MID	A	9	35	33	10	2	0	0	12	1	0	1	5	1	0	0	1	0	4	2	.303	.343	.364
87	CHW/SAL	A	68	278	250	78	14	1	5	109	17	1	4	40	1	4	3	14	4	44	35	.312	.361	.436
	PEN/CAR	A+	41	185	162	42	6	1	1	53	18	0	1	19	3	0	4	11	6	21	18	.259	.330	.327
88	TAM/FSL	A+	101	390	360	93	10	4	2	117	17	0	3	49	13	7	3	24	5	44	33	.258	.295	.325
90	VAN/PCL	AAA	130	554	508	135	20	4	3	172	27	0	5	63	14	6	10	7	7	77	45	.266	.306	.339
91	VAN/PCL	AAA	93	374	338	94	11	3	0	103	21	0	3	38	14	10	2	11	8	39	20	.278	.324	.305
92	VAN/PCL	AAA	135	544	497	143	12	7	0	169	29	1	2	44	11	14	2	29	12	72	29	.288	.328	.340
93	NAS/AMA	AAA	137	626	580	179	21	6	9	239	26	0	2	59	17	12	6	31	5	87	74	.309	.337	.412
	CHI/AL		8	15	14	5	0	0	0	5	1	0	0	1	0	0	0	0	0	3	2	.357	.400	.357

Martinez, Carlos Alberto Escobar — BR/TR — b.8/11/64 — POS 1B-206, 3B-146, DH-70, OF-11   NYA 11/17/83

YR	TM/LG	CL	G	TPA	AB	H	2B	3B	HR	TB	BB	IBB	HB	SO	GDP	SH	SF	SB	CS	R	RBI	BA	OBA	SA
84	YAN/GCL	R	31	100	91	14	1	1	0	17	6	0	0	15	1	2	1	3	0	9	4	.154	.204	.187
85	FL/FSL	A+	93	333	311	77	15	7	6	124	14	1	2	65	9	4	2	8	4	39	44	.248	.283	.399
86	FL/FSL	A+	5	16	16	1	0	0	0	1	0	0	0	6	1	0	0	0	0	1	0	.063	.063	.063
	ALB/EAS	AA	69	264	253	70	18	2	8	116	6	0	2	46	4	0	2	2	3	34	39	.277	.299	.458
	BUF/AMA	AAA	17	60	54	16	1	0	2	23	2	0	2	12	1	0	2	0	0	6	6	.296	.333	.426
87	HAW/PCL	AAA	83	322	304	75	15	1	3	101	14	1	0	50	8	1	3	3	2	32	36	.247	.277	.332
	BIR/SOU	AA	9	31	30	7	1	0	0	8	0	0	1	6	1	0	0	2	0	2	0	.233	.258	.267
88	BIR/SOU	AA	133	544	498	138	22	3	14	208	36	2	2	82	10	2	6	25	7	67	73	.277	.325	.418
	CHI/AL		17	55	55	9	1	0	0	10	0	0	0	12	1	0	0	1	0	5	0	.164	.164	.182
89	VAN/PCL	AAA	18	71	64	25	3	0	2	36	5	0	2	14	0	0	1	0	0	12	9	.391	.423	.563
	SB/MID	A	3	12	11	6	0	0	1	9	1	0	0	1	0	0	0	2	0	2	3	.545	.583	.818
	CHI/AL		109	379	350	105	22	0	5	142	21	2	1	57	14	6	1	4	1	44	32	.300	.340	.406
90	CHI/AL		92	283	272	61	6	5	4	89	10	2	0	40	7	4	1	0	1	18	24	.224	.252	.327
91	CAN/EAS	AA	80	326	295	97	22	2	11	156	22	3	2	47	7	0	7	11	4	48	73	.329	.371	.529
	CLE/AL		72	275	257	73	14	0	5	102	10	2	2	43	10	1	5	3	2	22	30	.284	.310	.397
92	CS/PCL	AAA	9	36	32	10	1	0	0	11	1	1	1	5	1	1	1	2	0	7	5	.313	.333	.344
	CLE/AL		69	241	228	60	9	1	5	86	7	0	1	21	5	1	4	1	2	23	35	.263	.283	.377
93	CLE/AL		80	285	262	64	10	0	5	89	20	3	0	29	5	0	2	6	1	26	31	.244	.295	.340
	CHW/INT	AAA	20	84	79	29	7	1	3	47	4	0	0	15	0	0	2	0	1	17	12	.367	.405	.595
6 YR TOTALS			439	1518	1424	372	62	6	24	518	68	9	4	202	43	9	13	10	10	138	152	.261	.294	.364

Martinez, Constantino "Tino" — BL/TR — b.12/7/67 — POS 1B-233, DH-58   SEA88 1/14

YR	TM/LG	CL	G	TPA	AB	H	2B	3B	HR	TB	BB	IBB	HB	SO	GDP	SH	SF	SB	CS	R	RBI	BA	OBA	SA
89	WIL/EAS	AA	137	577	509	131	29	2	13	203	59	13	0	54	11	1	8	7	1	51	64	.257	.330	.399
90	CAL/PCL	AAA	128	540	453	145	28	1	17	226	74	11	3	37	9	2	8	8	5	83	93	.320	.413	.499
	SEA/AL		24	78	68	15	4	0	0	19	9	0	0	9	0	0	1	0	0	4	5	.221	.308	.279
91	CAL/PCL	AAA	122	535	442	144	34	5	18	242	82	7	3	44	5	0	8	3	3	94	86	.326	.428	.548
	SEA/AL		36	125	112	23	2	0	4	37	11	0	0	24	2	0	1	0	0	11	9	.205	.272	.330
92	SEA/AL		136	513	460	118	19	2	16	189	42	5	9	77	24	1	2	2	1	53	66	.257	.316	.411
93	SEA/AL		109	464	408	108	25	1	17	186	45	9	1	56	7	2	1	0	0	48	60	.265	.343	.456
4 YR TOTALS			305	1180	1048	264	50	3	37	431	107	18	7	166	33	4	14	2	4	116	140	.252	.321	.411

Martinez, David "Dave" — BL/TL — b.9/26/64 — POS OF-839, 1B-21, P-1   TOR 8/23/84

YR	TM/LG	CL	G	TPA	AB	H	2B	3B	HR	TB	BB	IBB	HB	SO	GDP	SH	SF	SB	CS	R	RBI	BA	OBA	SA
84	QC/MID	A	12	51	41	9	2	2	0	15	9	0	1	13	1	0	0	3	4	6	5	.220	.373	.366
85	WIN/CAR	A+	115	454	386	132	14	4	5	169	62	5	3	35	9	1	2	38	14	52	54	.342	.435	.438
86	CHI/NL		53	116	108	15	1	1	1	21	6	0	1	22	1	0	1	4	2	13	7	.139	.190	.194
	IOW/AMA	AAA	83	362	318	92	11	5	5	128	36	1	1	34	2	4	3	42	5	52	32	.289	.360	.403
87	CHI/NL		142	520	459	134	18	8	8	192	57	4	2	96	4	1	1	16	8	70	36	.292	.372	.418
88	CHI/NL		75	283	256	65	10	1	4	89	21	5	2	46	2	0	4	7	3	27	34	.254	.311	.348
	MON/NL		63	211	191	49	3	5	2	68	17	3	0	48	1	2	1	16	6	24	12	.257	.316	.356
	YEAR		138	494	447	114	13	6	6	157	38	8	2	94	3	2	5	23	9	51	46	.255	.313	.351
89	MON/NL		126	396	361	99	16	7	3	138	27	2	0	57	1	7	1	23	4	41	27	.274	.324	.382
90	MON/NL		118	421	391	109	13	5	11	165	24	2	1	48	8	3	2	13	11	60	39	.279	.321	.422
91	MON/NL		124	427	396	117	18	5	7	166	20	3	3	54	3	5	3	16	7	47	42	.295	.332	.419
92	CIN/NL		135	445	393	100	20	5	3	139	42	4	0	54	6	6	4	12	8	47	31	.254	.323	.354
93	PHO/PCL	AAA	3	16	15	7	0	0	0	7	1	0	0	1	0	0	0	1	0	4	2	.467	.500	.467
	SF/NL		91	268	241	58	12	1	5	87	27	3	0	39	5	0	0	6	3	28	27	.241	.317	.361
8 YR TOTALS			**927**	**3087**	**2796**	**746**	**111**	**38**	**44**	**1065**	**241**	**26**	**9**	**464**	**31**	**24**	**17**	**113**	**52**	**357**	**255**	**.267**	**.325**	**.381**

Martinez, Domingo Emilio — BR/TR — b.8/4/67 — POS 1B-14, 3B-1   TOR 8/23/84

YR	TM/LG	CL	G	TPA	AB	H	2B	3B	HR	TB	BB	IBB	HB	SO	GDP	SH	SF	SB	CS	R	RBI	BA	OBA	SA
85	BJ/GCL	R	58	233	219	65	10	2	4	91	12	0	2	42	3	0	0	3	4	36	19	.297	.339	.416
86	VEN/CAL	A+	129	501	455	113	19	6	9	171	36	2	4	127	15	3	3	9	9	51	57	.248	.307	.376
87	DUN/FSL	A+	118	481	435	112	32	2	8	172	41	2	3	88	9	0	2	8	3	53	65	.257	.324	.395
88	KNO/SOU	AA	143	568	516	136	25	2	13	204	40	3	5	88	13	0	7	2	7	54	70	.264	.319	.395
89	KNO/SOU	AA	120	472	415	102	19	2	10	155	42	3	9	82	7	1	5	2	2	56	53	.246	.325	.373
90	KNO/SOU	AA	128	522	463	119	20	3	17	196	51	1	5	81	24	1	2	4	4	53	66	.257	.336	.423
91	SYR/INT	AAA	126	525	467	146	16	2	17	217	41	0	6	107	10	5	6	6	4	61	83	.313	.371	.465
92	SYR/INT	AAA	116	483	438	120	22	0	21	205	33	5	8	95	11	0	4	6	0	55	62	.274	.333	.468
	TOR/AL		7	8	8	5	0	0	1	8	0	0	0	1	0	0	0	0	0	2	3	.625	.625	1.000
93	SYR/INT	AAA	127	510	465	127	24	2	24	227	31	6	10	115	11	0	4	4	5	50	79	.273	.329	.488
	TOR/AL		8	15	14	4	0	0	1	7	1	0	0	7	0	0	0	0	0	2	3	.286	.333	.500
2 YR TOTALS			**15**	**23**	**22**	**9**	**0**	**0**	**2**	**15**	**1**	**0**	**0**	**8**	**0**	**0**	**0**	**0**	**0**	**4**	**6**	**.409**	**.435**	**.682**

Martinez, Edgar — BR/TR — b.1/2/63 — POS 3B-492, DH-57, 1B-2   SEA 12/19/82

YR	TM/LG	CL	G	TPA	AB	H	2B	3B	HR	TB	BB	IBB	HB	SO	GDP	SH	SF	SB	CS	R	RBI	BA	OBA	SA
84	WAU/MID	A	126	533	433	131	32	2	15	212	84	2	3	57	7	7	6	11	9	72	66	.303	.414	.490
85	CHT/SOU	AA	111	455	357	92	15	5	3	126	71	2	5	30	16	10	12	1	3	43	47	.258	.378	.353
	CAL/PCL	AAA	20	80	68	24	7	1	0	33	12	1	0	7	2	0	0	1	0	8	14	.353	.450	.485
86	CHT/SOU	AA	132	553	451	119	29	5	6	176	89	2	2	35	8	5	6	2	5	71	74	.264	.383	.390
87	CAL/PCL	AAA	129	531	438	144	31	1	10	207	82	2	2	48	10	6	3	3	5	75	66	.329	.434	.473
	SEA/AL		13	46	43	16	5	2	0	25	2	0	1	5	0	0	0	0	0	6	5	.372	.413	.581
88	CAL/PCL	AAA	95	407	331	120	19	4	8	171	66	6	3	40	9	2	5	9	1	63	64	.363	.467	.517
	SEA/AL		14	38	32	9	4	0	0	13	4	0	0	1	0	0	1	0	0	0	5	.281	.351	.406
89	CAL/PCL	AAA	32	141	113	39	11	0	3	59	22	1	3	13	1	1	2	2	2	30	23	.345	.457	.522
	SEA/AL		65	196	171	41	5	0	2	52	17	1	3	26	3	1	2	2	1	20	20	.240	.314	.304
90	SEA/AL		144	570	487	147	27	2	11	211	74	3	5	62	13	1	3	1	4	71	49	.302	.397	.433
91	SEA/AL		150	642	544	167	35	1	14	246	84	9	8	72	19	2	4	0	3	98	52	.307	.405	.452
92	SEA/AL		135	592	528	181	*46	3	18	287	54	2	4	61	15	1	5	14	4	100	73	*.343	.404	.544
93	JAC/SOU	AA	4	16	14	5	0	0	1	8	2	0	0	1	0	0	0	0	0	2	3	.357	.438	.571
	SEA/AL		42	165	135	32	7	0	4	51	28	1	0	19	4	1	1	0	0	20	13	.237	.366	.378
7 YR TOTALS			**563**	**2249**	**1940**	**593**	**129**	**8**	**49**	**885**	**263**	**16**	**21**	**252**	**54**	**8**	**17**	**17**	**12**	**315**	**217**	**.306**	**.391**	**.456**

Martinez, Reyenaldo Ignacio "Chito" — BL/TL — b.12/19/65 — POS OF-111, DH-10, 1B-1   KC84 6/148

YR	TM/LG	CL	G	TPA	AB	H	2B	3B	HR	TB	BB	IBB	HB	SO	GDP	SH	SF	SB	CS	R	RBI	BA	OBA	SA
84	EUG/NWL	A-	59	201	176	53	12	3	0	71	24	2	0	38	3	1	0	4	4	18	26	.301	.385	.403
85	FM/FSL	A+	76	284	248	65	9	5	0	84	31	3	1	42	8	1	3	11	5	35	29	.262	.343	.339
86	MEM/SOU	AA	93	330	283	86	16	5	11	145	42	4	2	58	2	2	1	4	4	48	44	.304	.396	.512
87	OMA/AMA	AAA	35	132	121	26	10	1	2	44	11	0	0	43	0	0	0	0	0	14	14	.215	.280	.364
	MEM/SOU	AA	78	319	283	74	10	3	9	117	33	0	1	94	6	0	2	5	3	34	43	.261	.339	.413
88	MEM/SOU	AA	141	560	485	110	16	4	13	173	66	4	1	130	6	2	6	20	3	67	65	.227	.317	.357
89	MEM/SOU	AA	127	471	399	97	20	2	23	190	63	7	1	137	8	4	4	3	4	55	62	.243	.345	.476
90	OMA/AMA	AAA	122	424	364	96	12	8	21	187	54	5	0	129	9	0	3	6	6	59	67	.264	.361	.514
91	ROC/INT	AAA	60	239	211	68	8	1	20	138	26	3	0	69	3	0	2	2	2	42	50	.322	.393	.654
	BAL/AL		67	228	216	58	12	1	13	111	11	0	0	51	2	0	1	1	1	32	33	.269	.303	.514
92	BAL/AL		83	235	198	53	10	1	5	80	31	4	2	47	4	0	2	3	0	26	25	.268	.366	.404
93	BAL/AL		8	19	15	0	0	0	0	0	4	2	0	4	0	0	0	0	0	0	0	.000	.211	.000
	BOW/EAS	AA	5	15	13	1	0	0	0	2	0	0	0	2	1	0	0	0	0	5	0	.077	.200	.077
	ROC/INT	AAA	43	158	145	38	11	0	5	64	11	0	0	34	2	0	0	0	0	14	23	.262	.314	.441
3 YR TOTALS			**158**	**482**	**429**	**111**	**22**	**2**	**18**	**191**	**46**	**6**	**2**	**102**	**11**	**0**	**5**	**1**	**2**	**58**	**58**	**.259**	**.330**	**.445**

Mattingly, Donald Arthur "Don" — BL/TL — b.4/20/61 — POS 1B-1412, OF-76, DH-75, 3B-3, 2B-1   NYA79 19/492

YR	TM/LG	CL	G	TPA	AB	H	2B	3B	HR	TB	BB	IBB	HB	SO	GDP	SH	SF	SB	CS	R	RBI	BA	OBA	SA
82	NY/AL		7	13	12	2	0	0	0	2	0	0	0	1	2	0	1	0	0	0	1	.167	.154	.167
83	NY/AL		91	305	279	79	15	4	4	114	21	5	1	31	8	2	2	0	0	34	32	.283	.333	.409
84	NY/AL		153	662	603	*207	*44	2	23	324	41	8	1	33	15	8	9	1	1	91	110	*.343	.381	.537
85	NY/AL		159	727	652	211	*48	3	35	*370	56	13	2	41	15	7	15	2	2	107	*145	.324	.371	.567
86	NY/AL		162	742	677	*238	*53	2	31	*388	53	11	1	35	17	1	10	0	0	117	113	.352	.394	*.573

(continued)

Mattingly, Donald Arthur "Don" (continued)

YR	TM/LG	CL	G	TPA	AB	H	2B	3B	HR	TB	BB	IBB	HB	SO	GDP	SH	SF	SB	CS	R	RBI	BA	OBA	SA
87	NY/AL		141	629	569	186	38	2	30	318	51	13	1	38	16	0	8	1	4	93	115	.327	.378	.559
88	NY/AL		144	651	599	186	37	0	18	277	41	14	3	29	13	0	8	1	0	94	88	.311	.353	.462
89	NY/AL		158	693	631	191	37	2	23	301	51	18	1	30	15	0	10	3	0	79	113	.303	.351	.477
90	NY/AL		102	428	394	101	16	0	5	132	28	13	3	20	13	0	3	1	0	40	42	.256	.308	.335
91	NY/AL		152	646	587	169	35	0	9	231	46	11	4	42	21	0	9	2	0	64	68	.288	.339	.394
92	NY/AL		157	686	640	184	40	0	14	266	39	7	1	43	11	0	6	3	0	89	86	.287	.327	.416
93	NY/AL		134	596	530	154	27	2	17	236	61	9	2	42	20	0	3	0	0	78	86	.291	.364	.445
	12 YR TOTALS		1560	6778	6173	1908	390	17	209	2959	488	122	20	385	166	13	84	14	7	886	999	**.309**	**.357**	**.479**

May, Derrick Brant — BL/TR — b.7/14/68 — POS OF-254 CHN86 1/9

YR	TM/LG	CL	G	TPA	AB	H	2B	3B	HR	TB	BB	IBB	HB	SO	GDP	SH	SF	SB	CS	R	RBI	BA	OBA	SA
86	WYT/APP	R+	54	197	178	57	6	1	0	65	16	1	2	15	3	0	1	17	4	25	23	.320	.381	.365
87	PEO/MID	A	128	487	439	131	19	8	9	193	42	4	1	106	5	0	5	5	7	60	52	.298	.357	.440
88	WIN/CAR	A+	130	532	485	148	29	9	8	219	34	4	5	82	3	0	5	13	8	76	65	.305	.357	.452
89	CHA/SOU	AA	136	530	491	145	26	5	9	208	33	4	5	76	8	1	0	19	7	72	70	.295	.346	.424
90	IOW/AMA	AAA	119	489	459	136	27	1	8	189	23	4	0	50	11	1	6	5	6	55	69	.296	.326	.412
	CHI/NL		17	63	61	15	3	0	1	21	2	0	0	7	1	0	0	1	0	8	11	.246	.270	.344
91	IOW/AMA	AAA	82	337	310	92	18	4	3	127	19	4	4	38	9	1	3	7	8	47	49	.297	.342	.410
	CHI/NL		15	25	22	5	2	0	1	10	2	0	0	1	1	0	1	0	0	4	3	.227	.280	.455
92	IOW/AMA	AAA	8	33	30	11	4	1	2	23	3	0	0	3	1	0	0	1	0	6	8	.367	.424	.767
	CHI/NL		124	371	351	96	11	0	8	131	14	4	3	40	10	2	1	5	3	33	45	.274	.306	.373
93	CHI/NL		128	503	465	137	25	2	10	196	31	6	1	41	15	0	6	10	3	62	77	.295	.336	.422
	4 YR TOTALS		284	962	899	253	41	2	20	358	49	10	4	89	27	2	8	16	6	107	136	**.281**	**.319**	**.398**

Mayne, Brent Danem — BL/TR — b.4/19/68 — POS C-215, 3B-8, DH-3 KC89 1/13

YR	TM/LG	CL	G	TPA	AB	H	2B	3B	HR	TB	BB	IBB	HB	SO	GDP	SH	SF	SB	CS	R	RBI	BA	OBA	SA
89	BC/FSL	A+	7	24	24	13	3	1	0	18	0	0	0	3	0	0	0	0	1	5	8	.542	.542	.750
90	MEM/SOU	AA	115	481	412	110	16	3	2	138	52	1	2	51	13	7	8	5	2	48	61	.267	.346	.335
	KC/AL		5	16	13	3	0	0	0	3	3	0	0	3	0	0	0	0	1	2	1	.231	.375	.231
91	KC/AL		85	259	231	58	8	0	3	75	23	4	0	42	6	2	3	2	4	22	31	.251	.315	.325
92	KC/AL		82	229	213	48	10	0	0	58	11	0	0	26	5	2	3	0	4	16	18	.225	.260	.272
93	KC/AL		71	227	205	52	9	1	2	69	18	7	1	31	6	3	0	3	2	22	22	.254	.317	.337
	4 YR TOTALS		243	731	662	161	27	1	5	205	55	11	1	102	17	7	6	5	11	62	72	**.243**	**.300**	**.310**

McCarty, David Andrew — BR/TL — b.11/23/69 — POS OF-67, 1B-36, DH-2 MIN91 1/3

YR	TM/LG	CL	G	TPA	AB	H	2B	3B	HR	TB	BB	IBB	HB	SO	GDP	SH	SF	SB	CS	R	RBI	BA	OBA	SA
91	VIS/CAL	A+	15	66	50	19	3	0	3	31	13	0	3	7	0	0	0	3	1	16	8	.380	.530	.620
	ORL/SOU	AA	28	100	88	23	4	0	3	36	10	0	2	20	1	0	0	0	1	18	11	.261	.350	.409
92	ORL/SOU	AA	129	526	456	124	16	2	18	198	55	5	8	89	8	1	6	6	6	75	79	.272	.356	.434
	POR/PCL	AAA	7	33	26	13	2	0	1	18	5	0	1	3	1	1	0	1	0	7	8	.500	.594	.692
93	POR/PCL	AAA	40	174	143	55	11	0	8	90	27	2	1	25	3	0	3	5	2	42	31	.385	.477	.629
	MIN/AL		98	371	350	75	15	2	2	100	19	0	1	80	13	1	0	2	6	36	21	.214	.257	.286

McClendon, Lloyd Glenn — BR/TR — b.1/11/59 — POS OF-240, 1B-99, C-50, 3B-9 NYN80 10/183

YR	TM/LG	CL	G	TPA	AB	H	2B	3B	HR	TB	BB	IBB	HB	SO	GDP	SH	SF	SB	CS	R	RBI	BA	OBA	SA
84	VER/EAS	AA	60	233	202	56	16	0	7	93	28	0	2	28	5	0	1	2	2	36	27	.277	.369	.460
	WIC/AMA	AAA	48	174	152	45	13	1	6	78	21	0	0	33	3	0	1	2	0	28	28	.296	.379	.513
85	DEN/AMA	AAA	114	436	379	105	18	5	16	181	51	4	3	56	6	0	3	4	4	57	79	.277	.365	.478
86	DEN/AMA	AAA	132	509	433	112	30	1	24	216	70	1	2	75	6	0	4	2	4	75	88	.259	.361	.499
87	NAS/AMA	AAA	26	105	84	24	6	0	3	39	17	0	2	15	1	0	2	1	1	11	14	.286	.410	.464
	CIN/NL		45	77	72	15	5	0	2	26	4	0	0	15	1	0	1	0	0	8	13	.208	.247	.361
88	NAS/AMA	AAA	2	8	7	1	0	0	0	1	1	0	0	1	0	0	0	0	0	0	0	.143	.250	.143
	CIN/NL		72	157	137	30	4	0	3	43	15	1	1	22	6	1	2	4	0	9	14	.219	.301	.314
89	IOW/AMA	AAA	34	131	109	35	10	0	4	57	21	1	0	19	3	0	1	4	1	18	13	.321	.427	.523
	CHI/NL		92	305	259	74	12	1	12	124	37	3	1	31	5	0	1	7	6	47	40	.286	.368	.479
90	IOW/AMA	AAA	25	102	91	26	2	0	2	34	8	1	2	19	3	0	1	3	1	14	10	.286	.353	.374
	CHI/NL		49	122	107	17	3	0	1	23	14	2	0	21	2	0	1	0	5	5	10	.159	.254	.215
	PIT/NL		4	3	3	1	0	0	1	4	0	0	0	1	0	0	0	0	0	1	2	.333	.333	1.333
	YEAR		53	125	110	18	3	0	2	27	14	2	0	22	2	0	1	0	5	6	12	.164	.256	.245
91	PIT/NL		85	183	163	47	7	0	7	75	18	0	0	23	2	0	1	1	0	24	24	.288	.366	.460
92	PIT/NL		84	224	190	48	11	1	3	67	24	2	0	24	5	1	3	1	3	26	20	.253	.350	.353
93	PIT/NL		88	207	181	40	11	1	2	59	23	1	0	17	4	1	2	0	3	21	19	.221	.306	.326
	7 YR TOTALS		519	1278	1112	272	50	3	31	421	139	7	7	154	23	4	16	15	11	141	142	**.245**	**.328**	**.379**

McGee, Willie Dean — BB/TR — b.11/2/58 — POS OF-1532, SS-1, DH-1 NYA77* S1/15

YR	TM/LG	CL	G	TPA	AB	H	2B	3B	HR	TB	BB	IBB	HB	SO	GDP	SH	SF	SB	CS	R	RBI	BA	OBA	SA
82	STL/NL		123	439	422	125	12	8	4	165	12	2	2	58	9	2	1	24	12	43	56	.296	.318	.391
83	STL/NL		147	631	601	172	22	8	5	225	26	2	0	98	8	1	3	39	8	75	75	.286	.314	.374
84	STL/NL		145	604	571	166	19	11	6	225	29	2	2	80	12	0	3	43	10	82	50	.291	.325	.394
85	STL/NL		152	652	612	*216	26	*18	10	308	34	2	3	86	3	1	5	56	16	114	82	*.353	.384	.503
86	STL/NL		124	539	497	127	22	7	7	184	37	7	1	82	8	0	4	19	16	65	48	.256	.306	.370
87	STL/NL		153	652	620	177	37	11	11	269	24	5	2	90	24	1	1	16	4	76	105	.285	.312	.434
88	STL/NL		137	600	562	164	24	6	3	209	32	5	1	84	10	2	3	41	6	73	50	.292	.329	.372
89	LOU/AMA	AAA	8	32	27	11	4	0	0	15	3	1	0	4	0	0	1	1	0	5	4	.407	.438	.556
	STL/NL		58	211	199	47	10	2	3	70	10	1	0	34	2	1	1	8	6	23	17	.236	.275	.352
90	STL/NL		125	542	501	168	32	5	3	219	38	6	1	86	9	0	2	28	9	76	62	*.335	.382	.437
	OAK/AL		29	123	113	31	3	2	0	38	10	0	0	18	4	0	0	3	0	23	15	.274	.333	.336

McGee, Willie Dean (continued)

YR	TM/LG	CL	G	TPA	AB	H	2B	3B	HR	TB	BB	IBB	HB	SO	GDP	SH	SF	SB	CS	R	RBI	BA	OBA	SA
	YEAR		154	665	614	199	35	7	3	257	48	6	1	104	13	0	2	31	9	99	77	.324	.373	.419
91	PHO/PCL	AAA	4	13	10	5	1	0	0	6	3	0	0	1	0	0	0	2	0	4	1	.500	.615	.600
	SF/NL		131	543	497	155	30	3	4	203	34	3	2	74	11	8	2	17	9	67	43	.312	.357	.408
92	SF/NL		138	510	474	141	20	2	1	168	29	3	1	88	7	5	1	13	4	56	36	.297	.339	.354
93	SF/NL		130	519	475	143	28	1	4	185	38	7	1	67	12	3	2	10	9	53	46	.301	.353	.389
12 YR TOTALS			1592	6565	6144	1832	285	84	61	2468	353	44	13	945	119	23	32	317	109	826	685	.298	.336	.402

McGriff, Frederick Stanley "Fred" — BL/TL — b.10/31/63 — POS 1B-927, DH-100   NYA81 9/233

YR	TM/LG	CL	G	TPA	AB	H	2B	3B	HR	TB	BB	IBB	HB	SO	GDP	SH	SF	SB	CS	R	RBI	BA	OBA	SA
84	KNO/SOU	AA	56	222	189	47	13	2	9	91	29	3	1	55	2	0	3	0	2	29	25	.249	.347	.481
	SYR/INT	AAA	70	266	238	56	10	1	13	107	26	0	0	89	3	1	1	0	1	28	28	.235	.309	.450
85	SYR/INT	AAA	51	204	176	40	8	2	5	67	23	0	4	53	2	1	0	0	0	19	20	.227	.330	.381
86	TOR/AL		3	5	5	1	0	0	0	1	0	0	0	2	0	0	0	0	0	1	0	.200	.200	.200
	SYR/INT	AAA	133	563	468	121	23	4	19	209	83	8	4	119	16	0	8	0	3	69	74	.259	.369	.447
87	TOR/AL		107	356	295	73	16	0	20	149	60	4	1	104	3	0	3	3	2	58	43	.247	.376	.505
88	TOR/AL		154	623	536	151	35	4	34	296	79	3	4	149	15	0	4	6	1	100	82	.282	.376	.552
89	TOR/AL		161	680	551	148	27	3	*36	289	119	12	4	132	14	1	5	7	4	98	92	.269	.399	.525
90	TOR/AL		153	658	557	167	21	1	35	295	94	12	2	108	14	0	4	5	3	91	88	.300	.400	.530
91	SD/NL		153	642	528	147	19	1	31	261	105	26	2	135	14	0	5	4	1	84	106	.278	.396	.494
92	SD/NL		152	632	531	152	30	4	*35	295	96	23	1	108	14	0	4	8	5	79	104	.286	.394	.556
93	SD/NL		83	349	302	83	11	1	18	150	42	4	1	55	9	0	1	1	3	52	46	.275	.361	.497
	ATL/NL		68	291	255	79	18	1	19	156	34	2	1	51	5	0	1	1	0	59	55	.310	.392	.612
	YEAR		151	640	557	162	29	2	37	306	76	6	2	106	14	0	5	5	3	111	101	.291	.375	.549
8 YR TOTALS			1034	4236	3560	1001	177	15	228	1892	629	86	16	844	81	2	29	38	20	622	616	.281	.389	.531

McGriff, Terence Roy "Terry" — BR/TR — b.9/23/63 — POS C-79   CIN81 8/197

YR	TM/LG	CL	G	TPA	AB	H	2B	3B	HR	TB	BB	IBB	HB	SO	GDP	SH	SF	SB	CS	R	RBI	BA	OBA	SA
81	BIL/PIO	R+	42	117	96	26	3	0	1	32	18	1	1	11	6	0	2	0	0	15	15	.271	.385	.333
82	EUG/NWL	A-	53	219	190	46	10	2	4	72	26	0	0	47	4	0	3	1	0	23	31	.242	.329	.379
83	TAM/FSL	A+	87	289	260	66	11	3	5	98	26	3	1	62	6	1	1	2	0	21	45	.254	.323	.377
84	TAM/FSL	A+	110	400	345	96	19	0	7	136	48	4	2	62	13	0	5	5	4	48	41	.278	.365	.394
85	VER/EAS	AA	110	421	363	92	10	4	13	149	54	2	3	81	6	0	1	1	0	54	54	.253	.354	.410
86	DEN/AMA	AAA	108	391	340	99	22	1	9	150	41	4	2	71	11	0	6	0	0	54	54	.291	.365	.441
87	NAS/AMA	AAA	67	258	228	62	11	3	10	109	25	5	0	47	10	0	5	0	0	36	33	.272	.337	.478
	CIN/NL		34	97	89	20	3	0	2	29	8	0	0	17	3	0	0	0	0	6	11	.225	.289	.326
88	NAS/AMA	AAA	35	108	97	21	3	1	1	29	10	0	2	15	4	0	1	0	0	8	12	.216	.287	.299
	CIN/NL		35	109	96	19	3	0	1	25	12	0	0	31	3	0	1	0	1	9	4	.198	.284	.260
89	NAS/AMA	AAA	102	366	335	94	24	1	5	135	29	3	1	68	12	1	0	0	1	42	28	.281	.340	.403
	CIN/NL		6	13	11	3	0	0	0	3	2	1	0	2	3	0	0	0	0	1	2	.273	.385	.273
90	NAS/AMA	AAA	94	373	325	91	17	0	9	135	38	1	2	46	8	2	6	2	2	44	54	.280	.353	.415
	CIN/NL		2	4	4	0	0	0	0	0	0	0	0	1	0	0	0	0	0	0	0	.000	.000	.000
	HOU/NL		4	5	5	0	0	0	0	0	0	0	0	3	0	0	0	0	0	0	0	.000	.000	.000
	YEAR		6	9	9	0	0	0	0	0	0	0	0	4	0	0	0	0	0	0	0	.000	.000	.000
91	TUC/PCL	AAA	51	167	146	42	15	1	0	59	16	0	3	20	6	0	2	0	1	18	24	.288	.365	.404
92	SYR/INT	AAA	21	66	56	14	2	0	2	22	9	0	0	11	2	0	1	1	0	4	7	.250	.348	.393
93	EDM/PCL	AAA	105	392	339	117	29	2	7	171	49	2	1	29	10	0	3	2	1	62	55	.345	.426	.504
	FLO/NL		3	8	7	0	0	0	0	0	1	0	0	2	0	0	0	0	0	0	0	.000	.125	.000
5 YR TOTALS			84	236	212	42	6	0	3	57	23	1	0	54	6	0	1	1	0	16	17	.198	.275	.269

McGwire, Mark David — BR/TR — b.10/1/63 — POS 1B-910, 3B-24, OF-4, DH-4   OAK84 1/10

YR	TM/LG	CL	G	TPA	AB	H	2B	3B	HR	TB	BB	IBB	HB	SO	GDP	SH	SF	SB	CS	R	RBI	BA	OBA	SA
84	MOD/CAL	A+	16	63	55	11	3	0	1	17	8	0	0	21	2	0	0	0	0	7	1	.200	.302	.309
85	MOD/CAL	A+	138	596	489	134	23	3	24	235	96	2	4	108	9	0	7	1	2	95	106	.274	.393	.481
86	HUN/SOU	AA	55	249	195	59	15	0	10	104	46	0	1	45	10	1	6	3	0	40	53	.303	.427	.533
	TAC/PCL	AAA	78	330	280	89	21	5	13	159	42	4	2	67	7	2	4	1	1	42	59	.318	.405	.568
	OAK/AL		18	58	53	10	1	0	3	20	4	0	1	18	0	0	0	0	1	10	9	.189	.259	.377
87	OAK/AL		151	641	557	161	28	4	*49	344	71	8	5	131	6	0	5	1	1	97	118	.289	.370	*.618
88	OAK/AL		155	635	550	143	22	1	32	263	76	4	4	117	15	0	4	0	0	87	99	.260	.352	.478
89	OAK/AL		143	587	490	113	17	0	33	229	83	5	3	94	23	0	11	1	1	74	95	.231	.339	.467
90	OAK/AL		156	650	523	123	16	0	39	256	*110	9	7	116	13	1	0	2	1	87	108	.235	.370	.489
91	OAK/AL		154	585	483	97	22	0	22	185	93	3	3	116	13	1	5	2	1	62	75	.201	.330	.383
92	OAK/AL		139	571	467	125	22	0	42	273	90	12	5	105	10	0	9	0	1	87	104	.268	.385	*.585
93	OAK/AL		27	107	84	28	6	0	9	61	21	5	2	19	0	0	0	0	1	16	24	.333	.467	.726
8 YR TOTALS			943	3834	3207	800	134	5	229	1631	548	46	29	716	80	3	47	6	7	520	632	.249	.359	.509

McIntosh, Timothy Allen "Tim" — BR/TR — b.3/21/65 — POS C-24, OF-21, 1B-8, DH-5   MIL86 3/61

YR	TM/LG	CL	G	TPA	AB	H	2B	3B	HR	TB	BB	IBB	HB	SO	GDP	SH	SF	SB	CS	R	RBI	BA	OBA	SA
86	BEL/MID	A	49	196	173	45	3	2	4	64	18	0	2	33	3	0	3	0	0	26	21	.260	.332	.370
87	BEL/MID	A	130	521	461	139	30	3	20	235	49	2	7	96	4	1	3	4	4	83	85	.302	.375	.510
88	STO/CAL	A+	138	598	519	147	32	6	15	236	57	1	11	96	6	6	5	10	5	81	92	.283	.363	.455
89	EP/TEX	AA	120	511	463	139	30	3	17	226	29	3	8	72	8	2	9	5	4	72	93	.300	.346	.488
90	DEN/AMA	AAA	116	466	416	120	21	3	18	201	26	0	14	59	9	3	7	6	2	72	74	.288	.346	.483
	MIL/AL		5	5	5	1	0	0	0	1	0	0	0	2	0	0	0	0	0	1	1	.200	.200	.800
91	DEN/AMA	AAA	122	517	462	135	14	3	9	182	37	3	1	60	15	0	7	6	5	69	91	.292	.354	.489
	MIL/AL		7	11	11	4	1	0	1	8	0	0	0	1	0	0	0	0	0	2	1	.364	.364	.727
92	MIL/AL		35	84	77	14	3	0	0	17	3	0	2	9	1	1	1	1	3	7	6	.182	.229	.221

(continued)

McIntosh, Timothy Allen "Tim" (continued)

YR	TM/LG	CL	G	TPA	AB	H	2B	3B	HR	TB	BB	IBB	HB	SO	GDP	SH	SF	SB	CS	R	RBI	BA	OBA	SA
93	OTT/INT	AAA	27	118	106	31	7	1	6	58	10	2	0	22	3	0	2	1	0	15	21	.292	.347	.547
	MIL/AL		1	0	0	0	0	0	0	0	0	0	0	0	0	0	0	0	0	0	0	.000	.000	.000
	MON/NL		20	21	21	2	1	0	0	3	0	0	0	7	0	0	0	0	0	2	2	.095	.095	.143
	YEAR		21	21	21	2	1	0	0	3	0	0	0	7	0	0	0	0	0	2	2	.095	.095	.143
4 YR TOTALS			68	121	114	21	5	0	2	32	3	0	2	22	1	1	1	1	3	12	10	.184	.217	.281

McKnight, Jefferson Alan "Jeff" — BB/TR — b.2/18/63 — POS 2B-38, 1B-37, SS-34, OF-16, 3B-13, DH-5, C-1   NYN83* S2/29

YR	TM/LG	CL	G	TPA	AB	H	2B	3B	HR	TB	BB	IBB	HB	SO	GDP	SH	SF	SB	CS	R	RBI	BA	OBA	SA
84	COL/SAL	A	95	280	251	64	10	1	1	79	26	2	1	17	5	1	1	9	1	31	27	.255	.326	.315
85	COL/SAL	A	67	183	159	42	6	1	1	53	21	1	1	18	2	0	2	6	2	26	24	.264	.350	.333
	LYN/CAR	A+	49	186	150	33	6	1	0	41	29	0	1	19	1	4	3	0	0	19	21	.220	.341	.273
86	JAC/TEX	AA	132	562	469	118	24	3	4	160	76	3	3	58	10	5	9	5	2	71	55	.252	.354	.341
87	JAC/TEX	AA	16	64	59	12	3	0	2	21	4	0	1	12	3	0	0	1	1	5	8	.203	.266	.356
	TID/INT	AAA	87	214	184	47	7	3	2	66	24	1	1	22	6	1	4	0	1	21	25	.255	.338	.359
88	TID/INT	AAA	113	385	345	88	14	0	2	108	36	5	0	32	3	1	1	0	4	36	25	.255	.323	.313
89	NY/NL		6	14	12	3	0	0	0	3	2	0	0	1	1	0	0	0	0	2	0	.250	.357	.250
	TID/INT	AAA	116	509	425	106	19	2	9	156	79	1	1	56	13	3	1	3	0	84	48	.249	.368	.367
90	ROC/INT	AAA	100	390	339	95	21	3	7	143	41	3	0	59	4	4	6	7	5	56	45	.280	.352	.422
	BAL/AL		29	84	75	15	2	0	1	20	5	0	1	17	3	0	0	0	0	11	4	.200	.259	.267
91	ROC/INT	AAA	22	96	81	31	7	0	2	45	14	0	0	10	3	0	1	1	2	19	18	.383	.469	.556
	BAL/AL		16	43	41	7	1	0	0	8	2	0	0	7	2	0	0	0	0	2	2	.171	.209	.195
92	TID/INT	AAA	102	406	352	108	21	1	4	143	51	3	0	52	14	1	1	3	3	43	43	.307	.395	.406
	NY/NL		31	87	85	23	3	1	2	34	2	0	0	8	2	0	0	0	1	10	13	.271	.287	.400
93	NY/NL		105	183	164	42	3	1	2	53	13	0	0	31	3	3	2	0	0	19	13	.256	.311	.323
5 YR TOTALS			187	411	377	90	9	2	5	118	24	0	2	64	8	6	2	1	1	44	32	.239	.286	.313

McLemore, Mark Tremell — BB/TR — b.10/4/64 — POS 2B-349, OF-124, DH-25, SS-14, 3B-13   CAL82 8/218

YR	TM/LG	CL	G	TPA	AB	H	2B	3B	HR	TB	BB	IBB	HB	SO	GDP	SH	SF	SB	CS	R	RBI	BA	OBA	SA
82	SAL/NWL	A-	55	210	165	49	6	2	0	59	39	0	2	38	2	1	3	14	6	42	25	.297	.431	.358
83	PEO/MID	A	95	393	329	79	7	3	0	92	53	0	2	64	3	6	3	15	11	42	18	.240	.346	.280
84	RED/CAL	A+	134	603	482	142	8	3	0	156	106	1	1	75	2	11	3	59	15	102	45	.295	.421	.324
85	MID/TEX	AA	117	534	458	124	17	6	2	159	66	4	1	59	4	6	3	31	16	80	46	.271	.362	.347
86	MID/TEX	AA	63	291	237	75	9	1	1	89	48	1	1	18	5	1	4	38	8	54	29	.316	.428	.376
	EDM/PCL	AAA	73	333	286	79	13	1	0	94	39	2	0	30	0	4	4	29	9	41	23	.276	.359	.329
	CAL/AL		5	6	4	0	0	0	0	0	1	0	0	2	0	1	0	1	0	0	0	.000	.200	.000
87	CAL/AL		138	499	433	102	13	3	3	130	48	0	0	72	7	15	3	25	8	61	41	.236	.310	.300
88	PS/CAL	A+	11	57	44	15	3	1	0	20	11	0	1	7	0	1	1	7	3	9	6	.341	.474	.455
	EDM/PCL	AAA	12	51	45	12	3	0	0	15	4	0	0	7	0	2	0	7	1	7	6	.267	.327	.333
	CAL/AL		77	265	233	56	11	2	2	77	25	0	0	28	6	5	2	13	7	38	16	.240	.312	.330
89	EDM/PCL	AAA	114	485	430	105	13	2	2	128	49	0	1	67	14	2	3	26	11	60	34	.244	.321	.298
	CAL/AL		32	115	103	25	3	1	0	30	7	0	1	19	2	3	1	6	1	12	14	.243	.295	.291
90	CAL/AL		20	53	48	7	2	0	0	9	4	0	0	9	1	1	0	1	0	4	2	.146	.212	.188
	EDM/PCL	AAA	9	45	39	10	2	0	0	12	6	0	0	10	1	0	0	3	0	4	3	.256	.356	.308
	PS/CAL	A+	6	25	22	6	0	0	0	6	3	0	0	7	0	0	0	2	0	3	2	.273	.360	.273
	CS/PCL		14	65	54	15	2	0	1	20	11	0	0	6	1	0	0	5	5	11	7	.278	.400	.370
	CLE/AL		8	12	12	2	0	0	0	2	0	0	0	6	0	0	0	1	0	2	2	.167	.167	.167
	YEAR		28	65	60	9	2	0	0	11	4	0	0	15	1	1	0	2	0	6	4	.150	.203	.183
91	HOU/NL		21	68	61	9	1	0	0	10	6	0	0	13	0	1	0	0	1	6	2	.148	.221	.164
	TUC/PCL	AAA	4	16	14	5	1	0	0	6	2	0	0	1	2	0	1	0	0	2	0	.357	.438	.429
	JAC/TEX	AA	7	28	22	5	3	0	1	11	6	0	0	3	0	0	0	1	0	6	4	.227	.393	.500
	ROC/INT	AAA	57	259	228	64	11	4	1	86	27	0	0	29	5	2	2	12	5	32	28	.281	.354	.377
92	BAL/AL		101	256	228	56	7	2	0	67	21	1	0	26	6	6	1	11	5	40	27	.246	.308	.294
93	BAL/AL		148	663	581	165	27	5	4	214	64	4	1	92	21	11	6	21	15	81	72	.284	.353	.368
8 YR TOTALS			550	1937	1703	422	64	13	9	539	176	5	2	267	44	42	14	77	38	244	174	.248	.317	.317

McNamara, James Patrick "Jim" — BL/TR — b.6/10/65 — POS C-34   SF86 5/110

YR	TM/LG	CL	G	TPA	AB	H	2B	3B	HR	TB	BB	IBB	HB	SO	GDP	SH	SF	SB	CS	R	RBI	BA	OBA	SA
86	EVE/NWL	A-	46	181	158	39	1	2	8	68	18	2	3	39	3	0	2	0	0	23	30	.247	.331	.430
87	CLI/MID	A	110	413	385	95	22	1	5	134	19	1	0	52	15	2	7	4	2	43	53	.247	.277	.348
88	SJ/CAL	A+	93	362	315	59	9	0	1	71	43	1	2	76	18	0	2	3	4	27	41	.187	.287	.225
89	SAL/CAL	A+	49	178	155	37	8	0	0	45	22	2	0	24	3	1	0	3	1	9	10	.239	.333	.290
	PHO/PCL	AAA	27	75	69	12	3	0	0	15	4	0	0	13	2	2	0	1	2	3	4	.174	.219	.217
	SJ/CAL	A+	19	67	65	18	2	0	1	23	1	0	0	13	3	0	1	0	1	2	8	.277	.284	.354
90	SJ/CAL	A+	53	179	158	32	2	2	1	41	18	0	0	30	3	1	1	0	4	20	22	.203	.287	.259
	PHO/PCL	AAA	6	23	20	9	0	0	0	9	2	0	0	4	0	0	1	0	0	2	1	.450	.522	.450
	SHR/TEX	AA	28	86	79	19	7	0	0	26	6	0	0	9	1	1	0	0	0	2	13	.241	.302	.329
91	PHO/PCL	AAA	17	60	53	9	1	0	0	10	6	0	0	12	1	1	0	0	0	3	2	.170	.254	.189
	SHR/TEX	AA	39	132	109	30	8	2	2	48	21	3	0	11	2	1	1	2	1	13	20	.275	.389	.440
92	SF/NL		30	82	74	16	1	0	1	20	6	2	0	25	1	2	0	0	0	6	9	.216	.275	.270
	PHO/PCL	AAA	23	81	67	14	3	0	0	17	14	3	0	13	5	0	0	0	0	5	3	.209	.346	.254
93	PHO/PCL	AAA	50	173	158	31	6	0	1	39	12	1	0	29	8	1	2	1	0	10	23	.196	.250	.247
	SF/NL		4	7	7	1	0	0	0	1	0	0	0	1	0	0	0	0	0	0	1	.143	.143	.143
2 YR TOTALS			34	89	81	17	1	0	1	21	6	2	0	26	1	2	0	0	0	6	10	.210	.264	.259

McNeely, Jeffrey Lavern "Jeff" — BR/TR — b.10/18/69 — POS OF-13, DH-3   BOS89 4/52

YR	TM/LG	CL	G	TPA	AB	H	2B	3B	HR	TB	BB	IBB	HB	SO	GDP	SH	SF	SB	CS	R	RBI	BA	OBA	SA
89	RS/GCL	R	9	40	32	13	1	1	0	16	7	0	0	3	1	0	1	5	1	10	4	.406	.500	.500

McNeely, Jeffrey Lavern "Jeff" (continued)

YR	TM/LG	CL	G	TPA	AB	H	2B	3B	HR	TB	BB	IBB	HB	SO	GDP	SH	SF	SB	CS	R	RBI	BA	OBA	SA
	ELM/NYP	A-	61	239	208	52	7	0	2	65	26	0	4	54	4	1	0	16	8	20	21	.250	.345	.313
90	WH/FSL	A+	16	65	62	10	0	0	0	10	3	0	0	19	1	0	0	7	1	4	3	.161	.200	.161
	ELM/NYP	A-	73	299	246	77	4	5	6	109	40	5	3	60	7	8	2	39	10	41	37	.313	.412	.443
91	LYN/CAR	A+	106	465	382	123	16	5	4	161	74	4	4	74	5	4	1	38	21	58	38	.322	.436	.421
92	NB/EAS	AA	85	293	261	57	8	4	2	79	26	0	2	78	10	4	0	10	5	30	11	.218	.294	.303
93	PAW/INT	AAA	129	556	498	130	14	3	2	156	43	1	3	102	4	10	2	40	7	65	35	.261	.322	.313
	BOS/AL		21	44	37	11	1	0	1	14	7	0	0	9	0	0	0	0	6	10	1	.297	.409	.378

McRae, Brian Wesley — BB/TR — b.8/27/67 — POS OF-496   KC85 1/17

YR	TM/LG	CL	G	TPA	AB	H	2B	3B	HR	TB	BB	IBB	HB	SO	GDP	SH	SF	SB	CS	R	RBI	BA	OBA	SA
85	ROY/GCL	R	60	253	217	58	6	5	0	74	28	0	2	34	7	4	2	27	12	40	23	.267	.353	.341
86	EUG/NWL	A-	72	355	306	82	10	3	1	101	41	1	5	49	6	1	2	28	4	66	29	.268	.362	.330
87	FM/FSL	A+	131	509	481	121	14	1	1	140	22	1	6	70	4	0	0	33	18	62	31	.252	.293	.291
88	BC/FSL	A+	30	121	107	33	2	0	1	38	9	0	3	11	2	0	0	8	4	18	11	.308	.378	.355
	MEM/SOU	AA	91	316	288	58	13	1	4	85	16	0	2	60	8	10	0	13	5	33	15	.201	.248	.295
89	MEM/SOU	AA	138	592	533	121	18	8	5	170	43	1	8	94	5	7	1	23	8	72	42	.227	.294	.319
90	MEM/SOU	AA	116	532	470	126	24	6	10	192	44	1	3	65	9	14	0	21	10	78	64	.268	.334	.409
	KC/AL		46	182	168	48	8	3	2	68	9	0	0	29	5	3	2	4	3	21	23	.286	.318	.405
91	KC/AL		152	663	629	164	28	9	8	234	24	1	6	99	12	3	5	20	11	86	64	.261	.288	.372
92	KC/AL		149	592	533	119	23	5	4	164	42	1	6	88	10	7	4	18	5	63	52	.223	.285	.308
93	KC/AL		153	685	627	177	28	9	12	259	37	1	4	105	8	14	3	23	14	78	69	.282	.325	.413
4 YR TOTALS			500	2122	1957	508	87	26	26	725	112	3	12	321	35	27	14	65	33	248	208	**.260**	**.302**	**.370**

McReynolds, Walter Kevin "Kevin" — BR/TR — b.10/16/59 — POS OF-1422, DH-2   SD81 1/6

YR	TM/LG	CL	G	TPA	AB	H	2B	3B	HR	TB	BB	IBB	HB	SO	GDP	SH	SF	SB	CS	R	RBI	BA	OBA	SA
83	SD/NL		39	155	140	31	3	1	4	48	12	1	0	29	1	0	3	2	1	15	14	.221	.277	.343
84	SD/NL		147	571	525	146	26	6	20	244	34	8	0	69	14	3	9	3	6	68	75	.278	.317	.465
85	SD/NL		152	616	564	132	24	4	15	209	43	6	3	81	17	2	4	4	0	61	75	.234	.290	.371
86	SD/NL		158	641	560	161	31	6	26	282	66	6	1	83	9	5	9	8	6	89	96	.287	.358	.504
87	NY/NL		151	639	590	163	32	5	29	292	39	5	1	70	13	1	8	14	1	86	95	.276	.318	.495
88	NY/NL		147	600	552	159	30	2	27	274	38	3	4	56	6	1	5	21	0	82	99	.288	.336	.496
89	NY/NL		148	599	545	148	25	3	22	245	46	10	1	74	8	0	7	15	7	74	85	.272	.326	.450
90	NY/NL		147	601	521	140	23	1	24	237	71	11	1	61	8	0	8	9	2	75	82	.269	.353	.455
91	NY/NL		143	578	522	135	32	1	16	217	49	7	2	46	8	1	4	6	6	65	74	.259	.322	.416
92	KC/AL		109	445	373	92	25	0	13	156	67	3	3	48	6	1	3	7	1	45	49	.247	.357	.418
93	KC/AL		110	393	351	86	22	4	11	149	37	6	1	56	8	1	3	2	2	44	44	.245	.316	.425
11 YR TOTALS			1451	5838	5243	1393	273	33	207	2353	502	66	14	673	98	14	65	91	32	704	786	**.266**	**.328**	**.449**

Meares, Patrick James "Pat" — BR/TR — b.9/6/68 — POS SS-111   MIN90 15/329

YR	TM/LG	CL	G	TPA	AB	H	2B	3B	HR	TB	BB	IBB	HB	SO	GDP	SH	SF	SB	CS	R	RBI	BA	OBA	SA
90	KEN/MID	A	52	229	197	47	10	2	4	73	25	2	4	45	1	2	1	2	1	26	22	.239	.335	.371
91	VIS/CAL	A+	89	393	360	109	21	4	6	156	24	0	5	63	11	0	4	15	5	53	44	.303	.351	.433
92	ORL/SOU	AA	81	320	300	76	19	0	3	104	11	1	7	57	6	0	2	5	5	42	23	.253	.294	.347
93	POR/PCL	AAA	18	60	54	16	5	0	0	21	3	0	1	11	0	2	0	0	0	6	3	.296	.345	.389
	MIN/AL		111	361	346	87	14	3	0	107	7	0	1	52	11	4	3	4	5	33	33	.251	.266	.309

Mejia, Roberto Antonio — BR/TR — b.4/14/72 — POS 2B-65   LA 11/21/88

YR	TM/LG	CL	G	TPA	AB	H	2B	3B	HR	TB	BB	IBB	HB	SO	GDP	SH	SF	SB	CS	R	RBI	BA	OBA	SA
91	GF/PIO	R+	23	93	84	22	6	2	2	38	7	0	1	22	0	0	1	3	1	17	14	.262	.323	.452
92	VB/FSL	A	96	374	330	82	17	1	12	137	37	4	2	60	6	0	5	14	10	42	40	.248	.324	.415
93	CS/PCL	AAA	77	313	291	87	15	2	14	148	18	0	1	56	6	0	3	12	5	51	48	.299	.339	.509
	COL/NL		65	248	229	53	14	5	5	92	13	1	1	63	2	4	1	4	1	31	20	.231	.275	.402

Melvin, Robert Paul "Bob" — BR/TR — b.10/28/61 — POS C-612, DH-23, 1B-7, 3B-1   DET81* S1/2

YR	TM/LG	CL	G	TPA	AB	H	2B	3B	HR	TB	BB	IBB	HB	SO	GDP	SH	SF	SB	CS	R	RBI	BA	OBA	SA
84	EVA/AMA	AAA	44	145	141	35	13	0	0	48	3	0	0	32	3	1	0	1	0	12	11	.248	.264	.340
	BIR/SOU	AA	69	293	271	73	14	1	2	95	18	2	0	47	12	2	2	1	0	34	33	.269	.313	.351
85	NAS/AMA	AAA	53	197	177	48	7	1	9	84	16	0	1	38	5	1	2	3	1	27	24	.271	.332	.475
	DET/AL		41	87	82	18	4	1	0	24	3	0	0	21	1	2	0	0	0	10	4	.220	.247	.293
86	SF/NL		89	289	268	60	14	2	5	93	15	1	0	69	7	3	3	3	2	24	25	.224	.262	.347
87	SF/NL		84	265	246	49	8	0	11	90	17	3	1	44	7	0	2	0	4	31	31	.199	.249	.366
88	PHO/PCL	AAA	21	84	75	23	5	0	2	34	8	0	1	13	4	0	0	0	0	11	9	.307	.381	.453
	SF/NL		92	288	273	64	13	1	8	103	13	0	1	46	5	1	1	0	2	23	27	.234	.268	.377
89	BAL/AL		85	301	278	67	10	1	1	82	15	3	1	53	10	7	1	1	4	22	32	.241	.279	.295
90	BAL/AL		93	318	301	73	14	1	5	104	11	0	1	53	4	3	1	3	0	30	37	.243	.267	.346
91	BAL/AL		79	245	228	57	10	1	1	70	11	2	1	46	5	5	1	3	0	11	23	.250	.279	.307
92	KC/AL		32	77	70	22	5	0	0	27	5	0	1	13	3	1	0	0	0	5	13	.314	.351	.386
93	BOS/AL		77	190	176	39	7	0	3	55	7	0	1	44	2	3	3	0	0	13	23	.222	.251	.313
9 YR TOTALS			672	2060	1922	449	85	6	34	648	97	10	1	389	48	20	20	4	13	169	208	**.234**	**.268**	**.337**

Merced, Orlando Luis — BB/TR — b.11/2/66 — POS 1B-261, OF-134, C-1   PIT 2/25/85

YR	TM/LG	CL	G	TPA	AB	H	2B	3B	HR	TB	BB	IBB	HB	SO	GDP	SH	SF	SB	CS	R	RBI	BA	OBA	SA
85	PIR/GCL	R	40	146	136	31	6	0	1	40	9	0	1	29	3	0	0	3	0	16	13	.228	.281	.294
86	MAC/SAL	A	65	188	173	34	4	1	2	46	12	0	1	38	3	0	2	5	3	20	24	.197	.250	.266
	WAT/NYP	A-	27	106	89	16	6	1	1	27	14	2	2	21	2	0	1	6	2	12	9	.180	.302	.303
87	MAC/SAL	A	4	5	4	0	0	0	0	0	0	0	0	3	0	0	1	0	0	1	0	.000	.200	.000
	WAT/NYP	A-	4	14	12	5	0	0	0	5	2	0	0	1	0	0	0	1	0	4	3	.417	.500	.583

(continued)

Merced, Orlando Luis (continued)

YR	TM/LG	CL	G	TPA	AB	H	2B	3B	HR	TB	BB	IBB	HB	SO	GDP	SH	SF	SB	CS	R	RBI	BA	OBA	SA
88	AUG/SAL	A	37	146	136	36	6	3	1	51	7	1	2	20	2	0	1	2	0	19	17	.265	.308	.375
	SAL/CAR	A+	80	332	298	87	12	7	7	134	27	1	1	64	7	1	5	13	3	47	42	.292	.347	.450
89	HAR/EAS	AA	95	380	341	82	16	4	6	124	32	6	2	65	6	1	4	13	3	43	48	.240	.306	.364
	BUF/AMA	AAA	35	139	129	44	5	3	1	58	7	1	0	26	2	2	1	0	1	18	16	.341	.372	.450
90	BUF/AMA	AAA	101	426	378	99	12	6	9	150	46	3	0	63	8	1	1	14	5	52	55	.262	.341	.397
	PIT/NL		25	25	24	5	1	0	0	6	1	0	0	9	1	0	0	0	0	3	0	.208	.240	.250
91	BUF/AMA	AAA	3	13	12	2	0	0	0	2	1	0	0	4	0	0	0	1	1	1	0	.167	.231	.167
	PIT/NL		120	478	411	113	17	2	10	164	64	4	1	81	6	1	0	1	8	4	83	50	.275	.373	.399
92	PIT/NL		134	465	405	100	28	5	6	156	52	8	2	63	6	1	5	5	4	50	60	.247	.332	.385
93	PIT/NL		137	527	447	140	26	4	8	198	77	10	1	64	9	0	2	3	3	68	70	.313	.414	.443
4 YR TOTALS			**416**	**1495**	**1287**	**358**	**72**	**11**	**24**	**524**	**194**	**22**	**4**	**217**	**22**	**2**	**8**	**16**	**11**	**204**	**180**	**.278**	**.372**	**.407**

Mercedes, Henry Felipe — BR/TR — b.7/23/69 — POS C-27, DH-1   OAK 6/10/87

YR	TM/LG	CL	G	TPA	AB	H	2B	3B	HR	TB	BB	IBB	HB	SO	GDP	SH	SF	SB	CS	R	RBI	BA	OBA	SA
88	ATH/ARI	R	2	5	5	2	0	0	0	2	0	0	0	0	0	0	0	0	0	1	0	.400	.400	.400
89	MAD/MID	A	51	178	152	32	3	0	2	41	22	1	1	46	1	3	0	0	0	11	13	.211	.314	.270
	MOD/CAL	A+	16	44	37	3	0	0	0	6	7	0	0	22	0	0	0	0	0	6	3	.081	.227	.162
	SO/NWL	A-	22	72	61	10	0	1	0	12	10	0	0	24	0	0	0	0	0	6	1	.164	.292	.197
90	TAC/PCL	AAA	12	36	31	6	1	0	0	7	3	0	0	7	2	2	0	0	1	3	2	.194	.265	.226
	MAD/MID	A	90	321	282	64	13	2	3	90	30	0	1	100	5	3	4	2	6	29	37	.227	.302	.319
91	MOD/CAL	A+	116	464	388	100	17	3	4	135	68	1	2	110	6	3	3	5	8	55	61	.258	.369	.348
92	TAC/PCL	AAA	85	276	246	57	9	2	0	70	26	0	0	60	8	4	0	1	3	36	20	.232	.305	.285
	OAK/AL		9	5	5	4	0	1	0	6	0	0	0	1	0	0	0	0	0	1	1	.800	.800	1.200
93	TAC/PCL	AAA	85	298	256	61	13	1	4	88	31	2	1	53	1	4	0	1	3	37	32	.238	.315	.344
	OAK/AL		20	50	47	10	2	0	0	12	2	0	1	15	0	0	0	1	1	5	3	.213	.260	.255
2 YR TOTALS			**29**	**55**	**52**	**14**	**2**	**1**	**0**	**18**	**2**	**0**	**1**	**16**	**0**	**0**	**0**	**1**	**1**	**6**	**4**	**.269**	**.309**	**.346**

Mercedes, Luis Roberto — BR/TR — b.2/15/68 — POS OF-44, DH-10   BAL 2/16/87

YR	TM/LG	CL	G	TPA	AB	H	2B	3B	HR	TB	BB	IBB	HB	SO	GDP	SH	SF	SB	CS	R	RBI	BA	OBA	SA
88	BLU/APP	R+	59	253	215	59	8	4	0	75	32	0	3	39	6	3	1	16	11	36	20	.274	.372	.349
89	FRE/CAR	A+	108	438	401	124	12	5	3	155	30	2	3	62	7	2	2	29	11	62	36	.309	.360	.387
90	HAG/EAS	AA	108	464	416	139	12	4	3	168	34	2	6	70	13	6	4	38	14	71	37	.334	.391	.404
91	ROC/INT	AAA	102	454	374	125	14	5	2	155	65	0	5	63	11	6	4	23	13	68	36	.334	.435	.414
	BAL/AL		19	59	54	11	2	0	0	13	4	0	0	9	1	1	0	0	0	10	2	.204	.259	.241
92	ROC/INT	AAA	103	460	409	128	15	1	3	154	44	2	1	56	11	3	3	35	14	62	29	.313	.379	.377
	BAL/AL		23	62	50	7	2	0	0	9	8	0	1	9	2	2	1	0	1	7	4	.140	.267	.180
93	PHO/PCL	AAA	70	286	244	71	5	3	0	82	36	0	4	30	5	1	1	14	6	28	15	.291	.389	.336
	BAL/AL		10	30	24	7	2	0	0	9	5	0	1	4	1	1	0	0	0	1	0	.292	.414	.375
	SF/NL		18	29	25	4	0	1	0	6	1	0	2	3	0	1	0	0	1	1	3	.160	.250	.240
	YEAR		28	59	49	11	2	1	0	15	6	0	2	7	1	2	0	0	1	2	3	.224	.333	.306
3 YR TOTALS			**70**	**180**	**153**	**29**	**6**	**1**	**0**	**37**	**18**	**0**	**3**	**25**	**4**	**5**	**1**	**1**	**3**	**19**	**9**	**.190**	**.286**	**.242**

Merullo, Matthew Bates "Matt" — BL/TR — b.8/4/65 — POS C-70, 1B-16, DH-14   CHA86 7/179

YR	TM/LG	CL	G	TPA	AB	H	2B	3B	HR	TB	BB	IBB	HB	SO	GDP	SH	SF	SB	CS	R	RBI	BA	OBA	SA
86	PEN/CAR	A+	64	231	208	63	12	2	3	88	19	3	1	16	5	0	3	1	0	21	35	.303	.359	.423
87	DB/FSL	A+	70	276	250	65	11	6	4	100	20	1	0	18	6	0	6	1	1	26	47	.260	.308	.400
	BIR/SOU	AA	48	173	167	46	7	0	2	59	6	0	0	20	5	0	0	1	0	13	17	.275	.301	.353
88	BIR/SOU	AA	125	496	449	117	26	0	6	161	40	3	3	50	9	1	3	3	2	58	60	.261	.323	.359
89	VAN/PCL	AAA	3	12	9	2	1	0	0	3	2	0	0	1	1	1	0	0	0	0	2	.222	.364	.333
	CHI/AL		31	90	81	18	1	0	1	22	6	0	0	14	2	1	2	0	0	5	8	.222	.273	.272
	BIR/SOU	AA	33	140	119	35	6	0	3	50	16	2	0	15	3	2	3	0	1	19	23	.294	.370	.420
90	BIR/SOU	AA	102	420	378	110	26	1	8	162	34	6	3	49	6	3	2	2	4	57	50	.291	.353	.429
91	BIR/SOU	AA	8	30	28	6	0	0	2	12	2	0	0	4	1	0	0	0	0	5	3	.214	.267	.429
	CHI/AL		80	154	140	32	1	0	4	48	5	0	1	18	1	1	4	0	0	8	21	.229	.268	.343
92	CHI/AL		24	53	50	9	1	1	1	14	2	1	0	8	0	0	1	0	0	3	3	.180	.208	.240
	VAN/PCL	AAA	14	46	45	8	1	1	1	14	1	0	0	2	3	0	0	1	0	2	4	.178	.196	.311
93	CHI/AL		8	21	20	1	0	0	0	1	0	0	0	1	1	1	0	0	0	1	0	.050	.050	.050
	NAS/AMA	AAA	103	386	352	117	30	1	12	185	28	6	3	47	12	1	2	0	1	50	65	.332	.384	.526
4 YR TOTALS			**143**	**318**	**291**	**60**	**3**	**1**	**6**	**83**	**16**	**1**	**1**	**41**	**4**	**4**	**6**	**0**	**1**	**17**	**32**	**.206**	**.245**	**.285**

Meulens, Hensley Filemon Acasio — BR/TR — b.6/23/67 — POS OF-120, DH-13, 3B-11, 1B-10   NYA 10/31/85

YR	TM/LG	CL	G	TPA	AB	H	2B	3B	HR	TB	BB	IBB	HB	SO	GDP	SH	SF	SB	CS	R	RBI	BA	OBA	SA
86	YAN/GCL	R	59	253	219	51	10	4	4	81	28	0	4	66	7	1	1	4	2	36	31	.233	.329	.370
87	PW/CAR	A+	116	498	430	129	23	2	28	240	53	3	9	124	7	0	6	14	3	76	103	.300	.384	.558
	FL/FSL	A+	17	65	58	10	3	0	0	13	7	0	0	25	0	0	0	0	0	2	2	.172	.262	.224
88	ALB/EAS	AA	79	316	278	68	9	1	13	118	37	2	1	97	7	0	0	3	3	50	40	.245	.335	.424
	CMB/INT	AAA	55	224	209	48	9	1	6	77	14	0	0	61	5	0	1	2	0	27	22	.230	.277	.368
89	ALB/EAS	AA	104	406	335	86	8	2	11	131	61	0	9	108	4	0	1	0	0	55	45	.257	.384	.391
	CMB/INT	AAA	14	53	45	13	4	0	1	20	8	0	0	13	2	0	1	0	2	8	3	.289	.396	.444
	NY/AL		8	30	28	5	0	0	0	5	2	0	0	8	2	0	0	0	0	2	1	.179	.233	.179
90	CMB/INT	AAA	136	559	480	137	20	5	26	245	66	4	7	132	12	1	5	6	4	81	96	.285	.376	.510
	NY/AL		23	95	83	20	7	0	3	36	9	0	3	25	3	0	0	0	0	12	10	.241	.337	.434
91	NY/AL		96	313	288	64	8	1	6	92	18	0	4	97	7	1	2	3	0	37	29	.222	.276	.319
92	CMB/INT	AAA	141	603	534	147	28	4	26	257	60	6	5	168	15	1	3	15	8	96	100	.275	.352	.481
	NY/AL		2	6	5	3	0	0	0	3	1	0	0	1	0	0	0	0	0	1	1	.600	.667	1.200
93	NY/AL		30	61	53	9	1	0	2	16	8	0	0	19	2	0	0	0	1	8	5	.170	.279	.340
	CMB/INT	AAA	75	317	279	57	14	0	14	113	32	0	3	92	1	0	3	6	2	39	45	.204	.290	.405
5 YR TOTALS			**159**	**505**	**457**	**101**	**16**	**2**	**12**	**157**	**38**	**1**	**7**	**149**	**15**	**1**	**2**	**4**	**2**	**60**	**46**	**.221**	**.290**	**.344**

Mieske, Matthew Todd "Matt" — BR/TR — b.2/13/68 — POS OF-22 — SD90 17/471

YR	TM/LG	CL	G	TPA	AB	H	2B	3B	HR	TB	BB	IBB	HB	SO	GDP	SH	SF	SB	CS	R	RBI	BA	OBA	SA
90	SPO/NWL	A-	76	349	291	99	20	0	12	155	45	3	6	43	6	1	6	26	12	59	63	.340	.431	.533
91	HD/CAL	A+	133	603	492	168	36	6	15	261	94	6	13	82	13	0	4	39	12	108	119	.341	.456	.530
92	DEN/AMA	AAA	134	575	524	140	29	11	19	248	39	2	3	90	15	4	5	13	9	80	77	.267	.319	.473
93	NO/AMA	AAA	60	251	219	57	14	2	8	99	27	3	3	46	5	2	0	6	4	36	22	.260	.349	.452
	MIL/AL		23	63	58	14	0	0	3	23	4	0	0	14	2	1	0	0	2	9	7	.241	.290	.397

Miller, Keith Alan — BR/TR — b.6/12/63 — POS 2B-222, OF-124, 3B-31, SS-22, DH-7 — NYN 9/6/84

YR	TM/LG	CL	G	TPA	AB	H	2B	3B	HR	TB	BB	IBB	HB	SO	GDP	SH	SF	SB	CS	R	RBI	BA	OBA	SA
85	LYN/CAR	A+	89	369	325	98	16	5	7	145	39	0	4	52	5	1	0	14	2	51	54	.302	.383	.446
	JAC/TEX	AA	46	180	165	37	8	1	3	56	12	0	1	38	6	1	1	8	1	17	22	.224	.279	.339
86	JAC/TEX	AA	94	424	353	116	23	4	5	162	62	1	7	55	5	2	0	28	5	80	36	.329	.438	.459
87	TID/INT	AAA	53	220	202	50	9	1	6	79	14	1	1	36	5	3	0	14	2	29	22	.248	.300	.391
	NY/NL		25	57	51	19	2	2	0	25	2	0	1	6	1	3	0	8	1	14	1	.373	.407	.490
88	TID/INT	AAA	42	187	171	48	11	1	1	64	12	1	2	20	0	0	2	8	5	23	15	.281	.332	.374
	NY/NL		40	79	70	15	1	1	1	21	6	0	0	10	1	3	0	0	5	9	5	.214	.276	.300
89	TID/INT	AAA	48	204	184	49	8	2	1	64	18	0	2	24	2	0	0	12	2	33	15	.266	.338	.348
	NY/NL		57	152	143	33	7	0	1	43	5	0	1	27	3	0	0	6	0	15	7	.231	.262	.301
90	NY/NL		88	262	233	60	18	0	1	71	23	1	2	46	2	2	2	16	3	42	12	.258	.327	.305
91	NY/NL		98	304	275	77	22	1	4	113	23	0	5	44	2	0	1	14	4	41	23	.280	.345	.411
92	KC/AL		106	464	416	118	24	4	4	162	31	0	14	46	1	1	2	16	6	57	38	.284	.352	.389
93	OMA/AMA	AAA	6	24	24	7	1	1	0	10	0	0	0	2	2	0	0	1	0	2	2	.292	.292	.417
	KC/AL		37	118	108	18	3	0	0	21	8	0	1	19	3	0	1	3	1	9	3	.167	.229	.194
7 YR TOTALS			**451**	**1436**	**1296**	**340**	**67**	**8**	**11**	**456**	**98**	**1**	**24**	**198**	**13**	**12**	**6**	**63**	**20**	**187**	**89**	**.262**	**.324**	**.352**

Millette, Joseph Anthony "Joe" — BR/TR — b.8/12/66 — POS SS-33, 3B-6, 2B-1 — PHI 9/4/88

YR	TM/LG	CL	G	TPA	AB	H	2B	3B	HR	TB	BB	IBB	HB	SO	GDP	SH	SF	SB	CS	R	RBI	BA	OBA	SA
89	BAT/NYP	A-	11	46	42	10	3	0	0	13	4	0	0	6	0	0	0	3	0	4	4	.238	.304	.310
	SPA/SAL	A	60	250	209	50	4	3	0	60	28	0	7	36	5	3	3	4	2	27	18	.239	.344	.287
90	CLE/FSL	A+	108	344	295	54	4	0	0	59	29	0	7	53	5	7	6	4	4	31	18	.183	.267	.200
91	CLE/FSL	A+	18	68	55	14	2	0	0	16	7	0	1	6	1	3	2	1	2	6	6	.255	.338	.291
	REA/EAS	AA	115	409	353	87	9	4	3	113	36	2	7	54	5	10	3	6	6	52	28	.246	.326	.320
92	SCR/INT	AAA	78	284	256	68	11	1	1	84	15	0	6	30	8	7	0	3	2	24	23	.266	.321	.328
	PHI/NL		33	87	78	16	0	0	0	16	5	2	2	10	8	2	0	1	0	5	2	.205	.271	.205
93	SCR/INT	AAA	107	375	343	77	15	2	1	99	19	2	5	56	9	7	1	5	4	27	24	.224	.274	.289
	PHI/NL		10	14	10	2	0	0	0	2	1	0	2	2	1	3	0	0	0	3	2	.200	.273	.200
2 YR TOTALS			**43**	**101**	**88**	**18**	**0**	**0**	**0**	**18**	**6**	**2**	**2**	**12**	**9**	**5**	**0**	**1**	**0**	**8**	**4**	**.205**	**.271**	**.205**

Milligan, Randy Andre — BR/TR — b.11/27/61 — POS 1B-554, DH-42, OF-20 — NYN81* 1/3

YR	TM/LG	CL	G	TPA	AB	H	2B	3B	HR	TB	BB	IBB	HB	SO	GDP	SH	SF	SB	CS	R	RBI	BA	OBA	SA
84	JAC/TEX	AA	62	252	193	53	5	0	9	85	53	4	4	39	4	0	2	15	7	32	34	.275	.437	.440
85	JAC/TEX	AA	119	453	391	121	22	2	13	186	53	5	4	78	12	1	4	11	6	60	77	.309	.394	.476
86	JAC/TEX	AA	78	332	269	85	11	3	7	123	60	3	2	42	10	0	1	13	6	53	53	.316	.443	.457
	TID/INT	AAA	21	69	60	5	0	0	0	5	9	0	0	15	2	0	0	0	0	3	3	.083	.203	.083
87	TID/INT	AAA	136	557	457	149	28	4	29	272	91	10	4	77	18	0	5	8	4	99	103	.326	.438	.595
	NY/NL		3	2	1	0	0	0	0	0	1	0	0	1	0	0	0	0	0	0	0	.000	.500	.000
88	PIT/NL		40	103	82	18	5	0	3	32	20	0	1	24	2	0	0	1	2	10	8	.220	.379	.390
	BUF/AMA	AAA	63	263	221	61	15	3	2	88	36	2	1	40	7	0	5	1	2	37	30	.276	.373	.398
89	BAL/AL		124	444	365	98	23	5	12	167	74	2	3	75	12	0	4	4	5	64	60	.268	.394	.458
90	BAL/AL		109	456	362	96	20	1	20	178	88	3	2	68	11	0	4	6	3	64	60	.265	.408	.492
91	BAL/AL		141	571	483	127	17	2	16	196	84	4	2	108	23	0	2	0	5	57	70	.263	.373	.406
92	BAL/AL		137	577	462	111	21	1	11	167	106	0	4	81	15	0	5	8	8	71	53	.240	.383	.361
93	CIN/NL		83	282	234	64	11	1	6	95	46	0	1	49	3	0	1	3	3	30	29	.274	.394	.406
	CLE/AL		19	61	47	20	7	0	0	27	14	0	0	4	0	0	0	0	1	7	7	.426	.557	.574
	YEAR		102	343	281	84	18	1	6	122	60	0	1	53	3	0	1	3	4	37	36	.299	.423	.434
7 YR TOTALS			**656**	**2496**	**2036**	**534**	**104**	**10**	**68**	**862**	**433**	**9**	**13**	**410**	**66**	**0**	**14**	**16**	**18**	**295**	**272**	**.262**	**.393**	**.423**

Mitchell, Kevin Darnell — BR/TR — b.1/13/62 — POS OF-655, 3B-235, DH-26, SS-25, 1B-3 — NYN 11/16/80

YR	TM/LG	CL	G	TPA	AB	H	2B	3B	HR	TB	BB	IBB	HB	SO	GDP	SH	SF	SB	CS	R	RBI	BA	OBA	SA
84	TID/INT	AAA	120	471	432	105	21	3	10	162	25	0	3	89	16	2	9	1	2	51	54	.243	.284	.375
	NY/NL		7	14	14	3	0	0	0	3	0	0	0	3	0	0	0	1	0	1	1	.214	.214	.214
85	TID/INT	AAA	95	385	348	101	24	2	9	156	32	1	2	60	14	0	3	3	1	44	43	.290	.351	.448
86	NY/NL		108	364	328	91	22	2	12	153	33	0	1	61	6	1	1	3	3	51	43	.277	.344	.466
87	SD/NL		62	217	196	48	7	1	7	78	20	3	0	38	5	0	1	0	0	19	26	.245	.313	.398
	SF/NL		69	298	268	82	13	1	15	142	28	1	2	50	5	0	9	9	6	49	44	.306	.376	.530
	YEAR		131	515	464	130	20	2	22	220	48	4	2	88	10	0	1	9	6	68	70	.280	.350	.474
88	SF/NL		148	566	505	127	25	7	19	223	48	7	5	85	9	1	7	5	5	60	80	.251	.319	.442
89	SF/NL		154	640	543	158	34	6	*47	*345	87	32	3	115	6	0	7	3	4	100	*125	.291	.387	*.635
90	SF/NL		140	589	524	152	24	2	35	285	58	6	2	87	6	0	5	4	7	90	93	.290	.360	.544
91	SF/NL		113	423	371	95	13	1	27	191	43	8	5	57	6	0	4	2	3	52	69	.256	.338	.515
92	SEA/AL		99	402	360	103	24	0	9	154	35	4	3	46	4	0	3	0	1	48	67	.286	.351	.428
93	CIN/NL		93	353	323	110	21	3	19	194	25	4	1	48	14	0	4	1	1	56	64	.341	.385	.601
9 YR TOTALS			**993**	**3866**	**3432**	**969**	**183**	**23**	**190**	**1768**	**377**	**68**	**22**	**590**	**63**	**2**	**33**	**27**	**31**	**525**	**612**	**.282**	**.354**	**.515**

Molitor, Paul Leo — BR/TR — b.8/22/56 — POS 3B-791, DH-555, 2B-400, 1B-154, SS-57, OF-50 — MIL77 1/3

YR	TM/LG	CL	G	TPA	AB	H	2B	3B	HR	TB	BB	IBB	HB	SO	GDP	SH	SF	SB	CS	R	RBI	BA	OBA	SA
78	MIL/AL		125	556	521	142	26	4	6	194	19	2	4	54	6	7	5	30	12	73	45	.273	.301	.372
79	MIL/AL		140	645	584	188	27	16	9	274	48	5	2	48	9	6	5	33	13	88	62	.322	.372	.469

(continued)

Molitor, Paul Leo (continued)

YR	TM/LG	CL	G	TPA	AB	H	2B	3B	HR	TB	BB	IBB	HB	SO	GDP	SH	SF	SB	CS	R	RBI	BA	OBA	SA
80	MIL/AL		111	512	450	137	29	2	9	197	48	4	3	48	9	6	5	34	7	81	37	.304	.372	.438
81	MIL/AL		64	284	251	67	11	0	2	84	25	1	2	29	3	5	0	10	6	45	19	.267	.341	.335
82	MIL/AL		160	751	666	201	26	8	19	300	69	1	1	93	9	10	5	41	9	*136	71	.302	.366	.450
83	MIL/AL		152	682	608	164	28	6	15	249	59	4	2	74	12	7	6	41	8	95	47	.270	.333	.410
84	MIL/AL		13	49	46	10	1	0	0	11	2	0	0	8	0	0	1	1	0	3	6	.217	.245	.239
85	MIL/AL		140	642	576	171	28	3	10	235	54	6	1	80	12	7	4	21	7	93	48	.297	.356	.408
86	MIL/AL		105	482	437	123	24	3	9	186	40	0	0	81	9	2	3	20	5	62	55	.281	.340	.426
87	MIL/AL		118	542	465	164	*41	5	16	263	69	2	2	67	4	5	1	45	10	*114	75	.353	.438	.566
88	MIL/AL		154	690	609	190	34	6	13	275	71	8	2	54	10	5	3	41	10	115	60	.312	.384	.452
89	MIL/AL		155	696	615	194	35	4	11	270	64	4	4	67	11	4	9	27	11	84	56	.315	.379	.439
90	BEL/MID	A	1	4	4	2	0	0	0	5	0	0	0	0	0	0	0	0	0	1	1	.500	.500	1.250
	MIL/AL		103	458	418	119	27	6	12	194	37	4	1	51	7	0	2	18	3	64	45	.285	.343	.464
91	MIL/AL		158	749	665	*216	32	*13	17	325	77	16	6	62	11	0	1	19	8	*133	75	.325	.399	.489
92	MIL/AL		158	700	609	195	36	7	12	281	73	12	3	66	13	4	11	31	6	89	89	.320	.389	.461
93	TOR/AL		160	725	636	*211	37	5	22	324	77	3	3	71	13	1	8	22	4	121	111	.332	.402	.509
16 YR TOTALS			2016	9163	8156	2492	442	91	182	3662	832	72	37	953	138	69	69	434	119	1396	901	.306	.370	.449

Mondesi, Raul Ramon — BR/TR — b.3/12/71 — POS OF-40   LA 6/6/88

YR	TM/LG	CL	G	TPA	AB	H	2B	3B	HR	TB	BB	IBB	HB	SO	GDP	SH	SF	SB	CS	R	RBI	BA	OBA	SA
90	GF/PIO	R+	44	189	175	53	10	4	8	95	11	1	2	30	0	0	1	30	7	35	31	.303	.349	.543
91	BAK/CAL	A+	28	115	106	30	7	2	3	50	5	1	3	21	0	0	1	9	4	23	13	.283	.330	.472
	SA/TEX	AA	53	228	213	58	11	5	5	94	8	0	4	47	1	0	3	8	3	32	26	.272	.307	.441
	ALB/PCL	AAA	2	9	9	3	0	1	0	5	0	0	0	1	0	0	0	1	0	3	0	.333	.333	.556
92	ALB/PCL	AAA	35	148	138	43	4	7	4	73	9	4	1	35	0	0	0	2	3	23	15	.312	.358	.529
	SA/TEX	AA	18	72	68	18	2	2	2	30	1	0	0	24	1	0	3	3	2	8	14	.265	.264	.441
93	ALB/PCL	AAA	110	450	425	119	22	7	12	191	18	4	2	85	4	0	5	13	10	65	65	.280	.309	.449
	LA/NL		42	91	86	25	3	1	4	42	4	0	0	16	1	1	0	4	1	13	10	.291	.322	.488

Montoyo, Jose Carlos "Charlie" — BR/TR — b.10/17/65 — POS 2B-3   MIL87 7/149

YR	TM/LG	CL	G	TPA	AB	H	2B	3B	HR	TB	BB	IBB	HB	SO	GDP	SH	SF	SB	CS	R	RBI	BA	OBA	SA
87	HEL/PIO	R+	13	58	45	13	1	2	0	18	12	0	0	3	0	0	1	2	1	12	2	.289	.431	.400
	BEL/MID	A	55	246	188	50	9	2	5	78	52	0	4	22	4	1	1	8	0	46	19	.266	.433	.415
88	STO/CAL	A+	132	619	450	115	14	1	3	140	156	0	5	93	7	6	2	16	6	103	61	.256	.450	.311
89	STO/CAL	A+	129	571	448	111	22	2	0	137	102	3	11	40	7	6	4	13	9	69	48	.248	.396	.306
90	EP/TEX	AA	94	405	322	93	15	3	3	123	72	1	8	43	9	1	2	9	0	71	44	.289	.428	.382
91	DEN/AMA	AAA	120	478	394	94	13	1	12	145	69	5	5	50	7	6	4	15	3	68	45	.239	.356	.368
92	DEN/AMA	AAA	84	310	259	84	7	4	2	105	47	0	1	36	10	2	3	3	5	40	34	.324	.429	.405
93	OTT/INT	AAA	99	405	319	89	18	2	1	114	71	0	4	37	11	6	5	0	0	43	43	.279	.411	.357
	MON/NL		4	5	5	2	1	0	0	3	0	0	0	0	0	0	0	0	0	1	3	.400	.400	.600

Morandini, Michael Robert "Mickey" — BL/TR — b.4/22/66 — POS 2B-357, SS-3   PHI88 4/120

YR	TM/LG	CL	G	TPA	AB	H	2B	3B	HR	TB	BB	IBB	HB	SO	GDP	SH	SF	SB	CS	R	RBI	BA	OBA	SA
89	SPA/SAL	A	63	275	231	78	19	1	1	102	35	0	3	45	3	4	2	18	9	43	30	.338	.428	.442
	CLE/FSL	A+	17	72	63	19	4	1	0	25	7	1	1	8	0	1		3	1	14	4	.302	.375	.397
	REA/EAS	AA	48	213	188	66	12	1	5	95	23	4	1	32	2	1	0	5	5	39	29	.351	.425	.505
90	SCR/INT	AAA	139	578	503	131	24	10	1	178	60	0	5	90	10	10	0	16	6	76	31	.260	.345	.354
	PHI/NL		25	87	79	19	4	0	1	26	6	0	0	19	1	2	0	3	0	9	3	.241	.294	.329
91	SCR/INT	AAA	12	52	46	12	4	0	1	19	5	0	0	6	0	1	2	3	0	7	9	.261	.327	.413
	PHI/NL		98	364	325	81	11	4	1	103	29	0	2	54	4	2	2	13	2	38	20	.249	.313	.317
92	PHI/NL		127	455	422	112	8	8	3	145	25	2	0	64	4	6	2	8	3	47	30	.265	.305	.344
93	PHI/NL		120	470	425	105	19	9	3	151	34	2	4	73	7	4	2	13	2	57	33	.247	.309	.355
4 YR TOTALS			370	1376	1251	317	42	21	8	425	94	4	7	201	19	18	6	37	7	151	86	.253	.308	.340

Morris, William Harold "Hal" — BL/TL — b.4/9/65 — POS 1B-417, OF-16, DH-2   NYA86 7/210

YR	TM/LG	CL	G	TPA	AB	H	2B	3B	HR	TB	BB	IBB	HB	SO	GDP	SH	SF	SB	CS	R	RBI	BA	OBA	SA
86	ONE/NYP	A-	36	149	127	48	9	2	3	70	18	2	1	15	3	2	1	1	1	26	30	.378	.456	.551
	ALB/EAS	AA	25	85	79	17	5	0	0	22	4	0	1	10	3	1	0	1	1	7	4	.215	.262	.278
87	ALB/EAS	AA	135	580	530	173	31	4	5	227	36	2	4	43	12	5	5	7	4	65	73	.326	.370	.428
88	CMB/INT	AAA	121	502	452	134	19	4	3	170	36	6	3	62	12	7	4	8	5	41	38	.296	.349	.376
	NY/AL		15	20	20	2	0	0	0	2	0	0	0	9	0	0	0	0	0	1	0	.100	.100	.100
89	CMB/INT	AAA	111	456	417	136	24	1	17	213	28	2	4	47	5	3	4	5	3	70	66	.326	.371	.511
	NY/AL		15	19	18	5	0	0	0	5	1	0	0	4	0	0	0	0	0	2	4	.278	.316	.278
90	NAS/AMA	AAA	16	72	64	22	5	0	1	30	5	1	2	10	2	0	1	1	1	8	10	.344	.403	.469
	CIN/NL		107	336	309	105	22	3	7	154	21	1	1	32	12	3	2	9	3	50	36	.340	.381	.498
91	CIN/NL		136	537	478	152	33	1	14	229	46	4	1	61	4	5	7	10	4	72	59	.318	.374	.479
92	NAS/AMA	AAA	2	8	6	1	0	0	0	2	2	0	0	2	0	0	0	0	1	1	0	.167	.375	.333
	CIN/NL		115	446	395	107	21	3	6	152	45	8	2	53	12	2	6	6	6	41	53	.271	.347	.385
93	IND/AMA	AAA	3	14	13	6	0	1	0	11	1	0	0	5	0	0	0	0	0	4	5	.462	.500	.846
	CIN/NL		101	421	379	120	18	5	7	159	34	4	2	51	5	0	6	2	2	48	49	.317	.371	.420
6 YR TOTALS			489	1779	1599	491	94	7	34	701	147	23	6	210	35	10	17	27	15	214	201	.307	.364	.438

Munoz, Pedro Javier — BR/TR — b.9/19/68 — POS OF-289, DH-6   TOR 5/31/85

YR	TM/LG	CL	G	TPA	AB	H	2B	3B	HR	TB	BB	IBB	HB	SO	GDP	SH	SF	SB	CS	R	RBI	BA	OBA	SA
85	BJ/GCL	R	40	160	145	38	3	6	0	47	9	0	4	20	4	1	1	4	1	14	17	.262	.321	.324
86	FLO/SAL	A	122	508	445	131	16	5	14	199	54	4	5	100	12	2	2	9	5	69	82	.294	.375	.447
87	DUN/FSL	A+	92	382	341	80	11	5	8	125	34	0	2	74	7	1	6	13	4	55	44	.235	.304	.367
88	DUN/FSL	A+	133	544	481	141	21	7	8	200	52	5	4	87	23	0	7	15	4	59	73	.293	.362	.416

Munoz, Pedro Javier (continued)

YR	TM/LG	CL	G	TPA	AB	H	2B	3B	HR	TB	BB	IBB	HB	SO	GDP	SH	SF	SB	CS	R	RBI	BA	OBA	SA
89	KNO/SOU	AA	122	468	442	118	15	4	19	198	20	2	2	85	11	0	4	10	4	54	65	.267	.299	.448
90	SYR/INT	AAA	86	346	317	101	22	3	7	150	24	3	1	64	12	1	3	16	7	41	56	.319	.365	.473
	POR/PCL	AAA	30	129	110	35	4	0	5	54	15	1	4	18	1	0	0	8	4	19	21	.318	.419	.491
	MIN/AL		22	90	85	23	4	1	0	29	2	0	0	16	3	1	2	3	0	13	5	.271	.281	.341
91	POR/PCL	AAA	56	233	212	67	19	2	5	105	19	3	1	42	6	0	1	9	5	33	28	.316	.373	.495
	MIN/AL		51	151	138	39	7	1	7	69	9	0	1	31	2	1	2	3	0	15	26	.283	.327	.500
92	MIN/AL		127	439	418	113	16	3	12	171	17	1	1	90	18	0	3	4	5	44	71	.270	.298	.409
93	MIN/AL		104	354	326	76	11	1	13	128	25	2	3	97	7	0	0	1	2	34	38	.233	.294	.393
4 YR TOTALS			**304**	**1034**	**967**	**251**	**38**	**6**	**32**	**397**	**53**	**3**	**5**	**234**	**30**	**2**	**7**	**11**	**7**	**106**	**140**	**.260**	**.299**	**.411**

Murphy, Dale Bryan — BR/TR — b.3/12/56 — POS OF-1853, 1B-209, C-85   ATL74 1/5

YR	TM/LG	CL	G	TPA	AB	H	2B	3B	HR	TB	BB	IBB	HB	SO	GDP	SH	SF	SB	CS	R	RBI	BA	OBA	SA
76	ATL/NL		19	72	65	17	6	0	3	23	7	0	0	9	0	0	0	0	0	3	9	.262	.333	.354
77	ATL/NL		18	76	76	24	8	1	2	40	0	0	0	8	3	0	0	0	1	5	14	.316	.316	.526
78	ATL/NL		151	583	530	120	14	3	23	209	42	3	3	145	15	3	5	11	7	66	79	.226	.284	.394
79	ATL/NL		104	429	384	106	7	2	21	180	38	5	2	67	12	0	5	6	1	53	57	.276	.340	.469
80	ATL/NL		156	633	569	160	27	2	33	290	59	9	1	133	8	2	2	9	6	98	89	.281	.349	.510
81	ATL/NL		104	416	369	91	12	1	13	144	44	8	0	72	10	1	2	14	5	43	50	.247	.325	.390
82	ATL/NL		162	698	598	168	23	2	36	303	93	9	3	134	10	0	4	23	11	113	*109	.281	.378	.507
83	ATL/NL		162	687	589	178	24	4	36	318	90	12	2	110	15	0	6	30	4	131	*121	.302	.393	*.540
84	ATL/NL		162	691	607	176	32	8	*36	*332	79	20	2	134	13	0	3	19	7	94	100	.290	.372	*.547
85	ATL/NL		162	712	616	185	32	2	*37	332	*90	15	1	141	14	0	3	7	7	*118	111	.300	.388	.539
86	ATL/NL		160	692	614	163	29	7	29	293	75	5	2	141	10	0	1	7	7	89	83	.265	.347	.477
87	ATL/NL		159	693	566	167	27	1	44	328	115	29	7	136	11	0	5	16	6	115	105	.295	.417	.580
88	ATL/NL		156	671	592	134	35	4	24	249	74	16	2	125	24	0	3	3	5	77	77	.226	.313	.421
89	ATL/NL		154	647	574	131	16	0	20	207	65	10	2	142	14	0	6	3	2	60	84	.228	.306	.361
90	ATL/NL		97	394	349	81	14	0	17	146	41	11	1	84	11	0	3	9	2	38	55	.232	.312	.418
	PHI/NL		57	235	214	57	9	1	7	89	20	3	0	46	11	0	1	0	1	22	28	.266	.328	.416
	YEAR		154	629	563	138	23	1	24	235	61	14	1	130	22	0	4	9	3	60	83	.245	.318	.417
91	PHI/NL		153	599	544	137	33	1	18	226	48	3	0	93	20	0	7	1	0	66	81	.252	.309	.415
92	PHI/NL		18	63	62	10	1	0	2	17	1	0	0	13	3	0	0	0	0	5	7	.161	.175	.274
93	COL/NL		26	49	42	6	1	0	0	7	5	1	0	15	5	0	2	0	0	1	7	.143	.224	.167
18 YR TOTALS			**2180**	**9040**	**7960**	**2111**	**350**	**39**	**398**	**3733**	**986**	**159**	**28**	**1748**	**209**	**6**	**60**	**161**	**68**	**1197**	**1266**	**.265**	**.346**	**.469**

Murray, Eddie Clarence — BB/TR — b.2/24/56 — POS 1B-2368, DH-200, 3B-6, OF-3   BAL73 3/63

YR	TM/LG	CL	G	TPA	AB	H	2B	3B	HR	TB	BB	IBB	HB	SO	GDP	SH	SF	SB	CS	R	RBI	BA	OBA	SA
77	BAL/AL		160	666	611	173	29	2	27	287	48	6	1	104	22	0	6	0	1	81	88	.283	.333	.470
78	BAL/AL		161	690	610	174	32	3	27	293	70	7	1	97	15	1	8	6	5	85	95	.285	.356	.480
79	BAL/AL		159	687	606	179	30	2	25	288	72	9	2	78	16	1	6	10	2	90	99	.295	.369	.475
80	BAL/AL		158	683	621	186	36	2	32	322	54	10	2	71	18	0	6	7	2	100	116	.300	.354	.519
81	BAL/AL		99	422	378	111	21	2	*22	202	40	10	1	43	10	0	3	2	3	57	*78	.294	.360	.534
82	BAL/AL		151	627	550	174	30	1	32	302	70	18	1	82	17	0	6	7	2	87	110	.316	.391	.549
83	BAL/AL		156	680	582	178	30	3	33	313	86	13	3	90	17	0	9	5	1	115	111	.306	.393	.538
84	BAL/AL		162	705	588	180	26	3	29	299	*107	25	2	87	9	0	8	10	2	97	110	.306	*.410	.509
85	BAL/AL		156	677	583	173	37	1	31	305	84	12	2	68	8	0	8	5	2	111	124	.297	.383	.523
86	BAL/AL		137	578	495	151	25	2	17	229	78	7	0	49	17	0	5	3	0	61	84	.305	.396	.463
87	BAL/AL		160	694	618	171	28	3	30	295	73	6	0	80	15	0	3	1	2	89	91	.277	.352	.477
88	BAL/AL		161	681	603	171	27	2	28	286	75	8	0	78	20	0	3	5	2	75	84	.284	.361	.474
89	LA/NL		160	690	594	147	29	1	20	238	87	24	2	85	11	0	7	7	2	66	88	.247	.342	.401
90	LA/NL		155	645	558	184	22	3	26	290	82	21	1	64	19	0	4	8	5	96	95	.330	.414	.520
91	LA/NL		153	639	576	150	23	1	19	232	55	17	0	74	17	0	8	10	3	69	96	.260	.321	.403
92	NY/NL		156	625	551	144	37	2	16	233	66	8	0	74	15	0	4	4	2	64	93	.261	.336	.423
93	NY/NL		154	659	610	174	28	1	27	285	40	4	0	61	24	0	9	2	2	77	100	.285	.325	.467
17 YR TOTALS			**2598**	**11048**	**9734**	**2820**	**490**	**33**	**441**	**4699**	**1187**	**205**	**18**	**1285**	**254**	**2**	**107**	**92**	**38**	**1420**	**1662**	**.290**	**.364**	**.483**

Myers, Gregory Richard "Greg" — BL/TR — b.4/14/66 — POS C-332, DH-9   TOR84 2/74

YR	TM/LG	CL	G	TPA	AB	H	2B	3B	HR	TB	BB	IBB	HB	SO	GDP	SH	SF	SB	CS	R	RBI	BA	OBA	SA
84	MH/PIO	R+	38	153	133	42	9	0	2	57	16	1	0	6	4	3	1	0	0	20	20	.316	.387	.429
85	FLO/SAL	A	134	539	489	109	19	2	5	147	39	0	2	54	12	2	7	0	0	52	62	.223	.279	.301
86	VEN/CAL	A+	124	502	451	133	23	4	20	224	45	5	2	46	10	1	5	9	4	65	79	.295	.355	.497
87	SYR/INT	AAA	107	370	342	84	19	1	10	135	22	3	1	46	5	3	2	3	3	35	47	.246	.292	.395
	TOR/AL		7	9	9	1	0	0	0	1	0	0	0	3	2	0	0	0	0	1	0	.111	.111	.111
88	SYR/INT	AAA	34	128	120	34	7	1	7	64	8	1	0	24	1	0	0	1	0	18	21	.283	.328	.533
89	KNO/SOU	AA	29	94	90	30	10	0	5	55	3	0	0	16	2	0	1	0	1	11	19	.333	.351	.611
	SYR/INT	AAA	24	94	89	24	6	0	1	33	4	0	0	9	3	1	0	0	1	8	11	.270	.301	.371
	TOR/AL		17	46	44	5	2	0	0	7	2	0	0	9	2	0	0	0	0	0	1	.114	.152	.159
90	SYR/INT	AAA	3	13	11	2	1	0	0	3	1	0	0	1	0	1	0	0	0	0	2	.182	.231	.273
	TOR/AL		87	277	250	59	7	1	5	83	22	0	0	33	12	1	4	0	1	33	22	.236	.293	.332
91	TOR/AL		107	333	309	81	22	0	8	127	21	4	0	45	13	0	3	0	0	25	36	.262	.306	.411
92	TOR/AL		22	68	61	14	6	0	1	23	5	0	0	12	3	0	2	0	0	4	13	.230	.279	.377
	CAL/AL		8	18	17	4	1	0	0	5	0	0	0	4	0	0	0	0	0	0	0	.235	.235	.294
	YEAR		30	86	78	18	7	0	1	28	5	0	0	11	2	1	2	0	0	4	13	.231	.271	.359
93	CAL/AL		108	315	290	74	10	0	7	105	17	2	2	47	8	3	3	3	3	27	40	.255	.298	.362
6 YR TOTALS			**356**	**1066**	**980**	**238**	**48**	**1**	**21**	**351**	**67**	**6**	**2**	**148**	**39**	**5**	**12**	**3**	**5**	**90**	**112**	**.243**	**.289**	**.358**

Naehring, Timothy James "Tim" — BR/TR — b.2/1/67 — POS SS-70, 2B-40, 3B-26, DH-14, OF-1 — BOS88 8/199

YR	TM/LG	CL	G	TPA	AB	H	2B	3B	HR	TB	BB	IBB	HB	SO	GDP	SH	SF	SB	CS	R	RBI	BA	OBA	SA
88	ELM/NYP	A-	19	73	59	18	3	0	1	24	8	0	1	11	1	1	4	0	0	6	13	.305	.375	.407
	WH/FSL	A+	42	164	141	32	7	0	0	39	19	1	3	24	1	0	1	1	1	17	10	.227	.329	.277
89	LYN/CAR	A+	56	236	209	63	7	1	4	84	23	0	0	30	7	1	3	2	0	24	37	.301	.366	.402
	PAW/INT	AAA	79	312	273	75	16	1	3	102	27	1	3	41	6	2	7	2	3	32	31	.275	.339	.374
90	PAW/INT	AAA	82	335	290	78	16	1	15	141	37	2	3	56	6	2	3	0	1	45	47	.269	.354	.486
	BOS/AL		24	93	85	23	6	0	2	35	8	1	0	15	2	0	0	0	0	10	12	.271	.333	.412
91	BOS/AL		20	65	55	6	1	0	0	7	6	0	0	15	0	4	0	0	0	1	3	.109	.197	.127
92	PAW/INT	AAA	11	43	34	10	1	0	2	16	8	0	1	6	1	0	1	0	1	7	5	.294	.442	.471
	BOS/AL		72	214	186	43	8	0	3	60	18	0	3	31	1	6	1	0	0	12	14	.231	.308	.323
93	PAW/INT	AAA	55	241	202	62	9	1	7	94	35	3	0	27	5	3	1	0	2	38	36	.307	.408	.465
	BOS/AL		39	141	127	42	10	0	1	55	10	0	0	26	3	3	1	1	0	14	17	.331	.377	.433
4 YR TOTALS			155	513	453	114	25	0	6	157	42	1	3	87	6	13	2	1	0	37	46	.252	.318	.347

Natal, Robert Marcel "Rob" — BR/TR — b.11/13/65 — POS C-42 — MON87 15/330

YR	TM/LG	CL	G	TPA	AB	H	2B	3B	HR	TB	BB	IBB	HB	SO	GDP	SH	SF	SB	CS	R	RBI	BA	OBA	SA
87	JAM/NYP	A-	57	198	180	58	8	4	7	95	12	1	3	25	3	0	3	6	4	26	32	.322	.369	.528
88	WPB/FSL	A+	113	431	387	93	17	0	6	128	29	0	9	50	8	3	3	3	2	47	51	.240	.306	.331
89	JAC/SOU	AA	46	155	141	29	8	1	0	39	9	0	0	24	1	2	3	2	1	12	11	.206	.248	.277
	WPB/FSL	A+	15	59	48	6	0	0	1	9	9	1	2	9	1	0	1	0	0	5	2	.125	.288	.188
90	JAC/SOU	AA	62	193	171	42	7	1	7	72	14	2	5	42	2	1	2	0	1	23	25	.246	.318	.421
91	IND/AMA	AAA	16	48	41	13	4	0	0	17	6	1	0	9	0	0	1	1	0	2	9	.317	.396	.415
	HAR/EAS	AA	100	400	336	86	16	3	13	147	49	3	8	90	5	2	5	1	1	47	53	.256	.359	.438
92	MON/NL		5	7	6	0	0	0	0	0	1	0	0	1	1	0	0	0	0	0	0	.000	.143	.000
	IND/AMA	AAA	96	380	344	104	19	3	12	165	28	1	1	42	7	1	3	3	0	50	50	.302	.359	.480
93	EDM/PCL	AAA	17	75	66	21	6	1	3	38	8	0	1	10	0	0	0	1	0	16	16	.318	.400	.576
	FLO/NL		41	131	117	25	4	1	1	34	6	0	4	22	6	3	1	1	0	3	6	.214	.273	.291
2 YR TOTALS			46	138	123	25	4	1	1	34	7	0	4	23	7	3	1	1	0	3	6	.203	.267	.276

Navarro, Norberto "Tito" — BB/TR — b.9/12/70 — POS SS-2 — NYN 9/2/87

YR	TM/LG	CL	G	TPA	AB	H	2B	3B	HR	TB	BB	IBB	HB	SO	GDP	SH	SF	SB	CS	R	RBI	BA	OBA	SA
88	KIN/APP	R+	54	210	172	42	3	2	0	49	30	0	3	27	4	2	3	3	4	26	23	.244	.361	.285
89	PIT/NYP	A-	46	179	157	44	6	2	0	54	18	0	0	30	8	3	1	13	13	26	14	.280	.352	.344
90	COL/SAL	A	136	582	497	156	25	4	0	189	69	1	2	55	14	7	7	50	14	86	54	.314	.395	.380
	JAC/TEX	AA	3	13	11	2	1	0	0	3	2	0	0	2	0	0	0	0	1	0	1	.182	.308	.273
91	WIL/EAS	AA	128	572	482	139	9	4	2	162	73	2	2	63	10	12	4	42	19	69	42	.288	.380	.336
93	MET/GCL	R	4	19	14	4	1	1	0	7	3	0	0	1	0	0	2	1	0	2	5	.286	.368	.500
	NOR/INT	AAA	96	315	273	77	11	1	0	90	33	1	0	39	10	7	2	19	3	35	16	.282	.357	.330
	NY/NL		12	18	17	1	0	0	0	1	0	0	0	1	0	0	0	0	0	1	1	.059	.059	.059

Neel, Troy Lee — BL/TR — b.9/14/65 — POS DH-94, 1B-36, OF-9 — CLE86* 9/208

YR	TM/LG	CL	G	TPA	AB	H	2B	3B	HR	TB	BB	IBB	HB	SO	GDP	SH	SF	SB	CS	R	RBI	BA	OBA	SA
86	BAT/NYP	A-	4	13	13	0	0	0	0	0	0	0	0	8	0	0	0	0	0	0	1	.000	.000	.000
87	BUR/APP	R+	59	225	192	54	17	0	10	101	25	4	3	59	3	0	5	0	0	36	59	.281	.364	.526
88	WAT/MID	A	91	378	331	96	20	1	8	142	38	3	6	76	11	0	3	0	1	49	57	.290	.370	.429
89	CAN/EAS	AA	124	469	404	118	21	2	21	206	51	6	9	87	10	0	5	5	9	58	73	.292	.380	.510
90	CS/PCL	AAA	98	337	288	81	15	0	6	114	43	1	2	52	5	0	4	5	4	39	50	.281	.374	.396
91	TAC/PCL	AAA	18	67	59	14	3	1	0	19	7	0	0	14	0	0	0	0	0	7	7	.237	.328	.322
	HUN/SOU	AA	110	458	364	101	21	0	23	191	82	18	6	75	7	0	5	3	3	64	68	.277	.410	.525
92	TAC/PCL	AAA	112	467	396	139	36	3	17	232	60	11	6	84	6	0	3	1	1	61	74	.351	.439	.586
	OAK/AL		24	59	53	14	0	0	3	26	5	0	1	15	1	0	0	0	0	8	9	.264	.339	.491
93	TAC/PCL	AAA	13	56	50	18	4	0	1	25	6	2	0	9	0	0	0	1	1	11	9	.360	.429	.500
	OAK/AL		123	482	427	124	21	0	19	202	49	5	4	101	7	0	2	3	5	59	63	.290	.367	.473
2 YR TOTALS			147	541	480	138	24	0	22	228	54	5	5	116	8	0	2	3	6	67	72	.287	.364	.475

Newfield, Marc Alexander — BR/TR — b.10/19/72 — POS DH-15, OF-5 — SEA90 1/6

YR	TM/LG	CL	G	TPA	AB	H	2B	3B	HR	TB	BB	IBB	HB	SO	GDP	SH	SF	SB	CS	R	RBI	BA	OBA	SA
90	MAR/ARI	R	51	221	192	60	13	0	6	95	25	0	2	20	3	0	2	4	4	34	38	.313	.394	.495
91	SB/CAL	A+	125	514	440	132	22	3	11	193	59	9	10	90	14	0	5	12	6	64	68	.300	.391	.439
	JAC/SOU	AA	6	27	26	6	3	0	0	9	0	0	0	8	0	0	0	0	0	4	2	.231	.259	.346
92	JAC/SOU	AA	45	179	162	40	12	0	4	64	12	0	3	34	3	1	1	1	5	15	19	.247	.309	.395
93	JAC/SOU	AA	91	377	336	103	18	0	19	178	33	1	5	35	12	0	3	1	1	48	51	.307	.374	.530
	SEA/AL		22	70	66	15	3	0	1	21	2	0	0	8	2	0	1	0	0	5	7	.227	.257	.318

Newson, Warren Dale — BL/TL — b.7/3/64 — POS OF-105, DH-17 — SD86* 4/90

YR	TM/LG	CL	G	TPA	AB	H	2B	3B	HR	TB	BB	IBB	HB	SO	GDP	SH	SF	SB	CS	R	RBI	BA	OBA	SA
86	SPO/NWL	A-	54	208	159	37	8	1	2	53	47	1	0	37	5	1	1	3	1	29	31	.233	.406	.333
87	CHS/SAL	A	58	246	191	66	12	2	7	103	52	1	0	35	5	2	1	13	7	50	32	.346	.484	.539
	REN/CAL	A+	51	207	165	51	7	2	6	80	39	0	0	34	1	2	1	2	6	44	28	.309	.439	.485
88	RIV/CAL	A+	130	548	438	130	23	7	22	233	107	3	0	102	11	0	3	36	19	99	91	.297	.432	.532
89	WIC/TEX	AA	128	536	427	130	20	6	18	216	103	10	0	99	9	1	5	20	9	94	70	.304	.436	.506
90	LV/PCL	AAA	123	492	404	123	20	6	13	188	83	3	0	110	10	1	4	13	5	80	58	.304	.420	.465
91	VAN/PCL	AAA	33	143	111	41	12	1	2	61	30	1	0	26	2	0	2	5	4	19	19	.369	.497	.550
	CHI/AL		71	160	132	39	4	0	4	56	28	1	0	34	4	0	0	3	2	20	25	.295	.419	.424
92	VAN/PCL	AAA	19	76	59	15	0	0	0	15	16	1	0	15	2	0	1	2	2	7	9	.254	.421	.254
	CHI/AL		63	173	136	30	3	0	1	36	37	2	0	38	4	0	0	0	0	19	11	.221	.387	.265
93	NAS/AMA	AAA	61	218	176	60	8	2	4	84	38	1	0	38	4	0	4	6	4	40	21	.341	.454	.477
	CHI/AL		26	49	40	12	2	0	1	17	9	0	0	12	2	0	0	0	0	9	6	.300	.429	.450
3 YR TOTALS			160	382	308	81	8	0	7	110	74	4	0	84	10	0	0	5	2	48	42	.263	.406	.357

Nieves, Melvin Ramos — BB/TR — b.12/28/71 — POS OF-21   ATL 5/20/88

YR	TM/LG	CL	G	TPA	AB	H	2B	3B	HR	TB	BB	IBB	HB	SO	GDP	SH	SF	SB	CS	R	RBI	BA	OBA	SA
88	BRA/GCL	R	56	200	176	30	6	0	1	39	20	0	2	53	2	1	1	5	4	16	12	.170	.261	.222
89	PUL/APP	R+	64	269	231	64	16	3	9	113	30	4	1	59	2	3	4	6	4	43	46	.277	.357	.489
90	SUM/SAL	A	126	531	459	130	24	7	9	195	53	4	9	125	7	1	9	10	6	60	59	.283	.362	.425
91	DUR/CAR	A+	64	247	201	53	11	0	9	91	40	2	5	53	1	0	1	3	8	31	25	.264	.397	.453
92	DUR/CAR	A+	31	129	106	32	9	1	8	67	17	3	2	33	1	0	4	4	2	18	32	.302	.395	.632
	GRE/SOU	AA	100	414	350	99	23	5	18	186	52	2	6	98	4	2	4	6	4	61	76	.283	.381	.531
	ATL/NL		12	21	19	4	1	0	0	5	2	0	0	7	0	0	0	0	0	0	1	.211	.286	.263
93	RIC/INT	AAA	78	302	273	76	10	3	10	122	25	4	2	84	4	1	1	4	3	38	36	.278	.342	.447
	LV/PCL	AAA	43	179	159	49	10	1	7	82	18	0	0	42	1	0	0	0	0	31	24	.308	.385	.516
	SD/NL		19	51	47	9	0	0	2	15	3	0	1	21	0	0	0	0	0	4	3	.191	.255	.319
2 YR TOTALS			**31**	**72**	**66**	**13**	**1**	**0**	**2**	**20**	**5**	**0**	**1**	**28**	**0**	**0**	**0**	**0**	**0**	**4**	**4**	**.197**	**.264**	**.303**

Nilsson, David Wayne "Dave" — BL/TR — b.12/14/69 — POS C-137, 1B-7, DH-6   MIL 1/28/87

YR	TM/LG	CL	G	TPA	AB	H	2B	3B	HR	TB	BB	IBB	HB	SO	GDP	SH	SF	SB	CS	R	RBI	BA	OBA	SA
87	HEL/PIO	R+	55	213	188	74	13	0	1	90	22	2	0	14	4	1	2	0	1	36	21	.394	.453	.479
88	BEL/MID	A	95	364	332	74	15	2	4	105	25	2	2	49	10	0	5	2	5	28	41	.223	.277	.316
89	STO/CAL	A+	125	532	472	115	16	6	5	158	51	1	1	75	20	4	4	2	1	59	56	.244	.316	.335
90	STO/CAL	A+	107	406	359	104	22	3	7	153	43	3	1	36	6	0	4	6	5	70	47	.290	.362	.426
91	EP/TEX	AA	65	279	249	104	24	3	5	149	27	4	1	14	4	0	2	4	0	52	57	.418	.473	.598
	DEN/AMA	AAA	28	112	95	22	8	0	1	33	17	0	0	16	2	0	0	1	1	10	14	.232	.348	.347
92	DEN/AMA	AAA	66	270	240	76	16	7	3	115	23	2	0	19	3	2	5	10	4	38	39	.317	.369	.479
	MIL/AL		51	183	164	38	8	0	4	58	17	1	0	18	1	2	0	2	2	15	25	.232	.304	.354
93	EP/TEX	AA	5	20	17	8	1	0	1	12	2	0	0	4	0	0	1	1	1	5	7	.471	.500	.706
	NO/AMA	AAA	17	68	61	21	6	0	1	30	5	0	0	6	1	1	1	0	1	9	9	.344	.388	.492
	MIL/AL		100	340	296	76	10	2	7	111	37	5	0	36	10	4	3	3	6	35	40	.257	.336	.375
2 YR TOTALS			**151**	**523**	**460**	**114**	**18**	**2**	**11**	**169**	**54**	**6**	**0**	**54**	**11**	**6**	**3**	**5**	**8**	**50**	**65**	**.248**	**.325**	**.367**

Nixon, Otis Junior — BB/TR — b.1/9/59 — POS OF-857, DH-18, SS-1   NYA79 S1/3

YR	TM/LG	CL	G	TPA	AB	H	2B	3B	HR	TB	BB	IBB	HB	SO	GDP	SH	SF	SB	CS	R	RBI	BA	OBA	SA
83	NY/AL		13	15	14	2	0	0	0	2	1	0	0	5	0	0	0	2	0	2	0	.143	.200	.143
84	CLE/AL		49	103	91	14	0	0	0	14	8	0	0	11	2	3	1	12	6	16	1	.154	.220	.154
	MAI/INT	AAA	72	305	253	70	5	1	0	77	44	0	0	45	2	6	2	39	10	42	22	.277	.381	.304
85	CLE/AL		104	174	162	38	4	0	3	51	8	0	0	27	2	4	0	20	11	34	9	.235	.271	.315
86	CLE/AL		105	110	95	25	4	1	0	31	13	0	0	12	1	2	0	23	6	33	8	.263	.352	.326
87	CLE/AL		19	20	17	1	0	0	0	1	0	0	0	4	0	0	0	2	3	2	1	.059	.200	.059
	BUF/AMA	AAA	59	283	249	71	13	4	2	98	34	0	0	30	3	0	0	36	7	51	23	.285	.371	.394
88	IND/AMA	AAA	67	282	235	67	6	3	0	79	43	1	3	28	1	3	1	40	14	52	19	.285	.394	.336
	MON/NL		90	305	271	66	8	2	0	78	28	0	4	42	0	2	2	46	13	47	15	.244	.312	.288
89	MON/NL		126	293	258	56	7	2	0	67	33	1	0	36	3	2	0	37	12	41	21	.217	.306	.260
90	MON/NL		119	263	231	58	6	2	1	71	28	0	0	33	2	3	1	50	13	46	20	.251	.331	.307
91	ATL/NL		124	460	401	119	10	1	0	131	47	3	2	40	1	7	3	72	21	81	26	.297	.371	.327
92	ATL/NL		120	502	456	134	14	2	2	158	39	0	0	54	4	5	2	41	18	79	22	.294	.348	.346
93	ATL/NL		134	532	461	124	12	3	1	145	61	2	0	63	10	5	1	47	13	77	24	.269	.351	.315
11 YR TOTALS			**1003**	**2777**	**2457**	**637**	**65**	**13**	**7**	**749**	**269**	**6**	**2**	**327**	**30**	**35**	**14**	**352**	**116**	**458**	**147**	**.259**	**.331**	**.305**

Nokes, Matthew Dodge "Matt" — BL/TR — b.10/31/63 — POS C-653, DH-124, OF-5, 3B-2   SF81 20/503

YR	TM/LG	CL	G	TPA	AB	H	2B	3B	HR	TB	BB	IBB	HB	SO	GDP	SH	SF	SB	CS	R	RBI	BA	OBA	SA
84	SHR/TEX	AA	97	340	308	89	19	2	11	145	30	0	0	34	9	2	0	2	2	32	61	.289	.350	.471
85	SHR/TEX	AA	105	396	344	101	24	1	14	169	41	2	2	47	11	2	7	2	0	52	56	.294	.365	.491
	SF/NL		19	55	53	11	2	0	2	19	1	0	1	9	2	0	0	0	0	3	5	.208	.236	.358
86	NAS/AMA	AAA	125	466	428	122	25	4	10	185	30	6	5	41	12	0	3	2	0	55	71	.285	.337	.432
	DET/AL		7	25	24	8	1	0	1	12	1	1	0	1	1	0	0	0	0	2	2	.333	.360	.500
87	DET/AL		135	508	461	133	14	2	32	247	35	2	6	70	13	3	3	2	1	69	87	.289	.345	.536
88	DET/AL		122	425	382	96	18	0	16	162	34	3	1	58	11	1	2	0	1	53	53	.251	.313	.424
89	DET/AL		87	290	268	67	10	0	9	104	17	1	2	37	7	1	2	1	0	15	39	.250	.298	.388
90	DET/AL		44	118	111	30	5	1	3	46	4	3	2	14	1	0	2	0	0	12	16	.270	.305	.414
	NY/AL		92	264	240	57	4	0	8	85	20	1	4	33	6	0	0	2	2	21	32	.237	.307	.354
	YEAR		136	382	351	87	9	1	11	131	24	4	6	47	7	0	2	2	2	33	40	.248	.306	.373
91	NY/AL		135	493	456	122	20	0	24	214	25	5	5	49	6	0	7	3	2	52	77	.268	.308	.469
92	NY/AL		121	430	384	86	9	0	22	163	37	11	3	62	13	0	6	0	1	42	59	.224	.293	.424
93	NY/AL		76	238	217	54	8	0	10	92	16	2	2	31	4	0	3	0	0	25	35	.249	.303	.424
9 YR TOTALS			**838**	**2846**	**2596**	**664**	**91**	**4**	**127**	**1144**	**190**	**31**	**26**	**364**	**68**	**10**	**24**	**8**	**7**	**294**	**397**	**.256**	**.310**	**.441**

Obando, Sherman Omar — BR/TR — b.1/23/70 — POS DH-21, OF-8   NYA 9/17/87

YR	TM/LG	CL	G	TPA	AB	H	2B	3B	HR	TB	BB	IBB	HB	SO	GDP	SH	SF	SB	CS	R	RBI	BA	OBA	SA
88	YAN/GCL	R	49	192	172	44	10	2	4	70	16	2	0	32	3	0	2	8	5	26	27	.256	.328	.407
89	ONE/NYP	A-	70	301	276	86	23	3	6	133	16	1	6	45	3	1	2	8	5	50	45	.312	.360	.482
90	PW/CAR	A+	121	498	439	117	24	6	10	183	42	1	11	85	7	0	6	5	3	67	67	.267	.341	.417
91	YAN/GCL	R	4	19	17	5	2	0	0	7	1	0	1	2	0	0	0	1	0	3	1	.294	.368	.412
	PW/CAR	A+	42	163	140	37	11	1	7	71	19	2	2	28	1	0	2	4	3	25	31	.264	.356	.507
92	ALB/EAS	AA	109	427	381	107	19	3	17	183	32	1	8	67	12	2	4	3	1	71	56	.281	.346	.480
93	BOW/EAS	AA	19	71	58	14	2	0	3	25	9	0	1	11	1	0	3	1	0	8	12	.241	.338	.431
	BAL/AL		31	97	92	25	6	0	3	36	4	0	1	26	1	0	0	0	0	8	15	.272	.309	.391

O'Brien, Charles Hugh "Charlie" — BR/TR — b.5/1/60 — POS C-398   OAK82 4/132

YR	TM/LG	CL	G	TPA	AB	H	2B	3B	HR	TB	BB	IBB	HB	SO	GDP	SH	SF	SB	CS	R	RBI	BA	OBA	SA
84	MOD/CAL	A+	9	37	32	9	2	0	1	14	2	0	3	4	1	0	0	0	0	8	5	.281	.378	.438

O'Brien, Charles Hugh "Charlie" (continued)

YR	TM/LG	CL	G	TPA	AB	H	2B	3B	HR	TB	BB	IBB	HB	SO	GDP	SH	SF	SB	CS	R	RBI	BA	OBA	SA
	TAC/PCL	AAA	69	237	195	44	11	1	9	82	28	0	6	31	1	8	0	0	1	33	22	.226	.341	.421
85	HUN/SOU	AA	33	135	115	24	5	0	7	50	16	0	2	20	6	1	1	0	1	20	16	.209	.313	.435
	MOD/CAL	A+	9	29	27	8	4	1	1	17	2	1	0	5	0	0	0	0	0	5	2	.296	.345	.630
	TAC/PCL	AAA	18	65	57	9	4	0	0	13	6	0	1	17	0	0	1	0	0	5	7	.158	.246	.228
	OAK/AL		16	14	11	3	1	0	0	4	3	0	0	3	0	0	0	0	0	3	1	.273	.429	.364
86	VAN/PCL	AAA	6	21	17	2	0	0	0	2	4	0	0	4	0	0	0	0	0	1	1	.118	.286	.118
	EP/TEX	AA	92	399	336	109	20	3	15	180	50	0	6	30	7	1	6	0	0	72	75	.324	.415	.536
87	MIL/AL		10	40	35	7	3	1	0	12	4	0	0	4	0	1	0	0	1	2	0	.200	.282	.343
	DEN/AMA	AAA	80	318	266	75	12	1	8	113	42	2	2	33	5	6	2	5	5	37	35	.282	.381	.425
88	DEN/AMA	AAA	48	182	153	43	5	0	4	60	19	1	4	19	6	5	1	1	2	16	25	.281	.373	.392
	MIL/AL		40	127	118	26	6	0	2	38	5	0	0	16	3	4	0	0	1	12	9	.220	.252	.322
89	MIL/AL		62	226	188	44	10	0	6	72	21	1	9	11	11	8	0	0	0	22	35	.234	.339	.383
90	MIL/AL		46	166	145	27	7	2	0	38	11	1	2	26	3	8	0	0	0	11	11	.186	.253	.262
	NY/NL		28	83	68	11	3	0	0	14	10	2	0	8	1	2	2	0	0	6	9	.162	.272	.206
	YEAR		74	249	213	38	10	2	0	52	21	3	3	34	4	10	2	0	0	17	20	.178	.259	.244
91	NY/NL		69	191	168	31	6	0	2	43	17	1	4	25	5	0	2	0	2	16	14	.185	.272	.256
92	NY/NL		68	177	156	33	12	0	2	51	16	1	1	18	4	4	0	0	1	15	13	.212	.289	.327
93	NY/NL		67	208	188	48	11	0	4	71	14	1	2	14	4	3	1	1	1	15	23	.255	.312	.378
8 YR TOTALS			**406**	**1232**	**1077**	**230**	**59**	**3**	**16**	**343**	**101**	**7**	**19**	**125**	**31**	**30**	**5**	**1**	**6**	**102**	**115**	**.214**	**.291**	**.318**

O'Brien, Peter Michael "Pete" — BL/TL — b.2/9/58 — POS 1B-1377, DH-120, OF-61   TEX79 15/381

YR	TM/LG	CL	G	TPA	AB	H	2B	3B	HR	TB	BB	IBB	HB	SO	GDP	SH	SF	SB	CS	R	RBI	BA	OBA	SA
82	TEX/AL		20	74	67	16	4	1	4	34	6	0	0	8	0	0	1	1	0	13	13	.239	.297	.507
83	TEX/AL		154	588	524	124	24	5	8	182	58	2	1	62	12	3	2	5	4	53	53	.237	.313	.347
84	TEX/AL		142	581	520	149	26	2	18	233	53	8	0	50	11	1	7	3	5	57	80	.287	.348	.448
85	TEX/AL		159	655	573	153	34	3	22	259	69	4	3	53	18	3	9	5	10	69	92	.267	.342	.452
86	TEX/AL		156	641	551	160	23	3	23	258	87	11	0	66	19	0	3	4	4	86	90	.290	.385	.468
87	TEX/AL		159	638	569	163	26	1	23	260	59	6	0	61	9	0	10	0	4	84	88	.286	.348	.457
88	TEX/AL		156	628	547	149	24	1	16	223	72	9	0	73	12	1	8	1	4	57	71	.272	.352	.408
89	CLE/AL		155	646	554	144	24	1	12	206	83	17	2	48	12	2	5	3	1	75	55	.260	.356	.372
90	SEA/AL		108	417	366	82	18	0	5	115	44	7	1	33	12	1	4	0	0	32	27	.224	.308	.314
91	SEA/AL		152	617	560	139	29	3	17	225	44	7	1	61	14	3	9	0	1	58	88	.248	.300	.402
92	SEA/AL		134	444	396	88	15	1	14	147	40	8	0	27	8	1	7	2	1	40	52	.222	.289	.371
93	SEA/AL		72	239	210	54	7	0	7	82	26	4	0	21	8	0	3	0	0	30	27	.257	.335	.390
12 YR TOTALS			**1567**	**6168**	**5437**	**1421**	**254**	**21**	**169**	**2224**	**641**	**77**	**7**	**563**	**133**	**15**	**68**	**24**	**34**	**654**	**736**	**.261**	**.336**	**.409**

Offerman, Jose Antonio — BB/TR — b.11/8/68 — POS SS-384   LA 7/24/86

YR	TM/LG	CL	G	TPA	AB	H	2B	3B	HR	TB	BB	IBB	HB	SO	GDP	SH	SF	SB	CS	R	RBI	BA	OBA	SA
88	VB/FSL	A+	4	16	14	4	2	0	0	6	2	0	0	0	0	0	0	0	0	4	2	.286	.375	.429
	GF/PIO	R+	60	293	251	83	11	5	2	110	38	1	2	42	3	1	1	57	10	75	28	.331	.421	.438
89	BAK/CAL	A+	62	283	245	75	9	4	2	98	35	2	2	48	5	0	1	37	13	53	22	.306	.396	.400
	SA/TEX	AA	68	322	278	80	6	3	2	98	40	4	1	39	1	3	0	32	13	47	22	.288	.379	.353
90	ALB/PCL	AAA	117	535	454	148	16	11	0	186	71	0	4	81	7	4	4	60	19	104	56	.326	.416	.410
	LA/NL		29	63	58	9	0	0	0	12	4	1	0	14	0	1	0	0	1	7	7	.155	.210	.207
91	ALB/PCL	AAA	79	340	289	86	8	4	0	102	47	3	0	58	5	4	0	32	15	58	29	.298	.396	.353
	LA/NL		52	140	113	22	2	0	0	24	25	2	1	32	5	0	3	2	2	10	3	.195	.345	.212
92	LA/NL		149	598	534	139	20	8	1	178	57	4	0	98	5	1	5	23	16	67	30	.260	.331	.333
93	LA/NL		158	696	590	159	21	6	1	195	71	7	2	75	12	25	8	30	13	77	62	.269	.346	.331
4 YR TOTALS			**388**	**1497**	**1295**	**329**	**43**	**14**	**3**	**409**	**157**	**14**	**3**	**219**	**22**	**32**	**10**	**57**	**31**	**161**	**102**	**.254**	**.334**	**.316**

O'Leary, Troy Franklin — BL/TL — b.8/4/69 — POS OF-19   MIL87 14/331

YR	TM/LG	CL	G	TPA	AB	H	2B	3B	HR	TB	BB	IBB	HB	SO	GDP	SH	SF	SB	CS	R	RBI	BA	OBA	SA
87	HEL/PIO	R+	3	5	5	2	0	0	0	2	0	0	0	0	0	0	0	0	0	0	1	.400	.400	.400
88	HEL/PIO	R+	67	243	203	70	11	1	0	83	30	1	3	32	4	3	5	10	8	40	27	.345	.425	.409
89	BEL/MID	A	42	130	115	21	4	0	0	25	15	1	0	20	3	0	0	1	8	7	8	.183	.277	.217
	HEL/PIO	R+	68	305	263	89	16	3	11	144	28	2	9	43	6	9	3	9	7	54	56	.338	.402	.548
90	BEL/MID	A	118	486	436	130	29	1	6	179	41	2	0	90	4	3	3	12	12	73	62	.298	.356	.411
	STO/CAL	A+	2	8	6	3	1	0	0	4	2	1	0	1	0	0	0	0	0	1	0	.500	.625	.667
91	STO/CAL	A+	126	500	418	110	20	4	5	153	73	5	5	96	6	1	3	4	9	63	46	.263	.377	.366
92	EP/TEX	AA	135	577	506	169	27	8	5	227	59	6	1	87	7	3	8	28	16	92	79	.334	.399	.449
93	NO/AMA	AAA	111	444	388	106	32	1	7	161	43	7	2	84	12	0	5	6	3	65	59	.273	.345	.415
	MIL/AL		19	49	41	12	3	0	0	15	5	0	0	9	1	0	0	0	0	3	3	.293	.370	.366

Olerud, John Garrett — BL/TL — b.8/5/68 — POS 1B-428, DH-113   TOR89 4/79

YR	TM/LG	CL	G	TPA	AB	H	2B	3B	HR	TB	BB	IBB	HB	SO	GDP	SH	SF	SB	CS	R	RBI	BA	OBA	SA
89	TOR/AL		6	8	8	3	0	0	0	3	0	0	0	3	0	0	0	0	0	2	0	.375	.375	.375
90	TOR/AL		111	421	358	95	15	1	14	154	57	6	1	75	5	1	4	0	2	43	48	.265	.364	.430
91	TOR/AL		139	541	454	116	30	1	17	199	68	9	6	84	12	3	10	0	2	64	68	.256	.353	.438
92	TOR/AL		138	537	458	130	28	0	16	206	70	11	1	61	15	1	7	1	0	68	66	.284	.375	.450
93	TOR/AL		158	679	551	200	*54	1	24	330	114	33	7	65	12	0	7	0	2	109	107	*.363	*.473	.599
5 YR TOTALS			**552**	**2186**	**1829**	**544**	**127**	**4**	**71**	**892**	**309**	**59**	**15**	**286**	**44**	**5**	**28**	**1**	**6**	**286**	**289**	**.297**	**.398**	**.488**

Oliver, Joseph Melton "Joe" — BR/TR — b.7/24/65 — POS C-529, 1B-13, OF-1   CIN83 3/41

YR	TM/LG	CL	G	TPA	AB	H	2B	3B	HR	TB	BB	IBB	HB	SO	GDP	SH	SF	SB	CS	R	RBI	BA	OBA	SA
84	CR/MID	A	102	363	335	73	11	0	3	93	17	1	4	83	11	4	3	2	2	34	29	.218	.262	.278
85	TAM/FSL	A+	112	428	386	104	23	2	7	152	32	3	1	75	9	4	5	1	5	38	62	.269	.323	.394
86	VER/EAS	AA	84	308	282	78	18	1	6	116	21	1	0	47	12	5	2	2	1	32	41	.277	.321	.411

Oliver, Joseph Melton "Joe" (continued)

YR	TM/LG	CL	G	TPA	AB	H	2B	3B	HR	TB	BB	IBB	HB	SO	GDP	SH	SF	SB	CS	R	RBI	BA	OBA	SA
87	VER/EAS	AA	66	264	236	72	13	2	10	119	17	2	3	30	2	1	7	0	3	31	60	.305	.350	.504
88	NAS/AMA	AA	73	244	220	45	7	2	4	68	18	1	3	39	9	1	2	0	1	19	24	.205	.272	.309
	CHT/SOU	AA	28	112	105	26	6	0	3	41	5	0	2	19	3	0	0	0	0	9	12	.248	.295	.390
89	NAS/AMA	AAA	71	255	233	68	13	0	6	99	13	1	3	35	3	1	5	0	0	22	31	.292	.331	.425
	CIN/NL		49	161	151	41	8	0	3	58	6	1	1	28	3	1	2	0	0	13	23	.272	.300	.384
90	CIN/NL		121	409	364	84	23	0	8	131	37	15	2	75	6	5	1	1	1	34	52	.231	.304	.360
91	CIN/NL		94	291	269	58	11	0	11	102	18	5	0	53	14	4	0	0	1	21	41	.216	.265	.379
92	CIN/NL		143	534	485	131	25	1	10	188	35	19	1	75	12	6	7	2	3	42	57	.270	.316	.388
93	CIN/NL		139	521	482	115	28	0	14	185	27	2	1	91	13	2	9	0	0	40	75	.239	.276	.384
5 YR TOTALS			**546**	**1916**	**1751**	**429**	**95**	**1**	**46**	**664**	**123**	**42**	**5**	**322**	**48**	**18**	**19**	**3**	**4**	**150**	**248**	**.245**	**.293**	**.379**

Olson, Gregory William "Greg" — BR/TR — b.9/6/60 — POS C-402, 3B-1   NYN82 7/163

YR	TM/LG	CL	G	TPA	AB	H	2B	3B	HR	TB	BB	IBB	HB	SO	GDP	SH	SF	SB	CS	R	RBI	BA	OBA	SA
84	JAC/TEX	AA	74	272	234	55	9	0	0	64	30	5	1	16	10	5	2	1	1	27	22	.235	.322	.274
85	JAC/TEX	AA	69	240	211	57	7	0	1	67	23	1	1	20	4	3	2	1	3	21	32	.270	.342	.318
86	JAC/TEX	AA	64	231	196	39	5	1	2	52	30	0	1	16	4	3	1	0	0	28	16	.199	.307	.265
	TID/INT	AAA	19	62	55	18	1	0	0	19	5	0	0	7	4	1	1	0	0	11	7	.327	.377	.345
87	TID/INT	AAA	47	138	120	34	8	1	2	50	14	1	0	13	1	2	2	0	0	15	15	.283	.353	.417
88	TID/INT	AAA	115	397	344	92	19	1	6	131	42	2	4	42	12	1	6	0	0	39	48	.267	.348	.381
89	MIN/AL		3	2	2	1	0	0	0	1	0	0	0	0	0	0	0	0	0	0	0	.500	.500	.500
	POR/PCL	AAA	79	303	247	58	8	2	6	88	45	2	3	27	10	3	5	3	2	38	38	.235	.353	.356
90	RIC/INT	AAA	3	7	7	0	0	0	0	0	0	0	0	0	0	0	0	0	0	0	0	.000	.000	.000
	ATL/NL		100	332	298	78	12	1	7	113	30	4	2	55	8	1	1	1	1	36	36	.262	.332	.379
91	ATL/NL		133	464	411	99	25	0	6	142	44	3	3	48	13	2	4	1	1	46	44	.241	.316	.345
92	ATL/NL		95	340	302	72	14	2	3	99	34	4	1	31	8	1	2	1	0	27	27	.238	.316	.328
93	ATL/NL		83	295	262	59	10	0	4	81	29	0	1	27	11	2	1	1	0	23	24	.225	.304	.309
5 YR TOTALS			**414**	**1433**	**1275**	**309**	**61**	**3**	**20**	**436**	**137**	**11**	**7**	**157**	**40**	**6**	**8**	**5**	**3**	**132**	**131**	**.242**	**.317**	**.342**

O'Neill, Paul Andrew — BL/TL — b.2/25/63 — POS OF-849, 1B-23, DH-2, P-1   CIN81 4/93

YR	TM/LG	CL	G	TPA	AB	H	2B	3B	HR	TB	BB	IBB	HB	SO	GDP	SH	SF	SB	CS	R	RBI	BA	OBA	SA
84	VER/EAS	AA	134	536	475	126	31	5	16	215	52	6	2	72	4	0	7	29	11	70	76	.265	.336	.453
85	DEN/AMA	AAA	137	545	509	155	32	3	7	214	28	4	1	73	11	1	6	5	7	63	74	.305	.338	.420
	CIN/NL		5	12	12	4	1	0	0	5	0	0	0	2	0	0	0	0	0	1	1	.333	.333	.417
86	CIN/NL		3	3	2	0	0	0	0	0	1	0	0	1	0	0	0	0	0	0	0	.000	.333	.000
	DEN/AMA	AAA	55	206	193	49	9	2	5	77	9	3	2	28	6	0	1	1	1	20	27	.254	.291	.399
87	NAS/AMA	AAA	11	43	37	11	0	0	3	20	5	0	0	5	3	0	1	1	0	12	6	.297	.372	.541
	CIN/NL		84	178	160	41	14	1	7	78	18	1	0	29	3	0	0	2	1	24	28	.256	.331	.488
88	CIN/NL		145	533	485	122	25	3	16	201	38	5	2	65	7	3	5	8	6	58	73	.252	.306	.414
89	NAS/AMA	AAA	4	15	12	4	0	0	0	4	3	0	0	1	0	0	0	1	1	1	0	.333	.467	.333
	CIN/NL		117	480	428	118	24	2	15	191	46	8	2	64	7		4	20	5	49	74	.276	.346	.446
90	CIN/NL		145	564	503	136	28	0	16	212	53	13	1	103	12	1	5	13	11	59	78	.270	.339	.421
91	CIN/NL		152	607	532	136	36	0	28	256	73	14	1	107	8	0	1	6	3	71	91	.256	.346	.481
92	CIN/NL		148	584	496	122	19	1	14	185	77	15	2	85	10	3	6	6	3	59	66	.246	.346	.373
93	NY/AL		141	547	498	155	34	1	20	251	44	5	2	69	13	0	3	2	4	71	75	.311	.367	.504
9 YR TOTALS			**940**	**3508**	**3116**	**834**	**181**	**8**	**116**	**1379**	**350**	**61**	**11**	**525**	**60**	**7**	**24**	**63**	**37**	**392**	**486**	**.268**	**.341**	**.443**

Oquendo, Jose Manuel — BB/TR — b.7/4/63 — POS 2B-571, SS-312, OF-62, 3B-56, 1B-23, P-3, C-1   NYN 4/15/79

YR	TM/LG	CL	G	TPA	AB	H	2B	3B	HR	TB	BB	IBB	HB	SO	GDP	SH	SF	SB	CS	R	RBI	BA	OBA	SA
83	NY/NL		120	353	328	70	7	0	1	80	19	2	2	60	10	3	1	8	9	29	17	.213	.260	.244
84	TID/INT	AAA	38	120	113	18	1	0	1	22	5	0	1	14	3	1	0	8	1	8	8	.159	.202	.195
	NY/NL		81	211	189	42	5	0	0	47	15	2	2	26	2	3	2	10	1	23	10	.222	.284	.249
85	LOU/AMA	AAA	133	432	384	81	8	1	1	94	24	0	5	41	9	15	4	13	4	38	30	.211	.264	.245
86	STL/NL		76	158	138	41	4	0	0	47	15	4	0	20	3	2	3	2	3	20	13	.297	.359	.341
87	STL/NL		116	312	248	71	9	0	1	83	54	6	0	29	6	4	4	4	4	43	24	.286	.408	.335
88	STL/NL		148	518	451	125	10	1	7	158	52	7	0	40	12	8	7	3	4	36	46	.277	.350	.350
89	STL/NL		163	650	556	162	28	7	1	207	79	7	0	59	12	8	3	3	5	59	48	.291	.375	.372
90	STL/NL		156	553	469	118	17	5	1	148	74	8	0	46	7	5	5	1	1	38	37	.252	.350	.316
91	STL/NL		127	441	366	88	11	4	1	110	67	13	1	48	5	4	5	2	1	37	26	.240	.357	.301
92	ARK/TEX	AA	2	7	7	3	0	0	0	3	0	0	0	0	0	0	0	0	0	3	1	.429	.429	.429
	LOU/AMA	AAA	20	76	64	17	2	0	0	19	11	0	0	3	3	0	1	0	0	3	8	.266	.368	.297
	STL/NL		14	40	35	9	3	1	0	14	5	1	0	3	0	0	0	0	0	3	3	.257	.350	.400
93	STL/NL		46	89	73	15	0	0	0	15	12	1	0	8	5	0	0	0	0	7	4	.205	.314	.205
10 YR TOTALS			**1047**	**3325**	**2853**	**741**	**94**	**19**	**12**	**909**	**392**	**51**	**5**	**339**	**58**	**45**	**30**	**33**	**31**	**295**	**228**	**.260**	**.347**	**.319**

Orsulak, Joseph Michael "Joe" — BL/TL — b.5/31/62 — POS OF-955, DH-13, 1B-4   PIT80 7/153

YR	TM/LG	CL	G	TPA	AB	H	2B	3B	HR	TB	BB	IBB	HB	SO	GDP	SH	SF	SB	CS	R	RBI	BA	OBA	SA
83	PIT/NL		7	12	11	2	0	0	0	2	0	0	0	1	0	1	0	0	1	0	1	.182	.167	.182
84	HAW/PCL	AAA	98	425	388	110	19	12	3	162	29	5	2	38	4	3	3	14	12	51	53	.284	.334	.418
	PIT/NL		32	73	67	17	1	2	0	22	1	0	1	7	0	0	3	3	1	12	3	.254	.271	.328
85	PIT/NL		121	436	397	119	14	6	0	145	26	3	1	27	5	9	3	24	11	54	21	.300	.342	.365
86	PIT/NL		138	437	401	100	19	6	2	137	28	2	1	38	4	6	1	24	11	60	19	.249	.299	.342
87	VAN/PCL	AAA	39	165	143	33	6	0	1	44	17	0	1	30	7	2	3	5	4	48	27	.288	.331	.422
88	BAL/AL		125	416	379	109	21	3	8	160	23	2	8	35	4	1	5	9	7	59	55	.288	.351	.421
89	BAL/AL		123	446	390	111	22	5	7	164	41	4	0	35	7	4	6	5	6	49	57	.285	.343	.420
90	BAL/AL		124	465	413	111	14	3	11	164	46	9	4	48	7	4	6	6	5	49	57	.269	.343	.397
91	BAL/AL		143	521	486	135	22	1	5	174	28	4	2	45	9	4	5	6	6	57	43	.278	.321	.358
92	BAL/AL		117	428	391	113	18	3	4	149	28	5	2	34	3	4	1	5	6	45	39	.289	.342	.381

(continued)

Orsulak, Joseph Michael "Joe" (continued)

YR	TM/LG	CL	G	TPA	AB	H	2B	3B	HR	TB	BB	IBB	HB	SO	GDP	SH	SF	SB	CS	R	RBI	BA	OBA	SA
93	NY/NL		134	441	409	116	15	4	8	163	28	1	2	25	6	0	2	5	4	59	35	.284	.331	.399
10 YR TOTALS			1064	3675	3344	933	146	33	45	1280	249	29	19	291	49	41	22	87	53	443	300	**.279**	**.330**	**.383**

Ortiz, Adalberto Colon "Junior" — BR/TR — b.10/24/59 — POS C-674, DH-3   PIT 1/18/77

YR	TM/LG	CL	G	TPA	AB	H	2B	3B	HR	TB	BB	IBB	HB	SO	GDP	SH	SF	SB	CS	R	RBI	BA	OBA	SA
82	PIT/NL		7	16	15	3	1	0	0	4	1	0	0	3	1	0	0	0	0	1	0	.200	.250	.267
83	PIT/NL		5	10	8	1	0	0	0	1	1	0	0	0	0	0	0	0	0	1	0	.125	.222	.125
	NY/NL		68	190	185	47	5	0	0	52	3	0	1	34	1	1	0	1	0	10	12	.254	.270	.281
	YEAR		73	200	193	48	5	0	0	53	4	0	1	34	1	2	0	1	0	11	12	.249	.268	.275
84	NY/NL		40	98	91	18	3	0	0	21	5	0	0	15	2	0	2	1	0	6	11	.198	.235	.231
85	PIT/NL		23	76	72	21	2	0	1	26	3	1	0	17	1	1	0	1	0	4	5	.292	.320	.361
86	PIT/NL		49	122	110	37	6	0	0	43	9	0	0	13	4	1	2	0	1	11	14	.336	.380	.391
87	PIT/NL		75	213	192	52	8	1	1	65	15	1	0	23	6	5	1	0	2	16	22	.271	.322	.339
88	PIT/NL		49	132	118	33	6	0	2	45	9	0	2	9	6	1	2	1	2	8	18	.280	.336	.381
89	PIT/NL		91	258	230	50	6	1	1	61	20	4	2	20	9	3	3	2	4	16	22	.217	.282	.265
90	MIN/AL		71	187	170	57	7	1	0	66	12	0	2	16	4	2	1	0	4	18	18	.335	.384	.388
91	MIN/AL		61	151	134	28	5	1	0	35	15	0	1	12	6	1	0	0	1	9	11	.209	.293	.261
92	CLE/AL		86	262	244	61	7	0	0	68	12	0	4	23	7	2	0	0	1	20	24	.250	.296	.279
93	CLE/AL		95	270	249	55	13	0	0	68	11	1	5	26	10	4	1	1	0	19	20	.221	.267	.273
12 YR TOTALS			720	1985	1818	463	69	4	5	555	116	7	17	211	57	22	12	8	17	139	177	**.255**	**.304**	**.305**

Ortiz, Luis Alberto — BR/TR — b.5/25/70 — POS 3B-5, DH-3   BOS91 11/226

YR	TM/LG	CL	G	TPA	AB	H	2B	3B	HR	TB	BB	IBB	HB	SO	GDP	SH	SF	SB	CS	R	RBI	BA	OBA	SA
91	RS/GCL	R	42	164	153	51	11	2	4	78	8	0	2	9	1	0	1	2	1	21	29	.333	.372	.510
92	LYN/CAR	A+	94	384	355	103	27	1	10	162	22	3	2	55	8	0	5	4	2	43	61	.290	.331	.456
93	PAW/INT	AAA	102	421	402	118	28	1	18	202	13	3	4	74	10	0	4	1	1	45	81	.294	.316	.502
	BOS/AL		9	12	12	3	0	0	0	3	0	0	0	2	0	0	0	0	0	0	1	.250	.250	.250

Orton, John Andrew — BR/TR — b.12/8/65 — POS C-153, DH-1, OF-1   CAL87 1/25

YR	TM/LG	CL	G	TPA	AB	H	2B	3B	HR	TB	BB	IBB	HB	SO	GDP	SH	SF	SB	CS	R	RBI	BA	OBA	SA
87	SAL/NWL	A-	51	218	176	46	8	1	8	80	32	1	7	61	5	1	2	6	2	31	36	.261	.392	.455
	MID/TEX	AA	5	16	13	2	1	0	0	3	2	0	1	3	0	0	0	0	0	1	0	.154	.313	.231
88	PS/CAL	A+	68	287	230	46	6	1	1	57	45	0	10	79	4	2	0	0	0	42	28	.200	.354	.248
89	MID/TEX	AA	99	401	344	80	20	6	10	142	37	1	7	102	5	6	7	2	2	51	53	.233	.314	.413
	CAL/AL		16	42	39	7	1	0	0	8	2	0	0	17	0	1	0	0	0	4	4	.179	.220	.205
90	EDM/PCL	AAA	50	195	174	42	8	0	6	68	19	1	0	63	7	1	1	4	2	29	26	.241	.314	.391
	CAL/AL		31	92	84	16	5	0	1	24	5	0	1	31	2	2	0	1	0	8	6	.190	.244	.286
91	EDM/PCL	AAA	76	287	245	55	14	1	5	86	31	0	4	66	4	4	2	5	5	39	32	.224	.322	.351
	CAL/AL		29	84	69	14	4	0	0	18	10	0	1	17	2	4	0	0	1	7	3	.203	.313	.261
92	EDM/PCL	AAA	49	186	149	38	9	2	1	62	28	0	3	32	3	4	2	3	5	28	25	.255	.379	.416
	CAL/AL		43	125	114	25	3	0	1	34	7	0	2	32	1	2	0	1	1	11	12	.219	.276	.298
93	CAL/AL		37	105	95	18	5	0	1	26	7	0	1	24	1	2	0	2	1	5	4	.189	.252	.274
	PS/CAL	A+	2	8	7	0	0	0	0	0	1	0	0	1	0	0	0	0	0	0	0	.000	.125	.000
5 YR TOTALS			156	448	401	80	18	0	4	110	31	0	5	121	6	11	0	2	5	35	29	**.200**	**.265**	**.274**

Owen, Spike Dee — BB/TR — b.4/19/61 — POS SS-1343, DH-9   SEA82 1/6

YR	TM/LG	CL	G	TPA	AB	H	2B	3B	HR	TB	BB	IBB	HB	SO	GDP	SH	SF	SB	CS	R	RBI	BA	OBA	SA
83	SEA/AL		80	340	306	60	11	3	2	83	24	0	2	44	2	5	3	10	6	36	21	.196	.257	.271
84	SEA/AL		152	590	530	130	18	8	3	173	46	0	3	63	5	9	2	16	8	67	43	.245	.308	.326
85	SEA/AL		118	393	352	91	10	6	6	131	34	0	0	27	5	5	2	11	5	41	37	.259	.322	.372
86	SEA/AL		112	446	402	99	22	6	0	133	34	1	1	42	11	7	2	11	3	46	35	.246	.305	.331
	BOS/AL		42	147	126	23	2	1	1	30	17	0	1	9	2	1	1	3	1	21	10	.183	.283	.238
	YEAR		154	593	528	122	24	7	1	163	51	1	2	51	13	8	3	14	4	67	45	.231	.300	.309
87	BOS/AL		132	504	437	113	17	7	2	150	53	2	1	43	9	9	4	11	8	50	48	.259	.337	.343
88	BOS/AL		89	294	257	64	14	1	5	95	27	0	2	27	7	7	1	0	1	40	18	.249	.324	.370
89	MON/NL		142	522	437	102	17	4	6	145	76	25	3	44	11	3	3	6	5	52	41	.233	.349	.332
90	MON/NL		149	533	453	106	24	5	5	155	70	12	3	60	6	5	2	8	6	55	35	.234	.333	.342
91	MON/NL		139	475	424	108	22	8	3	155	42	11	1	61	11	4	4	2	6	39	26	.255	.321	.366
92	MON/NL		122	446	386	104	16	3	7	147	50	3	0	30	10	6	4	9	4	52	40	.269	.348	.381
93	NY/AL		103	367	334	78	16	2	2	104	29	2	0	30	4	4	0	3	2	41	20	.234	.294	.311
11 YR TOTALS			1380	5057	4444	1078	189	54	42	1501	502	56	14	480	85	63	34	77	52	540	374	**.243**	**.319**	**.338**

Owens, Claude Jayhawk "J" — BR/TR — b.2/10/69 — POS C-32   MIN90 3/52

YR	TM/LG	CL	G	TPA	AB	H	2B	3B	HR	TB	BB	IBB	HB	SO	GDP	SH	SF	SB	CS	R	RBI	BA	OBA	SA
90	KEN/MID	A	66	270	216	51	9	2	5	79	39	0	13	59	8	1	1	15	7	31	30	.236	.383	.366
91	VIS/CAL	A+	65	278	233	57	17	1	6	94	35	1	8	70	4	0	2	14	6	33	33	.245	.360	.403
92	ORL/SOU	AA	102	382	330	88	24	0	4	124	36	0	11	67	5	0	5	10	2	50	30	.267	.353	.376
93	CS/PCL	AAA	55	203	174	54	11	3	6	89	21	0	5	56	4	0	3	6	3	24	43	.310	.394	.511
	COL/NL		33	94	86	18	5	0	3	32	6	1	2	30	1	0	0	0	1	12	6	.209	.277	.372

Pagliarulo, Michael Timothy "Mike" — BL/TR — b.3/15/60 — POS 3B-1111, 1B-5, SS-2, DH-2, 2B-1   NYA81 6/155

YR	TM/LG	CL	G	TPA	AB	H	2B	3B	HR	TB	BB	IBB	HB	SO	GDP	SH	SF	SB	CS	R	RBI	BA	OBA	SA
84	CMB/INT	AAA	58	169	146	31	5	1	7	59	18	0	0	30	2	3	0	0	0	24	25	.212	.293	.404
	NY/AL		67	219	201	48	15	3	7	90	15	0	0	46	5	0	3	0	0	24	34	.239	.288	.448
85	NY/AL		138	435	380	91	16	2	19	168	45	4	4	86	6	3	3	0	0	55	62	.239	.324	.442
86	NY/AL		149	565	504	120	24	3	28	234	54	10	4	120	10	1	2	4	1	71	71	.238	.316	.464
87	NY/AL		150	582	522	122	26	3	32	250	53	9	2	111	9	2	3	1	3	76	87	.234	.305	.479

Pagliarulo, Michael Timothy "Mike" (continued)

YR	TM/LG	CL	G	TPA	AB	H	2B	3B	HR	TB	BB	IBB	HB	SO	GDP	SH	SF	SB	CS	R	RBI	BA	OBA	SA
88	NY/AL		125	490	444	96	20	1	15	163	37	9	2	104	5		1	6	1	0	46	67	.216	.276	.367
89	NY/AL		74	244	223	44	10	0	4	66	19	0	2	43	2	0	0	1	1	1	19	16	.197	.266	.296
	SD/NL		50	168	148	29	7	0	3	45	18	4	1	39	3	1	0	2	0		12	14	.196	.287	.304
	YEAR		124	412	371	73	17	0	7	111	37	4	3	82	5	1	0	3	1	1	31	30	.197	.275	.299
90	SD/NL		128	446	398	101	23	2	7	149	39	3	3	66	12	2	4	1	3		29	38	.254	.322	.374
91	MIN/AL		121	393	365	102	20	0	6	140	21	3	3	55	9	2	2	1	2		38	36	.279	.322	.384
92	MIR/FSL	A+	6	24	20	4	2	0	0	6	4	0	0	2	1	0	0	1	0		2	2	.200	.333	.300
	MIN/AL		42	108	105	21	4	0	0	25	1	0	1	17	1	0	1	1	0		10	9	.200	.213	.238
93	MIN/AL		83	279	253	74	16	4	3	107	18	2	5	34	5	2	1	6	6		31	23	.292	.350	.423
	BAL/AL		33	126	117	38	9	0	6	65	8	0	1	15	2	0	0	0	0		24	21	.325	.373	.556
	YEAR		116	405	370	112	25	4	9	172	26	2	6	49	7	2	1	6	6		55	44	.303	.357	.465
10 YR TOTALS			**1160**	**4055**	**3660**	**886**	**190**	**18**	**130**	**1502**	**328**	**44**	**28**	**736**	**69**	**14**	**25**	**18**	**16**		**435**	**478**	**.242**	**.307**	**.410**

Pagnozzi, Thomas Alan "Tom" — BR/TR — b.7/30/62 — POS C-523, 1B-36, 3B-6   SL83 8/208

YR	TM/LG	CL	G	TPA	AB	H	2B	3B	HR	TB	BB	IBB	HB	SO	GDP	SH	SF	SB	CS	R	RBI	BA	OBA	SA
84	SPR/MID	A	114	442	396	112	20	4	10	170	31	3	4	75	9	4	7	3	4	57	68	.283	.336	.429
85	ARK/TEX	AA	41	153	139	43	7	1	5	67	13	1	0	21	8	1	0	0	0	15	29	.309	.368	.482
	LOU/AMA	AAA	76	296	268	72	13	2	5	104	21	1	3	47	11	0	4	0	1	29	40	.269	.324	.388
86	LOU/AMA	AAA	30	113	106	31	4	0	1	38	6	0	1	21	3	0	0	0	0	12	18	.292	.336	.358
87	LOU/AMA	AAA	84	359	320	100	20	2	14	166	30	0	3	50	16	0	6	0	0	53	71	.313	.370	.519
	STL/NL		27	53	48	9	1	0	2	16	4	2	0	13	1	0	1	0	0	8	9	.188	.250	.333
88	STL/NL		81	209	195	55	9	0	0	64	11	1	0	32	5	2	1	0	1	17	15	.282	.319	.328
89	STL/NL		52	88	80	12	2	0	0	14	6	2	1	19	7	0	1	0	0	3	3	.150	.216	.175
90	STL/NL		69	237	220	61	15	0	2	82	14	1	1	37	10	0	2	1	1	20	23	.277	.321	.373
91	STL/NL		140	510	459	121	24	5	2	161	36	4	6	63	10	6	5	9	13	38	57	.264	.319	.351
92	STL/NL		139	523	485	121	26	3	7	174	28	9	1	64	15	6	3	2	5	33	44	.249	.290	.359
93	LOU/AMA	AAA	12	45	43	12	3	0	1	18	2	0	0	3	1	0	0	0	0	5	1	.279	.311	.419
	STL/NL		92	355	330	85	15	1	7	123	19	6	1	30	7	0	5	1	0	31	41	.258	.296	.373
7 YR TOTALS			**600**	**1975**	**1817**	**464**	**92**	**9**	**20**	**634**	**118**	**27**	**8**	**258**	**44**	**15**	**17**	**14**	**19**	**150**	**192**	**.255**	**.301**	**.349**

Palmeiro, Rafael — BL/TL — b.9/24/64 — POS 1B-789, OF-212, DH-16   CHN85 1/22

YR	TM/LG	CL	G	TPA	AB	H	2B	3B	HR	TB	BB	IBB	HB	SO	GDP	SH	SF	SB	CS	R	RBI	BA	OBA	SA
85	PEO/MID	A	73	315	279	83	22	4	5	128	31	2	2	34	4	1	2	9	3	34	51	.297	.369	.459
86	PIT/EAS	AA	140	579	509	156	29	2	12	225	54	13	3	32	8	1	13	15	7	66	95	.306	.367	.442
	CHI/NL		22	78	73	18	4	0	3	31	4	0	1	6	4	0	1	1	1	9	12	.247	.295	.425
87	IOW/AMA	AAA	57	244	214	64	14	3	11	117	22	1	3	22	2	1	4	4	3	36	41	.299	.366	.547
	CHI/NL		84	244	221	61	15	1	14	120	20	1	1	26	4	0	2	2	2	32	30	.276	.336	.543
88	CHI/NL		152	629	580	178	41	5	8	253	38	6	3	34	11	2	6	12	6	75	53	.307	.349	.436
89	TEX/AL		156	632	559	154	23	4	8	209	63	3	6	48	18	2	4	4	3	76	64	.275	.354	.374
90	TEX/AL		154	651	598	*191	35	6	14	280	40	6	3	59	24	2	8	3	2	72	89	.319	.361	.468
91	TEX/AL		159	714	631	203	*49	3	26	336	68	10	6	72	17	2	7	4	2	115	88	.322	.389	.532
92	TEX/AL		159	701	608	163	27	4	22	264	72	8	10	83	10	5	6	2	3	84	85	.268	.352	.434
93	TEX/AL		160	686	597	176	40	2	37	331	73	22	5	85	8	2	9	22	3	*124	105	.295	.371	.554
8 YR TOTALS			**1046**	**4335**	**3867**	**1144**	**234**	**25**	**132**	**1824**	**378**	**56**	**35**	**413**	**96**	**15**	**40**	**50**	**20**	**587**	**526**	**.296**	**.360**	**.472**

Palmer, Dean William — BR/TR — b.12/27/68 — POS 3B-354, OF-30, DH-11, SS-2   TEX86 3/59

YR	TM/LG	CL	G	TPA	AB	H	2B	3B	HR	TB	BB	IBB	HB	SO	GDP	SH	SF	SB	CS	R	RBI	BA	OBA	SA
86	RAN/GCL	R	50	192	163	34	7	1	0	43	22	0	5	34	3	0	2	6	3	19	12	.209	.318	.264
87	GAS/SAL	A	128	527	484	104	16	0	9	147	36	1	6	126	16	0	1	4	4	51	54	.215	.277	.304
88	CHA/FSL	A+	74	324	305	81	12	1	4	107	15	1	1	69	12	0	3	3	0	38	35	.266	.299	.351
89	TUL/TEX	AA	133	550	498	125	32	5	25	242	41	4	4	152	6	3	4	15	5	82	90	.251	.311	.486
	TEX/AL		16	20	19	2	2	0	0	4	0	0	0	12	0	0	1	0	0	0	1	.105	.100	.211
90	TUL/TEX	AA	7	29	24	7	0	1	3	18	4	1	1	10	0	0	0	0	0	4	9	.292	.414	.750
	OC/AMA	AAA	88	343	316	69	17	4	12	130	20	0	4	106	2	0	3	2	4	33	39	.218	.271	.411
91	OC/AMA	AAA	60	259	234	70	11	4	22	151	20	2	3	61	2	1	2	4	6	45	59	.299	.357	.645
	TEX/AL		81	304	268	50	9	2	15	108	32	0	3	98	4	1	0	0	2	38	37	.187	.281	.403
92	TEX/AL		152	613	541	124	25	0	26	227	62	2	4	154	9	2	4	10	4	74	72	.229	.311	.420
93	TEX/AL		148	585	519	127	31	2	33	261	53	2	4	154	5	0	5	11	10	88	96	.245	.321	.503
4 YR TOTALS			**397**	**1522**	**1347**	**303**	**67**	**4**	**74**	**600**	**147**	**6**	**15**	**418**	**18**	**3**	**10**	**21**	**16**	**200**	**206**	**.225**	**.306**	**.445**

Pappas, Erik Daniel — BR/TR — b.4/25/66 — POS C-69, OF-16, 1B-2   CAL84 1/6

YR	TM/LG	CL	G	TPA	AB	H	2B	3B	HR	TB	BB	IBB	HB	SO	GDP	SH	SF	SB	CS	R	RBI	BA	OBA	SA
84	SAL/NWL	A-	56	215	177	43	3	3	1	55	31	0	3	26	1	3	1	10	5	24	15	.243	.363	.311
85	QC/MID	A	100	385	317	76	8	4	2	98	61	0	3	56	3	3	1	16	6	53	29	.240	.366	.309
86	PS/CAL	A+	74	310	248	61	16	2	5	96	56	1	1	58	7	1	4	9	5	40	38	.246	.382	.387
87	PS/CAL	A+	119	471	395	96	20	3	3	131	66	0	3	53	6	1	4	16	3	40	38	.243	.346	.332
88	MID/TEX	AA	83	314	275	76	17	2	4	109	29	0	4	53	6	4	4	4	3	40	38	.276	.345	.396
89	CHA/SOU	AA	119	434	354	106	31	1	16	187	66	1	8	50	8	4	2	7	8	69	49	.299	.419	.528
90	IOW/AMA	AAA	131	487	405	101	19	2	16	172	65	1	8	84	13	6	6	5	5	56	55	.249	.362	.425
91	CHI/NL		7	18	17	3	0	0	0	3	1	0	0	5	0	0	0	0	0	1	2	.176	.222	.176
	IOW/AMA	AAA	88	340	284	78	19	1	7	120	45	2	3	47	12	4	5	3	3	41	48	.275	.378	.423
92	OMA/AMA	AAA	45	166	138	30	8	1	4	52	23	0	3	23	3	1	2	0	0	17	17	.217	.333	.377
	VAN/PCL	AAA	37	117	98	27	4	0	4	43	14	0	2	17	3	1	2	0	0	19	13	.276	.371	.439
93	LOU/AMA	AAA	21	82	71	24	4	0	4	44	11	0	0	15	1	0	0	0	2	19	13	.338	.427	.620
	STL/NL		82	266	228	63	12	0	1	78	35	2	0	35	7	0	3	1	3	25	28	.276	.368	.342
2 YR TOTALS			**89**	**284**	**245**	**66**	**12**	**0**	**1**	**81**	**36**	**2**	**0**	**40**	**7**	**0**	**3**	**1**	**3**	**26**	**30**	**.269**	**.359**	**.331**

Paquette, Craig Howard — BR/TR — b.3/28/69 — POS 3B-104, OF-1, DH-1   OAK89 7/218

YR	TM/LG	CL	G	TPA	AB	H	2B	3B	HR	TB	BB	IBB	HB	SO	GDP	SH	SF	SB	CS	R	RBI	BA	OBA	SA
89	SO/NWL	A-	71	310	277	93	22	3	14	163	30	4	2	46	6	0	1	9	4	53	56	.336	.403	.588
90	MOD/CAL	A+	130	549	495	118	23	4	15	194	47	1	3	123	10	0	4	8	5	65	59	.238	.306	.392
91	HUN/SOU	AA	102	416	378	99	18	1	8	143	28	0	3	87	16	2	5	0	5	50	60	.262	.314	.378
92	HUN/SOU	AA	115	485	450	116	25	4	17	200	29	0	2	118	12	1	3	13	10	59	71	.258	.304	.444
	TAC/PCL	AAA	17	68	66	18	7	0	2	31	2	0	0	16	3	0	0	3	1	10	11	.273	.294	.470
93	TAC/PCL	AAA	50	200	183	49	8	0	8	81	14	0	0	54	6	0	2	3	3	29	29	.268	.320	.443
	OAK/AL		105	409	393	86	20	4	12	150	14	2	0	108	7	1	1	4	2	35	46	.219	.245	.382

Parent, Mark Alan — BR/TR — b.9/16/61 — POS C-190, 1B-1, DH-1   SD79 5/92

YR	TM/LG	CL	G	TPA	AB	H	2B	3B	HR	TB	BB	IBB	HB	SO	GDP	SH	SF	SB	CS	R	RBI	BA	OBA	SA
84	BEA/TEX		111	430	380	109	24	3	7	160	38	5	1	39	18	4	7	1	4	52	60	.287	.347	.421
85	LV/PCL	AAA	105	392	361	87	23	3	7	137	29	2	0	58	10	1	1	1	3	36	45	.241	.297	.380
86	LV/PCL	AAA	86	295	267	77	10	4	5	110	23	2	0	25	10	1	4	0	3	29	40	.288	.340	.412
	SD/NL		8	15	14	2	0	0	0	2	1	0	0	3	1	0	0	0	0	1	0	.143	.200	.143
87	LV/PCL	AAA	105	429	387	113	23	2	4	152	38	3	1	53	16	1	2	2	1	50	43	.292	.355	.393
	SD/NL		12	25	25	2	0	0	0	2	0	0	0	9	0	0	0	0	0	0	2	.080	.080	.080
88	SD/NL		41	125	118	23	3	0	6	44	6	0	0	23	1	0	1	0	0	9	15	.195	.232	.373
89	SD/NL		52	154	141	27	4	0	7	52	8	2	0	34	5	1	4	0	1	12	21	.191	.229	.369
90	SD/NL		65	208	189	42	11	0	3	62	16	3	1	29	2	1	3	0	1	13	16	.222	.283	.328
91	OC/AMA	AAA	5	9	8	2	0	0	0	2	0	0	0	1	0	0	1	0	0	0	1	.250	.222	.250
	TEX/AL		3	1	1	0	0	0	0	0	0	0	0	0	1	0	0	0	0	0	0	.000	.000	.000
92	ROC/INT	AAA	101	394	356	102	24	0	17	177	35	1	0	64	14	0	3	4	3	52	69	.287	.348	.497
	BAL/AL		17	40	34	8	1	0	2	15	3	0	0	7	0	2	0	0	0	4	4	.235	.316	.441
93	ROC/INT	AAA	92	373	332	82	15	0	14	139	40	0	0	71	12	0	2	0	0	47	56	.247	.327	.419
	BAL/AL		22	61	54	14	2	0	4	28	3	0	0	14	0	1	0	0	1	7	12	.259	.293	.519
8 YR TOTALS			**220**	**629**	**576**	**118**	**21**	**0**	**22**	**205**	**37**	**5**	**1**	**120**	**10**	**9**	**6**	**2**	**0**	**46**	**70**	**.205**	**.252**	**.356**

Parker, Richard Alan "Rick" — BR/TR — b.3/20/63 — POS OF-55, 2B-3, SS-2, 3B-1   PHI85 17/408

YR	TM/LG	CL	G	TPA	AB	H	2B	3B	HR	TB	BB	IBB	HB	SO	GDP	SH	SF	SB	CS	R	RBI	BA	OBA	SA
85	BEN/NWL	A-	55	252	205	51	9	1	2	68	40	0	4	42	2	0	3	14	7	45	20	.249	.377	.332
86	SPA/SAL	A	62	273	233	69	7	3	5	97	36	0	2	39	7	2	0	14	9	39	28	.296	.395	.416
	CLE/FSL	A+	63	246	218	51	10	2	0	65	21	1	2	29	2	3	2	8	9	24	15	.234	.305	.298
87	CLE/FSL	A+	101	369	330	83	13	3	3	111	31	3	3	36	4	2	3	6	9	56	34	.252	.319	.336
88	REA/EAS	AA	116	408	362	93	13	3	3	121	36	2	3	50	6	1	6	24	6	50	47	.257	.324	.334
89	REA/EAS	AA	103	440	388	92	7	9	3	126	42	0	5	62	8	2	3	17	13	59	32	.237	.317	.325
	PHO/PCL	AAA	18	72	68	18	2	2	0	24	2	1	0	14	1	1	0	1	2	5	11	.265	.296	.353
90	PHO/PCL	AAA	44	195	173	58	7	4	1	76	22	0	1	25	1	0	0	18	10	38	18	.335	.410	.439
	SF/NL		54	121	107	26	5	0	2	37	10	1	0	15	1	3	0	5	1	19	14	.243	.314	.346
91	SF/NL		13	15	14	1	0	0	0	1	1	0	0	5	0	0	0	0	0	0	1	.071	.133	.071
	PHO/PCL	AAA	85	331	297	89	10	9	6	135	26	1	2	35	7	0	6	16	3	41	41	.300	.353	.455
92	TUC/PCL	AAA	105	353	319	103	10	11	4	147	28	0	3	36	7	3	0	20	3	51	38	.323	.383	.461
93	TUC/PCL	AAA	29	134	120	37	9	3	2	58	14	1	0	20	2	1	0	6	2	28	12	.308	.381	.483
	HOU/NL		45	49	45	15	3	0	0	18	3	0	0	6	2	1	0	1	2	11	4	.333	.375	.400
3 YR TOTALS			**112**	**185**	**166**	**42**	**8**	**0**	**2**	**56**	**14**	**0**	**0**	**28**	**3**	**4**	**0**	**7**	**3**	**30**	**19**	**.253**	**.315**	**.337**

Parks, Derek Gavin — BR/TR — b.9/29/68 — POS C-14   MIN86 1/10

YR	TM/LG	CL	G	TPA	AB	H	2B	3B	HR	TB	BB	IBB	HB	SO	GDP	SH	SF	SB	CS	R	RBI	BA	OBA	SA
86	ELI/APP	R+	62	255	224	53	10	1	10	95	23	0	5	58	3	0	3	1	0	39	40	.237	.318	.424
87	KEN/MID	A	129	559	466	115	19	2	24	210	77	5	10	111	12	0	6	1	1	70	94	.247	.361	.451
88	ORL/SOU	AA	118	469	400	94	15	0	7	130	49	1	15	81	12	0	1	1	1	52	42	.235	.337	.325
89	ORL/SOU	AA	31	120	95	18	3	0	2	27	19	0	6	27	1	0	0	0	0	16	10	.189	.358	.284
90	POR/PCL	AAA	76	258	231	41	8	1	11	84	18	0	8	56	6	0	1	0	2	27	27	.177	.260	.364
91	ORL/SOU	AA	92	304	256	55	14	0	6	87	31	1	12	65	4	2	0	0	2	30	31	.215	.325	.340
92	POR/PCL	AAA	79	288	249	61	12	0	12	109	25	0	4	47	6	4	0	0	2	33	49	.245	.317	.438
	MIN/AL		7	8	6	2	0	0	0	2	1	0	1	0	1	0	0	0	0	1	0	.333	.500	.333
93	POR/PCL	AAA	107	421	363	113	23	1	17	189	48	1	6	57	12	0	4	0	0	63	71	.311	.392	.521
	MIN/AL		7	21	20	4	0	0	0	4	1	0	0	2	0	0	0	0	0	3	1	.200	.238	.200
2 YR TOTALS			**14**	**29**	**26**	**6**	**0**	**0**	**0**	**6**	**2**	**0**	**1**	**3**	**0**	**0**	**0**	**0**	**0**	**4**	**1**	**.231**	**.310**	**.231**

Parrish, Lance Michael — BR/TR — b.6/15/56 — POS C-1713, DH-122, 1B-29, OF-6   DET74 1/16

YR	TM/LG	CL	G	TPA	AB	H	2B	3B	HR	TB	BB	IBB	HB	SO	GDP	SH	SF	SB	CS	R	RBI	BA	OBA	SA
77	DET/AL		12	51	46	9	2	0	3	20	5	0	0	12	2	0	1	0	0	10	7	.196	.275	.435
78	DET/AL		85	304	288	63	11	3	14	122	11	0	0	71	8	1	1	0	0	37	41	.219	.254	.424
79	DET/AL		143	548	493	136	26	3	19	225	49	2	2	105	15	3	1	6	7	65	65	.276	.343	.456
80	DET/AL		144	592	553	158	34	6	24	276	31	3	3	109	24	1	3	6	4	79	82	.286	.325	.499
81	DET/AL		96	384	348	85	18	2	10	137	34	0	2	52	16	1	3	2	3	39	46	.244	.311	.394
82	DET/AL		133	529	486	138	19	2	32	257	40	5	1	99	5	0	2	3	4	75	87	.284	.338	.529
83	DET/AL		155	663	605	163	42	3	27	292	44	7	1	106	21	0	13	1	3	80	114	.269	.314	.483
84	DET/AL		147	629	578	137	16	2	33	256	41	6	2	120	12	2	1	2	3	75	98	.237	.287	.443
85	DET/AL		140	600	549	150	27	1	28	263	41	5	2	90	10	1	5	2	3	64	98	.273	.323	.479
86	DET/AL		91	374	327	84	6	1	22	158	38	3	5	83	3	1	3	0	0	53	62	.257	.340	.483
87	PHI/NL		130	518	466	114	21	0	17	186	47	2	1	104	23	0	4	0	0	42	67	.245	.313	.399
88	PHI/NL		123	478	424	91	17	2	15	157	47	7	3	93	11	0	4	0	0	44	60	.215	.293	.370
89	CAL/AL		124	482	433	103	12	1	17	168	42	6	4	104	10	1	2	0	2	48	50	.238	.306	.388
90	CAL/AL		133	523	470	126	14	0	24	212	46	4	5	107	12	0	2	0	1	54	70	.268	.338	.451
91	CAL/AL		119	445	402	87	12	0	19	156	35	2	5	117	3	1	2	0	3	38	51	.216	.285	.451
92	CAL/AL		24	90	83	19	4	0	3	33	5	1	4	22	1	0	1	0	0	7	11	.229	.270	.398

Parrish, Lance Michael (continued)

YR	TM/LG	CL	G	TPA	AB	H	2B	3B	HR	TB	BB	IBB	HB	SO	GDP	SH	SF	SB	CS	R	RBI	BA	OBA	SA
	SEA/AL		69	214	192	45	11	1	8	82	19	2	1	48	6	0	2	1	1	19	21	.234	.304	.427
	YEAR		93	304	275	64	13	1	12	115	24	3	1	70	7	1	3	1	1	26	32	.233	.294	.418
93	ALB/PCL	AAA	11	41	33	9	2	0	0	11	5	0	3	4	1	0	0	0	0	4	1	.273	.415	.333
	CLE/AL		10	24	20	4	1	0	1	8	4	0	0	5	2	0	0	1	0	2	2	.200	.333	.400
17 YR TOTALS			**1878**	**7448**	**6763**	**1712**	**291**	**27**	**317**	**3008**	**579**	**61**	**35**	**1447**	**188**	**16**	**55**	**27**	**36**	**831**	**1032**	**.253**	**.313**	**.445**

Pasqua, Daniel Anthony "Dan" — BL/TL — b.10/17/61 — POS OF-590, 1B-144, DH-116 NYA82 4/76

YR	TM/LG	CL	G	TPA	AB	H	2B	3B	HR	TB	BB	IBB	HB	SO	GDP	SH	SF	SB	CS	R	RBI	BA	OBA	SA
84	NAS/SOU	AA	136	561	460	112	14	3	33	231	95	7	3	148	8	0	3	5	2	78	91	.243	.374	.502
85	CMB/INT	AAA	78	339	287	92	16	5	18	172	48	2	2	62	10	0	2	5	0	52	69	.321	.419	.599
	NY/AL		60	166	148	31	3	1	9	63	16	4	1	38	1	0	1	0	0	17	25	.209	.289	.426
86	CMB/INT	AAA	32	142	110	32	3	3	6	59	32	0	0	29	2	0	0	1	1	25	20	.291	.451	.536
	NY/AL		102	332	280	82	17	0	16	147	47	3	3	78	4	0	1	2	0	44	45	.293	.399	.525
87	CMB/INT	AAA	23	92	85	29	6	0	6	53	5	0	1	21	1	1	0	2	0	16	15	.341	.385	.624
	NY/AL		113	362	318	74	7	1	17	134	40	3	1	99	7	2	1	0	2	42	42	.233	.319	.421
88	CHI/AL		129	475	422	96	16	2	20	176	46	5	3	100	10	0	4	1	2	48	50	.227	.307	.417
89	CHI/AL		73	277	246	61	9	1	11	105	25	1	1	58	0	1	4	1	2	26	47	.248	.315	.427
90	CHI/AL		112	369	325	89	27	3	13	161	37	7	2	66	4	0	5	1	1	43	58	.274	.347	.495
91	CHI/AL		134	484	417	108	22	5	18	194	62	4	3	86	9	1	1	0	2	71	66	.259	.358	.465
92	BIR/SOU	AA	3	10	8	1	0	0	0	1	2	0	0	2	0	0	0	0	0	1	0	.125	.300	.125
	CHI/AL		93	306	265	56	16	1	6	92	36	1	1	57	4	1	3	0	1	26	33	.211	.305	.347
93	CHI/AL		78	206	176	36	10	1	5	63	26	1	0	51	3	1	3	2	2	22	20	.205	.302	.358
9 YR TOTALS			**894**	**2977**	**2597**	**633**	**127**	**15**	**115**	**1135**	**335**	**29**	**15**	**633**	**42**	**9**	**21**	**7**	**10**	**339**	**386**	**.244**	**.331**	**.437**

Patterson, John Allen — BB/TR — b.2/11/67 — POS 2B-22, OF-5 SF88 25/594

YR	TM/LG	CL	G	TPA	AB	H	2B	3B	HR	TB	BB	IBB	HB	SO	GDP	SH	SF	SB	CS	R	RBI	BA	OBA	SA
88	EVE/NWL	A-	58	251	232	58	10	4	0	76	18	0	0	27	1	0	1	21	3	37	26	.250	.303	.328
90	SJ/CAL	A+	131	596	530	160	23	6	4	207	46	2	9	74	7	5	6	29	17	91	66	.302	.364	.391
91	SHR/TEX	AA	117	511	464	137	31	13	4	206	30	2	11	63	9	3	3	41	20	81	56	.295	.350	.444
92	PHO/PCL	AAA	93	402	362	109	20	6	2	147	33	4	5	45	3	0	2	58	18	52	37	.301	.366	.406
	SF/NL		32	109	103	19	1	1	0	22	5	0	1	24	2	0	0	5	1	10	4	.184	.229	.214
93	SJ/CAL	A+	16	77	68	16	7	1	0	26	7	1	2	12	0	0	0	6	0	8	14	.235	.325	.382
	SF/NL		16	16	16	3	0	0	1	6	0	0	0	5	0	0	0	0	1	1	2	.188	.188	.375
2 YR TOTALS			**48**	**125**	**119**	**22**	**1**	**1**	**1**	**28**	**5**	**0**	**1**	**29**	**2**	**0**	**0**	**5**	**2**	**11**	**6**	**.185**	**.224**	**.235**

Pecota, William Joseph "Bill" — BR/TR — b.2/16/60 — POS 3B-241, SS-177, 2B-156, OF-32, 1B-28, DH-14, P-2, C-1 KC81* 10/234

YR	TM/LG	CL	G	TPA	AB	H	2B	3B	HR	TB	BB	IBB	HB	SO	GDP	SH	SF	SB	CS	R	RBI	BA	OBA	SA
84	MEM/SOU	AA	145	655	543	131	19	2	9	181	99	2	3	72	11	7	3	43	15	84	50	.241	.360	.333
85	OMA/AMA	AAA	130	478	409	98	17	3	1	124	57	0	5	55	14	2	5	21	10	47	34	.240	.336	.303
86	OMA/AMA	AAA	139	529	474	125	26	2	4	167	37	3	8	45	8	7	3	21	8	48	54	.264	.326	.352
	KC/AL		12	34	29	6	2	0	0	8	3	0	1	3	1	0	1	0	2	3	2	.207	.294	.276
87	OMA/AMA	AAA	35	144	126	39	8	1	2	55	15	0	2	15	1	1	0	7	1	31	16	.310	.392	.437
	KC/AL		66	172	156	43	5	1	3	59	15	0	1	25	3	0	0	5	0	22	14	.276	.343	.378
88	KC/AL		90	206	178	37	3	3	1	49	18	0	2	34	1	7	1	7	2	25	15	.208	.286	.275
89	OMA/AMA	AAA	64	285	248	63	12	1	3	86	29	2	2	29	8	1	5	10	5	34	40	.254	.331	.347
	KC/AL		65	92	83	17	4	2	3	34	7	1	1	9	1	0	0	5	0	21	5	.205	.275	.410
90	OMA/AMA	AAA	29	137	116	35	6	0	4	53	17	1	3	11	1	0	1	11	1	30	13	.302	.401	.457
	KC/AL		87	280	240	58	15	2	5	92	33	0	1	39	5	6	0	8	7	43	20	.242	.336	.383
91	KC/AL		125	448	398	114	23	2	6	159	41	0	2	45	12	7	0	16	7	53	45	.286	.356	.399
92	NY/NL		117	302	269	61	13	2	2	80	25	3	1	40	7	5	2	9	3	28	26	.227	.293	.297
93	ATL/NL		72	65	62	20	2	1	0	24	2	0	0	5	1	0	1	1	1	17	5	.323	.344	.387
8 YR TOTALS			**634**	**1599**	**1415**	**356**	**67**	**11**	**20**	**505**	**144**	**10**	**9**	**200**	**33**	**27**	**4**	**51**	**20**	**212**	**132**	**.252**	**.324**	**.357**

Peltier, Daniel Edward "Dan" — BL/TL — b.6/30/68 — POS OF-65, 1B-5 TEX89 2/65

YR	TM/LG	CL	G	TPA	AB	H	2B	3B	HR	TB	BB	IBB	HB	SO	GDP	SH	SF	SB	CS	R	RBI	BA	OBA	SA
89	BUT/PIO	R+	33	148	122	49	7	1	7	79	25	2	1	16	4	0	0	10	1	35	28	.402	.507	.648
90	TUL/TEX	AA	117	497	448	125	20	4	11	186	40	2	6	67	8	1	2	10	6	66	57	.279	.345	.415
91	OC/AMA	AAA	94	392	345	79	16	4	3	112	43	2	0	71	8	2	2	6	5	38	32	.229	.313	.325
92	OC/AMA	AAA	125	517	450	133	30	7	7	198	60	3	1	72	14	1	1	7	7	65	53	.296	.381	.440
	TEX/AL		12	24	24	4	0	0	0	4	0	0	0	3	0	0	0	0	0	1	1	.167	.167	.167
93	OC/AMA	AAA	48	208	187	60	15	4	5	98	19	4	0	27	4	0	2	4	2	28	33	.321	.380	.524
	TEX/AL		65	183	160	43	7	1	1	55	20	1	0	27	3	1	2	0	4	23	17	.269	.352	.344
2 YR TOTALS			**77**	**207**	**184**	**47**	**7**	**1**	**1**	**59**	**20**	**0**	**1**	**30**	**3**	**1**	**1**	**0**	**4**	**24**	**19**	**.255**	**.330**	**.321**

Pena, Antonio Francisco "Tony" — BR/TR — b.6/4/57 — POS C-1714, 1B-13, OF-3, DH-1 PIT 7/22/75

YR	TM/LG	CL	G	TPA	AB	H	2B	3B	HR	TB	BB	IBB	HB	SO	GDP	SH	SF	SB	CS	R	RBI	BA	OBA	SA
80	PIT/NL		8	21	21	9	1	1	0	12	0	0	0	4	1	0	0	0	1	1	1	.429	.429	.571
81	PIT/NL		66	223	210	63	9	1	2	80	8	2	1	23	4	2	0	2	2	16	17	.300	.326	.381
82	PIT/NL		138	523	497	147	28	4	11	216	17	3	4	57	17	3	2	2	5	53	63	.296	.323	.435
83	PIT/NL		151	580	542	163	22	3	15	236	31	8	0	73	13	6	1	6	7	51	70	.301	.338	.435
84	PIT/NL		147	592	546	156	27	2	15	232	36	5	4	79	14	3	3	12	8	77	78	.286	.333	.425
85	PIT/NL		147	587	546	136	27	2	10	197	29	4	4	67	19	1	7	12	6	53	59	.249	.284	.361
86	PIT/NL		144	565	510	147	26	2	10	207	53	6	2	69	21	0	0	9	10	56	52	.288	.356	.406
87	LOU/AMA	AAA	2	8	8	3	0	0	0	3	0	0	0	0	0	0	0	0	0	0	0	.375	.375	.375
	STL/NL		116	425	384	82	13	4	5	118	36	9	1	54	19	2	2	6	1	40	44	.214	.281	.307
88	STL/NL		149	546	505	133	23	1	10	188	33	11	3	60	12	3	4	6	2	55	51	.263	.308	.372
89	STL/NL		141	464	424	110	17	2	4	143	35	19	2	33	19	2	1	5	6	36	37	.259	.318	.337

(continued)

Pena, Antonio Francisco "Tony" (continued)

YR	TM/LG	CL	G	TPA	AB	H	2B	3B	HR	TB	BB	IBB	HB	SO	GDP	SH	SF	SB	CS	R	RBI	BA	OBA	SA
90	BOS/AL		143	540	491	129	19	1	7	171	43	3	1	71	23	2	3	8	6	62	56	.263	.322	.348
91	BOS/AL		141	512	464	107	23	2	5	149	37	1	4	53	23	4	3	8	3	45	48	.231	.291	.321
92	BOS/AL		133	450	410	99	21	1	1	125	24	0	1	61	11	13	2	3	2	39	38	.241	.284	.305
93	BOS/AL		126	347	304	55	11	0	4	78	25	0	2	46	12	13	3	1	3	20	19	.181	.246	.257
14 YR TOTALS			**1750**	**6375**	**5854**	**1536**	**267**	**26**	**99**	**2152**	**407**	**71**	**22**	**750**	**208**	**61**	**31**	**79**	**61**	**604**	**633**	**.262**	**.311**	**.368**

Pena, Geronimo — BB/TR — b.3/29/67 — POS 2B-215, OF-4   SL 8/9/84

YR	TM/LG	CL	G	TPA	AB	H	2B	3B	HR	TB	BB	IBB	HB	SO	GDP	SH	SF	SB	CS	R	RBI	BA	OBA	SA
86	JC/APP	R+	56	259	202	60	7	4	3	84	46	4	7	33	1	1	3	27	3	55	20	.297	.438	.416
87	SAV/SAL	A	134	590	505	136	28	3	9	197	73	6	8	98	6	1	3	80	21	95	51	.269	.368	.390
88	SP/FSL	A+	130	593	484	125	25	10	4	182	88	3	8	103	5	8	5	35	18	82	35	.258	.378	.376
89	SP/FSL	A+	6	27	21	4	1	0	0	5	3	0	0	6	0	0	0	2	3	2	2	.190	.370	.238
	ARK/TEX	AA	77	320	267	79	16	8	9	138	38	3	3	68	0	3	4	14	6	61	44	.296	.394	.517
90	LOU/AMA	AAA	118	484	390	97	24	6	6	151	69	0	18	116	3	3	4	24	13	65	35	.249	.383	.387
	STL/NL		18	51	45	11	2	0	0	13	4	0	1	14	0	0	1	1	1	5	2	.244	.314	.289
91	STL/NL		104	212	185	45	8	3	5	74	18	1	5	45	0	1	3	15	5	38	17	.243	.322	.400
92	LOU/AMA	AAA	28	115	101	25	9	4	3	51	13	1	1	27	0	0	4	13	3	16	12	.248	.339	.505
	STL/NL		62	236	203	62	12	1	7	97	24	0	5	37	1	0	4	13	8	31	31	.305	.386	.478
93	LOU/AMA	AAA	7	26	23	4	1	0	0	5	1	0	1	4	0	1	0	0	0	4	0	.174	.240	.217
	STL/NL		74	289	254	65	19	2	5	103	25	0	4	71	1	3	4	13	5	34	30	.256	.330	.406
4 YR TOTALS			**258**	**788**	**687**	**183**	**41**	**6**	**17**	**287**	**71**	**1**	**15**	**167**	**4**	**5**	**10**	**42**	**19**	**108**	**80**	**.266**	**.344**	**.418**

Pendleton, Terry Lee — BB/TR — b.7/16/60 — POS 3B-1375, OF-1   SL82 7/179

YR	TM/LG	CL	G	TPA	AB	H	2B	3B	HR	TB	BB	IBB	HB	SO	GDP	SH	SF	SB	CS	R	RBI	BA	OBA	SA
84	LOU/AMA	AAA	91	358	330	98	23	5	4	143	24	1	0	51	4	1	3	6	7	52	44	.297	.342	.433
	STL/NL		67	283	262	85	16	3	1	110	16	3	0	32	7	0	5	20	5	37	33	.324	.357	.420
85	STL/NL		149	602	559	134	16	3	5	171	37	4	0	75	18	3	3	17	12	56	69	.240	.285	.306
86	STL/NL		159	626	578	138	26	5	1	177	34	10	1	59	12	6	7	24	6	56	59	.239	.279	.306
87	STL/NL		159	667	583	167	29	4	12	240	70	6	2	74	18	3	9	19	12	82	96	.286	.360	.412
88	STL/NL		110	421	391	99	20	2	6	141	21	4	2	51	9	4	3	3	1	44	53	.253	.293	.361
89	STL/NL		162	661	613	162	28	5	13	239	44	3	0	81	16	2	2	9	5	83	74	.264	.313	.390
90	STL/NL		121	484	447	103	20	2	6	145	30	8	1	58	12	0	6	7	5	46	58	.230	.277	.324
91	ATL/NL		153	644	586	*187	34	8	22	*303	43	8	1	70	16	7	7	10	2	94	86	*.319	.363	.517
92	ATL/NL		160	689	640	*199	39	1	21	303	37	8	0	67	16	5	7	5	2	98	105	.311	.345	.473
93	ATL/NL		161	682	633	172	33	1	17	258	36	5	3	97	18	3	7	5	1	81	84	.272	.311	.408
10 YR TOTALS			**1401**	**5759**	**5292**	**1446**	**261**	**34**	**104**	**2087**	**368**	**59**	**10**	**664**	**142**	**33**	**56**	**119**	**53**	**677**	**717**	**.273**	**.319**	**.394**

Pennyfeather, William Nathaniel "Will" — BR/TR — b.5/25/68 — POS OF-27   PIT 7/1/88

YR	TM/LG	CL	G	TPA	AB	H	2B	3B	HR	TB	BB	IBB	HB	SO	GDP	SH	SF	SB	CS	R	RBI	BA	OBA	SA
88	PIR/GCL	R	17	77	74	18	2	1	1	25	2	0	0	18	0	0	1	3	3	6	7	.243	.260	.338
	PRI/APP	R+	16	63	57	19	2	0	1	24	6	0	0	15	0	0	0	7	2	11	5	.333	.397	.421
89	WEL/NYP	A-	75	310	289	55	10	1	3	76	12	1	2	75	6	1	6	18	5	34	26	.190	.223	.263
90	AUG/SAL	A	122	497	465	122	14	4	4	156	23	0	3	85	7	3	3	21	12	69	48	.262	.300	.335
91	SAL/CAR	A+	81	331	319	85	17	3	8	132	8	0	1	52	9	1	2	11	8	35	46	.266	.285	.414
	CAR/SOU	AA	42	159	149	41	5	0	0	46	8	0	1	17	8	1	1	3	2	13	9	.275	.310	.309
92	CAR/SOU	AA	51	211	199	67	13	1	6	100	9	1	0	34	5	0	3	7	6	28	25	.337	.360	.503
	BUF/AMA	AAA	55	167	160	38	6	2	1	51	2	0	3	24	4	2	0	3	2	19	12	.237	.261	.319
	PIT/NL		15	10	9	2	0	0	0	2	0	0	0	6	0	0	1	0	0	2	0	.222	.222	.222
93	BUF/AMA	AAA	112	484	457	114	18	3	14	180	18	2	8	92	3	8	1	10	12	54	41	.249	.277	.394
	PIT/NL		21	34	34	7	1	0	0	8	0	0	0	6	1	0	0	0	1	4	2	.206	.206	.235
2 YR TOTALS			**36**	**44**	**43**	**9**	**1**	**0**	**0**	**10**	**0**	**0**	**0**	**6**	**2**	**1**	**0**	**0**	**1**	**6**	**2**	**.209**	**.209**	**.233**

Perez, Eduardo Atanasio — BR/TR — b.9/11/69 — POS 3B-45, DH-3   CAL91 1/17

YR	TM/LG	CL	G	TPA	AB	H	2B	3B	HR	TB	BB	IBB	HB	SO	GDP	SH	SF	SB	CS	R	RBI	BA	OBA	SA
91	BOI/NWL	A-	46	185	160	46	13	0	1	62	19	0	4	39	4	1	1	12	3	35	22	.287	.375	.387
92	PS/CAL	A+	54	233	204	64	8	4	3	89	23	0	3	33	5	0	3	14	3	37	35	.314	.386	.436
	MID/TEX	AA	62	262	235	54	8	1	3	73	22	1	1	49	7	1	3	19	7	27	23	.230	.295	.311
93	VAN/PCL	AAA	96	395	363	111	23	6	12	182	28	5	3	83	5	1	0	21	7	66	70	.306	.360	.501
	CAL/AL		52	192	180	45	6	2	4	67	9	0	2	39	4	0	1	5	4	16	30	.250	.292	.372

Perry, Gerald June — BL/TR — b.10/30/60 — POS 1B-632, OF-89, DH-68   ATL78 11/261

YR	TM/LG	CL	G	TPA	AB	H	2B	3B	HR	TB	BB	IBB	HB	SO	GDP	SH	SF	SB	CS	R	RBI	BA	OBA	SA
83	ATL/NL		27	45	39	14	2	0	1	19	5	0	0	4	1	0	1	0	1	5	6	.359	.422	.487
84	ATL/NL		122	419	347	92	12	2	7	129	61	5	2	38	9	2	7	15	12	52	47	.265	.372	.372
85	ATL/NL		110	262	238	51	5	0	3	65	23	1	0	28	7	0	1	9	5	22	13	.214	.282	.273
86	RIC/INT	AAA	107	449	384	125	30	5	10	195	58	8	4	41	13	0	3	22	11	69	75	.326	.416	.508
	ATL/NL		29	80	70	19	2	0	2	27	8	1	0	4	4	1	1	0	1	6	11	.271	.342	.386
87	ATL/NL		142	590	533	144	35	2	12	219	48	1	1	63	18	3	5	42	16	77	74	.270	.329	.411
88	ATL/NL		141	595	547	164	29	1	8	219	36	9	1	49	18	3	10	29	14	61	74	.300	.338	.400
89	ATL/NL		72	303	266	67	11	0	4	90	32	5	3	28	5	0	2	10	6	24	21	.252	.337	.338
90	KC/AL		133	512	465	118	22	2	8	168	39	4	0	56	14	0	5	17	4	57	57	.254	.313	.361
91	STL/NL		109	267	242	58	8	4	6	92	22	1	0	34	2	0	3	15	8	29	36	.240	.300	.380
92	STL/NL		87	161	143	34	5	1	0	45	15	4	1	23	3	0	2	1	3	13	18	.238	.311	.315
93	STL/NL		96	116	98	33	5	0	4	50	18	2	0	17	1	0	1	1	1	21	16	.337	.440	.510
11 YR TOTALS			**1068**	**3350**	**2988**	**794**	**139**	**11**	**56**	**1123**	**307**	**33**	**11**	**350**	**85**	**7**	**37**	**141**	**74**	**367**	**373**	**.266**	**.333**	**.376**

Petralli, Eugene James "Geno" — BL/TR — b.9/25/59 — POS C-574, DH-66, 3B-63, 2B-14, 1B-7, OF-3 TOR78* 3/53

YR	TM/LG	CL	G	TPA	AB	H	2B	3B	HR	TB	BB	IBB	HB	SO	GDP	SH	SF	SB	CS	R	RBI	BA	OBA	SA
82	TOR/AL		16	49	44	16	2	0	0	18	4	0	0	6	1	1	0	0	0	3	1	.364	.417	.409
83	TOR/AL		6	5	4	0	0	0	0	0	1	0	0	1	0	0	0	0	0	0	0	.000	.200	.000
84	TOR/AL		3	3	3	0	0	0	0	0	0	0	0	0	0	0	0	0	0	0	0	.000	.000	.000
	MAI/INT	AAA	23	96	83	18	3	0	0	21	13	2	0	10	5	0	0	0	2	9	5	.217	.323	.253
85	MAI/INT	AAA	2	8	7	1	0	0	0	1	0	0	0	1	0	0	0	0	0	0	1	.143	.143	.143
	OC/AMA	AAA	27	91	80	21	8	0	1	32	10	1	0	9	3	1	0	0	0	11	5	.262	.344	.400
	TEX/AL		42	116	100	27	2	0	0	29	8	0	1	12	4	3	4	1	0	7	11	.270	.319	.290
86	TEX/AL		69	142	137	35	9	3	2	56	5	0	0	14	7	0	0	3	0	17	18	.255	.282	.409
87	TEX/AL		101	232	202	61	11	2	7	97	27	2	2	29	4	0	0	0	2	28	31	.302	.388	.480
88	TEX/AL		129	400	351	99	14	2	6	138	41	5	2	52	12	1	5	0	0	35	36	.282	.356	.393
89	TUL/TEX	AA	5	15	13	3	0	0	1	6	2	0	0	2	0	0	0	0	0	2	1	.231	.333	.462
	TEX/AL		70	205	184	56	7	0	4	75	17	1	2	24	5	1	1	0	0	18	23	.304	.368	.408
90	TEX/AL		133	382	325	83	13	1	0	98	50	3	3	49	12	1	4	0	2	28	21	.255	.357	.302
91	OC/AMA	AAA	4	17	15	4	1	0	0	5	2	0	0	1	1	0	0	0	0	1	2	.267	.353	.333
	TEX/AL		87	228	199	54	8	1	2	70	21	1	0	25	4	7	1	2	1	21	20	.271	.339	.352
92	TEX/AL		94	213	192	38	12	0	1	53	20	2	0	34	8	0	1	0	0	11	18	.198	.274	.276
93	OC/AMA	AAA	6	23	20	4	1	0	1	8	3	0	0	3	1	0	0	2	0	2	1	.200	.304	.400
	TEX/AL		59	156	133	32	5	0	1	40	22	3	0	17	5	1	0	0	0	16	13	.241	.348	.301
12 YR TOTALS			**809**	**2131**	**1874**	**501**	**83**	**9**	**24**	**674**	**216**	**17**	**10**	**263**	**62**	**16**	**15**	**8**	**6**	**184**	**192**	**.267**	**.344**	**.360**

Phillips, Charles Gene "J. R." — BL/TL — b.4/29/70 — POS 1B-5 CAL88 3/91

YR	TM/LG	CL	G	TPA	AB	H	2B	3B	HR	TB	BB	IBB	HB	SO	GDP	SH	SF	SB	CS	R	RBI	BA	OBA	SA
88	BEN/NWL	A-	56	236	210	40	8	0	4	60	21	1	1	70	5	1	3	3	1	24	23	.190	.264	.286
89	QC/MID	A	125	503	442	85	29	1	8	140	49	2	4	146	5	4	4	3	3	41	50	.192	.277	.317
90	PS/CAL	A+	46	175	162	32	4	1	1	41	10	1	1	58	8	1	1	3	1	14	15	.198	.247	.253
	BOI/NWL	A-	70	260	237	46	6	0	10	82	20	0	0	78	4	1	2	1	2	30	34	.194	.255	.346
91	PS/CAL	A+	130	534	471	117	22	2	20	203	57	4	3	144	8	1	2	15	14	64	70	.248	.332	.431
92	MID/TEX	AA	127	536	497	118	32	4	14	200	32	4	2	165	9	1	4	5	3	58	77	.237	.284	.402
93	PHO/PCL	AAA	134	571	506	133	35	2	27	253	53	9	6	127	2	0	6	7	5	80	94	.263	.336	.500
	SF/NL		11	16	16	5	1	1	1	11	0	0	0	5	0	0	0	0	0	1	4	.313	.313	.688

Phillips, Keith Anthony "Tony" — BB/TR — b.4/25/59 — POS 2B-654, 3B-328, OF-295, SS-293, DH-66, 1B-4 MON78* S1/10

YR	TM/LG	CL	G	TPA	AB	H	2B	3B	HR	TB	BB	IBB	HB	SO	GDP	SH	SF	SB	CS	R	RBI	BA	OBA	SA
82	OAK/AL		40	100	81	17	2	2	0	23	12	0	2	26	0	5	0	2	3	11	8	.210	.326	.284
83	OAK/AL		148	476	412	102	12	3	4	132	48	1	2	70	5	11	3	16	5	54	35	.248	.327	.320
84	OAK/AL		154	505	451	120	24	3	4	162	42	1	0	86	5	7	5	10	6	62	37	.266	.325	.359
85	TAC/PCL	AAA	20	78	69	9	1	0	0	10	8	1	0	28	1	0	1	3	0	9	5	.130	.218	.145
	OAK/AL		42	178	161	45	12	2	4	73	13	0	0	34	1	3	1	3	2	23	17	.280	.331	.453
86	OAK/AL		118	532	441	113	14	5	5	152	76	2	0	82	2	9	3	15	10	76	52	.256	.367	.345
87	TAC/PCL	AAA	7	30	26	9	2	1	1	16	4	0	0	3	0	0	0	1	0	5	6	.346	.433	.615
	OAK/AL		111	441	379	91	20	0	10	141	57	1	0	76	9	2	3	7	6	48	46	.240	.337	.372
88	TAC/PCL	AAA	16	73	59	16	0	0	2	22	12	0	1	13	0	1	0	2	0	10	8	.271	.394	.373
	OAK/AL		79	251	212	43	8	4	2	65	36	0	1	50	6	1	1	0	2	32	17	.203	.320	.307
89	OAK/AL		143	524	451	118	15	6	4	157	58	2	3	66	17	5	5	3	8	48	47	.262	.345	.348
90	DET/AL		152	687	573	144	23	5	8	201	99	0	4	85	10	9	2	19	9	97	55	.251	.364	.351
91	DET/AL		146	655	564	160	28	4	17	247	79	5	3	95	8	3	6	10	5	87	72	.284	.371	.438
92	DET/AL		159	733	606	167	32	3	10	235	*132	5	1	93	13	5	7	12	10	*114	64	.276	.387	.388
93	DET/AL		151	707	566	177	27	0	7	225	*132	5	4	102	11	1	4	16	11	113	57	.313	.443	.398
12 YR TOTALS			**1443**	**5789**	**4897**	**1297**	**217**	**37**	**75**	**1813**	**766**	**17**	**23**	**865**	**87**	**61**	**42**	**113**	**77**	**765**	**507**	**.265**	**.364**	**.370**

Piazza, Michael Joseph "Mike" — BR/TR — b.9/4/68 — POS C-162, 1B-1 LA88 61/1390

YR	TM/LG	CL	G	TPA	AB	H	2B	3B	HR	TB	BB	IBB	HB	SO	GDP	SH	SF	SB	CS	R	RBI	BA	OBA	SA
89	SAL/NWL	A-	57	214	198	53	11	0	8	88	13	0	2	51	11	0	1	0	0	22	25	.268	.318	.444
90	VB/FSL	A+	88	285	272	68	20	0	6	106	11	0	1	68	6	0	1	0	0	27	45	.250	.281	.390
91	BAK/CAL	A+	117	506	448	124	27	2	29	242	47	2	3	83	19	0	8	0	3	71	80	.277	.344	.540
92	SA/TEX	AA	31	127	114	43	11	0	7	75	13	2	0	18	2	0	0	0	0	18	21	.377	.441	.658
	ALB/PCL	AAA	94	398	358	122	22	5	16	202	37	4	2	57	9	0	1	1	3	54	69	.341	.405	.564
	LA/NL		21	74	69	16	3	0	1	22	4	0	1	12	1	0	0	0	0	5	7	.232	.284	.319
93	LA/NL		149	602	547	174	24	2	35	307	46	6	3	86	10	0	6	3	4	81	112	.318	.370	.561
2 YR TOTALS			**170**	**676**	**616**	**190**	**27**	**2**	**36**	**329**	**50**	**6**	**4**	**98**	**11**	**0**	**6**	**3**	**4**	**86**	**119**	**.308**	**.361**	**.534**

Pirkl, Gregory Daniel "Greg" — BR/TR — b.8/7/70 — POS 1B-5, DH-2 SEA88 2/44

YR	TM/LG	CL	G	TPA	AB	H	2B	3B	HR	TB	BB	IBB	HB	SO	GDP	SH	SF	SB	CS	R	RBI	BA	OBA	SA
88	BEL/NWL	A-	65	266	246	59	6	0	6	83	12	0	6	59	8	0	2	1	1	22	35	.240	.289	.337
89	BEL/NWL	A-	70	295	265	68	6	0	8	98	23	2	3	51	8	1	3	4	1	31	36	.257	.320	.370
90	SB/CAL	A+	58	224	207	61	10	0	5	86	13	0	3	34	5	0	1	0	0	37	28	.295	.344	.415
91	PEN/CAR	A+	64	258	239	63	16	0	6	97	9	0	7	49	4	0	3	0	0	20	41	.264	.306	.406
	SB/CAL	A+	63	259	239	75	13	1	14	132	12	1	2	43	8	0	6	4	0	42	53	.314	.344	.552
92	JAC/SOU	AA	59	247	227	66	11	1	10	109	9	1	7	45	10	0	4	0	1	25	29	.291	.332	.480
	CAL/PCL	AAA	79	305	286	76	21	3	6	121	14	0	3	64	8	0	2	0	3	30	32	.266	.305	.423
93	SEA/AL		7	23	23	4	0	0	1	7	0	0	0	4	2	0	0	0	0	1	4	.174	.174	.304
	CAL/PCL	AAA	115	475	445	137	24	0	21	226	13	1	6	50	15	1	10	3	3	67	94	.308	.329	.508

Plantier, Phillip Alan "Phil" — BL/TR — b.1/27/69 — POS OF-251, DH-32 BOS87 12/292

YR	TM/LG	CL	G	TPA	AB	H	2B	3B	HR	TB	BB	IBB	HB	SO	GDP	SH	SF	SB	CS	R	RBI	BA	OBA	SA
87	ELM/NYP	A-	28	91	80	14	2	0	2	22	9	0	0	9	4	1	1	0	0	7	9	.175	.256	.275
88	WH/FSL	A+	111	399	337	81	13	1	4	108	51	6	6	62	4	3	0	2	0	29	32	.240	.346	.320

(continued)

Plantier, Phillip Alan "Phil" (continued)

YR	TM/LG	CL	G	TPA	AB	H	2B	3B	HR	TB	BB	IBB	HB	SO	GDP	SH	SF	SB	CS	R	RBI	BA	OBA	SA
89	LYN/CAR	A+	131	528	443	133	26	1	27	242	74	7	7	122	2	0	4	4	5	73	105	.300	.405	.546
90	PAW/INT	AAA	123	507	430	109	22	3	33	236	62	3	9	148	4	3	3	1	8	83	79	.253	.357	.549
	BOS/AL		14	21	15	2	1	0	0	3	4	0	1	6	1	0	1	0	0	1	3	.133	.333	.200
91	PAW/INT	AAA	84	368	298	91	19	4	16	166	65	2	5	64	4	0	0	6	1	69	61	.305	.438	.557
	BOS/AL		53	174	148	49	7	1	11	91	23	2	1	38	2	0	2	1	0	27	35	.331	.420	.615
92	PAW/INT	AAA	12	46	40	17	0	0	5	32	6	1	0	6	1	0	0	0	1	7	14	.425	.500	.800
	BOS/AL		108	399	349	86	19	0	7	126	44	8	2	83	9	2	2	2	3	46	30	.246	.332	.361
93	SD/NL		138	536	462	111	20	1	34	235	61	7	7	124	4	1	5	4	5	67	100	.240	.335	.509
4 YR TOTALS			**313**	**1130**	**974**	**248**	**47**	**2**	**52**	**455**	**132**	**17**	**11**	**251**	**16**	**3**	**10**	**7**	**8**	**141**	**168**	**.255**	**.347**	**.467**

Polidor, Gustavo Adolfo "Gus" — BR/TR — b.10/26/61 — POS SS-96, 3B-79, 2B-42, DH-3, OF-1 ␣␣␣␣ CAL 1/5/81

YR	TM/LG	CL	G	TPA	AB	H	2B	3B	HR	TB	BB	IBB	HB	SO	GDP	SH	SF	SB	CS	R	RBI	BA	OBA	SA
81	HOL/EAS	AA	130	521	479	119	17	3	2	148	31	0	3	62	23	6	2	5	4	46	47	.248	.297	.309
82	HOL/EAS	AA	56	217	208	47	7	0	2	60	5	0	1	23	4	2	1	2	5	17	23	.226	.247	.288
83	NAS/EAS	AA	105	356	329	69	7	2	0	80	17	2	1	32	11	8	1	4	6	32	21	.210	.250	.243
84	WAT/EAS	AA	119	431	394	88	11	1	1	104	25	1	1	32	12	10	1	3	7	42	32	.223	.271	.264
85	EDM/PCL	AAA	132	511	460	131	18	7	2	169	37	0	1	53	18	10	3	5	6	56	51	.285	.337	.367
	CAL/AL		2	1	1	1	0	0	0	1	0	0	0	0	0	0	0	0	0	1	0	1.000	1.000	1.000
86	EDM/PCL	AAA	119	518	476	143	27	5	5	195	29	1	1	41	9	9	3	7	9	72	61	.300	.340	.410
	CAL/AL		6	20	19	5	1	0	0	6	1	0	0	0	2	0	0	0	0	1	1	.263	.300	.316
87	CAL/AL		63	141	137	36	3	0	2	45	2	0	1	15	3	0	1	0	0	12	15	.263	.277	.328
88	EDM/PCL	AAA	11	37	33	12	4	0	0	16	2	0	0	3	1	0	1	0	0	6	7	.364	.405	.485
	CAL/AL		54	87	81	12	3	0	0	15	1	0	0	11	2	3	0	0	0	4	4	.148	.179	.185
89	MIL/AL		79	186	175	34	7	0	0	41	6	0	2	18	6	3	0	3	0	15	14	.194	.230	.234
90	MIL/AL		18	15	15	1	0	0	0	1	0	0	0	1	0	0	0	0	0	0	1	.067	.067	.067
	DEN/AMA	AAA	46	176	165	50	8	0	1	61	4	0	4	19	6	5	0	0	3	17	16	.303	.327	.370
91	DEN/AMA	AAA	30	113	103	28	2	1	0	32	4	0	0	8	7	6	0	0	3	8	5	.272	.299	.311
	TAC/PCL	AAA	53	207	182	54	8	4	0	70	12	1	2	15	6	9	2	0	0	22	14	.297	.343	.385
92	TAC/PCL	AAA	99	393	363	101	16	0	1	120	22	0	1	24	13	4	3	4	4	23	43	.278	.319	.331
93	EDM/PCL	AAA	72	274	249	71	16	2	3	100	17	3	2	17	11	5	1	1	1	26	40	.285	.335	.402
	FLO/NL		7	6	6	1	1	0	0	2	0	0	0	2	0	0	0	0	0	0	0	.167	.167	.333
7 YR TOTALS			**229**	**456**	**434**	**90**	**15**	**0**	**2**	**111**	**12**	**0**	**3**	**47**	**13**	**6**	**1**	**3**	**0**	**33**	**35**	**.207**	**.233**	**.256**

Polonia, Luis Andrew — BL/TL — b.10/12/64 — POS OF-756, DH-99 ␣␣␣␣ OAK 1/3/84

YR	TM/LG	CL	G	TPA	AB	H	2B	3B	HR	TB	BB	IBB	HB	SO	GDP	SH	SF	SB	CS	R	RBI	BA	OBA	SA
84	MAD/MID	A	135	601	528	162	21	10	8	227	57	7	5	95	5	9	2	55	24	103	64	.307	.378	.430
85	HUN/SOU	AA	130	584	515	149	15	18	2	206	59	3	0	54	5	6	4	39	20	82	36	.289	.360	.400
86	TAC/PCL	AAA	134	610	549	165	20	4	3	202	52	2	3	65	12	2	4	36	21	98	63	.301	.362	.368
87	TAC/PCL	AAA	14	71	56	18	1	2	0	23	14	1	0	6	1	0	1	4	2	18	8	.321	.451	.411
	OAK/AL		125	469	435	125	16	10	4	173	32	1	0	64	4	1	1	29	7	78	49	.287	.335	.398
88	TAC/PCL	AAA	65	287	254	85	13	5	2	114	29	1	1	28	0	3	31	15		58	27	.335	.401	.449
	OAK/AL		84	313	288	84	11	4	2	109	21	0	0	40	3	2	2	24	9	51	27	.292	.338	.378
89	OAK/AL		59	218	206	59	6	4	1	76	9	0	0	15	5	2	1	13	4	31	17	.286	.315	.369
	NY/AL		66	248	227	71	11	2	2	92	16	1	2	29	8	0	3	9	4	39	29	.313	.359	.405
	YEAR		125	466	433	130	17	6	3	168	25	1	2	44	13	2	4	22	8	70	46	.300	.338	.388
90	NY/AL		11	23	22	7	0	0	0	7	0	0	0	1	0	1	0	1	0	2	3	.318	.304	.318
	CAL/AL		109	413	381	128	7	9	2	159	25	1	1	42	8	3	3	20	14	50	32	.336	.376	.417
	YEAR		120	436	403	135	7	9	2	166	25	1	1	43	9	4	3	21	14	52	35	.335	.372	.412
91	CAL/AL		150	662	604	179	28	8	2	229	52	4	1	74	11	2	3	48	23	92	50	.296	.352	.379
92	CAL/AL		149	635	577	165	17	4	0	190	45	6	1	64	18	8	4	51	21	83	35	.286	.337	.329
93	CAL/AL		152	637	576	156	17	6	1	188	48	7	2	53	7	8	3	55	24	75	32	.271	.328	.326
7 YR TOTALS			**905**	**3618**	**3316**	**974**	**113**	**47**	**14**	**1223**	**248**	**20**	**7**	**382**	**65**	**26**	**21**	**250**	**106**	**501**	**274**	**.294**	**.342**	**.369**

Pose, Scott Vernon — BL/TR — b.2/11/67 — POS OF-10 ␣␣␣␣ CIN89 34/888

YR	TM/LG	CL	G	TPA	AB	H	2B	3B	HR	TB	BB	IBB	HB	SO	GDP	SH	SF	SB	CS	R	RBI	BA	OBA	SA
89	BIL/PIO	R+	60	267	210	74	7	2	0	85	54	3	1	31	2	1	1	26	3	52	25	.352	.485	.405
90	CHW/SAL	A	135	612	480	143	13	5	0	166	114	8	7	56	5	5	6	49	21	106	46	.298	.435	.346
91	NAS/AMA	AAA	15	58	52	10	0	0	0	10	2	0	2	9	0	2	0	3	1	7	3	.192	.250	.192
	CHT/SOU	AA	117	483	402	110	8	5	1	131	69	3	2	50	7	7	3	17	13	61	31	.274	.380	.326
92	CHT/SOU	AA	136	600	526	180	22	8	2	224	63	5	4	66	8	4	3	21	27	87	45	.342	.414	.426
93	EDM/PCL	AAA	109	447	398	113	8	6	0	133	42	3	1	36	8	5	1	19	9	61	27	.284	.353	.334
	FLO/NL		15	43	41	8	2	0	0	10	2	0	0	4	0	0	0	0	2	0	3	.195	.233	.244

Pratt, Todd Alan — BR/TR — b.2/9/67 — POS C-37 ␣␣␣␣ BOS85 6/153

YR	TM/LG	CL	G	TPA	AB	H	2B	3B	HR	TB	BB	IBB	HB	SO	GDP	SH	SF	SB	CS	R	RBI	BA	OBA	SA
85	ELM/NYP	A-	39	134	119	16	1	1	0	19	10	0	1	27	6	3	1	0	1	7	5	.134	.206	.160
86	GRE/SAL	A	107	435	348	84	16	0	12	136	74	0	5	114	10	4	4	0	1	63	56	.241	.378	.391
87	WH/FSL	A+	118	484	407	105	22	0	12	163	70	4	1	94	10	0	6	0	0	57	65	.258	.364	.400
88	NB/EAS	AA	124	446	395	89	15	2	8	132	41	2	3	110	7	1	6	1	4	41	49	.225	.299	.334
89	NB/EAS	AA	109	395	338	77	17	1	2	102	44	1	7	66	10	1	5	1	2	30	35	.228	.325	.302
90	NB/EAS	AA	70	218	195	45	14	1	2	67	18	0	0	56	7	1	5	1	0	15	22	.231	.293	.344
91	PAW/INT	AAA	68	250	219	64	16	1	11	113	23	2	3	42	9	1	5	0	3	27	41	.292	.367	.516
92	REA/EAS	AA	41	156	132	44	6	1	6	70	24	0	0	28	1	0	0	0	0	20	26	.333	.436	.530
	SCR/INT	AAA	41	158	125	40	9	1	7	72	30	0	1	14	5	1	2	1	0	20	28	.320	.446	.576
	PHI/NL		16	50	46	13	2	0	2	20	4	0	0	12	0	0	0	0	0	6	10	.283	.340	.435
93	SCR/INT	AAA	3	12	9	2	0	0	0	3	3	0	0	1	0	0	0	0	0	1	1	.222	.417	.333
	PHI/NL		33	95	87	25	6	0	5	46	5	0	1	19	2	1	1	0	0	8	13	.287	.330	.529
2 YR TOTALS			**49**	**145**	**133**	**38**	**7**	**0**	**7**	**66**	**9**	**0**	**1**	**31**	**4**	**1**	**1**	**0**	**0**	**14**	**23**	**.286**	**.333**	**.496**

Pride, Curtis John — BL/TR — b.12/17/68 — POS OF-2
NYN86 10/258

YR	TM/LG	CL	G	TPA	AB	H	2B	3B	HR	TB	BB	IBB	HB	SO	GDP	SH	SF	SB	CS	R	RBI	BA	OBA	SA
86	KIN/APP	R+	27	53	46	5	0	0	1	8	6	0	1	24	0	0	0	5	0	5	4	.109	.226	.174
87	KIN/APP	R+	31	123	104	25	4	0	1	32	16	0	1	34	0	2	0	14	5	22	9	.240	.347	.308
88	KIN/APP	R+	70	322	268	76	13	1	8	115	50	1	1	48	2	2	1	23	7	59	27	.284	.397	.429
89	PIT/NYP	A-	55	242	212	55	7	3	6	86	25	1	2	47	1	2	1	9	2	35	23	.259	.342	.406
90	COL/SAL	A	53	213	191	51	4	4	6	81	21	3	0	45	3	0	1	11	8	38	25	.267	.338	.424
91	SL/FSL	A+	116	440	392	102	21	7	9	164	43	4	2	94	8	3	0	24	5	57	37	.260	.336	.418
92	BIN/EAS	AA	118	440	388	88	15	3	10	139	47	1	4	110	5	0	1	14	11	54	42	.227	.316	.358
93	HAR/EAS	AA	50	200	180	64	6	3	15	121	12	0	4	36	2	2	2	21	6	51	39	.356	.404	.672
	OTT/INT	AAA	69	301	262	79	11	4	6	116	34	7	3	61	3	2	0	29	12	55	22	.302	.388	.443
	MON/NL		10	9	9	4	1	1	1	10	0	0	0	3	0	0	0	1	0	3	5	.444	.444	1.111

Prince, Thomas Albert "Tom" — BR/TR — b.8/13/64 — POS C-153, 1B-1, 3B-1
PIT84* S4/64

YR	TM/LG	CL	G	TPA	AB	H	2B	3B	HR	TB	BB	IBB	HB	SO	GDP	SH	SF	SB	CS	R	RBI	BA	OBA	SA
84	PIR/GCL	R	18	57	48	11	0	0	1	14	8	0	1	10	0	0	0	0	0	4	6	.229	.351	.292
	WAT/NYP	A-	23	80	69	14	3	0	2	23	9	0	1	13	1	1	0	0	0	6	13	.203	.304	.333
85	MAC/SAL	A	124	474	360	75	20	1	10	127	96	0	12	92	8	1	5	13	3	60	42	.208	.387	.353
86	PW/CAR	A+	121	457	395	100	34	1	10	166	50	1	7	74	5	2	4	5	5	59	47	.253	.346	.420
87	HAR/EAS	AA	113	430	365	112	23	2	6	157	51	2	8	46	16	4	2	6	3	41	54	.307	.401	.430
	PIT/NL		4	9	9	2	1	0	1	6	0	0	0	2	0	0	0	0	0	1	2	.222	.222	.667
88	BUF/AMA	AAA	86	338	304	79	16	0	14	137	23	2	7	53	6	3	1	3	6	35	42	.260	.325	.451
	PIT/NL		29	80	74	13	2	0	0	15	4	0	0	15	5	2	0	0	0	3	6	.176	.218	.203
89	PIT/NL		21	59	52	7	4	0	0	11	6	1	0	12	1	0	1	1	1	1	5	.135	.220	.212
	BUF/AMA	AAA	65	212	183	37	8	0	6	65	22	1	2	30	4	1	4	2	3	21	33	.202	.289	.355
90	BUF/AMA	AAA	94	334	284	64	13	0	7	98	39	0	5	46	6	3	3	4	7	38	37	.225	.326	.345
	PIT/NL		4	11	10	1	0	0	0	1	1	0	0	0	0	0	0	0	0	1	0	.100	.182	.100
91	BUF/AMA	AAA	80	270	221	46	8	3	6	78	37	1	7	31	5	2	3	3	4	29	32	.208	.336	.353
	PIT/NL		26	42	34	9	3	0	1	15	7	1	0	3	3	0	0	0	0	4	2	.265	.405	.441
92	BUF/AMA	AAA	75	278	244	64	17	0	9	108	20	1	8	35	5	2	4	2	3	34	35	.262	.333	.443
	PIT/NL		27	52	44	9	2	0	0	11	6	0	0	9	2	0	1	1	1	1	5	.091	.192	.136
93	PIT/NL		66	204	179	35	14	0	2	55	13	2	7	38	5	2	3	1	1	14	24	.196	.272	.307
7 YR TOTALS			**177**	**457**	**402**	**71**	**26**	**0**	**4**	**109**	**37**	**3**	**8**	**81**	**16**	**4**	**6**	**3**	**4**	**25**	**44**	**.177**	**.256**	**.271**

Puckett, Kirby — BR/TR — b.3/14/61 — POS OF-1492, DH-40, 2B-3, 3B-3, SS-2
MIN82 1/3

YR	TM/LG	CL	G	TPA	AB	H	2B	3B	HR	TB	BB	IBB	HB	SO	GDP	SH	SF	SB	CS	R	RBI	BA	OBA	SA
84	TOL/INT	AAA	21	87	80	21	2	0	1	26	4	0	0	14	4	2	1	8	2	9	5	.262	.294	.325
	MIN/AL		128	583	557	165	12	5	0	187	16	1	4	69	11	4	2	14	7	63	31	.296	.320	.336
85	MIN/AL		161	744	691	199	29	13	4	266	41	0	4	87	9	5	3	21	12	80	74	.288	.330	.385
86	MIN/AL		161	723	680	223	37	6	31	365	34	4	7	99	14	2	0	20	12	119	96	.328	.366	.537
87	MIN/AL		157	668	624	*207	32	5	28	333	32	7	6	91	16	0	6	12	7	96	99	.332	.367	.534
88	MIN/AL		158	691	657	*234	42	5	24	*358	23	4	2	83	17	0	9	6	7	109	121	.356	.375	.545
89	MIN/AL		159	684	635	*215	45	4	9	295	41	9	3	59	21	1	5	11	4	75	85	*.339	.379	.465
90	MIN/AL		146	615	551	164	40	3	12	246	57	11	3	73	15	1	3	5	4	82	80	.298	.365	.446
91	MIN/AL		152	661	611	195	29	6	15	281	31	4	4	78	27	8	7	11	5	92	89	.319	.352	.460
92	MIN/AL		160	696	639	*210	38	4	19	*313	44	13	6	97	17	1	6	17	7	104	110	.329	.374	.490
93	MIN/AL		156	682	622	184	39	3	22	295	47	7	7	93	15	1	5	8	6	89	89	.296	.349	.474
10 YR TOTALS			**1538**	**6747**	**6267**	**1996**	**343**	**54**	**164**	**2939**	**366**	**60**	**46**	**829**	**162**	**22**	**46**	**125**	**71**	**909**	**874**	**.318**	**.358**	**.469**

Pulliam, Harvey Jerome — BR/TR — b.10/20/67 — POS OF-42, DH-2
KC86 3/79

YR	TM/LG	CL	G	TPA	AB	H	2B	3B	HR	TB	BB	IBB	HB	SO	GDP	SH	SF	SB	CS	R	RBI	BA	OBA	SA
86	ROY/GCL	R	48	184	168	35	3	0	4	50	8	1	3	33	9	2	3	3	2	14	23	.208	.253	.298
87	APP/MID	A	110	428	395	109	20	1	9	158	26	0	3	79	10	1	3	21	7	54	55	.276	.323	.400
88	BC/FSL	A+	132	501	457	111	19	4	4	150	34	3	5	87	13	2	3	21	11	56	42	.243	.301	.328
89	OMA/AMA	AAA	7	25	22	4	2	0	0	6	3	0	0	6	0	0	0	0	0	3	2	.182	.280	.273
	MEM/SOU	AA	116	469	417	121	28	8	10	195	44	4	5	65	12	0	3	5	5	67	67	.290	.362	.468
90	OMA/AMA	AAA	123	494	436	117	18	5	16	193	49	0	8	82	14	2	4	9	3	72	72	.268	.343	.443
91	OMA/AMA	AAA	104	382	346	89	18	2	6	129	31	2	1	61	8	1	3	9	2	35	39	.257	.318	.373
	KC/AL		18	37	33	9	1	0	3	19	3	1	0	9	1	1	0	0	0	4	4	.273	.333	.576
92	KC/AL		4	6	5	1	1	0	0	2	1	0	0	3	0	0	0	0	0	2	0	.200	.333	.400
	OMA/AMA	AAA	100	401	359	97	12	2	16	161	32	1	6	53	15	1	3	4	4	55	60	.270	.338	.448
93	KC/AL		27	65	62	16	5	0	1	24	2	0	1	14	3	0	0	0	0	7	6	.258	.292	.387
	OMA/AMA	AAA	54	226	208	55	10	0	5	80	17	1	1	36	6	0	0	5	1	28	26	.264	.323	.385
3 YR TOTALS			**49**	**108**	**100**	**26**	**7**	**0**	**4**	**45**	**6**	**1**	**1**	**26**	**4**	**1**	**0**	**0**	**0**	**13**	**10**	**.260**	**.308**	**.450**

Quintana, Carlos Narcis — BR/TR — b.8/26/65 — POS 1B-340, OF-91, DH-9
BOS 11/26/84

YR	TM/LG	CL	G	TPA	AB	H	2B	3B	HR	TB	BB	IBB	HB	SO	GDP	SH	SF	SB	CS	R	RBI	BA	OBA	SA
85	ELM/NYP	A-	65	254	220	61	8	0	4	81	29	0	3	31	6	0	2	3	0	27	35	.277	.366	.368
86	GRE/SAL	A	126	546	443	144	19	4	11	204	90	1	4	54	16	3	6	26	9	97	81	.325	.438	.460
87	NB/EAS	AA	56	235	206	64	11	3	2	87	24	3	1	33	9	0	4	3	3	31	31	.311	.379	.422
88	PAW/INT	AAA	131	517	471	134	25	3	16	213	38	1	3	72	15	2	3	3	5	67	66	.285	.340	.452
	BOS/AL		5	8	6	2	0	0	0	2	2	0	0	3	0	0	0	0	0	1	2	.333	.500	.333
89	PAW/INT	AAA	82	330	272	78	11	2	11	126	53	1	0	39	7	0	6	4	3	45	52	.287	.397	.463
	BOS/AL		34	84	77	16	5	0	0	21	6	0	0	12	5	0	0	0	0	6	6	.208	.274	.273
90	BOS/AL		149	572	512	147	28	0	7	196	52	0	2	74	19	4	4	1	2	56	67	.287	.354	.383
91	BOS/AL		149	550	478	141	21	1	11	197	61	2	5	66	17	6	5	1	0	69	71	.295	.375	.412
93	BOS/AL		101	343	303	74	5	0	1	82	31	2	2	52	13	5	2	1	0	31	19	.244	.317	.271
5 YR TOTALS			**438**	**1557**	**1376**	**380**	**59**	**1**	**19**	**498**	**153**	**4**	**6**	**207**	**54**	**15**	**7**	**3**	**2**	**163**	**165**	**.276**	**.350**	**.362**

(continued)

Raines, Timothy "Tim" — BB/TR — b.9/16/59 — POS OF-1692, 2B-53, DH-33 MON77 5/106

YR	TM/LG	CL	G	TPA	AB	H	2B	3B	HR	TB	BB	IBB	HB	SO	GDP	SH	SF	SB	CS	R	RBI	BA	OBA	SA
79	MON/NL		6	0	0	0	0	0	0	0	0	0	0	0	0	0	0	2	0	3	0	.000	.000	.000
80	MON/NL		15	27	20	1	0	0	0	1	6	0	0	3	0	1	0	5	0	5	0	.050	.269	.050
81	MON/NL		88	363	313	95	13	7	5	137	45	5	2	31	7	0	3	*71	11	61	37	.304	.391	.438
82	MON/NL		156	731	647	179	32	8	4	239	75	9	2	83	6	6	1	*78	16	90	43	.277	.353	.369
83	MON/NL		156	720	615	183	32	8	11	264	97	9	2	70	12	2	4	*90	14	*133	71	.298	.393	.429
84	MON/NL		160	718	622	192	*38	9	8	272	87	7	2	69	7	3	4	*75	10	106	60	.309	.393	.437
85	MON/NL		150	665	575	184	30	13	11	273	81	13	3	60	9	3	3	70	9	115	41	.320	.405	.475
86	MON/NL		151	664	580	194	35	10	9	276	78	9	2	60	6	1	3	70	9	91	62	*.334	*.413	.476
87	MON/NL		139	627	530	175	34	8	18	279	90	26	4	52	9	0	5	50	5	*123	68	.330	.429	.526
88	MON/NL		109	488	429	116	19	7	12	185	53	14	2	44	8	0	4	33	7	66	48	.270	.350	.431
89	MON/NL		145	618	517	148	29	6	9	216	93	18	3	48	8	0	5	41	9	76	60	.286	.395	.418
90	MON/NL		130	538	457	131	11	5	9	179	70	8	3	43	9	0	8	49	16	65	62	.287	.379	.392
91	CHI/AL		155	709	609	163	20	6	5	210	83	9	5	68	7	9	3	51	15	102	50	.268	.359	.345
92	CHI/AL		144	644	551	162	22	9	7	223	81	4	0	48	5	4	8	45	6	102	54	.294	.380	.405
93	NAS/AMA	AAA	3	13	11	5	1	0	0	6	2	0	0	0	0	0	0	2	1	3	2	.455	.538	.545
	CHI/AL		115	486	415	127	16	4	16	199	64	4	3	35	7	2	2	21	7	75	54	.306	.401	.480
15 YR TOTALS			1819	7998	6880	2050	331	100	124	2953	1003	135	33	714	100	31	51	751	134	1213	710	.298	.387	.429

Ramirez, Manuel Aristides "Manny" — BR/TR — b.5/30/72 — POS DH-20, OF-1 CLE91 1/13

YR	TM/LG	CL	G	TPA	AB	H	2B	3B	HR	TB	BB	IBB	HB	SO	GDP	SH	SF	SB	CS	R	RBI	BA	OBA	SA
91	BUR/APP	R+	59	258	215	70	11	4	19	146	34	5	6	41	4	0	3	7	8	44	63	.326	.426	.679
92	KIN/CAR	A+	81	344	291	81	18	4	13	146	45	3	4	74	9	1	3	3	3	52	63	.278	.379	.502
93	CAN/EAS	AA	89	396	344	117	32	0	17	200	45	10	4	68	11	0	5	2	2	67	79	.340	.414	.581
	CHW/INT	AAA	40	177	145	46	12	0	14	100	27	1	2	35	1	0	3	1	1	38	36	.317	.424	.690
	CLE/AL		22	55	53	9	1	0	2	16	2	0	0	8	3	0	0	0	0	5	5	.170	.200	.302

Ready, Randy Max — BR/TR — b.1/8/60 — POS 2B-222, 3B-202, OF-171, DH-33, 1B-17 MIL80 7/155

YR	TM/LG	CL	G	TPA	AB	H	2B	3B	HR	TB	BB	IBB	HB	SO	GDP	SH	SF	SB	CS	R	RBI	BA	OBA	SA
83	MIL/AL		12	43	37	15	3	2	1	25	6	1	0	3	0	0	0	0	1	8	6	.405	.488	.676
84	MIL/AL		37	140	123	23	6	1	3	40	14	0	0	18	2	3	0	0	0	13	13	.187	.270	.325
	VAN/PCL	AAA	43	201	151	49	7	4	3	73	43	2	5	21	4	2	0	10	4	48	18	.325	.487	.483
85	VAN/PCL	AAA	52	222	190	62	12	3	4	92	30	2	0	14	3	0	2	14	3	33	29	.326	.414	.484
	MIL/AL		48	200	181	48	9	5	1	70	14	0	1	23	6	2	2	0	0	29	21	.265	.318	.387
86	MIL/AL		23	89	79	15	4	0	1	22	9	0	0	9	3	1	0	2	0	8	4	.190	.273	.278
	SD/NL		1	3	3	0	0	0	0	0	0	0	0	1	0	0	0	0	0	0	0	.000	.000	.000
	YEAR		24	92	82	15	4	0	1	22	9	0	0	10	3	1	0	2	0	8	4	.183	.264	.268
	LV/PCL	AAA	10	44	38	14	4	0	1	21	6	0	0	2	0	0	0	1	1	5	8	.368	.455	.553
87	SD/NL		124	423	350	108	26	6	12	182	67	7	2	44	7	2	1	7	3	69	54	.309	.423	.520
88	SD/NL		114	380	331	88	16	2	7	129	39	1	3	38	3	4	3	6	2	43	39	.266	.346	.390
89	SD/NL		28	80	67	17	2	1	0	21	11	0	0	6	2	1	1	0	0	4	5	.254	.354	.313
	PHI/NL		72	223	187	50	11	1	8	87	31	0	2	31	2	0	3	4	3	33	21	.267	.372	.465
	YEAR		100	303	254	67	13	2	8	108	42	0	2	37	4	1	4	4	3	37	26	.264	.368	.425
90	PHI/NL		101	253	217	53	9	1	1	67	29	0	1	35	3	3	3	3	2	26	26	.244	.332	.309
91	PHI/NL		76	258	205	51	10	1	1	66	47	3	1	25	1	1	4	2	1	32	20	.249	.385	.322
92	OAK/AL		61	154	125	25	2	0	3	36	25	1	0	23	1	2	2	1	0	17	17	.200	.329	.288
93	ROC/INT	AAA	84	360	305	88	17	3	9	138	50	2	1	37	7	1	3	4	0	48	46	.289	.387	.452
	MON/NL		40	159	134	34	8	1	1	47	23	0	1	8	4	1	0	2	1	22	10	.254	.367	.351
11 YR TOTALS			737	2405	2039	527	106	21	39	792	315	8	12	264	38	20	19	27	13	304	236	.258	.358	.388

Reboulet, Jeffrey Allen "Jeff" — BR/TR — b.4/30/64 — POS SS-98, 3B-57, 2B-24, OF-10, DH-2 MIN86 10/247

YR	TM/LG	CL	G	TPA	AB	H	2B	3B	HR	TB	BB	IBB	HB	SO	GDP	SH	SF	SB	CS	R	RBI	BA	OBA	SA
86	VIS/CAL	A+	72	316	254	73	13	3	0	88	54	1	1	33	4	5	2	14	11	54	29	.287	.412	.346
87	ORL/SOU	AA	129	486	422	108	15	1	1	128	58	0	1	56	9	5	0	9	5	52	35	.256	.347	.303
88	ORL/SOU	AA	125	504	439	112	24	2	4	152	53	0	3	55	9	7	2	18	8	57	41	.255	.338	.346
	POR/PCL	AAA	4	15	12	1	0	0	0	1	3	0	0	2	1	0	0	0	0	0	1	.083	.267	.083
89	POR/PCL	AAA	26	79	65	16	1	0	0	17	12	0	0	11	2	0	2	1	1	9	3	.246	.354	.262
	ORL/SOU	AA	81	346	291	63	5	1	0	70	49	0	1	33	7	2	3	11	6	43	26	.216	.328	.241
90	ORL/SOU	AA	97	355	287	66	12	2	2	88	57	1	2	37	5	5	4	10	5	43	28	.230	.357	.307
91	POR/PCL	AAA	134	469	391	97	27	1	3	139	57	2	2	52	10	17	2	5	2	50	46	.248	.345	.355
92	POR/PCL	AAA	48	202	161	46	11	1	2	65	35	0	1	18	7	4	1	3	3	21	21	.286	.414	.404
	MIN/AL		73	168	137	26	8	0	1	38	23	0	1	24	6	7	0	3	2	15	16	.190	.311	.277
93	MIN/AL		109	283	240	62	8	0	1	73	35	0	2	37	6	5	1	5	5	33	15	.258	.356	.304
2 YR TOTALS			182	451	377	88	15	1	2	111	58	0	3	63	6	12	1	8	7	48	31	.233	.339	.294

Redus, Gary Eugene — BR/TR — b.11/1/56 — POS OF-770, 1B-232, DH-7, 2B-1 CIN78 15/381

YR	TM/LG	CL	G	TPA	AB	H	2B	3B	HR	TB	BB	IBB	HB	SO	GDP	SH	SF	SB	CS	R	RBI	BA	OBA	SA
82	CIN/NL		20	89	83	18	3	2	1	28	5	0	0	21	0	0	1	11	2	12	7	.217	.258	.337
83	CIN/NL		125	531	453	112	20	9	17	201	71	4	3	111	6	2	2	39	14	90	51	.247	.352	.444
84	CIN/NL		123	455	394	100	21	3	7	148	52	3	1	71	4	3	5	48	11	69	22	.254	.338	.376
85	CIN/NL		101	294	246	62	14	4	6	102	44	2	1	52	0	2	1	48	12	51	28	.252	.366	.415
86	REA/EAS	AA	6	26	24	6	1	0	0	7	2	0	0	6	0	0	0	1	0	1	1	.250	.308	.292
	PHI/NL		90	392	340	84	22	4	11	147	47	4	3	78	2	1	1	25	7	62	33	.247	.343	.432
87	CHI/AL		130	554	475	112	26	6	12	186	69	0	7	90	7	3	7	52	11	78	48	.236	.328	.392
88	CHI/AL		77	304	262	69	10	4	6	105	33	1	2	52	5	0	7	26	2	42	34	.263	.342	.401
	PIT/NL		30	88	71	14	2	0	2	22	15	0	1	19	1	0	1	5	2	12	4	.197	.341	.310
	YEAR		107	392	333	83	12	4	8	127	48	1	3	71	6	0	8	31	4	54	38	.249	.342	.381
89	PIT/NL		98	324	279	79	18	7	6	129	40	3	1	51	5	1	3	25	6	42	33	.283	.372	.462

Redus, Gary Eugene (continued)

YR	TM/LG	CL	G	TPA	AB	H	2B	3B	HR	TB	BB	IBB	HB	SO	GDP	SH	SF	SB	CS	R	RBI	BA	OBA	SA
90	PIT/NL		96	268	227	56	15	3	6	95	33	0	2	38	1	1	5	11	5	32	23	.247	.341	.419
91	PIT/NL		98	288	252	62	12	2	7	99	28	2	3	39	0	1	4	17	3	45	24	.246	.324	.393
92	PIT/NL		76	193	176	45	7	3	3	67	17	0	0	25	1	0	0	11	4	26	12	.256	.321	.381
93	TEX/AL		77	248	222	64	12	4	6	102	23	1	0	35	3	0	3	4	4	28	31	.288	.351	.459
12 YR TOTALS			**1141**	**4028**	**3480**	**877**	**182**	**51**	**90**	**1431**	**477**	**20**	**17**	**682**	**35**	**14**	**40**	**322**	**83**	**589**	**350**	**.252**	**.342**	**.411**

Reed, Jeffrey Scott "Jeff" — BL/TR — b.11/12/62 — POS C-552   MIN80 1/12

YR	TM/LG	CL	G	TPA	AB	H	2B	3B	HR	TB	BB	IBB	HB	SO	GDP	SH	SF	SB	CS	R	RBI	BA	OBA	SA
84	TOL/INT	AAA	94	345	301	80	16	3	3	111	37	3	2	35	7	4	1	1	1	30	35	.266	.349	.369
	MIN/AL		18	24	21	3	3	0	0	6	2	0	0	6	0	1	0	0	0	3	1	.143	.217	.286
85	TOL/INT	AAA	122	483	404	100	15	3	5	136	59	3	5	49	13	9	6	1	1	53	36	.248	.346	.337
	MIN/AL		7	10	10	2	0	0	0	2	0	0	0	3	0	0	0	0	0	2	0	.200	.200	.200
86	TOL/INT	AAA	25	92	71	22	5	3	1	36	17	0	0	9	3	3	1	0	0	10	14	.310	.438	.507
	MIN/AL		68	185	165	39	6	1	2	53	16	0	1	19	2	3	0	1	0	13	9	.236	.308	.321
87	IND/AMA	AAA	5	19	17	3	0	0	0	3	1	0	0	2	0	1	0	0	0	0	0	.176	.222	.176
	MON/NL		75	228	207	44	11	0	1	58	12	1	1	20	8	4	4	0	0	15	21	.213	.254	.280
88	MON/NL		43	138	123	27	3	2	0	34	13	1	0	22	3	1	1	0	0	10	9	.220	.292	.276
	IND/AMA	AAA	8	24	22	7	3	0	0	10	2	0	0	2	0	0	0	0	0	1	1	.318	.375	.455
	CIN/NL		49	157	142	33	6	0	1	42	15	0	0	19	2	0	0	0	0	10	7	.232	.306	.296
	YEAR		92	295	265	60	9	2	1	76	28	1	0	41	5	1	1	0	0	20	16	.226	.299	.287
89	CIN/NL		102	330	287	64	11	0	3	84	34	5	2	46	6	3	4	0	0	16	23	.223	.306	.293
90	CIN/NL		72	205	175	44	8	1	3	63	24	5	0	26	4	5	1	0	0	12	16	.251	.340	.360
91	CIN/NL		91	300	270	72	15	2	3	100	23	3	1	38	6	1	5	0	1	20	31	.267	.321	.370
92	NAS/AMA	AAA	14	29	25	6	1	0	1	10	2	1	0	7	2	1	0	1	0	2	2	.240	.286	.400
	CIN/NL		15	26	25	4	0	0	0	4	1	1	0	4	1	0	0	0	0	2	2	.160	.192	.160
93	SJ/CAL	A+	4	11	10	5	1	0	0	6	1	0	0	0	0	0	0	0	0	2	2	.500	.545	.600
	SF/NL		66	136	119	31	3	0	6	52	16	4	0	22	2	0	1	0	1	10	12	.261	.346	.437
10 YR TOTALS			**606**	**1739**	**1544**	**363**	**66**	**6**	**19**	**498**	**156**	**20**	**5**	**225**	**34**	**18**	**16**	**2**	**3**	**113**	**131**	**.235**	**.304**	**.323**

Reed, Jody Eric — BR/TR — b.7/26/62 — POS 2B-628, SS-231, 3B-9, DH-4, OF-1   BOS84 8/198

YR	TM/LG	CL	G	TPA	AB	H	2B	3B	HR	TB	BB	IBB	HB	SO	GDP	SH	SF	SB	CS	R	RBI	BA	OBA	SA
84	WH/FSL	A+	77	334	273	74	14	1	0	90	52	3	0	19	5	6	3	9	8	46	20	.271	.384	.330
85	WH/FSL	A+	134	592	489	157	25	1	0	184	94	2	1	26	9	4	4	16	11	95	45	.321	.429	.376
86	NB/EAS	AA	60	275	218	50	12	1	0	64	52	1	0	9	5	3	2	10	5	33	11	.229	.375	.294
	PAW/INT	AAA	69	270	227	64	11	0	1	78	31	0	1	8	3	7	4	8	2	27	30	.282	.365	.344
87	PAW/INT	AAA	136	594	510	151	22	2	7	198	69	0	2	23	12	8	5	9	7	77	51	.296	.379	.388
	BOS/AL		9	35	30	9	1	1	0	12	4	0	0	0	0	1	0	1	1	4	8	.300	.382	.400
88	BOS/AL		109	400	338	99	23	1	1	127	45	1	4	21	5	11	2	1	3	60	28	.293	.380	.376
89	BOS/AL		146	619	524	151	42	2	3	206	73	0	4	44	12	13	5	4	5	76	40	.288	.376	.393
90	BOS/AL		155	691	598	173	*45	0	5	233	75	4	4	65	19	11	3	4	4	70	51	.289	.371	.390
91	BOS/AL		153	696	618	175	42	2	5	236	60	2	5	53	15	11	3	6	5	87	60	.283	.349	.382
92	BOS/AL		143	626	550	136	27	1	3	174	62	2	4	44	17	10	4	7	8	64	40	.247	.321	.316
93	LA/NL		132	504	445	123	21	2	2	154	38	10	1	40	16	7	3	1	1	48	31	.276	.333	.346
7 YR TOTALS			**847**	**3571**	**3103**	**866**	**201**	**9**	**19**	**1142**	**357**	**19**	**17**	**267**	**84**	**74**	**20**	**24**	**29**	**409**	**258**	**.279**	**.355**	**.368**

Reimer, Kevin Michael — BL/TR — b.6/28/64 — POS OF-223, DH-200   TEX85 10/265

YR	TM/LG	CL	G	TPA	AB	H	2B	3B	HR	TB	BB	IBB	HB	SO	GDP	SH	SF	SB	CS	R	RBI	BA	OBA	SA
85	BUR/MID	A	80	323	292	67	12	0	8	103	22	0	8	43	10	0	1	0	4	25	33	.229	.300	.353
86	SAL/CAR	A+	133	525	453	111	21	2	16	184	61	6	7	71	15	2	2	4	5	57	76	.245	.342	.406
87	CHA/FSL	A+	74	304	271	66	13	7	6	111	29	2	2	48	6	0	2	2	1	36	34	.244	.319	.410
88	TUL/TEX	AA	133	534	486	147	30	11	21	262	38	9	5	95	9	0	5	4	4	74	76	.302	.356	.539
	TEX/AL		12	26	25	3	0	0	1	6	0	0	0	6	0	0	1	0	0	2	2	.120	.115	.240
89	TEX/AL		3	5	5	0	0	0	0	0	0	0	0	0	0	0	0	0	0	0	0	.000	.000	.000
	OC/AMA	AAA	133	554	514	137	37	7	10	218	33	3	2	91	13	0	4	4	1	59	73	.267	.311	.424
90	OC/AMA	AAA	51	217	198	56	18	2	4	90	18	3	0	25	7	0	0	2	0	24	33	.283	.341	.455
	TEX/AL		64	111	100	26	6	1	2	43	10	0	1	22	3	0	0	0	0	5	15	.260	.333	.430
91	TEX/AL		136	440	394	106	22	0	20	188	33	6	7	93	10	0	5	0	0	46	69	.269	.332	.477
92	TEX/AL		148	547	494	132	32	2	16	216	42	5	10	103	10	0	1	2	0	56	58	.267	.336	.437
93	MIL/AL		125	477	437	109	22	1	13	172	30	4	5	72	12	1	4	5	4	53	60	.249	.303	.394
6 YR TOTALS			**488**	**1606**	**1455**	**376**	**85**	**4**	**52**	**625**	**115**	**15**	**23**	**297**	**36**	**1**	**12**	**7**	**12**	**162**	**204**	**.258**	**.320**	**.430**

Renteria, Richard Avina "Rich" — BR/TR — b.12/25/61 — POS 2B-53, 3B-31, DH-16, SS-12, OF-1   PIT80 1/20

YR	TM/LG	CL	G	TPA	AB	H	2B	3B	HR	TB	BB	IBB	HB	SO	GDP	SH	SF	SB	CS	R	RBI	BA	OBA	SA
80	BP/GCL	R	46	193	176	40	6	1	2	54	9	2	2	15	5	3	3	4	2	19	23	.227	.268	.307
81	GRN/SAL	A	127	559	510	146	19	5	4	187	26	3	10	53	16	6	7	8	5	90	48	.286	.329	.367
82	ALE/CAR	A+	127	546	508	168	24	5	14	244	24	2	4	54	19	3	7	12	9	80	100	.331	.361	.480
83	LYN/EAS	AA	115	464	424	121	25	0	4	158	33	2	4	45	14	2	3	3	2	47	40	.285	.338	.373
84	NAS/EAS	AA	113	488	443	121	22	7	0	160	39	2	1	43	8	3	2	21	15	63	34	.273	.332	.361
	HAW/PCL	AAA	19	84	77	19	3	1	0	24	6	0	0	7	3	1	0	1	0	8	11	.247	.301	.312
85	HAW/PCL	AAA	7	31	31	6	2	0	0	8	0	0	0	4	0	0	0	0	0	2	2	.194	.194	.258
86	HAW/PCL	AAA	112	423	389	122	20	9	1	163	22	1	2	29	13	8	2	3	3	51	51	.314	.346	.419
	PIT/NL		10	12	12	3	1	0	0	4	0	0	0	2	1	0	0	2	0	2	0	.250	.250	.333
87	SEA/AL		12	11	10	1	1	0	0	2	0	0	1	2	0	0	0	0	0	0	0	.100	.182	.200
	CAL/PCL	AAA	69	282	267	79	14	3	1	102	9	0	1	20	11	2	3	3	3	41	32	.296	.318	.382
88	SEA/AL		31	91	88	18	9	0	0	27	2	0	0	3	1	0	1	0	0	6	6	.205	.222	.307
	CAL/PCL	AAA	24	95	87	23	6	1	4	43	5	0	3	12	3	1	3	1	0	15	10	.264	.319	.494
89	CAL/PCL	AAA	65	257	234	69	17	0	5	101	15	1	1	11	8	1	6	4	3	34	36	.295	.332	.432

(continued)

Renteria, Richard Avina "Rich" (continued)

YR	TM/LG	CL	G	TPA	AB	H	2B	3B	HR	TB	BB	IBB	HB	SO	GDP	SH	SF	SB	CS	R	RBI	BA	OBA	SA
91	IND/AMA	AAA	20	79	72	17	5	0	1	25	6	0	0	9	4	0	1	0	0	6	5	.236	.291	.347
93	FLO/NL		103	290	263	67	9	2	2	86	21	1	2	31	8	3	1	0	0	27	30	.255	.314	.327
4 YR TOTALS			**156**	**404**	**373**	**89**	**20**	**2**	**2**	**119**	**24**	**1**	**2**	**45**	**12**	**4**	**1**	**2**	**5**	**37**	**37**	**.239**	**.287**	**.319**

Reynolds, Harold Craig — BB/TR — b.11/26/60 — POS 2B-1274, DH-3, OF-1   SEA80 S1/2

YR	TM/LG	CL	G	TPA	AB	H	2B	3B	HR	TB	BB	IBB	HB	SO	GDP	SH	SF	SB	CS	R	RBI	BA	OBA	SA
83	SEA/AL		20	63	59	12	4	1	0	18	2	0	0	9	1	1	1	0	2	8	1	.203	.226	.305
84	SLC/PCL	AAA	135	646	558	165	22	6	3	208	73	2	3	72	9	9	3	37	17	94	54	.296	.378	.373
	SEA/AL		10	12	10	3	0	0	0	3	0	0	1	1	0	1	0	1	1	3	0	.300	.364	.300
85	CAL/PCL	AAA	52	248	212	77	11	3	5	109	28	1	1	18	2	1	4	9	13	36	30	.363	.433	.514
	SEA/AL		67	122	104	15	3	1	0	20	17	0	0	14	0	1	0	3	2	15	6	.144	.264	.192
86	CAL/PCL	AAA	29	139	118	37	7	0	1	47	20	0	1	12	1	1	0	10	8	20	7	.314	.413	.398
	SEA/AL		126	486	445	99	19	4	1	129	29	0	3	42	6	9	0	30	12	46	24	.222	.275	.290
87	SEA/AL		160	584	530	146	31	8	1	196	39	0	2	34	7	8	5	*60	20	73	35	.275	.325	.370
88	SEA/AL		158	663	598	169	26	*11	4	229	51	1	2	51	9	10	2	35	29	61	41	.283	.340	.383
89	SEA/AL		153	677	613	184	24	9	1	226	55	1	3	45	4	3	3	25	18	87	43	.300	.359	.369
90	SEA/AL		160	737	642	162	36	5	5	223	81	3	3	52	9	5	6	31	16	100	55	.252	.336	.347
91	SEA/AL		161	728	631	160	34	6	3	215	72	2	5	63	11	14	6	28	8	95	57	.254	.332	.341
92	SEA/AL		140	521	458	113	23	3	3	151	45	1	3	41	12	11	4	15	12	55	33	.247	.316	.330
93	BAL/AL		145	570	485	122	20	4	4	162	66	3	4	47	4	10	5	12	11	64	47	.252	.343	.334
11 YR TOTALS			**1300**	**5163**	**4575**	**1185**	**220**	**52**	**21**	**1572**	**457**	**11**	**26**	**399**	**63**	**73**	**32**	**240**	**131**	**607**	**342**	**.259**	**.328**	**.344**

Rhodes, Karl Derrick — BL/TL — b.8/21/68 — POS OF-93   HOU86 3/68

YR	TM/LG	CL	G	TPA	AB	H	2B	3B	HR	TB	BB	IBB	HB	SO	GDP	SH	SF	SB	CS	R	RBI	BA	OBA	SA
86	AST/GCL	R	62	261	222	65	10	3	0	81	32	3	0	33	1	5	2	14	6	36	22	.293	.379	.365
87	ASH/SAL	A	129	501	413	104	16	4	3	137	77	6	0	82	4	3	8	43	14	62	50	.252	.363	.332
88	OSC/FSL	A+	132	546	452	128	4	2	1	139	81	4	2	58	7	6	5	65	23	69	34	.283	.391	.308
89	CMB/SOU	AA	143	619	520	134	25	5	4	181	93	3	3	105	13	6	3	18	12	81	63	.258	.372	.348
90	TUC/PCL	AAA	107	440	385	106	24	11	3	161	47	2	0	75	9	3	5	24	4	68	59	.275	.350	.418
	HOU/NL		38	101	86	21	6	1	1	32	13	3	0	12	1	1	1	4	1	12	3	.244	.340	.372
91	HOU/NL		44	152	136	29	3	1	1	37	14	3	0	26	3	0	1	2	2	7	12	.213	.289	.272
	TUC/PCL	AAA	84	355	308	80	17	1	1	102	38	1	0	47	11	5	4	5	8	45	46	.260	.337	.331
92	HOU/NL		5	4	4	0	0	0	0	0	0	0	0	2	0	0	0	0	0	0	0	.000	.000	.000
	TUC/PCL	AAA	94	400	332	96	16	10	2	138	55	5	2	63	6	4	7	8	8	62	54	.289	.386	.416
93	OMA/AMA	AAA	88	410	365	116	31	2	23	220	38	4	1	60	8	2	4	10	5	81	64	.318	.380	.603
	IOW/AMA	AAA	35	149	125	40	12	1	7	75	20	4	1	22	2	2	1	6	3	31	25	.320	.415	.600
	HOU/NL		5	2	2	0	0	0	0	0	0	0	0	0	0	0	0	0	0	0	0	.000	.000	.000
	CHI/NL		15	63	52	15	2	1	3	28	11	0	0	9	0	0	2	0	0	12	7	.288	.413	.538
	YEAR		20	65	54	15	2	1	3	28	11	0	0	9	0	0	2	0	0	12	7	.278	.406	.519
4 YR TOTALS			**107**	**322**	**280**	**65**	**11**	**3**	**5**	**97**	**38**	**6**	**1**	**49**	**4**	**1**	**2**	**8**	**3**	**31**	**22**	**.232**	**.324**	**.346**

Richardson, Jeffrey Scott "Jeff" — BR/TR — b.8/26/65 — POS SS-46, 3B-12, 2B-8   CIN86 7/176

YR	TM/LG	CL	G	TPA	AB	H	2B	3B	HR	TB	BB	IBB	HB	SO	GDP	SH	SF	SB	CS	R	RBI	BA	OBA	SA
86	BIL/PIO	R+	47	180	162	51	14	4	0	73	17	0	1	23	0	0	0	12	1	42	20	.315	.383	.451
87	TAM/FSL	A+	100	415	374	112	9	2	0	125	30	5	3	35	16	1	7	10	4	44	37	.299	.350	.334
	VER/EAS	AA	35	142	134	28	4	0	0	32	5	0	1	25	4	0	0	5	0	24	8	.209	.243	.239
88	CHT/SOU	AA	122	447	399	100	17	1	1	122	23	0	9	56	7	12	4	8	1	50	37	.251	.303	.306
89	NAS/AMA	AAA	88	313	286	78	19	2	1	104	17	4	4	42	13	6	3	3	1	36	25	.273	.313	.364
	CIN/NL		53	140	125	21	4	0	2	31	10	0	3	23	3	3	1	1	0	10	11	.168	.234	.248
90	BUF/AMA	AAA	66	183	164	34	4	0	1	41	14	0	2	21	7	3	0	1	0	15	15	.207	.278	.250
91	PIT/NL		6	4	4	1	0	0	0	1	0	0	0	3	0	0	0	0	0	0	0	.250	.250	.250
	BUF/AMA	AAA	62	218	186	48	16	2	1	71	18	8	2	29	3	9	3	5	3	21	24	.258	.325	.382
92	BUF/AMA	AAA	97	361	328	95	23	2	3	131	19	3	1	46	12	11	2	5	2	34	29	.290	.329	.399
93	BOS/AL		15	27	24	5	2	0	0	7	1	0	2	3	0	0	2	0	0	3	2	.208	.240	.292
	PAW/INT	AAA	9	31	28	9	1	0	0	10	1	0	0	6	1	1	1	0	0	2	1	.321	.333	.357
3 YR TOTALS			**74**	**171**	**153**	**27**	**6**	**0**	**2**	**39**	**11**	**0**	**1**	**29**	**3**	**5**	**1**	**1**	**0**	**13**	**13**	**.176**	**.235**	**.255**

Riles, Ernest "Ernie" — BL/TR — b.10/2/60 — POS SS-362, 3B-301, 2B-88, DH-21, 1B-10, OF-5   MIL81* S3/63

YR	TM/LG	CL	G	TPA	AB	H	2B	3B	HR	TB	BB	IBB	HB	SO	GDP	SH	SF	SB	CS	R	RBI	BA	OBA	SA
84	VAN/PCL	AAA	123	501	424	113	19	7	3	155	67	8	1	67	15	1	8	1	2	59	54	.267	.362	.366
85	VAN/PCL	AAA	30	138	118	41	7	1	2	56	17	4	1	13	1	0	2	2	2	19	20	.347	.428	.475
	MIL/AL		116	495	448	128	12	7	5	169	36	0	2	54	16	6	3	2	2	54	45	.286	.339	.377
86	MIL/AL		145	588	524	132	24	2	9	187	54	0	1	80	14	6	3	7	7	69	47	.252	.321	.357
87	EP/TEX	AA	41	183	153	52	10	0	6	80	28	1	0	24	4	0	2	1	1	45	24	.340	.437	.523
	MIL/AL		83	316	276	72	11	1	4	97	30	1	3	47	6	3	6	3	4	38	38	.261	.329	.351
88	MIL/AL		41	135	127	32	6	1	1	43	7	0	1	26	3	1	0	2	0	7	9	.252	.291	.339
	SF/NL		79	201	187	55	7	2	3	75	10	2	0	33	5	0	4	1	2	26	28	.294	.323	.401
	YEAR		120	336	314	87	13	3	4	118	17	2	1	59	8	1	4	3	4	33	37	.277	.310	.376
89	SF/NL		122	337	302	84	13	2	7	122	28	3	2	50	7	1	4	0	2	43	40	.278	.339	.404
90	SF/NL		92	184	155	31	2	1	8	59	26	3	0	26	2	1	1	0	0	22	21	.200	.313	.381
91	OAK/AL		108	321	281	60	8	4	5	91	31	3	4	42	8	4	4	3	2	30	32	.214	.290	.324
92	TUC/PCL	AAA	60	237	202	62	17	3	1	88	30	4	0	33	5	1	3	0	0	37	35	.307	.390	.436
	HOU/NL		39	64	61	16	1	1	0	20	2	0	0	11	0	0	1	0	0	5	4	.262	.281	.328
93	PAW/INT	AAA	6	23	18	5	0	0	2	11	3	0	2	5	0	0	0	0	0	3	3	.278	.348	.611
	BOS/AL		94	170	143	27	8	0	5	50	20	3	2	40	3	4	2	3	1	15	20	.189	.292	.350
9 YR TOTALS			**919**	**2811**	**2504**	**637**	**92**	**20**	**48**	**913**	**244**	**15**	**9**	**409**	**64**	**25**	**29**	**20**	**28**	**309**	**284**	**.254**	**.319**	**.365**

Ripken, Calvin Edwin Jr. "Cal" — BR/TR — b.8/24/60 — POS SS-1885, 3B-77   BAL78 4/78

YR	TM/LG	CL	G	TPA	AB	H	2B	3B	HR	TB	BB	IBB	HB	SO	GDP	SH	SF	SB	CS	R	RBI	BA	OBA	SA
81	BAL/AL		23	40	39	5	0	0	0	5	1	0	0	8	4	0	0	0	0	1	0	.128	.150	.128
82	BAL/AL		160	655	598	158	32	5	28	284	46	3	3	95	16	2	6	3	3	90	93	.264	.317	.475
83	BAL/AL		162	726	663	*211	*47	2	27	343	58	0	0	97	24	0	5	0	4	*121	102	.318	.371	.517
84	BAL/AL		162	716	641	195	37	7	27	327	71	1	2	89	16	0	2	2	1	103	86	.304	.374	.510
85	BAL/AL		161	718	642	181	32	5	26	301	67	1	1	68	32	0	8	2	3	116	110	.282	.347	.469
86	BAL/AL		162	707	627	177	35	1	25	289	70	1	4	60	19	0	6	4	2	98	81	.282	.355	.461
87	BAL/AL		162	717	624	157	28	3	27	272	81	0	1	77	19	0	11	3	5	97	98	.252	.333	.436
88	BAL/AL		161	689	575	152	25	1	23	248	102	7	2	69	10	0	10	2	2	87	81	.264	.372	.431
89	BAL/AL		162	712	646	166	30	0	21	259	57	5	3	72	22	0	6	3	2	80	93	.257	.317	.401
90	BAL/AL		161	695	600	150	28	4	21	249	82	17	5	66	12	0	7	3	1	78	84	.250	.341	.415
91	BAL/AL		162	717	650	210	46	5	34	*368	53	15	5	46	19	0	9	6	1	99	114	.323	.374	.566
92	BAL/AL		162	715	637	160	29	1	14	233	64	14	7	50	13	0	7	4	3	73	72	.251	.323	.366
93	BAL/AL		162	718	641	165	26	3	24	269	65	19	6	58	17	0	6	1	4	87	90	.257	.329	.420
13 YR TOTALS			1962	8525	7583	2087	395	37	297	3447	817	87	39	855	223	3	83	33	31	1130	1104	**.275**	**.345**	**.455**

Ripken, William Oliver "Billy" — BR/TR — b.12/16/64 — POS 2B-693, SS-18, DH-4, 3B-3   BAL82 11/286

YR	TM/LG	CL	G	TPA	AB	H	2B	3B	HR	TB	BB	IBB	HB	SO	GDP	SH	SF	SB	CS	R	RBI	BA	OBA	SA
84	HAG/CAR	A+	115	451	409	94	15	3	2	121	36	1	4	64	11	2	0	3	5	48	40	.230	.298	.296
85	CHA/SOU	AA	18	58	51	7	1	0	0	8	6	0	0	4	1	1	0	0	0	2	3	.137	.228	.157
	DB/FSL	A+	67	250	222	51	11	0	0	62	22	1	0	24	6	5	1	7	4	23	18	.230	.298	.279
	HAG/CAR	A+	14	50	47	12	0	1	0	14	1	0	2	2	0	0	0	0	2	9	0	.255	.300	.298
86	CHA/SOU	AA	141	564	530	142	20	3	5	183	24	2	1	47	21	7	2	9	4	58	62	.268	.300	.345
87	ROC/INT	AAA	74	266	238	68	15	0	0	83	21	0	0	23	9	7	0	7	2	32	11	.286	.344	.349
	BAL/AL		58	257	234	72	9	0	2	87	21	0	0	23	3	1	1	4	1	27	20	.308	.363	.372
88	BAL/AL		150	559	512	106	18	1	2	132	33	0	5	63	14	6	3	8	2	52	34	.207	.260	.258
89	BAL/AL		115	364	318	76	11	2	2	97	22	0	1	53	12	19	5	1	2	31	26	.239	.284	.305
90	BAL/AL		129	456	406	118	28	1	3	157	28	2	4	43	7	17	1	5	2	48	38	.291	.342	.387
91	FRE/CAR	A+	1	4	4	1	0	0	0	1	0	0	0	0	0	0	0	0	0	2	1	.250	.250	.250
	HAG/EAS	AA	1	5	5	3	0	0	0	3	0	0	0	0	0	0	0	0	0	1	0	.600	.600	.600
	BAL/AL		104	315	287	62	11	1	0	75	15	0	0	31	14	11	2	0	1	24	14	.216	.253	.261
92	BAL/AL		111	363	330	76	15	1	4	103	18	1	3	26	10	10	2	2	3	35	36	.230	.275	.312
93	TEX/AL		50	153	132	25	4	0	0	29	11	0	4	19	6	5	1	0	2	12	11	.189	.270	.220
7 YR TOTALS			717	2467	2219	535	96	5	13	680	148	3	16	258	66	69	15	20	13	229	179	**.241**	**.291**	**.306**

Rivera, Luis Antonio — BR/TR — b.1/3/64 — POS SS-637, 2B-32, DH-10, 3B-4, OF-1   MON 9/22/81

YR	TM/LG	CL	G	TPA	AB	H	2B	3B	HR	TB	BB	IBB	HB	SO	GDP	SH	SF	SB	CS	R	RBI	BA	OBA	SA
84	WPB/FSL	A+	124	497	439	100	23	0	6	141	50	5	5	79	16	0	3	14	2	54	43	.228	.312	.321
85	JAC/SOU	AA	138	598	538	129	20	2	16	201	44	1	7	69	7	3	6	18	15	74	72	.240	.303	.374
86	IND/AMA	AAA	108	447	407	100	17	5	7	148	29	0	4	68	12	1	6	18	8	60	43	.246	.298	.364
	MON/NL		55	187	166	34	11	1	0	47	17	0	0	33	1	1	1	2	1	20	13	.205	.285	.283
87	IND/AMA	AAA	108	473	433	135	26	3	8	191	32	2	2	73	4	3	3	24	11	73	53	.312	.360	.441
	MON/NL		18	33	32	5	2	0	0	7	1	0	0	0	0	0	0	0	0	0	1	.156	.182	.219
88	MON/NL		123	402	371	83	17	3	4	118	24	4	1	69	9	3	3	3	4	35	30	.224	.271	.318
89	PAW/INT	AAA	43	191	175	44	9	0	1	56	11	0	0	23	3	4	0	5	3	22	13	.251	.299	.320
	BOS/AL		93	349	323	83	17	1	5	117	20	1	1	60	7	4	1	2	3	35	29	.257	.301	.362
90	BOS/AL		118	385	346	78	20	2	7	119	25	0	1	58	10	12	1	4	3	38	45	.225	.279	.344
91	BOS/AL		129	468	414	107	22	3	8	159	35	0	3	86	10	12	4	4	3	64	40	.258	.318	.384
92	BOS/AL		102	322	288	62	11	1	0	75	26	0	3	56	5	5	0	4	2	17	29	.215	.287	.260
93	BOS/AL		62	145	130	27	8	1	1	40	11	0	1	36	2	2	1	1	0	13	7	.208	.273	.308
8 YR TOTALS			700	2291	2070	479	108	10	25	682	159	5	12	406	44	39	11	19	20	222	194	**.231**	**.289**	**.329**

Roberson, Kevin Lynn — BB/TR — b.1/29/68 — POS OF-51   CHN88 15/404

YR	TM/LG	CL	G	TPA	AB	H	2B	3B	HR	TB	BB	IBB	HB	SO	GDP	SH	SF	SB	CS	R	RBI	BA	OBA	SA
88	WYT/APP	R+	63	270	225	47	12	2	3	72	40	0	3	86	0	0	2	3	2	39	29	.209	.333	.320
89	CHW/SAL	A	126	509	429	109	19	1	13	169	70	4	5	149	1	1	3	3	6	49	57	.254	.363	.394
90	WIN/CAR	A+	85	344	313	84	23	3	5	128	25	0	3	70	6	1	2	7	3	49	45	.268	.327	.409
	CHA/SOU	AA	31	130	119	29	6	2	5	54	8	0	0	25	3	1	2	2	0	14	16	.244	.287	.454
91	CHA/SOU	AA	136	560	507	130	24	2	19	215	39	1	9	129	10	0	5	17	3	77	67	.256	.318	.424
92	IOW/AMA	AAA	51	206	197	60	15	4	6	101	5	1	2	46	4	1	0	0	1	25	34	.305	.327	.513
93	IOW/AMA	AAA	67	289	263	80	20	1	16	150	19	3	4	66	4	0	0	0	1	48	50	.304	.356	.570
	CHI/NL		62	195	180	34	4	1	9	67	12	0	3	48	2	0	0	0	1	23	27	.189	.251	.372

Roberts, Leon Joseph "Bip" — BB/TR — b.10/27/63 — POS 2B-279, OF-265, 3B-134, SS-33   PIT82 S1/13

YR	TM/LG	CL	G	TPA	AB	H	2B	3B	HR	TB	BB	IBB	HB	SO	GDP	SH	SF	SB	CS	R	RBI	BA	OBA	SA
84	PW/CAR	A+	134	552	498	150	25	5	8	209	44	3	3	63	4	2	5	50	13	81	77	.301	.358	.420
85	NAS/EAS	AA	105	442	401	109	19	5	1	141	29	2	6	43	6	4	2	40	12	64	23	.272	.329	.352
86	SD/NL		101	258	241	61	5	2	1	73	14	1	0	29	2	2	1	14	12	34	12	.253	.293	.303
87	LV/PCL	AAA	98	406	359	110	18	10	1	151	37	3	3	39	11	6	1	27	14	66	38	.306	.375	.421
88	LV/PCL	AAA	100	383	343	121	21	8	7	179	32	1	0	45	5	6	2	29	7	73	51	.353	.406	.522
	SD/NL		5	10	9	3	0	0	0	3	1	0	0	0	0	0	0	0	0	0	0	.333	.400	.333
89	SD/NL		117	387	329	99	15	8	3	139	49	0	1	45	3		2	21	11	81	25	.301	.391	.422
90	SD/NL		149	629	556	172	36	3	9	241	55	1	6	65	8	4	3	46	12	104	44	.309	.375	.433
91	SD/NL		117	472	424	119	13	3	3	147	37	0	4	71	6	4	3	26	11	66	32	.281	.342	.347
92	CIN/NL		147	601	532	172	34	6	4	230	62	4	2	54	7	1	4	44	16	92	45	.323	.393	.432
93	CIN/NL		83	336	292	70	13	0	1	86	38	2	0	46	2	0	3	26	6	46	18	.240	.330	.295
7 YR TOTALS			719	2693	2383	696	116	22	21	919	256	7	16	312	28	21	17	177	70	424	176	**.292**	**.362**	**.386**

Rodriguez, Henry Anderson — BL/TL — b.11/8/67 — POS OF-96, 1B-14 · LA 7/14/85

YR	TM/LG	CL	G	TPA	AB	H	2B	3B	HR	TB	BB	IBB	HB	SO	GDP	SH	SF	SB	CS	R	RBI	BA	OBA	SA
87	DOD/GCL	R	49	170	148	49	7	3	0	62	16	7	3	15	5	1	2	3	1	23	15	.331	.402	.419
88	SAL/NWL	A-	72	323	291	84	14	4	2	112	21	1	4	42	7	1	6	14	2	47	39	.289	.339	.385
89	VB/FSL	A+	126	490	433	123	33	1	10	188	48	11	2	58	12	1	6	7	6	53	73	.284	.354	.434
	BAK/CAL	A+	3	9	9	2	0	0	1	5	0	0	0	3	0	0	0	0	0	2	2	.222	.222	.556
90	SA/TEX	AA	129	573	495	144	22	9	28	268	61	9	2	66	11	1	14	5	4	82	109	.291	.362	.541
91	ALB/PCL	AAA	121	478	446	121	22	5	10	183	25	3	1	62	12	1	5	4	5	61	67	.271	.308	.410
92	ALB/PCL	AAA	94	409	365	111	21	5	14	184	31	5	1	57	11	2	10	1	5	59	72	.304	.351	.504
	LA/NL		53	156	146	32	7	0	3	48	8	0	0	30	2	1	1	0	0	11	14	.219	.258	.329
93	ALB/PCL	AAA	46	198	179	53	13	5	4	88	14	0	2	37	5	0	3	1	2	26	30	.296	.348	.492
	LA/NL		76	188	176	39	10	0	8	73	11	2	0	39	1	0	1	1	0	20	23	.222	.266	.415
2 YR TOTALS			**129**	**344**	**322**	**71**	**17**	**0**	**11**	**121**	**19**	**2**	**0**	**69**	**3**	**1**	**2**	**1**	**0**	**31**	**37**	**.220**	**.262**	**.376**

Rodriguez, Ivan — BR/TR — b.11/27/71 — POS C-338, DH-3 · TEX 7/27/88

YR	TM/LG	CL	G	TPA	AB	H	2B	3B	HR	TB	BB	IBB	HB	SO	GDP	SH	SF	SB	CS	R	RBI	BA	OBA	SA
89	GAS/SAL	A	112	418	386	92	22	1	7	137	21	0	2	58	6	5	4	2	5	38	42	.238	.278	.355
90	CHA/FSL	A+	109	432	408	117	17	7	2	154	12	2	7	50	6	1	4	1	0	48	55	.287	.316	.377
91	TUL/TEX	AA	50	188	175	48	7	2	3	68	6	0	1	27	5	1	5	1	2	16	28	.274	.294	.389
	TEX/AL		88	288	280	74	16	0	3	99	5	0	0	42	10	2	1	0	1	24	27	.264	.276	.354
92	TEX/AL		123	454	420	109	16	1	8	151	24	2	1	73	15	7	2	0	0	39	37	.260	.300	.360
93	TEX/AL		137	519	473	129	28	4	10	195	29	3	4	70	16	5	8	8	7	56	66	.273	.315	.412
3 YR TOTALS			**348**	**1261**	**1173**	**312**	**60**	**5**	**21**	**445**	**58**	**5**	**5**	**185**	**41**	**14**	**11**	**8**	**8**	**119**	**130**	**.266**	**.301**	**.379**

Ronan, Edward Marcus "Marc" — BL/TR — b.9/19/69 — POS C-6 · SL90 4/86

YR	TM/LG	CL	G	TPA	AB	H	2B	3B	HR	TB	BB	IBB	HB	SO	GDP	SH	SF	SB	CS	R	RBI	BA	OBA	SA
90	HAM/NYP	A-	56	186	167	38	6	0	1	47	15	0	1	37	3	0	3	1	2	14	15	.228	.290	.281
91	SAV/SAL	A	108	388	343	81	10	1	0	93	38	1	3	54	13	3	1	11	3	39	45	.236	.317	.271
92	SPR/MID	A	110	404	376	81	19	2	6	122	23	2	1	58	11	0	4	4	5	45	48	.215	.260	.324
93	SP/FSL	A+	25	98	87	27	5	0	0	32	6	0	0	10	1	3	2	0	0	13	6	.310	.347	.368
	ARK/TEX	AA	96	315	281	60	16	1	7	99	26	2	2	47	4	3	3	1	3	33	34	.214	.282	.352
	STL/NL		6	12	12	1	0	0	0	1	0	0	0	5	0	0	0	0	0	0	0	.083	.083	.083

Rossy, Elam Jose "Rico" — BR/TR — b.2/16/64 — POS SS-63, 2B-27, 3B-25 · BAL85 30/803

YR	TM/LG	CL	G	TPA	AB	H	2B	3B	HR	TB	BB	IBB	HB	SO	GDP	SH	SF	SB	CS	R	RBI	BA	OBA	SA
85	NEW/NYP	A-	73	283	246	53	14	2	3	80	32	1	1	22	13	3	1	17	7	38	25	.215	.307	.325
86	MIA/FSL	A+	38	166	134	34	7	1	1	46	24	0	1	8	4	6	1	10	6	26	9	.254	.369	.343
	CHA/SOU	AA	77	269	232	68	16	2	3	97	26	0	2	19	2	8	1	13	5	40	25	.293	.368	.418
87	CHA/SOU	AA	127	521	471	135	22	3	4	175	43	0	3	38	20	3	1	20	9	69	50	.287	.349	.372
88	BUF/AMA	AAA	68	201	187	46	4	0	1	53	13	0	0	18	4	0	1	1	5	12	20	.246	.294	.283
89	HAR/EAS	AA	78	270	238	60	16	1	2	84	27	0	3	19	5	0	2	2	4	20	25	.252	.333	.353
	BUF/AMA	AAA	38	131	109	21	5	0	0	26	18	1	1	11	4	1	2	4	0	11	10	.193	.308	.239
90	BUF/AMA	AAA	8	23	17	3	0	0	0	5	4	0	0	2	0	1	1	1	0	3	2	.176	.318	.294
	GRE/SOU	AA	5	22	21	4	1	0	0	5	1	0	0	2	1	0	0	0	2	4	0	.190	.227	.238
	RIC/INT	AAA	107	461	380	88	13	0	4	113	69	1	3	43	12	7	2	13	6	58	32	.232	.352	.297
91	RIC/INT	AAA	139	570	482	124	25	2	2	157	67	1	5	44	12	13	3	4	8	58	48	.257	.352	.326
	ATL/NL		5	1	1	0	0	0	0	0	0	0	0	0	0	0	0	0	0	0	0	.000	.000	.000
92	KC/AL		59	178	149	32	8	1	1	45	20	1	1	20	6	7	1	0	3	21	12	.215	.310	.302
	OMA/AMA	AAA	48	213	174	55	10	0	4	79	34	0	0	14	5	2	3	3	5	29	17	.316	.422	.454
93	OMA/AMA	AAA	37	155	131	39	10	1	5	66	20	1	1	19	1	0	3	1	3	25	21	.298	.400	.504
	KC/AL		46	97	86	19	4	0	2	29	9	0	1	11	0	1	0	0	3	10	12	.221	.302	.337
3 YR TOTALS			**110**	**276**	**236**	**51**	**12**	**1**	**3**	**74**	**29**	**1**	**2**	**32**	**6**	**8**	**1**	**0**	**3**	**31**	**24**	**.216**	**.306**	**.314**

Rowland, Richard Garnet "Rich" — BR/TR — b.2/25/67 — POS C-27, DH-8, 1B-1, 3B-1 · DET88 17/447

YR	TM/LG	CL	G	TPA	AB	H	2B	3B	HR	TB	BB	IBB	HB	SO	GDP	SH	SF	SB	CS	R	RBI	BA	OBA	SA
88	BRI/APP	R+	56	217	186	51	10	1	4	75	27	1	1	39	2	0	3	1	2	29	41	.274	.364	.403
89	FAY/SAL	A	108	438	375	102	17	1	9	148	54	2	3	98	8	3	3	4	1	43	59	.272	.366	.395
90	LON/EAS	AA	47	185	161	46	10	0	8	80	20	3	3	33	7	0	1	1	1	22	30	.286	.373	.497
	TOL/INT	AAA	62	213	192	50	12	0	7	83	15	0	1	33	3	3	2	2	3	28	22	.260	.314	.432
	DET/AL		7	21	19	3	1	0	0	4	2	1	0	4	1	0	0	0	0	3	0	.158	.238	.211
91	TOL/INT	AAA	109	447	383	104	26	0	13	169	60	3	3	77	8	0	1	4	2	56	68	.272	.374	.441
	DET/AL		4	4	4	1	0	0	0	1	0	0	0	2	0	0	0	0	0	0	1	.250	.333	.250
92	TOL/INT	AAA	136	536	473	111	19	1	25	207	56	6	3	112	20	0	4	1	3	75	82	.235	.317	.438
	DET/AL		6	17	14	3	0	0	0	3	3	0	0	3	0	0	0	0	0	2	0	.214	.353	.214
93	TOL/INT	AAA	96	382	325	87	24	2	21	178	51	3	3	72	11	0	3	1	0	58	59	.268	.369	.548
	DET/AL		21	52	46	10	3	0	0	13	5	0	0	16	1	1	0	0	0	2	4	.217	.294	.283
4 YR TOTALS			**38**	**96**	**83**	**17**	**4**	**0**	**0**	**21**	**11**	**1**	**0**	**25**	**3**	**1**	**1**	**0**	**0**	**7**	**5**	**.205**	**.295**	**.253**

Royer, Stanley Dean "Stan" — BR/TR — b.8/31/67 — POS 3B-20, 1B-6 · OAK88 1/16

YR	TM/LG	CL	G	TPA	AB	H	2B	3B	HR	TB	BB	IBB	HB	SO	GDP	SH	SF	SB	CS	R	RBI	BA	OBA	SA
88	SO/NWL	A-	73	326	286	91	19	3	6	134	33	1	2	71	6	1	4	1	0	47	48	.318	.388	.469
89	TAC/PCL	AAA	6	21	19	5	1	0	0	6	2	0	0	6	1	0	0	0	0	2	2	.263	.333	.316
	MOD/CAL	A+	127	539	476	120	28	1	11	183	58	3	1	132	11	2	2	3	2	54	69	.252	.333	.384
90	HUN/SOU	AA	137	585	527	136	29	3	14	213	43	0	3	113	13	8	4	4	1	69	89	.258	.315	.404
	LOU/AMA	AAA	4	17	15	4	1	0	0	5	1	0	0	2	0	1	0	0	1	0	4	.267	.353	.467
91	LOU/AMA	AAA	138	575	523	133	30	6	14	217	43	1	3	126	14	0	6	1	2	48	74	.254	.311	.415
	STL/NL		9	22	21	6	1	0	0	7	1	0	0	3	0	0	0	0	0	1	1	.286	.318	.333
92	LOU/AMA	AAA	124	488	444	125	31	2	11	193	32	2	4	74	17	4	4	1	0	55	77	.282	.333	.435
	STL/NL		13	33	31	10	2	0	2	18	1	0	0	4	0	0	0	1	0	6	9	.323	.333	.581

YR	TM/LG	CL	G	TPA	AB	H	2B	3B	HR	TB	BB	IBB	HB	SO	GDP	SH	SF	SB	CS	R	RBI	BA	OBA	SA
93	LOU/AMA	AAA	98	409	368	103	19	0	16	170	33	2	0	74	9	3	5	2	0	46	54	.280	.335	.462
	STL/NL		24	48	46	14	2	0	1	19	2	0	0	14	2	0	0	0	1	4	8	.304	.333	.413
3 YR TOTALS			**46**	**103**	**98**	**30**	**5**	**0**	**3**	**44**	**4**	**0**	**0**	**20**	**2**	**0**	**1**	**0**	**1**	**11**	**18**	**.306**	**.330**	**.449**

Russell, John William — BR/TR — b.1/5/61 — POS C-209, OF-119, DH-25, 1B-24, 3B-4, P-1   PHI82 1/13

YR	TM/LG	CL	G	TPA	AB	H	2B	3B	HR	TB	BB	IBB	HB	SO	GDP	SH	SF	SB	CS	R	RBI	BA	OBA	SA
82	REA/EAS	AA	77	295	263	53	10	5	6	91	23	3	4	84	8	2	3	3	2	26	30	.202	.273	.346
83	POR/PCL	AAA	128	491	445	113	23	3	27	223	42	1	2	109	3	0	2	3	3	71	76	.254	.320	.501
84	POR/PCL	AAA	93	403	350	101	22	5	19	190	44	0	6	91	10	0	3	1	0	75	77	.289	.375	.543
	PHI/NL		39	114	99	28	8	1	2	44	12	2	0	33	2	0	3	0	1	11	11	.283	.351	.444
85	POR/PCL	AAA	16	63	49	15	2	2	4	33	13	3	1	15	0	0	0	0	0	8	11	.306	.460	.673
	PHI/NL		81	234	216	47	12	0	9	86	18	0	0	72	5	0	0	0	0	22	23	.218	.278	.398
86	PHI/NL		93	348	315	76	21	2	13	140	25	2	3	103	6	1	4	0	1	35	60	.241	.300	.444
87	MAI/INT	AAA	44	167	143	29	6	1	7	58	22	0	0	37	7	1	1	2	3	15	24	.203	.307	.406
	PHI/NL		24	65	62	9	1	0	3	19	3	0	0	17	4	0	0	0	1	5	8	.145	.185	.306
88	MAI/INT	AAA	110	430	394	90	18	0	13	147	29	2	4	108	3	0	3	4	2	50	52	.228	.286	.373
	PHI/NL		22	53	49	12	1	0	2	19	3	0	0	15	2	0	0	0	0	5	4	.245	.302	.388
89	ATL/NL		74	169	159	29	2	0	2	37	6	2	1	53	4	0	1	0	0	16	8	.182	.225	.233
90	OC/AMA	AAA	6	24	22	9	4	0	2	19	2	0	1	2	0	0	0	0	0	7	6	.409	.458	.864
	TEX/AL		68	140	128	35	4	0	2	45	11	2	0	41	3	1	1	0	0	16	8	.273	.331	.352
91	TEX/AL		22	29	27	3	0	0	0	3	1	0	0	7	0	0	1	0	0	3	1	.111	.138	.111
92	TUL/TEX	AA	46	186	163	42	11	0	10	83	17	1	0	42	6	0	0	0	4	26	27	.258	.344	.509
	TEX/AL		7	13	10	1	0	0	0	1	1	0	0	4	0	0	0	1	2	1	3	.100	.231	.100
93	TEX/AL		18	24	22	5	1	0	1	9	2	0	0	10	0	0	0	0	0	1	3	.227	.292	.409
10 YR TOTALS			**448**	**1189**	**1087**	**245**	**50**	**3**	**34**	**403**	**84**	**7**	**6**	**355**	**26**	**2**	**10**	**3**	**3**	**113**	**129**	**.225**	**.282**	**.371**

Sabo, Christopher Andrew "Chris" — BR/TR — b.1/19/62 — POS 3B-749, SS-2   CIN83 2/30

YR	TM/LG	CL	G	TPA	AB	H	2B	3B	HR	TB	BB	IBB	HB	SO	GDP	SH	SF	SB	CS	R	RBI	BA	OBA	SA
84	VER/EAS	AA	125	495	441	94	19	1	5	130	44	1	4	62	11	2	4	10	5	44	38	.213	.288	.295
85	VER/EAS	AA	124	495	428	119	19	0	11	171	50	1	7	39	6	6	4	7	5	66	46	.278	.360	.400
86	DEN/AMA	AAA	129	492	432	118	26	2	10	178	48	2	3	53	9	3	6	9	2	83	60	.273	.346	.412
87	NAS/AMA	AAA	91	360	315	92	19	3	7	138	37	4	1	25	9	1	6	23	4	56	51	.292	.362	.438
88	CIN/NL		137	582	538	146	40	2	11	223	29	1	6	52	12	5	4	46	14	74	44	.271	.314	.414
89	NAS/AMA	AAA	7	30	30	5	2	0	0	7	0	0	0	0	4	0	0	0	0	0	3	.167	.167	.233
	CIN/NL		82	336	304	79	21	1	6	120	25	2	3	33	2	4	2	14	9	40	29	.260	.316	.395
90	CIN/NL		148	636	567	153	38	2	25	270	61	7	4	58	8	1	3	25	10	95	71	.270	.343	.476
91	CIN/NL		153	640	582	175	35	3	26	294	44	3	6	79	13	6	1	19	6	91	88	.301	.354	.505
92	NAS/AMA	AAA	3	14	11	4	0	0	1	7	1	0	2	1	0	0	0	0	0	3	1	.364	.500	.636
	CIN/NL		96	382	344	84	19	3	12	145	30	1	1	54	12	1	6	4	5	42	43	.244	.302	.422
93	CIN/NL		148	611	552	143	33	2	21	243	43	5	2	105	10	2	8	6	4	86	82	.259	.315	.440
6 YR TOTALS			**764**	**3187**	**2887**	**780**	**186**	**13**	**101**	**1295**	**232**	**19**	**24**	**381**	**57**	**18**	**26**	**114**	**48**	**428**	**357**	**.270**	**.327**	**.449**

Salmon, Timothy James "Tim" — BR/TR — b.8/24/68 — POS OF-161, DH-1   CAL89 3/69

YR	TM/LG	CL	G	TPA	AB	H	2B	3B	HR	TB	BB	IBB	HB	SO	GDP	SH	SF	SB	CS	R	RBI	BA	OBA	SA
89	BEN/NWL	A-	55	238	196	48	6	5	6	82	33	0	6	61	2	1	2	2	4	37	31	.245	.367	.418
90	PS/CAL	A+	36	143	118	34	6	0	2	46	21	0	4	44	1	0	0	11	1	19	21	.288	.413	.390
	MID/TEX	AA	27	117	97	26	3	0	3	40	18	0	1	38	1	0	1	0	0	17	16	.268	.385	.412
91	MID/TEX	AA	131	565	465	114	26	4	23	217	89	1	6	166	6	3	2	12	6	100	94	.245	.372	.467
92	EDM/PCL	AAA	118	510	409	142	38	4	29	275	91	11	6	103	9	0	4	9	7	101	105	.347	.469	.672
	CAL/AL		23	92	79	14	1	0	2	21	11	1	1	23	1	0	1	1	4	8	6	.177	.283	.266
93	CAL/AL		142	610	515	146	35	1	31	276	82	5	5	135	6	0	8	5	6	93	95	.283	.382	.536
2 YR TOTALS			**165**	**702**	**594**	**160**	**36**	**1**	**33**	**297**	**93**	**6**	**6**	**158**	**7**	**0**	**9**	**6**	**7**	**101**	**101**	**.269**	**.369**	**.500**

Samuel, Juan Milton — BR/TR — b.12/9/60 — POS 2B-1170, OF-190, 1B-6, 3B-5   PHI 4/29/80

YR	TM/LG	CL	G	TPA	AB	H	2B	3B	HR	TB	BB	IBB	HB	SO	GDP	SH	SF	SB	CS	R	RBI	BA	OBA	SA
83	PHI/NL		18	71	65	18	1	2	2	29	4	1	1	16	1	0	0	3	2	14	5	.277	.324	.446
84	PHI/NL		160	737	701	191	36	*19	15	310	28	2	7	168	6	0	5	72	15	105	69	.272	.307	.442
85	PHI/NL		161	709	663	175	31	13	19	289	33	2	6	141	8	2	5	53	19	101	74	.264	.303	.436
86	PHI/NL		145	633	591	157	36	12	16	265	26	3	8	142	8	1	7	42	14	90	78	.266	.302	.448
87	PHI/NL		160	726	655	178	37	*15	28	329	60	5	5	162	12	0	5	35	15	113	100	.272	.335	.502
88	PHI/NL		157	685	629	153	32	9	12	239	39	6	12	151	8	0	5	33	10	68	67	.243	.298	.380
89	PHI/NL		51	219	199	49	3	1	8	78	18	1	1	45	2	0	1	11	3	32	20	.246	.311	.392
	NY/NL		86	370	333	76	13	1	3	100	24	1	10	75	5	2	1	31	9	37	28	.228	.299	.300
	YEAR		137	589	532	125	16	2	11	178	42	2	11	120	7	2	2	42	12	69	48	.235	.303	.335
90	LA/NL		143	558	492	119	24	3	13	188	51	2	5	126	6	5	3	38	20	62	52	.242	.316	.382
91	LA/NL		153	659	594	161	22	6	12	231	49	4	3	133	8	8	3	23	8	74	58	.271	.328	.389
92	LA/NL		47	136	122	32	3	1	0	37	7	3	1	22	0	0	4	2	2	7	15	.262	.303	.303
	KC/AL		29	110	102	29	5	3	0	40	7	1	1	27	2	0	0	2	1	15	8	.284	.336	.392
	YEAR		76	246	224	61	8	4	0	77	14	4	2	49	2	0	4	4	3	22	23	.272	.318	.344
93	CIN/NL		103	289	261	60	10	4	4	90	23	3	2	53	2	0	2	9	7	31	26	.230	.298	.345
11 YR TOTALS			**1413**	**5902**	**5407**	**1398**	**253**	**89**	**132**	**2225**	**369**	**37**	**63**	**1261**	**70**	**24**	**39**	**358**	**125**	**749**	**600**	**.259**	**.311**	**.412**

Sanchez, Rey Francisco — BR/TR — b.10/5/67 — POS SS-176, 2B-6   TEX86 13/313

YR	TM/LG	CL	G	TPA	AB	H	2B	3B	HR	TB	BB	IBB	HB	SO	GDP	SH	SF	SB	CS	R	RBI	BA	OBA	SA
86	RAN/GCL	R	52	217	169	49	3	1	0	54	41	0	3	18	3	3	1	10	10	27	23	.290	.435	.320
87	GAS/SAL	A	50	187	160	35	1	2	1	43	22	0	2	17	9	3	0	6	3	19	10	.219	.321	.269
	BUT/PIO	R+	49	217	189	69	10	6	0	91	21	1	2	11	6	3	2	22	6	36	25	.365	.430	.481

(continued)

Sanchez, Rey Francisco (continued)

YR	TM/LG	CL	G	TPA	AB	H	2B	3B	HR	TB	BB	IBB	HB	SO	GDP	SH	SF	SB	CS	R	RBI	BA	OBA	SA
88	CHA/FSL	A+	128	462	418	128	6	5	0	144	35	4	5	24	14	1	3	29	11	60	38	.306	.364	.344
89	OC/AMA	AAA	134	495	464	104	10	4	1	125	21	0	2	50	14	5	3	4	4	38	39	.224	.259	.269
91	IOW/AMA	AAA	126	474	417	121	16	5	2	153	37	2	7	27	11	11	2	13	7	60	46	.290	.356	.367
	CHI/NL		13	27	23	6	0	0	0	6	4	0	0	3	0	0	0	0	0	1	2	.261	.370	.261
92	IOW/AMA	AAA	20	81	76	26	3	0	0	29	4	0	0	3	1	0	6	3	12	3	.342	.375	.382
	CHI/NL		74	275	255	64	14	3	1	87	10	1	3	17	7	5	2	2	1	24	19	.251	.285	.341
93	CHI/NL		105	373	344	97	11	2	0	112	15	7	3	22	8	9	2	1	1	35	28	.282	.316	.326
3 YR TOTALS			192	675	622	167	25	5	1	205	29	8	6	42	15	14	4	3	2	60	49	.268	.306	.330

Sandberg, Ryne Dee — BR/TR — b.9/18/59 — POS 2B-1666, 3B-133, SS-7   PHI78 20/511

YR	TM/LG	CL	G	TPA	AB	H	2B	3B	HR	TB	BB	IBB	HB	SO	GDP	SH	SF	SB	CS	R	RBI	BA	OBA	SA
81	PHI/NL		13	6	6	1	0	0	0	1	0	0	0	1	0	0	0	0	0	2	0	.167	.167	.167
82	CHI/NL		156	687	635	172	33	5	7	236	36	3	4	90	7	7	5	32	12	103	54	.271	.312	.372
83	CHI/NL		158	699	633	165	25	4	8	222	51	3	3	79	8	7	5	37	11	94	48	.261	.316	.351
84	CHI/NL		156	700	636	200	36	*19	19	331	52	3	3	101	7	5	4	32	7	*114	84	.314	.367	.520
85	CHI/NL		153	673	609	186	31	6	26	307	57	5	1	97	10	2	4	54	11	113	83	.305	.364	.504
86	CHI/NL		154	682	627	178	28	5	14	258	46	6	3	79	11	3	6	34	11	68	76	.284	.330	.411
87	CHI/NL		132	587	523	154	25	2	16	231	59	4	2	79	11	1	2	21	2	81	59	.294	.367	.442
88	CHI/NL		155	679	618	163	23	8	19	259	54	3	1	91	14	1	5	25	10	77	69	.264	.322	.419
89	CHI/NL		157	672	606	176	25	5	30	301	59	8	4	85	9	1	2	15	5	*104	76	.290	.356	.497
90	CHI/NL		155	675	615	188	30	3	*40	*344	50	8	1	84	8	0	2	25	7	*116	100	.306	.354	.559
91	CHI/NL		158	684	585	170	32	2	26	284	87	4	2	89	9	1	9	22	8	104	100	.291	.379	.485
92	CHI/NL		158	687	612	186	32	8	26	312	68	4	1	73	13	0	6	17	6	100	87	.304	.371	.510
93	DAY/FSL	A+	2	6	5	1	0	0	0	4	1	0	0	0	0	0	0	0	0	2	2	.200	.333	.800
	ORL/SOU	AA	4	12	9	2	0	0	0	2	3	0	1	0	0	0	0	1	0	1	1	.222	.417	.222
	CHI/NL		117	503	456	141	20	0	9	188	37	1	2	62	12	2	6	9	2	67	45	.309	.359	.412
13 YR TOTALS			1822	7934	7161	2080	340	67	240	3274	656	52	24	1010	119	30	63	323	92	1143	881	.290	.349	.457

Sanders, Deion Luwynn — BL/TL — b.8/9/67 — POS OF-235, DH-4   NYA88 27/781

YR	TM/LG	CL	G	TPA	AB	H	2B	3B	HR	TB	BB	IBB	HB	SO	GDP	SH	SF	SB	CS	R	RBI	BA	OBA	SA
88	YAN/GCL	R	17	79	75	21	4	2	0	29	2	0	1	10	1	0	1	11	2	7	6	.280	.304	.387
	FL/FSL	A+	6	23	21	9	2	0	0	11	1	0	1	3	1	1	0	2	0	5	2	.429	.455	.524
	CMB/INT	AAA	5	24	20	3	1	0	0	4	1	0	2	4	1	1	0	1	1	3	0	.150	.261	.200
89	ALB/EAS	AA	33	138	119	34	2	2	1	43	11	1	7	20	1	1	0	17	5	28	6	.286	.380	.361
	CMB/INT	AAA	70	289	259	72	12	7	5	113	22	1	1	48	8	4	3	16	7	38	30	.278	.333	.436
	NY/AL		14	50	47	11	0	0	2	19	3	1	0	8	0	0	0	1	0	7	7	.234	.280	.404
90	CMB/INT	AAA	22	105	84	27	7	1	2	42	17	0	2	15	1	1	1	9	1	21	10	.321	.442	.500
	NY/AL		57	149	133	21	2	2	3	36	13	0	1	27	2	1	0	8	3	24	9	.158	.236	.271
91	RIC/INT	AAA	29	141	130	34	6	3	5	61	10	0	0	28	2	0	1	12	4	20	16	.262	.312	.469
	ATL/NL		54	122	110	21	1	2	4	38	12	0	0	23	1	0	0	11	3	16	13	.191	.270	.345
92	ATL/NL		97	325	303	92	6	*14	8	150	18	0	2	52	5	1	2	26	9	54	28	.304	.346	.495
93	ATL/NL		95	294	272	75	18	6	6	123	16	3	3	42	3	1	2	19	7	42	28	.276	.321	.452
5 YR TOTALS			317	940	865	220	29	24	23	366	62	4	6	152	11	3	4	65	21	143	85	.254	.307	.423

Sanders, Reginald Laverne "Reggie" — BR/TR — b.12/1/67 — POS OF-256   CIN87 7/180

YR	TM/LG	CL	G	TPA	AB	H	2B	3B	HR	TB	BB	IBB	HB	SO	GDP	SH	SF	SB	CS	R	RBI	BA	OBA	SA
88	BIL/PIO	R+	17	72	64	15	1	1	0	18	6	0	0	4	1	1	1	10	2	11	3	.234	.296	.281
89	GRE/SAL	A	81	349	315	91	18	5	9	146	29	2	3	63	3	1	1	21	7	53	53	.289	.353	.463
90	CR/MID	A	127	532	466	133	21	4	17	213	59	2	4	97	8	2	1	40	15	89	63	.285	.370	.457
91	CHT/SOU	AA	86	349	302	95	15	8	8	150	41	5	1	67	5	1	4	15	2	50	49	.315	.394	.497
	CIN/NL		9	40	40	8	0	0	1	11	0	0	0	9	1	0	0	1	1	6	3	.200	.200	.275
92	CIN/NL		116	438	385	104	26	6	12	178	48	2	4	98	6	0	1	16	7	62	36	.270	.356	.462
93	CIN/NL		138	563	496	136	16	4	20	220	51	7	5	118	10	3	8	27	10	90	83	.274	.343	.444
3 YR TOTALS			263	1041	921	248	42	10	33	409	99	9	9	225	17	3	9	44	18	158	122	.269	.343	.444

Santiago, Benito — BR/TR — b.3/9/65 — POS C-914, OF-2   SD 9/1/82

YR	TM/LG	CL	G	TPA	AB	H	2B	3B	HR	TB	BB	IBB	HB	SO	GDP	SH	SF	SB	CS	R	RBI	BA	OBA	SA
84	REN/CAL	A+	114	464	416	116	20	6	16	196	36	4	4	75	11	2	6	5	2	64	83	.279	.338	.471
85	BEA/TEX	AA	101	401	372	111	16	6	5	154	16	1	2	59	6	8	3	12	2	55	52	.298	.328	.414
86	LV/PCL	AAA	117	461	437	125	26	3	17	208	17	1	1	81	12	2	4	19	7	55	71	.286	.312	.476
	SD/NL		17	65	62	18	2	0	3	29	2	0	0	12	0	0	1	0	1	10	6	.290	.308	.468
87	SD/NL		146	572	546	164	33	2	18	255	16	2	5	112	12	1	4	21	12	64	79	.300	.324	.467
88	SD/NL		139	527	492	122	22	2	10	178	24	2	1	82	18	1	5	15	7	49	46	.248	.282	.362
89	SD/NL		129	494	462	109	16	3	16	179	26	6	1	89	9	3	2	11	6	50	62	.236	.277	.387
90	LV/PCL	AAA	6	24	20	6	2	0	1	11	3	0	0	1	0	0	0	0	0	5	8	.300	.375	.550
	SD/NL		100	382	344	93	8	5	11	144	27	2	3	55	4	1	7	5	5	42	53	.270	.323	.419
91	SD/NL		152	614	580	155	22	3	17	234	23	5	4	114	21	0	7	8	10	60	87	.267	.296	.403
92	LV/PCL	AAA	4	14	13	4	0	0	1	7	1	1	0	0	0	0	0	0	0	3	2	.308	.357	.538
	SD/NL		106	411	386	97	21	0	10	148	21	1	0	52	14	0	4	2	5	37	42	.251	.287	.383
93	FLO/NL		139	515	469	108	19	6	13	178	37	2	5	88	9	0	4	10	7	49	50	.230	.291	.380
8 YR TOTALS			928	3580	3341	866	143	21	98	1345	176	20	19	604	87	10	34	72	53	361	425	.259	.297	.403

Santovenia, Nelson Gil — BR/TR — b.7/27/61 — POS C-263, 1B-9   MON82 S1/19

YR	TM/LG	CL	G	TPA	AB	H	2B	3B	HR	TB	BB	IBB	HB	SO	GDP	SH	SF	SB	CS	R	RBI	BA	OBA	SA
84	JAC/SOU	AA	90	305	255	55	9	0	5	79	44	2	0	30	12	2	3	0	3	27	29	.216	.329	.310
85	IND/AMA	AAA	28	83	75	16	2	0	0	18	7	0	0	11	0	0	1	1	1	5	4	.213	.277	.240
	JAC/SOU	AA	57	206	184	40	6	0	2	52	14	1	1	18	10	4	3	2	0	15	15	.217	.272	.283

Santovenia, Nelson Gil (continued)

YR	TM/LG	CL	G	TPA	AB	H	2B	3B	HR	TB	BB	IBB	HB	SO	GDP	SH	SF	SB	CS	R	RBI	BA	OBA	SA
86	JAC/SOU	AA	31	94	72	22	7	0	4	41	19	0	1	7	2	2	0	0	1	15	11	.306	.457	.569
	IND/AMA	AAA	18	63	57	12	1	0	1	16	5	0	0	13	1	1	0	0	0	6	2	.211	.274	.281
87	JAC/SOU	AA	117	439	394	110	17*	0	19	184	36	1	5	58	13	1	3	3	4	56	63	.279	.345	.467
	MON/NL		2	1	1	0	0	0	0	0	0	0	0	0	0	0	0	0	0	0	0	.000	.000	.000
88	IND/AMA	AAA	27	98	91	28	5	0	2	39	4	0	1	16	2	1	1	0	0	9	13	.308	.340	.429
	MON/NL		92	344	309	73	20	2	8	121	24	3	3	77	4	4	4	2	3	26	41	.236	.294	.392
89	MON/NL		97	337	304	76	14	1	5	107	24	2	3	37	12	2	4	2	1	30	31	.250	.307	.352
90	IND/AMA	AAA	11	47	44	14	2	0	1	19	1	0	1	7	3	0	1	0	0	3	10	.318	.340	.432
	MON/NL		59	176	163	31	3	1	6	54	8	0	0	31	5	0	5	0	3	13	28	.190	.222	.331
91	IND/AMA	AAA	61	218	195	51	7	1	6	78	21	1	0	25	11	0	2	0	1	23	26	.262	.330	.400
	MON/NL		41	102	96	24	5	0	2	35	2	2	0	18	4	0	4	0	0	7	14	.250	.255	.365
92	CHI/AL		2	3	3	1	0	0	0	4	0	0	0	0	0	0	0	0	0	1	2	.333	.333	1.333
	VAN/PCL	AAA	91	324	281	74	16	0	6	108	37	2	0	49	6	3	3	0	0	24	42	.263	.346	.384
93	OMA/AMA	AAA	81	296	274	65	13	0	11	111	12	1	3	50	4	0	7	0	1	33	42	.237	.270	.405
	KC/AL		4	9	8	1	0	0	0	1	1	0	0	2	0	0	0	0	0	0	0	.125	.222	.125
7 YR TOTALS			**297**	**972**	**884**	**206**	**42**	**4**	**22**	**322**	**59**	**7**	**6**	**165**	**25**	**6**	**17**	**4**	**7**	**77**	**116**	**.233**	**.281**	**.364**

Sasser, Mack Daniel "Mackey" — BL/TR — b.8/3/62 — POS C-271, OF-68, 1B-24, DH-19, 3B-2 — SF84* 5/114

YR	TM/LG	CL	G	TPA	AB	H	2B	3B	HR	TB	BB	IBB	HB	SO	GDP	SH	SF	SB	CS	R	RBI	BA	OBA	SA
84	CLI/MID	A	118	471	428	125	20	5	6	173	30	3	2	46	11	4	7	15	5	57	65	.292	.336	.404
	FRE/CAL	A+	16	67	62	17	1	1	0	20	3	0	0	6	1	1	1	1	0	8	6	.274	.303	.323
85	FRE/CAL	A+	133	548	497	168	27	4	14	245	36	4	3	35	12	3	9	3	3	79	102	.338	.380	.493
86	SHR/TEX	AA	120	498	441	129	29	5	5	183	44	13	2	36	12	2	9	4	2	52	72	.293	.353	.415
87	SF/NL		2	4	4	0	0	0	0	0	0	0	0	0	0	0	0	0	0	0	0	.000	.000	.000
	PHO/PCL	AAA	87	335	307	101	21	0	1	125	22	2	2	13	4	1	3	2	3	45	42	.329	.374	.407
	VAN/PCL	AAA	28	106	93	26	3	1	2	37	10	1	1	6	2	1	1	1	0	8	14	.280	.352	.398
	PIT/NL		12	23	23	5	0	0	0	5	0	0	0	2	1	0	0	0	0	2	2	.217	.217	.217
	YEAR		14	27	27	5	0	0	0	5	0	0	0	2	1	0	0	0	0	2	2	.185	.185	.185
88	NY/NL		60	131	123	35	10	1	1	50	4	0	0	9	4	0	4	0	0	9	17	.285	.313	.407
89	NY/NL		72	191	182	53	14	2	1	74	7	4	0	15	3	1	1	0	1	17	22	.291	.316	.407
90	NY/NL		100	288	270	83	14	0	6	115	15	9	1	19	7	0	2	0	0	31	41	.307	.344	.426
91	NY/NL		96	243	228	62	14	2	5	95	9	2	1	19	6	1	4	0	2	18	35	.272	.298	.417
92	NY/NL		92	149	141	34	6	0	2	46	3	0	0	10	4	0	5	0	0	7	18	.241	.248	.326
93	SEA/AL		83	208	188	41	10	2	1	58	15	6	1	30	7	0	4	1	0	18	21	.218	.274	.309
7 YR TOTALS			**517**	**1237**	**1159**	**313**	**68**	**7**	**16**	**443**	**55**	**25**	**3**	**104**	**32**	**2**	**18**	**1**	**3**	**102**	**156**	**.270**	**.300**	**.382**

Saunders, Douglas Long "Doug" — BR/TR — b.12/13/69 — POS 2B-22, 3B-4, SS-1 — NYN88 3/78

YR	TM/LG	CL	G	TPA	AB	H	2B	3B	HR	TB	BB	IBB	HB	SO	GDP	SH	SF	SB	CS	R	RBI	BA	OBA	SA
88	MET/GCL	R	16	75	64	16	4	1	0	22	9	0	0	14	0	2	0	2	3	8	10	.250	.342	.344
	LF/NYP	A-	29	107	100	30	6	1	0	38	6	0	0	15	2	1	0	1	4	10	11	.300	.340	.380
89	COL/SAL	A	115	422	377	99	18	4	4	137	35	2	3	78	5	4	3	5	5	53	38	.263	.328	.363
90	SL/FSL	A+	115	462	408	92	8	4	1	111	43	0	2	96	7	7	2	24	10	52	43	.225	.301	.272
91	SL/FSL	A+	70	264	230	54	9	2	2	73	25	0	4	43	6	5	0	5	6	19	18	.235	.320	.317
92	BIN/EAS	AA	130	497	435	108	16	2	5	143	52	0	1	68	9	5	4	8	12	45	38	.248	.327	.329
93	NOR/INT	AAA	105	411	356	88	12	6	2	118	44	1	3	63	13	7	1	6	5	37	24	.247	.334	.331
	NY/NL		28	73	67	14	2	0	0	16	3	0	0	4	2	3	0	0	0	8	0	.209	.243	.239

Sax, Stephen Louis "Steve" — BR/TR — b.1/29/60 — POS 2B-1673, OF-33, DH-26, 3B-7 — LA78 8/229

YR	TM/LG	CL	G	TPA	AB	H	2B	3B	HR	TB	BB	IBB	HB	SO	GDP	SH	SF	SB	CS	R	RBI	BA	OBA	SA
81	LA/NL		31	127	119	33	2	0	2	41	7	1	0	14	0	1	0	5	7	15	9	.277	.317	.345
82	LA/NL		150	699	638	180	23	7	4	229	49	1	2	53	10	10	0	49	19	88	47	.282	.335	.359
83	LA/NL		155	692	623	175	18	5	5	218	58	3	1	73	8	8	2	56	30	94	41	.281	.342	.350
84	LA/NL		145	622	569	138	24	4	1	173	47	3	1	53	12	3	3	34	19	70	35	.243	.300	.304
85	LA/NL		136	551	488	136	8	4	1	155	54	12	3	43	15	3	3	27	11	62	42	.279	.352	.318
86	LA/NL		157	704	633	210	43	4	6	279	59	5	1	58	12	4	3	40	17	91	56	.332	.390	.441
87	LA/NL		157	663	610	171	22	7	6	225	44	5	3	61	13	5	1	37	11	84	46	.280	.331	.369
88	LA/NL		160	687	632	175	19	4	5	217	45	6	1	51	11	7	2	42	12	70	57	.277	.325	.343
89	NY/AL		158	717	651	205	26	3	5	252	52	2	1	44	19	8	5	43	17	88	63	.315	.364	.387
90	NY/AL		155	680	615	160	24	2	4	200	49	3	4	46	13	6	6	43	9	70	42	.260	.316	.325
91	NY/AL		158	707	652	198	38	2	10	270	41	2	3	38	15	5	6	31	11	85	56	.304	.345	.414
92	CHI/AL		143	630	567	134	26	4	4	180	43	4	2	42	17	12	6	30	12	74	47	.236	.290	.317
93	CHI/AL		57	129	119	28	5	0	1	36	8	0	0	6	1	2	0	7	3	20	8	.235	.283	.303
13 YR TOTALS			**1762**	**7608**	**6916**	**1943**	**278**	**46**	**54**	**2475**	**556**	**47**	**24**	**582**	**146**	**75**	**37**	**444**	**178**	**911**	**549**	**.281**	**.335**	**.358**

Scarsone, Steven Wayne "Steve" — BR/TR — b.4/11/66 — POS 2B-28, 3B-10, 1B-6, SS-1 — PHI86* 2/34

YR	TM/LG	CL	G	TPA	AB	H	2B	3B	HR	TB	BB	IBB	HB	SO	GDP	SH	SF	SB	CS	R	RBI	BA	OBA	SA
86	BEN/NWL	A-	65	256	219	48	10	4	4	78	30	0	4	51	2	1	2	11	2	42	21	.219	.322	.356
87	CHW/SAL	A	95	296	259	56	11	2	0	72	31	0	3	64	1	1	0	8	5	35	17	.216	.307	.278
88	CLE/FSL	A+	125	494	456	120	21	4	8	173	18	0	8	93	3	6	6	14	4	51	46	.263	.299	.379
89	REA/EAS	AA	75	265	240	43	5	0	4	60	15	2	1	67	5	5	4	2	2	30	22	.179	.227	.250
90	CLE/FSL	A+	59	240	211	58	9	5	3	86	19	1	4	57	2	2	4	3	4	20	23	.275	.345	.408
	REA/EAS	AA	74	264	245	65	12	1	3	88	14	0	1	63	0	4	0	0	0	26	23	.265	.308	.359
91	REA/EAS	AA	15	53	49	15	4	0	0	23	4	0	0	15	0	0	0	1	0	6	3	.306	.358	.490
	SCR/INT	AAA	111	440	405	111	20	6	6	161	19	2	7	81	4	2	7	10	5	52	38	.274	.313	.398
92	PHI/NL		7	14	13	2	0	0	0	2	1	0	0	6	0	0	0	0	0	1	0	.154	.214	.154
	SCR/INT	AAA	89	361	325	89	23	4	11	153	24	3	4	74	7	5	3	10	7	43	48	.274	.329	.471
	ROC/INT	AAA	23	93	82	21	3	0	1	27	6	1	1	12	3	1	3	3	2	13	12	.256	.304	.329

(continued)

Scarsone, Steven Wayne "Steve" (continued)

YR	TM/LG	CL	G	TPA	AB	H	2B	3B	HR	TB	BB	IBB	HB	SO	GDP	SH	SF	SB	CS	R	RBI	BA	OBA	SA
	BAL/AL		11	19	17	3	0	0	0	3	1	0	0	6	0	1	0	0	0	2	0	.176	.222	.176
	YEAR		18	33	30	5	0	0	0	5	2	0	0	12	0	1	0	0	0	3	0	.167	.219	.167
93	PHO/PCL	AAA	19	80	70	18	1	2	3	32	8	1	2	21	0	0	0	0	2	13	9	.257	.350	.457
	SF/NL		44	112	103	26	9	0	2	41	4	0	0	32	0	4	1	0	1	16	15	.252	.278	.398
2 YR TOTALS			**62**	**145**	**133**	**31**	**9**	**0**	**2**	**46**	**6**	**0**	**0**	**44**	**0**	**5**	**1**	**0**	**1**	**19**	**15**	**.233**	**.264**	**.346**

Schofield, Richard Craig "Dick" — BR/TR — b.11/21/62 — POS SS-1231, 2B-2, DH-1   CAL81 1/3

YR	TM/LG	CL	G	TPA	AB	H	2B	3B	HR	TB	BB	IBB	HB	SO	GDP	SH	SF	SB	CS	R	RBI	BA	OBA	SA
83	CAL/AL		21	62	54	11	2	0	3	22	6	0	1	8	2	1	0	0	0	4	4	.204	.295	.407
84	CAL/AL		140	452	400	77	10	3	4	105	33	0	6	79	7	13	0	5	2	39	21	.192	.264	.262
85	CAL/AL		147	496	438	96	19	3	8	145	35	0	8	70	8	12	3	11	4	50	41	.219	.287	.331
86	CAL/AL		139	529	458	114	17	6	13	182	48	2	5	55	8	9	9	23	5	67	57	.249	.321	.397
87	CAL/AL		134	531	479	120	17	3	9	170	37	0	2	63	4	10	3	19	3	52	46	.251	.305	.355
88	CAL/AL		155	589	527	126	11	6	6	167	40	0	9	57	5	11	2	20	5	61	34	.239	.303	.317
89	CAL/AL		91	346	302	69	11	2	4	96	28	0	3	47	4	11	2	9	3	42	26	.228	.299	.318
90	EDM/PCL	AAA	5	21	18	7	1	0	1	11	3	0	0	4	0	0	0	0	0	4	4	.389	.476	.611
	CAL/AL		99	379	310	79	8	1	1	92	52	3	2	61	3	13	2	3	4	41	18	.255	.363	.297
91	CAL/AL		134	487	427	96	9	3	0	111	50	2	3	69	3	7	0	8	4	44	31	.225	.310	.260
92	CAL/AL		1	4	3	1	0	0	0	1	1	0	0	0	0	0	0	0	0	0	0	.333	.500	.333
	NY/NL		142	498	420	86	18	2	4	120	60	4	5	82	11	10	3	11	4	52	36	.205	.309	.286
	YEAR		143	502	423	87	18	2	4	121	61	4	5	82	11	10	3	11	4	52	36	.206	.311	.286
93	DUN/FSL	A+	11	35	30	6	2	0	0	8	3	0	0	7	1	2	0	0	1	4	4	.200	.273	.267
	TOR/AL		36	128	110	21	1	2	0	26	16	0	0	25	1	2	0	3	0	11	5	.191	.294	.236
11 YR TOTALS			**1239**	**4501**	**3928**	**896**	**123**	**31**	**52**	**1237**	**406**	**11**	**44**	**616**	**56**	**99**	**24**	**112**	**34**	**463**	**319**	**.228**	**.306**	**.315**

Segui, David Vincent — BB/TL — b.7/19/66 — POS 1B-317, OF-51, DH-9   BAL87 19/455

YR	TM/LG	CL	G	TPA	AB	H	2B	3B	HR	TB	BB	IBB	HB	SO	GDP	SH	SF	SB	CS	R	RBI	BA	OBA	SA
88	HAG/CAR	A+	60	219	190	51	12	4	3	80	22	3	3	23	7	0	4	0	0	35	31	.268	.347	.421
89	FRE/CAR	A+	83	332	284	90	19	0	10	139	41	3	4	32	4	0	3	2	1	43	50	.317	.407	.489
	HAG/EAS	AA	44	194	173	56	14	1	1	75	16	0	2	16	6	1	2	0	0	22	27	.324	.383	.434
90	ROC/INT	AAA	86	357	307	103	28	0	2	137	45	4	0	28	15	0	5	5	4	55	51	.336	.415	.446
	BAL/AL		40	136	123	30	7	0	2	43	11	2	1	15	12	1	0	0	0	14	15	.244	.311	.350
91	ROC/INT	AAA	28	115	96	26	2	0	1	31	15	1	1	6	6	0	3	2	2	9	10	.271	.365	.323
	BAL/AL		86	228	212	59	7	0	2	72	12	2	0	19	7	3	1	1	1	15	22	.278	.316	.340
92	BAL/AL		115	211	189	44	9	0	1	56	20	3	0	23	4	2	0	1	0	21	17	.233	.306	.296
93	BAL/AL		146	519	450	123	27	0	10	180	58	4	0	53	18	3	8	2	1	54	60	.273	.351	.400
4 YR TOTALS			**387**	**1094**	**974**	**256**	**50**	**0**	**15**	**351**	**101**	**11**	**1**	**110**	**41**	**9**	**9**	**4**	**2**	**104**	**114**	**.263**	**.330**	**.360**

Seitzer, Kevin Lee — BR/TR — b.3/26/62 — POS 3B-895, 1B-81, OF-16, 2B-15, DH-11, SS-7, P-1   KC83 11/283

YR	TM/LG	CL	G	TPA	AB	H	2B	3B	HR	TB	BB	IBB	HB	SO	GDP	SH	SF	SB	CS	R	RBI	BA	OBA	SA
84	CHS/SAL	A	141	617	489	145	26	5	8	205	118	2	3	70	15	1	6	23	5	96	79	.297	.432	.419
85	FM/FSL	A+	90	382	290	91	10	5	3	120	85	4	2	30	6	0	5	28	7	61	46	.314	.466	.414
	MEM/SOU	AA	52	218	187	65	6	2	1	78	25	1	5	21	2	1	0	9	3	26	20	.348	.438	.417
86	MEM/SOU	AA	4	18	11	3	0	0	0	3	7	0	0	1	0	0	0	2	1	4	1	.273	.556	.273
	OMA/AMA	AAA	129	540	432	138	20	11	13	219	89	4	9	57	6	1	9	20	13	86	74	.319	.438	.507
	KC/AL		28	116	96	31	4	1	2	43	19	0	1	14	0	0	0	0	0	16	11	.323	.440	.448
87	KC/AL		161	725	641	*207	33	8	15	301	80	0	2	85	18	1	1	12	7	105	83	.323	.399	.470
88	KC/AL		149	643	559	170	32	5	5	227	72	4	6	64	15	3	3	10	8	90	60	.304	.387	.406
89	KC/AL		160	715	597	168	17	2	4	201	102	7	5	76	16	4	7	17	8	78	48	.281	.387	.337
90	KC/AL		158	697	622	171	31	5	6	230	67	2	2	66	11	4	2	7	5	91	38	.275	.346	.370
91	KC/AL		85	267	234	62	11	3	1	82	29	3	2	21	4	1	1	4	1	28	25	.265	.350	.350
92	MIL/AL		148	615	540	146	35	1	5	198	57	4	2	44	16	7	9	13	11	74	71	.270	.337	.367
93	OAK/AL		73	289	255	65	10	2	4	91	27	1	1	33	7	2	4	4	7	24	27	.255	.324	.357
	MIL/AL		47	182	162	47	6	0	7	74	17	0	1	15	7	1	1	3	0	21	30	.290	.359	.457
	YEAR		120	471	417	112	16	2	11	165	44	1	2	48	14	3	5	7	7	45	57	.269	.338	.396
8 YR TOTALS			**1009**	**4249**	**3706**	**1067**	**179**	**27**	**49**	**1447**	**470**	**21**	**22**	**418**	**94**	**23**	**28**	**70**	**47**	**527**	**393**	**.288**	**.369**	**.390**

Servais, Scott Daniel — BR/TR — b.6/4/67 — POS C-169   HOU88 4/64

YR	TM/LG	CL	G	TPA	AB	H	2B	3B	HR	TB	BB	IBB	HB	SO	GDP	SH	SF	SB	CS	R	RBI	BA	OBA	SA
89	OSC/FSL	A+	46	176	153	41	9	0	2	56	16	2	2	35	1	0	5	0	2	16	23	.268	.335	.366
	CMB/SOU	AA	63	226	199	47	5	0	1	55	19	0	3	42	5	1	4	0	3	20	22	.236	.307	.276
90	TUC/PCL	AAA	89	332	303	66	11	3	5	98	18	1	4	61	6	3	4	0	0	37	37	.218	.267	.323
91	TUC/PCL	AAA	60	242	219	71	12	0	2	89	13	2	6	19	9	3	1	0	4	34	27	.324	.377	.406
	HOU/NL		16	42	37	6	3	0	0	9	4	0	0	8	0	1	0	0	0	0	6	.162	.244	.243
92	HOU/NL		77	227	205	49	9	0	0	58	11	2	5	25	7	6	0	0	0	12	15	.239	.294	.283
93	HOU/NL		85	291	258	63	11	0	11	107	22	2	5	45	6	3	3	0	0	24	32	.244	.313	.415
3 YR TOTALS			**178**	**560**	**500**	**118**	**23**	**0**	**11**	**174**	**37**	**4**	**10**	**78**	**13**	**10**	**3**	**0**	**0**	**36**	**53**	**.236**	**.300**	**.348**

Sharperson, Michael Tyrone "Mike" — BR/TR — b.10/4/61 — POS 3B-255, 2B-156, SS-41, 1B-19, OF-1   TOR81 S1/11

YR	TM/LG	CL	G	TPA	AB	H	2B	3B	HR	TB	BB	IBB	HB	SO	GDP	SH	SF	SB	CS	R	RBI	BA	OBA	SA
84	KNO/SOU	AA	140	596	542	165	25	7	4	216	48	2	1	66	10	4	1	20	13	86	48	.304	.361	.399
85	SYR/INT	AAA	134	616	536	155	19	7	1	191	71	1	3	75	5	3	4	14	15	86	59	.289	.372	.356
86	SYR/INT	AAA	133	600	519	150	18	9	4	198	69	15	4	67	14	4	1	17	13	86	45	.289	.379	.382
87	TOR/AL		32	105	96	20	4	1	0	26	7	0	1	15	2	1	1	2	0	4	9	.208	.269	.271
	SYR/INT	AAA	88	382	338	101	21	5	5	147	40	0	1	41	5	2	1	14	10	67	26	.299	.374	.435
	LA/NL		10	37	33	9	2	0	0	11	4	1	0	5	1	0	0	0	1	7	1	.273	.351	.333
	YEAR		42	142	129	29	6	1	0	37	11	1	1	20	3	1	1	2	1	11	10	.225	.291	.287

Sharperson, Michael Tyrone "Mike" (continued)

YR	TM/LG	CL	G	TPA	AB	H	2B	3B	HR	TB	BB	IBB	HB	SO	GDP	SH	SF	SB	CS	R	RBI	BA	OBA	SA
88	ALB/PCL	AAA	56	244	210	67	10	2	0	81	31	0	1	25	7	1	1	19	6	55	30	.319	.407	.386
	LA/NL		46	64	59	16	1	0	0	17	1	0	1	12	1	2	1	0	1	8	4	.271	.290	.288
89	ALB/PCL	AAA	98	434	359	111	15	7	3	149	66	2	2	46	9	4	3	17	12	81	48	.309	.416	.415
	LA/NL		27	34	28	7	3	0	0	10	4	1	0	7	1	1	1	0	1	2	5	.250	.333	.357
90	LA/NL		129	415	357	106	14	2	3	133	46	6	1	39	5	8	3	15	6	42	36	.297	.376	.373
91	LA/NL		105	252	216	60	11	2	2	81	25	0	1	24	2	10	0	1	3	24	20	.278	.355	.375
92	LA/NL		128	372	317	95	21	0	3	125	47	1	0	33	9	5	3	2	2	48	36	.300	.387	.394
93	LA/NL		73	97	90	23	4	0	2	33	5	0	1	17	2	0	1	2	0	13	10	.256	.299	.367
8 YR TOTALS			550	1376	1196	336	60	5	10	436	139	9	5	152	23	27	9	22	14	148	121	**.281**	**.356**	**.365**

Shave, Jonathan Taylor "Jon" — BR/TR — b.11/4/67 — POS SS-9, 2B-8   TEX90 5/144

YR	TM/LG	CL	G	TPA	AB	H	2B	3B	HR	TB	BB	IBB	HB	SO	GDP	SH	SF	SB	CS	R	RBI	BA	OBA	SA
90	BUT/PIO	R+	64	284	250	88	9	3	2	109	25	0	3	27	8	2	4	21	8	41	42	.352	.411	.436
91	GAS/SAL	A	55	237	213	62	11	0	2	79	20	0	1	26	3	3	0	11	9	29	24	.291	.355	.371
	CHA/FSL	A+	56	218	189	43	4	1	1	52	18	1	5	31	3	2	4	7	7	17	20	.228	.306	.275
92	TUL/TEX	AA	118	506	453	130	23	5	2	169	37	1	4	59	10	7	5	6	7	57	36	.287	.343	.373
93	TEX/AL		17	52	47	15	2	0	0	17	0	0	0	8	0	3	2	1	3	3	7	.319	.306	.362
	OC/AMA	AAA	100	431	399	105	17	3	4	140	20	0	2	60	12	9	1	4	3	58	41	.263	.301	.351

Sheaffer, Danny Todd — BR/TR — b.8/2/61 — POS C-90, 1B-7, 3B-3, OF-3, DH-3   BOS81* 1/20

YR	TM/LG	CL	G	TPA	AB	H	2B	3B	HR	TB	BB	IBB	HB	SO	GDP	SH	SF	SB	CS	R	RBI	BA	OBA	SA
81	BRI/EAS	AA	8	13	12	0	0	0	0	0	0	0	0	3	1	0	0	0	0	0	1	.000	.000	.000
	ELM/NYP	A-	62	225	198	57	9	0	8	90	23	1	1	38	9	3	0	2	0	39	29	.288	.365	.455
82	WH/FSL	A+	82	286	260	65	4	0	5	84	18	2	1	37	12	4	3	2	2	20	25	.250	.298	.323
83	WIN/CAR	A	112	430	380	105	14	2	15	168	36	1	3	50	7	3	8	1	1	48	63	.276	.337	.442
84	NB/EAS	AA	93	339	303	73	10	0	1	86	29	2	0	31	10	1	6	2	2	33	27	.241	.302	.284
85	PAW/INT	AAA	77	266	243	63	9	0	8	96	17	0	1	35	8	2	2	0	0	24	33	.259	.311	.395
86	PAW/INT	AAA	79	280	265	90	16	1	2	114	10	0	1	24	5	3	1	9	6	34	30	.340	.365	.430
87	PAW/INT	AAA	69	250	242	62	13	2	2	85	6	2	0	29	10	1	0	3	2	32	25	.256	.273	.351
	BOS/AL		25	68	66	8	1	0	1	12	0	1	0	14	2	1	1	0	0	1	6	.121	.119	.182
88	PAW/INT	AAA	98	329	299	82	17	1	1	104	18	1	3	32	10	8	1	1	9	30	28	.274	.321	.348
89	CLE/AL		7	19	16	1	0	0	0	1	2	0	0	2	2	0	0	0	0	1	0	.063	.167	.063
	CS/PCL	AAA	107	436	401	113	26	2	3	152	24	0	7	39	13	7	3	6	12	62	47	.282	.322	.379
90	BUF/AMA	AAA	55	158	144	35	7	0	2	48	11	1	1	14	7	1	1	4	1	23	19	.243	.299	.333
91	POR/PCL	AAA	93	367	330	100	14	2	1	121	26	1	5	35	12	3	3	2	6	46	43	.303	.360	.367
92	POR/PCL	AAA	116	472	442	122	23	4	5	168	21	3	2	36	19	3	4	3	5	54	56	.276	.309	.380
93	COL/NL		82	233	216	60	10	1	4	83	8	0	1	15	9	2	6	2	3	26	32	.278	.299	.384
3 YR TOTALS			114	320	298	69	10	1	5	96	10	0	1	31	11	4	7	2	3	32	37	**.232**	**.253**	**.322**

Sheets, Larry Kent — BL/TR — b.12/6/59 — POS DH-345, OF-328, 1B-11, C-6, 3B-2   BAL78 2/29

YR	TM/LG	CL	G	TPA	AB	H	2B	3B	HR	TB	BB	IBB	HB	SO	GDP	SH	SF	SB	CS	R	RBI	BA	OBA	SA
84	ROC/INT	AAA	134	489	431	130	26	4	13	203	54	4	1	73	8	0	3	0	0	76	67	.302	.378	.471
	BAL/AL		8	17	16	7	1	0	1	11	1	0	0	3	0	0	0	0	0	3	2	.438	.471	.688
85	BAL/AL		113	360	328	86	8	0	17	145	28	2	2	52	15	1	1	0	1	43	50	.262	.323	.442
86	BAL/AL		112	364	338	92	17	1	18	165	21	3	2	56	16	1	2	0	2	42	60	.272	.317	.488
87	BAL/AL		135	508	469	148	23	0	31	264	31	1	3	67	16	0	5	1	1	74	94	.316	.358	.563
88	BAL/AL		136	504	452	104	19	1	10	155	42	4	4	72	11	0	4	1	1	38	47	.230	.302	.343
89	BAL/AL		102	338	304	74	12	1	7	109	26	10	3	58	4	0	5	1	1	33	33	.243	.305	.359
90	DET/AL		131	390	360	94	17	2	10	145	24	2	3	42	13	0	4	1	3	40	52	.261	.308	.403
93	NO/AMA	AAA	127	506	457	128	28	1	18	212	31	9	7	52	10	1	10	3	6	60	98	.280	.329	.464
	SEA/AL		11	20	17	2	1	0	0	3	2	0	1	2	0	0	1	0	0	0	1	.118	.250	.176
8 YR TOTALS			748	2501	2284	607	98	5	94	997	175	22	19	351	77	2	21	6	12	273	339	**.266**	**.321**	**.437**

Sheffield, Gary Antonian — BR/TR — b.11/18/68 — POS 3B-466, SS-94, DH-9   MIL86 1/6

YR	TM/LG	CL	G	TPA	AB	H	2B	3B	HR	TB	BB	IBB	HB	SO	GDP	SH	SF	SB	CS	R	RBI	BA	OBA	SA
86	HEL/PIO	R+	57	253	222	81	12	2	15	142	20	2	3	14	3	1	7	14	5	53	71	.365	.413	.640
87	STO/CAL	A+	129	570	469	130	23	3	17	210	81	8	8	48	7	6	6	25	15	84	103	.277	.388	.448
88	EP/TEX	AA	77	343	296	93	19	3	19	175	35	0	3	41	9	4	5	5	4	70	65	.314	.386	.591
	DEN/AMA	AAA	57	244	212	73	9	5	9	119	21	1	5	22	3	1	5	5	1	42	54	.344	.407	.561
	MIL/AL		24	89	80	19	1	0	4	32	7	0	0	7	1	1	1	3	1	12	12	.237	.295	.400
89	DEN/AMA	AAA	7	32	29	4	1	1	0	7	2	0	0	1	1	0	0	0	0	3	0	.138	.194	.241
	MIL/AL		95	405	368	91	18	0	5	124	27	0	4	33	8	3	3	10	6	34	32	.247	.303	.337
90	MIL/AL		125	547	487	143	30	1	10	205	44	1	3	41	11	4	9	25	10	67	67	.294	.350	.421
91	MIL/AL		50	203	175	34	12	2	2	56	19	1	3	15	3	1	5	5	5	25	22	.194	.277	.320
92	SD/NL		146	618	557	184	34	3	33	*323	48	5	6	40	19	0	7	5	3	87	100	*.330	.385	.580
93	SD/NL		68	282	258	76	12	2	10	122	18	0	3	30	9	0	3	5	1	34	36	.295	.344	.473
	FLO/NL		72	275	236	69	8	3	10	113	29	6	6	34	2	0	4	12	4	33	37	.292	.378	.479
	YEAR		140	557	494	145	20	5	20	235	47	6	9	64	11	0	7	17	5	67	73	.294	.361	.476
6 YR TOTALS			580	2419	2161	616	115	11	74	975	192	13	25	200	53	9	32	65	33	292	306	**.285**	**.346**	**.451**

Shelton, Benjamin Davis "Ben" — BR/TL — b.9/21/69 — POS OF-6, 1B-2   PIT87 2/34

YR	TM/LG	CL	G	TPA	AB	H	2B	3B	HR	TB	BB	IBB	HB	SO	GDP	SH	SF	SB	CS	R	RBI	BA	OBA	SA
87	PIR/GCL	R	38	134	119	34	8	3	4	60	12	1	2	48	0	0	1	7	2	22	16	.286	.358	.504
88	AUG/SAL	A	38	161	128	25	4	0	4	46	30	0	2	72	1	0	1	3	2	25	20	.195	.354	.359
	PRI/APP	R+	63	254	204	45	7	3	4	70	42	1	5	82	1	0	3	8	3	34	20	.221	.362	.343
89	AUG/SAL	A	122	478	386	95	16	4	8	143	87	1	3	132	5	0	2	18	4	67	50	.246	.387	.370
90	SAL/CAR	A+	109	391	320	66	10	2	10	110	55	0	8	116	5	4	4	1	2	44	36	.206	.333	.344

(continued)

Shelton, Benjamin Davis "Ben" (continued)

YR	TM/LG	CL	G	TPA	AB	H	2B	3B	HR	TB	BB	IBB	HB	SO	GDP	SH	SF	SB	CS	R	RBI	BA	OBA	SA
91	SAL/CAR	A+	65	254	203	53	10	2	14	109	45	4	5	65	5	1	0	4	2	37	56	.261	.407	.537
	CAR/SOU	AA	55	203	169	39	8	3	1	56	29	0	4	57	2	0	1	2	1	19	19	.231	.355	.331
92	CAR/SOU	AA	115	447	368	86	17	0	10	133	68	1	8	117	11	0	3	4	3	57	51	.234	.362	.361
93	BUF/AMA	AAA	65	200	173	48	8	1	5	73	24	0	3	44	2	0	0	0	0	25	22	.277	.375	.422
	PIT/NL		15	27	24	6	1	0	2	13	3	0	0	3	2	0	0	0	0	3	7	.250	.333	.542

Sherman, Darrell Edward — BL/TL — b.12/4/67 — POS OF-26   SD89 5/156

YR	TM/LG	CL	G	TPA	AB	H	2B	3B	HR	TB	BB	IBB	HB	SO	GDP	SH	SF	SB	CS	R	RBI	BA	OBA	SA
89	SPO/NWL	A-	70	335	258	82	13	1	0	97	58	2	13	29	1	2	4	58	7	70	29	.318	.459	.376
90	RIV/CAL	A+	131	592	483	140	10	4	0	158	89	2	12	51	7	6	2	74	26	97	35	.290	.411	.327
	LV/PCL	AAA	4	13	12	0	0	0	0	0	1	0	0	0	0	0	0	1	0	1	1	.000	.077	.000
91	WIC/TEX	AA	131	593	502	148	17	3	3	180	74	1	9	28	6	2	6	43	21	93	48	.295	.391	.359
92	WIC/TEX	AA	64	273	220	73	11	2	6	106	40	2	9	25	4	2	2	26	7	60	25	.332	.450	.482
	LV/PCL	AAA	71	316	269	77	8	1	3	96	42	0	3	41	3	1	1	26	5	48	22	.286	.387	.357
93	LV/PCL	AAA	82	320	272	72	8	2	0	84	38	0	2	27	1	1	1	20	10	52	11	.265	.358	.309
	SD/NL		37	74	63	14	1	0	0	15	6	0	3	8	0	1	1	2	1	8	2	.222	.315	.238

Shields, Thomas Charles "Tommy" — BL/TR — b.8/14/64 — POS 2B-7, 3B-7, 1B-1, OF-1   PIT86 15/368

YR	TM/LG	CL	G	TPA	AB	H	2B	3B	HR	TB	BB	IBB	HB	SO	GDP	SH	SF	SB	CS	R	RBI	BA	OBA	SA
86	WAT/NYP	A-	43	181	153	44	6	1	4	64	17	0	7	36	3	1	3	15	6	25	25	.288	.378	.418
	PW/CAR	A+	30	128	112	31	7	1	1	43	9	0	5	16	5	1	1	4	1	17	12	.277	.354	.384
88	SAL/CAR	A+	45	181	156	49	5	0	3	63	16	0	6	24	5	1	2	10	3	20	25	.314	.394	.404
	HAR/EAS	AA	57	218	198	61	4	2	2	75	14	1	3	25	5	2	1	7	3	30	21	.308	.361	.379
89	HAR/EAS	AA	123	456	417	120	13	4	5	156	25	3	9	62	11	2	3	17	5	66	47	.288	.339	.374
90	BUF/AMA	AAA	123	412	380	94	20	3	2	126	21	1	2	72	12	3	5	12	7	42	30	.247	.288	.332
91	ROC/INT	AAA	116	463	412	119	18	3	6	161	32	1	11	73	11	5	3	16	8	69	52	.289	.354	.391
92	ROC/INT	AAA	121	475	431	130	23	3	10	189	30	1	6	72	5	4	4	13	7	58	59	.302	.352	.439
	BAL/AL		2	0	0	0	0	0	0	0	0	0	0	0	0	0	0	0	0	0	0	.000	.000	.000
93	IOW/AMA	AAA	84	350	314	90	16	1	9	135	26	1	6	46	9	2	2	10	6	48	48	.287	.351	.430
	CHI/NL		20	36	34	6	1	0	0	7	2	0	0	10	1	0	0	0	0	4	1	.176	.222	.206
2 YR TOTALS			**22**	**36**	**34**	**6**	**1**	**0**	**0**	**7**	**2**	**0**	**0**	**10**	**1**	**0**	**0**	**0**	**0**	**4**	**1**	**.176**	**.222**	**.206**

Shipley, Craig Barry — BR/TR — b.1/7/63 — POS SS-111, 3B-54, 2B-38, OF-5   LA 5/28/84

YR	TM/LG	CL	G	TPA	AB	H	2B	3B	HR	TB	BB	IBB	HB	SO	GDP	SH	SF	SB	CS	R	RBI	BA	OBA	SA
84	VB/FSL	A+	85	351	293	82	11	2	0	97	52	6	4	44	9	1	1	18	7	56	28	.280	.394	.331
85	ALB/PCL	AAA	124	443	414	100	9	2	0	113	22	3	1	43	12	3	3	24	6	50	30	.242	.280	.273
86	LA/NL		12	31	27	3	1	0	0	4	2	1	1	5	1	1	0	0	0	3	4	.111	.200	.148
	ALB/PCL	AAA	61	220	203	59	8	2	0	71	11	0	2	23	3	3	1	6	7	33	16	.291	.332	.350
87	ALB/PCL	AAA	49	154	139	31	6	1	1	42	13	0	1	19	3	1	0	6	2	17	15	.223	.294	.302
	SA/TEX	AA	33	134	127	30	5	3	2	47	5	0	1	17	0	1	1	1	0	14	9	.236	.269	.370
	LA/NL		26	35	35	9	1	0	0	10	0	0	0	6	2	0	0	0	0	3	2	.257	.257	.286
88	JAC/TEX	AA	89	363	335	88	14	3	6	126	24	2	3	40	9	0	1	6	5	41	41	.263	.317	.376
	TID/INT	AAA	40	159	151	41	5	0	1	49	4	0	1	15	3	2	2	0	0	12	13	.272	.287	.325
89	TID/INT	AAA	44	142	131	27	1	0	2	34	7	0	0	22	3	2	2	6	9	6	9	.206	.243	.260
	NY/NL		4	7	7	1	0	0	0	1	0	0	0	0	0	0	0	0	0	3	0	.143	.143	.143
90	TID/INT	AAA	4	3	3	0	0	0	0	0	0	0	0	1	0	0	0	0	0	1	0	.000	.000	.000
91	LV/PCL	AAA	65	248	230	69	9	5	5	103	10	1	4	32	7	4	0	2	2	27	34	.300	.340	.448
	SD/NL		37	95	91	25	3	0	1	31	2	0	1	14	1	1	0	6	6	6	6	.275	.298	.341
92	SD/NL		52	108	105	26	6	0	0	32	2	1	0	21	2	1	0	1	1	7	7	.248	.262	.305
93	SD/NL		105	245	230	54	9	0	4	75	10	0	3	31	3	1	1	12	3	25	22	.235	.275	.326
6 YR TOTALS			**236**	**521**	**495**	**118**	**20**	**0**	**5**	**153**	**16**	**2**	**5**	**78**	**9**	**4**	**1**	**13**	**5**	**47**	**41**	**.238**	**.269**	**.309**

Shumpert, Terrance Darnell "Terry" — BR/TR — b.8/16/66 — POS 2B-212, DH-4, SS-1   KC87 2/41

YR	TM/LG	CL	G	TPA	AB	H	2B	3B	HR	TB	BB	IBB	HB	SO	GDP	SH	SF	SB	CS	R	RBI	BA	OBA	SA
87	EUG/NWL	A-	48	218	186	54	16	1	4	84	27	0	3	41	1	0	2	16	4	38	21	.290	.385	.452
88	APP/MID	A	114	486	422	102	37	2	7	164	56	1	3	90	1	0	5	36	3	64	38	.242	.331	.389
89	OMA/AMA	AAA	113	398	355	88	29	2	4	133	25	0	10	63	5	7	1	23	7	54	22	.248	.315	.375
90	OMA/AMA	AAA	39	175	153	39	6	4	2	59	14	0	3	28	3	4	1	18	0	24	12	.255	.327	.386
	KC/AL		32	96	91	25	6	1	0	33	2	0	0	17	4	0	2	3	3	7	8	.275	.292	.363
91	KC/AL		144	417	369	80	16	4	5	119	30	1	0	75	10	10	3	17	11	45	34	.217	.283	.322
92	OMA/AMA	AAA	56	233	210	42	12	0	1	57	13	0	4	33	1	5	1	5	5	23	14	.200	.259	.271
	KC/AL		36	99	94	14	5	1	1	24	3	0	0	16	1	1	1	2	1	6	11	.149	.175	.255
93	OMA/AMA	AAA	111	487	413	124	29	1	14	197	41	0	6	62	7	7	21	6	36	8	70	59	.300	.367	.477
	KC/AL		8	12	10	1	0	0	0	1	2	0	0	2	0	0	0	1	0	0	0	.100	.250	.100
4 YR TOTALS			**220**	**624**	**564**	**120**	**27**	**6**	**6**	**177**	**37**	**0**	**6**	**111**	**16**	**12**	**5**	**23**	**16**	**58**	**53**	**.213**	**.266**	**.314**

Siddall, Joseph Todd "Joe" — BL/TR — b.10/25/67 — POS C-15, 1B-1, OF-1   MON 8/5/87

YR	TM/LG	CL	G	TPA	AB	H	2B	3B	HR	TB	BB	IBB	HB	SO	GDP	SH	SF	SB	CS	R	RBI	BA	OBA	SA
88	JAM/NYP	A-	53	199	178	38	5	1	1	52	14	0	1	29	3	4	5	2	4	18	16	.213	.272	.292
89	ROC/MID	A	98	354	313	74	15	2	4	105	26	1	6	56	3	5	4	8	5	36	38	.236	.304	.335
90	WPB/FSL	A+	106	382	349	78	12	1	0	92	20	0	1	55	7	10	2	6	7	29	32	.223	.266	.264
91	HAR/EAS	AA	76	264	235	54	6	1	1	65	23	1	1	53	7	2	3	8	3	28	23	.230	.298	.277
92	HAR/EAS	AA	95	324	288	68	12	0	2	86	29	1	1	55	7	1	3	4	4	26	27	.236	.310	.299
93	OTT/INT	AAA	48	160	136	29	6	0	1	38	19	5	0	33	6	3	2	0	2	14	16	.213	.306	.279
	MON/NL		19	21	20	2	1	0	0	3	0	0	0	5	0	1	0	0	0	0	1	.100	.143	.150

Sierra, Ruben Angel — BB/TR — b.10/6/65 — POS OF-1168, DH-42   TEX 11/21/82

YR	TM/LG	CL	G	TPA	AB	H	2B	3B	HR	TB	BB	IBB	HB	SO	GDP	SH	SF	SB	CS	R	RBI	BA	OBA	SA
84	BUR/MID	A	138	541	482	127	33	5	6	188	49	5	1	97	9	6	3	13	9	55	75	.263	.331	.390
85	TUL/TEX	AA	137	587	545	138	34	8	13	227	35	6	1	111	8	1	5	22	9	63	74	.253	.297	.417
86	OC/AMA	AAA	46	209	189	56	11	2	9	98	15	3	0	27	5	1	4	8	2	31	41	.296	.341	.519
	TEX/AL		113	411	382	101	13	10	16	182	22	3	1	65	8	1	5	7	8	50	55	.264	.302	.476
87	TEX/AL		158	696	643	169	35	4	30	302	39	4	2	114	18	0	12	16	11	97	109	.263	.302	.470
88	TEX/AL		156	668	615	156	32	2	23	261	44	10	1	91	15	0	8	18	4	77	91	.254	.301	.424
89	TEX/AL		162	689	634	194	35	*14	29	*344	43	2	2	82	7	0	10	8	2	101	*119	.306	.347	*.543
90	TEX/AL		159	666	608	170	37	2	16	259	49	13	1	86	15	0	8	9	0	70	96	.280	.330	.426
91	TEX/AL		161	726	661	203	44	5	25	332	56	7	0	91	17	0	9	16	4	110	116	.307	.357	.502
92	TEX/AL		124	539	500	139	30	6	14	223	31	6	0	59	9	0	8	12	4	66	70	.278	.315	.446
	OAK/AL		27	117	101	28	4	1	3	43	14	6	0	9	2	0	2	2	0	17	17	.277	.359	.426
	YEAR		151	656	601	167	34	7	17	266	45	12	0	68	11	0	10	14	4	83	87	.278	.323	.443
93	OAK/AL		158	692	630	147	23	5	22	246	52	16	0	97	17	0	10	25	5	77	101	.233	.288	.390
8 YR TOTALS			1218	5204	4774	1307	253	49	178	2192	350	67	7	694	108	1	72	113	38	665	774	.274	.320	.459

Silvestri, David Joseph "Dave" — BR/TR — b.9/29/67 — POS SS-10, 3B-3   HOU88 3/52

YR	TM/LG	CL	G	TPA	AB	H	2B	3B	HR	TB	BB	IBB	HB	SO	GDP	SH	SF	SB	CS	R	RBI	BA	OBA	SA
89	OSC/FSL	A+	129	529	437	111	20	1	2	139	68	1	6	72	15	8	10	28	13	67	50	.254	.355	.318
90	PW/CAR	A+	131	558	465	120	30	7	5	179	77	0	6	90	9	5	5	37	13	74	56	.258	.367	.385
	ALB/EAS	AA	2	7	7	2	0	0	0	2	0	0	0	1	0	0	0	0	0	0	2	.286	.286	.286
91	ALB/EAS	AA	140	601	512	134	31	8	19	238	83	3	2	126	18	2	2	19	13	97	83	.262	.366	.465
92	CMB/INT	AAA	118	491	420	117	25	5	13	191	58	1	0	110	10	0	5	19	11	83	73	.279	.373	.455
	NY/AL		7	13	13	4	0	2	0	8	0	0	0	3	1	0	0	0	0	3	1	.308	.308	.615
93	NY/AL		7	26	21	6	1	0	1	10	5	0	0	3	1	0	0	0	0	4	4	.286	.423	.476
	CMB/INT	AAA	120	503	428	115	26	4	20	209	68	4	3	127	10	0	4	6	9	76	65	.269	.370	.488
2 YR TOTALS			14	39	34	10	1	2	1	18	5	0	0	6	2	0	0	0	0	7	5	.294	.385	.529

Slaught, Donald Martin "Don" — BR/TR — b.9/11/58 — POS C-1053, DH-13, 3B-1   KC80 8/172

YR	TM/LG	CL	G	TPA	AB	H	2B	3B	HR	TB	BB	IBB	HB	SO	GDP	SH	SF	SB	CS	R	RBI	BA	OBA	SA
82	KC/AL		43	126	115	32	6	0	3	47	9	0	0	12	3	2	0	0	0	14	8	.278	.331	.409
83	KC/AL		83	290	276	86	13	4	0	107	11	0	0	27	8	1	2	3	1	21	28	.312	.336	.388
84	KC/AL		124	446	409	108	27	4	4	155	20	4	2	55	8	7	0	0	0	48	42	.264	.297	.379
85	TEX/AL		102	370	343	96	17	4	8	145	20	1	6	41	8	1	0	5	4	34	35	.280	.331	.423
86	OC/AMA	AAA	3	12	12	4	1	0	0	5	0	0	0	3	0	0	0	0	0	2	1	.333	.333	.417
	TEX/AL		95	341	314	83	17	1	13	141	16	0	5	59	8	3	3	3	2	39	46	.264	.308	.449
87	TEX/AL		95	266	237	53	15	2	8	96	24	3	1	51	7	4	0	0	3	25	16	.224	.298	.405
88	NY/AL		97	358	322	91	25	1	9	145	24	3	3	54	10	5	4	1	1	33	43	.283	.334	.450
89	NY/AL		117	392	350	88	21	3	5	130	30	3	5	57	9	2	5	1	1	34	38	.251	.315	.371
90	PIT/NL		84	267	230	69	18	3	4	105	27	2	3	27	2	3	4	0	1	27	29	.300	.375	.457
91	PIT/NL		77	250	220	65	17	1	1	87	21	1	3	32	6	5	1	1	0	19	29	.295	.363	.395
92	BUF/AMA	AAA	2	6	6	2	0	0	0	2	0	0	0	0	0	0	0	0	0	1	1	.333	.333	.333
	PIT/NL		87	285	255	88	17	3	4	123	17	5	2	23	6	6	5	2	2	26	37	.345	.384	.482
93	PIT/NL		116	420	377	113	19	2	10	166	29	2	6	56	13	4	4	2	1	34	55	.300	.356	.440
12 YR TOTALS			1120	3811	3448	972	212	28	69	1447	248	24	36	494	88	44	35	18	15	354	406	.282	.333	.420

Smith, John Dwight "Dwight" — BL/TR — b.11/8/63 — POS OF-377   CHN84 S3/62

YR	TM/LG	CL	G	TPA	AB	H	2B	3B	HR	TB	BB	IBB	HB	SO	GDP	SH	SF	SB	CS	R	RBI	BA	OBA	SA
84	PIK/APP	R+	61	253	195	46	6	2	1	59	52	1	4	47	2	2	0	39	7	42	17	.236	.406	.303
85	GEN/NYP	A-	73	265	232	67	11	2	4	94	31	3	1	33	1	0	1	30	10	44	32	.289	.374	.405
86	PEO/MID	A	124	537	471	146	22	11	11	223	59	2	3	92	4	2	2	53	19	92	57	.310	.389	.473
87	PIT/EAS	AA	130	573	498	168	28	10	18	270	67	6	2	79	8	2	4	60	18	111	72	.337	.415	.542
88	IOW/AMA	AAA	129	569	505	148	26	3	9	207	54	1	5	90	9	5	0	25	20	76	48	.293	.367	.410
89	IOW/AMA	AAA	21	91	83	27	7	3	2	46	7	0	0	11	2	1	0	6	2	11	7	.325	.378	.554
	CHI/NL		109	381	343	111	19	6	9	169	31	0	2	51	4	4	1	9	4	52	52	.324	.382	.493
90	CHI/NL		117	322	290	76	15	0	6	109	28	2	2	46	7	0	0	11	6	34	27	.262	.329	.376
91	CHI/NL		90	180	167	38	7	2	3	58	11	2	1	32	2	1	0	2	3	16	21	.228	.279	.347
92	IOW/AMA	AAA	3	10	8	2	1	0	0	3	2	0	0	0	0	0	0	0	0	1	1	.250	.400	.375
	CHI/NL		109	233	217	60	10	3	3	85	13	1	2	40	1	0	2	9	8	28	24	.276	.318	.392
93	DAY/FSL	A+	5	20	16	5	4	0	0	9	3	0	1	0	0	0	1	3	2	3	2	.313	.450	.563
	CHI/NL		111	342	310	93	17	5	11	153	25	1	3	51	3	1	3	9	5	51	35	.300	.355	.494
5 YR TOTALS			536	1458	1327	378	68	16	32	574	108	5	9	220	17	6	8	39	27	181	159	.285	.341	.433

Smith, Lonnie — BR/TR — b.12/22/55 — POS OF-1354, DH-30   PHI74 1/3

YR	TM/LG	CL	G	TPA	AB	H	2B	3B	HR	TB	BB	IBB	HB	SO	GDP	SH	SF	SB	CS	R	RBI	BA	OBA	SA
78	PHI/NL		17	8	4	0	0	0	0	0	4	0	0	3	0	0	0	4	0	6	0	.000	.500	.000
79	PHI/NL		17	31	30	5	2	0	0	7	1	0	0	7	0	0	0	2	1	4	3	.167	.194	.233
80	PHI/NL		100	331	298	101	14	4	3	132	26	2	4	48	5	1	2	33	13	69	20	.339	.397	.443
81	PHI/NL		62	202	176	57	14	3	2	83	18	1	5	14	1	3	0	21	10	40	11	.324	.402	.472
82	STL/NL		156	672	592	182	35	8	8	257	64	2	9	74	11	3	4	68	26	*120	69	.307	.381	.434
83	STL/NL		130	547	492	158	31	5	8	223	41	2	9	55	11	1	4	43	18	83	45	.321	.381	.453
84	STL/NL		145	590	504	126	20	4	6	172	70	4	9	90	7	3	4	50	13	77	49	.250	.349	.341
85	STL/NL		28	115	96	25	2	2	0	31	16	1	3	20	2	1	0	9	2	15	7	.260	.377	.323
	KC/AL		120	498	448	115	23	4	6	164	41	0	4	69	2	0	5	40	9	77	41	.257	.321	.366
	YEAR		148	613	544	140	25	6	6	195	56	1	7	89	4	1	5	52	13	92	48	.257	.332	.358
86	KC/AL		134	568	508	146	25	7	8	209	46	0	10	78	10	2	2	26	9	80	44	.287	.357	.411
87	OMA/AMA	AAA	40	172	149	49	9	1	7	81	18	0	2	24	4	0	2	9	4	36	33	.329	.395	.544
	KC/AL		48	197	167	42	7	1	3	60	24	0	4	31	1	0	2	9	2	26	8	.251	.355	.359

(continued)

Smith, Lonnie (continued)

YR	TM/LG	CL	G	TPA	AB	H	2B	3B	HR	TB	BB	IBB	HB	SO	GDP	SH	SF	SB	CS	R	RBI	BA	OBA	SA
88	RIC/INT	AAA	93	369	290	87	13	5	9	137	66	4	8	65	6	1	4	26	3	58	51	.300	.438	.472
	ATL/NL		43	125	114	27	3	0	3	39	10	0	0	25	0	1	4	2	1	14	9	.237	.296	.342
89	ATL/NL		134	577	482	152	34	4	21	257	76	3	11	95	7	1	7	25	12	89	79	.315	*.415	.533
90	ATL/NL		135	537	466	142	27	9	9	214	58	3	6	69	2	1	6	10	10	72	42	.305	.384	.459
91	ATL/NL		122	416	353	97	19	1	7	139	50	3	9	64	4	2	2	9	5	58	44	.275	.377	.394
92	ATL/NL		84	182	158	39	8	2	6	69	17	1	3	37	1	0	4	4	0	23	33	.247	.324	.437
93	PIT/NL		94	252	199	57	5	4	6	88	43	2	5	42	3	3	2	9	4	35	24	.286	.422	.442
	BAL/AL		9	32	24	5	1	0	2	12	8	0	0	10	0	0	0	0	0	5	3	.208	.406	.500
	YEAR		103	284	223	62	6	4	8	100	51	2	5	52	3	3	2	9	4	43	27	.278	.420	.448
16 YR TOTALS			1578	5880	5111	1476	270	58	98	2156	612	19	91	831	67	21	45	369	140	896	531	.289	.372	.422

Smith, Osborne Earl "Ozzie" — BB/TR — b.12/26/54 — POS SS-2322   SD77 4/86

YR	TM/LG	CL	G	TPA	AB	H	2B	3B	HR	TB	BB	IBB	HB	SO	GDP	SH	SF	SB	CS	R	RBI	BA	OBA	SA
78	SD/NL		159	668	590	152	17	6	1	184	47	0	0	43	11	28	3	40	12	69	46	.258	.311	.312
79	SD/NL		156	649	587	124	18	6	0	154	37	5	2	37	11	22	1	28	7	77	27	.211	.260	.262
80	SD/NL		158	712	609	140	18	5	0	168	71	1	5	49	9	23	4	57	15	67	35	.230	.313	.276
81	SD/NL		110	507	450	100	11	2	0	115	41	1	5	37	8	10	1	22	12	53	21	.222	.294	.256
82	STL/NL		140	567	488	121	24	1	2	153	68	12	2	32	10	4	5	25	5	58	43	.248	.339	.314
83	STL/NL		159	626	552	134	30	6	3	185	64	9	1	36	10	7	2	34	7	69	50	.243	.321	.335
84	STL/NL		124	484	412	106	20	5	1	139	56	5	2	17	8	11	3	35	7	53	44	.257	.347	.337
85	STL/NL		158	615	537	148	22	3	6	194	65	11	2	27	13	9	2	31	8	70	54	.276	.355	.361
86	STL/NL		153	609	514	144	19	4	0	171	79	13	2	27	9	11	3	31	7	67	54	.280	.376	.333
87	STL/NL		158	706	600	182	40	4	0	230	89	3	1	36	9	12	4	43	9	104	75	.303	.392	.383
88	STL/NL		153	669	575	155	27	1	3	193	74	2	1	43	7	12	7	57	9	80	51	.270	.350	.336
89	STL/NL		155	664	593	162	30	8	2	214	55	3	2	37	10	11	3	29	7	82	50	.273	.335	.361
90	STL/NL		143	592	512	130	21	1	1	156	61	2	4	33	8	7	10	32	6	61	50	.254	.330	.305
91	STL/NL		150	641	550	157	30	3	3	202	83	2	1	36	8	6	1	35	9	96	50	.285	.380	.367
92	STL/NL		132	590	518	153	20	2	0	177	59	4	0	34	11	12	1	43	9	73	31	.295	.367	.342
93	STL/NL		141	603	545	157	22	6	1	194	43	1	1	18	11	7	7	21	8	75	53	.288	.337	.356
16 YR TOTALS			2349	9902	8632	2265	369	63	23	2829	992	76	29	542	153	192	57	563	137	1154	734	.262	.338	.328

Snow, Jack Thomas "J.T." — BB/TL — b.2/26/68 — POS 1B-135, DH-1   NYA89 4/129

YR	TM/LG	CL	G	TPA	AB	H	2B	3B	HR	TB	BB	IBB	HB	SO	GDP	SH	SF	SB	CS	R	RBI	BA	OBA	SA
89	ONE/NYP	A-	73	311	274	80	18	2	8	126	29	6	2	35	9	4	4	4	1	41	51	.292	.359	.460
90	PW/CAR	A+	138	578	520	133	25	1	8	184	46	3	5	65	20	0	7	2	0	57	72	.256	.318	.354
91	ALB/EAS	AA	132	559	477	133	33	3	13	211	67	3	3	78	10	2	10	5	1	78	76	.279	.364	.442
92	CMB/INT	AAA	135	570	492	154	26	4	15	233	70	11	1	65	9	1	6	3	3	81	78	.313	.395	.474
	NY/AL		7	19	14	2	1	0	0	3	5	1	0	0	0	0	0	0	0	1	2	.143	.368	.214
93	VAN/PCL	AAA	23	106	94	32	9	1	5	58	10	0	1	13	1	0	1	0	0	19	24	.340	.410	.617
	CAL/AL		129	489	419	101	18	2	16	171	55	4	2	88	10	7	6	3	0	60	57	.241	.328	.408
2 YR TOTALS			136	508	433	103	19	2	16	174	60	5	2	93	10	7	6	3	0	61	59	.238	.329	.402

Snyder, James Cory "Cory" — BR/TR — b.11/11/62 — POS OF-827, SS-69, 1B-61, 3B-51, DH-7, 2B-4   CLE84 1/4

YR	TM/LG	CL	G	TPA	AB	H	2B	3B	HR	TB	BB	IBB	HB	SO	GDP	SH	SF	SB	CS	R	RBI	BA	OBA	SA
85	WAT/EAS	AA	139	575	512	144	25	3	28	255	44	2	4	123	12	3	12	5	9	77	94	.281	.336	.498
86	MAI/INT	AAA	49	214	192	58	19	0	9	104	17	1	1	39	5	1	2	3	3	25	32	.302	.357	.542
	CLE/AL		103	433	416	113	21	1	24	208	16	0	0	123	8	1	0	2	3	58	69	.272	.299	.500
87	CLE/AL		157	615	577	136	24	2	33	263	31	4	1	166	3	0	6	5	1	74	82	.236	.273	.456
88	CLE/AL		142	558	511	139	24	3	26	247	42	7	1	101	12	0	4	5	1	71	75	.272	.326	.483
89	CAN/EAS	AA	4	13	11	5	0	0	0	5	1	1	0	1	1	0	1	0	0	3	2	.455	.538	.455
	CLE/AL		132	518	489	105	17	0	18	176	23	1	2	134	11	0	4	6	5	49	59	.215	.251	.360
90	CLE/AL		123	468	438	102	27	3	14	177	21	3	2	118	11	1	6	1	4	46	55	.233	.268	.404
91	CHI/AL		50	126	117	22	4	0	3	35	6	1	0	41	5	3	0	0	0	10	11	.188	.228	.299
	SYR/INT	AAA	17	74	67	18	3	0	6	39	4	0	1	16	0	1	0	0	0	11	17	.269	.311	.582
	TOR/AL		21	54	49	7	1	0	0	9	3	0	0	19	1	1	1	0	0	4	6	.143	.189	.184
	YEAR		71	180	166	29	4	1	3	44	9	1	0	60	6	4	1	0	0	14	17	.175	.216	.265
92	SF/NL		124	420	390	105	22	2	14	173	23	2	2	96	10	2	3	4	4	48	57	.269	.311	.444
93	LA/NL		143	570	516	137	33	1	11	205	47	3	4	147	8	2	1	4	1	61	56	.266	.331	.397
8 YR TOTALS			995	3762	3503	866	172	13	143	1493	212	21	12	945	69	10	25	27	19	421	470	.247	.291	.426

Sojo, Luis Beltran — BR/TR — b.1/3/66 — POS 2B-226, SS-20, 3B-17, OF-6, DH-4   TOR 1/3/86

YR	TM/LG	CL	G	TPA	AB	H	2B	3B	HR	TB	BB	IBB	HB	SO	GDP	SH	SF	SB	CS	R	RBI	BA	OBA	SA
87	MB/SAL	A	72	245	223	47	5	4	2	66	17	0	0	18	9	4	1	5	1	23	15	.211	.266	.296
88	MB/SAL	A	135	586	536	155	22	5	5	202	35	1	2	35	18	7	6	14	9	83	56	.289	.332	.377
89	SYR/INT	AAA	121	513	482	133	20	5	3	172	21	0	1	42	9	4	5	9	14	54	54	.276	.305	.357
90	SYR/INT	AAA	75	324	297	88	12	3	6	124	14	0	1	23	8	3	9	4	2	39	25	.296	.321	.418
	TOR/AL		33	85	80	18	3	0	1	24	5	0	0	5	1	0	0	1	0	14	9	.225	.271	.300
91	CAL/AL		113	402	364	94	14	1	3	119	14	0	5	26	12	19	0	4	2	38	20	.258	.295	.327
92	EDM/PCL	AAA	37	161	145	43	9	1	1	57	9	0	1	17	5	4	2	4	2	22	24	.297	.338	.393
	CAL/AL		106	391	368	100	12	3	7	139	14	0	1	24	14	7	1	7	11	37	43	.272	.299	.378
93	TOR/AL		19	54	47	8	2	0	0	10	4	0	0	3	2	1	1	0	0	5	6	.170	.231	.213
	SYR/INT	AAA	43	154	142	31	7	2	1	45	8	0	0	12	6	2	1	1	2	17	12	.218	.260	.317
4 YR TOTALS			271	932	859	220	31	4	11	292	37	0	6	57	30	28	2	12	14	94	78	.256	.291	.340

Sorrento, Paul Anthony — BL/TR — b.11/17/65 — POS 1B-298, DH-42, OF-3   CAL86 8/108

YR	TM/LG	CL	G	TPA	AB	H	2B	3B	HR	TB	BB	IBB	HB	SO	GDP	SH	SF	SB	CS	R	RBI	BA	OBA	SA
86	QC/MID	A	53	204	177	63	11	2	6	96	24	0	2	40	4	0	1	0	0	33	34	.356	.436	.542

Sorrento, Paul Anthony (continued)

YR	TM/LG	CL	G	TPA	AB	H	2B	3B	HR	TB	BB	IBB	HB	SO	GDP	SH	SF	SB	CS	R	RBI	BA	OBA	SA
	PS/CAL	A+	16	66	62	15	3	0	1	21	4	1	0	15	3	0	0	0	1	5	7	.242	.288	.339
87	PS/CAL	A+	114	454	370	83	14	2	8	125	78	1	3	95	9	0	3	1	2	66	45	.224	.361	.338
88	PS/CAL	A+	133	582	465	133	30	6	14	217	110	5	2	101	10	0	5	3	4	91	99	.286	.421	.467
89	ORL/SOU	AA	140	604	509	130	35	2	27	250	84	7	7	119	7	0	4	1	1	81	112	.255	.366	.491
	MIN/AL		14	27	21	5	0	0	0	5	5	1	0	4	0	0	1	0	0	2	1	.238	.370	.238
90	POR/PCL	AAA	102	424	354	107	27	1	19	193	64	2	1	95	8	0	5	3	0	59	72	.302	.406	.545
	MIN/AL		41	135	121	25	4	1	5	46	12	0	1	31	3	0	1	1	1	11	13	.207	.281	.380
91	POR/PCL	AAA	113	485	409	126	30	2	13	199	62	5	8	65	15	0	6	1	0	59	79	.308	.404	.487
	MIN/AL		26	51	47	12	2	0	4	26	4	2	0	11	3	0	0	0	0	6	13	.255	.314	.553
92	CLE/AL		140	514	458	123	24	1	18	203	51	7	1	89	13	1	3	0	3	52	60	.269	.341	.443
93	CLE/AL		148	527	463	119	26	1	18	201	58	11	2	121	10	0	4	3	1	75	65	.257	.340	.434
5 YR TOTALS			**369**	**1254**	**1110**	**284**	**56**	**3**	**45**	**481**	**130**	**21**	**4**	**256**	**29**	**1**	**9**	**4**	**5**	**146**	**152**	**.256**	**.334**	**.433**

Sosa, Samuel Peralta "Sammy" — BR/TR — b.11/10/68 — POS OF-540, DH-8   TEX 7/30/85

YR	TM/LG	CL	G	TPA	AB	H	2B	3B	HR	TB	BB	IBB	HB	SO	GDP	SH	SF	SB	CS	R	RBI	BA	OBA	SA
86	RAN/GCL	R	61	253	229	63	19	1	4	96	22	0	0	51	4	0	2	11	3	38	28	.275	.336	.419
87	GAS/SAL	A	129	548	519	145	27	4	11	213	21	0	5	123	7	0	3	22	8	73	59	.279	.312	.410
88	CHA/FSL	A+	131	549	507	116	13	12	9	180	35	0	4	106	14	0	3	42	24	70	51	.229	.282	.355
89	TUL/TEX	AA	66	295	273	81	15	4	7	125	15	0	3	52	4	2	1	16	11	45	31	.297	.338	.458
	TEX/AL		25	88	84	20	3	0	1	26	0	0	0	20	3	4	0	0	2	8	3	.238	.238	.310
	OC/AMA	AAA	10	41	39	4	2	0	0	6	2	0	0	8	0	0	0	4	2	2	3	.103	.146	.154
	VAN/PCL	AAA	13	56	49	18	3	0	1	24	7	0	0	6	1	0	0	3	1	7	5	.367	.446	.490
	CHI/AL		33	115	99	27	5	0	3	41	11	2	2	27	3	1	2	7	5	19	10	.273	.351	.414
	YEAR		58	203	183	47	8	0	4	67	11	2	2	47	6	5	2	7	7	27	13	.257	.303	.366
90	CHI/AL		153	579	532	124	26	10	15	215	33	4	6	150	10	2	4	32	16	72	70	.233	.282	.404
91	VAN/PCL	AAA	32	137	116	31	7	2	3	51	17	0	1	32	2	0	3	9	3	19	19	.267	.358	.440
	CHI/AL		116	338	316	64	10	1	10	106	14	2	2	98	5	0	5	13	6	39	33	.203	.240	.335
92	IOW/AMA	AAA	5	21	19	6	2	0	0	8	1	1	0	2	0	1	0	5	0	3	1	.316	.350	.421
	CHI/NL		67	291	262	68	7	2	8	103	19	1	4	63	4	4	2	15	7	41	25	.260	.317	.393
93	CHI/NL		159	641	598	156	25	5	33	290	38	6	4	135	14	0	1	36	11	92	93	.261	.309	.485
5 YR TOTALS			**553**	**2052**	**1891**	**459**	**76**	**18**	**70**	**781**	**115**	**15**	**18**	**493**	**39**	**16**	**12**	**103**	**45**	**271**	**234**	**.243**	**.291**	**.413**

Spehr, Timothy Joseph "Tim" — BR/TR — b.7/2/66 — POS C-86   KC88 5/127

YR	TM/LG	CL	G	TPA	AB	H	2B	3B	HR	TB	BB	IBB	HB	SO	GDP	SH	SF	SB	CS	R	RBI	BA	OBA	SA
88	APP/MID	A	31	126	110	29	3	0	5	47	10	1	4	28	1	0	2	3	0	15	22	.264	.341	.427
89	BC/FSL	A+	18	71	64	16	5	0	1	24	5	0	1	17	1	2	1	0	0	8	7	.250	.304	.375
	MEM/SOU	AA	61	236	216	42	9	0	8	75	16	1	2	59	2	1	1	5	3	22	23	.194	.255	.347
90	OMA/AMA	AAA	102	366	307	69	10	2	6	101	41	0	10	88	4	6	2	5	5	27	26	.225	.333	.329
91	OMA/AMA	AAA	72	250	215	59	14	2	6	95	25	1	4	48	0	3	3	3	2	27	26	.274	.356	.442
	KC/AL		37	88	74	14	0	0	3	28	9	0	1	18	2	3	1	1	0	7	14	.189	.282	.378
92	OMA/AMA	AAA	109	413	336	85	22	0	15	152	61	0	11	89	5	4	1	4	2	48	42	.253	.384	.452
93	OTT/INT	AAA	46	162	141	28	6	1	4	48	14	1	6	35	4	0	1	2	1	15	13	.199	.296	.340
	MON/NL		53	99	87	20	6	0	2	32	6	1	2	20	1	2	3	2	2	14	10	.230	.281	.368
2 YR TOTALS			**90**	**187**	**161**	**34**	**11**	**0**	**5**	**60**	**15**	**1**	**2**	**38**	**2**	**6**	**3**	**3**	**0**	**21**	**24**	**.211**	**.282**	**.373**

Spiers, William James "Bill" — BL/TR — b.6/5/66 — POS SS-337, 2B-112, 3B-13, OF-8, DH-7, 1B-2   MIL87 1/13

YR	TM/LG	CL	G	TPA	AB	H	2B	3B	HR	TB	BB	IBB	HB	SO	GDP	SH	SF	SB	CS	R	RBI	BA	OBA	SA
87	HEL/PIO	R+	6	25	22	9	1	0	0	10	3	0	0	3	0	0	0	2	0	4	3	.409	.480	.455
	BEL/MID	A	64	278	258	77	10	1	3	98	15	0	3	38	6	2	0	11	5	43	26	.298	.344	.380
88	STO/CAL	A+	84	409	353	95	17	3	5	133	42	1	5	41	5	7	2	27	7	68	52	.269	.353	.377
	EP/TEX		47	186	168	47	5	2	3	65	15	0	1	20	7	0	1	4	1	22	21	.280	.344	.387
89	DEN/AMA	AAA	14	53	47	17	2	1	2	27	5	0	0	6	1	0	1	0	0	9	8	.362	.423	.574
	MIL/AL		114	373	345	88	9	3	4	115	21	1	1	63	2	4	2	10	1	44	33	.255	.298	.333
90	DEN/AMA	AAA	11	49	38	12	0	0	1	15	10	0	0	8	2	0	1	1	1	6	7	.316	.449	.395
	MIL/AL		112	389	363	88	15	3	2	115	16	0	1	45	12	6	4	11	6	44	36	.242	.274	.317
91	MIL/AL		133	464	414	117	13	6	8	166	34	2	0	55	9	10	4	14	8	71	54	.283	.337	.401
92	BEL/MID	A	16	63	55	13	3	0	0	16	7	0	0	7	2	0	1	4	0	9	7	.236	.317	.291
	MIL/AL		12	18	16	5	2	0	0	7	1	0	0	4	0	1	0	1	1	2	2	.313	.353	.438
93	MIL/AL		113	386	340	81	8	4	2	103	29	2	4	51	11	9	4	9	9	43	36	.238	.302	.303
5 YR TOTALS			**484**	**1630**	**1478**	**379**	**47**	**16**	**16**	**506**	**101**	**3**	**8**	**218**	**34**	**30**	**13**	**45**	**25**	**204**	**161**	**.256**	**.305**	**.342**

Sprague, Edward Nelson Jr. "Ed" — BR/TR — b.7/25/67 — POS 3B-186, 1B-26, C-17, DH-4   TOR88 1/25

YR	TM/LG	CL	G	TPA	AB	H	2B	3B	HR	TB	BB	IBB	HB	SO	GDP	SH	SF	SB	CS	R	RBI	BA	OBA	SA
89	DUN/FSL	A+	52	217	192	42	9	2	7	76	16	2	7	40	1	0	2	1	1	21	23	.219	.300	.396
	SYR/INT	AAA	86	315	288	60	14	1	5	91	18	2	5	73	1	1	3	0	0	23	33	.208	.264	.316
90	SYR/INT	AAA	142	567	519	124	23	5	20	217	31	1	10	100	9	3	4	4	2	60	75	.239	.293	.418
91	SYR/INT	AAA	23	102	88	32	8	0	5	55	10	0	2	21	1	0	2	0	0	24	25	.364	.431	.625
	TOR/AL		61	183	160	44	7	0	4	63	19	2	3	43	2	0	1	0	0	17	20	.275	.361	.394
92	SYR/INT	AAA	100	419	369	102	18	2	16	172	44	3	4	73	7	0	2	0	1	49	50	.276	.358	.466
	TOR/AL		22	50	47	11	0	0	1	16	3	0	0	7	0	0	0	0	0	6	7	.234	.280	.340
93	TOR/AL		150	596	546	142	31	1	12	211	32	1	10	85	23	2	6	1	0	50	73	.260	.310	.386
3 YR TOTALS			**233**	**829**	**753**	**197**	**40**	**1**	**17**	**290**	**54**	**3**	**13**	**135**	**25**	**2**	**7**	**1**	**3**	**73**	**100**	**.262**	**.319**	**.385**

Stahoviak, Scott Edmund — BL/TR — b.3/6/70 — POS 3B-19   MIN91 2/27

YR	TM/LG	CL	G	TPA	AB	H	2B	3B	HR	TB	BB	IBB	HB	SO	GDP	SH	SF	SB	CS	R	RBI	BA	OBA	SA
91	VIS/CAL	A+	43	185	158	44	9	1	1	58	22	1	2	28	3	2	0	9	5	29	25	.278	.377	.367
92	VIS/CAL	A+	110	496	409	126	26	3	5	173	82	2	3	66	6	0	2	17	6	62	68	.308	.425	.423

(continued)

Stahoviak, Scott Edmund (continued)

YR	TM/LG	CL	G	TPA	AB	H	2B	3B	HR	TB	BB	IBB	HB	SO	GDP	SH	SF	SB	CS	R	RBI	BA	OBA	SA
93	NAS/SOU	AA	93	393	331	90	25	1	12	153	56	2	1	95	5	1	4	10	2	40	56	.272	.375	.462
	MIN/AL		20	60	57	11	4	0	0	15	3	0	0	22	2	0	0	0	2	1	1	.193	.233	.263

Stairs, Matthew Wade "Matt" — BL/TR — b.2/27/68 — POS OF-11   MON 1/17/89

YR	TM/LG	CL	G	TPA	AB	H	2B	3B	HR	TB	BB	IBB	HB	SO	GDP	SH	SF	SB	CS	R	RBI	BA	OBA	SA
89	JAM/NYP	A-	14	46	43	11	1	0	1	15	3	0	0	5	0	0	0	1	2	8	5	.256	.304	.349
	WPB/FSL	A+	36	122	111	21	3	1	1	29	9	0	0	18	3	1	1	0	0	12	9	.189	.248	.261
	ROC/MID	A	44	161	141	40	9	2	2	59	15	3	2	29	4	2	1	5	4	20	14	.284	.358	.418
90	WPB/FSL	A+	55	231	183	62	9	3	3	86	41	4	5	19	5	0	2	15	2	30	30	.339	.468	.470
	JAC/SOU	AA	79	310	280	71	17	0	3	97	22	1	3	43	6	0	5	5	3	26	34	.254	.310	.346
91	HAR/EAS	AA	129	579	505	168	30	10	13	257	66	8	3	47	14	2	3	23	11	87	78	.333	.411	.509
92	IND/AMA	AAA	110	460	401	107	23	4	11	171	49	3	4	61	10	4	2	11	11	57	56	.267	.351	.426
	MON/NL		13	38	30	5	2	0	0	7	7	0	0	7	0	0	1	0	0	2	5	.167	.316	.233
93	OTT/INT	AAA	34	139	125	35	4	2	3	52	11	1	2	15	3	1	0	4	1	18	29	.280	.348	.416
	MON/NL		6	8	8	3	1	0	0	4	0	0	0	1	0	0	0	0	0	1	2	.375	.375	.500
2 YR TOTALS			**19**	**46**	**38**	**8**	**3**	**0**	**0**	**11**	**7**	**0**	**0**	**8**	**1**	**0**	**1**	**0**	**0**	**3**	**7**	**.211**	**.326**	**.289**

Stankiewicz, Andrew Neal "Andy" — BR/TR — b.8/10/64 — POS SS-82, 2B-40, 3B-4, DH-2   NYA86 11/314

YR	TM/LG	CL	G	TPA	AB	H	2B	3B	HR	TB	BB	IBB	HB	SO	GDP	SH	SF	SB	CS	R	RBI	BA	OBA	SA
86	ONE/NYP	A-	59	267	216	64	8	3	0	78	38	0	5	41	2	4	4	14	3	51	17	.296	.407	.361
87	FL/FSL	A+	119	530	456	140	18	7	2	178	62	1	4	84	9	7	1	26	13	80	47	.307	.394	.390
88	ALB/EAS	AA	109	473	414	111	20	2	1	138	39	0	9	53	6	9	2	15	10	63	33	.268	.343	.333
	CMB/INT	AAA	29	121	114	25	0	0	0	25	6	0	0	25	4	1	0	2	0	4	4	.219	.258	.219
89	ALB/EAS	AA	133	577	498	133	26	2	4	175	57	2	8	59	8	3	11	41	9	74	49	.267	.345	.351
90	CMB/INT	AAA	135	538	446	102	14	4	1	127	71	1	10	63	11	7	4	25	8	68	48	.229	.345	.285
91	CMB/INT	AAA	125	422	372	101	12	4	1	124	29	0	8	46	10	8	5	29	16	47	41	.272	.333	.333
92	NY/AL		116	451	400	107	22	2	2	139	38	0	5	43	12	4	2	9	5	52	25	.268	.338	.348
93	CMB/INT	AAA	90	370	331	80	12	5	0	102	29	0	3	46	5	4	3	12	8	45	32	.242	.306	.308
	NY/AL		16	10	9	0	0	0	0	0	1	0	0	1	0	0	0	0	0	5	0	.000	.100	.000
2 YR TOTALS			**132**	**461**	**409**	**107**	**22**	**2**	**2**	**139**	**39**	**0**	**5**	**43**	**13**	**7**	**1**	**9**	**5**	**57**	**25**	**.262**	**.333**	**.340**

Stanley, Robert Michael "Mike" — BR/TR — b.6/25/63 — POS C-452, DH-75, 1B-47, 3B-26, OF-3   TEX85 15/395

YR	TM/LG	CL	G	TPA	AB	H	2B	3B	HR	TB	BB	IBB	HB	SO	GDP	SH	SF	SB	CS	R	RBI	BA	OBA	SA
85	SAL/CAR	A+	4	10	9	5	0	0	0	5	1	0	0	1	0	0	0	0	0	2	3	.556	.600	.556
	BUR/MID	A	13	49	42	13	2	0	1	18	6	0	0	5	1	0	1	0	1	8	6	.310	.388	.429
	TUL/TEX	AA	46	193	165	51	10	0	3	70	24	0	2	18	4	1	1	6	2	24	17	.309	.401	.424
86	TUL/TEX	AA	67	276	235	69	16	2	6	107	34	0	2	26	2	1	4	5	3	41	35	.294	.382	.455
	OC/AMA	AAA	56	249	202	74	13	3	5	108	44	0	1	42	4	1	1	1	1	37	49	.366	.480	.535
	TEX/AL		15	33	30	10	3	0	1	16	3	0	0	7	0	0	0	0	0	4	1	.333	.394	.533
87	OC/AMA	AAA	46	216	182	61	8	3	13	114	29	1	3	36	7	0	2	2	0	43	54	.335	.431	.626
	TEX/AL		78	253	216	59	8	1	6	87	31	0	1	48	6	1	4	3	0	34	37	.273	.361	.403
88	TEX/AL		94	292	249	57	8	0	3	74	37	0	0	62	6	1	5	0	0	21	27	.229	.323	.297
89	TEX/AL		67	137	122	30	3	1	1	38	12	1	1	29	5	1	0	1	0	9	11	.246	.324	.311
90	TEX/AL		103	226	189	47	8	1	2	63	30	2	0	25	4	6	1	1	0	21	19	.249	.350	.333
91	TEX/AL		95	223	181	45	13	1	3	69	34	2	2	44	2	5	1	0	0	25	25	.249	.372	.381
92	NY/AL		68	207	173	43	7	0	8	74	33	0	1	45	6	0	0	0	0	24	27	.249	.372	.428
93	NY/AL		130	491	423	129	17	1	26	226	57	4	5	85	10	0	6	1	1	70	84	.305	.389	.534
8 YR TOTALS			**650**	**1862**	**1583**	**420**	**67**	**5**	**50**	**647**	**237**	**7**	**11**	**345**	**39**	**14**	**17**	**7**	**1**	**208**	**231**	**.265**	**.361**	**.409**

Staton, David Alan "Dave" — BR/TR — b.4/12/68 — POS 1B-12   SD89 4/130

YR	TM/LG	CL	G	TPA	AB	H	2B	3B	HR	TB	BB	IBB	HB	SO	GDP	SH	SF	SB	CS	R	RBI	BA	OBA	SA
89	SPO/NWL	A-	70	309	260	94	18	0	17	163	39	4	8	49	13	0	2	1	1	52	72	.362	.456	.627
90	RIV/CAL	A+	92	393	335	97	16	1	20	175	52	5	2	78	11	0	4	4	1	56	64	.290	.384	.522
	WIC/TEX	AA	45	188	164	50	11	0	6	79	22	0	1	36	6	0	1	0	0	26	31	.305	.388	.482
91	LV/PCL	AAA	107	425	375	100	19	1	22	187	44	4	3	89	11	0	3	1	0	61	74	.267	.346	.499
92	LV/PCL	AAA	96	380	335	94	20	0	19	171	34	2	6	95	14	0	5	1	0	47	76	.281	.353	.510
93	WIC/TEX	AA	5	14	12	5	3	0	0	8	2	0	0	4	0	0	0	0	0	2	2	.417	.500	.667
	RC/CAL	A+	58	253	221	70	21	0	18	145	30	1	1	52	6	0	1	0	0	37	58	.317	.399	.656
	LV/PCL	AAA	11	41	37	10	0	0	7	31	3	0	0	9	3	0	1	0	0	8	11	.270	.317	.838
	SD/NL		17	46	42	11	3	0	5	29	3	0	1	12	2	0	0	0	0	7	9	.262	.326	.690

Steinbach, Terry Lee — BR/TR — b.3/2/62 — POS C-709, DH-54, 1B-51, 3B-22, OF-15   OAK83 9/215

YR	TM/LG	CL	G	TPA	AB	H	2B	3B	HR	TB	BB	IBB	HB	SO	GDP	SH	SF	SB	CS	R	RBI	BA	OBA	SA
84	MAD/MID	A	135	535	474	140	24	6	11	209	49	1	1	59	12	4	7	5	6	57	79	.295	.358	.441
85	HUN/SOU	AA	128	515	456	124	31	3	9	188	45	2	3	36	9	4	7	4	1	64	72	.272	.337	.412
86	HUN/SOU	AA	138	611	505	164	33	2	24	273	94	1	5	74	12	0	7	10	9	113	132	.325	.430	.541
	OAK/AL		6	16	15	5	0	0	2	11	1	0	0	0	0	0	0	0	0	3	4	.333	.375	.733
87	OAK/AL		122	438	391	111	16	3	16	181	32	2	9	66	10	3	3	1	2	66	56	.284	.349	.463
88	OAK/AL		104	398	351	93	19	1	9	141	33	2	6	47	13	3	5	3	0	42	51	.265	.334	.402
89	OAK/AL		130	491	454	124	13	1	7	160	30	2	2	66	14	2	3	1	2	37	42	.273	.319	.352
90	OAK/AL		114	410	379	95	15	2	9	141	19	1	4	66	11	5	3	0	1	32	57	.251	.291	.372
91	OAK/AL		129	494	456	125	31	1	6	176	22	4	7	70	15	2	7	2	2	50	67	.274	.312	.386
92	OAK/AL		128	487	438	122	20	1	12	180	45	0	3	58	20	0	1	2	2	48	53	.279	.345	.411
93	OAK/AL		104	418	389	111	19	1	10	162	25	1	0	65	13	0	4	3	3	47	43	.285	.333	.416
8 YR TOTALS			**837**	**3152**	**2873**	**786**	**133**	**10**	**71**	**1152**	**207**	**15**	**32**	**438**	**96**	**13**	**27**	**12**	**13**	**325**	**373**	**.274**	**.327**	**.401**

Stillwell, Kurt Andrew — BB/TR — b.6/4/65 — POS SS-681, 2B-166, 3B-23 CIN83 1/2

YR	TM/LG	CL	G	TPA	AB	H	2B	3B	HR	TB	BB	IBB	HB	SO	GDP	SH	SF	SB	CS	R	RBI	BA	OBA	SA
84	CR/MID	A	112	461	382	96	15	1	4	125	70	1	1	53	3	3	5	24	9	63	33	.251	.365	.327
85	DEN/AMA	AAA	59	206	182	48	7	4	1	66	21	2	0	23	3	3	0	5	3	28	22	.264	.340	.363
86	DEN/AMA	AAA	10	32	30	7	0	0	0	7	2	0	0	4	2	0	0	2	0	2	2	.233	.281	.233
	CIN/NL		104	315	279	64	6	1	0	72	30	1	2	47	5	4	0	6	2	31	26	.229	.309	.258
87	CIN/NL		131	433	395	102	20	7	4	148	32	2	2	50	5	2	2	4	6	54	33	.258	.316	.375
88	KC/AL		128	518	459	115	28	5	10	183	47	0	3	76	7	6	3	6	5	63	53	.251	.322	.399
89	KC/AL		130	516	463	121	20	7	7	176	42	2	3	64	3	5	3	9	6	52	54	.261	.325	.380
90	KC/AL		144	560	506	126	35	4	3	178	39	1	4	60	11	4	7	0	2	60	51	.249	.304	.352
91	KC/AL		122	428	385	102	17	1	6	139	33	5	1	56	8	5	4	3	4	44	51	.265	.322	.361
92	SD/NL		114	416	379	86	15	3	2	113	26	2	4	58	6	4	4	4	1	35	24	.227	.274	.298
93	SD/NL		57	135	121	26	4	0	1	33	11	2	1	22	2	2	0	4	3	9	11	.215	.286	.273
	CAL/AL		22	68	61	16	2	2	0	22	4	0	0	11	2	1	2	2	0	2	3	.262	.299	.361
	YEAR		79	203	182	42	6	2	1	55	15	2	1	33	4	3	2	6	3	11	14	.231	.290	.302
8 YR TOTALS			**952**	**3389**	**3048**	**758**	**147**	**30**	**33**	**1064**	**264**	**22**	**17**	**444**	**49**	**33**	**27**	**38**	**29**	**350**	**306**	**.249**	**.310**	**.349**

Stocker, Kevin Douglas — BB/TR — b.2/13/70 — POS SS-70 PHI91 2/54

YR	TM/LG	CL	G	TPA	AB	H	2B	3B	HR	TB	BB	IBB	HB	SO	GDP	SH	SF	SB	CS	R	RBI	BA	OBA	SA
91	SPA/SAL	A	70	290	250	55	11	1	0	68	31	1	2	37	3	6	1	15	3	26	20	.220	.310	.272
92	CLE/FSL	A+	63	283	244	69	13	4	1	93	27	2	4	31	4	5	3	15	9	43	33	.283	.360	.381
	REA/EAS	AA	62	267	240	60	9	2	1	76	22	1	2	30	2	3	0	17	4	31	13	.250	.318	.317
93	SCR/INT	AAA	83	357	313	73	14	1	3	98	29	2	7	56	7	8	0	17	6	54	17	.233	.312	.313
	PHI/NL		70	302	259	84	12	3	2	108	30	11	8	43	8	1	5	1	0	46	31	.324	.409	.417

Strange, Joseph Douglas "Doug" — BB/TR — b.4/13/64 — POS 2B-156, 3B-99, SS-10, DH-1 DET85 7/184

YR	TM/LG	CL	G	TPA	AB	H	2B	3B	HR	TB	BB	IBB	HB	SO	GDP	SH	SF	SB	CS	R	RBI	BA	OBA	SA
85	BRI/APP	R+	65	258	226	69	16	1	6	105	22	1	3	30	6	4	3	6	0	43	45	.305	.370	.465
86	LAK/FSL	A+	126	546	466	119	29	4	2	162	65	5	2	59	18	7	6	18	6	59	63	.255	.345	.348
87	GF/EAS	AA	115	470	431	130	31	6	13	202	31	3	3	53	17	0	5	5	11	63	70	.302	.349	.469
	TOL/INT	AAA	16	51	45	11	2	0	1	16	4	0	1	7	1	1	1	3	2	7	5	.244	.300	.356
88	TOL/INT	AAA	82	292	278	56	8	2	6	86	8	0	2	46	5	1	2	9	1	23	19	.201	.228	.309
	GF/EAS	AA	57	243	218	61	11	1	1	77	16	2	0	28	5	1	2	11	1	32	36	.280	.318	.353
89	TOL/INT	AAA	83	344	304	75	15	2	8	118	34	2	2	49	11	2	4	3	3	38	42	.247	.325	.388
	DET/AL		64	217	196	42	4	1	1	51	17	0	1	36	6	3	0	3	3	16	14	.214	.280	.260
90	TUC/PCL	AAA	37	108	98	22	3	0	0	25	8	0	0	23	2	0	0	0	0	7	7	.224	.283	.255
	IOW/AMA	AAA	82	302	269	82	17	1	5	116	28	2	1	42	9	3	1	5	0	31	35	.305	.371	.431
91	IOW/AMA	AAA	131	573	509	149	35	3	8	218	49	10	3	75	12	7	5	10	5	76	56	.293	.352	.428
	CHI/NL		3	11	9	4	1	0	0	5	0	0	0	1	1	0	1	0	0	0	0	.444	.455	.556
92	IOW/AMA	AAA	55	227	212	65	16	1	4	95	9	0	1	32	4	1	4	3	3	32	26	.307	.332	.448
	CHI/NL		52	106	94	15	1	0	1	19	10	2	0	15	2	2	0	1	0	7	5	.160	.240	.202
93	TEX/AL		145	542	484	124	29	0	7	174	43	12	8	69	12	8	4	5	1	58	60	.256	.318	.360
4 YR TOTALS			**264**	**876**	**783**	**185**	**35**	**1**	**9**	**249**	**70**	**5**	**5**	**121**	**20**	**13**	**5**	**11**	**7**	**81**	**80**	**.236**	**.301**	**.318**

Strawberry, Darryl Eugene — BL/TL — b.3/12/62 — POS OF-1292 NYN80 1/1

YR	TM/LG	CL	G	TPA	AB	H	2B	3B	HR	TB	BB	IBB	HB	SO	GDP	SH	SF	SB	CS	R	RBI	BA	OBA	SA
83	NY/NL		122	473	420	108	15	7	26	215	47	9	4	128	5	0	2	19	6	63	74	.257	.336	.512
84	NY/NL		147	602	522	131	27	4	26	244	75	15	0	131	8	1	4	27	8	75	97	.251	.343	.467
85	NY/NL		111	470	393	109	15	4	29	219	73	13	1	96	9	3	3	26	11	78	79	.277	.389	.557
86	NY/NL		136	562	475	123	27	5	27	241	72	9	6	141	4	0	5	28	12	76	93	.259	.358	.507
87	NY/NL		154	640	532	151	32	5	39	310	97	1	37	122	4	0	5	36	12	108	104	.284	.398	.583
88	NY/NL		153	640	543	146	27	3	*39	296	85	21	3	127	6	0	9	29	14	101	101	.269	.366	*.545
89	NY/NL		134	541	476	107	26	1	29	222	61	13	1	105	4	3		11	4	69	77	.225	.312	.466
90	NY/NL		152	621	542	150	18	1	37	281	70	15	5	110	5	0	5	15	8	92	108	.277	.361	.518
91	LA/NL		139	588	505	134	22	4	28	248	75	24	0	125	8	0	5	10	3	86	99	.265	.361	.491
92	LA/NL		43	177	156	37	8	0	5	60	19	4	1	34	2	0	0	5	1	20	25	.237	.322	.385
93	ALB/PCL	AAA	5	21	19	6	2	0	1	11	2	0	0	5	0	0	0	0	0	3	2	.316	.381	.579
	LA/NL		32	120	100	14	2	0	5	31	16	1	2	19	1	0	2	1	0	12	12	.140	.267	.310
11 YR TOTALS			**1323**	**5434**	**4664**	**1210**	**219**	**34**	**290**	**2367**	**690**	**117**	**32**	**1138**	**56**	**1**	**47**	**205**	**84**	**780**	**869**	**.259**	**.356**	**.508**

Suero, Williams Urban "William" — BR/TR — b.11/7/66 — POS 2B-23, DH-2, SS-1, 3B-1 TOR 5/1/85

YR	TM/LG	CL	G	TPA	AB	H	2B	3B	HR	TB	BB	IBB	HB	SO	GDP	SH	SF	SB	CS	R	RBI	BA	OBA	SA
86	MH/PIO	R+	64	297	273	76	7	5	2	99	15	0	3	36	7	4	2	13	4	39	28	.278	.321	.363
87	SC/NYP	A-	77	336	297	94	12	4	4	126	35	1	1	35	3	2	1	23	11	43	24	.316	.389	.424
88	MB/SAL	A	125	555	493	140	21	6	6	191	49	2	4	72	4	3	6	21	7	88	52	.284	.350	.387
89	DUN/FSL	A+	51	226	206	60	10	5	2	86	16	0	3	32	3	1	0	6	3	35	17	.291	.351	.417
	KNO/SOU	AA	87	363	324	84	17	5	4	123	34	0	3	50	2	4	2	7	4	42	29	.259	.335	.380
90	KNO/SOU	AA	133	576	483	127	29	7	16	218	78	3	9	78	5	4	3	40	22	80	60	.263	.372	.451
91	SYR/INT	AAA	98	445	393	78	18	1	1	101	38	0	7	51	9	4	3	17	13	49	28	.198	.279	.257
	DEN/AMA	AAA	20	83	70	27	3	2	0	34	10	0	1	8	3	2	1	3	0	20	15	.386	.457	.486
92	MIL/AL		18	19	16	3	1	0	0	4	2	0	1	1	2	0	0	1	1	4	0	.188	.316	.250
	DEN/AMA	AAA	75	313	276	71	10	4	2	102	31	1	2	33	5	3	1	9	9	42	25	.257	.332	.370
93	NO/AMA	AAA	46	151	124	28	4	1	0	37	21	0	1	17	3	2	3	4	13	25	13	.226	.336	.298
	MIL/AL		15	15	14	3	1	0	0	4	0	0	0	3	1	0	0	1	0	4	0	.233	.324	.267
2 YR TOTALS			**33**	**34**	**30**	**7**	**1**	**0**	**0**	**8**	**3**	**0**	**1**	**4**	**3**	**0**	**0**	**1**	**2**	**4**	**0**	**.233**	**.324**	**.267**

Surhoff, William James "B.J." — BL/TR — b.8/4/64 — POS C-674, 3B-187, DH-35, OF-34, 1B-28, SS-1, 2B-1 MIL85 1/1

YR	TM/LG	CL	G	TPA	AB	H	2B	3B	HR	TB	BB	IBB	HB	SO	GDP	SH	SF	SB	CS	R	RBI	BA	OBA	SA
85	BEL/MID	A	76	318	289	96	13	4	7	138	22	0	0	35	3	2	5	10	9	39	58	.332	.373	.478

(continued)

Surhoff, William James "B.J." (continued)

YR	TM/LG	CL	G	TPA	AB	H	2B	3B	HR	TB	BB	IBB	HB	SO	GDP	SH	SF	SB	CS	R	RBI	BA	OBA	SA
86	VAN/PCL	AAA	116	502	458	141	19	3	5	181	28	5	8	31	16	3	5	22	8	71	59	.308	.355	.395
87	MIL/AL		115	445	395	118	22	3	7	167	36	1	0	30	13	5	9	11	10	50	68	.299	.350	.423
88	MIL/AL		139	541	493	121	21	0	5	157	31	9	3	49	12	11	3	21	6	47	38	.245	.292	.318
89	MIL/AL		126	477	436	108	17	4	5	148	25	1	3	29	8	3	10	14	12	42	55	.248	.287	.339
90	MIL/AL		135	530	474	131	21	4	6	178	41	5	1	37	8	7	7	18	7	55	59	.276	.331	.376
91	MIL/AL		143	553	505	146	19	4	5	188	26	2	0	33	21	13	9	5	8	57	68	.289	.319	.372
92	MIL/AL		139	543	480	121	19	1	4	154	46	8	2	41	9	5	10	14	8	63	62	.252	.314	.321
93	MIL/AL		148	599	552	151	38	3	7	216	36	5	2	47	9	4	5	12	9	66	79	.274	.318	.391
7 YR TOTALS			**945**	**3688**	**3335**	**896**	**157**	**19**	**39**	**1208**	**241**	**31**	**11**	**266**	**80**	**48**	**53**	**95**	**60**	**380**	**429**	**.269**	**.315**	**.362**

Sveum, Dale Curtis — BB/TR — b.11/23/63 — POS SS-410, 3B-139, 2B-49, 1B-25, DH-6, OF-1 MIL82 1/25

YR	TM/LG	CL	G	TPA	AB	H	2B	3B	HR	TB	BB	IBB	HB	SO	GDP	SH	SF	SB	CS	R	RBI	BA	OBA	SA
84	EP/TEX	AA	131	573	523	172	41	8	9	256	43	1	0	72	9	1	6	6	3	92	84	.329	.376	.489
85	VAN/PCL	AAA	122	468	415	98	17	3	6	139	48	6	1	79	17	1	2	4	5	42	48	.236	.317	.335
86	VAN/PCL	AAA	28	122	105	31	3	2	1	41	13	0	1	24	4	0	3	0	0	16	23	.295	.369	.390
	MIL/AL		91	356	317	78	13	2	7	116	32	0	1	63	7	5	1	4	3	35	35	.246	.316	.366
87	MIL/AL		153	586	535	135	27	3	25	243	40	4	1	133	11	5	5	2	6	86	95	.252	.303	.454
88	MIL/AL		129	495	467	113	14	4	9	162	21	0	1	122	6	3	3	1	0	41	51	.242	.274	.347
89	BEL/MID	A	6	20	15	2	1	0	0	3	5	2	0	6	0	0	0	0	0	0	2	.133	.350	.200
	STO/CAL	A+	11	50	43	8	0	0	1	11	6	1	0	14	2	0	1	0	0	5	5	.186	.280	.256
90	DEN/AMA	AAA	57	240	218	63	17	2	2	90	20	3	0	49	5	2	0	1	2	25	26	.289	.349	.413
	MIL/AL		48	133	117	23	7	0	1	33	12	0	1	30	2	0	2	0	1	15	12	.197	.278	.282
91	MIL/AL		90	308	266	64	19	1	4	97	32	0	1	78	8	5	4	2	4	33	43	.241	.320	.365
92	PHI/NL		54	153	135	24	4	0	2	34	16	4	0	39	5	5	2	0	1	13	16	.178	.261	.252
	CHI/AL		40	131	114	25	9	0	2	40	12	0	0	29	1	2	3	1	1	15	12	.219	.287	.351
	YEAR		94	284	249	49	13	0	4	74	28	4	0	68	6	2	5	1	1	28	28	.197	.273	.297
93	TAC/PCL	AAA	12	50	43	15	1	0	2	22	6	1	1	7	1	0	0	2	1	10	6	.349	.440	.512
	CAL/PCL	AAA	33	145	120	36	11	1	6	67	24	0	0	32	0	1	0	0	1	31	26	.300	.414	.558
	OAK/AL		30	96	79	14	2	1	2	24	16	1	0	21	2	1	0	0	0	12	6	.177	.316	.304
7 YR TOTALS			**635**	**2258**	**2030**	**476**	**95**	**11**	**52**	**749**	**181**	**9**	**6**	**515**	**42**	**21**	**20**	**10**	**15**	**250**	**270**	**.234**	**.296**	**.369**

Tackett, Jeffrey Wilson "Jeff" — BR/TR — b.12/1/65 — POS C-108, 3B-1, P-1 BAL84 2/53

YR	TM/LG	CL	G	TPA	AB	H	2B	3B	HR	TB	BB	IBB	HB	SO	GDP	SH	SF	SB	CS	R	RBI	BA	OBA	SA
84	BLU/APP	R+	34	123	98	16	2	0	0	18	23	0	0	28	1	0	2	1	1	9	12	.163	.317	.184
85	DB/FSL	A+	40	118	103	20	5	2	0	29	13	0	1	16	6	0	1	1	3	8	10	.194	.288	.282
	NEW/NYP	A-	62	215	187	39	6	0	0	45	22	0	2	33	4	3	1	2	2	21	22	.209	.297	.241
86	HAG/CAR	A+	83	288	246	70	15	1	0	87	36	0	5	36	2	0	1	16	5	53	21	.285	.385	.354
87	CHA/SOU	AA	61	221	205	46	6	1	0	54	12	0	2	34	2	1	1	5	5	18	13	.224	.273	.263
88	CHA/SOU	AA	81	317	272	56	9	0	0	65	42	0	2	46	7	0	1	6	4	24	18	.206	.315	.239
89	ROC/INT	AAA	67	223	199	36	3	1	2	47	19	0	1	45	3	3	2	3	1	13	17	.181	.253	.236
90	ROC/INT	AAA	108	363	306	73	8	3	4	99	47	0	7	50	3	3	3	3	8	37	33	.239	.353	.324
91	ROC/INT	AAA	126	496	433	102	18	2	6	142	54	0	2	59	15	4	3	3	3	64	50	.236	.321	.328
	BAL/AL		6	11	8	1	0	0	0	1	2	0	0	2	0	0	1	0	0	1	0	.125	.300	.125
92	BAL/AL		65	208	179	43	8	1	1	68	17	1	2	28	11	6	0	0	1	21	24	.240	.307	.380
93	ROC/INT	AAA	8	31	25	8	2	0	0	10	3	0	2	8	0	0	1	0	0	1	2	.320	.419	.400
	BAL/AL		39	103	87	15	3	0	0	18	13	0	0	28	5	2	1	0	0	8	9	.172	.277	.207
3 YR TOTALS			**110**	**322**	**274**	**59**	**11**	**1**	**5**	**87**	**32**	**1**	**2**	**58**	**16**	**9**	**5**	**0**	**0**	**30**	**33**	**.215**	**.297**	**.318**

Tarasco, Anthony Giacinto "Tony" — BL/TR — b.12/9/70 — POS OF-12 ATL88 17/372

YR	TM/LG	CL	G	TPA	AB	H	2B	3B	HR	TB	BB	IBB	HB	SO	GDP	SH	SF	SB	CS	R	RBI	BA	OBA	SA
88	IF/PIO	R+	7	15	10	0	0	0	0	0	5	0	0	2	1	0	0	1	0	1	1	.000	.333	.000
	BRA/GCL	R	21	73	64	15	6	1	0	23	7	0	1	7	4	0	1	3	2	10	4	.234	.319	.359
89	PUL/APP	R+	49	181	156	53	8	2	2	71	21	2	0	20	2	2	2	7	2	22	22	.340	.413	.455
90	SUM/SAL	A	107	401	355	94	13	3	3	122	37	2	1	57	6	5	3	9	5	42	37	.265	.333	.344
91	DUR/CAR	A+	78	277	248	62	8	2	12	110	21	2	1	64	3	4	3	11	9	31	38	.250	.308	.444
92	GRE/SOU	AA	133	527	489	140	22	2	15	211	27	2	1	84	9	3	3	33	19	73	54	.286	.321	.431
93	RIC/INT	AAA	93	414	370	122	15	7	15	196	36	3	1	54	1	3	3	19	11	73	53	.330	.388	.530
	ATL/NL		24	37	35	8	2	0	0	10	0	0	0	5	1	0	1	0	1	6	2	.229	.243	.286

Tartabull, Danilo "Danny" — BR/TR — b.10/30/62 — POS OF-746, DH-256, 2B-32, SS-24, 3B-5 CIN80 5/71

YR	TM/LG	CL	G	TPA	AB	H	2B	3B	HR	TB	BB	IBB	HB	SO	GDP	SH	SF	SB	CS	R	RBI	BA	OBA	SA
84	SLC/PCL	AAA	116	484	418	127	22	9	13	206	57	3	1	69	11	1	7	11	13	69	73	.304	.383	.493
	SEA/AL		10	24	20	6	1	0	2	13	2	0	1	3	0	0	1	0	0	3	7	.300	.375	.650
85	CAL/PCL	AAA	125	546	473	142	14	3	43	291	67	4	1	123	14	1	4	17	4	102	109	.300	.385	.615
	SEA/AL		19	69	61	20	7	1	1	32	8	0	0	14	1	0	0	1	0	8	7	.328	.406	.525
86	SEA/AL		137	578	511	138	25	6	25	250	61	2	1	157	10	2	3	4	8	76	96	.270	.347	.489
87	KC/AL		158	667	582	180	27	3	34	315	79	2	1	136	14	0	6	5	5	95	101	.309	.390	.541
88	KC/AL		146	593	507	139	38	3	26	261	76	4	4	119	10	0	6	8	5	80	102	.274	.369	.515
89	KC/AL		133	515	441	118	22	0	18	194	69	2	3	123	12	0	2	4	2	54	62	.268	.369	.440
90	KC/AL		88	352	313	84	19	0	15	148	36	0	0	93	9	0	3	1	1	41	60	.268	.341	.473
91	KC/AL		132	557	484	153	35	3	31	287	65	6	3	121	9	0	5	6	3	78	100	.316	.397	*.593
92	NY/AL		123	526	421	112	19	0	25	206	103	14	0	115	7	0	2	2	2	72	85	.266	.409	.489
93	NY/AL		138	611	513	128	33	2	31	258	92	9	2	156	8	0	6	2	0	87	102	.250	.363	.503
10 YR TOTALS			**1084**	**4492**	**3853**	**1078**	**226**	**18**	**208**	**1964**	**591**	**39**	**15**	**1037**	**80**	**2**	**31**	**35**	**25**	**594**	**722**	**.280**	**.375**	**.510**

Tatum, James Ray "Jim" — BR/TR — b.10/9/67 — POS 1B-12, 3B-11, OF-3   SD85 3/76

YR	TM/LG	CL	G	TPA	AB	H	2B	3B	HR	TB	BB	IBB	HB	SO	GDP	SH	SF	SB	CS	R	RBI	BA	OBA	SA
85	SPO/NWL	A-	74	311	281	64	9	1	1	78	20	0	5	60	7	4	1	0	1	21	32	.228	.290	.278
86	CHS/SAL	A	120	483	431	112	19	2	10	165	41	2	2	83	11	4	5	2	4	55	62	.260	.324	.383
87	CHS/SAL	A	128	535	468	131	22	2	9	184	46	2	8	65	16	4	9	8	5	52	72	.280	.348	.393
88	WIC/TEX	AA	118	446	402	105	26	1	8	157	30	2	5	73	5	6	3	2	3	38	54	.261	.318	.391
90	CAN/EAS	AA	30	115	106	19	6	0	2	31	6	1	1	19	2	0	2	1	0	6	11	.179	.226	.292
	STO/CAL	A+	70	285	260	68	16	0	12	120	13	0	8	49	1	0	4	4	5	41	59	.262	.312	.462
91	EP/TEX	AA	130	593	493	158	27	8	18	255	63	5	15	79	21	2	20	5	7	99	128	.320	.399	.517
92	DEN/AMA	AAA	130	556	492	162	36	3	19	261	40	3	9	87	11	4	11	8	9	74	101	.329	.382	.530
	MIL/AL		5	9	8	1	0	0	0	1	1	0	0	2	0	0	0	0	0	0	0	.125	.222	.125
93	CS/PCL	AAA	13	48	45	10	2	0	2	18	2	1	0	9	3	0	0	0	0	5	7	.222	.271	.400
	COL/NL		92	106	98	20	5	0	1	28	5	0	1	29	0	0	2	0	0	7	12	.204	.245	.286
2 YR TOTALS			**97**	**115**	**106**	**21**	**5**	**0**	**1**	**29**	**6**	**0**	**1**	**29**	**0**	**0**	**2**	**0**	**0**	**7**	**12**	**.198**	**.243**	**.274**

Taubensee, Edward Kenneth "Eddie" — BL/TR — b.10/31/68 — POS C-218   CIN86 6/150

YR	TM/LG	CL	G	TPA	AB	H	2B	3B	HR	TB	BB	IBB	HB	SO	GDP	SH	SF	SB	CS	R	RBI	BA	OBA	SA
86	RED/GCL	R	35	118	107	21	3	0	1	27	11	0	0	33	2	0	0	0	1	8	11	.196	.271	.252
87	BIL/PIO	R+	55	190	162	43	7	0	5	65	25	5	1	47	2	0	0	0	2	24	28	.265	.363	.401
88	CHT/SOU	AA	5	15	12	2	0	0	1	5	3	0	0	4	0	0	0	0	0	2	1	.167	.333	.417
	GRE/SAL	A	103	380	330	85	16	1	10	133	44	5	4	93	6	2	1	1	8	36	41	.258	.351	.403
89	CR/MID	A	59	223	196	39	5	0	8	68	25	4	2	55	3	0	0	4	1	25	22	.199	.296	.347
	CHT/SOU	AA	45	142	127	24	2	0	3	35	11	2	0	28	3	1	3	0	0	11	13	.189	.248	.276
90	CR/MID	A	122	477	417	108	21	1	16	179	51	5	4	98	7	4	11	4	4	57	62	.259	.342	.429
91	CS/PCL	AAA	91	318	287	89	23	3	13	157	31	5	0	61	6	0	0	0	0	53	39	.310	.377	.547
	CLE/AL		26	73	66	16	2	1	0	20	5	1	0	16	1	0	2	0	0	5	8	.242	.288	.303
92	TUC/PCL	AAA	20	83	74	25	8	1	1	38	8	1	0	17	0	1	0	0	0	13	10	.338	.402	.514
	HOU/NL		104	331	297	66	15	0	5	96	31	3	2	78	4	0	1	2	1	23	28	.222	.299	.323
93	HOU/NL		94	312	288	72	11	1	9	112	21	5	0	44	8	0	2	1	0	26	42	.250	.299	.389
3 YR TOTALS			**224**	**716**	**651**	**154**	**28**	**2**	**14**	**228**	**57**	**9**	**2**	**138**	**13**	**1**	**5**	**3**	**1**	**54**	**78**	**.237**	**.298**	**.350**

Tettleton, Mickey Lee — BB/TR — b.9/16/60 — POS C-816, DH-153, 1B-69, OF-61   OAK81 5/118

YR	TM/LG	CL	G	TPA	AB	H	2B	3B	HR	TB	BB	IBB	HB	SO	GDP	SH	SF	SB	CS	R	RBI	BA	OBA	SA
84	ALB/EAS	AA	86	339	281	65	18	0	5	98	52	1	0	52	8	0	6	2	1	32	47	.231	.345	.349
	OAK/AL		33	88	76	20	2	1	1	27	11	0	0	21	3	0	1	0	0	10	5	.263	.352	.355
85	MOD/CAL	A+	4	14	14	3	3	0	0	6	0	0	0	4	1	0	0	0	0	1	2	.214	.214	.429
	OAK/AL		78	246	211	53	12	0	3	74	28	0	2	59	6	5	0	2	0	23	15	.251	.344	.351
86	MOD/CAL	A+	15	62	42	10	1	0	2	17	19	1	1	9	1	0	0	2	0	14	8	.238	.484	.405
	OAK/AL		90	262	211	43	9	0	10	82	39	0	1	51	3	7	4	7	1	26	35	.204	.325	.389
87	MOD/CAL	A+	3	12	11	4	1	0	2	11	1	0	0	4	0	0	0	0	0	4	2	.364	.417	1.000
	OAK/AL		82	248	211	41	3	0	8	68	30	0	0	65	3	5	2	1	1	19	26	.194	.292	.322
88	ROC/INT	AAA	19	50	41	10	3	1	1	18	9	0	0	15	0	0	0	0	0	9	4	.244	.380	.439
	BAL/AL		86	316	283	74	11	1	11	120	28	2	2	70	9	1	3	3	2	31	37	.261	.330	.424
89	BAL/AL		117	489	411	106	21	2	26	209	73	4	1	117	8	0	3	3	2	72	65	.258	.369	.509
90	BAL/AL		135	559	444	99	21	2	15	169	106	3	5	160	7	0	4	2	4	68	51	.223	.376	.381
91	DET/AL		154	608	501	132	17	2	31	246	101	9	2	131	12	0	4	3	3	85	89	.263	.387	.491
92	DET/AL		157	654	525	125	25	0	32	246	*122	18	1	137	5	0	6	0	6	82	83	.238	.379	.469
93	DET/AL		152	637	522	128	25	4	32	257	109	12	0	139	5	0	6	3	1	79	110	.245	.372	.492
10 YR TOTALS			**1084**	**4107**	**3395**	**821**	**146**	**12**	**169**	**1498**	**647**	**48**	**14**	**950**	**61**	**19**	**32**	**21**	**27**	**495**	**516**	**.242**	**.363**	**.441**

Teufel, Timothy Shawn "Tim" — BR/TR — b.7/7/58 — POS 2B-806, 3B-99, 1B-83, DH-2, SS-1   MIN80 3/38

YR	TM/LG	CL	G	TPA	AB	H	2B	3B	HR	TB	BB	IBB	HB	SO	GDP	SH	SF	SB	CS	R	RBI	BA	OBA	SA
83	MIN/AL		21	82	78	24	7	1	3	42	2	0	0	8	1	2	0	0	0	11	6	.308	.325	.538
84	MIN/AL		157	652	568	149	30	3	14	227	76	8	2	73	18	2	4	1	3	76	61	.262	.349	.400
85	MIN/AL		138	496	434	113	24	3	10	173	48	2	3	70	14	7	4	4	2	58	50	.260	.335	.399
86	NY/NL		93	318	279	69	20	1	4	103	32	1	1	42	6	3	1	2	2	35	31	.247	.324	.369
87	NY/NL		97	350	299	92	29	0	14	163	44	2	2	53	7	3	3	2		55	61	.308	.398	.545
88	NY/NL		90	309	273	64	20	0	4	96	29	1	1	41	6	2	1	1		35	31	.234	.306	.352
89	NY/NL		83	254	219	56	7	0	6	73	32	1	1	50	4	0	2	1	1	27	15	.256	.350	.333
90	NY/NL		80	192	175	43	11	0	10	84	15	1	0	33	5	1	1	0	2	28	24	.246	.304	.480
91	NY/NL		20	36	34	4	0	0	1	7	2	0	0	9	0	0	0	0	0	2	2	.118	.167	.206
	SD/NL		97	363	307	70	16	0	11	119	49	4	1	69	8	2	4	2	8	39	42	.228	.334	.388
	YEAR		117	399	341	74	16	0	12	126	51	4	1	77	8	2	4	2	8	41	44	.217	.319	.370
92	SD/NL		101	279	246	55	10	0	6	83	31	3	1	45	7	0	1	2	1	23	25	.224	.312	.337
93	SD/NL		96	231	200	50	11	2	7	86	27	9	0	39	9	1	1	2	2	26	31	.250	.338	.430
11 YR TOTALS			**1073**	**3562**	**3112**	**789**	**185**	**12**	**86**	**1256**	**387**	**23**	**12**	**531**	**85**	**27**	**24**	**23**	**19**	**415**	**379**	**.254**	**.336**	**.404**

Thomas, Frank Edward — BR/TR — b.5/27/68 — POS 1B-415, DH-115   CHA89 1/7

YR	TM/LG	CL	G	TPA	AB	H	2B	3B	HR	TB	BB	IBB	HB	SO	GDP	SH	SF	SB	CS	R	RBI	BA	OBA	SA
89	WS/GCL	R	17	66	52	19	5	0	1	27	11	0	1	3	0	0	0	2	1	8	11	.365	.470	.519
	SAR/FSL	A+	55	223	188	52	9	1	4	75	31	0	3	33	6	0	1	0	1	27	30	.277	.386	.399
90	BIR/SOU	AA	109	474	353	114	27	5	18	205	112	2	5	74	13	0	3	0	5	85	71	.323	.487	.581
	CHI/AL		60	240	191	63	11	3	7	101	44	0	2	54	5	0	2	1	2	39	31	.330	.454	.529
91	CHI/AL		158	700	559	178	31	2	32	309	*138	13	1	112	20	0	2	1	2	104	109	.318	*.453	.553
92	CHI/AL		160	711	573	185	*46	2	24	307	*122	6	5	88	19	0	11	6	3	108	115	.323	*.439	.536
93	CHI/AL		153	676	549	174	36	0	41	333	112	23	2	54	10	0	13	4	2	106	128	.317	.426	.607
4 YR TOTALS			**531**	**2327**	**1872**	**600**	**124**	**7**	**104**	**1050**	**416**	**42**	**10**	**308**	**54**	**0**	**29**	**11**	**8**	**357**	**383**	**.321**	**.441**	**.561**

Thome, James Howard "Jim" — BL/TR — b.8/27/70 — POS 3B-114 — CLE89 12/333

YR	TM/LG	CL	G	TPA	AB	H	2B	3B	HR	TB	BB	IBB	HB	SO	GDP	SH	SF	SB	CS	R	RBI	BA	OBA	SA
89	IND/GCL	R	55	213	186	44	5	3	0	55	21	1	1	33	5	3	2	6	4	22	22	.237	.314	.296
90	BUR/APP	R+	34	149	118	44	7	1	4	89	27	3	4	18	2	0	0	6	3	31	34	.373	.503	.754
	KIN/CAR	A+	33	143	117	36	4	1	2	54	24	0	1	26	4	0	1	4	1	19	16	.308	.427	.462
91	CAN/EAS	AA	84	345	294	99	20	2	5	138	44	4	4	58	7	0	3	8	2	47	45	.337	.426	.469
	CS/PCL	AAA	41	166	151	43	7	3	2	62	12	0	0	29	4	0	3	0	0	20	28	.285	.331	.411
	CLE/AL		27	104	98	25	4	2	1	36	5	1	1	16	4	0	0	1	1	7	9	.255	.298	.367
92	CAN/EAS	AA	30	132	107	36	9	2	1	52	24	3	1	30	3	0	2	0	0	16	14	.336	.462	.486
	CLE/AL		40	131	117	24	3	1	2	35	10	2	1	34	3	0	2	2	0	8	14	.205	.275	.299
	CS/PCL	AAA	12	55	48	15	4	1	2	27	6	1	1	16	0	0	0	0	0	11	14	.313	.400	.563
93	CHW/INT	AAA	115	497	410	136	21	4	25	240	76	8	7	94	9	0	4	1	3	85	102	.332	.441	.585
	CLE/AL		47	192	154	41	11	0	7	73	29	1	4	36	3	0	5	2	1	28	22	.266	.385	.474
3 YR TOTALS			114	427	369	90	18	3	10	144	44	4	7	86	10	0	7	5	2	43	43	.244	.330	.390

Thompson, Milton Bernard "Milt" — BL/TR — b.1/5/59 — POS OF-926 — ATL79* 2/29

YR	TM/LG	CL	G	TPA	AB	H	2B	3B	HR	TB	BB	IBB	HB	SO	GDP	SH	SF	SB	CS	R	RBI	BA	OBA	SA
84	RIC/INT	AAA	134	593	503	145	11	3	4	174	83	3	3	86	9	2	2	47	17	91	40	.288	.391	.346
	ATL/NL		25	111	99	30	1	0	2	37	11	1	0	11	1	1	0	14	2	16	4	.303	.373	.374
85	RIC/INT	AAA	82	353	312	98	10	1	2	116	32	3	1	30	9	5	3	34	11	52	22	.314	.376	.372
	ATL/NL		73	193	182	55	7	2	0	66	7	3	0	36	1	5	0	9	4	17	6	.302	.339	.363
86	POR/PCL	AAA	41	179	161	56	6	1	1	73	15	1	1	20	3	1	1	20	3	26	16	.348	.404	.453
	PHI/NL		96	332	299	75	7	1	6	102	26	1	1	62	4	3	2	19	4	38	23	.251	.311	.341
87	PHI/NL		150	575	527	159	26	9	7	224	42	2	0	87	5	3	3	46	10	86	43	.302	.351	.425
88	PHI/NL		122	423	378	109	16	2	2	135	39	6	1	59	8	2	3	17	9	53	33	.288	.354	.357
89	STL/NL		155	591	545	158	28	8	4	214	39	5	4	91	12	0	3	27	8	60	68	.290	.340	.393
90	STL/NL		135	463	418	91	14	7	6	137	39	5	5	60	4	1	0	25	5	42	30	.218	.292	.328
91	STL/NL		115	361	326	100	16	5	6	144	32	7	0	53	4	2	1	16	9	55	34	.307	.368	.442
92	STL/NL		109	226	208	61	9	1	4	84	16	3	2	39	4	0	0	18	6	31	17	.293	.350	.404
93	PHI/NL		129	387	340	89	14	2	4	119	40	9	2	57	8	3	2	9	4	42	44	.262	.341	.350
10 YR TOTALS			1109	3662	3322	927	138	37	41	1262	291	39	18	555	50	17	14	200	61	440	302	.279	.339	.380

Thompson, Robert Randall "Robby" — BR/TR — b.5/10/62 — POS 2B-1091, SS-1 — SF83 S1/2

YR	TM/LG	CL	G	TPA	AB	H	2B	3B	HR	TB	BB	IBB	HB	SO	GDP	SH	SF	SB	CS	R	RBI	BA	OBA	SA
84	FRE/CAL	A+	102	383	325	81	11	3	8	116	47	1	5	85	8	1	5	21	7	53	43	.249	.348	.357
85	SHR/TEX	AA	121	527	449	117	20	7	9	178	65	0	5	101	8	3	5	28	7	85	40	.261	.358	.396
86	SF/NL		149	615	549	149	27	3	7	203	42	0	5	112	11	18	1	12	15	73	47	.271	.328	.370
87	SF/NL		132	474	420	110	26	5	10	176	40	3	8	91	8	6	0	16	11	62	44	.262	.338	.419
88	SF/NL		138	540	477	126	24	6	7	183	40	0	4	111	7	14	5	14	5	66	48	.264	.323	.384
89	SF/NL		148	620	547	132	26	*11	13	219	51	0	13	133	6	9	0	12	2	91	50	.241	.321	.400
90	SF/NL		144	549	498	122	22	3	15	195	34	1	6	96	9	3	4	14	4	67	56	.245	.299	.392
91	SF/NL		144	573	492	129	24	5	19	220	63	2	6	95	5	11	1	14	7	74	48	.262	.352	.447
92	SF/NL		128	505	443	115	25	1	14	184	43	1	8	75	8	7	4	5	9	54	49	.260	.333	.415
93	SF/NL		128	559	494	154	30	2	19	245	45	7	7	97	7	9	4	6	6	85	65	.312	.375	.496
8 YR TOTALS			1111	4435	3920	1037	204	36	104	1625	358	77	57	810	61	82	18	97	57	572	407	.265	.334	.415

Thompson, Ryan Orlando — BR/TR — b.11/4/67 — POS OF-105 — TOR87 13/335

YR	TM/LG	CL	G	TPA	AB	H	2B	3B	HR	TB	BB	IBB	HB	SO	GDP	SH	SF	SB	CS	R	RBI	BA	OBA	SA
87	MH/PIO	R+	40	116	110	27	3	1	1	35	6	0	0	34	1	0	0	1	2	13	9	.245	.284	.318
88	SC/NYP	A-	23	86	57	10	4	0	0	14	24	0	4	21	0	1	0	2	2	13	2	.175	.447	.246
	DUN/FSL	A+	17	32	29	4	0	0	1	7	2	0	1	12	0	0	0	2	2	2	2	.138	.219	.241
89	SC/NYP	A-	74	301	278	76	14	1	6	110	16	0	4	60	8	0	3	9	6	39	36	.273	.319	.396
90	DUN/FSL	A+	117	467	438	101	15	5	6	144	20	1	2	100	5	3	4	18	5	56	37	.231	.265	.329
91	KNO/SOU	AA	114	441	403	97	14	3	8	141	26	2	4	88	11	3	1	17	10	48	40	.241	.291	.350
92	SYR/INT	AAA	112	478	429	121	20	7	14	197	43	1	3	114	5	2	1	10	4	74	46	.282	.351	.459
	NY/NL		30	117	108	24	7	1	3	42	8	0	0	24	2	0	1	2	2	15	10	.222	.274	.389
93	NOR/INT	AAA	60	255	224	58	11	2	12	109	24	2	5	81	2	0	2	0	3	39	34	.259	.341	.487
	NY/NL		80	316	288	72	19	2	11	128	19	4	3	81	5	0	2	3	2	34	26	.250	.302	.444
2 YR TOTALS			110	433	396	96	26	3	14	170	27	4	3	105	7	5	2	4	9	49	36	.242	.294	.429

Thon, Richard William "Dickie" — BR/TR — b.6/20/58 — POS SS-1143, 2B-98, 3B-50, DH-29, 1B-1 — CAL 11/23/75

YR	TM/LG	CL	G	TPA	AB	H	2B	3B	HR	TB	BB	IBB	HB	SO	GDP	SH	SF	SB	CS	R	RBI	BA	OBA	SA
79	CAL/AL		35	62	56	19	3	0	0	22	5	0	0	10	2	1	0	0	0	6	8	.339	.393	.393
80	CAL/AL		80	285	267	68	12	2	0	84	10	0	1	28	5	5	2	7	5	32	15	.255	.282	.315
81	HOU/NL		49	105	95	26	6	0	0	32	9	1	0	13	1	0	0	6	1	13	3	.274	.337	.337
82	HOU/NL		136	540	496	137	31	*10	3	197	37	2	1	48	4	5	1	37	8	73	36	.276	.327	.397
83	HOU/NL		154	686	619	177	28	9	20	283	54	10	2	73	12	3	8	34	16	81	79	.286	.341	.457
84	HOU/NL		5	18	17	6	0	0	0	6	1	0	0	4	1	0	0	0	0	3	1	.353	.389	.471
85	HOU/NL		84	272	251	63	6	1	6	89	18	4	0	50	2	1	2	8	5	26	29	.251	.299	.355
86	HOU/NL		106	309	278	69	13	1	3	93	29	5	0	81	9	8	1	6	5	24	21	.248	.299	.335
87	TUC/PCL	AAA	14	56	48	13	4	0	0	17	6	0	1	12	1	1	0	1	1	10	6	.271	.364	.354
	HOU/NL		32	83	66	14	1	0	1	18	16	3	0	13	1	1	0	6	3	6	3	.212	.366	.273
88	SD/NL		95	296	258	68	12	2	1	87	33	2	0	49	4	2	2	19	4	36	18	.264	.347	.337
89	PHI/NL		136	472	435	118	18	4	15	189	33	6	0	81	6	1	0	6	3	45	60	.271	.321	.434
90	PHI/NL		149	595	552	141	20	4	8	193	37	10	3	77	14	1	2	12	5	54	48	.255	.305	.350
91	PHI/NL		146	570	539	136	18	4	9	189	25	4	0	84	9	1	3	11	9	54	44	.252	.283	.351
92	TEX/AL		95	303	275	68	15	3	4	101	20	1	0	40	2	2	4	12	6	30	37	.247	.293	.367
93	MIL/AL		85	275	245	66	10	1	1	81	22	3	0	39	4	2	1	12	12	23	33	.269	.324	.331
15 YR TOTALS			1387	4871	4449	1176	193	42	71	1666	348	51	9	658	77	30	35	167	63	496	435	.264	.317	.374

Thurman, Gary Montez — BR/TR — b.11/12/64 — POS OF-332, DH-23 KC83 1/21

YR	TM/LG	CL	G	TPA	AB	H	2B	3B	HR	TB	BB	IBB	HB	SO	GDP	SH	SF	SB	CS	R	RBI	BA	OBA	SA
84	CHS/SAL	A	129	571	478	109	6	8	6	149	81	1	8	127	6	1	3	44	17	71	51	.228	.347	.312
85	FM/FSL	A+	134	532	453	137	9	9	0	164	68	1	4	93	7	3	4	70	18	68	45	.302	.395	.362
86	MEM/SOU	AA	131	589	525	164	24	12	7	233	57	0	0	81	5	4	3	53	18	88	62	.312	.378	.444
	OMA/AMA	AAA	3	4	2	1	0	0	0	1	2	0	0	0	0	0	0	2	0	1	0	.500	.750	.500
87	OMA/AMA	AAA	115	509	450	132	14	9	8	188	48	0	3	84	4	5	3	58	7	88	39	.293	.363	.418
	KC/AL		27	90	81	24	2	0	0	26	8	0	0	20	1	1	0	7	2	12	5	.296	.360	.321
88	OMA/AMA	AAA	106	475	422	106	12	6	3	139	38	2	4	80	8	8	3	35	12	77	40	.251	.317	.329
	KC/AL		35	70	66	11	1	0	0	12	4	0	0	20	0	0	0	5	1	6	2	.167	.214	.182
89	OMA/AMA	AAA	17	71	64	14	3	2	0	21	7	0	0	18	0	0	0	5	4	5	3	.219	.296	.328
	KC/AL		72	105	87	17	2	1	0	21	15	0	0	26	0	2	1	16	0	24	5	.195	.311	.241
90	OMA/AMA	AAA	98	424	381	126	14	8	0	156	31	1	4	68	6	6	2	39	15	65	26	.331	.389	.409
	KC/AL		23	63	60	14	3	0	0	17	2	0	0	12	2	1	0	1	1	5	3	.233	.258	.283
91	KC/AL		80	200	184	51	9	0	2	66	11	0	1	42	4	1	1	15	5	24	13	.277	.320	.359
92	KC/AL		88	216	200	49	6	3	0	61	9	0	1	34	3	6	0	9	6	25	20	.245	.281	.305
93	DET/AL		75	102	89	19	2	2	0	25	11	0	0	30	2	1	1	7	0	22	13	.213	.297	.281
7 YR TOTALS			**400**	**846**	**767**	**185**	**25**	**6**	**2**	**228**	**60**	**0**	**2**	**184**	**12**	**14**	**3**	**60**	**15**	**118**	**61**	**.241**	**.297**	**.297**

Tingley, Ronald Irvin "Ron" — BR/TR — b.5/27/59 — POS C-198 SD77 10/242

YR	TM/LG	CL	G	TPA	AB	H	2B	3B	HR	TB	BB	IBB	HB	SO	GDP	SH	SF	SB	CS	R	RBI	BA	OBA	SA
77	WW/NWL	A-	21	38	33	5	0	0	1	8	2	0	2	9	1	0	0	0	0	8	3	.152	.243	.242
78	WW/NWL	A-	43	168	140	29	2	0	2	37	21	1	5	38	2	1	1	2	0	22	21	.207	.329	.264
79	SC/CAL	A+	52	166	143	29	4	1	0	35	18	0	0	37	2	3	2	0	3	11	17	.203	.288	.245
	AMA/TEX	AA	30	105	90	23	4	1	1	32	14	0	0	17	2	1	0	3	0	16	6	.256	.356	.356
80	REN/CAL	A+	65	243	204	61	3	3	3	79	33	1	0	35	4	4	2	1	0	37	35	.299	.393	.387
81	AMA/TEX	AA	116	446	379	109	9	10	13	177	52	0	4	98	4	8	1	4	1	45	42	.288	.376	.467
82	HAW/PCL	AAA	115	427	362	95	13	8	6	142	56	0	2	103	5	2	1	11	6	45	42	.262	.363	.392
	SD/NL		8	21	20	2	0	0	0	2	0	0	0	7	0	1	0	0	0	0	0	.100	.100	.100
83	LV/PCL	AAA	92	338	294	83	15	6	10	140	39	2	1	85	2	1	3	9	4	44	48	.282	.365	.476
85	CAL/PCL	AAA	83	311	277	70	11	3	11	120	30	1	2	74	11	0	2	3	4	36	47	.253	.330	.433
86	RIC/INT	AAA	9	24	23	4	0	0	0	4	0	0	0	9	0	1	0	0	0	1	1	.174	.174	.174
	MAI/INT	AAA	49	166	151	31	2	1	3	44	12	0	0	27	7	2	1	1	0	12	12	.205	.262	.291
87	BUF/AMA	AAA	57	197	167	45	8	5	3	78	25	1	4	42	3	0	1	1	2	27	30	.269	.376	.467
88	CS/PCL	AAA	44	148	130	37	5	1	3	53	12	0	2	23	4	1	3	1	0	11	20	.285	.347	.408
	CLE/AL		9	26	24	4	0	0	1	7	2	0	0	8	1	0	0	0	0	1	2	.167	.231	.292
89	CS/PCL	AAA	66	234	207	54	8	2	6	84	19	1	1	49	6	1	6	2	1	28	39	.261	.318	.406
	CAL/AL		4	4	3	1	0	0	0	1	0	0	0	0	0	0	1	0	0	0	0	.333	.500	.333
90	EDM/PCL	AAA	54	198	172	46	9	2	5	74	21	0	2	39	6	1	2	1	1	27	23	.267	.350	.430
	CAL/AL		5	4	3	0	0	0	0	0	1	0	0	1	1	0	0	0	0	0	0	.000	.250	.000
91	EDM/PCL	AAA	17	65	55	16	5	0	3	30	8	0	1	14	0	1	0	1	0	11	15	.291	.391	.545
	CAL/AL		45	128	115	23	7	0	1	33	8	0	1	34	1	4	0	1	1	11	13	.200	.258	.287
92	CAL/AL		71	147	127	25	2	1	3	38	13	0	2	35	4	5	0	0	1	15	8	.197	.282	.299
93	CAL/AL		58	104	90	18	1	2	0	25	9	0	1	22	4	3	1	1	2	7	12	.200	.277	.278
7 YR TOTALS			**200**	**434**	**382**	**73**	**16**	**1**	**5**	**106**	**34**	**0**	**4**	**107**	**11**	**13**	**1**	**2**	**4**	**34**	**35**	**.191**	**.264**	**.277**

Tinsley, Lee Owen — BB/TR — b.3/4/69 — POS OF-6, DH-2 OAK87 1/11

YR	TM/LG	CL	G	TPA	AB	H	2B	3B	HR	TB	BB	IBB	HB	SO	GDP	SH	SF	SB	CS	R	RBI	BA	OBA	SA
87	MED/NWL	A-	45	174	132	23	3	2	0	30	35	0	2	57	1	1	4	9	3	22	13	.174	.347	.227
88	SO/NWL	A-	72	329	256	64	8	2	3	85	66	1	1	106	1	1	1	42	10	56	28	.250	.412	.332
89	MAD/MID	A	123	477	397	72	10	2	6	104	67	1	9	177	6	3	1	19	11	51	31	.181	.312	.262
90	MAD/MID	A	132	570	482	121	14	12	12	195	78	7	5	175	3	3	2	44	11	88	59	.251	.360	.405
91	HUN/SOU	AA	92	363	303	68	7	6	2	93	52	1	3	97	6	1	4	36	14	47	24	.224	.340	.307
	CAN/EAS	AA	38	163	139	41	7	2	3	61	18	2	4	37	2	2	0	18	5	26	8	.295	.391	.439
92	CS/PCL	AAA	27	100	81	19	2	1	0	23	16	0	1	19	3	1	1	3	3	19	4	.235	.364	.284
	CAN/EAS	AA	96	400	349	100	7	2	5	140	42	4	2	82	1	2	5	18	5	65	38	.287	.365	.401
93	SEA/AL		11	21	19	3	1	0	1	7	2	0	0	9	1	0	0	1	0	4	1	.158	.238	.368
	CAL/PCL	AAA	111	509	450	136	25	18	10	227	50	5	2	98	3	4	3	34	11	94	63	.302	.372	.504

Tomberlin, Andy Lee — BL/TL — b.11/7/66 — POS OF-7 ATL 8/16/85

YR	TM/LG	CL	G	TPA	AB	H	2B	3B	HR	TB	BB	IBB	HB	SO	GDP	SH	SF	SB	CS	R	RBI	BA	OBA	SA
86	SUM/SAL	A	13	2	1	0	0	0	0	0	1	0	0	1	0	0	0	0	0	0	0	.000	.500	.000
	PUL/APP	R+	3	6	4	1	0	0	0	1	2	0	0	0	0	0	0	0	0	2	0	.250	.500	.250
87	PUL/APP	R+	14	7	7	2	0	0	0	2	0	0	0	0	0	0	0	0	0	1	1	.286	.286	.286
88	BUR/MID	A	43	160	134	46	7	3	3	68	22	2	2	33	0	1	1	7	4	24	18	.343	.440	.507
	DUR/CAR	A+	83	309	256	77	16	3	6	117	49	3	1	42	2	2	1	16	8	43	35	.301	.414	.457
89	DUR/CAR	A+	119	426	363	102	13	2	16	167	54	7	5	82	4	3	1	35	12	63	61	.281	.381	.460
90	GRE/SOU	AA	60	226	196	61	9	1	4	84	20	0	5	35	1	4	1	9	7	31	25	.311	.387	.429
	RIC/INT	AAA	80	329	283	86	19	3	4	123	39	7	1	43	7	4	2	11	4	36	31	.304	.388	.435
91	RIC/INT	AAA	93	388	329	77	13	2	9	100	41	3	6	85	6	9	1	10	6	47	24	.234	.332	.304
92	RIC/INT	AAA	118	467	406	110	16	5	9	163	41	1	8	102	2	10	2	12	12	69	47	.271	.348	.401
93	BUF/AMA	AAA	68	246	221	63	11	6	12	122	18	3	4	48	5	1	2	3	0	41	45	.285	.347	.552
	PIT/NL		27	45	42	12	2	0	1	17	2	0	0	14	0	0	1	0	0	4	5	.286	.333	.405

Trammell, Alan Stuart — BR/TR — b.2/21/58 — POS SS-1973, DH-42, 3B-35, OF-8 DET76 2/26

YR	TM/LG	CL	G	TPA	AB	H	2B	3B	HR	TB	BB	IBB	HB	SO	GDP	SH	SF	SB	CS	R	RBI	BA	OBA	SA
77	DET/AL		19	48	43	8	0	0	0	8	4	0	0	12	1	1	0	0	0	6	0	.186	.255	.186
78	DET/AL		139	504	448	120	14	6	2	152	45	0	2	56	12	6	3	3	1	49	34	.268	.335	.339
79	DET/AL		142	520	460	127	11	4	6	164	43	0	0	55	6	12	5	17	14	68	50	.276	.335	.357

(continued)

Trammell, Alan Stuart (continued)

YR	TM/LG	CL	G	TPA	AB	H	2B	3B	HR	TB	BB	IBB	HB	SO	GDP	SH	SF	SB	CS	R	RBI	BA	OBA	SA
80	DET/AL		146	652	560	168	21	5	9	226	69	2	3	63	10	13	7	12	12	107	65	.300	.376	.404
81	DET/AL		105	463	392	101	15	3	2	128	49	2	3	31	10	16	3	10	3	52	31	.258	.342	.327
82	DET/AL		157	556	489	126	34	3	9	193	52	0	0	47	5	9	6	19	8	66	57	.258	.325	.395
83	DET/AL		142	581	505	161	31	2	14	238	57	2	0	64	7	15	4	30	10	83	66	.319	.385	.471
84	DET/AL		139	626	555	174	34	5	14	260	60	2	3	63	8	6	2	19	13	85	69	.314	.382	.468
85	DET/AL		149	677	605	156	21	7	13	230	50	4	2	71	6	11	9	14	5	79	57	.258	.312	.380
86	DET/AL		151	653	574	159	33	7	21	269	59	4	5	57	7	11	4	25	12	107	75	.277	.347	.469
87	DET/AL		151	668	597	205	34	3	28	329	60	8	3	47	11	2	6	21	2	109	105	.343	.402	.551
88	DET/AL		128	523	466	145	24	1	15	216	46	8	4	46	14	0	7	7	4	73	69	.311	.373	.464
89	DET/AL		121	506	449	109	20	3	5	150	45	1	4	45	9	3	5	10	2	54	43	.243	.314	.334
90	DET/AL		146	637	559	170	37	1	14	251	68	7	3	55	11	3	6	12	10	71	89	.304	.377	.449
91	DET/AL		101	421	375	93	20	0	9	140	37	1	3	39	7	5	1	11	2	57	55	.248	.320	.373
92	DET/AL		29	120	102	28	7	1	1	40	15	0	1	4	6	1	1	2	2	11	11	.275	.370	.392
93	DET/AL		112	447	401	132	25	3	12	199	38	2	2	38	7	1	2	12	8	72	60	.329	.388	.496
17 YR TOTALS			**2077**	**8602**	**7580**	**2182**	**381**	**54**	**174**	**3193**	**797**	**43**	**36**	**793**	**137**	**118**	**71**	**224**	**108**	**1149**	**936**	**.288**	**.355**	**.421**

Treadway, Hugh Jeffery "Jeff" — BL/TR — b.1/22/63 — POS 2B-520, 3B-51, DH-4   CIN 1/29/84

YR	TM/LG	CL	G	TPA	AB	H	2B	3B	HR	TB	BB	IBB	HB	SO	GDP	SH	SF	SB	CS	R	RBI	BA	OBA	SA
84	TAM/FSL	A+	119	441	372	115	16	0	0	131	54	8	5	40	10	7	3	13	7	44	44	.309	.401	.352
85	VER/EAS	AA	129	514	431	130	17	1	2	155	71	2	2	40	10	5	5	6	5	63	49	.302	.399	.360
86	VER/EAS	AA	33	148	122	41	8	1	1	54	23	2	1	12	7	3	0	3	1	18	16	.336	.439	.443
	DEN/AMA	AAA	72	227	204	67	11	4	3	95	19	2	1	12	4	1	2	3	1	20	23	.328	.385	.466
87	NAS/AMA	AAA	123	472	409	129	28	5	7	188	52	3	3	41	8	2	6	2	1	66	59	.315	.391	.460
	CIN/NL		23	90	84	28	4	0	2	38	2	0	1	6	1	3	0	1	0	9	4	.333	.356	.452
88	CIN/NL		103	341	301	76	19	4	2	109	27	7	3	30	4	4	6	2	0	30	23	.252	.315	.362
89	ATL/NL		134	514	473	131	18	3	8	179	30	3	3	38	9	4	5	3	2	58	40	.277	.317	.378
90	ATL/NL		128	511	474	134	20	2	11	191	25	1	3	42	10	5	4	3	4	56	59	.283	.320	.403
91	ATL/NL		106	336	306	98	17	2	3	128	23	1	2	19	8	2	3	2	2	41	32	.320	.368	.418
92	GRE/SOU	AA	4	13	11	5	2	0	0	7	2	0	0	1	0	0	0	0	1	1	1	.455	.538	.636
	ATL/NL		61	136	126	28	9	4	0	36	9	4	0	16	3	1	0	1	2	5	5	.222	.274	.286
93	CLE/AL		97	240	221	67	14	1	2	89	14	2	2	21	6	1	1	2	1	25	27	.303	.347	.403
7 YR TOTALS			**652**	**2168**	**1985**	**562**	**98**	**13**	**28**	**770**	**130**	**18**	**11**	**172**	**41**	**22**	**20**	**13**	**11**	**224**	**190**	**.283**	**.328**	**.388**

Tubbs, Gregory Alan "Greg" — BR/TR — b.8/31/62 — POS OF-21   ATL84 22/565

YR	TM/LG	CL	G	TPA	AB	H	2B	3B	HR	TB	BB	IBB	HB	SO	GDP	SH	SF	SB	CS	R	RBI	BA	OBA	SA
84	BRA/GCL	R	18	74	58	21	4	3	0	31	15	0	0	5	0	0	1	5	2	13	3	.362	.486	.534
	AND/SAL	A	50	205	174	53	5	2	2	68	27	0	1	29	0	3	0	19	6	25	11	.305	.401	.391
85	SUM/SAL	A	61	278	239	85	11	7	6	128	33	0	2	36	2	1	3	30	18	53	36	.356	.433	.536
	DUR/CAR	A+	70	308	266	75	15	6	8	126	36	0	3	52	6	2	1	29	12	44	32	.282	.373	.474
86	GRE/SOU	AA	144	659	536	144	21	7	5	194	107	2	3	74	14	10	3	31	22	95	56	.269	.391	.362
87	GRE/SOU	AA	141	636	540	145	19	3	8	187	86	2	1	86	9	7	1	24	19	97	40	.269	.370	.346
88	GRE/SOU	AA	29	115	101	24	1	1	0	27	13	0	1	20	1	0	0	4	0	13	12	.238	.330	.267
	RIC/INT	AAA	78	261	228	56	14	2	2	80	28	0	1	38	5	3	1	8	8	43	11	.246	.329	.351
89	GRE/SOU	AA	11	35	27	5	0	0	0	5	8	0	0	4	0	0	0	3	0	4	1	.185	.371	.185
	RIC/INT	AAA	115	458	405	122	10	11	4	166	47	0	1	49	10	5	0	19	15	64	35	.301	.375	.410
90	RIC/INT	AAA	11	35	23	5	0	0	0	5	11	0	0	6	0	1	0	0	2	3	1	.217	.471	.217
	HAR/EAS	AA	54	238	213	60	6	5	3	85	23	0	0	35	7	1	1	8	1	35	21	.282	.350	.399
91	BUF/AMA	AAA	121	433	373	102	18	11	3	151	48	1	5	62	10	5	2	34	11	71	34	.273	.362	.405
92	BUF/AMA	AAA	110	495	430	126	20	5	7	177	57	2	3	64	6	3	2	20	19	69	42	.293	.378	.412
93	IND/AMA	AAA	97	382	334	102	21	4	10	161	42	3	2	65	4	1	3	15	11	59	45	.305	.383	.482
	CIN/NL		35	74	59	11	0	0	1	14	14	0	1	10	0	0	0	3	1	10	2	.186	.351	.237

Tucker, Eddie Jack — BR/TR — b.11/18/66 — POS C-27   SF88 7/126

YR	TM/LG	CL	G	TPA	AB	H	2B	3B	HR	TB	BB	IBB	HB	SO	GDP	SH	SF	SB	CS	R	RBI	BA	OBA	SA
88	EVE/NWL	A-	45	189	153	40	5	0	3	54	30	0	3	34	8	0	3	0	0	24	23	.261	.386	.353
89	CLI/MID	A	126	500	426	105	20	2	3	138	58	2	9	80	11	3	4	6	5	44	43	.246	.346	.324
90	SJ/CAL	A+	123	531	439	123	28	2	5	170	71	4	13	69	14	2	6	9	3	59	71	.280	.391	.387
91	SHR/TEX	AA	110	413	352	100	29	1	4	143	48	1	5	57	8	6	2	3	4	49	49	.284	.376	.406
92	TUC/PCL	AAA	83	322	288	87	15	1	2	107	28	1	3	35	12	1	2	5	1	36	29	.302	.368	.372
	HOU/NL		20	56	50	6	1	0	0	7	3	0	2	13	2	1	0	1	1	5	3	.120	.200	.140
93	TUC/PCL	AAA	98	371	318	87	20	2	1	114	47	8	2	37	7	2	2	1	5	54	37	.274	.369	.358
	HOU/NL		9	28	26	5	1	0	0	6	2	0	0	3	0	0	0	1	0	1	3	.192	.250	.231
2 YR TOTALS			**29**	**84**	**76**	**11**	**2**	**0**	**0**	**13**	**5**	**0**	**2**	**16**	**2**	**1**	**0**	**1**	**1**	**6**	**6**	**.145**	**.217**	**.171**

Turang, Brian Craig — BR/TR — b.6/14/67 — POS OF-38, 3B-2, 2B-1, DH-1   SEA89 50/1299

YR	TM/LG	CL	G	TPA	AB	H	2B	3B	HR	TB	BB	IBB	HB	SO	GDP	SH	SF	SB	CS	R	RBI	BA	OBA	SA
89	BEL/NWL	A-	60	254	207	59	10	3	4	87	33	0	12	50	1	2	0	9	6	42	11	.285	.413	.420
90	SB/CAL	A+	132	573	487	144	25	5	12	215	69	0	7	98	8	6	4	25	16	86	67	.296	.388	.441
	CAL/PCL	AAA	3	11	9	2	0	0	0	2	2	0	0	4	0	0	0	0	0	1	1	.222	.364	.222
91	JAC/SOU	AA	41	147	130	28	6	2	0	38	13	1	2	33	1	2	0	6	2	14	7	.215	.297	.292
	SB/CAL	A+	34	119	100	18	2	1	0	22	15	0	3	31	1	1	0	6	6	9	4	.180	.305	.220
92	JAC/SOU	AA	129	544	483	121	21	3	14	190	44	2	12	61	12	6	3	19	9	67	63	.251	.327	.393
93	CAL/PCL	AAA	110	475	423	137	20	11	8	203	40	2	3	48	7	5	4	24	8	84	54	.324	.383	.480
	SEA/AL		40	160	140	35	11	1	0	48	17	0	2	20	1	1	0	6	2	22	7	.250	.340	.343

Turner, Christopher Wan "Chris" — BR/TR — b.3/23/69 — POS C-25   CAL91 8/194

YR	TM/LG	CL	G	TPA	AB	H	2B	3B	HR	TB	BB	IBB	HB	SO	GDP	SH	SF	SB	CS	R	RBI	BA	OBA	SA
91	BOI/NWL	A-	52	204	163	37	5	0	2	48	32	0	2	32	3	2	5	10	1	26	29	.227	.351	.294
92	QC/MID	A	109	435	330	83	18	1	9	130	85	5	8	65	3	6	6	8	7	66	53	.252	.410	.394
93	VAN/PCL	AAA	90	348	283	78	12	1	4	104	49	1	3	44	7	8	5	6	1	50	57	.276	.382	.367
	CAL/AL		25	86	75	21	5	0	1	29	9	0	1	16	1	0	1	1	1	9	13	.280	.360	.387

Uribe, Jose Altagracia — BB/TR — b.1/21/59 — POS SS-1015, 2B-2   NYA 2/18/77

YR	TM/LG	CL	G	TPA	AB	H	2B	3B	HR	TB	BB	IBB	HB	SO	GDP	SH	SF	SB	CS	R	RBI	BA	OBA	SA
84	STL/NL		8	20	19	4	0	0	0	4	0	0	0	2	1	0	1	0	1	4	3	.211	.211	.211
85	SF/NL		147	513	476	113	20	4	3	150	30	8	2	57	5	5	0	8	2	46	26	.237	.285	.315
86	SF/NL		157	517	453	101	15	1	3	127	61	19	0	76	3	2	3	22	11	46	43	.223	.315	.280
87	SF/NL		95	340	309	90	16	5	5	131	24	9	1	35	1	5	1	12	2	44	30	.291	.343	.424
88	SF/NL		141	535	493	124	10	7	3	157	36	10	0	69	3	4	2	14	10	47	35	.252	.301	.318
89	SF/NL		151	497	453	100	12	6	1	127	34	12	0	74	7	4	6	6	6	34	30	.221	.273	.280
90	SF/NL		138	448	415	103	8	6	1	126	29	13	0	49	8	4	0	5	9	35	24	.248	.297	.304
91	SJ/CAL	A+	3	11	9	1	0	1	0	3	1	0	0	2	0	0	0	0	0	0	1	.111	.182	.333
	PHO/PCL	AAA	11	42	41	14	1	1	0	17	1	0	0	3	1	0	0	0	0	7	4	.341	.357	.415
	SF/NL		90	252	231	51	9	1	0	70	20	6	0	33	1	2	0	3	4	23	12	.221	.283	.303
92	SF/NL		66	181	162	39	9	1	2	56	14	3	0	25	3	4	1	2	2	24	13	.241	.299	.346
93	HOU/NL		45	66	53	13	1	0	0	14	8	4	1	5	1	1	0	1	0	4	3	.245	.355	.264
10 YR TOTALS			**1038**	**3369**	**3064**	**738**	**99**	**34**	**19**	**962**	**256**	**84**	**4**	**425**	**33**	**37**	**8**	**74**	**46**	**307**	**219**	**.241**	**.300**	**.314**

Valentin, John William — BR/TR — b.2/18/67 — POS SS-202   BOS88 5/121

YR	TM/LG	CL	G	TPA	AB	H	2B	3B	HR	TB	BB	IBB	HB	SO	GDP	SH	SF	SB	CS	R	RBI	BA	OBA	SA
88	ELM/NYP	A-	60	250	207	45	5	1	2	58	36	1	0	35	6	5	2	5	4	18	16	.217	.331	.280
89	WH/FSL	A+	55	234	215	58	13	1	3	82	13	0	1	29	7	2	3	4	4	27	18	.270	.310	.381
	LYN/CAR	A+	75	311	264	65	7	2	8	100	41	1	2	40	8	2	2	5	2	47	34	.246	.350	.379
90	NB/EAS	AA	94	351	312	68	18	1	2	94	25	1	0	46	5	11	3	1	2	20	31	.218	.274	.301
91	NB/EAS	AA	23	91	81	16	3	0	0	19	9	0	0	14	2	1	0	1	1	8	5	.198	.278	.235
	PAW/INT	AAA	100	399	329	87	22	4	9	144	60	2	0	42	9	6	4	1	1	52	49	.264	.374	.438
92	PAW/INT	AAA	97	388	331	86	18	1	9	133	48	1	3	50	9	5	1	1	2	47	29	.260	.358	.402
	BOS/AL		58	212	185	51	13	0	5	79	20	0	2	17	5	4	1	1	1	21	25	.276	.351	.427
93	PAW/INT	AAA	2	9	9	3	0	0	1	6	0	0	0	1	1	0	0	0	0	3	1	.333	.333	.667
	BOS/AL		144	539	468	130	40	3	11	209	49	2	2	77	9	16	4	3	4	50	66	.278	.346	.447
2 YR TOTALS			**202**	**751**	**653**	**181**	**53**	**3**	**16**	**288**	**69**	**2**	**4**	**94**	**14**	**20**	**5**	**4**	**4**	**71**	**91**	**.277**	**.347**	**.441**

Valentin, Jose Antonio — BB/TR — b.10/12/69 — POS SS-20, 2B-1   SD 10/12/86

YR	TM/LG	CL	G	TPA	AB	H	2B	3B	HR	TB	BB	IBB	HB	SO	GDP	SH	SF	SB	CS	R	RBI	BA	OBA	SA
87	SPO/NWL	A-	70	283	244	61	8	2	2	79	35	2	1	38	4	3	0	8	5	52	24	.250	.346	.324
88	CHS/SAL	A	133	505	444	103	20	1	6	143	45	1	3	83	10	9	4	11	4	56	44	.232	.304	.322
89	RIV/CAL	A+	114	430	381	74	10	5	10	124	37	1	5	93	4	5	2	8	7	40	41	.194	.273	.325
	WIC/TEX	AA	18	57	49	12	1	0	2	19	5	1	0	12	1	3	0	1	0	8	5	.245	.315	.388
90	WIC/TEX	AA	11	42	36	10	2	0	0	12	5	0	0	7	1	1	0	2	1	4	2	.278	.366	.333
91	WIC/TEX	AA	129	515	447	112	22	5	17	195	55	1	4	115	5	4	5	8	6	73	68	.251	.335	.436
92	DEN/AMA	AAA	139	565	492	118	19	11	3	168	53	2	5	99	8	9	6	9	4	78	45	.240	.317	.341
	MIL/AL		4	4	3	0	0	0	0	0	0	0	0	0	0	0	1	0	0	1	1	.000	.000	.000
93	NO/AMA	AAA	122	462	389	96	22	5	9	155	47	2	8	87	3	14	4	9	10	56	53	.247	.337	.398
	MIL/AL		19	63	53	13	1	2	0	21	7	1	1	16	1	2	1	1	0	10	7	.245	.344	.396
2 YR TOTALS			**23**	**67**	**56**	**13**	**1**	**2**	**0**	**21**	**7**	**1**	**1**	**16**	**1**	**2**	**1**	**1**	**0**	**11**	**8**	**.232**	**.323**	**.375**

Valle, David "Dave" — BR/TR — b.10/30/60 — POS C-798, DH-17, 1B-10, OF-1   SEA78 2/32

YR	TM/LG	CL	G	TPA	AB	H	2B	3B	HR	TB	BB	IBB	HB	SO	GDP	SH	SF	SB	CS	R	RBI	BA	OBA	SA
84	SLC/PCL	AAA	86	335	284	79	13	1	12	130	45	2	3	36	6	0	3	0	1	54	54	.278	.379	.458
	SEA/AL		13	28	27	8	1	0	1	12	1	0	0	5	0	0	0	0	0	4	4	.296	.321	.444
85	CAL/PCL	AAA	42	151	131	45	8	0	6	71	20	1	0	19	6	0	0	0	0	17	26	.344	.430	.542
	SEA/AL		31	73	70	11	1	0	0	12	1	0	1	17	1	1	0	0	2	4	2	.157	.181	.171
86	CAL/PCL	AAA	105	404	353	110	21	2	21	198	41	0	7	43	13	1	2	5	1	71	72	.312	.392	.561
	SEA/AL		22	60	53	18	3	0	5	36	7	0	0	7	2	0	0	0	0	10	15	.340	.417	.679
87	SEA/AL		95	346	324	83	16	3	12	141	15	2	3	46	13	0	3	1	0	40	53	.256	.292	.435
88	SEA/AL		93	322	290	67	10	2	10	116	18	0	9	38	14	0	5	0	0	29	50	.231	.295	.400
89	CAL/PCL	AAA	2	7	6	0	0	0	0	0	0	0	1	0	0	0	0	0	0	0	0	.000	.143	.000
	SEA/AL		94	355	316	75	10	3	7	112	29	1	6	32	13	1	1	1	0	32	34	.237	.311	.354
90	SEA/AL		107	364	308	66	15	0	7	102	45	4	7	48	11	4	0	1	2	37	33	.214	.328	.331
91	SEA/AL		132	376	324	63	8	1	8	97	34	0	9	49	19	6	3	1	2	38	32	.194	.286	.299
92	SEA/AL		124	410	367	88	16	1	9	133	27	1	8	58	7	7	1	0	0	39	30	.240	.305	.362
93	SEA/AL		135	500	423	109	19	1	13	167	48	1	17	56	18	0	8	4	5	48	63	.258	.354	.395
10 YR TOTALS			**846**	**2834**	**2502**	**588**	**104**	**10**	**72**	**928**	**225**	**9**	**60**	**356**	**97**	**30**	**17**	**4**	**5**	**279**	**318**	**.235**	**.311**	**.371**

Van Burkleo, Tyler Lee "Ty" — BL/TL — b.10/7/63 — POS 1B-12   MIL 12/19/81

YR	TM/LG	CL	G	TPA	AB	H	2B	3B	HR	TB	BB	IBB	HB	SO	GDP	SH	SF	SB	CS	R	RBI	BA	OBA	SA
92	EDM/PCL	AAA	135	541	458	125	28	7	19	224	75	6	5	100	10	0	3	20	5	83	88	.273	.379	.489
93	CAL/AL		12	39	33	5	3	0	1	11	6	0	0	9	0	0	0	1	0	2	1	.152	.282	.333
	VAN/PCL	AAA	105	419	361	99	19	2	6	140	51	3	2	89	9	1	2	6	0	47	56	.274	.364	.388

Vanderwal, John Henry — BL/TL — b.4/29/66 — POS OF-112, 1B-49   MON87 5/70

YR	TM/LG	CL	G	TPA	AB	H	2B	3B	HR	TB	BB	IBB	HB	SO	GDP	SH	SF	SB	CS	R	RBI	BA	OBA	SA
87	JAM/NYP	A-	18	73	69	33	12	3	3	60	3	0	0	14	2	0	1	3	2	24	15	.478	.493	.870
	WPB/FSL	A+	50	223	189	54	11	2	2	75	30	0	0	25	2	1	3	3	3	29	22	.286	.378	.397

(continued)

Vanderwal, John Henry (continued)

YR	TM/LG	CL	G	TPA	AB	H	2B	3B	HR	TB	BB	IBB	HB	SO	GDP	SH	SF	SB	CS	R	RBI	BA	OBA	SA
88	WPB/FSL	A+	62	272	231	64	15	2	10	113	32	2	3	40	0	3	3	11	4	50	33	.277	.368	.489
	JAC/SOU	AA	58	227	208	54	14	0	3	77	17	1	1	49	3	0	1	3	4	22	14	.260	.317	.370
89	JAC/SOU	AA	71	242	217	55	9	2	6	86	22	1	1	51	5	0	2	2	3	30	24	.253	.322	.396
90	JAC/SOU	AA	77	321	277	84	25	3	8	139	39	2	3	46	7	0	2	6	3	45	40	.303	.393	.502
	IND/AMA	AAA	51	148	135	40	6	0	2	52	13	0	0	28	3	0	0	0	1	16	14	.296	.358	.385
91	IND/AMA	AAA	133	564	478	140	36	8	15	237	79	4	2	118	10	1	4	8	1	84	71	.293	.393	.496
	MON/NL		21	63	61	13	4	1	1	22	1	0	0	18	1	0	1	0	0	4	8	.213	.222	.361
92	MON/NL		105	237	213	51	8	2	4	75	24	2	0	36	2	0	0	3	0	21	20	.239	.316	.352
93	MON/NL		106	244	215	50	7	4	5	80	27	2	1	30	4	0	1	6	3	34	30	.233	.320	.372
3 YR TOTALS			**232**	**544**	**489**	**114**	**19**	**7**	**10**	**177**	**52**	**4**	**1**	**84**	**8**	**0**	**2**	**9**	**3**	**59**	**58**	**.233**	**.307**	**.362**

Van Slyke, Andrew James "Andy" — BL/TR — b.12/21/60 — POS OF-1327, 1B-82, 3B-62 — SL79 1/6

YR	TM/LG	CL	G	TPA	AB	H	2B	3B	HR	TB	BB	IBB	HB	SO	GDP	SH	SF	SB	CS	R	RBI	BA	OBA	SA
83	STL/NL		101	361	309	81	15	5	8	130	46	5	1	64	4	2	3	21	7	51	38	.262	.357	.421
84	STL/NL		137	426	361	88	16	4	7	133	63	9	0	71	5	0	2	28	5	45	50	.244	.354	.368
85	STL/NL		146	475	424	110	25	6	13	186	47	6	2	54	7	1	1	34	6	61	55	.259	.335	.439
86	STL/NL		137	470	418	113	23	7	13	189	47	5	1	85	2	1	3	21	8	48	61	.270	.343	.452
87	PIT/NL		157	630	564	165	36	11	21	286	56	4	4	122	6	3	3	34	8	93	82	.293	.359	.507
88	PIT/NL		154	659	587	169	23	15	25	297	57	2	1	126	8	1	13	30	1	101	100	.288	.345	.506
89	PIT/NL		130	531	476	113	18	9	9	176	47	3	3	100	13	1	4	16	9	64	53	.237	.308	.370
90	PIT/NL		136	567	493	140	26	6	17	229	66	2	1	89	6	3	4	14	4	67	77	.284	.367	.465
91	PIT/NL		138	577	491	130	24	7	17	219	71	2	4	85	5	0	11	10	3	87	83	.265	.355	.446
92	PIT/NL		154	685	614	199	45	12	14	310	58	4	4	99	9	0	9	12	2	103	89	.324	.381	.505
93	CAR/SOU	AA	2	5	5	0	0	0	0	0	0	0	0	3	0	0	0	0	0	0	0	.000	.200	.000
	PIT/NL		83	353	323	100	13	4	8	145	24	5	2	40	13	0	4	11	2	42	50	.310	.357	.449
11 YR TOTALS			**1473**	**5734**	**5060**	**1408**	**264**	**86**	**152**	**2300**	**582**	**46**	**23**	**935**	**78**	**12**	**57**	**231**	**59**	**762**	**738**	**.278**	**.352**	**.455**

Varsho, Gary Andrew — BL/TR — b.6/20/61 — POS OF-162, 1B-3 — CHN82 6/107

YR	TM/LG	CL	G	TPA	AB	H	2B	3B	HR	TB	BB	IBB	HB	SO	GDP	SH	SF	SB	CS	R	RBI	BA	OBA	SA
84	MID/TEX	AA	128	486	429	112	15	6	8	163	49	2	1	86	4	4	3	27	8	65	50	.261	.336	.380
85	PIT/EAS	AA	115	469	418	101	14	6	3	136	40	1	5	53	3	1	1	40	8	62	37	.242	.315	.325
86	PIT/EAS	AA	107	444	399	106	18	5	13	173	38	4	3	52	1	1	3	45	11	75	44	.266	.332	.434
87	IOW/AMA	AAA	132	555	504	152	23	9	9	220	41	2	3	65	6	3	4	37	17	87	48	.302	.355	.437
88	IOW/AMA	AAA	66	257	234	65	16	5	4	103	18	0	2	38	1	1	2	8	2	46	26	.278	.332	.440
	CHI/NL		46	75	73	20	3	0	0	23	1	0	0	6	0	0	1	5	0	6	5	.274	.280	.315
89	IOW/AMA	AAA	31	125	112	26	3	1	2	37	9	2	2	21	2	0	2	6	3	13	13	.232	.296	.330
	CHI/NL		61	91	87	16	4	2	0	24	4	1	0	13	0	0	0	3	0	10	6	.184	.220	.276
90	IOW/AMA	AAA	63	259	229	69	9	0	7	99	25	2	3	35	2	0	2	18	7	35	33	.301	.375	.432
	CHI/NL		46	49	48	12	4	0	0	16	1	1	0	6	1	0	0	2	0	10	1	.250	.265	.333
91	PIT/NL		99	210	187	51	11	2	4	78	19	2	2	34	2	1	9	2		23	23	.273	.344	.417
92	PIT/NL		103	173	162	36	6	3	4	60	10	1	0	32	2	0	0	22	22		.222	.266	.370
93	IND/AMA	AAA	32	141	121	35	8	1	3	54	15	1	2	13	1	3	2	2	19	18		.289	.377	.446
	CIN/NL		77	109	95	22	6	0	2	34	9	0	1	19	1	3	1	0	8	11		.232	.302	.358
6 YR TOTALS			**432**	**707**	**652**	**157**	**34**	**7**	**10**	**235**	**44**	**5**	**3**	**110**	**6**	**4**	**4**	**25**	**4**	**79**	**68**	**.241**	**.290**	**.360**

Vaughn, Gregory Lamont "Greg" — BR/TR — b.7/3/65 — POS OF-490, DH-96 — MIL86 S1/4

YR	TM/LG	CL	G	TPA	AB	H	2B	3B	HR	TB	BB	IBB	HB	SO	GDP	SH	SF	SB	CS	R	RBI	BA	OBA	SA
86	HEL/PIO	R+	66	300	258	75	13	2	16	140	30	1	2	69	1	5	5	23	5	64	54	.291	.363	.543
87	BEL/MID	A	139	608	492	150	31	6	33	292	102	2	5	115	8	3	6	36	9	120	105	.305	.425	.593
88	EP/TEX	AA	131	579	505	152	39	2	28	279	63	3	3	120	11	4	4	22	5	104	105	.301	.379	.552
89	DEN/AMA	AAA	110	452	387	107	17	5	26	212	62	4	0	94	10	2	1	20	3	74	92	.276	.376	.548
	MIL/AL		38	128	113	30	3	0	5	48	13	0	0	23	0	0	2	4	1	18	23	.265	.336	.425
90	MIL/AL		120	429	382	84	26	2	17	165	33	1	0	91	11	7	6	7	4	51	61	.220	.280	.432
91	MIL/AL		145	614	542	132	24	5	27	247	62	2	1	125	5	2	7	2	2	81	98	.244	.319	.456
92	MIL/AL		141	573	501	114	18	2	23	205	60	1	5	123	8	2	5	15	15	77	78	.228	.313	.409
93	MIL/AL		154	667	569	152	28	2	30	274	89	14	5	118	6	0	4	10	7	97	97	.267	.369	.482
5 YR TOTALS			**598**	**2411**	**2107**	**512**	**99**	**11**	**102**	**939**	**257**	**18**	**12**	**480**	**30**	**11**	**24**	**38**	**29**	**324**	**357**	**.243**	**.325**	**.446**

Vaughn, Maurice Samuel "Mo" — BL/TR — b.12/15/67 — POS 1B-265, DH-55 — BOS89 2/23

YR	TM/LG	CL	G	TPA	AB	H	2B	3B	HR	TB	BB	IBB	HB	SO	GDP	SH	SF	SB	CS	R	RBI	BA	OBA	SA
89	NB/EAS	AA	73	275	245	68	15	0	8	107	25	3	3	47	7	1	1	1	3	28	38	.278	.350	.437
90	PAW/INT	AAA	108	438	386	114	26	1	22	208	44	2	6	87	11	0	2	3	2	62	72	.295	.374	.539
91	PAW/INT	AAA	69	301	234	64	10	0	14	116	60	7	3	44	6	0	4	2	1	35	50	.274	.422	.496
	BOS/AL		74	251	219	57	12	0	4	81	26	2	2	43	7	0	4	2	1	21	32	.260	.339	.370
92	PAW/INT	AAA	39	168	149	42	6	0	6	66	18	1	0	35	5	0	1	1	0	15	28	.282	.357	.443
	BOS/AL		113	408	355	83	16	2	13	142	47	1	3	67	5	0	3	3	3	42	57	.234	.326	.400
93	BOS/AL		152	633	539	160	34	1	29	283	79	23	8	130	14	0	7	4	3	86	101	.297	.390	.525
3 YR TOTALS			**339**	**1292**	**1113**	**300**	**62**	**3**	**46**	**506**	**152**	**32**	**13**	**240**	**30**	**0**	**14**	**9**	**7**	**149**	**190**	**.270**	**.360**	**.455**

Velarde, Randy Lee — BR/TR — b.11/24/62 — POS 3B-204, SS-178, OF-80, 2B-30, DH-4 — CHA85 19/345

YR	TM/LG	CL	G	TPA	AB	H	2B	3B	HR	TB	BB	IBB	HB	SO	GDP	SH	SF	SB	CS	R	RBI	BA	OBA	SA
85	NF/NYP	A-	67	254	218	48	7	3	1	64	35	2	1	72	10	0	0	8	3	28	16	.220	.331	.294
86	BUF/AMA	AAA	9	23	20	4	1	0	0	5	2	0	0	6	1	0	0	1	0	2	2	.200	.304	.250
	APP/MID	A	124	487	417	105	31	4	11	177	58	1	1	96	10	1	4	13	6	55	50	.252	.350	.424
87	ALB/EAS	AA	71	294	263	83	20	2	7	128	25	0	3	47	9	2	1	8	6	40	32	.316	.380	.487
	CMB/INT	AAA	49	204	185	59	10	6	2	96	14	0	4	36	2	0	1	2	2	21	33	.319	.377	.519
	NY/AL		8	22	22	4	0	0	0	4	0	0	0	6	1	0	0	0	0	1	1	.182	.182	.182

Velarde, Randy Lee (continued)

YR	TM/LG	CL	G	TPA	AB	H	2B	3B	HR	TB	BB	IBB	HB	SO	GDP	SH	SF	SB	CS	R	RBI	BA	OBA	SA
88	CMB/INT	AAA	78	321	293	79	23	4	5	125	25	1	1	71	7	0	2	7	5	39	37	.270	.327	.427
	NY/AL		48	125	115	20	6	0	5	41	8	0	2	24	3	0	0	1	1	18	12	.174	.240	.357
89	CMB/INT	AAA	103	431	387	103	26	3	11	168	38	0	5	105	8	1	0	3	5	59	53	.266	.340	.434
	NY/AL		33	111	100	34	4	2	2	48	7	0	1	14	0	3	0	0	3	12	11	.340	.389	.480
90	NY/AL		95	253	229	48	6	2	5	73	20	0	1	53	6	2	1	0	3	21	19	.210	.275	.319
91	NY/AL		80	210	184	45	11	1	1	61	18	0	3	43	6	5	0	3	1	19	15	.245	.322	.332
92	NY/AL		121	461	412	112	24	1	7	159	38	0	2	78	13	4	5	7	2	57	46	.272	.333	.386
93	ALB/EAS	AA	5	19	17	4	0	0	1	7	2	0	0	2	1	0	0	0	0	2	2	.235	.316	.412
	NY/AL		85	253	226	68	13	2	7	106	18	2	4	39	12	3	2	2	2	28	24	.301	.360	.469
7 YR TOTALS			**470**	**1435**	**1288**	**331**	**64**	**8**	**27**	**492**	**109**	**3**	**13**	**257**	**41**	**17**	**8**	**13**	**12**	**156**	**128**	**.257**	**.319**	**.382**

Velasquez, Guillermo — BL/TR — b.4/23/68 — POS 1B-41, OF-8   MEX 1986

YR	TM/LG	CL	G	TPA	AB	H	2B	3B	HR	TB	BB	IBB	HB	SO	GDP	SH	SF	SB	CS	R	RBI	BA	OBA	SA
87	CHS/SAL	A	102	312	295	65	12	0	3	86	16	0	0	65	13	1	0	2	0	32	30	.220	.260	.292
88	CHS/SAL	A	135	567	520	149	28	3	11	216	34	9	1	110	6	3	9	1	1	55	90	.287	.326	.415
89	RIV/CAL	A+	139	607	544	152	30	2	9	213	51	4	2	91	14	0	10	4	3	73	69	.279	.338	.392
90	WIC/TEX	AA	105	417	377	102	21	2	12	163	35	5	1	66	9	0	4	0	1	48	72	.271	.331	.432
91	WIC/TEX	AA	130	557	501	148	26	3	21	243	48	6	1	75	6	0	2	2	3	72	100	.295	.354	.485
92	LV/PCL	AAA	136	566	512	158	44	4	7	231	44	8	1	94	7	0	9	3	1	68	99	.309	.359	.451
	SD/NL		15	24	23	7	0	0	1	10	1	0	0	7	0	0	0	0	0	1	5	.304	.333	.435
93	LV/PCL	AAA	30	142	129	43	6	1	5	66	10	1	1	19	2	0	2	0	0	23	24	.333	.380	.512
	SD/NL		79	157	143	30	2	0	3	41	13	2	0	35	3	0	1	0	0	7	20	.210	.274	.287
2 YR TOTALS			**94**	**181**	**166**	**37**	**2**	**0**	**4**	**51**	**14**	**2**	**0**	**42**	**3**	**0**	**1**	**0**	**0**	**8**	**25**	**.223**	**.282**	**.307**

Ventura, Robin Mark — BL/TR — b.7/14/67 — POS 3B-626, 1B-38   CHA88 1/10

YR	TM/LG	CL	G	TPA	AB	H	2B	3B	HR	TB	BB	IBB	HB	SO	GDP	SH	SF	SB	CS	R	RBI	BA	OBA	SA
89	BIR/SOU	AA	129	563	454	126	25	2	3	164	93	12	6	51	9	4	6	9	7	75	67	.278	.403	.361
	CHI/AL		16	58	45	8	3	0	0	11	8	0	1	6	1	1	3	0	0	5	7	.178	.298	.244
90	CHI/AL		150	565	493	123	17	1	5	157	55	2	1	53	5	13	3	1	4	48	54	.249	.324	.318
91	CHI/AL		157	705	606	172	25	1	23	268	80	3	4	67	22	8	7	2	4	92	100	.284	.367	.442
92	CHI/AL		157	694	592	167	38	1	16	255	93	9	0	71	14	1	8	2	4	85	93	.282	.375	.431
93	CHI/AL		157	669	554	145	27	1	22	240	105	16	3	82	18	1	6	1	6	85	94	.262	.379	.433
5 YR TOTALS			**637**	**2691**	**2290**	**615**	**110**	**4**	**66**	**931**	**341**	**30**	**9**	**279**	**60**	**24**	**27**	**6**	**18**	**315**	**348**	**.269**	**.362**	**.407**

Villanueva, Hector — BR/TR — b.10/2/64 — POS C-123, 1B-26   CHN 3/26/85

YR	TM/LG	CL	G	TPA	AB	H	2B	3B	HR	TB	BB	IBB	HB	SO	GDP	SH	SF	SB	CS	R	RBI	BA	OBA	SA
85	PEO/MID	A	65	226	193	45	7	0	1	55	27	0	3	36	7	2	1	0	2	22	19	.233	.335	.285
86	WIN/CAR	A+	125	509	412	131	20	2	13	194	81	3	2	42	12	2	12	6	4	58	100	.318	.422	.471
87	PIT/EAS	AA	109	440	391	107	31	0	14	180	43	1	1	38	8	2	3	3	4	59	70	.274	.345	.460
88	PIT/EAS	AA	127	521	436	137	24	3	10	197	71	6	4	58	9	2	8	5	4	50	75	.314	.408	.452
89	IOW/AMA	AAA	120	480	444	112	25	1	12	175	32	2	1	95	6	1	2	1	1	46	57	.252	.303	.394
90	IOW/AMA	AAA	52	198	177	47	7	1	8	80	19	2	1	36	4	1	0	0	0	20	34	.266	.340	.452
	CHI/NL		52	120	114	31	4	1	7	58	4	2	2	27	3	0	0	1	0	14	18	.272	.308	.509
91	IOW/AMA	AAA	6	27	25	9	3	0	2	18	1	1	0	6	0	0	1	0	0	2	9	.360	.370	.720
	CHI/NL		71	214	192	53	10	1	13	104	21	1	0	30	3	0	0	0	0	23	32	.276	.346	.542
92	IOW/AMA	AAA	49	182	159	38	8	0	9	73	20	0	0	36	4	1	0	0	0	21	35	.239	.320	.459
	CHI/NL		51	123	112	17	6	0	2	29	11	2	0	24	5	0	0	0	0	9	13	.152	.228	.259
93	LOU/AMA	AAA	40	142	124	30	9	0	5	54	16	1	1	17	3	0	0	0	0	13	20	.242	.331	.435
	STL/NL		17	59	55	8	1	0	3	18	4	1	0	17	3	0	0	0	0	7	9	.145	.203	.327
4 YR TOTALS			**191**	**516**	**473**	**109**	**21**	**2**	**25**	**209**	**40**	**6**	**2**	**98**	**14**	**0**	**1**	**1**	**0**	**53**	**72**	**.230**	**.293**	**.442**

Vina, Fernando — BL/TR — b.4/16/69 — POS 2B-16, SS-4, DH-2   NYN90 9/253

YR	TM/LG	CL	G	TPA	AB	H	2B	3B	HR	TB	BB	IBB	HB	SO	GDP	SH	SF	SB	CS	R	RBI	BA	OBA	SA
91	COL/SAL	A	129	569	498	135	23	6	6	188	46	1	13	27	5	5	7	42	22	77	50	.271	.344	.378
92	TID/INT	AAA	11	33	30	6	0	0	0	6	0	0	0	2	1	2	1	0	0	3	2	.200	.194	.200
	SL/FSL	A+	111	462	421	124	15	5	1	152	32	2	3	26	7	4	2	36	17	61	42	.295	.347	.361
93	NOR/INT	AAA	73	303	287	66	6	4	4	92	7	2	4	17	12	4	1	16	11	24	27	.230	.258	.321
	SEA/AL		24	53	45	10	2	0	0	12	4	0	3	3	0	1	0	6	0	5	2	.222	.327	.267

Vizcaino, Jose Luis — BB/TR — b.3/26/68 — POS SS-180, 3B-130, 2B-54   LA 2/18/86

YR	TM/LG	CL	G	TPA	AB	H	2B	3B	HR	TB	BB	IBB	HB	SO	GDP	SH	SF	SB	CS	R	RBI	BA	OBA	SA
87	DOD/GCL	R	49	175	150	38	5	1	0	45	22	1	0	24	1	2	1	8	5	26	12	.253	.347	.300
88	BAK/CAL	A+	122	502	433	126	11	4	0	145	50	1	7	54	6	10	2	13	14	77	38	.291	.372	.335
89	ALB/PCL	AAA	129	483	434	123	10	4	1	144	33	2	1	41	10	12	3	16	14	60	44	.283	.333	.332
	LA/NL		7	11	10	2	0	0	0	2	0	0	0	1	0	1	0	0	0	2	0	.200	.200	.200
90	ALB/PCL	AAA	81	312	276	77	10	2	0	97	30	3	0	33	6	3	3	13	6	46	38	.279	.346	.351
	LA/NL		37	55	51	14	1	1	0	17	4	1	0	8	3	0	0	1	0	3	2	.275	.327	.333
91	CHI/NL		93	154	145	38	5	0	0	43	5	0	0	18	1	2	2	2	1	7	10	.262	.283	.297
92	CHI/NL		86	305	285	64	10	4	1	85	14	2	0	35	4	5	1	3	0	25	17	.225	.260	.298
93	CHI/NL		151	617	551	158	19	4	4	197	46	2	3	71	9	8	9	12	9	74	54	.287	.340	.358
5 YR TOTALS			**374**	**1142**	**1042**	**276**	**35**	**9**	**5**	**344**	**69**	**5**	**3**	**133**	**15**	**16**	**12**	**18**	**11**	**111**	**83**	**.265**	**.309**	**.330**

Vizquel, Omar Enrique — BB/TR — b.4/24/67 — POS SS-653, DH-2, 2B-1   SEA 4/1/84

YR	TM/LG	CL	G	TPA	AB	H	2B	3B	HR	TB	BB	IBB	HB	SO	GDP	SH	SF	SB	CS	R	RBI	BA	OBA	SA
84	BUT/PIO	R+	15	49	45	14	2	0	0	16	3	0	0	8	0	0	1	2	0	7	4	.311	.347	.356
85	BEL/NWL	A-	50	204	187	42	9	0	5	66	12	1	0	27	0	4	1	4	3	24	17	.225	.270	.353
86	WAU/MID	A	105	425	352	75	13	2	4	104	64	1	2	56	6	2	1	19	6	60	28	.213	.333	.295

(continued)

Vizquel, Omar Enrique (continued)

YR	TM/LG	CL	G	TPA	AB	H	2B	3B	HR	TB	BB	IBB	HB	SO	GDP	SH	SF	SB	CS	R	RBI	BA	OBA	SA
87	SAL/CAL	A+	114	474	407	107	12	8	0	135	57	1	0	56	5	6	4	25	19	61	38	.263	.350	.332
88	VER/EAS	AA	103	430	374	95	18	2	2	123	42	1	3	44	6	3	8	30	11	54	35	.254	.328	.329
	CAL/PCL	AAA	33	113	107	24	2	3	1	35	5	1	0	14	1	1	0	2	4	10	12	.224	.259	.327
89	CAL/PCL	AAA	7	32	28	6	2	0	0	8	3	0	1	4	1	0	0	0	2	3	3	.214	.313	.286
	SEA/AL		143	431	387	85	7	3	1	101	28	0	1	40	6	13	2	1	4	45	20	.220	.273	.261
90	SB/CAL	A+	6	31	28	7	0	0	0	7	3	0	0	1	0	0	0	1	2	5	3	.250	.323	.250
	CAL/PCL	AAA	48	176	150	35	6	2	0	45	13	0	2	10	3	9	2	4	3	18	8	.233	.299	.300
	SEA/AL		81	285	255	63	3	2	2	76	18	0	0	22	7	10	2	4	1	19	18	.247	.295	.298
91	SEA/AL		142	482	426	98	16	4	1	125	45	0	0	37	8	8	3	7	2	42	41	.230	.302	.293
92	CAL/PCL	AAA	6	24	22	6	1	0	0	7	1	0	1	3	3	0	0	0	1	0	2	.273	.333	.318
	SEA/AL		136	527	483	142	20	4	0	170	32	0	2	38	14	9	1	15	13	49	21	.294	.340	.352
93	SEA/AL		158	630	560	143	14	2	0	167	50	2	4	71	7	13	3	12	14	68	31	.255	.319	.298
5 YR TOTALS			**660**	**2355**	**2111**	**531**	**60**	**15**	**6**	**639**	**173**	**2**	**7**	**208**	**42**	**53**	**11**	**39**	**34**	**223**	**131**	**.252**	**.309**	**.303**

Voigt, John David "Jack" — BR/TR — b.5/17/66 — POS OF-43, DH-9, 1B-5, 3B-3   BAL87 10/221

YR	TM/LG	CL	G	TPA	AB	H	2B	3B	HR	TB	BB	IBB	HB	SO	GDP	SH	SF	SB	CS	R	RBI	BA	OBA	SA
87	NEW/NYP	A-	63	254	219	70	10	1	11	115	33	0	0	45	3	1	1	1	3	41	52	.320	.407	.525
	HAG/CAR	A+	2	10	9	1	0	0	0	1	1	0	0	4	0	0	0	0	0	0	1	.111	.200	.111
88	HAG/CAR	A+	115	444	367	83	18	2	12	141	66	2	6	92	7	3	2	5	2	62	42	.226	.351	.384
89	FRE/CAR	A+	127	479	406	107	26	5	10	173	62	4	4	106	1	5	2	17	2	61	77	.264	.363	.426
90	HAG/EAS	AA	126	499	418	107	26	2	12	173	59	1	5	97	7	6	11	5	3	55	70	.256	.347	.414
91	HAG/EAS	AA	29	108	90	22	3	0	4	25	15	1	2	19	2	1	0	6	3	15	6	.244	.364	.278
	ROC/INT	AAA	83	315	267	72	12	4	6	110	40	2	1	53	8	5	2	9	2	46	35	.270	.365	.412
92	ROC/INT	AAA	129	508	443	126	23	4	16	205	58	3	4	102	10	3	3	9	2	74	64	.284	.372	.463
	BAL/AL		1	0	0	0	0	0	0	0	0	0	0	0	0	0	0	0	0	0	0	.000	.000	.000
93	ROC/INT	AAA	18	70	61	22	6	1	3	39	9	0	0	14	1	0	0	1	0	16	11	.361	.443	.639
	BAL/AL		64	177	152	45	11	1	6	76	25	0	0	33	3	0	0	1	0	32	23	.296	.395	.500
2 YR TOTALS			**65**	**177**	**152**	**45**	**11**	**1**	**6**	**76**	**25**	**0**	**0**	**33**	**3**	**0**	**0**	**1**	**0**	**32**	**23**	**.296**	**.395**	**.500**

Walbeck, Matthew Lovick "Matt" — BB/TR — b.10/2/69 — POS C-11   CHN87 7/192

YR	TM/LG	CL	G	TPA	AB	H	2B	3B	HR	TB	BB	IBB	HB	SO	GDP	SH	SF	SB	CS	R	RBI	BA	OBA	SA
87	WYT/APP	R+	51	194	169	53	9	3	1	71	22	0	0	39	4	0	3	0	1	24	28	.314	.387	.420
88	CHW/SAL	A	104	352	312	68	9	0	2	83	30	1	3	44	8	6	1	1	5	28	24	.218	.292	.266
89	PEO/MID	A	94	368	341	86	19	0	4	117	20	1	3	47	7	1	3	5	2	38	47	.252	.297	.343
90	PEO/MID	A	25	75	66	15	1	0	0	16	5	0	2	7	1	2	0	1	0	2	5	.227	.301	.242
91	WIN/CAR	A+	91	295	260	70	11	0	3	90	20	1	3	23	7	3	10	3	2	25	41	.269	.315	.346
92	CHA/SOU	AA	105	425	385	116	22	1	7	161	33	3	2	56	6	3	2	2	2	48	42	.301	.358	.418
93	IOW/AMA	AAA	87	355	331	93	18	2	6	133	18	4	0	47	6	2	1	2	0	31	43	.281	.320	.402
	CHI/NL		11	31	30	6	2	0	1	11	1	0	0	6	0	0	0	0	0	2	6	.200	.226	.367

Walewander, James "Jim" — BB/TR — b.5/2/62 — POS 2B-89, 3B-22, DH-22, SS-18   DET83 9/225

YR	TM/LG	CL	G	TPA	AB	H	2B	3B	HR	TB	BB	IBB	HB	SO	GDP	SH	SF	SB	CS	R	RBI	BA	OBA	SA
83	BRI/APP	R+	73	325	285	91	14	2	4	121	34	2	1	29	1	2	3	35	4	56	28	.319	.390	.425
84	LAK/FSL	A+	137	583	502	136	16	2	0	156	64	2	6	40	15	8	3	47	18	70	36	.271	.358	.311
85	LAK/FSL	A+	129	556	499	141	13	7	0	168	48	4	2	28	7	1	6	30	10	80	36	.283	.344	.337
	BIR/SOU	AA	14	48	45	13	0	1	0	15	2	0	1	3	0	1	0	1	1	3	2	.289	.319	.333
86	GF/EAS	AA	124	491	440	107	10	6	1	132	43	4	2	54	11	4	2	25	11	59	31	.243	.312	.300
87	TOL/INT	AAA	59	240	210	57	9	1	0	68	28	1	1	31	3	1	0	18	11	27	12	.271	.360	.324
	DET/AL		53	63	54	13	3	1	0	21	7	0	0	6	2	2	0	2	1	24	4	.241	.328	.389
88	TOL/INT	AAA	4	15	11	5	2	0	0	7	3	0	0	3	0	1	0	2	1	4	2	.455	.571	.636
	DET/AL		88	198	175	37	5	0	0	42	12	0	0	26	1	10	0	11	4	23	6	.211	.261	.240
89	TOL/INT	AAA	133	560	484	109	15	3	0	151	60	3	6	72	9	4	4	32	10	53	38	.225	.316	.312
90	CMB/INT	AAA	131	479	368	92	14	5	1	119	90	1	11	67	4	6	4	49	13	80	31	.250	.408	.323
	NY/AL		9	5	5	1	0	0	0	1	0	0	0	0	0	0	0	1	1	1	1	.200	.200	.400
91	CMB/INT	AAA	126	492	408	92	11	3	3	118	69	1	5	66	5	7	3	54	19	81	38	.225	.342	.289
92	OC/AMA	AAA	44	148	124	26	7	0	0	33	17	0	2	18	1	3	2	20	10	20	10	.210	.310	.266
93	VAN/PCL	AAA	102	428	351	107	12	1	1	124	60	1	9	57	8	5	3	36	6	77	43	.305	.416	.353
	CAL/AL		12	14	8	1	0	0	0	1	5	0	1	1	0	0	1	1	1	2	3	.125	.429	.125
4 YR TOTALS			**162**	**280**	**242**	**52**	**9**	**1**	**1**	**66**	**24**	**0**	**0**	**33**	**3**	**12**	**2**	**15**	**7**	**50**	**14**	**.215**	**.284**	**.273**

Walker, Cleotha "Chico" — BB/TR — b.11/25/57 — POS OF-174, 3B-122, 2B-74, DH-7   BOS76 22/525

YR	TM/LG	CL	G	TPA	AB	H	2B	3B	HR	TB	BB	IBB	HB	SO	GDP	SH	SF	SB	CS	R	RBI	BA	OBA	SA
76	ELM/NYP	A-	22	39	28	5	1	2	0	10	11	0	0	10	0	0	0	1	0	9	1	.179	.410	.357
77	ELM/NYP	A-	64	263	227	50	4	3	1	63	29	3	0	39	2	0	0	10	1	26	14	.220	.307	.278
78	WH/FSL	A+	133	532	480	134	10	6	3	165	43	1	0	71	6	3	3	17	7	66	52	.279	.337	.344
79	BRI/EAS	AA	123	552	498	132	19	12	8	199	44	2	0	77	10	6	4	29	16	75	57	.265	.322	.400
80	PAW/INT	AAA	139	584	536	146	18	7	8	202	41	8	1	91	9	4	0	21	10	59	52	.272	.325	.377
	BOS/AL		19	66	57	12	0	0	1	15	6	1	0	10	1	1	1	3	2	3	5	.211	.292	.263
81	PAW/INT	AAA	138	596	535	148	21	5	17	230	49	6	0	110	13	9	3	24	12	50	68	.277	.336	.430
	BOS/AL		6	18	17	6	0	0	0	6	1	0	0	2	0	0	0	2	0	3	2	.353	.389	.353
82	PAW/INT	AAA	133	560	494	124	22	2	15	195	60	7	2	99	9	3	3	25	9	71	66	.251	.330	.395
83	PAW/INT	AAA	125	517	442	119	18	1	18	193	64	2	4	80	8	3	3	27	14	78	56	.269	.366	.437
	BOS/AL		4	5	5	2	0	0	0	2	0	0	0	1	0	0	0	2	0	2	1	.400	.400	1.200
84	BOS/AL		3	3	2	0	0	0	0	0	0	0	0	0	0	0	0	0	0	0	0	.000	.000	.000
	PAW/INT	AAA	130	587	499	131	26	5	18	221	80	9	0	88	6	4	4	42	17	91	51	.263	.362	.443
85	CHI/NL		21	12	12	1	0	0	0	1	0	0	0	5	0	0	0	0	0	3	0	.083	.083	.083
	IOW/AMA	AAA	89	388	331	94	17	8	5	142	50	1	2	60	9	4	1	42	11	47	46	.284	.380	.429

Walker, Cleotha "Chico" (continued)

YR	TM/LG	CL	G	TPA	AB	H	2B	3B	HR	TB	BB	IBB	HB	SO	GDP	SH	SF	SB	CS	R	RBI	BA	OBA	SA
86	IOW/AMA	AAA	138	599	530	158	30	11	16	258	62	2	0	68	7	1	6	67	22	97	65	.298	.368	.487
	CHI/NL		28	112	101	28	3	2	1	38	10	0	0	20	3	0	1	15	4	21	7	.277	.339	.376
87	IOW/AMA	AAA	90	383	315	77	13	3	8	120	65	3	0	52	8	0	3	28	9	64	31	.244	.371	.381
	CHI/NL		47	121	105	21	4	0	0	25	12	1	0	23	1	2	2	11	4	15	7	.200	.277	.238
88	CAL/AL		33	86	78	12	1	0	0	13	6	0	0	15	2	2	0	2	1	8	2	.154	.214	.167
	EDM/PCL	AAA	79	337	304	88	17	4	7	134	29	2	0	47	9	0	4	25	4	58	39	.289	.347	.441
89	SYR/INT	AAA	123	495	431	103	11	5	12	160	58	8	1	61	7	1	4	37	10	61	63	.239	.328	.371
90	CHA/SOU	AA	88	359	310	82	15	1	12	135	44	1	0	72	7	0	5	10	3	49	45	.265	.351	.435
	IOW/AMA	AAA	32	141	114	41	7	1	6	68	25	5	1	17	1	1	0	9	3	30	19	.360	.479	.596
91	CHI/NL		124	411	374	96	10	1	6	126	33	2	0	57	3	1	3	13	5	51	34	.257	.315	.337
92	CHI/NL		19	30	26	3	0	0	0	3	3	3	0	4	0	0	1	1	0	2	2	.115	.200	.115
	NY/NL		107	255	227	70	12	1	4	96	24	3	0	46	9	0	5	15	1	24	36	.308	.369	.423
	YEAR		126	285	253	73	12	1	4	99	27	3	0	50	9	0	5	15	1	26	38	.289	.351	.391
93	NY/NL		115	229	213	48	7	1	5	72	14	0	0	29	3	0	2	7	0	18	19	.225	.271	.338
11 YR TOTALS			526	1348	1217	299	37	7	17	401	109	7	1	212	22	6	15	67	19	150	116	.246	.305	.329

Walker, Larry Kenneth Robert — BL/TR — b.12/1/66 — POS OF-512, 1B-43   MON 11/14/84

YR	TM/LG	CL	G	TPA	AB	H	2B	3B	HR	TB	BB	IBB	HB	SO	GDP	SH	SF	SB	CS	R	RBI	BA	OBA	SA
85	UTI/NYP	A-	62	241	215	48	8	2	2	66	18	4	5	57	1	2	1	12	6	24	26	.223	.297	.307
86	BUR/MID	A	95	390	332	96	12	6	29	207	46	1	9	112	4	0	3	16	8	67	74	.289	.387	.623
	WPB/FSL	A+	38	142	113	32	7	5	4	61	26	2	2	32	2	0	1	2	2	20	16	.283	.423	.540
87	JAC/SOU	AA	128	553	474	136	25	7	26	253	67	5	9	120	6	0	3	24	3	91	83	.287	.383	.534
89	IND/AMA	AAA	114	456	385	104	18	2	12	162	50	8	9	87	6	5	7	36	6	68	59	.270	.361	.421
	MON/NL		20	56	47	8	0	0	0	8	5	0	1	13	0	3	0	1	1	4	4	.170	.264	.170
90	MON/NL		133	478	419	101	18	3	19	182	49	5	5	112	8	3	2	21	7	59	51	.241	.326	.434
91	MON/NL		137	539	487	141	30	2	16	223	42	2	5	102	7	0	4	14	9	59	64	.290	.349	.458
92	MON/NL		143	583	528	159	31	4	23	267	41	10	6	97	7	0	8	18	6	85	93	.301	.353	.506
93	MON/NL		138	582	490	130	24	5	22	230	80	20	6	76	8	0	6	29	7	85	86	.265	.371	.469
5 YR TOTALS			571	2238	1971	539	103	14	80	910	217	37	23	400	32	7	20	83	30	292	298	.273	.349	.462

Wallach, Timothy Charles "Tim" — BR/TR — b.9/14/57 — POS 3B-1754, 1B-90, OF-40, P-2, SS-1, 2B-1   MON79 1/10

YR	TM/LG	CL	G	TPA	AB	H	2B	3B	HR	TB	BB	IBB	HB	SO	GDP	SH	SF	SB	CS	R	RBI	BA	OBA	SA
80	MON/NL		5	12	11	2	0	0	1	5	1	0	0	5	0	0	0	0	0	1	2	.182	.250	.455
81	MON/NL		71	231	212	50	9	1	4	73	15	2	4	37	3	0	0	0	1	19	13	.236	.299	.344
82	MON/NL		158	645	596	160	31	3	28	281	36	4	4	81	15	5	4	6	4	89	97	.268	.313	.471
83	MON/NL		156	647	581	156	33	3	19	252	55	8	6	97	9	4	5	4	3	54	70	.269	.335	.434
84	MON/NL		160	643	582	143	25	4	18	230	50	6	7	101	12	0	4	9	7	55	72	.246	.311	.395
85	MON/NL		155	617	569	148	36	3	22	256	38	8	5	79	17	0	5	9	4	70	81	.260	.310	.450
86	MON/NL		134	539	480	112	22	1	18	190	44	8	10	72	16	0	5	8	4	50	71	.233	.308	.396
87	MON/NL		153	644	593	177	*42	4	26	305	37	5	7	98	6	0	7	9	5	89	123	.298	.343	.514
88	MON/NL		159	640	592	152	32	5	12	230	38	7	3	88	19	0	7	5	2	52	69	.257	.302	.389
89	MON/NL		154	639	573	159	*42	0	13	240	58	10	1	81	21	0	7	6	9	76	77	.277	.341	.419
90	MON/NL		161	678	626	185	37	5	21	295	42	11	3	80	12	0	7	6	9	69	98	.296	.339	.471
91	MON/NL		151	637	577	130	22	1	13	193	50	4	6	100	12	0	4	2	4	60	73	.225	.292	.334
92	MON/NL		150	602	537	120	29	1	9	178	50	2	8	90	10	0	7	2	2	53	59	.223	.296	.331
93	LA/NL		133	522	477	106	19	1	12	163	32	2	3	70	10	0	9	0	2	42	62	.222	.271	.342
14 YR TOTALS			1900	7696	7006	1800	379	32	216	2891	546	81	67	1079	162	6	71	50	63	779	967	.257	.314	.413

Walters, Daniel Gene "Dan" — BR/TR — b.8/15/66 — POS C-81   HOU84 6/123

YR	TM/LG	CL	G	TPA	AB	H	2B	3B	HR	TB	BB	IBB	HB	SO	GDP	SH	SF	SB	CS	R	RBI	BA	OBA	SA
85	ASH/SAL	A	15	30	28	1	0	0	0	1	1	0	0	11	1	1	0	0	0	1	1	.036	.069	.036
	AUB/NYP	A-	44	156	144	30	6	0	0	36	8	0	1	23	6	0	3	1	0	15	10	.208	.250	.250
86	ASH/SAL	A	101	384	366	96	21	0	8	143	14	0	1	59	12	1	2	1	1	42	46	.262	.290	.391
87	OSC/FSL	A+	99	381	338	84	8	0	1	95	33	2	0	42	15	5	5	2	4	23	30	.249	.311	.281
88	TUC/PCL	AAA	2	7	7	0	0	0	0	0	0	0	0	2	0	0	0	0	0	0	0	.000	.000	.000
	CMB/SOU	AA	98	341	305	71	10	1	7	104	26	1	3	42	11	3	4	1	0	31	28	.233	.296	.341
89	WIC/TEX	AA	89	333	300	82	15	1	5	115	25	2	3	31	5	3	0	0	2	30	45	.273	.333	.383
90	WIC/TEX	AA	58	223	199	59	12	0	7	92	21	1	0	21	8	0	2	0	0	25	40	.296	.363	.462
	LV/PCL	AAA	53	200	184	47	9	0	3	65	13	0	0	24	10	0	3	0	1	19	26	.255	.300	.353
91	LV/PCL	AAA	96	315	293	93	22	0	4	127	22	5	0	35	12	0	0	0	1	39	44	.317	.365	.433
92	LV/PCL	AAA	35	142	127	50	9	0	2	65	10	1	2	24	0	1	2	1	0	14	25	.394	.440	.512
	SD/NL		57	194	179	45	11	1	4	70	10	2	2	28	3	1	2	1	0	14	22	.251	.295	.391
93	LV/PCL	AAA	66	239	223	64	14	0	5	93	14	0	1	26	13	0	1	1	2	26	39	.287	.331	.417
	SD/NL		27	102	94	19	3	0	1	25	7	2	1	13	2	1	0	1	0	6	10	.202	.255	.266
2 YR TOTALS			84	296	273	64	14	1	5	95	17	4	2	41	5	1	2	2	0	20	32	.234	.281	.348

Walton, Jerome O'Terrell — BR/TR — b.7/8/65 — POS OF-339, DH-4   CHN86* 2/36

YR	TM/LG	CL	G	TPA	AB	H	2B	3B	HR	TB	BB	IBB	HB	SO	GDP	SH	SF	SB	CS	R	RBI	BA	OBA	SA
86	WYT/APP	R+	62	269	229	66	7	4	5	96	28	0	6	40	3	3	3	21	3	48	34	.288	.376	.419
87	PEO/MID	A	128	580	472	158	24	11	6	222	91	2	11	91	9	5	1	49	25	102	38	.335	.452	.470
88	PIT/EAS	AA	120	470	414	137	26	2	3	176	41	0	8	69	6	4	3	42	13	64	49	.331	.399	.425
89	IOW/AMA	AAA	4	19	18	6	1	0	1	10	1	0	0	5	0	0	0	2	1	4	4	.333	.368	.556
	CHI/NL		116	515	475	139	23	3	5	183	27	2	6	77	6	2	5	24	7	64	46	.293	.335	.385
90	IOW/AMA	AAA	4	18	16	3	0	0	0	3	2	0	0	4	0	0	0	1	0	3	1	.188	.278	.375
	CHI/NL		101	449	392	103	16	2	2	129	50	3	4	70	4	1	3	14	5	63	21	.263	.350	.329
91	CHI/NL		123	298	270	59	13	1	5	89	19	0	3	55	7	3	3	7	3	42	17	.219	.275	.330
92	IOW/AMA	AAA	7	31	27	8	2	1	0	12	4	0	0	6	0	0	0	0	0	8	3	.296	.387	.444

(continued)

Walton, Jerome O'Terrell (continued)

YR	TM/LG	CL	G	TPA	AB	H	2B	3B	HR	TB	BB	IBB	HB	SO	GDP	SH	SF	SB	CS	R	RBI	BA	OBA	SA
	CHI/NL		30	69	55	7	0	1	0	9	9	0	2	13	1	3	0	1	2	7	1	.127	.273	.164
93	VAN/PCL	AAA	54	202	176	55	11	1	2	74	16	0	1	24	6	8	1	5	4	34	20	.313	.371	.420
	CAL/AL		5	3	2	0	0	0	0	0	0	0	0	2	0	0	0	1	0	2	0	.000	.333	.000
5 YR TOTALS			375	1334	1194	308	52	7	12	410	106	2	15	217	18	9	10	47	19	178	85	.258	.324	.343

Ward, Turner Max — BB/TR — b.4/11/65 — POS OF-134, DH-1, 1B-1   NYA86 19/470

YR	TM/LG	CL	G	TPA	AB	H	2B	3B	HR	TB	BB	IBB	HB	SO	GDP	SH	SF	SB	CS	R	RBI	BA	OBA	SA
86	ONE/NYP	A-	63	259	221	62	4	1	1	71	31	1	2	39	4	2	3	6	6	42	19	.281	.370	.321
87	FL/FSL	A+	130	573	493	145	15	2	7	185	64	4	6	83	8	7	3	25	3	83	55	.294	.380	.375
88	CMB/INT	AAA	134	551	490	123	24	1	7	170	48	5	3	100	8	8	2	28	5	55	50	.251	.320	.347
89	IND/GCL	R	4	17	15	3	0	0	0	3	2	0	0	2	1	0	0	1	0	2	1	.200	.294	.200
	CAN/EAS	AA	30	108	93	28	5	1	0	35	15	0	0	16	2	0	0	2	1	19	3	.301	.398	.376
90	CS/PCL	AAA	133	585	495	148	24	9	6	208	72	1	4	70	16	5	9	22	15	89	65	.299	.386	.420
	CLE/AL		14	49	46	16	2	1	1	23	3	0	0	8	1	0	0	3	0	10	10	.348	.388	.500
91	CLE/AL		40	114	100	23	7	0	1	30	10	0	0	16	1	0	4	0	0	11	5	.230	.300	.300
	CS/PCL	AAA	14	58	51	10	1	1	1	16	6	0	0	9	1	1	0	2	1	5	3	.196	.281	.314
	SYR/INT	AAA	59	266	218	72	11	3	7	110	47	1	0	22	1	1	0	9	9	40	32	.330	.449	.505
	TOR/AL		8	14	13	4	0	0	0	4	1	0	0	1	0	0	0	1	0	1	2	.308	.357	.308
	YEAR		48	128	113	27	7	0	1	34	11	0	0	18	1	0	4	0	0	12	7	.239	.306	.301
92	SYR/INT	AAA	81	329	280	67	10	2	10	111	44	3	2	43	8	2	1	7	5	41	29	.239	.346	.396
	TOR/AL		18	33	29	10	3	0	1	16	4	0	0	4	1	0	0	1	0	7	3	.345	.424	.552
93	KNO/SOU	AA	7	30	23	6	2	0	0	8	7	0	0	3	0	0	0	3	0	6	2	.261	.433	.348
	TOR/AL		72	198	167	32	4	2	4	52	23	2	1	26	7	3	4	3	3	20	28	.192	.287	.311
4 YR TOTALS			152	408	355	85	16	3	6	125	41	2	1	56	11	7	4	6	4	49	48	.239	.317	.352

Webster, Leonard Irell "Lenny" — BR/TR — b.2/10/65 — POS C-127, DH-2   MIN85 21/535

YR	TM/LG	CL	G	TPA	AB	H	2B	3B	HR	TB	BB	IBB	HB	SO	GDP	SH	SF	SB	CS	R	RBI	BA	OBA	SA
86	KEN/MID	A	22	76	65	10	2	0	0	12	10	0	0	12	3	0	0	0	0	2	8	.154	.267	.185
	ELI/APP	R+	48	176	152	35	4	0	3	48	22	0	2	21	6	0	0	1	0	29	14	.230	.335	.316
87	KEN/MID	A	52	160	140	35	7	0	3	51	17	0	0	20	8	0	3	2	0	17	17	.250	.325	.364
88	KEN/MID	A	129	546	465	134	23	2	11	194	71	5	1	47	13	2	7	3	2	82	87	.288	.379	.417
89	VIS/CAL	A+	63	264	231	62	14	0	5	84	27	1	1	27	9	0	5	2	1	36	39	.268	.341	.364
	ORL/SOU	AA	59	242	191	45	7	0	2	58	44	1	3	20	3	2	2	0	0	29	17	.236	.383	.304
	MIN/AL		14	23	20	6	2	0	0	8	3	0	0	0	0	0	0	0	0	3	1	.300	.391	.400
90	ORL/SOU	AA	126	526	455	119	31	0	8	174	68	5	0	57	11	0	3	0	0	69	71	.262	.356	.382
	MIN/AL		2	7	6	2	0	0	0	3	1	0	0	1	0	0	0	0	0	1	0	.333	.429	.500
91	POR/PCL	AAA	87	353	325	82	18	0	7	121	24	2	1	32	14	0	1	0	0	43	34	.252	.303	.372
	MIN/AL		18	41	34	10	1	0	3	20	6	0	0	6	0	0	1	0	0	7	8	.294	.390	.588
92	MIN/AL		53	129	118	33	10	1	1	48	9	0	0	11	3	2	0	0	0	10	13	.280	.331	.407
93	MIN/AL		49	117	106	21	2	0	1	26	11	0	0	8	1	0	0	1	0	14	8	.198	.274	.245
5 YR TOTALS			136	317	284	72	16	1	5	105	30	1	0	32	6	2	1	1	2	35	30	.254	.324	.370

Webster, Mitchell Dean "Mitch" — BB/TL — b.5/16/59 — POS OF-931, DH-16, 1B-5   LA77 23/581

YR	TM/LG	CL	G	TPA	AB	H	2B	3B	HR	TB	BB	IBB	HB	SO	GDP	SH	SF	SB	CS	R	RBI	BA	OBA	SA
83	TOR/AL		11	12	11	2	0	0	0	2	1	0	0	1	0	0	0	0	0	2	0	.182	.250	.182
84	SYR/INT	AAA	95	420	360	108	22	5	3	149	51	4	0	36	4	9	0	16	4	60	25	.300	.387	.414
	TOR/AL		26	23	22	5	2	1	0	9	1	0	0	7	1	0	0	0	0	9	4	.227	.261	.409
85	TOR/AL		4	1	1	0	0	0	0	0	0	0	0	0	0	0	0	0	0	0	0	.000	.000	.000
	SYR/INT	AAA	47	215	189	52	5	3	3	72	20	1	1	24	3	4	1	5	4	32	23	.275	.346	.381
	MON/NL		74	234	212	58	5	2	11	103	20	3	0	33	3	1	1	15	9	32	23	.274	.335	.486
	YEAR		78	235	213	58	8	2	11	103	20	3	0	33	3	1	1	15	10	32	30	.272	.333	.484
86	MON/NL		151	645	576	167	31	*13	8	248	57	4	4	78	9	3	5	36	15	89	49	.290	.355	.431
87	MON/NL		156	676	588	165	30	8	15	256	70	5	6	95	6	8	4	33	10	101	63	.281	.361	.435
88	MON/NL		81	306	259	66	5	2	2	81	36	2	1	37	3	4	2	10	10	33	13	.255	.354	.313
	CHI/NL		70	289	264	70	11	6	4	105	19	2	0	50	2	1	2	10	4	36	26	.265	.319	.398
	YEAR		151	595	523	136	16	8	6	186	55	2	1	87	5	5	4	22	14	69	39	.260	.337	.356
89	CHI/NL		98	308	272	70	12	4	3	99	30	5	1	55	3	3	2	14	2	40	19	.257	.331	.364
90	CLE/AL		128	477	437	110	20	6	12	178	20	1	3	61	5	11	6	22	6	58	55	.252	.285	.407
91	CLE/AL		13	36	32	4	0	0	0	4	3	0	0	9	0	1	0	2	2	2	5	.125	.200	.125
	PIT/NL		36	106	97	17	3	4	1	31	9	1	0	31	0	0	0	9	9	9	9	.175	.245	.320
	LA/NL		58	84	74	21	5	1	0	31	9	0	0	21	0	1	0	0	0	12	10	.284	.361	.419
	YEAR		107	226	203	42	8	5	2	66	21	1	0	61	3	2	0	2	2	23	19	.207	.281	.325
92	LA/NL		135	304	262	70	12	5	2	110	27	3	2	49	1	8	5	11	5	33	35	.267	.334	.420
93	LA/NL		88	192	172	42	6	2	2	58	11	2	2	24	3	4	3	4	6	26	14	.244	.293	.337
11 YR TOTALS			1129	3693	3279	867	145	54	65	1315	313	26	26	551	39	45	30	159	71	482	327	.264	.331	.401

Wedge, Eric Michael — BR/TR — b.1/27/68 — POS DH-21, C-6   BOS89 5/83

YR	TM/LG	CL	G	TPA	AB	H	2B	3B	HR	TB	BB	IBB	HB	SO	GDP	SH	SF	SB	CS	R	RBI	BA	OBA	SA
89	ELM/NYP	A-	41	160	145	34	6	3	0	65	15	0	0	21	3	0	0	1	1	20	22	.234	.306	.448
	NB/EAS	AA	14	47	40	8	2	0	0	10	5	0	0	10	1	2	0	1	1	3	2	.200	.289	.250
90	NB/EAS	AA	103	396	339	77	13	1	5	107	50	2	2	54	14	0	5	1	3	36	47	.227	.326	.316
91	NB/EAS	AA	2	9	8	2	0	0	0	2	0	0	0	2	0	0	0	1	0	0	2	.250	.222	.250
	WH/FSL	A+	8	25	21	5	0	0	1	8	3	0	1	2	1	0	0	0	0	2	1	.238	.333	.381
	PAW/INT	AAA	53	196	163	38	14	1	1	57	25	0	1	26	3	0	2	1	0	24	18	.233	.330	.423
	BOS/AL		1	1	1	1	0	0	0	1	0	0	0	0	0	0	0	0	0	0	0	1.000	1.000	1.000
92	PAW/INT	AAA	65	247	211	63	9	1	11	105	32	1	1	40	6	0	3	0	1	28	40	.299	.389	.498
	BOS/AL		27	81	68	17	2	0	5	34	13	0	0	18	0	0	0	1	1	11	11	.250	.370	.500

Wedge, Eric Michael (continued)

YR	TM/LG	CL	G	TPA	AB	H	2B	3B	HR	TB	BB	IBB	HB	SO	GDP	SH	SF	SB	CS	R	RBI	BA	OBA	SA
93	CV/CAL	A+	6	25	23	7	0	0	3	16	2	1	0	6	1	0	0	0	0	6	11	.304	.360	.696
	CS/PCL	AAA	38	108	90	24	6	0	3	39	16	1	2	22	4	0	0	0	0	17	13	.267	.389	.433
	COL/NL		9	11	11	2	0	0	0	2	0	0	0	4	0	0	0	0	0	2	1	.182	.182	.182
3 YR TOTALS			**37**	**93**	**80**	**20**	**2**	**0**	**5**	**37**	**13**	**0**	**0**	**22**	**0**	**0**	**0**	**0**	**0**	**13**	**12**	**.250**	**.355**	**.463**

Wehner, John Paul — BR/TR — b.6/29/67 — POS 3B-73, 1B-13, OF-13, 2B-8

PIT88 7/174

YR	TM/LG	CL	G	TPA	AB	H	2B	3B	HR	TB	BB	IBB	HB	SO	GDP	SH	SF	SB	CS	R	RBI	BA	OBA	SA
88	WAT/NYP	A-	70	293	265	73	6	0	3	88	21	0	2	39	4	1	4	18	6	41	31	.275	.329	.332
89	SAL/CAR	A+	137	559	515	155	32	6	14	241	42	4	1	81	14	0	1	21	10	69	73	.301	.354	.468
90	HAR/EAS	AA	138	565	511	147	27	1	4	188	40	4	4	51	12	4	6	24	11	71	62	.288	.340	.368
91	CAR/SOU	AA	61	268	234	62	5	1	3	78	24	1	2	32	7	3	5	17	5	30	21	.265	.332	.333
	BUF/AMA	AAA	31	128	112	34	9	2	1	50	14	1	0	12	5	0	2	6	4	18	15	.304	.375	.446
	PIT/NL		37	113	106	36	7	0	0	43	7	0	0	17	0	0	0	3	0	15	7	.340	.381	.406
92	BUF/AMA	AAA	60	258	223	60	13	2	7	98	29	0	3	30	6	1	3	10	7	37	27	.269	.354	.439
	PIT/NL		55	137	123	22	6	0	0	28	12	2	0	22	4	2	0	3	0	11	4	.179	.252	.228
93	BUF/AMA	AAA	89	375	330	83	22	2	7	130	40	2	1	53	5	2	2	17	3	61	34	.252	.332	.394
	PIT/NL		29	43	35	5	0	0	0	5	6	1	0	10	0	2	0	0	0	3	0	.143	.268	.143
3 YR TOTALS			**121**	**293**	**264**	**63**	**13**	**0**	**0**	**76**	**25**	**3**	**0**	**49**	**4**	**4**	**0**	**6**	**0**	**29**	**11**	**.239**	**.304**	**.288**

Weiss, Walter William "Walt" — BB/TR — b.11/28/63 — POS SS-675, DH-2

OAK85 1/11

YR	TM/LG	CL	G	TPA	AB	H	2B	3B	HR	TB	BB	IBB	HB	SO	GDP	SH	SF	SB	CS	R	RBI	BA	OBA	SA
85	POC/PIO	R+	40	175	158	49	9	3	0	64	12	0	1	18	5	0	4	6	0	19	21	.310	.354	.405
	MOD/CAL	A+	30	135	122	24	4	1	0	30	12	0	0	20	4	1	0	3	3	17	7	.197	.269	.246
86	MAD/MID	A	84	362	322	97	15	5	2	128	33	1	1	66	7	0	6	12	5	50	54	.301	.362	.398
	HUN/SOU	AA	46	175	160	40	2	1	0	44	11	0	2	39	2	1	1	5	1	19	13	.250	.305	.275
87	HUN/SOU	AA	91	394	337	96	16	2	1	119	47	2	2	67	5	6	2	23	3	43	32	.285	.374	.353
	TAC/PCL	AAA	46	211	179	47	4	3	0	57	28	0	1	31	5	1	3	9	3	35	17	.263	.364	.318
	OAK/AL		16	29	26	12	4	0	0	16	2	0	0	2	0	1	1	1	2	3	1	.462	.500	.615
88	OAK/AL		147	511	452	113	17	3	3	145	35	1	9	56	9	8	7	4	4	44	39	.250	.312	.321
89	TAC/PCL	AAA	2	9	9	1	1	0	0	2	0	0	0	0	0	0	0	0	0	0	0	.111	.111	.222
	MOD/CAL	A+	5	14	8	3	0	0	0	3	4	0	1	1	1	1	1	0	0	1	0	.375	.571	.375
	OAK/AL		84	263	236	55	11	0	3	75	21	0	1	39	5	5	0	6	1	30	21	.233	.298	.318
90	OAK/AL		138	505	445	118	17	1	2	143	46	5	4	53	7	6	4	9	3	50	35	.265	.337	.321
91	OAK/AL		40	148	133	30	6	1	0	38	12	0	0	14	3	1	2	6	0	15	13	.226	.286	.286
92	TAC/PCL	AAA	4	16	13	3	1	0	0	4	2	0	0	1	0	1	0	1	0	2	3	.231	.313	.308
	OAK/AL		103	375	316	67	5	2	0	76	43	1	11	39	10	11	4	6	3	36	21	.212	.305	.241
93	FLO/NL		158	591	500	133	14	2	1	154	79	13	3	73	8	5	4	7	2	50	39	.266	.367	.308
7 YR TOTALS			**686**	**2422**	**2108**	**528**	**74**	**9**	**9**	**647**	**238**	**20**	**18**	**276**	**39**	**37**	**21**	**39**	**16**	**228**	**169**	**.250**	**.329**	**.307**

Whitaker, Louis Rodman "Lou" — BL/TR — b.5/12/57 — POS 2B-2162, DH-19

DET75 5/99

YR	TM/LG	CL	G	TPA	AB	H	2B	3B	HR	TB	BB	IBB	HB	SO	GDP	SH	SF	SB	CS	R	RBI	BA	OBA	SA
77	DET/AL		11	37	32	8	1	0	0	9	4	0	0	6	0	1	0	2	2	5	2	.250	.333	.281
78	DET/AL		139	567	484	138	12	7	3	173	61	0	1	65	9	13	8	7	7	71	58	.285	.361	.357
79	DET/AL		127	520	423	121	14	8	3	160	78	2	1	66	10	14	4	20	10	75	42	.286	.395	.378
80	DET/AL		145	568	477	111	19	1	1	135	73	0	0	79	9	12	6	8	4	68	45	.233	.331	.283
81	DET/AL		109	382	335	88	14	4	5	125	40	3	1	42	5	3	3	5	3	48	36	.263	.340	.373
82	DET/AL		152	619	560	160	22	8	15	243	48	4	2	58	8	6	4	11	3	76	65	.286	.341	.434
83	DET/AL		161	720	643	206	40	6	12	294	67	8	2	70	9	2	8	17	10	94	72	.320	.380	.457
84	DET/AL		143	629	558	161	25	1	13	227	62	5	0	63	9	4	5	6	4	90	56	.289	.357	.407
85	DET/AL		152	701	609	170	29	8	21	278	80	9	2	56	3	5	4	6	3	102	73	.279	.362	.456
86	DET/AL		144	651	584	157	26	6	20	255	63	5	6	70	20	6	4	13	8	95	73	.269	.338	.437
87	DET/AL		149	684	604	160	38	6	16	258	71	2	5	108	5	4	4	13	5	110	59	.265	.341	.427
88	DET/AL		115	477	403	111	18	2	12	169	66	5	0	61	6	6	2	2	0	54	55	.275	.376	.419
89	DET/AL		148	611	509	128	21	1	28	235	89	6	3	59	7	1	3	6	3	77	85	.251	.361	.462
90	DET/AL		132	552	472	112	22	2	18	192	74	7	0	71	10	1	5	8	2	75	60	.237	.338	.407
91	DET/AL		138	572	470	131	26	2	23	230	90	6	2	45	3	2	4	4	2	94	78	.279	.391	.489
92	DET/AL		130	544	453	126	26	0	19	209	81	9	1	46	9	5	4	6	4	77	71	.278	.386	.461
93	DET/AL		119	476	383	111	32	1	9	172	78	4	4	46	11	7	4	3	1	72	67	.290	.412	.449
17 YR TOTALS			**2214**	**9310**	**7999**	**2199**	**385**	**63**	**218**	**3364**	**1125**	**71**	**17**	**1011**	**129**	**86**	**83**	**137**	**75**	**1283**	**997**	**.275**	**.362**	**.421**

White, Derrick Ramon — BR/TR — b.10/12/69 — POS 1B-17

MON91 7/165

YR	TM/LG	CL	G	TPA	AB	H	2B	3B	HR	TB	BB	IBB	HB	SO	GDP	SH	SF	SB	CS	R	RBI	BA	OBA	SA
91	JAM/NYP	A-	72	320	271	89	10	4	6	125	40	0	7	46	8	0	2	8	3	46	50	.328	.425	.461
92	HAR/EAS	AA	134	544	495	137	19	2	13	199	40	3	7	73	16	0	2	17	3	63	81	.277	.338	.402
93	WPB/FSL	A+	6	26	25	5	0	0	0	5	1	0	0	2	0	0	0	2	0	1	1	.200	.231	.200
	OTT/INT	AAA	67	273	249	70	15	1	4	99	20	0	3	52	2	0	1	10	7	32	29	.281	.341	.398
	HAR/EAS	AA	20	86	78	18	1	0	2	25	5	0	2	17	2	0	1	2	0	14	12	.231	.291	.321
	MON/NL		17	52	49	11	0	3	0	2	2	0	0	20	0	0	0	0	0	6	4	.224	.269	.408

White, Devon Markes — BB/TR — b.12/29/62 — POS OF-1048, DH-2

CAL81 2/132

YR	TM/LG	CL	G	TPA	AB	H	2B	3B	HR	TB	BB	IBB	HB	SO	GDP	SH	SF	SB	CS	R	RBI	BA	OBA	SA
84	RED/CAL	A+	138	609	520	147	25	5	7	203	56	1	11	118	8	17	5	36	12	101	55	.283	.361	.390
85	MID/TEX	AA	70	310	260	77	10	4	4	107	35	2	6	46	2	3	6	38	8	52	35	.296	.384	.412
	EDM/PCL	AAA	66	309	277	70	16	5	4	108	24	0	4	47	3	1	3	21	9	53	39	.253	.318	.390
	CAL/AL		21	9	7	1	0	0	0	1	1	0	0	3	0	0	0	3	1	7	0	.143	.333	.143
86	EDM/PCL	AAA	112	497	461	134	25	10	14	221	31	8	3	90	2	1	1	42	12	84	60	.291	.339	.479
	CAL/AL		29	57	51	12	1	1	1	18	6	0	0	8	0	0	0	6	0	8	3	.235	.316	.353

(continued)

White, Devon Markes (continued)

YR	TM/LG	CL	G	TPA	AB	H	2B	3B	HR	TB	BB	IBB	HB	SO	GDP	SH	SF	SB	CS	R	RBI	BA	OBA	SA
87	CAL/AL		159	696	639	168	33	5	24	283	39	2	2	135	8	14	2	32	11	103	87	.263	.306	.443
88	CAL/AL		122	486	455	118	22	2	11	177	23	1	2	84	5	5	1	17	8	76	51	.259	.297	.389
89	CAL/AL		156	678	636	156	18	13	12	236	31	3	2	129	12	7	2	44	16	86	56	.245	.282	.371
90	EDM/PCL	AAA	14	62	55	20	4	4	0	32	7	2	0	12	1	0	0	4	2	9	6	.364	.435	.582
	CAL/AL		125	503	443	96	17	3	11	152	44	5	3	116	6	10	3	21	6	57	44	.217	.290	.343
91	TOR/AL		156	715	642	181	40	10	17	292	55	1	7	135	7	5	6	33	10	110	60	.282	.342	.455
92	TOR/AL		153	696	641	159	26	7	17	250	47	0	5	133	9	0	3	37	4	98	60	.248	.303	.390
93	TOR/AL		146	668	598	163	42	6	15	262	57	1	7	127	3	3	3	34	4	116	52	.273	.341	.438
9 YR TOTALS			**1067**	**4508**	**4112**	**1054**	**199**	**47**	**108**	**1671**	**303**	**13**	**29**	**870**	**50**	**44**	**20**	**227**	**60**	**661**	**413**	**.256**	**.310**	**.406**

White, Rondell Bernard — BR/TR — b.2/23/72 — POS OF-21   MON90 2/24

YR	TM/LG	CL	G	TPA	AB	H	2B	3B	HR	TB	BB	IBB	HB	SO	GDP	SH	SF	SB	CS	R	RBI	BA	OBA	SA
90	EXP/GCL	R	57	243	221	66	7	4	5	96	17	0	5	33	5	0	0	10	7	33	34	.299	.362	.434
91	SUM/SAL	A	123	534	465	122	23	6	13	196	57	3	7	109	8	4	1	50	17	80	68	.262	.349	.422
92	WPB/FSL	A+	111	505	450	142	10	12	4	188	46	4	5	78	7	3	1	42	16	80	41	.316	.384	.418
	HAR/EAS	AA	21	99	89	27	7	1	2	42	6	0	4	14	3	0	0	6	1	22	7	.303	.374	.472
93	OTT/INT	AAA	37	165	150	57	8	2	7	90	12	1	3	20	4	0	0	10	1	28	32	.380	.436	.600
	HAR/EAS	AA	91	403	373	122	16	10	12	194	22	1	5	72	3	0	3	21	6	72	52	.327	.370	.520
	MON/NL		23	83	73	19	3	1	2	30	7	0	0	16	1	2	1	1	2	9	15	.260	.321	.411

Whiten, Mark Anthony — BB/TR — b.11/25/66 — POS OF-431, DH-7   TOR86* 5/130

YR	TM/LG	CL	G	TPA	AB	H	2B	3B	HR	TB	BB	IBB	HB	SO	GDP	SH	SF	SB	CS	R	RBI	BA	OBA	SA
86	MH/PIO	R+	70	308	270	81	16	3	10	133	29	2	6	56	2	1	2	22	3	53	44	.300	.378	.493
87	MB/SAL	A	139	587	494	125	22	5	15	202	76	10	16	149	1	0	1	49	14	90	64	.253	.370	.409
88	DUN/FSL	A+	99	434	385	97	8	5	7	136	41	6	3	69	8	2	3	17	14	61	37	.252	.326	.353
	KNO/SOU	AA	28	121	108	28	3	1	2	39	12	1	1	20	5	0	0	6	2	20	9	.259	.339	.361
89	KNO/SOU	AA	129	496	423	109	13	6	12	170	60	1	11	114	7	0	2	11	10	75	47	.258	.363	.402
90	SYR/INT	AAA	104	434	390	113	19	4	14	182	37	5	3	72	8	0	4	14	6	65	48	.290	.353	.467
	TOR/AL		33	96	88	24	1	1	2	33	7	0	0	14	2	0	1	2	0	12	7	.273	.323	.375
91	TOR/AL		46	164	149	33	4	3	2	49	11	1	1	35	1	0	3	0	1	12	19	.221	.274	.329
	CLE/AL		70	281	258	66	14	4	7	109	19	1	2	50	8	0	2	4	2	34	26	.256	.310	.422
	YEAR		116	445	407	99	18	7	9	158	30	2	3	85	13	0	5	4	3	46	45	.243	.297	.388
92	CLE/AL		148	588	508	129	19	4	9	183	72	10	2	102	12	3	3	16	12	73	43	.254	.347	.360
93	STL/NL		152	626	562	142	13	4	25	238	58	9	2	110	11	0	4	15	8	81	99	.253	.323	.423
4 YR TOTALS			**449**	**1755**	**1565**	**394**	**51**	**16**	**45**	**612**	**167**	**21**	**7**	**311**	**38**	**3**	**13**	**37**	**23**	**212**	**194**	**.252**	**.324**	**.391**

Whitmore, Darrell Lamont — BL/TR — b.11/18/68 — POS OF-69   CLE90 3/46

YR	TM/LG	CL	G	TPA	AB	H	2B	3B	HR	TB	BB	IBB	HB	SO	GDP	SH	SF	SB	CS	R	RBI	BA	OBA	SA
90	BUR/APP	R+	30	124	112	27	3	2	0	34	9	0	0	30	0	0	1	9	5	18	13	.241	.306	.304
91	WAT/NYP	A-	6	22	19	7	2	1	0	11	3	0	0	0	0	0	0	0	0	2	3	.368	.455	.579
92	KIN/CAR	A+	121	509	443	124	22	2	10	180	56	5	5	92	8	0	5	17	9	71	52	.280	.363	.406
93	EDM/PCL	AAA	73	298	273	97	24	2	8	152	22	0	0	53	12	0	3	11	8	52	62	.355	.399	.557
	FLO/NL		76	267	250	51	8	2	4	75	10	0	5	72	8	2	0	4	2	24	19	.204	.249	.300

Wilkerson, Curtis Vernon — BB/TR — b.4/26/61 — POS SS-444, 2B-351, 3B-128, DH-10, OF-2   TEX80 4/92

YR	TM/LG	CL	G	TPA	AB	H	2B	3B	HR	TB	BB	IBB	HB	SO	GDP	SH	SF	SB	CS	R	RBI	BA	OBA	SA
83	TEX/AL		16	37	35	6	0	1	0	8	2	0	0	5	0	0	0	3	0	7	1	.171	.216	.229
84	TEX/AL		153	522	484	120	12	0	1	135	22	0	2	72	7	12	2	12	10	47	26	.248	.282	.279
85	TEX/AL		129	395	360	88	11	6	0	111	22	0	4	63	7	6	3	14	7	35	22	.244	.293	.308
86	TEX/AL		110	249	236	56	10	3	0	72	11	0	2	42	2	0	1	9	7	27	15	.237	.273	.305
87	TEX/AL		85	146	138	37	5	3	2	54	6	0	2	16	2	0	0	2	0	28	14	.268	.308	.391
88	TEX/AL		117	371	338	99	12	5	0	121	26	3	2	43	7	3	4	9	4	41	28	.293	.345	.358
89	CHI/NL		77	170	160	39	4	2	1	50	8	0	1	33	3	1	1	4	2	18	10	.244	.278	.313
90	CHI/NL		77	196	186	41	5	1	0	48	7	0	0	36	4	3	0	2	2	21	16	.220	.249	.258
91	PIT/NL		85	210	191	36	7	2	2	53	15	0	1	40	2	0	4	2	0	20	18	.188	.243	.277
92	KC/AL		111	326	296	74	10	1	2	92	18	3	1	47	4	7	4	7	7	27	29	.250	.292	.311
93	KC/AL		12	29	28	4	0	0	0	4	1	0	0	6	1	0	0	2	0	1		.143	.172	.143
11 YR TOTALS			**972**	**2651**	**2452**	**600**	**78**	**23**	**8**	**748**	**138**	**8**	**12**	**403**	**39**	**32**	**17**	**81**	**43**	**272**	**179**	**.245**	**.286**	**.305**

Wilkins, Richard David "Rick" — BL/TR — b.6/4/67 — POS C-288   CHN86 23/582

YR	TM/LG	CL	G	TPA	AB	H	2B	3B	HR	TB	BB	IBB	HB	SO	GDP	SH	SF	SB	CS	R	RBI	BA	OBA	SA
87	GEN/NYP	A-	75	302	243	61	8	2	8	97	58	8	1	40	3	0	0	7	2	35	43	.251	.397	.399
88	PEO/MID	A	137	575	490	119	30	1	8	175	67	6	7	110	12	2	9	4	6	54	63	.243	.337	.357
89	WIN/CAR	A+	132	512	445	111	24	1	12	173	50	6	8	87	11	2	5	3	5	61	54	.249	.331	.389
90	CHA/SOU	AA	127	501	449	102	18	1	17	173	43	5	9	95	9	1	3	4	5	48	71	.227	.300	.385
91	IOW/AMA	AAA	38	123	107	29	3	1	6	49	11	1	1	17	1	2	2	1	2	12	14	.271	.339	.458
	CHI/NL		86	235	203	45	9	0	6	72	19	2	6	56	1	2	4	0	1	21	22	.222	.307	.355
92	IOW/AMA	AAA	47	178	155	43	11	2	3	73	19	2	2	47	1	1	1	0	0	20	28	.277	.362	.471
	CHI/NL		83	274	244	66	9	1	8	101	28	7	0	53	6	1	1	0	0	20	22	.270	.344	.414
93	CHI/NL		136	500	446	135	23	1	30	250	50	13	3	99	6	0	1	2	1	78	73	.303	.376	.561
3 YR TOTALS			**305**	**1009**	**893**	**246**	**41**	**2**	**44**	**423**	**97**	**22**	**9**	**208**	**15**	**8**	**2**	**5**	**6**	**119**	**117**	**.275**	**.352**	**.474**

Williams, Bernabe "Bernie" — BB/TR — b.9/13/68 — POS OF-286   NYA 9/13/85

YR	TM/LG	CL	G	TPA	AB	H	2B	3B	HR	TB	BB	IBB	HB	SO	GDP	SH	SF	SB	CS	R	RBI	BA	OBA	SA
86	YAN/GCL	R	61	274	230	62	5	3	2	79	39	0	1	40	3	1	3	33	12	45	25	.270	.374	.343
87	FL/FSL	A+	25	94	71	11	3	0	0	14	18	1	3	22	1	2	1	5	1	11	4	.155	.348	.197
	ONE/NYP	A-	25	106	93	32	4	0	0	36	10	0	1	14	0	1	1	9	3	13	15	.344	.410	.387

Williams, Bernabe "Bernie" (continued)

YR	TM/LG	CL	G	TPA	AB	H	2B	3B	HR	TB	BB	IBB	HB	SO	GDP	SH	SF	SB	CS	R	RBI	BA	OBA	SA
88	PW/CAR	A+	92	408	337	113	16	7	7	164	66	6	4	66	5	0	1	29	11	72	45	.335	.449	.487
89	CMB/INT	AAA	50	194	162	35	8	1	2	51	25	1	2	38	3	3	2	11	5	21	16	.216	.325	.315
	ALB/EAS	AA	91	384	314	79	11	8	11	139	60	4	6	72	9	3	1	26	13	63	42	.252	.381	.443
90	ALB/EAS	AA	134	571	466	131	28	5	8	193	98	6	4	97	12	1	2	39	18	91	54	.281	.409	.414
91	CMB/INT	AAA	78	353	306	90	14	6	6	140	38	2	2	43	5	4	3	9	8	52	37	.294	.372	.458
	NY/AL		85	374	320	76	19	4	3	112	48	0	1	57	4	2	3	10	5	43	34	.237	.336	.350
92	CMB/INT	AAA	95	423	363	111	23	9	8	176	52	5	1	61	8	1	6	20	8	68	50	.306	.389	.485
	NY/AL		62	293	261	73	14	2	5	106	29	1	1	36	5	2	0	7	6	39	26	.280	.354	.406
93	NY/AL		139	628	567	152	31	4	12	227	53	4	4	106	17	1	3	9	9	67	68	.268	.333	.400
3 YR TOTALS			**286**	**1295**	**1148**	**301**	**64**	**10**	**20**	**445**	**130**	**5**	**6**	**199**	**26**	**5**	**6**	**26**	**20**	**149**	**128**	**.262**	**.339**	**.388**

Williams, Gerald Floyd — BR/TR — b.8/10/66 — POS OF-49 ·   NYA87 12/367

YR	TM/LG	CL	G	TPA	AB	H	2B	3B	HR	TB	BB	IBB	HB	SO	GDP	SH	SF	SB	CS	R	RBI	BA	OBA	SA
87	ONE/NYP	A-	29	132	115	42	6	2	2	58	16	0	1	18	3	0	0	6	2	26	29	.365	.447	.504
88	PW/CAR	A+	54	176	159	29	3	0	2	38	15	0	0	47	4	1	1	6	1	20	18	.182	.251	.239
	FL/FSL	A+	63	232	212	40	7	2	2	57	16	0	3	56	4	1	0	4	3	21	17	.189	.255	.269
89	PW/CAR	A+	134	518	454	104	19	6	13	174	51	1	7	120	7	5	1	15	10	63	69	.229	.316	.383
90	FL/FSL	A+	50	224	204	59	4	5	7	94	16	1	2	52	1	0	2	19	5	25	43	.289	.344	.461
	ALB/EAS	AA	96	365	324	81	17	2	13	141	35	1	1	74	7	1	3	18	5	54	58	.250	.324	.435
91	ALB/EAS	AA	45	197	175	50	15	0	5	80	18	2	0	26	5	1	3	18	3	28	32	.286	.347	.457
	CMB/INT	AAA	61	220	198	51	8	3	2	71	16	1	0	39	3	0	5	9	11	20	27	.258	.309	.359
92	CMB/INT	AAA	142	595	547	156	31	6	16	247	38	2	5	98	12	0	5	36	14	92	86	.285	.334	.452
	NY/AL		15	27	27	8	2	0	0	19	0	0	0	3	0	0	0	2	0	7	6	.296	.296	.704
93	CMB/INT	AAA	87	365	336	95	19	6	8	150	20	1	2	66	7	1	6	29	12	53	38	.283	.321	.446
	NY/AL		42	71	67	10	2	3	0	18	1	0	2	14	2	0	1	2	0	11	6	.149	.183	.269
2 YR TOTALS			**57**	**98**	**94**	**18**	**4**	**3**	**3**	**37**	**1**	**0**	**2**	**17**	**2**	**0**	**1**	**4**	**0**	**18**	**12**	**.191**	**.214**	**.394**

Williams, Matthew Derrick "Matt" — BR/TR — b.11/28/65 — POS 3B-735, SS-118   SF86 1/3

YR	TM/LG	CL	G	TPA	AB	H	2B	3B	HR	TB	BB	IBB	HB	SO	GDP	SH	SF	SB	CS	R	RBI	BA	OBA	SA
86	EVE/NWL	A-	4	19	17	4	0	1	1	9	1	0	0	4	0	0	1	0	0	3	10	.235	.263	.529
	CLI/MID		68	280	250	60	14	3	7	101	24	1	3	51	6	0	3	3	3	32	29	.240	.311	.404
87	PHO/PCL	AAA	56	235	211	61	15	2	6	98	19	3	0	53	2	3	2	6	2	36	37	.289	.345	.464
	SF/NL		84	266	245	46	9	2	8	83	16	4	1	68	5	3	1	4	3	28	21	.188	.240	.339
88	PHO/PCL	AAA	82	324	306	83	19	1	12	140	13	2	1	56	9	0	4	6	5	45	51	.271	.299	.458
	SF/NL		52	170	156	32	6	1	8	64	8	0	2	41	7	3	1	0	1	17	19	.205	.251	.410
89	PHO/PCL	AAA	76	320	284	91	20	2	26	193	32	4	3	51	8	0	1	9	3	61	61	.320	.394	.680
	SF/NL		84	311	292	59	18	1	18	133	14	1	2	72	5	1	2	1	2	31	50	.202	.242	.455
90	SF/NL		159	664	617	171	27	2	33	301	33	9	7	138	13	2	5	7	4	87	*122	.277	.319	.488
91	SF/NL		157	635	589	158	24	5	34	294	33	6	6	128	11	0	2	5	7	72	98	.268	.310	.499
92	SF/NL		146	576	529	120	13	5	20	203	39	11	6	109	15	0	2	7	7	58	66	.227	.286	.384
93	SF/NL		145	619	579	170	33	4	38	325	27	4	4	80	12	0	9	1	3	105	110	.294	.325	.561
7 YR TOTALS			**827**	**3241**	**3007**	**756**	**130**	**20**	**159**	**1403**	**170**	**35**	**28**	**636**	**68**	**9**	**27**	**25**	**25**	**398**	**486**	**.251**	**.295**	**.467**

Wilson, Craig — BR/TR — b.11/28/64 — POS 3B-60, 2B-24, OF-22, 1B-5   SL84 20/503

YR	TM/LG	CL	G	TPA	AB	H	2B	3B	HR	TB	BB	IBB	HB	SO	GDP	SH	SF	SB	CS	R	RBI	BA	OBA	SA
84	ERI/NYP	A-	72	318	282	83	18	4	7	130	29	0	4	27	8	1	2	10	4	53	46	.294	.366	.461
85	SPR/MID	A	133	562	504	132	16	4	8	180	47	0	1	67	12	4	6	33	14	64	52	.262	.323	.357
86	SPR/MID	A	127	575	496	136	17	6	1	168	65	0	1	49	11	9	4	44	12	106	49	.274	.357	.339
87	SP/FSL	A+	38	176	162	58	6	4	0	72	14	0	0	5	3	0	0	12	8	35	35	.358	.409	.444
	LOU/AMA	AAA	21	76	70	15	2	1	0	20	3	0	0	5	1	2	1	0	2	10	8	.214	.243	.286
	ARK/TEX	AA	66	274	238	69	13	1	1	87	30	1	1	19	5	3	2	9	6	37	26	.290	.369	.366
88	LOU/AMA	AAA	133	561	497	127	27	2	1	161	54	1	0	46	13	6	4	6	4	59	46	.256	.326	.324
89	ARK/TEX	AA	55	250	224	71	12	1	1	88	21	1	4	14	3	1	1	8	5	41	40	.317	.377	.393
	LOU/AMA	AAA	75	298	278	81	18	3	1	108	14	0	2	25	5	3	1	1	3	37	30	.291	.329	.388
	STL/NL		6	5	4	1	0	0	0	1	1	0	0	2	0	0	0	0	0	1	1	.250	.400	.250
90	LOU/AMA	AAA	57	244	204	57	9	2	2	76	28	0	1	15	3	5	6	5	3	30	23	.279	.360	.373
	STL/NL		55	131	121	30	2	0	0	32	8	0	0	14	7	0	2	0	2	13	7	.248	.290	.264
91	STL/NL		60	90	82	14	2	0	0	16	6	0	1	10	2	0	0	0	0	5	13	.171	.222	.195
92	LOU/AMA	AAA	20	87	81	24	5	0	0	31	5	0	0	8	1	0	1	3	0	13	5	.296	.337	.383
	STL/NL		61	119	106	33	6	0	0	39	10	2	0	18	4	1	2	0	2	13	13	.311	.368	.368
93	OMA/AMA	AAA	65	257	234	65	13	1	3	89	20	0	1	24	6	1	1	5	3	26	28	.278	.336	.380
	KC/AL		21	57	49	13	1	0	1	17	7	0	0	6	0	1	0	1	1	6	3	.265	.357	.347
5 YR TOTALS			**203**	**402**	**362**	**91**	**11**	**0**	**1**	**105**	**32**	**4**	**0**	**50**	**13**	**3**	**5**	**2**	**5**	**31**	**37**	**.251**	**.308**	**.290**

Wilson, Daniel Allen "Dan" — BR/TR — b.3/25/69 — POS C-44   CIN90 1/7

YR	TM/LG	CL	G	TPA	AB	H	2B	3B	HR	TB	BB	IBB	HB	SO	GDP	SH	SF	SB	CS	R	RBI	BA	OBA	SA
90	CHW/SAL	A	32	128	113	28	9	1	2	45	13	0	0	17	1	0	1	1	0	16	17	.248	.323	.398
91	CHW/SAL	A	52	225	197	62	11	1	3	84	25	0	0	21	6	0	1	1	5	25	29	.315	.396	.426
	CHT/SOU	AA	81	318	292	75	19	2	2	104	21	0	0	39	10	1	4	2	2	32	38	.257	.303	.356
92	NAS/AMA	AAA	106	405	366	92	16	1	4	122	31	3	2	58	7	2	4	1	4	27	34	.251	.310	.333
	CIN/NL		12	28	25	9	1	0	0	10	3	0	0	8	0	0	0	0	0	2	3	.360	.429	.400
93	IND/AMA	AAA	51	215	191	50	11	1	1	66	19	1	4	31	4	3	1	1	0	18	17	.262	.330	.346
	CIN/NL		36	88	76	17	3	0	0	20	9	4	0	24	4	2	1	0	0	6	8	.224	.302	.263
2 YR TOTALS			**48**	**116**	**101**	**26**	**4**	**0**	**0**	**30**	**12**	**4**	**0**	**24**	**4**	**2**	**1**	**0**	**0**	**8**	**11**	**.257**	**.333**	**.297**

Wilson, Glenn Dwight — BR/TR — b.12/22/58 — POS OF-1131, 1B-11, DH-6, 3B-4, P-1   DET80 1/18

YR	TM/LG	CL	G	TPA	AB	H	2B	3B	HR	TB	BB	IBB	HB	SO	GDP	SH	SF	SB	CS	R	RBI	BA	OBA	SA
82	DET/AL		84	342	322	94	15	1	12	147	15	0	0	51	8	3	2	2	3	39	34	.292	.322	.457
83	DET/AL		144	533	503	135	25	6	11	205	25	1	3	79	9	0	2	1	1	55	65	.268	.306	.408
84	PHI/NL		132	363	341	82	21	3	6	127	17	1	1	56	12	1	3	7	1	28	31	.240	.276	.372
85	PHI/NL		161	650	608	167	39	5	14	258	35	1	0	117	24	0	7	7	4	73	102	.275	.311	.424
86	PHI/NL		155	639	584	158	30	4	15	241	42	1	4	91	15	0	9	5	1	70	84	.271	.319	.413
87	PHI/NL		154	614	569	150	21	2	14	217	38	2	1	82	18	0	6	3	6	55	54	.264	.308	.381
88	SEA/AL		78	302	284	71	10	1	3	92	15	0	0	52	13	1	2	1	1	28	17	.250	.286	.324
	PIT/NL		37	134	126	34	8	0	2	48	3	1	1	18	4	2	2	0	0	11	15	.270	.288	.381
	YEAR		115	436	410	105	18	1	5	140	18	1	1	70	17	3	4	1	1	39	32	.256	.286	.341
89	PIT/NL		100	368	330	93	20	4	9	148	32	5	1	39	8	0	5	1	4	42	49	.282	.342	.448
	HOU/NL		28	108	102	22	6	0	2	34	5	0	0	14	3	0	1	0	1	8	15	.216	.250	.333
	YEAR		128	476	432	115	26	4	11	182	37	5	1	53	11	0	6	1	5	50	64	.266	.321	.421
90	HOU/NL		118	399	368	90	14	0	10	134	26	1	1	64	16	0	4	0	3	42	55	.245	.293	.364
91	RIC/INT	AAA	29	114	100	27	4	0	2	37	13	0	0	21	3	0	1	1	1	13	15	.270	.351	.370
93	BUF/AMA	AAA	61	224	201	56	14	1	12	108	16	2	3	38	8	0	4	0	1	32	43	.279	.335	.537
	PIT/NL		10	15	14	2	0	0	0	2	0	0	0	9	0	1	0	0	0	0	0	.143	.143	.143
10 YR TOTALS			1201	4467	4151	1098	209	26	98	1653	253	13	12	672	130	8	43	27	25	451	521	.265	.306	.398

Wilson, Nigel Edward — BL/TL — b.1/12/70 — POS OF-3   TOR 7/30/87

YR	TM/LG	CL	G	TPA	AB	H	2B	3B	HR	TB	BB	IBB	HB	SO	GDP	SH	SF	SB	CS	R	RBI	BA	OBA	SA
88	SC/NYP	A-	40	121	103	21	1	2	2	32	12	0	4	32	0	1	0	8	4	12	11	.204	.308	.311
89	SC/NYP	A-	42	177	161	35	5	2	4	56	11	0	4	50	0	1	0	8	2	17	18	.217	.284	.348
90	MB/SAL	A	110	480	440	120	23	9	16	209	30	3	6	71	4	2	2	22	12	77	62	.273	.326	.475
91	DUN/FSL	A+	119	504	455	137	18	13	12	217	29	4	9	99	4	4	7	27	11	64	55	.301	.350	.477
92	KNO/SOU	AA	137	565	521	143	34	7	26	269	33	5	7	137	2	2	2	13	8	85	69	.274	.325	.516
93	EDM/PCL	AAA	96	408	370	108	26	7	17	199	25	7	10	108	6	1	2	8	3	66	68	.292	.351	.538
	FLO/NL		7	16	16	0	0	0	0	0	0	0	0	11	0	0	0	0	0	0	0	.000	.000	.000

Wilson, Willie James — BB/TR — b.7/9/55 — POS OF-2021, DH-26   KC74 1/18

YR	TM/LG	CL	G	TPA	AB	H	2B	3B	HR	TB	BB	IBB	HB	SO	GDP	SH	SF	SB	CS	R	RBI	BA	OBA	SA
76	KC/AL		12	6	6	1	0	0	0	1	0	0	0	2	0	0	0	2	1	0	0	.167	.167	.167
77	KC/AL		13	37	34	11	2	0	0	13	1	0	0	8	1	2	0	6	3	10	1	.324	.343	.382
78	KC/AL		127	223	198	43	8	2	0	55	16	0	2	33	2	5	2	46	12	43	16	.217	.280	.278
79	KC/AL		154	640	588	185	18	13	6	247	28	3	7	92	1	13	4	*83	12	113	49	.315	.351	.420
80	KC/AL		161	745	705	*230	28	*15	3	297	28	3	6	81	4	5	1	79	10	*133	49	.326	.357	.421
81	KC/AL		102	465	439	133	10	7	1	160	18	3	4	42	5	3	1	34	8	54	32	.303	.335	.364
82	KC/AL		136	621	585	194	19	*15	3	252	26	2	6	81	4	2	2	37	11	87	46	*.332	.365	.431
83	KC/AL		137	611	576	159	22	8	2	203	33	2	1	75	4	1	0	59	8	90	33	.276	.316	.352
84	KC/AL		128	588	541	163	24	9	2	211	39	2	3	56	7	2	3	47	5	81	44	.301	.350	.390
85	KC/AL		141	642	605	168	25	*21	4	247	29	3	5	94	6	2	1	43	11	87	43	.278	.316	.408
86	KC/AL		156	675	631	170	20	7	9	231	31	1	9	97	6	3	1	34	8	77	44	.269	.313	.366
87	KC/AL		146	653	610	170	18	*15	4	230	32	2	6	88	9	4	1	59	11	97	30	.279	.320	.377
88	KC/AL		147	628	591	155	17	*11	1	197	22	1	2	106	5	8	5	35	7	81	37	.262	.289	.333
89	KC/AL		112	423	383	97	17	7	3	137	27	0	1	78	8	6	6	24	6	58	43	.253	.300	.358
90	KC/AL		115	345	307	89	13	3	2	114	30	1	2	57	4	3	3	24	6	49	42	.290	.354	.371
91	OAK/AL		113	318	294	70	14	4	0	92	18	1	4	43	11	1	1	20	5	38	28	.238	.290	.313
92	OAK/AL		132	437	396	107	15	5	0	132	35	2	1	65	11	2	3	28	8	38	37	.270	.329	.333
93	CHI/NL		105	237	221	57	11	3	1	77	11	1	3	40	2	1	1	7	2	29	11	.258	.301	.348
18 YR TOTALS			2137	8294	7710	2202	281	145	41	2896	424	27	62	1138	90	63	35	667	134	1165	585	.286	.327	.376

Winfield, David Mark "Dave" — BR/TR — b.10/3/51 — POS OF-2468, DH-304, 1B-8, 3B-2   SD73 1/4

YR	TM/LG	CL	G	TPA	AB	H	2B	3B	HR	TB	BB	IBB	HB	SO	GDP	SH	SF	SB	CS	R	RBI	BA	OBA	SA
73	SD/NL		56	154	141	39	4	1	3	54	12	1	0	19	5	0	1	0	0	9	12	.277	.331	.383
74	SD/NL		145	544	498	132	18	4	20	218	40	2	1	96	14	0	5	9	7	57	75	.265	.318	.438
75	SD/NL		143	591	509	136	20	2	15	205	69	14	3	82	11	3	7	23	4	74	76	.267	.354	.403
76	SD/NL		137	567	492	139	26	4	13	212	65	8	3	78	14	2	5	26	7	81	69	.283	.366	.431
77	SD/NL		157	678	615	169	29	7	25	287	58	10	0	75	12	0	5	16	7	104	92	.275	.335	.467
78	SD/NL		158	649	587	181	30	5	24	293	55	20	2	81	13	0	5	21	9	88	97	.308	.367	.499
79	SD/NL		159	686	597	184	27	10	34	*333	85	24	2	71	9	0	3	15	9	97	*118	.308	.395	.558
80	SD/NL		162	643	558	154	25	6	20	251	79	14	2	83	13	0	4	23	7	89	87	.276	.365	.450
81	NY/AL		105	440	388	114	25	1	13	180	43	3	1	41	13	1	7	11	1	52	68	.294	.360	.464
82	NY/AL		140	597	539	151	24	8	37	302	45	7	0	64	20	5	8	5	3	84	106	.280	.331	.560
83	NY/AL		152	664	598	169	26	8	32	307	58	2	2	77	30	0	6	15	6	99	116	.283	.345	.513
84	NY/AL		141	626	567	193	34	4	19	292	53	9	0	71	14	0	6	6	4	106	100	.340	.393	.515
85	NY/AL		155	689	633	174	34	6	26	298	52	8	0	96	17	0	4	19	7	105	114	.275	.328	.471
86	NY/AL		154	652	565	148	31	5	24	261	77	9	2	106	20	2	6	6	5	90	104	.262	.349	.462
87	NY/AL		156	655	575	158	22	1	27	263	76	9	0	96	20	1	3	5	6	83	97	.275	.358	.457
88	NY/AL		149	631	559	180	37	2	25	296	69	10	2	88	19	0	1	9	7	96	107	.322	.398	.530
90	NY/AL		20	67	61	13	3	0	2	22	4	0	1	13	2	0	1	0	1	7	6	.213	.269	.361
	CAL/AL		112	470	414	114	18	2	19	193	48	3	1	68	15	1	6	0	1	63	72	.275	.348	.466
	YEAR		132	537	475	127	21	2	21	215	52	3	2	81	17	1	7	0	1	70	78	.267	.338	.453
91	CAL/AL		150	633	568	149	27	4	28	268	56	4	1	109	21	2	6	7	2	75	86	.262	.326	.472
92	TOR/AL		156	670	583	169	33	3	26	286	82	10	1	106	15	0	3	2	3	92	108	.290	.377	.491
93	MIN/AL		143	594	547	148	27	2	21	242	45	2	0	106	15	0	3	2	3	72	76	.271	.325	.442
20 YR TOTALS			2850	11900	10594	3014	520	85	453	5063	1171	165	24	1609	307	18	93	220	95	1623	1786	.285	.354	.478

Womack, Anthony Darrell "Tony" — BL/TR — b.9/26/69 — POS SS-6   PIT91 8/201

YR	TM/LG	CL	G	TPA	AB	H	2B	3B	HR	TB	BB	IBB	HB	SO	GDP	SH	SF	SB	CS	R	RBI	BA	OBA	SA
91	WEL/NYP	A-	45	185	166	46	3	0	1	52	17	0	0	39	1	2	0	26	6	30	8	.277	.344	.313
92	AUG/SAL	A	102	432	380	93	8	3	0	107	41	0	5	59	2	4	2	50	25	62	18	.245	.325	.282
93	SAL/CAR	A+	72	322	304	91	11	3	2	114	13	0	2	34	2	2	1	28	14	41	18	.299	.331	.375
	CAR/SOU	AA	60	273	247	75	7	2	0	86	17	2	1	34	3	4	4	21	6	41	23	.304	.346	.348
	PIT/NL		15	28	24	2	0	0	0	2	3	0	0	3	0	1	0	2	0	5	0	.083	.185	.083

Wood, Edward Robert "Ted" — BL/TL — b.1/4/67 — POS OF-32   SF88 2/28

YR	TM/LG	CL	G	TPA	AB	H	2B	3B	HR	TB	BB	IBB	HB	SO	GDP	SH	SF	SB	CS	R	RBI	BA	OBA	SA
89	SHR/TEX	AA	114	419	349	90	13	1	0	105	51	2	6	72	8	10	8	9	7	44	43	.258	.359	.301
90	SHR/TEX	AA	131	543	456	121	22	11	17	216	74	5	7	76	8	4	2	17	8	81	72	.265	.375	.474
91	PHO/PCL	AAA	137	612	512	159	38	6	11	242	86	4	4	96	13	0	10	12	7	90	109	.311	.407	.473
	SF/NL		10	28	25	3	0	0	0	3	2	0	0	11	0	1	0	0	0	0	1	.120	.185	.120
92	PHO/PCL	AAA	110	477	418	127	24	7	7	186	48	4	4	74	5	2	5	9	9	70	63	.304	.377	.445
	SF/NL		24	67	58	12	1	0	1	17	6	0	0	15	4	2	0	0	0	5	3	.207	.292	.293
93	OTT/INT	AAA	83	274	231	59	11	4	1	81	38	3	2	54	4	2	1	12	2	39	21	.255	.364	.351
	MON/NL		13	32	26	5	1	0	0	6	3	1	0	3	0	3	0	0	0	4	3	.192	.276	.231
3 YR TOTALS			**47**	**127**	**109**	**20**	**3**	**0**	**1**	**26**	**11**	**1**	**1**	**29**	**4**	**6**	**0**	**0**	**0**	**9**	**7**	**.183**	**.264**	**.239**

Woodson, Tracy Michael — BR/TR — b.10/5/62 — POS 3B-141, 1B-46   LA84 3/77

YR	TM/LG	CL	G	TPA	AB	H	2B	3B	HR	TB	BB	IBB	HB	SO	GDP	SH	SF	SB	CS	R	RBI	BA	OBA	SA
84	VB/FSL	A+	76	293	256	56	9	0	4	77	27	2	6	41	5	0	4	7	4	29	36	.219	.304	.301
85	VB/FSL	A+	138	576	504	126	30	4	9	191	50	6	9	78	12	5	8	10	5	55	62	.250	.324	.379
86	SA/TEX	AA	131	535	495	133	27	3	18	220	33	7	5	59	11	1	1	4	1	65	90	.269	.320	.444
87	ALB/PCL	AAA	67	282	259	75	13	2	5	107	17	0	2	22	12	0	4	1	1	37	44	.290	.333	.413
	LA/NL		53	148	136	31	8	1	1	44	9	2	2	21	2	0	1	1	0	14	11	.228	.284	.324
88	ALB/PCL	AAA	85	359	313	100	21	1	17	174	39	4	2	48	8	1	4	1	3	46	73	.319	.394	.556
	LA/NL		65	183	173	43	4	1	3	58	7	1	1	32	4	0	2	1	2	15	15	.249	.279	.335
89	LA/NL		4	6	6	0	0	0	0	0	0	0	0	1	2	0	0	0	0	0	0	.000	.000	.000
	ALB/PCL	AAA	89	364	325	95	21	0	14	158	32	2	4	40	7	0	3	2	1	49	59	.292	.360	.486
90	VAN/PCL	AAA	131	541	480	128	22	5	17	211	50	2	6	70	18	0	5	6	4	70	81	.267	.340	.440
91	RIC/INT	AAA	120	482	441	122	20	3	6	166	28	1	3	43	18	3	8	1	4	43	56	.277	.317	.376
92	LOU/AMA	AAA	109	447	412	122	23	2	12	185	24	2	2	46	12	5	4	4	3	62	59	.296	.335	.449
	STL/NL		31	119	114	35	8	0	1	46	4	0	1	10	1	1	0	0	0	9	22	.307	.331	.404
93	STL/NL		62	79	77	16	2	0	0	18	1	0	0	14	1	0	1	0	0	4	2	.208	.215	.234
5 YR TOTALS			**215**	**535**	**506**	**125**	**22**	**2**	**5**	**166**	**20**	**3**	**4**	**78**	**10**	**1**	**4**	**2**	**3**	**42**	**50**	**.247**	**.279**	**.328**

Wrona, Richard James "Rick" — BR/TR — b.12/10/63 — POS C-69, 1B-1   CHN85 6/130

YR	TM/LG	CL	G	TPA	AB	H	2B	3B	HR	TB	BB	IBB	HB	SO	GDP	SH	SF	SB	CS	R	RBI	BA	OBA	SA
85	PEO/MID	A	6	18	16	4	1	0	0	5	2	0	0	5	2	0	0	0	0	2	2	.250	.333	.313
	WIN/CAR	A+	20	52	49	11	4	0	0	15	3	0	0	15	0	0	0	0	1	4	2	.224	.269	.306
86	WIN/CAR	A+	91	305	267	68	15	0	4	95	25	1	5	37	9	8	0	5	2	43	32	.255	.330	.356
87	PIT/EAS	AA	70	231	218	48	10	3	1	67	7	3	1	32	4	2	3	5	1	22	25	.220	.245	.307
88	PIT/EAS	AA	5	9	6	0	0	0	0	0	1	0	1	2	0	1	0	0	0	0	1	.000	.125	.000
	IOW/AMA	AAA	83	210	193	51	9	0	2	66	17	1	0	34	6	0	0	0	0	28	23	.264	.324	.342
	CHI/NL		4	6	6	0	0	0	0	0	0	0	0	1	0	0	0	0	0	0	0	.000	.000	.000
89	IOW/AMA	AAA	60	197	189	41	8	3	2	61	7	2	1	40	4	0	0	1	1	15	13	.217	.249	.323
	CHI/NL		38	97	92	26	2	1	2	36	2	1	1	21	1	0	2	0	0	11	14	.283	.299	.391
90	CHI/NL		16	32	29	5	0	0	0	5	2	1	0	11	0	1	0	0	0	3	0	.172	.226	.172
	IOW/AMA	AAA	58	160	146	33	4	0	2	43	10	1	1	35	7	3	0	0	0	16	15	.226	.280	.295
91	TUL/TEX	AA	27	87	82	13	0	1	3	24	5	0	0	18	4	0	0	2	1	4	7	.159	.207	.293
92	CIN/NL		11	23	23	4	0	0	0	4	0	0	0	3	2	0	0	0	0	0	1	.174	.174	.174
	NAS/AMA	AAA	40	125	118	29	8	2	2	47	5	0	0	21	2	1	0	1	1	16	10	.246	.282	.398
93	CHI/AL		4	8	8	1	0	0	0	1	0	0	0	4	0	0	0	0	0	0	1	.125	.125	.125
	NAS/AMA	AAA	73	204	184	39	13	0	3	61	11	0	4	35	1	4	3	0	1	24	22	.212	.260	.332
5 YR TOTALS			**73**	**166**	**158**	**36**	**2**	**1**	**2**	**46**	**4**	**2**	**1**	**40**	**3**	**1**	**2**	**1**	**0**	**14**	**15**	**.228**	**.248**	**.291**

Yelding, Eric Girard — BR/TR — b.2/22/65 — POS SS-130, OF-109, 2B-55, 3B-10   TOR84* 1/19

YR	TM/LG	CL	G	TPA	AB	H	2B	3B	HR	TB	BB	IBB	HB	SO	GDP	SH	SF	SB	CS	R	RBI	BA	OBA	SA
84	MH/PIO	R+	67	332	304	94	14	6	4	132	26	0	0	46	3	0	2	31	11	61	29	.309	.361	.434
85	KIN/CAR	A+	135	571	526	137	14	4	2	165	33	0	4	70	4	5	3	62	26	59	31	.260	.307	.314
86	VEN/CAL	A+	131	601	560	157	14	7	4	197	33	3	0	84	6	6	2	41	18	83	40	.280	.319	.352
87	KNO/SOU	AA	39	165	150	30	6	1	0	38	12	0	1	25	4	1	1	10	5	23	7	.200	.262	.253
	MB/SAL	A	88	384	357	109	12	2	1	128	18	0	4	30	5	1	4	73	13	53	31	.305	.342	.359
88	SYR/INT	AAA	138	594	556	139	15	2	1	161	36	3	0	102	4	3	0	59	23	69	38	.250	.296	.290
89	HOU/NL		70	102	90	21	2	0	0	23	7	0	1	19	2	2	2	11	5	19	9	.233	.290	.256
90	HOU/NL		142	559	511	130	9	5	1	152	39	1	0	87	11	4	5	64	25	69	28	.254	.305	.297
91	HOU/NL		78	293	276	67	11	1	1	83	13	1	3	46	4	1	3	11	9	19	20	.243	.276	.301
	TUC/PCL	AAA	11	49	43	17	3	0	0	20	4	0	2	4	0	0	0	4	2	10	5	.395	.469	.465
92	HOU/NL		9	8	8	2	0	0	0	2	0	0	0	2	0	0	0	0	0	1	1	.250	.250	.250
	TUC/PCL	AAA	57	234	218	63	8	5	0	81	13	0	0	50	6	2	1	17	9	30	23	.289	.328	.372
	VAN/PCL	AAA	36	139	120	26	3	0	0	29	13	0	2	17	2	4	0	6	2	17	6	.217	.289	.242
93	CHI/NL		69	123	108	22	5	1	1	32	11	2	0	22	3	4	0	10	4	14	10	.204	.277	.296
5 YR TOTALS			**368**	**1085**	**993**	**242**	**27**	**7**	**3**	**292**	**70**	**6**	**1**	**177**	**20**	**13**	**8**	**89**	**41**	**122**	**67**	**.244**	**.292**	**.294**

Young, Eric Orlando — BR/TR — b.5/18/67 — POS 2B-122, OF-52   LA89 46/1123

YR	TM/LG	CL	G	TPA	AB	H	2B	3B	HR	TB	BB	IBB	HB	SO	GDP	SH	SF	SB	CS	R	RBI	BA	OBA	SA
89	DOD/GCL	R	56	235	197	65	11	5	2	92	33	1	3	16	1	1	1	41	10	53	22	.330	.432	.467

(continued)

Young, Eric Orlando (continued)

YR	TM/LG	CL	G	TPA	AB	H	2B	3B	HR	TB	BB	IBB	HB	SO	GDP	SH	SF	SB	CS	R	RBI	BA	OBA	SA
90	VB/FSL	A+	127	544	460	132	23	7	2	175	69	1	6	35	4	5	4	76	16	101	50	.287	.384	.380
91	SA/TEX	AA	127	539	461	129	17	4	3	163	67	0	2	36	13	8	1	70	26	82	35	.280	.373	.354
	ALB/PCL	AAA	1	5	5	2	0	0	0	2	0	0	0	0	0	0	0	0	0	0	0	.400	.400	.400
92	ALB/PCL	AAA	94	407	350	118	16	5	3	153	33	0	4	18	10	13	7	28	11	61	49	.337	.393	.437
	LA/NL		49	144	132	34	1	0	1	38	8	0	0	9	3	4	0	6	1	9	11	.258	.300	.288
93	COL/NL		144	565	490	132	16	8	3	173	63	3	4	41	9	4	4	42	19	82	42	.269	.355	.353
2 YR TOTALS			**193**	**709**	**622**	**166**	**17**	**8**	**4**	**211**	**71**	**3**	**4**	**50**	**12**	**8**	**4**	**48**	**20**	**91**	**53**	**.267**	**.344**	**.339**

Young, Gerald Anthony — BB/TR — b.10/22/64 — POS OF-557   NYN82 5/111

YR	TM/LG	CL	G	TPA	AB	H	2B	3B	HR	TB	BB	IBB	HB	SO	GDP	SH	SF	SB	CS	R	RBI	BA	OBA	SA
81	BIL/PIO	R+	47	151	135	44	7	0	1	54	13	1	0	19	3	2	1	3	1	22	23	.326	.383	.400
84	COL/SAL	A	124	491	396	84	14	3	1	107	84	1	2	69	7	6	3	43	7	69	52	.212	.351	.270
85	OSC/FSL	A+	133	576	474	121	20	9	3	168	86	5	5	48	17	2	9	31	13	88	48	.255	.369	.354
86	CMB/SOU	AA	136	617	539	151	30	4	9	216	67	5	1	57	6	2	8	54	27	101	62	.280	.356	.401
87	TUC/PCL	AAA	86	394	340	99	15	5	2	130	47	0	3	32	6	2	2	43	12	59	31	.291	.380	.382
	HOU/NL		71	303	274	88	9	2	1	104	26	0	1	27	1	0	2	26	9	44	15	.321	.380	.380
88	HOU/NL		149	655	576	148	21	9	0	187	66	1	3	66	10	5	5	65	27	79	37	.257	.334	.325
89	HOU/NL		146	620	533	124	17	3	0	147	74	4	2	60	7	6	5	34	25	71	38	.233	.326	.276
90	TUC/PCL	AAA	49	227	183	61	7	4	0	76	40	1	0	18	5	2	2	14	11	37	24	.333	.449	.415
	HOU/NL		57	179	154	27	4	1	1	36	20	0	0	23	3	4	1	15	4	15	4	.175	.269	.234
91	TUC/PCL	AAA	24	95	79	24	2	3	0	32	14	1	0	8	2	1	1	3	1	14	17	.304	.404	.405
	HOU/NL		108	169	142	31	3	1	1	39	24	0	0	17	3	1	2	16	5	26	11	.218	.327	.275
92	TUC/PCL	AAA	20	90	74	23	2	1	0	27	14	1	1	4	2	1	0	13	6	15	2	.311	.427	.365
	HOU/NL		74	90	76	14	1	1	0	17	10	0	0	11	2	4	0	6	2	14	4	.184	.279	.224
93	COL/NL		19	23	19	1	0	0	0	1	4	0	0	1	0	0	0	0	1	5	1	.053	.217	.053
	IND/AMA	AAA	32	125	103	31	10	0	1	44	18	3	1	17	0	2	1	7	1	15	6	.301	.407	.427
	CAL/PCL	AAA	26	125	104	31	8	2	1	46	20	0	0	16	1	1	0	7	9	19	10	.298	.411	.442
7 YR TOTALS			**624**	**2039**	**1774**	**433**	**55**	**17**	**3**	**531**	**224**	**5**	**6**	**205**	**28**	**20**	**15**	**153**	**72**	**254**	**110**	**.244**	**.328**	**.299**

Young, Kevin Stacey — BR/TR — b.6/16/69 — POS 1B-136, 3B-13   PIT90 7/187

YR	TM/LG	CL	G	TPA	AB	H	2B	3B	HR	TB	BB	IBB	HB	SO	GDP	SH	SF	SB	CS	R	RBI	BA	OBA	SA
90	WEL/NYP	A-	72	281	238	58	16	2	5	93	31	2	7	36	4	0	5	10	2	46	30	.244	.342	.391
91	SAL/CAR	A+	56	231	201	63	12	4	6	101	20	0	7	34	5	0	3	3	2	38	28	.313	.390	.502
	CAR/SOU	AA	75	287	263	90	19	6	3	130	15	1	8	38	7	0	1	9	3	36	33	.342	.394	.494
	BUF/AMA	AAA	4	11	9	2	1	0	0	3	0	0	1	0	0	0	1	1	0	1	2	.222	.273	.333
92	BUF/AMA	AAA	137	579	490	154	29	6	8	219	67	0	11	67	11	8	3	18	12	91	65	.314	.406	.447
	PIT/NL		10	9	7	4	0	0	0	4	2	0	0	0	0	0	0	1	0	2	4	.571	.667	.571
93	PIT/NL		141	508	449	106	24	3	6	154	36	3	9	82	10	5	9	2	2	38	47	.236	.300	.343
2 YR TOTALS			**151**	**517**	**456**	**110**	**24**	**3**	**6**	**158**	**38**	**3**	**9**	**82**	**10**	**5**	**9**	**3**	**2**	**40**	**51**	**.241**	**.307**	**.346**

Yount, Robin R — BR/TR — b.9/16/55 — POS SS-1479, OF-1218, DH-138, 1B-12   MIL73 1/3

YR	TM/LG	CL	G	TPA	AB	H	2B	3B	HR	TB	BB	IBB	HB	SO	GDP	SH	SF	SB	CS	R	RBI	BA	OBA	SA
74	MIL/AL		107	364	344	86	14	5	3	119	12	0	1	46	4	5	2	7	7	48	26	.250	.276	.346
75	MIL/AL		147	607	558	149	28	2	8	205	33	3	1	69	8	10	5	12	4	67	52	.267	.307	.367
76	MIL/AL		161	690	638	161	19	3	2	192	38	3	0	69	13	8	6	16	11	59	54	.252	.292	.301
77	MIL/AL		154	663	605	174	34	4	4	228	41	1	2	80	11	11	4	16	7	66	49	.288	.333	.428
78	MIL/AL		127	545	502	147	23	9	9	215	24	1	1	43	5	13	6	16	5	66	71	.293	.323	.428
79	MIL/AL		149	626	577	154	26	5	8	214	35	3	1	52	15	10	3	11	8	72	51	.267	.308	.371
80	MIL/AL		143	647	611	179	*49	10	23	317	26	1	1	67	8	6	3	20	5	121	87	.293	.321	.519
81	MIL/AL		96	411	377	103	15	5	10	158	22	1	2	37	4	4	6	4	1	50	49	.273	.312	.419
82	MIL/AL		156	704	635	*210	*46	12	29	*367	54	2	1	63	19	4	10	14	3	129	114	.331	.379	*.578
83	MIL/AL		149	662	578	178	42	*10	17	291	72	6	3	58	11	1	8	12	5	102	80	.308	.383	.503
84	MIL/AL		160	702	624	186	27	7	16	275	67	7	1	67	22	1	9	14	4	105	80	.298	.362	.441
85	MIL/AL		122	527	466	129	26	3	15	206	49	3	2	56	8	1	9	10	4	76	68	.277	.342	.442
86	MIL/AL		140	595	522	163	31	7	9	235	62	7	4	73	9	5	2	14	5	82	46	.312	.388	.450
87	MIL/AL		158	723	635	198	25	9	21	304	76	10	1	94	9	6	5	19	9	99	103	.312	.384	.479
88	MIL/AL		162	696	621	190	38	*11	13	289	63	10	3	63	21	2	7	22	9	92	91	.306	.369	.465
89	MIL/AL		160	690	614	195	38	9	21	314	63	9	6	71	9	3	4	19	13	101	103	.318	.384	.511
90	MIL/AL		158	683	587	145	17	5	17	223	78	6	6	89	7	4	8	15	8	98	77	.247	.337	.380
91	MIL/AL		130	571	503	131	20	4	10	189	54	8	4	79	13	1	9	6	4	66	77	.260	.332	.376
92	MIL/AL		150	629	557	147	40	3	8	217	53	9	3	81	9	4	12	15	4	71	77	.264	.325	.390
93	MIL/AL		127	514	454	117	25	3	8	172	44	5	3	93	12	5	6	11	6	62	51	.258	.326	.379
20 YR TOTALS			**2856**	**12249**	**11008**	**3142**	**583**	**126**	**251**	**4730**	**966**	**95**	**48**	**1350**	**217**	**104**	**123**	**271**	**105**	**1632**	**1406**	**.285**	**.342**	**.430**

Zambrano, Eduardo Jose — BR/TR — b.2/1/66 — POS OF-4, 1B-2   BOS 11/1/84

YR	TM/LG	CL	G	TPA	AB	H	2B	3B	HR	TB	BB	IBB	HB	SO	GDP	SH	SF	SB	CS	R	RBI	BA	OBA	SA
85	GRE/SAL	A	115	493	443	120	17	3	1	146	31	0	13	61	15	1	5	1	1	63	51	.271	.333	.330
86	GRE/SAL	A	112	448	395	94	16	5	12	156	42	0	4	80	10	1	6	4	3	68	65	.238	.313	.395
87	WH/FSL	A+	69	263	225	60	16	1	11	111	27	0	5	47	7	3	1	1	1	33	32	.267	.354	.493
	NB/EAS	AA	33	132	118	29	11	1	2	48	10	1	2	21	1	1	1	2	1	16	11	.246	.313	.407
88	NB/EAS	AA	121	425	381	85	13	1	8	124	30	1	8	70	7	4	2	10	7	36	30	.223	.292	.325
89	NB/EAS	AA	54	191	169	37	8	1	3	56	14	0	4	27	3	4	0	3	1	15	11	.219	.294	.331
90	KIN/CAR	A+	63	237	204	50	7	2	3	70	29	1	0	36	6	1	2	6	1	26	30	.245	.339	.343
91	CAR/SOU	AA	83	304	269	68	17	3	3	100	22	0	4	56	4	2	4	7	4	28	39	.253	.311	.372
	BUF/AMA	AAA	48	169	144	49	8	5	3	76	17	1	3	25	4	1	4	3	2	19	35	.340	.408	.528
92	BUF/AMA	AAA	126	457	394	112	22	4	16	190	51	2	8	75	7	3	5	3	2	47	79	.284	.368	.482
93	IOW/AMA	AAA	133	538	469	142	29	2	32	271	54	11	6	93	10	2	7	10	7	95	115	.303	.377	.578
	CHI/NL		8	18	17	5	0	0	0	5	1	0	0	3	1	0	0	0	0	1	2	.294	.333	.294

Zeile, Todd Edward — BR/TR — b.9/9/65 — POS 3B-455, C-128, 1B-11, OF-1   SL86 3/55

YR	TM/LG	CL	G	TPA	AB	H	2B	3B	HR	TB	BB	IBB	HB	SO	GDP	SH	SF	SB	CS	R	RBI	BA	OBA	SA
86	ERI/NYP	A-	70	294	248	64	14	1	14	122	37	1	2	52	3	1	6	5	1	40	63	.258	.352	.492
87	SPR/MID	A	130	561	487	142	24	4	25	249	70	7	1	85	10	0	3	1	3	94	106	.292	.380	.511
88	ARK/TEX	AA	129	518	430	117	33	2	19	211	83	8	1	64	11	0	4	6	5	95	75	.272	.388	.491
89	LOU/AMA	AAA	118	506	453	131	26	3	19	220	45	1	1	78	10	0	7	0	1	71	85	.289	.350	.486
	STL/NL		28	93	82	21	3	1	1	29	9	1	0	14	1	1	1	0	0	7	8	.256	.326	.354
90	STL/NL		144	570	495	121	25	3	15	197	67	3	2	77	11	0	6	2	4	62	57	.244	.333	.398
91	STL/NL		155	638	565	158	36	3	11	233	62	3	5	94	15	0	6	17	11	76	81	.280	.353	.412
92	LOU/AMA	AAA	21	84	74	23	4	1	5	44	9	0	0	13	4	0	1	0	0	11	13	.311	.381	.595
	STL/NL		126	514	439	113	18	4	7	160	68	4	0	70	11	0	7	7	10	51	48	.257	.352	.364
93	STL/NL		157	647	571	158	36	1	17	247	70	5	0	76	15	0	6	5	4	82	103	.277	.352	.433
5 YR TOTALS			**610**	**2462**	**2152**	**571**	**118**	**12**	**51**	**866**	**276**	**16**	**7**	**331**	**53**	**1**	**26**	**31**	**29**	**278**	**297**	**.265**	**.347**	**.402**

Zupcic, Robert "Bob" — BR/TR — b.8/18/66 — POS OF-252, DH-10   BOS87 2/32

YR	TM/LG	CL	G	TPA	AB	H	2B	3B	HR	TB	BB	IBB	HB	SO	GDP	SH	SF	SB	CS	R	RBI	BA	OBA	SA
87	ELM/NYP	A-	66	262	238	72	12	2	7	109	17	0	2	35	5	3	2	5	4	39	37	.303	.351	.458
88	LYN/CAR	A+	135	565	482	143	33	5	13	225	60	4	8	64	6	7	8	10	6	69	97	.297	.378	.467
89	PAW/INT	AAA	27	99	94	24	7	1	1	36	3	0	0	15	2	0	2	1	3	8	11	.255	.273	.383
	NB/EAS	AA	94	375	346	75	12	2	2	97	19	0	1	55	7	7	2	15	1	37	28	.217	.258	.280
90	NB/EAS	AA	132	516	461	98	26	1	2	132	36	2	6	65	7	6	7	10	8	45	41	.213	.275	.286
91	PAW/INT	AAA	129	505	429	103	27	1	18	186	55	2	1	58	5	12	8	11	6	70	70	.240	.323	.434
	BOS/AL		18	27	25	4	0	0	1	7	1	0	0	6	0	1	0	0	0	3	3	.160	.192	.280
92	PAW/INT	AAA	9	34	25	8	1	0	2	15	8	0	0	6	0	0	1	0	1	3	5	.320	.471	.600
	BOS/AL		124	432	392	108	19	1	3	138	25	1	4	60	6	7	4	2	2	46	43	.276	.322	.352
93	BOS/AL		141	326	286	69	24	2	2	103	27	2	2	54	7	8	3	5	2	40	26	.241	.308	.360
3 YR TOTALS			**283**	**785**	**703**	**181**	**43**	**3**	**6**	**248**	**53**	**3**	**6**	**120**	**13**	**16**	**7**	**7**	**4**	**89**	**72**	**.257**	**.312**	**.353**

Abbott, James Anthony "Jim" — BL/TL — b.9/19/67　　CAL88 1/8

YR	TM/LG	CL	G	TBF	GS	CG	SHO	GF	IP	H	HR	BB	IBB	HB	SO	SH	SF	WP	BK	R	ER	W	L	PCT	SV	ERA
89	CAL/AL		29	788	29	4	2	0	181.1	190	13	74	3	4	115	11	5	8	2	95	79	12	12	.500	0	3.92
90	CAL/AL		33	925	33	4	1	0	211.2	246	16	72	6	5	105	9	6	4	3	116	106	10	14	.417	0	4.51
91	CAL/AL		34	1002	34	5	1	0	243.0	222	14	73	6	5	158	7	7	1	4	85	78	18	11	.621	0	2.89
92	CAL/AL		29	874	29	7	0	0	211.0	208	12	68	3	4	130	8	4	2	0	73	65	7	15	.318	0	2.77
93	NY/AL		32	906	32	4	1	0	214.0	221	22	73	4	3	95	12	4	9	0	115	104	11	14	.440	0	4.37
5 YR TOTALS			157	4495	157	24	5	0	1061.0	1087	77	360	22	21	603	47	26	24	9	484	432	58	66	.468	0	3.66

Abbott, Paul David — BR/TR — b.9/15/67　　MIN85 3/67

YR	TM/LG	CL	G	TBF	GS	CG	SHO	GF	IP	H	HR	BB	IBB	HB	SO	SH	SF	WP	BK	R	ER	W	L	PCT	SV	ERA
85	ELI/APP	R+	10	172	10	1	0	0	35.0	33	3	32	0	0	34	1	0	7	1	32	27	1	5	.167	0	6.94
86	KEN/MID	A	25	462	15	1	0	7	98.0	102	13	73	3	2	73	3	2	7	0	62	49	6	10	.375	0	4.50
87	KEN/MID	A	26	620	25	1	0	0	145.1	102	11	103	0	3	138	5	6	11	2	76	59	13	6	.684	0	3.65
88	VIS/CAL	A+	28	799	28	4	2	0	172.1	141	9	143	5	4	205	8	6	12	9	95	80	11	9	.550	0	4.18
89	ORL/SOU	AA	17	389	17	1	0	0	90.2	71	6	48	0	0	102	2	1	7	7	48	44	9	3	.750	0	4.37
90	POR/PCL	AAA	23	568	23	4	1	0	128.1	110	9	82	0	1	129	3	3	8	5	75	65	5	14	.263	0	4.56
	MIN/AL		7	162	7	0	0	0	34.2	37	0	28	0	1	25	1	1	1	0	24	23	0	5	.000	0	5.97
91	POR/PCL	AAA	8	193	8	1	1	0	44.0	36	2	28	0	0	40	0	1	1	0	19	19	2	3	.400	0	3.89
	MIN/AL		15	210	3	0	0	1	47.1	38	5	36	1	0	43	0	1	3	0	27	25	3	1	.750	0	4.75
92	POR/PCL	AAA	7	191	7	0	0	0	46.1	30	2	31	0	0	46	0	0	0	0	13	12	4	1	.800	0	2.33
	MIN/AL		6	50	0	0	0	5	11.0	12	1	5	0	1	13	0	1	1	0	4	4	0	0	.000	0	3.27
93	CLE/AL		5	84	5	0	0	0	18.1	19	5	11	0	0	7	0	0	1	0	15	13	0	1	.000	0	6.38
	CHW/INT	AAA	4	91	4	0	0	0	19.0	25	4	7	0	0	12	3	1	3	0	16	14	0	1	.000	0	6.63
	CAN/EAS	AA	13	315	12	1	0	0	75.1	71	4	28	2	1	86	1	0	6	0	34	34	4	5	.444	0	4.06
4 YR TOTALS			33	506	15	0	0	6	111.1	106	11	80	2	2	88	8	5	8	0	70	65	3	7	.300	0	5.25

Agosto, Juan Roberto — BL/TL — b.2/23/58　　BOS 8/29/74

YR	TM/LG	CL	G	TBF	GS	CG	SHO	GF	IP	H	HR	BB	IBB	HB	SO	SH	SF	WP	BK	R	ER	W	L	PCT	SV	ERA
81	CHI/AL		2	22	0	0	0	1	5.2	5	1	0	0	0	3	0	0	0	0	3	3	0	0	.000	0	4.76
82	CHI/AL		1	13	0	0	0	1	2.0	7	0	0	0	0	1	0	0	0	0	4	4	0	0	.000	0	18.00
83	CHI/AL		39	166	0	0	0	13	41.2	41	2	11	1	1	29	5	4	2	0	20	19	2	2	.500	1	4.10
84	CHI/AL		49	243	0	0	0	18	55.1	54	2	34	7	3	26	5	1	1	0	20	19	2	1	.667	7	3.09
85	BUF/AMA	AAA	6	52	0	0	0	5	12.2	13	0	2	0	0	11	1	0	0	0	3	3	0	0	.000	2	2.13
	CHI/AL		54	246	0	0	0	21	60.1	45	3	23	1	0	39	3	3	3	0	27	24	4	3	.571	1	3.58
86	CHI/AL		9	24	0	0	0	1	4.2	6	0	4	0	0	3	0	0	0	0	5	4	0	2	.000	0	7.71
	MIN/AL		17	115	1	0	0	3	20.1	43	1	14	0	2	9	2	0	1	0	25	20	1	2	.333	1	8.85
	YEAR		26	139	1	0	0	4	25.0	49	1	18	0	2	12	2	0	1	0	30	24	1	4	.200	1	8.64
	TOL/INT	AAA	21	149	0	0	0	18	35.0	33	0	14	0	1	29	1	0	4	0	11	9	4	3	.571	6	2.31
87	TUC/PCL	AAA	44	214	0	0	0	24	50.0	48	1	19	2	2	31	4	0	4	1	16	11	4	2	.667	7	1.98
	HOU/NL		27	118	0	0	0	13	27.1	26	1	10	1	0	20	6	3	0	1	12	8	1	1	.500	2	2.63
88	HOU/NL		75	371	0	0	0	33	91.2	74	6	30	13	2	33	9	5	5	5	27	23	10	2	.833	4	2.26
89	HOU/NL		71	361	0	0	0	28	83.0	81	3	32	10	2	46	5	6	4	1	32	27	4	5	.444	1	2.93
90	HOU/NL		*82	404	0	0	0	29	92.1	91	4	39	8	7	50	7	3	1	0	46	44	9	8	.529	4	4.29
91	STL/NL		72	377	0	0	0	22	86.0	92	4	39	4	3	34	11	3	6	0	52	46	5	3	.625	2	4.81
92	CAL/PCL	AAA	10	92	0	0	0	4	21.2	20	2	13	0	2	12	1	0	0	0	12	12	1	0	1.000	1	4.98
	STL/NL		22	143	0	0	0	10	31.2	39	2	9	2	3	13	2	2	0	0	24	22	2	4	.333	0	6.25
	SEA/AL		17	84	1	0	0	2	18.1	27	0	3	0	0	12	1	0	0	0	12	12	0	0	.000	0	5.89
	YEAR		39	227	1	0	0	12	50.0	66	2	12	2	3	25	3	2	0	0	36	34	2	4	.333	0	6.12
93	LV/PCL	AAA	19	78	0	0	0	5	18.0	21	2	5	2	1	15	0	0	0	0	8	8	2	0	1.000	4	4.00
	TUC/PCL	AAA	32	168	0	0	3	13	33.0	45	3	24	3	2	18	3	5	3	0	24	22	5	3	.625	6	6.00
	HOU/NL		6	26	0	0	0	3	6.0	8	1	3	0	0	3	0	0	0	0	4	4	0	0	.000	0	6.00
13 YR TOTALS			543	2713	2	0	0	198	626.1	639	30	248	47	30	307	55	28	21	7	313	279	40	33	.548	29	4.01

Aguilera, Richard Warren "Rick" — BR/TR — b.12/31/61　　NYN83 5/58

YR	TM/LG	CL	G	TBF	GS	CG	SHO	GF	IP	H	HR	BB	IBB	HB	SO	SH	SF	WP	BK	R	ER	W	L	PCT	SV	ERA
84	LYN/CAR	A+	13	364	13	6	3	0	88.1	72	3	28	1	6	101	3	2	6	2	29	23	8	3	.727	0	2.34
	JAC/TEX	AA	11	284	11	2	1	0	67.0	68	5	19	1	0	71	2	1	2	0	37	34	4	4	.500	0	4.57
85	TID/INT	AAA	11	314	11	2	1	0	79.0	64	5	17	0	1	55	1	3	1	2	24	22	6	4	.600	0	2.51
	NY/NL		21	507	19	2	0	1	122.1	118	8	37	2	2	74	7	4	5	2	49	44	10	7	.588	0	3.24
86	NY/NL		28	605	20	2	0	2	141.2	145	15	36	1	7	104	6	5	5	3	70	61	10	7	.588	0	3.88
87	TID/INT	AAA	3	47	3	0	0	0	13.0	8	0	1	0	0	10	0	0	0	0	2	1	1	1	.500	0	0.69
	NY/NL		18	494	17	1	0	0	115.0	124	12	33	2	3	77	7	2	9	0	53	46	11	3	.786	0	3.60
88	SL/FSL	A+	2	30	2	0	0	0	7.0	7	0	1	0	0	5	3	0	1	0	1	1	0	0	.000	0	1.29
	TID/INT	AAA	1	25	1	0	0	0	6.0	6	0	1	0	0	4	1	0	0	0	1	1	0	0	.000	0	1.50
	NY/NL		11	111	0	0	0	2	24.2	29	2	10	2	1	16	2	1	0	0	20	19	0	4	.000	0	6.93
89	NY/NL		36	284	0	0	0	19	69.1	59	3	21	3	2	80	1	5	0	0	19	18	6	6	.500	7	2.34
	MIN/AL		11	310	11	3	0	0	75.2	71	5	17	1	1	57	0	0	0	0	32	27	3	5	.375	0	3.21
	YEAR		47	594	11	3	0	19	145.0	130	8	38	4	3	137	1	5	0	0	51	45	9	11	.450	7	2.79
90	MIN/AL		56	268	0	0	0	54	65.1	55	5	19	6	4	61	2	4	0	0	27	20	5	3	.625	32	2.76
91	MIN/AL		63	275	0	0	0	60	69.0	44	3	30	4	1	61	1	3	0	0	20	18	4	5	.444	42	2.35
92	MIN/AL		64	273	0	0	0	61	66.2	60	7	17	4	1	52	2	5	0	0	28	21	2	6	.250	41	2.83
93	MIN/AL		65	287	0	0	0	61	72.1	60	9	14	1	1	59	2	1	0	0	25	25	4	3	.571	34	3.11
9 YR TOTALS			373	3414	70	8	0	260	822.0	765	69	234	30	23	641	33	18	36	9	343	299	55	49	.529	156	3.27

Aldred, Scott Phillip — BL/TL — b.6/12/68   DET86 16/411

YR	TM/LG	CL	G	TBF	GS	CG	SHO	GF	IP	H	HR	BB	IBB	HB	SO	SH	SF	WP	BK	R	ER	W	L	PCT	SV	ERA
87	FAY/SAL	A	21	485	20	0	0	0	111.0	101	5	69	0	3	91	2	7	8	1	56	44	4	9	.308	0	3.57
88	LAK/FSL	A+	25	583	25	1	1	0	131.1	122	6	72	1	8	102	3	3	5	4	61	52	8	7	.533	0	3.56
89	LON/EAS	AA	20	513	20	3	1	0	122.0	98	11	59	0	5	97	3	3	9	2	55	52	10	6	.625	0	3.84
90	TOL/INT	AAA	29	687	29	2	0	0	158.0	145	16	81	1	4	133	2	10	10	4	93	86	6	15	.286	0	4.90
	DET/AL		4	63	3	0	0	0	14.1	13	0	10	1	1	7	2	1	0	0	6	6	1	2	.333	0	3.77
91	TOL/INT	AAA	22	581	20	2	0	2	135.1	127	7	72	1	4	95	9	2	5	0	65	59	8	8	.500	1	3.92
	DET/AL		11	253	11	1	0	0	57.1	58	9	30	2	0	35	3	2	3	1	37	33	2	4	.333	0	5.18
92	TOL/INT	AAA	16	392	13	3	0	1	86.0	92	13	47	0	2	81	1	1	6	0	57	49	4	6	.400	0	5.13
	DET/AL		16	304	13	0	0	0	65.0	80	12	33	4	3	34	4	3	1	0	51	49	3	8	.273	0	6.78
93	COL/NL		5	40	0	0	0	1	6.2	10	1	9	1	1	5	2	0	1	0	10	8	0	0	.000	0	10.80
	MON/NL		3	25	0	0	0	1	5.1	9	1	1	0	0	4	0	0	1	0	4	4	1	0	1.000	0	6.75
	YEAR		8	65	0	0	0	2	12.0	19	2	10	1	1	9	2	0	2	0	14	12	1	0	1.000	0-	9.00
4 YR TOTALS			39	685	27	1	0	2	148.2	170	23	83	8	5	85	11	6	6	1	108	100	7	14	.333	0	6.05

Alvarez, Wilson Eduardo — BL/TL — b.3/24/70   TEX 9/23/86

YR	TM/LG	CL	G	TBF	GS	CG	SHO	GF	IP	H	HR	BB	IBB	HB	SO	SH	SF	WP	BK	R	ER	W	L	PCT	SV	ERA
87	GAS/SAL	A	8	153	6	0	0	1	32.0	39	5	23	0	4	19	0	1	0	0	24	23	1	5	.167	0	6.47
	RAN/GCL	R	10	193	10	0	0	0	44.2	41	4	21	0	3	46	1	1	3	0	29	26	2	5	.286	0	5.24
88	GAS/SAL	A	23	552	23	1	0	0	127.0	113	5	49	1	7	134	4	6	5	10	63	42	4	11	.267	0	2.98
	OC/AMA	AAA	5	71	3	0	0	1	16.2	17	2	6	0	1	9	0	2	0	0	8	7	1	1	.500	0	3.78
89	CHA/FSL	A+	13	331	13	3	2	0	81.0	68	2	21	0	4	51	3	3	4	0	29	19	7	4	.636	0	2.11
	TUL/TEX	AA	7	196	7	1	1	0	48.0	40	1	16	3	0	29	0	1	2	0	14	11	2	2	.500	0	2.06
	TEX/AL		1	5	1	0	0	0	0.0	3	2	2	0	0	0	0	0	0	0	3	3	0	1	.000	0	0.00
	BIR/SOU	AA	6	149	5	1	0	0	35.2	32	3	16	0	1	18	0	0	1	1	12	12	2	1	.667	0	3.03
90	VAN/PCL	AAA	17	350	15	1	0	0	75.0	91	7	51	0	4	35	2	3	1	2	54	50	7	7	.500	0	6.00
	BIR/SOU	AA	7	203	7	1	0	0	46.1	44	4	25	0	0	36	0	0	2	2	24	22	5	1	.833	0	4.27
91	BIR/SOU	AA	23	634	23	3	2	0	152.1	109	6	74	0	3	165	1	3	9	3	46	31	10	6	.625	0	1.83
	CHI/AL		10	237	9	2	1	0	56.1	47	9	29	0	0	32	3	1	1	0	26	22	3	2	.600	0	3.51
92	CHI/AL		34	455	9	0	0	4	100.1	103	12	65	2	4	66	3	4	2	0	64	58	5	3	.625	0	5.20
93	NAS/AMA	AAA	1	31	1	0	0	0	6.1	7	0	2	0	0	4	0	0	0	0	7	2	0	1	.000	0	2.84
	CHI/AL		31	877	31	1	1	0	207.2	168	14	122	8	7	155	13	6	2	1	78	68	15	8	.652	0	2.95
4 YR TOTALS			76	1574	50	3	2	4	364.1	321	37	218	10	11	253	19	11	6	1	171	151	23	14	.622	1	3.73

Andersen, Larry Eugene — BR/TR — b.5/6/53   CLE71 7/155

YR	TM/LG	CL	G	TBF	GS	CG	SHO	GF	IP	H	HR	BB	IBB	HB	SO	SH	SF	WP	BK	R	ER	W	L	PCT	SV	ERA
75	CLE/AL		3	23	0	0	0	1	5.2	4	0	2	0	0	4	0	1	2	0	3	3	0	0	.000	0	4.76
77	CLE/AL		11	62	0	0	0	7	14.1	10	1	9	3	0	8	3	0	1	0	7	5	0	0	.000	0	3.14
79	CLE/AL		8	77	0	0	0	4	16.2	25	3	4	0	0	7	1	2	0	0	14	14	0	0	.000	0	7.56
81	SEA/AL		41	273	0	0	0	23	67.2	57	4	18	2	2	40	0	3	0	0	27	20	3	3	.500	5	2.66
82	SEA/AL		40	354	1	0	0	14	79.2	100	16	23	1	4	32	3	3	2	0	56	53	0	0	.000	1	5.99
83	PHI/NL		17	106	0	0	0	4	26.1	19	0	9	1	0	14	1	1	1	1	7	7	1	0	1.000	0	2.39
84	PHI/NL		64	376	0	0	0	25	90.2	85	5	25	6	0	54	4	4	2	1	32	24	3	7	.300	4	2.38
85	PHI/NL		57	318	0	0	0	19	73.0	78	5	26	4	3	50	3	1	1	1	41	35	3	3	.500	4	4.32
86	PHI/NL		10	55	0	0	0	1	12.2	19	0	3	0	0	9	2	1	0	0	8	6	0	0	.000	0	4.26
	HOU/NL		38	268	0	0	0	7	64.2	64	2	23	10	1	33	2	1	2	0	22	20	2	1	.667	1	2.78
	YEAR		48	323	0	0	0	8	77.1	83	2	26	10	1	42	10	5	1	0	30	26	2	1	.667	1	3.03
87	HOU/NL		67	440	0	0	0	31	101.2	95	7	41	10	2	94	7	4	1	1	46	39	9	5	.643	5	3.45
88	HOU/NL		53	350	0	0	0	25	82.2	82	3	20	8	1	66	1	3	1	0	29	27	2	4	.333	5	2.94
89	HOU/NL		60	351	0	0	0	21	87.2	63	2	24	4	0	85	4	5	2	0	19	15	4	4	.500	3	1.54
90	HOU/NL		50	301	0	0	0	20	73.2	61	2	24	5	1	68	5	5	2	0	19	16	5	2	.714	6	1.95
	BOS/AL		15	86	0	0	0	4	22.0	18	0	3	1	0	25	0	0	0	0	3	3	0	0	.000	1	1.23
	YEAR		65	387	0	0	0	24	95.2	79	2	27	5	2	93	5	5	2	0	22	19	5	2	.714	7	1.79
91	SD/NL		38	188	0	0	0	24	47.0	39	4	13	3	0	40	4	2	1	0	13	12	3	4	.429	13	2.30
92	HD/CAL	A+	5	33	2	0	0	0	8.0	7	1	2	0	0	10	0	1	0	0	5	2	0	0	.000	0	2.25
	SD/NL		34	140	0	0	0	13	35.0	26	2	8	2	1	35	1	1	0	0	14	13	1	1	.500	2	3.34
93	PHI/NL		64	256	0	0	0	13	61.2	54	4	21	2	1	67	2	0	2	1	22	20	3	2	.600	0	2.92
16 YR TOTALS			670	4024	1	0	0	256	962.2	899	56	296	61	17	731	50	40	21	7	382	332	39	37	.513	49	3.10

Anderson, Brian James — BL/TL — b.4/16/72   CAL93 1/3

YR	TM/LG	CL	G	TBF	GS	CG	SHO	GF	IP	H	HR	BB	IBB	HB	SO	SH	SF	WP	BK	R	ER	W	L	PCT	SV	ERA
93	MID/TEX	AA	2	47	2	0	0	0	10.2	16	2	0	0	0	9	0	0	0	0	5	4	0	1	.000	0	3.38
	VAN/PCL	AAA	2	42	2	0	0	0	8.0	13	3	6	0	1	2	0	2	1	1	12	11	0	1	.000	0	12.38
	CAL/AL		4	45	1	0	0	3	11.1	11	1	2	0	0	4	0	0	0	0	5	5	0	0	.000	0	3.97

Anderson, Michael James "Mike" — BR/TR — b.7/30/66   CIN 6/10/88

YR	TM/LG	CL	G	TBF	GS	CG	SHO	GF	IP	H	HR	BB	IBB	HB	SO	SH	SF	WP	BK	R	ER	W	L	PCT	SV	ERA
88	RED/GCL	R	2	34	2	0	0	0	7.1	6	0	5	0	0	11	0	0	3	4	7	4	0	1	.000	0	4.91
	BIL/PIO	R+	17	192	4	0	0	12	44.1	36	1	21	1	2	52	0	4	4	0	17	16	3	1	.750	2	3.25
89	GRE/SAL	A	25	647	25	4	2	0	154.1	117	7	72	0	8	154	2	3	9	2	64	49	11	6	.647	0	2.86
90	CR/MID	A	23	613	23	2	0	0	138.1	134	6	62	0	5	101	4	7	10	0	67	52	10	5	.667	0	3.38
91	CHT/SOU	AA	28	698	26	3	3	1	155.1	142	8	93	2	8	115	4	4	17	1	94	76	10	9	.526	0	4.40
92	CHT/SOU	AA	28	716	26	4	4	1	171.2	155	4	61	1	7	149	0	3	15	3	59	48	13	7	.650	0	2.52
93	CHT/SOU	AA	2	54	2	0	0	0	15.0	10	0	8	0	0	14	1	1	0	0	3	2	1	1	.500	0	1.20
	IND/AMA	AAA	23	647	23	2	1	0	151.0	150	10	56	0	4	111	7	7	8	0	73	63	10	6	.625	0	3.75
	CIN/NL		3	30	0	0	0	0	5.1	12	3	3	0	0	4	0	0	0	0	11	11	0	0	.000	0	18.56

Appier, Robert Kevin "Kevin" — BR/TR — b.12/6/67 KC87 1/9

YR	TM/LG	CL	G	TBF	GS	CG	SHO	GF	IP	H	HR	BB	IBB	HB	SO	SH	SF	WP	BK	R	ER	W	L	PCT	SV	ERA
87	EUG/NWL	A-	15	340	15	0	0	0	77.0	81	2	29	0	2	72	5	6	7	1	43	26	5	2	.714	0	3.04
88	BC/FSL	A+	24	601	24	1	0	0	147.1	134	1	39	5	2	112	4	6	7	4	58	45	10	9	.526	0	2.75
	MEM/SOU	AA	3	75	3	0	0	0	19.2	11	0	7	0	0	18	0	1	1	0	5	4	2	0	1.000	0	1.83
89	KC/AL		6	106	5	0	0	0	21.2	34	3	12	1	0	10	0	3	0	0	22	22	1	4	.200	0	9.14
	OMA/AMA	AAA	22	594	22	3	2	0	139.0	141	6	42	1	2	109	2	4	5	1	70	61	8	8	.500	0	3.95
90	OMA/AMA	AAA	3	69	3	0	0	0	18.0	15	0	3	0	1	17	0	0	0	0	3	3	2	0	1.000	0	1.50
	KC/AL		32	784	24	3	3	1	185.2	179	13	54	2	6	127	5	9	6	1	67	57	12	8	.600	0	2.76
91	KC/AL		34	881	31	6	3	1	207.2	205	13	61	3	2	158	8	6	7	1	97	79	13	10	.565	0	3.42
92	KC/AL		30	852	30	3	0	0	208.1	167	10	68	5	2	150	8	3	4	0	59	57	15	8	.652	0	2.46
93	KC/AL		34	953	34	5	5	0	238.2	183	8	81	3	1	186	3	5	5	0	74	68	18	8	.692	0	*2.56
5 YR TOTALS			136	3576	124	17	7	2	862.0	768	47	276	14	11	631	24	26	22	2	319	283	59	38	.608	0	2.95

Aquino, Luis Antonio — BR/TR — b.5/19/64 TOR 6/19/82

YR	TM/LG	CL	G	TBF	GS	CG	SHO	GF	IP	H	HR	BB	IBB	HB	SO	SH	SF	WP	BK	R	ER	W	L	PCT	SV	ERA
84	KIN/CAR	A+	53	292	0	0	0	42	70.0	50	3	37	4	3	78	7	0	2	1	21	21	5	6	.455	20	2.70
	KNO/SOU	AA	3	19	0	0	0	2	4.0	3	1	3	1	1	7	0	1	0	1	4	4	0	0	.000	0	9.00
85	KNO/SOU	AA	50	336	0	0	0	42	83.0	58	4	32	0	0	82	5	3	1	0	29	24	5	7	.417	20	2.60
86	SYR/INT	AAA	43	351	6	0	0	27	84.1	70	7	34	2	1	60	1	2	5	0	30	27	3	7	.300	10	2.88
	TOR/AL		7	50	0	0	0	3	11.1	14	2	3	1	0	5	0	1	1	0	8	8	1	1	.500	0	6.35
87	SYR/INT	AAA	26	379	11	0	0	6	84.2	75	11	51	1	8	68	1	2	2	1	46	45	6	7	.462	0	4.78
	OMA/AMA	AAA	14	203	4	1	1	5	50.2	42	2	16	1	0	29	2	1	0	0	15	13	3	2	.600	1	2.31
88	OMA/AMA	AAA	25	525	16	1	1	3	129.1	106	3	50	3	5	93	3	3	1	0	43	41	8	3	.727	0	2.85
	KC/AL		7	136	5	1	1	0	29.0	33	1	17	0	1	11	0	1	1	0	15	9	1	0	1.000	0	2.79
89	KC/AL		34	591	16	2	1	4	141.1	148	6	35	4	4	68	2	4	0	0	62	55	6	8	.429	0	3.50
90	KC/AL		20	287	3	1	0	3	68.1	59	6	27	6	4	28	5	2	3	1	25	24	4	1	.800	0	3.16
91	KC/AL		38	661	18	1	1	9	157.0	152	10	47	5	4	80	2	7	1	0	67	60	8	4	.667	3	3.44
92	OMA/AMA	AAA	2	46	2	0	0	0	10.1	13	1	4	0	0	3	0	1	0	0	3	3	0	0	.000	0	2.61
	KC/AL		15	293	13	0	0	0	67.2	81	5	20	1	1	11	2	1	1	0	35	34	3	6	.333	0	4.52
93	FLO/NL		38	471	13	0	0	5	110.2	115	4	40	1	5	67	7	2	4	0	43	42	6	8	.429	3	3.42
7 YR TOTALS			159	2489	68	5	3	28	585.1	602	36	189	18	19	270	18	20	15	3	255	232	29	28	.509	3	3.57

Armstrong, Jack William — BR/TR — b.3/7/65 CIN87 1/18

YR	TM/LG	CL	G	TBF	GS	CG	SHO	GF	IP	H	HR	BB	IBB	HB	SO	SH	SF	WP	BK	R	ER	W	L	PCT	SV	ERA
87	BIL/PIO	R+	5	87	4	0	0	0	20.1	16	0	12	0	0	29	1	0	1	0	7	6	2	1	.667	0	2.66
	VER/EAS	AA	5	152	5	2	1	0	35.2	24	0	23	4	1	39	3	2	3	1	12	12	1	2	.333	0	3.03
88	NAS/AMA	AAA	17	476	17	4	1	0	120.0	84	6	38	1	2	116	5	6	3	2	44	40	5	5	.500	0	3.00
	CIN/NL		14	293	13	0	0	0	65.1	63	6	38	2	0	45	4	3	5	2	44	42	4	7	.364	0	5.79
89	NAS/AMA	AAA	25	738	24	12	6	0	182.2	144	10	58	2	6	152	10	3	2	5	63	59	13	9	.591	0	2.91
	CIN/NL		9	187	8	0	0	1	42.2	40	5	21	0	0	23	2	1	0	0	24	22	2	3	.400	0	4.64
90	CIN/NL		29	704	29	2	1	1	166.0	151	9	59	7	6	110	8	5	7	5	72	63	12	9	.571	0	3.42
91	NAS/AMA	AAA	6	143	6	2	1	0	37.1	31	4	15	1	3	28	1	3	0	0	14	11	2	0	1.000	0	2.65
	CIN/NL		27	611	24	1	0	1	139.2	158	25	54	2	2	93	6	9	7	0	90	85	7	13	.350	0	5.48
92	CLE/AL		35	735	23	1	0	5	166.2	176	23	67	0	3	114	6	6	6	3	100	86	6	15	.286	0	4.64
93	FLO/NL		36	879	33	0	0	2	196.1	210	29	78	6	7	118	8	10	7	2	105	98	9	17	.346	0	4.49
6 YR TOTALS			150	3409	128	4	1	10	776.2	798	99	317	21	18	503	34	35	25	13	435	396	40	64	.385	0	4.59

Arocha, Rene — BR/TR — b.2/24/66 SL 11/21/91

YR	TM/LG	CL	G	TBF	GS	CG	SHO	GF	IP	H	HR	BB	IBB	HB	SO	SH	SF	WP	BK	R	ER	W	L	PCT	SV	ERA
92	LOU/AMA	AAA	25	705	25	3	1	0	166.2	145	8	65	0	6	128	9	4	3	2	59	50	12	7	.632	0	2.70
93	STL/NL		32	774	29	1	0	0	188.0	197	20	31	2	3	96	8	5	3	1	89	79	11	8	.579	0	3.78

Ashby, Andrew Jason "Andy" — BR/TR — b.7/11/67 PHI 5/4/86

YR	TM/LG	CL	G	TBF	GS	CG	SHO	GF	IP	H	HR	BB	IBB	HB	SO	SH	SF	WP	BK	R	ER	W	L	PCT	SV	ERA
86	BEN/NWL	A-	16	0	6	0	0	4	60.0	56	3	34	1	2	45	0	0	3	1	40	33	1	2	.333	2	4.95
87	SPA/SAL	A	13	301	13	1	0	0	64.1	73	8	38	2	2	52	3	1	9	1	45	40	4	6	.400	0	5.60
	UTI/NYP	A-	13	264	13	0	0	0	60.0	56	3	36	3	1	51	2	1	7	0	38	27	3	7	.300	0	4.05
88	BAT/NYP	A-	6	174	6	2	1	0	44.2	25	3	16	0	1	32	2	0	0	2	11	8	3	1	.750	0	1.61
	SPA/SAL	A	3	68	3	0	0	0	16.2	13	0	7	0	0	16	0	0	2	0	7	5	1	1	.500	0	2.70
89	SPA/SAL	A	17	463	17	3	1	0	106.2	95	8	49	0	5	100	2	4	4	1	48	34	5	9	.357	0	2.87
	CLE/FSL	A+	6	173	6	2	1	0	43.2	28	0	14	0	1	44	1	0	4	1	9	6	1	4	.200	0	1.24
90	REA/EAS	AA	23	591	23	4	1	0	139.2	134	3	48	0	4	94	5	4	10	2	65	53	10	7	.588	0	3.42
91	SCR/INT	AAA	26	691	26	6	3	0	161.1	144	12	60	2	9	113	3	4	7	0	78	62	11	11	.500	0	3.46
	PHI/NL		8	186	8	0	0	0	42.0	41	5	19	0	3	26	1	3	6	0	28	28	1	5	.167	0	6.00
92	SCR/INT	AAA	7	133	7	0	0	0	33.0	23	4	14	0	3	18	1	1	4	0	13	11	2	0	.000	0	3.00
	PHI/NL		10	171	10	0	0	0	37.0	42	6	21	0	1	24	0	2	3	0	31	31	1	3	.250	0	7.54
93	CS/PCL	AAA	7	181	6	1	0	0	41.2	45	2	12	0	3	35	2	1	3	0	25	19	4	2	.667	0	4.10
	COL/NL		20	277	9	0	0	3	54.0	89	5	32	4	3	33	3	3	2	3	54	51	0	4	.000	0	8.50
	SD/NL		12	300	12	0	0	0	69.0	79	14	24	1	1	44	3	4	4	0	46	42	3	6	.333	0	5.48
	YEAR		32	577	21	0	0	3	123.0	168	19	56	4	7	77	6	7	6	3	100	93	3	10	.231	1	6.80
3 YR TOTALS			50	934	37	0	0	3	202.0	251	30	96	5	8	127	9	12	14	3	159	152	5	18	.217	1	6.77

Assenmacher, Paul Andre — BL/TL — b.12/10/60 ATL 7/10/83

YR	TM/LG	CL	G	TBF	GS	CG	SHO	GF	IP	H	HR	BB	IBB	HB	SO	SH	SF	WP	BK	R	ER	W	L	PCT	SV	ERA
84	DUR/CAR	A+	26	640	24	3	1	1	147.1	153	16	52	0	4	147	11	3	5	1	78	70	6	11	.353	0	4.28
85	DUR/CAR	A+	14	170	0	0	0	11	38.1	38	1	13	4	1	36	6	0	0	0	16	14	3	2	.600	1	3.29
	GRE/SOU	AA	29	212	0	0	0	21	52.2	47	0	11	3	1	59	3	1	1	0	16	15	6	0	1.000	4	2.56

Assenmacher, Paul Andre (continued)

YR	TM/LG	CL	G	TBF	GS	CG	SHO	GF	IP	H	HR	BB	IBB	HB	SO	SH	SF	WP	BK	R	ER	W	L	PCT	SV	ERA
86	ATL/NL		61	287	0	0	0	27	68.1	61	5	26	4	0	56	7	1	2	3	23	19	7	3	.700	7	2.50
87	RIC/INT	AAA	4	107	4	0	0	0	24.2	30	4	8	1	0	21	0	0	0	1	11	10	1	2	.333	0	3.65
	ATL/NL		52	251	0	0	0	10	54.2	58	8	24	4	1	39	2	1	0	0	41	31	1	1	.500	2	5.10
88	ATL/NL		64	329	0	0	0	32	79.1	72	4	32	11	1	71	8	1	7	0	28	27	8	7	.533	5	3.06
89	ATL/NL		49	247	0	0	0	14	57.2	55	2	16	7	1	64	7	2	3	1	26	23	1	3	.250	0	3.59
	CHI/NL		14	84	0	0	0	3	19.0	19	1	12	1	0	15	2	1	0	0	11	11	2	1	.667	0	5.21
	YEAR		63	331	0	0	0	17	76.2	74	3	28	8	1	79	9	3	3	1	37	34	3	4	.429	0	3.99
90	CHI/NL		74	426	1	0	0	21	103.0	90	10	36	8	1	95	10	3	2	0	33	32	7	2	.778	10	2.80
91	CHI/NL		75	427	0	0	0	31	102.2	85	10	31	6	3	117	8	4	4	0	41	37	7	8	.467	15	3.24
92	CHI/NL		70	298	0	0	0	23	68.0	72	6	26	5	3	67	1	2	4	0	32	31	4	4	.500	8	4.10
93	CHI/NL		46	166	0	0	0	15	38.2	44	5	13	3	0	34	0	0	0	0	15	15	2	1	.667	0	3.49
	NY/AL		26	71	0	0	0	6	17.1	10	0	9	3	1	11	4	0	0	0	6	6	2	2	.500	0	3.12
	YEAR		72	237	0	0	0	21	56.0	54	5	22	6	1	45	4	0	0	0	21	21	4	3	.571	0	3.38
8 YR TOTALS			**531**	**2586**	**1**	**0**	**0**	**182**	**608.2**	**566**	**51**	**225**	**52**	**11**	**569**	**49**	**15**	**22**	**4**	**256**	**232**	**41**	**32**	**.562**	**47**	**3.43**

Astacio, Pedro Julio — BR/TR — b.11/28/69 LA 11/21/87

YR	TM/LG	CL	G	TBF	GS	CG	SHO	GF	IP	H	HR	BB	IBB	HB	SO	SH	SF	WP	BK	R	ER	W	L	PCT	SV	ERA
89	DOD/GCL	R	12	321	12	1	1	0	76.2	77	3	12	0	4	52	4	2	4	2	30	27	7	3	.700	0	3.17
90	VB/FSL	A+	8	215	8	0	0	0	47.0	54	3	23	0	1	41	1	1	4	5	39	33	1	5	.167	0	6.32
	YAK/NWL	A-	3	79	3	0	0	0	20.2	9	0	4	0	2	22	0	0	3	0	8	4	2	0	1.000	0	1.74
	BAK/CAL	A+	10	213	7	1	0	0	52.0	46	3	15	1	3	34	1	1	2	1	22	16	5	2	.714	0	2.77
91	VB/FSL	A+	9	223	9	3	1	0	59.1	44	0	8	0	1	45	2	1	2	0	19	11	5	3	.625	0	1.67
	SA/TEX	AA	19	497	19	2	1	0	113.0	142	3	39	3	3	62	5	3	4	2	67	60	4	11	.267	0	4.78
92	ALB/PCL	AAA	24	442	15	1	0	4	98.2	115	8	44	1	2	66	3	1	6	1	68	60	6	6	.500	0	5.47
	LA/NL		11	341	11	4	4	0	82.0	80	1	20	4	2	43	3	2	1	0	23	18	5	5	.500	0	1.98
93	LA/NL		31	777	31	3	2	0	186.1	165	14	68	5	5	122	7	8	8	9	80	74	14	9	.609	0	3.57
2 YR TOTALS			**42**	**1118**	**42**	**7**	**6**	**0**	**268.1**	**245**	**15**	**88**	**9**	**7**	**165**	**10**	**10**	**9**	**9**	**103**	**92**	**19**	**14**	**.576**	**0**	**3.09**

Austin, James Parker "Jim" — BR/TR — b.12/7/63 SD86 6/144

YR	TM/LG	CL	G	TBF	GS	CG	SHO	GF	IP	H	HR	BB	IBB	HB	SO	SH	SF	WP	BK	R	ER	W	L	PCT	SV	ERA
86	SPO/NWL	A-	28	0	0	0	0	19	59.2	53	1	22	2	1	74	0	0	7	0	24	15	5	4	.556	5	2.26
87	CHS/SAL	A	31	642	21	2	1	3	152.0	138	10	56	2	1	123	4	1	20	1	89	71	7	10	.412	0	4.20
88	RIV/CAL	A+	12	333	12	2	1	0	80.0	65	5	35	0	2	73	2	3	2	0	31	24	6	2	.750	0	2.70
	WIC/TEX	AA	12	313	12	4	1	0	73.0	76	9	23	0	1	52	2	3	10	0	46	39	5	6	.455	0	4.81
89	STO/CAL	A+	7	204	7	0	0	0	48.1	51	3	14	0	4	44	2	1	2	0	19	14	3	3	.500	0	2.61
	EP/TEX	AA	22	406	13	2	0	5	85.0	121	4	34	1	4	69	2	3	4	0	60	55	3	10	.231	1	5.82
90	EP/TEX	AA	38	384	3	0	0	24	92.1	91	5	26	4	1	77	3	2	8	0	36	25	11	3	.786	6	2.44
91	DEN/AMA	AAA	20	184	3	0	0	10	44.0	35	4	24	3	2	37	0	2	1	0	12	12	6	3	.667	3	2.45
	MIL/AL		5	46	0	0	0	1	8.2	8	1	11	1	3	3	1	1	0	0	8	8	0	0	.000	0	8.31
92	MIL/AL		47	235	0	0	0	24	58.1	38	2	32	4	2	30	1	1	1	0	13	12	5	2	.714	0	1.85
93	MIL/AL		31	137	0	0	0	0	33.0	28	3	11	1	1	15	1	0	4	0	15	14	1	2	.333	0	3.82
	NO/AMA	AAA	8	72	0	0	0	0	16.0	17	3	7	0	0	7	0	1	4	1	11	9	1	2	.333	0	5.06
3 YR TOTALS			**83**	**418**	**0**	**0**	**0**	**21**	**100.0**	**74**	**6**	**56**	**8**	**6**	**48**	**4**	**2**	**6**	**0**	**36**	**34**	**6**	**4**	**.600**	**0**	**3.06**

Avery, Steven Thomas "Steve" — BL/TL — b.4/14/70 ATL88 1/3

YR	TM/LG	CL	G	TBF	GS	CG	SHO	GF	IP	H	HR	BB	IBB	HB	SO	SH	SF	WP	BK	R	ER	W	L	PCT	SV	ERA
88	PUL/APP	R+	10	249	10	3	2	0	66.0	38	2	19	0	1	80	1	1	5	1	16	11	7	1	.875	0	1.50
89	DUR/CAR	A+	13	337	13	3	1	0	86.2	59	5	20	1	1	90	5	0	4	1	22	14	6	4	.600	0	1.45
	GRE/SOU	AA	13	341	13	1	0	0	84.1	68	3	34	0	1	75	4	1	4	0	32	26	6	3	.667	0	2.77
90	RIC/INT	AAA	13	343	13	3	0	0	82.1	85	7	21	0	2	69	6	2	5	0	35	31	5	5	.500	0	3.39
	ATL/NL		21	466	20	1	1	1	99.0	121	7	45	2	2	75	14	4	4	1	79	62	3	11	.214	0	5.64
91	ATL/NL		35	868	35	3	1	0	210.1	189	21	65	0	3	137	8	4	4	1	89	79	18	8	.692	0	3.38
92	ATL/NL		35	969	35	2	2	0	233.2	216	14	71	3	0	129	12	8	7	3	95	83	11	11	.500	0	3.20
93	ATL/NL		35	891	35	3	1	0	223.1	216	14	43	5	0	125	12	8	3	1	81	73	18	6	.750	0	2.94
4 YR TOTALS			**126**	**3194**	**125**	**9**	**5**	**1**	**766.1**	**742**	**56**	**224**	**10**	**5**	**466**	**46**	**24**	**19**	**6**	**344**	**297**	**50**	**36**	**.581**	**0**	**3.49**

Ayala, Robert Joseph "Bobby" — BR/TR — b.7/8/69 CIN 6/27/88

YR	TM/LG	CL	G	TBF	GS	CG	SHO	GF	IP	H	HR	BB	IBB	HB	SO	SH	SF	WP	BK	R	ER	W	L	PCT	SV	ERA
88	RED/GCL	R	20	153	0	0	0	15	33.0	34	0	12	0	3	24	3	3	1	0	23	14	0	4	.000	3	3.82
89	GRE/SAL	A	22	467	19	1	0	1	105.1	97	7	50	0	4	70	2	3	10	2	73	48	5	8	.385	0	4.10
90	CR/MID	A	18	215	7	3	1	3	53.1	40	6	18	0	4	59	2	1	6	0	24	20	6	1	.600	1	3.38
	CHW/SAL	A	21	287	4	2	1	8	74.0	48	2	21	1	3	73	2	1	0	0	23	20	6	1	.857	2	2.43
91	CHT/SOU	AA	39	403	8	1	0	16	90.2	79	10	58	4	4	92	4	3	1	0	52	47	3	1	.750	4	4.67
92	CHT/SOU	AA	27	690	27	3	3	0	162.2	152	14	58	0	11	154	2	2	9	0	75	64	12	6	.667	0	3.54
	CIN/NL		5	127	5	0	0	0	29.0	33	1	6	2	1	23	2	0	0	0	15	14	2	1	.667	0	4.34
93	IND/AMA	AAA	5	123	5	0	0	0	27.0	36	1	12	1	1	19	3	0	1	0	19	17	0	2	.000	0	5.67
	CIN/NL		43	450	9	0	0	8	98.0	106	16	45	4	7	65	9	2	5	0	72	61	7	10	.412	3	5.60
2 YR TOTALS			**48**	**577**	**14**	**0**	**0**	**8**	**127.0**	**139**	**17**	**58**	**6**	**8**	**88**	**11**	**2**	**5**	**0**	**87**	**75**	**9**	**11**	**.450**	**3**	**5.31**

Ayrault, Robert Cunningham "Bob" — BR/TR — b.4/27/66 RENO 6/2/89

YR	TM/LG	CL	G	TBF	GS	CG	SHO	GF	IP	H	HR	BB	IBB	HB	SO	SH	SF	WP	BK	R	ER	W	L	PCT	SV	ERA
89	REN/CAL	A+	24	478	14	3	1	5	109.2	104	7	57	3	11	91	3	4	3	3	56	46	7	4	.636	0	3.78
	BAT/NYP	A-	4	93	3	2	1	1	26.0	13	1	7	0	2	20	1	0	0	0	5	4	2	1	.667	0	1.38
	REA/EAS	AA	2	33	1	0	0	0	8.2	3	0	4	0	0	4	0	0	0	0	1	1	0	0	.000	0	1.04
90	REA/EAS	AA	44	432	9	0	0	29	109.1	77	4	34	1	2	84	3	5	2	0	33	28	4	6	.400	10	2.30
91	SCR/INT	AAA	68	433	0	0	0	21	98.2	91	12	47	4	5	103	5	5	5	0	58	53	8	5	.615	3	4.83

(continued)

Ayrault, Robert Cunningham "Bob" (continued)

YR	TM/LG	CL	G	TBF	GS	CG	SHO	GF	IP	H	HR	BB	IBB	HB	SO	SH	SF	WP	BK	R	ER	W	L	PCT	SV	ERA
92	SCR/INT	AAA	20	110	0	0	0	14	25.1	19	4	15	3	1	30	3	2	0	0	15	14	5	1	.833	6	4.97
	PHI/NL		30	178	0	0	0	7	43.1	32	4	17	1	1	27	4	3	0	0	16	15	2	2	.500	2	3.12
93	SCR/INT	AAA	5	33	0	0	0	3	7.1	8	0	3	1	0	9	0	0	0	0	2	1	0	1	.000	0	1.23
	CAL/PCL	AAA	3	22	0	0	0	2	4.1	8	0	2	0	0	3	0	0	0	0	5	5	0	0	.000	1	10.38
	ALB/PCL	AAA	11	74	0	0	0	1	14.2	21	2	7	3	2	13	1	0	0	0	10	10	2	2	.500	0	6.14
	PHI/NL		10	59	0	0	0	3	10.1	18	1	10	1	1	8	0	0	0	1	11	11	2	0	1.000	0	9.58
	SEA/AL		14	80	0	0	0	6	19.2	18	1	6	1	0	7	1	2	0	0	8	7	1	1	.500	0	3.20
	YEAR		24	139	0	0	0	9	30.0	36	2	16	2	1	15	1	2	1	0	19	18	3	1	.750	0	5.40
2 YR TOTALS			**54**	**317**	**0**	**0**	**0**	**16**	**73.1**	**68**	**2**	**33**	**3**	**2**	**42**	**5**	**5**	**1**	**0**	**35**	**33**	**5**	**3**	**.625**	**0**	**4.05**

Bailey, Phillip Cory "Cory" — BR/TR — b.1/24/71
BOS91 18/408

YR	TM/LG	CL	G	TBF	GS	CG	SHO	GF	IP	H	HR	BB	IBB	HB	SO	SH	SF	WP	BK	R	ER	W	L	PCT	SV	ERA
91	RS/GCL	R	1	9	0	0	0	1	2.0	2	0	1	0	0	1	0	0	0	0	1	0	0	0	.000	1	0.00
	ELM/NYP	A-	28	151	0	0	0	25	39.0	19	2	12	0	3	54	1	0	2	0	10	8	2	4	.333	15	1.85
92	LYN/CAR	A+	49	272	0	0	0	43	66.1	43	3	30	2	2	87	6	2	5	0	20	18	5	7	.417	23	2.44
93	PAW/INT	AAA	52	264	0	0	0	40	65.2	48	1	31	3	1	59	2	2	5	1	21	21	4	5	.444	20	2.88
	BOS/AL		11	66	0	0	0	5	15.2	12	0	12	0	0	11	1	1	2	1	7	6	0	1	.000	0	3.45

Ballard, Jeffrey Scott "Jeff" — BL/TL — b.8/13/63
BAL85 4/177

YR	TM/LG	CL	G	TBF	GS	CG	SHO	GF	IP	H	HR	BB	IBB	HB	SO	SH	SF	WP	BK	R	ER	W	L	PCT	SV	ERA
85	NEW/NYP	A-	13	381	13	6	3	0	96.0	78	2	20	1	0	91	1	1	1	1	20	15	10	2	.833	0	1.41
86	HAG/CAR	A+	17	466	17	5	2	0	112.0	106	3	32	1	3	115	0	1	3	2	39	23	9	5	.643	0	1.85
	CHA/SOU	AA	10	261	10	0	0	0	59.2	70	7	20	1	0	35	0	0	0	1	29	22	5	2	.714	0	3.32
	ROC/INT	AAA	2	34	2	0	0	0	6.1	11	1	3	0	1	7	0	1	0	0	6	5	0	2	.000	0	7.11
87	ROC/INT	AAA	23	647	23	4	1	0	160.1	151	15	35	2	5	114	3	6	2	0	60	55	13	4	.765	0	3.09
	BAL/AL		14	327	14	0	0	0	69.2	100	15	35	1	0	27	0	1	0	0	60	51	2	8	.200	0	6.59
88	ROC/INT	AAA	9	247	8	3	1	0	60.2	56	4	11	0	1	32	1	1	3	1	26	20	4	3	.571	0	2.97
	BAL/AL		25	654	25	6	1	0	153.1	167	15	42	2	6	41	3	3	2	2	83	75	8	12	.400	0	4.40
89	BAL/AL		35	912	35	4	1	0	215.1	240	16	57	5	4	62	10	5	3	0	95	82	18	8	.692	0	3.43
90	BAL/AL		44	578	17	0	0	6	133.1	152	22	42	6	3	50	5	2	2	1	79	73	2	11	.154	0	4.93
91	ROC/INT	AAA	7	221	7	3	0	0	51.0	63	2	10	0	0	19	1	6	1	0	27	25	3	3	.500	0	4.41
	BAL/AL		26	540	22	0	0	1	123.2	153	16	28	2	0	37	1	3	3	1	91	77	6	12	.333	0	5.60
92	LOU/AMA	AAA	24	653	24	3	1	0	160.2	164	16	34	1	2	76	2	8	2	1	57	45	12	8	.600	0	2.52
93	BUF/AMA	AAA	12	311	12	1	0	0	74.2	79	4	17	0	2	40	3	3	0	0	22	19	6	1	.857	0	2.29
	PIT/NL		25	234	5	0	0	4	53.2	70	3	15	3	2	16	5	1	2	0	31	29	4	1	.800	0	4.86
6 YR TOTALS			**169**	**3245**	**118**	**10**	**2**	**11**	**749.0**	**882**	**87**	**219**	**19**	**17**	**233**	**24**	**15**	**12**	**5**	**439**	**387**	**40**	**52**	**.435**	**0**	**4.65**

Bankhead, Michael Scott "Scott" — BR/TR — b.7/31/63
KC84 1/16

YR	TM/LG	CL	G	TBF	GS	CG	SHO	GF	IP	H	HR	BB	IBB	HB	SO	SH	SF	WP	BK	R	ER	W	L	PCT	SV	ERA
85	MEM/SOU	AA	24	592	24	2	1	0	140.1	117	16	56	0	3	128	0	3	3	0	63	56	8	6	.571	0	3.59
86	OMA/AMA	AAA	7	187	7	2	0	0	48.1	31	2	14	1	0	34	0	0	1	3	11	8	2	2	.500	0	1.49
	KC/AL		24	517	17	0	0	2	121.0	121	14	37	7	3	94	5	5	1	0	66	62	8	9	.471	0	4.61
87	SEA/AL		27	642	25	2	0	1	149.1	168	35	37	0	3	95	3	6	2	2	96	90	9	8	.529	0	5.42
88	SB/CAL	A+	2	43	2	0	0	0	11.0	6	0	4	0	1	6	1	0	0	0	3	2	0	0	.000	0	1.64
	CAL/PCL	AAA	2	51	2	0	0	0	11.0	15	2	5	0	0	5	0	0	0	0	9	9	1	1	.500	0	7.36
	SEA/AL		21	557	21	2	1	0	135.0	115	8	38	5	1	102	3	1	3	1	53	46	7	9	.438	0	3.07
89	SEA/AL		33	862	33	3	2	0	210.1	187	19	63	1	3	140	4	8	2	0	84	78	14	6	.700	0	3.34
90	CAL/PCL	AAA	2	32	2	0	0	0	7.0	9	1	3	0	0	7	0	1	0	0	6	5	0	1	.000	0	6.43
	SEA/AL		4	63	4	0	0	0	13.0	18	2	7	0	0	10	0	2	1	0	16	16	0	2	.000	0	11.08
91	SB/CAL	A+	2	24	2	0	0	0	5.1	4	2	1	0	1	4	0	0	0	0	4	3	1	0	.000	0	5.06
	BEL/NWL	A-	1	14	0	0	0	1	4.0	1	0	1	0	0	8	0	0	0	0	0	0	1	0	1.000	0	0.00
	CAL/PCL	AAA	5	33	0	0	0	2	8.2	7	0	1	0	0	10	0	0	0	0	1	1	0	0	.000	1	1.04
	SEA/AL		17	271	9	0	0	2	60.2	73	8	21	2	1	28	0	2	2	0	35	33	3	6	.333	0	4.90
92	CIN/NL		54	299	0	0	0	10	70.2	57	4	29	5	3	53	3	3	6	0	26	23	10	4	.714	1	2.93
93	BOS/AL		40	272	0	0	0	4	64.1	59	7	29	3	0	47	3	4	1	0	28	25	2	1	.667	0	3.50
8 YR TOTALS			**220**	**3483**	**109**	**7**	**3**	**19**	**824.1**	**798**	**97**	**261**	**23**	**15**	**569**	**21**	**31**	**16**	**3**	**404**	**373**	**53**	**45**	**.541**	**1**	**4.07**

Banks, Willie Anthony — BR/TR — b.2/27/69
MIN87 1/3

YR	TM/LG	CL	G	TBF	GS	CG	SHO	GF	IP	H	HR	BB	IBB	HB	SO	SH	SF	WP	BK	R	ER	W	L	PCT	SV	ERA
87	ELI/APP	R+	13	332	13	0	0	0	65.2	73	3	62	0	3	71	3	4	28	3	71	51	1	8	.111	0	6.99
88	KEN/MID	A	24	580	24	0	0	0	125.2	109	3	107	2	4	113	2	5	14	2	73	52	10	10	.500	0	3.72
89	VIS/CAL	A+	27	723	27	7	4	0	174.0	122	5	85	0	10	173	2	7	22	1	70	50	12	9	.571	0	2.59
	ORL/SOU	AA	1	30	1	0	0	0	7.0	10	0	0	0	0	9	0	0	2	0	4	4	1	0	1.000	0	5.14
90	ORL/SOU	AA	28	737	28	1	0	0	162.2	161	15	98	0	7	114	1	8	6	1	93	71	7	9	.438	0	3.93
91	POR/PCL	AAA	25	653	24	1	1	1	146.1	156	6	76	2	4	63	2	4	14	2	81	74	9	8	.529	0	4.55
	MIN/AL		5	85	3	0	0	2	17.1	21	1	12	0	0	16	0	2	0	0	15	11	1	1	.500	0	5.71
92	POR/PCL	AAA	11	310	11	2	1	0	75.0	62	2	34	0	0	41	2	1	5	1	20	16	6	1	.857	0	1.92
	MIN/AL		16	324	12	0	0	2	71.0	80	6	37	0	2	37	2	2	5	0	46	45	4	4	.500	0	5.70
93	MIN/AL		31	754	30	0	0	0	171.1	186	17	78	2	3	138	4	9	9	5	91	77	11	12	.478	0	4.04
3 YR TOTALS			**52**	**1163**	**45**	**0**	**0**	**5**	**259.2**	**287**	**24**	**127**	**2**	**5**	**191**	**6**	**9**	**17**	**6**	**152**	**133**	**16**	**17**	**.485**	**0**	**4.61**

Barnes, Brian Keith — BL/TL — b.3/25/67
MON89 4/97

YR	TM/LG	CL	G	TBF	GS	CG	SHO	GF	IP	H	HR	BB	IBB	HB	SO	SH	SF	WP	BK	R	ER	W	L	PCT	SV	ERA
89	JAM/NYP	A-	2	33	2	0	0	0	9.0	4	0	3	0	0	15	0	0	1	1	1	1	1	0	1.000	0	1.00
	WPB/FSL	A+	7	187	7	4	3	0	50.0	25	0	16	0	0	67	3	1	4	0	9	4	4	3	.571	0	0.72
	IND/AMA	AAA	1	24	1	0	0	0	6.0	5	0	2	0	0	5	0	0	0	0	1	1	1	0	1.000	0	1.50

Barnes, Brian Keith (continued)

YR	TM/LG	CL	G	TBF	GS	CG	SHO	GF	IP	H	HR	BB	IBB	HB	SO	SH	SF	WP	BK	R	ER	W	L	PCT	SV	ERA
90	JAC/SOU	AA	29	828	28	3	1	0	201.1	144	12	87	2	9	213	7	5	8	1	78	62	13	7	.650	0	2.77
	MON/NL		4	115	4	1	0	0	28.0	25	2	7	0	0	23	2	0	2	0	10	9	1	1	.500	0	2.89
91	WPB/FSL	A+	2	27	2	0	0	0	7.0	3	0	4	0	0	6	0	0	3	0	0	0	0	0	.000	0	0.00
	IND/AMA	AAA	2	44	2	0	0	0	11.0	6	0	8	0	1	10	1	0	0	0	2	2	1	0	1.000	0	1.64
	MON/NL		28	684	27	1	0	0	160.0	135	16	84	2	6	117	9	5	5	1	82	75	5	8	.385	0	4.22
92	IND/AMA	AAA	13	338	13	2	1	0	83.0	69	8	30	1	1	77	1	2	2	2	35	34	4	4	.500	0	3.69
	MON/NL		21	417	17	0	0	2	100.0	77	9	46	1	3	65	5	1	1	2	34	33	6	6	.500	0	2.97
93	MON/NL		52	442	8	0	0	8	100.0	105	9	48	2	0	60	8	3	5	1	53	49	2	6	.250	3	4.41
4 YR TOTALS			**105**	**1658**	**56**	**2**	**0**	**10**	**388.0**	**342**	**36**	**185**	**5**	**9**	**265**	**24**	**9**	**13**	**4**	**179**	**166**	**14**	**21**	**.400**	**3**	**3.85**

Batchelor, Richard Anthony "Rich" — BR/TR — b.4/8/67   NYA89 37/987

YR	TM/LG	CL	G	TBF	GS	CG	SHO	GF	IP	H	HR	BB	IBB	HB	SO	SH	SF	WP	BK	R	ER	W	L	PCT	SV	ERA
90	GRE/SAL	A	27	200	0	0	0	18	51.1	39	1	14	1	0	38	0	2	2	0	15	9	2	2	.500	8	1.58
91	FL/FSL	A+	50	269	0	0	0	41	62.0	55	1	22	5	1	58	6	1	4	0	28	19	4	7	.364	25	2.76
	ALB/EAS	AA	1	9	0	0	0	1	1.0	5	0	1	0	0	0	1	0	0	0	5	5	0	0	.000	0	45.00
92	ALB/EAS	AA	58	320	0	0	0	34	70.2	79	5	34	3	6	45	1	2	4	0	40	33	4	5	.444	7	4.20
93	ALB/EAS	AA	36	162	0	0	0	32	40.1	27	1	12	0	1	40	1	0	3	0	9	4	1	3	.250	19	0.89
	CMB/INT	AAA	15	74	0	0	0	14	16.1	14	0	8	1	1	17	0	1	2	0	5	5	1	1	.500	6	2.76
	STL/NL		9	45	0	0	0	2	10.0	14	1	3	1	0	4	1	0	0	0	12	9	0	0	.000	0	8.10

Bautista, Jose Joaquin — BR/TR — b.7/25/64   NYN 4/25/81

YR	TM/LG	CL	G	TBF	GS	CG	SHO	GF	IP	H	HR	BB	IBB	HB	SO	SH	SF	WP	BK	R	ER	W	L	PCT	SV	ERA
81	KIN/APP	R+	13	0	11	3	2	0	66.0	84	0	17	0	0	34	0	0	0	0	54	34	3	6	.333	0	4.64
82	KIN/APP	R+	14	0	4	0	0	0	38.0	61	3	19	0	0	13	0	0	3	1	44	38	0	4	.000	0	9.00
83	MET/GCL	R	13	0	13	2	0	0	81.0	66	2	32	0	0	44	0	0	5	0	31	21	4	3	.571	0	2.33
84	COL/SAL	A	19	544	18	5	3	0	135.0	121	10	35	3	0	96	7	2	3	1	52	47	13	4	.765	0	3.13
85	LYN/CAR	A+	27	674	25	7	3	1	169.0	145	8	33	0	3	109	2	3	3	1	49	44	15	8	.652	1	2.34
86	JAC/TEX	AA	7	109	4	0	0	0	21.2	36	3	6	1	0	13	0	0	3	0	22	20	0	1	.000	0	8.31
	LYN/CAR	A+	18	486	18	5	1	0	118.2	120	12	24	1	3	62	4	3	4	3	58	52	8	8	.500	0	3.94
87	JAC/TEX	AA	28	712	25	2	1	2	169.1	174	9	43	3	4	95	3	6	4	5	76	61	10	5	.667	0	3.24
88	BAL/AL		33	721	25	3	0	5	171.2	171	21	45	3	7	76	2	3	4	5	86	82	6	15	.286	0	4.30
89	ROC/INT	AAA	15	398	13	3	1	1	98.2	84	10	26	1	3	47	3	4	1	0	41	31	4	4	.500	0	2.83
	BAL/AL		15	325	10	0	0	4	78.0	84	17	15	1	0	30	1	1	0	0	46	46	3	4	.429	0	5.31
90	ROC/INT	AAA	27	442	13	3	0	4	108.2	115	10	15	0	4	50	3	5	3	5	51	49	7	8	.467	2	4.06
	BAL/AL		22	112	0	0	0	9	26.2	28	4	7	3	0	15	1	1	2	0	15	12	1	0	1.000	0	4.05
91	OC/AMA	AAA	11	139	3	0	0	4	32.1	38	4	6	0	1	22	1	0	0	0	19	19	0	3	.000	0	5.29
	MIA/FSL	A+	11	293	11	4	3	0	76.1	63	5	11	0	1	69	1	0	1	1	23	23	8	2	.800	0	2.71
	BAL/AL		5	34	0	0	0	3	5.1	13	1	5	0	1	3	0	0	1	0	10	10	0	0	.000	0	16.88
	ROC/INT	AAA	2	56	0	0	0	5	15.1	8	1	3	2	0	7	2	0	0	0	1	1	1	0	1.000	1	0.59
92	OMA/AMA	AAA	40	476	7	1	0	16	108.1	125	7	28	0	2	60	2	4	1	0	66	59	2	10	.167	2	4.90
	MEM/SOU	AA	1	25	1	0	0	0	6.0	6	1	2	0	1	7	0	1	0	0	3	3	1	0	1.000	0	4.50
93	CHI/NL		58	459	7	1	0	14	111.2	105	11	27	3	5	63	4	3	4	1	38	35	10	3	.769	2	2.82
5 YR TOTALS			**133**	**1651**	**42**	**4**	**0**	**35**	**393.1**	**401**	**54**	**99**	**9**	**14**	**187**	**8**	**8**	**11**	**6**	**195**	**185**	**20**	**23**	**.465**	**2**	**4.23**

Beck, Rodney Roy "Rod" — BR/TR — b.8/3/68   OAK86 13/327

YR	TM/LG	CL	G	TBF	GS	CG	SHO	GF	IP	H	HR	BB	IBB	HB	SO	SH	SF	WP	BK	R	ER	W	L	PCT	SV	ERA
86	MED/NWL	A-	13	0	6	0	0	5	32.2	47	4	11	1	1	21	0	0	4	0	25	19	1	3	.250	1	5.23
87	MED/NWL	A-	17	431	12	2	0	1	92.0	106	5	26	0	4	69	4	0	12	1	74	53	5	8	.385	0	5.18
88	CLI/MID	A	28	706	23	5	1	1	177.0	177	11	27	2	0	123	4	1	3	5	68	59	12	7	.632	0	3.00
89	SJ/CAL	A+	13	402	13	4	0	0	97.1	91	5	26	1	3	88	1	3	2	1	29	26	11	2	.846	0	2.40
	SHR/TEX	AA	16	416	14	4	1	0	99.0	108	6	16	3	3	74	2	3	2	2	45	39	7	3	.700	0	3.55
90	PHO/PCL	AAA	12	345	12	2	0	0	76.2	100	8	18	1	1	43	2	4	6	0	51	42	4	7	.364	0	4.93
	SHR/TEX	AA	14	366	14	2	1	0	93.0	85	4	17	1	1	71	4	1	7	0	26	23	10	3	.769	0	2.23
91	PHO/PCL	AAA	23	280	5	3	0	14	71.1	56	3	13	2	2	35	2	4	3	0	18	16	4	3	.571	6	2.02
	SF/NL		31	214	0	0	0	10	52.1	53	4	13	4	2	38	4	2	0	0	22	22	1	1	.500	1	3.78
92	SF/NL		65	352	0	0	0	42	92.0	62	4	15	2	2	87	6	2	5	1	20	18	3	3	.500	17	1.76
93	SF/NL		76	309	0	0	0	71	79.1	57	11	13	4	3	86	6	3	4	0	20	19	3	1	.750	48	2.16
3 YR TOTALS			**172**	**875**	**0**	**0**	**0**	**123**	**223.2**	**172**	**19**	**41**	**8**	**6**	**211**	**16**	**7**	**9**	**2**	**62**	**59**	**7**	**5**	**.583**	**66**	**2.37**

Bedrosian, Stephen Wayne "Steve" — BR/TR — b.12/6/57   ATL78 3/53

YR	TM/LG	CL	G	TBF	GS	CG	SHO	GF	IP	H	HR	BB	IBB	HB	SO	SH	SF	WP	BK	R	ER	W	L	PCT	SV	ERA
81	ATL/NL		15	106	1	0	0	5	24.1	15	2	15	2	1	9	0	1	0	0	14	12	1	2	.333	0	4.44
82	ATL/NL		64	567	3	0	0	30	137.2	102	7	57	5	4	123	9	2	6	0	39	37	8	6	.571	11	2.42
83	ATL/NL		70	504	1	0	0	52	120.0	100	11	51	8	4	114	8	4	1	0	50	48	9	10	.474	19	3.60
84	ATL/NL		40	345	4	0	0	28	83.2	65	5	33	1	1	81	1	1	4	0	23	22	9	6	.600	11	2.37
85	ATL/NL		37	907	37	0	0	0	206.2	198	17	111	6	5	134	6	7	6	0	101	88	7	15	.318	0	3.83
86	PHI/NL		68	381	0	0	0	56	90.1	79	12	34	10	2	82	3	5	1	0	39	34	8	6	.571	29	3.39
87	PHI/NL		65	366	0	0	0	56	89.0	79	11	28	1	1	74	2	1	3	1	31	28	5	3	.625	*40	2.83
88	MAI/INT	AAA	5	28	0	0	0	2	6.2	6	0	2	0	0	6	0	0	0	0	0	0	0	0	.000	0	0.00
	PHI/NL		57	322	0	0	0	49	74.1	75	9	27	5	0	61	0	3	2	0	34	31	6	6	.500	28	3.75
89	PHI/NL		28	135	0	0	0	27	33.2	21	7	17	1	1	24	0	2	3	1	13	12	2	3	.400	6	3.21
	SF/NL		40	207	0	0	0	33	51.0	35	5	22	4	0	34	1	2	0	0	18	15	1	4	.200	17	2.65
	YEAR		68	342	0	0	0	60	84.2	56	12	39	5	1	58	1	4	3	1	31	27	3	7	.300	23	2.87
90	SF/NL		68	349	0	0	0	53	79.1	72	6	44	9	2	43	3	4	7	0	40	37	9	9	.500	17	4.20
91	MIN/AL		56	332	0	0	0	22	77.1	70	11	35	6	3	44	2	4	2	2	43	38	5	3	.625	6	4.42
93	ATL/NL		49	198	0	0	0	12	49.2	34	4	14	2	1	33	3	4	1	0	11	9	5	2	.714	0	1.63
12 YR TOTALS			**657**	**4719**	**46**	**0**	**0**	**423**	**1117.0**	**945**	**104**	**488**	**68**	**24**	**856**	**38**	**35**	**32**	**4**	**455**	**411**	**75**	**75**	**.500**	**184**	**3.31**

Belcher, Timothy Wayne "Tim" — BR/TR — b.10/19/61   NYA84* S1/1

YR	TM/LG	CL	G	TBF	GS	CG	SHO	GF	IP	H	HR	BB	IBB	HB	SO	SH	SF	WP	BK	R	ER	W	L	PCT	SV	ERA
84	MAD/MID	A	16	427	16	3	1	0	98.1	80	6	48	1	8	111	2	5	6	0	45	39	9	4	.692	0	3.57
	ALB/EAS	AA	10	242	10	2	0	0	54.0	37	2	41	0	3	40	0	3	2	1	30	20	3	4	.429	0	3.33
85	HUN/SOU	AA	29	688	26	3	1	1	149.2	145	12	99	0	7	90	0	12	11	2	99	78	11	10	.524	0	4.69
86	HUN/SOU	AA	9	176	9	0	0	0	37.0	50	3	22	1	0	25	0	2	3	0	28	27	2	5	.286	0	6.57
87	TAC/PCL	AAA	29	743	28	2	1	0	163.0	143	8	133	2	1	136	2	6	8	2	89	80	9	11	.450	0	4.42
	LA/NL		6	135	5	0	0	1	34.0	30	2	7	0	0	23	2	1	0	1	11	9	4	2	.667	0	2.38
88	LA/NL		36	719	27	4	1	5	179.2	143	8	51	7	2	152	6	1	4	0	65	58	12	6	.667	4	2.91
89	LA/NL		39	937	30	*10	*8	6	230.0	182	20	80	5	7	200	6	6	7	2	81	72	15	12	.556	1	2.82
90	LA/NL		24	627	24	5	2	0	153.0	136	17	48	0	2	102	5	6	4	1	76	68	9	9	.500	0	4.00
91	LA/NL		33	880	33	2	1	0	209.1	189	10	75	3	2	156	11	3	7	2	76	61	10	9	.526	0	2.62
92	CIN/NL		35	949	34	2	1	1	227.2	201	17	80	2	3	149	12	11	3	1	104	99	15	14	.517	0	3.91
93	CIN/NL		22	590	22	4	2	0	137.0	134	11	47	4	7	101	6	3	6	0	72	68	9	6	.600	0	4.47
	CHI/AL		12	296	11	1	1	0	71.2	64	8	27	0	1	34	2	1	0	0	36	35	3	5	.375	0	4.40
	YEAR		34	886	33	5	3	0	208.2	198	19	74	4	8	135	8	4	6	0	108	103	12	11	.522	0	4.44
7 YR TOTALS			**207**	**5133**	**186**	**28**	**16**	**13**	**1242.1**	**1079**	**93**	**415**	**21**	**24**	**917**	**50**	**32**	**33**	**5**	**521**	**470**	**77**	**63**	**.550**	**5**	**3.40**

Belinda, Stanley Peter "Stan" — BR/TR — b.8/6/66   PIT86 10/238

YR	TM/LG	CL	G	TBF	GS	CG	SHO	GF	IP	H	HR	BB	IBB	HB	SO	SH	SF	WP	BK	R	ER	W	L	PCT	SV	ERA
86	PIR/GCL	R	17	84	0	0	0	15	20.1	23	1	2	0	1	17	1	2	4	0	12	6	3	2	.600	7	2.66
	WAT/NYP	A-	5	29	0	0	0	5	8.0	5	1	2	0	0	5	0	0	0	0	3	3	0	0	.000	2	3.38
87	MAC/SAL	A	50	329	0	0	0	45	82.0	59	4	27	1	4	75	3	5	4	0	26	19	6	4	.600	16	2.09
88	SAL/CAR	A+	53	308	0	0	0	42	71.2	54	9	32	4	2	63	8	3	4	0	33	22	6	4	.600	14	2.76
89	HAR/EAS	AA	32	171	0	0	0	28	38.2	32	1	25	3	1	33	3	1	1	0	13	10	1	4	.200	13	2.33
	BUF/AMA	AAA	19	114	0	0	0	15	28.1	13	1	13	3	2	28	3	1	1	1	5	3	2	2	.500	9	0.95
	PIT/NL		8	46	0	0	0	2	10.1	13	0	2	0	1	10	0	0	1	0	8	7	0	1	.000	0	6.10
90	BUF/AMA	AAA	15	96	0	0	0	10	23.2	20	1	8	1	1	25	2	1	0	1	8	5	3	1	.750	5	1.90
	PIT/NL		55	245	0	0	0	17	58.1	48	4	29	3	1	55	2	2	1	0	23	23	3	4	.429	8	3.55
91	PIT/NL		60	318	0	0	0	37	78.1	50	10	35	4	4	71	4	3	2	0	30	30	7	5	.583	16	3.45
92	PIT/NL		59	299	0	0	0	42	71.1	58	8	29	5	0	57	4	6	1	0	26	25	6	4	.600	18	3.15
93	PIT/NL		40	171	0	0	0	37	42.1	35	4	11	4	1	30	1	2	0	0	18	17	3	1	.750	19	3.61
	KC/AL		23	116	0	0	0	7	27.1	30	2	6	0	1	25	1	0	2	0	13	13	1	1	.500	0	4.28
	YEAR		63	287	0	0	0	44	69.2	65	6	17	4	2	55	3	2	2	0	31	30	4	2	.667	19	3.88
5 YR TOTALS			**245**	**1195**	**0**	**0**	**0**	**142**	**288.0**	**234**	**28**	**112**	**16**	**7**	**248**	**13**	**13**	**7**	**0**	**118**	**115**	**20**	**16**	**.556**	**61**	**3.59**

Bell, Eric Alvin — BL/TL — b.10/27/63   BAL82 9/234

YR	TM/LG	CL	G	TBF	GS	CG	SHO	GF	IP	H	HR	BB	IBB	HB	SO	SH	SF	WP	BK	R	ER	W	L	PCT	SV	ERA
82	BLU/APP	R+	11	0	9	0	0	0	51.0	42	2	36	0	2	30	0	0	2	0	19	12	4	1	.800	0	2.12
83	NEW/NYP	A-	18	0	5	2	0	0	60.0	71	5	30	0	1	56	0	0	4	0	44	33	3	2	.600	6	4.95
84	HAG/CAR	A+	3	23	1	0	0	0	3.2	6	0	5	0	1	6	0	0	0	0	4	4	0	0	.000	0	9.82
	NEW/NYP	A-	15	424	15	4	1	0	102.1	82	6	26	0	2	114	0	2	8	1	40	28	8	3	.727	0	2.46
85	HAG/CAR	A+	26	664	26	5	2	0	158.1	141	7	63	0	1	162	3	3	4	0	73	55	11	6	.647	0	3.13
	BAL/AL		4	24	0	0	0	3	5.2	4	1	4	0	0	4	0	0	0	0	3	3	0	0	.000	0	4.76
86	CHA/SOU	AA	18	539	18	6	1	0	129.2	109	7	66	0	1	104	3	1	5	0	49	44	9	6	.600	0	3.05
	ROC/INT	AAA	11	323	11	4	0	0	76.2	68	3	35	1	0	59	0	1	7	0	26	26	7	3	.700	0	3.05
	BAL/AL		4	105	4	0	0	0	23.1	23	4	14	0	0	18	1	1	0	0	14	13	1	2	.333	0	5.01
87	BAL/AL		33	729	29	2	0	1	165.0	174	32	78	2	0	111	4	2	2	0	113	100	10	13	.435	0	5.45
88	ROC/INT	AAA	7	148	7	0	0	0	36.1	28	0	13	0	0	33	3	1	1	2	11	8	3	1	.750	0	1.98
89	HAG/EAS	AA	9	170	7	0	0	1	43.0	32	3	11	1	1	35	1	0	1	0	11	9	4	2	.667	1	1.88
	ROC/INT	AAA	7	172	7	0	0	0	39.2	40	5	15	0	0	27	1	1	2	0	24	22	1	2	.333	0	4.99
90	ROC/INT	AAA	27	667	27	3	0	0	148.0	168	16	65	0	4	90	4	8	11	1	90	80	9	6	.600	0	4.86
91	CAN/EAS	AA	18	402	16	1	0	0	93.1	82	1	37	1	2	84	3	5	6	0	47	30	9	5	.643	0	2.89
	CS/PCL	AAA	4	108	4	1	1	0	25.1	23	1	11	1	0	16	1	0	1	0	6	6	2	1	.667	0	2.13
	CLE/AL		10	61	0	0	0	3	18.0	5	0	5	0	1	9	0	1	0	0	2	1	4	0	1.000	0	0.50
92	CLE/AL		7	75	1	0	0	2	15.1	22	1	9	0	1	10	1	1	1	0	13	13	0	2	.000	0	7.63
	CS/PCL	AAA	26	575	18	5	0	0	137.2	161	10	30	1	0	56	0	6	3	2	64	57	10	7	.588	1	3.73
93	TUC/PCL	AAA	22	474	16	3	1	1	106.2	131	8	39	0	1	53	4	4	5	0	59	48	4	6	.400	0	4.05
	HOU/NL		10	34	0	0	0	2	7.1	10	0	2	0	0	2	0	0	1	0	5	5	0	1	.000	0	6.14
6 YR TOTALS			**68**	**1028**	**34**	**2**	**0**	**11**	**234.2**	**238**	**38**	**112**	**0**	**4**	**152**	**6**	**4**	**2**	**1**	**150**	**135**	**15**	**18**	**.455**	**0**	**5.18**

Benes, Andrew Charles "Andy" — BR/TR — b.8/20/67   SD88 1/1

YR	TM/LG	CL	G	TBF	GS	CG	SHO	GF	IP	H	HR	BB	IBB	HB	SO	SH	SF	WP	BK	R	ER	W	L	PCT	SV	ERA
89	WIC/TEX	AA	16	437	16	5	3	0	108.1	79	6	39	1	2	115	5	2	1	2	32	26	8	4	.667	0	2.16
	LV/PCL	AAA	5	133	5	0	0	0	26.2	41	8	12	0	1	29	2	0	2	2	29	24	2	1	.667	0	8.10
	SD/NL		10	280	10	0	0	0	66.2	51	7	31	0	1	66	6	2	0	3	28	26	6	3	.667	0	3.51
90	SD/NL		32	811	31	2	0	1	192.1	177	18	69	5	10	140	5	4	5	0	87	77	10	11	.476	0	3.60
91	SD/NL		33	908	33	4	1	0	223.0	194	23	59	7	4	167	3	4	4	1	76	75	15	11	.577	0	3.03
92	SD/NL		34	961	34	2	2	0	231.1	230	14	61	6	5	169	19	6	1	1	90	86	13	14	.481	0	3.35
93	SD/NL		34	968	34	4	2	0	230.2	200	23	86	7	4	179	10	6	14	2	111	97	15	15	.500	0	3.78
5 YR TOTALS			**143**	**3928**	**142**	**12**	**5**	**1**	**944.0**	**852**	**85**	**306**	**25**	**15**	**721**	**45**	**24**	**20**	**15**	**392**	**361**	**59**	**54**	**.522**	**0**	**3.44**

Bere, Jason Phillip — BR/TR — b.5/26/71   CHA90 37/952

YR	TM/LG	CL	G	TBF	GS	CG	SHO	GF	IP	H	HR	BB	IBB	HB	SO	SH	SF	WP	BK	R	ER	W	L	PCT	SV	ERA
90	WS/GCL	R	16	163	2	0	0	6	38.0	26	1	19	0	1	41	0	1	1	1	19	10	0	4	.000	1	2.37
91	SB/MID	A	27	686	27	2	1	0	163.0	116	8	100	0	5	158	7	4	11	1	66	52	9	12	.429	0	2.87
92	SAR/FSL	A+	18	458	18	1	1	0	116.0	84	3	34	3	1	106	4	3	6	0	35	31	7	2	.778	0	2.41
	BIR/SOU	AA	8	216	8	4	2	0	54.0	44	1	20	1	1	45	1	2	2	0	22	18	4	4	.500	0	3.00

Bere, Jason Phillip (continued)

YR	TM/LG	CL	G	TBF	GS	CG	SHO	GF	IP	H	HR	BB	IBB	HB	SO	SH	SF	WP	BK	R	ER	W	L	PCT	SV	ERA
	VAN/PCL	AAA	1	6	0	0	0	0	1.0	2	0	0	0	0	2	0	0	0	0	0	0	0	0	.000	0	0.00
93	NAS/AMA	AAA	8	206	8	0	0	0	49.1	36	1	25	1	1	52	3	2	2	0	19	13	5	1	.833	0	2.37
	CHI/AL		24	610	24	1	0	0	142.2	109	12	81	0	5	129	4	2	8	0	60	55	12	5	.706	0	3.47

Bergman, Sean Frederick — BR/TR — b.4/11/70   DET91 6/114

YR	TM/LG	CL	G	TBF	GS	CG	SHO	GF	IP	H	HR	BB	IBB	HB	SO	SH	SF	WP	BK	R	ER	W	L	PCT	SV	ERA
91	NF/NYP	A-	15	384	15	0	0	0	84.2	87	1	42	0	2	77	1	4	5	7	57	42	5	7	.417	0	4.46
92	LAK/FSL	A+	13	320	13	0	0	0	83.0	61	2	14	0	0	67	3	0	2	2	28	23	5	2	.714	0	2.49
	LON/EAS	AA	14	390	14	1	0	0	88.1	85	2	45	2	0	59	6	1	4	0	52	42	4	7	.364	0	4.28
93	DET/AL		9	189	6	1	0	1	39.2	47	6	23	3	1	19	3	2	3	1	29	25	1	4	.200	0	5.67
	TOL/INT	AAA	19	503	19	3	0	0	117.0	124	9	53	0	8	91	6	3	6	2	62	57	8	9	.471	0	4.38

Bielecki, Michael Joseph "Mike" — BR/TR — b.7/31/59   PIT79 S1/8

YR	TM/LG	CL	G	TBF	GS	CG	SHO	GF	IP	H	HR	BB	IBB	HB	SO	SH	SF	WP	BK	R	ER	W	L	PCT	SV	ERA
84	HAW/PCL	AAA	28	0	28	9	2	0	187.2	162	11	88	2	2	162	0	0	4	3	70	62	19	3	.864	0	2.97
	PIT/NL		4	17	0	0	0	1	4.1	4	0	0	0	0	1	1	0	0	1	0	0	0	0	.000	0	0.00
85	HAW/PCL	AAA	20	0	20	2	0	0	129.1	117	13	56	1	1	111	0	0	6	1	58	55	8	6	.571	0	3.83
	PIT/NL		12	211	7	0	0	1	45.2	45	5	31	1	1	22	4	0	1	1	26	23	2	3	.400	0	4.53
86	PIT/NL		31	667	27	0	0	0	148.2	149	10	83	3	6	83	7	6	7	5	87	77	6	11	.353	0	4.66
87	VAN/PCL	AAA	26	802	26	3	0	0	181.0	194	12	78	3	5	140	8	5	12	2	89	76	12	10	.545	0	3.78
	PIT/NL		8	192	8	2	0	0	45.2	43	6	12	0	1	25	5	2	3	0	25	24	2	3	.400	0	4.73
88	IOW/AMA	AAA	23	212	3	1	1	12	54.2	34	3	20	1	2	50	2	0	0	1	19	16	3	2	.600	5	2.63
	CHI/NL		19	215	5	0	0	7	48.1	55	4	16	1	0	33	1	4	3	0	22	18	2	2	.500	0	3.35
89	CHI/NL		33	882	33	4	3	0	212.1	187	16	81	8	0	147	9	3	9	4	82	74	18	7	*.720	0	3.14
90	CHI/NL		36	749	29	0	0	0	168.0	188	13	70	11	5	103	6	4	11	0	101	92	8	11	.421	1	4.93
91	CHI/NL		39	718	25	0	0	8	172.0	169	18	54	6	2	72	10	6	6	0	91	86	13	11	.542	0	4.50
	ATL/NL		2	9	0	0	0	1	1.2	2	0	2	0	0	3	0	0	0	0	0	0	0	0	.000	0	0.00
	YEAR		41	727	25	0	0	9	173.2	171	18	56	6	2	75	10	6	6	0	91	86	13	11	.542	0	4.46
92	ATL/NL		19	336	14	1	1	0	80.1	77	2	27	1	1	62	3	2	4	0	27	23	2	3	.333	0	2.57
93	ROC/INT	AAA	9	215	9	0	0	0	48.1	56	4	16	1	1	31	2	2	5	0	33	27	5	3	.625	0	5.03
	CLE/AL		13	317	13	0	0	0	68.2	90	8	23	3	2	38	0	2	1	0	47	45	4	5	.444	0	5.90
10 YR TOTALS			**216**	**4313**	**161**	**7**	**4**	**24**	**996.0**	**1009**	**82**	**399**	**34**	**14**	**589**	**56**	**29**	**45**	**14**	**508**	**462**	**57**	**57**	**.500**	**1**	**4.17**

Black, Harry Ralston "Bud" — BL/TL — b.6/30/57   SEA79 17/417

YR	TM/LG	CL	G	TBF	GS	CG	SHO	GF	IP	H	HR	BB	IBB	HB	SO	SH	SF	WP	BK	R	ER	W	L	PCT	SV	ERA
81	SEA/AL		2	7	0	0	0	0	1.0	2	0	3	1	0	0	0	0	1	0	0	0	0	0	.000	0	0.00
82	KC/AL		22	386	14	0	0	2	88.1	92	10	34	6	3	40	4	3	4	7	48	45	4	6	.400	0	4.58
83	KC/AL		24	672	24	3	0	0	161.1	159	19	43	1	2	58	4	5	4	0	75	68	10	7	.588	0	3.79
84	KC/AL		35	1045	35	8	1	0	257.0	226	22	64	2	4	140	6	1	2	2	99	89	17	12	.586	0	3.12
85	KC/AL		33	885	33	5	2	0	205.2	216	17	59	4	8	122	8	4	9	1	111	99	10	15	.400	0	4.33
86	KC/AL		56	503	4	0	0	26	121.0	100	14	43	5	7	68	4	4	2	2	49	43	5	10	.333	9	3.20
87	KC/AL		29	520	18	0	0	4	122.1	126	16	35	2	5	61	1	3	6	0	63	49	8	6	.571	1	3.60
88	KC/AL		17	98	0	0	0	5	22.0	23	2	11	2	0	19	1	0	0	2	12	12	2	1	.667	0	4.91
	WIL/EAS	AA	1	15	1	0	0	0	5.0	0	0	0	0	0	5	0	0	0	0	0	0	1	0	1.000	0	0.00
	CLE/AL		16	260	7	0	0	4	59.0	59	6	23	1	4	44	5	3	5	4	35	33	2	3	.400	1	5.03
	YEAR		33	358	7	0	0	9	81.0	82	8	34	3	4	63	6	3	5	6	47	45	4	4	.500	1	5.00
89	CLE/AL		33	912	32	6	3	0	222.1	213	14	52	0	1	88	9	5	13	5	95	83	12	11	.522	0	3.36
90	CLE/AL		29	796	29	5	2	0	191.0	171	17	58	1	4	103	4	5	6	1	79	75	11	10	.524	0	3.53
	TOR/AL		3	61	2	0	0	1	15.2	10	2	3	0	1	3	2	2	0	0	7	7	2	1	.667	0	4.02
	YEAR		32	857	31	5	2	1	206.2	181	19	61	1	5	106	6	7	6	1	86	82	13	11	.542	0	3.57
91	SF/NL		34	893	34	3	3	0	214.1	201	25	71	8	4	104	11	7	6	6	104	95	12	16	.429	0	3.99
92	PHO/PCL	AAA	3	81	3	1	1	0	21.0	21	5	5	0	1	10	0	1	0	0	3	2	2	0	1.000	0	0.86
	SF/NL		28	749	28	2	1	0	177.0	178	23	59	11	1	82	8	4	3	7	88	78	10	12	.455	0	3.97
93	SJ/CAL	A+	1	4	1	0	0	0	1.0	2	1	0	0	0	2	0	0	0	0	1	1	0	0	.000	0	9.00
	SF/NL		16	394	16	0	0	0	93.2	89	13	33	2	2	45	8	4	0	4	44	37	8	2	.800	0	3.56
13 YR TOTALS			**377**	**8181**	**276**	**32**	**12**	**42**	**1951.2**	**1865**	**200**	**591**	**46**	**46**	**977**	**75**	**50**	**61**	**41**	**909**	**813**	**113**	**112**	**.502**	**11**	**3.75**

Blair, William Allen "Willie" — BR/TR — b.12/18/65   TOR86 11/289

YR	TM/LG	CL	G	TBF	GS	CG	SHO	GF	IP	H	HR	BB	IBB	HB	SO	SH	SF	WP	BK	R	ER	W	L	PCT	SV	ERA
86	SC/NYP	A-	21	204	0	0	0	18	53.2	32	1	20	1	0	55	1	0	3	0	10	10	5	0	1.000	12	1.68
87	DUN/FSL	A+	50	375	0	0	0	45	85.1	99	5	29	0	1	72	5	6	9	0	51	42	2	9	.182	13	4.43
88	DUN/FSL	A+	4	26	0	0	0	3	6.2	5	0	4	1	0	5	1	2	2	0	2	2	2	0	1.000	0	2.70
	KNO/SOU	AA	34	429	9	0	0	14	102.0	94	7	35	2	4	76	1	5	4	2	49	41	5	5	.500	3	3.62
89	SYR/INT	AAA	19	451	17	3	1	0	106.2	94	10	38	1	2	76	2	1	2	1	55	47	5	6	.455	0	3.97
90	SYR/INT	AAA	3	83	3	0	0	0	19.0	20	1	8	0	0	6	1	1	0	0	13	10	0	2	.000	0	4.74
	TOR/AL		27	297	6	0	0	8	68.2	66	4	28	4	1	43	0	4	3	0	33	31	3	5	.375	0	4.06
91	CS/PCL	AAA	26	496	15	0	0	10	113.2	130	10	30	2	2	57	3	3	3	1	74	63	9	6	.600	4	4.99
	CLE/AL		11	168	5	0	0	1	36.0	58	7	10	0	1	13	1	2	1	0	27	27	2	3	.400	0	6.75
92	TUC/PCL	AAA	21	223	2	1	0	8	52.2	50	2	12	2	4	35	1	2	2	0	20	14	4	4	.500	2	2.39
	HOU/NL		29	331	8	0	0	8	78.2	74	9	25	2	2	48	4	3	2	0	47	35	5	7	.417	0	4.00
93	COL/NL		46	664	18	0	0	5	146.0	184	20	42	4	3	84	10	8	6	1	90	77	6	10	.375	0	4.75
4 YR TOTALS			**113**	**1460**	**37**	**1**	**0**	**15**	**329.1**	**382**	**36**	**105**	**10**	**7**	**188**	**15**	**17**	**12**	**1**	**197**	**170**	**16**	**25**	**.390**	**0**	**4.65**

Boddicker, Michael James "Mike" — BR/TR — b.8/23/57   BAL78 9/152

YR	TM/LG	CL	G	TBF	GS	CG	SHO	GF	IP	H	HR	BB	IBB	HB	SO	SH	SF	WP	BK	R	ER	W	L	PCT	SV	ERA
80	BAL/AL		1	34	1	0	0	0	7.1	6	1	5	0	0	4	0	0	0	0	6	5	0	1	.000	0	6.14

Boddicker, Michael James "Mike" (continued)

YR	TM/LG	CL	G	TBF	GS	CG	SHO	GF	IP	H	HR	BB	IBB	HB	SO	SH	SF	WP	BK	R	ER	W	L	PCT	SV	ERA
81	BAL/AL		2	25	0	0	0	1	5.2	6	1	2	0	0	2	0	0	2	0	4	3	0	0	.000	0	4.76
82	BAL/AL		7	110	0	0	0	4	25.2	25	2	12	2	0	20	1	0	0	0	10	10	1	0	1.000	0	3.51
83	BAL/AL		27	711	26	10	*5	1	179.0	141	13	52	1	0	120	4	3	5	0	65	55	16	8	.667	0	2.77
84	BAL/AL		34	1051	34	16	4	0	261.1	218	23	81	1	5	128	2	7	6	1	95	81	*20	11	.645	0	*2.79
85	BAL/AL		32	899	32	9	2	0	203.1	227	13	89	7	5	135	9	2	5	0	104	92	12	17	.414	0	4.07
86	BAL/AL		33	934	33	7	.0	0	218.1	214	30	74	4	11	175	3	6	7	0	125	114	14	12	.538	0	4.70
87	BAL/AL		33	950	33	7	2	0	226.0	212	29	78	4	7	152	7	4	10	0	114	105	10	12	.455	0	4.18
88	BAL/AL		21	636	21	4	0	0	147.0	149	14	51	5	11	100	3	8	3	4	72	63	6	12	.333	0	3.86
	BOS/AL		15	365	14	1	1	0	89.0	85	3	26	1	3	56	1	4	3	0	30	26	7	3	.700	0	2.63
	YEAR		36	1001	35	5	1	0	236.0	234	17	77	6	14	156	4	12	6	4	102	89	13	15	.464	0	3.39
89	BOS/AL		34	912	34	3	2	0	211.2	217	19	71	4	10	145	8	10	4	1	101	94	15	11	.577	0	4.00
90	BOS/AL		34	956	34	4	0	0	228.0	225	16	69	6	10	143	4	1	10	0	92	85	17	8	.680	0	3.36
91	KC/AL		30	775	29	1	0	1	180.2	188	13	59	0	13	79	1	1	1	0	89	82	12	12	.500	0	4.08
92	KC/AL		29	392	8	0	0	8	86.2	92	5	37	3	8	47	2	3	2	0	50	48	1	4	.200	3	4.98
93	OMA/AMA	AAA	3	66	3	0	0	0	15.2	18	3	4	0	0	12	0	0	0	0	9	8	0	2	.000	0	4.60
	BEL/MID	A	1	16	1	0	0	0	4.0	3	0	1	0	0	4	0	0	0	0	1	1	0	0	.000	0	2.25
	MIL/AL		10	249	10	1	0	0	54.0	77	6	15	1	4	24	1	1	0	0	35	34	3	5	.375	0	5.67
14 YR TOTALS			342	8999	309	63	16	15	2123.2	2082	188	721	39	87	1330	54	50	60	8	992	897	134	116	.536	3	3.80

Boever, Joseph Martin "Joe" — BR/TR — b.10/4/60   SL 6/25/82

YR	TM/LG	CL	G	TBF	GS	CG	SHO	GF	IP	H	HR	BB	IBB	HB	SO	SH	SF	WP	BK	R	ER	W	L	PCT	SV	ERA
84	ARK/TEX	AA	8	56	0	0	0	8	11.0	10	1	12	0	1	12	0	1	1	1	11	10	0	1	.000	3	8.18
	SP/FSL	A+	48	325	0	0	0	38	77.2	52	2	45	0	1	81	1	2	1	1	31	26	6	4	.600	14	3.01
85	ARK/TEX	AA	27	151	0	0	0	20	37.2	21	1	23	4	0	45	3	1	2	0	5	5	3	1	.750	9	1.19
	LOU/AMA	AAA	21	156	0	0	0	13	35.1	28	0	22	0	0	37	0	1	1	0	11	8	3	2	.600	1	2.04
	STL/NL		13	69	0	0	0	5	16.1	17	3	4	1	0	20	1	1	1	0	8	8	0	0	.000	0	4.41
86	LOU/AMA	AAA	51	375	0	0	0	26	88.0	71	1	48	6	2	75	7	5	10	1	25	22	4	5	.444	5	2.25
	STL/NL		11	93	0	0	0	4	21.2	19	2	11	0	0	8	0	0	1	0	5	4	0	1	.000	1	1.66
87	LOU/AMA	AAA	43	263	0	0	0	36	59.0	52	7	27	2	1	79	1	3	1	0	22	22	3	2	.600	21	3.36
	RIC/INT	AAA	6	38	0	0	0	4	9.0	8	0	4	1	1	8	0	0	0	0	1	1	1	0	1.000	0	1.00
	ATL/NL		14	93	0	0	0	10	18.1	29	4	12	1	0	18	1	1	1	0	15	15	1	0	1.000	0	7.36
88	RIC/INT	AAA	48	279	0	0	0	43	71.1	47	5	22	1	0	71	2	2	2	0	17	17	6	3	.667	22	2.14
	ATL/NL		16	70	0	0	0	13	20.1	12	1	1	0	1	7	2	0	0	0	4	4	0	2	.000	1	1.77
89	ATL/NL		66	349	0	0	0	53	82.1	78	6	34	5	1	68	5	0	5	0	37	36	4	11	.267	21	3.94
90	ATL/NL		33	198	0	0	0	21	42.1	40	6	35	10	2	35	2	2	2	0	23	22	1	3	.250	8	4.68
	PHI/NL		34	190	0	0	0	13	46.0	37	0	16	2	0	40	2	0	1	2	12	11	2	3	.400	6	2.15
	YEAR		67	388	0	0	0	34	88.1	77	6	51	12	2	75	4	2	3	2	35	33	3	6	.333	14	3.36
91	PHI/NL		68	431	0	0	0	27	98.1	90	10	54	11	0	89	3	4	6	2	45	42	3	5	.375	0	3.84
92	HOU/NL		*81	479	0	0	0	26	111.1	103	3	45	9	4	67	10	4	4	0	38	31	3	6	.333	2	2.51
93	OAK/AL		42	353	0	0	0	19	79.1	87	8	33	4	4	49	2	3	1	0	40	34	4	2	.667	3	3.86
	DET/AL		19	96	0	0	0	3	23.0	14	1	11	3	0	14	3	4	0	0	10	7	2	1	.667	3	2.74
	YEAR		61	449	0	0	0	22	102.1	101	9	44	7	4	63	5	7	1	0	50	41	6	3	.667	3	3.61
9 YR TOTALS			397	2421	0	0	0	194	559.1	526	44	256	46	10	415	31	21	22	3	237	214	20	34	.370	41	3.44

Bohanon, Brian Edward — BL/TL — b.8/1/68   TEX87 1/19

YR	TM/LG	CL	G	TBF	GS	CG	SHO	GF	IP	H	HR	BB	IBB	HB	SO	SH	SF	WP	BK	R	ER	W	L	PCT	SV	ERA
87	RAN/GCL	R	5	84	4	0	0	0	21.0	15	1	5	0	0	21	0	0	2	0	13	11	0	2	.000	0	4.71
88	CHA/FSL	A+	2	31	2	0	0	0	6.2	6	0	5	0	0	9	0	0	0	1	4	4	0	1	.000	0	5.40
89	CHA/FSL	A+	11	213	7	0	0	3	54.2	40	1	20	0	2	33	1	1	1	1	16	11	0	3	.000	1	1.81
	TUL/TEX	AA	11	297	11	1	1	0	73.2	59	3	27	0	3	44	3	2	1	1	20	18	5	0	1.000	0	2.20
90	TEX/AL		11	158	6	0	0	1	34.0	40	6	18	0	2	15	0	3	1	0	30	25	0	3	.000	0	6.62
	OC/AMA	AAA	14	135	4	0	0	4	32.0	35	2	8	0	0	22	2	1	2	0	16	13	1	2	.333	1	3.66
91	CHA/FSL	A+	2	47	2	0	0	0	11.2	6	0	4	0	2	7	0	2	1	0	5	5	1	0	1.000	0	3.86
	TUL/TEX	AA	2	54	2	0	0	0	11.2	9	0	11	0	0	6	1	0	0	0	8	3	0	1	.000	0	2.31
	OC/AMA	AAA	7	197	7	0	0	0	46.1	49	2	15	1	1	37	2	2	2	0	19	15	0	2	.000	0	2.91
	TEX/AL		11	273	11	0	0	0	61.1	66	4	23	0	2	34	2	5	3	1	35	33	4	3	.571	0	4.84
92	TUL/TEX	AA	6	120	6	1	0	0	28.1	25	0	9	0	3	25	0	0	4	0	7	4	2	2	.667	0	1.27
	OC/AMA	AAA	9	232	9	3	0	0	56.0	53	5	15	0	1	24	1	1	0	0	21	17	4	2	.667	0	2.73
	TEX/AL		18	220	7	0	0	3	45.2	57	7	25	0	1	29	0	2	0	0	38	32	1	1	.500	0	6.31
93	OC/AMA	AAA	2	31	2	0	0	0	7.0	7	1	5	0	0	7	0	0	1	0	6	5	0	1	.000	0	6.43
	TEX/AL		36	418	8	0	0	8	92.2	107	8	46	3	4	45	2	5	10	0	54	49	4	4	.500	0	4.76
4 YR TOTALS			76	1069	32	1	0	8	233.2	270	25	112	3	9	123	4	15	16	1	157	139	9	11	.450	0	5.35

Bolton, Rodney Earl — BR/TR — b.9/23/68   CHA90 14/348

YR	TM/LG	CL	G	TBF	GS	CG	SHO	GF	IP	H	HR	BB	IBB	HB	SO	SH	SF	WP	BK	R	ER	W	L	PCT	SV	ERA
90	UTI/NYP	A-	6	168	6	1	1	0	44.0	27	0	11	0	3	45	1	0	0	0	4	2	5	1	.833	0	0.41
	SB/MID	A	7	196	7	3	1	0	51.0	34	0	12	1	1	50	1	1	1	0	14	11	5	1	.833	0	1.94
91	SAR/FSL	A+	15	412	15	5	2	0	103.2	81	2	23	0	2	77	5	1	1	1	29	22	7	6	.538	0	1.91
	BIR/SOU	AA	12	360	12	3	2	0	89.0	73	3	21	1	8	57	0	2	3	0	26	16	8	4	.667	0	1.62
92	VAN/PCL	AAA	27	781	27	3	2	0	187.1	174	9	59	2	1	111	4	9	2		72	61	11	9	.550	0	2.93
93	CHI/AL		9	197	8	0	0	0	42.1	55	4	16	0	1	17	1	4	4	0	40	35	2	6	.250	0	7.44
	NAS/AMA	AAA	18	486	16	1	0	1	115.2	108	10	37	2	3	75	2	3	11	0	40	37	10	1	.909	1	2.88

Bolton, Thomas Edward "Tom" — BL/TL — b.5/6/62   BOS80 19/518

YR	TM/LG	CL	G	TBF	GS	CG	SHO	GF	IP	H	HR	BB	IBB	HB	SO	SH	SF	WP	BK	R	ER	W	L	PCT	SV	ERA
80	ELM/NYP	A-	23	237	1	1	1	15	56.0	43	4	22	0	0	43	1	0	1	0	26	15	6	2	.750	5	2.41

Bolton, Thomas Edward "Tom" (continued)

YR	TM/LG	CL	G	TBF	GS	CG	SHO	GF	IP	H	HR	BB	IBB	HB	SO	SH	SF	WP	BK	R	ER	W	L	PCT	SV	ERA
81	WH/FSL	A+	24	420	0	0	0	3	92.0	125	5	41	0	3	47	2	3	7	1	62	46	2	3	.400	0	4.50
82	WH/FSL	A+	28	682	25	4	0	1	163.0	161	3	63	0	2	77	6	4	7	4	67	54	9	8	.529	0	2.98
83	NB/EAS	AA	16	416	16	2	1	0	99.2	93	7	41	0	1	62	1	0	5	0	36	32	7	3	.700	0	2.89
	PAW/INT	AAA	6	144	6	0	0	0	29.0	33	4	25	0	1	20	1	0	1	1	26	21	0	5	.000	0	6.52
84	NB/EAS	AA	33	380	9	0	0	11	87.0	87	5	34	3	4	66	2	3	6	2	54	40	4	5	.444	1	4.14
85	NB/EAS	AA	34	437	10	1	0	14	101.0	106	4	40	1	2	74	5	3	3	2	53	48	5	6	.455	1	4.28
86	PAW/INT	AAA	29	356	7	1	0	11	86.0	80	6	25	2	0	58	9	2	1	1	30	26	3	4	.429	0	2.72
87	PAW/INT	AAA	5	93	4	0	0	1	21.2	25	0	12	1	0	8	0	1	1	0	14	13	2	1	.667	0	5.40
	BOS/AL		29	287	0	0	0	5	61.2	83	5	27	2	2	49	3	3	3	0	33	30	1	0	1.000	0	4.38
88	PAW/INT	AAA	18	81	0	0	0	8	19.1	17	0	10	0	1	15	0	0	2	0	7	6	3	0	1.000	0	2.79
	BOS/AL		28	140	0	0	0	8	30.1	35	1	14	1	0	21	2	1	2	1	17	16	1	3	.250	0	4.75
89	BOS/AL		4	83	4	0	0	0	17.1	21	1	10	1	0	9	0	1	1	0	18	16	0	0	.000	0	8.31
	PAW/INT	AAA	25	606	22	5	2	2	143.1	140	13	47	2	4	99	6	1	0	1	57	46	12	5	.706	1	2.89
90	PAW/INT	AAA	4	50	2	0	0	1	11.2	9	2	7	0	0	8	0	1	2	0	6	5	1	0	1.000	0	3.86
	BOS/AL		21	501	16	3	0	2	119.2	111	6	47	3	3	65	3	5	1	1	46	45	10	5	.667	0	3.38
91	BOS/AL		25	499	19	3	0	4	110.0	136	16	51	2	2	64	2	4	3	0	72	64	8	9	.471	0	5.24
92	BOS/AL		21	135	1	0	0	6	29.0	34	4	14	1	2	23	0	1	2	1	11	11	1	2	.333	0	3.41
	CIN/NL		16	210	8	0	0	3	46.1	52	9	23	2	2	27	1	1	3	1	28	27	3	5	.500	0	5.24
	YEAR		37	345	9	0	0	9	75.1	86	9	37	3	4	50	1	1	5	2	39	38	4	5	.444	0	4.54
93	DET/AL		43	462	8	0	0	9	102.2	113	5	45	10	7	66	7	2	5	1	57	51	6	6	.500	0	4.47
7 YR TOTALS			187	2317	56	3	0	37	517.0	585	43	231	22	17	324	18	17	20	5	282	260	30	32	.484	1	4.53

Bones, Ricardo Ricky "Ricky" — BR/TR — b.4/7/69 SD 5/13/86

YR	TM/LG	CL	G	TBF	GS	CG	SHO	GF	IP	H	HR	BB	IBB	HB	SO	SH	SF	WP	BK	R	ER	W	L	PCT	SV	ERA
86	SPO/NWL	A-	18	0	9	0	0	4	58.0	63	3	29	1	1	46	0	0	7	2	44	36	1	3	.250	0	5.59
87	CHS/SAL	A	26	729	26	4	1	0	170.1	183	9	45	4	6	130	4	1	5	2	81	69	12	5	.706	0	3.65
88	RIV/CAL	A+	25	742	25	5	2	0	175.1	162	11	64	3	4	129	2	2	14	5	80	71	15	6	.714	0	3.64
89	WIC/TEX	AA	24	611	24	2	0	0	136.1	162	22	47	5	2	88	4	3	7	3	103	87	10	9	.526	0	5.74
90	WIC/TEX	AA	21	591	21	2	1	0	137.0	138	15	45	0	5	96	7	5	6	4	66	53	6	4	.600	0	3.48
	LV/PCL	AAA	5	158	5	0	0	0	36.1	45	2	10	0	1	25	0	0	1	0	17	14	2	1	.667	0	3.47
91	LV/PCL	AAA	23	611	23	1	0	0	136.1	155	10	43	3	4	95	2	4	6	3	90	64	8	6	.571	0	4.22
	SD/NL		11	234	11	0	0	0	54.0	57	3	18	0	0	31	0	4	4	0	33	29	4	6	.400	0	4.83
92	MIL/AL		31	705	28	0	0	0	163.1	169	27	48	0	9	65	2	5	3	2	90	83	9	10	.474	0	4.57
93	MIL/AL		32	883	31	3	0	1	203.2	222	28	63	3	6	63	5	5	6	1	122	110	11	11	.500	0	4.86
3 YR TOTALS			74	1822	70	3	0	1	421.0	448	58	129	3	17	159	7	16	13	3	245	222	24	27	.471	0	4.75

Borbon, Pedro Felix — BR/TL — b.11/15/67 CHA 6/4/88

YR	TM/LG	CL	G	TBF	GS	CG	SHO	GF	IP	H	HR	BB	IBB	HB	SO	SH	SF	WP	BK	R	ER	W	L	PCT	SV	ERA
88	WS/GCL	R	16	299	11	1	1	2	74.2	52	1	17	0	2	67	3	3	5	14	28	20	5	3	.625	1	2.41
90	BUR/MID	A	14	381	14	6	2	0	97.2	73	3	23	0	3	76	0	0	4	1	25	16	11	3	.786	0	1.47
	DUR/CAR	A+	11	266	11	0	0	0	61.1	73	8	16	0	2	37	2	2	2	1	40	37	4	5	.444	0	5.43
91	DUR/CAR	A+	37	388	6	1	0	21	91.0	85	2	35	2	2	79	5	4	4	2	40	23	4	3	.571	5	2.27
	GRE/SOU	AA	4	120	4	0	0	0	29.0	23	1	10	0	3	22	1	0	2	0	12	9	1	0	.000	0	2.79
92	GRE/SOU	AA	39	384	10	0	0	14	94.0	73	6	42	1	3	79	1	3	2	0	36	32	8	2	.800	3	3.06
	ATL/NL		2	7	0	0	0	2	1.1	2	0	1	1	0	1	0	0	0	0	1	1	0	1	.000	0	6.75
93	RIC/INT	AAA	52	344	0	0	0	15	76.2	71	7	42	9	2	95	10	3	3	1	40	36	5	5	.500	1	4.23
	ATL/NL		3	11	0	0	0	0	1.2	3	0	3	0	1	0	0	0	0	0	4	4	0	0	.000	0	21.60
2 YR TOTALS			5	18	0	0	0	2	3.0	5	0	4	1	0	3	1	0	0	0	5	5	0	1	.000	0	15.00

Bosio, Christopher Louis "Chris" — BR/TR — b.4/3/63 MIL82* S2/44

YR	TM/LG	CL	G	TBF	GS	CG	SHO	GF	IP	H	HR	BB	IBB	HB	SO	SH	SF	WP	BK	R	ER	W	L	PCT	SV	ERA
84	BEL/MID	A	26	759	26	11	2	0	181.0	159	12	56	0	5	156	4	3	17	4	83	55	17	6	.739	0	2.73
85	EP/TEX	AA	28	780	25	6	1	3	181.1	186	14	49	4	4	155	9	6	4	5	108	77	11	6	.647	2	3.82
86	VAN/PCL	AAA	44	254	0	0	0	34	67.0	47	1	13	4	0	60	1	1	0	0	18	17	7	3	.700	16	2.28
	MIL/AL		10	154	4	0	0	3	34.2	41	4	13	0	0	29	1	0	2	1	27	27	0	4	.000	0	7.01
87	MIL/AL		46	734	19	2	0	8	170.0	187	18	50	3	1	150	3	3	14	2	102	99	11	8	.579	2	5.24
88	DEN/AMA	AAA	2	56	2	1	0	0	14.0	13	0	4	0	1	12	2	0	1	0	6	6	1	0	1.000	0	3.86
	MIL/AL		38	766	22	9	1	15	182.0	190	13	38	6	2	84	7	9	4	2	80	68	7	15	.318	6	3.36
89	MIL/AL		33	969	33	8	2	0	234.2	225	16	48	1	6	173	5	5	4	2	90	77	15	10	.600	0	2.95
90	BEL/MID	A	1	15	1	0	0	0	3.0	4	0	1	0	0	0	0	0	0	0	2	1	0	0	.000	0	3.00
	MIL/AL		20	557	20	4	1	0	132.2	131	15	38	1	3	76	4	4	7	0	67	59	4	9	.308	0	4.00
91	MIL/AL		32	840	32	5	1	0	204.2	187	15	58	0	8	117	2	6	5	0	80	74	14	10	.583	0	3.25
92	MIL/AL		33	937	33	4	2	0	231.1	223	21	44	1	4	120	6	5	8	2	100	93	16	6	.727	0	3.62
93	SEA/AL		29	678	24	3	1	2	164.1	138	14	59	3	6	119	4	5	5	0	75	63	9	9	.500	1	3.45
8 YR TOTALS			241	5635	187	35	9	28	1354.1	1322	121	348	15	30	868	35	36	46	9	621	560	76	71	.517	9	3.72

Boskie, Shawn Kealoha — BR/TR — b.3/28/67 CHN86* 1/10

YR	TM/LG	CL	G	TBF	GS	CG	SHO	GF	IP	H	HR	BB	IBB	HB	SO	SH	SF	WP	BK	R	ER	W	L	PCT	SV	ERA
86	WYT/APP	R+	14	268	12	1	0	0	54.0	42	4	57	1	7	40	1	0	15	0	41	32	4	4	.500	0	5.33
87	PEO/MID	A	26	657	25	1	0	0	149.0	149	12	56	2	17	100	4	5	7	5	91	72	9	11	.450	0	4.35
88	WIN/CAR	A+	27	825	27	4	2	0	186.0	176	9	89	1	17	164	4	7	14	4	83	70	12	7	.632	0	3.39
89	CHA/SOU	AA	28	813	28	5	0	0	181.0	196	10	84	3	19	164	1	8	11	0	105	88	11	8	.579	0	4.38
90	IOW/AMA	AAA	8	217	8	1	0	0	51.0	46	1	21	1	2	51	2	1	1	0	22	18	4	2	.667	0	3.18
	CHI/NL		15	415	15	0	0	0	97.2	99	8	31	3	1	49	8	2	3	2	42	40	5	6	.455	0	3.69
91	IOW/AMA	AAA	7	186	6	2	0	0	45.1	43	1	11	0	2	29	5	1	1	0	19	18	2	2	.500	0	3.57
	CHI/NL		28	582	20	0	0	2	129.0	150	14	52	4	5	62	8	6	1	1	78	75	4	9	.308	0	5.23

(continued)

Boskie, Shawn Kealoha (continued)

YR	TM/LG	CL	G	TBF	GS	CG	SHO	GF	IP	H	HR	BB	IBB	HB	SO	SH	SF	WP	BK	R	ER	W	L	PCT	SV	ERA
92	IOW/AMA	AAA	2	32	2	0	0	0	7.1	8	0	3	0	0	3	0	0	0	0	4	3	0	0	.000	0	3.68
	CHI/NL		23	393	18	0	0	2	91.2	96	14	36	3	4	39	9	6	5	1	55	51	5	11	.313	0	5.01
93	IOW/AMA	AAA	11	300	11	1	0	0	71.2	70	4	21	0	7	35	2	1	1	0	35	34	6	1	.857	0	4.27
	CHI/NL		39	277	2	0	0	10	65.2	63	7	21	2	7	39	4	1	5	0	30	25	5	3	.625	0	3.43
4 YR TOTALS			**105**	**1667**	**55**	**1**	**0**	**14**	**384.0**	**408**	**43**	**140**	**12**	**17**	**189**	**29**	**15**	**14**	**4**	**205**	**191**	**19**	**29**	**.396**	**0**	**4.48**

Bottenfield, Kent Dennis — BB/TR — b.11/14/68 — MON86 4/96

YR	TM/LG	CL	G	TBF	GS	CG	SHO	GF	IP	H	HR	BB	IBB	HB	SO	SH	SF	WP	BK	R	ER	W	L	PCT	SV	ERA
86	EXP/GCL	R	13	323	13	2	0	0	74.1	73	2	30	0	3	41	2	6	0	1	42	27	5	6	.455	0	3.27
87	BUR/MID	A	27	706	27	6	3	0	161.0	175	12	42	0	2	103	3	3	9	2	98	81	9	13	.409	0	4.53
88	WPB/FSL	A+	27	745	27	9	4	0	181.0	165	10	47	0	5	120	3	5	4	3	80	67	10	8	.556	0	3.33
89	JAC/SOU	AA	25	625	25	1	0	0	138.2	137	13	73	2	9	91	6	9	6	2	101	81	3	17	.150	0	5.26
90	JAC/SOU	AA	29	718	28	2	1	0	169.0	158	14	67	1	11	121	7	4	7	0	72	64	12	10	.545	0	3.41
91	IND/AMA	AAA	29	712	27	5	2	0	166.1	155	15	61	7	4	108	11	5	5	1	97	75	8	15	.348	0	4.06
92	IND/AMA	AAA	25	629	23	3	1	1	152.1	139	12	58	1	2	111	6	4	2	0	64	58	12	8	.600	0	3.43
	MON/NL		10	135	4	0	0	2	32.1	26	1	11	1	1	14	1	2	0	0	9	8	1	2	.333	1	2.23
93	MON/NL		23	373	11	0	0	2	83.0	93	11	33	2	5	33	11	1	4	1	49	38	2	5	.286	0	4.12
	COL/NL		14	337	14	1	0	0	76.2	86	13	38	1	1	30	10	3	0	0	53	52	3	5	.375	0	6.10
	YEAR		37	710	25	1	0	2	159.2	179	24	71	3	6	63	21	4	4	1	102	90	5	10	.333	0	5.07
2 YR TOTALS			**47**	**845**	**29**	**1**	**0**	**4**	**192.0**	**205**	**25**	**82**	**4**	**7**	**77**	**22**	**6**	**4**	**1**	**111**	**98**	**6**	**12**	**.333**	**1**	**4.59**

Boucher, Denis — BR/TL — b.3/7/68 — TOR 8/18/87

YR	TM/LG	CL	G	TBF	GS	CG	SHO	GF	IP	H	HR	BB	IBB	HB	SO	SH	SF	WP	BK	R	ER	W	L	PCT	SV	ERA
88	MB/SAL	A	33	809	32	1	0	0	196.2	161	11	63	1	8	169	7	6	15	21	81	62	13	12	.520	0	2.84
89	DUN/FSL	A+	33	675	28	1	1	1	164.2	142	6	58	2	6	117	3	8	13	8	80	56	10	10	.500	0	3.06
90	DUN/FSL	A+	9	226	9	2	2	0	60.0	45	1	8	0	2	62	0	0	4	0	8	5	7	0	1.000	0	0.75
	SYR/INT	AAA	17	449	17	2	1	0	107.2	100	7	37	2	2	80	4	4	6	0	52	46	8	5	.615	0	3.85
91	TOR/AL		7	162	7	0	0	0	35.1	39	6	16	1	2	16	3	1	0	4	20	18	0	3	.000	0	4.58
	SYR/INT	AAA	8	241	8	1	0	0	56.2	57	5	19	1	3	28	4	1	2	0	24	20	2	1	.667	0	3.18
	CLE/AL		5	108	5	0	0	0	22.2	35	6	8	0	0	13	0	0	1	0	21	21	1	4	.200	0	8.34
	YEAR		12	270	12	0	0	0	58.0	74	12	24	1	2	29	3	1	1	4	41	39	1	7	.125	0	6.05
	CS/PCL	AAA	3	59	3	0	0	0	14.1	14	1	2	0	0	9	0	1	0	0	8	8	1	0	1.000	0	5.02
92	CS/PCL	AAA	20	497	18	6	0	1	124.0	119	4	30	1	2	40	3	4	7	2	50	48	11	4	.733	0	3.48
	CLE/AL		8	184	7	0	0	0	41.0	48	9	20	0	1	17	1	3	1	0	29	29	2	2	.500	0	6.37
93	LV/PCL	AAA	24	331	7	1	0	2	70.0	101	12	27	3	6	46	4	1	4	1	59	50	4	7	.364	1	6.43
	OTT/INT	AAA	11	169	6	0	0	1	43.0	36	0	11	0	1	22	2	0	3	0	13	13	6	0	1.000	0	2.72
	MON/NL		5	111	5	0	0	0	28.1	24	1	3	1	0	14	0	3	2	0	7	6	3	1	.750	0	1.91
3 YR TOTALS			**25**	**565**	**24**	**0**	**0**	**0**	**127.1**	**146**	**22**	**47**	**2**	**3**	**60**	**4**	**7**	**2**	**6**	**77**	**74**	**6**	**10**	**.375**	**0**	**5.23**

Bowen, Ryan Eugene — BR/TR — b.2/10/68 — HOU86 1/13

YR	TM/LG	CL	G	TBF	GS	CG	SHO	GF	IP	H	HR	BB	IBB	HB	SO	SH	SF	WP	BK	R	ER	W	L	PCT	SV	ERA
87	ASH/SAL	A	26	704	26	6	2	0	160.1	143	12	78	1	5	126	7	4	8	2	86	72	12	5	.706	0	4.04
88	OSC/FSL	A+	4	65	4	0	0	0	13.2	12	0	10	0	1	12	1	0	2	0	8	6	1	0	1.000	0	3.95
89	CMB/SOU	AA	27	655	27	3	1	0	139.2	123	11	116	0	8	136	7	4	12	0	83	66	8	6	.571	0	4.25
90	TUC/PCL	AAA	10	177	7	0	0	0	34.2	41	5	38	1	0	29	2	0	0	0	36	36	1	3	.250	0	9.35
	CMB/SOU	AA	18	491	18	2	2	0	113.0	103	7	49	0	0	109	4	5	5	1	59	47	8	4	.667	0	3.74
91	TUC/PCL	AAA	18	450	18	2	2	0	98.2	114	3	56	2	3	78	3	0	9	0	56	48	5	5	.500	0	4.38
	HOU/NL		14	319	13	0	0	0	71.2	73	4	36	1	3	49	2	1	6	1	43	41	6	4	.600	0	5.15
92	TUC/PCL	AAA	21	555	20	1	1	0	122.1	128	7	64	1	5	94	6	2	8	0	68	56	7	6	.538	0	4.12
	HOU/NL		11	179	9	0	0	2	33.2	48	3	30	3	2	22	3	0	5	0	43	41	0	7	.000	0	10.96
93	FLO/NL		27	693	27	2	1	0	156.2	156	11	87	7	3	98	5	4	10	4	83	77	8	12	.400	0	4.42
3 YR TOTALS			**52**	**1191**	**49**	**2**	**1**	**2**	**262.0**	**277**	**23**	**153**	**11**	**8**	**169**	**10**	**10**	**23**	**5**	**169**	**159**	**14**	**23**	**.378**	**0**	**5.46**

Brantley, Jeffrey Hoke "Jeff" — BR/TR — b.9/5/63 — SF85 6/134

YR	TM/LG	CL	G	TBF	GS	CG	SHO	GF	IP	H	HR	BB	IBB	HB	SO	SH	SF	WP	BK	R	ER	W	L	PCT	SV	ERA
85	FRE/CAL	A+	14	0	13	3	0	0	94.2	83	4	37	0	1	85	0	0	7	0	39	35	8	2	.800	0	3.33
86	SHR/TEX	AA	26	686	26	8	3	0	165.2	139	13	68	0	6	125	5	3	11	2	78	64	8	10	.444	0	3.48
87	SHR/TEX	AA	2	48	2	0	0	0	11.2	12	1	4	0	1	7	0	0	1	0	7	4	0	1	.000	0	3.09
	PHO/PCL	AAA	29	761	28	2	0	0	170.1	187	13	82	3	11	111	5	5	5	2	110	88	6	11	.353	0	4.65
88	PHO/PCL	AAA	27	533	19	1	0	1	122.2	130	6	39	2	5	83	2	7	2	8	65	59	9	5	.643	0	4.33
	SF/NL		9	88	1	0	0	2	20.2	22	2	6	1	1	11	1	0	0	1	13	13	0	1	.000	1	5.66
89	PHO/PCL	AAA	7	56	0	0	0	5	14.1	6	1	4	0	1	20	1	0	0	0	2	2	1	1	.500	3	1.26
	SF/NL		59	422	1	0	0	15	97.1	101	10	37	8	2	69	7	3	3	2	50	44	7	1	.875	0	4.07
90	SF/NL		55	361	0	0	0	32	86.2	77	3	33	6	3	61	2	2	6	0	18	15	5	3	.625	19	1.56
91	SF/NL		67	411	0	0	0	39	95.1	78	8	52	10	5	81	4	4	6	0	27	26	5	2	.714	15	2.45
92	SF/NL		56	381	0	0	0	32	91.2	67	8	45	4	3	86	7	3	3	1	32	30	7	7	.500	7	2.95
93	SF/NL		53	496	12	0	0	0	113.2	112	11	46	2	7	76	5	5	5	5	60	54	5	6	.455	0	4.28
6 YR TOTALS			**299**	**2159**	**18**	**0**	**0**	**129**	**505.1**	**457**	**50**	**219**	**32**	**21**	**384**	**26**	**17**	**15**	**11**	**200**	**182**	**29**	**20**	**.592**	**42**	**3.24**

Brennan, William Raymond — BR/TR — b.1/15/63 — LA 9/1/84

YR	TM/LG	CL	G	TBF	GS	CG	SHO	GF	IP	H	HR	BB	IBB	HB	SO	SH	SF	WP	BK	R	ER	W	L	PCT	SV	ERA
85	VB/FSL	A+	22	616	21	5	1	0	142.0	121	1	59	1	5	74	8	6	11	2	64	45	10	9	.526	0	2.85
86	SA/TEX	AA	26	642	21	3	0	2	146.2	149	11	61	7	2	83	2	5	7	0	75	63	7	9	.438	0	3.87
87	ALB/PCL	AAA	28	747	28	4	0	0	171.1	188	9	67	0	5	95	9	3	20	0	95	82	10	9	.526	0	4.31
88	ALB/PCL	AAA	29	719	28	4	0	0	167.1	177	15	51	0	5	83	4	2	3	0	85	71	14	8	.636	0	3.82
	LA/NL		4	44	2	0	0	2	9.1	13	0	6	1	0	7	0	0	2	1	7	7	0	1	.000	0	6.75

Brennan, William Raymond (continued)

YR	TM/LG	CL	G	TBF	GS	CG	SHO	GF	IP	H	HR	BB	IBB	HB	SO	SH	SF	WP	BK	R	ER	W	L	PCT	SV	ERA
89	ALB/PCL	AAA	34	573	17	2	0	2	129.0	149	7	57	0	1	104	3	3	15	1	87	75	6	9	.400	0	5.23
90	TUC/PCL	AAA	41	521	8	2	0	5	110.1	104	5	89	3	10	88	5	3	10	1	68	58	8	7	.533	0	4.73
91	HAR/EAS	AA	21	162	0	0	0	6	34.2	35	1	30	1	4	33	2	1	9	0	21	12	3	2	.600	1	3.12
92	TOL/INT	AAA	12	130	3	0	0	4	26.2	29	1	23	0	2	28	0	0	8	0	29	24	0	4	.000	1	8.10
	IOW/AMA	AAA	19	147	1	0	0	9	29.2	43	4	12	1	2	34	0	0	3	0	27	21	1	4	.200	0	6.37
93	IOW/AMA	AAA	28	773	28	2	1	0	179.0	180	13	64	0	15	143	7	4	23	0	96	88	10	7	.588	0	4.42
	CHI/NL		8	65	1	0	0	0	15.0	16	2	8	1	1	11	0	1	0	0	8	7	2	1	.667	0	4.20
2 YR TOTALS			12	109	3	0	0	2	24.1	29	2	14	2	1	18	0	1	2	1	15	14	2	2	.500	0	5.18

Brewer, William Robert "Billy" — BL/TL — b.4/15/68   MON90 36/751

YR	TM/LG	CL	G	TBF	GS	CG	SHO	GF	IP	H	HR	BB	IBB	HB	SO	SH	SF	WP	BK	R	ER	W	L	PCT	SV	ERA
90	JAM/NYP	A-	11	115	2	0	0	4	27.2	23	0	13	0	0	37	1	0	2	0	10	9	2	2	.500	1	2.93
91	ROC/MID	A	29	176	0	0	0	16	41.0	32	1	25	0	1	43	2	1	6	0	12	9	3	3	.500	5	1.98
92	WPB/FSL	A+	28	144	0	0	0	20	36.1	27	0	14	1	2	37	1	0	2	0	10	7	2	2	.500	8	1.73
	HAR/EAS	AA	20	114	0	0	0	4	23.1	25	1	18	1	1	18	0	1	5	0	15	13	2	0	1.000	0	5.01
93	KC/AL		46	157	0	0	0	14	39.0	31	6	20	1	0	28	1	0	1	0	16	15	2	2	.500	0	3.46

Brink, Bradford Albert "Brad" — BR/TR — b.1/20/65   PHI86 1/7

YR	TM/LG	CL	G	TBF	GS	CG	SHO	GF	IP	H	HR	BB	IBB	HB	SO	SH	SF	WP	BK	R	ER	W	L	PCT	SV	ERA
86	REA/EAS	AA	5	107	4	0	0	0	23.2	22	2	20	2	1	8	3	1	0	0	12	10	0	4	.000	0	3.80
87	CLE/FSL	A+	17	418	17	2	1	0	94.1	99	5	39	0	2	64	4	5	1	0	50	40	4	7	.364	0	3.82
	REA/EAS	AA	12	308	11	1	1	0	72.0	76	7	23	2	5	50	2	4	3	2	42	40	3	2	.600	0	5.00
88	MAI/INT	AAA	17	375	17	3	1	0	86.0	100	8	21	0	4	58	2	3	4	2	43	41	5	5	.500	0	4.29
89	SCR/INT	AAA	3	49	3	0	0	0	11.0	11	0	6	0	0	3	1	0	1	0	7	5	0	1	.000	0	4.09
91	SPA/SAL	A	3	68	3	1	0	0	16.1	15	1	5	0	0	16	0	1	0	1	3	3	2	1	.667	0	1.65
	CLE/FSL	A+	2	46	2	0	0	0	13.0	6	1	3	0	1	10	1	0	0	1	1	1	2	0	1.000	0	0.69
	REA/EAS	AA	5	138	5	0	0	0	34.0	32	3	6	1	2	27	2	2	1	0	14	14	2	2	.500	0	3.71
92	REA/EAS	AA	3	59	3	0	0	0	13.2	14	0	3	0	0	12	1	0	0	0	6	5	1	1	.500	0	3.29
	SCR/INT	AAA	17	454	17	5	2	0	111.1	100	15	34	0	2	92	0	1	3	0	47	43	8	2	.800	0	3.48
	PHI/NL		8	187	7	0	0	0	41.1	53	2	13	2	1	16	1	0	0	0	27	19	0	4	.000	0	4.14
93	SCR/NT	AAA	18	445	18	2	2	0	106.2	104	10	27	1	5	89	6	0	0	0	53	50	7	7	.500	0	4.22
	PHI/NL		2	24	0	0	0	1	6.0	3	1	3	0	0	8	0	0	1	0	2	2	0	0	.000	0	3.00
2 YR TOTALS			10	211	7	0	0	1	47.1	56	3	16	2	1	24	1	0	1	0	29	21	0	4	.000	0	3.99

Briscoe, John Eric — BR/TR — b.9/22/67   OAK88 4/73

YR	TM/LG	CL	G	TBF	GS	CG	SHO	GF	IP	H	HR	BB	IBB	HB	SO	SH	SF	WP	BK	R	ER	W	L	PCT	SV	ERA
88	ATH/ARI	R	7	105	6	0	0	0	25.2	26	1	6	0	1	23	0	1	3	3	14	10	1	1	.500	0	3.51
89	MAD/MID	A	21	524	20	1	0	1	117.2	121	7	57	0	9	69	10	9	11	1	66	55	7	5	.583	0	4.21
90	MOD/CAL	A+	29	373	12	1	0	12	86.1	72	12	52	0	2	66	4	1	7	0	50	44	3	6	.333	4	4.59
	HUN/SOU	AA	3	30	0	0	0	0	4.2	9	1	7	0	0	7	0	0	1	0	7	7	0	0	.000	0	13.50
91	HUN/SOU	AA	2	19	0	0	0	2	4.1	1	0	2	0	0	6	0	0	0	0	2	0	2	0	1.000	0	0.00
	OAK/AL		11	62	0	0	0	9	14.0	12	3	10	0	1	9	0	1	3	0	11	11	0	0	.000	0	7.07
	TAC/PCL	AAA	22	342	9	0	0	6	76.1	73	7	44	1	5	66	2	2	3	0	35	31	3	5	.375	1	3.66
92	OAK/AL		2	40	2	0	0	0	7.0	12	0	9	0	0	4	1	0	2	0	6	5	0	1	.000	0	6.43
	TAC/PCL	AAA	33	368	6	0	0	11	78.0	78	7	68	5	1	66	5	2	6	0	62	51	2	5	.286	0	5.88
93	HUN/SOU	AA	30	158	0	0	0	28	38.2	28	3	16	1	1	62	3	0	0	0	14	13	4	0	1.000	16	3.03
	TAC/PCL	AAA	9	59	0	0	0	8	12.1	13	1	9	3	0	16	2	0	1	0	5	4	1	1	.500	6	2.92
	OAK/AL		17	122	0	0	0	6	24.2	26	2	26	3	0	24	0	2	5	0	25	22	1	0	1.000	0	8.03
3 YR TOTALS			30	224	2	0	0	15	45.2	50	5	45	3	0	37	1	3	10	0	42	38	1	1	.500	0	7.49

Brocail, Douglas Keith "Doug" — BL/TR — b.5/16/67   SD86* 1/12

YR	TM/LG	CL	G	TBF	GS	CG	SHO	GF	IP	H	HR	BB	IBB	HB	SO	SH	SF	WP	BK	R	ER	W	L	PCT	SV	ERA
86	SPO/NWL	A-	16	0	15	0	0	1	85.0	85	4	53	1	6	77	0	0	10	1	52	36	5	4	.556	0	3.81
87	CHS/SAL	A	19	393	18	0	0	0	92.1	94	6	28	0	1	68	3	3	4	0	51	42	2	6	.250	0	4.09
88	CHS/SAL	A	22	447	13	5	0	7	107.0	107	3	25	0	4	107	4	2	4	3	40	32	8	6	.571	2	2.69
89	WIC/TEX	AA	23	603	22	1	1	0	134.2	158	11	50	4	1	95	5	5	9	4	88	78	5	9	.357	0	5.21
90	WIC/TEX	AA	12	227	9	0	0	1	52.0	53	7	24	0	2	27	1	0	4	0	30	25	2	2	.500	0	4.33
91	WIC/TEX	AA	34	625	16	3	1	11	146.1	147	15	43	3	4	108	3	13	0	0	77	63	10	7	.588	6	3.87
92	LV/PCL	AAA	29	733	25	4	0	2	172.1	187	7	63	5	6	103	6	1	6	0	82	76	10	10	.500	0	3.97
	SD/NL		3	64	3	0	0	0	14.0	17	2	5	0	1	15	2	0	0	0	10	10	0	0	.000	0	6.43
93	LV/PCL	AAA	10	219	8	0	0	1	51.1	51	4	14	0	1	32	1	2	2	0	26	21	4	2	.667	1	3.68
	SD/NL		24	571	24	0	0	0	128.1	143	16	42	4	4	70	10	8	4	1	75	65	4	13	.235	0	4.56
2 YR TOTALS			27	635	27	0	0	0	142.1	160	18	47	4	4	85	12	8	4	1	85	75	4	13	.235	0	4.74

Bronkey, Jacob Jeffrey "Jeff" — BR/TR — b.9/18/65   MIN86 2/38

YR	TM/LG	CL	G	TBF	GS	CG	SHO	GF	IP	H	HR	BB	IBB	HB	SO	SH	SF	WP	BK	R	ER	W	L	PCT	SV	ERA
86	KEN/MID	A	14	221	6	1	0	5	49.1	41	5	30	3	4	25	4	2	5	0	24	21	4	6	.400	0	3.83
87	ORL/SOU	AA	24	239	4	1	0	16	48.2	70	5	28	1	4	23	1	5	0	0	40	34	1	6	.143	7	6.29
	VIS/CAL	A+	27	175	0	0	0	20	35.1	26	2	32	6	6	31	0	1	2	0	21	15	2	5	.286	5	3.82
88	VIS/CAL	A+	43	382	6	0	0	27	85.1	66	0	67	0	11	58	0	1	14	1	44	32	4	6	.400	9	3.38
89	ORL/SOU	AA	16	294	13	0	0	1	61.2	74	3	35	1	9	47	3	3	3	0	53	37	1	2	.333	0	5.40
90	OC/AMA	AAA	28	237	0	0	0	7	51.2	58	3	28	6	3	18	1	3	4	0	28	25	2	4	.333	0	4.35
91	OC/AMA	AAA	7	52	0	0	0	3	10.0	16	2	4	0	1	7	0	0	0	0	13	12	0	1	.000	0	10.80
	TUL/TEX	AA	4	39	0	0	0	3	7.2	11	0	5	0	1	5	0	0	0	0	9	8	0	0	.000	0	9.39
92	TUL/TEX	AA	45	286	0	0	0	34	70.2	51	0	25	4	3	58	6	2	4	0	27	20	2	7	.222	13	2.55
	OC/AMA	AAA	13	78	0	0	0	8	15.2	26	1	7	0	2	10	0	0	2	0	13	13	0	1	.000	3	7.47

(continued)

Bronkey, Jacob Jeffrey "Jeff" (continued)

YR	TM/LG	CL	G	TBF	GS	CG	SHO	GF	IP	H	HR	BB	IBB	HB	SO	SH	SF	WP	BK	R	ER	W	L	PCT	SV	ERA
93	OC/AMA	AAA	29	144	0	0	0	26	37.1	29	2	7	2	0	19	0	4	2	0	11	11	2	2	.500	14	2.65
	TEX/AL		21	152	0	0	0	6	36.0	39	4	11	4	1	18	1	2	2	0	20	16	1	1	.500	1	4.00

Bross, Terrence Paul "Terry" — BR/TR — b.3/30/66   NYN87 14/342

YR	TM/LG	CL	G	TBF	GS	CG	SHO	GF	IP	H	HR	BB	IBB	HB	SO	SH	SF	WP	BK	R	ER	W	L	PCT	SV	ERA
87	LF/NYP	A-	10	129	3	0	0	1	28.0	22	3	20	0	0	21	2	1	1	1	23	12	2	0	1.000	0	3.86
88	LF/NYP	A-	20	248	6	0	0	8	55.1	43	2	38	0	1	59	1	2	2	2	25	19	2	1	.667	1	3.09
89	SL/FSL	A+	35	234	0	0	0	26	58.0	39	1	26	3	1	47	0	4	3	1	21	18	8	2	.800	11	2.79
90	JAC/TEX	AA	58	290	0	0	0	48	71.2	46	4	40	5	2	51	5	3	4	4	21	21	3	4	.429	28	2.64
91	TID/INT	AAA	27	159	0	0	0	10	33.0	31	0	32	2	1	23	1	1	3	2	21	16	2	0	1.000	2	4.36
	WIL/EAS	AA	20	98	0	0	0	16	25.1	13	1	11	0	0	27	2	1	1	0	12	7	2	0	1.000	5	2.49
	NY/NL		8	39	0	0	0	4	10.0	7	1	3	0	0	5	1	0	0	0	2	2	0	0	.000	0	1.80
92	LV/PCL	AAA	49	356	0	0	0	12	85.2	83	4	30	3	0	42	5	6	5	1	36	31	7	3	.700	5	3.26
93	PHO/PCL	AAA	54	343	0	0	0	28	79.1	76	5	37	1	1	69	1	5	3	2	37	35	4	4	.500	5	3.97
	SF/NL		2	10	0	0	0	1	2.0	3	1	1	0	0	1	0	0	0	0	2	2	0	0	.000	0	9.00
2 YR TOTALS			**10**	**49**	**0**	**0**	**0**	**5**	**12.0**	**10**	**2**	**4**	**0**	**0**	**6**	**1**	**0**	**0**	**0**	**4**	**4**	**0**	**0**	**.000**	**0**	**3.00**

Brow, Scott John — BR/TR — b.3/17/69   TOR90 8/204

YR	TM/LG	CL	G	TBF	GS	CG	SHO	GF	IP	H	HR	BB	IBB	HB	SO	SH	SF	WP	BK	R	ER	W	L	PCT	SV	ERA
90	SC/NYP	A-	9	165	7	0	0	0	39.2	34	2	11	0	2	39	2	0	4	0	18	10	3	1	.750	0	2.27
91	DUN/FSL	A+	15	306	12	0	0	1	69.2	73	5	28	1	2	31	3	3	2	5	50	37	3	7	.300	0	4.78
92	DUN/FSL	A+	25	690	25	3	1	0	170.2	143	8	44	2	7	107	4	5	3	3	53	46	14	2	.875	0	2.43
93	KNO/SOU	AA	3	74	3	1	0	0	19.0	13	3	9	0	0	12	1	1	2	0	8	7	1	2	.333	0	3.32
	SYR/INT	AAA	20	510	19	2	0	0	121.1	119	8	37	1	6	64	1	6	8	2	63	59	6	8	.429	0	4.38
	TOR/AL		6	83	3	0	0	1	18.0	19	2	10	1	1	7	1	1	2	0	15	12	1	1	.500	0	6.00

Brown, James Kevin "Kevin" — BR/TR — b.3/14/65   TEX86 1/4

YR	TM/LG	CL	G	TBF	GS	CG	SHO	GF	IP	H	HR	BB	IBB	HB	SO	SH	SF	WP	BK	R	ER	W	L	PCT	SV	ERA
86	RAN/GCL	R	3	26	0	0	0	0	6.0	7	0	2	0	0	0	0	0	0	1	4	4	0	0	.000	0	6.00
	TUL/TEX	AA	3	47	2	0	0	0	10.0	9	0	5	0	0	10	1	0	0	1	7	5	0	0	.000	0	4.50
	TEX/AL		1	19	1	0	0	0	5.0	6	0	0	0	0	4	0	0	0	0	2	2	1	0	1.000	0	3.60
87	TUL/TEX	AA	8	193	8	0	0	0	42.0	53	3	18	1	1	26	0	2	1	0	36	34	1	4	.200	0	7.29
	OC/AMA	AAA	5	124	5	0	0	0	24.1	32	2	17	0	4	9	0	0	1	2	32	29	0	5	.000	0	10.73
	CHA/FSL	A+	6	153	6	1	0	0	36.1	33	1	17	0	0	21	0	0	0	0	14	11	0	0	.000	0	2.72
88	TUL/TEX	AA	26	741	26	5	0	0	174.1	174	5	61	1	10	118	3	0	13	8	94	68	12	10	.545	0	3.51
	TEX/AL		4	110	4	1	0	0	23.1	33	2	8	1	0	12	1	0	1	1	15	11	1	1	.500	0	4.24
89	TEX/AL		28	798	28	7	0	0	191.0	167	10	70	2	4	104	3	6	7	2	81	71	12	9	.571	0	3.35
90	TEX/AL		26	757	26	6	2	0	180.0	175	13	60	3	3	88	7	9	2	2	84	72	12	10	.545	0	3.60
91	TEX/AL		33	934	33	0	0	0	210.2	233	17	90	5	13	96	6	4	12	3	116	103	9	12	.429	0	4.40
92	TEX/AL		35	1108	35	11	1	0	*265.2	262	11	76	2	10	173	7	8	8	2	117	98	*21	11	.656	0	3.32
93	TEX/AL		34	1001	34	12	3	0	233.0	228	14	74	5	15	142	5	3	8	1	105	93	15	12	.556	0	3.59
7 YR TOTALS			**161**	**4727**	**161**	**37**	**6**	**0**	**1108.2**	**1104**	**67**	**378**	**17**	**46**	**619**	**24**	**28**	**45**	**10**	**520**	**450**	**71**	**55**	**.563**	**0**	**3.65**

Browning, Thomas Leo "Tom" — BL/TL — b.4/28/60   CIN82 11/233

YR	TM/LG	CL	G	TBF	GS	CG	SHO	GF	IP	H	HR	BB	IBB	HB	SO	SH	SF	WP	BK	R	ER	W	L	PCT	SV	ERA
84	WIC/AMA	AAA	30	801	28	8	1	1	189.1	169	24	73	1	6	160	5	5	2	0	88	83	12	10	.545	0	3.95
	CIN/NL		3	95	3	0	0	0	23.1	27	0	5	0	0	14	1	0	1	0	4	4	1	0	1.000	0	1.54
85	CIN/NL		38	1083	38	6	4	0	261.1	242	29	73	8	3	155	13	7	2	0	111	103	20	9	.690	0	3.55
86	CIN/NL		39	1016	39	4	2	0	243.1	225	26	70	6	1	147	14	12	3	0	123	103	14	13	.519	0	3.81
87	NAS/AMA	AAA	5	138	5	1	1	0	29.2	37	5	12	0	0	28	1	2	1	0	22	20	2	3	.400	0	6.07
	CIN/NL		32	791	31	2	0	0	183.0	201	27	61	7	5	117	10	7	2	4	107	102	10	13	.435	0	5.02
88	CIN/NL		36	1001	36	5	2	0	250.2	205	36	64	3	7	124	6	8	2	1	98	95	18	5	.783	0	3.41
89	CIN/NL		37	1031	37	9	2	0	249.2	241	31	64	10	3	118	12	6	2	0	109	94	15	12	.556	0	3.39
90	CIN/NL		35	957	35	2	1	0	227.2	235	24	52	13	5	99	13	5	5	1	98	96	15	9	.625	0	3.80
91	CIN/NL		36	983	36	1	0	0	230.1	241	32	56	4	4	115	8	4	1	0	124	107	14	14	.500	0	4.18
92	CIN/NL		16	386	16	0	0	0	87.0	108	6	28	7	2	33	5	4	3	1	49	49	6	5	.545	0	5.07
93	CIN/NL		21	505	20	0	0	0	114.0	159	15	20	2	1	53	4	2	1	0	61	60	7	7	.500	0	4.74
10 YR TOTALS			**293**	**7848**	**291**	**29**	**11**	**1**	**1870.1**	**1884**	**226**	**493**	**60**	**31**	**975**	**86**	**60**	**24**	**13**	**884**	**813**	**120**	**87**	**.580**	**0**	**3.91**

Brummett, Gregory Scott "Greg" — BR/TR — b.4/20/67   SF89 11/284

YR	TM/LG	CL	G	TBF	GS	CG	SHO	GF	IP	H	HR	BB	IBB	HB	SO	SH	SF	WP	BK	R	ER	W	L	PCT	SV	ERA
89	SJ/CAL	A+	2	49	2	0	0	0	9.2	15	2	8	0	1	3	0	1	0	0	7	6	0	1	.000	0	5.59
	EVE/NWL	A-	14	311	10	1	0	2	72.0	63	1	24	0	6	76	0	3	6	4	34	23	4	2	.667	0	2.88
90	CLI/MID	A	6	107	4	0	0	0	25.2	18	0	9	0	3	22	1	0	1	3	14	10	2	2	.500	0	3.51
91	CLI/MID	A	16	445	16	5	2	0	112.1	91	2	32	2	3	74	2	2	5	1	39	34	10	5	.667	0	2.72
92	SJ/CAL	A+	19	379	13	2	2	1	100.0	74	2	21	0	4	68	6	1	1	0	32	29	10	4	.714	0	2.61
	PHO/PCL	AAA	3	21	1	0	0	2	4.2	8	0	4	1	0	1	0	0	0	0	4	4	0	1	.000	0	7.71
93	PHO/PCL	AAA	18	454	18	0	0	0	107.0	114	3	27	3	2	84	1	2	3	3	56	44	7	7	.500	0	3.70
	SF/NL		8	196	8	0	0	0	46.0	53	9	13	1	0	20	1	2	2	2	25	24	2	3	.400	0	4.70
	MIN/AL		5	115	5	0	0	0	26.2	29	3	15	1	0	10	0	3	0	0	17	17	2	1	.667	0	5.74
	YEAR		13	311	13	0	0	0	72.2	82	12	28	2	0	30	1	5	2	2	42	41	4	4	.500	0	5.08
1 YR TOTALS			**13**	**311**	**13**	**0**	**0**	**0**	**72.2**	**82**	**12**	**28**	**2**	**0**	**30**	**1**	**5**	**2**	**2**	**42**	**41**	**4**	**4**	**.500**	**0**	**5.08**

Bullinger, James Eric "Jim" — BR/TR — b.8/21/65   CHN86 9/220

YR	TM/LG	CL	G	TBF	GS	CG	SHO	GF	IP	H	HR	BB	IBB	HB	SO	SH	SF	WP	BK	R	ER	W	L	PCT	SV	ERA
89	CHA/SOU	AA	2	14	0	0	0	2	3.0	2	0	3	0	0	5	0	0	1	0	0	0	0	0	.000	0	0.00

Bullinger, James Eric "Jim" (continued)

YR	TM/LG	CL	G	TBF	GS	CG	SHO	GF	IP	H	HR	BB	IBB	HB	SO	SH	SF	WP	BK	R	ER	W	L	PCT	SV	ERA
90	WIN/CAR	A+	14	392	13	3	0	0	90.0	81	5	46	0	7	85	3	2	6	1	43	37	7	6	.538	0	3.70
	CHA/SOU	AA	9	194	9	0	0	0	44.0	42	7	18	0	3	33	1	1	3	1	30	25	3	4	.429	0	5.11
91	CHA/SOU	AA	20	595	20	8	0	0	142.2	132	5	61	2	6	128	5	1	5	3	62	56	9	9	.500	0	3.53
	IOW/AMA	AAA	8	203	8	0	0	0	46.2	47	6	23	0	0	30	1	1	7	0	32	28	3	4	.429	0	5.40
92	IOW/AMA	AAA	20	91	0	0	0	20	22.0	17	0	12	3	0	15	1	1	2	1	6	6	1	2	.333	14	2.45
	CHI/NL		39	380	9	1	0	15	85.0	72	9	54	6	4	36	9	4	4	0	49	44	2	8	.200	7	4.66
93	IOW/AMA	AAA	49	326	3	0	0	37	73.2	64	3	43	5	4	74	2	3	13	0	29	28	4	6	.400	20	3.42
	CHI/NL		15	75	0	0	0	6	16.2	18	1	9	0	0	10	0	1	0	0	9	8	1	0	1.000	1	4.32
2 YR TOTALS			**54**	**455**	**9**	**1**	**0**	**21**	**101.2**	**90**	**10**	**63**	**6**	**4**	**46**	**9**	**5**	**4**	**0**	**58**	**52**	**3**	**8**	**.273**	**8**	**4.60**

Burba, David Allen "Dave" — BR/TR — b.7/7/66
SEA87 2/33

YR	TM/LG	CL	G	TBF	GS	CG	SHO	GF	IP	H	HR	BB	IBB	HB	SO	SH	SF	WP	BK	R	ER	W	L	PCT	SV	ERA
87	BEL/NWL	A-	5	97	5	0	0	0	23.1	20	0	3	0	0	24	0	0	4	0	10	5	3	1	.750	0	1.93
	SAL/CAL	A+	9	246	9	0	0	0	54.2	53	3	29	0	2	46	3	2	3	0	31	28	1	6	.143	0	4.61
88	SB/CAL	A+	20	485	20	1	0	0	114.0	106	4	54	1	4	102	4	2	5	2	41	34	5	7	.417	0	2.68
89	WIL/EAS	AA	25	651	25	5	1	0	156.2	138	7	55	0	3	89	5	3	4	5	69	55	11	7	.611	0	3.16
90	CAL/PCL	AAA	31	493	18	1	0	8	113.2	124	11	45	0	2	47	4	3	5	3	64	59	10	6	.625	2	4.67
	SEA/AL		6	35	0	0	0	2	8.0	8	0	2	0	0	4	0	0	0	0	6	4	0	0	.000	0	4.50
91	CAL/PCL	AAA	23	315	9	0	0	9	71.1	82	4	27	0	4	42	4	1	3	2	35	28	6	4	.600	4	3.53
	SEA/AL		22	153	2	0	0	11	36.2	34	6	14	3	0	16	0	1	0	1	16	15	2	2	.500	1	3.68
92	PHO/PCL	AAA	13	324	13	0	0	0	74.1	86	5	24	2	3	44	3	2	3	2	40	39	5	5	.500	0	4.72
	SF/NL		23	318	11	0	0	4	70.2	80	4	31	2	2	47	2	4	1	1	43	39	2	7	.222	0	4.97
93	SF/NL		54	408	5	0	0	9	95.1	95	14	37	5	2	88	6	3	6	0	49	45	10	3	.769	0	4.25
4 YR TOTALS			**105**	**914**	**18**	**0**	**0**	**26**	**210.2**	**217**	**24**	**84**	**10**	**6**	**155**	**10**	**7**	**6**	**1**	**114**	**103**	**14**	**12**	**.538**	**1**	**4.40**

Burgos, Enrique — BL/TL — b.10/7/65
TOR 1/31/83

YR	TM/LG	CL	G	TBF	GS	CG	SHO	GF	IP	H	HR	BB	IBB	HB	SO	SH	SF	WP	BK	R	ER	W	L	PCT	SV	ERA
84	FLO/SAL	A	2	7	0	0	0	0	1.0	2	0	1	0	1	0	0	0	1	0	2	2	0	0	.000	0	18.00
	BRA/GCL	R	12	319	10	1	0	0	71.2	74	1	22	0	1	38	6	2	9	1	37	19	4	5	.444	0	2.39
85	FLO/SAL	A	26	240	0	0	1	12	47.2	55	2	44	2	1	32	5	2	7	1	39	35	3	1	.750	0	6.61
	KIN/CAR	A+	7	47	1	0	0	1	8.1	12	1	10	0	0	5	0	2	1	0	11	11	0	2	.000	0	11.88
86	FLO/SAL	A	28	418	10	0	2	6	85.0	92	5	70	0	2	71	5	5	15	0	76	61	3	8	.273	0	6.46
	VEN/CAL	A+	9	205	9	0	0	0	45.2	46	1	31	0	0	37	1	4	5	1	27	20	1	3	.250	0	3.94
87	KNO/SOU	AA	17	222	5	0	1	6	45.1	33	4	55	0	1	45	2	1	3	1	27	22	2	3	.400	0	4.37
	MB/SAL	A	23	159	0	0	7	13	38.1	22	2	24	1	0	36	2	2	8	0	15	9	5	2	.714	0	2.11
88	SYR/INT	AAA	2	13	0	0	0	0	2.1	4	0	2	0	0	2	0	0	0	0	2	2	0	0	.000	0	7.71
	DUN/FSL	A+	33	239	4	0	0	13	49.2	61	0	37	2	0	55	3	1	9	3	28	26	1	5	.167	0	4.71
89	DUN/FSL	A+	8	59	0	0	0	3	12.2	8	0	7	0	0	15	1	2	1	1	7	3	1	0	1.000	0	2.13
	MIA/FSL	A+	15	92	1	0	0	10	20.2	20	0	13	0	0	18	1	1	4	1	14	9	1	1	.500	0	3.92
	MB/SAL	A	16	87	1	0	1	10	16.2	16	0	20	2	2	15	2	0	3	0	11	5	0	2	.000	0	2.70
93	OMA/AMA	AAA	48	263	0	0	0	26	62.1	36	4	37	0	1	91	0	1	6	0	26	22	2	4	.333	0	3.18
	KC/AL		5	28	0	0	0	3	5.0	5	0	6	1	1	6	0	0	1	0	5	5	0	1	.000	0	9.00

Burkett, John David — BR/TR — b.11/28/64
SF83 6/148

YR	TM/LG	CL	G	TBF	GS	CG	SHO	GF	IP	H	HR	BB	IBB	HB	SO	SH	SF	WP	BK	R	ER	W	L	PCT	SV	ERA
84	CLI/MID	A	20	553	20	2	0	0	126.2	128	5	38	1	6	83	7	3	9	1	81	61	7	6	.538	0	4.33
85	FRE/CAL	A+	20	0	20	1	1	0	109.2	98	3	46	0	6	72	0	0	6	0	43	35	7	4	.636	0	2.87
86	FRE/CAL	A+	4	118	4	0	0	0	24.2	34	2	8	0	2	14	0	0	2	0	19	15	0	0	.000	0	5.47
	SHR/TEX	AA	22	513	21	4	2	0	128.2	99	7	42	0	4	73	4	0	3	3	46	38	10	6	.625	0	2.66
87	SHR/TEX	AA	27	759	27	6	3	0	177.2	181	11	53	2	7	126	6	6	3	1	75	66	14	8	.636	0	3.34
	SF/NL		3	28	0	0	0	1	6.0	7	2	3	0	1	5	1	0	0	0	4	3	0	0	.000	0	4.50
88	SHR/TEX	AA	7	199	7	2	1	0	50.2	33	3	18	2	1	34	3	2	1	1	15	12	5	1	.833	0	2.13
	PHO/PCL	AAA	21	524	21	0	0	0	114.0	142	7	49	3	5	74	5	7	1	2	79	66	5	11	.313	0	5.21
89	PHO/PCL	AAA	28	745	28	2	1	0	167.2	197	19	59	3	8	105	6	6	2	2	111	94	10	11	.476	0	5.05
90	PHO/PCL	AAA	3	86	3	2	1	0	23.0	18	1	4	0	0	10	0	0	0	0	8	7	2	1	.667	0	2.74
	SF/NL		33	857	32	2	0	1	204.0	201	18	61	7	4	118	6	8	5	0	92	86	14	7	.667	1	3.79
91	SF/NL		36	890	34	3	1	0	206.2	223	19	60	2	10	131	8	8	5	0	103	96	12	11	.522	0	4.18
92	SF/NL		32	799	32	3	1	0	189.2	194	13	45	6	4	107	11	4	0	0	96	81	13	9	.591	0	3.84
93	SF/NL		34	942	34	2	1	0	231.2	224	18	40	4	11	145	8	4	1	2	100	94	*22	7	.759	0	3.65
5 YR TOTALS			**138**	**3516**	**132**	**10**	**3**	**2**	**838.0**	**849**	**70**	**209**	**19**	**30**	**506**	**34**	**21**	**9**	**5**	**395**	**360**	**61**	**34**	**.642**	**1**	**3.87**

Burns, Todd Edward — BR/TR — b.7/6/63
OAK84 7/168

YR	TM/LG	CL	G	TBF	GS	CG	SHO	GF	IP	H	HR	BB	IBB	HB	SO	SH	SF	WP	BK	R	ER	W	L	PCT	SV	ERA
84	MED/NWL	A-	22	0	0	0	0	18	36.1	21	0	12	0	0	63	0	0	0	0	4	2	3	0	1.000	8	0.50
	MAD/MID	A	10	55	0	0	0	9	14.0	11	1	3	0	0	20	3	0	0	0	4	4	3	2	.600	1	2.57
85	MAD/MID	A	20	506	19	5	3	0	123.0	109	8	40	0	4	94	1	3	12	0	55	50	8	8	.500	0	3.66
	HUN/SOU	AA	4	94	4	1	1	0	22.2	16	0	13	0	0	8	0	2	0	0	6	3	3	1	.750	0	1.19
86	HUN/SOU	AA	20	525	18	5	3	0	124.2	122	16	39	1	3	77	1	6	6	3	59	52	7	5	.500	0	3.75
	TAC/PCL	AAA	11	66	0	0	0	9	16.2	11	1	12	1	0	14	1	0	1	0	4	4	0	1	.000	2	2.16
87	HUN/SOU	AA	34	257	0	0	0	27	63.2	49	4	17	1	4	54	1	1	5	0	24	21	3	4	.429	7	2.97
	TAC/PCL	AAA	21	122	0	0	0	10	27.2	27	3	16	1	0	30	1	2	1	0	16	15	2	2	.500	1	4.88
88	TAC/PCL	AAA	21	310	5	1	0	3	73.1	74	4	26	2	1	59	3	2	0	0	39	30	4	3	.571	1	3.68
	OAK/AL		17	425	14	2	0	0	102.2	93	8	34	1	1	57	2	2	1	0	38	36	8	2	.800	0	3.16
89	OAK/AL		50	374	2	0	0	22	96.1	66	3	28	5	1	49	3	2	1	0	28	24	6	5	.545	8	2.24
90	OAK/AL		43	337	2	0	0	9	78.2	78	8	32	4	0	43	5	3	0	0	28	26	3	3	.500	3	2.97
91	MOD/CAL	A+	2	31	1	0	0	0	6.0	9	1	3	0	1	3	0	0	0	0	7	7	1	0	1.000	0	10.50

(continued)

Burns, Todd Edward (continued)

YR	TM/LG	CL	G	TBF	GS	CG	SHO	GF	IP	H	HR	BB	IBB	HB	SO	SH	SF	WP	BK	R	ER	W	L	PCT	SV	ERA
	OAK/AL		9	57	0	0	0	5	13.1	10	2	8	1	0	3	1	2	1	0	5	5	1	0	1.000	0	3.38
	TAC/PCL	AAA	13	112	0	0	0	4	25.1	30	5	7	2	0	24	1	3	2	0	16	15	0	2	.000	2	5.33
92	OC/AMA	AAA	8	169	7	0	0	1	42.1	32	3	13	0	0	16	0	1	1	1	15	12	3	2	.600	0	2.55
	TEX/AL		35	433	10	0	0	9	103.0	97	8	32	1	4	55	2	4	5	0	54	44	3	5	.375	1	3.84
93	TEX/AL		25	288	5	0	0	8	65.0	63	6	32	3	2	35	2	3	3	2	36	33	0	4	.000	0	4.57
	STL/NL		24	131	0	0	0	5	30.2	32	8	9	6	0	10	3	2	0	1	21	21	0	4	.000	0	6.16
	YEAR		49	419	5	0	0	13	95.2	95	14	41	9	2	45	5	5	3	3	57	54	0	8	.000	0	5.08
6 YR TOTALS			**203**	**2045**	**33**	**2**	**0**	**61**	**489.2**	**439**	**43**	**175**	**21**	**8**	**252**	**22**	**17**	**21**	**9**	**209**	**189**	**21**	**23**	**.477**	**13**	**3.47**

Bushing, Christopher Shaun "Chris" — BR/TR — b.11/4/67   BAL 6/14/86

YR	TM/LG	CL	G	TBF	GS	CG	SHO	GF	IP	H	HR	BB	IBB	HB	SO	SH	SF	WP	BK	R	ER	W	L	PCT	SV	ERA
86	BLU/APP	R+	13	104	1	0	0	7	26.1	14	1	12	0	0	30	0	2	4	0	5	4	2	0	1.000	2	1.37
87	BLU/APP	R+	20	157	0	0	0	11	37.0	27	2	18	0	1	51	1	0	1	1	20	15	2	0	1.000	6	3.65
89	PEN/CAR	A+	35	472	14	1	0	13	99.2	96	4	79	0	6	99	3	5	10	5	64	48	2	7	.222	3	4.33
90	ROC/MID	A	46	344	0	0	0	32	79.2	62	5	38	5	2	99	8	2	3	0	38	29	3	6	.333	12	3.28
91	WPB/FSL	A+	46	274	0	0	0	26	65.0	41	1	40	3	1	68	6	1	4	7	15	14	2	1	.667	9	1.94
	HAR/EAS	AA	3	37	1	0	0	0	8.2	3	0	8	0	1	7	0	0	2	0	2	1	1	0	1.000	0	1.04
92	REA/EAS	AA	22	305	8	0	0	2	70.1	68	9	30	0	2	72	2	3	4	0	38	34	3	6	.333	1	4.35
	NAS/AMA	AAA	5	42	0	0	0	1	10.1	8	1	6	0	0	6	1	1	0	0	4	4	1	0	1.000	0	3.48
93	CHT/SOU	AA	61	279	0	0	0	50	70.0	50	7	23	2	2	84	2	2	2	1	20	18	6	1	.857	29	2.31
	CIN/NL		6	25	0	0	0	2	4.1	9	1	4	0	0	3	0	1	2	0	7	6	0	0	.000	0	12.46

Butcher, Michael Dana "Mike" — BR/TR — b.5/10/65   KC86 S2/36

YR	TM/LG	CL	G	TBF	GS	CG	SHO	GF	IP	H	HR	BB	IBB	HB	SO	SH	SF	WP	BK	R	ER	W	L	PCT	SV	ERA
86	EUG/NWL	A-	14	0	14	1	0	0	72.1	51	2	49	0	7	68	0	0	5	1	39	31	5	4	.556	0	3.86
87	FM/FSL	A+	5	133	5	1	0	0	31.1	33	3	8	0	1	17	0	0	0	0	20	19	2	2	.500	0	5.46
	APP/MID	A	20	525	19	3	1	0	121.1	101	4	56	5	5	89	5	5	9	2	50	36	10	4	.714	0	2.67
88	BC/FSL	A+	6	143	6	0	0	0	32.2	32	2	10	1	2	20	1	4	1	0	19	14	1	4	.200	0	3.86
	APP/MID	A	4	73	4	0	0	0	18.0	17	0	5	0	2	7	1	1	3	0	7	6	0	1	.000	0	3.00
	QC/MID	A	3	28	0	0	0	0	6.0	6	0	4	0	2	7	1	0	1	0	3	3	0	0	.000	0	4.50
	PS/CAL	A+	7	199	7	0	0	0	42.2	57	3	19	0	4	37	0	1	6	0	33	27	3	2	.600	0	5.70
89	MID/TEX	AA	15	331	15	0	0	0	68.2	92	6	41	1	3	49	2	4	7	2	54	50	2	6	.250	0	6.55
90	MID/TEX	AA	35	413	8	0	0	6	87.0	109	7	55	2	3	84	6	3	3	1	68	60	3	7	.300	0	6.21
91	MID/TEX	AA	41	394	6	0	0	13	88.0	93	6	46	0	8	70	2	7	4	0	54	51	9	6	.600	3	5.22
92	EDM/PCL	AAA	26	130	0	0	0	16	29.1	24	2	18	2	2	32	5	1	1	0	12	10	5	2	.714	4	3.07
	CAL/AL		19	125	0	0	0	6	27.2	29	3	13	1	2	24	0	0	0	0	11	10	2	2	.500	0	3.25
93	VAN/PCL	AAA	14	108	1	0	0	5	24.1	21	3	12	0	1	12	2	1	3	2	16	12	2	3	.400	3	4.44
	CAL/AL		23	124	0	0	0	11	28.1	21	2	15	1	2	24	1	3	0	0	12	9	1	0	1.000	8	2.86
2 YR TOTALS			**42**	**249**	**0**	**0**	**0**	**17**	**56.0**	**50**	**5**	**28**	**2**	**4**	**48**	**1**	**3**	**0**	**0**	**23**	**19**	**3**	**2**	**.600**	**8**	**3.05**

Cadaret, Gregory James "Greg" — BL/TL — b.2/27/62   OAK83 11/267

YR	TM/LG	CL	G	TBF	GS	CG	SHO	GF	IP	H	HR	BB	IBB	HB	SO	SH	SF	WP	BK	R	ER	W	L	PCT	SV	ERA
84	MOD/CAL	A+	26	0	26	6	2	0	171.1	162	7	82	0	1	138	0	0	14	2	79	58	13	8	.619	0	3.05
85	HUN/SOU	AA	17	387	17	0	0	0	82.1	96	9	57	0	3	60	2	4	9	0	61	56	3	7	.300	0	6.12
	MOD/CAL	A+	12	0	12	1	1	0	61.1	59	4	54	0	1	43	0	0	10	0	50	40	3	9	.250	0	5.87
86	HUN/SOU	AA	28	666	28	1	0	0	141.1	166	6	98	0	3	113	1	4	15	0	106	85	12	5	.706	0	5.41
87	HUN/SOU	AA	24	172	0	0	0	21	40.1	31	1	20	3	0	48	1	0	6	1	16	13	5	2	.714	9	2.90
	TAC/PCL	AAA	7	57	0	0	0	4	13.0	5	1	13	1	2	0	0	0	0	0	6	5	1	2	.333	1	3.46
	OAK/AL		29	176	0	0	0	7	39.2	37	6	24	1	1	30	2	2	1	0	22	20	6	2	.750	0	4.54
88	OAK/AL		58	311	0	0	0	16	71.2	60	2	36	1	1	64	5	5	5	3	26	23	5	2	.714	3	2.89
89	OAK/AL		26	119	0	0	0	8	27.2	21	0	19	3	0	14	0	2	0	0	9	7	0	0	.000	0	2.28
	NY/AL		20	412	13	3	1	1	92.1	109	7	38	1	2	66	3	3	6	2	53	47	5	5	.500	0	4.58
	YEAR		46	531	13	3	1	7	120.0	130	7	57	4	2	80	3	5	6	2	62	54	5	5	.500	0	4.05
90	NY/AL		54	525	6	0	0	9	121.1	120	8	64	5	1	80	9	4	14	0	62	56	5	4	.556	3	4.15
91	NY/AL		68	517	5	0	0	17	121.2	110	8	59	6	2	105	6	3	3	1	52	49	8	6	.571	3	3.62
92	NY/AL		46	471	11	1	1	9	103.2	104	12	74	7	2	73	3	3	5	1	53	49	4	8	.333	1	4.25
93	CIN/NL		34	158	0	0	0	15	32.2	40	3	23	5	1	23	3	0	2	0	19	18	2	1	.667	1	4.96
	KC/AL		13	62	0	0	0	3	15.1	14	0	7	0	1	2	1	0	0	0	5	5	1	1	.500	0	2.93
	YEAR		47	220	0	0	0	18	48.0	54	3	30	5	2	25	4	0	2	0	24	23	3	2	.600	1	4.31
7 YR TOTALS			**348**	**2751**	**35**	**4**	**2**	**83**	**626.0**	**615**	**46**	**344**	**29**	**11**	**457**	**32**	**20**	**36**	**7**	**301**	**274**	**36**	**29**	**.554**	**11**	**3.94**

Campbell, Kevin Wade — BR/TR — b.12/6/64   LA86 5/126

YR	TM/LG	CL	G	TBF	GS	CG	SHO	GF	IP	H	HR	BB	IBB	HB	SO	SH	SF	WP	BK	R	ER	W	L	PCT	SV	ERA
86	GF/PIO	R+	15	0	15	3	0	0	85.0	99	5	32	0	3	66	0	0	6	0	62	44	5	6	.455	0	4.66
87	VB/FSL	A+	28	807	28	5	1	0	184.0	200	11	64	4	9	112	6	6	11	4	100	80	7	14	.333	0	3.91
88	VB/FSL	A+	26	677	26	5	1	0	163.2	166	6	49	2	3	115	10	4	6	1	67	50	8	12	.400	0	2.75
89	BAK/CAL	A+	31	255	0	0	0	17	60.1	43	0	28	1	1	63	2	5	3	0	23	17	5	3	.625	6	2.54
	SA/TEX	AA	17	127	0	0	0	7	27.0	29	3	16	1	0	28	2	2	1	0	22	20	1	5	.167	2	6.67
90	SA/TEX	AA	49	329	0	0	0	29	81.0	67	1	25	6	1	84	3	3	7	1	29	21	2	6	.250	3	2.33
91	TAC/PCL	AAA	35	304	0	0	0	12	75.0	53	5	35	1	3	56	5	3	4	0	18	15	9	2	.818	5	1.80
	OAK/AL		14	94	0	0	0	3	23.0	13	4	14	0	1	16	1	0	0	0	7	7	1	0	1.000	0	2.74
92	TAC/PCL	AAA	10	63	0	0	0	3	13.1	16	2	8	0	0	14	0	0	2	0	6	6	2	2	.500	0	4.05
	OAK/AL		32	297	5	0	0	6	65.0	66	4	45	3	0	38	3	3	2	0	39	37	2	3	.400	1	5.12
93	OAK/AL		11	77	0	0	0	4	16.0	20	1	11	1	1	9	0	1	0	0	13	13	0	0	.000	0	7.31
	TAC/PCL	AAA	40	230	0	0	0	28	55.2	42	5	24	2	2	46	3	2	3	0	19	17	3	5	.375	12	2.75
3 YR TOTALS			**57**	**468**	**5**	**0**	**0**	**12**	**104.0**	**99**	**9**	**70**	**4**	**2**	**63**	**4**	**3**	**2**	**0**	**59**	**57**	**3**	**3**	**.500**	**1**	**4.93**

Candelaria, John Robert "John" — BL/TL — b.11/6/53 — PIT72 2/47

YR	TM/LG	CL	G	TBF	GS	CG	SHO	GF	IP	H	HR	BB	IBB	HB	SO	SH	SF	WP	BK	R	ER	W	L	PCT	SV	ERA
75	PIT/NL		18	497	18	4	1	0	120.2	95	8	36	9	2	95	6	4	1	0	47	37	8	6	.571	0	2.76
76	PIT/NL		32	881	31	11	4	1	220.0	173	22	60	5	2	138	13	6	0	0	87	77	16	7	.696	1	3.15
77	PIT/NL		33	917	33	6	1	0	230.2	197	29	50	2	2	133	9	6	1	2	64	60	20	5	*.800	0	*2.34
78	PIT/NL		30	796	29	3	1	1	189.0	191	15	49	6	5	94	8	2	3	3	73	68	12	11	.522	1	3.24
79	PIT/NL		33	850	30	8	0	2	207.0	201	25	41	6	3	101	4	7	2	0	83	74	14	9	.609	0	3.22
80	PIT/NL		35	969	34	7	0	1	233.1	246	14	50	4	3	97	14	12	0	2	114	104	11	14	.440	1	4.01
81	PIT/NL		6	168	6	0	0	0	40.2	42	3	11	1	0	14	1	1	0	0	17	16	2	2	.500	0	3.54
82	PIT/NL		31	704	30	1	1	1	174.2	166	13	37	3	4	133	5	6	1	0	62	57	12	7	.632	1	2.94
83	PIT/NL		33	797	32	2	0	0	197.2	191	15	45	3	2	157	4	4	3	2	73	71	15	8	.652	0	3.23
84	PIT/NL		33	751	28	3	1	4	185.1	179	19	34	3	1	133	10	4	1	0	69	56	12	11	.522	2	2.72
85	PIT/NL		37	229	0	0	0	26	54.1	57	7	14	2	1	47	3	4	0	0	23	22	2	4	.333	9	3.64
	CAL/AL		13	301	13	1	1	0	71.0	70	7	24	1	3	53	4	3	2	0	33	30	7	3	.700	0	3.80
	YEAR		50	530	13	1	1	26	125.1	127	14	38	3	4	100	7	7	2	0	56	52	9	7	.563	9	3.73
86	PS/CAL	A+	2	27	2	0	0	0	7.0	4	0	2	0	0	8	0	0	0	0	2	2	0	0	.000	0	2.57
	CAL/AL		16	365	16	1	1	0	91.2	68	4	26	2	3	81	3	3	2	1	30	26	10	2	.833	0	2.55
87	CAL/AL		20	487	20	0	0	0	116.2	127	17	20	1	0	74	6	5	0	0	70	61	8	6	.571	0	4.71
	NY/NL		3	57	3	0	0	0	12.1	17	1	3	0	0	10	2	1	0	0	8	8	2	0	1.000	0	5.84
	YEAR		23	544	23	0	0	0	129.0	144	18	23	1	0	84	8	6	0	0	78	69	10	6	.625	0	4.81
88	NY/AL		25	640	24	6	2	1	157.0	150	18	23	2	2	121	4	6	2	12	69	59	13	7	.650	0	3.38
89	YAN/GCL	R	2	31	2	0	0	0	8.0	6	0	1	0	1	12	0	0	0	1	0	0	1	0	1.000	0	0.00
	NY/AL		10	206	6	1	0	1	49.0	49	8	12	1	0	37	2	2	2	1	28	28	3	3	.500	0	5.14
	MON/NL		12	68	0	0	0	2	16.1	17	3	4	2	0	14	1	3	0	0	8	6	0	2	.000	0	3.31
	YEAR		22	274	6	1	0	3	65.1	66	11	16	3	0	51	3	5	2	1	36	34	3	5	.375	0	4.68
90	MIN/AL		34	239	1	0	0	10	58.1	55	9	9	2	0	44	2	3	3	0	23	22	7	3	.700	4	3.39
	TOR/AL		13	106	2	0	0	5	21.1	32	2	11	3	2	19	0	3	2	0	13	13	0	3	.000	1	5.48
	YEAR		47	345	3	0	0	15	79.2	87	11	20	5	2	63	2	6	5	0	36	35	7	6	.538	5	3.95
91	LA/NL		59	138	0	0	0	10	33.2	31	3	11	2	0	38	1	3	1	1	16	14	1	1	.500	2	3.74
92	LA/NL		50	108	0	0	0	11	25.1	20	1	13	4	2	23	2	1	0	0	9	8	2	5	.286	5	2.84
93	PIT/NL		24	92	0	0	0	6	19.2	25	2	9	1	1	17	1	1	1	1	19	18	0	3	.000	1	8.24
19 YR TOTALS			**600**	**10366**	**356**	**54**	**13**	**82**	**2525.2**	**2399**	**245**	**592**	**63**	**37**	**1673**	**105**	**93**	**28**	**26**	**1038**	**935**	**177**	**122**	**.592**	**29**	**3.33**

Candiotti, Thomas Caesar "Tom" — BR/TR — b.8/31/57 — VICT 7/17/79

YR	TM/LG	CL	G	TBF	GS	CG	SHO	GF	IP	H	HR	BB	IBB	HB	SO	SH	SF	WP	BK	R	ER	W	L	PCT	SV	ERA
83	MIL/AL		10	233	8	2	1	1	55.2	62	4	16	0	2	21	0	2	0	0	21	20	4	4	.500	0	3.23
84	VAN/PCL	AAA	15	0	15	4	0	0	96.2	96	4	22	0	2	53	0	0	3	1	36	31	8	4	.667	0	2.89
	BEL/MID	A	2	49	2	0	0	0	10.0	12	1	5	0	0	12	1	0	1	0	5	3	1	0	1.000	0	2.70
	MIL/AL		8	147	6	0	0	0	32.1	38	5	10	0	0	23	0	0	1	0	21	19	2	2	.500	0	5.29
85	EP/TEX	AA	4	122	4	1	1	0	29.1	29	2	7	·1	0	16	2	0	0	0	11	9	1	0	1.000	0	2.76
	VAN/PCL	AAA	24	0	24	5	1	0	150.2	178	14	36	2	4	97	0	0	5	5	83	66	9	13	.409	0	3.94
86	CLE/AL		36	1078	34	*17	3	1	252.1	234	18	106	0	8	167	3	9	12	4	112	100	16	12	.571	0	3.57
87	CLE/AL		32	888	32	7	2	0	201.2	193	28	93	2	4	111	8	10	13	2	132	107	7	18	.280	0	4.78
88	CLE/AL		31	903	31	11	1	0	216.2	225	15	53	3	6	137	12	5	5	7	86	79	14	8	.636	0	3.28
89	CLE/AL		31	847	31	4	0	0	206.0	188	10	55	5	4	124	6	4	4	8	80	71	13	10	.565	0	3.10
90	CLE/AL		31	856	29	3	1	1	202.0	207	23	55	1	6	128	4	3	9	3	92	82	15	11	.577	0	3.65
91	CLE/AL		15	442	15	3	0	0	108.1	88	6	28	0	2	86	1	7	6	0	35	27	7	6	.538	0	2.24
	TOR/AL		19	539	19	3	0	0	129.2	114	6	45	1	4	81	3	4	11	0	47	43	6	7	.462	0	2.98
	YEAR		34	981	34	6	0	0	238.0	202	12	73	1	6	167	4	11	11	0	82	70	13	13	.500	0	2.65
92	LA/NL		32	839	30	6	2	1	203.2	177	13	63	5	3	152	20	6	9	2	78	68	11	15	.423	0	3.00
93	LA/NL		33	898	32	2	0	0	213.2	192	12	71	1	6	155	15	9	6	0	86	74	8	10	.444	0	3.12
10 YR TOTALS			**278**	**7670**	**267**	**58**	**10**	**4**	**1822.0**	**1718**	**140**	**595**	**18**	**45**	**1185**	**72**	**59**	**70**	**26**	**790**	**690**	**103**	**103**	**.500**	**0**	**3.41**

Carpenter, Cris Howell — BR/TR — b.4/5/65 — SL87 1/14

YR	TM/LG	CL	G	TBF	GS	CG	SHO	GF	IP	H	HR	BB	IBB	HB	SO	SH	SF	WP	BK	R	ER	W	L	PCT	SV	ERA
88	STL/NL		8	203	8	1	0	0	47.2	56	3	9	2	1	24	1	4	1	0	27	25	2	3	.400	0	4.72
	LOU/AMA	AAA	13	359	13	1	1	0	87.2	81	7	26	0	0	45	0	1	1	0	28	28	6	2	.750	0	2.87
89	LOU/AMA	AAA	27	154	0	0	0	23	36.2	39	3	9	0	0	29	1	2	1	0	17	13	5	3	.625	11	3.19
	STL/NL		36	303	5	0	0	10	68.0	70	4	26	9	2	35	4	4	1	0	30	24	4	4	.500	0	3.18
90	STL/NL		4	32	0	0	0	1	8.0	5	2	2	1	0	6	0	0	0	0	4	4	0	0	.000	0	4.50
	LOU/AMA	AAA	22	591	22	2	1	0	143.1	146	16	21	2	6	100	6	5	1	1	61	59	9	7	.556	0	3.70
91	STL/NL		59	266	0	0	0	19	66.0	53	6	20	9	4	47	3	2	5	0	29	29	10	4	.714	0	4.23
92	STL/NL		73	355	0	0	0	21	88.0	69	10	27	8	4	46	8	3	5	0	29	29	5	4	.556	1	2.97
93	FLO/NL		29	154	0	0	0	9	37.1	29	1	13	2	2	26	1	1	5	0	15	12	0	1	.000	2	2.89
	TEX/AL		27	139	0	0	0	8	32.0	35	4	12	1	2	27	1	3	2	0	15	15	4	1	.800	1	4.22
	YEAR		56	293	0	0	0	17	69.1	64	5	25	3	4	53	2	4	7	0	30	27	4	2	.667	1	3.50
6 YR TOTALS			**236**	**1452**	**13**	**1**	**0**	**68**	**347.0**	**317**	**30**	**109**	**32**	**11**	**211**	**18**	**17**	**15**	**0**	**151**	**140**	**25**	**17**	**.595**	**2**	**3.63**

Cary, Charles Douglas "Chuck" — BL/TL — b.3/3/60 — DET81 7/172

YR	TM/LG	CL	G	TBF	GS	CG	SHO	GF	IP	H	HR	BB	IBB	HB	SO	SH	SF	WP	BK	R	ER	W	L	PCT	SV	ERA
84	BIR/SOU	AA	22	484	20	3	0	1	108.1	118	10	46	1	1	62	4	6	9	3	61	58	6	4	.600	0	4.82
85	NAS/AMA	AAA	48	269	0	0	0	16	66.0	55	6	27	1	3	54	2	3	4	0	27	22	2	1	.667	8	3.00
	DET/AL		16	95	0	0	0	6	23.2	16	2	8	1	2	22	0	1	0	0	9	9	0	0	.000	2	3.42
86	NAS/AMA	AAA	22	126	0	0	0	13	26.1	29	3	15	2	0	19	1	2	2	0	18	16	1	4	.200	5	5.47
	DET/AL		22	140	0	0	0	6	31.2	33	4	15	4	0	21	2	2	1	0	18	12	1	2	.333	0	3.41
87	RIC/INT	AAA	40	454	9	0	0	16	105.2	104	12	43	0	0	128	5	4	8	0	64	55	4	6	.400	3	4.68
	ATL/NL		13	70	0	0	0	6	16.2	17	3	4	3	1	15	1	0	0	0	7	7	1	1	.500	1	3.78
88	BRA/GCL	R	4	51	4	0	0	0	12.0	11	0	2	0	0	18	0	1	2	1	10	5	0	2	.000	0	3.75

(continued)

Cary, Charles Douglas "Chuck" (continued)

YR	TM/LG	CL	G	TBF	GS	CG	SHO	GF	IP	H	HR	BB	IBB	HB	SO	SH	SF	WP	BK	R	ER	W	L	PCT	SV	ERA
	RIC/INT	AAA	5	26	0	0	0	2	6.1	4	0	2	0	1	3	0	0	0	0	1	1	0	0	.000	1	1.42
	ATL/NL		7	39	0	0	0	1	8.1	8	1	4	0	1	7	2	0	1	0	6	6	0	0	.000	0	6.48
89	CMB/INT	AAA	11	97	2	0	0	6	23.1	17	1	13	1	0	27	0	1	1	2	9	8	1	1	.500	0	3.09
	NY/AL		22	404	11	2	0	4	99.1	78	13	29	6	0	79	1	1	6	1	42	36	4	4	.500	0	3.26
90	NY/AL		28	661	27	2	0	1	156.2	155	21	55	1	1	134	3	5	11	2	77	73	6	12	.333	0	4.19
91	NY/AL		10	247	9	0	0	0	53.1	61	6	32	2	0	34	1	0	2	1	35	35	1	6	.143	0	5.91
	CMB/INT	AAA	8	207	8	0	0	0	45.2	44	9	26	0	1	27	2	0	6	2	31	29	5	3	.625	0	5.72
93	NAS/AMA	AAA	1	10	0	0	0	0	2.0	4	0	2	0	0	1	0	0	0	0	2	2	0	1	.000	0	9.00
	SB/MID	A	8	69	3	0	0	4	18.0	13	0	1	0	2	28	0	0	0	0	4	4	1	1	.500	0	2.00
	CHI/AL		16	96	0	0	0	4	20.2	22	1	11	0	3	10	1	4	4	0	12	12	1	0	1.000	0	5.23
8 YR TOTALS			**134**	**1752**	**47**	**4**	**0**	**28**	**410.1**	**390**	**50**	**158**	**17**	**8**	**322**	**11**	**13**	**26**	**5**	**206**	**190**	**14**	**26**	**.350**	**3**	**4.17**

Casian, Lawrence Paul "Larry" — BR/TL — b.10/28/65   MIN87 6/139

YR	TM/LG	CL	G	TBF	GS	CG	SHO	GF	IP	H	HR	BB	IBB	HB	SO	SH	SF	WP	BK	R	ER	W	L	PCT	SV	ERA
87	VIS/CAL	A+	18	400	15	2	1	3	97.0	89	3	49	0	7	96	1	2	7	0	35	27	10	3	.769	2	2.51
88	ORL/SOU	AA	27	723	26	4	1	0	174.0	165	14	62	1	7	104	6	4	12	8	72	57	9	9	.500	0	2.95
	POR/PCL	AAA	1	14	0	0	0	0	2.2	5	1	0	0	0	2	1	0	0	0	3	0	0	1	.000	0	0.00
89	POR/PCL	AAA	28	738	27	0	0	0	169.1	201	13	63	0	6	65	5	4	5	2	97	85	7	12	.368	0	4.52
90	POR/PCL	AAA	37	682	23	1	0	4	156.2	171	14	59	5	3	89	8	4	2	2	90	78	9	9	.500	0	4.48
	MIN/AL		5	90	3	0	0	1	22.1	26	2	4	0	0	11	0	1	0	0	9	8	2	1	.667	0	3.22
91	MIN/AL		15	87	0	0	0	4	18.1	28	4	7	2	1	6	0	1	0	2	16	15	0	1	.000	0	7.36
	POR/PCL	AAA	34	217	6	0	0	10	52.0	51	3	16	1	1	24	0	2	0	0	25	20	3	2	.600	1	3.46
92	POR/PCL	AAA	58	247	0	0	0	23	62.0	54	1	13	5	1	43	3	2	5	0	16	16	4	0	1.000	11	2.32
	MIN/AL		6	28	0	0	0	1	6.2	7	0	1	0	0	2	0	0	0	0	2	2	1	0	1.000	0	2.70
93	POR/PCL	AAA	7	31	0	0	0	5	7.2	9	0	2	1	0	2	0	0	0	0	1	0	1	0	1.000	2	0.00
	MIN/AL		54	241	0	0	0	8	56.2	59	1	14	2	1	31	3	3	2	0	23	19	5	3	.625	1	3.02
4 YR TOTALS			**80**	**446**	**3**	**0**	**0**	**14**	**104.0**	**120**	**7**	**26**	**4**	**2**	**50**	**3**	**4**	**4**	**0**	**50**	**44**	**8**	**4**	**.667**	**1**	**3.81**

Castillo, Antonio Jose "Tony" — BL/TL — b.3/1/63   TOR 2/16/83

YR	TM/LG	CL	G	TBF	GS	CG	SHO	GF	IP	H	HR	BB	IBB	HB	SO	SH	SF	WP	BK	R	ER	W	L	PCT	SV	ERA
83	BB/GCL	R	1		0	0	0	0	3.0	3	0	0	0	0	0	0	0	0	0	1	1	0	0	.000	1	3.00
84	FLO/SAL	A	25	592	24	4	1	0	137.1	123	11	50	0	0	96	2	2	4	0	71	52	11	8	.579	0	3.41
85	KIN/CAR	A+	36	546	12	0	0	8	127.2	111	5	48	3	3	136	5	0	2	0	44	27	11	7	.611	3	1.90
87	DUN/FSL	A+	39	293	0	0	0	18	69.2	62	2	19	1	5	62	3	1	4	0	30	26	6	2	.750	6	3.36
88	DUN/FSL	A+	30	166	0	0	0	23	42.2	31	0	10	0	1	46	4	2	0	2	9	7	4	3	.571	12	1.48
	KNO/SOU	AA	5	27	0	0	0	2	8.0	2	0	1	0	0	11	0	0	0	0	0	0	1	0	1.000	2	0.00
	TOR/AL		14	54	0	0	0	6	15.0	10	2	2	0	0	14	0	2	0	0	5	5	1	0	1.000	0	3.00
89	SYR/INT	AAA	27	171	0	0	0	19	41.2	33	7	15	2	0	37	3	1	1	1	15	13	1	3	.250	5	2.81
	TOR/AL		17	86	0	0	0	8	17.2	23	0	10	5	1	10	2	4	3	0	14	12	1	1	.500	1	6.11
	ATL/NL		12	41	0	0	0	5	9.1	8	0	4	1	0	5	1	0	0	0	5	5	0	1	.000	0	4.82
	YEAR		29	127	0	0	0	13	27.0	31	0	14	6	1	15	3	4	3	0	19	17	1	2	.333	1	5.67
90	RIC/INT	AAA	5	93	4	0	0	0	25.0	14	5	6	0	0	27	1	0	1	0	7	7	3	1	.750	0	2.52
	ATL/NL		52	337	3	0	0	7	76.2	93	5	20	3	1	64	4	4	2	2	41	36	5	1	.833	1	4.23
91	RIC/INT	AAA	23	463	17	0	0	0	118.0	89	4	32	0	1	78	5	2	2	2	47	38	5	6	.455	0	2.90
	ATL/NL		7	44	0	0	0	5	8.2	13	3	5	0	0	8	1	0	0	0	9	7	1	1	.500	0	7.27
	NY/NL		10	104	3	0	0	1	23.2	27	1	6	1	0	10	1	1	0	0	7	5	1	0	1.000	0	1.90
	YEAR		17	148	3	0	0	6	32.1	40	4	11	1	0	18	2	1	0	0	16	12	2	1	.667	0	3.34
92	TOL/INT	AAA	12	192	9	0	0	0	44.2	48	3	14	0	0	24	0	1	4	0	23	18	2	3	.400	2	3.63
93	SYR/INT	AAA	1	22	1	0	0	0	6.0	4	0	0	0	0	2	0	0	0	0	0	0	0	0	.000	0	0.00
	TOR/AL		51	211	0	0	0	10	50.2	44	4	22	5	0	28	5	2	1	0	19	19	3	2	.600	0	3.38
5 YR TOTALS			**163**	**877**	**6**	**0**	**0**	**38**	**201.2**	**218**	**15**	**69**	**15**	**2**	**139**	**14**	**13**	**6**	**2**	**100**	**89**	**12**	**6**	**.667**	**2**	**3.97**

Castillo, Frank Anthony — BR/TR — b.4/1/69   CHN87 5/140

YR	TM/LG	CL	G	TBF	GS	CG	SHO	GF	IP	H	HR	BB	IBB	HB	SO	SH	SF	WP	BK	R	ER	W	L	PCT	SV	ERA
87	WYT/APP	R+	12	372	12	5	0	0	90.1	86	4	21	0	5	83	3	2	2	1	31	23	10	1	.909	0	2.29
	GEN/NYP	A-	1	23	1	0	0	0	6.0	3	0	1	0	0	6	0	0	0	0	1	0	1	0	1.000	0	0.00
88	PEO/MID	A	9	186	8	2	2	0	51.0	25	1	10	0	1	58	0	0	0	0	5	4	6	1	.857	0	0.71
89	WIN/CAR	A+	18	521	18	8	1	0	129.1	118	5	24	1	3	114	2	1	1	1	42	36	9	6	.600	0	2.51
	CHA/SOU	AA	10	283	10	4	0	0	68.0	73	7	12	3	1	43	4	2	1	0	35	29	3	4	.429	0	3.84
90	CHA/SOU	AA	18	471	18	4	1	0	111.1	113	4	27	4	0	112	6	1	4	1	54	48	6	6	.500	0	3.88
91	IOW/AMA	AAA	4	98	4	1	0	0	25.0	20	0	7	0	1	20	0	1	0	0	7	7	3	1	.750	0	2.52
	CHI/NL		18	467	18	4	1	0	111.2	107	5	33	2	0	73	6	3	5	1	56	54	6	7	.462	0	4.35
92	CHI/NL		33	856	33	0	0	0	205.1	179	19	63	6	6	135	11	5	11	0	91	79	10	11	.476	0	3.46
93	CHI/NL		29	614	25	2	0	0	141.1	162	20	39	4	9	84	10	3	6	3	83	76	5	8	.385	0	4.84
3 YR TOTALS			**80**	**1937**	**76**	**6**	**0**	**0**	**458.1**	**448**	**44**	**135**	**12**	**15**	**292**	**27**	**11**	**21**	**4**	**230**	**209**	**21**	**26**	**.447**	**0**	**4.10**

Charlton, Norman Wood "Norm" — BB/TL — b.1/6/63   MON84 2/28

YR	TM/LG	CL	G	TBF	GS	CG	SHO	GF	IP	H	HR	BB	IBB	HB	SO	SH	SF	WP	BK	R	ER	W	L	PCT	SV	ERA
84	WPB/FSL	A+	8	187	8	0	0	0	39.1	51	2	22	1	0	27	2	3	1	1	27	20	1	4	.200	0	4.58
85	WPB/FSL	A+	24	571	23	5	2	0	128.0	135	7	79	1	4	71	4	4	9	0	79	65	7	10	.412	0	4.57
86	VER/EAS	AA	22	578	22	6	1	0	136.2	109	4	74	2	3	96	6	9	8	0	55	43	10	6	.625	0	2.83
87	NAS/AMA	AAA	18	426	17	3	1	0	98.1	97	8	44	1	1	74	6	2	7	2	57	47	2	8	.200	0	4.30
88	NAS/AMA	AAA	27	743	27	7	1	0	182.0	149	7	56	1	2	161	9	3	13	17	69	61	11	10	.524	0	3.02
	CIN/NL		10	259	10	0	0	0	61.1	60	6	20	2	0	39	1	2	2	0	27	27	4	5	.444	0	3.96
89	CIN/NL		69	393	0	0	0	27	95.1	67	5	40	7	2	98	9	2	7	2	38	31	8	3	.727	0	2.93
90	CIN/NL		56	650	16	1	1	13	154.1	131	10	70	4	4	117	7	2	9	1	53	47	12	9	.571	2	2.74

Charlton, Norman Wood "Norm" (continued)

YR	TM/LG	CL	G	TBF	GS	CG	SHO	GF	IP	H	HR	BB	IBB	HB	SO	SH	SF	WP	BK	R	ER	W	L	PCT	SV	ERA
91	CIN/NL		39	438	11	0	0	10	108.1	92	6	34	4	6	77	7	1	11	0	37	35	3	5	.375	1	2.91
92	CIN/NL		64	341	0	0	0	46	81.1	79	7	26	4	3	90	7	3	8	0	39	27	4	2	.667	26	2.99
93	SEA/AL		34	141	0	0	0	29	34.2	22	4	17	0	0	48	0	1	6	0	12	9	1	3	.250	18	2.34
6 YR TOTALS			**272**	**2222**	**37**	**1**	**1**	**125**	**535.1**	**451**	**38**	**207**	**21**	**17**	**469**	**31**	**11**	**39**	**7**	**206**	**176**	**32**	**27**	**.542**	**47**	**2.96**

Christopher, Michael Wayne "Mike" — BR/TR — b.11/3/63   NYA85 7/181

YR	TM/LG	CL	G	TBF	GS	CG	SHO	GF	IP	H	HR	BB	IBB	HB	SO	SH	SF	WP	BK	R	ER	W	L	PCT	SV	ERA
85	ONE/NYP	A-	15	317	9	2	2	3	80.1	58	2	22	0	3	84	1	1	3	0	21	13	8	1	.889	0	1.46
86	ALB/EAS	AA	11	273	11	2	0	0	60.2	75	6	12	1	3	34	2	4	3	0	48	34	3	5	.375	0	5.04
	FL/FSL	A+	15	421	14	3	1	0	102.2	92	2	36	0	1	56	4	2	1	1	37	30	7	3	.700	0	2.63
87	FL/FSL	A+	24	694	24	9	4	0	169.1	183	5	28	1	0	81	6	4	4	0	63	46	13	8	.619	0	2.44
88	ALB/EAS	AA	24	648	24	5	1	0	152.2	166	7	44	3	6	67	4	5	2	4	75	65	13	7	.650	0	3.83
89	CMB/INT	AAA	13	331	11	1	0	0	73.0	95	6	21	3	3	42	6	5	1	0	45	39	5	6	.455	0	4.81
	ALB/EAS	AA	8	213	8	3	0	0	53.2	48	1	7	1	0	33	0	1	0	0	17	15	6	1	.857	0	2.52
90	ALB/PCL	AAA	54	287	0	0	0	25	68.2	62	3	23	3	2	47	5	4	0	0	20	15	6	1	.857	8	1.97
91	ALB/PCL	AAA	63	334	0	0	0	34	77.1	73	4	30	5	3	67	1	4	3	0	25	21	7	2	.778	16	2.44
	LA/NL		3	15	0	0	0	2	4.0	2	0	3	0	0	2	0	0	0	0	0	0	0	0	.000	0	0.00
92	CS/PCL	AAA	49	240	0	0	0	45	58.2	59	2	13	6	0	39	5	4	3	0	21	19	4	4	.500	26	2.91
	CLE/AL		10	79	0	0	0	4	18.0	17	2	10	1	0	13	1	1	2	0	8	6	0	0	.000	0	3.00
93	CHW/INT	AAA	50	204	0	0	0	46	50.1	51	2	6	4	0	36	3	2	2	0	21	18	3	6	.333	22	3.22
	CLE/AL		9	51	0	0	0	3	11.2	14	3	2	1	0	8	0	0	0	0	6	5	0	0	.000	0	3.86
3 YR TOTALS			**22**	**145**	**0**	**0**	**0**	**9**	**33.2**	**33**	**5**	**15**	**2**	**0**	**23**	**1**	**1**	**2**	**0**	**14**	**11**	**0**	**0**	**.000**	**0**	**2.94**

Clark, Mark Willard — BR/TR — b.5/12/68   SL88 11/236

YR	TM/LG	CL	G	TBF	GS	CG	SHO	GF	IP	H	HR	BB	IBB	HB	SO	SH	SF	WP	BK	R	ER	W	L	PCT	SV	ERA
88	HAM/NYP	A-	15	385	15	2	0	0	94.1	88	10	32	2	0	60	4	3	2	1	39	32	6	7	.462	0	3.05
89	SAV/SAL	A	27	712	27	4	2	0	173.2	143	8	52	0	1	132	4	4	11	3	61	47	14	9	.609	0	2.44
90	SP/FSL	A+	10	254	10	1	1	0	62.0	63	3	14	0	1	58	2	2	3	1	33	21	3	2	.600	0	3.05
	ARK/TEX	AA	19	479	19	5	0	0	115.1	111	11	37	2	0	87	6	4	2	0	56	49	5	11	.313	0	3.82
91	ARK/TEX	AA	15	398	15	4	1	0	92.1	99	2	30	4	2	76	3	2	2	0	50	41	5	5	.500	0	4.00
	LOU/AMA	AAA	7	189	6	1	0	0	45.1	43	4	15	0	0	29	1	3	1	0	17	15	3	2	.600	0	2.98
	STL/NL		7	93	2	0	0	0	22.1	17	3	11	0	0	13	0	3	2	0	10	10	1	1	.500	0	4.03
92	LOU/AMA	AAA	9	250	9	4	3	0	61.0	56	4	15	1	0	38	4	0	2	0	20	19	4	4	.500	0	2.80
	STL/NL		20	488	20	1	1	0	113.1	117	12	36	2	0	44	7	4	3	0	59	56	3	10	.231	0	4.45
93	CHW/INT	AAA	2	52	2	0	0	0	13.0	9	0	2	0	0	12	0	1	0	0	5	3	1	0	1.000	0	2.08
	CLE/AL		26	454	15	1	0	1	109.1	119	18	25	1	1	57	1	1	1	0	55	52	7	5	.583	0	4.28
3 YR TOTALS			**53**	**1035**	**37**	**2**	**1**	**2**	**245.0**	**253**	**33**	**72**	**3**	**1**	**114**	**8**	**8**	**7**	**0**	**124**	**118**	**11**	**16**	**.407**	**0**	**4.33**

Clemens, William Roger "Roger" — BR/TR — b.8/4/62   BOS83 1/19

YR	TM/LG	CL	G	TBF	GS	CG	SHO	GF	IP	H	HR	BB	IBB	HB	SO	SH	SF	WP	BK	R	ER	W	L	PCT	SV	ERA
84	PAW/INT	AAA	7	189	6	3	1	1	46.2	39	3	14	0	0	50	3	1	0	0	12	10	2	3	.400	0	1.93
	BOS/AL		21	575	20	5	1	0	133.1	146	13	29	3	2	126	2	3	4	0	67	64	9	4	.692	0	4.32
85	BOS/AL		15	407	15	3	1	0	98.1	83	5	37	0	0	74	1	2	1	3	38	36	7	5	.583	0	3.29
86	BOS/AL		33	997	33	10	1	0	254.0	179	21	67	0	4	238	4	6	11	3	77	70	*24	4	*.857	0	*2.48
87	BOS/AL		36	1157	36	*18	*7	0	281.2	248	19	83	4	9	256	6	4	4	3	100	93	*20	9	*.690	0	2.97
88	BOS/AL		35	1063	35	*14	*8	0	264.0	217	17	62	4	6	*291	5	5	7	0	93	86	18	12	.600	0	2.93
89	BOS/AL		35	1044	35	8	3	0	253.1	215	20	93	5	8	230	9	5	7	0	101	88	17	11	.607	0	3.13
90	BOS/AL		31	920	31	7	*4	0	228.1	193	7	54	7	9	209	7	5	5	0	59	49	21	6	.778	0	*1.93
91	BOS/AL		35	1077	35	13	*4	0	*271.1	219	15	65	12	5	*241	8	6	5	0	93	79	18	10	.643	0	*2.62
92	BOS/AL		32	989	32	11	*5	0	246.2	203	11	62	5	9	208	5	5	3	0	80	66	18	11	.621	0	*2.41
93	PAW/INT	AAA	1	16	1	0	0	0	3.2	1	0	4	0	1	8	0	0	0	0	0	0	0	0	.000	0	0.00
	BOS/AL		29	808	29	2	1	0	191.2	175	17	67	4	11	160	5	7	3	1	99	95	11	14	.440	0	4.46
10 YR TOTALS			**302**	**9037**	**301**	**91**	**35**	**0**	**2222.2**	**1878**	**145**	**619**	**40**	**64**	**2033**	**51**	**48**	**51**	**17**	**807**	**726**	**163**	**86**	**.655**	**0**	**2.94**

Cone, David Brian — BL/TR — b.1/2/63   KC81 4/74

YR	TM/LG	CL	G	TBF	GS	CG	SHO	GF	IP	H	HR	BB	IBB	HB	SO	SH	SF	WP	BK	R	ER	W	L	PCT	SV	ERA
84	MEM/SOU	AA	29	804	29	9	1	0	178.2	162	9	114	1	5	110	6	9	27	4	103	85	8	12	.400	0	4.28
85	OMA/AMA	AAA	28	710	27	5	1	0	158.2	157	13	93	3	2	115	8	8	7	4	90	82	9	15	.375	0	4.65
86	OMA/AMA	AAA	39	296	2	2	0	33	71.0	60	3	25	2	2	63	2	6	6	1	23	22	8	4	.667	14	2.79
	KC/AL		11	108	0	0	0	5	22.2	29	2	13	1	1	21	0	0	1	0	14	14	0	0	.000	0	5.56
87	TID/INT	AAA	3	51	3	0	0	0	11.0	10	1	6	0	1	7	1	0	0	0	8	7	0	0	.000	0	5.73
	NY/NL		21	420	13	1	0	0	99.1	87	11	44	1	5	68	4	3	2	4	46	41	5	6	.455	1	3.71
88	NY/NL		35	936	28	8	4	0	231.1	178	10	80	7	5	213	11	5	10	10	67	57	20	3	*.870	0	2.22
89	NY/NL		34	910	33	7	2	0	219.2	183	20	74	6	4	190	6	4	14	4	92	86	14	8	.636	0	3.52
90	NY/NL		31	860	30	6	2	0	211.2	177	21	65	1	1	*233	3	7	10	4	84	76	14	10	.583	0	3.23
91	NY/NL		34	966	34	5	2	0	232.2	204	13	73	2	3	*241	6	6	13	6	95	85	14	14	.500	0	3.29
92	NY/NL		27	831	27	7	*5	0	196.2	162	12	82	5	9	214	6	7	9	2	75	63	13	7	.650	0	2.88
	TOR/AL		8	224	7	0	0	0	53.0	39	3	29	2	3	47	3	0	5	0	16	15	4	3	.571	0	2.55
	YEAR		35	1055	34	7	5	0	249.2	201	15	111	7	12	261	9	7	14	2	91	78	17	10	.630	0	2.81
93	KC/AL		34	1060	34	6	1	0	254.0	205	20	114	2	10	191	7	9	14	2	102	94	11	14	.440	0	3.33
8 YR TOTALS			**235**	**6315**	**206**	**40**	**16**	**9**	**1521.0**	**1264**	**112**	**574**	**27**	**42**	**1418**	**51**	**43**	**82**	**26**	**591**	**531**	**95**	**65**	**.594**	**1**	**3.14**

Converse, James Daniel "Jim" — BL/TR — b.8/17/71   SEA90 16/431

YR	TM/LG	CL	G	TBF	GS	CG	SHO	GF	IP	H	HR	BB	IBB	HB	SO	SH	SF	WP	BK	R	ER	W	L	PCT	SV	ERA
90	BEL/NWL	A-	12	281	12	0	0	0	66.2	50	1	32	0	2	75	0	1	2	9	31	29	2	4	.333	0	3.92
91	PEN/CAR	A+	26	643	26	1	0	0	137.2	143	12	97	2	2	137	3	4	9	2	90	76	6	15	.286	0	4.97

(continued)

Converse, James Daniel "Jim" (continued)

YR	TM/LG	CL	G	TBF	GS	CG	SHO	GF	IP	H	HR	BB	IBB	HB	SO	SH	SF	WP	BK	R	ER	W	L	PCT	SV	ERA
92	JAC/SOU	AA	27	677	26	2	0	0	159.0	134	9	82	1	5	157	3	4	8	1	61	47	12	7	.632	0	2.66
93	SEA/AL		4	93	4	0	0	0	20.1	23	0	14	2	0	10	0	1	0	0	12	12	1	3	.250	0	5.31
	CAL/PCL	AAA	23	565	22	4	0	0	121.2	144	6	64	1	3	78	2	7	8	0	86	73	7	8	.467	0	5.40

Cook, Andrew Bernard "Andy" — BR/TR — b.8/30/67   NYA88 8/287

YR	TM/LG	CL	G	TBF	GS	CG	SHO	GF	IP	H	HR	BB	IBB	HB	SO	SH	SF	WP	BK	R	ER	W	L	PCT	SV	ERA
88	ONE/NYP	A-	16	444	16	2	0	0	102.0	116	2	21	0	4	65	2	1	2	3	50	41	8	4	.667	0	3.62
89	PW/CAR	A+	25	621	24	5	1	0	153.0	123	7	49	0	6	83	4	2	6	7	68	56	8	12	.400	0	3.29
90	ALB/EAS	AA	24	648	24	5	0	0	156.2	146	12	52	2	4	53	5	5	6	5	69	60	12	8	.600	0	3.45
91	ALB/EAS	AA	14	360	14	1	0	0	82.0	94	2	27	0	0	46	0	3	1	0	46	36	6	3	.667	0	3.95
	CMB/INT	AAA	13	338	13	2	0	0	79.1	63	0	38	0	4	40	5	3	1	2	34	31	5	5	.500	0	3.52
92	CMB/INT	AAA	32	411	9	0	0	7	99.2	85	8	36	0	3	58	5	1	3	0	41	35	7	5	.583	2	3.16
93	NY/AL		4	28	1	0	0	3	5.1	4	1	7	0	0	4	1	0	2	0	3	3	0	1	.000	0	5.06
	CMB/INT	AAA	21	543	20	0	0	0	118.1	149	14	49	3	7	47	6	5	4	3	91	86	6	7	.462	0	6.54

Cook, Dennis Bryan — BL/TL — b.10/4/62   SF85 18/446

YR	TM/LG	CL	G	TBF	GS	CG	SHO	GF	IP	H	HR	BB	IBB	HB	SO	SH	SF	WP	BK	R	ER	W	L	PCT	SV	ERA
85	CLI/MID	A	13	343	13	1	0	0	83.0	73	7	27	0	2	40	0	4	5	4	35	31	5	4	.556	0	3.36
86	FRE/CAL	A+	27	735	25	1	2	2	170.0	141	16	100	1	5	173	5	6	7	3	92	75	12	7	.632	1	3.97
87	SHR/TEX	AA	16	426	16	1	1	0	105.2	94	1	20	1	1	98	3	2	4	3	32	25	9	2	.818	0	2.13
	PHO/PCL	AAA	12	277	11	1	0	0	62.0	72	8	26	2	1	24	1	1	4	4	45	36	2	5	.286	0	5.23
88	PHO/PCL	AAA	26	600	25	5	1	0	141.1	138	14	51	1	3	110	3	6	5	4	73	61	11	9	.550	0	3.88
	SF/NL		4	86	4	1	1	0	22.0	9	1	11	0	0	13	0	3	1	0	8	7	2	1	.667	0	2.86
89	PHO/PCL	AAA	12	319	12	3	1	0	78.0	73	4	19	0	1	85	1	4	4	2	29	27	7	4	.636	0	3.12
	SF/NL		2	58	2	1	0	0	15.0	13	1	5	0	0	9	0	0	1	0	3	3	1	0	1.000	0	1.80
	PHI/NL		21	441	16	1	1	1	106.0	97	17	33	6	2	58	5	2	3	2	56	47	6	8	.429	0	3.99
	YEAR		23	499	18	2	1	1	121.0	110	18	38	6	2	67	5	2	4	2	59	50	7	8	.467	0	3.72
90	PHI/NL		42	594	13	2	1	4	141.2	132	13	54	9	2	58	5	5	6	3	61	56	8	3	.727	1	3.56
	LA/NL		5	69	0	0	0	0	14.1	23	7	2	0	0	6	2	0	0	0	13	12	1	1	.500	0	7.53
	YEAR		47	663	13	2	1	4	156.0	155	20	56	9	2	64	7	5	6	3	74	68	9	4	.692	1	3.92
91	ALB/PCL	AAA	14	373	14	1	0	0	91.2	73	9	32	0	2	84	5	3	5	3	46	37	7	3	.700	0	3.63
	SA/TEX	AA	7	202	7	1	0	0	50.2	43	2	10	1	1	45	3	3	0	4	20	14	1	3	.250	0	2.49
	LA/NL		20	69	1	0	0	5	17.2	12	0	7	1	0	8	1	2	0	0	3	1	1	0	1.000	0	0.51
92	CLE/AL		32	669	25	1	0	1	158.0	156	29	50	2	2	96	3	3	4	5	79	67	5	7	.417	0	3.82
93	CLE/AL		25	233	6	0	0	6	54.0	62	9	16	1	2	34	3	2	0	1	36	34	5	5	.500	0	5.67
	CHW/INT	AAA	12	179	6	0	0	3	42.2	46	4	8	0	0	40	0	2	0	2	26	24	3	2	.600	0	5.06
6 YR TOTALS			**151**	**2219**	**70**	**6**	**3**	**13**	**528.2**	**504**	**77**	**178**	**20**	**8**	**282**	**19**	**19**	**15**	**11**	**259**	**227**	**29**	**25**	**.537**	**1**	**3.86**

Cook, Michael Horace "Mike" — BR/TR — b.8/14/63   CAL85 2/19

YR	TM/LG	CL	G	TBF	GS	CG	SHO	GF	IP	H	HR	BB	IBB	HB	SO	SH	SF	WP	BK	R	ER	W	L	PCT	SV	ERA
85	QC/MID	A	2	44	2	0	0	0	10.0	6	0	7	0	1	10	0	0	1	0	3	2	0	0	.000	0	1.80
86	MID/TEX	AA	15	453	15	2	0	0	105.1	101	2	52	0	2	82	1	4	10	2	54	41	4	6	.400	0	3.50
	CAL/AL		5	46	1	0	0	1	9.0	13	3	7	1	0	6	0	0	0	0	12	9	0	0	.000	0	9.00
	EDM/PCL	AAA	9	245	9	0	0	0	55.1	49	10	24	0	3	35	1	2	3	1	42	33	4	1	.800	0	5.37
87	CAL/AL		16	148	1	0	0	6	34.1	34	7	18	0	0	27	1	0	3	1	21	21	1	2	.333	0	5.50
	EDM/PCL	AAA	15	376	15	4	2	0	83.1	81	8	54	1	1	54	2	5	12	2	64	60	4	7	.364	0	6.48
88	EDM/PCL	AAA	51	402	5	0	0	34	91.0	93	11	41	6	2	84	4	3	6	0	56	49	5	9	.357	10	4.85
	CAL/AL		3	15	0	0	0	1	3.2	4	0	1	0	1	2	0	0	1	0	2	2	0	0	.000	0	4.91
89	POR/PCL	AAA	42	273	0	0	0	36	64.0	53	9	35	0	1	55	4	0	5	0	29	26	5	3	.625	12	3.66
	MIN/AL		15	102	0	0	0	5	21.1	22	4	17	1	1	15	0	2	2	0	12	12	0	1	.000	0	5.06
90	POR/PCL	AAA	19	496	19	2	1	0	115.1	105	8	59	0	5	63	4	4	5	0	54	41	6	8	.429	0	3.20
91	CAL/PCL	AAA	10	153	6	0	0	1	30.2	45	5	24	0	1	18	0	0	1	0	35	33	2	4	.333	0	9.68
92	LOU/AMA	AAA	43	259	0	0	0	8	58.2	58	5	31	4	1	56	1	2	3	0	31	30	3	2	.600	0	4.60
93	ROC/INT	AAA	57	373	0	0	0	38	81.1	77	3	48	9	5	74	7	1	11	0	39	28	6	7	.462	13	3.10
	BAL/AL		2	13	0	0	0	0	3.0	1	0	2	1	0	3	0	0	0	0	1	0	0	0	.000	0	0.00
5 YR TOTALS			**41**	**324**	**2**	**0**	**0**	**13**	**71.1**	**74**	**11**	**45**	**3**	**2**	**53**	**1**	**2**	**5**	**1**	**47**	**44**	**1**	**6**	**.143**	**0**	**5.55**

Cooke, Steven Montague "Steve" — BR/TL — b.1/14/70   PIT89 36/912

YR	TM/LG	CL	G	TBF	GS	CG	SHO	GF	IP	H	HR	BB	IBB	HB	SO	SH	SF	WP	BK	R	ER	W	L	PCT	SV	ERA
90	WEL/NYP	A-	11	188	11	0	0	0	46.0	36	2	17	0	2	43	0	1	6	1	21	12	2	3	.400	0	2.35
91	AUG/SAL	A	11	269	11	1	0	0	60.2	50	0	35	1	5	52	3	1	3	0	28	19	5	4	.556	0	2.82
	SAL/CAR	A+	2	57	2	0	0	0	13.0	14	0	2	0	1	6	0	0	4	1	8	7	1	0	1.000	0	4.85
	CAR/SOU	AA	9	223	9	1	1	0	55.2	39	2	19	0	4	46	1	1	5	0	21	14	3	3	.500	0	2.26
92	CAR/SOU	AA	6	143	6	0	0	0	36.0	31	1	12	1	3	38	0	1	1	0	13	12	2	2	.500	0	3.00
	BUF/AMA	AAA	13	325	13	0	0	0	74.1	71	2	36	2	4	54	5	5	3	1	35	31	6	3	.667	0	3.75
	PIT/NL		11	91	0	0	0	8	23.0	22	2	4	1	0	10	0	0	0	0	9	9	2	0	1.000	1	3.52
93	PIT/NL		32	882	32	3	1	0	210.2	207	22	59	6	6	132	13	6	3	3	101	91	10	10	.500	0	3.89
2 YR TOTALS			**43**	**973**	**32**	**3**	**1**	**8**	**233.2**	**229**	**24**	**63**	**5**	**3**	**142**	**13**	**6**	**3**	**3**	**110**	**100**	**12**	**10**	**.545**	**1**	**3.85**

Cormier, Rheal Paul — BL/TL — b.4/23/67   SL88 8/158

YR	TM/LG	CL	G	TBF	GS	CG	SHO	GF	IP	H	HR	BB	IBB	HB	SO	SH	SF	WP	BK	R	ER	W	L	PCT	SV	ERA
89	SP/FSL	A+	26	669	26	4	2	0	169.2	141	9	33	2	0	122	6	3	4	7	63	42	12	7	.632	0	2.23
90	ARK/TEX	AA	22	530	21	3	1	1	121.1	133	9	30	2	5	102	6	2	5	2	81	68	5	12	.294	0	5.04
	LOU/AMA	AAA	4	92	4	0	0	0	24.0	18	1	4	0	0	18	0	1	0	0	8	6	1	0	.500	0	2.25
91	LOU/AMA	AAA	21	543	21	3	3	0	127.2	140	5	31	2	6	74	10	6	6	1	64	60	7	9	.438	0	4.23
	STL/NL		11	281	10	2	0	1	67.2	74	5	12	1	3	38	1	3	2	1	35	31	4	5	.444	0	4.12

Cormier, Rheal Paul (continued)

YR	TM/LG	CL	G	TBF	GS	CG	SHO	GF	IP	H	HR	BB	IBB	HB	SO	SH	SF	WP	BK	R	ER	W	L	PCT	SV	ERA
92	LOU/AMA	AAA	1	20	1	0	0	0	4.0	8	0	0	0	0	1	0	0	0	0	4	3	0	1	.000	0	6.75
	STL/NL		31	772	30	3	0	1	186.0	194	15	33	2	5	117	11	3	4	2	83	76	10	10	.500	0	3.68
93	STL/NL		38	619	21	1	0	4	145.1	163	18	27	3	4	75	10	4	6	0	80	70	7	6	.538	0	4.33
3 YR TOTALS			**80**	**1672**	**61**	**6**	**0**	**6**	**399.0**	**431**	**38**	**68**	**6**	**11**	**230**	**22**	**10**	**12**	**3**	**198**	**177**	**21**	**21**	**.500**	**0**	**3.99**

Corsi, James Bernard "Jim" — BR/TR — b.9/9/61   NYA82 24/642

YR	TM/LG	CL	G	TBF	GS	CG	SHO	GF	IP	H	HR	BB	IBB	HB	SO	SH	SF	WP	BK	R	ER	W	L	PCT	SV	ERA
82	ONE/NYP	A-	1	4	0	0	0	0	3.0	5	0	2	0	0	6	0	0	0	0	0	0	0	0	.000	0	0.00
	PAI/APP	R+	8	0	4	0	0	0	31.0	32	0	13	0	0	20	0	0	0	1	11	10	0	2	.000	0	2.90
83	GRE/SAL	A	12	0	7	1	0	0	50.0	59	0	33	0	5	37	0	0	8	0	37	23	2	2	.500	1	4.14
	ONE/NYP	A-	11	0	10	2	0	0	59.0	76	1	21	0	1	47	0	0	2	0	38	28	3	6	.333	0	4.27
85	GRE/SAL	A	41	363	2	1	0	36	78.2	94	1	23	3	4	84	4	3	4	0	49	37	5	8	.385	9	4.23
86	NB/EAS	AA	29	220	0	0	0	19	51.1	52	2	20	5	3	38	6	0	2	0	13	13	2	3	.400	3	2.28
87	MOD/CAL	A+	19	121	0	0	0	10	30.0	23	1	10	1	1	45	1	0	4	0	16	12	3	1	.750	6	3.60
	HUN/SOU	AA	28	182	0	0	0	18	48.0	30	1	15	1	0	33	2	0	5	0	17	15	8	1	.889	4	2.81
88	TAC/PCL	AAA	50	247	0	0	0	45	59.0	60	2	23	10	1	48	4	1	5	2	25	18	2	5	.286	16	2.75
	OAK/AL		11	89	1	0	0	7	21.1	20	1	6	1	0	10	3	1	1	1	10	9	0	0	.000	0	3.80
89	TAC/PCL	AAA	23	131	0	0	0	18	28.1	40	1	9	4	1	23	1	2	2	0	17	13	2	3	.400	8	4.13
	OAK/AL		22	149	0	0	0	14	38.1	26	1	10	0	1	21	2	2	0	0	8	8	1	2	.333	0	1.88
90	TAC/PCL	AAA	5	26	0	0	0	2	6.0	9	0	1	0	0	3	0	0	0	0	2	1	0	0	.000	0	1.50
91	TUC/PCL	AAA	2	11	0	0	0	0	3.0	2	0	0	0	0	4	0	0	0	0	0	0	0	0	.000	0	0.00
	HOU/NL		47	322	0	0	0	15	77.2	76	6	23	5	0	53	3	2	1	1	37	32	0	5	.000	0	3.71
92	TAC/PCL	AAA	26	121	0	0	0	22	29.1	22	0	10	3	1	21	2	2	2	1	8	4	0	0	.000	12	1.23
	OAK/AL		32	185	0	0	0	16	44.0	44	2	18	2	0	19	4	2	0	0	12	7	4	2	.667	0	1.43
93	HD/CAL	A+	3	38	3	0	0	0	9.0	11	1	2	0	0	6	0	0	0	0	3	3	0	1	.000	0	3.00
	FLO/NL		15	97	0	0	0	6	20.1	28	1	10	3	0	7	3	1	0	0	15	15	0	2	.000	0	6.64
5 YR TOTALS			**127**	**842**	**1**	**0**	**0**	**58**	**201.2**	**194**	**12**	**67**	**11**	**1**	**110**	**15**	**10**	**2**	**2**	**82**	**71**	**5**	**12**	**.294**	**0**	**3.17**

Cox, Danny Bradford — BR/TR — b.9/21/59   SL81 12/319

YR	TM/LG	CL	G	TBF	GS	CG	SHO	GF	IP	H	HR	BB	IBB	HB	SO	SH	SF	WP	BK	R	ER	W	L	PCT	SV	ERA
81	JC/APP	R+	13	0	13	10	4	0	109.0	80	3	36	0	1	87	0	0	3	0	27	25	9	4	.692	0	2.06
82	SPR/MID	A	15	0	13	2	0	0	84.0	82	7	29	0	4	68	0	0	8	1	46	24	5	3	.625	0	2.57
83	ARK/TEX	AA	11	0	11	7	1	0	86.0	60	4	24	0	1	73	0	0	0	0	31	22	8	3	.727	0	2.30
	SP/FSL	A+	5	0	5	2	0	0	32.0	26	0	14	0	2	22	0	0	1	0	10	9	2	2	.500	0	2.53
	LOU/AMA	AAA	2	0	2	0	0	0	11.0	10	1	0	0	1	8	0	0	1	0	3	3	0	0	.000	0	2.45
	STL/NL		12	352	12	0	0	0	83.0	92	6	23	2	0	36	2	2	0	0	38	30	3	3	.333	0	3.25
84	LOU/AMA	AAA	6	168	6	4	0	0	42.1	34	3	7	0	0	34	2	1	0	1	16	10	4	1	.800	0	2.13
	STL/NL		29	668	27	1	1	0	156.1	171	9	54	6	7	70	10	5	2	4	81	70	9	11	.450	0	4.03
85	STL/NL		35	989	35	10	4	0	241.0	226	19	64	5	3	131	12	9	3	1	91	77	18	9	.667	0	2.88
86	STL/NL		32	881	32	8	0	0	220.0	189	14	60	6	2	108	8	3	3	4	85	71	12	13	.480	0	2.90
87	STL/NL		31	864	31	2	0	0	199.1	224	17	71	6	3	101	14	4	5	1	99	86	11	9	.550	0	3.88
88	LOU/AMA	AAA	3	50	3	0	0	0	11.2	11	1	6	0	0	7	1	0	0	2	7	4	0	0	.000	0	3.09
	STL/NL		13	361	13	0	0	0	86.0	89	1	25	7	1	47	5	3	4	3	40	38	3	8	.273	0	3.98
90	SPR/MID	A	1	16	1	0	0	0	5.0	1	0	0	0	0	3	0	0	0	0	0	0	0	0	.000	0	0.00
	ARK/TEX	AA	1	25	1	1	0	0	7.0	3	0	1	0	0	3	0	0	0	0	1	1	1	0	1.000	0	1.29
	LOU/AMA	AAA	4	68	3	0	0	0	11.0	22	3	10	0	0	6	1	0	8	3	20	19	0	3	.000	0	15.55
91	CLE/FSL	A+	3	62	3	0	0	0	18.0	4	0	4	0	0	15	0	0	0	0	3	0	1	0	1.000	0	0.00
	SCR/INT	AAA	1	24	1	0	0	0	6.0	5	0	1	0	0	3	1	0	0	0	2	2	1	0	1.000	0	3.00
	PHI/NL		23	433	17	0	0	0	102.1	98	14	39	2	1	46	6	7	7	1	57	52	4	6	.400	0	4.57
92	PHI/NL		9	178	7	0	0	0	38.1	46	3	19	1	0	30	1	3	2	0	28	23	2	2	.500	0	5.40
	BUF/AMA	AAA	8	166	6	0	0	0	42.1	28	0	18	0	0	30	1	3	2	2	11	8	1	1	.500	0	1.70
	PIT/NL		16	100	0	0	0	8	24.1	20	2	8	1	0	18	2	1	0	1	9	9	3	1	.750	3	3.33
	YEAR		25	278	7	0	0	8	62.2	66	5	27	2	0	48	3	1	2	1	37	32	5	3	.625	3	4.60
93	TOR/AL		44	348	0	0	0	13	83.2	73	8	29	5	2	84	0	1	5	0	31	29	7	6	.538	2	3.12
9 YR TOTALS			**244**	**5174**	**174**	**21**	**5**	**23**	**1234.1**	**1228**	**98**	**392**	**41**	**17**	**671**	**66**	**36**	**32**	**14**	**559**	**485**	**72**	**71**	**.503**	**5**	**3.54**

Crim, Charles Robert "Chuck" — BR/TR — b.7/23/61   MIL82 17/443

YR	TM/LG	CL	G	TBF	GS	CG	SHO	GF	IP	H	HR	BB	IBB	HB	SO	SH	SF	WP	BK	R	ER	W	L	PCT	SV	ERA
84	EP/TEX	AA	55	360	0	0	0	33	90.0	77	4	25	4	2	69	5	4	2	0	20	15	7	4	.636	17	1.50
85	VAN/PCL	AAA	48	0	5	0	0	23	106.2	110	8	38	3	4	68	0	0	3	4	58	54	3	6	.333	6	4.56
86	EP/TEX	AA	16	156	0	0	0	13	39.0	35	5	2	2	2	32	2	0	0	0	16	12	2	4	.333	0	2.77
	VAN/PCL	AAA	26	204	0	0	0	0	45.1	64	2	15	4	1	26	1	1	1	0	32	25	0	3	.000	1	4.96
87	MIL/AL		53	549	5	0	0	18	130.0	133	15	39	4	3	56	6	1	2	1	60	53	6	8	.429	12	3.67
88	MIL/AL		*70	425	0	0	0	25	105.0	95	11	28	3	2	58	4	6	9	2	38	34	7	6	.538	9	2.91
89	MIL/AL		*76	487	0	0	0	31	117.2	114	7	36	9	2	59	3	6	5	0	42	37	9	7	.563	7	2.83
90	BEL/MID	A	1	10	1	0	0	0	2.0	3	0	0	0	0	0	0	0	0	0	2	1	0	0	.000	0	4.50
	MIL/AL		67	367	0	0	0	25	85.2	88	7	23	4	2	39	6	3	3	1	39	33	3	5	.375	11	3.47
91	MIL/AL		66	408	0	0	0	29	91.1	115	9	25	9	2	39	1	3	3	3	52	47	8	5	.615	3	4.63
92	CAL/AL		57	383	0	0	0	16	87.0	100	11	29	6	4	30	3	4	0	0	56	50	7	6	.538	1	5.17
93	CAL/AL		11	67	0	0	0	3	15.1	17	2	5	1	2	10	1	0	0	0	11	10	2	2	.500	0	5.87
7 YR TOTALS			**400**	**2686**	**5**	**0**	**0**	**147**	**632.0**	**662**	**62**	**185**	**37**	**19**	**291**	**23**	**23**	**23**	**7**	**298**	**264**	**42**	**39**	**.519**	**43**	**3.76**

Cummings, John Russell — BL/TL — b.5/10/69   SEA90 8/215

YR	TM/LG	CL	G	TBF	GS	CG	SHO	GF	IP	H	HR	BB	IBB	HB	SO	SH	SF	WP	BK	R	ER	W	L	PCT	SV	ERA
90	BEL/NWL	A-	6	130	6	0	0	0	34.0	25	1	9	0	0	39	1	1	2	3	11	8	1	1	.500	0	2.12
	SB/CAL	A+	7	186	7	1	0	0	40.2	47	3	20	0	0	30	0	1	3	0	27	19	2	4	.333	0	4.20

(continued)

Cummings, John Russell — BL/TL (continued)

YR	TM/LG	CL	G	TBF	GS	CG	SHO	GF	IP	H	HR	BB	IBB	HB	SO	SH	SF	WP	BK	R	ER	W	L	PCT	SV	ERA
91	SB/CAL	A+	29	567	20	0	0	2	124.0	129	7	61	1	3	120	1	6	15	4	79	56	4	10	.286	1	4.06
92	PEN/CAR	A+	27	712	27	4	1	0	168.1	149	11	63	6	10	144	7	5	4	1	71	48	16	6	.727	0	2.57
93	JAC/SOU	AA	7	194	7	1	0	0	45.2	50	1	9	0	1	35	2	0	1	2	24	16	2	2	.500	0	3.15
	CAL/PCL	AAA	11	280	10	0	0	0	65.1	69	6	21	2	2	42	0	1	7	0	40	30	3	4	.429	0	4.13
	SEA/AL		10	207	8	1	0	0	46.1	59	6	16	2	2	19	0	2	1	1	34	31	0	6	.000	0	6.02

Daal, Omar Jesus — BL/TL — b.3/1/72   LA 4/24/90

YR	TM/LG	CL	G	TBF	GS	CG	SHO	GF	IP	H	HR	BB	IBB	HB	SO	SH	SF	WP	BK	R	ER	W	L	PCT	SV	ERA
92	ALB/PCL	AAA	12	54	0	0	0	4	10.1	14	1	11	1	0	9	2	0	0	2	9	9	0	2	.000	0	7.84
	SA/TEX	AA	35	257	5	0	0	16	57.1	60	3	33	1	4	52	6	2	7	3	39	32	2	6	.250	5	5.02
93	ALB/PCL	AAA	6	23	0	0	0	4	5.1	5	1	3	1	0	2	0	0	0	0	2	2	1	1	.500	0	3.38
	LA/NL		47	155	0	0	0	12	35.1	36	5	21	3	0	19	2	2	1	2	20	20	2	3	.400	0	5.09

Darling, Ronald Maurice "Ron" — BR/TR — b.8/19/60   TEX81 1/9

YR	TM/LG	CL	G	TBF	GS	CG	SHO	GF	IP	H	HR	BB	IBB	HB	SO	SH	SF	WP	BK	R	ER	W	L	PCT	SV	ERA
83	NY/NL		5	148	5	1	0	0	35.1	31	0	17	1	3	23	3	0	3	2	11	11	1	3	.250	0	2.80
84	NY/NL		33	884	33	2	2	0	205.2	179	17	104	2	5	136	7	6	7	1	97	87	12	9	.571	0	3.81
85	NY/NL		36	1043	35	4	2	1	248.0	214	21	114	1	3	167	13	4	7	1	93	80	16	6	.727	0	2.90
86	NY/NL		34	967	34	4	2	0	237.0	203	21	81	2	3	184	10	6	7	3	84	74	15	6	.714	0	2.81
87	NY/NL		32	891	32	2	0	0	207.2	183	24	96	3	3	167	5	3	6	3	111	99	12	8	.600	0	4.29
88	NY/NL		34	971	34	7	4	0	240.2	218	24	60	2	5	161	10	8	7	2	97	87	17	9	.654	0	3.25
89	NY/NL		33	922	33	4	0	0	217.1	214	19	70	7	3	153	7	13	12	4	100	85	14	14	.500	0	3.52
90	NY/NL		33	554	18	1	0	3	126.0	135	20	44	4	5	99	7	3	5	1	73	63	7	9	.438	0	4.50
91	NY/NL		17	427	17	0	0	0	102.1	96	9	28	1	6	58	7	4	9	0	50	44	5	6	.455	0	3.87
	MON/NL		3	81	3	0	0	0	17.0	25	6	5	0	1	11	0	0	4	0	16	14	0	2	.000	0	7.41
	OAK/AL		12	319	12	0	0	0	75.0	64	7	38	2	2	60	5	4	3	1	34	34	3	7	.300	0	4.08
	YEAR		32	827	32	0	0	0	194.1	185	22	71	3	9	129	12	8	16	5	100	92	8	15	.348	0	4.26
92	OAK/AL		33	866	33	4	3	0	206.1	198	15	72	5	4	99	4	3	13	0	98	84	15	10	.600	0	3.66
93	OAK/AL		31	793	29	3	0	1	178.0	198	22	72	5	5	95	5	6	3	1	107	102	5	9	.357	0	5.16
11 YR TOTALS			**336**	**8866**	**318**	**32**	**13**	**5**	**2096.1**	**1958**	**205**	**801**	**35**	**48**	**1413**	**83**	**60**	**86**	**23**	**971**	**864**	**122**	**98**	**.555**	**0**	**3.71**

Darwin, Daniel Wayne "Danny" — BR/TR — b.10/25/55   TEX 5/10/76

YR	TM/LG	CL	G	TBF	GS	CG	SHO	GF	IP	H	HR	BB	IBB	HB	SO	SH	SF	WP	BK	R	ER	W	L	PCT	SV	ERA
78	TEX/AL		3	36	1	0	0	2	8.2	11	0	1	0	0	8	0	1	0	0	4	4	1	0	1.000	0	4.15
79	TEX/AL		20	313	6	1	0	4	78.0	50	5	30	2	5	58	3	6	0	1	36	35	4	4	.500	0	4.04
80	TEX/AL		53	468	2	0	0	35	109.2	98	4	50	7	2	104	5	7	3	0	37	32	13	4	.765	8	2.63
81	TEX/AL		22	601	22	6	2	0	146.0	115	12	57	5	6	98	8	3	4	0	67	59	9	9	.500	0	3.64
82	TEX/AL		56	394	1	0	0	41	89.0	95	6	37	8	2	61	10	5	2	1	38	34	10	8	.556	7	3.44
83	TEX/AL		28	780	26	9	2	0	183.0	175	9	62	3	3	92	7	7	2	0	86	71	8	13	.381	0	3.49
84	TEX/AL		35	955	32	5	1	2	223.2	249	19	54	2	4	123	3	3	3	0	110	98	8	12	.400	0	3.94
85	MIL/AL		39	919	29	11	1	8	217.2	212	34	65	4	4	125	7	9	6	0	112	92	8	18	.308	2	3.80
86	MIL/AL		27	537	14	5	1	4	130.1	120	13	35	1	3	80	5	6	5	0	62	51	6	8	.429	0	3.52
	HOU/NL		12	222	8	1	0	2	54.1	50	3	9	0	0	40	1	2	0	0	19	14	5	2	.714	0	2.32
	YEAR		39	759	22	6	1	6	184.2	170	16	44	1	3	120	6	9	5	0	81	65	11	10	.524	0	3.17
87	HOU/NL		33	833	30	3	1	0	195.2	184	17	69	12	5	134	9	5	3	1	87	78	9	10	.474	0	3.59
88	HOU/NL		44	804	20	3	0	9	192.0	189	20	48	9	7	129	10	9	1	2	86	82	8	13	.381	3	3.84
89	HOU/NL		68	482	0	0	0	26	122.0	92	8	33	9	2	104	8	5	2	3	34	32	11	4	.733	7	2.36
90	HOU/NL		48	646	17	3	0	14	162.2	136	11	31	4	4	109	4	2	0	2	42	40	11	4	.733	2	*2.21
91	BOS/AL		12	292	12	0	0	0	68.0	71	15	15	1	4	42	1	2	2	0	39	39	3	6	.333	0	5.16
92	BOS/AL		51	688	15	2	0	21	161.1	159	11	53	9	5	124	7	5	5	0	76	71	9	9	.500	3	3.96
93	BOS/AL		34	919	34	2	0	0	229.1	196	31	49	8	3	130	6	9	5	1	93	83	15	11	.577	0	3.26
16 YR TOTALS			**585**	**9889**	**269**	**51**	**9**	**168**	**2371.1**	**2202**	**218**	**698**	**84**	**59**	**1561**	**93**	**85**	**42**	**12**	**1028**	**915**	**138**	**135**	**.505**	**32**	**3.47**

Davis, George Earl "Storm" — BR/TR — b.12/26/61   BAL79 6/175

YR	TM/LG	CL	G	TBF	GS	CG	SHO	GF	IP	H	HR	BB	IBB	HB	SO	SH	SF	WP	BK	R	ER	W	L	PCT	SV	ERA
82	BAL/AL		29	412	8	1	0	9	100.2	96	8	28	4	0	67	4	6	2	1	40	39	8	4	.667	0	3.49
83	BAL/AL		34	831	29	6	1	0	200.1	180	14	64	4	2	125	5	4	7	2	90	80	13	7	.650	0	3.59
84	BAL/AL		35	923	31	10	2	3	225.0	205	7	71	6	5	105	7	9	6	1	86	78	14	9	.609	0	3.12
85	BAL/AL		31	750	28	8	1	0	175.0	172	11	70	5	1	93	3	3	2	1	92	88	10	8	.556	0	4.53
86	HAG/CAR	A+	1	18	1	0	0	0	4.0	3	0	3	0	0	6	0	0	0	0	0	0	0	0	.000	0	0.00
	BAL/AL		25	657	25	2	0	0	154.0	166	16	49	2	6	96	3	2	5	0	70	62	9	12	.429	0	3.62
87	WIC/TEX	AA	1	17	1	0	0	0	4.0	4	0	0	0	0	2	0	0	0	0	3	0	1	0	1.000	0	0.00
	REN/CAL	A+	1	22	1	0	0	0	5.0	2	0	2	0	0	5	0	0	0	0	2	2	0	0	.000	0	3.60
	SD/NL		21	292	10	0	0	5	62.2	70	5	36	6	2	37	2	2	7	1	48	43	2	7	.222	0	6.18
	OAK/AL		5	128	5	0	0	0	30.1	28	3	11	0	0	28	0	1	2	0	13	11	1	1	.500	0	3.26
	YEAR		26	420	15	0	0	5	93.0	98	8	47	6	2	65	2	3	9	1	61	54	3	8	.273	0	5.23
88	OAK/AL		33	872	33	1	0	0	201.2	211	16	91	2	4	127	3	8	16	2	86	83	16	7	.696	0	3.70
89	OAK/AL		31	733	31	1	0	0	169.1	187	19	68	1	3	91	5	7	6	1	91	82	19	7	.731	0	4.36
90	KC/AL		21	498	20	0	0	0	112.0	129	9	35	1	0	62	1	3	4	1	66	59	7	10	.412	0	4.74
91	KC/AL		51	515	9	1	0	22	114.1	140	11	46	9	1	53	6	4	2	1	69	63	3	9	.250	2	4.96
92	BAL/AL		48	372	2	0	0	24	89.1	79	5	36	2	2	53	6	4	4	0	35	34	7	3	.700	4	3.43
93	OAK/AL		19	284	8	0	0	2	62.2	68	5	33	2	2	37	1	2	2	1	45	43	2	6	.250	0	6.18
	DET/AL		24	144	0	0	0	10	35.1	25	4	15	4	1	36	1	1	0	0	12	12	0	2	.000	4	3.06
	YEAR		43	428	8	0	0	12	98.0	93	9	48	6	3	73	2	3	2	1	57	55	2	8	.200	4	5.05
12 YR TOTALS			**407**	**7411**	**239**	**30**	**5**	**75**	**1732.2**	**1756**	**133**	**653**	**52**	**20**	**1010**	**47**	**56**	**71**	**10**	**843**	**777**	**111**	**92**	**.547**	**11**	**4.04**

Davis, Mark William — BL/TL — b.10/19/60 PHI79* S1/1

YR	TM/LG	CL	G	TBF	GS	CG	SHO	GF	IP	H	HR	BB	IBB	HB	SO	SH	SF	WP	BK	R	ER	W	L	PCT	SV	ERA
80	PHI/NL		2	30	1	0	0	0	7.0	4	0	5	0	0	5	0	0	0	0	2	2	0	0	.000	0	2.57
81	PHI/NL		9	194	9	0	0	0	43.0	49	7	24	0	0	29	2	4	1	0	37	37	1	4	.200	0	7.74
83	SF/NL		20	469	20	2	2	0	111.0	93	14	50	4	3	83	2	4	8	1	51	43	6	4	.600	0	3.49
84	SF/NL		46	766	27	1	0	6	174.2	201	25	54	12	5	124	10	10	8	4	113	104	5	17	.227	0	5.36
85	SF/NL		77	465	1	0	0	38	114.1	89	13	41	7	3	131	13	1	6	1	49	45	5	12	.294	7	3.54
86	SF/NL		67	342	2	0	0	20	84.1	63	6	34	7	1	90	5	5	3	0	33	28	5	7	.417	4	2.99
87	SF/NL		20	301	11	1	0	1	70.2	72	9	28	1	4	51	3	2	4	2	38	37	4	5	.444	0	4.71
	SD/NL		43	265	0	0	0	17	62.1	51	5	31	7	2	47	4	0	2	0	26	22	5	3	.625	2	3.18
	YEAR		63	566	11	1	0	18	133.0	123	14	59	8	6	98	7	2	6	2	64	59	9	8	.529	2	3.99
88	SD/NL		62	402	0	0	0	52	98.1	70	2	42	11	0	102	7	1	9	1	24	22	5	10	.333	28	2.01
89	SD/NL		70	370	0	0	0	65	92.2	66	6	31	1	2	92	3	4	8	0	21	19	4	3	.571	*44	1.85
90	KC/AL		53	334	3	0	0	28	68.2	71	9	52	3	4	73	2	2	6	0	43	39	2	7	.222	6	5.11
91	OMA/AMA	AAA	6	142	6	0	0	0	35.2	27	1	9	0	1	36	0	2	1	0	11	8	4	1	.800	0	2.02
	KC/AL		29	276	5	0	0	8	62.2	55	6	39	0	1	47	2	5	1	0	36	31	6	3	.667	1	4.45
92	KC/AL		13	176	6	0	0	4	36.1	42	3	28	0	0	19	1	4	1	0	31	29	1	3	.250	0	7.18
	ATL/NL		14	85	0	0	0	7	16.2	22	3	13	2	1	15	0	1	4	1	13	13	1	0	1.000	0	7.02
	YEAR		27	261	6	0	0	11	53.0	64	9	41	2	1	34	1	5	5	1	44	42	2	3	.400	0	7.13
93	PHI/NL		25	154	0	0	0	4	31.1	35	4	24	1	1	28	1	0	1	0	15	15	0	3	.000	0	3.52
	SD/NL		35	173	0	0	0	9	38.1	44	6	20	6	0	42	3	1	1	1	22	18	1	2	.333	4	4.26
	YEAR		60	327	0	0	0	13	69.2	79	10	44	7	1	70	4	1	2	1	37	33	1	5	.167	4	4.26
13 YR TOTALS			585	4802	85	4	2	259	1112.1	1027	121	516	62	27	978	58	44	63	12	554	504	51	83	.381	96	4.08

Dayley, Kenneth Grant "Ken" — BL/TL — b.2/25/59 ATL80 1/3

YR	TM/LG	CL	G	TBF	GS	CG	SHO	GF	IP	H	HR	BB	IBB	HB	SO	SH	SF	WP	BK	R	ER	W	L	PCT	SV	ERA
82	ATL/NL		20	313	11	0	0	3	71.1	79	9	25	2	0	34	7	5	2	0	39	36	5	6	.455	0	4.54
83	ATL/NL		24	436	16	0	0	3	104.2	100	12	39	2	2	70	3	3	3	0	59	50	5	8	.385	0	4.30
84	ATL/NL		4	92	4	0	0	0	18.2	28	5	6	1	1	10	1	0	0	0	18	11	0	3	.000	0	5.30
	RIC/INT	AAA	9	275	9	2	1	0	62.1	66	6	24	0	0	45	1	0	4	1	31	28	5	1	.833	0	4.04
	STL/NL		3	32	2	0	0	1	5.0	16	1	5	0	0	1	0	0	0	0	10	10	0	2	.000	0	18.00
	YEAR		7	124	6	0	0	1	23.2	44	6	11	1	1	11	1	0	0	0	28	21	0	5	.000	0	7.99
	LOU/AMA	AAA	13	386	13	3	0	0	96.1	86	6	22	1	2	79	6	0	3	1	42	35	4	6	.400	0	3.27
85	STL/NL		57	271	0	0	0	27	65.1	65	2	18	9	0	62	4	2	0	0	24	20	4	4	.500	11	2.76
86	STL/NL		31	170	0	0	0	13	38.2	42	1	11	3	1	33	4	1	0	0	19	14	0	3	.000	5	3.26
87	LOU/AMA	AAA	1	9	1	0	0	0	2.0	1	0	1	0	0	1	0	0	0	0	1	1	0	0	.000	0	4.50
	SPR/MID	A	2	14	2	0	0	0	3.2	1	0	1	0	0	3	0	0	0	0	0	0	0	0	.000	0	0.00
	STL/NL		53	260	0	0	0	29	61.0	52	2	33	8	2	63	2	1	0	0	21	18	9	5	.643	4	2.66
88	STL/NL		54	226	0	0	0	21	55.1	48	2	19	7	1	38	4	1	2	0	20	17	2	7	.222	5	2.77
89	STL/NL		71	310	0	0	0	28	75.1	63	3	30	10	0	40	3	1	2	1	26	24	4	3	.571	12	2.87
90	STL/NL		58	307	0	0	0	17	73.1	63	5	30	7	0	51	2	5	6	0	32	29	4	4	.500	2	3.56
91	DUN/FSL	A+	3	21	2	0	0	0	6.0	1	0	2	0	0	2	0	0	0	0	0	0	0	0	.000	0	0.00
	TOR/AL		8	26	0	0	0	3	4.1	7	1	6	0	3	0	1	1	0	0	3	3	0	0	.000	0	6.23
	SYR/INT	AAA	10	79	0	0	0	2	14.0	26	2	11	0	0	13	0	1	0	0	16	15	0	1	.000	1	9.64
92	SYR/INT	AAA	4	23	0	0	0	1	3.2	3	1	6	0	2	4	0	0	0	0	7	7	0	0	.000	0	17.18
93	ALB/PCL	AAA	9	55	1	0	0	0	10.1	14	1	12	1	0	9	0	0	5	1	15	14	0	0	.000	0	12.19
	TOR/AL		2	7	0	0	0	0	0.2	1	0	4	0	0	2	0	0	0	0	2	0	0	0	.000	0	0.00
11 YR TOTALS			385	2450	33	0	0	145	573.2	564	42	225	49	8	406	33	20	26	1	273	232	33	45	.423	39	3.64

DeLeon, Jose — BR/TR — b.12/20/60 PIT79 2/62

YR	TM/LG	CL	G	TBF	GS	CG	SHO	GF	IP	H	HR	BB	IBB	HB	SO	SH	SF	WP	BK	R	ER	W	L	PCT	SV	ERA
83	PIT/NL		15	438	15	3	2	0	108.0	75	5	47	2	1	118	4	3	5	2	36	34	7	3	.700	0	2.83
84	PIT/NL		30	795	28	5	1	0	192.1	147	10	92	5	3	153	7	7	2	2	86	80	7	13	.350	0	3.74
85	HAW/PCL	AAA	5	0	5	4	2	0	41.0	15	3	10	0	1	45	0	0	1	0	4	4	4	0	1.000	0	0.88
	PIT/NL		31	700	25	1	0	5	162.2	138	15	89	3	3	149	7	4	7	1	93	85	2	19	.095	3	4.70
86	PIT/NL		9	83	1	0	0	5	16.1	17	2	11	0	1	11	0	1	0	0	16	15	1	3	.250	1	8.27
	HAW/PCL	AAA	15	431	14	7	1	1	106.0	87	5	44	3	1	83	5	4	3	0	32	29	5	8	.385	0	2.46
	CHI/AL		13	325	13	1	0	0	79.0	49	7	42	0	4	68	4	1	0	0	30	26	4	5	.444	0	2.96
	YEAR		22	408	14	1	0	0	95.1	66	9	59	0	5	79	5	1	7	0	46	41	5	8	.385	1	3.87
87	CHI/AL		33	889	31	2	0	0	206.0	177	24	97	4	10	153	6	6	6	1	106	92	11	12	.478	0	4.02
88	STL/NL		34	940	34	3	1	0	225.1	198	13	86	7	2	208	10	7	3	0	95	92	13	10	.565	0	3.67
89	STL/NL		36	972	36	5	3	0	244.2	173	16	80	5	6	*201	11	5	3	2	96	83	16	12	.571	0	3.05
90	STL/NL		32	793	32	0	0	0	182.2	168	15	86	9	5	164	11	8	5	1	96	90	7	19	.269	0	4.43
91	STL/NL		28	679	28	1	0	0	162.1	144	15	61	1	4	118	6	4	5	0	57	49	5	9	.357	0	2.71
92	STL/NL		29	443	15	0	0	0	102.1	95	7	43	1	2	72	6	3	0	0	56	52	2	7	.222	0	4.57
	PHI/NL		3	63	3	0	0	0	15.0	16	0	5	0	0	7	0	0	0	0	7	5	0	1	.000	0	3.00
	YEAR		32	506	18	0	0	0	117.1	111	7	48	1	2	79	6	3	0	0	63	57	2	8	.200	0	4.37
93	PHI/NL		24	207	3	0	0	6	47.0	39	5	27	1	2	34	3	2	2	0	25	17	3	0	1.000	0	3.26
	CHI/AL		11	37	3	0	0	7	10.1	5	0	3	0	1	6	0	3	2	0	2	2	0	0	.000	0	1.74
	YEAR		35	244	6	0	0	7	57.1	44	5	30	1	3	40	3	5	2	0	27	19	3	0	1.000	0	2.98
11 YR TOTALS			328	7364	264	21	7	20	1754.1	1441	136	775	43	49	1462	69	51	57	7	801	722	78	113	.408	4	3.70

DeLucia, Richard Anthony "Rich" — BR/TR — b.10/7/64 SEA86 6/141

YR	TM/LG	CL	G	TBF	GS	CG	SHO	GF	IP	H	HR	BB	IBB	HB	SO	SH	SF	WP	BK	R	ER	W	L	PCT	SV	ERA
86	BEL/NWL	A-	13	0	11	1	1	1	74.0	44	4	24	0	1	69	0	0	2	2	20	14	8	2	.800	0	1.70
88	SB/CAL	A+	22	541	22	5	3	0	127.2	110	4	59	3	7	118	2	6	6	2	57	44	7	8	.467	0	3.10
89	WIL/EAS	AA	10	234	10	0	1	0	54.2	59	4	13	0	1	41	0	2	5	0	28	23	3	4	.429	0	3.79
90	SB/CAL	A+	5	116	5	1	0	0	30.2	19	4	3	0	4	35	1	0	1	0	9	7	4	1	.800	0	2.05

(continued)

DeLucia, Richard Anthony "Rich" (continued)

YR	TM/LG	CL	G	TBF	GS	CG	SHO	GF	IP	H	HR	BB	IBB	HB	SO	SH	SF	WP	BK	R	ER	W	L	PCT	SV	ERA
	WIL/EAS	AA	18	447	18	2	1	0	115.0	92	7	30	2	2	76	3	3	1	0	30	27	6	6	.500	0	2.11
	CAL/PCL	AAA	5	139	5	1	0	0	32.1	30	2	12	0	2	23	0	3	3	0	17	13	2	2	.500	0	3.62
	SEA/AL		5	144	5	1	0	0	36.0	30	2	9	0	0	20	2	0	0	0	9	8	1	2	.333	0	2.00
91	SEA/AL		32	779	31	0	0	0	182.0	176	31	78	4	4	98	5	14	10	0	107	103	12	13	.480	0	5.09
92	CAL/PCL	AAA	8	162	5	2	1	3	40.1	32	2	14	0	0	38	0	1	2	0	11	11	4	2	.667	1	2.45
	SEA/AL		30	382	11	0	0	6	83.2	100	13	35	1	2	66	2	2	1	0	55	51	3	6	.333	1	5.49
93	SEA/AL		30	195	1	0	0	11	42.2	46	5	23	3	1	48	1	1	4	0	24	22	3	6	.333	0	4.64
	CAL/PCL	AAA	8	192	7	0	0	0	44.0	45	6	20	1	0	38	0	0	4	0	30	28	1	5	.167	1	5.73
4 YR TOTALS			97	1500	48	1	0	17	344.1	352	51	145	8	7	232	10	17	15	0	195	184	19	27	.413	1	4.81

Deshaies, James Joseph "Jim" — BL/TL — b.6/23/60   NYA82 21/542

YR	TM/LG	CL	G	TBF	GS	CG	SHO	GF	IP	H	HR	BB	IBB	HB	SO	SH	SF	WP	BK	R	ER	W	L	PCT	SV	ERA
84	NAS/SOU	AA	7	196	7	1	0	0	45.0	33	3	29	1	1	42	2	0	1	3	20	14	3	2	.600	0	2.80
	NY/AL		2	40	2	0	0	0	7.0	14	1	7	0	0	5	0	1	0	0	9	9	0	1	.000	0	11.57
	CMB/INT	AAA	18	552	18	9	4	0	135.2	99	9	62	4	1	117	3	4	3	1	45	36	10	5	.667	0	2.39
85	CMB/INT	AAA	21	564	21	3	0	0	131.2	124	16	59	1	1	106	4	7	3	4	67	63	8	6	.571	0	4.31
	HOU/NL		2	10	0	0	0	0	3.0	1	0	0	0	0	2	0	0	0	0	0	0	0	0	.000	0	0.00
86	HOU/NL		26	599	26	1	0	0	144.0	124	16	59	2	2	128	4	3	0	7	58	52	12	6	.706	0	3.25
87	HOU/NL		26	648	25	1	0	0	152.0	149	22	57	0		104	9	3	4	5	81	78	11	6	.647	0	4.62
88	HOU/NL		31	847	31	3	2	0	207.0	164	20	72	5	2	127	8	13	1	6	77	69	11	14	.440	0	3.00
89	HOU/NL		34	928	34	6	3	0	225.2	180	15	79	8	4	153	11	5	8	0	80	73	15	10	.600	0	2.91
90	HOU/NL		34	881	34	2	0	0	209.1	186	21	84	9	8	119	17	12	3	3	93	88	7	12	.368	0	3.78
91	HOU/NL		28	686	28	1	0	0	161.0	156	19	72	5	0	98	4	1	0	5	90	89	5	12	.294	0	4.98
92	LV/PCL	AAA	18	242	8	0	0	2	58.0	60	6	17	0	2	46	4	0	3	2	28	26	6	3	.667	1	4.03
	SD/NL		15	395	15	0	0	0	96.0	92	6	33	2	1	46	3	2	1	2	40	35	4	7	.364	0	3.28
93	MIN/AL		27	693	27	1	0	0	167.1	159	24	51	1	6	80	4	7	0	4	85	82	11	13	.458	0	4.41
	SF/NL		5	77	4	0	0	1	17.0	24	2	6	0	1	5	1	0	1	0	9	8	2	2	.500	0	4.24
	YEAR		32	770	31	1	0	1	184.1	183	26	57	1	7	85	5	7	1	4	94	90	13	15	.464	0	4.39
10 YR TOTALS			230	5804	226	15	6	1	1389.1	1249	146	520	39	25	867	61	53	18	33	622	583	78	82	.488	0	3.78

DeSilva, John Reed — BR/TR — b.9/30/67   DET89 8/213

YR	TM/LG	CL	G	TBF	GS	CG	SHO	GF	IP	H	HR	BB	IBB	HB	SO	SH	SF	WP	BK	R	ER	W	L	PCT	SV	ERA
89	NF/NYP	A-	4	95	4	0	0	0	24.0	15	0	8	0	2	24	1	0	3	1	5	5	3	0	1.000	0	1.88
	FAY/SAL	A	9	215	9	1	0	0	52.2	40	4	21	0	0	54	1	2	2	3	23	16	2	2	.500	0	2.73
90	LAK/FSL	A+	14	349	14	0	0	0	91.0	54	4	25	0	4	113	1	2	3	1	18	15	8	1	.889	0	1.48
	LON/EAS	AA	14	375	14	1	1	0	89.0	87	4	27	0	2	76	1	3	3	0	47	38	5	6	.455	0	3.84
91	LON/EAS	AA	11	294	11	2	1	0	73.2	51	4	24	0	0	80	2	2	1	0	24	23	5	4	.556	0	2.81
	TOL/INT	AAA	11	251	11	1	0	0	58.2	62	10	21	0	1	56	0	1	1	0	33	30	5	4	.556	0	4.60
92	TOL/INT	AAA	7	89	2	0	0	3	19.0	26	5	8	0	0	21	1	0	1	0	18	18	0	3	.000	0	8.53
	LON/EAS	AA	9	216	9	1	1	0	52.1	51	4	13	0	1	53	1	2	2	1	24	24	2	4	.333	0	4.13
93	TOL/INT	AAA	25	675	24	1	0	0	161.0	145	13	60	2	0	136	5	3	1	1	73	66	7	10	.412	0	3.69
	DET/AL		1	4	0	0	0	1	1.0	2	0	0	0	0	0	0	0	1	0	1	1	0	0	.000	0	9.00
	LA/NL		3	23	0	0	0	2	5.1	6	0	1	0	0	6	0	0	0	0	4	4	0	0	.000	0	6.75
	YEAR		4	27	0	0	0	3	6.1	8	0	1	0	0	6	0	0	1	0	5	5	0	0	.000	0	7.11
1 YR TOTALS			4	27	0	0	0	3	6.1	8	0	1	0	0	6	0	0	1	0	5	5	0	0	.000	0	7.11

Dewey, Mark Alan — BR/TR — b.1/3/65   SF87 23/594

YR	TM/LG	CL	G	TBF	GS	CG	SHO	GF	IP	H	HR	BB	IBB	HB	SO	SH	SF	WP	BK	R	ER	W	L	PCT	SV	ERA
87	EVE/NWL	A-	19	365	10	1	0	5	84.2	88	2	26	1	2	67	2	6	1	2	39	31	7	3	.700	1	3.30
88	CLI/MID	A	37	474	7	1	0	11	119.1	95	5	14	0	8	76	2	1	1	5	36	19	10	4	.714	7	1.43
89	SJ/CAL	A+	59	301	0	0	0	57	68.2	62	2	23	5	7	60	5	1	3	0	35	24	1	6	.143	30	3.15
90	SHR/TEX	AA	33	157	0	0	0	32	38.1	37	1	10	2	3	23	3	0	1	0	11	8	1	5	.167	13	1.88
	PHO/PCL	AAA	19	130	0	0	0	17	30.1	26	2	10	2	2	27	2	1	0	0	14	9	2	3	.400	8	2.67
	SF/NL		14	92	0	0	0	5	22.2	22	1	5	1	0	11	2	0	0	1	7	7	1	1	.500	0	2.78
91	PHO/PCL	AAA	10	59	0	0	0	10	11.1	16	0	7	5	1	4	2	1	0	0	7	5	1	2	.333	4	3.97
	TID/INT	AAA	48	286	0	0	0	32	64.2	61	2	36	6	0	38	5	2	5	1	30	24	12	3	.800	9	3.34
92	TID/INT	AAA	43	238	0	0	0	32	54.1	61	5	18	6	0	55	6	0	5	0	29	26	5	7	.417	9	4.31
	NY/NL		20	143	0	0	0	6	33.1	37	2	10	2	0	24	1	0	0	0	16	16	1	0	1.000	0	4.32
93	BUF/AMA	AAA	22	114	0	0	0	11	29.1	21	2	5	0	3	17	0	0	0	0	9	4	2	0	1.000	6	1.23
	PIT/NL		21	108	0	0	0	17	26.2	14	0	10	1	3	14	3	1	0	0	8	7	1	2	.333	7	2.36
3 YR TOTALS			55	343	0	0	0	28	82.2	73	3	25	4	3	49	6	3	0	2	31	30	3	3	.500	7	3.27

Dibble, Robert Keith "Rob" — BL/TR — b.1/24/64   CIN83 S1/20

YR	TM/LG	CL	G	TBF	GS	CG	SHO	GF	IP	H	HR	BB	IBB	HB	SO	SH	SF	WP	BK	R	ER	W	L	PCT	SV	ERA
84	TAM/FSL	A+	15	279	11	2	0	1	64.2	59	2	29	4	1	39	1	3	5	0	31	21	5	2	.714	0	2.92
85	CR/MID	A	45	290	1	0	0	30	65.2	67	3	28	2	1	73	4	2	6	0	37	28	5	5	.500	12	3.84
86	VER/EAS	AA	31	246	1	0	0	20	55.1	53	0	28	3	0	37	1	1	5	1	29	19	3	2	.600	10	3.09
	DEN/AMA	AAA	5	27	0	0	0	3	6.2	9	0	2	0	0	3	0	0	0	1	4	4	1	0	1.000	0	5.40
87	NAS/AMA	AAA	44	276	0	0	0	19	61.0	72	5	27	4	1	51	4	2	5	1	34	32	2	4	.333	4	4.72
88	NAS/AMA	AAA	31	140	0	0	0	25	35.0	21	2	14	0	1	41	1	2	3	0	9	9	2	1	.667	13	2.31
	CIN/NL		37	235	0	0	0	6	59.1	43	2	21	5	1	59	2	3	3	0	12	12	1	1	.500	0	1.82
89	CIN/NL		74	401	0	0	0	18	99.0	62	4	39	11	3	141	3	5	4	0	23	23	10	5	.667	2	2.09
90	CIN/NL		68	384	0	0	0	29	98.0	62	3	34	3	1	136	4	6	5	0	22	19	8	3	.727	11	1.74
91	CIN/NL		67	334	0	0	0	57	82.1	67	5	25	2	0	124	5	3	5	0	32	29	3	5	.375	31	3.17
92	CIN/NL		63	286	0	0	0	49	70.1	48	3	31	2	2	110	2	2	3	0	26	24	3	5	.375	25	3.07
93	CIN/NL		45	196	0	0	0	37	41.2	34	8	42	0	0	49	1	0	4	0	33	30	1	4	.200	19	6.48
6 YR TOTALS			354	1836	0	0	0	196	450.2	316	25	192	23	9	619	17	18	28	3	148	137	26	23	.531	88	2.74

DiPino, Frank Michael — BL/TL — b.10/22/56   MIL 7/11/77

YR	TM/LG	CL	G	TBF	GS	CG	SHO	GF	IP	H	HR	BB	IBB	HB	SO	SH	SF	WP	BK	R	ER	W	L	PCT	SV	ERA
81	MIL/AL		2	10	0	0	0	2	2.1	0	0	3	0	0	3	0	0	0	0	0	0	0	0	.000	0	0.00
82	HOU/NL		6	122	6	0	0	0	28.1	32	1	11	1	0	25	3	2	0	0	20	19	2	2	.500	0	6.04
83	HOU/NL		53	279	0	0	0	32	71.1	52	2	20	5	1	67	1	3	3	0	21	21	3	4	.429	20	2.65
84	HOU/NL		57	329	0	0	0	44	75.1	74	3	36	11	1	65	5	2	3	1	32	28	4	9	.308	14	3.35
85	HOU/NL		54	329	0	0	0	29	76.0	69	7	43	6	2	49	3	3	4	1	44	34	3	7	.300	6	4.03
86	HOU/NL		31	167	0	0	0	14	40.1	27	5	16	1	2	27	5	1	3	0	18	16	1	3	.250	3	3.57
	CHI/NL		30	178	0	0	0	12	40.0	47	6	14	5	0	43	4	2	3	0	27	23	2	4	.333	0	5.17
	YEAR		61	345	0	0	0	26	80.1	74	11	30	6	2	70	9	3	3	0	45	39	3	7	.300	3	4.37
87	CHI/NL		69	343	0	0	0	20	80.0	75	7	34	2	1	61	6	4	5	0	31	28	3	3	.500	4	3.15
88	CHI/NL		63	398	0	0	0	23	90.1	102	6	32	1	1	69	2	6	6	1	54	50	2	3	.400	6	4.98
89	STL/NL		67	347	0	0	0	8	88.1	73	6	20	7	0	44	1	5	2	0	26	24	9	0	1.000	0	2.45
90	STL/NL		62	360	0	0	0	24	81.0	92	8	31	12	1	49	8	7	3	0	45	41	5	2	.714	3	4.56
91	LOU/AMA	AAA	2	7	0	0	0	0	1.0	0	0	3	0	0	0	0	0	0	0	4	4	0	0	.000	0	36.00
92	LOU/AMA	AAA	18	102	0	0	0	5	22.2	28	3	8	0	0	10	1	2	2	0	15	10	0	3	.000	0	3.97
	STL/NL		9	45	0	0	0	3	11.0	9	0	3	0	0	8	1	0	0	0	2	2	0	0	.000	0	1.64
93	OMA/AMA	AAA	15	90	0	0	0	8	22.2	21	3	4	1	2	9	1	0	0	0	9	7	1	2	.333	1	2.78
	KC/AL		11	74	0	0	0	5	15.2	21	2	6	0	2	5	0	2	0	0	12	12	1	1	.500	0	6.89
12 YR TOTALS			**514**	**2981**	**6**	**0**	**0**	**216**	**700.0**	**673**	**53**	**269**	**57**	**10**	**515**	**39**	**37**	**28**	**4**	**332**	**298**	**35**	**38**	**.479**	**56**	**3.83**

DiPoto, Gerard Peter "Jerry" — BR/TR — b.5/24/68   CLE89 2/71

YR	TM/LG	CL	G	TBF	GS	CG	SHO	GF	IP	H	HR	BB	IBB	HB	SO	SH	SF	WP	BK	R	ER	W	L	PCT	SV	ERA
89	WAT/NYP	A-	14	373	14	1	0	0	87.1	75	3	39	0	4	98	4	2	10	4	42	35	6	5	.545	0	3.61
90	KIN/CAR	A+	24	636	24	1	0	0	145.1	129	6	77	1	10	143	5	4	12	3	75	61	11	4	.733	0	3.78
	CAN/EAS	AA	3	59	2	0	0	0	14.0	11	0	4	0	2	12	0	0	1	0	5	4	1	0	1.000	0	2.57
91	CAN/EAS	AA	28	670	26	2	0	0	156.0	143	10	74	2	2	97	1	9	15	3	83	66	6	11	.353	0	3.81
92	CS/PCL	AAA	50	568	9	0	0	21	122.0	148	6	66	3	6	62	9	2	9	6	78	67	9	9	.500	2	4.94
93	CHW/INT	AAA	34	177	0	0	0	27	46.2	34	2	13	1	1	44	1	1	4	0	10	10	6	3	.667	12	1.93
	CLE/AL		46	247	0	0	0	26	56.1	57	0	30	7	1	41	3	2	0	0	21	15	4	4	.500	11	2.40

Dixon, Steven Ross "Steve" — BL/TL — b.8/3/69   SL89 31/796

YR	TM/LG	CL	G	TBF	GS	CG	SHO	GF	IP	H	HR	BB	IBB	HB	SO	SH	SF	WP	BK	R	ER	W	L	PCT	SV	ERA
89	JC/APP	R+	18	200	3	0	0	5	43.1	50	1	23	2	2	29	4	3	4	2	34	29	1	3	.250	0	6.02
90	SAV/SAL	A	64	355	0	0	0	21	83.2	59	1	38	5	4	93	8	0	4	0	34	18	7	3	.700	8	1.94
91	SP/FSL	A+	53	269	0	0	0	23	64.1	54	3	24	1	0	54	7	4	2	2	32	27	5	4	.556	1	3.78
92	ARK/TEX	AA	40	192	0	0	0	20	49.0	34	2	15	4	0	65	3	2	2	0	11	10	2	1	.667	2	1.84
	LOU/AMA	AAA	18	94	0	0	0	8	19.2	20	0	19	2	1	16	0	0	0	1	12	11	1	2	.333	1	5.03
93	LOU/AMA	AAA	57	292	0	0	0	41	67.2	57	8	33	7	4	61	4	2	2	0	38	37	5	7	.417	20	4.92
	STL/NL		4	20	0	0	0	0	2.2	7	1	5	0	0	2	2	0	0	0	10	10	0	0	.000	0	33.75

Doherty, John Harold — BR/TR — b.6/11/67   DET89 19/499

YR	TM/LG	CL	G	TBF	GS	CG	SHO	GF	IP	H	HR	BB	IBB	HB	SO	SH	SF	WP	BK	R	ER	W	L	PCT	SV	ERA
89	NF/NYP	A-	26	177	1	0	0	25	47.1	30	1	6	2	3	45	1	0	2	1	7	5	1	1	.500	14	0.95
90	FAY/SAL	A	7	50	0	0	0	3	9.1	17	0	1	0	1	6	1	0	1	0	12	6	1	0	1.000	1	5.79
	LAK/FSL	A+	30	153	0	0	0	20	41.0	33	1	5	2	1	23	2	1	0	4	7	5	5	1	.833	10	1.10
91	LON/EAS	AA	53	281	0	0	0	44	65.0	62	2	21	0	2	42	2	2	1	1	29	16	3	3	.500	15	2.22
92	DET/AL		47	491	11	0	0	9	116.0	131	4	25	5	4	37	3	2	5	0	61	50	7	4	.636	3	3.88
93	DET/AL		32	780	31	3	2	1	184.2	205	19	48	7	5	63	5	4	4	1	104	91	14	11	.560	0	4.44
2 YR TOTALS			**79**	**1271**	**42**	**3**	**2**	**10**	**300.2**	**336**	**23**	**73**	**12**	**9**	**100**	**8**	**6**	**9**	**1**	**165**	**141**	**21**	**15**	**.583**	**3**	**4.22**

Dopson, John Robert — BL/TR — b.7/14/63   MON82 1/45

YR	TM/LG	CL	G	TBF	GS	CG	SHO	GF	IP	H	HR	BB	IBB	HB	SO	SH	SF	WP	BK	R	ER	W	L	PCT	SV	ERA
84	JAC/SOU	AA	26	726	26	6	1	0	170.2	198	10	41	2	1	76	13	2	5	0	83	70	10	8	.556	0	3.69
85	JAC/SOU	AA	5	129	5	1	0	0	32.1	27	2	10	0	1	20	1	0	1	0	5	4	3	0	1.000	0	1.11
	IND/AMA	AAA	18	412	18	3	2	0	95.1	88	7	44	1	3	48	5	2	3	0	44	40	4	7	.364	0	3.78
	MON/NL		4	70	3	0	0	0	13.0	25	4	4	0	0	4	0	0	0	2	17	16	0	2	.000	0	11.08
86	WPB/FSL	A+	2	43	2	0	0	0	10.2	8	0	4	0	1	8	0	0	0	0	0	0	2	0	1.000	0	0.00
	IND/AMA	AAA	4	76	4	0	0	0	16.0	18	0	11	0	0	6	0	0	2	1	12	8	0	3	.000	0	4.50
87	JAC/SOU	AA	21	504	21	1	1	0	118.1	123	8	30	1	1	75	0	1	1	0	58	50	7	5	.583	0	3.80
88	IND/AMA	AAA	3	71	3	0	0	0	18.0	19	0	4	0	0	15	2	0	1	0	9	7	0	0	.000	0	3.50
	MON/NL		26	704	26	4	0	0	168.2	150	15	58	3	4	101	9	2	2	1	69	57	3	11	.214	0	3.04
89	PAW/INT	AAA	2	43	2	0	0	0	8.2	13	1	1	0	0	9	0	0	0	0	9	7	0	2	.000	0	7.27
	BOS/AL		29	727	28	2	0	0	169.1	166	14	69	0	2	95	9	4	7	15	84	75	12	8	.600	0	3.99
90	BOS/AL		4	75	4	0	0	0	17.2	13	2	9	0	0	9	0	0	0	0	7	4	0	0	.000	0	2.04
	PAW/INT	AAA	5	95	5	0	0	0	22.0	28	3	8	1	0	13	1	0	1	0	12	12	2	1	.667	0	4.91
91	WH/FSL	A+	6	116	6	0	0	0	26.2	26	1	8	0	1	26	0	1	1	0	14	10	2	2	.500	0	3.38
	BOS/AL		1	6	0	0	0	0	1.0	2	0	1	0	0	0	0	0	0	0	2	2	0	0	.000	0	18.00
92	PAW/INT	AAA	6	153	6	1	0	0	38.0	28	1	8	0	0	23	0	2	0	0	15	10	1	2	.333	0	2.37
	BOS/AL		25	598	25	0	0	0	141.1	159	17	38	2	2	55	2	2	3	3	78	64	7	11	.389	0	4.08
93	BOS/AL		34	681	28	1	1	3	155.2	170	16	59	12	2	89	8	4	2	3	93	86	7	11	.389	0	4.97
7 YR TOTALS			**123**	**2861**	**114**	**4**	**1**	**4**	**666.2**	**685**	**68**	**238**	**17**	**7**	**353**	**20**	**18**	**16**	**22**	**350**	**304**	**29**	**43**	**.403**	**0**	**4.10**

Downs, Kelly Robert — BR/TR — b.10/25/60   PHI79 26/661

YR	TM/LG	CL	G	TBF	GS	CG	SHO	GF	IP	H	HR	BB	IBB	HB	SO	SH	SF	WP	BK	R	ER	W	L	PCT	SV	ERA
84	POR/PCL	AAA	30	0	25	5	2	2	163.0	166	12	65	3	4	104	0	0	7	2	106	96	7	12	.368	0	5.30
85	PHO/PCL	AAA	37	0	19	2	1	6	137.0	138	9	56	4	1	109	0	0	7	4	69	61	9	10	.474	1	4.01
86	PHO/PCL	AAA	18	466	18	4	0	0	108.0	116	11	28	1	3	68	2	3	6	2	54	41	8	5	.615	0	3.42

(continued)

Downs, Kelly Robert (continued)

YR	TM/LG	CL	G	TBF	GS	CG	SHO	GF	IP	H	HR	BB	IBB	HB	SO	SH	SF	WP	BK	R	ER	W	L	PCT	SV	ERA
	SF/NL		14	372	14	1	0	0	88.1	78	5	30	7	3	64	4	4	3	2	29	27	4	4	.500	0	2.75
87	SF/NL		41	797	28	4	3	4	186.0	185	14	67	11	4	137	7	1	12	4	83	75	12	9	.571	1	3.63
88	SF/NL		27	685	26	6	3	0	168.0	140	11	47	8	3	118	4	9	7	4	67	62	13	9	.591	0	3.32
89	PHO/PCL	AAA	3	42	3	0	0	0	9.1	11	1	5	0	0	9	0	0	0	2	9	9	1	1	.500	0	8.68
	SJ/CAL	A+	1	21	1	0	0	0	5.0	1	0	4	0	0	7	0	0	0	0	0	0	0	0	.000	0	0.00
	SF/NL		18	349	15	0	0	1	82.2	82	7	26	4	1	49	4	4	3	3	47	44	4	8	.333	0	4.79
90	SJ/CAL	A+	1	19	1	0	0	0	5.0	5	0	0	0	1	3	0	0	0	0	2	1	0	1	.000	0	1.80
	PHO/PCL	AAA	1	20	1	0	0	0	5.0	5	1	0	0	0	4	1	0	0	0	3	1	0	0	.000	0	1.80
	SF/NL		13	265	9	0	0	1	63.0	56	2	20	4	2	31	2	1	2	1	26	24	3	2	.600	0	3.43
91	SF/NL		45	479	11	0	0	4	111.2	99	12	53	9	3	62	4	4	4	1	59	52	10	4	.714	0	4.19
92	SF/NL		19	272	7	0	0	5	62.1	65	4	24	0	3	33	7	2	4	0	27	24	1	2	.333	0	3.47
	OAK/AL		18	364	13	0	0	2	82.0	72	4	46	3	4	38	6	4	3	1	36	30	5	5	.500	0	3.29
	YEAR		37	636	20	0	0	7	144.1	137	8	70	3	7	71	13	6	7	1	63	54	6	7	.462	0	3.37
93	OAK/AL		42	539	12	0	0	12	119.2	135	14	60	8	2	66	3	4	4	1	80	75	5	10	.333	0	5.64
8 YR TOTALS			**237**	**4122**	**135**	**11**	**6**	**29**	**963.2**	**912**	**73**	**373**	**54**	**25**	**598**	**41**	**33**	**42**	**17**	**454**	**413**	**57**	**53**	**.518**	**1**	**3.86**

Drabek, Douglas Dean "Doug" — BR/TR — b.7/25/62   CHA83 11/279

YR	TM/LG	CL	G	TBF	GS	CG	SHO	GF	IP	H	HR	BB	IBB	HB	SO	SH	SF	WP	BK	R	ER	W	L	PCT	SV	ERA
84	APP/MID	A	1	21	1	0	0	0	5.0	3	0	3	0	0	6	0	0	0	0	1	1	1	0	1.000	0	1.80
	GF/EAS	AA	19	497	17	7	3	2	124.2	90	6	44	2	2	75	4	8	6	0	34	31	12	5	.706	0	2.24
	NAS/SOU	AA	4	131	4	2	0	0	31.0	30	1	10	0	2	22	0	3	2	1	11	8	1	2	.333	0	2.32
85	ALB/EAS	AA	26	777	26	9	2	0	192.2	153	12	55	2	6	153	7	6	2	0	71	64	13	7	.650	0	2.99
86	CMB/INT	AAA	8	198	8	0	0	0	42.0	50	9	25	0	0	23	0	1	3	0	36	34	1	4	.200	0	7.29
	NY/AL		27	561	21	0	0	1	131.2	126	13	50	1	3	76	5	2	7	0	64	60	7	8	.467	0	4.10
87	PIT/NL		29	721	28	3	1	0	176.1	165	22	46	2	0	120	3	4	5	1	86	76	11	12	.478	0	3.88
88	PIT/NL		33	880	32	3	1	0	219.1	194	21	50	4	6	127	7	5	4	1	83	75	15	7	.682	0	3.08
89	PIT/NL		35	994	34	8	5	0	244.1	215	21	69	3	3	123	13	7	3	0	83	76	14	12	.538	0	2.80
90	PIT/NL		33	918	33	9	3	0	231.1	190	15	56	2	5	131	10	3	6	0	78	71	*22	6	*.786	0	2.76
91	PIT/NL		35	977	35	5	2	0	234.2	245	16	62	6	3	142	15	2	6	0	92	80	15	14	.517	0	3.07
92	PIT/NL		34	1021	34	10	4	0	256.2	218	17	54	8	6	177	8	8	11	1	84	79	15	11	.577	0	2.77
93	HOU/NL		34	991	34	7	2	0	237.2	242	18	60	12	3	157	14	8	12	0	108	100	9	18	.333	0	3.79
8 YR TOTALS			**260**	**7063**	**251**	**43**	**18**	**3**	**1732.0**	**1595**	**143**	**447**	**38**	**27**	**1053**	**72**	**43**	**48**	**3**	**678**	**617**	**108**	**88**	**.551**	**0**	**3.21**

Drahman, Brian Stacy — BR/TR — b.11/7/66   MIL86 S2/30

YR	TM/LG	CL	G	TBF	GS	CG	SHO	GF	IP	H	HR	BB	IBB	HB	SO	SH	SF	WP	BK	R	ER	W	L	PCT	SV	ERA
86	HEL/PIO	R+	18	0	10	0	0	5	65.1	79	4	33	1	0	40	0	0	4	0	49	43	4	6	.400	2	5.92
87	BEL/MID	A	46	318	0	0	0	41	79.0	63	2	23	3	3	60	4	2	5	1	28	19	6	5	.545	18	2.16
88	STO/CAL	A+	44	266	0	0	0	40	62.1	57	2	27	1	1	50	1	0	3	0	17	14	4	5	.444	14	2.02
89	EP/TEX	AA	19	151	0	0	0	8	31.0	52	3	11	1	1	23	1	0	3	0	31	25	3	4	.429	2	7.26
	STO/CAL	A+	12	112	0	0	0	10	27.2	22	0	9	0	2	30	1	0	2	0	11	10	3	2	.600	4	3.25
	SAR/FSL	A+	7	73	2	0	0	3	16.2	18	1	5	1	1	9	0	0	1	0	9	6	0	0	.000	1	3.24
90	BIR/SOU	AA	50	383	1	0	0	31	90.1	90	6	24	3	3	72	9	4	12	1	50	41	6	4	.600	17	4.08
91	VAN/PCL	AAA	22	106	0	0	0	21	24.1	21	2	13	1	0	17	4	0	1	0	12	12	2	3	.400	12	4.44
	CHI/AL		28	125	0	0	0	8	30.2	21	4	13	1	0	18	2	1	0	0	12	11	3	2	.600	0	3.23
92	VAN/PCL	AAA	48	242	0	0	0	44	58.1	44	5	31	1	0	34	3	2	2	0	16	13	2	4	.333	30	2.01
	CHI/AL		5	29	0	0	0	2	7.0	6	0	3	0	0	1	0	0	0	0	3	2	0	0	.000	0	2.57
93	NAS/AMA	AAA	54	249	0	0	0	50	55.2	59	1	19	8	2	49	3	4	3	0	29	18	9	4	.692	20	2.91
	CHI/AL		5	23	0	0	0	1	5.1	7	2	0	3	0	3	0	0	0	0	0	0	0	0	.000	1	0.00
3 YR TOTALS			**38**	**177**	**0**	**0**	**0**	**14**	**43.0**	**34**	**4**	**17**	**1**	**0**	**22**	**2**	**1**	**1**	**0**	**15**	**13**	**3**	**2**	**.600**	**1**	**2.72**

Draper, Michael Anthony "Mike" — BR/TR — b.9/14/66   NYA88 23/677

YR	TM/LG	CL	G	TBF	GS	CG	SHO	GF	IP	H	HR	BB	IBB	HB	SO	SH	SF	WP	BK	R	ER	W	L	PCT	SV	ERA
88	ONE/NYP	A-	8	46	0	0	0	8	10.2	10	0	3	0	0	16	0	1	1	0	4	1	2	1	.667	3	0.84
	PW/CAR	A+	9	155	5	1	0	1	35.1	37	1	4	1	4	20	1	3	4	2	22	13	2	3	.400	0	3.31
89	PW/CAR	A+	25	646	24	6	1	0	153.1	147	7	42	4	6	84	3	4	12	1	66	53	14	8	.636	0	3.11
90	ALB/EAS	AA	8	196	8	0	0	0	43.1	51	4	19	0	2	15	0	1	0	0	34	31	2	2	.500	0	6.44
	FL/FSL	A+	14	389	14	1	1	0	96.0	80	4	22	0	3	52	5	3	0	0	30	24	9	1	.900	0	2.25
	PW/CAR	A+	5	107	4	1	0	0	22.2	31	2	9	0	2	8	1	3	4	0	20	16	0	2	.000	0	6.35
91	ALB/EAS	AA	36	555	14	1	1	6	131.1	125	6	47	4	6	71	5	3	10	1	58	48	10	6	.625	2	3.29
	CMB/INT	AAA	4	132	4	2	0	0	28.2	36	1	5	0	0	13	0	1	0	0	21	12	1	3	.250	0	3.77
92	CMB/INT	AAA	57	332	3	0	0	50	80.0	70	3	28	2	4	49	2	1	2	1	36	32	5	6	.455	37	3.60
93	NY/NL		29	184	1	0	0	11	42.1	53	2	14	3	0	16	3	5	0	1	22	20	1	1	.500	0	4.25

Dreyer, Steven William "Steve" — BR/TR — b.11/19/69   TEX90 8/225

YR	TM/LG	CL	G	TBF	GS	CG	SHO	GF	IP	H	HR	BB	IBB	HB	SO	SH	SF	WP	BK	R	ER	W	L	PCT	SV	ERA
90	BUT/PIO	R+	8	146	8	0	0	0	35.2	32	2	10	0	0	29	0	0	1	0	21	18	1	1	.500	0	4.54
91	GAS/SAL	A	25	661	25	3	1	0	162.0	137	5	62	1	5	122	5	4	4	0	51	42	7	10	.412	0	2.33
92	CHA/FSL	A+	26	675	26	4	3	0	168.2	164	8	37	2	6	111	10	4	4	0	54	45	11	7	.611	0	2.40
93	TUL/TEX	AA	5	128	5	1	1	0	31.1	26	4	9	1	0	27	0	1	0	0	13	13	2	2	.500	0	3.73
	OC/AMA	AAA	16	445	16	1	0	0	107.0	108	5	31	1	2	59	4	3	4	0	39	36	4	6	.400	0	3.03
	TEX/AL		10	186	6	0	0	0	41.0	48	7	20	1	1	23	0	0	0	0	26	26	3	3	.500	0	5.71

Eckersley, Dennis Lee — BR/TR — b.10/3/54   CLE72 3/50

YR	TM/LG	CL	G	TBF	GS	CG	SHO	GF	IP	H	HR	BB	IBB	HB	SO	SH	SF	WP	BK	R	ER	W	L	PCT	SV	ERA
75	CLE/AL		34	794	24	6	2	5	186.2	147	16	90	8	7	152	6	4	6	1	61	54	13	7	.650	2	2.60
76	CLE/AL		36	821	30	9	3	3	199.1	155	13	78	2	5	200	10	4	6	1	82	76	13	12	.520	1	3.43

Eckersley, Dennis Lee (continued)

YR	TM/LG	CL	G	TBF	GS	CG	SHO	GF	IP	H	HR	BB	IBB	HB	SO	SH	SF	WP	BK	R	ER	W	L	PCT	SV	ERA
77	CLE/AL		33	1006	33	12	3	0	247.1	214	31	54	11	7	191	11	6	3	0	100	97	14	13	.519	0	3.53
78	BOS/AL		35	1121	35	16	3	0	268.1	258	30	71	8	7	162	7	8	3	0	99	89	20	8	.714	0	2.99
79	BOS/AL		33	1018	33	17	2	0	246.2	234	29	59	4	6	150	10	6	1	1	89	82	17	10	.630	0	2.99
80	BOS/AL		30	818	30	8	0	0	197.2	188	25	44	7	2	121	7	8	0	0	101	94	12	14	.462	0	4.28
81	BOS/AL		23	649	23	8	2	0	154.0	160	9	35	2	3	79	6	5	0	0	82	73	9	8	.529	0	4.27
82	BOS/AL		33	926	33	11	3	0	224.1	228	31	43	3	2	127	4	4	1	0	101	93	13	13	.500	0	3.73
83	BOS/AL		28	787	28	2	0	0	176.1	223	27	39	4	6	77	1	5	1	0	119	110	9	13	.409	0	5.61
84	BOS/AL		9	270	9	2	0	0	64.2	71	10	13	2	1	33	3	3	2	0	38	36	4	4	.500	0	5.01
	CHI/NL		24	662	24	2	0	0	160.1	152	11	36	7	4	81	8	6	1	2	59	54	10	8	.556	0	3.03
	YEAR		33	932	33	4	0	0	225.0	223	21	49	9	5	114	11	9	3	2	97	90	14	12	.538	0	3.60
85	CHI/NL		25	664	25	6	2	0	169.1	145	15	19	4	3	117	6	2	0	3	61	58	11	7	.611	0	3.08
86	CHI/NL		33	862	32	1	0	0	201.0	226	21	43	3	3	137	13	10	2	5	109	102	6	11	.353	0	4.57
87	OAK/AL		54	460	2	0	0	33	115.2	99	11	17	3	3	113	3	3	1	0	41	39	6	8	.429	16	3.03
88	OAK/AL		60	279	0	0	0	53	72.2	52	5	11	2	1	70	1	3	0	2	20	19	4	2	.667	*45	2.35
89	OAK/AL		51	206	0	0	0	46	57.2	32	5	3	0	1	55	0	4	0	0	10	10	4	0	1.000	33	1.56
90	OAK/AL		63	262	0	0	0	61	73.1	41	2	4	1	0	73	0	1	0	0	9	5	4	2	.667	48	0.61
91	OAK/AL		67	299	0	0	0	59	76.0	60	11	9	3	1	87	1	0	1	0	26	25	5	4	.556	43	2.96
92	OAK/AL		69	309	0	0	0	65	80.0	62	5	11	6	2	93	3	0	0	0	17	17	7	1	.875	*51	1.91
93	OAK/AL		64	276	0	0	0	52	67.0	67	7	13	4	2	80	2	2	0	0	32	31	2	4	.333	36	4.16
19 YR TOTALS			**804**	**12489**	**361**	**100**	**20**	**377**	**3038.1**	**2814**	**314**	**692**	**84**	**65**	**2198**	**102**	**87**	**26**	**16**	**1256**	**1164**	**183**	**149**	**.551**	**275**	**3.45**

Edens, Thomas Patrick "Tom" — BR/TR — b.6/9/61   KC83 14/361

YR	TM/LG	CL	G	TBF	GS	CG	SHO	GF	IP	H	HR	BB	IBB	HB	SO	SH	SF	WP	BK	R	ER	W	L	PCT	SV	ERA
84	COL/SAL	A	16	409	15	4	1	1	95.1	65	1	58	1	1	60	2	4	10	1	44	33	7	4	.636	0	3.12
	LYN/CAR	A+	3	65	2	0	0	0	14.1	11	1	8	0	0	15	0	0	1	0	6	4	1	1	.500	0	2.51
85	LYN/CAR	A+	16	353	16	0	0	0	82.0	86	4	34	0	2	48	2	5	3	2	40	35	6	4	.600	0	3.84
86	JAC/TEX	AA	16	431	16	4	0	0	106.0	76	4	41	1	1	72	5	2	10	0	36	30	9	4	.692	0	2.55
	TID/INT	AAA	11	280	11	2	1	0	61.1	71	5	28	1	1	31	1	1	4	0	33	31	5	3	.625	0	4.55
87	NY/NL		2	42	2	0	0	0	8.0	15	2	4	0	0	4	2	0	0	0	6	6	0	0	.000	0	6.75
	TID/INT	AAA	25	605	22	0	0	1	138.0	140	10	55	0	7	61	6	6	2	1	69	55	9	7	.563	1	3.59
88	TID/INT	AAA	24	582	21	3	0	0	135.1	128	7	53	1	5	89	1	0	3	1	67	52	7	6	.538	0	3.46
89	TID/INT	AAA	18	295	8	0	0	3	65.0	76	3	28	2	4	31	0	2	2	0	43	38	1	5	.167	1	5.26
	SCR/INT	AAA	7	177	6	0	0	0	42.1	45	2	11	2	1	16	1	2	2	0	16	15	1	1	.500	0	3.19
90	DEN/AMA	AAA	19	154	0	0	0	9	36.2	32	3	22	0	0	26	1	1	3	0	23	22	1	1	.500	4	5.40
	MIL/AL		35	387	0	0	0	9	89.0	89	8	33	3	4	40	1	5	1	0	52	44	4	5	.444	2	4.45
91	POR/PCL	AAA	25	668	24	3	1	0	161.1	145	6	62	3	7	100	5	5	4	0	67	54	10	7	.588	0	3.01
	MIN/AL		8	143	6	0	0	0	33.0	34	2	10	1	0	19	0	1	1	0	15	15	2	2	.500	0	4.09
92	MIN/AL		52	317	0	0	0	14	76.1	65	1	36	3	2	57	4	0	5	0	26	24	6	3	.667	3	2.83
93	OSC/FSL	A+	3	17	1	0	0	0	4.0	5	0	1	0	1	4	0	0	0	0	0	0	1	0	1.000	0	0.00
	TUC/PCL	AAA	5	34	0	0	0	1	7.1	9	0	3	0	1	6	0	0	0	0	5	5	1	0	1.000	0	6.14
	HOU/NL		38	203	0	0	0	20	49.0	47	4	19	7	0	21	4	1	3	0	17	17	1	1	.500	0	3.12
5 YR TOTALS			**135**	**1092**	**14**	**0**	**0**	**43**	**255.1**	**250**	**17**	**102**	**14**	**6**	**141**	**16**	**5**	**12**	**0**	**116**	**106**	**13**	**11**	**.542**	**5**	**3.74**

Eichhorn, Mark Anthony — BR/TR — b.11/21/60   TOR79* 2/30

YR	TM/LG	CL	G	TBF	GS	CG	SHO	GF	IP	H	HR	BB	IBB	HB	SO	SH	SF	WP	BK	R	ER	W	L	PCT	SV	ERA
82	TOR/AL		7	171	7	0	0	0	38.0	40	4	14	1	0	16	1	2	3	0	28	23	0	3	.000	0	5.45
84	SYR/INT	AAA	36	541	18	3	1	7	117.2	147	13	51	0	4	54	3	3	8	0	92	78	5	9	.357	0	5.97
85	KNO/SOU	AA	26	473	10	2	1	2	116.1	101	11	34	2	4	76	5	4	2	1	49	39	5	1	.833	0	3.02
	SYR/INT	AAA	8	154	7	0	0	1	37.1	38	5	7	0	0	27	2	1	1	0	24	20	2	5	.286	0	4.82
86	TOR/AL		69	612	0	0	0	38	157.0	105	8	45	14	7	166	9	2	2	1	32	30	14	6	.700	10	1.72
87	TOR/AL		*89	540	0	0	0	27	127.2	110	14	52	13	6	96	7	4	3	1	47	45	10	6	.625	4	3.17
88	SYR/INT	AAA	18	162	1	0	0	4	38.1	35	0	15	5	4	34	0	2	0	0	9	5	4	4	.500	2	1.17
	TOR/AL		37	302	0	0	0	17	66.2	79	3	27	4	6	28	8	1	3	6	32	31	0	3	.000	1	4.18
89	RIC/INT	AAA	25	152	0	0	0	24	41.0	29	0	6	0	2	33	2	0	1	0	6	6	1	0	1.000	19	1.32
	ATL/NL		45	286	0	0	0	13	68.1	70	6	19	8	1	49	7	4	1	0	36	33	5	5	.500	0	4.35
90	CAL/AL		60	374	0	0	0	40	84.2	98	2	23	0	6	69	4	2	2	0	36	29	2	5	.286	13	3.08
91	CAL/AL		70	311	0	0	0	23	81.2	63	2	13	1	2	49	5	3	0	0	21	18	3	3	.500	1	1.98
92	CAL/AL		42	237	0	0	0	19	56.2	51	2	18	8	0	42	2	3	3	1	19	15	2	4	.333	2	2.38
	TOR/AL		23	135	0	0	0	7	31.0	35	1	7	0	2	19	1	2	2	0	15	15	2	0	1.000	0	4.35
	YEAR		65	372	0	0	0	26	87.2	86	3	25	8	2	61	3	5	5	1	34	30	4	4	.500	2	3.08
93	TOR/AL		54	309	0	0	0	16	72.2	76	3	22	7	3	47	3	2	2	0	26	22	3	1	.750	0	2.72
9 YR TOTALS			**496**	**3277**	**7**	**0**	**0**	**200**	**784.1**	**727**	**45**	**240**	**56**	**33**	**581**	**45**	**27**	**24**	**10**	**292**	**261**	**41**	**36**	**.532**	**31**	**2.99**

Eiland, David William "Dave" — BR/TR — b.7/5/66   NYA87 5/185

YR	TM/LG	CL	G	TBF	GS	CG	SHO	GF	IP	H	HR	BB	IBB	HB	SO	SH	SF	WP	BK	R	ER	W	L	PCT	SV	ERA
87	ONE/NYP	A-	5	109	5	0	0	0	29.1	20	1	3	0	0	16	0	1	0	0	6	6	4	0	1.000	0	1.84
	FL/FSL	A+	8	248	8	4	1	0	62.1	57	0	8	0	0	28	2	0	1	1	17	13	5	3	.625	0	1.88
88	ALB/EAS	AA	18	472	18	7	2	0	119.1	95	8	22	3	1	66	4	5	2	0	39	34	9	5	.643	0	2.56
	NY/AL		3	57	3	0	0	0	12.2	15	6	4	0	0	7	0	0	0	0	9	9	0	0	.000	0	6.39
	CMB/INT	AAA	4	106	4	0	0	0	24.1	25	4	6	0	1	13	0	1	1	0	8	7	1	1	.500	0	2.59
89	NY/AL		6	152	6	0	0	0	34.1	44	5	13	3	2	11	1	2	0	0	25	22	1	3	.250	0	5.77
	CMB/INT	AAA	18	427	18	2	0	0	103.0	107	10	21	0	0	45	1	3	1	1	47	43	9	4	.692	0	3.76
90	CMB/INT	AAA	27	706	26	11	3	0	175.1	155	8	32	0	3	96	3	1	2	2	63	56	16	5	.762	0	2.87
	NY/AL		5	127	5	0	0	0	30.1	31	2	5	0	0	16	0	0	0	0	14	12	2	1	.667	0	3.56
91	CMB/INT	AAA	9	244	9	2	0	0	60.0	54	5	7	0	0	18	1	1	0	0	22	16	6	1	.857	0	2.40
	NY/AL		18	317	13	0	0	4	72.2	87	10	23	1	3	18	3	0	0	0	51	43	2	5	.286	0	5.33

(continued)

Eiland, David William "Dave" (continued)

YR	TM/LG	CL	G	TBF	GS	CG	SHO	GF	IP	H	HR	BB	IBB	HB	SO	SH	SF	WP	BK	R	ER	W	L	PCT	SV	ERA
92	SD/NL		7	120	7	0	0	0	27.0	33	1	5	0	0	10	0	0	0	1	21	17	0	2	.000	0	5.67
	LV/PCL	AAA	14	276	14	0	0	0	63.2	78	4	11	2	0	31	7	6	0	0	43	37	4	5	.444	0	5.23
93	SD/NL		10	217	9	0	0	0	48.1	58	5	17	1	1	14	2	2	1	0	33	28	0	3	.000	0	5.21
	CHW/INT	AAA	8	154	8	0	0	0	35.2	42	8	12	0	1	13	1	0	0	0	22	21	1	3	.250	0	5.30
	OC/AMA	AAA	7	155	7	1	0	0	35.2	39	1	9	0	1	15	1	1	0	0	18	17	3	1	.750	0	4.29
6 YR TOTALS			**49**	**990**	**43**	**0**	**0**	**4**	**225.1**	**268**	**29**	**67**	**5**	**8**	**76**	**3**	**7**	**1**	**1**	**153**	**131**	**5**	**14**	**.263**	**0**	**5.23**

Eldred, Calvin John "Cal" — BR/TR — b.11/24/67　　　　　　　　　　　　　　MIL89 1/17

YR	TM/LG	CL	G	TBF	GS	CG	SHO	GF	IP	H	HR	BB	IBB	HB	SO	SH	SF	WP	BK	R	ER	W	L	PCT	SV	ERA
89	BEL/MID	A	5	127	5	0	0	0	31.1	23	0	11	1	1	32	1	0	2	2	10	8	2	1	.667	0	2.30
90	STO/CAL	A+	7	197	7	3	1	0	50.0	31	2	19	0	3	75	0	0	2	1	12	9	4	2	.667	0	1.62
	EP/TEX	AA	19	485	19	0	0	0	110.1	126	9	47	0	2	93	3	3	4	1	61	55	5	4	.556	0	4.49
91	DEN/AMA	AAA	29	784	29	3	1	0	185.0	161	13	84	2	12	168	4	8	8	2	82	77	13	9	.591	0	3.75
	MIL/AL		3	73	3	0	0	0	16.0	20	2	6	0	0	10	0	0	0	0	9	8	2	0	1.000	0	4.50
92	DEN/AMA	AAA	19	570	19	4	1	0	141.0	122	9	42	0	4	99	3	6	3	0	49	47	10	6	.625	0	3.00
	MIL/AL		14	394	14	2	1	0	100.1	76	4	23	0	2	62	1	0	3	0	21	20	11	2	.846	0	1.79
93	MIL/AL		36	1087	36	8	1	0	*258.0	232	32	91	5	10	180	5	12	2	0	120	115	16	16	.500	0	4.01
3 YR TOTALS			**53**	**1554**	**53**	**10**	**2**	**0**	**374.1**	**328**	**38**	**120**	**5**	**12**	**252**	**6**	**12**	**5**	**0**	**150**	**143**	**29**	**18**	**.617**	**0**	**3.44**

Erickson, Scott Gavin — BR/TR — b.2/2/68　　　　　　　　　　　　　　MIN89 4/112

YR	TM/LG	CL	G	TBF	GS	CG	SHO	GF	IP	H	HR	BB	IBB	HB	SO	SH	SF	WP	BK	R	ER	W	L	PCT	SV	ERA
89	VIS/CAL	A+	12	320	12	2	0	0	78.2	79	3	22	0	0	59	0	0	3	4	29	26	3	4	.429	0	2.97
90	ORL/SOU	AA	15	397	15	3	1	0	101.0	75	3	24	0	5	69	1	2	4	1	38	34	8	3	.727	0	3.03
	MIN/AL		19	485	17	1	0	1	113.0	108	9	51	4	5	53	5	2	3	0	49	36	8	4	.667	0	2.87
91	MIN/AL		32	851	32	5	3	0	204.0	189	13	71	3	6	108	5	7	4	0	80	72	*20	8	*.714	0	3.18
92	MIN/AL		32	888	32	5	3	0	212.0	197	18	83	8	8	101	9	7	6	1	86	80	13	12	.520	0	3.40
93	MIN/AL		34	976	34	1	0	0	218.2	266	17	71	1	10	116	10	13	5	0	138	126	8	19	.296	0	5.19
4 YR TOTALS			**117**	**3200**	**115**	**12**	**6**	**1**	**747.2**	**760**	**57**	**276**	**11**	**29**	**378**	**29**	**29**	**18**	**1**	**353**	**314**	**49**	**43**	**.533**	**0**	**3.78**

Ettles, Mark Edward — BR/TR — b.10/30/66　　　　　　　　　　　　　　DET89 33/863

YR	TM/LG	CL	G	TBF	GS	CG	SHO	GF	IP	H	HR	BB	IBB	HB	SO	SH	SF	WP	BK	R	ER	W	L	PCT	SV	ERA
89	NF/NYP	A-	5	66	0	0	0	3	17.2	12	0	2	0	0	21	0	0	1	1	3	2	3	0	1.000	1	1.02
	FAY/SAL	A	19	120	0	0	0	11	27.2	28	1	9	2	1	34	2	0	1	2	9	7	2	2	.500	2	2.28
90	LAK/FSL	A+	45	295	0	0	0	21	68.0	63	1	16	1	6	62	4	2	4	2	34	25	5	5	.500	3	3.31
91	LAK/FSL	A+	8	76	1	0	0	0	17.0	19	2	6	0	1	14	0	0	1	1	11	9	2	1	.667	0	4.76
	CHS/SAL	A	29	188	0	0	0	23	45.2	36	2	12	2	2	59	5	2	2	0	15	12	2	1	.667	12	2.36
	WAT/MID	A	14	60	0	0	0	14	16.0	6	2	6	2	0	24	0	0	0	0	5	4	1	2	.333	8	2.25
92	WIC/TEX	AA	54	283	0	0	0	43	68.1	54	6	23	6	4	86	4	1	8	1	23	21	3	8	.273	22	2.77
93	LV/PCL	AAA	47	224	0	0	0	41	49.2	58	2	22	6	2	29	3	1	13	0	28	26	3	6	.333	15	4.71
	SD/NL		14	81	0	0	0	5	18.0	23	4	4	1	0	9	0	2	3	0	16	13	1	0	1.000	0	6.50

Fajardo, Hector — BR/TR — b.11/16/70　　　　　　　　　　　　　　PIT 2/14/89

YR	TM/LG	CL	G	TBF	GS	CG	SHO	GF	IP	H	HR	BB	IBB	HB	SO	SH	SF	WP	BK	R	ER	W	L	PCT	SV	ERA
89	PIR/GCL	R	10	154	6	0	0	0	34.2	38	0	20	0	0	19	0	1	1	0	24	23	0	5	.000	0	5.97
90	PIR/GCL	R	5	92	4	0	0	0	21.0	23	0	8	0	0	17	0	1	1	1	10	9	1	1	.500	0	3.86
	AUG/SAL	A	7	173	7	0	0	0	39.2	41	1	15	0	2	28	1	0	0	1	18	17	2	2	.500	0	3.86
91	AUG/SAL	A	11	250	11	1	1	0	60.1	44	1	24	0	2	79	1	3	3	1	26	18	4	3	.571	0	2.69
	SAL/CAR	A+	1	30	1	1	0	0	7.2	4	1	1	1	0	7	1	0	0	0	3	2	0	0	.000	0	2.35
	CAR/SOU	AA	10	258	10	1	0	0	61.0	55	4	24	0	0	53	2	3	2	2	32	28	3	4	.429	0	4.13
	PIT/NL		2	35	2	0	0	0	6.1	10	0	7	0	0	4	0	0	0	0	7	7	0	0	.000	0	9.95
	BUF/AMA	AAA	8	36	0	0	0	4	9.1	6	0	3	0	0	12	0	0	0	0	1	1	1	0	1.000	1	0.96
	TEX/AL		4	84	3	0	0	1	19.0	25	2	4	1	0	15	0	3	0	0	13	12	0	2	.000	0	5.68
	YEAR		6	119	5	0	0	1	25.1	35	2	11	1	0	23	0	3	0	0	20	19	0	2	.000	0	6.75
92	RAN/GCL	R	1	27	1	0	0	0	6.1	5	0	2	0	1	9	0	0	1	0	4	4	0	1	.000	0	5.68
	CHA/FSL	A+	4	95	4	0	0	0	22.2	22	0	8	0	1	12	2	1	0	0	9	7	2	2	.500	0	2.78
	TUL/TEX	AA	5	99	4	0	0	0	25.0	19	2	7	0	0	26	0	1	0	0	8	6	1	2	.333	0	2.16
	OC/AMA	AAA	1	30	1	0	0	0	7.0	8	0	2	0	0	6	0	0	0	0	2	2	1	0	1.000	0	2.16
93	RAN/GCL	R	6	114	6	0	0	0	30.0	21	0	5	0	0	27	1	0	0	0	8	6	3	1	.750	0	1.80
	CHA/FSL	A+	2	21	1	0	0	0	5.0	5	0	1	0	0	3	0	0	0	0	1	1	0	0	.000	0	1.80
	TEX/AL		1	2	0	0	0	1	0.2	0	0	0	0	0	0	0	0	0	0	0	0	0	0	.000	0	0.00
2 YR TOTALS			**7**	**121**	**5**	**0**	**0**	**2**	**26.0**	**35**	**2**	**11**	**0**	**1**	**24**	**0**	**3**	**3**	**0**	**20**	**19**	**0**	**2**	**.000**	**0**	**6.58**

Farr, Steven Michael "Steve" — BR/TR — b.12/12/56　　　　　　　　　　　　　　PIT 12/13/76

YR	TM/LG	CL	G	TBF	GS	CG	SHO	GF	IP	H	HR	BB	IBB	HB	SO	SH	SF	WP	BK	R	ER	W	L	PCT	SV	ERA
84	MAI/INT	AAA	6	179	6	2	1	0	45.0	37	3	8	0	0	40	3	0	0	2	14	13	4	0	1.000	0	2.60
	CLE/AL		31	488	16	0	0	4	116.0	106	14	46	3	0	83	2	3	2	2	61	59	3	11	.214	1	4.58
85	OMA/AMA	AAA	17	532	16	7	3	0	133.2	105	6	41	0	3	98	3	2	1	2	36	30	10	4	.714	0	2.02
	KC/AL		16	164	3	0	0	5	37.2	34	2	20	4	2	36	1	2	2	0	15	13	2	1	.667	1	3.11
86	KC/AL		56	443	0	0	0	33	109.1	90	10	39	8	4	83	3	2	2	0	39	38	8	4	.667	8	3.13
87	OMA/AMA	AAA	8	50	0	0	0	8	12.2	6	0	6	1	0	15	0	0	0	1	3	2	0	0	.000	4	1.42
	KC/AL		47	408	0	0	0	19	91.0	97	9	44	4	2	88	3	2	2	0	47	42	4	3	.571	1	4.15
88	KC/AL		62	344	0	0	0	49	82.2	74	5	30	6	2	72	1	3	4	2	25	23	5	4	.556	20	2.50
89	KC/AL		51	279	2	0	0	23	63.1	75	5	22	5	1	56	0	3	1	0	35	29	2	5	.286	18	4.12
90	KC/AL		57	515	6	1	1	20	127.0	99	6	48	9	5	94	10	1	2	0	32	28	13	7	.650	1	1.98
91	NY/AL		60	285	0	0	0	48	70.0	57	4	20	3	5	60	3	5	2	0	19	17	5	5	.500	23	2.19

Farr, Steven Michael "Steve" (continued)

YR	TM/LG	CL	G	TBF	GS	CG	SHO	GF	IP	H	HR	BB	IBB	HB	SO	SH	SF	WP	BK	R	ER	W	L	PCT	SV	ERA
92	NY/AL		50	207	0	0	0	42	52.0	34	2	19	0	2	37	1	2	0	0	10	9	2	2	.500	30	1.56
93	NY/AL		49	211	0	0	0	37	47.0	44	8	28	4	2	39	3	4	2	0	22	22	2	2	.500	25	4.21
10 YR TOTALS			**479**	**3344**	**28**	**1**	**1**	**297**	**796.0**	**710**	**65**	**316**	**46**	**30**	**648**	**21**	**23**	**22**	**5**	**305**	**280**	**46**	**44**	**.511**	**128**	**3.17**

Farrell, John Edward — BR/TR — b.8/4/62   CLE84 2/32

YR	TM/LG	CL	G	TBF	GS	CG	SHO	GF	IP	H	HR	BB	IBB	HB	SO	SH	SF	WP	BK	R	ER	W	L	PCT	SV	ERA
84	WAT/MID	A	9	213	9	2	0	0	43.1	59	4	33	0	1	29	3	0	4	2	34	31	0	5	.000	0	6.44
	MAI/INT	AAA	5	117	5	0	0	0	26.1	20	2	20	2	1	12	1	2	1	0	11	11	2	1	.667	0	3.76
85	WAT/EAS	AA	25	678	25	5	1	0	149.0	161	8	76	1	5	75	8	6	7	1	106	86	7	13	.350	0	5.19
86	WAT/EAS	AA	26	732	26	9	3	0	173.1	158	15	54	2	10	104	4	4	3	0	82	59	9	10	.474	0	3.06
87	BUF/AMA	AAA	25	681	24	2	0	1	156.0	155	26	64	2	8	91	3	5	9	1	109	101	6	12	.333	0	5.83
	CLE/AL		10	297	9	1	0	0	69.0	68	7	22	1	5	28	3	1	1	1	29	26	5	1	.833	0	3.39
88	CLE/AL		31	895	30	4	0	1	210.1	216	15	67	3	9	92	9	6	2	3	106	99	14	10	.583	0	4.24
89	CLE/AL		31	895	31	7	2	0	208.0	196	14	71	4	7	132	8	6	4	0	97	84	9	14	.391	0	3.63
90	CAN/EAS	AA	2	46	2	0	0	0	10.0	13	1	2	0	1	5	0	0	0	0	8	8	1	1	.500	0	7.20
	CLE/AL		17	418	17	1	0	0	96.2	108	10	33	1	1	44	5	2	1	0	49	46	4	5	.444	0	4.28
93	VAN/PCL	AAA	12	363	12	2	0	0	85.2	83	7	28	1	8	71	2	2	4	0	44	38	4	5	.444	0	3.99
	CAL/AL		21	420	17	0	0	1	90.2	110	22	44	3	7	45	2	2	3	0	74	74	3	12	.200	0	7.35
5 YR TOTALS			**110**	**2925**	**104**	**13**	**2**	**2**	**674.2**	**698**	**68**	**237**	**12**	**29**	**341**	**27**	**17**	**11**	**4**	**355**	**329**	**35**	**42**	**.455**	**0**	**4.39**

Fassero, Jeffrey Joseph "Jeff" — BL/TL — b.1/5/63   SL84 22/554

YR	TM/LG	CL	G	TBF	GS	CG	SHO	GF	IP	H	HR	BB	IBB	HB	SO	SH	SF	WP	BK	R	ER	W	L	PCT	SV	ERA
84	JC/APP	R+	13	292	11	0	0	2	66.2	65	2	39	0	0	59	0	4	1	1	42	34	4	7	.364	1	4.59
85	SPR/MID	A	29	533	15	1	0	2	119.0	125	11	45	3	3	65	4	3	4	3	78	53	4	8	.333	1	4.01
86	SP/FSL	A+	26	720	26	6	1	0	176.0	156	5	56	4	0	112	7	3	5	3	63	48	13	7	.650	0	2.45
87	ARK/TEX	AA	28	674	27	2	1	0	151.1	168	16	67	7	1	118	10	2	7	1	90	69	10	7	.588	0	4.10
88	ARK/TEX	AA	70	375	1	0	0	36	78.0	97	1	41	13	3	72	7	2	5	2	48	31	5	5	.500	17	3.58
89	ARK/TEX	AA	6	174	6	2	1	0	44.0	32	1	12	0	1	38	1	0	1	1	11	8	4	1	.800	0	1.64
	LOU/AMA	AAA	22	511	19	0	0	0	112.0	136	13	47	1	2	73	8	3	8	4	79	65	3	10	.231	0	5.22
90	CAN/EAS	AA	61	281	0	0	0	30	64.1	66	5	24	1	0	61	5	0	9	0	24	20	5	4	.556	6	2.80
91	IND/AMA	AAA	18	71	0	0	0	11	18.1	11	1	7	3	1	12	1	0	1	0	3	3	3	0	1.000	4	1.47
	MON/NL		51	223	0	0	0	30	55.1	39	1	17	1	1	42	6	1	0	0	17	15	2	5	.286	8	2.44
92	MON/NL		70	368	0	0	0	22	85.2	81	1	34	6	2	63	5	2	7	1	35	27	8	7	.533	1	2.84
93	MON/NL		56	616	15	1	0	10	149.2	119	7	54	0	0	140	7	4	5	0	50	38	12	5	.706	1	2.29
3 YR TOTALS			**177**	**1207**	**15**	**1**	**0**	**62**	**290.2**	**239**	**9**	**105**	**7**	**3**	**245**	**18**	**6**	**16**	**1**	**102**	**80**	**22**	**17**	**.564**	**10**	**2.48**

Fernandez, Alexander "Alex" — BR/TR — b.8/13/69   CHA90 1/4

YR	TM/LG	CL	G	TBF	GS	CG	SHO	GF	IP	H	HR	BB	IBB	HB	SO	SH	SF	WP	BK	R	ER	W	L	PCT	SV	ERA
90	WS/GCL	R	2	43	2	0	0	0	10.0	11	0	1	0	2	16	0	1	1	2	4	4	1	0	1.000	0	3.60
	SAR/FSL	A+	2	59	2	0	0	0	14.2	8	0	3	0	0	23	0	1	1	0	4	3	1	1	.500	0	1.84
	BIR/SOU	AA	4	99	4	0	0	0	25.0	20	0	6	0	0	27	0	0	1	0	7	3	3	0	1.000	0	1.08
	CHI/AL		13	378	13	3	0	0	87.2	89	6	34	0	3	61	5	0	1	0	40	37	5	5	.500	0	3.80
91	CHI/AL		34	827	32	2	0	1	191.2	186	16	88	2	2	145	7	11	4	1	100	96	9	13	.409	0	4.51
92	VAN/PCL	AAA	4	109	3	2	1	0	28.2	15	0	6	1	0	27	1	0	0	0	8	3	2	1	.667	0	0.94
	CHI/AL		29	804	29	4	2	0	187.2	199	21	50	3	8	95	6	4	3	0	100	89	8	11	.421	0	4.27
93	CHI/AL		34	1004	34	3	1	0	247.1	221	27	67	5	6	169	9	3	8	0	95	86	18	9	.667	0	3.13
4 YR TOTALS			**110**	**3013**	**108**	**12**	**3**	**1**	**714.1**	**695**	**70**	**239**	**10**	**19**	**470**	**27**	**18**	**16**	**1**	**335**	**308**	**40**	**38**	**.513**	**0**	**3.88**

Fernandez, Charles Sidney "Sid" — BL/TL — b.10/12/62   LA81 4/73

YR	TM/LG	CL	G	TBF	GS	CG	SHO	GF	IP	H	HR	BB	IBB	HB	SO	SH	SF	WP	BK	R	ER	W	L	PCT	SV	ERA
83	LA/NL		2	33	1	0	0	0	6.0	7	0	7	0	1	9	0	0	0	0	4	4	0	1	.000	0	6.00
84	TID/INT	AAA	17	451	17	3	0	0	105.2	69	2	63	1	3	123	5	3	8	0	39	30	6	5	.545	0	2.56
	NY/NL		15	371	15	0	0	0	90.0	74	8	34	3	0	62	5	5	1	4	40	35	6	6	.500	0	3.50
85	TID/INT	AAA	5	142	5	1	0	0	35.1	17	2	21	0	0	42	0	1	0	0	8	8	4	1	.800	0	2.04
	NY/NL		26	685	26	3	0	0	170.1	108	14	80	3	2	180	4	3	3	2	56	53	9	9	.500	0	2.80
86	NY/NL		32	855	31	2	1	1	204.1	161	13	91	1	2	200	9	7	6	0	82	80	16	6	.727	1	3.52
87	NY/NL		28	665	27	3	1	0	156.0	130	16	67	8	8	134	3	4	2	0	75	66	12	8	.600	0	3.81
88	NY/NL		31	751	31	1	1	0	187.0	127	15	70	1	6	189	2	7	4	9	69	63	12	10	.545	0	3.03
89	NY/NL		35	883	32	6	2	0	219.1	157	21	75	3	6	198	4	4	1	3	73	69	14	5	.737	0	2.83
90	NY/NL		30	735	30	2	1	0	179.1	130	18	67	4	5	181	7	6	4	1	79	69	9	14	.391	0	3.46
91	SL/FSL	A+	1	11	1	0	0	0	3.0	1	0	0	0	0	4	0	0	0	0	0	0	0	0	.000	0	0.00
	WIL/EAS	AA	1	23	1	0	0	0	6.0	3	0	1	0	0	5	0	0	0	0	0	0	0	0	.000	0	0.00
	TID/INT	AAA	3	58	3	0	0	0	15.2	9	0	3	0	0	22	0	1	2	1	2	2	1	0	1.000	0	1.15
	NY/NL		8	177	8	0	0	0	44.0	36	4	9	0	0	31	5	1	0	0	18	14	1	3	.250	0	2.86
92	NY/NL		32	865	32	5	2	0	214.2	162	12	67	4	4	193	12	1	1	0	67	65	14	11	.560	0	2.73
93	SL/FSL	A+	1	16	1	0	0	0	4.0	3	1	1	0	0	1	0	0	0	0	2	2	0	1	.000	0	4.50
	BIN/EAS	AA	2	36	2	0	0	0	10.0	6	0	3	0	0	11	0	0	0	0	2	2	1	0	1.000	0	1.80
	NY/NL		18	469	18	1	1	0	119.2	82	17	36	0	3	81	3	1	2	0	42	39	5	6	.455	0	2.93
11 YR TOTALS			**257**	**6489**	**251**	**23**	**9**	**1**	**1590.2**	**1174**	**138**	**603**	**27**	**37**	**1458**	**54**	**51**	**20**	**18**	**605**	**557**	**98**	**79**	**.554**	**1**	**3.15**

Fetters, Michael Lee "Mike" — BR/TR — b.12/19/64   CAL86 4/27

YR	TM/LG	CL	G	TBF	GS	CG	SHO	GF	IP	H	HR	BB	IBB	HB	SO	SH	SF	WP	BK	R	ER	W	L	PCT	SV	ERA
86	SAL/NWL	A-	12	0	12	1	0	0	72.0	60	4	51	0	3	72	0	0	4	1	39	27	4	2	.667	0	3.38
87	PS/CAL	A+	19	518	19	2	0	0	116.0	106	2	73	0	6	105	4	5	22	1	62	46	9	7	.563	0	3.57
88	MID/TEX	AA	20	522	20	2	0	0	114.0	116	10	67	3	7	101	7	4	18	14	78	75	8	8	.500	0	5.92
	EDM/PCL	AAA	2	57	2	0	0	0	14.0	8	0	10	0	1	11	0	0	1	0	3	3	2	0	1.000	0	1.93

(continued)

Fetters, Michael Lee "Mike" (continued)

YR	TM/LG	CL	G	TBF	GS	CG	SHO	GF	IP	H	HR	BB	IBB	HB	SO	SH	SF	WP	BK	R	ER	W	L	PCT	SV	ERA
89	EDM/PCL	AAA	26	704	26	6	2	0	.168.0	160	11	72	2	7	144	1	1	16	2	80	71	12	8	.600	0	3.80
	CAL/AL		1	16	0	0	0	0	3.1	5	1	1	0	0	4	0	0	2	0	4	3	0	0	.000	0	8.10
90	EDM/PCL	AAA	5	116	5	1	1	0	27.1	22	0	13	0	1	26	1	0	1	0	9	3	1	1	.500	0	0.99
	CAL/AL		26	291	2	0	0	10	67.2	77	9	20	0	2	35	1	0	3	0	33	31	1	1	.500	1	4.12
91	EDM/PCL	AAA	11	264	11	1	0	0	61.0	65	5	26	0	3	43	1	1	2	3	39	33	2	7	.222	0	4.87
	CAL/AL		19	206	4	0	0	8	44.2	53	4	28	2	3	24	1	0	4	0	29	24	2	5	.286	0	4.84
92	MIL/AL		50	243	0	0	0	11	62.2	38	3	24	2	7	43	5	2	4	1	15	13	5	1	.833	2	1.87
93	MIL/AL		45	246	0	0	0	14	59.1	59	4	22	4	2	23	5	5	0	0	29	22	3	3	.500	0	3.34
5 YR TOTALS			141	1002	6	0	0	43	237.2	232	21	95	8	14	129	12	7	13	1	110	93	11	10	.524	3	3.52

Finley, Charles Edward "Chuck" — BL/TL — b.11/26/62   CAL85* S1/4

YR	TM/LG	CL	G	TBF	GS	CG	SHO	GF	IP	H	HR	BB	IBB	HB	SO	SH	SF	WP	BK	R	ER	W	L	PCT	SV	ERA
85	SAL/NWL	A-	18	0	0	0	0	12	29.0	34	1	10	0	0	32	0	0	4	0	21	15	3	1	.750	5	4.66
86	QC/MID	A	10	43	0	0	0	9	12.0	4	0	3	0	0	16	0	0	1	1	0	0	1	0	1.000	6	0.00
	CAL/AL		25	198	0	0	0	7	46.1	40	2	23	1	1	37	4	0	2	0	17	17	3	1	.750	0	3.30
87	CAL/AL		35	405	3	0	0	17	90.2	102	7	43	3	3	63	2	2	4	3	54	47	2	7	.222	0	4.67
88	CAL/AL		31	831	31	2	0	0	194.1	191	15	82	7	6	111	7	10	5	8	95	90	9	15	.375	0	4.17
89	CAL/AL		29	827	29	9	1	0	199.2	171	13	82	0	2	156	7	3	4	2	64	57	16	9	.640	0	2.57
90	CAL/AL		32	962	32	7	2	0	236.0	210	17	81	3	2	177	12	3	9	0	77	63	18	9	.667	0	2.40
91	CAL/AL		34	955	34	4	2	0	227.1	205	23	101	1	8	171	4	3	6	3	102	96	18	9	.667	0	3.80
92	CAL/AL		31	885	31	4	1	0	204.1	212	24	98	2	3	124	10	10	6	0	99	90	7	12	.368	0	3.96
93	CAL/AL		35	1065	35	*13	2	0	251.1	243	22	82	1	6	187	11	7	8	1	108	88	16	14	.533	0	3.15
8 YR TOTALS			252	6128	195	39	8	24	1450.0	1374	123	592	18	31	1026	57	38	44	17	616	548	89	76	.539	0	3.40

Fleming, David Anthony "Dave" — BL/TL — b.11/7/69   SEA90 3/79

YR	TM/LG	CL	G	TBF	GS	CG	SHO	GF	IP	H	HR	BB	IBB	HB	SO	SH	SF	WP	BK	R	ER	W	L	PCT	SV	ERA
90	SB/CAL	A+	12	328	12	4	0	0	79.2	64	0	30	1	1	77	1	1	5	5	29	23	7	3	.700	0	2.60
91	JAC/SOU	AA	21	567	20	6	1	0	140.0	129	7	25	2	2	109	5	2	6	0	50	41	10	6	.625	0	2.64
	CAL/PCL	AAA	3	60	2	1	0	0	16.0	11	1	3	0	0	16	0	1	0	0	2	2	2	0	1.000	0	1.13
	SEA/AL		9	73	3	0	0	3	17.2	19	3	3	0	3	11	0	0	1	0	13	13	1	0	1.000	0	6.62
92	SEA/AL		33	946	33	7	4	0	228.1	225	13	60	3	4	112	3	2	8	1	95	86	17	10	.630	0	3.39
93	JAC/SOU	AA	4	71	4	0	0	0	16.1	16	2	7	0	1	10	2	0	0	0	9	8	0	2	.000	0	4.41
	SEA/AL		26	737	26	1	1	0	167.1	189	15	67	6	6	75	4	8	2	0	84	81	12	5	.706	0	4.36
3 YR TOTALS			68	1756	62	8	5	3	413.1	433	31	130	9	13	198	7	10	11	1	192	180	30	15	.667	0	3.92

Flener, Gregory Alan "Huck" — BB/TL — b.2/25/69   TOR90 10/258

YR	TM/LG	CL	G	TBF	GS	CG	SHO	GF	IP	H	HR	BB	IBB	HB	SO	SH	SF	WP	BK	R	ER	W	L	PCT	SV	ERA
90	SC/NYP	A-	14	258	7	0	0	3	61.2	45	4	33	0	1	46	3	0	4	3	29	23	4	3	.571	1	3.36
91	MB/SAL	A	55	333	0	0	0	44	79.0	58	2	41	0	0	107	6	3	7	2	28	16	6	4	.600	13	1.82
92	DUN/FSL	A+	41	451	8	0	0	19	112.1	70	4	50	2	7	93	5	2	2	1	35	28	7	3	.700	8	2.24
93	KNO/SOU	AA	38	556	16	2	2	10	136.1	130	9	39	1	3	114	6	4	9	8	56	50	13	6	.684	4	3.30
	TOR/AL		6	30	0	0	0	1	6.2	7	0	4	1	0	2	0	0	1	0	3	3	0	0	.000	0	4.05

Fletcher, Edward Paul "Paul" — BR/TR — b.1/14/67   PHI88 39/1029

YR	TM/LG	CL	G	TBF	GS	CG	SHO	GF	IP	H	HR	BB	IBB	HB	SO	SH	SF	WP	BK	R	ER	W	L	PCT	SV	ERA
88	MAR/APP	R+	15	320	14	1	0	1	69.1	81	4	33	0	4	61	1	3	3	1	44	36	1	3	.250	1	4.67
89	BAT/NYP	A-	14	339	14	3	0	0	82.1	77	13	28	0	3	58	2	2	3	1	41	30	7	5	.583	0	3.28
90	SPA/SAL	A	9	207	9	1	0	0	49.1	46	3	18	0	2	53	1	1	7	1	24	18	2	4	.333	0	3.28
	CLE/FSL	A+	20	498	18	2	0	1	117.1	104	3	49	0	13	104	6	5	2	2	56	44	5	8	.385	1	3.38
91	CLE/FSL	A+	14	119	4	0	0	5	29.1	22	1	8	1	0	27	1	2	2	0	6	4	0	1	.000	1	1.23
	REA/EAS	AA	21	517	19	3	1	1	120.2	111	12	56	3	1	90	3	2	6	1	56	48	7	9	.438	0	3.58
92	REA/EAS	AA	22	521	20	3	1	0	127.0	103	10	47	2	5	103	1	1	2	1	45	40	9	4	.692	0	2.83
	SCR/INT	AAA	4	85	4	0	0	0	22.2	17	1	2	0	1	26	0	0	2	0	8	7	3	0	1.000	0	2.78
93	SCR/INT	AAA	34	625	19	2	1	5	140.0	146	21	60	3	9	116	4	4	21	0	99	88	4	12	.250	0	5.66
	PHI/NL		1	1	0	0	0	0	0.1	0	0	0	0	0	0	0	0	1	0	0	0	0	0	.000	0	0.00

Fossas, Emilio Antonio "Tony" — BL/TL — b.9/23/57   TEX79 12/303

YR	TM/LG	CL	G	TBF	GS	CG	SHO	GF	IP	H	HR	BB	IBB	HB	SO	SH	SF	WP	BK	R	ER	W	L	PCT	SV	ERA
79	RAN/GCL	R	10	0	9	1	0	0	60.0	54	2	26	0	3	49	0	0	0	0	28	20	6	3	.667	0	3.00
	TUL/TEX	AA	2	0	2	0	0	0	11.0	14	1	4	0	3	3	0	0	1	0	10	8	1	1	.500	0	6.55
80	ASH/SAL	A	30	0	27	8	2	0	197.0	187	11	69	0	5	140	0	0	14	7	64	69	12	8	.600	0	3.15
81	TUL/TEX	AA	38	0	12	1	1	0	106.0	113	4	44	0	3	57	0	0	4	2	65	49	5	6	.455	0	4.16
82	BUR/MID	A	25	0	18	10	1	0	146.0	121	4	33	0	7	115	0	0	4	0	63	50	8	9	.471	0	3.08
83	TUL/TEX	AA	24	0	16	6	1	0	133.0	123	11	46	0	3	103	0	0	2	0	77	62	8	7	.533	0	4.20
	OC/AMA	AAA	10	0	5	0	0	0	35.0	55	2	12	0	1	23	0	0	2	0	33	31	2	4	.333	0	7.97
84	TUL/TEX	AA	4	43	0	0	0	4	10.0	12	0	3	0	1	5	0	0	0	0	5	5	0	1	.000	0	4.50
	OC/AMA	AAA	29	529	15	3	0	3	121.0	143	12	34	1	2	74	0	2	9	0	65	58	5	9	.357	0	4.31
85	OC/AMA	AAA	30	465	13	2	0	8	110.0	121	6	36	1	0	49	7	4	2	0	65	58	7	6	.538	0	4.75
86	EDM/PCL	AAA	7	186	7	2	0	0	43.1	53	5	12	0	0	15	2	1	1	0	23	22	3	3	.500	0	4.57
87	EDM/PCL	AAA	40	520	15	1	0	9	117.1	152	8	29	7	8	54	6	5	8	2	76	65	6	8	.429	0	4.99
88	TEX/AL		5	28	0	0	0	1	5.2	11	0	2	0	0	4	0	0	0	0	3	3	0	0	.000	0	4.76
	OC/AMA	AAA	52	271	0	0	0	14	66.2	64	2	16	2	2	42	0	0	0	0	21	21	3	0	1.000	4	2.83
89	DEN/AMA	AAA	24	141	0	0	0	7	35.1	27	0	11	1	0	35	0	0	2	0	9	8	5	1	.833	6	2.04
	MIL/AL		51	256	0	0	0	16	61.0	57	3	22	7	0	42	1	1	4	0	27	24	2	2	.500	1	3.54
90	MIL/AL		32	146	0	0	0	9	29.1	44	4	10	0	0	24	2	1	0	0	23	21	2	3	.400	0	6.44
	DEN/AMA	AAA	25	141	0	0	0	14	35.2	29	1	10	3	1	34	3	0	4	0	8	6	5	2	.714	4	1.51

Fossas, Emilio Antonio "Tony" (continued)

YR	TM/LG	CL	G	TBF	GS	CG	SHO	GF	IP	H	HR	BB	IBB	HB	SO	SH	SF	WP	BK	R	ER	W	L	PCT	SV	ERA
91	BOS/AL		64	244	0	0	0	18	57.0	49	3	28	9	3	29	5	0	2	0	27	22	3	2	.600	1	3.47
92	BOS/AL		60	129	0	0	0	17	29.2	31	1	14	3	1	19	3	0	0	0	9	8	1	2	.333	2	2.43
93	BOS/AL		71	175	0	0	0	19	40.0	38	4	15	4	2	39	0	1	1	1	28	23	1	1	.500	0	5.17
6 YR TOTALS			283	978	0	0	0	80	222.2	230	16	91	25	7	153	17	5	5	4	117	101	9	10	.474	4	4.08

Foster, Kevin Christopher — BR/TR — b.1/13/69 MON87 31/746

YR	TM/LG	CL	G	TBF	GS	CG	SHO	GF	IP	H	HR	BB	IBB	HB	SO	SH	SF	WP	BK	R	ER	W	L	PCT	SV	ERA
90	EXP/GCL	R	4	47	0	0	0	1	10.2	9	0	6	0	1	11	1	0	0	0	6	6	2	0	1.000	0	5.06
	GC/PIO	R+	10	248	10	0	0	0	55.0	43	3	34	0	6	52	0	1	10	0	42	28	1	7	.125	0	4.58
91	SUM/SAL	A	34	443	11	1	1	9	102.0	62	3	68	1	9	111	1	5	5	4	36	31	10	4	.714	1	2.74
92	WPB/FSL	A+	16	279	11	0	0	2	69.1	45	4	31	1	3	66	0	2	1	1	19	15	7	2	.778	0	1.95
93	JAC/SOU	AA	12	278	12	1	1	0	65.2	53	2	29	0	4	72	0	2	4	1	32	29	4	4	.500	0	3.97
	SCR/INT	AAA	17	304	9	1	0	0	71.0	63	7	29	0	3	59	0	0	5	0	32	31	1	1	.500	0	3.93
	PHI/NL		2	40	1	0	0	0	6.2	13	3	7	0	0	6	0	0	2	0	11	11	0	1	.000	0	14.85

Foster, Stephen Eugene "Steve" — BR/TR — b.8/16/66 CIN88 11/306

YR	TM/LG	CL	G	TBF	GS	CG	SHO	GF	IP	H	HR	BB	IBB	HB	SO	SH	SF	WP	BK	R	ER	W	L	PCT	SV	ERA
88	BIL/PIO	R+	18	114	0	0	0	14	30.1	15	0	7	1	3	27	3	2	1	7	5	4	2	3	.400	7	1.19
89	CR/MID	A	51	245	0	0	0	47	59.0	46	2	19	6	5	55	2	1	5	5	16	14	0	3	.000	23	2.14
90	CHT/SOU	AA	50	277	0	0	0	42	59.0	69	6	33	4	4	52	3	8	3	2	38	35	5	10	.333	20	5.34
91	CHT/SOU	AA	17	64	0	0	0	16	15.2	10	0	4	0	3	18	1	0	2	1	4	2	0	0	.000	10	1.15
	NAS/AMA	AAA	41	237	0	0	0	25	54.2	46	4	29	5	1	52	3	0	0	0	17	13	2	3	.400	12	2.14
	CIN/NL		11	53	0	0	0	5	14.0	7	1	4	0	0	11	0	0	0	0	5	3	0	0	.000	0	1.93
92	NAS/AMA	AAA	17	212	7	0	0	6	50.1	53	3	22	0	1	28	4	0	0	1	20	15	5	3	.625	1	2.68
	CIN/NL		31	209	1	0	0	7	50.0	52	4	13	1	0	34	5	2	1	0	16	16	1	1	.500	2	2.88
93	CIN/NL		17	105	0	0	0	7	25.2	23	1	5	2	1	16	1	0	0	0	8	5	2	2	.500	0	1.75
3 YR TOTALS			59	367	1	0	0	19	89.2	82	6	22	3	1	61	6	2	1	0	29	24	3	3	.500	2	2.41

Franco, John Anthony — BL/TL — b.9/17/60 LA81 6/125

YR	TM/LG	CL	G	TBF	GS	CG	SHO	GF	IP	H	HR	BB	IBB	HB	SO	SH	SF	WP	BK	R	ER	W	L	PCT	SV	ERA
84	WIC/AMA	AAA	6	39	0	0	0	3	9.1	8	1	4	0	0	11	1	0	0	0	6	6	1	0	1.000	0	5.79
	CIN/NL		54	335	0	0	0	30	79.1	74	3	36	4	2	55	4	4	2	0	28	23	6	2	.750	4	2.61
85	CIN/NL		67	407	0	0	0	33	99.0	83	5	40	8	1	61	11	1	4	0	27	24	12	3	.800	12	2.18
86	CIN/NL		74	429	0	0	0	52	101.0	90	7	44	12	3	84	8	3	4	2	40	33	6	6	.500	29	2.94
87	CIN/NL		68	344	0	0	0	60	82.0	76	6	27	6	1	61	5	2	1	0	26	23	8	5	.615	32	2.52
88	CIN/NL		70	336	0	0	0	61	86.0	60	3	27	3	0	46	5	1	1	2	18	15	6	6	.500	*39	1.57
89	CIN/NL		60	345	0	0	0	50	80.2	77	3	36	8	0	60	7	3	2	2	35	28	4	8	.333	32	3.12
90	NY/NL		55	287	0	0	0	48	67.2	66	4	21	2	0	56	3	1	7	2	22	19	5	3	.625	*33	2.53
91	NY/NL		52	247	0	0	0	48	55.1	61	2	18	4	1	45	3	0	6	0	27	18	5	9	.357	30	2.93
92	NY/NL		31	128	0	0	0	30	33.0	24	1	11	2	0	20	1	0	2	0	6	6	6	2	.750	15	1.64
93	NY/NL		35	172	0	0	0	30	36.1	46	6	19	3	1	29	4	1	5	0	24	21	4	3	.571	10	5.20
10 YR TOTALS			566	3030	0	0	0	442	720.1	657	40	279	52	7	517	50	18	33	8	253	210	62	47	.569	236	2.62

Fredrickson, Scott Eric — BR/TR — b.8/19/67 SD90 14/390

YR	TM/LG	CL	G	TBF	GS	CG	SHO	GF	IP	H	HR	BB	IBB	HB	SO	SH	SF	WP	BK	R	ER	W	L	PCT	SV	ERA
90	SPO/NWL	A-	26	197	1	0	0	15	46.2	35	3	18	1	2	61	5	1	6	4	22	17	3	3	.500	8	3.28
91	WAT/MID	A	26	153	0	0	0	22	38.1	24	1	15	3	1	40	1	2	3	2	9	5	3	5	.375	6	1.17
	HD/CAL	A+	23	154	0	0	0	19	35.0	31	2	18	2	1	26	2	1	6	0	15	9	4	1	.800	7	2.31
92	WIC/TEX	AA	56	303	0	0	0	22	73.1	50	9	38	3	2	66	2	5	11	0	29	26	4	7	.364	5	3.19
93	CS/PCL	AAA	23	119	0	0	0	18	26.1	25	3	19	3	0	20	2	1	2	0	16	16	1	3	.250	7	5.47
	COL/NL		25	137	0	0	0	4	29.0	33	3	17	2	1	20	2	2	4	1	25	20	0	1	.000	0	6.21

Freeman, Marvin — BR/TR — b.4/10/63 PHI84 2/49

YR	TM/LG	CL	G	TBF	GS	CG	SHO	GF	IP	H	HR	BB	IBB	HB	SO	SH	SF	WP	BK	R	ER	W	L	PCT	SV	ERA
84	BEN/NWL	A-	15	0	15	2	1	0	89.2	64	1	52	0	1	79	0	0	7	0	41	26	8	5	.615	0	2.61
85	REA/EAS	AA	11	293	11	2	0	0	65.1	51	11	52	1	1	35	5	5	3	0	41	39	1	7	.125	0	5.37
	CLE/FSL	A+	14	366	13	3	3	1	88.1	72	0	36	1	1	55	1	4	7	1	32	30	6	5	.545	0	3.06
86	REA/EAS	AA	27	720	27	4	2	0	163.0	130	12	111	3	1	113	5	8	11	1	89	73	13	6	.684	0	4.03
	PHI/NL		3	61	3	0	0	0	16.0	6	0	10	0	0	7	0	1	0	0	4	4	2	0	1.000	0	2.25
87	MAI/INT	AAA	10	223	10	2	0	0	46.0	56	8	30	0	0	29	1	0	6	0	38	32	0	7	.000	0	6.26
	REA/EAS	AA	9	222	9	0	0	0	49.2	45	7	32	1	0	40	0	0	6	0	30	28	3	3	.500	0	5.07
88	MAI/INT	AAA	18	325	14	2	1	0	74.0	62	8	46	3	0	37	3	1	11	0	43	38	5	5	.500	0	4.62
	PHI/NL		11	249	11	0	0	0	51.2	55	2	43	1	0	37	1	3	3	1	36	35	2	3	.400	0	6.10
89	PHI/NL		1	16	1	0	0	0	3.0	2	1	1	0	0	4	0	0	0	0	2	2	0	0	.000	0	6.00
	SCR/INT	AAA	5	57	5	0	0	0	14.0	11	0	9	1	0	10	0	1	2	0	7	7	1	1	.500	0	4.50
90	SCR/INT	AAA	7	163	7	0	0	0	35.1	39	5	19	0	1	33	0	3	2	0	23	20	2	4	.333	0	5.09
	PHI/NL		16	147	3	0	0	4	32.1	34	5	14	2	1	26	1	0	0	0	21	20	0	2	.000	1	5.57
	RIC/INT	AAA	7	159	7	1	1	0	39.0	33	3	22	0	0	23	1	1	1	0	20	20	2	3	.400	0	4.62
	ATL/NL		9	60	0	0	0	5	15.2	7	3	3	0	0	12	1	0	1	0	3	3	1	0	1.000	0	1.72
	YEAR		25	207	3	0	0	5	48.0	41	8	17	2	1	38	2	0	1	0	24	23	1	2	.333	1	4.31
91	ATL/NL		34	190	0	0	0	9	48.0	37	2	13	1	2	34	1	1	1	0	19	16	1	0	1.000	0	3.00
92	ATL/NL		58	276	0	0	0	15	64.1	61	7	29	7	1	41	2	1	4	0	26	23	7	5	.583	3	3.22
93	RIC/INT	AAA	2	18	2	0	0	0	4.0	4	0	1	0	1	5	0	0	0	0	1	1	0	0	.000	0	2.25
	ATL/NL		21	103	0	0	0	5	23.2	24	1	10	2	1	25	0	0	0	0	16	16	2	0	1.000	0	6.08
7 YR TOTALS			153	1102	18	0	0	31	254.2	226	17	127	14	10	183	10	4	19	2	127	119	15	10	.600	5	4.21

Frey, Steven Francis "Steve" — BR/TL — b.7/29/63   NYA83 15/379

YR	TM/LG	CL	G	TBF	GS	CG	SHO	GF	IP	H	HR	BB	IBB	HB	SO	SH	SF	WP	BK	R	ER	W	L	PCT	SV	ERA
84	FL/FSL	A+	47	281	0	0	0	25	64.2	46	2	34	0	1	66	1	3	4	0	26	15	4	2	.667	4	2.09
85	FL/FSL	A+	19	89	0	0	0	13	22.1	11	0	12	0	1	15	1	0	0	0	4	3	1	1	.500	7	1.21
	ALB/EAS	AA	40	261	0	0	0	14	61.1	53	4	25	5	3	54	2	0	0	0	30	26	4	7	.364	3	3.82
86	CMB/INT	AAA	11	93	0	0	0	2	19.0	29	3	10	1	0	11	0	2	0	0	17	17	0	2	.000	0	8.05
	ALB/EAS	AA	40	287	0	0	0	26	73.0	50	5	18	1	2	62	2	4	2	0	25	17	3	4	.429	4	2.10
87	ALB/EAS	AA	14	111	0	0	0	10	28.0	20	0	7	1	0	19	1	0	1	0	6	6	0	2	.000	1	1.93
	CMB/INT	AAA	23	196	0	0	0	11	47.1	45	4	10	0	0	35	1	3	4	0	19	16	2	1	.667	3	3.04
88	TID/INT	AAA	58	230	1	0	0	22	54.2	38	3	25	6	3	58	4	2	1	3	23	19	6	3	.667	6	3.13
89	MON/NL		20	103	0	0	0	11	21.1	29	4	11	1	1	15	0	2	1	1	15	13	3	2	.600	0	5.48
	IND/AMA	AAA	21	97	0	0	0	8	25.1	18	1	6	1	0	23	2	0	0	0	7	5	2	1	.667	3	1.78
90	IND/AMA	AAA	2	10	0	0	0	1	3.0	0	0	1	0	0	3	0	0	0	0	0	0	0	0	.000	1	0.00
	MON/NL		51	236	0	0	0	21	55.2	44	4	29	6	1	29	3	2	0	0	15	13	8	2	.800	9	2.10
91	IND/AMA	AAA	30	145	0	0	0	15	35.2	25	1	15	2	1	45	1	0	1	1	6	6	3	1	.750	5	1.51
	MON/NL		31	182	0	0	0	5	39.2	43	3	23	4	1	21	3	2	3	1	31	22	0	1	.000	1	4.99
92	CAL/AL		51	193	0	0	0	20	45.1	39	6	22	3	2	24	2	3	1	0	18	18	4	2	.667	4	3.57
93	CAL/AL		55	212	0	0	0	28	48.1	41	1	26	1	3	22	4	1	3	0	20	16	2	3	.400	13	2.98
5 YR TOTALS			**208**	**926**	**0**	**0**	**0**	**85**	**210.1**	**196**	**18**	**111**	**15**	**8**	**111**	**12**	**10**	**8**	**2**	**99**	**82**	**17**	**10**	**.630**	**27**	**3.51**

Frohwirth, Todd Gerard — BR/TR — b.9/28/62   PHI84 13/335

YR	TM/LG	CL	G	TBF	GS	CG	SHO	GF	IP	H	HR	BB	IBB	HB	SO	SH	SF	WP	BK	R	ER	W	L	PCT	SV	ERA
84	BEN/NWL	A-	29	0	0	0	0	25	49.2	26	0	31	4	3	60	0	0	1	0	17	9	4	4	.500	11	1.63
85	PEN/CAR	A+	54	363	0	0	0	48	82.0	70	2	48	3	4	74	3	1	6	3	33	20	7	5	.583	18	2.20
86	CLE/FSL	A+	32	227	0	0	0	23	52.0	54	1	18	2	2	39	1	2	2	0	29	23	3	3	.500	10	3.98
	REA/EAS	AA	29	175	0	0	0	23	42.0	39	1	10	4	2	23	2	0	1	0	20	15	0	4	.000	12	3.21
87	MAI/INT	AAA	27	141	0	0	0	18	32.1	30	3	15	7	0	21	2	3	0	1	12	9	1	4	.200	3	2.51
	REA/EAS	AA	36	217	0	0	0	31	58.0	36	3	13	0	2	44	1	4	1	0	14	12	2	4	.333	19	1.86
	PHI/NL		10	43	0	0	0	2	11.0	12	0	2	0	0	9	0	0	0	0	0	0	1	0	1.000	0	0.00
88	PHI/NL		12	62	0	0	0	6	12.0	16	2	11	6	0	11	1	1	2	0	11	11	1	2	.333	0	8.25
	MAI/INT	AAA	49	258	0	0	0	38	62.2	52	3	19	3	5	39	5	0	3	0	21	17	7	3	.700	13	2.44
89	SCR/INT	AAA	21	134	0	0	0	17	32.1	29	1	11	3	1	29	2	0	0	0	11	8	3	2	.600	7	2.23
	PHI/NL		45	258	0	0	0	11	62.2	56	4	18	0	3	39	3	1	1	0	26	25	1	0	1.000	0	3.59
90	PHI/NL		5	12	0	0	0	0	1.0	3	0	6	2	0	1	0	0	1	0	2	2	0	1	.000	0	18.00
	SCR/INT	AAA	67	349	0	0	0	52	83.0	76	3	32	3	8	56	6	3	0	0	34	28	9	7	.563	21	3.04
91	ROC/INT	AAA	20	97	0	0	0	16	24.2	17	1	5	0	2	18	2	2	1	0	12	10	1	3	.250	8	3.65
	BAL/AL		51	372	0	0	0	10	96.1	64	2	29	3	1	77	4	1	3	0	24	20	7	3	.700	3	1.87
92	BAL/AL		65	444	0	0	0	23	106.0	97	4	41	4	3	58	7	1	2	0	33	29	4	3	.571	4	2.46
93	BAL/AL		70	411	0	0	0	30	96.1	91	7	44	8	3	50	7	2	1	0	47	41	6	7	.462	3	3.83
7 YR TOTALS			**258**	**1602**	**0**	**0**	**0**	**82**	**385.1**	**339**	**19**	**151**	**23**	**10**	**245**	**22**	**6**	**5**	**1**	**143**	**128**	**20**	**16**	**.556**	**10**	**2.99**

Garces, Richard Aron "Rich" — BR/TR — b.5/18/71   MIN 12/29/87

YR	TM/LG	CL	G	TBF	GS	CG	SHO	GF	IP	H	HR	BB	IBB	HB	SO	SH	SF	WP	BK	R	ER	W	L	PCT	SV	ERA
88	ELI/APP	R+	17	254	3	1	0	10	59.0	51	1	27	2	1	69	2	1	7	0	22	15	5	4	.556	5	2.29
89	KEN/MID	A	24	596	24	4	1	0	142.2	117	5	62	1	5	84	5	5	5	6	70	54	9	10	.474	0	3.41
90	VIS/CAL	A+	47	212	0	0	0	42	54.2	33	2	16	0	1	75	1	1	6	0	14	11	2	2	.500	28	1.81
	ORL/SOU	AA	15	81	0	0	0	14	17.1	17	0	14	2	0	22	1	0	2	0	4	4	2	1	.667	8	2.08
	MIN/AL		5	24	0	0	0	3	5.2	4	0	4	0	1	0	0	0	0	0	2	1	0	0	.000	2	1.59
91	POR/PCL	AAA	10	58	0	0	0	8	13.0	10	1	8	1	1	13	0	0	0	0	7	7	0	1	.000	3	4.85
	ORL/SOU	AA	10	75	0	0	0	0	16.1	12	0	14	2	2	17	2	1	0	0	6	6	2	1	.667	0	3.31
92	ORL/SOU	AA	58	334	0	0	0	42	73.1	76	6	39	2	2	72	8	7	6	0	46	37	3	3	.500	13	4.54
93	MIN/AL		3	18	0	0	0	1	4.0	4	0	2	0	0	4	0	0	0	0	2	0	0	0	.000	0	0.00
	POR/PCL	AAA	35	293	7	0	0	5	54.0	70	4	64	1	0	48	3	2	3	3	55	50	1	3	.250	0	8.33
2 YR TOTALS			**8**	**42**	**0**	**0**	**0**	**4**	**9.2**	**8**	**0**	**6**	**0**	**0**	**4**	**0**	**0**	**0**	**0**	**4**	**1**	**0**	**0**	**.000**	**2**	**0.93**

Gardiner, Michael James "Mike" — BB/TR — b.10/19/65   SEA87 18/449

YR	TM/LG	CL	G	TBF	GS	CG	SHO	GF	IP	H	HR	BB	IBB	HB	SO	SH	SF	WP	BK	R	ER	W	L	PCT	SV	ERA
87	BEL/NWL	A-	2	35	1	0	0	0	10.0	6	0	1	0	1	11	0	0	0	0	0	0	2	0	1.000	0	0.00
	WAU/MID	A	13	368	13	2	1	0	81.0	91	9	33	2	3	80	2	5	3	1	54	47	3	5	.375	0	5.22
88	WAU/MID	A	11	132	6	0	0	4	31.1	31	1	13	1	2	24	0	0	1	1	16	11	2	1	.667	1	3.16
89	WAU/MID	A	15	120	1	0	0	11	30.1	21	0	11	1	4	48	2	0	0	0	5	2	4	0	1.000	7	0.59
	WIL/EAS	AA	30	274	3	1	0	14	63.1	54	4	32	6	1	60	1	3	4	1	25	20	4	6	.400	2	2.84
90	WIL/EAS	AA	26	697	26	5	1	0	179.2	136	8	29	1	1	149	4	3	4	1	47	38	12	8	.600	0	1.90
	SEA/AL		5	66	3	0	0	0	12.2	22	1	5	2	0	6	0	1	1	0	17	15	0	0	.000	0	10.66
91	PAW/INT	AAA	8	220	8	2	1	0	57.2	39	2	11	0	1	42	3	2	0	0	16	15	7	1	.875	0	2.34
	BOS/AL		22	562	22	0	0	0	130.0	140	18	47	2	0	91	1	3	1	0	79	70	9	10	.474	0	4.85
92	PAW/INT	AAA	5	138	5	2	0	0	32.2	32	3	9	0	0	37	0	0	0	0	14	12	1	3	.250	0	3.31
	BOS/AL		28	566	18	0	0	0	130.2	126	12	58	2	2	79	3	5	3	0	78	69	4	10	.286	0	4.75
93	OTT/INT	AAA	5	101	5	0	0	0	25.0	17	2	9	0	0	25	5	1	2	0	6	6	1	1	.500	0	2.16
	TOL/INT	AAA	4	22	1	0	0	2	5.0	6	0	2	0	0	10	0	0	0	0	3	3	0	1	.000	0	5.40
	MON/NL		24	173	2	0	0	3	38.0	40	3	19	2	1	21	1	0	2	0	28	22	2	3	.400	0	5.21
	DET/AL		10	51	2	0	0	1	11.1	12	0	7	1	0	4	1	0	2	0	5	5	0	0	.000	0	3.97
	YEAR		34	224	4	0	0	4	49.1	52	3	26	3	1	25	2	0	4	0	33	27	2	3	.400	0	4.93
4 YR TOTALS			**89**	**1418**	**45**	**0**	**0**	**8**	**322.2**	**340**	**34**	**136**	**7**	**5**	**201**	**6**	**12**	**11**	**0**	**207**	**181**	**15**	**25**	**.375**	**0**	**5.05**

Gardner, Mark Allan — BR/TR — b.3/1/62   MON85 8/192

YR	TM/LG	CL	G	TBF	GS	CG	SHO	GF	IP	H	HR	BB	IBB	HB	SO	SH	SF	WP	BK	R	ER	W	L	PCT	SV	ERA
85	JAM/NYP	A-	3	54	3	0	0	0	13.0	9	0	4	0	1	16	1	0	0	1	4	4	0	0	.000	0	2.77

Gardner, Mark Allan (continued)

YR	TM/LG	CL	G	TBF	GS	CG	SHO	GF	IP	H	HR	BB	IBB	HB	SO	SH	SF	WP	BK	R	ER	W	L	PCT	SV	ERA
	WPB/FSL	A+	10	257	9	4	0	1	60.2	54	4	18	1	2	44	3	2	6	1	24	16	5	4	.556	0	2.37
86	JAC/SOU	AA	29	726	28	3	1	1	168.2	144	8	90	1	8	140	5	5	15	1	88	72	10	11	.476	0	3.84
87	IND/AMA	AAA	9	207	9	0	0	0	46.0	48	8	28	1	1	41	0	1	2	1	32	29	3	3	.500	0	5.67
	JAC/SOU	AA	17	434	17	1	0	0	101.0	101	13	42	0	0	78	5	3	4	0	50	47	4	6	.400	0	4.19
88	JAC/SOU	AA	15	443	15	4	2	0	112.1	72	4	36	0	5	130	3	1	2	0	24	20	6	3	.667	0	1.60
	IND/AMA	AAA	13	351	13	3	1	0	84.1	65	5	32	0	5	71	6	1	5	0	30	26	4	2	.667	0	2.77
89	IND/AMA	AAA	24	660	23	4	2	1	163.1	122	3	59	1	5	175	9	6	7	1	51	43	12	4	.750	0	2.37
	MON/NL		7	117	4	0	0	1	26.1	26	2	11	1	2	21	0	0	0	0	16	15	0	3	.000	0	5.13
90	MON/NL		27	642	26	3	3	1	152.2	129	13	61	5	9	135	4	7	2	4	62	58	7	9	.438	0	3.42
91	IND/AMA	AAA	6	133	6	0	0	0	31.0	26	3	16	0	3	38	0	2	2	0	13	12	2	0	1.000	0	3.48
	MON/NL		27	692	27	0	0	0	168.1	139	17	75	1	4	107	7	2	2	1	78	72	9	11	.450	0	3.85
92	MON/NL		33	778	30	0	0	0	179.2	179	15	60	2	9	132	12	7	2	0	91	87	12	10	.545	0	4.36
93	OMA/AMA	AAA	8	193	8	1	0	0	48.1	34	7	19	2	1	41	1	1	1	0	17	15	4	2	.667	0	2.79
	KC/AL		17	387	16	0	0	0	91.2	92	17	36	0	4	54	0	1	2	0	65	63	4	6	.400	0	6.19
5 YR TOTALS			**111**	**2616**	**103**	**3**	**3**	**3**	**618.2**	**565**	**64**	**243**	**9**	**28**	**449**	**24**	**23**	**8**	**5**	**312**	**295**	**32**	**39**	**.451**	**0**	**4.29**

Gibson, Paul Marshall — BL/TR — b.1/4/60   CIN78* 3/70

YR	TM/LG	CL	G	TBF	GS	CG	SHO	GF	IP	H	HR	BB	IBB	HB	SO	SH	SF	WP	BK	R	ER	W	L	PCT	SV	ERA
84	ORL/SOU	AA	27	529	12	3	1	7	121.0	125	9	54	0	1	64	4	2	6	0	71	52	7	7	.500	1	3.87
85	BIR/SOU	AA	36	615	14	2	2	5	144.1	135	13	63	1	0	79	4	4	4	0	73	66	8	8	.500	1	4.12
86	GF/EAS	AA	9	81	1	0	0	3	19.2	16	0	7	0	0	21	0	0	0	0	3	3	3	1	.750	1	1.37
	NAS/AMA	AAA	30	489	14	2	0	9	113.1	121	12	40	5	2	91	3	3	8	0	58	50	5	6	.455	2	3.97
87	TOL/INT	AAA	27	753	27	7	2	0	179.0	173	14	57	6	3	118	2	5	6	1	83	69	14	7	.667	0	3.47
88	DET/AL		40	390	1	0	0	18	92.0	83	4	34	8	2	50	3	5	3	1	33	30	4	2	.667	0	2.93
89	DET/AL		45	573	13	0	0	16	132.0	129	11	57	12	6	77	7	5	4	1	71	68	4	8	.333	0	4.64
90	DET/AL		61	422	0	0	0	17	97.1	99	10	44	12	1	56	4	5	1	1	36	33	5	4	.556	3	3.05
91	DET/AL		68	432	0	0	0	28	96.0	112	10	48	8	3	52	2	2	4	0	51	49	5	7	.417	8	4.59
92	TID/INT	AAA	2	14	0	0	0	1	3.0	3	0	2	1	0	2	0	0	0	0	1	1	0	0	.000	0	3.00
	NY/NL		43	273	0	0	0	12	62.0	70	7	25	0	0	49	3	1	1	0	37	36	0	1	.000	0	5.23
93	NOR/INT	AAA	14	79	0	0	0	11	21.0	10	0	5	0	0	29	1	0	0	0	2	2	1	1	.500	7	0.86
	CMB/INT	AAA	3	25	0	0	0	1	7.0	7	0	0	1	0	7	0	0	0	0	0	0	1	0	1.000	1	0.00
	NY/NL		8	42	0	0	0	1	8.2	14	1	2	0	1	12	0	0	1	0	6	5	1	1	.500	0	5.19
	NY/AL		20	142	0	0	0	9	35.1	31	4	9	0	0	25	0	3	0	0	15	12	2	0	1.000	0	3.06
	YEAR		28	184	0	0	0	10	44.0	45	5	11	0	1	37	0	3	1	0	21	17	3	1	.750	0	3.48
6 YR TOTALS			**285**	**2274**	**15**	**0**	**0**	**101**	**523.1**	**538**	**49**	**219**	**40**	**12**	**321**	**19**	**21**	**14**	**3**	**249**	**233**	**21**	**23**	**.477**	**11**	**4.01**

Glavine, Thomas Michael "Tom" — BL/TL — b.3/25/66   ATL84 2/47

YR	TM/LG	CL	G	TBF	GS	CG	SHO	GF	IP	H	HR	BB	IBB	HB	SO	SH	SF	WP	BK	R	ER	W	L	PCT	SV	ERA
84	BRA/GCL	R	8	141	7	0	0	1	32.1	29	0	13	0	1	34	2	1	12	0	17	12	2	3	.400	0	3.34
85	SUM/SAL	A	26	680	26	2	1	0	168.2	114	6	73	0	9	174	5	2	19	0	58	44	9	6	.600	0	2.35
86	GRE/SOU	AA	22	629	22	2	1	0	145.1	129	14	70	3	2	114	7	4	8	0	62	55	11	6	.647	0	3.41
	RIC/INT	AAA	7	186	7	1	1	0	40.0	40	4	27	0	2	12	1	2	3	0	29	25	1	5	.167	0	5.63
87	RIC/INT	AAA	22	643	22	4	1	0	150.1	142	15	56	3	5	91	7	2	8	0	70	56	6	12	.333	0	3.35
	ATL/NL		9	238	9	0	0	0	50.1	55	5	33	4	3	20	2	3	1	1	34	31	2	4	.333	0	5.54
88	ATL/NL		34	844	34	1	0	0	195.1	201	12	63	7	8	84	17	11	2	2	111	99	7	17	.292	0	4.56
89	ATL/NL		29	766	29	6	4	0	186.0	172	20	40	3	2	90	11	4	2	0	88	76	14	8	.636	0	3.68
90	ATL/NL		33	929	33	1	0	0	214.1	232	18	78	10	1	129	21	2	8	1	111	102	10	12	.455	0	4.28
91	ATL/NL		34	989	34	*9	1	0	246.2	201	17	69	6	2	192	7	6	10	2	83	70	*20	11	.645	0	2.55
92	ATL/NL		33	919	33	7	*5	0	225.0	197	6	70	7	2	129	8	4	5	0	81	69	*20	8	.714	0	2.76
93	ATL/NL		36	1014	36	4	2	0	239.1	236	16	90	7	2	120	10	2	4	0	91	85	*22	6	.786	0	3.20
7 YR TOTALS			**208**	**5699**	**208**	**28**	**12**	**0**	**1357.0**	**1294**	**94**	**443**	**44**	**20**	**764**	**70**	**34**	**32**	**6**	**599**	**532**	**95**	**66**	**.590**	**0**	**3.53**

Gohr, Gregory James "Greg" — BR/TR — b.10/29/67   DET89 1/21

YR	TM/LG	CL	G	TBF	GS	CG	SHO	GF	IP	H	HR	BB	IBB	HB	SO	SH	SF	WP	BK	R	ER	W	L	PCT	SV	ERA
89	FAY/SAL	A	4	50	4	0	0	0	11.1	11	3	6	0	1	10	0	1	1	0	9	9	0	2	.000	0	7.15
90	LAK/FSL	A+	25	577	25	0	0	0	137.2	125	0	50	0	5	90	2	1	11	6	52	40	13	5	.722	0	2.62
91	LON/EAS	AA	2	42	2	0	0	0	11.0	9	0	2	0	1	10	0	0	0	0	0	0	0	0	.000	0	0.00
	TOL/INT	AAA	26	627	26	2	1	0	148.1	125	11	66	0	3	96	9	5	14	3	86	76	10	8	.556	0	4.61
92	TOL/INT	AAA	22	551	20	2	1	0	130.2	124	9	46	1	3	94	3	3	5	1	65	58	4	10	.444	0	3.99
93	TOL/INT	AAA	18	484	17	2	0	0	107.0	127	16	38	2	5	77	1	8	5	0	74	69	3	10	.231	0	5.80
	DET/AL		16	108	0	0	0	9	22.2	26	1	14	2	2	23	1	1	1	0	15	15	0	0	.000	0	5.96

Gomez, Patrick Alexander "Pat" — BL/TL — b.3/17/68   CHN86 4/90

YR	TM/LG	CL	G	TBF	GS	CG	SHO	GF	IP	H	HR	BB	IBB	HB	SO	SH	SF	WP	BK	R	ER	W	L	PCT	SV	ERA
86	WYT/APP	R+	11	265	11	0	0	0	54.0	57	4	46	0	0	55	2	6	13	3	51	31	3	6	.333	0	5.17
87	PEO/MID	A	20	435	17	1	0	3	94.0	88	4	71	2	1	95	2	3	13	3	55	45	3	6	.333	0	4.31
88	CHW/SAL	A	36	357	9	0	0	14	78.2	75	1	52	0	3	97	5	1	14	3	53	47	2	7	.222	5	5.38
89	WIN/CAR	A+	23	579	21	3	1	0	137.2	115	6	60	2	5	127	7	3	8	6	59	42	11	6	.647	0	2.75
	CHA/SOU	AA	2	57	2	0	0	0	14.1	14	0	3	0	1	11	1	0	4	2	5	4	1	0	1.000	0	2.51
90	RIC/INT	AAA	4	74	4	0	0	0	15.1	19	1	10	1	0	9	0	0	3	1	16	15	1	1	.500	0	8.80
	GRE/SOU	AA	23	557	21	0	0	0	124.1	126	9	71	4	2	94	3	8	16	12	75	62	6	8	.429	0	4.49
91	GRE/SOU	AA	13	318	13	0	0	0	79.2	58	1	31	1	3	71	3	2	7	1	20	16	5	2	.714	0	1.81
	RIC/INT	AAA	16	376	14	0	0	0	82.0	99	8	41	0	2	41	3	2	9	1	55	40	2	9	.182	0	4.39
92	RIC/INT	AAA	23	330	11	0	0	3	71.0	79	10	42	2	2	48	1	3	8	0	47	43	3	5	.375	0	5.45
	GRE/SOU	AA	8	177	8	1	1	0	47.2	25	0	19	0	0	38	1	0	3	0	8	6	4	0	1.000	0	1.13
93	SD/NL		27	144	1	0	0	6	31.2	35	2	19	4	0	26	1	4	2	0	19	18	1	2	.333	0	5.12

Gooden, Dwight Eugene — BR/TR — b.11/16/64   NYN82 1/5

YR	TM/LG	CL	G	TBF	GS	CG	SHO	GF	IP	H	HR	BB	IBB	HB	SO	SH	SF	WP	BK	R	ER	W	L	PCT	SV	ERA
84	NY/NL		31	879	31	7	3	0	218.0	161	7	73	2	2	*276	3	2	3	7	72	63	17	9	.654	0	2.60
85	NY/NL		35	1065	35	*16	8	0	276.2	198	13	69	4	2	*268	6	2	6	2	51	47	*24	4	.857	0	*1.53
86	NY/NL		33	1020	33	12	2	0	250.0	197	17	80	4	4	200	10	8	4	4	92	79	17	6	.739	0	2.84
87	LYN/CAR	A+	1	15	1	0	0	0	4.0	2	0	2	0	0	3	0	0	0	0	0	0	0	0	.000	0	0.00
	TID/INT	AAA	4	96	4	1	0	0	22.0	20	0	9	0	2	24	0	1	0	0	7	5	3	0	1.000	0	2.05
	NY/NL		25	730	25	7	3	0	179.2	162	11	53	2	2	148	5	5	1	1	68	64	15	7	*.682	0	3.21
88	NY/NL		34	1024	34	10	3	0	248.1	242	8	57	4	6	175	10	6	5	5	98	88	18	9	.667	0	3.19
89	NY/NL		19	497	17	0	0	1	118.1	93	9	47	2	2	101	4	3	7	5	42	38	9	4	.692	1	2.89
90	NY/NL		34	983	34	2	1	0	232.2	229	10	70	3	7	223	10	7	6	3	106	99	19	7	.731	0	3.83
91	NY/NL		27	789	27	3	1	0	190.0	185	12	56	2	3	150	5	4	5	2	80	76	13	7	.650	0	3.60
92	NY/NL		31	863	31	3	0	0	206.0	197	11	70	7	3	145	5	7	3	1	93	84	10	13	.435	0	3.67
93	NY/NL		29	866	29	7	2	0	208.2	188	16	61	1	9	149	11	7	5	2	89	80	12	15	.444	0	3.45
10 YR TOTALS			298	8716	296	67	23	1	2128.1	1852	114	636	30	40	1835	74	51	45	32	791	718	154	81	.655	1	3.04

Gordon, Thomas "Tom" — BR/TR — b.11/18/67   KC86 6/157

YR	TM/LG	CL	G	TBF	GS	CG	SHO	GF	IP	H	HR	BB	IBB	HB	SO	SH	SF	WP	BK	R	ER	W	L	PCT	SV	ERA
86	ROY/GCL	R	9	184	7	2	1	1	44.0	31	0	23	1	0	47	0	1	7	1	12	5	3	1	.750	1	1.02
	OMA/AMA	AAA	1	12	0	0	0	0	1.1	6	0	2	0	0	3	0	0	0	0	7	7	0	0	.000	0	47.25
87	FM/FSL	A+	3	60	3	0	0	0	13.2	5	0	17	0	2	11	0	0	0	0	4	4	1	0	1.000	0	2.63
	EUG/NWL	A-	15	315	13	0	0	1	72.1	48	2	47	0	3	91	0	0	2	4	33	23	9	0	1.000	1	2.86
88	APP/MID	A	17	473	17	5	1	0	118.0	69	3	43	1	0	172	1	5	10	4	30	27	7	5	.583	0	2.06
	MEM/SOU	AA	6	174	6	2	2	0	47.1	16	1	17	0	1	62	0	0	1	0	3	2	6	0	1.000	0	0.38
	OMA/AMA	AAA	3	85	3	0	0	0	20.1	11	0	15	0	0	29	0	0	0	0	3	3	3	0	1.000	0	1.33
	KC/AL		5	67	2	0	0	0	15.2	16	1	7	0	0	18	0	0	0	0	9	9	0	2	.000	0	5.17
89	KC/AL		49	677	16	1	1	16	163.0	122	10	86	1	1	153	4	4	12	0	67	66	17	9	.654	1	3.64
90	KC/AL		32	858	32	6	1	0	195.1	192	17	99	1	3	175	8	2	11	0	99	81	12	11	.522	0	3.73
91	KC/AL		45	684	14	1	0	11	158.0	129	16	87	6	4	167	5	3	5	0	76	68	9	14	.391	1	3.87
92	KC/AL		40	516	11	0	0	13	117.2	116	9	55	4	4	98	2	6	5	2	67	60	6	10	.375	0	4.59
93	KC/AL		48	651	14	2	0	18	155.2	125	11	77	5	1	143	6	6	17	0	65	62	12	6	.667	1	3.58
6 YR TOTALS			219	3453	89	10	2	58	805.1	700	64	411	20	13	754	25	21	50	2	383	346	56	52	.519	3	3.87

Gossage, Richard Michael "Rich" — BR/TR — b.7/5/51   CHA70 9/198

YR	TM/LG	CL	G	TBF	GS	CG	SHO	GF	IP	H	HR	BB	IBB	HB	SO	SH	SF	WP	BK	R	ER	W	L	PCT	SV	ERA
72	CHI/AL		36	352	1	0	0	7	80.0	72	2	44	3	4	57	10	2	7	0	44	38	7	1	.875	2	4.28
73	CHI/AL		20	232	4	1	0	4	49.2	57	9	37	2	3	33	5	4	6	0	44	41	0	4	.000	0	7.43
74	CHI/AL		39	397	3	0	0	19	89.1	92	4	47	7	2	64	6	4	2	1	45	41	4	6	.400	1	4.13
75	CHI/AL		62	583	0	0	0	49	141.2	99	3	70	15	5	130	15	0	3	0	32	29	9	8	.529	*26	1.84
76	CHI/AL		31	956	29	15	0	1	224.0	214	16	90	3	9	135	8	7	6	0	104	98	9	17	.346	1	3.94
77	PIT/NL		72	523	0	0	0	55	133.0	78	9	49	6	2	151	7	6	2	0	27	24	11	9	.550	26	1.62
78	NY/AL		63	543	0	0	0	55	134.1	87	9	59	8	2	122	9	8	5	0	41	30	10	11	.476	*27	2.01
79	NY/AL		36	234	0	0	0	33	58.1	48	5	19	4	0	41	4	0	3	0	18	17	5	3	.625	18	2.62
80	NY/AL		64	401	0	0	0	58	99.0	74	5	37	3	1	103	8	4	4	0	29	25	6	2	.750	*33	2.27
81	NY/AL		32	173	0	0	0	30	46.2	22	1	14	1	1	48	1	1	1	0	6	4	3	2	.600	20	0.77
82	NY/AL		56	356	0	0	0	43	93.0	63	5	28	5	0	102	5	2	5	0	23	23	4	5	.444	30	2.23
83	NY/AL		57	367	0	0	0	47	87.1	82	5	25	5	1	90	5	6	0	0	27	22	13	5	.722	22	2.27
84	SD/NL		62	412	0	0	0	51	102.1	75	6	36	4	3	84	4	3	2	2	34	33	10	6	.625	25	2.90
85	SD/NL		50	308	0	0	0	38	79.0	64	1	17	1	1	52	3	4	0	0	21	16	5	3	.625	26	1.82
86	SD/NL		45	281	0	0	0	38	64.2	69	8	20	0	2	63	0	0	0	0	36	32	5	7	.417	21	4.45
87	SD/NL		40	217	0	0	0	30	52.0	47	4	19	6	0	44	2	3	2	0	18	18	5	7	.556	11	3.12
88	CHI/NL		46	194	0	0	0	33	43.2	50	7	15	5	3	30	1	3	2	2	23	21	4	4	.500	13	4.33
89	SF/NL		31	182	0	0	0	22	43.2	32	2	27	3	0	24	2	1	2	0	16	13	2	1	.667	4	2.68
	NY/AL		11	56	0	0	0	6	14.1	14	0	3	1	1	6	1	0	1	0	6	6	1	0	1.000	1	3.77
	YEAR		42	238	0	0	0	28	58.0	46	2	30	4	1	30	3	2	3	0	22	19	3	1	.750	5	2.95
91	OC/AMA	AAA	2	10	0	0	0	1	2.0	2	1	1	0	1	3	0	0	1	0	4	4	0	0	.000	0	18.00
	TEX/AL		44	167	0	0	0	16	40.1	33	4	16	1	3	28	3	0	3	0	16	16	4	2	.667	1	3.57
92	OAK/AL		30	163	0	0	0	13	38.0	32	5	19	4	2	26	1	2	0	0	13	12	0	2	.000	0	2.84
93	OAK/AL		39	213	0	0	0	12	47.2	49	6	26	2	1	40	0	2	4	0	24	24	4	5	.444	1	4.53
21 YR TOTALS			966	7310	37	16	0	660	1762.0	1453	113	717	89	44	1473	104	65	61	5	647	583	121	107	.531	309	2.98

Gott, James William "Jim" — BR/TR — b.8/3/59   SL77 4/84

YR	TM/LG	CL	G	TBF	GS	CG	SHO	GF	IP	H	HR	BB	IBB	HB	SO	SH	SF	WP	BK	R	ER	W	L	PCT	SV	ERA
82	TOR/AL		30	600	23	1	1	4	136.0	134	15	66	0	3	82	3	2	8	0	76	67	5	10	.333	0	4.43
83	TOR/AL		34	776	30	6	1	2	176.2	195	15	68	5	5	121	4	3	2	0	103	93	9	14	.391	0	4.74
84	TOR/AL		35	464	12	1	1	11	109.2	93	7	49	3	3	73	7	6	1	0	54	49	7	6	.538	2	4.02
85	SF/NL		26	629	26	2	0	0	148.1	144	10	51	3	1	78	6	4	3	2	73	64	7	10	.412	0	3.88
86	SF/NL		9	66	2	0	0	3	13.0	16	0	13	2	0	9	1	1	1	1	12	11	0	0	.000	1	7.62
	PHO/PCL	AAA	2	12	2	0	0	0	2.2	2	0	3	0	0	2	0	0	0	0	2	2	0	0	.000	0	6.75
87	SF/NL		30	253	3	0	0	8	56.0	53	4	32	5	2	63	1	1	1	0	32	28	1	0	1.000	0	4.50
	PIT/NL		25	129	0	0	0	22	31.0	28	0	8	2	0	27	1	1	1	0	11	5	0	2	.000	13	1.45
	YEAR		55	382	3	0	0	30	87.0	81	4	40	7	2	90	2	1	2	0	43	33	1	2	.333	13	3.41
88	PIT/NL		67	314	0	0	0	59	77.1	68	9	22	5	2	76	7	3	1	0	30	30	6	6	.500	34	3.49
89	PIT/NL		1	4	0	0	0	1	0.2	1	0	1	0	0	1	0	0	0	0	0	0	0	0	.000	0	0.00
90	BAK/CAL	A+	7	56	3	0	0	0	13.0	13	0	4	0	1	16	2	0	2	0	5	4	0	0	.000	0	2.77
	LA/NL		50	270	0	0	0	24	62.0	59	5	34	7	0	44	0	4	1	0	27	20	3	5	.375	3	2.90
91	LA/NL		55	322	0	0	0	26	76.0	63	5	32	7	1	73	6	1	9	0	28	25	4	3	.571	2	2.96
92	LA/NL		68	369	0	0	0	28	88.0	72	4	41	13	1	75	6	1	9	3	27	24	3	3	.500	6	2.45

Gott, James William "Jim" (continued)

YR	TM/LG	CL	G	TBF	GS	CG	SHO	GF	IP	H	HR	BB	IBB	HB	SO	SH	SF	WP	BK	R	ER	W	L	PCT	SV	ERA
93	LA/NL		62	313	0	0	0	45	77.2	71	6	17	5	1	67	7	2	5	0	23	20	4	8	.333	25	2.32
12 YR TOTALS			492	4509	96	10	3	232	1052.1	997	80	434	57	19	789	51	28	45	15	496	436	49	67	.422	86	3.73

Gozzo, Mauro Paul — BR/TR — b.3/7/66   NYN84 13/315

YR	TM/LG	CL	G	TBF	GS	CG	SHO	GF	IP	H	HR	BB	IBB	HB	SO	SH	SF	WP	BK	R	ER	W	L	PCT	SV	ERA
84	LF/NYP	A-	24	176	0	0	0	8	38.1	40	3	28	4	0	30	0	2	7	1	27	24	4	3	.571	2	5.63
85	COL/SAL	A	49	330	0	0	0	42	78.0	62	3	39	7	2	66	3	5	4	1	22	22	11	4	.733	14	2.54
86	LYN/CAR	A+	60	341	0	0	0	46	78.1	80	3	35	3	2	50	5	2	4	1	30	27	9	4	.692	9	3.10
87	MEM/SOU	AA	19	400	14	1	0	2	91.1	95	13	36	2	4	56	1	2	3	3	58	46	6	5	.545	0	4.53
88	MEM/SOU	AA	33	430	12	0	0	9	92.2	127	9	36	1	1	48	2	7	14	3	64	59	4	9	.308	3	5.73
89	KNO/SOU	AA	18	245	6	2	1	6	60.1	59	1	12	1	1	37	0	5	2	1	27	20	7	0	1.000	0	2.98
	SYR/INT	AAA	12	251	7	2	1	2	62.0	56	3	19	0	0	34	1	1	2	0	22	19	5	1	.833	2	2.76
	TOR/AL		9	133	3	0	0	2	31.2	35	4	9	1	0	10	0	2	0	0	19	17	4	1	.800	0	4.83
90	SYR/INT	AAA	34	409	10	0	0	19	98.0	87	5	44	3	3	62	3	1	3	1	46	39	3	8	.273	7	3.58
	CLE/AL		2	13	0	0	0	1	3.0	2	0	2	0	0	2	0	0	0	0	0	0	0	0	.000	0	0.00
91	CLE/AL		2	28	2	0	0	0	4.2	9	0	7	0	0	3	0	1	0	0	10	10	0	0	.000	0	19.29
	CS/PCL	AAA	25	588	20	3	0	4	130.1	143	9	68	3	6	81	3	7	7	4	86	76	10	6	.625	1	5.25
92	POR/PCL	AAA	37	644	19	3	2	11	155.2	155	11	50	3	3	108	6	0	2	0	61	58	10	9	.526	1	3.35
	MIN/AL		2	12	0	0	0	0	1.2	7	0	1	0	0	1	0	0	1	0	5	5	0	0	.000	0	27.00
93	NOR/INT	AAA	28	798	28	2	0	0	190.1	208	10	49	7	9	97	4	5	6	0	88	73	8	11	.421	0	3.45
	NY/NL		10	57	0	0	0	5	14.0	11	1	5	1	0	6	0	0	0	0	5	4	0	1	.000	1	2.57
5 YR TOTALS			25	243	5	0	0	8	55.0	64	4	23	2	1	22	0	3	3	0	39	36	4	2	.667	1	5.89

Grahe, Joseph Milton "Joe" — BR/TR — b.8/14/67   CAL89 2/39

YR	TM/LG	CL	G	TBF	GS	CG	SHO	GF	IP	H	HR	BB	IBB	HB	SO	SH	SF	WP	BK	R	ER	W	L	PCT	SV	ERA
90	MID/TEX	AA	18	519	18	1	0	0	119.0	145	10	34	1	4	58	2	2	11	1	75	70	7	5	.583	0	5.29
	EDM/PCL	AAA	5	159	5	2	0	0	40.0	35	4	11	0	0	21	0	0	0	0	10	6	3	0	1.000	0	1.35
	CAL/AL		8	200	8	0	0	0	43.1	51	3	23	1	3	25	0	0	1	0	30	24	3	4	.429	0	4.98
91	EDM/PCL	AAA	14	428	14	3	1	0	94.1	121	3	30	0	3	55	4	2	6	0	55	42	9	3	.750	0	4.01
	CAL/AL		18	330	10	1	0	2	73.0	84	2	33	0	3	40	1	1	2	0	43	39	3	7	.300	0	4.81
92	EDM/PCL	AAA	3	78	3	0	0	0	19.2	18	0	5	0	0	12	0	0	1	0	7	7	1	0	1.000	0	3.20
	CAL/AL		46	399	7	0	0	31	94.2	85	5	39	2	6	39	4	4	3	0	37	37	5	6	.455	21	3.52
93	VAN/PCL	AAA	4	26	2	0	0	0	6.0	4	1	2	0	0	5	1	0	1	0	3	3	1	1	.500	0	4.50
	CAL/AL		45	247	0	0	0	32	56.2	54	5	25	4	2	31	0	3	3	0	22	18	4	1	.800	11	2.86
4 YR TOTALS			117	1176	25	1	0	65	267.2	274	15	120	7	14	135	7	8	9	0	132	118	15	18	.455	32	3.97

Granger, Jeffrey Adam "Jeff" — BR/TL — b.12/16/71   KC93 1/5

YR	TM/LG	CL	G	TBF	GS	CG	SHO	GF	IP	H	HR	BB	IBB	HB	SO	SH	SF	WP	BK	R	ER	W	L	PCT	SV	ERA
93	EUG/NWL	A-	8	146	7	0	0	0	36.0	28	2	10	1	1	56	1	0	1	0	17	12	3	3	.500	0	3.00
	KC/AL		1	8	0	0	0	0	1.0	3	0	2	0	0	0	0	0	0	0	3	3	0	0	.000	0	27.00

Grant, Mark Andrew — BR/TR — b.10/24/63   SF81 1/10

YR	TM/LG	CL	G	TBF	GS	CG	SHO	GF	IP	H	HR	BB	IBB	HB	SO	SH	SF	WP	BK	R	ER	W	L	PCT	SV	ERA
84	PHO/PCL	AAA	17	0	17	4	1	0	111.1	102	7	61	2	1	78	0	0	8	0	64	49	5	7	.417	0	3.96
	SF/NL		11	231	10	0	0	1	53.2	56	6	19	0	1	32	2	3	3	0	40	38	1	4	.200	1	6.37
85	PHO/PCL	AAA	29	0	29	4	3	0	183.0	182	17	90	5	3	133	0	0	18	0	101	92	8	15	.348	0	4.52
86	PHO/PCL	AAA	28	785	27	10	3	0	181.2	204	13	46	2	9	93	2	9	8	0	105	99	14	7	.667	0	4.90
	SF/NL		4	39	1	0	0	3	10.0	6	0	5	0	0	5	0	0	0	0	4	4	1	0	.000	0	3.60
87	PHO/PCL	AAA	3	93	3	2	0	0	23.0	20	2	5	0	1	12	2	1	0	0	8	8	2	1	.667	0	3.13
	SF/NL		16	264	8	0	0	2	61.0	66	6	21	5	1	32	7	1	2	2	29	24	1	2	.333	1	3.54
	SD/NL		17	456	17	2	1	0	102.1	104	16	52	3	0	58	8	0	6	1	59	53	6	7	.462	0	4.66
	YEAR		33	720	25	2	1	2	163.1	170	22	73	8	1	90	15	1	8	3	88	77	7	9	.438	1	4.24
88	SD/NL		33	410	11	0	0	9	97.2	97	14	36	2	6	61	4	5	4	0	41	40	2	8	.200	3	3.69
89	SD/NL		50	466	0	0	0	19	116.1	105	11	32	6	3	69	5	2	2	0	45	43	8	2	.800	2	3.33
90	SD/NL		26	180	0	0	0	5	39.0	47	5	19	8	0	29	4	3	1	1	23	21	1	1	.500	0	4.85
	ATL/NL		33	231	1	0	0	16	52.1	61	4	18	3	1	40	2	2	1	0	30	27	1	2	.333	3	4.64
	YEAR		59	411	1	0	0	21	91.1	108	9	37	11	1	69	6	5	2	1	53	48	2	3	.400	3	4.73
91	RIC/INT	AAA	1	10	0	0	0	0	3.0	2	0	1	0	1	3	0	0	0	0	0	0	0	0	.000	0	0.00
92	JAC/SOU	AA	5	125	0	0	0	0	32.2	25	2	4	0	1	21	0	0	0	0	10	7	1	2	.333	0	1.93
	CAL/PCL	AAA	4	113	3	0	0	0	26.0	32	2	4	1	2	11	1	2	2	0	15	12	1	3	.250	0	4.15
	SEA/AL		23	352	10	0	0	4	81.0	100	6	22	2	2	42	5	1	1	0	39	35	2	4	.333	0	3.89
93	TUC/PCL	AAA	4	34	0	0	0	1	8.1	5	0	3	0	0	10	1	0	0	0	1	1	1	0	1.000	0	1.08
	VAN/PCL	AAA	1	8	0	0	0	1	2.0	0	0	2	0	0	1	1	0	0	0	0	0	0	0	.000	0	0.00
	HOU/NL		6	46	0	0	0	3	11.0	11	0	5	2	0	8	0	0	2	0	4	1	0	0	.000	0	0.82
	COL/NL		14	68	0	0	0	6	14.1	23	4	6	1	0	8	0	1	2	0	20	20	0	1	.000	1	12.56
	YEAR		20	114	0	0	0	9	25.1	34	4	11	3	0	14	0	1	4	0	24	21	0	1	.000	1	7.46
8 YR TOTALS			233	2743	58	2	1	68	638.2	676	72	235	36	10	382	39	18	24	5	334	306	22	32	.407	8	4.31

Grater, Mark Anthony — BR/TR — b.1/19/64   SL86 24/594

YR	TM/LG	CL	G	TBF	GS	CG	SHO	GF	IP	H	HR	BB	IBB	HB	SO	SH	SF	WP	BK	R	ER	W	L	PCT	SV	ERA
86	JC/APP	R+	24	163	0	0	0	19	41.1	25	2	14	2	3	46	0	2	7	0	14	11	5	2	.714	8	2.40
87	SAV/SAL	A	50	319	0	0	0	28	74.0	54	4	48	9	6	59	5	1	11	1	35	25	6	10	.375	6	3.04
88	SPR/MID	A	53	318	0	0	0	28	81.0	60	4	27	7	4	66	4	1	5	3	23	16	7	2	.778	11	1.78
89	SP/FSL	A+	56	279	0	0	0	49	67.1	44	0	24	4	7	59	4	3	2	0	23	14	3	8	.273	32	1.87
90	LOU/AMA	AAA	24	124	0	0	0	15	28.1	24	0	15	4	0	18	0	2	3	0	13	10	0	2	.000	3	3.18
	ARK/TEX	AA	29	182	0	0	0	22	44.0	31	1	18	0	4	43	1	1	6	0	18	14	2	0	1.000	17	2.86

(continued)

Grater, Mark Anthony (continued)

YR	TM/LG	CL	G	TBF	GS	CG	SHO	GF	IP	H	HR	BB	IBB	HB	SO	SH	SF	WP	BK	R	ER	W	L	PCT	SV	ERA
91	STL/NL		3	15	0	0	0	2	3.0	5	0	2	0	0	6	0	0	0	0	0	0	0	0	.000	0	0.00
	LOU/AMA	AAA	58	329	0	0	0	41	80.1	68	1	33	8	3	54	6	0	0	4	20	18	3	5	.375	12	2.02
92	LOU/AMA	AAA	54	314	0	0	0	45	76.0	74	2	15	2	3	46	6	1	0	2	26	18	7	8	.467	24	2.13
93	TOL/INT	AAA	28	145	0	0	4	20	31.0	42	8	12	0	1	31	0	1	0	2	31	28	1	1	.500	0	8.13
	CAL/PCL	AAA	9	62	0	0	0	7	11.2	19	1	6	0	2	4	0	0	0	2	10	10	0	1	.000	0	7.71
	DET/AL		6	25	0	0	0	1	5.0	6	0	4	1	0	4	0	0	1	0	3	3	0	0	.000	0	5.40
2 YR TOTALS			9	40	0	0	0	3	8.0	11	0	6	1	0	4	0	0	1	0	3	3	0	0	.000	0	3.38

Green, Tyler Scott — BR/TR — b.2/18/70   PHI91 1/10

YR	TM/LG	CL	G	TBF	GS	CG	SHO	GF	IP	H	HR	BB	IBB	HB	SO	SH	SF	WP	BK	R	ER	W	L	PCT	SV	ERA
91	BAT/NYP	A-	3	58	3	0	0	0	15.0	7	0	6	0	2	19	1	0	2	0	2	2	1	0	1.000	0	1.20
	CLE/FSL	A+	2	50	2	0	0	0	13.0	3	0	8	0	0	20	0	0	2	0	2	2	2	0	1.000	0	1.38
92	REA/EAS	AA	12	249	12	0	0	0	62.1	46	4	20	0	1	67	4	1	5	0	16	13	6	3	.667	0	1.88
	SCR/INT	AAA	2	50	2	0	0	0	10.1	7	1	12	0	1	15	0	0	1	0	7	7	0	1	.000	0	6.10
93	SCR/INT	AAA	28	496	14	4	0	6	118.1	102	8	43	2	5	87	3	4	8	2	62	52	6	10	.375	0	3.95
	PHI/NL		3	41	2	0	0	1	7.1	16	1	5	0	0	7	0	0	2	0	9	6	0	0	.000	0	7.36

Greene, Ira Thomas "Tommy" — BR/TR — b.4/6/67   ATL85 1/14

YR	TM/LG	CL	G	TBF	GS	CG	SHO	GF	IP	H	HR	BB	IBB	HB	SO	SH	SF	WP	BK	R	ER	W	L	PCT	SV	ERA
85	PUL/APP	R+	12	226	12	1	1	0	50.2	49	7	27	0	2	32	1	1	4	0	45	43	2	5	.286	0	7.64
86	SUM/SAL	A	28	758	28	5	3	0	174.2	162	17	82	3	8	169	4	3	15	7	95	91	11	7	.611	0	4.69
87	GRE/SOU	AA	23	590	23	4	2	0	142.1	103	13	66	1	4	101	4	2	7	2	60	52	11	8	.579	0	3.29
88	RIC/INT	AAA	29	765	29	4	3	0	177.1	169	10	70	1	3	130	7	8	5	8	98	94	7	17	.292	0	4.77
89	RIC/INT	AAA	26	638	26	2	1	0	152.0	136	9	50	0	2	125	9	5	10	0	74	61	9	12	.429	0	3.61
	ATL/NL		4	103	4	1	1	0	26.1	22	5	6	1	0	17	1	1	2	0	12	12	1	2	.333	0	4.10
90	ATL/NL		5	61	2	0	0	0	12.1	14	3	9	0	1	4	2	0	0	0	11	11	1	0	1.000	0	8.03
	RIC/INT	AAA	19	459	18	2	0	0	109.0	88	5	65	3	0	65	5	3	8	3	49	45	5	8	.385	0	3.72
	SCR/INT	AAA	1	27	1	0	0	0	7.0	5	0	2	0	0	4	0	0	0	0	0	0	0	0	.000	0	0.00
	PHI/NL		10	166	7	0	0	0	39.0	36	5	17	1	0	17	3	0	1	0	20	18	2	3	.400	0	4.15
	YEAR		15	227	9	0	0	0	51.1	50	8	26	1	1	21	5	0	1	0	31	29	3	3	.500	0	5.08
91	PHI/NL		36	857	27	3	2	3	207.2	177	19	66	4	3	154	9	11	9	1	85	78	13	7	.650	0	3.38
92	REA/EAS	AA	1	10	1	0	0	0	2.0	3	1	2	0	0	2	0	0	0	0	2	2	0	0	.000	0	9.00
	SCR/INT	AAA	5	86	5	1	1	0	21.2	15	3	4	0	1	21	0	0	0	0	7	6	2	1	.667	0	2.49
	PHI/NL		13	298	12	0	0	0	64.1	75	5	34	2	0	39	4	2	1	0	39	38	3	3	.500	0	5.32
93	PHI/NL		31	834	30	7	2	0	200.0	175	12	62	3	3	167	9	9	15	0	84	76	16	4	.800	0	3.42
5 YR TOTALS			99	2319	82	11	5	4	549.2	499	49	194	11	7	398	28	24	27	1	251	233	36	19	.655	0	3.82

Greer, Kenneth William "Kenny" — BR/TR — b.5/12/67   NYA88 7/261

YR	TM/LG	CL	G	TBF	GS	CG	SHO	GF	IP	H	HR	BB	IBB	HB	SO	SH	SF	WP	BK	R	ER	W	L	PCT	SV	ERA
88	ONE/NYP	A-	15	470	15	4	0	0	112.1	109	0	18	2	7	60	5	4	6	6	46	30	5	5	.500	0	2.40
89	PW/CAR	A+	29	461	13	3	1	7	111.2	101	3	22	0	7	44	2	2	4	1	56	52	7	3	.700	2	4.19
90	FL/FSL	A+	38	417	5	0	0	11	89.1	115	5	33	2	7	55	9	5	3	3	64	54	4	9	.308	1	5.44
	PW/CAR	A+	1	32	1	0	0	0	7.2	7	0	2	0	0	7	0	1	0	0	2	2	1	0	1.000	0	2.35
91	FL/FSL	A+	31	245	1	0	0	12	57.1	49	3	22	2	7	46	1	1	5	0	31	27	4	3	.571	0	4.24
92	PW/CAR	A+	13	112	1	0	0	6	27.0	25	1	9	0	1	30	0	0	1	0	11	11	1	2	.333	1	3.67
	ALB/EAS	AA	40	280	1	0	0	18	68.2	48	1	30	4	0	53	2	1	6	0	19	14	4	1	.800	4	1.83
	CMB/INT	AAA	1	7	0	0	0	1	1.0	3	0	1	0	0	1	0	0	0	0	2	1	0	0	.000	0	9.00
93	CMB/INT	AAA	46	347	0	0	0	21	79.1	78	5	36	6	2	50	4	2	6	0	41	39	9	4	.692	6	4.42
	NY/NL		1	3	0	0	0	0	1.0	0	0	0	0	0	0	0	0	0	0	0	0	1	0	1.000	0	0.00

Grimsley, Jason Alan — BR/TR — b.8/7/67   PHI85 11/252

YR	TM/LG	CL	G	TBF	GS	CG	SHO	GF	IP	H	HR	BB	IBB	HB	SO	SH	SF	WP	BK	R	ER	W	L	PCT	SV	ERA
85	BEN/NWL	A-	6	0	1	0	0	2	11.1	12	0	25	0	1	10	0	0	3	0	21	17	0	1	.000	0	13.50
86	UTI/NYP	A-	14	342	14	3	0	0	64.2	63	3	77	0	11	46	1	2	18	0	61	46	1	10	.091	0	6.40
87	SPA/SAL	A	23	380	9	3	0	7	88.1	59	4	54	2	6	98	2	5	12	0	48	31	7	4	.636	0	3.16
88	CLE/FSL	A+	16	422	15	2	0	1	101.1	80	2	37	1	9	90	4	4	12	2	48	42	4	7	.364	0	3.73
	REA/EAS	AA	5	98	4	0	0	1	21.1	20	1	13	1	0	14	1	1	1	0	19	17	1	3	.250	0	7.17
89	REA/EAS	AA	26	727	26	8	2	0	172.0	121	13	109	4	10	134	6	3	12	0	65	57	11	8	.579	0	2.98
	PHI/NL		4	91	4	0	0	0	18.1	19	2	19	1	0	15	0	1	3	0	13	12	1	3	.250	0	5.89
90	SCR/INT	AAA	22	563	22	0	0	0	128.1	111	7	78	1	4	99	4	6	18	3	68	56	8	5	.615	0	3.93
	PHI/NL		11	255	11	0	0	0	57.1	47	1	43	0	2	41	2	1	6	1	21	21	3	2	.600	0	3.30
91	PHI/NL		12	272	12	0	0	0	61.0	54	4	41	3	3	42	1	3	14	0	34	33	1	7	.125	0	4.87
	SCR/INT	AAA	9	231	9	0	0	0	51.2	48	3	37	2	2	43	3	0	2	0	28	25	2	3	.400	0	4.35
92	TUC/PCL	AAA	26	565	20	0	0	0	124.2	152	4	55	0	2	90	2	5	14	0	79	70	8	7	.533	0	5.05
93	CHW/INT	AAA	28	579	19	3	1	5	135.1	138	10	49	1	1	102	3	3	18	0	64	51	6	6	.500	0	3.39
	CLE/AL		10	194	6	0	0	0	42.1	52	3	20	1	1	27	1	1	6	0	26	25	3	4	.429	0	5.31
4 YR TOTALS			37	812	33	0	0	1	179.0	172	10	123	5	6	117	3	7	24	1	94	91	8	16	.333	0	4.58

Groom, Wedsel Gary "Buddy" — BL/TL — b.7/10/65   CHA87 12/297

YR	TM/LG	CL	G	TBF	GS	CG	SHO	GF	IP	H	HR	BB	IBB	HB	SO	SH	SF	WP	BK	R	ER	W	L	PCT	SV	ERA
87	WS/GCL	R	4	48	1	0	0	1	12.0	12	0	2	0	1	8	1	0	0	0	1	1	1	0	1.000	1	0.75
	DB/FSL	A+	11	290	10	2	0	0	67.2	60	4	33	1	2	29	1	0	2	0	30	27	7	2	.778	0	3.59
88	TAM/FSL	A+	27	801	27	8	0	0	195.0	181	4	51	1	6	118	2	10	11	6	69	55	13	10	.565	0	2.54
89	BIR/SOU	AA	26	735	26	7	3	0	167.1	172	13	78	1	2	94	10	8	11	3	101	84	13	8	.619	0	4.52
90	BIR/SOU	AA	20	519	20	3	0	0	115.1	135	10	48	1	2	66	3	1	6	0	81	65	6	8	.429	0	5.07
91	LON/EAS	AA	11	220	7	0	0	2	51.2	51	7	12	1	2	39	0	0	2	0	20	20	7	1	.875	0	3.48

Groom, Wedsel Gary "Buddy" (continued

YR	TM/LG	CL	G	TBF	GS	CG	SHO	GF	IP	H	HR	BB	IBB	HB	SO	SH	SF	WP	BK	R	ER	W	L	PCT	SV	ERA
	TOL/INT	AAA	24	320	6	0	0	4	75.0	75	7	25	2	4	49	5	2	1	1	39	36	2	5	.286	1	4.32
92	DET/AL		12	177	7	0	0	3	38.2	48	4	22	4	0	15	3	2	0	1	28	25	0	5	.000	1	5.82
	TOL/INT	AAA	16	443	16	1	0	0	109.1	102	8	23	1	1	71	3	4	5	0	41	34	7	7	.500	0	2.80
93	TOL/INT	AAA	16	421	15	0	0	0	102.0	98	5	30	1	3	78	1	2	2	0	34	31	9	3	.750	0	2.74
	DET/AL		19	170	3	0	0	8	36.2	48	4	13	5	2	15	2	4	2	1	25	25	0	2	.000	0	6.14
2 YR TOTALS			31	347	10	0	0	11	75.1	96	8	35	9	2	30	5	6	2	2	53	50	0	7	.000	1	5.97

Gross, Kevin Frank — BR/TR — b.6/8/61   PHI81* S1/11

YR	TM/LG	CL	G	TBF	GS	CG	SHO	GF	IP	H	HR	BB	IBB	HB	SO	SH	SF	WP	BK	R	ER	W	L	PCT	SV	ERA
83	PHI/NL		17	418	17	1	1	0	96.0	100	13	35	3	3	66	2	1	4	1	46	38	4	6	.400	0	3.56
84	PHI/NL		44	566	14	1	1	9	129.0	140	8	44	4	5	84	9	3	4	4	66	59	8	5	.615	1	4.12
85	PHI/NL		38	873	31	6	2	0	205.2	194	11	81	6	7	151	7	5	2	0	86	78	15	13	.536	0	3.41
86	PHI/NL		37	1040	36	7	2	0	241.2	240	28	94	2	8	154	8	5	2	0	115	108	12	12	.500	0	4.02
87	PHI/NL		34	878	33	3	1	1	200.2	205	26	87	7	10	110	8	5	2	0	107	97	9	16	.360	0	4.35
88	PHI/NL		33	989	33	5	1	0	231.2	209	18	89	5	11	162	9	4	5	0	101	95	12	14	.462	0	3.69
89	MON/NL		31	867	31	4	3	0	201.1	188	20	88	6	6	158	10	3	5	5	105	98	11	12	.478	0	4.38
90	MON/NL		31	712	26	2	1	3	163.1	171	9	65	7	4	111	6	9	4	1	86	83	9	12	.429	0	4.57
91	LA/NL		46	509	10	0	0	16	115.2	123	10	50	6	4	95	4	4	3	0	55	46	10	11	.476	3	3.58
92	LA/NL		34	856	30	4	3	0	204.2	182	11	77	10	3	158	14	6	4	2	82	72	8	13	.381	0	3.17
93	LA/NL		33	892	32	3	0	1	202.1	224	15	74	7	5	150	11	6	2	1	110	93	13	13	.500	0	4.14
11 YR TOTALS			378	8600	293	36	14	30	1992.0	1976	169	784	63	64	1399	90	52	38	33	959	867	111	127	.466	4	3.92

Gross, Kip Lee — BR/TR — b.8/24/64   NYN86 4/102

YR	TM/LG	CL	G	TBF	GS	CG	SHO	GF	IP	H	HR	BB	IBB	HB	SO	SH	SF	WP	BK	R	ER	W	L	PCT	SV	ERA
87	LYN/CAR	A+	16	379	15	2	0	0	89.1	92	1	22	1	6	39	2	3	1	1	37	27	7	4	.636	0	2.72
88	SL/FSL	A+	28	736	27	7	3	0	178.1	153	1	53	6	7	124	1	3	10	11	72	52	13	9	.591	0	2.62
89	JAC/TEX	AA	16	444	16	4	0	0	112.0	96	9	13	0	2	60	4	2	4	4	47	31	6	5	.545	0	2.49
	TID/INT	AAA	12	289	12	0	0	0	70.1	72	3	17	0	1	39	5	2	1	1	33	31	4	4	.500	0	3.97
90	NAS/AMA	AAA	40	521	11	2	1	11	127.0	113	6	47	3	7	62	6	2	6	3	54	47	12	7	.632	3	3.33
	CIN/NL		5	25	0	0	0	2	6.1	6	0	2	0	0	3	0	0	0	0	3	3	0	0	.000	0	4.26
91	NAS/AMA	AAA	14	195	6	1	1	3	47.2	39	3	16	0	4	28	0	2	3	1	13	11	5	3	.625	0	2.08
	CIN/NL		29	381	9	1	0	6	85.2	93	8	40	2	0	40	6	2	5	1	43	33	6	4	.600	0	3.47
92	ALB/PCL	AAA	31	437	14	2	0	16	107.2	96	1	36	5	2	58	4	4	3	1	48	42	6	5	.545	8	3.51
	LA/NL		16	109	1	0	0	7	23.2	32	1	10	1	0	14	0	0	1	0	14	11	1	1	.500	0	4.18
93	ALB/PCL	AAA	59	521	0	0	0	25	124.1	115	7	41	6	2	96	7	1	9	3	58	56	13	7	.650	13	4.05
	LA/NL		10	59	0	0	0	0	15.0	13	0	4	0	0	12	0	0	0	0	1	1	0	0	.000	0	0.60
4 YR TOTALS			60	574	10	1	0	15	130.2	144	9	56	3	0	69	6	3	6	2	61	48	7	5	.583	0	3.31

Guardado, Edward Adrain "Eddie" — BR/TL — b.10/2/70   MIN90 24/570

YR	TM/LG	CL	G	TBF	GS	CG	SHO	GF	IP	H	HR	BB	IBB	HB	SO	SH	SF	WP	BK	R	ER	W	L	PCT	SV	ERA
91	ELI/APP	R+	14	376	13	3	1	1	92.0	67	5	31	0	2	106	5	1	6	2	30	19	8	4	.667	0	1.86
92	KEN/MID	A	18	429	18	2	1	0	101.0	106	5	30	0	4	103	6	2	2	7	57	49	5	10	.333	0	4.37
	VIS/CAL	A+	7	195	7	1	1	0	49.1	47	1	10	0	0	39	2	1	0	0	13	9	7	0	1.000	0	1.64
93	NAS/SOU	AA	10	255	10	2	2	0	65.1	53	1	10	0	2	57	2	1	2	0	10	9	4	0	1.000	0	1.24
	MIN/AL		19	426	16	0	0	2	94.2	123	13	36	1	0	46	1	3	0	0	68	65	3	8	.273	0	6.18

Gubicza, Mark Steven — BR/TR — b.8/14/62   KC81 2/34

YR	TM/LG	CL	G	TBF	GS	CG	SHO	GF	IP	H	HR	BB	IBB	HB	SO	SH	SF	WP	BK	R	ER	W	L	PCT	SV	ERA
84	KC/AL		29	800	29	4	2	0	189.0	172	13	75	0	5	111	4	9	3	1	90	85	10	14	.417	0	4.05
85	KC/AL		29	760	28	0	0	0	177.1	160	14	77	0	5	99	4	9	12	0	88	80	14	10	.583	0	4.06
86	KC/AL		35	765	24	3	2	2	180.2	155	18	84	2	5	118	4	8	15	0	77	73	12	6	.667	0	3.64
87	KC/AL		35	1036	35	10	2	0	241.2	231	18	120	3	6	166	6	11	14	1	114	107	13	18	.419	0	3.98
88	KC/AL		35	1111	35	8	4	0	269.2	237	11	83	3	6	183	3	6	12	4	94	81	20	8	.714	0	2.70
89	KC/AL		36	1060	36	8	2	0	255.0	252	10	63	3	5	173	11	4	9	0	100	86	15	11	.577	0	3.04
90	KC/AL		16	409	16	2	0	0	94.0	101	5	38	4	4	71	6	4	2	1	48	47	4	7	.364	0	4.50
91	OMA/AMA	AAA	3	71	3	0	0	0	16.1	20	0	4	0	0	12	0	0	0	0	7	6	2	1	.667	0	3.31
	KC/AL		26	601	26	0	0	0	133.0	168	10	42	1	6	89	3	5	9	0	90	84	9	12	.429	0	5.68
92	KC/AL		18	470	18	2	1	0	111.1	110	8	36	3	1	81	5	3	5	1	47	46	7	6	.538	0	3.72
93	KC/AL		49	474	6	0	0	12	104.1	128	2	43	8	2	80	6	6	12	0	61	54	5	8	.385	2	4.66
10 YR TOTALS			308	7486	253	37	13	14	1756.0	1714	99	661	32	45	1171	49	66	89	8	809	743	109	100	.522	2	3.81

Guetterman, Arthur Lee "Lee" — BL/TL — b.11/22/58   SEA81 6/80

YR	TM/LG	CL	G	TBF	GS	CG	SHO	GF	IP	H	HR	BB	IBB	HB	SO	SH	SF	WP	BK	R	ER	W	L	PCT	SV	ERA
84	CHT/SOU	AA	24	652	24	5	2	0	157.0	174	7	38	2	4	47	6	2	5	1	68	59	11	7	.611	0	3.38
	SEA/AL		3	22	0	0	0	0	4.1	9	0	2	0	0	2	0	0	1	0	2	2	0	0	.000	0	4.15
85	CAL/PCL	AAA	20	0	18	2	0	1	110.1	138	7	44	0	1	48	0	0	3	0	86	71	5	8	.385	0	5.79
86	CAL/PCL	AAA	4	82	4	0	0	0	19.1	24	0	7	0	0	8	1	0	0	0	12	12	1	0	1.000	0	5.59
	SEA/AL		41	353	4	1	0	8	76.0	108	7	30	3	4	38	1	4	2	0	67	62	0	4	.000	0	7.34
87	CAL/PCL	AAA	16	186	2	1	0	5	44.0	41	1	17	1	1	29	1	2	3	0	14	14	5	1	.833	1	2.86
	SEA/AL		25	483	17	2	1	3	113.1	117	13	35	2	2	42	2	5	3	1	60	48	11	4	.733	0	3.81
88	CMB/INT	AAA	18	493	18	6	0	0	120.2	109	2	26	2	3	49	5	5	4	0	46	37	9	6	.600	0	2.76
	NY/AL		20	177	2	0	0	7	40.2	49	2	14	0	1	15	1	1	2	1	21	21	1	2	.333	0	4.65
89	NY/AL		70	412	0	0	0	38	103.0	98	6	26	9	0	51	4	4	5	0	31	28	5	5	.500	13	2.45
90	NY/AL		64	376	0	0	0	21	93.0	80	6	26	7	0	48	3	1	6	0	37	35	11	7	.611	2	3.39
91	NY/AL		64	376	0	0	0	37	88.0	91	5	25	3	0	35	4	4	3	0	42	36	3	4	.429	6	3.68
92	NY/AL		15	114	0	0	0	0	22.2	35	5	13	3	0	15	0	0	1	0	24	24	1	1	.500	0	9.53

(continued)

Guetterman, Arthur Lee "Lee" (continued)

YR	TM/LG	CL	G	TBF	GS	CG	SHO	GF	IP	H	HR	BB	IBB	HB	SO	SH	SF	WP	BK	R	ER	W	L	PCT	SV	ERA
	NY/NL		43	196	0	0	0	15	43.1	57	5	14	5	1	15	2	3	3	0	28	28	3	4	.429	2	5.82
	YEAR		58	310	0	0	0	22	66.0	92	10	27	8	1	20	2	5	4	0	52	52	4	5	.444	2	7.09
93	LOU/AMA	AAA	25	145	0	0	0	7	33.2	35	0	12	3	2	20	1	1	3	1	11	11	2	1	.667	2	2.94
	STL/NL		40	192	0	0	0	14	46.0	41	1	16	5	2	19	1	2	1	0	18	15	3	3	.500	1	2.93
9 YR TOTALS			**385**	**2701**	**23**	**3**	**1**	**151**	**630.1**	**685**	**51**	**201**	**39**	**13**	**270**	**25**	**27**	**22**	**1**	**330**	**299**	**38**	**34**	**.528**	**24**	**4.27**

Gullickson, William Lee "Bill" — BR/TR — b.2/20/59   MON77 1/2

YR	TM/LG	CL	G	TBF	GS	CG	SHO	GF	IP	H	HR	BB	IBB	HB	SO	SH	SF	WP	BK	R	ER	W	L	PCT	SV	ERA
79	MON/NL		1	4	0	0	0	1	1.0	2	0	0	0	0	0	0	0	0	0	0	0	0	0	.000	0	0.00
80	MON/NL		24	593	19	5	2	1	141.0	127	6	50	2	2	120	3	4	5	0	53	47	10	5	.667	0	3.00
81	MON/NL		22	640	22	3	2	0	157.1	142	3	34	4	4	115	5	2	4	0	54	49	7	9	.438	0	2.80
82	MON/NL		34	990	34	6	0	0	236.2	231	25	61	2	4	155	9	6	11	3	101	94	12	14	.462	0	3.57
83	MON/NL		34	990	34	10	1	0	242.1	230	19	59	4	4	120	4	7	4	1	108	101	17	12	.586	0	3.75
84	MON/NL		32	919	32	3	0	0	226.2	230	27	37	7	1	100	8	4	5	0	100	91	12	9	.571	0	3.61
85	MON/NL		29	759	29	4	1	0	181.1	187	8	47	9	1	68	12	8	1	1	78	71	14	12	.538	0	3.52
86	CIN/NL		37	1014	37	6	2	0	244.2	245	24	60	10	2	121	12	13	3	0	103	92	15	12	.556	0	3.38
87	CIN/NL		27	698	27	3	1	0	165.0	172	33	39	6	2	89	6	4	1	0	99	89	10	11	.476	0	4.85
	NY/AL		8	198	8	1	0	0	48.0	46	7	11	1	1	28	2	4	0	0	29	26	4	2	.667	0	4.88
	YEAR		35	896	35	4	1	0	213.0	218	40	50	7	3	117	8	8	1	0	128	115	14	13	.519	0	4.86
90	HOU/NL		32	846	32	2	1	0	193.1	221	21	61	14	2	73	9	8	3	2	100	82	10	14	.417	0	3.82
91	DET/AL		35	954	35	4	0	0	226.1	256	22	44	13	4	91	8	8	4	0	109	98	*20	9	.690	0	3.90
92	DET/AL		34	919	34	4	1	0	221.2	228	35	50	5	0	64	7	9	6	0	109	107	14	13	.519	0	4.34
93	LAK/FSL	A+	5	84	5	0	0	0	18.1	24	2	4	0	1	9	1	1	1	0	14	14	1	0	1.000	0	6.87
	TOL/INT	AAA	1	26	1	0	0	0	6.0	8	4	0	0	0	4	0	0	0	0	6	6	1	0	1.000	0	9.00
	DET/AL		28	699	28	2	0	0	159.1	186	28	44	3	3	70	6	7	2	0	106	95	13	9	.591	0	5.37
13 YR TOTALS			**377**	**10223**	**371**	**53**	**11**	**2**	**2444.2**	**2503**	**258**	**597**	**80**	**30**	**1214**	**88**	**84**	**52**	**8**	**1149**	**1042**	**158**	**131**	**.547**	**0**	**3.84**

Guthrie, Mark Andrew — BB/TR — b.9/22/65   MIN87 7/165

YR	TM/LG	CL	G	TBF	GS	CG	SHO	GF	IP	H	HR	BB	IBB	HB	SO	SH	SF	WP	BK	R	ER	W	L	PCT	SV	ERA
87	VIS/CAL	A+	4	48	1	0	0	1	12.0	10	0	5	1	0	9	2	0	2	0	7	6	2	1	.667	0	4.50
88	VIS/CAL	A+	25	742	25	4	1	0	171.1	169	6	86	1	3	182	5	3	14	7	81	63	12	9	.571	0	3.31
89	ORL/SOU	AA	14	382	14	0	0	0	96.0	75	4	38	0	2	103	4	0	3	6	32	21	8	3	.727	0	1.97
	POR/PCL	AAA	7	189	7	1	0	0	44.1	45	4	16	0	0	35	1	3	2	0	21	18	3	4	.429	0	3.65
	MIN/AL		13	254	8	0	0	2	57.1	66	7	21	1	1	38	1	1	5	0	32	29	2	4	.333	0	4.55
90	POR/PCL	AAA	9	178	8	1	0	1	42.1	47	1	12	0	2	39	1	1	0	1	19	14	1	3	.250	0	2.98
	MIN/AL		24	603	21	3	1	0	144.2	154	8	39	3	1	101	6	0	9	0	65	61	7	9	.438	0	3.79
91	MIN/AL		41	432	12	0	0	13	98.0	116	11	41	2	1	72	4	3	7	0	52	47	7	5	.583	2	4.32
92	MIN/AL		54	303	0	0	0	15	75.0	59	7	23	2	0	76	4	2	2	0	27	24	2	3	.400	5	2.88
93	MIN/AL		22	94	0	0	0	2	21.0	20	2	16	2	0	15	1	2	1	0	11	11	2	1	.667	0	4.71
5 YR TOTALS			**154**	**1686**	**41**	**3**	**1**	**32**	**396.0**	**415**	**35**	**140**	**15**	**3**	**302**	**16**	**12**	**20**	**3**	**187**	**172**	**20**	**22**	**.476**	**7**	**3.91**

Guzman, Jose Alberto — BR/TR — b.4/9/63   TEX 2/10/81

YR	TM/LG	CL	G	TBF	GS	CG	SHO	GF	IP	H	HR	BB	IBB	HB	SO	SH	SF	WP	BK	R	ER	W	L	PCT	SV	ERA
84	TUL/TEX	AA	25	597	25	7	1	0	140.1	137	6	55	1	0	82	1	8	8	0	75	65	7	9	.438	0	4.17
85	OC/AMA	AAA	25	606	23	4	1	2	149.2	131	11	40	0	2	76	5	6	2	2	60	52	10	5	.667	1	3.13
	TEX/AL		5	140	5	0	0	0	32.2	27	3	14	1	0	24	0	1	2	0	13	10	3	2	.600	0	2.76
86	TEX/AL		29	757	29	2	0	0	172.1	199	23	60	2	6	87	7	4	3	0	101	87	9	15	.375	0	4.54
87	TEX/AL		37	880	30	6	0	0	208.1	196	30	82	0	3	143	9	8	6	5	115	108	14	14	.500	0	4.67
88	TEX/AL		30	876	30	6	2	0	206.2	180	20	82	3	5	157	4	6	10	12	99	85	11	13	.458	0	3.70
90	CHA/FSL	A+	2	37	2	0	0	0	8.1	10	0	4	0	0	7	1	0	0	0	3	2	0	1	.000	0	2.16
	TUL/TEX	AA	1	12	1	0	0	0	3.0	3	0	0	0	0	2	0	0	0	0	2	2	0	1	.000	0	6.00
	OC/AMA	AAA	7	126	7	0	0	0	28.2	35	2	9	0	0	18	0	1	1	1	20	18	0	3	.000	0	5.65
91	OC/AMA	AAA	3	84	3	0	0	0	20.2	18	1	4	0	0	18	1	0	2	1	9	9	1	1	.500	0	3.92
	TEX/AL		25	730	25	5	1	0	169.2	152	10	84	1	4	125	2	3	8	1	67	58	13	7	.650	0	3.08
92	TEX/AL		33	947	33	5	0	0	224.0	229	17	73	0	4	179	9	7	6	0	103	91	16	11	.593	0	3.66
93	CHI/NL		30	819	30	2	0	0	191.0	188	25	74	6	3	163	8	5	6	5	98	92	12	10	.545	0	4.34
7 YR TOTALS			**189**	**5149**	**182**	**26**	**4**	**1**	**1204.2**	**1171**	**128**	**469**	**13**	**25**	**878**	**36**	**33**	**40**	**23**	**596**	**531**	**78**	**72**	**.520**	**0**	**3.97**

Guzman, Juan Andres — BR/TR — b.10/28/66   LA 3/16/85

YR	TM/LG	CL	G	TBF	GS	CG	SHO	GF	IP	H	HR	BB	IBB	HB	SO	SH	SF	WP	BK	R	ER	W	L	PCT	SV	ERA
85	DOD/GCL	R	21	189	3	0	0	12	42.0	39	2	25	3	1	43	3	2	15	3	26	18	5	1	.833	4	3.86
86	VB/FSL	A+	26	594	24	3	0	0	131.1	114	3	90	4	4	96	4	3	16	2	69	51	10	9	.526	0	3.49
87	BAK/CAL	A+	22	508	21	0	0	0	110.0	106	4	84	0	1	113	0	1	19	1	71	58	5	6	.455	0	4.75
88	KNO/SOU	AA	46	363	2	0	0	23	84.0	52	1	61	5	1	90	4	4	6	6	29	22	4	5	.444	6	2.36
89	SYR/INT	AAA	14	99	0	0	0	4	20.1	13	0	30	0	0	22	2	0	5	0	9	9	1	1	.500	0	3.98
	KNO/SOU	AA	22	232	8	0	0	7	47.2	34	2	60	0	2	50	2	1	8	5	36	33	1	4	.200	0	6.23
90	KNO/SOU	AA	37	685	21	0	0	7	157.0	145	10	80	5	3	138	6	11	21	8	84	74	11	9	.550	1	4.24
91	SYR/INT	AAA	12	287	11	0	0	0	67.0	46	4	42	0	2	67	1	3	7	2	39	30	4	5	.444	0	4.03
	TOR/AL		23	574	23	0	0	0	138.2	98	6	66	0	4	123	2	5	10	0	53	46	10	3	.769	0	2.99
92	SYR/INT	AAA	1	16	1	0	0	0	3.0	6	0	1	0	0	3	0	0	0	0	2	2	0	0	.000	0	6.00
	TOR/AL		28	733	28	1	0	0	180.2	135	6	72	2	1	165	5	3	14	2	56	53	16	5	.762	0	2.64
93	TOR/AL		33	963	33	2	1	0	221.0	211	17	110	2	3	194	5	9	26	1	107	98	14	3	.824	0	3.99
3 YR TOTALS			**84**	**2270**	**84**	**4**	**1**	**0**	**540.1**	**444**	**29**	**248**	**4**	**8**	**482**	**12**	**17**	**50**	**3**	**216**	**197**	**40**	**11**	**.784**	**0**	**3.28**

Haas, Robert David "Dave" — BR/TR — b.10/19/65 — DET88 15/395

YR	TM/LG	CL	G	TBF	GS	CG	SHO	GF	IP	H	HR	BB	IBB	HB	SO	SH	SF	WP	BK	R	ER	W	L	PCT	SV	ERA
88	FAY/SAL	A	11	243	11	0	0	0	54.2	59	0	19	1	6	46	1	1	2	4	20	11	4	3	.571	0	1.81
89	LAK/FSL	A+	10	247	10	1	0	1	62.0	50	1	16	0	6	46	0	1	1	1	16	14	4	1	.800	0	2.03
	LON/EAS	AA	18	460	18	2	1	0	103.2	107	13	51	1	11	75	5	2	5	1	69	65	3	11	.214	0	5.64
90	LON/EAS	AA	27	740	27	3	1	0	177.2	151	10	74	1	10	116	4	3	14	1	64	59	13	8	.619	0	2.99
91	TOL/INT	AAA	28	718	28	1	0	0	157.1	187	11	77	3	8	133	8	3	8	1	103	92	8	10	.444	0	5.26
	DET/AL		11	50	0	0	0	0	10.2	8	1	12	3	1	6	2	2	1	0	8	8	1	0	1.000	0	6.75
92	TOL/INT	AAA	22	636	22	2	0	0	148.2	149	11	53	1	9	112	5	5	5	0	72	69	9	8	.529	0	4.18
	DET/AL		12	264	11	1	1	1	61.2	68	8	16	1	1	29	1	0	2	0	30	27	5	3	.625	0	3.94
93	DET/AL		20	131	0	0	0	5	28.0	45	9	8	5	0	17	2	1	0	0	20	19	1	2	.333	0	6.11
	TOL/INT	AAA	2	27	2	0	0	0	4.1	8	0	6	0	1	2	0	0	1	0	9	9	0	0	.000	0	18.69
3 YR TOTALS			43	445	11	1	1	6	100.1	121	18	36	9	2	52	5	3	3	0	58	54	7	5	.583	0	4.84

Habyan, John Gabriel — BR/TR — b.1/29/63 — BAL82 3/78

YR	TM/LG	CL	G	TBF	GS	CG	SHO	GF	IP	H	HR	BB	IBB	HB	SO	SH	SF	WP	BK	R	ER	W	L	PCT	SV	ERA
82	BLU/APP	R+	12	0	12	2	1	0	81.0	68	3	24	0	1	55	0	0	4	1	35	32	9	2	.818	0	3.56
	HAG/CAR	A+	1	0	1	0	0	0	0.0	5	2	2	0	0	1	0	0	0	0	5	5	0	0	.000	0	0.00
83	HAG/CAR	A+	11	0	11	1	0	0	48.0	54	3	29	0	1	42	0	0	5	0	41	31	2	3	.400	0	5.81
	NEW/NYP	A-	11	0	11	1	1	0	71.0	68	6	29	0	2	64	0	0	4	0	34	27	5	3	.625	0	3.42
84	HAG/CAR	A+	13	342	13	4	1	0	81.1	64	5	33	0	1	81	4	1	5	0	41	32	9	4	.692	0	3.54
	CHA/SOU	AA	13	340	13	1	0	0	77.0	84	8	34	1	0	55	2	6	6	1	46	38	4	7	.364	0	4.44
85	CHA/SOU	AA	28	799	28	8	2	0	189.2	157	11	90	0	2	123	5	5	13	0	73	69	13	5	.722	0	3.27
	BAL/AL		2	12	0	0	0	1	2.2	3	0	0	0	0	2	0	0	0	0	1	0	1	0	1.000	0	0.00
86	ROC/INT	AAA	26	686	25	5	1	0	157.1	168	13	69	2	1	93	5	3	10	1	82	75	12	7	.632	0	4.29
	BAL/AL		6	117	5	0	0	1	26.1	24	1	18	2	0	14	2	1	1	0	17	13	1	3	.250	0	4.44
87	ROC/INT	AAA	7	209	7	2	1	0	49.0	47	5	20	0	1	39	0	2	2	0	23	21	3	2	.600	0	3.86
	BAL/AL		27	493	13	2	0	4	116.1	110	20	40	1	2	64	4	4	3	0	67	62	6	7	.462	1	4.80
88	BAL/AL		7	68	0	0	0	1	14.2	22	2	4	0	1	4	0	0	0	0	10	7	1	0	1.000	0	4.30
	ROC/INT	AAA	23	635	23	8	1	0	147.1	161	13	46	2	0	91	8	6	7	1	78	73	9	9	.500	0	4.46
89	ROC/INT	AAA	7	154	5	1	0	0	37.1	38	2	5	0	0	22	2	0	1	0	15	9	1	2	.333	0	2.17
	CMB/INT	AAA	8	207	8	2	0	0	46.1	65	2	9	0	1	30	2	3	2	0	29	28	2	3	.400	0	5.44
90	CMB/INT	AAA	36	459	11	2	0	11	112.0	99	9	30	4	1	77	4	5	5	0	52	40	7	7	.500	6	3.21
	NY/AL		6	37	0	0	0	1	8.2	10	0	2	0	1	4	0	1	0	0	2	2	0	0	.000	0	2.08
91	NY/AL		66	349	0	0	0	16	90.0	73	2	20	2	2	70	2	1	1	2	28	23	4	2	.667	2	2.30
92	NY/AL		56	316	0	0	0	20	72.2	84	6	21	5	2	44	5	3	2	1	32	31	5	6	.455	7	3.84
93	NY/AL		36	181	0	0	0	21	42.1	45	5	16	2	0	29	0	2	0	0	20	19	2	1	.667	1	4.04
	KC/AL		12	58	0	0	0	2	14.0	14	1	4	2	0	10	0	0	0	0	7	7	0	0	.000	0	4.50
	YEAR		48	239	0	0	0	23	56.1	59	6	20	4	0	39	0	2	0	0	27	26	2	1	.667	1	4.15
8 YR TOTALS			218	1631	18	0	0	67	387.2	385	39	125	14	7	241	13	13	9	6	184	164	20	19	.513	11	3.81

Hammond, Christopher Andrew "Chris" — BL/TL — b.1/21/66 — CIN86* 6/148

YR	TM/LG	CL	G	TBF	GS	CG	SHO	GF	IP	H	HR	BB	IBB	HB	SO	SH	SF	WP	BK	R	ER	W	L	PCT	SV	ERA
86	RED/GCL	R	7	176	7	1	0	0	41.2	27	0	17	1	0	53	1	0	5	0	21	13	3	2	.600	0	2.81
	TAM/FSL	A+	5	100	5	0	0	0	21.2	25	0	13	1	1	5	0	0	1	0	8	8	0	2	.000	0	3.32
87	TAM/FSL	A+	25	745	24	6	0	1	170.0	174	10	60	1	3	126	4	4	6	3	81	67	11	11	.500	0	3.55
88	CHT/SOU	AA	26	743	26	4	2	0	182.2	127	2	77	3	3	127	1	3	5	4	48	35	16	5	.762	0	1.72
89	NAS/AMA	AAA	24	697	24	3	1	0	157.1	144	7	96	1	3	142	6	4	9	2	69	59	11	7	.611	0	3.38
90	CIN/NL		3	56	3	0	0	0	11.1	13	2	12	1	0	4	1	0	1	0	9	8	0	2	.000	0	6.35
	NAS/AMA	AAA	24	611	24	5	3	0	149.0	118	7	63	1	5	149	1	5	9	0	43	36	15	1	.938	0	2.17
91	CIN/NL		20	425	18	0	0	0	99.2	92	4	48	3	2	50	6	1	3	0	51	45	7	7	.500	0	4.06
92	CIN/NL		28	627	26	0	0	1	147.1	149	13	55	6	3	79	5	3	6	0	75	69	7	10	.412	0	4.21
93	FLO/NL		32	826	32	0	0	0	191.0	207	18	66	2	1	108	10	2	6	0	106	99	11	12	.478	0	4.66
4 YR TOTALS			83	1934	79	1	0	1	449.1	461	37	181	12	6	241	22	6	20	8	241	221	25	31	.446	0	4.43

Hampton, Michael William "Mike" — BR/TL — b.9/9/72 — SEA90 6/161

YR	TM/LG	CL	G	TBF	GS	CG	SHO	GF	IP	H	HR	BB	IBB	HB	SO	SH	SF	WP	BK	R	ER	W	L	PCT	SV	ERA
90	MAR/ARI	R	14	292	13	0	0	0	64.1	52	0	40	0	4	59	1	2	10	6	32	19	7	2	.778	0	2.66
91	SB/CAL	A+	18	341	15	1	1	1	73.2	71	3	47	1	6	57	2	1	12	3	58	43	1	7	.125	0	5.25
	BEL/NWL	A-	9	225	9	0	0	0	57.0	32	0	26	0	0	65	2	0	6	3	15	10	5	2	.714	0	1.58
92	SB/CAL	A+	25	720	25	6	2	0	170.0	163	8	66	1	3	132	4	8	10	4	75	59	13	8	.619	0	3.12
	JAC/SOU	AA	2	42	2	1	0	0	10.1	13	0	1	0	0	6	0	0	0	0	5	5	1	0	.000	0	4.35
93	SEA/AL		13	95	3	0	0	2	17.0	28	3	17	3	0	8	1	1	1	1	20	18	1	3	.250	1	9.53
	JAC/SOU	AA	15	356	14	1	0	1	87.1	71	3	33	1	4	84	2	1	2	4	43	36	6	4	.600	0	3.71

Haney, Christopher Deane "Chris" — BL/TL — b.11/16/68 — MON90 9/51

YR	TM/LG	CL	G	TBF	GS	CG	SHO	GF	IP	H	HR	BB	IBB	HB	SO	SH	SF	WP	BK	R	ER	W	L	PCT	SV	ERA
90	JAM/NYP	A-	6	107	5	0	0	1	28.0	17	1	10	0	4	26	1	0	1	0	3	3	3	0	1.000	1	0.96
	ROC/MID	A	8	204	8	3	0	0	53.0	40	1	10	0	4	45	3	2	0	0	15	13	2	4	.333	0	2.21
	JAC/SOU	AA	1	25	1	0	0	0	6.0	6	0	3	0	0	6	0	0	0	0	0	0	1	0	1.000	0	0.00
91	HAR/EAS	AA	12	334	12	3	0	0	83.1	65	4	31	1	3	68	8	2	3	1	21	20	5	3	.625	0	2.16
	IND/AMA	AAA	2	50	2	0	0	0	10.1	14	2	6	0	1	4	0	0	0	0	10	5	1	1	.500	0	4.35
	MON/NL		16	387	16	0	0	0	84.2	94	6	43	1	1	51	6	1	9	0	49	38	3	7	.300	0	4.04
92	IND/AMA	AAA	15	368	15	0	0	0	84.0	88	4	42	0	3	61	3	2	2	0	50	48	5	2	.714	0	5.14
	MON/NL		9	165	6	1	1	0	38.0	40	6	10	4	0	27	3	3	5	1	25	23	2	3	.400	0	5.45
	KC/AL		7	174	7	1	0	0	42.0	35	5	16	2	0	27	0	6	0	0	18	18	2	3	.400	0	3.86
	YEAR		16	339	13	2	1	0	80.0	75	11	26	6	0	54	3	9	5	1	43	41	4	6	.400	0	4.61

(continued)

Haney, Christopher Deane "Chris" (continued)

YR	TM/LG	CL	G	TBF	GS	CG	SHO	GF	IP	H	HR	BB	IBB	HB	SO	SH	SF	WP	BK	R	ER	W	L	PCT	SV	ERA
93	OMA/AMA	AAA	8	185	7	2	0	0	47.2	43	2	14	0	1	32	0	1	2	0	13	12	6	1	.857	0	2.27
	KC/AL		23	556	23	1	1	0	124.0	141	13	53	2	3	65	3	4	6	1	87	83	9	9	.500	0	6.02
3 YR TOTALS			55	1282	52	3	3	2	288.2	310	30	122	5	8	170	9	11	20	2	179	162	16	22	.421	0	5.05

Hanson, Erik Brian — BR/TR — b.5/18/65   SEA86 2/36

YR	TM/LG	CL	G	TBF	GS	CG	SHO	GF	IP	H	HR	BB	IBB	HB	SO	SH	SF	WP	BK	R	ER	W	L	PCT	SV	ERA
86	CHT/SOU	AA	3	43	2	0	0	1	9.1	10	1	4	1	2	11	0	0	1	1	4	4	0	0	.000	0	3.86
87	CHT/SOU	AA	21	538	21	1	0	0	131.1	102	10	43	0	3	131	1	2	11	1	56	38	8	10	.444	0	2.60
	CAL/PCL	AAA	8	201	7	0	0	0	47.1	38	4	21	0	2	43	2	2	2	0	23	19	1	3	.250	0	3.61
88	CAL/PCL	AAA	27	691	26	2	1	1	161.2	167	9	57	0	0	154	2	5	10	4	92	76	12	7	.632	0	4.23
	SEA/AL		6	168	6	0	0	0	41.2	35	4	12	1	1	36	3	0	2	2	17	15	2	3	.400	0	3.24
89	CAL/PCL	AAA	8	175	8	1	0	0	38.0	51	1	11	0	2	37	1	1	4	0	30	29	4	2	.667	0	6.87
	SEA/AL		17	465	17	1	0	0	113.1	103	7	32	1	5	75	4	1	5	0	44	40	9	5	.643	0	3.18
90	SEA/AL		33	964	33	5	1	0	236.0	205	15	68	6	2	211	5	6	10	1	88	85	18	9	.667	0	3.24
91	CAL/PCL	AAA	1	21	1	0	0	0	6.0	1	0	2	0	1	5	1	0	1	0	1	1	0	0	.000	0	1.50
	SEA/AL		27	744	27	2	1	0	174.2	182	16	56	2	8	143	2	8	14	1	82	74	8	8	.500	0	3.81
92	SEA/AL		31	809	30	6	1	0	186.2	209	14	57	1	7	112	8	9	6	0	110	100	8	17	.320	0	4.82
93	SEA/AL		31	898	30	7	0	0	215.0	215	17	60	6	5	163	10	4	8	0	91	83	11	12	.478	0	3.47
6 YR TOTALS			145	4048	143	21	3	0	967.1	949	73	285	17	22	740	32	28	43	4	432	397	56	54	.509	0	3.69

Harkey, Michael Anthony "Mike" — BR/TR — b.10/25/66   CHN87 1/4

YR	TM/LG	CL	G	TBF	GS	CG	SHO	GF	IP	H	HR	BB	IBB	HB	SO	SH	SF	WP	BK	R	ER	W	L	PCT	SV	ERA
87	PEO/MID	A	12	343	12	3	0	0	76.0	81	3	28	2	6	48	6	2	2	3	45	30	2	3	.400	0	3.55
	PIT/EAS	AA	1	6	0	0	0	0	2.0	1	0	0	0	0	2	0	0	0	0	0	0	0	0	.000	0	0.00
88	PIT/EAS	AA	13	358	13	3	1	0	85.2	66	1	35	1	3	73	3	0	5	5	29	13	9	2	.818	0	1.37
	IOW/AMA	AAA	12	317	12	3	1	0	78.2	55	6	33	0	1	62	3	3	3	1	36	31	7	2	.778	0	3.55
	CHI/NL		5	155	5	0	0	0	34.2	33	0	15	3	2	18	5	0	2	1	14	10	0	3	.000	0	2.60
89	IOW/AMA	AAA	12	277	12	0	0	0	63.0	67	7	25	0	3	37	1	3	3	1	37	31	2	7	.222	0	4.43
90	CHI/NL		27	728	27	2	1	0	173.2	153	14	59	8	7	94	5	4	8	1	71	63	12	6	.667	0	3.26
91	CHI/NL		4	84	4	0	0	0	18.2	21	3	6	1	0	15	0	1	0	0	11	11	0	2	.000	0	5.30
92	PEO/MID	A	2	54	2	0	0	0	12.0	15	2	3	0	1	17	0	0	1	0	6	4	1	0	1.000	0	3.00
	IOW/AMA	AAA	4	101	4	0	0	0	22.2	21	3	13	0	4	16	1	3	3	0	15	14	0	1	.000	0	5.56
	CHA/SOU	AA	1	33	1	0	0	0	8.0	9	2	0	0	0	5	0	0	0	0	5	5	0	1	.000	0	5.63
	CHI/NL		7	159	7	0	0	0	38.0	34	4	15	0	1	21	1	2	3	1	13	8	4	0	1.000	0	1.89
93	ORL/SOU	AA	1	21	1	0	0	0	5.1	4	0	2	0	0	5	0	0	0	0	1	1	0	0	.000	0	1.69
	CHI/NL		28	676	28	1	0	0	157.1	187	17	43	4	3	67	8	8	1	3	100	92	10	10	.500	0	5.26
5 YR TOTALS			71	1802	71	3	1	0	422.1	428	38	138	16	13	215	19	15	15	6	209	184	26	21	.553	0	3.92

Harnisch, Peter Thomas "Pete" — BB/TR — b.9/23/66   BAL87 3/27

YR	TM/LG	CL	G	TBF	GS	CG	SHO	GF	IP	H	HR	BB	IBB	HB	SO	SH	SF	WP	BK	R	ER	W	L	PCT	SV	ERA
87	BLU/APP	R+	9	216	9	0	0	0	52.2	38	0	26	1	1	64	1	1	4	1	19	15	3	1	.750	0	2.56
	HAG/CAR	A+	4	91	4	0	0	0	20.0	17	0	14	0	0	18	0	1	3	1	7	5	1	2	.333	0	2.25
88	CHA/SOU	AA	20	552	20	4	2	0	132.1	113	6	52	0	4	141	1	3	4	4	55	38	7	6	.538	0	2.58
	ROC/INT	AAA	7	230	7	3	2	0	58.1	44	2	14	1	1	43	3	2	1	1	16	14	4	1	.800	0	2.16
	BAL/AL		2	61	2	0	0	0	13.0	13	1	9	1	0	10	2	0	1	0	8	8	0	2	.000	0	5.54
89	ROC/INT	AAA	12	354	12	3	1	0	87.1	60	7	35	0	4	59	4	5	3	2	27	25	5	5	.500	0	2.58
	BAL/AL		18	468	17	2	0	1	103.1	97	10	64	3	5	70	4	5	5	1	55	53	5	5	.357	0	4.62
90	BAL/AL		31	821	31	3	0	0	188.2	189	17	86	5	1	122	6	5	2	2	96	91	11	11	.500	0	4.34
91	HOU/NL		33	900	33	4	2	0	216.2	169	14	83	3	5	172	9	7	5	2	71	65	12	9	.571	0	2.70
92	HOU/NL		34	859	34	0	0	0	206.2	182	18	64	3	5	164	5	5	4	1	92	85	9	10	.474	0	3.70
93	HOU/NL		33	896	33	5	*4	0	217.2	171	20	79	5	6	185	4	3	1	1	84	72	16	9	.640	0	2.98
6 YR TOTALS			151	4005	150	14	6	1	946.0	821	80	385	20	22	723	35	26	20	7	406	374	53	50	.515	0	3.56

Harris, Greg Allen — BB/TR — b.11/2/55   NYN 9/17/76

YR	TM/LG	CL	G	TBF	GS	CG	SHO	GF	IP	H	HR	BB	IBB	HB	SO	SH	SF	WP	BK	R	ER	W	L	PCT	SV	ERA
81	NY/NL		16	300	14	0	0	2	68.2	65	8	28	2	2	54	4	1	3	2	36	34	3	5	.375	1	4.46
82	CIN/NL		34	398	10	1	0	9	91.1	96	12	37	1	2	67	5	3	2	2	56	49	2	6	.250	1	4.83
83	CIN/NL		1	9	0	0	0	0	1.0	2	0	3	2	1	1	0	0	0	0	3	3	0	0	.000	0	27.00
84	MON/NL		15	68	0	0	0	4	17.2	10	0	7	1	2	15	1	0	0	0	4	4	0	1	.000	2	2.04
	IND/AMA	AAA	14	199	6	0	0	4	44.2	44	7	29	0	3	45	1	2	3	0	27	22	4	4	.500	1	4.43
	SD/NL		19	158	1	0	0	10	36.2	28	3	18	0	2	30	1	3	3	0	14	11	2	1	.667	1	2.70
	YEAR		34	226	1	0	0	14	54.1	38	3	25	1	4	45	2	3	3	0	18	15	2	2	.500	3	2.48
85	TEX/AL		58	450	0	0	0	35	113.0	74	7	43	3	5	111	3	2	2	1	35	31	5	4	.556	11	2.47
86	TEX/AL		73	462	0	0	0	63	111.1	103	12	42	6	1	95	3	6	2	1	40	35	10	8	.556	20	2.83
87	TEX/AL		42	629	19	0	0	14	140.2	157	18	56	3	4	106	7	3	4	2	92	76	5	10	.333	0	4.86
88	MAI/INT	AAA	3	22	0	0	0	3	4.2	5	1	1	1	0	5	2	0	0	0	3	1	0	1	.000	1	1.93
	PHI/NL		66	446	1	0	0	19	107.0	80	7	52	14	4	71	6	2	8	2	34	28	4	6	.400	1	2.36
89	PHI/NL		44	324	0	0	0	17	75.1	64	7	43	7	2	51	3	2	10	0	34	30	2	2	.500	1	3.58
	BOS/AL		15	118	0	0	0	7	28.0	21	1	15	2	0	25	1	1	2	0	12	8	2	2	.500	0	2.57
	YEAR		59	442	0	0	0	24	103.1	85	8	58	9	2	76	4	3	12	0	46	38	4	4	.500	1	3.31
90	BOS/AL		34	803	30	1	0	3	184.1	186	13	77	7	6	117	8	9	8	1	90	82	13	9	.591	0	4.00
91	BOS/AL		53	731	21	0	0	15	173.0	157	13	69	5	5	127	4	6	5	0	79	74	11	12	.478	2	3.85
92	BOS/AL		70	459	2	0	0	22	107.2	82	6	60	11	4	73	8	5	5	0	38	30	4	9	.308	4	2.51
93	BOS/AL		*80	494	0	0	0	24	112.1	95	7	60	14	10	103	4	4	3	0	55	47	6	7	.462	8	3.77
13 YR TOTALS			620	5849	98	4	0	244	1368.0	1220	114	610	78	50	1046	65	49	63	13	622	542	69	82	.457	52	3.57

Harris, Gregory Wade "Greg" — BR/TR — b.12/1/63 — SD85 10/258

YR	TM/LG	CL	G	TBF	GS	CG	SHO	GF	IP	H	HR	BB	IBB	HB	SO	SH	SF	WP	BK	R	ER	W	L	PCT	SV	ERA
85	SPO/NWL	A-	13	0	13	1	0	0	87.1	80	5	36	0	3	90	0	0	6	0	36	33	5	4	.556	0	3.40
86	CHS/SAL	A	27	803	27	8	2	0	191.1	176	13	54	2	3	176	10	5	6	0	69	56	13	7	.650	0	2.63
87	WIC/TEX	AA	27	780	27	7	2	0	174.1	205	32	49	3	3	170	4	2	7	6	103	83	12	11	.522	0	4.28
88	LV/PCL	AAA	26	692	25	5	2	0	159.2	160	15	65	2	1	147	4	4	8	5	84	73	9	5	.643	0	4.11
	SD/NL		3	68	1	1	0	2	18.0	13	0	3	0	0	15	0	0	0	0	3	3	2	0	1.000	0	1.50
89	SD/NL		56	554	8	0	0	25	135.0	106	8	52	9	2	106	5	2	3	3	43	39	8	9	.471	6	2.60
90	SD/NL		73	488	0	0	0	33	117.1	92	6	49	13	4	97	7	2	3	3	35	30	8	8	.500	9	2.30
91	LV/PCL	AAA	4	92	4	0	0	0	20.2	24	1	8	2	0	16	0	0	2	1	20	17	1	2	.333	0	7.40
	SD/NL		20	537	20	3	2	0	133.0	116	16	27	6	1	95	9	2	2	0	42	33	9	5	.643	0	2.23
92	HD/CAL	A+	1	19	1	0	0	0	5.1	2	0	1	0	0	5	0	0	0	0	0	0	0	0	.000	0	0.00
	LV/PCL	AAA	2	56	2	0	0	0	16.0	8	0	1	0	0	15	0	0	0	0	1	1	1	0	1.000	0	0.56
	SD/NL		20	496	20	1	0	0	118.0	113	13	35	2	2	66	8	3	2	1	62	54	4	8	.333	0	4.12
93	SD/NL		22	639	22	4	0	0	152.0	151	18	39	4	3	83	8	2	2	3	65	62	10	9	.526	0	3.67
	COL/NL		13	336	13	0	0	0	73.1	88	15	30	3	4	40	6	2	4	3	62	53	1	8	.111	0	6.50
	YEAR		35	975	35	4	0	0	225.1	239	33	69	9	7	123	14	4	6	6	127	115	11	17	.393	0	4.59
6 YR TOTALS			**207**	**3118**	**84**	**9**	**2**	**60**	**746.2**	**679**	**76**	**235**	**39**	**16**	**502**	**45**	**18**	**15**	**13**	**312**	**274**	**42**	**47**	**.472**	**15**	**3.30**

Harris, Tyrone Eugene "Gene" — BR/TR — b.12/5/64 — MON86 5/122

YR	TM/LG	CL	G	TBF	GS	CG	SHO	GF	IP	H	HR	BB	IBB	HB	SO	SH	SF	WP	BK	R	ER	W	L	PCT	SV	ERA
86	JAM/NYP	A-	4	86	4	0	0	0	20.1	15	0	11	0	1	16	0	0	2	0	8	5	0	2	.000	0	2.21
	BUR/MID	A	7	210	6	4	3	0	53.1	37	1	15	0	1	32	0	3	2	2	12	8	4	2	.667	0	1.35
	WPB/FSL	A+	2	52	2	0	0	0	11.0	14	0	7	0	0	5	2	1	0	0	7	5	0	0	.000	0	4.09
87	WPB/FSL	A+	26	773	26	7	1	0	179.0	178	7	77	1	2	121	5	4	11	3	101	87	9	7	.563	0	4.37
88	JAC/SOU	AA	18	500	18	7	0	0	126.2	95	4	45	0	2	103	2	2	7	4	43	37	9	5	.643	0	2.63
89	MON/NL		11	84	0	0	0	7	20.0	16	1	10	0	1	17	1	3	0	0	11	11	1	1	.500	0	4.95
	IND/AMA	AAA	6	46	0	0	0	4	11.0	4	0	10	1	0	9	0	0	0	0	0	0	1	0	1.000	2	0.00
	CAL/PCL	AAA	5	20	0	0	0	4	6.0	4	0	1	0	0	4	0	0	0	0	0	0	0	0	.000	2	0.00
	SEA/AL		10	152	6	0	0	2	33.1	47	3	15	1	1	14	0	3	0	0	27	24	1	4	.200	0	6.48
	YEAR		21	236	6	0	0	9	53.1	63	4	25	1	1	25	1	4	1	0	38	35	2	5	.286	0	5.91
90	CAL/PCL	AAA	6	30	0	0	0	6	7.2	7	0	4	0	0	9	0	0	2	0	2	2	3	0	1.000	2	2.35
	SEA/AL		25	176	0	0	0	12	38.0	31	5	30	5	1	43	0	2	2	0	25	20	1	2	.333	0	4.74
91	CAL/PCL	AAA	25	152	0	0	0	18	35.0	37	2	11	1	1	23	1	3	2	1	16	13	4	0	1.000	4	3.34
	SEA/AL		8	66	0	0	0	3	13.1	15	1	10	3	0	6	1	0	1	0	8	6	0	0	.000	1	4.05
92	SEA/AL		8	40	0	0	0	2	9.0	8	3	6	0	0	6	0	0	0	0	7	7	0	0	.000	0	7.00
	LV/PCL	AAA	18	153	0	0	0	9	34.1	36	4	16	5	1	35	4	1	4	1	15	14	0	2	.000	4	3.67
	SD/NL		14	90	1	0	0	4	21.1	15	0	15	0	1	19	3	0	1	0	8	7	0	2	.000	0	2.95
	YEAR		22	130	1	0	0	4	30.1	23	3	15	0	1	25	3	0	1	0	15	14	0	2	.000	0	4.15
93	SD/NL		59	269	0	0	0	48	59.1	57	3	37	8	1	39	5	2	2	0	27	20	6	6	.500	23	3.03
5 YR TOTALS			**135**	**877**	**7**	**0**	**0**	**76**	**194.1**	**189**	**16**	**117**	**17**	**4**	**138**	**16**	**8**	**14**	**2**	**113**	**95**	**9**	**15**	**.375**	**25**	**4.40**

Hartley, Michael Edward "Mike" — BR/TR — b.8/31/61 — SL 11/27/81

YR	TM/LG	CL	G	TBF	GS	CG	SHO	GF	IP	H	HR	BB	IBB	HB	SO	SH	SF	WP	BK	R	ER	W	L	PCT	SV	ERA
84	SP/FSL	A+	31	622	23	4	1	1	139.1	142	3	84	10	4	88	7	2	16	2	81	65	8	14	.364	0	4.20
85	SPR/MID	A	33	516	12	0	0	10	114.1	119	9	62	2	8	100	7	6	9	0	77	65	2	7	.222	0	5.12
86	SPR/MID	A	8	82	0	0	0	5	15.0	22	4	14	1	1	10	1	2	2	0	17	16	0	0	.000	1	9.60
	SAV/SAL	A	39	248	0	0	0	25	56.0	38	0	37	1	7	55	0	1	9	0	31	18	5	7	.417	8	2.89
87	BAK/CAL	A+	33	236	0	0	0	27	56.0	44	3	24	5	4	72	4	0	4	0	19	16	5	4	.556	14	2.57
	SA/TEX	AA	25	161	0	0	0	19	41.0	21	2	18	5	2	37	4	1	6	0	8	6	3	4	.429	3	1.32
	ALB/PCL	AAA	2	14	0	0	0	0	2.2	5	0	3	1	0	3	0	0	0	0	3	2	0	1	.000	0	6.75
88	SA/TEX	AA	30	177	0	0	0	25	45.0	25	2	18	3	2	57	1	1	1	1	5	4	5	1	.833	9	0.80
	ALB/PCL	AAA	18	99	0	0	0	11	20.2	22	1	12	1	2	16	4	0	0	0	11	10	2	2	.500	3	4.35
89	ALB/PCL	AAA	58	315	0	0	0	50	77.1	53	4	34	2	2	76	3	2	2	0	31	24	7	4	.636	18	2.79
	LA/NL		5	20	0	0	0	3	6.0	2	0	3	0	0	4	0	0	0	0	1	1	0	1	.000	0	1.50
90	ALB/PCL	AAA	3	14	0	0	0	2	3.0	3	0	3	0	0	0	0	0	0	0	0	0	0	0	.000	0	0.00
	LA/NL		32	325	6	1	1	8	79.1	58	7	30	2	2	76	1	2	3	0	32	26	6	3	.667	1	2.95
91	LA/NL		40	258	0	0	0	11	57.0	53	7	37	7	3	44	1	1	3	1	29	28	2	1	1.000	1	4.42
	PHI/NL		18	110	0	0	0	5	26.1	21	4	10	1	3	19	1	0	7	1	11	11	2	1	.667	1	3.76
	YEAR		58	368	0	0	0	16	83.1	74	11	47	8	6	63	2	1	10	2	40	39	4	1	.800	2	4.21
92	SCR/INT	AAA	3	47	0	0	0	2	11.0	9	2	7	0	0	12	0	0	0	0	6	5	1	2	.333	0	4.09
	PHI/NL		46	243	0	0	0	15	55.0	54	5	23	6	2	53	5	1	3	1	23	21	7	6	.538	2	3.44
93	MIN/AL		53	359	0	0	0	21	81.0	86	4	36	3	7	57	4	6	8	0	38	36	1	2	.333	1	4.00
5 YR TOTALS			**194**	**1315**	**6**	**1**	**1**	**63**	**304.2**	**274**	**27**	**136**	**19**	**17**	**253**	**13**	**9**	**25**	**2**	**134**	**123**	**18**	**13**	**.581**	**4**	**3.63**

Harvey, Bryan Stanley — BR/TR — b.6/2/63 — CAL 8/20/84

YR	TM/LG	CL	G	TBF	GS	CG	SHO	GF	IP	H	HR	BB	IBB	HB	SO	SH	SF	WP	BK	R	ER	W	L	PCT	SV	ERA
85	QC/MID	A	30	345	7	0	0	17	81.2	66	5	37	0	2	111	5	2	4	2	37	32	5	6	.455	4	3.53
86	PS/CAL	A+	43	244	0	0	0	29	57.0	38	4	38	6	3	68	4	5	2	0	24	17	3	4	.429	15	2.68
87	MID/TEX	AA	43	225	0	0	0	36	53.0	40	1	28	5	0	78	4	0	10	0	14	12	2	2	.500	20	2.04
	CAL/AL		3	22	0	0	0	2	5.0	6	0	2	0	1	3	0	0	3	0	0	0	0	0	.000	0	0.00
88	EDM/PCL	AAA	5	30	0	0	0	5	5.2	7	0	4	0	1	10	0	0	0	0	2	2	0	0	.000	2	3.18
	CAL/AL		50	303	0	0	0	38	76.0	59	4	20	6	1	67	3	4	5	0	22	18	7	5	.583	17	2.13
89	CAL/AL		51	245	0	0	0	42	55.0	36	4	41	1	0	78	3	0	6	0	21	21	3	3	.500	25	3.44
90	CAL/AL		54	267	0	0	0	47	64.1	45	4	35	6	0	82	4	4	7	1	24	23	4	4	.500	25	3.22
91	CAL/AL		67	309	0	0	0	63	78.2	51	6	17	3	1	101	3	2	2	0	20	14	2	4	.333	*46	1.60
92	CAL/AL		25	122	0	0	0	22	28.2	22	4	11	4	0	34	0	2	0	0	12	9	0	4	.000	13	2.83
93	FLO/NL		59	264	0	0	0	54	69.0	45	4	13	2	0	73	1	2	1	0	14	13	1	5	.167	45	1.70
7 YR TOTALS			**309**	**1532**	**0**	**0**	**0**	**268**	**376.2**	**264**	**28**	**139**	**19**	**2**	**438**	**20**	**20**	**25**	**5**	**113**	**98**	**17**	**25**	**.405**	**171**	**2.34**

Hathaway, Hillary Houston "Hilly" — BL/TL — b.9/12/69   CAL89 35/903

YR	TM/LG	CL	G	TBF	GS	CG	SHO	GF	IP	H	HR	BB	IBB	HB	SO	SH	SF	WP	BK	R	ER	W	L	PCT	SV	ERA
90	BOI/NWL	A-	15	336	15	0	0	0	86.0	56	1	25	0	2	113	1	3	7	5	18	14	8	2	.800	0	1.47
91	QC/MID	A	20	545	20	1	0	0	129.0	126	5	41	1	7	110	4	1	11	3	58	48	9	6	.600	0	3.35
92	PS/CAL	A+	3	98	3	2	1	0	24.0	25	1	3	0	0	17	0	1	1	0	5	4	2	1	.667	0	1.50
	MID/TEX	AA	14	378	14	1	0	0	95.1	90	2	10	0	8	69	1	1	2	2	39	34	7	2	.778	0	3.21
	CAL/AL		2	29	1	0	0	0	5.2	8	1	3	0	0	1	1	1	0	0	5	5	0	0	.000	0	7.94
93	VAN/PCL	AAA	12	291	12	0	0	0	70.1	60	5	27	0	2	44	1	2	4	1	38	32	7	0	1.000	0	4.09
	CAL/AL		11	253	11	0	0	0	57.1	71	6	26	1	5	11	1	3	5	1	35	32	4	3	.571	0	5.02
2 YR TOTALS			**13**	**282**	**12**	**0**	**0**	**0**	**63.0**	**79**	**7**	**29**	**1**	**5**	**12**	**2**	**4**	**5**	**1**	**40**	**37**	**4**	**3**	**.571**	**0**	**5.29**

Heaton, Neal — BL/TL — b.3/3/60   CLE81 2/39

YR	TM/LG	CL	G	TBF	GS	CG	SHO	GF	IP	H	HR	BB	IBB	HB	SO	SH	SF	WP	BK	R	ER	W	L	PCT	SV	ERA
82	CLE/AL		8	142	4	0	0	0	31.0	32	1	16	0	0	14	1	2	4	0	21	18	0	2	.000	0	5.23
83	CLE/AL		39	637	16	4	3	19	149.1	157	11	44	10	1	75	3	5	1	0	79	69	11	7	.611	7	4.16
84	CLE/AL		38	880	34	4	1	2	198.2	231	21	75	5	0	75	6	10	3	1	128	115	12	15	.444	0	5.21
85	CLE/AL		36	921	33	5	1	2	207.2	244	19	80	2	7	82	7	8	2	2	119	113	9	17	.346	0	4.90
86	CLE/AL		12	324	12	2	0	0	74.1	73	8	34	4	1	24	2	0	2	0	42	35	3	6	.333	0	4.24
	MIN/AL		21	526	17	3	0	2	124.1	128	18	47	4	1	66	4	5	2	0	60	55	4	9	.308	1	3.98
	YEAR		33	850	29	5	0	2	198.2	201	26	81	8	2	90	6	5	4	0	102	90	7	15	.318	1	4.08
87	MON/NL		32	807	32	3	1	0	193.1	207	25	37	3	3	105	5	5	2	5	103	97	13	10	.565	0	4.52
88	MON/NL		32	415	11	0	0	7	97.1	98	14	43	5	3	43	5	5	2	0	54	54	3	10	.231	2	4.99
89	PIT/NL		42	620	18	1	0	5	147.1	127	12	55	12	6	67	12	3	4	5	55	50	6	7	.462	0	3.05
90	PIT/NL		30	599	24	1	0	2	146.0	143	17	38	1	2	68	10	6	4	1	66	56	12	9	.571	0	3.45
91	PIT/NL		42	293	1	0	0	5	68.2	72	6	21	2	4	34	3	3	0	1	37	33	3	3	.500	0	4.33
92	KC/AL		31	185	0	0	0	8	41.0	43	5	22	2	1	29	2	3	3	1	21	19	3	1	.750	0	4.17
	DEN/AMA	AAA	6	98	4	0	0	0	23.0	23	1	8	0	2	9	1	0	0	0	10	9	2	1	.667	0	3.52
	MIL/AL		1	4	0	0	0	1	1.0	0	0	1	0	0	2	0	0	0	0	0	0	0	0	.000	0	0.00
	YEAR		32	189	0	0	0	9	42.0	43	5	23	2	1	31	2	3	3	1	21	19	3	1	.750	0	4.07
93	NY/AL		18	128	0	0	0	9	27.0	34	6	11	1	3	15	0	1	2	0	19	18	1	0	1.000	0	6.00
12 YR TOTALS			**382**	**6481**	**202**	**22**	**6**	**62**	**1507.0**	**1589**	**163**	**524**	**51**	**32**	**699**	**60**	**54**	**30**	**21**	**804**	**732**	**80**	**96**	**.455**	**10**	**4.37**

Henke, Thomas Anthony "Tom" — BR/TR — b.12/21/57   TEX80 S4/67

YR	TM/LG	CL	G	TBF	GS	CG	SHO	GF	IP	H	HR	BB	IBB	HB	SO	SH	SF	WP	BK	R	ER	W	L	PCT	SV	ERA
82	TEX/AL		8	67	0	0	0	6	15.2	14	0	8	0	0	9	1	0	0	0	2	2	1	0	1.000	0	1.15
83	TEX/AL		8	65	0	0	0	5	16.0	16	1	4	0	0	17	0	0	0	0	6	6	1	0	1.000	1	3.38
84	OC/AMA	AAA	39	270	0	0	0	34	64.2	59	1	25	6	1	65	1	1	5	1	21	19	6	2	.750	7	2.64
	TEX/AL		25	141	0	0	0	13	28.1	36	0	20	1	0	25	1	4	2	2	21	20	1	1	.500	2	6.35
85	SYR/INT	AAA	39	185	0	0	0	32	51.1	13	2	18	2	1	60	2	3	1	0	5	5	2	1	.667	18	0.88
	TOR/AL		28	153	0	0	0	22	40.0	29	4	8	2	0	42	2	2	0	0	12	9	3	3	.500	13	2.03
86	TOR/AL		63	370	0	0	0	51	91.1	63	6	32	4	1	118	2	6	3	1	39	34	9	5	.643	27	3.35
87	TOR/AL		72	363	0	0	0	62	94.0	62	10	25	3	0	128	3	5	5	0	27	26	0	6	.000	*34	2.49
88	TOR/AL		52	285	0	0	0	44	68.0	60	6	24	2	4	66	4	2	0	0	23	22	4	4	.500	25	2.91
89	TOR/AL		64	356	0	0	0	56	89.0	66	5	25	4	2	116	4	4	3	2	20	19	8	3	.727	20	1.92
90	TOR/AL		61	297	0	0	0	58	74.2	58	8	19	2	1	75	4	1	6	0	18	18	2	4	.333	32	2.17
91	TOR/AL		49	190	0	0	0	43	50.1	33	4	11	2	0	53	0	0	3	0	13	13	0	2	.000	32	2.32
92	TOR/AL		57	228	0	0	0	50	55.2	40	5	22	2	0	46	0	3	0	4	19	14	3	2	.600	34	2.26
93	TEX/AL		66	302	0	0	0	60	74.1	55	7	27	3	1	79	3	3	3	0	25	24	5	5	.500	40	2.91
12 YR TOTALS			**553**	**2817**	**0**	**0**	**0**	**470**	**697.1**	**532**	**56**	**225**	**29**	**9**	**774**	**24**	**29**	**26**	**3**	**225**	**207**	**37**	**35**	**.514**	**260**	**2.67**

Henneman, Michael Alan "Mike" — BR/TR — b.12/11/61   DET84 4/104

YR	TM/LG	CL	G	TBF	GS	CG	SHO	GF	IP	H	HR	BB	IBB	HB	SO	SH	SF	WP	BK	R	ER	W	L	PCT	SV	ERA
84	BIR/SOU	AA	29	258	1	0	0	16	59.1	48	1	33	2	2	39	2	1	3	0	22	16	4	2	.667	6	2.43
85	BIR/SOU	AA	46	327	0	0	0	38	70.1	88	6	28	4	7	40	2	2	3	0	50	45	3	5	.375	9	5.76
86	NAS/AMA	AAA	31	254	0	0	0	18	58.0	57	5	23	1	4	39	3	6	5	1	27	19	2	5	.286	1	2.95
87	TOL/INT	AAA	11	62	0	0	0	9	18.1	5	0	3	0	0	19	0	1	1	0	3	3	1	1	.500	4	1.47
	DET/AL		55	399	0	0	0	28	96.2	86	8	30	5	3	75	2	2	7	0	36	32	11	3	.786	7	2.98
88	DET/AL		65	364	0	0	0	51	91.1	72	9	24	10	2	58	5	2	0	0	23	19	9	6	.600	22	1.87
89	DET/AL		60	401	0	0	0	35	90.0	84	4	51	15	5	69	7	3	0	1	46	37	11	4	.733	8	3.70
90	DET/AL		69	399	0	0	0	53	94.1	90	4	33	12	3	50	5	2	3	0	36	32	8	6	.571	22	3.05
91	DET/AL		60	358	0	0	0	50	84.1	81	2	34	8	0	61	5	2	0	0	29	27	10	2	.833	21	2.88
92	DET/AL		60	321	0	0	0	53	77.1	75	6	20	10	0	58	4	2	6	0	36	34	2	6	.250	24	3.96
93	DET/AL		63	316	0	0	0	50	71.2	69	4	32	8	2	58	4	2	4	0	28	21	5	3	.625	24	2.64
7 YR TOTALS			**432**	**2558**	**0**	**0**	**0**	**320**	**605.2**	**557**	**35**	**224**	**68**	**15**	**429**	**32**	**21**	**34**	**2**	**234**	**202**	**56**	**30**	**.651**	**128**	**3.00**

Henry, Dwayne Allen — BR/TR — b.2/16/62   TEX80 9/274

YR	TM/LG	CL	G	TBF	GS	CG	SHO	GF	IP	H	HR	BB	IBB	HB	SO	SH	SF	WP	BK	R	ER	W	L	PCT	SV	ERA
80	RAN/GCL	R	11	0	11	1	1	0	54.0	36	2	28	0	1	47	0	0	6	0	23	16	5	1	.833	0	2.67
81	ASH/SAL	A	25	0	25	1	0	0	134.0	120	21	58	0	4	86	0	0	8	0	81	66	8	7	.533	0	4.43
82	BUR/MID	A	4	0	4	0	0	0	18.0	6	0	6	0	1	25	0	0	2	0	2	0	2	0	1.000	0	0.00
83	TUL/TEX	AA	9	0	9	0	0	0	14.0	16	2	19	0	0	14	0	0	4	0	14	9	0	1	.000	0	5.79
	RAN/GCL	R	3	0	2	0	0	0	9.0	10	0	1	0	1	11	0	0	0	0	6	4	0	0	.000	0	4.00
84	TUL/TEX	AA	33	373	12	1	1	15	85.0	65	1	60	0	2	79	1	4	3	0	42	32	5	8	.385	8	3.39
	TEX/AL		3	25	0	0	0	1	4.1	5	0	7	0	0	4	0	0	1	0	4	4	0	1	.000	0	8.31
85	TUL/TEX	AA	34	339	11	0	0	19	81.1	51	1	44	3	1	97	3	2	7	0	32	24	7	6	.538	9	2.66
	TEX/AL		16	86	0	0	0	10	21.0	16	0	16	2	1	19	0	1	1	0	6	6	1	1	.500	3	2.57
86	OC/AMA	AAA	28	204	1	0	0	16	44.1	51	3	27	0	0	41	2	3	5	0	30	29	2	1	.667	5	5.89
	TEX/AL		19	93	0	0	0	4	19.1	14	1	22	0	1	17	1	2	7	1	11	10	1	0	1.000	4	4.66

Henry, Dwayne Allen (continued)

YR	TM/LG	CL	G	TBF	GS	CG	SHO	GF	IP	H	HR	BB	IBB	HB	SO	SH	SF	WP	BK	R	ER	W	L	PCT	SV	ERA
87	OC/AMA	AAA	30	317	8	0	0	15	69.0	66	11	50	3	0	55	1	3	3	0	39	38	4	4	.500	3	4.96
	TEX/AL		5	50	0	0	0	1	10.0	12	2	9	0	0	7	0	0	1	0	10	10	0	0	.000	0	9.00
88	OC/AMA	AAA	46	336	3	0	0	24	75.2	57	3	54	0	4	98	3	6	11	1	51	47	5	5	.500	7	5.59
	TEX/AL		11	59	0	0	0	5	10.1	15	1	9	1	3	10	0	1	3	1	10	10	0	1	.000	1	8.71
89	RIC/INT	AAA	41	359	6	0	0	20	84.2	43	4	61	3	3	101	3	3	7	0	28	23	11	5	.688	1	2.44
	ATL/NL		12	55	0	0	0	6	12.2	12	2	5	1	0	16	2	0	1	0	6	6	0	2	.000	1	4.26
90	RIC/INT	AAA	13	109	0	0	0	6	27.0	12	1	16	1	1	36	2	0	1	0	7	7	1	1	.500	2	2.33
	ATL/NL		34	176	0	0	0	14	38.1	41	3	25	0	0	34	0	1	2	1	26	24	2	2	.500	2	5.63
91	HOU/NL		52	282	0	0	0	25	67.2	51	7	39	7	2	51	6	2	5	0	25	24	3	2	.600	2	3.19
92	CIN/NL		60	352	0	0	0	11	83.2	59	4	44	6	1	72	7	3	12	0	31	31	3	3	.500	2	3.33
93	CIN/NL		3	26	0	0	0	1	4.2	6	0	4	1	0	2	0	0	1	0	8	2	0	1	.000	0	3.86
	SEA/AL		31	249	1	0	0	15	54.0	56	6	35	4	2	35	3	4	7	0	40	40	2	1	.667	2	6.67
	YEAR		34	275	1	0	0	16	58.2	62	6	39	5	2	37	3	4	8	0	48	42	2	2	.500	2	6.44
10 YR TOTALS			**246**	**1453**	**1**	**0**	**0**	**93**	**326.0**	**287**	**26**	**206**	**20**	**9**	**266**	**22**	**14**	**40**	**3**	**178**	**167**	**13**	**15**	**.464**	**9**	**4.61**

Henry, Floyd Bluford "Butch" — BL/TL — b.10/7/68   CIN87 15/388

YR	TM/LG	CL	G	TBF	GS	CG	SHO	GF	IP	H	HR	BB	IBB	HB	SO	SH	SF	WP	BK	R	ER	W	L	PCT	SV	ERA
87	BIL/PIO	R+	9	151	5	0	0	2	35.0	37	3	12	1	1	38	0	1	4	1	21	18	4	0	1.000	1	4.63
88	CR/MID	A	27	745	27	1	1	0	187.0	144	14	56	2	6	163	7	4	6	8	59	47	16	2	.889	0	2.26
89	CHT/SOU	AA	7	110	7	0	0	0	26.1	22	2	12	1	0	19	1	1	2	0	12	10	1	3	.250	0	3.42
90	CHT/SOU	AA	24	622	22	2	0	0	143.1	151	15	58	0	3	95	9	5	12	2	74	67	8	8	.500	0	4.21
91	TUC/PCL	AAA	27	671	27	2	0	0	153.2	192	10	42	2	1	97	8	5	5	4	92	82	10	11	.476	0	4.80
92	HOU/NL		28	710	28	2	1	0	165.2	185	16	41	7	1	96	12	7	2	2	81	74	6	9	.400	0	4.02
93	OTT/INT	AAA	5	125	5	1	0	0	31.1	34	2	1	0	0	25	0	1	0	0	15	13	3	1	.750	0	3.73
	COL/NL		20	390	15	1	0	1	84.2	117	14	24	2	1	39	6	5	1	0	66	62	2	8	.200	0	6.59
	MON/NL		10	77	1	0	0	3	18.1	18	1	4	0	0	8	0	1	0	0	10	8	1	1	.500	0	3.93
	YEAR		30	467	16	1	0	4	103.0	135	15	28	2	1	47	6	6	1	0	76	70	3	9	.250	0	6.12
2 YR TOTALS			**58**	**1177**	**44**	**3**	**1**	**4**	**268.2**	**320**	**31**	**69**	**9**	**2**	**143**	**18**	**13**	**3**	**2**	**157**	**144**	**9**	**18**	**.333**	**0**	**4.82**

Henry, Richard Douglas "Doug" — BR/TR — b.12/10/63   MIL85 8/185

YR	TM/LG	CL	G	TBF	GS	CG	SHO	GF	IP	H	HR	BB	IBB	HB	SO	SH	SF	WP	BK	R	ER	W	L	PCT	SV	ERA
86	BEL/MID	A	27	639	24	4	1	1	143.1	153	16	56	4	6	115	3	5	9	4	95	74	7	8	.467	1	4.65
87	BEL/MID	A	31	593	15	1	0	5	132.2	145	6	51	5	5	106	2	4	7	0	83	72	8	9	.471	2	4.88
88	STO/CAL	A+	23	280	1	1	0	14	70.2	46	1	31	1	1	71	1	1	5	4	19	14	7	1	.875	7	1.78
	EP/TEX	AA	14	182	3	3	1	1	45.2	33	4	19	0	1	50	0	1	3	3	16	16	4	0	1.000	0	3.15
89	EP/TEX	AA	1	11	1	0	0	0	2.0	3	1	3	0	0	0	0	0	0	0	3	3	0	0	.000	0	13.50
	STO/CAL	A+	4	43	3	0	0	0	11.0	9	0	3	0	0	9	0	0	0	0	4	0	0	1	.000	0	0.00
90	STO/CAL	A+	4	35	0	0	0	3	8.0	4	0	3	0	2	13	0	1	1	0	1	1	1	0	1.000	1	1.13
	EP/TEX	AA	15	131	0	0	0	12	30.2	31	1	11	0	0	25	0	1	0	2	13	10	1	0	1.000	9	2.93
	DEN/AMA	AAA	27	218	0	0	0	15	50.2	46	4	27	2	0	54	2	1	3	0	26	25	2	3	.400	8	4.44
91	DEN/AMA	AAA	32	234	0	0	0	27	57.2	47	4	20	3	3	47	4	2	4	2	16	14	3	2	.600	14	2.18
	MIL/AL		32	137	0	0	0	25	36.0	16	1	14	1	0	28	1	2	0	0	4	4	2	1	.667	15	1.00
92	MIL/AL		68	277	0	0	0	56	65.0	64	6	24	4	0	52	1	2	4	0	34	29	1	4	.200	29	4.02
93	MIL/AL		54	260	0	0	0	41	55.0	67	7	25	8	3	38	5	4	4	0	37	34	4	4	.500	17	5.56
3 YR TOTALS			**154**	**674**	**0**	**0**	**0**	**122**	**156.0**	**147**	**14**	**63**	**13**	**3**	**118**	**7**	**8**	**8**	**0**	**75**	**67**	**7**	**9**	**.438**	**61**	**3.87**

Hentgen, Patrick George "Pat" — BR/TR — b.11/13/68   TOR86 5/133

YR	TM/LG	CL	G	TBF	GS	CG	SHO	GF	IP	H	HR	BB	IBB	HB	SO	SH	SF	WP	BK	R	ER	W	L	PCT	SV	ERA
86	SC/NYP	A-	13	191	11	0	0	2	40.0	38	3	30	1	2	30	2	1	3	0	27	20	0	4	.000	1	4.50
87	MB/SAL	A	32	753	31	2	2	0	188.0	145	5	60	0	8	131	4	2	14	3	62	49	11	5	.688	0	2.35
88	DUN/FSL	A+	31	651	30	0	0	1	151.1	139	10	65	1	6	125	4	6	14	2	80	58	3	12	.200	0	3.45
89	DUN/FSL	A+	29	633	28	0	0	0	151.1	123	5	71	1	2	148	6	7	16	4	53	45	9	8	.529	0	2.68
90	KNO/SOU	AA	28	633	26	0	0	0	153.1	121	10	68	0	3	142	3	5	8	3	57	52	9	5	.643	0	3.05
91	SYR/INT	AAA	31	729	28	0	0	2	171.0	146	17	90	0	3	155	5	6	11	2	91	85	8	9	.471	0	4.47
	TOR/AL		3	30	1	0	0	1	7.1	5	1	3	0	2	3	1	0	1	0	2	2	0	0	.000	0	2.45
92	SYR/INT	AAA	4	81	4	0	0	0	20.1	15	1	4	0	0	17	2	0	0	1	6	6	1	2	.333	0	2.66
	TOR/AL		28	229	2	0	0	10	50.1	49	7	32	5	0	39	2	2	2	1	30	30	5	2	.714	0	5.36
93	TOR/AL		34	926	32	3	0	0	216.1	215	27	74	0	7	122	6	5	11	0	103	93	19	9	.679	0	3.87
3 YR TOTALS			**65**	**1185**	**35**	**3**	**0**	**11**	**274.0**	**269**	**35**	**109**	**5**	**9**	**164**	**9**	**7**	**14**	**2**	**135**	**125**	**24**	**11**	**.686**	**0**	**4.11**

Heredia, Gilbert "Gil" — BR/TR — b.10/26/65   SF87 9/230

YR	TM/LG	CL	G	TBF	GS	CG	SHO	GF	IP	H	HR	BB	IBB	HB	SO	SH	SF	WP	BK	R	ER	W	L	PCT	SV	ERA
87	EVE/NWL	A-	3	80	3	1	0	0	20.0	24	2	1	0	0	14	0	0	1	0	8	8	2	0	1.000	0	3.60
	FRE/CAL	A+	11	321	11	5	2	0	80.2	62	8	23	1	0	60	2	5	2	2	28	26	5	3	.625	0	2.90
88	SJ/CAL	A+	27	863	27	9	0	0	206.1	216	9	46	0	4	121	9	7	9	0	107	80	13	12	.520	0	3.49
89	SHR/TEX	AA	7	104	2	1	0	1	24.2	28	1	4	0	1	18	1	0	0	0	10	7	1	0	1.000	0	2.55
90	PHO/PCL	AAA	29	626	19	0	0	2	147.0	159	7	37	0	3	75	6	6	4	1	81	67	9	7	.563	1	4.10
91	PHO/PCL	AAA	33	592	15	0	0	7	140.1	155	3	28	5	2	75	9	2	4	0	60	44	9	11	.450	2	2.82
	SF/NL		7	126	4	0	0	0	33.0	27	1	6	1	3	13	2	0	0	2	14	14	0	2	.000	0	3.82
92	SF/NL		13	132	4	0	0	3	30.0	32	3	16	1	1	15	0	0	1	0	20	18	2	3	.400	0	5.40
	PHO/PCL	AAA	22	325	7	1	1	7	80.2	83	3	13	1	0	37	2	1	3	0	30	18	5	5	.500	2	2.01
	IND/AMA	AAA	3	72	3	1	0	0	17.2	18	1	3	0	0	9	0	0	0	0	2	2	1	0	1.000	0	1.02
	MON/NL		7	55	1	0	0	1	14.2	12	1	4	0	0	7	1	0	1	0	3	3	1	1	.500	0	1.84
	YEAR		20	187	5	0	0	4	44.2	44	4	20	1	1	22	1	0	2	0	23	21	3	4	.400	0	4.23
93	OTT/INT	AAA	16	429	16	1	0	0	102.2	97	7	26	2	3	66	4	6	6	0	46	34	8	4	.667	0	2.98
	MON/NL		20	246	9	0	0	2	57.1	66	4	14	2	2	40	4	3	2	1	28	25	4	2	.667	2	3.92
3 YR TOTALS			**47**	**559**	**18**	**1**	**0**	**7**	**135.0**	**137**	**12**	**41**	**5**	**3**	**75**	**8**	**3**	**2**	**0**	**65**	**60**	**6**	**7**	**.462**	**2**	**4.00**

Hernandez, Francis Xavier "Xavier" — BL/TR — b.8/16/65 TOR86 4/107

YR	TM/LG	CL	G	TBF	GS	CG	SHO	GF	IP	H	HR	BB	IBB	HB	SO	SH	SF	WP	BK	R	ER	W	L	PCT	SV	ERA
86	SC/NYP	A-	13	284	10	1	1	3	70.2	55	6	16	0	6	69	1	0	5	2	27	21	5	5	.500	0	2.67
87	SC/NYP	A-	13	242	11	0	0	0	55.0	57	4	16	0	4	49	1	1	2	0	39	31	3	3	.500	0	5.07
88	MB/SAL	A	23	585	22	2	2	1	148.0	116	5	28	1	7	111	1	3	10	4	52	42	13	6	.684	0	2.55
	KNO/SOU	AA	11	290	11	2	0	0	68.1	73	3	15	0	3	33	2	1	2	1	32	22	2	4	.333	0	2.90
89	KNO/SOU	AA	4	112	4	1	1	0	24.0	25	0	11	0	2	17	0	1	1	0	11	11	1	1	.500	0	4.13
	TOR/AL		7	101	0	0	0	2	22.2	25	2	8	0	1	7	0	2	1	0	15	12	1	0	1.000	0	4.76
	SYR/INT	AAA	15	411	15	2	1	0	99.1	95	7	22	0	2	47	4	4	4	2	42	39	5	6	.455	0	3.53
90	HOU/NL		34	268	1	0	0	10	62.1	60	8	24	5	4	24	0	4	6	0	34	32	2	1	.667	0	4.62
91	TUC/PCL	AAA	16	151	3	0	0	8	36.0	35	1	9	0	2	34	1	3	4	2	16	11	2	1	.667	4	2.75
	HOU/NL		32	285	6	0	0	8	63.0	66	6	32	7	0	55	1	1	0	0	34	33	2	7	.222	3	4.71
92	HOU/NL		77	454	0	0	0	25	111.0	81	5	42	7	3	96	3	2	5	0	31	26	9	1	.900	7	2.11
93	HOU/NL		72	389	0	0	0	29	96.2	75	6	28	3	1	101	3	3	6	0	37	28	4	5	.444	9	2.61
5 YR TOTALS			222	1497	7	0	0	74	355.2	307	27	134	22	9	283	9	12	18	0	151	131	18	14	.563	19	3.31

Hernandez, Jeremy Stuart — BR/TR — b.7/6/66 SL87 2/46

YR	TM/LG	CL	G	TBF	GS	CG	SHO	GF	IP	H	HR	BB	IBB	HB	SO	SH	SF	WP	BK	R	ER	W	L	PCT	SV	ERA
87	ERI/NYP	A-	16	412	16	1	0	0	99.1	87	7	41	3	2	62	3	3	7	1	36	31	5	4	.556	0	2.81
88	SPR/MID	A	24	615	24	3	1	0	147.1	133	8	34	2	7	97	0	3	4	8	73	58	12	6	.667	0	3.54
89	SP/FSL	A+	3	63	3	0	0	0	14.0	17	0	5	0	0	5	2	1	2	0	14	12	0	2	.000	0	7.71
	CHS/SAL	A	10	260	10	2	1	0	58.2	65	2	16	1	3	39	2	0	1	3	37	23	3	5	.375	0	3.53
	RIV/CAL	A+	9	264	9	4	1	0	67.0	55	2	11	0	4	65	0	0	2	0	17	13	5	2	.714	0	1.75
	WIC/TEX	AA	4	91	3	0	0	0	19.0	30	6	8	0	0	9	1	1	4	0	18	18	2	1	.667	0	8.53
90	WIC/TEX	AA	26	675	26	1	0	0	155.0	163	18	50	0	7	101	7	9	6	1	92	78	7	6	.538	0	4.53
91	LV/PCL	AAA	56	309	0	0	0	45	68.1	76	1	25	10	4	67	5	2	2	0	36	36	4	8	.333	13	4.74
	SD/NL		9	56	0	0	0	7	14.1	8	0	5	0	0	9	1	0	1	0	1	0	0	0	.000	2	0.00
92	LV/PCL	AAA	42	236	0	0	0	33	55.2	53	2	20	4	4	38	5	3	3	0	19	18	2	4	.333	11	2.91
	SD/NL		26	157	0	0	0	11	36.2	39	4	11	5	1	25	6	5	0	0	17	17	1	4	.200	1	4.17
93	SD/NL		21	146	0	0	0	9	34.1	41	2	7	1	0	26	2	1	2	0	19	18	0	2	.000	4	4.72
	CLE/AL		49	321	0	0	0	31	77.1	75	12	27	6	0	44	2	5	2	0	33	27	6	5	.545	8	3.14
	YEAR		70	467	0	0	0	31	111.2	116	14	34	7	0	70	4	6	2	0	52	45	6	7	.462	8	3.63
3 YR TOTALS			105	680	0	0	0	49	162.2	163	18	50	12	1	104	10	11	4	2	70	62	7	11	.389	11	3.43

Hernandez, Roberto Manuel — BR/TR — b.11/11/64 CAL86 1/16

YR	TM/LG	CL	G	TBF	GS	CG	SHO	GF	IP	H	HR	BB	IBB	HB	SO	SH	SF	WP	BK	R	ER	W	L	PCT	SV	ERA
86	SAL/NWL	A-	10	0	10	0	0	0	55.0	57	3	42	1	1	38	0	0	6	0	37	28	2	2	.500	0	4.58
87	QC/MID	A	7	102	6	0	0	1	21.0	24	2	12	0	2	21	0	0	5	0	21	16	2	3	.400	1	6.86
88	QC/MID	A	24	699	24	6	1	0	164.2	157	8	48	0	6	114	4	4	7	5	70	58	9	10	.474	0	3.17
	MID/TEX	AA	3	59	3	0	0	0	12.1	16	0	8	0	1	7	0	0	1	0	13	9	0	2	.000	0	6.57
89	MID/TEX	AA	12	305	12	0	0	0	64.0	94	4	30	0	2	42	1	5	4	1	57	49	2	7	.222	0	6.89
	PS/CAL	A+	7	188	7	0	0	0	42.2	49	2	16	0	2	33	3	1	4	0	27	22	1	4	.200	0	4.64
	SB/MID	A	4	95	4	0	0	0	24.1	19	1	7	0	0	17	2	0	0	0	9	9	1	1	.500	0	3.33
90	BIR/SOU	AA	17	469	17	1	0	0	108.0	103	6	43	0	2	62	5	5	3	1	57	44	8	5	.615	0	3.67
	VAN/PCL	AAA	11	329	11	3	1	0	79.1	73	4	26	0	2	49	3	3	3	0	33	25	3	5	.375	0	2.84
91	VAN/PCL	AAA	7	195	7	0	0	0	44.2	41	2	23	0	0	40	1	1	1	0	17	16	4	1	.800	0	3.22
	WS/GCL	R	1	18	1	0	0	0	6.0	2	0	0	0	0	7	0	0	0	0	0	0	0	0	.000	0	0.00
	BIR/SOU	AA	4	85	4	0	0	0	22.2	11	2	6	0	2	25	0	1	0	0	5	5	2	1	.667	0	1.99
	CHI/AL		9	69	3	0	0	0	15.0	18	1	3	0	0	6	0	1	0	0	15	13	1	0	1.000	0	7.80
92	VAN/PCL	AAA	9	86	0	0	0	9	20.2	13	0	11	1	1	23	0	0	2	0	9	6	3	3	.500	2	2.61
	CHI/AL		43	277	0	0	0	27	71.0	45	4	20	1	4	68	0	3	2	0	15	13	7	3	.700	12	1.65
93	CHI/AL		70	314	0	0	0	67	78.2	66	6	20	1	0	71	2	2	5	0	21	20	3	4	.429	38	2.29
3 YR TOTALS			122	660	3	0	0	95	164.2	129	11	47	2	4	145	2	5	5	0	51	46	11	7	.611	50	2.51

Hershiser, Orel Leonard Quinton — BR/TR — b.9/16/58 LA79 18/440

YR	TM/LG	CL	G	TBF	GS	CG	SHO	GF	IP	H	HR	BB	IBB	HB	SO	SH	SF	WP	BK	R	ER	W	L	PCT	SV	ERA
83	LA/NL		8	37	0	0	0	4	8.0	7	1	6	0	0	5	1	0	1	0	6	3	0	0	.000	1	3.38
84	LA/NL		45	771	20	8	*4	10	189.2	160	9	50	8	4	150	2	3	8	1	65	56	11	8	.579	2	2.66
85	LA/NL		36	953	34	9	5	1	239.2	179	8	68	5	6	157	5	4	5	0	72	54	19	3	*.864	0	2.03
86	LA/NL		35	988	35	8	1	0	231.1	213	13	86	11	5	153	14	6	12	3	112	99	14	14	.500	0	3.85
87	LA/NL		37	1093	35	10	1	2	*264.2	247	17	74	5	9	190	8	2	11	2	105	90	16	16	.500	1	3.06
88	LA/NL		35	1068	34	*15	*8	1	*267.0	208	18	73	10	4	178	19	6	8	5	73	67	*23	8	.742	1	2.26
89	LA/NL		35	1047	33	8	4	0	*256.2	226	9	77	14	3	178	19	6	8	4	75	66	15	15	.500	0	2.31
90	LA/NL		4	106	4	0	0	0	25.1	26	1	4	0	1	16	1	0	0	0	12	12	1	1	.500	0	4.26
91	ALB/PCL	AAA	1	19	1	0	0	0	5.0	5	0	4	0	0	5	0	0	1	0	0	0	0	0	.000	0	0.00
	BAK/CAL	A+	2	40	2	0	0	0	11.0	5	0	1	0	0	6	1	0	0	0	2	1	2	0	1.000	0	0.82
	SA/TEX	AA	1	31	1	0	0	0	7.0	11	0	1	0	0	5	0	0	0	0	3	2	0	0	.000	0	2.57
	LA/NL		21	473	21	0	0	0	112.0	112	3	32	6	5	73	2	1	4	0	43	43	7	2	.778	0	3.46
92	LA/NL		33	910	33	1	0	0	210.2	209	15	69	13	8	130	15	6	10	0	101	86	10	15	.400	0	3.67
93	LA/NL		33	913	33	5	1	0	215.2	201	17	72	13	7	141	12	4	7	0	106	86	12	14	.462	0	3.59
11 YR TOTALS			322	8359	282	64	24	18	2020.2	1788	111	611	85	52	1371	88	38	70	20	770	662	128	96	.571	5	2.95

Hesketh, Joseph Thomas "Joe" — BR/TL — b.2/15/59 MON80 2/50

YR	TM/LG	CL	G	TBF	GS	CG	SHO	GF	IP	H	HR	BB	IBB	HB	SO	SH	SF	WP	BK	R	ER	W	L	PCT	SV	ERA
84	IND/AMA	AAA	22	595	22	5	1	2	147.2	120	8	54	2	3	135	6	6	10	3	60	50	12	3	.800	0	3.05
	MON/NL		11	182	5	1	1	2	45.0	38	2	15	3	0	32	2	2	1	3	15	9	2	2	.500	1	1.80
85	MON/NL		25	618	25	2	1	0	155.1	125	10	45	2	0	113	2	3	3	3	52	43	10	5	.667	0	2.49
86	MON/NL		15	362	15	0	0	0	82.2	92	11	31	4	2	67	2	4	3	3	46	46	6	5	.545	0	5.01

Hesketh, Joseph Thomas "Joe" (continued)

YR	TM/LG	CL	G	TBF	GS	CG	SHO	GF	IP	H	HR	BB	IBB	HB	SO	SH	SF	WP	BK	R	ER	W	L	PCT	SV	ERA
87	EXP/GCL	R	2	20	1	0	0	0	4.1	7	0	0	0	0	8	0	0	1	0	4	4	0	0	.000	0	8.31
	JAC/SOU	AA	6	78	3	0	0	1	19.2	18	1	4	1	0	22	0	0	1	0	6	5	1	0	1.000	1	2.29
	MON/NL		18	128	0	0	0	3	28.2	23	2	15	3	2	31	2	0	1	0	12	10	0	0	.000	1	3.14
88	IND/AMA	AAA	8	47	0	0	0	3	11.0	10	1	5	0	0	16	0	0	0	0	5	4	0	0	.000	2	3.27
	MON/NL		60	304	0	0	0	23	72.2	63	1	35	9	0	64	5	4	5	1	30	23	4	3	.571	9	2.85
89	IND/AMA	AAA	5	40	1	0	0	3	9.1	11	0	5	0	0	9	0	1	1	0	4	4	0	0	.000	1	3.86
	MON/NL		43	219	0	0	0	17	48.1	54	5	26	6	0	44	6	2	1	3	34	31	6	4	.600	3	5.77
90	MON/NL		2	12	0	0	0	0	3.0	2	0	2	1	0	3	0	0	0	0	0	0	1	0	1.000	0	0.00
	ATL/NL		31	135	0	0	0	15	31.0	30	5	12	0	1	21	0	1	5	0	23	20	0	2	.000	5	5.81
	BOS/AL		12	122	0	0	0	4	25.2	37	2	11	1	0	26	0	0	3	0	12	10	0	4	.000	0	3.51
	YEAR		45	269	2	0	0	19	59.2	69	7	25	2	1	50	0	1	8	0	35	30	1	6	.143	5	4.53
91	BOS/AL		39	631	17	0	0	5	153.1	142	19	53	3	0	104	7	3	8	0	59	56	12	4	.750	0	3.29
92	BOS/AL		30	659	25	1	0	4	148.2	162	15	58	9	2	104	5	6	6	0	84	72	8	9	.471	1	4.36
93	BOS/AL		28	246	5	0	0	8	53.1	62	4	29	4	0	34	4	2	4	2	35	30	3	4	.429	1	5.06
10 YR TOTALS			**314**	**3618**	**94**	**4**	**2**	**78**	**847.2**	**830**	**76**	**332**	**45**	**7**	**643**	**41**	**24**	**41**	**15**	**399**	**350**	**52**	**42**	**.553**	**21**	**3.72**

Hibbard, James Gregory "Greg" — BL/TL — b.9/13/64　KC86 16/417

YR	TM/LG	CL	G	TBF	GS	CG	SHO	GF	IP	H	HR	BB	IBB	HB	SO	SH	SF	WP	BK	R	ER	W	L	PCT	SV	ERA
86	EUG/NWL	A-	26	0	1	0	0	15	39.0	30	2	19	0	2	44	0	0	0	0	23	15	5	2	.714	5	3.46
87	APP/MID	A	9	265	9	2	1	0	64.2	53	3	18	3	2	61	1	0	2	0	17	8	7	2	.778	0	1.11
	FM/FSL	A+	3	92	3	3	1	0	24.0	20	0	3	0	1	20	2	0	0	0	5	5	2	1	.667	0	1.88
	MEM/SOU	AA	16	431	16	3	1	0	106.0	102	7	21	1	2	56	3	3	1	0	48	38	7	6	.538	0	3.23
88	VAN/PCL	AAA	25	617	24	4	1	0	144.1	155	7	44	4	4	65	7	5	6	2	74	66	11	11	.500	0	4.12
89	VAN/PCL	AAA	9	231	9	2	1	0	58.0	47	3	11	0	1	45	1	3	5	0	24	17	2	3	.400	0	2.64
	CHI/AL		23	581	23	2	0	0	137.1	142	5	41	0	2	55	5	4	4	0	58	49	6	7	.462	0	3.21
90	CHI/AL		33	871	33	3	1	0	211.0	202	11	55	2	6	92	8	4	9	0	80	74	14	9	.609	0	3.16
91	VAN/PCL	AAA	1	24	1	0	0	0	5.1	6	0	3	0	0	3	0	1	0	0	3	2	0	0	.000	0	3.38
	CHI/AL		32	806	29	5	0	1	194.0	196	23	57	1	2	71	8	2	1	0	107	93	11	11	.500	0	4.31
92	CHI/AL		31	755	28	0	0	2	176.0	187	17	57	2	7	69	10	6	1	1	92	86	10	7	.588	1	4.40
93	CHI/NL		31	800	31	1	0	0	191.0	209	19	47	9	3	82	9	10	1	2	96	84	15	11	.577	0	3.96
5 YR TOTALS			**150**	**3813**	**144**	**11**	**1**	**3**	**909.1**	**936**	**75**	**257**	**14**	**20**	**369**	**40**	**32**	**9**	**4**	**433**	**386**	**56**	**45**	**.554**	**1**	**3.82**

Hickerson, Bryan David — BL/TL — b.10/13/63　MIN86 7/169

YR	TM/LG	CL	G	TBF	GS	CG	SHO	GF	IP	H	HR	BB	IBB	HB	SO	SH	SF	WP	BK	R	ER	W	L	PCT	SV	ERA
86	VIS/CAL	A+	11	302	11	3	0	0	72.1	72	3	25	1	1	69	9	3	2	0	37	34	4	3	.571	0	4.23
87	CLI/MID	A	17	371	10	2	1	3	94.0	60	1	37	0	1	103	3	1	5	0	17	13	11	0	1.000	1	1.24
	SHR/TEX	AA	4	70	3	0	0	0	16.0	20	0	4	0	1	23	1	1	1	0	7	7	1	2	.333	0	3.94
89	SJ/CAL	A+	21	561	21	1	1	0	134.0	111	1	57	0	1	110	6	5	3	2	52	38	11	6	.647	0	2.55
90	SHR/TEX	AA	27	294	6	0	0	7	66.0	71	2	26	2	1	63	4	2	2	2	37	31	3	6	.333	1	4.23
	PHO/PCL	AAA	12	162	4	0	0	3	34.1	48	2	16	2	0	26	2	2	0	1	25	21	0	4	.000	0	5.50
91	SHR/TEX	AA	23	165	0	0	0	6	39.0	36	2	14	3	0	41	6	0	2	1	15	13	3	4	.429	2	3.00
	PHO/PCL	AAA	12	97	0	0	0	7	21.1	29	1	5	1	0	21	1	1	1	0	10	9	1	1	.500	2	3.80
	SF/NL		17	212	6	0	0	4	50.0	53	3	17	3	0	43	2	2	5	0	20	20	2	2	.500	0	3.60
92	SF/NL		61	345	1	0	0	8	87.1	74	7	21	2	1	68	4	5	4	4	31	30	5	3	.625	0	3.09
93	SF/NL		47	525	15	0	0	5	120.1	137	14	39	3	1	69	11	4	4	0	58	57	7	5	.583	0	4.26
3 YR TOTALS			**125**	**1082**	**22**	**0**	**0**	**17**	**257.2**	**264**	**24**	**77**	**8**	**2**	**180**	**17**	**9**	**10**	**1**	**109**	**107**	**14**	**10**	**.583**	**0**	**3.74**

Higuera, Teodoro Valenzuela "Teddy" — BB/TL — b.11/9/58　MEX 1979

YR	TM/LG	CL	G	TBF	GS	CG	SHO	GF	IP	H	HR	BB	IBB	HB	SO	SH	SF	WP	BK	R	ER	W	L	PCT	SV	ERA
84	EP/TEX	AA	19	530	19	4	0	0	121.0	116	11	43	0	1	99	4	1	5	2	57	35	8	7	.533	0	2.60
	VAN/PCL	AAA	8	0	6	0	2	2	40.0	49	3	14	0	0	29	0	0	2	0	26	21	1	4	.200	0	4.72
85	MIL/AL		32	874	30	7	2	2	212.1	186	22	63	0	3	127	5	10	4	3	105	92	15	8	.652	0	3.90
86	MIL/AL		34	1031	34	15	4	0	248.1	226	26	74	5	3	207	7	11	3	0	84	77	20	11	.645	0	2.79
87	MIL/AL		35	1084	35	14	3	0	261.2	236	24	87	2	2	240	6	9	4	2	120	112	18	10	.643	0	3.85
88	MIL/AL		31	895	31	8	1	0	227.1	168	15	59	4	6	192	10	7	6	0	66	62	16	9	.640	0	2.45
89	EP/TEX	AA	1	21	1	0	0	0	5.0	5	0	1	0	0	4	0	0	0	0	2	1	0	0	1.000	0	1.80
	MIL/AL		22	567	22	2	1	0	135.1	125	9	48	2	4	91	6	5	0	1	56	52	9	6	.600	0	3.46
90	MIL/AL		27	720	27	4	1	0	170.0	167	16	50	2	3	129	10	4	2	1	80	71	11	10	.524	0	3.76
91	DEN/AMA	AAA	2	38	2	0	0	0	8.2	6	1	6	0	0	6	0	0	0	0	3	2	1	0	1.000	0	2.08
	MIL/AL		7	153	6	0	0	0	36.1	37	2	10	1	0	33	0	1	2	0	18	18	3	2	.600	0	4.46
92	BEL/MID	A	2	46	2	0	0	0	11.0	13	2	1	0	0	11	0	0	0	0	4	4	1	0	1.000	0	3.27
	EP/TEX	AA	1	20	1	0	0	0	5.0	4	0	2	0	0	3	1	0	0	0	2	2	0	0	.000	0	3.60
	DEN/AMA	AAA	2	42	2	0	0	0	8.2	7	0	4	0	0	4	1	0	0	0	5	4	1	0	1.000	0	4.15
93	NO/AMA	AAA	3	42	3	0	0	0	8.0	11	1	7	0	0	7	0	0	2	0	11	8	0	1	.000	0	9.00
	MIL/AL		8	148	8	0	0	0	30.0	43	4	16	2	1	27	1	1	1	0	24	24	1	3	.250	0	7.20
8 YR TOTALS			**196**	**5472**	**193**	**50**	**12**	**3**	**1321.1**	**1188**	**118**	**407**	**17**	**23**	**1046**	**45**	**48**	**13**	**16**	**553**	**508**	**93**	**59**	**.612**	**0**	**3.46**

Hill, Kenneth Wade "Ken" — BR/TR — b.12/14/65　DET 2/14/85

YR	TM/LG	CL	G	TBF	GS	CG	SHO	GF	IP	H	HR	BB	IBB	HB	SO	SH	SF	WP	BK	R	ER	W	L	PCT	SV	ERA
85	GAS/SAL	A	15	318	12	0	0	0	69.0	60	5	57	1	1	48	2	2	15	0	51	38	3	6	.333	0	4.96
86	GAS/SAL	A	22	524	16	1	0	4	122.2	95	4	80	0	5	86	2	5	14	1	51	38	9	5	.643	0	2.79
	GF/EAS	AA	1	31	1	0	0	0	7.0	4	1	6	0	0	4	0	0	3	0	4	4	0	1	.000	0	5.14
	ARK/TEX	AA	3	75	3	1	0	0	18.0	18	0	7	0	0	9	1	0	1	0	10	9	1	2	.333	0	4.50
87	ARK/TEX	AA	18	244	8	0	0	2	53.2	60	1	30	3	0	48	0	1	9	0	33	31	3	5	.375	0	5.20
	SP/FSL	A+	18	172	4	0	0	10	41.0	38	2	17	1	1	33	0	2	2	0	19	19	1	3	.250	2	4.17
88	ARK/TEX	AA	22	511	22	3	1	0	115.1	129	7	50	1	1	107	2	3	8	5	76	63	9	9	.500	0	4.92

(continued)

Hill, Kenneth Wade "Ken" (continued)

YR	TM/LG	CL	G	TBF	GS	CG	SHO	GF	IP	H	HR	BB	IBB	HB	SO	SH	SF	WP	BK	R	ER	W	L	PCT	SV	ERA
	STL/NL		4	62	1	0	0	0	14.0	16	0	6	0	0	6	0	0	1	0	9	8	0	1	.000	0	5.14
89	LOU/AMA	AAA	3	79	3	0	0	0	18.0	13	1	10	0	0	18	0	0	1	0	8	7	0	2	.000	0	3.50
	STL/NL		33	862	33	2	1	0	196.2	186	9	99	6	5	112	14	5	11	2	92	83	7	15	.318	0	3.80
90	LOU/AMA	AAA	12	326	12	2	1	0	85.1	47	6	27	1	1	104	4	1	2	0	20	17	6	1	.857	0	1.79
	STL/NL		17	343	14	1	0	1	78.2	79	7	33	1	1	58	5	5	5	0	49	48	5	6	.455	0	5.49
91	LOU/AMA	AAA	1	3	1	0	0	0	1.0	0	0	0	0	0	2	0	0	0	0	0	0	0	0	.000	0	0.00
	STL/NL		30	743	30	0	0	0	181.1	147	15	67	4	6	121	7	7	7	1	76	72	11	10	.524	0	3.57
92	MON/NL		33	908	33	3	3	0	218.0	187	13	75	4	3	150	15	3	11	4	76	65	16	9	.640	0	2.68
93	OTT/INT	AAA	1	13	1	0	0	0	4.0	1	0	1	0	0	0	0	0	0	0	0	0	0	0	.000	0	0.00
	MON/NL		28	780	28	2	0	0	183.2	163	7	74	7	6	90	9	7	6	2	84	66	9	7	.563	0	3.23
6 YR TOTALS			**145**	**3698**	**139**	**8**	**4**	**1**	**872.1**	**778**	**51**	**354**	**22**	**21**	**537**	**50**	**27**	**41**	**9**	**386**	**342**	**48**	**48**	**.500**	**0**	**3.53**

Hill, Milton Giles "Milt" — BR/TR — b.8/22/65   CIN87 28/726

YR	TM/LG	CL	G	TBF	GS	CG	SHO	GF	IP	H	HR	BB	IBB	HB	SO	SH	SF	WP	BK	R	ER	W	L	PCT	SV	ERA
87	BIL/PIO	R+	21	125	0	0	0	19	32.2	25	1	4	2	0	40	1	0	5	0	10	6	3	1	.750	7	1.65
88	CR/MID	A	44	300	0	0	0	38	78.1	52	3	17	7	1	69	3	1	4	8	21	18	9	4	.692	13	2.07
89	CHT/SOU	AA	51	281	0	0	0	42	70.0	49	4	28	6	0	63	1	5	1	4	19	16	6	5	.545	13	2.06
90	NAS/AMA	AAA	48	276	0	0	0	11	71.1	51	4	18	1	2	58	1	5	4	2	20	18	4	4	.500	3	2.27
91	NAS/AMA	AAA	37	269	0	0	0	16	67.1	59	3	15	1	0	62	3	3	3	3	26	22	3	3	.500	3	2.94
	CIN/NL		22	137	0	0	0	8	33.1	36	1	8	2	0	20	4	3	1	0	14	14	1	1	.500	0	3.78
92	NAS/AMA	AAA	53	292	0	0	0	39	74.1	56	7	17	4	1	70	3	1	4	1	30	22	0	5	.000	18	2.66
	CIN/NL		14	80	0	0	0	5	20.0	15	1	5	2	1	10	2	1	0	0	9	7	0	0	.000	1	3.15
93	CIN/NL		19	125	0	0	0	2	28.2	34	5	9	1	0	23	0	3	1	0	18	18	3	0	1.000	0	5.65
	IND/AMA	AAA	20	227	5	0	0	9	53.0	53	1	17	4	3	45	5	0	3	0	27	24	3	5	.375	2	4.08
3 YR TOTALS			**55**	**342**	**0**	**0**	**0**	**15**	**82.0**	**85**	**7**	**22**	**5**	**1**	**53**	**6**	**7**	**2**	**0**	**41**	**39**	**4**	**1**	**.800**	**1**	**4.28**

Hillegas, Shawn Patrick — BR/TR — b.8/21/64   LA84* S1/4

YR	TM/LG	CL	G	TBF	GS	CG	SHO	GF	IP	H	HR	BB	IBB	HB	SO	SH	SF	WP	BK	R	ER	W	L	PCT	SV	ERA
84	VB/FSL	A+	13	379	13	4	2	0	93.1	71	1	33	3	3	64	3	1	1	1	25	19	5	3	.625	0	1.83
85	SA/TEX	AA	23	606	23	3	0	0	139.1	134	6	67	1	3	56	9	5	5	3	72	49	4	10	.286	0	3.17
86	SA/TEX	AA	17	549	17	7	1	0	132.1	107	7	58	1	2	97	1	2	7	0	60	45	9	5	.643	0	3.06
	ALB/PCL	AAA	9	216	9	1	0	0	46.2	48	1	31	2	2	43	0	3	4	0	35	32	1	5	.167	0	6.17
87	ALB/PCL	AAA	24	709	24	4	1	0	165.2	172	4	64	1	0	105	6	6	7	1	79	62	13	5	.722	0	3.37
	LA/NL		12	252	10	0	0	0	58.0	52	5	31	0	0	51	4	1	4	0	27	23	4	3	.571	0	3.57
88	LA/NL		11	239	10	0	0	0	56.2	54	5	17	1	3	30	1	2	3	0	26	26	3	4	.429	0	4.13
	ALB/PCL	AAA	16	411	15	2	2	0	100.2	93	8	22	0	1	66	2	2	3	1	44	39	6	4	.600	0	3.49
	CHI/AL		6	166	6	0	0	0	40.0	30	4	18	0	1	26	0	2	0	1	16	14	3	2	.600	0	3.15
	YEAR		17	405	16	0	0	0	96.2	84	9	35	1	4	56	1	4	3	1	42	40	6	6	.500	0	3.72
89	CHI/AL		50	533	13	0	0	12	119.2	132	12	51	4	3	76	4	2	4	1	67	63	7	11	.389	3	4.74
90	VAN/PCL	AAA	36	261	0	0	0	23	67.1	49	4	15	0	1	52	4	3	2	1	22	13	5	3	.625	9	1.74
	CHI/AL		7	43	0	0	0	3	11.1	4	0	5	1	0	5	1	1	2	0	1	1	0	0	.000	0	0.79
91	CLE/AL		51	359	3	0	0	31	83.0	67	7	46	7	2	66	4	4	7	0	42	40	3	4	.429	7	4.34
92	FL/FSL	A+	1	22	1	0	0	0	6.0	3	0	1	0	0	2	0	0	0	0	0	0	1	0	1.000	0	0.00
	CMB/INT	AAA	4	114	4	0	0	0	27.1	24	0	10	0	2	20	0	0	2	0	10	10	2	0	1.000	0	3.29
	NY/AL		21	351	9	1	0	4	78.1	96	12	33	1	0	46	1	3	2	0	52	48	1	8	.111	0	5.51
	OAK/AL		5	34	0	0	0	2	7.2	8	1	4	1	0	3	1	0	0	0	5	2	0	0	.000	0	2.35
	YEAR		26	385	9	1	0	6	86.0	104	13	37	2	0	49	2	3	2	0	57	50	1	8	.111	0	5.23
93	OAK/AL		18	288	11	0	0	0	60.2	78	8	33	1	0	29	4	3	3	0	48	47	3	6	.333	0	6.97
	TAC/PCL	AAA	9	217	9	0	0	0	47.2	62	4	13	0	1	29	1	3	0	0	31	29	2	3	.400	0	5.48
7 YR TOTALS			**181**	**2265**	**62**	**1**	**1**	**57**	**515.1**	**521**	**54**	**238**	**16**	**13**	**332**	**19**	**20**	**21**	**1**	**284**	**264**	**24**	**38**	**.387**	**10**	**4.61**

Hillman, John Eric "Eric" — BL/TL — b.4/27/66   NYN87 17/420

YR	TM/LG	CL	G	TBF	GS	CG	SHO	GF	IP	H	HR	BB	IBB	HB	SO	SH	SF	WP	BK	R	ER	W	L	PCT	SV	ERA
87	LF/NYP	A-	13	346	13	2	1	0	79.0	84	4	30	2	3	80	2	5	8	1	44	37	6	4	.600	0	4.22
88	COL/SAL	A	17	320	13	0	0	4	73.0	54	2	43	0	6	60	1	2	5	3	45	32	1	6	.143	1	3.95
89	COL/SAL	A	9	151	7	0	0	2	33.2	28	1	21	0	4	33	1	2	1	0	17	7	2	1	.667	1	1.87
	SL/FSL	A+	19	404	14	1	0	0	88.1	96	3	53	0	3	67	3	2	15	1	59	54	6	6	.500	0	5.50
90	SL/FSL	A+	4	99	3	0	0	0	27.0	15	0	8	1	0	23	1	0	3	0	2	2	2	0	1.000	0	0.67
	JAC/TEX	AA	14	386	15	0	0	0	89.1	92	3	30	2	4	61	1	1	7	2	42	39	6	5	.545	0	3.93
91	TID/INT	AAA	27	710	27	2	0	0	161.2	184	8	58	0	10	91	15	6	13	2	89	72	5	12	.294	0	4.01
92	TID/INT	AAA	34	380	9	0	0	7	91.1	93	6	27	1	2	49	2	4	2	0	39	37	9	2	.818	3	3.65
	NY/NL		11	227	9	0	0	0	52.1	67	9	10	2	2	16	3	1	1	0	31	31	2	2	.500	0	5.33
93	NOR/INT	AAA	10	238	9	3	1	1	61.0	52	3	12	1	2	27	2	2	2	0	18	15	6	2	.750	0	2.21
	NY/NL		27	627	22	3	1	1	145.0	173	12	24	2	4	60	10	10	0	1	83	64	2	9	.182	0	3.97
2 YR TOTALS			**38**	**854**	**30**	**3**	**1**	**3**	**197.1**	**240**	**21**	**34**	**4**	**6**	**76**	**13**	**11**	**1**	**1**	**114**	**95**	**4**	**11**	**.267**	**0**	**4.33**

Hitchcock, Sterling Alex — BL/TL — b.4/29/71   NYA89 8/233

YR	TM/LG	CL	G	TBF	GS	CG	SHO	GF	IP	H	HR	BB	IBB	HB	SO	SH	SF	WP	BK	R	ER	W	L	PCT	SV	ERA
89	YAN/GCL	R	13	299	13	0	0	0	76.2	48	1	27	0	4	98	3	1	5	0	16	14	9	1	.900	0	1.64
90	GRE/SAL	A	27	694	27	6	5	0	173.1	122	7	60	1	8	171	5	4	5	2	68	56	12	12	.500	0	2.91
91	PW/CAR	A+	19	500	19	2	0	0	119.1	111	2	26	0	3	101	3	4	5	2	49	35	7	7	.500	0	2.64
92	ALB/EAS	AA	24	600	24	2	1	0	146.2	116	6	42	0	9	155	3	1	9	2	51	42	6	9	.400	0	2.58
	NY/AL		3	68	3	0	0	0	13.0	23	2	6	0	0	6	0	1	0	0	12	12	0	2	.000	0	8.31
93	ONE/NYP	A-	1	3	0	0	0	0	1.0	0	0	0	0	0	0	0	0	0	0	0	0	0	0	.000	0	0.00
	CMB/INT	AAA	16	334	16	0	0	0	76.2	80	8	28	0	6	85	0	0	1	0	43	41	3	5	.375	0	4.81
	NY/AL		6	135	6	0	0	0	31.0	32	4	14	1	1	26	0	1	3	2	18	16	1	2	.333	0	4.65
2 YR TOTALS			**9**	**203**	**9**	**0**	**0**	**0**	**44.0**	**55**	**6**	**20**	**1**	**2**	**32**	**0**	**2**	**3**	**2**	**30**	**28**	**1**	**4**	**.200**	**0**	**5.73**

Hoffman, Trevor William — BR/TR — b.10/13/67   CIN89 11/290

YR	TM/LG	CL	G	TBF	GS	CG	SHO	GF	IP	H	HR	BB	IBB	HB	SO	SH	SF	WP	BK	R	ER	W	L	PCT	SV	ERA
91	CR/MID	A	27	133	0	0	0	25	33.2	22	0	13	0	1	52	2	0	2	1	8	7	1	1	.500	12	1.87
	CHT/SOU	AA	14	59	0	0	0	13	14.0	10	0	7	1	0	23	0	0	1	0	4	3	1	0	1.000	8	1.93
92	CHT/SOU	AA	6	118	6	0	0	0	29.2	22	1	11	1	1	31	1	1	3	0	6	5	3	0	1.000	0	1.52
	NAS/AMA	AAA	42	278	5	0	0	23	65.1	57	6	32	3	1	63	1	0	4	0	32	31	4	6	.400	6	4.27
93	FLO/NL		28	152	0	0	0	13	35.2	24	5	19	7	0	26	2	1	3	0	13	13	2	2	.500	2	3.28
	SD/NL		39	239	0	0	0	13	54.1	56	5	20	6	1	53	2	4	2	0	30	26	2	4	.333	3	4.31
	YEAR		67	391	0	0	0	26	90.0	80	10	39	13	1	79	4	5	5	0	43	39	4	6	.400	5	3.90
1 YR TOTALS			**67**	**391**	**0**	**0**	**0**	**26**	**90.0**	**80**	**10**	**39**	**13**	**1**	**79**	**4**	**5**	**5**	**0**	**43**	**39**	**4**	**6**	**.400**	**5**	**3.90**

Holman, Bradly Thomas "Brad" — BR/TR — b.2/9/68   KC90 33/947

YR	TM/LG	CL	G	TBF	GS	CG	SHO	GF	IP	H	HR	BB	IBB	HB	SO	SH	SF	WP	BK	R	ER	W	L	PCT	SV	ERA
90	EUG/NWL	A-	17	184	4	0	0	3	43.1	43	3	17	0	4	31	2	0	4	2	28	23	0	3	.000	0	4.78
91	PEN/CAR	A+	47	334	0	0	0	35	78.1	70	4	33	7	2	71	5	5	5	3	34	28	6	6	.500	10	3.22
92	PEN/CAR	A+	13	74	0	0	0	12	17.2	15	0	4	1	0	19	0	0	2	0	8	6	1	1	.500	5	3.06
	JAC/SOU	AA	35	305	0	0	0	15	73.2	67	6	21	3	4	76	0	2	3	0	24	21	3	3	.500	4	2.57
93	CAL/PCL	AAA	21	427	13	1	0	2	98.2	109	5	42	0	3	54	3	6	7	1	59	52	8	4	.667	0	4.74
	SEA/AL		19	152	0	0	0	9	36.1	27	1	16	2	5	27	1	1	3	0	17	15	1	3	.250	3	3.72

Holmes, Darren Lee — BR/TR — b.4/25/66   LA84 16/415

YR	TM/LG	CL	G	TBF	GS	CG	SHO	GF	IP	H	HR	BB	IBB	HB	SO	SH	SF	WP	BK	R	ER	W	L	PCT	SV	ERA
84	GF/PIO	R+	18	0	6	1	0	4	44.2	53	5	30	1	2	29	0	0	3	3	41	33	2	5	.286	0	6.65
85	VB/FSL	A+	33	277	0	0	0	20	63.2	57	0	35	2	0	46	4	5	6	1	31	22	4	3	.571	2	3.11
86	VB/FSL	A+	11	288	10	0	0	1	64.2	55	0	39	2	3	59	3	0	5	0	30	21	3	6	.333	0	2.92
87	VB/FSL	A+	19	455	19	1	1	0	99.2	111	4	53	0	1	46	4	6	5	1	60	50	6	4	.600	0	4.52
88	ALB/PCL	AAA	2	22	1	0	0	0	5.1	6	0	1	0	0	1	0	0	0	0	3	3	0	1	.000	0	5.06
89	SA/TEX	AA	17	471	16	3	2	1	110.1	102	5	44	2	3	81	2	4	8	6	59	47	5	8	.385	1	3.83
	ALB/PCL	AAA	9	177	8	0	0	1	38.2	50	8	18	1	0	31	0	2	2	0	32	32	1	4	.200	0	7.45
90	ALB/PCL	AAA	56	389	0	0	0	30	92.2	78	3	39	2	4	99	0	4	5	2	34	32	12	2	.857	13	3.11
	LA/NL		14	77	0	0	0	6	17.1	15	1	11	3	0	19	1	2	2	0	10	10	0	1	.000	0	5.19
91	DEN/AMA	AAA	1	6	0	0	0	1	1.0	1	0	2	0	0	2	0	0	0	0	1	1	0	0	.000	0	9.00
	BEL/MID	A	2	6	0	0	0	2	2.0	0	0	0	0	0	3	0	0	0	0	0	0	0	0	.000	2	0.00
	MIL/AL		40	344	0	0	0	9	76.1	90	6	27	1	1	59	8	3	6	0	43	40	1	4	.200	3	4.72
92	DEN/AMA	AAA	12	48	0	0	0	12	13.0	7	1	1	0	1	9	0	0	0	0	2	2	0	0	.000	7	1.38
	MIL/AL		41	173	0	0	0	25	42.1	35	4	11	4	2	31	4	0	0	0	12	12	4	4	.500	6	2.55
93	CS/PCL	AAA	3	29	2	0	0	0	8.2	1	0	1	0	0	9	0	0	0	0	1	0	1	0	1.000	0	0.00
	COL/NL		62	274	0	0	0	51	66.2	56	6	20	1	2	60	0	0	2	1	31	30	3	3	.500	25	4.05
4 YR TOTALS			**157**	**868**	**0**	**0**	**0**	**86**	**202.2**	**196**	**14**	**69**	**9**	**5**	**169**	**13**	**5**	**9**	**1**	**96**	**92**	**8**	**12**	**.400**	**34**	**4.09**

Holzemer, Mark Harold — BL/TL — b.8/20/69   CAL87 6/109

YR	TM/LG	CL	G	TBF	GS	CG	SHO	GF	IP	H	HR	BB	IBB	HB	SO	SH	SF	WP	BK	R	ER	W	L	PCT	SV	ERA
88	BEN/NWL	A-	13	311	13	1	1	0	68.2	59	3	47	1	6	72	0	1	8	6	51	40	4	6	.400	0	5.24
89	QC/MID	A	25	603	25	3	1	0	139.1	122	4	64	1	5	131	3	5	12	4	68	52	12	7	.632	0	3.36
90	MID/TEX	AA	15	363	15	1	0	0	77.0	92	10	41	0	6	54	2	1	6	0	55	45	1	7	.125	0	5.26
91	MID/TEX	AA	2	28	2	0	0	0	6.1	3	0	5	0	1	7	1	0	2	0	2	1	0	0	.000	0	1.42
	PS/CAL	A+	6	98	6	0	0	0	22.0	15	1	16	1	1	19	2	1	1	1	14	7	0	4	.000	0	2.86
92	PS/CAL	A+	5	124	5	2	0	0	30.0	23	2	13	0	3	32	1	0	0	0	10	10	3	2	.600	0	3.00
	MID/TEX	AA	7	188	7	2	0	0	44.2	45	4	13	0	1	36	0	1	1	0	22	19	2	5	.286	0	3.83
	EDM/PCL	AAA	17	416	16	4	0	1	89.0	114	12	55	1	7	49	2	6	5	1	69	66	5	7	.417	0	6.67
93	VAN/PCL	AAA	24	642	23	4	0	1	145.2	158	9	70	2	4	80	4	5	5	5	94	78	9	6	.600	0	4.82
	CAL/AL		5	117	4	0	0	1	23.1	34	2	13	0	3	10	1	0	2	0	24	23	0	3	.000	0	8.87

Honeycutt, Frederick Wayne "Rick" — BL/TL — b.6/29/52   PIT76 17/405

YR	TM/LG	CL	G	TBF	GS	CG	SHO	GF	IP	H	HR	BB	IBB	HB	SO	SH	SF	WP	BK	R	ER	W	L	PCT	SV	ERA
77	SEA/AL		10	125	3	0	0	3	29.0	26	7	11	2	3	17	0	2	2	1	16	14	0	1	.000	0	4.34
78	SEA/AL		26	594	24	4	1	0	134.1	150	12	49	5	3	50	9	7	3	0	81	73	5	11	.313	0	4.89
79	SEA/AL		33	839	28	8	1	2	194.0	201	22	67	7	6	83	11	6	5	1	103	87	11	12	.478	0	4.04
80	SEA/AL		30	871	30	9	1	0	203.1	221	22	60	7	7	79	11	7	4	0	99	89	10	17	.370	0	3.94
81	TEX/AL		20	509	20	8	2	0	127.2	120	12	17	1	0	40	5	0	1	0	49	47	11	6	.647	0	3.31
82	TEX/AL		30	728	26	4	1	3	164.0	201	20	54	4	3	64	4	8	3	1	103	96	5	17	.227	0	5.27
83	TEX/AL		25	693	25	5	2	0	174.2	168	7	37	2	6	56	3	6	2	0	59	47	14	8	.636	0	*2.42
	LA/NL		9	172	7	1	0	0	39.0	46	6	13	4	2	18	2	0	1	0	26	25	2	3	.400	0	5.77
	YEAR		34	865	32	6	2	0	213.2	214	15	50	6	8	74	5	6	3	3	85	72	16	11	.593	0	3.03
84	LA/NL		29	762	28	6	2	0	183.2	180	11	51	11	2	75	4	2	5	2	72	58	10	9	.526	0	2.84
85	LA/NL		31	600	25	1	0	2	142.0	141	9	49	7	4	67	5	4	2	0	71	54	8	12	.400	1	3.42
86	LA/NL		32	713	28	0	0	2	171.0	164	9	45	4	3	100	5	5	4	1	71	63	11	9	.550	0	3.32
87	LA/NL		27	525	20	1	1	0	115.2	133	10	45	2	5	92	2	9	4	2	74	59	2	12	.143	0	4.59
	OAK/AL		7	106	4	0	0	1	23.2	25	3	9	0	2	10	3	1	1	1	17	14	1	4	.200	0	5.32
	YEAR		34	631	24	1	1	1	139.1	158	13	54	2	7	102	5	10	5	3	91	73	3	16	.158	0	4.72
88	OAK/AL		55	330	0	0	0	17	79.2	74	6	25	2	3	47	3	2	6	8	36	31	3	2	.600	7	3.50
89	OAK/AL		64	305	0	0	0	24	76.2	56	3	26	3	1	52	5	2	5	1	26	20	2	2	.500	12	2.35
90	OAK/AL		63	256	0	0	0	13	63.1	46	2	22	2	1	38	2	4	1	0	23	19	2	2	.500	7	2.70
91	MOD/CAL	A+	3	17	3	0	0	0	5.0	4	0	2	0	0	5	0	0	0	1	1	1	0	0	.000	0	1.80
	MAD/MID	A	1	7	1	0	0	0	1.0	4	0	0	0	0	1	0	0	0	0	2	2	0	0	.000	0	18.00
	OAK/AL		43	167	0	0	0	7	37.2	37	3	20	3	2	26	1	1	0	0	16	15	2	4	.333	0	3.58
92	OAK/AL		54	169	0	0	0	7	39.0	41	2	10	3	3	32	1	4	1	0	19	16	1	4	.200	3	3.69
93	OAK/AL		52	174	0	0	0	7	41.2	30	2	20	1	2	21	7	1	1	0	18	13	1	4	.200	1	2.81
17 YR TOTALS			**640**	**8638**	**268**	**47**	**11**	**88**	**2040.0**	**2060**	**172**	**630**	**77**	**47**	**967**	**86**	**69**	**43**	**20**	**979**	**840**	**101**	**139**	**.421**	**31**	**3.71**

Hope, John Alan — BR/TR — b.12/21/70 — PIT89 3/59

YR	TM/LG	CL	G	TBF	GS	CG	SHO	GF	IP	H	HR	BB	IBB	HB	SO	SH	SF	WP	BK	R	ER	W	L	PCT	SV	ERA
89	PIR/GCL	R	4	68	3	0	0	0	15.0	15	0	6	0	1	14	1	3	0	1	12	8	0	1	.000	0	4.80
91	WEL/NYP	A-	3	67	3	0	0	0	17.0	12	0	3	0	2	15	0	0	0	0	1	1	2	0	1.000	0	0.53
	AUG/SAL	A	7	188	7	0	0	0	46.1	29	1	19	0	4	37	0	1	2	1	20	18	4	2	.667	0	3.50
	SAL/CAR	A+	6	122	5	0	0	1	27.2	38	5	4	0	0	18	0	1	0	0	20	19	2	2	.500	0	6.18
92	SAL/CAR	A+	27	726	27	4	0	0	176.1	169	13	46	0	10	106	2	4	10	3	75	68	11	8	.579	0	3.47
93	CAR/SOU	AA	21	478	20	0	0	0	111.1	123	7	29	4	8	66	2	6	10	2	69	54	9	4	.692	0	4.37
	BUF/AMA	AAA	4	92	0	0	0	0	21.1	30	4	2	0	1	6	0	0	0	0	16	15	2	1	.667	0	6.33
	PIT/NL		7	166	7	0	0	0	38.0	47	2	8	3	2	8	5	1	1	0	19	17	0	2	.000	0	4.03

Horsman, Vincent Stanley Joseph "Vince" — BR/TL — b.3/9/67 — TOR 9/26/84

YR	TM/LG	CL	G	TBF	GS	CG	SHO	GF	IP	H	HR	BB	IBB	HB	SO	SH	SF	WP	BK	R	ER	W	L	PCT	SV	ERA
85	MH/PIO	R+	18	0	1	0	0	2	40.1	56	1	23	3	0	30	0	0	1	0	31	28	0	3	.000	1	6.25
86	FLO/SAL	A	29	419	9	1	1	10	90.2	93	8	49	0	1	64	1	6	5	4	56	41	4	3	.571	1	4.07
87	MB/SAL	A	30	621	28	0	0	1	149.0	144	20	37	2	2	109	6	5	5	2	74	55	7	7	.500	0	3.32
88	KNO/SOU	AA	20	260	6	1	0	6	58.1	57	5	28	3	3	40	4	4	4	1	34	30	3	2	.600	0	4.63
	DUN/FSL	A+	14	159	2	0	0	3	39.2	28	1	13	2	1	34	1	1	4	1	7	6	3	1	.750	1	1.36
89	DUN/FSL	A+	35	330	1	0	0	23	79.0	72	3	27	1	1	60	1	2	1	0	24	22	5	6	.455	8	2.51
	KNO/SOU	AA	4	19	0	0	0	3	5.0	3	0	2	1	0	3	0	0	0	0	1	1	0	0	.000	1	1.80
90	DUN/FSL	A+	28	209	0	0	0	14	50.0	53	0	15	2	1	41	2	2	0	0	21	18	4	7	.364	1	3.24
	KNO/SOU	AA	8	51	0	0	0	0	11.2	11	1	5	0	0	10	1	0	1	0	7	6	2	1	.667	0	4.63
91	KNO/SOU	AA	42	335	2	0	0	17	80.2	79	2	19	5	0	80	3	1	3	1	23	21	4	1	.800	3	2.34
	TOR/AL		4	16	0	0	0	0	4.0	2	0	3	1	0	2	1	0	0	0	0	0	0	0	.000	0	0.00
92	OAK/AL		58	180	0	0	0	9	43.1	39	3	21	4	0	18	3	1	1	0	13	12	2	1	.667	1	2.49
93	TAC/PCL	AAA	26	149	0	0	0	10	33.2	37	11	9	2	0	23	1	2	1	0	25	16	1	2	.333	3	4.28
	OAK/AL		40	116	0	0	0	5	25.0	25	2	15	1	3	17	0	1	0	0	15	15	2	0	1.000	0	5.40
3 YR TOTALS			102	312	0	0	0	16	72.1	66	5	39	6	3	37	4	1	2	0	28	27	4	1	.800	1	3.36

Hough, Charles Oliver "Charlie" — BR/TR — b.1/5/48 — LA66 8/159

YR	TM/LG	CL	G	TBF	GS	CG	SHO	GF	IP	H	HR	BB	IBB	HB	SO	SH	SF	WP	BK	R	ER	W	L	PCT	SV	ERA
70	LA/NL		8	79	0	0	0	5	17.0	18	7	11	0	0	8	0	0	0	0	11	10	0	0	.000	2	5.29
71	LA/NL		4	19	0	0	0	3	4.1	3	1	3	0	0	4	1	0	0	0	3	2	0	0	.000	0	4.15
72	LA/NL		2	13	0	0	0	2	2.2	2	0	2	0	0	4	0	0	0	0	1	1	0	0	.000	0	3.38
73	LA/NL		37	309	0	0	0	18	71.2	52	3	45	2	6	70	4	3	2	0	24	22	4	2	.667	5	2.76
74	LA/NL		49	389	0	0	0	16	96.0	65	12	40	2	4	63	6	8	4	0	45	40	9	4	.692	1	3.75
75	LA/NL		38	266	0	0	0	24	61.0	43	3	34	0	8	34	3	0	4	1	25	20	3	7	.300	4	2.95
76	LA/NL		77	600	0	0	0	55	142.2	102	6	77	3	8	81	4	1	9	0	43	35	12	8	.600	18	2.21
77	LA/NL		70	551	0	0	0	53	127.1	98	10	70	6	7	105	10	4	8	0	53	47	6	12	.333	22	3.32
78	LA/NL		55	390	0	0	0	31	93.1	69	6	48	4	5	66	0	4	3	0	38	34	5	5	.500	7	3.28
79	LA/NL		42	662	14	0	0	10	151.1	152	16	66	2	8	76	9	4	9	1	88	80	7	5	.583	0	4.76
80	LA/NL		19	156	1	0	0	5	32.1	37	4	21	0	2	25	3	3	3	0	21	20	1	3	.250	1	5.57
	TEX/AL		16	270	2	2	1	7	61.1	54	2	37	2	3	47	4	1	8	0	30	27	2	2	.500	0	3.96
	YEAR		35	426	3	2	1	12	93.2	91	6	58	2	5	72	7	4	11	0	51	47	3	5	.375	1	4.52
81	TEX/AL		21	330	5	2	0	9	82.0	61	4	31	1	3	69	1	1	4	0	30	27	4	1	.800	1	2.96
82	TEX/AL		34	954	34	12	2	0	228.0	217	21	72	5	7	128	7	4	9	0	111	100	16	13	.552	0	3.95
83	TEX/AL		34	1030	33	11	3	1	252.0	219	22	95	0	3	152	5	5	6	1	96	89	15	13	.536	0	3.18
84	TEX/AL		36	1133	36	*17	1	0	266.0	260	26	94	3	9	164	5	7	12	2	127	111	16	14	.533	0	3.76
85	TEX/AL		34	1018	34	14	1	0	250.1	198	23	83	1	7	141	7	1	11	3	102	92	14	6	.467	0	3.31
86	OC/AMA	AAA	1	22	1	0	0	0	5.0	7	1	1	0	0	3	0	0	1	0	5	5	0	1	.000	0	9.00
	TEX/AL		33	958	33	7	2	0	230.1	188	32	89	2	9	146	9	1	16	0	115	97	17	10	.630	0	3.79
87	TEX/AL		40	1231	40	13	0	0	*285.1	238	36	124	1	19	223	5	14	12	9	159	120	18	13	.581	0	3.79
88	TEX/AL		34	1067	34	10	0	0	252.0	202	20	126	1	12	174	8	8	10	10	111	93	15	16	.484	0	3.32
89	TEX/AL		30	795	30	5	1	0	182.0	168	28	95	2	6	94	3	6	7	5	97	88	10	13	.435	0	4.35
90	TEX/AL		32	950	32	5	0	0	218.2	190	24	119	2	11	114	2	11	4	0	108	99	12	12	.500	0	4.07
91	CHI/AL		31	858	29	4	1	1	199.1	167	21	94	0	11	107	8	16	5	1	98	89	9	10	.474	0	4.02
92	CHI/AL		27	751	27	4	0	0	176.1	160	19	66	2	7	76	2	6	10	1	88	77	7	12	.368	0	3.93
93	FLO/NL		34	876	34	0	0	0	204.1	202	20	71	2	8	126	11	7	11	4	109	97	9	16	.360	0	4.27
24 YR TOTALS			837	15655	419	106	12	240	3687.2	3165	366	1613	43	164	2297	111	117	170	38	1733	1517	211	207	.505	61	3.70

Howard, Christian "Chris" — BR/TL — b.11/18/65 — NYA 6/16/86

YR	TM/LG	CL	G	TBF	GS	CG	SHO	GF	IP	H	HR	BB	IBB	HB	SO	SH	SF	WP	BK	R	ER	W	L	PCT	SV	ERA
87	PW/CAR	A+	4	37	0	0	0	0	7.0	9	0	8	0	1	1	0	1	0	0	8	8	0	0	.000	0	10.29
88	ALB/EAS	AA	2	9	0	0	0	1	1.1	3	0	1	0	0	1	1	0	1	0	2	2	0	0	.000	0	13.50
	PW/CAR	A+	31	219	0	0	0	18	50.0	44	3	23	1	1	48	5	0	3	3	18	13	2	2	.500	3	2.34
89	FL/FSL	A+	13	106	0	0	0	6	25.1	19	1	13	1	0	25	0	2	0	0	6	5	2	0	1.000	0	1.78
	ALB/EAS	AA	24	145	0	0	0	10	34.0	29	4	17	2	0	33	0	1	0	0	14	13	0	0	.000	2	3.44
90	ALB/EAS	AA	2	30	0	0	0	0	5.0	9	0	7	0	0	2	0	0	0	0	8	8	0	0	.000	0	14.40
	KIN/CAR	A+	8	73	0	0	0	3	14.2	21	0	2	0	0	16	0	0	2	0	5	4	1	1	.500	0	2.45
91	BIR/SOU	AA	38	219	0	0	0	24	53.0	43	2	16	1	1	52	6	2	2	1	14	12	6	1	.857	9	2.04
92	WS/GCL	R	1	9	0	0	0	0	2.0	3	0	0	0	0	3	0	0	0	0	1	1	0	0	.000	0	4.50
	VAN/PCL	AAA	20	111	0	0	0	5	24.2	18	3	22	3	0	24	6	2	0	1	9	8	3	1	.750	0	2.92
93	NAS/AMA	AAA	43	271	0	0	0	17	66.2	55	9	16	4	0	53	3	5	1	0	32	25	4	3	.571	3	3.38
	CHI/AL		3	10	0	0	0	0	2.1	2	0	3	1	0	1	0	0	0	0	0	0	1	0	1.000	0	0.00

Howe, Steven Roy "Steve" — BL/TL — b.3/10/58 — LA79 1/16

YR	TM/LG	CL	G	TBF	GS	CG	SHO	GF	IP	H	HR	BB	IBB	HB	SO	SH	SF	WP	BK	R	ER	W	L	PCT	SV	ERA
80	LA/NL		59	359	0	0	0	36	84.2	83	1	22	10	2	39	8	3	1	0	33	25	7	9	.438	17	2.66

Howe, Steven Roy "Steve" (continued)

YR	TM/LG	CL	G	TBF	GS	CG	SHO	GF	IP	H	HR	BB	IBB	HB	SO	SH	SF	WP	BK	R	ER	W	L	PCT	SV	ERA
81	LA/NL		41	227	0	0	0	25	54.0	51	2	18	7	0	32	4	4	0	0	17	15	5	3	.625	8	2.50
82	LA/NL		66	393	0	0	0	41	99.1	87	3	17	11	0	49	10	3	1	0	27	23	7	5	.583	13	2.08
83	LA/NL		46	274	0	0	0	33	68.2	55	2	12	7	1	52	5	3	3	0	15	11	4	7	.364	18	1.44
85	LA/NL		19	104	0	0	0	14	22.0	30	2	5	2	1	11	2	2	2	0	17	12	1	1	.500	3	4.91
	MIN/AL		13	94	0	0	0	5	19.0	28	1	7	2	0	10	0	3	1	0	16	13	2	3	.400	0	6.16
	YEAR		32	198	0	0	0	19	41.0	58	3	12	4	1	21	2	5	3	0	33	25	3	4	.429	3	5.49
86	SJ/CAL	A+	14	190	8	0	0	5	49.0	40	0	5	0	2	37	1	2	1	0	14	8	3	2	.600	2	1.47
87	OC/AMA	AAA	7	85	3	0	0	1	20.2	26	1	5	0	1	14	1	1	1	0	8	8	2	2	.500	0	3.48
	TEX/AL		24	131	0	0	0	15	31.1	33	2	8	1	3	19	2	0	2	1	15	15	3	3	.500	1	4.31
90	SAL/CAL	A+	10	78	6	0	0	2	17.0	19	0	5	0	1	14	0	2	2	2	8	4	2	1	.000	0	2.12
91	CMB/INT	AAA	12	72	0	0	0	0	18.0	11	0	8	2	1	13	2	0	1	0	1	0	2	1	.667	5	0.00
	NY/AL		37	189	0	0	0	10	48.1	39	1	7	2	3	34	2	1	2	0	12	9	3	1	.750	3	1.68
92	NY/AL		20	79	0	0	0	10	22.0	9	1	3	1	0	12	1	1	1	0	7	6	3	0	1.000	6	2.45
93	CMB/INT	AAA	2	15	2	0	0	0	2.2	6	0	1	0	0	1	0	0	0	0	3	3	0	1	.000	0	10.13
	NY/AL		51	215	0	0	0	19	50.2	58	7	10	4	3	19	3	2	0	0	31	28	3	5	.375	4	4.97
9 YR TOTALS			376	2065	0	0	0	208	500.0	473	22	109	47	13	277	39	22	13	1	190	157	38	37	.507	73	2.83

Howell, Jay Canfield — BR/TR — b.11/26/55   CIN76 31/667

YR	TM/LG	CL	G	TBF	GS	CG	SHO	GF	IP	H	HR	BB	IBB	HB	SO	SH	SF	WP	BK	R	ER	W	L	PCT	SV	ERA
80	CIN/NL		5	19	0	0	0	1	3.1	8	0	0	0	1	1	0	1	0	0	5	5	0	0	.000	0	13.50
81	CHI/NL		10	97	2	0	0	1	22.1	23	3	10	2	2	10	1	1	0	0	13	12	2	0	1.000	0	4.84
82	NY/AL		6	138	6	0	0	0	28.0	42	1	13	0	0	21	0	2	1	0	25	24	2	3	.400	0	7.71
83	NY/AL		19	368	12	2	0	3	82.0	89	7	35	0	3	61	1	5	2	1	53	49	1	5	.167	0	5.38
84	NY/AL		61	426	1	0	0	23	103.2	86	5	34	3	0	109	3	3	4	0	33	31	9	4	.692	7	2.69
85	OAK/AL		63	414	0	0	0	58	98.0	98	8	31	3	1	68	3	4	4	1	32	31	9	8	.529	29	2.85
86	MOD/CAL	A+	2	12	2	0	0	0	2.0	5	1	1	0	0	1	0	0	0	0	3	3	0	0	.000	0	13.50
	OAK/AL		38	230	0	0	0	33	53.1	53	3	23	4	1	42	0	1	0	0	23	20	3	6	.333	16	3.38
87	OAK/AL		36	200	0	0	0	27	44.1	48	6	21	1	1	35	3	2	4	0	30	29	3	4	.429	16	5.89
88	LA/NL		50	262	0	0	0	38	65.0	44	1	21	2	1	70	4	2	3	0	16	15	5	3	.625	21	2.08
89	LA/NL		56	312	0	0	0	41	79.2	60	3	22	6	0	55	4	2	1	0	15	14	5	3	.625	28	1.58
90	LA/NL		45	271	0	0	0	35	66.0	59	5	20	3	0	59	1	0	4	1	17	16	5	5	.500	16	2.18
91	LA/NL		44	202	0	0	0	35	51.0	39	3	11	3	1	40	1	1	3	0	19	18	6	5	.545	16	3.18
92	VB/FSL	A+	5	32	0	0	0	0	6.2	9	2	3	0	1	4	1	0	0	0	6	6	0	0	.000	0	8.10
	BAK/CAL	A+	4	26	4	0	0	0	6.0	8	1	1	0	0	8	0	0	0	0	4	4	0	1	.000	0	6.00
	LA/NL		41	203	0	0	0	26	46.2	41	2	18	5	1	36	5	1	3	1	9	8	1	3	.250	4	1.54
93	ATL/NL		54	233	0	0	0	22	58.1	48	3	16	4	0	37	3	4	0	2	16	15	3	3	.500	0	2.31
14 YR TOTALS			528	3375	21	2	0	343	801.2	738	47	275	36	18	644	35	31	29	8	306	287	54	52	.509	153	3.22

Hurst, Bruce Vee — BL/TL — b.3/24/58   BOS76 1/22

YR	TM/LG	CL	G	TBF	GS	CG	SHO	GF	IP	H	HR	BB	IBB	HB	SO	SH	SF	WP	BK	R	ER	W	L	PCT	SV	ERA
80	BOS/AL		12	147	7	0	0	2	30.2	39	4	16	0	2	16	0	2	4	2	33	31	2	2	.500	0	9.10
81	BOS/AL		5	104	5	0	0	0	23.0	23	1	12	2	1	11	0	2	2	0	11	11	2	0	1.000	0	4.30
82	BOS/AL		28	535	19	0	0	3	117.0	161	16	40	2	3	53	2	7	5	0	87	75	3	7	.300	0	5.77
83	BOS/AL		33	903	32	6	2	0	211.1	241	22	62	5	3	115	3	4	1	2	102	96	12	12	.500	0	4.09
84	BOS/AL		33	958	33	9	2	0	218.0	232	25	88	3	6	136	3	4	1	1	106	95	12	12	.500	0	3.92
85	BOS/AL		35	973	31	6	1	0	229.1	243	31	70	4	3	189	6	4	3	4	123	115	11	13	.458	0	4.51
86	BOS/AL		25	721	25	11	4	0	174.1	169	18	50	2	3	167	3	6	0	0	63	58	13	8	.619	0	2.99
87	BOS/AL		33	1001	33	15	3	0	238.2	239	35	76	5	1	190	5	8	3	1	124	117	15	13	.536	0	4.41
88	BOS/AL		33	922	32	7	1	0	216.2	222	21	65	1	2	166	8	5	5	3	98	88	18	6	.750	0	3.66
89	SD/NL		33	990	33	*10	2	0	244.2	214	16	66	7	0	179	18	3	8	0	84	73	15	11	.577	0	2.69
90	SD/NL		33	903	33	9	*4	0	223.2	188	21	63	5	1	162	15	1	7	1	85	78	11	9	.550	0	3.14
91	SD/NL		31	909	31	4	0	0	221.2	201	17	59	3	3	141	8	4	5	1	89	81	15	8	.652	0	3.29
92	SD/NL		32	902	32	6	4	0	217.1	223	22	51	3	0	131	12	4	9	1	96	93	14	9	.609	0	3.85
93	LV/PCL	AAA	1	24	1	0	0	0	5.0	8	1	0	0	0	7	0	1	2	0	6	5	0	0	.000	0	9.00
	RC/CAL	A+	1	20	1	0	0	0	4.1	4	0	1	0	0	6	0	0	0	0	5	4	0	0	.000	0	8.31
	CS/PCL	AAA	3	67	3	0	0	0	14.2	22	0	4	1	0	8	2	0	0	0	13	12	1	1	.500	0	7.36
	SD/NL		2	26	2	0	0	0	4.1	9	0	3	0	0	3	1	0	0	0	7	6	0	1	.000	0	12.46
	COL/NL		3	34	3	0	0	0	8.2	6	1	3	0	0	6	0	0	0	1	5	5	0	1	.000	0	5.19
	YEAR		5	60	5	0	0	0	13.0	15	1	6	0	0	9	1	0	1	1	12	11	0	2	.000	0	7.62
14 YR TOTALS			371	10028	351	83	23	5	2379.1	2410	250	724	42	28	1665	86	51	55	19	1113	1022	143	112	.561	0	3.87

Hutton, Mark Steven — BR/TR — b.2/6/70   NYA 12/15/88

YR	TM/LG	CL	G	TBF	GS	CG	SHO	GF	IP	H	HR	BB	IBB	HB	SO	SH	SF	WP	BK	R	ER	W	L	PCT	SV	ERA
89	ONE/NYP	A-	12	283	12	0	0	0	66.1	70	1	24	0	1	62	2	4	5	2	39	30	6	2	.750	0	4.07
90	GRE/SAL	A	21	394	19	0	0	1	81.1	77	2	62	0	1	72	2	3	14	1	78	57	1	10	.091	0	6.31
91	FL/FSL	A+	24	606	24	3	0	0	147.0	98	5	65	5	11	117	6	1	4	4	54	40	5	8	.385	0	2.45
	CMB/INT	AAA	1	24	1	0	0	0	6.0	3	0	5	0	0	5	0	0	0	0	2	1	1	0	1.000	0	1.50
92	ALB/EAS	AA	25	703	25	1	0	0	165.1	146	6	66	1	11	128	2	3	2	1	75	66	13	7	.650	0	3.59
	CMB/INT	AAA	1	22	0	0	0	0	5.0	7	0	2	0	0	4	0	0	0	0	4	3	0	0	.000	0	5.40
93	CMB/INT	AAA	21	544	21	0	0	0	133.0	98	14	53	0	10	112	1	2	2	0	52	47	10	4	.714	0	3.18
	NY/AL		7	104	4	0	0	0	22.0	24	2	17	0	1	12	1	2	0	0	17	14	1	1	.500	0	5.73

Ignasiak, Michael James "Mike" — BB/TR — b.3/12/66   MIL88 8/211

YR	TM/LG	CL	G	TBF	GS	CG	SHO	GF	IP	H	HR	BB	IBB	HB	SO	SH	SF	WP	BK	R	ER	W	L	PCT	SV	ERA
88	HEL/PIO	R+	7	53	0	0	0	7	11.2	10	1	7	0	1	18	0	0	2	0	5	4	2	0	1.000	1	3.09
	BEL/MID	A	9	232	9	1	0	0	56.1	52	4	12	1	2	66	3	2	1	1	21	17	2	4	.333	0	2.72

(continued)

Ignasiak, Michael James "Mike" (continued)

YR	TM/LG	CL	G	TBF	GS	CG	SHO	GF	IP	H	HR	BB	IBB	HB	SO	SH	SF	WP	BK	R	ER	W	L	PCT	SV	ERA
89	STO/CAL	A+	28	763	28	4	4	0	179.0	140	4	97	0	5	142	4	5	12	1	67	54	11	6	.647	0	2.72
90	STO/CAL	A+	6	130	6	1	1	0	32.0	18	3	17	0	2	23	1	0	2	1	14	14	3	1	.750	0	3.94
	EP/TEX	AA	15	368	15	1	0	0	82.2	96	5	34	1	1	39	2	3	4	3	45	40	6	3	.667	0	4.35
91	DEN/AMA	AAA	24	587	22	1	0	1	137.2	119	14	57	2	6	103	1	1	4	1	68	65	9	5	.643	1	4.25
	MIL/AL		4	51	1	0	0	0	12.2	7	2	8	0	0	10	0	0	0	0	8	8	2	1	.667	0	5.68
92	DEN/AMA	AAA	62	388	0	0	0	34	92.0	83	4	33	4	1	64	8	2	3	3	37	30	7	4	.636	10	2.93
93	NO/AMA	AAA	35	220	0	0	0	18	57.2	26	4	20	2	1	61	4	3	3	1	10	7	6	0	1.000	9	1.09
	MIL/AL		27	158	0	0	0	4	37.0	32	2	21	4	2	28	1	1	0	1	17	15	1	1	.500	0	3.65
2 YR TOTALS			**31**	**209**	**1**	**0**	**0**	**4**	**49.2**	**39**	**4**	**29**	**4**	**2**	**38**	**1**	**1**	**0**	**0**	**25**	**23**	**3**	**2**	**.600**	**0**	**4.17**

Innis, Jeffrey David "Jeff" — BR/TR — b.7/5/62   NYN83 15/318

YR	TM/LG	CL	G	TBF	GS	CG	SHO	GF	IP	H	HR	BB	IBB	HB	SO	SH	SF	WP	BK	R	ER	W	L	PCT	SV	ERA
83	LF/NYP	A-	28	0	0	0	0	28	46.0	29	0	28	0	0	68	0	0	4	0	8	7	8	0	1.000	8	1.37
84	JAC/TEX	AA	42	283	0	0	0	27	59.1	65	3	40	4	0	63	4	0	6	1	34	28	6	5	.545	8	4.25
85	LYN/CAR	A+	53	311	0	0	0	39	77.0	46	2	40	1	1	91	6	2	3	0	26	20	6	3	.667	14	2.34
86	JAC/TEX	AA	56	359	0	0	0	48	92.0	69	2	24	3	1	75	3	6	2	0	30	25	4	5	.444	25	2.45
87	TID/INT	AAA	29	171	0	0	0	18	44.1	26	3	16	2	1	28	0	4	0	0	10	10	6	1	.857	5	2.03
	NY/NL		17	109	0	0	0	8	25.2	29	5	4	1	0	28	0	0	1	0	9	9	0	0	.000	0	3.16
88	NY/NL		12	80	0	0	0	7	19.0	19	0	2	1	0	14	0	0	0	0	6	4	1	1	.500	0	1.89
	TID/INT	AAA	34	213	0	0	0	19	48.1	43	3	25	8	0	43	3	0	1	0	22	19	0	5	.000	4	3.54
89	TID/INT	AAA	25	127	0	0	0	18	29.2	28	0	8	2	1	14	4	0	1	0	9	7	3	1	.750	10	2.12
	NY/NL		29	160	0	0	0	12	39.2	38	2	8	1	1	16	1	1	1	0	16	14	0	1	.000	0	3.18
90	TID/INT	AAA	40	209	0	0	0	33	52.2	34	1	17	5	3	42	4	1	1	0	11	10	5	2	.714	19	1.71
	NY/NL		18	104	0	0	0	12	26.1	19	4	10	3	1	12	0	2	1	0	9	7	1	3	.250	2	2.39
91	NY/NL		69	336	0	0	0	29	84.2	66	2	23	4	6	47	6	5	4	0	30	25	0	2	.000	0	2.66
92	NY/NL		76	373	0	0	0	28	88.0	85	4	36	4	6	39	7	4	1	0	32	28	6	9	.400	1	2.86
93	NY/NL		67	345	0	0	0	30	76.2	81	5	38	12	6	36	9	1	3	1	39	35	2	3	.400	3	4.11
7 YR TOTALS			**288**	**1507**	**1**	**0**	**0**	**126**	**360.0**	**337**	**22**	**121**	**27**	**15**	**192**	**24**	**14**	**10**	**3**	**141**	**122**	**10**	**20**	**.333**	**5**	**3.05**

Jackson, Danny Lynn — BR/TL — b.1/5/62   KC82* S1/1

YR	TM/LG	CL	G	TBF	GS	CG	SHO	GF	IP	H	HR	BB	IBB	HB	SO	SH	SF	WP	BK	R	ER	W	L	PCT	SV	ERA
83	KC/AL		4	87	3	0	0	0	19.0	26	1	6	0	0	9	0	0	0	0	12	11	1	1	.500	0	5.21
84	OMA/AMA	AAA	16	459	16	10	3	0	110.1	91	8	45	3	1	82	5	2	3	0	50	45	5	8	.385	0	3.67
	KC/AL		15	338	11	1	0	3	76.0	84	4	35	0	5	40	3	0	2	2	41	36	2	6	.250	0	4.26
85	KC/AL		32	893	32	4	3	0	208.0	209	7	76	2	6	114	5	4	4	2	94	79	14	12	.538	0	3.42
86	KC/AL		32	789	27	4	1	3	185.2	177	13	79	1	4	115	10	4	7	0	83	66	11	12	.478	1	3.20
87	KC/AL		36	981	34	11	2	1	224.0	219	11	109	1	7	152	8	7	5	0	115	100	9	18	.333	1	4.02
88	CIN/NL		35	1034	35	*15	6	0	260.2	206	13	71	6	2	161	13	5	5	2	86	79	*23	8	.742	0	2.73
89	CIN/NL		20	519	20	1	0	0	115.2	122	10	57	7	1	70	6	4	3	2	78	72	6	11	.353	0	5.60
90	CHW/SAL	A	1	12	1	0	0	0	3.0	2	0	1	0	0	2	0	0	0	0	2	2	0	0	.000	0	6.00
	NAS/AMA	AAA	2	45	2	0	0	0	11.0	9	0	4	0	0	3	1	0	0	0	0	0	1	0	1.000	0	0.00
	CIN/NL		22	499	21	0	0	0	117.1	119	11	40	4	2	76	4	5	3	1	54	47	6	6	.500	0	3.61
91	IOW/AMA	AAA	1	19	1	0	0	0	5.0	2	0	2	0	0	4	0	0	0	0	1	1	0	0	.000	0	1.80
	CHI/NL		17	347	14	0	0	0	70.2	89	8	48	4	1	31	8	2	1	1	59	53	1	5	.167	0	6.75
92	CHI/NL		19	501	19	0	0	0	113.0	117	5	48	3	3	51	11	5	5	2	59	53	4	9	.308	0	4.22
	PIT/NL		15	382	15	0	0	0	88.1	94	1	29	3	1	46	6	5	1	0	40	33	4	5	.500	0	3.36
	YEAR		34	883	34	0	0	0	201.1	211	6	77	6	4	97	17	10	2	2	99	86	8	13	.381	0	3.84
93	PHI/NL		32	919	32	2	1	0	210.1	214	12	80	2	4	120	14	8	4	0	105	88	12	11	.522	0	3.77
11 YR TOTALS			**279**	**7289**	**263**	**38**	**13**	**8**	**1688.2**	**1676**	**96**	**678**	**33**	**36**	**985**	**89**	**49**	**37**	**12**	**826**	**717**	**93**	**103**	**.474**	**1**	**3.82**

Jackson, Michael Ray "Mike" — BR/TR — b.12/22/64   PHI84* S2/44

YR	TM/LG	CL	G	TBF	GS	CG	SHO	GF	IP	H	HR	BB	IBB	HB	SO	SH	SF	WP	BK	R	ER	W	L	PCT	SV	ERA
84	SPA/SAL	A	14	352	14	0	0	0	80.2	53	8	50	0	7	77	3	1	4	1	35	24	7	2	.778	0	2.68
85	PEN/CAR	A+	31	554	18	0	0	0	125.1	127	11	53	1	5	96	2	4	6	7	71	64	7	9	.438	1	4.60
86	REA/EAS	AA	30	174	0	0	0	23	43.1	25	1	22	2	1	42	0	2	4	1	9	8	2	3	.400	6	1.66
	POR/PCL	AAA	17	100	0	0	0	10	22.2	18	2	13	4	1	23	2	1	5	0	8	8	3	1	.750	3	3.18
	PHI/NL		9	54	0	0	0	4	13.1	12	2	4	1	2	3	0	0	0	0	5	5	0	0	.000	0	3.38
87	MAI/INT	AAA	2	46	2	0	0	0	11.0	9	0	5	1	0	13	1	0	2	1	2	1	1	0	1.000	0	0.82
	PHI/NL		55	468	0	0	0	22	109.1	88	16	56	6	3	93	3	4	6	6	55	51	3	10	.231	1	4.20
88	SEA/AL		62	412	0	0	0	29	99.1	74	10	43	10	2	76	3	10	6	6	37	29	6	5	.545	4	2.63
89	SEA/AL		65	431	0	0	0	27	99.1	81	4	54	6	4	94	6	7	4	5	43	35	4	6	.400	7	3.17
90	SEA/AL		63	338	0	0	0	28	77.1	64	8	44	12	2	69	8	5	9	2	42	39	5	7	.417	3	4.54
91	SEA/AL		72	363	0	0	0	35	88.2	64	11	34	11	6	74	4	0	7	2	35	32	7	7	.500	14	3.25
92	SF/NL		67	346	0	0	0	24	82.0	76	4	33	10	4	80	5	2	6	1	35	34	6	6	.500	2	3.73
93	SF/NL		*81	317	0	0	0	17	77.1	58	7	24	11	2	70	4	2	6	2	28	26	6	6	.500	1	3.03
8 YR TOTALS			**474**	**2729**	**7**	**0**	**0**	**172**	**646.2**	**517**	**63**	**292**	**62**	**28**	**559**	**33**	**25**	**28**	**20**	**280**	**251**	**37**	**47**	**.440**	**32**	**3.49**

Jean, Domingo — BR/TR — b.1/9/69   CHA 5/8/89

YR	TM/LG	CL	G	TBF	GS	CG	SHO	GF	IP	H	HR	BB	IBB	HB	SO	SH	SF	WP	BK	R	ER	W	L	PCT	SV	ERA
90	WS/GCL	R	13	311	13	1	0	0	78.2	55	1	16	0	6	65	0	0	10	2	32	20	2	5	.286	0	2.29
91	SB/MID	A	25	680	25	2	0	0	158.0	121	7	65	0	10	141	4	7	18	5	75	58	12	8	.600	0	3.30
92	FL/FSL	A+	23	637	25	5	1	0	158.2	118	3	49	1	6	172	7	4	4	1	57	46	6	11	.353	0	2.61
	ALB/EAS	AA	1	17	1	0	0	0	4.0	3	0	1	0	0	5	0	0	0	0	2	1	0	0	.000	0	2.25
93	ALB/EAS	AA	11	257	11	1	0	0	61.0	42	4	33	0	4	41	1	1	4	0	24	17	5	3	.625	0	2.51
	CMB/INT	AAA	7	180	7	1	0	0	44.2	40	2	13	1	2	39	0	2	3	0	15	14	2	2	.500	0	2.82
	PW/CAR	A+	1	6	1	0	0	0	1.2	1	0	1	0	0	1	0	0	0	0	0	0	0	0	.000	0	0.00
	NY/AL		10	176	0	1	0	1	40.1	37	7	19	1	0	20	0	1	1	0	20	20	1	1	.500	0	4.46

Jimenez, Miguel Anthony — BR/TR — b.8/19/69   OAK91 14/333

YR	TM/LG	CL	G	TBF	GS	CG	SHO	GF	IP	H	HR	BB	IBB	HB	SO	SH	SF	WP	BK	R	ER	W	L	PCT	SV	ERA
91	SO/NWL	A-	10	159	9	0	0	0	34.2	22	0	34	0	2	39	0	0	6	6	21	12	0	2	.000	0	3.12
92	MAD/MID	A	26	514	19	2	1	0	120.1	78	3	78	1	8	135	2	2	12	14	48	39	7	7	.500	0	2.92
	HUN/SOU	AA	1	19	1	0	0	0	5.0	3	1	3	0	0	8	0	0	0	0	1	1	1	0	1.000	0	1.80
93	HUN/SOU	AA	20	476	19	0	0	0	107.0	92	10	64	0	4	105	2	1	6	2	49	35	10	6	.625	0	2.94
	TAC/PCL	AAA	8	164	8	0	0	0	37.2	32	4	24	0	1	34	2	1	3	0	23	20	2	3	.400	0	4.78
	OAK/AL		5	120	4	0	0	0	27.0	27	5	16	0	1	13	0	0	0	0	12	12	1	0	1.000	0	4.00

Johnson, David Wayne "Dave" — BR/TR — b.10/24/59   PIT 6/10/82

YR	TM/LG	CL	G	TBF	GS	CG	SHO	GF	IP	H	HR	BB	IBB	HB	SO	SH	SF	WP	BK	R	ER	W	L	PCT	SV	ERA
84	PW/CAR	A+	13	348	13	3	1	0	88.1	60	2	35	0	1	48	3	1	3	0	22	13	7	5	.583	0	1.32
	NAS/EAS	AA	12	366	12	4	0	0	83.2	95	2	31	1	3	47	1	4	7	1	52	45	1	8	.111	0	4.84
85	NAS/EAS	AA	34	624	18	4	1	9	153.0	129	9	45	1	2	84	11	2	6	0	66	53	6	9	.400	2	3.12
86	HAW/PCL	AAA	22	624	22	6	1	0	150.1	150	6	35	0	3	71	8	7	0	0	68	53	8	7	.533	0	3.17
87	PIT/NL		5	31	0	0	0	3	6.1	13	1	2	0	0	4	0	0	0	0	7	7	0	0	.000	0	9.95
	VAN/PCL	AAA	23	650	22	9	2	1	153.2	133	9	68	0	10	76	7	4	8	3	74	60	8	10	.444	0	3.51
88	BUF/AMA	AAA	29	829	29	9	2	0	192.1	213	6	55	2	2	90	6	7	5	7	93	75	15	12	.556	0	3.51
89	ROC/INT	AAA	18	444	14	2	0	2	105.0	104	4	31	2	4	60	3	3	4	1	45	38	7	6	.538	1	3.26
	BAL/AL		14	378	14	0	0	0	89.1	90	11	28	1	4	26	3	3	0	0	44	42	4	7	.364	0	4.23
90	BAL/AL		30	758	29	3	0	0	180.0	196	30	43	2	3	68	5	7	1	2	83	82	13	9	.591	0	4.10
91	HAG/EAS	AA	3	68	3	0	0	0	18.0	13	0	3	0	0	8	1	0	1	0	3	2	3	0	1.000	0	1.00
	ROC/INT	AAA	2	56	2	0	0	0	13.0	18	1	5	0	0	8	1	2	1	0	7	6	0	1	.000	0	4.15
	BAL/AL		22	393	14	0	0	4	84.0	127	18	24	3	4	38	0	1	0	0	68	66	4	8	.333	0	7.07
92	EDM/PCL	AAA	1	16	1	0	0	0	2.0	8	0	1	0	1	1	0	0	0	0	6	5	0	0	.000	0	22.50
	TOL/INT	AAA	25	223	5	1	0	11	52.2	60	4	17	1	1	29	0	4	2	0	27	25	4	4	.500	3	4.27
93	TOL/INT	AAA	9	60	0	0	0	1	17.1	6	0	5	1	0	8	2	0	0	0	0	0	1	0	1.000	0	0.00
	DET/AL		6	46	0	0	0	2	8.1	13	3	5	1	2	7	0	1	1	0	13	12	1	1	.500	0	12.96
5 YR TOTALS			**77**	**1606**	**57**	**7**	**0**	**9**	**368.0**	**439**	**63**	**102**	**7**	**13**	**143**	**8**	**12**	**2**	**4**	**215**	**209**	**22**	**25**	**.468**	**0**	**5.11**

Johnson, Randall David "Randy" — BR/TL — b.9/10/63   MON85 2/36

YR	TM/LG	CL	G	TBF	GS	CG	SHO	GF	IP	H	HR	BB	IBB	HB	SO	SH	SF	WP	BK	R	ER	W	L	PCT	SV	ERA
85	JAM/NYP	A-	8	130	8	0	0	0	27.1	29	2	24	0	0	21	1	4	3	1	22	18	0	3	.000	0	5.93
86	WPB/FSL	A+	26	535	26	2	1	0	119.2	89	3	94	0	6	133	10	4	13	4	49	42	8	7	.533	0	3.16
87	JAC/SOU	AA	25	629	24	0	0	0	140.0	100	10	128	0	9	163	1	1	12	2	63	58	11	8	.579	0	3.73
88	IND/AMA	AAA	20	489	19	0	0	0	113.1	85	6	72	0	3	111	4	3	8	20	52	41	8	7	.533	0	3.26
	MON/NL		4	109	4	1	0	0	26.0	23	3	7	0	0	25	0	0	0	0	8	7	3	0	1.000	0	2.42
89	MON/NL		7	143	6	0	0	1	29.2	29	2	26	1	0	26	3	4	2	2	25	22	0	4	.000	0	6.67
	IND/AMA	AAA	3	77	3	0	0	0	18.0	13	0	9	0	1	17	0	0	0	0	5	4	1	1	.500	0	2.00
	SEA/AL		22	572	22	2	0	0	131.0	118	11	70	1	3	104	7	9	5	5	75	64	7	9	.438	0	4.40
	YEAR		29	715	28	2	0	1	160.2	147	13	96	2	3	130	10	13	7	7	100	86	7	13	.350	0	4.82
90	SEA/AL		33	944	33	5	2	0	219.2	174	26	120	2	5	194	7	7	5	3	103	89	14	11	.560	0	3.65
91	SEA/AL		33	889	33	2	1	0	201.1	151	15	152	0	12	228	9	8	12	2	96	89	13	10	.565	0	3.98
92	SEA/AL		31	922	31	6	2	0	210.1	154	13	144	1	18	*241	3	8	13	1	104	88	12	14	.462	0	3.77
93	SEA/AL		35	1043	34	10	3	1	255.1	185	22	99	1	16	*308	8	7	8	2	97	92	19	8	.704	1	3.24
6 YR TOTALS			**165**	**4622**	**163**	**26**	**8**	**2**	**1073.1**	**834**	**92**	**618**	**6**	**54**	**1126**	**37**	**42**	**47**	**14**	**508**	**451**	**68**	**56**	**.548**	**1**	**3.78**

Johnson, William Jeffrey "Jeff" — BR/TL — b.8/4/66   NYA88 3/157

YR	TM/LG	CL	G	TBF	GS	CG	SHO	GF	IP	H	HR	BB	IBB	HB	SO	SH	SF	WP	BK	R	ER	W	L	PCT	SV	ERA
88	ONE/NYP	A-	14	371	14	0	0	0	87.2	67	2	39	0	2	91	3	3	3	2	35	29	6	1	.857	0	2.98
89	PW/CAR	A+	25	578	24	0	0	0	138.2	125	7	55	1	0	99	8	2	14	2	59	45	4	10	.286	0	2.92
90	FL/FSL	A+	17	439	17	1	0	0	103.2	101	2	25	0	3	84	5	2	5	2	55	42	6	8	.429	0	3.65
	ALB/EAS	AA	9	239	9	3	1	0	60.2	44	0	15	0	2	41	2	0	1	0	14	11	4	3	.571	0	1.63
91	CMB/INT	AAA	10	261	10	0	0	0	62.0	58	1	25	0	1	40	4	1	1	3	27	18	4	0	1.000	0	2.61
	NY/AL		23	562	23	0	0	0	127.0	156	15	33	1	6	62	7	4	5	1	89	84	6	11	.353	0	5.95
92	CMB/INT	AAA	11	229	11	0	0	0	58.0	41	0	18	0	2	38	2	3	3	0	15	14	2	1	.667	0	2.17
	NY/AL		13	245	8	0	0	3	52.2	71	4	23	0	4	22	1	1	2	1	44	39	2	3	.400	0	6.66
93	NY/AL		2	22	2	0	0	0	2.2	12	1	2	0	0	1	0	0	2	0	10	9	0	0	.000	0	30.38
	CMB/INT	AAA	19	500	17	3	1	0	114.2	125	7	47	2	5	59	6	2	6	1	55	44	7	6	.538	0	3.45
3 YR TOTALS			**38**	**829**	**33**	**0**	**0**	**3**	**182.1**	**239**	**20**	**58**	**1**	**8**	**76**	**6**	**6**	**6**	**1**	**143**	**132**	**8**	**16**	**.333**	**0**	**6.52**

Johnston, Joel Raymond — BR/TR — b.3/8/67   KC88 3/75

YR	TM/LG	CL	G	TBF	GS	CG	SHO	GF	IP	H	HR	BB	IBB	HB	SO	SH	SF	WP	BK	R	ER	W	L	PCT	SV	ERA
88	EUG/NWL	A-	14	295	14	0	0	0	64.0	64	1	34	0	7	64	4	3	7	6	49	37	4	7	.364	0	5.20
89	BC/FSL	A+	26	586	26	0	0	0	131.2	135	6	63	2	11	76	2	6	8	5	84	72	9	4	.692	0	4.92
90	MEM/SOU	AA	4	40	3	0	0	1	6.2	5	1	16	0	0	6	0	0	3	0	9	5	0	0	.000	0	6.75
	BC/FSL	A+	31	251	7	1	0	18	55.1	36	3	49	0	3	60	6	3	6	1	37	30	2	4	.333	7	4.88
	OMA/AMA	AAA	2	9	0	0	0	0	3.0	1	0	1	0	0	3	0	0	0	0	0	0	0	0	.000	0	0.00
91	OMA/AMA	AAA	47	318	0	0	0	27	74.1	60	12	42	2	1	63	4	0	6	0	43	43	4	7	.364	8	5.21
	KC/AL		13	85	0	0	0	1	22.1	9	0	9	3	0	21	1	1	1	0	1	1	1	0	1.000	0	0.40
92	KC/AL		5	13	0	0	0	1	2.2	3	2	2	0	0	0	1	0	1	0	4	4	0	0	.000	0	13.50
	OMA/AMA	AAA	42	342	0	0	0	22	74.2	80	9	45	2	4	48	5	5	3	0	54	53	5	2	.714	0	6.39
93	BUF/AMA	AAA	26	150	0	0	0	14	31.1	30	5	25	2	3	26	4	3	5	0	28	27	1	3	.250	1	7.76
	PIT/NL		33	210	0	0	0	16	53.1	38	7	19	5	0	31	4	0	1	0	20	20	2	4	.333	2	3.38
3 YR TOTALS			**51**	**308**	**0**	**0**	**0**	**18**	**78.1**	**50**	**9**	**30**	**8**	**0**	**52**	**5**	**0**	**2**	**0**	**25**	**25**	**3**	**4**	**.429**	**2**	**2.87**

Johnstone, John William — BR/TR — b.11/25/68
NYN87 21/524

YR	TM/LG	CL	G	TBF	GS	CG	SHO	GF	IP	H	HR	BB	IBB	HB	SO	SH	SF	WP	BK	R	ER	W	L	PCT	SV	ERA
87	KIN/APP	R+	17	144	1	0	0	4	29.0	42	3	20	0	0	21	0	3	4	1	28	24	1	1	.500	0	7.45
88	MET/GCL	R	12	314	12	3	0	0	74.0	65	4	25	0	4	57	1	3	5	1	29	22	3	4	.429	0	2.68
89	PIT/NYP	A-	15	444	15	2	1	0	104.0	101	4	28	1	3	60	1	3	4	1	47	32	11	2	.846	0	2.77
90	SL/FSL	A+	25	708	25	9	3	0	172.2	145	3	60	1	5	120	4	5	16	2	53	43	15	6	.714	0	2.24
91	WIL/EAS	AA	27	720	27	2	0	0	165.1	159	5	79	1	5	100	7	6	8	0	94	73	7	9	.438	0	3.97
92	BIN/EAS	AA	24	615	24	2	0	0	149.1	132	8	36	0	9	121	7	4	3	0	66	62	7	7	.500	0	3.74
93	EDM/PCL	AAA	30	645	21	1	0	6	144.1	167	16	59	2	6	126	5	8	9	2	95	83	4	15	.211	4	5.18
	FLO/NL		7	54	0	0	0	3	10.2	16	1	7	0	0	5	0	0	1	0	8	7	0	2	.000	0	5.91

Jones, Barry Louis — BR/TR — b.2/15/63
PIT84 3/69

YR	TM/LG	CL	G	TBF	GS	CG	SHO	GF	IP	H	HR	BB	IBB	HB	SO	SH	SF	WP	BK	R	ER	W	L	PCT	SV	ERA
84	WAT/NYP	A-	14	376	14	2	1	0	86.2	75	4	49	0	4	61	1	2	8	1	41	33	6	3	.667	0	3.43
85	PW/CAR	A+	28	154	0	0	0	23	37.1	26	0	19	3	0	42	6	0	9	0	7	5	3	2	.600	10	1.21
	NAS/EAS	AA	23	111	0	0	0	20	29.0	19	1	10	0	0	24	2	1	4	0	6	5	3	2	.600	12	1.55
	HAW/PCL	AAA	1	0	0	0	0	1	3.0	5	0	1	0	0	2	0	0	0	0	5	3	0	0	.000	0	9.00
86	HAW/PCL	AAA	35	203	0	0	0	32	48.0	41	3	20	4	2	28	5	1	0	0	20	19	3	6	.333	7	3.56
	PIT/NL		26	159	0	0	0	10	37.1	29	3	21	2	0	29	2	1	2	0	16	12	3	4	.429	3	2.89
87	VAN/PCL	AAA	20	112	0	0	0	20	25.1	21	2	14	1	0	27	0	2	0	0	9	9	1	2	.333	11	3.20
	PIT/NL		32	203	0	0	0	10	43.1	55	6	23	6	0	28	3	2	3	0	34	27	2	4	.333	1	5.61
88	PIT/NL		42	241	0	0	0	15	56.1	57	3	21	6	1	31	5	4	7	1	21	19	1	1	.500	2	3.04
	CHI/AL		17	106	0	0	0	10	26.0	15	3	17	1	0	17	0	1	6	1	7	7	2	2	.500	1	2.42
	YEAR		59	347	0	0	0	25	82.1	72	6	38	7	1	48	5	5	13	2	28	26	3	3	.500	3	2.84
89	WS/GCL	R	7	70	4	0	0	2	18.1	12	0	5	0	1	14	0	0	0	0	7	3	0	1	.000	1	1.47
	SB/MID	A	3	17	0	0	0	1	3.2	6	0	0	0	0	2	1	0	0	0	3	2	0	0	.000	0	4.91
	CHI/AL		22	121	0	0	0	8	30.1	22	2	17	4	2	17	4	2	1	0	12	8	3	2	.600	1	2.37
90	CHI/AL		65	310	0	0	0	9	74.0	62	2	33	7	1	45	7	5	4	1	20	19	11	4	.733	1	2.31
91	MON/NL		*77	353	0	0	0	46	88.2	76	8	33	8	1	46	7	3	1	1	35	33	4	9	.308	13	3.35
92	PHI/NL		44	243	0	0	0	10	54.1	65	3	24	4	2	19	2	1	5	0	30	28	5	6	.455	0	4.64
	NY/NL		17	76	0	0	0	7	15.1	20	0	11	3	0	11	1	2	0	0	16	16	2	0	1.000	1	9.39
	YEAR		61	319	0	0	0	17	69.2	85	3	35	7	2	30	3	3	2	0	46	44	7	6	.538	1	5.68
93	NAS/AMA	AAA	7	70	0	0	0	2	17.1	16	3	3	0	0	7	1	0	0	0	5	5	0	0	.000	2	2.60
	CHI/AL		6	38	0	0	0	1	7.1	14	2	3	0	0	7	1	0	0	0	8	7	0	1	.000	0	8.59
8 YR TOTALS			348	1850	0	0	0	126	433.0	415	32	194	37	6	250	32	21	22	6	199	176	33	33	.500	23	3.66

Jones, Douglas Reid "Doug" — BR/TR — b.6/24/57
MIL78* 3/59

YR	TM/LG	CL	G	TBF	GS	CG	SHO	GF	IP	H	HR	BB	IBB	HB	SO	SH	SF	WP	BK	R	ER	W	L	PCT	SV	ERA
82	MIL/AL		4	14	0	0	0	2	2.2	5	1	0	0	1	1	0	0	0	0	3	3	0	0	.000	0	10.13
84	VAN/PCL	AAA	3	0	0	0	0	0	8.0	9	3	3	0	1	2	0	0	2	0	9	9	1	0	1.000	0	10.13
	EP/TEX	AA	16	479	16	7	0	0	109.1	120	12	35	2	4	62	6	3	3	0	61	52	6	8	.429	0	4.28
85	WAT/EAS	AA	39	506	1	0	0	25	116.0	123	11	36	8	3	113	5	4	0	0	59	47	9	4	.692	7	3.65
86	MAI/INT	AAA	43	472	3	0	0	21	116.1	105	6	27	5	0	98	4	1	4	0	35	27	5	6	.455	9	2.09
	CLE/AL		11	79	0	0	0	5	18.0	18	0	6	1	1	12	1	1	1	0	5	5	1	0	1.000	1	2.50
87	BUF/AMA	AAA	23	240	0	0	0	20	61.2	49	3	12	0	0	61	3	1	4	0	18	14	5	2	.714	7	2.04
	CLE/AL		49	400	0	0	0	29	91.1	101	4	24	5	6	87	5	5	0	0	45	32	6	5	.545	8	3.15
88	CLE/AL		51	338	0	0	0	46	83.1	69	1	16	3	2	72	3	0	2	3	26	21	3	4	.429	37	2.27
89	CLE/AL		59	331	0	0	0	53	80.2	76	4	13	4	1	65	9	4	1	0	25	21	7	10	.412	32	2.34
90	CLE/AL		66	331	0	0	0	64	84.1	66	5	22	4	2	55	2	2	2	0	26	24	5	5	.500	43	2.56
91	CS/PCL	AAA	17	135	2	1	1	14	35.2	30	3	5	0	1	29	4	2	0	0	14	13	2	2	.500	7	3.28
	CLE/AL		36	293	4	0	0	29	63.1	87	7	17	5	0	48	2	2	1	0	42	39	4	8	.333	7	5.54
92	HOU/NL		80	440	0	0	0	70	111.2	96	5	17	5	5	93	9	2	1	0	29	23	11	8	.579	36	1.85
93	HOU/NL		71	381	0	0	0	60	85.1	102	7	21	6	6	66	9	4	3	0	46	43	4	10	.286	26	4.54
9 YR TOTALS			427	2607	4	0	0	358	620.2	620	34	137	33	22	499	39	20	11	5	247	211	41	50	.451	190	3.06

Jones, James Condia "Jimmy" — BR/TR — b.4/20/64
SD82 1/3

YR	TM/LG	CL	G	TBF	GS	CG	SHO	GF	IP	H	HR	BB	IBB	HB	SO	SH	SF	WP	BK	R	ER	W	L	PCT	SV	ERA
82	WW/NWL	A-	14	0	14	0	0	0	78.0	64	4	71	0	1	78	0	0	7	1	49	28	4	6	.400	0	3.23
83	REN/CAL	A+	17	0	17	6	1	0	116.0	96	0	49	0	3	79	0	0	3	0	50	35	7	5	.583	0	2.72
84	BEA/TEX	AA	13	354	13	0	0	0	85.2	63	5	39	0	4	49	7	3	4	0	28	20	7	2	.778	0	2.10
85	BEA/TEX	AA	16	389	16	1	0	0	85.0	84	3	66	3	0	57	3	5	5	5	51	44	7	5	.583	0	4.66
86	LV/PCL	AAA	28	696	27	4	2	0	157.2	168	10	72	0	1	114	6	5	9	0	84	77	9	10	.474	0	4.40
	SD/NL		3	65	3	0	0	0	18.0	10	1	3	0	0	11	1	0	0	0	6	5	2	0	1.000	0	2.50
87	LV/PCL	AAA	4	104	4	1	0	0	24.1	24	1	8	0	0	11	0	0	0	0	16	16	1	0	1.000	0	5.92
	SD/NL		30	639	22	2	1	4	145.2	154	14	54	5	3	51	5	3	2	1	85	67	9	7	.563	0	4.14
88	SD/NL		29	760	29	3	0	0	179.0	192	14	44	3	3	82	11	9	4	1	98	82	9	14	.391	0	4.12
89	CMB/INT	AAA	20	509	20	4	1	0	124.0	110	9	31	1	2	94	8	6	1	0	54	52	8	5	.571	0	3.77
	NY/AL		11	211	6	0	0	0	48.0	56	7	16	1	2	25	1	1	1	0	29	28	2	1	.667	0	5.25
90	CMB/INT	AAA	11	299	11	3	1	0	73.0	46	1	35	1	5	78	1	2	0	0	20	19	5	2	.714	0	2.34
	NY/AL		17	238	7	0	0	0	50.0	72	8	23	0	1	25	1	2	0	0	42	35	2	2	.333	0	6.30
91	HOU/NL		26	593	22	1	1	0	135.1	143	9	51	3	3	88	7	2	4	0	73	66	6	8	.429	0	4.39
92	JAC/TEX	AA	3	83	3	1	0	0	18.0	18	1	3	0	0	20	0	1	0	0	9	5	1	2	.333	0	2.50
	HOU/NL		25	579	23	0	0	0	139.1	135	13	39	3	5	69	7	4	3	0	64	63	10	6	.625	0	4.07
93	OTT/INT	AAA	3	59	3	0	0	0	15.0	10	0	4	0	0	12	1	0	1	0	11	9	1	0	1.000	0	1.20
	MON/NL		12	175	6	0	0	3	39.2	47	6	9	0	0	21	1	1	2	0	34	28	4	1	.800	0	6.35
8 YR TOTALS			153	3260	118	7	3	20	755.0	809	72	239	12	19	376	34	25	20	5	431	374	43	39	.524	0	4.46

Jones, Robert Joseph "Bobby" — BR/TR — b.2/10/70   NYN91 2/36

YR	TM/LG	CL	G	TBF	GS	CG	SHO	GF	IP	H	HR	BB	IBB	HB	SO	SH	SF	WP	BK	R	ER	W	L	PCT	SV	ERA
91	COL/SAL	A	5	98	5	0	0	0	24.1	20	2	3	0	2	35	1	0	0	4	5	5	3	1	.750	0	1.85
92	BIN/EAS	AA	24	625	24	4	4	0	158.0	118	5	43	0	8	143	4	6	3	1	40	33	12	4	.750	0	1.88
93	NOR/INT	AAA	24	671	24	6	3	0	166.0	149	9	32	2	11	126	3	5	11	0	72	67	12	10	.545	0	3.63
	NY/NL		9	265	9	0	0	0	61.2	61	6	22	3	2	35	5	3	1	0	35	25	2	4	.333	0	3.65

Jones, Todd Barton Givin — BL/TR — b.4/24/68   HOU89 2/27

YR	TM/LG	CL	G	TBF	GS	CG	SHO	GF	IP	H	HR	BB	IBB	HB	SO	SH	SF	WP	BK	R	ER	W	L	PCT	SV	ERA
89	AUB/NYP	A-	11	241	9	1	0	1	49.2	47	2	42	1	2	71	1	0	9	1	39	30	2	3	.400	0	5.44
90	OSC/FSL	A+	27	678	27	1	0	0	151.1	124	2	109	1	3	106	7	2	16	3	81	59	12	10	.545	0	3.51
91	OSC/FSL	A+	14	311	14	0	0	0	72.1	69	2	35	0	3	51	1	2	4	0	38	35	4	4	.500	0	4.35
	JAC/TEX	AA	10	258	10	0	0	0	55.1	51	2	39	1	4	37	2	1	6	2	37	30	4	3	.571	0	4.88
92	JAC/TEX	AA	61	295	0	0	0	48	66.0	52	3	44	3	2	60	5	0	5	1	28	23	3	7	.300	25	3.14
	TUC/PCL	AAA	3	23	0	0	0	2	4.0	1	0	10	1	0	4	0	0	1	0	2	2	0	1	.000	0	4.50
93	TUC/PCL	AAA	41	220	0	0	0	28	48.2	49	5	31	2	0	45	3	1	5	0	26	24	4	2	.667	12	4.44
	HOU/NL		27	150	0	0	0	8	37.1	28	4	15	2	1	25	2	1	1	1	14	13	1	2	.333	2	3.13

Juden, Jeffrey Daniel "Jeff" — BR/TR — b.1/19/71   HOU89 1/12

YR	TM/LG	CL	G	TBF	GS	CG	SHO	GF	IP	H	HR	BB	IBB	HB	SO	SH	SF	WP	BK	R	ER	W	L	PCT	SV	ERA
89	AST/GCL	R	9	177	8	0	0	0	39.2	33	0	17	0	3	49	1	3	7	2	21	15	1	4	.200	0	3.40
90	OSC/FSL	A+	15	390	15	2	0	0	91.0	72	2	42	0	5	85	3	1	7	4	37	23	10	1	.909	0	2.27
	CMB/SOU	AA	11	250	11	0	0	0	52.0	55	2	42	2	4	40	1	1	9	2	36	31	1	3	.250	0	5.37
91	JAC/TEX	AA	16	408	16	0	0	0	95.2	84	4	44	0	3	75	8	4	6	2	43	33	6	3	.667	0	3.10
	TUC/PCL	AAA	10	245	10	0	0	0	56.2	56	2	25	0	0	51	4	3	7	0	28	20	3	2	.600	0	3.18
	HOU/NL		4	81	3	0	0	0	18.0	19	3	7	1	0	11	2	3	0	1	14	12	0	2	.000	0	6.00
92	TUC/PCL	AAA	26	655	26	0	0	0	147.0	149	11	71	1	7	120	12	7	12	7	84	66	9	10	.474	0	4.04
93	TUC/PCL	AAA	27	755	27	0	0	0	169.0	174	8	76	0	9	156	5	5	15	0	102	87	11	6	.647	0	4.63
	HOU/NL		2	23	0	0	0	1	5.0	4	1	4	1	0	7	0	1	0	0	3	3	0	1	.000	0	5.40
2 YR TOTALS			**6**	**104**	**3**	**0**	**0**	**1**	**23.0**	**23**	**4**	**11**	**2**	**0**	**18**	**2**	**4**	**0**	**1**	**17**	**15**	**0**	**3**	**.000**	**0**	**5.87**

Kaiser, Jeffrey Patrick "Jeff" — BR/TL — b.7/24/60   OAK82 9/262

YR	TM/LG	CL	G	TBF	GS	CG	SHO	GF	IP	H	HR	BB	IBB	HB	SO	SH	SF	WP	BK	R	ER	W	L	PCT	SV	ERA
82	MED/NWL	A-	15	0	15	1	0	0	78.0	91	5	57	0	2	69	0	0	12	1	56	46	8	1	.889	0	5.31
83	MOD/CAL	A+	25	0	25	4	0	0	164.0	160	4	80	0	5	102	0	0	9	0	84	70	12	9	.571	0	3.84
84	ALB/EAS	AA	7	187	7	1	1	0	47.2	36	0	15	0	1	20	3	1	1	1	11	10	5	1	.833	0	1.89
	TAC/PCL	AAA	14	0	12	0	0	0	74.2	81	4	28	1	1	38	0	0	1	1	52	38	4	7	.364	0	4.58
85	TAC/PCL	AAA	27	0	4	0	0	11	46.1	33	3	18	4	0	36	0	0	2	1	10	9	4	2	.667	5	1.75
	OAK/AL		15	97	0	0	0	4	16.2	25	6	20	2	1	10	1	2	2	0	32	27	0	0	.000	0	14.58
86	TAC/PCL	AAA	34	498	18	2	1	10	110.2	123	5	52	2	5	63	2	4	6	5	70	53	4	4	.500	2	4.31
87	BUF/AMA	AAA	22	333	8	0	0	5	71.1	87	9	32	1	3	53	2	2	2	2	52	41	5	3	.625	1	5.17
	CLE/AL		2	18	0	0	0	0	3.1	4	1	3	0	1	2	0	0	0	0	6	6	0	0	.000	0	16.20
88	CLE/AL		3	11	0	0	0	0	2.2	2	0	1	0	0	0	0	0	0	0	0	0	0	0	.000	0	0.00
	CS/PCL	AAA	36	229	0	0	0	21	53.0	56	5	19	2	1	47	4	3	1	0	23	22	3	2	.600	6	3.74
89	CS/PCL	AAA	31	213	1	0	0	12	45.1	64	1	18	1	1	46	4	0	3	1	29	22	3	6	.333	3	4.37
	CLE/AL		6	22	0	0	0	1	3.2	5	1	5	0	0	4	0	1	1	0	5	3	0	0	.000	0	7.36
90	CLE/AL		5	60	0	0	0	0	12.2	16	2	7	1	0	9	0	1	0	0	5	5	0	0	.000	0	3.55
	CS/PCL	AAA	25	182	0	0	0	11	43.0	36	3	22	2	2	46	0	3	5	1	16	14	2	2	.500	3	2.93
91	DEN/AMA	AAA	8	85	1	0	0	0	18.2	16	0	13	1	1	12	2	1	1	0	9	8	0	1	.000	0	3.86
	TOL/INT	AAA	16	145	3	0	0	6	34.2	35	3	11	0	1	28	1	0	5	2	9	8	3	0	1.000	1	2.08
	DET/AL		10	26	0	0	0	2	5.0	6	1	5	2	0	4	0	0	0	0	5	5	0	0	.000	2	9.00
92	TOL/INT	AAA	28	129	0	0	0	15	30.2	25	2	12	1	0	33	1	1	0	1	12	8	1	0	1.000	5	2.35
93	IND/AMA	AAA	1	3	0	0	0	0	1.0	0	0	0	0	0	2	0	0	0	0	0	0	0	0	.000	0	0.00
	NOR/INT	AAA	21	95	0	0	0	15	22.1	23	4	6	0	3	23	0	1	1	0	15	14	1	1	.500	9	5.64
	CIN/NL		3	16	0	0	0	1	3.1	4	0	2	1	0	4	0	0	1	0	1	1	0	0	.000	0	2.70
	NY/NL		6	21	0	0	0	2	4.2	6	1	3	0	0	5	0	0	1	0	6	6	0	0	.000	0	11.57
	YEAR		9	37	0	0	0	3	8.0	10	1	5	1	0	9	0	0	2	0	7	7	0	0	.000	0	7.87
7 YR TOTALS			**50**	**271**	**0**	**0**	**0**	**13**	**52.0**	**68**	**12**	**46**	**6**	**2**	**38**	**3**	**6**	**3**	**0**	**60**	**53**	**0**	**2**	**.000**	**2**	**9.17**

Kamieniecki, Scott Andrew — BR/TR — b.4/19/64   NYA86 15/366

YR	TM/LG	CL	G	TBF	GS	CG	SHO	GF	IP	H	HR	BB	IBB	HB	SO	SH	SF	WP	BK	R	ER	W	L	PCT	SV	ERA
87	PW/CAR	A+	19	499	19	1	0	0	112.1	91	7	78	3	5	84	1	2	9	2	61	52	9	5	.643	0	4.17
	ALB/EAS	AA	10	176	7	0	0	1	37.0	41	0	33	3	1	19	5	0	3	1	25	22	1	3	.250	0	5.35
88	PW/CAR	A+	15	451	15	7	2	0	100.1	115	3	50	1	2	72	2	0	10	1	62	49	6	7	.462	0	4.40
	FL/FSL	A+	12	329	11	1	1	0	77.0	71	0	40	1	2	51	1	2	7	0	36	31	3	6	.333	0	3.62
89	ALB/EAS	AA	24	636	23	6	3	1	151.0	142	13	57	1	2	140	1	3	5	0	67	62	10	9	.526	1	3.70
90	ALB/EAS	AA	22	562	21	3	1	1	132.0	113	5	61	0	0	99	6	6	4	1	55	47	10	9	.526	0	3.20
91	CMB/INT	AAA	11	308	11	3	1	0	76.1	61	2	20	0	3	58	3	2	3	0	25	20	6	3	.667	0	2.36
	NY/AL		9	239	9	0	0	0	55.1	54	8	22	1	3	34	2	1	0	0	24	24	4	4	.500	0	3.90
92	FL/FSL	A+	1	28	1	1	0	0	7.0	8	0	0	0	0	3	0	0	0	0	1	1	1	0	1.000	0	1.29
	CMB/INT	AAA	2	50	2	0	0	0	13.0	6	1	4	0	0	12	0	0	0	0	1	1	1	0	1.000	0	0.69
	NY/AL		28	804	28	0	0	0	188.0	193	13	74	9	5	88	3	5	3	0	100	91	6	14	.300	0	4.36
93	CMB/INT	AAA	1	22	1	0	0	0	6.0	5	0	0	0	0	3	0	0	0	0	1	1	1	0	1.000	0	1.50
	NY/AL		30	659	20	2	2	0	154.1	163	17	59	7	3	72	5	1	4	0	73	70	10	7	.588	1	4.08
3 YR TOTALS			**67**	**1702**	**57**	**6**	**0**	**4**	**397.2**	**410**	**38**	**155**	**17**	**11**	**194**	**8**	**11**	**12**	**1**	**197**	**185**	**20**	**25**	**.444**	**1**	**4.19**

Karsay, Steven Andrew "Steve" — BR/TR — b.3/24/72   TOR90 1/22

YR	TM/LG	CL	G	TBF	GS	CG	SHO	GF	IP	H	HR	BB	IBB	HB	SO	SH	SF	WP	BK	R	ER	W	L	PCT	SV	ERA
90	SC/NYP	A-	5	90	5	0	0	0	22.2	11	0	12	0	0	25	0	0	0	3	4	2	1	1	.500	0	0.79
91	MB/SAL	A	20	460	20	0	0	0	110.2	96	7	48	0	5	100	4	3	8	5	58	44	4	9	.308	0	3.58
92	DUN/FSL	A+	16	334	16	3	2	0	85.2	56	6	29	0	4	87	1	1	2	3	32	26	6	3	.667	0	2.73
93	KNO/SOU	AA	19	434	18	1	0	0	104.0	98	9	32	1	6	100	3	3	5	2	42	39	8	4	.667	0	3.38
	HUN/SOU	AA	2	56	2	0	0	0	14.0	13	2	3	0	1	22	1	0	0	0	8	8	0	0	.000	0	5.14
	OAK/AL		8	210	8	0	0	0	49.0	49	4	16	1	2	33	0	2	1	0	23	22	3	3	.500	0	4.04

Key, James Edward "Jimmy" — BR/TL — b.4/22/61   TOR82 3/56

YR	TM/LG	CL	G	TBF	GS	CG	SHO	GF	IP	H	HR	BB	IBB	HB	SO	SH	SF	WP	BK	R	ER	W	L	PCT	SV	ERA
84	TOR/AL		63	285	0	0	0	24	62.0	70	8	32	8	1	44	6	1	3	1	37	32	4	5	.444	10	4.65
85	TOR/AL		35	856	32	3	0	0	212.2	188	22	50	1	2	85	5	5	6	1	77	71	14	6	.700	0	3.00
86	TOR/AL		36	959	35	4	2	0	232.0	222	24	74	1	3	141	10	6	3	0	98	92	14	11	.560	0	3.57
87	TOR/AL		36	1033	36	8	1	0	261.0	210	24	66	6	2	161	11	3	8	5	93	80	17	8	.680	0	*2.76
88	DUN/FSL	A+	4	83	4	0	0	0	21.1	15	0	1	0	0	11	1	0	0	1	2	0	2	0	1.000	0	0.00
	TOR/AL		21	551	21	2	2	0	131.1	127	13	30	2	5	65	4	3	1	0	55	48	12	5	.706	0	3.29
89	TOR/AL		33	886	33	5	1	0	216.0	226	18	27	2	3	118	9	9	4	1	99	93	13	14	.481	0	3.88
90	DUN/FSL	A+	3	77	3	0	0	0	18.0	21	0	3	0	0	14	0	1	1	0	7	5	2	0	1.000	0	2.50
	TOR/AL		27	636	27	0	0	0	154.2	169	20	22	2	1	88	5	6	0	1	79	73	13	7	.650	0	4.25
91	TOR/AL		33	877	33	2	2	0	209.1	207	12	44	3	3	125	10	5	1	0	84	71	16	12	.571	0	3.05
92	TOR/AL		33	900	33	4	2	0	216.2	205	24	59	0	4	117	2	7	5	0	88	85	13	13	.500	0	3.53
93	NY/AL		34	948	34	4	2	0	236.2	219	26	43	1	1	173	6	9	3	0	84	79	18	6	*.750	0	3.00
10 YR TOTALS			**351**	**7931**	**284**	**32**	**12**	**24**	**1932.1**	**1843**	**191**	**447**	**26**	**25**	**1117**	**68**	**54**	**34**	**9**	**794**	**724**	**134**	**87**	**.606**	**10**	**3.37**

Kiefer, Mark Andrew — BR/TR — b.11/13/68   MIL87 22/539

YR	TM/LG	CL	G	TBF	GS	CG	SHO	GF	IP	H	HR	BB	IBB	HB	SO	SH	SF	WP	BK	R	ER	W	L	PCT	SV	ERA
88	HEL/PIO	R+	15	296	9	2	0	4	68.0	76	3	17	0	6	51	3	0	4	3	30	20	4	4	.500	0	2.65
89	BEL/MID	A	30	533	15	7	2	5	131.2	106	4	32	2	8	100	1	4	6	0	44	34	9	6	.600	1	2.32
90	BRE/ARI	R	1	12	0	0	0	0	2.2	3	0	1	0	1	2	0	0	0	0	1	1	0	0	.000	0	3.38
	STO/CAL	A+	11	261	10	0	0	1	60.0	65	5	17	0	8	37	0	1	3	1	23	22	5	2	.714	0	3.30
91	EP/TEX	AA	12	325	12	0	0	0	75.2	62	4	43	2	1	72	2	2	6	0	33	28	7	1	.875	0	3.33
	DEN/AMA	AAA	17	448	17	3	2	0	101.1	104	7	41	0	9	68	4	1	6	0	55	52	9	5	.643	0	4.62
92	DEN/AMA	AAA	27	706	26	1	0	0	162.2	168	25	65	1	9	145	3	4	8	3	95	83	7	13	.350	0	4.59
93	EP/TEX	AA	11	221	11	0	0	0	51.2	48	5	19	0	2	44	1	0	6	3	29	23	3	4	.429	0	4.01
	NO/AMA	AAA	5	126	5	0	0	0	28.1	28	4	17	0	0	23	1	1	4	0	20	16	3	2	.600	0	5.08
	MIL/AL		6	37	0	0	0	0	9.1	3	0	5	0	1	7	1	0	0	0	0	0	0	0	.000	1	0.00

Kiely, John Francis — BR/TR — b.10/4/64   DET 9/7/87

YR	TM/LG	CL	G	TBF	GS	CG	SHO	GF	IP	H	HR	BB	IBB	HB	SO	SH	SF	WP	BK	R	ER	W	L	PCT	SV	ERA
88	BRI/APP	R+	8	53	0	0	0	6	11.2	9	0	7	0	0	14	2	0	2	0	9	8	2	2	.500	1	6.17
89	LAK/FSL	A+	36	267	0	0	0	22	63.2	52	2	27	4	0	56	4	3	1	2	26	17	4	3	.571	8	2.40
90	LON/EAS	AA	46	321	0	0	0	25	76.2	62	2	42	6	2	52	2	4	2	0	17	15	3	0	1.000	12	1.76
91	DET/AL		7	42	0	0	0	3	6.2	13	0	9	2	1	1	1	2	0	0	11	11	0	1	.000	0	14.85
	TOL/INT	AAA	42	301	0	0	0	27	72.0	55	1	35	3	3	60	4	2	2	0	25	17	4	2	.667	6	2.13
92	TOL/INT	AAA	21	125	0	0	0	17	31.2	25	1	9	0	0	31	0	0	1	0	11	10	1	1	.500	9	2.84
	DET/AL		39	231	0	0	0	20	55.0	44	2	28	3	0	18	4	1	3	0	14	13	4	2	.667	0	2.13
93	DET/AL		8	59	0	0	0	5	11.2	13	2	13	5	1	5	1	0	2	0	11	10	0	2	.000	0	7.71
	TOL/INT	AAA	37	261	0	0	0	16	58.0	65	8	25	1	1	48	1	2	3	0	34	25	3	4	.429	4	3.88
3 YR TOTALS			**54**	**332**	**0**	**0**	**0**	**28**	**73.1**	**70**	**4**	**50**	**10**	**2**	**24**	**7**	**4**	**3**	**0**	**36**	**34**	**4**	**5**	**.444**	**0**	**4.17**

Kile, Darryl Andrew — BR/TR — b.12/2/68   HOU87 30/782

YR	TM/LG	CL	G	TBF	GS	CG	SHO	GF	IP	H	HR	BB	IBB	HB	SO	SH	SF	WP	BK	R	ER	W	L	PCT	SV	ERA
88	AST/GCL	R	12	263	12	0	0	0	59.2	48	1	33	0	3	54	3	1	9	8	34	21	5	3	.625	0	3.17
89	CMB/SOU	AA	20	508	20	6	2	0	125.2	74	5	68	1	6	108	3	4	5	6	47	36	11	6	.647	0	2.58
	TUC/PCL	AAA	6	122	6	1	1	0	25.2	33	1	13	0	1	18	0	0	1	1	20	17	2	1	.667	0	5.96
90	TUC/PCL	AAA	26	575	23	1	0	0	123.1	147	16	68	1	5	77	2	5	13	4	97	91	5	10	.333	0	6.64
91	HOU/NL		37	689	22	0	0	5	153.2	144	16	84	4	6	100	9	5	5	4	81	63	7	11	.389	0	3.69
92	TUC/PCL	AAA	9	250	9	0	0	0	56.1	50	3	32	0	3	43	0	2	3	4	31	25	4	1	.800	0	3.99
	HOU/NL		22	554	22	2	0	0	125.1	124	8	63	4	4	90	5	6	3	2	61	55	5	10	.333	0	3.95
93	HOU/NL		32	733	26	4	2	0	171.2	152	12	69	1	15	141	5	7	4	1	73	67	15	8	.652	0	3.51
3 YR TOTALS			**91**	**1976**	**70**	**6**	**2**	**5**	**450.2**	**420**	**36**	**216**	**9**	**25**	**331**	**19**	**18**	**17**	**11**	**215**	**185**	**27**	**29**	**.482**	**0**	**3.69**

Kilgus, Paul Nelson — BL/TL — b.2/2/62   TEX84 43/821

YR	TM/LG	CL	G	TBF	GS	CG	SHO	GF	IP	H	HR	BB	IBB	HB	SO	SH	SF	WP	BK	R	ER	W	L	PCT	SV	ERA
84	TRI/NWL	A-	14	0	14	0	0	0	78.1	87	1	31	0	3	60	0	0	4	0	38	25	7	5	.583	0	2.87
85	SAL/CAR	A+	38	346	0	0	0	19	84.1	69	5	26	2	6	67	0	1	4	1	28	19	3	1	.750	10	2.03
86	TUL/TEX	AA	41	447	7	2	0	24	103.2	102	7	36	5	5	84	3	0	4	3	56	43	3	7	.300	8	3.73
87	OC/AMA	AAA	21	104	0	0	0	17	24.2	23	2	10	3	2	14	0	0	3	0	12	11	2	0	1.000	7	4.01
	TEX/AL		25	385	12	0	0	2	89.1	95	14	31	2	2	42	0	0	0	0	45	41	2	7	.222	0	4.13
88	TEX/AL		32	871	32	5	3	0	203.1	190	18	71	2	10	88	4	4	6	4	105	94	12	15	.444	0	4.16
89	IOW/AMA	AAA	1	37	1	0	0	0	9.0	9	0	2	0	0	5	1	1	2	0	3	3	1	0	1.000	0	3.00
	CHI/NL		35	642	23	0	0	5	145.2	164	9	49	6	5	61	5	4	3	0	90	71	6	10	.375	2	4.39
90	TOR/AL		11	74	0	0	0	0	16.1	19	2	7	1	1	7	2	1	0	0	11	11	0	0	.000	0	6.06
	SYR/INT	AAA	20	516	17	7	1	0	125.2	116	10	39	4	5	75	5	1	4	0	47	41	6	8	.429	0	2.94
91	BAL/AL		38	267	0	0	0	14	62.0	60	8	24	2	3	32	2	4	2	0	38	35	0	2	.000	1	5.08
	ROC/INT	AAA	9	202	6	0	0	2	45.1	58	3	10	0	0	29	0	1	0	0	32	29	2	2	.500	0	5.76
92	LOU/AMA	AAA	27	706	26	4	2	0	168.1	189	11	28	1	5	90	5	9	4	0	90	71	9	8	.529	0	3.80

Kilgus, Paul Nelson (continued)

YR	TM/LG	CL	G	TBF	GS	CG	SHO	GF	IP	H	HR	BB	IBB	HB	SO	SH	SF	WP	BK	R	ER	W	L	PCT	SV	ERA
93	LOU/AMA	AAA	9	275	9	4	1	0	68.0	59	10	19	0	1	54	2	0	3	0	21	20	7	1	.875	0	2.65
	STL/NL		22	109	1	0	0	7	28.2	18	1	8	1	1	21	0	0	0	0	2	2	1	0	1.000	1	0.63
6 YR TOTALS			163	2348	68	5	3	32	545.1	546	52	190	14	22	251	14	15	11	6	291	254	21	34	.382	4	4.19

King, Kevin Ray — BL/TL — b.2/11/69   SEA90 7/188

YR	TM/LG	CL	G	TBF	GS	CG	SHO	GF	IP	H	HR	BB	IBB	HB	SO	SH	SF	WP	BK	R	ER	W	L	PCT	SV	ERA
90	BEL/NWL	A-	6	140	6	0	0	0	32.0	37	3	10	0	0	27	1	0	1	1	18	17	3	2	.600	0	4.78
	PEN/CAR	A+	7	159	7	0	0	0	36.1	42	2	13	0	0	20	2	1	2	3	23	18	4	2	.667	0	4.46
91	PEN/CAR	A+	17	405	17	2	1	0	92.2	99	8	38	0	0	59	5	5	5	2	55	45	6	7	.462	0	4.37
92	SB/CAL	A+	27	744	27	0	0	0	165.2	226	14	55	0	2	101	2	11	10	2	118	98	7	16	.304	0	5.32
93	RIV/CAL	A+	25	184	0	0	0	14	46.0	37	0	20	1	1	46	0	1	3	0	10	10	2	0	1.000	1	3.14
	JAC/SOU	AA	16	116	0	0	0	8	28.2	25	3	7	2	1	13	3	1	3	0	8	8	0	1	.000	1	6.17
	SEA/AL		13	49	0	0	0	3	11.2	9	3	4	1	1	8	3	2	0	0	8	8	0	0	.000	0	6.17

Klink, Joseph Charles "Joe" — BL/TL — b.2/3/62   NYN83 38/801

YR	TM/LG	CL	G	TBF	GS	CG	SHO	GF	IP	H	HR	BB	IBB	HB	SO	SH	SF	WP	BK	R	ER	W	L	PCT	SV	ERA
84	COL/SAL	A	31	172	0	0	0	27	38.2	30	1	28	0	1	49	4	3	5	1	19	15	5	4	.556	11	3.49
85	LYN/CAR	A+	44	221	0	0	0	17	51.2	41	1	26	2	0	59	4	2	5	2	16	13	3	3	.500	5	2.26
86	ORL/SOU	AA	45	297	0	0	0	41	68.0	59	5	37	1	2	63	5	1	1	0	24	19	4	5	.444	11	2.51
87	MIN/AL		12	116	0	0	0	5	23.0	37	4	11	0	0	17	1	1	1	0	18	17	0	1	.000	0	6.65
	POR/PCL	AAA	12	107	0	0	0	7	23.0	25	1	13	1	0	14	1	3	1	0	14	11	0	0	.000	0	4.30
88	HUN/SOU	AA	21	143	0	0	0	12	34.2	25	0	14	1	0	30	0	0	3	0	6	3	1	2	.333	3	0.78
	TAC/PCL	AAA	27	185	0	0	0	15	38.2	48	0	17	1	1	32	5	3	3	6	29	22	2	1	.667	1	5.12
89	TAC/PCL	AAA	6	23	0	0	0	5	6.2	2	0	2	0	1	5	0	0	0	0	0	0	0	0	.000	0	0.00
	HUN/SOU	AA	57	249	0	0	0	53	60.2	46	2	23	0	2	59	3	4	6	5	19	19	4	4	.500	26	2.82
90	OAK/AL		40	165	0	0	0	19	39.2	34	1	18	0	0	19	1	0	3	1	9	9	0	0	.000	1	2.04
91	MOD/CAL	A+	3	19	3	0	0	0	5.0	4	2	1	0	0	5	0	0	0	0	2	2	0	0	.000	0	3.60
	OAK/AL		62	266	0	0	0	10	62.0	60	4	21	5	5	34	8	0	4	0	30	30	10	3	.769	2	4.35
93	FLO/NL		59	168	0	0	0	10	37.2	37	0	24	4	0	22	2	3	1	2	22	21	0	2	.000	0	5.02
4 YR TOTALS			173	715	0	0	0	44	162.1	168	9	74	9	5	92	12	4	9	3	79	77	10	6	.625	3	4.27

Knudsen, Kurt David — BR/TR — b.2/20/67   DET88 9/239

YR	TM/LG	CL	G	TBF	GS	CG	SHO	GF	IP	H	HR	BB	IBB	HB	SO	SH	SF	WP	BK	R	ER	W	L	PCT	SV	ERA
88	BRI/APP	R+	2	14	0	0	0	2	2.1	4	0	1	0	0	0	0	0	0	0	3	0	0	0	.000	0	0.00
	FAY/SAL	A	12	77	0	0	0	5	20.0	8	1	9	1	1	22	2	1	1	1	4	3	3	1	.750	1	1.35
	LAK/FSL	A+	7	39	0	0	0	4	9.1	7	0	7	0	0	6	0	0	0	0	2	1	0	0	.000	0	0.96
89	LAK/FSL	A+	45	225	0	0	0	26	54.1	43	1	22	7	1	68	5	2	2	3	16	13	3	2	.600	10	2.15
90	LAK/FSL	A+	14	253	8	0	0	5	67.0	42	2	22	0	0	70	1	1	5	2	18	17	5	0	1.000	3	2.28
	LON/EAS	AA	15	102	0	0	0	8	26.0	15	1	11	0	2	26	0	1	2	1	6	6	2	1	.667	1	2.08
91	LON/EAS	AA	34	226	0	0	0	18	51.2	42	1	30	2	1	56	0	4	3	0	29	20	2	3	.400	6	3.48
	TOL/INT	AAA	12	79	0	0	0	3	18.1	13	1	10	1	0	20	0	1	0	0	11	3	1	2	.333	1	1.47
92	TOL/INT	AAA	12	82	0	0	0	3	21.2	11	0	6	0	1	19	1	1	1	0	5	5	3	1	.750	1	2.08
	DET/AL		48	313	1	0	0	14	70.2	70	9	41	9	2	51	4	2	5	0	39	36	2	3	.400	5	4.58
93	TOL/INT	AAA	23	136	0	0	0	15	33.1	24	3	11	1	1	39	1	0	2	1	15	14	2	2	.500	6	3.78
	DET/AL		30	171	0	0	0	7	37.2	41	9	16	2	4	29	2	3	2	0	22	20	3	2	.600	2	4.78
2 YR TOTALS			78	484	1	0	0	21	108.1	111	18	57	11	5	80	6	5	7	0	61	56	5	5	.500	7	4.65

Knudson, Mark Richard — BR/TR — b.10/28/60   HOU82 3/69

YR	TM/LG	CL	G	TBF	GS	CG	SHO	GF	IP	H	HR	BB	IBB	HB	SO	SH	SF	WP	BK	R	ER	W	L	PCT	SV	ERA
84	CMB/SOU	AA	14	414	14	3	0	0	101.0	100	2	27	4	0	54	7	2	2	0	32	25	4	5	.444	0	2.23
	TUC/PCL	AAA	13	0	13	1	0	0	84.0	93	6	20	3	1	42	0	0	0	0	41	34	4	6	.400	0	3.64
85	TUC/PCL	AAA	24	0	22	4	2	0	146.0	171	10	37	1	1	68	0	0	0	0	69	65	8	5	.615	0	4.01
	HOU/NL		2	53	2	0	0	0	11.0	21	0	3	0	0	4	1	1	0	0	11	11	0	0	.000	0	9.00
86	HOU/NL		9	191	7	0	0	1	42.2	48	5	15	5	1	20	3	1	1	0	23	20	1	5	.167	0	4.22
	TUC/PCL	AAA	15	401	14	3	1	0	94.0	111	2	21	0	0	55	2	2	3	2	46	41	5	5	.500	0	3.93
	VAN/AMA	AAA	2	54	2	1	0	0	12.2	13	2	5	1	0	8	0	0	0	0	8	8	1	1	.500	0	5.68
	MIL/AL		4	82	1	0	0	1	17.2	22	4	5	1	0	9	0	0	1	0	15	15	0	1	.000	0	7.64
	YEAR		13	273	8	0	0	2	60.1	70	12	20	6	1	29	3	1	2	0	38	35	1	6	.143	0	5.22
87	DEN/AMA	AAA	14	345	14	1	0	0	78.1	89	11	30	0	2	37	3	1	4	1	53	51	7	2	.778	0	5.86
	MIL/AL		15	288	8	1	0	3	62.0	88	7	14	1	0	26	3	5	1	0	46	37	4	4	.500	0	5.37
88	DEN/AMA	AAA	24	677	22	6	0	1	164.1	180	4	33	1	5	66	1	9	6	4	67	62	11	8	.579	0	3.40
	MIL/AL		5	63	0	0	0	3	16.0	17	1	0	0	0	7	0	0	1	0	3	2	0	0	.000	0	1.13
89	MIL/AL		40	499	7	1	0	16	123.2	110	15	29	2	3	47	2	4	1	0	50	46	8	5	.615	0	3.35
90	MIL/AL		30	719	27	4	2	0	168.1	187	14	40	1	5	56	3	9	6	0	84	77	10	9	.526	0	4.12
91	MIL/AL		12	174	7	0	0	3	35.0	54	8	15	0	0	15	2	2	0	1	33	31	1	3	.250	0	7.97
	DEN/AMA	AAA	13	234	10	2	0	0	51.2	73	5	13	1	2	28	6	1	1	0	34	31	4	4	.500	1	5.40
92	LV/PCL	AAA	37	655	20	1	1	0	147.0	184	6	47	0	4	79	6	8	4	5	90	73	11	7	.611	3	4.47
93	CS/PCL	AAA	5	120	5	1	1	0	28.0	30	0	6	0	0	15	0	1	0	0	12	7	3	1	.750	0	2.25
	COL/NL		4	39	0	0	0	2	5.2	16	4	5	0	0	3	0	0	0	0	14	14	0	0	.000	0	22.24
8 YR TOTALS			121	2108	59	6	2	29	482.0	563	61	128	10	8	195	15	18	15	0	279	253	24	29	.453	0	4.72

Kramer, Thomas Joseph "Tom" — BB/TR — b.1/9/68   CLE87 4/125

YR	TM/LG	CL	G	TBF	GS	CG	SHO	GF	IP	H	HR	BB	IBB	HB	SO	SH	SF	WP	BK	R	ER	W	L	PCT	SV	ERA
87	BUR/APP	R+	12	292	11	2	1	0	71.2	57	2	26	0	1	71	0	1	0	0	31	24	7	3	.700	1	3.01
88	WAT/MID	A	27	814	27	10	2	0	198.2	173	9	60	3	4	152	10	3	5	3	70	56	14	7	.667	0	2.54
89	KIN/CAR	A+	18	527	17	5	1	1	131.2	97	7	42	4	5	89	5	3	4	1	44	38	9	5	.643	0	2.60
	CAN/EAS	AA	10	202	8	1	0	0	43.1	58	6	20	0	0	26	3	4	1	0	34	30	1	6	.143	0	6.23

(continued)

Kramer, Thomas Joseph "Tom" (continued)

YR	TM/LG	CL	G	TBF	GS	CG	SHO	GF	IP	H	HR	BB	IBB	HB	SO	SH	SF	WP	BK	R	ER	W	L	PCT	SV	ERA
90	KIN/CAR	A+	16	402	16	2	1	0	98.0	82	5	29	0	2	96	1	2	1	0	34	31	7	4	.636	0	2.85
	CAN/EAS	AA	12	287	10	2	0	0	72.0	67	3	14	1	0	46	2	1	1	0	25	24	6	3	.667	0	3.00
91	CAN/EAS	AA	35	320	5	0	0	13	79.1	61	5	34	3	1	61	6	1	3	0	23	21	7	3	.700	6	2.38
	CS/PCL	AAA	10	43	1	0	0	6	11.1	5	1	5	0	0	18	0	1	0	0	1	1	1	0	1.000	4	0.79
	CLE/AL		4	30	0	0	0	1	4.2	10	1	6	0	0	4	0	3	0	0	9	9	0	0	.000	0	17.36
92	CS/PCL	AAA	38	344	3	0	0	11	75.2	88	2	43	2	1	72	4	3	0	0	43	41	8	3	.727	3	4.88
93	CLE/AL		39	535	16	1	0	6	121.0	126	19	59	7	2	71	3	2	1	0	60	54	7	3	.700	0	4.02
2 YR TOTALS			43	565	16	1	0	7	125.2	136	20	65	7	2	75	3	5	1	0	69	63	7	3	.700	0	4.51

Krueger, William Culp "Bill" — BL/TL — b.4/24/58   OAK 7/12/80

YR	TM/LG	CL	G	TBF	GS	CG	SHO	GF	IP	H	HR	BB	IBB	HB	SO	SH	SF	WP	BK	R	ER	W	L	PCT	SV	ERA
83	OAK/AL		17	473	16	2	0	0	109.2	104	7	53	1	2	58	0	5	1	1	54	44	7	6	.538	0	3.61
84	TAC/PCL	AAA	5	0	5	2	0	0	31.2	29	3	21	0	20	0	0	0	0	0	17	13	2	2	.500	0	3.69
	OAK/AL		26	647	24	1	0	0	142.0	156	9	85	2	2	61	4	8	5	1	95	75	10	10	.500	0	4.75
85	TAC/PCL	AAA	2	0	2	0	0	0	9.2	12	2	6	0	0	10	0	0	0	0	10	10	0	1	.000	0	9.31
	OAK/AL		32	674	23	2	0	4	151.1	165	13	69	1	2	56	1	5	6	3	95	76	9	10	.474	0	4.52
86	MAD/MID	A	1	7	0	0	0	1	2.0	1	0	1	0	0	1	0	0	0	0	0	0	0	0	.000	0	0.00
	TAC/PCL	AAA	8	235	8	2	1	0	52.1	53	4	27	0	1	41	3	2	2	0	32	27	3	3	.500	0	4.64
	OAK/AL		11	149	3	0	0	4	34.1	40	4	13	0	0	10	1	2	3	1	25	23	1	2	.333	1	6.03
87	OAK/AL		9	33	0	0	0	0	5.2	9	0	8	1	0	2	0	0	1	0	7	6	0	1	.000	0	9.53
	TAC/PCL	AAA	10	273	10	2	1	0	62.1	64	2	27	2	4	37	0	0	0	2	26	24	3	3	.500	0	3.47
	ALB/PCL	AAA	14	376	14	5	1	0	84.0	94	3	39	0	1	60	0	3	0	0	48	42	6	4	.600	0	4.50
	LA/NL		2	13	0	0	0	0	2.1	3	0	1	0	0	2	0	0	0	0	2	0	0	0	.000	0	0.00
	YEAR		11	46	0	0	0	1	8.0	12	0	9	0	0	4	0	0	0	0	9	6	0	3	.000	0	6.75
88	LA/NL		1	14	1	0	0	0	2.1	4	0	2	1	0	1	0	0	0	0	3	3	0	0	.000	0	11.57
	ALB/PCL	AAA	27	747	26	7	4	0	173.1	167	14	69	1	0	114	4	6	8	1	74	58	15	5	.750	0	3.01
89	DEN/AMA	AAA	2	54	2	0	0	0	13.1	10	1	6	0	0	9	0	0	0	0	4	3	1	1	.500	0	2.03
	MIL/AL		34	403	5	0	0	8	93.2	96	9	33	3	0	72	1	1	0	0	43	40	3	2	.600	3	3.84
90	BEL/MID	A	1	20	1	0	0	0	6.0	4	0	0	0	0	6	0	0	0	0	1	1	1	0	1.000	0	1.50
	MIL/AL		30	566	17	0	0	4	129.0	137	10	54	4	3	64	3	10	8	0	70	57	6	8	.429	0	3.98
91	SEA/AL		35	751	25	1	0	2	175.0	194	15	60	4	4	91	6	9	10	0	82	70	11	8	.579	0	3.60
92	MIN/AL		27	684	27	2	2	0	161.1	166	18	46	2	3	86	4	1	11	0	82	77	10	6	.625	0	4.30
	MON/NL		9	81	2	0	0	0	17.1	23	0	7	0	1	13	0	0	0	0	13	13	0	2	.000	0	6.75
	YEAR		36	765	29	2	2	3	178.2	189	18	53	2	4	99	4	1	12	0	95	90	10	8	.556	0	4.53
93	TOL/INT	AAA	3	47	3	0	0	0	11.1	11	0	3	0	0	8	0	0	0	0	2	2	1	0	1.000	0	1.59
	DET/AL		32	356	7	0	0	7	82.0	90	6	30	5	4	60	3	3	8	0	43	31	6	4	.600	0	3.40
11 YR TOTALS			265	4844	150	8	2	33	1106.0	1187	91	461	28	22	576	27	44	63	9	614	515	63	61	.508	4	4.19

Lancaster, Lester Wayne "Les" — BR/TR — b.4/21/62   CHN 6/13/85

YR	TM/LG	CL	G	TBF	GS	CG	SHO	GF	IP	H	HR	BB	IBB	HB	SO	SH	SF	WP	BK	R	ER	W	L	PCT	SV	ERA
85	WYT/APP	R+	20	433	10	7	1	8	102.0	98	6	24	5	1	81	4	3	4	0	49	41	7	4	.636	3	3.62
86	WIN/CAR	A+	13	396	13	3	0	0	97.0	88	4	30	2	2	52	3	4	1	1	37	30	8	3	.727	0	2.78
	PIT/EAS	AA	14	389	14	2	0	0	88.0	105	4	34	2	5	49	2	4	2	1	46	41	5	6	.455	0	4.19
87	IOW/AMA	AAA	15	268	6	0	0	6	67.0	59	9	17	3	1	62	3	1	0	1	24	24	5	3	.625	4	3.22
	CHI/NL		27	578	18	0	0	4	132.1	138	14	51	5	1	78	5	6	7	8	76	72	8	3	.727	0	4.90
88	CHI/NL		44	371	3	0	0	15	85.2	89	4	34	7	1	36	3	7	3	3	42	36	4	4	.400	5	3.78
89	IOW/AMA	AAA	17	389	14	3	2	0	91.1	76	6	43	0	3	56	4	2	1	0	38	27	5	7	.417	0	2.66
	CHI/NL		42	288	0	0	0	15	72.2	60	2	15	1	0	56	3	4	2	1	12	11	4	2	.667	8	1.36
90	IOW/AMA	AAA	6	74	0	0	0	2	17.2	20	1	5	0	0	15	0	1	0	0	10	8	0	1	.000	1	4.08
	CHI/NL		55	479	6	1	1	26	109.0	121	11	40	8	1	65	6	5	7	0	57	56	9	5	.643	6	4.62
91	CHI/NL		64	653	11	1	0	21	156.0	150	13	49	7	4	102	9	4	2	2	68	61	9	7	.563	3	3.52
92	DET/AL		41	404	1	0	0	17	86.2	101	11	51	3	2	35	4	2	1	0	66	61	3	4	.429	0	6.33
93	STL/NL		50	259	0	0	0	12	61.1	56	5	21	5	1	36	5	1	5	0	24	20	4	1	.800	0	2.93
7 YR TOTALS			323	3032	39	3	1	110	703.2	715	60	261	45	11	408	33	31	28	14	345	317	41	28	.594	22	4.05

Landrum, Thomas William "Bill" — BR/TR — b.8/17/57   CHN 6/22/80

YR	TM/LG	CL	G	TBF	GS	CG	SHO	GF	IP	H	HR	BB	IBB	HB	SO	SH	SF	WP	BK	R	ER	W	L	PCT	SV	ERA
84	WIC/AMA	AAA	47	545	9	2	0	16	130.1	120	8	52	1	1	120	6	7	4	2	58	50	7	4	.636	2	3.45
85	DEN/AMA	AAA	29	596	19	3	1	6	138.0	148	9	49	1	3	88	7	2	4	7	72	61	6	6	.500	2	3.98
86	DEN/AMA	AAA	24	166	2	0	0	19	36.1	36	1	25	2	0	36	1	0	3	1	20	14	1	3	.250	8	3.47
	CIN/NL		10	65	0	0	0	4	13.1	23	0	4	0	1	14	1	1	0	0	11	10	0	0	.000	0	6.75
87	NAS/AMA	AAA	19	164	2	0	0	5	38.2	30	0	19	3	0	47	0	3	2	0	9	9	4	0	1.000	1	2.09
	CIN/NL		44	276	2	0	0	14	65.0	68	3	34	6	0	42	7	2	4	1	35	34	3	2	.600	2	4.71
88	CHI/NL		7	55	0	0	0	5	12.1	19	1	3	0	0	6	0	0	1	0	8	8	1	0	1.000	0	5.84
	IOW/AMA	AAA	9	81	0	0	0	6	21.1	13	2	6	1	0	22	0	0	1	1	7	7	1	0	1.000	3	2.95
89	BUF/AMA	AAA	5	91	3	1	0	0	25.1	16	0	6	0	0	20	0	0	1	0	2	2	3	0	1.000	0	0.71
	PIT/NL		56	325	0	0	0	40	81.0	60	2	28	4	0	51	3	2	1	0	18	15	2	3	.400	26	1.67
90	PIT/NL		54	292	0	0	0	41	71.2	69	4	21	5	0	39	5	3	1	0	22	17	7	3	.700	13	2.13
91	PIT/NL		61	322	0	0	0	43	76.1	76	4	19	5	0	45	1	1	3	2	32	27	4	4	.500	17	3.18
92	MON/NL		18	95	0	0	0	6	20.0	27	3	4	2	0	14	0	0	2	0	16	16	1	1	.500	0	7.20
	IND/AMA	AAA	14	109	5	0	0	0	27.1	27	4	4	0	0	23	0	1	1	0	15	12	1	1	.500	0	3.95
93	CIN/NL		18	86	0	0	0	6	21.2	18	1	4	1	0	14	2	0	0	0	9	9	0	0	.000	0	3.74
8 YR TOTALS			268	1516	2	0	0	159	361.1	360	18	124	27	2	218	20	9	11	5	151	136	18	15	.545	58	3.39

Langston, Mark Edward — BR/TL — b.8/20/60 · SEA81 3/35

YR	TM/LG	CL	G	TBF	GS	CG	SHO	GF	IP	H	HR	BB	IBB	HB	SO	SH	SF	WP	BK	R	ER	W	L	PCT	SV	ERA
84	SEA/AL		35	965	33	5	2	0	225.0	188	16	118	5	8	*204	13	7	4	2	99	85	17	10	.630	0	3.40
85	SEA/AL		24	577	24	2	0	0	126.2	122	22	91	2	2	72	3	2	3	3	85	77	7	14	.333	0	5.47
86	SEA/AL		37	1057	36	9	0	1	239.1	234	30	123	1	4	*245	5	8	10	3	142	129	12	14	.462	0	4.85
87	SEA/AL		35	1152	35	14	3	0	272.0	242	30	114	0	5	*262	12	6	9	2	132	116	19	13	.594	0	3.84
88	SEA/AL		35	1078	35	9	3	0	261.1	222	32	110	2	3	235	6	5	7	4	108	97	15	11	.577	0	3.34
89	SEA/AL		10	297	10	2	1	0	73.1	60	3	19	0	4	60	0	3	1	2	30	29	4	5	.444	0	3.56
	MON/NL		24	740	24	6	4	0	176.2	138	13	93	6	0	175	9	4	5	2	57	47	12	9	.571	0	2.39
	YEAR		34	1037	34	8	5	0	250.0	198	16	112	6	4	235	9	7	6	4	87	76	16	14	.533	0	2.74
90	CAL/AL		33	950	33	5	1	0	223.0	215	13	104	1	5	195	6	6	6	0	120	109	10	17	.370	0	4.40
91	CAL/AL		34	992	34	7	0	0	246.1	190	30	96	3	2	183	4	5	6	0	89	82	19	8	.704	0	3.00
92	CAL/AL		32	941	32	9	2	0	229.0	206	14	74	2	6	174	4	5	5	0	103	93	13	14	.481	0	3.66
93	CAL/AL		35	1039	35	7	0	0	256.1	220	22	85	2	1	196	3	8	10	2	100	91	16	11	.593	0	3.20
10 YR TOTALS			**334**	**9788**	**331**	**75**	**16**	**1**	**2329.0**	**2037**	**225**	**1027**	**24**	**40**	**2001**	**65**	**60**	**68**	**20**	**1065**	**955**	**144**	**126**	**.533**	**0**	**3.69**

Layana, Timothy Joseph "Tim" — BR/TR — b.3/2/64 · NYA86 2/80

YR	TM/LG	CL	G	TBF	GS	CG	SHO	GF	IP	H	HR	BB	IBB	HB	SO	SH	SF	WP	BK	R	ER	W	L	PCT	SV	ERA
86	ONE/NYP	A-	3	71	3	0	0	0	19.0	10	1	5	0	1	24	1	0	1	0	5	5	2	0	1.000	0	2.37
	FL/FSL	A+	11	276	10	3	1	1	68.1	59	1	19	1	4	52	2	0	5	1	19	17	5	4	.556	1	2.24
87	ALB/EAS	AA	8	195	7	1	0	1	46.1	51	4	18	0	2	19	2	1	1	1	28	26	2	4	.333	0	5.05
	PW/CAR	A+	7	111	3	0	0	2	22.2	29	3	11	0	1	17	1	2	5	2	22	16	2	1	.667	0	6.35
	CMB/INT	AAA	13	310	13	0	0	0	70.0	77	6	37	2	1	36	3	1	3	0	37	37	4	5	.444	0	4.76
88	ALB/EAS	AA	14	378	14	1	0	0	87.0	90	3	30	2	6	42	3	3	2	8	52	42	5	7	.417	0	4.34
	CMB/INT	AAA	11	216	9	0	0	0	47.2	54	2	25	0	6	25	0	1	2	4	34	32	1	7	.125	0	6.04
89	ALB/EAS	AA	40	261	1	0	0	37	67.2	53	2	15	3	3	48	5	1	2	4	17	13	7	4	.636	17	1.73
90	CIN/NL		55	344	0	0	0	17	80.0	71	7	44	5	2	53	4	3	5	4	33	31	5	3	.625	2	3.49
91	CIN/NL		22	95	0	0	0	9	20.2	23	1	11	0	0	14	1	0	3	0	18	16	0	2	.000	0	6.97
	NAS/AMA	AAA	26	210	2	0	0	4	47.1	41	3	28	0	4	43	3	0	6	1	17	17	3	1	.750	1	3.23
92	ROC/INT	AAA	41	323	3	0	0	28	72.1	79	3	38	6	4	48	4	4	14	0	45	43	3	3	.500	4	5.35
93	PHO/PCL	AAA	55	306	0	0	0	38	67.1	80	5	24	4	5	55	4	6	8	2	42	36	3	2	.600	9	4.81
	SF/NL		1	15	0	0	0	0	2.0	7	1	1	1	0	1	0	0	0	0	5	5	0	0	.000	0	22.50
3 YR TOTALS			**78**	**454**	**0**	**0**	**0**	**26**	**102.2**	**101**	**9**	**56**	**6**	**2**	**68**	**6**	**3**	**8**	**4**	**56**	**52**	**5**	**5**	**.500**	**2**	**4.56**

Leach, Terry Hester — BR/TR — b.3/13/54 · BATR 6/29/76

YR	TM/LG	CL	G	TBF	GS	CG	SHO	GF	IP	H	HR	BB	IBB	HB	SO	SH	SF	WP	BK	R	ER	W	L	PCT	SV	ERA
81	NY/NL		21	139	1	0	0	3	35.1	26	2	12	1	0	16	0	0	0	0	11	10	1	1	.500	0	2.55
82	NY/NL		21	194	1	1	1	12	45.1	46	2	18	5	0	30	5	1	0	0	22	21	2	1	.667	3	4.17
84	RIC/INT	AAA	12	78	1	0	0	10	14.2	28	3	3	1	1	6	1	1	0	0	16	15	1	2	.333	1	9.20
	TID/INT	AAA	31	329	0	0	0	16	80.1	70	3	27	4	0	53	2	1	0	0	26	17	10	2	.833	0	1.90
85	TID/INT	AAA	24	178	0	0	0	12	45.1	33	1	8	1	0	25	2	2	0	0	12	8	1	0	1.000	4	1.59
	NY/NL		22	226	4	1	1	4	55.2	48	3	14	1	1	30	5	2	0	0	19	18	3	4	.429	1	2.91
86	NY/NL		6	30	0	0	0	1	6.2	6	0	3	0	0	4	0	0	0	0	3	2	0	0	.000	0	2.70
	TID/INT	AAA	34	327	4	1	0	15	79.2	69	8	21	1	2	55	4	5	1	1	30	22	4	4	.500	7	2.49
87	NY/NL		44	542	12	1	1	7	131.1	132	14	29	5	1	61	8	1	0	1	54	47	11	1	.917	0	3.22
88	NY/NL		52	392	0	0	0	21	92.0	95	5	24	4	3	51	7	2	0	1	32	26	7	2	.778	3	2.54
89	NY/NL		10	85	0	0	0	4	21.1	19	1	4	0	1	2	1	0	0	0	11	10	0	0	.000	0	4.22
	KC/AL		30	328	3	0	0	6	73.2	78	4	36	9	1	34	6	1	0	1	46	34	5	6	.455	0	4.15
	YEAR		40	413	3	0	0	10	95.0	97	5	40	9	2	36	7	1	0	1	57	44	5	6	.455	0	4.17
90	MIN/AL		55	344	0	0	0	29	81.2	84	2	21	10	1	46	7	2	1	1	31	29	2	5	.286	2	3.20
91	MIN/AL		50	292	0	0	0	22	67.1	82	3	14	1	0	32	3	1	1	0	28	27	1	2	.333	0	3.61
92	CHI/AL		51	292	0	0	0	21	73.2	57	2	20	5	1	22	2	1	0	0	17	16	6	5	.545	1	1.95
93	CHI/AL		14	64	0	0	0	8	16.0	15	0	2	1	1	3	0	0	0	0	5	5	0	0	.000	1	2.81
	NAS/AMA	AAA	5	20	0	0	0	1	5.2	4	0	0	0	0	4	1	0	0	0	2	2	0	0	.000	1	3.18
	BIR/SOU	AA	4	19	0	0	0	1	4.1	4	0	2	1	0	3	0	0	0	0	2	2	0	0	.000	1	4.15
11 YR TOTALS			**376**	**2928**	**21**	**3**	**3**	**138**	**700.0**	**688**	**38**	**197**	**48**	**13**	**331**	**44**	**18**	**3**	**3**	**279**	**245**	**38**	**27**	**.585**	**10**	**3.15**

Leary, Timothy James "Tim" — BR/TR — b.12/23/58 · NYN79 1/2

YR	TM/LG	CL	G	TBF	GS	CG	SHO	GF	IP	H	HR	BB	IBB	HB	SO	SH	SF	WP	BK	R	ER	W	L	PCT	SV	ERA
81	NY/NL		1	7	1	0	0	0	2.0	0	0	1	0	0	3	0	0	1	0	0	0	0	0	.000	0	0.00
83	NY/NL		2	53	2	1	0	0	10.2	15	0	4	0	0	9	1	1	0	1	10	4	1	1	.500	0	3.38
84	TID/INT	AAA	10	241	10	0	0	0	53.1	47	4	42	0	3	27	0	3	4	0	26	24	4	4	.500	0	4.05
	NY/NL		20	237	7	0	0	3	53.2	61	2	18	3	2	29	1	2	3	3	28	24	3	3	.500	0	4.02
85	VAN/PCL	AAA	27	0	27	3	1	0	177.2	174	9	57	1	5	136	0	0	6	1	85	79	10	7	.588	0	4.00
	MIL/AL		5	146	5	0	0	0	33.1	40	5	8	1	1	29	0	0	0	0	18	15	1	4	.200	0	4.05
86	MIL/AL		33	817	30	4	2	0	188.1	216	20	53	4	7	110	4	6	7	0	97	88	12	12	.500	0	4.21
87	LA/NL		39	469	12	0	0	11	107.2	121	15	36	5	2	61	6	1	3	0	62	57	3	11	.214	1	4.76
88	LA/NL		35	932	34	9	6	0	228.2	201	13	56	4	6	180	7	3	9	6	87	74	17	11	.607	0	2.91
89	LA/NL		19	481	17	2	0	0	117.1	107	9	37	7	2	59	4	4	0	4	45	44	6	7	.462	0	3.38
	CIN/NL		14	393	14	0	0	0	89.2	98	8	31	8	3	64	3	4	6	0	39	37	2	7	.222	0	3.71
	YEAR		33	874	31	2	0	0	207.0	205	17	68	15	5	123	7	8	10	4	84	81	8	14	.364	0	3.52
90	NY/AL		31	881	31	6	1	0	208.0	202	20	78	1	7	138	7	4	7	2	105	95	9	19	.321	0	4.11
91	NY/AL		28	551	18	1	0	4	120.2	150	20	57	1	4	83	7	2	10	0	89	87	4	10	.286	0	6.49
92	NY/AL		18	414	15	2	0	0	97.0	84	9	57	4	4	34	4	4	4	0	62	60	5	6	.455	0	5.57
	SEA/AL		8	210	8	1	0	0	44.0	47	3	30	1	3	12	1	5	5	0	27	24	3	4	.429	0	4.91
	YEAR		26	624	23	3	0	0	141.0	131	12	87	5	7	46	5	9	9	0	89	84	8	10	.444	0	5.36
93	SEA/AL		33	746	27	0	0	6	169.1	202	21	58	5	8	68	5	5	11	3	110	95	11	9	.550	0	5.05
12 YR TOTALS			**286**	**6337**	**221**	**25**	**9**	**28**	**1470.1**	**1544**	**143**	**524**	**43**	**51**	**879**	**53**	**39**	**81**	**13**	**773**	**704**	**77**	**104**	**.425**	**1**	**4.31**

Lefferts, Craig Lindsay — BL/TL — b.9/29/57   CHN80 9/219

YR	TM/LG	CL	G	TBF	GS	CG	SHO	GF	IP	H	HR	BB	IBB	HB	SO	SH	SF	WP	BK	R	ER	W	L	PCT	SV	ERA
83	CHI/NL		56	367	5	0	0	10	89.0	80	13	29	3	2	60	7	0	2	0	35	31	3	4	.429	1	3.13
84	SD/NL		62	420	0	0	0	29	105.2	88	4	24	1	1	56	4	6	2	2	29	25	3	4	.429	10	2.13
85	SD/NL		60	345	0	0	0	24	83.1	75	7	30	4	0	48	7	1	2	0	34	31	7	6	.538	2	3.35
86	SD/NL		*83	446	0	0	0	36	107.2	98	7	44	11	1	72	9	5	1	1	41	37	9	8	.529	4	3.09
87	SD/NL		33	225	0	0	0	8	51.1	56	9	15	5	2	39	2	0	5	2	29	25	2	2	.500	2	4.38
	SF/NL		44	191	0	0	0	14	47.1	36	4	18	6	0	18	4	2	1	1	18	17	3	3	.500	4	3.23
	YEAR		77	416	0	0	0	22	98.2	92	13	33	11	2	57	6	2	6	3	47	42	5	5	.500	6	3.83
88	SF/NL		64	362	0	0	0	30	92.1	74	7	23	5	1	58	6	3	4	0	33	30	3	8	.273	11	2.92
89	SF/NL		70	430	0	0	0	32	107.0	93	11	22	5	1	71	4	4	4	1	38	32	2	4	.333	20	2.69
90	SD/NL		56	327	0	0	0	44	78.2	68	10	22	4	1	60	5	1	1	0	26	22	7	5	.583	23	2.52
91	SD/NL		54	290	0	0	0	40	69.0	74	5	14	3	1	48	10	5	3	1	35	30	1	6	.143	23	3.91
92	SD/NL		27	684	27	0	0	0	163.1	180	16	35	2	0	81	12	5	4	1	76	67	13	9	.591	0	3.69
	BAL/AL		5	136	5	1	0	0	33.0	34	3	6	0	0	23	2	1	1	0	19	15	1	3	.250	0	4.09
	YEAR		32	820	32	1	0	0	196.1	214	19	41	2	0	104	14	6	5	1	95	82	14	12	.538	0	3.76
93	OC/AMA	AAA	1	27	1	0	0	0	6.0	9	1	2	0	0	1	0	1	0	0	5	5	0	1	.000	0	7.50
	TEX/AL		52	373	8	0	0	9	83.1	102	17	28	3	1	58	6	3	0	1	57	56	3	9	.250	0	6.05
11 YR TOTALS			666	4596	45	1	0	276	1111.0	1058	113	310	52	11	692	78	36	30	10	470	418	57	71	.445	100	3.39

Leftwich, Philip Dale "Phil" — BR/TR — b.5/19/69   CAL90 1/64

YR	TM/LG	CL	G	TBF	GS	CG	SHO	GF	IP	H	HR	BB	IBB	HB	SO	SH	SF	WP	BK	R	ER	W	L	PCT	SV	ERA
90	BOI/NWL	A-	15	373	15	0	0	0	92.0	88	0	22	1	1	81	1	3	3	2	36	19	8	2	.800	0	1.86
91	QC/MID	A	26	716	26	5	1	0	173.0	158	6	59	0	3	163	7	2	8	2	70	63	11	9	.550	0	3.28
	MID/TEX	AA	1	27	1	0	0	0	6.0	5	0	5	0	0	3	0	0	0	0	2	2	1	0	1.000	0	3.00
92	MID/TEX	AA	21	546	21	0	0	0	121.0	156	10	37	1	4	85	6	3	2	1	90	79	6	9	.400	0	5.88
93	VAN/PCL	AAA	20	552	20	3	1	0	126.0	138	8	45	1	2	102	3	4	4	0	74	65	7	7	.500	0	4.64
	CAL/AL		12	343	12	1	0	0	80.2	81	5	27	1	3	31	3	1	1	0	35	34	4	6	.400	0	3.79

Leibrandt, Charles Louis "Charlie" — BR/TL — b.10/4/56   CIN78 9/225

YR	TM/LG	CL	G	TBF	GS	CG	SHO	GF	IP	H	HR	BB	IBB	HB	SO	SH	SF	WP	BK	R	ER	W	L	PCT	SV	ERA
79	CIN/NL		3	16	0	0	0	1	4.1	2	0	2	0	0	1	0	1	0	0	2	0	0	0	.000	0	0.00
80	CIN/NL		36	754	27	5	2	3	173.2	200	15	54	4	2	62	12	2	1	6	84	82	10	9	.526	0	4.25
81	CIN/NL		7	128	4	1	1	0	30.0	28	0	15	2	0	9	2	2	0	0	12	12	1	1	.500	0	3.60
82	CIN/NL		36	484	11	0	0	10	107.2	130	4	48	9	2	34	10	2	6	1	68	61	5	7	.417	1	5.10
84	OMA/AMA	AAA	9	278	9	4	3	0	72.2	51	4	16	2	3	38	1	0	0	0	14	10	7	1	.875	0	1.24
	KC/AL		23	621	23	0	0	0	143.2	158	11	38	2	3	53	3	7	5	1	65	58	11	7	.611	0	3.63
85	KC/AL		33	983	33	8	3	0	237.2	223	17	68	3	2	108	8	5	4	0	86	71	17	9	.654	0	2.69
86	KC/AL		35	975	34	8	1	0	231.1	238	18	63	0	4	108	14	5	2	1	112	105	14	11	.560	0	4.09
87	KC/AL		35	1015	35	8	3	0	240.1	235	23	74	2	1	151	6	5	9	3	104	91	16	11	.593	0	3.41
88	KC/AL		35	1002	35	7	2	0	243.0	244	20	62	3	4	125	5	7	10	4	98	86	13	12	.520	0	3.19
89	KC/AL		33	712	27	3	1	3	161.0	196	13	54	4	2	73	8	4	9	2	98	92	5	11	.313	0	5.14
90	GRE/SOU	AA	2	46	2	0	0	0	13.0	5	0	5	0	0	12	0	0	1	0	4	0	1	0	1.000	0	0.00
	ATL/NL		24	680	24	5	2	0	162.1	164	9	35	3	4	76	7	4	3	1	72	57	9	11	.450	0	3.16
91	ATL/NL		36	949	36	1	1	0	229.2	212	18	56	3	4	128	19	6	5	3	105	89	15	13	.536	0	3.49
92	ATL/NL		32	799	31	5	2	0	193.0	191	9	42	4	5	104	7	4	3	2	78	72	15	7	.682	0	3.36
93	TEX/AL		26	656	26	1	0	0	150.1	169	15	45	5	4	89	8	4	5	2	84	76	9	10	.474	0	4.55
14 YR TOTALS			394	9774	346	52	18	17	2308.0	2390	172	656	44	37	1121	110	60	63	31	1068	952	140	119	.541	2	3.71

Leiter, Alois Terry "Al" — BL/TL — b.10/23/65   NYA84 2/50

YR	TM/LG	CL	G	TBF	GS	CG	SHO	GF	IP	H	HR	BB	IBB	HB	SO	SH	SF	WP	BK	R	ER	W	L	PCT	SV	ERA
84	ONE/NYP	A-	10	250	10	0	0	0	57.0	52	1	26	0	2	48	2	4	5	1	32	23	3	2	.600	0	3.63
85	FL/FSL	A+	17	386	17	1	0	0	82.0	87	3	57	1	2	44	4	1	5	1	70	59	1	6	.143	0	6.48
	ONE/NYP	A-	6	157	6	2	0	0	38.0	27	0	25	0	0	34	4	1	5	0	14	10	3	2	.600	0	2.37
86	FL/FSL	A+	22	526	21	1	1	0	117.2	96	2	90	1	5	101	4	2	7	1	64	53	4	8	.333	0	4.05
87	ALB/EAS	AA	15	327	14	2	0	0	78.0	64	4	37	0	2	71	4	2	3	2	34	29	3	3	.500	0	3.35
	CMB/INT	AAA	5	101	5	0	0	0	23.1	21	1	15	0	0	23	1	1	3	0	18	16	1	4	.200	0	6.17
	NY/AL		4	104	4	0	0	0	22.2	24	2	15	0	0	28	1	0	4	0	16	16	2	2	.500	0	6.35
88	CMB/INT	AAA	4	58	4	0	0	0	13.0	5	0	14	0	3	12	0	0	1	2	7	5	0	2	.000	0	3.46
	NY/AL		14	251	14	0	0	0	57.1	49	7	33	0	5	60	1	0	1	4	27	25	4	4	.500	0	3.92
89	NY/AL		4	123	4	0	0	0	26.2	23	1	21	0	2	22	1	1	1	0	20	18	1	2	.333	0	6.07
	TOR/AL		1	31	1	0	0	0	6.2	9	1	2	0	0	4	0	0	0	0	3	3	0	0	.000	0	4.05
	YEAR		5	154	5	0	0	0	33.1	32	2	23	0	2	26	1	1	1	0	23	21	1	2	.333	0	5.67
	DUN/FSL	A+	3	39	3	0	0	0	8.0	11	0	5	0	0	4	0	0	0	1	5	5	0	2	.000	0	5.63
90	DUN/FSL	A+	6	99	6	0	0	0	24.0	18	1	12	0	0	14	0	1	2	1	8	7	0	0	.000	0	2.63
	SYR/INT	AAA	15	353	14	1	1	0	78.0	59	4	68	0	5	69	5	5	6	0	43	40	3	8	.273	0	4.62
	TOR/AL		4	22	0	0	0	2	6.1	1	0	2	0	0	5	0	0	0	0	0	0	0	0	.000	0	0.00
91	TOR/AL		3	13	1	0	0	0	1.2	3	0	5	0	1	1	0	0	0	0	5	5	0	0	.000	0	27.00
	DUN/FSL	A+	4	40	4	0	0	0	9.2	5	0	4	0	1	5	1	0	0	0	2	2	0	0	.000	0	1.86
92	SYR/INT	AAA	27	703	27	0	0	0	163.1	159	9	64	0	9	108	4	5	9	0	82	70	9	9	.471	0	3.86
	TOR/AL		1	7	0	0	0	0	1.0	1	0	2	0	0	0	0	0	0	0	1	1	0	0	.000	0	9.00
93	TOR/AL		34	454	12	1	1	4	105.0	93	8	56	2	4	66	3	3	2	2	52	48	9	6	.600	2	4.11
7 YR TOTALS			65	1005	35	1	1	7	227.1	203	19	136	2	11	186	7	4	9	7	124	116	16	14	.533	2	4.59

Leiter, Mark Edward — BR/TR — b.4/13/63   BAL83* 4/103

YR	TM/LG	CL	G	TBF	GS	CG	SHO	GF	IP	H	HR	BB	IBB	HB	SO	SH	SF	WP	BK	R	ER	W	L	PCT	SV	ERA
83	BLU/APP	R+	6	0	6	2	0	0	36.0	33	0	13	0	3	35	0	0	2	0	17	11	2	1	.667	0	2.75
	HAG/CAR	A+	8	0	8	0	0	0	36.0	42	0	28	0	3	18	0	0	3	0	31	29	1	5	.167	0	7.25

Leiter, Mark Edward (continued)

YR	TM/LG	CL	G	TBF	GS	CG	SHO	GF	IP	H	HR	BB	IBB	HB	SO	SH	SF	WP	BK	R	ER	W	L	PCT	SV	ERA
84	HAG/CAR	A+	27	643	24	5	1	2	139.1	132	13	108	2	8	105	6	4	13	1	96	87	8	13	.381	0	5.62
85	HAG/CAR	A+	34	351	6	1	0	22	83.1	77	2	29	3	7	82	4	4	3	0	44	32	2	8	.200	8	3.46
	CHA/SOU	AA	5	23	0	0	0	2	6.1	3	1	2	0	0	8	0	0	0	0	1	1	0	1	.000	1	1.42
89	FL/FSL	A+	6	143	4	1	0	1	35.1	27	1	5	0	2	22	0	0	1	0	9	6	2	2	.500	1	1.53
	CMB/INT	AAA	22	404	12	0	0	2	90.0	102	5	34	2	5	70	2	3	3	5	50	50	9	6	.600	0	5.00
90	CMB/INT	AAA	30	508	14	2	1	6	122.2	114	5	27	0	1	115	2	3	7	0	56	49	9	4	.692	1	3.60
	NY/AL		8	119	3	0	0	2	26.1	33	5	9	0	2	21	2	1	0	0	20	20	1	1	.500	0	6.84
91	TOL/INT	AAA	5	29	0	0	0	3	6.2	6	0	3	0	1	7	0	0	0	0	0	0	1	0	1.000	1	0.00
	DET/AL		38	578	15	1	0	7	134.2	125	16	50	4	6	103	5	6	2	0	66	63	9	7	.563	1	4.21
92	DET/AL		35	475	14	1	0	7	112.0	116	9	43	5	3	75	2	8	3	0	57	52	8	5	.615	0	4.18
93	DET/AL		27	471	13	1	0	4	106.2	111	17	44	5	3	70	3	5	5	0	61	56	6	6	.500	0	4.72
4 YR TOTALS			**108**	**1643**	**45**	**3**	**0**	**20**	**379.2**	**385**	**47**	**146**	**14**	**14**	**269**	**12**	**20**	**10**	**0**	**204**	**191**	**24**	**19**	**.558**	**1**	**4.53**

Leskanic, Curtis John "Curt" — BR/TR — b.4/2/68   CLE89 7/203

YR	TM/LG	CL	G	TBF	GS	CG	SHO	GF	IP	H	HR	BB	IBB	HB	SO	SH	SF	WP	BK	R	ER	W	L	PCT	SV	ERA
90	KIN/CAR	A+	14	303	14	2	0	0	73.1	61	6	30	1	2	71	2	2	10	8	34	30	6	5	.545	0	3.68
91	KIN/CAR	A+	28	730	28	0	0	0	174.1	143	10	91	0	3	163	1	1	16	1	63	54	15	8	.652	0	2.79
92	ORL/SOU	AA	26	664	23	3	0	1	152.2	158	15	64	0	9	126	2	3	10	1	84	73	9	11	.450	0	4.30
	POR/PCL	AAA	5	68	3	0	0	2	15.1	16	1	8	0	0	14	1	0	0	1	17	17	1	2	.333	0	9.98
93	WIC/TEX	AA	7	185	7	0	0	0	44.1	37	3	17	0	3	42	2	2	4	0	20	17	3	2	.600	0	3.45
	CS/PCL	AAA	9	195	7	1	1	1	44.1	39	3	26	0	2	38	2	1	2	2	24	22	4	3	.571	0	4.47
	COL/NL		18	260	8	0	0	1	57.0	59	7	27	1	2	30	5	4	8	2	40	34	1	5	.167	0	5.37

Lewis, Richie Todd — BR/TR — b.1/25/66   MON87 4/44

YR	TM/LG	CL	G	TBF	GS	CG	SHO	GF	IP	H	HR	BB	IBB	HB	SO	SH	SF	WP	BK	R	ER	W	L	PCT	SV	ERA
87	IND/AMA	AAA	2	19	0	0	0	2	3.2	6	2	2	0	1	3	0	0	0	0	4	4	0	0	.000	0	9.82
88	JAC/SOU	AA	12	275	12	0	0	0	61.1	37	2	56	0	3	60	0	3	7	4	32	23	5	3	.625	0	3.38
89	JAC/SOU	AA	17	414	17	0	0	0	94.1	80	2	55	0	2	105	7	1	8	2	37	27	5	4	.556	0	2.58
90	WPB/FSL	A+	10	68	0	0	0	6	15.0	12	0	11	0	1	14	1	0	1	0	8	5	1	0	.000	2	3.00
	JAC/SOU	AA	11	54	0	0	0	8	14.1	7	0	5	0	0	14	0	1	3	0	2	2	0	0	.000	5	1.26
91	HAR/EAS	AA	34	318	6	0	0	16	74.2	67	3	40	1	2	82	3	2	5	2	33	31	6	5	.545	5	3.74
	IND/AMA	AAA	5	131	4	0	0	0	27.2	35	1	20	1	0	22	0	1	2	0	12	11	1	0	1.000	0	3.58
	ROC/INT	AAA	2	62	2	0	0	0	16.0	13	1	7	0	0	18	0	0	1	0	5	5	1	0	1.000	0	2.81
92	BAL/AL		2	40	2	0	0	0	6.2	13	1	7	0	0	4	0	1	0	0	8	8	1	1	.500	0	10.80
	ROC/INT	AAA	24	668	23	6	1	1	159.1	136	15	61	2	3	154	1	4	15	2	63	58	10	9	.526	0	3.28
93	FLO/NL		57	341	0	0	0	14	77.1	68	7	43	6	1	65	8	5	9	1	37	28	6	3	.667	0	3.26
2 YR TOTALS			**59**	**381**	**2**	**0**	**0**	**14**	**84.0**	**81**	**8**	**50**	**6**	**1**	**69**	**8**	**5**	**9**	**1**	**45**	**36**	**7**	**4**	**.636**	**0**	**3.86**

Lewis, Scott Allen — BR/TR — b.12/5/65   CAL88 10/273

YR	TM/LG	CL	G	TBF	GS	CG	SHO	GF	IP	H	HR	BB	IBB	HB	SO	SH	SF	WP	BK	R	ER	W	L	PCT	SV	ERA
88	BEN/NWL	A-	9	262	9	2	0	0	61.2	63	3	12	0	5	53	1	3	3	2	33	24	5	3	.625	0	3.50
	QC/MID	A	3	85	3	1	0	0	21.1	19	0	5	0	0	20	1	0	1	2	12	11	1	2	.333	0	4.64
	PS/CAL	A+	2	37	1	0	0	0	8.0	12	3	2	0	0	7	0	0	0	0	5	5	0	1	.000	0	5.63
89	MID/TEX	AA	25	729	25	4	1	0	162.1	195	15	55	9	8	104	2	3	12	9	121	89	11	12	.478	0	4.93
90	EDM/PCL	AAA	27	749	27	6	0	0	177.2	198	16	35	1	7	124	4	3	2	0	90	77	13	11	.542	0	3.90
	CAL/AL		2	60	2	1	0	0	16.1	10	2	2	0	0	9	0	0	0	0	4	4	1	1	.500	0	2.20
91	EDM/PCL	AAA	17	489	17	4	0	0	110.0	132	7	26	2	8	87	4	4	5	3	71	55	3	9	.250	0	4.50
	CAL/AL		16	281	11	0	0	0	60.1	81	9	21	0	2	37	2	0	3	0	43	42	3	5	.375	0	6.27
92	EDM/PCL	AAA	22	630	22	5	0	0	146.2	159	9	40	2	7	88	5	3	7	2	74	68	10	6	.625	0	4.17
	CAL/AL		21	160	2	0	0	7	38.1	36	3	14	1	2	18	0	3	1	1	18	17	4	0	1.000	0	3.99
93	MID/TEX	AA	1	25	1	0	0	0	6.0	6	0	0	0	0	8	1	0	1	0	1	1	1	0	1.000	0	1.50
	VAN/PCL	AAA	24	156	0	0	0	18	39.1	31	1	9	2	2	38	2	1	1	0	7	6	3	1	.750	9	1.37
	CAL/AL		15	142	4	0	0	2	32.0	37	3	12	1	2	10	2	1	1	0	16	15	1	2	.333	0	4.22
4 YR TOTALS			**54**	**643**	**19**	**1**	**0**	**9**	**147.0**	**164**	**17**	**49**	**2**	**6**	**74**	**4**	**10**	**5**	**1**	**81**	**78**	**9**	**8**	**.529**	**0**	**4.78**

Lilliquist, Derek Jansen — BL/TL — b.2/20/66   ATL87 1/6

YR	TM/LG	CL	G	TBF	GS	CG	SHO	GF	IP	H	HR	BB	IBB	HB	SO	SH	SF	WP	BK	R	ER	W	L	PCT	SV	ERA
87	BRA/GCL	R	2	44	2	0	0	0	13.0	3	0	2	0	0	16	0	0	0	0	0	0	0	0	.000	0	0.00
	DUR/CAR	A+	3	94	3	2	0	0	25.0	13	1	6	0	1	29	1	0	0	0	9	8	2	1	.667	0	2.88
88	RIC/INT	AAA	28	716	28	2	0	0	170.2	179	11	36	1	6	80	6	7	5	6	70	64	10	12	.455	0	3.38
89	ATL/NL		32	718	30	0	0	0	165.2	202	16	34	5	2	79	3	4	3	3	87	73	8	10	.444	0	3.97
90	ATL/NL		12	279	11	0	0	1	61.2	75	10	19	4	1	34	6	4	0	2	45	43	2	8	.200	0	6.28
	RIC/INT	AAA	5	143	5	1	0	0	35.0	31	3	11	0	0	24	0	0	0	0	11	10	4	0	1.000	0	2.57
	SD/NL		16	258	7	1	1	2	60.1	61	6	23	1	2	29	3	1	2	1	29	29	3	3	.500	0	4.33
	YEAR		28	537	18	1	1	3	122.0	136	16	42	5	3	63	9	5	2	3	74	72	5	11	.313	0	5.31
91	LV/PCL	AAA	33	491	14	0	0	8	105.1	142	10	33	1	2	89	6	4	0	0	79	65	4	0	.000	0	5.38
	SD/NL		6	70	2	0	0	0	14.1	25	3	4	1	0	7	0	0	1	0	14	14	0	0	.000	0	8.79
92	CLE/AL		71	239	0	0	0	22	61.2	39	5	18	6	2	47	5	4	0	0	13	12	5	3	.625	6	1.75
93	CLE/AL		56	271	2	0	0	28	64.0	64	5	19	5	1	40	4	4	4	0	20	16	4	4	.500	10	2.25
5 YR TOTALS			**193**	**1835**	**52**	**1**	**1**	**54**	**427.2**	**466**	**45**	**117**	**22**	**8**	**236**	**28**	**14**	**9**	**6**	**208**	**187**	**22**	**30**	**.423**	**16**	**3.94**

Linton, Douglas Warren "Doug" — BR/TR — b.2/9/65   TOR86 43/878

YR	TM/LG	CL	G	TBF	GS	CG	SHO	GF	IP	H	HR	BB	IBB	HB	SO	SH	SF	WP	BK	R	ER	W	L	PCT	SV	ERA
87	MB/SAL	A	20	480	19	2	0	1	122.0	94	9	25	0	2	155	0	2	8	1	34	21	14	2	.875	1	1.55
	KNO/SOU	AA	1	15	1	0	0	0	3.0	5	0	1	0	1	1	0	0	1	0	3	3	0	0	.000	0	9.00
88	DUN/FSL	A+	12	111	0	0	0	6	27.2	19	0	9	1	0	28	1	1	2	0	5	5	2	1	.667	2	1.63

(continued)

Linton, Douglas Warren "Doug" (continued)

YR	TM/LG	CL	G	TBF	GS	CG	SHO	GF	IP	H	HR	BB	IBB	HB	SO	SH	SF	WP	BK	R	ER	W	L	PCT	SV	ERA
89	DUN/FSL	A+	9	117	1	0	0	5	27.1	27	1	9	0	0	35	0	1	1	0	12	9	1	2	.333	2	2.96
	KNO/SOU	AA	14	355	13	3	2	0	90.0	68	2	23	2	2	93	3	1	6	1	28	26	5	4	.556	0	2.60
90	SYR/INT	AAA	26	753	26	8	3	0	177.1	174	14	67	3	8	113	2	10	4	1	77	67	10	10	.500	0	3.40
91	SYR/INT	AAA	30	710	26	3	1	1	161.2	181	21	56	2	10	93	6	10	5	0	108	90	10	12	.455	0	5.01
92	TOR/AL		8	116	3	0	0	2	24.0	31	5	17	0	0	16	1	2	2	0	23	23	1	3	.250	0	8.63
	SYR/INT	AAA	25	741	25	7	1	0	170.2	176	17	70	3	7	126	5	4	12	1	83	71	12	10	.545	0	3.74
93	SYR/INT	AAA	13	206	7	0	0	4	47.1	48	11	14	3	3	42	0	1	2	0	29	28	2	6	.250	2	5.32
	TOR/AL		4	55	1	0	0	0	11.0	11	0	9	0	1	2	0	2	0	0	8	8	0	1	.000	0	6.55
	CAL/AL		19	123	0	0	0	6	25.2	35	8	14	1	0	19	0	1	2	0	22	22	2	0	1.000	0	7.71
	YEAR		23	178	0	0	0	6	36.2	46	8	23	1	1	23	0	3	2	0	30	30	2	1	.667	0	7.36
2 YR TOTALS			**31**	**294**	**4**	**0**	**0**	**8**	**60.2**	**77**	**13**	**40**	**1**	**1**	**39**	**1**	**5**	**4**	**0**	**53**	**53**	**3**	**4**	**.429**	**0**	**7.86**

Lloyd, Graeme John — BL/TL — b.4/9/67   TOR 1/26/88

YR	TM/LG	CL	G	TBF	GS	CG	SHO	GF	IP	H	HR	BB	IBB	HB	SO	SH	SF	WP	BK	R	ER	W	L	PCT	SV	ERA
88	MB/SAL	A	41	281	0	0	0	18	59.2	71	2	30	5	6	43	1	0	5	2	33	24	3	2	.600	2	3.62
89	DUN/FSL	A+	2	14	0	0	0	0	2.2	6	0	1	0	0	0	0	0	1	0	3	3	0	0	.000	0	10.13
	MB/SAL	A	1	21	1	0	0	0	5.0	5	1	0	0	1	3	0	0	1	0	4	3	0	0	.000	0	5.40
90	MB/SAL	A	19	216	6	0	0	8	49.2	51	3	16	1	0	42	0	0	1	1	20	15	5	2	.714	6	2.72
91	DUN/FSL	A+	50	260	0	0	0	39	60.1	54	2	25	2	1	39	2	0	4	0	17	15	2	5	.286	24	2.24
	KNO/SOU	AA	2	7	0	0	0	1	1.2	1	0	1	0	0	2	0	0	0	0	0	0	0	0	.000	0	0.00
92	KNO/SOU	AA	49	376	7	1	0	33	92.0	79	2	25	2	3	65	1	1	8	0	30	20	4	8	.333	14	1.96
93	MIL/AL		55	269	0	0	0	12	63.2	64	5	13	3	3	31	1	2	4	0	24	20	3	4	.429	0	2.83

Looney, Brian James — BL/TL — b.9/26/69   MON91 11/269

YR	TM/LG	CL	G	TBF	GS	CG	SHO	GF	IP	H	HR	BB	IBB	HB	SO	SH	SF	WP	BK	R	ER	W	L	PCT	SV	ERA
91	JAM/NYP	A-	11	246	11	2	1	0	62.1	42	0	28	0	0	64	2	2	6	0	12	8	7	1	.875	0	1.16
92	ROC/MID	A	17	141	0	0	0	5	31.1	28	0	23	0	1	34	2	0	1	0	13	11	3	1	.750	0	3.16
	ALB/SAL	A	11	265	11	1	1	0	67.1	51	1	30	0	0	56	1	3	4	0	22	16	3	2	.600	0	2.14
93	WPB/FSL	A+	18	451	16	0	0	1	106.0	108	2	29	0	5	109	7	3	2	1	48	37	4	6	.400	0	3.14
	HAR/EAS	AA	8	221	8	1	1	0	56.2	36	2	17	1	1	76	1	1	0	0	15	15	3	2	.600	0	2.38
	MON/NL		3	28	1	0	0	1	6.0	8	0	2	0	0	7	0	0	1	0	2	2	0	0	.000	0	3.00

Lopez, Albert Anthony "Albie" — BR/TR — b.8/18/71   CLE91 20/528

YR	TM/LG	CL	G	TBF	GS	CG	SHO	GF	IP	H	HR	BB	IBB	HB	SO	SH	SF	WP	BK	R	ER	W	L	PCT	SV	ERA
91	BUR/APP	R+	13	302	13	0	0	0	73.1	61	4	23	0	3	81	2	2	4	0	33	28	4	5	.444	0	3.44
92	CMB/SAL	A	16	402	16	1	0	0	97.0	80	4	33	0	2	117	0	3	9	7	41	31	7	2	.778	0	2.88
	KIN/CAR	A+	10	268	10	1	1	0	64.0	56	5	26	1	1	44	1	2	4	0	28	25	5	2	.714	0	3.52
93	CAN/EAS	AA	16	449	16	2	0	0	110.0	79	10	47	0	5	80	1	6	6	1	44	38	9	4	.692	0	3.11
	CHW/INT	AAA	3	47	2	0	0	0	12.0	8	1	2	0	2	7	0	0	0	0	3	3	1	0	1.000	0	2.25
	CLE/AL		9	222	9	0	0	0	49.2	49	7	32	1	1	25	1	1	0	0	34	33	3	1	.750	0	5.98

Luebbers, Larry Christopher — BR/TR — b.10/11/69   CIN90 8/216

YR	TM/LG	CL	G	TBF	GS	CG	SHO	GF	IP	H	HR	BB	IBB	HB	SO	SH	SF	WP	BK	R	ER	W	L	PCT	SV	ERA
90	BIL/PIO	R+	13	318	13	1	1	0	72.1	74	3	31	0	6	48	2	3	7	1	46	36	5	4	.556	0	4.48
91	CR/MID	A	28	781	28	3	0	0	184.2	177	8	64	5	10	98	12	6	11	4	85	64	8	10	.444	0	3.12
92	CR/MID	A	14	355	14	1	0	0	82.1	71	2	33	0	8	56	4	3	1	1	33	24	7	0	1.000	0	2.62
	CHT/SOU	AA	14	368	14	1	0	0	87.1	86	5	34	1	4	56	2	1	5	2	34	22	6	5	.545	0	2.27
93	IND/AMA	AAA	15	380	15	0	0	0	84.1	81	7	47	5	6	51	6	2	1	0	45	39	4	7	.364	0	4.16
	CIN/NL		14	332	14	0	0	0	77.1	74	4	38	3	1	38	4	5	5	0	49	39	2	5	.286	0	4.54

Mac Donald, Robert Joseph "Rob" — BL/TL — b.4/27/65   TOR87 19/491

YR	TM/LG	CL	G	TBF	GS	CG	SHO	GF	IP	H	HR	BB	IBB	HB	SO	SH	SF	WP	BK	R	ER	W	L	PCT	SV	ERA
87	SC/NYP	A-	1	20	1	0	0	0	4.0	8	0	0	0	0	4	0	0	0	0	4	2	0	0	.000	0	4.50
	MH/PIO	R+	13	109	0	0	0	9	24.2	22	0	12	1	1	26	1	0	5	0	13	8	3	1	.750	2	2.92
	MB/SAL	A	10	94	0	0	0	4	20.2	24	1	7	1	0	12	2	1	2	0	18	13	2	1	.667	0	5.66
88	MB/SAL	A	52	222	0	0	0	48	53.1	42	2	18	3	0	43	3	1	2	0	13	10	3	4	.429	15	1.69
89	KNO/SOU	AA	43	264	0	0	0	27	63.0	52	2	23	2	2	58	5	0	1	0	27	23	3	5	.375	9	3.29
	SYR/INT	AAA	12	75	0	0	0	4	16.0	16	0	6	0	1	12	1	1	0	0	10	10	1	0	1.000	0	5.63
90	KNO/SOU	AA	36	237	0	0	0	29	57.0	37	2	29	4	1	54	9	1	3	0	17	12	1	2	.333	15	1.89
	SYR/INT	AAA	9	35	0	0	0	4	8.1	4	1	9	0	0	6	0	1	0	0	5	5	0	0	.000	2	5.40
	TOR/AL		4	8	0	0	0	1	2.1	0	0	2	0	0	0	0	0	0	0	0	0	0	0	.000	0	0.00
91	SYR/INT	AAA	7	29	0	0	0	1	6.0	5	1	5	0	0	6	0	1	0	0	3	3	1	0	1.000	0	4.50
	TOR/AL		45	231	0	0	0	10	53.2	51	5	25	4	0	24	2	1	2	1	19	17	3	3	.500	1	2.85
92	SYR/INT	AAA	17	104	0	0	0	11	23.1	25	2	12	1	0	14	2	0	1	0	13	12	2	3	.400	2	4.63
	TOR/AL		27	204	0	0	0	9	47.1	50	4	16	3	1	26	1	1	0	0	24	23	1	0	1.000	0	4.37
93	DET/AL		68	293	0	0	0	24	65.2	67	4	33	5	1	39	4	5	3	1	42	39	3	3	.500	3	5.35
4 YR TOTALS			**144**	**736**	**0**	**0**	**0**	**44**	**169.0**	**168**	**17**	**76**	**12**	**2**	**89**	**7**	**8**	**4**	**2**	**85**	**79**	**7**	**6**	**.538**	**3**	**4.21**

Maddux, Gregory Alan "Greg" — BR/TR — b.4/14/66   CHN84 2/31

YR	TM/LG	CL	G	TBF	GS	CG	SHO	GF	IP	H	HR	BB	IBB	HB	SO	SH	SF	WP	BK	R	ER	W	L	PCT	SV	ERA
84	PIK/APP	R+	14	361	12	2	2	1	85.2	63	2	41	2	8	62	2	3	4	1	35	25	6	2	.750	0	2.63
85	PEO/MID	A	27	787	27	6	0	0	186.0	176	9	52	0	6	125	8	3	5	2	86	66	13	9	.591	0	3.19
86	PIT/EAS	AA	8	249	8	4	2	0	63.2	49	1	15	0	1	35	0	2	1	0	22	19	4	3	.571	0	2.69
	IOW/AMA	AAA	18	538	18	5	2	0	128.1	127	3	30	3	12	65	4	2	3	0	49	43	10	1	.909	0	3.02
	CHI/NL		6	144	5	1	0	1	31.0	44	3	11	2	1	20	1	0	4	5	20	19	2	4	.333	0	5.52
87	IOW/AMA	AAA	4	109	4	2	2	0	27.2	17	1	12	0	2	22	0	0	2	0	3	3	3	0	1.000	0	0.98

Maddux, Gregory Alan "Greg" (continued)

YR	TM/LG	CL	G	TBF	GS	CG	SHO	GF	IP	H	HR	BB	IBB	HB	SO	SH	SF	WP	BK	R	ER	W	L	PCT	SV	ERA
	CHI/NL		30	701	27	1	1	2	155.2	181	17	74	13	4	101	7	1	4	7	111	97	6	14	.300	0	5.61
88	CHI/NL		34	1047	34	9	3	0	249.0	230	13	81	16	9	140	11	2	3	6	97	88	18	8	.692	0	3.18
89	CHI/NL		35	1002	35	7	1	0	238.1	222	13	82	13	6	135	18	6	5	3	90	78	19	12	.613	0	2.95
90	CHI/NL		35	1011	35	8	2	0	237.0	242	11	71	10	4	144	18	5	3	3	116	91	15	15	.500	0	3.46
91	CHI/NL		37	1070	37	7	2	0	*263.0	232	18	66	9	8	198	16	3	6	3	113	98	15	11	.577	0	3.35
92	CHI/NL		35	1061	35	9	4	0	*268.0	201	7	70	7	14	199	15	3	5	0	68	65	*20	11	.645	0	2.18
93	ATL/NL		36	1064	36	*8	1	0	*267.0	228	14	52	7	6	197	15	7	5	1	85	70	20	10	.667	0	*2.36
8 YR TOTALS			**248**	**7100**	**244**	**50**	**14**	**3**	**1709.0**	**1580**	**96**	**507**	**77**	**50**	**1134**	**101**	**27**	**33**	**23**	**700**	**606**	**115**	**85**	**.575**	**0**	**3.19**

Maddux, Michael Ausley "Mike" — BL/TR — b.8/27/61   PHI82 5/119

YR	TM/LG	CL	G	TBF	GS	CG	SHO	GF	IP	H	HR	BB	IBB	HB	SO	SH	SF	WP	BK	R	ER	W	L	PCT	SV	ERA
84	REA/EAS	AA	20	527	19	4	0	2	116.0	143	10	49	2	2	77	9	4	12	0	82	65	3	12	.200	0	5.04
	POR/PCL	AAA	8	0	8	1	0	0	44.2	58	5	17	2	1	22	0	0	2	0	32	29	2	4	.333	0	5.84
85	POR/PCL	AAA	27	0	26	6	1	1	166.0	195	15	51	4	4	96	0	0	13	2	106	98	9	12	.429	0	5.31
86	POR/PCL	AAA	12	334	12	3	0	0	84.0	70	5	22	0	1	65	3	2	2	0	26	22	5	2	.714	0	2.36
	PHI/NL		16	351	16	0	0	0	78.0	88	6	34	4	3	44	3	3	4	2	56	47	3	7	.300	0	5.42
87	MAI/INT	AAA	18	446	16	3	1	1	103.1	116	9	23	2	1	71	2	2	5	1	58	50	6	6	.500	0	4.35
	PHI/NL		7	72	2	0	0	0	17.0	17	1	5	0	1	15	0	0	1	0	5	5	2	0	1.000	0	2.65
88	MAI/INT	AAA	5	109	3	1	0	0	23.2	25	3	10	0	2	18	1	0	2	0	18	11	0	2	.000	0	4.18
	PHI/NL		25	380	11	0	0	4	88.2	91	6	34	4	4	59	7	3	4	2	41	37	4	3	.571	0	3.76
89	SCR/INT	AAA	19	515	17	3	1	1	123.0	119	7	26	2	7	100	2	5	8	1	55	50	7	7	.500	0	3.66
	PHI/NL		16	191	4	2	1	1	43.2	52	3	13	3	2	26	3	1	3	1	29	25	1	3	.250	1	5.15
90	LA/NL		11	88	2	0	0	3	20.2	24	3	4	2	1	19	0	1	0	0	15	15	0	1	.000	0	6.53
	ALB/PCL	AAA	20	473	19	2	0	0	108.0	122	8	32	2	4	85	3	2	7	0	59	51	8	5	.615	0	4.25
91	SD/NL		64	388	1	0	0	27	98.2	78	4	27	3	1	57	5	2	5	0	30	27	7	2	.778	5	2.46
92	SD/NL		50	330	1	0	0	14	79.2	71	2	24	4	1	60	2	3	4	1	25	21	2	2	.500	5	2.37
93	NY/NL		58	320	0	0	0	31	75.0	67	3	27	7	4	57	7	6	4	1	34	30	3	8	.273	5	3.60
8 YR TOTALS			**247**	**2120**	**37**	**2**	**1**	**80**	**501.1**	**488**	**27**	**169**	**25**	**16**	**329**	**27**	**19**	**27**	**7**	**235**	**207**	**22**	**26**	**.458**	**16**	**3.72**

Magnante, Michael Anthony "Mike" — BL/TL — b.6/17/65   KC88 11/283

YR	TM/LG	CL	G	TBF	GS	CG	SHO	GF	IP	H	HR	BB	IBB	HB	SO	SH	SF	WP	BK	R	ER	W	L	PCT	SV	ERA
88	EUG/NWL	A-	3	59	3	0	0	0	16.0	10	0	2	0	0	26	0	0	0	0	6	1	1	1	.500	0	0.56
	APP/MID	A	9	199	8	0	0	0	47.2	48	3	15	0	0	40	4	1	3	0	20	17	3	2	.600	0	3.21
	BC/FSL	A+	4	95	4	1	0	0	24.0	19	1	8	0	0	19	1	0	0	0	12	11	1	1	.500	0	4.13
89	MEM/SOU	AA	26	659	26	4	1	0	157.1	137	10	53	3	9	118	6	2	8	0	70	64	8	9	.471	0	3.66
90	OMA/AMA	AAA	13	320	13	2	0	0	76.2	72	6	25	0	2	56	3	0	3	1	39	35	2	5	.286	0	4.11
91	OMA/AMA	AAA	10	264	10	2	0	0	65.2	53	2	23	0	1	50	2	2	2	0	23	22	6	1	.857	0	3.02
	KC/AL		38	236	0	0	0	10	55.0	55	3	23	3	2	42	2	1	1	0	19	15	0	0	.000	0	2.45
92	KC/AL		44	403	12	0	0	11	89.1	115	5	35	5	2	31	5	7	2	0	53	49	4	9	.308	0	4.94
93	OMA/AMA	AAA	33	428	13	0	0	5	105.1	97	7	29	2	4	74	2	2	1	0	46	43	2	6	.250	2	3.67
	KC/AL		7	145	6	0	0	0	35.1	37	3	11	1	1	16	1	1	1	0	16	16	1	2	.333	0	4.08
3 YR TOTALS			**89**	**784**	**18**	**0**	**0**	**21**	**179.2**	**207**	**11**	**69**	**9**	**3**	**89**	**8**	**9**	**4**	**0**	**88**	**80**	**5**	**12**	**.294**	**0**	**4.01**

Magrane, Joseph David "Joe" — BR/TL — b.7/2/64   SL85 1/18

YR	TM/LG	CL	G	TBF	GS	CG	SHO	GF	IP	H	HR	BB	IBB	HB	SO	SH	SF	WP	BK	R	ER	W	L	PCT	SV	ERA
85	JC/APP	R+	6	113	5	2	2	0	30.0	15	0	11	0	1	31	0	0	0	2	4	2	2	1	.667	0	0.60
	SP/FSL	A+	5	137	5	1	1	0	34.2	21	0	14	0	1	17	0	0	2	1	8	4	3	1	.750	0	1.04
86	ARK/TEX	AA	13	353	13	5	2	0	89.1	66	3	31	0	2	66	4	1	8	0	29	24	8	4	.667	0	2.42
	LOU/AMA	AAA	15	457	15	8	2	0	113.1	93	4	33	1	5	72	2	5	7	4	34	26	9	6	.600	0	2.06
87	LOU/AMA	AAA	3	88	3	1	1	0	23.1	16	1	3	0	0	17	0	0	1	0	7	5	1	0	1.000	0	1.93
	STL/NL		27	722	26	4	2	0	170.1	157	9	60	6	10	101	9	3	9	7	75	67	9	7	.563	0	3.54
88	LOU/AMA	AAA	4	86	4	1	0	0	20.0	19	1	7	0	2	18	0	1	4	0	7	7	2	1	.667	0	3.15
	STL/NL		24	677	24	4	3	0	165.1	133	6	51	4	2	100	8	4	8	8	57	40	5	9	.357	0	*2.18
89	STL/NL		34	971	33	9	3	1	234.2	219	11	72	7	6	127	14	8	14	5	81	76	18	9	.667	0	2.91
90	STL/NL		31	855	31	3	2	0	203.1	204	10	59	7	8	100	8	6	11	2	86	81	10	17	.370	0	3.59
92	SP/FSL	A+	3	70	3	0	0	0	18.0	14	0	5	0	1	15	1	0	2	0	4	3	0	1	.000	0	1.50
	LOU/AMA	AAA	10	248	10	0	0	0	53.1	60	3	29	1	3	35	6	1	3	1	32	32	3	4	.429	0	5.40
	STL/NL		5	143	5	0	0	0	31.1	34	2	15	0	2	20	3	1	4	0	15	14	1	2	.333	0	4.02
93	STL/NL		22	499	20	0	0	2	116.0	127	15	37	3	5	38	6	7	4	0	68	64	8	10	.444	0	4.97
	CAL/AL		8	209	8	0	0	0	48.0	48	4	21	0	0	24	4	3	4	0	27	21	3	2	.600	0	3.94
	YEAR		30	708	28	0	0	2	164.0	175	19	58	3	5	62	10	10	8	0	95	85	11	12	.478	0	4.66
6 YR TOTALS			**151**	**4076**	**147**	**20**	**10**	**3**	**969.0**	**922**	**51**	**315**	**27**	**33**	**510**	**52**	**32**	**54**	**21**	**409**	**363**	**54**	**56**	**.491**	**0**	**3.37**

Mahomes, Patrick Lavon "Pat" — BR/TR — b.8/9/70   MIN88 6/155

YR	TM/LG	CL	G	TBF	GS	CG	SHO	GF	IP	H	HR	BB	IBB	HB	SO	SH	SF	WP	BK	R	ER	W	L	PCT	SV	ERA
88	ELI/APP	R+	13	344	13	3	0	0	78.0	66	4	51	0	3	93	3	1	9	2	45	32	6	3	.667	0	3.69
89	KEN/MID	A	25	668	25	3	1	0	156.1	120	4	100	3	2	167	0	9	9	3	66	57	13	7	.650	0	3.28
90	VIS/CAL	A+	28	784	28	5	1	0	185.1	136	14	118	1	4	178	3	4	19	1	77	68	11	11	.500	0	3.30
91	ORL/SOU	AA	18	463	17	2	0	0	116.0	77	5	57	0	3	136	0	3	3	0	30	23	8	5	.615	0	1.78
	POR/PCL	AAA	9	244	9	2	0	0	55.0	50	2	36	1	0	41	2	3	4	0	26	21	3	5	.375	0	3.44
92	POR/PCL	AAA	17	455	16	2	0	0	111.0	97	7	43	1	0	87	0	0	3	0	43	42	9	5	.643	0	3.41
	MIN/AL		14	302	13	0	0	1	69.2	73	7	37	0	0	44	0	3	2	1	41	39	3	4	.429	0	5.04
93	MIN/AL		12	173	5	0	0	4	37.1	47	8	16	0	1	23	1	1	5	1	34	32	1	5	.167	0	7.71
	POR/PCL	AAA	17	467	16	3	1	1	115.2	89	11	54	0	1	94	4	2	5	1	47	39	11	4	.733	0	3.03
2 YR TOTALS			**26**	**475**	**18**	**0**	**0**	**5**	**107.0**	**120**	**13**	**53**	**0**	**1**	**67**	**1**	**6**	**5**	**1**	**75**	**71**	**4**	**9**	**.308**	**0**	**5.97**

Maldonado, Carlos Cesar — BB/TR — b.10/18/66   KC 4/28/86

YR	TM/LG	CL	G	TBF	GS	CG	SHO	GF	IP	H	HR	BB	IBB	HB	SO	SH	SF	WP	BK	R	ER	W	L	PCT	SV	ERA
86	ROY/GCL	R	10	136	4	0	0	2	34.1	29	1	10	1	0	16	1	1	3	0	10	7	0	2	.000	0	1.83
87	APP/MID	A	2	13	0	0	0	1	2.1	4	0	3	0	0	4	1	1	0	0	3	3	0	0	.000	0	11.57
	ROY/GCL	R	20	223	0	0	0	8	58.0	32	2	19	2	2	56	2	0	2	1	18	16	5	1	.833	4	2.48
88	BC/FSL	A+	16	242	7	0	0	2	52.2	46	5	39	0	7	44	2	1	3	0	35	31	1	5	.167	0	5.30
89	BC/FSL	A+	28	300	0	0	0	19	76.2	47	3	24	4	1	66	3	1	2	0	14	10	11	3	.786	9	1.17
90	MEM/SOU	AA	55	323	0	0	0	48	77.1	61	5	37	0	1	77	3	4	5	0	29	25	4	5	.444	20	2.91
	KC/AL		4	31	0	0	0	1	6.0	9	0	4	0	0	9	0	1	1	0	6	6	0	0	.000	0	9.00
91	KC/AL		5	43	0	0	0	2	7.2	11	0	9	1	0	1	1	0	4	0	9	7	0	0	.000	0	8.22
	OMA/AMA	AAA	41	282	1	0	0	31	61.0	67	6	42	1	2	46	3	2	6	0	31	29	1	1	.500	9	4.28
92	OMA/AMA	AAA	47	315	0	0	0	36	75.0	61	6	35	0	2	60	9	6	1	0	34	30	7	4	.636	16	3.60
93	NO/AMA	AAA	12	77	0	0	0	9	19.1	13	0	7	1	0	14	1	1	1	0	1	1	1	0	1.000	7	0.47
	MIL/AL		29	167	0	0	0	9	37.1	40	2	17	5	0	18	4	4	1	0	20	19	2	2	.500	1	4.58
3 YR TOTALS			**38**	**241**	**0**	**0**	**0**	**12**	**51.0**	**60**	**2**	**30**	**6**	**0**	**28**	**5**	**5**	**6**	**0**	**35**	**32**	**2**	**2**	**.500**	**1**	**5.65**

Manzanillo, Josias — BR/TR — b.10/16/67   BOS 2/1/83

YR	TM/LG	CL	G	TBF	GS	CG	SHO	GF	IP	H	HR	BB	IBB	HB	SO	SH	SF	WP	BK	R	ER	W	L	PCT	SV	ERA
83	ELM/NYP	A-	12	0	4	0	0	0	38.0	52	7	20	0	2	19	0	0	5	0	44	34	1	5	.167	0	8.05
84	ELM/NYP	A-	14	128	0	0	0	7	25.2	27	1	26	1	1	15	1	1	9	0	24	15	2	3	.400	1	5.26
85	GRE/SAL	A	7	62	0	0	0	2	12.0	12	1	18	0	0	10	0	0	2	0	13	13	1	1	.500	0	9.75
	ELM/NYP	A-	19	181	4	0	0	10	39.2	36	1	36	4	2	43	0	1	12	0	19	17	2	4	.333	1	3.86
86	WH/FSL	A+	23	601	21	3	2	2	142.2	110	3	81	0	3	102	6	4	9	0	51	36	13	5	.722	0	2.27
87	NB/EAS	AA	2	45	2	0	0	0	10.0	8	1	8	0	0	12	0	0	0	0	5	5	2	0	1.000	0	4.50
89	NB/EAS	AA	26	657	26	3	1	0	147.2	129	11	85	7	5	93	4	5	16	2	78	60	9	10	.474	0	3.66
90	NB/EAS	AA	12	317	12	2	1	0	74.0	66	3	37	1	2	51	1	0	7	3	34	28	4	4	.500	0	3.41
	PAW/INT	AAA	15	368	15	5	0	0	82.2	75	9	45	0	2	77	1	2	8	0	57	51	4	7	.364	0	5.55
91	NB/EAS	AA	7	212	7	0	0	0	49.2	37	0	28	1	1	35	5	0	2	1	25	16	2	2	.500	0	2.90
	PAW/INT	AAA	20	459	16	0	0	0	102.2	109	12	53	0	4	65	2	4	9	1	69	64	5	5	.500	0	5.61
	BOS/AL		1	8	0	0	0	1	1.0	2	0	3	0	0	1	0	0	0	0	2	2	0	0	.000	0	18.00
92	MEM/SOU	AA	2	33	0	0	0	0	7.1	6	0	6	0	1	8	0	0	2	0	6	6	0	2	.000	0	7.36
	OMA/AMA	AAA	26	603	21	0	0	2	136.1	138	12	71	0	7	114	0	7	8	1	76	66	7	10	.412	0	4.36
93	NO/AMA	AAA	1	4	0	0	0	1	1.0	1	1	0	0	0	3	0	0	0	0	1	1	0	0	.000	0	9.00
	NOR/INT	AAA	14	350	12	2	1	1	84.0	82	3	25	1	2	79	1	4	0	0	40	29	1	5	.167	0	3.11
	MIL/AL		10	86	1	0	0	4	17.0	22	1	10	3	2	10	2	1	0	0	20	18	1	1	.500	1	9.53
	NY/NL		6	54	0	0	0	2	12.0	8	1	9	0	0	11	1	0	0	0	7	4	0	0	.000	0	3.00
	YEAR		16	140	1	0	0	6	29.0	30	2	19	3	2	21	3	1	0	0	27	22	1	1	.500	1	6.83
2 YR TOTALS			**17**	**148**	**1**	**0**	**0**	**7**	**30.0**	**32**	**2**	**22**	**3**	**2**	**22**	**3**	**3**	**1**	**0**	**29**	**24**	**1**	**1**	**.500**	**1**	**7.20**

Martinez, Jose Dennis "Dennis" — BR/TR — b.5/14/55   BAL 12/10/73

YR	TM/LG	CL	G	TBF	GS	CG	SHO	GF	IP	H	HR	BB	IBB	HB	SO	SH	SF	WP	BK	R	ER	W	L	PCT	SV	ERA
76	BAL/AL		4	106	2	1	0	1	27.2	23	1	8	0	0	18	1	0	1	0	8	8	1	2	.333	0	2.60
77	BAL/AL		42	709	13	5	0	19	166.2	157	10	64	5	8	107	8	8	5	0	86	76	14	7	.667	4	4.10
78	BAL/AL		40	1140	38	15	2	0	276.1	257	20	93	4	3	142	8	7	8	0	121	108	16	11	.593	0	3.52
79	BAL/AL		40	1206	39	*18	3	0	*292.1	279	28	78	1	1	132	12	12	9	2	129	119	15	16	.484	0	3.66
80	BAL/AL		25	428	12	2	0	8	99.2	103	12	44	6	2	42	1	3	0	1	44	44	6	4	.600	1	3.97
81	BAL/AL		25	753	24	9	2	0	179.0	173	10	62	1	2	88	2	5	6	1	84	66	*14	5	.737	0	3.32
82	BAL/AL		40	1093	39	10	2	0	252.0	262	30	87	3	7	111	11	7	7	1	123	118	16	12	.571	0	4.21
83	BAL/AL		32	688	25	4	0	3	153.0	209	21	45	0	7	71	3	5	2	0	108	94	7	16	.304	0	5.53
84	BAL/AL		34	599	20	2	0	4	141.2	145	26	37	2	5	77	0	5	5	0	81	79	6	9	.400	0	5.02
85	BAL/AL		33	789	31	3	1	1	180.0	203	29	63	3	4	68	0	11	4	1	110	103	13	11	.542	0	5.15
86	BAL/AL		4	33	0	0	0	1	6.2	11	0	2	0	0	2	0	1	0	0	5	5	0	0	.000	0	6.75
	ROC/INT	AAA	4	83	4	0	0	0	19.1	18	5	9	0	0	14	0	1	0	0	14	13	2	1	.667	0	6.05
	MON/NL		19	416	15	1	1	1	98.0	103	11	28	4	3	63	8	5	3	0	52	50	3	6	.333	0	4.59
	YEAR		23	449	15	1	1	2	104.2	114	11	30	4	3	65	8	6	3	0	57	55	3	6	.333	0	4.73
87	MIA/FSL	A+	3	89	3	0	0	0	19.0	21	0	3	0	3	11	0	1	2	0	14	13	1	1	.500	0	6.16
	IND/AMA	AAA	7	161	7	1	1	0	38.1	32	5	13	1	0	30	3	1	0	2	20	19	3	2	.600	0	4.46
	MON/NL		22	599	22	2	1	0	144.2	133	9	40	2	6	84	4	3	4	2	59	53	11	4	.733	0	3.30
88	MON/NL		34	968	34	9	2	0	235.1	215	21	55	3	6	120	2	6	5	10	94	71	15	13	.536	0	2.72
89	MON/NL		34	950	33	5	2	1	232.0	227	21	49	4	7	142	4	4	3	0	88	82	16	7	.696	0	3.18
90	MON/NL		32	908	32	7	2	0	226.0	191	16	49	9	6	156	11	3	1	0	80	74	10	11	.476	0	2.95
91	MON/NL		31	905	31	*9	*5	0	222.0	187	9	62	3	4	123	7	3	0	0	70	59	14	11	.560	0	*2.39
92	MON/NL		32	900	32	6	0	0	226.1	172	12	60	3	9	147	12	5	2	0	75	62	16	11	.593	0	2.47
93	MON/NL		35	945	34	2	0	1	224.2	211	27	64	7	11	138	10	4	2	4	110	96	15	9	.625	1	3.85
18 YR TOTALS			**558**	**14135**	**476**	**110**	**23**	**40**	**3384.0**	**3261**	**313**	**990**	**59**	**91**	**1831**	**108**	**91**	**74**	**27**	**1527**	**1367**	**208**	**165**	**.558**	**6**	**3.64**

Martinez, Pedro Aquino — BL/TL — b.11/29/68   SD 9/30/86

YR	TM/LG	CL	G	TBF	GS	CG	SHO	GF	IP	H	HR	BB	IBB	HB	SO	SH	SF	WP	BK	R	ER	W	L	PCT	SV	ERA
87	SPO/NWL	A-	18	240	5	1	0	4	51.2	57	1	36	1	0	42	3	2	5	0	31	22	4	1	.800	0	3.83
88	SPO/NWL	A-	15	433	15	1	0	0	99.2	108	1	32	0	2	89	2	6	4	5	55	47	8	3	.727	0	4.24
89	CHS/SAL	A	27	750	27	5	2	0	187.0	147	5	64	1	2	158	4	5	4	2	53	41	14	8	.636	0	1.97
90	WIC/TEX	AA	24	576	23	2	0	0	129.1	139	15	70	2	2	88	5	2	4	0	83	69	6	10	.375	0	4.80
91	WIC/TEX	AA	26	677	26	3	2	0	156.2	169	21	57	2	3	95	8	4	5	0	99	91	11	10	.524	0	5.23
92	WIC/TEX	AA	26	694	26	3	1	0	168.1	153	12	52	0	3	142	4	4	4	0	66	56	11	7	.611	0	2.99
93	LV/PCL	AAA	15	381	14	1	0	0	87.2	94	8	40	4	2	65	2	4	3	1	49	46	3	5	.375	0	4.72
	SD/NL		32	148	0	0	0	9	37.0	23	4	13	1	1	32	0	0	0	0	11	10	3	1	.750	0	2.43

Martinez, Pedro Jaime — BR/TR — b.7/25/71 — LA 6/18/88

YR	TM/LG	CL	G	TBF	GS	CG	SHO	GF	IP	H	HR	BB	IBB	HB	SO	SH	SF	WP	BK	R	ER	W	L	PCT	SV	ERA
90	GF/PIO	R+	14	345	14	0	0	0	77.0	74	5	40	1	8	82	2	2	6	1	39	31	8	3	.727	0	3.62
91	BAK/CAL	A+	10	243	10	0	0	0	61.1	41	3	19	0	5	83	0	2	1	1	17	14	8	0	1.000	0	2.05
	SA/TEX	AA	12	310	12	4	3	0	76.2	57	1	31	1	3	74	5	0	5	1	21	15	7	5	.583	0	1.76
	ALB/PCL	AAA	6	157	6	0	0	0	39.1	28	3	16	0	0	35	1	1	3	0	17	16	3	3	.500	0	3.66
92	ALB/PCL	AAA	20	527	20	3	1	0	125.1	104	10	57	0	9	124	4	2	2	0	57	53	7	6	.538	0	3.81
	LA/NL		2	31	1	0	0	1	8.0	6	0	1	0	0	8	0	0	0	0	2	2	0	1	.000	0	2.25
93	ALB/PCL	AAA	1	11	1	0	0	0	3.0	1	0	1	0	0	4	0	0	0	0	1	1	0	0	.000	0	3.00
	LA/NL		65	444	0	0	0	20	107.0	76	5	57	4	4	119	0	5	3	1	34	31	10	5	.667	2	2.61
2 YR TOTALS			**67**	**475**	**3**	**0**	**0**	**21**	**115.0**	**82**	**5**	**58**	**4**	**4**	**127**	**0**	**5**	**3**	**1**	**36**	**33**	**10**	**6**	**.625**	**2**	**2.58**

Martinez, Ramon Jaime — BR/TR — b.3/22/68 — LA 9/1/84

YR	TM/LG	CL	G	TBF	GS	CG	SHO	GF	IP	H	HR	BB	IBB	HB	SO	SH	SF	WP	BK	R	ER	W	L	PCT	SV	ERA
85	DOD/GCL	R	23	254	6	0	0	6	59.0	57	1	23	0	1	42	5	2	5	0	30	17	4	1	.800	1	2.59
86	BAK/CAL	A+	20	494	20	2	1	0	106.0	119	3	63	2	2	78	6	5	4	2	73	56	4	8	.333	0	4.75
87	VB/FSL	A+	25	699	25	6	1	0	170.1	128	3	78	1	4	148	5	2	5	2	45	41	16	5	.762	0	2.17
88	SA/TEX	AA	14	392	14	2	1	0	95.0	79	2	34	2	1	89	3	2	2	8	29	26	8	4	.667	0	2.46
	ALB/PCL	AAA	10	249	10	1	1	0	58.2	43	3	32	0	1	49	1	2	5	4	24	18	5	2	.714	0	2.76
	LA/NL		9	151	6	0	0	0	35.2	27	0	22	1	0	23	0	1	3	0	17	15	1	3	.250	0	3.79
89	ALB/PCL	AAA	18	476	18	2	1	0	113.0	92	6	50	0	1	127	2	2	5	4	40	35	10	2	.833	0	2.79
	LA/NL		15	410	15	2	2	0	98.2	79	11	41	1	5	89	4	0	1	0	39	35	6	4	.600	0	3.19
90	LA/NL		33	950	33	*12	3	0	234.1	191	22	67	5	4	223	7	5	3	0	89	76	20	6	.769	0	2.92
91	LA/NL		33	916	33	6	4	0	220.1	190	18	69	4	7	150	8	4	6	0	89	80	17	13	.567	0	3.27
92	LA/NL		25	662	25	1	1	0	150.2	141	11	69	4	5	101	12	5	9	0	82	67	8	11	.421	0	4.00
93	LA/NL		32	918	32	4	3	0	211.2	202	15	104	9	4	127	12	5	2	2	88	81	10	12	.455	0	3.44
6 YR TOTALS			**147**	**4007**	**144**	**25**	**13**	**0**	**951.1**	**830**	**77**	**372**	**24**	**25**	**713**	**47**	**15**	**22**	**5**	**404**	**354**	**62**	**49**	**.559**	**0**	**3.35**

Mason, Roger Le Roy — BR/TR — b.9/18/58 — DET 9/21/80

YR	TM/LG	CL	G	TBF	GS	CG	SHO	GF	IP	H	HR	BB	IBB	HB	SO	SH	SF	WP	BK	R	ER	W	L	PCT	SV	ERA
81	MAC/SAL	A	26	0	26	4	1	0	148.0	153	10	50	0	7	105	0	0	4	0	77	64	10	10	.500	0	3.89
82	LAK/FSL	A+	22	0	22	5	0	0	132.0	124	9	52	0	6	72	0	0	7	0	60	51	7	7	.500	0	3.48
83	BIR/SOU	AA	17	0	17	4	1	0	126.0	116	10	43	0	7	83	0	0	3	0	45	29	7	4	.636	0	2.07
	EVA/AMA	AAA	11	0	11	2	0	0	78.0	84	6	21	0	0	43	0	0	4	0	39	37	5	5	.500	0	4.27
84	EVA/AMA	AAA	25	651	25	6	2	0	151.2	175	10	64	1	1	88	5	2	6	1	78	64	9	7	.563	0	3.80
	DET/AL		5	97	2	0	0	2	22.0	23	1	10	0	0	15	0	2	2	0	11	11	1	1	.500	1	4.50
85	PHO/PCL	AAA	24	0	24	5	2	0	167.1	145	12	72	6	4	120	0	0	6	0	67	62	12	1	.923	0	3.33
	SF/NL		5	128	5	1	1	0	29.2	28	1	11	1	0	26	2	0	0	0	13	7	1	3	.250	0	2.12
86	PHO/PCL	AAA	1	22	1	0	0	0	6.0	2	0	1	0	0	2	0	0	0	0	0	0	1	0	1.000	0	0.00
	SF/NL		11	262	11	1	0	0	60.0	56	1	30	3	3	43	2	3	1	0	35	32	3	4	.429	0	4.80
87	SF/NL		5	110	5	1	0	0	26.0	30	4	10	0	0	18	1	0	1	1	15	13	1	1	.500	0	4.50
	PHO/PCL	AAA	10	265	10	1	0	0	61.0	62	4	20	0	0	49	2	3	1	0	34	28	5	1	.833	0	4.13
88	PHO/PCL	AAA	19	397	17	1	0	2	90.2	90	9	38	2	4	62	1	1	2	0	62	49	2	9	.182	0	4.86
89	TUC/PCL	AAA	25	621	25	5	1	0	155.0	125	7	46	1	2	105	6	6	5	0	71	61	7	12	.368	0	3.54
	HOU/NL		2	8	0	0	0	1	1.1	2	0	2	0	0	3	0	0	0	0	3	3	0	0	.000	0	20.25
90	BUF/AMA	AAA	29	325	2	0	0	6	77.0	78	2	25	4	1	45	4	1	2	1	21	18	3	5	.375	3	2.10
91	BUF/AMA	AAA	34	521	15	2	1	6	122.2	115	11	44	1	6	80	6	4	2	0	47	42	9	5	.643	0	3.08
	PIT/NL		24	114	0	0	0	6	29.2	21	2	6	1	1	21	1	1	2	0	11	10	3	2	.600	3	3.03
92	PIT/NL		65	374	0	0	0	26	88.0	80	11	33	2	4	56	4	2	2	0	41	40	5	7	.417	8	4.09
93	SD/NL		34	207	0	0	0	14	50.0	43	1	18	2	2	39	6	3	1	0	20	18	0	7	.000	3	3.24
	PHI/NL		34	210	0	0	0	15	49.2	47	9	16	1	0	32	1	2	1	3	28	27	5	5	.500	0	4.89
	YEAR		68	417	0	0	0	29	99.2	90	10	34	3	2	71	7	5	2	3	48	45	5	12	.294	0	4.06
8 YR TOTALS			**185**	**1510**	**23**	**2**	**1**	**64**	**356.1**	**330**	**34**	**136**	**18**	**10**	**253**	**21**	**15**	**11**	**4**	**177**	**161**	**19**	**30**	**.388**	**12**	**4.07**

Mauser, Timothy Edward "Tim" — BR/TR — b.10/4/66 — PHI88 2/68

YR	TM/LG	CL	G	TBF	GS	CG	SHO	GF	IP	H	HR	BB	IBB	HB	SO	SH	SF	WP	BK	R	ER	W	L	PCT	SV	ERA
88	SPA/SAL	A	4	88	3	0	0	0	23.0	15	0	5	0	0	18	2	2	1	0	6	5	2	1	.667	0	1.96
	REA/EAS	AA	5	120	5	0	0	0	28.1	27	4	6	0	2	17	2	0	0	0	14	11	2	3	.400	0	3.49
89	CLE/FSL	A+	16	457	16	5	0	0	107.0	105	4	40	0	5	73	2	0	2	1	40	32	6	7	.462	0	2.69
	REA/EAS	AA	11	302	11	4	2	0	72.0	62	5	33	0	1	54	0	2	0	0	36	29	7	4	.636	0	3.62
90	REA/EAS	AA	8	194	8	1	0	0	46.1	35	2	15	0	3	40	2	0	4	0	20	17	3	4	.429	0	3.30
	SCR/INT	AAA	16	395	16	4	1	0	98.1	75	10	34	1	3	54	1	1	3	0	48	40	5	7	.417	0	3.66
91	PHI/NL		3	53	0	0	0	1	10.2	18	3	3	0	0	6	1	0	0	0	10	9	0	0	.000	0	7.59
	SCR/INT	AAA	26	544	18	1	0	3	128.1	119	11	55	3	2	75	4	4	4	0	66	53	6	11	.353	0	3.72
92	SCR/INT	AAA	45	427	5	0	0	15	100.0	87	6	45	4	0	75	6	6	4	0	37	33	8	6	.571	4	2.97
93	SCR/INT	AAA	19	79	0	0	0	19	20.2	10	1	5	0	0	25	1	0	4	0	2	2	2	0	1.000	10	0.87
	PHI/NL		8	71	0	0	0	1	16.1	15	1	7	1	0	14	0	0	0	0	9	9	0	0	.000	0	4.96
	SD/NL		28	164	0	0	0	15	37.2	36	5	17	5	2	32	1	1	1	0	19	15	0	1	.000	0	3.58
	YEAR		36	235	0	0	0	16	54.0	51	6	24	5	1	46	1	1	2	0	28	24	0	1	.000	0	4.00
2 YR TOTALS			**39**	**288**	**0**	**0**	**0**	**17**	**64.2**	**69**	**9**	**27**	**5**	**1**	**52**	**2**	**1**	**2**	**0**	**38**	**33**	**0**	**1**	**.000**	**0**	**4.59**

Maysey, Matthew Samuel "Matt" — BR/TR — b.1/8/67 — SD85 7/180

YR	TM/LG	CL	G	TBF	GS	CG	SHO	GF	IP	H	HR	BB	IBB	HB	SO	SH	SF	WP	BK	R	ER	W	L	PCT	SV	ERA
85	SPO/NWL	A-	7	0	4	0	0	2	29.0	27	3	16	0	1	18	0	0	5	0	18	15	0	3	.000	0	4.66
86	CHS/SAL	A	18	196	5	0	0	11	43.0	43	5	24	2	0	39	3	0	5	2	28	24	3	2	.600	1	5.02
87	CHS/SAL	A	41	623	18	5	0	21	150.1	112	11	59	4	5	143	8	7	13	3	71	53	14	11	.560	7	3.17
88	WIC/TEX	AA	28	789	28	4	0	0	187.0	180	15	68	1	5	120	7	6	18	5	88	77	9	9	.500	0	3.71
89	LV/PCL	AAA	28	773	28	4	1	0	176.1	173	19	84	3	2	96	3	1	12	3	94	80	8	12	.400	0	4.08

(continued)

Maysey, Matthew Samuel "Matt" (continued)

YR	TM/LG	CL	G	TBF	GS	CG	SHO	GF	IP	H	HR	BB	IBB	HB	SO	SH	SF	WP	BK	R	ER	W	L	PCT	SV	ERA
90	LV/PCL	AAA	26	634	25	1	0	1	137.2	155	10	88	5	5	72	6	5	12	1	97	86	6	10	.375	0	5.62
91	HAR/EAS	AA	15	419	15	2	2	0	104.2	90	3	28	0	2	86	2	3	8	0	26	22	6	5	.545	0	1.89
	IND/AMA	AAA	12	272	12	0	0	0	63.0	60	1	33	2	2	45	0	1	6	0	45	36	3	6	.333	0	5.14
92	MON/NL		2	12	0	0	0	1	2.1	4	1	0	0	1	1	0	0	0	0	1	1	0	0	.000	0	3.86
	IND/AMA	AAA	35	286	1	0	0	14	67.0	63	9	28	5	0	38	4	2	2	1	32	32	5	3	.625	5	4.30
93	NO/AMA	AAA	29	215	5	0	0	6	52.1	48	8	14	1	0	40	1	2	2	1	25	24	0	3	.000	2	4.13
	MIL/AL		23	105	0	0	0	12	22.0	28	4	13	1	1	10	2	2	4	0	14	14	1	2	.333	1	5.73
2 YR TOTALS			25	117	0	0	0	13	24.1	32	5	13	1	2	11	2	2	4	0	15	15	1	2	.333	1	5.55

McCaskill, Kirk Edward — BR/TR — b.4/9/61 CAL82 4/88

YR	TM/LG	CL	G	TBF	GS	CG	SHO	GF	IP	H	HR	BB	IBB	HB	SO	SH	SF	WP	BK	R	ER	W	L	PCT	SV	ERA
84	EDM/PCL	AAA	24	0	22	2	0	0	143.0	162	19	74	1	1	75	0	0	1	2	104	91	7	11	.389	0	5.73
85	EDM/PCL	AAA	3	0	3	0	0	0	17.2	17	1	6	0	0	18	0	0	0	0	7	4	1	1	.500	0	2.04
	CAL/AL		30	807	29	6	1	0	189.2	189	23	64	1	4	102	2	5	5	0	105	99	12	12	.500	0	4.70
86	CAL/AL		34	1013	33	10	2	1	246.1	207	19	92	1	5	202	6	5	10	2	98	92	17	10	.630	0	3.36
87	PS/CAL	A+	2	35	2	0	0	0	10.0	4	0	3	0	0	7	0	0	0	0	1	0	2	0	1.000	0	0.00
	EDM/PCL	AAA	1	24	1	0	0	0	6.0	3	0	4	0	0	4	0	1	0	0	2	2	1	0	1.000	0	3.00
	CAL/AL		14	334	13	1	1	0	74.2	84	14	34	0	2	56	3	1	1	0	52	47	4	6	.400	0	5.67
88	CAL/AL		23	635	23	4	2	0	146.1	155	9	61	3	1	98	1	6	13	2	78	70	8	6	.571	0	4.31
89	CAL/AL		32	864	32	6	4	0	212.0	202	16	59	1	3	107	4	4	7	2	73	69	15	10	.600	0	2.93
90	CAL/AL		29	738	29	2	1	0	174.1	161	9	72	1	2	78	3	1	5	0	77	63	12	11	.522	0	3.25
91	CAL/AL		30	762	30	1	0	0	177.2	193	19	66	1	3	71	6	6	6	0	93	84	10	19	.345	0	4.26
92	CHI/AL		34	911	34	0	0	0	209.0	193	11	95	5	6	109	7	7	6	2	116	97	12	13	.480	0	4.18
93	SB/MID	A	1	25	1	0	0	0	6.0	3	0	3	0	0	5	0	0	0	0	2	1	1	0	1.000	0	1.50
	CHI/AL		30	502	14	0	0	6	113.2	144	12	36	6	1	65	2	3	6	0	71	66	4	8	.333	2	5.23
9 YR TOTALS			256	6566	237	30	11	7	1543.2	1528	132	579	19	27	888	33	38	60	9	763	687	94	95	.497	2	4.01

McClure, Robert Craig "Bob" — BR/TL — b.4/29/52 KC73 S3/30

YR	TM/LG	CL	G	TBF	GS	CG	SHO	GF	IP	H	HR	BB	IBB	HB	SO	SH	SF	WP	BK	R	ER	W	L	PCT	SV	ERA
75	KC/AL		12	66	0	0	0	4	15.1	4	0	14	2	0	15	0	0	0	2	0	0	1	0	1.000	1	0.00
76	KC/AL		8	22	0	0	0	0	4.0	3	0	8	0	0	3	0	0	0	0	4	4	0	0	.000	0	9.00
77	MIL/AL		68	302	0	0	0	31	71.1	64	2	34	5	1	57	5	5	1	2	25	20	2	1	.667	6	2.52
78	MIL/AL		44	283	0	0	0	29	65.0	53	8	30	4	6	47	7	2	1	1	30	27	2	6	.250	9	3.74
79	MIL/AL		36	229	0	0	0	16	51.0	53	6	24	0	3	37	2	3	5	0	29	22	5	2	.714	5	3.88
80	MIL/AL		52	390	5	2	1	23	90.2	83	6	37	2	2	47	1	5	0	2	34	31	5	8	.385	10	3.08
81	MIL/AL		4	34	0	0	0	1	7.2	7	1	4	1	0	6	0	0	0	0	3	3	0	0	.000	0	3.52
82	MIL/AL		34	734	26	5	0	5	172.2	160	21	74	4	4	99	6	4	5	5	90	81	12	7	.632	0	4.22
83	MIL/AL		24	625	23	4	0	0	142.0	152	11	68	1	5	68	0	4	4	0	75	71	9	9	.500	0	4.50
84	MIL/AL		39	616	18	1	0	5	139.2	154	9	52	4	2	68	8	8	1	3	76	68	4	8	.333	1	4.38
85	MIL/AL		38	370	1	0	0	12	85.2	91	10	30	2	3	57	3	2	0	0	43	41	4	1	.800	3	4.31
86	MIL/AL		13	75	0	0	0	7	16.1	18	2	10	1	1	11	1	0	0	0	7	7	2	1	.667	0	3.86
	MON/NL		52	257	0	0	0	15	62.2	53	2	23	2	1	42	3	2	1	1	22	21	2	5	.286	6	3.02
	YEAR		65	332	0	0	0	22	79.0	71	4	33	3	1	53	4	3	1	1	29	28	4	6	.400	6	3.19
87	MON/NL		52	222	0	0	0	16	52.1	47	8	20	3	0	33	5	2	0	1	30	20	6	1	.857	5	3.44
88	MON/NL		19	87	0	0	0	8	19.0	23	3	6	0	1	12	3	2	0	3	13	13	1	3	.250	2	6.16
	NY/NL		14	46	0	0	0	5	11.0	12	1	2	0	1	7	0	0	1	0	5	5	1	0	1.000	0	4.09
	YEAR		33	133	0	0	0	13	30.0	35	4	8	0	2	19	3	2	1	3	18	18	2	3	.400	3	5.40
89	CAL/AL		48	205	0	0	0	27	52.1	39	2	15	1	1	36	1	4	2	2	14	9	6	1	.857	3	1.55
90	PS/CAL	A+	2	10	1	0	0	0	3.0	3	0	1	0	0	6	0	0	0	0	0	0	0	0	.000	0	0.00
	CAL/AL		11	30	0	0	0	1	7.0	7	0	4	0	0	3	0	0	0	0	6	5	2	0	1.000	0	6.43
91	CAL/AL		13	48	0	0	0	2	9.2	13	3	5	0	1	5	0	1	2	1	11	10	0	0	.000	0	9.31
	STL/NL		32	98	0	0	0	9	23.0	24	1	8	2	1	15	1	3	0	0	8	8	1	1	.500	0	3.13
	YEAR		45	146	0	0	0	11	32.2	37	4	13	2	2	20	1	4	2	1	19	18	1	1	.500	0	4.96
92	STL/NL		71	230	0	0	0	16	54.0	52	6	25	5	2	24	1	3	1	0	21	19	2	2	.500	0	3.17
93	FLO/NL		14	36	0	0	0	0	6.1	13	2	5	1	0	6	0	0	0	0	5	5	1	1	.500	0	7.11
19 YR TOTALS			698	5005	73	12	1	233	1158.2	1125	104	497	39	34	701	48	51	29	30	551	490	68	57	.544	52	3.81

McDonald, Larry Benard "Ben" — BR/TR — b.11/14/67 BAL89 1/1

YR	TM/LG	CL	G	TBF	GS	CG	SHO	GF	IP	H	HR	BB	IBB	HB	SO	SH	SF	WP	BK	R	ER	W	L	PCT	SV	ERA
89	FRE/CAR	A+	2	35	2	0	0	0	9.0	10	0	0	0	0	9	0	0	1	2	2	2	0	0	.000	0	2.00
	BAL/AL		6	33	0	0	0	2	7.1	8	2	4	0	0	3	0	1	1	1	7	7	1	0	1.000	0	8.59
90	HAG/EAS	AA	3	48	3	0	0	0	11.0	11	1	3	0	1	15	0	0	0	0	8	8	0	1	.000	0	6.55
	ROC/INT	AAA	7	183	7	0	0	0	44.0	33	4	21	1	2	37	2	0	4	0	18	14	3	3	.500	0	2.86
	BAL/AL		21	472	15	3	2	2	118.2	88	9	35	0	0	65	3	5	5	0	36	32	8	5	.615	0	2.43
91	ROC/INT	AAA	2	36	2	0	0	0	7.0	10	1	5	0	0	7	0	0	0	0	7	6	0	0	.000	0	7.71
	BAL/AL		21	532	21	0	0	0	126.1	126	16	43	2	1	85	2	3	3	0	71	68	6	8	.429	0	4.84
92	BAL/AL		35	958	35	4	2	0	227.0	213	32	74	5	9	158	6	6	3	2	113	107	13	13	.500	0	4.24
93	BAL/AL		34	914	34	7	1	0	220.1	185	17	86	4	5	171	7	4	7	1	92	83	13	14	.481	0	3.39
5 YR TOTALS			117	2909	105	15	5	4	699.2	620	76	242	11	15	482	18	19	19	4	319	297	41	40	.506	0	3.82

McDowell, Jack Burns — BR/TR — b.1/16/66 CHA87 1/5

YR	TM/LG	CL	G	TBF	GS	CG	SHO	GF	IP	H	HR	BB	IBB	HB	SO	SH	SF	WP	BK	R	ER	W	L	PCT	SV	ERA
87	WS/GCL	R	2	28	1	0	0	1	7.0	4	0	1	0	1	12	0	1	0	0	3	2	0	1	.000	0	2.57
	BIR/SOU	AA	4	89	4	1	0	0	20.2	19	5	8	0	1	17	0	0	3	0	20	18	1	2	.333	0	7.84
	CHI/AL		4	103	4	0	0	0	28.0	16	1	6	0	2	15	0	0	0	0	6	6	3	0	1.000	0	1.93
88	CHI/AL		26	687	26	1	0	0	158.2	147	12	68	5	7	84	6	7	11	1	85	70	5	10	.333	0	3.97

McDowell, Jack Burns (continued)

YR	TM/LG	CL	G	TBF	GS	CG	SHO	GF	IP	H	HR	BB	IBB	HB	SO	SH	SF	WP	BK	R	ER	W	L	PCT	SV	ERA
89	WS/GCL	R	4	93	4	0	0	0	24.0	19	0	4	0	1	25	0	0	0	0	2	2	2	0	1.000	0	0.75
	VAN/PCL	AAA	16	397	16	1	0	0	86.2	97	6	50	0	3	65	3	4	2	1	60	59	5	6	.455	0	6.13
90	CHI/AL		33	866	33	4	0	0	205.0	189	20	77	0	7	165	1	5	7	1	93	87	14	9	.609	0	3.82
91	CHI/AL		35	1028	35	*15	3	0	253.2	212	19	82	2	4	191	8	8	10	1	97	96	17	10	.630	0	3.41
92	CHI/AL		34	1079	34	*13	1	0	260.2	247	21	75	9	7	178	8	6	6	0	95	92	20	10	.667	0	3.18
93	CHI/AL		34	1067	34	10	*4	0	256.2	261	20	69	6	3	158	8	6	6	0	104	96	*22	10	.688	0	3.37
6 YR TOTALS			**166**	**4830**	**166**	**43**	**8**	**0**	**1162.2**	**1072**	**93**	**377**	**22**	**30**	**791**	**31**	**28**	**42**	**4**	**480**	**447**	**81**	**49**	**.623**	**0**	**3.46**

McDowell, Roger Alan — BR/TR — b.12/21/60 NYN82 3/59

YR	TM/LG	CL	G	TBF	GS	CG	SHO	GF	IP	H	HR	BB	IBB	HB	SO	SH	SF	WP	BK	R	ER	W	L	PCT	SV	ERA
84	JAC/TEX	AA	3	32	2	0	0	0	7.1	9	0	1	0	0	8	0	0	0	0	3	3	0	0	.000	0	3.68
85	NY/NL		62	516	2	0	0	36	127.1	108	9	37	8	1	70	6	2	6	2	43	40	6	5	.545	17	2.83
86	NY/NL		75	524	0	0	0	52	128.0	107	4	42	5	3	65	7	3	3	3	48	43	14	9	.609	22	3.02
87	NY/NL		56	384	0	0	0	45	88.2	95	7	28	4	2	32	5	5	3	1	41	41	7	5	.583	25	4.16
88	NY/NL		62	378	0	0	0	41	89.0	80	1	31	7	3	46	3	5	6	1	31	26	5	5	.500	16	2.63
89	NY/NL		25	156	0	0	0	15	35.1	34	1	16	2	2	15	3	1	3	1	21	13	1	5	.167	4	3.31
	PHI/NL		44	231	0	0	0	41	56.2	45	2	22	5	1	32	3	0	0	0	15	7	5	5	.500	19	1.11
	YEAR		69	387	0	0	0	56	92.0	79	3	38	8	3	47	6	1	3	1	36	20	6	8	.333	23	1.96
90	PHI/NL		72	373	0	0	0	60	86.1	92	2	35	9	2	39	10	4	1	1	41	37	6	8	.429	22	3.86
91	PHI/NL		38	271	0	0	0	16	59.0	61	1	32	12	2	28	7	1	1	0	28	21	3	6	.333	7	3.20
	LA/NL		33	174	0	0	0	18	42.1	39	3	16	4	0	22	4	2	0	1	12	12	6	3	.667	7	2.55
	YEAR		71	445	0	0	0	34	101.1	100	4	48	20	2	50	11	3	1	1	40	33	9	9	.500	10	2.93
92	LA/NL		65	393	0	0	0	39	83.2	103	3	42	13	1	50	10	4	3	1	46	38	6	10	.375	14	4.09
93	LA/NL		54	300	0	0	0	19	68.0	76	3	30	10	2	27	3	1	5	0	32	17	5	3	.625	2	2.25
9 YR TOTALS			**586**	**3700**	**2**	**0**	**0**	**382**	**864.1**	**840**	**35**	**331**	**84**	**19**	**426**	**61**	**27**	**33**	**10**	**358**	**295**	**62**	**62**	**.500**	**151**	**3.07**

McElroy, Charles Dwayne "Chuck" — BL/TL — b.10/1/67 PHI86 8/192

YR	TM/LG	CL	G	TBF	GS	CG	SHO	GF	IP	H	HR	BB	IBB	HB	SO	SH	SF	WP	BK	R	ER	W	L	PCT	SV	ERA
86	UTI/NYP	A-	14	386	14	5	1	0	94.2	85	4	28	0	2	91	8	2	2	0	40	31	4	6	.400	0	2.95
87	SPA/SAL	A	24	535	21	5	2	0	130.1	117	6	48	2	0	115	4	1	7	1	51	45	14	4	.778	0	3.11
	CLE/FSL	A+	2	27	2	0	0	0	7.1	1	0	4	0	1	7	0	1	0	0	1	0	1	0	1.000	0	0.00
88	REA/EAS	AA	28	698	26	4	2	0	160.0	173	9	70	2	2	92	6	2	4	1	89	80	9	12	.429	0	4.50
89	REA/EAS	AA	32	188	0	0	0	24	47.0	39	0	14	2	3	39	3	2	3	0	14	14	3	1	.750	12	2.68
	SCR/INT	AAA	14	68	0	0	0	9	15.1	13	1	11	1	1	12	1	1	0	0	6	5	1	2	.333	3	2.93
	PHI/NL		11	46	0	0	0	4	10.1	12	1	4	1	0	8	0	0	0	0	2	2	0	0	.000	0	1.74
90	SCR/INT	AAA	57	324	1	0	0	26	76.0	62	6	34	4	5	78	7	2	3	0	24	23	6	8	.429	7	2.72
	PHI/NL		16	76	0	0	0	8	14.0	24	0	10	2	0	16	0	0	0	0	13	12	0	1	.000	0	7.71
91	CHI/NL		71	419	0	0	0	12	101.1	73	7	57	10	0	92	9	6	1	0	33	22	6	2	.750	3	1.95
92	CHI/NL		72	369	0	0	0	30	83.2	73	5	51	10	0	83	5	5	3	0	40	33	4	7	.364	6	3.55
93	IOW/AMA	AAA	9	73	0	0	0	4	15.2	19	1	9	0	1	13	0	0	1	0	10	8	0	1	.000	2	4.60
	CHI/NL		49	214	0	0	0	11	47.1	51	4	25	1	0	31	5	1	3	0	30	24	2	2	.500	0	4.56
5 YR TOTALS			**219**	**1124**	**0**	**0**	**0**	**65**	**256.2**	**233**	**17**	**147**	**25**	**1**	**230**	**19**	**13**	**7**	**0**	**118**	**93**	**12**	**12**	**.500**	**9**	**3.26**

McGehee, George Kevin "Kevin" — BR/TR — b.1/18/69 SF90 11/230

YR	TM/LG	CL	G	TBF	GS	CG	SHO	GF	IP	H	HR	BB	IBB	HB	SO	SH	SF	WP	BK	R	ER	W	L	PCT	SV	ERA
90	EVE/NWL	A-	15	333	14	1	0	0	73.2	74	6	38	0	4	86	3	2	16	5	47	39	4	8	.333	0	4.76
91	SJ/CAL	A+	26	735	26	2	0	0	174.0	129	1	87	2	8	171	5	6	11	2	58	45	13	6	.684	0	2.33
92	SHR/TEX	AA	25	654	24	1	0	0	158.1	146	10	42	0	5	140	3	7	8	1	61	52	9	7	.563	0	2.96
93	PHO/PCL	AAA	4	104	4	0	0	0	22.0	28	1	8	1	5	16	1	3	1	0	16	12	0	3	.000	0	4.91
	ROC/INT	AAA	20	551	20	2	0	0	133.2	124	14	37	1	7	92	1	3	3	0	53	44	7	6	.538	0	2.96
	BAL/AL		5	75	0	0	0	1	16.2	18	5	7	2	2	7	1	1	1	0	11	11	0	0	.000	0	5.94

McMichael, Gregory Winston "Greg" — BR/TR — b.12/1/66 CLE88 9/163

YR	TM/LG	CL	G	TBF	GS	CG	SHO	GF	IP	H	HR	BB	IBB	HB	SO	SH	SF	WP	BK	R	ER	W	L	PCT	SV	ERA
88	BUR/APP	R+	3	86	3	1	1	0	21.0	17	0	4	0	0	20	0	1	1	1	9	6	2	0	1.000	0	2.57
	KIN/CAR	A+	11	307	11	2	0	0	77.1	57	3	18	1	3	35	3	6	4	1	31	23	4	2	.667	0	2.68
89	CAN/EAS	AA	26	704	26	8	5	0	170.0	164	10	64	1	6	101	3	5	9	1	81	66	11	11	.500	0	3.49
90	CAN/EAS	AA	13	172	4	0	0	4	40.1	39	3	17	1	1	19	2	2	3	0	17	15	2	3	.400	0	3.35
	CS/PCL	AAA	12	279	12	1	1	0	59.0	72	5	30	0	4	34	2	4	6	0	45	38	2	3	.400	0	5.80
91	DUR/CAR	A+	36	350	6	0	0	13	79.2	83	3	29	3	8	82	6	2	6	2	34	32	5	6	.455	2	3.62
92	GRE/SOU	AA	15	186	4	0	0	4	46.1	37	2	13	2	0	53	1	2	2	0	7	4	2	2	.667	1	1.36
	RIC/INT	AAA	19	382	13	0	0	2	90.1	89	5	34	1	1	86	6	2	1	1	52	44	6	5	.545	2	4.38
93	ATL/NL		74	365	0	0	0	40	91.2	68	3	29	4	0	89	4	2	6	1	22	21	2	3	.400	19	2.06

Meacham, Russell Loren "Rusty" — BR/TR — b.1/27/68 DET87 33/858

YR	TM/LG	CL	G	TBF	GS	CG	SHO	GF	IP	H	HR	BB	IBB	HB	SO	SH	SF	WP	BK	R	ER	W	L	PCT	SV	ERA
88	FAY/SAL	A	6	117	5	0	0	0	24.2	37	3	6	1	2	16	0	1	2	5	19	17	0	3	.000	0	6.20
	BRI/APP	R+	13	303	9	2	2	1	75.1	55	1	22	0	7	85	1	1	5	1	14	12	9	1	.900	0	1.43
89	FAY/SAL	A	16	413	15	2	0	1	102.0	103	4	23	1	6	74	1	4	2	3	33	26	10	3	.769	0	2.29
	LAK/FSL	A+	11	259	9	4	2	1	64.2	59	3	12	2	2	39	3	0	0	0	15	14	5	4	.556	0	1.95
90	LON/EAS	AA	26	722	26	9	3	0	178.0	161	11	36	0	4	123	4	3	5	0	70	62	15	9	.625	0	3.13
91	DET/AL		10	126	4	0	0	0	27.2	35	4	11	0	0	14	1	1	3	0	17	16	2	1	.667	0	5.20
	TOL/INT	AAA	26	517	17	3	1	1	125.1	117	8	40	3	1	70	2	5	3	2	53	43	7	9	.563	2	3.09
92	KC/AL		64	412	0	0	0	20	101.2	88	5	21	5	1	64	3	9	4	0	39	31	10	4	.714	2	2.74
93	OMA/AMA	AAA	7	37	0	0	0	2	9.1	10	1	0	0	0	10	0	0	0	0	5	5	0	0	.000	0	4.82
	KC/AL		15	104	0	0	0	11	21.0	31	2	5	5	0	20	1	1	2	0	15	13	2	2	.500	0	5.57
3 YR TOTALS			**89**	**642**	**4**	**0**	**0**	**32**	**150.1**	**154**	**11**	**37**	**6**	**4**	**91**	**4**	**13**	**4**	**1**	**71**	**60**	**14**	**7**	**.667**	**2**	**3.59**

Melendez, Jose Luis — BR/TR — b.9/2/65   PIT 8/29/83

YR	TM/LG	CL	G	TBF	GS	CG	SHO	GF	IP	H	HR	BB	IBB	HB	SO	SH	SF	WP	BK	R	ER	W	L	PCT	SV	ERA
84	WAT/NYP	A-	15	372	15	3	1	0	91.0	61	6	40	0	6	68	1	2	4	2	37	28	5	7	.417	0	2.77
85	PW/CAR	A+	9	180	8	1	0	1	44.1	25	2	26	0	0	41	0	3	2	0	17	12	3	2	.600	1	2.44
86	PW/CAR	A+	28	768	27	6	1	0	186.1	141	9	81	1	2	146	7	5	6	5	75	54	13	10	.565	0	2.61
87	HAR/EAS	AA	6	91	6	0	0	0	18.1	28	4	11	0	0	13	1	0	0	1	24	22	1	3	.250	0	10.80
	SAL/CAR	A+	20	493	20	1	1	0	116.1	96	17	56	0	8	86	0	5	4	0	62	59	9	6	.600	0	4.56
88	SAL/CAR	A+	8	233	8	2	1	0	53.2	55	10	19	1	1	50	0	0	2	1	26	24	4	2	.667	0	4.02
	HAR/EAS	AA	22	274	4	2	2	6	71.1	46	2	19	1	1	38	2	3	3	4	20	18	5	3	.625	1	2.27
89	WIL/EAS	AA	11	295	11	0	0	0	73.1	54	7	22	1	2	56	1	2	0	6	23	20	3	4	.429	0	2.45
	CAL/PCL	AAA	17	184	2	0	0	4	40.2	42	6	19	2	3	24	2	3	1	0	27	26	1	2	.333	0	5.75
90	CAL/PCL	AAA	45	525	1	0	0	14	124.2	119	11	44	2	6	95	2	5	2	1	61	54	11	4	.733	2	3.90
	SEA/AL		3	28	0	0	0	1	5.1	8	2	3	0	1	7	0	0	1	0	8	7	0	0	.000	0	11.81
91	LV/PCL	AAA	9	238	8	1	0	1	58.2	54	8	11	0	3	45	1	4	0	0	27	26	7	0	1.000	0	3.99
	SD/NL		31	381	9	0	0	10	93.2	77	11	24	3	1	60	2	6	3	2	35	34	8	5	.615	3	3.27
92	SD/NL		56	363	3	0	0	18	89.1	82	9	20	7	3	82	7	4	1	1	32	29	6	7	.462	0	2.92
93	BOS/AL		9	63	0	0	0	5	16.0	10	4	5	3	0	14	2	0	0	0	4	4	2	1	.667	0	2.25
	PAW/INT	AAA	19	156	0	0	0	10	35.0	37	7	7	0	2	31	2	2	2	0	24	21	2	3	.400	2	5.40
4 YR TOTALS			**99**	**835**	**12**	**0**	**0**	**34**	**204.1**	**177**	**24**	**52**	**13**	**5**	**163**	**9**	**12**	**5**	**3**	**79**	**74**	**16**	**13**	**.552**	**3**	**3.26**

Menendez, Antonio Gustavo "Tony" — BR/TR — b.2/20/65   CHA84 1/20

YR	TM/LG	CL	G	TBF	GS	CG	SHO	GF	IP	H	HR	BB	IBB	HB	SO	SH	SF	WP	BK	R	ER	W	L	PCT	SV	ERA
84	WS/GCL	R	6	148	6	0	0	0	37.0	26	2	13	0	0	30	0	1	2	0	19	13	3	2	.600	0	3.16
85	BUF/AMA	AAA	1	15	1	0	0	0	2.1	9	0	1	1	0	2	0	0	0	0	5	5	0	1	.000	0	19.29
	APP/MID	A	24	620	24	2	0	0	148.0	134	8	55	0	4	100	6	3	11	1	67	45	13	4	.765	0	2.74
86	PEN/CAR	A+	11	279	10	1	1	0	63.0	58	9	29	0	4	43	1	6	6	0	35	32	4	4	.500	0	4.57
	BIR/SOU	AA	17	470	17	0	0	0	96.1	132	17	50	0	7	52	0	3	14	0	71	61	7	8	.467	0	5.70
87	BIR/SOU	AA	27	776	27	4	1	0	173.1	193	19	76	1	7	102	3	7	12	2	111	93	10	10	.500	0	4.83
88	BIR/SOU	AA	24	642	24	3	0	0	153.0	131	14	64	0	2	112	4	8	6	4	79	67	6	11	.353	0	3.94
89	BIR/SOU	AA	27	596	18	2	1	6	144.0	123	14	53	2	4	115	5	1	7	2	61	51	10	4	.714	1	3.19
90	VAN/PCL	AAA	24	307	9	2	1	2	72.2	63	6	28	1	6	48	3	5	1	0	34	30	2	5	.286	0	3.72
91	TUL/TEX	AA	3	54	2	0	0	0	14.0	9	0	4	0	0	14	0	0	0	0	2	2	3	0	1.000	0	1.29
	OC/AMA	AAA	21	504	19	0	0	1	116.0	107	6	62	2	6	82	5	8	8	1	70	67	5	5	.500	0	5.20
92	CIN/NL		3	15	0	0	0	1	4.2	1	1	0	0	0	5	0	0	0	0	1	1	1	0	1.000	0	1.93
	NAS/AMA	AAA	50	458	2	0	0	11	106.2	98	10	47	6	3	92	8	5	3	0	53	48	3	5	.375	1	4.05
93	BUF/AMA	AAA	54	255	0	0	0	39	63.1	50	5	21	2	3	48	1	3	5	0	20	17	4	5	.444	24	2.42
	PIT/NL		14	85	0	0	0	3	21.0	20	4	4	0	1	13	1	1	0	0	8	7	2	0	1.000	0	3.00
2 YR TOTALS			**17**	**100**	**0**	**0**	**0**	**4**	**25.2**	**21**	**5**	**4**	**0**	**1**	**18**	**1**	**1**	**0**	**0**	**9**	**8**	**3**	**0**	**1.000**	**0**	**2.81**

Mercker, Kent Franklin — BL/TL — b.2/1/68   ATL86 1/5

YR	TM/LG	CL	G	TBF	GS	CG	SHO	GF	IP	H	HR	BB	IBB	HB	SO	SH	SF	WP	BK	R	ER	W	L	PCT	SV	ERA
86	BRA/GCL	R	9	203	8	0	0	1	47.1	37	1	16	1	0	42	2	0	6	1	21	13	4	3	.571	0	2.47
87	DUR/CAR	A+	3	49	3	0	0	0	11.2	11	1	6	0	0	14	0	0	1	0	8	7	0	1	.000	0	5.40
88	DUR/CAR	A+	19	527	19	5	0	0	127.2	102	5	47	0	2	159	0	1	7	1	44	39	11	4	.733	0	2.75
	GRE/SOU	AA	9	207	9	0	0	0	48.1	36	2	26	1	1	60	1	0	2	2	20	18	3	1	.750	0	3.35
89	RIC/INT	AAA	27	698	27	4	0	0	168.2	107	17	95	4	3	144	7	7	7	2	66	60	9	12	.429	0	3.20
	ATL/NL		2	26	1	0	0	1	4.1	8	0	6	0	0	4	0	0	0	0	6	6	0	0	.000	0	12.46
90	RIC/INT	AAA	12	260	10	0	0	1	58.1	60	1	27	1	1	69	0	1	5	1	30	23	5	4	.556	1	3.55
	ATL/NL		36	211	0	0	0	28	48.1	43	6	24	3	2	39	1	2	2	0	22	17	4	7	.364	7	3.17
91	ATL/NL		50	306	0	0	0	28	73.1	56	5	35	3	1	62	2	4	5	3	23	21	5	3	.625	6	2.58
92	ATL/NL		53	289	0	0	0	18	68.1	51	4	35	1	3	49	4	1	6	0	27	26	3	2	.600	6	3.42
93	ATL/NL		43	283	6	0	0	9	66.0	52	7	36	3	2	59	0	0	5	0	24	21	3	1	.750	0	2.86
5 YR TOTALS			**184**	**1115**	**11**	**0**	**0**	**84**	**260.1**	**210**	**17**	**136**	**10**	**8**	**213**	**7**	**5**	**17**	**2**	**102**	**91**	**15**	**13**	**.536**	**19**	**3.15**

Merriman, Brett Alan — BR/TR — b.7/15/66   CLE88 11/215

YR	TM/LG	CL	G	TBF	GS	CG	SHO	GF	IP	H	HR	BB	IBB	HB	SO	SH	SF	WP	BK	R	ER	W	L	PCT	SV	ERA
88	BUR/APP	R+	8	190	8	0	0	0	45.1	39	1	13	1	1	45	2	2	6	4	20	13	0	4	.000	0	2.58
89	MIA/FSL	A+	5	105	5	0	0	0	19.0	30	1	17	0	4	8	1	3	3	0	21	17	0	4	.000	0	8.05
	WAT/NYP	A-	14	402	14	2	2	0	92.0	75	1	44	0	8	64	5	2	3	0	50	27	7	5	.583	0	2.64
90	PS/CAL	A+	24	460	16	0	0	0	100.2	106	2	55	2	1	53	3	1	8	0	60	42	3	10	.231	0	3.75
	MID/TEX	AA	2	18	0	0	0	1	4.0	7	0	0	0	0	1	0	0	0	0	1	1	1	0	1.000	0	2.25
91	PS/CAL	A+	34	188	0	0	0	24	41.1	36	0	30	5	2	23	1	1	4	0	20	9	4	1	.800	2	1.96
92	MID/TEX	AA	38	214	0	0	0	27	53.1	49	3	10	1	.3	32	1	2	1	0	26	16	3	4	.429	9	2.70
	EDM/PCL	AAA	22	136	0	0	0	14	31.2	31	0	10	3	2	19	1	0	2	0	10	5	1	3	.250	1	1.42
93	POR/PCL	AAA	39	206	0	0	0	33	48.0	46	0	18	0	3	29	1	2	0	0	19	16	5	0	1.000	15	3.00
	MIN/AL		19	135	0	0	0	10	27.0	36	3	23	2	3	14	0	2	1	0	29	29	1	1	.500	0	9.67

Mesa, Jose Ramon Nova — BR/TR — b.5/22/66   TOR 10/31/81

YR	TM/LG	CL	G	TBF	GS	CG	SHO	GF	IP	H	HR	BB	IBB	HB	SO	SH	SF	WP	BK	R	ER	W	L	PCT	SV	ERA
84	FLO/SAL	A	7	177	7	0	0	0	38.1	38	3	25	0	0	35	1	2	2	1	24	16	4	3	.571	0	3.76
	KIN/CAR	A+	10	221	9	0	0	0	50.2	51	2	28	0	0	24	1	1	2	1	23	22	5	2	.714	0	3.91
85	KIN/CAR	A+	30	508	20	0	0	5	106.2	110	11	79	0	9	71	1	10	12	1	89	73	5	10	.333	1	6.16
86	VEN/CAL	A+	24	614	24	2	1	0	142.1	141	6	58	0	1	113	2	1	9	2	71	61	10	6	.625	0	3.86
	KNO/SOU	AA	9	190	8	2	1	0	41.1	40	6	23	0	2	30	0	2	2	0	32	20	2	2	.500	0	4.35
87	KNO/SOU	AA	35	881	35	4	2	0	193.1	206	19	104	0	3	115	0	8	13	0	131	112	10	13	.435	0	5.21
	BAL/AL		6	143	5	0	0	0	31.1	38	7	15	0	0	17	0	0	0	0	23	21	1	3	.250	0	6.03
88	ROC/INT	AAA	11	81	3	0	0	5	15.2	21	1	14	0	2	15	0	0	1	0	20	15	0	0	.000	0	8.62
89	HAG/EAS	AA	3	51	3	0	0	0	13.0	9	0	4	0	0	12	0	0	0	0	2	2	0	0	.000	0	1.38

Mesa, Jose Ramon Nova (continued)

YR	TM/LG	CL	G	TBF	GS	CG	SHO	GF	IP	H	HR	BB	IBB	HB	SO	SH	SF	WP	BK	R	ER	W	L	PCT	SV	ERA
	ROC/INT	AAA	7	45	1	0	0	4	10.0	10	2	6	0	0	3	0	0	1	0	6	6	0	2	.000	0	5.40
90	HAG/EAS	AA	15	333	15	3	1	0	79.0	77	4	30	0	1	72	3	1	2	0	35	30	5	5	.500	0	3.42
	ROC/INT	AAA	4	106	4	0	0	0	26.0	21	2	12	0	0	23	0	0	3	0	11	7	1	2	.333	0	2.42
	BAL/AL		7	202	7	0	0	0	46.2	37	2	27	2	1	24	2	2	1	1	20	20	3	2	.600	0	3.86
91	ROC/INT	AAA	8	216	8	1	1	0	51.1	37	4	30	0	2	48	1	1	3	1	25	22	3	3	.500	0	3.86
	BAL/AL		23	566	23	2	1	0	123.2	151	11	62	2	3	64	5	4	3	0	86	82	6	11	.353	0	5.97
92	BAL/AL		13	300	12	0	0	1	67.2	77	9	27	1	2	22	0	3	2	0	41	39	3	8	.273	0	5.19
	CLE/AL		15	400	15	1	1	0	93.0	92	5	43	0	2	40	2	2	0	0	45	43	4	4	.500	0	4.16
	YEAR		28	700	27	1	1	1	160.2	169	14	70	1	4	62	2	5	2	0	86	82	7	12	.368	0	4.59
93	CLE/AL		34	897	33	3	0	0	208.2	232	21	62	2	7	118	9	9	8	2	122	114	10	12	.455	0	4.92
5 YR TOTALS			**98**	**2508**	**95**	**6**	**2**	**1**	**571.0**	**627**	**55**	**236**	**7**	**15**	**285**	**18**	**20**	**18**	**3**	**337**	**319**	**27**	**40**	**.403**	**0**	**5.03**

Miceli, Daniel "Danny" — BR/TR — b.9/9/70   KC 3/7/90

YR	TM/LG	CL	G	TBF	GS	CG	SHO	GF	IP	H	HR	BB	IBB	HB	SO	SH	SF	WP	BK	R	ER	W	L	PCT	SV	ERA
90	ROY/GCL	R	27	227	0	0	0	13	53.0	45	0	29	5	2	48	4	1	4	0	27	23	3	4	.429	4	3.91
91	EUG/NWL	A-	25	135	0	0	0	21	33.2	18	1	18	0	1	43	1	1	2	0	8	8	0	1	.000	10	2.14
92	APP/MID	A	23	89	0	0	0	22	23.1	12	0	4	1	1	44	1	0	1	0	6	5	1	1	.500	9	1.93
	MEM/SOU	AA	32	145	0	0	0	16	37.2	20	5	13	0	1	46	2	4	1	0	9	8	4	0	1.000	4	1.91
93	MEM/SOU	AA	40	271	0	0	0	29	58.2	54	4	39	3	4	68	2	3	4	1	30	30	6	4	.600	7	4.60
	CAR/SOU	AA	13	51	0	0	0	12	12.1	11	2	4	1	0	19	0	0	0	0	8	7	0	2	.000	10	5.11
	PIT/NL		9	25	0	0	0	1	5.1	6	0	3	0	0	4	0	0	0	1	3	3	0	0	.000	0	5.06

Milacki, Robert "Bob" — BR/TR — b.7/28/64   BAL83 S2/29

YR	TM/LG	CL	G	TBF	GS	CG	SHO	GF	IP	H	HR	BB	IBB	HB	SO	SH	SF	WP	BK	R	ER	W	L	PCT	SV	ERA
84	HAG/CAR	A+	15	339	13	1	0	1	77.2	69	2	48	0	0	62	1	2	6	0	35	29	4	5	.444	0	3.36
85	DB/FSL	A+	8	167	6	2	0	1	38.1	32	0	26	0	0	24	2	3	7	1	23	17	1	4	.200	0	3.99
	HAG/CAR	A+	7	174	7	1	0	0	40.2	32	1	22	0	2	37	0	0	0	0	16	12	3	2	.600	0	2.66
86	HAG/CAR	A+	13	292	12	1	1	0	60.2	69	4	37	2	1	46	1	4	6	1	59	32	4	5	.444	0	4.75
	MIA/FSL	A+	12	297	11	0	0	0	67.1	70	1	27	2	2	41	2	4	6	0	36	28	4	4	.500	0	3.74
	CHA/SOU	AA	1	28	1	0	0	0	5.1	7	0	4	0	0	6	1	0	2	0	4	4	0	1	.000	0	6.75
87	CHA/SOU	AA	29	662	24	2	0	2	148.0	168	10	66	0	3	101	2	3	10	0	86	75	11	9	.550	1	4.56
88	CHA/SOU	AA	5	150	5	1	0	0	37.2	26	1	12	1	3	29	1	1	1	1	11	10	3	1	.750	0	2.39
	ROC/INT	AAA	24	747	24	11	3	0	176.2	174	8	65	1	1	103	2	2	6	1	62	53	12	8	.600	0	2.70
	BAL/AL		3	91	3	1	1	0	25.0	9	1	9	0	0	18	0	0	0	0	2	2	2	0	1.000	0	0.72
89	BAL/AL		37	1022	36	3	2	0	243.0	233	21	88	4	2	113	7	6	1	1	105	101	14	12	.538	0	3.74
90	BAL/AL		27	594	24	1	1	0	135.1	143	18	61	2	0	60	5	5	2	1	73	67	5	8	.385	0	4.46
91	HAG/EAS	AA	3	67	3	0	0	0	17.0	14	1	3	0	0	16	0	0	0	0	3	2	3	0	1.000	0	1.06
	BAL/AL		31	758	26	3	1	1	184.0	175	17	53	3	1	108	7	5	1	2	86	82	10	9	.526	0	4.01
92	ROC/INT	AAA	9	253	9	3	0	0	61.0	57	9	21	0	2	35	1	4	3	0	33	31	7	1	.875	0	4.57
	BAL/AL		23	525	20	1	1	0	115.2	140	16	44	2	2	51	3	3	7	1	78	75	6	8	.429	1	5.84
93	CHW/INT	AAA	21	288	7	0	0	8	71.2	59	6	19	1	0	46	2	2	4	0	31	27	4	3	.571	4	3.39
	CLE/AL		5	74	2	0	0	1	16.0	19	3	11	0	0	9	0	2	1	0	8	6	1	1	.500	0	3.38
6 YR TOTALS			**126**	**3064**	**111**	**8**	**5**	**3**	**719.0**	**719**	**76**	**266**	**11**	**5**	**357**	**22**	**19**	**11**	**5**	**352**	**333**	**38**	**38**	**.500**	**1**	**4.17**

Militello, Sam Salvatore — BR/TR — b.11/26/69   NYA90 6/165

YR	TM/LG	CL	G	TBF	GS	CG	SHO	GF	IP	H	HR	BB	IBB	HB	SO	SH	SF	WP	BK	R	ER	W	L	PCT	SV	ERA
90	ONE/NYP	A-	13	332	13	3	2	0	88.2	53	2	24	0	1	119	0	2	0	2	14	12	8	2	.800	0	1.22
91	PW/CAR	A+	16	397	16	1	0	0	103.1	65	1	27	1	4	113	1	4	1	1	19	14	12	2	.857	0	1.22
	ALB/EAS	AA	7	191	7	0	0	0	46.0	40	3	19	0	3	55	1	1	0	0	14	12	2	2	.500	0	2.35
92	CMB/INT	AAA	22	576	21	3	2	0	141.1	104	5	46	1	11	152	2	5	4	1	45	36	12	2	.857	0	2.29
	NY/AL		9	255	9	0	0	0	60.0	43	6	32	1	2	42	0	0	1	0	24	23	3	3	.500	0	3.45
93	NY/AL		3	46	2	0	0	0	9.1	10	1	7	1	2	5	0	0	0	0	8	7	1	1	.500	0	6.75
	CMB/INT	AAA	7	151	7	0	0	0	33.0	36	7	20	0	1	39	1	0	4	0	22	21	1	3	.250	0	5.73
2 YR TOTALS			**12**	**301**	**11**	**0**	**0**	**0**	**69.1**	**53**	**7**	**39**	**2**	**4**	**47**	**0**	**0**	**1**	**0**	**32**	**30**	**4**	**4**	**.500**	**0**	**3.89**

Miller, Paul Robert — BR/TR — b.4/27/65   PIT87 53/1199

YR	TM/LG	CL	G	TBF	GS	CG	SHO	GF	IP	H	HR	BB	IBB	HB	SO	SH	SF	WP	BK	R	ER	W	L	PCT	SV	ERA
87	PIR/GCL	R	12	292	12	1	1	0	70.1	55	3	26	0	2	62	4	1	3	0	34	25	3	6	.333	0	3.20
88	AUG/SAL	A	15	374	15	2	2	0	90.1	80	3	28	1	4	51	3	5	8	5	34	29	6	5	.545	0	2.89
89	SAL/CAR	A+	26	599	20	2	1	0	133.2	138	17	64	0	8	82	2	4	8	1	86	62	6	12	.333	0	4.17
90	SAL/CAR	A+	22	628	22	5	1	0	150.2	145	6	33	1	7	83	3	6	5	2	58	41	8	6	.571	0	2.45
	HAR/EAS	AA	5	148	5	2	1	0	37.0	27	1	10	0	2	11	1	2	0	0	9	9	2	1	.667	0	2.19
91	CAR/SOU	AA	15	369	15	1	0	0	89.1	69	4	35	4	3	69	7	1	5	1	29	24	7	2	.778	0	2.42
	PIT/NL		1	21	1	0	0	0	5.0	4	0	3	0	0	2	0	0	0	0	3	3	0	0	.000	0	5.40
	BUF/AMA	AAA	10	272	10	2	0	0	67.0	41	2	29	0	5	30	4	0	1	1	17	11	5	2	.714	0	1.48
92	PIT/NL		6	46	0	0	0	1	11.1	11	0	1	0	0	5	1	1	1	0	3	3	1	0	1.000	0	2.38
	BUF/AMA	AAA	8	150	7	0	0	0	32.1	38	3	16	0	1	19	2	0	2	0	23	14	2	3	.400	0	3.90
93	CAR/SOU	AA	6	152	6	0	0	0	38.1	31	1	12	1	0	33	1	1	4	1	15	12	2	2	.500	0	2.82
	BUF/AMA	AAA	10	220	10	0	0	0	52.1	57	2	14	1	1	25	2	0	0	0	28	26	3	1	.750	0	4.47
	PIT/NL		3	47	3	0	0	1	10.0	15	2	2	0	0	2	2	0	1	0	6	6	0	0	.000	0	5.40
3 YR TOTALS			**10**	**114**	**3**	**0**	**0**	**2**	**26.1**	**30**	**2**	**6**	**0**	**0**	**9**	**3**	**1**	**2**	**0**	**12**	**12**	**1**	**0**	**1.000**	**0**	**4.10**

Mills, Alan Bernard — BR/TR — b.10/18/66   CAL86 S1/8

YR	TM/LG	CL	G	TBF	GS	CG	SHO	GF	IP	H	HR	BB	IBB	HB	SO	SH	SF	WP	BK	R	ER	W	L	PCT	SV	ERA
86	SAL/NWL	A-	14	0	14	1	0	0	83.2	77	1	60	0	5	50	0	0	5	0	58	43	6	6	.500	0	4.63
87	PW/CAR	A+	35	424	8	0	0	11	85.2	102	7	64	3	4	53	7	0	9	0	75	58	2	11	.154	1	6.09

Mills, Alan Bernard (continued)

YR	TM/LG	CL	G	TBF	GS	CG	SHO	GF	IP	H	HR	BB	IBB	HB	SO	SH	SF	WP	BK	R	ER	W	L	PCT	SV	ERA
88	PW/CAR	A+	42	416	5	0	0	19	93.2	93	4	43	2	5	59	5	5	6	1	56	43	3	8	.273	4	4.13
89	FL/FSL	A+	22	140	0	0	0	15	31.0	40	0	9	1	4	25	3	3	3	2	15	13	1	4	.200	6	3.77
	PW/CAR	A+	26	155	0	0	0	26	39.2	22	0	13	1	5	44	1	2	6	0	5	4	6	1	.857	7	0.91
90	CMB/INT	AAA	17	123	0	0	0	13	29.1	22	0	14	0	2	30	1	1	2	0	11	11	3	3	.500	6	3.38
	NY/AL		36	200	0	0	0	18	41.2	48	4	33	6	1	24	4	1	3	0	21	19	1	5	.167	0	4.10
91	CMB/INT	AAA	38	522	15	0	0	18	113.2	109	3	75	1	6	77	5	6	12	1	65	56	7	5	.583	8	4.43
	NY/AL		6	72	2	0	0	3	16.1	16	1	8	0	0	11	0	1	2	0	9	8	1	1	.500	0	4.41
92	ROC/INT	AAA	3	23	0	0	0	3	5.0	6	1	2	0	0	8	0	0	0	0	3	3	0	1	.000	1	5.40
	BAL/AL		35	428	3	0	0	12	103.1	78	5	54	10	1	60	6	5	2	0	33	30	10	4	.714	2	2.61
93	BAL/AL		45	421	0	0	0	18	100.1	80	14	51	5	4	68	4	6	3	0	39	36	5	4	.556	4	3.23
4 YR TOTALS			**122**	**1121**	**5**	**0**	**0**	**51**	**261.2**	**222**	**24**	**146**	**21**	**6**	**163**	**14**	**13**	**10**	**0**	**102**	**93**	**17**	**14**	**.548**	**6**	**3.20**

Minchey, Nathan Derek "Nate" — BR/TR — b.8/31/69   MON87 3/36

YR	TM/LG	CL	G	TBF	GS	CG	SHO	GF	IP	H	HR	BB	IBB	HB	SO	SH	SF	WP	BK	R	ER	W	L	PCT	SV	ERA
87	EXP/GCL	R	12	252	11	2	0	0	54.2	62	1	28	0	2	61	0	0	6	0	45	30	3	4	.429	0	4.94
88	ROC/MID	A	28	673	27	0	0	0	150.1	148	4	87	1	8	63	4	8	14	5	93	80	11	12	.478	0	4.79
89	ROC/MID	A	15	395	15	0	0	0	87.0	85	2	54	0	3	53	4	2	14	1	51	46	3	6	.333	0	4.76
	BUR/MID	A	11	294	11	1	0	0	69.0	69	6	28	0	2	34	2	5	8	0	37	35	2	6	.250	0	4.57
90	DUR/CAR	A+	25	579	24	2	2	0	133.0	143	11	46	0	5	100	4	3	13	2	75	56	4	11	.267	0	3.79
91	MIA/FSL	A+	13	378	13	4	1	0	95.1	81	1	31	0	4	61	2	1	2	2	31	20	5	3	.625	0	1.89
	DUR/CAR	A+	15	354	12	3	0	0	88.2	72	3	29	0	3	77	0	1	6	0	31	28	6	6	.500	0	2.84
92	GRE/SOU	AA	28	684	25	5	4	1	172.0	137	7	40	2	7	115	3	3	9	0	51	44	13	6	.684	0	2.30
	PAW/INT	AAA	2	23	0	0	0	0	7.0	3	0	0	0	0	4	0	0	0	0	0	0	2	0	1.000	0	0.00
93	PAW/INT	AAA	29	814	29	7	2	0	194.2	182	22	50	1	10	113	7	5	8	0	103	87	7	14	.333	0	4.02
	BOS/AL		5	141	5	1	0	0	33.0	35	5	8	2	0	18	1	0	2	0	16	13	1	2	.333	0	3.55

Minor, Blas — BR/TR — b.3/20/66   PIT88 6/148

YR	TM/LG	CL	G	TBF	GS	CG	SHO	GF	IP	H	HR	BB	IBB	HB	SO	SH	SF	WP	BK	R	ER	W	L	PCT	SV	ERA
88	PRI/APP	R+	15	77	0	0	0	14	16.1	18	2	5	0	0	23	0	0	0	0	10	8	0	1	.000	7	4.41
89	SAL/CAR	A+	39	377	4	0	0	25	86.2	91	6	31	6	2	62	4	1	3	1	43	35	3	5	.375	0	3.63
90	HAR/EAS	AA	38	391	6	0	0	23	94.0	81	5	29	7	0	98	8	4	3	1	41	32	6	4	.600	5	3.06
	BUF/AMA	AAA	1	12	0	0	0	0	2.2	2	0	2	0	0	2	0	0	0	0	1	1	0	1	.000	0	3.38
91	BUF/AMA	AAA	17	168	3	0	0	3	36.0	46	7	15	0	0	25	2	1	1	0	27	23	2	2	.500	0	5.75
	CAR/SOU	AA	3	52	2	0	0	0	12.2	9	1	7	0	0	18	1	0	1	0	4	4	0	0	.000	0	2.84
92	PIT/NL		1	9	0	0	0	0	2.0	3	0	0	0	0	0	0	0	1	0	2	1	0	0	.000	0	4.50
	BUF/AMA	AAA	45	379	7	0	0	29	96.1	72	7	26	2	1	60	4	2	2	1	30	26	5	4	.556	18	2.43
93	PIT/NL		65	398	0	0	0	18	94.1	94	8	26	3	4	84	6	4	5	0	43	43	8	6	.571	2	4.10
2 YR TOTALS			**66**	**407**	**0**	**0**	**0**	**18**	**96.1**	**97**	**8**	**26**	**3**	**4**	**84**	**6**	**4**	**6**	**0**	**45**	**44**	**8**	**6**	**.571**	**2**	**4.11**

Minutelli, Gino Michael — BL/TL — b.5/23/64   TRICIT 5/19/85

YR	TM/LG	CL	G	TBF	GS	CG	SHO	GF	IP	H	HR	BB	IBB	HB	SO	SH	SF	WP	BK	R	ER	W	L	PCT	SV	ERA
85	TRI/NWL	A-	20	0	10	0	0	7	57.0	61	3	57	0	6	79	0	0	6	0	57	51	4	8	.333	0	8.05
86	CR/MID	A	27	671	27	3	2	0	152.2	133	14	76	1	5	149	4	6	16	2	73	62	15	5	.750	0	3.66
87	TAM/FSL	A+	17	461	15	5	1	1	104.1	98	4	48	4	5	70	10	3	13	1	51	44	7	6	.538	0	3.80
	VER/EAS	AA	6	168	6	0	0	0	39.2	34	3	16	0	2	39	0	0	2	1	15	14	4	1	.800	0	3.18
88	CHT/SOU	AA	2	27	2	0	0	0	5.2	6	0	4	0	1	3	0	0	0	2	2	1	0	0	.000	0	1.59
89	RED/GCL	R	1	4	1	0	0	0	1.0	0	0	0	0	0	0	0	0	0	1	0	0	0	0	.000	0	0.00
	CHT/SOU	AA	14	140	6	0	0	0	29.0	28	1	23	0	0	20	0	1	8	4	19	17	1	1	.500	0	5.28
90	CHT/SOU	AA	17	467	17	3	0	0	108.1	106	9	46	1	2	75	5	2	5	13	52	48	9	5	.643	0	3.99
	NAS/AMA	AAA	11	315	11	3	0	0	78.1	65	5	31	0	1	61	1	1	0	0	34	28	5	2	.714	0	3.22
	CIN/NL		2	6	0	0	0	0	1.0	0	0	2	0	1	0	0	0	0	0	1	1	0	0	.000	0	9.00
91	CHW/SAL	A	2	28	2	0	0	0	8.0	2	0	4	0	0	8	0	0	0	0	0	0	1	0	1.000	0	0.00
	NAS/AMA	AAA	13	325	13	1	1	0	80.1	57	3	35	2	1	64	6	2	6	0	25	17	4	7	.364	0	1.90
	CIN/NL		16	124	3	0	0	2	25.1	30	5	18	1	0	21	0	2	3	0	17	17	0	2	.000	0	6.04
92	NAS/AMA	AAA	29	722	29	1	0	0	158.0	177	18	76	1	5	110	13	5	11	1	96	75	4	12	.250	0	4.27
93	PHO/PCL	AAA	49	235	0	0	0	34	53.2	55	1	26	0	0	57	1	3	6	1	28	24	2	2	.500	11	4.02
	SF/NL		9	64	0	0	0	4	14.1	7	2	15	0	0	10	1	2	1	0	9	6	0	1	.000	0	3.77
3 YR TOTALS			**27**	**194**	**3**	**0**	**0**	**6**	**40.2**	**37**	**7**	**35**	**1**	**1**	**31**	**1**	**4**	**5**	**0**	**27**	**24**	**0**	**3**	**.000**	**0**	**5.31**

Miranda, Angel Luis — BL/TL — b.11/9/69   MIL 3/4/87

YR	TM/LG	CL	G	TBF	GS	CG	SHO	GF	IP	H	HR	BB	IBB	HB	SO	SH	SF	WP	BK	R	ER	W	L	PCT	SV	ERA
87	BUT/PIO	R+	12	91	0	0	0	5	21.2	15	3	10	1	2	28	1	0	1	1	13	9	1	1	.500	0	3.74
	HEL/PIO	R+	13	95	0	0	0	5	21.2	12	1	16	2	0	32	1	0	0	0	9	6	0	0	.000	3	2.49
88	STO/CAL	A+	16	139	0	0	0	5	26.1	20	1	37	0	2	36	2	0	7	0	30	21	0	1	.000	2	7.18
	HEL/PIO	R+	14	284	11	0	0	1	60.2	54	2	58	0	2	75	0	1	6	3	32	26	5	2	.714	0	3.86
89	BEL/MID	A	43	264	0	0	0	40	63.0	39	1	32	6	1	88	7	5	3	1	13	6	6	5	.545	16	0.86
90	STO/CAL	A+	52	443	9	2	1	40	108.1	75	7	49	1	2	138	6	4	2	2	37	32	9	4	.692	24	2.66
91	EP/TEX	AA	38	317	0	0	0	24	74.1	55	2	41	1	1	86	1	4	8	0	27	21	4	2	.667	11	2.54
	DEN/AMA	AAA	11	60	0	0	0	8	11.2	10	0	17	1	0	14	2	0	1	0	9	8	0	1	.000	2	6.17
92	DEN/AMA	AAA	28	714	27	1	1	0	160.1	183	16	77	0	1	122	6	3	9	6	100	85	6	12	.333	0	4.77
93	NO/AMA	AAA	9	72	2	0	0	0	18.1	11	3	10	0	0	24	1	0	1	0	8	7	1	0	1.000	0	3.44
	MIL/AL		22	502	17	0	0	0	120.0	100	12	52	4	2	88	3	4	2	2	53	44	4	5	.444	0	3.30

Mlicki, David John "Dave" — BR/TR — b.6/8/68   CLE90 19/460

YR	TM/LG	CL	G	TBF	GS	CG	SHO	GF	IP	H	HR	BB	IBB	HB	SO	SH	SF	WP	BK	R	ER	W	L	PCT	SV	ERA
90	BUR/APP	R+	8	81	1	0	0	2	18.0	16	1	6	0	1	17	0	1	0	0	11	7	3	1	.750	0	3.50

Mlicki, David John "Dave" (continued)

YR	TM/LG	CL	G	TBF	GS	CG	SHO	GF	IP	H	HR	BB	IBB	HB	SO	SH	SF	WP	BK	R	ER	W	L	PCT	SV	ERA
	WAT/NYP	A-	7	139	4	0	0	3	32.0	33	3	11	0	0	28	0	1	0	0	15	12	3	0	1.000	0	3.38
91	CMB/SAL	A	22	516	19	2	0	1	115.2	101	3	70	1	6	136	1	1	10	2	70	54	8	6	.571	0	4.20
92	CAN/EAS	AA	27	720	27	2	0	0	172.2	143	8	80	3	3	146	5	7	9	1	77	69	11	9	.550	0	3.60
	CLE/AL		4	101	4	0	0	0	21.2	23	3	16	0	1	16	0	1	1	0	14	12	0	2	.000	0	4.98
93	CAN/EAS	AA	6	92	6	0	0	0	23.0	15	0	8	0	2	21	0	1	2	0	2	1	2	1	.667	0	0.39
	CLE/AL		3	58	3	0	0	0	13.1	11	2	6	0	2	7	0	0	2	0	6	5	0	0	.000	0	3.38
2 YR TOTALS			7	159	7	0	0	0	35.0	34	5	22	0	3	23	2	0	3	0	20	17	0	2	.000	0	4.37

Moeller, Dennis Michael — BR/TL — b.9/15/67 KC86 17/443

YR	TM/LG	CL	G	TBF	GS	CG	SHO	GF	IP	H	HR	BB	IBB	HB	SO	SH	SF	WP	BK	R	ER	W	L	PCT	SV	ERA
86	EUG/NWL	A-	14	0	11	0	0	0	61.2	54	1	34	0	2	65	0	0	7	2	22	21	4	0	1.000	0	3.06
87	APP/MID	A	18	292	13	0	0	0	55.0	72	5	45	3	1	49	2	3	6	0	63	44	2	5	.286	0	7.20
88	APP/MID	A	20	421	18	0	0	1	99.0	94	4	34	1	4	88	4	3	5	2	46	35	3	5	.375	0	3.18
89	BC/FSL	A+	12	280	11	2	0	1	71.0	59	2	20	1	1	64	0	3	1	1	17	14	9	0	1.000	0	1.77
	MEM/SOU	AA	5	100	5	0	0	0	25.1	16	2	10	0	1	21	2	0	0	0	9	8	1	1	.500	0	2.84
90	MEM/SOU	AA	14	307	14	0	0	0	67.2	79	11	30	1	2	42	3	3	3	2	55	47	7	6	.538	0	6.25
	OMA/AMA	AAA	11	274	11	1	1	0	65.0	63	9	30	1	0	53	1	0	0	5	29	29	5	2	.714	0	4.02
91	MEM/SOU	AA	10	224	10	0	0	0	53.0	52	6	21	0	1	54	1	1	1	1	24	15	4	5	.444	0	2.55
	OMA/AMA	AAA	14	342	14	0	0	0	78.1	70	4	40	0	3	51	3	1	3	3	36	28	7	3	.700	0	3.22
92	OMA/AMA	AAA	23	496	16	3	1	2	120.2	121	9	34	1	4	56	3	1	5	3	36	33	8	5	.615	2	2.46
	KC/AL		5	89	4	0	0	1	18.0	24	5	11	0	0	6	3	3	1	2	17	14	0	3	.000	0	7.00
93	BUF/AMA	AAA	24	326	11	0	0	4	76.2	85	13	21	3	1	38	5	5	4	5	43	37	3	4	.429	0	4.34
	PIT/NL		10	82	0	0	0	3	16.1	26	2	7	1	1	13	1	0	1	2	20	18	1	0	1.000	0	9.92
2 YR TOTALS			15	171	4	0	0	4	34.1	50	7	18	3	1	19	4	3	2	3	37	32	1	3	.250	0	8.39

Mohler, Michael Ross "Mike" — BR/TL — b.7/26/68 OAK89 41/1101

YR	TM/LG	CL	G	TBF	GS	CG	SHO	GF	IP	H	HR	BB	IBB	HB	SO	SH	SF	WP	BK	R	ER	W	L	PCT	SV	ERA
90	MAD/MID	A	42	280	2	0	0	10	63.1	56	2	32	0	2	72	8	2	4	1	34	24	1	1	.500	1	3.41
91	MOD/CAL	A+	21	505	20	1	0	0	122.2	106	5	45	1	2	98	2	3	7	1	48	39	9	4	.692	0	2.86
	HUN/SOU	AA	8	225	8	0	0	0	53.0	55	5	20	0	2	27	2	0	3	0	22	21	4	2	.667	0	3.57
92	HUN/SOU	AA	44	346	6	0	0	19	80.1	72	5	39	1	3	56	5	4	2	1	41	32	3	8	.273	3	3.59
93	OAK/AL		42	290	9	0	0	4	64.1	57	10	44	3	2	42	5	2	0	1	45	40	1	6	.143	0	5.60

Monteleone, Richard "Rich" — BR/TR — b.3/22/63 DET82 1/20

YR	TM/LG	CL	G	TBF	GS	CG	SHO	GF	IP	H	HR	BB	IBB	HB	SO	SH	SF	WP	BK	R	ER	W	L	PCT	SV	ERA
82	BRI/APP	R+	12	0	12	2	0	0	71.0	66	8	23	0	1	52	0	0	4	1	41	31	4	6	.400	0	3.93
83	LAK/FSL	A+	24	0	24	1	0	0	142.0	146	6	80	0	3	124	0	0	12	0	80	65	9	8	.529	0	4.12
	BIR/SOU	AA	3	0	3	0	0	0	15.0	25	4	6	0	0	9	0	0	0	0	12	12	1	1	.500	0	7.20
84	BIR/SOU	AA	19	537	19	4	0	0	123.2	116	9	67	0	4	74	2	5	11	2	69	64	7	8	.467	0	4.66
	EVA/AMA	AAA	11	279	11	2	0	0	64.0	64	7	36	0	2	42	1	2	0	1	33	32	5	3	.625	0	4.50
85	NAS/AMA	AAA	27	652	26	3	0	0	145.1	149	14	87	2	2	97	7	3	11	0	89	82	6	12	.333	0	5.08
86	CAL/PCL	AAA	39	728	21	0	0	14	158.2	177	16	89	5	1	101	7	8	8	3	108	93	8	12	.400	5	5.28
87	SEA/AL		3	34	0	0	0	1	7.0	10	2	4	0	1	2	0	0	0	0	5	5	0	0	.000	0	6.43
	CAL/PCL	AAA	51	309	0	0	0	33	65.1	59	5	63	0	2	38	7	3	4	0	45	40	6	13	.316	15	5.51
88	CAL/PCL	AAA	10	56	0	0	0	3	9.1	21	4	4	0	1	5	0	1	0	3	19	13	0	0	.000	0	12.54
	EDM/PCL	AAA	20	478	16	3	1	1	113.0	120	10	23	0	4	92	4	3	3	4	65	56	4	7	.364	0	4.46
	CAL/AL		3	20	0	0	0	2	4.1	4	0	1	1	1	3	0	0	0	0	0	0	0	0	.000	0	0.00
89	EDM/PCL	AAA	13	234	8	2	0	4	57.0	50	3	16	1	2	47	6	0	1	0	23	22	3	6	.333	0	3.47
	CAL/AL		24	170	0	0	0	3	39.2	39	3	13	1	1	27	1	2	2	0	15	14	2	2	.500	0	3.18
90	EDM/PCL	AAA	5	52	1	0	0	1	14.0	7	1	4	0	0	9	1	0	0	0	3	3	1	0	1.000	1	1.93
	CMB/INT	AAA	38	265	0	0	0	27	64.1	51	4	23	4	1	60	5	3	0	0	17	16	4	4	.500	9	2.24
	NY/AL		5	31	0	0	0	2	7.1	8	0	2	0	0	8	0	0	0	0	5	5	0	0	.000	0	6.14
91	CMB/INT	AAA	32	182	0	0	0	25	46.2	36	1	7	0	0	52	1	1	1	0	15	11	1	3	.250	17	2.12
	NY/AL		26	201	0	0	0	10	47.0	42	5	19	3	0	34	2	1	3	0	27	19	3	1	.750	0	3.64
92	NY/AL		47	380	0	0	0	15	92.2	82	7	27	3	0	62	3	1	0	3	35	34	7	3	.700	0	3.30
93	NY/AL		42	369	0	0	0	11	85.2	85	14	35	10	0	50	4	5	1	0	52	47	7	4	.636	0	4.94
7 YR TOTALS			150	1205	0	0	0	49	283.2	270	31	101	18	3	186	10	10	4	5	139	124	19	11	.633	0	3.93

Montgomery, Jeffrey Thomas "Jeff" — BR/TR — b.1/7/62 CIN83 10/212

YR	TM/LG	CL	G	TBF	GS	CG	SHO	GF	IP	H	HR	BB	IBB	HB	SO	SH	SF	WP	BK	R	ER	W	L	PCT	SV	ERA
84	TAM/FSL	A+	31	190	0	0	0	28	44.1	29	1	30	6	0	56	2	2	1	0	15	12	5	3	.625	14	2.44
	VER/EAS	AA	22	112	0	0	0	11	25.1	14	0	24	2	0	20	3	0	1	1	7	6	1	0	1.000	2	2.13
85	VER/EAS	AA	53	405	1	0	0	33	101.0	63	6	48	4	1	89	6	0	2	0	25	23	5	3	.625	9	2.05
86	DEN/AMA	AAA	30	652	22	2	1	4	151.2	162	13	57	0	3	78	4	5	11	3	88	74	11	7	.611	0	4.39
87	NAS/AMA	AAA	24	594	21	1	0	0	139.0	132	17	51	3	3	121	3	4	3	4	76	64	8	5	.615	0	4.14
	CIN/NL		14	89	1	0	0	6	19.1	25	2	9	1	0	13	0	0	1	0	15	14	2	2	.500	0	6.52
88	OMA/AMA	AAA	20	106	0	0	0	18	28.1	15	1	11	0	0	36	1	0	0	0	6	6	2	2	.333	13	1.91
	KC/AL		45	271	0	0	0	13	62.2	54	6	30	1	2	47	3	2	3	6	25	24	7	2	.778	1	3.45
89	KC/AL		63	363	0	0	0	39	92.0	66	3	25	4	2	94	1	1	2	1	16	14	7	3	.700	18	1.37
90	KC/AL		73	400	0	0	0	59	94.1	81	6	34	6	3	94	2	2	1	0	36	25	6	5	.545	24	2.39
91	KC/AL		67	376	0	0	0	55	90.0	83	6	28	2	3	77	3	2	2	0	32	29	4	4	.500	33	2.90
92	KC/AL		65	333	0	0	0	62	82.2	61	5	27	2	3	69	2	2	1	2	23	20	1	6	.143	39	2.18
93	KC/AL		69	347	0	0	0	63	87.1	65	3	23	4	2	66	5	1	3	0	22	22	7	5	.583	*45	2.27
7 YR TOTALS			396	2179	1	0	0	297	528.1	435	31	176	22	16	460	21	10	24	8	169	148	34	27	.557	160	2.52

Moore, Marcus Braymont — BB/TR — b.11/2/70   CAL89 17/429

YR	TM/LG	CL	G	TBF	GS	CG	SHO	GF	IP	H	HR	BB	IBB	HB	SO	SH	SF	WP	BK	R	ER	W	L	PCT	SV	ERA
89	BEN/NWL	A-	14	373	14	1	0		81.2	84	2	51	1	5	74	4	4	14	6	55	41	2	5	.286	0	4.52
90	QC/MID	A	27	717	27	2	1	0	160.1	150	6	106	0	3	160	2	7	13	9	83	59	16	5	.762	0	3.31
91	DUN/FSL	A+	27	694	25	2	0	1	160.2	139	3	99	3	4	115	9	5	12	9	78	66	6	13	.316	0	3.70
92	KNO/SOU	AA	36	493	14	1	0	18	106.1	110	10	79	0	5	85	3	7	17	5	82	66	5	10	.333	0	5.59
93	CV/CAL	A+	8	53	0	0	0	8	12.0	7	0	9	0	0	15	1	0	1	0	3	1	1	0	1.000	2	0.75
	CS/PCL	AAA	30	209	0	0	0	14	44.1	54	3	29	0	1	38	3	1	4	0	26	22	1	5	.167	4	4.47
	COL/NL		27	128	0	0	0	8	26.1	30	4	20	0	1	13	0	0	4	0	25	20	3	1	.750	0	6.84

Moore, Michael Wayne "Mike" — BR/TR — b.11/26/59   SEA81 1/1

YR	TM/LG	CL	G	TBF	GS	CG	SHO	GF	IP	H	HR	BB	IBB	HB	SO	SH	SF	WP	BK	R	ER	W	L	PCT	SV	ERA
82	SEA/AL		28	651	27	1	1	0	144.1	159	21	79	0	2	73	8	4	6	0	91	86	7	14	.333	0	5.36
83	SEA/AL		22	556	21	3	2	1	128.0	130	10	60	4	3	108	1	6	7	0	75	67	6	8	.429	0	4.71
84	SEA/AL		34	937	33	6	0	0	212.0	236	16	85	10	5	158	5	6	7	2	127	117	7	17	.292	0	4.97
85	SEA/AL		35	1016	34	14	2	1	247.0	230	18	70	2	4	155	2	7	10	3	100	95	17	10	.630	0	3.46
86	SEA/AL		38	1145	37	11	1	1	266.0	279	28	94	6	12	146	10	6	4	1	141	127	11	13	.458	1	4.30
87	SEA/AL		33	1020	33	12	0	0	231.0	268	29	84	3	0	115	9	8	4	2	145	121	9	19	.321	0	4.71
88	SEA/AL		37	918	32	9	3	3	228.2	196	24	63	6	3	182	3	3	4	1	104	96	9	15	.375	1	3.78
89	OAK/AL		35	976	35	6	3	0	241.2	193	14	83	1	2	172	5	6	17	0	82	70	19	11	.633	0	2.61
90	OAK/AL		33	862	33	3	0	0	199.1	204	14	84	2	3	73	4	7	13	0	113	103	13	15	.464	0	4.65
91	OAK/AL		33	887	33	3	1	0	210.0	176	11	105	1	5	153	5	4	14	0	75	69	17	8	.680	0	2.96
92	OAK/AL		36	982	36	2	0	0	223.0	229	20	103	0	8	117	7	11	22	0	113	102	17	12	.586	0	4.12
93	DET/AL		36	942	36	4	3	0	213.2	227	35	89	10	3	89	4	8	9	0	135	124	13	9	.591	0	5.22
12 YR TOTALS			400	10892	390	74	16	6	2544.2	2527	240	999	50	50	1541	63	76	117	11	1301	1177	145	151	.490	2	4.16

Morgan, Michael Thomas "Mike" — BR/TR — b.10/8/59   OAK78 1/4

YR	TM/LG	CL	G	TBF	GS	CG	SHO	GF	IP	H	HR	BB	IBB	HB	SO	SH	SF	WP	BK	R	ER	W	L	PCT	SV	ERA
78	OAK/AL		3	60	3	1	0	0	12.1	19	1	8	0	0	0	1	0	0	0	12	10	0	3	.000	0	7.30
79	OAK/AL		13	368	13	2	0	0	77.1	102	7	50	0	3	17	4	4	7	0	57	51	2	10	.167	0	5.94
82	NY/AL		30	661	23	2	0	2	150.1	167	15	67	5	2	71	2	4	6	0	77	73	7	11	.389	0	4.37
83	TOR/AL		16	198	4	0	0	2	45.1	48	6	21	0	2	22	0	1	3	0	26	26	0	3	.000	0	5.16
84	SYR/INT	AAA	34	803	28	10	4	4	185.2	167	11	100	3	2	105	6	5	11	0	101	84	13	11	.542	1	4.07
85	SEA/AL		2	33	2	0	0	0	6.0	11	2	5	0	0	2	0	0	1	0	8	8	1	1	.500	0	12.00
	CAL/PCL	AAA	1	0	1	0	0	0	2.0	3	0	0	0	0	0	0	0	0	0	1	1	0	0	.000	0	4.50
86	SEA/AL		37	951	33	9	1	2	216.1	243	24	86	3	4	116	7	3	8	1	122	109	11	17	.393	1	4.53
87	SEA/AL		34	898	31	8	2	2	207.0	245	25	53	3	5	85	8	5	11	0	117	107	12	17	.414	0	4.65
88	ROC/INT	AAA	3	74	3	0	0	0	17.0	19	1	6	0	0	7	0	1	1	0	10	9	0	2	.000	0	4.76
	BAL/AL		22	299	10	2	0	6	71.1	70	6	23	1	1	29	1	0	5	0	45	43	1	6	.143	1	5.43
89	LA/NL		40	604	19	0	0	7	152.2	130	6	33	8	2	72	6	6	6	0	51	43	8	11	.421	0	2.53
90	LA/NL		33	891	33	6	*4	0	211.0	216	19	60	5	5	106	11	4	4	0	100	88	11	15	.423	0	3.75
91	LA/NL		34	949	33	5	1	1	236.1	197	12	61	10	3	140	10	4	6	0	85	73	14	10	.583	1	2.78
92	CHI/NL		34	966	34	6	1	0	240.0	203	14	79	10	3	123	10	5	11	0	80	68	16	8	.667	0	2.55
93	CHI/NL		32	883	32	1	0	0	207.2	206	15	74	8	7	111	11	5	8	2	100	93	10	15	.400	0	4.03
13 YR TOTALS			330	7761	270	42	10	22	1833.2	1857	152	620	53	35	894	73	41	76	4	880	792	93	127	.423	3	3.89

Morris, John Scott "Jack" — BR/TR — b.5/16/55   DET76 5/98

YR	TM/LG	CL	G	TBF	GS	CG	SHO	GF	IP	H	HR	BB	IBB	HB	SO	SH	SF	WP	BK	R	ER	W	L	PCT	SV	ERA
77	DET/AL		7	189	6	1	0	0	45.2	38	4	23	0	0	28	3	1	2	0	20	19	1	1	.500	0	3.74
78	DET/AL		28	469	7	0	0	10	106.0	107	8	49	5	3	48	8	9	4	0	57	51	3	5	.375	0	4.33
79	DET/AL		27	806	27	9	1	0	197.2	179	19	59	4	4	113	3	6	9	1	76	72	17	7	.708	0	3.28
80	DET/AL		36	1074	36	11	2	0	250.0	252	20	87	5	4	112	10	13	6	2	125	116	16	15	.516	0	4.18
81	DET/AL		25	798	25	15	1	0	198.0	153	14	78	11	2	97	8	9	2	2	69	67	*14	7	.667	0	3.05
82	DET/AL		37	1107	37	17	3	0	266.1	247	37	96	7	0	135	4	5	10	0	131	120	17	16	.515	0	4.06
83	DET/AL		37	1204	37	20	1	0	*293.2	257	30	83	5	3	*232	8	9	18	0	117	109	20	13	.606	0	3.34
84	DET/AL		35	1015	35	9	1	0	240.1	221	20	87	7	2	148	5	3	6	0	108	96	19	11	.633	0	3.60
85	DET/AL		35	1077	35	13	4	0	257.0	212	21	110	2	5	191	11	7	15	3	102	95	16	11	.593	0	3.33
86	DET/AL		35	1092	35	15	*6	0	267.0	229	40	82	7	0	223	6	3	12	0	105	97	21	8	.724	0	3.27
87	DET/AL		34	1101	34	13	0	0	266.0	227	39	93	7	1	208	6	5	24	0	111	100	18	11	.621	0	3.38
88	DET/AL		34	997	34	10	2	0	235.0	225	20	83	7	4	168	12	3	11	11	115	103	15	13	.536	0	3.94
89	LAK/FSL	A+	3	30	3	0	0	0	8.0	7	0	0	0	0	9	2	0	0	0	2	2	0	0	.000	0	2.25
	DET/AL		24	743	24	10	0	0	170.1	189	23	59	3	2	115	6	7	12	1	102	92	6	14	.300	0	4.86
90	DET/AL		36	1073	36	*11	3	0	249.2	231	26	97	13	6	162	7	10	16	2	144	125	15	18	.455	0	4.51
91	MIN/AL		35	1032	35	10	2	0	246.2	226	18	92	5	5	163	5	8	15	1	107	94	18	12	.600	0	3.43
92	TOR/AL		34	1005	34	6	1	0	240.2	222	18	80	2	10	132	4	7	9	2	114	108	*21	6	.778	0	4.04
93	TOR/AL		27	702	27	4	1	0	152.2	189	18	65	12	3	103	4	5	14	1	116	105	7	12	.368	0	6.19
17 YR TOTALS			526	15484	504	174	28	10	3682.2	3404	375	1323	97	54	2378	111	110	193	27	1719	1569	244	180	.575	0	3.83

Moyer, Jamie — BL/TL — b.11/18/62   CHN84 6/135

YR	TM/LG	CL	G	TBF	GS	CG	SHO	GF	IP	H	HR	BB	IBB	HB	SO	SH	SF	WP	BK	R	ER	W	L	PCT	SV	ERA
84	GEN/NYP	A-	14	407	14	5	2	0	104.2	59	5	31	0	5	120	1	1	7	1	27	22	9	3	.750	0	1.89
85	WIN/CAR	A+	12	391	12	6	2	1	94.0	82	1	22	1	5	94	7	3	0	3	36	24	8	2	.800	0	2.30
	PIT/EAS	AA	15	419	15	3	0	0	96.2	99	4	32	1	5	51	3	4	4	1	49	40	7	6	.538	0	3.72
86	PIT/EAS	AA	6	162	6	0	0	0	41.0	27	2	16	0	0	42	1	0	3	1	10	4	3	1	.750	0	0.88
	IOW/AMA	AAA	6	165	6	2	0	0	42.1	25	0	11	0	0	25	0	0	0	0	14	12	3	2	.600	0	2.55
	CHI/NL		16	395	16	1	0	0	87.1	107	10	42	1	3	45	3	3	3	0	52	49	7	4	.636	0	5.05
87	CHI/NL		35	899	33	1	0	1	201.0	210	28	97	4	5	147	14	5	11	2	127	114	12	15	.444	0	5.10
88	CHI/NL		34	855	30	3	1	1	202.0	212	20	55	7	4	121	14	4	4	0	84	78	9	15	.375	0	3.48

Moyer, Jamie (continued)

YR	TM/LG	CL	G	TBF	GS	CG	SHO	GF	IP	H	HR	BB	IBB	HB	SO	SH	SF	WP	BK	R	ER	W	L	PCT	SV	ERA
89	RAN/GCL	R	3	42	3	0	0	0	11.0	8	0	3	0	0	18	1	0	1	0	4	2	1	0	1.000	0	1.64
	TUL/TEX	AA	2	53	2	1	1	0	12.1	16	1	3	0	0	9	0	0	1	1	8	7	1	1	.500	0	5.11
	TEX/AL		15	337	15	1	0	0	76.0	84	10	33	0	2	44	1	4	1	0	51	41	4	9	.308	0	4.86
90	TEX/AL		33	447	10	1	0	6	102.1	115	6	39	4	4	58	1	7	1	0	59	53	2	6	.250	0	4.66
91	STL/NL		8	142	7	0	0	1	31.1	38	5	16	0	1	20	4	2	2	1	21	20	0	5	.000	0	5.74
	LOU/AMA	AAA	20	536	20	1	0	0	125.2	125	16	43	4	3	69	6	3	9	3	64	53	5	10	.333	0	3.80
92	TOL/INT	AAA	21	566	20	5	0	1	138.2	128	8	37	3	0	80	7	2	5	0	48	44	10	8	.556	0	2.86
93	ROC/INT	AAA	8	217	8	1	1	0	54.0	42	2	13	0	3	41	1	1	0	0	13	10	6	0	1.000	0	1.67
	BAL/AL		25	630	25	3	1	0	152.0	154	11	38	2	6	90	3	1	1	1	63	58	12	9	.571	0	3.43
7 YR TOTALS			166	3705	136	10	3	9	852.0	920	90	320	23	25	525	40	28	23	7	457	413	46	63	.422	0	4.36

Mulholland, Terence John "Terry" — BR/TL — b.3/9/63   SF84 2/24

YR	TM/LG	CL	G	TBF	GS	CG	SHO	GF	IP	H	HR	BB	IBB	HB	SO	SH	SF	WP	BK	R	ER	W	L	PCT	SV	ERA
84	EVE/NWL	A-	3	0	3	0	0	0	19.0	10	0	4	0	1	15	0	0	1	0	2	0	1	0	1.000	0	0.00
	FRE/CAL	A+	9	0	9	0	0	0	42.2	32	1	36	0	0	39	0	0	1	0	17	14	5	2	.714	0	2.95
85	SHR/TEX	AA	26	761	26	8	3	0	176.2	166	9	87	2	2	122	8	1	6	0	79	57	9	8	.529	0	2.90
86	PHO/PCL	AAA	17	482	17	3	0	0	111.0	112	6	56	4	1	77	7	2	4	4	60	55	8	5	.615	0	4.46
	SF/NL		15	245	10	0	0	1	54.2	51	3	35	2	1	27	5	1	6	0	33	30	1	7	.125	0	5.07
87	PHO/PCL	AAA	37	799	29	3	0	4	172.1	200	6	90	0	4	94	5	7	17	3	124	97	7	12	.368	1	5.07
88	PHO/PCL	AAA	19	447	14	3	2	1	100.2	116	2	44	0	0	57	3	2	5	4	45	40	7	3	.700	0	3.58
	SF/NL		9	191	6	2	1	1	46.0	50	3	7	0	1	18	5	0	1	0	20	19	2	1	.667	0	3.72
89	PHO/PCL	AAA	13	313	10	3	0	0	78.1	67	3	26	2	3	61	5	2	2	3	30	26	4	5	.444	0	2.99
	SF/NL		5	51	1	0	0	2	11.0	15	0	4	0	0	6	0	0	0	0	5	5	0	0	.000	0	4.09
	PHI/NL		20	462	17	2	1	2	104.1	122	8	32	3	4	60	7	1	3	0	61	58	4	7	.364	0	5.00
	YEAR		25	513	18	2	1	4	115.1	137	8	36	3	4	66	7	1	3	0	66	63	4	7	.364	0	4.92
90	SCR/INT	AAA	1	27	1	0	0	0	6.0	9	0	2	0	0	2	0	0	0	0	4	2	0	1	.000	0	3.00
	PHI/NL		33	746	26	6	1	2	180.2	172	15	42	7	2	75	7	12	7	2	78	67	9	10	.474	0	3.34
91	PHI/NL		34	956	34	8	3	0	232.0	231	15	49	2	3	142	11	6	3	0	100	93	16	13	.552	0	3.61
92	PHI/NL		32	937	32	*12	2	0	229.0	227	14	46	3	3	125	10	7	3	0	101	97	13	11	.542	0	3.81
93	PHI/NL		29	786	28	7	2	0	191.0	177	20	40	2	3	116	5	4	5	0	80	69	12	9	.571	0	3.25
7 YR TOTALS			177	4374	154	37	10	8	1048.2	1045	78	255	19	17	569	50	31	28	2	478	438	57	58	.496	0	3.76

Munoz, Michael Anthony "Mike" — BL/TL — b.7/12/65   LA86 3/74

YR	TM/LG	CL	G	TBF	GS	CG	SHO	GF	IP	H	HR	BB	IBB	HB	SO	SH	SF	WP	BK	R	ER	W	L	PCT	SV	ERA
86	GF/PIO	R+	14	0	14	2	2	0	81.1	85	4	38	0	1	49	0	0	3	0	44	29	4	4	.500	0	3.21
87	BAK/CAL	A+	52	524	12	2	0	23	118.0	125	5	43	3	0	80	11	2	6	1	68	49	8	7	.533	8	3.74
88	SA/TEX	AA	56	302	0	0	0	35	71.2	63	0	24	-1	1	71	5	1	6	0	18	8	7	2	.778	14	1.00
89	ALB/PCL	AAA	60	345	0	0	0	27	79.0	72	2	40	8	0	81	6	3	6	0	32	27	6	4	.600	6	3.08
	LA/NL		3	14	0	0	0	1	2.2	5	1	2	0	0	3	0	0	0	0	5	5	0	0	.000	0	16.88
90	LA/NL		8	24	0	0	0	3	5.2	6	0	3	0	2	1	0	0	0	0	2	2	0	1	.000	0	3.18
	ALB/PCL	AAA	49	258	0	0	0	14	59.1	65	8	19	3	0	40	4	2	3	1	33	28	4	1	.800	6	4.25
91	DET/AL		6	46	0	0	0	4	9.1	14	0	5	0	3	3	0	1	0	0	10	10	0	0	.000	0	9.64
	TOL/INT		38	235	1	0	0	19	54.0	44	0	35	4	0	38	2	1	3	0	30	23	2	3	.400	8	3.83
92	DET/AL		65	210	0	0	0	15	48.0	44	3	25	6	0	23	4	2	2	0	16	16	1	2	.333	2	3.00
93	CS/PCL	AAA	40	167	0	0	0	13	37.2	46	0	9	0	0	30	3	2	2	0	10	7	1	2	.333	3	1.67
	DET/AL		8	19	0	0	0	3	3.0	4	1	6	1	0	0	0	0	0	0	2	2	0	0	.000	0	6.00
	COL/NL		21	82	0	0	0	7	18.0	21	1	9	3	0	16	3	2	2	0	12	9	2	1	.667	0	4.50
	YEAR		29	101	0	0	0	10	21.0	25	2	15	4	0	17	3	2	2	0	14	11	2	2	.500	0	4.71
5 YR TOTALS			111	395	0	0	0	33	86.2	94	6	50	10	0	48	8	5	5	0	47	44	3	5	.375	2	4.57

Munoz, Roberto "Bobby" — BR/TR — b.3/3/68   NYA88 12/391

YR	TM/LG	CL	G	TBF	GS	CG	SHO	GF	IP	H	HR	BB	IBB	HB	SO	SH	SF	WP	BK	R	ER	W	L	PCT	SV	ERA
89	YAN/GCL	R	2	41	2	0	0	0	10.1	5	0	4	0	0	13	0	0	1	1	4	4	1	1	.500	0	3.48
	FL/FSL		3	58	3	0	0	0	11	16	2	7	0	0	12	0	1	0	1	7	6	1	2	.333	0	4.72
90	GRE/SAL	A	25	581	24	0	0	0	132.2	133	4	58	1	5	100	2	2	4	6	70	55	5	12	.294	0	3.73
91	FL/FSL	A+	19	443	19	4	2	0	108.0	91	4	40	0	4	53	2	4	6	2	45	28	5	8	.385	0	2.33
	CMB/INT	AAA	1	21	1	0	0	0	3.0	8	0	3	0	0	2	0	0	0	0	8	8	0	1	.000	0	24.00
92	ALB/EAS	AA	22	491	22	0	0	0	112.1	96	2	70	0	4	66	2	4	8	0	55	41	7	5	.583	0	3.28
93	CMB/INT	AAA	22	124	1	0	0	18	31.1	24	0	8	0	0	16	1	0	1	0	6	5	1	3	.750	10	1.44
	NY/AL		38	208	0	0	0	12	45.2	48	1	26	0	0	33	1	2	0	0	27	27	3	3	.500	0	5.32

Murphy, Robert Albert "Rob" — BL/TL — b.5/26/60   CIN81* S1/3

YR	TM/LG	CL	G	TBF	GS	CG	SHO	GF	IP	H	HR	BB	IBB	HB	SO	SH	SF	WP	BK	R	ER	W	L	PCT	SV	ERA
84	VER/EAS	AA	45	313	1	0	0	25	69.2	57	0	35	3	1	69	9	4	7	0	23	21	2	3	.400	15	2.71
85	DEN/AMA	AAA	41	395	0	0	0	18	84.0	94	8	57	4	2	66	5	2	8	0	55	43	5	5	.500	5	4.61
	CIN/NL		2	12	0	0	0	2	3.0	2	1	2	0	0	1	0	0	0	0	2	2	0	0	.000	0	6.00
86	DEN/AMA	AAA	27	180	0	0	0	16	42.2	33	0	21	0	0	36	3	1	0	0	12	9	3	4	.429	7	1.90
	CIN/NL		34	195	0	0	0	12	50.1	26	0	21	0	0	36	3	3	5	0	4	4	6	0	1.000	1	0.72
87	CIN/NL		87	415	0	0	0	21	100.2	91	7	32	5	0	99	1	2	1	0	37	34	8	5	.615	3	3.04
88	CIN/NL		*76	350	0	0	0	28	84.2	69	3	38	6	1	74	9	1	5	1	31	29	0	6	.000	3	3.08
89	BOS/AL		74	438	0	0	0	27	105.0	97	7	41	8	1	107	7	3	6	0	38	32	5	7	.417	9	2.74
90	BOS/AL		68	285	0	0	0	20	57.0	85	10	32	4	1	54	4	4	4	0	46	40	0	6	.000	7	6.32
91	SEA/AL		57	211	0	0	0	26	48.0	47	5	19	4	1	34	3	0	1	0	17	16	0	1	.000	4	3.00
92	HOU/NL		59	242	0	0	0	6	55.2	56	2	21	4	0	42	3	4	3	0	28	25	3	1	.750	0	4.04
93	STL/NL		73	279	0	0	0	23	64.2	73	8	20	6	1	41	4	2	5	0	37	35	5	7	.417	1	4.87
9 YR TOTALS			530	2427	0	0	0	165	569.0	546	42	226	38	5	488	34	18	34	1	240	217	27	33	.450	28	3.43

Mussina, Michael Cole "Mike" — BR/TR — b.12/8/68   BAL90 1/20

YR	TM/LG	CL	G	TBF	GS	CG	SHO	GF	IP	H	HR	BB	IBB	HB	SO	SH	SF	WP	BK	R	ER	W	L	PCT	SV	ERA
90	HAG/EAS	AA	7	168	7	2	1	0	42.1	34	1	7	0	0	40	1	1	3	1	10	7	3	0	1.000	0	1.49
	ROC/INT	AAA	2	50	2	0	0	0	13.1	8	2	4	0	0	15	0	0	0	0	2	2	0	0	.000	0	1.35
91	ROC/INT	AAA	19	497	19	3	1	0	122.1	108	9	31	0	2	107	3	1	6	1	42	39	10	4	.714	0	2.87
	BAL/AL		12	349	12	2	0	0	87.2	77	7	21	0	1	52	3	2	3	1	31	28	4	5	.444	0	2.87
92	BAL/AL		32	957	32	8	4	0	241.0	212	16	48	2	2	130	13	6	6	0	70	68	18	5	*.783	0	2.54
93	BOW/EAS	AA	2	30	2	0	0	0	8.0	5	0	1	0	0	10	0	0	0	0	2	2	1	0	1.000	0	2.25
	BAL/AL		25	693	25	3	2	0	167.2	163	20	44	2	3	117	6	4	5	0	84	83	14	6	.700	0	4.46
3 YR TOTALS			69	1999	69	13	6	0	496.1	452	43	113	4	6	299	22	12	14	1	185	179	36	16	.692	0	3.25

Mutis, Jeffrey Thomas "Jeff" — BL/TL — b.12/20/66   CLE88 3/27

YR	TM/LG	CL	G	TBF	GS	CG	SHO	GF	IP	H	HR	BB	IBB	HB	SO	SH	SF	WP	BK	R	ER	W	L	PCT	SV	ERA
88	BUR/APP	R+	3	79	3	0	0	0	22.0	8	0	6	0	0	20	0	0	1	2	1	1	3	0	1.000	0	0.41
	KIN/CAR	A+	1	24	1	0	0	0	5.2	6	0	3	0	0	2	1	0	1	0	1	1	1	0	1.000	0	1.59
89	KIN/CAR	A+	16	406	15	5	2	1	99.2	87	6	20	0	2	68	1	4	3	2	42	29	7	3	.700	0	2.62
90	CAN/EAS	AA	26	702	26	7	3	0	165.0	178	6	44	2	3	94	3	2	5	1	73	58	11	10	.524	0	3.16
91	CLE/AL		3	68	3	0	0	0	12.1	23	1	7	1	0	6	2	1	0	1	16	16	0	3	.000	0	11.68
	CAN/EAS	AA	25	682	24	7	4	0	169.2	138	0	51	1	2	89	8	4	3	1	42	34	11	5	.688	0	1.80
92	CLE/AL		3	64	2	0	0	0	11.1	24	4	6	0	0	8	0	2	2	0	14	12	0	2	.000	0	9.53
	CS/PCL	AAA	25	652	24	4	0	0	145.1	177	4	57	1	5	77	5	3	4	0	99	82	9	9	.500	0	5.08
93	CHW/INT	AAA	12	315	11	3	0	0	75.2	64	1	25	3	3	59	1	2	1	0	27	22	6	0	1.000	0	2.62
	CLE/AL		17	364	13	1	1	1	81.0	93	14	33	2	2	29	0	2	1	0	56	52	3	6	.333	0	5.78
3 YR TOTALS			23	496	18	1	1	1	104.2	140	19	46	3	7	43	2	5	4	0	86	80	3	11	.214	0	6.88

Myers, Randall Kirk "Randy" — BL/TL — b.9/19/62   NYN82 S1/9

YR	TM/LG	CL	G	TBF	GS	CG	SHO	GF	IP	H	HR	BB	IBB	HB	SO	SH	SF	WP	BK	R	ER	W	L	PCT	SV	ERA
84	LYN/CAR	A+	23	641	22	7	1	1	157.0	123	7	61	0	3	171	5	1	11	0	46	36	13	5	.722	0	2.06
	JAC/TEX	AA	5	148	5	1	1	0	35.0	29	2	16	1	0	35	2	2	1	0	14	8	2	1	.667	0	2.06
85	JAC/TEX	AA	19	517	19	2	1	0	120.1	99	4	69	1	1	116	5	5	8	1	61	53	4	8	.333	0	3.96
	TID/INT	AAA	8	184	7	0	0	0	44.0	40	1	20	1	0	25	1	1	4	0	13	9	1	1	.500	0	1.84
	NY/NL		1	7	0	0	0	0	2.0	0	0	1	0	0	2	0	0	0	0	0	0	0	0	.000	0	0.00
86	TID/INT	AAA	45	278	0	0	0	35	65.0	44	2	44	3	2	79	3		3	0	19	17	6	7	.462	12	2.35
	NY/NL		10	53	0	0	0	5	10.2	11	1	9	1	1	13	0	0	0	0	5	5	0	0	.000	0	4.22
87	TID/INT	AAA	5	33	0	0	0	4	7.1	6	0	4	0	1	13	1	0	0	0	4	4	0	0	.000	3	4.91
	NY/NL		54	314	0	0	0	18	75.0	61	6	30	5	0	92	7	6	3	0	36	33	3	6	.333	6	3.96
88	NY/NL		55	261	0	0	0	44	68.0	45	5	17	2	2	69	3	2	2	0	15	13	7	3	.700	26	1.72
89	NY/NL		65	349	0	0	0	47	84.1	62	6	40	4	0	88	6	2	3	0	23	22	7	4	.636	24	2.35
90	CIN/NL		66	353	0	0	0	59	86.2	59	6	38	3	2	98	4	2	1	0	24	20	4	6	.400	31	2.08
91	CIN/NL		58	575	12	0	0	18	132.0	116	8	80	5	1	108	8	6	2	0	61	52	6	13	.316	6	3.55
92	SD/NL		66	348	0	0	0	57	79.2	84	7	34	2	1	66	7	5	5	0	38	38	3	6	.333	38	4.29
93	CHI/NL		73	313	0	0	0	69	75.1	65	7	26	2	1	86	1	2	3	0	26	26	2	4	.333	*53	3.11
9 YR TOTALS			448	2573	12	1	0	318	613.2	503	44	275	30	9	622	36	25	20	2	228	209	32	42	.432	184	3.07

Nabholz, Christopher William "Chris" — BL/TL — b.1/5/67   MON88 3/49

YR	TM/LG	CL	G	TBF	GS	CG	SHO	GF	IP	H	HR	BB	IBB	HB	SO	SH	SF	WP	BK	R	ER	W	L	PCT	SV	ERA
89	ROC/MID	A	24	654	23	3	3	0	161.1	132	6	41	0	0	149	5	4	11	2	54	39	13	5	.722	0	2.18
90	JAC/SOU	AA	11	304	11	0	0	0	74.1	62	6	27	0	1	77	1	1	6	1	28	25	7	2	.778	0	3.03
	IND/AMA	AAA	10	274	10	0	0	0	63.1	66	7	28	0	1	44	1	6	3	0	38	34	0	0	.000	0	4.83
	MON/NL		11	282	11	1	1	0	70.0	43	6	32	1	2	53	1	2	1	0	23	22	6	2	.750	0	2.83
91	IND/AMA	AAA	4	74	4	0	0	0	19.1	13	2	5	0	0	16	1	0	0	0	5	4	2	2	.500	0	1.86
	MON/NL		24	631	24	1	0	0	153.2	134	5	57	4	2	99	2	4	3	0	66	62	8	7	.533	0	3.63
92	MON/NL		32	812	32	1	1	0	195.0	176	11	74	2	5	130	7	4	5	0	80	72	11	12	.478	0	3.32
93	OTT/INT	AAA	5	109	5	0	0	0	26.2	24	1	7	0	0	20	1	1	1	0	15	13	1	1	.500	0	4.39
	MON/NL		26	505	21	1	0	2	116.2	100	9	63	4	8	74	7	4	4	0	57	53	9	8	.529	0	4.09
4 YR TOTALS			93	2230	88	4	2	2	535.1	453	31	226	11	17	356	17	14	16	3	226	209	34	29	.540	0	3.51

Nagy, Charles Harrison — BL/TR — b.5/5/67   CLE88 2/17

YR	TM/LG	CL	G	TBF	GS	CG	SHO	GF	IP	H	HR	BB	IBB	HB	SO	SH	SF	WP	BK	R	ER	W	L	PCT	SV	ERA
89	KIN/CAR	A+	13	373	13	6	4	0	95.1	69	0	24	0	4	99	1	3	3	0	22	16	8	4	.667	0	1.51
	CAN/EAS	AA	15	400	14	2	0	0	94.0	102	4	32	0	2	65	3	2	1	0	44	35	4	5	.444	0	3.35
90	CAN/EAS	AA	23	694	23	9	0	0	175.0	132	9	39	0	4	99	4	4	3	3	62	49	13	8	.619	0	2.52
	CLE/AL		9	208	8	0	0	1	45.2	58	7	21	0	1	26	1	1	1	1	31	30	2	4	.333	0	5.91
91	CLE/AL		33	914	33	6	1	0	211.1	228	15	66	7	6	109	5	9	6	2	103	97	10	15	.400	0	4.13
92	CLE/AL		33	1018	33	10	3	0	252.0	245	11	57	1	2	169	6	6	5	0	91	83	17	10	.630	0	2.96
93	CAN/EAS	AA	2	32	2	0	0	0	8.0	8	0	2	0	0	4	0	0	0	0	1	1	0	0	.000	0	1.13
	CLE/AL		9	223	9	1	0	0	48.2	66	6	13	1	2	30	2	1	2	0	38	34	2	6	.250	0	6.29
4 YR TOTALS			84	2363	83	17	4	1	557.2	597	39	157	9	11	334	14	20	16	3	263	244	31	35	.470	0	3.94

Navarro, Jaime — BR/TR — b.3/27/67   MIL87 4/71

YR	TM/LG	CL	G	TBF	GS	CG	SHO	GF	IP	H	HR	BB	IBB	HB	SO	SH	SF	WP	BK	R	ER	W	L	PCT	SV	ERA
87	HEL/PIO	R+	13	356	13	3	0	0	85.2	87	5	18	1	1	95	2		5	2	37	34	4	3	.571	0	3.57
88	STO/CAL	A+	26	727	26	4	1	0	174.2	148	6	74	1	6	151	4	1	22	2	70	60	15	5	.750	0	3.09
89	EP/TEX	AA	11	316	11	1	0	0	76.2	61	3	35	1	2	78	1	0	5	1	29	21	5	2	.714	0	2.47
	DEN/AMA	AAA	3	87	3	1	0	0	20.0	24	0	7	0	0	15	1	1	1	0	8	8	1	1	.500	0	3.60
	MIL/AL		19	470	19	1	1	0	109.2	119	6	32	3	1	56	5	2	1	1	47	38	7	8	.467	0	3.12
90	DEN/AMA	AAA	6	176	6	1	0	0	40.2	41	1	14	0	0	28	1	0	2	0	27	19	2	4	.400	0	4.20
	MIL/AL		32	654	22	3	0	2	149.1	176	11	41	3	4	75	4	5	6	5	83	74	8	7	.533	1	4.46

Navarro, Jaime (continued)

YR	TM/LG	CL	G	TBF	GS	CG	SHO	GF	IP	H	HR	BB	IBB	HB	SO	SH	SF	WP	BK	R	ER	W	L	PCT	SV	ERA
91	MIL/AL		34	1002	34	10	2	0	234.0	237	18	73	3	6	114	7	9	10	0	117	102	15	12	.556	0	3.92
92	MIL/AL		34	1004	34	3	3	0	246.0	224	14	64	4	6	100	9	13	6	0	98	91	17	11	.607	0	3.33
93	MIL/AL		35	955	34	5	1	0	214.1	254	21	73	4	11	114	6	17	11	0	135	127	11	12	.478	0	5.33
5 YR TOTALS			**154**	**4085**	**141**	**24**	**6**	**3**	**953.1**	**1010**	**70**	**283**	**17**	**28**	**459**	**31**	**45**	**36**	**5**	**480**	**432**	**58**	**50**	**.537**	**1**	**4.08**

Neagle, Dennis Edward "Denny" — BL/TL — b.9/13/68   MIN89 3/85

YR	TM/LG	CL	G	TBF	GS	CG	SHO	GF	IP	H	HR	BB	IBB	HB	SO	SH	SF	WP	BK	R	ER	W	L	PCT	SV	ERA
89	ELI/APP	R+	6	91	3	0	0	3	22.0	20	1	8	0	1	32	1	1	1	1	11	11	1	2	.333	1	4.50
	KEN/MID	A	6	166	6	1	1	0	43.2	25	3	16	0	1	40	5	1	1	0	9	8	2	1	.667	0	1.65
90	VIS/CAL	A+	10	241	10	0	0	0	63.0	39	2	16	0	0	92	1	1	0	2	13	10	8	0	1.000	0	1.43
	ORL/SOU	AA	17	486	17	4	1	0	121.1	94	11	31	0	5	94	4	2	2	0	40	33	12	3	.800	0	2.45
91	POR/PCL	AAA	19	438	17	1	1	1	104.2	101	6	32	1	2	94	4	2	4	0	41	38	9	4	.692	0	3.27
	MIN/AL		7	92	3	0	0	2	20.0	28	3	7	2	0	14	0	0	1	0	9	9	0	0	.000	0	4.05
92	PIT/NL		55	380	6	0	0	8	86.1	81	9	43	8	3	77	4	3	3	0	46	43	4	6	.400	2	4.48
93	BUF/AMA	AAA	3	14	0	0	0	1	3.1	3	0	2	0	0	6	0	0	0	0	0	0	0	0	.000	0	0.00
	PIT/NL		50	360	7	0	0	13	81.1	82	10	37	3	3	73	1	1	5	0	49	48	3	5	.375	1	5.31
3 YR TOTALS			**112**	**832**	**16**	**0**	**0**	**23**	**187.2**	**191**	**22**	**87**	**13**	**5**	**164**	**5**	**4**	**9**	**2**	**104**	**100**	**7**	**12**	**.368**	**3**	**4.80**

Nelson, Jeffrey Allan "Jeff" — BR/TR — b.11/17/66   LA84 22/569

YR	TM/LG	CL	G	TBF	GS	CG	SHO	GF	IP	H	HR	BB	IBB	HB	SO	SH	SF	WP	BK	R	ER	W	L	PCT	SV	ERA
84	GF/PIO	R+	1	0	0	0	0	0	0.2	3	1	3	0	1	1	0	0	0	0	4	4	0	0	.000	0	54.00
	DOD/GCL	R	9	56	0	0	0	3	13.1	6	0	6	0	1	7	0	0	1	1	3	2	0	0	.000	0	1.35
85	DOD/GCL	R	14	242	7	0	0	3	47.1	72	1	32	0	0	31	0	1	8	1	50	29	0	5	.000	0	5.51
86	GF/PIO	R+	3	0	0	0	0	2	2.0	5	0	4	0	0	5	0	0	1	0	3	3	0	0	.000	0	13.50
	BAK/CAL	A+	24	412	11	0	0	6	71.1	79	9	84	1	4	37	1	9	10	0	83	53	0	7	.000	0	6.69
87	SAL/CAL	A+	17	389	16	1	0	0	80.0	80	2	71	0	4	43	4	3	17	0	61	51	3	7	.300	0	5.74
88	SB/CAL	A+	27	677	27	1	1	0	149.1	163	9	91	2	8	94	2	4	20	0	115	92	8	9	.471	0	5.54
89	WIL/EAS	AA	15	392	15	2	0	0	92.1	72	2	53	1	4	61	0	3	8	1	41	34	7	5	.583	0	3.31
90	WIL/EAS	AA	10	203	10	0	0	0	43.1	65	2	18	1	2	14	0	2	2	0	35	31	1	4	.200	0	6.44
	PEN/CAR	A+	18	247	7	1	0	8	60.0	47	5	25	1	1	49	1	0	2	0	21	21	2	2	.500	6	3.15
91	JAC/SOU	AA	21	113	0	0	0	20	28.1	23	0	9	0	0	34	0	2	0	0	5	4	4	0	1.000	12	1.27
	CAL/PCL	AAA	28	146	0	0	0	21	32.1	39	1	15	3	0	26	2	3	2	1	19	14	3	4	.429	7	3.90
92	CAL/PCL	AAA	2	10	0	0	0	2	3.2	0	0	1	0	0	0	0	0	0	0	0	0	1	0	1.000	0	0.00
	SEA/AL		66	352	0	0	0	27	81.0	71	7	44	12	6	46	9	3	2	0	34	31	1	7	.125	6	3.44
93	CAL/PCL	AAA	5	31	0	0	0	4	7.2	6	0	2	0	1	6	1	0	2	0	1	1	1	0	1.000	1	1.17
	SEA/AL		71	269	0	0	0	13	60.0	57	5	34	10	8	61	2	4	2	0	30	29	5	3	.625	1	4.35
2 YR TOTALS			**137**	**621**	**0**	**0**	**0**	**40**	**141.0**	**128**	**12**	**78**	**22**	**14**	**107**	**11**	**7**	**4**	**0**	**64**	**60**	**6**	**10**	**.375**	**7**	**3.83**

Nelson, Wayland Eugene "Gene" — BR/TR — b.12/3/60   TEX78 34/690

YR	TM/LG	CL	G	TBF	GS	CG	SHO	GF	IP	H	HR	BB	IBB	HB	SO	SH	SF	WP	BK	R	ER	W	L	PCT	SV	ERA
81	NY/AL		8	179	7	0	0	0	39.1	40	5	23	1	1	16	0	2	2	0	24	21	3	1	.750	0	4.81
82	SEA/AL		22	545	19	2	1	2	122.2	133	16	60	1	2	71	4	2	4	2	70	63	6	9	.400	0	4.62
83	SEA/AL		10	153	5	1	0	2	32.0	38	6	21	2	1	11	2	0	1	0	29	28	0	3	.000	0	7.87
84	SLC/PCL	AAA	17	0	17	6	1	0	112.0	138	15	54	3	5	89	0	0	11	1	75	70	6	8	.429	0	5.63
	CHI/AL		20	304	9	2	0	4	74.2	72	9	17	0	1	36	1	2	4	1	38	37	3	5	.375	1	4.46
85	CHI/AL		46	643	18	1	0	11	145.2	144	23	67	4	7	101	9	2	11	1	74	69	10	10	.500	2	4.26
86	CHI/AL		54	488	1	0	0	26	114.2	118	7	41	5	3	70	7	1	3	0	52	49	6	6	.500	6	3.85
87	OAK/AL		54	530	6	0	0	15	123.2	120	12	35	0	5	94	3	5	7	0	58	54	6	5	.545	3	3.93
88	OAK/AL		54	456	1	0	0	20	111.2	93	9	38	4	3	67	3	4	6	0	42	38	9	6	.600	3	3.06
89	OAK/AL		50	335	0	0	0	15	80.0	60	5	30	3	2	70	3	4	5	0	33	29	3	5	.375	3	3.26
90	OAK/AL		51	291	0	0	0	17	74.2	55	5	17	1	3	38	1	5	1	0	14	13	3	3	.500	5	1.57
91	OAK/AL		44	229	0	0	0	11	48.2	60	12	23	1	3	23	3	4	0	0	38	37	1	5	.167	0	6.84
92	OAK/AL		28	234	2	0	0	8	51.2	68	5	22	5	2	23	4	5	2	0	37	37	3	1	.750	0	6.45
93	CAL/AL		46	231	0	0	0	20	52.2	50	5	23	4	2	31	3	4	1	0	25	18	0	5	.000	4	3.08
	TEX/AL		6	34	0	0	0	2	8.0	10	1	1	1	0	4	0	0	1	0	3	3	0	0	.000	1	3.38
	YEAR		52	265	0	0	0	22	60.2	60	3	24	5	2	35	3	4	2	0	28	21	0	5	.000	5	3.12
13 YR TOTALS			**493**	**4652**	**68**	**6**	**1**	**153**	**1080.0**	**1061**	**117**	**418**	**32**	**33**	**655**	**43**	**40**	**46**	**10**	**537**	**496**	**53**	**64**	**.453**	**28**	**4.13**

Nen, Robert Allen "Robb" — BR/TR — b.11/28/69   TEX87 34/831

YR	TM/LG	CL	G	TBF	GS	CG	SHO	GF	IP	H	HR	BB	IBB	HB	SO	SH	SF	WP	BK	R	ER	W	L	PCT	SV	ERA
87	RAN/GCL	R	2	13	0	0	0	0	2.1	4	0	3	1	0	4	0	0	0	0	2	2	0	0	.000	0	7.71
88	GAS/SAL	A	14	269	10	0	0	1	48.1	69	5	45	0	2	36	1	4	5	2	57	40	0	5	.000	0	7.45
	BUT/PIO	R+	14	257	13	0	0	0	48.1	65	4	45	0	1	30	0	2	12	1	55	47	4	5	.444	0	8.75
89	GAS/SAL	A	24	580	24	1	1	0	138.1	96	7	76	0	6	146	2	4	15	4	47	37	7	4	.636	0	2.41
90	CHA/FSL	A+	11	231	11	0	0	0	53.2	44	1	36	0	0	38	2	2	6	0	28	22	1	4	.200	0	3.69
	TUL/TEX	AA	7	120	7	0	0	0	26.2	23	1	21	0	2	21	1	2	3	0	20	15	0	5	.000	0	5.06
91	TUL/TEX	AA	6	124	6	0	0	0	28.0	24	6	20	0	2	23	1	2	2	0	21	18	0	2	.000	0	5.79
92	TUL/TEX	AA	4	98	4	1	0	0	25.0	21	1	10	1	0	14	0	0	4	0	7	6	1	1	.500	0	2.16
93	OC/AMA	AAA	6	141	5	0	0	0	28.1	45	3	18	0	2	23	1	2	2	0	22	21	0	2	.000	0	6.67
	TEX/AL		9	113	3	0	0	3	22.2	28	1	26	0	0	12	0	1	1	1	17	16	1	1	.500	0	6.35
	FLO/NL		15	159	1	0	0	2	33.1	35	5	20	0	0	27	1	1	4	0	28	26	1	0	1.000	0	7.02
	YEAR		24	272	4	0	0	5	56.0	63	6	46	0	0	39	1	2	5	1	45	42	2	1	.667	0	6.75
1 YR TOTALS			**24**	**272**	**4**	**0**	**0**	**5**	**56.0**	**63**	**6**	**46**	**0**	**0**	**39**	**1**	**2**	**6**	**1**	**45**	**42**	**2**	**1**	**.667**	**0**	**6.75**

Nichols, Rodney Lea "Rod" — BR/TR — b.12/29/64   CLE85 5/115

YR	TM/LG	CL	G	TBF	GS	CG	SHO	GF	IP	H	HR	BB	IBB	HB	SO	SH	SF	WP	BK	R	ER	W	L	PCT	SV	ERA
85	BAT/NYP	A-	13	361	13	3	0	0	84.0	74	10	33	0	3	93	0	2	6	0	40	28	5	5	.500	0	3.00
86	WAT/MID	A	20	493	20	3	1	0	115.1	128	8	21	1	13	83	3	4	3	1	56	52	8	5	.615	0	4.06
87	KIN/CAR	A+	9	231	8	1	1	1	56.0	53	3	14	0	1	61	0	2	4	0	27	25	4	2	.667	0	4.02
	WIL/EAS	AA	16	441	16	1	0	0	100.0	107	9	33	0	9	60	2	3	5	1	53	41	4	3	.571	0	3.69
88	KIN/CAR	A+	4	109	4	0	0	0	24.0	26	1	15	0	0	19	0	2	2	0	13	12	3	1	.750	0	4.50
	CS/PCL	AAA	10	256	9	2	0	1	58.2	69	8	17	2	3	43	1	2	3	2	41	37	2	6	.250	0	5.68
	CLE/AL		11	297	10	3	0	0	69.1	73	5	23	1	2	31	2	2	2	3	41	39	1	7	.125	0	5.06
89	CS/PCL	AAA	10	274	10	2	1	0	65.1	57	2	30	0	1	41	1	3	1	2	28	26	8	1	.889	0	3.58
	CLE/AL		15	315	11	0	0	2	71.2	81	9	24	0	2	42	3	2	0	0	42	35	4	6	.400	0	4.40
90	CLE/AL		4	79	2	0	0	0	16.0	24	5	6	0	2	3	1	0	0	0	14	14	0	3	.000	0	7.87
	CS/PCL	AAA	22	602	22	4	2	0	133.1	160	12	48	3	11	74	0	4	3	2	84	76	12	9	.571	0	5.13
91	CLE/AL		31	578	16	3	1	4	137.1	145	6	30	3	6	76	6	4	3	0	63	54	2	11	.154	1	3.54
92	CS/PCL	AAA	9	233	9	1	0	0	54.0	65	6	16	1	1	35	0	4	4	1	39	34	3	3	.500	0	5.67
	CLE/AL		30	456	9	0	0	5	105.1	114	13	31	1	2	56	1	5	3	0	58	53	4	3	.571	0	4.53
93	ALB/PCL	AAA	21	552	21	3	1	0	127.2	132	16	50	3	3	79	6	3	9	3	68	61	8	5	.615	0	4.30
	LA/NL		4	28	0	0	0	2	6.1	9	1	2	2	0	3	1	0	0	0	5	4	0	1	.000	0	5.68
6 YR TOTALS			**95**	**1753**	**48**	**6**	**1**	**14**	**406.0**	**446**	**39**	**116**	**7**	**14**	**211**	**14**	**13**	**8**	**3**	**223**	**199**	**11**	**31**	**.262**	**1**	**4.41**

Nied, David Glen — BR/TR — b.12/22/68   ATL87 14/350

YR	TM/LG	CL	G	TBF	GS	CG	SHO	GF	IP	H	HR	BB	IBB	HB	SO	SH	SF	WP	BK	R	ER	W	L	PCT	SV	ERA
88	SUM/SAL	A	27	701	27	3	1	0	165.1	156	15	53	1	12	133	7	3	6	2	78	69	12	9	.571	0	3.76
89	DUR/CAR	A+	12	275	12	0	0	0	58.1	74	10	23	1	5	38	2	1	1	0	47	43	5	2	.714	0	6.63
	BUR/MID	A	13	341	12	2	1	0	80.0	78	3	23	0	5	73	3	2	3	1	38	34	5	6	.455	0	3.83
90	DUR/CAR	A+	10	176	10	0	0	0	42.1	38	3	14	0	1	27	2	1	4	0	19	18	1	1	.500	0	3.83
	BUR/MID	A	10	252	9	1	1	1	64.0	55	2	10	0	1	66	2	2	3	0	21	16	5	3	.625	0	2.25
91	DUR/CAR	A+	13	312	12	2	2	1	80.2	46	3	23	0	3	77	1	1	0	0	19	14	8	3	.727	0	1.56
	GRE/SOU	AA	15	367	15	1	0	0	89.2	79	0	20	3	6	101	3	2	1	0	26	24	7	3	.700	0	2.41
92	RIC/INT	AAA	26	680	26	7	2	0	168.0	144	15	44	2	3	159	8	7	1	0	73	53	14	9	.609	0	2.84
	ATL/NL		6	83	2	0	0	0	23.0	10	0	5	0	0	19	1	0	1	0	3	3	3	0	1.000	0	1.17
93	CV/CAL	A+	1	16	1	0	0	0	3.0	3	0	0	0	0	3	0	0	0	0	2	1	0	1	.000	0	3.00
	CS/PCL	AAA	3	73	3	0	0	0	15.0	24	3	4	0	1	11	0	1	0	0	17	15	0	2	.000	0	9.00
	COL/NL		16	394	16	1	0	0	87.0	99	8	42	4	1	46	9	7	1	1	53	50	5	9	.357	0	5.17
2 YR TOTALS			**22**	**477**	**18**	**1**	**0**	**0**	**110.0**	**109**	**8**	**47**	**4**	**1**	**65**	**10**	**7**	**1**	**1**	**56**	**53**	**8**	**9**	**.471**	**0**	**4.34**

Nielsen, Gerald Arthur "Jerry" — BL/TL — b.8/5/66   NYA88 15/469

YR	TM/LG	CL	G	TBF	GS	CG	SHO	GF	IP	H	HR	BB	IBB	HB	SO	SH	SF	WP	BK	R	ER	W	L	PCT	SV	ERA
88	ONE/NYP	A-	19	158	1	0	0	8	38.0	27	0	18	0	3	35	3	0	0	4	6	3	6	2	.750	0	0.71
89	PW/CAR	A+	39	198	0	0	0	16	49.1	26	0	25	0	6	45	2	4	6	0	14	12	3	2	.600	4	2.19
90	PW/CAR	A+	26	665	26	1	1	0	151.2	149	9	79	1	11	119	4	2	9	2	76	66	7	12	.368	0	3.92
91	FL/FSL	A+	42	275	0	0	0	14	64.2	50	2	31	4	3	66	5	5	7	0	29	20	3	3	.500	4	2.78
	ALB/EAS	AA	6	38	0	0	0	2	8.0	9	1	8	1	0	5	1	0	0	0	6	5	0	1	.000	0	5.63
92	ALB/EAS	AA	36	207	0	0	0	21	53.0	38	1	15	2	1	59	1	0	5	0	8	7	3	5	.375	11	1.19
	CMB/INT	AAA	4	18	0	0	0	2	5.0	2	0	2	0	1	5	0	1	0	0	1	1	0	0	.000	1	1.80
	NY/AL		20	90	0	0	0	12	19.2	17	1	18	2	0	12	1	1	1	0	10	10	1	0	1.000	0	4.58
93	CAL/AL		10	62	0	0	0	3	12.1	18	1	4	0	1	8	1	3	0	0	13	11	0	0	.000	0	8.03
	VAN/PCL	AAA	33	252	5	0	0	10	55.2	70	4	20	3	0	45	7	2	2	1	32	26	2	5	.286	0	4.20
2 YR TOTALS			**30**	**152**	**0**	**0**	**0**	**15**	**32.0**	**35**	**2**	**22**	**2**	**1**	**20**	**2**	**4**	**1**	**1**	**23**	**21**	**1**	**0**	**1.000**	**0**	**5.91**

Novoa, Rafael Angel — BL/TL — b.10/26/67   SF89 9/232

YR	TM/LG	CL	G	TBF	GS	CG	SHO	GF	IP	H	HR	BB	IBB	HB	SO	SH	SF	WP	BK	R	ER	W	L	PCT	SV	ERA
89	EVE/NWL	A-	3	73	3	0	0	0	15.0	20	2	8	0	1	20	0	1	0	3	11	8	0	1	.000	0	4.80
	CLI/MID	A	13	267	10	0	0	0	63.2	58	1	18	1	4	61	9	1	1	6	20	18	5	4	.556	0	2.54
90	CLI/MID	A	15	397	14	3	1	0	97.2	73	6	30	0	4	113	3	3	2	2	32	26	9	2	.818	0	2.40
	SHR/TEX	AA	11	297	10	2	1	1	71.2	60	3	25	0	2	65	1	2	4	0	21	21	5	4	.556	0	2.64
	SF/NL		7	88	2	0	0	2	18.2	21	3	13	1	0	14	0	1	0	0	14	14	0	1	.000	1	6.75
91	PHO/PCL	AAA	17	450	17	0	0	0	93.2	135	16	37	3	5	46	5	6	3	1	83	62	6	6	.500	0	5.96
92	EP/TEX	AA	22	617	21	6	0	1	146.1	143	6	48	3	9	124	4	3	8	1	63	53	10	7	.588	0	3.26
93	NO/AMA	AAA	20	471	18	2	1	0	113.0	105	20	38	3	5	74	1	3	4	1	55	43	10	5	.667	0	3.42
	MIL/AL		15	249	7	2	0	0	56.0	58	7	22	2	4	17	2	2	1	0	32	28	0	3	.000	0	4.50
2 YR TOTALS			**22**	**337**	**9**	**2**	**0**	**2**	**74.2**	**79**	**10**	**35**	**3**	**4**	**31**	**4**	**3**	**1**	**0**	**46**	**42**	**0**	**4**	**.000**	**1**	**5.06**

Nunez, Edwin — BR/TR — b.5/27/63   SEA 3/17/79

YR	TM/LG	CL	G	TBF	GS	CG	SHO	GF	IP	H	HR	BB	IBB	HB	SO	SH	SF	WP	BK	R	ER	W	L	PCT	SV	ERA
79	BEL/NWL	A-	6	0	6	2	0	0	39.0	39	0	5	0	0	30	0	0	0	0	14	9	4	1	.800	0	2.08
80	WAU/MID	A	22	0	19	8	2	0	138.0	145	0	58	0	0	91	0	0	0	0	71	57	9	7	.563	0	3.72
81	WAU/MID	A	25	0	25	13	0	0	186.0	143	0	58	0	0	205	0	0	0	0	61	51	16	3	.842	0	2.47
82	SEA/AL		8	153	5	0	0	0	35.1	36	7	16	0	0	27	3	0	0	0	18	18	1	2	.333	0	4.58
	SLC/PCL	AAA	11	0	8	1	0	0	55.0	40	0	23	0	0	42	0	0	0	0	26	21	4	3	.571	0	3.44
83	SEA/AL		14	170	5	0	0	4	37.0	40	3	22	1	3	35	1	2	3	0	21	18	0	4	.000	0	4.38
	SLC/PCL	AAA	14	0	12	3	0	0	77.0	99	0	36	0	0	52	0	0	0	0	70	61	4	4	.500	0	7.13
84	SLC/PCL	AAA	18	0	0	0	0	13	27.2	24	2	12	1	0	26	0	0	0	0	12	11	3	2	.600	3	3.58
	SEA/AL		37	280	0	0	0	23	67.2	55	8	21	2	0	57	1	3	0	0	26	24	2	2	.500	7	3.19
85	SEA/AL		70	378	0	0	0	53	90.1	79	13	34	5	0	58	4	3	1	0	36	31	7	3	.700	16	3.09
86	CAL/PCL	AAA	6	65	1	1	0	4	14.0	19	2	4	0	0	9	0	1	1	0	13	11	1	2	.333	0	7.07
	SEA/AL		14	93	0	0	0	6	21.2	25	5	5	1	0	17	0	0	0	0	15	14	1	2	.333	0	5.82
87	SEA/AL		48	198	0	0	0	40	47.1	45	7	18	3	1	34	3	4	2	0	20	20	3	4	.429	12	3.80

Nunez, Edwin (continued)

YR	TM/LG	CL	G	TBF	GS	CG	SHO	GF	IP	H	HR	BB	IBB	HB	SO	SH	SF	WP	BK	R	ER	W	L	PCT	SV	ERA
88	CAL/PCL	AAA	3	65	3	0	0	0	15.1	15	0	4	0	1	12	0	0	0	0	9	8	2	0	1.000	0	4.70
	SEA/AL		14	145	3	0	0	2	29.1	45	4	14	3	2	19	2	4	0	1	33	26	1	4	.200	0	7.98
	NY/NL		10	65	0	0	0	4	14.0	21	1	3	0	0	8	0	0	1	0	7	7	1	0	1.000	0	4.50
	YEAR		24	210	3	0	0	6	43.1	66	5	17	3	2	27	2	4	1	1	40	33	2	4	.333	0	6.85
89	TOL/INT	AAA	13	239	8	1	0	3	59.1	47	7	18	2	2	53	3	1	1	3	20	17	1	5	.167	1	2.58
	DET/AL		27	238	0	0	0	12	54.0	49	6	36	13	0	41	6	3	2	1	33	25	3	4	.429	1	4.17
90	DET/AL		42	343	0	0	0	15	80.1	65	4	37	6	2	66	5	1	4	0	26	20	3	1	.750	6	2.24
91	BEL/MID	A	5	37	1	0	0	3	9.0	9	1	0	0	1	9	0	0	1	0	5	4	0	1	.000	1	4.00
	MIL/AL		23	119	0	0	0	18	25.1	28	6	13	2	0	24	3	2	0	1	20	17	2	1	.667	8	6.04
92	MIL/AL		10	58	0	0	0	5	13.2	12	1	6	0	0	10	0	0	0	0	5	4	1	1	.500	0	2.63
	TEX/AL		39	205	0	0	0	11	45.2	51	5	16	0	2	39	0	4	5	0	29	28	0	2	.000	3	5.52
	YEAR		49	263	0	0	0	16	59.1	63	6	22	0	2	49	0	4	5	0	34	32	1	3	.250	3	4.85
93	OAK/AL		56	341	0	0	0	16	75.2	89	7	29	2	6	58	5	2	4	2	36	32	3	6	.333	1	3.81
12 YR TOTALS			**412**	**2786**	**14**	**0**	**0**	**209**	**637.1**	**640**	**72**	**270**	**38**	**19**	**493**	**33**	**26**	**21**	**10**	**325**	**284**	**28**	**36**	**.438**	**54**	**4.01**

O'Donoghue, John Preston — BL/TL — b.5/26/69   BAL 6/28/90

YR	TM/LG	CL	G	TBF	GS	CG	SHO	GF	IP	H	HR	BB	IBB	HB	SO	SH	SF	WP	BK	R	ER	W	L	PCT	SV	ERA
90	BLU/APP	R+	10	200	6	2	2	3	49.1	50	2	10	0	1	67	2	0	2	1	13	11	4	2	.667	0	2.01
	FRE/CAR	A+	1	18	1	0	0	0	4.0	5	0	0	0	0	3	0	0	0	0	2	2	0	1	.000	0	4.50
91	FRE/CAR	A+	22	567	21	2	1	1	133.2	131	6	50	2	2	128	0	2	8	1	55	43	7	8	.467	0	2.90
92	HAG/EAS	AA	17	459	16	2	0	1	112.1	78	6	40	0	4	87	4	2	7	4	37	28	7	4	.636	0	2.24
	ROC/INT	AAA	13	282	10	3	1	1	69.2	60	5	19	1	0	47	4	0	5	0	31	25	5	4	.556	0	3.23
93	ROC/INT	AAA	22	543	20	2	1	1	127.2	122	11	41	0	3	111	8	3	3	0	60	55	7	4	.636	0	3.88
	BAL/AL		11	90	1	0	0	3	19.2	22	4	10	1	1	16	0	0	1	0	12	10	0	1	.000	0	4.58

Ojeda, Robert Michael "Bob" — BL/TL — b.12/17/57   BOS 5/20/78

YR	TM/LG	CL	G	TBF	GS	CG	SHO	GF	IP	H	HR	BB	IBB	HB	SO	SH	SF	WP	BK	R	ER	W	L	PCT	SV	ERA
80	BOS/AL		7	122	7	0	0	0	26.0	39	2	14	1	0	12	0	0	1	0	20	20	1	1	.500	0	6.92
81	BOS/AL		10	267	10	2	0	0	66.1	50	6	25	2	2	28	3	1	0	0	25	23	6	2	.750	0	3.12
82	BOS/AL		22	352	14	0	0	6	78.1	95	13	29	0	1	52	0	1	5	0	53	49	4	6	.400	0	5.63
83	BOS/AL		29	746	28	5	0	0	173.2	173	15	73	2	3	94	6	11	2	0	85	78	12	7	.632	0	4.04
84	BOS/AL		33	928	32	8	*5	0	216.2	211	17	96	2	2	137	8	6	0	1	106	96	12	12	.500	0	3.99
85	BOS/AL		39	671	22	5	0	10	157.2	166	11	48	9	2	102	10	3	3	3	74	70	9	11	.450	1	4.00
86	NY/NL		32	871	30	7	2	1	217.1	185	15	52	3	2	148	10	3	2	1	72	62	18	5	*.783	0	2.57
87	NY/NL		10	192	7	0	0	0	46.1	45	5	10	1	0	21	3	1	1	0	23	20	3	5	.375	0	3.88
88	NY/NL		29	752	29	5	5	0	190.1	158	6	33	2	4	133	6	6	4	7	74	61	10	13	.435	0	2.88
89	NY/NL		31	824	31	5	2	0	192.0	179	16	78	5	2	95	6	7	3	1	83	74	13	11	.542	0	3.47
90	NY/NL		38	500	12	0	0	9	118.0	123	10	40	4	2	62	3	3	2	3	53	48	7	6	.538	0	3.66
91	LA/NL		31	802	31	2	1	0	189.1	181	15	70	9	3	120	15	9	4	2	78	67	12	9	.571	0	3.18
92	LA/NL		29	731	29	2	1	0	166.1	169	8	81	8	1	94	11	4	3	0	80	67	6	9	.400	0	3.63
93	CLE/AL		9	194	7	0	0	0	43.0	48	5	21	0	0	27	4	3	3	0	22	21	2	1	.667	0	4.40
14 YR TOTALS			**349**	**7952**	**289**	**41**	**16**	**26**	**1881.1**	**1822**	**144**	**670**	**48**	**24**	**1125**	**85**	**61**	**30**	**19**	**848**	**756**	**115**	**98**	**.540**	**1**	**3.62**

Olivares, Omar — BR/TR — b.7/6/67   SD 9/15/86

YR	TM/LG	CL	G	TBF	GS	CG	SHO	GF	IP	H	HR	BB	IBB	HB	SO	SH	SF	WP	BK	R	ER	W	L	PCT	SV	ERA
87	CHS/SAL	A	31	744	24	5	0	3	170.1	182	9	57	4	7	86	6	10	3	1	107	87	4	14	.222	0	4.60
88	CHS/SAL	A	24	746	24	10	3	0	185.1	166	3	43	2	3	94	5	7	9	7	63	46	13	6	.684	0	2.23
	RIV/CAL	A+	4	96	3	1	0	0	23.1	18	2	9	0	2	16	1	0	1	1	9	3	3	0	1.000	0	1.16
89	WIC/TEX	AA	26	771	26	6	1	0	185.2	175	10	61	6	10	79	3	8	10	1	87	70	12	11	.522	0	3.39
90	LOU/AMA	AAA	23	643	23	5	2	0	159.1	127	9	59	1	9	88	4	2	6	2	58	50	10	11	.476	0	2.82
	STL/NL		9	201	6	0	0	0	49.1	45	2	17	0	2	20	1	0	1	1	17	16	1	1	.500	0	2.92
91	LOU/AMA	AAA	6	158	6	0	0	0	36.1	39	1	16	1	1	27	1	1	2	1	15	14	1	2	.333	0	3.47
	STL/NL		28	688	24	0	0	2	167.1	148	11	61	1	5	91	11	3	3	1	72	69	11	7	.611	1	3.71
92	STL/NL		32	818	30	1	0	1	197.0	189	20	63	5	4	124	8	7	2	0	84	84	9	9	.500	0	3.84
93	STL/NL		58	537	9	0	0	11	118.2	134	10	54	7	9	63	4	4	4	1	60	55	5	3	.625	1	4.17
4 YR TOTALS			**127**	**2244**	**69**	**1**	**0**	**14**	**532.1**	**516**	**45**	**195**	**13**	**20**	**298**	**24**	**13**	**10**	**5**	**233**	**224**	**26**	**20**	**.565**	**2**	**3.79**

Oliver, Darren Christopher — BR/TL — b.10/6/70   TEX88 3/63

YR	TM/LG	CL	G	TBF	GS	CG	SHO	GF	IP	H	HR	BB	IBB	HB	SO	SH	SF	WP	BK	R	ER	W	L	PCT	SV	ERA
88	RAN/GCL	R	12	216	9	0	0	0	54.1	39	0	18	0	2	59	2	1	3	2	16	13	5	1	.833	0	2.15
89	GAS/SAL	A	24	525	23	2	1	0	122.1	86	4	82	1	5	108	3	3	15	2	54	43	8	7	.533	0	3.16
90	RAN/GCL	R	3	21	3	0	0	0	6.0	1	0	1	0	1	7	0	0	1	0	0	0	0	0	.000	0	0.00
	GAS/SAL	A	1	11	1	0	0	0	2.0	1	0	1	0	0	2	0	0	0	0	3	3	0	0	.000	0	13.50
91	CHA/FSL	A+	2	33	1	0	0	0	8.0	6	1	3	0	0	12	0	0	1	0	4	4	0	1	.000	0	4.50
92	CHA/FSL	A+	8	95	1	1	1	2	25.0	11	0	10	2	2	33	0	0	3	0	2	2	1	0	1.000	2	0.72
	TUL/TEX	AA	3	66	3	0	0	0	14.1	15	1	4	0	0	14	1	0	0	0	9	5	0	1	.000	0	3.14
93	TUL/TEX	AA	46	315	0	0	0	25	73.1	51	1	41	5	9	77	5	1	9	0	18	16	7	5	.583	6	1.96
	TEX/AL		2	14	0	0	0	1	3.1	2	1	1	0	0	4	0	0	1	1	1	1	0	0	.000	0	2.70

Olson, Greggory William "Gregg" — BR/TR — b.10/11/66   BAL88 1/4

YR	TM/LG	CL	G	TBF	GS	CG	SHO	GF	IP	H	HR	BB	IBB	HB	SO	SH	SF	WP	BK	R	ER	W	L	PCT	SV	ERA
88	HAG/CAR	A+	8	33	0	0	0	8	9.0	5	1	2	0	0	9	1	0	0	1	2	2	1	0	1.000	4	2.00
	CHA/SOU	AA	8	78	0	0	0	3	15.1	24	2	6	0	0	22	1	1	0	0	13	10	0	1	.000	1	5.87
	BAL/AL		10	51	0	0	0	6	11.0	10	1	10	1	0	9	0	1	0	1	4	4	1	1	.500	0	3.27
89	BAL/AL		64	356	0	0	0	52	85.0	57	1	46	10	1	90	4	1	9	3	17	16	5	2	.714	27	1.69
90	BAL/AL		64	305	0	0	0	58	74.1	57	3	31	3	3	74	1	2	5	0	20	20	6	5	.545	37	2.42

(continued)

Olson, Greggory William "Gregg" (continued)

YR	TM/LG	CL	G	TBF	GS	CG	SHO	GF	IP	H	HR	BB	IBB	HB	SO	SH	SF	WP	BK	R	ER	W	L	PCT	SV	ERA
91	BAL/AL		72	319	0	0	0	62	73.2	74	1	29	5	1	72	5	1	8	1	28	26	4	6	.400	31	3.18
92	BAL/AL		60	244	0	0	0	56	61.1	46	3	24	0	0	58	0	2	4	0	14	14	1	5	.167	36	2.05
93	BAL/AL		50	188	0	0	0	45	45.0	37	1	18	3	0	44	2	2	5	0	9	8	0	2	.000	29	1.60
6 YR TOTALS			**320**	**1463**	**0**	**0**	**0**	**277**	**350.1**	**281**	**10**	**158**	**22**	**5**	**347**	**12**	**8**	**31**	**5**	**92**	**88**	**17**	**21**	**.447**	**160**	**2.26**

Ontiveros, Steven "Steve" — BR/TR — b.3/5/61   OAK82 1/54

YR	TM/LG	CL	G	TBF	GS	CG	SHO	GF	IP	H	HR	BB	IBB	HB	SO	SH	SF	WP	BK	R	ER	W	L	PCT	SV	ERA
84	TAC/PCL	AAA	2	0	2	0	0	0	11.1	18	3	5	0	1	6	0	0	0	0	11	10	1	1	.500	0	7.94
	MAD/MID	A	5	122	5	2	0	0	30.2	23	0	6	0	1	26	1	1	1	0	10	7	3	1	.750	0	2.05
85	TAC/PCL	AAA	15	0	0	0	0	7	33.2	26	1	21	2	2	30	0	0	1	0	13	11	3	0	1.000	2	2.94
	OAK/AL		39	284	0	0	0	18	74.2	45	4	19	2	2	36	2	2	1	0	17	16	1	3	.250	8	1.93
86	OAK/AL		46	305	0	0	0	27	72.2	72	10	25	3	1	54	1	6	4	0	40	38	2	2	.500	10	4.71
87	TAC/PCL	AAA	1	12	1	0	0	0	3.0	1	0	2	0	0	1	0	1	1	0	1	1	0	0	.000	0	3.00
	OAK/AL		35	645	22	2	1	6	150.2	141	19	50	3	4	97	6	2	4	1	78	67	10	8	.556	1	4.00
88	OAK/AL		10	241	10	0	0	0	54.2	57	4	21	0	0	30	0	0	5	5	32	28	3	4	.429	0	4.61
89	SCR/INT	AAA	1	15	1	0	0	0	3.1	3	0	3	0	0	0	0	0	0	0	0	0	0	0	.000	0	0.00
	PHI/NL		6	134	5	0	0	0	30.2	34	2	15	1	0	12	1	0	0	0	15	13	2	1	.667	0	3.82
90	CLE/FSL	A+	3	29	3	0	0	0	7.2	4	0	3	0	0	2	0	0	0	0	2	2	0	0	.000	0	2.35
	REA/EAS	AA	2	29	2	0	0	0	6.0	7	0	2	0	2	8	0	0	0	0	6	6	0	0	.000	0	9.00
	PHI/NL		5	43	0	0	0	0	10.0	9	1	3	0	0	6	0	0	0	0	3	3	0	0	.000	0	2.70
91	SCR/INT	AAA	7	127	7	0	0	0	31.0	29	2	10	0	0	21	0	1	2	0	11	10	2	1	.667	0	2.90
93	POR/PCL	AAA	20	418	16	2	0	2	103.1	90	5	20	1	4	73	2	6	5	2	40	33	7	6	.538	0	2.87
	SEA/AL		14	72	0	0	0	8	18.0	18	0	6	2	0	13	1	0	0	0	3	2	0	2	.000	0	1.00
7 YR TOTALS			**155**	**1724**	**37**	**2**	**1**	**60**	**411.1**	**376**	**40**	**139**	**12**	**7**	**248**	**16**	**10**	**17**	**6**	**188**	**167**	**18**	**20**	**.474**	**19**	**3.65**

Oquist, Michael Lee "Mike" — BR/TR — b.5/30/68   BAL89 14/323

YR	TM/LG	CL	G	TBF	GS	CG	SHO	GF	IP	H	HR	BB	IBB	HB	SO	SH	SF	WP	BK	R	ER	W	L	PCT	SV	ERA
89	ERI/NYP	A-	15	402	15	1	1	0	97.2	86	7	25	0	3	109	2	1	1	1	43	39	7	4	.636	0	3.59
90	FRE/CAR	A+	25	678	25	3	1	0	166.1	134	11	48	3	4	170	6	6	9	1	64	52	9	8	.529	0	2.81
91	HAG/EAS	AA	27	717	26	1	0	1	166.1	168	15	62	4	0	136	4	7	7	1	82	75	10	9	.526	0	4.06
92	ROC/INT	AAA	26	665	24	5	0	0	153.1	164	17	45	1	5	111	9	5	4	1	80	70	10	12	.455	0	4.11
93	ROC/INT	AAA	28	617	21	2	1	1	149.1	144	20	41	1	2	128	5	1	5	0	62	58	9	8	.529	0	3.50
	BAL/AL		5	50	0	0	0	2	11.2	12	0	4	1	0	8	0	0	0	0	5	5	0	0	.000	0	3.86

Orosco, Jesse Russell — BR/TL — b.4/21/57   MIN78* 2/41

YR	TM/LG	CL	G	TBF	GS	CG	SHO	GF	IP	H	HR	BB	IBB	HB	SO	SH	SF	WP	BK	R	ER	W	L	PCT	SV	ERA
79	NY/NL		18	154	2	0	0	6	35.0	33	4	22	0	2	22	3	0	0	0	20	19	1	2	.333	0	4.89
81	NY/NL		8	69	0	0	0	4	17.1	13	2	6	2	0	18	2	0	0	1	4	3	0	1	.000	1	1.56
82	NY/NL		54	451	2	0	0	22	109.1	92	7	40	2	2	89	5	4	3	2	37	33	4	10	.286	4	2.72
83	NY/NL		62	432	0	0	0	42	110.0	76	3	38	7	1	84	4	3	1	2	27	18	13	7	.650	17	1.47
84	NY/NL		60	355	0	0	0	52	87.0	58	7	34	6	2	85	3	3	1	0	29	25	10	6	.625	31	2.59
85	NY/NL		54	331	0	0	0	39	79.0	66	6	34	7	0	68	1	1	0	0	26	24	8	6	.571	17	2.73
86	NY/NL		58	338	0	0	0	40	81.0	64	6	35	3	2	62	3	2	0	1	23	21	8	6	.571	21	2.33
87	NY/NL		58	335	0	0	0	41	77.0	78	5	31	9	2	78	5	4	2	0	41	38	3	9	.250	16	4.44
88	LA/NL		55	229	0	0	0	21	53.0	41	4	30	4	3	43	3	3	1	0	18	16	3	2	.600	9	2.72
89	CLE/AL		69	312	0	0	0	29	78.0	54	7	26	4	2	79	8	3	0	0	20	18	3	4	.429	3	2.08
90	CLE/AL		55	289	0	0	0	28	64.2	58	9	38	7	0	55	5	3	1	0	35	28	5	4	.556	2	3.90
91	CLE/AL		47	202	0	0	0	20	45.2	52	4	15	8	1	36	1	1	3	1	20	19	2	0	1.000	0	3.74
92	MIL/AL		59	158	0	0	0	14	39.0	33	5	13	1	1	40	0	2	2	0	15	14	3	1	.750	1	3.23
93	MIL/AL		57	233	0	0	0	27	56.2	47	2	17	3	1	67	1	2	4	1	25	20	3	5	.375	8	3.18
14 YR TOTALS			**714**	**3888**	**4**	**0**	**0**	**385**	**932.2**	**765**	**71**	**379**	**62**	**21**	**826**	**43**	**34**	**21**	**8**	**340**	**296**	**66**	**63**	**.512**	**130**	**2.86**

Osborne, Donovan Alan — BB/TL — b.6/21/69   SL90 1/13

YR	TM/LG	CL	G	TBF	GS	CG	SHO	GF	IP	H	HR	BB	IBB	HB	SO	SH	SF	WP	BK	R	ER	W	L	PCT	SV	ERA
90	HAM/NYP	A-	4	86	4	0	0	0	20.0	21	0	5	1	0	14	1	1	1	2	8	8	0	2	.000	0	3.60
	SAV/SAL	A	6	169	6	1	0	0	41.1	40	2	7	0	3	28	1	1	2	3	20	12	2	2	.500	0	2.61
91	ARK/TEX	AA	26	696	26	3	0	0	166.0	178	6	43	3	4	130	9	4	4	4	82	67	8	12	.400	0	3.63
92	STL/NL		34	754	29	0	0	2	179.0	193	14	38	2	2	104	7	4	6	0	91	75	11	9	.550	0	3.77
93	STL/NL		26	657	26	1	0	0	155.2	153	18	47	4	7	83	6	2	4	0	73	65	10	7	.588	0	3.76
2 YR TOTALS			**60**	**1411**	**55**	**1**	**0**	**2**	**334.2**	**346**	**32**	**85**	**6**	**9**	**187**	**13**	**6**	**10**	**0**	**164**	**140**	**21**	**16**	**.568**	**0**	**3.76**

Osuna, Alfonso "Al" — BR/TL — b.8/10/65   HOU87 16/418

YR	TM/LG	CL	G	TBF	GS	CG	SHO	GF	IP	H	HR	BB	IBB	HB	SO	SH	SF	WP	BK	R	ER	W	L	PCT	SV	ERA
87	AUB/NYP	A-	8	75	0	0	0	3	15.2	16	1	14	0	0	20	0	0	0	0	16	10	1	0	1.000	0	5.74
	ASH/SAL	A	14	81	0	0	0	7	19.2	20	0	6	0	0	20	0	0	0	3	6	6	2	0	1.000	2	2.75
88	OSC/FSL	A+	8	58	0	0	0	2	11.2	12	1	9	1	0	5	0	1	0	0	9	9	0	1	.000	0	6.94
	ASH/SAL	A	31	212	0	0	0	19	50.0	41	1	25	2	2	41	0	4	9	9	19	11	6	1	.857	3	1.98
89	OSC/FSL	A+	46	283	0	0	0	26	67.2	50	2	27	4	2	62	7	2	5	5	27	20	3	4	.429	7	2.66
90	CMB/SOU	AA	60	289	0	0	0	26	69.1	57	4	33	2	3	82	3	1	6	0	30	26	7	5	.583	6	3.38
	HOU/NL		12	48	0	0	0	2	11.1	10	1	6	1	3	6	0	0	0	0	6	6	2	0	1.000	0	4.76
91	HOU/NL		71	353	0	0	0	32	81.2	59	3	46	5	0	68	6	5	0	0	39	31	7	6	.538	12	3.42
92	HOU/NL		66	270	0	0	0	17	61.2	52	8	38	5	1	37	5	4	3	0	29	29	6	3	.667	0	4.23
93	TUC/PCL	AAA	13	133	4	0	0	3	30.0	26	1	17	0	5	38	0	1	4	0	16	15	3	1	.750	1	4.50
	HOU/NL		44	107	0	0	0	6	25.1	17	3	13	2	1	21	4	0	0	0	10	9	1	1	.500	2	3.20
4 YR TOTALS			**193**	**778**	**0**	**0**	**0**	**57**	**180.0**	**138**	**17**	**103**	**13**	**8**	**132**	**15**	**17**	**12**	**2**	**84**	**75**	**16**	**10**	**.615**	**14**	**3.75**

Otto, David Alan "Dave" — BL/TL — b.11/12/64 — OAK85 2/39

YR	TM/LG	CL	G	TBF	GS	CG	SHO	GF	IP	H	HR	BB	IBB	HB	SO	SH	SF	WP	BK	R	ER	W	L	PCT	SV	ERA
85	MED/NWL	A-	11	0	11	0	0	0	42.1	42	1	22	0	2	27	0	0	5	0	27	19	2	2	.500	0	4.04
86	MAD/MID	A	26	724	26	6	1	0	169.0	154	9	71	0	2	125	10	5	6	1	72	50	13	7	.650	0	2.66
87	MAD/MID	A	1	11	1	0	0	0	3.0	2	0	0	0	0	2	0	0	0	0	0	0	0	0	.000	0	0.00
	HUN/SOU	AA	9	192	8	1	0	0	50.0	36	1	11	0	0	25	0	1	4	0	14	13	4	1	.800	0	2.34
	OAK/AL		3	24	0	0	0	3	6.0	7	1	1	0	0	3	0	0	0	0	6	6	0	0	.000	0	9.00
88	TAC/PCL	AAA	21	564	21	2	0	0	127.2	124	7	63	3	0	80	1	4	7	4	71	50	4	9	.308	0	3.52
	OAK/AL		3	43	2	0	0	1	10.0	9	0	6	0	0	7	0	0	0	1	2	2	0	0	.000	0	1.80
89	TAC/PCL	AAA	29	714	28	2	1	0	169.0	164	6	61	3	1	122	3	4	18	2	84	69	10	13	.435	0	3.67
	OAK/AL		1	26	1	0	0	0	6.2	6	0	2	0	0	4	0	0	0	0	2	2	0	0	.000	0	2.70
90	OAK/AL		2	13	0	0	0	2	2.1	3	0	3	0	0	2	0	0	0	0	3	2	0	0	.000	0	7.71
	TAC/PCL	AAA	2	10	0	0	0	0	2.0	3	0	1	0	0	1	0	0	0	0	1	1	0	0	.000	0	4.50
91	CS/PCL	AAA	17	418	15	1	0	1	94.2	110	7	43	2	1	62	3	3	7	3	56	50	5	6	.455	0	4.75
	CLE/AL		18	425	14	1	0	0	100.0	108	7	27	6	4	47	8	4	3	0	52	47	2	8	.200	0	4.23
92	CAN/EAS	AA	1	9	1	0	0	0	3.0	1	0	1	0	0	1	0	0	0	0	0	0	0	0	.000	0	0.00
	CS/PCL	AAA	6	166	6	1	0	0	43.2	35	0	10	1	1	11	2	1	3	1	14	14	3	2	.600	0	2.89
	CLE/AL		18	368	16	0	0	0	80.1	110	12	33	0	1	32	3	1	5	0	64	63	5	9	.357	0	7.06
93	PIT/NL		28	306	8	0	0	7	68.0	85	9	28	1	3	30	4	4	4	0	40	38	3	4	.429	0	5.03
7 YR TOTALS			73	1205	41	1	0	13	273.1	328	29	100	7	8	125	18	6	12	1	169	160	10	21	.323	0	5.27

Painter, Lance Telford — BL/TL — b.7/21/67 — SD90 25/681

YR	TM/LG	CL	G	TBF	GS	CG	SHO	GF	IP	H	HR	BB	IBB	HB	SO	SH	SF	WP	BK	R	ER	W	L	PCT	SV	ERA
90	SPO/NWL	A-	23	280	1	0	0	10	71.2	45	4	15	0	2	104	4	1	3	3	18	12	7	3	.700	3	1.51
91	WAT/MID	A	28	788	28	7	4	0	200.0	162	14	57	7	2	201	5	4	3	1	64	51	14	8	.636	0	2.30
92	WIC/TEX	AA	27	680	27	1	1	0	163.1	138	11	55	1	10	137	8	3	6	3	74	64	10	5	.667	0	3.53
93	CS/PCL	AAA	23	610	22	4	1	0	138.0	165	10	44	2	5	91	10	5	6	2	90	66	9	7	.563	0	4.30
	COL/NL		10	166	6	1	0	2	39.0	52	5	9	0	0	16	1	2	0	0	26	26	2	2	.500	0	6.00

Pall, Donn Steven — BR/TR — b.1/11/62 — CHA85 23/579

YR	TM/LG	CL	G	TBF	GS	CG	SHO	GF	IP	H	HR	BB	IBB	HB	SO	SH	SF	WP	BK	R	ER	W	L	PCT	SV	ERA
85	WS/GCL	R	13	342	13	4	2	0	86.0	68	2	10	0	0	63	3	5	3	3	34	16	7	5	.583	0	1.67
86	APP/MID	A	11	317	11	3	1	0	78.0	71	2	14	1	4	51	2	0	4	0	29	20	5	5	.500	0	2.31
	BIR/SOU	AA	21	313	9	0	0	6	73.0	77	9	27	3	2	41	3	2	5	2	38	36	3	4	.429	1	4.44
87	BIR/SOU	AA	30	718	23	3	0	3	158.0	173	18	63	4	8	139	3	8	9	2	100	75	8	11	.421	0	4.27
88	VAN/PCL	AAA	44	293	0	0	0	25	72.2	61	2	20	2	3	41	2	1	2	1	21	18	5	2	.714	10	2.23
	CHI/AL		17	130	0	0	0	6	28.2	39	1	8	1	0	16	1	1	0	0	11	11	0	2	.000	0	3.45
89	SB/MID	A	2	12	0	0	0	0	3.1	1	0	0	0	0	4	0	0	0	0	0	0	0	0	.000	0	0.00
	CHI/AL		53	370	0	0	0	27	87.0	90	9	19	3	8	58	8	2	4	1	35	32	4	5	.444	6	3.31
90	CHI/AL		56	306	0	0	0	11	76.0	63	7	24	8	4	39	4	2	2	0	33	28	3	5	.375	2	3.32
91	CHI/AL		51	282	0	0	0	7	71.0	59	7	20	3	3	40	4	0	2	0	22	19	7	2	.778	0	2.41
92	CHI/AL		39	323	0	0	0	12	73.0	79	9	27	8	2	27	1	3	1	2	43	40	5	2	.714	1	4.93
93	CHI/AL		39	251	0	0	0	9	58.2	62	5	11	2	3	29	6	1	3	1	25	21	2	3	.400	1	3.22
	PHI/NL		8	69	0	0	0	2	17.2	15	1	3	0	0	11	1	0	1	0	7	5	1	0	1.000	0	2.55
	YEAR		47	320	0	0	0	11	76.1	77	6	14	3	2	40	7	1	4	1	32	26	3	3	.500	1	3.07
6 YR TOTALS			263	1731	0	0	0	74	412.0	407	39	112	26	19	220	26	9	13	4	176	156	22	19	.537	10	3.41

Parrett, Jeffrey Dale "Jeff" — BR/TR — b.8/26/61 — MIL83 9/236

YR	TM/LG	CL	G	TBF	GS	CG	SHO	GF	IP	H	HR	BB	IBB	HB	SO	SH	SF	WP	BK	R	ER	W	L	PCT	SV	ERA
84	BEL/MID	A	29	413	5	1	1	6	91.2	76	8	71	1	1	95	5	6	13	0	50	46	4	3	.571	2	4.52
85	STO/CAL	A+	45	0	2	0	0	21	127.2	97	5	75	2	1	120	0	0	7	2	50	39	7	4	.636	11	2.75
86	MON/NL		12	91	0	0	0	6	20.1	19	3	13	0	0	21	0	1	2	0	11	11	0	1	.000	0	4.87
	IND/AMA	AAA	25	297	8	0	0	7	69.0	54	3	35	2	0	76	3	3	7	0	44	38	2	5	.286	2	4.96
87	IND/AMA	AAA	20	91	0	0	0	19	22.1	15	0	13	0	0	17	1	0	3	0	5	5	2	1	.667	9	2.01
	MON/NL		45	267	0	0	0	26	62.0	53	8	30	4	0	56	5	1	6	1	33	29	7	6	.538	6	4.21
88	MON/NL		61	369	0	0	0	34	91.2	66	8	45	9	1	62	9	4	6	1	29	27	12	4	.750	6	2.65
89	PHI/NL		72	444	0	0	0	34	105.2	90	6	44	13	0	98	7	5	7	3	43	35	12	6	.667	6	2.98
90	PHI/NL		47	355	0	0	0	14	81.2	92	10	36	8	1	69	3	1	1	1	51	47	4	9	.308	1	5.18
	ATL/NL		20	124	0	0	0	5	27.0	27	1	19	2	1	17	4	4	2	0	11	9	1	1	.500	1	3.00
	YEAR		67	479	5	0	0	19	108.2	119	11	55	10	2	86	7	5	1	5	62	56	5	10	.333	2	4.64
91	ATL/NL		18	109	0	0	0	9	21.1	31	2	12	0	0	14	2	0	4	0	18	15	1	2	.333	1	6.33
	RIC/INT	AAA	19	352	14	0	0	2	79.2	72	2	46	1	1	88	2	2	5	0	45	40	2	7	.222	0	4.52
92	OAK/AL		66	410	0	0	0	14	98.1	81	7	42	3	2	78	4	4	11	1	35	33	9	1	.900	1	3.02
93	COL/NL		40	341	6	0	0	13	73.2	78	6	45	9	2	66	4	5	11	1	47	44	3	3	.500	1	5.38
8 YR TOTALS			381	2510	11	0	0	155	581.2	537	51	286	50	7	481	38	27	52	7	278	250	49	33	.598	22	3.87

Patterson, Kenneth Brian "Ken" — BL/TL — b.7/8/64 — NYA85 3/77

YR	TM/LG	CL	G	TBF	GS	CG	SHO	GF	IP	H	HR	BB	IBB	HB	SO	SH	SF	WP	BK	R	ER	W	L	PCT	SV	ERA
85	ONE/NYP	A-	6	103	6	0	0	0	22.1	23	0	14	0	2	21	1	0	1	0	14	12	2	2	.500	0	4.84
86	FL/FSL	A+	5	100	5	0	0	0	18.2	30	2	16	0	3	13	0	0	2	0	20	16	0	2	.000	0	7.71
	ONE/NYP	A-	15	399	15	5	4	0	100.1	67	0	45	0	4	102	1	1	7	1	25	15	9	3	.750	0	1.35
87	FL/FSL	A+	9	202	9	0	0	0	42.2	46	0	31	0	2	36	1	2	5	1	34	30	1	3	.250	0	6.33
	ALB/EAS	AA	24	272	8	1	0	14	63.2	59	2	31	1	2	47	3	3	4	0	31	28	3	6	.333	5	3.96
	HAW/PCL	AAA	3	14	0	0	0	3	3.1	1	0	3	0	0	5	0	0	0	0	0	0	0	0	.000	2	0.00
88	VAN/PCL	AAA	55	349	4	1	0	23	86.1	64	4	36	7	2	89	5	4	7	2	37	31	6	5	.545	13	3.23
	CHI/AL		9	92	2	0	0	0	20.2	25	2	7	0	0	8	0	1	1	0	11	11	0	1	.000	1	4.79
89	VAN/PCL	AAA	2	35	2	0	0	0	9.0	6	0	4	0	0	17	1	1	2	0	2	1	0	0	.000	0	1.00
	CHI/AL		50	284	1	0	0	18	65.2	64	11	28	3	2	43	1	4	3	1	37	33	6	1	.857	0	4.52

(continued)

Patterson, Kenneth Brian "Ken" (continued)

YR	TM/LG	CL	G	TBF	GS	CG	SHO	GF	IP	H	HR	BB	IBB	HB	SO	SH	SF	WP	BK	R	ER	W	L	PCT	SV	ERA
90	CHI/AL		43	283	0	0	0	15	66.1	58	6	34	1	2	40	2	5	2	0	27	25	2	1	.667	2	3.39
91	CHI/AL		43	265	0	0	0	13	63.2	48	5	35	1	1	32	3	2	2	0	22	20	3	0	1.000	1	2.83
92	PEO/MID	A	2	16	0	0	0	1	3.0	5	0	2	0	0	5	0	0	0	0	4	4	0	0	.000	0	12.00
	IOW/AMA	AAA	1	11	0	0	0	0	1.2	4	2	1	0	1	1	0	0	0	0	4	4	0	1	.000	0	21.60
	CHI/NL		32	191	1	0	0	4	41.2	41	7	27	6	1	23	6	4	3	1	25	18	2	3	.400	0	3.89
93	CAL/AL		46	255	0	0	0	9	59.0	54	7	35	5	0	36	2	1	2	0	30	30	1	1	.500	1	4.58
6 YR TOTALS			**223**	**1370**	**4**	**0**	**0**	**62**	**317.0**	**290**	**38**	**166**	**16**	**6**	**182**	**14**	**16**	**13**	**3**	**152**	**137**	**14**	**8**	**.636**	**5**	**3.89**

Patterson, Robert Chandler "Bob" — BR/TL — b.5/16/59   SD82 21/524

YR	TM/LG	CL	G	TBF	GS	CG	SHO	GF	IP	H	HR	BB	IBB	HB	SO	SH	SF	WP	BK	R	ER	W	L	PCT	SV	ERA
84	LV/PCL	AAA	60	0	7	1	0	41	143.1	129	12	37	7	1	97	0	0	3	0	63	52	8	9	.471	13	3.27
85	LV/PCL	AAA	42	0	20	7	1	16	186.1	187	19	52	5	1	146	0	0	5	2	80	65	10	11	.476	6	3.14
	SD/NL		3	26	0	0	0	2	4.0	13	2	3	0	0	1	0	0	0	1	11	11	0	0	.000	0	24.75
86	HAW/PCL	AAA	25	653	21	6	1	2	156.0	146	9	44	0	1	137	6	4	3	0	68	59	9	6	.600	1	3.40
	PIT/NL		11	159	5	0	0	2	36.1	49	0	5	2	0	20	1	1	0	1	20	20	2	3	.400	0	4.95
87	VAN/PCL	AAA	14	348	12	5	1	1	89.0	62	5	30	0	0	92	2	0	2	1	21	21	5	2	.714	0	2.12
	PIT/NL		15	201	7	0	0	2	43.0	49	5	22	4	1	27	6	3	1	0	34	32	1	4	.200	0	6.70
88	BUF/AMA	AAA	4	120	4	1	0	0	31.0	26	0	4	0	0	20	2	0	1	0	12	8	2	1	1.000	0	2.32
89	BUF/AMA	AAA	31	725	25	4	1	3	177.1	177	13	35	2	2	103	8	5	3	0	69	66	12	6	.667	1	3.35
	PIT/NL		12	109	3	0	0	1	26.2	23	3	8	2	0	20	1	1	0	0	13	12	4	3	.571	1	4.05
90	PIT/NL		55	386	5	0	0	19	94.2	88	9	21	7	3	70	5	3	1	2	33	31	8	5	.615	5	2.95
91	PIT/NL		54	270	1	0	0	19	65.2	67	7	15	1	0	57	2	2	2	0	32	30	4	3	.571	2	4.11
92	PIT/NL		60	268	0	0	0	26	64.2	59	7	23	6	0	43	3	2	3	0	22	21	6	3	.667	9	2.92
93	TEX/AL		52	224	0	0	0	29	52.2	59	8	11	0	1	46	1	2	0	0	28	28	2	4	.333	1	4.78
8 YR TOTALS			**262**	**1643**	**21**	**0**	**0**	**101**	**387.2**	**407**	**41**	**108**	**22**	**5**	**284**	**19**	**14**	**5**	**4**	**193**	**185**	**27**	**25**	**.519**	**18**	**4.29**

Pavlik, Roger Allen — BB/TR — b.10/4/67   TEX86 2/32

YR	TM/LG	CL	G	TBF	GS	CG	SHO	GF	IP	H	HR	BB	IBB	HB	SO	SH	SF	WP	BK	R	ER	W	L	PCT	SV	ERA
87	GAS/SAL	A	15	303	14	0	0	0	67.1	66	3	42	0	5	55	1	4	6	0	46	37	2	7	.222	0	4.95
88	GAS/SAL	A	18	408	16	0	0	1	84.1	94	3	58	2	6	89	4	0	10	3	65	43	2	12	.143	0	4.59
	BUT/PIO	R+	8	223	8	1	1	0	49.0	45	2	34	0	7	56	2	1	3	0	29	25	4	0	1.000	0	4.59
89	CHA/FSL	A+	26	511	22	1	1	2	118.2	92	5	72	1	8	98	4	4	12	4	60	45	3	8	.273	1	3.41
90	CHA/FSL	A+	11	279	11	1	0	0	66.1	50	1	40	2	5	76	2	0	6	1	21	18	5	3	.625	0	2.44
	TUL/TEX	AA	16	418	16	2	1	0	100.1	66	4	71	2	5	91	3	1	7	2	29	26	6	5	.545	0	2.33
91	OC/AMA	AAA	8	126	7	0	0	0	26.0	19	1	26	1	1	43	0	1	5	1	21	15	0	0	.000	0	5.19
92	OC/AMA	AAA	18	485	18	0	0	0	117.2	90	7	51	0	4	104	3	8	14	1	44	39	7	5	.583	0	2.98
	TEX/AL		13	275	12	1	0	0	62.0	66	3	34	0	3	45	0	2	9	0	32	29	4	4	.500	0	4.21
93	OC/AMA	AAA	6	150	6	0	0	0	37.0	26	1	14	0	2	32	0	0	2	0	12	7	3	2	.600	0	1.70
	TEX/AL		26	712	26	2	0	0	166.1	151	18	80	3	5	131	6	4	6	0	67	63	12	6	.667	0	3.41
2 YR TOTALS			**39**	**987**	**38**	**3**	**0**	**0**	**228.1**	**217**	**21**	**114**	**3**	**8**	**176**	**6**	**6**	**15**	**0**	**99**	**92**	**16**	**10**	**.615**	**0**	**3.63**

Pennington, Brad Lee — BL/TL — b.4/14/69   BAL89 13/297

YR	TM/LG	CL	G	TBF	GS	CG	SHO	GF	IP	H	HR	BB	IBB	HB	SO	SH	SF	WP	BK	R	ER	W	L	PCT	SV	ERA
89	BLU/APP	R+	15	319	14	0	0	0	64.1	50	2	74	0	6	81	1	3	14	8	58	47	2	7	.222	0	6.58
90	WAU/MID	A	32	523	18	1	0	0	106.0	81	12	121	1	4	142	6	4	10	1	89	61	4	9	.308	0	5.18
91	KC/MID	A	23	112	0	0	0	19	23.0	16	1	25	0	0	43	0	0	4	0	17	15	0	2	.000	4	5.87
	FRE/CAR	A+	36	203	0	0	0	27	43.2	32	4	44	0	2	58	3	2	4	0	23	19	1	4	.200	13	3.92
92	FRE/CAR	A+	8	38	0	0	0	6	9.0	5	0	4	0	1	16	1	1	1	0	3	2	1	0	1.000	2	2.00
	HAG/EAS	AA	19	121	0	0	0	16	28.1	20	0	17	0	3	33	4	3	4	0	9	8	1	2	.333	7	2.54
	ROC/INT	AAA	29	158	0	0	0	17	39.0	12	2	33	2	1	56	1	1	1	0	10	9	1	3	.250	5	2.08
93	ROC/INT	AAA	17	73	0	0	0	14	15.2	12	0	13	0	0	19	0	0	1	1	11	6	1	2	.333	8	3.45
	BAL/AL		34	158	0	0	0	16	33.0	34	7	25	0	2	39	1	1	3	0	25	24	3	2	.600	4	6.55

Perez, Melido Turpen Gross — BR/TR — b.2/15/66   KC 7/22/83

YR	TM/LG	CL	G	TBF	GS	CG	SHO	GF	IP	H	HR	BB	IBB	HB	SO	SH	SF	WP	BK	R	ER	W	L	PCT	SV	ERA
84	CHS/SAL	A	16	387	15	0	0	0	89.0	99	9	19	0	2	55	2	2	4	1	52	43	5	7	.417	0	4.35
85	EUG/NWL	A-	17	0	15	2	0	1	101.0	116	13	35	2	1	88	0	0	4	2	65	61	6	7	.462	0	5.44
86	BUR/MID	A	28	712	23	13	1	5	170.1	148	15	49	3	3	153	5	2	8	1	83	70	10	12	.455	0	3.70
87	FM/FSL	A+	8	247	8	5	1	0	64.1	51	3	7	0	0	51	3	1	3	0	20	17	4	3	.571	0	2.38
	MEM/SOU	AA	20	538	20	5	2	0	133.2	125	13	20	1	0	126	1	1	4	0	60	51	8	5	.615	0	3.43
	KC/AL		3	53	3	0	0	0	10.1	18	2	5	0	0	5	0	0	0	0	12	9	1	1	.500	0	7.84
88	CHI/AL		32	836	32	3	1	0	197.0	186	26	72	0	2	138	5	8	13	3	105	83	12	10	.545	0	3.79
89	CHI/AL		31	810	31	2	0	0	183.1	187	23	90	3	3	141	6	5	12	5	106	102	11	14	.440	0	5.01
90	CHI/AL		35	833	35	3	3	0	197.0	177	14	86	1	2	161	4	6	8	4	111	101	13	14	.481	0	4.61
91	CHI/AL		49	553	8	0	0	16	135.2	111	15	52	0	1	128	4	1	11	1	49	47	8	7	.533	1	3.12
92	NY/AL		33	1013	33	10	2	0	247.2	212	16	93	5	5	218	6	8	13	0	94	79	13	16	.448	0	2.87
93	NY/AL		25	718	25	0	0	0	163.0	173	22	64	5	1	148	4	2	3	1	103	94	6	14	.300	0	5.19
7 YR TOTALS			**208**	**4816**	**167**	**18**	**5**	**16**	**1134.0**	**1064**	**118**	**462**	**14**	**14**	**939**	**28**	**29**	**60**	**14**	**580**	**515**	**64**	**76**	**.457**	**1**	**4.09**

Perez, Michael Irvin "Mike" — BR/TR — b.10/19/64   SL86 13/312

YR	TM/LG	CL	G	TBF	GS	CG	SHO	GF	IP	H	HR	BB	IBB	HB	SO	SH	SF	WP	BK	R	ER	W	L	PCT	SV	ERA
86	JC/APP	R+	18	314	8	2	0	6	72.2	69	3	22	0	5	72	1	2	1	0	35	24	3	5	.375	3	2.97
87	SPR/MID	A	58	321	0	0	0	51	84.1	47	2	21	2	4	119	3	2	2	0	12	8	6	2	.750	41	0.85
88	ARK/TEX	AA	11	75	0	0	0	4	14.1	18	2	13	2	1	17	1	2	2	3	18	18	1	3	.250	0	11.30
	SP/FSL	A+	35	173	0	0	0	28	43.1	24	0	16	1	4	45	2	3	2	0	12	10	2	4	.500	17	2.08
89	ARK/TEX	AA	57	329	0	0	0	51	76.2	68	5	32	2	2	74	0	2	3	1	34	31	4	6	.400	33	3.64

Perez, Michael Irvin "Mike" (continued)

YR	TM/LG	CL	G	TBF	GS	CG	SHO	GF	IP	H	HR	BB	IBB	HB	SO	SH	SF	WP	BK	R	ER	W	L	PCT	SV	ERA
90	LOU/AMA	AAA	57	298	0	0	0	50	67.1	64	9	33	4	2	69	4	1	3	0	34	32	7	7	.500	31	4.28
	STL/NL		13	55	0	0	0	7	13.2	12	0	3	0	0	5	0	2	0	0	6	6	1	0	1.000	1	3.95
91	STL/NL		14	75	0	0	0	2	17.0	19	1	7	2	1	7	1	0	0	0	11	11	0	2	.000	0	5.82
	LOU/AMA	AAA	37	224	0	0	0	23	47.0	54	5	25	6	2	39	5	2	4	0	38	32	3	5	.375	4	6.13
92	STL/NL		77	377	0	0	0	22	93.0	70	4	32	9	1	46	7	4	4	0	23	19	9	3	.750	0	1.84
93	ARK/TEX	AA	4	19	0	0	0	0	3.2	7	0	0	0	1	4	1	0	0	0	3	3	0	0	.000	0	7.36
	STL/NL		65	298	0	0	0	25	72.2	65	4	20	1	1	58	5	5	2	0	24	20	7	2	.778	7	2.48
4 YR TOTALS			**169**	**805**	**0**	**0**	**0**	**56**	**196.1**	**166**	**9**	**62**	**12**	**3**	**116**	**13**	**11**	**6**	**1**	**64**	**56**	**17**	**7**	**.708**	**8**	**2.57**

Petkovsek, Mark Joseph — BR/TR — b.11/18/65   TEX87 3/29

YR	TM/LG	CL	G	TBF	GS	CG	SHO	GF	IP	H	HR	BB	IBB	HB	SO	SH	SF	WP	BK	R	ER	W	L	PCT	SV	ERA
87	RAN/GCL	R	3	26	1	0	0	0	5.2	4	0	0	2	0	7	0	0	0	0	2	2	0	0	.000	0	3.18
	CHA/FSL	A+	11	249	10	0	0	1	56.0	67	2	17	0	0	23	3	3	5	1	36	25	3	4	.429	0	4.02
88	CHA/FSL	A+	28	708	28	7	5	0	175.2	156	5	42	2	3	95	6	7	11	4	71	58	10	11	.476	0	2.97
89	OC/AMA	AAA	6	147	6	0	0	0	30.2	39	3	18	1	3	8	1	1	2	0	27	25	0	4	.000	0	7.34
	TUL/TEX	AA	21	585	21	0	1	0	140.0	144	7	35	0	3	66	6	7	5	0	63	54	8	5	.615	0	3.47
90	OC/AMA	AAA	28	669	28	0	0	0	151.0	187	9	42	1	4	81	3	2	8	0	103	88	7	14	.333	0	5.25
91	TEX/AL		4	53	1	0	0	0	9.1	21	4	4	0	0	6	0	1	2	0	16	15	0	1	.000	0	14.46
	OC/AMA	AAA	25	646	24	3	1	0	149.2	162	9	38	2	7	67	5	9	8	1	89	82	9	8	.529	0	4.93
92	BUF/AMA	AAA	32	632	22	1	0	1	150.1	150	9	44	1	7	49	12	3	5	0	76	59	8	8	.500	0	3.53
93	BUF/AMA	AAA	14	291	11	1	0	0	70.2	74	8	16	0	2	27	2	1	4	0	38	34	3	4	.429	0	4.33
	PIT/NL		26	145	0	0	0	8	32.1	43	7	9	2	0	14	4	1	6	0	25	25	3	0	1.000	0	6.96
2 YR TOTALS			**30**	**198**	**1**	**0**	**0**	**9**	**41.2**	**64**	**11**	**13**	**2**	**0**	**20**	**4**	**2**	**6**	**0**	**41**	**40**	**3**	**1**	**.750**	**0**	**8.64**

Pichardo, Hipolito Antonio — BR/TR — b.8/22/69   KC 12/16/87

YR	TM/LG	CL	G	TBF	GS	CG	SHO	GF	IP	H	HR	BB	IBB	HB	SO	SH	SF	WP	BK	R	ER	W	L	PCT	SV	ERA
88	ROY/GCL	R	1	9	0	0	0	0	1.1	3	0	1	0	1	3	0	0	0	0	2	2	0	0	.000	0	13.50
89	APP/MID	A	12	300	12	2	0	0	75.2	58	4	18	0	5	50	2	1	5	4	29	25	5	4	.556	0	2.97
90	BC/FSL	A+	11	201	10	0	0	0	45.0	47	1	25	0	1	40	2	2	4	2	28	19	1	6	.143	0	3.80
91	MEM/SOU	AA	34	447	11	0	0	5	99.0	116	4	38	5	4	75	7	4	6	1	56	47	3	11	.214	0	4.27
92	MEM/SOU	AA	2	55	2	0	0	0	14.0	13	0	1	0	0	10	1	0	0	0	2	1	0	0	.000	0	0.64
	KC/AL		31	615	24	1	1	0	143.2	148	9	49	1	3	59	4	5	3	1	71	63	9	6	.600	0	3.95
93	KC/AL		30	720	25	2	0	2	165.0	183	10	53	2	6	70	3	8	5	3	85	74	7	8	.467	0	4.04
2 YR TOTALS			**61**	**1335**	**49**	**3**	**1**	**2**	**308.2**	**331**	**19**	**102**	**3**	**9**	**129**	**7**	**13**	**8**	**4**	**156**	**137**	**16**	**14**	**.533**	**0**	**3.99**

Plantenberg, Erik John — BB/TL — b.10/30/68   BOS90 15/443

YR	TM/LG	CL	G	TBF	GS	CG	SHO	GF	IP	H	HR	BB	IBB	HB	SO	SH	SF	WP	BK	R	ER	W	L	PCT	SV	ERA
90	ELM/NYP	A-	16	185	5	0	0	4	40.1	44	2	19	0	0	36	6	1	4	1	26	18	2	3	.400	1	4.02
91	LYN/CAR	A+	20	461	20	0	0	0	103.0	116	3	51	1	4	73	4	2	8	0	59	43	11	5	.688	0	3.76
92	LYN/CAR	A+	21	384	12	0	0	4	81.2	112	7	36	0	5	62	2	4	6	0	69	47	2	3	.400	0	5.18
93	JAC/SOU	AA	34	182	0	0	0	13	44.2	38	0	14	1	0	49	1	0	1	0	11	10	2	1	.667	1	2.01
	SEA/AL		20	53	0	0	0	4	9.2	11	0	12	1	1	7	0	0	1	0	7	7	0	0	.000	1	6.52

Plesac, Daniel Thomas "Dan" — BL/TL — b.2/4/62   MIL83 1/26

YR	TM/LG	CL	G	TBF	GS	CG	SHO	GF	IP	H	HR	BB	IBB	HB	SO	SH	SF	WP	BK	R	ER	W	L	PCT	SV	ERA
84	STO/CAL	A+	16	0	16	2	0	0	108.1	106	7	50	0	2	101	0	0	3	2	51	40	6	6	.500	0	3.32
	EP/TEX	AA	7	171	7	0	0	0	39.0	43	2	16	0	0	24	1	1	2	0	19	15	2	2	.500	0	3.46
85	EP/TEX	AA	25	662	24	2	0	0	150.1	171	12	68	1	0	128	5	5	13	1	91	83	12	5	.706	0	4.97
86	MIL/AL		51	377	0	0	0	33	91.0	81	5	29	1	0	75	6	5	4	0	34	30	10	7	.588	14	2.97
87	MIL/AL		57	325	0	0	0	47	79.1	63	8	23	4	3	89	1	2	6	0	30	23	5	6	.455	23	2.61
88	MIL/AL		50	211	0	0	0	48	52.1	46	2	12	2	0	52	2	0	4	0	14	14	1	2	.333	30	2.41
89	MIL/AL		52	242	0	0	0	51	61.1	47	6	17	1	0	52	0	4	2	0	16	16	3	4	.429	33	2.35
90	MIL/AL		66	299	0	0	0	52	69.0	67	5	31	6	3	65	2	2	2	0	36	34	3	7	.300	24	4.43
91	MIL/AL		45	402	10	0	0	25	92.1	92	12	39	1	4	61	3	7	2	1	49	44	2	7	.222	8	4.29
92	MIL/AL		44	330	4	0	0	13	79.0	64	9	35	5	3	54	4	1	2	0	28	26	5	4	.556	1	2.96
93	CHI/NL		57	276	0	0	0	12	62.2	74	10	21	6	0	47	4	3	5	2	37	33	2	1	.667	0	4.74
8 YR TOTALS			**422**	**2462**	**14**	**0**	**0**	**281**	**587.0**	**534**	**53**	**207**	**23**	**12**	**495**	**26**	**27**	**26**	**10**	**244**	**220**	**31**	**38**	**.449**	**133**	**3.37**

Plunk, Eric Vaughn — BR/TR — b.9/3/63   NYA81 4/103

YR	TM/LG	CL	G	TBF	GS	CG	SHO	GF	IP	H	HR	BB	IBB	HB	SO	SH	SF	WP	BK	R	ER	W	L	PCT	SV	ERA
84	FL/FSL	A+	28	791	28	7	1	0	176.1	153	5	123	1	6	152	5	8	17	7	85	56	12	12	.500	0	2.86
85	HUN/SOU	AA	13	347	13	2	1	0	79.1	61	9	56	0	2	68	1	3	4	1	36	30	8	2	.800	0	3.40
	TAC/PCL	AAA	11	0	10	0	0	0	53.0	51	3	50	3	2	43	0	0	4	3	41	34	0	5	.000	0	5.77
86	TAC/PCL	AAA	6	147	6	0	0	0	32.2	25	4	33	0	3	31	2	3	3	2	18	17	2	3	.400	0	4.68
	OAK/AL		26	537	15	0	0	2	120.1	91	14	102	3	5	98	2	5	9	2	75	71	4	7	.364	0	5.31
87	TAC/PCL	AAA	24	140	0	0	0	19	34.2	21	1	17	2	0	56	1	0	6	0	8	6	1	1	.500	9	1.56
	OAK/AL		32	432	11	0	0	11	95.0	91	8	62	3	0	90	3	5	5	2	53	50	4	2	.400	2	4.74
88	OAK/AL		49	331	0	0	0	22	78.0	62	6	39	4	2	79	2	1	6	7	27	26	7	2	.778	5	3.00
89	OAK/AL		23	113	0	0	0	12	28.2	17	1	12	0	1	24	1	0	4	1	7	7	1	1	.500	1	2.20
	NY/AL		27	332	7	0	0	5	75.2	65	9	52	2	0	61	2	2	4	0	36	31	7	5	.583	0	3.69
	YEAR		50	445	7	0	0	17	104.1	82	10	64	2	1	85	3	4	8	1	43	38	8	6	.571	1	3.28
90	NY/AL		47	310	0	0	0	16	72.2	58	6	43	4	2	67	7	0	6	0	27	22	6	3	.667	0	2.72
91	NY/AL		43	521	8	0	0	5	111.2	128	18	62	1	0	103	6	4	6	0	69	59	2	5	.286	0	4.76
92	CAN/EAS	AA	9	63	0	0	0	3	15.2	11	0	5	0	0	19	2	0	1	0	4	3	1	2	.333	0	1.72
	CLE/AL		58	309	0	0	0	20	71.2	61	6	38	2	0	50	3	2	5	0	31	29	9	6	.600	4	3.64
93	CLE/AL		70	306	0	0	0	40	71.0	61	6	30	4	0	77	1	4	9	2	29	22	4	5	.444	15	2.79
8 YR TOTALS			**375**	**3191**	**41**	**0**	**0**	**134**	**724.2**	**634**	**72**	**440**	**22**	**12**	**649**	**31**	**24**	**49**	**22**	**354**	**317**	**44**	**40**	**.524**	**27**	**3.94**

Poole, James Richard "Jim" — BL/TL — b.4/28/66   LA88 8/218

YR	TM/LG	CL	G	TBF	GS	CG	SHO	GF	IP	H	HR	BB	IBB	HB	SO	SH	SF	WP	BK	R	ER	W	L	PCT	SV	ERA
88	VB/FSL	A+	10	63	0	0	0	6	14.1	13	0	9	1	1	12	1	1	1	0	7	6	1	1	.500	0	3.77
89	VB/FSL	A+	60	306	0	0	0	50	78.1	57	0	24	7	2	93	5	0	3	0	16	14	11	4	.733	19	1.61
	BAK/CAL	A+	1	7	0	0	0	1	1.2	2	0	0	0	0	1	0	0	0	0	1	0	0	0	.000	0	0.00
90	SA/TEX	AA	54	278	0	0	0	35	63.2	55	3	27	5	2	77	8	0	6	0	31	17	6	7	.462	16	2.40
	LA/NL		16	46	0	0	0	4	10.2	7	1	8	4	0	6	0	0	1	0	5	5	0	0	.000	0	4.22
91	OC/AMA	AAA	10	41	0	0	0	7	12.1	4	0	1	0	0	14	0	2	0	0	0	0	0	0	.000	3	0.00
	TEX/AL		5	31	0	0	0	2	6.0	10	0	3	0	0	4	0	0	0	0	4	3	0	0	.000	0	4.50
	ROC/INT	AAA	27	123	0	0	0	19	29.0	29	1	9	0	0	25	0	1	3	0	11	9	3	2	.600	9	2.79
	BAL/AL		24	135	0	0	0	3	36.0	19	3	9	2	0	34	3	2	2	0	10	8	3	2	.600	0	2.00
	YEAR		29	166	0	0	0	5	42.0	29	3	12	2	0	38	3	2	2	0	14	11	3	2	.600	1	2.36
92	HAG/EAS	AA	7	52	3	0	0	0	13.0	14	0	1	0	2	4	1	0	0	0	4	4	0	1	.000	0	2.77
	ROC/INT	AAA	32	180	0	0	0	19	42.1	40	8	18	1	1	30	1	4	3	0	26	25	1	6	.143	10	5.31
	BAL/AL		6	14	0	0	0	1	3.1	3	0	1	0	0	3	0	0	0	0	3	0	0	0	.000	0	0.00
93	BAL/AL		55	197	0	0	0	11	50.1	30	2	21	5	0	29	3	2	0	0	18	12	2	1	.667	2	2.15
4 YR TOTALS			**106**	**423**	**0**	**0**	**0**	**21**	**106.1**	**69**	**6**	**42**	**11**	**0**	**76**	**6**	**5**	**3**	**0**	**40**	**28**	**5**	**3**	**.625**	**3**	**2.37**

Portugal, Mark Steven — BR/TR — b.10/30/62   MIN 10/23/80

YR	TM/LG	CL	G	TBF	GS	CG	SHO	GF	IP	H	HR	BB	IBB	HB	SO	SH	SF	WP	BK	R	ER	W	L	PCT	SV	ERA
84	ORL/SOU	AA	27	849	27	10	3	0	196.0	171	16	113	2	3	110	4	3	9	0	80	65	14	7	.667	0	2.98
85	TOL/INT	AAA	19	547	19	5	1	0	128.2	129	10	60	0	0	89	2	2	4	3	60	54	8	5	.615	0	3.78
	MIN/AL		6	105	4	0	0	0	24.1	24	3	14	0	0	12	0	2	1	1	16	15	1	3	.250	0	5.55
86	TOL/INT	AAA	6	191	6	3	1	0	45.0	34	2	23	0	2	30	0	2	1	0	15	13	5	1	.833	0	2.60
	MIN/AL		27	481	15	3	0	7	112.2	112	10	50	1	1	67	5	3	5	0	56	54	6	10	.375	1	4.31
87	MIN/AL		13	204	7	0	0	3	44.0	58	13	24	1	1	28	0	1	1	0	40	38	1	3	.250	0	7.77
	POR/PCL	AAA	17	451	16	2	0	1	102.0	108	9	50	0	0	69	1	3	5	0	75	68	1	10	.091	0	6.00
88	POR/PCL	AAA	3	80	3	1	1	0	19.2	15	0	8	0	0	9	2	2	1	0	3	3	2	0	1.000	0	1.37
	MIN/AL		26	242	0	0	0	9	57.2	60	11	17	1	1	31	2	3	2	2	30	29	3	3	.500	3	4.53
89	TUC/PCL	AAA	17	480	17	5	0	0	116.2	107	6	32	1	3	90	2	1	3	0	55	49	7	5	.583	0	3.78
	HOU/NL		20	440	15	3	0	1	108.0	91	7	37	0	2	86	8	1	3	0	34	33	7	1	.875	0	2.75
90	HOU/NL		32	831	32	6	3	0	196.2	187	21	67	4	4	136	7	6	6	0	90	79	11	10	.524	0	3.62
91	HOU/NL		32	710	27	1	0	3	168.1	163	19	59	5	2	120	6	6	4	1	91	84	10	12	.455	1	4.49
92	HOU/NL		18	405	16	1	1	0	101.1	76	7	41	3	1	62	5	1	1	1	32	30	6	3	.667	0	2.66
93	HOU/NL		33	876	33	1	1	0	208.0	194	10	77	3	4	131	11	3	9	2	75	64	18	4	*.818	0	2.77
9 YR TOTALS			**207**	**4294**	**149**	**9**	**3**	**23**	**1021.0**	**965**	**101**	**386**	**18**	**16**	**673**	**44**	**26**	**33**	**7**	**464**	**426**	**63**	**49**	**.563**	**5**	**3.76**

Powell, Dennis Clay — BR/TL — b.8/13/63   LA 5/17/83

YR	TM/LG	CL	G	TBF	GS	CG	SHO	GF	IP	H	HR	BB	IBB	HB	SO	SH	SF	WP	BK	R	ER	W	L	PCT	SV	ERA
84	VB/FSL	A+	4	106	4	0	0	0	26.0	19	0	12	1	1	14	2	1	3	0	7	4	1	1	.500	0	1.38
	SA/TEX	AA	24	721	24	5	2	0	168.0	153	8	87	0	2	82	3	4	3	2	81	63	9	8	.529	0	3.38
85	ALB/PCL	AAA	18	0	17	3	0	0	111.2	106	5	48	0	1	55	0	6	6	2	40	34	9	0	1.000	0	2.74
	LA/NL		16	133	2	0	0	6	29.1	30	7	13	3	1	19	4	1	3	0	19	17	1	1	.500	1	5.22
86	ALB/PCL	AAA	7	176	7	0	0	0	41.2	45	3	15	0	0	27	0	1	1	0	23	19	3	3	.500	0	4.10
	LA/NL		27	272	6	0	0	5	65.1	65	5	25	7	1	31	5	2	7	0	32	31	2	7	.222	0	4.27
87	CAL/PCL	AAA	20	538	20	2	1	0	117.1	145	12	48	1	2	65	4	3	3	1	80	64	4	8	.333	0	4.91
	SEA/AL		16	147	3	0	0	1	34.1	32	3	15	0	0	17	2	2	0	0	13	12	1	3	.250	0	3.15
88	SEA/AL		12	95	2	0	0	1	18.2	29	2	11	2	2	15	0	2	0	0	20	18	1	3	.250	0	8.68
	CAL/PCL	AAA	21	481	18	2	1	1	108.0	116	9	49	1	1	81	4	3	1	0	57	50	6	4	.600	1	4.17
89	CAL/PCL	AAA	18	109	0	0	0	14	25.1	21	0	12	0	1	15	0	2	0	0	10	6	3	2	.600	6	2.13
	SEA/AL		43	201	1	0	0	9	45.0	49	6	21	0	0	27	3	3	1	0	25	25	2	2	.500	2	5.00
90	SEA/AL		2	17	0	0	0	0	3.0	5	0	2	0	1	0	1	1	1	0	3	3	0	0	.000	0	9.00
	MIL/AL		9	197	7	0	0	1	39.1	59	6	19	0	1	23	2	2	2	0	37	30	0	4	.000	0	6.86
	YEAR		11	214	7	0	0	2	42.1	64	6	21	0	2	23	2	2	2	0	40	33	0	4	.000	0	7.02
	DEN/AMA	AAA	11	263	11	2	0	0	62.1	63	6	21	0	0	46	2	2	3	1	34	25	4	4	.500	0	3.61
91	CAL/PCL	AAA	27	761	26	5	1	0	173.2	200	20	59	0	6	96	5	6	12	1	90	80	9	8	.529	0	4.15
92	SEA/AL		49	243	0	0	0	11	57.0	49	5	29	2	3	35	5	0	2	0	30	29	4	2	.667	0	4.58
93	SEA/AL		33	197	2	0	0	7	47.2	42	5	24	2	1	32	5	2	0	0	22	22	0	0	.000	0	4.15
	CAL/PCL	AAA	12	164	4	0	0	2	40.0	37	3	19	1	1	30	1	0	0	0	16	16	3	2	.600	1	3.60
8 YR TOTALS			**207**	**1502**	**23**	**0**	**0**	**42**	**339.2**	**360**	**35**	**159**	**16**	**12**	**199**	**26**	**14**	**17**	**2**	**201**	**187**	**11**	**22**	**.333**	**3**	**4.95**

Powell, Ross John — BL/TL — b.1/24/68   CIN89 3/80

YR	TM/LG	CL	G	TBF	GS	CG	SHO	GF	IP	H	HR	BB	IBB	HB	SO	SH	SF	WP	BK	R	ER	W	L	PCT	SV	ERA
89	CR/MID	A	13	319	13	1	1	0	76.1	68	4	23	0	1	58	1	1	4	3	37	30	7	4	.636	0	3.54
90	CHT/SOU	AA	29	783	27	6	1	1	185.0	172	10	57	5	6	132	11	8	11	2	89	73	8	14	.364	0	3.55
	NAS/AMA	AAA	3	9	0	0	0	1	2.2	1	0	0	0	0	4	2	0	0	0	1	1	0	0	.000	0	3.38
91	NAS/AMA	AAA	24	568	24	1	0	0	129.2	125	10	63	1	2	82	5	2	4	0	74	63	8	8	.500	0	4.37
92	CHT/SOU	AA	14	224	5	0	0	0	57.1	43	2	17	1	0	56	3	1	1	0	9	8	4	1	.800	1	1.26
	NAS/AMA	AAA	25	403	12	0	0	4	93.1	89	5	42	1	3	84	2	2	3	0	37	35	4	3	.333	0	3.38
93	IND/AMA	AAA	28	764	27	4	0	1	179.2	159	27	71	1	5	133	1	2	13	2	89	82	10	10	.500	0	4.11
	CIN/NL		9	66	1	0	0	1	16.1	13	1	6	0	0	17	2	0	1	0	8	8	0	3	.000	0	4.41

Power, Ted Henry — BR/TR — b.1/31/55   LA76 5/115

YR	TM/LG	CL	G	TBF	GS	CG	SHO	GF	IP	H	HR	BB	IBB	HB	SO	SH	SF	WP	BK	R	ER	W	L	PCT	SV	ERA
81	LA/NL		5	66	2	0	0	1	14.1	16	0	7	2	1	7	0	2	0	0	6	5	1	3	.250	0	3.14
82	LA/NL		12	160	4	0	0	4	33.2	38	4	23	1	0	15	4	1	3	3	27	25	1	1	.500	0	6.68
83	CIN/NL		49	480	6	1	0	14	111.0	120	10	49	4	0	57	4	6	1	0	62	56	5	6	.455	2	4.54
84	CIN/NL		*78	456	0	0	0	42	108.2	93	4	46	8	0	81	9	8	3	0	37	34	9	7	.563	11	2.82

Power, Ted Henry (continued)

YR	TM/LG	CL	G	TBF	GS	CG	SHO	GF	IP	H	HR	BB	IBB	HB	SO	SH	SF	WP	BK	R	ER	W	L	PCT	SV	ERA
85	CIN/NL		64	342	0	0	0	50	80.0	65	2	45	8	1	42	6	4	1	0	27	24	8	6	.571	27	2.70
86	CIN/NL		56	537	10	0	0	30	129.0	115	13	52	10	1	95	9	6	5	1	59	53	10	6	.625	1	3.70
87	CIN/NL		34	887	34	2	1	0	204.0	213	28	71	7	3	133	8	7	3	2	115	102	10	13	.435	0	4.50
88	KC/AL		22	360	12	2	2	3	80.1	98	7	30	3	3	44	2	4	3	0	54	53	5	6	.455	0	5.94
	DET/AL		4	83	2	0	0	0	18.2	23	1	8	4	0	13	0	0	1	0	13	12	1	1	.500	0	5.79
	YEAR		26	443	14	2	2	3	99.0	121	8	38	7	3	57	2	4	4	0	67	65	6	7	.462	0	5.91
89	LOU/AMA	AAA	8	152	7	1	1	0	37.0	29	3	15	1	2	36	0	1	1	0	13	13	4	3	.571	0	3.16
	STL/NL		23	407	15	0	0	2	97.0	96	7	21	3	1	43	5	3	1	0	47	40	7	7	.500	0	3.71
90	PIT/NL		40	218	0	0	0	25	51.2	50	5	17	6	0	42	3	2	1	0	23	21	1	3	.250	7	3.66
91	CIN/NL		68	371	0	0	0	22	87.0	87	6	31	5	2	51	6	4	6	1	37	35	5	3	.625	3	3.62
92	CLE/AL		64	409	0	0	0	16	99.1	88	7	35	9	4	51	7	8	2	1	33	28	3	3	.500	0	2.54
93	CLE/AL		20	101	0	0	0	6	20.0	30	2	8	3	0	11	2	1	1	0	17	16	0	2	.000	0	7.20
	SEA/AL		25	105	0	0	0	18	25.1	27	1	9	1	0	16	1	1	1	0	11	11	2	2	.500	13	3.91
	YEAR		45	206	0	0	0	24	45.1	57	3	17	4	0	27	3	2	2	0	28	27	2	4	.333	13	5.36
13 YR TOTALS			**564**	**4982**	**85**	**5**	**3**	**233**	**1160.0**	**1159**	**97**	**452**	**74**	**17**	**701**	**66**	**57**	**32**	**10**	**568**	**515**	**68**	**69**	**.496**	**70**	**4.00**

Pugh, Timothy Dean "Tim" — BR/TR — b.1/26/67   CIN89 6/160

YR	TM/LG	CL	G	TBF	GS	CG	SHO	GF	IP	H	HR	BB	IBB	HB	SO	SH	SF	WP	BK	R	ER	W	L	PCT	SV	ERA
89	BIL/PIO	R+	13	333	13	2	0	0	77.2	81	4	25	0	5	72	6	2	4	6	44	34	2	6	.250	0	3.94
90	CHW/SAL	A	27	733	27	8	2	0	177.1	142	5	56	0	7	153	5	3	10	0	58	38	15	6	.714	0	1.93
91	CHT/SOU	AA	5	143	5	0	0	0	38.1	20	2	11	0	4	24	1	1	0	0	7	7	3	1	.750	0	1.64
	NAS/AMA	AAA	23	612	23	3	1	0	148.2	130	9	56	2	10	89	3	4	5	0	68	63	7	11	.389	0	3.81
92	NAS/AMA	AAA	27	725	27	3	2	0	169.2	165	10	65	3	8	117	6	5	4	0	75	67	12	9	.571	0	3.55
	CIN/NL		7	187	7	0	0	0	45.1	47	2	13	3	1	18	2	1	0	0	15	13	4	2	.667	0	2.58
93	CIN/NL		31	738	27	3	1	3	164.1	200	19	59	1	7	94	6	5	3	2	102	96	10	15	.400	0	5.26
2 YR TOTALS			**38**	**925**	**34**	**3**	**1**	**3**	**209.2**	**247**	**21**	**72**	**4**	**8**	**112**	**8**	**6**	**3**	**2**	**117**	**109**	**14**	**17**	**.452**	**0**	**4.68**

Quantrill, Paul John — BL/TR — b.11/3/68   BOS89 8/163

YR	TM/LG	CL	G	TBF	GS	CG	SHO	GF	IP	H	HR	BB	IBB	HB	SO	SH	SF	WP	BK	R	ER	W	L	PCT	SV	ERA
89	RS/GCL	R	2	18	0	0	0	2	5.0	2	0	0	0	0	5	0	0	0	0	0	0	0	0	.000	2	0.00
	ELM/NYP	A-	20	326	7	5	0	7	76.0	90	5	12	2	6	57	4	3	1	2	37	29	5	4	.556	2	3.43
90	WH/FSL	A+	7	182	7	1	0	0	45.2	46	3	6	0	0	14	0	2	3	0	24	21	2	5	.286	0	4.14
	NB/EAS	AA	22	549	22	1	1	0	132.2	148	3	23	2	4	53	4	7	3	2	65	52	7	11	.389	0	3.53
91	NB/EAS	AA	5	142	5	1	0	0	35.0	32	2	8	0	1	18	3	1	0	0	14	8	2	1	.667	0	2.06
	PAW/INT	AAA	25	645	23	6	2	0	155.2	169	14	30	1	4	75	9	2	2	2	81	77	10	7	.588	0	4.45
92	PAW/INT	AAA	19	504	18	4	1	1	119.0	143	16	20	1	4	56	6	8	4	2	63	59	6	8	.429	0	4.46
	BOS/AL		27	213	0	0	0	10	49.1	55	1	15	5	1	24	4	2	1	0	18	12	2	3	.400	1	2.19
93	BOS/AL		49	594	14	1	1	8	138.0	151	13	44	14	2	66	4	2	0	1	73	60	6	12	.333	1	3.91
2 YR TOTALS			**76**	**807**	**14**	**1**	**1**	**18**	**187.1**	**206**	**14**	**59**	**19**	**3**	**90**	**8**	**4**	**1**	**1**	**91**	**72**	**8**	**15**	**.348**	**2**	**3.46**

Radinsky, Scott David — BL/TL — b.3/3/68   CHA86 3/75

YR	TM/LG	CL	G	TBF	GS	CG	SHO	GF	IP	H	HR	BB	IBB	HB	SO	SH	SF	WP	BK	R	ER	W	L	PCT	SV	ERA
86	WS/GCL	R	7	122	7	0	0	0	26.2	24	0	17	0	0	18	1	3	2	1	20	10	1	0	1.000	0	3.38
87	PEN/CAR	A+	12	187	8	0	0	2	39.0	43	2	32	0	3	37	2	2	3	1	30	25	1	7	.125	0	5.77
	WS/GCL	R	11	249	10	0	0	0	58.1	43	1	39	0	4	41	2	2	5	1	23	15	3	3	.500	0	2.31
88	WS/GCL	R	5	17	0	0	0	2	3.1	2	0	4	0	0	7	0	0	1	2	2	2	0	0	.000	0	5.40
89	SB/MID	A	53	248	0	0	0	49	61.2	39	1	19	2	5	83	4	2	2	2	21	12	7	5	.583	31	1.75
90	CHI/AL		62	237	0	0	0	18	52.1	47	1	36	1	2	46	2	2	2	0	18	16	6	1	.857	4	4.82
91	CHI/AL		67	289	0	0	0	19	71.1	53	4	23	2	1	49	4	4	0	0	18	16	5	5	.500	8	2.02
92	CHI/AL		68	261	0	0	0	33	59.1	54	3	34	5	2	48	2	1	3	0	21	18	3	7	.300	15	2.73
93	CHI/AL		73	250	0	0	0	24	54.2	61	3	19	1	1	44	2	0	0	4	33	26	8	2	.800	4	4.28
4 YR TOTALS			**270**	**1037**	**0**	**0**	**0**	**94**	**237.2**	**215**	**11**	**112**	**11**	**6**	**187**	**10**	**7**	**5**	**5**	**101**	**88**	**22**	**15**	**.595**	**31**	**3.33**

Rapp, Patrick Leland "Pat" — BR/TR — b.7/13/67   SF89 15/388

YR	TM/LG	CL	G	TBF	GS	CG	SHO	GF	IP	H	HR	BB	IBB	HB	SO	SH	SF	WP	BK	R	ER	W	L	PCT	SV	ERA
89	POC/PIO	R+	16	333	12	1	0	1	73.0	90	5	29	1	8	40	3	2	6	0	54	43	4	6	.400	0	5.30
90	CLI/MID	A	27	692	26	4	0	1	167.1	132	2	79	2	7	132	6	2	8	3	60	49	14	10	.583	0	2.64
91	SJ/CAL	A+	16	396	15	1	0	0	90.0	88	1	37	0	10	73	1	2	2	2	41	25	7	5	.583	0	2.50
	SHR/TEX	AA	10	257	10	1	0	0	60.1	52	1	22	0	3	46	3	2	1	0	23	18	6	2	.750	0	2.69
92	SF/NL		3	43	2	0	0	0	10.0	8	0	6	1	1	3	2	0	0	0	8	8	0	2	.000	0	7.20
	PHO/PCL	AAA	39	516	12	2	1	17	121.0	115	2	40	3	2	79	8	10	1	1	54	41	8	9	.467	3	3.05
93	EDM/PCL	AAA	17	440	17	4	1	0	107.2	89	8	34	0	1	93	7	5	2	1	45	41	8	3	.727	0	3.43
	FLO/NL		16	412	16	1	0	0	94.0	101	7	39	1	2	57	8	4	6	0	49	42	4	6	.400	0	4.02
2 YR TOTALS			**19**	**455**	**18**	**1**	**0**	**1**	**104.0**	**109**	**7**	**45**	**2**	**3**	**60**	**10**	**4**	**6**	**0**	**57**	**50**	**4**	**8**	**.333**	**0**	**4.33**

Rasmussen, Dennis Lee — BL/TL — b.4/18/59   CAL80 1/17

YR	TM/LG	CL	G	TBF	GS	CG	SHO	GF	IP	H	HR	BB	IBB	HB	SO	SH	SF	WP	BK	R	ER	W	L	PCT	SV	ERA
83	SD/NL		4	58	1	0	0	1	13.2	10	1	8	1	0	13	0	0	1	0	5	3	0	0	.000	0	1.98
84	CMB/INT	AAA	6	177	6	3	1	0	43.2	24	1	27	0	0	30	1	1	8	0	15	15	4	1	.800	0	3.09
	NY/AL		24	616	24	1	1	0	147.2	127	16	60	1	4	110	3	5	2	0	79	75	9	6	.600	0	4.57
85	CMB/INT	AAA	7	196	7	1	0	0	45.0	41	1	25	0	1	43	3	2	1	0	22	20	3	5	.375	0	3.80
	NY/AL		22	429	16	2	0	2	101.2	97	10	42	1	1	63	1	5	3	0	56	45	3	5	.375	0	3.98
86	NY/AL		31	819	31	3	1	0	202.0	160	28	74	2	1	131	4	3	3	1	91	87	18	6	.750	0	3.88
87	CMB/INT	AAA	1	26	1	0	0	0	7.0	5	0	0	0	0	4	0	1	0	0	1	1	1	0	1.000	0	1.29
	NY/AL		26	627	25	2	0	0	146.0	145	31	55	1	4	89	5	5	6	0	78	77	9	7	.563	0	4.75
	CIN/NL		7	187	7	0	0	0	45.1	39	5	12	0	1	39	1	1	2	0	22	20	4	1	.800	0	3.97

(continued)

Rasmussen, Dennis Lee (continued)

YR	TM/LG	CL	G	TBF	GS	CG	SHO	GF	IP	H	HR	BB	IBB	HB	SO	SH	SF	WP	BK	R	ER	W	L	PCT	SV	ERA
	YEAR		33	814	32	2	0	0	191.1	184	36	67	1	5	128	8	6	7	2	100	97	13	8	.619	0	4.56
88	CIN/NL		11	255	11	1	1	0	56.1	68	8	22	4	2	27	2	2	1	5	36	36	2	6	.250	0	5.75
	SD/NL		20	599	20	6	0	0	148.1	131	9	36	0	2	85	8	2	6	0	48	42	14	4	.778	0	2.55
	YEAR		31	854	31	7	1	0	204.2	199	17	58	4	4	112	10	4	7	5	84	78	16	10	.615	0	3.43
89	SD/NL		33	799	33	1	0	0	183.2	190	18	72	6	3	87	9	11	4	2	100	87	10	10	.500	0	4.26
90	SD/NL		32	825	32	3	1	0	187.2	217	28	62	4	3	86	14	4	9	1	110	94	11	15	.423	0	4.51
91	LV/PCL	AAA	5	114	5	1	0	0	26.1	23	2	15	0	2	12	1	1	1	1	18	16	1	3	.250	0	5.47
	SD/NL		24	633	24	1	1	0	146.2	155	12	49	3	2	75	4	6	1	1	74	61	6	13	.316	0	3.74
92	ROC/INT	AAA	9	208	9	1	0	0	46.0	49	3	22	0	0	33	1	1	1	0	33	29	0	7	.000	0	5.67
	IOW/AMA	AAA	2	52	2	0	0	0	11.1	15	0	3	0	1	6	1	1	0	0	7	6	1	1	.500	0	4.76
	CHI/NL		3	24	1	0	0	1	5.0	7	2	2	1	0	6	0	0	0	0	6	6	0	0	.000	0	10.80
	OMA/AMA	AAA	11	205	6	3	2	1	50.2	37	3	17	2	0	44	4	1	0	1	14	8	3	3	.500	0	1.42
	KC/AL		5	134	5	1	1	0	37.2	25	0	6	0	0	12	1	0	0	3	7	6	4	1	.800	0	1.43
	YEAR		8	158	6	1	1	1	42.2	32	2	8	1	0	12	1	1	0	3	13	12	4	1	.800	0	2.53
93	OMA/AMA	AAA	17	451	17	3	1	0	105.2	124	16	27	0	1	59	4	5	4	2	68	59	7	8	.467	0	5.03
	KC/AL		9	138	4	0	0	3	29.0	40	4	14	1	1	12	0	1	1	0	25	24	1	2	.333	0	7.45
11 YR TOTALS			**251**	**6143**	**234**	**21**	**5**	**6**	**1450.2**	**1411**	**172**	**514**	**21**	**26**	**829**	**51**	**50**	**50**	**14**	**737**	**663**	**91**	**76**	**.545**	**0**	**4.11**

Reardon, Jeffrey James "Jeff" — BR/TR — b.10/1/55   NYN 6/14/77

YR	TM/LG	CL	G	TBF	GS	CG	SHO	GF	IP	H	HR	BB	IBB	HB	SO	SH	SF	WP	BK	R	ER	W	L	PCT	SV	ERA
79	NY/NL		18	81	0	0	0	10	20.2	12	2	9	3	0	10	2	1	1	0	7	4	1	2	.333	2	1.74
80	NY/NL		61	475	0	0	0	35	110.1	96	10	47	15	3	101	8	5	2	0	36	32	8	7	.533	6	2.61
81	NY/NL		18	124	0	0	0	14	28.2	27	2	12	4	1	28	1	1	1	0	11	11	1	0	1.000	2	3.45
	MON/NL		25	155	0	0	0	19	41.2	21	3	9	0	1	21	3	0	1	0	6	6	2	0	1.000	6	1.30
	YEAR		43	279	0	0	0	33	70.1	48	5	21	4	2	49	3	1	1	0	17	17	3	0	1.000	8	2.18
82	MON/NL		75	444	0	0	0	53	109.0	87	6	36	4	4	86	8	4	2	0	28	25	7	4	.636	26	2.06
83	MON/NL		66	403	0	0	0	53	92.0	87	7	44	9	1	78	8	2	2	0	34	31	7	9	.438	21	3.03
84	MON/NL		68	363	0	0	0	58	87.0	70	5	37	7	3	79	3	2	4	0	31	28	7	7	.500	23	2.90
85	MON/NL		63	356	0	0	0	50	87.2	68	7	26	4	1	67	3	1	2	0	31	31	2	8	.200	*41	3.18
86	MON/NL		62	368	0	0	0	58	89.0	83	12	26	2	1	67	9	1	0	0	42	39	7	9	.438	35	3.94
87	MIN/AL		63	337	0	0	0	58	80.1	70	14	28	4	3	83	1	3	2	0	41	40	8	8	.500	31	4.48
88	MIN/AL		63	299	0	0	0	58	73.0	68	6	15	2	2	56	4	1	0	3	21	20	2	4	.333	42	2.47
89	MIN/AL		65	297	0	0	0	61	73.0	68	8	12	3	3	46	1	5	1	1	33	33	5	4	.556	31	4.07
90	BOS/AL		47	210	0	0	0	37	51.1	39	5	19	4	1	33	1	1	0	0	19	18	5	3	.625	21	3.16
91	BOS/AL		57	248	0	0	0	51	59.1	54	9	16	3	1	44	0	2	0	0	21	21	1	4	.200	40	3.03
92	BOS/AL		46	183	0	0	0	39	42.1	53	6	7	0	1	32	0	0	0	0	20	20	2	2	.500	27	4.25
	ATL/NL		14	62	0	0	0	11	15.2	14	0	2	1	1	7	1	2	0	0	2	2	3	0	1.000	3	1.15
	YEAR		60	245	0	0	0	50	58.0	67	6	9	1	2	39	2	2	0	0	22	22	5	2	.714	30	3.41
93	CIN/NL		58	267	0	0	0	32	61.2	66	4	10	0	5	35	4	4	2	0	34	28	4	6	.400	8	4.09
15 YR TOTALS			**869**	**4672**	**0**	**0**	**0**	**687**	**1122.2**	**983**	**106**	**355**	**65**	**27**	**873**	**57**	**34**	**20**	**4**	**417**	**388**	**72**	**77**	**.483**	**365**	**3.11**

Reed, Richard Allen "Rick" — BR/TR — b.8/16/64   PIT86 26/644

YR	TM/LG	CL	G	TBF	GS	CG	SHO	GF	IP	H	HR	BB	IBB	HB	SO	SH	SF	WP	BK	R	ER	W	L	PCT	SV	ERA
86	PIR/GCL	R	8	96	3	0	0	1	24.0	20	0	6	0	0	15	1	3	0	1	12	10	0	2	.000	0	3.75
	MAC/SAL	A	1	26	1	0	0	0	6.1	5	0	2	0	0	1	1	0	0	0	3	2	0	0	.000	0	2.84
87	MAC/SAL	A	46	388	0	0	0	20	93.2	80	6	29	3	4	92	3	4	4	0	38	26	8	4	.667	7	2.50
88	SAL/CAR	A+	15	294	8	4	1	2	72.1	56	4	17	1	5	73	0	1	3	1	28	22	6	2	.750	0	2.74
	HAR/EAS	AA	2	60	2	0	0	0	16.0	11	0	4	0	0	17	0	0	2	0	2	2	1	0	1.000	0	1.13
	PIT/NL		2	47	2	0	0	0	12.0	10	1	2	0	0	6	0	0	0	0	4	4	1	0	1.000	0	3.00
	BUF/AMA	AAA	10	301	9	3	2	0	77.0	62	9	12	2	1	50	6	1	1	1	15	14	5	2	.714	0	1.64
89	BUF/AMA	AAA	20	522	20	3	0	0	125.2	130	9	28	0	1	75	6	3	3	0	58	52	9	8	.529	0	3.72
	PIT/NL		15	232	7	0	0	2	54.2	62	5	11	3	2	34	2	2	0	3	35	34	1	4	.200	0	5.60
90	PIT/NL		13	238	8	1	1	2	53.2	62	6	12	6	1	27	2	2	1	0	32	26	2	3	.400	1	4.36
	BUF/AMA	AAA	15	369	15	2	2	0	91.0	82	4	21	0	6	63	6	0	1	0	37	35	7	4	.636	0	3.46
91	PIT/NL		1	21	1	0	0	0	4.1	8	1	1	0	0	2	0	0	0	0	6	5	0	0	.000	0	10.38
	BUF/AMA	AAA	25	660	25	5	2	0	167.2	151	3	26	2	2	102	9	6	2	1	45	40	14	4	.778	0	2.15
92	OMA/AMA	AAA	11	259	10	3	0	1	62.0	67	8	12	0	4	35	2	2	0	0	33	30	5	4	.556	1	4.35
	KC/AL		19	419	18	1	1	0	100.1	105	10	20	3	5	49	2	5	0	0	47	41	3	7	.300	0	3.68
93	OMA/AMA	AAA	19	502	19	3	1	0	128.1	116	19	14	1	2	58	1	5	1	0	48	44	11	4	.733	0	3.09
	OC/AMA	AAA	5	144	5	1	0	0	34.1	43	2	2	0	1	21	1	1	1	0	20	16	1	3	.250	0	4.19
	KC/AL		1	18	0	0	0	0	3.2	6	0	1	0	1	3	0	0	0	0	4	4	0	0	.000	0	9.82
	TEX/AL		2	18	0	0	0	0	4.0	6	1	0	0	0	2	0	0	0	0	1	1	1	0	1.000	0	2.25
	YEAR		3	36	0	0	0	0	7.2	12	1	1	0	1	5	0	0	0	0	5	5	1	0	1.000	0	5.87
6 YR TOTALS			**53**	**993**	**36**	**2**	**2**	**4**	**232.2**	**259**	**24**	**48**	**12**	**10**	**123**	**8**	**9**	**0**	**3**	**129**	**115**	**8**	**14**	**.364**	**1**	**4.45**

Reed, Steven Vincent "Steve" — BR/TR — b.3/11/66   SF 6/24/88

YR	TM/LG	CL	G	TBF	GS	CG	SHO	GF	IP	H	HR	BB	IBB	HB	SO	SH	SF	WP	BK	R	ER	W	L	PCT	SV	ERA
88	POC/PIO	R+	31	192	0	0	0	29	46.0	42	3	8	1	2	49	3	2	0	1	20	13	4	1	.800	13	2.54
89	CLI/MID	A	60	370	0	0	0	50	94.2	54	1	38	10	7	104	4	5	0	0	16	11	5	3	.625	26	1.05
	SJ/CAL	A+	2	7	0	0	0	1	2.0	0	0	1	0	0	3	0	0	0	0	0	0	0	0	.000	0	0.00
90	SHR/TEX	AA	45	255	0	0	0	28	60.1	53	2	20	6	2	59	2	1	1	0	20	11	3	1	.750	8	1.64
91	SHR/TEX	AA	15	81	0	0	0	14	21.2	17	1	4	0	0	26	0	0	0	0	2	2	2	0	1.000	7	0.83
	PHO/PCL	AAA	41	241	0	0	0	24	56.1	62	5	12	0	2	46	3	2	0	0	33	27	2	3	.400	4	4.31
92	SHR/TEX	AA	27	105	0	0	0	25	29.0	18	1	0	0	0	33	0	1	0	0	3	2	1	0	1.000	23	0.62
	PHO/PCL	AAA	29	128	0	0	0	28	31.0	27	2	10	3	0	30	1	2	0	0	13	12	0	0	.000	20	3.48
	SF/NL		18	63	0	0	0	2	15.2	13	2	3	0	1	11	0	0	0	0	5	4	1	0	1.000	0	2.30

Reed, Steven Vincent "Steve" (continued)

YR	TM/LG	CL	G	TBF	GS	CG	SHO	GF	IP	H	HR	BB	IBB	HB	SO	SH	SF	WP	BK	R	ER	W	L	PCT	SV	ERA
93	CS/PCL	AAA	11	49	0	0	0	10	12.1	8	0	3	1	1	10	1	0	1	0	1	0	0	0	.000	7	0.00
	COL/NL		64	347	0	0	0	14	84.1	80	13	30	5	3	51	2	3	1	0	47	42	9	5	.643	3	4.48
2 YR TOTALS			82	410	0	0	0	16	100.0	93	15	33	5	4	62	2	3	1	0	52	46	10	5	.667	3	4.14

Reynolds, Richard Shane "Shane" — BR/TR — b.3/26/68   HOU89 5/72

YR	TM/LG	CL	G	TBF	GS	CG	SHO	GF	IP	H	HR	BB	IBB	HB	SO	SH	SF	WP	BK	R	ER	W	L	PCT	SV	ERA
89	AUB/NYP	A-	6	150	6	1	1	0	35.0	36	1	14	0	4	23	1	0	1	1	16	9	3	2	.600	0	2.31
	ASH/SAL	A	8	224	8	2	1	0	51.1	53	2	21	0	1	33	2	2	1	4	25	21	5	3	.625	0	3.68
90	CMB/SOU	AA	29	710	27	2	1	1	155.1	181	14	70	1	5	92	11	5	6	6	104	83	9	10	.474	0	4.81
91	JAC/TEX	AA	27	673	27	2	0	0	151.0	165	8	62	1	2	116	8	7	4	2	93	75	8	9	.471	1	4.47
92	TUC/PCL	AAA	25	605	22	2	0	1	142.0	156	4	34	2	4	106	3	4	4	1	73	58	9	8	.529	1	3.68
	HOU/NL		8	122	5	0	0	0	25.1	42	3	6	1	0	10	6	1	1	1	22	20	1	3	.250	0	7.11
93	TUC/PCL	AAA	25	584	20	2	0	1	139.1	147	4	21	0	3	106	6	5	4	0	74	56	10	6	.625	1	3.62
	HOU/NL		5	49	1	0	0	0	11.0	11	0	6	1	0	10	0	0	1	0	4	1	0	0	.000	0	0.82
2 YR TOTALS			13	171	6	0	0	0	36.1	53	2	12	2	0	20	6	1	1	1	26	21	1	3	.250	0	5.20

Reynoso, Armando Martin — BR/TR — b.5/1/66   MEX 3/15/89

YR	TM/LG	CL	G	TBF	GS	CG	SHO	GF	IP	H	HR	BB	IBB	HB	SO	SH	SF	WP	BK	R	ER	W	L	PCT	SV	ERA
90	RIC/INT	AAA	4	102	3	0	0	0	24.0	26	3	7	0	0	15	1	1	0	3	7	6	3	1	.750	0	2.25
91	RIC/INT	AAA	22	544	19	3	3	1	131.0	117	9	39	1	10	97	7	3	9	6	44	38	10	6	.625	0	2.61
	ATL/NL		6	103	5	0	0	1	23.1	26	4	10	1	3	10	3	0	2	0	18	16	2	1	.667	0	6.17
92	RIC/INT	AAA	28	693	27	4	1	1	169.1	156	12	52	6	7	108	3	5	8	5	65	50	12	9	.571	0	2.66
	ATL/NL		3	32	1	0	0	0	7.2	11	2	2	1	1	2	1	0	0	0	4	4	1	0	1.000	1	4.70
93	CS/PCL	AAA	4	93	4	0	0	0	22.1	19	1	8	0	1	22	2	2	2	0	10	8	2	1	.667	0	3.22
	COL/NL		30	830	30	4	0	0	189.0	206	22	63	7	9	117	5	8	7	6	101	84	12	11	.522	0	4.00
3 YR TOTALS			39	965	36	4	0	2	220.0	243	28	75	9	13	129	9	8	9	6	123	104	15	12	.556	1	4.25

Rhodes, Arthur Lee "Arthur Lee" — BL/TL — b.10/24/69   BAL88 3/34

YR	TM/LG	CL	G	TBF	GS	CG	SHO	GF	IP	H	HR	BB	IBB	HB	SO	SH	SF	WP	BK	R	ER	W	L	PCT	SV	ERA
88	BLU/APP	R+	11	155	7	0	0	3	35.1	29	1	15	0	1	44	0	1	9	2	17	13	3	4	.429	0	3.31
89	ERI/NYP	A-	5	115	5	1	0	0	31.0	13	1	10	0	0	45	0	0	2	1	7	4	2	0	1.000	0	1.16
	FRE/CAR	A+	7	109	6	0	0	0	24.1	19	2	19	0	0	28	0	1	4	1	16	14	2	2	.500	0	5.18
90	FRE/CAR	A+	13	322	13	4	0	0	80.2	62	6	21	0	1	103	0	1	3	1	25	19	4	6	.400	0	2.12
	HAG/EAS	AA	12	303	12	0	0	0	72.1	62	3	39	0	0	60	1	0	3	5	32	30	3	4	.429	0	3.73
91	HAG/EAS	AA	19	428	19	2	2	0	106.2	73	2	47	1	0	115	1	0	3	10	37	32	7	4	.636	0	2.70
	BAL/AL		8	174	8	0	0	0	36.0	47	4	23	1	3	23	1	3	2	0	35	32	0	3	.000	0	8.00
92	ROC/INT	AAA	17	434	17	1	0	0	101.2	84	7	46	0	0	115	3	2	3	4	48	42	6	6	.500	0	3.72
	BAL/AL		15	394	15	2	1	0	94.1	87	6	38	2	1	77	5	1	2	1	39	38	7	5	.583	0	3.63
93	ROC/INT	AAA	6	115	6	0	0	0	26.2	26	5	15	0	0	33	0	0	5	1	12	12	1	1	.500	0	4.05
	BAL/AL		17	387	17	0	0	0	85.2	91	16	49	1	1	49	2	3	2	0	62	62	5	6	.455	0	6.51
3 YR TOTALS			40	955	40	2	1	0	216.0	225	26	110	3	2	149	8	7	6	1	136	132	12	14	.462	0	5.50

Righetti, David Allan "Dave" — BL/TL — b.11/28/58   TEX77* 1/9

YR	TM/LG	CL	G	TBF	GS	CG	SHO	GF	IP	H	HR	BB	IBB	HB	SO	SH	SF	WP	BK	R	ER	W	L	PCT	SV	ERA
79	NY/AL		3	67	3	0	0	0	17.1	10	2	10	0	0	13	1	1	0	1	7	7	0	1	.000	0	3.63
81	NY/AL		15	422	15	2	0	0	105.1	75	1	38	0	0	89	0	2	1	1	25	24	8	4	.667	0	*2.05
82	NY/AL		33	804	27	4	0	3	183.0	155	11	108	4	6	163	8	5	9	5	88	77	11	10	.524	1	3.79
83	NY/AL		31	900	31	7	2	0	217.0	194	12	67	2	2	169	10	4	10	1	96	83	14	8	.636	0	3.44
84	NY/AL		64	400	0	0	0	53	96.1	79	5	37	7	0	90	4	4	0	1	29	25	5	6	.455	31	2.34
85	NY/AL		74	452	0	0	0	60	107.0	96	5	45	9	0	92	6	3	7	0	36	33	12	7	.632	29	2.78
86	NY/AL		74	435	0	0	0	68	106.2	88	4	35	7	2	83	5	4	1	0	31	29	8	8	.500	*46	2.45
87	NY/AL		60	419	0	0	0	54	95.0	95	9	44	4	2	77	6	5	1	3	45	37	8	6	.571	31	3.51
88	NY/AL		60	377	0	0	0	41	87.0	86	5	37	2	1	70	4	0	2	0	35	34	5	5	.500	25	3.52
89	NY/AL		55	300	0	0	0	53	69.0	73	6	26	6	1	51	7	2	0	0	32	23	2	6	.250	25	3.00
90	NY/AL		53	235	0	0	0	47	53.0	48	8	26	2	2	43	1	1	2	0	24	21	1	1	.500	36	3.57
91	SF/NL		61	304	0	0	0	49	71.2	64	4	28	0	3	51	4	2	1	1	29	27	2	7	.222	24	3.39
92	SF/NL		54	340	4	0	0	23	78.1	79	4	36	5	0	46	6	4	5	2	47	44	2	7	.222	3	5.06
93	SF/NL		51	210	0	0	0	15	47.1	58	11	17	1	0	31	2	0	1	0	31	30	1	1	.500	1	5.70
14 YR TOTALS			688	5665	80	13	2	466	1334.0	1200	84	554	48	20	1069	64	37	40	19	555	494	79	76	.510	252	3.33

Rijo, Jose Antonio — BR/TR — b.5/13/65   NYA 8/1/80

YR	TM/LG	CL	G	TBF	GS	CG	SHO	GF	IP	H	HR	BB	IBB	HB	SO	SH	SF	WP	BK	R	ER	W	L	PCT	SV	ERA
84	NY/AL		24	289	5	0	0	8	62.1	74	5	33	1	1	47	6	1	2	1	40	33	2	8	.200	2	4.76
	CMB/INT	AAA	11	294	11	0	0	0	65.1	67	7	40	0	1	47	0	1	4	1	35	32	3	3	.500	0	4.41
85	TAC/PCL	AAA	24	0	24	3	1	0	149.0	116	6	108	3	0	179	0	0	4	11	64	48	7	10	.412	0	2.90
	OAK/AL		12	272	9	0	0	1	63.2	57	6	28	2	1	65	5	0	0	0	26	25	2	4	.600	0	3.53
86	OAK/AL		39	856	26	4	0	9	193.2	172	24	108	7	4	176	10	6	9	4	116	100	9	11	.450	0	4.65
87	TAC/PCL	AAA	9	230	8	2	0	0	54.2	44	5	28	1	0	67	1	0	8	2	27	24	2	4	.333	0	3.95
	OAK/AL		21	394	14	1	0	3	82.1	106	10	41	1	2	67	3	5	2	2	67	54	2	7	.222	0	5.90
88	CIN/NL		49	653	19	0	0	12	162.0	120	7	63	9	3	160	8	5	1	4	47	43	13	8	.619	0	2.39
89	CIN/NL		19	464	19	1	0	0	111.0	101	6	48	3	2	86	3	4	0	0	39	35	7	6	.538	0	2.84
90	NAS/AMA	AAA	1	19	1	0	0	0	4.1	5	0	2	0	0	4	0	0	0	0	4	4	0	0	.000	0	8.31
	CIN/NL		29	801	29	7	1	0	197.0	151	10	78	1	2	152	9	2	2	0	65	59	14	8	.636	0	2.70
91	CIN/NL		30	825	30	3	1	0	204.1	165	8	55	4	3	172	4	0	3	0	69	57	15	6	*.714	0	2.51
92	CIN/NL		33	836	33	2	0	0	211.0	185	15	44	3	3	171	4	2	4	0	67	60	15	10	.600	0	2.56
93	CIN/NL		36	1029	36	2	0	0	257.1	218	19	62	2	2	*227	13	3	0	1	76	71	14	9	.609	0	2.48
10 YR TOTALS			292	6419	220	20	4	33	1544.2	1349	110	560	29	23	1323	66	40	24	25	612	537	97	77	.557	3	3.13

Risley, William Charles "Bill" — BR/TR — b.5/29/67   CIN87 14/362

YR	TM/LG	CL	G	TBF	GS	CG	SHO	GF	IP	H	HR	BB	IBB	HB	SO	SH	SF	WP	BK	R	ER	W	L	PCT	SV	ERA
87	RED/GCL	R	11	226	11	0	0	0	52.1	38	0	26	3	3	50	3	9	6	2	24	11	1	4	.200	0	1.89
88	GRE/SAL	A	23	515	23	3	3	0	120.1	82	2	84	0	11	135	3	9	9	19	60	55	8	4	.667	0	4.11
89	CR/MID	A	27	581	27	2	0	0	140.2	87	9	81	2	6	128	1	9	19	8	72	61	9	10	.474	0	3.90
90	CR/MID	A	22	579	22	7	1	0	137.2	99	8	68	1	7	123	6	4	13	3	51	43	8	9	.471	0	2.81
91	CHT/SOU	AA	19	465	19	3	0	0	108.1	81	3	60	2	9	77	3	6	5	5	48	38	5	7	.417	0	3.16
	NAS/AMA	AAA	8	199	8	1	0	0	44.0	45	4	26	2	1	32	1	1	4	0	27	24	3	5	.375	0	4.91
92	MON/NL		1	19	1	0	0	0	5.0	4	1	0	1	0	2	1	0	0	0	1	1	1	0	1.000	0	1.80
	IND/AMA	AAA	25	434	15	0	0	1	95.2	105	11	47	0	4	64	3	5	2	4	69	68	5	8	.385	0	6.40
93	OTT/INT	AAA	41	277	0	0	0	12	63.2	51	7	34	3	3	74	6	3	5	0	26	18	2	4	.333	1	2.54
	MON/NL		2	14	0	0	0	1	3.0	2	1	2	0	1	2	1	0	0	0	3	2	0	0	.000	0	6.00
2 YR TOTALS			**3**	**33**	**1**	**0**	**0**	**1**	**8.0**	**6**	**1**	**3**	**0**	**1**	**4**	**2**	**0**	**0**	**0**	**4**	**3**	**1**	**0**	**1.000**	**0**	**3.38**

Rivera, Bienvenido Santana "Ben" — BR/TR — b.1/11/69   ATL 11/15/85

YR	TM/LG	CL	G	TBF	GS	CG	SHO	GF	IP	H	HR	BB	IBB	HB	SO	SH	SF	WP	BK	R	ER	W	L	PCT	SV	ERA
87	BRA/GCL	R	16	220	5	0	0	2	49.2	55	0	19	1	2	29	1	2	2	2	26	18	1	5	.167	0	3.26
88	SUM/SAL	A	27	724	27	3	2	0	173.1	167	12	52	1	9	99	2	5	6	7	77	61	9	11	.450	0	3.17
89	DUR/CAR	A+	23	462	22	1	0	0	102.1	113	6	51	1	5	58	4	3	10	3	55	51	5	7	.417	0	4.49
90	GRE/SOU	AA	13	243	13	0	0	0	52.0	68	6	26	0	3	32	2	1	10	0	40	38	1	4	.200	0	6.58
	DUR/CAR	A+	16	327	13	0	0	3	75.0	69	7	33	1	5	64	3	2	4	2	41	30	5	3	.625	1	3.60
91	GRE/SOU	AA	26	683	26	3	2	0	158.2	155	13	75	4	3	116	3	1	8	4	76	63	11	8	.579	0	3.57
92	ATL/NL		8	78	0	0	0	3	15.1	21	1	13	2	1	11	0	1	0	0	8	8	0	1	.000	0	4.70
	SCR/INT	AAA	2	41	2	1	1	0	12.0	4	0	2	0	1	10	0	0	0	0	0	0	2	0	1.000	0	0.00
	PHI/NL		20	409	14	4	1	4	102.0	78	8	32	2	2	66	5	1	5	0	32	32	7	3	.700	0	2.82
	YEAR		28	487	14	4	1	7	117.1	99	9	45	4	4	77	5	2	5	0	40	40	7	4	.636	0	3.07
93	PHI/NL		30	742	28	1	1	1	163.0	175	16	85	4	6	123	5	5	13	0	99	91	13	9	.591	0	5.02
2 YR TOTALS			**58**	**1229**	**42**	**5**	**2**	**8**	**280.1**	**274**	**25**	**130**	**8**	**10**	**200**	**10**	**7**	**18**	**0**	**139**	**131**	**20**	**13**	**.606**	**0**	**4.21**

Robertson, Richard Wayne "Rich" — BL/TL — b.9/15/68   PIT90 9/241

YR	TM/LG	CL	G	TBF	GS	CG	SHO	GF	IP	H	HR	BB	IBB	HB	SO	SH	SF	WP	BK	R	ER	W	L	PCT	SV	ERA
90	WEL/NYP	A-	16	293	13	0	0	0	64.1	51	4	55	2	1	80	1	2	6	2	34	22	3	4	.429	0	3.08
91	SAL/CAR	A+	12	210	11	0	0	0	45.2	34	2	42	0	3	32	1	0	4	0	32	25	2	4	.333	0	4.93
	AUG/SAL	A	13	348	12	1	0	1	74.0	73	4	51	0	1	62	1	1	3	1	52	41	4	7	.364	0	4.99
92	SAL/CAR	A+	6	152	6	0	0	0	37.0	29	6	10	0	1	27	0	1	1	1	18	14	3	0	1.000	0	3.41
	CAR/SOU	AA	20	534	20	1	1	0	124.2	127	7	41	2	4	107	1	2	4	1	51	42	6	7	.462	0	3.03
93	BUF/AMA	AAA	23	569	23	2	0	0	132.1	141	9	52	4	2	71	3	5	10	1	67	63	9	8	.529	0	4.28
	PIT/NL		9	44	0	0	0	3	9.0	15	0	4	0	0	4	0	0	0	0	6	6	0	1	.000	0	6.00

Rodriguez, Richard Anthony "Rich" — BL/TL — b.3/1/63   NYN84 9/211

YR	TM/LG	CL	G	TBF	GS	CG	SHO	GF	IP	H	HR	BB	IBB	HB	SO	SH	SF	WP	BK	R	ER	W	L	PCT	SV	ERA
84	LF/NYP	A-	25	171	1	0	0	6	35.1	28	0	36	7	1	27	4	2	3	0	21	11	2	1	.667	0	2.80
85	COL/SAL	A	49	365	3	0	0	19	80.1	89	4	36	2	1	71	6	1	7	1	41	36	6	3	.667	6	4.03
86	JAC/TEX	AA	13	161	5	1	0	2	33.0	51	5	15	2	0	15	2	1	1	0	35	33	3	4	.429	0	9.00
	LYN/CAR	A+	36	184	0	0	0	16	45.1	37	2	19	0	1	38	1	1	4	1	20	18	2	1	.667	3	3.57
87	LYN/CAR	A+	69	291	0	0	0	30	68.0	69	3	26	0	0	59	1	1	2	1	23	21	3	1	.750	5	2.78
88	JAC/TEX	AA	47	335	1	0	0	25	78.1	66	3	42	6	1	68	9	4	6	5	35	25	2	7	.222	6	2.87
89	WIC/TEX	AA	54	319	0	0	0	38	74.1	74	3	37	11	2	40	2	2	3	2	30	30	8	3	.727	8	3.63
90	LV/PCL	AAA	27	243	0	0	0	13	59.0	50	5	22	1	1	46	1	4	3	1	24	23	3	4	.429	3	3.51
	SD/NL		32	201	0	0	0	15	47.2	52	2	16	4	1	22	2	0	1	0	17	15	1	1	.500	1	2.83
91	SD/NL		64	335	1	0	0	15	80.0	66	8	44	8	0	40	7	2	1	0	31	29	3	1	.750	0	3.26
92	SD/NL		61	369	1	0	0	15	91.0	77	4	29	4	0	64	2	2	1	1	28	24	6	3	.667	0	2.37
93	SD/NL		34	133	0	0	0	10	30.0	34	2	9	3	1	22	2	0	1	0	15	11	2	3	.400	2	3.30
	FLO/NL		36	198	0	0	0	11	46.0	39	8	24	5	1	21	3	0	1	0	23	21	0	1	.000	1	4.11
	YEAR		70	331	0	0	0	21	76.0	73	10	33	8	2	43	5	0	2	0	38	32	2	4	.333	3	3.79
4 YR TOTALS			**227**	**1236**	**2**	**0**	**0**	**70**	**294.2**	**268**	**24**	**122**	**24**	**3**	**169**	**16**	**3**	**4**	**0**	**114**	**100**	**12**	**9**	**.571**	**4**	**3.05**

Rogers, Charles Kevin "Kevin" — BB/TL — b.8/20/68   SF88 11/230

YR	TM/LG	CL	G	TBF	GS	CG	SHO	GF	IP	H	HR	BB	IBB	HB	SO	SH	SF	WP	BK	R	ER	W	L	PCT	SV	ERA
88	POC/PIO	R+	13	314	13	1	0	0	69.2	73	4	35	0	2	71	0	3	5	4	51	48	2	8	.200	0	6.20
89	CLI/MID	A	29	722	28	4	0	0	169.1	128	4	78	1	6	168	6	4	5	1	74	48	13	8	.619	0	2.55
90	SJ/CAL	A+	28	732	26	1	1	1	172.0	143	9	68	1	11	186	6	8	19	4	86	69	14	5	.737	0	3.61
91	SHR/TEX	AA	22	528	22	2	0	0	118.0	124	7	54	4	2	108	5	5	12	2	63	44	4	6	.400	0	3.36
92	SHR/TEX	AA	16	413	16	2	2	0	101.0	87	3	29	0	4	110	1	1	4	0	34	29	8	5	.615	0	2.58
	PHO/PCL	AAA	11	287	11	1	1	0	69.2	63	0	22	1	1	62	5	3	2	1	34	31	3	3	.500	0	4.00
	SF/NL		6	148	6	0	0	0	34.0	37	4	13	1	1	26	2	1	0	0	17	16	0	2	.000	0	4.24
93	SF/NL		64	334	0	0	0	24	80.2	71	3	28	1	1	62	0	1	3	0	28	24	2	2	.500	0	2.68
2 YR TOTALS			**70**	**482**	**6**	**0**	**0**	**24**	**114.2**	**108**	**7**	**41**	**6**	**5**	**88**	**2**	**1**	**5**	**0**	**45**	**40**	**2**	**4**	**.333**	**0**	**3.14**

Rogers, Kenneth Scott "Kenny" — BL/TL — b.11/10/64   TEX82 38/816

YR	TM/LG	CL	G	TBF	GS	CG	SHO	GF	IP	H	HR	BB	IBB	HB	SO	SH	SF	WP	BK	R	ER	W	L	PCT	SV	ERA
84	BUR/MID	A	39	396	4	1	1	16	92.2	87	9	33	3	4	93	5	5	8	0	52	41	4	7	.364	3	3.98
85	DB/FSL	A+	6	54	0	0	0	1	10.0	12	0	11	1	1	9	1	1	0	0	9	8	0	1	.000	0	7.20
	BUR/MID	A	33	411	4	2	0	12	95.0	67	3	62	0	6	76	4	1	9	1	34	30	2	5	.286	4	2.84
86	SAL/CAR	A+	12	297	12	0	0	0	66.0	75	9	26	0	1	46	2	2	5	1	54	46	2	7	.222	0	6.27
	TUL/TEX	AA	10	135	0	0	0	8	26.1	39	4	18	1	0	23	0	1	3	0	30	29	0	3	.000	0	9.91
87	CHA/FSL	A+	5	76	3	0	0	0	17.0	17	1	8	0	1	14	1	0	0	0	13	9	0	3	.000	0	4.76
	TUL/TEX	AA	28	316	6	0	0	8	69.0	80	5	35	3	2	59	3	1	14	0	51	41	1	5	.167	2	5.35

Rogers, Kenneth Scott "Kenny" (continued)

YR	TM/LG	CL	G	TBF	GS	CG	SHO	GF	IP	H	HR	BB	IBB	HB	SO	SH	SF	WP	BK	R	ER	W	L	PCT	SV	ERA
88	CHA/FSL	A+	8	138	6	0	0	1	35.1	22	1	11	0	2	26	0	2	1	2	8	5	2	0	1.000	1	1.27
	TUL/TEX	AA	13	354	13	2	0	0	83.1	73	6	34	0	3	76	3	1	3	4	43	37	4	6	.400	0	4.00
89	TEX/AL		73	314	0	0	0	24	73.2	60	2	42	9	4	63	6	3	6	0	28	24	3	4	.429	2	2.93
90	TEX/AL		69	428	3	0	0	46	97.2	93	6	42	5	1	74	7	4	5	0	40	34	10	6	.625	15	3.13
91	TEX/AL		63	511	9	0	0	20	109.2	121	14	61	7	6	73	9	5	3	1	80	66	10	10	.500	5	5.42
92	TEX/AL		*81	337	0	0	0	38	78.2	80	7	26	8	0	70	4	1	4	1	32	27	3	6	.333	6	3.09
93	TEX/AL		35	885	33	5	0	0	208.1	210	18	71	2	4	140	7	5	6	5	108	95	16	10	.615	0	4.10
5 YR TOTALS			321	2475	45	5	0	128	568.0	564	47	242	31	15	420	33	18	24	7	288	246	42	36	.538	28	3.90

Rojas, Melquiades "Mel" — BR/TR — b.12/10/66   MON 11/7/85

YR	TM/LG	CL	G	TBF	GS	CG	SHO	GF	IP	H	HR	BB	IBB	HB	SO	SH	SF	WP	BK	R	ER	W	L	PCT	SV	ERA
86	EXP/GCL	R	13	261	12	1	0	1	55.1	63	0	37	0	2	34	3	3	4	0	39	30	4	5	.444	0	4.88
87	BUR/MID		25	686	25	4	1	0	158.2	146	10	67	1	3	100	4	6	8	0	84	67	8	9	.471	0	3.80
88	ROC/MID	A	12	302	12	3	0	0	73.1	52	3	29	0	2	72	3	1	3	2	30	20	6	4	.600	0	2.45
	WPB/FSL	A+	2	19	2	0	0	0	5.0	4	1	0	0	0	4	0	0	0	0	2	2	1	0	1.000	0	3.60
89	JAC/SOU	AA	34	447	12	1	1	17	112.0	62	1	57	0	5	104	7	4	8	1	39	31	10	7	.588	5	2.49
90	IND/AMA	AAA	17	412	17	0	0	0	97.2	84	9	47	3	1	64	5	2	3	1	42	34	2	4	.333	0	3.13
	MON/NL		23	173	0	0	0	5	40.0	34	5	24	4	2	26	2	0	2	0	17	16	3	1	.750	1	3.60
91	IND/AMA	AAA	14	221	10	0	0	2	52.2	50	4	14	1	1	55	5	1	4	1	29	24	4	2	.667	1	4.10
	MON/NL		37	200	0	0	0	13	48.0	42	4	13	1	1	37	0	2	3	0	21	20	3	3	.500	6	3.75
92	IND/AMA	AAA	4	37	0	0	0	1	8.1	10	0	3	0	0	7	0	0	1	0	5	5	2	1	.667	0	5.40
	MON/NL		68	399	0	0	0	26	100.2	71	2	34	8	2	70	4	2	5	0	17	16	7	1	.875	10	1.43
93	MON/NL		66	378	0	0	0	25	88.1	80	6	30	3	4	48	8	6	5	0	39	29	5	8	.385	10	2.95
4 YR TOTALS			194	1150	0	0	0	69	277.0	227	17	101	16	9	181	14	10	12	0	94	81	18	13	.581	27	2.63

Roper, John Christopher — BR/TR — b.11/21/71   CIN90 12/324

YR	TM/LG	CL	G	TBF	GS	CG	SHO	GF	IP	H	HR	BB	IBB	HB	SO	SH	SF	WP	BK	R	ER	W	L	PCT	SV	ERA
90	RED/GCL	R	13	281	13	0	0	0	74.0	41	1	31	0	3	76	0	0	2	0	10	8	7	2	.778	0	0.97
91	CHW/SAL	A	27	741	27	5	3	0	186.2	135	5	67	0	4	189	1	5	8	1	59	47	14	9	.609	0	2.27
92	CHT/SOU	AA	20	513	20	1	1	0	120.2	115	11	37	2	4	99	5	6	15	5	57	55	10	9	.526	0	4.10
93	IND/AMA	AAA	12	248	12	0	0	0	54.2	56	12	30	1	3	42	0	0	2	2	33	27	3	5	.375	0	4.45
	CIN/NL		16	360	15	0	0	0	80.0	92	10	36	3	4	54	5	3	5	1	51	50	2	5	.286	0	5.63

Rueter, Kirk Wesley — BL/TL — b.12/1/70   MON91 19/477

YR	TM/LG	CL	G	TBF	GS	CG	SHO	GF	IP	H	HR	BB	IBB	HB	SO	SH	SF	WP	BK	R	ER	W	L	PCT	SV	ERA
91	EXP/GCL	R	5	76	4	0	0	0	19.0	16	0	4	0	0	19	2	1	1	0	5	2	1	1	.500	0	0.95
	SUM/SAL	A	8	160	5	0	0	1	40.2	32	3	10	0	0	27	1	0	1	0	8	6	3	1	.750	0	1.33
92	ROC/MID	A	26	697	26	6	2	0	174.1	150	5	36	2	1	153	10	3	4	1	68	50	11	9	.550	0	2.58
93	HAR/EAS	AA	9	225	8	1	1	1	59.2	47	4	7	0	0	36	2	0	1	0	10	9	5	0	1.000	0	1.36
	OTT/INT	AAA	7	174	7	0	0	0	43.1	46	3	7	0	0	27	1	1	0	0	20	13	4	2	.667	0	2.70
	MON/NL		14	341	14	0	0	0	85.2	85	5	18	1	0	31	1	0	0	0	33	26	8	0	1.000	0	2.73

Ruffcorn, Scott Patrick — BR/TR — b.12/12/69   CHA91 1/25

YR	TM/LG	CL	G	TBF	GS	CG	SHO	GF	IP	H	HR	BB	IBB	HB	SO	SH	SF	WP	BK	R	ER	W	L	PCT	SV	ERA
91	WS/GCL	R	4	49	2	0	0	1	11.1	8	0	5	0	0	15	0	0	1	1	7	4	0	0	.000	0	3.18
	SB/MID	A	9	193	9	0	0	0	43.2	35	1	25	0	2	45	2	1	1	2	26	19	1	3	.250	0	3.92
92	SAR/FSL	A+	25	642	24	2	0	0	160.1	122	7	39	0	3	140	4	5	3	1	53	39	14	5	.737	0	2.19
93	BIR/SOU	AA	20	563	20	3	3	0	135.0	108	6	52	0	4	141	5	0	7	0	47	41	9	4	.692	0	2.73
	NAS/AMA	AAA	7	172	6	1	0	0	45.0	30	5	8	1	0	44	2	1	3	0	16	14	2	2	.500	0	2.80
	CHI/AL		3	46	2	0	0	1	10.0	9	2	10	0	0	2	1	1	1	0	11	9	0	2	.000	0	8.10

Ruffin, Bruce Wayne — BB/TL — b.10/4/63   PHI85 2/34

YR	TM/LG	CL	G	TBF	GS	CG	SHO	GF	IP	H	HR	BB	IBB	HB	SO	SH	SF	WP	BK	R	ER	W	L	PCT	SV	ERA
85	CLE/FSL	A+	14	399	14	3	1	0	97.0	87	2	34	1	2	74	2	1	3	1	33	31	5	5	.500	0	2.88
86	REA/EAS	AA	16	380	13	4	2	0	90.1	89	3	26	1	0	68	1	4	2	0	41	33	8	4	.667	0	3.29
	PHI/NL		21	600	21	6	0	0	146.1	138	6	44	6	2	70	2	4	0	1	53	40	9	4	.692	0	2.46
87	PHI/NL		35	884	35	3	1	0	204.2	236	17	73	4	0	93	8	10	6	0	118	99	11	14	.440	0	4.35
88	PHI/NL		55	646	15	3	0	14	144.1	151	7	80	6	3	82	10	3	12	0	86	71	6	10	.375	3	4.43
89	SCR/INT	AAA	9	225	9	0	0	0	50.0	44	2	39	1	2	44	2	2	9	0	28	26	5	1	.833	0	4.68
	PHI/NL		24	576	23	1	0	0	125.2	152	10	62	6	0	70	8	1	8	0	69	62	6	10	.375	0	4.44
90	PHI/NL		32	678	25	2	1	1	149.0	178	14	62	7	1	79	10	6	3	2	99	89	6	13	.316	0	5.38
91	SCR/INT	AAA	13	337	13	1	0	0	75.1	82	4	41	0	0	50	1	4	4	0	43	39	4	5	.444	0	4.66
	PHI/NL		31	508	15	1	1	2	119.0	125	6	38	3	1	85	6	4	4	0	52	50	4	7	.364	0	3.78
92	MIL/AL		25	272	6	1	0	6	58.0	66	3	41	3	0	45	3	4	3	2	43	43	1	6	.143	0	6.67
	DEN/AMA	AAA	4	119	4	1	0	0	28.2	28	4	8	1	0	17	1	0	0	1	12	3	3	0	1.000	0	0.94
93	COL/NL		59	619	12	0	0	8	139.2	145	10	69	9	1	126	4	5	8	0	71	60	6	5	.545	2	3.87
8 YR TOTALS			282	4783	152	17	3	31	1086.2	1191	77	469	44	9	650	51	36	43	3	591	514	49	69	.415	5	4.26

Ruffin, Johnny Renando — BR/TR — b.7/29/71   CHA88 4/93

YR	TM/LG	CL	G	TBF	GS	CG	SHO	GF	IP	H	HR	BB	IBB	HB	SO	SH	SF	WP	BK	R	ER	W	L	PCT	SV	ERA
88	WS/GCL	R	13	246	11	1	0	1	58.2	43	3	22	0	4	31	1	2	9	2	27	15	4	2	.667	0	2.30
89	UTI/NYP	A-	15	376	15	0	0	0	88.1	67	3	46	0	1	92	5	1	8	0	43	33	4	8	.333	0	3.36
90	SB/MID	A	24	568	24	0	0	0	123.0	117	7	82	0	3	92	4	2	17	4	86	57	7	6	.538	0	4.17
91	SAR/FSL	A+	26	655	26	6	2	0	158.2	126	9	62	0	5	117	3	5	10	2	68	57	11	4	.733	0	3.23
92	BIR/SOU	AA	10	228	10	0	0	0	47.2	51	3	34	0	0	44	1	1	4	0	48	32	0	7	.000	0	6.04
	SAR/FSL	A+	23	290	8	0	0	6	62.2	56	5	41	0	4	61	2	1	10	2	46	41	3	7	.300	0	5.89

(continued)

Ruffin, Johnny Renando (continued)

YR	TM/LG	CL	G	TBF	GS	CG	SHO	GF	IP	H	HR	BB	IBB	HB	SO	SH	SF	WP	BK	R	ER	W	L	PCT	SV	ERA
93	BIR/SOU	AA	11	92	0	0	0	10	22.1	16	2	9	1	0	23	2	1	0	0	9	7	0	4	.000	2	2.82
	NAS/AMA	AAA	29	242	0	0	0	11	60.0	48	5	16	4	1	69	2	2	10	0	24	22	3	4	.429	1	3.30
	IND/AMA	AAA	3	25	0	0	0	3	6.2	3	0	2	1	0	6	1	0	0	0	1	1	1	1	.500	1	1.35
	CIN/NL		21	159	0	0	0	5	37.2	36	4	11	1	1	30	1	0	2	0	16	15	2	1	.667	2	3.58

Ruskin, Scott Drew — BR/TL — b.6/8/63   PIT86 S3/64

YR	TM/LG	CL	G	TBF	GS	CG	SHO	GF	IP	H	HR	BB	IBB	HB	SO	SH	SF	WP	BK	R	ER	W	L	PCT	SV	ERA
89	SAL/CAR	A+	14	359	13	3	0	1	84.2	71	5	33	0	4	92	1	1	6	4	35	21	4	5	.444	1	2.23
	HAR/EAS	AA	12	278	10	2	0	0	63.0	64	5	32	0	1	56	2	3	2	2	38	34	2	3	.400	0	4.86
90	PIT/NL		44	221	0	0	0	8	47.2	50	2	28	3	2	34	3	2	3	1	21	16	2	2	.500	2	3.02
	MON/NL		23	115	0	0	0	4	27.2	25	2	10	3	0	23	2	0	0	0	7	7	1	0	1.000	0	2.28
	YEAR		67	336	0	0	0	12	75.1	75	4	38	6	2	57	5	2	3	1	28	23	3	2	.600	2	2.75
91	MON/NL		64	275	0	0	0	24	63.2	57	4	30	2	3	46	5	0	5	0	31	30	4	4	.500	6	4.24
92	CIN/NL		57	234	0	0	0	19	53.2	56	6	20	4	1	43	7	2	1	0	31	30	4	3	.571	2	5.03
93	IND/AMA	AAA	49	245	2	0	0	42	56.0	60	8	22	3	0	41	1	1	1	0	34	32	1	5	.167	28	5.14
	CIN/NL		4	8	0	0	0	0	1.0	3	1	2	0	0	0	0	0	0	0	2	2	0	0	.000	0	18.00
4 YR TOTALS			**192**	**853**	**0**	**0**	**0**	**55**	**193.2**	**191**	**15**	**90**	**12**	**6**	**146**	**17**	**4**	**9**	**1**	**92**	**85**	**11**	**9**	**.550**	**8**	**3.95**

Russell, Jeffrey Lee "Jeff" — BR/TR — b.9/2/61   CIN79 8/126

YR	TM/LG	CL	G	TBF	GS	CG	SHO	GF	IP	H	HR	BB	IBB	HB	SO	SH	SF	WP	BK	R	ER	W	L	PCT	SV	ERA
83	CIN/NL		10	282	10	2	0	0	68.1	58	7	22	3	0	40	6	5	1	1	30	23	4	5	.444	0	3.03
84	CIN/NL		33	787	30	4	2	1	181.2	186	15	65	8	4	101	8	3	3	3	97	86	6	18	.250	0	4.26
85	DEN/AMA	AAA	16	440	16	1	1	0	102.1	94	5	46	1	1	81	4	6	5	3	51	48	6	4	.600	0	4.22
	OC/AMA	AAA	2	53	2	0	0	0	13.0	11	1	5	0	0	13	0	0	1	0	4	4	1	0	1.000	0	2.77
	TEX/AL		13	295	13	0	0	0	62.0	85	10	27	1	2	44	1	3	2	0	55	52	3	6	.333	0	7.55
86	OC/AMA	AAA	11	306	11	1	0	0	70.2	63	5	38	0	2	34	4	2	1	1	32	31	4	1	.800	0	3.95
	TEX/AL		37	338	0	0	0	9	82.0	74	11	31	2	1	54	1	2	5	0	40	31	5	2	.714	2	3.40
87	CHA/FSL	A+	2	44	2	0	0	0	11.0	8	1	5	0	0	3	0	1	0	0	3	3	0	0	.000	0	2.45
	OC/AMA	AAA	4	53	2	0	0	0	6.1	5	0	1	0	0	5	1	0	0	0	1	1	0	0	.000	0	1.42
	TEX/AL		52	442	2	0	0	12	97.1	109	9	52	5	2	56	0	5	4	0	56	48	5	4	.556	3	4.44
88	TEX/AL		34	793	24	5	0	1	188.2	183	15	66	3	4	88	4	3	5	7	86	80	10	9	.526	0	3.82
89	TEX/AL		71	278	0	0	0	66	72.2	45	4	24	5	3	77	1	3	6	0	21	16	6	4	.600	*38	1.98
90	CHA/FSL	A+	1	1	0	0	0	0	0.0	1	0	0	0	0	0	0	0	0	0	1	1	0	1	.000	0	0.00
	TEX/AL		27	111	0	0	0	22	25.1	23	1	16	1	0	16	1	1	2	0	15	12	1	5	.167	10	4.26
91	TEX/AL		68	336	0	0	0	56	79.1	71	11	26	1	1	52	3	4	5	0	36	29	6	4	.600	30	3.29
92	TEX/AL		51	241	0	0	0	42	56.2	51	3	22	3	2	43	1	2	3	0	14	12	2	3	.400	28	1.91
	OAK/AL		8	35	0	0	0	4	9.2	4	0	3	0	0	5	0	0	0	0	0	0	2	0	1.000	2	0.00
	YEAR		59	276	0	0	0	46	66.1	55	3	25	3	2	48	1	2	3	0	14	12	4	3	.571	30	1.63
93	BOS/AL		51	189	0	0	0	48	46.2	39	1	14	1	1	45	1	2	4	0	16	14	1	4	.200	33	2.70
11 YR TOTALS			**455**	**4127**	**79**	**11**	**2**	**261**	**970.1**	**928**	**87**	**368**	**37**	**23**	**621**	**29**	**35**	**41**	**12**	**466**	**403**	**51**	**64**	**.443**	**146**	**3.74**

Ryan, Kenneth Frederick "Ken" — BR/TR — b.10/24/68   BOS 6/16/86

YR	TM/LG	CL	G	TBF	GS	CG	SHO	GF	IP	H	HR	BB	IBB	HB	SO	SH	SF	WP	BK	R	ER	W	L	PCT	SV	ERA
86	ELM/NYP	A-	13	103	1	0	0	10	21.2	20	0	21	1	1	22	0	1	2	0	14	14	2	2	.500	0	5.82
87	GRE/SAL	A	28	554	19	2	0	8	121.1	139	10	63	8	3	75	1	7	10	3	88	74	3	12	.200	0	5.49
88	LYN/CAR	A+	19	344	14	0	0	2	71.1	79	4	45	1	3	49	2	1	5	3	51	49	2	7	.222	0	6.18
89	WH/FSL	A+	24	586	22	3	0	1	137.0	114	5	81	0	7	78	4	4	8	4	58	48	8	8	.500	0	3.15
90	LYN/CAR	A+	28	735	28	3	1	0	161.1	182	10	82	0	6	109	6	5	19	1	104	92	6	14	.300	0	5.13
91	WH/FSL	A+	21	213	1	0	0	11	52.2	40	1	19	0	2	53	0	0	3	1	15	12	1	3	.250	1	2.05
	NB/EAS	AA	14	116	0	0	0	6	26.0	23	2	12	1	1	26	4	0	2	0	7	5	1	2	.333	1	1.73
	PAW/INT	AAA	9	80	0	0	0	4	18.1	15	2	11	1	1	14	2	1	2	0	11	10	1	0	1.000	1	4.91
92	NB/EAS	AA	44	220	0	0	0	42	50.2	44	0	24	2	1	51	0	2	4	0	17	11	1	4	.200	22	1.95
	PAW/INT	AAA	9	36	0	0	0	6	8.2	6	1	4	0	0	6	0	0	0	0	2	2	1	0	1.000	7	2.08
	BOS/AL		7	30	0	0	0	6	7.0	4	0	5	0	0	5	1	1	0	0	5	5	0	0	.000	1	6.43
93	PAW/INT	AAA	18	112	0	0	0	15	25.1	18	1	17	0	2	22	3	1	2	1	9	7	0	2	.000	2	2.49
	BOS/AL		47	223	0	0	0	26	50.0	43	2	29	3	3	49	4	4	3	0	23	20	7	2	.778	1	3.60
2 YR TOTALS			**54**	**253**	**0**	**0**	**0**	**32**	**57.0**	**47**	**4**	**34**	**5**	**3**	**54**	**5**	**5**	**3**	**0**	**28**	**25**	**7**	**2**	**.778**	**2**	**3.95**

Ryan, Lynn Nolan "Nolan" — BR/TR — b.1/31/47   NYN65 10/182

YR	TM/LG	CL	G	TBF	GS	CG	SHO	GF	IP	H	HR	BB	IBB	HB	SO	SH	SF	WP	BK	R	ER	W	L	PCT	SV	ERA
66	NY/NL		2	17	1	0	0	0	3.0	5	1	3	1	0	6	0	0	1	0	5	5	0	1	.000	0	15.00
68	NY/NL		21	559	18	3	0	1	134.0	93	12	75	4	4	133	12	4	7	0	50	46	6	9	.400	1	3.09
69	NY/NL		25	375	10	2	0	4	89.1	60	3	53	3	1	92	2	1	2	3	38	35	6	3	.667	1	3.53
70	NY/NL		27	570	19	5	2	4	131.2	86	10	97	2	4	125	8	4	8	0	59	50	7	11	.389	1	3.42
71	NY/NL		30	705	26	3	0	1	152.0	125	8	116	4	15	137	3	0	6	1	78	67	10	14	.417	0	3.97
72	CAL/AL		39	1154	39	20	*9	0	284.0	166	14	157	4	10	*329	11	3	18	0	80	72	19	16	.543	0	2.28
73	CAL/AL		41	1355	39	26	4	2	326.0	238	18	162	2	7	*383	2	7	15	0	113	104	21	16	.568	1	2.87
74	CAL/AL		42	1392	41	26	3	0	*332.2	221	18	202	3	9	*367	12	4	9	0	127	107	22	16	.579	0	2.89
75	CAL/AL		28	864	28	10	5	0	198.0	152	13	132	0	7	186	6	7	12	0	90	76	14	12	.538	0	3.45
76	CAL/AL		39	1196	39	21	*7	0	284.1	193	13	183	2	5	*327	13	4	5	2	117	106	17	18	.486	0	3.36
77	CAL/AL		37	1272	37	*22	4	0	299.0	198	12	204	7	9	*341	22	10	21	3	110	92	19	16	.543	0	2.77
78	CAL/AL		31	1008	31	14	3	0	234.2	183	11	148	7	3	*260	11	14	13	2	106	97	10	13	.435	0	3.72
79	CAL/AL		34	937	34	17	*5	0	222.2	169	15	114	3	2	*223	8	10	9	0	104	89	16	14	.533	0	3.60
80	HOU/NL		35	982	35	4	2	0	233.2	205	10	98	3	2	200	7	7	10	1	100	87	11	10	.524	0	3.35
81	HOU/NL		21	605	21	5	3	0	149.0	99	2	68	3	1	140	5	3	16	2	34	28	11	5	.688	0	*1.69
82	HOU/NL		35	1050	35	10	3	0	250.1	196	20	109	3	8	245	9	3	18	2	100	88	16	12	.571	0	3.16

Ryan, Lynn Nolan "Nolan" (continued)

YR	TM/LG	CL	G	TBF	GS	CG	SHO	GF	IP	H	HR	BB	IBB	HB	SO	SH	SF	WP	BK	R	ER	W	L	PCT	SV	ERA
83	HOU/NL		29	804	29	5	2	0	196.1	134	9	101	3	4	183	7	5	5	1	74	65	14	9	.609	0	2.98
84	HOU/NL		30	760	30	5	2	0	183.2	143	12	69	2	4	197	4	6	6	3	78	62	12	11	.522	0	3.04
85	HOU/NL		35	983	35	4	0	0	232.0	205	12	95	8	9	209	11	12	14	2	108	98	10	12	.455	0	3.80
86	HOU/NL		30	729	30	1	0	0	178.0	119	14	82	5	4	194	5	4	15	0	72	66	12	8	.600	0	3.34
87	HOU/NL		34	873	34	0	0	0	211.2	154	14	87	2	4	*270	9	1	10	2	75	65	8	16	.333	0	*2.76
88	HOU/NL		33	930	33	4	1	0	220.0	186	18	87	6	7	*228	10	8	10	7	98	86	12	11	.522	0	3.52
89	TEX/AL		32	988	32	6	2	0	239.1	162	17	98	3	9	*301	9	5	19	1	96	85	16	10	.615	0	3.20
90	TEX/AL		30	818	30	5	2	0	204.0	137	18	74	2	7	*232	3	5	9	1	86	78	13	9	.591	0	3.44
91	TEX/AL		27	683	27	2	2	0	173.0	102	12	72	0	5	203	3	9	8	0	58	56	12	6	.667	0	2.91
92	TEX/AL		27	675	27	2	0	0	157.1	138	9	69	0	12	157	6	7	9	0	75	65	5	9	.357	0	3.72
93	TEX/AL		13	291	13	0	0	0	66.1	54	5	40	0	1	46	2	2	3	0	47	36	5	5	.500	0	4.88
27 YR TOTALS			**807**	**22575**	**773**	**222**	**61**	**13**	**5386.0**	**3923**	**321**	**2795**	**78**	**158**	**5714**	**205**	**146**	**277**	**33**	**2178**	**1911**	**324**	**292**	**.526**	**3**	**3.19**

Saberhagen, Bret William — BR/TR — b.4/11/64   KC82 19/480

YR	TM/LG	CL	G	TBF	GS	CG	SHO	GF	IP	H	HR	BB	IBB	HB	SO	SH	SF	WP	BK	R	ER	W	L	PCT	SV	ERA
84	KC/AL		38	634	18	2	1	9	157.2	138	13	36	4	2	73	8	5	7	1	71	61	10	11	.476	1	3.48
85	KC/AL		32	931	32	10	1	0	235.1	211	19	38	1	1	158	9	7	1	3	79	75	20	6	.769	0	2.87
86	KC/AL		30	652	25	4	2	4	156.0	165	15	29	1	2	112	3	3	1	1	77	72	7	12	.368	0	4.15
87	KC/AL		33	1048	33	15	4	0	257.0	246	27	53	2	6	163	8	5	6	1	99	96	18	10	.643	0	3.36
88	KC/AL		35	1089	35	9	0	0	260.2	271	18	59	5	4	171	8	10	9	0	122	110	14	16	.467	0	3.80
89	KC/AL		36	1021	35	*12	4	0	*262.1	209	13	43	6	2	193	9	6	8	1	74	63	*23	6	*.793	0	*2.16
90	KC/AL		20	561	20	5	0	0	135.0	146	9	28	1	1	87	4	4	1	0	52	49	5	9	.357	0	3.27
91	KC/AL		28	789	28	7	2	0	196.1	165	12	45	5	9	136	3	3	8	1	76	67	13	8	.619	0	3.07
92	NY/NL		17	397	15	1	1	0	97.2	84	6	27	1	4	81	3	3	1	2	39	38	3	5	.375	0	3.50
93	NY/NL		19	556	19	4	1	0	139.1	131	11	17	4	3	93	6	6	2	2	55	51	7	7	.500	0	3.29
10 YR TOTALS			**288**	**7678**	**260**	**69**	**16**	**13**	**1897.1**	**1766**	**143**	**375**	**30**	**34**	**1267**	**66**	**52**	**44**	**12**	**744**	**682**	**120**	**90**	**.571**	**1**	**3.24**

Salkeld, Roger William — BR/TR — b.3/6/71   SEA89 1/3

YR	TM/LG	CL	G	TBF	GS	CG	SHO	GF	IP	H	HR	BB	IBB	HB	SO	SH	SF	WP	BK	R	ER	W	L	PCT	SV	ERA
89	BEL/NWL	A-	8	168	6	0	0	1	42.0	27	0	10	0	4	55	1	1	3	3	17	6	2	2	.500	0	1.29
90	SB/CAL	A+	25	677	25	2	0	0	153.1	140	3	83	0	3	167	7	1	9	2	77	58	11	5	.688	0	3.40
91	JAC/SOU	AA	23	634	23	5	0	0	153.2	131	9	55	1	10	159	5	5	12	2	56	52	8	8	.500	0	3.05
	CAL/PCL	AAA	4	90	4	0	0	0	19.1	18	2	13	0	1	10	1	0	1	0	16	11	2	1	.667	0	5.12
93	JAC/SOU	AA	14	334	14	0	0	0	77.0	71	8	29	1	5	56	3	5	2	1	39	28	4	3	.571	0	3.27
	SEA/AL		3	61	2	0	0	0	14.1	13	0	4	1	0	10	0	0	0	0	4	4	0	0	.000	0	2.51

Sampen, William Albert "Bill" — BR/TR — b.1/18/63   PIT85 12/294

YR	TM/LG	CL	G	TBF	GS	CG	SHO	GF	IP	H	HR	BB	IBB	HB	SO	SH	SF	WP	BK	R	ER	W	L	PCT	SV	ERA
85	WAT/NYP	A-	5	48	0	0	0	2	10.0	9	0	7	0	1	11	1	1	2	0	3	2	0	0	.000	1	1.80
86	WAT/NYP	A-	9	130	5	0	0	3	29.2	27	0	13	0	1	29	1	2	3	0	18	14	0	3	.000	2	4.25
87	SAL/CAR	A+	26	650	26	2	1	0	152.1	126	16	72	1	7	137	5	5	3	2	77	65	9	8	.529	0	3.84
88	SAL/CAR	A+	8	217	8	1	0	0	51.1	47	4	14	0	0	59	1	1	1	2	22	19	3	3	.500	0	3.33
	HAR/EAS	AA	13	349	12	3	0	0	82.2	72	3	27	1	2	65	1	2	2	2	38	34	6	3	.667	0	3.70
89	HAR/EAS	AA	26	691	26	6	0	0	165.2	148	8	40	3	5	134	5	8	6	0	75	59	11	9	.550	0	3.21
90	MON/NL		59	394	4	0	0	26	90.1	94	7	33	6	2	69	5	3	4	0	34	30	12	7	.632	2	2.99
91	IND/AMA	AAA	7	170	7	0	0	0	39.2	33	1	19	0	1	41	1	1	1	0	13	9	4	0	1.000	0	2.04
	MON/NL		43	409	8	0	0	8	92.1	96	13	46	7	3	52	4	4	3	1	49	41	9	5	.643	0	4.00
92	MON/NL		44	267	0	0	0	10	63.1	62	4	29	4	1	23	1	1	2	2	22	22	1	4	.200	0	3.13
	IND/AMA	AAA	2	16	0	0	0	0	3.0	3	0	3	0	0	4	0	0	0	0	2	2	1	1	.500	0	6.00
	KC/AL		8	81	1	0	0	3	19.2	21	0	3	1	0	14	1	1	2	1	10	8	0	2	.000	0	3.66
	YEAR		52	348	2	0	0	13	83.0	83	4	32	7	4	37	6	3	2	1	32	30	1	6	.143	0	3.25
93	KC/AL		18	89	0	0	0	3	18.1	25	1	9	0	4	9	0	2	2	0	12	12	2	2	.500	0	5.89
	OMA/AMA	AAA	33	160	0	0	0	28	37.0	37	6	13	1	2	34	0	0	1	0	16	14	1	2	.333	8	3.41
4 YR TOTALS			**172**	**1240**	**14**	**0**	**0**	**50**	**284.0**	**298**	**25**	**120**	**20**	**13**	**167**	**17**	**10**	**11**	**3**	**127**	**113**	**24**	**20**	**.545**	**2**	**3.58**

Sanders, Scott Gerald — BR/TR — b.3/25/69   SD90 2/32

YR	TM/LG	CL	G	TBF	GS	CG	SHO	GF	IP	H	HR	BB	IBB	HB	SO	SH	SF	WP	BK	R	ER	W	L	PCT	SV	ERA
90	SPO/NWL	A-	3	70	3	0	0	0	19.0	12	0	5	0	2	21	1	0	4	1	3	2	2	1	.667	0	0.95
	WAT/MID	A	7	166	7	0	0	0	37.0	43	2	21	0	1	29	1	2	2	0	21	20	2	2	.500	0	4.86
91	WAT/MID	A	4	102	4	0	0	0	26.1	17	0	6	0	1	18	1	0	0	0	2	2	3	0	1.000	0	0.68
	HD/CAL	A+	21	569	21	4	2	0	132.2	114	7	72	2	7	93	4	2	8	2	72	54	9	6	.600	0	3.66
92	WIC/TEX	AA	14	377	14	0	0	0	87.2	85	7	37	2	4	95	5	4	4	0	35	34	7	5	.583	0	3.49
	LV/PCL	AAA	14	340	12	1	1	0	72.0	97	7	31	1	3	51	4	0	9	0	49	44	3	6	.333	0	5.50
93	LV/PCL	AAA	24	687	24	4	0	0	152.1	170	19	62	2	6	161	13	4	6	1	101	84	5	10	.333	0	4.96
	SD/NL		9	231	9	0	0	0	52.1	54	4	23	1	3	37	1	2	0	0	32	24	3	3	.500	0	4.13

Sanderson, Scott Douglas — BR/TR — b.7/22/56   MON77 3/54

YR	TM/LG	CL	G	TBF	GS	CG	SHO	GF	IP	H	HR	BB	IBB	HB	SO	SH	SF	WP	BK	R	ER	W	L	PCT	SV	ERA
78	MON/NL		10	251	9	1	1	1	61.0	52	3	21	0	1	50	3	2	2	0	20	17	4	2	.667	0	2.51
79	MON/NL		34	696	24	5	3	3	168.0	148	16	54	4	3	138	5	7	2	3	69	64	9	8	.529	1	3.43
80	MON/NL		33	875	33	7	3	0	211.1	206	18	56	3	3	125	11	5	6	0	76	73	16	11	.593	0	3.11
81	MON/NL		22	560	22	4	1	0	137.1	122	10	31	2	1	77	7	4	2	0	50	45	9	7	.563	0	2.95
82	MON/NL		32	922	32	7	1	0	224.0	212	24	58	5	6	158	14	2	5	0	98	86	12	12	.500	0	3.46
83	MON/NL		18	346	16	0	0	0	81.1	98	12	20	0	0	55	2	1	3	0	50	42	6	7	.462	1	4.65
84	LOD/CAL	A+	1	0	0	0	0	0	5.0	7	1	0	0	0	6	0	0	0	0	2	2	0	1	.000	0	3.60
	CHI/NL		24	571	24	3	0	0	140.2	140	5	24	3	2	76	6	8	3	2	54	49	8	5	.615	0	3.14

(continued)

Sanderson, Scott Douglas (continued)

YR	TM/LG	CL	G	TBF	GS	CG	SHO	GF	IP	H	HR	BB	IBB	HB	SO	SH	SF	WP	BK	R	ER	W	L	PCT	SV	ERA
85	CHI/NL		19	480	19	2	0	0	121.0	100	13	27	4	0	80	7	7	1	0	49	42	5	6	.455	0	3.12
86	CHI/NL		37	697	28	1	1	2	169.2	165	21	37	2	2	124	6	5	3	1	85	79	9	11	.450	1	4.19
87	CHI/NL		32	631	22	0	0	5	144.2	156	23	50	5	3	106	4	5	1	0	72	69	8	9	.471	2	4.29
88	PEO/MID	A	1	20	1	0	0	0	5.0	4	0	0	0	0	3	0	0	0	2	1	0	0	0	.000	0	0.00
	IOW/AMA	AAA	3	55	3	0	0	0	13.1	13	1	2	0	1	4	0	0	0	0	7	7	1	0	1.000	0	4.72
	CHI/NL		11	62	0	0	0	3	15.1	13	1	3	1	0	6	0	0	3	0	9	9	1	2	.333	0	5.28
89	CHI/NL		37	611	23	2	0	2	146.1	155	16	31	6	2	86	8	3	1	3	69	64	11	9	.550	0	3.94
90	OAK/AL		34	885	34	2	1	0	206.1	205	27	66	2	4	128	4	8	3	1	99	89	17	11	.607	0	3.88
91	NY/AL		34	837	34	2	2	0	208.0	200	22	29	0	3	130	5	5	4	1	95	88	16	10	.615	0	3.81
92	NY/AL		33	851	33	2	1	0	193.1	220	28	64	5	5	104	3	11	4	1	116	106	12	11	.522	0	4.93
93	CAL/AL		21	576	21	4	1	0	135.1	153	15	27	5	5	66	6	3	1	2	77	67	7	11	.389	0	4.46
	SF/NL		11	201	8	0	0	1	48.2	48	12	7	2	1	36	3	2	0	3	20	19	4	2	.667	0	3.51
	YEAR		32	777	29	4	1	1	184.0	201	27	34	7	6	102	9	10	1	5	97	86	11	13	.458	0	4.21
16 YR TOTALS			442	10052	382	42	14	18	2412.1	2393	266	605	49	37	1545	89	90	39	18	1108	1008	154	134	.535	5	3.76

Sanford, Meredith Leroy "Mo" — BR/TR — b.12/24/66   CIN88 31/826

YR	TM/LG	CL	G	TBF	GS	CG	SHO	GF	IP	H	HR	BB	IBB	HB	SO	SH	SF	WP	BK	R	ER	W	L	PCT	SV	ERA
88	RED/GCL	R	14	217	11	0	0	1	53.0	34	6	25	1	0	64	0	1	3	4	24	19	3	4	.429	1	3.23
89	GRE/SAL	A	25	629	25	3	1	0	153.2	112	8	64	1	0	160	4	2	2	6	52	48	12	6	.667	0	2.81
90	CR/MID	A	25	628	25	2	1	0	157.2	112	15	55	1	4	180	3	2	8	1	50	48	13	6	.765	0	2.74
91	CHT/SOU	AA	16	395	16	1	1	0	95.1	69	7	55	2	1	124	4	3	1	0	37	29	7	4	.636	0	2.74
	NAS/AMA	AAA	5	140	5	2	2	0	33.2	19	0	22	0	1	38	0	0	4	0	7	6	3	0	1.000	0	1.60
	CIN/NL		5	118	5	0	0	0	28.0	19	3	15	1	1	31	0	0	4	0	14	12	1	2	.333	0	3.86
92	CHT/SOU	AA	4	101	4	1	1	0	26.2	13	2	6	0	2	29	0	0	1	0	5	4	4	0	1.000	0	1.35
	NAS/AMA	AAA	25	549	25	0	0	0	122.0	128	22	65	1	3	129	4	4	5	2	81	77	8	8	.500	0	5.68
93	CS/PCL	AAA	20	456	17	0	0	0	105.0	103	8	57	2	4	104	4	4	3	3	64	61	3	6	.333	0	5.23
	COL/NL		11	166	6	0	0	1	35.2	37	4	27	0	0	36	4	2	1	1	25	21	1	2	.333	0	5.30
2 YR TOTALS			16	284	11	0	0	1	63.2	56	7	42	1	1	67	4	2	6	1	39	33	2	4	.333	0	4.66

Scanlan, Robert Guy "Bob" — BR/TR — b.8/9/66   PHI84 25/636

YR	TM/LG	CL	G	TBF	GS	CG	SHO	GF	IP	H	HR	BB	IBB	HB	SO	SH	SF	WP	BK	R	ER	W	L	PCT	SV	ERA
84	PHI/GCL	R	13	173	6	0	0	2	33.1	43	0	30	0	0	17	0	3	2	4	31	24	0	2	.000	0	6.48
85	SPA/SAL	A	26	669	25	4	1	0	152.1	160	7	53	0	4	108	3	6	8	0	95	70	8	12	.400	0	4.14
86	CLE/FSL	A+	24	559	22	5	0	0	125.2	146	1	45	4	5	51	6	4	4	1	73	58	8	12	.400	0	4.15
87	REA/EAS		27	718	26	3	1	0	164.0	187	12	55	3	11	91	9	4	1	0	98	93	15	5	.750	0	5.10
88	MAI/INT	AAA	28	713	27	4	1	0	161.0	181	10	50	7	8	79	13	7	17	8	110	100	5	18	.217	0	5.59
89	REA/EAS	AA	31	531	17	4	1	0	118.1	124	9	58	1	5	63	5	5	12	1	88	76	6	10	.375	0	5.78
90	SCR/INT	AAA	23	565	23	1	0	0	130.0	128	11	59	3	7	74	3	4	3	0	79	70	8	11	.421	0	4.85
91	IOW/AMA	AAA	4	79	3	0	0	0	18.1	14	0	10	1	0	15	2	0	3	0	8	6	2	0	1.000	0	2.95
	CHI/NL		40	482	13	0	0	16	111.0	114	5	40	3	3	44	8	6	5	1	60	48	7	8	.467	1	3.89
92	CHI/NL		69	360	0	0	0	41	87.1	76	4	30	6	1	42	4	2	6	4	32	28	3	6	.333	14	2.89
93	CHI/NL		70	323	0	0	0	13	75.1	79	6	28	7	3	44	2	6	0	2	41	38	4	5	.444	0	4.54
3 YR TOTALS			179	1165	13	0	0	70	273.2	269	15	98	16	7	130	14	14	11	7	133	114	14	19	.424	15	3.75

Schilling, Curtis Montague "Curt" — BR/TR — b.11/14/66   BOS86* 2/39

YR	TM/LG	CL	G	TBF	GS	CG	SHO	GF	IP	H	HR	BB	IBB	HB	SO	SH	SF	WP	BK	R	ER	W	L	PCT	SV	ERA
86	ELM/NYP	A-	16	399	15	2	1	1	93.2	92	3	30	1	2	75	4	1	4	2	34	27	7	3	.700	0	2.59
87	GRE/SAL	A	29	777	28	7	3	1	184.0	179	10	65	8	2	189	5	3	10	2	96	78	8	15	.348	0	3.82
88	NB/EAS	AA	21	440	17	4	1	1	106.0	91	3	40	0	1	62	4	3	2	6	44	35	8	5	.615	0	2.97
	CHA/SOU	AA	7	189	7	2	1	0	45.1	36	2	23	0	0	32	0	3	2	0	19	16	5	2	.714	0	3.18
	BAL/AL		4	76	4	0	0	0	14.2	22	3	10	1	1	4	0	3	0	0	19	16	0	3	.000	0	9.82
89	ROC/INT	AAA	27	762	27	9	3	0	185.1	176	11	59	0	1	109	4	3	6	5	76	66	13	11	.542	0	3.21
	BAL/AL		5	38	1	0	0	0	8.2	10	2	3	0	0	6	0	0	1	0	6	6	0	1	.000	0	6.23
90	ROC/INT	AAA	15	374	14	1	0	0	87.1	95	10	25	1	2	83	4	0	0	2	46	38	4	4	.500	0	3.92
	BAL/AL		35	191	0	0	0	16	46.0	38	1	19	0	0	32	2	4	0	0	13	13	1	2	.333	3	2.54
91	TUC/PCL	AAA	13	99	0	0	0	7	23.2	16	0	12	1	0	21	1	0	1	0	9	9	0	1	.000	0	3.42
	HOU/NL		56	336	0	0	0	34	75.2	79	2	39	7	0	71	5	1	4	1	35	32	3	5	.375	8	3.81
92	PHI/NL		42	895	26	10	4	10	226.1	165	11	59	4	1	147	6	3	9	3	67	59	14	11	.560	2	2.35
93	PHI/NL		34	982	34	7	2	0	235.1	234	23	57	6	6	186	9	7	9	3	114	105	16	7	.696	0	4.02
6 YR TOTALS			176	2518	65	17	6	60	606.2	548	42	187	18	6	446	23	23	20	4	254	231	34	29	.540	13	3.43

Schooler, Michael Ralph "Mike" — BR/TR — b.8/10/62   SEA85 3/35

YR	TM/LG	CL	G	TBF	GS	CG	SHO	GF	IP	H	HR	BB	IBB	HB	SO	SH	SF	WP	BK	R	ER	W	L	PCT	SV	ERA
85	BEL/NWL	A-	10	0	10	0	0	0	55.1	42	5	15	0	2	48	0	0	1	1	24	18	4	3	.571	0	2.93
86	WAU/MID	A	26	700	26	6	1	0	166.1	166	20	44	0	4	171	3	3	10	2	83	62	12	10	.545	0	3.35
87	CHT/SOU	AA	28	748	28	3	2	0	175.0	183	14	48	1	6	144	2	5	4	7	87	77	13	8	.619	0	3.96
88	CAL/PCL	AAA	26	139	0	0	0	21	33.2	33	2	6	1	0	47	1	1	5	1	19	12	4	4	.500	3	3.21
	SEA/AL		40	214	0	0	0	33	48.1	45	4	24	4	1	54	5	1	1	0	21	19	5	8	.385	15	3.54
89	SEA/AL		67	329	0	0	0	60	77.0	81	2	19	3	2	69	3	1	6	1	27	24	1	7	.125	33	2.81
90	SEA/AL		49	229	0	0	0	45	56.0	47	5	16	5	1	45	1	0	2	0	18	14	1	4	.200	30	2.25
91	JAC/SOU	AA	11	50	2	0	0	3	11.1	13	2	1	0	1	9	1	0	0	0	9	7	1	1	.500	0	5.56
	SEA/AL		34	138	0	0	0	23	34.1	25	2	10	0	0	33	3	0	1	0	14	14	3	3	.500	7	3.67
92	CAL/PCL	AAA	1	8	0	0	0	0	2.0	1	0	2	0	0	3	0	0	0	0	1	1	0	0	.000	0	3.67
	BEL/NWL	A-	2	12	1	0	0	0	3.0	1	0	0	0	1	4	0	0	0	0	0	0	0	0	.000	0	0.00
	SEA/AL		53	232	0	0	0	36	51.2	55	7	24	6	1	33	4	4	1	2	29	27	2	7	.222	13	4.70
93	OC/AMA	AAA	28	205	0	0	0	20	45.2	59	3	11	0	0	31	1	1	5	2	33	30	1	3	.250	5	5.91

Schooler, Michael Ralph "Mike" (continued)

YR	TM/LG	CL	G	TBF	GS	CG	SHO	GF	IP	H	HR	BB	IBB	HB	SO	SH	SF	WP	BK	R	ER	W	L	PCT	SV	ERA
	TEX/AL		17	111	0	0	0	0	24.1	30	3	10	1	0	16	2	0	1	0	17	15	3	0	1.000	0	5.55
6 YR TOTALS			260	1253	0	0	0	197	291.2	283	23	103	19	5	248	15	10	14	3	126	113	15	29	.341	98	3.49

Schourek, Peter Alan "Pete" — BL/TL — b.5/10/69   NYN87 3/56

YR	TM/LG	CL	G	TBF	GS	CG	SHO	GF	IP	H	HR	BB	IBB	HB	SO	SH	SF	WP	BK	R	ER	W	L	PCT	SV	ERA
87	KIN/APP	R+	12	336	12	2	0	0	78.1	70	7	34	0	2	57	4	1	2	1	37	32	4	5	.444	0	3.68
89	COL/SAL	A	27	593	19	5	1	3	136.0	120	11	66	2	2	131	7	4	5	3	66	43	5	9	.357	1	2.85
	SL/FSL	A+	2	16	1	0	0	1	4.0	3	0	2	0	1	4	0	0	0	0	1	1	0	0	.000	0	2.25
90	TID/INT	AAA	2	54	2	1	1	0	14.0	9	0	5	0	1	14	2	0	0	0	4	4	1	0	1.000	0	2.57
	SL/FSL	A+	5	143	5	2	2	0	37.0	29	1	8	0	2	28	0	1	0	0	4	4	4	1	.800	0	0.97
	JAC/TEX	AA	19	519	19	1	0	0	124.1	109	8	39	2	5	94	5	7	5	1	53	42	11	4	.733	0	3.04
91	TID/INT	AAA	4	100	4	0	0	0	25.0	18	3	10	0	1	17	1	0	0	0	7	7	1	1	.500	0	2.52
	NY/NL		35	385	8	1	1	7	86.1	82	7	43	4	2	67	5	4	1	0	49	41	5	4	.556	2	4.27
92	TID/INT	AAA	8	228	8	2	1	0	52.2	46	2	23	0	0	42	0	1	3	1	20	16	2	5	.286	0	2.73
	NY/NL		22	578	21	0	0	0	136.0	137	9	44	6	2	60	4	4	4	2	60	55	6	8	.429	0	3.64
93	NY/NL		41	586	18	0	0	6	128.1	168	13	45	7	3	72	3	8	1	2	90	85	5	12	.294	0	5.96
3 YR TOTALS			98	1549	47	1	1	13	350.2	387	29	132	17	7	199	12	16	6	4	199	181	16	24	.400	2	4.65

Schwarz, Jeffrey William "Jeff" — BR/TR — b.5/20/64   CHN82 25/597

YR	TM/LG	CL	G	TBF	GS	CG	SHO	GF	IP	H	HR	BB	IBB	HB	SO	SH	SF	WP	BK	R	ER	W	L	PCT	SV	ERA
82	CUB/GCL	R	11	0	9	0	0	0	43.0	47	3	37	0	2	24	0	0	8	4	39	29	2	5	.286	0	6.07
83	PIK/APP	R+	13	0	13	1	0	0	69.0	73	7	45	0	4	61	0	0	10	0	61	40	3	8	.273	0	5.22
84	QC/MID	A	27	606	24	2	0	1	130.0	106	11	111	2	11	123	11	3	17	0	88	73	4	14	.222	0	5.05
85	PEO/MID	A	27	605	19	6	2	3	143.1	99	4	79	2	9	140	3	7	9	0	60	51	7	9	.438	0	3.20
86	WIN/CAR	A+	4	57	2	0	0	1	12.0	10	3	12	0	1	11	0	0	3	2	10	10	0	1	.000	0	7.50
87	PEO/MID	A	20	418	13	2	1	1	92.1	79	7	59	1	8	91	6	6	9	1	59	47	5	7	.417	0	4.58
88	WIN/CAR	A+	24	689	24	2	2	0	151.1	133	10	110	1	6	153	3	8	12	4	93	76	7	12	.368	0	4.52
	PIT/EAS	AA	3	72	3	0	0	0	14.1	19	1	11	0	0	5	0	0	1	0	9	9	0	1	.000	0	5.65
89	HAG/EAS	AA	17	311	9	0	0	5	69.0	66	3	41	0	4	78	1	1	9	0	45	30	0	0	.000	1	3.91
	ROC/INT	AAA	9	62	0	0	0	4	12.1	5	0	16	0	1	12	2	0	2	0	9	8	0	2	.000	0	5.84
90	ROC/INT	AAA	5	60	1	0	0	0	12.2	10	1	19	0	0	4	0	3	4	0	10	10	0	0	.000	0	7.11
	STO/CAL	A+	19	265	8	0	0	3	56.1	59	1	36	0	9	59	2	0	5	1	36	30	3	3	.500	2	4.79
91	EP/TEX	AA	27	649	24	3	1	1	141.2	139	11	97	1	8	134	7	7	19	3	91	77	11	8	.579	0	4.89
92	BIR/SOU	AA	21	147	0	0	0	16	38.2	16	1	9	2	4	53	0	0	2	0	5	5	2	1	.667	6	1.16
	VAN/PCL	AAA	23	162	0	0	0	17	36.0	26	0	31	4	0	42	1	1	5	0	18	12	1	3	.250	3	3.00
93	NAS/AMA	AAA	7	43	0	0	0	2	11.0	1	0	12	1	0	8	0	2	3	1	3	3	0	0	.000	0	2.45
	CHI/AL		41	218	0	0	0	10	51.0	35	4	38	2	3	41	0	3	5	1	21	21	2	2	.500	0	3.71

Scott, Darryl Nelson — BR/TR — b.8/6/68   CAL 6/13/90

YR	TM/LG	CL	G	TBF	GS	CG	SHO	GF	IP	H	HR	BB	IBB	HB	SO	SH	SF	WP	BK	R	ER	W	L	PCT	SV	ERA
90	BOI/NWL	A-	27	221	0	0	0	11	53.2	41	3	20	1	2	57	0	1	5	0	11	8	2	1	.667	6	1.34
91	QC/MID	A	47	285	0	0	0	36	75.1	35	2	26	4	1	123	1	2	9	1	18	13	4	3	.571	19	1.55
92	MID/TEX	AA	27	126	0	0	0	22	29.2	20	0	14	1	2	35	2	2	4	0	9	6	1	1	.500	7	1.82
	EDM/PCL	AAA	31	164	0	0	0	17	36.1	41	1	21	0	0	48	0	3	4	2	21	21	0	2	.000	6	5.20
93	VAN/PCL	AAA	46	206	0	0	0	33	51.2	35	4	19	2	1	57	1	1	3	0	12	12	7	1	.875	15	2.09
	CAL/AL		16	90	0	0	0	2	20.0	19	1	11	1	1	13	0	2	0	0	13	13	1	2	.333	0	5.85

Scott, Timothy Dale "Tim" — BR/TR — b.11/16/66   LA84 2/51

YR	TM/LG	CL	G	TBF	GS	CG	SHO	GF	IP	H	HR	BB	IBB	HB	SO	SH	SF	WP	BK	R	ER	W	L	PCT	SV	ERA
84	GF/PIO	R+	13	0	13	3	2	0	78.0	90	4	38	1	2	44	0	0	5	2	58	38	5	4	.556	0	4.38
85	BAK/CAL	A+	12	0	10	1	0	2	63.2	84	4	28	0	1	31	0	0	2	4	46	41	3	4	.429	0	5.80
86	VB/FSL	A+	20	418	13	3	1	2	95.1	113	2	34	2	2	37	4	9	5	5	44	36	5	4	.556	0	3.40
87	SA/TEX	AA	2	33	2	0	0	0	5.1	14	2	2	0	1	6	0	0	1	0	10	10	0	1	.000	0	16.88
	BAK/CAL	A+	7	137	5	1	0	1	32.1	33	2	10	1	1	29	0	1	2	0	19	16	2	3	.400	0	4.45
88	BAK/CAL	A+	36	272	2	0	0	25	64.1	52	3	26	5	2	59	4	4	2	0	34	26	4	7	.364	7	3.64
89	SA/TEX	AA	48	308	0	0	0	28	68.0	71	3	36	5	0	64	5	3	1	4	30	28	4	2	.667	4	3.71
90	ALB/PCL	AAA	17	73	0	0	0	9	15.0	14	2	14	2	0	15	0	0	0	0	9	7	2	1	.667	3	4.20
	SA/TEX	AA	30	186	0	0	0	20	47.1	35	5	14	1	0	52	0	1	1	0	17	15	3	3	.500	7	2.85
91	SD/NL		2	5	0	0	0	0	1.0	2	0	0	0	0	1	0	0	0	0	2	1	0	0	.000	0	9.00
	LV/PCL	AAA	41	497	11	0	0	9	111.0	133	8	39	8	1	74	5	7	2	0	78	64	8	8	.500	0	5.19
92	LV/PCL	AAA	24	106	0	0	0	23	28.0	20	1	3	0	1	25	3	1	0	0	8	7	1	2	.333	15	2.25
	SD/NL		34	173	0	0	0	16	37.2	39	4	21	6	1	30	4	1	0	0	24	22	4	1	.800	0	5.26
93	SD/NL		24	169	0	0	0	2	37.2	38	1	15	0	4	30	2	2	1	0	13	10	2	0	1.000	0	2.39
	MON/NL		32	148	0	0	0	16	34.0	31	3	19	2	0	35	1	0	0	2	15	14	5	2	.714	1	3.71
	YEAR		56	317	0	0	0	18	71.2	69	4	34	2	4	65	3	2	1	2	28	24	7	2	.778	1	3.01
3 YR TOTALS			92	495	0	0	0	34	110.1	110	8	55	8	5	96	7	3	2	2	54	47	11	3	.786	1	3.83

Scudder, William Scott "Scott" — BR/TR — b.2/14/68   CIN86 1/17

YR	TM/LG	CL	G	TBF	GS	CG	SHO	GF	IP	H	HR	BB	IBB	HB	SO	SH	SF	WP	BK	R	ER	W	L	PCT	SV	ERA
86	BIL/PIO	R+	12	0	8	0	0	1	52.2	42	1	36	0	3	38	0	0	8	0	34	28	1	3	.250	0	4.78
87	CR/MID	A	26	660	26	0	0	0	153.2	129	16	76	0	7	128	8	2	15	3	86	70	7	12	.368	0	4.10
88	CR/MID	A	16	405	15	0	0	0	102.1	61	3	41	0	2	126	0	1	6	0	30	23	7	3	.700	0	2.02
	CHT/SOU	AA	11	290	11	0	0	0	70.0	53	4	30	0	1	52	1	3	2	0	24	23	5	2	.714	0	2.96
89	NAS/AMA	AAA	12	339	12	3	0	0	80.2	54	6	48	0	3	64	2	2	5	0	27	24	6	2	.750	0	2.68
	CIN/NL		23	451	17	0	0	3	100.1	91	14	61	11	1	66	7	2	2	0	54	50	4	9	.308	0	4.49
90	NAS/AMA	AAA	11	315	11	1	0	0	80.2	53	1	32	0	0	60	1	0	6	3	27	21	7	1	.875	0	2.34

(continued)

Scudder, William Scott "Scott" (continued)

YR	TM/LG	CL	G	TBF	GS	CG	SHO	GF	IP	H	HR	BB	IBB	HB	SO	SH	SF	WP	BK	R	ER	W	L	PCT	SV	ERA
	CIN/NL		21	316	10	0	0	3	71.2	74	12	30	3	3	42	3	1	2	2	41	39	5	5	.500	0	4.90
91	CIN/NL		27	443	14	0	0	4	101.1	91	6	56	4	6	51	8	3	7	0	52	49	6	9	.400	0	4.35
92	CS/PCL	AAA	1	14	1	0	0	0	3.0	4	0	2	0	0	1	0	0	1	0	3	2	0	1	.000	0	6.00
	CLE/AL		23	509	22	0	0	0	109.0	134	10	55	0	2	66	6	4	7	0	80	64	6	10	.375	0	5.28
93	CLE/AL		2	20	1	0	0	0	4.0	5	0	4	0	1	1	0	0	0	0	4	4	0	1	.000	0	9.00
	CHW/INT	AAA	23	597	22	2	0	0	136.0	148	21	52	1	7	64	0	7	5	0	92	76	7	7	.500	0	5.03
5 YR TOTALS			**96**	**1739**	**64**	**0**	**0**	**11**	**386.1**	**395**	**42**	**206**	**19**	**13**	**226**	**24**	**10**	**16**	**3**	**231**	**206**	**21**	**34**	**.382**	**1**	**4.80**

Seanez, Rudy Caballero — BR/TR — b.10/20/68   CLE86 4/83

YR	TM/LG	CL	G	TBF	GS	CG	SHO	GF	IP	H	HR	BB	IBB	HB	SO	SH	SF	WP	BK	R	ER	W	L	PCT	SV	ERA
86	BUR/APP	R+	13	318	12	1	1	1	76.0	59	5	32	0	3	56	1	3	6	0	37	27	5	2	.714	0	3.20
87	WAT/MID	A	10	159	10	0	0	0	34.2	35	6	23	0	1	23	0	2	2	2	29	26	0	4	.000	0	6.75
88	WAT/MID	A	22	505	22	1	1	0	113.1	98	10	68	0	6	93	2	2	14	2	69	59	6	6	.500	0	4.69
89	KIN/CAR	A+	25	539	25	1	0	0	113.0	94	0	111	1	5	149	1	1	13	1	66	52	8	10	.444	0	4.14
	CS/PCL	AAA	1	4	0	0	0	1	1.0	1	0	0	0	0	0	0	0	0	0	0	0	0	0	.000	0	0.00
	CLE/AL		5	20	0	0	0	2	5.0	1	0	4	1	0	7	0	2	1	1	2	2	0	0	.000	0	3.60
90	CAN/EAS	AA	15	68	0	0	0	11	16.2	9	0	12	0	1	27	0	0	0	0	4	4	1	0	1.000	5	2.16
	CLE/AL		24	127	0	0	0	12	27.1	22	2	25	1	1	24	0	1	5	0	17	17	2	1	.667	0	5.60
	CS/PCL	AAA	12	59	0	0	0	10	12.0	15	2	10	0	0	7	0	1	3	0	10	9	1	4	.200	0	6.75
91	CAN/EAS	AA	25	161	0	0	0	18	38.1	17	2	30	1	1	73	0	1	1	0	12	11	4	2	.667	7	2.58
	CS/PCL	AAA	16	86	0	0	0	11	17.1	17	2	22	0	1	19	0	1	5	0	14	14	0	0	.000	0	7.27
	CLE/AL		5	33	0	0	0	2	5.0	10	2	7	0	0	2	0	0	2	0	12	9	0	0	.000	0	16.20
93	CV/CAL	A+	5	46	1	0	0	1	8.1	9	0	11	0	0	12	1	0	1	0	9	9	0	2	.000	0	9.72
	CS/PCL	AAA	3	13	0	0	0	1	3.0	3	1	1	0	0	5	0	0	0	0	3	3	0	0	.000	0	9.00
	LV/PCL	AAA	14	90	0	0	0	8	19.2	24	2	11	0	0	14	0	1	7	1	15	14	0	1	.000	0	6.41
	SD/NL		3	20	0	0	0	3	3.1	8	1	2	0	0	1	1	0	0	0	6	5	0	0	.000	0	13.50
4 YR TOTALS			**37**	**200**	**0**	**0**	**0**	**17**	**40.2**	**41**	**5**	**38**	**2**	**1**	**39**	**1**	**3**	**8**	**1**	**37**	**33**	**2**	**1**	**.667**	**0**	**7.30**

Sele, Aaron Helmer — BR/TR — b.6/25/70   BOS91 1/23

YR	TM/LG	CL	G	TBF	GS	CG	SHO	GF	IP	H	HR	BB	IBB	HB	SO	SH	SF	WP	BK	R	ER	W	L	PCT	SV	ERA
91	WH/FSL	A+	13	304	11	4	0	1	69.0	65	2	32	2	6	51	2	0	5	6	42	38	3	6	.333	1	4.96
92	LYN/CAR	A+	20	535	19	2	1	0	127.0	104	5	46	0	14	112	3	2	5	3	51	41	13	5	.722	0	2.91
	NB/EAS	AA	7	162	6	1	0	0	33.0	43	2	15	0	5	29	1	0	4	1	29	23	2	1	.667	0	6.27
93	PAW/INT	AAA	14	373	14	2	1	0	94.1	74	8	23	0	5	87	2	0	1	0	30	23	8	2	.800	0	2.19
	BOS/AL		18	484	18	0	0	0	111.2	100	5	48	2	7	93	2	5	5	0	42	34	7	2	.778	0	2.74

Seminara, Frank Peter — BR/TR — b.5/16/67   NYA88 9/313

YR	TM/LG	CL	G	TBF	GS	CG	SHO	GF	IP	H	HR	BB	IBB	HB	SO	SH	SF	WP	BK	R	ER	W	L	PCT	SV	ERA
88	ONE/NYP	A-	16	350	13	0	0	2	78.1	86	2	32	2	5	60	3	2	11	6	49	38	4	7	.364	1	4.37
89	PW/CAR	A+	21	158	0	0	0	12	36.2	26	0	22	3	5	23	1	3	5	4	23	15	2	4	.333	2	3.68
	ONE/NYP	A-	11	280	10	3	1	0	70.0	51	0	18	0	3	70	3	0	1	3	25	16	7	2	.778	0	2.06
90	PW/CAR	A+	25	692	25	4	2	0	170.1	136	5	52	1	10	132	1	2	12	2	51	36	16	8	.667	0	1.90
91	WIC/TEX	AA	27	761	27	6	1	0	176.0	173	10	68	0	9	107	9	5	12	3	86	66	15	10	.600	0	3.38
92	LV/PCL	AAA	13	357	13	1	1	0	80.2	92	2	33	3	3	48	2	4	2	5	46	37	6	4	.600	0	4.13
	SD/NL		19	435	18	0	0	0	100.1	98	5	46	3	3	61	3	2	1	1	46	41	9	4	.692	0	3.68
93	LV/PCL	AAA	21	518	19	0	0	1	114.1	136	15	52	1	4	99	6	4	2	2	79	69	8	5	.615	1	5.43
	SD/NL		18	212	7	0	0	0	46.1	53	5	21	3	3	22	6	2	1	0	30	23	3	3	.500	0	4.47
2 YR TOTALS			**37**	**647**	**25**	**0**	**0**	**0**	**146.2**	**151**	**10**	**67**	**6**	**6**	**83**	**9**	**4**	**2**	**1**	**76**	**64**	**12**	**7**	**.632**	**0**	**3.93**

Service, Scott David — BR/TR — b.2/26/67   PHI 8/24/85

YR	TM/LG	CL	G	TBF	GS	CG	SHO	GF	IP	H	HR	BB	IBB	HB	SO	SH	SF	WP	BK	R	ER	W	L	PCT	SV	ERA
86	SPA/SAL	A	14	281	9	1	0	1	58.2	68	3	34	0	7	49	2	1	6	1	44	38	1	6	.143	0	5.83
	UTI/NYP	A-	10	299	10	2	0	0	70.2	65	1	18	0	5	43	3	2	5	1	30	21	5	4	.556	0	2.67
	CLE/FSL	A+	4	105	4	1	1	0	25.1	20	2	15	0	0	19	1	0	1	1	10	9	1	2	.333	0	3.20
87	REA/EAS	AA	5	95	4	0	0	0	19.2	22	5	16	0	1	12	0	0	1	0	19	17	0	0	.000	0	7.78
	CLE/FSL	A+	21	557	21	5	2	0	137.2	127	8	32	0	4	73	2	3	1	1	46	38	13	4	.765	0	2.48
88	REA/EAS	AA	10	240	9	1	1	0	56.2	52	4	22	2	0	39	1	1	1	6	25	18	3	4	.429	0	2.86
	MAI/INT	AAA	19	470	18	1	1	0	110.1	109	10	31	3	2	87	6	6	8	8	51	45	8	8	.500	0	3.67
	PHI/NL		5	23	1	0	0	1	5.1	7	0	1	0	1	6	0	0	0	0	1	1	0	0	.000	0	1.69
89	REA/EAS	AA	23	349	10	1	1	9	85.2	71	8	23	0	8	82	1	3	3	0	36	31	6	6	.500	1	3.26
	SCR/INT	AAA	23	148	0	0	0	15	33.1	27	2	23	6	2	23	4	0	0	0	8	8	3	1	.750	6	2.16
90	SCR/INT	AAA	45	428	9	0	0	11	96.1	96	10	44	1	5	94	2	2	4	0	56	51	5	4	.556	2	4.76
91	IND/AMA	AAA	18	477	17	3	1	1	121.1	83	7	39	0	6	91	2	3	5	1	42	40	6	7	.462	0	2.97
92	IND/AMA	AAA	13	95	0	0	0	7	24.1	12	0	9	0	3	25	2	0	1	0	3	2	2	0	1.000	0	0.74
	MON/NL		5	41	0	0	0	0	7.0	15	1	5	0	0	11	0	0	0	0	11	11	0	0	.000	0	14.14
	NAS/AMA	AAA	39	299	2	0	0	15	70.2	54	2	35	3	2	87	4	0	2	0	22	18	6	2	.750	4	2.29
93	IND/AMA	AAA	21	133	0	0	0	13	30.1	25	5	17	3	0	28	3	1	1	0	16	15	4	2	.667	2	4.45
	COL/NL		3	24	0	0	0	0	4.2	8	1	1	0	1	3	0	0	1	0	5	5	0	0	.000	0	9.64
	CIN/NL		26	173	0	0	0	7	41.1	36	5	15	4	1	40	2	2	2	0	19	17	2	2	.500	0	3.70
	YEAR		29	197	0	0	0	7	46.0	44	6	16	4	2	43	2	2	2	0	24	22	2	2	.500	0	4.30
3 YR TOTALS			**39**	**261**	**0**	**0**	**0**	**8**	**58.1**	**66**	**7**	**22**	**4**	**3**	**60**	**2**	**4**	**0**	**0**	**36**	**34**	**2**	**2**	**.500**	**2**	**5.25**

Shaw, Jeffrey Lee "Jeff" — BR/TR — b.7/7/66   CLE86* 1/1

YR	TM/LG	CL	G	TBF	GS	CG	SHO	GF	IP	H	HR	BB	IBB	HB	SO	SH	SF	WP	BK	R	ER	W	L	PCT	SV	ERA
86	BAT/NYP	A-	14	367	12	3	1	1	88.2	79	5	35	0	5	71	3	4	10	0	32	24	8	4	.667	0	2.44
87	WAT/MID	A	28	788	28	6	4	0	184.1	192	15	56	0	6	117	4	6	8	5	89	72	11	11	.500	0	3.52

Shaw, Jeffrey Lee "Jeff" (continued)

YR	TM/LG	CL	G	TBF	GS	CG	SHO	GF	IP	H	HR	BB	IBB	HB	SO	SH	SF	WP	BK	R	ER	W	L	PCT	SV	ERA
88	WIL/EAS	AA	27	718	27	6	1	0	163.2	173	11	75	1	10	61	10	10	12	4	94	66	5	19	.208	0	3.63
89	CAN/EAS	AA	30	661	22	6	3	3	154.1	134	9	67	3	14	95	5	7	7	0	84	62	7	10	.412	0	3.62
90	CS/PCL	AAA	17	438	16	4	0	0	98.2	98	7	52	0	3	55	4	5	5	0	54	47	10	3	.769	0	4.29
	CLE/AL		12	229	9	0	0	0	48.2	73	11	20	0	0	25	1	3	3	0	38	36	3	4	.429	0	6.66
91	CS/PCL	AAA	12	329	12	1	0	0	75.2	77	9	25	0	4	55	0	2	1	1	47	39	6	3	.667	0	4.64
	CLE/AL		29	311	1	0	0	9	72.1	72	6	27	5	4	31	1	4	6	0	34	27	0	5	.000	1	3.36
92	CLE/AL		2	33	1	0	0	1	7.2	7	2	4	0	0	3	2	0	0	0	7	7	0	1	.000	0	8.22
	CS/PCL	AAA	25	673	24	1	0	0	155.0	174	11	45	2	10	84	0	7	5	0	88	82	10	5	.667	0	4.76
93	OTT/INT	AAA	2	18	1	0	0	0	4.0	5	0	2	0	1	0	0	0	0	0	0	0	0	0	.000	0	0.00
	MON/NL		55	404	8	0	0	13	95.2	91	12	32	2	7	50	5	2	2	0	47	44	2	7	.222	0	4.14
4 YR TOTALS			**98**	**977**	**19**	**0**	**0**	**23**	**224.1**	**243**	**31**	**83**	**7**	**11**	**109**	**9**	**9**	**11**	**0**	**126**	**114**	**5**	**17**	**.227**	**1**	**4.57**

Shepherd, Keith Wayne — BR/TR — b.1/21/68   PIT86 11/264

YR	TM/LG	CL	G	TBF	GS	CG	SHO	GF	IP	H	HR	BB	IBB	HB	SO	SH	SF	WP	BK	R	ER	W	L	PCT	SV	ERA
86	PIR/GCL	R	8	78	2	0	0	4	16.1	16	0	15	0	1	12	2	3	3	1	17	11	0	4	.000	0	6.06
87	WAT/NYP	A-	17	318	13	1	1	0	70.2	66	0	42	0	5	57	6	2	4	1	40	33	5	2	.714	0	4.20
88	AUG/SAL	A	16	378	16	1	1	0	85.0	71	3	50	0	8	49	1	1	10	1	45	38	7	3	.700	0	4.02
	SAL/CAR	A+	8	144	5	0	0	0	29.1	26	2	29	0	1	15	1	0	3	1	24	19	2	3	.400	0	5.83
89	BC/FSL	A+	11	216	10	0	0	0	47.1	45	3	32	0	2	20	2	2	3	0	33	26	1	7	.125	0	4.94
	KIN/CAR	A+	8	124	2	0	0	3	28.1	25	2	15	0	0	23	1	2	2	0	11	9	1	2	.333	0	2.86
90	REN/CAL	A+	5	120	5	0	0	0	25.0	22	1	18	0	2	16	3	1	6	1	25	15	1	4	.200	0	5.40
	WAT/NYP	A-	24	235	0	0	0	19	54.1	41	1	29	1	4	55	4	0	9	1	22	15	3	3	.500	3	2.48
91	SB/MID	A	31	140	0	0	0	21	35.1	17	0	19	2	1	38	3	0	5	1	4	2	1	2	.333	10	0.51
	SAR/FSL	A+	18	166	0	0	0	8	39.2	33	0	20	0	2	24	3	1	1	0	16	12	1	1	.500	2	2.72
92	BIR/SOU	AA	40	282	0	0	0	30	71.1	50	1	20	2	1	64	4	1	7	1	19	17	3	3	.500	7	2.14
	REA/EAS	AA	4	87	3	0	0	1	22.2	17	1	4	1	1	9	2	0	0	0	7	7	0	1	.000	0	2.78
	PHI/NL		12	91	0	0	0	6	22.0	19	0	6	1	0	10	4	3	1	0	10	8	1	1	.500	2	3.27
93	CS/PCL	AAA	37	339	1	0	0	20	67.2	90	2	44	2	4	57	2	4	15	0	61	51	3	6	.333	8	6.78
	COL/NL		14	85	1	0	0	3	19.1	26	4	10	1	1	17	1	1	1	0	16	15	1	3	.250	1	6.98
2 YR TOTALS			**26**	**176**	**1**	**0**	**0**	**9**	**41.1**	**45**	**4**	**10**	**1**	**1**	**17**	**5**	**4**	**2**	**0**	**26**	**23**	**2**	**4**	**.333**	**3**	**5.01**

Shinall, Zakary Sebastien "Zak" — BR/TR — b.10/14/68   LA87 29/742

YR	TM/LG	CL	G	TBF	GS	CG	SHO	GF	IP	H	HR	BB	IBB	HB	SO	SH	SF	WP	BK	R	ER	W	L	PCT	SV	ERA
87	GF/PIO	R+	1	15	0	0	0	0	1.1	4	1	5	0	1	0	0	0	0	1	8	7	0	0	.000	0	47.25
	DOD/GCL	R	8	131	6	0	0	1	30.1	27	0	15	1	0	29	2	0	4	0	17	17	1	2	.333	0	5.04
88	BAK/CAL	A+	28	526	19	1	1	3	113.0	90	1	104	0	4	63	3	6	20	3	65	53	7	8	.467	0	4.22
89	VB/FSL	A+	47	352	4	1	0	23	86.0	71	4	29	7	2	69	5	3	4	2	32	24	5	7	.417	7	2.51
90	SA/TEX	AA	20	390	15	0	0	3	91.1	93	2	41	1	1	43	5	0	6	1	44	36	6	3	.667	0	3.55
91	SA/TEX	AA	25	234	5	0	0	19	54.2	53	4	21	2	0	29	3	1	1	3	31	18	2	4	.333	9	2.96
	ALB/PCL	AAA	29	176	0	0	0	11	41.0	48	3	10	2	2	22	2	0	3	0	15	14	2	0	1.000	1	3.07
92	ALB/PCL	AAA	64	363	0	0	0	32	82.0	91	7	37	11	2	46	7	2	4	0	38	30	13	5	.722	6	3.29
93	CHW/INT	AAA	1	6	0	0	0	0	0.2	3	0	1	0	0	0	0	0	0	0	4	4	0	0	.000	0	54.00
	CAL/PCL	AAA	33	211	0	0	0	19	46.2	55	6	18	3	4	25	2	1	4	0	29	26	2	1	.667	5	5.01
	SEA/AL		1	14	0	0	0	0	2.2	4	1	2	0	0	0	0	0	0	0	1	1	0	0	.000	0	3.38

Shouse, Brian Douglas — BL/TL — b.9/26/68   PIT90 13/349

YR	TM/LG	CL	G	TBF	GS	CG	SHO	GF	IP	H	HR	BB	IBB	HB	SO	SH	SF	WP	BK	R	ER	W	L	PCT	SV	ERA
90	WEL/NYP	A-	17	177	1	0	0	7	39.2	50	2	7	0	3	39	3	2	1	2	27	23	4	3	.571	2	5.22
91	AUG/SAL	A	26	124	0	0	0	25	31.0	22	1	9	1	3	32	1	1	5	0	13	11	2	3	.400	8	3.19
	SAL/CAR	A+	17	147	0	0	0	9	33.2	35	2	15	2	0	25	2	0	1	0	12	11	2	1	.667	3	2.94
92	CAR/SOU	AA	59	323	0	0	0	33	77.1	71	3	28	4	2	79	8	2	4	1	31	21	5	6	.455	4	2.44
93	BUF/AMA	AAA	48	218	0	0	0	14	51.2	54	7	17	2	2	45	0	3	1	0	24	22	1	0	1.000	2	3.83
	PIT/NL		6	22	0	0	0	1	4.0	7	1	2	0	0	3	0	1	0	0	4	4	0	0	.000	0	9.00

Slocumb, Heathcliff — BR/TR — b.6/7/66   NYN 7/10/84

YR	TM/LG	CL	G	TBF	GS	CG	SHO	GF	IP	H	HR	BB	IBB	HB	SO	SH	SF	WP	BK	R	ER	W	L	PCT	SV	ERA
84	KIN/APP	R+	1	3	0	0	0	0	0.1	0	0	0	0	0	1	0	0	0	0	1	0	0	0	.000	0	0.00
	LF/NYP	A-	4	51	1	0	0	0	9.0	8	0	16	0	1	10	0	0	4	0	11	11	0	0	.000	0	11.00
85	KIN/APP	R+	11	232	9	0	0	0	52.1	47	0	31	0	1	29	2	1	15	0	32	22	3	2	.600	0	3.78
86	LF/NYP	A-	25	186	0	0	0	13	43.2	24	3	36	1	0	41	1	0	8	0	17	8	3	1	.750	1	1.65
87	WIN/CAR	A+	9	135	4	0	0	1	27.1	26	1	26	0	0	27	2	3	0	1	25	19	1	2	.333	0	6.26
	PEO/MID	A	16	455	16	3	1	0	103.2	97	2	42	3	3	81	0	2	15	0	44	30	10	4	.714	0	2.60
88	WIN/CAR	A+	25	567	19	2	1	3	119.2	122	5	90	1	3	78	2	5	19	2	75	66	6	6	.500	1	4.96
89	PEO/MID	A	49	233	0	0	0	43	55.2	31	0	33	4	1	52	5	3	6	0	16	11	5	3	.625	22	1.78
90	CHA/SOU	AA	43	232	0	0	0	37	50.1	50	0	32	5	3	37	6	2	4	0	20	12	3	1	.750	12	2.15
	IOW/AMA	AAA	20	115	0	0	0	10	27.0	16	1	18	2	2	21	2	1	3	0	10	6	2	1	.600	1	2.00
91	IOW/AMA	AAA	12	59	0	0	0	6	13.1	10	0	9	1	0	9	1	0	1	0	8	6	1	0	1.000	0	4.05
	CHI/NL		52	274	0	0	0	21	62.2	53	3	30	6	5	34	6	6	9	0	29	24	2	1	.667	1	3.45
92	IOW/AMA	AAA	36	177	1	0	0	23	41.2	36	3	16	1	0	47	1	1	4	0	13	12	1	3	.250	7	2.59
	CHI/NL		30	174	0	0	0	11	36.0	52	3	21	3	1	27	2	2	2	0	27	26	0	3	.000	0	6.50
93	IOW/AMA	AAA	10	48	0	0	0	10	12.0	7	0	8	0	0	10	1	0	0	0	2	2	1	0	1.000	0	1.50
	CHW/INT	AAA	23	129	0	0	0	9	30.1	25	2	11	0	0	25	4	0	2	0	14	12	3	2	.600	0	3.56
	CHI/NL		10	42	0	0	0	4	10.2	7	0	4	0	0	9	1	0	0	0	5	4	1	0	1.000	0	3.38
	CLE/AL		20	122	0	0	0	5	27.1	28	3	16	2	0	18	1	1	1	0	14	13	1	0	.750	0	4.28
	YEAR		30	164	0	0	0	9	38.0	35	3	20	2	0	22	1	1	3	0	19	17	4	1	.800	0	4.03
3 YR TOTALS			**112**	**612**	**0**	**0**	**0**	**41**	**136.2**	**140**	**9**	**71**	**11**	**4**	**83**	**9**	**11**	**10**	**0**	**75**	**67**	**6**	**5**	**.545**	**2**	**4.41**

Part 5: Career Records — Pitcher Register   493

Slusarski, Joseph Andrew "Joe" — BR/TR — b.12/19/66 — OAK88 3/46

YR	TM/LG	CL	G	TBF	GS	CG	SHO	GF	IP	H	HR	BB	IBB	HB	SO	SH	SF	WP	BK	R	ER	W	L	PCT	SV	ERA
89	MOD/CAL	A+	27	753	27	4	1	0	184.0	155	15	50	0	8	160	5	3	13	1	78	65	13	10	.565	0	3.18
90	HUN/SOU	AA	17	471	17	2	0	0	108.2	114	9	35	0	3	75	2	9	5	0	65	54	6	8	.429	0	4.47
	TAC/PCL	AAA	9	241	9	0	0	0	55.2	54	3	22	0	2	37	1	3	1	1	24	21	4	2	.667	0	3.40
91	TAC/PCL	AAA	7	182	7	0	0	0	46.1	42	4	10	0	0	25	0	0	0	2	20	14	4	2	.667	0	2.72
	OAK/AL		20	486	19	1	0	0	109.1	121	14	52	1	4	60	3	3	4	0	69	64	5	7	.417	0	5.27
92	TAC/PCL	AAA	11	249	10	0	0	0	57.1	67	6	18	1	1	26	0	5	1	0	30	24	2	4	.333	0	3.77
	OAK/AL		15	338	14	0	0	1	76.0	85	15	27	0	6	38	1	5	0	1	52	46	5	5	.500	0	5.45
93	OAK/AL		2	43	1	0	0	0	8.2	9	1	11	3	0	1	2	0	0	0	5	5	0	0	.000	0	5.19
	TAC/PCL	AAA	24	501	21	1	1	0	113.1	133	6	40	1	1	61	3	7	2	0	67	60	7	5	.583	0	4.76
3 YR TOTALS			**37**	**867**	**34**	**1**	**0**	**1**	**194.0**	**215**	**30**	**90**	**4**	**10**	**99**	**3**	**8**	**4**	**1**	**126**	**115**	**10**	**12**	**.455**	**0**	**5.34**

Smiley, John Patrick — BL/TL — b.3/17/65 — PIT83 12/300

YR	TM/LG	CL	G	TBF	GS	CG	SHO	GF	IP	H	HR	BB	IBB	HB	SO	SH	SF	WP	BK	R	ER	W	L	PCT	SV	ERA
84	MAC/SAL	A	21	553	19	2	0	2	130.0	119	12	41	1	2	73	4	4	4	1	73	57	5	11	.313	1	3.95
85	PW/CAR	A+	10	259	10	0	0	0	56.0	64	3	27	0	4	45	4	3	3	2	36	32	2	2	.500	0	5.14
	MAC/SAL	A	16	384	16	1	1	0	88.2	84	12	37	0	2	70	5	2	4	1	55	46	3	8	.273	0	4.67
86	PW/CAR	A+	48	371	2	0	0	36	90.0	64	2	40	1	1	93	5	1	9	1	35	31	2	4	.333	14	3.10
	PIT/NL		12	42	0	0	0	2	11.2	4	2	4	0	0	9	0	0	0	0	6	5	1	0	1.000	0	3.86
87	PIT/NL		63	336	0	0	0	19	75.0	69	7	50	4	0	58	0	1	3	0	49	48	5	5	.500	4	5.76
88	PIT/NL		34	835	32	5	1	0	205.0	185	15	46	4	3	129	11	8	4	1	81	74	13	11	.542	0	3.25
89	PIT/NL		28	835	28	8	1	0	205.1	174	22	49	5	4	123	5	7	5	2	78	64	12	8	.600	0	2.81
90	PIT/NL		26	632	25	2	0	0	149.1	161	15	36	1	2	86	5	4	2	2	83	77	9	10	.474	0	4.64
91	PIT/NL		33	836	32	2	1	0	207.2	194	17	44	0	3	129	5	4	9	1	78	71	*20	8	*.714	0	3.08
92	MIN/AL		34	970	34	5	2	0	241.0	205	17	65	0	6	163	4	9	4	0	93	86	16	9	.640	0	3.21
93	CIN/NL		18	455	18	2	0	0	105.2	117	15	31	0	2	60	10	3	2	1	69	66	3	9	.250	0	5.62
8 YR TOTALS			**248**	**4941**	**169**	**24**	**5**	**21**	**1200.2**	**1109**	**110**	**325**	**18**	**20**	**757**	**46**	**38**	**27**	**13**	**537**	**491**	**79**	**60**	**.568**	**4**	**3.68**

Smith, Bryn Nelson — BR/TR — b.8/11/55 — BAL 12/18/74

YR	TM/LG	CL	G	TBF	GS	CG	SHO	GF	IP	H	HR	BB	IBB	HB	SO	SH	SF	WP	BK	R	ER	W	L	PCT	SV	ERA
81	MON/NL		7	53	0	0	0	1	13.0	14	1	3	0	0	9	0	0	2	0	4	4	1	0	1.000	0	2.77
82	MON/NL		47	335	1	0	0	16	79.1	81	5	23	5	0	50	1	4	5	1	43	37	2	4	.333	3	4.20
83	MON/NL		49	636	12	5	3	17	155.1	142	13	43	6	5	101	14	2	5	3	51	43	6	11	.353	3	2.49
84	MON/NL		28	751	28	4	2	0	179.0	178	15	51	7	3	101	7	2	2	2	72	66	12	13	.480	0	3.32
85	MON/NL		32	890	32	4	2	0	222.1	193	12	41	3	1	127	13	4	1	0	85	72	18	5	.783	0	2.91
86	MON/NL		30	807	30	1	0	0	187.1	182	15	63	6	6	105	10	3	4	2	101	82	10	8	.556	0	3.94
87	WPB/FSL	A+	4	76	4	0	0	0	17.2	19	2	1	0	3	16	1	0	1	0	10	8	0	2	.000	0	4.08
	MON/NL		26	643	26	2	0	0	150.1	164	16	31	4	2	94	7	5	1	1	81	73	10	9	.526	0	4.37
88	MON/NL		32	791	32	1	0	0	198.0	179	15	32	2	10	122	7	6	2	5	79	66	12	10	.545	0	3.00
89	MON/NL		33	864	32	3	1	0	215.2	177	16	54	4	4	129	7	5	3	1	76	68	10	11	.476	0	2.84
90	STL/NL		26	605	25	0	0	0	141.1	160	11	30	1	4	78	7	5	2	0	81	67	9	8	.529	0	4.27
91	STL/NL		31	818	31	3	0	0	198.2	188	16	45	3	4	94	10	7	3	3	95	85	12	9	.571	0	3.85
92	LOU/AMA	AAA	2	39	2	0	0	0	10.0	6	0	2	0	2	2	1	0	0	0	2	2	1	0	1.000	0	1.80
	STL/NL		13	91	1	0	0	3	21.1	20	3	5	1	3	9	2	0	0	0	11	11	4	2	.667	0	4.64
93	COL/NL		11	150	5	0	0	2	29.2	47	2	11	1	3	9	2	4	1	0	29	28	2	4	.333	0	8.49
13 YR TOTALS			**365**	**7434**	**255**	**23**	**8**	**39**	**1791.1**	**1725**	**140**	**432**	**43**	**48**	**1028**	**87**	**47**	**33**	**16**	**808**	**702**	**108**	**94**	**.535**	**6**	**3.53**

Smith, Lee Arthur — BR/TR — b.12/4/57 — CHN75 2/28

YR	TM/LG	CL	G	TBF	GS	CG	SHO	GF	IP	H	HR	BB	IBB	HB	SO	SH	SF	WP	BK	R	ER	W	L	PCT	SV	ERA
80	CHI/NL		18	97	0	0	0	6	21.2	21	0	14	5	0	17	1	1	0	0	9	7	2	0	1.000	0	2.91
81	CHI/NL		40	280	1	0	0	12	66.2	57	2	31	8	1	50	8	2	7	1	31	26	3	6	.333	1	3.51
82	CHI/NL		72	480	5	0	0	38	117.0	105	5	37	5	3	99	6	5	6	1	38	35	2	5	.286	17	2.69
83	CHI/NL		66	413	0	0	0	56	103.1	70	5	41	14	1	91	9	2	5	2	23	19	4	10	.286	*29	1.65
84	CHI/NL		69	428	0	0	0	59	101.0	98	6	35	7	0	86	4	5	6	0	42	41	9	7	.563	33	3.65
85	CHI/NL		65	397	0	0	0	57	97.2	87	9	32	6	1	112	3	1	4	0	35	33	7	4	.636	33	3.04
86	CHI/NL		66	372	0	0	0	59	90.1	69	7	42	11	0	93	6	3	2	0	32	31	9	9	.500	31	3.09
87	CHI/NL		62	360	0	0	0	55	83.2	84	4	32	5	0	96	4	0	2	0	30	29	4	10	.286	36	3.12
88	BOS/AL		64	363	0	0	0	57	83.2	72	7	37	6	1	96	3	2	2	0	34	26	4	5	.444	29	2.80
89	BOS/AL		64	290	0	0	0	50	70.2	53	6	33	6	0	96	2	1	0	0	30	28	6	1	.857	25	3.57
90	BOS/AL		11	64	0	0	0	8	14.1	13	0	9	2	0	17	0	0	0	0	4	3	2	1	.667	4	1.88
	STL/NL		53	280	0	0	0	45	68.2	58	3	20	5	0	70	2	3	3	0	20	16	3	4	.429	27	2.10
	YEAR		64	344	0	0	0	53	83.0	71	3	29	7	0	87	2	3	3	0	24	19	5	5	.500	31	2.06
91	STL/NL		67	300	0	0	0	61	73.0	70	5	13	5	0	67	1	1	1	0	19	19	6	3	.667	*47	2.34
92	STL/NL		70	310	0	0	0	55	75.0	62	4	26	4	0	60	2	1	2	0	28	26	4	9	.308	*43	3.12
93	STL/NL		55	206	0	0	0	48	50.0	49	11	9	1	0	49	2	2	1	0	25	25	2	4	.333	43	4.50
	NY/AL		8	33	0	0	0	8	8.0	4	0	5	1	0	11	0	0	0	0	0	0	0	0	.000	3	0.00
	YEAR		63	239	0	0	0	56	58.0	53	11	14	2	0	60	2	2	1	0	25	25	2	4	.333	46	3.88
14 YR TOTALS			**850**	**4673**	**6**	**0**	**0**	**674**	**1124.2**	**972**	**74**	**416**	**91**	**7**	**1110**	**55**	**31**	**43**	**4**	**400**	**364**	**67**	**78**	**.462**	**401**	**2.91**

Smith, Peter John "Pete" — BR/TR — b.2/27/66 — PHI84 1/21

YR	TM/LG	CL	G	TBF	GS	CG	SHO	GF	IP	H	HR	BB	IBB	HB	SO	SH	SF	WP	BK	R	ER	W	L	PCT	SV	ERA
84	PHI/GCL	R	8	155	8	0	0	0	37.0	28	0	16	0	0	35	3	1	2	0	11	6	1	2	.333	0	1.46
85	CLE/FSL	A+	26	663	25	4	1	0	153.0	135	2	80	1	2	86	1	7	3	1	68	56	12	10	.545	0	3.29
86	GRE/SOU	AA	24	499	19	0	1	1	104.2	117	11	78	0	4	64	7	4	2	1	88	68	1	8	.111	0	5.85
87	GRE/SOU	AA	29	744	25	5	1	2	177.1	162	10	67	0	3	119	4	4	11	2	76	66	9	9	.500	1	3.35
	ATL/NL		6	143	6	0	0	0	31.2	39	3	14	0	0	11	0	2	3	1	21	17	1	2	.333	0	4.83
88	ATL/NL		32	837	32	5	3	0	195.1	183	15	88	3	1	124	12	4	5	7	89	80	7	15	.318	0	3.69

Smith, Peter John "Pete" (continued)

YR	TM/LG	CL	G	TBF	GS	CG	SHO	GF	IP	H	HR	BB	IBB	HB	SO	SH	SF	WP	BK	R	ER	W	L	PCT	SV	ERA
89	ATL/NL		28	613	27	1	0	0	142.0	144	13	57	2	0	115	4	5	3	7	83	75	5	14	.263	0	4.75
90	ATL/NL		13	327	13	3	0	0	77.0	77	11	24	2	0	56	4	3	2	1	45	41	5	6	.455	0	4.79
	GRE/SOU	AA	2	12	2	0	0	0	3.1	1	0	0	0	0	2	0	0	0	0	0	0	0	0	.000	0	0.00
91	MAC/SAL	A	3	45	3	0	0	0	9.2	15	1	2	0	0	14	0	0	2	0	11	9	0	0	.000	0	8.38
	RIC/INT	AAA	10	239	10	1	0	0	51.0	66	10	24	0	0	41	1	5	2	1	44	41	3	3	.500	0	7.24
	ATL/NL		14	211	10	0	0	2	48.0	48	5	22	3	0	29	2	4	1	4	33	27	1	3	.250	0	5.06
92	RIC/INT	AAA	15	415	15	4	1	0	109.1	75	6	24	0	4	93	2	1	1	0	27	26	7	4	.636	0	2.14
	ATL/NL		12	323	11	2	1	0	79.0	63	3	28	2	0	43	4	1	2	1	19	18	7	0	1.000	0	2.05
93	ATL/NL		20	390	14	0	0	2	90.2	92	15	36	3	2	53	6	5	1	1	45	44	4	8	.333	0	4.37
7 YR TOTALS			**125**	**2844**	**113**	**11**	**4**	**4**	**663.2**	**646**	**65**	**269**	**15**	**3**	**431**	**32**	**24**	**17**	**22**	**335**	**302**	**30**	**48**	**.385**	**0**	**4.10**

Smith, Zane William — BL/TL — b.12/28/60   ATL82 3/63

YR	TM/LG	CL	G	TBF	GS	CG	SHO	GF	IP	H	HR	BB	IBB	HB	SO	SH	SF	WP	BK	R	ER	W	L	PCT	SV	ERA
84	GRE/SOU	AA	9	239	9	3	1	0	60.0	47	0	23	0	1	35	2	1	1	0	13	11	7	0	1.000	0	1.65
	RIC/INT	AAA	19	534	19	3	0	0	123.2	113	11	65	1	3	68	7	3	7	1	62	57	7	4	.636	0	4.15
	ATL/NL		3	87	3	0	0	0	20.0	16	1	13	2	0	16	1	0	0	0	7	5	1	0	1.000	0	2.25
85	ATL/NL		42	631	18	2	2	3	147.0	135	4	80	5	3	85	16	1	2	0	70	62	9	10	.474	1	3.80
86	ATL/NL		38	889	32	3	1	2	204.2	209	4	105	6	5	139	13	6	8	0	109	92	8	16	.333	1	4.05
87	ATL/NL		36	1035	36	9	3	0	242.0	245	19	91	6	5	130	12	5	5	1	130	110	15	10	.600	0	4.09
88	ATL/NL		23	609	22	3	0	0	140.1	159	8	44	4	3	59	15	2	2	2	72	67	5	10	.333	0	4.30
89	ATL/NL		17	432	17	0	0	0	99.0	102	5	33	3	2	58	10	5	3	0	65	49	1	12	.077	0	4.45
	MON/NL		31	202	0	0	0	10	48.0	39	2	19	4	1	35	5	0	1	0	11	8	0	1	.000	2	1.50
	YEAR		48	634	17	0	0	10	147.0	141	7	52	7	3	93	15	5	4	0	76	57	1	13	.071	2	3.49
90	MON/NL		22	578	21	1	0	0	139.1	141	11	41	3	3	80	2	2	1	0	57	50	6	7	.462	0	3.23
	PIT/NL		11	282	10	3	2	1	76.0	55	4	9	1	0	50	1	1	1	0	20	11	6	2	.750	0	1.30
	YEAR		33	860	31	4	2	1	215.1	196	15	50	4	3	130	3	3	2	0	77	61	12	9	.571	0	2.55
91	PIT/NL		35	916	35	6	3	0	228.0	234	15	29	3	2	120	7	5	1	0	95	81	16	10	.615	0	3.20
92	PIT/NL		23	566	22	4	3	0	141.0	138	8	19	3	2	56	12	4	0	0	56	48	8	8	.500	0	3.06
93	CAR/SOU	AA	4	85	4	1	0	0	20.2	20	1	5	0	1	13	0	2	1	0	10	7	1	2	.333	0	3.05
	PIT/NL		14	353	14	1	0	0	83.0	97	5	22	3	0	32	6	0	2	0	43	42	3	7	.300	0	4.55
10 YR TOTALS			**295**	**6580**	**230**	**32**	**14**	**16**	**1568.1**	**1570**	**90**	**505**	**43**	**26**	**860**	**100**	**31**	**26**	**3**	**735**	**625**	**78**	**93**	**.456**	**3**	**3.59**

Smithberg, Roger Craig — BR/TR — b.3/21/66   SD87 2/42

YR	TM/LG	CL	G	TBF	GS	CG	SHO	GF	IP	H	HR	BB	IBB	HB	SO	SH	SF	WP	BK	R	ER	W	L	PCT	SV	ERA
88	RIV/CAL	A+	15	426	15	5	0	0	103.1	90	2	32	0	2	72	1	0	12	3	52	38	9	2	.818	0	3.31
89	LV/PCL	AAA	22	604	22	4	0	0	137.0	159	9	35	2	4	58	7	4	3	4	79	68	7	7	.500	0	4.47
90	RIV/CAL	A+	3	53	3	0	0	0	13.0	12	1	2	0	0	5	0	1	0	1	7	6	1	1	.333	0	4.15
	LV/PCL	AAA	13	325	13	0	0	0	66.0	91	8	39	0	6	30	0	4	6	1	63	51	2	7	.222	0	6.95
91	HD/CAL	A+	3	75	3	0	0	0	18.0	12	0	6	0	1	11	2	1	0	0	6	3	1	1	.500	0	1.50
	WIC/TEX	AA	7	190	7	0	0	0	41.1	49	3	16	1	1	23	2	1	3	0	28	22	2	3	.400	0	4.79
	LV/PCL	AAA	17	374	15	1	0	0	79.0	112	8	33	1	3	34	5	4	8	0	65	58	3	7	.300	0	6.61
92	REN/CAL	A+	10	80	0	0	0	5	16.2	23	0	10	3	0	11	1	2	0	0	10	6	2	1	.667	0	3.24
	HUN/SOU	AA	20	159	0	0	0	8	36.0	42	4	12	1	2	19	2	2	1	0	17	16	3	3	.500	1	4.00
93	HUN/SOU	AA	27	162	0	0	0	13	36.2	34	3	16	1	2	36	2	2	2	0	15	9	4	2	.667	0	2.21
	TAC/PCL	AAA	28	211	0	0	0	12	50.2	50	1	11	1	2	25	5	3	2	0	14	10	3	3	.500	4	1.78
	OAK/AL		13	76	0	0	0	9	19.2	13	2	7	2	1	4	2	0	1	0	7	6	1	2	.333	3	2.75

Smoltz, John Andrew — BR/TR — b.5/15/67   DET85 22/574

YR	TM/LG	CL	G	TBF	GS	CG	SHO	GF	IP	H	HR	BB	IBB	HB	SO	SH	SF	WP	BK	R	ER	W	L	PCT	SV	ERA
86	LAK/FSL	A+	17	395	14	2	1	0	96.0	86	7	31	0	5	47	0	4	2	6	44	38	7	8	.467	0	3.56
87	GF/EAS	AA	21	582	21	0	0	0	130.0	131	17	81	2	7	86	3	2	6	8	89	82	4	10	.286	0	5.68
	RIC/INT	AAA	3	76	3	0	0	0	16.0	17	2	11	0	1	5	0	0	1	1	11	11	0	1	.000	0	6.19
88	RIC/INT	AAA	20	552	20	3	0	0	135.1	118	5	37	1	2	115	4	3	6	2	49	42	10	5	.667	0	2.79
	ATL/NL		12	297	12	0	0	0	64.0	74	10	33	4	2	37	0	2	2	0	40	39	2	7	.222	0	5.48
89	ATL/NL		29	847	29	5	0	0	208.0	160	15	72	2	2	168	10	7	8	3	79	68	12	11	.522	0	2.94
90	ATL/NL		34	966	34	6	2	0	231.1	206	20	90	3	1	170	9	8	14	3	109	99	14	11	.560	0	3.85
91	ATL/NL		36	947	36	5	0	0	229.2	206	16	77	1	3	148	9	9	20	1	101	97	14	13	.519	0	3.80
92	ATL/NL		35	1021	35	9	3	0	246.2	206	17	80	5	5	*215	7	8	17	1	90	78	15	12	.556	0	2.85
93	ATL/NL		35	1028	35	3	1	0	243.2	208	23	100	12	6	208	13	4	13	1	104	98	15	11	.577	0	3.62
6 YR TOTALS			**181**	**5106**	**181**	**28**	**6**	**0**	**1223.1**	**1060**	**101**	**452**	**27**	**19**	**946**	**50**	**36**	**74**	**11**	**523**	**479**	**72**	**65**	**.526**	**0**	**3.52**

Spradlin, Jerry Carl — BB/TR — b.6/14/67   CIN88 18/488

YR	TM/LG	CL	G	TBF	GS	CG	SHO	GF	IP	H	HR	BB	IBB	HB	SO	SH	SF	WP	BK	R	ER	W	L	PCT	SV	ERA
88	BIL/PIO	R+	17	201	5	0	0	2	47.2	45	2	14	1	2	23	1	2	3	0	25	17	4	1	.800	0	3.21
89	GRE/SAL	A	42	389	1	0	0	22	94.2	88	5	23	0	4	56	3	7	4	0	35	29	7	2	.778	2	2.76
90	CR/MID	A	5	57	0	0	0	0	12.0	13	1	5	1	0	6	1	0	0	0	8	4	1	0	.000	0	3.00
	CHW/SAL	A	43	308	1	0	0	34	74.1	74	5	17	5	2	39	4	1	3	1	23	21	3	4	.429	17	2.54
91	CHT/SOU	AA	48	406	1	0	0	22	96.0	95	2	32	7	4	73	1	5	9	0	38	33	7	3	.700	4	3.09
92	CR/MID	A	1	11	0	0	0	0	2.1	5	0	0	0	0	4	0	0	0	0	2	2	1	0	1.000	0	7.71
	CHT/SOU	AA	59	248	0	0	0	53	65.1	52	1	13	2	0	35	6	1	3	0	11	10	3	3	.500	34	1.38
93	IND/AMA	AAA	34	239	0	0	0	8	56.2	58	4	12	2	0	46	2	0	2	0	24	22	3	2	.600	1	3.49
	CIN/NL		37	193	0	0	0	16	49.0	44	4	9	0	0	24	3	1	0	0	20	19	2	2	.667	2	3.49

Springer, Russell Paul "Russ" — BR/TR — b.11/7/68   NYA89 6/181

YR	TM/LG	CL	G	TBF	GS	CG	SHO	GF	IP	H	HR	BB	IBB	HB	SO	SH	SF	WP	BK	R	ER	W	L	PCT	SV	ERA
89	YAN/GCL	R	6	95	6	0	0	0	24.0	14	0	10	0	1	34	0	0	1	0	8	4	3	0	1.000	0	1.50

(continued)

Springer, Russell Paul "Russ" (continued)

YR	TM/LG	CL	G	TBF	GS	CG	SHO	GF	IP	H	HR	BB	IBB	HB	SO	SH	SF	WP	BK	R	ER	W	L	PCT	SV	ERA
90	YAN/GCL	R	4	62	4	0	0	0	15.0	10	0	4	0	0	17	0	0	1	1	6	2	0	2	.000	0	1.20
	GRE/SAL	A	10	249	10	0	0	0	56.1	51	3	31	0	1	51	0	1	3	1	33	23	2	3	.400	0	3.67
91	FL/FSL	A+	25	634	25	2	0	0	152.1	118	9	62	1	6	139	5	6	6	3	68	59	5	9	.357	0	3.49
	ALB/EAS	AA	2	60	2	0	0	0	15.0	9	0	6	1	0	16	0	0	0	0	4	3	1	0	1.000	0	1.80
92	CMB/INT	AAA	20	499	20	1	0	0	123.2	89	11	54	0	5	95	1	3	4	0	46	37	8	5	.615	0	2.69
	NY/AL		14	75	0	0	0	5	16.0	18	0	10	0	1	12	0	0	1	0	11	11	0	0	.000	0	6.19
93	VAN/PCL	AAA	11	263	9	1	0	1	59.0	58	5	33	1	0	40	2	1	3	0	37	28	5	4	.556	0	4.27
	CAL/AL		14	278	9	1	0	3	60.0	73	11	32	1	3	31	1	1	6	0	48	48	1	6	.143	0	7.20
2 YR TOTALS			**28**	**353**	**9**	**1**	**0**	**8**	**76.0**	**91**	**11**	**42**	**1**	**4**	**43**	**1**	**1**	**6**	**0**	**59**	**59**	**1**	**6**	**.143**	**0**	**6.99**

Stanton, William Michael "Mike" — BL/TL — b.6/2/67   ATL87 13/324

YR	TM/LG	CL	G	TBF	GS	CG	SHO	GF	IP	H	HR	BB	IBB	HB	SO	SH	SF	WP	BK	R	ER	W	L	PCT	SV	ERA
87	PUL/APP	R+	15	354	13	3	2	1	83.1	64	7	42	0	3	82	3	4	2	0	37	30	4	8	.333	0	3.24
88	BUR/MID	A	30	675	23	1	1	3	154.0	154	7	69	2	1	160	4	3	16	1	86	62	11	5	.688	0	3.62
	DUR/CAR	A+	2	55	2	1	1	0	12.1	14	0	5	0	0	14	0	0	1	1	3	2	1	0	1.000	0	1.46
89	GRE/SOU	AA	47	207	0	0	0	36	51.1	32	1	31	3	0	58	5	2	4	0	10	9	4	1	.800	19	1.58
	RIC/INT	AAA	13	77	0	0	0	11	20.0	6	0	13	1	0	20	1	0	0	0	0	0	2	0	1.000	8	0.00
	ATL/NL		20	94	0	0	0	10	24.0	17	0	8	1	0	27	4	0	1	0	4	4	0	1	.000	7	1.50
90	ATL/NL		7	42	0	0	0	4	7.0	16	1	4	2	1	7	0	0	1	0	16	14	0	3	.000	2	18.00
	GRE/SOU	AA	4	27	4	0	0	0	5.2	7	1	3	0	0	4	0	0	0	0	1	1	0	1	.000	0	1.59
91	ATL/NL		74	314	0	0	0	20	78.0	62	6	21	1	1	54	6	0	0	0	27	25	5	5	.500	7	2.88
92	ATL/NL		65	264	0	0	0	23	63.2	59	6	20	2	1	44	3	2	3	0	32	29	5	4	.556	8	4.10
93	ATL/NL		63	236	0	0	0	41	52.0	51	4	29	7	0	43	5	2	1	0	35	27	4	6	.400	27	4.67
5 YR TOTALS			**229**	**950**	**0**	**0**	**0**	**98**	**224.2**	**205**	**17**	**82**	**18**	**4**	**175**	**17**	**4**	**6**	**0**	**114**	**99**	**14**	**19**	**.424**	**51**	**3.97**

Stewart, David Keith "Dave" — BR/TR — b.2/19/57   LA75 16/384

YR	TM/LG	CL	G	TBF	GS	CG	SHO	GF	IP	H	HR	BB	IBB	HB	SO	SH	SF	WP	BK	R	ER	W	L	PCT	SV	ERA
78	LA/NL		1	6	0	0	0	1	2.0	1	0	0	0	0	1	0	0	0	0	0	0	0	0	.000	0	0.00
81	LA/NL		32	184	0	0	0	14	43.1	40	3	14	5	0	29	7	3	4	0	13	12	4	3	.571	6	2.49
82	LA/NL		45	616	14	0	0	9	146.1	137	14	49	11	2	80	10	5	3	0	72	62	9	8	.529	1	3.81
83	LA/NL		46	328	1	0	0	25	76.0	67	4	33	7	2	54	7	3	2	0	28	25	5	2	.714	8	2.96
	TEX/AL		8	237	8	2	0	0	59.0	50	2	17	0	2	24	2	1	1	0	15	14	5	2	.714	0	2.14
	YEAR		54	565	9	2	0	25	135.0	117	6	50	7	4	78	9	4	3	0	43	39	10	4	.714	8	2.60
84	TEX/AL		32	847	27	3	0	2	192.1	193	26	87	3	4	119	4	4	5	12	106	101	7	14	.333	0	4.73
85	TEX/AL		42	361	5	0	0	29	81.1	86	13	37	5	2	64	5	2	5	1	53	49	0	6	.000	4	5.42
	PHI/NL		4	22	0	0	0	3	4.1	5	0	4	2	0	2	0	0	2	0	4	3	0	0	.000	0	6.23
	YEAR		46	383	5	0	0	32	85.2	91	13	41	5	2	66	5	2	7	1	57	52	0	6	.000	4	5.46
86	PHI/NL		8	56	0	0	0	2	12.1	15	1	4	0	0	9	0	3	1	3	9	9	0	0	.000	0	6.57
	TAC/PCL	AAA	1	13	0	0	0	0	3.0	4	0	1	0	0	3	0	0	0	0	1	0	0	0	.000	0	0.00
	OAK/AL		29	644	17	4	1	2	149.1	137	15	65	2	3	102	4	4	9	0	67	62	9	5	.643	0	3.74
	YEAR		37	700	17	4	1	4	161.2	152	16	69	2	3	111	4	7	10	0	76	71	9	5	.643	0	3.95
87	OAK/AL		37	1103	37	8	1	0	261.1	224	24	105	2	6	205	7	5	11	0	121	107	*20	13	.606	0	3.68
88	OAK/AL		37	1156	37	*14	2	0	*275.2	240	14	110	2	3	192	7	9	14	16	111	99	21	12	.636	0	3.23
89	OAK/AL		36	1081	36	8	0	0	257.2	260	23	69	4	6	155	9	10	13	0	105	95	21	9	.700	0	3.32
90	OAK/AL		36	1088	36	*11	*4	0	*267.0	226	16	83	1	5	166	10	10	8	0	84	76	22	11	.667	0	2.56
91	OAK/AL		35	1014	35	2	1	0	226.0	245	24	105	1	9	144	5	15	13	0	135	130	11	11	.500	0	5.18
92	OAK/AL		31	838	31	2	0	0	199.1	175	25	79	1	8	130	5	3	3	1	96	81	12	10	.545	0	3.66
93	TOR/AL		26	687	26	0	0	0	162.0	146	23	72	0	4	96	3	4	4	0	86	80	12	8	.600	0	4.44
14 YR TOTALS			**485**	**10268**	**310**	**54**	**9**	**87**	**2415.1**	**2247**	**227**	**933**	**41**	**56**	**1572**	**85**	**87**	**105**	**22**	**1105**	**1005**	**158**	**114**	**.581**	**19**	**3.74**

Stieb, David Andrew "Dave" — BR/TR — b.7/22/57   TOR78 5/106

YR	TM/LG	CL	G	TBF	GS	CG	SHO	GF	IP	H	HR	BB	IBB	HB	SO	SH	SF	WP	BK	R	ER	W	L	PCT	SV	ERA
79	TOR/AL		18	563	18	7	1	0	129.1	139	11	48	3	4	52	4	4	3	1	70	62	8	8	.500	0	4.31
80	TOR/AL		34	1004	32	14	4	0	242.2	232	12	83	6	6	108	12	9	6	2	108	100	12	15	.444	0	3.71
81	TOR/AL		25	748	25	11	2	0	183.2	148	10	61	2	11	89	5	7	1	2	70	65	11	10	.524	0	3.19
82	TOR/AL		38	1187	38	*19	*5	0	*288.1	271	27	75	4	5	141	9	3	5	1	116	104	17	14	.548	0	3.25
83	TOR/AL		36	1141	36	14	4	0	278.0	223	21	93	6	14	187	6	9	5	1	105	94	17	12	.586	0	3.04
84	TOR/AL		35	1085	35	11	2	0	*267.0	215	19	88	1	11	198	8	6	2	0	87	84	16	8	.667	0	2.83
85	TOR/AL		36	1087	36	8	2	0	265.0	206	22	96	3	9	167	14	2	4	1	89	73	14	13	.519	0	*2.48
86	TOR/AL		37	919	34	1	1	2	205.0	239	29	87	1	15	127	6	5	6	0	128	108	7	12	.368	0	4.74
87	TOR/AL		33	789	31	3	1	1	185.0	164	16	87	4	7	115	5	5	5	0	92	84	13	9	.591	0	4.09
88	TOR/AL		32	844	31	8	4	0	207.1	157	15	79	0	13	147	3	4	4	5	76	70	16	8	.667	0	3.04
89	TOR/AL		33	850	33	3	2	0	206.2	164	12	76	2	13	101	3	3	2	0	83	77	17	8	.680	0	3.35
90	TOR/AL		33	861	33	2	2	0	208.2	179	11	64	0	10	125	3	5	0	0	73	68	18	6	.750	0	2.93
91	TOR/AL		9	244	9	1	0	0	59.2	52	4	23	2	0	29	4	1	0	0	22	21	4	3	.571	0	3.17
92	DUN/FSL	A+	2	50	2	0	0	0	12.2	7	0	4	0	2	11	1	0	0	0	6	3	1	1	.500	0	2.13
	TOR/AL		21	415	14	0	0	3	96.1	98	9	43	3	4	45	6	1	1	0	58	54	4	6	.400	0	5.04
93	SAR/FSL	A+	2	61	2	0	0	0	12.1	18	2	2	0	1	14	0	0	0	0	10	8	1	1	.500	0	5.84
	NAS/AMA	AAA	1	29	1	0	0	0	7.0	9	0	2	0	0	3	0	0	0	0	3	3	0	1	.000	0	3.86
	OMA/AMA	AAA	9	217	8	1	0	0	47.2	63	10	12	0	2	18	1	2	0	0	37	34	3	3	.500	0	6.42
	CHI/AL		4	107	4	0	0	0	22.1	27	1	14	0	0	11	2	1	1	0	17	15	1	3	.250	0	6.04
15 YR TOTALS			**424**	**11844**	**409**	**103**	**30**	**7**	**2845.0**	**2514**	**219**	**1017**	**35**	**124**	**1642**	**98**	**68**	**51**	**14**	**1194**	**1079**	**175**	**135**	**.565**	**1**	**3.41**

Stottlemyre, Todd Vernon — BL/TR — b.5/20/65   TOR85 S1/3

YR	TM/LG	CL	G	TBF	GS	CG	SHO	GF	IP	H	HR	BB	IBB	HB	SO	SH	SF	WP	BK	R	ER	W	L	PCT	SV	ERA
86	VEN/CAL	A+	17	428	17	2	0	0	103.2	76	4	36	0	2	104	4	1	7	2	39	28	9	4	.692	0	2.43

Stottlemyre, Todd Vernon (continued)

YR	TM/LG	CL	G	TBF	GS	CG	SHO	GF	IP	H	HR	BB	IBB	HB	SO	SH	SF	WP	BK	R	ER	W	L	PCT	SV	ERA
	KNO/SOU	AA	18	432	18	1	0	0	99.0	93	5	49	1	1	81	2	5	4	2	56	46	8	7	.533	0	4.18
87	SYR/INT	AAA	34	827	34	1	0	0	186.2	189	14	87	3	6	143	2	10	10	1	103	92	11	13	.458	0	4.44
88	SYR/INT	AAA	7	187	7	1	0	0	48.1	36	1	8	0	0	51	1	1	2	2	12	11	5	0	1.000	0	2.05
	TOR/AL		28	443	16	0	0	2	98.0	109	15	46	5	4	67	5	3	2	3	70	62	4	8	.333	0	5.69
89	SYR/INT	AAA	10	233	9	2	0	1	55.2	46	4	15	0	2	45	1	0	0	0	23	20	3	2	.600	0	3.23
	TOR/AL		27	545	18	0	0	4	127.2	137	11	44	4	5	63	3	7	4	1	56	55	7	7	.500	0	3.88
90	TOR/AL		33	866	33	4	0	0	203.0	214	18	69	4	8	115	3	5	6	1	101	98	13	17	.433	0	4.34
91	TOR/AL		34	921	34	1	0	0	219.0	194	21	75	3	12	116	0	8	4	0	97	92	15	8	.652	0	3.78
92	TOR/AL		28	755	27	6	2	0	174.0	175	20	63	4	10	98	2	11	7	0	99	87	12	11	.522	0	4.50
93	TOR/AL		30	786	28	1	1	0	176.2	204	11	69	5	3	98	5	11	7	1	107	95	11	12	.478	0	4.84
6 YR TOTALS			**180**	**4316**	**156**	**12**	**3**	**6**	**998.1**	**1033**	**96**	**366**	**25**	**42**	**557**	**18**	**45**	**30**	**6**	**530**	**489**	**62**	**63**	**.496**	**0**	**4.41**

Sutcliffe, Richard Lee "Rick" — BL/TR — b.6/21/56   LA74 1/21

YR	TM/LG	CL	G	TBF	GS	CG	SHO	GF	IP	H	HR	BB	IBB	HB	SO	SH	SF	WP	BK	R	ER	W	L	PCT	SV	ERA
76	LA/NL		1	17	1	0	0	0	5.0	2	0	1	0	0	3	0	0	0	0	0	0	0	0	.000	0	0.00
78	LA/NL		2	9	0	0	0	0	1.2	2	0	1	0	1	0	0	0	0	0	0	0	0	0	.000	0	0.00
79	LA/NL		39	1016	30	5	1	2	242.0	217	16	97	6	2	117	16	9	8	6	104	93	17	10	.630	0	3.46
80	LA/NL		42	491	10	1	1	19	110.0	122	10	55	2	1	59	4	3	4	5	73	68	3	9	.250	5	5.56
81	LA/NL		14	197	6	0	0	5	47.0	41	5	20	2	2	16	1	2	0	0	24	21	2	2	.500	0	4.02
82	CLE/AL		34	887	27	6	1	3	216.0	174	16	98	2	4	142	7	8	6	1	81	71	14	8	.636	1	*2.96
83	CLE/AL		36	1061	35	10	2	0	243.1	251	23	102	5	6	160	8	9	7	3	131	116	17	11	.607	0	4.29
84	CLE/AL		15	428	15	2	0	0	94.1	111	7	46	3	2	58	4	3	3	1	60	54	4	5	.444	0	5.15
	CHI/NL		20	602	20	7	3	0	150.1	123	9	39	0	1	155	1	1	3	2	53	45	16	1	*.941	0	2.69
	YEAR		35	1030	35	9	3	0	244.2	234	16	85	3	3	213	5	4	6	3	113	99	20	6	.769	0	3.64
85	CHI/NL		20	549	20	6	3	0	130.0	119	12	44	3	3	102	3	4	6	0	51	46	8	8	.500	0	3.18
86	CHI/NL		28	764	27	4	1	0	176.2	166	18	96	8	1	122	6	2	13	1	92	91	5	14	.263	0	4.64
87	CHI/NL		34	1012	34	6	1	0	237.1	223	24	106	14	4	174	9	8	9	4	106	97	*18	10	.643	0	3.68
88	CHI/NL		32	958	32	12	2	0	226.0	232	18	70	9	2	144	17	5	11	0	97	97	13	14	.481	0	3.86
89	CHI/NL		35	938	34	5	1	0	229.0	202	18	69	8	2	153	15	10	12	6	98	93	16	11	.593	0	3.66
90	IOW/AMA	AAA	2	62	2	0	0	0	12.2	18	2	7	0	0	12	0	1	0	0	13	11	0	0	.000	0	7.82
	CHI/NL		5	97	5	0	0	0	21.1	25	2	12	0	0	7	1	2	4	0	14	14	0	2	.000	0	5.91
91	PEO/MID	A	1	40	1	0	0	0	9.0	12	0	2	0	1	6	1	1	0	0	6	6	0	0	.000	0	6.00
	IOW/AMA	AAA	3	65	2	0	0	1	13.0	23	3	6	0	0	8	0	1	2	1	14	14	1	2	.333	0	9.69
	CHI/NL		19	422	18	0	0	0	96.2	96	4	45	2	0	52	5	8	2	2	52	44	6	5	.545	0	4.10
92	BAL/AL		36	1018	36	5	2	0	237.1	251	20	74	4	7	109	6	11	7	2	123	118	16	15	.516	0	4.47
93	BAL/AL		29	763	28	3	0	0	166.0	212	23	74	5	6	80	4	3	1	0	112	106	10	10	.500	0	5.75
17 YR TOTALS			**441**	**11229**	**378**	**72**	**18**	**29**	**2630.0**	**2569**	**225**	**1049**	**73**	**44**	**1653**	**107**	**88**	**96**	**37**	**1271**	**1174**	**165**	**135**	**.550**	**6**	**4.02**

Swan, Russell Howard "Russ" — BL/TL — b.1/3/64   SF86 9/214

YR	TM/LG	CL	G	TBF	GS	CG	SHO	GF	IP	H	HR	BB	IBB	HB	SO	SH	SF	WP	BK	R	ER	W	L	PCT	SV	ERA
86	EVE/NWL	A-	7	0	7	2	0	0	46.0	30	2	22	0	1	45	0	0	1	1	17	11	5	0	1.000	0	2.15
	CLI/MID	A	7	179	7	2	1	0	43.2	36	2	8	0	1	37	0	2	1	1	18	15	3	3	.500	0	3.09
87	FRE/CAL	A+	12	274	12	0	0	0	64.0	54	5	29	0	1	59	4	0	4	0	40	27	6	3	.667	0	3.80
88	SJ/CAL	A+	11	301	11	2	1	0	76.2	53	2	26	0	1	62	7	0	2	0	28	19	7	0	1.000	0	2.23
89	SHR/TEX	AA	11	304	11	0	0	0	75.1	62	2	22	1	1	56	1	1	3	2	25	22	2	3	.400	0	2.63
	SF/NL		2	34	2	0	0	0	6.2	11	4	4	0	2	2	2	0	0	0	10	8	0	2	.000	0	10.80
	PHO/PCL	AAA	14	348	13	1	0	0	83.0	75	8	29	0	3	49	5	2	2	3	37	31	4	3	.571	0	3.36
90	SF/NL		2	18	2	0	0	0	2.1	6	0	4	0	0	1	0	0	0	0	4	1	0	0	.000	0	3.86
	PHO/PCL	AAA	6	153	6	0	0	0	33.2	41	1	15	0	2	21	1	1	1	1	17	13	2	4	.333	0	3.48
	CAL/PCL	AAA	5	105	5	0	0	0	23.0	28	0	12	0	0	14	1	0	3	0	18	15	1	2	.333	0	5.87
	SEA/AL		11	195	8	0	0	0	47.0	42	3	18	2	0	15	2	3	0	0	22	19	2	3	.400	0	3.64
	YEAR		13	213	9	0	0	0	49.1	48	3	22	2	0	16	2	3	1	0	26	20	2	4	.333	0	3.65
91	SEA/AL		63	336	0	0	0	11	78.2	81	8	28	7	0	33	6	1	8	0	35	30	6	2	.750	2	3.43
92	SEA/AL		55	457	9	1	0	26	104.1	104	8	45	3	0	45	7	5	6	0	60	55	3	10	.231	9	4.74
93	CAL/PCL	AAA	9	51	0	0	0	3	10.2	14	1	8	0	0	7	0	0	0	0	11	10	2	1	.667	0	8.44
	SEA/AL		23	100	0	0	0	6	19.2	25	2	18	1	2	10	1	0	0	0	20	20	3	3	.500	0	9.15
5 YR TOTALS			**156**	**1140**	**20**	**1**	**0**	**43**	**258.2**	**269**	**25**	**117**	**17**	**5**	**106**	**18**	**9**	**15**	**1**	**151**	**133**	**14**	**21**	**.400**	**11**	**4.63**

Swift, William Charles "Bill" — BR/TR — b.10/27/61   SEA84 1/2

YR	TM/LG	CL	G	TBF	GS	CG	SHO	GF	IP	H	HR	BB	IBB	HB	SO	SH	SF	WP	BK	R	ER	W	L	PCT	SV	ERA
85	CHT/SOU	AA	7	166	7	0	0	0	39.0	34	2	21	0	2	21	2	2	3	0	16	16	2	1	.667	0	3.69
	SEA/AL		23	532	21	0	0	0	120.2	131	8	48	5	5	55	6	3	5	3	71	64	6	10	.375	0	4.77
86	CAL/PCL	AAA	10	240	8	3	1	2	57.0	57	5	22	2	2	29	1	1	2	0	33	25	4	4	.500	1	3.95
	SEA/AL		29	534	17	1	0	3	115.1	148	5	55	2	7	55	5	3	2	1	85	70	2	9	.182	0	5.46
87	CAL/PCL	AAA	5	95	5	0	0	0	18.1	32	2	13	1	0	5	0	2	2	1	22	18	0	0	.000	0	8.84
88	SEA/AL		38	757	24	6	1	4	174.2	199	10	65	3	8	47	3	5	2	1	99	89	8	12	.400	0	4.59
89	SB/CAL	A+	2	36	2	0	0	0	10.0	8	0	2	0	0	4	0	0	0	0	1	0	1	0	1.000	0	0.00
	SEA/AL		37	551	16	0	0	7	130.0	140	5	38	4	2	45	4	3	4	1	72	64	7	3	.700	0	4.43
90	SEA/AL		55	533	0	0	0	18	128.0	135	4	21	6	7	42	5	4	8	3	46	34	6	4	.600	6	2.39
91	SEA/AL		71	359	0	0	0	30	90.1	74	3	26	4	1	48	2	0	2	1	22	20	1	2	.333	17	1.99
92	SF/NL		30	655	22	3	2	2	164.2	144	6	43	3	3	77	5	2	0	1	41	38	10	4	.714	1	*2.08
93	SF/NL		34	928	34	1	1	0	232.2	195	18	55	5	6	157	4	2	4	0	82	73	21	8	.724	0	2.82
8 YR TOTALS			**317**	**4849**	**142**	**11**	**4**	**64**	**1156.1**	**1166**	**61**	**351**	**32**	**39**	**526**	**36**	**20**	**31**	**12**	**518**	**452**	**61**	**52**	**.540**	**25**	**3.52**

Swindell, Forest Gregory "Greg" — BR/TL — b.1/2/65   CLE86 1/2

YR	TM/LG	CL	G	TBF	GS	CG	SHO	GF	IP	H	HR	BB	IBB	HB	SO	SH	SF	WP	BK	R	ER	W	L	PCT	SV	ERA
86	WAT/MID	A	3	68	3	0	0	0	18.0	12	1	3	0	0	25	0	0	0	0	2	2	2	1	.667	0	1.00
	CLE/AL		9	255	9	1	0	0	61.2	57	9	15	0	1	46	3	1	3	2	35	29	5	2	.714	0	4.23
87	CLE/AL		16	441	15	4	1	0	102.1	112	18	37	1	1	97	4	3	0	1	62	58	3	8	.273	0	5.10
88	CLE/AL		33	988	33	12	4	0	242.0	234	18	45	3	1	180	9	5	5	0	97	86	18	14	.563	0	3.20
89	CLE/AL		28	749	28	5	2	0	184.1	170	16	51	1	0	129	4	4	3	1	71	69	13	6	.684	0	3.37
90	CLE/AL		34	912	34	3	0	0	214.2	245	27	47	2	1	135	8	6	3	2	110	105	12	9	.571	0	4.40
91	CLE/AL		33	971	33	7	0	0	238.0	241	21	31	1	3	169	13	8	3	1	112	92	9	16	.360	0	3.48
92	CIN/NL		31	867	30	5	3	0	213.2	210	14	41	4	2	138	9	7	3	2	72	64	12	8	.600	0	2.70
93	HOU/NL		31	818	30	1	1	0	190.1	215	24	40	3	1	124	13	3	2	2	98	88	12	13	.480	0	4.16
8 YR TOTALS			**215**	**6001**	**212**	**38**	**11**	**0**	**1447.0**	**1484**	**147**	**307**	**15**	**10**	**1018**	**63**	**37**	**22**	**11**	**657**	**591**	**84**	**76**	**.525**	**0**	**3.68**

Swingle, Paul Christopher — BR/TR — b.12/21/66   CAL89 29/747

YR	TM/LG	CL	G	TBF	GS	CG	SHO	GF	IP	H	HR	BB	IBB	HB	SO	SH	SF	WP	BK	R	ER	W	L	PCT	SV	ERA
89	BEN/NWL	A-	9	81	0	0	0	2	18.1	7	0	19	0	0	26	1	0	5	1	9	6	1	0	1.000	0	2.95
90	BOI/NWL	A-	14	52	0	0	0	12	13.2	5	0	4	1	0	25	1	0	0	0	1	1	0	1	.000	6	0.66
91	PS/CAL	A+	43	268	0	0	0	28	57.0	51	2	41	8	1	63	3	3	11	0	37	28	5	4	.556	10	4.42
92	MID/TEX	AA	25	648	25	2	0	0	149.2	158	14	51	1	6	104	3	6	8	2	88	78	8	10	.444	0	4.69
93	VAN/PCL	AAA	37	318	4	0	0	11	67.2	85	4	32	1	1	61	2	4	3	1	61	52	2	9	.182	1	6.92
	CAL/AL		9	49	0	0	0	2	9.2	15	2	6	0	0	6	0	1	0	0	9	9	0	1	.000	0	8.38

Tanana, Frank Daryl — BL/TL — b.7/3/53   CAL71 1/13

YR	TM/LG	CL	G	TBF	GS	CG	SHO	GF	IP	H	HR	BB	IBB	HB	SO	SH	SF	WP	BK	R	ER	W	L	PCT	SV	ERA
73	CAL/AL		4	108	4	2	1	0	26.1	20	2	8	0	0	22	0	0	2	0	11	9	2	2	.500	0	3.08
74	CAL/AL		39	1127	35	12	4	2	268.2	262	27	77	4	8	180	10	4	4	2	104	93	14	19	.424	0	3.12
75	CAL/AL		34	1029	33	16	5	1	257.1	211	21	73	6	7	*269	13	4	8	1	80	75	16	9	.640	0	2.62
76	CAL/AL		34	1142	34	23	2	0	288.1	212	24	73	5	9	261	14	3	5	0	88	78	19	10	.655	0	2.43
77	CAL/AL		31	973	31	20	*7	0	241.1	201	19	61	2	12	205	8	7	8	1	72	68	15	9	.625	0	*2.54
78	CAL/AL		33	1014	33	10	4	0	239.0	239	26	60	7	9	137	8	10	5	8	108	97	18	12	.600	0	3.65
79	CAL/AL		18	382	17	2	1	0	90.1	93	9	25	0	2	46	1	2	6	1	44	39	7	5	.583	0	3.89
80	CAL/AL		32	870	31	7	0	1	204.0	223	18	45	0	8	113	4	4	3	1	107	94	11	12	.478	0	4.15
81	BOS/AL		24	596	23	5	2	0	141.1	142	17	43	4	4	78	1	4	2	0	70	63	4	10	.286	0	4.01
82	TEX/AL		30	832	30	7	0	0	194.1	199	16	55	10	7	87	13	4	0	1	102	91	7	18	.280	0	4.21
83	TEX/AL		29	667	22	3	0	1	159.1	144	14	49	5	7	108	7	3	6	1	70	56	7	9	.438	0	3.16
84	TEX/AL		35	1054	35	9	1	0	246.1	234	30	81	3	6	141	6	5	12	4	117	89	15	15	.500	0	3.25
85	TEX/AL		13	340	13	0	0	0	77.2	89	15	23	2	1	52	2	4	3	0	53	51	2	7	.222	0	5.91
	DET/AL		20	567	20	4	0	0	137.1	131	13	34	6	2	107	3	4	2	1	59	51	10	7	.588	0	3.34
	YEAR		33	907	33	4	0	0	215.0	220	28	57	8	3	159	5	8	5	1	112	102	12	14	.462	0	4.27
86	DET/AL		32	812	31	3	1	1	188.1	196	23	65	9	3	119	6	5	5	1	95	87	12	9	.571	0	4.16
87	DET/AL		34	924	34	5	3	0	218.2	216	27	56	5	5	146	8	11	6	0	106	95	15	10	.600	0	3.91
88	DET/AL		32	876	32	2	0	0	203.0	213	25	64	7	4	127	3	6	0	0	105	95	14	11	.560	0	4.21
89	DET/AL		33	955	33	6	1	0	223.2	227	21	74	8	7	147	7	10	8	0	105	89	10	14	.417	0	3.58
90	DET/AL		34	763	29	1	0	0	176.1	190	25	66	7	9	114	3	7	5	1	104	104	9	8	.529	1	5.31
91	DET/AL		33	920	33	3	2	0	217.1	217	26	78	9	2	107	12	3	3	0	98	91	13	12	.520	0	3.77
92	DET/AL		32	818	31	3	0	0	186.2	188	22	90	9	7	91	7	10	11	1	102	91	13	11	.542	0	4.39
93	NY/NL		29	784	29	0	0	0	183.0	198	26	48	7	9	104	12	4	7	2	100	91	7	15	.318	0	4.48
	NY/AL		3	88	3	0	0	0	19.2	18	2	7	1	0	12	0	0	0	0	10	7	0	2	.000	0	3.20
	YEAR		32	872	32	0	0	0	202.2	216	28	55	8	9	116	12	4	7	2	110	98	7	17	.292	0	4.35
21 YR TOTALS			**638**	**17641**	**616**	**143**	**34**	**10**	**4188.1**	**4063**	**448**	**1255**	**116**	**129**	**2773**	**165**	**117**	**119**	**27**	**1910**	**1704**	**240**	**236**	**.504**	**1**	**3.66**

Tapani, Kevin Ray — BR/TR — b.2/18/64   OAK86 2/40

YR	TM/LG	CL	G	TBF	GS	CG	SHO	GF	IP	H	HR	BB	IBB	HB	SO	SH	SF	WP	BK	R	ER	W	L	PCT	SV	ERA
86	MED/NWL	A-	2	0	2	0	0	0	8.1	6	0	3	0	0	9	0	0	0	0	3	0	1	0	1.000	0	0.00
	TAC/PCL	AAA	1	14	1	0	0	0	2.1	5	1	1	0	0	1	0	0	0	0	6	4	0	1	.000	0	15.43
	MOD/CAL	A+	11	293	11	1	0	0	69.0	74	2	22	1	1	44	6	1	0	0	26	19	6	1	.857	0	2.48
	HUN/SOU	AA	1	26	1	0	0	0	6.0	8	0	1	0	0	2	0	0	0	0	4	4	1	0	1.000	0	6.00
87	MOD/CAL	A+	24	627	24	6	1	0	148.1	122	14	60	2	5	121	6	1	21	0	74	62	10	7	.588	0	3.76
88	SL/FSL	A+	3	76	3	0	0	0	19.0	17	1	4	0	0	11	0	0	2	0	5	3	1	0	1.000	0	1.42
	JAC/TEX	AA	24	248	5	0	0	9	62.1	46	1	19	2	0	35	5	2	1	3	23	19	5	1	.833	3	2.74
89	NY/NL		3	31	0	0	0	1	7.1	5	1	4	0	0	2	0	1	0	0	3	3	0	0	.000	0	3.68
	TID/INT	AAA	17	459	17	2	1	0	109.0	113	6	25	2	1	63	1	2	3	1	49	42	7	5	.583	0	3.47
	POR/PCL	AAA	6	170	6	0	0	0	41.0	38	4	12	1	0	30	1	1	0	0	15	10	4	2	.667	0	2.20
	MIN/AL		5	138	5	0	0	0	32.2	34	2	8	1	0	21	1	1	0	0	15	14	2	2	.500	0	3.86
	YEAR		8	169	5	0	0	0	40.0	39	3	12	1	0	23	1	2	0	0	18	17	2	2	.500	0	3.83
90	MIN/AL		28	659	28	1	1	0	159.1	164	12	29	2	2	101	3	4	1	0	75	72	12	8	.600	0	4.07
91	MIN/AL		34	974	34	4	1	0	244.0	225	23	40	0	2	135	9	6	3	3	84	81	16	9	.640	0	2.99
92	MIN/AL		34	911	34	4	1	0	220.0	226	17	48	2	5	138	8	11	4	0	103	97	16	11	.593	0	3.97
93	MIN/AL		36	964	35	3	1	0	225.2	243	21	57	1	6	150	5	3	4	2	123	111	12	15	.444	0	4.43
5 YR TOTALS			**140**	**3677**	**136**	**12**	**4**	**0**	**889.0**	**897**	**76**	**186**	**6**	**15**	**547**	**24**	**28**	**12**	**4**	**403**	**378**	**58**	**45**	**.563**	**0**	**3.83**

Tavarez, Julian — BR/TR — b.5/22/73   CLE 2/22/90

YR	TM/LG	CL	G	TBF	GS	CG	SHO	GF	IP	H	HR	BB	IBB	HB	SO	SH	SF	WP	BK	R	ER	W	L	PCT	SV	ERA
92	BUR/APP	R+	14	370	14	2	2	0	87.1	86	3	12	0	10	69	2	1	5	1	41	26	6	3	.667	0	2.68
93	KIN/CAR	A+	18	489	18	2	0	0	119.0	102	6	28	0	7	107	3	4	3	1	48	32	11	5	.688	0	2.42
	CAN/EAS	AA	3	69	2	1	1	0	19.0	14	0	1	0	2	11	0	0	0	0	2	2	2	1	.667	0	0.95
	CLE/AL		8	172	7	0	0	0	37.0	53	7	13	2	2	19	0	1	3	1	29	27	2	2	.500	0	6.57

Taylor, Kerry Thomas — BR/TR — b.1/25/71   MIN 6/26/89

YR	TM/LG	CL	G	TBF	GS	CG	SHO	GF	IP	H	HR	BB	IBB	HB	SO	SH	SF	WP	BK	R	ER	W	L	PCT	SV	ERA
89	ELI/APP	R+	9	157	8	0	0	0	36.0	26	1	22	0	2	24	3	1	1	0	11	6	3	0	1.000	0	1.50
90	TWI/GCL	R	14	275	13	1	1	1	63.0	57	2	33	0	4	59	0	4	5	4	37	25	3	1	.750	0	3.57
91	KEN/MID	A	26	586	26	2	1	0	132.0	121	4	84	1	10	84	2	5	11	1	74	56	7	11	.389	0	3.82
92	KEN/MID	A	27	733	27	2	1	0	170.1	150	3	68	0	10	158	6	2	11	1	71	52	10	9	.526	0	2.75
93	SD/NL		36	326	7	0	0	9	68.1	72	5	49	0	4	45	10	3	4	0	53	49	0	5	.000	0	6.45

Taylor, Rodney Scott "Scott" — BL/TL — b.8/2/67   BOS88 28/719

YR	TM/LG	CL	G	TBF	GS	CG	SHO	GF	IP	H	HR	BB	IBB	HB	SO	SH	SF	WP	BK	R	ER	W	L	PCT	SV	ERA
88	ELM/NYP	A-	2	16	0	0	0	1	3.2	2	0	3	0	0	8	0	0	0	0	0	0	1	0	1.000	0	0.00
89	LYN/CAR	A+	19	332	9	0	0	4	81.0	61	7	25	3	1	99	2	2	3	3	33	26	5	3	.625	1	2.89
90	LYN/CAR	A+	13	372	13	1	0	0	89.0	76	2	30	2	2	120	3	0	7	3	36	27	5	6	.455	0	2.73
	NB/EAS	AA	5	117	5	0	0	0	27.1	23	0	13	0	1	27	3	0	1	0	8	5	0	2	.000	0	1.65
91	NB/EAS	AA	4	109	4	0	0	0	29.0	20	0	9	0	0	38	0	0	1	0	2	2	2	0	1.000	0	0.62
	PAW/INT	AAA	7	161	7	1	0	0	39.0	32	3	17	0	1	35	0	2	1	1	19	15	3	3	.500	0	3.46
92	PAW/INT	AAA	26	694	26	5	0	0	162.0	168	16	61	1	2	91	3	5	17	0	73	66	9	11	.450	0	3.67
	BOS/AL		4	57	1	0	0	1	14.2	13	4	4	0	0	7	0	0	0	0	8	8	1	1	.500	0	4.91
93	PAW/INT	AAA	47	533	8	0	0	10	122.2	132	12	48	0	3	88	7	2	2	1	61	55	7	7	.500	1	4.04
	BOS/AL		16	59	0	0	0	3	11.0	14	1	12	1	0	8	1	0	0	0	10	10	0	1	.000	0	8.18
2 YR TOTALS			**20**	**116**	**1**	**0**	**0**	**4**	**25.2**	**27**	**5**	**16**	**3**	**1**	**15**	**1**	**0**	**0**	**0**	**18**	**18**	**1**	**2**	**.333**	**0**	**6.31**

Telford, Anthony Charles — BR/TR — b.3/6/66   BAL87 4/65

YR	TM/LG	CL	G	TBF	GS	CG	SHO	GF	IP	H	HR	BB	IBB	HB	SO	SH	SF	WP	BK	R	ER	W	L	PCT	SV	ERA
87	NEW/NYP	A-	6	72	2	0	0	3	17.2	16	0	3	0	0	27	0	0	0	0	2	2	1	0	1.000	0	1.02
	HAG/CAR	A+	2	46	2	0	0	0	11.1	9	0	5	0	1	10	0	0	0	0	2	2	1	0	1.000	0	1.59
	ROC/INT	AAA	1	9	0	0	0	0	2.0	0	0	3	0	0	3	0	0	1	0	0	0	0	0	.000	0	0.00
88	HAG/CAR	A+	1	24	1	0	0	0	7.0	3	0	0	0	0	10	0	0	0	0	1	0	1	0	1.000	0	0.00
89	FRE/CAR	A+	9	116	5	0	0	2	25.2	25	1	12	0	2	19	1	2	2	0	15	12	2	1	.667	1	4.21
90	FRE/CAR	A+	8	207	8	1	0	0	53.2	35	1	11	1	4	49	0	0	4	0	15	10	4	2	.667	0	1.68
	HAG/EAS	AA	14	384	13	0	1	1	96.0	80	3	25	1	3	73	5	3	4	0	26	21	10	2	.833	0	1.97
	BAL/AL		8	168	6	0	0	0	36.1	43	4	19	0	1	20	0	2	1	0	22	20	3	3	.500	0	4.95
91	ROC/INT	AAA	27	665	25	3	0	0	157.1	166	17	48	2	4	115	5	3	7	2	82	69	12	9	.571	0	3.95
	BAL/AL		9	109	1	0	0	4	26.2	27	1	6	1	0	24	0	1	1	0	12	12	0	0	.000	0	4.05
92	ROC/INT	AAA	27	766	26	3	0	1	181.0	183	15	64	0	6	129	4	4	9	2	89	84	12	7	.632	0	4.18
93	BAL/AL		3	34	0	0	0	2	7.1	11	3	1	0	1	6	0	0	1	0	8	8	0	0	.000	0	9.82
	ROC/INT	AAA	38	397	6	0	0	12	90.2	98	10	33	3	3	66	2	4	6	0	51	43	7	7	.500	2	4.27
3 YR TOTALS			**20**	**311**	**9**	**0**	**0**	**6**	**70.1**	**81**	**10**	**26**	**1**	**2**	**50**	**0**	**3**	**3**	**0**	**42**	**40**	**3**	**3**	**.500**	**0**	**5.12**

Telgheder, David William "Dave" — BR/TR — b.11/11/66   NYN89 31/814

YR	TM/LG	CL	G	TBF	GS	CG	SHO	GF	IP	H	HR	BB	IBB	HB	SO	SH	SF	WP	BK	R	ER	W	L	PCT	SV	ERA
89	PIT/NYP	A-	13	233	7	4	1	4	58.2	43	2	9	1	2	65	1	1	2	1	18	16	5	3	.625	2	2.45
90	COL/SAL	A	14	380	13	5	1	1	99.1	79	2	10	0	0	81	0	0	0	1	22	17	9	3	.750	0	1.54
	SL/FSL	A+	14	382	14	3	0	0	96.0	84	3	14	0	1	77	3	4	3	0	38	32	9	4	.692	0	3.00
91	WIL/EAS	AA	28	711	26	1	0	1	167.2	185	7	33	3	5	90	7	11	4	1	81	67	13	11	.542	0	3.60
92	TID/INT	AAA	28	698	27	3	2	1	169.0	173	16	36	4	0	118	4	7	1	1	87	79	6	14	.300	0	4.21
93	NOR/INT	AAA	13	313	12	0	0	1	76.1	81	6	19	1	3	52	3	0	1	0	29	25	7	3	.700	1	2.95
	NY/NL		24	325	7	0	0	7	75.2	82	10	21	2	4	35	2	1	1	0	40	40	6	2	.750	0	4.76

Tewksbury, Robert Alan "Bob" — BR/TR — b.11/30/60   NYA81 19/493

YR	TM/LG	CL	G	TBF	GS	CG	SHO	GF	IP	H	HR	BB	IBB	HB	SO	SH	SF	WP	BK	R	ER	W	L	PCT	SV	ERA
81	ONE/NYP	A-	14	0	14	6	1	0	90.0	85	8	37	0	2	62	0	0	5	1	43	34	7	3	.700	0	3.40
82	FL/FSL	A+	24	0	23	13	5	0	182.0	146	6	47	0	5	92	0	0	11	1	46	38	15	4	.789	0	1.88
83	FL/FSL	A+	2	0	2	1	0	0	16.0	6	0	1	0	0	5	0	0	0	0	0	0	2	0	1.000	0	0.00
	NAS/SOU	AA	7	0	7	3	0	0	51.0	49	6	10	0	1	15	0	0	0	0	20	16	5	1	.833	0	2.82
84	NAS/SOU	AA	26	724	26	6	0	0	172.0	185	8	42	3	4	78	3	4	4	1	69	54	11	9	.550	0	2.83
85	ALB/EAS	AA	17	434	17	4	2	0	106.2	101	9	19	0	2	63	3	3	2	1	48	42	6	5	.545	0	3.54
	CMB/INT	AAA	6	160	6	1	1	0	44.0	22	2	5	0	0	21	0	0	0	1	5	5	3	0	1.000	0	1.02
86	CMB/INT	AAA	2	37	2	0	0	0	10.0	6	0	2	0	0	4	0	0	0	1	3	3	1	0	1.000	0	2.70
	NY/AL		23	558	20	2	0	0	130.1	144	8	31	0	5	49	4	7	3	2	58	48	9	5	.643	0	3.31
87	CMB/INT	AAA	11	300	11	0	0	0	74.2	68	5	11	0	1	32	2	1	0	2	23	21	6	1	.857	0	2.53
	NY/AL		8	149	6	0	0	1	33.1	47	5	7	0	1	12	0	0	0	0	26	25	1	4	.200	0	6.75
	CHI/NL		7	93	3	0	0	3	18.0	32	1	13	3	0	10	3	1	1	2	15	13	0	4	.000	0	6.50
	YEAR		15	242	9	0	0	4	51.1	79	6	20	3	1	22	3	1	1	2	41	38	1	8	.111	0	6.66
88	CHI/NL		1	18	1	0	0	0	3.1	6	1	2	0	0	1	0	0	0	0	5	3	0	0	.000	0	8.10
	IOW/AMA	AAA	10	277	10	2	2	0	67.0	73	8	10	0	2	43	1	2	1	6	28	28	4	2	.667	0	3.76
89	LOU/AMA	AAA	28	767	28	2	1	1	189.0	170	9	34	1	2	72	8	1	1	0	63	51	13	5	.722	0	2.43
	STL/NL		7	125	4	1	1	2	30.0	25	2	10	2	2	17	1	1	0	0	12	11	1	0	1.000	0	3.30
90	LOU/AMA	AAA	6	159	6	2	0	0	40.2	41	2	3	0	2	22	1	0	0	0	15	11	3	2	.600	0	2.43
	STL/NL		28	595	20	3	2	1	145.1	151	7	15	3	3	50	5	7	2	0	67	56	10	9	.526	1	3.47
91	STL/NL		30	798	30	3	0	0	191.0	206	13	38	2	5	75	12	10	0	0	86	69	11	12	.478	0	3.25
92	STL/NL		33	915	32	5	0	1	233.0	217	15	20	0	3	91	9	7	2	0	63	56	16	5	*.762	0	2.16
93	STL/NL		32	907	32	2	0	0	213.2	258	15	20	1	6	97	15	9	2	0	99	91	17	10	.630	0	3.83
8 YR TOTALS			**169**	**4158**	**148**	**16**	**3**	**8**	**998.0**	**1086**	**67**	**156**	**12**	**25**	**402**	**51**	**43**	**10**	**4**	**431**	**372**	**65**	**49**	**.570**	**1**	**3.35**

Thigpen, Robert Thomas "Bobby" — BR/TR — b.7/17/63　　　　　　　　　　　CHA85 4/85

YR	TM/LG	CL	G	TBF	GS	CG	SHO	GF	IP	H	HR	BB	IBB	HB	SO	SH	SF	WP	BK	R	ER	W	L	PCT	SV	ERA
85	NF/NYP	A-	28	211	1	0	0	25	52.1	30	0	19	2	1	74	1	1	2	0	12	10	2	3	.400	9	1.72
	APP/MID	A	1	11	0	0	0	0	2.2	1	0	1	1	0	4	0	0	0	0	1	0	1	0	1.000	0	0.00
86	BIR/SOU	AA	25	707	25	5	0	0	159.2	182	12	54	1	11	90	3	7	4	2	97	83	8	11	.421	0	4.68
	CHI/AL		20	142	0	0	0	14	35.2	26	1	12	0	1	20	1	1	0	0	7	7	2	0	1.000	7	1.77
87	HAW/PCL	AAA	9	234	9	2	1	0	52.2	72	5	14	1	1	17	1	1	0	1	38	36	2	3	.400	0	6.15
	CHI/AL		51	369	0	0	0	37	89.0	86	10	24	5	3	52	6	0	0	0	30	27	7	5	.583	16	2.73
88	CHI/AL		68	398	0	0	0	59	90.0	96	6	33	3	4	62	4	5	6	2	38	33	5	8	.385	34	3.30
89	CHI/AL		61	336	0	0	0	56	79.0	62	10	40	3	1	47	5	5	2	1	34	33	2	6	.250	34	3.76
90	CHI/AL		*77	347	0	0	0	73	88.2	60	5	32	3	1	70	4	3	2	0	20	18	4	6	.400	*57	1.83
91	CHI/AL		67	309	0	0	0	58	69.2	63	10	38	8	4	47	7	3	2	0	32	27	7	5	.583	30	3.49
92	CHI/AL		55	253	0	0	0	40	55.0	58	4	33	5	3	45	1	4	0	0	29	29	1	3	.250	22	4.75
93	CHI/AL		25	166	0	0	0	11	34.2	51	5	12	0	5	19	0	3	0	0	25	22	0	0	.000	1	5.71
	PHI/NL		17	88	0	0	0	5	19.1	23	2	9	1	1	10	2	1	0	1	13	13	3	1	.750	0	6.05
	YEAR		42	254	0	0	0	16	54.0	74	7	21	1	6	29	2	4	0	1	38	35	3	1	.750	1	5.83
8 YR TOTALS			**441**	**2408**	**0**	**0**	**0**	**353**	**561.0**	**525**	**53**	**233**	**28**	**23**	**372**	**31**	**25**	**12**	**4**	**228**	**209**	**31**	**34**	**.477**	**201**	**3.35**

Timlin, Michael August "Mike" — BR/TR — b.3/10/66　　　　　　　　　　　TOR87 5/127

YR	TM/LG	CL	G	TBF	GS	CG	SHO	GF	IP	H	HR	BB	IBB	HB	SO	SH	SF	WP	BK	R	ER	W	L	PCT	SV	ERA
87	MH/PIO	R+	13	326	12	2	0	0	75.1	79	4	26	0	5	66	1	2	9	5	50	43	4	8	.333	0	5.14
88	MB/SAL	A	35	653	22	0	0	1	151.0	119	4	77	2	19	106	2	2	8	4	68	48	10	6	.625	0	2.86
89	DUN/FSL	A+	33	397	7	1	0	16	88.2	90	2	36	1	5	64	9	3	10	3	44	32	5	8	.385	7	3.25
90	DUN/FSL	A+	42	203	0	0	0	40	50.1	36	0	16	2	1	46	3	0	3	0	11	8	7	2	.778	22	1.43
	KNO/SOU	AA	17	105	0	0	0	15	26.0	20	0	7	1	1	21	0	0	0	0	6	5	1	2	.333	8	1.73
91	TOR/AL		63	463	3	0	0	17	108.1	94	6	50	11	1	85	6	2	0	0	43	38	11	6	.647	3	3.16
92	DUN/FSL	A+	6	39	1	0	0	1	10.0	9	0	2	0	0	7	0	0	1	0	2	1	0	0	.000	1	0.90
	SYR/INT	AAA	7	51	1	0	0	4	11.1	15	3	5	1	0	7	0	0	0	0	11	11	0	1	.000	3	8.74
	TOR/AL		26	190	0	0	0	14	43.2	45	3	20	5	1	35	2	1	0	0	23	20	0	2	.000	1	4.12
93	DUN/FSL	A+	4	30	0	0	0	2	9.0	4	0	0	0	0	8	0	0	0	0	1	1	0	0	.000	1	1.00
	TOR/AL		54	254	0	0	0	27	55.2	63	7	27	3	1	49	1	2	0	0	32	29	4	2	.667	1	4.69
3 YR TOTALS			**143**	**907**	**3**	**0**	**0**	**58**	**207.2**	**202**	**13**	**97**	**19**	**3**	**169**	**9**	**6**	**6**	**0**	**98**	**87**	**15**	**10**	**.600**	**5**	**3.77**

Toliver, Freddie Lee — BR/TR — b.2/3/61　　　　　　　　　　　NYA79 3/77

YR	TM/LG	CL	G	TBF	GS	CG	SHO	GF	IP	H	HR	BB	IBB	HB	SO	SH	SF	WP	BK	R	ER	W	L	PCT	SV	ERA
84	WIC/AMA	AAA	32	725	23	6	0	4	164.0	142	19	116	1	2	113	3	4	5	3	90	88	11	6	.647	0	4.83
	CIN/NL		3	42	1	0	0	0	10.0	7	0	7	0	0	4	1	0	0	0	2	1	0	0	.000	0	0.90
85	DEN/AMA	AAA	19	508	19	5	2	0	122.1	113	6	56	0	1	84	3	3	6	1	50	44	11	3	.786	0	3.24
	PHI/NL		11	117	3	0	0	4	25.0	27	2	17	1	0	23	0	1	0	0	15	13	0	4	.000	1	4.68
86	POR/PCL	AAA	6	123	6	0	0	0	26.2	31	1	14	0	1	15	1	2	0	1	23	22	1	3	.250	0	7.43
	PHI/NL		5	112	5	0	0	0	25.2	28	0	11	0	0	20	3	0	1	0	14	10	0	2	.000	0	3.51
87	MAI/INT	AAA	22	543	21	2	0	0	124.2	114	15	67	6	2	80	2	2	3	1	70	64	6	9	.400	0	4.62
	PHI/NL		10	139	4	0	0	2	30.1	34	2	17	2	1	25	2	2	1	1	19	19	1	1	.500	0	5.64
88	POR/PCL	AAA	13	385	13	4	1	0	95.0	79	4	35	0	1	54	3	1	1	2	42	33	7	2	.778	0	3.13
	MIN/AL		21	491	19	0	0	0	114.2	116	8	52	1	1	69	3	3	0	1	57	54	7	6	.538	0	4.24
89	POR/PCL	AAA	8	204	8	2	1	0	50.1	44	2	14	0	1	35	0	1	3	2	22	15	4	2	.667	0	2.68
	MIN/AL		7	140	5	0	0	0	29.0	39	2	15	1	0	11	1	0	0	0	26	25	1	3	.250	0	7.76
	SD/NL		9	65	0	0	0	3	14.0	17	5	9	1	0	14	1	0	0	0	14	11	0	0	.000	0	7.07
	YEAR		16	205	5	0	0	3	43.0	56	7	24	2	0	25	2	0	0	0	40	36	1	3	.250	0	7.53
	LV/PCL	AAA	5	145	5	2	1	0	33.2	28	0	17	0	1	37	0	0	2	0	10	9	4	1	1.000	0	2.41
90	PS/CAL	A+	7	63	1	0	0	3	15.2	15	1	6	2	1	5	1	0	1	0	5	5	0	1	.000	0	2.87
	EDM/PCL	AAA	13	293	12	0	0	0	67.2	71	9	28	0	3	45	0	1	0	0	34	30	8	2	.800	0	3.99
91	EDM/PCL	AAA	18	411	18	2	1	0	95.1	89	6	49	1	0	68	1	5	11	2	48	44	7	4	.636	0	4.15
92	SAL/CAL	A+	20	535	20	3	1	0	123.2	125	5	47	2	3	104	8	5	3	0	63	48	5	8	.385	0	3.49
	CAR/SOU	AA	15	92	0	0	0	10	19.1	22	2	10	1	2	24	1	1	2	0	11	9	1	2	.333	3	4.19
93	CAR/SOU	AA	33	170	0	0	0	24	40.0	32	2	24	4	3	48	5	1	3	1	16	14	2	2	.500	12	3.15
	BUF/AMA	AAA	13	59	0	0	0	10	12.1	13	0	9	4	0	11	1	1	0	0	5	5	1	3	.250	1	3.65
	PIT/NL		12	90	0	0	0	3	21.2	20	2	8	0	2	14	2	3	0	0	10	9	1	0	1.000	0	3.74
7 YR TOTALS			**78**	**1196**	**37**	**0**	**0**	**12**	**270.1**	**288**	**21**	**136**	**5**	**6**	**180**	**17**	**8**	**13**	**2**	**157**	**142**	**10**	**16**	**.385**	**1**	**4.73**

Tomlin, Randy Leon — BL/TL — b.6/14/66　　　　　　　　　　　PIT88 18/460

YR	TM/LG	CL	G	TBF	GS	CG	SHO	GF	IP	H	HR	BB	IBB	HB	SO	SH	SF	WP	BK	R	ER	W	L	PCT	SV	ERA
88	WAT/NYP	A-	15	407	15	5	2	0	103.1	75	4	25	1	6	87	3	3	4	2	31	25	7	5	.583	0	2.18
89	SAL/CAR	A+	21	582	21	3	2	0	138.2	131	11	43	0	3	99	2	2	7	0	60	50	12	6	.667	0	3.25
	HAR/EAS	AA	5	119	5	0	0	0	32.0	18	0	6	0	1	31	1	3	0	0	6	3	2	2	.500	0	0.84
90	BUF/AMA	AAA	3	33	1	0	0	0	8.0	12	1	1	0	0	3	0	1	0	0	3	3	0	0	.000	0	3.38
	HAR/EAS	AA	19	521	18	4	3	0	126.1	101	3	34	6	6	92	4	2	4	1	43	32	9	6	.600	0	2.28
	PIT/NL		12	297	12	2	0	0	77.2	62	5	12	1	1	42	2	5	0	0	24	22	4	4	.500	0	2.55
91	PIT/NL		31	736	27	4	2	0	175.0	170	9	54	4	6	104	5	2	2	3	75	58	8	7	.533	0	2.98
92	PIT/NL		35	866	33	1	1	0	208.2	226	11	42	4	5	90	13	5	7	0	85	79	14	9	.609	0	3.41
93	CAR/SOU	AA	2	41	0	0	0	0	12.0	7	1	1	0	0	9	0	1	0	0	1	1	1	0	1.000	0	0.75
	PIT/NL		18	411	18	1	0	0	98.1	109	11	15	0	4	44	0	4	2	2	57	53	4	8	.333	0	4.85
4 YR TOTALS			**96**	**2310**	**90**	**8**	**3**	**0**	**559.2**	**567**	**36**	**123**	**9**	**17**	**280**	**28**	**17**	**14**	**10**	**241**	**212**	**30**	**28**	**.517**	**0**	**3.41**

Torres, Salomon — BR/TR — b.3/11/72　　　　　　　　　　　SF 9/15/89

YR	TM/LG	CL	G	TBF	GS	CG	SHO	GF	IP	H	HR	BB	IBB	HB	SO	SH	SF	WP	BK	R	ER	W	L	PCT	SV	ERA
91	CLI/MID	A	28	814	28	8	3	0	210.1	148	4	47	2	9	214	4	4	9	1	48	33	16	5	.762	0	1.41
92	SHR/TEX	AA	25	680	25	4	2	0	162.1	167	10	34	2	2	151	4	5	9	1	93	76	6	10	.375	0	4.21

Torres, Salomon (continued)

YR	TM/LG	CL	G	TBF	GS	CG	SHO	GF	IP	H	HR	BB	IBB	HB	SO	SH	SF	WP	BK	R	ER	W	L	PCT	SV	ERA
93	SHR/TEX	AA	12	324	12	2	1	0	83.1	67	6	12	0	3	67	1	1	3	0	27	25	7	4	.636	0	2.70
	PHO/PCL	AAA	14	437	14	4	1	0	105.1	105	5	27	0	2	99	3	2	7	2	43	41	7	4	.636	0	3.50
	SF/NL		8	196	8	0	0	0	44.2	37	5	27	3	1	23	7	1	3	1	21	20	3	5	.375	0	4.03

Trachsel, Stephen Christopher "Steve" — BR/TR — b.10/31/70   CHN91 7/215

YR	TM/LG	CL	G	TBF	GS	CG	SHO	GF	IP	H	HR	BB	IBB	HB	SO	SH	SF	WP	BK	R	ER	W	L	PCT	SV	ERA
91	GEN/NYP	A-	2	52	2	0	0	0	14.1	10	0	6	0	0	7	0	0	0	1	2	2	1	0	1.000	0	1.26
	WIN/CAR	A+	12	312	12	1	0	0	73.2	70	3	19	0	1	69	5	1	1	3	38	30	4	4	.500	0	3.67
92	CHA/SOU	AA	29	768	29	5	2	0	191.0	180	19	35	3	4	135	6	3	7	1	76	65	13	8	.619	0	3.06
93	IOW/AMA	AAA	27	703	26	1	1	1	170.2	170	20	45	0	6	135	4	4	4	1	78	75	13	6	.684	0	3.96
	CHI/NL		3	78	3	0	0	0	19.2	16	4	3	0	0	14	1	1	1	0	10	10	0	0	.000	0	4.58

Trlicek, Richard Alan "Ricky" — BR/TR — b.4/26/69   PHI87 3/104

YR	TM/LG	CL	G	TBF	GS	CG	SHO	GF	IP	H	HR	BB	IBB	HB	SO	SH	SF	WP	BK	R	ER	W	L	PCT	SV	ERA
87	UTI/NYP	A-	10	177	8	1	1	0	37.1	43	2	31	2	1	22	0	0	5	1	28	17	2	5	.286	0	4.10
88	BAT/NYP	A-	8	151	8	0	0	0	31.2	27	2	31	0	4	26	0	3	7	2	32	26	2	3	.400	0	7.39
89	SUM/SAL	A	15	385	15	0	0	0	93.2	73	7	40	1	4	72	3	3	3	3	40	27	6	5	.545	0	2.59
	DUR/CAR	A+	1	30	1	0	0	0	8.0	3	0	1	0	1	4	0	0	2	0	2	1	0	0	.000	0	1.13
90	DUN/FSL	A+	26	649	26	0	0	0	154.1	128	2	72	0	6	125	6	3	22	6	74	64	5	8	.385	0	3.73
91	KNO/SOU	AA	41	218	0	0	0	38	51.1	36	3	22	3	0	55	2	3	4	0	26	14	2	5	.286	16	2.45
92	TOR/AL		2	9	0	0	0	0	1.2	2	0	2	0	0	1	0	0	0	0	2	2	0	0	.000	0	10.80
	SYR/INT	AAA	35	195	0	0	0	23	43.1	37	2	31	1	0	35	2	2	8	1	22	21	1	1	.500	10	4.36
93	LA/NL		41	267	0	0	0	18	64.0	59	3	21	4	2	41	2	0	4	1	32	29	1	2	.333	1	4.08
2 YR TOTALS			**43**	**276**	**0**	**0**	**0**	**18**	**65.2**	**61**	**3**	**23**	**4**	**2**	**42**	**2**	**0**	**4**	**1**	**34**	**31**	**1**	**2**	**.333**	**1**	**4.25**

Trombley, Michael Scott "Mike" — BR/TR — b.4/14/67   MIN89 14/373

YR	TM/LG	CL	G	TBF	GS	CG	SHO	GF	IP	H	HR	BB	IBB	HB	SO	SH	SF	WP	BK	R	ER	W	L	PCT	SV	ERA
89	KEN/MID	A	12	202	3	0	0	6	49.0	45	1	13	0	3	41	1	0	4	3	23	17	5	1	.833	2	3.12
	VIS/CAL	A+	6	165	6	2	1	0	42.0	31	2	11	0	3	36	2	0	2	0	12	10	2	2	.500	0	2.14
90	VIS/CAL	A+	27	739	25	3	1	1	176.0	163	12	50	0	11	164	3	3	8	1	79	67	14	6	.700	0	3.43
91	ORL/SOU	AA	27	773	27	7	2	0	191.0	153	12	57	2	7	175	7	6	2	1	65	54	12	7	.632	0	2.54
92	POR/PCL	AAA	25	695	25	2	0	0	165.0	149	18	58	1	6	138	5	2	1	2	70	67	10	8	.556	0	3.65
	MIN/AL		10	194	7	0	0	0	46.1	43	5	17	0	2	38	2	0	0	0	20	17	3	2	.600	0	3.30
93	MIN/AL		44	506	10	0	0	8	114.1	131	15	41	4	3	85	3	7	5	0	72	62	6	6	.500	2	4.88
2 YR TOTALS			**54**	**700**	**17**	**0**	**0**	**8**	**160.2**	**174**	**20**	**58**	**4**	**4**	**123**	**5**	**7**	**5**	**0**	**92**	**79**	**9**	**8**	**.529**	**2**	**4.43**

Tsamis, George Alex — BR/TL — b.6/14/67   MIN89 15/399

YR	TM/LG	CL	G	TBF	GS	CG	SHO	GF	IP	H	HR	BB	IBB	HB	SO	SH	SF	WP	BK	R	ER	W	L	PCT	SV	ERA
89	VIS/CAL	A+	15	387	13	3	0	1	94.1	85	10	34	0	2	87	3	0	9	3	36	32	6	3	.667	0	3.05
90	VIS/CAL	A+	26	731	26	4	3	0	183.2	168	4	61	0	4	145	3	2	7	1	62	45	17	4	.810	0	2.21
91	ORL/SOU	AA	1	28	1	0	0	0	7.0	3	0	4	0	0	5	0	0	0	0	2	0	0	0	.000	0	0.00
	POR/PCL	AAA	29	716	27	2	1	0	167.2	183	11	66	0	5	71	8	6	7	1	75	61	10	8	.556	0	3.27
92	POR/PCL	AAA	39	700	22	4	1	6	163.2	195	12	51	1	5	71	3	5	2	0	78	71	13	4	.765	1	3.90
93	POR/PCL	AAA	3	74	3	0	0	0	14.0	27	2	5	0	0	10	0	0	1	0	15	13	1	2	.333	0	8.36
	MIN/AL		41	309	0	0	0	18	68.1	86	9	27	5	3	30	2	6	1	1	51	47	1	2	.333	1	6.19

Turner, William Matthew "Matt" — BR/TR — b.2/18/67   ATL 5/21/86

YR	TM/LG	CL	G	TBF	GS	CG	SHO	GF	IP	H	HR	BB	IBB	HB	SO	SH	SF	WP	BK	R	ER	W	L	PCT	SV	ERA
86	PUL/APP	R+	18	229	5	0	0	7	48.2	55	6	28	1	2	48	1	2	2	0	36	25	1	3	.250	2	4.62
87	SUM/SAL	A+	39	423	9	0	0	17	93.2	91	8	48	2	5	102	5	4	8	6	61	49	2	3	.400	1	4.71
88	BUR/MID	A	7	161	6	0	0	0	34.1	43	9	16	0	3	26	0	1	0	3	27	25	1	3	.250	0	6.55
	SUM/SAL	A	7	65	0	0	0	4	15.2	17	0	3	0	2	7	0	0	1	0	8	8	1	0	1.000	0	4.60
89	DUR/CAR	A+	53	499	3	0	0	19	118.0	95	11	47	9	5	114	3	5	5	3	38	32	9	9	.500	1	2.44
90	GRE/SOU	AA	40	289	0	0	0	26	67.2	59	6	29	2	3	60	1	1	4	2	24	20	6	4	.600	4	2.66
	RIC/INT	AAA	22	175	1	0	0	11	42.0	44	6	16	1	2	36	1	1	7	1	20	18	2	3	.400	2	3.86
91	RIC/INT	AAA	23	161	0	0	0	17	36.0	33	5	20	0	2	33	2	4	4	0	21	19	1	3	.250	5	4.75
	TUC/PCL	AAA	13	115	0	0	0	5	26.0	27	0	14	2	1	25	0	1	1	1	12	12	1	1	.500	1	4.15
92	TUC/PCL	AAA	63	436	0	0	0	38	100.0	93	2	40	3	2	84	7	4	5	3	52	39	2	8	.200	14	3.51
93	EDM/PCL	AAA	12	51	0	0	0	12	13.2	9	1	2	0	0	15	0	1	0	0	1	1	0	0	.000	10	0.66
	FLO/NL		55	279	0	0	0	26	68.0	55	7	26	9	1	59	6	4	6	1	23	22	4	5	.444	0	2.91

Urbani, Thomas James "Tom" — BL/TL — b.1/21/68   SL90 14/357

YR	TM/LG	CL	G	TBF	GS	CG	SHO	GF	IP	H	HR	BB	IBB	HB	SO	SH	SF	WP	BK	R	ER	W	L	PCT	SV	ERA
90	JC/APP	R+	9	217	9	0	0	0	48.1	43	2	15	0	1	40	1	0	4	0	35	18	4	3	.571	0	3.35
	HAM/NYP	A-	5	125	5	0	0	0	26.1	33	4	15	1	3	17	0	2	3	1	26	18	0	4	.000	0	6.15
91	SPR/MID	A	8	195	8	0	0	0	47.2	45	2	6	0	2	42	0	2	1	1	20	11	3	2	.600	0	2.08
	SP/FSL	A+	19	476	19	2	1	0	118.2	109	4	25	0	2	64	3	5	1	0	39	31	8	7	.533	0	2.35
92	ARK/TEX	AA	10	263	10	2	1	0	65.1	49	3	15	1	2	41	3	0	1	0	23	14	4	6	.400	0	1.93
	LOU/AMA	AAA	16	384	16	2	0	0	88.2	91	9	37	1	7	46	4	2	5	0	50	46	4	5	.444	0	4.67
93	LOU/AMA	AAA	18	377	13	0	0	2	94.2	86	4	23	1	2	65	3	2	0	0	29	26	9	5	.643	1	2.47
	STL/NL		18	283	9	0	0	2	62.0	73	4	26	2	0	33	4	1	1	0	44	32	1	3	.250	0	4.65

Valdez, Sergio Sanchez — BR/TR — b.9/7/64   MON 1/20/83

YR	TM/LG	CL	G	TBF	GS	CG	SHO	GF	IP	H	HR	BB	IBB	HB	SO	SH	SF	WP	BK	R	ER	W	L	PCT	SV	ERA
83	CAL/PIO	R+	13	0	13	0	0	0	72.0	88	7	31	0	2	41	0	0	4	0	55	45	6	3	.667	0	5.63
84	WPB/FSL	A+	5	54	0	0	0	2	11.1	15	2	8	0	0	6	0	0	1	1	11	11	0	0	.000	0	8.74

(continued)

Valdez, Sergio Sanchez (continued)

YR	TM/LG	CL	G	TBF	GS	CG	SHO	GF	IP	H	HR	BB	IBB	HB	SO	SH	SF	WP	BK	R	ER	W	L	PCT	SV	ERA
	JAM/NYP	A-	13	340	12	5	1	1	76.0	78	3	33	0	1	46	5	3	4	1	47	34	2	7	.222	0	4.03
85	UTI/NYP	A-	15	454	15	5	0	0	105.2	98	6	36	1	1	86	2	4	8	3	53	36	6	5	.545	0	3.07
86	WPB/FSL	A+	24	589	24	6	4	0	145.2	119	9	46	0	4	108	1	1	3	5	48	40	16	6	.727	0	2.47
	MON/NL		5	120	5	0	0	0	25.0	39	2	11	0	1	20	0	0	2	0	20	19	0	4	.000	0	6.84
87	IND/AMA	AAA	27	714	27	2	2	0	158.1	191	14	64	4	7	128	5	6	8	2	108	90	10	7	.588	0	5.12
88	IND/AMA	AAA	14	351	14	0	0	0	84.0	80	8	28	0	2	61	2	2	1	4	38	32	5	4	.556	0	3.43
89	IND/AMA	AAA	19	374	12	0	0	3	90.2	78	4	26	2	5	81	4	2	5	4	38	33	6	3	.667	1	3.28
	ATL/NL		19	145	1	0	0	8	32.2	31	5	17	3	0	26	2	0	2	0	24	22	1	2	.333	0	6.06
90	ATL/NL		6	26	0	0	0	3	5.1	6	0	3	0	0	3	1	0	1	0	4	4	0	0	.000	0	6.75
	CS/PCL	AAA	7	195	7	2	1	0	43.1	55	7	13	0	1	33	0	0	1	0	29	25	4	3	.571	0	5.19
	CLE/AL		24	440	13	0	0	4	102.1	109	17	35	2	1	63	4	5	3	0	62	54	6	6	.500	0	4.75
	YEAR		30	466	13	0	0	7	107.2	115	17	38	2	1	66	5	5	4	0	66	58	6	6	.500	0	4.85
91	CLE/AL		6	70	0	0	0	1	16.1	15	3	5	1	0	11	1	1	1	0	11	10	1	0	1.000	0	5.51
	CS/PCL	AAA	26	542	15	4	0	6	131.1	139	12	27	6	7	71	3	4	9	2	67	60	4	12	.250	0	4.11
92	IND/AMA	AAA	13	254	8	0	0	1	62.1	59	3	13	1	1	41	2	2	2	0	29	26	4	2	.667	0	3.75
	MON/NL		27	148	0	0	0	9	37.1	25	2	12	1	0	32	1	0	4	0	12	10	0	2	.000	0	2.41
93	OTT/INT	AAA	30	350	4	0	0	6	83.2	77	3	22	2	6	53	1	3	7	0	31	29	5	3	.625	1	3.12
	MON/NL		4	14	0	0	0	1	3.0	3	1	1	0	0	2	0	0	0	0	4	3	0	0	.000	0	9.00
6 YR TOTALS			**91**	**963**	**19**	**0**	**0**	**26**	**222.0**	**229**	**30**	**84**	**7**	**2**	**157**	**9**	**6**	**13**	**0**	**137**	**122**	**8**	**14**	**.364**	**0**	**4.95**

Valenzuela, Fernando — BL/TL — b.11/1/60

MEX 1978

YR	TM/LG	CL	G	TBF	GS	CG	SHO	GF	IP	H	HR	BB	IBB	HB	SO	SH	SF	WP	BK	R	ER	W	L	PCT	SV	ERA
80	LA/NL		10	66	0	0	0	4	17.2	8	0	5	0	0	16	1	1	0	1	2	0	2	0	1.000	1	0.00
81	LA/NL		25	758	25	*11	*8	0	*192.1	140	11	61	4	1	*180	9	3	4	0	55	53	13	7	.650	0	2.48
82	LA/NL		37	1156	37	18	4	0	285.0	247	13	83	12	2	199	19	6	4	0	105	91	19	13	.594	0	2.87
83	LA/NL		35	1094	35	9	4	0	257.0	245	16	99	10	3	189	27	5	12	1	122	107	15	10	.600	0	3.75
84	LA/NL		34	1078	34	12	2	0	261.0	218	14	106	4	2	240	11	7	11	1	109	88	12	17	.414	0	3.03
85	LA/NL		35	1109	35	14	5	0	272.1	211	14	101	5	1	208	13	8	10	1	92	74	17	10	.630	0	2.45
86	LA/NL		34	1102	34	*20	3	0	269.1	226	18	85	5	1	242	15	3	13	0	104	94	*21	11	.656	0	3.14
87	LA/NL		34	1116	34	*12	1	0	251.0	254	25	124	4	4	190	18	2	14	1	120	111	14	14	.500	0	3.98
88	LA/NL		23	626	22	3	0	1	142.1	142	11	76	4	0	64	15	5	7	1	71	67	5	8	.385	1	4.24
89	LA/NL		31	852	31	3	0	0	196.2	185	11	98	6	2	116	11	3	6	4	89	75	10	13	.435	0	3.43
90	LA/NL		33	900	33	5	2	0	204.0	223	19	77	4	0	115	11	4	13	1	112	104	13	13	.500	0	4.59
91	PS/CAL	A+	1	19	1	0	0	0	4.0	4	0	3	0	0	2	0	0	0	0	1	0	0	0	.000	0	0.00
	CAL/AL		2	36	2	0	0	0	6.2	14	3	3	0	0	5	1	1	2	0	10	9	0	2	.000	0	12.15
	MID/TEX	AA	4	93	4	1	1	0	23.0	18	1	6	0	1	17	2	0	5	0	5	5	3	1	.750	0	1.96
	EDM/PCL	AAA	7	170	7	0	0	0	36.2	48	9	17	1	1	36	0	2	0	0	34	29	3	3	.500	0	7.12
93	ROC/INT	AAA	1	18	1	0	0	0	3.1	6	0	3	0	0	1	0	0	0	0	4	4	0	1	.000	0	10.80
	BOW/EAS	AA	1	22	1	0	0	0	6.0	4	0	0	0	1	4	1	0	0	0	1	1	0	0	.000	0	1.50
	BAL/AL		32	768	31	5	2	0	178.2	179	18	79	2	4	78	4	7	8	0	104	98	8	10	.444	0	4.94
13 YR TOTALS			**365**	**10661**	**353**	**112**	**31**	**5**	**2534.0**	**2292**	**173**	**997**	**60**	**20**	**1842**	**151**	**59**	**103**	**11**	**1095**	**971**	**149**	**128**	**.538**	**2**	**3.45**

Valera, Julio Enrique — BR/TR — b.10/13/68

NYN 3/6/86

YR	TM/LG	CL	G	TBF	GS	CG	SHO	GF	IP	H	HR	BB	IBB	HB	SO	SH	SF	WP	BK	R	ER	W	L	PCT	SV	ERA
86	KIN/APP	R+	13	356	13	2	1	0	76.1	91	5	29	2	0	64	4	0	4	1	58	44	3	10	.231	0	5.19
87	COL/SAL	A	22	522	22	2	2	0	125.1	114	7	31	0	4	97	2	1	6	0	53	39	8	7	.533	0	2.80
88	COL/SAL	A	30	775	27	8	0	3	191.0	171	8	51	3	4	144	5	7	9	6	77	68	15	11	.577	1	3.20
89	SL/FSL	A+	6	173	6	3	2	0	45.0	34	1	6	1	0	45	2	0	0	0	5	5	4	2	.667	0	1.00
	JAC/TEX	AA	19	566	19	6	1	0	137.1	123	4	36	2	8	107	7	3	10	0	47	38	10	6	.625	0	2.49
	TID/INT	AAA	2	52	2	0	0	0	13.0	8	1	5	0	1	10	0	1	0	0	3	3	1	1	.500	0	2.08
90	TID/INT	AAA	24	648	24	9	2	0	158.0	146	12	39	3	5	133	6	5	7	5	66	53	10	10	.500	0	3.02
	NY/NL		3	64	3	0	0	0	13.0	20	1	7	0	0	4	2	0	2	0	11	10	1	1	.500	0	6.92
91	NY/NL		2	11	0	0	0	0	2.0	1	0	4	1	0	3	0	0	0	0	0	0	0	0	.000	0	0.00
	TID/INT	AAA	26	739	26	3	1	0	176.1	152	12	70	4	6	117	8	4	4	0	79	75	10	10	.500	0	3.83
92	TID/INT	AAA	1	25	1	0	0	0	6.0	5	0	2	0	0	2	0	1	0	0	6	6	0	1	1.000	0	0.00
	CAL/AL		30	792	28	4	2	0	188.0	188	15	64	5	2	113	6	2	5	0	82	78	8	11	.421	0	3.73
93	CAL/AL		19	246	5	0	0	8	53.0	77	8	15	2	2	28	4	1	2	0	44	39	3	6	.333	4	6.62
4 YR TOTALS			**54**	**1113**	**36**	**4**	**2**	**9**	**256.0**	**286**	**24**	**90**	**8**	**4**	**148**	**10**	**3**	**7**	**0**	**137**	**127**	**12**	**18**	**.400**	**4**	**4.46**

Van Poppel, Todd Matthew — BR/TR — b.12/9/71

OAK90 1/14

YR	TM/LG	CL	G	TBF	GS	CG	SHO	GF	IP	H	HR	BB	IBB	HB	SO	SH	SF	WP	BK	R	ER	W	L	PCT	SV	ERA
90	SO/NWL	A-	5	92	5	0	0	0	24.0	10	1	9	0	2	32	1	0	1	0	5	3	1	1	.500	0	1.13
	MAD/MID	A	3	61	3	0	0	0	13.2	8	0	10	0	1	17	0	1	0	0	11	6	2	1	.667	0	3.95
91	HUN/SOU	AA	24	608	24	1	1	0	132.1	118	2	90	0	6	115	4	6	12	1	69	51	6	13	.316	0	3.47
	OAK/AL		1	21	1	0	0	0	4.2	7	1	2	0	0	6	0	0	0	0	5	5	0	0	.000	0	9.64
92	TAC/PCL	AAA	9	202	9	0	0	0	45.1	44	4	35	0	1	29	3	4	1	1	22	20	4	2	.667	0	3.97
93	TAC/PCL	AAA	16	355	16	0	0	0	78.2	67	5	54	0	4	71	3	2	6	0	53	51	4	8	.333	0	5.83
	OAK/AL		16	380	16	0	0	0	84.0	76	10	62	0	2	47	1	2	3	0	50	47	6	6	.500	0	5.04
2 YR TOTALS			**17**	**401**	**17**	**0**	**0**	**0**	**88.2**	**83**	**11**	**64**	**0**	**2**	**53**	**1**	**2**	**3**	**0**	**55**	**52**	**6**	**6**	**.500**	**0**	**5.28**

Viola, Frank John — BL/TL — b.4/19/60

MIN81 2/37

YR	TM/LG	CL	G	TBF	GS	CG	SHO	GF	IP	H	HR	BB	IBB	HB	SO	SH	SF	WP	BK	R	ER	W	L	PCT	SV	ERA
82	MIN/AL		22	543	22	3	1	0	126.0	152	22	38	2	0	84	2	0	4	1	77	73	4	10	.286	0	5.21
83	MIN/AL		35	949	34	4	0	0	210.0	242	34	92	1	8	127	1	2	6	2	141	128	7	15	.318	0	5.49
84	MIN/AL		35	1047	35	10	4	0	257.2	225	28	73	1	4	149	1	5	6	1	101	92	18	12	.600	0	3.21
85	MIN/AL		36	1059	36	9	0	0	250.2	262	26	68	3	2	135	5	6	6	2	136	114	18	14	.563	0	4.09

Viola, Frank John (continued)

YR	TM/LG	CL	G	TBF	GS	CG	SHO	GF	IP	H	HR	BB	IBB	HB	SO	SH	SF	WP	BK	R	ER	W	L	PCT	SV	ERA
86	MIN/AL		37	1053	37	7	1	0	245.2	257	37	83	0	3	191	4	5	12	0	136	123	16	13	.552	0	4.51
87	MIN/AL		36	1037	36	7	1	0	251.2	230	29	66	1	6	197	7	3	1	1	91	81	17	10	.630	0	2.90
88	MIN/AL		35	1031	35	7	2	0	255.1	236	20	54	2	3	193	6	6	5	1	80	75	*24	7	*.774	0	2.64
89	MIN/AL		24	731	24	7	1	0	175.2	171	17	47	1	3	138	9	4	5	1	80	74	8	12	.400	0	3.79
	NY/NL		12	351	12	2	1	0	85.1	75	5	27	3	1	73	3	2	3	0	35	32	5	5	.500	0	3.38
	YEAR		36	1082	36	9	2	0	261.0	246	22	74	4	4	211	12	6	8	1	115	106	13	17	.433	0	3.66
90	NY/NL		35	1016	35	7	3	0	*249.2	227	15	60	2	2	182	13	3	11	0	83	74	20	12	.625	0	2.67
91	NY/NL		35	980	35	3	0	0	231.1	259	25	54	4	1	132	15	5	6	1	112	102	13	15	.464	0	3.97
92	BOS/AL		35	999	35	6	1	0	238.0	214	13	89	4	7	121	7	10	12	2	99	91	13	12	.520	0	3.44
93	BOS/AL		29	787	29	2	1	0	183.2	180	12	72	5	6	91	8	7	5	0	76	64	11	8	.579	0	3.14
12 YR TOTALS			**406**	**11583**	**405**	**74**	**16**	**0**	**2760.2**	**2730**	**283**	**823**	**35**	**46**	**1813**	**85**	**57**	**82**	**12**	**1247**	**1123**	**174**	**145**	**.545**	**0**	**3.66**

Wagner, Paul Alan — BR/TR — b.11/14/67   PIT89 13/314

YR	TM/LG	CL	G	TBF	GS	CG	SHO	GF	IP	H	HR	BB	IBB	HB	SO	SH	SF	WP	BK	R	ER	W	L	PCT	SV	ERA
89	WEL/NYP	A-	13	220	10	0	0	1	50.1	54	4	15	0	1	34	1	1	4	0	34	25	4	5	.444	0	4.47
90	AUG/SAL	A	35	313	1	0	0	20	72.0	71	3	30	3	2	71	3	3	7	0	30	22	7	7	.500	4	2.75
	SAL/CAR	A+	11	159	4	0	0	3	36.0	39	7	17	1	0	28	0	1	3	0	22	20	0	1	.000	2	5.00
91	SAL/CAR	A+	25	660	25	5	2	0	158.2	124	14	60	0	9	113	4	2	11	1	70	55	11	6	.647	0	3.12
92	CAR/SOU	AA	19	513	19	2	1	0	121.2	104	3	47	1	3	101	6	5	6	0	52	41	6	6	.500	0	3.03
	BUF/AMA	AAA	8	181	8	0	0	0	39.1	51	1	14	0	1	19	2	1	2	0	27	24	3	3	.500	0	5.49
	PIT/NL		6	52	1	0	0	1	13.0	9	0	5	0	0	5	0	0	1	0	1	1	2	0	1.000	0	0.69
93	PIT/NL		44	599	17	1	1	9	141.1	143	15	42	2	1	114	6	7	12	0	72	67	8	8	.500	2	4.27
2 YR TOTALS			**50**	**651**	**18**	**1**	**1**	**10**	**154.1**	**152**	**15**	**47**	**2**	**1**	**119**	**6**	**7**	**13**	**0**	**73**	**68**	**10**	**8**	**.556**	**2**	**3.97**

Wainhouse, David Paul "Dave" — BL/TR — b.11/7/67   MON88 1/19

YR	TM/LG	CL	G	TBF	GS	CG	SHO	GF	IP	H	HR	BB	IBB	HB	SO	SH	SF	WP	BK	R	ER	W	L	PCT	SV	ERA
89	WPB/FSL	A+	13	286	13	0	0	0	66.1	75	4	19	0	8	26	3	2	6	3	35	30	1	5	.167	0	4.07
90	WPB/FSL	A+	12	327	12	2	1	0	76.2	68	1	34	0	5	58	0	3	2	3	28	18	6	3	.667	0	2.11
	JAC/SOU	AA	17	428	16	2	0	0	95.2	97	7	47	2	4	59	3	2	0	0	59	46	7	7	.500	0	4.33
91	HAR/EAS	AA	33	224	0	0	0	27	52.0	49	1	17	2	4	46	2	1	3	0	17	15	2	2	.500	11	2.60
	MON/NL		2	14	0	0	0	1	2.2	2	0	4	0	0	1	0	0	1	0	2	2	0	1	.000	0	6.75
	IND/AMA	AAA	14	127	0	0	0	8	28.2	28	1	15	1	3	13	2	1	4	0	14	13	2	0	1.000	1	4.08
92	IND/AMA	AAA	44	208	0	0	0	41	46.0	48	4	24	6	2	37	2	2	4	0	22	21	5	4	.556	21	4.11
93	SEA/AL		3	20	0	0	0	0	2.1	7	1	5	0	1	2	0	0	0	0	7	7	0	0	.000	0	27.00
	CAL/PCL	AAA	13	62	0	0	0	10	15.2	10	2	7	1	1	7	2	2	2	0	7	7	0	1	.000	5	4.02
2 YR TOTALS			**5**	**34**	**0**	**0**	**0**	**1**	**5.0**	**9**	**1**	**9**	**0**	**1**	**3**	**0**	**1**	**2**	**0**	**9**	**9**	**0**	**1**	**.000**	**0**	**16.20**

Wakefield, Timothy Stephen "Tim" — BR/TR — b.8/2/66   PIT88 8/200

YR	TM/LG	CL	G	TBF	GS	CG	SHO	GF	IP	H	HR	BB	IBB	HB	SO	SH	SF	WP	BK	R	ER	W	L	PCT	SV	ERA
89	WEL/NYP	A-	18	168	1	0	0	11	39.2	30	1	21	0	2	42	2	1	9	0	17	15	1	1	.500	2	3.40
90	SAL/CAR	A+	28	824	28	2	0	0	190.1	187	24	85	2	10	127	7	6	11	0	109	100	10	14	.417	0	4.73
91	BUF/AMA	AAA	1	23	1	0	0	0	4.2	8	3	1	0	0	4	0	0	0	0	6	6	0	1	.000	0	11.57
	CAR/SOU	AA	26	741	25	8	1	1	183.0	155	13	51	6	9	123	4	6	3	2	68	59	15	8	.652	0	2.90
92	BUF/AMA	AAA	20	559	20	6	1	0	135.1	122	10	51	1	3	71	3	7	9	0	52	46	10	3	.769	0	3.06
	PIT/NL		13	373	13	4	1	0	92.0	76	3	35	1	1	51	6	4	3	1	26	22	8	1	.889	0	2.15
93	CAR/SOU	AA	9	265	9	1	0	0	56.2	68	5	22	0	5	36	2	4	3	0	48	44	3	5	.375	0	6.99
	PIT/NL		24	595	20	3	2	1	128.1	145	14	75	2	9	59	7	5	6	0	83	80	6	11	.353	0	5.61
2 YR TOTALS			**37**	**968**	**33**	**7**	**3**	**1**	**220.1**	**221**	**17**	**110**	**3**	**10**	**110**	**13**	**9**	**9**	**1**	**109**	**102**	**14**	**12**	**.538**	**0**	**4.17**

Walk, Robert Vernon "Bob" — BR/TR — b.11/26/56   PHI7 S3/52

YR	TM/LG	CL	G	TBF	GS	CG	SHO	GF	IP	H	HR	BB	IBB	HB	SO	SH	SF	WP	BK	R	ER	W	L	PCT	SV	ERA
80	PHI/NL		27	673	27	2	0	0	151.2	163	8	71	2	2	94	5	5	6	3	82	77	11	7	.611	0	4.57
81	ATL/NL		12	189	8	0	0	1	43.1	41	6	23	0	1	16	2	0	1	0	25	22	1	4	.200	0	4.57
82	ATL/NL		32	717	27	3	1	1	164.1	179	19	59	2	6	84	8	5	7	0	101	89	11	9	.550	0	4.87
83	ATL/NL		1	20	1	0	0	0	3.2	7	0	2	0	0	1	0	0	0	0	3	3	0	0	.000	0	7.36
84	HAW/PCL	AAA	18	0	18	5	3	0	127.1	100	3	42	0	2	85	0	0	2	3	39	32	9	5	.643	0	2.26
	PIT/NL		2	44	2	0	0	0	10.1	8	1	4	1	0	10	0	0	1	0	5	3	1	1	.500	0	2.61
85	HAW/PCL	AAA	24	0	24	12	1	0	173.0	143	10	61	1	4	124	0	0	12	4	57	51	16	5	.762	0	2.65
	PIT/NL		9	248	9	1	1	0	58.2	60	3	18	2	0	40	3	1	2	0	27	24	2	3	.400	0	3.68
86	PIT/NL		44	592	15	1	1	7	141.2	129	14	64	7	3	78	6	5	12	1	66	59	7	8	.467	2	3.75
87	PIT/NL		39	498	12	1	1	6	117.0	107	11	51	2	3	78	6	2	7	3	52	43	8	2	.800	0	3.31
88	PIT/NL		32	881	32	2	1	0	212.2	183	6	65	5	2	81	14	5	13	0	75	64	12	10	.545	0	2.71
89	PIT/NL		33	843	31	2	0	0	196.0	208	15	65	1	4	83	4	2	4	4	106	96	13	10	.565	0	4.41
90	PIT/NL		26	549	24	1	1	0	129.2	136	17	36	2	3	73	3	3	5	3	59	54	7	5	.583	1	3.75
91	CAR/SOU	AA	1	19	1	0	0	0	5.0	5	0	2	0	0	3	0	0	0	0	1	1	0	0	.000	0	1.80
	PIT/NL		25	484	20	1	0	0	115.0	104	10	35	2	5	67	4	1	11	2	53	46	9	2	.818	0	3.60
92	PIT/NL		36	567	19	1	0	7	135.0	132	10	43	5	4	60	5	1	7	2	54	48	10	6	.625	2	3.20
93	PIT/NL		32	822	32	3	0	0	187.0	214	23	70	5	5	80	10	9	7	3	121	118	13	14	.481	0	5.68
14 YR TOTALS			**350**	**7127**	**259**	**16**	**6**	**24**	**1666.0**	**1671**	**143**	**606**	**36**	**40**	**848**	**74**	**42**	**80**	**33**	**829**	**746**	**105**	**81**	**.565**	**5**	**4.03**

Walton, Bruce Kenneth — BR/TR — b.12/25/62   OAK85 16/403

YR	TM/LG	CL	G	TBF	GS	CG	SHO	GF	IP	H	HR	BB	IBB	HB	SO	SH	SF	WP	BK	R	ER	W	L	PCT	SV	ERA
85	POC/PIO	R+	18	0	9	0	0	6	76.2	89	2	27	1	1	69	0	0	7	0	46	35	3	7	.300	3	4.11
86	MOD/CAL	A+	27	778	27	4	0	0	176.0	204	16	41	3	9	107	10	5	7	1	96	80	13	7	.650	0	4.09
	MAD/MID	A	1	21	1	0	0	0	5.0	5	0	1	0	0	1	0	1	0	0	3	3	0	0	.000	0	5.40
87	MOD/CAL	A+	16	437	16	3	1	0	106.1	97	6	27	0	4	84	1	3	2	0	44	34	8	6	.571	0	2.88

(continued)

Walton, Bruce Kenneth (continued)

YR	TM/LG	CL	G	TBF	GS	CG	SHO	GF	IP	H	HR	BB	IBB	HB	SO	SH	SF	WP	BK	R	ER	W	L	PCT	SV	ERA
	HUN/SOU	AA	18	248	2	0	0	6	58.0	61	4	13	1	1	40	2	3	4	2	24	20	2	2	.500	2	3.10
88	HUN/SOU	AA	42	502	3	0	0	17	116.1	126	10	23	7	5	82	5	3	2	6	64	59	4	5	.444	3	4.56
89	TAC/PCL	AAA	32	461	14	1	1	7	107.2	118	7	27	1	1	76	4	4	3	2	59	45	8	6	.571	0	3.76
90	TAC/PCL	AAA	46	403	5	0	0	21	98.1	103	12	23	5	2	67	4	7	1	5	42	34	5	5	.500	7	3.11
91	TAC/PCL	AAA	38	184	0	0	0	38	46.2	39	0	5	1	0	49	2	0	2	0	11	7	1	1	.500	20	1.35
	OAK/AL		12	56	0	0	0	5	13.0	11	3	6	0	1	10	0	1	3	0	9	9	1	0	1.000	0	6.23
92	OAK/AL		7	49	0	0	0	2	10.0	17	1	3	0	0	7	0	1	0	1	11	11	0	0	.000	0	9.90
	TAC/PCL	AAA	35	333	7	2	1	22	81.1	76	6	21	4	3	60	1	2	1	0	29	25	8	2	.800	8	2.77
93	MON/NL		4	32	0	0	0	3	5.2	11	1	3	0	0	2	2	0	0	0	6	6	0	0	.000	0	9.53
	OTT/INT	AAA	40	167	0	0	0	38	42.2	32	2	8	2	0	40	2	1	0	0	12	5	4	4	.500	16	1.05
	TUC/PCL	AAA	13	59	0	0	0	12	15.0	12	0	3	1	0	14	0	1	1	0	4	3	2	0	1.000	7	1.80
3 YR TOTALS			23	137	0	0	0	10	28.2	39	5	12	0	1	17	2	2	3	1	26	26	1	0	1.000	0	8.16

Ward, Roy Duane "Duane" — BR/TR — b.5/28/64　　ATL82 1/9

YR	TM/LG	CL	G	TBF	GS	CG	SHO	GF	IP	H	HR	BB	IBB	HB	SO	SH	SF	WP	BK	R	ER	W	L	PCT	SV	ERA
84	GRE/SOU	AA	21	471	20	4	0	0	104.2	108	9	57	0	2	54	4	6	8	1	71	58	4	9	.308	0	4.99
85	GRE/SOU	AA	28	671	24	3	0	1	150.0	141	4	105	1	4	100	3	5	9	0	83	70	11	10	.524	0	4.20
	RIC/INT	AAA	5	30	1	0	0	3	5.1	8	1	8	0	1	3	0	0	0	0	9	7	0	1	.000	0	11.81
86	ATL/NL		10	73	0	0	0	6	16.0	22	2	8	0	0	8	2	0	0	1	13	13	0	1	.000	0	7.31
	RIC/INT	AAA	6	158	6	0	0	0	34.2	34	0	23	0	1	17	3	0	0	0	13	13	1	1	.500	0	3.38
	SYR/INT	AAA	14	359	14	0	0	0	83.0	91	9	29	0	2	50	2	1	1	0	43	39	6	4	.600	0	4.23
	TOR/AL		2	15	1	0	0	1	2.0	3	0	4	0	1	1	0	0	1	0	4	3	0	1	.000	0	13.50
	YEAR		12	88	1	0	0	7	18.0	25	2	12	0	1	9	2	0	1	1	17	16	0	2	.000	0	8.00
87	SYR/INT	AAA	46	319	3	0	0	29	76.1	59	7	42	1	2	67	2	2	2	0	35	33	2	2	.500	14	3.89
	TOR/AL		12	57	0	0	0	4	11.2	14	0	12	2	0	10	1	1	0	0	9	9	1	0	1.000	0	6.94
88	TOR/AL		64	487	0	0	0	32	111.2	101	5	60	8	5	91	4	5	10	3	46	41	9	3	.750	15	3.30
89	TOR/AL		66	494	0	0	0	39	114.2	94	4	58	11	5	122	12	11	13	0	55	48	4	10	.286	15	3.77
90	TOR/AL		73	508	0	0	0	39	127.2	101	9	42	10	1	112	6	2	5	0	51	49	2	8	.200	11	3.45
91	TOR/AL		*81	428	0	0	0	46	107.1	80	3	33	3	2	132	3	4	6	0	36	33	7	6	.538	23	2.77
92	TOR/AL		79	414	0	0	0	35	101.1	76	5	39	3	1	103	3	4	7	0	27	22	7	4	.636	12	1.95
93	TOR/AL		71	282	0	0	0	70	71.2	49	4	25	2	1	97	0	2	7	0	17	17	2	3	.400	*45	2.13
8 YR TOTALS			458	2758	2	0	0	272	664.0	540	32	281	39	16	676	31	29	49	4	258	235	32	36	.471	121	3.19

Watson, Allen Kenneth — BL/TL — b.11/18/70　　SL91 2/21

YR	TM/LG	CL	G	TBF	GS	CG	SHO	GF	IP	H	HR	BB	IBB	HB	SO	SH	SF	WP	BK	R	ER	W	L	PCT	SV	ERA
91	HAM/NYP	A-	8	156	8	0	0	0	39.1	22	2	17	0	0	46	0	1	1	0	15	11	1	1	.500	0	2.52
	SAV/SAL	A	3	62	3	0	0	0	13.2	16	1	8	0	0	12	0	2	1	1	7	6	1	1	.500	0	3.95
92	SP/FSL	A+	14	374	14	2	0	0	89.2	81	0	18	2	2	80	4	1	1	0	31	19	5	4	.556	0	1.91
	ARK/TEX	AA	14	376	14	3	1	0	96.1	77	4	23	1	2	93	4	0	0	3	24	23	8	5	.615	0	2.15
	LOU/AMA	AAA	2	53	2	0	0	0	12.1	8	1	5	0	0	9	0	0	2	0	4	2	1	0	1.000	0	1.46
93	LOU/AMA	AAA	17	483	17	2	0	0	120.2	101	13	31	0	4	86	5	0	2	3	46	39	5	4	.556	0	2.91
	STL/NL		16	373	15	0	0	1	86.0	90	11	28	2	3	49	4	2	3	0	53	44	6	7	.462	0	4.60

Wayne, Gary Anthony — BL/TL — b.11/30/62　　MON84 5/93

YR	TM/LG	CL	G	TBF	GS	CG	SHO	GF	IP	H	HR	BB	IBB	HB	SO	SH	SF	WP	BK	R	ER	W	L	PCT	SV	ERA
84	WPB/FSL	A+	13	342	12	2	0	0	74.1	70	1	49	0	3	46	3	2	9	2	38	32	3	5	.375	0	3.87
85	JAC/SOU	AA	21	471	20	2	0	0	102.0	108	3	70	3	1	62	2	4	11	1	67	60	3	12	.200	0	5.29
	WPB/FSL	A+	8	147	4	0	0	0	30.2	37	1	22	0	0	18	5	1	5	0	23	19	2	2	.500	0	5.58
86	WPB/FSL	A+	47	255	0	0	0	41	61.1	48	1	25	2	1	55	2	2	3	1	16	11	2	5	.286	25	1.61
87	JAC/SOU	AA	56	324	0	0	0	28	80.1	56	4	35	0	0	78	2	2	2	1	23	21	5	1	.833	10	2.35
88	IND/AMA	AAA	8	33	0	0	0	2	7.1	9	0	3	0	0	6	0	1	3	1	5	5	0	0	.000	1	6.14
89	MIN/AL		60	302	0	0	0	21	71.0	55	4	36	4	1	41	4	2	7	0	28	26	3	4	.429	1	3.30
90	POR/PCL	AAA	22	134	0	0	0	13	31.2	29	1	13	1	0	30	1	2	4	0	14	12	2	4	.333	5	3.41
	MIN/AL		38	166	0	0	0	12	38.2	38	5	13	0	1	28	1	2	4	1	19	18	1	1	.500	1	4.19
91	POR/PCL	AAA	51	296	0	0	0	32	67.2	63	4	31	4	1	66	4	4	4	2	27	21	4	5	.444	8	2.79
	MIN/AL		8	52	0	0	0	2	12.1	11	1	4	0	1	7	1	1	0	0	7	7	1	0	1.000	0	5.11
92	POR/PCL	AAA	14	93	0	0	0	7	23.0	23	1	1	0	0	20	0	0	1	0	11	6	0	1	.000	5	2.35
	MIN/AL		41	210	0	0	0	13	48.0	46	2	19	5	2	29	8	3	1	1	18	14	3	3	.500	2	2.63
93	COL/NL		65	283	0	0	0	21	62.1	68	8	26	8	1	49	3	7	9	1	40	35	5	3	.625	1	5.05
5 YR TOTALS			212	1013	0	0	0	69	232.1	218	20	98	17	7	154	17	15	21	2	112	100	13	11	.542	4	3.87

Weathers, John David "Dave" — BR/TR — b.9/25/69　　TOR88 3/82

YR	TM/LG	CL	G	TBF	GS	CG	SHO	GF	IP	H	HR	BB	IBB	HB	SO	SH	SF	WP	BK	R	ER	W	L	PCT	SV	ERA
88	SC/NYP	A-	15	267	12	0	0	2	62.2	58	3	26	0	2	36	2	0	5	4	30	21	4	4	.500	0	3.02
89	MB/SAL	A	31	759	31	2	0	0	172.2	163	3	86	2	7	111	5	2	12	1	99	74	11	13	.458	0	3.86
90	DUN/FSL	A+	27	675	27	2	0	0	158.0	158	2	59	0	9	96	4	7	10	9	82	65	10	7	.588	0	3.70
91	KNO/SOU	AA	24	575	22	5	2	0	139.1	121	4	49	1	8	114	1	3	7	2	51	38	10	7	.588	0	2.45
	TOR/AL		15	79	0	0	0	4	14.2	15	1	17	3	2	13	2	0	0	0	9	8	1	0	1.000	0	4.91
92	TOR/AL		2	15	0	0	0	0	3.1	5	1	2	0	0	3	0	0	0	0	3	3	0	0	.000	0	8.10
	SYR/INT	AAA	12	215	10	0	0	1	48.1	48	3	21	2	2	30	1	2	0	0	29	25	1	4	.200	0	4.66
93	EDM/PCL	AAA	22	611	22	3	1	0	141.0	150	12	47	2	2	117	5	3	4	1	77	60	11	4	.733	0	3.83
	FLO/NL		14	202	6	0	0	0	45.2	57	3	13	1	1	34	1	0	6	0	26	26	2	3	.400	0	5.12
3 YR TOTALS			31	296	6	0	0	6	63.2	77	5	32	4	3	50	4	1	6	0	38	37	3	3	.500	0	5.23

Wegman, William Edward "Bill" — BR/TR — b.12/19/62   MIL81 5/124

YR	TM/LG	CL	G	TBF	GS	CG	SHO	GF	IP	H	HR	BB	IBB	HB	SO	SH	SF	WP	BK	R	ER	W	L	PCT	SV	ERA
84	EP/TEX	AA	10	265	10	4	0	0	64.0	62	5	15	0	3	42	1	0	1	0	25	19	4	5	.444	0	2.67
	VAN/PCL	AAA	6	0	3	0	0	2	27.2	30	0	8	0	1	16	0	0	0	1	11	6	0	3	.000	1	1.95
85	VAN/PCL	AAA	28	0	28	8	2	0	188.0	187	21	52	5	5	113	0	0	2	0	93	84	10	11	.476	0	4.02
	MIL/AL		3	73	3	0	0	0	17.2	17	3	3	0	0	6	0	1	0	1	8	7	2	0	1.000	0	3.57
86	MIL/AL		35	836	32	2	0	1	198.1	217	32	43	2	7	82	4	5	5	2	120	113	5	12	.294	0	5.13
87	MIL/AL		34	934	33	7	0	0	225.0	229	31	53	2	6	102	4	6	0	2	113	106	12	11	.522	0	4.24
88	MIL/AL		32	847	31	4	1	0	199.0	207	24	50	5	4	84	3	10	1	1	104	91	13	13	.500	0	4.12
89	MIL/AL		11	240	8	0	0	1	51.0	69	6	21	2	0	27	0	4	2	0	44	38	2	6	.250	0	6.71
90	DEN/AMA	AAA	3	54	3	0	0	0	13.2	10	0	7	0	0	14	1	1	0	0	5	5	1	0	1.000	0	3.29
	MIL/AL		8	132	5	1	1	0	29.2	37	6	6	1	0	20	1	1	0	0	21	16	2	2	.500	0	4.85
	BEL/MID	A	1	7	1	0	0	0	2.0	1	0	0	0	0	2	0	0	0	0	0	0	0	0	.000	0	0.00
91	BEL/MID	A	3	45	3	0	0	0	11.0	11	0	1	0	2	12	0	0	2	0	5	2	0	0	.000	0	1.64
	DEN/AMA	AAA	1	26	1	0	0	0	7.0	6	0	1	0	0	1	0	0	0	0	2	2	0	0	.000	0	2.57
	MIL/AL		28	785	28	7	2	0	193.1	176	16	40	0	7	89	6	4	6	0	76	61	15	7	.682	0	2.84
92	MIL/AL		35	1079	35	7	0	0	261.2	251	28	55	3	9	127	7	4	1	2	104	93	13	14	.481	0	3.20
93	MIL/AL		20	514	18	5	0	0	120.2	135	13	34	5	2	50	3	11	0	0	70	60	4	14	.222	0	4.48
9 YR TOTALS			**206**	**5440**	**193**	**33**	**4**	**2**	**1296.1**	**1338**	**159**	**305**	**20**	**35**	**587**	**28**	**46**	**15**	**8**	**660**	**585**	**68**	**79**	**.463**	**0**	**4.06**

Welch, Robert Lynn "Bob" — BR/TR — b.11/3/56   LA77 1/20

YR	TM/LG	CL	G	TBF	GS	CG	SHO	GF	IP	H	HR	BB	IBB	HB	SO	SH	SF	WP	BK	R	ER	W	L	PCT	SV	ERA
78	LA/NL		23	439	13	4	3	6	111.1	92	6	26	2	1	66	4	6	2	2	28	25	7	4	.636	3	2.02
79	LA/NL		25	349	12	1	0	10	81.1	82	7	32	4	3	64	4	1	0	0	42	36	5	6	.455	5	3.98
80	LA/NL		32	889	32	3	2	0	213.2	190	15	79	6	3	141	12	10	7	5	85	78	14	9	.609	0	3.29
81	LA/NL		23	601	23	2	1	0	141.1	141	11	41	0	3	88	9	4	2	0	56	54	9	5	.643	0	3.44
82	LA/NL		36	965	36	9	3	0	235.2	199	19	81	5	5	176	7	4	5	1	94	88	16	11	.593	0	3.36
83	LA/NL		31	828	31	4	3	0	204.0	164	13	72	4	3	156	8	7	4	6	73	60	15	12	.556	0	2.65
84	LA/NL		31	771	29	3	1	0	178.2	191	11	58	7	2	126	10	2	4	2	86	75	13	13	.500	0	3.78
85	VB/FSL	A+	3	65	3	0	0	0	17.0	15	0	1	0	0	9	1	0	0	0	4	4	0	0	.000	0	2.12
	LA/NL		23	675	23	8	3	0	167.1	141	16	35	2	6	96	6	2	7	4	49	43	14	4	.778	0	2.31
86	LA/NL		33	981	33	7	3	0	235.2	227	14	55	6	7	183	7	8	2	1	95	86	7	13	.350	0	3.28
87	LA/NL		35	1027	35	6	*4	0	251.2	204	21	86	6	4	196	10	6	4	4	94	90	15	9	.625	0	3.22
88	OAK/AL		36	1034	36	4	2	0	244.2	237	22	81	1	10	158	12	8	3	13	107	99	17	9	.654	0	3.64
89	OAK/AL		33	884	33	1	0	0	209.2	191	13	78	3	6	137	3	4	5	0	82	70	17	8	.680	0	3.00
90	OAK/AL		35	979	35	2	2	0	238.0	214	26	77	4	5	127	6	5	2	2	90	78	*27	6	*.818	0	2.95
91	OAK/AL		35	950	35	7	1	0	220.0	220	25	91	3	11	101	6	6	3	2	124	112	12	13	.480	0	4.58
92	OAK/AL		20	513	20	0	0	0	123.2	114	13	43	0	2	47	3	2	1	0	47	45	11	7	.611	0	3.27
93	OAK/AL		30	746	28	0	0	0	166.2	208	25	56	5	7	63	10	3	1	0	102	98	9	11	.450	0	5.29
16 YR TOTALS			**481**	**12631**	**454**	**61**	**28**	**16**	**3023.1**	**2815**	**257**	**991**	**58**	**78**	**1925**	**117**	**79**	**52**	**42**	**1254**	**1137**	**208**	**140**	**.598**	**8**	**3.38**

Wells, David Lee — BL/TL — b.5/20/63   TOR82 2/30

YR	TM/LG	CL	G	TBF	GS	CG	SHO	GF	IP	H	HR	BB	IBB	HB	SO	SH	SF	WP	BK	R	ER	W	L	PCT	SV	ERA
84	KIN/CAR	A+	7	192	7	0	0	0	42.0	51	1	19	1	1	44	1	2	4	1	29	22	1	6	.143	0	4.71
	KNO/SOU	AA	8	239	8	3	1	0	59.0	58	3	17	0	0	34	0	1	1	0	22	17	3	2	.600	0	2.59
86	FLO/SAL	A	4	54	1	0	0	0	12.2	7	1	9	0	0	14	0	1	1	0	6	5	0	0	.000	0	3.55
	VEN/CAL	A+	5	72	2	0	0	1	19.0	13	0	4	0	0	26	2	1	0	0	5	4	2	1	.667	0	1.89
	KNO/SOU	AA	10	174	7	1	0	2	40.0	42	1	18	0	1	32	2	3	4	0	24	18	1	3	.250	0	4.05
	SYR/INT	AAA	3	17	0	0	0	1	3.2	6	0	1	0	0	4	0	0	0	1	4	4	0	1	.000	0	9.82
87	SYR/INT	AAA	43	453	12	0	0	17	109.1	102	9	32	0	0	106	3	3	9	1	49	47	4	6	.400	5	3.87
	TOR/AL		18	132	2	0	0	6	29.1	37	0	12	0	0	32	1	0	4	0	14	13	4	3	.571	1	3.99
88	SYR/INT	AAA	6	28	0	0	0	3	5.2	5	0	2	1	0	4	0	0	0	0	1	0	0	0	.000	3	0.00
	TOR/AL		41	279	0	0	0	15	64.1	65	12	31	9	2	56	2	2	6	2	36	33	3	5	.375	4	4.62
89	TOR/AL		54	352	0	0	0	19	86.1	66	5	28	7	0	78	3	2	6	3	25	23	7	4	.636	2	2.40
90	TOR/AL		43	759	25	0	0	8	189.0	165	14	45	3	2	115	9	2	7	1	72	66	11	6	.647	3	3.14
91	TOR/AL		40	811	28	2	0	3	198.1	188	24	49	1	2	106	6	6	10	3	88	82	15	10	.600	1	3.72
92	TOR/AL		41	529	14	0	0	14	120.0	138	16	36	6	8	62	3	4	3	0	84	72	7	9	.438	2	5.40
93	DET/AL		32	776	30	0	0	0	187.0	183	26	42	6	7	139	3	3	13	0	93	87	11	9	.550	0	4.19
7 YR TOTALS			**269**	**3638**	**99**	**2**	**0**	**65**	**874.1**	**842**	**97**	**243**	**32**	**21**	**588**	**27**	**19**	**49**	**10**	**412**	**376**	**58**	**46**	**.558**	**13**	**3.87**

Wendell, Steven John "Turk" — BB/TR — b.5/19/67   ATL88 7/112

YR	TM/LG	CL	G	TBF	GS	CG	SHO	GF	IP	H	HR	BB	IBB	HB	SO	SH	SF	WP	BK	R	ER	W	L	PCT	SV	ERA
88	PUL/APP	R+	14	418	14	6	1	0	101.0	85	3	30	0	6	87	5	2	7	6	50	43	3	8	.273	0	3.83
89	BUR/MID	A	22	643	22	9	5	0	159.0	127	7	41	1	3	153	2	0	1	6	63	39	9	11	.450	0	2.21
	GRE/SOU	AA	1	19	1	0	0	0	3.2	7	3	1	0	0	3	0	0	0	0	5	4	0	0	.000	0	9.82
	DUR/CAR	A+	3	89	3	1	0	0	24.0	13	0	6	0	0	27	0	0	0	0	4	3	2	0	1.000	0	1.13
90	GRE/SOU	AA	36	434	13	1	1	13	91.0	105	5	48	2	11	85	5	6	8	2	70	58	4	9	.308	2	5.74
	DUR/CAR	A+	6	154	5	1	0	0	38.2	24	3	15	1	2	26	0	0	2	0	10	8	1	3	.250	0	1.86
91	GRE/SOU	AA	25	613	20	1	1	3	147.2	130	4	51	5	6	122	2	2	11	0	47	42	11	3	.786	0	2.56
	RIC/INT	AAA	3	97	3	1	0	0	21.0	20	3	6	1	3	18	1	0	2	0	12	8	0	0	.000	0	3.43
92	IOW/AMA	AAA	4	107	4	0	0	0	25.0	17	3	15	0	0	12	2	1	1	0	7	4	2	0	1.000	0	1.44
93	IOW/AMA	AAA	25	639	25	5	2	0	148.2	148	9	47	0	6	110	4	6	9	3	88	76	10	8	.556	0	4.60
	CHI/NL		7	98	4	0	0	1	22.2	24	0	8	1	0	15	0	2	0	0	13	11	1	2	.333	0	4.37

Wertz, William Charles "Bill" — BR/TR — b.1/15/67   CLE89 30/801

YR	TM/LG	CL	G	TBF	GS	CG	SHO	GF	IP	H	HR	BB	IBB	HB	SO	SH	SF	WP	BK	R	ER	W	L	PCT	SV	ERA
89	IND/GCL	R	12	282	11	1	1	0	66.0	57	0	36	0	4	56	1	4	11	0	23	23	4	3	.571	0	3.14
90	REN/CAL	A+	17	295	9	0	0	1	61.1	61	6	52	0	5	52	3	4	12	0	58	45	1	3	.250	0	6.60

(continued)

Wertz, William Charles "Bill" (continued)

YR	TM/LG	CL	G	TBF	GS	CG	SHO	GF	IP	H	HR	BB	IBB	HB	SO	SH	SF	WP	BK	R	ER	W	L	PCT	SV	ERA
	WAT/NYP	A-	14	431	14	2	0	0	100.2	81	3	48	0	4	92	2	2	6	0	39	32	10	2	.833	0	2.86
91	CMB/SAL	A	49	391	0	0	0	31	91.0	81	6	32	3	6	95	6	4	5	0	41	30	6	8	.429	9	2.97
92	CAN/EAS	AA	57	382	0	0	0	24	97.1	75	1	30	6	3	69	3	2	3	0	16	13	8	4	.667	8	1.20
93	CHW/INT	AAA	28	207	1	0	0	9	50.2	42	4	14	4	1	47	3	0	1	0	18	11	7	2	.778	0	1.95
	CLE/AL		34	262	0	0	0	7	59.2	54	5	32	2	1	53	1	1	0	0	28	24	2	3	.400	0	3.62

West, David Lee — BL/TL — b.9/1/64
NYN83 6/84

YR	TM/LG	CL	G	TBF	GS	CG	SHO	GF	IP	H	HR	BB	IBB	HB	SO	SH	SF	WP	BK	R	ER	W	L	PCT	SV	ERA
84	COL/SAL	A	12	288	12	0	0	0	60.2	41	2	68	1	2	60	4	1	14	1	47	42	3	5	.375	0	6.23
	LF/NYP	A-	13	290	11	0	0	1	62.0	43	1	62	0	1	79	3	4	16	2	35	23	6	4	.600	0	3.34
85	COL/SAL	A	26	677	25	5	2	0	150.0	105	6	111	1	9	194	6	3	23	3	97	76	10	9	.526	0	4.56
86	LYN/CAR	A+	13	343	13	1	0	0	75.0	76	3	53	0	3	70	5	3	4	1	50	43	1	6	.143	0	5.16
	COL/SAL	A	13	403	13	3	1	0	92.2	74	4	56	1	3	101	3	3	14	2	41	30	10	3	.769	0	2.91
87	JAC/TEX	AA	25	730	25	4	2	0	166.2	152	5	81	1	4	186	4	4	5	3	67	52	10	7	.588	0	2.81
88	TID/INT	AAA	23	675	23	7	1	0	160.1	106	5	97	1	9	143	11	3	5	3	42	32	12	4	.750	0	1.80
	NY/NL		2	25	1	0	0	0	6.0	6	0	3	0	0	3	0	0	0	2	2	2	1	0	1.000	0	3.00
89	TID/INT	AAA	12	343	12	5	1	0	87.1	60	9	29	0	2	69	6	4	3	1	31	23	7	4	.636	0	2.37
	NY/NL		11	112	2	0	0	0	24.1	25	4	14	2	1	19	0	1	2	0	20	20	0	2	.000	0	7.40
	MIN/AL		10	182	5	0	0	4	39.1	48	5	19	1	2	31	2	2	1	0	29	28	3	2	.600	0	6.41
	YEAR		21	294	7	0	0	4	63.2	73	9	33	3	3	50	2	3	3	0	49	48	3	4	.429	0	6.79
90	MIN/AL		29	646	27	2	0	0	146.1	142	21	78	1	4	92	6	3	4	1	88	83	7	9	.438	0	5.10
91	ORL/SOU	AA	1	1	1	0	0	0	0.1	0	0	0	0	0	0	0	0	0	0	0	0	0	0	.000	0	0.00
	POR/PCL	AAA	4	68	4	0	0	0	15.2	12	3	12	0	0	15	1	1	0	0	11	11	1	1	.500	0	6.32
	MIN/AL		15	305	12	0	0	0	71.1	66	13	28	0	1	52	3	3	3	0	37	36	4	4	.500	0	4.54
92	POR/PCL	AAA	19	444	18	1	0	0	101.2	88	6	65	1	2	87	4	2	9	1	51	50	7	6	.538	0	4.43
	MIN/AL		9	139	4	0	0	1	28.1	32	3	20	1	0	19	0	1	2	0	24	22	1	3	.250	0	6.99
93	PHI/NL		76	375	0	0	0	27	86.1	60	6	51	4	5	87	8	2	3	0	37	28	6	4	.600	3	2.92
6 YR TOTALS			**152**	**1784**	**50**	**2**	**0**	**32**	**402.0**	**379**	**52**	**213**	**8**	**14**	**303**	**18**	**14**	**14**	**3**	**237**	**219**	**22**	**24**	**.478**	**3**	**4.90**

Weston, Michael Lee "Mickey" — BR/TR — b.3/26/61
NYN82 12/293

YR	TM/LG	CL	G	TBF	GS	CG	SHO	GF	IP	H	HR	BB	IBB	HB	SO	SH	SF	WP	BK	R	ER	W	L	PCT	SV	ERA
82	LF/NYP	A-	17	0	13	2	0	0	92.0	105	16	22	0	4	67	0	0	0	0	63	52	7	6	.538	0	5.09
83	COL/SAL	A	37	0	1	0	0	0	74.0	87	5	22	0	1	46	0	0	8	0	48	36	2	2	.500	6	4.38
84	COL/SAL	A	32	272	2	0	0	20	63.2	58	2	27	6	2	40	6	1	5	0	27	13	6	5	.545	2	1.84
85	LYN/CAR	A+	49	407	3	1	1	24	100.1	81	4	22	2	0	62	3	2	4	1	29	24	6	5	.545	10	2.15
86	JAC/TEX	AA	34	308	4	0	0	7	70.2	73	9	27	3	4	36	3	2	3	0	40	34	4	4	.500	2	4.33
87	JAC/TEX	AA	58	346	1	0	0	21	82.0	96	4	18	5	1	50	0	1	6	1	39	31	8	4	.667	3	3.40
88	JAC/TEX	AA	30	507	14	1	1	4	125.1	127	3	20	4	0	61	8	5	4	0	50	31	8	5	.615	0	2.23
	TID/INT	AAA	4	115	4	2	1	0	29.2	21	0	5	1	1	16	0	0	0	0	6	5	2	1	.667	0	1.52
89	ROC/INT	AAA	23	445	14	2	1	7	112.0	103	6	19	0	1	51	2	0	2	0	30	26	8	3	.727	4	2.09
	BAL/AL		7	55	0	0	0	2	13.0	18	1	2	0	1	7	0	0	0	0	8	8	1	0	1.000	1	5.54
90	ROC/INT	AAA	29	432	12	2	0	13	109.1	93	3	22	0	0	58	1	2	3	0	36	24	11	1	.917	6	1.98
	BAL/AL		9	94	2	0	0	4	21.0	28	6	6	1	0	9	1	0	1	0	20	18	0	1	.000	0	7.71
91	TOR/AL		2	8	0	0	0	0	2.0	1	0	1	1	0	1	0	0	0	0	0	0	0	0	.000	0	0.00
	SYR/INT	AAA	27	710	25	3	0	1	166.0	193	7	36	1	3	60	4	5	10	0	85	69	12	6	.667	0	3.74
92	PHI/NL		1	19	1	0	0	0	3.2	7	1	1	0	1	0	0	0	0	0	5	5	0	1	.000	0	12.27
	SCR/INT	AAA	26	683	24	2	1	1	170.2	165	12	29	2	3	79	5	5	4	1	65	59	10	6	.625	1	3.11
93	NOR/INT	AAA	21	542	20	3	0	1	127.1	149	10	18	2	2	41	3	2	2	0	77	60	10	9	.526	0	4.24
	NY/NL		4	30	0	0	0	1	5.2	11	0	1	0	1	2	0	0	0	0	5	5	0	0	.000	0	7.94
5 YR TOTALS			**23**	**206**	**3**	**0**	**0**	**8**	**45.1**	**65**	**8**	**11**	**2**	**3**	**19**	**1**	**0**	**1**	**0**	**38**	**36**	**1**	**2**	**.333**	**1**	**7.15**

Wetteland, John Karl — BR/TR — b.8/21/66
LA85* S2/39

YR	TM/LG	CL	G	TBF	GS	CG	SHO	GF	IP	H	HR	BB	IBB	HB	SO	SH	SF	WP	BK	R	ER	W	L	PCT	SV	ERA
85	GF/PIO	R+	11	0	2	0	0	3	20.2	17	0	15	1	0	23	0	0	0	0	10	9	1	1	.500	0	3.92
86	BAK/CAL	A+	15	313	12	4	0	1	67.0	71	6	46	1	1	38	2	4	10	1	50	43	0	7	.000	0	5.78
	GF/PIO	R+	12	0	12	1	0	0	69.1	70	8	40	0	3	59	0	0	7	1	51	42	4	3	.571	0	5.45
87	VB/FSL	A+	27	759	27	7	2	0	175.2	150	11	92	0	4	144	3	4	17	0	81	61	12	7	.632	0	3.13
88	SA/TEX	AA	25	684	25	3	1	0	162.1	141	10	77	1	1	140	7	5	22	2	74	70	10	8	.556	0	3.88
89	ALB/PCL	AAA	10	286	10	1	0	0	69.0	61	11	20	0	0	73	2	0	0	0	28	28	5	3	.625	0	3.65
	LA/NL		31	411	12	0	0	7	102.2	81	8	34	4	0	96	4	2	16	1	46	43	5	8	.385	1	3.77
90	ALB/PCL	AAA	8	120	5	1	0	2	29.0	27	5	13	0	0	26	1	1	0	0	19	18	2	2	.500	0	5.59
	LA/NL		22	190	5	0	0	7	43.0	44	6	17	3	4	36	1	1	4	0	28	23	2	4	.333	0	4.81
91	ALB/PCL	AAA	41	245	4	0	0	34	61.1	48	5	26	1	1	55	4	3	1	0	22	19	4	3	.571	20	2.79
	LA/NL		6	36	0	0	0	3	9.0	5	0	3	0	1	9	0	1	1	0	2	0	1	0	1.000	0	0.00
92	MON/NL		67	347	0	0	0	58	83.1	64	6	36	3	2	99	5	1	4	0	27	27	4	4	.500	37	2.92
93	WPB/FSL	A+	2	9	2	0	0	0	3.0	0	0	0	0	0	6	0	0	0	0	0	0	0	0	.000	0	0.00
	MON/NL		70	344	0	0	0	58	85.1	58	3	28	3	2	113	5	1	7	0	17	13	9	3	.750	43	1.37
5 YR TOTALS			**196**	**1328**	**17**	**0**	**0**	**133**	**323.1**	**252**	**23**	**118**	**13**	**11**	**353**	**15**	**6**	**36**	**1**	**120**	**106**	**21**	**19**	**.525**	**81**	**2.95**

Whitehurst, Walter Richard "Wally" — BR/TR — b.4/11/64
OAK85 3/65

YR	TM/LG	CL	G	TBF	GS	CG	SHO	GF	IP	H	HR	BB	IBB	HB	SO	SH	SF	WP	BK	R	ER	W	L	PCT	SV	ERA
85	MED/NWL	A-	14	0	14	2	0	0	88.0	92	6	29	1	7	91	0	0	11	2	51	35	7	5	.583	0	3.58
	MOD/CAL	A+							10.0	10	1	5	0	1	5	0	0	0	0	3	2	1	0	1.000	0	1.80
86	MAD/MID	A	8	234	8	5	4	0	61.0	42	4	16	0	1	57	1	0	4	0	8	4	6	1	.857	0	0.59
	HUN/SOU	AA	19	468	19	2	0	0	104.2	114	4	46	3	7	54	5	2	12	3	66	54	9	5	.643	0	4.64
87	HUN/SOU	AA	28	766	28	5	3	0	183.1	192	12	42	3	2	106	6	6	9	0	104	81	11	10	.524	0	3.98

Whitehurst, Walter Richard "Wally" (continued)

YR	TM/LG	CL	G	TBF	GS	CG	SHO	GF	IP	H	HR	BB	IBB	HB	SO	SH	SF	WP	BK	R	ER	W	L	PCT	SV	ERA
88	TID/INT	AAA	26	664	26	3	1	0	165.0	145	7	32	3	8	113	8	4	10	9	65	56	10	11	.476	0	3.05
89	TID/INT	AAA	21	551	20	3	1	1	133.0	123	5	32	2	1	95	3	2	3	2	54	48	8	7	.533	0	3.25
	NY/NL		9	64	1	0	0	4	14.0	17	2	5	0	0	9	0	1	1	0	7	7	0	1	.000	0	4.50
90	TID/INT	AAA	2	34	2	0	0	0	9.0	7	0	1	0	1	10	0	0	0	0	2	2	1	0	1.000	0	2.00
	NY/NL		38	263	0	0	0	16	65.2	63	5	9	2	0	46	3	0	2	0	27	24	1	0	1.000	0	3.29
91	NY/NL		36	556	20	0	0	6	133.1	142	12	25	3	4	87	6	3	3	4	67	62	7	12	.368	1	4.18
92	NY/NL		44	421	11	0	0	7	97.0	99	4	33	5	4	70	6	3	2	1	45	39	3	9	.250	0	3.62
93	WIC/TEX	AA	4	80	4	0	0	0	21.1	11	1	5	0	0	14	0	0	4	1	4	3	1	0	1.000	0	1.27
	SD/NL		21	441	19	0	0	1	105.2	109	11	30	5	3	57	5	8	5	1	47	45	4	7	.364	0	3.83
5 YR TOTALS			**148**	**1745**	**51**	**0**	**0**	**34**	**415.2**	**430**	**34**	**102**	**15**	**11**	**269**	**20**	**15**	**13**	**6**	**193**	**177**	**15**	**29**	**.341**	**3**	**3.83**

Whiteside, Matthew Christopher "Matt" — BR/TR — b.8/8/67   TEX90 25/678

YR	TM/LG	CL	G	TBF	GS	CG	SHO	GF	IP	H	HR	BB	IBB	HB	SO	SH	SF	WP	BK	R	ER	W	L	PCT	SV	ERA
90	BUT/PIO	R+	18	256	5	0	0	5	57.1	57	4	25	0	9	45	0	0	4	6	33	22	4	4	.500	2	3.45
91	GAS/SAL	A	48	255	0	0	0	42	62.2	43	1	21	0	5	71	1	3	3	0	19	15	3	1	.750	29	2.15
92	TUL/TEX	AA	33	134	0	0	0	32	33.2	31	2	3	1	1	30	0	0	2	0	9	9	0	1	.000	21	2.41
	OC/AMA	AAA	12	44	0	0	0	12	11.1	7	1	3	1	0	13	0	0	0	0	1	1	1	0	1.000	8	0.79
	TEX/AL		20	118	0	0	0	8	28.0	26	1	11	2	0	13	1	0	1	0	8	6	1	1	.500	4	1.93
93	OC/AMA	AAA	8	55	0	0	0	6	11.1	17	1	8	4	0	10	1	0	1	1	7	7	2	1	.667	1	5.56
	TEX/AL		60	305	0	0	0	10	73.0	78	7	23	6	1	39	2	1	0	2	37	35	2	1	.667	1	4.32
2 YR TOTALS			**80**	**423**	**0**	**0**	**0**	**18**	**101.0**	**104**	**8**	**34**	**8**	**1**	**52**	**2**	**2**	**2**	**2**	**45**	**41**	**3**	**2**	**.600**	**5**	**3.65**

Wickander, Kevin Dean — BL/TL — b.1/4/65   CLE86 2/30

YR	TM/LG	CL	G	TBF	GS	CG	SHO	GF	IP	H	HR	BB	IBB	HB	SO	SH	SF	WP	BK	R	ER	W	L	PCT	SV	ERA
86	BAT/NYP	A-	11	194	9	0	0	2	46.1	30	4	27	0	1	63	0	0	2	0	19	14	3	4	.429	0	2.72
87	KIN/CAR	A+	25	621	25	2	1	0	147.1	128	7	75	2	7	118	5	6	14	0	69	56	9	6	.600	0	3.42
88	WIL/EAS	AA	24	113	0	0	0	24	28.2	14	0	9	0	4	33	1	0	0	1	3	2	1	0	1.000	16	0.63
	CS/PCL	AAA	19	167	0	0	0	9	32.2	44	4	27	3	2	22	1	1	5	0	30	26	0	2	.000	0	7.16
89	CLE/AL		2	15	0	0	0	1	2.2	6	0	2	1	0	0	0	0	0	0	1	1	0	0	.000	0	3.38
	CS/PCL	AAA	45	200	0	0	0	26	42.2	40	2	27	5	4	41	3	5	1	2	14	14	1	3	.250	11	2.95
90	CLE/AL		10	53	0	0	0	3	12.1	14	0	4	0	1	10	0	2	2	0	6	5	0	0	.000	0	3.65
91	CS/PCL	AAA	11	44	0	0	0	6	11.0	8	0	5	2	0	9	0	1	1	0	3	3	1	0	1.000	2	2.45
	CAN/EAS	AA	20	108	0	0	0	7	25.0	24	0	13	1	1	21	3	0	1	0	14	11	1	2	.333	0	3.96
92	CS/PCL	AAA	8	42	0	0	0	4	11.0	4	0	6	0	0	13	0	1	0	0	2	2	0	0	.000	2	1.64
	CLE/AL		44	187	0	0	0	10	41.0	39	1	28	3	4	38	2	2	1	0	14	14	2	0	1.000	1	3.07
93	IND/AMA	AAA	1	11	1	0	0	0	3.0	2	0	1	0	0	2	0	0	0	0	0	0	0	0	.000	0	0.00
	CLE/AL		11	44	0	0	0	1	8.2	15	3	3	0	3	3	0	1	0	0	7	4	0	0	.000	0	4.15
	CIN/NL		33	126	0	0	0	8	25.1	32	5	19	1	2	20	1	0	4	1	20	19	1	0	1.000	0	6.75
	YEAR		44	170	0	0	0	9	34.0	47	8	22	1	2	23	1	1	5	1	27	23	1	0	1.000	0	6.09
4 YR TOTALS			**100**	**425**	**0**	**0**	**0**	**23**	**90.0**	**106**	**9**	**56**	**5**	**7**	**71**	**3**	**4**	**6**	**2**	**48**	**43**	**3**	**1**	**.750**	**1**	**4.30**

Wickman, Robert Joe "Bob" — BR/TR — b.2/6/69   CHA90 2/44

YR	TM/LG	CL	G	TBF	GS	CG	SHO	GF	IP	H	HR	BB	IBB	HB	SO	SH	SF	WP	BK	R	ER	W	L	PCT	SV	ERA
90	WS/GCL	R	2	42	2	0	0	0	11.0	7	0	4	0	0	15	0	1	2	3	4	3	2	0	1.000	0	2.45
	SAR/FSL	A+	2	61	2	0	0	0	13.2	17	0	4	0	0	8	0	1	0	0	7	3	0	1	.000	0	1.98
	SB/MID	A	9	256	9	3	0	0	65.1	50	1	16	0	1	50	3	0	0	3	16	10	7	2	.778	0	1.38
91	SAR/FSL	A+	7	188	7	1	1	0	44.0	43	2	11	0	1	32	1	0	2	0	16	10	5	1	.833	0	2.05
	BIR/SOU	AA	20	572	20	4	1	0	131.1	127	5	50	0	5	81	3	5	4	2	68	52	6	10	.375	0	3.56
92	CMB/INT	AAA	23	641	23	0	0	0	157.0	131	6	55	0	5	108	3	2	10	1	61	51	12	5	.706	0	2.92
	NY/AL		8	213	8	0	0	0	50.1	51	2	20	0	2	21	1	3	3	0	25	23	6	1	.857	0	4.11
93	NY/AL		41	629	19	1	1	9	140.0	156	13	69	7	5	70	4	1	2	0	82	72	14	4	.778	4	4.63
2 YR TOTALS			**49**	**842**	**27**	**1**	**1**	**9**	**190.1**	**207**	**15**	**89**	**7**	**7**	**91**	**5**	**4**	**5**	**0**	**107**	**95**	**20**	**5**	**.800**	**4**	**4.49**

Williams, Brian O'Neal — BR/TR — b.2/15/69   HOU90 2/31

YR	TM/LG	CL	G	TBF	GS	CG	SHO	GF	IP	H	HR	BB	IBB	HB	SO	SH	SF	WP	BK	R	ER	W	L	PCT	SV	ERA
90	AUB/NYP	A-	3	34	3	0	0	0	6.2	6	0	6	0	1	7	1	0	1	1	5	3	0	0	.000	0	4.05
91	OSC/FSL	A+	15	378	15	0	0	0	89.2	72	0	40	1	2	67	3	6	3	5	41	29	6	4	.600	0	2.91
	JAC/TEX	AA	3	66	3	0	0	0	15.0	17	1	7	0	0	15	0	0	3	0	8	7	2	1	.667	0	4.20
	TUC/PCL	AAA	7	177	7	0	0	0	38.1	39	3	22	0	2	29	0	0	3	4	25	21	0	1	.000	0	4.93
	HOU/NL		2	49	2	0	0	0	12.0	11	2	4	0	1	4	0	0	0	0	5	5	0	1	.000	0	3.75
92	TUC/PCL	AAA	12	315	12	0	0	0	70.0	78	3	26	0	6	58	3	4	5	4	37	35	6	1	.857	0	4.50
	HOU/NL		16	413	16	0	0	0	96.1	92	10	42	1	0	54	7	3	2	1	44	42	7	6	.538	0	3.92
93	TUC/PCL	AAA	2	11	0	0	0	0	3.0	1	0	0	0	0	3	0	0	0	0	0	0	1	0	1.000	0	0.00
	HOU/NL		42	357	5	0	0	12	82.0	76	7	38	4	4	56	5	3	9	2	48	44	4	4	.500	3	4.83
3 YR TOTALS			**60**	**819**	**23**	**0**	**0**	**12**	**190.1**	**179**	**19**	**84**	**5**	**5**	**114**	**12**	**6**	**11**	**3**	**97**	**91**	**11**	**11**	**.500**	**3**	**4.30**

Williams, Gregory Scott "Woody" — BR/TR — b.8/19/66   TOR88 28/732

YR	TM/LG	CL	G	TBF	GS	CG	SHO	GF	IP	H	HR	BB	IBB	HB	SO	SH	SF	WP	BK	R	ER	W	L	PCT	SV	ERA
88	SC/NYP	A-	12	294	12	2	0	0	76.0	48	1	21	0	3	58	0	1	4	1	22	13	8	2	.800	0	1.54
	KNO/SOU	AA	6	120	4	0	0	0	28.1	27	1	12	0	0	25	0	0	1	0	13	12	2	2	.500	0	3.81
89	DUN/FSL	A+	20	325	9	0	0	8	81.1	63	3	27	1	2	60	1	3	5	0	26	21	3	5	.375	3	2.32
	KNO/SOU	AA	14	302	12	2	2	0	71.0	61	6	33	2	2	51	3	4	1	0	32	28	3	5	.375	1	3.55
90	SYR/INT	AAA	3	46	0	0	0	0	9.0	15	1	4	0	0	9	0	1	0	0	10	10	0	1	.000	0	10.00
	KNO/SOU	AA	42	519	12	0	0	19	126.0	111	7	39	3	2	74	3	4	6	4	55	44	7	9	.438	5	3.14
91	KNO/SOU	AA	18	177	1	0	0	8	42.2	42	1	14	1	1	37	0	1	0	0	18	17	3	2	.600	3	3.59
	SYR/INT	AAA	31	243	0	0	0	16	54.2	52	2	27	3	3	37	4	1	4	1	27	25	3	4	.429	6	4.12

(continued)

Williams, Gregory Scott "Woody" (continued)

YR	TM/LG	CL	G	TBF	GS	CG	SHO	GF	IP	H	HR	BB	IBB	HB	SO	SH	SF	WP	BK	R	ER	W	L	PCT	SV	ERA
92	SYR/INT	AAA	25	503	16	1	0	3	120.2	115	4	41	0	3	81	2	5	2	5	1	46	42	6	8	.429	1	3.13
93	SYR/INT	AAA	12	67	0	0	0	11	16.1	15	2	5	3	0	16	0	1	0	0	0	5	4	1	1	.500	3	2.20
	DUN/FSL	A+	2	14	0	0	0	0	4.0	0	0	2	0	0	2	0	0	0	0	0	0	0	0	0	.000	0	0.00
	TOR/AL		30	172	0	0	0	9	37.0	40	2	22	3	1	24	2	1	2	1		18	18	3	1	.750	0	4.38

Williams, Michael Darren "Mike" — BR/TR — b.7/29/69   PHI90 14/374

YR	TM/LG	CL	G	TBF	GS	CG	SHO	GF	IP	H	HR	BB	IBB	HB	SO	SH	SF	WP	BK	R	ER	W	L	PCT	SV	ERA
90	BAT/NYP	A-	27	195	0	0	0	21	47.0	39	0	13	4	1	42	3	3	1	1	17	12	2	3	.400	11	2.30
91	CLE/FSL	A+	14	348	14	2	1	0	93.1	65	5	14	0	3	76	3	1	2	6	23	18	7	3	.700	0	1.74
	REA/EAS	AA	15	404	15	2	1	0	100.0	92	1	34	0	2	50	3	3	2	0	43	41	7	5	.583	0	3.69
92	REA/EAS	AA	3	68	3	0	0	0	15.2	17	1	7	0	0	12	0	1	3	0	10	9	1	2	.333	0	5.17
	PHI/NL		5	121	5	1	0	0	28.2	29	3	7	0	0	5	1	1	1	0	20	17	1	1	.500	0	5.34
	SCR/INT	AAA	16	381	16	3	1	0	92.2	84	4	30	2	0	59	4	0	2	0	26	25	9	1	.900	0	2.43
93	SCR/INT	AAA	14	385	13	1	1	1	97.1	93	7	16	0	2	53	4	2	2	0	34	31	9	2	.818	0	2.87
	PHI/NL		17	221	4	0	0	2	51.0	50	5	22	2	0	33	1	0	2	0	32	30	1	3	.250	0	5.29
2 YR TOTALS			22	342	9	1	0	2	79.2	79	8	29	2	0	38	2	1	2	0	52	47	2	4	.333	0	5.31

Williams, Mitchell Steven "Mitch" — BL/TL — b.11/17/64   SD82 7/187

YR	TM/LG	CL	G	TBF	GS	CG	SHO	GF	IP	H	HR	BB	IBB	HB	SO	SH	SF	WP	BK	R	ER	W	L	PCT	SV	ERA
84	REN/CAL	A+	26	0	26	3	1	0	164.0	163	11	127	.	9	165	.	0	19	3	113	91	9	8	.529	0	4.99
85	SAL/CAR	A+	22	471	21	1	0	1	99.0	57	6	117	0	6	138	2	2	12	1	64	60	6	9	.400	0	5.45
	TUL/TEX	AA	6	165	6	0	0	0	33.0	17	1	48	0	2	37	2	1	3	1	24	17	2	2	.500	0	4.64
86	TEX/AL		*80	435	0	0	0	38	98.0	69	8	79	8	11	90	1	3	5	5	39	39	8	6	.571	8	3.58
87	TEX/AL		85	469	1	0	0	32	108.2	63	9	94	7	7	129	1	3	4	2	47	39	8	6	.571	6	3.23
88	TEX/AL		67	296	0	0	0	51	68.0	48	4	47	3	6	61	3	4	5	6	38	35	2	7	.222	18	4.63
89	CHI/NL		*76	365	0	0	0	61	81.2	71	6	52	4	8	67	2	5	6	4	27	25	4	4	.500	36	2.76
90	CHI/NL		59	310	2	0	0	39	66.1	60	4	50	6	1	55	5	3	4	2	38	29	1	8	.111	16	3.93
91	PHI/NL		69	386	0	0	0	60	.88.1	56	4	62	5	8	84	4	4	4	1	24	23	12	5	.706	30	2.34
92	PHI/NL		66	368	0	0	0	56	81.0	69	4	64	2	6	74	8	3	5	3	39	34	5	8	.385	29	3.78
93	PHI/NL		65	281	0	0	0	57	62.0	56	3	44	1	2	60	4	2	6	0	30	23	3	7	.300	43	3.34
8 YR TOTALS			567	2910	3	0	0	394	654.0	492	42	492	36	49	620	31	27	39	23	282	247	43	51	.457	186	3.40

Williamson, Mark Alan — BR/TR — b.7/21/59   SD82 4/83

YR	TM/LG	CL	G	TBF	GS	CG	SHO	GF	IP	H	HR	BB	IBB	HB	SO	SH	SF	WP	BK	R	ER	W	L	PCT	SV	ERA
84	REN/CAL	A+	56	0	1	0	0	46	93.0	105	2	23	10	2	69	0	0	4	0	41	30	10	12	.455	15	2.90
85	BEA/TEX	AA	42	333	0	0	0	32	78.2	72	1	23	7	2	64	6	2	3	0	27	25	10	9	.526	8	2.86
86	LV/PCL	AAA	65	445	0	0	0	36	104.1	103	10	36	10	4	81	3	5	2	1	47	39	10	3	.769	16	3.36
87	ROC/INT	AAA	1	18	0	0	0	1	4.0	6	0	1	0	0	1	0	0	0	0	3	3	0	1	.000	0	6.75
	BAL/AL		61	520	2	0	0	36	125.0	122	12	41	15	3	73	5	3	3	0	59	56	8	9	.471	3	4.03
88	ROC/INT	AAA	12	131	3	1	0	8	29.2	38	2	5	2	0	25	0	0	3	0	11	11	2	3	.400	2	3.34
	BAL/AL		37	507	10	2	0	11	117.2	125	14	40	2	2	69	4	2	5	3	70	64	5	8	.385	2	4.90
89	BAL/AL		65	445	0	0	0	38	107.1	105	4	30	2	2	55	7	3	0	0	35	35	10	5	.667	9	2.93
90	BAL/AL		49	343	0	0	0	15	85.1	65	8	28	2	0	60	6	1	2	1	25	21	8	2	.800	1	2.21
91	BAL/AL		65	357	0	0	0	21	80.1	87	9	35	7	0	53	1	1	2	1	42	40	5	5	.500	4	4.48
92	HAG/EAS	AA	6	57	5	0	0	0	14.2	13	1	2	0	0	8	0	0	1	0	9	8	0	1	.000	0	4.91
	ROC/INT	AAA	4	12	0	0	0	3	3.2	2	0	0	0	0	1	0	0	0	0	0	0	0	0	.000	2	0.00
	BAL/AL		12	78	0	0	0	5	18.2	16	1	10	1	0	14	1	0	1	0	3	2	0	0	.000	1	0.96
93	BAL/AL		48	386	1	0	0	12	88.0	106	5	25	8	0	45	6	4	2	3	54	48	7	5	.583	0	4.91
7 YR TOTALS			337	2636	13	2	0	138	622.1	626	53	209	50	7	369	30	26	19	3	288	266	43	34	.558	20	3.85

Willis, Carl Blake — BL/TR — b.12/28/60   DET83 23/581

YR	TM/LG	CL	G	TBF	GS	CG	SHO	GF	IP	H	HR	BB	IBB	HB	SO	SH	SF	WP	BK	R	ER	W	L	PCT	SV	ERA
83	BRI/APP	R+	2	0	0	0	0	0	2.0	0	0	4	0	0	3	0	0	0	0	1	1	0	1	.000	0	4.50
	LAK/FSL	A+	4	0	0	0	0	0	9.0	6	0	5	0	0	7	0	0	0	0	0	0	3	0	1.000	0	0.00
	BIR/SOU	AA	14	0	0	0	0	0	20.0	16	0	7	0	0	13	0	0	0	0	9	9	3	1	.750	2	4.05
84	DET/AL		10	74	0	0	0	4	16.0	25	1	5	2	0	4	0	0	0	0	13	13	0	2	.000	0	7.31
	EVA/AMA	AAA	40	242	1	0	0	32	60.1	59	5	20	2	0	27	3	2	3	3	26	25	5	3	.625	16	3.73
	CIN/NL		7	39	0	0	0	1	9.2	8	1	2	0	0	3	1	0	0	0	4	4	0	1	.000	1	3.72
	YEAR		17	113	2	0	0	5	25.2	33	2	7	2	0	7	1	0	0	0	17	17	0	3	.000	1	5.96
85	DEN/AMA	AAA	37	338	0	0	0	24	78.0	82	7	30	2	1	27	1	6	8	1	39	36	4	4	.500	8	4.15
	CIN/NL		11	69	0	0	0	6	13.2	21	3	5	0	0	6	1	2	1	0	18	14	1	0	1.000	0	9.22
86	DEN/AMA	AAA	20	139	0	0	0	16	32.2	29	3	16	1	1	16	2	0	2	0	22	17	1	3	.250	4	4.68
	CIN/NL		29	233	0	0	0	7	52.1	54	4	32	4	1	24	1	1	5	0	29	26	1	3	.250	0	4.47
87	NAS/AMA	AAA	53	369	0	0	0	25	83.2	97	5	30	5	2	54	3	1	4	0	39	31	6	4	.600	5	3.33
88	CHI/AL		6	55	0	0	0	0	12.0	17	3	7	1	0	6	0	1	2	0	12	11	0	0	.000	0	8.25
	VAN/PCL	AAA	40	285	0	0	0	21	64.0	77	3	16	0	0	44	1	1	1	0	36	30	4	4	.500	4	4.22
89	EDM/PCL	AAA	36	493	10	0	0	12	112.1	137	9	36	3	1	47	3	1	4	0	54	46	5	7	.417	5	3.69
90	CS/PCL	AAA	41	457	6	0	0	16	98.2	136	9	32	3	1	42	4	0	6	0	80	70	5	3	.625	2	6.39
91	POR/PCL	AAA	3	41	0	0	0	0	11.0	5	0	0	0	0	5	0	0	0	0	4	2	1	1	.500	0	1.64
	MIN/AL		40	355	0	0	0	9	89.0	76	4	19	1	0	53	4	0	2	0	31	26	8	3	.727	2	2.63
92	MIN/AL		59	313	0	0	0	21	79.1	73	4	11	1	0	45	2	3	0	0	25	24	7	3	.700	1	2.72
93	POR/PCL	AAA	2	19	0	0	0	0	4.0	8	0	0	0	0	3	0	0	0	0	2	1	0	0	.000	0	2.25
	MIN/AL		53	236	0	0	0	21	58.0	56	2	11	0	0	44	2	1	3	0	23	20	3	0	1.000	5	3.10
7 YR TOTALS			215	1374	2	0	0	69	330.0	330	22	98	19	2	185	14	12	15	3	155	138	20	12	.625	10	3.76

Wilson, Stephen Douglas "Steve" — BL/TL — b.12/13/64 — TEX85 3/83

YR	TM/LG	CL	G	TBF	GS	CG	SHO	GF	IP	H	HR	BB	IBB	HB	SO	SH	SF	WP	BK	R	ER	W	L	PCT	SV	ERA
85	BUR/MID	A	21	317	10	0	0	4	72.2	71	11	27	1	2	76	5	4	1	3	44	37	3	5	.375	0	4.58
86	TUL/TEX	AA	24	617	24	2	0	0	136.2	117	10	103	0	7	95	5	8	12	6	83	74	7	13	.350	0	4.87
87	CHA/FSL	A+	20	442	17	1	1	1	107.0	81	5	44	0	3	80	0	2	5	2	41	29	9	5	.643	0	2.44
88	TUL/TEX	AA	25	698	25	5	3	0	165.1	147	14	53	1	8	132	6	4	3	1	72	58	15	7	.682	0	3.16
	TEX/AL		3	31	0	0	0	1	7.2	7	1	4	1	0	1	0	0	0	0	5	5	0	0	.000	0	5.87
89	CHI/NL		53	364	8	0	0	9	85.2	83	6	31	5	1	65	5	4	7	0	43	40	6	4	.600	2	4.20
90	CHI/NL		45	597	15	0	0	5	139.0	140	17	43	6	2	95	9	3	2	1	77	74	4	9	.308	1	4.79
91	CHI/NL		8	53	0	0	0	2	12.1	13	1	5	1	0	9	0	1	0	0	7	6	0	0	.000	0	4.38
	IOW/AMA	AAA	25	482	16	1	0	4	114.0	102	11	45	2	7	84	0	1	9	0	55	49	3	8	.273	0	3.87
	LA/NL		11	28	0	0	0	3	8.1	1	0	4	0	0	5	0	1	0	0	0	0	0	0	.000	0	0.00
	YEAR		19	81	0	0	0	5	20.2	14	1	9	1	0	14	0	1	0	0	7	6	0	0	.000	0	2.61
92	LA/NL		60	301	0	0	0	18	66.2	74	6	29	7	1	54	5	4	7	0	37	31	2	5	.286	0	4.18
93	ALB/PCL	AAA	13	220	12	0	0	0	51.1	57	5	14	0	2	44	4	1	4	2	29	25	0	3	.000	0	4.38
	LA/NL		25	120	0	0	0	4	25.2	30	2	14	4	1	23	1	0	3	0	13	13	1	0	1.000	1	4.56
6 YR TOTALS			**205**	**1494**	**23**	**1**	**0**	**42**	**345.1**	**348**	**33**	**130**	**24**	**5**	**252**	**20**	**12**	**12**	**2**	**182**	**169**	**13**	**18**	**.419**	**6**	**4.40**

Wilson, Trevor Kirk — BL/TL — b.6/7/66 — SF85 8/186

YR	TM/LG	CL	G	TBF	GS	CG	SHO	GF	IP	H	HR	BB	IBB	HB	SO	SH	SF	WP	BK	R	ER	W	L	PCT	SV	ERA
85	EVE/NWL	A-	17	0	7	0	0	8	55.1	67	2	26	0	1	50	0	0	6	2	36	26	2	4	.333	3	4.23
86	CLI/MID	A	34	569	21	0	0	7	130.2	126	6	64	1	6	84	3	3	5	2	70	62	6	11	.353	2	4.27
87	CLI/MID	A	26	668	26	3	2	0	161.1	130	3	77	0	6	146	2	6	9	2	60	36	10	6	.625	0	2.01
88	SHR/TEX	AA	12	291	11	0	0	0	72.2	55	0	23	1	0	53	2	3	1	13	19	15	5	4	.556	0	1.86
	PHO/PCL	AAA	11	233	9	0	0	0	51.2	49	3	33	2	0	49	3	1	1	4	35	29	2	3	.400	0	5.05
	SF/NL		4	96	4	0	0	0	22.0	25	1	8	0	1	15	3	1	0	1	14	10	0	2	.000	0	4.09
89	PHO/PCL	AAA	23	504	20	2	0	2	115.1	109	5	76	1	2	77	3	4	5	7	49	40	7	7	.500	0	3.12
	SF/NL		14	167	4	0	0	2	39.1	28	2	24	0	4	22	3	1	0	1	20	19	2	3	.400	0	4.35
90	PHO/PCL	AAA	11	290	10	2	1	0	66.0	63	2	44	2	0	45	4	3	1	3	31	28	5	5	.500	0	3.82
	SF/NL		27	457	17	3	2	3	110.1	87	11	49	1	6	66	6	1	5	3	52	49	8	7	.533	0	4.00
91	SF/NL		44	841	29	2	1	6	202.0	173	13	77	4	5	139	14	5	5	3	87	80	13	11	.542	0	3.56
92	SF/NL		26	661	26	1	1	0	154.0	152	18	64	5	6	88	11	6	2	7	82	72	8	14	.364	0	4.21
93	SJ/CAL	A+	2	35	2	0	0	0	10.0	4	0	3	0	0	8	0	0	1	0	0	0	1	0	1.000	0	0.00
	SF/NL		22	455	18	1	0	1	110.0	110	8	40	3	2	57	6	3	0	0	45	44	7	5	.583	0	3.60
6 YR TOTALS			**137**	**2677**	**98**	**7**	**4**	**12**	**637.2**	**575**	**53**	**262**	**15**	**22**	**387**	**43**	**18**	**12**	**14**	**300**	**274**	**38**	**42**	**.475**	**0**	**3.87**

Witt, Michael Atwater "Mike" — BR/TR — b.7/20/60 — CAL78 3/92

YR	TM/LG	CL	G	TBF	GS	CG	SHO	GF	IP	H	HR	BB	IBB	HB	SO	SH	SF	WP	BK	R	ER	W	L	PCT	SV	ERA
81	CAL/AL		22	555	21	7	1	1	129.0	123	9	47	4	11	75	3	4	2	0	60	47	8	9	.471	0	3.28
82	CAL/AL		33	748	26	5	1	2	179.2	177	8	47	2	7	85	8	5	8	1	77	70	8	6	.571	0	3.51
83	CAL/AL		43	683	19	2	0	15	154.0	173	14	75	7	6	77	5	7	8	0	90	84	7	14	.333	5	4.91
84	CAL/AL		34	1032	34	9	2	0	246.2	227	17	84	3	5	196	7	7	7	1	103	95	15	11	.577	0	3.47
85	CAL/AL		35	1049	35	6	1	0	250.0	228	22	98	6	4	180	4	5	11	1	115	99	15	9	.625	0	3.56
86	CAL/AL		34	1071	34	14	3	0	269.0	218	22	73	2	3	208	3	5	6	0	95	85	18	10	.643	0	2.84
87	CAL/AL		36	1065	34	16	3	0	247.0	252	34	84	4	4	192	6	6	6	0	128	110	16	14	.533	0	4.01
88	CAL/AL		34	1080	34	12	2	0	249.2	263	14	87	7	5	133	11	10	9	2	130	115	13	16	.448	0	4.15
89	CAL/AL		33	937	33	5	0	0	220.0	252	26	48	1	2	123	10	13	7	0	119	111	9	15	.375	0	4.54
90	CAL/AL		10	92	0	0	0	4	20.1	19	1	13	2	1	14	1	1	1	0	9	4	0	3	.000	1	1.77
	NY/AL		16	406	16	2	1	0	96.2	87	8	34	2	4	60	0	5	6	0	53	48	5	6	.455	0	4.47
	YEAR		26	498	16	2	1	4	117.0	106	9	47	4	5	74	1	6	7	0	62	52	5	9	.357	1	4.00
91	CMB/INT	AAA	1	22	1	0	0	0	4.0	7	0	3	0	1	5	0	0	1	0	4	4	0	0	.000	0	9.00
	NY/AL		2	26	2	0	0	0	5.1	8	1	1	0	0	4	0	0	0	0	7	6	0	0	.000	0	10.13
	ALB/EAS	AA	1	10	1	0	0	0	2.0	2	0	2	0	0	2	0	0	0	0	2	2	0	0	.000	0	9.00
92	YAN/GCL	R	3	45	3	0	0	0	12.0	7	0	2	0	0	13	0	0	2	0	1	0	1	0	1.000	0	0.00
93	NY/AL		9	183	9	0	0	0	41.0	39	7	22	0	3	30	1	0	1	0	26	24	3	2	.600	0	5.27
	ALB/EAS	AA	1	8	0	0	0	0	2.0	2	0	2	0	0	0	0	0	0	0	0	0	0	0	.000	0	0.00
	CMB/INT	AAA	3	55	3	0	0	0	13.2	11	1	5	0	0	11	0	0	0	0	3	3	1	0	1.000	0	1.98
12 YR TOTALS			**341**	**8927**	**299**	**72**	**11**	**22**	**2108.1**	**2066**	**183**	**713**	**40**	**55**	**1373**	**59**	**68**	**73**	**5**	**1012**	**898**	**117**	**116**	**.502**	**6**	**3.83**

Witt, Robert Andrew "Bobby" — BR/TR — b.5/11/64 — TEX85 1/3

YR	TM/LG	CL	G	TBF	GS	CG	SHO	GF	IP	H	HR	BB	IBB	HB	SO	SH	SF	WP	BK	R	ER	W	L	PCT	SV	ERA
85	TUL/TEX	AA	11	167	8	0	0	1	35.0	26	1	44	0	1	39	0	1	7	1	26	25	0	6	.000	0	6.43
86	TEX/AL		31	741	31	0	0	0	157.2	130	18	143	2	3	174	3	9	22	3	104	96	11	9	.550	0	5.48
87	OC/AMA	AAA	1	23	1	0	0	0	5.0	5	1	3	0	0	2	0	1	0	0	5	5	1	0	1.000	0	9.00
	TUL/TEX	AA	1	28	1	0	0	0	5.0	5	1	6	0	0	2	0	1	0	0	9	3	0	1	.000	0	5.40
	TEX/AL		26	673	25	0	0	0	143.0	114	10	140	1	3	160	5	5	7	2	82	78	8	10	.444	0	4.91
88	OC/AMA	AAA	11	341	11	3	0	0	76.2	69	1	47	0	2	70	3	2	4	0	42	37	4	6	.400	0	4.34
	TEX/AL		22	736	22	13	2	0	174.1	134	13	101	2	1	148	7	4	16	8	83	76	8	10	.444	0	3.92
89	TEX/AL		31	869	31	5	1	0	194.1	182	14	114	3	2	166	11	8	7	4	123	111	12	13	.480	0	5.14
90	TEX/AL		33	954	32	7	1	1	222.0	197	12	110	3	4	221	5	6	11	2	98	83	17	10	.630	0	3.36
91	OC/AMA	AAA	2	35	2	0	0	0	8.0	3	0	8	0	0	12	0	0	1	1	1	1	1	1	.500	0	1.13
	TEX/AL		17	413	16	1	0	0	88.2	84	4	74	1	1	82	0	6	7	1	66	60	3	7	.300	0	6.09
92	TEX/AL		25	708	25	0	0	0	161.1	152	14	95	1	2	100	3	8	6	1	87	80	9	13	.409	0	4.46
	OAK/AL		6	140	6	0	0	0	31.2	31	2	19	1	0	25	4	1	3	0	12	12	1	1	.500	0	3.41
	YEAR		31	848	31	0	0	0	193.0	183	16	114	2	2	125	7	9	9	1	99	92	10	14	.417	0	4.29
93	OAK/AL		35	950	33	5	1	0	220.0	226	16	91	5	3	131	9	8	8	1	112	103	14	13	.519	0	4.21
8 YR TOTALS			**226**	**6184**	**221**	**32**	**6**	**1**	**1393.0**	**1250**	**103**	**887**	**19**	**19**	**1207**	**50**	**56**	**88**	**21**	**767**	**699**	**83**	**86**	**.491**	**0**	**4.52**

Wohlers, Mark Edward — BR/TR — b.1/23/70   ATL88 10/190

YR	TM/LG	CL	G	TBF	GS	CG	SHO	GF	IP	H	HR	BB	IBB	HB	SO	SH	SF	WP	BK	R	ER	W	L	PCT	SV	ERA
88	PUL/APP	R+	13	275	9	1	0	4	59.2	47	0	50	0	0	49	1	3	6	2	37	22	5	3	.625	0	3.32
89	SUM/SAL	A	14	326	14	0	0	0	68.0	74	3	59	0	4	51	3	3	10	1	55	49	2	7	.222	0	6.49
	PUL/APP	R+	14	219	8	0	0	2	46.0	48	5	28	0	2	50	1	0	2	0	36	28	1	1	.500	0	5.48
90	SUM/SAL	A	37	208	2	0	0	16	52.2	27	1	20	0	4	85	1	2	0	2	13	11	5	4	.556	5	1.88
	GRE/SOU	AA	14	72	0	0	0	11	15.2	14	0	14	0	1	20	0	1	1	0	7	7	0	1	.000	6	4.02
91	GRE/SOU	AA	28	116	0	0	0	27	31.1	9	0	13	0	0	44	3	2	3	0	4	2	0	0	.000	21	0.57
	RIC/INT	AAA	23	111	0	0	0	21	26.1	23	1	12	1	1	22	4	0	1	0	4	3	1	0	1.000	11	1.03
	ATL/NL		17	89	0	0	0	4	19.2	17	1	13	3	2	13	2	1	0	0	7	7	3	1	.750	2	3.20
92	RIC/INT	AAA	27	151	2	0	0	20	34.1	32	5	17	3	0	33	4	1	6	0	16	15	0	2	.000	9	3.93
	ATL/NL		32	140	0	0	0	16	35.1	28	0	14	4	1	17	5	1	1	0	11	10	1	2	.333	4	2.55
93	RIC/INT	AAA	25	122	0	0	0	20	29.1	21	0	11	0	1	39	2	0	2	0	7	6	1	3	.250	4	1.84
	ATL/NL		46	199	0	0	0	13	48.0	37	2	22	3	1	45	5	1	0	0	25	24	6	2	.750	6	4.50
3 YR TOTALS			95	428	0	0	0	33	103.0	82	3	49	10	4	75	12	3	1	0	43	41	10	5	.667	6	3.58

Worrell, Timothy Howard "Tim" — BR/TR — b.7/5/67   SD89 19/520

YR	TM/LG	CL	G	TBF	GS	CG	SHO	GF	IP	H	HR	BB	IBB	HB	SO	SH	SF	WP	BK	R	ER	W	L	PCT	SV	ERA
90	CHS/SAL	A	20	478	19	3	0	0	110.2	120	6	28	2	1	68	4	4	9	1	65	57	5	8	.385	0	4.64
91	WAT/MID	A	14	359	14	3	2	0	86.1	70	5	33	0	3	83	0	1	1	1	36	32	8	4	.667	0	3.34
	HD/CAL	A+	11	283	11	2	0	0	63.2	65	2	33	0	2	70	3	2	3	0	32	30	5	2	.714	0	4.24
92	WIC/TEX	AA	19	508	19	1	1	0	125.2	115	4	32	0	2	109	1	3	1	3	46	40	8	6	.571	0	2.86
	LV/PCL	AAA	10	266	10	1	1	0	63.1	61	4	19	0	3	32	4	3	1	0	32	30	4	2	.667	0	4.26
93	LV/PCL	AAA	15	382	14	2	0	0	87.0	102	13	26	1	2	89	2	5	2	0	61	53	5	6	.455	0	5.48
	SD/NL		21	443	16	0	0	1	100.2	104	11	43	5	0	52	8	5	3	0	63	55	2	7	.222	0	4.92

Worrell, Todd Roland — BR/TR — b.9/28/59   SL82 1/21

YR	TM/LG	CL	G	TBF	GS	CG	SHO	GF	IP	H	HR	BB	IBB	HB	SO	SH	SF	WP	BK	R	ER	W	L	PCT	SV	ERA
84	ARK/TEX	AA	18	474	18	5	0	0	100.1	109	8	67	4	0	88	7	4	8	1	72	50	3	10	.231	0	4.49
	SP/FSL	A+	8	209	7	2	0	0	47.1	41	0	24	2	0	33	2	0	4	0	22	11	3	2	.600	0	2.09
85	LOU/AMA	AAA	34	532	17	2	1	15	127.2	114	8	47	1	4	126	2	6	5	1	59	51	8	6	.571	11	3.60
	STL/NL		17	88	0	0	0	11	21.2	17	2	7	2	0	17	0	2	2	0	7	7	3	0	1.000	5	2.91
86	STL/NL		74	430	0	0	0	60	103.2	86	9	41	16	1	73	7	6	1	0	29	24	9	10	.474	*36	2.08
87	STL/NL		75	395	0	0	0	54	94.2	86	8	34	11	0	92	4	2	3	0	29	28	8	6	.571	33	2.66
88	STL/NL		68	366	0	0	0	54	90.0	69	7	34	14	1	78	3	5	6	2	32	30	5	9	.357	32	3.00
89	LOU/AMA	AAA	1	3	0	0	0	0	1.0	0	0	0	0	0	0	0	0	0	0	0	0	0	0	.000	0	0.00
	STL/NL		47	219	0	0	0	39	51.2	42	4	26	13	0	41	3	1	3	0	21	17	3	5	.375	20	2.96
91	LOU/AMA	AAA	3	16	0	0	0	0	3.0	4	1	3	0	0	4	0	0	0	0	6	6	0	0	.000	0	18.00
92	STL/NL		67	256	0	0	0	14	64.0	45	4	25	5	1	64	3	5	3	0	15	15	5	3	.625	3	2.11
93	BAK/CAL	A+	2	7	2	0	0	0	2.0	1	0	0	0	0	5	0	0	0	0	0	0	0	0	.000	0	0.00
	ALB/PCL	AAA	7	37	2	0	0	1	8.2	7	1	2	0	1	13	0	0	0	0	2	1	1	0	1.000	1	1.04
	LA/NL		35	167	0	0	0	22	38.2	46	6	11	1	0	31	3	6	1	0	28	26	1	1	.500	5	6.05
7 YR TOTALS			383	1921	0	0	0	254	464.1	391	40	178	62	3	396	23	22	15	6	161	147	34	34	.500	134	2.85

Young, Anthony Wayne — BR/TR — b.1/19/66   NYN87 39/978

YR	TM/LG	CL	G	TBF	GS	CG	SHO	GF	IP	H	HR	BB	IBB	HB	SO	SH	SF	WP	BK	R	ER	W	L	PCT	SV	ERA
87	LF/NYP	A-	14	247	9	0	0	0	53.2	58	6	25	2	1	48	2	2	4	0	37	27	3	4	.429	0	4.53
88	LF/NYP	A-	15	304	10	4	0	2	73.2	51	1	34	0	0	75	1	3	9	1	33	18	3	5	.375	0	2.20
89	COL/SAL	A	21	548	17	8	1	2	129.0	115	5	55	1	4	127	1	3	7	3	60	50	9	6	.600	0	3.49
90	JAC/TEX	AA	23	632	23	3	1	0	158.0	116	3	52	5	3	95	1	2	7	1	38	29	15	3	.833	0	1.65
91	TID/INT	AAA	25	702	25	3	1	0	164.0	172	13	67	2	1	93	9	5	6	1	74	68	7	9	.438	0	3.73
	NY/NL		10	202	8	0	0	2	49.1	48	4	12	1	1	20	1	1	1	0	20	17	2	5	.286	0	3.10
92	NY/NL		52	517	13	1	0	26	121.0	134	8	31	5	1	64	11	4	3	1	66	56	2	14	.125	15	4.17
93	NOR/INT	AAA	3	60	3	0	0	0	16.0	14	1	5	0	0	8	0	0	0	0	2	2	1	1	.500	0	1.13
	NY/NL		39	445	10	1	0	19	100.1	103	8	42	9	1	62	11	3	0	2	62	42	1	16	.059	3	3.77
3 YR TOTALS			101	1164	31	2	0	47	270.2	285	20	85	15	3	146	23	8	4	3	148	115	5	35	.125	18	3.82

Young, Bryan Owen "Pete" — BR/TR — b.3/19/68   MON89 6/150

YR	TM/LG	CL	G	TBF	GS	CG	SHO	GF	IP	H	HR	BB	IBB	HB	SO	SH	SF	WP	BK	R	ER	W	L	PCT	SV	ERA
89	JAM/NYP	A-	18	269	10	0	0	8	65.0	63	2	14	0	5	62	0	1	6	0	18	14	5	2	.714	4	1.94
90	WPB/FSL	A+	39	453	12	0	0	25	109.1	106	3	27	1	2	62	3	0	1	0	36	30	8	3	.727	19	2.47
91	SUM/SAL	A	1	5	0	0	0	0	1.0	1	0	1	0	0	2	0	0	0	0	1	1	0	0	.000	0	9.00
	HAR/EAS	AA	54	368	0	0	0	29	90.0	82	9	24	4	2	74	1	1	7	0	28	26	7	5	.583	13	2.60
92	MON/NL		13	85	0	0	0	6	20.1	18	0	9	2	1	11	0	2	1	0	9	9	0	0	.000	0	3.98
	IND/AMA	AAA	36	216	0	0	0	20	48.2	53	5	21	3	1	34	4	2	5	0	19	19	6	2	.750	7	3.51
93	OTT/INT	AAA	48	311	0	0	0	16	72.1	63	5	33	10	6	46	5	4	2	0	32	30	4	5	.444	1	3.73
	MON/NL		4	20	0	0	0	2	5.1	4	1	0	0	0	3	0	0	0	0	2	2	1	0	1.000	0	3.38
2 YR TOTALS			17	105	0	0	0	8	25.2	22	1	9	2	1	14	0	2	1	0	11	11	1	0	1.000	0	3.86

Young, Clifford Raphael "Cliff" — BL/TL — b.8/2/64   MON83 6/120

YR	TM/LG	CL	G	TBF	GS	CG	SHO	GF	IP	H	HR	BB	IBB	HB	SO	SH	SF	WP	BK	R	ER	W	L	PCT	SV	ERA
83	CAL/PIO	R+	13	0	13	4	0	0	79.0	98	8	32	0	0	72	0	0	0	0	55	45	7	1	.875	0	5.13
84	GAS/SAL	A	24	614	24	7	2	0	144.1	117	10	68	2	1	121	7	7	4	0	77	67	8	10	.444	0	4.18
85	WPB/FSL	A+	25	664	25	7	0	0	153.2	149	13	57	0	6	112	4	7	5	4	77	68	15	5	.750	0	3.98
86	KNO/SOU	AA	31	880	31	11	0	0	203.2	232	25	71	1	2	121	3	4	5	5	111	88	12	14	.462	0	3.89
87	KNO/SOU	AA	42	541	12	0	0	10	119.1	148	15	43	5	3	76	1	3	6	0	76	59	4	7	.471	4	4.45
88	SYR/INT	AAA	33	608	18	4	1	7	147.1	133	13	32	0	3	75	2	5	3	0	68	56	6	9	.600	3	3.42
89	EDM/PCL	AAA	31	591	21	0	2	1	139.0	158	16	32	1	5	89	6	4	3	4	80	74	8	9	.471	0	4.79

Young, Clifford Raphael "Cliff" (continued)

YR	TM/LG	CL	G	TBF	GS	CG	SHO	GF	IP	H	HR	BB	IBB	HB	SO	SH	SF	WP	BK	R	ER	W	L	PCT	SV	ERA
90	EDM/PCL	AAA	30	208	0	0	0	14	52.0	45	1	10	1	1	30	6	1	0	2	15	14	7	4	.636	4	2.42
	CAL/AL		17	137	0	0	0	5	30.2	40	2	7	1	1	19	2	4	1	0	14	12	1	1	.500	0	3.52
91	EDM/PCL	AAA	34	328	8	0	0	15	71.2	88	2	25	1	4	39	4	3	8	0	53	39	4	8	.333	5	4.90
	CAL/AL		11	49	0	0	0	6	12.2	12	3	3	1	0	6	0	0	0	0	6	6	1	0	1.000	0	4.26
92	EDM/PCL	AAA	28	639	20	5	1	2	143.1	174	14	42	4	4	104	8	4	2	2	94	89	10	8	.556	0	5.59
93	CHW/INT	AAA	5	141	5	1	1	0	37.2	30	4	2	0	0	21	0	0	0	0	10	9	3	1	.750	0	2.15
	CLE/AL		21	271	7	0	0	3	60.1	74	9	18	1	3	31	1	1	0	0	35	31	3	3	.500	1	4.62
3 YR TOTALS			**49**	**457**	**7**	**0**	**0**	**14**	**103.2**	**126**	**14**	**28**	**3**	**4**	**56**	**3**	**5**	**1**	**0**	**55**	**49**	**5**	**4**	**.556**	**1**	**4.25**

Young, Curtis Allen "Curt" — BR/TL — b.4/16/60   OAK81 5/92

YR	TM/LG	CL	G	TBF	GS	CG	SHO	GF	IP	H	HR	BB	IBB	HB	SO	SH	SF	WP	BK	R	ER	W	L	PCT	SV	ERA
83	OAK/AL		8	50	2	0	0	0	9.0	17	1	5	0	1	5	0	0	1	0	17	16	0	1	.000	0	16.00
84	TAC/PCL	AAA	14	0	14	5	1	0	95.1	88	8	28	1	1	61	0	0	5	0	45	40	6	4	.600	0	3.78
	OAK/AL		20	475	17	2	1	0	108.2	118	9	31	0	8	41	1	4	3	0	53	49	9	4	.692	0	4.06
85	MOD/CAL	A+	2	0	2	0	0	0	5.2	7	0	6	0	1	3	0	0	0	0	4	3	0	0	.000	0	4.76
	TAC/PCL	AAA	3	0	3	0	0	0	15.0	10	1	7	0	0	8	0	0	0	0	7	6	2	0	1.000	0	3.60
	OAK/AL		19	214	7	0	0	5	46.0	57	15	22	0	1	19	0	1	1	0	38	37	0	4	.000	0	7.24
86	TAC/PCL	AAA	4	99	4	1	0	0	27.0	16	1	6	0	0	28	0	0	0	0	7	6	4	0	1.000	0	2.00
	OAK/AL		29	826	27	5	2	0	198.0	176	19	57	1	7	116	8	9	7	2	88	76	13	9	.591	0	3.45
87	OAK/AL		31	828	31	6	0	0	203.0	194	38	44	0	3	124	6	4	2	1	102	92	13	7	.650	0	4.08
88	OAK/AL		26	651	26	1	0	0	156.1	162	23	50	3	5	69	3	5	3	6	77	72	11	8	.579	0	4.14
89	OAK/AL		25	495	20	1	0	2	111.0	117	10	47	2	3	55	1	0	4	4	56	46	5	9	.357	0	3.73
90	OAK/AL		26	527	21	0	0	0	124.1	124	17	53	1	2	56	4	3	3	0	70	67	9	6	.600	0	4.85
91	OAK/AL		41	306	1	0	0	6	68.1	74	8	34	2	2	27	3	1	2	1	38	38	4	2	.667	0	5.00
92	OMA/AMA	AAA	2	44	2	0	0	0	10.0	15	1	2	0	1	6	0	1	0	0	6	6	0	1	.000	0	5.40
	KC/AL		10	107	2	0	0	2	24.1	29	1	7	1	0	7	0	1	0	0	14	14	1	2	.333	0	5.18
	CMB/INT	AAA	3	67	3	0	0	0	16.0	16	1	6	0	0	2	0	0	0	0	6	6	3	0	1.000	0	3.38
	NY/AL		13	188	5	0	0	3	43.1	51	1	10	1	2	13	3	2	0	0	21	16	3	0	1.000	0	3.32
	YEAR		23	295	7	0	0	5	67.2	80	2	17	2	2	20	3	3	0	0	35	30	4	2	.667	0	3.99
93	TAC/PCL	AAA	10	262	10	1	0	0	65.1	53	2	16	0	1	31	2	2	1	2	23	14	6	1	.857	0	1.93
	OAK/AL		3	64	3	0	0	0	14.2	14	5	6	0	0	4	0	0	0	0	7	7	1	1	.500	0	4.30
11 YR TOTALS			**251**	**4731**	**162**	**15**	**3**	**18**	**1107.0**	**1133**	**147**	**366**	**11**	**33**	**536**	**29**	**29**	**26**	**14**	**581**	**530**	**69**	**53**	**.566**	**0**	**4.31**

Young, Matthew John "Matt" — BL/TL — b.8/9/58   SEA80 2/32

YR	TM/LG	CL	G	TBF	GS	CG	SHO	GF	IP	H	HR	BB	IBB	HB	SO	SH	SF	WP	BK	R	ER	W	L	PCT	SV	ERA
83	SEA/AL		33	851	32	5	2	0	203.2	178	17	79	2	7	130	4	8	4	2	86	74	11	15	.423	0	3.27
84	SLC/PCL	AAA	6	0	6	0	0	0	41.2	32	0	20	0	2	37	0	0	4	0	9	7	6	0	1.000	0	1.51
	SEA/AL		22	524	22	1	0	0	113.1	141	11	57	3	1	73	1	5	3	1	81	72	6	8	.429	0	5.72
85	SEA/AL		37	951	35	5	2	2	218.1	242	23	76	3	7	136	7	3	6	2	135	119	12	19	.387	1	4.91
86	SEA/AL		65	458	5	1	0	32	103.2	108	9	46	2	8	82	4	3	7	1	50	44	8	6	.571	13	3.82
87	LA/NL		47	234	0	0	0	31	54.1	62	3	17	5	0	42	1	1	3	0	30	27	5	8	.385	11	4.47
89	MOD/CAL	A+	3	50	3	0	0	0	12.0	9	0	6	0	0	13	0	0	1	0	1	1	0	0	.000	0	0.75
	TAC/PCL	AAA	2	45	2	0	0	0	11.0	8	0	5	0	0	6	0	1	0	0	4	3	1	1	.500	0	2.45
	OAK/AL		26	183	4	0	0	1	37.1	42	2	31	2	0	27	4	1	5	0	31	28	1	4	.200	0	6.75
90	SEA/AL		34	963	33	7	1	0	225.1	198	15	107	7	6	176	7	7	16	0	106	88	8	18	.308	0	3.51
91	PAW/INT	AAA	2	38	2	0	0	0	8.0	8	0	6	0	0	7	0	0	0	0	4	4	1	0	1.000	0	4.50
	BOS/AL		19	404	16	0	0	1	88.2	92	4	53	2	2	69	1	2	5	0	55	51	3	7	.300	0	5.18
92	BOS/AL		28	321	8	1	0	4	70.2	69	7	42	2	3	57	4	3	2	0	42	36	0	4	.000	0	4.58
93	CHW/INT	AAA	3	68	3	1	0	0	17.2	11	1	5	0	3	17	0	0	0	0	5	5	1	0	1.000	0	2.55
	SYR/INT	AAA	7	125	5	0	0	0	31.2	22	1	14	0	2	38	1	0	0	0	10	8	2	1	.667	0	2.27
	CLE/AL		22	347	8	0	0	2	74.1	75	8	57	0	3	65	4	1	5	1	45	43	1	6	.143	0	5.21
10 YR TOTALS			**333**	**5236**	**163**	**20**	**5**	**73**	**1189.2**	**1207**	**99**	**565**	**28**	**37**	**857**	**37**	**34**	**56**	**7**	**661**	**582**	**55**	**95**	**.367**	**25**	**4.40**

Part 6 | 1994 Season Projections

If you've purchased previous editions of the *Stat Book*, you'll know that this part of the book is completely new. Instead of devoting a substantial amount of space in the Career Registers to minor-league prospects, this year's book includes two new reports.

Even though the career registers in the 1993 *Stat Book* included 250 minor-league prospects (as well as scores of other prospects who had a "cup of coffee" in the majors in 1992), many of the prospects who made their big-league debuts in 1993 ended up not being included. Although expansion had much to do with this, the fact is that it has proven impossible to predict six months in advance which minor-leaguers will be playing in the majors next season—especially without the benefit of analyzing off-season transactions, free-agent signings, and spring-training performances.

Therefore, this edition includes extensive information which is applicable to all players, major-league or minor-league, regardless of which prospects actually end up playing in 1994. The data in this section should prove extremely useful when you are evaluating the 1993 performances of top prospects and when you are projecting 1994 performances for all players.

1994 PROJECTIONS AND 1993 MINOR LEAGUE PARK FACTORS

The first new report consists of Pete Palmer's 1994 projections for 770 active major-league players. While these projections won't be perfectly accurate, I'm confident that they are as good or better than anything else on the market.

The second new report consists of detailed analysis for all minor-league parks for the 1993 season. The statistics come from Howe Sportsdata in Boston, the official statisticians for all 18 U.S.-based minor leagues. The report also includes the league averages so that you can accurately compare your favorite prospect's performance in one league to another prospect's performance in another league. If you've ever been surprised at how well mediocre hitters in the International League (about 4.5 runs per game in 1993) can hit in the big leagues, or if you've ever wondered about a pitching prospect with a sky-high ERA in the Pacific Coast League (almost 5.5 runs per game in 1993), you should appreciate the ability to systematically compare both individual park effects and the huge differences between minor leagues.

Most of you are probably familiar with Pete Palmer's credentials. For those who are not, here is a brief summary. Pete is co-editor (with John Thorn) of the massive encyclopedia *Total Baseball*, which is now in its third edition. Quite simply, it is far and away the best baseball encyclopedia ever published—and I assure you that I was saying the same thing when it was being published by a competitor of HarperCollins a few years ago. *Total Baseball* is now in its third print edition; a new CD-ROM version will also be published this spring. Pete was also co-author (again with John Thorn) of one of the seminal works of modern baseball analysis, *The Hidden Game of Baseball*—now, sadly, out of print. He is a longtime member of the Society for American Baseball Research and chaired SABR's statistical analysis committee for many years. He was a member of the board of directors of Project Scoresheet and served for years as a consultant to the official statisticians for the American League. Pete has been published in many major sports periodicals, has contributed to more than a dozen baseball reference books, and was honored by SABR with the Bob Davids Award in 1989.

The projections in this section include all batters who had 100 or more plate appearances in the majors in 1993. All starting pitchers who made least 10 starts or pitched 50 or more innings in 1993 are included; all relief pitchers who relieved in 25 or more games or pitched in 30 games total are included as well.

As with almost all such systems, the projections for both batters and pitchers are solidly anchored on their career major-league performance to date. The primary factors considered are a player's career averages, his age, his recent playing time, and a weighted average of his three most recent seasons. A basic assumption of the system is that player performance will tend to move toward the league average; that is, players who have especially good or bad seasons are not likely to repeat such extremes. If a player performs well, the system projects an increase in his playing time the following year; if he plays badly, the system will decrease his expected playing time.

For pitchers, the expected offensive level of their 1994 team is also factored in when projecting statistics such as wins and losses. This means, of course, that pitcher projections will change more dramatically than batter projections when off-season trades and free-agent signings are considered.

This projection system has been tested by comparing it to others which have been published in recent years, and these tests have indicated that it is as accurate as or more accurate than the other prominent projections. I'm confident that you will find these projections generally interesting and informative, and I'm certain that they will be useful when planning your draft strategy if you play in a fantasy or boardgame league. Pete has been working on the system for several years, testing and refining it as needed. Publishing the projections will almost certainly result in much criticism and praise, the former for the inevitable mistakes and the latter for the inevitable (we hope!) projections which are on-target.

Pete and I are now working on a system of projections for minor-league players. Of course, it is much more problematic to predict performance for minor-leaguers who have no big-league track record that to make predictions for major-leaguers. We expect to have this system tested and ready by spring training. If you would like to receive information about these minor-league projections, write to The Baseball Workshop at the address on the back page of the book. If you purchase this edition of the *Stat Book*, you will be eligible to receive a free set of projections for top minor-league prospects.

MINOR LEAGUE PARK AND LEAGUE STATISTICS

The data contained in this report are pretty straightforward. The minor leagues are grouped by classification (see the introduction to Part 5 if you aren't sure of the classifications for the lower minors), and the runs and home runs per game are shown after the league name. League totals and averages are shown also: Be sure to keep in mind these sometimes large differences within each classification when comparing prospects across leagues.

There are two lines for each 1993 minor-league team. The first line ("home") shows the combined statistics for *both the home and visiting teams* when playing in that park; the second line ("road") shows the park factor in each category. These park factors are expressed as a ratio between the home totals and the road totals for both the home and visiting teams—if the ratio is less than 1.00, the home park favored pitchers in that category; if the ratio is greater than 1.00, it favored batters.

These park factors were normalized for the number of games played at home and on the road, as you can see by looking at the games column. The most important columns are the overall runs and the slugging and on-base averages, but you can get a good idea of how a given level of offense was generated by looking at the home run, hit, walk, and strikeout factors.

I trust that you will find this new information as useful as I have. While knowledgable fans have been making such adjustments for years now, having the exact information in front of you is always preferable when making educated guesses. As you can easily see, there are very large differences between various minor league parks and between leagues; moreover, these differences are always in flux. Just as in the majors, league offensive levels can rise and fall for many reasons. Armed with these park factors and league averages, your educated guesses should be more educated than before.

1994 SEASON PROJECTIONS

BATTERS

NAME	BA	G	AB	R	H	HR	RBI	SA	OBA
Mike Aldrete	.255	106	251	36	64	7	30	.390	.356
Luis Alicea	.269	126	375	47	101	3	46	.373	.350
Roberto Alomar	.305	161	620	106	189	13	86	.448	.386
Sandy Alomar	.268	74	250	24	67	4	30	.368	.314
Moises Alou	.280	147	489	71	137	16	83	.466	.331
Rich Amaral	.287	112	366	51	105	1	41	.363	.344
Brady Anderson	.259	137	514	79	133	13	61	.418	.360
Eric Anthony	.248	142	468	62	116	16	70	.402	.316
Alex Arias	.280	105	279	32	78	2	22	.333	.356
Brad Ausmus	.260	71	231	26	60	7	18	.416	.287
Carlos Baerga	.307	155	623	95	191	19	102	.454	.346
Kevin Baez	.207	62	150	13	31	0	9	.287	.287
Jeff Bagwell	.290	146	541	75	157	18	84	.466	.369
Harold Baines	.283	119	413	58	117	17	71	.455	.362
Bret Barberie	.272	117	383	43	104	4	35	.358	.355
Skeeter Barnes	.285	73	137	22	39	2	22	.401	.322
Kevin Bass	.270	90	222	27	60	4	29	.405	.332
Kim Batiste	.273	107	238	21	65	6	37	.395	.290
Bill Bean	.257	100	183	20	47	4	29	.383	.293
Derek Bell	.263	147	502	69	132	18	65	.412	.311
Jay Bell	.287	156	614	96	176	10	54	.414	.360
George Bell	.251	86	343	37	86	13	58	.414	.283
Juan Bell	.231	126	368	49	85	5	36	.323	.313
Albert Belle	.271	162	609	87	165	36	123	.511	.342
Freddie Benavides	.280	94	254	25	71	3	29	.390	.306
Mike Benjamin	.206	73	160	23	33	4	17	.344	.274
Todd Benzinger	.272	82	195	22	53	4	25	.400	.313
Sean Berry	.258	138	333	52	86	14	49	.441	.338
Damon Berryhill	.246	115	334	25	82	9	45	.395	.292
Dante Bichette	.290	145	531	77	154	17	77	.473	.325
Craig Biggio	.279	155	599	92	167	14	53	.422	.365
Lance Blankenship	.218	95	252	44	55	2	24	.298	.377
Jeff Blauser	.284	162	545	95	155	15	68	.426	.379
Mike Blowers	.266	139	403	55	107	15	55	.447	.341
Tim Bogar	.249	89	233	22	58	3	29	.361	.304
Wade Boggs	.292	128	489	70	143	4	49	.372	.375
Frank Bolick	.218	90	202	24	44	4	23	.337	.304
Barry Bonds	.300	162	547	117	164	39	114	.594	.425
Bobby Bonilla	.258	139	496	76	128	27	82	.480	.348
Bret Boone	.247	87	316	37	78	14	44	.430	.292
Pat Borders	.260	130	446	39	116	10	53	.390	.297
Mike Bordick	.269	151	501	58	135	3	46	.333	.345
Daryl Boston	.259	131	294	44	76	12	37	.442	.331
Jeff Branson	.268	138	377	43	101	3	27	.342	.302
Sid Bream	.261	100	261	28	68	8	38	.418	.334
Rod Brewer	.284	117	183	19	52	2	23	.372	.351
Greg Briley	.250	82	152	16	38	3	11	.349	.294
Hubie Brooks	.256	46	133	13	34	3	18	.383	.306
Scott Brosius	.252	82	230	30	58	7	28	.400	.298
Jarvis Brown	.229	83	170	32	39	0	9	.324	.333
Jerry Browne	.268	86	269	31	72	2	26	.338	.333
Jacob Brumfield	.264	115	288	44	76	6	24	.410	.318
Tom Brunansky	.230	59	183	19	42	6	27	.393	.313
Steve Buechele	.265	125	437	50	116	13	60	.416	.337
Jay Buhner	.255	158	550	81	140	27	90	.451	.354
Ellis Burks	.265	139	483	69	128	16	67	.431	.340
Jeromy Burnitz	.238	102	311	57	74	15	44	.466	.332
Brett Butler	.296	134	506	72	150	1	34	.366	.391
Francisco Cabrera	.242	94	120	12	29	6	20	.450	.305
Ivan Calderon	.249	65	205	25	51	3	25	.371	.316
Ken Caminiti	.271	130	491	66	133	12	66	.405	.329
Casey Candaele	.250	53	116	12	29	1	9	.336	.307
Jose Canseco	.250	63	236	37	59	13	47	.470	.328
Chuck Carr	.273	131	491	69	134	3	37	.338	.336
Mark Carreon	.275	86	211	24	58	7	33	.427	.320
Joe Carter	.257	136	530	79	136	28	101	.487	.311
Vinny Castilla	.262	118	363	40	95	10	33	.413	.293
Andujar Cedeno	.265	158	532	66	141	11	57	.397	.326
Wes Chamberlain	.269	97	316	37	85	12	48	.456	.308
Archi Cianfrocco	.250	104	308	33	77	12	49	.412	.291
Dave Clark	.262	118	282	42	74	11	47	.433	.352
Jerald Clark	.267	133	449	52	120	12	60	.421	.312
Phil Clark	.312	127	298	37	93	10	38	.483	.347

NAME	AVG	G	AB	R	H	HR	RBI	SLG	OBP
Will Clark	.283	126	463	70	131	15	70	.449	.362
Royce Clayton	.276	156	548	55	151	6	65	.365	.326
Greg Colbrunn	.269	78	193	18	52	4	27	.394	.300
Alex Cole	.270	121	345	51	93	0	22	.325	.352
Vince Coleman	.281	89	342	59	96	2	25	.374	.335
Darnell Coles	.269	69	197	26	53	4	26	.401	.321
Jeff Conine	.289	151	547	68	158	10	71	.399	.348
Scott Cooper	.280	161	514	62	144	8	59	.395	.354
Joey Cora	.268	157	518	89	139	2	45	.346	.355
Wil Cordero	.260	148	496	61	129	10	58	.395	.319
Rod Correia	.273	86	172	17	47	0	12	.314	.328
Tim Costo	.241	50	158	21	38	4	19	.380	.275
Henry Cotto	.270	84	204	27	55	4	20	.377	.296
Chad Curtis	.278	148	539	83	150	7	55	.369	.357
Milt Cuyler	.248	82	254	45	63	1	22	.343	.309
Doug Dascenzo	.256	56	125	17	32	1	8	.328	.304
Darren Daulton	.246	153	521	85	128	25	104	.466	.371
Chili Davis	.255	138	491	66	125	21	88	.442	.345
Eric Davis	.239	121	414	58	99	16	59	.399	.327
Butch Davis	.250	52	132	21	33	3	17	.424	.277
Andre Dawson	.274	100	379	40	104	14	60	.446	.312
Rob Deer	.216	112	402	60	87	23	54	.428	.314
Delino DeShields	.284	129	503	77	143	4	39	.370	.372
Orestes Destrade	.254	139	481	51	122	17	72	.401	.323
Mike Devereaux	.261	116	472	62	123	15	68	.428	.313
Mario Diaz	.280	83	211	26	59	2	25	.365	.310
Gary Disarcina	.260	124	407	44	106	3	43	.334	.298
Chris Donnels	.244	98	213	20	52	2	24	.352	.325
Rob Ducey	.257	61	136	20	35	2	11	.412	.322
Mariano Duncan	.281	121	477	65	134	10	61	.415	.304
Lenny Dykstra	.292	155	617	124	180	16	60	.444	.397
Damion Easley	.298	94	299	39	89	2	27	.385	.369
Jim Eisenreich	.302	134	348	43	105	5	44	.408	.346
Alvaro Espinoza	.273	104	264	31	72	3	22	.367	.297
Mike Felder	.257	109	300	36	77	2	20	.330	.311
Junior Felix	.256	62	227	29	58	5	29	.392	.296
Felix Fermin	.280	133	436	46	122	1	40	.335	.325
Tony Fernandez	.280	132	504	66	141	4	48	.381	.347
Cecil Fielder	.253	139	525	73	133	29	106	.459	.345
Steve Finley	.280	127	482	64	135	6	42	.400	.327
Darrin Fletcher	.259	140	406	32	105	8	59	.377	.318
Scott Fletcher	.279	123	441	68	123	4	47	.385	.337
Tom Foley	.246	87	179	16	44	2	19	.352	.287
Julio Franco	.290	135	500	81	145	13	72	.430	.361
Lou Frazier	.288	127	215	31	62	1	18	.353	.342
Travis Fryman	.279	162	648	93	181	22	99	.451	.347
Gary Gaetti	.246	88	301	33	74	11	40	.409	.298
Greg Gagne	.276	156	503	63	139	9	52	.400	.315
Andres Galarraga	.312	129	484	63	151	19	81	.502	.349
Dave Gallagher	.272	97	202	30	55	4	26	.401	.336
Mike Gallego	.271	118	387	58	105	9	46	.393	.356
Ron Gant	.262	155	580	98	152	29	102	.474	.332
Carlos Garcia	.271	140	516	73	140	11	45	.401	.317
Jeff Gardner	.264	142	398	52	105	1	23	.354	.339
Brent Gates	.288	140	538	64	155	7	69	.388	.355
Bob Geren	.235	57	136	9	32	3	10	.338	.297
Kirk Gibson	.253	103	360	56	91	12	52	.419	.334
Bernard Gilkey	.290	150	552	89	160	14	64	.444	.356
Joe Girardi	.286	97	325	33	93	3	28	.369	.342
Dan Gladden	.263	83	315	46	83	9	43	.403	.311
Chris Gomez	.257	80	222	20	57	0	20	.329	.313
Leo Gomez	.232	75	254	32	59	10	30	.394	.324
Rene Gonzales	.260	112	315	37	82	3	31	.346	.353
Juan Gonzalez	.277	156	595	97	165	44	117	.556	.330
Luis Gonzalez	.277	157	537	72	149	15	73	.434	.336
Mark Grace	.303	146	561	75	170	11	79	.435	.373
Craig Grebeck	.258	73	198	24	51	2	19	.348	.345
Mike Greenwell	.297	143	529	70	157	11	69	.437	.359
Ken Griffey	.295	162	611	100	180	37	107	.550	.377
Marquis Grissom	.286	147	590	92	169	15	74	.422	.336
Ozzie Guillen	.291	130	444	46	129	4	50	.383	.302

NAME	BA	G	AB	R	H	HR	RBI	SA	OBA
Ricky Gutierrez	.255	138	455	80	116	5	27	.334	.339
Tony Gwynn	.328	121	485	67	159	6	51	.447	.372
Chris Gwynn	.294	118	299	38	88	2	28	.391	.344
Chip Hale	.315	89	238	30	75	3	33	.399	.383
Darryl Hamilton	.304	132	494	71	150	7	53	.399	.360
Dave Hansen	.273	135	238	24	65	6	35	.378	.357
Brian Harper	.304	136	490	52	149	10	69	.420	.344
Lenny Harris	.274	81	168	19	46	1	14	.333	.332
Bill Haselman	.259	82	193	28	50	7	22	.415	.315
Billy Hatcher	.279	126	451	59	126	6	47	.384	.326
Charlie Hayes	.279	162	580	75	162	22	88	.466	.323
Scott Hemond	.253	116	257	38	65	6	29	.397	.347
Dave Henderson	.234	94	338	37	79	16	47	.429	.292
Rickey Henderson	.271	132	465	100	126	18	54	.441	.410
Carlos Hernandez	.269	68	145	10	39	3	13	.366	.305
Phil Hiatt	.222	89	261	34	58	8	40	.372	.291
Kevin Higgins	.230	75	191	19	44	0	14	.267	.305
Glenallen Hill	.254	95	287	34	73	15	45	.470	.302
Chris Hoiles	.278	146	478	78	133	29	76	.515	.379
Dave Hollins	.265	144	535	96	142	20	86	.443	.363
Thomas Howard	.269	113	324	43	87	5	34	.380	.313
Kent Hrbek	.245	112	372	54	91	19	69	.441	.355
Tim Hulett	.289	88	253	35	73	3	25	.383	.349
David Hulse	.296	121	422	74	125	1	28	.372	.337
Todd Hundley	.237	136	422	42	100	11	53	.367	.282
Pete Incaviglia	.261	119	380	51	99	19	73	.474	.311
Darrin Jackson	.249	64	225	25	56	7	27	.391	.285
Bo Jackson	.242	82	277	36	67	16	47	.455	.305
John Jaha	.261	143	472	71	123	16	61	.405	.333
Dion James	.307	124	349	58	107	6	36	.430	.371
Chris James	.256	81	203	23	52	7	27	.424	.311
Stan Javier	.273	110	264	35	72	2	27	.364	.346
Gregg Jefferies	.308	153	588	81	181	14	81	.435	.368
Reggie Jefferson	.260	116	381	37	99	10	36	.388	.315
Howard Johnson	.237	68	232	35	55	8	32	.405	.343
Lance Johnson	.299	137	501	66	150	1	43	.383	.339
Chris Jones	.269	112	234	33	63	6	31	.436	.306
Brian Jordan	.274	86	292	37	80	11	50	.486	.315
Ricky Jordan	.290	81	186	24	54	5	24	.430	.316
Terry Jorgensen	.256	60	156	16	40	1	14	.321	.304
Felix Jose	.277	126	447	57	124	8	50	.391	.330
Wally Joyner	.282	130	476	69	134	13	62	.437	.356
David Justice	.259	157	567	87	147	33	106	.481	.350
Ron Karkovice	.235	132	391	56	92	18	55	.422	.298
Eric Karros	.255	136	517	62	132	19	73	.422	.298
Pat Kelly	.264	132	413	51	109	7	47	.387	.316
Bobby Kelly	.290	85	335	46	97	9	39	.430	.334
Jeff Kent	.263	146	498	70	131	20	81	.442	.317
Jeff King	.278	149	564	74	157	11	87	.397	.335
Wayne Kirby	.271	131	428	70	116	6	56	.376	.328
Joe Kmak	.222	54	117	10	26	0	8	.274	.321
Chuck Knoblauch	.284	140	545	80	155	2	43	.350	.364
Randy Knorr	.251	72	183	19	46	7	35	.437	.312
Chad Kreuter	.273	131	403	59	110	13	50	.444	.355
John Kruk	.300	146	520	88	156	13	77	.450	.403
Tim Laker	.250	71	136	11	34	0	14	.309	.283
Tom Lampkin	.214	79	168	24	36	4	25	.333	.303
Ray Lankford	.258	121	423	64	109	10	52	.397	.356
Mike Lansing	.288	140	486	64	140	3	45	.370	.354
Barry Larkin	.300	109	417	62	125	10	56	.444	.376
Gene Larkin	.267	55	150	18	40	2	18	.360	.343
Manuel Lee	.255	69	208	28	53	1	17	.303	.330
Mark Lemke	.252	158	465	50	117	7	42	.340	.334
Darren Lewis	.261	126	456	74	119	2	40	.329	.320
Mark Lewis	.275	34	120	13	33	1	10	.358	.313
Jim Leyritz	.279	108	283	42	79	14	52	.473	.378
Jose Lind	.269	118	386	35	104	0	37	.319	.302
Nelson Liriano	.286	64	203	34	58	2	18	.389	.354
Pat Listach	.272	99	372	57	101	2	32	.341	.341
Greg Litton	.268	98	224	27	60	4	30	.406	.332
Scott Livingstone	.295	104	319	41	94	3	41	.373	.331
Kenny Lofton	.303	146	564	105	171	2	40	.383	.383
Torey Lovullo	.250	119	368	41	92	6	30	.351	.322
Scott Lydy	.233	60	150	17	35	3	11	.340	.299

NAME	AVG	G	AB	R	H	HR	RBI	SLG	OBP
Kevin Maas	.227	63	181	24	41	9	26	.409	.321
Mike Macfarlane	.256	127	410	55	105	19	62	.473	.335
Shane Mack	.287	122	460	67	132	11	58	.437	.350
Dave Magadan	.271	125	414	46	112	4	44	.350	.379
Candy Maldonado	.245	66	188	21	46	7	28	.410	.329
Kirt Manwaring	.271	132	428	43	116	5	45	.350	.339
Albert Martin	.274	151	492	85	135	18	65	.472	.331
Carlos Martinez	.266	77	256	26	68	5	34	.371	.307
Tino Martinez	.258	117	418	48	108	16	60	.433	.330
Dave Martinez	.259	87	247	30	64	4	25	.377	.326
Edgar Martinez	.297	47	172	29	51	5	19	.459	.384
Don Mattingly	.287	123	488	67	140	13	71	.424	.347
Derrick May	.289	143	477	59	138	11	74	.411	.329
Brent Mayne	.258	88	244	25	63	2	27	.336	.315
David McCarty	.228	98	351	38	80	2	22	.302	.272
Lloyd McClendon	.245	72	151	19	37	3	17	.358	.333
Willie McGee	.304	118	425	50	129	3	38	.384	.351
Fred McGriff	.274	147	530	91	145	33	95	.519	.367
Mark McGwire	.250	46	148	24	37	11	30	.527	.372
Jeff McKnight	.269	98	171	20	46	2	16	.345	.317
Mark McLemore	.280	152	533	78	149	3	65	.356	.348
Brian McRae	.271	142	561	72	152	9	61	.390	.317
Kevin McReynolds	.247	96	320	40	79	10	41	.422	.330
Pat Meares	.264	117	364	36	96	0	36	.324	.279
Roberto Mejia	.237	80	283	39	67	6	25	.410	.279
Bob Melvin	.258	64	151	11	39	2	19	.344	.290
Orlando Merced	.283	144	463	68	131	8	68	.413	.378
Hensley Meulens	.219	41	96	14	21	3	10	.365	.299
Randy Milligan	.265	92	283	38	75	7	35	.392	.391
Kevin Mitchell	.299	99	344	52	103	17	64	.515	.354
Paul Molitor	.314	149	593	102	186	17	89	.472	.383
Mickey Morandini	.263	121	418	54	110	3	32	.361	.320
Hal Morris	.299	106	385	47	115	7	49	.413	.359
Pedro Munoz	.256	111	351	38	90	13	50	.413	.305
Eddie Murray	.274	129	492	60	135	19	81	.443	.326
Greg Myers	.262	114	309	28	81	7	44	.385	.305
Tim Naehring	.282	74	216	19	61	2	23	.375	.342
Rob Natal	.233	47	129	4	30	1	7	.310	.301
Troy Neel	.280	131	439	59	123	19	64	.462	.356
Dave Nilsson	.254	114	342	39	87	8	48	.377	.333
Otis Nixon	.285	116	407	72	116	1	22	.332	.357
Matt Nokes	.245	76	233	27	57	12	38	.438	.301
Charlie O'Brien	.243	69	181	16	44	3	20	.365	.310
Pete O'Brien	.250	59	184	22	46	6	26	.397	.319
Jose Offerman	.270	154	556	73	150	1	50	.335	.347
John Olerud	.311	162	553	93	172	21	92	.510	.413
Joe Oliver	.254	134	453	39	115	13	67	.397	.296
Greg Olson	.243	77	243	24	59	3	24	.337	.322
Paul O'Neill	.279	140	487	64	136	18	71	.454	.352
Joe Orsulak	.288	122	389	52	112	6	35	.391	.337
Junior Ortiz	.254	76	201	17	51	0	19	.303	.304
John Orton	.222	42	108	9	24	1	8	.315	.294
Spike Owen	.257	98	311	39	80	3	24	.354	.326
Mike Pagliarulo	.288	119	364	49	105	7	41	.426	.337
Tom Pagnozzi	.264	92	322	28	85	5	38	.376	.305
Rafael Palmeiro	.280	152	575	102	161	29	89	.497	.356
Dean Palmer	.233	149	524	82	122	30	86	.466	.313
Erik Pappas	.275	96	265	29	73	1	33	.340	.367
Craig Paquette	.226	107	402	37	91	13	49	.396	.254
Dan Pasqua	.226	63	164	21	37	5	21	.390	.325
Dan Peltier	.265	87	211	29	56	1	23	.336	.345
Tony Pena	.232	93	254	23	59	3	22	.315	.294
Geronimo Pena	.264	92	284	41	75	7	35	.419	.340
Terry Pendleton	.289	135	533	74	154	16	76	.439	.328
Eduardo Perez	.256	64	223	20	57	5	38	.381	.298
Gerald Perry	.273	88	121	18	33	3	18	.413	.355
Geno Petralli	.240	59	129	13	31	1	13	.318	.333
Tony Phillips	.289	145	547	101	158	9	56	.388	.408
Mike Piazza	.299	162	591	81	177	35	112	.525	.351
Phil Plantier	.242	147	484	68	117	28	87	.467	.333
Luis Polonia	.287	128	491	69	141	1	31	.344	.341
Todd Pratt	.282	63	170	17	48	9	27	.500	.330
Tom Prince	.206	70	170	14	35	2	24	.324	.291
Kirby Puckett	.300	141	563	82	169	18	83	.465	.349
Carlos Quintana	.276	93	293	35	81	4	32	.348	.352

NAME	BA	G	AB	R	H	HR	RBI	SA	OBA
Tim Raines	.287	109	407	71	117	10	44	.420	.378
Randy Ready	.241	50	137	22	33	2	13	.336	.364
Jeff Reboulet	.252	120	254	34	64	1	19	.307	.355
Gary Redus	.274	75	201	28	55	5	23	.428	.339
Jeff Reed	.257	74	152	12	39	5	16	.401	.327
Jody Reed	.274	114	412	49	113	2	32	.352	.338
Kevin Reimer	.260	121	407	48	106	14	56	.420	.320
Rich Renteria	.261	98	249	26	65	2	28	.341	.317
Harold Reynolds	.258	127	434	59	112	3	40	.343	.343
Ernie Riles	.213	82	141	15	30	4	18	.355	.296
Cal Ripken	.265	143	567	75	150	20	78	.425	.333
Billy Ripken	.238	43	122	13	29	1	12	.295	.299
Luis Rivera	.239	55	142	15	34	1	13	.331	.306
Kevin Roberson	.197	67	193	26	38	10	30	.383	.258
Bip Roberts	.281	82	292	48	82	2	21	.360	.358
Henry Rodriguez	.233	83	202	22	47	8	26	.411	.278
Ivan Rodriguez	.274	148	504	56	138	10	62	.401	.314
Rico Rossy	.231	52	108	14	25	2	13	.333	.320
Chris Sabo	.261	135	501	75	131	19	72	.447	.318
Tim Salmon	.265	152	547	92	145	30	93	.497	.362
Juan Samuel	.257	83	241	29	62	3	25	.369	.317
Rey Sanchez	.288	111	365	38	105	0	30	.345	.325
Ryne Sandberg	.297	109	421	65	125	13	51	.447	.358
Deion Sanders	.276	106	304	49	84	7	30	.457	.323
Reggie Sanders	.267	139	490	85	131	18	71	.441	.340
Benito Santiago	.251	128	450	48	113	13	53	.398	.301
Mackey Sasser	.249	86	177	16	44	2	23	.356	.290
Steve Sax	.267	30	101	15	27	1	8	.356	.312
Steve Scarsone	.259	64	143	22	37	3	19	.392	.287
Dick Schofield	.222	36	108	13	24	1	8	.287	.328
David Segui	.269	162	431	50	116	8	54	.381	.344
Kevin Seitzer	.270	115	400	48	108	7	53	.385	.340
Scott Servais	.246	101	293	24	72	9	33	.386	.312
Danny Sheaffer	.274	82	215	26	59	4	31	.377	.296
Gary Sheffield	.290	143	517	71	150	23	79	.485	.353
Craig Shipley	.260	103	223	24	58	3	21	.350	.297
Ruben Sierra	.260	132	527	71	137	18	84	.425	.311
Don Slaught	.304	114	358	32	109	8	51	.436	.358
Dwight Smith	.285	133	326	48	93	9	36	.451	.337
Lonnie Smith	.264	94	208	36	55	7	28	.423	.385
Ozzie Smith	.292	117	452	66	132	1	39	.358	.355
J.T. Snow	.242	129	414	59	100	16	57	.406	.331
Cory Snyder	.264	139	469	56	124	12	56	.407	.322
Paul Sorrento	.260	141	443	64	115	17	61	.436	.339
Sammy Sosa	.257	155	565	86	145	28	80	.457	.306
Tim Spehr	.228	71	123	18	28	4	18	.390	.295
Bill Spiers	.261	117	348	50	91	3	41	.342	.326
Ed Sprague	.265	145	502	48	133	11	69	.392	.318
Mike Stanley	.279	151	448	68	125	24	80	.484	.370
Terry Steinbach	.283	106	382	44	108	9	46	.411	.335
Kurt Stillwell	.251	70	195	18	49	2	17	.333	.307
Kevin Stocker	.314	87	322	55	101	2	37	.404	.398
Doug Strange	.258	145	450	54	116	7	55	.360	.323
Darryl Strawberry	.223	27	94	14	21	5	15	.404	.327
B.J. Surhoff	.276	141	511	64	141	6	72	.380	.323

NAME	AVG	G	AB	R	H	HR	RBI	SLG	OBP
Dale Sveum	.212	37	99	13	21	2	12	.333	.313
Jeff Tackett	.223	42	103	12	23	2	13	.311	.317
Danny Tartabull	.253	135	491	80	124	29	95	.493	.368
Eddie Taubensee	.249	108	321	28	80	8	43	.377	.310
Mickey Tettleton	.237	150	507	76	120	30	94	.469	.366
Tim Teufel	.240	83	192	23	46	6	26	.396	.329
Frank Thomas	.298	162	580	103	173	34	118	.540	.410
Jim Thome	.247	83	267	38	66	9	34	.416	.348
Milt Thompson	.277	127	314	43	87	4	37	.376	.350
Robby Thompson	.283	133	491	75	139	18	58	.456	.352
Ryan Thompson	.249	88	317	39	79	12	29	.442	.303
Dickie Thon	.270	74	226	22	61	2	28	.358	.316
Gary Thurman	.250	62	104	19	26	0	12	.327	.307
Alan Trammell	.302	112	401	66	121	11	57	.454	.365
Jeff Treadway	.295	103	241	25	71	2	25	.390	.341
Brian Turang	.253	51	178	28	45	0	9	.348	.345
John Valentin	.274	153	497	53	136	12	69	.437	.344
Dave Valle	.248	134	400	45	99	11	51	.380	.336
John Vanderwal	.238	114	235	33	56	5	30	.374	.321
Andy VanSlyke	.300	80	310	46	93	8	46	.458	.358
Greg Vaughn	.248	152	556	89	138	28	92	.451	.341
Mo Vaughn	.272	160	545	77	148	25	94	.470	.363
Randy Velarde	.281	86	249	32	70	6	26	.418	.342
Guillermo Velasquez	.237	85	152	8	36	4	24	.322	.299
Robin Ventura	.265	152	554	81	147	19	89	.424	.369
Jose Vizcaino	.283	162	545	68	154	3	50	.354	.332
Omar Vizquel	.273	148	513	61	140	1	30	.326	.335
Jack Voigt	.285	97	228	46	65	9	33	.478	.383
Chico Walker	.261	76	157	16	41	3	17	.363	.314
Larry Walker	.272	141	507	80	138	21	84	.465	.356
Tim Wallach	.237	106	384	38	91	9	50	.357	.298
Dan Walters	.241	35	116	9	28	2	14	.353	.294
Turner Ward	.220	75	168	22	37	4	26	.345	.313
Lenny Webster	.244	55	119	15	29	2	12	.336	.313
Mitch Webster	.252	71	139	20	35	2	15	.374	.312
Walt Weiss	.260	150	473	50	123	1	37	.300	.358
Lou Whitaker	.274	112	372	66	102	12	60	.444	.388
Devon White	.266	130	534	95	142	14	48	.427	.331
Mark Whiten	.253	143	514	73	130	18	75	.405	.328
Darrell Whitmore	.215	72	237	24	51	4	19	.316	.262
Rick Wilkins	.279	161	502	73	140	28	70	.498	.353
Bernie Williams	.267	129	524	66	140	10	61	.397	.337
Matt Williams	.267	150	580	88	155	33	97	.497	.307
Willie Wilson	.270	64	159	19	43	0	12	.352	.324
Dave Winfield	.270	114	433	59	117	18	66	.453	.335
Eric Yelding	.239	69	134	16	32	1	12	.321	.301
Eric Young	.271	145	480	76	130	3	42	.350	.353
Kevin Young	.249	134	417	37	104	6	47	.360	.315
Robin Yount	.263	108	396	53	104	7	51	.386	.330
Todd Zeile	.270	150	540	73	146	13	85	.411	.351
Bob Zupcic	.262	129	302	41	79	2	31	.368	.321

PITCHERS

NAME	W	L	PCT	ERA	G	GS	IP	H	BB	SO
Jim Abbott	12	8	.600	3.83	26	26	181.0	184	61	93
Rick Aguilera	5	3	.625	3.15	66	0	71.1	61	18	56
Wilson Alvarez	14	9	.609	3.56	39	29	209.2	183	128	148
Larry Andersen	4	2	.667	3.13	60	0	60.1	53	19	61
Kevin Appier	16	10	.615	2.88	35	34	237.2	199	82	173
Luis Aquino	5	6	.455	3.72	29	13	96.2	103	33	48
Jack Armstrong	7	11	.389	4.54	32	27	168.1	178	66	107
Rene Arocha	10	9	.526	3.92	30	27	177.0	188	30	89
Andy Ashby	4	8	.333	5.50	26	18	103.0	121	43	72
Paul Assenmacher	4	3	.571	3.72	64	0	58.0	57	22	53
Pedro Astacio	11	9	.550	3.46	29	29	182.1	168	64	112
Jim Austin	3	2	.600	3.40	44	0	50.1	40	26	23
Steve Avery	15	10	.600	3.25	35	35	221.1	216	55	122
Bobby Ayala	4	5	.444	5.00	33	8	81.0	85	36	57
Bob Ayrault	3	3	.500	4.50	37	0	48.0	49	23	27
Scott Bankhead	4	3	.571	3.58	40	1	65.1	61	28	45
Willie Banks	9	9	.500	4.33	31	29	164.1	179	77	125
Brian Barnes	5	5	.500	3.98	31	10	86.0	80	41	55
Jose Bautista	6	5	.545	3.40	55	6	100.2	101	27	55
Rod Beck	6	3	.667	2.40	69	0	82.1	63	15	79
Steve Bedrosian	4	2	.667	3.30	50	0	57.1	48	23	34
Tim Belcher	10	9	.526	4.10	27	27	171.1	159	61	113
Stan Belinda	4	4	.500	3.80	59	0	68.2	60	23	55
Andy Benes	11	11	.500	3.69	30	30	202.1	186	67	150
Jason Bere	10	7	.588	3.62	25	25	151.2	118	88	134
Sean Bergman	4	5	.444	5.42	18	12	81.1	94	46	40
Mike Bielecki	5	5	.500	4.52	20	16	93.2	104	31	54
Bud Black	6	6	.500	3.95	18	18	109.1	107	38	51
Willie Blair	7	8	.467	4.59	44	16	135.1	162	39	78
Mike Boddicker	4	6	.400	4.74	20	13	87.1	102	29	42
Joe Boever	6	4	.600	3.43	58	0	89.1	88	40	56
Brian Bohanon	4	5	.444	4.85	30	9	81.2	93	39	44
Rodney Bolton	3	6	.333	6.33	17	15	79.2	95	28	35
Tom Bolton	5	5	.500	4.54	35	9	85.1	96	39	55
Ricky Bones	8	11	.421	4.63	28	27	167.1	177	51	59
Chris Bosio	10	8	.556	3.66	26	24	162.1	149	48	100
Shawn Boskie	4	4	.500	4.28	27	7	67.1	69	24	35
Kent Bottenfield	7	9	.438	4.64	34	22	141.2	152	61	57
Denis Boucher	4	4	.500	4.28	13	13	69.1	73	21	32
Ryan Bowen	6	10	.375	4.80	28	27	148.0	150	84	96
Jeff Brantley	6	4	.600	3.77	48	7	90.2	83	41	68
Billy Brewer	3	3	.500	3.67	64	0	54.0	44	29	38
Doug Brocail	6	8	.429	4.56	24	24	126.1	140	41	73
Jeff Bronkey	3	3	.500	3.98	30	0	52.0	56	16	26
Kevin Brown	13	10	.565	3.75	29	29	206.1	210	68	122
Tom Browning	6	7	.462	4.54	20	19	111.0	140	25	51
Greg Brummett	5	6	.455	4.90	18	18	101.0	112	38	42
Dave Burba	5	5	.500	4.31	43	7	85.2	87	34	71
John Burkett	12	10	.545	3.91	32	31	202.2	205	42	122
Todd Burns	4	5	.444	4.48	36	5	78.1	75	30	39
Mike Butcher	3	2	.600	3.26	38	0	49.2	43	26	41
Greg Cadaret	3	3	.500	4.14	37	3	54.1	56	34	37
Tom Candiotti	12	9	.571	3.19	30	29	197.2	180	66	139
Cris Carpenter	4	3	.571	3.63	57	0	69.1	61	24	46
Larry Casian	4	3	.571	3.54	58	0	61.0	68	16	31
Tony Castillo	4	2	.667	3.75	48	1	57.2	59	22	35
Frank Castillo	7	8	.467	4.32	25	23	133.1	137	39	83
Norm Charlton	4	2	.667	2.92	39	1	52.1	45	21	56
Mark Clark	6	7	.462	4.30	26	17	117.1	124	31	56
Roger Clemens	10	8	.556	3.64	23	23	163.1	145	50	135
David Cone	14	11	.560	3.38	30	30	221.1	186	98	187
Steve Cooke	11	10	.524	3.99	32	28	191.2	191	53	117
Rheal Cormier	8	7	.533	4.06	30	21	137.1	150	24	77
Danny Cox	5	3	.625	3.89	35	4	78.2	74	30	66
John Cummings	4	6	.400	5.61	19	15	86.2	106	29	36
Omar Daal	2	4	.333	4.99	70	0	52.1	53	31	29
Ron Darling	7	8	.467	4.40	23	23	139.0	143	52	76
Danny Darwin	12	10	.545	3.67	38	27	201.1	184	50	122
Storm Davis	4	4	.500	4.61	37	5	80.0	78	36	54
Mark Davis	3	4	.429	4.82	48	2	65.1	72	43	60
Rich DeLucia	3	3	.500	4.72	22	6	53.1	56	24	44
Jim Deshaies	9	9	.500	4.29	27	27	159.1	156	53	77
Mark Dewey	3	2	.600	3.31	34	0	49.0	39	17	28
Rob Dibble	3	3	.500	4.47	49	0	50.1	39	33	71
Jerry DiPoto	5	2	.714	2.56	51	0	63.1	67	35	44
John Doherty	10	8	.556	4.33	37	25	164.1	183	41	55
John Dopson	7	8	.467	4.61	28	24	136.2	149	47	71
Kelly Downs	4	5	.444	4.59	28	10	84.1	87	41	46
Doug Drabek	12	10	.545	3.54	28	28	200.2	199	50	129
Mike Draper	3	3	.500	4.31	37	1	54.1	68	18	20
Steve Dreyer	4	6	.400	5.38	20	12	82.0	93	39	47
Dennis Eckersley	4	3	.571	3.48	57	0	62.0	58	11	71
Tom Edens	4	3	.571	3.38	39	1	56.0	54	24	31
Mark Eichhorn	6	2	.750	2.97	55	0	72.2	74	21	46
Dave Eiland	4	6	.400	4.97	20	17	88.2	103	27	27
Cal Eldred	12	11	.522	3.81	29	29	208.0	187	71	140
Scott Erickson	9	10	.474	4.41	26	26	165.1	181	57	85
Steve Farr	4	2	.667	3.23	52	0	53.0	45	26	41
John Farrell	4	6	.400	5.12	18	16	91.1	97	36	50
Jeff Fassero	8	5	.615	2.61	60	9	120.2	103	46	102
Alex Fernandez	14	10	.583	3.68	33	32	222.1	213	66	143
Sid Fernandez	8	6	.571	3.03	19	19	127.2	95	40	96
Mike Fetters	4	3	.571	3.21	45	1	61.2	57	26	30
Chuck Finley	13	12	.520	3.59	32	32	223.1	223	87	155
Dave Fleming	9	8	.529	4.09	25	24	156.1	170	54	73
Tony Fossas	3	3	.500	4.29	85	0	50.1	48	21	41
Steve Foster	3	2	.600	2.45	31	0	47.2	47	12	30
John Franco	3	3	.500	3.83	47	0	49.1	55	22	37
Scott Fredrickson	2	4	.333	5.74	41	0	47.0	52	27	34
Steve Frey	3	3	.500	3.61	62	0	57.1	51	31	27
Todd Frohwirth	6	4	.600	3.38	57	0	85.1	79	36	47
Mark Gardner	4	6	.400	4.81	18	16	97.1	92	36	65
Paul Gibson	3	3	.500	4.33	36	0	54.0	59	19	41
Tom Glavine	15	9	.625	3.19	33	33	220.1	212	78	120
Pat Gomez	2	4	.333	5.04	43	2	50.0	55	30	42
Dwight Gooden	11	11	.500	3.66	28	28	194.1	183	61	137
Tom Gordon	9	9	.500	3.94	49	14	157.2	135	79	143
Rich Gossage	3	3	.500	4.01	43	0	51.2	49	27	40
Jim Gott	5	3	.625	2.68	60	0	77.1	70	26	64
Joe Grahe	4	3	.571	3.50	37	3	61.2	61	27	30
Mark Grant	2	3	.400	4.78	23	3	43.1	52	15	26
Tommy Greene	12	9	.571	3.74	31	29	192.1	177	66	150
Jason Grimsley	4	5	.444	4.64	18	14	83.1	85	48	56
Buddy Groom	2	3	.400	5.29	23	6	51.0	61	20	22
Kevin Gross	10	10	.500	3.92	32	26	174.1	183	66	130
Eddie Guardado	4	7	.364	5.75	20	17	101.2	128	37	51
Mark Gubicza	4	5	.444	4.54	29	0	85.1	99	31	64
Lee Guetterman	3	3	.500	4.42	46	0	55.0	59	19	20
Bill Gullickson	7	7	.500	4.66	22	22	131.1	144	32	51
Jose Guzman	9	9	.500	4.07	25	25	166.0	166	64	135
Juan Guzman	13	8	.619	3.70	29	29	192.1	172	92	167
Dave Haas	2	3	.400	4.86	22	4	46.1	60	14	26
John Habyan	3	3	.500	3.86	47	0	58.1	61	18	39
Chris Hammond	7	11	.389	4.46	29	28	163.1	171	59	91
Chris Haney	5	8	.385	5.11	21	20	111.0	116	44	65
Erik Hanson	12	10	.545	3.97	30	29	199.1	209	59	142
Mike Harkey	7	9	.438	4.75	24	24	136.1	155	38	62
Pete Harnisch	13	10	.565	3.34	33	33	212.2	177	77	170
Greg A. Harris	6	5	.545	3.65	56	3	91.1	78	48	73
Greg W. Harris	9	10	.474	4.26	28	28	177.1	181	52	100
Gene Harris	4	3	.571	3.47	58	0	62.1	60	39	41
Mike Hartley	4	4	.500	3.96	52	0	75.0	77	35	57
Bryan Harvey	5	3	.625	2.09	63	0	73.1	52	17	78
Hilly Hathaway	4	6	.400	4.82	19	19	97.0	117	43	19
Neal Heaton	2	3	.400	4.80	31	0	45.0	50	19	27
Tom Henke	5	3	.625	2.86	67	0	72.1	55	27	70
Mike Henneman	5	3	.625	3.28	59	0	71.1	71	28	54
Dwayne Henry	3	3	.500	4.77	36	0	54.2	48	32	41
Butch Henry	5	7	.417	4.88	24	17	103.1	122	26	54
Doug Henry	3	3	.500	4.58	55	0	55.0	58	23	41
Pat Hentgen	12	9	.571	4.10	39	27	193.1	193	73	112
Xavier Hernandez	6	4	.600	2.86	64	1	91.1	74	32	85
Jeremy Hernandez	6	5	.545	3.67	61	0	95.2	99	29	60

NAME	W	L	PCT	ERA	G	GS	IP	H	BB	SO
Roberto Hernandez	6	3	.667	2.50	63	0	79.1	65	22	68
Orel Hershiser	11	10	.524	3.75	30	30	189.2	185	63	120
Greg Hibbard	10	10	.500	4.19	29	28	174.0	188	48	71
Bryan Hickerson	6	5	.545	3.97	44	9	95.1	102	29	61
Teddy Higuera	3	4	.429	4.86	13	12	63.0	70	23	54
Ken Hill	11	9	.550	3.31	28	28	182.1	163	71	102
Milt Hill	2	3	.400	4.53	32	0	47.2	50	13	34
Shawn Hillegas	4	6	.400	5.24	31	12	89.1	99	43	53
Eric Hillman	7	9	.438	4.19	27	22	144.0	174	24	57
Sterling Hitchcock	4	4	.500	4.88	14	14	72.0	80	31	57
Trevor Hoffman	4	5	.444	3.96	62	0	84.0	75	37	72
Brad Holman	3	3	.500	3.88	28	0	53.1	40	24	25
Darren Holmes	4	4	.500	3.92	57	0	66.2	60	20	55
Rick Honeycutt	3	2	.600	3.31	66	0	51.2	45	23	31
John Hope	5	4	.556	4.06	15	15	82.0	102	17	17
Vince Horsman	2	3	.400	4.20	67	0	45.0	43	25	25
Charlie Hough	8	10	.444	4.18	26	26	161.1	153	60	90
Steve Howe	3	3	.500	4.02	51	0	53.2	53	10	24
Jay Howell	5	2	.714	2.54	55	0	60.1	52	19	39
Mike Ignasiak	3	3	.500	4.05	36	1	53.1	44	31	40
Jeff Innis	4	4	.500	3.61	62	0	72.1	73	32	33
Danny Jackson	12	9	.571	4.04	30	30	187.1	196	75	99
Mike Jackson	5	3	.625	3.42	72	0	76.1	63	27	68
Domingo Jean	5	4	.556	4.46	21	12	82.2	76	39	42
Randy Johnson	14	10	.583	3.58	31	30	216.1	161	112	252
Joel Johnston	4	3	.571	3.47	38	0	59.2	42	22	35
Doug Jones	4	4	.500	3.87	57	0	74.1	83	16	58
Jimmy Jones	4	5	.444	4.72	17	12	76.1	80	22	42
Bobby Jones	6	6	.500	3.81	15	15	104.0	105	38	58
Todd Jones	3	3	.500	3.31	39	0	54.1	42	23	35
Scott Kamieniecki	9	7	.563	4.19	26	20	148.1	155	57	70
Steve Karsay	5	5	.500	4.12	15	15	94.0	95	31	63
Jimmy Key	15	9	.625	3.33	32	32	218.2	211	47	140
Darryl Kile	10	9	.526	3.77	33	27	171.1	160	78	130
Paul Kilgus	3	2	.600	3.38	35	1	50.2	43	18	30
Joe Klink	2	3	.400	4.44	65	0	50.2	49	25	28
Kurt Knudsen	3	3	.500	4.61	39	0	52.2	54	26	40
Tom Kramer	7	7	.500	4.23	41	16	123.1	130	62	74
Les Lancaster	4	3	.571	4.12	38	1	63.1	64	26	35
Mark Langston	13	11	.542	3.48	31	31	222.1	196	77	165
Tim Leary	7	9	.438	4.97	27	22	139.1	153	58	60
Craig Lefferts	4	4	.500	4.61	28	8	68.1	77	18	42
Phil Leftwich	6	6	.500	3.89	17	17	111.0	113	38	42
Charlie Leibrandt	8	7	.533	4.02	22	22	134.1	141	36	75
Al Leiter	7	6	.538	4.21	38	13	115.1	102	63	72
Mark Leiter	6	6	.500	4.40	30	13	110.1	112	44	75
Curt Leskanic	4	6	.400	5.17	30	13	94.0	96	44	51
Richie Lewis	4	4	.500	3.76	55	1	76.2	72	45	63
Scott Lewis	2	3	.400	4.47	22	6	50.1	57	18	22
Derek Lilliquist	5	3	.625	2.63	65	2	68.1	66	21	43
Doug Linton	2	3	.400	5.18	27	3	48.2	51	26	38
Graeme Lloyd	4	3	.571	2.97	57	0	66.2	69	14	31
Albie Lopez	4	6	.400	5.58	16	16	90.1	86	56	47
Larry Luebbers	5	6	.455	4.49	19	19	106.1	102	52	53
Rob MacDonald	3	3	.500	4.60	56	0	62.2	62	28	36
Greg Maddux	19	10	.655	2.67	35	35	260.0	225	60	184
Mike Maddux	4	4	.500	3.24	51	0	72.1	65	25	51
Mike Magnante	4	4	.500	4.18	31	10	75.1	87	27	34
Joe Magrane	7	9	.438	4.35	26	24	147.0	154	51	62
Pat Mahomes	3	5	.375	5.42	20	12	74.2	80	33	51
Carlos Maldonado	2	3	.400	4.78	40	0	52.2	58	27	26
Josias Manzanillo	2	4	.333	5.55	26	2	47.0	44	29	34
Dennis Martinez	11	9	.550	3.45	28	27	185.1	167	53	111
Pedro A. Martinez	4	2	.667	2.62	47	0	55.0	36	20	45
Pedro J. Martinez	7	4	.636	2.82	61	2	102.0	76	55	109
Ramon Martinez	12	11	.522	3.68	31	31	200.2	191	93	123
Roger Mason	5	4	.556	4.06	60	0	84.1	76	29	58
Tim Mauser	3	4	.429	4.32	37	0	58.1	59	25	48
Kirk McCaskill	6	6	.500	4.57	22	16	108.1	118	41	57
Ben McDonald	13	10	.565	3.90	32	32	205.1	184	76	151
Jack McDowell	15	10	.600	3.49	30	30	224.2	224	65	143
Roger McDowell	4	3	.571	3.07	54	0	70.1	82	34	32
Chuck McElroy	3	3	.500	3.74	50	0	55.1	52	32	45
Greg McMichael	7	3	.700	2.26	74	0	91.2	72	31	85
Kent Mercker	5	3	.625	3.26	48	4	69.0	56	38	56

NAME	W	L	PCT	ERA	G	GS	IP	H	BB	SO
Jose Mesa	8	9	.471	4.59	27	26	160.2	172	54	85
Alan Mills	6	4	.600	3.31	38	1	92.1	75	49	58
Nate Minchey	5	4	.556	3.72	11	11	75.0	82	19	40
Blas Minor	5	5	.500	4.11	58	0	85.1	86	23	74
Angel Miranda	8	7	.533	3.48	24	19	132.0	113	59	94
Mike Mohler	2	4	.333	5.43	40	9	61.1	53	41	41
Rich Monteleone	5	4	.556	4.28	38	0	75.2	72	28	47
Jeff Montgomery	6	4	.600	2.61	67	0	86.1	69	26	65
Marcus Moore	2	4	.333	5.98	48	0	46.2	50	33	24
Mike Moore	9	8	.529	4.52	26	26	155.1	157	68	77
Mike Morgan	11	9	.550	3.55	26	26	177.1	167	60	93
Jack Morris	7	6	.538	4.76	18	18	115.1	121	43	74
Jamie Moyer	9	7	.563	3.86	29	24	149.1	157	43	88
Terry Mulholland	12	8	.600	3.65	27	27	185.0	182	39	107
Bobby Munoz	3	3	.500	5.10	45	0	54.2	56	30	40
Rob Murphy	3	3	.500	4.45	68	0	60.2	66	20	41
Mike Mussina	10	7	.588	3.73	22	22	154.1	146	37	96
Jeff Mutis	4	7	.364	5.38	21	16	100.1	115	39	41
Randy Myers	5	4	.556	3.63	60	1	74.1	69	32	72
Chris Nabholz	7	7	.500	3.86	23	21	121.1	108	56	78
Charles Nagy	5	4	.556	4.01	13	13	85.1	94	22	53
Jaime Navarro	8	10	.444	4.44	24	24	160.0	171	50	78
Denny Neagle	4	5	.444	4.79	45	6	73.1	72	33	67
Jeff Nelson	4	3	.571	3.98	63	0	61.0	56	34	50
Gene Nelson	3	3	.500	4.38	48	1	61.2	68	25	33
Robb Nen	2	5	.286	6.05	24	4	55.0	59	43	40
David Nied	5	7	.417	4.63	20	18	105.0	110	47	60
Rafael Novoa	5	6	.455	4.67	27	12	96.1	100	41	36
Edwin Nunez	4	4	.500	4.21	56	0	72.2	83	28	57
Bob Ojeda	5	4	.556	3.89	15	14	81.0	85	38	48
Omar Olivares	5	5	.500	4.11	30	11	96.1	100	38	55
Gregg Olson	5	2	.714	2.31	61	0	58.1	51	24	54
Jesse Orosco	4	3	.571	3.38	65	0	58.2	52	19	62
Donovan Osborne	9	8	.529	3.86	27	26	156.1	162	43	85
Al Osuna	3	2	.600	3.86	58	0	46.2	36	27	34
Lance Painter	3	6	.333	5.65	20	12	78.0	101	18	33
Donn Pall	5	3	.625	3.58	45	0	75.1	77	19	36
Jeff Parrett	3	4	.429	4.48	40	3	66.1	65	35	56
Ken Patterson	3	3	.500	4.25	45	0	59.1	54	36	34
Bob Patterson	3	3	.500	4.12	51	0	54.2	57	14	44
Roger Pavlik	11	8	.579	3.69	28	27	168.1	160	84	128
Brad Pennington	2	3	.400	5.88	51	0	49.0	48	35	62
Melido Perez	9	7	.563	4.17	24	19	140.1	135	54	126
Mike Perez	5	3	.625	2.54	64	0	74.1	66	24	48
Mark Petkovsek	2	3	.400	4.81	37	1	48.2	55	11	28
Hipolito Pichardo	9	9	.500	4.10	31	25	160.1	175	53	67
Dan Plesac	3	3	.500	4.18	44	2	60.1	62	23	43
Eric Plunk	5	3	.625	3.61	59	1	72.1	68	35	67
Jim Poole	5	2	.714	2.43	63	0	59.1	39	25	36
Mark Portugal	13	10	.565	3.18	34	33	206.1	193	79	127
Dennis Powell	3	3	.500	4.55	38	2	55.1	52	27	35
Ted Power	3	3	.500	3.93	41	0	50.1	54	18	28
Tim Pugh	7	9	.438	4.75	26	23	140.1	165	48	79
Paul Quantrill	6	5	.545	3.82	41	9	106.0	118	34	50
Scott Radinsky	4	3	.571	3.53	71	0	58.2	60	24	45
Pat Rapp	5	7	.417	4.22	20	19	113.0	120	48	66
Jeff Reardon	3	3	.500	3.86	57	0	58.1	64	10	36
Steve Reed	4	5	.444	4.29	61	0	77.2	73	27	48
Armando Reynoso	9	10	.474	4.13	29	28	174.1	192	59	105
Arthur Lee Rhodes	5	6	.455	5.11	18	18	98.2	97	49	68
Dave Righetti	3	3	.500	4.73	46	1	51.1	53	20	34
Jose Rijo	17	10	.630	2.74	36	36	249.1	221	61	205
Ben Rivera	8	8	.500	4.47	29	23	145.0	146	70	106
Rich Rodriguez	4	4	.500	3.45	60	0	73.0	68	31	43
Kevin Rogers	6	3	.667	3.20	56	2	81.2	78	30	61
Kenny Rogers	10	10	.500	4.13	60	23	180.2	186	66	126
Mel Rojas	6	4	.600	2.71	62	0	86.1	75	30	50
John Roper	4	7	.364	5.33	21	19	103.0	116	45	71
Kirk Rueter	8	5	.615	2.95	19	19	119.0	123	26	41
Bruce Ruffin	5	6	.455	4.23	42	10	104.1	110	52	89
Johnny Ruffin	3	3	.500	3.76	31	0	55.0	54	16	43
Jeff Russell	4	2	.667	2.70	55	0	56.2	50	19	44
Ken Ryan	3	3	.500	3.79	54	0	57.0	49	34	55
Bret Saberhagen	9	8	.529	3.47	21	21	145.1	135	26	100

NAME	W	L	PCT	ERA	G	GS	IP	H	BB	SO
Scott Sanders	5	6	.455	4.14	16	16	95.2	99	42	67
Scott Sanderson	9	9	.500	4.36	27	26	159.0	172	35	89
Mo Sanford	4	5	.444	4.68	21	13	75.0	69	51	80
Bob Scanlan	4	4	.500	3.97	55	2	70.1	70	26	36
Curt Schilling	13	9	.591	3.65	37	25	197.1	185	53	146
Pete Schourek	5	8	.385	4.80	32	16	114.1	132	40	64
Jeff Schwarz	4	3	.571	3.79	46	0	57.0	40	43	45
Tim Scott	4	4	.500	3.72	59	0	72.2	73	37	63
Aaron Sele	9	5	.643	2.96	21	21	130.2	122	59	105
Scott Service	3	3	.500	4.75	36	0	55.0	57	20	55
Jeff Shaw	4	5	.444	4.20	46	6	85.2	82	30	43
Heathcliff Slocumb	3	3	.500	4.42	43	0	53.0	55	28	33
John Smiley	6	6	.500	4.14	16	16	104.1	102	28	65
Lee Smith	4	3	.571	3.57	58	0	58.0	53	16	53
Pete Smith	7	5	.583	3.86	23	17	109.2	106	43	62
Zane Smith	6	5	.545	3.84	17	17	103.0	112	19	43
John Smoltz	14	10	.583	3.60	31	31	212.2	186	82	173
Jerry Spradlin	3	3	.500	3.63	43	0	57.0	53	11	27
Russ Springer	3	7	.300	5.50	28	12	90.0	95	43	56
Mike Stanton	3	3	.500	4.15	63	0	56.1	53	24	43
Dave Stewart	9	7	.563	4.34	23	23	143.0	133	62	89
Todd Stottlemyre	9	8	.529	4.52	25	24	151.1	161	56	84
Rick Sutcliffe	7	7	.500	4.89	21	21	127.0	145	49	62
Bill Swift	16	9	.640	2.83	43	29	219.2	194	56	130
Greg Swindell	10	9	.526	3.70	25	25	165.1	179	32	108
Frank Tanana	10	8	.556	4.29	26	26	163.2	170	56	88
Kevin Tapani	10	10	.500	4.12	28	28	181.1	190	42	115
Julian Tavarez	3	6	.333	6.08	17	15	77.0	106	26	42
Kerry Taylor	2	5	.286	5.83	33	6	63.1	64	43	43
Dave Telgheder	5	7	.417	4.67	33	10	104.0	112	29	48
Bob Tewksbury	12	9	.571	3.45	27	27	185.1	211	20	77
Bobby Thigpen	3	3	.500	4.83	47	0	54.0	63	25	36
Mike Timlin	4	3	.571	4.21	46	0	57.2	60	27	48
Randy Tomlin	6	6	.500	3.94	19	18	107.1	115	21	50
Salomon Torres	5	5	.500	4.08	16	16	90.1	76	55	46
Ricky Trlicek	3	4	.429	4.27	42	0	65.1	61	22	42
Mike Trombley	5	5	.500	4.53	32	9	91.1	100	32	69
George Tsamis	2	5	.286	5.78	38	0	62.1	76	24	28
Matt Turner	4	4	.500	3.17	57	0	71.0	59	28	59

NAME	W	L	PCT	ERA	G	GS	IP	H	BB	SO
Tom Urbani	5	6	.455	4.64	29	14	99.0	116	41	53
Fernando Valenzuela	8	8	.500	4.75	26	25	147.2	150	62	71
Todd VanPoppel	5	7	.417	4.86	20	20	107.1	96	76	64
Frank Viola	11	9	.550	3.51	27	27	179.1	179	66	89
Paul Wagner	8	7	.533	4.12	43	16	135.1	135	41	107
Tim Wakefield	6	7	.462	4.56	20	18	116.1	120	61	57
Bob Walk	7	8	.467	4.70	27	22	136.0	145	47	62
Duane Ward	6	2	.750	2.42	65	0	74.1	56	28	86
Allen Watson	6	6	.500	4.54	20	19	109.0	113	35	62
Gary Wayne	3	4	.429	4.40	58	0	59.1	62	24	44
Dave Weathers	4	6	.400	4.87	32	10	88.2	106	30	69
Bill Wegman	7	6	.538	3.80	18	17	118.1	122	29	52
Bob Welch	7	8	.467	4.59	23	22	133.1	149	47	53
David Wells	10	9	.526	4.31	35	25	167.0	168	41	111
Bill Wertz	4	3	.571	3.73	36	0	62.2	57	34	54
David West	5	4	.556	3.78	60	3	83.1	67	49	76
John Wetteland	7	3	.700	2.01	73	0	89.1	67	34	108
Wally Whitehurst	6	7	.462	3.95	32	18	116.1	122	33	70
Matt Whiteside	4	4	.500	4.06	57	0	71.0	75	23	37
Kevin Wickander	2	3	.400	4.78	59	0	49.0	59	31	39
Bob Wickman	8	7	.533	4.47	37	19	135.0	148	64	66
Brian Williams	4	5	.444	4.38	29	8	76.0	71	34	48
Woody Williams	3	3	.500	4.33	42	0	52.0	56	31	34
Mike Williams	5	6	.455	5.03	27	9	91.1	88	35	52
Mitch Williams	4	3	.571	3.52	59	0	64.0	55	48	59
Mark Williamson	4	4	.500	4.42	45	1	75.1	87	25	42
Carl Willis	4	3	.571	3.15	46	0	60.0	58	14	39
Steve Wilson	2	3	.400	4.30	43	0	46.0	51	22	38
Trevor Wilson	7	6	.538	3.87	23	20	121.0	119	47	68
Mike Witt	4	4	.500	4.76	18	15	79.1	74	36	54
Bobby Witt	10	11	.476	4.35	30	29	184.0	184	90	116
Mark Wohlers	3	3	.500	3.99	53	0	56.1	45	26	45
Tim Worrell	5	7	.417	4.84	23	17	109.2	112	46	57
Todd Worrell	3	3	.500	4.20	47	0	49.1	47	18	43
Anthony Young	5	5	.500	3.87	34	9	88.1	93	31	50
Cliff Young	3	3	.500	4.37	25	6	59.2	71	17	32
Matt Young	5	6	.455	4.66	30	12	96.2	93	64	84

MINOR LEAGUE PARK AND LEAGUE STATISTICS

AMERICAN ASSOCIATION — 1993 (Runs per game 4.743, home runs per game .918)

TEAM	H/R	G	AB	R	H	2B	3B	HR	BB	SO	BA	SA	OBA
Buffalo	Home	144	4763	608	1224	253	36	83	435	742	.257	.377	.319
	Road	1.000	.991	.818	.911	.951	.947	.480	.950	.923	.919	.823	.932
Indianapolis	Home	142	4787	691	1280	290	30	134	494	877	.267	.424	.336
	Road	.986	1.024	1.097	1.049	1.069	.895	1.007	1.044	1.049	1.024	1.013	1.021
Iowa	Home	144	4832	692	1294	277	15	143	463	959	.268	.420	.332
	Road	1.000	.991	1.033	.993	.945	.484	1.202	.998	1.107	1.002	1.017	1.003
Louisville	Home	144	4868	627	1259	241	43	162	444	900	.259	.426	.321
	Road	1.000	.998	.918	.926	.873	1.387	1.421	1.110	1.135	.928	1.018	.962
Nashville	Home	144	4848	686	1296	262	26	131	454	907	.267	.413	.330
	Road	1.014	1.011	1.001	1.024	1.009	.884	1.017	.955	1.033	1.013	1.005	.999
New Orleans	Home	144	4663	609	1241	257	34	126	448	783	.266	.417	.330
	Road	1.000	.977	.853	.966	1.012	.829	1.086	.924	1.020	.989	1.011	.982
Oklahoma City	Home	144	4968	812	1451	307	54	99	489	762	.292	.435	.356
	Road	1.000	1.040	1.210	1.147	1.181	1.929	.728	.955	.853	1.103	1.046	1.058
Omaha	Home	144	4698	730	1298	255	28	178	455	720	.276	.456	.340
	Road	1.000	.969	1.108	.998	.973	.824	1.309	1.099	.887	1.030	1.085	1.044
LEAGUE	TOTAL	1150	38427	5455	10343	2142	266	1056	3682	6650	.269	.421	.333

INTERNATIONAL LEAGUE — 1993 (Runs per game 4.559, home runs per game .838)

TEAM	H/R	G	AB	R	H	2B	3B	HR	BB	SO	BA	SA	OBA
Charlotte	Home	142	4816	696	1318	220	30	187	402	877	.274	.448	.330
	Road	1.014	.988	.969	1.014	.919	.739	1.336	.939	.994	1.027	1.072	1.012
Columbus	Home	142	4682	673	1233	273	43	119	536	907	.263	.416	.339
	Road	1.014	.987	.964	.966	1.051	1.285	.876	1.003	1.023	.979	.982	.988
Norfolk	Home	140	4649	516	1175	204	40	63	376	796	.253	.354	.309
	Road	.986	.980	.829	.929	.976	.811	.603	.937	.983	.948	.892	.953
Ottawa	Home	142	4752	632	1251	252	33	65	504	843	.263	.371	.334
	Road	1.000	1.027	1.048	1.049	1.200	1.000	.586	1.175	.910	1.021	.954	1.041
Pawtucket	Home	142	4932	698	1281	234	12	182	477	966	.260	.423	.325
	Road	1.000	1.058	1.231	1.075	1.059	.316	2.220	1.175	1.077	1.016	1.136	1.031
Richmond	Home	142	4760	667	1267	207	47	113	441	959	.266	.401	.328
	Road	1.000	.993	.974	.992	.855	1.382	.796	.915	.930	.999	.954	.985
Rochester	Home	140	4796	709	1287	258	44	124	484	1001	.268	.418	.335
	Road	.986	1.004	1.120	1.049	1.283	1.275	.939	.959	1.060	1.044	1.054	1.023
Scranton-Wilkes-Barre	Home	142	4715	619	1191	251	50	93	416	815	.253	.386	.313
	Road	1.000	.993	.978	.972	.980	1.923	.853	.893	.989	.979	.986	.966
Syracuse	Home	142	4590	612	1188	215	49	119	398	936	.259	.405	.318
	Road	1.000	.972	.962	.955	.850	.961	1.102	.928	1.022	.983	.994	.979
Toledo	Home	142	4702	634	1246	209	44	122	455	870	.265	.406	.330
	Road	1.000	1.001	.956	1.006	.897	.846	.992	1.112	1.020	1.005	.980	1.022
LEAGUE	TOTAL	1416	47394	6456	12437	2323	392	1187	4489	8970	.262	.403	.326

PACIFIC COAST LEAGUE — 1993 (Runs per game 5.476, home runs per game .739)

TEAM	H/R	G	AB	R	H	2B	3B	HR	BB	SO	BA	SA	OBA
Albuquerque	Home	144	5164	958	1606	293	47	151	487	868	.311	.474	.370
	Road	1.014	1.054	1.379	1.177	1.086	.828	1.551	1.154	1.065	1.117	1.138	1.104
Calgary	Home	138	4703	802	1406	315	33	128	501	740	.299	.462	.366
	Road	.972	.995	1.034	1.007	1.166	.485	1.220	.982	.871	1.012	1.031	1.007
Colorado Springs	Home	142	4832	875	1495	287	64	122	525	851	.309	.471	.377
	Road	1.014	1.030	1.198	1.121	1.064	1.191	1.415	1.076	.884	1.088	1.122	1.072
Edmonton	Home	138	4727	763	1408	304	62	124	425	798	.298	.467	.356
	Road	.958	1.008	1.147	1.063	1.154	1.406	1.391	1.001	.917	1.055	1.127	1.041
Las Vegas	Home	144	5103	870	1540	287	57	145	492	964	.302	.466	.363
	Road	1.014	1.045	1.185	1.086	1.037	1.061	1.324	1.002	1.114	1.040	1.067	1.023
Phoenix	Home	144	5122	770	1486	274	70	94	515	996	.290	.426	.355
	Road	1.014	1.048	1.015	1.063	1.027	1.278	.806	1.060	1.146	1.015	.981	1.013
Portland	Home	144	4672	680	1268	260	69	98	513	810	.271	.420	.343
	Road	1.014	.955	.781	.845	.849	1.334	.812	.994	1.087	.886	.904	.922
Tacoma	Home	142	4622	672	1275	285	29	89	474	893	.276	.408	.343
	Road	.986	.922	.807	.861	1.047	.452	.799	.866	1.030	.935	.924	.942
Tuscon	Home	144	5051	818	1478	289	104	49	494	899	.293	.420	.356
	Road	1.014	1.000	1.015	1.022	.956	2.182	.447	.928	.960	1.022	.977	1.004
Vancouver	Home	140	4530	568	1159	206	21	49	503	860	.256	.343	.330
	Road	1.000	.948	.625	.794	.680	.344	.471	.982	.959	.837	.746	.886
LEAGUE	TOTAL	1420	48526	7776	14121	2800	556	1049	4929	8679	.291	.436	.356

EASTERN LEAGUE — 1993 (Runs per game 4.526, home runs per game .673)

TEAM	H/R	G	AB	R	H	2B	3B	HR	BB	SO	BA	SA	OBA
Albany	Home	136	4432	637	1149	227	30	82	485	897	.259	.380	.332
	Road	.971	.993	.994	1.016	1.003	.702	.918	1.067	.981	1.023	.990	1.031
Binghamton	Home	140	4626	660	1251	215	51	113	476	820	.270	.412	.338
	Road	1.000	1.006	1.093	1.040	1.039	1.500	1.314	1.053	1.011	1.034	1.092	1.033
Bowie	Home	140	4492	559	1140	188	34	78	430	833	.254	.363	.319
	Road	1.000	.946	.880	.906	.931	1.030	.813	.885	.940	.958	.950	.957
Canton-Akron	Home	136	4419	645	1164	203	34	85	478	797	.263	.382	.335
	Road	.971	.950	.939	.930	.981	.946	.803	.865	.905	.979	.963	.967
Harrisburg	Home	140	4687	685	1201	182	40	122	534	1051	.256	.390	.332
	Road	1.029	1.009	.970	.984	.759	.827	.964	1.015	1.010	.975	.936	.984
London	Home	140	4883	672	1320	254	33	102	502	931	.270	.399	.338
	Road	1.029	1.065	1.122	1.133	1.116	1.105	1.339	1.024	1.081	1.063	1.087	1.037
New Britain	Home	140	4684	527	1139	224	28	61	483	951	.243	.342	.314
	Road	1.000	1.017	.871	.984	1.037	.667	.701	1.134	1.082	.967	.916	.997
Reading	Home	140	4618	648	1203	222	46	105	423	848	.261	.397	.323
	Road	1.000	1.017	1.170	1.021	1.168	1.533	1.296	1.000	.991	1.004	1.078	1.000
LEAGUE	TOTAL	1112	36841	5033	9567	1715	296	748	3811	7128	.260	.383	.329

SOUTHERN LEAGUE — 1993 (Runs per game 4.521, home runs per game .711)

TEAM	H/R	G	AB	R	H	2B	3B	HR	BB	SO	BA	SA	OBA
Birmingham	Home	142	4500	498	1052	185	23	56	431	1006	.234	.322	.301
	Road	1.000	.959	.716	.843	.797	.535	.491	.921	1.068	.879	.793	.904
Carolina	Home	140	4709	680	1234	269	47	102	434	965	.262	.404	.324
	Road	.986	1.006	1.229	1.052	1.337	1.766	1.310	1.038	1.181	1.046	1.139	1.039
Chattanooga	Home	144	4716	653	1244	223	34	100	449	962	.264	.389	.328
	Road	1.043	.992	1.121	1.038	.958	1.253	.958	1.109	.907	1.047	1.029	1.055
Greenville	Home	140	4609	657	1219	239	32	92	542	892	.264	.390	.342
	Road	.972	1.005	1.173	1.073	1.171	1.062	1.140	1.102	.990	1.068	1.089	1.066
Huntsville	Home	144	4635	605	1154	202	25	92	520	997	.249	.363	.325
	Road	1.043	.973	.774	.874	.803	1.141	.832	.874	1.034	.899	.888	.909
Jacksonville	Home	140	4812	645	1203	231	19	147	501	876	.250	.398	.321
	Road	.986	1.064	.994	.990	1.006	.507	1.569	1.081	1.006	.930	.998	.952
Knoxville	Home	142	4704	713	1380	249	46	84	417	855	.293	.419	.351
	Road	1.000	1.021	1.251	1.178	1.203	1.438	.944	.863	.890	1.155	1.131	1.080
Memphis	Home	136	4550	618	1210	213	28	118	485	786	.266	.403	.337
	Road	.944	.997	.984	.978	.936	.926	1.343	1.178	.927	.981	1.027	1.015
Nashville	Home	142	4784	654	1254	235	22	97	509	977	.262	.381	.333
	Road	1.000	.998	.978	.994	1.022	.688	.740	1.081	1.097	.996	.938	1.012
Orlando	Home	144	4808	669	1312	217	37	117	442	875	.273	.406	.334
	Road	1.029	.988	.943	1.007	.872	1.160	.989	.836	.926	1.019	1.003	.984
LEAGUE	TOTAL	1414	46827	6392	12262	2263	313	1005	4730	9191	.262	.388	.330

TEXAS LEAGUE — 1993 (Runs per game 4.433, home runs per game .693)

TEAM	H/R	G	AB	R	H	2B	3B	HR	BB	SO	BA	SA	OBA
Arkansas	Home	134	4187	499	1038	200	23	104	397	847	.248	.381	.313
	Road	.971	.953	.883	.947	.892	.911	1.082	1.056	.879	.993	1.009	1.014
El Paso	Home	136	4661	744	1357	255	69	62	459	802	.291	.415	.355
	Road	1.015	1.015	1.234	1.136	1.132	2.060	.671	1.087	1.020	1.119	1.081	1.100
Jackson	Home	134	4270	573	1092	197	14	99	399	975	.256	.378	.319
	Road	.985	.967	.950	.926	.909	.444	.922	1.015	1.081	.957	.937	.976
Midland	Home	138	4799	872	1473	324	41	120	468	842	.307	.467	.369
	Road	1.030	1.033	1.445	1.221	1.639	.971	1.324	1.077	1.012	1.182	1.231	1.141
San Antonio	Home	134	4449	459	1032	170	37	73	381	901	.232	.336	.293
	Road	.985	.981	.723	.840	.728	.894	.734	.916	1.017	.856	.827	.881
Shreveport	Home	136	4330	462	1044	189	36	45	382	847	.241	.333	.303
	Road	1.000	.969	.821	.883	.747	1.200	.517	.946	1.052	.911	.846	.929
Tulsa	Home	136	4480	602	1159	243	24	137	395	984	.259	.415	.319
	Road	1.015	1.046	1.084	1.073	1.197	.657	1.483	1.019	1.116	1.027	1.090	1.015
Wichita	Home	136	4576	594	1172	180	31	111	422	873	.256	.382	.319
	Road	1.000	1.036	.877	.977	.887	.886	1.306	.896	.866	.944	.977	.934
LEAGUE	TOTAL	1084	35752	4805	9367	1758	275	751	3303	7071	.262	.390	.324

CALIFORNIA LEAGUE — 1993 (Runs per game 5.366, home runs per game .704)

TEAM	H/R	G	AB	R	H	2B	3B	HR	BB	SO	BA	SA	OBA
Bakersfield	Home	136	4655	603	1157	213	11	106	540	989	.249	.367	.327
	Road	1.000	1.013	.836	.927	1.029	.289	1.140	.920	1.001	.915	.933	.923
Central Valley	Home	136	4654	765	1296	227	28	97	671	958	.278	.402	.369
	Road	1.000	1.010	1.234	1.123	1.091	.966	1.183	1.139	.980	1.112	1.111	1.101
High Desert	Home	138	4840	986	1456	252	67	163	617	873	.301	.482	.380
	Road	1.015	1.042	1.346	1.179	1.188	2.641	1.890	1.061	1.012	1.132	1.274	1.093
Modesto	Home	136	4401	702	1147	200	15	120	655	914	.261	.395	.356
	Road	1.000	.954	.983	.907	.917	.429	1.304	1.012	1.089	.951	.996	.981
Palm Springs	Home	136	4544	582	1164	172	50	21	554	793	.256	.330	.337
	Road	1.000	.955	.736	.852	.754	1.190	.210	1.018	.962	.892	.794	.935
Rancho Cucamonga	Home	136	4748	852	1402	292	44	115	574	862	.295	.448	.371
	Road	1.000	1.008	1.145	1.076	1.090	.898	1.402	.949	.887	1.068	1.102	1.034
Riverside	Home	136	4715	699	1329	236	34	50	459	780	.282	.378	.346
	Road	.986	1.016	.919	1.064	.954	1.190	.497	.779	.876	1.048	.946	.983
San Bernandino	Home	136	4741	829	1304	236	22	166	604	1019	.275	.439	.357
	Road	1.000	1.019	1.184	1.071	1.009	.733	1.694	1.062	1.098	1.051	1.132	1.043
San Jose	Home	136	4534	614	1134	206	34	55	601	898	.250	.347	.338
	Road	1.000	.992	.803	.895	.900	1.030	.509	.985	1.174	.902	.841	.933
Stockton	Home	136	4609	676	1237	227	33	66	628	767	.268	.375	.356
	Road	1.000	.993	.891	.936	1.086	1.179	.564	1.081	.952	.943	.898	.978
LEAGUE	TOTAL	1362	46441	7308	12626	2261	338	959	5903	8853	.272	.397	.354

CAROLINA LEAGUE — 1993 (Runs per game 4.583, home runs per game .761)

TEAM	H/R	G	AB	R	H	2B	3B	HR	BB	SO	BA	SA	OBA
Durham	Home	138	4694	668	1232	251	24	129	437	1072	.262	.409	.325
	Road	1.000	1.034	1.059	1.055	1.230	.667	1.418	.926	1.057	1.020	1.080	.994
Frederick	Home	144	4738	582	1163	213	32	88	482	1076	.245	.360	.315
	Road	1.059	1.009	.956	.992	.963	1.259	1.052	.996	1.082	.983	.996	.985
Kinston	Home	140	4598	554	1126	210	27	79	495	1098	.245	.354	.318
	Road	1.029	1.001	.867	.971	1.010	.971	.775	1.069	1.125	.970	.940	.992
Lynchburg	Home	138	4610	619	1190	223	28	99	429	990	.258	.383	.321
	Road	.986	.984	.922	.927	.870	.676	.851	.961	.994	.942	.910	.953
Prince William	Home	136	4432	560	1072	203	42	60	409	919	.242	.347	.306
	Road	.944	.962	.813	.876	.919	1.085	.572	.873	.926	.911	.871	.918
Salem	Home	140	4932	799	1375	248	28	187	477	1024	.279	.454	.342
	Road	1.000	1.083	1.382	1.249	1.319	1.037	2.174	1.097	1.044	1.153	1.292	1.112
Wilmington	Home	138	4499	542	1104	187	51	41	394	889	.245	.337	.306
	Road	.986	.955	.860	.888	.886	2.352	.322	.992	.929	.930	.845	.953
Winston-Salem	Home	140	4737	782	1339	206	22	165	475	854	.283	.440	.348
	Road	1.000	.978	1.199	1.079	.896	.629	1.222	1.100	.847	1.104	1.096	1.098
LEAGUE	TOTAL	1114	37240	5106	9601	1741	254	848	3598	7922	.258	.387	.323

FLORIDA STATE LEAGUE — 1993 (Runs per game 4.293, home runs per game .399)

TEAM	H/R	G	AB	R	H	2B	3B	HR	BB	SO	BA	SA	OBA
Charlotte	Home	134	4347	492	1082	169	34	44	477	756	.249	.334	.323
	Road	1.000	.964	.875	.904	.813	.919	1.222	1.030	.909	.938	.949	.968
Clearwater	Home	142	4704	640	1292	235	32	61	456	741	.275	.377	.339
	Road	1.109	.957	.986	.962	.981	.848	1.000	.998	.953	1.006	1.007	1.011
Daytona Beach	Home	134	4512	651	1208	191	60	70	447	755	.268	.383	.334
	Road	1.015	1.040	1.201	1.095	1.113	2.111	1.254	1.064	1.042	1.053	1.109	1.042
Dunedin	Home	130	4340	713	1187	220	45	97	559	790	.274	.412	.356
	Road	.970	1.031	1.447	1.121	1.311	.947	1.562	1.283	.983	1.087	1.150	1.108
Ft. Lauderdale	Home	124	4186	562	1134	173	30	44	412	697	.271	.358	.336
	Road	.899	.994	1.019	1.053	1.058	.696	.710	.848	.914	1.060	.998	1.011
Ft. Myers	Home	136	4610	581	1155	208	36	38	472	833	.251	.336	.320
	Road	1.030	.999	.967	.912	.874	1.059	.738	.994	1.045	.913	.898	.935
Lakeland	Home	130	4197	528	1123	178	50	49	437	709	.268	.369	.337
	Road	1.016	.953	.933	.996	.855	1.538	1.027	.908	.883	1.045	1.052	1.022
Osceola	Home	130	4359	557	1153	190	58	33	402	734	.265	.357	.327
	Road	1.000	1.026	.982	1.025	1.145	1.234	.559	.995	1.025	.999	.972	.994
St. Lucie	Home	124	4087	487	1088	166	32	45	347	612	.266	.356	.324
	Road	.912	1.011	.932	1.006	1.084	.747	1.148	.885	.941	.995	1.000	.974
St. Petersburg	Home	130	4411	489	1149	187	26	36	433	768	.260	.339	.327
	Road	.956	1.037	.890	1.049	.927	.877	.697	.960	1.071	1.011	.954	.993
Sarasota	Home	130	4295	533	1059	180	38	45	454	761	.247	.338	.319
	Road	.942	1.020	1.003	1.011	1.098	1.186	.853	1.170	.957	.991	.992	1.021
Vero Beach	Home	138	4647	696	1259	224	29	101	499	920	.271	.397	.342
	Road	1.078	1.030	1.157	1.088	1.259	.791	2.285	.947	1.147	1.057	1.162	1.022
West Palm Beach	Home	142	4536	472	1045	175	27	25	467	975	.230	.297	.302
	Road	1.092	.947	.696	.818	.703	.575	.388	.969	1.123	.864	.785	.906
LEAGUE	TOTAL	1724	57231	7401	14934	2496	497	688	5862	10051	.261	.358	.330

MIDWEST LEAGUE — 1993 (Runs per game 4.544, home runs per game .581)

TEAM	H/R	G	AB	R	H	2B	3B	HR	BB	SO	BA	SA	OBA
Appleton	Home	138	4477	694	1185	255	39	79	513	1046	.265	.392	.340
	Road	1.045	1.011	1.147	1.068	1.167	.910	.922	1.093	1.042	1.057	1.039	1.056
Beloit	Home	138	4611	750	1255	231	34	88	548	1044	.272	.394	.349
	Road	1.062	1.054	1.172	1.158	1.139	1.001	.975	1.075	1.071	1.099	1.061	1.071
Burlington	Home	132	4259	612	1009	191	13	117	527	1095	.237	.370	.321
	Road	.957	1.003	1.068	.948	.904	.324	1.799	1.148	1.049	.945	1.013	.991
Cedar Rapids	Home	134	4374	627	1060	152	26	97	549	1022	.242	.356	.327
	Road	1.000	1.016	.915	.938	.724	.929	1.183	1.109	1.086	.923	.932	.965
Clinton	Home	134	4142	587	1036	181	39	62	511	1004	.250	.358	.332
	Road	1.000	.965	.902	.988	.963	1.300	.602	.952	1.012	1.024	.956	1.013
Ft. Wayne	Home	140	4553	568	1100	184	37	63	513	1073	.242	.340	.318
	Road	1.077	.972	.886	.924	.850	1.011	.914	.947	.987	.950	.943	.960
Kane County	Home	134	4433	566	1080	192	29	65	502	1019	.244	.344	.321
	Road	.957	1.042	.992	.992	.924	1.082	1.191	1.014	1.124	.952	.967	.961
Madison	Home	128	4109	520	945	200	31	70	465	1010	.230	.345	.308
	Road	.901	1.014	.906	.926	1.088	.732	.844	.998	1.076	.913	.909	.937
Peoria	Home	140	4524	620	1161	252	37	51	456	962	.257	.363	.325
	Road	1.029	1.018	1.000	1.035	1.108	1.634	.643	1.002	.996	1.017	.987	1.009
Quad City	Home	118	3768	553	978	165	15	85	390	856	.260	.379	.329
	Road	.831	.987	1.029	1.013	.978	.501	1.346	1.034	.965	1.027	1.046	1.028
Rockford	Home	134	4268	591	1106	213	43	38	452	945	.259	.356	.330
	Road	1.031	.985	.995	.971	1.082	1.438	.595	.888	1.011	.986	.972	.970
South Bend	Home	138	4482	635	1230	209	65	64	433	809	.274	.393	.338
	Road	1.030	.971	1.016	1.068	.931	1.706	.740	1.008	.775	1.100	1.060	1.080
Springfield	Home	146	4597	663	1158	222	45	123	404	1080	.252	.400	.312
	Road	1.159	.977	1.046	1.008	.973	1.553	1.434	.777	.891	1.032	1.112	.978
Waterloo	Home	130	3928	574	997	203	15	92	463	864	.254	.383	.332
	Road	.956	.983	.944	.962	1.186	.424	1.094	.984	.943	.979	1.001	.986
LEAGUE	TOTAL	1884	60525	8560	15300	2850	468	1094	6726	13829	.253	.370	.328

SOUTH ATLANTIC LEAGUE — 1993 (Runs per game 4.557, home runs per game .502)

TEAM	H/R	G	AB	R	H	2B	3B	HR	BB	SO	BA	SA	OBA
Albany	Home	142	4664	608	1129	212	42	38	553	968	.242	.330	.322
	Road	1.000	1.007	.923	.958	.887	1.448	.396	1.154	1.018	.952	.867	.995
Asheville	Home	140	4686	743	1320	278	10	101	494	897	.282	.410	.350
	Road	1.014	1.014	1.122	1.152	1.251	.224	1.580	.914	.897	1.137	1.150	1.072
Augusta	Home	140	4704	676	1214	225	51	38	433	1016	.258	.352	.321
	Road	.986	1.010	1.036	1.021	1.037	1.724	.453	1.056	1.048	1.011	.955	1.016
Capital City	Home	140	4543	672	1156	259	36	47	610	1043	.254	.358	.343
	Road	.986	.981	1.025	.981	1.233	.811	.722	1.148	1.130	1.000	.992	1.034
Charleston, SC	Home	142	4690	626	1133	207	43	87	550	989	.242	.360	.321
	Road	1.000	.994	.969	.944	.950	1.303	1.475	1.040	.938	.950	1.022	.975
Charleston, WV	Home	138	4534	617	1086	204	42	29	599	999	.240	.322	.328
	Road	.972	1.004	.881	.995	.986	1.168	.293	.994	.919	.992	.873	.992
Columbus	Home	142	4747	661	1190	218	34	104	443	994	.251	.377	.315
	Road	1.000	1.019	1.118	1.087	1.095	1.214	1.507	.908	.979	1.067	1.127	1.023
Fayetteville	Home	140	4550	604	1080	168	26	63	564	1051	.237	.327	.321
	Road	.986	.950	.859	.870	.707	.613	.888	.904	.954	.916	.882	.933
Greensboro	Home	142	4731	710	1195	249	34	103	563	1031	.253	.385	.332
	Road	1.014	1.009	1.020	1.014	.948	.798	1.410	.927	.959	1.005	1.034	.985
Hagerstown	Home	142	4741	689	1224	240	43	102	482	1029	.258	.391	.327
	Road	1.000	1.020	1.124	1.055	1.034	1.433	1.397	1.017	.963	1.035	1.089	1.024
Hickory	Home	144	4795	620	1139	210	45	71	554	1068	.238	.345	.317
	Road	1.059	1.015	.957	1.001	1.012	1.250	1.099	1.036	1.096	.986	1.010	.995
Macon	Home	140	4578	566	1098	207	29	73	439	1100	.240	.346	.306
	Road	.986	1.001	1.000	.991	1.060	.613	1.277	.928	1.081	.990	1.007	.978
Savannah	Home	142	4644	559	1102	159	37	66	548	1085	.237	.330	.318
	Road	1.000	.993	.959	.971	.694	1.276	1.015	1.094	1.060	.978	.955	1.006
Spartanburg	Home	142	4676	653	1207	252	30	69	456	900	.258	.369	.324
	Road	1.000	.987	1.043	.980	1.189	1.000	1.380	.927	.996	.992	1.057	.983
LEAGUE	TOTAL	1976	65283	9004	16273	3088	502	991	7288	14170	.249	.357	.325

NEW YORK-PENN LEAGUE — 1993 (Runs per game 4.683, home runs per game .472)

TEAM	H/R	G	AB	R	H	2B	3B	HR	BB	SO	BA	SA	OBA
Auburn	Home	78	2656	442	691	128	24	30	302	570	.260	.360	.336
	Road	1.054	1.036	1.263	1.107	1.191	1.518	.769	1.165	.992	1.069	1.050	1.073
Batavia	Home	76	2511	303	583	88	32	18	238	502	.232	.314	.299
	Road	.974	.995	.997	.913	.684	1.729	.770	.989	.909	.918	.907	.939
Elmira	Home	76	2589	362	655	130	9	41	282	542	.253	.358	.326
	Road	1.027	1.034	.976	1.003	1.082	.674	1.051	1.125	1.021	.970	.976	.995
Erie	Home	78	2700	412	656	126	10	78	245	587	.243	.384	.306
	Road	1.026	1.022	1.160	1.026	1.216	.325	2.111	1.016	1.077	1.003	1.107	1.001
Geneva	Home	78	2521	408	655	123	8	48	284	555	.260	.372	.335
	Road	1.026	.965	1.069	1.064	1.090	.312	1.417	.948	.926	1.102	1.103	1.065
Glens Falls	Home	76	2590	352	674	128	20	30	253	516	.260	.360	.326
	Road	.974	1.006	1.041	1.034	1.018	.892	.933	1.003	.965	1.028	1.008	1.019
Jamestown	Home	76	2481	351	615	100	39	40	249	554	.248	.368	.316
	Road	.974	.985	.968	.949	.862	2.001	.838	1.018	.974	.964	.980	.980
Niagara Falls	Home	78	2558	317	596	113	15	28	290	616	.233	.322	.311
	Road	1.000	.966	.834	.931	1.027	.625	1.273	1.028	1.062	.964	.986	.988
Oneonta	Home	76	2526	331	630	87	49	21	249	544	.249	.348	.317
	Road	1.000	1.012	.840	.986	.737	2.042	.447	.801	.954	.975	.917	.936
Pittsfield	Home	76	2427	311	577	85	24	26	227	577	.238	.325	.303
	Road	1.027	.978	.926	.967	.739	1.375	1.266	.863	1.012	.989	.997	.967
St. Catherines	Home	78	2433	269	532	89	10	39	230	563	.219	.312	.286
	Road	1.000	.922	.733	.805	.848	.455	.750	.913	.929	.873	.851	.906
Utica	Home	74	2499	404	658	131	17	42	288	570	.263	.380	.339
	Road	.949	1.046	1.238	1.124	1.151	.527	1.302	1.292	1.071	1.075	1.054	1.097
Watertown	Home	78	2570	400	663	135	19	39	257	610	.258	.371	.325
	Road	1.000	.987	.966	1.003	1.154	.864	1.026	.816	1.099	1.017	1.032	.974
Welland	Home	76	2598	368	659	126	26	27	250	562	.254	.353	.319
	Road	.974	1.054	1.043	1.118	1.333	1.906	.630	1.172	1.023	1.060	1.037	1.064
LEAGUE	TOTAL	1074	35659	5030	8844	1589	302	507	3644	7868	.248	.352	.318

NORTHWEST LEAGUE — 1993 (Runs per game 5.094, home runs per game .582)

TEAM	H/R	G	AB	R'	H	2B	3B	HR	BB	SO	BA	SA	OBA
Bellingham	Home	76	2526	332	558	87	11	46	326	545	.221	.319	.310
	Road	1.000	.991	.874	.903	.719	.688	1.438	.860	.970	.911	.937	.911
Bend	Home	76	2626	412	713	116	11	55	346	566	.272	.387	.356
	Road	1.000	1.067	1.237	1.273	1.318	.611	1.058	1.231	.969	1.193	1.133	1.161
Boise	Home	76	2574	422	632	103	28	50	364	575	.246	.366	.339
	Road	1.000	1.040	1.141	1.008	.880	2.154	1.000	1.052	1.069	.970	.984	.983
Eugene	Home	76	2366	272	526	102	16	30	274	616	.222	.317	.303
	Road	1.000	.933	.741	.828	.919	.941	.638	.794	1.011	.888	.872	.891
Everett	Home	76	2544	396	621	115	12	50	396	679	.244	.358	.346
	Road	1.000	.963	.975	.952	.950	.667	1.064	.936	1.228	.990	.995	.987
Southern Oregon	Home	76	2545	444	672	141	19	55	369	508	.264	.399	.357
	Road	1.000	.993	1.102	1.015	1.175	.679	1.719	1.122	.909	1.023	1.096	1.043
Spokane	Home	76	2535	448	676	126	30	42	375	476	.267	.390	.361
	Road	1.000	1.004	1.140	1.119	1.326	1.667	1.000	1.033	.810	1.115	1.143	1.079
Yakima	Home	76	2581	371	622	104	19	26	406	564	.241	.326	.344
	Road	1.000	1.015	.834	.940	.860	1.056	.500	1.041	1.052	.926	.851	.960
LEAGUE	TOTAL	608	20297	3097	5020	894	146	354	2856	4529	.247	.358	.340

APPALACHIAN LEAGUE — 1993 (Runs per game 5.353, home runs per game .693)

TEAM	H/R	G	AB	R	H	2B	3B	HR	BB	SO	BA	SA	OBA
Bluefield	Home	66	2347	434	647	.123	10	59	306	531	.276	.412	.359
	Road	.943	1.072	1.205	1.193	1.388	.816	1.098	1.111	1.159	1.113	1.104	1.083
Bristol	Home	72	2409	391	624	113	26	56	317	551	.259	.397	.345
	Road	1.161	1.028	.999	1.058	1.145	1.866	.846	1.026	.997	1.029	1.017	1.019
Burlington	Home	66	2183	340	535	96	13	28	278	447	.245	.339	.330
	Road	.943	1.009	1.033	.952	.952	.862	.560	1.006	.937	.943	.871	.961
Danville	Home	70	2290	300	529	99	24	18	245	496	.231	.319	.305
	Road	1.061	.968	.837	.881	.864	1.886	.499	.996	.901	.911	.889	.942
Elizabethton	Home	64	2040	348	509	100	16	46	239	430	.250	.382	.328
	Road	.914	.953	1.034	.960	1.003	1.029	.932	.944	.962	1.007	1.010	1.003
Huntington	Home	70	2188	350	560	94	16	40	285	474	.256	.368	.342
	Road	1.061	.918	.842	.912	.844	.580	.673	1.101	.974	.994	.916	1.035
Johnson City	Home	68	2209	357	530	95	16	58	270	531	.240	.376	.323
	Road	1.000	.974	1.053	.897	.812	.640	1.487	.941	1.060	.921	.976	.939
Kingsport	Home	66	2198	361	604	115	9	62	217	417	.275	.420	.340
	Road	.943	1.010	1.029	1.066	1.034	.597	1.241	.865	.857	1.055	1.065	1.009
Martinsville	Home	68	2376	405	628	121	14	77	279	555	.264	.424	.342
	Road	1.000	1.038	1.038	1.036	1.080	.636	2.081	1.134	1.204	.998	1.112	1.016
Princeton	Home	68	2293	343	584	86	35	26	255	455	.255	.357	.329
	Road	1.000	1.035	.948	1.066	.989	1.750	.867	.885	.960	1.029	1.033	.986
LEAGUE	TOTAL	678	22533	3629	5750	1042	179	470	2691	4887	.255	.380	.335

PIONEER LEAGUE — 1993 (Runs per game 5.524, home runs per game .620)

TEAM	H/R	G	AB	R	H	2B	3B	HR	BB	SO	BA	SA	OBA
Billings	Home	76	2457	345	606	110	14	36	273	502	.247	.347	.322
	Road	1.027	1.015	.838	.901	1.071	.545	.730	.883	1.038	.888	.862	.896
Butte	Home	74	2452	502	780	131	38	60	319	463	.318	.476	.397
	Road	.974	1.028	1.174	1.133	1.246	1.858	1.044	1.146	.982	1.102	1.128	1.093
Great Falls	Home	74	2513	401	647	117	23	28	310	579	.257	.356	.339
	Road	1.057	1.057	1.126	1.119	1.203	1.674	.828	.987	1.014	1.059	1.052	1.023
Helena	Home	72	2331	345	584	80	13	51	306	588	.251	.362	.338
	Road	.973	.940	.769	.835	.587	.418	1.008	.944	1.068	.888	.854	.924
Idaho Falls	Home	76	2646	499	785	141	29	48	321	553	.297	.426	.373
	Road	1.000	1.046	1.152	1.123	1.369	1.160	.941	1.180	1.053	1.074	1.073	1.076
Lethbridge	Home	72	2266	340	540	87	10	39	270	525	.238	.337	.319
	Road	.973	.950	.865	.845	.758	.447	.891	.998	1.071	.889	.865	.933
Medicine Hat	Home	74	2384	361	608	95	18	48	238	460	.255	.370	.323
	Road	1.028	1.010	1.052	1.029	.915	.973	1.262	.938	.823	1.018	1.033	.998
Salt Lake City	Home	74	2441	477	741	120	31	57	328	534	.304	.448	.386
	Road	.974	.962	1.063	1.040	1.036	1.676	1.361	.960	.962	1.081	1.147	1.054
LEAGUE	TOTAL	592	19490	3270	5291	881	176	367	2365	4204	.271	.391	.350

ARIZONA LEAGUE — 1993 (Runs per game 5.235, home runs per game .228)

TEAM	H/R	G	AB	R	H	2B	3B	HR	BB	SO	BA	SA	OBA
Angels	Home	58	1813	235	431	63	32	6	193	388	.238	.318	.311
	Road	1.074	.961	.826	.976	.875	1.490	.430	.739	.901	1.016	1.002	.951
Athletics	Home	56	1906	333	491	88	22	41	244	415	.258	.391	.342
	Road	1.037	1.007	1.039	.980	1.048	.786	3.954	1.314	1.018	.973	1.102	1.035
Brewers	Home	56	1896	316	499	63	25	6	264	416	.263	.332	.353
	Road	1.000	1.001	.952	1.035	.926	1.000	.400	1.163	.902	1.034	.976	1.057
Cardinals	Home	54	1772	236	435	67	25	8	173	455	.245	.325	.313
	Road	1.038	.968	.845	.933	1.241	.777	.770	.825	1.141	.964	.966	.944
Giants	Home	56	1878	316	480	69	25	11	267	467	.256	.337	.348
	Road	1.037	.978	1.040	.972	.802	1.148	.884	.998	1.077	.994	.978	1.001
Mariners	Home	52	1750	358	468	68	35	14	232	398	.267	.370	.353
	Road	.929	1.024	1.500	1.164	1.046	1.346	1.256	1.173	.974	1.137	1.146	1.123
Padres	Home	54	1810	269	406	73	18	11	218	482	.224	.303	.308
	Road	.964	1.039	1.049	.975	1.328	.667	1.426	.946	1.075	.938	.961	.938
Rockies	Home	52	1717	230	403	67	18	3	179	367	.235	.300	.307
	Road	.929	1.024	.820	.971	.902	.969	.162	.922	.928	.948	.864	.943
LEAGUE	TOTAL	438	14542	2293	3613	558	200	100	1770	3388	.248	.335	.330

GULF COAST LEAGUE — 1993 (Runs per game 4.394, home runs per game .186)

TEAM	H/R	G	AB	R	H	2B	3B	HR	BB	SO	BA	SA	OBA
Astros	Home	60	1964	273	472	89	21	6	222	426	.240	.316	.317
	Road	1.034	.950	.996	.877	1.049	1.015	.580	1.262	1.110	.923	.940	.998
Blue Jays	Home	60	2035	321	535	90	32	17	221	404	.263	.364	.335
	Road	1.000	1.057	1.284	1.166	.938	1.778	2.833	1.122	.931	1.103	1.150	1.084
Braves	Home	60	1955	272	463	74	12	11	218	418	.237	.304	.313
	Road	1.071	.997	.958	1.005	1.114	.862	.733	.978	1.013	1.008	.993	1.001
Cubs	Home	60	1981	305	523	71	16	11	216	324	.264	.333	.336
	Road	1.034	1.021	1.057	1.076	.967	.672	.818	.985	.868	1.054	.997	1.030
Expos	Home	56	1851	229	423	62	15	9	217	367	.229	.293	.309
	Road	.933	.999	.947	.910	.874	.699	.742	1.081	1.024	.911	.882	.955
Marlins	Home	60	2061	284	549	90	20	8	186	403	.266	.341	.327
	Road	1.000	1.044	1.040	1.130	1.098	.952	.727	.834	.988	1.082	1.048	1.014
Mets	Home	58	1903	275	478	78	26	18	216	377	.251	.348	.328
	Road	.967	.985	1.023	1.011	1.062	2.690	2.069	.963	1.096	1.027	1.136	1.013
Orioles	Home	56	1844	233	411	55	20	8	192	346	.223	.287	.296
	Road	.933	1.050	1.145	1.069	.982	.893	1.071	.918	.864	1.018	.994	.980
Pirates	Home	60	1999	286	519	90	22	11	211	392	.260	.343	.330
	Road	1.034	1.043	1.257	1.245	1.500	1.063	1.063	.953	.987	1.193	1.197	1.106
Rangers	Home	60	1960	288	514	74	30	22	224	385	.262	.364	.338
	Road	1.000	1.030	1.112	1.140	.892	1.875	2.750	1.057	1.156	1.107	1.175	1.078
Red Sox	Home	60	1937	219	444	89	25	12	214	417	.229	.320	.306
	Road	1.000	.975	.936	.951	1.271	1.786	1.000	1.039	1.000	.975	1.057	.997
Royals	Home	60	1982	249	474	57	21	7	186	368	.239	.300	.304
	Road	1.034	1.014	1.047	1.034	.648	1.450	.752	1.051	.969	1.020	.972	1.022
Twins	Home	60	1910	242	420	70	12	8	249	383	.220	.282	.310
	Road	1.034	.974	.752	.853	.940	.464	.516	.999	.940	.876	.831	.924
White Sox	Home	58	1801	219	377	71	10	7	241	414	.209	.272	.303
	Road	.967	.921	.858	.769	.942	.383	.557	1.001	1.124	.836	.811	.910
Yankees	Home	58	1864	198	398	69	10	10	180	468	.214	.277	.283
	Road	.967	.952	.711	.842	.915	.431	.739	.850	.992	.884	.855	.896
LEAGUE	TOTAL	886	29047	3893	7000	1129	292	165	3193	5892	.241	.317	.316

NORTHERN LEAGUE — 1993 (Runs per game 4.881, home runs per game .579)

TEAM	H/R	G	AB	R	H	2B	3B	HR	BB	SO	BA	SA	OBA
Duluth-Superior	Home	72	2472	364	688	136	20	25	267	422	.278	.380	.349
	Road	1.000	1.004	1.034	1.042	1.283	2.222	.543	.967	.938	1.038	1.014	1.020
Rochester	Home	70	2428	429	670	115	7	83	307	450	.276	.432	.357
	Road	.946	1.065	1.463	1.141	1.241	.617	2.194	1.229	.965	1.071	1.205	1.079
St. Paul	Home	72	2441	372	693	117	5	35	289	404	.284	.379	.360
	Road	1.029	1.015	1.116	1.094	1.149	.405	.972	1.085	.977	1.077	1.049	1.067
Sioux City	Home	74	2508	309	623	104	15	31	266	467	.248	.339	.320
	Road	1.057	.985	.792	.869	.827	.946	.733	.957	.988	.883	.862	.910
Sioux Falls	Home	72	2522	357	709	118	14	50	278	433	.281	.398	.353
	Road	1.000	.976	.842	.956	.855	1.167	1.020	.942	1.072	.979	.980	.979
Thunder Bay	Home	70	2222	268	573	90	13	25	227	469	.258	.344	.327
	Road	.972	.955	.861	.922	.771	.955	.659	.843	1.074	.965	.910	.952
LEAGUE	TOTAL	430	14593	2099	3956	680	74	249	1634	2645	.271	.379	.344

1993 MINOR LEAGUE TEAM INDEX

This index is an alphabetical list of all 1993 minor-league teams (except for the Arizona, Gulf Coast, and Northern Leagues), showing their league and their major-league affiliation. State abbreviations are shown only where two cities with the same name have teams (except for Nashville, TN, these pairs of cities are in different states). League abbreviations and classifications can be found on page 278.

Independent or Co-op teams have their affiliation listed as IND. Arizona League and Gulf Coast League team affiliations are the same as their team names. All Northern League teams are independents. Since the Northern League operates outside of the National Association, it has no classification.

TEAM	LG	AFFIL	TEAM	LG	AFFIL	TEAM	LG	AFFIL	TEAM	LG	AFFIL
Albany, GA	SAL	BAL	Columbus, OH	INT	NYA	Knoxville	SOU	TOR	Rochester	INT	BAL
Albany-Colonie, NY	EAS	NYA	Danville	APP	ATL	Lakeland	FSL	DET	Rockford	MID	KC
Albuquerque	PCL	LA	Daytona Beach	FSL	CHN	Las Vegas	PCL	SD	Salem	CAR	PIT
Appleton	MID	SEA	Dunedin	FSL	TOR	Lethbridge	PIO	IND	Salt Lake	PIO	IND
Arkansas	TEX	SL	Durham	CAR	ATL	London	EAS	DET	San Jose	CAL	SF
Asheville	SAL	HOU	Edmonton	PCL	FLO	Louisville	AMA	SL	San Bernandino	CAL	IND
Auburn	NYP	HOU	El Paso	TEX	MIL	Lynchburg	CAR	BOS	San Antonio	TEX	LA
Augusta	SAL	PIT	Elizabethton	APP	MIN	Macon	SAL	ATL	Sarasota	FSL	CHA
Bakersfield	CAL	LA	Elmira	NYP	FLO	Madison	MID	OAK	Savannah	SAL	SL
Batavia	NYP	PHI	Erie	NYP	TEX	Martinsville	APP	PHI	Scranton-Wilkes-Barre	INT	PHI
Bellingham	NWL	SEA	Eugene	NWL	KC	Medicine Hat	PIO	TOR	Shreveport	TEX	SF
Beloit	MID	MIL	Everett	NWL	SF	Memphis	SOU	KC	South Bend	MID	CHA
Bend	NWL	COL	Fayetteville	SAL	DET	Midland	TEX	CAL	Southern Oregon	NWL	OAK
Billings	PIO	CIN	Frederick	CAR	BAL	Modesto	CAL	OAK	Spartanburg	SAL	PHI
Binghamton	EAS	NYN	Ft. Myers	FSL	MIN	Nashville, TN	AMA	CHA	Spokane	NWL	SD
Birmingham	SOU	CHA	Ft. Wayne	MID	MIN	Nashville, TN	SOU	MIN	Springfield	MID	SL
Bluefield	APP	BAL	Ft. Lauderdale	FSL	BOS	New Orleans	AMA	MIL	St. Petersburg	FSL	SL
Boise	NWL	CAL	Geneva	NYP	CHN	New Britain	EAS	BOS	St. Catherines	NYP	TOR
Bowie	EAS	BAL	Glens Falls	NYP	SL	Niagara Falls	NYP	DET	St. Lucie	FSL	NYN
Bristol	APP	DET	Great Falls	PIO	LA	Norfolk	INT	NYN	Stockton	CAL	MIL
Buffalo	AMA	PIT	Greensboro	SAL	NYA	Oklahoma City	AMA	TEX	Syracuse	INT	TOR
Burlington, IA	MID	MON	Greenville	SOU	ATL	Omaha	AMA	KC	Tacoma	PCL	OAK
Burlington, NC	APP	CLE	Hagerstown	SAL	BAL	Oneonta	NYP	NYA	Toledo	INT	DET
Butte	PIO	IND	Harrisburg	EAS	MON	Orlando	SOU	CHN	Tulsa	TEX	TEX
Calgary	PCL	SEA	Helena	PIO	MIL	Osceola	FSL	HOU	Tuscon	PCL	HOU
Canton-Akron	EAS	CLE	Hickory	SAL	CHA	Ottawa	INT	MON	Utica	NYP	BOS
Capital City	SAL	NYN	High Desert	CAL	FLO	Palm Springs	CAL	CAL	Vancouver	PCL	CAL
Carolina	SOU	PIT	Huntington	APP	CHN	Pawtucket	INT	BOS	Vero Beach	FSL	LA
Cedar Rapids	MID	CAL	Huntsville	SOU	OAK	Peoria	MID	CHN	Waterloo	MID	SD
Central Valley	CAL	COL	Idaho Falls	PIO	ATL	Phoenix	PCL	SF	Watertown	NYP	CLE
Charleston, WV	SAL	CIN	Indianapolis	AMA	CIN	Pittsfield	NYP	NYN	Welland	NYP	PIT
Charleston, SC	SAL	TEX	Iowa	AMA	CHN	Portland	PCL	MIN	West Palm Beach	FSL	MON
Charlotte, FL	FSL	TEX	Jackson	TEX	HOU	Prince William	CAR	NYA	Wichita	TEX	SD
Charlotte, NC	INT	CLE	Jacksonville	SOU	SEA	Princeton	APP	CIN	Wilmington	CAR	KC
Chattanooga	SOU	CIN	Jamestown	NYP	MON	Quad City	MID	HOU	Winston-Salem	CAR	CIN
Clearwater	FSL	PHI	Johnson City	APP	SL	Rancho Cucamonga	CAL	SD	Yakima	NWL	LA
Clinton	MID	SF	Kane County	MID	FLO	Reading	EAS	PHI			
Colorado Springs	PCL	COL	Kingsport	APP	NYN	Richmond	INT	ATL			
Columbus, GA	SAL	CLE	Kinston	CAR	CLE	Riverside	CAL	SEA			

INDEX

The first page number shown is where to locate that player's situational statistics; the second page number is the player's career records.

Players shown in ALL CAPS are regulars; non-regulars are in lower case. Players who made their major-league debuts in 1993 are italicized.

FOR BASEBALL ENTHUSIASTS ONLY

PROJECT SCORESHEET

Project Scoresheet no longer operates a volunteer scoring network, but its valuable data and publications are still available. The Project scored all major-league games from 1984 through 1990, and the Project's data base has been updated with the addition of data from the Baseball Workshop for the 1991 and 1992 seasons. Researchers should take note that the play-by-play data base is unavailable from any other source.

Data available from Project Scoresheet can be ordered on either IBM or Macintosh computer disks. Three separate data bases and two series of books are available. The price for the data varies from $25–$100 per set; the books range from $13–$20 each. Brief information on each type of product follows; if you write for an order form, you will also get more detailed descriptions of each product.

Play-by-play data for all 1984–92 games. Team rosters for each year and a master roster for 1984–92 are included with the complete record of every play for every game. The play-by-play data are in a format that is easy to import into any commercial spreadsheet or data base program, and they come packaged with utility programs to help analyze the data.

Major-league career data for all players who have played in the majors since the start of the 1980 season. Similar in content to the career registers in this *Stat Book*, these data include every official batting and pitching statistic as well as extensive demographic information for the players. If a player played in any game in the 1980s or 1990s, his complete career record is shown, team-by-team and year-by-year, whether he played in only one season or whether his career started in the 1950s (e.g., Jim Kaat).

Situational data for all seasons from 1984 to the present. For each year, complete situational breakdowns are included for every major-league player, whether he appeared in one game or 162 games. All categories shown for regular players in this *Stat Book* are included for every player, and a few minor categories (like batting with bases loaded) are also included.

Game Account Books for the American and National Leagues for the 1984–92 seasons. These books are approximately 300 pages each in a spiral-bound, self-published format. Each book contains account-form box scores for that season, giving a complete, coded play-by-play description of each AL or NL game.

Previous editions of *The Great American Baseball Stat Book* for the 1986–92 seasons. The format and contents of each edition varies, but they are all approximately 500 pages. Each book contains situational statistics for the previous year, as well as situational totals from 1984 onward. The 1987 *Stat Book* and 1988 *Stat Book* (covering the 1986 and 1987 seasons) were published by Random House; the 1989, 1990 and 1991 Stat Books were self-published by the Project and are spiral-bound. The 1992–93 editions of the *The Great American Baseball Stat Book* were published by Harper-Collins; they are very similar to the 1993 *Stat Book*.

If you would like a current order form for Project Scoresheet products, write to P.O. Box 27614, Philadelphia, PA 19118.

RETROSHEET

Long-time Society for American Baseball Research member and former Project Scoresheet board member David W. Smith is collecting pre-1984 scoresheets and compiling a computerized data base of these games. David teaches at the University of Delaware, and he has started a new organization called Retrosheet to publish the resulting data. Retrosheet is a noncommercial, volunteer effort, and all data collected will be made publicly available.

Retrosheet has already collected more than 70,000 scoresheets for games prior to 1984. These have come from many sources: fans, sportswriters, broadcasters, and major-league teams. Dozens of people are currently engaged in translating these old scoresheets and inputting these games, and data for the 1967 season will soon be available.

Retrosheet provides all materials and software needed by its volunteers. If you'd like to pitch in and help out with Retrosheet, you can write to 6 Penncross Circle, Newark, DE 19702. You can also call David Smith at 302-731-1570.

THE BASEBALL WORKSHOP

The Baseball Workshop is a baseball research and consulting company which was founded in 1992 to collect and publish baseball statistics and analysis. It provides these to fans, the media, teams, and professionals such as player agents. The Workshop continues to update the Project Scoresheet data base under a licensing agreement.

The Workshop is currently seeking baseball fans who would like to score major-league games during the 1994 season. The Workshop pays fans in each city to score each game on a pitch-by-pitch and play-by-play basis. Scorers then fax their scoresheets to a toll-free number where they are promptly input, checked, and compiled.

The Great American Baseball Stat Book is produced using the statistics derived from these scoresheets.

If you are a knowledgeable baseball fan who would like to participate, write to:

> The Baseball Workshop
> 619 Wadsworth Avenue
> Philadelphia, PA 19119

You will be contacted in February, 1994 by telephone, and an instructional package will be sent to you in March.

THE GREAT AMERICAN BASEBALL REPORT

This new monthly periodical will be the thinking baseball fan's year-round companion. It will be published ten times a year: 16-page monthly issues plus two 32-page issues during the off-season. The premiere issue will appear in January 1994. Edited by Gary Gillette, author of *The Great American Baseball Stat Book* and president of The Baseball Workshop, the Report will take advantage of the unique baseball data bases used to produce *The Great American Baseball Stat Book* and *Total Baseball*.

Among its features:

- In-depth articles and research reports on players and teams, performance, and predictions—information available nowhere else, published for the first time for the Report's subscribers.
- Extensive coverage of the pennant races, trades, and labor-management negotiations.
- Contemporary and historical analysis from noted baseball analysts and historians like Pete Palmer and Steve Mann.
- Rankings and ratings of major-league players and minor-league prospects.
- Thought-provoking commentary from noted baseball writers.
- Insightful interviews with baseball players, coaches, managers, executives, and authors.
- Book reviews, tough trivia contests, and an annual index for easy retrieval.

If you would like to subscribe to *The Great American Baseball Report* or have your name added to a mailing list to receive information on future products and publications, write to:

> The Baseball Workshop
> 619 Wadsworth Avenue
> Philadelphia, PA 19119

For one-year subscriptions to *The Great American Baseball Report*, please enclose $39.95 by check, money order or credit card authorization. Sample copies are $6.00; if you choose to subscribe, the sample copy price will be applied to your subscription payment.

Baseball Workshop Survey and Order Form

_____ Please send me FREE rankings of 1994's Top Prospects (available March 1994).

_____ Please send me information about the new computer disk version of *The Great American Baseball Stat Book*. (Purchasers of the Stat Book receive a substantial discount on the electronic version, which can search the database and respond to customized queries.)

You can help make the *Great American Stat Book* better by giving us your opinion:

1. Rate these features of the *1994 Great American Baseball Stat Book* from 10 (excellent) to 1 (poor):

   _____ regular players situational statistics   _____ fielding reports
   _____ non-regular players situational statistics   _____ career records
   _____ team/league statistics   _____ 1994 projections
   _____ special pitching reports   _____ minor league park factors
   _____ special baserunning reports   _____ user's guide

2. Do you use the information in the *Stat Book* for fantasy league analysis?   ☐ yes   ☐ no

3. Any comments or suggestions for improving the next edition of the *Great American Baseball Stat Book*?

   _____

   _____

   _____

4. When and where did you buy the 1994 Stat Book?
   Date _____ Store _____

5. If you would like further information on any of the items described in the previous pages, please check below:

   _____ Please send me the **Project Scoresheet** order form (Game Account Book, 1984–90 season data on disk, previous *Stat Book* editions).

   _____ Please send me **The Baseball Workshop** order form 1991–93 season data on disk, minor league player records, new computer version of the 1994 Stat Book).

   _____ Please have **Retrosheet** contact me about its ongoing research.

   _____ Please contact me regarding scoring for the 1994 baseball season.

Mail to:
The Baseball Workshop
619 Wadsworth Avenue
Philadelphia, PA 19119
or call/fax our toll-free number to leave your name, address, and request
800-275-9899